# BREWER'S

DICTIONARY OF
## MODERN PHRASE
## & FABLE

# BREWER'S

## DICTIONARY OF
## MODERN PHRASE
## & FABLE

Second Edition by
**JOHN AYTO & IAN CROFTON**

WEIDENFELD & NICOLSON

First published 2000
Second edition 2006

Weidenfeld & Nicolson
The Orion Publishing Group Ltd
Orion House
5 Upper Saint Martin's Lane
London WC2H 9EA
www.orionbooks.co.uk

1 3 5 7 9 10 8 6 4 2

**British Library Cataloguing in Publication Data**
A catalogue record for this book is available from the British Library

ISBN-13    978 0 304 36809 9
ISBN-10    0 304 36809 1

Typeset in Palatino by Gem Graphics, Trenance, Cornwall
Printed in Finland by WS Bookwell Ltd

The Orion Publishing Group's policy is to use papers that are
natural, renewable and recyclable products and made from wood
grown in sustainable forests. The logging and manufacturing
processes are expected to conform to environmental regulations of the
country of origin.

# CONTENTS

# INTRODUCTION

In the 850-plus pages that follow, Dr Ebenezer Cobham Brewer, redoubtable Victorian scholar and the compiler of the original *Brewer's Dictionary of Phrase and Fable* (1870), strides confidently into the 21st century. Exactly what he would have made of it – with its 'celebrity culture', its 'phishing' and 'phreaking', and its 'freedom fries' – is anybody's guess. But his lexicographic whiskers would surely have twitched at the wealth of striking and intriguing new phraseology the millennium has brought with it. This new edition of *Brewer's Dictionary of Modern Phrase and Fable* captures it on the wing.

The dictionary's overall scope remains that of its first edition, published just as the 20th century expired. It endeavours not only to tell the etymological 'stories' behind thousands of words, names, titles and phrases, but also to deliver information, eloquently, that is not normally found in the more conventional works of general reference. Just as importantly, it seeks to bring together in a single book a range of information that is rarely found within the pages of just one reference work. The effect is to create a book with a markedly demotic flavour, one that allows slang usages to live alongside technical terms, and where iconic products of 'high' art, such as literary novels, jostle with popular-cultural productions, such as television sitcoms. 'Mrs Dalloway' can thus cohabit with 'Beavis and Butthead', 'Disgusted of Tunbridge Wells' with 'Lady Chatterley's Lover', and the devious 'Tricky Dicky' of modern political folklore with his more dignified operatic avatar, 'Nixon in China'.

But the world has changed much in the first years of this millennium, and dictionary compilers must run to keep up. From the nodal point of '9/11', terminological ripples have spread out in all directions. Hyperbole has been in the air: the 'Clash of Civilizations', the 'War on Terror', the 'Axis of Evil'. Hand in hand with it comes its more disreputable partner, euphemism: 'assymetric warfare', 'decapitation strategy', 'extraordinary rendition', 'regime change'. In this new world we have learned the subtle distinctions in the camp of the sole remaining superpower ('chickenhawks', 'crusaders', 'neocons') and noted its insults ('Old Europe', 'surrender monkeys'). '7/7' brought matters closer to the present editors' home, a city some call 'Londonistan'.

The intensification of celebrity, personified by 'Posh and Becks' and the 'King of Chavs' (not to mention the 'Wags'), has been another key trend. Everyone can have a go, via 'reality TV' – a prospect to raise the enthusiasm even of the 'Whatever Generation'. And technology continues to transform. If you want celebrity (or pretty much anything else), why not bypass the middleman, head for your computer, write up your 'blog' and you might just show up on 'Google'. And you may even want to display your worldly goods on 'eBay'. The 'iPod' has added its layer to our personal cocoons, and we can 'phone a friend' with a recording of our latest 'happy slapping' escapade. But beware 'identity theft'!

In the sphere of politics and its media attentions, shifts of popularity and personnel have introduced us to (in Britain) 'Blatcherism' and 'Worcester woman', 'UKIP' and 'Veritas', 'Metro-Tories', the 'Notting Hill set' and 'Cameroonians', 'Champagne Charlie' and 'Ming the Merciless'. Not forgetting, further afield, 'Dubya' (or if you live in Iraq, the 'idiot son'), the 'Governator', *'Le Bulldozer'* and *'il Cavaliere'*.

But of course the constant inventiveness of the English language trans-cends categorizations, and this new edition of *Brewer's Dictionary of Modern Phrase and Fable* casts its net wide, over such choice items as the 'elephant in the corner', the 'killer fact', the 'bunny-boiler', the 'terrible twos' and the 'Croydon facelift'. These join the likes of 'yummy mummies', 'go commando', 'willy waving', 'as cheap as chips' and 'too posh to push' among the hundreds of colourful neologisms in the following pages.

Not that novelty is by any means the sole criterion for new admission. The remit of the dictionary covers the entire life of the 20th century as well as the growing infant of the 21st, and phraseology from earlier decades has been added ('D-Day Dodgers', 'Edward the Caresser', 'officers' raincoats', 'White Rose'). The editors have paid especial attention to increasing the coverage of phraseology from other, non-British varieties of English: from the United States in particular ('hide the weenie', 'hog heaven', 'hurtin' for certain') and also Australia ('bum to mum', 'the rough end of the pineapple', 'shoot through like a Bondi tram') and New Zealand ('Darth Vader's pencil box', 'sausage sizzle').

Another category whose coverage has been considerably strengthened is nicknames. We have already mentioned some politicals; but you can also meet, or re-acquaint yourself with, 'Bonking Boris' (two versions thereof), 'Chemical Ali' (not forgetting 'Comical Ali'), 'Eric the Eel', the 'Incredible Sulk', 'Madge', 'Needless Markup', 'Princess Pushy' and a host of others.

The editors are greatly indebted to Richard Milbank, *quondam* reference publisher at Weidenfeld & Nicolson, who commissioned this second edition of *Brewer's Dictionary of Modern Phrase and Fable* and made many important contributions to it. The overall editorial project was most ably managed by Mark Hawkins-Dady (who also contributed invaluably to the text), with the indispensable help of Rosie Anderson (on all fronts) and earlier in the project's life, assistant-editor Catherine Cleare. *Brewer's* regulars Patrick Heenan and David Pickering honed the text at proof-reading, and Gordon Galsworthy at Gem Graphics typeset the book with his usual maximum care and patience. The Publishers are grateful to Librios for their provision of database software.

Last, and most, this book would not exist without Adrian Room, the compiler of the first edition. Not only does his edifice still stand, but most of its original bricks are still in place, and his successor editors can but hope to have constructed an elegant and useful extension.

*John Ayto*
*Ian Crofton*
London, August 2006

# NOTES ON USING THE DICTIONARY

Entries are arranged in alphabetical order on a letter-by-letter basis. Thus, for example, 'Radio Caroline' comes after 'Radiocarbon dating', and 'Tub of lard' after 'Tube Alloys'.

Entries beginning 'Mr' or 'Mrs' are alphabetized on the basis of these abbreviated forms, while entries beginning 'Dr' and 'St' are positioned as if spelled out (Doctor, Saint).

Entries, including phrases, are positioned according to their first meaningful word, thus ignoring any initial 'The', 'A/An' or, in verbal phrases, 'To'. For example, the phrase 'to scare the living daylights out of someone' will be found under 'scare'.

Entries on named individuals, fictional or real, are normally alphabetized under surnames.

Entries containing numbers in their headwords (e.g. 9/11) are positioned as if the numbers are spelled out (Nine/eleven).

Cross-references, wherever they occur, are indicated by SMALL CAPITALS.

# THE DICTIONARY

# A

**Abba.** *See* NAME OF THE GAME; ROCK GROUP NAMES; 'WATERLOO'.

**Abbey Road.** An album by The BEATLES, released in the UK in September 1969 and featuring, among others, the songs 'Come Together', 'Something', 'OCTOPUS'S GARDEN', 'Here Comes the Sun', 'MAXWELL'S SILVER HAMMER', 'Mean Mr Mustard' and 'Polythene Pam'. The last-mentioned two tracks form part of a 16-minute 'Long Medley' of fragmentary and longer songs on the second side of the original LP. The album's celebrated cover photograph, with no title or text, was taken on the morning of 8 August 1969 and features the four Beatles, including a shoeless Paul McCartney, on a ZEBRA CROSSING outside the EMI Abbey Road Studios in St John's Wood, an inner suburb of northwest London. The photograph gave rise to bizarre rumours that McCartney was dead, fanatics claiming that the album's cover image carried clues to this effect. Absurdly, the registration number of a Volkswagen car captured in the photograph – LMW 281F – was identified as signifying that McCartney would have been '28 IF' he had lived. The car's number plates were stolen by hunters of Beatles memorabilia on several occasions thereafter, and the car itself was sold by auction at Sotheby's in 1986.

**Abbey Theatre.** Ireland's national theatre, on Lower Abbey Street, Dublin, where it was founded in 1904. It was built at the instigation of the Celtic revivalists W.B. Yeats (1865–1939) and Lady Gregory (1852–1932) and soon gained prestige for its productions of Irish playwrights such as Yeats himself, J.M. Synge and Sean O'Casey. Some stagings have caused controversy and even riots, notably the first productions of Synge's *The* PLAYBOY OF THE WESTERN WORLD (1907) and O'Casey's *The* PLOUGH AND THE STARS (1926). The latter questioned the motivations of the revered martyrs of the EASTER RISING and thus discredited the romanticized vision of Ireland that Yeats had helped to create. The original theatre was destroyed by fire in 1951, and the present building holds two auditoriums, the main one upstairs devoted to the Irish classics and new work by dramatists such as Brian Friel, and the Peacock Theatre downstairs, which is largely given over to experimental drama.

**Abby Singer shot.** In film production a nickname for the penultimate shot of the day. The name is that of Abby Singer, an assistant director at Universal Studios in the 1950s, who constantly promised that after the current shot only one more shot remained before the crew would move to another part of the studio or the day's shooting would end. *See also* MARTINI SHOT.

**Abdication Crisis.** The constitutional upheaval in which Edward VIII (1894–1972) renounced the British throne in order to marry Mrs Wallis Simpson (1896–1986), an American divorcee.

Edward became king on 20 January 1936 amid rumours of an existing romantic attachment. In the autumn came the news that the king intended to marry Mrs Simpson, who in 1927 had divorced her first husband, a US navy officer, and that same year married a London stockbroker, Ernest Simpson. The national objection to any marriage was not that Mrs Simpson was an American, or that she was a commoner, but that she was a divorcee, which would put in question Edward's relationship with the Church of England, which officially censured the whole idea of divorce. But events took their course, and on 27 October 1936 Mrs Simpson was granted a decree nisi. The king was now faced with four options: (1) he could marry Mrs Simpson and make her queen; (2) he could contract a morganatic marriage, so that neither Mrs Simpson nor any children of the marriage would share royal status or property; (3) he could abdicate and then marry; (4) he could abandon Mrs Simpson. He chose the third option, and by the Declaration of Abdication Act, 10 December 1936,

Edward VIII renounced the throne and was succeeded by his brother, George VI, who created him Duke of Windsor. The marriage took place in France on 3 June 1937.

Edward VIII thus had the shortest reign of any British monarch except that of his namesake, Edward V (1470–83), one of the 'Princes in the Tower'.

**Abendland.** (German, 'evening land'.) The West, especially Western civilization regarded as in decline. The word became familiar from the title of Oswald Spengler's book *Der Untergang des Abendlandes* ('The Decline of the West'; 1918–22) in which he argued that civilizations undergo a thousand-year cycle of growth and decline.

**Aberfan.** A mining village in South Wales where, on 21 October 1966, a coal tip subsided on the local school, killing 116 children and 28 adults. The collapse was believed to have been caused by water pouring into the tip from a previously unknown natural spring. The subsequent enquiry blamed the tragedy on the lack of any tipping policy by the National Coal Board.

**Abergele Martyrs.** The name given to two members of the clandestine Welsh organization MUDIAD AMDDIFFYN CYMRU, William Alwyn Jones and George Francis Taylor, of Abergele, Denbighshire (now Conwy), who were killed when the explosive devices they were carrying were accidentally detonated on 1 July 1969, the day of the investiture of the Prince of Wales at Caernarfon Castle. Their deaths were commemorated by several poets, and their graves have become the focus for an annual ceremony.

**'Abide with Me'.** This well-known hymn by Henry Francis Lyte (1793–1847), probably written in 1847, has been sung at FA cup finals since 1927, when it was introduced at the suggestion of the FA secretary, Frederick Wall. Earlier it was much parodied by soldiers in the First World War, one common version beginning: 'We've had no beer, we've had no beer today.' The hymn gave much comfort to Edith Cavell (1865–1915), the British nurse imprisoned and condemned to death by the Germans for helping wounded soldiers to escape, and the night before she was shot, she sat in her cell singing it with a British chaplain.

**Able and Baker.** The names of the first animals to survive being sent into space by the United States. They were, respectively, a rhesus monkey and a squirrel monkey and were sent aloft in the nose cone of a Jupiter rocket at Cape Canaveral, Florida, on 28 May 1959. They splashed down after 90 minutes near Antigua. Their names represent the words for the letters A and B in the 1942 signalling alphabet. *See also* LAIKA.

**Ableism.** Discrimination in favour of able-bodied people or against the disabled (the latter also being termed 'disablism'). The concept arose in the 1980s. *See also* POLITICAL CORRECTNESS.

**ABM.** The abbreviation for anti-ballistic missile, a weapon designed to destroy incoming nuclear-armed missiles (*see* ICBM). Both the United States and the USSR deployed ABMs from the 1960s to give them the capacity to survive a nuclear attack and retaliate, so eroding the effectiveness of the strategy of mutually assured destruction (MAD). On 26 March 1972 the two countries signed an ABM treaty that restricted the numbers of such missiles, so maintaining the power of deterrence. The SALT I treaty was signed on the same day.

**Abominable No-Man.** The punning nickname of Sherman L. Adams (1899–1986), chief White House aide to President Eisenhower, referring to his regular annotation 'no' on documents. The allusion is, of course, to the ABOMINABLE SNOWMAN.

**Abominable Snowman.** The popular name for the yeti, a large manlike or apelike animal said to inhabit the Himalayas. The term was popularized by climbing expeditions in the 1950s, and in 1960 Sir Edmund Hillary found footprints resembling those of a large bear. The phrase translates the Tibetan *metohkangmi*, from *metoh*, 'foul', and *kangmi*, 'snowman'.

***Absalom! Absalom!*** A novel (1936) by William Faulkner (1897–1962), recounting, from three different points of view, the ultimately doomed efforts of Thomas Sutpen to become accepted in Mississippi society and found a dynasty. At the climax of this tale of dark passions, destructive relationships and murder, Sutpen's son, Henry, now old, dies in the family home, which has been set alight by his African American half-sister, leaving the line to be carried on only by Henry's idiot African American great-nephew. The title recalls the lament of David for Absalom: 'O my son Absalom, my son, my son Absalom! would God I had died for thee, O Absalom, my son, my son!' (2 Samuel 18:33).

***Absolute Beginners.*** A novel (1959) by Colin MacInnes (1914–76). The second book in the author's 'London Trilogy', the story, whose climax is the Notting Hill race riots of 1958, is narrated by a 19-year-old VESPA-riding teenager, one of the happy-go-lucky generation who are the 'absolute beginners' of the title. The other books in the trilogy are *City of Spades* (1957) and *Mr Love and Justice* (1960). A film version of *Absolute Beginners* (1986) was directed as a musical by Julien Temple.

**Absolutely Fabulous.** A television SITCOM screened on BBC2 from 1992 to 1995 and from 2001 to 2003 and centring on the lives of Edina ('Eddy') Monsoon, a jet-setting PR agent and single mother, played by Jennifer Saunders, and Patsy Stone, her chain-smoking, hard-drinking, drug-taking former schoolfriend, played by Joanna Lumley. Their outrageous behaviour is set off by Edina's strait-laced, disapproving daughter, Saffron (Saffy), played by Julia Sawalha, and reflected in the title, colloquially abbreviated to *Ab Fab*, a typical upper-class eulogistic utterance, here employed ironically. Any notion of POLITICAL CORRECTNESS is noticeably absent.

**Abstract expressionism.** The dominant movement in US painting in the late 1940s and 1950s, characterized by the conveying of powerful emotions through the sensuous qualities of paint. The term was originally used in 1919 to describe certain paintings by Wassily Kandinsky (1866–1944), but in its current sense was first used by Robert Coates, art critic of *The New Yorker*, in 1946. Leading artists of the genre were Jackson Pollock (1912–56), Willem de Kooning (1904–97), Clyfford Still (1904–80), Mark Rothko (1903–70), Barnett Newman (1905–70), Franz Kline (1910–62), Arshile Gorky (1904–48), Robert Motherwell (1915–91) and Adolph Gottlieb (1903–74).

**Absurd, Theatre of the.** *See* THEATRE OF THE ABSURD.

**Abuse.** Literally, misuse, and a word current in English from the 16th century. In the latter half of the 20th century it became associated with specific areas of improper or harmful activity, notably alcohol abuse, drug abuse and solvent abuse on the one hand, as the illegal or excessive use of these substances, and child abuse on the other, as the maltreatment of a child, especially by physical violence or sexual interference. In this last sense the term effectively replaced what was earlier known as child molesting, while the subjection of very young children to physical violence was earlier familiar as 'baby battering' (*see* BATTERED BABY). All these terms are now in regular use, although certain official publications prefer 'misuse' when referring to substances. In the field of sports the word can apply to the misuse of physical equipment, so that tennis players who throw their rackets about in anger or frustration can be cautioned for 'racket abuse'.

**Abwehr.** (German, 'repulse'.) The German military intelligence organization created in 1921 as part of the Ministry of Defence. It was divided into three sections – reconnaissance, cipher and radio monitoring, and counter-espionage – and although relatively efficient in the early stages of the Second World War was continually undermined by the SS. It ceased to exist in 1944. The German word literally means 'warding off'.

**Abyssinia.** A fanciful alteration of 'I'll be seeing you', popular as a parting shot among hep-cats in the United States in the 1930s.

**Acacia Avenue.** A street name evocative of suburban MIDDLE ENGLAND and its middle-class values. As the acacia flourishes in warm climates, the implication is that the street that bears its name is likely to be in the 'soft' South of England rather than the 'tough' Midlands or North. The *Greater London Street Atlas* (1998) lists a dozen genuine streets so named.

> Sales of newspapers boomed as the *Daily Mirror* went for the mass working class and the *Daily Express* for Acacia Avenue's Walter Mitty dream of success, sophistication and romance.
> *The Times* (21 January 2000)

**ACAS.** An acronym for Advisory, Conciliation and Arbitration Service, a UK QUANGO established by the Employment Protection Act of 1975. It can act as a mediator and/or arbitrator in industrial disputes, if both sides agree, and also advises unions and employers on a wide range of industrial-relations and employment issues.

**Acceptable face.** The acceptable face of something is its positive or reasonable side, as distinct from what are regarded as its negative or unpopular aspects. The expression arose in the late 1970s as the converse of an 'unacceptable face', itself popularized by Edward Heath's UNACCEPTABLE FACE OF CAPITALISM.

> Bit by bit … I was becoming the almost acceptable face of homosexuality.
> QUENTIN CRISP: *How to Become a Virgin*, ch. 6 (1981)

**Acceptable level of violence, An.** A phrase associated, to his cost, with the Conservative politician Reginald Maudling (1917–79). As home secretary he visited Northern Ireland on 15 December 1971, and he concluded:

> I don't think one can speak of defeating the IRA, of eliminating them completely, but it is the design of the security forces to reduce their level of violence to something like an acceptable level.

**Accidental Death of an Anarchist.** A play, *Morte accidentale di un anarchico*, by the Italian playwright and actor Dario Fo (b.1926). First performed in 1970, it is about the inquiry following the death of a political activist after he falls from the window of Milan police station while being interrogated about terrorist bomb explosions. The play was based on real events, the original anarchist being Giuseppe Pinelli, a railway worker and political extremist who died in the same manner while being questioned about a terrorist bomb attack on a Milan bank in 1969. The play had to be altered on a nightly basis during its first run as more facts about the Pinelli case leaked out.

**Accident waiting to happen.** A potentially disastrous situation, typically caused by negligent or faulty procedures. The term is also used of a person likely to cause trouble.

> Accidents are often said to be 'waiting to happen'. It does not take much imagination to see that the chaotic start to the Whitbread round-the-world race ... could easily have ended in tragedy.
>
> *The Times* (23 September 1997)

**AC/DC.** A slang adjective, originally dating from the 1940s, meaning bisexual. The term derives from the abbreviations for the opposite types of electric current (alternating current and direct current). *See also* ROCK GROUP NAMES.

**Ace boon coon.** In African American slang, one's bosom friend. The origins of the expression are far from clear, although the 'boon' may be as in 'boon companion'. It seems unlikely that 'coon' is the same word as the opprobrious term for a black person, although it may be that some subversive reclaiming of an insulting epithet has been at work. It came to prominence in the early 1960s, although there is some anecdotal evidence for plain 'boon coon' from the 1930s.

**Ace in the hole.** A plan or piece of information kept hidden until the right time to use it. The expression relates to US stud poker, in which an ace, as the most valuable card, is dealt face down and not revealed. The 'hole' is simply a place of concealment. The phrase was popularized as the title of a US film of 1951 in which a journalist delays the rescue of a man (the 'ace') in a cave (the 'hole') in order to prolong the story and so boost the sales of his newspaper.

**Acid.** *See* LSD.

**Acid Bath Murders.** A sensational series of murders, which came to light in 1946 when John George Haigh (1909–49) was tried and convicted for the murder of an elderly widow whose body he had dissolved in a bath of sulphuric acid. He had committed similar murders and claimed to have drunk a cup of blood from each of his victims before annihilating them.

**Acid house.** The name of the synthesized dance music, popular in the late 1980s, is associated with 'acid' as slang for the drug LSD, although initially acid house dancers were more specifically fuelled by ECSTASY. A spin-off was acid jazz. *See also* HOUSE.

**Acid rain.** Rainfall made so acidic by atmospheric pollution that it causes environmental damage, mainly to forests, lakes and soils, but also to the fabric of older stone buildings. The pollution is primarily caused by the emission of sulphur dioxide and oxides of nitrogen from combustion plants that burn fossil fuels, such as coal-fired power stations, and, in the case of the latter, gases from road vehicles. The problem became acute in the 1970s. Subsequent emission controls began to benefit the environment generally, although the recovery of the more sensitive ecosystems has been disappointingly slow.

**Ack-ack.** A colloquial term for anti-aircraft fire in the Second World War, from the signallers' term for the letters AA. The name also happens to be imitative of machine-gun fire. *See also* PIP EMMA; ROGER.

**Acol.** The Standard British system of natural bidding in bridge. The system was devised in the mid-1930s by Jack Marx, S.J. Simon, Harrison Gray and Iain Macleod at the Acol Bridge Club in Hampstead, London. The system has continued to evolve since its inception.

**Acronymic aptness.** A tendency arose in the 20th century for the names of certain organizations, movements, charities and so on to spell out a meaningful or punning acronym rather than simply a meaningless word. The following are some examples.

ADAPT: Access for Disabled People to Art Today

CAMPFIRE: Communal Area Management Programmes for Indigenous Resources

CHIME: Churches' Initiative in Musical Education

EUREKA: European Research Cooperation Agency

FOCUS: Financial Outstation Central Unified System

HOLMES: Home Office Large Major Enquiry System (a police computer)

SEALS: Sea, Air and Land Service

SERENDIP: Search for Extraterrestrial Radio Emissions from Nearby Developed Intelligent Populations

SMART: Special Measures Action Reform Team

STEP: Special Temporary Employment Programme

TRACE: test equipment for rapid automatic checkout and evaluation

Equally creative are the humorous reinterpretations of acronymic names of airlines, as:

Alitalia: always late in take-off, always late in arriving

BOAC: better on a camel

Qantas: quite a nice trip, all survived

Sabena: such a bloody experience, never again

**Across the board.** Embracing all classes or categories; applying equally to all in a group. The expression is of US origin and dates from the 1950s. The allusion is to horse racing, where the term is used of a bet that covers all possible ways of winning money on a race: win (first), place (second) or show (third).

**Action française.** (French, 'French action'.) A far-right, proto-fascist political group in France that wielded considerable influence in the first half of the 20th century. The group expressed its ideas in *L'Action française*, a review first published in 1899, which became a daily newspaper from 1908 to 1944. The movement, led by the writer Charles Maurras (1868–1952), was anti-democratic, anti-republican and anti-Semitic, favouring instead the restoration of the monarchy and 'integral nationalism'. Its support among many Catholics was eroded when the newspaper and some of Maurras's books were placed on the Index of prohibited books by the papacy in 1926. During the Second World War the movement was closely associated with the collaborationist VICHY regime. It ceased to exist after 1944, when Maurras was given a life sentence, although he was released in 1952 on grounds of ill-health.

**Action man.** A man who flaunts his physical prowess by both word and deed. The phrase originates in the popular 'Action Man' toy figure, created in 1965 (originally as GI JOE) as the scale model of a soldier in battle dress. Prior to his marriage in 1981 Prince Charles (b.1948) was dubbed 'Action Man' in allusion to his keen interest in many areas of sport, and more recently the name has been applied to Paddy Ashdown (b.1941), former leader of the LIBERAL DEMOCRATS, partly for his 'no-nonsense' manner but also specifically for his military background (he served in the Special Boat Squadron of the Royal Marines, the navy's equivalent of the SAS).

> Is he [William Hague, Conservative politician] Action Man in flesh and blood, happier on the judo mat or walking in the Yorkshire Dales than stuck in a suit in the endless meetings that go with the job of Leader of Her Majesty's Opposition?
> *The Times* (16 August 1999)

**Action painting.** A technique of abstract painting in which paint is splashed or thrown at random on to the canvas. A famous exponent of the style was the US artist Jackson Pollock (1912–56), nicknamed 'Jack the Dripper', whose working methods have been captured on film by Hans Namuth (1915–90).

> At a certain point American painters, one after the other, began to consider the canvas as an arena in which to act, instead of a space in which to reproduce, redraw, analyse or

'express' a present of imagined object. Thus the canvas was no longer the support of a picture, but an event.
> HAROLD ROSENBERG: quoted in Tomassoni, *Pollock* (1968)

*See also* ABSTRACT EXPRESSIONISM.

**Action stations.** The positions or posts taken up by military personnel in preparation for action. The term, frequently used as a command or a signal for action, dates from the First World War. *See also* PANIC STATIONS.

**Action this day.** An annotation used on documents by Winston Churchill during the Second World War, both while at the Admiralty and subsequently as prime minister.

> There were the years as war leader, when he demanded 'action this day' and sometimes seemed willing to support any scheme, however hare-brained, that promised blood and thunder.
> JOHN KEEGAN: in *Daily Telegraph* (29 August 2002)

**ACT-UP.** The punning acronym of AIDS Coalition to Unleash Power, a direct-action protest group formed in the United States in 1987 to mount an urgent response to the AIDS crisis. The movement became noted for its guerrilla-style demonstrations, 'die-ins' and 'zaps' (sudden, coordinated acts). In 1989 members infiltrated the New York Stock Exchange and brought trading to a halt.

**Ada.** *See* PROGRAMMING LANGUAGES.

**Adam International Review.** A literary quarterly published in London since 1941. Its name is an acronym for *Arts, Drama, Architecture, Music* and its first editor was Miron Grindea, a Romanian who settled in England in 1939. It came to be regarded as a showcase for good writing and its contributors have included Anthony Powell, Max Beerbohm, W.H. Auden, H.G. Wells, Thomas Mann and André Gide.

**Addams Family.** A macabre family in the cartoons of the US artist Charles Addams (1912–88), whose work first appeared in *The New Yorker* in 1935. A television series of the mid-1960s starred the gruesome group, with John Astin playing Gomez Addams, Carolyn Jones as Morticia and an ageing Jackie Coogan in the role of Uncle Fester. There are also two film spin-offs: *The Addams Family* (1991) and *Addams Family Values* (1993), the latter more a series of gags than a movie.

**Adidas.** The proprietary name of a make of athletic equipment, and especially footwear and garments. It is that of Adolf ('Adi') *Das*sler (1900–78), the German manufacturer who in 1946 founded the company that produces them.

**'Adlestrop'.** A poem (1915) by Edward Thomas (1878–1917)

evoking in rhapsodic manner the sights and sounds of the English summer. Thomas was inspired to write the poem when the train on which he was travelling stopped at the Gloucestershire village station of Adlestrop, the name of which originally meant 'outlying farmstead of a man called Tætel':

> Yes; I remember Adlestrop –
> The name, because one afternoon
> Of heat the express-train drew up there
> Unwontedly. It was late June.

**Admass.** A term coined by J.B. Priestley in *Journey down a Rainbow* (1955) to describe the vast mid-20th-century proliferation of commercial advertising and high-pressure salesmanship, especially in the United States. The now dated word came to denote the vast mass of the general public to which advertisers addressed their publicity.

> Economics I do not pretend to understand, and sometimes I suspect that nobody does. But I understand people, and I know that the system I christened Admass, which we borrowed from America and did not improve, and constant inflation have made people unhappy.
> J.B. PRIESTLEY: in *Punch* (16 July 1962)

**Admirable Crichton, The.** A play (1902) by J.M. Barrie (1860–1937) about a resourceful manservant who proves the salvation of his social superiors when they are all cast away on a desert island. It was filmed (1957) under the same title, with Kenneth More in the title role, and earlier provided the basis for the Hollywood musical *We're Not Dressing* (1934), with Bing Crosby and Carole Lombard. The original of Barrie's character was the Scots adventurer, scholar, linguist and poet James 'The Admirable' Crichton (1560–82), whose brief but eventful life, culminating in his death in a brawl in Mantua, was the subject of Sir Thomas Urquhart's *Ekskubalauron; or, The Discoverie of a Exquisite Jewel* (1651) and of Harrison Ainsworth's novel *Crichton* (1837). The idea of a social inferior proving the better man on a desert island may have been suggested to Barrie by Sir Arthur Conan Doyle.

**Admiral's Cup.** An international yachting trophy presented in 1957 by the Royal Ocean Racing Club to encourage foreign yachts to race in British coastal waters. The event is the unofficial world championship of offshore yacht racing and is held every other summer. The admiral of the title is the head of the RORC, who presents the prize.

**Admiralty Arch.** The imposing structure at the terminal point of The Mall in London, leading into Trafalgar Square and adjoining the Admiralty, in Whitehall. It was erected in 1910 as a memorial to Queen Victoria and consists of three identical, deep arches, each with iron-wrought gates, those

in the central arch being opened only on ceremonial occasions. Offices in the south wing were occupied by the Ministry of Defence until 1994, while the north wing has two flats, one originally for the use of the First Lord of the Admiralty, the other for the First Sea Lord. One of the flats is currently used as a residence by the Labour deputy prime minister, John Prescott (*see* TWO JAGS); the fact that council tax for it had, since 1997, come out of public funds caused political embarrassment in January 2006 and prompted an apology (Prescott then being the cabinet member responsible for council tax arrangements).

**Adoration of Captain Shit and the Legend of the Black Star Part Two, The.** A painting by the black British artist Chris Ofili (b.1968). Given that it was neither an installation nor a video, it was something of a surprise when this relatively conventional work won the Turner Prize in 1998 – although the judges were no doubt impressed that the piece incorporated some elephant dung. The award attracted the usual blusterings:

> J.M.W. Turner would be spinning in his grave at the thought of his name being used even remotely in connection with Ofili's complete lack of taste.
> *The Times*, letter to the editor (19 December 1998)

**Adrian Mole.** *See* Adrian MOLE.

**Advent calendar.** A calendar celebrating the approach of Christmas, with little flaps or windows that are designed to be opened each day to reveal a picture or present. The enterprise was adopted from similar calendars in Germany and Austria and first emerged in Britain in the 1950s. It was soon divorced from any religious content and is now simply part of the 'Christmas countdown', which in supermarkets usually begins in September. Nowadays the windows often open to reveal chocolates or other goodies that are tempting to children.

**Adverse, Anthony.** The hero of the bestselling historical novel of 1934 named after him by Hervey Allen. He has various romantic adventures and misadventures in 19th-century Europe and America and thus lives up to his name. In a film of the same title (1936) he was played by Fredric March.

**Advertising slogans of the 20th and 21st centuries.** The ever-pervasive media of the 20th and 21st centuries has etched several advertising slogans on the collective consciousness, even when no actual interest is individually shown in the particular product. The most powerful have undoubtedly been those shown in television commercials, although the printed advertisements of the first half of the

20th century also generated many memorable phrases. Rhymes, puns and wordplay are often evident. The following is a selection of some of the best known, with the name of the product and, in brackets, the date of first use, where known, and the name of the originator, if known.

Abbey National building society (now bank): 'Get the Abbey habit' (late 1970s)

Access credit card: 'Access takes the waiting out of wanting' (c.1973)

Adler Elevated Shoes: 'Build up your ego, amigo' (1940s, Shirley Polykoff)

Ajax laundry detergent: 'Stronger than dirt' (1960s)

Alka-Seltzer stomach powder: 'I can't believe I ate the whole thing' (1972, Howie Cohen and Bob Pasqualine)

Allinson wholemeal bread: 'Bread wi' nowt taken out' (1985)

Amami hair products: 'Friday night is Amami night' (1920s)

AMERICAN EXPRESS credit card: 'Don't leave home without it' (1981) (see also THAT'LL DO NICELY, SIR)

Amplex breath purifier: 'Someone isn't using Amplex' (1950s)

Anadin analgesic tablets: 'Nothing acts faster than Anadin' (1960s)

Andrews Liver Salts laxative: 'Inner cleanliness' (1950s)

Andrex toilet tissue: 'Soft, strong and very long' (1981)

Armour & Co. meat products: 'The ham what am' (1917)

Aspro headache pills: 'One degree under' (1960s)

Audi cars: VORSPRUNG DURCH TECHNIK (1971)

Automobile Association: '… But I know a man who can' (1980s)

Avis Rent-A-Car: 'When you're only No. 2 [as against Hertz], you try harder' (1963)

Babycham sparkling drink: 'I'd love a Babycham' (1955)

Badedas bath additive: 'Things happen after a Badedas bath' (1966)

Barratt shoes: 'Walk the Barratt way' (early 1940s)

BENETTON clothing: 'United colors of Benetton' (late 1980s)

Benson & Hedges cigarettes: 'Pure gold' (1964)

Bic lighters: 'Flick your Bic' (1975, Charlie Moss)

BIRDS EYE peas: 'Sweet as the moment when the pod went 'pop'' (c.1965)

Bisto gravy browning: 'Ahh Bisto!' (1919)

Blue Band margarine: 'Spreads straight from the fridge' (late 1960s)

BMW automobiles: 'The ultimate driving machine' (1981)

Bounty chocolate and coconut bar: 'Bounty – the taste of paradise' (1960s)

Bournvita night drink: 'Sleep sweeter, Bournvita' (1960s)

BOVRIL: 'Bovril prevents that sinking feeling' (1920, H.H. Harris)

Braniff airline: 'When you got it, flaunt it' (1969)

Braniff airline: 'The end of the plain plane' (1985, Charlie Moss and Phil Parker)

British Airways: 'The world's favourite airline' (1983)

British Fruit Trades Federation: 'Eat more fruit' (1923)

British Gas: 'Don't you just love being in control?' (1991)

British Post Office: 'Someone, somewhere, wants a letter from you' (1960s)

British Rail: 'Let the train take the strain' (1970, Rod Allen)

British Rail: 'This is the age of the train' (1980)

British Rail: 'We're getting there' (1985)

British Telecom: 'It's for yoo-hoo!' (c.1985)

British Telecom: 'It's good to talk' (1994)

Brooke Bond P.G. Tips tea: 'The tea you can really taste' (1960s)

Brook Street secretarial agency: 'Brook Street Bureau got big by bothering' (1980s)

Brut aftershave: 'Splash it all over' (c.1974)

Brylcreem hair cream: 'A little dab'll do ya' (1949)

Budweiser beer: 'Where there's life there's Bud' (1959)

Buick automobiles: 'It makes you feel like the man you are' (1950s)

Burger King hamburger chain: 'Burger King – the home of the whopper' (1981)

BVDs underwear: 'Next to myself I like BVD's best' (c.1920)

Cadbury's Dairy Milk chocolate: 'Award yourself the C.D.M' (1967)

Cadbury's Drinking Chocolate: 'Hot chocolate, drinking chocolate – the late, late drink' (1960s)

Cadbury's Flake chocolate: 'Sixpence worth of heaven' (1965)

Cadbury's Fruit and Nut chocolate: 'Everyone's a Fruit and Nut case' (1964)

Cadbury's Milk Tray chocolates: 'And all because the lady loves Milk Tray' (1968)

Cadbury's Roses chocolates: 'Roses grow on you' (mid-1960s)

Cadbury's Snack confectionery: 'Bridge that gap with Cadbury's Snack' (1967, Mogens Olsen)

Calvin Klein jeans: 'You know what comes between me and my Calvins? Nothing!' (1980)

Camay soap: 'You'll look a little lovelier every day / With fabulous pink Camay' (c.1960)

Camel cigarettes: 'I'd walk a mile for a Camel' (early 1900s)

Campari aperitif : 'The first time is never the best' (1981)

Canada Dry tonics and mixers: 'Emigrate to Canada Dry (for the sake of your Scotch)' (1980)

Carling Black Label lager: 'I bet he drinks Carling Black Label' (1990)

Carlsberg lager: 'Probably the best lager in the world' (1973)

Carnation milk: 'Milk from contented cows' (1906)

Castlemaine XXXX lager: 'Australians wouldn't give a XXXX for anything else' (1986)

Castrol motor oil: 'Castrol. Liquid engineering' (1977)

Cerebos salt: 'See how it runs' (1919)

Chesterfield cigarettes: 'Blow some my way' (1926)

Chevrolet automobiles: 'Eye it – try it – buy it!' (1940)

Chock Full O'Nuts coffee: 'Chock Full O'Nuts is that heavenly coffee' (1950s)

Chrysler Plymouth automobiles: 'Look at all three [low-priced cars]!' (1932)

Clairol hair colouring: 'Does she … or doesn't she?'(1955)

Colgate Dental Cream: 'Cleans your breath while it cleans your teeth' (1946)

Colman's mustard: 'C'mon Colman's, light my fire' (1979)

Comfort fabric conditioner: 'Softness is a thing called Comfort' (late 1960s, Barry Day)

Commercial Union Assurance: 'We won't make a drama out of a crisis' (early 1980s)

Condor pipe tobacco: 'It's that Condor moment' (1970)

Consulate menthol cigarettes: 'Cool as a mountain stream' (early 1960s)

Coppertone sun lotion: 'Tan – don't burn' (1953)

Courage Tavern beer: 'Take Courage' (1966)

Courage Tavern beer: 'It's what your right arm's for' (c.1972)

Courvoisier brandy: 'The brandy of Napoleon' (1909)

Craven 'A' cigarettes: 'For your throat's sake, smoke Craven 'A'' (1920s)

Croft Original sherry: 'One instinctively knows when something is right' (1982)

Cyril Lord carpets: 'This is luxury you can afford by Cyril Lord' (early 1960s)

*Daily Mail* newspaper: '*Daily Mail*, million sale' (1920s)

*Daily Mirror* newspaper: 'Forward with the people' (c.1935)

De Beers Consolidated Mines: 'A diamond is forever' (1940s, Frances Gerety)

Del Monte canned fruit and fresh fruit: 'The man from Del Monte says 'yes'' (1985)

Dewar's Scotch whisky: 'It never varies' (1922)

Dial soap: 'People who like people like Dial' (1965)

Domestos bleach: 'Kills all known germs' (1959)

Double Diamond beer: 'A Double Diamond works wonders' (1952)

Double Diamond beer: 'I'm only here for the beer' (1971, Ros Levenstein)

Dr Collis Browne's Compound stomach medicine: 'There is no substitute' (c.1900)

Dr Pepper soft drink: 'Good for life!' (1937)

Egg Marketing Board: 'Go to work on an egg' (1957, perhaps Fay Weldon or Mary Gowing)

Electricity Council storage heaters: 'Poor cold Fred' (1969)

Eno's fruit salts laxative: 'First thing every morning renew your health with Eno's' (1927)

Esso motoring fuel: 'The Esso sign means happy motoring' (1950s) (*see also* TIGER IN ONE'S TANK)

Ex-Lax chocolate laxative: 'Keep 'regular' with Ex-Lax' (1934)

Fairy Liquid washing-up soap: 'For hands that do dishes' (1981)

Fiat Strada cars: 'Designed by computer. Silenced by laser. Built by robot' (1970s)

Firestone tyres: 'Where the rubber meets the road' (1976)

Fisk Rubber Co. tyres: 'Time to re-tire' (1907)

Fry's chocolate bars: 'Big Fry' [as distinct from small fry] (mid-1960s)

Fry's Turkish Delight: 'Full of eastern promise' (late 1950s)

F.W. Woolworth & Co. stores: 'Nothing over sixpence' (1910s)

Gas Council: 'High speed gas' (1960s, William Camp)

Gibbs S.R. toothpaste: 'It's tingling fresh' (mid-1950s)

Gillette razor blades: 'Good mornings begin with Gillette' (c.1952)

Glaxo dried skimmed milk: 'Glaxo builds bonny babies' (1913)

Gleem toothpaste: 'For people who can't brush their teeth after every meal' (1957)

Gloria Vanderbilt jeans by Murjani: 'My bottoms are tops' (1980)

Golden Wonder salted peanuts: 'Jungle fresh' (late 1970s)

Goodyear tyres: 'Out front. Pulling away' (1980)

Gordon's gin: 'It's got to be Gordon's' (1977)

Guinness stout: 'Guinness is good for you' (1929, Oswald Greene)

Guinness stout: 'My goodness, my Guinness' (1935, Dicky Richards)

Guinness stout: 'Pure genius' (1985)

Haig whisky: 'Don't be vague – ask for Haig' (c.1936)

Harp lager: 'Harp puts out the fire' (c.1976, Keith Ravenscroft)

Harpic lavatory cleaner: 'Cleans round the bend' (1930s)

Harvey's Bristol Cream: 'The best sherry in the world' (1981)

Hat Council: 'If you want to get ahead, get a hat' (1965)

Heineken lager: 'Heineken refreshes the parts other beers cannot reach' (1975, Terry Lovelock)

Heinz beans: 'Beanz meanz Heinz' (c.1967, Maurice Drake)

Homepride flour: 'Graded grains make finer flour' (1968)

HOOVER vacuum cleaners: 'It beats as it sweeps as it cleans' (1919, Gerald Page-Wood)

Horlicks malted milk powder drink: 'Horlicks guards against night starvation' (1930s) (*see also* NIGHT STARVATION)

Hovis bread: 'Don't say brown – say Hovis' (mid-1930s)

*The Independent* newspaper: '*Independent*. It is. Are you?' (1986)

John B. Stetson Co. hats: 'Step out with a Stetson' (1930s)

John Lewis stores: 'Never knowingly undersold' (1930s, John Lewis)

John Player & Sons cigarettes: 'Player's please' (1927, George Green)

Johnnie Walker whisky: 'Born 1820 – still going strong' (1910)

Keith Prowse ticket agency: 'You want the best seats, we have them' (1925)

Kellogg's Cornflakes: 'The best to you each morning' (1953)

Kellogg's Rice Krispies: 'Snap! Crackle! Pop!' (c.1928)

Kentucky Fried Chicken: 'It's finger lickin' good' (1952) (*see also* KFC)

Knirps umbrellas: 'You can't k-nacker a K-nirps' (1981, Dave Trott)

Kruschen health salts: 'I've got that Kruschen feeling' (1920s)

*Ladies' Home Journal*: 'Never underestimate the power of a woman' (c.1941)

Lady Clairol hair colourant: 'Is it true … blondes have more fun?' (1957)

Lay's potato chips: 'Bet you can't eat just one' (1981)

Lifebuoy soap: 'Stops body odour' (1933) (*see also* B.O)

Life-Savers mints: 'The mint with the hole' (1920)

Listerine mouthwash: 'Often a bridesmaid but never a bride' (c.1923, Milton Feasley)

Lord Calvert custom-blended whiskey: 'For men of distinction' (1945)

Lucas cycle lamps and batteries: 'King of the road' (1920s)

Lucky Strike cigarettes: 'It's toasted' (late 1920s)

Lucozade health drink: 'Lucozade aids recovery' (c.1986)

Lux toilet soap: 'Nine out of ten screen stars use Lux toilet soap for their priceless smooth skins' (1927)

Lyle's Golden Syrup: 'Out of the strong came forth sweetness' [from Judges 14:14] (1930s)

Lyons Corner Houses: 'Where's George? He's gone to Lyonch' (1936)

Mackeson beer: 'It looks good, tastes good and, by golly, it does you good' (1950s)

Maclean's toothpaste: 'Did you Maclean your teeth today?' (1934)

Maidenform brassieres: 'I dreamed I went walking [or variant] in my Maidenform bra' (1949)

Maltesers chocolates: 'Chocolates with the less fattening centres' (1965)

Marlboro cigarettes: 'Come to where the flavor is. Come to Marlboro Country' (mid-1950s)

MARS BAR: 'A Mars a day helps you work, rest and play' (c.1960, Norman Gaff)

Mary Quant cosmetics: 'Make-up to make love in' (early 1970s)

Maxwell House coffee: 'Good to the last drop' (1907)

MCDONALD'S restaurants: 'Nobody can do it like McDonald's can' (1970s)

MG motor cars: 'Mother wouldn't like it' (1972)

Midland Bank: 'Come and talk to the listening bank' (1980)

Milk Marketing Board: 'Drinka pinta milka day' (1958, Bertrand Whitehead)

Milky Way confectionery: 'The sweet you can eat between meals' (1960)

Morton Salt Co.: 'When it rains, it pours' (1911)

Mr Kipling Cakes: 'Mr Kipling does make exceedingly good cakes' (early 1970s)

Murray Mints: 'Too-good-to-hurry mints' (late 1950s)

National Airlines: 'I'm Mandy [or variant]. Fly me' (1971)

National Benzole petrol: 'The getaway people' (1963)

National Canine Defence League: 'A dog is for life, not just for Christmas' (late 1980s)

*News of the World* newspaper: 'All human life is there' (c.1958)

NIKE running shoes: 'Just do it' (1989)

Odorono toilet water: 'Within the curve of a woman's arm' (1919)

Oldham car batteries: 'I told 'em, Oldham' (late 1950s, Joan Bakewell)

Omo washing powder: 'Omo adds brightness to whiteness' (late 1950s)

Orange mobile phones: 'The future's bright, the future's Orange' (1996)

L'Oreal hair and beauty products: 'Because I'm worth it' (1967)

Oxo beef extract: 'Oxo gives a meal man-appeal' (1958)

Packard cars: 'Ask the man who owns one' (1902)

Pears' Soap: 'Preparing to be a beautiful lady' (1932)

Pebeco toothpaste: 'The toothpaste for thinking people' (1931)

Pedigree Chum dog food: 'Top breeders recommend it' (1964)

Penguin chocolate biscuits: 'P–P–P–Pick up a Penguin' (1960)

Pepsi Cola: 'Come alive – you're in the Pepsi generation' (1964)

Pepsodent toothpaste: 'You'll wonder where the yellow went / When you brush your teeth with Pepsodent' (1950s)

Persil washing powder: 'Persil washes whiter' (1970s) (*see also* WHITER THAN WHITE)

Peter Stuyvesant cigarettes: 'The international passport to smoking pleasure' (1960s)

Philips electronics: 'Simply years ahead' (c.1973)

Phyllosan tonic: 'Phyllosan fortifies the over-forties' (late 1940s)

Prudential Assurance Co.: 'The man from the Pru' (late 1940s)

Quaker Puffed Wheat and Puffed Rice: 'Food shot from guns' (c.1900, Claude C. Hopkins)

Qualcast Concorde lawnmowers: 'It's a lot less bovver than a hover' [i.e. than a Flymo] (1981)

Remington electric razors: 'I liked the razor so much I [US businessman Victor Kiam] bought the company' (1979)

Renault cars: 'What's yours called?' (1985)

Rolls-Royce motors: 'At 60 miles an hour the loudest noise in this new Rolls-Royce comes from the electric clock' (1958)

Ronseal wood preservatives: 'Does exactly what it says on the tin' (a registered trademark, c.1988)

Rothman's cigarettes: 'The best money can buy' (1981)

Rowntree's fruit gums: 'Don't forget the fruit gums, Mum' (1958)

Rowntree's Kit-Kat chocolate biscuit: 'Have a break, have a Kit-Kat' (c.1955)

Rowntree's Polo mints: 'The mint with the hole' (1947)

SCHWEPPES: 'Schh … you-know-who' (1960s, Royston Taylor)

Schweppes tonic waters and mixers: 'What is the secret of Schhh?' (c.1963)

7-Up soft drinks: 'Freshen up with 7-Up' (1962)

Senior Service cigarettes: 'Senior Service satisfy' (1981)

Sharp's toffee: 'Sharp's the word for toffee' (1927)

Shell motor fuel: 'You can be sure of Shell' (c.1931)

Shell motor fuel: 'That's Shell – that was!' (late 1930s)

Shell motor fuel: 'Go well – go Shell' (late 1940s)

Shredded Wheat breakfast cereal: 'Bet you can't eat three' (1982)

Singapore Airlines: 'A great way to fly' (1980)

Skoda cars: 'It's a Skoda. Honest' (2000)

Smarties chocolate buttons: 'Wot a lot I got' (c.1958)

Smash instant mashed potato: 'For mash get Smash' (1967)

Smirnoff vodka: 'I thought it was the 8.29 every morning [or variant] until I discovered Smirnoff' (c.1973)

Smuckers preserves: 'With a name like Smuckers it has to be good' (c.1960)

Society of American Florists: 'Say it with flowers' (1917, Henry Penn and Patrick O'Keefe)

START-RITE: 'Children's shoes have far to go' (1946)

Statler hotels: 'A room with a bath for a dollar and a half' (c.1900, Ellsworth M. Statler)

Steinway pianos: 'The instrument of the immortals' (1919, Raymond Rubicam)

Stopette spray deodorant: 'Make your armpit your charm pit' (early 1950s)

Stork margarine: 'Can you tell Stork from butter?' (c.1956)

Strand cigarettes: 'You're never alone with a Strand' (1960, John May)

Stripe toothpaste: 'Looks like fun, cleans like crazy' (1958)

Summer County margarine: 'Makes you feel like a queen' (1960s)

*The Sun* newspaper: 'Are you getting it every day?' (1979)

Sun Oil motor oil: 'I can be very friendly' (1973, Mary Lawrence)

Sunblest bread: 'Fresh to the last slice' (early 1960s)

*Sunday Mail* newspaper: 'If it's going on, it's going in' (1983)

*Sunday Times* newspaper: 'Sunday isn't Sunday without *The Sunday Times*' (1968, Frank Page)

Surf washing powder: 'Hold it up to the light, not a stain and shining bright' (late 1950s)

Tango orange drink: 'You know when you've been tangoed' (1994)

Tetley's tea: 'Tetley make tea-bags make tea' (1970s)

*The Times* newspaper: 'Top people take *The Times*' (1957)

Thunderbird wine: 'What's the good word? Thunderbird' (1957)

Tide washing powder: 'Tide's in, dirt's out' (1950s)

Tizer soft drink: 'Drink Tizer, the appetizer' (1920s)

Toni home perms: 'Which twin has the Toni – and which twin has the expensive perm?' (1951)

Tootal shirts: 'Looks even better on a man' [illustrated on a woman] (1961)

Treets confectionery: 'Melts in your mouth, not in your hand' (1967)

Triumph undergarments: 'Triumph has the bra for the way you are' (c.1977)

*TV Times* television listings magazine: 'I never knew it had so much in it' (1970s)

TYPHOO tea: 'Join the tea-set' (1970s)

Virginia Slims cigarettes: 'You've come a long way baby (to get where you got to today)' (1968)

Volkswagen automobiles: 'Think small' (c.1959)

Wall's ice cream: 'Stop me and buy one' (1922, perhaps Lionel and Charles Rodd)

Watneys beer: 'What we want is Watneys' (1940s)

Welgar Shredded Wheat: 'That 'good-morning' feeling' (mid-1940s)

Wendy hamburger restaurants: 'Ain't no reason to go anyplace else' (1981)

Wheaties breakfast cereal: 'Breakfast of champions' (1950)

Whiskas cat food: 'Eight out of ten cats prefer it' (1980s)

White Horse whisky: 'You can take a White Horse anywhere' (1969, Len Heath)

WONDERBRA brassiere: 'Hello boys' (1994, Nigel Rose)

Woodbury's Facial Soap: 'The skin you love to touch' (1910)

Woolwich Equitable building society: 'We're with the Woolwich' (late 1970s)

Wrigley's Doublemint chewing gum: 'Double your pleasure, double your fun' (1959)

YELLOW PAGES: 'Let your fingers do the walking' (1960s)

Zubes cough sweets: 'Zubes are good for your tubes' (1960s)

*See also* ALL BRAN; CLUNK CLICK; FLEXIBLE FRIEND; GERTCHA!; NAUGHTY BUT NICE; NICE ONE; OVALTINE; SCHOOLGIRL COMPLEXION; SUNNY JIM; WHERE'S THE BEEF?

**Aerial pingpong.** A nickname for Australian Rules football, a variety of the game on the lines of rugby football. Players attempt to kick the ball, similar to a rugby ball, between two goalposts, which, as distinct from rugby, have no crossbars. Points may also be scored for kicking the ball between either of two outer posts and the main goalposts. The ball can be kicked or punched, and players can run with it provided that they bounce it every 9.1m (10 yards). The ball thus spends much of the time being propelled back and forth through the air, which explains the name.

**Aerobics.** This physical fitness programme, designed to increase the efficiency of the body's intake of oxygen, was pioneered by the US doctor Kenneth H. Cooper, a former US Airforce flight surgeon, and popularized in his books *Aerobics* (1968) and *The Aerobics Way* (1977). He took the term from the existing word 'aerobic', meaning 'existing on oxygen in the air', from Greek *aer*, 'air', and *bios*, 'life'.

**Afferbeck Lauder.** *See* STRINE.

**Affinity card.** A cheque card or credit card for which the issuing bank donates a proportion of the money spent to a particular charity. The affinity card is a US concept, and the term primarily applies to a card owned by a member of an affinity group, i.e. a group of people having a common aim or interest, such as a club or college, whom it entitles to a range of discounts and other benefits. The affinity card relating specifically to charity dates from the late 1980s.

**Affluent society.** A phrase, in vogue from the 1950s, denoting the overall growth in material prosperity of British society as evidenced by the increasingly widespread ownership of cars, televisions, washing machines and the like. The term was popularized by the title of US economist J.K. Galbraith's (1908–2006) book *The Affluent Society* (1958). *See also* CONVENTIONAL WISDOM.

> This so-called affluent society is an ugly society still. It is a vulgar society. It is a society in which priorities have gone all wrong.
>
> ANEURIN BEVAN: speech in Blackpool (29 November 1959)

**Afghan Ron.** A nickname of the Scottish socialist politician Ron Brown (b. 1940), so named because of his links with the Soviet-backed regime in Afghanistan in the 1980s. He also maintained links with the Libyan leader Colonel Gaddafi. Brown was Labour MP for Edinburgh Leith from 1979 to 1992 but was deselected following a sex scandal involving his research assistant and her underwear.

**A4.** A standard European size of paper, slightly narrower and longer than standard US letter paper. The basis of the series of sizes is a rectangle with an area of one square metre, the sides of which are in the proportion of $1:\sqrt{2}$. The basic size of the A series is A0 (A zero), 841 × 1189mm. If this is halved, or the sheet folded in two, it produces A1, 594 × 841. Half A1 gives A2, 420 × 594, half A2 is A3, 297 × 420, and half A3 is A4, 210 × 297. This division and sub-division continues down to A10, 26 × 37. The A4 size is commonly found for standard business letters or even personal correspondence, as written, typed or computer-printed.

> Writing your [stage act] lines on your arm and sticking them to the wall on bits of A4 looks like you think the audience can just clear off.
>
> *Sunday Times* (15 August 1999)

**African American.** From the later 20th century, the ethnic term of respect for North Americans of African descent. As such it replaced 'black', which was current in the 1960s, which had in turn replaced 'negro', now regarded as derogatory. Its formulation matches the term NATIVE AMERICAN.

**African National Congress.** *See* ANC.

**African Queen, The.** A film (1951) adapted by James Agee from the novel *The African Queen* (1935) by C.S. Forester (1899–1966). It depicts the changing relationship between hard-living tramp steamer skipper Charlie Allnut (played in the film by Humphrey Bogart) and domineering missionary spinster Rose Sayer (played by Katharine Hepburn) as they try to escape the Germans on the River Ulonga-Bora in Africa in 1915. Director John Huston's autocratic attitude to his actors and his preoccupation with shooting an elephant instead of getting on with the film (allegedly his reason for insisting upon filming on location in the then Belgian Congo) was chronicled in the film *White Hunter, Black Heart* (1990), directed by and starring Clint Eastwood, based on a book by Peter Viertel (who worked on the screenplay of Huston's film). *African Queen* was the name of Bogart's boat. Katharine Hepburn's account of the making of the film was published as *The Making of the African Queen, or How I Went to Africa with Bogart, Bacall and Huston and Almost Lost my Mind* (1987).

**Afrika Korps.** The German army force that arrived in North Africa in February 1941 under General Rommel (*see* DESERT FOX) to reinforce the Italians against the British.

**Afro.** In terms of coiffure, the hairstyle in which naturally short, curly black hair is allowed to grow out in a bush around the head. The style became popular from the 1970s among those of African, African American and Afro-Caribbean descent. The name is popularly abbreviated to ''fro'.

**After the Fall.** A play (1964) by Arthur Miller (1915–2005) about the relationships between a twice-divorced lawyer and the women in his life. The character of the recently dead Maggie excited particular interest when the play was first performed, as she appeared to bear many similarities to the author's own former wife, the film actress

Marilyn MONROE, from whom he was divorced in 1961 and who died in 1962. The title of the play suggests the central character's notion of Maggie having robbed him, like the biblical Eve, of his Adam-like innocence and their consequent fall from God's favour. The 'Fall' in the title also evokes the fallen stone tower of the German concentration camp in which the lawyer's lover, Holga, was incarcerated (the main feature of the stage set), although links have also been made with the Depression, mental illness and the winter of the soul.

> I always preferred *This is Your Life* as a television show.
> NOËL COWARD: after the Broadway premiere of *After the Fall*

**Aga.** A brand of heavy, large, expensive heat-retaining cooking stove, which became a permanent fixture in many British kitchens from the 1930s, especially in VILLAGE ENGLAND. It is of Swedish origin, the letters forming an acronym of its manufacturer, *Svenska Aktiebolaget Gasackumulator* (Swedish Gas Accumulator Company). It has been valued for its dependability and appreciated for its cosiness, and Agas are still found in a number of middle-class homes, especially of those who savour the good life.

**Aga saga.** A type of popular novel, typically set in VILLAGE ENGLAND and devolving on the domestic and emotional lives of middle-class characters, who are likely to have an AGA stove in their homes. A doyenne of the genre is the writer Joanna Trollope (b.1943), whose novels include *A Village Affair* (1989) and *The Rector's Wife* (1991).

**Age Concern.** This pressure group on behalf of the aged evolved from the Old People's Welfare Committees that were first set up in 1940 to cope with the problem of the elderly in the Second World War. It adopted its present name in 1971.

**Ageism.** Discrimination against someone on the grounds of age, the implication being that they are too old for a position. Awareness of ageism arose in the 1970s when problems associated with increased longevity were first posed and when early retirement began to cause hitherto unfamiliar personal difficulties. The term was coined in 1969 by Dr Robert Butler, a US specialist in geriatrics. In the early 21st century social and economic pressures to encourage people to work longer threw the issue of ageism in the workplace into relief, and politicians began discussing making such discrimination illegal.

**Agenbite of inwit.** The remorse of conscience. The expression was a literary revival by James Joyce in *Ulysses* (1922) of the title, *Ayenbite of Inwyt*, of Dan Michel of Northgate's translation (1340) of a French medieval moral treatise.

*Ayenbite* is a Middle English translation (literally meaning 'again-bite') of Medieval Latin *remorsum*, the source of English 'remorse', and *Inwyt* a similar translation of Latin *conscientia*, the source of modern 'conscience'.

> His hands plunged and rummaged in his trunk while he called for a clean handkerchief. Agenbite of inwit.
> JAMES JOYCE: *Ulysses*, I (1922)

**Agent Orange.** A type of herbicide containing a deadly toxin (dioxin), notorious from its use by the US forces in the Vietnam War (1964–75) in order to defoliate trees that might provide cover for the VIET CONG and North Vietnamese forces and also to destroy crops that might feed the enemy. The substance affects not only plant life but also humans (although the users were not aware of this at the time), as a result of which much of Vietnam's agricultural economy was ruined and infant birth defects subsequently appeared, both in Vietnam and in the United States among military families. The name derives from the distinctive orange stripe on the preparation's packaging. Similarly colour-coded herbicides are Agent White, Agent Purple and Agent Blue.

**Age of Aquarius.** In NEW AGE terminology, the period that began in the 1960s when peace, freedom, brotherhood and the conquest of space all seemed perfectly feasible.

> When the moon is in the seventh house
> And Jupiter aligns with Mars,
> Then peace will guide the planets,
> And love will steer the stars;
> This is the dawning of the age of Aquarius,
> The age of Aquarius.
> JAMES RADO and GERMONE RAGNI: the musical *Hair* (1966)

**Age of consent.** The age at which consent to sexual intercourse (heterosexual or homosexual) is legal. In English and Scottish law it is 16. The age of consent to homosexual intercourse in private was set at 21 in 1967 and lowered to 18 in 1994. A government vote in favour of a further lowering of the latter age to 16 was overturned in 1998 by the House of Lords but again passed on a second reading in 1999. It was rejected for a second time by the Lords that same year, but once again passed by the Commons in 2000, when the government announced its intention to invoke the Parliament Act to force it into law, which duly came about. In the United States the age of consent varies from 14 to 18, depending on the individual state.

**Age of criminal responsibility.** In England and Wales a child of 10 is deemed to be sufficiently mature to be prosecuted for an offence. In Scotland the equivalent age is eight, while in Ireland it is only seven. In many other countries the age of criminal responsibility is significantly higher. In Canada it is 12, in France 13, in Germany 14 and in Spain 16.

**Age of Innocence, The.** A novel by Edith Wharton (1862–1937), published in 1920. The book is set in 1870s New York, and the title is tinged with irony. Wharton portrays a time when established society is anxious to keep out 'the "new people" whom New York was beginning to dread and yet be drawn to'. The story concerns the love of a successful lawyer, Newland Archer, for the unconventional, witty and experienced *femme du monde*, Ellen Olenska, separated wife of a Polish count. ('There is no woman in American literature as fascinating as the doomed Madame Olenska', opined Gore Vidal.) However:

> … what was or was not 'the thing' played a part as important in Newland Archer's New York as the inscrutable totem terrors that had ruled the destinies of his forefathers thousands of years ago.

In the end, social pressure obliges Archer to marry his eminently suitable and beautiful fiancée, May Welland.

Martin Scorsese directed a star-studded and reasonably well-received film of the novel (1993).

**Age of puberty.** In English law the age at which puberty begins is usually reckoned as 14 in boys and 12 in girls. In practice it usually occurs between the ages of 10 and 15 in both sexes, and there are exceptions either side of this range.

**Agitprop.** The purveying of left-wing (usually communist) propaganda by means of theatre, cinema, art and the like. The word derives from a borrowing of the Russian *agitprop*, itself from the phrase *agitatsiya i propaganda* ('agitation and propaganda'). The Russian term was first used by the Marxist writer Georgy Plekhanov (1856–1918), who defined and compared the two. His ideas were developed by LENIN in his 1902 pamphlet *What is to be Done?* After the 1917 OCTOBER REVOLUTION special propaganda trains were sent all over the country, and in the 1920s Agitprop was the name given to the bureau of the Central Committee of the Communist Party of the Soviet Union responsible for propaganda. Subsidiary agitprop units were established throughout the USSR.

Outside the specific Soviet context, the word came to be used more loosely for any not-too-subtle attempt to get across a socially or politically radical message in plays, films, etc., for example in the counter-cultural movements of the 1960s and 1970s.

**Agonizing reappraisal.** A reassessment of a policy or stance that has been painfully forced on one by a radical change of circumstance or by a realization of what the existing

circumstances actually are. The expression comes from a speech by the US statesman and international lawyer John Foster Dulles:

> If … the European Defence Community should not become effective; if France and Germany remain apart … that would compel an agonizing reappraisal of basic United States policy.
>
> Speech to Nato Council, 14 December 1953, quoted in
> *New York Times* (15 December 1953)

**Agony and the Ecstasy, The.** A fictional biography (1961) by Irving Stone (1903–89) of Michelangelo (1475–1564), sculptor, painter, poet and the architect of St Peter's in Rome, in which latter capacity he had to combat fierce political infighting to achieve his aims. The book is prefaced with a quotation from Michelangelo:

> The best of artists have no thought to show which the rough stone in its superfluous shell doth not include; to break the marble spell is all the hand that serves the brain can do.

The title echoes the sonnet on liberty 'To Toussaint L'Ouverture' by William Wordsworth (1770–1850):

> Thy friends are exultation, agonies,
> And love, and man's unconquerable mind.

It also recalls Walter Pater (1839–94):

> To burn always with this hard gem-like flame, to maintain this ecstasy, is success in life.
>
> From *Studies in the History of the Renaissance*.

A film (1965), directed by Carol Reed and loosely based on Stone's novel, depicted the artistic clashes between Michelangelo, played by Charlton Heston, and Pope Julius II, played by Rex Harrison, during the painting of the Sistine Chapel. The original version of the film, now rarely seen, included a 15-minute introduction about the works of Michelangelo, so that audiences would not confuse him with any other artist of the same name.

**Agony aunt.** A person, traditionally a woman, who conducts an advice column or page in newspapers or magazines (especially those targeted at women), answering correspondents who seek help with their problems. Many of the letters are from female readers and are concerned with such matters as family relationships, marital problems, sex and boyfriends. The male equivalent is an 'agony uncle', and a recent development in some publications has been to have both and 'uncle' and an 'aunt' replying to questions, presumably for balance.

**Agree to disagree.** To cease discussion because neither side will compromise; to agree to differ.

**Aha reaction.** In psychiatric jargon the sudden achievement of insight or illumination, especially in creative thinking. The allusion is to the involuntary exclamation 'Aha!' on making some discovery. The term dates from the 1970s and replaced the earlier 'aha experience' of the 1950s. Similar is the 'aha moment', as the instant when such an insight occurs or the discovery is made.

**Ahead of the game.** To 'keep or stay ahead of the game' is to maintain an advantage over others in a competitive situation. The 'game' here is literally sporting but is usually understood as meaning a business or interest, as in 'What's your game?' The phrase dates from the 1970s.

**AIDS.** The acronym of acquired immune deficiency syndrome, a disease in which the body loses most of its cellular immunity, so lowering the resistance to infection and malignancy. The cause is a virus known as HIV (human immunodeficiency virus) transmitted in blood and sexual fluids, and there is a lengthy incubation period. The disease was initially always fatal, although there are now effective drug treatments. It was first identified in the early 1980s and has affected millions of people worldwide, initially spreading in the West among homosexuals, intravenous drug users and recipients of infected blood transfusions. Its prevalence in the Western world has, until very recently, overshadowed its epidemic devastation in Africa, where it is transmitted chiefly through heterosexual contact, and where the availability of effective drugs is severely limited. *See also* GRID; HIV-POSITIVE.

**Aiken's Solution.** A strategy regarding the Vietnam War, encapsulated by the press as 'Claim victory and retreat', suggested in a speech to the US Senate in 1966 by the Republican George Aiken (1892–1984):

> The United States could well declare unilaterally that this stage of the Vietnam War is over – that we have 'won' in the sense that our Armed Forces are in control of most of the field and no potential enemy is in a position to establish its authority over South Vietnam.

Of the eventual withdrawal of US forces in 1973, Aiken commented: 'What we got was essentially what I recommended … we said we had won and we got out.'

**AIM.** The initials of American Indian Movement, a militant civil rights organization in the United States and Canada, founded in 1968, which sought the restoration of property and other rights granted by treaties.

**Aircraft names.** Many 20th-century aircraft became familiar as much from their names as from their role or appearance. The following is a selection of some of the better known, with reasons for the adoption. The first word is the manufacturer's name, with which the aircraft name often intentionally alliterates. The date is that of the aircraft's first flight.

Avro *Anson* (1933): for Sir George Anson (1697–1762), admiral and circumnavigator

Avro *Lancaster* (1941): for the Wars of the Roses between the Houses of Lancaster and York

Avro *Vulcan* (1952): for the Roman god of fire, an appropriate name for the heavy bomber

Bristol *Beaufighter* (1939): from the Bristol *Beaufort* torpedo bomber (1938) and 'fighter'

Bristol *Blenheim* (1936): for the English defeat of the French at the Battle of Blenheim (1704)

Bristol *Bulldog* (1927): an appropriate name for the single-seater fighter

de Havilland *Gipsy Moth* (1931): Sir Geoffrey de Havilland (1882–1965) was a lepidopterist

de Havilland *Mosquito* (1940): for the bomber's 'sting' (its bombs) and the whine of its engine

English Electric *Lightning* (1958): for the fighter's high speed and strike power

Fairey *Swordfish* (1934): for the naval aircraft's role as a torpedo bomber

Gloster *Gladiator* (1934): an appropriate name for the biplane fighter

Gloster *Meteor* (1943): for the jet fighter's speed and strike power

Handley Page *Halifax* (1939): for the historic Yorkshire city

Hawker *Harrier* (1966): for the fighter's ability to hunt its prey like a harrier (dog or bird)

Hawker *Hunter* (1951): for the fighter's aggressive role and speed of search for its prey

Hawker *Hurricane* (1935): for the fighter's speed and strength

Sopwith *Camel* (1916): for the distinctive 'hump' in front of the pilot's cockpit

Supermarine *Southampton* (1921): for Southampton Water, site of the manufacturer's works

Supermarine *Spitfire* (1936): for the fighter's aggressive role and fire power

Vickers *Vimy* (1917): for the Canadian victory at Vimy Ridge, France, in the First World War

Vickers *Wellington* (1936): for Arthur Wellesley, Duke of Wellington (1769–1852)

Westland *Lysander* (1936): for Lysander (d.395 BC), Spartan naval and military commander

*See also* AIR FORCE ONE.

**Airey house.** A house built from precast concrete sections.

Houses of this type were first constructed in the 1920s by the firm of William Airey & Son Ltd, a Leeds engineering company founded by Sir Edwin Airey (1878–1955).

**Air Force One.** The official aircraft of the president of the United States. A film thriller (1997) of this title, depicting a fictitious hijacking of Air Force One by Russian terrorists, was directed by Wolfgang Petersen and starred Harrison Ford as President James Marshall.

When in 2005 Tony Blair suggested that a similar aircraft be purchased for the use of himself and other government ministers (rather than chartering aircraft on an ad hoc basis), the proposed airliner was inevitably dubbed 'Blair Force One'.

**Air freshener.** A substance or device for making the air in a room smell fresh and clean on the one hand and masking unpleasant odours on the other, particularly in bathrooms and kitchens. Air fresheners are of US origin and were in some cases misapplied when introduced in Britain in the 1950s.

The manufacturers of Airwick, a freshener operated by withdrawing and exposing an impregnated pad from a bottle of liquid, found it necessary to include in the instructions for use: 'Do not try to light wick. Wick will not burn.'

**Air guitar.** In a literal sense, an imaginary guitar that one goes through the motions of playing, as rock fans took to doing in the 1980s at HEAVY METAL concerts. Since the mid-1990s the World Air Guitar Championships have been held at the Oulu Music Festival in Finland, and the event is promoted as a means of furthering world peace: the Festival's website features a cartoon of Osama BIN LADEN and George W. Bush (DUBYA) playing air guitar.

In a figurative sense an air guitarist is a speaker of empty rhetoric or one who makes hollow promises.

> Tony Blair has always been the air-guitarist of political rhetoric, standing in front of the mirror of publicity while aping the convictions of others.
> *Independent on Sunday* (3 October 1999)

**Airhead.** A silly or foolish person, who has 'nothing up top'. The term arose as US teenage slang in the 1970s. *See also* BIMBO; HIMBO; VALLEY GIRL.

**Air Miles.** A proprietary incentive scheme launched in the early 1980s by which points equivalent to miles of free air travel are awarded to purchasers of airline tickets or other products such as groceries from supermarkets.

**Airmiss.** An instance of two aircraft in flight on different routes being less than a prescribed distance apart. Such incidents were an increasing cause for concern from the 1960s. An example is that of June 1999 when a Korean Air freight flight came within 183m (200 yards) of a British Airways JUMBO JET flying from London to Hong Kong. Only rapid evading action by the latter averted disaster.

**Airport novel.** A light novel, such as a thriller, sold at airports for passengers to purchase and read during their flight. Similar novels are sold at railway stations. The term is also applied to the genre of such fiction.

**Air raids.** The first offensive use of aircraft was by the Italians in Libya in 1911. The first raid on a town by a German ZEPPELIN followed in 1914, when Lunéville, France, was attacked in this way, and the first air raid on Britain by German aeroplanes came soon after. In the Second World War daily German air raids on Britain began on 18 June 1940 (*see* the BLITZ). Attacks by V-1s followed in 1944. The Allies mounted their first heavy raids on German targets in 1943, and air raids have formed a part of almost every subsequent engagement, such as the Arab–Israeli conflicts of 1948–94, the FALKLANDS WAR, the GULF WAR, the Balkan conflicts of the 1990s, and the invasions of Afghanistan (2001–2) and Iraq (2003). However, mass bombing ('carpet bombing'), especially of civilian targets, has generally given way to the precision-guided weaponry such as the SMART BOMB. *See also* DRESDEN; GUERNICA.

**Aka.** The abbreviation of 'also known as', as 'Cassius Clay, aka Muhammad Ali'. It dates from the early 1970s but had previously long been used in law and business and especially by police departments in the United States instead of 'alias', which denotes a false or assumed name, whereas 'aka' merely indicates another name that may or may not be used by someone to conceal his or her original identity. It is sometimes used to denote a synonym, especially when explaining slang terms or jargon, as 'rug, aka wig'.

**Akela.** The adult leader of a pack of Cub Scouts (formerly WOLF CUBS). The word is the name of the 'great grey Lone Wolf, who led all the Pack by strength and cunning' in Rudyard Kipling's *Jungle Books* (1894, 1895), the name itself being the Hindi word for 'single', 'solitary'.

**AK-47.** *See* KALASHNIKOV.

**Aladdin Sane.** *See* ZIGGY STARDUST.

**Alamein, El.** A town on the northern coast of Egypt, about 80km (50 miles) west of Alexandria, which gave its name to one of the most decisive battles of the Second World War. In June 1942 the British 8th Army, under the command of Claude Auchinleck (*see* AUK), took up a defensive position along a 65-km (40-mile) line between El Alamein and the impassable Qattara Depression. The first Battle of Alamein (1–3 July) saw the 8th Army successfully repel an attack by the German AFRIKA KORPS under Erwin Rommel (*see* DESERT FOX), so preventing the Germans from reaching the Nile Delta. The British reinforced the defences through the summer, and in August Bernard Montgomery (*see* MONTY) was put in charge of the 8th Army, with Harold Alexander (1891–1969) replacing Auchinleck as overall commander in chief in the Middle East. In the second Battle of Alamein, also known as the Battle of Alam Halfa (30 August– 6 September), the 8th Army again repelled a German advance. In the third and most significant battle (23 October–4 November) the 8th Army went on the offensive, defeating Rommel's AXIS forces and pursuing them westwards. On 8 November Allied forces landed in northwest Africa, and Rommel became caught between two large enemy armies.

> It may almost be said, 'Before Alamein we never had a victory. After Alamein we never had a defeat.'
>
> WINSTON CHURCHILL: *Second World War*, vol. 4, ch. 33 (1951)

**Alarmed.** Fitted with an automatic alarm. The word in this usage dates from the 1960s but can still read strangely in a notice such as: 'This door is alarmed.'

**Albatross.** A source of misfortune or guilt; a burden. The use of the word in this sense is first recorded in the 1930s, but the allusion is to Samuel Taylor Coleridge's poem *The Rime of the Ancient Mariner* (1798) in which the Ancient Mariner shoots the albatross, a 'pious bird of good omen'. As a result, the ship is becalmed, all suffer, and his companions hang the bird around his neck as a punishment.

> This [Victoria and Albert] museum was founded on radical principles, but then got weighed down by its huge collection, which has become like an albatross round its neck.
>
> *The Times* (13 October 1999)

**Albert Herring.** An unusually comic opera by Benjamin Britten (1913–76) with a libretto by Eric Crozier, based on the short story 'Le Rosier de Mme Husson' (1888) by Guy de Maupassant (1850–93). It was first performed at Glyndebourne in 1947 to a mixed reception, *The Times* commenting: 'Mr Britten is still pursuing his old problem of seeing how much indigestible material he can dissolve in music … the result is a charade.' Albert Herring is a young shopkeeper who is dominated by his mother. As he is more virtuous than the local girls he is made May King, becomes drunk and liberates himself from his mother and other local puritans. In Maupassant's version the hero dies of alcoholism.

**Alcatraz.** (Spanish *Isla de los Alcatraces*, 'island of the

pelicans'.) A notorious US prison on the rocky island of the same name in San Francisco Bay. First used as a place of detention for military offenders in 1868, it later accommodated civilian prisoners. From 1934 it housed the most dangerous civilian criminals, including such figures of infamy as Al CAPONE, George 'Machine Gun' Kelly and Robert Stroud, the BIRDMAN OF ALCATRAZ. A shortage of water eventually led to the abandonment of the penitentiary in 1963. Following subsequent abortive Sioux Native American claims on the island, it became part of the Golden Gate National Recreation Area in 1972 and is now open to visitors. The name has been adopted for any secure or forbidding prison or place of confinement.

**Alcock and Brown.** The two British aviators, John Alcock (1892–1919) and Arthur Brown (1886–1948), who made the first non-stop flight across the Atlantic (14–15 June 1919). They made the flight in a converted Vickers Vimy bomber, taking off from Newfoundland and landing in a bog in Ireland 16 hours and 12 minutes later, having covered a distance of 3040km (1824 miles). The two men were knighted and received a £10,000 prize from the *Daily Mail*. A few months later Alcock died after a plane crash.

**Alcoholics Anonymous.** This self-help organization for those fighting the 'battle of the bottle' was founded in the United States in 1935 by William G. Wilson ('Bill W') and Robert H. Smith ('Dr Bob'). A branch was established in Britain in 1947, and in 2002 there were 100,000 groups registered in 150 countries. Members identify themselves only by first name at meetings. Its abbreviation is AA; and in spite of it being confusable in the UK with the identically abbreviated Automobile Association, the drinkers' 'AA' is still in common usage.

**Alcopop.** A blend of 'alcohol' and 'pop', like the drinks themselves, consisting of lemonade or some other soft drink to which alcohol has been added. Alcopops emerged on the market in the mid-1990s to tempt the younger drinker and predictably drew criticism that resulted in a lowering of the alcohol content in some brands and a modification of the description in others. Many brands of alcopops bear names that smack of raffishness, such as Hooch, Two Dogs, Wildbrew, Lemonhead or Barking Frog, although more recent brands aim for something 'cooler', such as Smirnoff Ice and Bacardi Breezer. The drinks companies refer to these products generically as FABs (flavoured alcoholic beverages) or RTDs (ready-to-drinks).

**Aldeburgh Festival.** The annual music festival in this small Suffolk resort was established in 1948 by Benjamin Britten (1913–76), who took up residence in the town after the

Second World War. For 20 years the event was held in local village halls and churches, but in 1967 Britten and his lifelong partner, the tenor Peter Pears (1910–86), bought the Maltings, a riverside barn in the nearby village of Snape, and converted it into a concert hall. It was destroyed by fire on its opening night but was rebuilt in time for the following year's festival. Many of Britten's works were written to be performed at Aldeburgh, and the festival soon became an international event and place of pilgrimage for lovers of its founder's music. Owing to the sexual orientation of Britten and Pears, a mischievous William Walton gave Aldeburgh the nickname 'Aldebugger' (*see also* BUGGER'S OPERA).

**Aldermaston.** *See* CND.

**Aldwych farce.** One of 10 farces by Ben Travers (1886–1980), staged at the Aldwych Theatre, London. The first was *A Cuckoo in the Nest* (1925). *Rookery Nook* (1927) followed, and the series ended with *Dirty Work* (1932) and *A Bit of a Test* (1933). The plays combined absurdly improbable situations, eccentric characters and broad humour with social satire. Most were filmed.

**Aleatory music.** (Latin *alea*, 'dice'.) A term used in modern music for a work in which the composer deliberately allows for chance occurrences or choices by performers. The concept was introduced by the US composer Charles Ives (1874–1954), some of whose scores incorporate an intentional randomness or even unrealizable notations that invite the performer to find a solution. Other composers to adopt the construct include Karlheinz Stockhausen (b.1928), Pierre Boulez (b.1925) and, taking the technique to its extremity, John Cage (1912–92).

**Alexander technique.** A system of ALTERNATIVE treatment designed to improve a patient's posture so that the body can work in a more relaxed and efficient manner. It arose in the 1930s and is named after Frederick Alexander (1869–1955), the Australian-born actor who developed it.

**Alexandra Rose Day.** A day in June when rose emblems are sold for the hospital fund inaugurated on 26 June 1912 by Queen Alexandra (1844–1925), Danish consort of Edward VII, to celebrate the 50th year of her residence in England.

**Alf.** In Australia, the archetype of the ordinary working-class bloke, conservative-to-reactionary in attitudes. A coinage of the late 1950s, it exploits the old-fashionedness of the male name 'Alf(red)'. *See also* ROY.

**Al Fatah.** (Arabic, 'the victory'.) A Palestinian political and military organization founded in 1958 by Yasser Arafat (1929–2004) with the aim of creating a Palestinian state. The PLO evolved from it. Al Fatah lost its hold on power in the

Palestinian Authority following a surprise defeat by the more militant Hamas in 2006.

**Alf Garnett.** *See* Alf GARNETT.

**Alfie.** A film (1966) based on a play by Bill Naughton (1910–92). Starring Michael Caine as the cheeky cockney misogynist, Alfie, who is permanently on the look-out for more 'birds' to add to his collection of sexual conquests, the film, with its frank confessions to camera, was considered a daring exploration of sexual morals in London of the SWINGING SIXTIES, and for a time the very title was synonymous with the so-called 'permissive society'. A sequel, *Alfie Darling* (1975), starring Alan Price in the lead role, failed to match the provocative exuberance of its predecessor. Even less notable was the 2004 remake of *Alfie*, starring Jude Law.

**ALGOL.** *See* PROGRAMMING LANGUAGES.

**Algonquin Round Table.** An informal group of American literary people who met daily for lunch on weekdays at a large round table at the Algonquin Hotel, New York, in the 1920s and 1930s. The Algonquin Round Table first met in 1919, and its members soon included some of the best-known writers, journalists and artists in New York, among them Dorothy Parker (1893–1967), Alexander Woollcott (1887–1943), Heywood Broun (1888–1939), Robert Benchley (1889–1945), Robert Sherwood (1896–1955), George S. Kaufman (1889–1961), Franklin P. Adams (1881–1960), Marc Connelly (1890–1980), Harold Ross (1892–1951), Harpo Marx (*see* MARX BROTHERS) and Russel Crouse (1893–1966). The gathering gradually thinned, however, and the last meeting was held in 1943.

**Alice band.** A flexible band used to hold back the hair, as worn by Alice in John Tenniel's illustrations for Lewis Carroll's *Through the Looking-Glass* (1872), but not those for *Alice in Wonderland* (1865), in which her hair falls free. Alice bands are favoured by female SLOANE RANGERS, and (at least for a period in 2003) by footballer David Beckham (*see* POSH AND BECKS).

**Alice blue.** A light greenish-blue colour, as that of the dresses worn at the turn of the 20th century by the dashing young American socialite Alice Lee Roosevelt (1884–1980), daughter of Theodore Roosevelt. The popular song 'Alice Blue Gown' (1919), by Joseph McCarthy and Harry Tierney, further promoted the fashion for the colour.

**Alice in Wonderland.** A nickname in royal circles for Princess Alice, Countess of Athlone (1883–1981), granddaughter of Queen Victoria, who was an avid reader of Lewis Carroll's books.

**Alien.** A well-regarded SCIENCE FICTION horror film (1979) starring Sigourney Weaver as Ripley, the human opponent of a lethal and apparently invulnerable species of alien monster. The success of the film inspired the sequels, *Aliens* (1986) and *Alien 3* (1992). While the second film was considered to be on a par with the first, the third was relatively poorly received. By the end of the series one critic was moved to parody the slogan under which the films were publicized, 'In space no one can hear you scream', as 'In space no one can hear you snore'. Actors in the third film, set in a space penal colony, informally renamed the movie *Skinheads in Space*. There was another (again rather weak) sequel, *Alien Resurrection*, in 1997.

**Alienation effect.** *See* EPIC THEATRE.

**Aliens.** A blanket term for the creatures or beings from outer space that are believed by the credulous to have invaded earth at various times from the 19th century or that are expected to do so at any moment in the future. LITTLE GREEN MEN are one fairly innocuous type, but others are much more sinister and destructive, like those in SCIENCE FICTION or HORROR MOVIES. One of the latter, ALIEN (1979), was a great commercial success and did much to popularize the term. Reports of human beings (in almost every case Americans) abducted by aliens have mostly been met with equal scepticism, although some individual accounts of the experience have intrigued a gullible public. Budd Hopkins's book *Witnessed: The True Story of the Brooklyn Bridge Abduction* (1996) describes his investigations into the claimed abduction of Linda Cortile from a high-rise Manhattan apartment block in 1989. *See also* CLOSE ENCOUNTER; MEN IN BLACK; SETI; UFO.

> There is the problem that from H.G. Wells's *War of the Worlds* onwards there has been only one plot: aliens arrive, wreak havoc, catastrophe imminent, Achilles' heel discovered, world saved.
>
> *The Times* (11 May 1998)

**Ali G.** The painfully supercool HIP-HOP character created by the comedian Sacha Baron Cohen (b.1971) for Channel 4's *Eleven O'Clock Show* in 1998. He subsequently had his own programme, *Da Ali G Show* (2000). He talks the mysterious talk and wears the right gear, but comes from a decidedly uncool suburban background (his gang is the West Staines MASSIVE); his comicality is based on the incongruities thus set up. His interviews, in which he put embarrassing questions to celebrities apparently unaware that he was a fictional character, made him a cult figure, and caused confusion when he was given a series in the United States. He ventured into the cinema with *Ali G Indahouse* (2002).

Since the success of Ali G, Cohen has created Borat, a moustachioed television reporter from Kazakhstan, whose comments on his native land's 'culture' (in Borat's world, a comical cocktail of macho primitivism and unusual practices with animals) have enraged the Kazakh authorities.

**A-line.** The shape of a garment, especially a dress or skirt, which is flared from the shoulder or waist and which thus looks like a capital letter A. The design was created in the mid-1950s by the French couturier Christian Dior. *See also* DIOR LOOK.

**A-list.** A potential or actual list of the most famous or socially sought-after people, the whole forming a super-elite or 'crème de la crème'. The letter A implies a hierarchy, so that in theory there could be a B-list, a C-list, etc., and even a Z-list consisting of the least desirable individuals. Dubbing someone a 'C-list celebrity' is usually regarded as a fairly crushing put-down. The concept is of US origin and dates from the mid-1980s.

> The other 12 [television channels] consist entirely of F-list celebrities going up the Nile in mismatched leisure-wear for various lifestyle and travel causes.
>
> *The Times* (19 November 1999)

*See also* CELEBRITY CULTURE; HELLO!; REALITY TV.

**Alive and well.** Flourishing, despite suggestions to the contrary. The 19th-century phrase came to be extended from the 1950s to include a place-name, as 'Alive and well and living in Luton' (or wherever). This formula was popularized by the title of the cabaret-style revue celebrating the songs of the Belgian composer and writer Jacques Brel, *Jacques Brel is Alive and Well and Living in Paris*, which opened OFF-BROADWAY at the Village Gate, New York, on 22 January 1968.

**Al-Jazeera.** (Arabic, 'the island', 'the peninsula'.) An Arabic-language satellite-television news broadcaster, based in and funded by the state of Qatar, in the Persian Gulf. Its name refers to the Arabian peninsula. Established in 1996, it achieved particular prominence as the conduit through which AL-QAIDA addressed itself, via clandestinely produced videos, to the West.

Al-Jazeera disclaims any links to terrorist organizations, but it nevertheless became a bugbear to President George W. Bush. It was alleged in 2005 that Bush has expressed a desire to bomb its headquarters, even though they were based in a country friendly to the United States. It has also managed to annoy a number of Middle Eastern regimes who would prefer their citizens to be exposed to state-controlled news media only.

***All About Eve.*** A film (1950) adapted by Joseph L. Mankiewicz from the short story 'The Wisdom of Eve' by Mary Orr. The plot concerns the vicious rivalry that develops between a fading Broadway star (Bette Davis) and the ruthless younger actress (Anne Baxter) who seeks to supplant her. Eve is not, in fact, the Davis character as might be expected, but Baxter's role. The story was later (1970) turned into a musical, *Applause*, which opened in New York with Lauren Bacall in Davis's role of Margo Channing.

> Margo (Bette Davis): Fasten your seat belts, it's going to be a bumpy night.
>
> JOSEPH L. MANKIEWICZ: *All About Eve*

**All-American boy.** *See* Jack ARMSTRONG.

**All animals are equal, but some are more equal than others.** *See* ANIMAL FARM.

**All Blacks.** The nickname of the New Zealand international rugby union team. It refers to the colour of their strip and was first made public by the *Daily Mail* at the beginning of their 1905 tour of Britain. The story goes that a reporter met the team as they landed at Plymouth and asked the colour of their shirts, shorts and socks. A player answered 'Black' to each of these, and then added by way of emphasis, 'we're all black'. The newspaper headline the following morning was: 'The All Blacks have arrived!' According to another account, the name originated during the same tour when a reporter dubbed the players 'all backs', which was subsequently misprinted. If their strip clashes with that of an opposing team the All Blacks reluctantly resort to an alternative in the form of white shirts and black shorts. This has happened when they have played against the dark colours of Scotland and in seven-a-side competitions. *See also* BLACK CAPS; BLACK FERNS; TALL BLACKS.

**All Bran.** The proprietary name of a breakfast cereal invented in the 1920s by John L. Kellogg, son of W.K. Kellogg (1860–1951), founder of the Kellogg Company. The cereal arose as a convenient way of using up the bran left over from other products. It has long been discreetly promoted for its laxative properties, using euphemistic slogans such as 'Join the "regulars" with Kellogg's All-Bran'.

**All dressed up and nowhere to go.** Ready for action but not required. The source of the line is the title of a song by Silvio Hein and Benjamin Burt, 'When You're All Dressed Up and No Place to Go'. The song was part of Raymond Hitchcock's musical *The Beauty Shop*, first staged at the Astor Theatre on Broadway in 1913 and produced in London in 1916. 'No place', rather than 'nowhere', betrays the song's US origin.

**Allen charge.** In US law a charge or instruction to a hung jury, in which the judge urges dissenting jurors to reconsider their views out of deference to the majority and at the same time to do their best to reach a verdict. The reference is to the case of Allen *v.* United States (1897) in which the charge was first used. The term itself dates from the 1950s.

**Allergy.** Properly, a medical term for a damaging immune response by the body to a substance to which it has become hypersensitive. Foods such as eggs, shellfish and nuts cause allergies in some people as often do 'fluffy' substances such as pollen, fur or dust. The word has come to be used colloquially to denote an antipathy to something, and the corresponding adjective 'allergic' is frequently found in this role, as: 'He's allergic to work'. The term itself dates from the early 20th century and arose from German *Allergie*, in turn from Greek *allos*, 'different', and *ergon*, 'action'. It was not until about the 1950s, however, that the word became generally familiar in English.

**Alley cat.** A cat that lives wild in a town. The term is of US origin, so an alley here approximates to an English mews. The expression became current in the 1920s for a promiscuous woman: an alley cat scrounges for food as a prostitute touts for clients. The best-known example of a literal alley cat is the eponymous hero of the US animated series *Top Cat* (1961–2), produced by the Hanna-Barbera Studio.

**Alleyn, Roderick.** The Old Etonian policeman who is the central character in over 30 crime novels by the New Zealand writer Ngaio Marsh (1899–1982), beginning with *A Man Lay Dead* (1934). He ages realistically throughout the series, and in *Last Ditch* (1977) his son Ricky takes over the role of detective.

**All Gas and Gaiters.** A television SITCOM broadcast in five series between 1967 and 1971 and making gentle fun of the church. The plot centres on the ecclesiastical rivalry at St Oggs cathedral with Derek Nimmo in the key role as a naive and accident-prone cleric. The title, expressing pompousness, comes from Dickens. Gaiters are part of a bishop's traditional costume.

**All girls together.** Women on terms of close friendship with one another, or engaged in intimate or revealing conversation. The phrases implies a collective enterprise that for each woman, individually, would seem unlikely.

***All God's Chillun Got Wings.*** A play (1924) by the US playwright Eugene O'Neill (1888–1953) about the marriage of an African American man and a white American woman. The play provoked a violent reaction when it was first presented in New York, with one outraged newspaper carrying the headline: 'White Actress Kisses Negro's Hand.'

The title refers to the truth that all humans are equal in God's eyes, no matter what their colour.

**Alliance.** The name used by the Liberal Party and the Social Democrats when campaigning together from 1983 until the two merged in 1988 as the LIBERAL DEMOCRATS.

**All men are rapists.** An assertion by a character in *The Women's Room* (1977), a novel by the US writer Marilyn French (b.1929), and since taken up by feminists of the more separatist, SCUM-ish persuasion.

> Whatever they may be in public life, whatever their relations with men, in their relations with women, all men are rapists, and that's all they are. They rape us with their eyes, their laws, and their codes.

French has made it clear that these are not necessarily her own beliefs. The feminist Andrea Dworkin (1946–2005) expressed similar sentiments to French's character in a speech in New York in 1976:

> Seduction is often difficult to distinguish from rape. In seduction, the rapist bothers to buy a bottle of wine.

**All mouth and trousers.** Boastful and blustering; all talk and no action. A phrase commonly used by women about men, who may be loud-mouthed and who wear the male garment mentioned. Confusingly, 'all mouth and no trousers', a common variant, means exactly the same. *See also* FUR COAT AND NO KNICKERS.

**All My Sons.** A play (1947) by the US playwright Arthur Miller (1915–2005) about an aircraft manufacturer, Joe Keller, whose family life falls apart after revelations that his company knowingly allowed faulty cylinder heads to be fitted to P-40 fighters, leading to the deaths of 21 pilots in the US Air Force. One of Keller's two sons has already committed suicide from shame at his father's treachery, but the 'sons' of the title is understood to refer more widely to all the young pilots who have died.

**Allnutt, Charlie.** The hero of C.S. Forester's gripping novel *The* AFRICAN QUEEN (1935). He is a good-for-nothing riverboat engineer in Africa at the outbreak of the First World War and is persuaded by Rose Sayer, a missionary's wife, to join combat. They turn their leaky old craft, the *African Queen*, into a 'torpedo' and finally ram and sink a German gunboat. The role of Allnutt in the film of the book (1951) was memorably played by Humphrey Bogart.

**All one's Christmases have come at once.** One has been specially lucky or unusually favoured. Normally Christmas comes but once a year' and its pleasures are thus infrequent. *See also* CHRISTMAS HAS COME EARLY.

> I have recently found the man of my dreams … I'm in orbit and feel as if all my Christmases have come at once.
>
> TARA PALMER-TOMKINSON: in *Sunday Times* (8 August 1999)

**All Passion Spent.** A novel (1931) by Vita Sackville-West (1892–1962). Dedicated to her two sons 'Benedict and Nigel, who are young, the story of people who are old', it is a study of ageing and of independence in old age. The title comes from *Samson Agonistes* (1671) by John Milton:

> His servants he, with new acquist
> Of true experience from this great event,
> With peace and consolation hath dismissed,
> And calm of mind, all passion spent.

**All Power to the Soviets!** An article by Lenin, which appeared in *Pravda* on 18 July 1917, in which he declared:

> During the several months that have passed since February 27 the will of the majority of the workers and peasants, of the overwhelming majority of the country's population, has become clear in more than a general sense. Their will has found expression in mass organizations – the Soviets of Workers', Soldiers' and Peasants' Deputies. How, then, can anyone oppose the transfer of all power in the state to the Soviets? Such opposition means nothing but renouncing democracy!

'All power to the Soviets' became the slogan of the revolutionary workers of Petrograd (subsequently Leningrad, and now St Petersburg again). The Soviets duly took power in the OCTOBER REVOLUTION later that year.

**All Quiet on the Western Front.** A novel (1929; in German as *Im Westen Nichts Neues*, 1929) of the First World War by Erich Maria Remarque (1898–1970). Brutally realistic and written in the first person, it is prefaced with a statement: 'This book is to be neither an accusation nor a confession, and least of all an adventure, for death is not an adventure to those who stand face to face with it. It will try simply to tell of a generation of men who, even though they may have escaped its shells, were destroyed by the war.' In 1933 the book was publicly burned by the Nazis as being 'defeatist', and Remarque was deprived of his citizenship. The title is ironic. It refers to the fact that a whole generation of his countrymen was destroyed while newspapers reported that there was 'no news in the west'. The film version (1930), directed by Lewis Milestone and starring Lew Ayres, was a landmark of US cinema.

**All-singing, all-dancing.** Possessing a wealth of desirable attributes or features, like an elaborate musical show. The term came to be particularly associated with technical gadgetry. Its origin may ultimately lie in a series of posters produced in the latter half of the 1920s to promote the new 'talking' cinema. One such poster advertised the first HOLLYWOOD musical film *Broadway Melody* (1929) with the words 'All talking All singing All dancing'.

**All Souls' Parish Magazine.** *The Times* was so nicknamed during the editorship (1923–41) of G.G. Dawson, fellow of All Souls, Oxford. He and some of his associates, who were also fellows of the college, frequently met there for discussions.

**All systems go.** Everything is ready for immediate action. The catchphrase was popularized in the 1960s by broadcast commentaries of the launches of US spacecraft. 'Go' does not mean 'depart' but 'correctly functioning'.

**All that jazz.** All that sort of thing; and so on. A phrase usually following a list of examples. 'Jazz' here has a tone of disparagement.

> I offers you this handkerchief, now set
> your left foot by my right foot,
> shoulder to shoulder, all that jazz,
> arm in arm, by the beautiful sea.
> JOHN BERRYMAN: *The Dream Songs*, 'Dream Song 76' (1969)

*All That Jazz* is also the title of a partly autobiographical film musical (1979) written and directed by Bob Fosse.

**All the President's Men.** A film (1976) directed by Alan J. Pakula about the uncovering of the WATERGATE scandal, based on a book (1974) of the same title by the *Washington Post* journalists Bob Woodward and Carl Bernstein (played respectively by Robert Redford and Dustin Hoffman). The president of the title is Richard M. Nixon, and the title refers to the attempts of the president and others in the White House to cover up the scandal.

> We are the President's men and we must behave accordingly.
> HENRY KISSINGER: at the time of the illegal bombing and invasion of Cambodia, quoted in M. and B. Kalb, *Kissinger* (1974)

There is also an obvious echo of the nursery rhyme:

> Humpty Dumpty sat on a wall.
> Humpty Dumpty had a great fall.
> All the king's horses and all the king's men
> Couldn't put Humpty together again.

*See also* DEEP THROAT.

**All This and Heaven Too.** A romantic film melodrama (1940) starring Charles Boyer and Bette Davis, based on the bestselling novel (1938) by the US writer Rachel Field (1894–1942) about a French aristocrat who falls in love with the governess and murders his wife. The title phrase originates

with the otherwise obscure English clergyman, Philip Henry (1631–96), whose words 'All this, and heaven too!' were quoted in Matthew Henry's *Life of Mr Philip Henry* (1698). The title is played on in a film collage (1977) of the Second World War, *All This and World War Two*, directed by Susan Winslow.

**'All You Need is Love'.** A musically undistinguished song by The BEATLES, credited to John Lennon and Paul McCartney (but mostly by Lennon), and written specifically for a television programme entitled *Our World*, which linked 24 countries by global satellite in June 1967. Released as a single the following month (it reached Number 1 in the charts in both the UK and United States), its message of sing-along idealism and optimism made it an appropriate anthem for the SUMMER OF LOVE. Of passing interest are the musical 'quotations' contained in the song, from 'La Marseillaise' (the French national anthem), a keyboard piece by J.S. Bach, 'Greensleeves' and Glenn Miller's 'In the Mood', as well as its oddly alternating bars of three and four beats (which cover versions tend to simplify).

> There's nothing you can do that can't be done
> Nothing you can sing that can't be sung
> Nothing you can say but you can learn how to
>     play the game
> It's easy.

**Ally Pally.** The nickname of Alexandra Palace in Muswell Hill, North London, as the original headquarters of BBC Television. The first transmission was on 26 August 1936 as *Here's Looking at You*, a variety show introduced by Leslie Mitchell, and the nickname followed soon after.

**Almeida Theatre.** The 300-seat London theatre of this name, the brainchild of Pierre Audi, opened in Upper Street, Islington, in 1981 in the restored Islington Literary and Scientific Institute, built in 1837 and later a Salvation Army hostel. The theatre takes its name from Almeida Street, a short street off Upper Street here whose own name commemorates the Battle of Almeida (1811) in the Peninsular War. Since 1990, when the actors Ian McDiarmid and Jonathan Kent took over its artistic direction, the theatre has attracted leading British and overseas players, such as Alan Bates, Ian Holm, Glenda Jackson, Diana Rigg, Juliette Binoche and Kevin Spacey. At the beginning of the 21st century it closed for a radical rebuild, and reopened in 2003.

**Aloha State.** A nickname for Hawaii, which became the 50th state of the United States of America in 1959. 'Aloha' is a Hawaiian word meaning 'love', used to express affection or kind wishes as a greeting or farewell. An 'aloha party' is thus one held on the occasion of an arrival or departure, while an 'aloha shirt' is a loose and brightly coloured sports shirt, often worn by US tourists or holidaymakers.

**Along for the ride.** To be, come or go along for the ride is to do so for pleasure or interest rather than active participation. The image is that of a passive passenger. The expression is of US origin; it dates from the 1950s.

**Alphabet City.** In local parlance, the nickname for the Lower East Side of New York City, to the east of First Avenue. The sobriquet, first recorded in 1980, reflects the prominence of four local thoroughfares called Avenues A, B, C and D. It is a decidedly insalubrious quarter, the haunt of drug dealers and other criminals.

**Alphabet soup.** A type of clear soup containing pasta in the shape of letters. (In the 1930s Heinz first produced the brand Alphabetti Spaghetti of pasta in tomato sauce.) In the figurative sense alphabet soup is an incomprehensible or confusing language, especially when containing numerous abbreviations or symbols. *See also* ANIMAL CRACKERS.

**Al-Qaida.** (Arabic, 'the base', often transliterated as 'Al-Qaeda', especially in a US context.) The name of an anti-Western Islamic terrorist network founded in the early 1990s by Osama BIN LADEN, members of which are believed to have been among those responsible for the attacks on the WORLD TRADE CENTER and the PENTAGON on 11 September 2001 (*see* 9/11). Al-Qaida, which operates through a network of cells and training camps in a number of different countries, is also thought to have been behind an earlier attack on the World Trade Center in 1993, and the bombings of the US embassies in Nairobi (Kenya) and Dar-es-Salaam (Tanzania) in July 1998, which killed more than 200 people. Al-Qaida, or groups linked to it or inspired by it, have also been responsible for a range of other terrorist attacks on 'soft' Western targets: outrages include the Bali bombings of 2002 and 2005, the Madrid train bombings of 2004, and the London bombings in July 2005 (*see* 7/7). Since the overthrow of Saddam Hussein by Anglo-American forces in 2003, Iraq has also become a focus of Al-Qaida activity.

The network's extreme fundamentalist ideology is global in its aspirations for a world governed under religious 'Sharia' law, and it therefore finds itself in opposition to almost all manifestations of Western influence as well as to existing state borders and political regimes (particularly in the Middle East) as well as other religions. Such wide-ranging antipathies give Al-Qaida a unique flavour (and, in the eyes of most, lend it an air of dangerous derangement), in contrast to the often narrow and specific grievances of other terrorist groups.

**Also-ran.** An inferior or mediocre person or thing. Properly an 'also-ran' is a horse in a race that does not get a 'place', i.e. come second, third or fourth. The term gained its figurative sense in the 1920s.

**Altamont.** More fully Altamont Speedway, the site near San Francisco in California of a nightmarish concert by The ROLLING STONES in December 1969, regarded by some aficionados of popular culture (together with the MANSON MURDERS of the same year) as sounding a death-knell for the carefree optimism of the 1960s. The free concert, staged as a kind of second WOODSTOCK, turned to tragedy when three people died. The demise of one of the victims, stabbed to death by Hell's Angels acting as 'security guards' after he had aimed a gun at Mick Jagger as he sang 'SYMPATHY FOR THE DEVIL', was captured on camera. The concert can be seen in the film *Gimme Shelter* (1970).

**Alte, Der.** (German, 'The Old One'.) A nickname for Konrad Adenauer (1876–1967), the Christian Democrat chancellor of West Germany, who was 73 years old when he took office in 1949 and who served for a further 14 years.

**Alternative.** A word fairly consistently in vogue from the late 1960s to express some cultural or other value that differs from the norm. It had its roots in the 'alternative society', associated with the world of the HIPPIES, which was dubbed 'counter-culture' by academics but 'underground' by the media. 'Alternative medicine' also appeared at this time, favouring such procedures and remedies as homeopathy and acupuncture and today having its devotees among those who have become disillusioned with traditional medicine (but *see also* COMPLEMENTARY MEDICINE). The early 1970s saw the emergence of 'alternative technology' in a bid to conserve natural resources and prevent damage to the environment. Favoured renewable energy sources in this field were wind and solar power and more recently 'ground source' energy.

The 1980s saw the evolution of both 'alternative comedy' and 'alternative therapy'. The former, eschewing conventional comedy in favour of black or surreal humour, has been popularized on television by such performers as Dawn French and Jennifer Saunders or Vic Reeves and Bob Mortimer. Alternative therapy, a progression of alternative medicine, involves special psychiatric (or quasi-psychiatric) techniques, such as REBIRTHING, group counselling and other practices based on simplified Freudian theories and applications.

**Altmark.** In the Royal Navy an opprobrious synonym for a ship or an establishment with a reputation for very strict discipline. It derives from a famous naval exploit of

February 1940, when Captain (later Admiral of the Fleet) Philip Vian, commanding the destroyer HMS *Cossack*, entered Norwegian territorial waters to effect the release of 299 British prisoners of war from the German supply ship *Altmark*, which had taken refuge in Jossingfjord.

**Always the bridesmaid, never the bride.** A proverbial lament of those who fruitlessly long for connubial bliss. It may have originated in the 1917 song 'Why Am I Always the Bridesmaid?' by Charles Collins, Fred W. Leigh and Lily Morris:

> Why am I always the bridesmaid,
> Never the blushing bride?

**Amadeus Quartet.** One of Britain's best-known string quartets in the years after the Second World War. Three of its members, Norbert Brainin, Siegmund Nissel and Peter Schidlof, were teenage refugees from Vienna in 1938 and first met in an Isle of Man internment camp in the early years of the war. The quartet was formed in 1947 with Martin Lovett as the fourth member, and it continued until Schidlof's death in 1987. Brainin died in 2005. The name of the quartet was a tribute to Wolfgang Amadeus Mozart, whose first name furnished 'the Wolf Gang' as an affectionate nickname for the four. *See also* STRING QUARTETS.

**Amazon.** *See* NET BOOK AGREEMENT.

**Ambling Alp.** A nickname of the Italian-born American champion heavyweight boxer Primo Carnera (1906–67), alluding to his style and country of origin.

**Ambush marketing.** The practice of one company intruding itself into a promotion, sponsored event, etc. staged by another company in order to obtain free advertising for its own goods or services. An example in the summer of 2005 was a large poster for the Southern Electricity company prominently displayed within view of television cameras outside the Oval cricket ground during the playing of the fifth Test match against Australia, sponsored by npower (another electricity company).

**America, Captain.** *See* CAPTAIN AMERICA.

**American Beauty.** A variety of climbing rose, with deep pink flowers. It has made a number of appearances in popular culture. 'American Beauty Rag', a piece of classic ragtime by Joseph Lamb, was published in 1913. Later in the century Frank Sinatra sang a song called 'American Beauty Rose' (by David/Evans/Altman):

> Daisy is darling, Iris is sweet
> Lily is lovely, Blossom's a treat
> Of all the sweethearts a guy could meet
> Well I finally chose an American beauty rose.

In 1970 The Grateful Dead (*see* DEADHEADS) released an album entitled *American Beauty* (although the word 'beauty' on the cover, beneath a painting of a rose, could be read as 'reality'). Songs on it included 'Sugar Magnolia' and 'Truckin'' (*see* KEEP ON TRUCKING). The 1999 film *American Beauty*, directed by Sam Mendes, stars Kevin Spacey as a frustrated middle-aged man, in whose fantasies his daughter's schoolfriend is seen naked apart from a covering of rose petals.

**American Buffalo.** A classic modern American play (1975) by David Mamet (b.1947) about the bungled attempts of three small-time crooks to steal a coin collection. The title of the play, which effectively lampoons modern capitalism, refers to an old US buffalo-head nickel that one of them produces in the second act, a symbol of their preoccupation with financial gains and their perverted sense of the AMERICAN DREAM. Mamet wrote the screenplay for the film version (1996), which starred Dustin Hoffman, Dennis Franz and Sean Nelson.

**American Caesar.** A nickname for the US general Douglas MacArthur (1880–1964), commander of the Southwest Pacific Area Theatre in the Second World War, supreme allied commander in occupied Japan and then commander of the US and United Nations forces during the opening months of the Korean War (1950–53). The allusion was largely to his exaggerated accounts of his own accomplishments, on the lines of those of Julius Caesar ('I came, I saw, I conquered').

**American dream.** The concept that the US social, economic and political system makes success possible for every American. The expression appears to have been coined by the American historian James T. Adams in *The Epic of America* (1931). It was subsequently popularized by the titles of such works as Edward Albee's play *The American Dream* (1961) and Norman Mailer's novel *An American Dream* (1965), and the ambiguities and contradictions inherent in the theme have been dealt with in such works as Arthur Miller's DEATH OF A SALESMAN and David Mamet's AMERICAN BUFFALO.

> The American dream turned belly up, turned green, bobbed to the scummy surface of cupidity unlimited, filled with gas, went *bang* in the noonday sun.
> KURT VONNEGUT: *God Bless You, Mr Rosewater* (1965)

> In the beginning was the American Dream, and the American Dream said: you can have anything your heart desires. It's yours by right. Guess what? You can't. It isn't.
> ERICA WAGNER: in *The Times* (11 March 1999)

**American Express.** The Amex credit card, as it is often

known, was first issued in 1956 by the American Express Company, founded in 1850 as a company specializing in the express transportation of goods, valuables and specie between New York and Buffalo. Its first president and secretary were, respectively, Henry Wells (1805–75) and William G. Fargo (1818–81), later of Wells Fargo fame. *See also* ADVERTISING SLOGANS OF THE 20TH AND 21ST CENTURIES; THAT'LL DO NICELY, SIR.

**American Gothic.** Perhaps the most reproduced (and most parodied) American work of art of the 20th century was painted by Grant Wood (1891–1942) in 1930. Largely self-taught, Wood worked mainly in his native Iowa. The painting purports to be a portrait of a stern farmer-preacher and his daughter, the former holding a pitchfork, while behind is their house, with a simple Gothic window set in the gable end. Actually, Wood used his sister, Nan, and his dentist, B.H. McKeeby, as models for the painting. The title has been taken as satirical, although Wood's avowed intention was to reflect the values of provincial American life. The hard, cold style reflects the influence of north European Renaissance painting, which Wood absorbed during a visit to Munich in 1928.

A forgettable 1988 horror film (UK/Canada) shared the title *American Gothic*. 'American Gothic' is sometimes used as an alternative for 'Southern Gothic', the kind of 20th-century fetidly atmospheric novel set in the American South and often featuring characters on the margins of society. The genre was exemplified in the work of Carson McCullers (1917–67), such as *The Ballad of the Sad Café* (1951).

**American Graffiti.** An Oscar-winning teenage rites-of-passage film comedy (1973) directed by George Lucas and starring Richard Dreyfuss. It concerns the activities of a group of teenagers in a small American town in the early 1960s and was based on the director's own experiences of growing up in Modesto, in California's Central Valley. It features an array of nostalgic pop hits of the 1960s, the rights for which constituted a significant proportion of the film's entire budget.

**American in Paris, An.** A classic musical film (1951) that ranks among the most popular MGM productions of the golden age of the American musical. Directed by Vincente Minnelli, it stars Gene Kelly as a frustrated artist (thereby providing an excuse for lots of backdrops based on famous French paintings) and Leslie Caron. The film was based on the tone poem 'An American in Paris' (1928) by George Gershwin, and Ira Gershwin allowed the piece's title to be used for the film provided that his brother provided all the music for the movie. The title echoes the long-established

adage 'Good Americans, when they die, go to Paris', credited by Oliver Wendell Holmes to Thomas Appleton (1812–84). It was this saying that prompted Oscar Wilde in *A Woman of No Importance* (1893) to suggest that if good Americans went to Paris when they died, then bad Americans undoubtedly went to America. Ironically, the film was shot in the United States against specially built sets.

**'American Pie'.** The classic pop song of this name by Don McLean (b.1945), released in 1971 as a double-sided single lasting 8½ minutes, was a tribute to Buddy Holly (1936–59) and is full of allusions to other performers. The song is, in essence, a chronological account of American youth through the 1960s, with the emphasis on the latter years of the decade. Of the individual references, 'the Jester' is Bob Dylan; 'the King' is Elvis Presley; 'the Quartet' are The BEATLES; 'Jack Flash' is Mick Jagger of The ROLLING STONES; 'a girl who sang the blues' is Janis Joplin; and 'the Father, Son and Holy Ghost' are the three singers who died on Holly's plane (Holly himself, Richie Valens and J.P. Richardson, the 'Big Bopper') as well as the three most prominent US assassination victims of the 1960s, Martin Luther King, Robert Kennedy and John F. Kennedy (*see* KENNEDY CURSE). The song's non-musical allusions are less straightforward, although 'The players tried to take the field, / The marching band refused to yield' probably refers to the riots of 1968 at the Democrats' Chicago convention, while 'there we were all in one place' is almost certainly a reference to WOODSTOCK. When asked the meaning of the song, Don MacLean is wont to reply: 'It means I'll never have to work again if I don't want to.'

> So, bye, bye, Miss American Pie,
> Drove my Chevy to the levee but the levee was dry.
> Them good old boys was drinkin' whiskey and rye
> Singin' 'This'll be the day that I die.'
> DON MCLEAN: 'American Pie' (song) (1971)

*American Pie* is also the title of a comic and sometimes serious rite-of-passage film (1999) directed by Paul Weitz and with a screenplay by Adam Herz, in which four teenage boys attempt to lose their virginity before they graduate. Like the famous song, the title refers to the saying 'As American as mom's apple pie'. In the film, mom's apple pie finds a novel role as a masturbatory aid for the frustrated Jim. His concerned father – who dispenses facts-of-life advice with the aid of pornographic magazines (at one point explaining the nature of a 'beaver shot') – catches Jim and the pie *in flagrante delicto*, and points out the unsatisfactory nature of such a relationship. (Jim's father acknowledges his own youthful self-stimulation, but has to acknowledge he never resorted to 'baked goods'.) There have been several less-subtle sequels.

**American Psycho.** A deeply controversial novel (1991) by Bret Easton Ellis (b.1964), recounting the murderous activities of Patrick Bateman, a 26-year-old Manhattan broker by day and psychopathic YUPPIE serial killer by night. The novel's graphic portrayal of sadistic violence against women (including torture, flaying and cannibalism) led to intense criticism from women's groups, but others chose to see the novel as a satire on the materialistic excesses of the 1980s. The novel was rejected by Simon and Schuster when they saw the manuscript, but it was eventually published by Vintage. A film version, starring Christian Bale as Bateman, was released in 2000.

**American Tragedy, An.** A novel (1925) by Theodore Dreiser (1871–1945), written as an argument that society is at fault for allowing the environment of the slums to breed a criminal instinct that is born of material ambition. The actual event on which the novel is based is one of 16 cases that Dreiser studied of a young man murdering his pregnant girlfriend in order to marry a rich girl, tragic circumstances that he felt were peculiarly American. A film version (1931), directed by Josef von Sternberg, is a worthy adaptation of the original; a remake, *A Place in the Sun* (1951), starring Montgomery Clift and Elizabeth Taylor, is less compelling.

**Am I bothered?** *See* the WHATEVER GENERATION.

**Amityville Horror.** *See under* FAKES.

**Amnesty International.** The organization of this name was founded in 1961 when a British lawyer, Peter Benenson, wrote an article in *The Observer* announcing the launch of an 'Appeal for Amnesty', the aim being to campaign for the release of political prisoners, meaning those imprisoned for their beliefs who had not used or advocated violence. It was the first human rights group systematically to catalogue human rights abuses worldwide, and in the 1980s it became a household name through its staging of concert tours with the participation, and implied endorsement, of celebrity performers. It publishes an annual *Report on Torture and Political Persecution around the World* and has refined its definition of human rights over the years to include social issues, such as rape and the persecution of homosexuals. *See also* PRISONER OF CONSCIENCE.

**Amos 'n' Andy.** A popular US radio programme performed by two blackface clowns five nights a week during the late 1920s and early 1930s and continuing on both television and radio until 1958. Amos was eager and industrious, while Andy was a doltish slacker. In the original radio version the

two were played respectively by Freeman S. Gosden and Charles V. Correll.

> Announcer: Amos and Andy, two lifelong buddies, from Dixie, have spent most of their life on a farm just outside of Atlanta, Georgia. Amos is a hard-working little fellow who tries to do everything he can to help others and to make himself progress, while his friend Andy is not especially fond of hard work and often has Amos to assist him in his own duties. As the curtain goes up we find the boys returning to the farmhouse with a bucket of milk.
>
> WMAQ RADIO: first episode of *Amos 'n' Andy* (19 March 1928)

**Amritsar Massacre.** An incident on 13 April 1919 (sometimes also referred to as the Jallianwallah Bagh Massacre) in which 379 people died after British troops opened fire on unarmed nationalist demonstrators in the city of Amritsar in the Punjab, India. A further 1200 were injured. The British commander, Brigadier General Reginald Dyer (1864–1927), was condemned for his actions by a subsequent commission of inquiry. The incident bolstered the nationalist cause in India.

**Amstrad.** The home computers of this name evolved from the company originally called A.M.S. Trading set up in 1968 by the Cockney entrepreneur *Alan M(ichael) Sugar* (b.1947), who began his business by selling car aerials from the back of a van. By 1980 he was dealing in audio and television goods, always adhering to a 'no frills' policy to keep down costs, and in 1985 he achieved a major breakthrough when he launched a word processor for the (then) absurdly low price of £399. The following year he shook the electronics market again when he produced a home computer for a third of the price of that marketed by IBM. The hugely successful Amstrad PC1512, launched in 1986, made IBM standard computing, previously restricted to the US market, accessible to the European home user for the first time. In the 1990s, overtaken in the computer field by the falling prices of other 'IBM-compatible' manufacturers, Amstrad moved away from home computing into various telecommunications devices, such as set-top boxes for satellite or digital television. Amstrad enthusiasts like to point out that the registered name is an anagram of 'smart ad'.

**Amtorg.** A Soviet cover organization for a spy operation run in the United States between the world wars. Its origins date from 1921 when the US businessman Armand Hammer (1899–1990) travelled to Moscow with a letter of introduction to LENIN. Lenin eased Hammer into what would become a long and profitable business arrangement with the Soviet Union, and in 1924 this led to the official establishment of Amtorg as a joint Soviet-American trading organization, its name a dual acronym for *Am*erican *T*rading *Org*anization and Russian *amerikansky torg*, 'American trade'. It remained active for many years after the United States recognized the Soviet regime in 1933. *See also* ARCOS AFFAIR.

**Amtrak.** The US public corporation of this name, officially the National Railroad Passenger Corporation, was set up in 1970 to run the essential intercity rail services, using federal funds that private enterprise was unable to provide. It began to run its train services in May 1971. The name is a shortening of '*Am*erican *tra*vel by track'.

**Anabolic steroids.** The drugs so designated, available from the 1960s, have an anabolic (protein-building) effect similar to testosterone and other male sex hormones. They are used in medicine to build tissue, promote muscle recovery following injury and help strengthen bones, but they have been widely abused by athletes, sports players and others wishing to improve their strength and stamina, a controversial practice that has serious risks to health.

**Anal-retentive.** A term from psychoanalytical jargon adopted generally to apply to someone who is unnaturally tidy or fussy. Properly it applies to a person with a fixation for excessive orderliness and parsimony, explained as having become thus as the result of fixation at the anal stage of development, i.e. the period lasting from about the age of 18 months to three years when a child undergoes toilet training.

> My mother said, 'You're an anal retentive, aren't you?' and my father said, 'You're tight-fisted, and you've always got your perfectly groomed head in a book.'
> SUE TOWNSEND: *The Growing Pains of Adrian Mole* (1984)

**Anarchy in the UK.** *See* NEVER MIND THE BOLLOCKS, HERE'S THE SEX PISTOLS.

**Anastasia.** The youngest daughter (1901–18) of the last tsar of Russia, Nicholas II. She was executed along with the rest of her family at Yekaterinburg after the revolution by the BOLSHEVIKS (confirmed in a post-Soviet Russian investigation of 1994). In the intervening years, however, several women claimed to be the grand duchess, saying that they had escaped from Russia, and laid claim to the Romanov fortune held in Swiss banks. One of the most notable claimants was one Anna Anderson (possibly a Polish woman called Franziska Schanzkowski), whose claim was finally rejected by a West German court in 1970. She died in 1984. The idea that Anastasia might have survived provides the theme of the US film *Anastasia* (1956), for which Ingrid Bergman won an Oscar. The film was based on a French play (1954) by Marcelle Maurette. This work's disregard for history is as nothing compared with that of the 1997 full-length cartoon of the same name.

**Anatomy is destiny.** A phrase originating with Sigmund Freud, and found in his *Collected Writings* (1924). Freud argued that gender was a fundamental determinant of personality traits: for example, 'penis envy' led women to regard themselves as inferior to men. The pioneering female psychologist Karen Horney (1885–1952), although regarding herself as a disciple of Freud, rejected these aspects of his teaching, arguing for nurture over nature, for culture over biology. Many feminists since have regarded Freudian psychoanalysis as a means of furthering patriarchy.

**ANC.** The African National Congress, the leading political party in South Africa. The ANC was founded in 1912 (by Gandhi among others) as the South African Native National Congress. The name echoed that of the Indian National Congress, founded in 1885. When APARTHEID was introduced in 1948 the ANC became one of its leading opponents, and the organization was banned in 1960. At this point it adopted a policy of armed resistance, and its leaders were either put in jail (as happened to Nelson Mandela) or were obliged to direct its activities from exile (as did Oliver Tambo). On his release from prison in 1990 Mandela took over the presidency of the just-legalized ANC from Tambo. In 1994 the ANC won South Africa's first fully democratic elections, and Mandela (b.1918) became president on 10 May 1994 until he retired in 1999, to be succeeded by Thabo Mbeki (b.1942).

**Ancient monument.** An official designation for a building or site of special architectural, historical or archaeological interest that is protected by Act of Parliament from damage or destruction. In England such monuments are cared for by English Heritage, in Scotland by Historic Scotland, and in Wales by Cadw. There are around 30,000 scheduled sites in England alone, plus a further 450,000 or so listed buildings. It is forbidden by law to demolish, extend or alter the character of the latter without prior consent from the local planning authority, although in some cases permission may be given retrospectively.

**And?** In teenage slang, a sarcastic conversational comeback, mostly invoked by them when bored with their interlocutor's (often a parent's) chat, to imply 'So, what else?'

**And counting.** A modern cliché indicating that the number mentioned is increasing and is likely to continue to do so. It originated as part of the formula used for counting down to the moment for a particular event, notably the launching of a missile or rocket.

Ten years of *D-Lib Magazine* and counting. I could not have predicted the degree of success that was to be achieved by the small set of dedicated folks who helped to launch *D-Lib Magazine* and to nurture it over the first ten years of its existence.

*D-Lib Magazine* (July / August 2005)

**Anderson shelter.** A small prefabricated air-raid shelter. It became a familiar sight in many British gardens during the Second World War. It took the form of a curved steel hut that was partly buried in the ground and covered with 60–90cm (2–3ft) of earth to protect the occupants against explosions. The shelters were the invention of a Scottish engineer, William Paterson, and took their name from Sir John Anderson (1882–1958), who was home secretary and minister for home security in the opening years of the war. *See also* MORRISON SHELTER.

**And finally....** A phrase associated with ITN's *News at Ten*, and used by its newsreaders to introduce the final item, usually something of a trivial yet life-affirming nature, so that viewers may finish their OVALTINE and retire to bed in good heart. The phrase is particularly associated with Martyn Lewis (who wrote a book of that title, in 1984) and Trevor McDonald, and few headline writers passed over the opportunity of using it in stories announcing McDonald's retirement in December 2005.

**And how!** A general exclamation of agreement, made at the end of another's statement, as: 'I really enjoyed that!' 'Me too! And how!' The phrase dates from the 1920s and echoes German *und wie!* By the end of the 20th century its fashionability had waned.

**And now for something completely different.** A catch-phrase used to link entirely unrelated sketches in the anarchic television comedy series MONTY PYTHON'S FLYING CIRCUS (1969–74). It would usually be uttered by John Cleese, as a television announcer in evening dress, at a desk in an incongruous location, for example on a seashore. The catchphrase picked up on a link used frequently by the presenters of the BBC's children's magazine programme BLUE PETER throughout the 1960s, by means of which the presenters would attempt to segue from Valerie Singleton making a doll out of a doily and a squeezy bottle (HERE'S ONE I MADE EARLIER) to John Noakes skydiving into a bowl of shark-infested custard (for example). The phrase is said to have been originated by Christopher Trace, one of the earliest of the Blue Peter presenters.

***And Quiet Flows the Don.*** The English title (1934) of a two-part translation of the four-volume work *Tikhy Don* ('The Quiet Don', 1928–40), by the Russian author Mikhail Sholokhov (1905–84). The second part was *The Don Flows Home to the Sea* (1940), published in the United States as *Seeds of Tomorrow* (1935) and *Harvest on the Don* (1960). The River Don flows through central Russia into the Black Sea. The complete work covers the years 1912–22 and reflects with objectivity the effect during peace and war of the Russian Revolution on the Cossack communities in the region. Sholokhov received the NOBEL PRIZE for literature in 1965, despite charges of plagiarism levelled by, among others, Alexander Solzhenitsyn.

**Andrews, Archie.** The cheeky schoolboy dummy who appeared on radio from 1944 to 1960. Despite the apparent contradiction of a ventriloquist's dummy that cannot be seen, the series of programmes in which he featured proved extremely popular, the most memorable being *Educating Archie*. He was the creation of Ted Kavanagh, who gave him his name, and his operator was Peter Brough (1916–99). Many subsequently famous comedians and singers played opposite Archie Andrews, including Beryl Reid as his girlfriend.

**Andromeda strain.** A term for any strain of bacteria, viruses or other micro-organisms whose accidental release from a laboratory could have catastrophic effects because of its unknown biochemical composition. The term derives from *The Andromeda Strain* (1969), a SCIENCE FICTION novel by the US writer Michael Crichton (b.1942), in which an unknown type of bacteria, picked up in outer space, accidentally escapes from a returning space probe, killing a town's inhabitants and threatening to contaminate the world. A film (1970) based on the novel and directed by Robert Wise made a successful and suspenseful thriller.

**And that's official.** A journalistic tag to give authority to newly published facts or information, as: 'Hospital waiting lists are at an all-time high. And that's official.'

**Andy Capp.** *See* Andy CAPP.

**Andy Pandy.** A popular puppet, in a blue and white striped suit and matching floppy hat, which first appeared in the 1950s on the children's television programme WATCH WITH MOTHER. He was alone at first, but was later joined by a teddy bear and a rag doll called Looby Loo, with whom he shared a basket. Only 26 programmes were made, but they were repeated until the 1970s.

As little has been heard for several decades of the star of BBC TV's *Watch with Mother*, he is presumed to be examining his priorities in a Celebrity Clinic.

HERMIONE EYRE and WILLIAM DONALDSON: *The Dictionary of National Celebrity* (2005)

In 2002–3 Cosgrove Hall Films revived the character in a new stop-motion animated series, shown on the BBC's CBeebies digital channel.

**Angel.** In Second World War RAF slang a height of 300m (1000ft), reasonably close to heaven. For obvious reasons the word is usually found in the plural, as in the title of the film *Angels One Five* (1952) (i.e. 15,000ft) about the BATTLE OF BRITAIN.

In the theatre, an 'angel' is a backer who comes up with cash to invest in a new show.

**Angel dust.** A hippy nickname for the drug phencyclidine hydrochloride (PCP). Developed as an animal tranquillizer, it enjoyed widespread use in the 1970s as an (illegal) hallucinogen.

**Angel in the house.** A mainly ironic term for a woman who is completely devoted to her husband. It comes from the title of Coventry Patmore's *The Angel in the House* (1854–63), a sequence of poems in praise of married love, and was introduced by Virginia Woolf in the 1930s.

> You who come of a younger and happier generation may not have heard of her – you may not know what I mean by the Angel in the House. I will describe her as shortly as I can. She was intensely sympathetic. She was immensely charming. She was utterly unselfish. She excelled in the difficult arts of family life. She sacrificed herself daily. If there was a chicken, she took the leg; if there was a draught she sat in it – in short she was so constituted that she never had a mind or a wish of her own, but preferred to sympathize always with the minds and wishes of others.
>
> VIRGINIA WOOLF (1931): in Michèle Barret, *Virginia Woolf: Women & Writing* (1979)

**Angel of Death.** (German, *Todesengel*.) The nickname of Joseph Mengele (1911–79), the Nazi doctor who worked at AUSCHWITZ between 1943 and 1945. His 'racial experiments', especially on twins, involved the most hideous cruelty. After the war he lived in hiding and then escaped to South America around 1949, living in Uruguay, Paraguay and Brazil under assumed identities. In 1985 an international team of forensic experts determined that the body of a man who had drowned in Brazil in 1979 was in fact Mengele.

**Angel of the North.** A huge sculpture of an angel with outstretched wings by Antony Gormley (b.1950), and Britain's best-known recent work of public art. It was erected on a hillside next to the A1 near Gateshead in the northeast of England in 1998. The angel is 20m high, and its wingspan is 54m. The structure – erected with the help of major engineering firms – celebrates the region's industrial past (the wings are those of an early aeroplane) and also marks the boundary of a different country, the lands of the Venerable Bede (*c*.673–735) and St Columba (*c*.521–597). Gormley has said of his work:

> The hilltop site is important and has the feeling of being a megalithic mound. When you think of the mining that was done underneath the site, there is a poetic resonance. Men worked beneath the surface in the dark. Now in the light, there is a celebration of this industry.

Gateshead Council's only Conservative Party member commented:

> I think it is ruining a piece of nice countryside.

**Angels of Mons.** The 3rd and 4th Divisions of the OLD CONTEMPTIBLES under the command of General H.L. Smith-Dorrien were hard pressed in their retreat from Mons (26–27 August 1914). On 29 September that year the *London Evening News* published Arthur Machen's fantasy story *The Bowmen*, crediting their preservation to St George and the angels, who, clad in white, held back the might of the German First Army by wielding longbows and raining arrows on the enemy. For some, the imaginary became a reality, and the 'Angels of Mons' became a legendary phrase.

**Anglepoise.** The proprietary name of a popular and innovative desk lamp, designed by George Carwardine, a motor engineer, and launched in 1933. The design used hinges that mimicked the action of a human arm, making the lamp flexible and balanced and able to hold a pose at almost any angle.

**Anglia, Ford.** *See* FORD ANGLIA.

**Anglo-Saxon Attitudes.** A novel (1956) by Angus Wilson (1913–91), whose central theme is an archaeological fraud. It is also a partly satirical, partly realistic dissection of attitudes that the author sees as being prevalent among a particular group within middle-class society in England. The title comes from a remark made by the King to Alice in Lewis Carroll's *Through the Looking-Glass* (1872) as the Messenger approaches 'skipping up and down, and wriggling like an eel, with his great hands spread out like fans on each side': 'He's an Anglo-Saxon Messenger – and those are Anglo-Saxon attitudes.'

**Angry Brigade.** An urban guerrilla organization responsible for various acts of terrorism in the late 1960s and early 1970s. Some of their number were jailed following a bomb attack on the home of Robert Carr, the employment secretary, in January 1971, and they earlier claimed responsibility for machine-gunning the Spanish embassy in London and for planting bombs near a BBC van during the MISS WORLD contest. Their name was a loose rendering of French *Les Enragés*, a radical group of *sans-culottes* at the time of the French Revolution.

**Angry Penguins.** An Australian avant-garde quarterly magazine devoted to art and literature. It was first published in Adelaide in 1940 by the poet and critic Max Harris (1921–96), who named it after a line in one of his own poems. In 1944 it was the subject of an embarrassing hoax when it devoted its autumn issue to the poems of the non-existent 'Ern Malley', whose works were concocted by two traditional poets who thought the journal pretentious and wanted to test the critical judgement of its editors. The sources from which they drew quotations included an army report on mosquito control. The journal never really recovered from the adverse publicity and it closed in 1946.

**Angry Young Man.** A name applied to certain modern British writers, and in particular to John Osborne (1929–94), whose play LOOK BACK IN ANGER (first performed 1956) prompted the reporter George Fearon to apply the term to him, although it had already occurred in 1951 as the title of a book by the Irish writer Leslie Paul. Those so dubbed were typically young and of provincial lower-middle class or working-class origin, and they gained notoriety for their satirical treatment and criticism of the ESTABLISHMENT, with its false or outmoded social, moral, political and intellectual values. The name is also sometimes applied to some US writers of protest. *See also* LUCKY JIM.

**Anik.** The name of one of a number of communications satellites launched by Canada in the 1970s to provide television, radio and telephone services to the country. The word is Inuit (Eskimo) for 'brother' and was proposed by a Montreal girl in a nationwide competition.

**Animal crackers.** Small, semi-sweet biscuits in the shape of animals, popular among American children. The confection was popularized outside the United States by Ray Henderson and Ted Koehler's song 'Animal crackers in My Soup', sung with saccharine sentiment by seven-year-old Shirley Temple in the film *Curly Top* (1935). *See also* ALPHABET SOUP.

*Animal Crackers* was already the title of a MARX BROTHERS film (1930) based on their stage show of the same title, in which the brothers have fun at the expense of American high society. Groucho plays the part of Captain Spaulding the explorer. Highlights of the movie include some classic insults aimed at the perpetually nonplussed Margaret Dumont.

> You're the most beautiful woman I've ever seen, which doesn't say much for you.
>
> GROUCHO MARX: *Animal Crackers*

**Animal Farm.** A satire in fable form by George ORWELL, published in 1945 and depicting a totalitarian regime like that of the Soviet Union under STALIN. The story describes how the pigs, by cunning, treachery and ruthlessness, come to dominate the more honest, gullible and hardworking animals. The leader of the pigs is Napoleon, representing Stalin, and at the end the pigs are in cahoots with the humans, even beginning to totter around on two legs – despite the animals' revolutionary slogan 'Four legs good, two legs bad.' The pigs' ultimate slogan is: 'All animals are equal, but some animals are more equal than others.'

Orwell first submitted his satire for publication in 1944, when Britain was allied with the Soviet Union in the fight against Nazi Germany, and for this reason it was rejected by both Jonathan Cape and Faber and Faber (where T.S. Eliot, a director of the firm, wrote that 'what was needed … was more public-spirited pigs'). Orwell had similar difficulties in the United States, where the Dial Press claimed that it was 'impossible to sell animal stories in the USA'. However, in 1945, after the end of the Second World War and with the onset of the Cold War, publishers took a different view, and the book became a great success, becoming a modern classic. *See also* FIRST LINES OF NOVELS.

**Animated Meringue.** A media nickname for the hugely coiffeured, pink-coutured and white-pancaked Barbara Cartland (1901–2000), prolific writer of light romantic fiction and champion of healthy eating. The name also alludes to her 'chalky' style of writing, and her fondness for driving around in a pink and white ROLLS-ROYCE. She was first so dubbed by the journalist Arthur Marshall (1910–89). She did not resent the sobriquet, and actually dispatched a telegram expressing her gratitude.

**Animatronics.** The technique of constructing lifelike models of humans or animals for use in films or other entertainment. The term originated in the 1970s as a shortening of animated electronics.

> To me, the kids looked like animatronics figures, robots from a ride at Disneyland.
>
> ARMISTEAD MAUPIN: *Maybe the Moon*, ch. 5 (1992)

**Anime.** A genre of Japanese film and television animation, also known as Japanimation. The drawing is highly stylized and bears the hallmark of mass production, the work of any one artist being indistinguishable from that of any other. Characters typically have child-like figures and faces, and enormous eyes. Anime often has a SCIENCE FICTION theme and sometimes includes violent or explicitly sexual material. It is usually adapted from popular MANGA comic books and in the 1990s accounted for one of the fastest growing US video markets. Its influence is not confined to the realm of pornography: the feature-length *Spirited Away* won joint first prize at the 2002 Berlin Film Festival as well as that year's OSCAR for best animated feature. The word is pronounced 'animay'.

**Ankle-biter.** A jocular but not altogether friendly term for a small child, reflecting the anarchic violence of which such diminutive persons have been deemed capable. It is first recorded in 1963, in American English, although since the early 1980s it has also become a popular term in Australia.

> Upon entering the bathroom ankle biter number two claimed sole use of the 'bottom shower', something she was not challenged over.
>
> www.dooyoo.co.uk/hotels-international (26 October 2005)

**Annabel's.** A famous nightclub in Berkeley Square, London. It was opened in 1963 by Mark Birley and named after his wife, Lady Annabel Tempest-Vane-Stewart (b.1934), an Anglo-Irish heiress who in 1978 married the millionaire Sir James Goldsmith (1933–1997). Its heyday was in the 1970s, when Lady Annabel persuaded many of her well-connected friends to become members. More recently it has witnessed the goings-on of the likes of David Blunkett, the former left-wing firebrand turned New Labour socialite, who in 2005 was criticized for accepting free membership at the club. *See also* MODELIZER.

**Anne of Green Gables.** The young red-haired heroine of the novel of this name (1908) by the Canadian children's author L.M. Montgomery (1874–1942). Her full name is Anne Shirley and she is taken on by an elderly couple, making herself useful on their farm. She is somewhat precocious and outspoken, but she is winning and winsome and was described by Mark Twain as 'the dearest and most loveable child in fiction since the immortal Alice'. Her adventures have been adopted for stage, film and television, and the US child film actress Dawn Paris (1918–93) legally adopted her name after playing her in *Anne of Green Gables* (1934). The unfortunately titled sequel, with the same star, was called *Anne of Windy Poplars* (1940).

**Annie Get Your Gun.** A musical comedy (1946) with a score by Irving Berlin (1888–1989) about the sharpshooter Annie Oakley (1860–1926), one of the stars of Buffalo Bill's Wild West Show. The show contains many memorable numbers, including 'There's no Business Like Show Business' and 'The Girl That I Marry', but although Oakley was a real person, the plot of the musical is largely fictional. In US

theatrical slang an 'Annie Oakley' became a nickname for a complimentary ticket, the punched appearance of these being reminiscent of the playing cards that the sharpshooter used to pepper with bullet-holes during her act.

**Annie Hall.** A film comedy (1977) portraying the angst of modern Manhattan residents. Written by, directed by and starring Woody Allen (b.1935), it featured Diane Keaton as the eponymous Annie Hall, the object of Allen's desire both on and off screen (and whose outfits in the film influenced a generation). The screenplay included some of Allen's best-known and most often repeated one-liners, not least his reflections on sex ('It was the most fun I ever had without laughing') and masturbation ('Don't knock it, it's sex with someone you love').

**Ann Summers party.** A women's social gathering held in the home in which sex aids, 'sensual lingerie', 'naughty novelties' and similar products of the UK chain of sex shops are sold, rather like an adult version of a TUPPERWARE party. The company took its name from the secretary of the firm's founder, and the 'party plan' was launched in 1981.

**Annus horribilis.** (Latin, 'horrible year'.) Any disastrous or unpleasant year. Such for the British royal family was 1992, which saw the divorce of Princess Anne, the Princess Royal, the separation of the Duke and Duchess of York, newspaper photographs of the latter topless and a terrible fire at Windsor Castle. Queen Elizabeth used the phrase in a speech to guests at a banquet in the Guildhall that year (24 November):

> In the words of one of my more sympathetic correspondents, it has turned out to be an 'annus horribilis'.

The expression is itself based on Latin *annus mirabilis*, 'wonderful year', a phrase made famous by John Dryden in his long poem, *Annus Mirabilis* (1667), referring to 1666, the year of the Fire of London and of continuing war with the Dutch.

**Anorak.** A word of Greenland Inuit (Eskimo) origin for a type of waterproof jacket with a hood, as originally worn in polar regions. The garment's popularity, practicality and relative cheapness caused it to be widely adopted for a number of outdoor uses, from walking to train-spotting. The latter pastime in particular gave it a 'nerdish' image, and as a result the word passed to denote a (usually male) boring person or SQUARE, especially one with solitary interests. *See also* NERD.

**Another fine mess.** What Oliver Hardy frequently claimed Stan Laurel had gotten him into, in the many Laurel and Hardy films of the 1930s and 1940s. The line, scripted by

Stan Laurel (1890–1965), first appeared in *Another Fine Mess* (1930) in the form:

> Another nice mess you've gotten me into.

**Another Munich.** *See* MUNICH.

**Anschluss.** In a historical context this German word, meaning 'junction' or 'union', refers to the annexation of Austria by NAZI Germany in March 1938, part of Hitler's drive to create a new German empire.

**Answer's a lemon.** The reply is unsatisfactory or does not exist. The saying derives from 'lemon' as a term for anything unsatisfactory, perhaps originally referring to the least valuable symbol in a FRUIT MACHINE.

**Answers on a postcard.** There is no neat or simple answer. The catchphrase refers to competitions in which contestants have to send in their answers on a postcard. Inevitably, there is little space for any detailed or lengthy answer, which the setters aim to deter in any case.

> What … are Vanessa [Feltz]'s talents, unique or otherwise? And how much of your money and mine is being spent on discovering a treatment that will fit them or even cure them? Answers on a postcard, please.
>
> *Sunday Times* (20 June 1999)

**Answer to a maiden's prayer.** An eligible bachelor, ideally young, handsome and wealthy, or generally anything that exactly meets requirements. The expression dates from the 1930s.

> You're the answer to a maiden's prayer, dear heart. No need for you to do a stroke of work, you can marry money and live the life of a gentleman.
>
> JOAN M. FLEMING: *Maiden's Prayer*, II (1957)

**Anthony dollar.** A US one-dollar coin with raised inner borders, issued in 1979, which bore a likeness of the American social reformer and women's suffrage leader Susan B. Anthony (1820–1906). Some people initially complained that in look and feel the coin was too much like a quarter (25 cents).

**Anthony Eden.** A black Homburg hat of the type worn in the 1940s by Sir Anthony Eden (1897–1977) when he was foreign secretary and one of the best dressed members of the House of Commons.

**Antic Hay.** A novel by Aldous Huxley (1894–1963) (*see also* BRAVE NEW WORLD), published in 1923. The book is a satire on intellectual posturing in London's bohemia in the years after the First World War. The title comes from Marlowe:

> My men, like satyrs grazing on the lawns,
> Shall with their goat feet dance an antic hay.
>
> CHRISTOPHER MARLOWE: *Edward II* (1593), I.i

'Antic' is an archaic word for 'fantastical' or 'grotesque', while a 'hay' was an old country dance in which the dancers weave in and out of a circle. Thus the title sums up what Huxley thought of the goings-on of his contemporaries.

> There are few who would not rather be taken in adultery than in provincialism.
>
> ALDOUS HUXLEY: *Antic Hay*, ch. 10

**Anti-novel.** A novel that dispenses with conventional structures and characteristics. Such novels first came to the fore in France in the 1950s (where the genre is known as the *nouveau roman*), rejecting the orderly presentation of plot and characters as not conforming to the reality of experience. Instead, the anti-novel concentrated on the prosaic description of things, the theory being that the reader is thereby able to participate directly, not vicariously, and so understand the mental state of the characters. Key figures in the evolution of the *nouveau roman* were Alain Robbe-Grillet (b.1922), Nathalie Sarraute (1900–99), Michel Butor (b.1926), Claude Simon (1913–2005) and Robert Pinget (1919–97).

**Anton Piller order.** In legal terminology a court order requiring the defendant in proceedings to permit the plaintiff or his representatives to enter the defendant's premises in order to obtain evidence essential to the case. The name is that of a German firm of electric motor manufacturers, which in 1975 was involved in legal proceedings in which such an order was granted.

**Ants in one's pants.** A state of nervousness or restlessness; the fidgets or 'jitters'. A phrase of US origin, so that 'pants' here are trousers.

**Anyone for tennis?** A general query based on what is regarded as a typical line in a 1920s drawing-room comedy and uttered by a well-dressed young man entering the room carrying a tennis racket. The precise provenance of the phrase is uncertain, although it has a clear pre-echo in G.B. Shaw's play *Misalliance* (1910) in which one of the characters, Johnny Tarleton, a young businessman, rises from a swinging chair and asks the assembled company: 'Anybody on for a game of tennis?' The phrase was adopted as the title of a 1968 television play by J.B. Priestley and was pastiched in John Wells's farce *Anyone for Denis?* (1981), guying Margaret Thatcher's husband.

**Any Questions?** A long-running radio discussion programme, first broadcast in 1948 and transmitted weekly from a series of halls around Britain. Four people, often politicians, form a panel to answer questions on a variety of topics put by a local audience. The series came to be associated particularly with its first two chairmen, Freddie

Grisewood (1948–67) and David Jacobs (1967–84), and a selection of listeners' responses to what has been said forms the basis of the following day's complementary programme, *Any Answers?* The current chairman is Jonathan Dimbleby, whose brother David hosts the BBC television equivalent, *Question Time.*

**Anything Goes.** A musical comedy (1934), with a score by Cole Porter and book by Guy Bolton and P.G. Wodehouse, about a variety of characters on board an ocean liner in the 1920s. Perfectly capturing the carefree vitality of 1920s youth, the show was originally to be called *Bon Voyage* and then *Hard to Get*, with the main event in the action being a shipwreck, but the title was changed and extensive alterations to the plot were necessitated by a tragic shipwreck in real life. The phrase subsequently became uniquely associated with its time. In addition to the title song, the show contains 'I Get a Kick Out of You' and 'You're the Top'. Bing Crosby and Ethel Merman (reprising her role in the original stage show) starred in the first film version (1936).

> In olden days, a glimpse of stocking
> Was looked on as something shocking,
> But now, Heaven knows,
> Anything goes.
> COLE PORTER: 'Anything Goes'

**Anzac.** A word coined in 1915 from the initials of the Australian and New Zealand Army Corps. It was also applied to the cove and beach in GALLIPOLI where they landed. Anzac Day, commemorating the landing, is celebrated on 25 April, while an Anzac biscuit from New Zealand is one made with butter, golden syrup, rolled oats and coconut, named in honour of the First World War forces. *See also* DIGGER; PEACEHAVEN.

**Anzac Pact.** The agreement reached between Australia and New Zealand in 1944 to cooperate in their policies with regard to armistices with the AXIS powers, the postwar settlement and certain other matters.

**Anzus Pact.** A defence treaty between Australia, New Zealand and the United States, signed in 1951. The agreement was put under strain in 1984 when New Zealand banned all nuclear-powered vessels, and vessels carrying nuclear weapons, from its ports. The United States strongly objected, but New Zealand's determination was further strengthened after the French secret service blew up the anti-nuclear GREENPEACE ship *Rainbow Warrior* in Auckland Harbour in 1985. Thereafter, the US government withdrew its treaty obligations towards New Zealand, and the pact effectively split into two separate security agreements: between Australia and the United States, and between New Zealand and Australia. *See also* NUCLEAR-FREE ZONE.

**A-OK.** Excellent; in good order. A US space age expression, supposedly standing for 'all systems OK'. The term is said to be the invention of a NASA public relations officer, Colonel 'Shorty' Powers, who used it during the suborbital flight on 5 May 1961 of the astronaut Alan Shepard. Powers misheard a simple 'OK' from Shepard as 'A-OK' and relayed it to reporters and radio listeners. Astronauts themselves are not recorded as actually using the term.

**Apartheid.** (Afrikaans, 'separateness'.) A policy adopted by the Afrikaner National Party in 1948 to ensure the dominance of the white minority. It divided South Africa into separate areas for whites and blacks, leading to the country's withdrawal from the British Commonwealth in 1961 and rioting, repression and isolation from other nations. Limited constitutional rights were granted to non-whites in 1985, and the remaining apartheid laws were repealed in 1991. The first multiracial elections were held in 1994. *See also* PASS LAWS.

**Apartment, The.** An OSCAR-winning bitter-sweet comedy film (1960) directed by Billy Wilder and starring Jack Lemmon and Shirley MacLaine. The apartment in question belongs to Baxter, a lonely insurance clerk, who lets his superiors use the apartment to conduct their extramarital affairs.

**Apgar score.** A criterion for measuring the well-being of a baby one minute after birth. A check is made of respiratory effort, heart rate, skin colour, muscle tone and any reflex reaction to an olfactory stimulation of the nose, and each of these five signs is rated between 0 and 2, giving a maximum of 10. The resultant score is an instant indicator of whether the baby is likely to be healthy or require medical assistance. The score is named after the US obstetric anaesthetist Virginia Apgar (1909–74), who devised it in the early 1950s and published it in 1953. It has remained the world's standard assessment of newborn babies.

**Apocalypse Now.** A film (1979) loosely based on the short story 'HEART OF DARKNESS' (1902) by Joseph Conrad (1857–1924). Directed by Francis Ford Coppola and starring Martin Sheen as a US Army captain detailed to assassinate the renegade Colonel Kurtz, played by Marlon Brando, it was set against the backdrop of the Vietnam War and astonished cinema audiences with such epic set-pieces as a helicopter assault conducted to the accompaniment of Wagner's 'The Ride of the Valkyries'. The massive cost of the film, which was shot in the Philippines and complicated when Martin Sheen suffered a heart attack, was compounded by the extent to which it went over schedule. In the film business it became known by the alternative title *Apocalypse Later* or *Apocalypse When?* During filming Coppola referred to the film as his 'Idiodyssey'. He later said:

> We made *Apocalypse* the way Americans made war in Vietnam. There were too many of us, too much money and equipment – and little by little we went insane.

In 2001 Coppola released his own cut, *Apocalypse Now Redux* (*redux* is Latin for 'brought back', 'restored'), which included the fabled 'French plantation sequence', the existence of which had been rumoured among fans for years.

**Apollo.** The NASA space programme for landing astronauts on the moon. The programme was announced in May 1961, but the first step of manned lunar exploration was not realized until 11 October 1968, when a team of three orbited the moon. Apollo 11 brought the step-by-step procedure to a climax on 20 July 1969 when Neil Armstrong became the first human to set foot on the moon. Remaining Apollo missions carried out extensive exploration of the lunar surface, and the programme came to an end with the flight of Apollo 17 in December 1972. *See also* GEMINI.

**Apologies to….** A conventional acknowledgement by an artist, illustrator or cartoonist that their work is based on that of a famous predecessor, as 'Apologies to Tenniel'. The formula is usually placed after the artist's own signature.

**Apparatchik.** A member of an organization who servilely does the bidding of its leadership. The term was borrowed from Russian in the mid-20th century, and originally denoted specifically a member of the administrative staff (the 'apparat') of the Communist Party. *See also* ORGANIZATION MAN.

**Appeasement.** The conciliatory foreign policy pursued by the British and French governments in the face of the European dictators in the late 1930s, culminating in the MUNICH agreement. In this sense, the term 'appeasement' was probably first coined by the Marquess of Lothian in a letter to *The Times* (4 May 1934):

> The only lasting solution is that Europe itself should gradually find its way to an internal equilibrium and a limitation of armaments by political appeasement.

The word was actually used by the British prime minister Neville Chamberlain himself to describe his dealings with Hitler and Mussolini, but it has come to have entirely negative connotations, denoting weakness in the face of bullying.

> Appeasement has never won a race yet. It is a bad horse, bred by good intentions out of paralysis of will.
>
> SIR GODFREY NICHOLSON: in the House of Commons (1956), at the time of the SUEZ CRISIS

*See also* CLIVEDEN SET.

**Appleby, Inspector.** The erudite police detective, with full name John Appleby, created by Michael Innes (J.I.M. Stewart; 1906–94) for a long series of novels, beginning with *Death at the President's Lodging* (1936). He usually comes up with an appropriate literary quotation and solves every complex case with calm ingenuity.

**Apple Macintosh.** A popular make of personal computer and the first to replace typed commands with a graphical user interface, i.e. a mouse for pointing and clicking at windows and icons. It was introduced in 1984 by Apple Computers, founded in a garage in California in 1976 by the US computer engineers Steve Jobs (b.1955) and Stephen Wozniak (b.1950). The company was the first computer firm not to use its name as its corporate identity. The idea of selling a computer under the name and image of a fruit was conceived by Jobs, and the company motif of a multi-coloured apple with a bite taken out of it is a reference to the biblical story of Adam and Eve, in which the apple (though not identified as such) represents the fruit of the Tree of Knowledge. The Macintosh model is similarly named after an American apple variety and soon became colloquially known as 'Mac'. The futuristic-looking iMac computer, launched in 1998, further promoted the name, and the company went on to create the hugely successful IPOD. In 2006 the 'Macbook', a new laptop computer, was launched.

**Après-midi d'un faune, L'.** A ballet choreographed by Vaslav Nijinksy (1890–1950) using the music of the tone poem *Prélude à l'Après-midi d'un faune* by Claude Debussy (1862–1918). The ballet was first performed by Diaghilev's BALLETS RUSSES in 1912. Debussy's piece, which was first performed in 1894, had been intended as the first of three pieces, but the planned *Interlude* and *Paraphrase finale* were never written. Debussy described his piece as an 'orchestral impression' of *L'Après-midi d'un faune* (1865), a long Symbolist poem by Stéphane Mallarmé (1842–98). The title means 'the afternoon of a faun', and the poem evokes frustrated sexual desire.

**Aqua Libra.** (Latin, 'water balance'.) The proprietary name of a soft drink based on a mixture of mineral water and fruit juices with herbal and other flavourings. It was first sold in the late 1980s and is promoted as an aid to good digestion and alkaline balance.

**Aquarius, Age of.** *See* AGE OF AQUARIUS.

**Arab League.** Formally the League of Arab States, this organization was founded in 1945 in Cairo to ensure cooperation among its member states while protecting their independence and sovereignty. Egypt's membership was suspended in 1979, when the headquarters moved from Cairo to Tunis, but it was readmitted in 1989. The PLO was admitted to full membership in 1976.

**Arbeit macht frei.** (German, 'Work sets free'.) These bitterly ironical words were inscribed on the gates of DACHAU concentration camp in 1933 and subsequently on those of AUSCHWITZ in the Second World War. Their authorship is unknown.

**Archers, The.** The world's longest-running radio serial, broadcast five days a week from 1951 (and from 1998, six days), with an 'omnibus' repeat on Sunday. It was initially devised to convey useful information to the farming community, and continues to introduce themes of topical interest to its audience. The original Archers were Dan and Doris, of Brookfield Farm in Ambridge, in the fictional county of Borsetshire, and their descendants remain the core characters. The news digest *The Week* helpfully carries a printed summary of the last six days' goings-on for any listeners who have missed out on an episode. *See also* BARWICK GREEN.

**Archie Bunker.** *See* Archie BUNKER.

**Archies.** A nickname for anti-aircraft guns and batteries in the First World War, probably from the popular song by George Robey, John L. St John and Alfred Glover, 'Archibald, Certainly Not!' (1909).

**Arcos Affair.** A diplomatic contretemps between Britain and the Soviet Union in 1927. It came about when MI5 suspected that personnel working for the All Russian Cooperative Society (ARCOS) in London were intelligence officers. A raid was made on ARCOS warehouses and offices and alleged evidence of espionage was found, as a result of which diplomatic ties were severed with the USSR. Britain had broken off relations three years previously after the ZINOVIEV LETTER incident (*see under* FAKES). A similar Soviet operation in the United States was run under the umbrella of AMTORG.

**Areas.** A piece of cricketing jargon which emerged in the early 21st century, denoting the places in which the bowler pitches the ball, especially in the context of causing maximum discomfiture to the batsman by the pressure of accuracy. Coaches exhort their charges to 'bowl it in the right areas'. *See also* CORRIDOR OF UNCERTAINTY.

> I got the ball in the right areas, which was the way to bowl on this pitch … When the pitch is slow it is often better to get the ball in the right area and swing it rather than just flat out. At times you've got to use your noodle.
>
> SIMON JONES: in *The Independent* (30 August 2005)

> These guys can put the ball in the areas we ask them to over a long period of time.
>
> DUNCAN FLETCHER (England coach): in *The Times* (31 August 2005)

**Are we downhearted? No!** A catchphrase adopted by British troops during the First World War:

> For two days the finest troops England has ever sent across the sea have been marching through the narrow streets of old Boulogne in solid columns of khaki … waving as they say that new slogan of Englishmen: 'Are we downhearted? … Nooooo!' 'Shall we win? … Yessss!'

The phrase was worked into a number of popular wartime songs, for example this from 1914 by Charles Knight and Kenneth Lyle:

> When there's trouble brewing,
> When there's something doing,
> Are we downhearted?
> No! Let 'em all come!

There is also this from 1917, by Ray Sherwood and Will Donaldson:

> Are we downhearted? No! No! No!
> We are ready to go, go go.
> Goodbye sweetheart, for a little while,
> Goodbye mother, let me see you smile.
> Soon the bugle will blow, blow, blow.
> Duty calls, we know,
> And we'll hang the Kaiser to a sour apple tree,
> Are we downhearted? No! No! No!

**Are You Being Served?** A rude and racy television SITCOM running from 1973 to 1985 and centring on the antics of the staff at Grace Brothers, an old-fashioned department store. Much of the humour derives from unsubtle innuendo in the style of the CARRY ON FILMS. The main characters include the brash and brassy head of ladies' fashion, Mrs Slocombe, played by Mollie Sugden, the smooth and silky-voiced floorwalker, Captain Peacock, played by Frank Thornton, the effete senior sales assistant in the menswear department, Mr Humphries, memorably camped up by John Inman, and Mrs Slocombe's glamorous assistant, Miss Brahms, played by Wendy Richard. The many *double entendres* in the script are extended to the title itself.

**Are you decent?** Are you dressed? This catchphrase

originated in the theatre and accompanied a knock on the door of an actor's or (in particular) actress's dressing-room. It later applied to anyone who might not be fully or appropriately dressed to receive a visitor. The first part of the phrase in this wider sense is obviously variable.

**Are you sitting comfortably? Then I'll begin.** The standard introduction used by Julia Lang to the BBC radio programme LISTEN WITH MOTHER.

**Argue the toss.** To dispute a decision already made. The phrase dates from the 1920s and alludes to a dispute over a decision reached by tossing a coin.

**Argument of the broken window pane.** The policy of violence against property undertaken by the SUFFRAGETTE movement in the years prior to the First World War. The phrase was coined by the movement's leader, Emmeline Pankhurst (1858–1928):

> The argument of the broken window pane is the most valuable argument in modern politics.
>
> Quoted in George Dangerfield, *The Strange Death of Liberal England* (1936)

*See also* CAT AND MOUSE ACT.

**Arica.** A training programme in self-development devised by the Bolivian-born mystic Oscra Ichaza. The Arica Institute to further the method was founded in New York in 1972, following a visit by a group of Americans to Ichaza in Arica, Chile. Hence the name. The programme is effectively a synthesis of several disciplines and is also known as 'scientific mysticism'.

**Arkham.** An imaginary city in Massachusetts in H.P. Lovecraft's fantasy tales *The Outsider and Others* (1939) and *Beyond the Wall of Sleep* (1943). It was founded in the 17th century but has changed very little since. It is crossed by the gloomy Miskatonic River and has a famous university, specializing in the occult. Travellers visit the city at their own risk.

**Arkle.** The most famous racehorse in history was foaled in Ireland in 1957 and won the Cheltenham Gold Cup three years in a row (1964–6), ridden by Pat Taaffe. His name was taken from that of a rocky mountain in the far northwest of Highland (formerly in Sutherland), some 30 km (19 miles) south of Cape Wrath, near which his owner, the Duchess of Westminster, had a home. He was a big bay gelding, fast and fluid over the jumps, and was a superb sprinter on the stretch. He dominated the British steeplechasing scene until a small fracture ended his career after his 35th race in December 1966. The Nottinghamshire and England

cricketer Derek Randall (b.1951) was also known as 'Arkle' for his impressive turn of speed in the field.

**Armalite.** The proprietary name (in the United States) of a type of lightweight, small-calibre assault rifle. The name, based on 'arm' and 'light', was registered in 1958, and the first such rifle, the AR–10, was a 7.62mm gas-operated weapon. This paved the way for the highly successful AR–15, adopted as the standard US Army rifle known as the M16. The AR–18, similar to it, was produced in Britain but with a simpler design, enabling it to be readily manufactured in less-developed countries. The Armalite became particularly familiar as the weapon favoured by the IRA. The 'Armalite and the ballot box' was, notoriously, the stated strategy of the Irish Republican movement in the 1980s, its twin elements being violence committed against British forces by the Provisional IRA and electoral advances made by the IRA's political wing, SINN FÉIN. *See also* the BULLET AND THE BALLOT BOX.

**Arm and a leg.** An extremely large amount of money, as: 'It cost me an arm and a leg to get here.'

**Arm candy.** A US colloquialism of the 1990s for a pretty girl or good-looking young man whose sole role is to adorn the arm of their companion of the moment. She might possibly end up as a TROPHY WIFE. *See also* EYE CANDY.

**Armistice Day.** 11 November, the day set aside to commemorate the fallen in the First World War, marked by a TWO-MINUTE SILENCE at 11 a.m. and religious ceremonies. The armistice ending the war, signed at 5 a.m., came into effect at 11 a.m. on 11 November 1918, the 11th hour of the 11th month. In 1946 the name was changed to REMEMBRANCE DAY. The United States has VETERANS DAY on 11 November as a legal holiday, while France celebrates its *Fête de la Victoire* (Victory Day).

**Armstrong, Jack.** The young, sports-loving hero of *Jack Armstrong, the All-American Boy*, a radio series first broadcast in the United States in 1933 and running to 1951. He was the creation of scriptwriter Robert Hardy Andrews, who sends him on a series of adventures around the world with the help of his Uncle Jim. He also appeared in a comic book of the 1940s in which his motto is: 'To keep myself straight and strong and clean, in mind as well as in body.'

**Army Game, The.** A popular television comedy series screened from 1957 to 1961 and based on the film *Private's Progress* (1956). Recruits at a remote transit camp included Private 'Excused Boots' Bisley, so called because he was allowed to wear plimsolls on parade, Private 'Cupcake' Cook and moronic Private 'Popeye' Popplewell, whose refrain 'I only asked' became a national catchphrase. A later addition was Company Sergeant-Major Claude Snudge, played by Bill Fraser, who, with Alfie Bass's Bisley, subsequently appeared in the spin-off BOOTSIE AND SNUDGE.

**Arndale Centre.** The shopping malls so named arose from the business set up in Bradford in 1931 by Samuel Chippindale (1909–90), an estate agent specializing in shops. This grew into the Arndale Property Trust, taking its name from a blend of Chippindale's own name and the first name of his partner, Arnold Hargenbach. The first Arndale Centre opened in Leeds in 1967, its architecture based on a US design. The bulldozing of various town centres to make way for the malls horrified many, although the later buildings regained some of the panache of Victorian glass and wrought-iron shopping arcades. Manchester's Arndale Centre, derisively dubbed 'the longest lavatory in Europe' for its expanses of yellow tiling, was destroyed in 1996 by an IRA bomb, which devastated the city centre, but it was completely revamped and reopened in 1999.

**Arnhem.** *See* BRIDGE TOO FAR.

**Aromatherapy.** The art or science of promoting 'health and beauty' by aromatic oils extracted from plants is of French origin and was first taken up in Britain in the 1960s. Practitioners claim that it can be used to treat a wide range of disorders, especially stress-related conditions. The word itself was coined in 1937 (as French *aromathérapie*) by the chemist and perfume manufacturer René-Maurice Gattefossé.

**Arrogance of power.** A catchphrase used to impugn the policies of a country or organization on the grounds that they stem from the arrogance that comes from having too much power. The phrase was coined by Senator William Fulbright in the 1960s and used by him as the title of a book (1967) in which he questioned the validity of US intervention in the affairs of foreign countries.

**Arsenal of democracy.** The United States, prior to its armed involvement in the Second World War. In his 'Fireside Chat' radio broadcast of 29 December 1940, US president Franklin D. Roosevelt (1882–1945) told the American people:

We must be the great arsenal of democracy.

Restrained from declaring war by the strong isolationist sentiment in the United States, Roosevelt did all he could via LEND-LEASE to support Britain's fight against Nazi Germany.

**Arsenic and Old Lace.** The film comedy (1941 but released in 1944) of this name was based on a play (1941) by Joseph Kesselring, which was a huge success on Broadway. The plot

revolves around two kindly but deranged old ladies (hence the 'old lace') who poison (hence the 'arsenic') elderly gentlemen who visit their home, wishing to relieve them of their loneliness. They bury the bodies in their cellar. The film, which was directed by Frank Capra, starred Cary Grant as the ladies' hapless and appalled nephew, Mortimer Brewster. The title of Kesselring's play was suggested by that of Myrtle Reed's novel LAVENDER AND OLD LACE (1902), criticized by reviewers of the day for its saccharine sentimentality.

**Art deco.** A decorative style in painting, glass, pottery, silverware, furniture, architecture and the like, at its height in the 1930s. It is distinguished by bold colours, geometrical shapes, stylized natural forms and symmetrical designs. The name comes from French *art décoratif*, 'decorative art', itself from the *Exposition internationale des arts décoratifs et industriels modernes* held in Paris in 1925 as the first major international exhibition of decorative art since the First World War.

**Arte povera.** (Italian, 'impoverished art'.) A term coined in 1967 by the Italian critic Germano Celant to describe a form of art in which the materials used, such as soil, twigs or newspaper, are deliberately chosen for their 'worthlessness' as a reaction against the commercialization of the art world. Leading Italian or Italian-based artists in the movement are Jannis Kounellis (b.1936) and Mario Merz (1925–2003), the latter making 'igloos' of metal armatures covered in nets, mud, twigs and so on. The use of such materials has been said to have a liberating effect on the artists concerned.

**Artex.** A type of plaster applied to walls and ceilings to give a textured finish, usually in decorative patterns. The general effect is necessarily repetitive but blandly pleasing. The name dates from the 1950s and derives from a blend of 'art' and 'texture'. Very popular in the 1970s, and useful in its ability to conceal cracks, it has slipped in and out of fashion since.

**Artist formerly known as Prince, The.** A common way of referring to the African American pop musician Prince (originally Prince Rogers Nelson b.1958), who, between 1993 and 2000, adopted an unpronounceable symbol for a name. The formula has been much adapted by those of a satirical bent.

**Art nouveau.** (French, 'new art'.) A decorative style of art flourishing in most of western Europe and the United States from the late 19th century to the outbreak of the First World War. As its name implies, it was a deliberate attempt to create a new style in reaction to the reproduction of historical forms that had been such a prominent feature of 19th-century architecture and design. Its most characteristic theme was the use of sinuous, asymmetrical lines based on plant forms, and frequent motifs were flowers, leaves and tendrils as well as female figures with flowing hair. The name itself came from a shop called *La Maison d'Art Nouveau*, opened in Paris in 1895 by the German-born art dealer Siegfried Bing (1838–1905). The genre has different names in different countries. Among English speakers it is sometimes known as 'Modern Style', while in Germany it was called *Jugendstil* (after the journal *Die Jugend*, 'Youth', founded in 1896), in Austria *Sezessionstil* (after the Vienna *Sezession*, a group of artists who had 'seceded' or broken away from the established academies), in Spain *Modernista* and in Italy *Stile Liberty* (after the Regent Street store that played an important part in promoting its designs).

**Art of the possible.** Politics, according to a saying sometimes attributed to the Conservative politician R.A. Butler (*see* RAB), who entitled his memoirs (1971) *The Art of the Possible*. However, variants of the saying have been traced to Camus, Bismarck, Cavour and Pindar.

> Politics is not the art of the possible. It consists in choosing between the disastrous and the unpalatable.
> J.K. GALBRAITH: letter to President J.F. Kennedy (March 1962)

**Art on Legs.** A nickname applied to the vast, bald, distinctly unglamorous transvestite performance artist Leigh Bowery (1961–94), who became one of the painter Lucien Freud's favourite nude models. Bowery was born in Australia, but moved to Britain in 1980. *See also* SEX ON LEGS.

**As and when.** When possible; eventually, as: 'I'll be in touch with you as and when.'

**As Australian as a meat pie.** Quintessentially Australian. Meat pies were long regarded as archetypal Australian fare, until the country discovered the joys of Pacific Rim cuisine towards the end of the 20th century. *See also* PIE-EATER.

**Asbo.** Acronymic shorthand for 'antisocial-behaviour order', a measure introduced in the UK at the end of the 20th century in an attempt to counter various low-level societal nuisances (e.g. noisy neighbours, out-of-control children with vandalistic tendencies) that had hitherto escaped the official notice of the law and were perceived to be on the increase. It is a civil measure (inaugurated in the Crime and Disorder Act 1998 and reinforced in England and Wales by the Anti-Social Behaviour Act 2003), but anyone who breaks an order served on them becomes liable to criminal proceedings and may end up in prison. Though doubts persist about their effectiveness, asbos have established a place for themselves in British popular culture – as witness the following verse circulating on the Web in the early 21st century:

> Wee Willie Winkie running through the town,
> Upstairs, downstairs, in his night gown.
> So they slapped an asbo on him.

***Ascent of F6, The.*** A play (1937) by W.H. Auden (1907–73) and Christopher Isherwood (1904–86) about an ill-fated British mountaineering expedition to a fictional peak identified simply as F6, on the frontier between the equally fictional British Sudoland and Ostnian Sudoland. The expedition leader, Michael Ransom, was based on the real-life soldier and writer T.E. Lawrence (1888–1935).

The name F6 echoes the style used by the 19th-century Survey of India, where native names or English names had not been established for remote mountains in the Himalaya. Today, K2 (the world's second-highest mountain) is one of the few peaks to retain its 'temporary' designation, which indicated that it was the second mountain in the Karakoram range to be measured (in 1856).

***Ascent of Man, The.*** A pioneering 13-part television series broadcast in 1973 and telling the story of man's discoveries in agriculture, technology and science. It was written by the Polish-born scientist Jacob Bronowski (1908–74) and presented by him with a compelling intensity, opening the eyes of many to the broad sweep of scientific history. Bronowski's book based on the series spread far and wide his fame as an expositor and thinker. A book of the series followed.

> Among the multitude of animals which scamper, fly, burrow and swim around us, man is the only one who is not locked into his environment. His imagination, his reason, his emotional subtlety and toughness, make it possible for him not to accept the environment but to change it. And that series of inventions, by which man from age to age has remade his environment, is a different kind of evolution – not biological, but cultural evolution. I call that brilliant sequence of cultural peaks *The Ascent of Man*.
> JACOB BRONOWSKI: *The Ascent of Man*, ch. 1 (1973)

**As cheap as chips.** Very inexpensive. The expression is particularly associated with the antiques expert David Dickinson, presenter of the BBC television programme *Bargain Hunt*, first broadcast in 2000.

> Cheap as chips enterprises such as the Macmillan New Writing imprint saturate the market and harm the prestige of publication.
> TIM CLARE: 'The Reading Experience' (internet blog) (20 August 2005)

**ASCII.** The acronym of American Standard Code for Information Interchange, representing the code of bits (binary digits) of 1s and 0s that is used in computer technology. With a particular series of bits representing the same numbers, letters and visuals, the code allows a standard exchange of files written in different computer languages.

**As flat as a tack.** Utterly drained, exhausted or low-spirited, having expended all one's energy or vitality. The image is of a tack that has been hammered in to the point of invisibility.

**As game as a meat ant.** In Australian English, very courageous. The meat ant is a truculent Australian insect of the genus *Iridomyrmex*, which is capable of inflicting an extremely painful nip.

**Ashcan School.** A group of American realist painters active from 1908 until the First World War. The most prominent members were those originally known as 'The Eight': Arthur B. Davies (1862–1928), William J. Glackens (1870–1938), Robert Henri (1865–1929), Ernest Lawson (1873–1939), George Luks (1867–1933), Maurice Prendergast (1859–1924), Everett Shinn (1876–1953) and John Sloan (1871–1951). Other painters who have been described as members include George Bellows (1882–1925), Glenn Coleman (1887–1932), Eugene Higgins (1874–1958), Edward Hopper (1882–1967) and Jerome Myers (1867–1940). Their style was traditional but their subjects daringly original, such as the vulgar crowds of Broadway, drunks in seedy bars and the sordid denizens of the waterfront. Hence their name, originally given derisively in a book edited by Holger Cahill and Alfred H. Barr entitled *Art in America in Modern Times* (1934). 'Ashcan' is an Americanism for a dustbin.

**Ashenden.** The secret agent in short stories by William Somerset Maugham (1874–1965), collected in *Ashenden, or The British Agent* (1928). The scenes are set in the First World War and are based on the author's own experience in British intelligence. Ashenden himself is something of a new type of spy in English fiction, humdrum rather than heroic. The film *The Secret Agent* (1936), starring John Gielgud and directed by Alfred Hitchcock, is based loosely on his exploits.

**Ashington Group.** A group of amateur artists active in Ashington, Northumberland, from 1934 to 1984. The group originated when Robert Lyon (1894–1978), an art lecturer at King's College, Newcastle upon Tyne, then part of Durham University, was asked to run an extramural class in the nearby mining town of Ashington under the auspices of the Workers' Educational Association. Lyon encouraged members to 'paint what you know', and their paintings were mainly of scenes drawn from their working, domestic and social lives.

**As I Walked out One Midsummer Morning.** An autobiographical account (1969) of his youth by the poet Laurie Lee (1914–97). The work is a sequel to CIDER WITH ROSIE and describes how the young Lee leaves his Gloucestershire village with little more than a fiddle. He first travels to London, and then to Spain on the eve of civil war. A third volume of memoirs, *A Moment of War*, was published in 1991. 'As I Walked out One Midsummer Morning' is a traditional – and very beautiful – English folk song, in which the singer meets a maid.

> Old men in the pubs sang, 'As I Walked Out', then walked out and never came back ... .
>
> LAURIE LEE: *Cider with Rosie* (1959), 'Last Days'

**As I Was Going Down Sackville Street.** The first volume of memoirs (1937) of the Irish poet and surgeon Olive St John Gogarty (1878–1957). Sackville Street (previously Drogheda Street) in central Dublin is now called O'Connell Street, in honour of 'the great liberator', Daniel O'Connell (1775–1847), who did much to achieve Catholic Emancipation in the Westminster Parliament. O'Connell Street is the location of the General Post Office, which was the rebel headquarters during the 1916 Easter Rising, and one of the few buildings to survive the fighting then and during the TROUBLES in 1922. For many years Nelson's Pillar stood opposite, but was blown up in 1966, presumably by nationalists who regarded it as an affront.

Gogarty himself was associated with leading figures of the Irish literary renaissance, such as W.B. Yeats (who included 17 of his poems in his 1936 *Oxford Book of Modern Verse*), George Moore and George Russell (Æ), but he resented the appearance of his student self as 'stately plump Buck Mulligan' in James Joyce's ULYSSES. He published two other volumes of memoirs, *Tumbling in the Hay* (1939) and *It Isn't This Time of Year at All* (1954). The title of the latter comes from the following exchange recorded in the book:

> I said, 'It is most extraordinary weather for this time of year.'
> He replied, 'Ah, it isn't this time of year at all.'

**A6 murder.** In August 1961 Michael Gregsten and his lover Valerie Storie were shot in their car in a lay-by off the A6 between Luton and Bedford. Gregsten died, but Storie survived, paralysed from the waist down. The first suspect was Peter Alphon, a travelling salesman, but at an identity parade Storie picked out another man, known to be innocent. The next suspect was James Hanratty, a petty criminal. Storie picked him out from an identity parade, and her identification led to his being hanged in April 1961. The journalist Paul Foot investigated the case and in *Who Killed Hanratty?* (1971), concluding that Hanratty was innocent; Foot also revealed that Alphon had repeatedly told him he was the murderer. However, in 2001 DNA evidence seemed to confirm Hanratty's guilt, although questions were then posed about the possible contamination of the evidence.

**Ask me another.** I don't know. The implication is that I don't know the answer to your present question, but I might know the answer to another. *Ask Me Another* was the title of an American television quiz show of the early 1950s in which panellists had to guess the identity of concealed sports celebrities by asking them questions.

**Aslan.** The great lion who is a central character in the NARNIA children's books by C.S. Lewis (1898–1963). His death and resurrection in the first book identify him as a deific or even specifically Christ-like figure. His name, which is the Turkish word for 'lion', is said to have come from Lewis's reading of the *Arabian Nights Entertainments*.

**Asleep at the wheel.** Inattentive; not concentrating on the task in hand. The allusion is to falling asleep while driving a car. A US equivalent of 19th-century origin is 'asleep at the switch', referring to the points lever ('switch') on a railway. The US country band Asleep at the Wheel, formed in 1970, took a name that referred to their non-stop concert travelling, much of it involving all-night drives.

**As mad as a box of frogs.** Completely deranged or unhinged, or utterly furious. The expression seems to have arisen towards the end of the 20th century, and to have no more rationale to it than that a boxful of frogs might well be a scene of chaos.

> He [Tom Baker] is allegedly as mad as a box of frogs. Was he showing any sign of that?
> www.20six.co.uk (26 October 2005)

**As mad** or **silly as a two-bob watch.** In Australian English, utterly feather-brained or out of touch with reality (a two-bob watch – costing two shillings – is cheap and unreliable). The expression is first recorded in 1954.

**Asphalt Jungle, The.** A FILM NOIR (1950) based on the novel (1949) of the same name by W.R. Burnett. Directed by John Huston and starring Sterling Hayden and Louis Calhern, it depicted the disintegration of a gang of thieves following a daring robbery attempt. The title of the film conveyed appropriate overtones of savagery in a bleak urban setting, where the paving is asphalt and the 'law of the jungle' prevails. *See also The* BLACKBOARD JUNGLE; CONCRETE JUNGLE.

**Aspidistra.** A very tolerant member of the Convallariaceae family, with broad, lance-shaped leaves and small, inconspicuous flowers borne at soil level. It was a popular houseplant from late Victorian times until the 1920s because of its ability to survive in gas-lit rooms, and it became a symbol of lower middle-class philistinism and dull respectability. George ORWELL wrote a novel called KEEP THE ASPIDISTRA FLYING (1936), and a song by Jimmy Harper, Tommie Connor and Will E. Haines, 'The Biggest Aspidistra in the World' (1938), was widely popularized by Gracie Fields (1898–1979).

**As rough as bags.** In Australian English, of a person or their behaviour, coarse, unrefined, 'common'. The expression reflects the characteristic Australian use of 'bag' to designate a container or other object made out of hessian sacking.

> 'Rough as bags', people said of Raelene, and in the same breath, 'heart of gold'.
> MARIAN ELDRIDGE: *Walking the Dog* (1984)

**As seen on TV.** A stock advertising recommendation for a product that has appeared in a television commercial or documentary programme. By extension, the phrase can also apply to any TIE-IN relating to a television programme.

> The biggest section in the new Waterstone's [bookshop] in Piccadilly is devoted to the section 'As Seen On TV'. You can't move for Channel 4 and BBC books.
> *The Times* (17 December 1999)

**Asses of Evil.** *See* AXIS OF EVIL.

**Asset stripping.** The practice of taking over a company in financial difficulties and selling each of its assets separately at a profit without regard for its future. The activity is legal but regarded with disfavour as it smacks of opportunism. The term became familiar in the 1970s but the practice itself is older.

**Asterix.** The comic French cartoon hero who first appeared in 1959 as the creation of the writer René Goscinny and the artist Albert Uderzo. He is a pint-sized, moustachioed Gaul who lives in Armorica (Brittany) and does his best to keep the Romans at bay. The stories include gentle and amusing caricatures of different European peoples, ranging from stolid tea-drinking Britons, professing delight in their diet of lamb and mint sauce, to knife-wielding Corsicans. His friends include the obtuse and obese Obelix and the Druid Getafix. First appearing in a weekly comic, he has since featured in a number of books and animated cartoons. His name (properly *Astérix*) is based on French *astérisque*, 'asterisk', with a final *-rix* found in typical Gaulish names such as that of the Gallic chieftain Vercingetorix (d.44 BC).

The names of the characters, both in the French originals and in the many translations, involve an array of puns. For example, Asterix, the asterisk (*), is the star of the stories, while his sidekick the mighty Obelix is a deliverer of standing stones (i.e. obelisks); and in footnotes, the obelisk or dagger sign is used after the asterisk. In the English translations by Anthea Bell and Derek Hockridge, subsidiary characters have names such as Geriatrix, Vitalstatistix and Fulliautomatix.

There have been a number of animated films based on the stories, the most recent released in 2006 as *Asterix and the Vikings*. A live-action feature film, *Astérix et Obélix contre César* ('Asterix and Obelix take on Caesar'), featuring Gérard Depardieu as Obelix and directed by Claude Zidi, was released in 1999.

**As the bishop said to the actress.** A response to an unintentional *double entendre*. The phrase dates from the music-hall era, when stand-up comedy abounded in 'bishop and actress' jokes. The association of the two types is either so unlikely or so potentially scandalous that the interpretation of a remark will be either innocuous or indecent. The rejoinder is often prompted by an entirely innocent reference, as: 'I've got something special to show you' ('As the bishop said to the actress'). The secondary meaning is not necessarily always improper. In the appropriate context (e.g. 'That's a big one.'), the phrase 'As the actress said to the bishop' may also be deployed. *See also* TOM SWIFTIES.

> Faint heart ne'er won fair lady, as the Bishop said to the Actress.
>
> 'ANON': *A Writer's Notebook* (1946)

**As thick as a plank** or **two planks** or **two short planks.** Very dull and stupid. The various versions date from the 1970s.

**As Time Goes By.** *See* PLAY IT AGAIN SAM.

**Aston University.** The Birmingham university was formed from a college of advanced technology in 1966 and was so named to be distinguished from the existing University of Birmingham, founded in 1901. It is not actually in Aston, a district 3km (2 miles) to the north, but in Gosta Green, near the city centre, and it took the name so as to be at the top of the alphabetical list of new universities and so readily catch the eye of the University Grants Committee.

**Astronaut.** (Greek *astron*, 'star', and *nauts*, 'sailor'.) A voyager in interstellar space. This word, first used in 1929, gained popular acceptance after the first manned space flight by Major Yuri Gagarin (1934–68) of the USSR on 12 April 1961.

He landed safely after orbiting the earth in 108 minutes at altitudes reaching a maximum of 327km (203 miles). *See also* COSMONAUT.

**Astroturf.** The proprietary name of a kind of artificial grass surface for a sports pitch. It was first developed by Monsanto in 1966 to provide a pitch for the Astrodome indoor sports stadium at Houston, Texas, where grass would not grow. Hence the name, which is sometimes taken up in other contexts, as for 'Astroturf Blonde', the journalistic byname of Alyson Rudd, writer on football for *The Times* in the 1990s.

**Asylum seeker.** Someone who tries to obtain political asylum in another country. The term is first recorded in 1959, but it was not until around the end of the 20th century that controversy over the motivations of would-be immigrants into the UK (were they really fleeing persecution or merely trying to better themselves financially?) set up the polar opposites of ECONOMIC MIGRANT and 'asylum seeker', the latter taking over much of the terminological territory hitherto held by 'refugee'.

**Asymmetric warfare** or **asymmetrical warfare.** A technical term, with more than a whiff of euphemism, for warfare between combatants of widely differing strength. Such encounters are nothing new, and indeed victories of David over Goliath (as of the English over the numerically superior French at Agincourt in 1415) are the stuff of heroic tales. It was not until the second half of the 20th century, though, as the idea of warfare as a battlefield clash between two roughly equal-sized armies began to fade into history, that the term came into its own. The Vietnam War demonstrated anew that asymmetric warfare is not necessarily won by the theoretically more powerful side. There, irregular forces using guerrilla tactics had overcome US military might, and in subsequent decades 'asymmetric warfare' came increasingly to be applied to a situation in which regular forces were being opposed by insurgents or 'terrorists'. The term has had a particularly high profile since 9/11.

> Rear Admiral Harry Harris, commander of the Joint Task Force Guantanamo, said the men were dedicated terrorists and jihadists. 'This [the suicide of three detainees at the US Navy base on Guantanamo Bay] was not an act of desperation, but an act of asymmetric warfare committed against us.'
>
> *Sunday Times* (11 June 2006)

**At all at all.** A supposedly typical Irish expression added for emphasis at the end of a sentence.

> Whenever she said that she always threw her eyes up to

heaven as if she didn't know what she was going to do about it at all at all at all.

PATRICK MCCABE: *The Dead School* (1995)

It is often used in a stage mock Irish context.

**Atatürk.** (Turkish, 'father of the Turks', from *ata*, 'father', and *Türk*, 'Turks'.) A surname adopted in 1934 by Mustapha Kemal (1881–1938), the maker of modern Turkey, when all Turks were made to assume surnames. In the First World War he held the Dardanelles and subsequently ruthlessly set out to Westernize the republic he had established in 1923. European dress was imposed, polygamy was abolished, women were enfranchised and the Latin script replaced the Arabic. Atatürk died at 9.05 a.m. on 10 November 1938, and his death has been commemorated in Turkey by a minute's silence at that time each year ever since.

**'At five in the afternoon'.** The translation of '*A las cinco de la tarde*', the dirge-like refrain of Federico García Lorca's great elegy, *Llanto por Ignacio Sánchez Mejías* ('Lament for Ignacio Sánchez Mejías'), in memory of a bullfighter who had been gored to death in 1934. The poem was published in 1935, and the following year Lorca himself was assassinated by nationalists shortly after the outbreak of the Spanish Civil War. The American abstract expressionist Robert Motherwell (1915–91) gave the title *At Five in the Afternoon* (1949) to one of his series of paintings, ELEGIES TO THE SPANISH REPUBLIC.

**Athlete's foot.** A popular or euphemistic name for *tinea pedis*, dating from the 1920s. The condition, a type of fungal infection, is characterized by peeling and broken skin, particularly between the toes. Its name alludes to its association with sweaty feet encased in shoes or boots, although it is frequently found among people who are anything but athletic. It is estimated that 80 per cent of the adult population of Britain suffer from it.

**Atkins, Tommy.** The once-common name of the archetypal British private soldier, often shortened to Tommy (plural Tommies). The name comes from the use of the name 'Thomas Atkins' on specimen forms in the British Army in the 19th century. Tommy makes an early appearance in a poem of the same name (1892) by Rudyard Kipling (1865–1936):

> For it's Tommy this, an' Tommy that, an' 'Chuck him out, the brute!'
> But it's 'Saviour of 'is country' when the guns begin to shoot.

**Atkins diet.** A diet devised by the US physician Dr Robert Atkins (1932–2003), in which the dieter may eat liberal amounts of meat, cheese, butter, cream and so on, as long as he or she keeps off carbohydrates (potatoes, bread, pasta, rice, sugary foods, etc.). The diet became briefly fashionable among skeletal celebrities in the early 21st century, although the estranged partners of some dieters reported that it made their breath smell like a week-old corpse. Atkins himself reportedly weighed 160kg (25 stone) at the time of his death, and had suffered a heart attack in 2002.

**Atlantic, Battle of the.** *See* BATTLE OF THE ATLANTIC.

**Atlantic Charter.** During the Second World War US President Roosevelt and Winston Churchill, the British prime minister, met on a warship in Placentia Bay, Newfoundland, on the western side of the Atlantic (11 August 1941) and made this eight-point declaration of the principles on which peace was to be based, consequent upon Allied victory. As the United States had not yet entered the war, Churchill was desperate for US support, and part of his plan was to draw America into the conflict. A keynote among the generalities of the Charter, which can be compared to President Wilson's FOURTEEN POINTS, was that after the war 'all men shall be enabled to live in freedom from fear and want'. Other points included opposition to further territorial expansion or territorial changes without the agreement of the inhabitants, the assertion that people should choose their own form of government, the establishment of international economic cooperation, and the disarmament of the aggressor nations. Britain also proposed a successor to the LEAGUE OF NATIONS, although the United States at this stage would not commit to joining such a body. However, the points enunciated in the Charter were to form the basis of the UNITED NATIONS.

**Atlantic Wall.** The name given by the Germans in the Second World War to their defences along the Atlantic coast of Europe, which were built to resist invasion. *See also* FORTRESS EUROPE.

***Atmospheric Skull Sodomizing a Grand Piano.*** A calm painting of a small Spanish village by Salvador Dalí (1904–89), the peace disturbed only by the event described in the title. One rather feels for the piano, only one of whose legs remains on the ground, such is the force of the skull's phallically extended jawbone. It is to paintings such as these that James Thurber was no doubt referring when he wrote in 1945: 'The naked truth about me is to the naked truth about Salvador Dali as an old ukulele in the attic is to a piano in a tree, and I mean a piano with breasts.'

**ATS.** Members of the Auxiliary Territorial Service, a women's army corps formed in 1938 and serving in the Second World

War. In 1949 it was succeeded by the WRAC (*see* WAAC). A single member was known as an AT.

> When shall I see the Thames again?
> The prow-promoted gems again,
> As beefy ATS
> Without their hats
> Come shooting through the bridge?
>
> JOHN BETJEMAN: *New Bats in Old Belfries*, 'Henley-on-Thames' (1945)

*See also* OFFICERS' GROUNDSHEETS.

**At Swim-Two-Birds.** A modernist novel (1939) by Flann O'Brien (one of several pseudonyms of Brian O'Nolan; 1911–66). It hovers between burlesque and parody of popular fiction, and also of Irish legend, such as had been promoted in the Irish Literary Revival. Snáimh-dá-en ('two-birds') was one of the resting-places of Mad Sweeney, hero of the Early Irish legend, *Buile Shuibne* ('The Frenzy of Suibne'), and is Devenish Island, between Clonmacnois and Shannonbridge, near where O'Brien spent part of his childhood. *See also* FIRST LINES OF NOVELS.

**Attaboy.** (Probably from 'That's the boy!'.) An exclamation of enthusiastic approval or encouragement, originating in the United States and widely used in the 1930s by young people in the English-speaking world. 'Attagirl' also exists when the one encouraged is female.

> 'Look at that little mite with *Attaboy*
> Printed across her paper sailor hat.
> Disgusting, isn't it? Who *can* they be,
> Her parents, to allow such forwardness?'
>
> JOHN BETJEMAN: *Selected Poems*, 'Beside the Seaside' (1948)

**At the end of the day.** When all is said and done; when everything has been taken into account. A now hackneyed phrase that first became current in the 1970s. It was the title of the sixth volume (1973) of Harold Macmillan's monumental memoirs (1966–75), the other six being *Winds of Change* (1966), *The Blast of War* (1967), *Tides of Fortune* (1969), *Riding the Storm* (1971), *Pointing the Way* (1972) and *The Past Masters* (1975). *See also* WIND OF CHANGE.

> 'At the end of the day,' he stated, 'this verifies what I have been saying against the cuts in public expenditure.'
>
> *South Nottinghamshire Echo* (16 December 1976)

**At the stroke of the midnight hour.** *See* MIDNIGHT'S CHILDREN.

**At this moment in time.** Now; these days. A near meaningless phrase favoured by representatives of trade unions, sports teams and the like when interviewed by the media. The following is an example of the usage in a statement by England's football manager, Glenn Hoddle (b.1957):

> I have never said that … At this moment in time, if that changes in years to come I don't know, but what happens here today and changes as we go along that is part of life's learning and part of your inner beliefs. But at this moment in time I did not say them things and at the end of the day I want to put that on record because it has hurt people.
>
> *The Times* (report of television interview) (2 February 1999)

**Attila the Hen.** A nickname of Margaret Thatcher (b.1923), Conservative prime minister from 1979 to 1990, so called for her uncompromising attitudes in punning reference to Attila (406–453), king of the Huns, noted for his ruthlessness. It may have been coined by the then Conservative minister Norman St John Stevas. *See also* BLESSED MARGARET; IRON LADY; LEADERENE; TINA.

**Attitude.** In the 1970s this word gained a new turn of meaning to denote a resentful or antagonistic manner and hence a self-possessed stance or assertive swagger. To have the latter is thus to 'have attitude' or to be 'with attitude'. Both senses are of US origin.

> In this job, you gotta have attitude, hang loose, ready for anything.
>
> *Police Review* (28 September 1990)

**Audi.** The car of this name was launched in 1909 by Dr August Horch (1868–1951), founder of the German company of Horch-Werke in Zwickau. He originally manufactured the car under his own name but lost control of the company and for legal reasons could not give his name to another car. He therefore ingeniously translated his surname, as if German *horch!*, 'hark!', into Latin *audi*. *See also* VORSPRUNG DURCH TECHNIK.

**Auf Wiedersehen, Pet.** A television comedy series screened from 1983 to 1986 and relating the misadventures of three Geordies, Denis, Neville and Oz, persuaded by local unemployment to seek work on a Düsseldorf building site. They are joined by Cockney lothario Wayne, Bristol ex-boxer Bomber, boring Brummie Barry and Liverpudlian arsonist Moxey. The disparate characters were soon ingrained on the national consciousness, and Oz in particular, played by ex-convict Jimmy Nail, was elevated to cult status. The title represents the lads' farewell to their German girlfriends. A new series was broadcast in 2004.

**Auk.** The regular nickname of Field-Marshal Sir C.J.E. Auchinleck (1884–1981), Commander-in-Chief in India during the Second World War. As a shortening of his surname, it derived from the bird so called and arose as an army nickname some time before the war.

**Aum Shinrikyo.** A Japanese cult inspired by certain Buddhist, Taoist and Hindu scriptures, which in 1995 was responsible for a attack on the Tokyo underground in which 12 people died from the effects of sarin nerve gas, and thousands were made ill. The Aum leader, Shoko Asahara, was sentenced to death in 2004, but went on to lodge an appeal.

*Aum* is a syllable representing the universe in the Hindu religion, and the second part is Japanese: *shin* 'truth', *ri* 'justice', *kyo* 'teaching, doctrine'. In 2000 the cult seems to have changed its name to 'Aleph'.

**Aunt Edna.** A typical theatre-goer of conservative taste. The playwright Terence Rattigan introduced the character in the preface to the second volume of his *Collected Works* (1953), describing her as an average attender of matinees whom playwrights must take into account:

> A nice, respectable, middle-class, middle-aged maiden lady, with time on her hands and the money to help her pass it … Let us call her Aunt Edna … Aunt Edna is universal, and to those who may feel that all the problems of the modern theatre might be solved by her liquidation, let me add that … she is also immortal.

Critics subsequently adopted the invention when complaining about the middle-class, middle-brow nature of his own plays.
*See also* Edna EVERAGE.

**Aunt Emma.** An unenterprising croquet player. The appellation dates from the 1960s.

**Auntie.** The BBC, regarded as a conservative or 'nannyish' organization, especially by comparison with the more populist and permissive commercial television. The BBC has itself accepted the nickname and exploited it punningly in such programme titles as *Auntie's Bloomers*, a selection of mishaps during filming. In the media the tag often serves as a simple synonym. *See also* the BEEB.

**Aunt Jane.** An African American nickname for an evangelical, HAPPY CLAPPY female worshipper.

> Black Christians must relearn the whole-hearted involvement with religion that typifies the churches' 'Aunt Janes'.
> *Time* (6 April 1970)

**Aunt Minnies.** A US nickname for photographs taken by commercial photographers or amateurs that happen to show an object of military intelligence interest behind the human subjects. In the Second World War US intelligence officers scoured antique shops for photographs and

postcards of this type, so called because someone's Aunt Minnie usually appeared in the picture.

**Aunt Thomasina.** A US nickname, current in the 1970s, for an obsequious African American woman, especially one who did not support the cause of WOMEN'S LIB. The analogy was with 'Uncle Tom' as a name for an African American man obsequious to whites, from the central character of Harriet Beecher Stowe's anti-slavery novel *Uncle Tom's Cabin* (1852).

**Au pair.** (French, 'on an equal footing'.) A young foreign person, typically female, who joins a family to take on housework and help with young children in exchange for board and lodging and a modest weekly wage. She usually does so to learn the language or to improve her knowledge of it, although some are perhaps drawn by the prospect of male company and the potential for a British boyfriend. The allure may well work the other way round, and the Swedish au pair, in particular, has come to be stereotyped as a high ranker in the sex stakes.

**Auschwitz.** The German name for the small town of Oświęcim in southern Poland, notorious as the site of one of the biggest Nazi death camps in the Second World War. A small camp for political prisoners (Auschwitz I) was established here in 1940, followed by a much larger camp (Auschwitz II) in 1941 close to the nearby village of Brzezinka (called Birkenau in German; hence the whole complex is sometimes called Auschwitz-Birkenau). A third camp, Auschwitz III, was a slave-labour camp. Auschwitz II was designed specifically as an extermination camp for Jews, gypsies and others. Estimates of the overall number of deaths at Auschwitz vary between 1 million and 2.5 million, and may have been as high as 4 million. So powerful is the name that it stands, metonymically, for the HOLOCAUST as a whole. *See also* ANGEL OF DEATH; BELSEN; DACHAU; FINAL SOLUTION.

**Aussie.** A familiar name for an Australian, first in use among Australian soldiers in the First World War. Their own colloquial name for themselves was DIGGER. *See also* STRINE.

**Austerity.** The label attached to the period 1945–51 immediately following the Second World War, in which rationing continued, and in some cases was even tightened. Although the period saw the introduction of the National Health Service, free secondary education for all and many other improvements in welfare provision (*see* WELFARE STATE), the defeat in 1951 of the Labour government that introduced these measures is often attributed to continuing austerity. The period was celebrated thus by Noël Coward, in ironic homage to 'The WHITE CLIFFS OF DOVER', which, as sung by Vera Lynn, had expressed the nation's hopes for the future in the darkest days of the war:

> There'll be blackbirds over
> The greyish cliffs of Dover …
>
> NOËL COWARD: 'There Are Bad Times Just around the Corner' (1952)

**Austin, Steve.** The 'bionic man' hero of Martin Caidon's novel *Cyborg* (1972). He is a test pilot who crashes, is badly injured, then rebuilt as part man, part machine. As he acclimatizes to his new body he discovers that he has superbly enhanced physical powers, which he uses to pursue various villains. The novel formed the basis of *The Six Million Dollar Man* (1973–8), a successful television series, in which Austin was played by Lee Majors (b.1940). This led to a spin-off series, *The Bionic Woman* (1976–8), with Lindsay Wagner playing the heroine, Jaime Sommers.

**Australian Living Treasures.** *See* NATIONAL TREASURE.

**Austrian Corporal.** A nickname of Adolf Hitler (1889–1945), the Nazi FÜHRER. Hitler was born in Austria, but moved to Munich in 1913. Although summoned for examination by the Austrian army in February 1914 he was rejected as unfit. When the First World War broke out he joined the 16th Bavarian Reserve Infantry Regiment as a volunteer. He spent much of the war serving as a runner on the front line and was wounded in 1916 and gassed in 1918. He was awarded the Iron Cross Second Class in 1914 and the Iron Cross First Class in 1918, but never rose above the rank of corporal. *See also* HERRENVOLK; Herr SCHICKLGRUBER.

**Austrian Oak, The.** A nickname given to the US bodybuilder, actor and now politician Arnold Schwarzenegger (b.1947) on account of his acting skills. His father was an Austrian Nazi, and Arnold himself has been Republican governor of California since 2003 (*see* The GOVERNATOR).

**Automatic pilot.** To do something on automatic pilot is to do it mechanically, without conscious awareness. The allusion is to the automatic pilot or autopilot that keeps an aircraft on a set course without the aid of the pilot. *See also* FLY BLIND.

**Avengers, The.** A British television comedy thriller series screened from 1961 to 1968 in a blend of the chic, the sexy, the violent and the self-mocking. The hero, elegant secret agent John Steed, with bowler hat and cane, was played by Patrick MacNee, while his female, leather-clad, judo-practising sidekick was first Cathy Gale, played by Honor Blackman, then Emma PEEL, played memorably by Diana Rigg, and finally Tara King, played by Linda Thorson. It became a worldwide hit, and with James BOND and The BEATLES it helped convince the world that Britain was modern and fashionable. In 1976 MacNee returned in *The New Avengers* with Joanna Lumley. A film version called *The Avengers* (1998), starring Ralph Fiennes as Steed and Uma Thurman as Emma Peel, flopped.

**Avenue of the Americas.** The official name given in the 1940s to Sixth Avenue, New York, to honour the Latin American countries. Few New Yorkers use the appellation, preferring the briefer numerical name. The street runs from Canal Street in the south to Central Park in the north, and for many years its length was followed by an elevated 'subway' or 'el' train.

**Aversion therapy.** A type of behaviour therapy introduced in the 1950s. Its aim was to make a patient abandon a habit or addiction by associating it with something unpleasant, such as an electric shock. It has been used to treat self-injurious behaviour in the mentally handicapped but has now mostly been superseded by other forms of therapy.

**Avon lady.** A woman who calls at private houses selling cosmetics on behalf of Avon Products Inc., a US firm founded in 1886 by David H. McConnell as the California Perfume Company. The firm's advertising jingle, 'Ding dong, this is Avon calling', soon became familiar in many homes, and some of its reps have risen to impressive heights in their careers. In Britain alone 4 million women were Avon ladies in the last half of the 20th century, but the setting up of the firm's INTERNET site in 1998 was seen as a threat to the thousands still doing the domestic rounds at doorstep level. In the film *Edward Scissorhands* (1990) an intrepid Avon lady acts as good fairy to the isolated freak boy Edward and gives him a cosy home in a Florida suburb.

> In one of her most memorable cases, she discovered that an errant wife was using her job as an Avon lady to betray her husband.
>
> *The Times* (26 May 1999)

*See also* TUPPERWARE.

**AWACS.** The acronym of *a*irborne *w*arning *a*nd *c*ontrol *s*ystem, a system of the US Air Force for the early detection of enemy bombers. As developed by the USAF, it was carried in a specially modified Boeing 707 aircraft, with its main RADAR antenna mounted on a turntable housed in a circular rotodome. The first production-model AWACS entered service with the USAF in 1977 and was taken up by the RAF soon after.

**Awesome Welles.** A not entirely flattering nickname for the overweight actor Orson Welles (1915–85) given him by his fellow American actor Tony Curtis. Towards the end of his career Welles is said to have weighed 181kg (399lb or 28½ stone).

**Awfully big adventure, An.** Dying, according to J.M. Barrie in Act 3 of PETER PAN (1904):

> To die will be an awfully big adventure.

This may have influenced the last words of Charles Frohman (1860–1915) before he went down with the torpedoed passenger liner *Lusitania* on 7 May 1915:

> Why fear death? It is the most beautiful adventure in life.

**Awkward age.** Adolescence, as a period of instability between childhood and adulthood. The term dates from the turn of the 20th century and may have been borrowed from French *l'âge ingrat*. Henry James has a novel of the English title (1899) about a young woman's emergence into an understanding of the world.

**AWOL.** The acronym of *a*bsent *w*ith*o*ut *l*eave (popularly, *w*ithout *o*fficial *l*eave), a military term originating in the First World War for a serviceman absent without permission from his place of duty or quarters but not intending to desert. 'To go AWOL' is to be absent thus, and the phrase can now apply to anyone or anything missing, as: 'Oh dear, Tiggy's gone AWOL again.'

**Axe-handles across the arse.** A colloquial Australian unit of measurement for the size of someone's posterior. Its use is highly impressionistic, multiplicity being the key: a broad-in-the-beam woman might be described modestly as 'two axe-handles across the arse' or, with more bravura, as 'six axe-handles across the arse'.

**Axis.** A collective term for Germany, Italy, Japan and their allies in the Second World War. The term was coined by the Italian fascist leader Benito Mussolini to describe the military alliance with NAZI Germany (also known as the Pact of Steel or the Rome–Berlin Axis) of 22 May 1939. The roots of the Axis go back further: Germany signed the Anti-Comintern Pact with Japan in 1936 and with Italy in 1937. In September 1940 the three countries signed the Tripartite Pact, committing them to a 10-year military alliance. During the Second World War Hungary, Bulgaria, Romania, Slovakia and Croatia all fought on the side of the Axis powers.

**Axis of Evil.** The term used by US President George W. Bush (*see* DUBYA) in his 2002 State of the Union address to Congress to designate a set of ROGUE STATES armed with WEAPONS OF MASS DESTRUCTION (WMD) and evil intentions towards the West. The original reference comprised Iran, Iraq and North Korea, but membership of the informal grouping is flexible.

> States like these, and their terrorist allies, constitute an axis of evil, arming to threaten the peace of the world. By seeking weapons of mass destruction, these regimes pose a grave and growing danger. They could provide these arms to terrorists, giving them the means to match their hatred. They could attack our allies or attempt to blackmail the United States. In any of these cases, the price of indifference would be catastrophic.

The term was partly derived from David Frum, one of Bush's speechwriters, who came up with 'axis of hatred'. This was adapted by Bush's chief speech writer, Michael Gerson, and it echoed Ronald Reagan's designation in the 1980s of the Soviet Union as the EVIL EMPIRE.

In the 2004 presidential election, following the Iraq War and the failure to find WMD there, the Democrats further elaborated the slogan, producing a bumper sticker with pictures of Bush, Vice-President Dick Cheney and Secretary of Defense Donald Rumsfeld, with the words 'Asses of Evil'.

**Axis Sally.** The name given by US servicemen to the radio propagandist Mildred Elizabeth Gillars (1900–88), the first woman in US history to be convicted of treason. Her career began in the Second World War on German radio, when in a sultry voice she tried to persuade the homesick soldiers that Germany was unbeatable, that their chances of surviving death were slim and that some draft dodger back in the United States was making off with their girlfriend. After the war she was convicted for treason for a single broadcast that she made on 11 May 1944, on the eve of the Normandy invasion. She was sentenced to 10 to 30 years' imprisonment and in 1950 was sent to the Federal Reformatory for Women in Alderson, West Virginia, where TOKYO ROSE also served part of her sentence. Gillars converted to Catholicism in 1960, was released on parole the following year and spent the rest of her working days teaching languages and music at a convent school. *See also* Lord HAW-HAW.

**Ayatollah.** A title given to any of a class of Shi'ite religious leaders in Iran, most notably the fiercely anti-Western Ayatollah Ruholla Khomeini (1902–89), leader of the 1979 Islamic revolution. Since then the ayatollahs have wielded considerable political power. The term is also sometimes pejoratively used for any sinisterly powerful political or morally prescriptive figure. The word derives from the Arabic for 'miraculous sign of God'. *See also* FATWA; GREAT SATAN; *The* SATANIC VERSES.

**Azania.** The African name of South Africa, introduced by the African National Congress. It is of classical origin and initially applied to East Africa. Its origin lies in the root word, meaning 'land of blacks', that gave the name of Zanzibar. In Evelyn Waugh's novel *Black Mischief* (1932) Azania is an imaginary island empire off the east coast of

Africa, its name and location clearly inspired by those of Zanzibar. Its capital is Debra-Dowa and it has many churches and places of worship of all denominations.

**Aziz, Dr.** The gentle Indian doctor in E.M. Forster's novel *A* PASSAGE TO INDIA (1924). He is accused of assaulting the Englishwoman Adela Quested in the Marabar Caves and is made to stand trial. He is acquitted, but remains permanently embittered. Forster based him on his friend Syed Ross Masood (1889–1937), director of public education in Hyderabad State from 1916 to 1928. In the 1984 film of the novel he is played by Victor Bannerjee.

**Azkaban.** The austere prison to which seriously errant wizards are despatched by the Ministry of Magic in the Harry POTTER books. Here they are guarded by hideous, ghostly beings called Dementors, who, as their name suggests, tend to make their prisoners lose the will to live. Azkaban is naturally where those discovered to be DEATH EATERS are sent, and it is supposedly inescapable – a rumour disproved by the titular character of *The Prisoner of Azkaban* (1999).

**AZT.** The abbreviation of azidothymidine, the tradename of zidovudine, an antiviral drug used in the treatment of AIDS. It was introduced in 1986.

**Aztec two-step.** *See* MONTEZUMA'S REVENGE.

# B

**Baa-Baas.** An affectionate nickname for the Barbarians, a unique rugby union football club that distinguished players are invited to join. The Barbarians' philosophy is based on adventure and attack, and matches involving the club are generally high-scoring affairs. Founded in 1890 in Bradford, the club has no clubhouse or ground of its own. There are typically six fixtures a year, including matches against England, Scotland, Wales and Ireland, and since 1948 international teams have usually concluded a tour of Britain with a game against the Barbarians. The Barbarians' 1973 match against the ALL BLACKS, won 23-11 by the Baa-Baas, has acquired almost mythic status in rugby circles, adorned as it was by an astounding try by the Welsh scrum-half Gareth Edwards, the culmination of a move that began deep in the Barbarians' half of the pitch and involved multiple passes.

**Baader-Meinhof Gang.** A German terrorist group active from 1968 to 1998 against US and German capitalist targets. It was also known as the Red Army Faction and was named after two of its founders, Andreas Baader (1943–77) and Ulrike Meinhof (1934–76). Both were arrested and jailed. Meinhof hanged herself in her cell. Baader and two other gang members were found shot in their cells, presumably suicides. Their deaths on 18 October 1977 came the day after West German commandos stormed a hijacked Lufthansa plane in Mogadishu, Somalia, and blocked a ransom attempt to free the terrorists. *See also* URBAN GUERRILLA.

**Babar.** The elegantly dressed African elephant in the books for young children by the French writer and illustrator Jean de Brunhoff (1899–1937), first published in 1931 with the author's handwritten text and original watercolours. Other characters include Céleste, whom Babar marries, and her cousin Arthur. Babar has inspired works in unexpected quarters, including a sequence of piano pieces by Francis Poulenc (1899–1963) and a study by the Marxist critic Ariel

Dorfman entitled *The Empire's Old Clothes* (1983). His name appears to derive from Hindi *babar*, 'lion'.

**Babbitt.** The leading character in the novel of this name (1922) by Sinclair Lewis (1885–1951). He is a prosperous realtor (estate agent) in the western city of Zenith, a simple, likeable fellow, with faint aspirations to culture that are forever smothered in the froth and futile hustle of US business life. Drive (which takes him nowhere), hustle (by which he saves no time) and efficiency (which does not enable him to do anything) are the keynotes of his life. Babbitt came to typify the business man of orthodox outlook and virtues, with no interest in cultural values, and the name has become a synonym for a certain type of American Philistinism.

**Babbling brook.** In Australian and New Zealand rhyming slang, a cook, especially one in an institution, mining camp or farm. It is commonly contracted to 'babbler', which is actually first recorded (1904) earlier than the full form.

**Babe, The.** George Herman 'Babe' Ruth (1895–1948), a US professional baseball player, was so known when he joined his first team, the Baltimore Orioles. He was a record-breaking hitter for the Boston Red Sox from 1914 to 1919 and thereafter for the New York Yankees (1920–34). The Yankee stadium, built shortly after he joined the club, has since been known as the 'House that Ruth Built'.

**Babelicious.** Stunningly sexually attractive. The outlandish epithet (standardly, but not exclusively, applied to young women) was launched on to an unsuspecting America in the 'Wayne's World' sketch on NBC's *Saturday Night Live* show in the early 1990s, and caught on in teen slang for a while, further bolstered by appearances in the films *Wayne's World* (1992) and *Wayne's World 2* (1993). It is a blend of 'babe' (in the sense 'sexually attractive woman') and 'delicious'.

Their commercial success notwithstanding, these movie

remakes also attracted media attention for the hot babelicious stars that hogged the headlines.

www.mtvasia.com

*See also* BOOTYLICIOUS.

**Baby blues.** Mood changes that mothers can suffer from after giving birth. Also a nickname (first recorded in 1972) for eyes, irrespective of their colour.

> I was shakin' in my shoes
> Whenever she flashed those baby blues.
> J. GEILS BAND: 'Centrefold' (song) (1981)

**Baby boom.** A sudden increase in births in the period following the Second World War, when husbands and fathers returned home and there was a sudden rise or 'boom' in the birth rate. A person born at this time is sometimes known as a 'baby boomer'.

> They are stressing the importance of the baby-boomers, roughly the generation now over 25 and under 40.
> *The Observer* (5 January 1986)

**Baby Born.** One of the most popular and commercially successful dolls of the 1990s, designed by Victor M. Pracas and made by Zapf Creation of Germany. It was created to resemble a real baby and had a realistic appeal in its multitude of 'bodily functions', which included eating, crying and soiling its nappy. Joints at its hips, shoulders and neck also gave realistic flexibility and movement.

**Baby Doc.** *See* PAPA DOC.

**Baby doll dress.** A short, high-waisted, short-sleeved, diaphanous dress, such as worn by a doll or young child. Young women who took to wearing such dresses in the early 1990s were seen as making a somewhat ambivalent statement about fashion and gender roles.

**Babygro.** The all-in-one stretch garment for babies was the invention in the 1950s of the Viennese businessman Walter Artzt, who also designed the fabric. The suit was designed for comfort and practicality and given a name to denote its prime function.

**Baby-kisser.** A US nickname for a politician, especially a campaigning one, who meets families and admires their babies (but without necessarily kissing them).

**Baby M.** The label name of the baby girl who was the centre of a court case of 1987. Her real name was either Melissa Stern or Sara Whitehead. Matters began when a New Jersey couple, William and Elizabeth Stern, engaged Mary Beth Whitehead as a SURROGATE MOTHER to bear Mr Stern's child via artificial insemination. When the child was born in 1986, however, Whitehead refused to part with her. The Sterns sued, and the resultant case raised important questions about business ethics and the bond between mother and child. The judge originally decided for the Sterns, but the New Jersey Supreme Court overturned the decision, granting Mr Stern custody and Whitehead parental rights, while at the same time declaring surrogacy contracts illegal.

**Baby snatcher.** Someone who enters into an amorous relationship with a much younger person. The expression is first recorded early in the 20th century, preceding the later 'cradle snatcher'.

**Baby Yar.** A large ravine near Kiev in Ukraine that became the site of a mass grave of more than 100,000 victims, mainly Jews but also Communist Party officials and Russian prisoners of war, killed by German SS squads (*see* EINSATZGRUPPEN) between 1941 and 1943. The massacre was carried out partly in obedience to Hitler's order to exterminate all Jews and Soviet officials, but partly also in retaliation for an explosion earlier in 1941 that had rocked the German command post in Kiev, killing many German soldiers. When the Germans subsequently retreated from the Soviet Union, they attempted to hide the evidence of the slaughter. The massacre was depicted in novels by Ilya Ehrenburg and Anatoly Kuznetsov and was the subject of Yevgeny Yevtushenko's moving poem 'Baby Yar' (1961).

**Bachelor gay.** A former stock term for a young man of independent means who lived mainly for 'wine, women and song'. The expression was popularized by a song of this title by James W. Tate from Harold Fraser-Simson's musical *The Maid of the Mountains* (1916). The change in sense of GAY essentially killed any currency that the phrase retained, except in frivolous or facetious use.

**Bachelor girl.** A now somewhat dated term for an unmarried professional young woman. The expression dates from the early 20th century.

**Bach Flower Remedies.** A form of ALTERNATIVE medicine using a series of 38 preparations made from wild flowers and plants to treat 'negative emotions' that manifest themselves as illness. The treatment was devised by the Harley Street homeopathist Dr Edward Bach (1880–1936).

**Backbeat.** *See* FIFTH BEATLE.

**Back in one's box.** If you tell someone to 'get back in their box', you mean that they should take a lower profile, stop being so obstreperous or opinionated, be a little less full of themselves – in other words, 'pipe down'. The underlying image may be of a jack-in-the-box that has just burst forth to general consternation.

All those critics of Charles Darwin University, get back in your box. That's the message CDU is promoting in the wake of its performance in The Good Universities' Guide and 'news of mammoth grants for seven research projects'… The university recently issued a media release with the headline 'CDU Nay-Sayers Put Back in The Box'. Funny thing is we didn't know they had any until they advertised it.

www.theaustralian.news.com.au (7 December 2005)

**'Back in the USSR'.** A rollicking rock 'n' roll song by The BEATLES, credited to John Lennon and Paul McCartney (but mainly by the latter). It appears on the so-called WHITE ALBUM, released in November 1968. The title of the song was originally to have been I'M BACKING BRITAIN (inspired by the slogan of a contemporary pro-British industry campaign) but was playfully turned on its head to become 'Backing the USSR' and finally 'Back in the USSR' (probably by analogy with Chuck Berry's 1959 hit 'Back in the USA'). Released in the year that the Soviet Union invaded Czechoslovakia (*see* PRAGUE SPRING), the song and its title led to The Beatles being accused by the extreme right-wing JOHN BIRCH SOCIETY of promoting communism.

**Back of a bus.** To look like, or have a face like, the back of a bus is to be at best unprepossessing and at worst plain or ugly: on the basis that the back of a bus, with its dirt and exhaust fumes, is an unpleasant public sight.

**Backroom boys.** A name given to the unpublicized scientists and technicians in the Second World War who contributed much to the development of scientific warfare and war production, and since applied generally to any BOFFINS of this kind. Nigel Balchin's novel *The* SMALL BACK ROOM (1943) is an exciting story of such research, with its many challenges and frustrations. It was filmed in 1948 by Michael Powell and Emeric Pressburger. The ultimate source of the phrase was the song 'See What the Boys in the Back Room Will Have', sung by Marlene Dietrich in the film DESTRY RIDES AGAIN (1939). Her spirited rendering of this inspired Lord Beaverbrook to use the words in a speech on war production (24 March 1941):

Now who is responsible for this work of development on which so much depends? To whom must the praise be given? To the boys in the back rooms. They do not sit in the limelight. But they are the men who do all the work. Many of them are Civil Servants.

**Back-seat driver.** One who criticizes without responsibility or who attempts to control from a subordinate position or without entitlement, like a passenger in the back seat of a car who tries to direct the driver. The phrase originated in the United States in the 1920s, when many cars were chauffeur-driven and their passengers sat in the back seat, quite legitimately directing the chauffeur where to go.

**Backstage.** This word's sense of 'behind the scenes' dates only from the 1920s. Originally the back stage was a recess in the rear wall of a stage used for pieces of scenery in a deep-set vista or otherwise for storage. The term then came to apply to all parts of the theatre behind the stage, including the actors' dressing rooms.

**Back story.** A history that is invented for the characters, places, etc. in a story, play or film, which accounts for their part in the narrative but is not necessarily explicitly recounted. The term is first recorded in 1982.

There's not a lot in the book [*Bleak House*] about Jarndyce's past, but Nigel [Stafford-Clark, producer] and Andrew [Davies, writer] put together a little imaginary back-story for him, so I had a bit more to hold on to. They reckoned his first wife had died from TB while still a young girl, and Jarndyce had never really recovered from the shock.

*Radio Times* (19 November 2005)

The Hollywood habit of creating 'prequels' for successful films might be seen as attempts to create back stories writ large.

**Back to basics.** A return to 'ground rules' and traditional values. The catch-all slogan was coined by the then prime minister, John Major, at the Conservative Party Conference of 1993. A succession of minor sex scandals involving Tory MPs in the months that followed gave the dictum an unfortunate resonance (*see*, for example, SHAGGER NORRIS).

It is time to get back to basics: to self-discipline and respect for the law, to consideration for others, to accepting responsibility for yourself and your family, and not shuffling it off on the state.

JOHN MAJOR: speech at Conservative Party Conference (8 October 1993)

*See also* VICTORIAN VALUES.

**Back to Methuselah.** A play (1921) by the Irish playwright George Bernard Shaw (1856–1950) consisting of five loosely linked dramas on a variety of philosophical themes, including that of old age. Methuselah is the oldest man mentioned in the Bible, in which he is said to have lived to the age of 969. Shaw himself lived to the age of 94. He once ascribed his long life to the location of his home in the village of Ayot St Lawrence, Hertfordshire, explaining that he had decided 'this is the place for me' after spotting a gravestone with the legend: 'Jane Eversley. Born 1825. Died 1895. Her time was short.'

**Back to square one.** Back to where one started. The expression is often linked with an explanatory device employed in the early days of broadcast commentaries on football matches when, in order to make the course of the game easier to follow, a diagram of the pitch, divided into numbered squares, was printed in the *Radio Times*, and from time to time the commentator's assistant would call out which square the ball was in: 'square one' was to one side of one of the goals. However, the phrase is not recorded before 1960, a quarter of a century after the 'squares' idea was abandoned, and it seems more plausible that the idea may have derived from earlier board games such as SNAKES AND LADDERS.

**Back to the drawing board.** Back to begin again, especially after the aborting of an enterprise. The implication is that the venture was not properly or adequately planned. The expression may have originated with aircraft designers in the Second World War, when tests revealed faults in some models.

**Back to the land.** A slogan that first emerged at the end of the 19th century to encourage people to return from the overcrowded cities to the countryside. Thus wags claimed that the slogan of the LAND GIRLS of the Second World War, allegedly a promiscuous lot, should be 'Backs to the land'. From the later 1960s, as a by-product of the HIPPIE and NEW AGE movements, a new back-to-the-land tendency emerged, with the emphasis on self-sufficiency in food and energy.

**Bad boy.** The bad boy of a particular field of activity is the man who disregards all its rules, creates trouble, etc.: its male *enfant terrible*. The expression is first recorded in the title of the composer George Antheil's book *Bad Boy of Music* (1945). Rock stars and other (often over-remunerated, high-living) popular-culture celebrities tend to have the description applied to them.

> 'It doesn't take much effort to be the bad boy of British bowls, believe me,' admits Sanders.
>
> *The Guardian* (22 August 2003)

**Badger.** A nickname for Alistair Darling, a leading Blairite in the NEW LABOUR government since 1997, alluding to his prematurely silver hair and black eyebrows, formerly also accompanied by a black beard; also a nickname for the Conservative politician Norman Lamont, chancellor of the exchequer 1990–3, on account of his silver quiff.

**Bad hair day.** A day on which nothing seems to go right, as when one's hair proves to be quite unmanageable. The expression dates from the 1980s, and originated among women, but has since been adopted widely irrespective of gender.

**Bad news.** An unpleasant person or thing. More specifically, in US usage, the bad news is the bill in a café or restaurant, as: 'OK, let's see what the bad news is.' *See also* GOOD NEWS AND THE BAD NEWS.

**Bad trip.** A bad or frightening experience while taking psychedelic drugs. The phrase dates from the 1960s.

**Baedeker raid.** A phrase originating in 1942 to describe a German air attack on a historic or culturally important British city, and specifically one listed in a Baedeker guidebook, such as Bath, Canterbury or Norwich. The raids were made in reprisal for British raids on Cologne and Lübeck. The guides themselves were originally issued by Karl Baedeker (1801–59) in Coblenz.

**BAFTA award.** An annual award of the British Academy of Film and Television Arts, founded in 1976 to promote British films and television. It is subdivided into categories such as 'best actress', 'best actor', 'best original screenplay' and the like. The awards ceremony is televised live by the BBC as a glittering show overlaid with a gloss of mutual admiration and mawkish sentimentality. *See also* OSCAR.

**Baggins, Bilbo.** The hero of J.R.R. Tolkien's children's novel *The* HOBBIT (1937). He is a small, hairy-footed being who, accompanied by the wizard GANDALF and a dozen 'dwarves', helps slay a dragon and recover a lost treasure. He reappears in *The* LORD OF THE RINGS (1954–5). *See also* FRODO.

**Baggy green.** The green cap worn by members of the Australian cricket team. Its somewhat voluminous design contrasts with the sleeker Corinthian version standardly worn (before the days of helmets and baseball caps) by cricketers from other countries. With the accession to the Australian captaincy in 1999 of Steve Waugh, who made a point of invoking Australian history (cricketing and otherwise) as a way of instilling pride and passion into his team, the baggy green took on an added dimension as a symbol of the Australian cricketing heritage.

> I asked what he [Shane Warne] had missed most about cricket while suspended. To my pleasant surprise, he did not have immediate recourse to the stupefying cult of the baggy green.
>
> GIDEON HAIGH: *Ashes 2005* (2005)

**Baghdad Blogger.** *See* BLOG.

**Baghdad Bob.** *See* COMICAL ALI.

**Bag lady.** A homeless woman who wanders the streets carrying all her possessions in shopping bags. The phrase originated in the United States.

**Bag of boiled sweets.** The 'only safe pleasure for a parliamentarian', according to Julian Critchley (1930–2000), maverick Conservative member of parliament, in *The Listener*, 10 June 1982, referring to yet another 'Tory MP in Sex Scandal' scandal.

**Bag of nerves.** *See* BUNDLE OF NERVES.

**Bagpuss.** An award-winning children's television cartoon, first shown in 1974, in which Emily, a Victorian girl who owns a magic shop, leaves various objects for her beloved eponymous cloth cat and his friends to mend. After the item was restored to its former glory, it was put in the window for its owner to collect. The pink-and-white striped Bagpuss, so named because he was 'baggy and a bit loose at the seams', would then yawn and go to sleep until the next episode. The character was created by Peter Firmin and Oliver Postgate.

**Bag some Zs** or **bag Zs.** To get some sleep. An American expression (first recorded in 1968), so the Zs (representing the sound of snoring) are 'zees' rather than 'zeds'. *See also* ZZZ.

**Bail bandit.** A colloquialism of the 1990s for a person who commits a crime while on bail awaiting trial.

**Bailey bridge.** A temporary bridge made of prefabricated steel parts that can be erected speedily, invented by the engineer Sir Donald Bailey (1901–85). In the Second World War such bridges were a major factor in the rapidity of Allied advances, especially in northwestern Europe.

**Bailie Vass.** A nickname used by *Private Eye* for Sir Alec Douglas-Home (1903–95), Conservative prime minister (1963–4). The nickname arose from a miscaptioning of a photograph in a Scottish newspaper (a bailie is a municipal magistrate in Scotland). To everybody's surprise Douglas-Home succeeded Harold Macmillan (SUPERMAC) as prime minister when the latter resigned at the time of the PROFUMO AFFAIR. To do so he renounced his title of 14th Earl of Home, and the Labour leader Harold Wilson (1916–95) observed. 'The whole process of democracy has ground to a halt with a fourteenth earl.' Douglas-Home responded: 'I suppose, if you come to think of it, Mr Wilson is the fourteenth Mr Wilson.' In 1974 Alec Douglas-Home became a life peer as Baron Home of the Hirsel.

**Bait and switch.** A deceptive and generally illegal commercial ruse by which customers are induced to visit a store by an advertised sale item (the 'bait'), only to be told that it is out of stock or that it is inferior to some more expensive item (the 'switch'). The expression dates from the 1920s.

**Baked Alaska.** The name of this tasty dessert, combining hot meringue and cold ice cream on a sponge cake base, is first recorded in the 1909 edition of Fannie Farmer's *Boston Cookery Book*. It existed some time before this, however, and is said by some to have been created by the chef Charles Ranhofer, who called it 'Alaska, Florida' in his cookbook of 1893.

**Bakelite.** The material course of modern life was altered significantly in 1909 when Leo Baekeland (1863–1944), a Belgian-born American chemist, announced his invention of Bakelite, the first synthetic polymer, basing its name on his own. It was hard, indissoluble, able to be moulded into different shapes and, above all, inexpensive. Commercial production began within a year, and soon everything from billiard balls to electrical insulators was made from the new plastic.

**Baker days.** A former term for days set aside in term time for teacher training in state schools. Such days, now known as INSET (in-service training), were introduced in 1987 by Kenneth Baker (b.1934), secretary of state for education, to acquaint teachers with new policies and classroom practice and to prepare them for the National Curriculum. With the pupils absent, some schools have taken advantage of such days to send teachers on 'educational' visits to museums or even on day trips abroad by way of 'team-building exercises'.

**Bakerloo Line.** A line of the London Underground that, when opened in 1906, ran only between Baker Street and Waterloo. Hence its portmanteau name, said to have been coined by 'Quex' (G.H.F. Nichols) of the *Evening News*.

**Bakewell tart.** A sweet tart containing a layer of jam beneath a topping made from ground almonds, sugar, eggs and butter. The connection with Bakewell is not known for certain, although legend has it that the original was created by accident in the early 19th century, when a chef at the Rutland Arms Hotel, in the centre of the Derbyshire town, made a mistake over a recipe. The 'tart' is a relatively new element. In the 19th century the confection was known as 'Bakewell pudding' (the earliest known reference to this is in Meg Dods's *The Cook and Housewife's Manual* of 1826), and the name 'Bakewell tart' is not recorded before the 20th century.

**Balance of terror.** A state of equilibrium between nations based on their mutual possession of nuclear weapons or some other means of mass terror. The expression dates from the COLD WAR and is said to have been coined in 1955 by the Canadian prime minister, Lester Pearson. *See also* MAD.

**Balcombe Street Gang.** An IRA group, which terrorized

London in the early 1970s in a campaign of bombings and shootings. The name is that of the Marylebone street where the four gunmen, Joseph O'Connell, Harry Duggan, Eddie Butler and Hugh Doherty, took a husband and wife hostage in December 1975 following a car chase and running gun battle in the West End. The men were jailed for life in 1977.

**Bald Eagle of Foggy Bottom.** A nickname of Robert A. Lovett (1895–1986), US secretary of state and under-secretary of defense under President Truman. The name alludes to his baldness, but also invites comparison with the bald eagle that is the national symbol of the United States. The latter part of the name refers to his time in the State Department, known as FOGGY BOTTOM.

**Baldilocks.** A nickname awarded by *Private Eye* to the Labour politician Gerald Kaufman (b.1930), a senior figure in the shadow cabinet in the 1980s and early 1990s, playing on Goldilocks and Kaufman's pate.

***Bald Prima Donna, The.*** A one-act play (*La Cantatrice chauve*) by the Romanian-born French playwright Eugène Ionesco (1912–94), which was first performed in Paris in 1950 to an audience of three. Described by the author as an 'anti-play', it is an apparently nonsensical entertainment in which the words exchanged by the characters seem to have no relation to each other, and it owed its genesis to the author's fascina-tion with examples of bizarre English phrases in language books. The 'bald prima donna' herself is the subject of just one obscure reference in the text, which actually came about in rehearsal when the Fire-chief garbled the words Ionesco had originally written. *See also* THEATRE OF THE ABSURD.

> *Fire-chief*: By the way, what about the Bald Prima Donna?
> *Mr Smith*: Ssh!
> *Mrs Smith*: She always wears her hair the same way!

**Balfour Declaration.** A letter expressing the views of the British government, written on 2 November 1917 by the foreign secretary Arthur Balfour (1848–1930) to Lionel Walter, 2nd Baron Rothschild (1868–1937), chairman of the British Zionist Federation (*see* ZIONISM). The letter stated the British government's support for 'the establishment in Palestine of a national home for the Jewish people' but specified that 'nothing shall be done which may prejudice the civil and religious rights of existing non-Jewish communities in Palestine' and that the political status of Jews in other countries should not be compromised. The Balfour Declaration was incorporated into the British man-date over Palestine (formerly part of the Turkish Ottoman Empire) awarded by the League of Nations in 1922, but the British abandoned the policy in 1939 and severely limited further Jewish immigration.

**Balfour's poodle.** The House of Lords. From 1906 the Conservative leader Arthur Balfour (1848–1930) exploited his party's majority in the Lords to block the legislation of Campbell-Bannerman's Liberal government, which had an overwhelming majority in the House of Commons. When the Lords rejected the Licensing Bill of 1908, Henry Chaplin, MP, claimed that the House of Lords was the 'watchdog of the constitution', to which Lloyd George replied: 'It is the right honourable gentleman's poodle. It fetches and carries for him. It barks for him. It bites anybody that he sets it on.' The expression was popularized by the title of Roy Jenkins's book *Mr Balfour's Poodle* (1954), an account of the struggle between the House of Lords and Asquith's government. This came to a head when the Lords vetoed Lloyd George's 'radical budget' of 1909 and led to the Parliament Bill of 1911, ending the power of the upper house to veto. *See also* BUSH'S POODLE.

**Ballboy** or **ballgirl.** A young person employed to retrieve balls that go out of play in tennis or some other game. Ballboys and ballgirls are particularly associated with the annual international tennis championships at Wimbledon, where they are constantly in the public eye. They were long recruited from Barnardo's foster homes but are now selected from year 10 (14- and 15-year-olds) at local comprehensive schools. They receive six months of disciplined coaching, including instruction in rolling and feeding balls to the players, and are now issued with smart Ralph Lauren-designed blue uniforms (replacing the green of old). For many years only boys were engaged. They were joined by their female counterparts in 1979, but girls were not admitted into the elite Centre Court team of 12 until 1985. In the 21st century, invidious sexual distinctions are blurred by the demotic 'ballkids'.

**Ball-breaker** or **ball-buster.** Originally, in US slang of the 1950s, a situation, task, etc. that is particularly burdensome or annoying. The expression also came to denote someone who sets uncomfortably exacting standards of work, but it was in the 1970s that it took on the meaning for which its wincingly graphic imagery ('ball' being 'testicle') seemed perfect: a domineering woman who destroys a man's self-confidence. An alternative formulation is 'ball-tearer'.

**Ballet Rambert.** *See* RAMBERT DANCE COMPANY.

**Ballets Russes.** The world's first modern ballet company was born on 18 March 1909 at the Théâtre du Châtelet, Paris, when a troupe of top-class Russian dancers, brought by Sergei Diaghilev (1872–1929) from St Petersburg and Moscow, staged *Le Pavillon d'Armide*, the *Polovtsian Dances* from *Prince Igor* and *Le Festin*. The event was a sensation with the public and launched Diaghilev himself as the greatest producer and impresario of the modern theatrical world. The company dissolved in 1929 following Diaghilev's death, and in 1932 it was succeeded by the Ballets Russes de Monte Carlo, with Colonel de Basil (originally Vasili Voskresensky; 1888–1951) as director.

**Ballgirl.** *See* BALLBOY.

**Ball is in your court, The.** It is up to you to make the next move. A metaphor from tennis dating from the 1950s.

**Ballpark figure.** An approximate figure, especially of a financial amount. A ballpark is a US baseball stadium. Since the playing area is large, a ballpark figure will not be narrowly defined. The term, which dates from the 1950s, equally relates to the practice of estimating the crowd attendance at a baseball game. *See also* IN THE RIGHT BALLPARK.

**Ball-tampering.** In cricket, the illegal alteration of the surface of a ball to affect its motion through the air when bowled. 'Tampering' of this kind is usually effected by fingering the seams of the ball or roughing up one side of it (polishing the ball is not illegal as long as it is done by the bowler). The practice is no doubt as old as cricket itself, but the term came to prominence in the early 1990s following a series of high-profile and controversial incidents in Test cricket, notably the accusations laid against the England captain Mike Atherton of rubbing earth on the ball during a match against South Africa in 1994.

**Ball-tearer.** A BALL-BREAKER. In the 1960 and 1970s the expression took off in Australian English as a term for something outstanding or impressive of its (bad) type (as in 'I've had a real ball-tearer of a day').

**Ball the jack.** To travel fast; to hurry. The expression originated in US railway jargon, in which a 'highball' was a signal to get under way or to increase speed and 'jack' was a locomotive. 'Ballin' the Jack', by Roy Burris, was a popular song in the ZIEGFELD FOLLIES 1913 revue.

> No sooner were we out of town than Eddie started to ball that jack ninety miles an hour out of sheer exuberance.
> JACK KEROUAC: *On the Road*, Pt I, ch. 3 (1957)

**Ballyhoo.** Fuss and bother. The word is of US origin and caught on in the early 20th century. Its source is disputed. A connection with the name of Ballyhooly, a village in Co. Cork, Ireland, has not been sustained, and even less likely is a blend of 'ballet' and 'whoop'. It is possible the initial 'bally' may be the same as the now old-fashioned euphemism for 'bloody'.

***Ballykissangel.*** A popular and picturesque television comedy series, first screened on BBC1 in 1996 and set in the fictional Irish village of the title name, supposedly meaning 'town of the banished angel' but in fact based on the name of the real Irish village of Ballykissan in Co. Kerry. However, the location filming was carried out in the Wicklow village of Avoca. *Ballykissangel* is a clerical comedy centring originally on the triumphs of a newly arrived English priest, Peter Clifford, whose secular travails include the landlady Assumpta Fitzgerald and the local fixer and businessman Brian Quigley. The series happened to coincide with an explosion of interest in things Irish, and 'Bally-K', as it came to be affectionately known, opened the eyes of many viewers to the changing role of religion in Irish society at the close of the 20th century, as typified by the loss of faith in many of the characters. The last (sixth) series was broadcast in 2001.

**Baloney** or **boloney.** Nonsense. The word dates from the 1920s and is said on dubious ground to derive from the Bologna sausage. The connection between the two remains obscure, although the sausage so named is traditionally said to have originally been stuffed with odds and ends ('rubbish') from slaughterhouses. When the US went off the gold standard in 1933 the devalued dollar was nicknamed the 'baloney dollar', the reasoning being that no matter how thinly the sausage is sliced it still retains its basic characteristics. During the 1936 presidential election the US Democratic politician Al Smith (1873–1944) criticized Franklin D. Roosevelt's NEW DEAL thus:

> No matter how thin you slice it, it's still baloney.

In 1943, in her maiden speech to the House of Representatives, the American writer, Republican politician and diplomat Clare Booth Luce (1903–87) criticized Vice President Henry A. Wallace's ideas about the postwar world thus:

> Much of what Mr Wallace calls his global thinking is, no matter how you slice it, still globaloney. Mr Wallace's warp of sense and his woof of nonsense is very tricky cloth out of which to cut the pattern of a postwar world.

The coinage 'globaloney' has since proved popular with journalists.

**Bambi.** A young deer who lives in a German forest. He originated as the creation of Felix Salten (real name Sigmund Salzmann) in his gentle children's novel *Bambi* (1926), which is a more or less realistic depiction of forest life. Bambi gained his greatest fame, however, from the Walt Disney feature-length cartoon named after him, released in 1942. His name, a shortening of Italian *bambino*, 'baby', was applied by the media to Tony Blair when he became leader of the Labour Party and, later, prime minister. The allusion was to his youthfully innocent appearance (*see also* THUMPER). After the 2003 Iraq war *The Guardian*'s cartoonist Steve Bell depicted this Bambi as blood-stained and with its pants on fire (as in the children's rhyme 'Liar, liar, pants on fire'), reflecting allegations that he had misled the British public about the reasons for going to war.

> Walt Disney made no more drastic or mistaken change than when he showed Bambi as a cute, lisping celluloid puppet titupping through a rainbow-hued landscape. A child who came to the book after seeing Disney's cartoon would find it hard to believe that Salten's young deer was the same character.
>
> MARGERY FISHER: *Who's Who in Children's Books* (1975)

**Bamboo Curtain.** Formed by analogy with IRON CURTAIN to denote the veil of secrecy and mistrust drawn between the Chinese communist bloc and the non-communist nations. The expression dates from the late 1940s. *See also* GARLIC WALL.

**Banality of evil, The.** A phrase coined by the political philosopher Hannah Arendt (1906–75), who left Nazi Germany in 1933, living first in France and then the United States. She used the phrase in *Eichmann in Jerusalem: A Report on the Banality of Evil* (1963), her book about the SS officer Adolf Eichmann, who after the 1941 Wannsee Conference was put in charge of implementing the FINAL SOLUTION. Eichmann escaped to Argentina after the Second World War, but was abducted by Israeli agents in 1961 and taken for trial in Jerusalem. He was executed for crimes against humanity in 1962. Arendt's point was that Eichmann and his colleagues were not inhuman monsters, but ordinary human beings.

> It was as though in those last minutes he was summing up the lessons that this long course in human wickedness had taught us – the lesson of the fearsome, word-and-thought-defying banality of evil.

**Banana.** A derogatory term for an Asian who has chosen to adopt white, Western values. Such a person is 'yellow outside but white inside'. The term dates from the 1960s.

**Banana belt.** A US term for a winter resort with a relatively mild climate. It was originally applied on Baffin Island in the 1960s to mainland North America as a region ('belt') regarded as being warm enough to grow bananas.

**Banana-bender.** A colloquial Australian nickname for a native of Queensland (which itself is facetiously known as 'Bananaland', from the local importance of bananas as a crop). Other Australians' view of their northeastern compatriots can be gauged by the use of 'Banana-bender' from the 1990s to mean also 'fool'.

**Banana King.** Roger Ackerley (1863–1929), chief salesman of the banana importers Elders & Fyffes, was so known. He did much to make Britain 'banana-conscious' in the early 20th century.

**Banana oil.** A phrase used colloquially in Australia and the United States for 'nonsense' or 'insincere talk'.

**Banana republic.** A small state, especially one in Central America, whose economy centres solely on the export of bananas. In consequence, the country is heavily dependent on foreign capital. The expression, which dates from the mid-1930s, came to gain a pejorative ring, and is now applied to any country regarded as third-rate, politically unstable and often ruled by a corrupt regime.

> Present policies are leading us to the status of a banana republic that has run out of bananas.
>
> RICHARD MARSH: quoted in *Daily Telegraph* (6 September 1978)

**Banana skin.** A cause of upset and humiliation. Fake banana skins are stock devices in pantomime for causing a 'pratfall'.

> The man who slips on the cunningly placed banana-skin does not laugh so soon as those who set the harmless trap and so, from the first, observe the whole scene.
>
> JOHN RUSSELL BROWN: *Shakespeare's Plays in Performance*, ch. 10 (1966)

**Band Aid.** A series of charity projects undertaken by the rock singer Bob Geldof after seeing a television documentary about the famine in Ethiopia in 1984. He contacted Midge Ure of the group Ultravox and they booked an array of stars from the world of pop to record a song of their own composition, 'Do They Know It's Christmas?'. Profits from the sales of the single, together with those from related projects such as the sale of T-shirts and videos, went to the famine victims. Geldof went to Ethiopia himself in 1985, then on 13 July 1985, under the name of Live Aid, arranged a huge simultaneous concert linking the Wembley Stadium in London with Philadelphia. The money raised by all this amounted to some £60 million by mid-1987. Meanwhile a similar US enterprise, American Band Aid, released the hit song 'We Are the World' on 1 April 1985. The name itself puns on 'Band Aid', the proprietary name of a US brand of adhesive sticking plaster similar to ELASTOPLAST.

Twenty years on a re-run of the event, named Live 8, was held worldwide on 2 July 2005 to coincide with that year's G8 summit in Edinburgh. Events took place in London, Paris, Berlin, Rome, Philadelphia, Barrie (Canada), Tokyo,

Johannesburg, Moscow, and Cornwall's Eden Project. It sought to raise awareness of THIRD WORLD poverty. *See also* COMIC RELIEF.

**B & D.** *See under* FEMIDOM.

**Bandit Country.** A name given to the southern part of the county of Armagh, Northern Ireland, by the then Labour secretary of state for Northern Ireland, Merlyn Rees, in November 1975. Rees used the name in a statement after the shooting by the IRA of three British soldiers at Drummuckavall, near Crossmaglen:

> There has never been a cease-fire in South Armagh for a variety of reasons – the nature of the countryside and the nature of the people. It is an unusual area – there is little support for the security forces in South Armagh. The government is not trying to buy off terrorism by the release of detainees as the number of terrorists arrested and charged shows. The release of detainees has nothing to do with the violence of the bandit country of South Armagh. There is wholesale gangsterism there.

The term was resented by nationalists, who saw it as typical of British efforts to portray as the actions of thugs and outlaws what they regarded as blows for Irish freedom. Some Republicans, however, revelled in it as a 'badge of honour' and as triumphant proof of the effectiveness of the IRA's military strategy in the area.

South Armagh is bordered on three sides by the Irish Republic and its largely Catholic population is historically sympathetic to the Republican cause. From the outset of the TROUBLES it was dominated by the Provisional IRA, who operated here with a greater freedom of action than in any other part of Northern Ireland. Attacks by the local brigade of the IRA included the sectarian massacre at Kingsmills, near Newry, in January 1976 of 12 Protestants (itself a revenge attack for the slaughter of three Catholics by Loyalists), the ambush and murder of 18 British soldiers at Narrow Water, near Warrenpoint, in August 1979, and the mysterious abduction and assassination in 1977 of Captain Robert Nairac, a maverick Grenadier Guards officer, whose body has never been found. *See also* NO-GO AREA; PROVOS.

**Bandito, El.** A nickname given by the Argentinian press to the Manchester United and England footballer Nobby Stiles (b.1942) on account of the supposed brutality of his tackling in Argentina's quarter-final defeat by England in the 1966 World Cup. The unprepossessing Stiles was also known as the 'Toothless Tiger' because of his committed style of play and his wearing of false teeth. Stiles is affectionately remembered for his dancing a spontaneous jig of delight

around Wembley stadium after England's victory over West Germany in the 1966 World Cup Final.

**B and K.** A shorthand used by journalists to refer to the Soviet leaders Nikolai Bulganin (1895–1975) and Nikita Khrushchev (1894–1971) when they visited the UK in 1956.

**Bangers and mash.** Sausages and mashed potatoes. The former are presumably so called because their skins are liable to burst when they are being cooked. The dish is popularly regarded as quintessentially British, although other nations equally enjoy the combination. 'Bangers' as a word for sausages has been current from the early 20th century, but the vogue for bangers and mash themselves began mainly after the Second World War.

**Bangkok Hilton.** The nickname of the jail in Bangkok, Thailand, that houses, among others, foreigners convicted of drug offences. It was the subject of *Bangkok Hilton*, an Australian TV mini-series first broadcast in 1989. *See also* HANOI HILTON.

**Bang to rights.** Caught in the act; arrested with positive proof of guilt. The slang expression is of US origin, dating from the 1920s, and derives from 'bang', denoting a sudden action, in this case the apprehending of a criminal, and 'to rights', meaning 'according to the law', 'good and proper'.

**Banker's hours.** Short working hours. The allusion is to the former usual opening hours of a bank, in Britain 9.30 a.m. to 3.30 p.m., in the United States 10.00 a.m. to 2.00 p.m. Bankers themselves actually work longer hours.

**Bankroll.** To provide financial backing for a project, as if offering rolls of bank notes. The term is of US origin and dates from the 1920s.

**Ban the bomb.** An anti-nuclear slogan of the 1950s of US origin, adopted subsequently by the CND. The alliterative brevity of the phrase made it memorable.

**Bantustan.** The name given to each of the supposedly independent areas set aside for black people in South Africa in the 1970s on the basis of ethnic and linguistic groupings. The first of the homelands, as they were also known, was Transkei, set up in 1976. Bophuthatswana followed in 1977, Venda in 1979, and Ciskei in 1981. Their independence did not receive international recognition since the areas were clearly set up to allow the white government to control the black population and exclude them from the political process. Further black states, containing approximately a third of South Africa's total black population, were 'self-governing' but non-independent: Gazankulu, KwaZulu, Lebowa, KwaNdebele, KaNgwane and Qwaqwa. Since

1994 all the Bantustans have rejoined the 'new' South Africa under the democratically elected black-majority government led by the African National Congress. Bantustan meant 'Bantu country', just as Hindustan means 'Hindu country'.

**Banzai.** In the Second World War a nickname for a reckless military attack by the Japanese. The word represents the shout or cheer given by the Japanese when greeting the emperor or going into battle. The literal meaning is '10,000 years', as a wish that the person may live that long. *Banzai* was also the title of a spoof Japanese game show, broadcast in 2001–4.

**Bara, Theda.** The exotic US film actress who became intimately associated with the term VAMP was born Theodosia Goodman in Cincinnati, Ohio, *c*.1885, the daughter of Bernard Goodman, an immigrant Polish Jew, and Pauline Louise de Coppet, a Frenchwoman. Her press agents put it about that she was born an Arab princess in the Sahara desert, further claiming that her name was an anagram of 'Arab Death'. However, the Goodman family were already calling themselves Bara when she began her career, taking the name from Coppet's Swiss father, Francis Bara de Coppet, and Theda was simply a pet form of the actress's first name. She died in 1955.

**Barbarella.** The blonde space voyager in a comic strip by Jean-Claud Forest, originally published in the French *V Magazine* from 1962. Her piquant adventures were collected in a 1964 book of her name that was translated into several languages. A film of the same title directed by Roger Vadim was produced in 1967 in which she was played by Jane Fonda.

**Barbarossa.** The code name for the German invasion of the Soviet Union on 22 June 1941. It was originally to have been called Fritz, but on 18 December 1940 Hitler renamed the operation after the byname, meaning 'Redbeard', of Emperor Frederick I (*c*.1123–90), who it was said would rise from his deathlike sleep and restore Germany to power. Early in the morning of 22 June, as the massive invasion got under way, the German foreign minister, Joachim von Ribbentrop, summoned the Soviet ambassador to Berlin and explained that the military activity along the Soviet border was merely a matter of 'defensive measures'. In fact, the intention was to capture three key cities, LENINGRAD, Moscow and Archangel, and then sweep down to the Caucasus, the oil-rich Caspian Sea and the Middle East. Although the operation began with tactical gains, it ultimately failed. Leningrad never fell, the Germans were checked before Moscow, and Hitler's forces were totally

unprepared for the onset of winter. *See also* SECOND WORLD WAR OPERATIONAL CODE NAMES; STALINGRAD.

**Barbershop.** A popular style of close harmony singing, revived in the 1930s in the United States from its former 19th-century vogue. The origins of the name are somewhat obscure. It may date from a time when US barber's shops were social and musical centres for the males of the locality or else refer back to British 'barber's music', meaning an extempore performance put on by patrons in a barber's shop as they waited their turn to be shaved.

**Barbican.** The word is most familiar as the proper name of the London Barbican, a complex of high-rise apartment blocks grouped around the Barbican Centre, a large and brutalist-style building opened in 1982 as a major cultural and exhibition centre. The complex takes its name from a former street, which was itself named after a watchtower in the city walls. The word represents Medieval Latin *barbacana*, but the origin of this is unknown.

**Barbie doll.** The progenitor of the curvaceous blonde doll was the German toy manufacturer Rolf Hausser, who launched her on the market on 12 August 1955, basing his creation on a cartoon character called Lili, who had first appeared in the German newspaper *Bild Zeitung* in 1952. In 1956 Ruth and Elliot Handler, co-founders of the US toy manufacturers Mattel, were on holiday in Lucerne with their daughter Barbara and son Ken when Barbara, then aged 15, pointed out the Lili doll in a shop window. Mrs Handler bought one and took it home. A manufacturer for a clone was found, and on 9 March 1959 Barbara Millicent Roberts, otherwise Barbie, named after the young girl who had spotted her prototype, was launched at the American Toy Fair in New York. In 1961 she was joined by a 'boyfriend', Ken, named after Barbara's brother.

**Barcelona chair.** A stainless steel chair with leather cushions and usually without arms. A chair of this type was originally exhibited in Barcelona in 1929 by the German architect Ludwig Mies van der Rohe, who designed it.

**Barcode.** The first machine-readable code in the form of figures and parallel lines was introduced in supermarkets in 1973. All countries have their individual authority for numbering, and each uses the first two or three digits for the full sequence of 13 figures. In Britain the prefix is 50. When a company seeks a barcode for a branded product it is given a number beginning with 50 followed by five more digits. The company then allocates a further five figures, making a total of 12. The 13th digit is a check, calculated from the other 12 to ensure that the overall number is correct.

**Barcoo salute.** An ironic Australian term for the characteristic Australian outback gesture of brushing flies away from one's face. Barcoo is an upcountry region of western Queensland, around the Barcoo River.

**Barefoot doctor.** A paramedical worker with basic medical training, especially one working in rural China. The phrase, dating from the 1970s, directly translates the Chinese.

**Barefoot in the Park.** A play (1963) by the US playwright Neil Simon (b.1927) about a newly married couple who experience their first fallings-out as they move into their first home, a tiny flat at the top of five flights of stairs. The title relates to the wife's complaint that her lawyer-husband is too strait-laced when he turns down an invitation to walk barefoot in the park in the freezing weather (he subsequently does so, despite a raging cold). Simon also wrote the screenplay for the film (1967), which starred Jane Fonda and Robert Redford as Corle and Paul Bratter and Ethel Banks as Corle's mother, Mildred.

> *Ethel*: I feel like we've died and gone to heaven – only we had to climb up.

**Barf.** To vomit. The verb, and its companion noun, are particularly associated with US college students, whose alcoholic consumption it is assumed makes them connoisseurs of the subject. It is not known where it came from; it seems unlikely to have been, as has been suggested, from German *werfen* 'throw' or its Yiddish descendant *varfn*, since neither of them is known to have been used to mean 'vomit'. It seems to have originated in the mid-1940s.

The noun 'barf' has been reapplied metaphorically to disgusting food: 'barf on a board' is a dish of reconstituted dried beef on toast.

**Barfly.** A person who spends much time in a bar, as if 'buzzing' around it.

**Bargaining chip** or **counter**. A potential concession or other factor that can be used to advantage in negotiations. The expression dates from US diplomatic usage of the mid-1960s and relates to the gambling chip. A poker player or gambler will obviously be at an advantage if he has a good supply of chips when bluffing or bidding against other players. The term became prominent during arms limitation talks between the United States and the USSR.

**Barking mad.** Completely crazy. The allusion (often abbreviated to simply 'barking') is to an uncontrollable dog. The nickname 'Daggers' supposedly awarded to the British prime minister Margaret Thatcher by unsympathetic members of her own cabinet was an abbreviation of 'Dagenham' – Dagenham being three stops on (on the District line) from Barking (as in 'barking mad').

**Barmy army.** The name given to the band of ardent and highly vocal cricket fans who follow the England team, especially on overseas tours. It was first bestowed in the course of the Ashes tour of Australia in 1994–5. It has subseqently also been applied to groups of supporters of other sports. A Scottish equivalent is the TARTAN ARMY.

**Barnacle Bailey.** The nickname of the Essex and England cricketer Trevor Bailey (b.1923), a notably obdurate and 'clinging' batsman, whose celebrated partnership with Willie Watson to save England from defeat against Australia in the 1953 Ashes series made him a national hero. In his later career as a cricket commentator he became better known by his other nickname, 'Boil', which appears to have originated in a mispronunciation of his surname by the stadium announcer at a football match he was playing in on the Continent.

**Barrel of fun** or **of laughs**. A source of much fun or merriment. The expression is mostly found in the negative, as: 'It wasn't exactly a barrel of laughs.' A barrel contains beer, which is conducive to merriment. The expression is of US origin.

> Roll out the barrel,
> We'll have a barrel of fun!
> JAROMIR VEYVODA, WLADIMIR TIMM and LEW BROWN: 'The Beer Barrel Polka' (song) (1939)

**Barrow Boy.** A nickname, punning on his surname, of the colourful Conservative politician Sir Gerald Nabarro (1913–73), MP for Kidderminster from 1950 to 1973 and owner of several cars with a CHERISHED NUMBER beginning NAB.

**Barrow Poets.** A group of poets founded in 1951 with the aim of selling their books of verse from street barrows in London during the FESTIVAL OF BRITAIN. When refused a licence for outdoor trading they turned to poetry readings in pubs and other places of public entertainment. By 1969 they had become sufficiently accepted to give a lunchtime reading in Westminster Abbey and had official approval to sell from their barrows in the Queen Elizabeth Hall on the SOUTH BANK.

**Barton, Dick.** The doughty hero of the BBC's first daily radio serial, *Dick Barton – Special Agent!*, running from 1946 to 1951. With the help of his trusted sidekicks, Snowey White and Jock Anderson, he foiled a host of criminal enterprises in a stream of thrilling adventures. A short television series based on the stories was screened in 1979. The series had a memorable signature tune in the form of Charles Williams's pounding 'Devil's Galop' (1944).

I like Dick Barton and listen to him when I get the chance. I listen because I like it, which seems a good reason for doing a thing provided you don't get yourself into trouble. There are too many people going round publicly trying to psycho-analyse other people.

> HERBERT MORRISON: quoted in E.S. Turner, *Boys Will Be Boys*, ch. 17 (1948)

**Bart Simpson.** *See* Bart SIMPSON.

**Barwick Green.** The catchy signature tune to the radio series *The* ARCHERS, one of the most familiar pieces of music in the whole of British broadcasting. It is the last segment of Arthur Wood's four-part suite *My Native Heath* (1922), composed in honour of his native Yorkshire.

**Baseball Annie.** A colloquial US term for a baseball groupie, a young female fan who follows baseball teams around and offers sex in return for proximity to her heroes. The term dates from the mid-1960s; the contemporary synonym 'Baseball Sadie' has not survived so well.

**Base** or **BASE jump.** A parachute jump from a high point on land, such as the roof of a tall building or a clifftop, instead of from an aircraft. The acronym represents four such points: 'building, antenna tower (of a radio station), span (of a bridge), earth'. The sport evolved in the US in the 1970s. One of its champions was the daredevil parachutist Thor Alex Kapperfjell (1967–99), known as the 'Human Fly', who once jumped from the Eiffel Tower. His favourite launch sites were Manhattan's tallest buildings, and his conquests included the Empire State Building, World Trade Center, Chrysler Building and Trump Tower. He was planning a leap from Chicago's Sears Tower when he was killed in an accident on a cliff in Norway after losing his bearings in fog.

**Bash Street Kids.** A group of unruly schoolchildren in a picture strip in the BEANO comic.

**BASIC.** *See* PROGRAMMING LANGUAGES.

**Basic English.** A fundamental selection of 850 English words designed in the 1920s by C.K. Ogden (1889–1957) as a common first step in the teaching of English and as an auxiliary language. The name comes from the initials of the words British, American, Scientific, International, Commercial.

**Basic Instinct.** *See* FATAL ATTRACTION.

**Basil Brush.** A fox puppet possessed of a gap-toothed grin, an upper-class voice and a prominent, highly mobile tail. Basil Brush first appeared on British television in 1964 and had his own Saturday children's show from 1968 to 1980, accompanied by a variety of straight men. His hallmark was a raucous cry of 'boom boom', which accompanied his usually execrable jokes. His operator was Ivan Owen.

Mr Brush's career revived in 2001, with the launch of a new series of his show.

**Basin Street.** A street in the red light district of the French quarter of New Orleans, which is possibly the original home of US JAZZ. The well-known 'Basin Street Blues' was composed by Spencer Williams in 1928.

**Basket case.** Originally, a soldier who had lost all four limbs in the First World War and thus had to be carried in a litter ('basket'). Hence, generally, any useless or incapable person or thing, especially when needing the support of others.

**Basket of currencies.** A group or range of currencies, especially as used for calculating values in certain international financial transactions. The term is economic jargon and dates from the 1970s. The image is presumably of a shopping basket that holds a collection of similar things.

**Bataan Death March.** The forced march of some 70,000 US and Filipino prisoners of war, captured by the Japanese in the Philippines in the early stages of the Second World War. The march started on 9 April 1941 at Mariveles, at the southern end of the Bataan Peninsula, and covered 88km (55 miles) to San Fernando. From there the marchers were taken by rail to Capas, from where they marched the final 13km (8 miles) to Camp O'Donnell. The marchers were constantly starved and beaten, and many who fell by the wayside were bayoneted. Only 54,000 reached the camp. After the war, the Japanese commander of the invasion forces in the Philippines, Lieutenant-General Homma Masaharu, was charged with responsibility for the death march, tried by a US military commission and executed on 3 April 1946.

**Bat a thousand.** In US slang, to be completely and consistently successful. The expression, first recorded in 1920, alludes to the batting record of a particularly successful baseball hitter. Conversely someone who is doing dreadfully could be said to be 'batting zero'.

**Bates, Norman.** The mad murderer in charge of a lonely motel in Robert Bloch's novel PSYCHO (1959). He believes that he is his own mother and in a fit of sexual frenzy kills a young woman who has unwittingly aroused him. The story was the basis for one of Alfred Hitchcock's most memorable movies (1960), in which Bates is played by Anthony Perkins. In *Psycho 2* (1982), Bloch's sequel to his original novel, Bates escapes from the hospital for the criminally insane in which he has been confined and once more goes on the rampage. A film loosely based on this was produced in 1983, again starring Perkins, and he also played him in a further sequel, *Psycho 3* (1986), with himself as director.

**Bates method.** A system of simple eyesight exercises designed to keep the eyes strong and healthy without the use of lenses or surgery. The technique was devised in the 1920s by the US ophthalmologist William H. Bates (1860–1931).

**Bathing beauty.** An attractive young woman in a bathing costume, especially one taking part in a beauty contest at a seaside resort. The now dated expression arose in the 1920s. An alternative was 'bathing belle'.

**Bathing Towel.** A punning nickname dating from his Charterhouse schooldays for Lord Baden-Powell (1857–1941), founder of the BOY SCOUTS. He in fact held bathing in high esteem and recommended its merits to his charges and followers in SCOUTING FOR BOYS (1908).

**Bathroom breaks, Presidential.** *See* BLADDER DIPLOMACY.

**Batman.** The costumed superhero of US comics, in popular regard almost as famous as SUPERMAN himself. He first appeared in 1939, conceived and drawn by Bob Kane (1915–98) for *Detective Comics*, issue number 37. His real name is Bruce Wayne, and in day-to-day life he is a Gotham City socialite, but dons his special bat suit, with cape and mask, in order to unmask villains (such as The Joker and The Penguin) incognito. His assistant is Robin, the Boy Wonder, alias Dick Grayson. He has appeared in most popular media, including books, films and television, and has inspired a female equivalent, Batgirl, alias Babs Gordon, who made her debut in *Detective Comics* in 1967. Batman's heroic deeds and escapades can be said to have classical antecedents in heroes such as Hercules (Heracles) and Ulysses (Odysseus). *See also* CAPED CRUSADER.

**Battenberg cake.** The name of this distinctively coloured cake, with its alternating squares of pink and yellow sponge, is first recorded in 1903. It must have existed earlier, however, and the cake itself is said to have been created to mark the marriage in 1884 of Princess Victoria of Hesse-Darmstadt, granddaughter of Queen Victoria, to Prince Louis of Battenberg. The Prince later took British nationality and in 1917 anglicized his name to Mountbatten. One of their four children was Earl Louis Mountbatten of Burma (1900–79).

**Batten down the hatches.** To prepare for trouble. The term originated in naval parlance, when a ship's crew would prepare for a storm by fastening tarpaulins over hatches with battens (strips of wood).

**Battered baby.** A young child who has been subjected to repeated injuries by one or more parents or some other adult. The injuries typically include bruises, burns and fractures, but their full extent may not be apparent until the child is examined medically and the complete skeleton X-rayed. The syndrome was first identified by social workers in the early 1960s. The concept was later extended to the battered wife and, although to a lesser extent, battered husband. *See also* ABUSE.

**Battered Cherub.** An amusingly descriptive nickname for the miner and trade union leader Joe Gormley, later Baron Gormley (1917–93), who used it as the title of his autobiography (1982).

**Battery acid.** An epithet conferred on any unpalatably tart liquid. In British English it tends to be applied to any thin sharp cheap wine. Americans use it particularly for bad coffee, and also for low-quality acidulous lemonade or grapefruit juice.

**Battleaxe.** A colourful term of US origin dating from the turn of the 20th century for a formidably aggressive and typically middle-aged or even elderly woman, who is figuratively seen as hacking her way through opponents and obstacles by wielding an axe. According to Christine Hamilton's *The Book of British Battleaxes* (1997), listing 33 representatives of the class (including herself), examples include the Conservative prime minister Margaret Thatcher (*see* IRON LADY), the dog trainer Barbara Woodhouse (*see* WALKIES!), Queen Victoria (1819–1901), Viscountess Rothermere (*see* BUBBLES), the brothel-keeper Cynthia Payne (*see* MADAM CYN), and the fictional Ena Sharples, played by Violet Carson in the SOAP OPERA CORONATION STREET.

> The term Battleaxe was first used around 1910 and it referred then to a very closely defined type: elderly, probably a spinster, aggressive, resentful towards the world, thoroughly unpleasant and pretty ugly to boot! Cast aside that image! For the purposes of this book, the word Battleaxe covers a multitude of talents, attributes and attitudes.
>
> CHRISTINE HAMILTON: *The Book of British Battleaxes*, Introduction (1997)

**Battlebus.** The special bus in which a political leader tours marginal and other key constituencies in order to rouse the electorate in the run-up to a general election. *See also* WHISTLE-STOP TOUR.

**Battle of Britain.** The attempt of the German LUFTWAFFE by their prolonged attack on southeastern England (August to October 1940) to defeat the RAF, as a prelude to invasion. RAF Fighter Command gained the victory and won universal admiration. The name arose from Sir Winston Churchill's speech (18 June 1940): 'What General Weygand called the Battle of France is over. I expect that the Battle of

Britain is about to begin.' The words 'The Battle of Britain is about to begin' appeared in the order of the day for RAF pilots on 10 July. *See also* FEW WELL-CHOSEN WORDS; SEA LION.

**Battle of Highbury.** The nickname of the so-called friendly football match between England and Italy at Highbury on 14 November 1934, which England won 3–2. The name alludes to the behaviour of the Italian team, who, promised exemption from military service if they won, resorted to physical confrontation, leaving a number of English players injured and provoking retaliation.

**Battle of the Atlantic.** The struggle for control of the sea routes between North America and Europe, and around the British Isles, during the Second World War. By 1943 the Allies had won the battle, by a combination of an improved convoy system and the cracking of the German ENIGMA codes, the latter enabling the position of U-BOATS to be pinpointed.

**Battle of the Bogside.** The name given to the savage rioting that took place in the Catholic BOGSIDE area of Londonderry on 12–15 August 1969, during the first 'long hot summer' of Northern Ireland's modern TROUBLES. Sectarian clashes arising from the annual march of the (Protestant) Apprentice Boys of Derry turned into a serious confrontation between the ROYAL ULSTER CONSTABULARY and Catholics. When the police, accompanied by Protestant rioters, chased Catholics back into the Bogside, they were attacked by a hail of petrol bombs from enraged residents. The intervention of the B SPECIALS, hated by Catholics, exacerbated an already volatile situation. A semblance of order was restored when a British Army regiment stationed nearby took over the police lines. The 'Battle of the Bogside' was the first time that CS gas was used as a riot control in the UK. Rioting erupted elsewhere in Northern Ireland, particularly Belfast, where hundreds of Catholics were burned out of their homes on the night of 14 August.

The events of 12–15 August led directly to the despatch of British troops to Northern Ireland, partly in response to the pleadings of moderate nationalist politicians for protection for their communities.

**Battle of the Bulge.** The final chief German counter-offensive in the Second World War, also known as the Ardennes Offensive, when the Allied forces were pushed back into Belgium in 1944, the 'bulge' being the wedge driven into their lines. The Germans were repulsed by the end of January 1945.

The expression is also in colloquial use for a struggle to lose weight, a 'fight against flab'.

**Battle of the Somme.** *See* SOMME.

**Battleship Potemkin, The.** A film (1925) commissioned by the Russian BOLSHEVIK regime to commemorate the 20th anniversary of the unsuccessful 1905 Revolution. Director Sergei Eisenstein focused on a single crucial episode of the 1905 Revolution, namely the mutiny of sailors on board the battleship *Potemkin* in the seaport of Odessa. The ruthless crushing of the rebellion by tsarist troops was encapsulated in the most famous scene of Eisenstein's film, that of the massacre of civilians on the ODESSA STEPS (one of the most famous images in 20th-century cinema). In fact, this and many other scenes in the film diverged sharply from historical fact, and there is little real evidence of any such massacre taking place outside the imagination of Bolshevik propagandists.

**Batty, Nora.** *See* LAST OF THE SUMMER WINE; NORA.

**Bauhaus.** One of the 20th century's most important movements in art and design opened in 1919 when the German architect Walter Gropius (1883–1969) established the school of this name in Weimar. His aim was to return to first principles in every form and so end the 19th-century division into 'art' on the one hand and 'craft' on the other. The name itself means literally 'house of building'.

**Bay of Pigs.** (Spanish *Bahía de los Cochinos*.) A bay on the southwest coast of Cuba, which on 17 April 1961 was the scene of an abortive invasion by a large group of anti-Castro dissidents. The operation was financed by the US government, which had been planning it for some months. The incident led to the installation of Soviet missile sites on Cuba and to the threat of nuclear war between the superpowers in October 1962. The so-called Cuban Missile Crisis was resolved only when Russia agreed to dismantle the rocket bases and ship them home (*see* HAWKS AND DOVES).

**Bayonet is a weapon with a worker at both ends, A.** A saying attributed to Lenin, and picked up by the Industrial Workers of the World in Australia during the First World War, when they campaigned successfully against compulsory conscription. The slogan continued to be used by pacifists and anti-war socialists in the Second World War, especially prior to the entry of the Soviet Union into the conflict in 1941.

**Baywatch.** This highly popular and melodramatic US television series, with its sun-drenched beaches, swimwear-bursting bathing beauties and mainly moralistic but wholly sexless plots, was first screened in 1990. It centres on a group of male and female Malibu lifeguards and has unsurprisingly generated a number of lucrative commercial spin-offs.

**Bazooka.** (1) A trombone-like instrument invented by the US comedian Bob Burns (1896–1956). The name is perhaps modelled on 'bazoo' or 'kazoo', a once popular, submarine-shaped toy producing sounds of the 'comb and paper' variety.

(2) A portable, tubular rocket-launcher used as an anti-tank weapon in the Second World War. This sense of the word was introduced in 1943 by Major Zeb Hastings of the US Army to name the new rocket gun, which when fired went 'bazoooom'.

(3) In the plural, a woman's breasts: a slang usage first recorded in the early 1960s.

> What a pair of bazookas that dame's packing.
> T. SANCHEZ: *Zoot-Suit* (1978)

**B.B.** The pseudonym of the British writer and illustrator Denys James Watkins-Pitchford (1905–90), the author of the fantasy novel *The* LITTLE GREY MEN (1942). Watkins-Pitchford chose the initialism for *The Sportsman's Bedside Book* (1937) and derived it from the designation of the particular size of lead shot he used for shooting wild geese, BB being 0.18 inches in diameter.

**BBC.** The British Broadcasting Company, as it was originally called, was formed by six electrical companies and broadcast its first programme, a news bulletin, at 6 p.m. on 14 November 1922 from 2LO, a studio in Savoy Hill, London. Two days later this was followed by the first entertainment programme. It lasted an hour, opening with Leonard Hawke, a baritone, performing 'Duke Goes West' and 'Tick' and concluding with Dorothy Chalmers performing 'Hymn to the Sun' and Schubert's *Rosamunde* on the violin. Its charter expired on 31 December 1926, and the following year it became a corporation. Television was first broadcast from Alexandra Palace (ALLY PALLY) in 1936, and foreign broadcasts began the following year. The BBC's television monopoly was broken in 1954 with the introduction of the first commercial channel, and its radio monopoly was similarly lost in the 1970s. The BBC's contribution and finances are governed by royal charter, and its broadcasting is funded by an annual television licence fee. Increasing competition from commercial channels has latterly obliged the BBC to lighten its 'fuddy-duddy' image without losing its long-held respected public status.

**BCBG.** *See* BON CHIC, BON GENRE.

**Beachcomber.** The pseudonym of the British humorist J.B.

Morton (1893–1975). He inherited the name from his predecessors in 1924 when he took over the 'By the Way' column in the *Daily Express*, which had started in 1917. Morton continued to write the column until the year of his death. His eccentric and absurdist humour appealed to a wide audience, and influenced British comic writing from *The Goon Show* and *Private Eye* to MONTY PYTHON'S FLYING CIRCUS.

> One disadvantage of being a hog is that at any moment some blundering fool may try to make a silk purse out of your wife's ear.
> *By the Way* (1931)

Among Beachcomber's creations was Mr Justice Cocklecarrot and DR STRABISMUS (WHOM GOD PRESERVE) OF UTRECHT. His writings became the basis of series on both television (1968–9, with Spike Milligan) and radio (from 1989, with Richard Ingrams and others).

**Beached whale.** A stock epithet for a large and ungainly person. A real whale in this situation is more likely to be described as 'stranded' or 'left high and dry'.

> He [R.A. Butler] seemed like a benign and decent beached whale washed up on the harder shores of modern Conservatism.
> PETER HENNESSY: in *The Independent* (8 May 1987)

**Beaches, Fight them on the.** *See* WE SHALL NEVER SURRENDER.

**Bead shoes.** A type of ornate women's shoes in fashion at the turn of the 20th century. They combined a high upper with the slightly waisted heel of a COURT SHOE, and the pattern cut into the leather was enhanced by an arrangement of tiny steel beads.

**Be afraid. Be very afraid.** The flesh-creeping catchphrase promulgated by the publicists of the 1986 US film *The Fly*, starring Jeff Goldblum as a scientist who accidentally transforms himself into a half human-half fly while experimenting with matter transmission (it was a remake of a possibly even more unpleasant 1958 film of the same name). The phrase caught on, and is often invoked at moments of potentially looming terror.

**Beagle 2.** An unmanned British spacecraft, part of the European Space Agency's Mars Express programme, intended to land on Mars and carry out various experiments on its surface. Designed by a team led by Professor Colin Pillinger (b.1943), it was launched on 2 June 2003 and landed on Mars on 25 December. Unfortunately it appeared to have been damaged on landing, and it failed to send back any signals to earth. It was named in honour of the original

*Beagle*, the ship on which Charles Darwin made his voyage of discovery in the 1830s.

**Béal na mBláth.** (Irish, 'the mouth of flowers'.) A valley in West Cork, Ireland, between Bandon and Macroom, notorious in Irish folk memory as the location of the assassination on 22 August 1922 of the nationalist leader Michael Collins (1890–1922). As commander of the army of the newly created Irish Free State (*see* FREE-STATERS), Collins had travelled to the west of Ireland, where Republican 'Irregulars' opposed to the treaty that he had signed with Britain, which had brought the new state into being, were holding out against the forces of the Free State government. Travelling in an armoured convoy, Collins was ambushed and killed in a gun battle with anti-treaty IRA men, plunging Ireland into mourning and exacerbating the bitterness of the civil war. The assassination was graphically and movingly recreated in Neil Jordan's film *Michael Collins* (1996).

Collins's near-legendary status in nationalist Ireland and the dramatic circumstances of his death, ensured that myth and controversy attached to the events of 22 August 1922. In particular, the presence in the vicinity of Béal na mBláth at the time of Collins's death of Éamon de Valera, Collins's former comrade-in-arms, Republican arch-opponent of the Anglo-Irish Treaty and future Irish prime minister (*see* DEV; TAOISEACH), gave rise to conspiracy theories implicating de Valera in the assassination, but these have long since been discredited. *See also* BIG FELLA.

**Beam me up, Scotty!** Get me out of this! An expression of the desire to be elsewhere, originating on US campuses in the 1960s. The phrase quotes Captain Kirk's supposed habitual request to the chief engineer, Lieutenant Commander 'Scotty' Scott, in the television series STAR TREK, to activate a 'beam' that can return him from a planet to the starship *Enterprise*. According to 'Trekkers', however, he never actually says this, his nearest equivalent words being 'Beam us up, Mr Scott'.

**Beam someone up.** To extricate someone from a difficult situation. The allusion is to the misquotation BEAM ME UP, SCOTTY!, from STAR TREK.

> 'Life on the road is very, very tough,' says Olson … 'But this is the way the chips fell, and, until they can find a way to beam us up, we're just going to have to deal with it.'
> *The Times* (10 December 1999)

**Beanie.** A small, close-fitting hat worn on the back of the head, something like a skullcap. The word dates from the 1940s and presumably derives from 'bean' as a slang term for the head.

**Beanie Babies.** Soft, bean-filled toys launched in 1994. They existed in about 200 different types of animals and characters and became an all-consuming craze for collectors, first in the United States, where they originated, then in Britain. Each type had a different name, such as Quackers the Duck, Chilly the Polar Bear and Waddle the Penguin, and collectors attended regular Beanie Fairs or traded their toys on the INTERNET. In 1999 their creator, Ty Warner, unexpectedly discontinued the toys, whose immense popularity had made him the richest toy-maker in the world.

**Beano.** A popular children's comic, published weekly since 1938 by the Dundee publishers D.C. Thomson. Its memorable characters include the little terror DENNIS THE MENACE, who first appeared in 1951, the BASH STREET KIDS, and, at the top of the social scale, the top-hatted Lord Snooty. The latter was disposed of in 1992, however, in the interests of POLITICAL CORRECTNESS.

**Bean Town.** A nickname for Boston, Massachusetts, where the staple diet is supposedly Boston baked beans, i.e. baked beans with salt pork and molasses.

**Bear, The.** *See* STORMIN' NORMAN.

**Bear of Very Little Brain, A.** A description of himself by WINNIE-THE-POOH:

> When you are a Bear of Very Little Brain, and you Think of Things, you find sometimes that a Thing which seemed very Thingish inside you is quite different when it gets out into the open and has other people looking at it.
> A.A. MILNE: *The House at Pooh Corner* (1928)

The phrase is often used in self-deprecating contexts by those of an incorrigibly cutesy disposition.

**Beast of Belsen.** In the Second World War the name given to Josef Kramer (1906–45), commandant of the infamous BELSEN concentration camp. Kramer was hanged on 13 December 1945 after being tried by a British military court.

**Beast of Bodmin Moor.** The nickname for a wild animal, possibly a black panther, that has attacked sheep and calves on farms in the region of Bodmin Moor, Cornwall, since the early 1980s. It was first sighted in 1983 but has still not been captured or even fully identified. Speculation exists that the beast may be a big cat released into the countryside by its former owner when it grew too big to be kept as a pet. A legendary beast of Dartmoor forms the subject of Sir Arthur Conan Doyle's tale *The* HOUND OF THE BASKERVILLES (1902). *See also* RUTLAND PANTHER.

**Beast of Bolsover.** The nickname given by parliamentary correspondents to Dennis Skinner (b.1932), the hard-line, left-wing Labour MP since 1970 for Bolsover, Derbyshire, notorious for his forthright and sometimes 'unParliamentary' language in the Commons. He has more than once been asked by the Speaker to withdraw his comments and even to leave the Chamber. Skinner describes himself in *Who's Who* as of 'good working-class mining stock' and he is generally held in public affection, even gaining admiration for his integrity and honesty.

**Beast of Jersey.** A journalistic nickname for E.J.L. (Ted) Paisnel, convicted of 13 sex offences against children in Jersey, Channel Islands, and sentenced to 30 years' imprisonment in 1971. The name was applied to him during the 11 years in which he evaded arrest on the island.

**Beat a path to someone's door.** To seek them out as important or of interest. The image is of trampling down the undergrowth to gain access to the remote home of a person who normally lives a quiet or anonymous life but who has suddenly become 'hot news'.

**Beat Generation.** The generation of the 1950s and early 1960s, who rejected traditional Western values by turning to drugs, living communally and generally adopting an anarchic attitude towards society. More specifically, the name refers to a group of US writers at this time, among the most notable of whom were Jack Kerouac (1922–69), Allen Ginsberg (1926–97) and William Burroughs (1914–97). The use of 'beat' in this sense is generally said to have been coined by Kerouac, who related it to the word 'beatitude'. Recent authorities, however, claim it was the creation of the writer and drug addict Herbert Huncke (1916–96). He was the template for Elmer Hassel in Kerouac's ON THE ROAD (1957), for an 'angel-headed hipster' in Ginsberg's HOWL and for Herman in Burroughs's *Junkie* (1953). *See also* BEATNIK; *The* NAKED LUNCH.

**Beatlemania.** A term that entered into the English language in 1963 to describe the frenziedly enthusiastic popular response to The BEATLES and their music, especially among teenage girls. The term was specifically coined by the *Daily Mirror* in the aftermath of a successful appearance by The Beatles on *Sunday Night At The London Palladium* on 13 October 1963, which was seen by an estimated 15 million television viewers in the UK. 'Beatlemania' soon became an established word. It was also briefly considered as a possible title for the film that eventually came to be called *A* HARD DAY'S NIGHT.

**Beatles, The.** Probably the world's most famous pop group, formed in 1959 by four young Liverpool musicians: Paul McCartney (b.1942), John Lennon (1940–80), George Harrison (1943–2001) and Ringo Starr, real name Richard Starkey (b.1940). They broke up in 1970, but the demand for their music has continued unabated. In their day they were worshipped by the young, respected by the not so young, and even compared by one music critic (William Mann, of *The Times*) to Schubert. Their name, while punning on 'beetle', perhaps partly in reference to their black jackets, was more obviously an allusion to the 'beat' of popular music, and to the BEAT GENERATION with which their heyday coincided.

> Dark, damp and smelly. I regretted my decision immediately, the noise was deafening.
>> BRIAN EPSTEIN: diary entry (1961), on first seeing The Beatles in the Cavern Club, Liverpool. Epstein later became their manager.

> I guess if you're going to be in a rock group it might as well be The Beatles.
>> GEORGE HARRISON: cited on www.bbc.co.uk/news/ (30 November 2001)

*See also* ABBEY ROAD; BEATLEMANIA; FIFTH BEATLE; LET IT BE; REVOLVER; RUBBER SOUL; RUTLAND; SERGEANT PEPPER'S LONELY HEARTS CLUB BAND; WHITE ALBUM.

**Beatnik.** A member of the BEAT GENERATION or, loosely, any person with long hair and scruffy clothes. The Yiddish suffix *-nik* is of Russian origin, as for SPUTNIK.

**Beat** or **scare the living daylights out of someone.** To beat or scare them severely. The daylights were originally the eyes but the word then came to be understood as meaning any vital organ.

***Beau Geste.*** A novel (1924) by P.C. Wren (1875–1941) about the French Foreign Legion, in which he himself served. The three GESTE brothers, Michael (Beau), John and Digby, have joined the Legion, taking upon themselves the opprobrium of having stolen a diamond that their aunt has sold and replaced by a fake so that she can preserve the reputation of her wastrel husband. The novel opens with an account of how a French officer, going to the relief of a desert fort manned by legionnaires, which has been surrounded by rebel Tuaregs, finds it defended only by corpses. The sequels included *Beau Sabreur* (1926) and *Beau Ideal* (1928). A silent film version (1926) of the original book was directed by Herbert Brenon. A stylish sound version directed by William Wellman followed in 1939. It starred Gary Cooper as Beau, Ray Milland as John and Robert Preston as Digby and was filmed in Buttercup Valley, west of Yuma, Arizona, not Africa. A 1966 remake, starring Telly Savalas and Guy Stockwell, stressed the violence of the original and allowed Beau to survive at the end.

*Beau geste* means literally 'fine gesture' in French, and denotes a display of magnanimity.

**Beaujolais nouveau.** (French, 'new Beaujolais'.) The annual promotion of young Beaujolais, sold in the same year of its vintage, crossed from France to Britain and then to the United States in the 1970s. Beaujolais sold within the first few months of a vintage is known as Beaujolais *primeur*, 'early season Beaujolais'. When demand for Beaujolais *nouveau* in Britain reached its peak in 1992 nearly half of all regular Beaujolais was sold in this youthful state for immediate consumption, thereby generating a welcome cash flow for the producer.

**Beautiful game.** In modern parlance, football; the description is attributed to the Brazilian footballer Pelé (b.1940), who autobiography was entitled *My Life and the Beautiful Game* (1977). Earlier in the 20th century, however, the same sobriquet was applied to cricket:

> A time will come, a time will come,
> When the people will sit with a peaceful heart,
> Watching the beautiful, beautiful game,
> That is battle and service and sport and art.
>
> ARNOLD WALL: 'A Time Will Come', quoted in John Atkinson (ed.), *In Praise of Cricket* (1946)

*See also* FUNNY OLD GAME.

**Beautiful people.** Originally, a nickname for the colourfully dressed HIPPIES of the 1960s, but subsequently a term for those moving in fashionable or glamorous circles.

> How does it feel to be one of the beautiful people,
> Now that you know who you are?
>
> JOHN LENNON and PAUL McCARTNEY: 'Baby You're a Rich Man' (song) (1967)

**Beauty contest.** In the context of US politics, a primary election contest in which the actual selection of delegates to the nominating convention is determined by party caucuses rather than votes. The term evolved in the 1960s from the use of the phrase for a competition of women for a prize awarded to the most beautiful. *See also* CATTLE SHOW.

**Beauty in the Bath.** A media nickname for the long unsolved murder of Cynthia Bolshaw, a 50-year-old beauty consultant of Heswall, Merseyside (now Wirral), found dead in her bath in 1983. In 1999 advances in DNA profiling techniques enabled police to charge John Taft, a 49-year-old company director, with the crime. He was jailed for life.

**Beaver.** An early 20th-century children's game, which involved being the first to spot a bearded man and shout 'Beaver!'. The word was earlier a nickname for a beard, probably referring to the animal's thick fur.

**Beaver, The.** The name given in journalistic circles to Lord Beaverbrook (William Maxwell Aitken; 1879–1964), Canadian-born politician and newspaper magnate. The term obviously derives from his title, but according to Tom Driberg, then 'William Hickey' columnist on Beaverbrook's *Daily Express*, it was equally apt as 'a zoological symbol of tireless industry'.

**Beavers.** Young boys, aged from six to eight, who are members of the youngest group in the Scout Association. The group was inaugurated in 1971 in Canada, a country where beavers are well known and where they were formerly exploited for their fur. *See also* BOY SCOUTS; EAGER BEAVER.

**Beavis and Butt-head.** The two teenagers who are the central characters of the television cartoon series that bears their name. They first appeared in 1992 as the creation of the former US musician, Mike Judge, who provides most of the voices. Their keynote is their sneering cynicism, regularly applied to the television and videos that they are invariably watching. In this role they are essentially caricatures of US youth and its obsession with these particular media.

**Bebop.** (Also 'bop' or 'rebop'.) A style of jazz that emerged in New York towards the end of the Second World War, characterized by dissonance, complex rhythms and sustained improvisation. Exponents included Charlie Parker (*see* BIRD), Dizzie Gillespie and Miles Davis. Bebop marked the birth of modern jazz. It was anathema to an older generation of jazzmen:

> Playing Bop is like playing Scrabble with all the vowels taken out.
>
> DUKE ELLINGTON: interview in *Look* (10 August 1954)

**Because it's there.** The answer famously given in March 1923 by the British mountaineer George Mallory (1886–1924) when asked why he wanted to climb Mount Everest. The following year he and his companion Andrew Irvine were last seen at a height of over 28,000 feet heading for the summit of Everest along the Northeast Ridge. Then they were hidden by cloud. Mallory's body, mummified in the cold, dry conditions, was found by climbers on the North Face in 1999. He had apparently fallen from the ridge, and it is thought unlikely that he and Irvine made the top. *See also* WELL, WE KNOCKED THE BASTARD OFF.

**Beckingham Palace.** The nickname of David and Victoria Beckham's Hertfordshire mansion, a former orphanage near Sawbridgeworth acquired after their marriage in 1999, and extensively – and expensively – renovated by them to a level of luxuriousness suited to media royalty. *See also* BUCK HOUSE; POSH AND BECKS.

**Bed and breakfast.** In Stock Exchange parlance 'to bed and breakfast' shares is to sell them after hours one evening and buy them back as soon as the market opens the following morning. The procedure establishes a loss for tax purposes.

**Bed-hopping.** A succession of casual sexual encounters. *See also* JUMP INTO BED WITH SOMEONE.

**Bed-In, John and Yoko's.** *See* 'GIVE PEACE A CHANCE'.

**Bedknob and Broomstick.** A novel by the British children's author Mary Norton (1903–92) concerning the relationship between three village children and Miss Price, a spinster who is training to be a witch. It was originally published in two parts, *The Magic Bedknob* (1945) and *Bonfires and Broomsticks* (1947), appearing as one volume with the title *Bedknob and Broomstick* in 1957. A musical film based on the book, *Bedknobs and Broomsticks*, was released by the Disney studios in 1971 starring Angela Landsbury as Miss Price.

**Bed of nails.** In the figurative sense an extremely difficult or uncomfortable situation. The term dates from the 1960s, when it was used by Ray Gunter (1909–77), minister of labour under Harold Wilson from 1964 to 1968, to describe the ministry itself. The phrase puns on 'bed of roses' while alluding to the literal bed of nails on which fakirs lie.

**Bedroom eyes.** Eyes expressing a sensual or sexual invitation. The phrase dates from the 1950s.

**Bedroom farce.** A popular play in which sexual infidelity and amorous escapades both in and out of marriage are normally required ingredients. The type owes much to the works of the French playwrights Eugène Labiche (1815–88) and Georges Feydeau (1862–1921), and the latter's name is synonymous with the French genre.

**Beeb, The.** A familiar nickname for the BBC, from the pronunciation of the initials. It is often used by the media as a simple synonym. *See also* AUNTIE.

**Beeching Axe.** The drastic modernization and 'rationalization' of Britain's railways in the 1960s, executed by Dr (later Lord) Richard Beeching (1913–85) when chairman of the British Railways Board (1963–5). Britain had previously been traversed by a dense network of railway lines that reached even the smallest towns. Many of the lines were barely profitable, while others had simply been allowed to deteriorate or been abandoned. The answer was a radical reorganization of the system. Beeching called for the closure of 2128 stations in a single sweep, decimating the service and all but erasing the rural railways that served the country's less populous communities. The operation was traumatic but highly effective, saving the exchequer millions of pounds. Some of the closed stations were

later converted into private houses as an unusual type of DES RES.

> No more will I go to Blandford Forum and Moretehoe
> On the slow train from Midsomer Norton and Mumby Road
> No churns, no porter, no cat on a seat
> At Chorlton-cum-Hardy or Chester-le-Street
> We won't be meeting again
> On the slow train.
>
> MICHAEL FLANDERS and DONALD SWANN: 'The Slow Train' (1964)

**Beefcake.** A colloquial term for pictures or photographs of men displayed for their muscular bodies or 'hunkiness'. It may also refer to such men themselves. *See also* CHEESECAKE.

**Beef Wellington.** A dish dating from the 1960s in the form of roasted fillet of beef traditionally covered with pâté de foie gras and a duxelles of mushrooms, and baked in a pastry crust. It is presumably named after the Duke of Wellington (1769–1852), who is known to have enjoyed a hearty meaty meal.

**Beefy.** A nickname given to the swashbuckling Somerset, Worcestershire, Durham and England cricketer Ian Botham (b.1955). A powerfully built all-rounder, Botham's batting and bowling feats in the Ashes series of 1981 (and in particular his performance in what became known as 'Botham's match' in the third test match of the series at Headingley), made him a national hero. He was also known, more prosaically, as 'Both' (pronounced as in 'moth'), and as 'Guy the Gorilla' (after the male silverback gorilla (d.1978) who was one of the most popular attractions at London Zoo).

**Beehive.** A woman's domed and lacquered hairstyle in fashion in the 1960s, so named as suggesting the appearance of a beehive. It gained the nickname in the southern United States of 'B-52', after the huge US Air Force bomber so called.

**Been there, done that.** A stereotyped phrase indicating that the speaker already has personal experience or knowledge of the thing mentioned, such as a visit to a place abroad or a new type of sport. An extended form, 'Been there, done that, bought the T-shirt', introduces a jaded touristic touch.

> Severed cows' heads? Pickled sharks? Elephant dung? Darling, we have been there, done that, bought the T-shirt – or at least a mop and bucket.
>
> *The Times* (28 September 1999)

**Beer and sandwiches.** Informal negotiations. The phrase became associated with last-ditch talks between trade unionists and politicians at 10 Downing Street when a strike or stoppage was in the offing, as frequently happened in the 1960s and 1970s. The named fare is regarded as typical of the negotiators. *See also* SMOKE-FILLED ROOM.

**Beer belly.** A stomach that protrudes as a result of the excessive consumption of beer. The unpleasant spectacle is also known as a 'beer gut'.

**Beer goggles.** US campus slang for the condition that results from an excess of beer drinking, when hitherto unremarkable people start to look sexually alluring. The expression dates from the 1980s.

**Beer Hall Putsch.** A failed NAZI rising in Munich on 8–9 November 1923, led by Adolf Hitler. It is also known as the Munich Putsch, *Putsch* being the German word for a sudden, violent political uprising. In association with General Erich Ludendorff (1865–1937), the right-wing military strong man who had become the 'silent dictator' of Germany towards the end of the First World War, Hitler and his small Nazi Party successfully persuaded a right-wing meeting in a Munich beer hall to join them in marching on Berlin to seize power, as Mussolini had done the previous year with his MARCH ON ROME. The next day some 3000 marchers set off for the centre of Munich, but were stopped when the police opened fire, killing 16 marchers. Realizing that the government was not going to cave in, the marchers abandoned their project. Ludendorff was acquitted at the subsequent trial, while Hitler received the minimum five-year sentence for treason. He served only eight months, however, during which he wrote MEIN KAMPF.

**Bee's knees.** Said of someone or something excellent or outstanding. The term, in the singular, was earlier used of a small or insignificant thing, but in the 1920s, in the plural, gained its present sense. The reference may be to the pollen containers on a bee's legs. The process of removing the pollen involves much bending of the bee's knees and is performed with great precision.

**Bee-stung lips.** Lips, especially a woman's, that are full, red and pouting, as if swollen from a bee-sting. The US film actress Mae Murray, whose real name was Marie Adrienne Koenig (1889–1965), was known as 'The girl with the bee-stung lips', and this was the title of an article about her by Alfred A. Cohn in the November 1917 number of *Photoplay*.

**Beetle.** An affectionate name for the Volkswagen saloon car. The name, suggested by the vehicle's rounded body, is a translation of German *Käfer*, additionally a word for an attractive girl or young woman, something like English 'chick'. The Volkswagen (German, 'people's car') had first been conceived in 1937 as an affordable mass-produced car

for the citizens of the Third Reich, and was originally known as the KdF-Wagen, after Kraft durch Freude ('strength through joy'), the Nazi leisure organization. In 1938 Ferdinand Porsche was put in charge of production, but the new factory was diverted into the manufacture of military vehicles, and in the war came to rely on slave labour. The Beetle itself did not enter production until after the Second World War. A 'new look' Beetle was launched in 1999.

> Men of all ages, it seems, cannot resist curves. Or a well-rounded bottom. Or buxom front. Or wide-eyed look. Or a brash red exterior. And the new VW Beetle has them all.
> *The Times* (22 May 1999)

**Beetle drive.** A session of the game of beetle, in which a picture of this insect is drawn or assembled. The build-up of the image is determined by the throw of a dice, six giving a body, five a head, four two eyes, three two feelers, two six legs and one a tail. A player must throw a six before beginning, but cannot draw eyes or feelers until a five is thrown. Play stops as soon as one player completes a picture. The game was first popular in the 1930s.

**Be good!** A friendly exhortation not to misbehave, usually said on parting. It is sometimes expanded to: 'If you can't be good, be careful!' Another addition is: 'Don't do anything I wouldn't do!'

**Beguine.** A popular dance in bolero rhythm of the 1930s originating in Martinique. It was the inspiration for Cole Porter's song 'Begin the Beguine' (1935) and takes its name from French *béguin*, 'flirtation', 'fancy', itself perhaps from the cap worn by members of the Beguine sisterhood of nuns.

> When they begin the Beguine
> It brings back the sound of music so tender,
> It brings back a night of tropical splendour,
> It brings back a memory ever green.

**Behind the bike shed.** Secretly; illicit. The reference is to a school bicycle shed, behind which clandestine sexual encounters and furtive smoking sessions are or were carried on. 'Bike shed' alone may suffice for the allusion.

**Behind the eight ball.** In a dangerous position from which it is impossible to escape. The phrase comes from the game of pool, in one variety of which all the balls must be pocketed in a certain order, except the black ball, numbered eight. If another ball touches the eight ball, the player is penalized. Therefore, if the eight ball is in front of the one which he intends to pocket, he is in a hazardous position. The expression dates from the 1930s.

**Behind the sofa.** The place from which one supposedly watches a scary television programme. A DOCTOR WHO fan club among Bristol University students calls itself 'Behind The Sofa'.

**Beirut.** The name of Lebanon's capital city became synonymous with bloody internecine strife during Lebanon's devastating civil war (1975–90), which not only involved an array of domestic factions but also attracted baleful interventions by outside parties including Israel, Syria and the United States. Until the mid-1970s Beirut had been an international financial centre, but subsequent struggles for power between left-wing Muslims and conservative Christian groups (mainly members of the PHALANGE) devastated the city. There was also conflict between pro-Iranian Shi'ite Muslims and Syrian-backed Druse (an Islamic sect). An already chaotic situation was exacerbated by the presence in Lebanon of the forces of the Palestine Liberation Organization (*see* PLO), who used southern Lebanon as a base for guerrilla raids into northern Israel. In 1976 Syria was invited by the Lebanese government to intervene in the fighting. The presence of the PLO and the Syrians led to a horrific escalation of the conflict in the early 1980s, when Israel invaded Lebanon (1982) and demanded the removal of Syrian and Palestinian forces from Beirut. An evacuation was overseen by a US-led international force but, following its departure, Israel moved into Muslim West Beirut and sent Christian Phalangist militias into the Palestinian refugee camps of Sabra and Chatila, where they killed hundreds of civilians, provoking an international outcry. The nightmare continued in 1983 as 300 US servicemen were killed in an attack on the US military headquarters by a suicide bomber of the militant Islamic Jihad faction after the US navy had shelled Muslim positions in Beirut.

The year 1984 saw a new and sinister development: the abduction of Europeans and Americans in Beirut by Muslim extremists. Prominent among those abducted were the US journalist Terry Anderson, the British journalist John McCarthy, the Irish teacher Brian Keenan and the Archbishop of Canterbury's envoy Terry Waite. Keenan later wrote a book about his experiences, *An Evil Cradling* (1992). In the 21st century renewed self-confidence in Lebanon forced the withdrawal of Syrian forces. But in July 2006 Israeli air and sea forces bombed Beirut again in their struggle with Hezbollah militants. *See also* GREEN LINE.

A graphic eye-witness account of the savagery of the Lebanese civil war and its effect on Beirut was provided by *Pity the Nation* (1990), by the journalist Robert Fisk. *See also* LONDONISTAN.

**Belfast Child.** A folk-influenced song by the Scottish rock group Simple Minds, released in 1989 and based on a traditional Irish air entitled 'She Moves Through the Fair'.

The creative prompting for the song was the TROUBLES in Northern Ireland and, in particular, the deaths at Enniskillen in 1987 of 11 people in the Remembrance Day bomb attack by the IRA. The song's wistful refrain, bracketing an apocalyptic middle section, looks forward to a peaceful time beyond the Troubles: 'One day we'll return here, when the Belfast Child sings again.' The song is the longest, other than The Beatles' 'HEY JUDE', to reach Number 1 in the UK singles charts.

**Believe it or not.** Said of something that seems incredible but that is actually true. The US illustrator Robert L. Ripley (1893–1949) gained considerable popularity with his syndicated newspaper features entitled *Believe It or Not!* His first contribution appeared in the New York *Globe* of 19 December 1918 in the form of nine small drawings of sports oddities, including a Canadian who ran 200 yards backwards in 14 seconds, a Frenchman who remained under water for 6 minutes and 29.8 seconds, and an Australian who skipped 11,810 times in four hours. They appeared under the heading 'Believe It or Not!' and launched Ripley into his lucrative career.

**Be like Dad, keep Mum.** This punning security slogan was launched by the Ministry of Information in the Second World War, the message being that younger members of a family should follow the example of the serviceman father and not talk about war-related matters. *See also* CARELESS TALK COSTS LIVES; LOOSE LIPS SINK SHIPS.

**Belisha beacon.** A flashing light in an amber-coloured globe mounted on a black-and-white banded pole, the sign of a pedestrian crossing. It is named after Leslie Hore-Belisha (1893–1957), minister of transport from 1934 to 1937, who introduced it.

**Belle of the ball.** The most beautiful girl or woman at a particular event or in a particular group. The French word *belle*, 'beautiful', came into English in the 17th century but the alliterative phrase quoted here dates from much later and was popularized by G.W. Hunt's song *The Belle of the Balle* (1873) as sung by George Leybourne. Modern usage may be ironic.

**Bell jar.** An environment in which one is protected or isolated from the outside world, as in the laboratory bell-shaped glass cover of the name, used for preserving samples. The figurative sense derives from Sylvia Plath's novel *The Bell Jar* (1963), published under the pseudonym Victoria Lucas, telling of the mental breakdown, attempted suicide and eventual recovery of a college girl, and based on the author's own experiences.

**Bells and smells.** Anglo-Catholic or High Church. The allusion is to the use of altar bells and incense in the service of the Eucharist, in the Roman Catholic manner.

**Bells and whistles.** In computing jargon, additional attractive features, gimmicks or 'gizmos'. The allusion is to a fairground organ with its multiplicity of bells and whistles. *See also* VANILLA.

**Belly dance.** A dance originating in the Middle East, usually performed by a woman and involving undulating movements of the belly and rapid gyration of the hips. The English name dates from the turn of the 20th century for the dance that is more properly known as *raqs sharqi*, 'oriental dance'. There are belly-dancing circles in Britain and elsewhere in the Western world.

**Bel Paese.** (Italian, 'beautiful country'.) This well-known Italian cheese was not made until the 20th century. It was the creation of Egidio Galbani in 1906 at Melzo, near Milan. The name does not allude directly to the beauty of the north Italian landscape, as many suppose, but was taken from the title of a book, *Il bel paese* (1875), by Antonio Stoppani (1824–91), an Italian priest, geologist and writer. The book does, however, describe the charms of the local countryside. The cheese wrapper depicts the head of Abbot Stoppani and a map of Italy. The Bel Paese made in the United States has what appears to be the same wrapper but its map is actually that of America.

**Belsen.** A Nazi concentration camp near the villages of Belsen and Bergen in Hanover, northwest Germany. It was also known as Bergen-Belsen. Although not built as an extermination camp, some 37,000 inmates, including Anne FRANK, died there during the Second World War as a result of starvation, disease or exhaustion. Its particular notoriety derives from the fact that it was the first such camp liberated by the Western Allies (on 15 April 1945). *See also* AUSCHWITZ; BEAST OF BELSEN; DACHAU; FINAL SOLUTION; HOLOCAUST.

**Belshazzar's Feast.** A noisy oratorio by William Walton (1902–83) setting words from the Bible that had been selected by Sacheverell Sitwell (1897–1988). It was first performed in 1931 and at the time must have seemed daringly modernist, but now rather seems to strain for its effects. Belshazzar, the last king of Babylon, was the son of Nebuchadnezzar. At the king's feast an unseen hand writes the words 'Mene, mene, tekel, upharsin' on the wall, which the prophet Daniel claims is a divine warning of the destruction of Babylon and Belshazzar's own death (Daniel 5:25).

**Belt and braces.** Doubly safe; extra secure. The phrase is usually said of a policy offering twofold security. Trousers that are kept up by both belt and braces are hardly likely to fall down. The expression dates from the 1920s.

**Belt out.** To sing or play loudly or vigorously. The term dates from the 1950s.

**Beltway.** A US term for a ring road, and in particular a nickname for the ring road around Washington, D.C., used allusively for Washington itself, especially with regard to the perceived insularity of the US government.

> [Presidential contender Pat] Buchanan's declaration yesterday was framed as a 'last chance' by the pugnacious rightwinger. 'Let me say to the money boys and the Beltway elite, who think that at long last they have pulled up the drawbridge and locked us out forever, you don't know this peasant army,' he said.
> *The Times* (26 October 1999)

Avaricious government contractors or consultants are known in US political slang as 'Beltway bandits'.

**Be my guest.** Do as you wish; help yourself. The expression dates from the 1950s, when it was a slogan advertising Hilton hotels. The words were also used as the title of a book of 1957 by the company's founder, Conrad Hilton (1887–1979).

**Bend** or **lean over backwards.** To make every effort to accommodate someone or something; to do all one can to be fair. The image is of a person who deliberately adopts a stance contrary to their natural 'inclination'. The expression dates from the 1920s.

**Bend someone's ear.** To talk to them at length or in order to request a favour. The image is of getting the person to incline their ear towards one's mouth. The phrase dates from the 1940s.

**Benetton.** A fashion-wear company that began as a small family enterprise producing woollen jumpers in a depressed postwar Italy. The nominal founder of the business was Luciano Benetton, a truck driver from Treviso, who died of malaria in 1945. His eldest son, Luciano, obtained work at the age of 15 in a fabric shop, while the youngest child, 13-year-old Giuliana, worked in a garment shop, knitting sweaters by night to sell to customers. Orders started coming in and by 1965 the Benettons had enough money to start a firm of their own. The company gained notoriety in the 1990s with its controversial advertisements, featuring giant photographs of a dead AIDS victim, an unwashed newborn baby, a black woman nursing a white baby, a man on death row, etc., accompanied only by the slogan 'United Colors of Benetton'. The man behind these campaigns was the photographer Oliviero Toscani, who had been given a free hand by Benetton.

**Ben-Hur.** A film epic (1959) based on a novel (1880) by Lew Wallace. Directed by William Wyler for MGM, it told the story of a rebellion against the Romans led by gladiator Ben-Hur. Starring Charlton Heston, it won particular acclaim for its breathtaking chariot race sequence, in which it was widely (but erroneously) believed that one participant was killed (legend has it that crew members can be seen racing to the stricken chariot in the film itself). A cash prize was put up for the charioteers hired for the film to encourage them to take greater risks. The full title of the original novel was *Ben-Hur: A Tale of the Christ*.

**Bennies.** An uncomplimentary nickname for inhabitants of the Falkland Islands, introduced by members of the British forces stationed there during the FALKLANDS WAR. The name derives from a 'loveable half-wit' character called Benny played by Paul Henry in the television SOAP OPERA *Crossroads* (1964–88).

**Benny Hill Show, The.** A consistently popular television comedy show, first screened on ITV in 1969 and featuring the cheerfully risqué comedian Benny Hill (1925–92). It was in the revue tradition, combining visual gags, slapstick sketches and corny jokes, and was the making of Hill, who won worldwide fame in consequence. Hill's lecherous leers at the bevies of scantily clad women brought mounting criticism, however, and although he claimed his humour was in the mould of Donald McGill's SEASIDE POSTCARDS (a trifle disingenuously, since the girls chased Hill, not Hill the girls), the show was eventually cancelled in 1989.

**Be prepared.** The motto of the BOY SCOUTS and GIRL GUIDES, taken from the initials of the movement's founder, Sir Robert Baden-Powell, known familiarly as 'B.P.'

**Bergen-Belsen.** *See* BELSEN.

**Berlin Airlift.** The operation by British and US aircraft to airlift food and supplies to Berlin in 1948, when the Soviet occupying army in eastern Germany blockaded all road, rail and water links between Berlin and the West. The Russians had taken this action in retaliation for the Western powers' decision to unite their German occupation zones into a single economic entity. When the blockade was lifted in 1949 the city was formally divided into East and West.

**Berliner.** A German word for a kind of doughnut, a lexical curiosity that escaped President J.F. Kennedy (JFK) when he gave his famous COLD WAR speech in Berlin on 26 June 1963: 'All free men, wherever they may live, are citizens of Berlin,

and, therefore, as a free man, I take pride in the words *Ich bin ein Berliner*.'

'Berliner' is also the name of a newspaper production format, approximately 470 mm. by 315 mm. (smaller than broadsheet but slightly larger than tabloid). It, along with its two sister formats, 'North German' and 'French', was established in the early 20th century, and is used by several newspapers on the continent of Europe, including *Le Monde* in France and *La Reppublica* in Italy. Its profile was raised in the UK when it was adopted by *The Guardian* in 2005 and by its Sunday relative *The Observer* in 2006. *See also* TABLOID.

**Berlin Wall.** On 13 August 1961 the East German authorities sealed off the border between East and West Berlin and began constructing a barrier along it. The purpose was to halt the large number of defections from East to West and to prevent impoverished East Berliners from travelling to relatively wealthy West Berlin. The original barbed wire was eventually replaced by concrete topped with wire. Would-be escapers were shot on sight, one tragic example being that of 18-year-old Peter Fechter, who was machine-gunned in the back as he tried to climb the wall in August 1962 and left to bleed to death while the East German guards looked on. On 9 November 1989, after hundreds of East Germans had fled to the West through Hungary and Czechoslovakia, the beleaguered East German regime lifted travel restrictions and, within days, began dismantling the wall. By January 1990 the authorities were selling large slabs of it for hard currency and had set December that year for its total demolition. In October, however, East Germany was formally absorbed into the German Federal Republic and only short sections of the wall remained standing as memorials. The name became emblematic for any disuniting barrier or artificial divide. *See also* CHECKPOINT CHARLIE.

**Bermuda shorts.** Casual knee-length shorts, as originally worn by US tourists on the island of Bermuda in the 1950s.

**Bermuda Triangle.** The triangular sea area between Bermuda, Florida and Puerto Rico, said to be a region of profound danger for anyone venturing into it. The story began in December 1944 when five bombers of the US Navy were lost while on a routine training mission from the Fort Lauderdale air base. A sensational book by Charles Berlitz, *The Bermuda Triangle* (1974), brought this to the attention of the public. Various other ships and aircraft were subsequently said to have vanished in the area. However, these either did not exist, or sank or capsized elsewhere, or simply went down from natural causes, such as the violent storms and rough seas for which the Bermuda Triangle is notorious. Mystics and occultists believe that the lost world of Atlantis lies beneath the Bermuda Triangle, and that the fire crystals that powered the city still emit energy beams that send ships and aircraft to their doom.

**Berni Inns.** These popular steakhouses or restaurants were the inspiration of Aldo Berni (1909–97), the son of an Italian-born café proprietor in South Wales. He spent some years working for his father but in 1948, together with his brother Frank (1903–2000), opened his first restaurant at Hort's in Bristol. From there the two went from strength to strength, buying up and transforming old coaching inns such as the Mitre at Oxford and the Rummer in Bristol. The latter became their first Berni Inn steakhouse in 1955. They went on to build up an empire of more than 300 restaurants, becoming the biggest chain outside the United States, and their enterprise brought 'dining out' within reach of many in 1950s Britain. The chain was sold to Grandmet in 1970 and then to Beefeater in 1992.

**Bertie Wooster of Marxism, The.** A phrase, possibly coined by the novelist Malcolm Bradbury (1932–2000), describing the Labour politician Tony Benn (b.1925), known for his wide-eyed enthusiasm for left-wing causes and for his upper-class background (*see* Bertie WOOSTER). Benn, originally Anthony Wedgwood Benn, was elected to parliament in 1950, but in 1960, when he inherited his father's title and became the 2nd Viscount Stansgate, he was disbarred from sitting in the House of Commons. Following the Peerage Act of 1963 Benn was able to renounce his title and resume his seat. In the Wilson and Callaghan governments of the 1960s and 1970s he held a number of positions: postmaster general, minister for technology, secretary of state for industry, and secretary of state for energy. In 1981 he unsuccessfully stood against Denis Healey for the deputy leadership of the party. Benn, who sees himself as an inheritor of the Christian socialist tradition, is a teetotaller and a prolific tea-drinker and diarist. In 2001 he retired from parliament in order 'to devote more time to politics', and was prominent in the opposition to the war in Iraq (though his son, the MP Hilary Benn, elected in a 1999 by-election, is a loyal supporter of NEW LABOUR.) His other nicknames include 'Loony Benn' (punning on 'loony bin', a mental hospital, and the so-called LOONY LEFT) and 'Wedgie'.

**Bertram Mills.** At one time Britain's best-known circus, founded by Bertram Mills (1873–1938), owner of a coach-building firm, after a bet with a friend that he could put on a better show than that currently available at Olympia in London. From 1920 his circus was the regular Christmas show at Olympia, and from 1929 it toured annually in a big

top. It was continued after his death by his two sons, Cyril and Bernard, and held its final season in the winter of 1966.

**Beslan Massacre.** A massacre in September 2004 at a school in Beslan, a town in North Ossetia, part of the Russian Federation. Some 30 Islamist fighters from Chechnya and elsewhere had seized the school, taking teachers, parents and pupils hostage. After three days fighting broke out between the hostage-takers and the security forces. Nearly all of the hostage-takers were killed, but so were some 330 civilians, more than half of them children. In addition, 11 members of the Russian special forces died. *See also* MOSCOW THEATRE SIEGE.

**Best and the brightest, The.** The intellectual cream of society, especially those young men and women selected to serve in influential positions. Traditionally they would have been recruited from Oxbridge in the UK, and the Ivy League universities in the United States. David Halberstam's book *The Best and the Brightest* (1972) is the story of the young idealists in the administration of President John F. Kennedy (*see* NEW FRONTIER), and their role in the escalation of the Vietnam War. *See also* ESTABLISHMENT; GREAT AND THE GOOD.

**Best-before date.** The date by which a food product must be used to ensure that it is still in good condition. In 1980 new regulations were introduced in Britain for the labelling of foodstuffs, and it became obligatory for perishable goods to be marked with the 'best-before' formula and a date. It was later realized that the phrase was too vague for certain perishables, and 'use-by' or 'sell-by' was preferred instead. Even so, the term is still widely used. The phrase has subsequently been adopted to indicate the age constraints on the employability of some job applicants, who thus have a 'best-before date' after which they will seem less attractive to employers. *See also* SELL-BY DATE.

**Best boy.** In cinematography a name for the principal assistant to the chief electrician or 'gaffer' in a film crew. The term is of US origin.

**Best of British luck.** An ironic wish to someone in an enterprise that is expected to fail. The expression, also abbreviated as 'the best of British', arose as a military catchphrase in the Second World War.

**Best prime minister we never had, The.** A sobriquet awarded to the Conservative politician R.A. (RAB) Butler (1902–82), who thrice failed to gain the party leadership. In 1955 the leadership went to Anthony Eden, while in 1957 it passed to Harold Macmillan. On Macmillan's resignation from the premiership in 1963 he made sure the succession went to Alec Douglas-Home rather than Butler. Butler himself, in 1955, had hastily given a positive answer to a reporter's question regarding Eden, 'Mr Butler, would you say that this is the best Prime Minister we have?' This apparent damnation with faint praise came to haunt him.

More recently, the phrase 'the best prime minister we never had' has been applied to John Smith, leader of the Labour Party from 1992 until his sudden death in 1994.

**Best thing since sliced bread.** The best thing or person ever. A general term of commendation dating from the late 1960s and referring, tongue in cheek, to the great technological innovation that enabled bread to be bought wrapped and already sliced. Sliced bread was first produced in 1930, in the United States, under the brand name Wonder Bread, the bread-slicing machine having been invented by Otto Rohwedder.

**Best Years of Our Lives, The.** An Oscar-winning film (1946) directed by William Wyler about three war veterans returning to civilian life in a middle-American town after war service in the Second World War. The film is critical of the casual attitude held by many Americans to the sacrifices made on their behalf. The film was based on a novel, *Glory For Me*, by MacKinlay Kantor.

**Betamax.** A video format introduced by SONY in the 1970s. It soon lost out to Matsushita's VHS (video home system), which became standard. The name represents Japanese *beta*, 'all over' and English *maximum*.

**Bête blanche.** (French, 'white beast'.) A slight cause of aversion; a minor annoyance. The term dates from the 1960s as a variant on the familiar *bête noire* ('black beast') as a particularly disliked person or thing.

**Better 'ole.** Old Bill, a disillusioned old soldier with a WALRUS MOUSTACHE in the First World War, portrayed by Captain Bruce Bairnsfather (1887–1959), artist and journalist, in his publications *Old Bill* and *The Better 'Ole*. As depicted in the *Bystander* of 24 November 1915, a younger Bill, cowering in a wet and muddy shell hole in the midst of a withering bombardment, says to his pal Bert, 'Well, if you knows of a better 'ole, go to it.' The joke and Old Bill struck the public fancy, and Old Bill became the embodiment of a familiar type of patient old grouser. It is probably from this that the 'Old Bill', or simply the BILL, became a nickname for the police, and the Metropolitan Police in particular. The precise connection is uncertain, but it may be either because many ex-servicemen joined the Metropolitan Police after the war or because such servicemen were recruited by posters showing Bairnsfather's Old Bill in a Special Constable's uniform.

**Better red than dead.** Better to live under communist domination than be exterminated. The phrase arose among nuclear disarmament campaigners in the late 1950s. The words may have been an inversion of a counter-cliché, 'Better dead than red'. A similar sentiment was expressed by the US revolutionary and statesman Patrick Henry in a speech to the Virginia Convention on 25 March 1775: 'I know not what course others may take; but as for me, give me liberty or give me death.' The international chain of shoe shops Red or Dead, presumably inspired by the phrase, was founded in 1982 by Wayne and Geraldine Hemingway and grew from a market stall in London. Kurt Cobain, the American grunge artiste, echoed the phrase when he sung 'I'd rather be dead than cool' in his 1991 song 'Stay Away'. *See also* PEACENIKS.

**Better than sex.** Very good or exciting. A general term of approval dating from around the 1950s, the comparison notionally being with an act of sexual intercourse.

**Betty Boop.** *See* Betty BOOP.

**Between a rock and a hard place.** In a dilemma; faced with a difficult decision. The expression has a biblical ring but is of US origin and first recorded in the 1920s. The image is of being caught or crushed between two rocks.

**Between the sticks.** Football jargon for the position of the goalkeeper, between the goalposts. The phrase dates from the 1950s.

**Beulah.** The cheery African American housemaid who first appeared in the US radio show *Fibber McGee and Molly* in 1944. Her voice was, in fact, provided by a white male actor, Marlin Hurt. She soon graduated to her own radio series, then moved to television. Her persona would subsequently be seen as a racial stereotype, but she was nevertheless one of the most popular comedy characters of the 1940s and 1950s.

**Beveridge Report.** The popular name of *Social Insurance and Allied Services*, a report written in 1942 by Lord Beveridge (1879–1963) that became the basis for the social-reform legislation of the Labour government of 1945–50. It identified five prime 'giants', illness, ignorance, disease, squalor and want, and proposed a scheme of social insurance 'from the cradle to the grave', recommending a national health service, social insurance and assistance, family allowances and policies to implement full employment.

**Beverly Hills.** A fashionable district of Los Angeles, near HOLLYWOOD, famous for its individualistic or extrovertly eccentric residences, the homes of film and television stars and of millionaires of all kinds. Its opulent mansions and winding drives form an elegant oasis of some 31,000 residents, cocooned from the hurly-burly of downtown Los Angeles, which completely surrounds it. It adopted its present name in 1911, before which it was simply Beverly. The name comes from Beverly Farms, where in 1906 a newspaper report claimed President Taft was staying. The name has become associated with various TV shows and films. *The Beverley Hillbillies* was a US sitcom (1962–71) about a family of hicks who hit it rich when oil is discovered on their farm, enabling them to move to Beverley Hills, bringing their rustic ways with them. The comedy film *Beverley Hills Cop* (1984) stars Eddie Murphy as a fast-talking streetwise Detroit cop whose mission to find his friend's murderer takes him to Los Angeles. The popular SOAP OPERA *Beverly Hills 90210*, about a group of well-heeled high school students, was first shown in 1990; the number in the title is the highly desirable ZIP CODE of their residential quarter.

**Bevin Boys.** A nickname for the young men directed to work in coal mines in the Second World War instead of doing military service. The name comes from that of Ernest Bevin (1881–1951), minister of labour and national service, who devised the scheme. Some 21,000 men were conscripted, the figure at the end of their call-up number determining their selection as miners rather than military men. The nearest they thus got to a uniform was the miner's helmet and safety lamp, and they were denied the protection of the buttonhole badge that identified members of the Merchant Navy. Although literally out of the public eye, their contribution to the war effort was fully recognized by Winston Churchill:

> One will say: 'I was a fighter pilot'; another will say: 'I was in the Submarine Service'; another: 'I marched with the Eighth Army'; a fourth will say: 'None of you could have lived without the convoys and the Merchant seamen'; and you, in your turn, will say, with equal pride and with equal right: 'We cut the coal.'
>
> Report (22 April 1943)

**Bewitched.** A classic US SITCOM running from 1964 to 1972 and depicting the adventures of an 'ordinary guy', Darrin Stephens, played by Dick York and Dick Sargent, and his wife, Samantha, who happens to be a witch, played by Elizabeth Montgomery. The immensely popular series, also shown in Britain, did much to promote a vogue for the names Darren and Samantha and to a lesser extent for Tabitha, the Stephens's magical daughter. A generally derided feature film inspired by the sitcom, starring Nicole Kidman, was released in 2005.

**Bewitched, bothered and bewildered.** A line from a Lorenz Hart song 'Bewitched', from the show *Pal Joey* (1941), encapsulating the experience of falling in love:

> I'm wild again
> Beguiled again
> A simpering, whimpering child again,
> Bewitched, bothered and bewildered am I.

**Beyond a reasonable doubt.** In the law of many countries, a judge and/or jury must be convinced of the accused's guilt 'beyond a reasonable doubt' before finding against them. There might still be an element of doubt, but if it would be unreasonable to discount all the other evidence favouring conviction, then a guilty verdict is called for. *Beyond a Reasonable Doubt* is the title of a 1956 US film directed by Fritz Lang, in which a writer is persuaded by a newspaper to fake evidence linking him to a murder.

**Beyond the black stump.** *See* BLACK STUMP.

**Beyond the Fringe.** The pioneering satirical show, which was first staged in 1960, owed its inspiration to Robert Ponsonby, director of the annual Edinburgh Festival, who sought a way of beating the FRINGE at its own game. Accordingly he invited four young Oxbridge writers and performers, Alan Bennett (b.1934), Dudley Moore (1935–2002), Peter Cook (1937–95) and Jonathan Miller (b.1936), to present a revue show. The result was a smash hit, and the show's vein of quirky satire established the four as the dominant force in British comedy for the following decade.

> I go to the theatre to be entertained, I want to be taken out of myself, I don't want to see lust and rape and incest and sodomy and so on, I can get all that at home.
>
> ALAN BENNETT: *Beyond the Fringe*, 'Man of Principles' (1963)

**B–52.** A giant US long-range strategic bomber, manufactured by Boeing. In full it is the B–52 Stratofortress (on the model of the Second World War B–17 FLYING FORTRESS), and it has served with the US air force since 1954, seeing action from Vietnam to Afghanistan and Iraq – although only in its conventional, rather than nuclear, role. In the southern United States the BEEHIVE hairdo became known as a B–52, which in turn inspired the name of The B–52s, the US pop group formed in 1976, whose two female members, Kate Pierson and Cindy Wilson, sported outsize bouffant hairdos.

**B-girls.** Bar girls, as young women employed by a bar to mix with male customers, chat to them and encourage them to buy drinks. B-girls were prevalent in US bars in the Second World War.

**Biafra.** The name of a short-lived West African state. Fears that the Nigerian government was becoming dominated by the rival Hausa tribe led to the secession of the predominantly Ibo Eastern Region of Nigeria in 1967. In the ensuing civil war federal Nigerian forces confined the Biafrans to a shrinking area of the interior by 1968 and by 1970 Biafra had ceased to exist. The sufferings of the Biafrans led to their name becoming synonymous with the ravages of warfare, famine and disease.

**Bible.** *See* GOOD NEWS BIBLE; JERUSALEM BIBLE; REVISED STANDARD VERSION.

**Bible-basher.** An aggressive evangelical preacher, so called from his blows on his Bible as he rams home his text. Alternative names are Bible-thumper and Bible-puncher.

**Bible Belt.** A name emerging in the 1920s for those areas of the southern and midwestern United States and western Canada where Protestant fundamentalism is widely practised. Nashville, Tennessee, is generally reckoned to be the capital of the US Bible Belt, and several Protestant religious denominations have publishing headquarters there, including the United Methodist Publishing House, one of the largest of its kind in the world.

**Bic.** *See* BIRO.

**Bicycle shot.** In football a shot made by a player kicking the ball back over his head with both legs off the ground when facing away from the goal. The effect somewhat resembles the motion of the legs when pedalling a bicycle.

**Bidonville.** (French, 'container town'.) A term applied in the 1950s to a shanty town built of oil drums or other metal containers, especially on the outskirts of a North African city, and typically an oil port such as Mohammedia in Morocco. *See also* CARDBOARD CITY.

**Biffo.** A nickname given to the Tory politician John Biffen (b.1930), who, despite being to the left of Margaret Thatcher, served in the IRON LADY's cabinet from 1979 to 1987 (as leader of the House of Commons from 1982). He then served as a backbencher until he was awarded a peerage in 1997. The name derives from Biffo the Bear, a cartoon character in *The* DANDY. The name was also applied to the rightwing Tory backbencher Geoffrey Dickens by the Labour MP Joe Ashton (b.1933), who explained it as an acronym for 'Big ignorant fool from Oldham'. In Ireland, the nickname denotes the Fianna Fáil politician Brian Cowen (b.1960), and in this case it is an acronym for 'Big ignorant fucker from Offaly'.

**Big Apple.** New York City. The name was first popularized in the 1920s by John J. FitzGerald, a reporter for the *Morning Telegraph*, who used it to refer to the city's racetracks and who claimed to have heard it used by black stable-hands in New Orleans in 1921. African American jazz musicians in the 1930s took up the name to refer to the city (and especially Harlem) as the jazz capital of the world. The nickname then faded from use but was revived in 1971 as part of a publicity campaign by Charles Gillett, president of the New York Convention and Visitors Bureau. The general allusion is to a city that is the 'big apple' or (punningly) 'apple core' sought as an ultimate prize by anyone after world fame.

**Big band.** The big band era of popular music dates from the 1930s, the age of SWING, when augmented dance and jazz bands came into vogue, with reed and brass sections having separate parts and playing against one another while leaving space for soloists. The style was perfected by the US bandleader and composer Don Redman (1900–64).

**Big Bang.** (1) In cosmology a theory explaining the origin of the universe. It postulates that a small, superdense mass exploded, hurling matter in all directions in a cataclysmic explosion. As the fragments slowed down, the stars and galaxies formed, although the universe is still expanding.

(2) The major modernization of the Stock Exchange, in the City of London, which took place on 27 October 1986, was also known as the Big Bang. The distinction between stockjobber and stockbroker was abolished, and operations became fully computerized. The aim was to maintain London's position as a leading international financial centre.

(3) During the COLD WAR, when the doctrine of MAD prevailed, 'the big bang' denoted the end world in a thermonuclear conflagration.

> If the big bang does come, and we all get killed off, it won't be in aid of the old-fashioned grand design. It'll be for the Brave New-nothing-very-much thank-you.
>
> JOHN OSBORNE: *Look Back in Anger* (1956)

**Big beast.** A politician who, in cricketing parlance, would be described as a 'big hitter'. He (occasionally she) has a variety of characteristics: considerable governmental experience at a senior level, robustness as a debater, intellectual vigour, gravitas (but not necessarily humourlessness). When (unsuccessfully) running for the Tory leadership in 2005, Kenneth Clarke (*see* PIE, PINT AND PANATELLA MAN) told an interviewer:

> I've got to persuade the [Conservative Party] conference that they've only got one big beast in the party at the moment – against the big beast in the Labour Party [i.e. Gordon Brown] that is going to take over from Blair.
>
> Quoted in *The Observer* (2 October 2005)

Others who have typified the big beast in the past include the likes of Michael Heseltine, Margaret Thatcher, Denis Healey and Jim Callaghan.

**Big Bertha.** The name given by the French to the large howitzers used by the Germans against Liège and Namur in 1914. They were made at the Škoda works, but were mistakenly assumed to be manufactured by Krupp, the famous German armament firm. Hence the allusion to Bertha Krupp (1886–1957), great-granddaughter of the firm's founder, Friedrich Krupp (1787–1826), to whom control of the works had passed on her father's death in 1902. In 1918 Paris was shelled from a range of 122km (76 miles) by the 142-ton 'Paris' gun, to which the name Big Bertha was again applied.

**Big Blue, The.** A nickname applied in the 1980s to the IBM corporation of America, which at that time bestrode the world of computers like a colossus. It arose originally as the nickname of a particular model of IBM machine, the 360 mainframe computer, which had a blue casing.

**Big Blunkett.** A nickname given to David Blunkett, New Labour home secretary 2001–4, until forced to resign, then work and pensions secretary from May 2005 until forced to resign again in November of that year. The nickname refers to BIG BROTHER (itself an alternative nickname for Blunkett), awarded because of Blunkett's championing of such measures as national identity cards, detention without charge or trial, and the dropping of jury trials. Blunkett is more affectionately known as 'Blunko'.

**Big Brother.** A person or organization that exercises dictatorial control, supposedly for one's own welfare and in one's best interests. The name is that of the invisible state machinery in George ORWELL's *Nineteen Eighty-Four* (1949) (*see* 1984), representing the real-life political leader of the USSR:

> On each landing, opposite the lift shaft, the poster with the enormous face gazed from the wall. It was one of those pictures which are so contrived that the eyes follow you about when you move. BIG BROTHER IS WATCHING YOU, the caption beneath it ran.
>
> ch. 1

Round-the-clock scrutiny by unseen watchers became a reality for contestants in the voyeuristic television game show *Big Brother*, series after series of which have enjoyed success in Britain and many other countries since 2000, with participants in each successive series fuelled by ever-increasing amounts of alcohol and seemingly shedding more and more inhibitions in front of an eager public, in the hope, presumably, of launching a brief career as a D-list celebrity. The format was invented by the Dutch TV executive John de Mol, and it has made his company Endemol large sums of money. A more recent development

is *Celebrity Big Brother*, featuring those who have already made it onto the D-list and publicity-hungry figures such as GORGEOUS GEORGE Galloway.

> Nobody in their right mind would volunteer to run the Big Brother gamut of social vivisection, with the result that nobody in their right mind appears on it.
>
> PETE CLARK: review of *Big Brother* in *Evening Standard* (19 May 2006)

> Re Big Brother: is this the pinnacle of more than four billion years of evolution?
>
> DR FRANK FAULKNER: letter to *The Guardian* (11 January 2006)

*See also* REALITY TV; VOYEURVISION.

**Big bug.** A BIG WHEEL.

**Big C.** Cancer, which one is reluctant to name in full.

> Shortly after an appearance at the Academy Awards ceremony in April … [John] Wayne succumbed to what he had termed 'The Big C'.
>
> JOHN H. LENIHAN: in *American National Biography* (1999)

**Big cheese.** The boss or someone in an important position. 'Cheese' here is either an alteration of 'chief' or a borrowing via Urdu from Persian *chiz*, 'thing'.

**Big Cyril.** A friendly nickname for Cyril Smith (b.1928), the genial and generously proportioned Liberal (and subsequently Liberal Democrat) MP for Rochdale for 20 years from 1972.

**Big Daddy.** The nickname of Idi Amin (1925–2003), the massively built Ugandan president (1971–9), known to his people as Idi Amin Dada. Amin seized power in Uganda in 1971 and committed numerous gruesome atrocities against his own people until overthrown in 1979. The nickname was also sometimes applied to President Lyndon Johnson (*see* LBJ).

Big Daddy was also the professional name of the powerfully figured all-in wrestler Shirley Crabtree (1930–97).

**Big day.** The day of an important or decisive event, and especially that of a marriage or wedding. The mental, moral, emotional, physical and social preparations involved for the latter can combine to make it the 'biggest' of a lifetime.

**Big deal!** An ironic exclamation belittling a supposedly fine offer or proposal. *See also* NO BIG DEAL.

**Big Dog.** *See* SLICK WILLIE.

**Big E.** An unceremonious dismissal or rejection; 'the push'. The 'E' stands for 'elbow'.

**Big Ears.** Originally the name of NODDY's sidekick. The name is now disrespectfully but accurately applied to Charles Clarke, New Labour secretary of state for education 2002–4 and home secretary 2004–6 (until a scandal over the failure to deport foreign criminals prompted his return to the backbenches in the BLAIR DITCH PROJECT). In 2003 a schoolboy visitor to his office did a 'bunny ears' sign behind the minister's back, possibly at the prompting of a news cameraman. Another nickname is 'No Trousers Charlie'. Apparently this name dates from the 1980s, when Clarke worked at Hackney council, and the name was awarded 'after he invited a date back to his place for coffee one night, went into the kitchen to make it, and duly returned with two steaming mugs of Nescafé – but no trousers. Bafflingly, his date screamed and ran' (*The Guardian*, 17 December 2004). Another *ad hominem* nickname is DUMBO.

**Big Easy, The.** The nickname of New Orleans, Louisiana, referring to the city's laid-back, easygoing lifestyle. It seems to have originated as the title of a 1970 novel by James Conaway. The 1986 film based on it featured Dennis Quaid as the hero, a New Orleans detective. The name seemed poignantly inappropriate after New Orleans was devastated by Hurricane Katrina in the autumn of 2005.

The sobriquet has also been applied to the 1.9m (6ft 3 in) South African golfer Ernie Els (b.1969), who is renowned for his relaxed style of play.

**Big Enchilada.** The nickname of John M. Newton (1913–88), US attorney general, who led President Nixon's re-election campaign in 1972 and was subsequently jailed for his role in the WATERGATE affair. An enchilada is a Mexican dish. The name was given by a Nixon aide, John Erlichman, during a taped conversation of 1973 when he sought to describe the size of the 'sacrificial lamb' who was being thrown to the wolves. The British would probably have seen him in terms of a BIG CHEESE.

**Big Fella.** A nickname of the Irish nationalist guerrilla leader and politician Michael Collins (1890–1922), so called for his impressive physical stature. *See also* BÉAL NA MBLÁTH; DEV; FREE-STATERS.

**Big fish in a small pond.** A person regarded as important only within the limited scope of their own social or other group.

**Big Four.** The four main Allied powers and/or their leaders at the Paris Peace Conference after the First World War: the USA / Woodrow Wilson; Britain / Lloyd George (WELSH WIZARD); France / Georges Clemenceau (*see* the TIGER); Italy / Vittorio Orlando.

The name was revived for the four major Allied powers in the Second World War and/or their leaders: the USA / Franklin Roosevelt (FDR); the USSR / Stalin (UNCLE JOE); the UK / Churchill (FORMER NAVAL PERSON; WINNIE); China /

Chiang Kai-shek (General CASH-MY-CHEQUE). It was these four powers that drew up the Charter of the United Nations at the San Francisco Conference in April 1945. *See also* BIG THREE.

**Big Freeze.** A nickname for the unusually cold winter of 1962–3 in Britain. It seriously disrupted the football league programme, and many matches were either cancelled or postponed.

**Big Frisbee, The.** A New Zealanders' nickname for Australia, presumably with reference to its shape (*see* FRISBEE), which might with a large stretch of the imagination be called circular. The expression dates from the 1990s.

**Bigger bang for your buck, A.** A phrase, meaning better value for money (US slang *buck*, 'dollar'), that originated in the COLD WAR. In 1954 President Eisenhower's secretary of state, John Foster Dulles, described to the Council on Foreign Relations his policy of massive retaliation should the Soviet Union mount a first nuclear strike against the United States: 'It is now possible to get, and share, more basic security at less cost.' His colleague, defense secretary Charles E. Wilson (1890–1961), who had been president of General Motors, described this as 'a bigger bang for a buck' (William Safire, *The New Language of Politics*, 1968). The phrase may owe something to an earlier slogan, an advertisement for fizzy drinks: 'More bounce to the ounce'. *See also* MILITARY-INDUSTRIAL COMPLEX; WHAT'S GOOD FOR GENERAL MOTORS IS GOOD FOR THE COUNTRY.

**Bigger Splash, A.** The best known of the many swimming-pool pictures by David Hockney (b.1937), painted in 1967. It was the third of a series, which explains the title, as Hockney himself recalls: '*The Little Splash*, which is a tiny painting … was the first of three paintings … from a photograph I found in a book about how to build swimming pools I found on a news stand in Hollywood. It was a nice little subject, a splash … And I thought, it's worth making this bigger, doing it a little differently, and so I did a slightly bigger one, *The Splash*, and I took a bit more care with it. But then I thought the background was perhaps slightly fussy, the buildings were a little too complicated, not quite right. So I decided I'd do a third version, a big one using a very simple building and strong light.'

**Biggin Hill.** The site near Westerham in Kent (now in southeastern Greater London) of an RAF aerodrome that played a major part in the BATTLE OF BRITAIN. The airfield was first established in the First World War and was affectionately known as 'Biggin on the Bump'. The name later became a byword for the heroic spirit of 1940. *See also* FEW WELL-CHOSEN WORDS; MOVING CHURCH.

**Big girl.** A teenage girl whose physical development suggests that she is older than she really is.

**Big girl's blouse.** A weakling; an ineffectual person. The expression originated in the north of England in the 1960s and was popularized by northern-based television programmes such as the SITCOM *Nearest and Dearest* (1968–72), featuring Hylda Baker and Jimmy Jewel as brother and sister Nellie and Eli Pledge who inherit a pickle-bottling factory. *See also* BIG GIRL.

> I find it bizarre that, while men are praised to the skies every time they come over all big girl's blouse, women are still penalized for getting in touch with their masculine side.
>
> INDIA KNIGHT: in *Sunday Times* (17 October 1999)

**Biggles.** The most famous aviator in boys' fiction was the creation of Captain W.E. Johns (1893–1968), who drew on memories of his experiences in the Royal Flying Corps during the First World War. His hero's full name is James Bigglesworth, DSO, DFC, MC, and he made his bow in magazine stories of the early 1930s. He also starts his flying career in the First World War and eventually becomes commander of a flying squadron. In the Second World War he plays a major role in the BATTLE OF BRITAIN. His GUNG-HO exploits continued until his creator's death.

**Big government.** A phrase used pejoratively (especially in the United States) of a central government that is regarded as having excessive powers and too great a bureaucracy. Although Henry David Thoreau, in his essay 'Civil Disobedience' (1849), argued 'That government is best which governs not at all', hostility towards 'big government' in the United States has tended to come from the right, who object to government regulation of business, the state's involvement in the provision of welfare, and, above all, taxes.

> If the government is big enough to give you everything you want, it is big enough to take away everything you have.
>
> GERALD FORD: quoted in John F. Parker, *If Elected* (1960).
> Ford, a Republican politician, became 38th president on the resignation of Richard Nixon in 1974.

**Big hair.** A bouffant hairstyle, especially one that has been teased, permed or sprayed to produce an impressive profusion. The term and style arose in the United States in the 1970s, and continued through the 1980s, popularized by glamorous American TV soaps such as *Dallas* and *Dynasty*.

> In eighties Britain, women wore in-yer-face shoulder pads and big hair to demonstrate their enthusiasm for money, power and the yuppie dream.
>
> *Sunday Express* (27 February 2000)

**Big-hearted Arthur.** The comedian Arthur Askey (1900–82) so called himself, alluding to his cheery willingness to help where no others would, and the name was generally adopted for him in billings.

**Big Heat, The.** A film (1953) adapted by Sidney Boehm from a mystery novel by William P. McGivern (1924–83). It starred Glenn Ford as Sergeant Dave Bannion, a police officer and family man determined to wreak vengeance on the gangsters who had killed his wife in mistake for him. Directed by Fritz Lang, it caused a considerable stir at the time for its violent content, notably an incident (not actually shown to the audience) in which gangster Lee Marvin throws scalding coffee in heroine Gloria Grahame's face. The title refers to the heat generated by the police as a result of US Senate crime investigations against organized crime in the early 1950s.

**Big Issue.** A magazine launched by John Bird and Dave Bulldog in 1991 to 'help the homeless help themselves'. The homeless make money by selling the magazine on town and city streets. In content it deals with the arts and current affairs as well as issues relating to housing and unemployment, which are implicitly the key subject of its punning title. There are now regional and internationals editions.

**Big lie.** A gross distortion or misrepresentation of the facts, especially when used by a politician or political party. Before and during the Second World War the expression was specifically applied to NAZI propaganda as disseminated by Hitler and Goebbels, the theory being that the bigger the lie and the more often it is told, the greater the number of people who will accept it. *See also* Protocols of the Elders of Zion *under* FAKES.

> The broad mass of a nation … will more easily fall victim to a big lie than to a small one.
>
> ADOLF HITLER: *Mein Kampf* (1925)

**Big Look.** A fashion in women's clothes introduced in 1974 and characterized by loose, broad, voluminous designs. It involved the elimination of linings and interfacings and meant that the clothes could be worn on top of one another in layers without making the wearer look unduly huge.

**Big Mac.** A proprietary name for a large hamburger served by MCDONALD'S fast-food outlets. *See also* MCJOB; MAC OUT; MCMANSION.

**Big Mal.** A nickname for anyone called Malcolm who is outstanding in some way, either physically or in status. Two so known are Malcolm Allison (b.1927), manager of Manchester City football club and later of Crystal Palace and Middlesbrough, and Malcolm Fraser (b.1930), prime minister of Australia from 1975 to 1983, who is over 1.8m (6ft) tall.

**Big Man.** The great Scottish football manager Jock Stein (John Stein; 1922–85), who led Glasgow Celtic to nine consecutive Scottish League championships (1966–74) and the European Cup (1967). The name is sometimes used in Northern Ireland of the militant Unionist politician the Rev. Ian Paisley (*see* PAISLEYITES).

**Big man on campus.** A US term for a male college student leader or idol. The phrase is usually abbreviated to BMOC.

**Big Momma.** A not unkind nickname for the champion golfer Laura Davies (b.1964), who is 1.7m (5ft 10in) tall and who when the name was given in the early 1980s weighed 73kg (161lb or 11½ stone).

**Bigmouth.** A noisy or indiscreet person.

**Big noise.** A BIG WHEEL.

**Big-note oneself.** In Australian slang, dating from the 1940s, to boast about oneself, to exaggerate one's achievements. 'Big note' in this context implies a high-value banknote (in British slang of the late 20th century, a 'big note' was a £100 note), and the expression's subtext is the vanity of the (newly) wealthy.

**Big ...-o.** A formula applied to a particular landmark decade birthday: for example, one's 50th birthday is 'the big five-o'. It dates from the 1980s.

**Big O.** The nickname of the US singer Roy Orbison (1936–88). Also the nickname of the US basketball player Oscar Robertson (b.1938), a prodigiously talented guard for the Cincinatti Royals from 1960 to 1970 and later for the Milwaukee Bucks.

**Big of you.** Generous of you. A phrase invariably used ironically, as: 'So you won't charge me for the stamp? That's big of you!' The phrase dates from the 1940s.

**Big one.** Something promoted to be bigger and better than any of its kind before. Also, a major or daunting under-taking, typically prefaced by a remark such as: 'This is the big one.'

**Big pot.** A BIG WHEEL.

**Big shot.** A BIG WHEEL.

**Big Sleep, The.** The first crime novel (1939) by the US writer Raymond Chandler (1888–1959). It is set in Los Angeles and introduces the detective Philip MARLOWE, a man of sentiment, wit and morality, as well as toughness. Chandler's aim was to present criminals as they really were,

not as the writers of detective novels represented them. The title refers to a passage at the end of the book: 'What did it matter where you lay once you were dead? … You were dead, you were sleeping the big sleep.' A complex but pacy film version (1946), with Humphrey Bogart as Marlowe, was directed by Howard Hawks. A remake (1978), directed by Michael Winner and starring Robert Mitchum, lacked the subtlety of Howard Hawks's version.

**Big stick diplomacy.** The backing of negotiations with the threat of military force. The term was popularized by Theodore Roosevelt's declaration in 1900 that he had always been fond of the West African proverb 'speak softly and carry a big stick'. He used such tactics successfully (1902–4) in the Alaskan boundary dispute and the second Venezuelan crisis.

**Big tent.** A phrase applied to the non-ideological politics of consensus that Tony Blair attempted after his election as New Labour prime minister in May 1997, in an effort to draw other parties of the centre into his PROJECT. Blair planned to bring the Liberal Democrats, led by Paddy Ashdown, into government, but this was opposed by other senior Labour figures. Before long the Lib Dems realized they were, in reality, to the left of New Labour, proposing increases in income tax and, under their next leader Charles Kennedy, rigorously opposing the 2003 invasion of Iraq.

> Blair can never decide whether he is her [Margaret Thatcher's] heir or the man who liberated the country from 18 years of Thatcherite captivity. But when it comes to popularity, he is no Thatcherite. She regarded popularity as capital to be invested and expended. Blair has been a miser of popularity, never happier than when sitting in his big tent counting his gold, desperate to ensure that not a single coin escapes.
> BRUCE ANDERSON: in *The Independent* (2003)

Big-tent politics have also been ascribed to politicians such as Kenneth Clarke and Ken Livingstone. The idea of the political leader in his tent presumably goes back to medieval kings on campaign. The image was robustly deployed by President Lyndon Johnson (1908–73) in discussing J. Edgar Hoover, the dangerously powerful head of the FBI:

> Better to have him inside the tent pissing out, than outside pissing in.

**Big Three.** Winston Churchill, Franklin D. Roosevelt and Joseph Stalin, heads of government of Britain, the United States and the Soviet Union, were so called when they met at the YALTA CONFERENCE in 1945. *See also* BIG FOUR.

**Big time.** Success in a profession, especially show business. Also, since the early 1980s, an adverb meaning 'to a considerable extent' (as in 'You're in trouble big time').

> The Shands have got the shag gene. No question. Big time.
> GYLES BRANDRETH: *Charles & Camilla: Portrait of a Love Affair* (2005)

**Big Train.** The nickname of the tall and well-built US baseball player and manager Walter Johnson (1887–1946), so called from the power of his deliveries. He first received the name in 1910.

**Big wheel.** An important or conceited person.

**Big white chief.** An important person, or the head or leader of an organization. The expression dates from the 1930s and supposedly represents Native American speech.

**Big Yin.** The regular nickname of the Scottish comedian Billy Connolly (b.1942), as Scots dialect for 'Big One'.

**Bikini.** This atoll in the Marshall Islands, the scene of US nuclear weapon testing in 1946, gave its name to a scanty two-piece swimming costume worn by women. The allusion is supposedly to the devastation of the atom-bomb test and the 'explosive' effect caused by a woman wearing such a costume (*see also* BLONDE BOMBSHELL; SEX BOMB). The garment was pioneered in the year of the test by the French couturiers Jacques Heim and Louis Réard, and the term first appeared in the magazine *Le Monde Illustré* in 1947. The initial 'bi-' was later amusingly taken to mean 'two', with reference to the two parts of the costume, so that a one-piece or topless swimsuit (the lower half of a bikini) came to be called a monokini. There is also a trikini, with two top parts. A more recent development is the 'tankini', a combination of a TANK TOP and a bikini.

> A bikini is like a barbed-wire fence. It protects the property without obstructing the view.
> JOEY ADAMS

**Bikini line.** The area of the thigh along the bottom edge of a BIKINI, especially with regard to its cosmetic depilatory treatment. The term need not specifically apply to the wearing of a bikini. *See also* BRAZILIAN WAX.

> While investigating the new, superbly thorough Brazilian bikini wax you should maintain a roughly natural outline on your bikini line.
> *The Times* (26 June 1999)

**Biko Affair.** A scandal arising from the death while in police custody of Steve Biko (1946–77), founder of the Black Consciousness Movement in South Africa. Biko's death came after 24 days during which he was held naked and shackled and suffered three brain lesions. Despite a postmortem finding that these were caused by 'application of force to his head', the subsequent inquest absolved the police from any responsibility for his death. This led to an international outcry, and to Biko becoming an important martyr in the anti-APARTHEID cause. The affair featured in Richard Attenborough's 1987 film *Cry Freedom*.

**Bilbo Baggins.** *See* Bilbo BAGGINS.

**Bilko.** The bespectacled US Army master sergeant played by Phil Silvers in the anarchic television comedy series *You'll Never Get Rich*, later known as *The Phil Silvers Show* and *Bilko* (1955–9). With the full name Ernest G. Bilko, he is a loveable conman who is forever fooling his superior officers. His creator was Nat Hiken. The show became cult viewing, and some enthusiasts regard Sergeant Bilko as the most memorable comic creation on US television.

**Bill, The.** The police force, or a member of it. The term is a shortening of OLD BILL (*see aslo* BETTER 'OLE) and was adopted as the title of a long-running television crime series about the lives and loves of personnel at the fictional Sun Hill police station in London's East End, first screened in 1984.

**Billi-bi.** A type of soup made from fresh mussels, cream and white wine. Its name is of French origin and dates from the 1960s, when it was complimented by Billy B. Leeds, a US businessman who was a regular diner at Maxim's in Paris, where the soup was served.

**Bill We'll Be Paying for Years, The.** *See* SLICK WILLIE.

**Billy Budd.** An all-male nautical opera by Benjamin Britten (1913–76) with a libretto by the novelist E.M. Forster and Eric Crozier, based on the novel *Billy Budd* (1891; not published until 1924) by Herman Melville (1819–91). It was first performed in London in 1951, and, because of the sexuality of its creators, became known among the politically incorrect as 'The Bugger's Opera' (in reference to the 18th-century *Beggar's Opera* of John Gay) . Billy Budd is an innocent sailor on board an 18th-century man-of-war. He is tormented by Claggart, the master at arms, whom he accidentally kills, and then goes willingly to his execution. There is another opera on the subject by Giorgio Ghedini (1892–1965), with a libretto by the Nobel laureate Salvatore Quasimodo (1901–68); it was first performed in 1949. There is also a film (1962) written and directed by Peter Ustinov (1921–2004), who starred alongside Terence Stamp (b.1940) as Billy.

**Billy Bunter.** *See* Billy BUNTER.

**Billy Williams' Cabbage Patch.** The English Rugby Football Union's ground at Twickenham, the headquarters of the game, also known as Twickers. It is popularly so called after William (Billy) Williams (1860–1951), who discovered the site and who persisted until it was acquired for rugby in 1907. The latter part of the name refers to the ground's former use as a market garden. The first match played there, on 2 October 1909, was between Harlequins and Richmond, and the first international was England v. Wales the following year. The nearby Railway Tavern changed its name to the Cabbage Patch in 1959 when England and Wales played Scotland and Ireland in a centenary match. The ground is now also the site of the Museum of Rugby, and tours of the stadium are held six days a week.

> Billy Williams's cabbage patch has never staged a more momentous game than this afternoon's match between England and the All Blacks.
> *The Times* (9 October 1999)

**Bimbo.** A superficially attractive but essentially shallow or unintelligent young woman. The word, from the Italian for 'baby', was first used in the 1920s as a derogatory term for a person of either sex. It then came to apply to a 'loose' woman before gaining its present nuance in the 1980s and duly spawning the HIMBO as a male equivalent.

**Bindle.** The henpecked husband in a series of comic novels by Herbert Jenkins, beginning with the one that bears his name (1916). Joseph Bindle spends much of his time on the dole and his wife is forever berating him with the cry of 'Lorst yer job?'

**Bing Boys.** The nickname of the Canadian troops in the First World War, from the name of their commanding officer, Lord Byng of Vimy (1862–1935). The name was also popularized by the revue, *The Bing Boys Are Here*, which opened at the Alhambra in 1915.

**Bingo.** A lastingly popular gambling game, played typically by pensioners in bingo halls converted from cinemas. The game is simple. Players have a card printed with a selection of numbers, and they cover the numbers as they are announced at random by a caller. The player who first covers all the numbers on his or her card calls 'Bingo' (or 'House') and wins a prize. The allure of the game is in its conviviality and in the caller's patter, which until electronic technology took over had traditional rhymes for the various numbers, such as 'legs eleven' for 11, 'dinkie doos' for 22, 'all the threes' for 33, 'clickety-click' for 66 and 'two fat ladies' for 88. The usual call at the start of the game is 'Eyes down, look in!' The word bingo itself probably imitates the 'ping' of a bell formerly rung to announce a win.

The game in its simplest form goes back at least to the 18th century, when it was called 'lotto'. It was in the 1930s that it became a mass popular entertainment, originally known in Britain usually as 'housey-housey' (from the notion of getting a full 'house' on one's card). The name 'bingo' originated in the US around the same time, and spread to Britain in the 1960s.

In the early 21st century bingo has increased its popularity, spreading beyond the traditional confines of retirees, with big money at stake.

**Binkie.** The regular first name, perhaps originally a childhood nickname, adopted by Hugh (originally Hughes) Beaumont (1908–73), managing director of the theatre group H.M. Tennant and an influential force in West End theatre. He was always known thus in theatrical circles.

**Bin Laden, Osama.** A Saudi-Arabian-born millionaire businessman and Islamic fundamentalist (b.1957) of the puritanical Wahabi sect, who uses his fortune to fund the terror network AL-QAIDA, operatives of which are widely believed to have been responsible for the attacks on the WORLD TRADE CENTER and the PENTAGON on 11 September 2001. A CIA-backed *mujahid* in the war against the Soviet army in Afghanistan in the 1980s (*see* MUJAHEDIN), Bin Laden turned against his American allies from the early 1990s. His fanatical opposition to US policy in the Middle East – especially US backing of the State of Israel, and the presence of US forces in his native Saudi Arabia – led him to instigate a worldwide campaign of attacks on US, European, Israeli, and other interests. Expelled from a base in Sudan under US and Egyptian pressure in 1996, Bin Laden returned to Afghanistan to live under the protection of the TALIBAN regime. When that was overthrown following American intervention in 2001, Bin Laden disappeared, and is believed to be hiding in the remote mountains on the border with Pakistan. The capture of Bin Laden, dead or alive, and the destruction of Al-Qaida, are stated aims of the WAR ON TERROR launched by US President George W. Bush.

**Biodiversity.** A BUZZWORD of the 1980s for the variety of plant and animal life in a particular location or even as taken worldwide. Generally speaking, a high level of biodiversity is regarded as both desirable and important, and its implementation often involves conservation action, especially in areas where particular plants or animals are close to extinction. In Britain the establishment of the NATIONAL FOREST is just one part of the programme.

**Biofeedback.** In a literal sense, biofeedback is simply feedback about the body, such as may be obtained by weighing oneself on the bathroom scales or taking one's temperature with a thermometer. 'Feedback' itself is a term that first gained currency among radio pioneers at the turn of the 20th century and that was defined by the US mathematician Norbert Wiener as 'a method of controlling a system by reinserting into it the results of its past performance'. In the light of this, biofeedback is now used for the electronic monitoring of a person's normally automatic bodily function, such as blood pressure, in order to train them to acquire voluntary control of that function. Once this is done, the procedure can have various beneficial applications. The biofeedback of BRAINWAVE activity, for example, can aid insomniacs and epileptics.

**Biological clock.** A supposed natural mechanism inside the body that controls the rhythm of the body's functions, whether they occur on a daily basis, such as sleeping, monthly, such as the menstrual cycle, or seasonally, such as the growth rate of children. The term is popularly misunderstood to denote the inexorable 'ticking away' of a woman's fertile years. *See also* CIRCADIAN RHYTHMS.

> My biological clock is ticking so loud I'm nearly deafened by it. They search me going into planes.
> MARIAN KEYES: 'Late Opening in the Last Chance Saloon' (1997)

**Bionic Woman.** *See* Steve AUSTIN.

**Bird.** The nickname (originally Yardbird) of Charlie Parker (1920–55), the jazz saxophonist. Known for his frenetic solos ('I was always in a panic', he said), Parker was one of the key innovators of the BEBOP style. After his early death, brought on by drug and alcohol abuse, the graffito 'Bird Lives!' spread around the world. It first appeared in the New York subways, and is said to have been the creation of the jazz trumpeter, poet and painter Ted Joans (1928–2003).

> Music is your own experience, your thoughts, your wisdom. If you don't live it, it won't come out of your horn.
> CHARLIE PARKER: quoted in Stearns, *The Story of Jazz* (1956)

*See also* BIRDLAND.

**Bird flu.** A type of flu, the H5N1 strain, among domesticated and wild birds, which is fatal to humans in a sizeable percentage of cases, although there are anti-viral treatments. It was widely publicized in the UK from 2005, as isolated incidents in East and Southeast Asia were increasing in number and spreading westwards, into the Middle East and Western Europe, giving rise to dire predictions of a catastrophic human pandemic should the virus mix with 'traditional' human flu strains and become contagious. Some doctors believed this mutation to be inevitable, and

some countries began stockpiling medicine to combat it. *See also* SPANISH FLU.

**Birdie.** A hole at golf that the player has completed in one stroke less than par (the standard for the course). Two strokes less is an eagle. Three strokes less is an albatross.

The story goes that one day in 1903 A.B. ('Ab') Smith was enjoying a game of golf in Atlantic City, United States. Endeavouring to improve his already good game, he made a shot that enabled him to sink his ball one under par. The success prompted his cry of delight, 'That's a bird of a shot!' The term caught on and in due course became affectionately known as a 'birdie'. The eagle and the albatross followed logically, since a stroke two under par is rare, like the eagle, and one three under par even rarer, like the albatross.

**Birdland.** A former famous jazz club in New York, named after the saxophonist Charlie 'BIRD' Parker, who played there. It opened in a Broadway basement in 1949 and was a venue for many leading jazz musicians. Rising rents forced it to close in 1965. It gave its name to George Shearing's song 'Lullaby of Birdland' (1952), and the name was subsequently appropriated by an unrelated jazz club at another Broadway address.

**Birdman of Alcatraz.** The US murderer Robert Stroud (1887–1963) was so called from his scientifically admired studies of the birds that flew to his prison window while he was awaiting execution in ALCATRAZ. His sentence was commuted in 1916 and he died of old age in prison. He was the subject of a 1962 film of the same name starring Burt Lancaster.

**Birds and the bees.** A euphemism for sexual activity or reproduction, alluding to the fanciful stories told to young children on the subject.

> Ten years ago, my friend was listening to his parents explaining the 'birds and the bees', now he finds himself extolling the virtues of the Femidom and ISAs to an astounded, clueless mother.
> *Sunday Times* (15 August 1999)

**Birds Eye.** The proprietary name of a make of frozen foods, from Clarence Birdseye (1886–1956), a US fur trapper, who, while trading in furs in Labrador over the five years from 1912, noticed that frozen fish and caribou meat tasted as good as fresh food even after being frozen for several months. He experimented with re-creating the natural conditions of freezing at his home, and in the early 1920s devised a system of quick-freezing that could have commercial applications. In 1924, at Gloucester, Massachusetts, he founded the General Seafoods Corporation, and a development of this was Birdseye Frosted Foods, formed in 1930. The first products to appear under the name were first commercially available in 1932. In Britain, Birds Eye products aimed at children, especially fish fingers, have for the last few decades been promoted on TV by a bearded nautical type known as Captain Birdseye.

**Birds of a Feather.** A popular television SITCOM first broadcast on the BBC in 1989 and based on the sibling rivalry and affection that exists between Sharon Theodopolopoudos and Tracey Stubbs, two ESSEX GIRL types, played by the real-life friends Pauline Quirke and Linda Robson. The series did much to promote the stereotypes associated with the names SHARON and TRACY.

**Birdwatching.** The practice or hobby of watching birds in their natural habitat. The term is first recorded as the title of a book by E. Selous, *Bird Watching* (1901), as a 'homelier' equivalent of the specifically scientific ornithology, and it in turn prompted various other 'watching' activities, such as those studied by the ethologist Desmond Morris in *Manwatching* (1977), *Bodywatching* (1985), *Catwatching* (1986) and even *Christmas Watching* (1992).

**Birmingham Six.** The six Irishmen who were arrested following the IRA bombing of two crowded Birmingham pubs on 21 November 1974, killing 21 and wounding more than 150. Billy Power, Gerry Hunter, Hugh Callaghan, John Walker, Paddy Joe Hill and Dick McIlkenny were tried in 1975, convicted on 21 murder counts and sentenced to life imprisonment. Subsequent appeals against the sentence failed until 1991, when they were judged to have been wrongly convicted and freed. Among the less wise pronouncements by Lord Denning, the senior judge, was this:

> We shouldn't have all these campaigns to get the Birmingham Six released if they'd been hanged. They'd have been forgotten and the whole community would be satisfied.
>
> *The Spectator*, 18 August 1990

*See also* BRIDGEWATER THREE; GUILDFORD FOUR; WINCHESTER THREE.

**Biro.** A name that soon became generic for any make of ball-point pen but that began with the commercial model introduced in 1945 by the Hungarian László Biró (1899–1985), who had patented his invention two years before. Working with a magazine, he had realized the advantage of quick-drying ink, and in 1940 had moved to Argentina on the rise of Nazism to perfect his idea. The Frenchman Marcel Bich (1914–94) took over the invention in 1958 and created a disposable version, the Bic. As with its predecessor, the name soon came to be used for any ball-point.

**Birthday honours.** The honours awarded on the date that is the sovereign's official birthday (as distinct from the actual one). For Elizabeth II, this is a Saturday in June. Most of the honours, in the form of peerages, knighthoods, military and civilian awards, are made from a list drawn up by the prime minister, which includes about 50 individuals recommended 'for political services'. The vast majority of those honoured, however, receive an OBE (ORDER OF THE BRITISH EMPIRE). The BEM (British Empire Medal) was also awarded until 1993, when it was discontinued. Only the highest honours are received personally from the sovereign, and the junior award is presented by royal representatives. A similar system operates for the New Year honours.

**Birthday Party, The.** A play (1958) by the British playwright Harold Pinter (b.1930) in which two menacing strangers disrupt the banality of life in an ordinary seaside boarding house. The celebration of the birthday of the lodger Stanley (including present-giving and party games) provides a connecting theme for the drama, as well as the title.

**Birth of a Nation, The.** An early film epic (1915), directed by D.W. Griffith and based on a racist novel, *The Clansman*, by the Southern Baptist minister Thomas Dixon. In bald cinematic terms *The Birth of a Nation* is a film following the fortunes of two families during the American Civil War (1861–5), and it was the most ambitious motion picture released to date. Ideologically, it is probably the most controversial film ever released in the United States, justifying and celebrating the white South's 'redemption' from Reconstruction (the liberal political reorganization of the Southern states (1865–77) that followed the Northern victory in the Civil War), the end of which process saw the disenfranchising of the African American population and the imposition of rigid racial segregation in the southern states of the old Confederacy. The nation 'born' in the title is thus a white-dominated society that has turned its back on the perceived fratricidal folly of the Civil War and the supposed African American despotism of Reconstruction. The film portrays the KU KLUX KLAN as triumphant defenders of white America, and the African American population as an inferior race.

> It is like writing history with lightning. And my only regret is that it is all so terribly true.
>
> PRESIDENT WOODROW WILSON: at the White House
> (18 February 1915)

**Birtism.** The style of management and organizational culture named after John Birt (b.1944), who was director general of the BBC from 1993 to March 2000. Birt was much criticized for stifling creativity by excessive layers of management and by the introduction of an internal market within the BBC, all at great expense, although with the intention of ensuring a culture of accountability.

**Biscuit cough.** A cough caused by a mere irritation or 'tickle' in the throat, as from biscuit crumbs. The term was popularized, or even invented, by A.A. Milne.

> 'Nasty cold day,' said Rabbit, shaking his head. 'And you were coughing this morning' … 'It was a Biscuit Cough', said Roo, 'not one you tell about.'
>
> A.A. MILNE: *The House at Pooh Corner* (1928)

**Bish-bash-bosh.** A phrase descriptive of any rapid or routine manual or mechanical operation, as: 'The double-glazing people put the new window in bish-bash-bosh.' The implication is generally that the operation was efficient, although taken individually the three elements of the phrase suggest the opposite. The *Daily Mirror* redeployed the expression with witty irony as a front-page splash (4 November 2005) to draw attention to the arrest of Rebekah Wade, editor of rival tabloid *The Sun*, for assaulting her husband, the actor Ross Kemp.

**Bismarck.** The Second World War German battleship, named after the 'Iron Chancellor' Otto von Bismarck (1815–98), who played the leading role in unifying Germany in the mid-19th century. Intended as a commerce raider, the immensely powerful *Bismarck* was completed in 1940. It made its first foray into the Atlantic in May 1941, accompanied by the heavy cruiser *Prinz Eugen*. A British fleet anticipated their course and met up with them in the north Atlantic on 24 May, when, during a brief encounter, the German ships sank the Royal Navy battleship *Hood* and damaged another, the *Prince of Wales*. The British heavy cruisers *Norfolk* and *Suffolk* continued to shadow the *Bismarck*, and later that day an attack by Fairey Swordfish torpedo-bombers from the carrier *Victorious* failed to inflict much damage on the German battleship. Then the British lost contact with the *Bismarck*, which was heading south, until it was spotted again on 26 May. Another attack by torpedo-bombers from the *Ark Royal* damaged the *Bismarck*'s steering gear. The next morning the battleships *King George V* and *Rodney*, together with the *Norfolk*, caught up with the *Bismarck* and reduced it to a blazing wreck. It was then dispatched to the bottom by a torpedo from the cruiser *Dorsetshire*. All but 110 of the *Bismarck*'s crew died. The German claim that it was scuttled is not generally accepted. The epic British pursuit of the German battleship was the subject of the 1960 film *Sink the Bismarck* starring Kenneth More.

**Bisto.** The proprietary name of a gravy powder first sold in 1910. It was popularized by the 'Bisto Kids', a group of urchin children who breathe 'Ah! Bisto!' as they savour the gravy's aroma. The name is probably arbitrary but has been explained as an anagrammatized acronym of the product's advertising slogan, 'Browns, Seasons, Thickens In One'.

**Bitch, The.** A nickname of the film actress Joan Collins (b.1933), partly from the reputation she has gained in her colourful private life, as a five-times married MANEATER, partly from the image of herself that she has projected in the films *The Stud* (1978) and *The Bitch* (1979) and as 'superbitch' Alexis Colby in the television melodrama DYNASTY. Collins became what she described as 'a patron' of the UK Independence Party in 2004, but rejoined the Conservative Party the following year. Having three grandchildren, she has been described in the press as a 'glam-ma'.

> Joan Collins is NOT 'The Bitch'. You'd better believe it. Or she will chew you into small pieces, spit you out and stamp on you. Then she'll sue the pants off you. That's official.
>
> CHRISTINE HAMILTON: *The Book of British Battleaxes* (1997)

**Bitch goddess.** Material or worldly success as an object of attainment. The phrase comes from a letter of 11 September 1906 written by William James to H.G. Wells, in which he refers to 'a symptom of the moral flabbiness born of the exclusive worship of the bitch-goddess *success*'.

**Bite the scenery.** In theatrical slang, to become very overwrought; to have a tantrum.

**Bits and bobs.** Odds and ends; small diffuse amounts. Weather forecasters sometimes refer to 'bits and bobs of rain' meaning scattered showers.

**Bitten by a bug.** Keenly interested in an activity. The phrase usually names the bug in question, as 'bitten by the railway bug'. The expression dates from the 1930s but 'bug' as a word for an enthusiast goes back to the 19th century.

> I was bitten by the bug in my native California at the age of 12 when a girlfriend taught me to body surf with flippers. I've been a wave rider ever since.
>
> *Independent on Sunday* (3 October 1999)

**Blackadder.** A wise-cracking but cynical character created by Rowan Atkinson in successive television series, each set in a different historical period. The first, *The Black Adder* (1983), was supposedly during the War of the Roses. The second, *Blackadder II* (1985), was a comic version set in Elizabethan times. In the third, *Blackadder the Third* (1987), Blackadder is butler to the Prince Regent in the period 1762–1815. The saga ended magnificently with *Blackadder Goes Forth* (1989), bringing the tale into the 20th century and set in the First

World War. In all of these Blackadder's long-suffering, dim-witted servant, Baldrick, is played by Tony Robinson.

**Black and Tans.** The name of a pack of hounds in County Limerick, applied to the specially recruited armed force of ex-servicemen sent to Ireland by the British government in 1920 during the Anglo-Irish War (War of Independence) to supplement the Royal Irish Constabulary. This force was so called from the colour of the mixed uniforms, which consisted of army khaki combined with the black belts and dark green caps of the RIC. Their main objective was to put down Republican rebels, which they proceeded to do with much bloodshed. The Irish for their part were merciless in their treatment of crown forces or suspected informers. *See also* IRA; SINN FÉIN; TROUBLES.

***Black and White Minstrel Show, The.*** A popular Saturday night BBC television variety show running for 20 years from 1958 and featuring white men blacked up as AFRICAN AMERICAN minstrels. The show finally faded from the screen when its incongruously racist nature was realized.

**Black bag job.** A US slang term for the surreptitious entry of an office or home in order to obtain files or other materials of intelligence interest. Although such break-ins were illegal, they were undertaken by the FBI in the interwar years, mainly for the benefit of code-breakers who wanted photographs of code books or diagrams of cipher machines. Another purpose was the installation of 'bugs' and telephone wire-taps. Black bag jobs, so called from the notional black (i.e. secret) carrier used, were outlawed by J. Edgar Hoover in 1966 but were again sanctioned in 1981 by President Reagan as long as they were conducted against a foreign power or its agents.

**BlackBerry.** A brand of 'personal digital assistant' (PDA), i.e. a handheld device that allows users to engage in a number of electronic tasks, in particular (via a small keyboard and wireless connection to mobile phone networks) to be able to use E-MAIL on the move. It was developed by the Canadian company Research in Motion. The device was apparently so-named by branding consultants as a punchier version of 'strawberry', after the miniature buttons on its keyboard evoked in one observer that particular fruit.

***Blackboard Jungle, The.*** The first novel (1954) of the US writer Evan Hunter (1926–2005) was based on his personal experience. It is a somewhat sensationalized account of an American urban high school where the boys are rough, the headmaster a bully, and the teachers overworked and plagued additionally by personal problems. As a result of the book, the expression blackboard jungle became a popular idiom for any undisciplined school of this type. A film version (1955), directed by Richard Brooks, was more notable for its introduction of Bill Haley and The Comets' 'ROCK AROUND THE CLOCK' behind the credits than for any intrinsic interest. *See also The* ASPHALT JUNGLE; CONCRETE JUNGLE; ROCK 'N' ROLL.

**Black bottom.** A popular dance of the 1920s, of US origin. It involved a sinuous rotation of the hips ('bottom').

**Black box.** An aircraft's flight data recorder, today usually orange in colour, not black. The term has a broader sense to apply to any complex piece of equipment whose workings remain a mystery. Here 'black' alludes to the arcane nature of its functions.

**Black Bradman.** A nickname of the Jamaica and West Indies cricketer George Headley (1909–83), whose batting feats in the 1930s led to inevitable comparisons with Australia's champion batsman, Don Bradman (*see* DON CAMILLO).

**Black cab.** A licensed London taxi, whether black in colour or not. Their drivers are required to be proficient in the KNOWLEDGE.

**Black Caps, The.** The New Zealand cricket team, which wears black caps with a silver fern motif on the front. For many decades the team laboured under the disadvantage (compared with rugby's ALL BLACKS) of having no settled nickname, but this one was eventually settled on by the marketing people in the 1990s.

**Black Dahlia, The.** The journalistic sobriquet assigned to Elizabeth Short, a young actress who was the victim of a brutal and still unsolved murder in Los Angeles in 1947. She had black hair and habitually wore black, and the name was further suggested by Raymond Chandler's *The Blue Dahlia*, the film of which had appeared the previous year. *The Black Dahlia* (1987), a hard-boiled crime novel by James Ellroy, was based on the case.

**Black dog.** Winston Churchill's name for the severe depressions to which he was sometimes prone. The term originally dates from the 18th century, being deployed by Dr Johnson in a letter to Mrs Thrale (28 June 1783):

> When I rise my breakfast is solitary, the black dog waits to share it, from breakfast to dinner he continues barking … Night comes at last, and some hours of restlessness and confusion bring me again to a day of solitude. What shall exclude the black dog from a habitation like this?

The black dog also appears in the writings of Sir Walter Scott and Robert Louis Stevenson, among others.

**Black Ferns.** The nickname of the New Zealand women's

rugby union team: black from the colour of their strip (as with the ALL BLACKS), and the silver fern being a New Zealand national symbol. It was introduced at the end of the 20th century (the alternative name 'Gal Blacks', provocatively touted in the media at the time, never stood a realistic chance).

**Black Forest gateau.** A rich chocolate sponge cake with layers of morello cherries or cherry jam and whipped cream, topped with chocolate icing. The name translates German *Schwarzwälder Kirschtorte*, the latter word referring to the kirsch with which the cake layers are sometimes sprinkled. The confection is said to have originated in Berlin in the 1930s and its name almost certainly alludes to its dark colour rather than to the Black Forest itself.

**Black Friday.** 15 April 1921 in Britain, when the alliance between the three main trade unions broke down over the refusal of transport workers and railwaymen to strike in sympathy with the miners. The miners thus struck alone but were forced to return to work in June. The decision of two of the main workforces not to join the strike marked a watershed in postwar industrial relations. *See also* RED FRIDAY.

**Black Hand.** The popular name of the Balkan terrorist organization that was founded in 1911 with the aim of uniting Serbia with Bosnia and Herzegovina and was largely responsible for contriving the assassination of the Archduke Franz Ferdinand in SARAJEVO on 28 June 1914. This was the event that precipitated the First World War. The name was also that of a group of Sicilian blackmailers and terrorists operating in the United States in the early 20th century.

**Blackhawk.** The US vigilante hero of *Military Comics* and of his own book, *Blackhawk*, from 1941 to 1969. He begins his career as an anti-NAZI freedom fighter and ends it as a CIA agent. He was the creation of Chuck Cuidera, and was perpetuated by Reed Crandall and other artists. He appeared on radio in the 1940s and was played by Kirk Allyn in a film serial, *Blackhawk* (1952).

The Sikorsky UH60, the main US tactical transport helicopter which entered service in 1978, is named the 'Black Hawk'. It achieved its fifteen minutes of fame in *Black Hawk Down*, the 2001 film (based on a 1999 book by Mark Bowden) about the abortive US raid on Mogadishu, Somalia in 1993.

**Black hole.** In astronomy a hypothetical region of collapsed stars whose gravitational pull is so extreme that not even light can escape. In 1974 the physicist and cosmologist Stephen Hawking caused a stir in scientific circles by asserting that small black holes emit radiation. The term 'black hole' is often used figuratively, e.g. for a an expensive project that sucks away money.

**Black is beautiful.** An AFRICAN AMERICAN civil rights slogan of US origin, dating from the mid-1960s. The words have a biblical resonance: 'I am black, but comely, O ye daughters of Jerusalem, as the tents of Kedar, as the curtains of Solomon' (Song of Solomon 1:5).

**Black Jack.** General John J. Pershing (1860–1948), commander of the American Expeditionary Force in the First World War. In the 1890s Pershing commanded the 10th Cavalry, one of the 'Buffalo Soldier' regiments comprising AFRICAN AMERICAN soldiers commanded by white officers. Later, as an instructor at West Point, his harsh discipline earned him the nickname 'Nigger Jack' from the cadets. US reporters covering the First World War turned this into 'Black Jack'.

**Black knight.** The converse of a WHITE KNIGHT, as an individual or company making an unwelcome takeover bid for another company. The term dates from the 1980s.

> Lance was styling himself as a 'friendly suitor' for the moment, but he would turn into a 'black knight' if he got an unfavorable answer from the boss.
>
> MILTON MOSKOWITZ, MICHAEL KATZ and ROBERT LEVERING (eds): *Everybody's Business*, ch. 15 (1980)

**Black Lubyanka.** *See* LUBYANKA.

**Black Martyrs.** A general name for the 22 Africans of Uganda who died for their Christian faith in the late 1880s. They included Joseph Mkasa, who reproached the ruler, Mwanga, for debauchery and for murdering a missionary bishop, James Hannington, in 1885, Charles Lwanga, in charge of the royal pages, most of whom were also killed, Matthias Murumba, a judge, and Andrew Kagwa, a catechist. They were all canonized in 1964 and their feast-day of 3 June was included in the Roman calendar of 1969 as that of the protomartyrs of Black Africa. *See also* FORTY MARTYRS.

**Black Mischief.** *See* AZANIA.

**Black mist.** A corrupt business or political practice. The term dates from the 1960s and specifically applies to such practices in Japan, so translates Japanese *kuroi kiri*, from *kuroi*, 'black', and *kiri*, 'fog', 'mist'. A black mist obscures the vision and thus figuratively serves as an intentional cover-up of such a practice.

**Black Monday.** 19 October 1987, when £50 billion was wiped off the value of publicly quoted companies. The crash followed Wall Street's panic performance the previous Friday and heavy selling in Tokyo. In the United States the fall was the greatest since the GREAT DEPRESSION. Black Monday was also the nickname given by Conservative right-wingers to 3 February 1960, the day when Harold Macmillan gave his WIND OF CHANGE speech in Cape Town. *See also* MONDAY CLUB.

**Black Muslims.** *See* NATION OF ISLAM.

**Black October.** A nickname among economists for the time of year when there is often a financial crisis. During the 13 years from 1986 to 1999 there were six such stock market panics or 'mini-crashes', including BLACK MONDAY. BLACK THURSDAY was also in October, and BLACK WEDNESDAY the previous month. The incidence is linked to the perception that autumn is, in effect, a 'new year' after the summer holiday, when personal strategies and life plans are reviewed.

**Blackout.** The term was first used in the theatre, when the lighting was extinguished to darken the whole stage. It is now mainly associated with its use in the Second World War as an air-raid precaution. From the outbreak of war (3 September 1939) until 23 April 1945 (coastal areas, 11 May), it was obligatory throughout Britain to cover all windows, skylights and the like before dark so that no gleam of light could be seen from outside. Moving vehicles were allowed only the dimmest of lights.

**Black Panther.** A nickname applied by the popular press to Donald Neilsen, convicted in 1975 of the kidnap and murder of the young heiress Lesley Whittle and of the killing of three sub-post office officials. The name referred to the black hood worn by Neilsen during the nine-month police search for him.

**Black Panthers.** A US political group-cum-militia set up to fight for the rights of African Americans. The organization was founded in 1966 in Oakland, California, by Huey Newton (1942–89) and Bobby Seale (b.1936) and began by setting up armed 'self-defence' patrols to resist police harassment.

> I suggested that we use the panther as our symbol and call our political vehicle the Black Panther Party. The panther is a fierce animal, but he will not attack until he is backed into a corner; then he will strike out.
> HUEY NEWTON: *Revolutionary Suicide* (1973)

There was a scandal at a medal ceremony during the 1968 Olympics in Mexico City, when two African American US athletes, Tommie Smith and John Carlos, winners of the gold and bronze in the 200m sprint, raised their fists in black

gloves – the Black Panther salute – while bowing their heads in protest against racism in the United States. *See also* BLACK POWER; BLACK PRIDE.

**Black paper.** An unofficial paper criticizing or censuring an official document or policy. The contrast is with the White Paper, an official government report in Britain giving information or proposals on a particular issue. The term originated in the notorious 1969 *Black Paper* attacking liberal/progressive approaches to education and the comprehensive-school system. It was written by two academics, Brian Cox and A.E. Dyson, and its vocal supporters included Dr Rhodes Boyson, a teacher-turned-Tory-MP. A second *Black Paper* appeared in 1971.

> Yet, as spending on education rises, so, too, does public concern or bafflement about its aims and method, as shown in the acrimonious debate initiated by the Black Paper on education.
> *The Times* (30 December 1970)

**Black Pearl.** The great Brazilian footballer Pelé (Edson Arantes do Nascimento; b.1940), regarded by many as the most talented player of all time. *See also* BRAZILIAN FOOTBALLERS.

**Blackpool.** The north of England resort's earthy name derives from a peaty pool that existed here before the present town arose in the 19th century. In some ways it evokes the down-to-earth pleasures and entertainments that are on offer. They include the golden sands of its Pleasure Beach; the famous Blackpool Tower, a scaled-down version of the Eiffel Tower, housing a zoo, a circus, a ballroom and a large organ; and a promenade, the GOLDEN MILE, thronged with holidaymakers and trundling trams by day and illuminated by strings of gaudy lights at night, when it is often populated by drunks and prostitutes. The Pleasure Beach, with its four ROLLER COASTERS, including the famous Pepsi Max Big One, is the apotheosis of sheer corporeal pleasure. Blackpool is in many ways the Brighton of the north, and on the serious side shares with its southern counterpart the privilege of hosting major political and trade union conferences.

> Blackpool is less cool Britannia than gruel Britannia. It is 1960s Britain minus the rock'n'roll.
> *Sunday Times* (10 October 1999)

**Black Power.** A concept originating among certain sections of AFRICAN AMERICAN opinion in the United States since 1966. Its advocates aim at redressing racial injustice by militant black nationalism.

> The adoption of the concept of Black Power is one of the most legitimate and healthy developments in American

politics and race relations in our time … It is a call for black people in this country to unite, to recognize their heritage, to build a sense of community. It is a call for black people to begin to define their own goals, to lead their own organizations and to support those organizations. It is a call to reject the racist institutions and values of this society.

STOKELY CARMICHAEL and CHARLES VERNON HAMILTON: *Black Power* (1967)

*See also* BLACK PANTHERS; NATION OF ISLAM.

**Black pride.** A loose movement – perhaps more an attitude than a movement – originating in the mid-1960s, at the time of the birth of the BLACK POWER movement and the formation of the BLACK PANTHERS. While the earlier civil rights movement had looked for equality and cooperation with the white population, the new movement was more radical and separatist.

Say It Loud, 'I'm Black and I'm Proud'

JAMES BROWN: title of song (1968)

**Black Sash.** An organization of black South African women founded in 1955 to sponsor research into racial questions and oppose APARTHEID. Their original official title was the Women's Defence of the Constitution, but they soon came to be known by their nickname, alluding to the broad black diagonal sash that they wore during picketing or other demonstrations.

**Black September.** A Palestinian terrorist group formed when the Palestine Liberation Organization (*see* PLO) was driven from Jordan in September 1970. Among other actions, Black September was responsible for the kidnap and assassination of 11 Israeli athletes in Munich, during the 1972 Olympic Games.

**Blackshirt.** The gentleman thief or amateur cracksman, real name Richard Verrell, in Bruce Graeme's bestselling novel named after him (1925). He is always scrupulously dressed in black, his evening dress complemented by black hood, black silk gloves, black shoes, black socks and black shirt. He has a special pocket from which, after his derring-do, he springs out an opera hat to set rakishly on his head as he sets out for home. The elegant hero appeared in many more books by Graeme, whose real name was Graham Montague Jeffries, and after the Second World War Graeme's son, writing as Roderic Graeme, began a new series of Blackshirt tales.

**Blackshirts.** Mussolini's Italian Fascists, who wore black shirts, as did their English imitators. The name was also used in NAZI Germany for Himmler's SS, by contrast with the Brownshirts (*see* SA). *See also* FASCISM; MOSLEYITES; WAFFEN SS.

**Black Sox scandal.** A scandal in the world of sport when in 1919 eight members of the Chicago White Sox, subsequently nicknamed the 'Black Sox', were accused of accepting bribes to lose the World Series that year to the Cincinnati Reds. The eight were acquitted through insufficient evidence but were later banned from baseball for life. *See also* JOE BLOGGS; SAY IT AIN'T SO, JOE.

**Black spot.** A place on a road where accidents often occur, such as a bend or crossing. *See also* CATSEYES.

**Black stump, The.** A notional tree stump, blackened by bush-fires, that in Australia marks the boundary between civilization and the lawless limbo of the remote outback. Hence 'beyond the black stump', an expression first recorded in 1965, implies the sparsely populated interior that lies beyond the narrow rim of 'European' Australia.

**Black Thursday.** 24 October 1929, the first day of the WALL STREET CRASH, when nearly 13 million shares changed hands. The panic continued on Black Monday (28 October) and Black Tuesday (29 October), when 16 million shares were traded and the stock market collapsed completely, leading to the GREAT DEPRESSION.

**Black Wednesday.** 16 September 1992, when Britain pulled out of the Exchange Rate Mechanism (ERM), allowing sterling to float. The crisis was largely due to currency speculators, such as George Soros (who made an estimated $1 billion in the process), selling large numbers of pounds. In response, in an effort to prop up sterling, the chancellor of the day, Norman Lamont, raised interest rates by 2 per cent and then by a further 3 per cent (to 15 per cent), but without improving sterling's value. It was reported that Lamont was heard whistling 'JE NE REGRETTE RIEN' in the bath that evening. Lamont promptly offered his resignation to prime minister John Major, but this was refused, and Lamont held on to office until May 1993. Black Wednesday was subsequently dubbed White Wednesday by those opposed to Britain's entry to the ERM. *See also* GREEN SHOOTS.

**Bladder diplomacy.** A ploy to extract a concession from the other party in a discussion. The hapless visitor is plied with drinks until he feels constrained to agree to the point at issue in order to excuse himself. The ruse was notoriously resorted to by President Assad of Syria (1930–2000) who, in an apparently generous gesture, offered his guests small cups of black coffee to this end. Presidents, secretaries of state and foreign ministers alike were all subjected to the treatment. Similar degrees of suffering have been experienced in other diplomatic settings. In September 2005 a photographer at a UN meeting snapped a note that President George W. Bush had just penned for his secretary of state, Condoleeza Rice. It read:

> I think I MAY NEED A BATHroom break? Is this possible?

***Blade Runner.*** A bleak SCIENCE FICTION film (1982) directed by Ridley Scott, starring Harrison Ford and Rutger Hauer, and set in Los Angeles in the year 2019. Ford plays a detective who is hunting down escaped androids or 'replicants'. It is based on a short story by Philip K. Dick entitled *Do Androids Dream of Electric Sheep?*

**Blah.** A representation of words that are too tedious or obvious to give in full, the degree of tedium or obviousness usually indicated by repetition. The word itself dates from the early years of the 20th century and is simply imitative while suggesting 'blather' or 'blether'.

> Yes, I know sexy clothes perpetuate sexual stereotypes and can be hell to wear, blah, blah, blah.
> *The Times* (20 September 1999)

**Blair Babes.** Originally a derisory term for the women Labour MPs supposedly cosseted by Tony Blair and devoted to him as fawning loyalists after Labour's victory in the 1997 general election. The phrase was suggested by a subsequent photocall, one of whose shots showed a grinning Blair amid a large group of such MPs looking up adoringly. The term was later extended to all backbenchers who were ON-MESSAGE and unquestioningly loyal to Blair and his policies. *See also* STEPFORD WIVES.

> Blair babes threaten to quit the Commons.
> *The Times*, headline (3 April 2000)

**Blair Ditch Project.** The name given by the *Daily Mirror* to Tony Blair's cabinet reshuffle of 6 May 2006, following poor Labour local election results. Among other casualties, Charles BIG EARS Clarke (*see also* TURKEY TWIZZLER) lost his post as home secretary, John TWO JAGS Prescott was relieved of his departmental responsibilities, Jack Straw, the long-serving foreign secretary, was demoted to leader of the Commons, and Geoff Hoon (*see* GEOFF WHO?) was bumped outside the cabinet. The name puns on the hit US horror film, unrelated to politics, *The Blair Witch Project* (1998). *See also* NIGHT OF THE LONG KNIVES.

**Blair Force One.** *See* AIR FORCE ONE.

**Blairism.** The political and economic policies of Tony Blair (b.1953), leader of the LABOUR PARTY from 1994 and prime minister from 1997. The personalized term corresponded largely in import to the general party policy implicit in the designation NEW LABOUR. *See also* BLATCHERISM.

**B.L.A.I.R.1.** *See* BUSH'S POODLE.

**Blaise, Modesty.** The strip cartoon adventuress created by Peter O'Donnell made her maiden bow in the *Evening Standard* in 1963. She is popularly regarded as a sort of female James BOND, and she rose to fame in the 1960s, when spy fiction was all the rage. She 'wrote' a number of novels (the author was actually O'Donnell), the first of which, *Modesty Blaise*, appeared in 1965. She featured in a single somewhat uncharacteristic film of this name (1966), directed by Joseph Losey, in which she was played by Monica Vitti. Her cartoon adventures continue to be syndicated in newspapers around the world.

**Blake, Sexton.** A fictional detective who first appeared in the adventure paper MARVEL in 1893. The first author to write a Sexton Blake story was Harry Blyth (1852–98), writing under the pen-name Hal Meredith. According to *The Oxford Companion to Children's Literature* over 100 writers have written stories featuring Sexton Blake, and he appeared in a wide variety of magazines, adventure papers and popular novels in the first half of the 20th century. Blake's appearance and manner gradually came to resemble that of Sherlock Holmes. 'Sexton Blake' is rhyming slang for 'fake', and also for 'cake' and 'snake'.

***Blake's 7.*** A cult television SCIENCE FICTION serial screened from 1978 to 1981. It followed the fortunes of a band of freedom fighters against the Terran Foundation led by Roj Blake in the second century of the third calendar. The motley 'magnificent seven' in question were Blake himself, played by Gareth Thomas, smuggler Jenna Jannis, computer expert Kerr Avon, thief Vila Restal, alien warrior Cally, 'gentle giant' Gan and the master computer of Blake's ship, Zen.

**Blame game.** Someone who 'plays the blame game' adopts a strategy of apportioning blame (to others) when things go wrong, rather than trying to put them right. The expression is first recorded in 1958 (in the writings of the critic Kenneth Tynan (1927–80), although it is not clear whether he originated it).

> Things go right for them and when they don't, they pick themselves up … They don't play the blame game.
> *newWitch* (2003)

**Blanket Protest.** A protest beginning in 1980 by IRA prisoners in Northern Ireland's MAZE Prison during the TROUBLES. The protest aimed at achieving political status for the prisoners and involved a refusal to wear prison clothing, the prisoners wrapping themselves in prison blankets instead. Some prisoners went on to hold a DIRTY PROTEST.

The protest culminated in a hunger strike in 1981 in which Bobby Sands, followed by nine more Republican prisoners, died, the British government having refused to give in to their demands. Nevertheless, the protests served to increase nationalist support for the Republican cause.

**Blankety Blank.** A weekly television GAME SHOW screened from 1979 to 1990 in which members of the public had to guess the missing word, the 'blank' of the title, in a given sentence and hope that the six celebrity guests present had written the same. The winner would receive a rather tawdry prize. The show was originally hosted with Irish geniality by Terry Wogan, then by a world-weary, sarcastic Les Dawson, a kind of anti-game show host. In 1997–9 and 2001–2 the show was revived and hosted by the drag artist and comedian Lily Savage (real name Paul O'Grady). The title reflects the stock euphemistic oath, as: 'I wish you'd leave my blankety-blank pen alone.'

**Blast.** The title of a British Modernist magazine (*see* MODERNISM), of which only two issues were produced, both in 1914. The magazine was founded by the British writer and painter Percy Wyndham Lewis (1882–1957) and the American poet Ezra Pound (1885–1972) and was subtitled 'the Review of the Great English Vortex' (Lewis being heavily involved in VORTICISM). The magazine was noted for its aggressive geometrical graphics, innovative typography and wild challenges to received ideas and values, echoing FUTURISM and in some ways anticipating DADAISM.

**Blast from the past.** Anything suddenly or powerfully nostalgic, especially an old pop song (which may alternatively be known as a 'rave from the grave').

> These thigh-length leather boots are a real blast from my past. I bought them in Chester in the 1970s because my friend had a pair, so I just had to follow suit.
> *Sunday People Magazine* (25 April 1999)

**Blatcherism.** A compound of BLAIRISM and THATCHERISM. The word implies a criticism of NEW LABOUR's adoption of Thatcherite values in the economic and social sphere.

> Policing cannot be expected to underpin a social order whose foundations have been eroded by Blatcherite neoliberalism.
> ROBERT REINER (professor of criminology at the London School of Economics): in *The Guardian* (24 November 2005)

*See also* BUTSKELLISM.

**Blaue Reiter, Der.** (German, 'The Blue Rider'.) A group of German expressionist painters formed in 1911 and based in Munich. Leading members were Wassily Kandinsky (1866–1944), Franz Marc (1880–1916) and Paul Klee

(1879–1940), and the organization took its name from Kandinsky's drawing of a blue horseman on the cover of an *Almanac* published in May 1912 as the first number of a proposed annual although in fact the only issue to appear. *See also* BLAUE VIER, DIE.

**Blaue Vier, Die.** (German, 'The Blue Four'.) A group of four painters formed in 1924 at the instigation of the German art dealer Galka Scheyer (1889–1945) with the aim of promoting their work abroad. They were Lyonel Feininger (1871–1956), Alexei von Jawlensky (1864–1941), Wassily Kandinsky (1866–1944) and Paul Klee (1879–1940), and their name indicated their association with the BLAUE REITER.

**Blaxpoitation.** A blend of 'black' and 'exploitation', with particular reference to films made with black (i.e. AFRICAN AMERICAN) performers and aimed at black audiences but usually made by white producers. Such films were popular in the 1970s. They took the form of every established genre but were particularly prominent in the form of violent crime films such as *Shaft* (1971), in which an African American PRIVATE EYE, played by Richard Roundtree, finds himself at odds with a racketeer. The US actress Pam Grier (b.1949) is generally regarded as the 'blaxploitation icon' of the period.

**Bleeding heart.** A person regarded as being excessively soft-hearted, especially in terms of financial generosity or political liberalism.

> Cut-throat competition in the credit card market has meant that it is even possible for conspicuous consumers and bleeding hearts [holding AFFINITY CARDS] to benefit from the lower rates.
> *The Times* (28 June 1999)

**Bleedin' obvious, The.** Something so painfully obvious that to state it is the acme of superfluousness. The expression is one of many catchphrases originated by MONTY PYTHON'S FLYING CIRCUS.

> Politics: Stating the bleedin' obvious – UK teenagers don't know much about politics, and have little interest in it. So why the surprise?
> www.blogcritics.org (17 January 2005)

**Bleed someone white.** To submit them to extortion, so depriving them of all their money ('blood'). The expression dates from the 1930s.

**Bless!** A somewhat cloying exclamation current from the 1990s in response to a tweely touching sight or utterance, especially one involving a young child or pet. It is a shortening of 'bless you', 'bless her heart', 'bless his little cotton socks' or some similar soppiness.

**Blessed Margaret.** A nickname given Margaret Thatcher (b.1923), Conservative prime minister from 1979 to 1990, by the Conservative politician and prominent Roman Catholic Norman St John Stevas, later Lord St John of Fawsley (b.1929), while Leader of the House and arts minister. He saw her as the saviour of Britain from socialism. *See also* ATTILA THE HEN.

**B. Liar.** *See* BUSH'S POODLE.

**Bliar, Tony.** *See* BUSH'S POODLE.

**Blighty.** A colloquial name for England used by soldiers serving overseas in the First World War but originating among those who had served in India some years before. It represents Urdu *bilāyatī*, 'foreign', from Arabic *wilāyat*, 'dominion'. A highly popular song during the First World War was A.J. Mills, Fred Godfrey and Bennett Scott's 'Take Me Back to Dear Old Blighty' (1916). A magazine called *Blighty*, specializing in PIN-UPS and cartoons, was a former favourite with the troops, particularly in and after the two world wars. Its last issue appeared in 1958. *See also* FIRST WORLD WAR SLANG.

> As far as ageing romantics are concerned Dover is the only way to return to good old Blighty.
> *The Times* (17 August 1999)

**Blimp.** (Apparently a coinage based on *limp*, perhaps from the code name *Type B-limp*.) A word originally applied to an observation balloon in the First World War. 'Colonel Blimp' was created after the war by the cartoonist David Low as a plump, pompous ex-officer who was rigidly and blindly opposed to anything new. Hence Colonel Blimp or blimp as a now rather dated term for a military officer, or any person with stuffy or reactionary views. *See also The* LIFE AND DEATH OF COLONEL BLIMP.

> He [Tony Blair] must also be the first party leader since Neville Chamberlain … to have the whole-hearted support of Colonel Blimp. What can one hear the old boy saying? 'Gad sir, it's good to have a public school man back at the helm.'
> WILLIAM REES-MOGG: in *The Times* (29 August 1994)

**Blind date.** An appointment to meet a person whom one has never met before, the expectation adding excitement to the romantic allure. The popular television programme *Blind Date* was screened from 1985 to 2003 as a sort of combined dating service and GAME SHOW. In the world of espionage a blind date is a meeting by an intelligence officer and an agent at the time and place of the latter's choosing.

**Blind someone with science.** To confuse or overawe them with technical jargon or learned talk.

**Bling** or **bling bling.** A slang term, emerging at the end of the 20th century, for ostentatious and (relatively) cheap jewellery or similarly flashy personal adornment. It has been claimed that it was coined by the New Orleans rap family Cash Money Millionaires in the late 1990s, and that it first came to public attention in the United States via a song by the Cash Money artiste BG called 'Bling Bling'. *See also* SULTANS OF BLING.

**Bliss out.** To achieve a state of such supreme content that one is oblivious to all else. The phrase dates from the 1960s and the drug-infused world of HIPPIES.

> Still slightly blissed-out after a shave and face massage, I acquiesce. The guy is John Major's barber, after all.
> *The Times* (21 August 1999)

**Blithe Spirit.** A play (1941) and film (1945) by British playwright, actor and composer Noël Coward (1899–1973). The plot revolves around the haunting of novelist Charles Condomine by the ghost of his first wife. The film, directed by David Lean, starred Rex Harrison as Charles, Kay Hammond as Elvira, the first Mrs Condomine, Constance Cummings as Ruth, the second Mrs Condomine, and Margaret Rutherford as the wholly memorable medium Madame Arcati. The title of the play is a quotation from Percy Bysshe Shelley's 'To a Skylark' (1820), with a pun on 'spirit':

> Hail to thee, blithe Spirit!
> Bird thou never wert,
> That from Heaven, or near it,
> Pourest thy full heart
> In profuse strains of unpremeditated art.

**Blitz, The.** The name (an abbreviation of BLITZKRIEG) given to the intensive German air raids on London during the Second World War. The bombardment was initiated by Hitler in retaliation for RAF attacks on Berlin and began on 7 September 1940, when 450 people were killed by a raid over the East End. The raids continued almost nightly until 10 May 1941, by which time there was an estimated casualty rate of over 1000 civilian deaths a day. Londoners were not the only ones to suffer, and most of Britain's major cities were bombed, COVENTRY suffering particularly badly. The final toll was an estimated 40,000 civilians killed and 46,000 injured. More than a million homes were destroyed and an immense amount of damage caused to industrial installations. A second Blitz took place in 1944–5, with raids on southeast England by V-1 and V-2 weapons. *See also* BAEDEKER RAID; BATTLE OF BRITAIN; BLACKOUT; EVACUEE; WIREWALKERS.

**Blitzkrieg.** (German, 'lightning war'.) A concentrated

military offensive designed to produce a knockout blow, deploying tanks, mechanized infantry and air support. The term was particularly applied to the attacks by Hitler's Germany on various European countries between 1939 and 1941. In 1940 the PHONEY WAR in western Europe ended with Blitzkrieg attacks on Norway, the Low Countries and France: the Germans captured Copenhagen on 9 April, Oslo on 10 April, The Hague on 14 May, Brussels on 17 May and Paris on 14 June, resulting in the British withdrawal at DUNKIRK. *See also* SHOCK AND AWE.

**Blobbo.** A nickname of the powerfully built US professional golfer Jack Nicklaus (b.1940), widely regarded as the greatest golfer of all time.

**Blockbuster.** Anything of great power or size, such as an epic film or a bestseller. The term derives from the heavy high-explosive bombs dropped in the Second World War, which were capable of destroying a whole block of buildings.

**Blog.** A personal website recounting the author's day-to-day existence, plus comments and links to other sites. The word (first recorded in 1999) is an abbreviation of 'web log'. A notorious recent blogger (a person who writes a blog) was Belle de Jour, whose site purported to recount the quotidian doings of a high-class hooker. Another famous pseudonymous blog was that of Salam Pax (respectively the Arabic and Latin words for 'peace'), the so-called Baghdad Blogger, who reported on his life and that of his friends at the time of the 2003 Iraq War. Blogs are increasingly being used for political comment, creating a new genre of journalism (but without the benefit of an editor). The environment in which bloggers operate has been termed the 'blogosphere'.

**Blonde bombshell.** A dated term for a strikingly good-looking, fair-haired young woman, especially when exuding a lively sexuality. The allusion is to her 'explosive' effect (*see also* BIKINI). The expression dates from the 1930s and was notable applied to the film actress Jean Harlow (1911–37), one of whose films was actually titled *Blonde Bombshell* (1933). The actress Betty Hutton (b.1921) was also sometimes so known. One of her own films was *Incendiary Blonde* (1945).

> Do you remember that 1960s school sitcom, Please Sir!? The one with John Alderton as the nice teacher who'd get into a … tizzy when confronted by the blonde bombshell of 5C?
>
> *Sunday Times* (17 October 1999)

**Blondie.** The heroine of the US cartoon strip of the same name by Chic Young, first published in 1930. She began as the flapper Blondie Boopadoop, but subsequently became the wife of the ineffectual Dagwood Bumstead and mother of the precocious Baby Dumpling. Her domestic dramas burgeoned into a series of more than 20 films with Blondie in the title, such as *Blondie Brings up Baby* (1939) and starring Penny Singleton. The last was *Blondie's Hero* (1950), after which she moved to television.

The name of the US rock group Blondie (formed in 1975) was directly associated with its charismatic blonde lead singer Deborah Harry (b.1945), although she never adopted the name for herself.

**Blood, Captain.** The medical doctor turned pirate captain in Rafael Sabatini's historical novel *Captain Blood* (1922) and its sequels. His full name is Peter Blood. Unjustly sentenced by Judge Jeffreys, Dr Blood is transported to the Spanish Main but there escapes captivity and becomes a privateer. The film of the same name (1935) was a great success and made a star of its leading man, Errol Flynn. Further films followed, with *Son of Captain Blood* (1962) appropriately starring Sean Flynn, Errol's son.

**Blood and Guts.** A nickname given by the soldiers in the Second World War to the US General George Smith Patton (1885–1945), with reference to his ungovernable temper. The origin of the nickname lies in a misquotation by a reporter of a statement by Patton that it takes blood and *brains* to win a war. The name is also a disrespectful term for the red ensign. A spectacular film, *Patton*, dealing with Patton's military career from 1943 to 1945, was released in 1970. It was directed by Franklin J. Schaffner and starred George C. Scott as Patton.

***Blood and Guts in High School.*** An anarchically witty experimental novel (1984) by the US writer Kathy Acker (1948–97), evoking the traumas of adolescence. Acker described herself as 'Post-Modern Literature's Girl Wonder'.

**Bloodbath.** The earliest sense of the word, dating from the 19th century, was a literal bath in warm blood taken by a debilitated person as a supposed tonic. The term then came to denote a massacre, borrowing the sense from German *Blutbad*. In the 20th century a figurative meaning evolved for a mass dismissal of employees or wholesale sacking of staff.

> I hear of a bloodbath in Crédit Lyonnais, which has just fired eight analysts.
>
> *The Times* (8 December 1999)

**Blood group.** A classification of blood according to the two types of antigens, known as A and B, on the surface of blood cells. According to whether a person's blood contains one or other of the two types, both or neither, it is classified as type A, B, AB or O. In Britain, the most common group is A, followed by O, then B, and finally AB.

**Blood on the carpet.** A heated debate or verbal wrangle, as if a fierce fight causing bloodshed. *Blood on the Carpet* was the title of a BBC2 TV documentary series about troubled businesses. It won a BAFTA in 2000.

**Blood Orange.** The partly punning, partly descriptive nickname of Lieutenant-General Sir George Gorringe (1868–1945), given by soldiers in the First World War on the grounds that he needlessly expended men's lives on the WESTERN FRONT.

**Blood, toil, tears and sweat.** A key phrase from Winston Churchill's first address as prime minister to the House of Commons, 13 May 1940, three days after Nazi Germany's onslaught on the Low Countries and the resignation of Neville Chamberlain:

> I would say to the House, as I said to those who have joined this Government, 'I have nothing to offer but blood, toil, tears, and sweat.'

He continued:

> What is our policy? … to wage war against a monstrous tyranny, never surpassed in the dark, lamentable catalogue of human crime … What is our aim? … Victory, victory at all costs, victory in spite of all terror; victory, however long and hard the road may be; for without victory, there is no survival.

**Blood Wedding.** The play, *Bodas de sangre*, by the Spanish playwright Federico García Lorca (1898–1936), first performed in 1933. It is about the tragedy and bloodshed that result after a bride elopes with a former lover on the day fixed for her marriage to another man. Lorca based his story on a real incident reported in the newspapers of Almería in 1928, in which a bride and her lover were hunted down by the family of the thwarted bridegroom. It was first staged in New York in 1935 under the title *Bitter Oleander* and subsequently in London as *The Marriage of Blood*.

**Bloody Friday.** 21 July 1972, when 11 people were killed and 130 injured by IRA bombs in Belfast.

**Bloody Maria.** A drink made with tequila and tomato juice. The name dates from the 1970s as a variant on the earlier BLOODY MARY.

**Bloody Mary.** The cocktail of vodka and tomato juice is said to have gained its name in 1927 when the US vaudeville comic, George Jessel (1898–1981), mixed a mid-morning tomato drink for himself in a Palm Beach bar. He offered a taste to Mary Brown Warburton, a Philadelphia socialite, who promptly spilt it down the front of her white gown, 'thereby christening herself and the drink "Bloody Mary"'

(*American National Biography*, 1999). The allusion is to Mary I (1516–58) of England and Ireland, nicknamed 'Bloody Mary' for her persecution of Protestants.

**Bloody Saturday.** 15 August 1998, when an IRA splinter group planted a car bomb that killed 29 and injured more than 200 in Omagh, Northern Ireland.

**Bloody Sunday.** (1) 22 January 1905. A deputation of workers led by Father Gapon marched to the Winter Palace in St Petersburg to present a petition to the Tsar. After giving warnings to disperse, the troops fired into the crowd. More than 100 people were killed and many hundreds more wounded.

(2) 21 November 1920. Fourteen undercover British intelligence agents were shot by SINN FÉIN in Dublin, and in the afternoon of the same day the BLACK AND TANS opened fire on a Gaelic football crowd at Croke Park, killing 12.

(3) 30 January 1972. Paratroops of the British Army opened fire on a banned civil rights march in Londonderry, killing 13. BLOODY FRIDAY followed six months later. *See also* BOGSIDE.

A wry twist to the term was given by the title of the award-winning film *Sunday, Bloody Sunday* (1971), written by Penelope Gilliatt and starring Glenda Jackson as a businesswoman and Peter Finch as a Jewish doctor who share the sexual favours of the same man.

> Didn't I know there was a famous Irish Bloody Sunday … Didn't I know about the Russian Bloody Sunday? Yes, I said. But it still wasn't the English bloody Sunday.
>
> PENELOPE GILLIATT: *Making Sunday Bloody Sunday*, Introduction (1986)

**Bloom, Leopold.** *See* BLOOMSDAY; ULYSSES.

**Bloomsbury Group.** The name given to a group of writers, artists and intellectuals, who lived and worked in Bloomsbury, central London, from about 1907 to 1930. They included Leonard (1880–1969) and Virginia (1882–1941) Woolf, Clive (1881–1964) and Vanessa (1879–1961) Bell, Roger Fry (1866–1934), E.M. Forster (1879–1970), Lytton Strachey (1880–1932), Duncan Grant (1885–1978) and John Maynard Keynes (1883–1946). They saw themselves as advocates of a new rational, civilized society and many of them had Cambridge links. They have been criticized by some as an overexposed group of serial adulterers and second-raters who, famously, 'lived in squares and loved in triangles', but the honesty of their intentions to some extent redeems them from such charges. They were influenced by the anti-Hegelian G.E. Moore's *Principia Ethica* (1903), which analysed the moral concept of goodness and commended the value of friendship and aesthetic experience.

**Bloomsday.** 16 June 1904, the day in the life of Leopold Bloom described by James Joyce in his novel ULYSSES (1922). It is marked annually in Dublin with a tour of pubs, hotels and shops where Bloom stopped, beginning with the South Bank Restaurant in Sandycove. It was David Norris, a senior lecturer in English at Trinity College, Dublin, who in the late 1960s revived interest in Bloom's journey:

> I dressed up in a straw hat and, with a silver cane, walked through Dublin and read from the book. Everyone thought I was mad, but it seems to have caught on.
>
> *The Times* (17 June 1994)

**Blot one's copybook.** To commit an error that spoils one's hitherto unblemished record or stains one's reputation. A copybook was originally a book containing models of handwriting for young people to copy. The expression dates from the 1930s.

**Blot on the landscape.** Anything that mars the beauty or perfection of something. 'Blot' as a blemish has been current since at least the time of Shakespeare, but the full phrase emerged only in the early 20th century. The reference is to a mark or stain that spoils a painted landscape. The term was punningly adapted by Tom Sharpe for his black farce *Blott on the Landscape* (1975), in which Blott is a handyman who halts the construction of a motorway through the grounds of a stately home. A televised version by Malcolm Bradbury was screened in 1985.

**Blow a fuse.** To explode with rage, especially unexpectedly, as when the fuse in an electric circuit suddenly melts through overloading. The expression dates from the 1920s.

> One of my teachers has an irritating habit. After teaching us very difficult pieces of information she asks, 'Does anyone have any questions?' Then if any confused pupil raises their hand … the teacher automatically blows a fuse! Now everyone is so terrified to ask a question that they're left confused, and when test time arrives she blows another fuse at the fact that we got it wrong!
>
> *The Times* (11 September 1999)

**Blow a raspberry.** To show contempt for someone or something by putting one's tongue between closed lips and expelling air forcibly with a resulting rude noise. The action is also known as a BRONX CHEER. 'Raspberry' is short for 'raspberry tart', rhyming slang for 'fart'. The expression is frequently applied figuratively. *See also* GOLDEN RASPBERRY.

> She [singer Shelby Lynne] finally blew a raspberry to the country music fame factory, went back home, and at 30, has recorded an album of monumental versatility and élan.
>
> *The Times* (4 October 1999)

**Blow away the cobwebs.** To banish a condition of lethargy; to refresh or reinvigorate oneself. 'Cobweb' as a metaphor for an accretion that needs to be cleared dates from the 16th century.

**Blow by blow account.** One describing events in minute detail. The expression is of US origin and comes from radio boxing match commentaries, where one would have 'a left to the body, a right to the chin' and so on.

**'Blowin' in the Wind'.** A song by Bob Dylan, one of the most famous protest songs of the 1960s, released in 1963 on the album *The Freewheelin' Bob Dylan*. Its gentle and wistful melody, sung to guitar and harmonica accompaniment, is based on the tune of the African American spiritual 'No More Auction Block For Me'. The song asks nine questions about peace and civil rights (including 'How many years can some people exist before they're allowed to be free?'), all of which are answered by the forlorn response 'The answer, my friend, is blowin' in the wind, the answer is blowin' in the wind.' The song became an anthem of the civil rights movement in the United States.

**Blow one's top.** To lose one's temper; to become angry. There are various alternatives for 'top' in this phrase, all originating in the 20th century, and including 'cool', 'cork', 'gaff', 'lid', 'roof', 'stack'. The general image is of a volcano erupting. *See also* FLIP ONE'S LID.

> When … [David] Mellor heard what had occurred, he blew his top. A few days later an account of his temper tantrum appeared in *The Observer*.
>
> *The Times* (17 November 1999)

**Blow someone out.** To cancel an engagement at short notice. An expression dating from the 1960s.

> We had a girl … who came up and said, 'Ooh, is this [the television dating show] *Streetmate*? Can I do it? Can I do it?' So we found her someone, and she blew us out the next day.
>
> *heat* (16 December 1999–5 January 2000)

**Blow someone's mind.** To induce hallucinatory experiences by means of drugs; to impress or affect keenly.

**Blow someone's socks off.** *See* KNOCK SOMEONE'S SOCKS OFF.

**Blow the whistle on.** To inform on someone; to bring a stop to something. The allusion is either to the policeman's whistle or to that of the referee in a football match. *See also* WHISTLE-BLOWER.

> Professor Davies was also found guilty of asking a junior colleague … to 'violate' study protocol, threatening him that he would be 'finished' if he blew the whistle on his boss.
>
> *The Times* (2 October 1999)

**Bludger.** An Australian term of abuse for someone drawing unemployment pay; the equivalent of the British 'scrounger'. The word is a shortened form of 'bludgeoner', originally meaning someone who lives off the earnings of a prostitute.

**Blue Angel, The.** A film (1930) adapted by Carl Zuckmayer from the novel *Professor Unrat* (1905) by Heinrich Mann (the brother of Thomas Mann). Shot under the direction of Joseph von Sternberg simultaneously in German and English (the German title is *Der blaue Engel*), the film made an international star of Marlene Dietrich, playing nightclub singer Lola, who was subsequently sometimes referred to as 'the blue angel'. Today it is best remembered for Dietrich's memorable rendition of 'Falling in Love Again', one of the tunes with which she was destined to become most closely associated.

**Blue baby.** A baby with a blue complexion resulting from a lack of oxygen in the blood. The cause is usually a congenital defect of the heart or the major blood vessels.

**Bluebell Girls.** A troupe of high-kicking young women in the Folies-Bergère tradition, established in the 1930s by the Anglo-Irish dancer Margaret Kelley (1910–2004), known as Miss Bluebell from the colour of her eyes as a baby. They actually began their career at the Folies-Bergère and still perform mainly in Paris, although many of the troupe are British.

**Blue Berets.** A nickname for members of the multinational UNITED NATIONS Peacekeeping Force, whose uniform includes such headgear. The UN Security Council has established several such forces since its foundation, each known by an acronymic name, e.g. UNPROFOR (United Nations Protection Force), which served in the former Yugoslavia in the 1990s.

**Blue bird of happiness.** A visionary concept elaborated from Maurice Maeterlinck's play *L'Oiseau bleu* (1908), first produced in London as *The Blue Bird* in 1910. It tells the story of a boy and girl seeking 'the blue bird', which brings 'the great secret of things and of happiness'.

**Blue chip.** Said of anything dependable or of high quality, with particular reference to a company or its shares when regarded as a reliable investment. The source is in gambling games such as poker, in which the blue chip usually has the highest value. The term dates from the early years of the 20th century and is now frequently found in job advertisements.

> Blue Chip Secretary for Blue Chip Co.
> *The Times*, advertisement heading (21 July 1999)

**Blue-collar worker.** A manual industrial worker, who at one time traditionally wore blue overalls. The term dates from the 1950s and arose from a contrast with the WHITE-COLLAR WORKER. *See also* GREY-COLLAR WORKER; PINK-COLLAR WORKER.

**Blue corner.** One of the two opponents ('corners') in a boxing match, the other being the red corner. The terms are used metaphorically for any two views or approaches, not necessarily in opposition.

> Roll up, roll up, for what promises to be one of the most entertaining fights in British banking history. In the blue corner we have one of Edinburgh's financial elite, Peter Burt; while in the red, there is the career banker from Newcastle, Derek Wanless.
> *The Times* (25 September 1999)

**Blue flu.** In the United States, a form of organized industrial protest in which employees en masse call in sick on a particular day and therefore do not go to work. The term originally referred to police officers (and still mainly does), the colour of whose uniforms may perhaps account for the 'blue'. The expression is first recorded in 1967.

**Bluegrass.** A form of COUNTRY MUSIC influenced by JAZZ and BLUES. It represents the earliest, traditional style of HILLBILLY string bands and is most familiar from its high-harmony vocals. It takes its name from the bluegrass grown for fodder in the southern states of the United States and especially in Kentucky and Virginia, the former of which is nicknamed the Bluegrass State (bluegrass, *Poa compressa* or *pratensis*, is as green as any other grass; it gets its name from the colour of its blossoms). *See also* COUNTRY MUSIC.

**Blue Guides.** The well-known series of guidebooks to Britain and foreign countries was launched in 1915, when Finlay and James Muirhead published their *Blue Guide to London and its Environs*. This was later issued by Hachette in French as a *Guide Bleu*. Hachette then went on to produce its own *Guide Bleu* to Paris, which was in turn published by Muirhead in English. The two-way arrangement lasted until 1933. The series has since continued, and is now published by Somerset Books.

**Blue Meanie.** Originally, one of a number of bizarre malevolent ogres in The BEATLES' cartoon film 'YELLOW SUBMARINE' (1968). The name was subsequently transferred to anyone thought of as ill disposed towards oneself, and in particular the police.

**Blue movie.** A pornographic film. The name is fancifully derived from the custom of Chinese brothels being painted blue externally.

**Blue on blue.** In British military jargon, an incident in which one side accidentally fires, drops bombs, etc. on its own positions or personnel – in other words, a form of FRIENDLY FIRE. The phrase alludes to the use of blue on maps and other documents to designate one's own side in a battle, exercise, etc.

> Sturgeon fired three blue-on-blue torpedoes at Sword-fish, happily without result.
>
> *Navy News* (September 2001)

**Blue orchid.** In Australian and New Zealand Second World War slang, a derisive soldier's term for a member of the air force, who wore a blue uniform and was regarded as having a relatively cosseted existence.

**Blue Peter.** One of the longest lasting and best of children's television programmes, broadcast by the BBC from 1958. Aimed mainly at the under-12s, it covers a wide range of subjects, many of them practical, and has made charitable appeals a special feature. Some of its presenters were almost family friends, such as Valerie Singleton (1962–71), John Noakes (1965–79) and Peter Purves (1967–79). Animals regularly featured, and the mongrel Petra, who first appeared in 1962, was a firm favourite until her death in 1977. The programme takes its name from the blue peter, a blue flag with a white centre, which a ship flies when about to leave port. *See also* AND NOW FOR SOMETHING COMPLETELY DIFFERENT; CHILDREN'S HOUR; HERE'S ONE I MADE EARLIER.

> *Blue Peter presenters.* Either shovelling cocaine up their noses or standing behind an elephant when it relieves itself.
>
> HERMIONE LEE and WILLIAM DONALDSON: *The Dictionary of National Celebrity* (2005)

**Blue plaque.** A blue ceramic plaque set into the facade of a building in London where a famous person lived, giving the relevant dates and details. The first was placed by the London County Council in 1903 on the house, Holly Lodge, Kensington, in which Thomas Macaulay died. In recent years plaques have commemorated events as well as lives. One set on an East End railway bridge in 1988 reads: 'The first Flying Bomb on London fell here, 13 June 1944.' In the 21st century the scheme was extended beyond London.

**Blueprint.** Strictly, a photographic print of a detailed plan, technical drawing or the like, in white lines on a blue background. The word is now used generally for any project, scheme or design.

**Blue Riband.** The liner gaining the record for the fastest Atlantic crossing was said to hold the Blue Riband of the Atlantic, and from 1907 to 1929 it was held by the Cunard liner *Mauretania*. It then passed to the *Europa* (1930) and

*Bremen* (1933) of Germany, to the *Rex* of Italy (1933), and to the French liner *Normandie* in 1935. After that it was held by the *Queen Mary* of Britain from 1938 until its capture by the American-owned *United States* in 1952. A trophy offered in 1935 by H.K. Hales (1868–1942) was first accepted by the United States Lines in 1952.

**Blue rinse brigade.** A slighting term for elderly, well-to-do women, who sometimes use a special rinse to give their grey or white hair a temporary blue tint. The phrase gained currency towards the end of the Second World War and came to be particularly associated with women at the annual Conservative Party Conference, partly because of the party's identifying colour. The use of 'brigade' implies that those so designated are a force to be reckoned with.

> He also goes traipsing across the United States … reciting poems to the blue-rinsed brigade.
>
> *Manchester Guardian Weekly* (1 August 1970)

> None of them [elderly ladies attending the 2005 Conservative party conference] dyes their hair blue because no woman in Britain has done that for 20 years and the phrase 'blue-rinse brigade' is a hackneyed old tag that means absolutely nothing.
>
> *The Observer* (9 October 2005)

**Blues.** A traditional form of US folksong, expressive of the unhappiness of the African American population in the southern states. The usual subject matter is love, the troubles that beset the singer or a nostalgic longing for home, coupled with an acceptance of life as it is. Blues usually consist of 12 bars made up of three four-bar phrases in 4/4 time. They can be vocal or instrumental and have had significant influence on JAZZ.

**Blues and twos.** In British police jargon, the flashing blue lights and siren (two-tone – whence 'twos') deployed by a vehicle of the emergency services when speeding on its way to an incident.

**Blueshirts.** An Irish fascist organization under General Eoin O'Duffy, former Commissioner of the Garda, which developed from the Army Comrades Association in the early 1930s. A Blueshirt battalion led by O'Duffy fought for General Franco in the Spanish Civil War (1936–9). *See also* FASCISM.

**Blue Sky Laws.** In the United States laws passed to protect the inexperienced buyer of stocks and bonds against fraud. The name is said to have its origin in a phrase used by one of the supporters of the earliest of these laws, who said that certain business operators were trying to capitalize 'the blue skies'.

**Blue-sky thinking.** Original or creative thinking, unfettered by conventional assumptions or models. A favourite of 21st-century management consultants, the expression can be traced back to the use of 'blue sky' as a verb in American English from the middle of the 20th century to denote thinking or talking about things in an untrammelled, speculative manner, as if day-dreaming while gazing at the sky. *See also* OUT OF THE BOX.

**'Blue Suede Shoes'.** A classic pop song about teenage fashion, written and sung by the country singer Carl Perkins and released in 1956. The song's title has its roots in an incident at a dance in which Perkins heard a boy tell a girl not to tread on his blue suede shoes. He wrote the song immediately afterwards. There was an almost simultaneous version of the song by Elvis Presley.

**Bluetooth.** A short-range radio frequency system developed by Ericsson, which allows for wireless connections between devices, as with the wireless earpiece that allows mobile phone users to have conversations without seeming to be on the phone (notwithstanding that in doing so they often appear to passers-by simply to be talking to themseleves). A 2006 episode of DOCTOR WHO traded on the earpieces' sinister quality by having them double as mind-controlling mechanisms under the sway of an evil megalomaniac.

The name 'Bluetooth' was adopted from Harold Bluetooth (translating Danish *Harold Blåtand*), Harold I (911–*c*.986), son of Gorm the Old, king of Denmark from 958 and of Norway from *c*.970. He united the two Scandinavian kingdoms and established Christianity there. His bizarre cognomen referred to his dark complexion; it had nothing to do, as is sometimes claimed, with a fondness for blueberries.

**Blunko.** *See* BIG BLUNKETT.

**Blurb.** A publisher's promotional description on the dust jacket or cover of a book. The word is said to have originated from the name 'Miss Belinda Blurb', coined in 1907 by the US humorist Gelett Burgess for the figure of a pulchritudinous young lady on a comic book jacket. Burgess later defined the word as follows:

1. A flamboyant advertisement; an inspired testimonial.
2. Fulsome praise; a sound like a publisher.

   *Burgess Unabridged* (1914)

**B-movie** or **B-picture.** A low-budget film of poor quality and often cheaply sensational content made as a supporting feature for the main film (the implied 'A-movie') in a cinema programme. A good example of the type is Val Newton's *I Walked With a Zombie* (1943), with a plot that is a tongue-in-cheek adaptation of Charlotte Brontë's *Jane Eyre* (1847).

It could be a scene from a B movie. Picture a remote comprehensive school in the bleak industrial valleys of Wales. It is 5 pm, the children have gone home and the site is deserted. The deputy head is finishing his paperwork when suddenly two burly men barge into his office.

*The Times* (3 November 1999)

**B.O.** Body odour, caused by the bacterial decomposition of sweat in unwashed areas of the body, especially the armpits and feet. The euphemistic abbreviation was invented and promoted by the manufacturers of Lifebuoy soap in the 1930s, originally in the United States. Hence 'B.O. juice' as US campus slang for deodorant.

A club-less man is sure to be regarded with some misgiving. Was he blackballed? Doesn't he know anyone to put him up? Has he B.O.?

GUY EGMONT: *The Art of Egmontese*, ch. 1 (1961)

**Boanerges.** (Greek, 'sons of thunder'.) The name given by T.E. Lawrence, LAWRENCE OF ARABIA, to the Brough Superior motorbike on which he was killed in an accident in 1935. Boanerges was originally the nickname given by Jesus to the apostles James and John (Mark 3:17), perhaps because of their excessive zeal (as in Mark 9:38 and Luke 9:54).

**Boarding-house reach.** Reaching across fellow diners for food instead of asking them to pass it. The term is of US origin and dates from the early 20th century, alluding to the former boarding-house practice of seating all the residents at a single large table, where some would rudely stretch across others to help themselves.

**Boat people.** A group term for refugees who have left their native country by sea. The expression became particularly associated with those Vietnamese who fled in small boats to Hong Kong, Australia and elsewhere following the conquest of South VIETNAM by North Vietnam in 1975.

**Bob-a-Job Week.** A fund-raising week instituted by the BOY SCOUTS in 1949. All kinds of jobs were undertaken, some for their publicity value, for the payment of one shilling. It became an annual effort but with the declining value of the 'bob' and the advent of DECIMAL CURRENCY Scout Job Week took its place in 1972.

**Bobbetty.** A nickname of the Conservative politician Robert Cecil, Lord Cranbourne (1893–1972), later the 5th Marquess of Salisbury, who resigned from Baldwin's government in 1938 over its appeasement policy, but later served as leader of the Lords until 1957.

**Bobbsey Twins.** Two sets of twins in a long series of books for young children by Laura Lee Hope, beginning with *Bobbsey Twins; or, Merry Days Indoors and Out* (1904). The older pair are called Bert and Nan, the younger Freddie and Flossie. The books have been read by generations of American children and in 1950 Hope revised the original, amending its genteel racism.

**Bobby socks.** White ankle-length socks commonly worn by teenage girls in the United States in the 1940s and 1950s. Hence bobby-soxers for the adolescent girls who wore such socks, especially as fans of popular singers. 'Bobby' here denotes the length of the socks, as if cut short or 'bobbed'.

> Fair Elaine the bobby-soxer,
>
> Fresh-complexioned with Innoxa.
>
> JOHN BETJEMAN: *A Few Late Chrysanthemums*, 'Middlesex' (1954)

**Bob the Builder.** The eponymous hero of a BBC animated series for very young children. The storylines generally involve the characters (many of whom are anthropomorphized machines) finding positive outcomes to various problems. The theme song 'Can we fix it? *Yes we can!*' was the Number-1 Christmas hit in the UK in 2000. Does Bob suffer from BUILDER'S BUM? *No, he does not!*

**Boche.** A FIRST WORLD WAR SLANG word for a German, or the Germans collectively, from a French word originating as a shortening of *Alboche*, an alteration of *Allemoche*, an argot form of *Allemand*, 'German'. The '*b*' is from *caboche*, a slang word for 'head', or from *tête de boche*, 'wooden head'.

**Bodgie.** In Australia in the 1950s, a young working-class male who wore extravagant clothing, occasionally got into trouble and worried the older generation – in effect, the Australian equivalent of the TEDDY BOY. The term came from Australian English 'bodger', denoting something fake or worthless (itself a derivative of the standard English verb 'bodge', meaning 'to make a bad job of something'), possibly inspired by the 'fake' US accents many such young men affected. *See also* WIDGIE.

**Bodice-ripper.** A sexually explicit romantic novel or film in a historical setting, the latter serving as a supposedly acceptable vehicle for the lubriciously narrated or portrayed seduction. The bodice is the old-fashioned type of undergarment worn by the heroine and torn by her lover in his passion.

**Bodmin Moor, Beast of.** *See* BEAST OF BODMIN MOOR.

**Body, The.** A promotional name for the US film actress and former model Marie McDonald (1923–65). Her physical allure first drew the public in *Pardon My Sarong* (1942). Not surprisingly, the tag has also been applied to other actresses and models, notably the US actress Victoria Principal

(b.1945), prominent in the television series DALLAS, and the Australian SUPERMODEL and actress Elle MacPherson, real name Eleanor Gow (b.1964).

**Body art.** A type of art in which the artist's own body is the medium. Much of it is overtly sexual or sadomasochistic in nature, an example of the former being the American Vito Acconci's *Seedbed* (1972), involving a daily display of masturbatory activity, and of the latter being the Italian Gina Pane's *Nourishment* (1971), in which she forced herself to regurgitate meat. Extreme examples of the genre have been exploited by the Californian Chris Burden, who in the name of art was kicked down two flights of concrete stairs in 1974. The term itself is also used for BODY PIERCING, as a public exhibition of a similar form of potentially harmful self-expression.

**Body bag.** A bag for carrying a corpse from the scene of warfare or an accident, such as a plane crash. In the plural the term has become something of a journalistic euphemism for war casualties, and US strategy and tactics in the Second GULF WAR clearly recognized in advance the importance of the so called 'body bag factor' and the need to limit one's own losses at all cost.

**Body beautiful.** An ideal of physical beauty. The form of the phrase, with inverted noun and adjective, suggests a patterning on a legal term such as 'the body politic'.

**Body blow.** In boxing a punch to the body; figuratively, therefore, a shattering blow, a severe setback or shock.

**Bodybuilding.** The carrying out of regular exercises designed to enhance the body's muscular development. The modern form of the practice grew out of 19th-century strong-man theatrical and circus acts. The first US physique contest took place in New York in 1903, staged by the physical culturist Bernarr Macfadden (1868–1955), dubbed 'the most perfectly developed man in America'. (He was born Bernard McFadden but respelled his name to make it sound 'stronger'.) The activity was widely promoted through mail-order lessons from the 1920s by Charles Atlas, original name Angelo Siciliano (1894–1972), and more recently the premier figure in the art was the Austrian-born US film actor, later governor (*see* GOVERNATOR) of California, Arnold Schwarzenegger (b.1947), formerly Mr Universe. Women bodybuilders began to emerge in the 1970s.

**Body count.** A tally of the people present or of those participating in a particular situation. The term originated in the VIETNAM War (1955–75) when it was used for the count of enemy soldiers killed by US and Allied forces. The HORROR MOVIE *Friday the 13th Part II* (1981) was advertised with the words 'The body count continues', referring to its forerunner, *Friday the 13th* (1980).

**Body double.** A stand-in for a film actor or actress in a stunt or nude scene. Thus Shelley Michelle was Julia Roberts's body double in certain scenes in *Pretty Woman* (1990).

> The film [*The Thomas Crown Affair*] makes only brief use of body doubles – the well-toned stand-ins who earn their living imitating someone else's body – but not, apparently, for reasons of vanity.
>
> *Sunday Times* (22 August 1999)

**Body language.** The use of movements of the body or gestures, mostly unconsciously, to convey a meaning or information. Thus crossing the legs and folding the arms are defensive gestures, expressing the desire to protect oneself. Different races have differing body languages. The term itself dates from the 1960s and apparently arose as a translation of French *langage corporel*.

**Bodyline bowling.** In cricket fast bowling aimed at the batsman's body rather than the wicket. Such bowling was originally known as leg theory, the aim being to bowl short and fast so that the batsman was obliged to use his bat as a shield to protect his upper body and in so doing lob a catch to a knot of expectant fielders on the leg side. In England's 1932–3 tour of Australia the captain, Douglas Jardine, encouraged his fast bowlers, Harold Larwood and Bill Voce, to use bodyline tactics as a counter to the threat posed by the prodigious Australian batsman Don Bradman. The strategy won the Ashes for England but aroused such a storm of indignation in Australia that diplomatic relations between the two countries were almost suspended. One positive result was a modification in the laws of cricket. *See also* DON CAMILLO; PULL A FAST ONE.

**Body piercing.** The piercing of holes in parts of the body other than the ear lobes in order to insert rods, rings and other objects, a form of adornment fashionable among young people since the 1990s. Visible organs favoured for the treatment include the nostril, the eyebrow, the lip and, among females, the navel. The tongue and nipple may also be so embellished, and for the enhancement of sexual pleasure more intimate parts. The art became socially acceptable but the risk of serious infection can make it medically hazardous. *See also* BODY ART.

**Body popping.** A dance popular in the 1980s, involving jerky and robotic arm and head movements and originating as a form of urban street display among Los Angeles teenagers in the late 1970s.

**Body search.** A search, especially by customs officials or the police, of a person's body for illicit weapons, drugs, and the like. The procedure can be unpleasant and degrading.

> I have considerable sympathy for [popular singer] Ms Diana Ross's outrage about the body search she endured at Heathrow. It is a revolting experience, and quite unnecessary.
>
> *The Times*, letter to the editor (24 September 1999)

**Body Shop.** The cosmetics company and shops of this name owe their origin to Anita Roddick (b.1942) who in 1976, together with her husband, Gordon Roddick, opened a shop in Brighton under this name to sell cosmetics made from natural materials and 'stripped of the hype'. The name was not original, but had been suggested by a car bodywork repair shop called 'The Body Shop' that Roddick had seen in the United States. Following the opening of the shop, two undertakers with premises in the same street, Kensington Gardens, sent Roddick a solicitor's letter claiming that her enterprise would adversely affect their business. The local paper ran a story that she, a defenceless woman, was being harassed, and the incident served instead as welcome start-up publicity.

In 2006 the Roddicks sold the business to L'Oréal, a move criticized by some concerned that they had 'sold out' in terms of the company's ethical policies.

**Body stocking.** A woman's undergarment covering the torso and legs. It is similar to a bodysuit, or body, a close-fitting one-piece garment worn for sports and exercising.

**Boer Wars.** Two wars (1880–1 and 1899–1902), also known as the South African Wars, fought between the British and the Boers (or Afrikaners) for mastery in southern Africa. The second conflict began with early British reverses that culminated in three celebrated sieges, at Ladysmith, Mafeking and Kimberley, the relief of which entered British imperial folklore (*see* MAFEKING NIGHT). Thereafter the British used scorched-earth tactics to quash the Boer COMMANDOS and CONCENTRATION CAMPS to intern their families. The war was ended by the Treaty of Vereeniging (1902), which included a British promise to the defeated Boers that they would deny the franchise to Africans until the Boer republics were returned to representative government.

**Boffin.** A nickname used by the RAF in the Second World War for a research scientist, one of the BACKROOM BOYS. It passed into general use in the 1940s. Its origin is uncertain. One theory derives it from an obsolete torpedo bomber, the Blackburn Baffin, itself named after the navigator William Baffin (*c*.1584–1622), discoverer in 1616 of Baffin Bay in the

North Atlantic. The word has now passed into school slang to mean a studious person or 'swot'.

**Bofors gun.** A light, rapid-firing 40-mm anti-aircraft (AA) gun, usually mounted as a pair, made by the Swedish firm of Bofors (named after the town of Bofors in south-central Sweden). Regarded as the most effective light AA gun of the Second World War, it was widely used by both British and US forces, both on land and at sea. In 1987 a political corruption scandal erupted in India when it was discovered that the Bofors firm had been involved in giving financial kickbacks in return for arms orders. *Events While Guarding the Bofors Gun* is the title of a play (1966) by the Scottish playwright John McGrath (b.1935).

**B of the Bang, The.** A new and controversial sculpture designed by Thomas Heatherwick, situated in Alan Turing Way, Manchester, and intended to commemorate the Commonwealth Games held in the city in 2002. At 56m (184ft) it is the tallest sculpture in Britain, and comprises a long pole leaning at 30 degrees (a tilt ten times that of the Leaning Tower of Pisa), with a burst of spikes at the end, somewhat resembling the less friendly sort of sea urchin. Those who feel the erection is in the worst tradition of civic kitsch were scandalized by the expenditure of £1.42 million of public money on the thing. It was officially opened in January 2005 by the sprinter Linford Christie, and its title reflects Christie's dictum that one should always try to start a race on 'the b of the bang' of the starter's gun.

**Bogan.** In Australian and New Zealand slang, an uncouth person, or a social misfit, a NERD. The term originated in Australia in the 1980s, and was popularized by Kylie Mole, a surly schoolgirl character in the Australian television comedy series *The Comedy Company* (first broadcast in 1988). It is unclear where it came from, although there may be some link with the Bogan River in the wilds of western New South Wales.

The controversial Australian leg-spinner Shane Warne was once described as 'the Bogan from Black Rock' (a suburb of Melbourne whence he hails).

**BOGOF.** 'Buy one get one free': an acronym in the retailing industry for a marketing ploy by which for each item bought (e.g. a tin of beans) the purchaser is given another identical one free. It is first recorded in 1985. A 2005 advertising campaign for McWilliams's wines humorously subverted the formula with such slogans as 'Buy one, get one' and 'Buy one or else'.

**BOGSAT.** A pungent acronym denoting decision-making by committee. It is variously interpreted as 'bunch of guys sitting around talking *or* around a table'.

Usually I dread the G-8. For a journalist it's the ultimate BOGSAT.

J.F.O. MCALLISTER: www.time.com (26 June 2005)

**Bogside.** One of the most resonant place-names in the geography of Northern Ireland's TROUBLES, sometimes colloquially shortened to 'the Bog'. The Bogside is a low-lying area beneath the city walls of Londonderry (Derry), and one of two Catholic estates that dominate the city (the other being the Creggan). Police incursions into the Bogside after a civil rights march from Belfast to Londonderry in October 1968 led to the birth of 'Free Derry', the Bogside becoming a NO-GO AREA for the security forces. The BATTLE OF THE BOGSIDE in August 1969 led to the deployment of British troops on the streets of Northern Ireland. On 29 March 1970, following a commemoration of the 1916 EASTER RISING, young Catholics were involved in clashes with the British army and the police, who replied to bricks and petrol bombs with tear gas, rubber bullets and Saracen armoured cars. The district was subsequently sealed off, and on 10 April the army announced the adoption of a 'get tough' policy in Northern Ireland, adding that anyone throwing a petrol bomb after a warning would be shot dead in the street. The Bogside was also the scene of the horrific events of BLOODY SUNDAY in January 1972. *See also* STROKE CITY.

**Bog-standard.** Ordinary and unremarkable. The origins of the expression have encouraged much speculation, but despite ingenious attempts to link it with 'bog' in various senses (e.g. 'lavatory'), the likeliest explanation is that it is a variation on 'box-standard', first recorded in this sense around the same time (the early 1980s) and implying a product in the state in which it emerges from the manufacturer's box, and with no later refinements or modifications.

In 2001 Tony Blair caused something of a furore when he referred disparagingly to the 'bog-standard comprehensive' (a phrase coined by a speechwriter, Peter Hayman) to signal the government's wish to create a greater diversity of secondary school types.

**'Bohemian Rhapsody'.** A flamboyant and operatic rock song, with teasingly allusive lyrics, by the pop group Queen. One of the most commercially successful pop releases of all time, it remained at Number 1 in the UK charts for nine weeks in 1975–6 and again in 1991 when it was re-released following the death of the group's lead singer Freddie Mercury from AIDS. The song appeared on the album, *A Night at the Opera*. Its lyrics, heavily overlaid with images of death, and including allusions to fictional and historical characters (Scaramouche and Galileo), have long intrigued the public.

Freddie Mercury said of the song: 'People should listen to it, think about it, and make up their own minds as to what it says to them.' *See also* ROCK GROUP NAMES.

**Boho.** An abbreviation of 'Bohemian' current from the 1950s to describe anyone with an unconventional lifestyle or a strikingly unusual or theatrical mode of dress.

> All that boho tragedy and minimalism of the Nineties [fashions] never sat very happily in Milan.
>
> *The Times* (28 February 2000)

**Bokmål.** (Norwegian, literally 'book language'.) The written language derived from Danish that is now the more common of the two official languages of Norway, the other being Nynorsk ('new Norwegian'). The name was officially adopted in 1929 to replace the earlier *Riksmål* ('state language'). Nynorsk was itself known before this date as *Landsmål* ('language of the land'). Plans to merge the two tongues into a common Norwegian language remain highly controversial.

**Boldly go where no man has gone before.** The mission of the starship *Enterprise*, as announced at the beginning of each episode of the first series of STAR TREK. The much-parodied words were those of the creator of the series, Gene Roddenberry (1921–91), whose daring split of the infinitive has been widely admired as a blow against pedantry.

**Boléro.** A long, slow and mesmeric orchestral crescendo by Maurice Ravel (1875–1937), unremittingly utilizing the rhythm of the traditional Spanish dance of the same name. Originally the music was for a ballet (1928), but it immediately became a very popular concert piece. *Boléro* featured on the soundtrack of the romantic film comedy *10* (1979), in which Dudley Moore lusts after Bo Derek, and was also used by the British ice-dancers Jayne Torvill and Christopher Dean (*see* TORVILL AND DEAN) in their performance at the 1984 Winter Olympics, for which they won the gold medal.

**Bolivian marching powder.** A facetious nickname for cocaine. Bolivia is a major producer.

**Bollinger Bolshevik.** *See* CHAMPAGNE SOCIALIST.

**Bolly.** Bollinger champagne. The casual colloquialism conceals the prestigious origin of the top quality wine, taking its name from Jacques Joseph Placide Bollinger, the youngest son of a noblewoman and a legal officer in Württemberg, who in 1829 formed a partnership with Amiral Comte Athanase Louis Emmanuel de Villermont and Paul-Joseph Renaudin to form the house of Champagne Renaudin, Bollinger & Cie. In 1837 Bollinger married de

Villermont's daughter, Louise Charlotte, and became a French citizen. The champagne is a favourite for a celebratory occasion.

> And to drink? For someone [pop singer Gabrielle] with a recent number one single and album to celebrate, perhaps a bottle of Bolly? 'Herbal tea, please,' she says.
>
> *heat* (2–8 March 2000)

**Bollywood.** A nickname for the Indian popular film industry, which is based in Mumbai (formerly named Bombay). The word is a blend of 'Bombay' and HOLLYWOOD. The standard product of such companies as Bombay Talkies Ltd was originally garish imitation of Hollywood entertainment.

> The new productions are pure Bollywood from the studios of Bombay. There are battle scenes and Pakistanis dying by the platoon. But there is also singing, dancing and romancing in the meadows.
>
> *The Times* (17 July 1999)

The Pakistani equivalent of Bollywood is Lollywood, the film industry in that country being based in Lahore.

> Lollywood movie posters displayed sultry actresses dancing with handsome, brown-skinned men in fields of marigolds.
>
> KHALED HOSSEINI: *The Kite Runner* (2003)

**Boloney.** *See* BALONEY.

**Bolshevik.** Properly a member of the Russian Revolutionary Party under LENIN, which seized power in 1917, aiming at the establishment of the supreme power of the proletariat and declaring war on capitalism. The Bolsheviks were so called from the fact that at the party conferences of 1902–3 the Leninists were the majority group (Russian *bol'she*, 'more'). The defeated minority were called MENSHEVIKS. *See also* WHITE RUSSIAN.

**Bolshie** or **Bolshy.** A contraction of BOLSHEVIK, used to denote a person with left-wing tendencies, or a rebellious or 'difficult' person generally.

**Bolsover, Beast of.** *See* BEAST OF BOLSOVER.

**BOLTOP.** *See* LOVERS' ACRONYMS.

**Bomba.** The hero of the novel *Bomba the Jungle Boy* (1926) by 'Roy Lockwood', a member of Edward L. Stratemeyer's writing syndicate, and of its many sequels. He lives in the Amazon basin and engages in exploits similar to those undertaken by TARZAN. He was played by Johnny Sheffield in the low-budget film *Bomba the Jungle Boy* (1949) and 11 sequels.

**Bomb Alley.** A description applied in the Second World War to a corridor through Kent and Sussex that was badly damaged by German V-1 flying bombs aimed at London in 1944–5. The hits were either caused by the DOODLEBUGS' notorious inaccuracy or as a result of being shot down by RAF fighters or anti-aircraft fire (out of 9521 fired at southern England, 4621 suffered this fate).

**Bomber Harris.** The apt nickname of Marshal of the RAF Sir Arthur Harris, Bt (1892–1984), commander-in-chief of Bomber Command in the Second World War and advocate of strategic bombing. He directed a huge bombing offensive in the form of a relentless nightly attack on German cities and manufacturing centres, ports and railways. His aggressive tactics have since been criticized and the effectiveness of the assault questioned. In 1992 demonstrators marred the unveiling by the Queen Mother of a statue to Harris at St Clement Danes, London, a church handed over to the RAF after the war and now a memorial to those killed in air battles. *See also* DRESDEN.

**Bomber jacket.** A short jacket tightly gathered at the waist and cuffs and usually having a front zip. It was modelled on the flight jackets worn by US Air Force crews. Hence the name.

> Both my three-year-old son and my father wear bomber jackets and jeans and I go to parties where 60-year-olds chat to 20-year-olds on something like equal terms.
>
> JOHN DIAMOND: in *The Times Magazine* (1 January 2000)

**Bomber Short.** A nickname given to Clare Short (b.1946), a leading left-winger and minister for overseas development in Tony Blair's New Labour government (1997–2003). Although Short opposed the war in Iraq, she failed to resign from the government until after 'REGIME CHANGE' had been violently completed. She is also known as Chief Sitting Bull, from a fancied resemblance to the Native American leader.

**Bomb-happy.** An expression current in the Second World War to describe someone in a state of near-hysteria induced by bombing, which often took the form of irrational euphoria. *See also* TRIGGER-HAPPY.

**'Bombs Away' LeMay.** *See* BOMB THEM BACK INTO THE STONE AGE.

**Bomb them back into the Stone Age.** The threat made to the North Vietnamese in 1965 by General Curtis E. LeMay (1906–90):

> They've got to draw in their horns and stop their aggression, or we're going to bomb them back into the Stone Age.

LeMay, nicknamed by his subordinates 'Iron Ass' and by his critics 'Bombs Away' LeMay, had masterminded the long-range bombing of Japanese cities by the US air force in 1944–5 (accounting for the deaths of anything between 300,000 and 1 million Japanese civilians) and served as air force chief of staff from 1961 to 1965. He was a notably hawkish Cold War Warrior, and in DR STRANGELOVE he was caricatured as General Buck Turgidson (played by George C. Scott). In the 1968 presidential election LeMay was chosen as his running mate by George C. Wallace of the right-wing, segregationist Independent Party.

A more successful candidate for high office, Ronald Reagan, suffered from a similar hubris regarding Vietnam, telling a reporter from the *Fresno Bee* in 1965:

> It's silly talking about how many years we will have to spend in the jungles of Vietnam when we could pave the whole country and put parking stripes on it and still be home for Christmas

That turned out to be Christmas 1973.

*See also* COLD WAR WARRIOR; HANOI JANE.

**Bomfog.** Pompous rhetoric. The term was coined in the 1970s by Vice-President Nelson A. Rockefeller as an acronym of '*b*rotherhood *o*f *m*an and *f*atherhood *o*f *G*od', a phrase said to be frequently used by preachers.

**Bon chic, bon genre.** (French, 'good style, good form'.) Well-bred and elegant; smart and stylish; PREPPY. The phrase describes the sophisticated, understated style of dress and manner seen in the British SLOANE RANGER. In France itself the expression is usually abbreviated as *BCBG*.

> She was a little unsure about it when I wrote the story a few months back, unconvinced that she wanted to share … our bilious bust-ups with the UK's well-heeled *bon chic, bon genre*.
>
> *Sunday Times* (24 October 1999)

**Bond, James.** The ultimate superspy, famous from the novels by Ian Fleming (1908–64) and from the gripping films based on them or inspired by them. He is intelligent and resourceful, a technological adept, a lover of fast cars and a wily seducer. Wherever his adventures and misadventures take him, he is always ultimately the victor and the avenger. Raymond Chandler described the character as 'what every man would like to be and what every woman would like between her sheets'. Bond first appears in *Casino Royale* (1953). His persona is an amalgam of some of the men whom Fleming met when he was serving in British Naval Intelligence in the Second World War. The 'double-O' prefix of his secret agent number, 007, declares he is 'licensed to kill'. His name, more prosaically, was taken from that of James Bond, ornithologist author of *Birds of the West Indies*, who was one of Fleming's neighbours in Jamaica. The title of the 19th Bond film, *The World Is Not Enough* (1999), neatly epitomizes his appeal to his fantasy-struck fans, for whom the real world is never enough. The words are the 1658 motto of the wealthy financier Sir Thomas Bond (d.1685), who gave his name to Bond Street, London, and they appear on the dust cover of Ian Fleming's novel *On Her Majesty's Secret Service* (1963), in which Bond comments that 'it is an excellent motto which I shall certainly adopt'. The words themselves translate Latin *Non sufficit orbis*, the tag end of a cynical line in Juvenal's *Satires* (2nd century ADA), about Alexander the Great: *Unus Pellaeo juveni non sufficit orbis*, 'For a young fellow from Pella a single world was not enough.' Juvenal in turn derived the phrase from the poet Lucan, who put the words in the mouth of Julius Caesar in a passage in his *Civil War* (1st century ADA) in which Caesar quells a mutiny in the ranks. Bond can thus claim a classical pedigree of a sort. *See also* DIAMONDS ARE FOREVER; DR NO; FROM RUSSIA WITH LOVE; GOLDFINGER; KISS KISS BANG BANG; NEVER SAY NEVER AGAIN; *A* VIEW TO A KILL; YOU ONLY LIVE TWICE.

**Bondage trousers.** Black leather trousers hung with chains, safety pins, zips and the like, of the kind favoured by PUNK rockers and others in the 1970s. Vivienne Westwood and Malcom McLaren's boutique, Sex, in the King's Road, London, was one of the first shops to sell them.

**Boneless Wonder.** A nickname given by Winston Churchill on 28 January 1931 to Ramsay MacDonald (*see* RAMSAY MAC) while the latter headed the Labour government of 1929–31. Churchill recalled that as a child he had been prevented by his parents from viewing an exhibit at Barnum's Circus known as 'the Boneless Wonder': 'My parents judged that the spectacle would be too revolting for my youthful eyes, and I have waited fifty years to see the Boneless Wonder sitting on the Treasury bench.'

**Bonfire of the Vanities, The.** A novel (1987) by Tom Wolfe (b.1931). It is a panoramic study of aspects of New York society, embracing Manhattan and the ghettoes of the Bronx, the art world, journalism, socialites and the legal profession. The title refers to the two occasions in the 1490s when, at the urging of the reformer Girolamo Savonarola (1452–98), the citizens of Florence made a huge 'bonfire of vanities' on which they immolated their worldly goods. A misguided attempt at a film version (1990) was directed by Brian de Palma.

**Bongo Bongo Land.** The term notoriously applied to the Third World collectively by the laid-back lothario of the Conservative Party, Alan Clark (1928–99). His use of the term while serving in Margaret Thatcher's government in the 1980s caused an uproar. As it happens, there is a Massif des Bongos in the Central African Republic, the bongo being a species of antelope.

***Bonjour Tristesse.*** The first novel (1954; in English, 1955) by Françoise Sagan (pen-name of Françoise Quoirez; b.1935). The title translates as 'Good morning, sadness', and the book, written in less than three months in a deserted family apartment after a tiff with her mother, is about the self-discovery of a precocious 17-year-old girl, Cécile, who is obsessed with life and love. The title quotes words from a poem by Paul Éluard:

> Adieu tristesse
> Bonjour tristesse
> Tu es inscrite dans les lignes du plafond
> Tu es inscrite dans les yeux que j'aime
> Tu n'es pas tout à fait la misère
> Car les lèvres les plus pauvres te dénoncent
> Par un sourire
> Bonjour tristesse.
>
> (Farewell sadness/Good morning sadness/You are written in the lines of the ceiling/You are written in the eyes that I love/You are not entirely misery/For your weakest lips betray you/By a smile/Good morning sadness)
>
> PAUL ÉLUARD: 'La Vie immédiate' (1932)

**Bonk.** To engage in an act of sexual intercourse. The sense evolved in the 1970s from the earlier meaning 'to hit' and has had various claimed originators.

> 'I [television personality Jeremy Beadle] remember the Sun headlines used to claim that the Sun created the word bonking, but *I* used to use the word bonking *regularly* on my show [in the late 1970s]
>
> … I used to say to callers, Done any good bonking lately? It was a real laugh. It's a bit much of the Sun to take credit for putting that word in the dictionary.'
>
> Q (March 1990)

Both the tennis player Boris Becker (b.1967) and the journalist and Conservative MP Boris Johnson have earned the tabloid nickname 'BONKING BORIS'. *See also* BONKBUSTER.

**Bonkbuster.** A type of popular novel, often with a female author, in which high-class, powerful or socially aspirant characters engage in many (and often illicit) sexual encounters (*see* BONK), the details being conveyed with suitable comprehensiveness. A pioneer of the genre was the US writer Jacqueline Susann, as in *The Love Machine* (1969) and *Once is Not Enough* (1973), while leading British exponents have been Jilly Cooper (b.1937) and Jackie Collins (b.1941). The word itself puns on BLOCKBUSTER. *See also* SEX AND SHOPPING; SHOPPING AND FUCKING.

A quick romp through the sexual fantasies of politicos can be exhausting, but writing a bonkbuster is at least a way of becoming noticed.

*The Times* (15 November 1999)

**Bonkers.** Mad; crazy. The colloquial term dates from the 1950s and perhaps came from the identical naval slang word meaning 'slightly drunk', itself probably alluding to a 'bonk' on the head. The term tends to be used by politicians of one another. 'Stark raving bonkers' is an elaboration.

In a series of 'foul remarks' about Baroness Thatcher, Mr Major described her as 'bonkers', 'mad' and 'loopy', according to a secret diary kept by one of his closest aides.

*The Times* (20 September 1994)

**Bonking Boris.** A nickname first given to the former German tennis star Boris Becker (b.1967), winner of the men's singles championship at Wimbledon in 1985, 1986 and 1989. The name arose after the amiable Becker (also nicknamed Boom Boom, from his powerful service) impregnated a Russian-African trainee investment banker and model, Angela Ermakova, in a broom cupboard while dining at London's fashionable Nobu restaurant in 1999. Becker had just had a tiff with his wife Barbara, whom he later divorced, and Ermakova was working as a waitress in the restaurant. Becker denied paternity of Ermakova's baby Anna, born the following year, until a DNA test proved otherwise, at which point he explained that Ermakova had performed oral sex on him, and alleged that she had transferred his sperm from her mouth without his knowledge or permission, as part of a blackmail plot by the Russian Mafia. The courts were not impressed, and in 2001 Becker agreed to pay Ermakova $5 million.

The nickname was subsequently given by the British tabloid press to flop-haired blond Tory MP Alexander Boris de Pfeffel Johnson, better known as plain Boris Johnson (b.1964), or sometimes as 'Bo-Jo'. The frequent media appearances and faux-buffoonery of the Old Etonian have done much to enhance the gaiety of nations. He earned the nickname Bonking Boris in 2004, following allegations that Johnson, a married man and father of four, had had a three-year affair with the former deputy-editor of *The Spectator*, Petronella Wyatt. Johnson dismissed the allegations as a 'pyramid of piffle'. He went on: 'I haven't had an affair with Petronella. It's balderdash. It's all completely untrue and ludicrous conjecture.' When it turned out that it was, *au contraire*, all completely true, he was sacked from his post as shadow arts minister by Tory Party leader Michael Howard – not because of the affair, insisted Howard, but because of the false denial.

**Bonnie and Clyde.** The first names of the American bandits Bonnie Parker (1911–34) and Clyde Barrow (1909–34). They first met in 1930 and moved into a small room in Dallas, Texas. Soon afterwards, Barrow was arrested for robbery and sentenced to two years in jail. He escaped with the aid of a pistol, probably smuggled in by Parker, but was recaptured and sent to a more secure unit. He was released on parole in 1932 and later that year the pair began a criminal career, taking a number of hostages, robbing banks and killing those who seemed to pose a threat. This continued until February 1934, when the head of the Texas prison system hired Frank Hamer, a former Texas ranger, to hunt the pair down. On 23 May 1934 a trap was set up on a road near Gibsland, Louisiana, and when the two arrived at the site Hamer and his posse riddled their vehicle with gunfire, killing them instantly. The exploits of the pair both appalled and enthralled America.

A film (1967) with a screenplay by Robert Benton and David Newman and directed by Arthur Penn was loosely based on their escapades, although the real robbers were much less attractive than their cinematic equivalents, played in the film by Faye Dunaway and Warren Beatty. The romance between them, suggested in the movie, was rendered unlikely by virtue of Barrow's homosexuality. The couple's murderous progress across the American Midwest has long been the subject of modern legend and has inspired several other movies, among them *You Only Live Once* (1937), *They Live by Night* (1948), *Gun Crazy* (1949), *The Bonnie Parker Story* (1958) and *Thieves Like Us* (1974).

**Bonus Army.** A gathering of unemployed American war veterans who in 1932 set up camp in Washington, D.C., and vowed to stay put until Congress authorized the immediate distribution of bonuses for military service in the First World War, although these were not scheduled for payment until 1945. They were dispersed by cavalrymen and their shantytown demolished.

**Bonzo.** The comically shaped puppy in the drawings by George E. Studdy, the first of which appeared in *The Sketch* for 8 November 1922. The name was invented by Captain Bruce Ingram, editor of *The Sketch*, and gained a place in the public consciousness as a typical dog name long after its original bearer had vanished from the printed page.

It was further popularized by the eccentric musical group known as the Bonzo Dog (Doo Dah) Band, formed in 1965. They issued a series of comically surreal and satirical LPs in a variety of musical styles, from trad jazz to rock, and obtained a cult status. Their only chart hit, 'The Urban Spaceman', was produced by 'Apollo C. Vermouth' – in reality, Paul McCartney of BEATLES fame. Their vocalist and moving spirit was Vivian Stanshall (1943–95).

**Boob tube.** An expression of two meanings: first, a television set, as watched by a boob or COUCH POTATO; second, a woman's tight-fitting strapless top, encasing the 'boobs' or breasts. It is likely the latter sense arose (in the 1970s) as a pun on the former, which dates from the 1950s.

> If you want to do the tube top thing, a word of advice: boob tubes tend to be too tight and ultra tarty.
>
> *The Times* (31 July 1999)

**Boogaloo.** A popular dance of US origin that arose in the 1960s. It is (or was) performed to ROCK 'N' ROLL music with swivelling and shuffling movements of the body and presumably bases its name on BOOGIE-WOOGIE.

**Boogie-woogie.** A style of piano JAZZ in which the left hand maintains a heavy repetitive pattern of eight beats to the bar while the right hand improvises. It was probably developed in the American Midwest early in the 20th century. The name seems to have originated in Clarence 'Pinetop' Smith's 'Pinetop's Boogie-Woogie' (1928). Boogie already existed as a slang word for a party. Its origin is uncertain. Woogie was then added as a rhyming element. *See also* BLUES; SWING.

**Boojie.** In African American slang, a dismissive term characterizing a person or thing as pretentiously middle-class or 'stuck up'. It is a distillation of the word 'bourgeois', and dates from around 1970.

**Booker Prize.** The leading British annual literary prize, launched in 1968 by the food-distribution firm Booker McConnell Ltd (now Booker plc, and part of The Big Food Group plc) and in 2005 worth £50,000. From 2002 it has been sponsored by the Man Group, a British hedge fund, and known officially as the Man Booker Prize. It is for a novel first published between 1 October and 30 September in the year of the award and since 1981 has been presented live on television. A winner did not enter the bestseller lists until 1982, when Salman Rushdie's MIDNIGHT'S CHILDREN was the choice. Some awards have been controversial, such as that of 1995 for James Kelman's *How Late It Was, How Late*, with its proliferation of FOUR-LETTER WORDS. More generally, criticism has been expressed regarding the quality of the selected writing, and Ian McEwen's short novel *Amsterdam*, awarded the prize in 1998, was felt by many to be inferior to earlier works such as *The Comfort of Strangers* (1981), *The Child in Time* (1987) and *Black Dogs* (1992). The only double winners to date are the South African writer J.M. Coetzee, for LIFE AND TIMES OF MICHAEL K (1983) and *Disgrace* (1999), and the Australian Peter Carey for OSCAR AND LUCINDA (1988) and *True History of the Kelly Gang* (2001).

**Boom box.** A large portable radio-cum-tape-recorder, characteristically played (as its name suggests) very loudly in public; a GHETTO-BLASTER. The term is first recorded in the United States in 1981.

**Boondocks.** A US colloquialism for rough or isolated country. The term dates from the 1940s when it was adopted by US Marines from Tagalog *bundok*, 'mountain', to apply to any remote region where they were required to operate.

**Boondoggle.** A verb of US origin meaning to do useless or futile work. The word is of uncertain origin. According to one account it was invented in the 1930s by an American scoutmaster, Robert H. Link, for a type of braided lanyard. This took time or trouble to make, hence the word passed to a futile task in general.

**Boop, Betty.** A supposedly sexy star of short cartoon films produced by Max Fleischer in the 1920s and 1930s. She had big sparkling eyes, a button nose and a squeaky voice and often appeared in various degrees of undress. Her tagline was 'Boop-Boop-a-Doop'. She was the first cartoon character to be censored and by the mid-1930s had abandoned her provocative garter, short skirt and décolletage.

**Bootsie and Snudge.** An army private and his irascible sergeant, played by Alfie Bass and Bill Fraser in the popular television series *The* ARMY GAME. The pair also appeared in the film *I Only Arsked* (1958) and subsequently had their own series, *Bootsie and Snudge* (1960–63). Their humour was very much in the mould of the CARRY ON FILMS.

**Boot stamping on a human face.** The image used by George Orwell to encapsulate the dystopian world of *1984* (1949):

> If you want a picture of the future, imagine a boot stamping on a human face – for ever.
>
> Pt III, ch. 3

The jackboot (especially the Nazi jackboot) as a symbol of totalitarian oppression had become current during the Second World War, and persists as a powerful image.

> Every woman adores a Fascist,
> The boot in the face, the brute
> Brute heart of a brute like you.
>
> SYLVIA PLATH: 'Daddy' (1963)

**Bootylicious.** Originally in African American slang, of a woman, highly sexually attractive, especially by virtue of shapely buttocks. The word, which is first recorded in 1994, is a blend of 'booty', meaning 'buttocks' (probably an alteration of 'botty'), and 'delicious' (*see also* BABELICIOUS).

In 2001 it was the name of the title track of an album by 'Destiny's Child'.

**Booze-and-bash fiction.** A term formerly applied to novels in which drunkenness and violence prevailed, such as a number of American crime novels, the James BOND stories of Ian Fleming and certain realistic novels in vogue after the Second World War, such as Alan Sillitoe's SATURDAY NIGHT AND SUNDAY MORNING (1958).

**Booze cruise.** A one-day visit to France by ship to stock up with alcoholic drink and tobacco at favourable prices. The traditional route for the enterprise, because it is the shortest, is Dover to Calais.

> Last-minute 'booze cruises' to buy cheap drink for Christmas and millennium parties are leading many motorists to risk their lives in search of a bargain, warn police.
> *The Times* (18 December 1999)

**Bore the pants off someone.** To bore them to a state of desperation. The expression, which dates from the 1930s, may be a variant of 'to charm the pants off', meaning to ingratiate oneself with a person. The implication is that they will do anything for you, even take their trousers off. If the charmer is female, as seems the most likely scenario, the guile will have achieved its purpose.

**Boring old gits to wed.** *See* the ROTTWEILER.

**Bork.** To criticize a political opponent, rival candidate, etc. bitterly and unrelentingly, especially via the media. This piece of US political jargon was inspired by the case of Judge Robert H. Bork, whose appointment to the US Supreme Court was blocked in 1987 as a result of a persistent media campaign against him.

> I wonder, though, how many members of the opposition were 'borked' by [Harriet] Miers so that she would get the nomination [to the US Supreme Court].
> www.confirmthem.com (13 October 2005)

**Borley Rectory.** *See under* FAKES.

**Borrowers, The.** The family of little people who live beneath the floorboards in Mary Norton's highly rated children's novel that bears their name (1952). Individually they are Homily, Pod and little Arriety, and they are so called as they survive by 'borrowing' essentials from the household above. There were four sequels (*The Borrowers Afield* (1955), *The Borrowers Afloat* (1959), *The Borrowers Aloft* (1961) and *The Borrowers Avenged* (1982)), there have been US and British television versions and a feature film called *The Borrowers* appeared in 1997.

**Borscht Belt.** A showbusiness nickname dating from the 1930s for a Jewish resort area in the Catskill Mountains, New York State, so called from the popularity of borscht (Russian-style beetroot soup) among Jews of eastern European origin.

> The Borscht Belt, they call this corridor of kosher kitsch, dotted with holiday bungalow complexes and resort hotels famous for generations for their matchmakers, big dinners, and fast-talking comedians.
> HOWARD JACOBSON: in *Sunday Times* (29 August 1999)

**Borstal.** A prison or detention centre for young male offenders, since 1982 officially designated a youth custody centre and subsequently a young offender institution. The centres took their name from the location of the first, which opened at Borstal, near Rochester, Kent, in 1902. By a strange linguistic coincidence, the Anglo-Saxon place-name Borstal means 'security place'. Brendan Behan's *Borstal Boy* (1958) gives a vivid fictionalized autobiographical account of life in such a centre.

**Bosie.** An Australian nickname for the GOOGLY in cricket, after the name of its inventor, the Middlesex player B.J.T. Bosanquet (1877–1936). Bosie was also the nickname of Oscar Wilde's lover, Lord Alfred Douglas (1870–1945).

**BOSS.** The sinisterly appropriate acronym for the Bureau of State Security, formerly a branch of the South African security police. It was notorious for its ruthless campaigns, including assassinations, against anti-APARTHEID activists at home and abroad.

**Boss, The.** A nickname that has been applied to a number of political figures, including Margaret Thatcher (*see* IRON LADY), Franklin Roosevelt (*see* FDR), Charles Haughey (prime minister of Ireland 1979–81, 1982, 1987–92), and to his wife by Harry S. Truman (*see* GIVE-'EM-HELL HARRY).

**Boston Pops.** The US orchestra of this name is drawn from members of the Boston Symphony Orchestra, founded in 1881. It began giving an annual series of light music concerts in 1885 and from 1900 these were known simply as 'Pops', short for 'Popular Concerts'. The name then passed to the orchestra itself.

**Boston Strangler.** Albert de Salvo (1933–73), who strangled 13 women in Boston, Massachusetts, in the early 1960s. He was jailed for life and stabbed to death by a fellow prisoner.

**Both oars in the water.** Personal equilibrium in one's life. Thus someone who can keep both oars in the water can lead a straightforward and relatively stress-free existence. The metaphor is from rowing: if you have only one oar in the water, you go round in circles.

Sometimes a midlife crisis can teach a man how to keep both oars in the water for the rest of his life.

www.news.cornell.edu (8 April 1999)

**Bottle bank.** A large metal container in which empty bottles are deposited (as if in a bank) by the public so that the glass can be recycled. There are also 'paper banks' for newspapers and magazines, 'can banks' for used drinks cans and 'clothes banks' for old clothing, curtains and the like.

**Bottleneck.** A narrow stretch of road where the smooth flow of traffic is impeded; any impediment that holds up production or trade.

**Bottle out.** To lose one's nerve or 'bottle'. The latter word apparently comes from 'bottle and glass', rhyming slang for 'arse', perhaps with a reference to the temporary incontinence experienced by an apprehensive or 'shit-scared' person.

**Bottle party.** A party to which guests are expected to bring a bottle of wine or some similar drinkable contribution.

**Bottom line.** The grand total; the final assessment. The expression arose in the 1970s as a translation of Yiddish *di untershte sture*, meaning the final profit or loss figure on an account.

That is apparently what motivates Mr Michael Ashcroft. That is the bottom line. Not political convictions … Not public interest, but the ruthless pursuit of his bottom line – of his profit.

PETER BRADLEY: speech in House of Commons, 21 July 1999, in *The Times* (22 July 1999)

**Bottom out.** To reach the lowest point before stabilizing or recovering. The phrase is typically associated with a country's economy or with a person's or organization's popularity ratings.

In the last 18 months of 'phoney war' election run-up the Tories have constantly sought evidence that they have 'bottomed out'.

ROBIN OAKLEY: in *The BBC News General Election Guide* (1997)

**Bottoms up!** A drinking toast of naval origin. The bottoms are those of the glasses as they are tilted up over the drinkers' mouths.

**Boudoir biscuits.** The sponge biscuits or sponge fingers now so known were originally eaten at funerals. In the early 20th century they received their present name, from a much more agreeable association with a lady's boudoir. The name is often found embossed on the bottom of the biscuit.

**Bounce an idea off someone.** To put it to them in order to

get their reaction or opinion. The degree of 'bounce' will indicate its potential.

**Bounce back.** To recover well after a setback or difficulty. The analogy is more with a toy figure that rights itself after being pushed over rather than with a rebounding ball.

Elton [John] has bounced back so many times he is pop's original India Rubber Man.

*The Times* (6 September 1999)

**Bouncing Czech.** A punning nickname applied to (among others) the crooked and litigious media tycoon Robert Maxwell (1923–91), who was born in Czechoslovakia as Jan Ludvik Hoch. He was also known as Captain Bob, and featured as such in a long-running cartoon strip in *Private Eye*. Maxwell was Labour MP for Buckingham (1964–70). Although a 1973 report by the Department of Trade and Industry had declared that he was unfit to hold the stewardship of a public company, he went on to build a huge publishing empire. The full depths of his fraudulent dealings, including the embezzlement of the Mirror Group's pension funds, did not emerge fully until after his apparent suicide. *See also* RUBBER CHEQUE.

**Bouncy castle.** A large inflatable toy castle for children to play on, chiefly by jumping and bouncing. The device was a standard attraction of the British fete from the late 1980s.

**Bounding Basque.** The nickname of the French tennis player Jean Borotra (1898–1994), one of the FOUR MUSKETEERS. He was born in the département of Basse-Pyrénées in the French Basque country and was known for the swiftness of his movement over the tennis court.

**Bourbon biscuits.** The chocolate-flavoured 'sandwich' biscuits have no connection with the French royal house of Bourbon apart from bearing its name, which is first recorded for them in the 1930s.

**Bovril.** This well-known concentrated beef extract was the invention in 1889 of John Lawson Johnston (1839–1900), a Scot who had studied with a view to entering the medical profession but who instead turned his attention to dietetics. He named his new food from a combination of Latin *bos*, *bovis*, 'ox', and Vril, a substance described in Lord Lytton's novel *The Coming Race* (1871) as an 'electric fluid … capable of being raised and disciplined into the mightiest agency of all forms of matter'. This name itself suggests Latin *virilis*, 'manly', so that the overall name implies 'beefiness'.

**Bovver boots.** Heavy laced boots extending to the mid-calf, as typically worn by BOVVER BOYS and SKINHEADS or any young male out to cause 'bovver', a Cockney pronunciation of 'bother'.

**Bovver boy.** A young hooligan of the SKINHEAD type prevalent in the 1960s, especially one wearing BOVVER BOOTS.

**Bowler hat.** In the armed forces, 'to get one's bowler hat' is to be demobilized and return to civilian life, a bowler hat at one time being regarded as an essential accoutrement of a civil servant.

**Bowles, Sally.** An English nightclub singer in Germany just before the coming of the NAZIS in Christopher Isherwood's novella named after her (1937). Although very young, she cultivates a brash air of sexual sagacity. Isherwood's work was subsequently incorporated in the volume GOODBYE TO BERLIN (1939), itself made into a stage play of 1951 by John Van Druten and a film of 1955 directed by Henry Cornelius, both bearing the title *I Am a Camera*. The film starred Julie Harris as Sally. Following another title change, to CABARET, the rather slight story became a stage musical of 1961 and a highly praised musical film of 1972. In the latter Sally was played with great verve and nervous vitality by Liza Minnelli.

**Bowl of cherries.** A pleasant or enjoyable situation or experience. The expression is frequently used ironically in the catchphrase 'Life is a bowl of cherries', popularized by Lew Brown's song 'Life is Just a Bowl of Cherries' (1931). The ironic twist is already present in the title of Erma Bombeck's humorous book *If Life is a Bowl of Cherries, What Am I Doing in the Pits* (1979).

**Box clever.** To act so as to outwit someone. A boxer has to use his wits to deliver and dodge punches. The metaphor dates from the 1930s.

**Boxed in.** Restricted in one's movements or ability to act, as if enclosed in a box.

> He [former prime minister John Major] urged the Tory leader [William Hague] to widen the appeal of his party … and not allow himself to be boxed in by either wing of the party.
>
> *The Times* (30 December 1999)

**Boxers.** Members of a nationalistic Chinese secret society, which took a prominent part in the rising against foreigners in 1900 and which was suppressed by joint European action. The group practised certain boxing and callisthenic rituals in the belief that this gave them supernatural powers and even made them impervious to bullets. Their Chinese name was accordingly *Yìhéquán*, 'righteous harmony fists', and it was the last word of this that gave their English name of Boxers.

**Box junction.** An area at a road junction marked out with a yellow grid. Drivers are supposed to enter the box only if their exit is clear. However, a driver may enter if intending to turn right and only prevented from doing so by oncoming traffic or by other vehicles waiting to turn right.

**Boy band.** A purpose-created pop group whose members are young, male, clean-cut and likely to appeal to adolescent (and younger) girls. Examples of the boy band are Take That, highly successful in the early 1990s, and, more recently, the Irish groups Boyzone and Westlife.

**Boy David, the.** A *Private Eye* nickname for David (now Lord) Steel (b.1938), leader of the Liberal Party (1976–88). He was the youngest MP in the Commons when returned at a by-election in 1965, and was only 38 when he took over the leadership of his party. The nickname was justified by his enduringly boyish looks, and the phrase alludes to the biblical David, who as a youth slew Goliath (1 Samuel 17), a giant-killing feat that Steel and his party never quite managed to pull off. The direct source of the name was perhaps the title of J.M. Barrie's play *The Boy David* (1936). More recently, the nickname has been applied to David Cameron (b.1966), youthful leader of the Tory Party since 2005.

**Boy in the boat, The.** A euphemistic name for the clitoris, drawing not unpoetically on its anatomical setting. It is first recorded in 1916, but probably goes back well beyond that.

**Boyo.** A boy or young man, especially a Welsh one, or a Welshman of any age. The term is mildly deprecatory. In UNDER MILK WOOD (1954) Dylan Thomas has a character Nogood Boyo: 'I want to be *good* Boyo, but nobody'll let me.'

> Who could really blame him [Welsh popular singer Tom Jones] for occasionally fancying what the tabloids invariably describe as a 'boyo-loving blonde' on the side?
>
> *Sunday Times* (28 November 1999)

**Boy racer.** Originally, in the 1940s, a nickname given to the AJS Model 7R racing motorcycle, which was manufactured for the mass market in 1948. Then, in the 1990s, it began to be used as a dismissive term for the type of flash young man who drives fast and aggressively (a customized Vauxhall Nova is his archetypal vehicle of choice) and indulges in illegal street races and various ostentatious and noisy manoeuvres, such as wheel-spins and 'donuts' (circles of burnt rubber left on the road after spinning on the spot), much to the annoyance of the local populace.

In New Zealand, the Land Transport (Unauthorised Street and Drag Racing) Amendment Act 2003 was nicknamed the 'Boy Racer' Act.

An anti-social dispersal zone giving police the power to move on 'boy racers' causing noise and nuisance on Aberdeen's Beach Boulevard has ended. The order was introduced to tackle so-called 'Bouley Bashers' driving high-powered cars, after complaints from local residents.

www.bbc.co.uk/news/ (29 August 2005)

*See also* PETROLHEAD.

**Boy Scouts** or **Scouts.** A popular youth movement started by General Sir Robert Baden-Powell (Lord Baden-Powell of Gilwell) in 1908. The aim was to train boys to be good citizens with high ideals of honour, service to others, cleanliness and self-reliance, based essentially on training in an outdoor setting. The movement became worldwide. There are four branches: Beaver Scouts (aged 6 to 8), Cub Scouts, formerly WOLF CUBS (8 to 10½), Scouts (10½ to14) and Explorer Scouts, formerly Venture Scouts (14 to 18). Girls are now admitted to the Scouts, and membership of the movement stands at 500,000 (with the first increase in 2006 for 13 years). *See also* BEAVERS; BE PREPARED; GIRL GUIDES.

**Boysenberries.** The hybrid of blackberries, loganberries and raspberries takes its name from Rudolph Boysen (d.1950), the US horticulturist who developed it in California in 1920.

**Boys from Brazil.** A film (1978) based on a novel by Ira Levin. Although the title suggests a light-hearted musical about samba players, the 'boys from Brazil' are in fact clones of Adolf Hitler prepared by Dr Josef Mengele (played by Gregory Peck), a real-life Nazi doctor known as the 'ANGEL OF DEATH', who escaped to South America after the Second World War. In the film he is pursued by Ezra Lieberman (played by Laurence Olivier), a character reminiscent of the real-life Nazi hunter Simon Wiesenthal.

**Boys from the Black Stuff, The.** *See* YOSSER.

**Boys in blue.** The police, from the colour of their uniforms.

**Boy's Own Paper, The.** Known as the *BOP*, this boys' magazine appeared from 1879 to 1967. First published by the Religious Tract Society, the *BOP* strove to provide its mainly middle-class readership with such appropriately uplifting subject matter as historical and military adventure stories, articles on sport and natural history as well as puzzles and competitions. Its prevailing white, Christian and imperialist ethos was memorably summed up by the writer Wyndham Lewis, who described the *BOP* as being: 'full of tough, hairy, conquering Nordics plundering through trackless forests and lethal swamps, wrestling with huge apes and enormous cobras, foiling villains of Latin origin, crammed with experience and philosophy and knowing practically everything.' The last issue of the *BOP*

was published in February 1967. That its Baden-Powellish values had long since ceased to be fashionable is reflected with unconscious irony in the *BOP* having as its final cover feature the 21-year-old Manchester United footballer George Best, described as a role model who 'doesn't smoke, drinks only occasionally and restricts his card-playing to sessions which ease the boredom of travelling'. The title of the *BOP* is ironically reflected in the gay rites-of-passage novel *A* BOY'S OWN STORY by the US writer Edmund White, and punningly in Boyzone, the name of a highly successful Irish BOY BAND of the 1990s. *See also The* GIRL'S OWN PAPER; RIPPING YARNS.

**Boy's Own Story, A.** The first (1982) in a trilogy of semi-autobiographical novels by the US novelist Edmund White (b.1940). It charts a boy's growing awareness of his homosexuality. The others are *The Beautiful Room is Empty* (1988) and *The Farewell Symphony* (1997). *See also The* BOY'S OWN PAPER.

**Boystown.** A nickname for the predominantly gay neighbourhood in West Hollywood, California. In 1985 the city was the first in the United States to elect a council with a majority of openly gay or lesbian members. The name itself puns on BOYS TOWN.

**Boys Town.** This unusual settlement near Omaha, Nebraska, was the brainchild of Father Edward J. Flanagan (1886–1948), an Irish-born Roman Catholic priest who was ordained in Austria in 1912. In 1913 he was appointed assistant pastor at St Patrick's Church, Omaha, and began to devote his life to improving the lot of the destitute and delinquent young people he saw on the streets. In 1917 he founded a home for homeless youths and when it became crowded moved outside the town to establish Boys Town the following year. Despite financial difficulties, the undertaking was a success and brought Flanagan worldwide fame as an expert on juvenile delinquency. The village is governed by the boys themselves and maintained by voluntary contributions. Girls were first admitted in 1979 and by the end of the 20th century Boys Town numbered some 800 residents. The enterprise was introduced to a wide public by the MGM film *Boys Town* (1938), with Spencer Tracy as Father Flanagan and Mickey Rooney as a troubled youth.

**Boy toy.** *See* TOY BOY.

**Boy Wonder.** A nickname dating from the 1920s for an exceptionally talented young man or boy, especially when in the public eye. The jockey Lester Piggott (b.1935) was so known after riding his first winner in 1948, while more recently the nickname has been applied, ironically, to the youthful but deep-voiced New Labour politician Ruth Kelly (b.1968), who became education secretary in December 2004, the youngest woman ever to enter the cabinet (she was reshuffled to become secretary for communities and local government in May 2006). The term suggests a variant on the earlier 'wonder boy'.

**B-picture.** *See* B-MOVIE.

**Bra.** An abbreviation of brassière first current in the 1930s, originally in the form 'bras'. 'Brassière' itself dates from the early years of the 20th century, and in 1914 Mary Phelps Jacobs used two handkerchiefs with ribbon straps as a basic design for a garment to flatten the bust. 'Burn your bra' was an American Women's Liberation slogan of the 1970s and bra-burning itself became the image most widely associated with feminism on both sides of the Atlantic. The analogy was with the burning of a draft card as a protest against the Vietnam War (1955–75).

> Just as the scale and coherence of suffragette militancy had been hidden from view, so the smokescreen of the 'burning bra' helped to obscure the real nature of the women's liberation movement.
>
> ANNA COOTE and BEATRIX CAMPBELL: *Sweet Freedom: The Struggle for Women's Liberation* (1982)

*See also* BRA WARS.

**Bradbury.** A £1 note, as issued by the Treasury in 1914–28, bearing the signature of J.S. Bradbury (1st Baron Bradbury), who launched the issue as Joint Permanent Secretary to the Treasury.

**Bradshaw.** A famous British railway guide, first issued in Manchester in 1839 by George Bradshaw (1801–53), a printer and engraver. The 'Monthly Guide' was first issued in January 1842, and consisted of 32 pages, giving tables of 43 railway lines. Publication ceased in 1961.

> 'There are difficulties, Watson. The vocabulary of Bradshaw is nervous and terse, but limited. The selection of words would hardly lend itself to the sending of general messages. We will eliminate Bradshaw.'
>
> SIR ARTHUR CONAN DOYLE: *The Valley of Fear*, Pt I, ch. 1 (1915)

**Brady Bunch, The.** A US television comedy series running from 1969 to 1974 and subsequently syndicated. Its story line centred on two broken families, a widower with three sons and a widow with three daughters. The six children of various ages mix and match to heal the break and the two adults marry. The plot was predictable but the programme struck a chord in a generation with a high divorce rate, and almost every young viewer could identify with one or other

of the characters. A series of increasingly improbable spin-offs, including *The Brady Brides* (1981), was less successful. In 1995 a film version updated the family to the 1990s, though they still exuded a whiff of the 1970s.

**Brain drain.** A phrase used to denote the drift abroad, which occurred from the early 1960s, of British-trained scientists, technologists, doctors and university teachers (especially to the United States), attracted by higher salaries and often better facilities for their work. *See also* BRAIN GAIN.

**Brain gain.** An increase in the professional and skilled workforce of a country as a result of the immigration of foreign scientists and scholars seeking better jobs. The term dates from the 1960s and puns on BRAIN DRAIN.

**Brainiac.** A contemptuous US term for someone who is considered far too clever – a know-all. It is an adoption of 'Brainiac' (blending, presumably, 'brain' and 'maniac'), the name of a highly intelligent but evil alien who began to appear in the SUPERMAN comics in the late 1950s.

**Brain of Britain.** A radio quiz show first broadcast in 1967 with mostly abstruse general knowledge questions put to selected members of the public. The overall annual winner is deemed 'Brain of Britain'.

**Brains Trust.** The name was originally applied by James M. Kieran of the *New York Times* to the advisers of Franklin D. Roosevelt (1882–1945) in his election campaign. It was later used for the group of college professors who advised him in administering the NEW DEAL. In Britain it was the name of a popular BBC programme (1941–9), in which a regular panel of Dr Julian Huxley, Professor C.E.M. Joad and Commander A.B. Campbell aired their views on questions submitted by listeners. Joad became famous for beginning his answers with 'IT ALL DEPENDS WHAT YOU MEAN BY ...' The term is now in general use for any such panel or team that answers questions.

**Brainwashing.** The subjection of someone to an intensive course of indoctrination in order to transform their opinions and political loyalties.

**Brainwave.** 'Brain wave' was originally a term for a hypothetical telepathic vibration in the brain that announced the occurrence of a remote event. This 19th-century sense evolved into the 20th-century 'brainwave' that is a sudden idea or 'flash of inspiration'. In the 1930s 'brainwaves' became a scientific term for the electrical impulses in the brain, as now measured by the electro-encephalogram, an essential tool in BIOFEEDBACK. Four frequency bands of such waves have been classified: delta, with a frequency of 0.5–3.5 cycles per second (c/s), as occurring in sleep; theta, 4–7 c/s, as in dozing or deep meditation; alpha, 8–12 c/s, as in relaxed wakefulness or meditation; and beta, 13–22 c/s, as in thinking or when focusing on the external world.

**Branch Davidians.** *See* WACO.

**Brand image.** The impression that a commercial product or brand makes in the mind of consumers, whether actual or potential. The term arose as advertising jargon in the late 1950s with reference to the enhancement of a product's image at the expense of its true description or actual value. The general aim of the brand image is to link words, statements, pictures, sounds and even smells to the brand in question.

> Ray Kroc's vision was to establish in the consciousness of all McDonald's customers a brand image whose essential characteristics and appeal never wavered.
>
> ANDREW TAYLOR: in *Brands* (1998)

**Branding.** The 20th-century business of selecting brand names for new products is fraught with problems. One hazard is the meaning of a name in a language other than that of the manufacturer. In 1992 the London advertising agency Euro RSCG ran an advertisement with pictures of a can of French orange drink named 'Pschitt', a packet of Spanish bubble-gum called 'Bang Bang', a roll of Swedish toilet paper called 'Kräpp' and a packet of Turkish biscuits named 'Bum!' Yet all these are simply imitative words except the Swedish name, which means 'crêpe'.

**Brand X.** An arbitrary designation for an unnamed brand when contrasted unfavourably with a product of the same type that is currently being promoted. The term dates from the 1930s.

**Branestawm, Professor.** The absent-minded, spectacles-bedecked professor who is always building crazy, impractical machines in Norman Hunter's children's book *The Incredible Adventures of Professor Branestawm* (1933), which was perfectly illustrated by William HEATH ROBINSON. Many more stories followed, and he was still going strong in *Professor Branestawm's Perilous Pudding* (1980), which was written when Hunter was 81.

**Brasília.** The purpose-built capital of Brazil, and one of the world's finest architectural realizations of the 20th century. It lies on the banks of an artificial lake near the geographical centre of the country and was designed by Lúcio Costa in 1957. It has the outline of an aeroplane, with the federal and civic buildings as the fuselage, the residential areas as the wings and the triangular Square of Three Powers as the nose. The executive, judicial and legislative buildings are grouped around the square, and the federal government began its move there from Rio de Janeiro in 1960. It is purely an administrative city, and has no industry of any kind.

**Brassed off.** Fed up, as if reprimanded by a senior officer or 'brass hat'.

**Brass monkey weather.** Weather that is 'cold enough to freeze the balls off a brass monkey'. The phrase goes back at least to the 19th century, but its origins remain obscure. The often touted notion that 'brass monkey' was a term for the plate on a warship's deck where cannon balls were stacked, and that in cold weather, the brass would contract, causing the stack to collapse, is completely fallacious. A more plausible source may be the brass figures of the 'Three Wise Monkeys', who saw no evil, heard no evil and spoke no evil, which were once popular.

**Brat, The.** *See* SUPERBRAT.

**Brat pack.** A group or clique of rowdy or ostentatious young people. The term originally applied to Hollywood stars of the mid-1980s such as Emilio Estevez, Matt Dillon, Patrick Swayze and Tom Cruise and is a pun on RAT PACK. The term itself was coined in 1985 by David Blum in an article about the film *St Elmo's Fire* (1985), in which one of the characters was played by Estevez.

**Braveheart.** The title of a film (1995) about the Scottish national hero William Wallace (*c.* 1270–1305), directed by the Australian-born actor Mel Gibson, who also played the title role. The film, although broadly faithful to Wallace's story (including his gruesome hanging, drawing and quartering in London), took considerable historical liberties. For example, it portrayed Wallace as the son of a Highland peasant, whereas his father was Sir Malcolm Wallace, a small landowner in Renfrewshire, in the Central Lowlands. The film also inaccurately depicts Wallace dallying romantically with Isabella of France, wife of the future Edward II of England. Nevertheless, the film struck a chord in Scotland, and became something of an icon of national pride and resistance at a time when most Scots felt oppressed by almost two decades of Conservative government from London. The term 'Braveheart spirit' has been used in relation to Scottish national football and rugby teams. The film won Oscars for best picture and best director.

**Brave New World.** A dystopian (*see* DYSTOPIA) novel (1932) by Aldous Huxley (1894–1963). Its portrayal of an imagined future world state in which men and women are processed into standardized batches by genetic engineering and lifelong conditioning was originally conceived as a challenge to the claims of H.G. Wells (1866–1946) for the desirability of eugenics. The title derives from Miranda's exclamation in Shakespeare's *The Tempest*:

O brave new world,
That has such people in't!
V.i

Huxley's title has had its own literary influences: in John Osborne's LOOK BACK IN ANGER, Jimmy PORTER talks despairingly of the absence of 'any good, brave causes', and of the world ending in nuclear holocaust, not for some 'grand design', but 'for the Brave New-nothing-very-much thank-you'.

*See also* FIRST LINES OF NOVELS.

**Bra Wars.** The name given by the press (on the model of STAR WARS) to the 2005 trade dispute between the EU and China over the import of low-cost Chinese clothing (including women's underwear) into Europe.

**Brazil, Angela.** The prolific author (1869–1947) of girls' school stories. Her name (stressed on the first syllable, like 'Basil') is now associated with the schoolgirl crushes and adventures with which her novels, rejoicing in titles such as *A Terrible Tomboy* (1904) and *A Fourth Form Friendship* (1911), were crammed. The schoolgirl slang used by Brazil's heroines, typified by words and phrases such as 'blossomy', 'top-hole' and 'jinky', provoked the censure of contemporary educationists and the mirth of posterity.

**Brazilian footballers.** Many Brazilian footballers play under nicknames. The following are some of the best known.

*Bebeto*: José Roberto Gama de Oliveira (b.1964)
*Didi*: Valdir Pereira (b.1928)
*Garrincha*: Manoel Francisco dos Santos (1933–83)
*Jaïrzinho*: Jaïr Ventura Filho (b.1944)
*Juninho*: Giulio Botelho (b.1929)
*Pelé*: Edson Arantes do Nascimento (b.1940)
*Robinho*: Robson do Sousa (b.1986)
*Ronaldinho*: Ronaldo de Assis Moreira (b.1980)
*Tostão*: Eduardo Gonçalves de Andrade (b.1947)
*Vava*: Edvaldo Izidio Neto (b.1934)
*Zico*: Artur Antunes Coimbra (b.1953)
*Zito*: José Eli de Miranda (b.1932)

**Brazilian wax.** A cosmetic depilatory treatment of the female pubic and genital area that involves the removal of all hair (sometimes with a small tuft left above the vulva as an artistic flourish). The name reflects its country of origin, such drastic measures being essential for those wishing to sport an exiguous thong on the beaches of Copacabana.

**Bread-and-butter letter.** A term of US origin dating from the turn of the 20th century for a letter expressing thanks for hospitality. One's host has provided one with sustenance, a basic form of which is bread and butter.

**Bread and Butter State.** A nickname for the state of Minnesota. It originated in 1901 at the time of the Pan-American Exposition in Buffalo, New York, where wheat and dairy products from Minnesota were displayed, giving the impression that the state was the 'nation's granary'. Agriculture still plays an important part in Minnesota's economy, although manufacturing displaced it in the early 1950s as the major source of income.

**Break a leg!** Good luck! A traditional wish to an actor going on stage in the theatre. The expression is said to relate to the assassination of Abraham Lincoln in his private box at Ford's Theatre, Washington, D.C., on 14 April 1865. The murderer, John Wilkes Booth, a Shakespearean actor of some repute, made good his escape after firing the shot by leaping down onto the stage, breaking his leg. 'Break a leg!' then arose as an example of black humour. This story is dismissed by many, if only on the grounds that the phrase is not recorded before the 20th century. It may be a translation of German *Hals und Beinbruch*, 'Neck and leg break'. Other languages have their equivalents, extended to good luck wishes in general, such as Italian *In bocca di lupo*, 'Into the wolf's mouth', and Russian *Ni pukha ni pera*, 'Neither fur nor feather'.

**Break-dancing.** This style of street dancing, both energetic and acrobatic, evolved among African Americans in the 1970s. It was typically danced to HIP-HOP and was so called as it was designed to fill a gap or break in a piece of rap music.

**Breakfast at Tiffany's.** A novella (1958) by the US writer Truman Capote (1924–84) about the uninhibited exploits in New York of 18-year-old Holly GOLIGHTLY. She has a homespun cure for the 'reds', worse than the mere 'blues [which] are because you're getting fat or maybe it's been raining too long':

Reds are horrible. You're afraid and you sweat like hell … something bad is going to happen and you don't know what.

The remedy is 'to get into a taxi and go to Tiffany's', the upmarket jewellery store. A bland, asexual film version (1961), directed by Blake Edwards, starred Audrey Hepburn as Holly.

**Breaking the mould.** What the foundation of the Social Democratic Party in 1981 was supposed to do to British politics. The one-time Labour cabinet minister Roy Jenkins

(1920–2003; *see* WOY) heralded the party that he was to co-found in a speech to the Parliamentary Press Gallery on 9 June 1980:

> The politics of the left and centre of this country are frozen in an out-of-date mould which is bad for the political and economic health of Britain and increasingly inhibiting for those who live within the mould. Can it be broken?

The image of breaking the mould can be traced back to the Italian poet Ludovico Ariosto (1474–1533), who, in a rather different context in his epic *Orlando Furioso* (1532), wrote:

> *Natura il fece, e poi rope la stampa.*
>
> (Nature made him, and then broke the mould.)
>
>    Canto 10

**Break it down!** In Australian English, stop! – an injunction to desist from bad or annoying behaviour. It dates from the 1930s.

**Breath.** The sparest play (1969) of the increasingly minimalist playwright Samuel Beckett (1906–89). Life, the universe and everything is pared down to a 30-second drama in which a stage covered with rubbish is accompanied by a breath, and then a cry. In the same year Beckett refused to go to Stockholm to receive his Nobel Prize in person because he did not wish to make a speech.

**Breathe down someone's neck.** To pursue them closely; to watch or monitor them constantly. The two senses date from the 1940s.

**Breathless.** An influential film (1959) based on a story suggested by François Truffaut (1932–84). The first film of the French NOUVELLE VAGUE director Jean-Luc Godard and well known under its French title, *À Bout de souffle*, it starred Jean-Paul Belmondo and Jean Seberg in a largely improvised (and indeed 'breathless') plot about small-time gangsterism and helped to establish a new genre in European cinema. A lacklustre 1983 remake with the same title, directed by James McBride, starred Richard Gere and transferred the action to Los Angeles.

**Breath of fresh air.** A refreshing change. The figurative sense of the literal term evolved in the mid-20th century. 'Breath' should be understood as a wafting of fresh air, not an inhalation of it.

**Breckenridge, Myra.** The transsexual who narrates her lurid adventures in Gore Vidal's novel that bears her name (1968) and in its sequel, *Myron* (1975). Both deal with HOLLYWOOD myths. A film of the first book was released in 1970 with Raquel Welch in the title role.

**Brenda.** A *Private Eye* nickname for Queen Elizabeth II (b.1926), who came to the throne in 1952. The name represents a deliberate down-grading of the royal status. A similar suburbanization was arranged for her husband, KEITH, her sister, YVONNE, her eldest son, BRIAN, and for his first wife CHERYL.

**Bren gun.** The lightweight quick-firing machine-gun made its first appearance in the years immediately preceding the Second World War. It was originally made in Brno, Czechoslovakia, then in Enfield, England. Bren is a blend of Brno and Enfield. *See also* STEN GUN.

**Bretton Woods.** The idyllic resort in the US state of New Hampshire, where in the summer of 1944 economic ambassadors of 44 countries met to negotiate the shape of postwar world trade. The resulting Bretton Woods agreements established the WORLD BANK. *See also* IMF.

**Brewer's droop.** Impotence resulting from the consumption of alcohol. This and brewer's goitre are expressions of Australian origin.

**Brewer's goitre.** A BEER BELLY.

**Brewster, Bobby.** The boy hero of a series of children's books, published between the 1940s and 1970s, by the British writer H.E. Todd (1908–88), who is visited by strange and magical happenings.

**Brezhnev doctrine.** A policy formulated by the Soviet leader Leonid Brezhnev (1906–82). The Brezhnev doctrine declared the right of the Soviet Union and its allies to intervene in Eastern Europe to 'defend socialism', where 'the essential common interests of other socialist countries are threatened by one of their number'. This doctrine was used to justify the Warsaw Pact invasion of Czechoslovakia in 1968 (*see* PRAGUE SPRING).

**Brian.** A male forename sometimes used to evoke an earnest but tedious person or a lower-middle-class nonentity. Examples are common in the media, as in joking references to the television sports commentator Brian Moore (1932–2001), who always seemed to be interviewing a footballer of the same name, so that the conversation was peppered with 'Well, Brian …', 'Yes, Brian …' and so on. The television comedy series MONTY PYTHON'S FLYING CIRCUS has a famous sketch centring on the name, and the programme's creators further exploited it in their film *Monty Python's Life of Brian* (1979), in which Brian is taken to be Jesus and crucified instead of him. And the magazine *Private Eye* refers to Charles, Prince of Wales as Brian (*see* BRENDA). *See also The* MAGIC ROUNDABOUT.

Winston Churchill, the grandson of the Prime Minister and former Conservative MP, might have chosen a different and happier career path had he been christened Brian.

*The Times* (17 July 1999)

**Bric.** An acronym in use from the early years of the 21st century for the fast-growing economies of *Brazil, Russia, India* and *China*. The term was coined by the Goldman Sachs global economics team:

If things go right, in less than 40 years, the BRICs economies together could be larger than the G6 in US dollar terms. By 2025 they could account for over half the size of the G6. Of the current G6, only the US and Japan may be among the six largest economies in US dollar terms in 2050.

'Dreaming with BRICs: The Path to 2050' (Goldman Sachs, Global Economics Paper No. 99, October 2003)

**Brick it.** To be extremely apprehensive or fearful. The expression evolved in the 1990s as a euphemistic variation on 'shit bricks *or* a brick' (dating from the 1930s), which invokes the laxative effects of fear.

**Bricks and clicks.** A nickname of US origin arising in the 1990s for the two basic types of business company. 'Bricks' companies do not use the INTERNET and rely on traditional 'bricks and mortar' business methods. 'Clicks' companies, named after the click of a computer mouse, use nothing but the Internet. A third type are the 'bricks and clicks' companies that combine online and traditional methods. Analysts believe that eventually there will be only 'bricks' and 'clicks' companies, all others having been eliminated by competition or bought by rivals. *See also* CLICKS AND MORTAR.

**Brideshead Revisited.** A family saga novel (1945) by Evelyn Waugh (1903–66) about the aristocracy and the Catholic faith in the years 1923–39, subtitled 'The Sacred and Profane Memories of Captain Charles Ryder'. It is told in retrospect by Charles Ryder, whose army unit in the Second World War is billeted at Brideshead Castle, seat of the Marchmain family. When he was a student at Oxford, Charles was romantically involved with Sebastian Flyte, the charming but dissolute younger Marchmain son, owner of a TEDDY BEAR called Aloysius. In his letters, Waugh referred to the evolving novel as his 'M.O.' (Magnum Opus) and 'G.E.C.' (Great English Classic). A lavish and highly acclaimed television version was broadcast in 1981.

**Brides in the Bath.** In 1915 a Bristol antiques dealer, George Joseph Smith, was sentenced to death for the murder of three young women. He had bigamously married each one, using an alias, then insured his new wife's life or persuaded her to make a will in his favour. As the final stage in his plan he took each to a different lodging house and drowned her in the bath. A colourful story was long current that while the body of one of his victims was still in the bath, Smith went into the next room and played 'Nearer, my God to Thee' on the harmonium.

**Bride Stripped Bare by Her Bachelors, Even, The.** This painting on two large panels of glass by the Dadaist (*see* DADAISM) Marcel Duchamp (1887–1968) is also called *The Large Glass*. The work consists of meticulously painted but indecipherable fragments of machinery (although a coffee grinder is apparent). Duchamp worked on the piece between 1915 and 1923, in search of an ideal of 'painting of precision and beauty of indifference'. The painting is said by some to satirize the frustrations of physical love, and by others to satirize the cult of the machine.

**Bridge of San Luis Rey, The.** A novel (1927) by the US writer Thornton Wilder (1897–1975), which won the PULITZER PRIZE for fiction. 'On Friday noon, July the twentieth, 1714, the finest bridge in all Peru broke and precipitated five travellers into the gulf below.' Brother Juniper, a witness to the accident, works for six years, 'knocking at all the doors in Lima, asking thousands of questions', to investigate why God should have chosen those five to die. In the end his book is burned and he goes to the stake for heresy. The conclusion of the abbess, who as a nun brought up one of the victims, is that: 'There is a land of the living and a land of the dead, and the bridge is love, the only survival, the only meaning.' An interminable film version (1944) was directed by Rowland V. Lee.

**Bridge on the River Kwai, The.** A film (1957) adapted by Carl Foreman and Michael Wilson from the novel *The Bridge over the River Kwai* by Pierre Boulle. Directed by David Lean, it starred Alec Guinness as Colonel Nicholson, the commanding officer of British prisoners of war forced by the Japanese to build a railway bridge over the River Kwai in Burma during the Second World War. Nicholson was based on the real Lieutenant-Colonel Philip Toosey (d.1975), who was the senior officer in a Japanese prisoner of war camp at Tamarkan. Unlike the film character, Toosey actively assisted those who tried to escape and sanctioned various attempts to sabotage the two bridges his men were obliged to build. The two bridges, one wood and one metal, were disabled by Allied bombers but never totally destroyed as they are in the film.

**'Bridge Over Troubled Water'.** The title of a song and album by Simon and Garfunkel, released in 1970. The song, a gospel-influenced pop classic written by Paul Simon and sung by the angelic-sounding tenor of Art Garfunkel, can be compared with a number of late 1960s pop anthems (The Beatles' LET IT BE, Cat Stevens's 'Morning Has Broken' and George Harrison's 'My Sweet Lord') for its striving after a tone of almost religious tranquillity (the song had the working title of 'Hymn'). The title comes from the phrase 'I'll be your bridge over deep water', which Paul Simon had heard in a version of the gospel song 'Mary Don't You Weep' sung by the Rev. Claude Jeter and the Swan Silvertones.

**Bridges of Madison County, The.** A romantic novel (1993) by the US writer Robert James Waller (b.1939). The story, a novel within a novel, concerns Francesca, a housewife whose life is suddenly transformed, while her family is away, by Robert Kincaid, a man who asks for directions. He has come to Madison County, Iowa, to photograph the seven covered bridges in the location. They have a fleeting affair. Blaise Aguirre's *The Fridges of Madison County* (1997) is a parody. A handsomely crafted film version (1995) was directed by Clint Eastwood, who also took the role of Kincaid, playing opposite Meryl Streep. Many judged it an improvement on the original.

**Bridget Jones.** *See* Bridget JONES.

**Bridge too far.** A position reached that is too risky; a step that is 'one too many'. The phrase comes from the title of Cornelius Ryan's book *A Bridge too Far* (1974), made into a memorable film (1977), about the 1944 Allied airborne landings in Holland. These were intended to capture 11 bridges needed for the Allied invasion of Germany but the enterprise failed grievously at Arnhem. In advance of the operation General Frederick Browning is said to have protested to Field-Marshal Montgomery, who was in overall command: 'But, sir, we may be going a bridge too far.' The cliché is mainly found in journalistic use, and the formula 'an X too far' has taken on a life of its own, denoting something taken to excess:

> An empire too far.
> *Christian Science Monitor*, headline (13 February 2003)

> It was a scoop of truly global proportions … Last week, however, it was looking like a scoop too far. Former al-Jazeera television correspondent Alouni was sent to jail for seven years by a Spanish court, which deemed he had not just cultivated al-Qaeda connections … but had actively collaborated with them.
> *Mail & Guardian Online* (15 October 2005)

**Bridgewater Three.** Michael Hickey, Vincent Hickey and Jimmy Robinson, on the basis of evidence of a fourth man, Patrick Molloy, were jailed in 1978 for the murder of a 13-year-old newspaper boy, Carl Bridgewater, when he

disturbed their alleged robbery at Yew Tree Farm, Staffordshire. Molloy died in custody in 1981. The remaining three were released in 1997 when their convictions were declared unsafe following the discovery that the police had forged Vincent Hickey's signature. *See also* BIRMINGHAM SIX; GUILDFORD FOUR; WINCHESTER THREE.

**Brief Encounter.** A romantic film (1945) based on the play *Still Life* by Noël Coward, and with a screenplay by Coward, David Lean, Ronald Neame and Anthony Havelock-Allan. Directed by David Lean, it starred Trevor Howard and Celia Johnson as star-crossed lovers who meet by chance on a railway station but subsequently deny themselves the opportunity to share an extra-marital affair. Such was the iconic status of the film with postwar British audiences that the very phrase 'brief encounter' became virtually synonymous with a short-lived sexual liaison.

**Brief History of Time, A.** A book (1988), subtitled 'From the Big Bang to Black Holes', by the British theoretical physicist Stephen Hawking (b.1942), which attempts to explain to a lay audience his ideas about the beginning of the universe, the nature of space-time and black holes, and the possible synthesis of quantum mechanics with the theory of relativity. In it the author asks such questions as 'Why does the universe go to all the bother of existing?' In the final chapter Hawking concludes:

> If we find the answer to that [the reason for the existence of the universe, and of humanity], it would be the ultimate triumph of human reason – for then we would know the mind of God.

The book was a surprise success, remaining on the UK bestseller list for more than three years. Some readers even managed to finish it.

> His brain is the best in the world. I wanted to talk to him about the universe but he just wanted to watch the girls.
> PETER STRINGFELLOW: recalling a visit Hawking had made to his London club, quoted in *The Observer* (12 December 2004)

**Brigadoon.** The imaginary village in the Scottish Highlands that is the setting of the musical play by Frederick Loewe and Alan Jay Lerner of the same name (1947). It is a strange place of the past, discovered by two American tourists on the one day of its reawakening in the 20th century, when one of its inhabitants, disappointed in love, tries to leave it. Its name suggests a blend of 'Bridge of Doon', a genuine-sounding Scottish place-name (Brig o' Doon in Alloway, Ayrshire, features in Robert Burns's 'Tam o' Shanter'), and 'rigadoon', a lively dance for couples.

**Bright-eyed and bushy-tailed.** Alert and lively; RARIN' TO GO. The phrase, dating from the 1940s, is a stereotypical image of a squirrel. It was popularized by Bob Merrill's song 'Bright Eyed and Bushy Tailed' (1953), which has the lines:

> If the fox in the bush and the squirr'l in the tree be,
> Why in the world can't you and me be
> Bright eyed and bushy tailed and sparkelly as we
> can be.

**Bright lights.** The glitter and glamour of city life, especially as a lure to the country dweller. The phrase, of US origin and dating from the 1920s, is familiar from the film *Bright Lights* (1935) and from Jay McInerney's novel *Bright Lights, Big City* (1984), about the frenzied life of a young, coke-snorting fact checker in Manhattan. The latter was filmed under the same title in 1988.

**Brighton Rock.** An 'entertainment' (1938) by Graham Greene (1904–91), centring on crime and corruption in the seaside resort of Brighton, Sussex, with Pinkie, a young scarfaced hoodlum, as the antihero. It was the first of Greene's novels to explore the dilemmas he experienced in observing the Catholic faith, to which he had converted in 1926 in order to marry. 'Rock' here is the confection in the form of a cylindrical stick of hard peppermint-flavoured sugar, often pink on the outside, sold at holiday resorts, with the name of the place worked round the inside all the way down the stick. A successfully 'seedy' film version (1947), to whose script Greene contributed, was directed by John Boulting, with Richard Attenborough in the role of Pinkie. *See also* FIRST LINES OF NOVELS.

**Brighton Run.** An annual rally for veteran cars (*see* VINTAGE CAR) from Hyde Park in London to the promenade at Brighton in Sussex, a distance of 85km (53 miles). It is held on the first Sunday in November and commemorates the so-called 'Emancipation Run' made by 33 motorists between the two towns on 14 November 1896, the day of repeal of the Locomotive Act of 1865, limiting the speed of steam carriages to 6.4kph (4mph) in the country and 3.2kph (2mph) in the town, and raising it to 23kph (14mph). The run is commemorated in the film GENEVIEVE.

On the 1996 centenary run, a record 600 cars took part, of which 540 finished. Speeds ranged from just over 11kph (7mph) by an 1896 Lutzman to almost 121kph (75mph) by a 1903 Mercedes.

**Brighton School.** A group of pioneer film-makers who were based in the Brighton area at the beginning of the 20th century, among them G.A. Smith (1864–1959) and J.A. Williamson (1855–1933). They attached great importance to the close-up and are best remembered for *Rescued by Rover* (1905), a seven-minute drama showing a collie rescuing his master's baby from kidnappers.

**Brighton trunk murders.** A series of murders between the First and Second World Wars in which the victims were secreted in trunks and dispatched to the left-luggage office at Brighton railway station. The term is applied particularly to the murder of Violette Kaye, for which Tony Mancini (under whose bed Miss Kaye and her trunk were found) was tried and acquitted in 1933.

> In the 1920s and 1930s it was highly unusual in Brighton for a week to pass without the body of a dead woman turning up in a trunk.
> WILLIAM DONALDSON: *Brewer's Rogues, Villains and Eccentrics* (2002)

**Bright young things.** The YOUNG THINGS or FLAPPERS who originally made their presence known in fashionable society in the 1920s and 1930s. They were 'bright' in meretriciousness rather than mentality, and their heirs continue to thrive in the form of PARTY GIRLS and other 21st-century socialites.

> By 8pm on Friday the mood in the club has completely transformed. The main bar is spilling over with bright young things ordering vodka martinis.
> *The Times* (7 January 2000)

**Brilliant pebbles.** A code name for small heat-seeking missiles designed to intercept and destroy enemy weapons. The term originated as part of the STAR WARS vocabulary of the late 1980s, when a series of code names was employed to indicate the different levels of intelligence shown by weapons of different sizes. The largest and least intelligent were thus 'moronic mountains', the smaller and more intelligent were 'smart rocks' (*see* SMART BOMB), and those yet smaller and smarter were 'brilliant pebbles'. A fourth category in the series was 'savant sand'.

> The Pentagon has been pushing the smart rocks, while Congress has been championing the ground-based missiles. Mr Edward Teller advocates 'brilliant pebbles'.
> *The Economist* (4 February 1989)

**Brillo Pad.** The nickname of the right-wing Scottish journalist Andrew Neil (b.1949), editor of *The Sunday Times* (1983–94) and from 1996 to 2005 editor-in-chief of the newspaper group that owned *The Scotsman*. The nickname, awarded by *Private Eye*, refers to Neil's hair (said to resemble the brand of scouring pad) and to his abrasive manner.

**Bring home the bacon.** To provide the necessities of life; to achieve success. The suggestion is of earning enough to feed one's family. The expression dates from the 1920s but may allude to a much older game of catching a greased pig at a country fair, the winner gaining the pig.

**Bring Me the Head of Alfredo Garcia.** A Western (1974) directed by Samuel Peckinpah. The head in question belongs to the man who seduced a rich Mexican's daughter. As Gene Shalit wrote, 'Bring me the head of the studio that released this one.' The 2001 remake, more ploddingly entitled *The Mexican*, met with more muted critical acclaim.

**Bring something** or **someone on.** To introduce something or someone into the action. The usage probably had its origins in the notion of bringing something on to a stage or other public arena, but by the end of the 20th century it had carved a particular niche for itself in American English as a challenge or dare to those issuing a threat, as if to say 'Do your worst! I can handle it. In fact I'd welcome it.'

> If he [President George W. Bush] wants to have a debate about our service in Vietnam, here is my answer: 'Bring it on'.
>
> SENATOR JOHN KERRY: quoted in www.townhall.com
> (27 August 2004)
>
> President Bush said [on] Wednesday that American troops under fire in Iraq aren't about to pull out, and he challenged those tempted to attack US forces, 'Bring them on'.
>
> www.usatoday.com (2 July 2003)

The Hollywood teen film *Bring It On* (2000), starring Kirsten Dunst, is an uplifting tale of a squad of college cheerleaders in their quest for the US national championship. It was followed in 2004 by *Bring It On Again*.

**Bring tears to someone's eyes.** To evoke such sympathy or empathy from them that they weep. The phrase is frequently used ironically.

**Brinkmanship.** A term coined by the US Democratic politician Adlai Stevenson (1900–65) in 1956 (although he disclaimed originality), with particular reference to the policy of the Republican secretary of state J. Foster Dulles (a noted COLD WAR WARRIOR) as leading to the brink of war. In 1956 Dulles was quoted by *Life* magazine (16 January) as saying:

> The ability to get to the verge without getting into the war is the necessary art … We walked to the brink and we looked it in the face.

On 25 February, Stevenson said in a speech at Hartford, Connecticut:

> We hear the secretary of state boasting of his brinkmanship – the art of bringing us to the edge of the abyss.

The term, based on Stephen Potter's GAMESMANSHIP, found a subsequent general application in the field of politics, or in any area of negotiation.
*See also* EYEBALL TO EYEBALL.

**Brink's-Mat robbery.** A robbery that took place in November 1983 when a gang stole gold bars worth £26 million, belonging to Johnson Matthey, a firm of dealers in precious metals, from the Brink's-Mat security warehouse at Heathrow Airport. It was Britain's biggest robbery at the time. The confession of a corrupt security guard gave police their first lead in an investigation which lasted almost ten years and resulted in charges against some 30 people.

**Britain, Battle of.** *See* BATTLE OF BRITAIN.

**Britain, Festival of.** *See* FESTIVAL OF BRITAIN.

**Britain can take it.** These morale-boosting words were promulgated by the Ministry of Information during the early months of the Second World War. They were regarded as patronizing, however, and as portraying Britons in a humourless 'stiff upper lip' stereotype, and the slogan was soon dropped.

**Britain plc.** Business jargon for Britain regarded as a unified commercial concern or 'corporation' formed from all its registered companies. UK PLC is similarly used. *See also* PLC.

**Brit Art.** A media-created label (alternatively rendered as 'Britart') for a group of young British conceptual artists (including Damien Hurst, Rachel Whiteread and Tracey Emin) who rose to prominence during the 1990s with their often deliberately shocking works (exhibited, for example, in the Royal Academy's *Sensation* exhibition in 1997). Their main patron was the millionaire advertising magnate, Charles Saatchi. Several of these artists' works, owned by Saatchi, went up in flames in a 2004 warehouse fire. The exponents of Brit Art are also known as YBAs (Young British Artists). *See also* EVERYONE I'VE EVER SLEPT WITH 1963–95; PHYSICAL IMPOSSIBILITY OF DEATH IN THE MIND OF SOMEONE LIVING; STUCKISM.

**Brit Awards.** Annual awards made in various categories for British pop and rock music, with 'Brit' both short for 'British' and an acronym of 'British Record Industry'. The first awards were held as the British Record Industry 'Britannia Centenary' Awards at the Wembley Conference Centre on 18 October 1977, the winners receiving recognition for their achievements over the previous 25 years. They included the groups Queen and Procol Harum, the cellist Jacqueline du Pré and the singers Cliff Richard and Julie Covington. It was intended to hold the ceremony annually, but this happened only from 1982. The formal title British Record Industry Awards was shortened to its present form in 1989. The occasion that year, televised live, was something of an embarrassment, with the presenters confusing stars, talking over videos and battling with lengthy pauses, but in the 1990s the event became much slicker and more high-profile. The awards are colloquially known as 'the Brits'.

The Brits have gone from a national laughing-stock to a must-be-there event … Appear on The Brits and you are guaranteed to sell albums.

*Sunday Express* (27 February 2000)

**British bulldog.** A team game popular among boys, particularly of the scouting variety (and sometimes among girls, of the guiding variety). Members of one team dash across a field or other space and attempt to break through a line formed by the other team, who in turn attempt to catch them. A caught player is hoisted off the ground with the cry 'British bulldog!' and then joins the opposing team. The name dates from the jingoistic days of the early 20th century, but the game was still being played in the 1960s.

**British disease.** An uncomplimentary term used abroad with reference to the prevalence of strikes and industrial action in Britain during the 1970s.

**British invasion.** The transformation of the US popular music scene by British performers in the 1960s, especially The BEATLES and The ROLLING STONES. Some acts, such as Chad and Jeremy, were famous in the United States but almost unknown at home. The 'second British invasion' was by PUNK ROCK and NEW WAVE in the early 1980s.

**British Legion.** An organization for promoting the welfare of ex-service personnel, especially the aged, sick and disabled. It was founded in 1921 largely through the exertions of Field Marshal Earl Haig (1861–1928), and it became the Royal British Legion in 1971. There are many local branches, and much of the money is raised by the sale of artificial poppies on POPPY DAY. *See also* ARMISTICE DAY; REMEMBRANCE DAY.

**British Library.** The British national library, formed in 1973 from the British Museum library. It opened in new premises at St Pancras, London, in 1998.

**British National Party.** *See* NATIONAL FRONT.

**British restaurant.** A government-subsidised restaurant operating in Britain in the Second World War. The designation 'Communal Feeding Centre' was originally proposed, but Winston Churchill suggested 'British restaurant' as more appropriate and attractive.

**Britpop.** British pop music, particularly of the type that emerged among the young bands of the mid-1990s such as Oasis and Blur, which were influenced by The BEATLES.

There is an eagerness to accept that our national culture is exemplified by Britpop, even at a time when the 'Brit' is as meaningless as the pop.

ROGER SCRUTON: in *The Times* (14 April 1999)

**Brittas Empire, The.** A television SITCOM screened from 1991 to 1996. It is set in a leisure centre and depicts the goings-on among the staff under the manager and his wife, the unlikeable and disaster-prone Gordon Brittas, played by Chris Barrie, and his dazed and confused wife, Helen, played by Pippa Haywood. The punning title contains a rather obvious historical allusion.

**Broadband.** A fast way of connecting to the INTERNET, which may be wireless or may utilize ordinary telephone lines, but which uses (literally) a wider bandwidth to allow more information to flow at greater speeds. In an age where large files of information are traded across the Internet – software downloads, music downloads, PODCASTS, even feature-film downloads – broadband has comprehensively superseded the earlier, slower dial-up connections. In mid-2006 *The Times* estimated that 10 million homes in the UK possessed the technology, a surge hastened by the sharp reductions in price for broadband services offered by ISP companies in stiff competition.

**Broad in the beam.** Well fleshed around the hips and buttocks. The expression dates from the 1940s and derives from the nautical expression for a ship that is 'wide in the waist'.

**Broadway Boogie-Woogie.** This painting (1942–3) represented a major stylistic breakthrough for the Dutch painter Piet Mondrian (1872–1944). For decades Mondrian had been painting 'neo-plasticist' abstracts consisting of no more than a few rectangles and lines with provocative titles such as *Composition in Yellow and Blue* (1929). Indeed, latterly colour itself had begun to absent itself from his works. Then, when the Second World War forced him to New York in 1940, the shock of being separated from his native polders seems to given him a much-needed shot in the arm. The daringly entitled *Broadway Boogie-Woogie* not only brings back primary colours, but includes more lines and rectangles than you could count in one glance. It is regarded as one of his finest works. Mondrian was to become even less inhibited in his *Victory Boogie-Woogie*, in which the geometrical shapes are much more loosely painted. This work was unfinished at the time of Mondrian's death.

**Brockton Bomber.** The nickname of the US heavyweight boxer Rocky MARCIANO, who hailed from Brockton, Massachusetts. He was also known as the Blockbuster and as the Rock from Brockton.

**Brompton cocktail.** A powerful painkiller and sedative consisting of vodka or other liquor laced with morphine and sometimes also with cocaine. The preparation is used to relieve pain caused by cancer and is said to be named after Brompton Hospital, London, where it was first applied to this end.

**Bronx cheer.** The rude sound made by those who BLOW A RASPBERRY to express their contempt. The allusion is to the uncouth behaviour of residents of the Bronx, New York. The expression dates from the 1920s.

**Brooklands.** The site of the world's first custom-built motor-racing circuit, near Weybridge in Surrey. It was the enterprise of Hugh Locke-King, a Surrey landowner, who in 1907 paid £150,000 to build a concrete racetrack in the form of an oval course with heavily banked curves. It was soon widely used by car manufacturers for testing new models. In its first year a record was set up by Selwyn Edge for travelling 2546km (1582 miles) in 24 hours at an average speed of 106kph (66mph), a figure that remained unbeaten for 18 years. Racing continued until the Second World War, during which the track was given over to aircraft production. It was not restored subsequently.

**Brooklyn Dodgers.** This famous baseball team was formed in Brooklyn, New York, in 1883. Around the turn of the 20th century it added the name 'Dodgers', from 'Trolley Dodgers', a general nickname for the residents of Brooklyn, referring to their reputed skill at evading ('dodging') the streetcars on the growing trolley system. Other names for the team included the Bridegrooms, following a run of marriages by team members in 1889; the Superbas, from 'Hanlon's Superbas', a popular theatrical group at the turn of the century, as a compliment to Ned Hanlon, their manager at this time; and the Robins, after their manager from 1914 to 1931, Wilbert Robinson.

**Brothel creepers.** Soft-soled suede shoes, suitable for creeping into and out of a brothel. Footwear of this type was popular among TEDDY BOYS in the 1950s.

> Look at photographs of [violinist Nigel] Kennedy six years ago and you see a straight-laced young chap with awfully sensible hair and polite shoes (none of the brothel creepers or cowboy boots he favours today).
>
> Q (September 1990)

**Brother Cadfael.** *See* Brother CADFAEL.

**'Brother Can You Spare a Dime?'** A song (1932) by Yip Harburg (1898–1981) and Jay Gorney that became an iconic evocation of Depression-era America. The narrator, an American Everyman who is now unemployed and reduced to begging, tells how he fought for his country, ploughed the fields and helped to build railroads and skyscrapers. Harburg himself wrote of him:

> He's bewildered. Here is a man who had built his faith and hope in this country … Then came the crash. Now he can't accept the fact that the bubble has burst. He still believes. He still has faith. He just doesn't understand what could have happened to make everything go so wrong.

**Brown, Father.** The priest and detective who appears in the short stories by G.K. Chesterton (1874–1936), which were collected in *The Innocence of Father Brown* (1911) and other books. Although outwardly meek and modest, he has a shrewd understanding of the criminal mind. His most fearsome adversary is the French thief Flambeau. His most powerful assistant is his God. Chesterton based him on the Irish priest Monsignor John O'Connor (1870–1952), a well-known figure in Catholic literary circles and the author's lifelong friend.

**Brown, William.** *See* WILLIAM.

**Brown bagger.** An Americanism for a person who carries their lunch to school or work in a brown paper bag. Brown-bagging is also the carrying of drink in such a bag to a club or restaurant, a concealment necessary to conform to the law in some states.

**Brown Bomber.** Joe Louis (1914–81), undefeated heavyweight champion of the world from 1937 until his retirement in 1949. On his return in 1950 he was defeated by Ezzard Charles and Rocky MARCIANO. He turned professional in 1934, winning 27 fights, all but 4 by knockouts. The phrase comes from his being an AFRICAN AMERICAN and from the great power of his punches.

**Browned off.** Fed up, disgruntled, disheartened. The slang phrase became popular in the Second World War. The reference is probably to a dish that has been overcooked. *See also* CHEESED OFF.

**Brown envelope.** An anonymous envelope in which personal or intimate information is delivered or illicit cash payments made, the latter typically to MOONLIGHTERS.

> Michael Stacpoole handed [Monica] Coghlan a sealed brown envelope containing £2000 in £50 notes to help her leave the country.
>
> *Sunday Times* (21 November 1999)

**Brownfield site.** A site for potential building development that has already had some development on it, as distinct from a GREENFIELD SITE. The green grass has gone, leaving the brown earth.

**Brownie.** A make of box camera manufactured by Kodak. The first model was introduced in 1900 and was named by George Eastman, the founder of Kodak, from the

'Brownies', the miniature humanoids who populated the children's books of the Canadian-born writer and illustrator Palmer Cox (1840–1928). Eastman's camera was cheap, simple and easy to operate and was especially aimed at children. Hence the appropriate name. *See also* BROWNIES.

**Brownie points.** Notional credit for something done to please or win favour. The expression probably relates to BROWN-NOSE but has become popularly associated with the BROWNIES, and is thus often spelt with a capital letter.

**Brownies.** Members of the junior section of the GIRL GUIDES, ostensibly so named from the colour of their uniform (originally all brown), but apparently originally alluding to the benevolent elves of Scottish folklore so called who haunted houses and carried out housework by night. Such duties would have accorded with the domestic tasks and 'good deeds' that the modern uniform wearers would have been encouraged to carry out.

**Browning Version, The.** A play (1949) by the British playwright Terence Rattigan (1911–77) about an ailing public school teacher who is humiliated both by his failure in his career and by his wife's infidelity. The title refers to a copy of Browning's translation of Aeschylus' *Agamemnon* that is presented to the teacher, Andrew Crocker-Harris, by one of his few admiring pupils. The character of Crocker-Harris was based on one of Rattigan's teachers at Harrow School, Coke Norris, who was similarly presented with a copy of the 'Browning version' (although possibly not by Rattigan himself). The role of Crocker-Harris was memorably played by Michael Redgrave in the 1951 film version and, less memorably, by Albert Finney in the 1994 remake.

**Brown-nose.** To curry favour; to behave sycophantically. The term relates to 'arse-licking'. *See also* BROWNIE POINTS.

**Brown Owl.** The name of the adult leader of a group of BROWNIES, her assistant being Tawny Owl. The names still popularly persist, although the two posts have been formally designated Brownie Leader and Assistant Brownie Leader respectively. The idea is that owls are wise, while brown (or tawny) is the colour of the Brownie uniform. Brown owl and tawny owl are alternative names for the same bird, *Strix aluco*.

**Brownshirts.** *See* SA.

**Brown sugar.** An African American slang term for an attractive black woman which crossed over into white slang vocabulary following the success of a rock song of the same title by The ROLLING STONES. The term also came to denote the drug HEROIN. The song, credited to Mick Jagger and Keith Richards, appears on the album STICKY FINGERS, released in 1971.

Gold coast slave ship bound for cotton fields
Sold in a market down in New Orleans
Scarred old slaver knows he's doing alright
Hear him whip the women, just around midnight
Ah, brown sugar how come you taste so good?
Ah, brown sugar just like a young girl should.

**Brown v. Board of Education of Topeka.** A legal case in which on 17 May 1954 the US Supreme Court ruled unanimously that racial segregation in public schools violated the 14th Amendment to the Constitution, which says that no state may deny equal protection of the laws to any person within its jurisdiction. Although the decision was limited to the public schools, it was believed to imply that segregation was not permissible in other public facilities.

**Browser.** *See* SURF THE NET.

**Brücke, Die.** (German, 'The Bridge'.) A group of German expressionist artists founded in Dresden in 1913 by four students of architecture: Fritz Bleyl (1880–1966), Erich Heckel (1883–1970), Ernst Ludwig Kirchner (1880–1938) and Karl Schmidt-Rottluff (1884–1976). The name was suggested by this last with reference to the group's admiration for the philosopher Nietzsche, who in *Also sprach Zarathustra* (1883–92) wrote: 'What is great about man is that he is a bridge and not a goal.' This dictum indicated the faith of the four in a happier and more creative future, to which their own work would lead as a bridge.

**Bruderhof.** (German, 'band of brothers'.) A Christian sect founded in Germany in 1921 who stressed the importance of communal property. They journeyed to Gloucestershire in England in 1937 when they were driven out by the NAZIS but to avoid internment in the Second World War left for Paraguay in 1941. They re-established themselves in Sussex in 1971. The men wore beards and dark trousers with braces. They supported themselves by making quality wooden toys in community workshops, and the women were clad in long skirts and headscarves or caps. Children first left the community at the secondary school stage. They later became known simply as the Christian Community. There are four other groups in the eastern United States.

**Bruges Group.** A group of anti-European (mainly Conservative MPs), named after a strongly worded speech made on 20 September 1988 by Margaret Thatcher, the IRON LADY, in Bruges, Belgium, in which she spoke out against closer European integration. In the 1992 general election some of the group stood as 'anti-federalists' against Conservative candidates. *See also* F-WORD.

**Brutalism.** A style of architecture created by the French architect Le Corbusier and his fellow modernist the German-born Ludwig Mies van der Rohe. It demanded a strictly functional approach to architectural design and was so named in 1954 by the English architects Peter and Alison Smithson with reference to Le Corbusier's post-1930 style, with its use of monumental sculptural shapes and raw, unfinished moulded concrete (the French for 'raw concrete' is *beton brut*, which is what the term 'brutalism' was based on, but the incidental connotations of cruel and heavy-handed overbearingness are often given precedence). Typical of the style are the buildings of the SOUTH BANK, especially the National Theatre (1976), and the Smithsons' own Hunstanton secondary modern school, Norfolk, built in 1950–3. By the end of the 1970s the style had fallen out of favour in many quarters.

**Brylcreem Boy.** The Middlesex and England cricketer and Arsenal footballer Denis Compton (1918–97), who became one of the first British sportsman to boost his appeal by appearing in advertisements, in his case for the hair preparation Brylcreem. Compton was one half of the MIDDLESEX TWINS.

**Brylcreem Boys.** A nickname for young Royal Air Force officers in the Second World War, famous for their well-groomed appearance and dashing exploits. One such young officer was pictured in advertisements for the named brand of hair cream. Hence the name, chiefly current among their army counterparts. *See also* GLAMOUR BOYS.

**BSE.** *See* MAD COW DISEASE.

**B Specials.** Members of the Ulster Special Constabulary, created in 1920 during the Anglo-Irish War (War of Independence) of 1919–21, and drawing many of its recruits from Edward Carson's Ulster Volunteers. They were paid an allowance for their one night's duty a week and were retained until late 1969, when following the outbreak of the TROUBLES they were disbanded and replaced by the ULSTER DEFENCE REGIMENT. There were also A Specials, on regular duty and full pay, and C Specials, unpaid auxiliaries. *See also* ROYAL ULSTER CONSTABULARY; ULSTER VOLUNTEER FORCE.

**BTM.** A colloquialism for the posterior, from 'bottom' as if written euphemistically 'b–t–m'. The term dates from the early years of the 20th century.

> No friendly wallop on the B.T.M.
> No loving arm-squeeze and no special look.
> JOHN BETJEMAN: *Selected Poems*, 'Beside the Seaside' (1948)

**Bubble dancer.** A woman who dances as if in the nude but actually covered by one or more balloons. A noted performer was the US actress Sally Rand, originally Helen

Gould Beck (1904–79), who was long a fan dancer, using large fans made of ostrich feathers, before creating an alternative dance with 1.5m (5ft) elastic 'bubbles'.

**Bubblegum music.** Bland or repetitive pop music, designed to appeal to children and young teenagers, who blow bubblegum. Middle of the Road's 'Chirpy Chirpy Cheep Cheep' (1971) is an example. Bubblegum itself was first on sale in the United States in 1928, as Fleer's 'Dubble Bubble'.

> Pop tends to divide between the highly commercial 'bubble-gum' songs, which almost exclusively have lyrics of complete banality, and the heavy or progressive rock in which the singer is there but his lyrics cannot be made out.
> PETER COLE: in *Anatomy of Pop* (1970)

**Bubbles.** A childish substitution for the first name Beverly, as for the US soprano Beverly Sills (b.1929) and the actress Beverley Brooks, otherwise Patricia, Viscountess Rothermere (1929–92).

**Buchmanism.** An alternative name for MORAL REARMAMENT, from the name of the movement's founder, Frank Buchman (1878–1961).

**Bucket shop.** A firm or travel agency that sells cheap airline tickets, especially illegally. The term originated as US slang in the 1970s but has a much longer history, a bucket shop earlier being an unauthorized stockbroking firm that speculates fraudulently with its clients' funds. The original bucket shops of the late 19th century were low-class liquor stores selling small quantities of spirits that had been dubiously distilled in buckets.

**Buck House.** SLOANE RANGER jargon for Buckingham Palace. The expression, with its pun on 'buck' as a devilish dandy and its degrading of 'palace' to 'house', is vulgar rather than voguish, although the palace actually was Buckingham House originally. *See also* BECKINGHAM PALACE.

**Buck Rogers.** The famous spaceman hero was created by Philip Francis Nowlan for his magazine serial 'Armageddon: 2419' in *Amazing Stories* in 1928. The cartoonist Dick Calkins then seized on the character for his newspaper strip 'Buck Rogers in the 25th Century', and this ran continuously from 1929 until the late 1960s, becoming so well known that he essentially personified the whole SCIENCE FICTION genre. In 1932 Buck made the transition to radio and subsequently to a cinema serial (1939), starring Buster Crabbe. His avowed intent, while planet warred against planet with death rays, fleets of spaceships and the like, was to save the universe from total destruction.

**Buck stops here.** The responsibility rests with me. The expression dates from the 1940s and alludes to the 19th-century phrase 'to pass the buck', meaning to evade blame or responsibility or shift it on to someone else. The US term comes from the game of poker, in which it is said to refer to the buckhorn knife that was placed in front of a player to indicate that he was the next dealer. When he had dealt, he 'passed the buck' to another player. President Harry S. Truman famously had a sign on his desk in the Oval Office saying 'The buck stops here.'

**Buck the trend.** To oppose or run counter to a general tendency, as of a company whose shares rise on the market while most are falling. There is an allusion to 'buck' as a male horned animal such as a deer or (originally) a goat, and probably also to 'butt', the way in which such an animal combats another. The term is usually applied positively and approvingly.

**Buddha of Suburbia, The.** A novel (1990) by Hanif Kureishi (b.1954) about racial attitudes in southeast London. The Buddha of the title is the narrator's Indian father, who precipitates a round of sexual musical chairs by leaving his English wife and setting up home with another English-woman, regarded as a guru at her parties in the suburbs of south London. Karim, the novel's bisexual narrator, becomes an actor, goes to New York, but yearns for London, to which he eventually returns, full of hope for a less complicated future. A television adaptation (1993) caused controversy for its alleged sexual explicitness.

**Buddy movie.** A US term dating from the 1960s for a film centring on comradeship between two men, i.e. between 'buddies'. Good examples are *Butch Cassidy and the Sundance Kid* (1969) and *The* STING (1973), both directed by George Roy Hill and both starring Paul Newman and Robert Redford.

**Buff-Hoon.** *See* GEOFF WHO?

**Buffy the Vampire Slayer.** A young American girl who wants to be normal but instead has been chosen as 'The Slayer', and given the power to hunt and destroy vampires. Her full name is Buffy Summers, and she first appeared in the rather feeble film of this name (1992), in which she was played by Kristy Swanson. She made a much more effective transfer to the television screen in 1997, with her role taken by the 'scream queen' Sarah Michelle Gellar and the location changed from Los Angeles to Sunnydale. Here, in between homework and dating, she wrangles with bloodsuckers, Inca mummies and the like. A spin-off, *Angel* (1999), followed the trail of the eponymous vampire who had now renounced evil to become Buffy's main love interest. Buffy's television career ended after seven series in 2003, whilst *Angel* ran until 2004.

**Bugger Bognor!** A retort allegedly made by George V in his last illness when a courtier, seeking to lift His Majesty's spirits, remarked that if he continued to make good progress he would soon be able to enjoy a few weeks' recuperation at Bognor Regis, a salubrious seaside resort in West Sussex. The town was originally plain Bognor but in 1929 was granted its royal suffix, Latin for 'of the king', as a token of appreciation by the king after spending an earlier period of convalescence there. The king's 'official' last words were 'How is the Empire?'

**Bugger's Opera, The.** An unknown wag thus dubbed the all-male opera *Billy Budd*, created by the gay triumvirate of Benjamin Britten, E.M. Forster and Eric Crozier, and with Britten's partner Peter Pears singing in the first performance in 1951. The nickname plays on John Gay's *The Beggar's Opera* (1728), produced by the theatre manager John Rich. It was said that the enormous success of the latter work 'made Gay rich and Rich gay'. *See also* ALDEBURGH FESTIVAL.

**Buggins' turn.** The principle of awarding promotion by rotation rather than on individual merit. Buggins is a supposedly common surname, but there were only two in the 1980 London telephone directory. The term was certainly current by 1917, when Lord Fisher used it in a letter in regard to an appointment. It may go back to 1861, when Trollope gave the name Buggins to a civil servant in *Framley Parsonage*.

The name itself is familiar in another context from 'Grandma Buggins', a tiresome old lady played by Mabel Constanduros in a radio series that ran from 1925 to the late 1940s.

**Bughouse Square.** A US nickname for any city park or centre where tramps, vagrants and the mentally disturbed gather. The sobriquet is particularly associated with Union Square, New York, and Washington Square Park, Chicago. The latter gained fame in the 1920s and 1930s for its numerous public speakers on political and philosophical subjects, with the orators standing on boxes or crates to be better seen and heard over the heads of the listeners and participants below. *See also* SPEAKERS' CORNER.

**Bugs Bunny.** The cartoon rabbit made his first appearance in a Warner Brothers animated short in 1938. He was the creation of Chuck Jones and Tex Avery, and his inimitable voice was produced by Mel Blanc. He went on to star in comics and on television. His catchphrase, 'What's up, Doc?', was used for the title of a comedy film of 1972. He was to have been called Jack Rabbit, but in the end was named after the infamous West Coast gangster, Benjamin 'Bugsy' Siegel (*c*.1906–47), whose colourful life and violent death were the subject of the film *Bugsy* (1991).

**Builder's bum.** The exposure to public view of the upper part of a person's buttocks, including the upper part of the inter-cheek fissure, especially as occasioned by incautious bending over. The term, which is first recorded in 1988, reflects a perception that workers on building sites are particularly prone to such revelations. An alternative in the same vein is 'plumber's bum' (or, in American English, 'plumber's butt').

> In a move to make the 'builder's bum' and unsightly beer bellies a distant memory, the contractor Amec issued its staff … with a strict dress code.
>
> *The Independent* (6 August 2001)

**Builder's tea.** Strong tea of a standard proprietary blend, as favoured by those with (in the opinion of Earl Grey drinkers) less sophisticated palates. In the merry-go-round of the English class system, manual workers such as builders are assumed to have undiscriminating tastes.

> Builder's tea generally is orange, with super-high levels of tannin – optionally drunk with three sugars.
>
> www.onegoodmove.org (26 May 2003)

**Built-in obsolescence.** *See* PLANNED OBSOLESCENCE.

**Bulge, Battle of the.** *See* BATTLE OF THE BULGE.

**Bull Connor.** A nickname of Eugene Connor, Commissioner of Public Safety in Birmingham, Alabama, whose brutal line with civil-rights protestors in 1963 caused a national outcry among liberal elements in the United States.

***Bulldog Drummond.*** An adventure thriller (1920), the first in a series, by Sapper (pen-name, from his war service in the Royal Engineers, known as Sappers, of Lieutenant-Colonel H.C. McNeile; 1888–1937). Subtitled 'The Adventures of a Demobilized Officer Who Found Peace Dull', it features a hard-drinking, athletic, ex-army, amateur anti-crime agent of the Robin Hood school, who always manages somehow to keep on the right side of the law, although his actions and attitudes are hopelessly racist, protofascist and anti-Semitic. The nickname Bulldog (his real name is Hugh), denoting tenacity, comes from 'We are the boys of the bulldog breed', in a jingoistic music-hall song of the times by Ian Colquhoun and Arthur Reece, 'Sons of the Sea, All British Born' (1897). Drummond was based on the soldier and writer Gerard Fairlie (*c*.1900–83), but his character also displays traits of 'Sapper' himself. A silent film version (1922), with Carlyle Blackwell in the title role, was followed by a lengthy series of British and US Bulldog Drummond films of varying quality. The last was *Some Girls Do* (1970), a feeble sequel to *Deadlier than the Male* (1967), with Richard Johnson as Drummond played *à la* James BOND, for whom he was undoubtedly the inspiration.

Sapper, Buchan, Dornford Yates, practitioners in that school of Snobbery with Violence that runs like a thread of good-class tweed through twentieth-century literature.

> ALAN BENNETT: *Forty Years On* (1969)

**Bulldozer, Le.** A nickname given to Jacques Chirac (b.1932), president of France since 1995 (and ex-officio co-prince of Andorra), on account of his *modus operandi* – dogged determination rather than flair, according to some commentators. It was Georges Pompidou, prime minister of France under President de Gaulle in the 1960s, who first dubbed Chirac 'mon bulldozer' when he was on Pompidou's personal staff. Chirac's ways with women have also earned him the nickname 'Jumping Jacky'.

**Bullet and the ballot box, The.** A phrase that encapsulates the policy of Sinn Féin in Northern Ireland from 1981 until the ceasefire of 1997. Another version is 'the ARMALITE and the ballot box', which is closer to the origin of the policy as enunciated by Danny Morrison (b.1953), Sinn Féin's director of publicity, at the party's annual conference in Dublin on 31 October 1981:

> Who here really believes that we can win the war through the ballot box? But will anyone here object if, with a ballot paper in one hand and the Armalite in the other, we take power in Ireland?

The policy emerged in the wake of the increase in support for the IRA and Sinn Féin in the wake of the deaths of the IRA hunger strikers that year.

The collocation of ballots and bullets precedes all this by more than a century, however:

> To give victory to the right, not bloody bullets, but peaceful ballots only, are necessary
>
> ABRAHAM LINCOLN: speech (18 May 1858)

The version of Lincoln's speech usually quoted is: 'The ballot is stronger than the bullet.'

**Bullet train.** A type of Japanese high-speed train, so nick-named in the West because of its shape. The first such train ran on the *Shinkansen* ('new trunk line') between Osaka and Tokyo in 1964. There are two types of service: the fast limited-stop trains called *Hikari* ('Lightning') and the fast stopping trains called *Kodama* ('Echo').

**Bullfrog of the Pontine Marshes.** A derisive nickname used by Winston Churchill in the Second World War for the Italian Fascist leader Benito Mussolini (1883–1945). *See also* DUCE.

**Bullying-Manner.** A nickname of Sir Reginald Manningham-Buller (later Lord Dilhorne, 1905–80), the Conservative attorney general from 1954 to 1962.

**Bumfuck, Egypt.** In US military slang, an extremely remote place, to which, if one is very unlucky, one will be posted. First recorded in 1972, it is often abbreviated for euphemistic purposes to 'B.F.E.'

**Bummery.** *See* WOBBLIES.

**Bump and grind.** The thrusting of the pelvis and rotating of the hips by a dancer, typically a striptease artist, imitating an act of sexual intercourse.

**Bump off.** To murder. The allusion is to giving someone a 'push'. The expression originated in the US underworld in the early years of the 20th century.

**Bum rap.** A false accusation; an unfair criminal sentence. The expression arose as US underworld slang in the 1920s. 'Bum' means 'bad', and 'rap' is the charge with which one is 'hit'.

**Bums on seats.** A paying audience viewed as a source of income.

> The massed Partick Thistle fans in the audience were ecstatic, everyone else looked a mite baffled. But that's your fragmented post-modern culture, isn't it? It makes no claims to universality; just puts neatly-labelled bums on seats.
> *The Guardian* (11 May 1993)

**Bum's rush.** Forcible ejection from a room or building. An expression of US origin with reference to the throwing out of an undesirable customer (as a bum might be) from a bar. To give someone the bum's rush is by extension to dismiss a person regarded as unsuitable or useless.

**Bum to mum.** A motto for sexual abstinence before an important sporting occasion, as promulgated by the management among Australian Rules footballers in the 1970s. To unpack the somewhat dense imagery, in the conjugal bed the player's back must remain turned towards his wife ('mum') (it was assumed in those more innocent days that his partner would be married to him, and indeed female).

**Bundle of fun** or **laughs.** Something amusing, cheerful or enjoyable. The expression is mostly encountered in the negative.

> There is no way in which Poulenc's opera [*The Carmelites*] can be dressed up in a review as a bundle of laughs. Quite the opposite.
> *The Times* (22 May 1999)

**Bundle of joy.** A baby, especially one not yet born and lovingly longed for.

**Bundle of laughs.** *See* BUNDLE OF FUN.

**Bundle** or **bag of nerves.** In a tense or apprehensive state, as: 'He was a real bundle of nerves before his driving test.'

**Bungalow Bill.** A nickname of the Conservative politician Bill Wiggin, appointed shadow Welsh Secretary in 2003 (although he was born in London and represents Leominster) and shadow minister for agriculture and fisheries in 2005. The nickname plays on Buffalo Bill, and the fact that his critics accuse Wiggin of having 'nothing upstairs'. *See also* WHITE ALBUM.

**Bungee-jumping.** An EXTREME SPORT that came into vogue in the early 1990s, consisting of jumping off a bridge or other high point with a strong elastic cord tied to one's ankles. The potentially lethal activity soon spread commercially to fair and amusement park operators, who used construction cranes to raise up metal cages for the jumpers. The word derives from bungie or bungy as a familiar term for an India rubber or eraser at the turn of the 20th century, the name itself perhaps being imitative of the object's 'squashiness'. Bungee-jumping is said to have had its beginnings on Pentecost Island in the South Pacific, where vines were used for similar jumps made by native boys in an ancient rite of passage.

**Bun in the oven.** A foetus in the womb. The concept is of having something 'cooking' within. *See also* IN THE CLUB; UP THE DUFF.

**Bunker, Archie.** The US equivalent of Alf GARNETT in the television comedy series *All in the Family* (1971–9) and the subsequent *Archie Bunker's Place* (1979–83). He is a loudmouthed bigot who is not slow to voice his low opinion of ethnic minorities. His impact on American viewers was if anything more shocking than Garnett's on his British counterparts.

**Bunny-boiler.** A deranged woman who stalks or otherwise persecutes a former lover who jilted her. The term, which is first recorded in 1990, alludes to a character (played by Glenn Close) in the 1987 Adrian Lyne film *Fatal Attraction* who kills the pet rabbit belonging to the daughter of her former lover and boils it in a saucepan.

**Bunny girl.** A nightclub hostess whose somewhat skimpy costume includes a fluffy, rabbit-like tail and a head-dress with long ears, like those of a rabbit. They were introduced by Hugh Hefner and Victor Lownes in the PLAYBOY Club on Park Lane, London, in 1966. Thousands of young women applied for the £34-a-week job, which involved wearing the cruelly boned costume, serving drinks with a special 'Bunny Dip', retaining a fixed smile for hours on end and keeping the fluffy tail fluffy. Miscreants were made to stand in a corner facing the wall. The name apparently derived from the notion that the girls provided male clients with an evening's chase.

Hugh Hefner might never have made it to the big time if he had called his girls rabbits instead of bunnies. He probably chose bunny because he wanted something close to, but not quite so obvious as, kitten or cat – the all-time winners for connotating female sexuality.

ALLEEN PACE NILSEN: *Sexism and Language* (1977)

**Bunny hug.** A type of dance in ragtime rhythm in which the couple hold each other closely, popular in the United States in the early 20th century.

**Bunny-hugger.** A disparaging term for animal lovers of a sentimental bent, as opposed to hard-nosed conservationists. Bunny-huggers will object to any proposed cull of animals that have become pests, such as introduced hedgehogs in the Outer Hebrides (which threaten the breeding birds), or grey squirrels (*see* RATS WITH GOOD PR) anywhere in Britain (which threaten the continued existence of the native red), or those so troubled by the fate of farmed minks that they release them into the wild, where they decimate the indigenous wildlife. Some regard the term as a badge of honour:

A bunnyhugger? The term is meant to be derogatory, as a description of anyone who cares about justice for animals, who has compassion for animals, who supports the concepts of establishing rights for animals, or is opposed to legal or institutionalized cruelty toward animals. I don't believe I've ever literally hugged a bunny, as a hug of any intensity would undoubtedly hurt them. But I plead guilty on all counts to being a bunnyhugger.

BARRY KENT MACKAY: on the website of the Animal Liberation Front

**Bunter, Billy.** A fat or greedy boy or man. The name is that of the fat and greedy schoolboy in the stories by 'Frank Richards' (Charles Hamilton) published between 1908 and 1961. His full name is William George Bunter. He is bespectacled, wears check trousers and attends GREYFRIARS, where he is known to his friends as the Fat Owl of the Remove. His favourite exclamation is 'Yarooooh!' He has a sister, Bessie Bunter, whose adventures are chronicled separately.

**Bupkis.** (Yiddish, 'beans'). In US slang, absolutely nothing at all. The word came into English, via Jewish American speakers, in the early 1940s.

BTW [By the way], the Gore endorsement means bupkis to me. I thought the guy was a weenie in 2000.

*Scripting News* (9 December 2003)

**Burberry.** *See* CHAV.

**Burgess and Maclean.** Two notorious British traitors, Guy Burgess (1911–63) and Donald Maclean (1913–83), who secretly worked as agents of the Soviet Union while serving as diplomats in the Foreign Office. Both had been recruited to the communist cause while at Cambridge in the 1930s (*see* CAMBRIDGE SPY RING), and served Soviet interests throughout the Second World War and the early part of the COLD WAR. Warned in 1951 that British and US agents were becoming suspicious of Maclean, both men disappeared, nothing being heard of them until 1956 when they emerged in Moscow. It turned out in 1963 that they had been warned by a 'third man' from their Cambridge circle, the intelligence officer Kim Philby (1912–88), who that year defected to the Soviet Union.

In 1979 it was made public that a 'fourth man' from the same Cambridge circle, Anthony Blunt (1907–83), had confessed in 1964 to helping to arrange the flight of Burgess and Maclean. Blunt had served in MI5 during the war, before resuming a career as a distinguished art historian and becoming surveyor of the Queen's pictures. There was a public outcry that his role had been kept secret while he was still serving the Queen, and he was stripped of his knighthood. In 1991 John Cairncross, who had served in the Treasury, at Bletchley Park (*see* ULTRA) and with MI6 during the Second World War, confessed to being the FIFTH MAN in the spy ring, Soviet intelligence sources having spoken of 'the magnificent five'. *See also* the MAGNIFICENT SEVEN.

**Burlington Bertie.** A would-be elegant 'man-about-town' or 'masher', personified by Vesta Tilley in a popular song of this name by Harry B. Norris (1900). The song below is a parody, written by William Hargreaves for his wife, the male impersonator Ella Shields.

I'm Burlington Bertie:
I rise at ten thirty
And saunter along
Like a toff;
I walk down the Strand
With my gloves on my hand,
And I walk down again
With them off.

WILLIAM HARGREAVES: 'Burlington Bertie from Bow' (1914)

**BURMA.** *See* LOVERS' ACRONYMS.

**Burma Road.** The route that was made in 1937–9 to open up the western interior of China by communication with the sea and that ran from Lashio to Kunming in Yunnan, a distance of 1240km (770 miles). It was the chief highway for supplies to China during the Second World War until the Japanese cut it in 1941. It was recaptured in 1945.

**Burn, baby, burn.** An AFRICAN AMERICAN extremist slogan

current during the riots of August 1965 in the Watts district of Los Angeles, in which 34 people were killed and whole blocks destroyed by fire. The words were adopted for the title of a popular song of 1974 by the duo Hudson-Ford, but here they had a sexual connotation.

**Burn bag.** A receptacle for secret documents that are to be officially destroyed by burning. The term has long been in use in intelligence work but was brought before the public in connection with the WATERGATE investigations.

**Burnham scale.** The standard salary scale for teachers in state schools, named after Harry Lawson Webster Levy-Lawson, 1st Viscount Burnham (1862–1933), chairman of the Standing Joint Committee of Education Authorities and Teachers that was set up on 12 September 1919.

**Burp gun.** In US slang, a machine gun. During the Second World War, the term was applied particularly to a type of machine pistol used by the German army, and later, in the 1950s, it was transferred to a kind of Soviet-manufactured submachine gun.

**Burrell Collection.** In 1944 the shipping magnate William Burrell (1861–1958) endowed Glasgow with a magnificent collection of 9000 artefacts and paintings, ranging from Greek and Egyptian antiquities to European medieval stained glass and paintings spanning 500 years. The bequest, one of the greatest to a city, stipulated that the works be displayed in a rural setting close to Glasgow. Since 1983 they have been housed in a museum designed to admit natural light and afford parkland views through high glass walls.

**Bury My Heart at Wounded Knee.** A historical study (1971) by Dee Brown (1908–2002) of the conquest of the American West and the destruction of the Native American tribes. The title comes from the last verse of a poem, 'American Names' (1927), by Stephen Vincent Benét:

I shall not rest quiet in Montparnasse.
I shall not lie easy in Winchelsea.
You may bury my body in Sussex grass,
You may bury my tongue at Champmédy.
I shall not be there, I shall rise and pass.
Bury my heart at Wounded Knee.

Wounded Knee was the site of the battle between US army forces and Native Americans on the Sioux reservation in South Dakota in 1890, in the course of which Chief Sitting Bull was killed.

**Busboy.** In the United States a young man who clears dirty dishes from tables in a restaurant or cafe, so called from the

four-wheeled cart or trolley that he manoeuvres, as if driving a bus.

**Busby's Babes.** A nickname for the younger members of Manchester United football team, coached into a new winning side by Matt (later Sir Matthew) Busby (1909–94) after the loss of eight of their number in an air crash at Munich on 6 February 1958. Busby was himself badly injured in the disaster.

**Bush Doctrine.** A policy enunciated by President George W. Bush (see DUBYA) in the wake of the 9/11 attacks, vis à vis his WAR ON TERROR. It can be summarized in a line from a speech he gave to a joint session of Congress on 20 September 2001:

Either you are with us, or you are with the terrorists.

By early in the next year he was saying (or threatening):

Many nations are realizing when we say you're either with us or against us, we mean it.

Bush appeared to extend this message to those countries that refused to support his war on Iraq in 2003 (see also BUSH'S POODLE). In November 2005 former President Jimmy Carter criticized this unilateralist stance in an article for the *Los Angeles Times*:

Even with our troops involved in combat and America facing the threat of additional terrorist attacks, our declaration of 'you are either with us or against us' has replaced the forming of alliances based on a clear comprehension of mutual interests, including the threat of terrorism.

**Bush's Poodle.** A disparaging nickname for Tony Blair, NEW LABOUR prime minister since 1997 (see also BLAIRISM; BLATCHERISM). The reference is to Blair's apparently unquestioning subservience to US president George W. Bush (see DUBYA) in foreign affairs, particularly concerning the Iraq War of 2003. At a press conference during Blair's visit to the newly re-elected Bush in Washington D.C., November 2004, the President was asked if he regarded Bush as his poodle, Blair interjected 'Don't answer that question.' In this respect, satirists also hold that Bush calls Blair 'My Little Tony' (punning on the equine equivalent of a Barbie doll, MY LITTLE PONY).

Suggestions that Blair had misled the British public in the run-up to the Iraq War led to a number of other nicknames, such as 'Tony Bliar' and 'B.Liar'. His dislike of ideology (especially democratic socialism) and reputation as the 'King of spin' have earned him the appellation 'Phoney Tony', while his (to some) creepily pious, gushily enthusiastic manner ('Trust me on this one') led *Private Eye* to turn him, in its spoof *St Albion Parish News*, into 'the Rev. A.R.P. Blair MA (Oxon)' (in this context, Bush is 'the Rev.

Dubya Bush of the Church of Latter Day Morons'). *Private Eye* also refers to him as 'the Dear Leader', the title more properly awarded to North Korea's dictator, Kim Jong-Il. In the comic *2000 AD* he is depicted as 'B.L.A.I.R. 1', a futuristic crime buster controlled by a Doctor Spin.

*See also* BAMBI.

**Business as usual.** A phrase indicating that normal business carries on as best it can under difficult circumstances. The expression was current before the First World War but became familiar in the Second World War when shops and businesses aimed to keep going in bomb-damaged premises. The term is something of a hyperbole, since conditions were hardly usual. The expression is also used, sometimes ironically, of any recurring event.

**Business of America is business, The.** *See* WHAT'S GOOD FOR GENERAL MOTORS IS GOOD FOR THE COUNTRY.

**Busted flush.** A person or thing that shows signs of great promise and fulfilment but that ultimately lets one down as a failure. The term comes from the game of poker, in which a busted flush is a flush (a hand of five cards all of the same suit) that one fails to complete.

> An insider said yesterday that a decision to limit [Mo] Mowlam's media appearances [as cabinet office minister] had already been taken. 'Mo is a busted flush,' he said.
>
> *Sunday Times* (6 February 2000)

**Buster.** A US nickname for a boy or young man, especially a 'beefy' one. The name sometimes replaces an individual's first name, as for the actor Buster Keaton (1895–1966), whose original names were Joseph Francis, the swimmer Buster Crabbe (1908–83), originally Clarence, and Buster Edwards (1931–94), one of the gang involved in the GREAT TRAIN ROBBERY, born Ronald Edwards; or it may complement it, as in the case of the US heavyweight boxer James 'Buster' Douglas (b.1960). Then there is Buster Gonad, the character with the 'unfeasibly' large testicles in the humorous comic VIZ.

**Butcher of Baghdad.** A nickname given by the Western press to Saddam Hussein (b.1937), president of Iraq from 1979 to 2003, after his invasion of Kuwait in 1990, which was purportedly accompanied by widespread atrocities.

**Butcher of Broadway.** The nickname of the feared and corpulent New York drama critic Alexander Woollcott (1887–1943), described by *Life* magazine as 'testy as a wasp and much more poisonous' (30 October 1939).

**Butcher of Kurdistan.** *See* CHEMICAL ALI.

**Butcher of Lyons.** (French *boucher de Lyon*.) Klaus Barbie (1913–91), head of the GESTAPO in Lyons from 1942 to 1944, was so nicknamed because of his alleged torture and murder of French Resistance fighters and others (*see* MAQUIS). Barbie was held responsible for the deaths of 4000 people, including French Resistance leader Jean Moulin (1899–1943), and the deportation of 7500 others. He was sentenced to life imprisonment by a French court in 1987, having been extradited from Bolivia.

**Butcher of Prague.** *See* the HANGMAN.

**Butcher of the Balkans.** A nickname given to Slobodan Milosevic (1941–2006), president of Serbia (1989–97) and of the Federal Republic of Yugoslavia (i.e. Serbia and Montenegro) (1997–2000). A former communist, he fanned the flames of Serbian nationalism in the 1990s, leading to wars in Croatia and Bosnia and attempts to expel the ethnic Albanian population of the Serbian province of Kosovo (*see* ETHNIC CLEANSING), the latter prompting NATO airstrikes against Serbia. In 1999 he was indicted by the UN's International Criminal Tribunal for the Former Yugoslavia for genocide in Bosnia, violations of the Geneva Conventions in Croatia and Bosnia, and crimes against humanity in Kosovo. After he was toppled from power by a peaceful revolution in 2000, he was handed over to the international war crimes tribunal in the Hague, where he insisted on defending himself, while denying the authority of the court. He died of a heart attack while in custody, before the completion of the trial.

**Butlin's.** The popular holiday camps of this name were the enterprise of Sir William ('Billy') Butlin (1899–1980), who came over from Canada in 1921. He opened the first holiday camp on the site of a former sugarbeet field near Skegness, Lincolnshire, on Easter Saturday, 11 April 1936 with capacity of 1000. The camps evolved into modern holiday centres, with a variety of amenities and entertainments on tap for both residents and visitors, reaching a peak in 1972 with one million bookings. Regular features were the broadcast call 'Wakey, Wakey!' to begin the day and the presence of REDCOATS to entertain and organize.

**Butskellism.** Consensus politics characteristic of the 1960s and 1970s, when there was a measure of agreement between the left wing of the Conservative Party and the right wing of the LABOUR PARTY. The name combines two representative MIDDLE OF THE ROAD figures, RAB Butler and the Labour leader Hugh Gaitskell (1906–63). *See also* BLATCHERISM.

**Butterflies in one's stomach** or **tummy.** A nervous fluttering sensation in one's body experienced before a formidable venture. The expression dates from the turn of the 20th century and is often shortened to simply 'butterflies'.

> 'I always have butterflies when I open Parliament,' she [Queen Elizabeth II] said.
>
> *Sunday Times* (25 January 1959)

**Butterfly effect.** The notion, in CHAOS THEORY, that a very small difference in the initial state of a physical system can make a significant difference to the state at some later time. The allusion is to the title of a paper delivered by the US meteorologist and mathematician Edward N. Lorenz to the American Association for the Advancement of Science on 29 December 1979 in Washington: 'Predictability: Does the flap of a butterfly's wings in Brazil set off a tornado in Texas?'

**Buy the farm.** To die. The expression is of US origin and dates from the Second World War. The origin may lie with fighter pilots, whose pipe dream was to give up flying, buy a farm and settle into peaceful retirement. Alternatively, the allusion may be to training flights crashing in a farmer's field, causing the farmer to sue for damages. As the pilot usually dies in such a crash, he has effectively bought the farm with his life.

**Buzz bomb.** A nickname for the V-1 flying bomb in the Second World War, so called either from the buzzing of its engine or because it came in at a low altitude, like an aircraft 'buzzing' the ground. *See also* DOODLEBUG.

**Buzz Lightyear.** *See* Buzz LIGHTYEAR.

**Buzz off.** To go away quickly, like a busy, buzzing bee. As an imperative ('Buzz off!'), the phrase has a connotation of abruptness or even vulgarity, perhaps from its suggestion of 'bugger off' or the somewhat similar-sounding 'piss off'.

**Buzzword.** A fashionable or vogue word, especially one originating as a technical term. Many terms from computer technology have become buzzwords, such as 'mainframe' and 'peripheral'. Even 'buzzword' has become a buzzword.

The word itself relates chiefly to 'buzz' in the sense of being excited or purposeful, but the influence of 'business' is also probably present. Those using buzzwords in their everyday speech are usually happily ignorant of the original technical sense.

**BVDs.** A type of lightweight long underwear for men, popular in the first half of the 20th century. They are of US origin and the abbreviated name is that of the manufacturers, Bradley, Vorhees and Day Co., although popularly interpreted as 'babies' ventilated diapers'. They now exist as a type of boxer shorts.

***By Grand Central Station I Sat Down and Wept.*** A novel (1945), in the form of a prose poem, by the Canadian novelist Elizabeth Smart (1913–86). It reflects some of the circumstances of her long-term affair with the British poet, George Barker (1913–91), with whom she had four children while Barker was married to another woman. The title plays on the first verse of Psalm 137: 'By the rivers of Babylon, there we sat down, yea, we wept, when we remembered Zion.' It refers to the narrator's reaction at Grand Central Station in New York when a meeting is missed and the affair appears to be over. There are further biblical references, drawn from the Song of Solomon, in an exchange between the police and the narrator, who has been arrested, with her lover, on a charge of crossing a state boundary for an immoral purpose.

***Byker Grove.*** A phenomenally popular teenage SOAP OPERA first screened in 1989 and set in the youth centre of the title, located in the Byker district of Newcastle upon Tyne. Its story lines included such themes as puppy love, anguished bereavement, drug-taking, 'girl-only nights' and arson attacks, and in 1995 it outraged the tabloid press by featuring a gay kiss. It also spawned the pop duo Ant and Dec (Ant McPartlin and Declan Donnelly) who returned in 1995 with a chat show series, *The Ant and Dec Show*, and who later presented *I'm a Celebrity, Get Me Out of Here!* (*see* REALITY TV). The BBC announced the last series for September 2006.

# C

**C.** *See* PROGRAMMING LANGUAGES.

**'C'.** The traditional code name for the head of MI6, deriving from the name of its first director, Captain Mansfield Cumming (1859–1923), whose agents during the First World War included the novelists Somerset Maugham and John Buchan. The names of the heads of MI6 were kept secret until the 1990s.

**Cabaret.** A stage musical (1968) and film (1972) adapted from John Van Druten's stage play *I am a Camera* (1951), which was in turn based on the short stories published as GOODBYE TO BERLIN (1939) by Christopher Isherwood. Drawing parallels between the overt decadence of the Berlin cabaret scene in the early 1930s and the more sinister moral decadence of the growing NAZI movement, the film starred Liza Minnelli as the cabaret singer Sally BOWLES to whom a young Englishman (Michael York) is attracted. Isherwood drew heavily for his book on his own memories of the years (1929–34) he spent in Berlin, supporting himself by giving English lessons. The original for Sally Bowles was Jean Ross (1912–73), the daughter of a Scottish cotton merchant who rebelled after a childhood in Egypt and went to Berlin to sing in cabaret.

**Cabbage Patch dolls.** Dough-faced, chinless dolls, representing children born from the heart of a cabbage, that were all the rage of 1983 in the United States and to a lesser extent in Britain. They were created by Xavier Roberts of the Original Appalachian Artworks, Inc. in Cleveland, Georgia, and were commercially marketed as Cabbage Patch Kids. In 1996 Mattel updated and relaunched them for a new generation.

**Cabbages and Kings.** The first volume of stories (1904) by O. Henry (pen-name of William Sydney Porter; 1862–1910). They are set in Latin America, where Porter took refuge from justice after having been accused of embezzling funds from the chaotically organized bank for which he worked. He returned home because of his wife's illness and gave himself up to the authorities in 1897 when she died. Found guilty on a technicality, he served three years in prison, and he began writing stories to support his young daughter during this period.

The title of the first collection is from 'The Walrus and the Carpenter' by Lewis Carroll (1832–98) in *Through the Looking-Glass* (1872):

> 'The time has come,' the Walrus said,
> 'To talk of many things:
> Of shoes – and ships – and sealing wax –
> Of cabbages – and kings.'

Francis Spufford's 1989 book of 'Lists in Literature' was titled *Cabbages and Kings*.

**Cabinet of Dr Caligari, The.** *See Doctor* CALIGARI.

**Cabin fever.** A colloquial term of US origin dating from the early 20th century for the lassitude, irritability and similar symptoms that result from long confinement or isolation indoors during the winter.

> Nobody has attempted a year in cyberspace. Some observers believe that after a few months DotComGuy's perception of reality will become distorted and he will suffer cabin fever.
> *Sunday Times* (19 December 1999)

**Cab-rank rule.** In legal parlance the rule by which barristers are expected to accept any instructions offered to them at a fair and proper fee, and not select the clients for whom they act. The analogy is with a taxi rank, where a passenger is expected to hire the next vehicle available.

> Alun Jones, QC, is the barrister instructed by the Crown Prosecution Service (CPS) on behalf of the Spanish Government on the extradition of General Augusto Pinochet. How did you get the case? The CPS asked me to conduct it after the arrest. Why did you agree to take it on? By virtue of the

cab-rank principle. I specialize in extradition and I was given instructions.

*The Times* (12 October 1999)

**Cactus Jack.** A nickname of John Nance Garner (1868–1967), the Texan Democrat who was speaker of the House of Representatives (1931–3) and Franklin D. Roosevelt's vice-president (1933–41).

**Cadfael, Brother.** The medieval Welsh monk in the series of historical detective novels by Ellis Peters (real name Edith Pargeter), beginning with *A Morbid Taste for Bones* (1977). He lives at Shrewsbury Abbey where he tends the herb garden and uses his wise powers of deduction to solve murder mysteries. The stories were transferred to television in 1994 with Derek Jacobi in the role of Brother Cadfael.

**Caesar salad.** A salad of cos lettuce and croutons served with a dressing of olive oil, lemon juice, raw egg, Worcestershire sauce and seasoning, the whole the invention in 1924 at Tijuana, Mexico, of the restaurateur Caesar Cardini.

**Café culture.** An affluent urban environment, such as was observed to flourish in London, Manchester, and other British cities from the 1980s and 1990s. Its connotations are more metaphorical than literal: it includes the sense of CAFÉ SOCIETY, but it is a term more generally suggestive of a time and place of leisure and money.

**Café society.** A term of US origin dating from the 1930s for the frequenters of fashionable restaurants and nightclubs.

**Caffè latte.** (Italian, 'milk coffee'.) A drink of frothy steamed milk to which a shot of espresso coffee has been added, popular from the 1960s and often known simply as 'latte'.

**Cagney and Lacey.** The female American cops, 'First Ladies of the New York Police Department', played respectively by Loretta Swit and Tyne Daly in the television movie *Cagney and Lacey* (1981) and in the popular subsequent television series of this title (1982–8), in which Cagney was played by Meg Foster and Sharon Gless but Lacey still by Daly. Detective Mary Christine Cagney and Detective Mary Beth Lacey are THIRTY-SOMETHING professionals whose remit takes them out of the squad room into areas such as alcoholism, DATE RAPE and other social evils.

**Caine Mutiny, The.** A novel (1951) by Herman Wouk (b.1915), which won the PULITZER PRIZE for fiction. It centres on the court martial of a naval officer who has been persuaded to take command of the minesweeper USS *Caine* on the grounds that its paranoid captain is unfit to continue at his post. It was made into a play (1953) by Wouk, and a film version (1954), directed by Edward Dmytryk, starred Humphrey Bogart as Captain Queeg.

**Cairo crud.** *See* MONTEZUMA'S REVENGE.

**Cakes and Ale.** A novel (1930) by W. Somerset Maugham (1874–1965), in which the author satirized the British literary establishment. Of the novelists portrayed, Edward Driffield was said to be based on Thomas Hardy (1840–1928), Grand Old Man of Literature, and Alroy Kear on Hugh Walpole (1884–1941), while Willie ASHENDEN is in some respects Maugham's alter ego. The title comes from a remark by Toby Belch to the Clown in Shakespeare's *Twelfth Night*:

> Dost thou think, because thou art virtuous, there shall be no more cakes and ale?
>
> II.iii

**Calamity Jane.** A nickname for anyone with a permanently gloomy outlook or doom-ridden view of life. It comes from the popular name of Martha Jane Burke, née Cannary (*c*.1852–1903), an American frontierswoman famed for her skill at riding and shooting, particularly during the Gold Rush days in the Black Hills of Dakota. It is claimed that she threatened 'calamity' to any man who tried to woo her, although she did in fact marry. She became the heroine of the Western musical film *Calamity Jane* (1953), starring Doris Day in the title role.

**'California über Alles'.** The title of the debut single of the American PUNK rock group, The Dead Kennedys, released in 1979. The title plays on the words *Deutschland über alles* ('Germany above all'), which used to appear in the German national anthem. The song's lyrics, written by the group's lead singer, Jello Biafra, savage the perceived NEW AGE modishness of life in the Golden State ('You will jog for the master race / and always wear the happy face'). The song appears on an album entitled *Fresh Fruit for Rotting Vegetables* (1980), the snarling anti-bourgeois invective of which is epitomized by such tracks as 'I Kill Children' and 'Let's Lynch the Landlord'.

**Caligari, Doctor.** The mysterious villain of the famous German HORROR MOVIE *The Cabinet of Dr Caligari* (1919). He is a magician and hypnotist who uses a sleepwalking victim to commit murders on his behalf, and was played by Werner Krauss. A later US film, *The Cabinet of Caligari* (1962), bore little relationship to the original.

**Callanetics.** A system of physical exercises based on small repeated muscular movements and squeezes, designed to improve muscle tone. It takes its name from Callan Pinckney (b.1939), the fitness trainer who devised it, and was the subject of a book of the same name published in 1984, subtitled 'Ten Years Younger in Ten Hours'. Although perhaps partly based on 'athletics', the name overall also fortuitously suggests 'callisthenics', gymnastic exercises to achieve gracefulness and strength, from Greek *kallos*, 'beauty', and *sthenos*, 'strength'.

**Calling bird.** From the late 20th century an increasingly common replacement for the colly bird in the familiar 'Twelve Days of Christmas' rhyme, giving thus 'four calling birds' in the countdown. The colly bird, as a dialect name for the blackbird (literally 'coaly bird'), was presumably felt to be too obscure to hold its place. However, a calling bird lacks the specificity of the other birds in the verselets: the three French hens, the two turtle doves and the single partridge in a pear tree.

***Call Me Madam.*** A musical comedy (1950) with a book by Howard Lindsay (1889–1968) and Russel Crouse (1893–1966) and a score by Irving Berlin (1888–1989) about the domineering Sally Adams, US ambassador to the tiny country of Lichtenburg. Made immortal by Ethel Merman, Sally Adams was based originally on the Washington society hostess Perla Mesta, who served as an ambassador under Harry S. Truman and instructed her staff to 'call her madam' when they asked how she should be addressed. Ethel Merman was much irritated by changes that Irving Berlin continued to make to the score very late in rehearsal for the show: when he tried to introduce a new verse for one of the songs she refused point-blank to take it on board, with the quip: 'Call me Miss Bird's Eye. The show is frozen.'

**Call me stupid.** A phrase, usually followed by 'but', used to point out a truth that others seem to have overlooked. The speaker implies that the adjective, although at other times perhaps applicable, is not so in this instance. The adjective itself is variable.

> Call me old-fashioned, but it seems to me that one of the great things to be said for being married is the combination of company and privacy.
>
> LIBBY PURVES: in *The Times* (12 January 1999)

***Call of the Wild, The.*** An animal novella (1903) by the US writer Jack London (1876–1916) about a domestic dog, Buck, which is kidnapped from a life of luxury in California and taken to the Klondike, where he becomes a sledge dog. After his master's death, he answers the call of the wild and joins a pack of wolves.

**Call the shots.** To dictate a course of action; to be in charge. The allusion is to dice gambling. The phrase dates from the 1960s.

**Cambridge Mafia.** A term of the early 1990s for a group of senior Conservatives who were at Cambridge together in the early 1960s and active there in university politics. Five were in John Major's cabinet of 1992: Kenneth Clarke, John Gummer, Michael Howard, Norman Lamont and Peter Lilley. A sixth, Norman Fowler, was then party chairman. Yet another of the group, Leon Brittan, was in the cabinet somewhat earlier (1981–6). *See also* PORTILLISTAS.

**Cambridge Spy Ring.** The popular name for the spies recruited by the NKVD (*see* KGB) at Cambridge University in the 1930s. The five main agents were Kim Philby (1912–88), Donald Maclean (1913–83), Guy Burgess (1911–63), John Cairncross (1913–95) and Anthony Blunt (1907–83). Most accounts consider the first recruit to have been Blunt, who in turn won over Cairncross, although their Soviet handler, Yuri Modin, in his book *My Five Cambridge Friends* (1994), says that Burgess was the man who recruited Blunt. According to Modin, code names for the five were Söhnchen ('Sonny'), Tom and Stanley for Philby; Mädchen ('Missy') and Hicks for Burgess; Johnson, Tom and Yan for Blunt; and Stuart, Wise, Lyric and Homer for Maclean. These last three were members of the Apostles, a secret Cambridge society founded in 1826 and including such famous figures as Roger Fry, Bertrand Russell, Desmond MacCarthy, Lytton Strachey, E.M. Forster, Leonard Woolf and J.M. Keynes. The Apostles sequestered themselves from their fellow students, not only because they believed in their intellectual superiority but also because many espoused Marxism and were homosexuals. *See also* BURGESS AND MACLEAN; George SMILEY.

**Camden Town Group.** A group of artists formed in 1911 by Walter Sickert (1860–1942), who had painted many of his nude studies in drab boarding-house rooms in Camden Town, then a largely working-class area of North London. In the group's first show he included two such paintings, *Camden Town Murder Series No. 1* and *No. 2*, although the link with any recent murder was more for publicity than for actuality. Other members of the group were Robert Bevan (1865–1925), Harold Gilman (1876–1919), Charles Ginner (1878–1952), Spencer Gore (1878–1914), Augustus John (1878–1961) and Wyndham Lewis (1882–1957). They had no real identity of style although most shared Sickert's liking for everyday subjects. In 1913 they merged with others to form the larger and more disparate LONDON GROUP.

**Camelot.** A nickname in the early 1960s for the members of John F. Kennedy's administration (*see* JACK THE ZIPPER; JFK), casting the stylish young US president himself in the role of King Arthur and his glamorous wife as Queen Guinevere. Kennedy's inauguration in 1961 gave promise of brighter and better things to come after the sober Eisenhower years (*see* BEST AND THE BRIGHTEST). Although ultimately deriving from the medieval legend, the name was directly prompted by the Lerner and Loewe musical *Camelot*, depicting King

Arthur's court, which had opened on Broadway the previous year:

> Don't let it be forgot
> That once there was a spot
> For one brief shining moment that was known
> As Camelot.

Camelot was later familiar in Britain as the name of the consortium operating the NATIONAL LOTTERY from 1994. The same associations of glamour and glitter are present, but there is also a verbal pun on 'lottery' and perhaps even on 'came a lot'.

> At several Cambridge dinner parties one heard faculty-types discuss ... institutional politics, the glory days in Washington when Camelot reigned, their books or research career frustrations.
>
> Harper's (October 1970)

**Camel's nose.** A small part of something very large, especially when difficult or unpleasant to deal with; the TIP OF THE ICEBERG. The term is of US origin, dating from the 1960s, and derives from the fuller phrase 'to let the camel's nose into the tent'.

**Cameroonians.** The nickname of the supporters of David Cameron (see BOY DAVID), who was elected leader of the Conservative Party in December 2005. They evolved out of the so-called NOTTING HILL SET (see also METRO-TORY). The term itself appears to have evolved out of an earlier form:

> To be a supporter of David Cameron, one learns from his cheerleaders, is to be one of the 'Cameroons'. Which proves one thing, at least: that the Etonian candidate for the Tory leadership hasn't looked at an up-to-date atlas for some time. 'After the first world war, the country was handed to Britain and France under a League of Nations mandate,' a representative of the Cameroon embassy explains, patiently. 'The English part of it was called the Cameroons. And one part of that voted to join Nigeria after independence, and the other joined French Cameroun.'
>
> MICHAEL HANN: in The Guardian (18 October 2005)

Whether the Cameroons deliberately avoided calling themselves 'Cameronians' is a ticklish point. Did they perhaps realize that the Cameronians were an extreme group of Scottish Covenanters (a.k.a. Whigs) in the 17th century? In any case, the press soon enough settled down to calling them Cameroonians, rather than either Cameroons or Cameronians.

**Camford.** A blend of the names of Oxford and Cambridge to suggest a university city, on the lines of the currently more familiar 'Oxbridge'. Both were used by Thackeray in

*Pendennis* (1848) but Camford also features in Conan Doyle's story 'The Adventure of the Creeping Man' in *The Case Book of Sherlock Holmes* (1927), in which it is famous for its chair of Comparative Anatomy, held in 1903 by Professor Presbury. Holmes duly reveals the secret of the professor's claim that a man can be transformed into an ape by being injected with monkey serum.

**Camillagate.** The name given to the revelation of the Prince of Wales's long-running affair to Camilla Parker Bowles (see the ROTTWEILER), especially the leaking of a taped 1989 telephone conversation between the two (while the Prince was still married to Diana, Princess of Wales), in which Charles expressed his desire to be reincarnated as Camilla's tampon. The name itself is modelled on WATERGATE. *See also* SQUIDGYGATE.

**Camillo, Don.** The tough rural priest in a series of humorous stories by the Italian writer Giovanni Guareschi (1908–68). His adversary is Peppone, the local Communist Party mayor. The stories first appeared in the Italian magazine *Candido* in the late 1940s and were subsequently collected in a number of books. The first of these in English translation was *The Little World of Don Camillo* (1950), and film and television versions have followed.

**Camp.** Ostentatiously and extravagantly effeminate; exaggerated or theatrical in style or manner. The origin of the word in this sense is uncertain, and it is not likely to derive directly from the military camp. A connection with French *se camper*, 'to adopt a proud pose', has been suggested.

> Not only is there a Camp vision, a Camp way of looking at things. Camp is as well a quality discoverable in objects and the behavior of persons. There are 'campy' movies, clothes, furniture, popular songs, novels, people, buildings.
>
> SUSAN SONTAG: 'Notes on Camp', *Partisan Review* (Fall 1964)

**Campbell's Soup.** The well-known brand of comestible was multiply immortalized by Andy Warhol (1928–87) in his 1962 stencilled picture *100 Cans of Campbell's Soup* and again in *Four Campbell's Soup Cans* (1965). Typically, Warhol's idea was not original: in 1960 Jasper Johns (b.1930) had made his sculpture of two cans of Ballantine Ale entitled *Painted Bronze*. But then, as Warhol predicted in 1963: 'Some day everybody will be thinking alike.'

**Camp David.** The rural retreat of US presidents, in Catoctin Mountain Park, Maryland, some 112km (70 miles) from Washington, D.C. It was established under the name SHANGRI LA in 1942 by F.D. Roosevelt and was made an official retreat by Harry S. Truman in 1945. In 1953 Dwight D. Eisenhower renamed it Camp David after his grandson (b.1947), who grew up to marry Richard M. Nixon's younger daughter Julie (b.1948).

**Camp David Agreements** or **Accords.** The two agreements between Israel and Egypt that led to a negotiated peace between those two countries, the first between Israel and any of its Arab neighbours. The agreements were signed on 17 September 1978 by the Israeli prime minister, Menachem Begin, and the Egyptian president, Anwar Sadat, under the aegis of the US president, Jimmy Carter, at his government retreat, CAMP DAVID. Hence the name.

**Camp Delta.** *See* CAMP X-RAY.

**Camp Fire Girls.** A youth organization for girls founded in the United States in 1910, the same year as the British GIRL GUIDES. As the name implies, camping is an important activity. Boys have been admitted since 1975 and the organization is now called Camp Fire USA.

**Campion, Albert.** The upper-class detective in the crime novels of Margery Allingham, beginning with *The Crime at Black Dudley* (1929). He is initially a somewhat foppish character but grows in strength and maturity as the series progresses.

**Campus classic.** A novel whose phenomenal success is due to its cult adoption by university students. The attraction is usually in a mix of entertainment with philosophy or of profundity with naivety. Examples of writers who produced such books are Hermann Hesse (*see* NARZISS UND GOLDMUND), J.R.R. Tolkien (*see The* LORD OF THE RINGS), Mervyn Peake (*see* GORMENGHAST) and J.D. Salinger (*see The* CATCHER IN THE RYE).

**Camp X-Ray.** A nickname given to Camp Delta, the detention centre run by the US military at its base at Guantánamo Bay, Cuba. 'X-Ray' was originally just part of a letter-sequence borrowed from the NATO phonetic alphabet, but was also taken to refer to the open cages in which prisoners were originally held. The original Camp X-Ray was a temporary facility, closed in April 2002, but the name came to be applied to the whole detention facility at Guantánamo Bay – known as 'Gitmo' by US soldiers. Camp Delta has been used to hold suspected terrorists as part of the US WAR ON TERROR, many such detainees having been seized during the US overthrow of the TALIBAN regime in Afghanistan in 2001. Detainees, who wear orange uniforms, include many 'foreign fighters', i.e. non-Afghani Islamists, some of them AL-QAIDA members, who fought alongside the Taliban. Some of those detained claimed they were visiting Afghanistan for legitimate reasons and had no connection with terrorist training camps. In relation to those it holds at

Guantánamo Bay the United States has not observed the Geneva Conventions regarding the detention and treatment of prisoners of war, describing the detainees instead as 'illegal combatants'. It has proposed to try detainees by special military tribunals, outside the normal processes of US justice, Guantánamo Bay not being located on US sovereign territory. There has been much international concern about the fate of the prisoners, their lack of legal representation and their general treatment by their captors. The motto over the gates of the camp reads: 'Honour Bound to Defend Freedom'. *See also* EXTRAORDINARY RENDITION.

**Canada Dry.** The oldest brand of ginger ale, first produced in the late 19th century by John J. McLaughlin, a pharmacist and chemist in Toronto, Ontario.

> I saw a notice which said 'Drink Canada Dry' and I've just started.
> BRENDAN BEHAN: attributed remark

**Canard Enchaîné, Le.** (French, 'The Fettered Duck'.) A French satirical weekly, first published in 1915, when it arose from an anti-militarist tract of troops in the trenches. It is famous for its exposés of scandals and abuses of power in political and business life and is the *bête noire* of the authorities, who bugged its new offices in the 1970s. Its name alludes to its beleaguerment.

**Candid camera.** An unseen camera used to photograph an unsuspecting subject. Candid camera shots have long been used in pictorial journalism. In the 1950s a US television series of the name, subsequently taken up in Britain, set up scenes putting people in an embarrassing situation and then filming their reaction.

The British version ran from 1960 to 1967 with Jonathan Routh as the host and returned briefly in 1974 under Peter Dulay. The stunts varied. In one scenario a secretary on her first day at work found the office collapsing around her, while in another a man was asked to hold up a wall for moment, then abandoned. In one classic example a car without an engine was 'driven' to a garage with a request for a repair to be carried out.

**'Candle in the Wind'.** A eulogy in song for the sex symbol Marilyn MONROE produced by the successful combination of Bernie Taupin (an avid collector of Monroe memorabilia, who wrote the lyrics) and Elton John (who wrote the music). Released in 1973, the song appeared on the album *Goodbye Yellow Brick Road*. The inspiration for the title appears to have come from Taupin's reading a description of the hell-raising rock star Janis Joplin as a 'candle in the wind', an allusion to the vulnerability of the latter's lifestyle (Joplin 'blew herself out' with drink and drugs at an early age).

After the death in a car crash of Diana, Princess of Wales in 1997, Taupin (at Elton John's suggestion) revised the lyrics to create a eulogy for the PEOPLE'S PRINCESS. The resulting version of the song (in which the original opening line 'Goodbye Norma Jean' becomes 'Goodbye England's rose') was sung by Elton John at Diana's funeral and went on to become the world's fastest-selling, bestselling single ever.

**Candy.** The innocent heroine of Terry Southern and Mason Hoffenberg's comic-cum-pornographic novel named after her (1958). As her name implies, she is a latter-day Candide-style character in a modern, sexually liberated setting. A film of the book was produced in 1968 with Ewa Aulin in the title role.

**Canned laughter.** Pre-recorded laughter that is dubbed on to radio and television comedy programmes. It is the modern equivalent of the claques who were hired to clap and cheer at theatre performances and is a device of US origin. It was first heard in Britain in the US television comedy show *I Love Lucy*, starring Lucille Ball, screened when ITV began broadcasting on 22 September 1955.

> The trend in TV has been to the canned laugh, a laugh reproduced by recording from some previous happy crowd, or synthetically manufactured.
>
> VANCE PACKARD: *The Hidden Persuaders*, ch. 18 (1957)

**Canned music.** Music recorded and reproduced, as opposed to live music played by musicians present in person. The comparison is with canned foods, since such music can be stored and used when required.

**Cannibal, Hannibal the.** *See* HANNIBAL THE CANNIBAL.

**Cannibal, The.** The nickname of the Belgian cyclist Eddie Merckx (b.1945), five times winner of the Tour de France and probably the greatest cyclist ever. He owed his nickname to his ability to 'eat up' his opponents through a combination of speed and strength.

**Cannot come. Lie follows.** A telegram sent by M. de Guermantes in *Time Regained* (1926), the last volume in Marcel Proust's novel sequence, REMEMBRANCE OF THINGS PAST. The real Lord Charles Beresford (1846–1919) is said to have sent a telegraph along similar lines to the Prince of Wales (the future Edward VII) in response to a last-minute invitation to dine: 'Very sorry can't come. Lie follows by post.'

**Can of worms.** A complex and unappetizing situation. The phrase dates from the 1950s and is found in the fuller form 'to open a can of worms', meaning to reveal a situation that is bound to lead to trouble. The image is of a container of maggots for use as fish bait.

**Can't do something for toffee.** Cannot do it at all. Said of someone who quite clearly lacks a particular ability, as: 'He can't sing for toffee.' 'For toffee' may have evolved as a variant of 'for nuts', referring to the bruised nuts that are a proper ingredient of toffee (hence walnut toffee and the like).

**Canteen culture.** A term for the male chauvinist and racist attitudes that are said to exist within the ranks of the British police force. The phrase dates from the late 1980s and alludes to the off-duty expression and exchange of opinions of this type in police station canteens.

**Can't pay, won't pay.** This doughty device was adopted in 1990 by those objecting to the new COMMUNITY CHARGE or 'poll tax', as well as by some other protest groups. The words were adopted from the title of Lino Pertile's English translation (1981) of Dario Fo's Italian play *Non si paga! Non si paga!* (1974).

**Canyoning.** An EXTREME SPORT that consists in launching oneself, appropriately clad in protective clothing, down a series of natural rapids and waterfalls. The undertaking is hazardous if proper precautions are not taken, and in 1999 21 participants were swept to their deaths by a swollen stream in the Swiss Alps after ignoring a severe storm warning.

**Caped crusader.** A sobriquet applied to BATMAN, and sometimes also to his sidekick Robin, both of whom don capes to combat villainy. Hence the term can be applied metaphorically to any person who fights to uphold moral right and decency and who champions the underdog.

> In the past, caped crusaders fought for truth, justice and the American way. Now gay rights will be added to their muscle-bound repertoire. The 21st-century gender pioneers are called Apollo and Midnighter, a loving couple who cohabit in a giant spaceship.
>
> *Sunday Times* (27 February 2000)

**Capone, Al.** A notorious Chicago gangster of Sicilian origin (1899–1947). He rose to power in the PROHIBITION era and made himself master of the rackets in the city by organizing the killing of most of the rival gunmen. After the ST VALENTINE'S DAY MASSACRE of 1929 he was left in supreme control of the protection rackets, speakeasies, brothels and so on. The suburb of Cicero was completely dominated by him. He was eventually jailed in 1931 for tax evasion. Capone's career has inspired many films, including

LITTLE CAESAR, SCARFACE (Capone's nickname) and *The* UNTOUCHABLES.

**Capp, Andy.** The cloth-capped working man from the northeast of England who is the lazy and loutish anti-hero of the popular comic newspaper strip by Reg Smythe (1917–98). He and his nagging wife, Flo, first appeared in the *Daily Mirror* in 1957. He survives today, but with a nod in the direction of POLITICAL CORRECTNESS, so that, for example, a cigarette no longer dangles from his lower lip. But he still keeps his cap on indoors, even when snoozing on the sofa. His name is an obvious pun on 'handicap', a racing word instantly appreciated by his gambling cronies.

**Capri, Ford.** *See* FORD CORTINA.

**Capri pants.** Tight-fitting trousers for women, with tapering legs ending below the knee. They were first in vogue in the 1950s, when they were worn by fashion-conscious visitors to the Italian island of Capri and other Mediterranean resorts.

**Captain America.** The costumed superhero of this name was the creation of Joe Simon and Jack Kirby for a comic book that first appeared in 1941. He begins as a weakling by the name of Steve Rogers, but is then injected with a wonder drug, acquires mighty muscles and starts to set about the NAZIS. He goes on to win the Second World War almost single-handed. His usual dress is a Stars-and-Stripes costume and a tight-fitting hood with a letter A on the brow. He rather lost direction after the war but then reappeared in various Marvel Comics.

**Captain Blood.** *See* Captain BLOOD.

**Captain Bob.** *See* BOUNCING CZECH.

**Captain Corelli's Mandolin.** A novel (1994) by Louis de Bernières (b.1954), set on the Greek island of Cephalonia. The major part of the action takes place during the Second World War and concerns the romance between the local doctor's daughter and Captain Antonio Corelli, a member of the occupying Italian forces, who is a skilled performer on the mandolin. A survey in 2000 revealed that the book was one of the ten sources most used for readings at weddings. A much-criticized film version (2001) was directed by John Madden and starred Nicholas Cage and Penelope Cruz. *See also* FIRST LINES OF NOVELS.

**Captain Future.** The space-travelling hero of the SCIENCE FICTION pulp magazine that bears his name (1940–4). His real name is Curt Newton, and his main task is to pursue interstellar criminals, which he does accompanied by a robot, an android and a 'living brain'. Most of the stories in which he features were written by Edmond Hamilton, sometimes using the pen-name Brett Sterling.

**Captain Marvel.** The red-suited, tough-muscled superhero of US comics, nicknamed 'the Big Red Cheese'. He first appeared in Fawcett's *Whiz* comics in 1940. His real name is Billy Batson, implying that he is a son of BATMAN, who made his debut the previous year. He begins as a weedy youth but is transformed when he meets a wizard who gives him a magic word to say. This is 'Shazam', an acronym of the names of six traditional heroes: Solomon, Hercules, Atlas, Zeus, Achilles and Mercury.

Captain Marvel is also the nickname of the West Bromwich Albion, Manchester United and England footballer Bryan Robson (b.1957), a talented midfielder of great stamina and courage during the 1980s and early 1990s. He made 89 appearances for England, earning his nickname by analogy with the US comic-strip superhero by captaining the side on 45 occasions.

**Captain Midnight.** A US radio hero created by Robert M. Burtt and Wilfred G. Moore. He is a daredevil pilot of the Secret Squadron and his 'real' name is Captain Jim 'Red' Albright. His chief role is as a NAZI-hunter and crime-buster, and his adventures livened the airwaves from 1940 to 1953. He also appeared in film and television serials as well as in comic books and strips.

**Captain Pugwash.** A cartoon pirate created by the British illustrator John Ryan (b.1921). Pugwash first appeared in picture books and on television (1957–75). The bombastic and cowardly captain of the ramshackle vessel the *Black Pig* is terrified of his mortal enemy, the villainous Black Jake, and has to be rescued by the cabin boy, Tom.

**Captain's chair.** A style of wooden chair with a saddle seat, a low curved back and arms supported on vertical spindles, the whole having a somewhat magisterial or 'commanding' appearance. Such chairs came into vogue from the 1970s and are mainly sought after by the aspiring and affluent.

**Cap the Knife.** A nickname given to Caspar Weinberger (1917–2006) because of his slashing of spending and lowering of taxes when running the finances of California during Ronald Reagan's governorship (1966–74). Once he became secretary of defense in Reagan's cabinet in 1981, however, the enormous hike in military expenditure earned him the nick-name Cap the Ladle. *See also* GREAT COMMUNICATOR; MAC THE KNIFE.

**Car bomb.** A terrorist weapon consisting of a car packed with explosives parked near to the target and detonated by timer or remote control. Car bombs were used by the IRA during the TROUBLES, both in Northern Ireland and in Great Britain. Car bombs became the suicide bomber's weapon of choice in Iraq following the 2003 invasion.

**Carbuncles, monstrous.** *See* MONSTROUS CARBUNCLE.

**Cardboard City.** A grimly descriptive nickname for an area on London's SOUTH BANK, in particular its concrete undercroft, neighbouring railway arches and 'Bull Ring' subway, which in the 1980s became the home of the homeless, who devised a makeshift residence in discarded cardboard cases and other packing materials. The term came to apply to similar 'cities' elsewhere. *See also* BIDONVILLE.

**Care in the community.** The policy of giving care and treatment to patients, especially the infirm and those suffering from mental illness, in their own homes rather than in an institution. In the 1960s the value, and indeed the morality, of the UK's large Victorian mental hospitals began to be questioned. Psychotropic drugs developed from the 1950s gave promise of more effective control of mental illness, and a programme began of closing such hospitals down and resettling their patients in a domestic setting (the number of psychiatric beds halved between the mid-1950s and the mid-1970s). Disquiet over the effectiveness of the new approach began to grow in the 1980s, particularly after several murders committed by former inmates, and procedures were reformed under the terms of the National Health Service and Community Care Act 1990. Nevertheless, the phrase 'care in the community', with its heavy whiff of patronizing euphemism, is still regarded with cynicism in some quarters, among both those who regard the whole exercise as mainly a way of saving money and those who see little evidence of community-mindedness in its operation.

**Careless talk costs lives.** A government slogan introduced in February 1940 and printed on half a million posters with artworks by the *Punch* cartoonist 'Fougasse' (Kenneth Bird), in which indiscreet gossips are overheard by Adolf Hitler. The posters were displayed in shops, offices, pubs and other public places around Britain, and the idea was that loose talk could give valuable information to enemy spies. The slogan was generally regarded as an improvement on the Ministry of Information's previous effort: 'Do not discuss anything which might be of national importance. The consequence of any such indiscretion may be the loss of many lives.' Later variants on the theme included 'BE LIKE DAD, KEEP MUM', 'LOOSE LIPS SINK SHIPS', 'Keep it under your hat' and 'Keep mum – she's not so dumb' (this last accompanying a painting of a trio of officers flirting with an alluring blonde).

**Caretaker, The.** A play (1960) by Harold Pinter (b.1930) about the disruption that ensues when two brothers befriend a rascally tramp and offer him shelter in the room they share. The title refers to the post of caretaker that the brothers independently offer the tramp, who rewards them by trying to drive them apart. *See also* THEATRE OF THE ABSURD.

**Carjacking.** A crime, said to have begun in Detroit, in which a car driver is ordered out of their car at knife or gun point and the vehicle driven off by the 'jacker'. *See also* JOYRIDING.

**Carlos.** *See* the JACKAL.

**Carmina Burana.** The highly rhythmic and lyrical 'scenic cantata' by Carl Orff (1895–1982) was first performed in 1937. The title means 'Songs of Beuron', and the subtitle *'cantiones profanae'* means 'profane songs'. The text consists of poems in Old French, Old German and Latin about love, drink and other pleasures; they come from a 13th-century manuscript found in the Benedictine monastery of Beuron in Bavaria. In Britain the work is usually given in a concert version, but in Germany it is often staged.

**Carnaby Street.** In the SWINGING SIXTIES the much publicized clothing centre for fashion-conscious young people, east of London's Regent Street. Its connection with youthful fashion began in the late 1950s, when John Stephens, John Vince and Andrea Spyropoulos opened Vince, a boutique selling colourful clothes to young people of both sexes. It subsequently became associated with trendy UNISEX costumes generally. It was showily refurbished by Westminster City Council in 1973, but its popularity had declined by 1975 when boutiques in the King's Road, Chelsea, began to attract this type of custom.

**Carnation revolution.** *See* REVOLUTION NAMES.

**Carpetbagger.** Originally a US term for a political candidate in an area where they had no local connections but simply a 'carpet bag' of personal belongings, the word subsequently came to be used generally of an unscrupulous opportunist, especially in politics or the financial markets. Its recent application to building society members dates from 1995, when it was adopted by Peter Robinson, a former building society executive, to describe speculators who joined a society purely in the hope of a 'windfall' payment made when it converted from a mutual organization to a bank.

> Societies may have more than enough carpetbaggers to defeat loyalists who favour remaining as mutuals owned by their members, rather than by shareholders.
>
> *Financial Times* (16 January 1999)

**Carpetbaggers, The.** A novel (1961) by Harold Robbins

(born Francis Kane; when he was adopted in 1927 he took the name Harold Rubin, which he later changed to Robbins; 1916–97). 'And behind the Northern Armies came another body of men. They came by the hundreds, yet each travelled alone … And on their back, or across their saddle, or on top of their wagon was the inevitable faded multicoloured bag made of worn and ragged remnants of carpet into which they had crammed all their worldly possessions. It was from these bags that they got their name. The Carpetbaggers.'

The novel is about big business and sex and is clearly based on the career of the US industrialist, film producer and aviator Howard Hughes (1905–76). The action, set between 1925 and 1945, with flashbacks, mainly concerns Jonas Cord, whose outward interests are 'airplanes, explosives and money and, when the spirit moves him, occasionally [making] a motion picture'. A melodramatic film version (1964) was directed by Edward Dmytryk and starred George Peppard.

**Carpet bombing.** The systematic intensive bombing of an area. Hence, in less serious vein, the delivery by the postman of unsolicited advertising matter ('junk mail') or any other relentless 'bombardment'.

> [The television quiz show *Who Wants to Be a*] *Millionaire*'s power isn't in its individual figures though, more its carpet-bombing of 12 consecutive nights of rival output.
> *heat* (23–29 September 1999)

**Carpet treader.** Estate agents' jargon for a person who asks to look round a house for sale with neither the inclination nor the money to buy.

**Carrie.** *See* PROM QUEEN.

**Carrot and stick.** A method of coercion that consists in alternating or combining the offer of an enticement with the threat of a punishment. The allusion is to the proverbial method of persuading a donkey to move by dangling a carrot before it one moment and beating it with a stick the next. The expression dates from the early 20th century.

**Carry a torch for someone.** To suffer from unrequited love for them. The picture is of a 'light of love' that still burns. A torch is also an emblem of marriage, from the old custom of forming wedding processions in the evening by torchlight.

**Carry On films.** A long-running series of film comedies that began with *Carry On Sergeant* in 1958. Their humour was mostly unsubtle or even 'blue', but they won a loyal following and still have their devotees, despite their complete lack of POLITICAL CORRECTNESS. There were 31 in the sequence, almost all with titles beginning *Carry On*, such as *Carry On Doctor* (1960) and *Carry On up the Khyber* (1968),

and regular members of the cast included Kenneth Williams, Charles Hawtrey, Sid James, Joan Sims, Barbara Windsor and Hattie Jacques. The latter two, in their respective roles as busty blonde nurse and formidable hospital matron, long etched the stereotypes in the public consciousness. The series proper ended in 1978 although the formula was temporarily revived for *Carry on Columbus* (1992), in which Julian Clary injected his own brand of CAMP. In 2006 it was announced that a new film, *Carry on London*, would be made, its plot revolving around a fleet of celebrity-carrying limousines.

**Carry the can.** To take the responsibility or blame for the mistakes or misdeeds of others. The phrase dates from the 1920s and is said to refer to the can of beer that a soldier carried for all his companions.

**Carry the flag.** *See* SHOW THE FLAG.

***Carve Her Name with Pride.*** A film (1958) based on the heroic wartime career and ultimate death of Violette Szabo, who was executed in 1945 by the Germans as an Allied spy following her capture on active service in France during the Second World War. The film starred Virginia McKenna as Szabo, and the title refers to the carving of Violette Szabo's name on a memorial after the war. Szabo, who was awarded a posthumous George Cross, was the daughter of a London taxi driver and a French woman. She was recruited into the Special Operations Executive (SOE) and was only 23 years old when she was executed. The screenwriter Leo Marks wrote a poem by which her radio messages from France were recognized:

> The life that I have
> Is all that I have
> And the life that I have
> Is yours.
> The love that I have
> Of the life that I have
> Is yours and yours and yours …

**Carve-up.** A distribution of spoils or ill-gotten gains. The term dates from the 1930s.

***Casablanca.*** A classic romantic melodrama (1942), based on a script by Julius and Philip Epstein, largely set in a bar in wartime Casablanca. Starring Humphrey Bogart as bar-owner Rick and Ingrid Bergman as his old flame, the film defied all expectations for its success. Originally intended as a vehicle for George Raft, it was demoted to a B-MOVIE when he was unavailable, and the parts were passed to Bogart and Bergman only after being first offered to Ronald Reagan and Ann Sheridan. The performers were the key to the film's success rather than the plot. A remake in 1983, starring David Soul, was greeted with derision, as was another version in 1990, when Sydney Pollack produced *Havana*, set in Cuba and starring Robert Redford. *See also* PLAY IT AGAIN SAM; USUAL SUSPECTS.

> *Rick*: We'll always have Paris.
>
> JULIUS AND PHILIP EPSTEIN: *Casablanca*

**Casablanca Conference.** From 14 to 24 January 1943 Winston Churchill and Franklin D. Roosevelt met at Casablanca, Morocco, to determine Allied strategy as the Second World War took its course. STALIN refused to attend as he was overseeing operations at STALINGRAD. The prospect of opening a SECOND FRONT in northern France was discussed, but Churchill considered this premature. Instead, the invasion of Sicily ('Operation Husky') was planned. Agreement was also reached to increase the bombing of Germany and to give priority to defeating the U-BOATS in the North Atlantic.

**Case the joint.** To survey a building such as a store with the aim of subsequently robbing it. 'Case' here has the sense 'cover', while 'joint', although now applied to any building or premises, was earlier one where criminals met or joined up. The phrase dates from the early 20th century.

**Casey Brown.** In US African American culture in the early part of the 20th century, a mythical figure who fought for African American rights and against racism. The first part of his name was also realized as 'K.C.'

**Cash cow.** A business or investment that provides a steady income or profit, like a cow that yields a regular supply of milk. The expression dates from the 1970s.

**Cash for questions.** A phrase arising from a series of parliamentary incidents in the mid-1990s, when a number of Conservative MPs admitted having received money from private individuals in return for asking specific questions in the House of Commons. In 1997 the Parliamentary Commissioner investigated claims that the Conservative MP Neil Hamilton had taken cash for questions from Mohamed al Fayed, the multi-millionaire owner of Harrods, and Hamilton lost his seat at the 1997 general election (*see* WHITE-SUIT CANDIDATE). More allegations followed, and in 1999 Hamilton lost a sensational libel action against al Fayed. *See also* SLEAZE FACTOR.

**Cash-my-cheque, General.** A nickname given to General Chiang Kai-shek (1887–1975), the Chinese Nationalist leader who headed the KUOMINTANG government of China from 1925 until defeated by the communists in 1949. He subsequently set up a government-in-exile in Taiwan. The nickname was originally a joke by the GOONS.

**Casper.** The cute little ghost of this name first appeared in the short animated film *The Friendly Ghost* (1945), based on a short story by Seymour Reitt. His search for a hospitable American family to haunt is continued in later films and in his own comic book from 1949.

**Casper Milquetoast.** A nickname for a timid person. The name is that of the central character in H.T. Webster's cartoon 'The Timid Soul', first published in the *New York World* in May 1924.

**Cassidy, Hopalong.** *See* HOPALONG CASSIDY.

**Casualty.** A top-ranking television medical drama screened on BBC1 since 1986 and set in the accident and emergency department of the fictional Holby City Hospital (Holby is a thinly disguised version of Bristol). Most episodes open with an innocent member of the public about to experience a tragedy that puts them in hospital. The series is noted for its frequent changes of cast with the exception of the caring charge nurse, Charlie Fairhead, played by Derek Thompson. A spin-off serial drama called *Holby City* was first screened in 1999.

**Cat, The.** The Chelsea and England goalkeeper Peter Bonetti (b.1941), famed for the feline agility that allowed him to save apparently unreachable shots. Bonetti is unfortunately remembered for letting in the three goals that West Germany scored against England in the quarter-finals of the 1970 World Cup, which removed England from the competition.

'The Cat' was also the nickname in his playing days of the Middlesex and England left-arm spinner Phil Tufnell (b.1966), who was known for his fondness for a cat-nap in the dressing room.

**Cat and Mouse Act.** The popular name of the Prisoners (Temporary Discharge for Ill Health) Act of 1913, which was passed by the Liberal government during the SUFFRAGETTE disturbances to prevent the imprisoned lawbreakers from achieving martyrdom through hunger strikes. They were released on licence when necessary, subject to re-arrest when their health recovered. To play cat and mouse with someone is to treat them cruelly or teasingly before a final act of cruelty. A suffragette poster of the day depicted a cat with a drooping suffragette in its mouth, like a mouse, and the caption: 'The Liberal Cat. Electors Vote Against Him! Keep the Liberal Out!'

***Cat and the Canary, The.*** A stage thriller (1922) by John Willard (1885–1942) that has inspired a host of film adaptations and imitations. As mourners gather for the reading of a will in an old, dark house, several of them fall victim to the maniac who haunts its spooky corridors, preying on them as a cat might tease and kill a canary. Most film adaptations played the story for laughs, including the best-known 1939 version, which did much to establish comedian Bob Hope as a major star.

**Catbird seat.** A favourable position. The US expression is said to derive from James Thurber's short story 'The Catbird Seat' (1942) where the phrase 'sitting in the catbird seat' is explained as referring to a baseball player in the fortunate position of having no strikes and therefore three balls still to play. The phrase came into common usage in the 1940s when the Mississippi-born sports commentator Red Barber used it. The image is rather of a cat perched in a tree eyeing a bird below as its potential prey than of the bird actually called a catbird (*Dumetella carolinensis*).

> I get you. If we swing it, we'll be sitting pretty. In the catbird seat.
>
>      P.G. WODEHOUSE: *Cocktail Time*, ch. 13 (1958)

**Cat burglar.** A thief who enters a building by climbing to an upper storey. Cats are famed for their ability to negotiate heights. The term dates from the early 20th century.

**Catch a tiger by the tail.** *See* RIDE A TIGER.

**Catcher in the Rye, The.** The first novel (1951) by J. D. Salinger (b.1919), about a mixed-up teenager called Holden CAULFIELD. The character first appeared in a story published in *The New Yorker* in 1946, in which year Salinger withdrew an earlier version of the book. The title of this CAMPUS CLASSIC is alluded to in Chapter 22, when Holden's younger sister goads him into naming 'something you'd like to be'. It transpires that he has misread the line in the song by Robert Burns (1759–96), 'Gin a body meet a body / Comin thro' the rye', as 'catch a body':

> 'I keep picturing all these little kids playing some game in this big field of rye … And I'm standing on the edge of some crazy cliff … I have to catch everybody if they start to go over the cliff … I'd just be the catcher in the rye. I know it's crazy.'

*See also* FIRST LINES OF NOVELS.

**Catch-23.** A colloquial term for a situation that is new to or more intricate than that of CATCH-22.

> The speech showed that Kissinger … has come to accept what Washington insiders call the 'Catch-23' of the oil business. Put simply, the idea is that to escape the political clutches of the cartel, the West will have to develop vast new sources of energy … The catch is that the very act of producing all this new energy may lead to a glut of oil.
>
>      *Newsweek* (17 February 1975)

**Catch-22.** A 'no-win' situation: whichever alternative you choose, you will lose or be in trouble. *Catch-22* was originally the title of a novel (1961) by Joseph Heller (1923–99). The story centres on Captain Yossarian of the 256th United States (Army) bombing squadron in the Second World War, whose main aim is to avoid being killed. Heller defined Catch-22 in chapter 5 of the novel:

> There was only one catch and that was Catch-22, which specified that a concern for one's own safety in the face of dangers that were real and immediate was the process of a rational mind. Orr was crazy and could be grounded. All he had to do was to ask; and as soon as he did, he would no longer be crazy and have to fly more missions. Orr would be crazy to fly more missions and sane if he didn't, but if he was sane he had to fly them. If he flew them he was crazy and didn't have to; but if he didn't want to he was sane and had to.

Heller's original title had been *Catch-18*, but his editor Robert Gottlieb pointed out that they were publishing Leon Uris's *Mila 18* in the same season. Heller later recalled:

> I thought of *Catch-Eleven*, because it's the only other number to start with an open vowel sound. I guess we doubled that.

A film version (1970) with Alan Arkin as Yossarian was directed by Mike Nichols.

> When I read something saying I've not done anything as good as *Catch-22* I'm tempted to reply, 'Who has?'
>
>      JOSEPH HELLER: quoted in *The Times*, 9 June 1993

**Category A.** In the British system of justice the highest category of security, for the most dangerous type of prisoner. Category B is for prisoners who should not be allowed to escape, C for those who are unlikely to attempt a difficult escape, and D for those suitable for open prison.

**Caterpillar Club.** An unofficial club started by the Irvin Parachute Company during the Second World War. The caterpillar is that of the silkworm, which supplied the material from which parachutes were formerly made. The company presented a small gold caterpillar pin to any RAF airman who had baled out in action, on his supplying the number of the parachute that had saved his life. Similarly the Goldfish Club existed for those who had been forced to resort to their rubber dinghies. Since then, similar clubs have been formed to encourage the wearing of protective clothing by industrial workers.

**Cathedral of Commerce.** *See* WOOLWORTH BUILDING.

**Cathedral of light.** The lighting effects, using searchlights, designed by Hitler's personal architect, Albert Speer (1905–81), for the 1934 NUREMBERG RALLY. It is this rally that is featured in Leni Reifenstahl's film, *The Triumph of the Will* (1936).

**Cat on a Hot Tin Roof.** A play (1955) by Tennessee Williams (1911–83) that was subsequently turned into a successful film (1958) starring Elizabeth Taylor, Paul Newman and Burl Ives. The title echoes the old English saying 'like a cat on hot bricks', which dates back to at least the 17th century, and this link is interestingly furthered by the fact that one of the main characters in Williams's story is named Brick. The play began life as a short story entitled 'Three Players of a Summer Game', but Williams changed it when he developed the tale for the stage, during the course of which he first introduced Brick's wife Maggie ('Maggie the Cat'). The author later claimed that his own father had coined the phrase, habitually complaining to his wife that she made him 'nervous as a cat on a hot tin roof'.

**Cats.** A musical comedy (1981) with a score by Andrew Lloyd Webber (b.1948) in which all the main characters are cats. It was based on poems from T.S. Eliot's *Old Possum's Book of Practical Cats* (1939).

**Catseyes.** The proprietary name of reflective studs set in rubber pads in the road as a guide to drivers when it is dark or foggy. They were the invention of Percy Shaw (1889–1975). The first 50 were laid at Brightlington crossroads, a notorious BLACK SPOT near Bradford, Yorkshire, in 1934. 'Cat's Eyes Cunningham' was the nickname given to Group Captain John Cunningham (1917–2002), RAF night fighter pilot in the Second World War. Even when flying without navigational aids he managed to shoot down some 12 German aircraft.

**Cat's pyjamas.** Something excellent or praiseworthy. The term dates from the 1920s and is often attributed to the US cartoonist and sportswriter Tad Dorgan (1877–1929), who has been credited with the coining of a number of colourful expressions (*see also* HOT DOG). A similar expression is the BEE'S KNEES. *See also* CAT'S WHISKERS.

**Catsuit.** A one-piece, close-fitting trouser suit, so called from its resemblance to the costume worn by a pantomime cat.

**Cat's whisker.** In the old 'crystal' wireless sets or radio receivers, this was the name given to the very fine pointed wire that made contact with the crystal.

**Cat's whiskers.** An excellent person or thing. There is a real allusion to the whiskers of a cat, since their extreme sensitivity enable it to pass through narrow spaces in total darkness. *See also* DOG'S BOLLOCKS.

**Cattle show.** In US politics a term for a public gathering of

presidential candidates running in a primary election campaign. *See also* BEAUTY CONTEST.

**Catwalk.** A narrow pathway or gangway over a theatre stage or along a bridge. Also an extended stage at a fashion show. Cats are able to walk safely along a raised narrow surface such as the top of a wall.

> Bare all you dare is the message from the New York catwalk.
> *The Times* (20 September 1999)

**Caucasian Chalk Circle, The.** A play (1948) by Bertolt Brecht (1898–1956), with the German title *Der kaukasische Kreidekreis*, set in the Caucasus in the aftermath of the Second World War. In it, peasants enact the legend whereby the competing claims of a child's biological mother and its foster mother are decided by a bogus judge (actually a thief and poacher). The judge, Azdak, orders that the matter be settled by the two women having a tug of war with the child within a chalk circle. The foster mother lets go first, fearing the child will be hurt, thus demonstrating her greater love, and is granted custody of the child. *See also* EPIC THEATRE.

**Caudillo.** The title adopted by General Franco, head of the Falangist government in Spain, in imitation of Mussolini's DUCE and Hitler's FÜHRER. Like them it means 'leader'. The slogan *Una Patria, Un Estado, Un Caudillo* ('one people, one state, one leader'), in imitation of the Nazi slogan EIN VOLK, EIN REICH, EIN FÜHRER, was invented for Franco by Millan Astráy (*see* EL GLORIOSO MUTILADO). *See also* FALANGE.

**Caught with one's pants down.** Caught unprepared or in an embarrassing situation. Pants (trousers) are normally lowered for two private purposes, one in the bedroom, the other in the bathroom. Despite this origin, the expression, which dates from the 1930s, is not considered vulgar. *See also* PADDY PANTSDOWN.

**Caulfield, Holden.** The young protagonist of J.D. Salinger's CAMPUS CLASSIC *The* CATCHER IN THE RYE (1951). He runs away from school and has a number of adventures and encounters in New York. He narrates his experiences in a part-cynical, part-innocent style and expresses his dismay at the 'phoniness' of everything. Salinger, a well-known recluse, has not permitted any film or television version of the novel to be made.

**Caution.** In its modern sense a formal warning given by a police officer to someone suspected of an offence. The warning in use from the 1960s was: 'You do not have to say anything unless you wish to do so but what you say may be given in evidence.' In 1995 a modified version was introduced, under the terms of the Police and Criminal

Evidence (PACE) Act (1984): 'You do not have to say anything. But it may harm your defence if you do not mention when questioned something which you later rely on in court. Anything you do say may be given in evidence.'

**Caution, Lemmy.** The G-man hero (*see* G-MEN) of a series of pseudo-American thrillers by the British writer Peter Cheyney, beginning with *This Man is Dangerous* (1936). He is notable for his willingness to use violence and he subsequently appeared in various French films of the 1950s, as well as in Jean-Luc Godard's unusual SCIENCE FICTION movie *Alphaville* (1965), in which he is played by Eddie Constantine.

***Cautionary Tales for Children.*** A book of comic tales in verse (1907) by the French-born British writer Hilaire Belloc (1870–1953), with illustrations by 'B.T.B.' (Belloc's friend Lord Basil Blackwood). Belloc's stories are a conscious parody of 19th-century 'cautionary tales', 'improving' parables intended to demonstrate the dangers that lie in wait for children who act disobediently.

In Belloc's verses an array of often minor childhood misdemeanours attract comically severe punishments. The stories include the tales of 'Jim, Who ran away from his nurse, and was eaten by a lion', 'Henry King, Who chewed bits of String, and was early cut off in Dreadful Agonies', 'Matilda, Who Told Lies, and was Burned to Death', 'Lord Lundy, Who was too Freely Moved to Tears, and thereby Ruined his Political Career', 'Rebecca, Who slammed doors for Fun and Perished Miserably' and 'George, Who played with a dangerous Toy, and suffered a Catastrophe of considerable Dimensions'. The last memorably describes the destruction of a wealthy town house and most of its residents by the explosion of a balloon purchased for George by his doting grandmother:

> The Lights went out! The Windows broke!
> The Room was filled with reeking smoke.
> And in the darkness screams and yells
> Were mingled with electric bells,
> And falling masonry and groans,
> And crunching, as of broken bones,
> And dreadful shrieks, when, worst of all,
> The house itself began to fall!
> It tottered, shuddering to and fro,
> Then crashed into the street below –
> Which happened to be Savile Row.

**Cavaliere, Il.** (Italian, 'the cavalier'.) An admiring nickname given to Silvio Berlusconi (b.1936), the Italian business-man, media tycoon and prime minister of Italy from 1994 to 1995 and 2001 to 2006 (when he lost the election, albeit by a slim and disputed margin, and some of his sheen to the decidedly uncharismatic Romano Prodi and his left-wing alliance). The name alludes to his supposedly dashing style – *il Berlusconismo*. In 2004 he had a hair implant. *See also* SULTANS OF BLING.

**Cavern Club.** A cellar-club in Liverpool that owes its prin-cipal fame to the many lunch-time appearances made there by The BEATLES in the early 1960s and which led to their attracting a cult following.

**C-B.** A nickname for Sir Henry Campbell-Bannerman (1836–1908), British Liberal prime minister (1905–8).

**CB radio.** Citizens' Band radio originated in the United States in 1958 as a narrow airwave band for businesses and emergencies. It was taken up by truckdrivers in the mid-1970s and soon became a national craze, developing its own idiosyncratic language. Typically, a CB-er might broadcast the alert that there were 'smokies' (police) ahead, avoid going over 'double nickel' (55mph/88kph) and receive a '10–4' (affirmative acknowledgement). A hit song devoted to the system was 'Convoy' (1976) by the country singer C.W. McCall. Its words were in CB jargon and the record was released with a printed 'translation' so that DJs could pass on the meaning to their listeners.

**Ceci n'est pas une pipe.** (French, 'this is not a pipe'.) The words written below a painting of a pipe by the Belgian surrealist René Magritte (1898–1967). The words are literally true, as it is a painting of a pipe, not a real pipe. The actual title of the work, which dates from 1928–9, is *La Trahison des images* ('The Treachery of Images').

**Ceiling.** The term is figuratively applied to the maximum height to which an aircraft can rise under certain conditions, or to an upper limit for prices or wages. In meteorology, the ceiling is the highest level from which the earth's surface can be seen, which is effectively the height of the cloud base above ground level.

**Ceiling zero.** An expression meaning that the clouds or mist are down to ground level.

**Celebrity culture.** A condemnatory term for the adulation afforded in the late 20th and early 21st centuries to those who are famous for reasons perceived as being unworthy of adulation. The shaft is aimed particularly at products of popular culture such as film stars, pop singers and foot-ballers (*see* POSH AND BECKS), whose lives are chronicled in minute and intimate detail on television, in the tabloid press, in celebrity magazines (*see* HELLO!), etc. Beyond such often modest talents, the term also encompasses those who have no particular achievement to their name, but are famous merely for being famous (e.g. the American heiress and socialite Paris Hilton and the talent-show judge Sharon Osbourne), and even those who are famous for being bad at something (e.g. William Hung, who achieved celebrity in the United States for his execrable singing audition/ performance on the television show *American Idol* in 2004). The phenomenon avidly recycles those who are already well known, inviting them to cash in on their celebrity in self-revelations beyond their normal comfort zone (e.g. in the television programmes *I'm a Celebrity ... Get Me Out of Here!* (2002– ), *Strictly Come Dancing* (2004– ) and *Dancing on Ice* (2006; *see* TORVILL AND DEAN)), and also draws in those who dream of a quick route to fame via REALITY TV and talent shows such as *The X Factor* (2004– ).

Thus is Andy Warhol's prophecy (*see* FAMOUS FOR 15 MINUTES) well on its way to realization. There is a superficial resemblance to the HOLLYWOOD-driven 'star' cult of the middle years of the 20th century, but the crucial distinction is, in the words of James F. English (*The Economy of Prestige*, 2005), 'a logic of exaggerated intimacy rather than exaggerated distance'. *See also* BIG BROTHER; KING OF CHAVS; MCMANSION; WANNABE.

**Cellulite.** A substance made up of fat, water and wastes that is supposed to form unsightly lumpy pockets beneath the skin or dimples on its surface like orange peel, especially on women's hips and thighs. Methods of removing it are varied but it cannot generally be burned off by dieting since it remains after slimming. The word dates from the 1970s and was coined by the French dietician Nicole Ronsard, from French *cellule*, 'cell'.

**Celtic Sea.** This area is formally defined as 'that part of the continental shelf lying between the 200 fathom contour, southern Ireland, the southwestern tip of Wales, Land's End and Ushant'. The term derives from the surrounding Celtic areas, i.e. Brittany, Cornwall, Wales and Ireland, and was first used by E.W.L. Holt in 1921.

**Celtic Twilight.** One of the main elements of the Irish Literary Revival of the later 19th and early 20th centuries, positing a special poetic vision for the residual Celts (lost, it was implied, by the Anglo-Saxons). The term originated as the title of a book of folk and supernatural writings, mainly by W.B. Yeats, which was published in 1893. Some cultural commentators feel that the murk of the Celtic Twilight cast too long and too kitschy a shadow across Irish art and letters in the 20th century.

**Cement Garden, The.** A novella (1978) by Ian McEwan (b.1948). The death of the teenage narrator's father, and then of his mother, leaves him, his two sisters and their small brother alone. Rather than tell anyone, with the risk that they will be taken into care and separated, they conceal their mother's body in the cellar in a tin trunk, filled with cement ('the cement garden'). A gamut of sexual deviation propels the action to its dark denouement. An unsettling film version (1993) was directed by Andrew Birkin.

**Cenotaph.** (Greek *kenotaphion*, from *kenos*, 'empty', and *taphos*, 'tomb'.) A monument raised to the memory of a person or persons buried elsewhere. By far the most noteworthy to the British is that in Whitehall, designed by Sir Edwin Lutyens, which was dedicated on 11 November 1920 to those who fell in the First World War. It is a slightly curved block of Portland stone, adorned with the flags of the three services and the merchant navy, and with the simple inscription 'To the Glorious Dead'. It has been adapted to commemorate the fallen of the Second World War as well.

**Central Powers.** A term for the coalition in the First World War formed mainly of the German Empire and Austria–Hungary, as the 'central' European states that were at war from 1914 against France and Britain on the WESTERN FRONT and against Russia on the Eastern Front. The term also encompassed Germany's other allies, Bulgaria and Turkey. *See also* SARAJEVO.

**Centrefold.** A printed and usually illustrated sheet that has been folded to form the centre spread of a magazine. The term was extended to the model, usually naked or at best skimpily clad, whose photograph features there. This sense became specifically associated with Hugh Hefner's PLAY-BOY, where the spread first appeared in February 1954, the subject being Margaret Scott.

> The concept of the centerfold became world famous and added a new word to the language. 'Centerfold' became another way of referring to a picture of a beautiful girl, just as 'pin-up' had the decade before.
>
> HUGH HEFNER: in Gretchen Edgren, *The Playmate Book*, Introduction (1996)

**Centre 42.** An organization of writers, painters, composers, actors and others set up by the playwright Arnold Wesker in 1961 to promote festivals of the arts, exhibitions of craft work and other activities designed for working people. It had trade union support and took its name from the numerical position it held on the agenda of a trades union meeting that solicited greater union involvement in artistic work. Its base was the building that became the ROUND-HOUSE theatre. It closed in 1970.

**Century of the Common Man.** The 20th century, the age of democracy. *The Century of the Common Man* (1943) was the title of a book by Henry A. Wallace, vice-president of the United States (1941–5) under F.D. Roosevelt. Wallace first used the phrase in a speech on 8 May 1942, articulating America's war aims and upholding the values of democracy, which he defined as 'the only true political expression of Christianity'. He deliberately contrasted the 'the century of the common man' with the hubristic THOUSAND-YEAR REICH of the 'Satan-inspired Führer':

> Some have spoken of the 'American Century'. I say that the century on which we are entering – The century which will come out of this war – can be and must be the century of the common man.

The phrase speedily became popular on both sides of the Atlantic and was much favoured by Nancy, Viscountess Astor. Taking up the theme, the American composer Aaron Copland produced his *Fanfare for the Common Man* (1942), of which the stirring trumpet tune has since prefaced many a ceremonial occasion.

**CGI.** Computer-generated imagery in film and television, which began in the mid-1970s and is now ubiquitous.

**Cha-cha** or **Cha-cha-cha.** This popular dance of the 1950s, like the MAMBO from which it evolved, was of Latin American origin. Its small steps and swaying hip movements, as well as its infectious music, made it a craze on both sides of the Atlantic.

**Chad.** Small pieces of paper or card that are the detritus of a hole-punching machine. Although its origins are obscure, the word has been well established in American English since at least the 1940s. It never made much headway in Britain, though, so when it enjoyed its moment of notoriety in 2000 it caused more than usual interest there. The US presidential election of November 2000 was extremely closely fought, which gave rise in some cases to arguments over the interpretation of punched ballot papers. An abstruse mini-vocabulary of 'chad' was revealed, including 'dimple chad' (a slight indentation), 'hanging chad' (with one corner hanging off slightly) and 'pregnant chad' (bulging but not completely punched through).

**Chad** or **Mr Chad.** A character whose bald head and large nose were depicted appearing over a wall and inquiring, 'Wot, no [word filled in to suit the circumstances]?', as a comment on a shortage of some commodity during and after the Second World War. Chad was particularly popular among the forces and offered scope for light relief in many a difficult situation. He was the creation in 1938 of the cartoonist 'Chat' (George Edward Chatterton). *See also* GRAFFITI; KILROY.

**Chaff.** In modern usage, 'chaff' was adopted in the Second World War as a term for the thin strips of metallic foil that were released into the atmosphere from aircraft to deflect radar signals and prevent detection. The strips were scattered in the air like chaff blown in the wind.

**Chain letter.** A letter, frequently anonymous, that the recipient is asked to copy and send to a stated number of friends or acquaintances, requesting them to do likewise, the aim being to secure a large sum of money or some other material reward. The pernicious practice seems to have begun at the turn of the 20th century, and the *Daily Chronicle* for 27 July 1906 tells how a Miss Audrey Griffin of Hurstville, New South Wales, Australia, initiated such a letter with the aim of collecting a million used postage stamps. By the end of the century the chain letter had become a chain E-MAIL, and *The Times* of 13 May 1999 relates how a brewer offered to give away 2 million SIX-PACKS for the MILLENNIUM if a message by this method reached the same number of recipients. The initiator was purportedly one Gary D. Anderson, but no such person existed.

**Chain reaction.** A series of events in which each event is caused by the previous one. The expression is of scientific origin, applied first in the 1920s to a chemical reaction in which the products themselves promote the reaction, which may in some cases accelerate dramatically, and second in the 1940s to a process of nuclear fission that occurs in nuclear reactors and bombs.

**Chain smoker.** One who smokes continuously, lighting a new cigarette from the one being finished, so that they form a chain. The term dates from the 1930s.

**Chalet School.** The fictional international school in the Austrian Tyrol that features in a series of girls' stories by Elinor Brent-Dyer (1895–1969). The first in the series was *The School at the Chalet* (1925); the last, published posthumously, was *Prefects of the Summer School* (1970).

**Chalk and talk.** The traditional method of teaching, with the teacher using the blackboard to illustrate what he or she says, as distinct from more informal or interactive methods. The phrase dates from the 1930s or even earlier.

**Challenged.** A word used euphemistically to indicate that a person has a disability or impairment in a particular respect, its precise application being indicated by a preceding adverb. The original intention was to introduce a term that was more positive than 'handicapped' or 'disabled' in an expression such as 'physically challenged'. The usage was mocked by the media, however, who applied it whimsically to other areas, so that a short person was 'vertically challenged', one with bad teeth was 'dentally challenged', and a bald man was 'follicularly challenged'. The original usage arose in the United States in the 1980s. *See also* POLITICAL CORRECTNESS.

> [The US television series] *Freaks [and Geeks]* tells it like it really was, giving centre stage to the misfits, losers and athletically challenged.
>
> *heat* (23–29 September 1999)

**Challenger.** The name of the US space shuttle that on 28 January 1986 exploded 73 seconds after blast-off from Cape Canaveral, instantly killing all seven astronauts, including a high-school teacher, Christa McAuliffe, the first private citizen to take part in the US shuttle programme. The US public was shocked to see such a disaster take place live on their TV screens but was comforted by the words of the GREAT COMMUNICATOR, President Ronald Reagan, who in a national television broadcast quoted (without crediting his source) from the 1941 sonnet 'High Flight' by John Gillespie Magee (1922–41), a US-born pilot who served with the Royal Canadian Air Force in the Second World War and died while on a bombing raid over Germany:

> Oh! I have slipped the surly bonds of earth,
> And danced the skies on laughter-silvered wings …
> And, while with silent lifting mind I've trod
> The high, untrespassed sanctity of space,
> Put out my hand and touched the face of God.

The inquiry into the disaster, headed by the distinguished physicist and Nobel laureate Richard Feynman (1918–88), found that the rubber seals in the booster rocket had failed because of low temperatures on the Cape the night before the launch. The shuttle programme was suspended for two years until the fault was rectified.

On 1 February 2003 the space shuttle *Columbia* broke up on re-entry, killing all seven astronauts on board, including the first Israeli in space. The disaster was traced to the damage caused to insulating tiles when they were hit by a piece of insulation foam that became detached from an external fuel tank during the launch.

**Challenger, Professor.** The irascible black-bearded scientist created by Arthur Conan Doyle as the central character of his novel *The Lost World* (1912). Together with the explorer Lord John Roxton and the young newspaper reporter Edward Malone he goes in search of MAPLE WHITE LAND, where they discover living dinosaurs and ape-men. He subsequently appeared in two further novels, *The Poison Belt* (1913) and *The Land of Mist* (1926).

**Chambersisms.** Such may be called the idiosyncratic definitions that have regularly appeared in the various

editions of *Chambers Dictionary* since its original publication in 1901. Their number has declined over the years, presumably under the constraints of POLITICAL CORRECTNESS or simply on grounds of accuracy, but the following remain in the 2003 edition:

*double-locked*: locked by two turns of the key, as in some locks and many novels

*éclair*: a cake, long in shape but short in duration

*he-man*: a man of exaggerated or extreme virility, or what some women consider to be virility

*Japanese cedar*: a very tall Japanese conifer (*Cryptomeria japonica*) often dwarfed by Japanese gardeners

*jaywalker*: a careless pedestrian whom motorists are expected to avoid running down

*middle-aged*: between youth and old age, variously reckoned to suit the reckoner

*Pict*: one of a dwarfish race of underground dwellers, to whom (with the Romans, the Druids and Cromwell) ancient monuments are generally attributed

*picture restorer*: a person who cleans and tries to restore old pictures

*sea serpent*: an enormous marine animal of serpent-like form frequently seen and described by credulous sailors, imaginative landsmen and common liars

**Champagne Charlie.** A nickname given Charles Kennedy (b.1959), leader of the Liberal Democrats (1999–2006), on account of his fondness for a dram – to the extent that in January 2006 he admitted to a drinking problem, and was pressured into resigning (*see* MING THE MERCILESS). His bonhomie and appearances on TV earned him the alternative nicknames of Good Time Charlie and Chat Show Charlie. While a student debater he was known as Taxi Kennedy, after it was revealed that he had taken a cab from St Andrews to Edinburgh to catch a flight to a debate in Ireland. Kennedy's noted antipathy to exercise has ensured that the name has stuck. Kennedy was also dubbed Red Charlie by the press, after he wooed the trade unions at the TUC conference in Blackpool in 2002. He was generally regarded as more union-friendly than Labour leader Tony Blair.

**Champagne socialist.** A person who practises and advocates socialist beliefs while patently seen to be a consumer of the best things in life. The writer John Mortimer (b.1923), the Labour MP Barbara Follett (b.1942) and the newspaper tycoon Robert Maxwell (1923–91) are examples of the type cited in the media. The term came to be more generally associated with the NEW LABOUR image promoted by Tony Blair following the 1997 general election.

In a time which has given bachelors a bad name, he [Labour MP Frank Field] has preserved his good one. In a party of champagne socialists, he is the champagne monk.

*The Times* (31 July 1998)

The epithet 'Bollinger Bolshevik' had earlier been hurled at the Labour politician Aneurin Bevan (1897–1960) by Brendan Bracken:

You Bollinger Bolshevik, you ritzy Robespierre, you lounge-lizard Lenin. Look at you, swilling Max's champagne and calling yourself a socialist.

Quoted by Randolph Churchill in *Evening Standard* (8 August 1958)

*See also* LIMOUSINE LIBERAL.

**Chan, Charlie.** The Chinese-American detective who works for the Honolulu Police was created by the US writer Earl D. Biggers and first appeared in *The House Without a Key* (1925). He was allegedly based on Chang Apana, a real Hawaiian police detective. He is wise and impassive and solves many murder mysteries, usually with the help of his 'Number-One Son'. He went on to feature in a number of popular films and was memorably played by the Swedish actor Warner Oland in *Charlie Chan Carries On* (1931) and its many sequels. His translation to British television in the late 1950s (in the series *The New Adventures of Charlie Chan*, played by J. Carrol Naish) was rather less successful.

**Chance would be a fine thing.** If only…. A phrase expressing the speaker's regret that the desired opportunity is unlikely to present itself. The expression is a stock reply by a married woman to a single who says that she does not wish to marry.

**Chanel No. 5.** Possibly the most famous perfume ever, created in 1921 for the French fashion designer Coco Chanel (1883–1971). The world's bestselling fragrance is made from ylang-ylang from the Comoro Islands, jasmine from Grasse in the south of France and May rose – 'a true olfactory symphony', according to Chanel. It is a scent that has become associated with the world's most glamorous women. When the American film actress Marilyn Monroe was asked in the 1950s what she wore in bed, she replied 'Chanel No. 5'. In 2004 Nicole Kidman starred as the new face of Chanel No. 5 in the what is rumoured to be the most expensive TV and cinema commercial ever made, a love story filmed in Sydney and directed by Baz Luhrmann (who directed Kidman in *Moulin Rouge*, 2001).

**Changi.** A notorious Japanese prisoner of war camp in the Second World War, near the town of this name in eastern occupied Singapore. In 1945 the prisoners were released by the British, who stripped the Japanese guards of their uniforms and made them kneel naked and kowtowing in submission before the liberators.

**Channel Tunnel.** A plan to link Britain and France by a tunnel under the English Channel had been discussed long before 1986, when an Anglo-French agreement was signed and work began. French and British teams met up in 1990 and the official opening took place in 1994, attended by Queen Elizabeth II and President Mitterrand of France. The route runs from Folkestone to Sangatte near Calais and there are three tunnels, each 50km (31 miles) long, two for rail traffic and a third in the centre for services and security. The enterprise has been not without cost. Six British workers died during construction, and a fire closed the tunnel for two weeks in 1996.

**Chaos theory.** A branch of mathematics that deals with so-called chaotic systems, an example of one such system being an engineered structure such as an oil platform that is subjected to irregular and unpredictable wave stress. The science is also sometimes known as chaology. *See also* BUTTERFLY EFFECT.

**Chaplinesque.** In the style of the highly popular film actor Charlie Chaplin (1889–1977), whose roles usually involved an affecting blend of comedy and pathos, especially in the depiction of unrequited love. His most memorable character and mythic alter ego was the Tramp.

**Chappaquiddick.** A tiny island off the Massachusetts coast that gained worldwide notoriety on 18 July 1969 when Senator Edward Kennedy, brother of the late President John F. Kennedy, was involved in an accident in which a 28-year-old woman, Mary Jo Kopechne, was trapped and drowned when a car he was driving ran off a small bridge. After an initial attempt to conceal the whole incident, Kennedy was eventually exonerated, despite a legal ruling that he had probably been driving negligently and had thus contributed to Miss Kopechne's death. Popular opinion claimed that Kennedy had escaped penalty through his social standing and political power, and the whole episode left a bitter taste in the mouth of the US public. *See also* KENNEDY CURSE.

**Chariots Offiah.** The rugby league and union wing Martin Offiah (b.1966). His nickname, punning on the title of the film CHARIOTS OF FIRE, reflects his speed and strength as a runner.

**Chariots of Fire.** A film (1981) about the rivalry between two British runners competing in the 1924 Olympics. Written by Colin Welland (b.1934) and starring Ben Cross and Ian Charleson, it featured a memorable soundtrack by Vangelis, which quickly became a signature tune for sporting enthusiasts everywhere. The title came from William Blake's poem 'Jerusalem', the preface to his epic poem *Milton* (1804–08), which is best known today as an anthemic hymn with strong patriotic overtones:

> Bring me my bow of burning gold!
> Bring me my arrows of desire!
> Bring me my spear! O clouds, unfold!
> Bring me my chariot of fire!
>
> WILLIAM BLAKE: 'Jerusalem'

**Charismatic movement.** A fundamentalist movement within many leading Christian churches that emphasizes group worship and the exercise of the spiritual 'gifts' of divine healing and glossolalia, or 'speaking in tongues'. It began in North America in the 1960s and is now worldwide. It has much in common with Pentecostalism, although since the 1970s its 'enthusiastic' features have become less evident. By the early 1980s it had become one of the main lay movements in the Roman Catholic Church, as well as the Church of England, and was recognized as such by the Vatican. Underlying the movement is an implicit understanding of 'charisma' itself as a word that in the original Greek means 'gift of grace'.

**Charity mugger.** *See* CHUGGER.

**Charleston.** A dance popular in the first half of the 1920s, apparently originating as a back-kicking dance among young African Americans in South Carolina, where Charleston is the main seaport. Dancers swivelled on the balls of their feet, swayed their body from side to side and knocked their knees with their hands in a furious frenzy, motions condemned by some killjoys as 'immoral'.

**Charlie.** *See* VICTOR CHARLIE.

**Charlie and the Chocolate Factory.** A fantasy novel (1964) by Roald Dahl (1916–90), in which Charlie Buckett wins a ticket that allows him to visit a chocolate factory owned by Mr Willy Wonka and manned by pygmies called Oompa-Loompas. It was filmed as *Willy Wonka and the Chocolate Factory* (1971), with Gene Wilder as Willy Wonka, and again as *Charlie and the Chocolate Factory* (2005), with Johnny Depp in the main part.

**Charlie's Angels.** A popular US television crime drama series screened from 1977 to 1982. It centred on three glamorous PRIVATE EYES, played by Farrah Fawcett-Majors, Kate Jackson and Jaclyn Smith, who are sent out 'crime-busting' by Charlie Townsend, the wealthy head of Townsend Investigations. The series was derided by many for its blatant sexism, and each episode opened with the following foreword: 'Once upon a time there were three little girls who went to the police academy and they were each assigned very hazardous duties, but I took them away from all that and they now work for me. My name is Charlie.' Viewers never saw Charlie, who communicated with his trio by office intercom. In 2000 a feature-film version of *Charlie's Angels* was released, starring Cameron Diaz, Drew Barrymore and Lucy Liu. A sequel, *Charlie's Angels: Full Throttle*, came out in 2003.

**Charlotte's Web.** A classic children's novel (1952) by the American writer E.B. White, about a young pig and a wise and motherly spider. An animated feature film of the story was released in 1972.

**Charm and cheek.** A disarming combination of 'niceness and nerve' that is popularly believed to enhance a person's prospects in an enterprise, especially in politics. *See also* CHARM OFFENSIVE.

**Charm bracelet.** A bracelet hung with charms, as small ornaments or trinkets fancifully believed to protect the wearer on the one hand and attract admirers on the other.

**Charm offensive.** The calculated use of personal charm or assumed amiability to achieve a particular end, especially in politics. The expression dates from the 1970s.

**Charm school.** An educational establishment where young women are taught social graces such as deportment and etiquette. Such schools burgeoned in the 1950s at a time when the Western world was anxious to return to civilized values after the brutalization and degradation of the Second World War.

**Charter 88.** A pressure group that in 1988 published a document arguing that several specific reforms were needed in Britain. Among them were a written constitution, a bill of rights, devolution to a Scottish assembly, proportional representation and freedom of information. Some of these aims are no longer mere aspirations. Proportional representation was adopted for the European elections of 1999, and that same year saw the opening of a Scottish parliament. A Freedom of Information Act was passed in 2000, and another for Scotland in 2002. The group's name relates both to the year in which its charter appeared and to 1688, the year of the Glorious Revolution, which introduced constitutional monarchy.

**Charter 77.** A petition drawn up in Czechoslovakia in January 1977 by a group of intellectuals, listing their grievances over the human-rights abuses of the communist regime. Many of the signatories were subsequently detained by the authorities, but the group remained active over the next decade or so, and played a key role in the Velvet Revolution (*see under* REVOLUTION NAMES) that toppled the communist regime in late 1989. Among the signatories was the playwright Václav Havel (b.1936), who during the revolution became spokesman for the main opposition group, Civic Forum, and by the end of the year had become president.

**Chase one's tail.** To indulge in a futile pursuit; to go round in circles. Dogs when excited or frenzied may literally chase their tails. The expression dates from the 1960s.

**Chase the dragon.** To smoke HEROIN. The drug is placed on a folded piece of tinfoil, which is heated with a taper. As the fumes are inhaled through a tube or roll of paper, they waft up and down the tinfoil with movements resembling the undulating tail of a dragon. Hence the term, reputedly translated from the Chinese.

**Chat room.** An area on the INTERNET or other computer network where users can communicate with one another, typically on a particular topic. See also INSTANT MESSAGING.

**Chat Show Charlie.** *See* CHAMPAGNE CHARLIE.

**Chatterbox.** A British children's magazine published between 1866 and 1948. Its contents included a mixture of 'improving' material such as factual articles and religious instruction.

**Chattering classes.** A slighting term for educated people, especially those in academic, artistic or media circles, who enjoy 'chattering' in print on issues of topical interest. The implication is that although writing extensively on such matters they have little or no first-hand knowledge of them. The phrase dates from the early 1980s, when it was applied to the city-oriented, left-wing intelligentsia who held forth over the dinner table. Its coinage has been attributed to the political columnist Alan Watkins (b.1933), although the earliest record of it in the *OED* is from Clive James's *Falling towards England* (1985), and it also became particularly associated with the writer Auberon Waugh. *See also* HAMPSTEAD SET.

**Chatterley, Lady.** The repressed aristocratic woman who finds sexual release with her gamekeeper, Oliver Mellors, in D.H. Lawrence's often misunderstood novel LADY CHATTERLEY'S LOVER (1928). Her name subsequently entered the language as something of a smutty joke. She is said to have been based on Lady Cynthia Asquith (1887–1960).

**Chat-up line.** An enquiry or remark used as a flirtatious or seductive gambit, such as the hackneyed 'Do you come here often?'

The Shaftesbury Theatre is hosting a singles night for its musical *Rent*, a chance for audiences in search of a partner to try their best chat-up lines.

*The Times* (6 September 1999)

**Chav.** A materialistic British working-class youth with a fondness for fashionable clothes and ostentatious jewellery (*see* BLING). The term, which is first recorded in 1998, is unisex, but a female of the species can also be a 'chavette'. It probably comes from the old Polari word 'chavy', meaning 'child', which in turn goes back to Romani *chavi*, but other derivations have been suggested, including Chatham, a Kentish town that is home to many chavs, and the northeastern dialect term 'charver' or 'charva', which in the 1990s was applied to a young male of the chav type.

> Chavs are the non-respectable working classes. Key chav characteristics apparently include being called Jasmine, Tiffany or Wayne, driving a souped-up Vauxhall Nova, and wearing 'prison-white' trainers and FCUK zip-up tops. Chav is, in short, Essex girl and the beshellsuited scouser, all rolled into one great Burberry-patterned beast.
>
> *The Guardian* (24 October 2004)

As the above quotation suggests, a distinguishing sartorial feature of the chav is his/her fondness for Burberry, a brand of clothing characterized by a fawn and red check pattern, and traditionally favoured by SLOANE RANGERS and others of that ilk (the public-school-educated Tony Blair has been photographed wearing a Burberry-collared shirt). Many pubs and bars now ban anyone wearing Burberry. Another sartorial affectation of the chav is the fondness for tucking the legs of his tracksuit into his Umbro socks, while the chavette delights in large hooped earrings and hair done in a CROYDON FACELIFT. Popular accessories include baseball caps and Staffordshire bull terriers. Chavs, once they get behind the wheel of a car (typically a Vauxhall Nova), metamorphose into BOY RACERS.

Inevitably, the phenomenon (like that of the ESSEX GIRL) has given rise to a number of jokes, for example:

> *Q.* What do you call a chavette in a white tracksuit? *A.* The bride.

> *Q.* If you pass two chavs in a car and you can't hear any music, who's driving? *A.* The police.

In some parts of the UK chavs are known by different names, for example, 'ned' (Glasgow), 'scally' (Liverpool) and 'TOWNIE' (London).

*See also* KING OF CHAVS; SHELL SUIT.

**Cheap and cheerful.** Simple and inexpensive but not unattractive, as of a garment or fashion detail but also applied to a restaurant.

**Cheap shot.** An unworthy or unfair critical remark. The term seems to have originated in US sporting slang, denoting a blow delivered unfairly or against an unprepared opponent, but it was being used in its current, much more general sense by the early 1970s.

> The cheap-shot kid. Clinton jabs at Bush for cutting taxes. How quick he forgets. If things are so bad, then why are they so good?
>
> LARRY KUDLOW: *National Review Online* (28 July 2004)

**Check.** An exclamation of assent or agreement, with a sense on the lines of 'OK', 'That's right' or 'Just as I thought'. It is of US origin and dates from the 1920s.

> The main murder victim is someone disliked by many people with varied motives. Check. Poirot sports foolish facial fur and refers to himself in the third person. Check. Someone with vital information gets a knife in the neck, just as they are about to blab. Check.
>
> *heat*, review of television drama *Poirot: Lord Edgware Dies* (17–23 February 2000)

**Check out the plumbing.** A US euphemism, one of many, meaning to visit the toilet.

**Checkpoint Charlie.** The most notorious of the official crossing-points between East and West Berlin, at the junction of Friedrichstrasse and Kochstrasse in the US sector. It took its name from the NATO phonetic code for the letter C, as it was the third crossing point in order. The others were Checkpoint Alpha, at Helmstedt–Marienborn, and Checkpoint Bravo, at Dreilinden–Drewitz. Checkpoint Charlie was the only crossing-point to be open round the clock. It became familiar to the public at large as much from spy fiction and thrillers such as Len Deighton's *Funeral in Berlin* (1965) as from its real existence in the COLD WAR. It was dismantled in 1990. That year, the British foreign secretary Dougland Hurd, speaking in Berlin, said:

> We should not forget the reason for which Checkpoint Charlie stood here for so many years, but no one can be sorry that it is going. At long last we are bringing 'Charlie' in from the cold.

*See also* BERLIN WALL; *The* SPY WHO CAME IN FROM THE COLD.

**Cheeky Chappie.** A billboard byname for the comedian Max Miller, whose original name was Thomas Henry Sargent (1894–1963), alluding to his JACK THE LAD persona and his love of innuendo and double entendres. His PLUS FOURS, black and white CO-RESPONDENT SHOES, snow-white HOMBURG and gaudy KIPPER TIE enhanced his brash image.

**Cheerio!** Goodbye! A parting expression of good wishes dating from the early years of the 20th century. The word derives from 'to cheer' in the sense 'to take courage', but later became associated with 'cheery'. A use as a friendly wish before drinking was also current but has now been largely superseded by 'cheers!'

> And 'cheerioh' and 'cheeri-bye'
> Across the waste of waters die.
>
> JOHN BETJEMAN: *New Bats in Old Belfries*, 'Henley-on-Thames' (1945)

**Cheerleaders.** In the United States, a team of girls who, as their name implies, 'lead the cheers' or perform organized cheering, chanting and dancing in support of a sports team at a match. Every high school has such a team, with members chosen for their looks, ability and enthusiasm, and professional sports teams have similar supporters in the form of well-paid dancers. Their colourful costumes with eye-catching MINISKIRTS or HOT PANTS provide much of the attraction. The cheerleaders of the Dallas Cowboys American football team are particularly noted for their poise and panache. *See also* RA-RA SKIRT.

**Cheese and wine party.** A social gathering at which cubelets of cheese and glasses of wine are served but where the emphasis is on business rather than pleasure, as at a fundraising event.

> The disclosure of Mr Dyke's presence at the most expensive cheese and wine party in British political history will be seized on by opponents of his candidacy within the BBC.
>
> *The Times* (17 May 1999)

The cheese and wine party became fashionable in the 1960s, but barely survived the 1970s.

**Cheesecake.** Pictures or photographs of women displayed for their sex appeal (*see* BEEFCAKE). A literal cheesecake is a type of rich tart, filled with a mixture of cream cheese, cream, sugar, and sometimes fruit, with or without a fruit topping. The colloquial equation of sweet and succulent food with attractive women is common. This particular example dates from the 1930s, while others are 'cookie', 'crumpet' and 'cupcake'. *See also* TWINKIE.

**Cheesed off.** Fed up, disgusted, disgruntled, like milk that has gone sour in the process of becoming cheese. *See also* BROWNED OFF.

**Cheese-eating.** *See* SURRENDER-MONKEY.

**Cheka.** *See* KGB.

**Chelsea Flower Show.** An annual summer display organized by the Royal Horticultural Society in the grounds of the Royal Hospital, Chelsea, since 1913. The exhibits range from prize vegetables to whole gardens, all housed on the 4.5ha (11 acres) of lawn. Opening night is a major occasion, attended by members of the royal family and other celebrities. The event lasts four days and on the final day a bell is rung at 5 p.m., when remaining exhibits are sold to the public.

**Chelsea tractor.** A derisive early 21st-century nickname for fuel-inefficient 4×4 off-road vehicles, designed for rough terrain, as used by the Chelsea set and YUMMY MUMMIES (or their nannies/au pairs) for doing the shopping, taking their children to school (hence an alternative designation, 'mum trucks'), driving to lunch, etc. London Mayor Ken Livingstone described their drivers as 'complete idiots'. *See also* SPORT-UTILITY VEHICLE.

**Chemical Ali.** The nickname of the Iraqi general, Ali Hassan al-Majid (b.1941), a cousin of Saddam Hussein, and defence minister in his government. His nickname refers to the belief that it was he who ordered the notorious chemical attack on the Kurdish town of Halabja in 1988, which resulted in the deaths of some 5000 people. Also known as the Butcher of Kurdistan, he was arrested by US occupation forces in August 2003. *See also* COMICAL ALI.

**Chemin des Dames.** (French, 'Ladies' Way'.) A ridge between the rivers Aisne and Ailette in northern France that was the scene of desperate fighting in the First World War. On 16 April 1917 the French advance under General Nivelle met with failure here after earlier successes at Laffaux, Hurtebise and Berry-au-Bac, in which French tanks were used for the first time, and on 27 May 1918 the German advance towards the Marne under General Ludendorff finally won through here. The ridge itself, an old Roman road, is said to take its name from the daughters of Louis XV (1710–74), the 'Ladies of France'. *See also* TIGER.

**Cheongsam.** (Chinese, 'long dress'.) A figure-hugging traditional Chinese dress that came into vogue among Western women in the mid-1990s as stylish evening wear. It is usually made from lustrous flower-patterned silk, closed in front by a 'frog' closure and topped with a round mandarin collar.

**Cheque-book journalism.** A phrase first current in the 1960s for the practice of securing exclusive rights to newspaper stories by offering large sums of money to anyone who can provide them, with scant regard for any ethical or moral considerations.

> Newspapers … should … come to a self-denying ordinance to abandon the cheque-book journalism of confession stories by criminals, prominent divorcees and others who have won notoriety.
>
> *New Statesman* (24 May 1963)

**Cheque is in the post, The.** A time-honoured excuse for failure to make a payment.

> When you are owed £200, you hear that great lie about the cheque being in the post a lot. When you are owed £20,000, the cheque is posted early. £2 million and they will probably send it by courier with a bouquet.
>
> *The Times* (17 January 2000)

However, in these days of online banking, debit cards, BACS payments, etc., the excuse is becoming ever less plausible.

**Chequers.** The official country residence of the prime minister, in the Chilterns near Wendover, Buckinghamshire, was presented to the nation for this purpose by Lord Lee of Fareham in 1917 and was first so used by Lloyd George in 1921. The house itself is Tudor in origin but with Victorian additions and substantial remodelling by Lee over the period 1909–12. Its formal name is Chequers Court and the Tudor house was built on the site of a 13th-century one owned by Laurence de Scaccario, whose own name probably meant that he was an official of the medieval Court of Exchequer, the court of law that dealt with matters of revenue. 'Scaccario' was thus rendered as the medieval equivalent of modern 'Exchequer' and subsequently shortened to 'Chequers'. The history of the name is in the event appropriate, since the prime minister is also First Lord of the Treasury.

**Cherished number.** A vehicle registration number that has been specially selected by the vehicle's owner to represent some personal whim or characteristic, as expressed by a legally prescribed combination and arrangement of letters and figures. The latter are often exploited as letters, so that 0 is O, 1 is I or L, 2 is Z, 5 is S, 6 is G, 13 is B and so on. CLA55Y could thus be seen as 'classy'. The most common device is to represent one's own name or initials.

A pioneer of the game was the Scottish comedian Harry Tate (1872–1940) who had T8 on his old Ford. Lord Brabazon of Tara (1884–1964), the first pilot to obtain the Royal Aero Club Flying Certificate, later secured FLY1, while Brigadier-General A.C. Critchley (1890–1963) acquired all the numbers GRA1 to GRA36 for himself and his Greyhound Racing Association colleagues. Celebrities continue to adopt the dodge, so that the comedian Jimmy Tarbuck is COM 1C, and when the flamboyant Conservative MP Jeffrey Archer made his first appearance in parliament in 1969 his personalized number plate was SOM 1 while that of his wife was ANY 1. Cars of ambassadors and high commissioners in Britain usually have a registration number 1 before or after the country's abbreviated name. Thus Australia has AUS 1, Canada has CAN 1, France has FRA 1, Norway has 1 NWY and so on. Spain, truer to the spirit, has SPA 1N. *See also* NAB; VANITY PLATE.

**Chernobyl.** A town near Kiev, Ukraine, where the world's worst nuclear accident occurred on 26 April 1986. Huge amounts of radioactive material were released into the atmosphere when one of a nuclear power station's four reactors exploded during attempts to install a safety system. The accident caused the deaths of 30 and radiation sickness among a further 200, some of whom later died. The radioactivity was spread by the wind over Belarus and Ukraine, and traces of it reached as far as France and Italy. The disaster dealt a grave blow to the Soviet Union's nuclear power programme.

**Cherry on the cake.** The finishing touch to something that is already agreeable. An iced cake is often decorated with a single cherry on top.

**Cherry-picker.** A name given to any of various sorts of crane, especially one with a small platform on top of an extendable arm, on which someone can stand to do work high above ground (as it were, picking cherries from a tree). The term is first recorded in 1945.

**Cherry reds.** A colloquial term for DOC MARTENS or BOVVER BOOTS, especially those of this colour worn by a SKINHEAD as part of his 'uniform'.

> Their ['skinheads'] hair is shaved within an eighth of an inch from the scalp, and they are dressed in oversized workpants, thin red suspenders and hobnailed, steeltoed boots costing about $10 and known as 'cherry reds'.
> *Time* (8 June 1970)

**Cheryl.** A nickname given to Princess Diana (*see* PEOPLE'S PRINCESS) by *Private Eye* (*compare* BRENDA).

**Chew the carpet.** To lose emotional control; to suffer a tantrum. The image is of a person falling to the floor and biting the carpet in anger or frustration. The expression is of US origin and dates from the 1950s.

**Chiantishire.** A media name for the area of Tuscany in Italy where Chianti wine is produced, especially in its role as a holiday resort for the English middle classes, who may even purchase homes there. The term is sometimes attributed to the writer and barrister John Mortimer (b.1923).

> The British are coming, flooding into Pisa airport, known as Pizza to the BA hostesses. They're invading Tuscany, part of Italy which has become part of England, so that it's known as Chiantishire to the natives.
> JOHN MORTIMER: in *Mortimer in Tuscany* (television programme) (17 May 1988)

**Chicago Bears.** A record-breaking professional American football team, with a home base at Wrigley Field, Chicago. They hold the record for the greatest number of consecutive wins, 18 (twice), in the National Football League, and their star player, George Blanda, played in a record 340 games in a record 26 seasons between 1949 and 1958.

**Chicago Seven.** The seven defendants convicted in 1970 of conspiracy to incite a riot following disturbances during the Democratic National Convention at Chicago in 1968: Rennie David, David T. Dellinger, John Froines, Thomas Hayden, Abbie Hoffman, Jerry C. Rubin and Lee Weiner. They were originally dubbed the Chicago Eight but an eighth defendant, Bobby Seale, was tried separately. The name set a pattern for subsequent groups of protesters or activists, especially when (actually or allegedly) wrongly convicted. *See also* BIRMINGHAM SIX; GUILDFORD FOUR; WINCHESTER THREE.

**Chicken à la King.** Cooked chicken breast served in a cream sauce with mushrooms and peppers. The name is said to compliment E. Clark King, the New York hotel proprietor who devised the dish at the turn of the 20th century.

**Chicken-and-egg situation.** An unresolved problem as to which of two things caused the other. The allusion is to the old riddle: 'Which came first, the chicken or the egg?' If the answer is 'chicken', then how was it hatched? If the answer is 'egg', then how was it laid? 'Chicken and egg' in this sense arose in the 1950s. An earlier equivalent dating from the 1930s was 'hen and egg'.

**Chickenhawks.** US Republicans who support military action abroad (especially against Iraq in 2003) – and are thus dubbed 'hawks' (*see* HAWKS AND DOVES) – but who have themselves avoided active service – and are hence 'chicken', i.e. cowardly. During the Vietnam War George W. Bush found a post at home with the National Guard, Dick Cheney had 'other priorities' at the time, Richard Perle attended the University of Chicago and John Ashcroft postponed his tour in Vietnam while he taught business education.

> We know who the chickenhawks are. They talk tough on national defense and military issues and cast aspersions on others. When it was their turn to serve where were they? AWOL, that's where they were … the lead chickenhawk against Senator Kerry [is] the vice president of the United States, Vice President Cheney.
> SENATOR FRANK LAUTENBERG: speaking in the US Senate (28 April 2004)

*See also* NEOCON.

**Chicken Kiev.** Chicken breast fried or baked and filled with garlic butter. The dish first emerged in the 1960s and was one of the first successful supermarket ready-made meals. The original name was 'chicken cutlet Kiev', translating Russian *kotlety po-kievski*, 'cutlets in the Kiev manner'.

**Chicken out.** To back down through fear or loss of nerve. The chicken is traditionally regarded as a nervous or cowardly creature. Hens will flee clucking in panic if approached unless the approacher is bringing their regular feed.

**Chicken ranch.** A brothel, especially an out-of-town brothel in Texas. The term is said to have been originally applied to such an establishment in La Grange, Texas, which supposedly could trace its history back to the 1840s and which became famous as the setting of the 1978 Broadway musical *The Best Little Whorehouse in Texas*. (In French, *poule* 'chicken' is used metaphorically for 'prostitute', and English 'chicken' can denote a young inexperienced prostitute.)

**Chicken run.** A term of the mid-1990s for the abandonment by a sitting MP of a marginal seat for a safer one. The specific application was to Conservative MPs who fled to safer seats in this way in anticipation of a rough ride in the forthcoming general election (1997). The phrase puns on 'chicken' in the sense of coward, a chicken run normally being an enclosure for domestic fowls. An earlier chicken run existed as a derisory term used in Rhodesia (now Zimbabwe) for the flight from the country of whites in the 1970s in anticipation of black rule.

***Chicken Soup with Barley.*** A play (1958) by the British playwright Arnold Wesker (b.1932) about the life of the Jewish Kahn family in East London in the 1930s. The first part of a trilogy, completed by *Roots* (1959) and *I'm Talking About Jerusalem* (1960), in which the central theme is that of caring, the play owed its title to the chicken soup young Ada Kahn is brought by a kind neighbour when she is ill.

Chicken soup is traditional Jewish comfort food, as in the bestselling American collection of spiritually uplifting stories, *Chicken Soup for the Soul* (1993), by Jack Canfield and Mark Victor Hansen. This has spawned numerous successors and turned into a major industry, to the extent that Chicken Soup is now a registered trademark.

**Chick flick.** A colloquialism for a TEARJERKER with an all-female cast and a story line involving much expression of emotion, mainly in the form of weeping, laughing, hugging and the like. Examples of such films, also known as 'sisterhood dramas', are *Boys on the Side* (1995), *The First Wives Club* (1996), *A Thousand Acres* (1997), *Hanging Up* (1999) and *Mona Lisa Smile* (2003). In a broader sense the term is often applied in general to ROM-COMS and films

focused around love, boy-meets-girl and friendship as opposed to action, death and destruction, which are assumed to be traits men look for in their cinematic entertainment. *Dirty Dancing* (1987), *Pretty Woman* (1990), *Sleepless in Seattle* (1993) and *Clueless* (1995), for example, would all be classed as chick flicks.

**Chick lit.** A journalistic term for the rash of urban novels since the 1990s that are meant to appeal strongly to (mainly younger) female readers, and which are mostly written by women. The term usually implies a lightness of touch, and comedies of manners concerning confused and bewildered TWENTY-SOMETHINGS and THIRTY-SOMETHINGS abound, almost invariably ending with the still endearingly confused heroine finding and keeping her Mr Right. Prominent authors include Helen Fielding (*see* Bridget JONES), Kathy Lette and Wendy Holden, and the genre tends to be identifiable in bookshops by the identikit colourful covers favoured by its publishers.

**Chief, The.** The nickname of Herbert Hoover (1874–1964), 31st US president. The hardly original name for a boss or leader here specifically related to Hoover's influence as secretary of commerce (1917–21). The public appearance of a US president is traditionally greeted with 'Hail to the Chief', James Sanderson's music to verses from Sir Walter Scott's *The Lady of the Lake* (1810), beginning with the line: 'Hail to the Chief who in triumph advances!'

**Chief Sitting Bull.** *See* BOMBER SHORT.

***Chien Andalou, Un.*** *See* SURREALISM.

**Child-bearing hips.** Broad hips, which in a girl or young woman popularly promise the birth of several children. The term is really a misnomer, since all girls at puberty develop wider hips than boys to provide for the future bearing of children.

***Child of Our Time, A.*** A wartime oratorio by Michael Tippett (1905–98) with a libretto by the composer. The work was written in 1939–41 and first performed in 1944. The 'child' of the title is Herschel Grynszpan, a Polish-Jewish student whose assassination in Paris of the German diplomat Ernst vom Rath on 7 November 1938 led to *Kristallnacht*, a night of violence against Jews and their property in Germany (*see* HOLOCAUST). Escalating official persecution followed. Tippett uses Negro spirituals at important points in the score, as Bach had used chorales in his Passions.

***Children of a Lesser God.*** A play (1979) by the US playwright Mark Medoff (b.1940) about the efforts of a hearing therapist to develop a relationship with a profoundly deaf young woman who refuses all offers of help. The title comes from Tennyson:

For why is all around us here

As if some lesser god had made the world,

But had not force to shape it as he would.

*Idylls of the King*, 'The Passing of Arthur' (1869)

**Children of all ages.** Everyone, including adults. A jocular formula popular with local radio broadcasters and first current in the 1950s. 'From nine to ninety' is sometimes added.

Obscenities are so frequently used on television that they are regarded as acceptable parlance; children of all ages and classes use obscene language in public.

*Daily Telegraph*, letter to the editor (16 May 1994)

**Children of God.** A controversial religious group that grew out of the JESUS MOVEMENT of the 1960s. It was founded in 1968 in California by David Berg and from the first its DROPOUT members adopted a strict communal lifestyle. Centres were set up in cities across the United States, but then some of the 'Children' made their way to London, and the group set up its headquarters there in 1971, using donated properties. The 'communities' or colonies formed the foundation of the group's activities and total commitment was required by each member. Emphasis was placed on the sharing of everything, and all members were expected to give up their personal possessions in accordance with the teaching of Jesus. Their political platform was 'godly socialism' and their creed that the world was in the 'last days'. The collapse of the United States in particular was prophesied.

**Children's Corner.** The set of six charming piano pieces by Claude Debussy (1862–1918) was dedicated to his daughter and written in 1906–8. The titles of the pieces are in English, presumably influenced by the family's English governess. The first piece is 'Doctor Gradus ad Parnassum', a parody of a series of studies by Clementi from 1817 (*Gradus ad Parnassum* is Latin for 'steps to Parnassus', the home of the classical Greek muses); the other pieces are 'Jimbo's Lullaby' (thought to be an error for 'Jumbo', given that Jimbo is a toy elephant), 'Serenade for the Doll', 'The Snow is Dancing', 'The Little Shepherd' and 'Golliwogg's Cakewalk'. A cakewalk was a kind of African American competitive dance with complex steps, for which a cake was awarded as a prize, and the 'Golliwogg's Cakewalk' includes a satirical musical quotation from Wagner's love-and-death music drama, *Tristan und Isolde* (1865).

**Children's Hour.** A popular radio programme for children, broadcast continuously by the BBC from 1922, the first year of its existence, to 1964. It went out early each weekday evening and for many years had regional editions. Its

presenters came to seem like members of the family, and were accordingly known as Aunt or Uncle. The best known was UNCLE MAC, in real life Derek McCulloch (1897–1967), and it was he who played LARRY THE LAMB in the programme's famous TOYTOWN. There were protests from adults and children alike when the programme was brought to an end, but audiences were falling as a result of the rise of television and the success of programmes such as BLUE PETER. The 'hour' of the title was not intended literally and the programme lasted a true hour for only two years. The title came from the first verse of a poem by Longfellow:

Between the dark and the daylight,

When the night is beginning to lower,

Comes a pause in the day's occupations,

That is known as the Children's Hour.

H.W. LONGFELLOW: *Birds of Passage*, Flight the Second, 'The Children's Hour' (1860)

In the later Victorian and Edwardian period, the 'children's hour' was the time between afternoon tea and dressing for dinner, when children might be seen, if not necessarily heard.

**Children's Hour, The.** A play (1934) by US playwright Lillian Hellman (1905–84) about the scandal that erupts after a teacher is accused of lesbianism by a vengeful pupil. Filmed in 1936, the play was based on a real case that was reported in Scotland in the 19th century, pointed out to the author by her close friend, the crime novelist Dashiell Hammett.

**Children's Newspaper, The.** A newspaper for children published from 22 March 1919 until 1 May 1965 and edited by Arthur Mee (1875–1943) until his death. Mee was also editor of *The Children's Encyclopaedia*, also published by Alfred Harmsworth's (Lord Northcliffe's) Amalgamated Press. Like *The Children's Encyclopaedia*, *The Children's Newspaper* concentrated on stories of heroism and individual achievement and also featured serial stories, photo pages and maps.

**Chill out.** To relax; to take it easy. The phrase was originated by African American US teenagers in the 1970s but later spread to black and white youths on both sides of the Atlantic. The concept is of being COOL. At RAVES and clubs, 'chill-out rooms' are often provided, where dancers may relax and literally cool down, listening to laid-back 'chill-out music' and drinking water, before re-entering the frenetic fray on the dance floor.

**Chilly bom-bom.** A pleasant phrase to indicate that it is unpleasantly cold. The words come from Cliff Friend's song 'I Love My Chili Bom-Bom' (1923), which also gave the name of the actress Chili Bouchier (1909–99), born Dorothy Boucher, on beginning her career as a teenage model.

**Chinaman.** A cricketing term (not to be confused with GOOGLY) denoting an offbreak bowled by a left-handed bowler to a right-handed batsman. It is said that the name derives from the Trinidadian bowler Ellis Achong (1904–86), who, although he played for the West Indies, was actually Chinese and who practised this kind of bowling, although not the first to do so. The term first became current in the 1930s.

**China syndrome.** A hypothetical series of events following the meltdown of a nuclear reactor, the fantastic premise being that the meltdown would pass through the earth's core from the United States and come out on the opposite side of the world in China. The term was popularized by the film *The China Syndrome* (1979) about attempts to conceal a nuclear danger, and the catastrophe at CHERNOBYL in 1986 gave it greater relevance.

**Chindits.** The long-range penetration force commanded by the maverick Major General Orde Wingate in the Second World War. In 1943 they entered Japanese-held Burma from the west, crossed the River Chindwin and, with supplies dropped by air, conducted guerrilla operations against the Japanese until they reached the River Irrawaddy. Finding the terrain unfavourable on crossing that river, however, they were obliged to make a circuitous return to India. They took their name from the *chinthe*, the fabulous lion that guards Burmese pagodas, and adopted the creature as their emblem. The name of the Chindwin itself may have influenced the choice.

**Chinese burn.** In the terminology of the school playground, a form of child-on-child torture that involves grasping the victim's arm tightly with both hands and twisting them in opposite directions. The expression is first recorded in 1956.

**Chinese Girl, The.** A work by the Siberian-born South African painter Vladimir Tretchikoff (1913–2006) of a young oriental woman with a blue-green face. Derided by the critics as hyper-kitsch, it is the bestselling print of all time, and adorned millions of sitting-room walls in the 1960s and 1970s.

**Chinese restaurant.** A restaurant specializing in Chinese 'take-away' dishes, a regular outlet on the British High Street. The first Chinese restaurant in Europe opened in London in 1908, when Chung Koon, a Chinese ship's cook, left his vessel and, marrying an English girl, set up an eating establishment in Piccadilly Circus. The restaurant, the Cathay, catered mainly for old colonial types who had returned to England from the Orient. Its popularity increased in the Second World War, when US GIs began taking their girlfriends there. Other family-run restaurants started to open elsewhere in London and in cities such as Liverpool and Manchester, their chief clientèle after the war being British soldiers who had returned from the Far East. The aroma of CHOP SUEY and CHOW MEIN is now familiar in even the smallest market town.

**Chinese restaurant syndrome.** A short-lived malady that can appear in a small number of people after eating in a CHINESE RESTAURANT. Symptoms include headache, dizziness and flushing and the cause is an excessive use of the flavouring agent monosodium glutamate. The illness is also known as Kwok's disease, after Robert Kwok, the US doctor who first described it in the 1960s.

**Chinese slavery.** Virtual slavery in the form of much hard work for negligible rewards. The phrase became widely used as a political slogan by the Liberals from 1903, when Arthur Balfour's Conservative government (1902–5) introduced coolies from China to combat the shortage of 'Kaffir' labour in the Rand gold mines after the dislocation caused by the South African War. They were kept in compounds and allowed out only under permit.

**Chinese wall.** On the Stock Exchange and in banks, a ban on the passing or leak of confidential financial information from one department to another, especially when detrimental to a client. The allusion is to the Great Wall of China.

**Chinese water torture.** A form of torture in which water drips steadily onto a bound victim's forehead with the aim of driving him insane.

**Chinese whispers.** Mistakes caused by faulty communication. The reference is to the party game in which a message is passed in a whisper to all the participants in turn. By the time it reaches the last player, it is so distorted that it might as well be in Chinese. A famous example is the military message 'Send reinforcements, we are going to advance', which emerged as 'Send three and fourpence, we are going to a dance.'

**Chingford Skinhead** or **Strangler.** A media nickname for Norman (now Lord) Tebbit (b.1931), the rightwing populist Europhobe MP for Chingford from 1974 (he had previously represented Epping, 1970–4) until his elevation to the peerage in 1992. He is known for his abrasive manner and robust invective and was a leading figure in the cabinets of Margaret Thatcher in the 1980s. He famously told the unemployed to get on their bikes to find work, as his own father had done in the GREAT DEPRESSION. *See also* SEMI-HOUSETRAINED POLECAT; SKINHEAD.

**Chinless wonder.** A vacuous upper-class male, who typically or supposedly has a receding chin, a feature that when firm is indicative of strength or determination. The expression dates from the 1960s and probably puns on the BONELESS WONDER, the contortionist of classic circus repute.

**Chin music.** Originally, in early 19th-century American English, talk, especially of an impudent or presumptuous variety. In the 1960s the expression was put to more evocative use in baseball, to denote a pitch thrown near a batter's chin, and it was enthusiastically adopted by West Indian cricket followers for the sort of short-pitched deliveries that their fast bowlers sent humming past batsmen's faces.

**Chip and PIN.** A verification system for credit- and debit-card transactions, in which the cards are embedded with a microchip and authenticated using a PIN (a 4-digit *p*ersonal *i*dentification *n*umber). The traditional credit or debit card had a magnetic stripe and required a signature for authentication. Chip and PIN was trialled, in Britain, in Northampton from May 2003 before it went nationwide in 2004. When someone did not know their PIN, the cashier could implement a PIN bypass requiring a signature. From 14 February 2006 – Valentine's Day – this facility was discouraged. New cards issued by banks have both a magnetic strip and a chip.

**Chippendales, The.** The US male striptease group was formed in 1979 by Somen Banerjee, an Indian garage owner from Los Angeles, who in 1975 had bought a failing bar called Destiny II and turned it into a nightclub. It is uncertain what gave him the inspiration for the enterprise, but he realized the potential of such a show following an initial 'male exotic dance night for ladies only' at the club, which he renamed Chippendales, for its mock-English furnishings. The name was in turn adopted by the hunky he-men. Their act is 'strip' and 'tease' in equal measure, and although full frontal nudity is strictly speaking off limits there are times when a view beyond the veil is apparently or even actually afforded, to the delight of the delirious female audience.

**Chips, Mr.** The archetypal bachelor public schoolmaster, who devotes his life to his school and his boys, and is fondly regarded by all. His full name is Arthur Chipping, and he was the creation of James Hilton (1900–54), who introduced him in the sentimental story GOODBYE, MR CHIPS (1934), in which his life is told in flashback. Long a bachelor, he had once met a young woman on a mountaineering holiday and married her, but she died after two years. He is an amalgam of Hilton's own headmaster father and a housemaster at the Leys School, Cambridge, which Hilton had attended.

**Chips Channon.** The nickname of Sir Henry Channon (1897–1958), American-born Conservative MP for Southend-on-Sea, better known as a London society figure and diarist. The reason for the name remains uncertain. One unlikely suggestion attributes it to the potato chips he introduced at a cocktail party. Another claims that he once shared bachelor quarters with a friend named or nicknamed Fish.

***Chips With Everything.*** A play (1962) by Arnold Wesker (b.1932), which examines what happens when young men from different classes are thrown together during National Service. 'Chips with everything' was a common description of the cuisine on offer in the British armed forces, and, indeed, in Britain generally.

> Coming back to Britain is always something of an ordeal. It ought not to be, but it is. And you don't have to be a snob to feel it. It isn't just the food, the sauce bottles on the cafe tables, and the chips with everything. It isn't just saying goodbye to wine, goodbye to sunshine …
>
> LINDSAY ANDERSON: *Declaration* (1957)

**Chisanbop.** (Korean, 'finger counting'.) The proprietary name of a system of calculating by using the fingers and thumbs. It was invented by the Korean mathematician Sung Jin Pai in the 1970s and adopted in particular for the teaching of basic arithmetic. The fingers are used to count to 99 with larger numbers carried over by memory or written down. The right-hand thumb stands for one unit with a place value of five, while each finger represents an additional unit. The left-hand thumb stands for 50, with each finger representing 10.

**Chitlin circuit.** In US show-business slang, the round of clubs, bars and other assorted one-horse venues to which an African American entertainer tends to be restricted before (hopefully) making the break-through into more general show-business success. The term is said to have been coined by the singer Lou Rawls (1933–2006) (chitlins, or chitterlings, are cooked pigs' intestines, a characteristic dish of southern African Americans).

**Chitty-Chitty-Bang-Bang.** A 3-part children's novel (1964) about a magical car by the thriller writer Ian Fleming (1908–64), creator of James BOND. Chitty-Chitty-Bang-Bang is a 'supercharged Paragon Panther', boasting 12 cylinders and owned by the inventor Commander Caractacus Potts. It is capable of flying and can perform exciting stunts. A successful film version, with a screenplay by Roald Dahl, was released in 1967, and in 2002 a stage-musical adaptation of the film was produced in London.

**Chopper.** A helicopter. The colloquialism or military jargon is part alteration of 'helicopter' (or 'copter'), part reference to the machine's 'chopping' blades. Other colloquial uses of the word include, in the plural, 'teeth' and, in the singular, 'penis'. *See also* 'Chopper Harris' *at* SPORTING NICKNAMES.

**Chop-socky.** A colloquial adjective designating an Asian-style martial-arts film featuring abundant violent action. First recorded in 1972, it is a pun on 'chop suey'.

**Chop suey.** A Chinese-style dish of meat, bean sprouts and the like, served with rice. From Chinese *tsap sui*, 'mixed bits'.

***Chorus Line, A.*** A musical (1975) with a score by Marvin Hamlisch (b.1944) and lyrics by Edward Kleban (1939–87) about the trials and tribulations of the hopeful actors and actresses as they present themselves for an audition. The show was based on a collection of taped interviews made with 24 dancers in 1974. It was filmed, not entirely successfully, in 1985.

**Chow mein.** A Chinese-style dish of fried noodles with shredded meat or shrimps and vegetables. The name represents Chinese *chao miàn*, 'fried flour'.

**Christ and Carrots.** A nickname given by Winston Churchill to the Labour politician Sir Stafford Cripps (1889–1952) on account of his Christian socialism and asceticism, which were reflected in the rigorous austerity of his policies during his time as chancellor of the exchequer (1947–50). Churchill is also reported as having remarked, vis à vis Cripps, 'There, but for the grace of God, goes God.'

***Christina's World.*** One of the best known and most popular works of the US artist Andrew Wyeth (b.1917), *Christina's World* (1948) depicts an eerily lit, sharply delineated but featureless farm landscape, with two farm buildings on the high horizon, while in the foreground is the mysterious figure of Christina, a thin-limbed girl propping herself up on the grass. Christina, whose view of the landscape we share, was a crippled neighbour of Wyeth's in the Brandywine Valley, Pennsylvania.

**Christingle.** A lighted candle, often set in an orange, that symbolizes Christ as the light of the world and which is given to children in a special children's service held during Advent. The custom originated in the Moravian Church but was taken up in the mid-20th century by other churches and in particular by the Church of England Children's Society. The name probably derives from German dialect *Christkindl*, 'Christ child', meaning Baby Jesus, who brings presents to children on Christmas Eve. The second part of the word has probably been influenced by 'ingle'. *See also* MIRACLE ON 34TH STREET.

**Christmas disease.** Not the consequence of an annual festive overindulgence but a serious condition that can make life difficult all the year round for its sufferer. It is a rare type of bleeding disorder, also known as haemophilia B, and is caused by a defect in the blood coagulation mechanism. It takes its name from Stephen Christmas, one of the first patients to be diagnosed with it in 1952.

**Christmas has come early.** An unexpected bonus or benefit has been received. The catchphrase often applies to the provision of something usually associated with the materialistic side of Christmas, such as money, food or drink. *See also* ALL ONE'S CHRISTMASES HAVE COME AT ONCE.

**Christmas tree bill.** In US political jargon, a legislative bill that provides benefits for various special-interest groups, especially as a result of numerous amendments not directly related to the main part of the proposed law. The term was originally applied to a tax bill affecting foreign investors that was passed in 1966 and signed 'with reservations' by President Lyndon B. Johnson (*see* LBJ), who noted that it would 'confer special tax windfalls and benefits [like Christmas presents] upon certain groups'.

**Christmas truce.** The spontaneous and unofficial truce that broke out along much of the WESTERN FRONT on the first Christmas of the First World War, in 1914. At various places along the line soldiers of both sides emerged out of their trenches into no-man's land to exchange small gifts and sing carols together. Between Frelinghien and Houplines the Seaforth Highlanders and a Saxon regiment played each other at football (the Scots losing 2–3). However, such fraternization was frowned on by senior officers, who made sure that such contact between their troops never occurred again for the rest of the war. The 1914 truce is the subject of the French feature film *Joyeux Noël* (*Happy Christmas*; 2004).

**Christopher Robin.** The little boy who shares adventures with WINNIE-THE-POOH and other animal friends in the stories and poems by A.A. Milne. He represents Milne's son, Christopher Robin Milne (1920–96), who was also the model for E.H. Shepard's illustrations. In his autobiography *The Enchanted Places* (1974) the original Christopher Robin tells the reader how he grew up to wish his name were Charles Robert.

**Chubby-chaser.** A man who is sexually attracted to fat women (or, if gay, to fat men). The term is of US origin, and dates from around the mid-1970s.

> I think it is a lot easier for a chubby chaser these days now that there are big girl night-clubs and, of course, BELLY magazine.

RICHARD WELLS: www.sizenet.com (25 November 1999)

**Chuck it down.** To rain heavily, as distinct from the more common steady or gentle fall of rain.

**Chuffed.** A word of opposite meanings, both current from the 1950s: on the one hand pleased or satisfied, on the other displeased or disgruntled. The former sense is commoner. *See also* JANUS WORD.

**Chugger.** A British colloquialism for someone employed by or on behalf of a charity to accost people in the street and ask them to commit to regular donations. First recorded in 2002, it is a blend based on 'charity mugger', which reflects a widely held view of the chuggers' importunate methods.

**Chump change.** A small or insignificant amount of money, i.e. small change fit only for a chump or fool. The expression arose from African-American English in the 1960s.

**Chums.** A magazine for boys, along the lines of *The* BOY'S OWN PAPER, published from 1892 until 1934.

**Chunder.** In Australian slang, one of a number of strange and colourful euphemisms for 'to vomit' (*see also* GO FOR THE BIG SPIT; TECHNICOLOR YAWN). This one, which dates from around 1950, is probably a shortening of rhyming slang 'Chunder Loo', for 'spew', which in turn was based on a cartoon character called 'Chunder Loo of Akin Foo'. He was created by the cartoonist Norman Lindsay (1879–1969), and appeared in advertisements for Cobra boot polish in the Sydney *Bulletin* between 1909 and 1920.

**Chunnel.** A nickname for the CHANNEL TUNNEL first recorded in 1928, almost 70 years before the long projected project finally became a reality.

**Church in Wales.** Following lengthy agitation, an Act of 1914 finally disestablished the Church in Wales and this took effect in 1920, when a separate province was created. The Church in Wales is thus no longer *Eglwys Loegr* (the 'English Church'), over-dependent on the landowners, and it provides regular services in Welsh as well as in English. After 1920 it increased in both numbers and influence.

**CIA.** The Central Intelligence Agency, established by President Truman to coordinate US intelligence in 1947. It became a global agency for collecting and evaluating intelligence and for extending US influence through covert action, especially in the early years of the COLD WAR, when it was still largely unknown to the US public. Although subject to fiascos, such as the BAY OF PIGS, the CIA performed well during the Cuban Missile Crisis (*see* HAWKS AND DOVES). Its reputation was badly tarnished, however, in the WATERGATE scandal, and it was almost annihilated in the revelations of abuses of power that followed. In 1995 President Clinton redefined its mission as the countering of WEAPONS OF MASS DESTRUCTION, drug trafficking and international organized crime, a brief far removed from its original mission of combating communism.

**Cicciolina, La.** (Italian, 'the little plump one'.) The nickname of Hungarian-born Italian porn star and politician Ilona Staller (b.1955), who campaigned with the slogan 'less nuclear energy, more sexual energy', and became a Radical Party member of the Italian parliament in 1987.

**Cider with Rosie.** An autobiographical account (1959) of his early years by the poet Laurie Lee (1914–97), evoking the landscape and innocent rural life of the Slad valley in Gloucestershire where he was born and brought up. He and Rosie Burdock 'sat very close, breathing the same hot air. We kissed only once, so shy and dry, it was like two leaves colliding in the air. … Rosie, having baptized me with her cidrous kisses, married a soldier, and I lost her for ever.' Whether or not Rosie actually existed Lee would never reveal. *See also* AS I WALKED OUT ONE MIDSUMMER MORNING; FIRST LINES OF NOVELS.

**Cigarette cards.** Picture cards on various thematic subjects inserted by manufacturers into cigarette packets. They first emerged in the late 19th century and remained a strong promotional device until well after the Second World War. The collection of complete sets of cards became a popular pastime and specialists in the subject became known as cartophilists, a designation coined by C.L. Bagnall in the April 1936 issue of *Cigarette Card News*.

**Cilice.** An instrument of fleshly mortification consisting of a band of interlinked metal rings with sharp points on the inside, that is worn typically around the upper thigh. Its use is associated particularly with the controversial Catholic organization OPUS DEI. The word originally denoted a hair shirt (it comes from Latin *cilicium*, which referred specifically to a covering of goat's hair that originated in Cilicia, a Roman province in southeastern Asia Minor), but in the 20th century was transferred to this more metallic means of discomfort.

**Cinderella services.** A US term for medical and social services provided to the mentally and physically handicapped, the aged and the chronically sick. The expression dates from the 1970s and alludes to the name of the fairy-tale heroine as a term for a neglected or despised person.

**Cinecittà.** (Italian, 'Cine-city'.) A complex of film studios opened in 1937 on the outskirts of Rome and the source of such BLOCKBUSTERS as BEN-HUR (1959) and *Cleopatra* (1963).

**CinemaScope.** A patent cinematographic process using

anamorphic lenses to compress a wide image into a standard frame and then expand it again during projection. The result is a picture almost two and half times as wide as it is high. The system was introduced by Twentieth Century-Fox in 1953 with its production of *The Robe* and the technique itself was based on that of Henri Chrétien (1879–1958), French inventor of the anamorphic lens.

**Cinéma verité.** An approach to the making of documentary films that arose in the late 1950s and early 1960s, characterized by a naturalistic approach and the absence of voiceover narration. The documentary makers themselves were not necessarily absent from their films, and such devices as the use of hand-held cameras drew attention to the fact that one was watching a film. The approach was also applied to fiction films, in which, in addition, improvised dialogue was used to suggest the inarticulateness of real life. A noted example is Francois Truffaut's autobiographical *Les Quatre Cent Coups* (1959), about a young boy who ends up in a detention centre. The term itself, French for 'cinema truth', is a direct translation of the Russian *Kino-Pravda*, the name the Russian director Dziga Vertov gave to his newsreel series reflecting Soviet life in the 1920s.

**Cinerama.** A wide-screen cinematographic technique created by the US research technician Fred Waller (1886–1954), who saw it open commercially only two years before his death in *This is Cinerama* (1952). The system employed three projectors, each projecting on a separate third of the huge 'wraparound' screen that filled the viewer's peripheral vision, giving the sense of being in the centre of the scene and actually involved in the action. One famous scene was a thrilling rollercoaster ride that invariably elicited screams of terrified delight from the audience.

**Circadian rhythms.** The daily periodicity of physiological processes and states such as metabolism, sleep patterns and variation in body temperature as controlled by the BIOLOGICAL CLOCK. The term arose in the 1950s and derives from Latin *circa*, 'about', and *dies*, 'day'.

**Circuit breaker.** A US term for a rebate on property tax or income tax granted by a state to a low-income homeowner or renter to help them cope with rising property taxes. The term dates from the 1970s and derives from the name for the automatic device that stops the flow of current in an electric circuit as a safety measure.

**Circular file.** An ironic name for a wastepaper basket, in which unwanted items are 'filed' away. The phrase is of US origin, and seems to have arisen in the Second World War period.

**Circus, The.** A nickname for M16, aka the Secret Intelligence Service, allegedly from Cambridge Circus, London, although the organization's headquarters were actually at Broadway from 1924 to 1966. The similarity between 'Circus' and 'Service' may have further prompted the name, which was made familiar to the public by the novels of John Le Carré such as *The Honourable Schoolboy* (1977). *See also* George SMILEY.

**Cirrhosis by the Sea.** The joky name given to a beach house in Malibu, California shared in the 1930s and 1940s by the film star Errol Flynn (1909–59) and fellow actor David Niven (1909–83) (Flynn being a heroic consumer of alcohol, and cirrhosis of the liver the drunkard's frequent fate).

**Cisco Kid.** A romantic Latin cowboy and Robin Hood of the American Southwest, who first appeared as a Mexican bandit in 'The Caballero's Way', a short story by O. Henry included in *Heart of the West* (1907). The character became a long-running hero of HOLLYWOOD silent and sound films and in the 1950s featured in a radio show and in television serials named after him.

**Citius, altius, fortius.** (Latin, 'faster, higher, stronger'.) The motto of the OLYMPIC GAMES, introduced *c*.1908 by Baron Pierre de Coubertin, founder of the modern games. He apparently spotted the words over the entrance to a French school, although they have also been attributed to the Rev. P. Didon, a friend and colleague of Coubertin.

**Citizen Kane.** A film (1941) based on a screenplay by Herman J. Mankiewicz (1897–1953) that looks back on the life and career of fictional newspaper magnate Charles Foster Kane (played by Orson Welles, who was also the director). Commonly listed among the best films ever made, it was a thinly disguised biography of the real-life media baron William Randolph Hearst (1863–1951). Hearst was sharply aware of this fact, particularly of the similarity between the relationship between Kane and his wife, who dreams of a career in opera, and that between himself and his wife, the actress Marion Davies. He tried to prevent the film's release but failed when Welles himself threatened to sue RKO Pictures if they withheld his masterpiece.

> There, but for the Grace of God, goes God.
>
> HERMAN J. MANKIEWICZ: referring to Orson Welles during the filming of *Citizen Kane*

**Citizen's arrest.** Any British citizen has the legal right to arrest someone committing or suspected of committing an arrestable offence, i.e. one carrying a prison sentence of five years or more. In practice the right is rarely exercised and usually hits local or even national headlines when it is.

**Citizen's Charter.** The document so named was launched by the Conservative government in 1991 as a statement of the British citizen's rights of redress in cases where a public service failed to meet a certain standard. The aim was to raise that standard and make the service more responsive to its users. In 1998 the LABOUR PARTY launched its successor, known as Service First. The term was originally coined by C.E. Innes and used in 1913 as the title of a book in which he set forth his 'scheme of national organization'.

**Cittabella.** The imaginary city of uncertain location that is the setting of Lia Wainstein's Italian novel *Viaggio in Drimonia* (1965). It is full of holes of various shapes and sizes, but despite this considerable hazard has a name that is Italian for 'beautiful city'.

**City of Dreadful Knights.** Cardiff. After the First World War Lloyd George, prime minister of the COALITION GOVERN-MENT, made lavish grants of honours in a cynical and blatant fashion. In 1922 Lord Salisbury opened an attack, and it was alleged that the government had fixed prices for the sale of titles, the money being put into party political funds. The Conservatives profited, as did Lloyd George's private party chest. As a consequence, a Royal Commission was set up in 1922 to recommend future procedure. Three people connected with prominent South Wales newspapers were among the recipients of these honours, hence Cardiff was dubbed the City of Dreadful Knights, a punning allusion to James Thomson's poem 'The City of Dreadful Night' (1874).

**City of Perspiring Dreams.** Cambridge, playing on 'the City of Dreaming Spires', a sobriquet of Oxford deriving from Matthew Arnold's *Thyrsis* (1866):

> And that sweet City with her dreaming spires …

The inversion originates in Frederic Raphael's TV drama series *The* GLITTERING PRIZES (novelized in 1976):

> 'So this is the city of dreaming spires,' Sheila said.
> 'Theoretically that's Oxford,' Adam said. 'This is the city of perspiring dreams.'

**Civil disobedience.** *See* NON-VIOLENCE.

**Civvy Street.** Civilian life, especially as reverted to after military service or on 'demob'. The phrase dates from the Second World War, but 'civvy' in combination with other words, such as 'civvy life', dates from the First World War, and 'civvies' as civilian clothes are of similar vintage.

**CJD.** *See* MAD COW DISEASE.

**Clam-diggers.** Casual trousers reaching to the middle of the calf, so called because they were originally worn for digging clams. The term dates from the 1940s and was revived when the trousers (pants) were again in fashion from the 1970s.

> These boots are perfect for showing off dance-toned calves. Whether you team them with an A-line skirt or clam-diggers, they're bold, bare and beautiful.
> *heat* (23–29 September 1999)

**Clangers, The.** A children's television puppet programme screened from 1969 to 1974. The Clangers were a band of pink, knitted, mouse-like creatures who inhabited a small blue moon, which they shared with the Soup Dragon and the Froglets. They wore small suits of gold armour and communicated in whistles, and they were so named from the sound the metal dustbin-lid entrances to their burrows made when they dived inside to escape meteorites. One of their favourite pastimes was eating Blue String Pudding.

**Clapped-out.** Worn out from age or heavy use. A term usually applied to something mechanical, such as a car. The suggestion is that it has been disabled or disempowered by the clap, or venereal disease. The expression dates from the 1940s.

**Clash of civilizations.** A phrase heard particularly since 9/11 to denote a perceived battle-to-the-death between the Christian (and/or liberal, democratic) West and the world of Islam in its most fundamentalist manifestations. The phrase was coined by Bernard Lewis in an article entitled 'The Roots of Muslim Rage' in *Atlantic Monthly* (September 1990), and picked up by Samuel P. Huntingdon in an article for the US journal *Foreign Affairs* (Summer 1993) entitled 'The Clash of Civilizations?', in which he predicted, contrary to Francis Fukayama's theory of the END OF HISTORY, that the 21st century would be marked by conflicts emerging out of cultural and religious differences, rather than over ideological and economic issues:

> In this emerging era of cultural conflict the United States must forge alliances with similar cultures and spread its values wherever possible. With alien civilizations the West must be accommodating if possible, but confrontational if necessary.

Huntingdon expanded his ideas in a book, *The Clash of Civilizations and the Remaking of World Order* (1996). Huntingdon himself identified a larger number of cultures in potential conflict than the Christian and Muslim ones, additionally listing the Hindu, Sinic (Chinese and Indochinese), Sub-Saharan, Buddhist and Japanese civilizations.

*See also* CULTURE WAR.

**Class act.** A generalized term of approbation for someone (or occcasionally something) considered to be of the highest degree of excellence. The phrase emerged from the language of the US entertainment industry in the mid-1970s. (The punningly titled US film *Class Act* (1992) concerned two high-school students who swopped identities.)

> Howard [Sherman]'s conclusion: 'Tori Spelling, you're a class act, even if your personal assistant signed your name'.
>
> www.newyorkish.com (16 March 2004)

**Claudine.** The lively young heroine of four semi-auto-biographical novels by Colette, in their English versions known as *Claudine at School* (1900), *Claudine in Paris* (1901), *Claudine Married* (1902) and *Claudine and Annie* (1903).

**Clause Four.** A clause originally in the LABOUR PARTY's constitution of 1918. It was written by Sidney Webb and embodied an affirmation of the party's commitment to the common ownership of industry and services:

> To secure for the workers by hand or brain the full fruits of their industry and the most equitable distribution thereof that may be possible upon the basis of the common ownership of the means of production, distribution and exchange.

Tony Blair, in his PROJECT to transform the Labour Party into NEW LABOUR, wanted to ditch the clause:

> Those who seriously believe we cannot improve on the words written for the world of 1918 when we are now in 1995 are not learning from our history but living it.

The clause was duly rewritten, and the commitment to common ownership was dropped from the party's constitution at a special conference on 29 April 1995. The new Clause Four talked instead of:

> A community in which power, wealth and opportunity are in the hands of the many not the few, where the rights we enjoy reflect the duties we owe … in which the enterprise of the market and the rigour of competition are joined with the forces of partnership and cooperation.

*See also* BLATCHERISM.

**Clause 28.** The designation by which SECTION 28 was known before its enactment.

**Claymore mine.** A type of anti-personnel mine introduced by the US Army in the 1960s. It was horseshoe-shaped and produced a directionalized, fan-shaped pattern of fragments. It was so named on an analogy with the claymore, a large double-edged broadsword formerly used by Scottish Highlanders.

**Clayton's.** In Australian English, something illusory, something much spoken of but nonexistent. The expression dates from the early 1980s, and was inspired by an advertising slogan for Clayton's Tonic, an Australian non-alcoholic drink made from kola nuts and citrus essences: 'It's the drink I have when I'm not having a drink.' This was dreamed up by Noel Delbridge, creative director of ad agency D'Arcy, McManus & Masius.

**Clean one's act up.** To improve one's conduct or way of life. The phrase dates from the 1970s.

**Clean someone's clock.** To beat or defeat them decisively. The term is of US military origin and arose in the Second World War. A person's 'clock' is probably their face ('dial').

**Clear blue water.** A tag touted by Conservative leaders in the mid-1990s to express the ideological gap between themselves and other parties, and especially the LABOUR PARTY. The phrase blends 'clear water', the distance between two boats, with 'blue water', the open sea, while rather obviously evoking blue as the traditional colour of the Conservative Party, then in power. The expression subsequently appeared in other contexts.

> The once-great Marks & Spencer is finding it increasingly difficult to show clear blue water between itself and leading rivals.
>
> *Sunday Times* (29 August 1999)

**Clear one's desk.** To leave one's job, usually as a result of dismissal. The phrase may have been suggested by the much older 'to clear the decks'.

> The *Mirror* share-tipping scandal claimed its first casualty last night when the broker who bought £20,000 shares for the Editor was asked to clear his desk.
>
> *The Times* (18 February 2000)

**Cleckheckmondsedge.** A semi-serious portmanteau name for the former Yorkshire (now Kirklees) conurbation of Cleckheaton, Heckmondwike and Liversedge, south of Bradford.

**Clerihew.** The name given to a particular kind of humorous verse invented by E. Clerihew Bentley (1875–1956). It is usually satirical and often biographical, consisting of four rhymed lines of uneven length. The first examples of the genre appeared in Bentley's book *Biography for Beginners* (1905), published under the name of 'E. Clerihew', and the name was applied to the form soon after by some unknown reader. A classic specimen from this first collection is:

> Sir Christopher Wren
> Said 'I am going to dine with some men.
> If anybody calls,
> Say I'm designing St Paul's.'

A more recent clerihew, not by Bentley, is:

Prime Minister John Major
Was hardly an old stager;
He cut little ice
By simply being nice.

A.R.

**Clicks and mortar.** In computer jargon a commercial operation that combines a retail store with an online business using the INTERNET. The 'clicks' are those of the mouse to exploit the latter; the 'mortar' is that of the bricks and mortar (on which the phrase puns) of the actual retail store. *See also* BRICKS AND CLICKS; E-BAY.

**Cliffhanger.** Figuratively, a state of affairs producing anxiety. The term derives from early US serialized adventure films, in which the hero or heroine was left in a perilous plight at the end of an episode in order to whet the audience's appetite for the next instalment. A classic exponent of the art was Pearl White, the star of *The Perils of Pauline* (1914), who frequently finished up dangling from the Palisades over the Hudson River. The suspense, in both senses of the word, made sure that the audience returned.

**Climb the walls.** To be beside oneself with pent-up anger, anxiety, frustration, etc. The phrase, first recorded in the United States in the early 1970s, perhaps conjures up a picture of a lunatic attempting to scale the walls of his cell.

What to do when it's freezing outside, you're stuck inside and everyone is ready to climb the walls?

www.osv.com (1 January 2005)

**Clio.** A statuette presented annually in the United States as an award for the best production, acting or the like in commercial advertisements during the year's television. It was first awarded in 1967 and takes its name from the Greek muse of history.

**Clippies.** Bus conductresses in London and other large cities were so known in the Second World War when they took over the clipping of tickets from male conductors. The occupation was continued by women for some time after the war.

**Cliveden set.** A collective name (coined by the left-wing journalist Claude Cockburn) for the right-wing politicians and journalists who gathered for weekend parties at Cliveden, the Buckinghamshire home of Lord and Lady Astor, in the late 1930s. They included Geoffrey Dawson, editor of *The Times* (and self-styled 'secretary-general of the Establishment'), and Lord Lothian. They favoured APPEASEMENT with Nazi Germany. It was said that government policy was decided at Cliveden, a proposition with which

the members of the set would no doubt have concurred (their self-delusion was conclusively demonstrated when Winston Churchill, rather than their preferred candidate, Lord Halifax, was chosen to succeed Neville Chamberlain as prime minister in 1940). A more derisive name for the set was 'God's Truth Ltd.'

We talk of … how terrible has been the influence of the Cliveden set.

HAROLD NICOLSON: *Diary* (19 September 1938)

**Cloche hat.** A woman's close-fitting bell-shaped hat, in fashion in the EDWARDIAN ERA and undergoing periodic revival since, for example in the 1950s.

**Clock in** or **on.** To start work; to begin a session of activity. The literal sense is to register one's arrival at a workplace by recording the time on a clock-like device. The converse is 'to clock out' or 'to clock off'. *See also* LOG IN.

***Clockwork Orange, A.*** A futuristic, dystopian (*see* DYSTOPIA) novel (1962) by Anthony Burgess (pen-name of John Anthony Burgess Wilson; 1917–93). Told in the first person in NADSAT, it describes an attempt to turn its young criminal hero, Alex, into a 'mechanical man' by means of therapy and brainwashing. The title derives from the Cockney expression 'queer as a clockwork orange', meaning 'homosexual'. The relevance of this to the novel or any of its characters is uncertain, although in the narrative itself it is the title of a book being typed up by a writer whose house Alex and his mates burst into. A film version of the novel was directed by Stanley Kubrick (1971). Burgess had reservations about changes made in the film adaptation of his novel and suggested that it should be retitled *Clockwork Marmalade*. Withdrawn in the UK after its original release, the film was re-released in 2000. *See also* COPYCAT KILLING.

Then I looked at its top sheet, and there was the name – A CLOCKWORK ORANGE – and I said: 'That's a fair gloopy [silly] title. Who ever heard of a clockwork orange?' Then I read a malenky [little] bit out loud in a sort of very high type preaching goloss [voice]: ' – The attempt to impose upon man, a creature of growth and capable of sweetness, to ooze juicily at the last round the bearded lips of God, to attempt to impose, I say, laws and conditions appropriate to a mechanical creation, against this I raise my sword-pen –'

*A Clockwork Orange*, ch. 2

**Close, but no cigar.** A formula for a commiseration or 'nice try'. The allusion is to the 'Highball', a fairground 'try-your-strength' machine with a pivot that the contestant hits with a hammer in the hope of sending a projectile up high enough to ring a bell. Those who succeed are awarded a cigar by the proprietor. The expression, like the machine itself, derives from US carnivals. *See also* RING A BELL.

**Closed book.** A person or thing about which one knows nothing, as distinct from an 'open book', about which one knows everything The analogy is with an unopened book whose contents remain undiscovered. The phrase dates from the early years of the 20th century and is sometimes taken to refer to an awkward or delicate matter, as if a book that one hesitates to open.

**Close encounter.** Journalistic jargon for any meeting, whether personal or professional. The phrase was popularized by the title of Steven Spielberg's SCIENCE FICTION film *Close Encounters of the Third Kind* (1977), itself referring to contact with ALIENS from a UFO. The film's slogan was 'We are not alone …' A 'close encounter of the first kind' is thus simply a sighting of a UFO, while a 'close encounter of the second kind' is evidence of an alien landing. A 'close encounter of the fourth kind' is an abduction by aliens. The categories were proposed in J. Allen Hynek's *The UFO Experience: A Scientific Enquiry* (1972).

**Closet queen.** A clandestine male homosexual who has not COME OUT OF THE CLOSET. 'Queen' as a term for a male homosexual dates from the late 19th century.

**Close your eyes and think of England.** Advice reputedly given to young brides in the earlier part of the 20th century, said to derive from the following journal entry made by Lady Hillingdon in 1912 (although the original has not been tracked down):

> I am happy now that Charles calls on my bedchamber less frequently than of old. As it is, I now endure but two calls a week and when I hear his steps outside my door I lie down on my bed, close my eyes, open my legs and think of England.

A variant on this was supplied by Alan Ayckbourn in his play *Bedroom Farce* (1978):

> My mother used to say, Delia, if S-E-X ever rears its ugly head, close your eyes before you see the rest of it.

**Cloth cap.** A man's flat woollen cap with a peak, regarded from the 1950s as an essential attribute of a working-class person. Andy CAPP always wears one in his day-to-day doings, even indoors. *See also* FLAT CAP.

> Today … new Labour celebrates that great event [the founding of the LABOUR PARTY 100 years earlier]. Don't expect too many cloth caps or misting NHS specs among the cheesy grins.
>
> *Sunday Times* (27 February 2000)

**Cloth ears.** To be cloth-eared is to be unable to hear or understand clearly, as if one's ears were made of cloth. The derogatory term dates from the early 20th century. *See also* TIN EAR.

**Cloud nine.** To be on cloud nine is to be elated or very happy. The expression derives from terminology used by the US Weather Bureau. Clouds are divided into classes, and each class into nine types. Cloud nine is cumulonimbus, a cumulus cloud of great vertical extent, topped with shapes of mountains or towers.

**Clouseau, Inspector.** The accident-prone French police inspector enjoyably played by Peter Sellers in the comedy film *The* PINK PANTHER (1963). He appeared in four sequels, with Sellers continuing in the role in the first three and Alan Arkin taking the part in the fourth. After Sellers' death in 1980, a final Clouseau film, *Trail of the Pink Panther* (1982), was stitched together from footage left over from the earlier movies. In 2006 Steve Martin took the role of Clouseau in a new Pink Panther film.

**Club car.** A railway coach furnished as a lounge, often with a refreshment bar. Club cars, reserved for passengers paying a premium over the season ticket rate, were formerly provided on so-called club trains, long-distance commuter trains operating until the Second World War between Manchester and the North Wales coast, Manchester and the Fylde coast, and Manchester and the Lake District, among other routes.

**Club 18–30.** A British travel company that provides package holidays for young people in search of SUN, SEA AND SAND, especially if the 'a' in 'sea' becomes an 'x'. Holiday destinations are mostly around the Mediterranean, in resorts where there are plenty of bars and clubs.

**Club Med.** The popular short name of the *Club Méditerranée*, 'Mediterranean Club', a French holiday firm founded in 1950 and a pioneer in the all-inclusive or 'package' holiday. It has established holiday camps or *villages* worldwide, but primarily on the Mediterranean coast of North Africa. Although now international in scope, the French flavour remains. The camp director is the *chef de village* and the camp staff, the equivalent of REDCOATS at BUTLIN'S, are *GOs* or *gentils organisateurs*, 'gentle organizers'. The name has become a byword for SUN, SEA AND SAND and all that goes with it, or for hedonism generally.

**Club sandwich.** A US term for a 'three decker' sandwich of meat (especially chicken and bacon), tomato, lettuce and mayonnaise, usually with two layers of filling between the three layers of bread (or toast). The comestible dates from the turn of the 20th century.

**Cluedo.** This classic WHODUNIT board game was the invention in 1949 of Anthony Pratt, an English solicitor's clerk, later a concert pianist. The object is to discover which of six suspects, using which of six weapons, murdered Dr Black, found dead after a dinner party, and in which of the nine rooms of his country house the murder took place. The characters, their names representing their colours, are the actress Miss Scarlett, aged 29; the retired Colonel Mustard, 66; the village vicar Reverend Green, 48; the socialite Mrs Peacock, 41; the archaeologist Professor Plum, 38; and Dr Black's housekeeper and cook Mrs White, 57. The weapons are a dagger, a length of lead piping, a candlestick, a rope, a spanner and a revolver; the rooms are the kitchen, the lounge, the ballroom, the billiard room, the hall, the dining room, the study, the library and the conservatory. In the United States the game is known as Clue and the victim is Mr Boddy.

**Clueless.** *See* POPSOCKS; VALSPEAK.

**Clunk click.** An onomatopoeic expression intended to represent the sound of a car door closing and a seat belt being secured. It figured in 'Clunk click every trip', the motto of a 1971 Royal Society for the Prevention of Accidents campaign to persuade car drivers and passengers to use their seat belts. It was fronted by the disc jockey Jimmy Savile. Wearing seatbelts in the front of cars only became compulsory in the UK in 1983. In 1989 it became mandatory for children in the back seats to wear seatbelts, and this was extended to adults in 1991.

**Cluster bomb.** A type of anti-personnel bomb containing numerous mini-bombs which radiate over a wide range on impact. It evolved in the mid-1960s as a 'refinement' of the conventional bomb during the VIETNAM War (1964–75). The name does not mean that such bombs are dropped in 'clusters', like sticks of incendiary bombs, but refers to the mass of projectiles discharged. Cluster bombs were controversially widely used in the Kosovo War of 1999, and in Iraq in 2003.

**Clydesiders.** A loose association of left-wing MPs representing Glasgow and Clydeside constituencies, who enlivened British politics and parliament from 1922 until they were much diminished in numbers following the 1931 general election. Notable among them were John Wheatley, of Housing Act fame, Campbell Stephen, Emanuel Shinwell and, best known of all, James Maxton (1885–1946), who became chairman of the Independent Labour Party,

founded by Keir Hardie in 1893. They acted as a ginger group for the LABOUR PARTY and were noted champions of the poor and unemployed.

The term 'Red Clydeside' is generally applied to the strongly socialist working-class movement in and around Glasgow, particularly associated with the (now largely defunct) ship-building industry. Revolutionary socialism first appeared on Clydeside during the First World War, when a number of left-wingers were jailed after they called for strike action. Early heroes of the movement included the pacifist Maxton, who was one of those imprisoned, and the communist school teacher John Maclean. In January 1919 English troops and tanks were deployed in Glasgow in the expectation of an imminent Bolshevik revolution. Red Clydeside again came to national notice in the early 1970s, when workers at one of the shipyards, led by the shop steward Jimmy Reid, staged a work-in to stop the yard being closed down. A right-wing perspective on Red Clydeside unrest in the First World War is to be found in John Buchan's novel MR STANDFAST (1919).

**CND.** The Campaign for Nuclear Disarmament was launched in 1958 and immediately gained prominence with its BAN THE BOMB marches between London and the Atomic Weapons Research Establishment at Aldermaston, Berkshire. Its first chairman (to 1964) was Canon Collins and its first president Bertrand Russell. The latter resigned in 1960, however, to form the more militant Committee of 100. The CND was committed to UNILATERAL NUCLEAR DISARMAMENT and the banning (or removal) of US cruise missiles from Britain, but its influence waned after the end of the COLD WAR and even further following the demise of the Soviet Union in 1991. The CND symbol is an inverted V bisected by a vertical line within a circle. The inverted V represents the semaphore signal for the letter N (both flags held down at an angle of 45 degrees from the horizontal), and the vertical line that for D (one flag held straight up and the other straight down), i.e. ND, the initials of *n*uclear *d*isarmament.

**CNN.** The first 24-hour TV news channel, founded in 1980 by Ted Turner and Reese Schonfeld. It is based in Atlanta, Georgia, and is now part of Time Warner. The initials stand for Cable News Network, or, according to some, Chicken Noodle News.

**Coalition government.** A government formed by normally opposed parties, usually in times of crisis, when party differences are set aside. Examples in the 20th century are Liberals, Unionists and Labour under Asquith (1915–16) (re–formed under Lloyd George, 1916–22), MacDonald's

NATIONAL GOVERNMENTS (1931–5) and Winston Churchill's wartime Coalition Government (1940–45).

**Coalition of the Willing.** President George W. Bush's (*see* DUBYA) name for those countries who supported the action of the United States in the Iraq War of 2003. The phrase actually goes back to the 1980s, to denote a group of countries acting together militarily without the sanction of the United Nations. In the 2003 war, although 48 countries were technically part of the coalition, only the UK (and to a lesser extent Australia) offered a significant military contribution (*see* BUSH'S POODLE). Many of the other countries, which generally sent merely symbolic contingents, were actually poor nations in need of US aid, leading the *New York Times* to refer to the 'Coalition of Welfare States', while Senator Robert Byrd used the acronym COW, suggesting that the United States was being 'milked'.

**Coastal Command.** The RAF command that operated over the sea from coastal bases in Britain in the Second World War.

**Cobber-dobber.** In Australian slang, someone who informs on their mates to the authorities. 'Cobber' is a long-standing Australian term for a friend (it probably comes from the British dialect verb 'cob', meaning 'to take a liking to', or from Hebrew/Yiddish *chaver*, 'chum'), and to 'DOB SOMEONE IN' is to incriminate them; the combination dates from the 1960s.

**COBOL.** *See* PROGRAMMING LANGUAGES.

**COBRA.** An acronym for Cabinet Office Briefing Room A, and hence the name of the UK government committee that meets in times of national emergency to coordinate local or national action. The composition of the committee varies according to the nature of the crisis, whether it be the fuel protests of 2000 or the London bombings of July 2005 (*see* 7/7). The facility itself provides secure communications between the prime minister and the armed forces, the police, the emergency services, hospitals and various government departments.

**Cobra.** A group of expressionist painters formed in Paris in 1948 by various Dutch and Scandinavian artists. Leading figures among the founders were the Dutchman Karel ppel (1921–2006), the Belgian Corneille (full name Corneille Beverloo) (b.1922) and the Dane Asger Jorn (1914–73). They aimed to give free expression to the unconscious, unimpeded and undirected by the intellect, and set store by spontaneous gesture. Their name derives from the first letters of the capital cities of the three countries of the artists involved: Co*p*enhagen, *Br*ussels and Amsterdam.

**Coca-Cola.** The carbonated drink was the invention in 1886 of John S. Pemberton, a US pharmacist. It is uncertain how he concocted the blend of ingredients that first went into the product, but his bookkeeper, Frank Robinson, devised a name that indicated the source of two of the extracts: coca leaves and the cola nut. Coca leaves yield cocaine, a form of which was originally present in Coca-Cola. Hence the curative claims initially made for it, so that people took it for dyspepsia, headaches and similar malaises. The drink came to be nicknamed Coke, and the manufacturers registered this as an alternative name in 1920 as their exclusive property. Thus, while 'cola' can be used as a general name for any carbonated drink made from cola nuts, Coca-Cola and Coke cannot. *See also* PEPSI-COLA; the REAL THING.

**Cochran revues.** The impresario Charles Blake Cochran (1872–1951) started his career in the United States but back in England soon became famous for his intimate revues, beginning with *Odds and Ends* (1914) at the Ambassadors Theatre. In 1918 he began a remarkable run of revues at the London Pavilion, including Noël Coward's *On With the Dance* (1925) and *This Year of Grace* (1928). The former was the first to star Cochran's famous 'Young Ladies'. His revues were distinctive from those of the EDWARDIAN ERA in that they relied more on witty dialogue than on dress and dancing.

***Cockaigne.*** The boisterous concert overture by Sir Edward Elgar (1857–1934) is subtitled 'In London Town'. It was first performed in 1901 and was intended to be an evocation of Edwardian London. 'Cockaigne' or 'Cockayne' (from which the word 'Cockney' is popularly derived) refers to a land of idleness and luxury that features in medieval European folklore that is the subject of a painting by the Flemish painter Pieter Bruegel the Elder (*c*.1525–69). The word derives via Old French *pais de cokaigne*, 'land of cakes', from Middle Low German *kokenje*, 'small cake', from which the houses in this idyllic land were supposed to be made. The idea is a persistent one: in the 1930s Depression in the United States, hobo lore evoked the land of the 'Big Rock Candy Mountain'. Despite expectations, the word 'Cockaigne' bears no etymological relationship to 'cocaine'; the latter derives from 'coca', as in COCA-COLA.

***Cocktail Party, The.*** A poetic drama (1949) by the Anglo-American poet T.S. Eliot (1888–1965) in which the personal relationships among a small group of friends are explored and discussed. The drama begins with a cocktail party hosted by Edward Chamberlayne shortly after his wife Lavinia has left him; it ends with another cocktail party with Edward and Lavinia reunited and their various friends having moved on in their lives. The cocktail party itself thus becomes a symbol of human existence, full of compromise and banality.

**Cock-up.** A muddle; a mess-up. An allusion to something that is turned from the true, with a suggestion of the vulgar sense of 'cock'.

**Coconut ice.** The name of this confection of grated coconut and sugar syrup dates from the early years of the 20th century. The precise sense of 'ice' is uncertain. The confection is not frozen, and it is not made with or served with ice or even ice cream. The allusion may perhaps be to its natural colour or its somewhat crystalline texture.

**Coffee-table book.** A large, expensive and lavishly illustrated book, supposedly placed on a low table in a sitting-room to be glanced at rather than read or to impress a visitor. The term dates from the early 1960s and may have originally been intended to mean a book that was simply too large to be shelved normally. Such books were earlier sometimes known as 'grand-piano books'. In 1999 the German art publishers Taschen published a limited edition of a book of 400 photographs by Helmut Newton that was so large and heavy that it came with its own coffee table.

**Cog in the wheel** or **machine.** A person who holds a small but necessary post in a large organization. The allusion is to the cog on a small wheel that engages with that on a larger wheel, which in turn may engage with that on an even larger wheel. The expression dates from the 1930s.

**Colbred sheep.** This highly fertile sheep, a cross between the Border Leicester, Clun, Friesland and Dorset Horn, takes its name from the Gloucestershire company of H.A. Colburn and Son, who first had the idea of developing such a breed in 1954. The process took nine years, and the first Colbred was shown by H.A. Colburn himself in 1963 at the Royal Show, Newcastle upon Tyne.

**Cold calling.** The calling of someone by telephone in an attempt to sell them something. The usual culprits are double-glazing firms. The call is 'cold' because the one called is unprepared for it.

***Cold Comfort Farm.*** A novel (1932) by Stella Gibbons (1902–89), parodying the rural novels of D.H. Lawrence (1885–1930) and Mary Webb (1881–1927), and in particular the latter's PRECIOUS BANE (1924). The author noted in her foreword: 'Because I have in mind all those thousands of persons not unlike myself … who are not always sure whether a sentence is Literature or whether it is just sheer flapdoodle, I have adopted the method perfected by the late Herr Baedeker, and firmly marked what I consider the finer

passages with one (*), two (**) or three (***) stars.' The title was suggested to the author by the writer Elizabeth Coxhead, who took the name from a real farm so called near her home at Hinckley, Leicestershire. Farms of the name still exist today, and 'cold comfort' as a phrase for little cheer goes back to medieval times. A film version (1995), written by Malcolm Bradbury and directed by John Schlesinger, was shown on television in Britain as an enjoyable comedy that never quite captured the spirit of the original.

> If she intended to tidy up life at Cold Comfort, she would find herself opposed at every turn by the influence of Aunt Ada … Persons of Aunt Ada's temperament were not fond of a tidy life.
> ch. 5

**Cold Duck.** A US name for an inexpensive mixture of sparkling burgundy and champagne. The name translates German *Kalte Ente*, 'cold duck', a fanciful alteration of *kalte Ende*, 'cold ends', meaning left-over wines mixed and served at the end of a party.

**Colditz.** A byword for a bleak prison or for any generally forbidding or unwelcoming edifice. Colditz Castle, in the town of this name about 48km (30 miles) from Leipzig, Germany, was a notorious prisoner of war camp in the Second World War and the site of many daring escape bids by Allied officers. The building and its name became widely known to the post-war generation from the highly popular television series *Colditz* (1972–4). Its 28 episodes were based on the books by Major Pat Reid and re-enacted the ruses devised by British officers to effect a breakout.

**Cold turkey.** The unpleasant effect produced by suddenly and completely giving up a drug to which one has been addicted. The reference is perhaps to a cold and unappetizing uncooked turkey by comparison with a warm and appetizing cooked one, although when this particular sense emerged in the 1920s 'cold turkey' already existed to mean 'directly', 'without any warning', and this may be the actual source. *See also* WITHDRAWAL SYMPTOMS.

**Cold War.** A state of tension, distrust and mutual hostility between states or groups of countries, without recourse to actual warfare. The state existed between the Soviet bloc countries and the Western world from the end of the Second World War until 1990. The superpowers did not fight each other directly, but on many occasions took on the other's allies or proxies, or supported their enemies (for example, in Vietnam and Afghanistan). The term was first used in a speech made on 16 April 1947 by the US financier Bernard Baruch (1870–1965), when US ambassador to the United Nations Atomic Energy Commission:

Let us not be deceived – we are today in the midst of a cold war.

The phrase is said to have been suggested to him by Herbert B. Swope, former editor of the *New York World*. By 1948, as the international situation grew more tense, Baruch was telling a Senate committee:

We are in the midst of a cold war which is getting warmer.

*See also* COLD WAR WARRIOR; DÉTENTE; EISENHOWER DOCTRINE; END OF HISTORY; HAWKS AND DOVES; McCARTHYISM; NATO; NEW WORLD ORDER; PEACEFUL COEXISTENCE; REAGAN DOCTRINE; TRUMAN DOCTRINE; WARSAW PACT.

**Cold War Warrior** or **Cold Warrior.** A term for a US politician or other prominent person who took a hawkish stance (*see* HAWKS AND DOVES) in the COLD WAR. The term first arose in the late 1950s. Notable Cold War Warriors have included Edward Teller, 'the Father of the H-bomb' (and the partial inspiration of DR STRANGELOVE), General Curtis 'Bombs Away' LeMay (*see* BOMB THEM BACK INTO THE STONE AGE), General Douglas MacArthur (the AMERICAN CAESAR), Ronald Reagan (the GREAT COMMUNICATOR; *see also* EVIL EMPIRE) and Margaret Thatcher (the IRON LADY). In STAR TREK VI (1991) Chang famously tells the captian 'all warriors are cold warriors'.

**Colemanballs.** *Private Eye*'s column in which it quotes tautologous, self-contradictory or otherwise fatuous utterances made by sports commentators. The term derives from the doyen of postwar British commentators, David Coleman (b.1926), responsible for such immortal lines as

He just can't believe what isn't happening to him

and

That's the fastest time ever run – but it's not as fast as the world record

and

Lasse Viren, the champion, came in fifth and ran a champion's race.

In the ranks of the otiose remark, it is perhaps the motor-racing commentator Murray Walker who wears the laurels with his immortal

With half the race gone, there is half the race still to go.

But it is the cricket commentators who hold pride of place with the (unintentional?) double entendre, for example this from Christopher Martin-Jenkins:

It is extremely cold here. The England fielders are keeping their hands in their pockets between balls.

**Collateral damage.** A euphemism for unintended casualties and damage caused among civilians in the course of a military operation. The term is of US origin and arose during

the VIETNAM War (1964–75). More recently it was again before the public in the First GULF WAR of 1991 and the Second Gulf War of 2003.

**College of cardinals.** Properly the College of Cardinals is the Roman Catholic body of cardinals responsible for electing the pope. In a general sense the term is also used for any select group of people authorized to elect a person as their leader, especially in politics.

**Colombey-les-deux-Églises.** A village in eastern France, where the French soldier and statesman Charles de Gaulle (1890–1970) had his private residence. As the location of de Gaulle's periodic withdrawals from political life, first in 1946, then again from 1953 until 1958, when he returned to national politics first as prime minister then as president at the height of the Algerian crisis, it has become synonymous with the voluntary exile of the elder statesman, waiting in landed isolation for his country's call. *See also* FIGHTING FRENCH; GAULLIST.

**Colombian necktie.** A euphemism for a particularly unpleasant method of killing whereby the throat is cut below the chin and the tongue then pulled through the resulting gash. The drastic measure is usually inflicted on someone who has betrayed the killer or his boss, and originated in the Colombian drug wars of the 1980s.

**Colonel Bogey.** A bracing march tune composed in 1914 by a military bandmaster, Kenneth Alford, whose real name was Frederick Ricketts (1881–1945). It is familiar in its whistled form from the film *The* BRIDGE ON THE RIVER KWAI (1957), set in the Second World War, and in the war itself was enthusiastically adopted for an anonymous bawdy quatrain about the NAZI leadership:

Hitler has only got one ball,
Goering has two but very small,
Himmler is somewhat similar,
But poor old Goebbels has no balls at all.

**Colonels, The.** *See* GREEK COLONELS.

*Color Purple, The.* A novel (1982), written in the form of letters, by the US writer Alice Walker (b.1944), which won the PULITZER PRIZE for fiction. A young African American woman, Celie, having been raped as a child by her father and borne him two children, who are then taken away from her, is married off to a violent bully. She is helped by her husband's mistress, a blues singer, to appreciate herself, the pleasures of sexual love and the role of God in the proliferation of love and beauty. His presence is especially evident in the colour purple:

I think it really pisses God off if you walk by the color purple in a field somewhere and don't notice it.

A film version (1985) was directed by Steven Spielberg, with Whoopi Goldberg as Celie.

**Colourless green ideas sleep furiously.** The famous example offered by the linguistics expert Noam Chomsky (b.1928) in his book *Syntactic Structures* (1957) of a sentence that is grammatically impeccable and yet completely meaningless.

**Columbia disaster.** *See* CHALLENGER.

**Columbia Pictures.** A US film company founded in 1924 by Harry Cohn (1891–1958), a former song plugger in vaudeville. It produced many B-MOVIES but also had its share of successful major features, especially films directed by Frank Capra in the 1930s and starring Rita Hayworth in the 1940s. Elia Kazan's ON THE WATERFRONT (1954) and David Lean's LAWRENCE OF ARABIA (1962) were both Columbia films. Cohn's second wife, Joan Perry, provided the face of the statue of Columbia that serves as the studio's logo on pictures.

**Columbine Massacre.** On 20 April 1999 two teenagers ran amok in Columbine High School, Littleton, Colorado, killing 12 students and a teacher before turning the gun on themselves. Many of their victims were shot at random, but the killers specially picked out 'jocks' (athletes) and blacks. The pair were obsessed with the NAZIS and timed the shooting to coincide with Hitler's birthday. The massacre rekindled the bitter debate about gun control in the United States. Michael Moore's 2002 polemical documentary film *Bowling for Columbine* took the incident as the starting point for an exploration of the nature and causes of violence in modern America. *See also* DUNBLANE MASSACRE; HUNGERFORD MASSACRE.

**Columbo.** The dishevelled, one-eyed Italian-American police lieutenant in the television series of the 1970s named after him, played by Peter Falk. His trademarks are his shabby raincoat and his trick of talking inconsequentially about his dragon wife, then turning back at the door to ask one final, vital question.

**Column inches.** Press publicity. A column inch is properly a one-inch length of a column in a news-paper or magazine. The greater the number of inches, either in a single issue or over several, the greater the prominence of the subject of the article or report.

> In the month she vanished there were 492 women and 544 men reported as missing … but Suzy [Lamplugh] got the column inches.
>
> *The Times* (7 December 1999)

**Come a gutzer.** In Australian slang, to fail utterly and calamitously; to 'come a cropper'. A 'gutzer' is a heavy fall, originally on one's stomach (in other words, a 'bellyflop'), and hence any disappointment, misfortune or failure. The expression is first recorded in 1918.

**Come** or **fall apart at the seams.** To lose emotional control. The image is of a disintegrating costume as a garment representing one's physical figure. The expression dates from the 1940s.

**Comeback kid.** Anyone who returns to their former activity, especially in the world of sport or entertainment or the media generally. President Bill Clinton so described himself after coming second in the New Hampshire primary in the 1992 presidential election. (Since 1952, no presidential candidate had won the election without first winning in New Hampshire.) Clinton successfully overcame allegations of sexual impropriety, draft-dodging and cannabis use ('I didn't inhale') to win the presidential election. His nickname continued to be justified by his riding of such storms as the WHITEWATER AFFAIR real-estate scandal and the MONICA Lewinsky affair, the latter leading to an unsuccessful attempt to impeach him in February 1999.

**Come clean.** To confess to a crime; to tell the whole truth. The phrase, of US origin and dating from the early 20th century, became a cliché in murder mysteries. A similar expression of earlier origin is 'to make a clean breast of'.

**Come from behind.** To win after lagging; to advance from a losing position. The metaphor originated in horse racing and has a general application in sport as well as a figurative usage.

**Come-hither look.** A flirtatious or seductive look. The second part of the phrase is variable.

> They make, in front of their looking-glasses, haughty or come-hithering faces for the young men in the street outside.
>
> DYLAN THOMAS: *Under Milk Wood* (1954)

**Come in from the cold.** To return to shelter and safety; to be welcomed back to a group. The expression has a literal origin but is almost always used figuratively. It was popularized by the title of John Le Carré's novel *The* SPY WHO CAME IN FROM THE COLD (1963).

**Come out of the closet.** To admit something openly; to let it be known that one is homosexual. The 'closet' is the metaphorical cupboard in which one keeps one's private information. The expression is commonly shortened to simply 'come out'. *See also* CLOSET QUEEN; OUTING.

Celebrity make-up artist Kevyn Aucoin [is] calling for more gay stars to come out of the closet.

*heat* (16 December 1999–5 January 2000)

**Come out of the kitchen.** To abandon one's traditional domestic role as a housewife for a career as a business-woman, especially when successful and of senior status.

**Come out of the woodwork.** To be revealed; to emerge from obscurity. The expression is frequently used in connection with someone or something unpleasant. The allusion is to beetles, cockroaches and other 'creepy-crawlies', which are seen only when they emerge from their hidden habitat (not necessarily woodwork). The converse is to vanish or disappear into the woodwork. The phrase dates from the 1970s.

**Come the acid.** To be unpleasant or offensive; to speak in a sarcastic or caustic manner. The expression dates from the 1920s.

**Come the raw prawn on** or **over someone.** To attempt to deceive them or impose on them. The Australian expression dates from the 1940s and derives from 'raw prawn' as an act of deception. A raw prawn is hard to swallow.

**Come to a grinding halt.** *See* GRIND TO A HALT.

**Come up and see me sometime.** A common cod chat-up line, based on a line spoken by American double-entendrice Mae West (1892–1980) in the film *She Done Him Wrong* (1933):

Why don't you come up sometime, and see me?

In the form 'Why don't you come up and see me some time?', the line is spoken *to* Mae West by W.C. Fields in *My Little Chickadee* (1939).

**Come up roses.** To develop favourably; to turn out perfectly. The phrase dates from the 1960s and derives from the song 'Everything's Coming Up Roses' from Stephen Sondheim's musical GYPSY (1959), based on the life of the dancer and STRIPTEASE artist Gypsy Rose Lee (1914–70). *See also* COME UP SMELLING OF ROSES.

**Come up smelling of roses.** To emerge unscathed from an unpleasant experience and find oneself in a better position than before. The image is of a person who has fallen into the mire but been 'fertilized' in the process of clambering out of it. Roses grow well in enriched soil. *See also* COME UP ROSES.

**Comfort food.** Food that comforts because it is associated with one's childhood or home cooking. The word can be used in similar applications, so that a comfort book is one that was perhaps first read some time ago but that is now reread with pleasure, especially if one is feeling 'low'.

**Comical Ali.** The nickname of Mohammed Saeed al-Sahhaf (b.1940), Iraqi information minister in Saddam Hussein's government. He earned the nickname (modelled on CHEMICAL ALI) at the time of the Second GULF WAR in 2003, for his continued insistence to journalists that the Iraqi army was annihilating the invading US and British forces. Even on 7 April 2003, as American tanks rolled along the streets of Baghdad within half a kilometre of where he was giving a press conference, he insisted that vast numbers of US troops were committing suicide at the gates of the city, unable to make an entry. In June 2003 a spokeswoman for the US army in the country said, 'He is an interesting story teller and we look forward to hearing what he has got to say.' He was questioned, but later released. In the US press he was known as Baghdad Bob.

**Comic Relief.** The first television programme so titled was screened in 1986, the aim being to entertain the viewer while raising money for famine relief. Many famous comedians were involved, offering their services free. The concept sprang from the charity BAND AID, organizers of Bob Geldof's rock-music event Live Aid staged for the same purpose the previous year. Subsequent Comic Relief programmes have been of marathon length with the scope widened to raise money for all kinds of needy causes both at home and abroad. *See also* RED NOSE DAY.

**Comics.** Although comic strips had been appearing in US newspapers since the closing years of the 19th century, it was not until the 1930s that comic books were published in non-newspaper form. The first, a newspaper-style Sunday section containing only comics, was a failure. The second, a 68-page publication introduced by the Dell Publishing Company in 1934, was a success. It was called *Famous Funnies*, promised 'games, puzzles, magic' and cost 10 cents. It was through SUPERMAN that the world of comics subsequently burgeoned into films and television.

**Coming out of one's ears.** In great abundance; very plenti-ful. The notion is that one is so full that one overflows through the only orifice that does not normally serve as an outlet. The phrase is of US origin and dates from the 1960s.

**Comintern.** The popular name of the Third (Communist) International (1919–43), formed in Moscow by the Soviet leader LENIN. From 1933 the Comintern advocated a POPULAR FRONT of communists, socialists and liberals against the German dictator Adolf Hitler. Germany signed the Anti-Comintern Pact with Japan in 1936 and with Italy in 1937 (*see* AXIS). The Internationals were coordinating bodies established by labour and socialist organizations. The First International or International Working Men's Association, formed in London under Karl Marx, lasted from 1864 until 1872; and the Second International, founded in Paris, from 1889 until 1940. An abortive Trotskyist Fourth International was founded in 1938.

**Commando.** (Afrikaans *kommando*, from Dutch *commando*, 'command'.) Originally, an armed unit of Boer horsemen on military service active in the Kaffir or Frontier Wars (1779–1877). Boer commandos raided isolated British units and lines of communication in the Second BOER WARS (1899–1902). In the Second World War the name was adopted for a member of the specially trained British assault troops formed from volunteers to undertake particularly hazardous tasks and originally, in 1940, to repel a German invasion of England.

> Plans should be studied to land secretly by night on the islands and kill or capture the invaders. This is exactly one of the exploits for which the Commandos would be suited.
> WINSTON CHURCHILL: *The Second World War*, vol. 2 (1948: these words written in 1940)

*See also* GO COMMANDO.

**Commercial inventions.** The years since 1900 have seen the emergence of several now familiar household names and branded products. The following chronological list, showing year of introduction, is a selection of 60. *See also* ROWNTREE MACKINTOSH.

Gillette safety razor (1901)

Crayola crayons (1902)

Campbell's pork and beans (1904)

Palmolive soap (1905)

L'Oréal perfume (1907)

Ex-Lax chocolate-flavoured laxative (1908)

Lipton's tea (1909)

Hallmark greetings cards (1910)

Hellmann's mayonnaise (1912)

Quaker Puffed Wheat (1913)

Wrigley's Doublemint chewing gum (1914)

PYREX (1915)

Lucky Strike cigarettes (1916)

BMW cars (1917)

Kotex sanitary towels (1918)

Bentley cars (1919)

Maidenform bras (1923)

Wonder bread (1927)

Lithiated Lemon (now 7-Up) (1929)

Snickers chocolate bars (1930)

Alka-Seltzer (1931)

Ritz crackers (by Nabisco) (1933)

Toyota cars (1935)

Tampax tampons (1936)

SPAM (1937)

Nescafé instant coffee (1938)

M&Ms chocolates (1940)

Cheerios (1941)

TUPPERWARE (1945)

Timex watches (1946)

Ajax cleanser (1947)

VELCRO (1948)

LEGO (1949)

Tropicana products (1951)

No-Cal ginger ale (1952)

Kentucky Fried Chicken (1955) (*see* KFC)

Pampers disposable nappies (1956)

BankAmericard (now VISA) (1958)

BARBIE DOLL (1959)

Pentel felt-tip pens (1960)

Coffee-Mate coffee whitener (1961)

Kodak Instamatic camera (1963)

Nutra-Sweet artificial sweetener (1965)

ACTION MAN figure (1965)

MasterCharge credit card (now MasterCard) (1966)

JACUZZI bath (1968)

NIKE shoes (1972)

Miller Lite beers (1975)

Pot Noodle snack food (1979)

WALKMAN (1979)

POST-IT NOTES (1980)

APPLE MACINTOSH (1984)

Microsoft Windows computer operating system (1985)

Motorola portable phone (1985)

PROZAC (1988)

Cyber-shot digital camera (1996)

SMART CAR (1998)

VIAGRA (1998)

IPOD (2001)

CHIP AND PIN (2003)

**Common Market.** The former popular name for the economic association of certain European countries that has now grown to be the EUROPEAN UNION.

**Community Charge.** The official euphemistic name for the controversial local tax introduced by the Conservative government in 1990. It was levied on every adult in a community and took no account of ability to pay, apart from a few categories of people eligible for an 80 per cent reduction. Popularly dubbed the 'poll tax', a term dating from medieval times, it led to a riot in West London in the spring of 1990 followed by an orchestrated campaign of non-payment. It was abandoned in 1993 in favour of the more equitable 'council tax', similar in structure to the earlier 'rates'. *See also* CAN'T PAY, WON'T PAY.

**Companion of Honour.** An order instituted in 1917 by George V for recognized services of national importance, sometimes regarded as a junior class of the ORDER OF MERIT. It may be conferred on men or women and restricts its membership to 65, excluding honorary members.

**Company, The.** The colloquial American nickname for the Central Intelligence Agency, the CIA. First recorded in 1967, it was largely inspired by *Cia.*, the abbreviation of Spanish *compañía* 'company'.

**Compassion fatigue.** Indifference to charitable appeals brought about by the frequency or number of such appeals. The expression dates from the early 1980s and came to reflect a concern that repeated images of starving and suffering people would lead to a deadening of the public's sympathy and generosity, especially towards THIRD WORLD countries affected by famine.

**Compensation culture.** A term denoting the increasing inclination of members of the public to sue employers, local authorities, doctors, schools and so on – in fact, any institution or person thought to be responsible for the litigant's accident or other misfortune. The compensation culture has long been a factor in US society, but its arrival in the UK (encouraged by lawyers offering no-win-no-fee deals) dates to the 1990s. Cases brought by Britons include a woman who sued a tour operator when a coconut fell on her head while on holiday in the West Indies. In 2005 *The Scotsman* newspaper reported that an insurance underwriter at Norwich Union's Perth office was suing her employer after she fell over a file filled with accident claims.

**Comper.** A fanatic or devotee of 'comps' or competitions, especially those of the type advertised on the back of products such as breakfast cereals. At the close of the 20th century the British 'comper king' was 78-year-old Leslie Jerman, a retired journalist, who over a three-year period alone won 150 prizes, from holidays to champagne. Many 'comps' involve the writing of original or punning advertising slogans, and Mr Jerman won a microwave oven from Iceland Frozen Foods for 'It's the finest food you ever thaw.'

**Compiègne.** A town about 65km (40 miles) northeast of Paris. It was in the adjacent forest of Compiègne, in the railway carriage of Marshal Foch, the Allied commander-in-chief, that on 10 November 1918 a delegation of moderate German politicians agreed to the punitive armistice terms set out by the Allies to end the First World War. All hostilities ceased the next day, at 11 a.m. on the eleventh day of the eleventh month (*see* ARMISTICE DAY). In the Second World War, after the fall of France, Hitler deliberately chose to re-enact the ceremony in reverse, and Foch's railway carriage was brought from a museum to the forest of Compiègne for General Jodl to dictate the German armistice terms to the French delegation on 22 June 1940. *See also* PÉTAINISTS; VICHY.

**Complementary medicine.** A term that has come to supersede 'ALTERNATIVE medicine', the connotation being that techniques such as acupuncture, homeopathy and reflexology complement rather than replace orthodox medical practice.

**Comstockery.** The rigid suppression of books, plays and other literature deemed to be salacious or corrupting, as advocated by the New York Society for the Suppression of Vice, whose moving spirit was the moral crusader Anthony Comstock (1844–1915). The word was coined in 1905 by George Bernard Shaw, writing in the *New York Times* of 26 September, when he defined it as 'the world's standing joke at the expense of the United States'.

**Conan the Barbarian.** The mighty-muscled warrior from Cimmeria created by the Texan writer Robert E. Howard and first appearing in short stories written for *Weird Tales* magazine in the early 1930s. He is big on brawn and small of brain, and slashes his way with his trusty sword through a fantastic world of magic and monsters. He has continued to appear in a large number of later stories and cartoon strips, most of them written by other hands.

The Austrian-born bodybuilder, Arnold Schwarzenegger (once the AUSTRIAN OAK, later the GOVERNATOR), the son of a Nazi, became a star after playing the eponymous hero in John Milius's 1982 film *Conan the Barbarian*:

> In this handsome, portentous, sword-and-sorcery epic set in a mythical Dark Age, Arnie is pitted against James Earl Jones, leader of a marauding snake cult, and establishes the superiority of Nietzsche over nurture. Milius is a brilliant filmmaker, but this is a tale told by an ideologue, full of sound and Führer signifying nothing.
>
> PHILIP FRENCH: in *The Observer* (7 November 2004)

**Concentration camp.** A guarded camp for non-military (usually political) prisoners. Concentration camps were first used by the British to intern Boer families in the Second BOER WAR (1899–1902), but the most infamous were the camps set up by the NAZIS after 1933 for the detention and persecution of their political opponents. *See also* HOLOCAUST.

**Concept album.** An oft-ridiculed development in the history of the pop music album, in which the tracks on the album, rather than being a series of discrete songs, together form a supposedly coherent series of songs on a related theme. The ROCK OPERA can be seen as a further development of the idea. *See also* PROG ROCK; SERGEANT PEPPER'S LONELY HEARTS CLUB BAND; ZIGGY STARDUST.

**Concert pitch.** The pitch, internationally agreed in 1939 and renewed and extended in 1960, to which musical instruments are usually tuned, a frequency of 440 hertz (vibrations per second) for the A above middle C. It replaced the standard of 435 Hz fixed in Paris in 1859 and confirmed in Vienna in 1885. Figuratively, 'concert pitch' is a state of alertness or keen readiness.

**Concorde.** The world's first supersonic passenger aircraft was built jointly by Britain and France at a cost of some £360 million. The French aircraft, Concorde 001, made its maiden flight on 2 March 1969, and the British version, 002, a month later, on 9 April. It entered regular service on 21 January 1976. The name represented the combined Anglo-French enterprise. The most popular route for the aircraft was the transatlantic, the flight from London to New York taking about 3 hours 40 minutes, roughly half the time required by a conventional jet. The first fatal accident involving Concorde occurred on 25 July 2000 when a French Concorde, bound from Paris to New York, crashed 60 seconds after take-off, killing all 109 people on board. The Concorde fleets of British Airways and Air France were grounded for modifications, but although they later returned to regular operations it was clear that the Concorde's days were numbered, and it was finally withdrawn from service in 2003.

**Concordski.** A media nickname, especially in the tabloid press, for the Soviet Tupolev Tu–144 supersonic transport aircraft, particularly at the time of its crash at the Paris Air Show on 23 June 1973. The name is a 'russified' version of CONCORDE.

***Concord Sonata.*** A strikingly discordant work for piano, with solos for viola and flute, by Charles Ives (1874–1954). It was composed between 1909 and 1915. The title refers not to the harmoniousness of the piece, which is highly experimental and features note-clusters, but to Concord, Massachusetts, home of the New England transcendentalists. The

full title of the work is *Sonata No. 2 (Concord Mass., 1840–1860)*, and the four movements are 'Emerson', 'Hawthorne', 'The Alcotts' and 'Thoreau'.

**Concrete jungle.** An expression dating from the 1960s for a city, or area of a city, with a high proportion of large, unattractive, modern buildings, making it unpleasant as a living environment. The term was popularized by the ethologist Desmond Morris. *See also The* ASPHALT JUNGLE; *The* BLACKBOARD JUNGLE.

> The city is not a concrete jungle, it is a human zoo.
>
> DESMOND MORRIS: *The Human Zoo*, Introduction (1969)

**Concrete poetry.** A form of poetry arising in the 1960s in which the meaning or effect is conveyed partly or even entirely by visual means, either by using patterns of words or letters or by drawing on other typographical devices. British exponents include Edwin Morgan (b.1920), George MacBeth (1932–92) and Bob Cobbing (b.1920). The technique was to some extent foreshadowed by the US poet e.e. cummings (1894–1962).

***Confederacy of Dunces, A.*** A satirical comedy (1980) by the US novelist John Kennedy Toole (1937–1969). Thanks to the efforts of his mother it was published more than ten years after he committed suicide, and won the PULITZER PRIZE for fiction. It is set in New Orleans, and the central character, Ignatius Reilly, is an overweight, argumentative layabout, who interrelates with a cast of equally eccentric and accident-prone characters. The title comes from Jonathan Swift:

> When a true genius appears in the world, you may know him by this sign, that the dunces are all in confederacy against him.
>
> *Thoughts on Various Subjects, Moral and Diverting* (1711)

**Confessional poetry.** A term used mainly by literary critics for a distinctive type of autobiographical poetry that emerged in the United States in the 1960s. The designation was first applied to Robert Lowell's *Life Studies* (1959), in which he wrote of his marital problems, his psychiatric difficulties and his sometimes ambivalent feelings towards his family. Later examples of the genre are Anne Sexton's *To Bedlam and Part of the Way Back* (1960), describing her depressive illness, and Sylvia Plath's *Ariel* (1965), whose 40 poems express her personal responses to the world about and within her.

**Congestion charge.** A charge levied on drivers using their vehicles in a particular urban area within prescibed times, with the aim of deterring them from entering the area and thus reducing traffic congestion. The term is first recorded as long ago as 1965, but it did not become widely known until such a scheme was introduced in Central London in 2003. Vehicle registration numbers are checked via remote cameras and matched with the list of charge-payers for that day. The initial fee was £5. Those who have omitted to pay are liable to a fine.

**Conjuring trick with bones, A.** The description of the Resurrection by David Jenkins (b.1925), Bishop of Durham (1984–94).

> I am not clear that God manoeuvres physical things ... After all, a conjuring trick with bones only proves that it is as clever as a conjuring trick with bones.
> On BBC Radio's *Poles Apart* (4 October 1984)

Jenkins also expressed scepticism about the virgin birth and other supernatural tenets of the faith. Traditionalists in the Church of England were aghast, and some regarded the lightning strike on York Minster in the same year and the subsequent damaging fire as an expression of divine displeasure with the Archbishop of York, who had appointed Jenkins.

**Conk out.** To fail or stop running suddenly, as of an engine or motor. The word 'conk' here is of uncertain origin. It may be simply onomatopoeic. The verb also means to collapse suddenly, as from exhaustion, or even to die. The actor John Le Mesurier, familiar as Sergeant Wilson in the DAD'S ARMY television series, arranged for the following announcement to be placed in *The Times* on his death (in 1983): 'John Le Mesurier wishes it to be known that he conked out on November 15th. He sadly misses family and friends.'

**Conscientious objector.** A person who objects to serving in the armed forces on grounds of conscience. The expression in this sense dates from the First World War. Colloquial names for a conscientious objector are 'CO' or (sometimes disparagingly) 'conchie' ('conchy').

**Conservative Party at prayer.** A gibe at the Church of England:

> The Church should go forward along the path of progress and be no longer satisfied only to represent the Conservative Party at prayer.
> MAUDE RODEN: speech in London, 16 July 1917

There was a certain degree of truth in the observation at that time, when Nonconformists were more likely to support either the Liberals or the Labour Party.

**Conservative with a small 'c'.** Favouring traditional attitudes and values coupled with an aversion to change, as distinct from Conservative, belonging to the Conservative

Party, which also espouses such attitudes and values but claims to do so selectively in order to conserve the best. *See also* WITH A CAPITAL.

**Conspicuous consumption.** The purchase and display of luxurious goods and services in an effort to impress. The phrase was coined by the US economist and social scientist Thorstein Veblen (1857–1929) in *The Theory of the Leisure Class* (1899) and has arguably been the leitmotif and driving force of the consumer society of the capitalist West ever since. Veblen argued that conspicuous consumption contributed to social unrest and posed a threat to economic competitiveness and long-term development.

> From the foregoing survey of conspicuous leisure and consumption, it appears that the utility of both alike for the purposes of reputability lies in the element of waste that is common to both. In the one case it is a waste of time and effort, in the other it is a waste of goods.
> *The Theory of the Leisure Class* (1899)

**Constructivism.** A movement or trend in abstract art that originated in Russia *c*.1914, became dominant there after the 1917 Revolution and spread to the West in the 1920s, where it has had considerable influence on a wide spectrum of artists. The founding father of the style, in which assorted mechanical objects are combined into abstract mobile structural forms, was Vladimir Tatlin (1885–1953), but his gigantic *Monument to the Third International*, intended to celebrate his faith in a communist society, never progressed beyond a wooden model, exhibited in 1920.

**Contemptibles, Old.** *See* OLD CONTEMPTIBLES.

**Continental day.** A school day common in many countries of mainland Europe, in which the timetable runs from early morning to early afternoon, typically 8 a.m. to 2 p.m. A day of this kind was adopted by some British schools from the 1980s, one prime advantage being the availability of greater time for after-school activities.

**Continuity girl.** The technique of filming allows a scenario to be shot in scenes that are not necessarily in sequence, and each shot may even be made several times. It is the task of the continuity girl to ensure that all details of costume, make-up, scenery and the like are correctly and consistently repeated each time. If this is done well the audience will be carried smoothly from one scene to the next without disturbing breaks or lapses of detail. The post has traditionally been held by a woman.

**Contras.** Members of a guerrilla force in Nicaragua that opposed the left-wing SANDINISTAS government of 1979 to 1990 and was supported by the United States for much of that time. The force became widely known from the 'Iran-Contra' affair or Irangate of 1986 (*see under* GATE). It was officially disbanded in 1990, following the Sandinistas' electoral defeat. The name is an abbreviation of Spanish *contrarrevolucionario*, 'counter-revolutionary'.

**Control freak.** A person obsessed with controlling and manipulating others. The expression is of US origin and dates from the 1960s. In British politics the term has been particularly applied since the mid-1990s to the SPIN DOCTORS of NEW LABOUR, who are determined that all their charges should be ON MESSAGE and SING FROM THE SAME HYMN SHEET.

> Knock knock.
> Who's there?
> Control freak. And now you say, 'Control freak who?'

**Conventional wisdom.** An ironic term for a widely held belief on which most people act. The expression comes from J.K. Galbraith's *The Affluent Society* (1958) to describe economic ideas that are familiar and predictable and therefore accepted by the general public, or as he put it: 'the beliefs that are at any time assiduously, solemnly and mindlessly traded between the conventionally wise'. *See also* AFFLUENT SOCIETY.

> According to conventional wisdom, oppositions do well when governments run into trouble.
> *Sunday Express* (27 February 2000)

**Convict # 2273.** A name applied to himself by the US socialist Eugene Debs (1855–1926) during his campaign for the presidency in 1920 (his fifth attempt). He ran this campaign from Atlanta Penitentiary, where he was serving a ten-year sentence for a 1918 speech in which he had defended three socialists who refused to serve in the First World War; this was judged a violation of the 1917 Espionage Act. Despite these difficulties, Debs still won nearly a million votes. The following year President Harding released Debs from jail, but his US citizenship was not restored until 1976, 50 years after his death.

**Coochy coochy coo.** A nonsense phrase expressing affection as one tickles or cossets a young child or, depending on the circumstances, an adult. The words have a vaguely sexual suggestion, partly by association with the type of belly dance known as the hootchy-kootchy.

**Cookie Lady Affair.** In 1970 US naval intelligence was informed that a Vietnamese national working at the US Navy offices in Saigon was selling discarded Navy documents to a woman who sold cookies (biscuits) on a nearby street corner. Expecting to uncover the early stages of a major spy ring, the Naval Investigative Service sent an officer to look the lady over. He bought three cookies from her, and she obligingly wrapped them in what the officer immediately recognized as a US Navy confidential message. It turned out that the cookie lady had been buying scrap paper from the employee to wrap her cookies, and that neither of them spoke a word of English. Security was subsequently tightened following this embarrassing blunder.

**Cookie pusher.** In US slang, a term of contempt for someone in an official position who is time-serving and incompetent. The insult is often directed specifically at State Department officials. It seems to have originated in the 1920s as a fanciful name for a young man who errs on the 'feminine side of life' – tea parties (where he presumably pushes cookies absent-mindedly around on his plate), conversation, the niceties of dress and of gossip, art, rather than sport, etc.

**Cook with gas.** To be on the right lines; to be on the road to success. An American colloquialism first recorded in 1942. At the time various alternative formulations were tried out, such as 'cook with electricity' and 'cook with radar', but it was 'gas' that won out.

**Cool.** Fashionably attractive; smartly up to date and desirable. The colloquialism seems to have evolved in the 1930s from jazz slang, alluding to jazz that is restrained and relaxed, as distinct from 'hot' jazz, which is strongly rhythmical and played with verve. A record of Charlie Parker's *Cool Blues* was released in 1947. The word found a place in the youth slang of the 1950s, but not surprisingly the following generation found it unutterably passé, and it almost vanished from the scene. In the 1990s, however, it staged a remarkable comeback, and by the 21st century had become a widely used, broadly generalized adjective of approval. It even, in an interesting shift of semantic focus, came to indicate that a person approved of or was comfortable with something, as in the quotation below:

> Jude Law: cool with nudity? 'I have no problem with nudity,' Jude Law once remarked. 'My friend Ewan and I are starkers in most of our films.'
> www.anecdotage.com

**Cool Britannia.** A phrase, punning on the patriotic song 'Rule, Britannia', briefly in vogue after youthful-looking, guitar-playing Tony Blair came to power in Britain in May 1997 at the head of a 'NEW LABOUR' government. The phrase actually occurred 30 years earlier, in a 1967 send-up of both the traditional song and contemporary British grooviness as recorded by the Bonzo Dog (Doo Dah) Band (*see under* BONZO):

Cool Britannia,

Britannia you are cool (take a trip!),

Britons ever, ever, ever

Shall be hip!

VIVIAN STANSHALL: 'Cool Britannia', from the album *Gorilla* (1967)

The new government in 1997 wooed, and was for a while wooed by, fashionable young artists and musicians, and the term suggested a revitalized and rejuvenated Britain after 18 years of Conservative rule. However, as the prime-ministerial coiffure thinned and his government adopted, in the eyes of many, increasingly illiberal policies the inevitable disillusion set in, and 'Cool Britannia' became nothing more than an embarrassing memory.

When I think of Cool Britannia, I think of old people dying of hypothermia.

TONY BENN: speech to the Labour Party conference (September 1998)

**Cooling-off period.** A period in which two sides in a dispute consider their position before resuming negotiations or discussions. The term is also used for the period of 14 days in which the signatory to a contract or agreement has the right to cancel. *See also* COOL IT.

**Cool it.** Relax, calm down. An injunction to someone who has become overheated. *See also* COOL.

**Cop.** An old verb meaning 'to catch' that in the 20th century formed a number of phrases, many of them of African American origin. Examples are 'cop a drag', to smoke a cigarette; 'cop a nod', to have a nap; 'cop a packet', to be killed or wounded; 'cop a squat', to sit down; 'cop a steal', to steal. *See also* COP A FEEL; COP A PLEA.

**Copacabana.** A famous New York nightclub on East 60th Street, opened in 1940. For the next two decades it was a glamorous venue for performances by such well-known names as Frank Sinatra, Ella Fitzgerald, Nat King Cole and Jimmy Durante. It then declined in popularity and closed in 1973. The name is that of the main beach of Rio de Janeiro in Brazil, a magnet for foreign tourists.

**Copacetic.** In US slang, fine, first-rate. Its origins are obscure. It has been assumed to be Italian, while Hebrew and Louisiana French derivations have also been suggested, but none carries conviction. Another tenuous candidate is Chinook Jargon *copasenee* 'everything is satisfactory'. It appears to have emerged in African-American English towards the end of the 19th century, which does not sit well with any of its proposed sources.

**Cop a feel.** To fondle sexually or to FEEL UP. *See also* COP.

**Cop a plea.** To engage in plea bargaining, i.e. to plead guilty to a lesser charge in return for the dropping of a greater one. The device is a peculiarity of the US legal system. *See also* COP.

**Cop off.** In modern British slang, to cop off is to leave one's place of work or school, usually before the proper time. To cop off with someone is to have sexual contact (anything from mild snogging to sexual intercourse) with them.

Vince tried to cop off with some guy only to find out something rather nasty.

www.queerasfolk.uk.com

**Cop out.** To abandon an attempt; to go back on one's word; to avoid one's responsibility. Hence a cop-out as a cowardly or feeble evasion.

**Copper's copper.** A senior police officer respected and trusted by his men, who see him as 'one of us'. The phrase may have arisen by contrast with 'copper's nark', a police informer, who is obviously not to be trusted.

[Sir John Stevens, Metropolitan Commissioner of Police] … variously described as 'the best detective in the country', 'a man with a CV to die for' and 'a copper's copper'.

*Sunday Times* (30 January 2000)

**Copycat killing.** A killing carried out in imitation of another, whether real or fictional. The increasing incidence of murders of this type in the latter half of the 20th century raised concern about the lurid publicity lavished on such crimes by the media, and generated debate regarding the extent to which scenes of violence on television and in the cinema are capable of influencing the young and susceptible. Stanley Kubrick's controversial film version of Anthony Burgess's novel *A* CLOCKWORK ORANGE (1962), first screened in 1971, was banned by Kubrick in 1973 in response to criticism that it could lead to copycat killings, and several rapes and murders were linked to the film. A gang chanting 'Singing in the Rain', a tune accompanying a vicious mugging in the film, was said to have raped a girl in Lancashire, and a judge condemned the film after a teenage boy wearing the 'droog' uniform of white overalls and black bowler hat beat a younger child. The film was re-released only in 2000. *See also* NADSAT.

**Coral Gables.** A superb example of a planned city adjoining Miami, Florida. It was developed by George E. Merrick on his family's farmland and at its incorporation in 1925 was named after the family's house of coral rock walls and gables. It is noted for its blend of Spanish and contemporary architecture and for its unique 'villages' with houses built in

French, South African Dutch and Chinese styles. Although originally exclusively residential it now contains several offices of large corporations, especially those trading with Latin America. To a large degree it is a visible realization of Merrick's ambition to build 'a place where castles in Spain are made real'.

**Co-respondent shoes.** Men's two-toned shoes, fashionable in the 1930s. They were so called because they were supposedly worn by a man cited in a divorce case, in other words by a 'cad'. They are sometimes erroneously called 'correspondent shoes', e.g. in Michael Tambini's study of 20th-century design, *The Look of the Century* (1999), presumably for their matching tones.

> In no circumstances should he [the 'Egmonter', or well-mannered male] wear 'co-respondent's shoes'.
>
> GUY EGMONT: *The Art of Egmontese*, ch. 5 (1961)

**Corgi and Bess.** A broadcasters' nickname for the Christmas message given annually on radio and television by Queen Elizabeth II, noted for her pet corgis, the pun being on PORGY AND BESS.

**Corn circles.** *See* CROP CIRCLES.

**Cornelia Gray.** *See* Cornelia GRAY.

***Corn is Green, The.*** A play (1938) by the British playwright Emlyn Williams (1905–87) about the experiences of a schoolmistress in the Welsh valleys at the turn of the century. The title evokes not only the rural surroundings but also the 'unripeness' of Miss Moffat's star pupil, Morgan Evans, and his preparation by her for the great deeds she hopes he will perform in later life. Williams himself played the schoolboy in the first production, recreating on stage the close relationship he himself had had as a boy with his own teacher, Miss Cooke, who nurtured his burgeoning talents.

**Cornish Alps.** A humorous local nickname for the clay spoil tips that are a prominent feature of the landscape surrounding St Austell in Cornwall. Viewed on a sunny day they do in fact bear a fancied resemblance to snow-covered peaks.

**Cornish Riviera.** A touristic name, based on that of the French Riviera, for the southern coast of Cornwall, and in particular Mounts Bay, from Penzance in the west to the Lizard in the east. The name is familiar from the Cornish Riviera express train from Paddington to Penzance. It first ran in 1904, when it was named the Riviera Express by J.C. Inglis, General Manager of the Great Western Railway. The south Devon and Dorset coast, further east, is sometimes similarly known as the English Riviera.

**Cornrow.** A style of tonsorial adornment in which the hair is plaited tightly to the scalp in a pattern of rows. It originated with African Americans, as a deliberate adaptation of styles favoured among African women.

> Always an icon, Rio Ferdinand's sudden discovery of the art of goalscoring makes his cornrow hairstyle *the* must-have look for the new year.
>
> *The Guardian* (30 December 2005)

**Coronation chicken.** Cold chicken with a curry sauce, accompanied by a salad of rice and peas and named for the coronation of Elizabeth II in 1953. The supreme advantage of the cold dish was that it would avoid the need for cooking on the day.

***Coronation Street.*** An enduringly popular television SOAP OPERA about working-class life in the (fictional) Manchester district of Weatherfield, first screened on 9 December 1960. The locale is the street so named, and most of the action takes place in a pub, the Rover's Return, at one end and a corner shop at the other. The cast and the characters they play have become household names, and the series has been lauded by prime ministers (Harold Wilson) and poets (John Betjeman). Its early story lines tended to be largely devoid of political or social issues, their content mostly concentrating on tales of petty scandals and illicit relationships, but in recent years social issues as diverse as teenage pregnancy and trans-sexualism have found their way into the programme. Fans nickname the programme 'Corrie'. Its original working title was *Florizel Street*.

**Corridor of uncertainty.** An item of cricketing jargon (often abbreviated to simply 'the corridor') popularized in the 1990s by the commentator and former Yorkshire and England batsman Geoffrey Boycott (b.1940). It refers to the area (*see* AREAS) just outside the batsman's off stump: a ball bowled on that line will cause the maximum doubt about whether to try to hit it or leave it alone, and therefore optimizes the chance of a dismissal.

**Corridors of power.** A collective term for the ministries in Whitehall with their top-ranking civil servants. The phrase was popularized (but not invented) by C.P. Snow in his novel *Homecomings* (1956):

> The official world, the corridors of power, the dilemmas of conscience and egotism – she disliked them all.

The phrase subsequently gained wide acceptance. He later used it for the title of the novel *Corridors of Power* (1964).

> Boffins at daggers drawn in corridors of power.
>
> *The Times*, headline (8 April 1965)

**Corrie.** The affectionate nickname bestowed on CORONATION STREET by its fans.

**Cortina.** *See* FORD CORTINA.

**Cosa Nostra.** (Italian, 'our thing'.) A name for the Mafia crime syndicate in the United States. It was originally used as a secret name but was made public by the informer Joseph Valachi in 1962.

> A former member of organized crime's ruling body, Mr Joseph Valachi, has named names and drawn a master plan of the Syndicate (which the underworld refers to as *Cosa Nostra*).
>
> *The Economist* (17 August 1963)

**Cosmetic surgery.** An operation performed to enhance an individual's appearance rather than to cure disease. It is chiefly undergone by women and typically involves an alteration of the size or shape of the nose (rhinoplasty), breasts (mammoplasty) or chin (mentoplasty) or a FACELIFT. The first two of these are known colloquially and respectively as a 'nose job' and a 'boob job'.

**Cosmic Bob.** A nickname given to Senator Bob Kerrey (b.1943) of Nebraska owing to his interest in otherworldly matters. He briefly and unsuccessfully ran for the Democratic presidential nomination in 1992.

**Cosmonaut.** (Russian *kosmonavt*, from Russian *kosmos*, 'space', and Greek *nautēs*, 'sailor'.) A Soviet ASTRONAUT. The word was first popularized in the late 1950s, when the USSR and the United States began their rivalry for space, and continued to be used for Russian astronauts in the post-Soviet era.

**Costa Book Awards.** *See* WHITBREAD AWARDS.

**Costa del Crime.** A nickname for the southeast coast of Spain, used by several British criminals as a bolt-hole from the law. The name punningly reflects those of various stretches of holiday coastline such as *Costa Brava* or *Costa del Sol*. The expression was the invention of the popular press and dates from the 1980s. The Costa Brava itself was so named in 1918 by the Spanish poet and journalist Ferran Aguiló in recognition of its ruggedness.

> Jack Took … said he expected that Harry Harris was at that very moment living it up on the Costa del Criminal [*sic*] with Miss Eddon Gurney.
>
> FAY WELDON: *The Heart of the Country* (1987)

**Costa Geriatrica.** A jocular name dating from the 1980s for the south coast of England, as a region with a large residential population of old and retired people, who seek sunny summers, sea air and mild winters. The name imitates those of Spanish coastal regions such as *Costa Brava*.

> Affectionately derided for decades as the 'Costa Geriatrica', even by the geriatric residents themselves, the Dorset resort [Bournemouth] must now have more nightclubs than Manhattan.
>
> *The Times* (29 July 1999)

**Cost an arm and a leg.** To be very expensive. The loss of both an arm and a leg is clearly too great a price to pay.

**Cosy up to.** To ingratiate oneself by creating a mutually agreeable or 'cosy' relationship. The expression is of US origin and dates from the 1930s.

> The BBC will do itself no harm by cosying up to the culture secretary.
>
> *Sunday Times* (6 June 1999)

**Cot death.** The unexplained death of a baby in its sleep, more formally known as sudden infant death syndrome (SIDS). It is the most common form of death between the ages of one month and one year, and is slightly more common among boys, among second children, and in winter. There may be no single cause for the death, which often cannot be explained even after autopsy.

**Cottage industry.** An industry in which employees work in their own homes, using their own equipment. The term dates from the 1920s.

**Cottaging.** In gay jargon the act of waiting or loitering in a public toilet or 'cottage' for the purpose of a sexual encounter. The adoption of this particular word is said to derive from the particulars of an eccentric 19th-century will in which the testator left a large sum to be expended on the construction of 'cottages of convenience', so called as public lavatories are small buildings. The verbal noun dates from the 1960s.

**Cottingley fairies.** *See under* FAKES.

**Couch potato.** A person who prefers lounging at home watching television to engaging in any purposeful activity, especially if it involves any physical effort. The expression is of US origin (it was reputedly coined by Tom Iacino) and probably puns on BOOB TUBE as slang for a television, the potato being a plant tuber. There may further be a punning reference to the fact that such a person is 'all eyes'.

**Couéism.** A system of therapy by auto-suggestion popular in the 1920s. It was propounded by the French pharmacist and hypnotist Émile Coué (1857–1926) and was encapsulated in the formula familiar in English as: 'Every day, in every way, I am getting better and better.' Coué recommended his patients mouth the mantra 15 to 20 times every morning and evening.

5

*Tous les jours, à tous points de vue, je vais de mieux en mieux*
('Every day, from every point of view, I am getting better and better').

ÉMILE COUÉ: *De la suggestion et de ses applications*
('On Suggestion and its Applications') (1915)

**Countdown.** A simple light entertainment television programme first screened in 1982 that somewhat curiously became cult afternoon viewing. Two contestants are required first to construct as long a word as possible from nine randomly drawn letters of the alphabet and then to manipulate numbers, also randomly selected, to arrive at a stated total. Part of the attraction lay in the cheerfully bumbling banter of the original host, Richard Whiteley (1943–2005), on the one hand, and the photogenic charms of the letters-and-numbers drawer, Carol Vorderman, on the other. Following Whiteley's sudden death, his role was assumed by the smooth-talking sports presenter and housewives' favourite, Des ('Call me Des') Lynam.

**Counted them all out...** *See* I COUNTED THEM ALL OUT AND I COUNTED THEM ALL BACK.

**Count one's blessings.** To be grateful for what one has. Edith Temple and Reginald Morgan's song 'Count Your Blessings One by One' became a hit in the late 1940s through such singers as Josef Locke, Harry Secombe and the Luton Girls Choir.

**Countries of the world.** Most of the nation-states in the world gained their independence as republics or sovereign states in the 20th century. The following is a tally of the situation at the beginning of the 21st century, with the year in which each nation-state gained or declared independence and a brief note on the circumstances of the change of status. There were two great waves in this respect: the liberation from colonial rule in the WIND OF CHANGE that blew across Africa from the late 1950s, and the establishment of independent states in eastern Europe and central Asia resulting from the formal dissolution of the Soviet Union in 1991. Some states, notably in Africa, took a new name on gaining independence, such as Ghana, formerly Gold Coast.

Albania (1912): independence from the Ottoman Empire

Algeria (1962): independence from France

Andorra (1993): Andorra's first formal constitution

Angola (1975): independence from Portugal

Antigua and Barbuda (1981): independence from Britain

Armenia (1991): secession from the Soviet Union; Armenia was briefly independent 1918–20 after Turkish (16th century) then Russian (1916) conquests

Austria (1955): recognition of Austrian sovereignty by the former Allied powers; Austria had previously become a republic in 1920 following the collapse of the Austro-Hungarian Empire, but was absorbed into the German Reich 1938–45

Azerbaijan (1991): secession from the Soviet Union; Azerbaijan became an independent republic in 1918 but was occupied by Russia in 1920

Bahamas (1973): independence from Britain

Bahrain (1971): independence from Britain

Bangladesh (1971): secession from PAKISTAN, of which Bangladesh was formerly the eastern section

Barbados (1966): independence from Britain

Belarus (1991): secession from the Soviet Union; Belarus was a Soviet Republic from 1919 (as Byelorussia)

Belize (1981): full independence from Britain

Benin (1960): independence from France (Benin was known as Dahomey until 1975)

Bosnia-Herzegovina (1992): international recognition of Bosnia's secession from Yugoslavia, of which it had been a constituent part since 1918

Botswana (1966): independence from Britain

Brunei (1984): full independence from Britain

Bulgaria (1946): proclamation of a communist republic; Bulgaria had previously been an independent kingdom from 1908 after 500 years of Turkish domination

Burkina Faso (1960): independence from France

Burma *see* Myanmar

Burundi (1962): independence from Belgium

Cambodia (1953): independence from France; known as Kampuchea 1976–89

Cameroon (1960): independence from France

Cape Verde (1975): independence from Portugal

Central African Republic (1960): independence from France

Chad (1960): independence from France

Comoros (apart from Mayotte) (1975): independence from France

Congo (1960): independence from Belgium; full name Democratic Republic of Congo; known as Zaire 1971–97

Congo-Brazzaville (1960): independence from France

Côte d'Ivoire (1960): independence from France

Croatia (1991): secession from Yugoslavia, of which it had been a constituent part since 1918

Cuba (1901): proclamation of republic; Cuba had been ceded to the United States by Spain in 1898 and was administered by the USA 1898–1901 and 1906–9

Cyprus (1960): independence from Britain

Czech Republic (1993): became a sovereign state when Slovakia (*see below*) seceded from Czechoslovakia, which had existed since 1918

Djibouti (1977): independence from France

Dominica (1978): independence from Britain

Egypt (1953): proclamation of republic; Egypt was granted nominal independence by Britain in 1922

Equatorial Guinea (1968): independence from Spain

Eritrea (1993): secession from Ethiopia

Estonia (1991): secession from the Soviet Union, of which it had been a constituent republic since 1945; previously Estonia had been a democratic republic 1919–40 and was occupied by Germany 1941–44

Fiji (1970): independence from Britain

Finland (1917): independence from Russia, which had ruled Finland since 1809

Gabon (1960): independence from France

Gambia (1965): independence from Britain

Georgia (1991): secession from the Soviet Union, of which it had been a constituent republic since 1922

Ghana (1957): independence from Britain

Grenada (1974): independence from Britain

Guinea (1958): independence from France

Guinea-Bissau (1974): independence from Portugal

Guyana (1966): independence from Britain

Hungary (1918): became an independent republic, stripped of much of its former territory, after the collapse of the Austro-Hungarian Empire

Iceland (1944): independence from Denmark

India (1947): independence from Britain; the partition of British India created the states of India and PAKISTAN

Indonesia (1949): independence from the Netherlands

Iran (1979): proclamation of an Islamic republic

Ireland (1921): limited independence as a dominion of the British Empire; constitution of 1937 declared Ireland to be a sovereign nation (*see* EIRE); became the Republic of Ireland in 1949

Israel (1948): proclamation of the State of Israel after the end of the British LEAGUE OF NATIONS mandate in Palestine (*see* MANDATE)

Jamaica (1962): independence from Britain

Jordan (1946): independence as the Kingdom of Jordan; as Transjordan it had been a British MANDATE 1920–3, then a separate emirate.

Kazakhstan (1991): secession from the Soviet Union

Kenya (1963): independence from Britain

Kiribati (1979): independence from Britain

Kyrgyzstan (1991): secession from the Soviet Union

Laos (1954): independence from France

Latvia (1991): secession from the Soviet Union, of which it had been a constituent republic since 1945; previously Latvia had been an independent republic 1919–40 and was occupied by Germany 1941–44

Lebanon (1944): independence from France, which had ruled the area under a LEAGUE OF NATIONS mandate since 1920 (*see* MANDATE)

Lesotho (1966): independence from Britain

Libya (1951): independence gained after Italian rule (from 1911) and Anglo-French administration after the Second World War

Lithuania (1991): secession from the Soviet Union, of which it had been a constituent republic since 1945; previously Lithuania had been an independent state 1919–40 and was occupied by Germany 1941–44

Macedonia (1992): secession from Yugoslavia

Madagascar (1960): independence from France

Malawi (1964): independence from Britain

Malaysia (1963): formed from a group of former British colonies which had gained independence in 1957 as the Federation of Malaya, plus territories in northwestern Borneo and Singapore (*see below*)

Maldives (1965): independence from Britain

Mali (1960): independence from France

Malta (1964): independence from Britain

Mauritania (1960): independence from France

Mauritius (1968): independence from Britain

Micronesia (1990): recognition of independence

Moldova (1991): secession from the Soviet Union

Mongolia (1924): establishment of republic following centuries of Chinese domination

Montenegro (2006): secession from Serbia

Morocco (1956): independence from France

Mozambique (1975): independence from Portugal

Myanmar (Burma) (1948): independence from Britain; the country's name was changed to Myanmar in 1989

Namibia (1990): independence from South Africa, which in 1966 had ignored the cancellation by the United Nations of the MANDATE under which South Africa had ruled Namibia since 1919

Nauru (1968): recognition of independence

Niger (1960): independence from France

Nigeria (1960): independence from Britain

North Korea (1948): declaration of a People's Republic; the state was created from the zone north of the 38th parallel occupied by Soviet troops after Japan's surrender at the end of the Second World War

Pakistan (1947): independence from Britain (*see also* India *above*)

Panama (1903): independence (with US support) from Spain

Papua New Guinea (1975): recognition of independence

Philippines (1946): independence from the United States, of which it had been a colony since 1898

Poland (1918): restoration of statehood after the First World War; Poland had been carved up between Russia, Austria and Prussia in the second half of the 18th century

Rwanda (1962): independence from Belgium

St Lucia (1979): independence from Britain

St Vincent and the Grenadines (1979): independence from Britain

Samoa (1962): recognition of independence

São Tomé e Príncipe (1975): independence from Portugal

Saudi Arabia (1932): state created from the kingdoms of Najd and Hejaz; Arab rulers had fought over the area after the demise of the Ottoman Empire in 1918

Senegal (1960): independence from France

Serbia (2003): formerly the rump (with Montenegro, *see above*) of the Federal Republic of Yugoslavia

Seychelles (1976): independence from Britain

Sierra Leone (1961): independence from Britain

Singapore (1965): secession from the Federation of Malaysia (*see* Malaysia *above*)

Slovakia (1993): secession from Czechoslovakia (*see* Czech Republic *above*)

Slovenia (1991): secession from Yugoslavia, of which it had been a constituent part since 1918

Solomon Islands (1978): independence from Britain

Somalia (1960): creation of an independent republic by a merger of former British Somaliland and Italian Somaliland

South Africa (1961): declaration of a republic outside the British Commonwealth; South Africa achieved independence within the British Empire in 1910

South Korea (1948): republic formed out of the zone south of the 38th parallel of latitude, the area occupied by US troops after Japan's surrender in 1945 at the end of the Second World War

Sri Lanka (1948): independence from Britain (as Ceylon)

Sudan (1955): independence from Britain; under Anglo-Egyptian administration from 1899

Suriname (1975): independence from the Netherlands

Swaziland (1968): independence from Britain

Syria (1946): independence from France, which had ruled the area as a LEAGUE OF NATIONS mandate since 1920 (*see* MANDATE)

Tajikistan (1991): secession from the Soviet Union

Tanzania (1961): independence from Britain as Tanganyika, which united with Zanzibar to become Tanzania in 1964

Timor-Leste (formerly East Timor) (2002): independence from Indonesia

Togo (1960): independence from France

Tonga (1970): independence from Britain

Trinidad and Tobago (1962): independence from Britain

Tunisia (1956): independence from France

Turkey (1923): proclamation of a Turkish republic

Turkmenistan (1991): secession from the Soviet Union

Tuvalu (1978): independence from Britain

Uganda (1962): independence from Britain

Ukraine (1991): secession from the Soviet Union

United Arab Emirates (1971): independence from Britain

Uzbekistan (1991): secession from the Soviet Union

Vanuatu (1980): recognition of independence

Vatican (1929): the Vatican City State came into being through the LATERAN TREATY of 1929

Vietnam (1976): proclamation of the unified Socialist Republic of Vietnam after the VIETNAM War

Yemen (1990): merging of North and South Yemen; previously the North became independent of Turkey in 1918, and the South independent of Britain in 1967

Zambia (1964): independence from Britain

Zimbabwe (1980): independence from Britain

**Country.** The 20th century saw the burgeoning of this word as the name for a geographical region associated with a particular writer or artist. Shakespeare Country is thus the region around Stratford-upon-Avon, Hardy Country is historical Wessex, where Thomas Hardy's novels are set, and Constable Country is the Stour Valley, Suffolk, where John Constable lived and painted. More recent than any of these is Catherine Cookson Country, or South Tyneside, where the prolific and long-lived popular novelist lived. Charles G. Harper's *The Hardy Country* appeared as early as 1904 in a series published by A. & C. Black that also included *The Burns Country*, *The Dickens Country* and *The Scott Country*. These regions are also promoted by local tourist authorities, as are such obvious literary shrines as the Brontë Country around Haworth, near Bradford, while famous persons have given rise to themed areas such as Captain Cook Country between Whitby, North Yorkshire, and Middlesbrough. Many recent 'Countries' have drawn tourists as the settings of filmed fiction. Herriot Country is thus the region around Askrigg in North Yorkshire where the televised version of James Herriot's novel of veterinary life *All Creatures Great and Small* (1972) was filmed. *See also* TELETOURISM.

> Small is beautiful. Never have these words been more apt than when applied to the Forster Country of North Hertfordshire, which adjoins Rooks Nest, childhood home of the writer E.M. Forster.
> MARGARET ASHBY: *Forster Country*, Introduction (1991)

**Country and western.** A form of COUNTRY MUSIC that in the 1940s and 1950s added cowboy songs to the generally rural music of southern American states. The name is popularly abbreviated to C&W. *See also* WESTERN.

**Country fit for heroes.** A phrase derived from a speech that the British prime minister David Lloyd George, the WELSH WIZARD, made at Wolverhampton on 24 November 1918, less than two weeks after the end of the First World War. His exact words were slightly different: 'What is our task? To make Britain a fit country for heroes to live in.' Lloyd George's COALITION GOVERNMENT swept back to power in the general election the following month. However, the phrase came to have a notoriously hollow ring, as, once the brief postwar economic boom was over, many former servicemen found themselves without a job, to the apparent indifference of those in power.

**Country mile.** A very long way. A mile in the country can take longer to traverse than in the town. The term originated in the United States around the middle of the 20th century.

**Country music.** A form of popular or folk music originating in the southern states of the United States in the early 20th century. It can be ultimately traced back to British immigrants who brought with them a tradition of narrative Celtic ballads and string-instrument playing, especially fiddling, and came to be known by different genre names depending on dominant elements or geographical factors. *See also* BLUEGRASS; COUNTRY AND WESTERN; HILLBILLY.

**Countryside Alliance.** A UK pressure group (CA for short) formed in 1998 out of the British Field Sports Society, the Countryside Business Group and the Countryside Movement. That year the CA held a demonstration in London to protest against certain government policies and proposals that would adversely affect the rural way of life. Chief among its concerns were a possible ban on blood sports (especially fox-hunting), the prospect of more building on GREEN BELT land and the hesitant handling of the MAD COW DISEASE crisis. Protesters also called for an end

to the decline of rural services such as village shops and country buses. The government's handling of the 2001 foot-and-mouth outbreak was also criticized by the CA. In 2002 the CA held a 'Liberty and Livelihood March' in London, but this and other activities failed to prevent a legal ban on hunting with hounds coming into force in 2005.

**Count sheep.** To imagine sheep crossing an obstacle and count them one by one as a supposed aid to inducing sleep. The dodge was known to the Victorians but became popular as an insomniac's soporific recourse only in the 20th century. The choice of this particular animal for the purpose may have arisen from a verbal association between 'sheep' and 'sleep'.

**Count to ten.** To pause when heated or angry in order to recover one's composure. The idea is that a mental count of one to ten will give one enough time to cool down. The expression is often used as an imperative, sometimes to oneself, as: 'He was a proper – count to ten! – rascal.'

**County Hall.** This impressive building on the south bank of the Thames in London was opened by George V in 1922 to house the London County Council, which until then had occupied crowded premises off Trafalgar Square. Construction took 13 years, partly because of the size of the building, partly because marshland on the site had to be reclaimed. On the demise of the LCC in 1965 County Hall became home to its successor, the Greater London Council, until that body in turn ceased to exist in 1986, leaving London as the only European city without any elected authority. The future of the building remained uncertain for some years until it was reopened in 1998 as a luxury hotel, complete with conference facilities, an aquarium and a health and fitness club. Until 2005 it was also home to Charles Saatchi's collection of BRIT ART.

**Couples.** A novel (1968) by the US writer John Updike (b.1932) about eight couples in suburban Massachusetts. Piet, who is married to Angela, has an affair with Georgene, and also with a pregnant Foxy, whom he impregnates immediately after she has had the baby. Georgene's husband lusts after Angela, who agrees to sleep with him in return for his having procured an abortion for Foxy. And so on. In the end, some normality is achieved. Piet and Foxy, now married to each other, 'live in Lexington, where, gradually, among people like themselves, they have been accepted, as another couple'.

**Coupon Election.** During the general election of 1918 Prime Minister David Lloyd George and Chancellor of the Exchequer Bonar Law sent a certificate or coupon to all candidates supporting the COALITION GOVERNMENT. The coupon was not accepted by the Asquith Liberals or by the Labour Party. A 'couponeer' was a politician who accepted the coupon.

**Courtesy.** A word applied variously to a product or service provided with the intention of being helpful or solicitous. A 'courtesy car' is thus one supplied free of charge by a commercial organization to someone already paying for other services, while a 'courtesy phone' in a supermarket or hotel enables customers or guests to call a taxi or hire a car, which itself may have a 'courtesy light', automatically switching on when a door is open. A 'courtesy call' is a telephone call made by a commercial organization to a private individual with the aim of selling something, usually double glazing, and as such is often intrusive and so anything but courteous.

**Court shoes.** Low-cut shoes for women, without laces or straps, and so called from their use as part of court dress. The US equivalent name for such shoes is 'pumps'.

> 'Elfine, *whatever* you do, always wear court shoes. Remember – c-o-u-r-t.'
> STELLA GIBBONS: *Cold Comfort Farm*, ch. 11 (1932)

**Coventry.** A city in the English Midlands, which during the Second World War was a centre for the manufacture of military vehicles, munitions and armaments. On the night of 14 November 1940 the city was extensively damaged by 449 Luftwaffe bombers in an operation code-named Moonlight. Over 1000 civilians were killed or badly injured, 50,000 houses were damaged, and the famous medieval cathedral was almost completely destroyed (the Germans gloatingly coined the verb *coventrieren* to denote intensive bombing, which was rendered into English as 'Coventrate'). Another raid followed in April 1941. The remains of the cathedral now stand alongside the new cathedral, designed by Sir Basil Spence (1907–76), which was consecrated in 1962. *See also* WAR REQUIEM.

**Cover girl.** A now dated term for an attractive young woman whose photograph appears, or deserves to appear, on the front cover of a magazine. The phrase is of US origin and dates from the early years of the 20th century.

**Cowboy.** An unqualified and usually unscrupulous provider of goods and services, especially in the building trade. The word in this sense dates from the 1960s and derives from an earlier term for a reckless driver, especially a lorry driver. This in turn goes back to a US slang term of the 1930s for any reckless young man, comparing him to the 'wild and woolly' original cowboys who were the cattle-herders of the American West. *See also* WHITE VAN MAN.

**Crack a fat.** In Australian slang, to have an erection. The expression dates from the 1940s, and received a considerable boost in the 1960s from Barry McKenzie, an Australian character of large sexual and alcoholic appetites created by Barry Humphries.

**Crack down on something.** To repress it; to take strong measures against it. The expression dates from the 1930s.

**Cracker factory.** In US slang, a hospital for the mentally ill. A decidedly non-PC usage, first recorded in 1981, it punningly combines 'crackers', in the sense 'mad', with the notion of a factory where crackers (dry non-sweet biscuits) are made.

**Crackerjack.** A long-running children's television programme screened from 1955 to 1984. It based its content largely on the music hall, and mixed slapstick sketches with pop music numbers, interspersed with 'boys v. girls' competitions. Many of its presenters, such as Eamonn Andrews, Leslie Crowther and Michael Aspel, subsequently became famous on adult television. 'Crackerjack' itself is an evocative slang word for anyone or anything regarded as excellent.

**Cracker night.** In Australia, a night marked by public and private firework displays (akin to Guy Fawkes' night in Britain). Originally it coincided with Empire Day (later Commonwealth Day), but in the latter part of the 20th century the occasion for the celebration was transferred to the Queen's official birthday.

> One cracker night Thommo and his uncle let off a few plugs of dynamite.
> Q. WILD: *The Honey Wind* (1981)

**Crack on to someone.** In Australian slang, to find someone sexually attractive, or to chat them up. The usage dates back to the mid-1950s.

**Crammer.** A type of private (independent) secondary school that concentrates on preparing its students for examinations and university entry. They are so called since they 'cram' their fee-paying candidates with the appropriate subject knowledge and the 'tricks of the trade'. They are less in evidence now than they once were, but are by no means defunct, since there are always schools where pupils are poorly taught and always pupils who lack application or intellect.

**Cramp someone's style.** To prevent them from acting freely or naturally. The image is of physically restricting one's manner of writing. The expression dates from the early 20th century.

**Crash and burn.** To fail disastrously in a romance or some other experience or enterprise. The allusion is to an aircraft or car that crashes and catches fire. The phrase is of US campus origin and dates from the 1970s.

**Crash out.** To go to sleep, especially suddenly or in a place other than one's usual bed.

**Crash pad.** A place where one can CRASH OUT.

**Crawley Food Mountain.** A description of the generously dimensioned Tory MP Nicholas Soames (a.k.a. FATTY SOAMES) by the Labour MP Tony Banks (1943–2006), Crawley being in Soames's Mid-Sussex constituency:

> The amiable Crawley food mountain clearly loves his grub. At the dispatch box he could probably persuade MPs that arsenic is quite palatable if suitably chilled.
>
> *Hansard*, April 1993

**Crazy Foam.** The proprietary name of a type of foam for children sold as a pressurized foam in an aerosol container and a popular toy or joke device in the 1960s.

**Crazy Gang.** The lunatic lot so named first formed up in 1932 for a performance of the revue *Crazy Month* at the London Palladium. It consisted of three pairs of already famous comics: Flanagan and Allen, otherwise Bud Flanagan (Robert Wintrop, originally Reuben Weintrop) (1896–1968) and Chesney Allen (1894–1982); Nervo and Knox, viz. Jimmy Nervo (James Henry Holloway) (1897–1975) and Teddy Knox (1896–1974); and the Scots pair Naughton and Gold, i.e. Charlie Naughton (1887–1976) and Jimmy Gold (James McGonigal) (1886–1967). 'Monsewer' Eddie Gray (1898–1969) often appeared with them, but was never more than a semidetached member of the gang. They remained together until 1960. The name Crazy Gang was applied in the 1980s and 1990s to the players of Wimbledon Football Club, for their vigorous style of play and antics both on and off the football field.

**Crazy golf.** A form of putting in which balls have to negotiate a number of obstacles such as humps, tunnels, bends and bridges in order to reach the hole.

> Until recently crazy golf was regarded as a quaint relic of the 1950s: now, with a glut in conventional 18-hole courses, long-nurtured plans for wilder alternatives are beginning to emerge.
>
> *Sunday Times* (26 July 1998)

**Crazy like a fox.** Very shrewd or cunning. A paradoxical simile of US origin, and the title of an anthology of prose pieces by the American humorist S.J. Perelman published in 1944.

**Crazy mixed-up kid.** A young person whose mind is confused by conflicting emotions. The expression dates from the 1950s.

**Crazy name, crazy guy!** A catchphrase prompted by the mention of a man with a (to the ears of English-speakers) unusual-sounding and probably foreign name, suggesting that his personality is equally outlandish. Mocking the hyperbole of gushing female gossip-columnists, it began life in the pages of *Private Eye* magazine and spread outwards from there.

> Emil Zatopek – crazy name, crazy guy! Paula Radcliffe – I'm amazed that bobble hat stayed on for so long in Chicago.
>
> www.letsrun.com (21 July 2003)

**Crazy paving.** Paving composed of irregularly shaped stone or concrete slabs, used for ornamental effect on terraces, garden paths and the like.

**Cream of the crop.** The best of anything. The alliterative phrase may owe something to the similarly alliterative and virtually synonymous French CRÈME DE LA CRÈME.

**Cream one's jeans.** To be overwhelmed with extreme delight, enthusiasm or excitement. A metaphorical extension, dating from at least the mid-1940s, of a US slang expression that originally denoted untoward vaginal moistening or male orgasm when fully clothed.

**Cream tea.** Afternoon tea that includes scones with clotted cream and jam. The name of the meal is first recorded only in the mid-1960s but must have existed some time before this. The homeland of the cream tea is the southwest of England, hence its alternative name of 'Devon cream tea', but the repast is now found in all parts of the British Isles as a leading staple in a variety of teashops.

**Creationism in a cheap tuxedo.** *See* INTELLIGENT DESIGN.

**Creature of habit.** A person who follows an unvarying routine. The implication is that the one so described is governed by the routine and cannot break free of it.

**Credibility gap.** The disparity that can exist between a claim or statement on the one hand and the reality of the situation on the other. If this is constantly experienced, it results in a loss of confidence in those making such statements. President Nixon created a credibility gap in the 1960s when he asked African Americans 'to judge him by his deeds and not his words'. They did, and were disappointed.

**CREEP.** An acronym for Committee for the Re-Election of the President, the inner circle that organized President Richard Nixon's campaign for a second term in the White House in 1972. After the WATERGATE scandal broke CREEP was revealed to have been involved in various illegal activities, such as funding the actual burglars. *See also* TRICKY DICKY.

**Crème de la crème.** The 'cream of the cream', literally translated from the French, in other words the pick of the bunch, the elite, the best. The phrase is famously used by the eponymous schoolmistress to her charges in Muriel Spark's 1961 novel *The* PRIME OF MISS JEAN BRODIE:

> I am putting old heads on your young shoulders ... all my pupils are the *crème de la crème*.

*See also* CREAM OF THE CROP.

**Crest of a wave.** To be on the crest of a wave is to be 'riding high' or making good progress in one's affairs, while more generally it is to be optimistic or OVER THE MOON. Ralph Reader's song 'Riding Along on the Crest of a Wave' (1937) was the theme tune of his GANG SHOW.

**Crew cut.** A form of haircut popularized by US athletes, particularly college rowing crews at Harvard and Yale universities, in the decade following the Second World War. The hair is closely cropped and brushed upright.

**Crew neck.** A close-fitting round neckline on a sweater. Its origin is similar to that of the CREW CUT.

**Cricket in Times Square, The.** A children's novel (1960) and the best-known book by the US writer George Selden (1929–89). It tells the story of Chester, a cricket, who travels to New York from rural Connecticut. *See also* TIMES SQUARE.

**Cricket test.** A hypothetical indicator of the national loyalty of new immigrants to Britain, and of their degree of integration into the British way of life. The phrase was prompted by a controversial contribution by Norman Tebbit (*see* CHINGFORD SKINHEAD) in April 1990 to a debate in the House of Commons on immigration from Hong Kong. He suggested that a way of determining whether immigrants from the Indian subcontinent were fully integrated into British society was to see whether they supported England or their country of origin in cricket matches between the two.

> Those right-wing ideologues – who define patriotism by a 'cricket test' – completely fail to understand our true strengths.
>
> GORDON BROWN: in *The Times* (10 January 2000)

**Crimbo.** Christmas. A child's word adopted in the 1980s by adults, especially those in the armed services and the popular media, who took to wishing all and sundry a 'Happy Crimbo'. Variants are Crimble and even just Crim.

> What with their Boxing Day feast of fun and this video for

new single *Say You'll Be Mine*, Steps are going to be ever-present this Crimble.
>
> *heat* (16 December 1999–5 January 2000)

**Crime doesn't pay.** A 20th-century propagandistic proverb, insisting (in the face of a certain amount of evidence to the contrary) that those who commit crime will inevitably suffer for it sooner or later, and will not in the long run profit from it. It is first recorded in 1927, and was popularized in the 1930s by its use in a US radio crime drama series 'The Shadow'.

> The Proceeds of Crime Act 2002 helps us to drive home the message that crime does not pay. By using the full range of powers available to us we can pursue those who try to profit from criminal activity.
>
> www.scotland.gov.uk (30 June 2005)

**Cringe-making.** Embarrassing enough to produce a physical reaction, as if cringing. The expression dates from the 1980s.

> A New Year's Eve show from my childhood ... is seared on my memory as one of the most cringe-making in television history.
>
> *The Times* (16 April 1999)

**Crippen, Dr.** The still resonant name of Hawley Harvey Crippen (1862–1910), an American doctor whose poisoning of his wife, an amateur music-hall artiste calling herself Belle Elmore, was one of the most sensational cases of the early 20th century. The remains of her body were discovered in 1910 in the coal cellar at 39 Hilldrop Crescent, North London, where Crippen had been living with his mistress, Ethel Le Neve. The pair had meanwhile fled to Canada on board the SS *Montrose*, Crippen calling himself Mr Robinson and Le Neve disguising herself as his son. The ship's captain was suspicious, however, and sent a message to Scotland Yard by wireless telegraphy. Chief Inspector Dew set off in pursuit in another ship and boarded the *Montrose* in the St Lawrence River. The use of telegraphy, the first known use of radio in making an arrest, meant that newspapers were able to report every stage of the chase before the murderer was even aware that he had been discovered. Crippen was hanged but Le Neve was acquitted, living until 1967.

**Crisis? What crisis?** The *Sun* newspaper's version of a comment made by Labour prime minister Jim Callaghan on his return from a meeting in Guadeloupe on 10 January 1979 during the so-called WINTER OF DISCONTENT. What Callaghan actually said was: 'I don't think other people in the world would share the view there is mounting chaos.' Callaghan lost the May 1979 election to Margaret Thatcher, who gave the editor of *The Sun* a knighthood.

**Crisp packet option.** A cheap and shoddy alternative to a proper or genuine article. The allusion is to crisp packets as one of the cheapest forms of packaging, serving simply as a basic container for its rapidly consumed contents.

**Crispy critter.** A blackly humorous US military slang expression for someone who has been burned to death or who has suffered extremely serious burns. It first appeared on the scene at the time of the Vietnam War, when napalm flowed like water.

**Croft, Lara.** The feisty, busty heroine of the *Tomb Raider* computer game series. She is the dreamchild of Jeremy Heath-Smith, who created her in 1996, and is produced by his company, Core Design. In the manner of her kind she has a fantasy 'biography', which records that she was born on 14 February (St Valentine's Day) in Wimbledon, the daughter of Lord Henshingley Croft, attended Wimbledon High School for Girls, GORDONSTOUN and a Swiss finishing school, and went out in the world with the occupation of 'adventurer'. In 1998 the model Nell McAndrew assumed her PIN-UP persona for a promotional tour in Europe. Lara was portrayed by Angelina Jolie in the 2001 film of *Tomb Raider*, directed by Simon West. A sequel, *The Cradle of Life* directed by Jan de Bont, followed in 2003.

> There is no doubt that Lara Croft is a lot more than a mere computer character. She has touched a nerve in the same way that James Bond does, and has become the first icon of the digital age.
>
> *The Times* (27 November 1999)

**Cronyism.** The preferential treatment of one's friends or colleagues, and especially the awarding of political posts through friendship rather than on ability. The charge of cronyism was levelled at Tony Blair, Labour prime minister from 1997, whose INNER CABINET members were dubbed TONY'S CRONIES by the media.

**Crooning.** A sentimental type of humming or singing in a low subdued voice, with much swooping between notes, that originated in the United States in the 1920s and that soon became popular. The word itself is ultimately imitative.

> The principle of crooning is to use as little voice as possible and instead to make a sentimental appeal by prolonged moaning somewhere near the written notes, but preferably never actually on those notes.
>
> ERIC BLOM: *Everyman's Dictionary of Music* (1947)

**Crop circles.** Also known as corn circles, these are circular areas of standing crops that have been neatly but mysteriously flattened, apparently by some kind of scything motion or vortex. They first appeared in the early 1980s in the South of England and have baffled scientists. They have

been ascribed to supernatural forces, to UFOS, to freak whirlwinds and to the orchestrated handiwork of hoaxers, but no explanation for their appearance has been fully convincing or conclusive. The phenomenon subsequently surfaced in other countries.

**Croque-monsieur.** (French, literally 'munch-sir'.) The French equivalent of a toasted cheese and ham sandwich. When served with a fried egg on top, it is known as a *croque-madame*. It is said to have first appeared in the early 20th century on the menu of a café on the Boulevard des Capucines in Paris. The name itself may have arisen as a whimsical variant of *croque-mitaine*, literally 'munch-mitten', a term for a bogeyman or ugly monster formerly used by French nurses and parents to frighten children into good behaviour.

**Cross of Lorraine.** *See* MAQUIS.

**Cross one's heart.** To promise or pledge. The words are often accompanied by a sign of the cross made over the heart.

> 'Let's both swear.' 'Cross my heart and hope to die. Now what about bed?'
>
> ROSE MACAULAY: *Crewe Train*, ch. 10 (1926)

**Crossover.** A hybrid genre, especially in music, in which elements of two or more distinct styles or schools are blended. The term came to the fore in the late 20th century in two contrasting musical applications. In the world of 'serious' music it denotes, not without a hint of hostility, a classically trained artiste who performs 'popular' music (the underlying negative image is of an opera singer making a cloth-eared hash of a popular standard number or a song from a musical that he or she has recorded simply for the money). However, it can also apply to a less deliberate (and less cynical) process in which elements of one genre come to be popular with devotees of another and are incorporated into it (examples include Afro-crossover and rhythm-crossover). By the 21st century the latter was such an established format that its successes were chronicled in 'crossover charts'.

**Crossword.** The popular pastime or obsession has its origins in the puzzle devised in 1913 by the British-born American editor Arthur Wynne for the Christmas issue of the 'Fun' supplement to the *New York Sunday World*. It appeared on 21 December as a diamond-shaped device with 31 words to be entered and straightforward clues such as 'What bargain hunters enjoy' ('sales'). The First World War hampered the spread of the new craze, but it was taken up soon after in Britain and continental Europe, and on 1 February 1930 *The Times* published its 'Crossword Puzzle No. 1', compiled by the rural novelist Adrian Bell, who was paid 3 guineas a puzzle. Its clues were rather more sophisticated, one being 'The final crack' ('doom') and another 'Retunes (anag.)' ('tureens'). Cryptic clues soon became a regular feature of most British crosswords, based on the compiler's classic principle, 'I need not mean what I say, but I must say what I mean', a tenet first propounded by 'Afrit' (A.F. Ritchie). An example of such a clue, in *The Times* crossword No. 21,302 for 3 January 2000, is 'Not feeling pain in leg, as broken in two areas', in which 'in leg as' is 'broken' (anagrammatized) between two letters 'a', the mathematical abbreviation for 'area', producing 'analgesia', defined as 'not feeling pain'. Crosswords that have become institutions include the cryptic 'Everyman' and harder 'Mephisto' in the *Sunday Times*, and the notoriously difficult *Listener* crossword, published weekly in *The Times* after that journal's demise in 1991.

**Croucher, The.** The nickname of the Gloucestershire and England cricketer Gilbert Laird Jessop (1874–1955), so called for his idiosyncratic stance at the crease. Jessop was probably the consistently fastest scorer in the history of cricket.

**Crow.** A sequence of poems (1970) by the British poet Ted Hughes (1930–98). The image of a mocking, predatory crow runs through the poems, which are mostly on the themes of birth and creation. The symbol of the crow was originally suggested to Hughes by a meeting with the US illustrator Leonard Baskin, with whom he had worked on several previous publications.

**Crown Court.** A court of criminal jurisdiction for England and Wales, set up in 1971, when it superseded the assize courts and quarter sessions. It deals with the most serious offences, such as murder, manslaughter, rape and robbery, amounting to some 3 per cent of all criminal cases, and is presided over by a judge sitting with a jury of 12 members of the public. Lesser offences, such as burglary and some assaults, are tried by magistrates.

**Croydon facelift.** A slang expression of the early 21st century for hair that is scraped back so tightly into a ponytail that it pulls back the skin on the wearer's cheekbones – a style supposedly favoured by the proles of Croydon, on the southern edge of Greater London.

> According to legend, one chavette scraped hair back so tightly and for so long, that when she finally let it down, her over-stretched forehead sort of drooped over her eyes, and looked like a bulldog. She then used it as an excuse to skive off school for two weeks.
>
> www.chavtowns.co.uk

*See also* CHAV.

**Crucible, The.** A historical drama (1953) by the US playwright Arthur Miller (1915–2005) about the witchcraft hysteria that swept through Salem, Massachusetts, in 1692. As well as suggesting the cauldrons and other utensils indispensable to traditional magic-making, the title also suggests that the incident should be attributed largely to the social conditions that prevailed at the time (fear of war with France, a bad winter, a smallpox epidemic, raids by pirates and the like) and the unconscious desire to find scapegoats to blame for such ills. Treated by Miller as a parallel for the McCarthyite (*see* MCCARTHYISM) investigations of the 1950s, the original witchcraft trials created a furore at the time and several of the jurors involved went so far as to publish a public 'Confession of Error':

> We confess that we ourselves were not capable to understand, nor able to withstand, the mysterious delusions of the Powers of Darkness and Prince of the Air; but were, for want of knowledge in ourselves and better information from others, prevailed with to take up such evidence against the accused, as on further consideration and better information we justly fear was insufficient for the touching the lives of any.
>
> A film adaptation, with the screenplay by Arthur Miller, appeared in 1996, directed by Nicholas Hyter.

**Crucible Theatre.** This noted Sheffield theatre opened in 1971 as a new building to replace the old Sheffield Playhouse, which had been set up in a converted British Legion hall. It takes its name from the crucible process of steel production, which was invented in Sheffield by Benjamin Huntsman in 1740, and has staged many memorable productions. The semicircular shape of the building, with its steeply rising banks of seats, further suggest an actual crucible as well as a metaphorical theatrical 'melting pot'. The theatre is also the venue for the world professional snooker championship.

**Cruella De Vil.** *See* Cruella DE VIL.

**Cruellest month.** T.S. Eliot's memorable phrase 'April is the cruellest month' in *The* WASTE LAND (1922) has been freely adopted and adapted by journalists for application to other months. One of the more frequent substitutions is 'August' for 'April', either because that month, although traditionally in the 'silly season', often chances to be newsworthy, or else by confusion with the title of Edna O'Brien's novel *August is a Wicked Month* (1965). There may also be a false association of sound between the second syllable of 'August' and that of 'cruellest'.

> June is the cruellest month in politics.
>
> *The Times* (5 June 1993)

**Cruel Sea, The.** A novel (1951) by Nicholas Monsarrat, about the officers and men, and their wives, of HMS *Compass Rose*, a corvette on convoy duties in the Second World War, and, after its sinking, HMS *Saltash*. 'The men are the stars of this story. The only heroines are the ships: and the only villain the cruel sea itself.' Monsarrat himself commanded a frigate during the war, and was mentioned in dispatches. A memorable and successful film version (1953) was directed by Charles Frend.

**Cruelty, Theatre of.** *See* THEATRE OF CRUELTY.

**Cruelty-free.** A BUZZWORD of the 1980s for consumer goods produced without involving any cruelty to animals in their manufacture or development.

**Cruising for a bruising.** Asking for trouble. A US phrase current from the 1940s.

**Crusaders.** A term of abuse applied by militant Muslims to the West in general, and to the United States and its allies in particular, especially in regard to their military interventions in the mainly Muslim countries of Afghanistan (since 2001) and Iraq (since 2003). The presence of US forces in Saudi Arabia, the land of the Prophet, since the 1991 First Gulf War has also caused considerable resentment. The reference is to the Christian Crusaders of the Middle Ages, who sought to retake what they called the Holy Land from Muslin rule, and in the process caused much bloodshed.

**Crush bar.** A bar in a theatre or opera house where members of the audience can buy a drink in the interval, so named because people are pressed close together in its confined area.

**Crusties.** A nickname of the 1990s for the homeless and vagrant young people who live by begging in towns and cities. They typically wear rough, dirty clothes, have matted or dreadlocked hair and are often visibly unwashed. Several have a dog on a string lead, and a number play rudimentary musical instruments in the hope of eliciting a few pennies from pedestrians. The name alludes to the patina of grime that characterizes their appearance.

**Crying game.** An exaggerated show of grief or mourning in order to win sympathy. The expression was popularized by Neil Jordan's acclaimed film *The Crying Game* (1992), a moving study of the ambiguity of human relationships against the background of Northern Ireland's TROUBLES. The public expression of grief following the death of Diana, Princess of Wales, in 1997 was felt by some to be contrived or media-enhanced and so little more than a 'crying game'.

**Cryonics.** The practice of deep-freezing the bodies of people who have died with the aim of bringing them back to life in the future if and when medical knowledge makes this possible. It is practised in particular in cases where someone has died of an incurable disease, and arose in the 1960s. The term itself is a contraction of 'cryogenics', the first element meaning 'cold' and deriving from Greek *kruos*, 'frost'.

**Crystal-gazing.** Attempting to forecast the future, as a fortune teller or clairvoyant does when gazing into her crystal ball.

> M&S is still buying nine months into the future. They are still crystal ball-gazing there at Baker Street.
> *The Times* (3 November 1999)

**Cry, the Beloved Country.** A novel (1948) by the South African writer Alan Paton (1903–88), in which he suggested a Christian resolution of the problem of racial APARTHEID in South Africa. It was influential also in promoting an awareness abroad of the country's political policies. The beloved country is Africa. A recurring motif is the 'forlorn crying' of the titihoya, a bird of the veldt. A film version (1951; US title *African Fury*) was directed by Zoltan Korda.

**C2.** A skilled manual worker. The term is a socio-economic category taken from a five-point scale that runs from A as top management, through B as middle management and C1 as supervisory and clerical workers, to D as unskilled and semi-skilled workers. C2s were the subject of special debate by political commentators in the 1980s and early 1990s, when their defection from a traditional Labour allegiance to THATCHERISM was held to be a major factor in successive Labour defeats.

> The C2s, regarded by pollsters and political parties as 'crucial' to electoral success, are important because they are the point where Mr Pooter gives way to Alf Garnett.
> DOMINIC HOBSON: *The Wealth of the Nation* (1999)

**Cuban Missile Crisis.** *See* HAWKS AND DOVES.

**Cubism.** The style of an early 20th-century school of painters who depicted surfaces, figures, tints, light and shade, and so on, by means of a multiplicity of shapes of a cubical and geometrical character. The name was introduced in 1908 by the French art critic Louis Vauxcelles, who took up a remark attributed to Matisse about Braque's 'little cubes'. The genre was essentially abstract and divorced from realism. It rejected any attempt to depict actual appearances and turned its back on traditional canons of art. It paved the way for much of modern art subsequently. Its chief exponents were Georges Braque (1882–1963), André Derain (1880–1954), Fernand Léger (1881–1955) and, notably, Pablo Picasso (1881–1973). *See also* DADAISM; FAUVISM; FUTURISM;

MODERNISM; ORPHISM; RURALISM; SURREALISM; SYN-
CHROMISM; TACHISM; VORTICISM.

**Cuckoo in the nest.** An unwelcome intruder. The allusion is
to the cuckoo's habit of laying its eggs in the nests of other
birds, who then incubate them as their own. After hatching,
the young cuckoos eject their adoptive parents' own eggs
and chicks and so effectively 'rule the roost'.

> The growth of offshore finance has been so dramatic that
> some micro-states risk it emerging as a cuckoo in the nest,
> not only crowding out existing industries, but also
> dominating the state apparatus.
>
> *The World Today* (August/September 1999)

**Cullinan Diamond.** The largest known diamond, named
after Sir Thomas Major Cullinan (1862–1936), chairman of
the Premier Diamond Mine, Johannesburg, where it was
found in 1905. Its uncut weight was 3025¾ carats (about
624g or 1lb 6oz). It was presented to King Edward VII by the
South African government and was cut into a number of
stones (the largest weighing some 516 carats), which now
form part of the Crown Jewels.

**Cult of personality.** The almost-religious adulation of the
supreme leader (i.e. dictator) in totalitarian states. The term
seems to have been first used by Soviet leader Nikita
Khrushchev, in his denunciation of his predecessor, Josef
Stalin, in a speech to the 20th Party Congress, 25 February
1956. The cult of Stalin was as nothing, however, compared
to the later cults of Mao in China and Kim Il-sung ('The
Great Leader') and his son Kim Jung-il ('The Dear Leader')
in North Korea, to whom godlike achievements and
qualities were/are ascribed.

**Cultural cringe.** A sense of inferiority experienced when
comparing one's own culture with that of a supposedly
more culturally 'advanced' nation or group of nations. The
expression was coined in a 1950 essay entitled 'The Cultural
Cringe' by the Australian literary critic A.A. Phillips
(1900–85) with reference to Australians and their alleged
perception of the low status of their culture when compared
especially with that of Britain and the rest of western
Europe:

> Above our writers – and other artists – looms the
> intimidating mass of Anglo-Saxon culture. Such a situation
> almost inevitably produces the characteristic Australian
> Cultural Cringe – appearing either as the Cringe Direct, or as
> the Cringe Inverted, in the attitude of the Blatant
> Blatherskite, the God's-Own-Country and I'm-a-better-
> man-than-you-are Australian bore.

The phrase has subsequently been used also of, among

others, Canada in relation to the United States, and New
Zealand in relation to Australia.

In 1992 the Australian prime minister Paul Keating (the
LIZARD OF OZ) addressed conservative anglophiles in the
Australian House of Representatives:

> Even as it [the UK] walked out on you and joined the
> Common Market, you were still looking for your MBEs and
> your knighthoods, and all the rest of the regalia that comes
> with it. You would take Australia right back down the time
> tunnel to the cultural cringe where you have always come
> from.

**Cultural Revolution.** The political upheaval in China of
1966–9, largely promoted by the youthful RED GUARD,
apparently aimed to effect a return to revolutionary Maoist
doctrines. It involved attacks on intellectuals, a wide-
ranging purge in party posts and a burgeoning personality
cult of Mao himself. It resulted in economic disruption and
dislocation, and was eventually stemmed by the Chinese
prime minister Chou En-lai.

**Culture shock.** A feeling of disorientation on being suddenly
subjected to an unfamiliar culture, such as a Westerner in the
Far East or a country-dweller in a city. The theme has been
variously treated in fiction, and was amusingly presented in
the film 'Crocodile' Dundee (1986), about the experiences of an
outbacker in New York. *See also* FUTURE SHOCK.

> Bill Bryson found himself suffering the indignity of culture
> shock when he took his English wife and kids to live in his
> homeland, America, after an absence of nearly 20 years.
>
> *The Times* (11 September 1999)

**Culture vulture.** A person obsessively interested in the arts.
The expression dates from the 1940s.

> There is a vulture
> Who circles above
> The carcass of culture.
>
> OGDEN NASH: *Free Wheeling* (1931)

**Culture war.** A term applied to the ideological conflict in the
United States between liberals and the right (especially of
the evangelical Christian variety) over such matters as
school prayers, the banning of books such as the Harry
POTTER series from school libraries (in this case, on the
grounds that they promote witchcraft), gay rights, abortion,
the teaching of creationism in science lessons (*see* INTELLI-
GENT DESIGN), multiculturalism and other forms of
POLITICAL CORRECTNESS. Even President George W. Bush
was condemned by the Christian right (his normal
supporters) at Christmas 2005, over the message in the
White House card, which simply read 'Best wishes for a

holiday season of hope and happiness'. Many of these controversies have at their core the principles of free speech and the separation of church and state enshrined in the US Constitution.

The term 'culture war' itself derives from the *Kulturkampf* ('cultural struggle') in Germany in the 1870s, when Chancellor Otto von Bismarck in alliance with the liberals sought to diminish the power and influence of the Roman Catholic Church in such areas as education, while the Vatican for its part condemned such institutions as civil marriage and declared the principle of papal infallibility. *See also* CLASH OF CIVILIZATIONS.

**Curate's delight.** *See* CURATE'S FRIEND.

**Curate's friend** or **delight.** A cakestand with two or more tiers, as at one time placed next to a curate when visiting a family and offered afternoon tea. The expression dates from the EDWARDIAN ERA. The otherwise puzzling stage direction below abbreviates the term.

> [*They sit down, ill at ease, whilst he places the tray on the table. He then goes out for the curate*].
>
> GEORGE BERNARD SHAW: *Fanny's First Play*, III (1911)

**Curl the mo.** In colloquial Australian English, to succeed spectacularly or triumphantly. 'Mo' is short for 'moustache', and the underlying image is of a man twirling the ends of his mustachios in satisfaction. The verbal phrase, which apparently dates from the 1920s, is often used adjectivally, to denote something excellent or first-rate (e.g. 'curl-the-mo mazuma', a large amount of money).

**Curl up.** To shrink with shame, horror, embarrassment or the like. The reference is either to the pose adopted by a young child when shocked or scolded, or to the similar instinctive reaction of an animal or insect such as a hedgehog or woodlouse. An extended form of the phrase, 'to curl up and die', again alludes to animals (a blackly humorous respelling, 'Curl Up and Dye', is the punning name of many a hairdressing establishment). The expression dates from the early 20th century.

**Curragh Mutiny.** In March 1914 a number of officers at the Curragh camp near Dublin offered their resignations rather than face the possibility of being ordered to act against Ulstermen to impose the Irish HOME RULE Bill. They succeeded in obtaining a written assurance from their commander-in-chief that they would not be expected to do this. The following month a successful gun-running operation provided arms for the ULSTER VOLUNTEER FORCE.

**Curse, The.** A euphemism for menstruation, dating from the 1920s. The reference is apparently to the curse that God put on Eve when she ate the forbidden fruit in the Garden of Eden (Genesis 3).

**Curtains.** The end; death. An allusion to the closing of the stage curtains at the end of a theatrical performance.

> That two minutes of compelling television [a viewer's grilling of Margaret Thatcher] in 1983 may well have meant curtains for *Nationwide* and the spirit of Lime Grove.
>
> *The Times* (15 October 1999)

**Custard pie.** A pie – or more correctly an open flan or tart – containing custard. Over the course of the 20th century it virtually vanished as an item of food, having transformed itself into a staple of slapstick comedy. The 'custard pies' with which (more or less) unsuspecting victims are slapped in the face, and other portions of their anatomy, are now routinely made with a substance (e.g. shaving foam) that presents fewer cleaning problems than custard and pastry.

**Customer is always right.** A general rule of retail tacitly adopted by most shops and stores from the turn of the 20th century, and explicitly stated by Gordon Selfridge, founder in 1909 of the London department store that bears his name (*see also* SHOPPING DAYS TO CHRISTMAS). A year or two earlier the Swiss hotelier César Ritz (*see* RITZY) was quoted as saying, '*Le client n'a jamais tort*' ('The customer is never wrong'), which amounts to exactly the same thing.

**Cut and dried.** Completely settled; finally arranged. The term arose in the early 20th century from an earlier literal sense applied to herbs sold in herbalists' shops, as distinct from fresh, growing herbs.

**Cut and paste.** Patched-up; rough and ready. An allusion to the simple artwork done by children in which pictures or shapes are cut out and glued (pasted) to paper. In computer jargon to cut and paste is to delete (and save) a section of text from a page or document and insert it elsewhere.

**Cut a rug.** To dance, especially when jitterbugging. The image is of one's vigorous steps gashing or tearing the floor covering. The expression comes from 1930s jive talk.

**Cuthbert.** A name coined by 'Poy' (Percy Hutton Fearon; 1874–1945), cartoonist of the London *Evening News* from 1913 to 1935, for the fit men who avoided military service in the First World War by securing a post in a government office or in the Civil Service. He depicted them as frightened-looking rabbits. The particular name perhaps intentionally echoes the children's taunt of 'cowardy custard', while its lisping sound suggests a womanish wimpishness. *See also* PERCY.

**Cut it.** To perform to an adequate standard; to do what is required. The expression is probably a reduced version of 'to CUT THE MUSTARD'.

> Could you cut it as a spy?
> www.dailymail.co.uk (29 October 2005)

**Cut it out!** Stop it! That's enough! To cut an action is to stop it. To cut it out is to stop it for good.

**Cut someone some slack.** To ease the pressure on someone, to allow them to relax somewhat. The expression originated in African American slang of the 1960s.

> Young women are considered to be more responsible than young men, so why should we cut them far more slack than we would, for example, a male drunk driver?
> *Sunday Times* (27 November 2005)

**Cut the mustard.** To do something well and efficiently, especially when it is suspected that one may lack the ability. The expression derives from 'mustard' as a slang word for a thing that is the best and the 'cutting' refers to the harvesting of the plant, garnering the best. *See also* HOT STUFF.

**Cutting edge.** The forefront of new developments. The analogy is with the sharp edge of a knife or tool. The term arose in the field of scientific and technological research in the 1950s.

> Something has changed. Sex … is no longer at the cutting edge of politics, especially for women.
> *The Guardian* (14 March 1989)

**Cut to the chase.** To come to the point. The allusion is to a silent film in which the preliminary action is edited (cut) so that one immediately gets to the exciting chase scene.

> Do you want to cut to the chase, Dennis? Tell us where the money's really from.
> *The Bill* (18 August 2005)

**C-word.** *See* FOUR-LETTER WORD.

**Cybercafé.** A café where customers can sit at computer terminals and log on to the INTERNET while enjoying a drink or a snack.

**Cybernetics.** This name for the science of communications and automatic control systems, in both machines and animate beings, was the invention of the US mathematician Norbert Wiener, who introduced it in his book, *Cybernetics: Control and Communication in the Animal and the Machine* (1948). Its derivation is from the Greek word for 'helmsman'. It was cybernetics that brought terms such as 'feedback' and 'input' into common usage, and it has itself spawned such offspring as CYBERCAFÉ, CYBERPUNK, CYBERSEX and CYBERSPACE.

**Cyberpunk.** A literary movement of the 1980s as a form of SCIENCE FICTION in which typically the human mind or body is invaded and controlled by computer-generated forces. The scenario is usually that of a lawless subculture, and the characters are often hackers or computer freaks. The term itself, combining CYBERNETICS and PUNK, was first used in the early 1980s by Gardner Dazois, editor of *Isaac Asimov's Science Fiction Magazine*.

**Cybersex.** Sexual arousal obtained by exchanging messages with another person on the INTERNET or by using VIRTUAL REALITY techniques, both erotic diversions of the 1990s. *See also* CYBERNETICS.

> Most [chat] rooms seem to be about sex. Far from being full of nerdy sociopaths, they are overrun by married men … looking for cybersex.
> *The Times* (29 June 1999)

**Cyberspace.** The notional environment in which communication over computer networks occurs. It is conventionally perceived as being 'space' inside the computer system but in fact has no real existence. The concept evolved in the 1980s. *See also* CYBERNETICS.

**Cybersquatter.** In computer jargon a person who registers the DOMAIN name of an existing company or individual with the aim of forcing the rightful owner to pay an exorbitant price for it. The practice is banned in US law as are variant ruses. When the oil companies Exxon and Mobil announced in 1998 that they were in merger talks, for example, five speculators registered addresses that joined their names in combinations such as 'exxonmobil.com', 'mobilexxon.com', 'exxon-mobil.net' and 'exxon-mobil. org'. There are also cybersquatters who deliberately try to mislead INTERNET users by registering names that are very close to existing names and that may be accidentally accessed by a slip of the finger on the keyboard. Thus 'wwwcitibank.com', as distinct from 'www.citibank.com', led to a lurid eyeful before Citibank closed it. Similarly 'microsift.com', rather than 'microsoft.com', used the adjacency of 'i' to 'o' on the keyboard to take the hasty to a site called 'geek-guy.com' run by a 24-year-old GEEK in SILICON VALLEY.

**Cymru am byth.** (Welsh, 'Wales for ever'.) The motto of the Welsh Guards, formed in 1915. The words are also generally in use as a rallying call for the principality as a whole.

**Czar.** *See* DRUG CZAR.

# D

**DA.** *See* DUCK'S ARSE.

**Dachau.** The first Nazi concentration camp, built near the town of Dachau in Bavaria in 1933, with the slogan ARBEIT MACHT FREI ('work brings freedom') over the gateway. Dachau became the model for later camps, and controlled a network of sub-camps throughout southern Germany and Austria. Although it was not an extermination camp, some 32,000 prisoners died from starvation, disease, maltreatment and the effects of horrendous medical experiments. Many of the inmates were transported on to death camps such as AUSCHWITZ. *See also* BELSEN; FINAL SOLUTION; HOLOCAUST.

**Dack up.** In New Zealand slang, to light up or smoke a marijuana joint. First recorded in 1991, the expression comes from 'dacca', an Australian slang term for marijuana, which itself came via Afrikaans *dagga* from *dachab*, a word in the Khoikhoi language of Namibia.

**Dadaism.** An anarchic and iconoclastic art movement, which began at Zurich in 1916, and arose from indignation and despair at the catastrophe of the First World War. Its supporters, writers and painters, sought to free themselves from all artistic conventions and what they considered cultural shams. Dadaism was influenced by CUBISM and FUTURISM, and after about 1922 it was succeeded by SURREALISM. The origin of the name is surrounded in confusion, but one of the more plausible accounts tells how the German poets Hugo Ball (1886–1927) and Richard Huelsenbeck (1892–1974) were leafing through a German–French dictionary when they came across the French word *dada*, meaning 'hobbyhorse'. Partly because of its nonsensical sound and partly through its associations with the freedom of childhood, they decided to adopt it. Jean Arp (1888–1966), Max Ernst (1891–1976) and Marcel Janco (1895–1984) were among their number. There was a similar wave in New York at the same time associated with Marcel Duchamp (1887–1968), Francis Picabia (1879–1953) and Man Ray (1890–1977). A plaque showing a human navel was unveiled in Zurich in 1966 to commemorate the 50th anniversary of the movement. *See also* FAUVISM; MERZ; ORPHISM; RURALISM; SYNCHROMISM; TACHISM; VORTICISM.

**Daddy, The.** The dominant male in a group, institution, etc.; the 'boss'. The expression dates back at least to the 1940s, but was popularized by Alan Clarke's film *Scum* (1979), in which the character Carlin, played by Ray Winstone, establishes his sway over his fellow inmates in a BORSTAL. His challenging mantra 'Who's the daddy?' was widely imitated.

> Americans live in Saddam's palaces and the Brits in his knocking shop. So who's the daddy and who's the Yankie bitch?
>
> A.A. GILL: *Sunday Times Magazine* (6 November 2005)

**Dad's Army.** A nickname for the HOME GUARD, many of whose members were middle-aged fathers. The name was popularized by the enjoyably nostalgic television comedy series so titled, screened on BBC from 1968 to 1977 and centring on the Second World War adventures of a disparate group of men who formed part of Britain's 'last line of defence' in the fictional south-coast town of Walmington-on-Sea. Memorable characters included Arthur Lowe as the pompous Captain Mainwaring, John Le Mesurier as the vague but cultured Sergeant Wilson, Clive Dunn as the madcap Lance-Corporal Jones, John Laurie as the pessimistic Private Frazer and Arnold Ridley as the frail Private Godfrey. The theme song of the series, 'Who do you think you are kidding, Mister Hitler?', was written by Jimmy Perry. 'Dad's army' is now used for any body of middle-aged or elderly volunteers. *See also* CONK OUT.

**Dagenham Yanks.** The nickname given to workers in the

Ford Motor Company's works in Cork, Ireland, who in the 1930s were transferred to the company's main factory in Dagenham, Essex.

**Daggers.** A nickname supposedly awarded to Margaret Thatcher, the IRON LADY, by members of her cabinet, not because she 'looked daggers' at them, but as an abbreviation for Dagenham, 'two stops on from Barking' (as in BARKING MAD).

**Dagwood.** A large thick sandwich of mixed ingredients, of the type made by Dagwood Bumstead, the lazy husband of BLONDIE in the cartoon strip by Chic Young.

**Dáil.** The lower house of the parliament of the Republic of Ireland, in full *Dáil Éireann* (Irish, 'Assembly of Ireland'). It was first established in 1919, when SINN FÉIN proclaimed an independent Irish republic.

**Daily double.** A mainly US term for a bet on the winners of two stated horseraces, usually the first and second, on a particular day of a meeting.

**Daily dozen.** A short session of daily physical exercises, traditionally performed in sets of 12. The phrase originally referred to a set of 12 callisthenic exercises devised by the famous Yale University American football coach Walter C. Camp (1859–1925) and came into general use in the early 20th century.

**Daisy chain.** Originally referring to a garland made by threading daisies together through slits in their stalks, the term has subsequently come to apply to various kinds of linked arrangements. One such is a group of dealers who agree to buy and sell a particular commodity, typically crude oil, among themselves as a way of inflating the price at which it is finally sold to an outside buyer. Another is a group of people who act as partners to each another simultaneously in sexual activity. A series of computer peripherals linked serially is also described as a daisy chain.

**Daisy-cutter.** In cricket, a ball that is rolled along the ground towards the wicket or that, on pitching, bounces very low.

'Daisy-cutter' is also the nickname for the largest conventional bomb in current use, the BLU-82B, a 7000 kg (15,000 lb) weapon that will reportedly kill anything within a radius of 90m / 300ft (270m / 900ft in some reports) – hence its nickname. It was first deployed by the US Air Force in VIETNAM, where it was nicknamed Commando Vaulter and used to make clearings in the jungle. In Afghanistan in 2001–2 it was used as an anti-personnel weapon and as a means of intimidating the enemy.

*See also* GRAND SLAM.

**Daleks.** The tin robots, resembling pepperpots on wheels, in the children's television series DOCTOR WHO, made their first appearance in 1963. They were the invention of the scriptwriter Terry Nation, who denied a claim that their name came arbitrarily from an encyclopedia volume titled DAL–LEK. They are famous for their threatening vocalization 'Exterminate! Exterminate!' and their ability to floor a foe with a ray beamed from their antennae. It used to be claimed that their plans to conquer and subjugate the universe were foiled only by their inability to climb stairs; but in the 2005 revival of the series, their ability to 'elevate' was revealed.

**Daley, Arthur.** *See* HER INDOORS; MINDER; NICE LITTLE EARNER.

**Dallas.** A US television melodrama screened from 1978 to 1991 that rapidly gained worldwide cult status. It centred on the everyday life of the Ewings, a Texan oil-rich family, consisting of patriarch Jock, matriarch Miss Ellie, and sons JR, Gary and Bobby. The show soon focused on JR, a scheming businessman and seducer of women, married to the alcoholic Sue Ellen, and the high point of the series was his attempted murder in 1980. The would-be assassin was subsequently revealed to be Sue Ellen's sister, Kristin, pregnant with JR's child.

**Dalloway, Mrs.** *See* MRS DALLOWAY.

**Dalton Plan.** A US system of secondary education based on individual learning. It divided each subject into monthly assignments, with pupils free to plan their own work schedules. The scheme was developed by Helen Parkhurst in 1919 and first used at a school for the handicapped. It was then introduced in 1920 at a high school in Dalton, Massachusetts.

**Damaged goods.** A derogatory term for a person who is inadequate or impaired in some way and specifically for an unmarried woman who is no longer a virgin. The phrase is literally applied to goods that have been damaged and are reduced in value. The expression dates from the early 20th century.

**Damart.** The thermal underwear of this name was the creation in the 1950s of three French brothers named Despature, who had a weaving business in the town of Roubaix. They experimented with a new type of chlorofibre that had good insulation and water-repellent properties and that also generated triboelectricity, a form of static electricity generated when fibres rub during wear. This latter attribute was believed by some to have therapeutic value in the treatment of rheumatism, arthritis and muscular complaints generally. They called their new material 'Thermolactyl', from 'thermo-', the Greek root meaning 'warm', and 'lactyl', a chemical radical derived from lactic acid used in the manufacturing process. The name of the product itself is said to come from the Rue Dammartine, where the three sat in a café discussing their breakthrough, while the red 'lightning flash' through the 'D' of the name represents a charge of triboelectricity.

**Dam Busters.** This special squadron of the RAF derived its name from the bombing raid it undertook in May 1943 to destroy the Sorpe, Eder and Moehne dams and so flood the Ruhr valley and disrupt German industry. The specially fitted Lancaster bombers achieved their aim, quite literally, with a unique 'bouncing bomb' designed by Sir Barnes Wallis (1887–1979). The mission was not an unqualified success, however, as the dams were soon repaired and 42 per cent of the bombers were lost. On the ground at least 1500 people died, many of them foreign 'slave' labourers. A film of the same name reconstructing the exploit was released in 1954.

**Damsel in distress.** A mainly humorous term for a young woman in difficulties, especially when of a trivial or mildly embarrassing nature. The image is of the imprisoned maiden or captive princess of medieval stories and fairy tales who was rescued by a KNIGHT IN SHINING ARMOUR. *See also* WHITE KNIGHT.

**Dance of the Seven Veils.** The popular title of Salome's sensuous dance before Herod in Richard Strauss's opera *Salome* (1905), in which she removes her seven veils one by one, in a sort of oriental striptease. There is no evidence of such a dance in the Bible, which does not refer to Salome by name, although Matthew 14:6 states that 'the daughter of Herodias danced before them'. The particular dance of this kind is, however, specified in Oscar Wilde's play *Salomé* (1893), on which the opera is based. In her role as Salome at a Covent Garden performance in 1988 the US mezzo-soprano Maria Ewing performed the sequence to its logical conclusion.

**Dances with Wolves.** A film (1990) about a US army officer who wins the trust of the Sioux Indians he has been sent to fight. It was directed by and starred Kevin Costner (b.1955). As well as winning acceptance by the Sioux, Lieutenant Dunbar (played by Costner) also wins the friendship of a wolf, hence the name given to him by the Sioux and the title of the film. While the film was still in production many people in the film business doubted that it would enjoy the success it eventually did, and it was commonly referred to as *Kevin's Gate*, drawing parallels with the disastrous HEAVEN'S GATE (1980).

**Dance to the Music of Time, A.** A *roman fleuve* (1951–75) by Anthony Powell (1905–2000). The title of the 12-novel sequence is that of the painting so known by Nicolas Poussin (1594–1665). The starting point of the first novel, *A Question of Upbringing*, is the narrator, Nicholas Jenkins, seeing in the attitude of some workmen gathered around a bucket of coke a suggestion of 'Poussin's scene in which the Seasons, hand in hand, facing outward, tread in rhythm to the notes of the lyre that the winged and naked greybeard plays'. The books have a chronological framework corresponding to Powell's own experience and times, and verge between the tragic and the comic. Poussin's painting was given its title by the Italian art theorist and collector Giovanni Pietro Bellori, originally: *Le quattro stagioni che ballano al suono del tempo* ('The four seasons that dance to the music of time'). Powell has described how the painting inspired him:

> I found myself in the Wallace Collection, standing in front of Nicolas Poussin's picture there given the title *A Dance to the Music of Time*. An almost hypnotic spell seems cast by this masterpiece on the beholder. I knew at once that Poussin had expressed at least one important aspect of what the novel must be.
>
> ANTHONY POWELL: *To Keep the Ball Rolling* (1976–82)

*See also* FIRST LINES OF NOVELS.

**Dan Dare.** The space pilot in the boys' comic EAGLE from 1950 to 1967. He serves as a colonel in the Interplanetary Space Fleet and has adventures on Venus and beyond. His great enemy is the dread MEKON. The cartoon strips featuring him were the work of Frank Hampson. Attempts to revive Dan Dare in comics of the 1970s and 1980s proved disappointing. In 2002 Dan Dare became the star of a computer-animated TV series.

**Dandy.** A British comic first published in December 1937. Its most famous character is DESPERATE DAN. *See also* KEYHOLE KATE.

**Dangerous dog.** A dog legally defined as dangerous to the public by the Dangerous Dogs Act 1991, which set out restrictions on the importation, breeding and keeping of a number of named breeds, notably pit-bull terriers, following a series of attacks on children by such dogs.

**Daniel Day, The.** A nickname for LUAS, Dublin's new tram system, opened in 2004. *Luas* is the Irish word for speed, the capitalization being just a piece of marketing-executive nonsense. Other nicknames include 'the Jerry Lee', 'the C.S.' and 'the Train in the Lane'. The references are to the Anglo-Irish actor Daniel Day Lewis (b.1957), the Narnia writer and

Christian apologist C.S. Lewis (1898–1963), and the American rock-and-roll musician Jerry Lee Lewis (b.1935).

**Danish Dentist on the Job.** (1976). The archetypical Scandinavian skin flick of the 1970s, although believed by some to be an apocryphal title. At this period Denmark and Sweden had a frolicsomely relaxed attitude to the erotic arts, prompting an investigative trip to Copenhagen in the 1970s by Lord Longford (*see* LORD PORN), anxious to establish the extent to which Scandinavian filth threatened British morals.

**Danny the Red.** A nickname of Daniel Cohn-Bendit (b.1945), one of the leaders of the student revolt in Paris in May 1968. He was subsequently deported to his native West Germany.

**Dansette.** A make of record player found in many households in the 1950s at a time when popular music had become a major industry. With the advent of ROCK 'N' ROLL, commercial opportunities were beginning to emerge for the growing teenage culture, and the player, with its colourful modern styling, appealed to many youthful music fans, its name suggesting its purpose.

**Dark energy.** A mysterious antigravitational energy invoked to account for the fact that the expansion of the universe is accelerating, rather than slowing down. It was in the late 1990s that observations of far distant supernovae indicated that something mysterious was happening at the edges of the universe, leading the US cosmologist Michael Turner to coin the term 'dark energy'. *See also* DARK MATTER.

**Dark matter.** Hypothetical, unobserved material in the universe posited by astrophysicists to account for certain gravitational effects. It is thought that the amount of dark matter in the universe could dictate the future of the universe. If there is insufficient mass, the universe will go on expanding indefinitely, until, according to the law of entropy, it will suffer a 'heat death' (all particles of matter would be evenly distributed and the temperature approaching absolute zero). If there is enough dark matter, once the momentum of the BIG BANG gives out the universe would contract in a 'big crunch', leading in turn to another big bang. However, the possible existence of DARK ENERGY may cast doubt on the possibility of this latter scenario.

The idea of dark matter is played with in Philip Pullman's HIS DARK MATERIALS.

**Darkness at Noon.** A novel (1940) by Arthur Koestler (1905–83), originally written in German. It draws on his experience as a member of the Communist Party from 1931 to 1938, during which time he was commissioned by the Communist International to write a book on the first FIVE-YEAR PLAN in Russia. The novel follows an earlier one, *The Gladiators* (1939), in which Spartacus is doomed because he did not apply the 'law of detours', whereby leaders should be 'pitiless for the sake of pity' and execute dissidents. In *Darkness at Noon* an elderly BOLSHEVIK follows the 'law' and sends people to their execution without compunction, until he himself is deemed expendable and is forced to sign a confession that consigns him to his death. The title echoes words from Milton's *Samson Agonistes* (1671) relating to the blindness of Samson:

> O dark, dark, dark, amid the blaze of noon,
> Irrecoverably dark, total eclipse
> Without all hope of day!

Another possible source is Cowper's 'The Progress of Error' (1782):

> Judgement drunk, and brib'd to lose his way
> Winks hard, and talks of darkness at noon-day.

An anonymous booklet was published in Boston in 1806 and entitled *Darkness at Noon, or the Great Solar Eclipse of the 16th June 1806*, and possibly Koestler was aware of this.

**Dark Side of the Moon, The.** A commercially successful album by the rock group Pink Floyd, released in 1973. Its cover, featuring a prism that creates a spectrum of colours, is one of the best known of all pop album sleeves. The bleak and portentous title introduces a suite of songs that dwell on the themes of materialism, madness, ageing and death, and include 'Time', 'Brain Damage', 'Money' and 'Us and Them'. *See also* ROCK GROUP NAMES.

**Darling Buds of May, The.** A comic novel (1958) by H.E. Bates (1905–74), the first of several about the carefree LARKIN FAMILY in rural England. Other titles featuring the Larkin family are the faintly punning *A Breath of French Air* (1959) and *Hark, Hark, the Lark* (1960), *Oh! To be in England* (1963) and *A Little of What You Fancy* (1970). In 1991–3 the books became the basis of a successful television series ('Perfick!' (perfect), constantly in the mouth of 'Pop' Larkin (played by David Jason), became a popular catchphrase for a time). The title comes from Shakespeare:

> Rough winds do shake the darling buds of May,
> And summer's lease hath all too short a date.
> Sonnet 18 (1609)

*See also* SUMMER'S LEASE.

**Darling Daisy.** Frances Evelyn Greville, Countess of Warwick (1861–1938), adulterous wife of the 5th Earl of Warwick and for nine years mistress of Edward VII, whom he often addressed in his letters to her as 'My Darling Daisy wife'. In

1914 she sought to make money by threatening to publish her memoirs, which would include the late king's letters. This was prevented by three prominent courtiers acting on behalf of George V. Her entry in earlier editions of the *Dictionary of National Biography* makes no mention of her infidelity, preferring instead to praise her beauty, her interest in socialism and her love of animals.

**Darren.** A forename that came to be regarded as rather NAFF in the 1980s. It is of 20th-century origin and was popularized by the husband in the US television comedy series BEWITCHED (1964–71). He was actually 'Darrin', but British viewers took to the name, assuming it was typically American, and respelled it 'Darren'. As such, it seemed a suitable male counterpart to the female SHARON and Karen, then rising in favour. However, the US film actor Darren McGavin (1922–2006) was an earlier bearer of the name and possibly the first to be emulated.

**Darth Vader.** *See* STAR WARS.

**Darth Vader's pencil box.** A facetious nickname applied to the Bank of New Zealand Head Office building in Wellington, New Zealand. It dates from the early 1980s, when George Lucas's initial STAR WARS films were at the height of their success, and the building's shape and sinister black non-reflective cladding called to mind their chief villain.

**Darwin Awards.** According to its own website (www.darwinawards.com):

> The Darwin Awards salute the improvement of the human genome by honoring those who accidentally kill themselves in really stupid ways.

Candidates are submitted by the public (largely in the United States), who come across the stories in local newspapers. As an example, the 2002 winner was a Colorado man who, having been pulled over by a police patrol car for erratic driving, decided to make a run for it. He then attempted to dissuade the policemen from pursuing him by firing a pistol over his shoulder. Unfortunately his ability to run and shoot at the same time was somewhat limited, and his fourth bullet penetrated his own head, thus bringing the chase to a conclusion. He died in hospital the following day. Other winners include the leader of a Christian cult in California who tried to teach himself the art of walking on water in his bath, then slipped on a piece of soap and killed himself. In 2005 the Awards honoured, among others, the Welshman who swore while watching Wales play England at rugby that 'If Wales wins, I'll cut my balls off.' Wales won, and he was true to his word, so removing himself from the gene pool.

**Date rape.** Rape by a person whom the subject is dating or with whom she (or he) has gone on a date. Although hardly a new phenomenon, date rape first emerged as a particular issue on US college campuses in the early 1980s. There may be fine legal implications in the act, since to an extent the person dated has implicitly or explicitly agreed to 'go with' the potential rapist.

The 1990s saw the emergence of so-called 'date-rape drugs', a range of sedative or euphoria-inducing drugs, notably Rohypnol, Ketamine and GHB (gama hydroxybutyric acid), that are used to spike the drink of a potential but probably unwilling sexual partner (usually but not exclusively female) and induce them to acquiesce in sexual intercourse or be subjected to it without their knowledge.

***Da Vinci Code.*** *The* best-selling book (along with the Harry POTTER series) of the early 21st century, written by Dan Brown, a US author, and published in 2003. It is a fictional pot-pourri of biblical interpretation, anti-Catholic conspiracy theory, French medieval history and pseudo art history, all laced with enough artful credibility to blur the borders between history and fiction, and to grip the imaginations of millions of readers.

The basic conceit is that a rather too human Jesus begat children via Mary Magdalene and through the resulting blood line created the Merovingian royal dynasty in France – and the Catholic Church knows it and has been covering it up for two millennia. Along the way various people in the know have left various clues, including Leonardo Da Vinci in his fresco *The Last Supper*. The investigation by one Professor Langdon of the mysterious death of a curator in the Louvre kicks off the plotline that unravels the details.

The basic theories and allusions are as old, in essence, as the Gnostic Gospels, which first put forward the idea of the Jesus–Mary union, but in 2005 a high-profile court case saw Dan Brown having to defend his work, under English law, for breach of the copyright of an earlier (supposedly) non-fiction work (*Holy Blood, Holy Grail* (1982) by Michael Baigent, Michael Leigh and Henry Lincoln). Brown won comprehensively, although the plaintifs are appealing.

The book has spawned much in its wake – imitative books, television documentaries (several of a debunking bent), a surge in tourism at the sites Brown mentions, credulous acceptance on the one hand and vehement pro-Catholic indignation on the other, and amused bewilderment or outraged scorn on the part of some professional historians. A feature film based on the book, unveiled at Cannes in 2006, was roundly jeered at by critics for being dull – an irrelevance, since the book's fan base ensured a healthy profit margin.

*See also* OPUS DEI.

**Davis Cup.** The international tennis trophy of this name was donated in 1900 by the US doubles champion Dwight F. Davis (1879–1945), the first tie being played between the United States and Britain on 7 August that year at the Longwood Cricket Club in Boston, Massachusetts. The cup is competed for annually on a knockout basis by teams from different countries, but has not been won by Britain since a triumph over Australia in 1936.

**Dawes Plan.** An arrangement for Germany's payment of reparations after the First World War. On the initiative of the British and US governments a committee of experts, presided over by Charles G. Dawes (1865–1951), a US financier, produced a report on the question of reparations for Germany's presumed liability for the war. The report was accepted by both the former Allies and Germany on 16 August 1924, and payments began. The scheme worked so well that by 1929 it was felt reasonable to remove the stringent controls over Germany and fix total reparations instead.

**Dawn raid.** A surprise visit by police at daybreak, usually made when searching for criminals or illicit goods or weapons. In stock exchange parlance, however, a dawn raid is an operation in which a large proportion of a company's shares are suddenly bought at the start of a day's trading at a price higher than their prevailing market rate, usually as a preliminary to a takeover bid.

**Day in the Death of Joe Egg, A.** A play (1967) by Peter Nichols (b.1927) about the struggles of a man and woman to cope with life with a severely disabled daughter. Based largely upon Nichols's own experiences as the father of a similarly handicapped child, the play took its title from a children's rhyme:

> Joe Egg's a fool,
> He tied his stocking to a stool.

**'Day in the Life, A'.** A highly imaginative and moving song, ending with a famous 42-second chord, that appears on the celebrated BEATLES album SERGEANT PEPPER'S LONELY HEARTS CLUB BAND. Credited to John Lennon and Paul McCartney, it is sometimes described as their finest musical achievement. The first verse of the song was inspired by the death in a car crash of The Beatles' society friend Tara Browne and, more famously, an item in the *Daily Mail* newspaper concerning holes in the roads in the Lancashire town of Blackburn.

> There are 4000 holes in the road in Blackburn, Lancashire, or one twenty-sixth of a hole per person, according to a council survey. If Blackburn is typical, there are two million holes in Britain's roads and 300,000 in London.
>
> *Daily Mail* (17 January 1967)

Like 'LUCY IN THE SKY WITH DIAMONDS', the song was banned by the BBC for its alleged references to drugs. The song has been the subject of enormous critical attention, focusing on such matters as disenchantment with the limits of conventional perception and the alienating effects of the media.

**Daylight robbery.** A blatantly excessive charge. The analogy is with a robbery committed in broad daylight, with no attempt at concealment or subterfuge. The expression dates from the 1940s.

**Daylight saving.** *See* SUMMER TIME.

**Day of Infamy.** Sunday 7 December 1941, the day that Japan mounted its surprise attack on the US naval base at PEARL HARBOR, so bringing the United States into the Second World War. The following day President Franklin D. Roosevelt (1882–1945) addressed Congress thus:

> Yesterday, December 7, 1941 – a date which will live in infamy – the United States of America was suddenly and deliberately attacked by the naval and air forces of the Empire of Japan.

*Day of Infamy* was the title of Walter Lord's 1957 account of the attack, based on interviews with over 600 of the participants. The phrase has also been applied to 11 September 2001; *see* 9/11.

**Day of the … .** A popular formula for a novel title, especially when indicating some sinister person or force. Examples are Nathanael West's *The* DAY OF THE LOCUST (1930), John Wyndham's *The* DAY OF THE TRIFFIDS (1951), Paul Scott's *The Day of the Scorpion* (1968) and Frederick Forsyth's *The* DAY OF THE JACKAL (1971).

**Day of the Jackal, The.** The first novel (1971) by Frederick Forsyth (b.1938). This thriller established his basic formula: an international crisis and a mixture of fictional and historical characters. The narrative follows the progress of an international plot to kill the French President, General de Gaulle (1890–1970), at the hands of a professional killer known as the JACKAL. An exciting film version (1973) was directed by Fred Zinnemann. A less exciting remake, *The Jackal*, appeared in 1997.

**Day of the Locust, The.** A dark novel (1939) by the US writer Nathanael West (1903–40). The work explores the seamy underside of Hollywood (where West had himself worked as a scriptwriter), and shows how it eats away at people's better selves. At the end Homer, a harmless but unexciting accountant, knocks down a boy who attacks him, and is in turn overwhelmed by a crowd of people (like a swarm of locusts) who are waiting for the arrival of stars at a premiere.

> I will restore to you the years that the locust hath eaten, the cankerworm, and the caterpillar, and the palmerworm, my great army which I sent among you.
>
> Joel 2:25

John Schlesinger's 1975 film of West's book, with Donald Sutherland and Karen Black, is highly regarded.

**Day of the Triffids, The.** A SCIENCE FICTION novel (1951) by John Wyndham (1903–69). An agricultural experiment has produced giant, man-eating, perambulating plants, which threaten a civilization that has already been hit by blindness after a stellar explosion. Wyndham himself invented the word 'triffid' for the plants, apparently basing it on 'trifid', meaning 'divided into three parts', since he describes the plants as being supported on 'three bluntly-tapered projections extending from the lower part [of their bodies]'. An unsubtle film version (1962) was directed by Steve Sekely.

**Day one.** The beginning, as: 'I never liked him from day one.' The concept is of the first ever day.

> From Day 1, fashion has dictated that women's tender toes be squeezed into a pointed-toe shoe that ignores the realities of human anatomy.
>
> *New York Times Magazine* (2 February 1979)

**Day person.** Someone who is at their best in the day and who tires early in the evening. The opposite is a 'night person', who finds it hard to function in the morning. There is also a 'morning person' and an 'evening person'. Every person is to an extent an amalgam of these. *See also* LARKS AND OWLS.

**Dayton Agreement.** The agreement on measures aimed at ending hostilities in the former Yugoslavia, reached in Dayton, Ohio, in November 1995. The accord was signed by the presidents of the three countries involved, Bosnia, Serbia and Croatia.

**Dazed and confused.** Bemused; disturbed; disconcerted. The phrase was in vogue in the 1990s as an expression of the turbulence of the social and cultural scene and of general unease concerning the approaching MILLENNIUM with its attendant MILLENNIUM BUG. The words were widely popularized as the title of a film of 1993 about a group of 1960s US high school students who celebrate their last day by victimizing their juniors. They also became familiar as the title of a CUTTING EDGE music, fashion and arts

magazine, first published in 1992. A similar sense of uncertainty and insecurity was voiced half a century earlier by Lorenz Hart's song 'Bewitched' (1941) with its memorable line 'BEWITCHED, BOTHERED AND BEWILDERED am I'.

> Appearing somewhat dazed and confused, Keith Richards, the hell-raising Rolling Stones guitarist, accepted a lifetime achievement honour at the tenth annual *Q Magazine* awards.
>
> *The Times* (4 November 1999)

**D-Day.** In the Second World War the day appointed for the Allied invasion of Europe and the opening of the long-awaited second front. It was eventually fixed for 5 June 1944 but because of impossible weather conditions was postponed at the last moment until 6 June. D simply stands for Day. *See also The* LONGEST DAY; OVERLORD; SECOND WORLD WAR OPERATIONAL CODE NAMES.

**D-Day Dodgers.** A pejorative term, said to have been coined in 1944 by Lady Astor MP, referring to those fighting in Italy while the Allied invasion of Normandy was taking place. The members of the US 5th and British 8th Armies thoroughly resented the moniker, as they fought bitter battles for every ridge and river crossing up the Italian peninsula. They even composed a rueful song, 'We Are the D-Day Dodgers', sung to the tune of 'LILI MARLENE'. The song ends with the verse:

> Look around the hillsides, through the mist and rain,
> See the scattered crosses, some that bear no name.
> Heartbreak and toil and suffering gone,
> The lads beneath, they slumber on.
> They are the D-Day Dodgers, who'll stay in Italy.

*See also* FORGOTTEN ARMY.

**Dead cat bounce.** In stock exchange jargon a temporary recovery in share prices after a substantial fall, caused by speculators buying to cover their positions. A live cat on falling will spring up or 'bounce back', but a dead one will not, although it may seem to do so.

**Dead end kids.** Children from poverty-stricken back streets for whom the future seems to hold little promise. The Dead End Kids were a popular group of young US film actors who first appeared as 'hooligans' in *Dead End* (1937). This was set in New York's East Side, where slum kids and gangsters lived next to a luxury apartment block. They went on to appear in such films as *Angels with Dirty Faces* (1938) and *On Dress Parade* (1939). They subsequently split up into the Little Tough Guys, the East Side Kids and the Bowery Boys. The original Dead End Kids were Billy Halop, Leo Gorcey, Bernard Punsley, Huntz Hall, Bobby Jordan and Gabriel Dell.

**Dead from the neck up.** Noticeably stupid. Such a person is 'brain-dead'.

**Deadheads.** Fans of The Grateful Dead, with a play on 'head', a consumer of recreational drugs. The Grateful Dead (simply 'The Dead' to their fans) were a US West Coast psychedelic rock band, formed in San Francisco in 1965, who continued to perform and record until the death of lead guitarist Jerry Garcia in 1995. Their influences included jazz, blues, rock and roll, country and bluegrass. *See also* AMERICAN BEAUTY; KEEP ON TRUCKING; ROCK GROUP NAMES.

**Dead heart.** The remote interior of Australia. The phrase comes from the title of J.W. Gregory's book *The Dead Heart of Australia* (1906).

**Dead in the water.** Unable to function effectively. The reference is not to a drowned person but to a boat or a ship that is unable to move for some reason, either because there is no current or no wind or because her engine has failed.

**Dead letter.** A law or regulation no longer acted upon. A letter that the post office has been unable to deliver either because of an incorrect address or because the person addressed is untraceable.

**Dead letter box** or **drop.** In espionage, a place where messages can be left by one person for another without either of them meeting. In 1985 Chief Warrant Officer John A. Walker Jr, a retired US naval officer, was arrested following months of observation by the FBI during which he left 129 classified documents at a dead drop in Poolsville, Maryland, for a KGB agent. The plan involved Walker dropping a 7-Up can at a prearranged spot to signal that he had placed the material at the drop, near a specified tree. On seeing the signal the agent was to proceed to the drop, pick up the bag and leave Walker a packet of cash. Walker was tried and sentenced to life imprisonment in a case that was one of the most damaging spy episodes in the history of the US Navy.

**Deadly Derek.** The nickname of the Kent and England cricketer Derek Underwood (b.1945), a left-arm medium-pace spin bowler whose bowling was unplayable on any wicket that was conducive to spin.

**Dead man's handle.** A handle on the controls of an electric train, so designed that it cuts off the current and applies the brakes if the driver releases his pressure from illness or some other cause. It is now officially called a driver's safety device and is usually in the form of a plate depressed by the foot. It was invented in 1902 by the American Frank J. Sprague.

**Dead man walking.** In the United States, an announcement called out by a prison guard as he escorts a condemned man to his execution. It was brought to public attention by the 1995 film *Dead Man Walking*, based on a book (1993) of the same name by Sister Helen Prejean, which tells of her correspondence with and visits to a murderer on Death Row. It subsequently acquired some metaphorical currency, denoting someone still 'alive' but as good as 'dead' (for example, the phrase was applied to the Liberal Democrat leader Charles Kennedy after his admission of alcoholism in January 2006).

**Dead meat.** To be dead meat is to be in serious trouble, as if as good as dead. 'Dead meat' is 19th-century slang for a corpse. *See also* ROAD KILL.

> It was taken for granted by news editors that by 9 am we had read our own paper, its main rival and a couple of the broadsheets. We were dead meat if we hadn't.
> *The Times* (1 October 1999)

**Dead Poets Society.** A film (1989) written by Tom Schulman and directed by Peter Weir about the disturbing events that unfold after an unconventional English teacher (played by Robin Williams) arrives at a conservative Vermont prep school in 1959. Inspired by their teacher to develop an interest in literature, the pupils assemble their own anarchic 'Dead Poets Society', which becomes a focus of their rebellion against the educational establishment.

**Dead president.** A humorous name for a US banknote. First recorded in 1944, it alludes to the US law that forbids the showing of the likeness of any living person on such a note.

**Dead Sea scrolls.** In 1947 a Bedouin goatherd made the first scroll discoveries in a cave at the northwest end of the Dead Sea, since when some hundreds more have been found. The scrolls are in Hebrew and Aramaic, and most scholars accept them as originating from the monastery of the Jewish sect of the Essenes at Qumran. There is still much controversy over their interpretation. In 1991 RADIOCARBON DATING established that most of the scrolls date to the last two centuries BC, making them the earliest extant manuscripts of the Old Testament and the Apocrypha.

**Dead sheep.** A description of the then shadow chancellor Geoffrey Howe, MOGADON MAN, by chancellor of the exchequer Denis Healey, the GROMYKO OF THE LABOUR PARTY. Healey used the phrase in a Commons debate in 1978, when he declared that 'That part of his speech was rather like being savaged by a dead sheep.' Healey claimed the phrase was derived from Winston Churchill's likening of an attack by Clement Attlee, LORD LOVE-A-DUCK OF

LIMEHOUSE, to 'being savaged by a pet lamb'. *See also* GROCER'S DAUGHTER; SHEEP IN SHEEP'S CLOTHING.

**Dead soldier.** An expression of US origin for an empty bottle, answering to the earlier 'dead Marine'. Full bottles, especially in the mass, suggest soldiers on parade, but when they are empty they are isolated and abandoned.

**Dead white European male.** The stereotype on which literary, cultural and philosophical studies have been traditionally centred, as distinct from (say) a living black African female. The expression became familiar in the 1990s in the acronymic form DWEM.

**Deafening silence.** An oxymoronic term for a significant or 'pregnant' silence, especially in a situation where one would have expected to hear something, such as a response to a question or a comment on a particular matter. The expression is first recorded in the 1960s.

**Dear John.** A letter ending a personal relationship. The expression dates from the Second World War, when US servicemen were separated from their partners, who then wrote to terminate the relationship. The words, a typical opening, have served as the title of various US and British comedies in which a hapless husband arrives home to find such a letter awaiting his return.

> 'Dear John,' the letter began. 'I have found someone else whom I think the world of. I think the only way out is for us to get a divorce,' it said. They usually began like that, those letters that told of infidelity on the part of the wives of servicemen.
> *Democrat and Chronicle* (Rochester, New York)
> (17 August 1945)

**Dear Leader.** *See* BUSH'S POODLE.

**Death, Angel of.** *See* ANGEL OF DEATH.

**Death by a thousand cuts.** A succession of slight injuries whose cumulative effect is fatal. The expression comes from one of the 'thoughts' in Chairman Mao's LITTLE RED BOOK: 'He who is not afraid of death by a thousand cuts dares to unhorse the emperor.'

**Death Eater.** In the Harry POTTER books, any of the wizards who are attracted enough to the Dark Arts to throw in their lot with the evil genius Lord Voldemort and become one of his faithful followers. While many of them end up imprisoned in AZKABAN, many more remain at large, concealing their true allegiance, awaiting a chance to flex their wands and use the taboo 'unforgivable curses', the worst of which is 'avada kedavra', the death curse. The term first occurs in *Harry Potter and the Goblet of Fire* (2000), and it

suggests the degree to which these fanatics metaphorically gorge on everything that is evil.

**Death in Venice.** A novella, originally *Der Tod in Venedig* (1912), by the German novelist Thomas Mann (1875–1955), which was published in Britain in 1928. It is a study, overlaid with symbolism, of the fatal attraction of an ailing and ageing writer, Gustav von Aschenbach, for a beautiful 13-year-old boy, Tadzio. He remains in Venice even in the face of a cholera epidemic, in which he dies. In the notable film version (1971) von Aschenbach, sensitively played by Dirk Bogarde, is reimagined as a composer. The latter is transparently based on Gustav Mahler, and the moving *Adagietto* from his fifth symphony (1901) accompanies the slow evolution of the story. Tadzio was played by the young Swedish actor Björn Andresen (b.1955), and the boy's mother by Silvana Mangano. *See also* FIRST LINES OF NOVELS.

**Deathless prose.** Immortal prose. The cliché, which dates from the 1960s, is almost always used ironically.

> I had imagined that my jumbled speech would be translated into deathless prose.
> QUENTIN CRISP: *How to Become a Virgin*, ch. 5 (1981)

**Death of a Salesman.** The PULITZER PRIZE-winning play (1949) by US playwright Arthur Miller (1915–2005) is about the tortured relationships between the failed salesman Willy Loman and his two sons, the self-justifying fantasies people need to survive, and, in a wider context, when the promise of the AMERICAN DREAM turns sour. The play, which culminates in Loman's suicide, was originally titled *The Inside of His Head*, a reference to the salesman's delusions about himself and his family.

The British theatre critic Kenneth Tynan thought it the best play to have emerged from the United States (partly because, in his view, it said so much *about* that country), and a certain pre-eminence still attaches to it, attracting leading actors to the role of Willy Loman.

**Death of Klinghofer, The.** An opera by the US composer John Adams (b.1947), with a libretto by Alice Goodman, first performed in 1991. The story concerns the Palestinian hijacking in October 1985 of the Italian cruise ship *Achille Lauro*, and the murder of Leon Klinghofer, one of the passengers.

**Death on the Nile.** A detective novel (1937) by Agatha Christie (1890–1976), involving Hercule POIROT. The setting is a cruise ship and the background stemmed from the author's interest in the work of her archaeologist husband, Max Mallowan (1904–78), whom she married in 1930 after a divorce from her first husband. A film version (1978) was capably directed by John Guillermin and starred Peter Ustinov as Poirot.

**Death on the Rock.** A popular name, from a television documentary on the incident, for the killing by the SAS of three IRA members, Sean Savage, Daniel McCann and Mairead Farrell, in Gibraltar on 6 March 1988. In 1995 the European Court of Human Rights condemned the killing. The undercover SAS men claimed that the three had been about to detonate a car bomb.

**Death row.** A 20th-century Americanism, but hardly a euphemism, for the section of a prison that contains the condemned cells. These days the inmates can spend decades on death row, as appeal follows appeal.

**Death squad.** A term that was first applied in the 1970s in Latin America to groups of military or police personnel who, working out of uniform and with or without official sanction, eliminate anybody perceived as a threat to the government in power. Death squads usually operate under military regimes; notable examples include Argentina in the period 1976–83 (*see* the DISAPPEARED) and El Salvador in the 1980s, where the death squads' victims included Archbishop Oscar Romero, assassinated in 1980. Sometimes the victims have been the target of a personal grudge, and in Brazil death squads have operated against homeless children.

**Debs' delight.** An eligible or elegant young man in fashionable society. 'Debs' are debutantes.

**Debunk.** To expose the falseness of; to reduce the inflated reputation of. The word, based on 'bunk', was invented by the US editor and writer William E. Woodward (1874–1950) in his book *Bunk* (1923). The new verb was adopted unwillingly by some Britons.

> The origin of *to debunk* is doubtless the same as that of American jargon in general – the inability of an ill-educated and unintelligent democracy to assimilate long words. Its intrusion in our own tongue is due partly to the odious novelty of the word itself, and partly to the prevailing fear that to write exact English nowadays is to be put down as a pedant and a prig.
>
> *Daily Telegraph* (2 March 1935)

**Decapitation strategy.** A military euphemism defined thus by Major Scott Walker in his paper 'A Unified Field Theory of Coercive Airpower' (*Aerospace Power Journal*, Summer 1997):

> Decapitation strategy … targets the enemy leadership and C2 command apparatus and may include direct attack aimed at killing the leadership of an enemy nation. The

mechanism may be either denial or punishment in nature. By destroying the enemy C2 network, we may deny him the ability to control his military units or provide them intelligence, resulting in an easy victory for our fielded forces. Additionally, most leaders place high value on their personal survival, even if capable successors exist. The new dictator, whose predecessor was turned into a smoking hole by a laser-guided bomb, may quickly adjust his personal cost/benefit analysis of continuing the war. This allows decapitation to work through a risk mechanism as well, since the new leader is likely deterred by fear of future cost to his own life. It should be noted here that many nations adhere to a policy of not targeting specific individual leaders; this was the stated policy of the United States during the Gulf War.

The policy had changed a decade later. In March 2003, prior to the main offensive on Iraq, US forces hit a building in which Saddam Hussein and his sons were thought to be hiding with two 2000 lb bombs. It turned out they were no longer there.

The idea of 'decapitation' has since been applied more figuratively in the realm of domestic politics. In the 2005 UK general election the Liberal Democrats targeted the marginal seats of leading Tories such as Oliver Letwin, Theresa May and David Davis in an attempted 'decapitation strategy' – or at least so the press described it. The Lib Dems' chief strategist Chris Lennard said, 'We never use the phrase actually … because this is not personally vindictive.' In any case, they were largely unsuccessful.

*See also* SHOCK AND AWE; WHITE-SUIT CANDIDATE.

**Decimal currency.** This was introduced in Britain on 15 February 1971, the new pound consisting of 100 pence. The new coins were the seven-sided 50p piece, the 10p piece (the same size as the former florin), the 5p piece (the same size as the former shilling), the 2p piece, the 1p piece and the ½p piece. The first three coins were silver in colour and the remainder copper-coloured. The ½p piece was taken out of circulation in 1984, and the 5p, 10p and 50p coins were made smaller in 1990, 1992 and 1997 respectively. The pound coin was introduced in 1983, and the two-pound coin entered general circulation in 1997.

The introduction of a decimal currency was first mooted in 1816 by the Tory MP John Croker.

***Decline and Fall.*** The first novel (1928) by Evelyn Waugh (1903–66), a comic, but embroidered and extended, reprise of some of the author's own experiences at Oxford University and as a teacher at a private school. A theological student, Paul Pennyfeather, innocently embroiled in a drunken incident, is sent down from Scone College, Oxford and becomes a master at an eccentric public school. Further misfortune follows when, on the morning of his wedding to the glamorous Margot Beste-Chetwynde (*see* METROLAND), he is arrested and imprisoned for his wife-to-be's involvement in the white slave-trade. An escape is engineered that allows Pennyfeather to resume his studies in the guise of a distant cousin. The title echoes that of *The Decline and Fall of the Roman Empire* by Edward Gibbon (1737–94). An only moderately amusing film version (1968), with Robin Phillips as Paul Pennyfeather, was directed by John Krish. *See also* FIRST LINES OF NOVELS.

**Decommissioning.** Generally, the process of putting something out of commission or closing it down, such as a nuclear power plant. More specifically the word has been applied to the handing over or destruction of weapons held by the various paramilitary groups in Northern Ireland under the terms of the GOOD FRIDAY AGREEMENT.

**Deely Bobbers.** These bobbing headsets resembling insect antennae were all the rage of 1982. They were the invention of John Mincove, a US novelty manufacturer. The origin of their name remains a mystery.

**Deep North.** A condescending nickname (modelled on the 'Deep South' of the United States) applied by sophisticates in the southern states of Australia to Queensland, viewed as staid and conservative. It is first recorded in 1972.

**Deep six.** 'To deep six' is to get rid of; to destroy. The phrase originated as US naval jargon for 'to throw overboard'. The reference is ultimately to SIX FEET UNDER.

**Deep Throat.** A code name for the anonymous source in the White House during the presidency of Richard M. Nixon who supplied *Washington Post* journalists Carl Bernstein and Bob Woodward with information that aided them in their WATERGATE investigations of 1972–4. The rumour that 'Deep Throat' did not in fact exist was hotly denied by Woodward, and in June 2005, Mark Felt, deputy director of the FBI in the early 1970s, revealed that he had been Deep Throat. One reason that he had not been caught at the time was that he himself was in charge of the FBI search for the source of the leaks. The name came from the title of a celebrated pornographic movie of 1972 starring Linda Lovelace. *See also* ALL THE PRESIDENT'S MEN; CREEP; TRICKY DICKY.

**Default.** In computer jargon a pre-selected option that a program will adopt if none other is selected by the user or programmer. The specialized sense dates from the 1960s and can bemuse neophytes, since the word normally denotes a failure and suggests 'falter' and even more 'fault'.

**Defcon.** An acronym for *Def*ense Readiness *Con*dition, a scale used by the US military to indicate the degree of threat in a given situation, ranging from Defcon 5 (ordinary peacetime readiness) to Defcon 1 (maximum force readiness, in response to an imminent or ongoing attack by a foreign military power). Defcon 1 has never been declared, but during the Cuban Missile Crisis (*see* HAWKS AND DOVES) the Strategic Air Command went to Defcon 2. At that time the rest of the US armed forces went to Defcon 3, which has also been ordered on two other occasions: during the 1973 YOM KIPPUR WAR and during the 9/11 terrorist attacks in 2001.

The United States also uses the Homeland Security Advisory System, to denote the level of domestic terrorist threat, ranging from green (low risk) through blue (general risk), yellow (significant risk), orange (high risk) to red (severe risk). Different levels of threat initiate different levels of security, for example at airports. The system was introduced in 2002, after the 9/11 attacks. The UK has a similar system, consisting of black, black special, amber and red, although the security services do not explain their meanings.

*See also* COBRA; RED ALERT.

**Defence of the Realm Acts.** *See* DORA.

**Defensive measures.** The phrase used by the German foreign minister Joachim von Ribbentrop early in the morning of 22 June 1941 to the Soviet ambassador in Berlin to describe the Nazi invasion of the Soviet Union then under way.

**Deferred success.** A euphemistic formulation with which some early 21st-century educationists sought to replace 'failure'. It hit the headlines in 2005, when a move to give it the stamp of official approval at a teaching union's conference provoked, perhaps understandably, howls of derision.

> Lots of coverage in this morning's headlines about a motion before the annual gathering of the Professional Association of Teachers to 'delete the word "fail" from the educational vocabulary to be replaced with the concept of "deferred success"'.
>
> ANDREW LEWIN: The Standard Site, Department for Education and Skills (20 July 2005)

**Defining moment.** An event that typifies or determines all subsequent related occurrences. The term gained common currency from the 1980s.

**Def jam.** Excellent music. 'Def' may be short for 'definitive' or possibly a Jamaican English form of 'death' as a general intensifier. A television programme for younger viewers,

*DEF II*, first shown on BBC 2 in 1988, introduced the word to an initially baffled British audience.

**Deir Yassin.** The name of a Palestinian village (in what is now the State of Israel) that was the scene of a massacre, on the morning of 9 April 1948, of 254 Arab civilians by IRGUN and STERN GANG terrorists, who included amongst their number the future prime minister of Israel, Menachem Begin (1913–92). Deir Yassin was situated outside the area assigned by the United Nations to the Jewish State. However, it was located in the 'corridor' between Tel Aviv and Jerusalem and was targeted for occupation by the HAGANAH, who authorized the Irgun and the Stern Gang to carry out the takeover. The panic engendered by the massacre contibuted to the exodus from Palestine of hundreds of thousands of Arabs. After the attack the leaders of the Haganah distanced themselves from the events at Deir Yassin and issued a statement denouncing the dissidents of Irgun and Stern Gang, as they had done after the attack on the King David Hotel in July 1946. Menachem Begin himself recalled:

> Arabs throughout the country, induced to believe wild takes or Irgun 'butchery', were seized with limitless panic and started to flee for their lives. This mass flight soon developed into a maddened, uncontrollable stampede. The political and economic significance of this development can hardly be overestimated.

**Déjà lu.** (French, 'already read'.) A phrase dating from the 1960s for the feeling that one may have read the present passage before, or an identical passage elsewhere. The phrase is based on *déjà vu*, 'already seen', as a term for the illusory feeling of having experienced the present situation before.

**Delaney amendment** or **clause.** An amendment to the US Food, Drug and Cosmetic Act that forbids the use of any food additive that has been shown to cause cancer in animals or people. The name is that of the US Congressman James J. Delaney (1901–87), the amendment's author. Although some 20 years old at the time, the amendment became the centre of controversy in the 1970s when scientists pointed out that minute quantities of an additive might not necessarily be harmful and could, in fact, be useful. Others maintained that even the smallest quantities of such substances should be banned.

**Delhi belly.** *See* MONTEZUMA'S REVENGE.

**Delia.** A name synonymous with good, simple cooking (rather than *haute cuisine*), from Delia Smith (b.1941), author and broadcaster on the subject from the 1970s. Guests invited to dinner may welcome or sample a dish with an enquiry on the lines of 'Is this Delia?' Considerable media interest was aroused when the name was adjudged to have a sufficiently high profile to warrant inclusion in the 2001 edition of the *Collins English Dictionary*, along with various associated phrases, including 'doing a Delia'. This originally denoted cooking a dish based on a Delia Smith recipe, but it took on a new connotation in 2005 when Smith, in her role as chairman of Norwich City football club, took to the pitch at half time after the team had surrendered a two-goal lead against Manchester City in order to berate the home fans, in somewhat febrile and overemotional style, for not supporting their team fervently enough. 'Where are you?' she cried. 'Let's be 'aving you!'

> Colin Youngjohns has ruled out 'doing a Delia' and taking to the field to rally fans for Saturday's crunch clash with Rushden.
>
> www.archive.thisisworcestershire.co.uk (17 March 2005)

**Deliver the goods.** To come up with what was expected; to fulfil one's promise.

**Delta of Venus.** A collection of erotic stories (published posthumously in 1977) by the French-born author Anaïs Nin (1903–77), one time mistress and life-long friend of Henry Miller. She had written them on commission when down on her luck in the early 1940s. The title none too subtly suggests the triangular shape of the female pubic region.

**Delusions of grandeur.** An exaggerated estimation of one's own importance; megalomania. The term dates from the early 20th century.

**Democratic Unionist Party.** *See* PAISLEYITES; ULSTER UNIONIST PARTY.

**Demoiselles d'Avignon, Les.** It was with this stunning canvas that Pablo Picasso (1881–1973) heralded the arrival of CUBISM. The austere simplicity of the work, painted in 1907, incorporates Picasso's discovery of African and ancient Iberian art: it features five nudes, four of whom are standing, and three of whom have mask-like faces. Surprisingly, given that the painting has become such an icon of modernism, the work was not reproduced until 1925 and not exhibited in public until 1937. The title was jokingly given to the work by the critic André Salmon, who suggested that the young ladies in the painting might be *demoiselles* ('young ladies') in a brothel in the Carré d'Avinyo (Avignon Street) in Barcelona.

**Denishawn School of Dancing.** This dance school and company opened in Los Angeles in 1915, taking its name from its founders, Ruth St Denis (1879–1968) and her husband, Ted Shawn (1891–1972). Its main attention was devoted to modern dance, and it fostered such leading modern dancers as Martha Graham (1894–1991), Doris Humphrey (1895–1958) and Charles Weidman (1901–75). The company closed in 1931 after St Denis and Shawn separated.

**Dennis the Menace.** There are two cartoon characters of this name and title, one British, the other American. The British Dennis has featured in the BEANO since 1951 and was the creation of cartoonist David Law. He has a shock of black hair, wears a red striped jersey and is accompanied by a fearsome dog called Gnasher. His female counterpart is Beryl the Peril. His US namesake was created the same year by artist Hank Ketcham as a four-year-old brat. He has appeared in various cartoon stories, including a televised version in the early 1960s and a feature film in 1993.

**Denver boot.** A wheel clamp used to immobilize an illegally parked car. The colloquialism is now dated but was current in Britain from the late 1960s when this solution to illegal parking was first discussed. The allusion is to Denver, Colorado, where wheel clamping was introduced in 1949.

**Derek and Clive.** *See* NOT ONLY... BUT ALSO....

**Derivative.** In financial market parlance, a financial contract whose value derives from, and is dependent on, the value of an underlying variable asset, such as a commodity, a currency or a security. Many such contracts are highly speculative, since an investor can potentially make a huge profit by a minimal outlay. In consequence, some banks and individuals have made and lost vast sums in such speculations, one of which led to the collapse of Barings Bank in 1995.

**Desaparecidos, Los.** *See* the DISAPPEARED.

**Desert Fox.** The nickname of Field Marshal Erwin Rommel (1891–1944), German commander of the AFRIKA KORPS in North Africa in the Second World War. The allusion was to his audacious surprise attacks, which won him early successes in 1941–2. The name was used equally by the Germans as *Der Wüstenfuchs*. There is no actual such animal. *See also* El ALAMEIN; DESERT RATS.

**Desert Island Discs.** The enduringly popular radio programme was created in 1942 by Roy Plomley (1914–85) and had its 2000th 'castaway' (the actor John Thaw) in 1990. Each celebrity is allowed to choose eight gramophone records and a single luxury and book (except the Bible and Shakespeare) that they would wish to have on their desert island. The first subject was the comedian Vic Oliver, and the only celebrity to be 'shipwrecked' four times was the comedian Arthur Askey. Plomley himself presented the programme until his death. Michael Parkinson replaced Plomley as presenter, and was succeeded in turn by Sue Lawley (1988–2006) and Kirsty Young.

**Desert Rats.** The name associated with the British 7th Armoured Division in the Second World War, whose divisional sign was the desert rat (jerboa), which was adopted during its 'scurrying and biting' tactics in Libya. The final design of the badge was a red rat outlined on a black background. The division served throughout the North Africa campaign of 1941–2 and in northwestern Europe from Normandy to Berlin. The name was later associated with the 7th Armoured Brigade, and was again to the fore when this force was in action in the Middle East during the First GULF WAR.

**Desert Shield.** The name adopted for the US contribution to the UN military coalition against Iraq in the First GULF WAR. *See also* DESERT STORM.

**Desert Storm.** The name of the air and land campaign waged by the US-led UN military coalition against Iraq in the First GULF WAR. In some contexts the name is used for the land battle only.

**Desiccated calculating machine.** A phrase coined by Aneurin Bevan in 1954, usually thought to refer to Hugh Gaitskell (1906–63), his successful rival for the LABOUR PARTY leadership in 1955. Although Bevan denied that he was referring to Gaitskill, the name stuck. Earlier, when Gaitskell was chancellor of the exchequer in 1950–1, Tory politician Iain Macleod (1913–70) had dubbed Gaitskell 'Mr Rising Price'. *See also* NYE.

**Designer drug.** A drug deliberately synthesized ('designed') to circumvent drug laws. A structure is used that is not illegal but mimics the chemistry and effects of an existing banned drug.

> Some of these people obviously use cocaine, marijuana and some exotic designer drugs.
> *New York Times* (23 September 1989)

**Designer label.** A label on an expensive or modish item of clothing that bears the name of a famous fashion designer, such as that of Calvin Klein on the back of jeans in the 1970s.

**Designer stubble.** The short hairs and beard on a man's face that has been deliberately left unshaven for a day or so with the aim of appearing attractively macho. The fashion became current from the late 1980s among models and media celebrities.

> A 20th-century Jack-the-lad, all designer stubble, shy smiles and off-the-shoulder shifts – an expert at pulling birds.
> *The Times* (11 October 1999)

**Design for Living.** A play (1933) by Noël Coward (1899–1973) about a successful *ménage à trois* established by three friends, Leo (a writer), Otto (a painter) and Gilda (a designer). The idea of writing about such a threesome was suggested to Coward both by Eugene O'Neill's *Strange Interlude* (1928) and by his own close friendship with the actors Alfred Lunt and Lynn Fontanne.

**Desire Street.** A street in New Orleans made famous by Tennessee Williams's play *A* STREETCAR NAMED DESIRE (1947), in which the central character, Blanche DuBois, visits her sister Stella, who lives with her husband Jack in the French Quarter of the city near the stop of two streetcars (trams) that run on the same track. Each is named for its destination, respectively 'Desire' and 'Cemetery', and these names are taken symbolically, Blanche contending that Stella's marriage is a product of lust, as aimless as the 'streetcar named Desire' that shuttles through the narrow streets. The name of the street does not denote a place of pleasure but derives from the French girl's name Désirée. A monument, the 'Streetcar Named Desire', now stands on the site near the French Market.

**Desktop.** In computer jargon the working area of a computer screen thought of as the equivalent of a desktop and containing ICONS representing items such as files and a waste bin, as normally found respectively on and under a conventional desk.

**Desperate Dan.** The brawny, stubble-chinned westerner who has appeared in the DANDY comic (which his name matches) since 1937 (he 'left' the comic briefly in 1997, as part of the storyline, but returned in triumph for the 60th anniversary edition). His favourite dish is cow pie, which he eats with the horns protruding from the pastry. He was the creation of the artist Dudley D. Watkins. There is a statue to him in Dundee, where the *Dandy* is published.

In 2004 the Labour Party produced a poster portraying Conservative leader Michael Howard as Desperate Dan, but was obliged to withdraw it after complaints from Dan's publisher, D.C. Thomson, from whom permission had not been sought.

**Desperate Housewives.** A blackly comic US television drama (2004– ), created by Marc Cherry, that mixes slapstick and suicide, modern manners and murder. The first season introduced the suburban inhabitants of the affluent Wisteria Lane (an American ACACIA AVENUE) via the unusual technique of a voiceover by a character who has committed suicide. Gradually the reasons for her suicide are revealed, though not without numerous plots twists, digressions and improbable coincidences. At the centre of the goings on are four variously neurotic 'housewives': Bree (played by Marcia Cross), an uptight pro-Republican WASP whose family is disintegrating; Lynette (played by Felicity Huffman), a married mother struggling to balance family, work and self; Susan (played by Terri Hatcher), a haphazard and immature divorcée and single mother, looking for love; and Gabrielle (played by Eva Longoria), a glamorous but selfish former model who worships money and her body. The device of the four central friends is a nod towards SEX AND THE CITY, though the characters in the latter tend not to have to contend with killings, kidnaps, child molestation, arson, fistfights with nuns, and a host of other difficulties that beset the denizens of Wisteria Lane.

**Desperately Seeking Susan.** A 1985 romantic comedy film starring Rosanna Arquette as a bored housewife who decides to spice up her life by following up the small ads. One reading 'Desperately Seeking Susan' leads her to the eponymous and mysterious Susan (played by Madonna). The title has become something of a journalistic formula: 'Desperately Seeking WMDs' (i.e. WEAPONS OF MASS DESTRUCTION) was a common headline following the invasion of Iraq in 2003.

**Des res.** A 'desirable residence', former estate agents' jargon for any house that they wish to sell. Since the mid-1980s the expression has generally been an ironic colloquialism.

> The ultra rich and famous can now leave dry land for the ultimate des res – an apartment on the ResidenSea liner.
> *heat* (18–24 November 1999)

**Destry Rides Again.** A WESTERN (1939) directed by George Marshall and adapted from a novel of the same title (1930) by Max Brand about peace-loving marshal Tom Destry, who relies on his wits rather than his gun to keep law and order in the unruly town of Bottleneck. He refuses to carry a gun, much to the alarm of the inhabitants, and his favourite tipple is sarsaparilla. The film starred James Stewart and Marlene Dietrich, but this was not the first time Destry had 'ridden again': Brand's novel had already been filmed in 1932, starring Tom Mix, and in 1954 it was adapted for the screen once more, in a film called simply *Destry* and starring Audie Murphy. *See also* BACKROOM BOYS.

**Détente.** (French, 'relaxation'.) A term describing the reduction in COLD WAR tension between the United States and the Soviet Union during the 1970s. Attempts to achieve a measure of peaceful co-existence began in 1968 during the VIETNAM War peace talks, and in 1972 President Richard Nixon re-established friendly relations between the United States and communist China. This Sino-US rapprochement in turn led the Soviet Union to improve its relations with the

United States. Among the results of *détente* were the ABM and SALT treaties, in which the United States and the Soviet Union agreed to limitations in the nuclear arms race. *See also* NIXON IN CHINA.

**Dev.** A nickname of the Irish politician Éamon de Valera (1882–1975), prime minister of Ireland (1932–48, 1951–4 and 1957–9) and president (1959–73). Born in the United States of a Spanish father, de Valera was also called the 'Long Fellow' because of his tall and gaunt appearance. A biography of de Valera by the Irish journalist Tim Pat Coogan was entitled *De Valera: Long Fellow, Long Shadow* (1993). *See also* BIG FELLA.

**De Vil, Cruella.** The wicked anti-heroine of Dodie Smith's children's novel *The* HUNDRED AND ONE DALMATIANS (1956), who kidnaps puppies with the aim of turning their fur into coats for humans. Her name, subsequently a byword for female heartlessness, implies that she is a cruel villain or cruel devil. The story was made into a popular Disney cartoon film, *One Hundred and One Dalmatians* (1961), and subsequently into a live-action film, *101 Dalmatians* (1996), in which Ms De Vil was played by Glenn Close.

Cruella De Vil was also a nickname given to the Conservative politician Edwina Currie (b.1946). Currie's appearance in the Commons provoked in one Tory minister a 'brief batsqueak of desire'. Her short career in government (1986–8) ended when, as a junior health minister, she announced, to the fury of the farming lobby, that most of the UK's egg production was infected with the salmonella bacteria. She has subsequently had a successful career as a radio broadcaster and writer of political BONKBUSTERS, while continuing to sit on the back benches. The nation's collective eyebrow was raised momentarily in 2002 when she published her diaries and therein confessed to an affair in the 1980s with future prime minister John Major.

**Devil's Dictionary, The.** A glossary of aphorisms (1911), first published as *The Cynic's Word Book* (1906) by Ambrose Bierce (1842–?1914). Typical entries are:

APOLOGIZE, *v.* To lay the foundation for a future offence.

INSURANCE, *n.* An ingenious modern game of chance in which the player is permitted to enjoy the comfortable conviction that he is beating the man who keeps the table.

MARRIAGE, *n.* The state or condition of a community consisting of a master, a mistress and two slaves, making two in all.

Bierce is believed to have died in battle at the age of 71, having been caught in Ojinaga, on the Rio Grande, when it was besieged and taken by rebels.

**Devil's Island.** (French *Isle du Diable*.) A former French penal colony, notorious for the harshness of its conditions, situated on a tiny island off the coast of French Guiana. The island's most famous prisoner was Albert Dreyfus (1859–1935), wrongly convicted of espionage and held there from 1895 to 1899 (*see also* DREYFUSARD). In 1969 another prisoner, Henri Charrière (1906–73), published a bestselling book, *Papillon* (the title referring to his own nickname), about his attempts to escape from the island, the last try in 1944 being successful. The 1973 film version, starring Steve McQueen and Dustin Hoffman, drew the following barb from one critic: '*Papillon* offers torture as entertainment but winds up making entertainment a form of torture.' The penal settlement was closed down in 1953, and the island is now a tourist resort.

**Devolution.** A term adopted in the 20th century for the transfer of certain powers from central government to assemblies in Scotland and Wales. In 1974 the Labour government proposed setting up a new Scottish parliament and a Welsh assembly. Referendums were held in 1979, with the Welsh voting against. The Scots narrowly voted in favour, but the support of at least 40 per cent of the electorate was required and was not obtained, so no action resulted. The intervening Conservative governments stood fast against devolution, but in 1997 the NEW LABOUR government held new referendums. This time both countries voted in favour. The Scottish parliament and the Welsh assembly, both elected in 1999, received legislative power over domestic issues, such as health, housing and social services, while Westminster retained control over defence, economic policy, employment, taxation and foreign affairs.

Despite occasional political grumblings for greater English regional autonomy, and the continued relevance of the WEST LOTHIAN QUESTION, a referendum for an assembly in the Northeast (2004) garnered little interest. However, under New Labour London did in 2000 get back a city-wide body, the Greater London Authority, albeit not with New Labour's chosen APPARATCHIK as mayor (*see* RED KEN).

**Di, Lady.** *See* LADY DI.

**Diamond Lil.** A nickname of the US film actress Mae West (1892–1980), from her play thus titled (1928) in which she took the main role. The heroine is so called because of the large amount of 'ice' (jewellery) her pimp has lavished on her.

**Diamonds Are Forever.** The eighth film (1971) in the James BOND series, starring Sean Connery as Bond and based on a book of the same title by Ian Fleming (1908–64). The title (which was reinforced by a theme tune sung by Shirley Bassey) was inspired by a slogan devised in 1939 by US advertising writer B.J. Kidd on behalf of De Beers Consolidated Mines in South Africa as part of a campaign to promote diamond engagement rings.

**Diamond system.** A system of play in football in which the formation of the midfield players is in the shape of a diamond. One player operates at the tip in the role of part-midfielder, part-striker, two players take up wider positions behind, and an anchor midfielder locates himself at the base in front of the defence. The task of the middle two players is to push forward when in possession of the ball and track back when the opposition has it.

**Dianetics.** A system that clamed to relieve or remove psycho-somatic disorders by cleansing the mind of harmful images. It was developed in 1950 by L. Ron Hubbard (1911–86), founder of the Church of SCIENTOLOGY, who took its name from Greek *dianœtikos*, 'relating to thought'.

**Dice with death.** To take serious risks. The expression dates from the 1940s and was long a journalistic cliché used in connection with motor-racing. The concept is of playing a game of dice with Death. If he wins, one will lose one's life.

**Dick Emery Show, The.** A long-running television comedy series screened from 1963 to 1981 and starring Dick Emery (1918–84) in a series of enjoyable impressions that included a toothy vicar, an ageing BOVVER BOY and a bouncy blonde, Mandy, who always ended a radio interview by giving her interviewer a saucy punch and saying: 'Ooh, you are awful – but I like you.'

**Dickless Tracy.** A derisive canteen nickname among male police officers for a female colleague. Originating in the United States in the 1960s, it puns on 'dick' in the sense 'penis' and the name of the fictional detective Dick TRACY.

**Dicky bow.** A bow tie. The name alludes to 'dicky' as a former slang term for a shirt collar and a still current colloquialism for a false shirt front.

**Dictatorship of the proletariat.** The form of government that would be established after the revolution, according to Karl Marx (1818–83). Marx himself attributed the phrase to the French revolutionary socialist Auguste Blanqui (1805–81). In Marx's theory the dictatorship of the proletariat was a key period in which bourgeois opposition to the revolution was to be crushed and the class relations of capitalist production were to be destroyed. The dictatorship of the proletariat – the industrial working class, conceived of as the majority – was to be followed by the withering away of the state and the establishment of true communism. Soviet Russia never managed to get past the dictator-ship phase, and its leaders, starting with Lenin, used the

concept of the dictatorship of the proletariat to justify their totalitarian rule, ostensibly on behalf of the workers.

> What I did that was new was to prove … that the class struggle necessarily leads to the dictatorship of the proletariat.
>
> KARL MARX: letter to Georg Weydemeyer (5 March 1852)

**Die for.** *See* TO DIE FOR.

**Dief the Chief.** A nickname awarded by his colleagues to Canadian politician John G. Diefenbaker (1895–1979), who became prime minister (1957–63) following his Progressive Conservative Party's landslide victory over the Liberals.

**Die Hard.** A film thriller (1988) starring Bruce Willis as a New York policeman pitted against a ruthless gang of terrorists with whom he is trapped in a high-rise Los Angeles office block (actually the headquarters building of 20th Century-Fox, makers of the film). The title of the film, and its sequels *Die Hard 2* (1990) and *Die Hard with a Vengeance* (1995), had been used previously in a variety of contexts over the years. 'Die Hard' was, for instance, the regimental nickname bestowed on the 57th Foot, later the 1st Battalion Middlesex Regiment and later still the 4th Battalion The Queen's Regiment, after their heroic but bloody stand at the Battle of Albuera in 1811. As the French enemies attacked, Colonel Inglis exhorted his men: 'Die hard, my men, die hard.'

> Die harder.
>
> Publicity slogan for *Die Hard 2*

**Diehards.** The nickname of those Conservative lords who rebelled against the party line in 1911 to vote against the Parliament Act, saying they would 'die fighting' the provisions of the act that restricted the veto power of the House of Lords. Their actions led to the resignation of party leader Arthur Balfour. *See also* BALFOUR'S POODLE; HEDGERS AND DITCHERS.

**Dien Bien Phu.** A village in VIETNAM, some 320km (200 miles) west of Hanoi, near the border with Laos. It was chosen as the site of a heavily fortified forward base by the French in their war against the nationalist and communist VIET MINH, who had been fighting for Vietnamese independence since 1946. The Viet Minh, having cut off all roads into Dien Bien Phu, began in March 1954 to besiege the base, which now could only be supplied from the air. The Viet Minh artillery outgunned that of the French, who, in the words of one soldier, were in a chamber pot, with the enemy in the process of unfastening his trousers. A series of offensives culmi-nated in an all-out Viet Minh attack launched on 1 May, and on 7 May the base was completely overrun. It was the end of French rule in Vietnam, and the former colony was divided into communist North Vietnam and US-sponsored South Vietnam.

**Dietrickery.** A nickname for the women's fashion for wearing men's clothes inspired in the 1930s by the German-born American actress Marlene Dietrich (1901–92). Amelia Bloomer's attempt to introduce trousers for women at the close of the 19th century had largely ended in failure, but 40 years on Dietrich set a trend popular with her female fans when she took to wearing men's clothes in public, typically in the form of a suit and tie topped by a slanting hat. Women did not wear trousers on a daily basis until after the Second World War, and by the 1960s women were buying more trousers than skirts.

**Different strokes.** A short form of 'different strokes for different folks', meaning that different people have different requirements. There is probably a sexual reference here. The phrase is of African American origin. *Diff'rent Strokes* (1978–86) was a US television comedy, shown subsequently in Britain, about a millionaire white widower who adopts two African American boys.

**Difficult we do immediately; the impossible takes a little longer, The.** A slogan adopted by various branches of the US armed forces, for example by the US Army Corps of Engineers and the US Army Air Force during the Second World War. The memorial in Washington, D.C., to the US Naval Construction Battalions has the following inscription:

> With willing hearts and skilful hands, the difficult we do at once, the impossible takes a little longer.

The construction was earlier used by the Norwegian polar explorer Fridtjof Nansen (1861–1930):

> Never stop because you are afraid – you are never so likely to be wrong. Never keep a line of retreat: it is a wretched invention. The difficult is what takes a little time; the impossible is what takes a little longer.

The boast goes back at least as far as the 18th century, when the French statesman Charles Alexandre de Calonne (1734–1802) replied to Marie Antoinette, who wondered whether a request she had made might be too difficult:

> *Madame, si c'est possible, c'est fait; impossible? cela fera.*

**Dig for victory.** A Ministry of Food exhortation disseminated from the earliest days of the Second World War, when the shortage of foodstuffs was an immediate concern. One consequence was a rise in the number of allotments from 815,000 in 1939 to 1.4 million in 1943. In the United States the equivalent call was 'Garden for victory', but somehow the British byword was beefier.

**Digger.** An Australian. The name was in use before 1850, consequent upon the discovery of gold, and was applied to ANZAC troops fighting (and digging in) in Flanders in the First World War and again in the Second World War.

> Burly, slouch-hatted, independent and profane, the Digger bestrides the battlefields of Gallipoli and the Western Front just as jauntily as his bronze monument looks down from Mont St Quentin above Péronne. It is integral to the Australian sense of nationhood and national character.
>
> *Times Literary Supplement* (review of Alistair Thomson, *Anzac Memories*) (16 September 1994)

*See also* DIRTY DIGGER.

**Digital age.** A nickname for the period starting in the 1990s, in which rapid advances in technology have resulted in the transfer of many items of electrical or electronic equipment to digital operation, among them compact discs (CDs), digital cameras, digital radio, digital video discs (DVDs) and DIGITAL TELEVISION. The revolution owed much to the burgeoning of the INTERNET, which enables people to download digital images, information, music and the like, and to switch to HOME SHOPPING and online banking.

**Digital television** or **DTV.** Television in which sound and images come to a screen via a digital (as distinct from analogue) signal broadcast from space. The result is an improvement in sound and picture quality, and the possibility of interactive services such as HOME SHOPPING or banking or the sending of E-MAILS without the use of a computer. Digital television came to Britain in the late 1990s and can be received by dish (satellite), aerial (terrestrial) or cable. It was at first regarded with caution by the public, who were wary of this revolution in their favourite medium.

**Dig one's own grave.** To cause one's own downfall. The phrase is first recorded in the 1930s.

> Far from staging a renaissance, the Conservatives dug their own grave last week.
>
> *Independent on Sunday* (10 October 1999)

**Dilbert.** The comic strip character of this name, an engineer NERD working for The Company, is the invention of the US cartoonist Scott Adams. He appears with his dog Dogbert, much smarter than he is, his mother Dilmom, a SCRABBLE addict, his colleagues Wally, Alice and Loud Howard, and The Pointy-Haired Boss. The strip is one of the most popular in the world, reaching 150 million readers daily, with spin-off bestsellers and its own WORLD WIDE WEB site, which attracts 4 million visits a month.

**Dimbledom.** A nickname for the dominant role played by three members of the Dimbleby family in British radio and television for half a century. Richard Dimbleby (1913–65) was a noted radio reporter in the Second World War, and it was his voice that listeners heard describing airborne forces taking off for Normandy and the horrors of BELSEN. He subsequently presented the current-affairs programme PANORAMA on BBC TV and provided commentary during the television presentation of solemn state occasions (*see* GOLD MICROPHONE IN WAITING). His elder son, David (b.1938), took over the presentation of *Panorama* for many years and anchored the BBC coverage of every general election from 1979 to 2005. David's brother, Jonathan (b.1944), became associated with major documentary programmes, including a report on the Ethiopian famine in 1973 and a documentary on Prince Charles, *Public Person, Private Man*, in 1994. He has chaired *Any Questions* on BBC Radio since 1987 and presented ITV's general election coverage since 1997.

**Diminished responsibility.** A legal term from the Homicide Act 1957, which exempts a person suffering from an unbalanced mental state from full liability for a crime, especially murder.

**Dimsie.** A fictional schoolgirl of the traditional JOLLY HOCKEYSTICKS type. She loves games and forms an 'Anti-Soppist Society' opposed to love, sentimentality and the use of cosmetics. She appeared in a lengthy series of stories by Dorita Fairlie Bruce, beginning with *The Senior Prefect* (1921), and was very popular among schoolgirl readers in the 1920s and 1930s. Her full name is Dorothy Maitland.

**Dinerese.** American diners of the 1940s were a source of many colourful expressions relating to customers' orders. Several are still current. A selection follows:

*Abbott and Costello*: frankfurters and beans (after the comedy film partners)

*Adam and Eve on a raft*: two poached eggs on toast

*All the way*: a sandwich with 'the works', i.e. every condiment in the kitchen

*BLT*: bacon, lettuce and tomato sandwich

*Bowl of red*: a serving of chilli

*Burn it*: cook it until well done

*Cowboy with spurs*: a western omelette (with minced ham and onions) with French fries (chips)

*Eve with the lid on*: apple pie

*Haystack*: strawberry pancakes ('hay' for 'straw')

*High and dry*: a sandwich without any condiments

*Hold the grass*: without lettuce

*Hold the mayo*: without mayonnaise

*Murphy carrying a wreath*: ham and potatoes (murphies) with cabbage

*On the hoof*: rare meat

OVER EASY

*Put out the lights and cry*: liver and onions (to put out someone's lights is to punch them in the liver)

*Red lead*: tomato ketchup

*Sunny side up*: *see* OVER EASY.

*Wreck a pair*: two scrambled eggs

**Diners Club.** The first all-purpose credit card came into being in 1950. It was launched by a US business executive, Francis X. McNamara, who embarrassingly discovered he had left his wallet at home on coming to settle the bill after entertaining clients to lunch at a fashionable Manhattan restaurant.

**Dingbat.** A North American and Australian term for a stupid or eccentric person. The origin may be in 'ding' in the sense 'to beat' with 'bat' subsequently associated with 'batty'. The word has also been used for various rather vaguely specified objects. In printing and computer jargon dingbats are special characters and symbols, i.e. those that differ from the standard letters and numerals.

**Dingle Dolphin, The.** A solitary dolphin that began to appear regularly in the harbour of Dingle, County Kerry, in 1984. He was christened Fungie, and attracted both NEW AGE and mainstream tourists.

**Dingo baby case.** An extraordinary Australian legal case originating in an incident at a campsite near Uluru (Ayer's Rock), Alice Springs, in 1980, when a young baby, Azaria Chamberlain, disappeared from her parents' tent. Initially it was thought that the baby must have been taken by a dingo (the Australian wild dog), but various pieces of circumstantial evidence led to suspicion falling on the mother, Lindy Chamberlain. Suspicion was increased by the fact that Azaria's parents belonged to the millenarian Seventh-Day Adventist cult, and it was said that the name they had given their daughter, Azaria, meant 'carrier of sin' (although the conventional meaning of the Hebrew Azariah is 'helped by God'). From this the rumour emerged that the mother might have sacrificed her daughter in some bizarre ritual. Lindy Chamberlain was arrested, tried, convicted and sentenced to hard labour for life. However, many believed that there had been a gross miscarriage of justice and the case was reopened in 1986, resulting in the release and pardon of Lindy Chamberlain. The story became the subject of the 1989 film *A Cry in the Dark*, starring Meryl Streep and Sam Neill.

**Dingo's breakfast.** A jocular Australian periphrasis employed by someone who has failed to break their fast. The official definition is 'a piss and a look around'. The term dates from the 1960s.

**Dinky Toys.** The model vehicles and figures so named were the creation of Frank Hornby, the inventor of MECCANO. They were introduced in 1934 as 'Modelled Miniatures' for use with Hornby's toy railway system but soon gained a distinct identity among their delighted schoolboy owners.

**Dinner lady.** A term current from the 1960s for a woman who serves meals and supervises children at mealtimes in a school. The term derives from young children themselves, for whom a midday meal is 'dinner' and any adult woman a 'lady'. *Dinner Ladies* was the title of a successful 1990s TV SITCOM written and featuring Victoria Wood, but in this case the dinner ladies worked in the canteen of a factory.

**Dionne quins.** The five daughters, Marie, Émilie, Yvonne, Cécile and Annette, born prematurely on 28 May 1934 to Oliva and Elzire Dionne near Callander, Ontario. They became wards of the state in 1935 and were exploited by the government for promotional purposes but their father regained control in 1941. Émilie died in 1954 and Marie in 1970. In 1998 the three surviving sisters accepted a settlement of $2.8 million from the Ontario government and promises of an inquiry into their treatment during their childhood.

**Dior Look.** The narrow-waisted, tightly fitting bodices and full-pleated skirts designed by the French couturier Christian Dior (1905–57) were launched in Paris on 12 February 1947, as the first postwar fashion fad, later known as the NEW LOOK.

The British comedy actress Beatrice Lillie (1894–1989) famously told a waiter who had spilt soup on her:

Never darken my Dior again!

*Every Other Inch a Lady* (1973)

*See also* A-LINE.

**Dip one's wick.** Of a man, to engage in sexual intercourse. To dip a wick in the literal sense is to make a candle by immersing a wick repeatedly in hot wax. The phrase has come to be associated in some minds with 'Hampton Wick', rhyming slang for 'prick' (although that 'Wick' has no etymological connection with the candle 'wick').

**Dip out.** In Australian English, someone who 'dips out on' an opportunity fails to take advantage of it. The expression dates from around 1950.

**Directoire knickers.** Straight, full, knee-length knickers with elastic at waist and knee. They are a development of the late Victorian 'Directoire' style of dress adopted from that worn at the time of the French Directory (1795–9), itself characterized by extravagance of design and imitative of Greek and Roman costume. The garment is still worn by some women, especially the elderly.

**Direct Rule.** The direct government of Northern Ireland from Westminster, introduced in 1972, the year of BLOODY SUNDAY, following the outbreak of the TROUBLES four years earlier. Direct rule was abandoned in December 1999 as an outcome of discussions proceeding from the signing of the GOOD FRIDAY AGREEMENT and the setting up of the Northern Ireland Assembly. It was reimposed in February 2000 amid bitter recriminations between SINN FÉIN and the British authorities over the issue of the DECOMMISSIONING of paramilitary weapons. The Assembly recommenced its functions, however, in the summer of 2000. It was suspended once more in October 2002, following allegations of a Sinn Féin spy plot in STORMONT.

**Dire straits.** Desperate trouble; impecuniosity. The phrase is probably based on the older 'dire necessity' and was popularized by the pop group of this name formed in 1977. *See also* ROCK GROUP NAMES.

**Dirty dancing.** A form of dancing to pop or disco music involving gyratory movements and hip-to-hip contact. It was a craze in the 1980s and was popularized by a film of 1987 of this title starring Jennifer Grey and Patrick Swayze. The LAMBADA was a natural development.

**Dirty Den.** The nickname of Dennis Watts, a character in the BBC television soap opera EASTENDERS. Watts, played by Leslie Grantham, was the landlord of the *Queen Vic* pub, and became a nationally known villain for his serial womanizing. In 1989 he was apparently murdered by a hitman, but made a miraculous reappearance in the programme in 2003. Alas, his second coming was shortlived, for he was murdered again in 2005 and is now officially dead.

**Dirty Digger, The.** The nickname used in *Private Eye* for the Australian-born, born-again right-wing US newspaper proprietor and media tycoon Rupert Murdoch (b.1931). 'Digger' is a slang term for an Australian, while 'dirty' refers to the page three girls who continue to adorn Murdoch's British tabloid newspaper, *The Sun*. Murdoch's News International Corporation also owns the London *Times*, *The Australian* (Australia's only national paper), the *New York Post*, 20th Century Fox, the publishers HarperCollins, Sky satellite TV, and much more. Murdoch has been accused of trying to monopolize media ownership, and of having an excessive influence on UK politics: for some decades, whichever party *The Sun* has supported in a general election has won. 'It's the *Sun* wot won it,' the newspaper's headline read on 11 April 1992, just after the election of that year. *See also* CRISIS? WHAT CRISIS?

**Dirty Dozen, The.** A war film (1967) directed by Robert Aldrich and adapted from a novel of the same title by E.M. Nathanson about a squad of 12 military prisoners who are challenged to perform a suicidal mission in occupied France during the Second World War in exchange for the chance of freedom. Starring Lee Marvin and Telly Savalas, among others, the film's title deliberately evoked the classic western *The* MAGNIFICENT SEVEN, made seven years earlier.

**Dirty dozens.** A ritual game among African Americans of insulting various relatives, especially their mothers, with 12 'rounds' of attack. The barbs are usually sexual or scatological. Hence 'dirty'.

**Dirty Harry.** The nickname of the violently inclined San Francisco detective Harry Callahan, played in a series of films by Clint Eastwood. In the first, *Dirty Harry* (1971), written by John Milius and directed by Don Siegel, his method of dealing with undesirables was expounded in a laconic speech that has become a cinema classic:

> I know what you're thinking, punk. You're thinking, 'Did he fire six shots or only five?' Now, to tell you the truth, in all this excitement, I've kind of lost track myself. But being as this is a .44 Magnum, the most powerful handgun in the world, and would blow your head clean off, you've got to ask yourself one question: 'Do I feel lucky?' Well, do ya, punk?

It was in a later sequel, *Sudden Impact* (1983), that he memorably challenged a criminal at gunpoint to 'Go ahead, MAKE MY DAY!'

**Dirty mac** or **raincoat brigade.** A term for men who frequent sex shops, watch BLUE MOVIES in seedy cinemas and buy pornographic magazines from the TOP SHELF of newsagents. The name alludes to the dirty macintosh they supposedly wear to achieve anonymity. The expression dates from the 1970s.

> Much has been made of the sex and nudity in the film [*Eyes Wide Shut*], but the dirty raincoat brigade will be disappointed if they hope for rampant coupling all the way through.
>
> *The Times* (1 September 1999)

**Dirty money.** Money acquired by dishonest or disreputable means. Such money can be decriminalized by 'laundering' it through a legitimate business such as a bank.

**Dirty old man.** A lecherous one, not necessarily old.

**Dirty protest.** A form of protest by mainly Republican paramilitary prisoners in Northern Ireland in the 1970s. They refused to wash and fouled their cells with the aim of gaining political, as opposed to criminal, status. *See also* BLANKET PROTEST; MAZE.

**Dirty raincoat brigade.** *See* DIRTY MAC BRIGADE.

**Dirty realism.** A term and concept introduced in 1987 by Bill Buford, editor of *Granta*, in an issue devoted to contemporary US fiction. 'Dirty realist' fiction typically includes laconic dialogue, seedy settings, explicit descriptions of violence and sordid sex, and characters who are downbeat and drearily hopeless. Leading writers of the genre are Raymond Carver (1938–88), Richard Ford (b.1944) and Tobias Wolff (b.1945).

**Dirty tricks.** A term dating from the 1940s for undercover or clandestine operations and deceitful schemes in politics and espionage. 'Dirty' here means 'unethical'. The term originally applied to covert intelligence operations carried out by the CIA, whose planning directorate was nicknamed the 'Department of Dirty Tricks'. The expression was subsequently extended to underhand activities aimed at undermining political opponents or commercial rivals.

**Dirty War.** *See* DISAPPEARED.

**Dirty weekend.** A weekend spent with someone other than one's spouse or with one's spouse but without one's children. 'Dirty' expresses a Victorian or puritanical attitude to sex. The phrase dates from the 1930s.

**Dirty work.** Although literally meaning an unpleasant or distasteful physical task, in which one is covered in dirt, the phrase more usually refers to an underhand or dishonourable action, in which the dirt is metaphorical. A fuller form is 'dirty work at the crossroads', perhaps alluding to the crossroads as a place where suicides were buried. The expression dates from the early years of the 20th century.

**Disappeared, The.** (Spanish *los desaparecidos*.) Those persons who disappeared in Argentina during the so-called 'Dirty War' under the military government of 1976–1983. The Dirty War was aimed at suspected left-wing guerrillas, the MONTONEROS, but widened to target anybody regarded as an enemy of the state. The disappeared, numbering between 6000 and 15,000 people, are assumed to have been murdered by state-sponsored DEATH SQUADS. 'The disappeared' is also used to refer to those people murdered by the IRA during the Northern Ireland TROUBLES who were buried in unknown places.

**Disaster movie.** A film in which a group of people are involved in a natural or 'manmade' disaster of some kind. Classic examples are *The Poseidon Adventure* (1972), with passengers trapped inside a capsized luxury liner, *Airport 1975* (1974), in which a stewardess has to manoeuvre a jumbo jet to safety after it collides with another plane, *Earthquake* (1974), set in Los Angeles, and *The Towering Inferno* (1974), in which the world's tallest building is destroyed by fire on the night of its inauguration. *See also* HORROR MOVIE.

**Disco Di.** A nickname given to Princess Diana (PRINCESS OF HEARTS, a.k.a. the PEOPLE'S PRINCESS), who was a prominent fan of the prancing pop duo called Wham!, comprising Andrew Ridgeley and George Michael.

**Discovery.** The bright green and crimson apple of this name is so called because of a chance discovery by an amateur grower. It was first marketed commercially in the 1970s.

**Discworld.** The setting of the comic fantasies by the novelist Terry Pratchett (b.1948), a flat planet supported by four elephants riding through space on a giant tortoise. There is no central character in the stories, although Death appears in most and is prominent in several. The first book in the sequence, *The Colour of Magic* (1983), is essentially a parody of H.P. Lovecraft (1890–1937) and other fantasy writers, but the series went on to create a world of its own, each of the volumes being self-contained. Much of the enjoyment of the stories derives from the strange names of characters and places, such as the wizard Igneous Cutwell, the kingdom of Djelibeybi, the Unseen University in Ankh-Morpork, Discworld's most ancient city, and Lady Sybil Deirdre Olgivanna Ramkin, the latter's richest resident, married to Commander Samuel Vimes.

**Disgusted, Tunbridge Wells.** A byname for a disgruntled resident of the named Kent town, a respectable community famed as a bastion of morality and decency. The name is supposedly used by those penning anonymous letters of complaint to the press, especially on any matter relating to falling standards. It is first recorded in 1978 (as the title of a BBC Radio programme), although according to a local journalist it was coined in the 1950s when, faced with a shortage of readers' letters, the editor of the *Tunbridge Wells Advertiser* got one of his reporters to make some up.

**Dish the dirt.** To reveal or spread malicious gossip. 'To dish' is to dish up or serve to an eager audience, while the 'dirt' is the damaging information. The phrase dates from the 1950s.

> A close friend of Sir Edward Heath is planning to dish the dirt on Baroness Thatcher.
>
> *The Times* (19 November 1999)

**Dishy.** Very attractive. The notion is that the person so described is 'tasty' or 'good enough to eat'. The term dates from the 1960s and can also be applied to things, such as a 'dishy car' or a 'dishy dress'.

> 'Mm, is *that* him?' said the girl, all velvet. 'He's dishy.'
>
> JOHN GARDNER: *The Liquidator*, ch. 3 (1964)

**Disneyland.** One of various THEME PARKS centring on the world created by the US animator and film producer Walt Disney (1901–66) and thus featuring MICKEY MOUSE and DONALD DUCK, among other characters, as well as replicas of the fairytale world of the cartoons themselves. The first such park of the name was opened in Anaheim, California, in 1955, with themes including Frontierland, tropical exploration, fairy tales, and space travel and the future. A second, larger complex, Walt Disney World (now Walt Disney World Resort), was opened near Orlando, Florida, in 1971. In 1983 a Japanese version, Tokyo Disneyland (now Tokyo Disney Resort), opened near Tokyo. Its themes replicated all those at Anaheim except Frontierland, which became Western-land, stocked with cowboys and Indians in retro fancy dress. In 1992 Disneyland Paris (now officially Disneyland Resort Paris, and commonly known as Euro Disney) opened its gates at Marne-la-Vallée, east of Paris, and in September 2005 Hong Kong Disneyland Resort joined the party.

> Some refer to it as a cultural Chernobyl. I think of it as a cultural Stalingrad.
>
> J.G. BALLARD: on Euro Disney, quoted in *Daily Telegraph* (2 July 1994).

It was the French theatre director Ariane Mnouchkine (b.1939) who described Euro Disney as 'a cultural Chernobyl'.

From the early 1960s onwards various US military institutions have been given the nickname (alluding to the original Disneyland's Californian location) of 'Disneyland East', suggesting a certain lack of contact with reality. They include the PENTAGON, the US Air Force Academy and the headquarters of the US Military Assistance Command in Vietnam.

The de Isney family gave its name to a field in Usselby, Lincolnshire, known in 1386 as *Disneyland*, some years before those in California, Florida and Paris (Walt was a descendant of a junior branch).

**Displaced persons.** A phrase applied to the millions of homeless and uprooted people in Europe and Asia whose misfortunes resulted from the havoc produced by the Second World War and subsequent events. They were colloquially referred to as DPs.

**Ditchers.** *See* HEDGERS AND DITCHERS.

**Divine Callas.** The American-born operatic soprano of Greek parentage Maria Callas (1923–77) was so known, the descriptive being traditional for a grand (or temperamental) opera singer. Her original surname was Kalageropoulos.

**Divino, Il.** The nickname of the Brazilian footballer Paolo Roberto Falcao (b.1953), one of the best players in the world in the early 1980s. *See also* BRAZILIAN FOOTBALLERS.

**Dixiecrats.** The nickname of a group of southern conservatives from 'Dixie' (the American South) who left the Democratic Party because of President GIVE-'EM-HELL HARRY Truman's policy of desegregation. In the 1948 US presidential election they put forward Strom Thurmond as a candidate, but he was overwhelmingly defeated by Truman.

**Dixie Dean.** The popular footballer William R. Dean (1907–80) was so nicknamed from a rhyme on 'sixty', the number of goals he scored for Everton in the 1927–8 season.

***Dixon of Dock Green.*** The longest-running police series on British television, shown on the BBC from 1955 to 1976. Its star was the kindly police constable George Dixon, played by Jack Warner, who had first appeared in the feature film *The Blue Lamp* (1950). The programme provided cosy, non-violent family entertainment: each episode opened with Dixon saluting the viewer with the words 'Evening, all' and closed with a homily from him to the effect that crime does not pay.

**Dizzy heights.** In the figurative sense, a position of worldly importance, as: 'He reached the dizzy heights of company director.' The usage is often ironic.

**DNA.** *See* DOUBLE HELIX.

**D notice.** An official notice sent to newspapers and the media generally forbidding them from publishing or broadcasting particular security information. D is the initial of the Defence, Press and Broadcasting Committee, the government body that sends out the notice. There have been suspicions that the security in question might be that of the government rather than that of the nation.

**Do a disappearing act.** To vanish suddenly, as: 'When the children saw the policeman looking they did a disappearing act.' The reference is to the familiar magician's trick of making people and objects disappear. The phrase dates from the early 20th century.

**Do a foreigner.** To work for one's own gain in one's employer's time or using their materials or facilities, or to do so without declaring one's earnings to the relevant authorities, such as the tax office. The expression originated in Second World War military slang and implies a betrayal of one's normal allegiance to one's employer and the state.

**Do a Melba.** To return (usually repeatedly) to one's career having previously retired. The expression is commonly used in the context of show business, where such serial retirements, often accompanied by ostentatious 'farewell' tours or performances, are far from infrequent. The practice was made infamous by the Australian soprano Dame Nellie Melba (1861–1931; real name Helen Mitchell – she based her stage name on 'Melbourne'), who found it impossible to keep away from the concert platform for long.

**Do a number on someone** or **something.** In US slang, to act with forcible harmful effect on someone or something. The usage originated in African-American English in the 1960s.

> It's enough to bring weak drills to a stop and will definitely do a number on your hand if you just try to hold it.
> www.cs.cmu.edu (2004)

**Do a runner.** To abscond from the police; to run away; to leave without paying. The expression spread from semi-criminal jargon in the 1970s.

**Do bears shit in the woods?** A sarcastic rhetorical question meaning 'Don't ask me stupid questions' or 'Obviously.' It goes back to the 1910s in the United States. The basic formula has various more or less scabrous variations, mainly based on the typical behaviour of animals, one of the more innocuous being 'Can a duck swim?' Religious sensitivities are encroached on in 'Is the pope a Catholic?'

**Do bird.** To serve a prison sentence. 'Bird' is short for 'birdlime', rhyming slang for 'time'. The phrase dates from the 1920s. 'Birdlime' is itself old slang for a thief, who has 'sticky fingers'.

**Dob someone in.** In colloquial Australian English, to inform on someone to the authorities. The expression dates from the 1950s. 'Dob' probably comes from a British dialect verb meaning 'to put or throw down'. *See also* COBBER-DOBBER.

**Dobson, Zuleika.** The young woman who wins the hearts of Oxford undergraduates in Max Beerbohm's novel ZULEIKA DOBSON (1911). Her beaux are so smitten that they all drown themselves in sorrow. She is said to have been based on the actress Constance Collier (1880–1955), who was briefly engaged to Beerbohm and who spent the summer of 1903 with him in Dieppe.

**Dockers' KC.** A press nickname for the Labour Minister Ernest Bevin (1881–1951) when he was national organizer of the dockers' union during the period 1910–21. 'KC' is 'King's Counsel'.

**Docklands.** London's dockland region has changed dramatically since the flourishing trade of the 18th and 19th centuries, when the British Empire was expanding and the Thames was full of cargo vessels of all types, with the enclosed docks handling hundreds of ships a year. The docks were originally in private hands but were taken over by the Port of London Authority in 1909. By the end of the 1960s the docks began to close, partly as a result of the demise of the empire but also because of competition from other ports, labour troubles and other adverse factors. In the mid-1970s it was proposed to redevelop the dockland site for commercial and residential use, and in 1981 the London Docklands Development Corporation was set up to oversee this. By 1990 areas such as the Surrey Commercial Docks and the Isle of Dogs were transformed, as had Canary Wharf, now a massive office development. The area is served by the Docklands Light Railway, which was opened in 1987 and is linked with the Underground system. The whole enterprise has not been without its financial fiascos, exacerbated by the recession of the early 1990s, and some developers were unable to sell their completed schemes.

**Doc Martens.** A type of footwear invented in 1945 by Klaus Maertens, a German doctor who needed a comfortable shoe after a skiing accident. He formed a rubber sole from a tyre and sealed it to an upper, so trapping a cushion of air. The boots were first produced in England under licence in 1960 by R. Griggs & Co. and were soon adopted by SKINHEADS, who saw their potential when 'putting the boot in'. PUNK rockers revived the fashion for 'Docs' in the 1970s, and the shoes subsequently became a youth-culture fashion staple and simultaneous anti-fashion statement.

**Dr Aziz.** *See* Dr AZIZ.

**Doctor Caligari.** *See* Doctor CALIGARI.

**Dr Death.** A media nickname for a murderer, especially a real or sham doctor who kills elderly people for financial or material gain. An example was the confidence trickster Sydney Noble, imprisoned in 1978 for drugging old ladies in order to ransack their homes. Another was the genuine family doctor Harold Shipman (1946–2004), Britain's worst SERIAL KILLER, convicted in 2000 of murdering 15 women patients and suspected of killing 100 during his 30-year career as a GP. The name owes its impact to its alliterative sound and oxymoronic sense. Doctors are expected to preserve life, not deprive their patients of it. The politician David Owen (b.1938), a Labour foreign minister and one of the founders of the Social Democrats (*see* LIBERAL DEMOCRATS), was known as Dr Death in *Private Eye*, because he was a medical doctor and for his dark looks. A character

called Dr Death, who has the power to reanimate the corpses of those he kills, was the central figure of the film *Dr Death: Seeker of Souls* (1973).

**Dr Dolittle.** *See* Dr DOLITTLE.

**Doctor Faustus.** *See* DOKTOR FAUSTUS.

**Dr Feelgood.** A nickname for a doctor who readily dispenses mood-enhancing drugs, such as amphetamines, for non-medicinal use. Hence also a term for a doctor who provides short-term palliatives rather than a more efficacious treatment or cure. The term was apparently first used, although not in the sense described, as a designation for himself by the US blues pianist Piano Red (real name William Perryman), who recorded 'Dr. Feelgood and the Interns' in 1962. The current sense is implicit, however, in the words of a song recorded soon after by the US soul singer Aretha Franklin and her husband and manager, Ted White, and this popularized the term.

> Don't send me no doctor
> Filling me up with all those pills
> Got a man named Dr Feelgood
> That man takes care of all my pains and my ills.
> ARETHA FRANKLIN and TED WHITE: 'Dr Feelgood' (1967)

**Dr J.** The nickname of the flamboyant and articulate US basketball player Julius Winfield Erving II (b.1950). A star player with the Philadelphia 76s from 1976, he acquired his nickname when playing for the University of Massachusetts early in his career.

**Dr Kildare.** *See* Dr KILDARE.

**Dr No.** A thriller (1958) by Ian Fleming (1908–64), set largely on an island in the Caribbean, where he had a second home, and featuring the agent James BOND. Bond's adversary is known as Dr No. The book is notable because Fleming, having killed off Bond at the end of FROM RUSSIA WITH LOVE, (1957), by having him ingeniously hacked with a poisoned toe-cap, had to resurrect him, as Conan Doyle did with Sherlock Holmes. The film of *Dr No* (1962), produced by Harry Saltzman and Albert R. Broccoli, was the first of a long series and marked the first appearance as Bond of Sean Connery.

**Doctor Pignose.** A nickname applied to the right-wing Conservative politician Dr Liam Fox (b.1961), an unsuccessful candidate for the party leadership in 2005. He was so dubbed by the *Guardian* cartoonist Steve Bell, in reference to his prominent nostrils.

**Doctors and nurses.** A game played by very young children, involving make-believe treatment such as bandaging or massaging on the one hand or rudimentary sexual investigation on the other.

**Dr Seuss.** *See* Dr SEUSS.

**Dr Spock.** *See* Dr SPOCK.

**Dr Strabismus (Whom God Preserve) of Utrecht.** A creation of BEACHCOMBER (the British humorist J.B. Morton). The good doctor was forever coming up with ingenious inventions:

> The ingenuity of Christmas gifts has inspired Dr Strabismus (Whom God Preserve) of Utrecht. He has invented the perfect gift for anyone who knows what he doesn't want. It is described in an advertisement as an oblong wooden peg which props up a built-in sieve. The angle of the sieve makes it possible to sift things sideways, so that what falls through goes into a bucket clamped vertically to the wall.

**Dr Strangelove.** A film (1963) based on the novel *Red Alert* by Peter George about the threat of global nuclear destruction. Titled in full *Dr Strangelove: or, How I Learned to Stop Worrying and Love the Bomb*, it was directed by Stanley Kubrick and starred Peter Sellers in three roles: Group Captain Lionel Mandrake (an upper-class British liaison officer), the ineffectual but decent President Merkin Muffley (loosely based on Adlai Stevenson) and the mad scientist Dr Strangelove himself (based on an amalgam of the 'Father of the H-bomb' Edward Teller, the rocket scientist Werner von Braun and Henry Kissinger). The character of General 'Buck' Turgidson (played by George C. Scott) is based on General Curtis 'Bombs Away' LeMay (*see* BOMB THEM BACK INTO THE STONE AGE). Such was the success of the film that subsequently any militaristic leader or defender of nuclear weapons was liable to dismissed as a 'Strangelove'. *See also* COLD WAR WARRIOR.

**Dr Syn.** A fictional 18th-century smuggler/priest, the creation in 1915 of Russell Thorndike. After a career as a pirate under his real name, Captain Clegg, he returns to his native village of Dymchurch, in the Romney Marshes, to live a simple life as a vicar under the appropriate but unsettling pseudonym Dr Christopher Syn. However, he soon reverts to type, assuming the guise of 'the Scarecrow' as leader of the Romney Marsh smugglers. His most famous film incarnation was by George Arliss in 1937.

**Doctor Who.** The Time Lord hero of the eponymous BBC children's television SCIENCE FICTION series, which began in 1963. Hailing from the planet Gallifrey, he travels through time and space in the TARDIS and is invariably accompanied by one or more female assistants from earth. He combats the forces of intergalactic evil, chief among them being the deadly DALEKS, the Cybermen (robots with human brains and no emotions), and other ugly aliens and mysterious forces. The first actor to take the role of the Doctor was William Hartnell, who portrayed him as a testy elderly academic. One of the most memorable depictions was by Tom Baker, whose Doctor was a tousle-headed eccentric sporting a long scarf. The series was originally intended as a children's educational programme.

The Doctor's ability to regenerate his face and body when it is mortally threatened helpfully works the periodic cast changes into the fiction. In 2005 *Doctor Who* returned to the small screen in touchier, feelier, wittier and much glossier form after an absence of 16 years. Christopher Eccleston played the Doctor and Billy Piper his feistier-than-the-norm female friend; the title role was subsequently taken by David Tennant, who reintroduced some of Baker's range of emotion and oddness. The scripts of the revived *Doctor Who*, by Russell T. Davies and others, have generally been admired.

**Doctor Zhivago.** A historical film epic (1965), lasting over 190 minutes, based on a novel of the same title (1957) by the Russian writer Boris Pasternak (1890–1960). Set against the background of the Russian Revolution and the ensuing civil war, it was filmed with Omar Sharif as the poet and physician Zhivago, whose love for the beautiful Lara (Julie Christie) causes pain for all involved. Many critics accused the film, directed by David Lean, of being too pretentious for its own good and saw MGM's insistence that the word 'Dr' be spelled out in full in the title as symptomatic of this weakness. The book brought Pasternak himself little happiness. Following his award of the NOBEL PRIZE for Literature, he was pilloried by literary rivals, who accused him of plagiarizing other works, and his companion Olga Ivinskaya, on whom Lara was based, was thrown into prison by the Soviets. The first publication of the novel in the Soviet Union did not take place until 1987. *See also* FIRST LINES OF NOVELS.

**Dodgems.** Bumper cars at a funfair. The name dates from the 1920s and originated in the United States as the proprietary term 'Dodg'em', so called because the aim is to avoid the other cars ('dodge 'em') while simultaneously trying to bump them.

**Dodge the column.** To shirk one's duty; to avoid work. The original reference was to the avoidance of military service in the First World War.

**Dodgy Dossier, The.** A derisive nickname that quickly attached itself to 'Iraq: Its Infrastructure of Concealment, Deception and Intimidation', a compendium of information about the WEAPONS OF MASS DESTRUCTION supposedly possessed by Iraq and the threat they presented to the civilized world, issued to the press by Alastair Campbell on behalf of the British government on 3 February 2003, once it was discovered that it was an ill-digested farrago of facts, non-facts and speculation, much of it simply lifted from uncredited sources (most notably a postgraduate thesis by a student at California State University). The intention had been to convince public opinion that it was right, just and necessary to invade Iraq, but once the dossier's true character had been revealed and its nickname had become a media cliché, the opposite effect was then achieved. The term went on to have a life of its own.

> He [Harold Macmillan] appended a dossier of what purported to be the opinions of Cabinet ministers, MPs, peers and party workers...; and, in the parlance of a later political generation, a distinctly dodgy dossier it was.
>
> GEOFFREY WHEATCROFT: *The Strange Death of Tory England* (2005)

*See also* SEPTEMBER DOSSIER.

**Does my bum look big in this?** A stereotypical question of the anxious female FASHION VICTIM. It was used as the title of a book (1997), subtitled 'The Diary of an Insecure Woman', by the comic writer and performer Arabella Weir, who frequently invoked the line while playing a character in the 1990s BBC television sketch series *The* FAST SHOW.

**Dog and pony show.** An elaborate display or presentation, as for a political party's new manifesto. The allusion is to a travelling variety show in which the performers are the named animals. The expression dates from the 1950s.

***Dog Day Afternoon.*** A film (1975) written by Frank Pierson and directed by Sidney Lumet about a bisexual man (played by Al Pacino) who stages a bank robbery in order to fund a sex-change operation for his transsexual lover (played by Chris Sarandon). The plot was based on an article about a real incident. The 'dog days' have been identified since Roman times as the hottest days of the summer, between early July and mid-August, when the dog star Sirius is reputed to add its heat to that of the sun.

**Dogger Bank.** The Battle of the Dogger Bank, during the First World War, was fought in the North Sea on 24 January 1915 when a raiding force of German battle cruisers was intercepted and shelled by a British squadron under the command of Admiral Beatty. The action convinced the Germans that they had been right to adopt a cautious strategy.

An earlier 'battle' – known as the Dogger Bank Incident – had taken place in 1904 when the Russian Baltic fleet, en route to the Far East to take on the Japanese, mistook some Hull trawlers for Japanese gunboats and opened fire. One trawler was sunk.

**Dogging.** Al fresco sexual exhibitionism, often conducted in cars in secluded rural locations. Both those who participate (in couples, threesomes or more varied combinations) and those who witness the act are said to be dogging. Such liaisons are often arranged by prior agreement via the internet or text messaging. Dogging became something of a craze in Britain in the early years of the 21st century. Scholars are divided as to what W.E. 'bloody but unbowed' Henley had in mind when he wrote:

> Madam Life's a piece in bloom
> Death goes dogging everywhere …
> 'To W.R.' (1877)

However, these lines do give a clue as to the etymology of the word, which originally denoted 'stalking' or 'pursuing', as in dogging someone's footsteps, and in the 1970s was applied to the practice of sneaking up on couples in remote places to secretly watch them having sex. *See also* ROASTING.

**Doggy bag.** A bag provided by some restaurants for customers to put uneaten food in, ostensibly to take home for their pet dog. The phrase and practice date from the 1960s.

**Dog is for life, not just for Christmas, A.** The slogan of the Dogs Trust (founded in 1891 as the National Canine Defence League), seen widely on stickers in the back windows of cars. The slogan was first introduced in 1978 to make people aware that a new puppy should not be regarded as some kind of 'living toy', to be discarded when no longer wanted.

**Dogsbody.** A person who does all the menial jobs that no one else wants to do, typically a young person or trainee employee. The term dates from the 1920s and presumably alludes to the simple tasks such as fetching and carrying that a dog can perform.

> I worked as a receptionist, general dogsbody and teamaker … I was 18 at the time and in charge of the phones, photocopiers, plants, fridge, dishwasher, couriers and fruit bowl.
> *The Times* (10 January 2000)

**Dog's bollocks, The.** The very best or most outstanding. The British slang expression emerged in the 1980s and was initially associated particularly with the humorous magazine *Viz*. Its creation may have been inspired partly by the notion of conspicuousness, but doubtless there is also a connection with such longstanding models as the CAT'S WHISKERS.

**Dog's dinner** or **breakfast.** A mess; a confused mixture. A dog's meal is often a mishmash of scraps. The expression dates from the 1930s. *See also* DRESSED UP LIKE A DOG'S DINNER.

**Dogs of War, The.** A thriller (1974) by Frederick Forsyth (b.1938). The theme is the attempt by a band of mercenaries to overthrow an African dictator. The title comes from Shakespeare: 'Cry *Havoc*, and let slip the dogs of war' (*Julius Caesar* III.i). A film version (1980), directed by John Irvin, lacks the tension of the original.

**Dog whistle.** A late 20th-century term for an approach to political campaigning in which potentially voter-attractive but sensitive topics are not mentioned directly but are subtly or indirectly alluded to in a way that only the target audience will notice. It originated in Australian politics around 1997 and was probably inspired by the use by Australian sheep-farmers of a high-pitched dog whistle, audible to dogs but not to people, to control their sheep dogs. The tactic supposedly won the Australian conservative leader John Howard much electoral success, and in 2005 it was brought to Britain by the Australian political strategist Lynton Crosby and used in the general election by the Conservative Party, led by Howard's British namesake Michael. On that occasion, however, the dogs failed to come to heel.

> Dog-whistle politics explains why the Conservative leader, Michael Howard, has been making such a big thing out of illegal gypsy and traveller encampments this week and why the Tories are determined to keep up the attack on the government's immigration policies.
> *The Economist* (23 March 2005)

**Doing a Ratner.** A phrase used to describe any own-goal in business. British entrepreneur Gerald Ratner (b.1949) had built his chain of jewellery shops into a business with a turnover of £1.2 billion. It all unravelled when he addressed the Institute of Directors in the Albert Hall, London, on 23 April 1991. In his speech he described a sherry decanter sold by his chain as 'total crap'. Once in his hole, he went on digging:

> We even sell a pair of earrings for under £1, which is cheaper than a prawn sandwich from Marks & Spencers. But I have to say the earrings probably won't last as long.

The value of the company plunged, his shareholders were mortified and Ratner was slung out on his ear.

**Do it.** In euphemistic usage, to engage in sexual intercourse.

*See also* 'IT' GIRL.

> Everybody's Doin' It Now.
> IRVING BERLIN: (song title) (1911)

In The BEATLES' 1968 song 'Why Don't We Do It in the Road?' (written by Paul McCartney) the reference in the title is not made explicit, but is widely assumed to be sexual intercourse. In the late 1970s a craze developed for car bumper and windscreen stickers bearing such witty legends as 'Windsurfers do it standing up.'

**Do-it-yourself.** A post-1945 phrase applied primarily to the efforts of the amateur house repairer, home improver and the like, but also more widely applied to many forms of self-help. A do-it-yourself (DIY) shop is one that caters for the needs of people who like making and repairing things themselves rather than having someone else do it for them.

**Doktor Faustus.** A novel (1947) by the German Nobel laureate Thomas Mann (1875–1955). The Faust of this complex and densely wrought work, which includes passages from the original 1587 *Faustbuch*, is Adrian Leverkühn, a modern composer who rejects tonality, expressiveness and the struggle of the artist to create. Instead he embraces an abstract, emotion-free system of composition – in fact based on the 12-note system devised by Arnold Schoenberg. At one point Leverkühn writes:

> Take Beethoven's notebooks. There is no thematic conception there as God gave it. He remoulds it and adds 'Meilleur' [better]. Scant confidence in God's prompting, scant respect for it is expressed in that 'Meilleur' – itself not very enthusiastic either. A genuine inspiration, immediate, absolute, unquestioned, ravishing, where there is no choice, no tinkering, no possible improvement; where all is as a sacred mandate, a visitation received by the possessed one with faltering and stumbling step, with shudders of awe from head to foot, with tears of joy blinding his eyes: no, that is not possible with God, who leaves the understanding too much to do. It comes but from the divel [*sic*], the true master and giver of such rapture.

Leverkühn's story parallels that of Germany, which gave up its soul and the whole of the Western humanist tradition in favour of unquestioning acceptance of the nihilistic 'rapture' offered by the Nazis, only to pay the price of destruction in the Second World War. The price that Leverkühn himself pays is isolation and, ultimately, madness and death.

**Dolby.** The tradename of an electronic noise-reduction system used in tape recording to reduce hiss. It accomplishes this by compressing the sound range during recording and decoding the signal by expansion during playback at a level greater than the level of the hiss. It was developed in the 1970s by the US engineer Ray A. Dolby (b.1933) of the Ampex Corporation, and found a ready application in the provision of stereophonic sound for cinemas and television sets.

**Dolce Vita, La.** A film (1960) co-written and directed by Federico Fellini (1920–93) about the meaninglessness of an Italian gossip writer's life among the rich, bored young of Rome. The title, meaning 'the soft life', is an ironical reference to the apparent ease and comfort of life among the jet-set. *See also* PAPARAZZI.

**Dolittle, Dr.** The genial and eccentric doctor who is the central character in the stories by Hugh Lofting (1886–1947). He has the special gift of speaking the language of most animals and eventually gives up his human practice to become an 'animal doctor'. He lives in Puddleby on the Marsh, but his adventures take him all over the world and even as far as the moon. His companions include Polynesia the Parrot, Chee Chee the Monkey and Gub Gub the Pig. The first book in the series is *The Story of Doctor Dolittle* (1920) and the middle volumes of the series are generally regarded as the best. Lofting illustrated the stories himself. The character's name may have come from Eliza DOOLITTLE, the heroine of George Bernard Shaw's PYGMALION.

In the 1967 film version Dr Dolittle is played by Rex Harrison, while in the 1998 version – which bears very little resemblance to the original indeed – Eddie Murphy takes the title role.

**Dollar Bill.** A nickname given to Bill Clinton (the COMEBACK KID), from the large sums he earned from giving lectures after he had finished being president.

**Dollar diplomacy.** A term applied to governmental support and furtherance of commercial interests abroad for both political and economic ends. The phrase, popular with critics of US policy, stems from the time of the Taft administration (1909–13), which fostered such policies in the Far East and Latin America. Their intention was to control as well as to promote enterprise abroad by substituting dollars for bullets and lending 'all proper support to every legitimate and beneficial American enterprise abroad'.

**Dolly.** The world's first cloned sheep, born on 5 July 1996 at the Roslin Institute near Edinburgh. She was grown from an embryo created from an egg cell whose nucleus had been replaced by the nucleus of a cell from an adult Finn-Dorset ewe, and was named after the full-figured US country singer Dolly Parton (b.1946) because the cell was taken from the sheep's udder. The scientific breakthrough raised the real possibility of the cloning of human beings. Dolly died in 2003. She was subsequently stuffed and mounted, and put on display in the Royal Museum, Edinburgh.

**Dolly-bird.** An attractive and stylish young woman, considered only with regard to her appearance. She was an essential ingredient of the SWINGING SIXTIES and was typically a secretary or shop assistant in her late teens or early 20s. The usage is thus now chiefly historical.

**Dolly mixture.** A mixture of small sweets of various shapes and colours, such as a doll might eat.

**Domain.** In computing, the sequence of words, abbreviations and the like that identifies a specific computer or network on the INTERNET and that serves as its address. A domain name appears in the form 'computer.domain', and common organizational domains are 'com' (commercial organization), 'edu' (educational organization), 'gov' (governmental organization), 'int' (international organization), 'net' (network organization) and 'org' (non-profit organization). For countries other than the United States country domains may be combined with organization domains, e.g. 'co.uk' (UK commercial organization), 'edu.ca' (Canadian educational organization). The tiny Pacific-island nation of Tuvalu has reputedly earned large sums of money for allowing non-Tuvalu media companies and the like to 'borrow' its domain name, 'tv'. Domain names have been the object of fanciful and mostly illegal manipulation by CYBERSQUATTERS.

**Do me** or **us a favour!** You must be joking! Do you think I would do that? A phrase denying the implications of a situation, as: 'So will you be living abroad?' 'No way! Do us a favour!'

**Dome Secretary.** *See* MANDY.

**Domino effect.** A phrase first coined in the early 1950s by the American political commentator Joseph Alsop to suggest that if one country fell to communism, its neighbours would fall in turn, like a row of upended dominoes. The theory was picked up by President Eisenhower, who in 1954 applied it to the possibility of communist victory over the French colonial power in Vietnam. This idea was echoed by Graham Greene in his novel *The Quiet American* (1955), set during the war of independence in Indochina:

'If Indo-China goes ...'

'I know the record. Siam goes. Malaya goes. Indonesia goes. What does "go" mean? If I believed in your God and another life, I'd bet my future harp against your golden crown that in five hundred years there may be no New York or London, but they'll be growing paddy in these fields, they'll be carrying their produce to market on long poles wearing their pointed hats. ...'

In the 1960s US strategists used the theory to justify armed intervention in the VIETNAM War. They were to some extent justified, as the communist victory in Vietnam in 1975 was followed by victories in Laos and Cambodia. But the domino effect spread no further than these other former parts of French Indochina.

The collapse of the communist regimes in eastern Europe one after the other in 1989 has been described as a 'reverse domino effect'.

**Don, The.** The Australian batsman Sir Donald Bradman (1908–2001), whose prodigious feats of run-making in the 1930s make him the greatest batsman who ever lived. Bradman was also known as the 'Little Master' on account of his diminutive size.

**Donald Duck.** The ill-tempered cartoon duck in a sailor suit, second in fame only to MICKEY MOUSE, was created by the Walt Disney studios in 1934, his first appearance being in the *Silly Symphony* cartoon *The Wise Little Hen*. His popularity was due in no small measure to his distinctive quacking voice, the creation of Clarence Nash.

**Don Camillo.** *See* Don CAMILLO.

**Done and dusted.** Completed, with no more left to do, as: 'Now the big project's all done and dusted I can take the holiday I'm owed!' The literal sense could relate either to a clearing and cleaning procedure or to a culinary one, where a cake, for example, has been dusted with icing sugar. The former is the more likely, but the duality is possible due to the contrary meanings of 'to dust': on the one hand to remove dust, on the other to add it. An occasional variation on the theme is 'home and hosed'.

**Donkey jacket.** A thick jacket, often dark blue in colour, worn by manual workers as a protection against the weather. The name alludes to the donkey as a working animal. The jacket was first adopted in the 1920s and was later turned into a general fashion garment.

**Donkey vote, The.** In Australian English, the practice of voting, in a ballot conducted on the preferential system, by simply listing one's preferences in the order (alphabetical or otherwise) in which they occur on the ballot paper. The term, picking up on the supposed stupidity of the donkey, is first recorded in 1962.

**Donmar Warehouse.** The London theatre of this name, known for its experimental productions, opened in 1960 in a warehouse for ripening bananas and was at first known simply as the Warehouse. 'Donmar' was then added from the names of its original purchasers, Donald Albery (1914–88) and his friend Margot Fonteyn (1919–91), the ballet

dancer. Albery was the son of Bronson Albery (1881–1971), who gave his name to the Albery Theatre, and step-grandson of Charles Wyndham (1837–1919), after whom Wyndham's Theatre is named.

**Don't ask.** Do not question me about it. The question may be merely potential rather than actual, and the unspoken answer left to the imagination, as: 'We found it was a nudist beach. Don't ask.'

**Don't ask, don't tell.** A pithy summary of the US military policy on homosexuality adopted in 1994, whereby personnel are not asked about their sexual orientation, and gays and lesbians are allowed to serve providing they do not openly reveal their sexuality. The usage has spread subsequently to other areas.

**Don't ask me.** A statement disclaiming knowledge or responsibility, as: 'I wonder how that happened?' 'Don't ask me. I wasn't there.'

**Don't call us, we'll call you.** A traditional expression of dismissal, arising from the formula of rejection used by producers or directors when auditioning actors. They naturally never do call.

**Don't die of ignorance.** The slogan of the 1987 UK government Aids-awareness campaign, and the title of a pamphlet delivered to every household in the country. The slogan was perhaps somewhat ironic in the light of the reported reaction of the health secretary, Norman Fowler, when told the previous year by his civil servants about the number of people who practise oral sex. 'Oh cwikey!' was apparently all he could manage. In the same year Fowler is said to have asked Romola Christopherson, Head of Information at the Department of Health, 'Womola, what's a vibwator? What do people use it for?' Despite these difficulties, the campaign is generally regarded as having been a success. In France a similar slogan was used: 'Silence = Mort [death]'.

**Don't drink and drive.** The slogan of repeated UK government campaigns to persuade people not to drive after having drunk alcohol. The original slogan, 'Don't ask a man to drink and drive', dates from 1964 (presumably in those days it was quite acceptable for women to drive while completely sozzled). Statutory breathalyser tests were introduced in October 1967.

**Don't frighten the horses.** *See* FRIGHTEN THE HORSES.

**Don't get mad, get even.** The principle that revenge is a better response to a slight than impotent rage ('mad' here has its originally US sense 'angry'). The adage was a favourite of the US businessman and diplomat Joseph

Kennedy (1888–1969), and came to be closely associated with the Kennedy clan, particularly JFK. It is often used with reference to affairs of the heart, counselling the jilted or abandoned partner to exact an exquisite vengeance (among notable claimed examples are the woman who soaked off and swapped around all the labels in her unfaithful husband's wine cellar, and the woman who secreted prawns inside the curtain rail in her former boyfriend's bedroom). On her divorce, Ivana Trump is said to have declared 'Don't get mad, get everything!'

**Don't give me that.** That's no excuse. You can't fool me. A phrase from the 1920s.

**Don't give up the day job.** Don't take up another career at which you might not succeed. The 'day job' is one's regular NINE-TO-FIVE JOB. The catchphrase is often humorously directed at someone who thinks they can make their fortune by pursuing a hobby or alternative interest, particularly one that might put them in the limelight, such as acting or rock music.

**Don't go there.** *See* GO THERE.

**Don't hold your breath.** Don't expect the thing in question to happen immediately. The implication is that it may not happen at all. The phrase is of US origin and dates from the 1970s.

**Don't let the bastards grind you down.** An injunction to persevere as cheerfully as possible despite the obstacles and discouragements placed in one's way by those in authority ('THEY'). It can be a reaction to a particular situation, or a more general encouragement to lead a 'keep smiling' kind of life. The US General Joseph 'Vinegar Joe' Stillwell (1883–1946) adopted it as his motto. A cod-Latin version is offered: ILLEGITIMI NON CARBORUNDUM.

> I can't get enough of this glorious, beautiful world and its colourful people and animals. I love Britain – it's just a bit too tame for me. Follow your dreams, and don't let the bastards grind you down! Love, Brian [Blessed].
> www.guardian.co.uk (22 August 2001)

**Don't make me laugh.** Don't be stupid. A stock ironic phrase from the 1920s.

**Dontopedology.** *See* FOOT-IN-MOUTH DISEASE.

**Don't strain yourself.** A stock ironic caution addressed to someone who is conspicuously failing to pull their weight.

**Doobrie.** Anything for which one cannot remember the name. The word originated in army slang in the 1950s, and was lifted from the crowd of similar synonyms ('doodah',

'dohickey', etc.) by its frequent use in the 1970s and '80s by the DJ and television performer Kenny Everett.

**Doodlebug.** A nickname in the Second World War for the V-1 flying bomb. The word itself goes back to the 19th century and combines *doodle*, 'ninny', with *bug*. *See also* BUZZ BOMB.

**Doolally.** An army expression of the early 20th century for an unbalanced state of mind or mental derangement. British time-expired soldiers in India were formerly sent to a camp at Deolali, near Bombay, to await passage home. There were often long, frustrating delays, when boredom and the climate may have led to some odd behaviour, which caused some of them to become 'doolally'. The full phrase was 'doolally tap', the latter word being Urdu *dap*, 'fever'.

**Doolittle, Eliza.** The Cockney heroine of G.B. Shaw's play PYGMALION (1914). She is a simple FLOWER GIRL until she is taken in hand by Professor Henry Higgins, who gives her an intensive course in elocution and introduces her to high society. The story was adapted as the successful Lerner and Loewe stage musical MY FAIR LADY (1945), and this was in turn made into a film of the same title (1964) with Audrey Hepburn in the leading role.

> *Higgins*: Eliza: you are to live here for the next six months, learning how to speak beautifully, like a lady in a florist's shop. If youre good and do whatever youre told, you shall sleep in a proper bedroom, and have lots to eat, and money to buy chocolates and take rides in taxis. If youre naughty and idle you will sleep in the back kitchen among the black beetles, and be walloped by Mrs Pearce with a broomstick.
> GEORGE BERNARD SHAW: *Pygmalion*, II (1914)

**Doom and gloom** or **gloom and doom.** Despondency and despair; a state of depression regarding the future. The expression and its variant are of US origin and arose in or soon after the Second World War. Both were given prominence by their occurrence in E.Y. 'Yip' Harburg's popular stage musical FINIAN'S RAINBOW (1947).

**Doomsday Machine.** A hypothetical machine designed to trigger automatic nuclear destruction under certain conditions without the possibility of human intervention to stop it. The term dates from the 1960s, after the concept of such a machine was first formulated by Herman Kahn in *On Thermonuclear War* (1960).

**Do one.** To run away, especially in order to evade capture; to scarper. The slang expression originated (possibly as an abbreviation of DO A RUNNER) in Liverpool and surrounding areas of Lancashire, and was probably introduced to a wider British public by the Channel 4 soap *Brookside*. It is first recorded in 1990.

We leg it back, grab the swag and do one.

    *Big Issue* (20 March 2000)

**Do one's best.** To do all one can. The call of a WOLF CUB leader to the assembled pack was 'Dyb, dyb, dyb, dyb!' standing for 'Do your best'. The chanted reply was 'We'll dob, dob, dob, dob!' ('Do our best').

**Do one's bit.** To make a useful contribution to an effort or cause. The expression first came to the fore in the First World War when it specifically related to serving in the armed forces. G.B. Shaw used the phrase in this sense in the title of his play *Augustus Does His Bit* (1919), as at a different level did Richmal Crompton in *William Does His Bit?* (1940) (*see* WILLIAM). It then broadened to apply to any public-spirited action. In 1999 the government embarked on a publicity campaign called 'Are You Doing Your Bit?' to encourage simple methods of environmental management.

**Doonesbury.** The NERD college graduate hero of a satirical comic strip by the US artist Garry Trudeau. He first appeared in the *Yale Daily News* in 1968 but two years later went national. His full name is Mike Doonesbury, his surname being a combination of 'Doone', Yale slang for an amiable fool, and 'Pillsbury', Trudeau's New Haven roommate. Other characters include the star American football player B.D. (named after the real Yale quarterback Brian Dowling) and the would-be radical Megaphone Mark. It was the first comic strip to win a PULITZER PRIZE (1975).

    'Say, B.D., as your new *roommate*, I'm most naturally very curious to learn what your interests are.' 'I play football.' '*Oh, wow! Really*? Football! Just think of that! *Wow! Boy*, what a pair we're going to make! A football player and a *lover boy*! I could get you girls, and you could get me football tickets. It certainly has *amazing advantages*.'

    GARRY TRUDEAU: *Doonesbury* (extract) (26–28 October 1970)

**Do one's head** or **nut in.** To harass; to aggravate; to bemuse or confuse. The sense is that one's mental processes become disturbed or deranged. The expression dates from the 1970s and is of US student origin. *See also* DO ONE'S NUT.

    The pop star Shaun Ryder was so high on drugs that he could not be bothered with a contract's small print. 'It did his nut in,' the Court of Appeal was told.

    *The Times* (16 December 1999)

**Do one's homework.** To make adequate preparation for the task facing one, especially to acquaint oneself thoroughly with the relevant material for a discussion, debate or speech, as a school pupil is expected to do work at home for the following day or later in the week. The expression dates from the 1930s.

**Do one's lolly.** In Australian slang, the equivalent of DO ONE'S NUT ('lolly', like 'nut', means 'head'). The expression dates from the early 1950s.

**Do one's nut.** To lose one's temper; to fly into a rage; to become worked up. The 'nut' is the head. The expression dates from the early 20th century.

**Do one's nut in.** *See* DO ONE'S HEAD IN.

**Doosra.** (Hindi, 'second', 'other'.) A mystery delivery introduced by spin bowlers from the Indian subcontinent towards the end of the 20th century. Dubbed 'the off-spinner's GOOGLY', it is bowled with a normal finger-spinner's action but with the hand reversed, so that the ball turns the opposite way from expected on pitching. It is particularly associated with the Sri Lankan off-spinner Muttiah Muralitharan (b.1972).

**Dora.** The popular name of the Defence of the Realm Acts (DORA), which imposed many temporary restrictions. The first of the series was passed in 1914 and the legislation was extended to the supply and sale of liquor in 1921. The name passed into common speech after being used in the law courts by Mr Justice Scrutton (1856–1934). In newspaper cartoons Dora was often portrayed as a long-nosed elderly female, the personification of restriction.

**Doris Karloff.** *See* Doris KARLOFF.

**Dormitory town.** A town on the outskirts of a large city or conurbation that serves as (and may have been built or developed specifically as) a place of residence for those who work in the city. The term (and its first cousin 'dormitory suburb') date from the period after the First World War when such agglomerations of sleeping quarters were springing up rapidly around London and other cities, to house the commuters who were travelling to and fro on the fast expanding railways.

**Dorothy bag.** A woman's handbag gathered at the top by a drawstring and slung by loops from the wrist. Such bags came into vogue in the early years of the 20th century. The identity of the Dorothy in question, if she ever existed, is unknown.

**Dorothy Dix.** Originally, in Australian political jargon, a planted parliamentary question, a fairly juicy lob served up by a compliant backbencher for the minister to smash safely away. The inspiration for the term came from 'Dorothy Dix', the pen-name of the US journalist E.M. Gilmer (1870–1951), who wrote a popular question-and-answer column.

    The political usage dates from the early 1960s, but in the 1970s Dix's name, often shortened to simply 'Dorothy', was redeployed as Australian rhyming slang for 'six' (of the sort hit over the boundary line in cricket).

> That is a Dorothy – and a big one at that.
> RICHIE BENAUD: *One-Day Cricket*, Channel 4 (2001)

**Do's and don'ts.** Recommendations what to do and what not to do. The phrase dates from the early 20th century. A more recent equivalent is 'do's and taboos', especially with reference to international etiquette, business procedures and the like.

**Do someone in.** To injure or kill them.

***Dot and the Kangaroo.*** An Australian fantasy novel, much influenced by Lewis Carroll, by Ethel C. Pedley (*c*.1860–98). Although it was published in Britain in 1899, it was not published in Australia until 1906. It tells the tale of a little girl, Dot, who is befriended by the Kangaroo when she becomes lost in the outback. With the Kangaroo's assistance she eventually reaches home, a double satisfaction since the Kangaroo discovers that her lost baby is being kept by Dot's parents after a kangaroo hunt. The novel is critical of the brutality of humans towards animals and features a 'trial' of Dot by assorted animals for crimes committed against them by white settlers.

**Dot-com.** A colloquialism for a company with a site on the INTERNET, alluding to its DOMAIN name, which includes 'com' (for 'commercial') preceded by a dot, such as the booksellers Amazon.com.

> Unlike established advertisers such as household goods and car manufacturers, the dot-coms care more about being on air [on television] by a certain date than the cost.
> *The Times* (10 December 1999)

Fevered speculation in the shares of dot-com companies – those doing business on the Internet – led to the so-called Dot-Com Bubble of the late 1990s, which was followed by a crash and a general depression in share values and among the workers of SILICON VALLEY.

**Do tell.** Is that so? Really? A phrase of opposite meanings: on the one hand, as an ironic response to a piece of information in which one has no interest; on the other, as an exhortation to the speaker to impart a piece of juicy gossip. Both date from the 1950s.

**Do the decent** or **right thing.** To behave honourably or appropriately, especially when the action is not in one's own interest.

**Do the dirty on someone.** To cheat or betray them. The implication is that one plays a dirty trick on them. The expression dates from the First World War.

**Do the math.** An invitation or injunction to make a simple calculation and come to the obvious conclusion (as in $2 + 2 = 4$). The expression seems to have originated in American English in the early 1990s; elsewhere in the English-speaking world, American 'math' is usually replaced by British 'maths'. An alternative way of saying the same thing is 'Go figure!'

> There are currently two manufacturers of number plates in Zimbabwe, and one of them belongs to a member of the ruling party … go do the maths!
> *The Zimbabwean* (6 May 2005)

**Double helix.** The structure of the DNA molecule, which consists of two linked spirals. The molecular structure of DNA, the 'blueprint of life', was established by Francis Crick (1916–2004) and James Watson (b.1928) in 1953 while working at Cambridge University. As Watson said: 'A structure this pretty just had to exist.' Their exposition demonstrated how the molecule could carry the genetic code unique to every individual organism. The discovery marked the foundation of modern genetics. The two men shared the NOBEL PRIZE for their work in 1962, along with Maurice Wilkins (1916–2004), who developed the method of X-ray diffraction that helped in their discovery. A fourth scientist, Rosalind Franklin (1920–58), is thought by many to have played an equally important role, but she died of cancer before the Nobel prize was awarded. In 1968 Watson published a popular account of the discovery under the title *The Double Helix*.

***Double Indemnity.*** A classic FILM NOIR (1944) adapted by Raymond Chandler and Billy Wilder (who also directed) from a novel of the same title by James M. Cain (1892–1977). It starred Fred MacMurray as the insurance salesman who becomes the lover of the scheming Barbara Stanwyck. She persuades him to help her to murder her husband for the insurance money she will receive, but does not allow for the interference of insurance investigator Edward G. Robinson. The title refers to the clause in the insurance policy that promises payment of a double benefit in the case of accidental death. The plot was based on an actual murder case, the notorious Snyder Gray affair of 1927.

**Double take.** An actor's trick in which one looks away from the person who has addressed a remark to one and then looks back at them quickly when the purport of the remark sinks in. The term is also used for a second look prompted by surprise or admiration. The phrase dates from the 1930s.

**Doublethink.** A term used by George ORWELL in his *Nineteen Eighty-Four* (1949) (*see* 1984) to describe what unscrupulous propagandists achieved by NEWSPEAK. It denotes the mental ability to hold simultaneously two entirely conflicting views or beliefs, a state achieved by political indoctrination.

His mind slid away into the labyrinthine world of doublethink. To know and not to know, to be conscious of complete truthfulness while telling carefully constructed lies, to hold simultaneously two opinions which cancelled out, knowing them to be contradictory and believing in both of them, to use logic against logic, to repudiate morality while laying claim to it, to believe that democracy was impossible and that the Party was the guardian of democracy.

GEORGE ORWELL: *Nineteen Eighty-Four*, Pt I, ch. 3 (1949)

**Double whammy.** A twofold blow ('wham') or setback. The phrase became familiar in the UK following the general election campaign of 1992, when the Conservatives produced a poster showing a pair of boxing gloves and headlined 'Labour's Double Whammy', explaining that this comprised 'more taxes, higher prices'. The impact of the poster was, however, muted, as few British people were then familiar with the US phrase – although it is now in common use in the UK. The term itself featured in Al Capp's strip LI'L ABNER, in which the character Evil-Eye Fleegle explains it:

Evil-Eye Fleegle is th' name, an' th' '*whammy*' is my game. Mudder Nature endowed me wit' eyes which can putrefy citizens t' th' spot! ... There is th' '*single whammy*'! *That*, friend, is th' full, *pure power* o' *one* o' my evil eyes! It's *dynamite*, friend, an' I do not t'row it around lightly! ... And, lastly – th' '*double whammy*' – namely, th' *full power* o' *both eyes* – which I hopes I never *hafta* use.

*Al Capp's Li'l Abner* (July 1951)

**Doughnutting.** The practice whereby MPs in the House of Commons sit close to an MP making a speech while the proceedings are being televised. The aim is to give the viewer the impression that the speaker is well supported or that the House is well attended, although the clustering MPs may simply wish to be seen on television themselves. The term is said to have been originally used of televised debates in the Canadian parliament. It became current in Britain after 1989 when parliamentary proceedings were first televised. The allusion is presumably to the circular shape of a ring doughnut, the speaker being at its centre.

**Do us a favour.** *See* DO ME A FAVOUR!

**Dover Patrol.** A naval patrol based in Dover that was formed in the First World War to maintain communications across the English Channel, comprising a varied collection of warships and fishing vessels. Both *Dover Patrol* and *L'Attaque* later became the names of popular board games.

**Dowager's hump.** A term for a forward curvature of the spine caused by osteoporosis. It is more common in older women than in men (hence its name) and can be avoided or retarded if the person concerned receives enough calcium in their adult diet.

**Down and dirty.** On the scale of decency, fairness, modesty, etc., at the no-holds-barred level. If it's a fight, vicious; if it's a sexual encounter, earthily uninhibited. The usage originated in the US in the early 1980s.

In a nut-shell, it [a book] contains some down and dirty (but totally legal) tips and tricks that you need to know if you expect to compete on the Internet.

www.aawebmasters.com (22 April 2002)

**Down and Out in Paris and London.** The autobiographical study (1933) by George ORWELL was the author's first published book. It is an account of working with the poor in London's East End, and doing menial jobs in a working-class district of Paris, while trying to get his writing published.

**Down below.** *See* DOWN THERE.

**Downing Street Declaration.** An agreement between the British and Irish governments, formulated in 1993 and intended as the basis of a peace initiative in Northern Ireland. The declaration, issued from the Prime Minister's residence at 10 Downing Street, was a further step along the road initiated by the Anglo-Irish Agreement of 1985. *See also* GOOD FRIDAY AGREEMENT.

**Down memory lane.** A nostalgic reminiscence or sentimental journey into the past. Some local newspapers run a regular feature under this heading. *Down Memory Lane* (1949) was the title of a compilation of Mack Sennett comedy shorts, while earlier 'Memory Lane' (1924) was a popular waltz by Buddy De Sylva, Larry Spier and Con Conrad.

Since I was a child, my fantasies have been fueled by the images of beautiful women in newspapers, magazines and on the movie screen. But this book is more than that. It is a trip down memory lane.

HUGH HEFNER: in Gretchen Edgren, *The Playmate Book*, Introduction (1996)

**Downshifter.** A person who changes a financially rewarding but stressful career or lifestyle for one that is less pressurized and less well paid but more fulfilling. The trend for downshifting arose in the United States during the early 1990s, when those in stressful occupations such as in the computer industry started to re-evaluate their priorities. The general conclusion was that quality equated with simplicity, so that people began moving to smaller houses and halving their workloads.

**Downside.** *See* UPSIDE.

**Down the hatch!** A drinking toast of nautical origin, dating from the 1930s. The hatch is the throat.

**Down there** or **down below.** A maidenish euphemism for the genital and excretory region. *See also* NETHER REGIONS.

> A programme devoted to problems 'down there' was too shy for anything but innuendo.
>
> *Radio Times*, letter to the editor (12–18 September 1998)

**Down to the wire.** Said of a situation in which the outcome is not known until the last minute. The allusion is to the imaginary line marking the end of a horse race, where the winners notionally pass 'under the wire'. The phrase is also heard in the variant 'up to the wire'.

> Cannes went right down to the wire last night in one of the most surprising and dramatic finishes in the [film] festival's history.
>
> *The Times* (24 May 1999)

**Down Your Way.** A BBC radio programme first broadcast in 1946 in which the presenter visited a different town or village in Britain each week and talked to colourful local figures about their community and its history. In return they were rewarded with the playing of their favourite piece of music. For many *Down Your Way* became regular Sunday teatime listening. There were only four presenters during the programme's long run: Stewart MacPherson (1946–50), Richard Dimbleby (1950–5), Franklin Engelmann (1955–72) and Brian Johnston (1972–87).

**DP.** *See* DISPLACED PERSONS.

**Drag.** Female dress worn by men; transvestite clothes. The allusion is probably to a long dress, which drags along the ground. The term originated as theatrical slang in the early 20th century.

> You would never have the fag
> Of dressing up in drag,
> You'd be a woman at the weekend.
>
> JOHN OSBORNE: *The World of Paul Slickey*, II, x (1959)

**Dragged kicking and screaming into the 20th century.** A phrase applied to any person or institution that is reluctant to modernize or resistant to progress. In current usage '21st century' is often used instead.

> [Listening to ragtime] he felt literally dragged out of the nineteenth into the 20th century.
>
> J.B. PRIESTLEY: in *London Opinion*, 1913

> A change, slight but unmistakable, has taken place; the English theatre has been dragged, as Adlai Stevenson once

said of the Republican Party, kicking and screaming into the 20th century.

> KENNETH TYNAN: *Curtains* (1961)

**Dragon boat.** A long and slender rowing boat with a dragon's head at its bows, used for racing with a mixed crew of 18. The sport of dragon-boat racing became popular around the world in the 1990s, especially in Canada, and was adopted from the much older annual contests held in China and Hong Kong on the fifth day of the fifth lunar month as an occasion for driving off evil spirits. Britain first hosted the world championships in 1999.

**Dragon lady.** A domineering or fearsome woman. The image is oriental, and the phrase had its origin in the name of the mysterious Asian chieftainess in Milton Caniff's popular cartoon strip *Terry and the Pirates* (1934–73), featuring Terry LEE. The name was also used as a nickname for the American U-2 strategic reconnaissance aircraft.

**Drain, The.** A nickname for the Waterloo and City Line on the London Underground, opened in 1898. The designation, at first derogatory but now almost affectionate, dates from the 1920s and refers to the deep and dingy route. It was the only Underground line run by British Rail (from 1948 to 1994).

**Drainpipes.** Narrow-legged, tight-fitting trousers, an essential part of the garb of TEDDY BOYS in the 1950s.

**Drake brass plate.** *See under* FAKES.

**Drake's Drum.** A drum that once belonged to the Elizabethan sea dog and English national hero Sir Francis Drake (1540–96), who played a key role in the defeat of the Spanish Armada in 1588. As he died Drake apparently ordered that the drum be taken back to his home at Buckland Abbey near Plymouth. As Sir Henry Newbolt (1862–1938) put it in 'Drake's Drum' (1897):

> Take my drum to England, hang et by the shore,
> Strike et when your powder's runnin' low;
> If the Dons [Spaniards] sight Devon, I'll quit the port o'
>   Heaven,
> An' drum them up the Channel as we drummed them long
>   ago.

The drum is said to have sounded on three momentous occasions in the 20th century. It was reportedly heard on the outbreak of the First World War in 1914, and again at the end of the war in 1918, when it apparently sounded aboard the *Royal Oak*, flagship of the British Grand Fleet anchored at SCAPA FLOW in the Orkneys while the German fleet arrived to surrender. Finally, a drum roll was heard during the desperate British evacuation from DUNKIRK in 1940.

**Drama queen.** Someone who makes a huge fuss over trivial matters, turning contretemps into tragedies. The term is said to have originated in gay slang in the 1960s, and to have referred exclusively to men, but it has long since become completely unisex.

> My daughter is such a drama queen on every level. Everything at 13 for her has to be perfect. Can anyone relate?
> http://boards.glamour.com (4 May 2005)

**Draw a line in the sand.** To define a limit or boundary; to state a level of tolerance beyond which one will not go. The expression is perhaps an elaboration of 'to draw the line' and was first current in the United States in the 1970s. It was seized on gratefully by politicians and diplomats, one of whom was probably responsible for the added imagery in the first place.

**Draw the crabs.** In Australian military slang dating from the First World War, to attract enemy fire ('crabs' is short for 'crab shells', an ironic reference to shells of the explosive variety). Later the application of the phrase broadened out to signify the attracting of any unwanted attention, particularly from the police.

**Draw the crow.** In Australian slang, to come off worst, especially in a share-out or division of spoils, labour, prizes, etc. The expression, which is first recorded in 1942, was inspired by an anecdote in which a number of shot birds are to be distributed by lottery, and one unlucky individual gets the crow (rather than the choice partridges, pheasants, etc. on offer).

**Dreaded lurgy.** An illness or indisposition of uncertain or unstated nature. The phrase became popular in the 1950s following its use by the GOONS in *The Goon Show*. The origin of 'lurgy' is unknown, although it suggests a thing that lurks on the one hand or an ALLERGY on the other. A spelling 'lergy' also exists to support the latter association.

> The Goon Show ... Poor Arnold Fringe is suddenly stricken with the Dreaded Lurgi.
> *Radio Times* (4 November 1954)

**Dreadlocks.** The hairstyle favoured by RASTAFARIANS, in which the hair is washed but not combed and then twisted while wet into braids or ringlets that hang down on all sides. Rastafarians outlawed the combing or cutting of hair in obedience to the biblical injunction: 'They shall not make baldness upon their head, neither shall they shave off the corner of their beard' (Leviticus 21:5), and they coined the term 'dreadlocks' to mock the aversion of non-believers to the look.

**Dreadnought.** A battleship launched on 18 February 1906 as the prototype of a class of Royal Navy battleships so named. They were larger and faster than their predecessors and equipped entirely with large-calibre guns. The introduction of the class initiated a hotting up of the naval arms race with Germany, and a jingoistic British public clamoured for more with the slogan 'We want eight and we won't wait.' Admiral Fisher, who as First Sea Lord had been responsible for the programme, adopted the motto 'Fear God and dread nought' when he was elevated to the peerage in 1909. That same year, when the chancellor of the exchequer David Lloyd George was battling with the House of Lords over his PEOPLE'S BUDGET, he made a speech in Newcastle in which he said:

> A fully equipped duke costs as much to keep up as two Dreadnoughts; and dukes are just as great a terror and they last longer.

The name *Dreadnought* had been used for a succession of Royal Navy ships since Elizabethan times. In 1960 the name passed to the first British nuclear-powered submarine.

**Dreamboat.** A very attractive person, especially a man from the point of view of a woman, as the 'vessel of one's dreams'. The expression, redolent of HOLLYWOOD, dates from the 1940s. Alma Cogan's 'Dreamboat' was a hit song of 1955.

**Dream come true.** A journalistic cliché for any stroke of luck or success experienced by a member of the public. It is equally resorted to by such people when interviewed by the media.

> But the Sheikh's first words after [winning] the race [the Derby] were not for himself. He said: 'This is a dream come true, but my thoughts are now of Alex.'
> *Independent on Sunday* (11 June 1995)

**Dream machine.** A nickname for the television industry. The term derives from *The Great American Dream Machine* (1971), a US television programme of topical satire. *See also* AMERICAN DREAM.

**Dream of Gerontius, The.** A choral piece (the composer rejected the label 'oratorio') by Edward Elgar (1857–1934) uses a text taken from a long mystical poem by Cardinal Newman (1801–90). The work was first performed in 1900 at the Birmingham Festival. Newman's poem, published in 1866, concerns the agonizing death of Gerontius and his experiences in the afterlife. A copy of the poem was found near the body of Gordon of Khartoum, covered in Gordon's jottings, and it was a copy of this annotated text that inspired Elgar. Newman's poem includes such tin-eared lines as:

> They sing of thy approaching agony,
> Which thou so eagerly didst question of

which Elgar nevertheless managed to set to music. Elgar's *Dream* has always excited strongly polarized opinions, many of them animated by religious prejudice (Catholic or anti-Catholic): George Moore described it as 'Holy water in a German beer barrel', while Charles Villiers Stanford complained that it was 'stinking of incense'; Frederick Delius opined that '*Gerontius* is a nauseating work', although Pope Pius XII believed it to be 'a sublime masterpiece'.

**Dream team.** A team or group of assembled individuals that is ideal in every respect. The term dates back at least to the early 1970s in American English, but it really came to the fore when it was applied to the US basketball team that won the gold medal at the Barcelona Olympics in 1992. Among the team's members were such basketball legends as 'Magic' Johnson, Michael Jordan and Larry Bird.

**Dresden.** A city in eastern Germany that was destroyed by bombing during the Second World War. It was formerly one of the world's most beautiful cities, referred to as 'the Florence on the Elbe', but on the night of 13–14 February 1945 a massive raid by 800 RAF bombers created a firestorm in the city that killed between 30,000 and 60,000 civilians (some estimates go as high as 135,000). During daylight on 14 February 400 USAAF bombers took over from the RAF, followed by 200 the next day, 400 on 2 March and 572 on 17 April. The raid has been the subject of controversy ever since. It was part of an Allied strategy, requested by the Soviet Union, to block the movement of German troops by bombing major cities such as Berlin, Chemnitz, Leipzig and Dresden. However, critics point out that the destruction of Dresden achieved little militarily and claim that the actual intention was to terrorize the German population into submission, so that they would not resist following the imminent Allied military victory. It has also been suggested that the Western Allies used the raid as a demonstration to the Soviet Union of the strength of their air power. In 1999 some citizens of Dresden objected when a statue of Arthur BOMBER HARRIS, wartime head of RAF Bomber Command, was raised in London.

**Dresden china.** A term used of anyone or anything delicately pretty or attractive, the comparison being with the fine porcelain so called, made originally at Dresden or at nearby Meissen. The figurative sense dates from the turn of the 20th century and is mostly used of women.

**Dress down.** To dress informally. Dressing down at work or in the office on Fridays arose as a US innovation, the idea being that the wearing of casual clothes would improve staff morale and increase productivity. Psychologists deny any connection, however, and for many employees, especially the more mature, obligatory dressing down can be an imposition. The practice is sometimes coupled with a fund-raising effort for charity, and school students may also have the occasional 'non-uniform day' set aside for this purpose. UNICEF capitalized on the trend by setting aside the first Friday in February as 'Non-Uniform Day' with the aim of encouraging schools to raise funds for needy children around the world.

**Dressed up like a dog's dinner.** Dressed in smart but ostentatious clothes. The allusion is to a (literal) DOG'S DINNER that outwardly looks appetizing but that is really a mishmash of scraps. The expression dates from the 1930s.

**Dreyfusard.** An advocate of the innocence of Capt. Alfred Dreyfus (1859–1935), a French artillery officer of Jewish descent who was convicted in 1894 on a charge of betraying military secrets to Germany and sent to DEVIL'S ISLAND. In 1898 Clemenceau and Zola took up his case and Zola wrote his famous open letter *J'accuse*. In 1899 he was retried and again condemned, but shortly afterwards he was pardoned. In 1906 the proceedings were finally quashed.

**Drink-driving.** The criminal offence of driving a vehicle with an excess of alcohol in the blood. In 2006 in Britain the legal blood alcohol limit for drivers was 80 milligrams per 100 millilitres. The expression itself dates from the 1960s.

**Drink with the flies.** In colloquial Australian English, to drink on one's own, especially in a pub or other place usually associated with convivial drinking in groups. The expression dates back to the 1910s.

**Drive a coach and horses through something.** To nullify its effectiveness. The earlier form of the phrase, which dates from the 17th century, was invariably 'to drive a coach and six (or four) through', and in 1672 Sir Stephen Rice, a Roman Catholic Chief Baron of the Exchequer, is quoted as saying: 'I will drive a coach and six horses through the Act of Settlement.' The present form of the expression arose in the 20th century and still frequently has a political or legalistic reference.

> 'The school's code of conduct is to respect the right of others to learn. This is a child who drives a coach and horses through that code.'
> *The Times* (7 December 1999)

**Drive by the seat of one's pants.** *See* FLY BY THE SEAT OF ONE'S PANTS.

**Drive** or **send someone up the wall.** To frustrate or infuriate them. The suggestion is that they are driven insane and attempt to climb the wall in order to escape.

**Drongo.** In colloquial Australian English, a fool or simpleton. The term was originally applied, during the Second World War, to a new recruit to the Royal Australian Air Force, but it soon broadened out in meaning. Ultimately of Malagasy origin, it is the name of a bird (*Dicrurus bracteata*) native to New Guinea and northern Australia, but its slang application may have been prompted by the fact that a notably unsuccessful Australian racehorse of the 1920s was called 'Drongo'.

**Droop-snoot.** (An aircraft with) a nose-section that points downwards or that can be adjusted to point downwards. The term originated as a nickname for the Lockheed P-38 Lightning, an American Second World War fighter-bomber, and was subsequently applied to the supersonic CONCORDE airliner, which was given an adjustable nose-cone to resolve visibility problems for the pilot on take-off and landing.

**Droopy drawers.** A nickname for a sloppy, depressing or dull person. 'Drawers' are knickers or underpants.

**Drop a bombshell.** To deliver unpleasant or disappointing news, especially when the opposite was expected. The expression dates from the First World War, when bombs were dropped by hand from aeroplanes.

> Jean loved dropping bombshells. Sometimes he thought she kept him for the sake of dropping them and watching him jump. …
> 'Harrix went bust,' she told him.
> FAY WELDON: *The Heart of the Country* (1987)

**Drop a brick.** To make an indiscreet or embarrassing remark. The expression is said to relate to a group of builders in Cambridge who dropped their bricks in surprise on seeing an extraordinarily inept column of student volunteers on the march one day in 1905. The actor and playwright Robert Morley edited an entertaining collection of verbal gaffes in *Robert Morley's Book of Bricks* (1978).

**Drop a clanger.** To commit a social gaffe or an embarrassing blunder which draws ringing attention to itself. Enjoyable examples of 'clangers' are those depicted by the cartoonist H.M. Bateman (1887–1970) in his drawings with titles beginning 'The Man Who … ', such as 'The Man Who Lit His Cigar Before the Loyal Toast' or 'The Man Who Threw a Snowball at St Moritz'.

**Drop a dime on someone.** To inform on them or betray them. The expression is of US origin and dates from the 1960s, when a public telephone call cost 10 cents (a dime). Such a call could be made by an informer to the police.

**Drop dead!** An expression of irritation or contempt, short for 'Why don't you drop dead?'

**Drop-dead.** Strikingly beautiful; excellent. The term dates from the 1970s and is frequently encountered with the adjective 'gorgeous'. The stunning effect is enough to make one drop dead.

> [Popular singer Shania] Twain is a bit of a conundrum. In the flesh, she is petite and slim … and pretty rather than the drop-dead stunner of her photos and videos.
> *The Times Magazine* (11 September 1999)

**Drop one's trousers.** To lower one's trousers, especially in a public place for purposes of urination or defecation.

**Dropout.** A student who fails to complete a college or university course, or more generally a person who has 'opted out' of conventional society.

> An international gathering of misfits and drop-outs, smoking pot and meditating in the Buddhist temples.
> *New Statesman* (15 December 1967)

**Drop someone in it.** To do or say something, often deliberately, that places another in difficulties. 'It' is tacitly understood as 'the shit'.

**Drop the dead donkey.** To abandon a project. The phrase was popularized or even originally introduced by the television satirical SITCOM *Drop the Dead Donkey* (1990–4), set in a newsroom, where the reference was to a last-minute decision to drop a news story.

**Drug Czar.** The popular title of the Anti-Drugs Coordinator, appointed by the Labour government in 1997 to coordinate the fight against drug abuse in Britain. The first to hold the post was Keith Hellawell. This particular use of 'czar' (or 'tsar') is of US origin. The designation was subsequently extended to officials with similar responsibilities in other areas.

> The Government will appoint a cancer 'czar' today to take charge of efforts to bring about big improvements in the way Britain treats people who have the disease.
> *The Times* (25 October 1999)
> Booze tsar set to tackle drunk yobs.
> *Metro* (23 August 2005)
> Blair orders Clarke to fund anti-yob czar.
> *Sunday Times* (4 September 2005)
> Britain's rail czar [the director general of railways at the Department for Transport] has been questioned by police over allegations that he assaulted a restaurant steward on an inter-city express service.
> *Sunday Times* (4 December 2005)
> Reid told ministers that he backed the respect 'czar', Louise Casey, who reports directly to the prime minister.
> *Sunday Times* (11 June 2006)

**Drug nicknames.** Drug users and dealers have evolved a jargon of their own, and most drugs, whether legal or not, have their individual nicknames. They include the following:

Amphetamine: bennies, dexies, goof balls, ice, speed

Cannabis (marijuana): baby, black, boo, bush, doobie, draw, ganja, grass, green, hash, hemp, joint, Mary Jane, pot, reefer, shit, skunk, spliff, tea, weed

Cocaine: bernies, C, Charlie, coke, crack, dust, flake, freebase, leaf, nose, rock, snow

HEROIN: beast, black tar, H, horse, poison, scag, scat, schmeck, smack, stuff, sugar

LSD: A, acid, chief, purple

MDMA: Adam, E, ECSTASY, XTC

Phencyclidine: angel dust, corn flakes, goon, hog, loopy dust, rocket fuel

**Drum majorette.** A girl or young woman who marches at the head of a procession, twirling and tossing a baton. Her uniform and prominent position to some extent mirror those of a drum major, who commands the corps of drums of a military band. She first made her appearance in the United States in the 1930s.

**Drummond, Bulldog.** *See* BULLDOG DRUMMOND.

**Drum 'n' bass.** A style of popular music, electronically mixing bass lines from REGGAE with speeded-up drum rhythms from HIP-HOP. Initially known as 'jungle', it emerged in the 1990s.

**Drunk Man Looks at the Thistle, A.** A long, 2500-line poem (1926) by the Scottish poet Hugh MacDiarmid (C.M. Grieve, 1892–1978), written in a variety of the Scots language synthesized from his own upbringing in the Scottish Borders and from Jamieson's *Etymological Dictionary of the Scottish Language* (1808). The framework story of the poem – reminiscent of Burns's phantasmagoric 'Tam o'Shanter' – is that a Scots drunk has stumbled into a ditch in the dark on the way back from the pub to his wife Jean, and there sees a thistle (the symbol of Scotland) in the moonlight. However, MacDiarmid's aim was to create a work as modernist as T.S. Eliot's *The* WASTE LAND and at the same time to return Scots literature from a parochial 'kailyard' to the international stage as it had been during the Renaissance – hence his slogan 'Not Burns – Dunbar!'.

> A Scottish poet maun assume
> The burden o' his people's doom,
> And dee to brak' their livin' tomb.

**Dry out.** To undergo treatment for alcoholism or drug abuse; to go into 'rehab'.

**Dry run.** A rehearsal of a performance or procedure before the actual one. It is 'dry' because it is unproductive, just as a dry cow yields no milk. The term is of US military origin and was first used in the Second World War for simulated bombings in which no bombs were dropped.

**Dry White Season, A.** A novel (1979) by the South African writer André Brink (b.1935), originally written and published in Afrikaans as *'n Droë wit seisoen*, and translated by himself. It is one of six novels he wrote between 1958 and 1967, using modern narrative techniques, as a counterblast to those Afrikaans novels that he described as a 'literature of drought and poor whites'. The message of this one, in which a white teacher, believing himself to be apolitical, embarks on a quest for justice after the death in custody of a black colleague, is that in the prevailing situation in South Africa it was impossible for anyone to remain politically uncommitted. A passionate film version (1989) was directed by Euzhan Palcy.

**DSK.** The abbreviation of 'Dvorak simplified keyboard'. In 1932 Dr August Dvorak, professor of education and director of research at the University of Washington, Seattle, devised a simplified typewriter keyboard which, he claimed, would accelerate the speed of typing compared to the traditional QWERTY arrangement by some 35 per cent. He based it on the frequency of letters in English, which is generally agreed to be as follows: E T A O N R I S H D L F C M U G Y P W B V K X J Q Z. The vowels A E I O U make up 39 per cent of all letters used and the five most common consonants are H N R S T. Dr Dvorak's layout was thus PYFGCRL in the top row, AOEUIDHTNS in the middle row, and QJKXBMWVZ in the bottom row. Despite the apparent advantages, however, the simplified keyboard never caught on and modern computer keyboards still adhere to the awkward and illogical QWERTY display.

**DTV.** *See* DIGITAL TELEVISION.

**Dub dub dub.** Black youth slang for the Internet, from the Web address prefix 'www' (standing for WORLD WIDE WEB).

**Dubois, Blanche.** The most memorable character from Tennessee Williams' play *A* STREETCAR NAMED DESIRE (1949), a study in mental decline and a modern archetype of a self-deluded down-at-heel gentility. Throwing herself on the charity of her sister Stella in her humble backstreet dwelling, she must share the space with Stella's brutally down-to-earth partner, Stanley Kowalski, a man whose blue-collar uncouthness repels her but whose raw physicality is compelling. After Stanley takes things too far and sexually assaults her, Blanche is tipped over the edge of reason, unable to make her realities and fantasies, past and present, coexist. The first film version (1951), with Vivian Leigh as Blanche and Marlon Brando as Stanley, oozes the sweaty heat and neon of New Orleans, a fitting backdrop. Blanche's vulnerability, with its sexual undertow, infuses her most famous line, delivered (ironically) as she is led away by a doctor at the end of the play (scene 11):

I have always depended on the kindness of strangers.

*See also* DESIRE STREET.

**Dubya.** A nickname of George W. Bush (b.1946 ), governor of Texas (1995–2000), and from 2001 the 43rd president of the United States. A Republican like his father George Bush (the 41st president; 1989–93), the gaffe-prone younger Bush defeated his Democratic rival, Vice-President Al Gore, in a close-run and controversial election whose result was disputed in the courts before Gore finally conceded victory. (Bush's victory over Democratic contender John Kerry in 2005 was, however, unquestionable.) Bush's nickname represents a drawling, Texas-accented pronunciation of his middle initial, and is said to emphasize his Southern ordinariness and plain-dealing in contrast with the sleaziness of his presidential predecessor (*see* COMEBACK KID; SLICK WILLIE). Bush reinforces his GOOD OLE BOY image with what one journalist has called his 'bandy-legged, jaw-jutting swagger'. By his opponents he is often referred to as 'the Village Idiot', as in the line found on T-shirts, bumper stickers, etc.: 'Somewhere in Texas a village is missing its idiot.' In *Private Eye*'s spoof column of British politics, *St Albion Parish News*, Bush is the Rev. Dubya Bush of the Church of Latter Day Morons. *See also* the IDIOT SON.

**Duce.** (Italian, 'leader'.) The title adopted by Benito Mussolini (1883–1945), the Fascist dictator of Italy from 1922 to 1943. *See also* CAUDILLO; FASCISM.

**Duchess of Pork.** *See* FERGIE.

**Duck, I forgot to.** *See* I FORGOT TO DUCK.

**Duck, looking, walking and quacking like a.** *See* IF IT LOOKS LIKE A DUCK, WALKS LIKE A DUCK AND QUACKS LIKE A DUCK, THEN IT JUST MAY BE A DUCK.

**Duck and dive.** To use one's ingenuity to escape from an undesirable or difficult situation. The metaphor may come from a boxer's agile attempts to avoid his opponent's blows, although the expression has also been explained as rhyming slang on 'skive'.

He [MP Neil Hamilton] was on the wrong side of the wavering line of decency … Worst of all, he became involved with the emir of duckers and divers [Harrods owner Mohamed al Fayed].
*Sunday Times* (26 December 1999)

**Duck or grouse.** A standing pleasantry for a notice on a low lintel warning people not to bump their heads on passing beneath. A variant at one time in an Oxford bookshop was 'Mind Your Egghead'.

**Ducks.** US Army-sponsored amphibious vehicles active in the Second World War. Their name arose as a fortuitous adaptation of the official designation DUKW, representing the factory code letters D for boat, U for lorry body and KW for lorry chassis. The vehicle moved on rubber tyres ashore and was propeller-driven when afloat.

**Duck's arse** or **DA.** A men's hairstyle in which the hair is swept back to a point at the nape of the neck, so that it looks like a duck's tail. The style was popular among TEDDY BOYS in the 1950s.

**Duck soup.** An easy task; a 'doddle' or 'cinch'. The allusion may be to a 'sitting duck' as an easy target. The expression is of US origin and was popularized by the MARX BROTHERS' film *Duck Soup* (1933).

**Duckworth–Lewis method.** An intricate method of revising targets in one-day cricket matches when rain stops play, devised in the 1990s by Frank Duckworth, a statistician, and Tony Lewis, a mathematics lecturer (not to be confused with the cricketer Tony Lewis (b.1938)). The system is based on the principle that the teams must know two figures in order to make as many runs as they can, namely the number of overs they have still to receive and the number of wickets they have in hand. The new targets are reached using a table and a calculator.

The system has baffled the media and the public as well as official scorers, but was adopted as the 'rain rule' for the 1999 World Cup, hosted by the England and Wales Cricket Board.

**Duff someone up.** To beat them up. The verb is probably Scottish dialect *duff*, 'to hit'.

**'Dulce et Decorum Est'.** A poem (1918) by the WAR POET Wilfred Owen (1893–1918) in which he describes the horrors of a gas attack in the trenches of the First World War. The poem was informed by Owen's personal experiences of the trenches and made doubly poignant by his own death in the last week of the war, when he was himself killed in action on the Sambre Canal. The title, with which the poem also ends, is a quotation from Horace's *Odes*, usually translated as: 'It is sweet and becoming to die for one's country.'

If you could hear, at every jolt, the blood
Come gargling from the froth-corrupted lungs,
Obscene as cancer,
Bitter as the cud

Of vile, incurable sores on innocent tongues, –
My friend, you would not tell with such high zest
To children ardent for some desperate glory,
The old Lie: *Dulce et decorum est*
*Pro patria mori.*

WILFRED OWEN: *'Dulce et Decorum Est'* (1918)

**Dullsville.** A dull state or condition, as if caused by living in a town so named. The term dates from the 1960s.

**Dumbarton Oaks.** The 'little concerto in the style of the Brandenburg Concertos' by Igor Stravinsky (1882–1971) was commissioned in 1938 by Mr and Mrs R.W. Bliss, who lived in the mansion of Dumbarton Oaks in Georgetown, near Washington, D.C. Between 21 August and 7 October 1944 the same mansion played host to a conference of Allied powers (China, the Soviet Union, the United States and the United Kingdom) that laid the foundations of what was to become the UNITED NATIONS.

**Dumb blonde.** This now rather dated expression for a conspicuously attractive but stupid young blonde woman, the BIMBO of today, seems a contradiction in terms, since such a female is not normally noted for her silence. The term was used to typecast the film actress Marilyn MONROE (1926–62) but was in fact an unfair stereotype that troubled her throughout her career. The first word of the US phrase has probably been influenced by German *dumm*, 'stupid'.

> Aged just seventeen and the daughter of a Blackpool landlady, she [film and television personality Sabrina] was the original dumb blonde. Indeed, part of her gimmick was that she never said a word on screen.
>
> HILARY KINGSLEY and GEOFF TIBBALLS: *Box of Delights* (1989)

**Dumb cluck.** A stupid person. 'Dumb' suggests German *dumm*, 'stupid' and 'cluck' Yiddish *klotz*, 'blockhead', the phrase as a whole perhaps influenced by German *Dummkopf*, 'idiot'.

**Dumb down.** To reduce to a lower level of understanding. As a transitive verb 'dumb down' dates from the 1930s, but it was in the mid-1980s that the intransitive practice of 'dumbing down' began to be perceived by some as increasingly pervasive in the media, where 'serious' newspapers represented their material in a more populist fashion while the more subtle points of television dramas and documentaries were demotically 'spelled out' for the benefit of the hedonistic viewer.

**Dumbledore, Albus.** *See* Harry POTTER.

**Dumbo.** A baby elephant whose large ears enable him to fly. The Walt Disney cartoon film of 1941 was based on the book

*Dumbo, the Flying Elephant* by Helen Aberson and Harold Pearl. In addition to Dumbo, the film introduced the Crows, who have the best song in the movie, 'When I See an Elephant Fly', and Dumbo's savvy 'manager' Timothy Mouse. Subsequently the nickname Dumbo has been applied to any person with large ears, such as New Labour's one-time home secretary Charles Clarke (*see* BIG EARS).

**Dunblane Massacre.** On 13 March 1996 a lone gunman, Thomas Hamilton, a former Scout leader, entered the local primary school at Dunblane, central Scotland, killing 16 young children and their teacher before turning the gun on himself. The massacre led to the banning of all privately held handguns in Britain and further tightening of the gun laws. *See also* COLUMBINE MASSACRE; HUNGERFORD MASSACRE.

**Dungeons and Dragons.** A fantasy role-playing computer game created in 1973 by Gary Gygax and Dave Arneson. Players can assume the role of any of various medieval-style fantasy characters (a brave young warrior, a beautiful princess, a crafty wizard, etc.) and negotiate their way computationally through the various obstacles that come in their way. The game quickly became a huge commercial success and proved to be the inspiration for a whole new genre.

**Dunkirk.** This once notorious haunt of pirates and privateers in northern France has acquired fresh associations since the Second World War. The name is now used figuratively to denote a forced military evacuation by sea to avoid disaster, a speedy and complete withdrawal, an entire abandonment of a position. The allusion is to the heroic evacuation of the main British expeditionary force (26 May to 4 June 1940), in the face of imminent disaster, by Vice-Admiral Ramsay's motley force of destroyers, yachts and other craft (*see* LITTLE SHIPS), with essential air cover from RAF Fighter Command. The phrase 'Dunkirk spirit' gained general currency to describe any sudden confrontation or crisis, especially one that is handled by 'rising to the occasion'.

> I have always deprecated – perhaps rightly, perhaps wrongly – in crisis after crisis, appeals to the Dunkirk spirit as an answer to our problems because what is required in our economic situation is not a brief period of inspired improvisation, work and sacrifice, such as we had under the leadership of the Rt Hon. Member for Woodford [Winston Churchill], but a very long, hard prolonged period of reorganization and redirection. It is the long haul, not the inspired spirit that we need.
>
> HAROLD WILSON: speech to the House of Commons while in opposition, 26 July 1961

I believe that the spirit of Dunkirk will once again carry us through to success.

HAROLD WILSON: speech to the Labour Party Conference (12 December 1964), after becoming prime minister

**Dunroamin.** A typical punning name for the home of a family that has finally found its nest or niche. Names of this type proliferated in the housing boom of the interwar years, when families sought a secure and comfortable base after the disruption and destruction of the First World War. Such names are still found today for the suburban semi and the country cottage, but council estates and retirement homes mostly eschew the characteristically British label in favour of a faceless number.

Dunroamin – a declaration to the world that a family has settled in the home of its choice; an innocent exposure of poor taste and puerile humour; or the epitome of middle-class bourgeois complacency?

PAUL OLIVER, IAN DAVIS and IAN BENTLEY: *Dunroamin*, Introduction (1981)

**Dunsterforce.** The nickname during the First World War of a 1000-strong British and Commonwealth force, under the command of General L.C. Dunsterville (1865–1946), which in January 1918 marched north from Persia to support the establishment of an independent Transcaucasia. The aim was to keep the oil-rich region free from the BOLSHEVIK Russians, Turks and Germans and to prevent any German–Turkish invasion of India. Dunsterville himself was a Russian speaker, a childhood friend of Rudyard Kipling, and the model for Corkran in Kipling's *Stalky & Co.* (1899), and the expedition was a notable episode in the GREAT GAME. By August, after various adventures, Dunsterforce had reached Baku (now the capital of Azerbaijan) but was obliged to withdraw on 14 September as 14,000 Turkish troops prepared to attack. Although Dunsterville reoccupied Baku after the armistice, he was ordered to withdraw. The region was subsequently absorbed by the Soviet Union.

**Durex.** The proprietary name of a well-known make of condom. The name, presumably based on 'durable', was registered in 1932 and was coined by A.R. Reid, chairman of the London Rubber Company, its manufacturers (it is said that he thought of it while travelling home by train one evening). The name offers a potential pitfall for Australian visitors to Britain, since in their home country 'Durex' is the equivalent of SELLOTAPE.

**Dust and ashes.** A disappointment or disillusionment. The expression dates from the turn of the 20th century and alludes to the legend of the Dead Sea Fruit or Apples of Sodom, as the fruit of trees reputed to grow on the shores of the Dead Sea, described by Josephus as of fair appearance externally but dissolving, when grasped, into smoke and ashes.

**Dust Bowl.** An area of Oklahoma and other prairie states of the United States. The name arose from the severe drought that affected the region in the early 1930s. Thousands of families (*see* OKIES) were forced to leave the area at the height of the GREAT DEPRESSION.

**Dust bunny.** An Americanism for a ball of dust and fluff, as found in an undusted area of the home, typically under a bed. A more graphic synonym is GHOST TURD.

**Dust something down** or **off.** To bring it out again for use after a long period of neglect. The expression dates from the 1940s.

A similar argument [that pornography corrupts] has often been used on behalf of the fairer sex. Most famously, it was dusted off in the *Lady Chatterley's Lover* obscenity trial 39 years ago, when the jury was asked: 'Is it a book you would wish your wife or your servants to read?'

*The Times* (31 July 1999)

**Dutch.** A nickname of President Ronald Reagan (1911–2004). According to his autobiography, the name was given him as a baby when his father described him as 'a little bit of a fat Dutchman' (*Where's the Rest of Me?*, 1965). Edmund Morris's *Dutch* (1999) is a memoir of Reagan. *See also* GIPPER; TEFLON.

**Dutch cap.** A contraceptive diaphragm for women, so named because the shape it assumes when in position bears some resemblance to the cap with triangular flaps that forms part of Dutch women's national dress.

**Dutch disease.** A term used by economists for the failure of a country's economy to develop properly as a result of the plundering of its natural resources, a situation typified by the Netherlands following the discovery of massive reserves of natural gas in 1959. The immediate effect of the find was to boost the economy but it was subsequently depressed when capital was diverted away from more productive investments, in particular manufacturing.

**Dutch elm disease.** The popular name of *Ceratocystis ulmi*, a disease in which a suffocating fungus grows beneath the bark of elm trees to be spread by beetles. It was first identified in the Netherlands in 1919 and was particularly virulent in Britain in the 1970s, so that by the early 1980s two out of three British elms had perished as a result of the infestation. When the disease killed the elms it produced forests of suckers from the roots, and these may be seen in hedgerows across Britain. The suckers grow to at least

6m (20ft), by which time they have developed a heavy enough bark to attract the beetles that carry the fungus. The cycle then recurs: the stems are re-infected and die, and the plants once again start from suckers.

**Dutching.** The practice of sending food destined for the British market for irradiation (exposure to gamma rays to kill micro-organisms) in a country where this is permitted, such as the Netherlands, in order to mask any bacterial contamination before it is put on sale. The technique was first applied in the 1980s.

**DVM.** Dead vegetable matter, a derisive nickname for the mass of dried flowers, dyed leaves, curling bark, twisted willow twigs, desiccated fruit and the like proliferating as supposedly essential accessories in the homes of the affluent. The term was introduced by the sociologist Tony Chapman in his study of new homes in Britain, *Stage Sets for Ideal Lives* (1999).

**Dvorak simplified keyboard.** *See* DSK.

**Dweeb.** A contemptible or puny person; a NERD. The term is of US origin and suggests a blend of 'dwarf' and 'feeble'.

**DWEM.** *See* DEAD WHITE EUROPEAN MALE.

**Dwile flonking.** A supposedly ancient but in reality entirely modern rustic contest that might otherwise be known as 'flannel flinging'. It became a nationwide craze in the 1960s after it featured on the television programme *It's a Square World* and is still held intermittently in Suffolk and elsewhere. Its rules and entertainingly esoteric vocabulary involve the formation of a 'girter' (circle) by one team, who dance round a member of the opposition, the 'flonker'. He holds a 'driveller' (stick) on the end of which is a 'dwile' (cloth) soaked in 'flonk' (ale). When the music stops the flonker flings the dwile and tries to hit the girter, scoring points depending on which part of their body is struck. If he fails to score the flonker is faced with the penalty of rapidly downing six pints. In 1967 in a match between Beccles and Bungay, the latter won 16–1.

**Dying Swan, The.** A ballet dance that became intimately associated with the great Anna Pavlova (1881–1931), for whom it was created by Michel Fokine, and danced to *Le Cygne* from Camille Saint-Saëns's *Le Carnaval des animaux* (1886). Based on the poignant poem of the same name by Alfred, Lord Tennyson about the final struggle for life of a dying bird, Pavlova first danced it at a gala performance in St Petersburg on 22 December 1907. She interpreted the role dramatically but simply, using her arms to simulate the beating of the swan's wings as its struggled helplessly to fly, while the quivering movements of her body and head suggested its death throes. At the end the fluttering ceased and the dancer slowly sank upon the stage. *See also* PAVLOVA.

**Dyke.** A lesbian. The word, dating from the 1940s, is of disputed origin. It may be a shortening of *morphodyke*, a dialect form and sub-standard pronunciation of 'hermaphrodite'.

**Dynasty.** A US television melodrama on the lines of DALLAS, screened from 1982 to 1989 and centring on the Carringtons, a Colorado oil-rich family comprising the slick, smooth Blake Carrington, his beautiful new wife Krystle and a mixed bag of offspring. Blake's ex-wife, Alexis (played by Joan Collins, the BITCH), had a key role as the 'villain of the piece'.

**Dystopia.** A modern coinage denoting the opposite of Utopia, the imaginary island in Sir Thomas More's political romance of the same name (1516) where all is perfect (*dys-* signifying 'bad', it was presumably based on the notion that *Utopia* was formed with *eu-* 'good', but in fact it incorporates Greek *ou* 'not'). The word is often used to describe the nightmare futures depicted in such novels as BRAVE NEW WORLD and *Nineteen Eighty-Four* (*see* 1984).

# E

**E-.** In the age of the INTERNET and the WORLD WIDE WEB, the prefix (standing for 'electronic') denoting transactions and services carried out across computer networks. The most widely known manifestation is E-MAIL, but other usages include e-commerce, e-banking, E-LEARNING and the astonishingly popular online auction site EBAY.

**E = mc².** Perhaps the most famous formula ever, in which 'E' is energy, 'm' is mass and 'c' is the speed of light. It was first proposed by Albert Einstein in 1905, as an adjunct to his special theory of relativity, in this form:

> If a body releases the energy L in the form of radiation, its mass is decreased by $L/V^2$.
>
> *Annalen der Physik* (1905)

Einstein's realization that mass can be transformed into energy is the basis of nuclear power, peaceful or otherwise. It was a discovery that he lived to regret, writing in 1946:

> The unleashed power of the atom has changed everything save our modes of thinking and we thus drift towards unparalleled catastrophe.

**Eager beaver.** A US expression in the Second World War for an over-zealous recruit whose keenness was marked by volunteering on every possible occasion. It was subsequently applied in civilian life to any glutton for work. The beaver is noted for its industry and hard work, but not specifically for its eagerness.

> It would be futile to play that game against Republican Earl Warren, one of the foremost spokesmen of the eager-beaver West.
>
> *Time* (5 July 1948)

**Eagle.** A British comic published between 1950 and 1969. It was initiated by the Rev. Marcus Morris and the illustrator Frank Hampson, and it was under Hampson's influence that *Eagle* moved away from the Christianity-imbued BOY'S OWN PAPER that Morris had envisaged to something more exciting. It featured the character DAN DARE, Pilot of the Future, and the villainous MEKON, as well as a comic-strip version of PC 49. An equivalent for girls had the imaginative title *Girl*. *See also The* BOY'S OWN PAPER.

**Eagle Has Landed, The.** A film (1976) adapted by Tom Mankiewicz from a bestselling novel by Jack Higgins (1975) about a fictional Nazi plot to kill Winston Churchill during the Second World War. The film starred Donald Sutherland as the Irish Republican hitman detailed to execute the assassination. In the original novel Heinrich Himmler receives the message that 'the eagle has landed' and thereby knows that his agent is safely on British soil. Higgins himself claimed that at least half of his story was based on truth, but left it to the reader to decide what was true and what was fiction. Coincidentally, in 1969 the phrase became the first words spoken by a human being on the surface of the moon, when it was quoted by US astronaut Neil Armstrong reporting the safe touchdown of the lunar module *Eagle*:

> Tranquillity Base here – the Eagle has landed.
>
> NEIL ARMSTRONG: radio transmission (1969)

A wry variation on the original formulation is 'The ego has landed', used to signal the arrival of someone of more than usual self-conceit. It was used as the title of a 1999 Robbie Williams album.

**Eagle of the Ninth, The.** A children's historical novel (1954) by Rosemary Sutcliff (1920–92), describing the search north of Hadrian's Wall by a retired centurion, Marcus, for a lost legion (the Ninth) and its standard (a silver eagle).

**Eagle's Nest.** Adolf Hitler's private retreat high on the Obersalzberg mountain above Berchtesgaden in Bavaria, near the Austrian border. It was linked by a lift cut through the rock to Hitler's mountain chalet, the Berghof, home to his mistress Eva Braun from 1936 until she joined him in

Berlin in 1945. Although the Eagle's Nest was private, Hitler used the Berghof for important meetings, such as that with Neville Chamberlain in mid-September 1938, before the MUNICH Agreement. The Berghof was destroyed by Allied bombing in April 1945, and the ruins were levelled in 1952 to prevent the site from becoming a shrine. However, the Eagle's Nest survives as a tea room. *See also* FÜHRER.

**Ealing comedies.** Comedy films produced by the Ealing Studios, West London, from the late 1940s. They typically feature a downtrodden group rebelling against authority and are regarded as quintessentially 'English'. Among the best are PASSPORT TO PIMLICO (1948), in which, following the discovery of an ancient treaty, Pimlico is found to belong to Burgundy, and cocks a snook at England; WHISKY GALORE (1948), in which a ship with a cargo of whisky is wrecked on a small Scottish island; *The* LAVENDER HILL MOB (1951), centring on a timid clerk who plans and executes a bullion robbery; *The Man in the White Suit* (1951), a story centred on the invention of a cloth that will never wear out, in which a range of satirical targets are hit; and *The* LADYKILLERS (1955), in which a gang of robbers take refuge in a little old lady's house, but end up falling victim to her guilelessness.

Ealing Studios itself was founded in 1907 and five years later its studios were the biggest in Britain. The company's fortunes began to fail in the 1950s, when tastes were changing, and after releasing *The Ladykillers* it sold its studios to the BBC. Film stages and offices were subsequently rented out for independent productions, and in 1995 the site was sold to the National Film and Television School. *See also* ELSTREE STUDIOS.

**Ear candy.** Uncomplicated, EASY LISTENING pop music, of a type calculated to appeal as much (or more) to parents as to teenagers. The term originated in the United States around 1984 (roughly contemporary with EYE CANDY).

**Early bath.** If a sports player is ordered to have an early bath he is sent off the pitch before the end of the game for an infringement. The reference is to the bath or shower taken by players at the end of the game, with perhaps also a hint of a child sent to bed early for misbehaving.

**Early doors.** At an early point in the proceedings. The expression probably originated in northern England, perhaps referring to the early opening of the doors of a place of entertainment or refreshment (and especially the reopening of a pub at 5.30 after its afternoon closure), and began to be more widely disseminated through television sports commentaries in the 1970s. At the end of the 20th century it came to be particularly associated with the colourful vocabulary of football boss and television guru Ron 'Big Ron' Atkinson. The BBC television sitcom *Early Doors*, set in a northern pub, was first broadcast in 2003.

**Early Learning Centre.** The firm of this name, running shops to sell educational toys for pre-school children and give advice to their parents, was set up in 1974 by the educationalist John Beale (b.1945), when the first shop so called opened in Reading. The name itself is an Americanism for a pre-school centre. A second shop followed in 1977, a third in 1978 and many more subsequently. Beale sold the business off to Fine Art Development in 1984 and two years later founded Past Times, a firm also with a chain of shops specializing in historical replicas and nostalgic artefacts.

**Early music.** A name originating in the 1940s for medieval, renaissance and baroque music, especially as revived and played on 'authentic' instruments of the appropriate period. A pioneer in the field was David Munrow (1942–76), founder of the Early Music Consort in 1967.

**Early night.** An occasion on which one goes to bed earlier than usual, especially in order to catch up on sleep. The term is necessarily subjective, since what is 'early' for one person will be normal for another. The same holds for a late night.

**Early retirement.** Retirement from one's occupation earlier than the statutory pension age. From the 1980s many have been able to retire early on favourable terms. At the turn of the 21st century the pension age was 65 for men and 60 for women, but in 1995 legislation was introduced to equalize the age for both sexes at 65. The change will be phased in over two years starting from 2010.

**Earthsea.** The fictional archipelago that is the setting of Ursula LeGuin's fantasy quartet *A* WIZARD OF EARTHSEA (1968), *The Tombs of Atuan* (1971), *The Farthest Shore* (1972) and *Tehanu* (1990). It is roughly circular and at its heart lies the group known as the Inner Isles, which cluster round the Inmost Sea. To the north of this sea lies Havnor, the seat of the King of all the Isles. To the south is Wathort, a key post for trading with the southern islands. At the heart of the Inmost Sea is Roke, the centre for the teaching of the magic that is crucially important to the life of Earthsea.

**Earth Shoes.** The proprietary name of a type of square-toed shoes with soles that are thicker in the front than at the back, the aim being to lower the heel for greater comfort. They are so called because they were first imported to the United States from Denmark, their country of origin, on 22 April 1970, the first Earth Day, a day set aside by environmentalists to promote the importance of pollution control.

**Earth Summit.** An unofficial name for the United Nations Conference on Environment and Development, held in Rio de Janeiro in 1992. The basic purpose of the summit conference was to discuss matters of environment and development regarded as essential to the future of the earth, such as BIODIVERSITY. A follow-up conference of the same name was held in Johannesburg, South Africa ten years later.

**Earth to ....** A sarcastic formula used to gain the attention of someone wrapped up in their own thoughts or out of touch with reality, or to pour scorn on a wildly impractical or eccentric thought or idea someone has uttered. First recorded in the 1970s, it mimics the opening words of a radio operator sending a message to deep space in mid-20th-century science fiction.

> Earth to Bush: the breaching of the levees had been foreseen for decades. If anyone wanted evidence that this president was completely divorced from reality, that statement was Exhibit A.
>
> www.commondreams.com (30 October 2005)

**EastEnders.** A BBC SOAP OPERA launched in 1985 and soon challenging and even bettering the veteran CORONATION STREET in viewing figures. As its title implies, it is set in the East End of London, in the (fictitious) borough of Walford, and centres on Albert Square and its Queen Vic pub, originally run by Den Watts and his wife Angie. The chief theme of the series has been the love triangle, and an early story line involved the seduction of a schoolgirl by the lecherous 'DIRTY DEN'. The episode in which Den gave Angie divorce papers for Christmas was watched by a record 30 million viewers. The soap's success has been largely due to its bold treatment of 'tough' issues such as rape, prostitution, unemployment, HIV infection, abortion and homosexuality.

**Eastern Approaches.** *See* WESTERN APPROACHES.

**Easter Rising.** The most dramatic of the events in the struggle for HOME RULE in Ireland. The uprising had been planned by a number of radical nationalist groups and began with the seizing of the General Post Office in O'Connell Street, Dublin, on Easter Monday, 24 April 1916. From its pillared portico Patrick Pearse, a leader of the Irish Republican Brotherhood, read out a proclamation announcing the birth of the Irish republic. British troops soon arrived to put down the rebellion and for almost a week Dublin was paralyzed by street fighting. British artillery bombardments compelled Pearse and his colleagues to surrender on 29 April, and he and 14 other leaders of the rebellion were subsequently court-martialled and executed, their martyrdom creating much sympathy for their cause. The rebellion was a contributory factor in the establishment of the Irish Free State in 1921 (*see* FREE-STATERS).

W.B. Yeats's (1865–1939) poem 'Easter 1916' was inspired by the Rising, and mythologized its very considerable impact on modern Irish history.

> I write it out in a verse – Macdonagh and MacBride
> And Connolly and Pearse
> Now and in time to be,
> Wherever green is worn
> Are changed, changed utterly:
> A terrible beauty is born.

The phrase 'terrible beauty' is frequently quoted as a pithy yet poetic encapsulation of the violent nature of Ireland's ascent to nationhood, and makes regular appearances in the titles of books on Irish themes, such as *Ireland:A Terrible Beauty* (1976), by Jill and Leon Uris. *See also* ABBEY THEATRE; IRA; PROVOS; TROUBLES.

**East of Eden.** A novel (1952) by John Steinbeck (1902–68). The story follows two families in the Salinas Valley, California, through three generations of discord. It centres on Adam Trask, his murderous wife Kathy, who abandons her family and becomes the madam of a brothel, and their twin sons, Aron and Caleb, whose rivalry recalls the biblical story of Cain and Abel. The title is drawn from that account: 'And Cain went out from the presence of the Lord, and dwelt in the land of Nod, on the east of Eden' (Genesis 4:16). A rousing film version (1955), starring James Dean, was somewhat over-directed by Elia Kazan.

**Easy listening.** A term dating from the 1960s for recordings of popular music that are undemanding to listen to and that thus serve well for background music in a working or social environment. The style is typified by the US singer Andy Williams (b.1927) with songs such as 'Music to Watch Girls By' and 'On the Street Where You Live'.

**Easy on the eye.** Pleasing to look at. A phrase dating from the 1920s and usually applied to a beautiful girl or woman. A somewhat earlier equivalent was 'easy to look at'.

**Easy-peasy.** Childishly simple. The second word is simply a rhyming jingle. The phrase dates from the 1970s.

> But do I hear our ludic masochist asking for more? Univocalics? Easy. Lipograms? Peasy.
>
> DAVID CRYSTAL: *Language Play*, ch. 3 (1998)

**Easy rider.** A sexually satisfying lover. The reference is to 'riding' one's partner. The title of the acclaimed film *Easy Rider* (1969), in which two dropouts ride across the United States on motorcycles, has overtones of the earlier sense.

**Easy street.** A secure and comfortable life; a place or position where living is easy. The US expression dates from the turn of the 20th century.

**Eat, drink and sleep something.** To be fully and continuously absorbed in it, not only in one's every waking moment but also as if when asleep. The expression is usually applied to an all-consuming occupation or interest. In 1996 COCA-COLA was promoted during the European Championship football tournament in England with the slogan 'Eat football, sleep football, drink Coca-Cola', and the same formula was subsequently used with regard to cricket in India.

> 'I've seen what a physically and mentally grinding job the leadership [of the Liberal Democrats] is to do. It is a job that you can only do if you eat, drink and sleep it.'
>
> CHARLES KENNEDY: in *The Times* (10 August 1999)

**Eat my shorts!** An exclamation of scorn and contempt. It originated (in the late 1970s) among US college students, so 'shorts' are male underpants, no doubt in unsavoury condition. It was popularized by Bart SIMPSON, whose catchphrase it became. In the UK, a British Asian version appeared in the shape of 'Eat my chuddies!' ('chuddies' are underwear; the expression was brought to a wider public by the BBC comedy series *Goodness Gracious Me* (first broadcast in 1998) and *The Kumars at No. 42*).

**Eat out of someone's hand.** To be entirely submissive or obedient. The allusion is to a pet or tame animal, which will eat from a human hand. The expression dates from the early 20th century.

**Eat someone for breakfast.** *See* HAVE SOMEONE FOR BREAKFAST.

**eBay.** An INTERNET business that manages online auctions and other forms of shopping. It was founded in California in 1995. By 2004 its annual revenue had risen to $3.27 billion. The name originates in the Echo Bay Technology Group, a web consultancy group set up by the founder of eBay, Pierre Omidyar, who chose the name because it 'sounded cool'. He could not register EchoBay.com, as that was taken by Echo Bay Mines, so plumped for eBay (the lower-case 'e' being a common abbreviation for 'electronic' in the world of computing, as in E-MAIL).

Millions of people around the world buy and sell on eBay daily, and objects for sale can vary from the apparently worthless (a NutriGrain bar in the shape of E.T sold for A$1035 in 2004) to the extremely expensive (a 17th-century edition of Shakespeare's *Pericles* sold for £5 million). It is a particularly important market for collectibles. In 2005 Bob Geldof described eBay as a 'cyber pimp', after it had allowed free tickets to that summer's Live 8 (*see* BAND AID) concerts to be offered for sale for substantial sums. The relevant auctions were subsequently removed by eBay. Among the other items banned for sale are tobacco, alcohol, Nazi memorabilia, firearms, human organs and soiled underwear.

**E-boat.** In the Second World War an abbreviation for enemy torpedo boat, i.e. a German one. *See also* U-BOAT.

**E-boat Alley.** The name given to the coastal convoy route off the coast of East Anglia, which was the scene of much successful E-BOAT activity in the early years of the Second World War.

**Ebonics.** African-American English regarded as a language in its own right rather than as a dialect of English. In 1996 it was recognized as a legitimate language variety by school officials in Oakland, California. The term combines 'ebony' and 'phonics'. *See also* LYIN' AND TESTIFYIN'.

**Ecky Thump.** A fictitious Lancashire martial art involving hitting people over the head with black puddings. The invention of Bill Oddie (b.1941), it was introduced in *The Goodies* episode 'Kung Fu Capers' in 1975 (*see under* GOODIES). 'Ecky' derives from the traditional North Country ejaculation 'By heck!'

**Ecological footprint.** A term dating from the early 1990s for the amount of land required to sustain a particular society or the human race in general. 'Footprint' as a word for the area covered by something, such as that under a vehicle or aircraft, dates from the 1960s.

**Economical with the truth.** A euphemism for untruthful, brought before the public in 1986 as a result of a statement by the then cabinet secretary, Sir Robert Armstrong, to the Supreme Court, New South Wales, Australia, in the SPYCATCHER TRIAL. Referring to a letter, Sir Robert said: 'It contains a misleading impression, not a lie. It was being economical with the truth' (*Daily Telegraph*, 19 November 1986).

The phrase can be traced back to a similar statement by Edmund Burke: 'Falsehood and delusion are allowed in no case whatsoever. But, as in the exercise of all the virtues, there is an economy of truth' (*Two Letters of Proposals for Peace*, 1796). Cross-examined at the Old Bailey in 1992, the Conservative politician Alan Clark referred to 'our old friend economical … with the *actualité*'.

**Economic migrant.** Someone who emigrates to another country for the purpose of economic advancement. The term dates back at least to the 1960s, but it came to particular prominence in the early 21st century in specific (and usually disadvantageous) contrast with 'ASYLUM SEEKER' (those who seek to better themselves financially being regarded as less morally worthy than those who flee persecution).

Education and 'suitable' marriage … are perhaps the most important vehicles for the social and economic migrant.

A.G. FRANK: in *Monthly Review* (November 1962)

**Eco-tourism.** Tourism directed towards an exotic natural environment, especially one under threat such as the Amazon rainforest, in order to support conservation efforts and view wildlife. Such tourism is distinct from the conventional kind, which frequently despoils the natural environment.

**Eco-warrior.** An activist who takes direct and often illegal action on an environmental issue, 'eco-' representing 'ecology'. Like 'eco-terrorist', the term has two diametrically opposed senses: on the one hand, one who takes action to further environmental ends; on the other, one who wreaks politically motivated damage to the natural environment. Both terms date from the 1990s.

The ring road plan sparked massive protests. Dr Margaret Jones abandoned her academic career to become a full-time eco-warrior to fight the road scheme.

*Sunday Express* (27 February 2000)

**Ecstasy.** The name of a drug that acts as a stimulant and can cause hallucinations, as a state of supposed ecstasy. Its chemical name is methylenedioxymethamphetamine, usually abbreviated as MDMA. It was originally designed in 1917 as an appetite suppressant, but in the late 1980s played a key role in the rise of RAVE culture in Britain, and in the early 1990s in California.

**Eddie the Eagle.** The nickname of Eddie Edwards (b.1964), a short-sighted Gloucestershire plasterer who without any official back-up competed for Britain in the ski-jumping event in the 1988 Winter Olympics at Calgary. To no one's great surprise he came last, but the eagle had momentarily soared, winning the instinctive support of thousands for the plucky underdog.

**Edge of one's seat.** To sit or be on the edge of one's seat is to be in a state of attentive or expectant excitement, as when watching an absorbing spectacle. The phrase may be hyphenated as a synonym for 'exciting', 'thrilling'.

This [Mozart's opera *Don Giovanni*] is an edge-of-your-seat production, definitely worth catching in London this week.

*The Times* (11 October 1999)

**Edinburgh Group.** A group of Scottish painters who exhibited together in 1912, 1913, 1919, 1920 and 1921. Leading members were John R. Barclay (1884–1963), William Oliphant Hutchison (1889–1970), Dorothy Johnstone (1892–1980), Mary Newbery (1892–1985), Eric Robertson (1887–1941), J.G. Spence Smith (1880–1951), A.R. Sturrock

(1885–1953), who was married to Newbery, D.M. Sutherland (1883–1973) and Cecile Walton (1891–1956). They painted in a variety of figurative styles and attracted a good deal of public and critical attention, not least because of the notoriously involved love lives of many of their number, notably Robertson.

**Edinburgh Tattoo.** A display of military music and marching, one of the more popular entertainments on offer at the annual Edinburgh Festival, although not officially part of it. It was introduced in 1947 as a celebration of ethnic piping and dancing, organized by the Army's Scottish Command, and in 1950 was officially retitled the Edinburgh Military Tattoo. The show is held on the esplanade of Edinburgh Castle, the core of the entertainment being provided by pipes and drums. A lone piper concludes the programme.

To you it may be taboo
To poo-poo the Tattoo.
But to me the Tattoo
Is something to say ta-ta to.

JOHN HEGLEY: 'Edinburgh' (1986)

**Edsel.** A nickname for a manufactured product that is old-fashioned or that does not answer to the requirements of its time. The allusion is to the Ford Edsel, an unpopular make of Ford car made from 1957 to 1962 and named after the US car manufacturer Edsel B. Ford (1893–1943), only son of Henry Ford, founder of the Ford Motor Company. It did not help that the name suggests German *Esel*, 'donkey'.

**Educated guess.** A guess based on knowledge and past experience, and therefore likely to be correct. Many guesses are random or at best speculative, so lack the attributes of any kind of education.

**Educating Archie.** *See* Archie ANDREWS.

**Education, education, education.** The avowed priority of NEW LABOUR in the mid-1990s, as declared by its leader Tony Blair at the Labour Party Conference on 1 October 1996: 'Ask me my three main priorities for government and I tell you: education, education and education.' Inevitably, party priorities became more diffuse following Labour's election to power in 1997, although education remained, at least nominally, a front runner. It is uncertain to what extent the pronouncement was based on that of an earlier labourite, LENIN, who in an article of 1923 advocating the importance of scientific education in the furtherance of communism, voiced the prime objectives of the *apparat* as: 'first – to study, second – to study and third – to study.' The threefold clarion call became a slogan of Soviet youth in its pursuit of politically correct learning.

**Edutainment.** An activity or product in an electronic medium such as a video or computer game that is intended to be educational as well as enjoyable. The term is a blend of 'education' and 'entertainment' and arose in the 1980s on an analogy both with 'docutainment', as a documentary film that seeks to inform as well as entertain, and with 'infotainment', as any kind of broadcast material that seeks to inform and entertain at the same time.

**Edwardian era.** The decade of the reign of King Edward VII (1901–10), an age of fashion and style, of households with servants, of personal maids, of comfortable trains, of grand hotels, of richly stocked department stores, and of general opulence and leisure. The period has been regarded with nostalgia by many ever since, and accounts for the popularity of such television series as UPSTAIRS, DOWNSTAIRS, and of the meticulous re-creations of MERCHANT IVORY FILMS. *See also* SERVANT PROBLEM; TEDDY BOYS.

**Edward the Caresser.** A nickname for Edward VII (reigned 1901–10), renowned for his liaisons with a variety of women (with a pun on Edward the Confessor). His love of food earned another nickname, 'Tum-Tum', while for his role in the Entente Cordiale with France (1904) he was called 'Edward the Peacemaker'. Another sobriquet was 'the Uncle of Europe', his mother Queen Victoria being 'the Grandmother of Europe', so many of her children and grandchildren having married into the royal families of the continent.

**Ee bah gum.** A supposedly characteristic Yorkshire exclamation, made up of *ee*, a northern form of 'oh', and *bah gum*, 'by God', with the '*u*' pronounced short as in 'good'. Although widely known, the phrase was curiously absent from dictionaries until the *Concise Oxford Dictionary* included it in its 1999 edition. A Second World War pleasantry had a Yorkshireman emerging from an air-raid shelter with the rueful words: 'Bah gum, chum, ma bum's numb.'

> Eeeh bah gum, Bradford's glum.
> *Independent on Sunday*, headline (28 November 1999)

**Eejit.** A fool, as a spelling representing a supposedly typical Irish pronunciation of 'idiot'.

> He could have phoned someone downstairs at the reception desk and asked: 'Where's the minibar?' But he'd have felt like an eejit.
> DERMOT BOLGER (ed): *Finbar's Hotel*, 'Room 101 – Benny does Dublin' (1997)

**Effing and blinding.** Swearing; using coarse language. 'Effing' is using the F-WORD (*see also* FOUR-LETTER WORD); 'blinding' is using a word based on 'blind' such as 'blimey' or 'gorblimey'.

**Egghead.** An academic or intellectual, popularly envisaged as having a head as bald as an egg. The term is of US origin and dates from the early years of the 20th century.

> Egghead weds hourglass.
>> The headline supposedly used by *Variety* in 1956 to announce the marriage of the playwright Arthur Miller and the glamorous film star Marilyn Monroe.
>
> Eggheads of the world, arise – I was even going to add that you have nothing to lose but your yolks.
> ADLAI STEVENSON: speech in Oakland (1 February 1956)

*See also* POINTY HEAD.

**Egg on one's face.** An appearance of embarrassment or foolishness resulting from a gaffe. Eating a soft-boiled egg may well leave yolk stains around the mouth. The expression dates from the 1950s.

> Fondly remembered are the technical hitches … 'Night after night we were left with egg on our faces. But we persisted,' Barratt recalls.
> *The Times* (15 October 1999)

**EGYPT.** *See* LOVERS' ACRONYMS.

**'Eight Days a Week'.** A song by The BEATLES, credited to John Lennon and Paul McCartney and released in Britain in December 1964. The title is based on the casual use by the group's drummer, Ringo Starr, of a Liverpudlian phrase denoting hard work.

**Eighteenth law.** Common sense. The laws (not rules) of football have been condensed to 17 in number and the modern referee is expected to be familiar with all of them, not least the addition.

**8th Army.** The most familiar of the seven British armies during the Second World War, formed in Egypt in 1941 for the North African and subsequent Italian campaigns. The others were the 1st Army, formed in Britain to invade North Africa in 1942, the 2nd Army, also formed in Britain and taking part in northwest European campaigns, the 9th Army, formed behind the 8th Army in the Levant, the 10th Army, formed in Iraq in 1941 and controlling Syria, Persia and Iraq, and the 12th Army, raised in Burma in 1945 and joining the 14th Army, also raised there, in retaking Burma and Malaya.

> The numbering defies logic and is generally seen as a way of duping the enemy into thinking there were more fighting men than was actually the case. *See also* El ALAMEIN; FORGOTTEN ARMY; MONTY.

> Eighth Army Push Bottles Up Germans.
>> Ambiguous and possibly apocryphal headline, sometimes said to have appeared in the *News Chronicle* in 1942

**Eight-page.** Sexually titillating; 'steamy'. The allusion is to the eight-page pornographic booklets of the 1930s in which cartoon characters such as MICKEY MOUSE, POPEYE and BLONDIE were depicted in smutty scenarios far removed from their usual 'good clean fun'.

> A truck-load of movie offers followed on from *Wild Things*, including … the Lara Croft gig in *Tomb Raider*. 'And lots of films with eight-page lesbian scenes', she [Denise Richards] adds.
>
> *heat* (18–24 November 1999)

**Eighty-six.** In US restaurants and 'eateries' an expression indicating that the requested item is 'off' or not available, or that the customer is not to be served. The number is probably simply rhyming slang for 'nix'.

**Einsatzgruppen.** (German, 'task forces'.) The groups of SS troops formed in 1939 to follow the German armies into Poland, with the purpose of killing national leaders and rounding up Jews. By the time Hitler invaded the Soviet Union the Einsatzgruppen were 12,000 strong and were charged with the 'resettlement' (i.e. extermination) of all Jews and Soviet political commissars and the elimination of civilian resistance. The initial method was shooting, and then other methods were tried, such as pumping exhaust fumes into sealed lorries in which the victims were locked. By 1943 more than 600,000 Soviet Jews had been 'resettled' by the Einsatzgruppen, but their productivity did not satisfy the Nazi hierarchy, who decided it would be more efficient to build purpose-built extermination camps. *See also* FINAL SOLUTION.

**Ein Volk, ein Reich, ein Führer.** A NAZI slogan meaning 'One people, one realm, one leader'. It also appears in the form *ein Reich, ein Volk, ein Führer*. *See also* CAUDILLO; FÜHRER.

**Eire.** A former name of Southern Ireland. The new Irish constitution of 1937 changed the name of the country from the Irish Free State (*see* FREE-STATERS) to Eire (the Gaelic name for Ireland). In 1949, when Southern Ireland became a republic and withdrew from the Commonwealth, it became the Republic of Ireland.

**Eisenhower Doctrine.** A foreign policy pronouncement by President Dwight D. Eisenhower on 5 January 1957, during the COLD WAR period. It promised military or economic aid to any Middle Eastern country needing help in resisting communist aggression and was intended to check the increase of Soviet influence in the Middle East resulting from the supply of arms to Egypt by communist countries, as well as from strong communist support of Arab states against an Israeli, French and British attack on Egypt in October 1956 (*see* SUEZ CRISIS). The pronouncement did not represent a radical change in US policy, since the TRUMAN DOCTRINE had pledged similar support to Greece and Turkey ten years before.

**El Alamein.** *See* El ALAMEIN.

**Elastoplast.** The proprietary name of a type of adhesive sticking plaster for covering cuts and wounds, first put on the market in 1928 by the firm of Smith and Nephew, founded in 1856. The name simply denotes an 'elastic plaster'.

**El Beatle.** *See* FIFTH BEATLE.

**El cheapo.** Very cheap; shoddy. The pseudo-Spanish expression came into vogue in the 1960s. Spanish *el*, 'the', has long been familiar to English speakers from its occurrence in personal and place-names such as *El Cid, El Greco, El Paso, El Dorado*. *See also* EL NIÑO.

**Elder statesman.** While now denoting a respected and experienced politician, the term originally specifically applied in the 1920s to a member of the Japanese *Genro*, a body of retired statesmen consulted when necessary by the emperor. The Japanese word itself means 'principal elders', from *gen*, 'root', and *ro*, 'old'.

**'Eleanor Rigby'.** A poignant lyric (to the accompaniment of a string quartet) by The BEATLES, credited to John Lennon and Paul McCartney and released in Britain in August 1966 on the album REVOLVER. Eleanor Rigby is a lonely spinster who dies alone without ever having been able to tell anyone about her feelings of personal despair. The name may derive from the name of a clothes shop in Bristol combined with the first name of the actress Eleanor Bron, or may alternatively be taken from a real-life Eleanor Rigby (1895–1939) who lived in Liverpool. The song's lyrics have a depth and resonance unusual for a pop single. Particularly memorable is the image of Eleanor keeping her face 'in a jar by the door', an expression of her stoic refusal to show her real emotions publicly.

**E-learning.** 'Electronic' learning. Since the 1990s it is an increasingly common form of teaching, at further and higher-education level, which takes advantage of computer technology, the INTERNET and the WORLD WIDE WEB to deliver learning materials, thus replacing traditional classes, lectures, seminars, etc. Courses may combine traditional campus learning and electronic elements ('blended learning') or may be wholly e-learning in structure, in which case they are a form of distance learning. In theory, the latter may be accessed from a computer anywhere in the world.

**Elective dictatorship.** A phrase often applied to the British system of government, especially where the governing party has a large majority (such as the governments of Margaret Thatcher and Tony Blair), in which circumstances the scrutinizing power of parliament and of dissenting backbench MPs tends to be reduced. The people themselves only have their say every four or five years, when a general election turns up. However, the government's powers may be constrained by, for example, judicial interpretations of the Human Rights Act of 1998, which came into effect in 2000, or by the House of Lords, to a limited extent.

The phrase originates in the title of a Dimbleby Lecture given on 19 October 1976 by the Tory politician Quintin Hogg (Lord Hailsham; 1907–2001).

> I – we – the government …
>
> TONY BLAIR: addressing the press the day after the general election of 5 May 2005

**Electra complex.** The psychoanalytical term for a daughter's feelings of sexual attraction towards her father and hostility towards her mother. The allusion is to Electra in Greek tragedy, the daughter of Agamemnon and Clytemnestra, who incited her brother Orestes to kill their mother in revenge for the latter's murder of their father. *See also* OEDIPUS COMPLEX.

**Electricification of the Soviet Union, The.** An opera by Nigel Osborne (b.1948) with a libretto by Craig Raine (b.1944), based on Russian sources by Boris Pasternak. It was first performed in 1987 at Glyndebourne. The story concerns a young poet's loves and his response to society, and the title comes from Lenin's famous practical definition of communism, from his report to the 8th party congress of 1920:

> Communism is Soviet power plus the electrification of the whole country.

**Electric Kool-Aid Acid Test, The.** *See* MERRY PRANKSTERS.

**Elegies to the Spanish Republic.** The title of a series of paintings by the great abstract expressionist Robert Motherwell (1915–91), characterized by vertical bands and ovals in black, white and subdued colours. Motherwell began the series in 1949, on the tenth anniversary of the final defeat of the Spanish Republic by Franco's Nationalists. Over the next three decades he painted almost 150 of these *Elegies. See also* 'AT FIVE IN THE AFTERNOON'.

**Elephant in the corner.** A significant issue that is perfectly obvious to everyone, but which they carefully avoid discussing or acknowledging. The expression, which is often alternatively formulated as 'the elephant in the living room', commonly occurs (and may have originated) in the terminology of alcoholism or drug addiction and recovery, connoting denial of the problem by friends and family of the addict.

> The bland-seeming question, What is news? turns out to be complicated, political and important. In the lives of most journalists, it is the elephant in the corner, huge and mildly embarrassing, but rarely openly discussed.
>
> ANDREW MARR: *My Trade* (2004)

**Elephant Man, The.** A much-admired film (1980), shot in black and white and directed by David Lynch, about a man whose elephantine features (resulting from disease) sentence him to a life as a carnival-show freak until he attracts the attention of a sympathetic member of the medical establishment. The film, starring John Hurt, was based on the life story of the real Joseph Merrick (1867–90), who was thus disfigured and who became the subject of medical curiosity in Victorian England. In the late 1980s Merrick's affliction was diagnosed as Proteus syndrome, a rare genetic disorder that results in overgrowths on one side of the body, enlarged hands and feet and tumour-like growths under the skin.

**Eleven-plus.** The name formerly given to the examination set to primary schoolchildren at the age of 11 or 12 and used as a means of judging their suitability for the various types of secondary education provided by the Education Act of 1944 (secondary modern, secondary technical, secondary grammar, etc). The unreliability of testing children at this age and so determining the type of school to which they should be sent resulted in the 1976 Education Act, which compelled local authorities to draw up plans for comprehensive reorganization, although this was later repealed. The term is still loosely used for the age at which children leave primary school.

**Eleventh commandment.** An ironical addition to the Ten Commandments, usually interpreted as 'Thou shalt not be found out'.

**Elidor.** A fantasy (1965) for children by Alan Garner (b.1934). A collection of everyday objects becomes the means of saving the mythical world of Elidor, to which four children have been transported from the back streets of Manchester. The name of Elidor suggests that of El Dorado, the fictitious country or city abounding in gold, at one time believed to exist in South America.

**Eligible bachelor.** A bachelor who is considered desirably available for marriage, as distinct from a 'confirmed bachelor', who for reasons known or unknown is not.

**Eliza Doolittle.** *See* Eliza DOOLITTLE.

**Elk Hills scandal.** *See* TEAPOT DOME SCANDAL.

**Elm Street.** The fictional location of a hugely successful series of SLASHER MOVIES that began with *A Nightmare on Elm Street* (1984), directed by Wes Craven. Five similarly blood-spattered sequels followed. The films centre around the nightmarish events that take place at 1428 Elm Street, involving the terrorizing of a group of suburban teenagers by the hideously scarred figure of Freddy Krueger (played by Robert Eklund), who has knives for fingernails.

**El Niño.** The irregularly occurring weather system that is characterized by warm ocean temperatures in the Equatorial Pacific. Its name is short for Spanish *El Niño de Navidad*, 'the Christmas Child', since it warms the water off the north Peruvian coast at Christmas. The name became generally familiar in the latter half of the 20th century when marked changes in the global climate became a matter of increasing concern. *See also* LA NIÑA.

**Elstree Studios.** Films at Elstree date from 1914, when Neptune Studios opened on the rural Hertfordshire site, chosen for its proximity to London. They closed in 1917 but were succeeded by a sprawling complex of studios soon dubbed 'the British HOLLYWOOD'. The first British 'talkie', *Blackmail*, was directed by Alfred Hitchcock at Elstree in 1929 and in the 1930s a stream of thrillers, comedies and musicals poured from the site. Following the Second World War Elstree produced such British classics as *The* DAM BUSTERS (1954) and also attracted American stars such as Gregory Peck in *Moby Dick* (1954) and Cary Grant in *Indiscreet* (1957). Its fortunes then flagged, but Stanley Kubrick kept the studios busy with 2001: A SPACE ODYSSEY (1968) and George Lucas even more so with STAR WARS (1976). The huge success of *The* FULL MONTY (1997), also shot at Elstree, ensured financial stability for the studios into the 21st century.

**Elvis Lives.** An anagrammatical slogan claiming the immortality, at least in spirit, of the extraordinarily popular singer Elvis Presley (1935–77). So-called 'Elvis sightings', or supposed physical manifestations of 'the KING', were still being proclaimed by devotees some 20 years on.

**Elvis the Pelvis.** A rhyming nickname of Elvis Presley (*see* ELVIS LIVES), alluding to the gyration of his hips on stage. It was sometimes shortened to simply 'Pelvis'. *See also* GRACELAND.

**E-mail.** 'Electronic mail', sent by one computer user to one or more others over a network. Communications sent by e-mail have attracted their own etiquette – 'netiquette' – differing from that of letters sent by SNAIL MAIL and in some ways closer to that of a telephone call. It is bad form to 'shout', i.e. use capital letters unnecessarily. Irony or sarcasm is frowned upon and gossip risks being forwarded to the wrong person. To aid those in the know, and to confuse those who are not, there is also a vocabulary of 'emoticons' (*see* SMILEY FACE): the characters and symbols of the keyboard used in such combinations as to convey emotions of pleasure, astonishment, etc., and which sometimes replace the standard signing-off phrases of regular letters.

The prefix 'e-' is also applied to other areas such as e-trade and e-commerce, meaning trade or commerce over the INTERNET. *See also* EBAY; E-LEARNING.

***Emergency – Ward 10.*** The first British medical television SOAP OPERA, screened on ITV from 1957 to 1967. It was set in the (fictitious) Oxbridge General Hospital and was initially to have been titled *Calling Nurse Roberts* after the original main character, Nurse Pat Roberts, played by Rosemary Miller.

***Emil and the Detectives.*** A novel, originally *Emil und die Detektive* (1929), by the German writer Erich Kästner (1899–1974). A much-imitated 'children-against-villains' tale, it tells the tale of 10-year-old Emil Tischbein who, travelling from Neustadt to Berlin to stay with relations, is robbed of his money on a train. He embarks on a hunt for the thief with the assistance of a group of children. The thief turns out to be notorious bank-robber, long sought by the police, and Emil is handsomely rewarded for his efforts.

**Emily's list.** A group launched in the United States in 1985 to raise funds for women wishing to become Democratic candidates, especially those who are pro-abortion. The name is an acronym of 'Early Money Is Like Yeast', the last word of this being a punning allusion to an agent that makes 'dough rise'. The movement spread to Britain in the early 1990s with the aim of increasing the representation of women in the LABOUR PARTY.

**Eminent Victorian.** A 20th-century term for any famous or worthy Briton active in the reign of Queen Victoria (1837–1901). The expression derives from Lytton Strachey's groundbreaking work of biographical MODERNISM *Eminent Victorians* (1918), containing studies of Cardinal Manning (1808–92), Florence Nightingale (1820–1910), Thomas Arnold (1795–1842) and General Gordon (1833–85). Strachey's title had a touch of irony about it, since part of his purpose was to deflate the conventions of obsequious Victorian biography. *See also* LEGEND IN ONE'S LIFETIME.

**Emmanuelle.** The eponymous heroine, played by Sylvia Kristel, of a soft-core French pornographic film, released in 1974. Emmanuelle, the bored wife of a French diplomat based in Thailand, is urged by her friends to embark on a journey of sexual discovery. The film spawned a number of equally tawdry sequels.

**Emmets.** An expression commonly applied in Cornwall to tourists and holidaymakers. 'Emmet' is an old word for an ant, and such insects swarm everywhere. *See also* GROCKLES.

**Emmy.** The television equivalent of the OSCAR, first awarded by the American Academy of Television Arts and Sciences in 1949. The awards, in the form of winged statuettes, are divided into comedy series, drama series and mini-series, with each of these subdivided into individual actors and actresses. The name itself is a form of Immy, a nickname for the image orthicon camera tube that formed part of early television sets. *See also* GRAMMY.

**Emoticon.** *See* SMILEY FACE.

**Empire Day.** A memorial day instituted by the Earl of Meath in 1902, after the end of the second Boer War, as a way to encourage schoolchildren to be aware of their duties and responsibilities as citizens of the British Empire. The day set aside was 24 May, Queen Victoria's birthday. In 1916 it was given official recognition in the United Kingdom, and it was renamed Commonwealth Day in 1958. Since 1977 this has been observed on the second Monday in March.

**Empire of the Senses.** (Japanese title: *Ai No Corrida*; also called *Empire of the Passions* and *In the Realm of the Senses*.) A notorious Japanese film (1976) written and directed by Nagisa Oshima (b.1932). The graphic sex – the story concerns the passionate affair between a servant girl and her master, and ends in the former killing and mutilating the latter – ensured that the film did not receive a certificate for public exhibition in Britain until 1991. Oshima was inspired by an incident in 1936 in which a woman was found wandering around Tokyo with her lover's severed penis.

One of the English titles was parodied by self-styled 'Post-Modern Literature's Girl Wonder', US writer Kathy Acker (1948–97), in her experimental novel *Empire of the Senseless* (1988). This is set in a Paris of the near future, and features the terrorists and occasional lovers Thivai, a pirate, and Abhor, a semi-human robot.

**Empire Strikes Back, The.** The second film (1980) in George Lucas's first STAR WARS trilogy. It was this title that is thought to have inspired the infamous description by President Ronald Reagan (who frequently confused reality with the movies) of the Soviet Union as 'the EVIL EMPIRE'.

**Empty nester.** A parent whose children have grown up and left home or 'flown the nest'. The expression is of US origin and dates from the 1960s. *See also* HOME ALONE.

**Emsworth, Lord.** The pig-loving peer who resides at Blandings Castle in the novels and short stories of P.G. Wodehouse (1881–1975). In his full glory he is Clarence Threepwood, 9th Earl of Emsworth, and he and his idiotic son, the Hon. Freddie Threepwood, first appear in the novel *Something Fresh* (1915). Many of the stories involve daring plots to abduct the Empress of Blandings, Lord Emsworth's prize pig.

**Emu parade.** An Australian colloquialism for a group of people assigned the task of cleaning up litter in a given area (who bend over and bob up and down like emus as they do their work). As the second part of the term suggests, it originated in the military.

**'End, The'.** A song by The Doors. *See* THIS IS THE END.

**Endgame.** A play (1957) by the Irish playwright Samuel Beckett (1906–89) in which four enigmatic characters, Hamm, Clov, Nagg and Nell (the last two of whom are encased in dustbins), inhabit a bare room with just two small curtained windows. The play is said to be the author's favourite among his works. Its meaning is obscure, but the title refers to chess, in which the endgame is the final series of moves in which a victor completes his opponent's inevitable defeat.

**End in tears.** To have an unhappy or painful outcome. The phrase is often by way of a warning: 'It will all end in tears.'

> Where almost nobody will speak to her, she falls for a middle-aged poacher who does at least involve her in his murderous rivalry with a gamekeeper. You can be sure it will all end in tears.
>
> *Sunday Times* (12 September 1999)

**End is nigh.** Traditional doom-laden words familiar from the placards of religious fanatics. The precise source of the prediction is uncertain, and although 'nigh' is very much a biblical word, the statement is not found in the Bible. Approximations exist, however, in: 'But the end of all things is at hand' (1 Peter 4:7), 'The day of the Lord cometh, for it is nigh at hand' (Joel 2:1), and 'Know ye that the kingdom of God is nigh at hand' (Luke 21:31).

**End of civilization as we know it.** The total collapse of ordered society. The expression, a supposed cinematic cliché uttered in a SCIENCE FICTION movie when the world is threatened by invasion from outer space, appears to originate in a line from the film CITIZEN KANE (1941) spoken by the newspaper magnate Charles Foster Kane at a press conference before the Second World War:

> 'I've talked with the responsible leaders of the Great Powers – England, France, Germany and Italy. They're too intelligent to embark on a project which would mean the end of civilization as we now know it. You can take my word for it: there'll be no war!'

**End of History, The.** A book (1992) by the American think-tanker Francis Fukuyama (b.1952), which argued that, with the end of the Cold War and the collapse of the Soviet Union, the global triumph of capitalism and liberal democracy are inevitable. The book's full title is *The End of History and the Last Man*, and it had its origins in a paper Fukuyama published in 1989. His thesis – that 'a remarkable consensus concerning the legitimacy of liberal democracy as a system of government [has] emerged throughout the world' – was somewhat compromised by the events of 9/11, which suggested that such a consensus was by no means universal. *See also* CLASH OF CIVILIZATIONS.

**End of story.** There is nothing more to add. A phrase indicating that the speaker has said all that needs to be said and that further words are superfluous. Colloquially it is sometimes shortened to 'end of'. *See also* FULL STOP.

**End of the Affair, The.** A novel (1951) by Graham Greene (1904–91) about a wartime love affair during the BLITZ. It is said to have been inspired by Greene's own extra-marital affair with Catherine Walston (1916–78), the promiscuous wife of a wealthy banker, Henry Miles, whose first name was the same as that of the cuckolded husband in the novel. In the novel Sarah, the wife, ends the affair, and dies from the complications of a cold, aggravated by the harassment of her former lover, who is a novelist. The affair between Greene and Walston carried on until the late 1950s. There have been two films: in 1954, directed by Edward Dmytryk, and 2000, directed by Neil Jordan.

**End of the beginning.** Winston Churchill's characterization of the victory at El Alamein (*see* El ALAMEIN), in a speech given at the Mansion House, London, 10 November 1942:

> This is not the end. It is not even the beginning of the end. But it is, perhaps, the end of the beginning.

**End of the world.** To say that something is not the end of the world is to recognize that although apparently calamitous, it is not finally disastrous. The expression dates from the beginning of the 20th century.

> *Lomax* [*with studied coolness*]: My good fellow: you neednt get into a state of nerves. Nothing's going to happen to you; and I suppose it wouldnt be the end of the world if anything did.
> GEORGE BERNARD SHAW: *Major Barbara*, III (1907)

**Enduring Freedom.** The operational code name of the US-led military operation in Afghanistan in 2001–2 to overthrow the TALIBAN regime and destroy AL-QAIDA bases in the country following the events of 9/11. The operation was originally to be called Infinite Justice, until it was realized this would offend Muslims, for whom 'infinite justice' is the sole prerogative of Allah. *See also* CAMP X-RAY; FREEDOM FRIES; FREEDOM TOWER; IRAQI FREEDOM; PATRIOT ACT; WAR ON TERROR.

**Enemy within.** Margaret Thatcher's characterization of the National Union of Mineworkers, under their leader Arthur Scargill (KING ARTHUR), at the time of the 1984–5 Miners' Strike:

> We had to fight the enemy without in the Falklands. We always have to be aware of the enemy within which is more difficult to fight and more dangerous to liberty.
> Speech to the 1922 Committee of Tory backbenchers
> (19 July 1984)

*See also* FALKLANDS FACTOR.

**Engineers of human souls.** STALIN's description of writers. In a speech to a group of writers at Maxim Gorky's house on 26 October 1932 he said:

> There are various forms of production: artillery, automobiles, lorries. You also produce 'commodities', 'works', 'products'. Such things are highly necessary. Engineering things. For people's souls. 'Products' are highly necessary too. 'Products' are very important for people's souls. You are engineers of human souls.

Gorky himself used the phrase in a speech to the Writers' Congress in 1934:

> The proletarian state must bring up thousands of excellent 'mechanics of culture', 'engineers of the 'soul'.

As might be expected, the phrase was not popular in the West:

> In free society art is not a weapon … Artists are not engineers of the soul.
> JOHN F. KENNEDY: speech at Amherst College, Massachusetts
> (26 October 1963).

The phrase was somewhat ironically borrowed as the title of *The Engineer of Human Souls* (1984), a rambling comic novel interweaving the present and the past by the Czech writer Josef Skvorecky, who was exiled to Canada after the failure of the PRAGUE SPRING. Skvorecky subtitles his novel 'An Entertainment on the Old Themes of Life, Women, Fate, Dreams, the Working Class, Secret Agents, Love and Death'.

**English disease.** A term current in continental Europe in the 1960s and 1970s (French, *la maladie anglaise*) to explain the sluggish state of the British economy. The symptoms were seen as strikes, restrictive practices, absenteeism and extended tea breaks. The same term was applied in the 1980s to soccer hooligans and LAGER LOUTS. Historically 'English disease' was a term current in continental Europe for melancholy or 'spleen' and also for rickets, a disease first identified in 17th-century England.

**English Patient, The.** A novel (1992) by Michael Ondaatje (b.1943), which was joint winner of the BOOKER PRIZE with *Sacred Hunger* by Barry Unsworth (b.1930). It is set in a battered Tuscan villa surrounded by unexploded mines, as World War II draws to a close in 1945. Four characters inhabit the villa: Kip, an Indian bomb-disposal expert; Caravaggio, a Canadian spy and thief; Hana, a young nurse; and her charge, the 'English patient', who has been appallingly burnt in a plane crash in North Africa. Little by little we come to find out more about this character's history. He is in fact a Hungarian, Count Almasy, and Ondaatje based him on the real Count Laszlo Almasy, the explorer of the Libyan Desert, who, during the war, used his geographical knowledge to infiltrate two German agents into Egypt. Ondaatje's characters from the English patient's past, Geoffrey and Katherine Clifton, are loosely based on Sir Robert and Lady Clayton East Clayton. Sir Robert died in 1932, at the age of 24, shortly after returning from an expedition with Almasy. Lady Clayton East Clayton (née Dorothy Mary Durrant) was a noted explorer and aviator, and met her death while flying at Brooklands in 1933. A glossily romantic film version (1996), with Ralph Fiennes in the title role, was directed by Anthony Minghella.

**English rose.** This term for a typically attractive light-complexioned English girl dates from the turn of the 20th century and is found in Basil Hood's poetic drama *Merrie England* (1902) in which he describes a garden where 'women are the flow'rs' and in which 'the sweetest blossom' or 'fairest Queen' is 'the perfect English rose'. The phrase has subsequently been associated with royal princesses, fair-skinned portrait posers and fine-boned film actresses, among others.

**English sunbathing.** Sitting fully clothed in the sunshine. A bemusedly ironic New Zealand term of the 1970s inspired by the curious habits of British immigrants.

**Enigma.** Germany's device for the encoding of strategic messages before and during the Second World War. The Enigma machine had a set of revolving drums that could scramble the alphabet into millions of combinations, generating a mass of gibberish that could be decoded only by another Enigma. A Polish mechanic working on the machine in 1928 took notes of the components before being repatriated, and with the help of the British and French secret services constructed a wooden mock-up. Later, a British cryptographer managed to smuggle a completely new Enigma machine to England, where a team of decoders found a way of cracking the ciphers. In 1939 the secret service set up the Ultra project at Bletchley Park, Buckinghamshire, for the purpose of intercepting the Germans' Enigma signals. The intelligence received was crucial in the BATTLE OF BRITAIN, the DUNKIRK evacuation, the BATTLE OF THE ATLANTIC and the Normandy landings on D-DAY. The Ultra project provided the subject-matter for *Enigma* (1995), a successful thriller by Robert Harris. A film version of Harris's novel, directed by Micheal Apted and starring Kate Winslet, appeared in 2001.

**Enjoy your meal.** A stock expression of goodwill made by a waiter in a restaurant after serving an opening course at table. The formula is virtually meaningless and is intended to suggest that whatever the reality the meal will indeed be a success and that the waiter will benefit as a result. *See also* HAVE A NICE DAY.

**Enola Gay.** The name of the Boeing B-29 Superfortress bomber that on 6 August 1945 dropped 'Little Boy', the atomic bomb that destroyed HIROSHIMA, killing nearly 80,000 people instantly. It was piloted by Colonel Paul Tibbets (b.1915) and was named after the pilot's mother. A second bomb, 'Fat Man', was dropped by *Bock's Car*, another B-29, on Nagasaki three days later. Shortly afterwards Japan surrendered, ending the Second World War. *Enola Gay* has been restored and is now on display at the Smithsonian's National Air and Space Museum in Washington, D.C. A life-size replica of 'Little Boy' was on display in the museum at Los Alamos until 9/11, after which it was hidden away deep underground, 300 feet beneath the town's MCDONALD'S.

A film, *Fat Man and Little Boy*, about the political pressures on scientists to create weapons of mass destruction, was released in 1989. It was directed by Roland Joffe and starred Paul Newman and Dwight Schultz.

**Enosis.** (Greek, 'union'.) The campaign of this name for the union of Cyprus and Greece originated in 1912 and continued until the establishment of the Republic of Cyprus in 1960. *See also* EOKA.

**Ensa.** The Entertainments National Service Association, which in the Second World War provided concerts and shows for British troops abroad and for camps and factories at home. Many famous figures in the entertainment world took part, greatly helping to boost morale. The acronym was affectionately interpreted as Every Night Something Awful.

**Entente Cordiale.** (French, 'cordial understanding'.) The agreement signed between Britain and France in 1904, forming the basis of Anglo-French cooperation in the First World War. It covered matters ranging from policies in North Africa to fishing rights off Newfoundland and proved that the former enemies could work together after all in the face of German military expansion. *See also* SARAJEVO.

**Entertaining Mr Sloane.** A play (1964) by the British playwright Joe Orton (1933–67) about an attractive young murderer whose attempts to establish a comfortable life for himself in the home of a doting woman and her brother only results in him becoming their sexual plaything. Sloane is the murderer 'entertained' by the brother and sister. This was the first of Orton's full-length plays, and its transfer to the West End of London was largely due to the efforts of Terence Rattigan, an apparently unlikely supporter. A film version appeared in 1969.

**E-numbers.** Code numbers preceded by the letter E on food products denote additives numbered in accordance with EUROPEAN UNION directives. There are just over 300 listed additives and about 3000 flavourings. E-numbers are divided into five groups: colourings (E100–180), preservatives (E200–290), antioxidants (E300–321), emulsifiers (E322–394) and sweeteners (E420–421). E-numbers are popularly associated with JUNK FOOD, which has many additives and flavourings.

**EOKA.** The Cypriot guerrilla force organized in 1954 to fight for ENOSIS. It was active until the mid-1970s. The name is an acronym of Greek *Ethnikē Organōsis Kupriakou Agōnos*, 'National Organization of Cypriot Struggle'.

**Epic theatre.** A type of anti-naturalistic theatre developed in the 1920s by the German director-dramatists Erwin Piscator and Bertolt Brecht. In plays such as MOTHER COURAGE AND HER CHILDREN and *The* CAUCASIAN CHALK CIRCLE, Brecht sought deliberately to distance audiences from the characters and action on stage through stylized dialogue and the use of songs, thereby encouraging them to focus on understanding the political contexts of the action. Brecht later described this technique as the *Verfremdungseffekt* (German, 'alienation effect').

**Equivalent VIII.** *See* TATE BRICKS.

**Equus.** A play (1973) by the British playwright Peter Shaffer (b.1926) about a young stable boy who undergoes psychiatric analysis after he blinds six horses following a frustrated sexual liaison. The play was based on an actual case, reported in the press in 1973, in which a young man blinded several horses apparently without motive. The play was filmed in 1977 starring Richard Burton as the psychiatrist. The young man's obsession with horses is reflected in the title, which is Latin for 'horse'.

**ER.** A television medical drama series of US origin, devised by Michael Crichton and first screened on Channel 4 in 1995. It is set in the Emergency Room (ER) of Cook County Hospital, Chicago, and its draw lies in its frantic pace, gory scenes and high emotional tension, with most of the action centring on the doctors and nurses rather than the patients.

**Eric the Eel.** The nickname of Eric Moussambani (b.1978), the natatorially challenged swimmer from Equatorial Guinea who entered the 100 metres freestyle in the Sydney Olympic Games of 2000 and finished last in his race in a time of 1 minute 52.72 seconds (which would not have won him a medal in the 200 metres), thereby achieving instant celebrity. Despite clocking the slowest ever Olympic time, Moussambi won his race – his two competitors having been disqualified for jumping the gun. 'That's what the Olympics are all about,' said the BBC commentator. The nickname was probably modelled on that of EDDIE THE EAGLE, another Olympic trier whose reach exceeded his grasp.

**ERNIE.** The Premium Bonds genius, more formally designated the *e*lectronic *r*andom *n*umber *i*ndicator *e*quipment. ERNIE is thus not a computer, as it is sometimes described. The first prize was drawn in 1956, and ERNIE was still in high favour with 'investors' 40 years on, despite the competing allure of the National Lottery from 1994. At the turn of the 21st century ERNIE offered thousands of prizes ranging from £50 to a single top prize of £1 million.

**Err is human, but to really foul things up takes a computer, To.** A modern proverb, first recorded in the *Farmer's Almanac for 1978*. It plays on a line from Alexander Pope's *Essay on Criticism* (1711):

> To err is human; to forgive, divine.

The proverb has been adapted by Robert Orben:

> To err is human – and to blame it on a computer is even more so.

**Escape film.** A film whose main story deals with some kind of entrapment. A narrative of this type has long been popular in the cinema since its effect is naturally enhanced by the confined area of the auditorium and even the spatial restriction of the screen, creating a sense of oppression for the audience and their own increased desire for freedom. Examples of such films are Jean Renoir's *La Grande Illusion* (1937), about three French pilots captured by the Germans in the First World War, and John Sturges's *The* GREAT ESCAPE (1963), in which Allied prisoners break out of a German prison camp. *See also* COLDITZ.

**Eskimo pie.** A proprietary name for a bar of chocolate-coated ice cream introduced in the United States in 1921.

**Essex girl.** A type of unintelligent and materialistic young woman who emerged in the late 1980s as the female equivalent of ESSEX MAN. Her supposed promiscuity and tarty appearance (short skirt, clunking gold jewellery, white stiletto heels) made her the butt of a variety of politically incorrect jokes (example: 'How does an Essex girl turn the light on after sex?' 'She kicks the car door open'). *See also* BIRDS OF A FEATHER; SHARON.

> It was soon obvious I had a blue-green algae problem. The stuff spreads faster than an Essex girl joke in a bar full of salesmen.
>
> *Practical Fishkeeping* (April 1992)

**Essex man.** A type of socially ungraced and culturally deprived Conservative voter, typically a self-made businessman, who lives in Essex or southeast England and who in the late 1980s worshipped the consumer-oriented gospel of THATCHERISM. The coining of the expression is generally attributed to the late left-wing Conservative MP Julian Critchley (who once opined that 'Essex is so right-wing that even the newsagents are white'), although the claim to authorship is contested by the journalist Simon Heffer. But whoever thought of the name, the species was definitively described in an unsigned profile headed 'Mrs Thatcher's bruiser' that appeared in the *Sunday Telegraph* for 7 October 1990:

> He [Essex man] is discovered in his original state and in the greatest abundance in the triangle between Brentwood, Southend and the Dagenham Marshes.

He is a ruthlessly self-interested, philistine, lager-swilling racist and the potential owner of a Rottweiler, if only he had time to walk it. One might add an element of Jack-the-Laddery to the mix. The specific link with Essex is that the south and southwest of the county had been the recipient of a wave of working-class immigrants from East London after the Second World War. Hitherto solid Labour voters, in the 1980s they discovered en masse the joys of unfettered capitalism. The Essex town of Basildon reinforced the stereotype when, in the 1992 general election, it was the first constituency to declare a result that accurately implied a stronger level of Conservative support in the country than the polls had predicted. *See also* ESSEX GIRL.

Essex Man, one of Britain's most strident class warriors with his mobile phone, Ford Escort XR3i and 'loadsamoney' mentality, is a doyen among consumers.

GREG HADFIELD and MARK SKIPWORTH: *Class*, ch. 8 (1994)

*See also* LOADSAMONEY.

**Establishment, The.** A term long used to denote in particular the established Church of England, but now a popular designation for the group or class of people who have authority within a society, especially, in Britain, those who control not only the Church of England but the government, the Civil Service and the armed forces. It has a somewhat derogatory significance associated with reaction, privilege and 'stuffiness'. The journalist Henry Fairlie is generally credited with bringing it into wide currency, in the *Spectator* article quoted below.

> By the 'Establishment' I do not mean only the centres of official power – though they are certainly part of it – but rather the whole matrix of official and social relations within which power is exercised … the 'Establishment' can be seen at work in the activities of, not only the Prime Minister, the Archbishop of Canterbury and the Earl Marshal, but of such lesser mortals as the Chairman of the Arts Council, the Director-General of the BBC, and even the editor of the *Times Literary Supplement*, not to mention dignitaries like Lady Violet Bonham Carter.
>
> HENRY FAIRLIE: in *The Spectator* (23 September 1955)

In the early 1960s, Peter Cook's ironically named London club The Establishment became a hot-bed of the anti-Establishment satire boom of that era. In October 1982, Harold Macmillan (a prime target of the 1960s satirists) told the Carlton Club:

> After a long life I have come to the conclusion that when all the establishment is united it is always wrong.

**Estádio da Luz.** The home ground of the Portuguese football club Benfica, on the outskirts of Lisbon, where it was opened in 1954. The name happens to mean 'Stadium of Light' but actually derives from the suburb, Luz, in which the ground and its surrounding sports facilities are located. *See also* STADIUM OF LIGHT.

**Estuary English.** A type of English accent identified as spreading out from London to the southeast of England, the area of the Thames Estuary, and containing a blend of received (standard) pronunciation and that of Cockney or London speech. The term was coined in 1984 by the linguist David Rosewarne. The accent is regarded as typical of a supposedly growing classless society. *See also* MOCKNEY.

In contrast with Eliza Doolittle, who had to re-engineer her accent to become socially acceptable, the prime minister [Tony Blair] descended into estuary English in an attempt to reach out to the masses.

*Sunday Times* (7 June 1998)

**E.T.** The gentle but rather grotesque creature from outer space, which befriends the children of a Californian household in Steven Spielberg's SCIENCE FICTION fantasy film *E.T.: The Extra-Terrestrial* (1982). He comes to earth looking for plant specimens but is stranded. The children care for him, and he teaches them how to fly. He then devises equipment enabling him to phone home. He finally falls ill and apparently dies, but is reborn just before a spacecraft arrives to take him back. The sentimental story, which has a quasi-religious undertone, is curiously moving.

**ETA.** An armed Basque separatist organization that aims to create a Basque state made up of four northern Spanish provinces and parts of southwest France. It arose in 1959 from the Basque Nationalist Party and has bases in both France and Spain but since 1968 has made the Spanish side its main battleground. It has pursued a campaign of violence in various parts of Spain, but a plot to assassinate King Juan Carlos in 1995 was unsuccessful. It declared a unilateral ceasefire in 1998 (and again in 2006) but in 1999 restarted its campaign of bombings, shootings and kidnappings. The name is an acronym of Basque *Euzkadi ta Azkatasuna*, 'Basque homeland and liberty'.

**Eternal triangle.** The comic or tragic situation of the amorous involvement of one of a married couple with another member of the opposite sex. The phrase occurred as the title of a book review in the *Daily Chronicle* for 5 December 1907: 'Mrs. Dudeney's novel … deals with the eternal triangle, which, in this case, consists of two men and one woman.' 'Eternal' implies that the situation dates from times of old.

**Ethical investment.** Investment in companies that meet ethical criteria specified by the investor. Typical areas of exclusion are the arms industry, tobacco manufacture, trade with a country that operates an oppressive regime, as formerly South Africa in the days of APARTHEID, or with a country that damages or despoils the natural environment, as the rainforests of South America. The term is of US origin and arose in the early 1980s.

**Ethnic cleansing.** A euphemistic term (translating Serbo-Croat *etničko čišćenje*) for the mass expulsion or extermination of people from a minority ethnic group within a particular country or region. The phrase came to be particularly associated with the bitter fighting between Bosnian Serbs and Bosnian Muslims in the former Yugoslavia in the 1990s and with the mass expulsion by ethnic Serbs of ethnic Albanians from Kosovo in 1999.

**Eton crop.** A short boyish hairstyle, fairly popular among English women in the 1920s, called after the boys at Eton College. The name was doubtless prompted by the Eton jacket, Eton collar and Eton suit, originally worn by the younger Eton boys but adopted and adapted for feminine wear before the First World War and returning to fashion after it.

Sylvia was wearing Etons at Monckley's suggestion.

COMPTON MACKENZIE: *Sylvia Scarlett*, I, ii (1918)

**Etrog.** An award presented annually since 1967 by the Canadian Film Awards Committee for film-making achievements. It is in the form of a gold-coated statuette mounted on a marble base and takes its name from the statuette's designer, the Romanian-born Canadian sculptor Sorel Etrog (b.1933).

**E-type.** A stylish model of Jaguar car launched in 1961. It became the instant motif of the SWINGING SIXTIES, attracting celebrity owners such as George Harrison of The BEATLES and the film actor Peter Sellers. It was produced until 1974 and although still sought after as a male dream car in the 1980s had generally declined as an object of desire by the close of the century, when even so speculation persisted about a revival.

The name evolved as a serial letter. The E-type was originally intended to be a racing replacement for the D-type of 1955–7, which in turn replaced the C-type, itself designed as a special racing two-seater for the 1951 LE MANS race. Because its engine and transmission were based on those of the XK120, the latter was originally called the XK120C, with C standing for 'Competition'. Enthusiasts began calling it the 'C-type', however, and the name stuck.

**Eurhythmics.** (Greek, 'good rhythm'.) A method of expressing the rhythmic aspects of music by physical movement, essentially a blend of dance and gymnastics. It was developed *c*.1905 by Émile Jaques-Dalcroze (1865-1950), a Swiss music teacher, composer and professor of harmony, who first applied it to schoolchildren. In 1910 he established an institute near Dresden in Germany and others followed in various European capitals and also in New York. The method still has its adherents and has influenced modern ballet and the dance of the theatre.

Eurythmics was later familiar as the name of a highly successful British pop duo formed in 1980 by Annie Lennox and David Stewart.

**Euro.** The name of the single currency that in 1999 was introduced alongside the national currencies of 12 countries (Austria, Belgium, Finland, France, Germany, Greece, Ireland, Italy, Luxembourg, the Netherlands, Portugal and Spain, but not Britain, Denmark or Sweden) in the EUROPEAN UNION and that replaced those currencies in 2002. It was first minted as a coin by France in 1998.

**Euroland.** A term fairly briefly in vogue from 1999 to denote a hypothetical political unit consisting of those countries within the EUROPEAN UNION that adopted the EURO as an official currency in that year. It had a rather earlier outing as an American name for the European Union as the 'superpower of the future'.

**European Pelé.** The Portuguese footballer Eusébio Ferreira da Silva (b.1942). A star forward, he appeared for the Portuguese club Benfica during the 1960s and early 1970s. Eusébio was, in fact, African, and was born in Portuguese East Africa (now Mozambique).

**European Union.** The economic grouping of western European countries (abbreviation, EU) that evolved in 1993 from the old European Community (EC), itself incorporating (and alternatively known as) the European Economic Community (EEC), or Common Market, which itself came into being in 1958 following ratification of the Treaty of Rome. It originally consisted of Belgium, France, West Germany, Italy, Luxembourg and the Netherlands, collectively known as the SIX. These were joined by Britain, Denmark and Ireland in 1973, by Greece in 1981, by Spain and Portugal in 1986, by the former East Germany in 1990, by Austria, Sweden and Finland in 1995 and by Cyprus, the Czech Republic, Estonia, Hungary, Latvia, Lithuania, Malta, Poland, Slovakia and Slovenia in 2004. *See also* EURO.

**Europhile.** Any person who is in favour of the EUROPEAN UNION (EU) and of closer European integration. A Eurosceptic is any person who is generally sceptical about the benefits of EU membership, and about the desirability of closer European integration, while a Europhobe is completely hostile to all things relating to the EU, seeing the organization as a threat to national sovereignty and national identity. *See also* F-WORD.

**Eurosceptic.** *See* EUROPHILE.

**Eurostar.** The high-speed passenger service provided by the railways of Belgium, Britain and France to link London with Paris, Brussels and other cities via the CHANNEL TUNNEL. The service first operated in 1994, and the journey from Waterloo to Paris Nord takes about four hours.

**Eurotrash.** An epithet originally applied to rich foreigners living in the United States, especially those from titled or ancient families. The term was popularized and personally epitomized by the society writer Taki Theodoracopoulos ('Taki') (b.1937) in columns for *Vanity Fair* and the *Spectator*. By the 1990s, however, the word came to be used for any 'foreign-looking' person, such as one who spoke with a foreign accent, whose clothing was markedly different from the norm, who sported a deep tan, who frequented fashionable nightclubs, or who displayed un-British (or un-American) signs of affectation or preciousness. *Eurotrash* was also the title of a teasingly tasteless Channel 4 programme, introduced by Antoine de Caunes.

**Eurovision Song Contest.** This popular but much-ridiculed annual television event, in which a number of European countries compete for the best song of the year, was first seen on the Eurovision network in 1956, but Britain did not enter until 1957, when 10 countries took part. By the end of the century this figure had more than quadrupled. Each country awards points from 0 to 12 to the others, the results being announced in French and English. The ability of some countries to be awarded *nul points* (pseudo-French for *nul point*) is always possible, a disgrace associated with Norway's song 'Mil etter mil' ('Mile after Mile') in the 1978 when it failed to pick up a single vote. Since then, such humiliation has been bestowed on other nations, and in 2003 it was the UK's turn to join the *nul points* club, when it came 26th (out of 26) with a song called 'Cry Baby' by Jemini. However, blatantly political voting patterns tend to ensure arbitrary outcomes anyway, thus Greece and Turkey rarely vote for each other, Ireland tends not to vote for the UK, while Germany (a country hosting many Turkish 'guest workers') often lauds Turkey's song. In 2006 the various former-Yugoslav countries voted for each other in an act of post-civil-war solidarity.

Although not in Europe, Israel and Morocco participate by virtue of their membership of the European Broadcasting Union. Ireland is the only nation to have won three times consecutively and it holds the record for most wins (7). In 2006 there was a break with the traditional bland Euro-pop and Finland's heavy metal band, Lordi, complete with reptilian monster outfits, won with the highest number of points in the history of the contest.

***Eustace and Hilda.*** A novel (1947), and also the title of a trilogy of which it is the third part, by L.P. Hartley (1895–1972). The trilogy follows the course of the relationship between the sickly Eustace and his elder sister, symbolically represented in the first book, *The Shrimp and the Anemone* (1944), when Hilda tears a shrimp from the grip of an anemone, killing the shrimp and disabling the anemone.

The second volume, *The Sixth Heaven* (1946), continues their story, and at the end of the third novel, Eustace dies in his sleep, and Hilda, whom he has cured from psychosomatic paralysis after a disastrous affair, retires into a nunnery.

**Euston Road School.** A name coined in 1938 by the art writer Clive Bell for a group of British painters centred round the School of Drawing and Painting that opened in a studio at 12 Fitzroy Street, London, in 1937, soon transferring to nearby 316 Euston Road. Founding members were William Coldstream (1908–87), Victor Pasmore (1908–98) and Claude Rogers (1907–79). They advocated a move away from modernist styles to a more straightforward naturalism and laid stress on the training of observation in the teaching of art. *See also* FITZROVIA.

**Evacuee.** A person who has been moved from a place of danger to one of safety. The word first became familiar in Britain on the eve of the Second World War, when the government decided that more than 2 million children could be killed if left in the cities and organized their evacuation. Operation Pied Piper began at 7.30 p.m. on 1 September 1939, two days before war broke out. Children gathered at schools ready to be taken to the country, their parents equipping them with spare clothing, a toothbrush, comb, handkerchief, their gas mask and enough food for the day. Billeting was compulsory, and all evacuees were found homes within three days. Fosterers were often shocked by the poverty of their new charges, many of whom were lice-ridden and innocent of basic hygiene. Evacuation was voluntary, but over 3 million went.

**Evans of the Broke.** The byname of Admiral Edward Evans, 1st Baron Mountevans (1881–1957), famed in the First World War for defeating six German destroyers when in command of HMS *Broke*. The ship herself was named for Rear-Admiral Sir Philip Broke (1776–1841), a post captain commanding the frigate *Shannon* in a famous duel with the US frigate *Chesapeake* in 1813.

**Evening, all.** *See* DIXON OF DOCK GREEN.

**Eventide home.** A euphemism for a home for the elderly, who are in the evening of their lives. In *My Commonplace Book* (1970) Baroness Stocks famously described the House of Lords as 'a perfect eventide home'.

**Events, dear boy, events.** A response attributed to the British prime minister Harold Macmillan (1894–1986) when asked by a journalist after a long dinner what caused him the most difficulty. The phrase has been used extensively by political journalists when commenting on how an un-expected event can derail a political policy or even a career.

Macmillan also reportedly spoke, on other occasions, of 'the opposition of events'.

**Everage, Edna.** Dame Edna Everage, a falsetto-voiced, larger-than-life Australian matron, with butterfly-winged spectacles, is the persona of the comedian Barry Humphries (b.1934). She was originally the aunt of Barry MCKENZIE. She (he) first appeared on television in the 1970s, and shocked a delighted audience by the way she alternately teased and insulted the star guests invited on her show. Her sidekick is Madge Allsop, a little woman who is as dour and dumb as Edna is cheery and chatty. Humphries was also the creator of the gross Sir Les PATTERSON.

**Ever closer union, An.** A phrase used in the Treaty of Rome (1957), which established the European Economic Commu-nity. The preamble to the treaty declared that the signatories (France, West Germany, Italy, the Netherlands, Belgium and Luxembourg) were 'determined to lay the foundations of an ever closer union among the peoples of Europe'. The phrase also occurs in the 1992 Maastricht Treaty, which turned the European Community into the EUROPEAN UNION. The preamble to the treaty talked of 'a new stage in the process of creating an ever closer union among the peoples of Europe'. The phrase is guaranteed to bring Europhobes out in a rash of angry pustules.

**Everyman Cinema.** London's oldest repertory cinema, in Holly Bush Vale, Hampstead. It specializes in double and triple bills of classic or cult films and opened on Boxing Day 1933 in the former Everyman Theatre here, established in 1919 and named for Ben Jonson's comedy *Every Man in His Humour* (1598).

**Everyman's Library.** This popular standard edition of reprints of masterpieces of world literature was first published by J.M. Dent in 1906. The first volume to appear was Boswell's *Life of Johnson*, originally published in 1791. The following words spoken by Knowledge in the 15th-century morality play *Everyman* were the inspiration for the name and appear in every volume:

> Everyman, I will go with thee, and be thy guide,
> In thy most need to go by thy side.

**Everyone I've Ever Slept With 1963–95.** A tent constructed by Britart *enfant terrible* Tracey Emin (b.1963), embroidered with the names of the 102 people she had ever shared a bed with. The work dates from 1995, and was destroyed in an accidental fire in 2004. In 1999 Emin's piece *My Bed* – featuring soiled sheets, empty vodka bottles and used condoms – failed to win the Turner Prize.

**Every picture tells a story.** An evocative truism

popularized by the caption for an advertisement of 1904 for Doan's Backache Kidney Pills, showing a person bent over with pain. The phrase may have been current before this but has been put to good use ever since, as for the title of John Hadfield's illustrated commentary on a selection of Victorian paintings, published in 1985.

**Every position must be held to the last man.** The order of British commander-in-chief Earl Haig (1861–1928) on 12 April 1918, during the German Spring Offensive.

> Every position must be held to the last man: there must be no retirement. With our backs to the wall, and believing in the justice of our cause, each one of us must fight on to the end.

**Everything but the kitchen sink.** Everything imaginable. The expression apparently arose in the Second World War as a humorous reference to the varied uses to which different articles could be imaginatively put in times of need. A kitchen usually has the widest range of such objects, but the uses to which the sink can be put are limited, if only on account of its size and fixedness.

**Everything in the garden is lovely.** All is well. The catch-phrase originated in a song of 1898 by John P. Harrington and George Le Brunn popularized in the early 20th century by Marie Lloyd.

**Everything you always wanted to know about sex but were afraid to ask.** This formulaic phrase, as the title of a book of 1970 by David Reuben, spawned a host of similar mesmeric strings and titles. Among the latter, of books published down to 1984, are the following:

*Everything That Linguists Have Always Wanted to Know About Logic But Were Ashamed to Ask*

*Everything You Always Wanted to Know About Drinking Problems And Then a Few Things You Didn't Want to Know*

*Everything You Always Wanted to Know About Elementary Statistics But Were Afraid to Ask*

*Everything You Always Wanted to Know About Mergers, Acquisitions and Divestitures But Didn't Know Whom to Ask*

*Everything You Wanted to Know About Stars But Didn't Know Where to Ask*

*Everything You Wanted to Know About the Catholic Church But Were Too Pious to Ask*

*Everything You Wanted to Know About the Catholic Church But Were Too Weak to Ask*

**Everywoman.** A typical woman; the prototype of womanhood. The word arose in the 1960s as a variant of 'Everyman', the name of the hero of a 15th-century morality play.

A political wife, in a sense, is a contradiction in terms … She must be the model of purity and probity at home, but she must be Everywoman outside, with a ready smile and a cheerful word for all the importuning bores on the campaign trail.

*Time* (7 October 1974)

**Evil Empire.** A description of the Soviet Union coined by President Ronald Reagan, the GREAT COMMUNICATOR, in a speech to US evangelical church leaders in March 1983:

> In your discussions of the nuclear freeze proposals, I urge you to beware the temptation of pride – the temptation blithely to declare yourselves above it all and label both sides equally at fault, to ignore the facts of history and the aggressive impulses of an evil empire.

The phrase, summing up the Manichaean approach to the COLD WAR of the US religious right, is assumed to have been drawn from the STAR WARS films, especially *The Empire Strikes Back* (1980). Earlier, in 1981, Reagan made an equally undiplomatic gaffe: while believing he was testing a radio microphone prior to a live broadcast he announced: 'My fellow Americans, I have signed legislation to outlaw Russia for ever. We begin bombing in five minutes.' Unfortunately, he was on air. After 1985 Reagan found himself able to do business with the new Soviet leader, Mikhail Gorbachev, GORBY, as the Cold War drew to a close.

***Evita.*** A musical (1978) with a score by Andrew Lloyd Webber (b.1948) and words by Tim Rice (b.1944) depicting the life and death of María Eva de Perón (1919–52), the wife of General Juan Perón, president of Argentina. Her sympathy with the poor, whom she called *los descamisados* ('the shirt-less ones'), helped her husband to win the 1946 election, but after her death from cancer his popularity declined. Evita was her nickname, and the musical touches on her rise from being a minor actress and model to her death, when she was regarded as almost a saint and idolized by the poor. The film version (1996) starred Jonathan Pryce as Perón and Madonna as Evita, with Antonio Banderas as Che Guevara, taking the part of a Greek chorus.

**Exclusion zone.** A term dating from the 1970s for an area where an authority has banned a particular activity. The original application was to a maritime zone forbidden to enemy ships (as in the FALKLANDS WAR). The sense was then extended to an area out of bounds because a hazardous substance has been released, as at CHERNOBYL in 1986. Finally, the term was taken up for any generally 'unacceptable' area.

**Executioner's Song, The.** A 'true life' novel (1979) by Norman Mailer (b.1923), which won the PULITZER PRIZE for fiction. Gary Gilmore (1941–77) was paroled from prison in 1976 and immediately committed two murders. He was rearrested and demanded the death penalty, which was carried out by firing squad. He was the first person to be executed in the United States for more than 10 years. Mailer fashioned a narrative of the affair and a portrait of Gilmore from more than a thousand hours of taped interviews with those involved in the case and hundreds of pages of notes. The title recalls the quotation from John Donne: 'I am mine own executioner', from *Devotions Upon Emergent Occasions*, Meditation No. 17 (1624).

**Exhibit A.** The chief evidence; the prime proof. The allusion is to the first document or object, labelled 'A', produced for the inspection of the court in a court case, or shown to a witness when giving evidence.

> My sister's Exhibit A for favouritism in our grown-up lives … is that my mother sent parcels of second-hand baby clothes to me when I had my children.
>
> *Sunday Times* (24 October 1999)

**Existence before essence.** The slogan of French existentialism, derived from the proposition by Jean-Paul Sartre (1905–80) in *Being and Nothingness* (1943):

> Existence precedes and rules essence. The idea is that in a godless universe humans consist solely of the sum of their choices and actions. There is no such thing as 'human nature', for humans do not have any prior or transcendent essence that dictates the course of their lives. There is only the freedom to choose; 'I am condemned to be free.'

**Exit.** The popular name of the Voluntary Euthanasia Society, formed in 1935 by a group of doctors. Their purpose was to campaign for a change in the law so that doctors could legally help terminally ill patients who wanted to die. Suicide ceased to be illegal in Britain in 1961, but it remains a criminal offence to assist anyone to commit suicide. The society distributes a LIVING WILL. The whole subject of voluntary euthanasia remains highly controversial and continues to remain a topic of impassioned debate in the media.

**Exocet.** The British public first became aware of this French-made guided anti-ship missile in 1982 when it was launched by Argentina against British ships in the FALKLANDS WAR. Its name derives from Greek *ekokoitos*, 'fish that comes up on the beach' (literally 'out of bed'). Exocoetidae is the family name of the various species of flying fish, *Exocoetus volans* being one of the most widely distributed.

**Exorcist, The.** A notorious HORROR MOVIE (1973), directed by William Friedkin, about the satanic possession of a 12-year-old girl and the efforts of various priests to drive the Devil out of her body. The film, which provoked huge controversy at the time of its release, was based on a bestselling novel (1970) by William Peter Blatty, who also wrote the screenplay.

**Experience.** A BUZZWORD from the 1980s for a range of promotional ventures, especially those regarded as coming under the umbrella of HERITAGE. Thus Land's End has a trivializing display called the 'Land's End Experience', Whitby, North Yorkshire, has the 'Dracula Experience' as a sort of 'horror show', and for the MILLENNIUM London drew many to the 'Millennium Experience' by the Thames. In its issue for 27 August 1995 *The Observer* had an advertisement inviting readers to 'leave your worries and the traffic behind and enjoy the Cotswold Experience'. The fashion for the word may owe something to The Jimi Hendrix Experience, the 1960s rock group.

**Expletive deleted.** A US expression indicating the omission in a printed text of an obscene word or phrase. The term dates from the 1970s. Transcripts of President Nixon's testimony during the WATERGATE enquiry contain many editorial amendments using this annotation.

> To an outsider to the field of astronomy, the range of reactions to the term 'Janus', listed in many references as the 10th moon of Saturn, is often a bit of a shock. Responses range from acceptance to tolerant smiles to expletive deleted.
>
> *Science News* (29 January 1977)

**Explore every avenue.** To investigate every possibility; to try all ways of reaching a solution. The trees that line an avenue can conceal its course and one may need to explore several before finding the one that leads to the desired destination. The expression is first recorded in the 1920s and the issue of *Punch* for 2 December 1931 had a cartoon captioned: 'Fancy picture of an eminent politician in search of a formula, leaving no stone unturned while exploring every avenue.'

**Expressionism.** *See* Der BLAUE REITER; Die BLAUE VIER; Die BRÜCKE.

**Extraordinary events.** A term used by the authorities in the Soviet Union during the Second World War to denote 'treasonous behaviour' on the part of military personnel, such as desertion, cowardice, changing sides, self-inflicted wounds, etc.

**Extraordinary rendition.** The US euphemism for the seizure by agents of the CIA's Special Removal Unit of terror suspects on foreign soil, and their dispatch to a third country, often one where torture is routinely used. The practice became more prevalent after 9/11. When it was reported in 2005 that some of the CIA flights concerned were making stop-offs in airports in western Europe, there was something of a furore.

> Hitherto … 'rendition' conjured up images of musical actors dressed in brightly coloured clothes crying 'hey, let's do a song about it!' In its qualified state, it would indicate someone garnering critical acclaim for said rendering, as in 'That really was an extraordinary rendition of Memory from Cats.' Now it turns out the phrase refers to sitting on the tarmac at Glasgow Prestwick airport while your CIA interrogators stock up on fuel before exporting you to some facility that doesn't show up on any Romanian Ordnance Survey maps … Certainly the dictionary has once again been left with egg on its face … Not one word about being cellophaned to a ducking stool in the former eastern bloc.
>
> MARINA HYDE: in *The Guardian* (6 December 2005)

**Extra-virgin.** A commercial term for olive oil that is not only 'virgin', i.e. obtained from the first pressing of the olives, but 'extra', i.e. of an especially fine grade.

**Extreme sport.** A term coined in the early 1990s for any sport involving a high risk. Many extreme sports evolved as variants of already existing standard sports, examples being snowboarding (from skiing), sky-surfing (from parachuting), free climbing (without the aid of climbing devices) and barefoot water-skiing (without skis). Others, such as BUNGEE-JUMPING and ZORBING, arose independently. *See also* CANYONING; PARKOUR.

***Exxon Valdez.*** While leaving the port of Valdez, the terminus of the Alaskan oil pipeline, on 25 March 1989, the tanker of this name ran aground on a reef in Prince William Sound, holing her hull and releasing 238,000 barrels of crude oil into the sea. The resulting damage to the rich marine wildlife was considerable. The subarctic environment severely hampered clean-up operations and Exxon, the company responsible, was further criticized for its allegedly slow response to the disaster. The spillage was the worst in US history. *See also* TORREY CANYON.

**Eyeball to eyeball.** Face to face. The image is of two people staring aggressively at each another without either giving way. The expression is of US origin and dates from the 1950s. At the time of the 1962 Cuban Missile Crisis (*see* HAWKS AND DOVES), US Secretary of State Dean Rusk (1909–94) told journalists:

> We're eyeball to eyeball and the other fellow just blinked.

The confrontation between the two superpowers at this juncture is noted as a piece of BRINKMANSHIP.

**Eye candy.** A US term originating in the 1980s for visual images that are attractive and enjoyable but intellectually undemanding. The term has been applied to elegantly or scantily dressed women in advertisements and to various television programmes, notably scenically attractive ones such as BAYWATCH, which are both entertaining and EASY ON THE EYE. *See also* ARM CANDY; EAR CANDY.

**Eye in the sky.** A term for an electronic ground surveillance apparatus used in aircraft or artificial satellites. The name dates from the 1960s and while descriptively appropriate may have been suggested by PIE IN THE SKY.

***Eyeless in Gaza.*** A novel (1936) by Aldous Huxley (1894–1963), in which some of the circumstances reflect those of the author; its writing heralded his final, philosophical phase, in which pacifism and mysticism are predominant influences. The novel's theme is that freedom without values is a form of blindness. It follows the journey of an able man, who is incapable of forming personal relationships, to self-discovery in the unlikely environment of a revolution in Mexico. The title is from *Samson Agonistes* (1671) by John Milton:

> Ask for this great deliverer now, and find him
> Eyeless in Gaza at the mill with slaves.

**Eyes out on stalks.** Eyes figuratively or even actually protruding through inquisitiveness, amazement, fear or other strong emotion or reaction. The allusion is to the eyes of a snail, which are at the end of retractable stalks and suggest alertness. The phrase dates from the 1930s.

# F

**Faber and Faber.** In 1924 Geoffrey Faber (1889–1961) was invited to become chairman of the Scientific Press. The following year he established his own publishing firm of Faber and Gwyer, the latter name representing the original owners of the Scientific Press. In 1929 the firm was reconstituted under its present name, the Gwyer interest being entirely withdrawn. The second Faber was fictional, and rumour has it that the repetition of the name was suggested by the writer Walter de la Mare, father of Richard de la Mere, one of the original directors, 'because you can't have too much of a good thing!'

> So if you 'ave business with Faber – or Faber –
> I'll give you this tip, and it's worth a lot more:
> You'll save yourself time, and you'll spare yourself labour
> If jist you make friends with the Cat at the door.
>
> T.S. ELIOT: *Old Possum's Book of Practical Cats*, 'Cat Morgan Introduces Himself' (1939). Eliot himself was a director of the firm.

**Fab Four.** A nickname for The BEATLES at the height of their fame in the 1960s. It is said to have been coined by Tony Barrow, who was head of The Beatles' press office between 1962 and 1968. 'Fab' is 'fabulous'.

**Façade.** The series of technically brilliant, supposedly avant-garde but fundamentally facile poems by Edith Sitwell (1887–1964), which are intended to be recited to music by William Walton (1902–83). The first performance was in 1923, but considerable revisions and rearrangements followed. A few lines will suffice to give a taste of the fun:

> When
> Sir
> Beelzebub called for his syllabub in the hotel in Hell
> Where Proserpine first fell …

**Face fits.** If one's face fits a situation figuratively one is judged as being suitable for it. The expression typically relates to a job application or interview. The idea is that one's credentials or qualifications are acceptable but that one needs to complete the picture with the right 'image'.

**Facelift.** An operation by COSMETIC SURGERY to smooth out wrinkles and lift sagging skin on an ageing face to make it look younger. It is commonest among women and produces a result that usually lasts about five years, when it may need to be repeated. Metaphorically, one can also give the front of a building, or a piece of furniture, etc., a facelift. *See also* CROYDON FACELIFT.

**Factor.** A vogue word from the 1980s for any influential force or agent, beginning with the FALKLANDS FACTOR, whose alliterative appeal may have encouraged similar coinings. *See also* FEEL-GOOD FACTOR; FUDGE FACTOR; KRYPTON FACTOR; SLEAZE FACTOR.

**Fag hag.** A slighting term of US origin dating from the 1960s for a heterosexual woman ('hag') who prefers or seeks out the company of a homosexual man ('fag').

***Fahrenheit 451.*** A fantasy of the near future by Ray Bradbury (b.1920). It was the author's first published novel, appearing in 1953. The theme is the triumph of the imagination under the threat of obliteration, and in particular the destruction by fire of all books. The title represents the temperature at which book paper is said to ignite and burn. Dissidents respond by memorizing the texts. A futuristic film version (1966) was directed by François Truffaut.

The book inspired the title of *Fahrenheit 9/11*, Michael Moore's documentary about the connections of the Bush family with the Saudi BIN LADEN family, one of whose members was behind AL-QAIDA and the 9/11 terrorist attacks on the United States. Moore released the film in 2004, in a vain attempt to persuade the American public not to re-elect George W. Bush as president. *See also* MIRAMAX.

***Fahrenheit 9/11.*** *See* FAHRENHEIT 451.

**Fail-safe.** A seemingly oxymoronic term that arose in aeronautical jargon of the 1940s to apply to a mechanism that can revert to a safe condition in the event of breakdown. In the COLD WAR the term was extended to apply to precautions and procedures agreed beforehand to ensure against escalation to a nuclear war. More recently the expression has found wider application.

> The Prime Minister was looking at proposals … to toughen the so-called 'fail-safe' mechanisms to ensure that Sinn Fein does not continue in government if the IRA fails to disarm.
> *The Times* (14 July 1999)

**Fair crack of the whip.** A reasonable chance to attempt something or prove oneself. The allusion is to having a chance to drive a horse-drawn vehicle. The expression dates from the 1920s and is first recorded in Australia.

**Fair Deal.** The liberal domestic reform programme of the US president Harry S. Truman (*see* GIVE-'EM-HELL HARRY), originally outlined by him as early as 1945. In his first postwar message to Congress that year, Truman called for expanded social security, new legislation on working hours and wages and a permanent Fair Employment Practices Act that would prevent racial or religious discrimination in the engagement of workers. Congress paid little attention at the time but the following year did pass the Employment Act, clearly stating the government's responsibility for maintaining full employment and establishing a Council of Economic Advisers to help assure a continuing healthy national economy. Truman reasserted his reform proposals in 1949 under the catchphrase, but Congress agreed to legislation on only some of his recommendations.

**Fairies at the bottom of the garden.** Said of anything seemingly ideal or idyllic, especially of a place to live or stay. The phrase comes from the opening line of Rose Fyleman's best-known poem 'The Fairies' (1918): 'There are fairies at the bottom of our garden!'

**Fairy cycle.** A type of small-wheeled low bicycle for children, first seen in the 1920s. Its small size and 'dinkiness' suggested the fancy that it might have been made for fairies to ride, just as a fairy cake is a small cake and fairy lights are small coloured lights.

**Fakes.** The difference between a fake and a forgery is a fine one. Generally speaking a fake is a thing that is not genuine, whether its perpetrator intended to deceive or not, whereas a forgery is an attempt to pass off as genuine some piece of spurious work or writing with the intent to deceive or defraud. All the following are 20th-century fakes or hoaxes,

although some are more patently forgeries. *See also* ANGRY PENGUINS; FALSE MEMORY SYNDROME.

  **Amityville Horror**. A sensational case of an alleged diabolical presence in a house at Amityville, Long Island, New York. The Lutz family of five moved into a large Dutch colonial house in the village of Amityville on 18 December 1975, undisturbed by the report that it had been the scene of a mass murder the previous year. They were soon subjected to a series of ghostly apparitions and other evil manifestations, forcing them to flee on 14 January 1976. A lurid account of their experiences was published by Jay Anson as *The Amityville Horror* in 1977, becoming an instant bestseller and spawning a top-grossing film of 1979 as well as a host of similar stories and movies based on the theme of a possessed house. It eventually emerged that the Lutzes had fabricated some of the ghoulish scenario (if not all of it) with a view to having a book published and reaping the reward of the ensuing publicity. The case resulted in a string of lawsuits. No problems have been reported from later owners of the house.

  **Borley Rectory**. The rectory at Borley, Essex, near the Suffolk border, was the subject of an exhaustive series of 'ghost hunts' conducted between 1929 and 1938 by Harry Price, founder of the National Laboratory of Psychical Research. The manifestations were supposedly in the form of poltergeist activity, with interest in the phenomena first fuelled by the *Daily Mail*. Price himself stayed at the rectory for a year from 1937 and assiduously documented his investigations using remote-control cine-cameras, still cameras, fingerprinting paraphernalia and other equipment. The rectory burned down in 1939 and the following year Price published his sensational account *The Most Haunted House in England*. Critics pointed out, however, that the incumbents of the rectory had not reported any unusual incidents, and Price was accused of having faked or fabricated them. Legends of the hauntings lingered even so, and the site continues to draw the curious.

  **Cottingley fairies**. In 1917 two little girls living at Bingley, Yorkshire, Elsie Wright and her cousin Frances, claimed they had seen fairies in nearby Cottingley Dell and said they had even taken photographs of them. The story came to the attention of Sir Arthur Conan Doyle, by then a convert to spiritualism. He believed the girls and vouched for the veracity of the photographs, even taking lantern slides made from them to America as part of a lecture tour. In 1983 Frances Griffiths, now aged 76, admitted that the pictures had been faked by photographing cut-outs of fairies from *Princess Mary's Gift Book*, a popular children's book. Two films have recreated the events, the British-made *Photographing Fairies* (1997) and the US *Fairytale: A True Story*

(1997), the former on a more philosophical plane than the latter.

**Drake brass plate**. Sir Francis Drake, during his voyage of circumnavigation (1577–80), anchored off the Californian coast in 1579 and set up a brass plate naming the territory New Albion and claiming it in the name of Queen Elizabeth I. In 1936 the plate was said to have been found near San Francisco and the inscription seemed to be reasonably authentic, although some authorities expressed doubt. A replica was, in due course, presented to Queen Elizabeth II, which is kept in Buckland Abbey, Drake's Devonshire property, now a museum. In 1977 a reported analysis of the composition of the brass by the Lawrence Berkeley Institute of the University of California and the Research Laboratory for Archaeology at Oxford found that it was of late 19th- or early 20th-century manufacture.

**Hitler diaries**. In April 1983 the *Sunday Times* reported the discovery of 60 volumes of Hitler's diaries, which had been acquired by the Hamburg magazine *Stern* for £2,460,000 and delivered to them by their reporter Gerd Heidemann. They were said to have been salvaged from an aircraft wrecked in 1945 and found in a hayloft. Professor Hugh Trevor-Roper (Lord Dacre) had vouched for their authenticity and the *Sunday Times* (after paying *Stern* for publication rights) obtained two volumes (1932 and 1935) for testing. Dr Julius Grant, a chemical expert, proved that the paper in the diaries was not in use until after the Second World War. Two weeks after their alleged discovery the Bonn government also declared them to be forgeries. Heidemann revealed that he had obtained them from a Stuttgart dealer in military relics, Peter Fischer, real name Konrad Kujau, and the latter confessed to forgery. Both were imprisoned in May 1983, brought to trial in August 1984 and sentenced in July 1985. Kujau was jailed for 4 years 6 months for forgery and Heidemann for 4 years 8 months for fraud. A black television comedy, *Selling Hitler*, based on Robert Harris's book of the same title about the hoax (1987), was screened in 1991.

**Piltdown man.** In 1908 and 1911 Charles Dawson of Lewes, Sussex, 'found' two pieces of a highly mineralized human skull in a gravel bed at Piltdown near Lewes. By 1912 he and Sir Arthur Smith Woodward had discovered the whole skull. This was thought to be that of a new genus of man and was called *Eoanthropus dawsoni*. It came to be accepted as such by prehistorians, archaeologists and others, although a few were sceptical. In 1953 J.S. Weiner, K.P. Oakley and W.E. Le Gros Clark issued a report (*Bulletin of the British Museum* (Natural History), vol. II, no. 3) announcing that the Piltdown mandible was a fake, in reality the jaw of a modern ape, the rest of the skull being

that of *Homo sapiens*. The hoax, which duped most of the experts, was apparently planned by William Sollas, Professor of Geology at Oxford, through his dislike of Woodward.

**Protocols of the Elders of Zion**. Forged material published by Serge Nilus in Russia in 1905 and based on an earlier forgery of 1903, purporting to outline secret Jewish plans for achieving world power by undermining Gentile morality, family life and health and by securing a monopoly in international finance, among other things. Their falsity was first exposed by Philip Graves, *The Times* correspondent in Constantinople, in 1921 and later judicially, at Bern (1934–5). Their influence in inciting anti-Semitism, notably among the Russians, and later providing Hitler and his associates with an excuse they knew to be a myth, provide tragic evidence of the power of the BIG LIE.

**Tom Keating's pictures**. Keating (1918–84), beginning as a picture restorer, produced about 2000 drawings and paintings and sold them as originals by Samuel Palmer (1805–81) and other English artists. He admitted his works were fakes in 1976, and in the last years of his life enjoyed brief fame on television as an expert on painting generally and Impressionism in particular.

**Turin Shroud**. The shroud of twill linen kept in Turin Cathedral since 1578 and claimed to be the one in which the body of Christ was wrapped after the crucifixion. The pope agreed to RADIOCARBON DATING in 1987, and in 1988 the archbishop of Turin appointed the Oxford Research Laboratory for Archaeology, the Department of Physics of Arizona University and the Swiss Federal Institute of Technology at Zurich to date the shroud, pieces of which were given to these institutes in April 1988. The results were announced on 13 October and the cloth was dated to the 14th century. There is no firm historical evidence that it was known earlier than this. Although not accepted by all, the general conclusion is that the shroud is a medieval fake.

**Vermeer forgeries**. Hans (Henri) van Meegeren (1889–1947) began his series of brilliant fakes of Dutch masters in 1937 with *Christ at Emmaus*, which was sold as a 'Vermeer' for 550,000 gulden. Experts duly acclaimed it. His intention seems to have been to indulge his contempt and hatred of the art critics by a superlative hoax, but the financial success of his first fake led to others, mostly Vermeers. Discovery came only in 1945 when Allied commissioners were seeking to restore to their former owners the art treasures that had found their way to Germany during the Second World War. Among Goering's collection was an unknown Vermeer, *The Woman taken in Adultery*, and its original vendor was found to be van Meegeren. Sale of such a work of national importance involved a charge of collaboration with the enemy. To escape the heavy penalty, van Meegeren confessed to faking 14 Dutch masterpieces, nine of which had been sold for a total of 7,167,000 gulden, and to prove his story agreed to paint another 'old masterpiece' in prison in the presence of the experts. He was sentenced to one year's imprisonment in October 1947 but died on 30 December.

**Vinland Map.** In *c*.1000 the Norse explorer Leif Eriksson visited and named an area of wooded land in North America. According to the Norse Saga, *Flateyjarbók*: 'When spring came they made ready and left, and Leif named the land after its fruits, and called it Vinland.' In 1957 the discovery of a map of the northeast American coast was announced and said to be the most exciting cartographic find of the century. Supposedly drawn *c*.1440, it substantially preceded the voyages of Columbus (1492) and of John Cabot (1497), thus conclusively establishing the extent of the Viking explorations. It was presented to Yale University by an anonymous donor in 1965. In 1974 Yale announced that it was a fake. The pigment of the ink with which it was drawn was found to contain titanium dioxide, first used in the 1920s.

**Zinoviev Letter.** A letter purportedly signed by the Russian Communist leader Grigory Zinoviev (1883–1936), president of the COMINTERN. It summoned the British Communist Party to intensify its revolutionary activities and to subvert the armed forces, and after being leaked to the *Daily Mail* it was published on 25 October 1924, four days before a general election. It helped to promote a 'red scare' and contributed to the fall of Ramsay MacDonald's first Labour government. Many Labour leaders held it to be a forgery, and its authenticity was denied by the Russians. In December 1966 the *Sunday Times* published an article establishing that the letter was a forgery perpetrated by a group of WHITE RUSSIAN *émigrés*. At the same time it was suggested that certain leaders at the Conservative Central Office knew that it was a fake, although the Conservative Party as a whole assumed it to be genuine. The 'informant' was paid for his services. The letter itself, headed 'VERY SECRET' and dated 15 September 1924, had the following opening paragraph:

> Dear Comrades, The time is approaching for the Parliament of England to consider the Treaty concluded between the Governments of Great Britain and the S.S.S.R. [*sic*] for the purpose of ratification. The fierce campaign raised by the British bourgeoisie around the question shows that the majority of the same, together with reactionary circles, are against the Treaty for the purpose of breaking off an agreement consolidating the ties between the proletariats of the two countries leading to the restora-

tion of normal relations between England and the S.S.S.R.

**Falange.** (Spanish, 'phalanx'.) At first the title of a right-wing party in Spain formed in 1933 by José Antonio Primo de Rivera (1903–36) to uphold his father's memory against republican criticism but later adopted by General Franco as the name of the one official party in the state. Basically, it represented a combination of European FASCISM and Spanish nationalism and was used to counterbalance royalist, army and church influence. In 1937 it forced the Carlists to join with it. The Falange lost its unique position after the CAUDILLO's death in 1975 and was formally disbanded in 1977.

In Lebanon, the 'Phalange' is a right-wing Christian militia, the political and military force of the Maronite Christian Church in Lebanon, formed in 1936 on the model of Franco's movement. The resistance of the Phalange to the introduction of democratic institutions in Lebanon contributed greatly to that country's civil war (1975–90). *See also* BEIRUT.

**Falkirk Triangle.** The name given by the press in recent years to the area around Falkirk, near Stirling in Scotland, and in particular to Bonnybridge, because of the number of UFO sightings reported there. The area is on the flightpath for Edinburgh and Glasgow airports, and the sky at night is lit up by the flares and lights of the huge oil refinery at nearby Grangemouth.

**Falklands factor.** The effect of the FALKLANDS WAR on the popularity of political parties, and in particular the impetus at the 1983 general election it was believed to give to Margaret Thatcher and her Conservative administration, which had previously been experiencing a period of unpopularity. Thatcher herself used the term in a slightly different way in a speech in Cheltenham on 3 July 1982:

> We have to see that the spirit of the South Atlantic – the real spirit of Britain – is kindled not only by war but can now be fired by peace. We have the first prerequisite. We know that we can do it – we haven't lost the ability. That is the Falklands Factor.

Thatcher proceeded to turn her attention to the so-called ENEMY WITHIN.

**Falklands War.** The brief, and – in the eyes of some – needless, armed conflict between Britain and Argentina in 1982. It was sparked off when General Galtieri's military junta sent Argentinian forces to invade the Falkland Islands, the British Crown Colony in the South Atlantic, in support of Argentina's claim to sovereignty. (The Argentinians know the islands as the Malvinas.) In response Britain sent a TASK FORCE of ships and aircraft, which forced the Argentinians to surrender six weeks after its arrival. Major losses included Argentina's only cruiser, the GENERAL BELGRANO, with the loss of 362 lives, and Britain's HMS *Sheffield*, sunk by an EXOCET missile, with a loss of 21. The overall death toll was 652 on the Argentinian side and 255 on the British. *See also* GOTCHA!

> The Falklands thing was a fight between two bald men over a comb.
>
> JORGE LUIS BORGES: quoted in *Time* (14 February 1983)

*See also* I COUNTED THEM ALL OUT AND I COUNTED THEM ALL BACK.

**Fall about.** To collapse in laughter. The expression is of US origin and dates from the 1960s.

**Fall apart at the seams.** *See* COME APART AT THE SEAMS.

**Fall guy.** A person who is made to take the blame (and punishment) for the misdeeds of another. A classic example is Gutman's hapless boy-henchman Wilmer Cook (played by Elisha Cook Jnr) in the film *The* MALTESE FALCON (1941), who is sacrificed to the police by his partners in crime.

**Fall off the back of a lorry.** Said of stolen goods, or of something acquired fortuitously or by somewhat dubious means. The allusion is to the traditional bogus excuse given to the police by someone caught in possession of stolen goods.

**Fall off the roof.** A euphemism, originating among US college students in the 1930s, for 'to begin one's menstrual period'.

**Fall off the wagon.** To resume drinking after a period of being ON THE WAGON.

**Fall on one's sword.** To commit metaphorical suicide; to step down from a post. The phrase is curiously absent from dictionaries and the *Oxford English Dictionary* has only the literal sense, as in the biblical original: 'Then said Saul unto his armourbearer, Draw thy sword, and thrust me through therewith … But his armourbearer would not; for he was sore afraid. Therefore Saul took a sword, and fell upon it. And when his armourbearer saw that Saul was dead, he fell likewise upon his sword, and died with him' (1 Samuel 31:4–5).

> Yesterday's reshuffle tipped the balance to those who believe in Mr Blair's project … Jack Cunningham, with due decency, fell on his sword.
>
> *The Times* (12 October 1999)

**Fallout.** The descent of radioactive dust from a nuclear explosion. Figuratively, fallout is used of the (usually negative) secondary consequences of some action.

**Falls Road.** An almost exclusively Catholic working-class street of industrial West Belfast in Northern Ireland and a potent element, like the nearby Protestant SHANKILL ROAD, in the sectarian geography of the city. During the TROUBLES 'the Falls', the road and its adjacent streets, became synonymous with hard-line republicanism. The Divis Flats, a flashpoint in the early years of the Troubles, lie in the 'Lower Falls', at its eastern end. *See also* BOGSIDE.

**False memory syndrome.** A term, often abbreviated FMS, that came into use in the 1990s following many cases in which individuals 'recall' child or adult sexual abuse or ritual satanic abuse that has not actually taken place. Such 'memories' have been coaxed out of children or those accused of abusing children by over-eager therapists or prosecutors, with the result that many lives have been blighted, not least those of parents, falsely implicated by their adult children. Cases of FMS first came to light in the United States in the late 1980s, when 22-year-old Ericka Ingram, of East Olympia, Washington, was obliged to 'admit' that she had been abused as a child by her father, an accusation supposedly supported by her 18-year-old sister, Julie, who 'evidenced' tales of satanic rituals involving their family and their father's friends. In 1993 Robert Kelly, of Edenton, North Carolina, was found guilty of some of the 183 charges of satanic paedophilia he was accused of committing at his day-care centre, despite the fact that some of the tales involved children being microwaved or thrown into tanks full of ravenous sharks. Most of the accusations came from stay-at-home mothers, and no one visiting the centre had ever noticed anything unusual. That same year 35-year-old Peter Ellis, of New Zealand, was accused of abusing over 50 young children at a similar centre. Much of the children's evidence was shown to be patently false, but Ellis was found 'guilty' of sexual violation and indecent assault and jailed for ten years. The whole murky pheno-menon subsequently surfaced in Britain, where in 1996 a man was acquitted of sexually abusing a woman thanks to psychological assessments concluding that the plaintiff was probably suffering from FMS, and that her 'memories' had in fact been suggested by story lines in television dramas.

**Falun Gong.** A Chinese method of spiritual healing intro-duced by Li Hongzhi (b.1951) in China in 1992. It is based on the ancient mystical and healing principles of *qigong* (literally 'energy exercise') said to balance and enhance the body's *qi* or energy force and takes its name from the *falun* ('law wheel'), a wheel of energy believed to revolve continuously inside the lower abdomen of its practitioners, who are exhorted to abstain from such 'vices' as homosexuality, premarital sex and even marital sex unless for procreation, as well as alcohol and tobacco. Its bible, written by its founder, is *Zhuan Falun* ('Rotating the Law Wheel'). In 1999 the Chinese government outlawed Falun Gong as an 'evil and dangerous cult' and issued a warrant for the arrest of Li, by then living in New York, on a charge of disruption of public order and conspiring to undermine the country's communist hegemony, a crime that carries the death penalty.

**Family Favourites.** A popular weekly record request show on the BBC's Light Programme linking London with the British Forces Network in Germany. *Family Favourites* began in 1945 and went out for an hour at Sunday lunchtime, thereby becoming intimately associated with the aroma of roast meat and gravy wafting from the kitchen. The programme was presented by Jean Metcalfe in London and Cliff Michelmore in Germany, but the two did not meet until 1949. They married the following year. The title became *Two-Way Family Favourites* in 1960 and the programme continued until 1984.

**Family hour.** A US term for a television viewing period, usually from 7 p.m. to 9 p.m., when only programmes suitable for family viewing are shown. In British terms this generally equates to viewing time before the WATERSHED.

**Family jewels.** A euphemism dating from the 1960s for the male genitalia, as the precious means of generating a new family.

In the world of US espionage the Family Jewels was the nickname of a list of illegal activities carried out by the Central Intelligence Agency (*see* CIA). It was compiled at the direction of James Schlesinger in 1973, appointed head of the CIA in the wake of the WATERGATE scandal, and first went to William E. Colby, Schlesinger's successor. The preliminary summary was called 'Potential Flap Activities', and the CIA's director of security, passing his files to the inspector general for inclusion in the report, jokingly called them 'the Family Jewels'. The name caught on and was soon applied to the entire list.

**Family newspaper.** Any regular newspaper regarded as an unsuitable medium for explicit sexual language. In some cases the phrase is introduced expressly to titillate the prurient reader.

> The neurotic nature of the British can be seen in the colourful lexicon we've developed to cope with bodily functions. … New to me this month is the gay phrase 'taking a trip up

Shaftesbury Avenue' and (for women only) 'riding the cotton pony'. This is a family newspaper. You work it out.
> *Evening Standard* (27 September 1999)

Where the mention of a taboo word is unavoidable, most British newspapers protect their readers' delicate sensibilities with a well placed asterisk or two ('f**k') (just a few top-of-the-market dailies and Sundays, such as *The Guardian* and *The Observer*, usually bare all: sophisticates cannot be shocked). By contrast, red-top tabloids make no bones about printing prurient pictures of naked women.

**Family Reunion, The.** A poetic drama (1939) by T.S. Eliot (1888–1965) about a husband's sense of guilt over his wife's mysterious death. The play was based upon the *Oresteia* of Aeschylus, in which Clytemnestra kills her husband Agamemnon after he returns from the Trojan War, and is in turn killed by her son Orestes, with the encouragement of his sister Electra (*see also* MOURNING BECOMES ELECTRA). All this is partially as a result of the curse on the House of Atreus.

> Round and round the circle
> Completing the charm
> So the knot be unknotted
> The cross be uncrossed
> The crooked made straight
> And the curse be ended.
> *The Family Reunion*, II.iii

**Family that prays together, stays together, The.** A slogan created in the 1940s for the Roman Catholic Family Rosary Crusade in the United States. It has been attributed to both Al Scarpone and Father Patrick Peyton, 'the Rosary Priest'. It has continued to be popular among Christian groups of various denominations, especially American ones. Disrespectful variants include 'The family that shoots together loots together.'

**Family values.** A catch-all phrase for social conservatism, chiefly embodying a range of 'anti-' attitudes, such as opposition to abortion, gay rights, feminism and sexual freedoms – in short, the constituents of the PERMISSIVE SOCIETY. In many ways the term has become the antonym of ALTERNATIVE. *See also* BACK TO BASICS; CULTURE WAR; NEW MORALITY; VICTORIAN VALUES.

**Famous Five, The.** The four children and their dog who have unlikely 'adventures', as they call them, at various holiday locations around Britain in the novels of Enid Blyton (1897–1968). They are the two brothers Julian (the eldest) and Dick, their younger sister, Anne, and their tomboy cousin Georgina, an only child known as 'George', together with her mongrel dog Timmy. They first appeared in *Five on a Treasure Island* (1942) and continued their exploits in a further 20 volumes, all with a title beginning *Five*.

Resolutely mid-century middle-class in attitudes and behaviour, the children encounter assorted ne'er-do-wells intent on nefarious deeds, who are often flagged as such by being dirty/Gypsies/Cockneys/poor/uneducated, etc.: the novels thus became an obvious target of POLITICAL CORRECTNESS years later. The adventures were also the inspiration for television farces in the *Comic Strip Presents …* series of the 1980s, the first being *Five Go Mad in Dorset* (1982). *See also* the SECRET SEVEN.

**Famous for 15 minutes.** Enjoying a brief period of fame before slipping back into obscurity. The expression comes from a remark made by the US artist Andy Warhol: 'In the future everybody will be world famous for 15 minutes' (*Andy Warhol*, 1968). Brief celebrity is thus sometimes referred to as '15 minutes of fame'. In 1988 BBC Radio 4 presented a series entitled *Famous for Fifteen Minutes* in which people who had tasted instant fame spoke of its effect on their lives and the obscurity to which they mostly returned. The first interviewee was Erika Roe, a Hampshire second-hand bookshop assistant, who became a sensation overnight when she ran topless across the pitch at Twickenham during a rugby international in 1982 (*see* STREAKING). She revealed that she had earned only £8000 during the whole six-year period from her fame and that she was now living on social security. BIG BROTHER; CELEBRITY CULTURE; REALITY TV; WANNABE.

**Famous last words.** A phrase now used as an ironical or facetious comment on an over-confident statement that may well be proved wrong by events, as: 'I'm bound to pass my driving test first time – famous last words!' Many 'famous last words' in the sense of dying utterances are either apocryphal or have survived in inaccurate versions. The following, spoken or written at or shortly before the named person's death, are among the more noteworthy of the 20th century:

William S. Burroughs (1914–97; US writer): 'Love? What is it? Most natural painkiller. What there is … love.'

Edith Cavell (1865–1915; English nurse) before facing the German firing party: 'Patriotism is not enough. I must have no hatred or bitterness towards anyone.'

Anton Chekhov (1860–1904; Russian dramatist and short story writer): 'It's been so long since I've had champagne.'

Erskine Childers (1870–1922; Anglo-Irish writer and nationalist) to the firing squad at his execution: 'Come closer, boys. It will be easier for you.'

Stephen Crane (1871–1900; US writer): 'When you come to the hedge that we must all go over, it isn't so bad. You feel sleepy, you don't care. Just a little dreamy anxiety, which world you're really in, that's all.'

Isadora Duncan (1877–1927; US dancer) uttered in French when her shawl caught in a car wheel in Nice, breaking her neck: 'Farewell, my friends, I go to glory.'

Kathleen Ferrier (1912–53; English contralto): 'Now I'll have eine kleine Pause.'

Charles Frohman (1860–1915; US theatre manager) before drowning in the *Lusitania*: 'Why fear death? It is the most beautiful adventure in life.'

George V (1865–1936; king of Britain) to his private secretary on the morning of his death: 'How's the Empire?' (*See also* BUGGER BOGNOR!)

O. Henry (1862–1910; US author; real name William Sydney Porter): 'Turn up the lights. I don't want to go home in the dark.'

Timothy Leary (1920–96; US drug-culture GURU): 'Why not, why not, why not. Yeah.'

Katherine Mansfield (1888–1923; New Zealand writer): 'I believe … I'm going to die. I love the rain. I want the feeling of it on my face.'

Lawrence Oates (1880–1912; English polar explorer): 'I am just going outside and may be some time.' (*See also* I MAY BE SOME TIME; VERY GALLANT GENTLEMAN.)

Sylvia Plath (1932–63; US poet) in the opening lines of her last poem, written a week before her suicide: 'The woman is perfected / Her dead / Body wears the smile of accomplishment.'

Dennis Potter (1935–94; English dramatist) in the face of imminent death from cancer: 'The nowness of everything is absolutely wondrous.'

Alan Pryce-Jones (1908–2000; English editor and conversationalist): 'What are they saying?'

Cecil John Rhodes (1853–1902; British colonial administrator): 'So little done, so much to do.'

Ken Saro-Wiwa (1941–95; Nigerian writer and minority rights activist) when about to be hanged: 'Lord take my soul, but the struggle continues.'

Robert Falcon Scott (1868–1912; English polar explorer) in his last diary entry: 'For God's sake look after our people.'

Lytton Strachey (1880–1932; English writer): 'If this is dying, then I don't think much of it.'

Hunter S. Thompson (1939–2005; US writer): 'Counselor' – the word was typed in the centre of a sheet of paper on the table by which Thompson shot himself.

Queen Victoria (1819–1901; queen of Britain) referring to the Boer War then in progress: 'Oh, that peace may come.'

Sergei Yesenin (Russian poet; 1895–1925) writing in his own blood the day before he hanged himself: 'In this life there's nothing new in dying, / But nor, of course, is living any newer.'

**Fan club.** An organization catering for the admirers of a celebrity, usually one in a field such as the cinema or pop music. Devotees send their adulatory comments and requests to a given address, where they may or may not be passed on and replied to by the idol in question. In modern times most such 'celebs' have their individual web site on the INTERNET. The first fan club is generally reckoned to be the Keen Order of Wallerites, founded in London in 1902 for fans of the popular actor-manager Lewis Waller (1860–1916). Members wore a badge showing on one side Waller in a powdered wig as Monsieur Beaucaire and on the other his favourite flower, a pansy. *See also* CELEBRITY CULTURE.

**Fancy Dan.** A flashy or pretentious man; a show-off. The expression is first recorded in the US in the 1920s, and was originally applied specifically to a sportsman who talked a good game but usually failed to finish first. The more generalized meaning was probably in place by the late 1930s.

> Cookbooks by Fancy-Dan chefs can be problematic – often beautiful to look at and contemplate, but totally impractical for most home cooks.
> www.ochef.com (accessed 2005)

**Fannie Mae.** An acronym based on the name of the Federal National Mortgage Association, set up by the US government in 1938 to trade in mortgages. It is now privately owned. *See also* FREDDIE MAC; GINNIE MAE.

**Fantasia.** An animated film (1940) produced by Walt Disney to the music of Bach, Tchaikovsky, Stravinsky, Mussorgsky, Ponchielli, Schubert, Beethoven and Paul Dukas. The project was acclaimed for its ambitious scope, if not for the kitschy nature of many of the images, but in reality the film was not originally intended to be of feature length. Disney's original project was to render an animated version of 'The Sorcerer's Apprentice', with Leopold Stokowski conducting Dukas's music and MICKEY MOUSE as the over-ambitious apprentice, but when this went badly over-budget, Disney realized the only way to get his money back was to make it part of a full-length work. The sorcerer's name is Yen Sid.

**Fantastic realism.** A style of painting that developed in Vienna in the late 1940s. Its adherents, mainly pupils of Albert Paris von Gütersloh (1887–1973), depicted a fairy-tale world of fantasy and imagination with minute detail, the paintings themselves often being literary and anecdotal by nature. The best-known representative of the genre is Ernst Fuchs (b.1930).

**Fantasy football.** A competition in which entrants select imaginary teams of real football players in an actual league and score points according to the actual performance of the players selected. The concept arose in the United States in the 1980s using American football players, but it soon spread across the Atlantic to British soccer teams. The *Daily Telegraph* was the first national newspaper to publish a fantasy football league, and its first season, in 1993, attracted around 300,000 entries. The contest has since been extended to other sports, such as cricket and basketball.

**Fantomas.** A French master criminal who turns over a new leaf and decides to use his skills for good causes instead of bad. He first appears in the novel (1911) named after him by Pierre Souvestre and Marcel Allain. His fame became international when he was played by René Navarre in 1913 in a series of silent films, and there have been various comic books and strips starring him. His name is based on French *fantôme*, 'phantom', 'ghost'.

**FAQ.** In computing jargon the abbreviation or acronym of 'frequently asked questions', as a text file containing a list of questions and answers relating to a particular subject. Many commercial or public information websites now contain FAQ sections. The term dates from the early 1990s.

**Faraway country, A.** British prime minister Neville Chamberlain's description of Czechoslovakia at the time of the German annexation of the Sudetenland.

> How horrible, fantastic, incredible it is that we should be digging trenches and trying on gas-masks here because of a quarrel in a faraway country between people of whom we know nothing.
> BBC Radio broadcast (27 September 1938)

Three days later Chamberlain returned from Munich proclaiming 'Peace for our time' (*see* PEACE IN OUR TIME).

**Farewell, My Lovely.** A crime novel (1940) by Raymond Chandler (1888–1959), of which the theme is police corruption. He originally intended it to be called 'The Second Murderer' from Shakespeare's *Richard III*, in which that character, after showing some reluctance to carry out his commission, steels himself: 'Zounds, he dies: I had forgot the reward.' After his publisher had rejected this title and the author's second choice, 'Zounds, He Dies', Chandler settled for *Farewell, My Lovely*, referring to the suicide of a character who has caused his hero, Philip MARLOWE, a great deal of trouble. It was made into a masterful FILM NOIR (1944), directed by Edward Dmytryk and with Dick Powell as Marlowe. A remake (1975), with Robert Mitchum as Marlowe, was tightly directed by Dick Richards.

**Farewell to Arms, A.** A tragically romantic or romantically tragic novel (1929) by Ernest Hemingway, drawing on his own experiences in Italy during the First World War. The novel's hero is an American serving with the Italians, who falls in love with a nurse and eventually deserts to flee with her up the lake to Switzerland – hence the title. Somewhat arbitrarily, the beloved then dies in childbirth.

**Fascism.** Originally an Italian political movement, taking its name from the old Roman *fasces*, a bundle of rods with a projecting axe blade carried by a lictor as a symbol of a magistrate's power. It was founded in 1919 by Benito Mussolini (1883–1945), who took advantage of the discontent in Italy after the First World War to form a totalitarian nationalist party against left-wing radicalism and socialism. In 1922 the Fascists marched on Rome and demanded power, and Victor Emmanuel III made Mussolini prime minister. He styled himself DUCE (leader) and made himself dictator in 1925, suppressing all other political parties the following year. The Fascists controlled Italy until 1943. The term soon came to be applied to similar totalitarian movements in other countries. Ruthlessness, inhumanity and dishonest and disreputable practices were notable characteristics of its adherents. *See also* FALANGE; FÜHRER; HITLERISM; IRON GUARD; MARCH ON ROME; NAZI.

> Benito Mussolini provided Italy with a new theme of government which, while it claimed to save the Italian people from Communism, raised himself to dictatorial power. As Fascism sprang from Communism, so Nazism developed from Fascism.
>
> WINSTON CHURCHILL: *The Second World War*, vol. I, *The Gathering Storm*, ch. 1 (1948)

**Fashion victim.** A person who blindly follows or adopts the latest fashion merely for the sake of it. The term dates from the 1980s.

**Fast** or **quick buck.** To make a fast or quick buck is to make money easily and quickly, also possibly illicitly. A buck is a dollar. The origin of the word is uncertain, but it may be a shortening of 'buckskin', as deerskins were used as a unit of exchange by Native Americans and frontiersmen in 19th-century America.

**Fast food.** Takeaway or eat-in food that can be served up fast, since it requires little preparation or is produced by heating up foods that have been pre-processed in a factory. Most types of cooked JUNK FOOD are available at fast food outlets.

Implicit in the speedy concept is that individual customer variations on standard fare are often not allowed or slow or difficult to achieve, such as ordering a BIG MAC without gherkins. In Britain there have been signs, in the 21st century, of a waning in popularity of the 'traditional' fast food outlets, as against an increase in the popularity of sandwich bars and other options; while at the other end of the scale is the international slow food movement, which began in Italy, and which promotes local produce, high nutrition values, and loving preparation.

**Fast forward.** The control that rapidly advances the tape on a tape or video player. The term is used figuratively to denote a jump ahead in a narrative, as: 'Fast forward to a London café a few months later' (*The Times*, 2 October 1999).

**Fast lane.** The outer, right-hand lane of a motorway, where traffic overtakes or travels at high speed. Metaphorically, to be or live in the fast lane is to have a busy or hectic lifestyle.

**Fast Show, The.** A fast-paced television comedy show first screened on BBC2 in 1994 and consisting of a series of brief unrelated sketches based on individual characters who reappear in their clearly identifiable roles every week. It was created and compiled by Paul Whitehouse and Charlie Higson, who took most of the main roles, one of the most memorable being the repressed homosexual country squire Lord Ralph Mayhew, played by Higson, and his Irish estate worker, Ted, played by Whitehouse. Many of the show's catchphrases, such as 'Suits you, Sir!' and 'Which was nice', soon became part of the national vocabulary.

**Fast track.** Metaphorically, a route or method that provides rapid results or promotion in business, especially when up against keen competition. The expression evolved from a US term for a racing track that is hard and dry, enabling horses to run fast.

**Fast worker.** A colloquialism for a person who achieves quick results, especially in a love affair.

**Fatal Attraction.** A film thriller (1987) directed by Adrian Lyne that depicted the vengeance wreaked on a successful lawyer and family man (Michael Douglas) by his lover (Glenn Close) after he refused to have any more to do with her after their ONE-NIGHT STAND. The ferocity of the tale caused a furore on the film's release and was alleged to have led to a sharp (if short-lived) drop in such extramarital activity on both sides of the Atlantic. The film encouraged a late 20th-century trend for sex thrillers featuring predatory females, such as the lurid Joe Eszterhas-scripted *Basic Instinct* (1992), directed by Paul Verhoeven and starring all parts of Sharon Stone, and *Disclosure* (1994), with Demi

Moore. Both films also co-starred Michael Douglas, and the press relished reports that the actor was being treated for 'sex addiction'.

**Fat Boy of Peckham, The.** The sobriquet of Johnny Trunley (1898–1944), who at the age of 5 weighed 70kg (11 stone) and was put on display as a freak at fairs, music halls, etc. By the time he was 18 he weighed 210kg (33 stone), and was said to be the heaviest man in England. The title was regularly invoked in the middle years of the 20th century when giving a dire warning of the dangers of obesity.

**Fat cat.** A rich and influential person, especially a businessman, politician or civil servant. In Britain in the 1990s the term came to be particularly associated with directors of privatized public utilities, some of whom were awarded spectacularly large pay rises or pay-offs. A fat cat is one that gets the 'cream'.

**Fat city.** Success or wealth, especially from criminal activity. The phrase dates from the 1940s and was popularized by the film *Fat City* (1972), about a boxer who makes a final bid for success.

**Fat Controller.** A derogatory nickname for any heavyweight manager or supervisor. The name is that of the boss of THOMAS THE TANK ENGINE in the children's picture books by the Rev. W. Awdry (1911–97) and his son, first published in 1946.

**Fat farm.** A US colloquialism for a health farm for overweight people.

**Fat-finger syndrome.** The name given to a keyboarding error that leads to undesirable consequences. It is particularly used in relation to mistakes made on the world's stock exchanges. There was a notorious case in Japan in December 2005, when a trader, instead of offering 1 share at 610,000 yen, mistakenly offered 610,000 shares at 1 yen each. The Tokyo Stock Exchange duly processed the trade, even though the company in question had only issued 14,000 shares. The error led to the brokerage firm responsible losing £128 million, and caused shockwaves across the stock markets of Asia.

**Father and Son.** An autobiography (1907) of his early years, subtitled 'A Study of Two Temperaments', by the literary critic Edmund Gosse (1849–1928). Gosse was the only son of Philip Gosse (1810–88), the Fundamentalist (*see* FUNDAMENTALISM) writer on zoology, with whom, after his mother's death in 1857, Gosse went to live in Devon. The book explores the conflict between generations caused by a restricted upbringing. *See also* OSCAR AND LUCINDA.

**Father Brown.** *See* Father BROWN.

**Father's Day.** A day devoted to fathers in the annual calendar, falling on the third Sunday in June. Britain imported the occasion from the United States, where it was devised by Mrs John Bruce Dodd of Spokane, Washington, in 1910 as a counterpart to MOTHER'S DAY. It was not widely observed, however, until almost a quarter of a century later.

**Fathers of the 20th century.** The title 'Father of' has long been traditionally applied to a leader, inventor or pioneer of some kind, such as Hippocrates (460–377 BC), the Father of Medicine, or George Washington (1732–99), the Father of America. The following are some modern 'Fathers' in various fields (in order of subject area):

Father of American Music: Charles Ives (1874–1954), US composer

Father of Australia: Sir Edmund Barton (1849–1920), the first Australian prime minister (1901–3)

Father of Country Music: Jimmie Rodgers (1897–1933), US singer and guitarist

Father of Daylight Saving: William Willett (1856–1915), English advocate of SUMMER TIME

Father of English Football: Sir Stanley Rous (1895–1986), sixth president of FIFA (1961–74)

Father of Europe: Jean Monnet (1888–1979), French proposer of a plan for the European Community (*see* EUROPEAN UNION)

Father of Geomorphology: William M. David (1850–1934), US geographer and geologist who discovered the cycle of erosion of land masses

Father of Greyhound Racing: Brigadier-General Alfred Critchley (1890–1964), who built the first track at Belle Vue, Manchester, in 1926

Father of Indian Nationalism: Dababhai Naoroji (1925–1917), who in 1906 claimed the right of India to self-government

Father of Modern American Gangsterism: Johnny Torrio (1882–1957), US bootlegger, brothel-keeper and killer

Father of Modern English Criminology: Dr Hermann Mannheim (1889–1974), German-born British founder of the study of criminology

Father of Modern Navigation: Admiral of the Fleet Sir Henry Oliver (1865–1965), English sailor

Father of Nuclear Physics: Ernest Rutherford, 1st Baron Rutherford (1871–1939), New Zealand physicist who split the atom

Father of Published Ragtime: Irving Berlin (1888–1989), US composer

Father of Ragtime: Scott Joplin (1886–1917), US jazz pianist and composer

Father of Television: John Logie Baird (1888–1946), Scottish electrical engineer, the first demonstrator of a television image (1926)

Father of the Atomic Bomb: Dr Robert Oppenheimer (1904–67), US physicist who supervised the construction of the atomic bomb in the Second World War

Father of the Blues: William C. Handy (1873–1958), US composer of 'The Memphis Blues' (1909); the title was also that of his autobiography (1941)

Father of the Chin: Major-General Sir John Bagot Glubb (1897–1987), English commander of the Arab Legion in Transjordan (1938–56), also known as 'Glubb Pasha'; he was badly wounded in the jaw in 1917. The sense of 'Father' here derives from Arabic usage, and the English title is a loose translation of the Arabic original, *Abu Hunaik*, literally 'Father of the Little Jaw'

Father of the Comic Strip: Richard Outcault (1863–1928), US creator of the 'Yellow Kid' (*see* YELLOW PRESS)

Father of the Computer: Alan Turing (1912–54), English mathematician and inventor of computer programming who, during the Second World War, led the efforts that broke the German ENIGMA codes

Father of the Four-letter Word: Henry Miller (1891–1980), US author of *Tropic of Cancer* (1934) and *Tropic of Capricorn* (1938), novels notorious for their explicit sexual content; *see also* FOUR-LETTER WORD

Father of the Gossip Column: Walter Winchell (1897–1972), US journalist, who began such a column in the *Evening Graphic* in 1924

Father of the Helicopter: Igor Sikorsky (1889–1972), Russian-born US aeronautical engineer, who constructed his first helicopter in 1909

Father of the Hydrogen Bomb: Edward Teller (1908–2003), Hungarian-born US physicist

Father of the Irish Republic: Éamon de Valera (1882–1975), Irish president of SINN FÉIN, which set up the first (unrecognized) Irish Republic in 1919; *see also* DEV

Father of the King's African Rifles: Frederick Lugard, 1st Baron Lugard (1858–1945), English soldier and colonial administrator, who raised the regiment of this name in 1891

Father of the Royal Air Force: Air Marshal Hugh Trenchard, 1st Viscount Trenchard (1873–1956), English officer, who helped found the RAF in 1918

Father of the Twentieth Amendment: Senator George W. Norris (1861–1944), who advocated the amendment to the Constitution that the inauguration of the president should take place on 20 January instead of 4 March (1933); the amendment ended 'lame-duck' sessions of Congress

Father of the United Nations: Cordell Hull (1871–1955), US secretary of state (1933–43), whose proposals at the Moscow conference of 1943 led to the formation of the UNITED NATIONS in 1945; his endeavours won him the NOBEL PRIZE for Peace in 1944

Father of Westerns: Thomas Ince (1882–1924), US film producer who introduced the WESTERN to the film industry (*War on the Plains*, 1912)

Father of the WORLD WIDE WEB: Sir Tim Berners Lee (b.1955)

**Father Ted.** The Irish Roman Catholic priest, played by Dermot Morgan, who was the central character of the television SITCOM named after him, first screened in 1995. It was written by Graham Linehan and Arthur Mathews. The action took place in the priests' home on the remote and fictional Craggy Island, off the west coast of Ireland, where Father Ted was forever struggling to control his two fellow priests, the young and naive Father Dougal (played by Ardal O'Hanlon) and the old and alcoholic Father Jack (Frank Kelly), forever shouting 'Drink!' Overseeing the three was the larger-than-life housekeeper, Mrs Doyle (Pauline McLynn), always determined to thrust a cup of tea into the hands of any visitor, with the words 'Go on, go on, go on, go on …'. Another catchphrase from the series was the word 'feck', a bowdlerization of the most popular FOUR-LETTER WORD. Morgan died, aged 45, in 1998, soon after filming of the last episode.

> An interesting footnote: 'Fek!' is Esperanto for 'shit!'
> www.feck.net (accessed 2006), the website devoted to the series

**Fatima.** The small town of this name in west central Portugal became a centre of Roman Catholic pilgrimage after the reported sighting of the Virgin Mary in 1917. On 13 May that year three country children, Lucia dos Santos and her two cousins, Francisco and Jacinta, claimed to have seen a vision of a woman standing on a cloud in an evergreen tree. In a conversation heard only by the two girls, the woman asked the children to return to the site on the 13th of each month until October. Despite attempts to refute the children's evidence, the story drew increasing numbers of devotees, so that by October 50,000 pilgrims assembled with the children at the site. Many claimed to have witnessed a 'miracle of the sun', but the woman herself was visible only to the children, identifying herself as 'Our Lady of the Rosary'. In 1930 the bishop of Leira proclaimed the legitimacy of the apparitions and authorized the cult of Our Lady of Fatima.

The name itself is remote from Christianity as it derives from a 12th-century Moorish princess, a namesake of Fatima (*c.*606–632), youngest daughter of the prophet Muhammad.

**Fat is a Feminist Issue.** A 1978 anti-diet book by the American psychotherapist Susie Orbach (b.1946), concerned with women's problems with eating and body image. Among other things, Orbach argues that fat women are using their fat to keep men from pestering them. In 1982 she published a sequel, *Fat is a Feminist Issue II*. Orbach has subsequently blamed the obesity crisis hitting the West on the diet industry and our guilt over our consumption of the world's resources.

**Fat lady, The.** *See* the OPERA ISN'T OVER UNTIL THE FAT LADY SINGS.

**Fat Man.** *See* ENOLA GAY.

**Fat Owl of the Remove.** *See* Billy BUNTER.

**Fatty Pang.** A nickname given to Chris Patten (b.1944) while governor of Hong Kong (1992–7), prior to the handover of the colony to the People's Republic of China. The comfortably but by no means excessively built Patten had been chairman of the Conservative Party, but lost his seat in the 1992 general election. In 1998–9, following the GOOD FRIDAY AGREEMENT, he chaired an independent commission into policing in Northern Ireland, which resulted in the replacement of the Royal Ulster Constabulary with the Police Service of Northern Ireland. Patten subsequently became a European commissioner (2000–4), and in 2003 was elected chancellor of Oxford University.

**Fattypuffs and Thinifers.** The English title of *Patapoufs et Filifers* (1930) by the French writer André Maurois (1885–1967). It tells of two brothers, one fat, one thin, who discover two contrasting nations beneath the surface of the earth. The suitably obese Fattypuffs do little but eat and sleep, while the slender and fastidious Thinifers work six days a week and do without lunch. An invasion of the land of the Fattypuffs by the Thinifers sets in train a reconciliation between the two peoples, who eventually agree to unite.

**Fatty Soames.** A descriptive nickname given to the Conservative politician Nicholas Soames (b.1948), grandson of Sir Winston Churchill, and armed services minister in John Major's government. He was shadow defence spokesman 2003–5. He has also been referred to as the CRAWLEY FOOD MOUNTAIN. The indiscreet diaries of Conservative former minister Alan Clark (1928–99) often evoke grand dining in Soames's company.

**Fatwa.** A legal decision given by a Muslim religious leader. The word became familiar in the West in 1989 when AYATOLLAH Khomeini of Iran issued a fatwa sentencing the writer Salman Rushdie (b.1947) to death for publishing *The SATANIC VERSES* (1988), a novel condemned as blasphemous and highly offensive. The Arabic word, which does not itself specifically mean a death sentence, is related to 'mufti'.

**Fauvism.** The name given to the work of a group of young French artists of the first decade of the 20th century, whose leader was Henri Matisse (1869–1954), and which included André Derain (1880–1954), Georges Braque (1882–1963), Maurice de Vlaminck (1876–1958), Raoul Dufy (1877–1953), Albert Marquet (1875–1947), Othon Friesz (1879–1949) and Georges Rouault (1871–1958). The corresponding German movement was *Die* BRÜCKE. The French school derives from the influence of Van Gogh, and the work was characterized by the imaginative use of brilliant colour, decorative simplicity, vitality and gaiety. The name Fauves ('wild beasts') arose from a remark of the French art critic Louis Vauxcelles, *'Donatello au milieu des fauves!'* ('Donatello among the wild beasts'), occasioned by the sight of a quattrocento-like statue amid their spectacularly coloured paintings at an exhibition of their work in 1905. *See also* CUBISM; DADAISM; FUTURISM; ORPHISM; RURALISM; SURREALISM; SYNCHROMISM; TACHISM; VORTICISM.

**Fave rave.** A now dated term for an infatuation with a popular performer, especially a singer. 'Fave' is 'favourite'. *See also* RAVE.

> As soon as he [singer David Cassidy] was seen on screen he was snatched by the US fan magazine market, always at the ready to replace a current fave rave.
> *The Times* (30 July 1973)

**Fawlty Towers.** A classic television SITCOM that has long claimed an indelible place in the British collective memory. It consisted of 12 half-hour programmes, the first series of 6 screened in 1975, the second in 1979. It was written by John Cleese and Connie Booth, married at the time, with Cleese playing Basil Fawlty, the manic, hen-pecked owner of the hotel of the title, and Booth taking the part of the winsome waitress Polly. Prunella Scales played Basil's formidable wife Sybil, while Andrew Sachs was the spectacularly incompetent but well-meaning Spanish waiter Manuel. The glory of the series lay in its beautifully crafted plots, its realistic dialogue with many memorable lines, and its perfectly cast characters, in both major and minor roles. The programme had its genesis in an occasion in 1971 when Cleese and some other members of the MONTY PYTHON'S FLYING CIRCUS team stayed at the Gleneagles Hotel in Torquay, which had a highly irascible manager by the name of Donald Sinclair (1919–78).

**FBI.** The Federal Bureau of Investigation evolved in 1935, under the leadership of the colourful J. Edgar Hoover (1895–1972), from a Department of Justice force of 'special agents' set up in 1908 as the Bureau of Investigation. Its new powers allowed its agents, the G-MEN, to be armed, to make arrests, and the organization was able to become a significant force against organized crime. It played a prominent part in the rooting out of supposed communist subversion in the early years of the COLD WAR (Hoover was virulently anti-communist), but its role in counter-espionage was gradually taken over by the CIA from the 1960s. Hoover remained director until his death, an extraordinarily long tenure enabled, it has been suggested, by the undisclosed information the FBI collected on the US presidents during this period.

**FDR.** An affectionate nickname of Franklin Delano Roosevelt (1882–1945), the Democratic statesman who was elected an unprecedented four times to be president of the United States (1933–45), and who led America through the GREAT DEPRESSION and the Second World War. He was also known as Franklin D. His high-spending NEW DEAL policies to deal with the Depression earned him the hostile nickname Franklin Deficit Roosevelt. Alistair Cooke (*see* LETTER FROM AMERICA) later observed that he 'saved the capitalist system by simply forgetting to balance the books'. In his secret communications with Winston Churchill before America's entry into the Second World War Roosevelt adopted the code name POTUS (President of the United States), while Churchill was FORMER NAVAL PERSON. *See also* JFK; LBJ; ONLY THING WE HAVE TO FEAR IS FEAR ITSELF.

**Fear and Loathing in Las Vegas.** An off-beat account (1972) by the 'gonzo journalist' (*see* GONZO JOURNALISM) Hunter S. Thompson (1939–2005) of an assignment to cover the 'Mint 400', an off-road motorbike race outside Las Vegas. The work is subtitled 'A Savage Journey to the Heart of the American Dream' (*see* AMERICAN DREAM). Accompanied by Dr Gonzo, his lawyer, Thompson (using the alias Raoul Duke) – himself much of the time under the influence of a range of recreational drugs, and therefore achieving little (or nothing) in the way of sporting reportage – confronts casino operators, bartenders, tourists, police officers and other members of the community. The opening gives some feel of the drug- and reality-fuelled fear and loathing that is to follow:

> We were somewhere around Barstow on the edge of the desert when the drugs began to take hold. I remember saying something like 'I feel a bit lightheaded; maybe you should drive …' And suddenly there was a terrible roar all around us and the sky was full of what looked like huge bats, all swooping and screeching and diving around the car, which was going about a hundred miles an hour with the top down to Las Vegas. And a voice was screaming: 'Holy Jesus! What are these goddamn animals?'

A film version (1998), directed by Terry Gilliam and starring Johnny Depp, is appropriately off the wall, but inevitably lacks Thompson's mastery of what has subsequently been dubbed 'gonzo' prose.

**Fear of Flying.** The first novel (1973) by Erica Jong (b.1942). It achieved a cult status in its time, as a work of female sexual liberation and a celebration of the FOUR-LETTER WORD. Isadora Wing (29), who is scared stiff of aeroplanes, flies with her psychiatrist husband to a convention in Vienna. From there she embarks with a lover on a sexual odyssey, fantasizing about the 'zipless fuck', which 'has all the swift compression of a dream and is seemingly free of all remorse or guilt; because there is no talk of her late husband or of his fiancé; because there is no talk at all'. At the end Isadora returns to her husband, having survived her adventures and conquered her fear. The title works on a deeper level than mere travel in an aircraft, however, since although sex for Isadora is a means of 'flying', it is an illusory escape from reality and an illusory freedom and one that she fears.

**Fearsome foursome.** A nickname for any formidable quartet. In sport the designation was used of Roosevelt Grier, Deacon Jones, Lamar Lundy and Merlin Olsen, members of the defensive line of the Los Angeles Rams American football team in the mid-1960s.

**Federast.** *See* F-WORD.

**Fédération internationale de football association.** *See* FIFA.

**Feeding frenzy.** A concentrated period of frantic commercial competition or rivalry, as in the media for readers, listeners or viewers or among firms aiming at an identical market. The allusion is to sharks or piranhas, which launch an aggressive and competitive group attack on their prey. The figurative phrase dates from the 1970s.

**Feed the fishes.** To vomit over the side of a ship when suffering from seasickness. The euphemism is a 20th-century US addition to the earlier colloquial sense to die by drowning.

**Feel-good factor.** A feeling of well-being in people, especially in a financial or material context. It may have little substance to underpin it. The phrase is frequently used in the media by political commentators with regard to an economic recovery following a downturn of some kind, the theory being that the political party in power during such a recovery will make the electorate feel good and so win their votes.

**Feel** or **look like death warmed up.** To feel (look) very unwell. It is an expression often used by those suffering from a hangover and dates from the 1930s.

**Feel no pain.** To be drunk, so that one is insensitive to physical hurt.

**Feel someone's collar.** To arrest them, in allusion to a policeman's grip on a person's collar.

**Feel the earth move.** To experience sexual ecstasy. The expression is first found in Ernest Hemingway's FOR WHOM THE BELL TOLLS (1940):

> 'Oh,' she said. 'I die each time. Do you not die?'
> 'No. Almost. But did thee feel the earth move?'
> 'Yes. As I died. Put thy arm around me, please.'
> ch. 13

**Feel up.** To fondle sexually, especially surreptitiously or without the subject's permission.

> It is no accident, I have often thought, that men seem so exceptionally keen on feeling one up while one is bent over a sink full of washing up in one's yellow rubber gloves.
> *The Times* (22 September 1999)

**Feldenkrais method.** A system designed to promote bodily and mental efficiency. It involves the analysis of neuromuscular activity through special exercises and was devised in the 1930s by the Russian-born physicist Moshe Feldenkrais (1904–84).

**Felix the Cat.** The feline hero of early animated film cartoons produced by Pat Sullivan in the 1920s. Throughout his many adventures, 'Felix kept on walking', and thus originated the formerly familiar catchphrase. Felix was introduced in the film *Feline Follies* (1919) and was designed and animated by Sullivan's associate, Otto Messmer, who stated that he based his black tomcat's mannerisms on those of Charlie Chaplin. His name was intended to suggest 'felicity', by contrast with the bad luck normally associated with black cats. For other animated felines, *see* TOM AND JERRY; TOP CAT.

**Fellow traveller.** A person in sympathy with a group, faction or political party but not a member of it. The term, which came to be chiefly used of communist sympathizers, is a translation of Russian *poputchik*, first used by Trotsky in this sense to refer to non-communist writers who sympathized with the Revolution. *See also* SPUTNIK.

**Female Eunuch, The.** A book (1970) by the Australian academic Germaine Greer (b.1939) that became one of the key texts of modern feminism. In particular, Greer championed female sexual freedom and decried the sexually passive role imposed both by society and by women themselves.

> You can now see the Female Eunuch the world over … spreading herself wherever blue jeans and Coca-Cola may go. Wherever you see nail varnish, lipstick, brassieres and high heels, the Eunuch has set up her camp.

**Femidom.** A proprietary name for a contraceptive sheath worn by women. Hence the name, a shortening of 'feminine condom'. The word should not be confused with 'femdom', the term for a dominatrix or dominating female in a sexual practice such as bondage and discipline (B & D).

**Feng shui.** In Chinese thought a system of good and evil influences in the natural surroundings, now increasingly taken into account in the West when designing buildings or simply when deciding where to sit. The words represent Chinese *fēng*, 'wind' and *shui*, 'water', and the whole is pronounced 'fung shway'. For the Chinese *feng shui* is both an art and a science, the former as a means of counteracting evil influences by good ones, the latter by determining the desirability of sites from the configuration of natural objects such as rivers, trees and hills. Many Chinese were at first concerned that the introduction of railways and telegraph lines would seriously damage the *feng shui* or prosperity of the districts through which they were laid.

**Ferdinand the Bull.** The gentle, peace-loving bull in the children's tale *The Story of Ferdinand* (1936) by Munro Leaf. He is chosen for the bullring, but the matador is disappointed when all that Ferdinand wants to do is to sniff the scent of the flowers in the hats of the women spectators. An award-winning Disney cartoon, *Ferdinand the Bull* (1938), was based on the story, which has a simple moral: peace and gentleness are better than fighting and death.

**Fergie.** A nickname of Sarah Ferguson (b.1959), who married Queen Elizabeth II's second son, Andrew, in 1986, becoming Duchess of York. Known for her extravagant lifestyle and fullish figure, she has also unkindly been dubbed the Duchess of Pork. Her marriage to the Duke of York ended in divorce in 1996.

> I couldn't believe it the other day when I picked up a British newspaper and read that 82 per cent of men would rather sleep with a goat than me.
> THE DUCHESS OF YORK: quoted in *The Observer* (25 March 2001)

**'Ferry Across the Mersey'.** A nostalgic Liverpudlian pop anthem by Gerry Marsden, performed by Gerry and the Pacemakers and released in 1964 when that city's pop groups were speeding along in the slipstream of The BEATLES. The name of the song was chosen as the title of a film about Gerry and the Pacemakers by Tony Warren, creator of the title CORONATION STREET for the popular soap opera.

**Festival of Britain.** This grand, government-sponsored celebration was staged on an area of derelict ground on

London's SOUTH BANK in 1951 ostensibly to mark the centenary of the Great Exhibition of 1851. In reality it was a morale-boosting exercise, a gesture of faith in a brighter future for Britain after the deprivations of the Second World War and the years of austerity that followed. Three of its most striking structures were the Dome of Discovery, the world's largest dome at the time; the SKYLON, and the Royal Festival Hall, the only permanent building and now one of London's main concert venues. See also BRUTALISM; MILLENNIUM.

> We believe in the right to strike,
> But now we've bloody well got to like
> Our own dear Festival of Britain.
>
> NOËL COWARD: *The Lyric Revue*, 'Don't Make Fun of the Fair' (1951)

**Fettuccine Alfredo.** A dish made with fettuccine (pasta shapes), butter, Parmesan cheese, black pepper and cream. The name slightly alters the Italian original, *fettucine all'Alfredo*, taking its name from Alfredo, the owner of a restaurant in Rome noted for the dish.

**Fever Pitch.** A popular sociological study (1992) by Nick Hornby (b.1957), subtitled 'A Story of Football and Obsession'. It charts the author's personal relationship with the game as a fan (from the age of 10) of Arsenal Football Club. The book, which soon became a bestseller, gave an insight into the thinking and attitude of the typical NEW LAD. The title has obvious punning connotations. A film version (1996), directed by David Evans and starring Colin Firth, presented the original as a romantic comedy. An Americanized version (2005) concerned actor Ben Fallon's character's obsession with the Boston Red Sox. See also HIGH FIDELITY.

**Few, The.** The RAF pilots of the BATTLE OF BRITAIN, so called from Winston Churchill's memorable tribute in the House of Commons on 20 August 1940: 'Never in the field of human conflict was so much owed by so many to so few.' A myth centring on the devil-may-care courage of the fur-collared British public-school airman was disseminated by the film *First of the Few* (1942) starring David Niven. In reality, British victory in the Battle of Britain owed just as much to the efforts of non-commissioned sergeants of the Volunteer Reserve and to the skills and bravery of the many foreign nationals, Czechs, Poles and others, who flew with the RAF.

**Few well-chosen words.** This phrase originally meant what it said in a positive or approbatory sense. In the 20th century, however, it took on an ironic tone. The words were still well-chosen but selected in order to reprehend, denounce or abuse.

**FFI.** (*Forces françaises de l'intérieur*, 'French Forces of the Interior'.) The grouping together in February 1944 of the various forces fighting for liberation after the fall of France in 1940. They were subsequently merged with the army (November 1944). See also MAQUIS.

**FFL.** (*Forces françaises libres*, 'Free French Forces'.) The forces organized by General de Gaulle from June 1940, after the German occupation of France, to continue the struggle in cooperation with the Allies. They were later called the FIGHTING FRENCH. See also MAQUIS.

**Fianna Fáil.** One of the two main political parties in Ireland, sometimes loosely called the Republican Party. It was formally constituted in 1926 under Éamon de Valera as a grouping of those opposed to the terms of the treaty with Great Britain that in 1921 brought the Irish Free State into existence. Its name derives from Irish *fianna*, 'band of warriors' and *Fáil*, the genitive form of *Fál*, an old name of Ireland, popularly understood to mean 'Destiny'. See also DEV; FINE GAEL; FREE-STATERS; SINN FÉIN; TAOISEACH.

**Fickle finger.** A capricious quasi-supernatural agency that controls events. Although many other combinations are possible, the term appears most often in the expression 'the fickle finger of fate', denoting the unseen hand of destiny. This was popularized by 'The Flying Fickle Finger of Fate', a mock talent-show award presented on the US television comedy show ROWAN AND MARTIN'S LAUGH-IN, and it reappeared (although not so named) in Britain in the 1990s as the logo of the National Lottery.

**Fiddler on the Roof.** A stage musical (1964) and film (1971), with a book by Joseph Stein, score by Jerry Bock and lyrics by Sheldon Harnick, that relate the story of a Jewish milkman who is forced to leave pre-revolutionary Russia and emigrate to the United States. Based on the short story collection *Tevye and His Daughters* by Sholom Aleichem, the significance of the title is obscure. It may be based on a proverbial expression meaning to 'eat, drink and be merry', but it may be taken generally to signify a person who cheerfully makes the best of things, whatever the circumstances.

**Fidel Castro in a miniskirt.** A description of the fiery young Northern Irish civil rights campaigner Bernadette Devlin (now McAliskey; b.1947) as she made her striking maiden speech in the House of Commons in 1969, having been elected a Unity Party MP for Mid-Ulster. The phrase was coined by the Ulster Unionist MP Stratton Mills (b.1932). The identification with the Cuban communist politician Fidel Castro (b.1927) reflects the perceived radicalism of her politics.

**Fido.** The name of a system developed by the Allies in the Second World War for dispersing fog by means of petrol burners on the ground. It is an acronym of *fog intensive dispersal operation* and was probably suggested by the dog's name Fido, meaning 'I trust'.

**Fiery Fred.** A nickname of the fast-bowling Yorkshire and England cricketer Freddie Trueman (1931–2006), whose first autobiography was titled *Ball of Fire* (1976).

**FIFA.** The Fédération Internationale de Football Association, the world governing body of football, named after the Football Association (FA) created in 1863 to standardize the rules of the game. By the end of the 19th century it became clear that football needed a governing body to encourage international development. The English, who had pioneered modern football, were not keen on the globalization of the game when a Dutch banker, C.A.W. Hirschmann, first proposed such a federation in 1902. They were equally cautious when a similar suggestion was made the following year by the Union des Sociétés Françaises de Sports Athlétiques. The English were thus absent when, on 21 May 1904, delegates from Belgium, Denmark, France, Holland, Spain, Sweden and Switzerland met in Paris to found FIFA. In due course England relented, and D.B. Woodfall became FIFA's second president. It was his French successor from 1921, Jules Rimet, who in 1932 moved FIFA to its present neutral headquarters in Zurich.

**Fifth Beatle.** A nickname used for a number of individuals associated with the four BEATLES.The original and most 'authentic' Fifth Beatle may be said to be Stuart Sutcliffe, the group's original bass guitarist, who left the group in 1961. Sutcliffe, a talented painter, died in Hamburg in 1962 at the age of 21 and later became the subject of a film, *Backbeat* (1993). Brian Epstein (1934–67), The Beatles' manager, was so dubbed in 1964 by the US disc jockey 'Murray the K' (Murray Kaufman), but he did not readily take to the appellation. George Martin (b.1926), The Beatles' producer, was also so named. The term was subsequently applied to anyone who missed out on success.

The Northern Irish and Manchester United footballer George Best (1946–2005) was also dubbed the Fifth Beatle, not because he missed out on success, but because in his mop-topped prime he was the subject of an equal degree of female adoration as the Fab Four. Another of Best's nicknames was 'El Beatle', awarded by the press after he took part in Manchester United's 5–1 defeat of Benfica at the Stadium of Light in the 1966 European Cup.

> Best ... was as much a part of the 60s as the Beatles, Carnaby Street, Mary Quant, flower power and the pill.
> DAVID LACEY: in *The Guardian* (25 November 2005)

**Fifth Column.** Traitors, those within a country who are working for the enemy, often by infiltrating into key positions and seeking to undermine the body politic from within. The phrase is attributed to General Emilio Mola, who, in the Spanish Civil War (1936–9), said that he had four columns encircling Madrid and a fifth column (Spanish *quinta columna*) working for him in the city.

**Fifth Estate.** Jocularly applied to various 'authorities', such as the BBC, the trade unions, and so on, following on from the Fourth Estate as a term for the press. The term dates from the 1960s.

**Fifth Man.** In 1991 John Cairncross (1913–95) was identified as the long-sought 'Fifth Man' in the CAMBRIDGE SPY RING. His role as a 'masterspy' was described in various books in the 1980s, but he always denied having been the Fifth Man. He was backed in his rebutment by Graham Greene, who, like Cairncross, had acted as an agent for MI6 in the Second World War, but the evidence against him was conclusive.

**Fifth Republic.** *See* FOURTH REPUBLIC.

**Fifty-fifty.** In equal amounts or proportion; 50 per cent each. The expression dates from the early 20th century and has been adopted untranslated by other languages, such as French and German *fifty-fifty*, Russian *fifti-fifti*.

**Fifty-first state.** An epithet for Puerto Rico, a commonwealth whose citizens have US citizenship. Hawaii was formerly so known until it became the 50th US state in 1959. The name is also sometimes applied to Britain, seen as following the fashions and trends of the United States – or as following unquestioningly US foreign policy initiatives (*see* BUSH'S POODLE), in which context Britain is sometimes referred to as 'America's biggest aircraft carrier'. The ordinal number may vary in this sense, especially in British use. *See also* SPECIAL RELATIONSHIP.

**Fifty million Frenchman can't be wrong.** This catchphrase was popular with US troops in the First World War, the stated number being that of the population of France. When the US nightclub personality Texas Guinan and her troupe were refused entry into France in 1931, she was quoted as saying: 'Fifty million Frenchmen *can* be wrong.' She promptly renamed her revue *Too Hot for Paris* and toured the United States with it instead.

**Fighting French.** (French *La France Combattante*.) All those Frenchmen at home and abroad who combined with the Allied nations in their war against the AXIS powers after the fall of France (June 1940). General de Gaulle and others escaped to England and he formed them into the FFL. The name was later changed to the Fighting French (14 July

1942). One of their most noted feats was the march of General Leclerc's column across the Sahara, from Lake Chad, to join the 8TH ARMY in Libya. These men were honoured by being the first formation to enter Paris on 23 August 1944. The Fighting French supported the Allies in Africa, Italy and elsewhere and together with the FFI made a valuable contribution to the liberation of France.

**Fight or flight.** The instinctive physiological response to a threatening situation, which alerts a human or animal either to mount an instant vigorous defence or to run away. It was first described in Walter Cannon's *The Wisdom of the Body* (1914).

**Fig newton.** A facetious American alteration of 'figment' (as in 'a figment of one's imagination'), inspired by the brand-name of a type of fig roll (which in turn was a tribute to the town of Newton, Massachusetts, near which the fig roll was originally manufactured). It is still alive and more or less kicking in the early 21st century.

> A significant part of the Democrat agenda is the war on individuality. This was no fig newton of my imagination. Master Democrat Ted Kennedy has made reference to this war in just these terms.
> www.boortz.com (26 April 2005)

**Figure of eight.** An outline of the figure 8, especially as traced in the ice by a skater or flown by an aircraft in the air. The figure can be repeated endlessly without a break. Hence the adoption of a horizontal figure of eight ($\infty$) as the symbol for infinity in mathematics.

**Fill one's boots.** To avail oneself to the full of an opportunity that presents itself; a British slang expression dating from the 1970s.

> You could be opening yourself up to a new culinary experience. Come on, fill your boots, young 'un.
> CHRISSIE GLAZEBROOK: *Madolescents* (2001)

**Fill someone in.** To inform them more fully in a particular matter. The concept is of filling in the blanks in the know-ledge. The expression dates from the 1940s.

**Fill someone's shoes.** To assume their role and fulfil it perfectly. One identifies with the other person not just by wearing their shoes but also by sharing their shoe size.

**Film noir.** (French, 'black film'.) A term, coined by the critic Frank Nino in 1946, denoting a genre of film developed in HOLLYWOOD in the 1940s and early 1950s that was charac-terized by an atmosphere of urban anxiety and alienation and featured cynical or world-weary anti-heroes. It evolved out of the crime, gangster and detective movies of the 1930s,

and its largely monochrome photography was marked by the use of strong light-and-shadow contrast (something it took from German Expressionist cinema of the 1930s). Many of the films were based on the work of such crime-writers as Raymond Chandler and Dashiell Hammett. John Huston's *The Maltese Falcon* (1941) is often cited as the first *film noir*, and LAURA (1944) and DOUBLE INDEMNITY (1944) are other early examples of the genre, but it really got under way in the second half of the 1940s, with *Mildred Pierce* (1945), *The Big Sleep* (1946), *The Postman Always Rings Twice* (1946), *Gilda* (1946) and *The Killers* (1946). A slightly later notable *film noir* is Huston's *The Asphalt Jungle* (1950).

**Film star nicknames.** Many stars of the silver screen gained one or more nicknames, some more ephemeral than others. The names were not usually given by the public but mostly originated as promotional labels. The following is a selection.

America's Boy Friend: Charles 'Buddy' Rogers (1904–99)

America's Sweetheart: *see* World's Sweetheart *below*

Anatomic Bomb: Silvana Pampanini (b.1927)

AUSTRIAN OAK, The

Biograph Girl: Florence Lawrence (1886–1938)

BODY, The

BODY ART

Bogey: Humphrey Bogart (1899–1957)

Brazilian Bombshell: Carmen Miranda (1913–55)

Clothes Horse: Joan Crawford (1904–77), who 'suffered in mink'

Empress of Emotion: Elissa Landi (1904–48)

FIRST GENTLEMAN OF THE SCREEN

First Lady of the Screen: Norma Shearer (1900–83)

Handsomest Man in the World: Francis X. Bushman (1883–1966)

HANOI JANE

ICEBERG, The

IRON BUTTERFLY

'IT' GIRL

KING OF HOLLYWOOD

King of the Cowboys: (1) Tom Mix (1880–1940); (2) Roy Rogers (1912–98)

King of the Serials: Buster Crabbe (1907–83), the original FLASH GORDON in serials

Lolla, La: Gina Lollabrigida (b.1927)

Magnificent Wildcat: Pola Negri (1897–1987)

Man of a Thousand Faces: Lon Chaney (1883–1930), a master of macabre make-up

MAN YOU LOVE TO HATE

OOMPH Girl

PEEKABOO Girl

PLATINUM BLONDE

SEX KITTEN

Sex Thimble: Dudley Moore (1935–2002), a mere 5ft 2½in tall

Sexy Rexy: Rex Harrison (1908–90)

Singing Capon: Nelson Eddy (1901–67), partner of the IRON BUTTERFLY

SWEATER GIRL

Threat: Lizabeth Scott (b.1922), a sultry leading lady of the 1940s

World's Greatest Actor: John Barrymore (1882–1942)

World's Greatest Actress: Marie Dressler (1869–1934)

World's Sweetheart: Mary Pickford (1893–1979), originally America's Sweetheart

*See also* the GOVERNATOR.

**Filofax.** The loose-leaf notebook or personal organizer so called, as a respelling of 'file of facts', dates from 1930, when the name was registered by its inventor, Grace Scurr, a 36-year-old shorthand typist with a London firm of printers. The product was originally a personal filing system, and as such was in demand by clerics, scientists and certain regiments. In the Second World War Filofaxes were standard issue at Sandhurst, and in military circles they were often known as vade-mecums. In the early 1980s Filofaxes suddenly became a necessary item for business people or an indispensable fashion accessory for YUPPIES. By the mid-1990s, however, they had largely been superseded by various computerized gadgets.

**Final Solution.** (German *die Endlösung*.) The term coined by the NAZIs for the extermination of the Jews of Europe. The term emerged at the Wannsee Conference, held on 20 January 1942 in the Berlin suburb of Grossen-Wannsee. The conference, attended by 15 senior Nazis headed by Reinhard Heydrich (the HANGMAN), was called to determine 'the final solution of the Jewish question'. Heydrich had received his orders on 31 July 1941 from Hermann Goering:

> I herewith commission you to carry out all preparations with regard to … a *total solution* of the Jewish question in those territories of Europe that are under German influence.

Heydrich himself addressed the conference thus:

> Now the rough work has been done we begin the period of finer work. We need to work in harmony with the civil administration. We count on you gentlemen as far as the final solution is concerned.

Although EINSATZGRUPPEN extermination squads had been active in eastern Europe since the beginning of the Second World War, their rate of killing did not satisfy the Nazi leadership, who now set in motion the mass transportation of European Jews to specially built death camps such as AUSCHWITZ, where extermination could be carried out on an industrial scale (*see* ZYKLON-B). Those deemed fit to work would be used as slave labour until they were exhausted, at which point they would be killed. The strategy was carried out with ruthless efficiency, resulting in the deaths of some 6 million Jews, the HOLOCAUST.

**Fine and dandy.** Excellent; perfect. The phrase is frequently applied ironically.

**Fine Gael.** One of the two main political parties of Ireland, together with FIANNA FÁIL, its name being Irish for 'tribe of Gaels'. It arose in 1933 from William Thomas Cosgrave's *Cumann na nGaedheal* (Society of Gaels), whose members had supported the terms of the Anglo-Irish treaty of 1921 that brought the Irish Free State into existence. Little now separates it politically from FIANNA FÁIL, of which it is even so a distinctive rival. *See also* FREE-STATERS.

**Fine** or **small print.** In the strict sense, printed matter in small type. The phrase subsequently came to denote the disadvantageous details of a situation. The specific allusion is to the conditions stipulated in an agreement or contract, which are often printed in such small print that they may be overlooked at the time of signing.

**Finest hour.** The words from a celebrated speech by Winston Churchill (18 June 1940), given at the time when the collapse of France was imminent and the BATTLE OF BRITAIN waged by the FEW was about to begin.

> Let us therefore brace ourselves to our duty, and so bear ourselves that, if the British Commonwealth and its Empire lasts for a thousand years, men will still say, 'This was their finest hour.'

**Finger on the pulse.** To have or keep one's finger on the pulse is to be aware of all the latest news or developments, just as the rate of a person's heartbeat and so the state of their health can be monitored by feeling their pulse with one's fingertips.

**Fingers** or **hand in the till.** To have one's fingers or hand in the till is to appropriate money from one's place of work.

**Finger trouble.** A colloquial term for an error caused by operating a control wrongly or pressing a wrong key on an electronic instrument, such as a television or a computer. *In extremis* this can result in FAT-FINGER SYNDROME.

***Fings Ain't Wot They Used T'Be.*** A musical (1959) with a score and lyrics by Lionel Bart (1930–99) and book by Frank Norman about the gamblers and prostitutes who inhabit low-life London. The success of the title song, which reflects the changes that overtake the lives of all the main characters, was enough to establish it as a popular catchphrase.

**Finian's Rainbow.** A musical comedy (1947) with a score by Burton Lane (1912–97) and book by E.Y. Harburg (1898–1981) and Fred Sady about an Irish immigrant to the United States called Finian McLonergan, who tries to get rich by burying a crock of gold he has stolen from a leprechaun. The title refers not only to the legend of the crock of gold at the end of the rainbow but also to the fact that Finian buries his crock of gold, hoping it will multiply, in a place called Rainbow Valley.

**Finnegans Wake.** A Modernist (*see* MODERNISM) novel (1939) by James Joyce (1882–1941). He began work on it in 1922 but was too superstitious to reveal the title; sections of it were published (1927–30) in New York as 'Work in Progress'. Whereas ULYSSES is concerned with a single day, *Finnegans Wake* is a record of a night, in which the mind of the sleeping H.C. Earwicker is interpreted with great virtuosity and invention of language. Joyce illustrated his literary method by saying that he was tunnelling through a mountain from two sides. And all the while he added layers of meaning. The structure largely follows the Italian philosopher Giovanni Battista Vico (1668–1744), who divided human history into three ages, divine, heroic and human, to which Joyce added a fourth, return, emphasizing Vico's theory of evolutionary cycles in civilizations. The punning title derives from an Irish-American ballad about Tim Finnegan, a drunken hod-carrier who falls from his ladder and is killed. A splash of whiskey at his wake awakes him, and he exclaims, 'Do ye think I'm dead then?' It also suggests the return of Fionn mac Cumhaill, mythical hero of the Ossianic cycle of stories. *See also* FIRST LINES OF NOVELS.

**Fireball.** The nickname of the fast and furious US motor-racing champion Edward G. Roberts (1929–64). He lived up to his name, dying of burns following a crash on a circuit in North Carolina.

**Fire blanks.** Of a man, to be infertile (e.g. because of a vasectomy).

> So to summarise: ... I am now firing blanks – and Grethe can come off the pill.
> www.owen.org (25 May 2004)

**Fire in one's belly.** Ambition; 'drive'. The belly is popularly regarded as the 'engine' that drives the body and the emotions, food being the fuel that 'stokes' it.

**Fire on all cylinders.** To work at peak level. The allusion is to an internal combustion engine, in which a cylinder 'fires'

when the fuel inside it is ignited. A fuller form of the phrase is 'to fire on all four cylinders'. Hence 'to fire on one cylinder' in the sense to work badly.

**Fireside chats.** The name adopted by President F.D. Roosevelt (*see* FDR) for his broadcasts to the American people on topics of national interest and importance. They began in 1933 and became customary during his administration.

**Fire watcher.** The name given to those volunteers in Britain who kept watch for fires started by enemy air raids during the Second World War.

**Firm, The.** A nickname for any influential or authoritative organization, especially as current among its members, such as the Royal Family or the CIA. The former was reputedly first so called by George VI, and here 'the Firm' has sometimes acquired the connotations of a public-relations exercise (principally on behalf of itself and in defence of its inherited privileges).

**First Gentleman of the Screen.** A nickname of the English-born US film actor George Arliss (1868–1946), so called from his elegance and the monocle that he sported.

**First Lady.** A name applied to the wife of the president of the United States. The term came into general use in the early 20th century. Eleanor Roosevelt (1884–1962), wife of FDR, became known as the First Lady of the World, owing to her work on behalf of peace and the poor with the UNITED NATIONS after her husband's death. She was perhaps the most influential and politically involved first lady prior to Hillary Rodham Clinton (b.1947), long-suffering wife of Bill Clinton, the COMEBACK KID.

Away from US politics, the title 'First lady of ... ' has been given to the following, among others:

First Lady of Broadway: a nickname of the US actress Katherine Cornell (1893–1974)

First Lady of Country Music: the nickname of the US singer Tammy Wynette, born Virginia Wynette Pugh (1942–98)

First Lady of Fleet Street: the nickname of the journalist Jean Rook (1931–91), chief columnist and assistant editor of the *Daily Express*

First Lady of Hollywood Fashion: the nickname of the US costume designer Edith Head (1907–81), who created opulent dresses for many famous HOLLYWOOD actresses as well as the stylish suits worn by Robert Redford and Paul Newman in *The Sting* (1973)

First Lady of the Screen: *see under* FILM STAR NICKNAMES

First Lady of the Stage: the US actress Helen Hayes (1900–93), who won an OSCAR in 1932, an EMMY in 1954 and a TONY in

1958; she was also known as 'The First Lady of the American Theatre'

**First light.** A term used in the armed forces for the earliest time (roughly dawn) at which light is sufficient for the movement of ships or for military operations to begin. Similarly last light is the latest time when such movements can take place. The expression was current in the Second World War.

**First lines of novels.** There follows a selective list of the first lines of some of the most celebrated novels and other works of fiction, in alphabetical order, written since 1900. Novel titles in small capital letters indicate that a separate entry for the novel or work in question can be found elsewhere in the dictionary.

*Age of Innocence, The* (1920) by Edith Wharton: 'On a January evening of the early seventies, Christine Nilsson was singing in Faust at the Academy of Music in New York.'

*All the Pretty Horses* (1992) by Cormac McCarthy: 'The candle-flame and the image of the candleflame caught in the pierglass twisted and righted when he entered the hall and again when he shut the door.'

ANIMAL FARM (1945) by George Orwell: 'Mr Jones, of the Manor Farm, had locked the hen-houses for the night, but was too drunk to remember to shut the pop-holes.'

AT SWIM-TWO-BIRDS (1939) by Flann O'Brien: 'Having placed in my mouth sufficient bread for three minutes' chewing, I withdrew my powers of sensual perception and retired into the privacy of my mind, my eyes and face assuming a vacant and preoccupied expression.'

BRAVE NEW WORLD (1932) by Aldous Huxley: 'A squat grey building of only thirty-four storeys.'

BREAKFAST AT TIFFANY'S (1958) by Truman Capote: 'I am always drawn back to the places where I have lived, the houses and their neighborhoods.'

BRIDESHEAD REVISITED (1945) by Evelyn Waugh: '"I have been there before," I said; I had been there before; first with Sebastian more than twenty years ago on a cloudless day in June, when the ditches were creamy with meadowsweet and the air heavy with all the scents of summer; it was a day of peculiar splendour, and though I had been there so often, in so many moods, it was to that first visit that my heart returned on this, my latest.'

BRIGHTON ROCK (1938) by Graham Greene: 'Hale knew, before he had been in Brighton three hours, that they meant to murder him.'

*Call It Sleep* (1934) by Henry Roth: 'The small white steamer, Peter Stuyvesant, that delivered the immigrants from the stench and throb of the steerage to the stench and throb of

New York tenements, rolled slightly on the water beside the stone quay in the lee of the weathered barracks and the new brick buildings of Ellis island.'

*Cancer Ward* (1968) by Alexander Solzhenitsyn: 'On top of it all, the cancer wing was "number thirteen".'

CAPTAIN CORELLI'S MANDOLIN (1994) by Louis de Bernières: 'Dr Iannis had enjoyed a satisfactory day in which none of his patients had died or got any worse.'

*Casino Royale* (1953) by Ian Fleming (the first James BOND book): 'The scent and smoke and sweat of a casino are nauseating at three in the morning.'

*Castle, The* (1926) by Franz Kafka: 'It was late evening when K. arrived.'

CATCH-22 (1961) by Joseph Heller: 'It was love at first sight.' (Yossarian falls in love with the Chaplain.)

CATCHER IN THE RYE, THE (1951) by J.D. Salinger: 'If you really want to hear about it, the first thing you'll probably want to know is where I was born, and what my lousy childhood was like, and how my parents were occupied and all before they had me, and all that David Copperfield kind of crap, but I don't feel like going into it, if you want to know the truth.'

CIDER WITH ROSIE (1959) by Laurie Lee: 'I was set down from the carrier's cart at the age of three; and there with a sense of bewilderment and terror my life in the village began.'

COLD COMFORT FARM (1932) by Stella Gibbons: 'The education bestowed on Flora Poste by her parents had been expensive, athletic and prolonged; and when they died within a few weeks of one another during the annual epidemic of the influenza or Spanish Plague which occurred in her twentieth year, she was discovered to possess every art and grace save that of earning her own living.'

*Corrections, The* (2001) by Jonathan Franzen: 'The madness of an autumn prairie cold front coming through.'

DANCE TO THE MUSIC OF TIME, A, vol. 1, *A Question of Upbringing* (1951) by Anthony Powell: 'The men at work at the corner of the street had made a kind of camp for themselves, where, marked out by tripods hung with red hurricane-lamps, an abyss in the road led down to a network of subterranean drain-pipes.'

DEATH IN VENICE (1912) by Thomas Mann: 'Gustave Aschenbach – or von Aschenbach, as he had been known officially since his fiftieth birthday – had set out alone from his house in Prince Regent Street, Munich, for an extended walk.'

DECLINE AND FALL (1928) by Evelyn Waugh: 'Mr Sniggs, the Junior Dean, and Mr Postlethwaite, the Domestic Bursar, sat alone in Mr Sniggs's rooms overlooking the garden quad at Scone College.'

DOCTOR ZHIVAGO (1957) by Boris Pasternak: 'On they went,

singing "Eternal Memory", and whenever they stopped, the sound of their feet, the horses and the gusts of wind seemed to carry on their singing.'

*Earthly Powers* (1980) by Anthony Burgess: 'It was the afternoon of my eighty-first birthday, and I was in bed with my catamite when Ali announced that the archbishop had come to see me.'

*Edwardians, The* (1930) by Vita Sackville-West: 'Among the many problems that beset the novelist, not the least weighty is the choice of moment at which to begin his novel.'

*Farewell to Arms, A* (1929) by Ernest Hemingway: 'In the late summer of that year we lived in a house in a village that looked across the river and the plain to the mountains.'

FINNEGANS WAKE (1939) by James Joyce: 'riverrun, past Eve and Adam's, from swerve of shore to bend of bay, brings us by a commodius vicus of recirculation back to Howth Castle and Environs.'

*Glass Bead Game, The* (1943) by Hermann Hesse: 'It is our intention to preserve in these pages what scant biographical material we have been able to collect concerning Joseph Knecht, or Ludi Magister Josephus III, as he is called in the Archives of the Glass Bead Game.'

*Good Soldier, The* (1915) by Ford Madox Ford: 'This is the saddest story I have ever heard.'

*Grand Meaulnes, The* (1913) by Alain-Fournier: 'He appeared at our house on a Sunday in November 189….'

GRAVITY'S RAINBOW (1973) by Thomas Pynchon: 'A screaming comes across the sky.'

GREAT GATSBY, THE (1925) by F. Scott Fitzgerald: 'In my younger and more vulnerable years my father gave me some advice that I've been turning over in my mind ever since.'

*Handmaid 's Tale, The* (1985) by Margaret Atwood: 'We slept in what had once been the gymnasium.'

*Harry Potter and the Philosopher's Stone* (see Harry POTTER) (1997) by J.K. Rowling: 'Mr. and Mrs. Dursley, of number four, Privet Drive, were proud to say that they were perfectly normal, thank you very much.'

'HEART OF DARKNESS' (1902) by Joseph Conrad: '*Nellie*, a cruising yawl, swung to her anchor without a flutter of sails, and was at rest.'

HERZOG (1964) by Saul Bellow: 'If I am out of my mind, it's all right with me, thought Moses Herzog.'

HITCH-HIKER'S GUIDE TO THE GALAXY, THE (1979): 'Far out in the unchartered backwaters of the unfashionable end of the Western Spiral arm of the galaxy lies a small unregarded yellow sun.'

HOBBIT, *The* (1937) by J.R.R. Tolkien: 'In a hole in the ground there lived a hobbit.'

*Honorary Consul, The* (1973) by Graham Greene: 'Doctor

Eduardo Plarr stood in the small port on the Paraná, among the rails and yellow cranes, watching where a horizontal plume of smoke stretched over the Chaco.'

*House at Pooh Corner, The* (1928) by A.A. Milne: 'An Introduction is to introduce people, but Christopher Robin and his friends, who have already been introduced to you, are now going to say Good-bye.' (Opening sentence of the introductory 'Contradiction'.)

*Invisible Man* (1952) by Ralph Ellison: 'I am an invisible man.'

*Jazz* (1992) by Toni Morrison: 'Sth, I know that woman.'

JEWEL IN THE CROWN, THE (1966), first novel of the *Raj Quartet* by Paul Scott: 'Imagine, then, a flat landscape, dark for the moment, but even so conveying to a girl running in the still deeper shadow cast by the wall of the Bibighar Gardens an idea of immensity, of distance, such as years before Miss Crane had been conscious of standing where a lane ended and cultivation began: a different landscape but also in the alluvial plain between the mountains of the north and the plateau of the south.'

*Kind of Loving, A* (1960) by Stan Barstow: 'It really begins with the wedding – the Boxing Day Chris got married – because that was the day I decided to *do* something about Ingrid Rothwell besides gawp at her like a love-sick cow or something whenever she came in sight.'

LADY CHATTERLEY'S LOVER (1928) by D.H. Lawrence: 'Ours is essentially a tragic age, so we refuse to take it tragically.' (*See also* Lady CHATTERLEY; LADY CHATTERLEY TRIAL.)

*Light in August* (1932) by William Faulkner: 'Sitting beside the road, watching the wagon mount the hill toward her, Lena thinks, "I have come from Alabama: a fur piece. All the way from Alabama a-walking. A fur piece."'

LION, THE WITCH AND THE WARDROBE, THE (1950) by C.S. Lewis: 'Once there were four children whose names were Peter, Susan, Edmund and Lucy. This story is about something that happened to them when they were sent away from London during the war because of the air-raids.'

LOLITA (1955) by Vladimir Nabokov: 'Lolita, light of my life, fire of my loins.'

*Look Homeward, Angel* (1929) by Thomas Wolfe: 'A destiny that leads the English to the Dutch is strange enough; but one that leads from Epsom into Pennsylvania, and thence into the hills that shut in Altamont over the proud coral cry of the cock, and the soft stone smile of an angel, is touched by that dark miracle of chance which makes new magic in a dusty world.'

LORD OF THE FLIES (1954) by William Golding: 'The boy with fair hair lowered himself down the last few feet of rock and began to pick his way towards the lagoon.'

LORD OF THE RINGS, THE, vol. 1, *The Fellowship of the Ring* (1954) by J.R.R. Tolkien: 'When Mr Bilbo Baggins of Bag End announced that he would shortly be celebrating his eleventy-first birthday with a party of special magnificence, there was much talk and excitement in Hobbiton.' The Prologue prior to Chapter 1 begins: 'This book is largely concerned with hobbits ....'

LUCKY JIM (1954) by Kingsley Amis: '"They made a silly mistake, though," the professor of history said, and his smile, as Dixon watched, gradually sank beneath the surface of his features at the memory.'

MAGIC MOUNTAIN, THE (1924) by Thomas Mann: 'An unassuming young man was travelling, in midsummer, from his native city of Hamburg, to Davos-Platz in the Canton of the Grisons, on a three weeks' visit.'

*Magus, The* (1966/1977) by John Fowles: 'I was born in 1927, the only child of middle-class parents, both English, and themselves born in the grotesquely elongated shadow, which they never rose sufficiently above history to leave, of that monstrous dwarf Queen Victoria.'

*Malone Dies* (1951) by Samuel Beckett: 'I shall soon be quite dead at last in spite of all.'

*Man Without Qualities, The*, vol. 1 (1930) by Robert Musil: 'There was a depression over the Atlantic.'

*Men at Arms* (1952), the first of *The Sword of Honour Trilogy* by Evelyn Waugh: 'When Guy Crouchback's grandparents, Gervase and Hermione, came to Italy on their honeymoon, French troops manned the defences of Rome, the Sovereign Pontiff drove out in an open carriage and Cardinals took their exercise side-saddle on the Pincian Hill.'

*Metamorphosis* (1915) by Franz Kafka: 'When Gregor Samsa awoke one morning from troubled dreams he found himself transformed in his bed into a monstrous insect.'

MIDNIGHT'S CHILDREN (1981) by Salman Rushdie: 'I was born in the city of Bombay ... once upon a time.'

MORE PRICKS THAN KICKS (1934) by Samuel Beckett: 'It was morning and Belacqua was stuck in the first of the canti in the moon.'

MRS DALLOWAY (1925) by Virginia Woolf: 'Mrs Dalloway said she would buy the flowers herself.'

MYRA BRECKENRIDGE (1968) by Gore Vidal: 'I am Myra Breckinridge whom no man will ever possess.'

NAKED AND THE DEAD, THE (1948) by Norman Mailer: 'Nobody could sleep.'

NAKED LUNCH, THE (1959) by William Burroughs: 'I awoke from The Sickness at the age of forty-five, calm and sane, and in reasonably good health except for a weakened liver and the look of borrowed flesh common to all who survive The Sickness.'

*Nights at the Circus* (1984) by Angela Carter: '"Lor' love you, sir!" Fevvers sang out in a voice that clanged like dustbin lids.'

*Nineteen Eighty-Four* (1949) by George ORWELL: It was a bright cold day in April, and the clocks were striking thirteen.' (*See also* 1984.)

OF MICE AND MEN (1937) by John Steinbeck: 'A few miles south of Soledad, the Salinas River drops in close to the hill-side bank and runs deep and green.'

ON THE ROAD (1958) by Jack Kerouac: 'I first met Dean not long after my wife and I split up.'

*One Hundred Years of Solitude* (1967) by Gabriel García Marquez: 'Many years later, as he faced the firing squad, Colonel Aureliano Buendía was to remember that distant afternoon when his father took him to discover ice.'

OSCAR AND LUCINDA (1988) by Peter Carey: 'If there was a bishop, my mother would have him to tea.'

*Our Lady of the Flowers* (1943) by Jean Genet: 'Weidmann appeared before you in a five o'clock edition, his head swathed in white bands, a nun and yet a wounded pilot fallen into the rye one September day like the day when the world came to know the name of Our Lady of the Flowers.'

PASSAGE TO INDIA, A (1924) by E.M. Forster: 'Except for the Marabar Caves – and they are twenty miles off – the city of Chandrapore presents nothing extraordinary.'

PETER PAN (1911) by J.M. Barrie: 'All children, except one, grow up.'

*Plague, The* (1947) by Albert Camus: 'The unusual events described in this chronicle occurred in 194..., at Oran.'

PORTRAIT OF THE ARTIST AS A YOUNG MAN, A (1916) by James Joyce: 'Once upon a time and a very good time it was there was a moocow coming down along the road and this moocow that was coming down along the road met a nicens little boy named baby tuckoo ....'

RAILWAY CHILDREN, THE (1906) by E. Nesbit: 'They were not railway children to begin with.'

REBECCA (1938) by Daphne du Maurier: 'Last night I dreamt I went to Manderley again.'

*Remains of the Day, The* (1989) by Kazuo Ishiguro: 'It seems increasingly likely that I will undertake the expedition that has been preoccupying my imagination now for some days.'

REMEMBRANCE OF THINGS PAST, vol. 1, *Swann's Way* (1913) by Marcel Proust: 'For a long time I used to go to bed early.'

RIDDLE OF THE SANDS, THE (1903) by Erskine Childers: 'I have read of men who, when forced by their calling to live for long periods in utter solitude – save for a few black faces – have made it a rule to dress regularly for dinner in order to maintain their self-respect and prevent a relapse into barbarism.'

ROOM AT THE TOP (1957) by John Braine: 'I came to Warley on a wet September morning with the sky the grey of Guiseley sandstone.'

*Sabbath's Theater* (1995) by Philip Roth: 'Either forswear fucking others or the affair is over.'

SATANIC VERSES, THE (1988) by Salman Rushdie: '"To be born again," sang Gibreel Farishta tumbling from the heavens, "first you have to die."'

*Scoop* (1938) by Evelyn Waugh: 'While still a young man, John Courteney Boot had, as his publisher proclaimed, "achieved an assured and enviable position in contemporary letters".'

SEA, THE SEA, THE (1978) by Iris Murdoch: 'The sea which lies before me as I write glows rather than sparkles in the bland May sunshine.'

*Sons and Lovers* (1913) by D.H. Lawrence: '"The Bottoms" succeeded to "Hell Row".'

SWALLOWS AND AMAZONS (1930) by Arthur Ransome: 'Roger, aged seven, and no longer the youngest of the family, ran in wide zigzags, to and fro, across the steep field that sloped up from the lake to Holly Howe, the farm where they were staying for part of the summer holidays.'

'Tailor of Gloucester, The' (1902) by Beatrix Potter: 'In the time of swords and periwigs and full-skirted coats with flowered lappets – when gentlemen wore ruffles, and gold-laced waistcoats of paduasoy and taffeta – there lived a tailor in Gloucester.'

'Tale of Samuel Whiskers, The' (1908) by Beatrix Potter: 'Once upon a time there was an old cat, called Mrs Tabitha Twitchit, who was an anxious parent.'

'Tale of the Flopsy Bunnies, The' (1909) by Beatrix Potter: 'It is said that the effect of eating too much lettuce is "soporific".'

'Tale of Tom Kitten, The' (1907) by Beatrix Potter: 'Once upon a time there were three little kittens, and their names were Mittens, Tom Kitten, and Moppet.'

THIRTY-NINE STEPS, THE (1915) by John Buchan: 'I returned from the City about three o'clock on that May afternoon pretty well disgusted with life.'

TIN DRUM, THE (1959) by Günter Grass: 'Granted: I am an inmate of a mental hospital; my keeper is watching me, he never lets me out of his sight; there's a peephole in the door, and my keeper's eye is the shade of brown that can never see through a blue-eyed type like me.'

*Titus Groan* (1946), the first of the GORMENGHAST trilogy by Mervyn Peake: 'Gormenghast, that is, the main massing of the original stone, taken by itself would have displayed a certain ponderous architectural quality were it possible to have ignored the circumfusion of those mean dwellings that swarmed like an epidemic around its outer walls.'

TOWERS OF TREBIZOND, THE (1957) by Rose Macaulay: '"Take my camel, dear," said my aunt Dot, as she climbed down from this animal on her return from High Mass.'

TRAINSPOTTING (1993) by Irvine Welsh: 'The sweat wis lashing oafay Sick Boy; he wis trembling.'

ULYSSES (1922) by James Joyce: 'Stately, plump Buck Mulligan came from the stairhead, bearing a bowl of lather on which a mirror and a razor lay crossed.'

*Unnamable, The* (1953) by Samuel Beckett: 'Where now?'

WATERSHIP DOWN (1972) by Richard Adams: 'The primroses were over.'

*White Teeth* (2000) by Zadie Smith: 'Early in the morning, late in the century, Cricklewood Broadway.'

*Wonderful* WIZARD OF OZ, *The* (1900) by L. Frank Baum: 'Dorothy lived in the midst of the great Kansas prairies, with Uncle Henry, who was a farmer, and Aunt Em, who was the farmer's wife.'

WORLD ACCORDING TO GARP, THE (1976) by John Irving: 'Garp's mother, Jenny Fields, was arrested in Boston in 1942 for wounding a man in a movie theater.'

**First Nations.** *See* NATIVE AMERICAN.

**First Night of the Proms.** The first evening of the annual Promenade Concerts at the Royal Albert Hall, London, in July, an eagerly awaited event for many concert-goers. The music chosen varies from year to year, and thus lacks the predictability of the pieces at the LAST NIGHT OF THE PROMS.

**First past the post.** Said of a voting system in which a candidate is elected by means of a simple majority. British parliamentary elections are run on the first-past-the-post system. The allusion is to horse-racing, in which the horse that reaches the winning post first is the one that wins.

**First World War.** For the origins of this name, *see* GREAT WAR.

**First World War slang.** British troops in France and Belgium during the First World War picked up certain French phrases and corrupted them after their own fashion. The following examples are from Basil Hargrave's *Origins and Meanings of Popular Phrases and Names* (1925):

'Ally toot sweet' (*Allez tout de suite*): Go away; clear off. (A *Punch* cartoon of 5 December 1917 showed a 'Tommy' shooing away a group of inquisitive French children with the words: 'Nah, then, alley toot sweet, an' the tooter the sweeter.')

'Apree ler gare finee' (*Après la guerre finie*, or more correctly *Après que la guerre sera finie*): After the war; when the war is over

'Aunt Mary Ann': a variant of *Sanfaryan*

'Come on tally plonk?' (*Comment allez-vous*?): How are you getting on?

'Cum-sah' (*Comme ça*): What's-its-name

'Na-poo'd' (*Il n'y en a plus*): Done for; put out of action; killed (*see* NAPOO)

'Sally-fairy-ann' (*Cela ne fait rien*): a variant of *Sanfaryan*

'Sanfaryan' (*Ça ne fait rien*): It doesn't matter

'Tres beans' (*Très bien*): Very good; very well

'Wulla' (*Voilà*): There you are

*See also* WIPERS.

**Fish Called Wanda, A.** A film comedy (1988) written by and starring John Cleese (b.1939) and based on a story by Cleese and Charles Crichton about a repressed English barrister who becomes chaotically involved in a jewel robbery. Wanda is the sexually alluring thief Wanda Gershwitz (played by Jamie Lee Curtis), for whom Cleese's character develops a passion (although a pet fish does also play a significant role in the convoluted plot). Kevin Kline, as a jealously violent and stupid co-conspirator and Cleese's fellow ex-MONTY PYTHON Michael Palin, as an animal-loving stuttering hitman, memorably augmented the goings on. A 'follow-up', *Fierce Creatures* (1997), featuring the same actors as different characters, flopped.

**Fish dive.** A position in ballet in which the male dancer holds the ballerina almost vertically upside down, as if diving towards the floor. It is particularly effective for a *pas de deux*, such as that in Act III of *The Sleeping Beauty*. The term dates from the 1940s and is known in French as *pas poisson*.

**Fishing expedition.** An attempt to find information by asking questions at random rather than directly. A fisherman hopes for a catch but may not have one. The expression is of US origin and dates from the 1930s. *See also* PHISHING.

**Fistful of Dollars, A.** A Western (1964), written and directed by Sergio Leone (1921–89), about a nameless gunfighter (played by Clint Eastwood) who becomes involved in the struggle for power between two rival families. The title refers to the gunfighter's mercenary status, hired first by one family and then by the other. The basic plot of the film, which helped establish the SPAGHETTI WESTERN genre and spawned the sequels *For a Few Dollars More* (1965) and *The* GOOD, THE BAD AND THE UGLY (1967), was derived from Akira Kurosawa's *Yojimbo* (1961), in which the mysterious stranger is a samurai warrior. *See also* MAN WITH NO NAME.

**Fit the frock.** Of a woman, to wear conventional female dress, or more generally to conform to the supposedly traditional feminine norm. The expression is often found in the negative.

I was always a tomboy at heart, so there were times when I didn't really feel like I fitted the frocks. It wasn't too much of a problem, though, because I love clothes.

    KIM WILDE: in *heat* (6–12 January 2000)

**Fitzrovia.** A region of London north of Oxford Street and west of Tottenham Court Road, so called after Fitzroy Square there. The name became associated in the 1930s with impecunious artists and writers and gained a somewhat dubious reputation.

After leaving school he emigrated into what he calls Fitzrovia – a world of outsiders, down-and-outs, drunks, sensualists, homosexuals and eccentrics.

    *Times Literary Supplement* (10 January 1958)

Bloomsbury (*see* BLOOMSBURY GROUP) lies to the other side of Tottenham Court Road.

**Five-finger discount.** US teenagers' slang for shoplifting, in which one puts the five fingers to nefarious use. The expression dates from the 1960s.

**Five-finger exercise.** Anything easy or straightforward. The allusion is to a piece of music composed specially to give a piano player practice in using all five fingers. This invariably involves running up and down a series of five notes and the execution of scales, as entertainingly exampled by the piece 'Pianists' in Camille Saint-Saëns' *The Carnival of the Animals* (1886).

**Five o'clock shadow.** The beginnings of a new beard on a man's clean-shaven face, visible at about this time of day. The expression dates from the 1930s when it was first used in an advertising campaign for Gem razor blades. One such advertisement contained the lines: 'Gem Blades are made by the makers of your Gem Razor. They fit *precisely*. This famous combination positively prevents "5 o'clock Shadow"; it's the last word in shaving comfort.' *See also* TRICKY DICKY.

**Five Percenters.** An offshoot of the black Muslim NATION OF ISLAM, who see themselves as possessing 'self-knowledge' of the racial superiority of blacks. They take their name from their belief that enlightened followers of Islam make up just 5 per cent of the population, a minority charged with educating the majority 85 per cent, who are oppressed by the remaining 10 per cent of corrupt 'white devils'. Their credo became the theme of many African American RAP MUSIC artists in the 1990s.

**Five-star.** Of the highest standard or class. The reference is to the system used to grade hotels. Sometimes crowns are substituted for stars, especially for hotels, but otherwise the system can be adopted for any type of rating. In some gradings the highest is four-star.

> Five stars denote large, luxury hotels offering the highest international standards of accommodation, facilities, services and cuisine.
>
> *AA All-In-One Guide: London* (1998)

**Five Towns.** Towns in the Potteries, in Staffordshire, that Arnold Bennett (1867–1931) used as the scene of the best known of his novels and stories, one of the earliest being *Anna of the Five Towns* (1902). They are Tunstall, Burslem, Hanley, Stoke-on-Trent, Longton and Fenton. These actually number six, but for artistic purposes Bennett called them five, giving them the respective fictional names of Turnhill, Bursley, Hanbridge, Knype and Longshaw. All are now part of Stoke-on-Trent.

**Five-year plan.** In the former USSR and its satellites, any of a series of plans for developing the whole of the nation's economy in a coordinated effort by a five-year programme. The first such plan was launched by STALIN in 1929 with the aim of making the Soviet Union self-supporting. Further plans followed, and the example was copied by some other countries, including India. The strategy was subsequently discredited and abandoned after the dissolution of the USSR in 1991.

**Fizzbo.** An Americanism for the selling of a house without the services of a real-estate broker (estate agent). The word is an attempt at pronouncing the abbreviation 'fsbo', standing for 'for sale by owner'.

***Flag.*** The painting of the US flag by Jasper Johns (b.1930), dating from 1954, is regarded by some as marking the beginning of the POP ART movement. Although clearly depicting the Stars and Stripes, the work's richly textured encaustic surface raises the question as to whether it is a painting or a flag. Johns later recalled (in a 1972 documentary): 'One night I dreamt I painted a large American flag, and the next morning I went out and bought the materials to begin it.'

**Flag of convenience.** The national flag flown by a ship that has registered in that country in order to avoid legal or tax commitments. The phenomenal growth in the mid-1950s of merchant fleets registered under the flags of such non-maritime countries as Liberia and Panama caused considerable concern. The ownership of such vessels was mainly vested in Greek and American countries as well as citizens of other nationalities. As a result of this system Panama had the world's largest merchant fleet in the mid-1990s while less than one-third of British shipping was actually registered in Britain.

**Flak.** Anti-aircraft fire. The expressive word is an abbreviation of German *Fliegerabwehrkanone*, literally 'flyer defence cannon'. A development was the flak-jacket, worn as protection against gunfire. Later came the figurative flak-catcher, as a person who deals with and deflects hostile comments or questions aimed at another. The word is sometimes spelt 'flack'.

**Flaky.** Liable to behave eccentrically; unreliable. The term is of US origin and became current in the 1960s. The suggestion is that the person could 'flake' or 'fall apart'. The word became widely known following President Reagan's use of it in a speech at the beginning of January 1986 to describe the Libyan head of state, Colonel Gadaffi.

**Flambards.** A fictional house in Essex that lends its name to the first (1967) of a series of novels for teenagers by K.M. Peyton (b.1929). The books were later (1979) adapted for television.

**Flaming.** The act of being verbally rude or inflammatory on-line, as in an E-MAIL. It is definitely not good NETIQUETTE.

**Flaming fury.** A colloquial Australian term (first recorded in 1960) for a basic outdoor privy. From time to time the contents were disposed of by pouring petrol or the like over them and setting fire to them – whence the name.

**Flannelled fools.** Cricketers. This term, used derisively or humorously, is taken from Rudyard Kipling:

> Then ye returned to your trinkets; then ye contented your souls
> With the flannelled fools at the wicket or the muddied oafs at the goals.
>
> 'The Islanders' (1903)

**Flapper.** A term applied in the early years of the 20th century to a teenage girl, from her plaited pigtail tied at the end with a large bow. As she walked along, the pigtail flapped on her back. Her hair was subsequently 'put up' in a bun or other hairstyle. Flappers later became synonymous with the BRIGHT YOUNG THINGS of the 1920s and 1930s. The term gained an added punning sense since it referred to a young woman who was 'flighty'. *See also* YOUNG THING.

**Flapper vote.** A contemptuous name for the vote granted to women of 21 by the Equal Franchise Act of 1928, sponsored by Stanley Baldwin's Conservative government. *See also* FLAPPER.

**Flash.** Ostentatious or gaudy, as: a 'flash wedding', a 'flash hotel'.

**Flashback.** A scene in a film or novel set earlier than the current action. It is a useful narrative device that allows a writer to be flexible in the temporal structure of the plot. Some films have a flashback within a flashback. In *The Barefoot Contessa* (1954) Humphrey Bogart, while attending Ava Gardner's funeral (in the present), reminisces about the night when she visited his hotel (flashback) to tell him about her wedding night (flashback within a flashback). *The Locket* (1946) famously has a fourfold flashback, i.e. a flashback within a flashback within a flashback within a flashback.

In psychotherapy a flashback is a disturbing sudden vivid memory of an event in the past, especially as the result of a psychological trauma such as that resulting from an accident. A flashback of this kind may be accompanied by hallucinations and can be precipitated by circumstances similar to those of the original event. Thus for a person who has undergone a wartime experience, a flashback might be induced by a clap of thunder.

**Flash Gordon.** The spaceman hero created in imitation of Buck ROGERS by the American strip cartoonist Alex Raymond in 1934. Together with his girlfriend, Dale Arden, he has a series of adventures on the planet Mongo (ruled by MING THE MERCILESS) and elsewhere. He subsequently moved to other media, notably cinema serials (1936–40) and a feature film *Flash Gordon* (1980), directed by Mike Hodges, but also novels. Flash Gordon was parodied in the rather rude film comedy *Flesh Gordon* (1974), which features such characters as Dale Ardor, Dr Flexi Jerkoff and Emperor Wang the Perverted.

**Flash Harry.** A name for a loudly dressed and usually boorish man. The nickname was applied more kindly and specifically to the orchestral conductor Sir Malcolm Sargent (1895–1967), famous for his debonair manner and dapper appearance. Sargent himself claimed the name referred to the way he flashed round the world. When Sir Thomas Beecham heard that Sargent was conducting in Tokyo, he is said to have remarked, 'Ah! Flash in Japan!' It was also the name of the 'spiv' character played by George Cole in the ST TRINIAN'S films of the 1950s.

> 'He's no Flash Harry,' says a friend. 'You won't see a fleet of Ferraris in his drive.'
>
> *heat* (13–19 January 2000)

**Flash mob.** A phenomenon of the early 21st century consisting of a crowd that suddenly assembles in a place, engages briefly in a co-ordinated and apparently gratuitous activity (e.g. a pillow fight) and then as suddenly disperses. The first such happening is said to have taken place in Macy's department store in New York City on 3 June 2003, when about 100 people turned up and attempted to buy a particular rug. Britain's first flash mob, later the same

summer, assembled in a London store and conversed without using words containing the letter 'o'. The organizing of such events is greatly facilitated by the use of E-MAIL and mobile phones. The term was probably inspired by the use of 'flash' to characterize something sudden and overwhelming (as in 'flash flood').

**Flat cap.** A man's cloth cap with a peak, similar to a CLOTH CAP but unlike it worn by an upper-class male or a member of the aristocracy. The names differentiate the two types of wearer.

> A Barbour, green wellies and a flat cap are perfectly sensible garb for the country but they also convey a certain set of Countryside Alliance values, of a person at ease with old landowner hierarchies.
>
> *Sunday Express* (27 February 2000)

**Flat Earth Society.** An ALTERNATIVE scientific organization that emerged at the turn of the 20th century from the 19th-century Universal Zetetic Society and that developed under the guidance or misguidance of Samuel Shenton (d.1971), an Englishman. Members hold that the earth is patently flat, as one can see with one's own eyes, that there are many references to the fact in the Bible, in which the Old Testament implies that the earth is flat and in which the New Testament tells how Jesus 'ascended' into heaven, that one has long spoken of 'the four corners of the earth' and that the landings on the moon in the 1960s were faked by HOLLYWOOD. The North Pole is thus at the centre of the earth and not, as its name implies, at its most northern point. The society is often regarded as the epitome of phoney science, or unscientific thinking. *See also* INTELLIGENT DESIGN.

**Flatland.** The setting of Edwin A. Abbott's novel of the same name (1952). It is a land where all objects, both animate and inanimate, appear two-dimensional. It has no sun and its houses are windowless, since light mysteriously appears inside and out, day or night. The size and shape of the inhabitants depend on age and status. Women, at the bottom of the social stratum, are straight lines, while the rest of society vary from soldiers and workmen, as isosceles triangles, to priests, who are perfect circles. The mathematician Ian Stewart has written a sequel called *Flatterland* (2001).

**Flatliner.** Medical jargon for a person whose heart has stopped beating. The reference is to the flat line that appears on an electrocardiograph screen when this occurs. The term was popularized by the film *Flatliners* (1990), in which medical students experiment to see if there is life after death.

**Flat spin.** To be in a 'flat spin' is to be very flurried, to be in a panic. In flying, a flat spin is when the longitudinal axis of an aircraft inclines downwards at an angle of less than 45°. In the early days of manned flight this inevitably involved loss of control. It later came to be an aerial manoeuvre performed at low level in air combat, as an evasive action.

**Flat top.** A style of haircut in which the hair is cut short on the top of the head so that it stands up and appears flat.

**Flattop.** A colloquial US term for an aircraft carrier.

**Flaubert's Parrot.** A novel (1984) by Julian Barnes (b.1946), in which the life and literary pursuits of the French novelist Gustave Flaubert (1821–80) are investigated by Geoffrey Braithwaite, a retired English doctor, as a means of coming to terms with the suicide of his wife. Parallels are drawn between Flaubert's eight-year affair with the poet Louise Colet (1810–76) and the unfaithfulness of Braithwaite's wife. The title refers to a stuffed parrot that Flaubert borrowed from a museum and set on his desk while writing the story 'Un Cœur Simple', in which a parrot, alive and then stuffed, is an object of reverence to the heroine.

**Flavour of the month.** A person or thing that is temporarily fashionable or in favour. The term evolved in the 1970s from an advertising phrase of the 1940s aimed at US ice cream consumers.

> When last she worked there she had been young, attractive, unattached. She had been 'flavour of the month'. But returning she was in a rather different situation: 'married, a mother, with outside commitments'.
>
> *The Times* (2 June 1998)

**Fleadh.** (Irish, 'feast', 'banquet'.) A festival of Irish or Celtic music, dancing and culture, as staged in various parts of Britain. The best known is the one first held in Finsbury Park, London, in 1990 (and is still held there) and now has its equivalent in New York and other US cities. It attracts top Irish bands and performers, as well as non-Irish bands, and was the creation of the Irish rock promoter Vince Power (b.1947). The word is pronounced 'flah'.

**Flea market.** A street market selling second-hand goods and the like, so called because the clutter of bric-à-brac and old clothes is conducive to fleas. The term was adopted in the 1920s from the French *marché aux puces*, the oldest and best known being that at St Ouen, on the northern edge of Paris, which has stalls selling clothes, shoes, records, books and junk of all kinds, as well as expensive antiques. *See also* FLEA PIT.

**Flea pit.** A colloquialism dating from the 1930s for a cinema, some of which were cheaply constructed and poorly furnished with dusty seats and floor coverings that literally bred fleas.

**Fleet's lit up.** One of the earliest and most famous of broadcasting gaffes came in 1937, when Lieutenant Commander Tommy Woodrooffe (1899–1978) commentated live for the BBC on the Spithead Naval Review. The commander, who appears from the recording to a be a little the worse for wear ('lit up' in the slang of the time), slurred: 'At the present moment the whole fleet is lit up. When I say "lit up" I mean lit up by fairy lamps. It's fantastic. It isn't a fleet at all … it's Fairyland. The whole fleet is in Fairyland,' and so on for a few more moments, during which the lights went off and Woodrooffe appeared to be convinced that the fleet had actually disappeared into thin air, at which point the broadcast cut to the studio announcer. This did not quite end Woodrooffe's broadcasting career. Commentating on the FA Cup Final in 1938 he announced 'If there's another goal now I'll eat my hat.' There was, and he kept his word. *See also* COLEMANBALLS; TIRED AND EMOTIONAL.

**Fleming's rules.** Memory aids for recalling the relative directions of the magnetic field, current and motion in an electric generator or motor, using one's fingers. Extend the hand vertically with the thumb pointing upwards, the first finger forwards, and the second finger at right angles to it. The three directions are represented by the thumb (*m* for *m*otion), first finger or forefinger (*f* for *f*ield) and second finger (*c* for *c*urrent). The left hand is used for motors, and the right for generators and dynamos. The devices were the invention of the English physicist John Fleming (1849–1945).

**Flesh Gordon.** *See under* FLASH GORDON.

**Flexible friend.** A punning name for a credit card, which is 'flexible' because it allows its bearer to negotiate varying amounts of money and because the PLASTIC of which it is made can be bent. The phrase originated in the early 1980s as an advertising slogan for the Access credit card.

**Flicks.** The cinema, a film show, an expression deriving from the early days of such shows in the 1920s, when the pictures 'flickered' on the screen. 'Flick' is still current as a colloquial term for a film, particularly the down-at-heel variety, such as a horror flick (supernatural thriller) or SKIN FLICK.

**Flimsy.** An old journalists' term for newspaper copy, arising from the thin paper (often used with a sheet of carbon paper to take a copy) on which reporters and others wrote up their matter for the press. The white £5 Bank of England note, which ceased to be legal tender in March 1961, was also known as a flimsy. In the Royal Navy the name is given to the brief certificate of conduct issued to an officer by his captain on the termination of his appointment to a ship or establishment. The derivation is again from the thin-quality paper.

**Flintstones, The.** The animated television series of this name (1960–66), a Hanna-Barbera production, recounted the day-to-day adventures of the Stone Age couple Fred and Wilma Flintstone and their neighbours, Barney and Betty Rubble, who lead a suburban existence in a world of Palaeolithic vehicles and dinosaur-powered machines. There have been various comic books and strips – and even two live-action feature films (1994 and 2000) – continuing the stories, and Fred Flintstone, in particular, is remembered for his exultant cry, 'Yabba-dabba-doo!' His name inspired dressing-room wits to nickname the Lancashire and England cricketer Andrew Flintoff as 'Freddie'.

**Flip one's lid.** To throw a fit of temper; to lose one's self-control. The image is that of a pot boiling over. The phrase dates from the 1940s. *See also* BLOW ONE'S TOP.

**Flip side.** The converse; the undesirable aspect of something. The allusion is to the reverse or less important side of a gramophone record, especially a pop single, as the side the listener 'flips' over to after hearing the main side. The original sense dates from the late 1940s.

**Flirty fishing.** A method of attracting potential members to a religious cult by beguiling them with expressions of love and friendship, as a sort of CHARM OFFENSIVE. The modern colloquialism in fact has biblical overtones: 'I will make you fishers of men' (Matthew 4:19). A more direct equivalent expression for such recruitment is LOVE-BOMBING.

**Float like a butterfly, sting like a bee.** The motto of the boxer Muhammad Ali (b. Cassius Clay, 1942), said to have originated with his trainer, Drew 'Bundini' Brown, who spoke the following lines on 25 February 1964 at the weigh-in before a title fight with Sonny Liston in Miami, Florida:

> Float like a butterfly, sting like a bee;
> His hands can't hit what his eyes can't see.

*See also* RUMBLE IN THE JUNGLE.

**Float someone's boat.** To appeal to them or excite them. The picture is of a grounded boat being freed by rising water or the incoming tide, an image that is perhaps ultimately sexual.

> Sitting … on one's own eating microwaveable Swedish meatballs washed down with aquavit does not exactly float my boat.
>
> *Sunday Times* (21 November 1999)

'Whatever floats his/her/your boat' thus means, liberally-spirited, 'whatever he/she/you prefer(s) is fine with me'.

**Flogging and whipping.** Powers of the British courts to pass a sentence of corporal punishment were abolished by the

Criminal Justice Act 1948, both for adults and juvenile offenders. *See also* the HANGING AND FLOGGING BRIGADE.

**Flook.** A bear-like beast with a trumpet-like snout and magical powers created for his strip cartoons in the *Daily Mail* by the artist Wally Fawkes (b.1924) under the pen-name 'Trog'. He appeared from 1949 to 1984 when he was transferred for a time to the *Daily Mirror*. The series was originally intended for children but soon evolved into a vehicle of adult satire and comedy at the expense of SWINGING LONDON.

**Floozie in the Jacuzzi, The.** A nickname for the fountain entitled *Anna Livia Plurabelle*, which was commissioned from Sean Mulcahy and Eamonn O'Doherty for Dublin's millennium in 1998. The work featured a reclining female figure in a watery setting. (*Anna Livia* is a Latinized form of *Anna Liffey*, a personification of the River Liffey. *Anna Livia Plurabelle* was James Joyce's name for her.)

**Florida Flambée.** *See* OLD SPARKY.

**Flower children.** The supporters of FLOWER POWER in the mid-1960s who advocated peace and love as against war and materialism. Also known as the BEAUTIFUL PEOPLE, they were a new form of HIPPIE movement, characterized by the wearing of bells and flowers. They appeared in Britain in 1967, taking their pattern from San Francisco.While not literally 'children' for the most part, the designation was apt, for it suggested a certain deliberate innocence and vulnerability.

**Flower girl.** Originally a woman or girl who sold flowers in the streets, such as Eliza DOOLITTLE, but more recently a young girl who carries flowers at a wedding or scatters them before the bride.

**'Flower of Scotland'.** A song written and performed in the late 1960s by the Corries, a Scottish folk music duo, and taken up as the favourite song at football and rugby matches north of the border, replacing SCOTLAND THE BRAVE as the unofficial Scottish national anthem. In 1998 the *Herald* newspaper of Glasgow ran a competition for a new Scottish anthem. The winner, announced in January 1999, was William Jackson's 'Land of Light'.

**Flowerpot Men, The.** Two flowerpot-dwelling identical puppets named Bill and Ben who first appeared on BBC children's television in 1952–4 as part of the WATCH WITH MOTHER programmes. They have since achieved a kind of cult status. Bill and Ben emerge from their pots to play when the gardener goes home for lunch and are warned of his imminent return by their friend Little Weed. The Flowerpot Men speak in a kind of gibberish, involving frequent use of the nonsense word 'flobbalot', said by one of the programme's creators to have been inspired by the sound of breaking wind in the bath. The unamused accused the BBC of subverting the efforts of infants to learn English, in much the same way as they were later to lambast the TELETUBBIES. A new series, named *Bill and Ben*, was launched in 2001, with a range of additional characters.

**Flower power.** The power of the FLOWER CHILDREN, based on the precept 'MAKE LOVE, NOT WAR'. The term itself may have been suggested by BLACK POWER. *See also* SUMMER OF LOVE.

**Fluff.** The nickname of the Australian-born veteran disc jockey Alan Freeman (b.1927), not as might be supposed for his 'fluffs' or mistakes on air but apparently from the old fluffy pullover that he wore.

**Flutter one's eyelashes at someone.** To flirt with someone, usually said of a woman. The eyes play an important role in the art of seduction.

**Fly a desk.** In RAF parlance, to take up a civil service or other office job after retiring as a pilot.

**Fly blind.** To pilot an aircraft solely by means of instruments, the opposite of visual navigation. It is not, however, quite the same as flying on AUTOMATIC PILOT.

**Flyby.** A flight past a particular object, especially for purposes of observation, as a spacecraft past a planet or satellite.

**Fly** or **drive by the seat of one's pants.** To rely on instinct rather than on knowledge. The phrase originated with US Air Force pilots in the Second World War. The concept is of sitting in the pilot's or driver's seat but being unprepared for what one may encounter as one proceeds.

**Flyer, The.** *See* KITTY HAWK.

**Flying bedstead.** A nickname of the experimental wingless and rotorless VTOL (vertical takeoff and landing) jet aircraft demonstrated in Britain in 1954. Its official designation was the Rolls-Royce Thrust Measuring Rig (TMR). The nickname was inspired by its appearance.

**Flying bishop.** An informal term dating from the 1990s for an Anglican bishop appointed to minister in another bishop's diocese to those who do not accept the ordination of women. The formal title of such bishops is 'Provincial Episcopal Visitors'. The analogy is with a FLYING PICKET.

**Flying circus.** An exhibition of aerobatics, as by aircraft at an air show. *See also* MONTY PYTHON'S FLYING CIRCUS.

**Flying Duchess.** Mary du Caurroy Russell, Duchess of Bedford (1865–1937). After making record-breaking return flights to India (1929) and South Africa (1930) with Captain Barnard, she obtained an 'A' pilot's licence in 1933 and disappeared on a solo flight over the North Sea in March 1937.

**Flying Finn.** The Finnish runner Paavo Nurmi (1897–1973) earned this apt nickname following his successes in the 1924 Olympics in Paris, in which he won five gold medals (he won nine Olympic golds in all in the 1920s). More recently the title has been accorded to Hannu Mikkola (b.1942), world rally champion in 1983. The name has since been adopted for almost any famous Finn, especially one who travels a lot, such as the conductor and composer Esa-Pekka Salonen (b.1958).

**Flying fornicator.** A facetious nickname applied in the early years of the 20th century to the last express train of the night from London to a provincial town, on which it was luridly supposed that most seats were taken up by necking couples. In Australia in the 1970s it was applied specifically to the last train from Sydney to Wollongong on Saturday nights.

**Flying Fortress.** A nickname for the Boeing B–17, a US long-range bomber developed in the 1930s and widely deployed in the Second World War. *See also* SWOOSE.

**Flying Peacemaker.** US Secretary of State Henry Kissinger (b.1923) was so dubbed by the press in the 1970s from his frequent journeys to world trouble spots and his SHUTTLE DIPLOMACY in the Middle East and Africa.

**Flying picket.** A picket that moves from one site to another in an industrial dispute. In the miners' strike of 1984 many flying pickets went to Nottinghamshire to support their colleagues in Britain's second largest coalfield. As a result of their activities, flying pickets were declared illegal under the 1980 Employment Act, and striking miners were confined to their own pits. *See also* KING ARTHUR.

**Flying saucers.** Mysterious objects supposedly resembling revolving, partially luminous discs that shoot across the sky at a high velocity and at a great height. They were largely brought to public attention by the US writer George Adamski, who in books such as *Flying Saucers Have Landed* (1953) told of travelling into space with extraterrestrials. The landing or sighting of flying saucers was reported on several occasions in the 1950s and 1960s, but their cult has now mostly faded.

The term itself is said to owe its origin to the American Kenneth Arnold, who after seeing a formation of objects in the Cascade Mountains in Washington (June 1947) described them as moving 'like a saucer would if you skipped it across water'. A local reporter picked up the phrase and coined the term 'flying saucer'. *See also* UFO.

**Flying Scotsman.** Designed by Sir Nigel Gresley, locomotive No. 4472 of this name was built in 1923 in Doncaster, Yorkshire, for the London and North-Eastern Railway. It was soon breaking new ground, and on 1 May 1928 made the first non-stop express run from London to Edinburgh in eight hours and three minutes. Its moment of glory came on 30 November 1934, when on a test run between London and Leeds it reached a speed of 160kph (100mph) over a stretch of 548m (600 yards) between Grantham and Peterborough. It was withdrawn in 1963 and after touring the United States for four years was bought by Sir William McAlpine of the building firm. It proved prohibitive to run, however, and in 1995 was retired with a cracked firebox before being rescued and lovingly restored by Tony Marchington, a computer software millionaire. On 4 July 1999, its expensive renovation completed, it once again steamed out of King's Cross station bearing its familiar engine number. The name *Flying Scotsman* had been in use for the service itself since 1862. *See also* TITLED TRAINS.

**Flying squad.** A police detachment able to proceed rapidly to the scene of a crime such as a robbery. In the Metropolitan Police, the Flying Squad became the best-known department of Scotland Yard. It was set up in 1918 to patrol dangerous areas of London and in 1920 acquired two motor vans to help in the task. These brought it the name of Flying Squad. The department was reorganized in 1978 as the Central Robbery Squad, but its old name is still in use. *See also* SWEENEY.

> Macavity's a Mystery Cat: he's called the Hidden Paw –
> For he's the master criminal who can defy the Law.
> He's the bafflement of Scotland Yard, the Flying Squad's despair:
> For when they reach the scene of the crime – *Macavity's not there!*
> T.S. ELIOT: *Old Possum's Book of Practical Cats*, 'Macavity: The Mystery Cat' (1939)

**Fly low.** To have one's trouser fly undone or gaping. A punning but rather dated phrase.

**Fly on the wall.** A hidden observer, who can overhear discussions or watch events unnoticed. A fly-on-the-wall technique, recording events as they happen without any overt artistic direction, is used by some makers of film and television documentaries. A pioneer example of the genre was the BBC's *The Family* (1974), a 12-part serial following the day-to-day life of the Wilkins family of Reading. The phrase dates from the 1940s. The premise of the BBC's comedy hit *The* OFFICE was that a fly-on-the-wall team were observing life unfold in the office environment.

**Flyover zone.** A virtual synonym for MIDDLE AMERICA, consisting of states that the urban sophisticates of California, New York, Washington and New England pass over (and never actually visit) as they jet from coast to coast. Psephologically, the 'flyover people' tend to vote Republican, while those living on the east and west coasts tend to vote for Democrats. They have not always been sympathetically defined.

> These people are simple farmers, people of the land, the common clay of the New West. You know – morons.
> MEL BROOKS: screenplay for *Blazing Saddles* (1974)

**Flypast.** A ceremonial flight of aircraft over a particular building or area, such as on major royal occasions.

**Flyposting.** The posting of bills or advertisements on unauthorized places, such as the windows of empty shops. The expression presumably alludes to the fact that the people who post them fly as soon as they have stuck up their bills. *See also* FLY-TIPPING.

**Fly the flag.** *See* SHOW THE FLAG.

**Fly-tipping.** The tipping of refuse in unauthorized sites. *See also* FLYPOSTING.

**FMS.** *See* FALSE MEMORY SYNDROME.

**Foggy Bottom.** A nickname for the US State Department, whose headquarters, to the southwest of the White House in Washington, D.C., are in a locality subject to fogs from the neighbouring Potomac River. The name has become punningly synonymous with political routine and government bureaucracy. *See also* BALD EAGLE OF FOGGY BOTTOM.

**Foleys.** In film-making a slang term for sound effects, especially as devised by the US expert Jack Foley, who established modern techniques for creating sounds recorded to fit the images on the screen. Most films now credit their 'Foley artists', who, among other ruses, might walk on boxes of gravel or starch to represent the sound of someone walking on gravel or snow out of doors.

**Fond farewell.** A tender or affectionate (or affecting) parting. The phrase owes much to its alliterative appeal and appears to have become popular only in the 20th century, when it became associated with funerals and memorial services. The *Daily Mirror* of 2 May 1995 tells how more than 500 admirers of the satirist and humorist Peter Cook 'gathered for the fond farewell in a London church'.

**Fonz.** The teenage hero of the US SITCOM *Happy Days* (1974–84), in full Arthur Fonzarelli. With his black leather jacket, slangy speech and 'thumbs up' gesture he was the epitome of 1950s COOL. He was played by Henry Winkler.

**Foo fighter.** In US Air Force slang of the Second World War, an unidentified flying object (*see* UFO). In a dress rehearsal for the UFO craze of the late 1940s and 1950s, American pilots in the final years of the War often reported encountering strange luminous objects in the sky during operations over Germany. At the time it was speculated that they were some sort of Nazi secret weapon. 'Foo' is a nonsense word that originated in the comic strip *Smoky Stover*, featuring a firefighter whose catchphrase was 'Where there's foo there's fire.' *See also* ROCK GROUP NAMES.

**'Fool on the Hill, The'.** A song about isolation by The BEATLES, credited to John Lennon and Paul McCartney (but mostly by McCartney) and released in Britain in November 1967. The Fool on the Hill is a kind of *idiot savant*, a 'man with a foolish grin' living 'alone on the hill' in a world of childlike ignorance. His intrinsic wisdom of the ways of the world is implied by the words of the chorus:

> But the fool on the hill
> Sees the sun going down,
> And the eyes in his head,
> See the world spinning round.

The song appeared in the film of MAGICAL MYSTERY TOUR.

**Football club nicknames.** Several English football clubs have nicknames that are not of immediately obvious origin. The following is a selection of those in use at some time in the 20th/21st century. The majority of the clubs themselves were founded in the late 19th century, and the year of formation is given in brackets after the club name. Each name is usually preceded by 'The'.

Addicks: Charlton Athletic (1905). A corruption of the second word of the club name. *See also* Latics *below*.

Baggies: West Bromwich Albion (1879). Said to refer to the baggy working clothes worn because of the heat by supporters from the local ironworks. *See also* Throstles *below*.

Bantams: Bradford City (1903). From the club's colours, supposedly those of a Bantam chicken.

Bees: Brentford (1889). 'B' for 'Brentford', as well as the insect, with its deadly sting.

Biscuitmen: Reading (1871). For the Huntley and Palmer biscuit factory in the town until 1974.

Blades: Sheffield United (1889). For the city's famous steel industry, and especially its cutlery.

Blues: (1) Ipswich Town (1878); (2) Manchester City (1894); (3) Chelsea (1905). From the clubs' colours. Other club sides thus nicknamed include Birmingham City, Carlisle United and Chester City.

Canaries: Norwich City (1902). From the city's former fame as a centre for the breeding and exhibition of canaries and other cage birds, reflected in the team's yellow and green strip.

Chairboys: Wycombe Wanderers (1884). From High Wycombe's furniture-making industry.

Cherries: AFC Bournemouth (1899). From the team's red and black strip.

Clarets: Burnley (1882). From the team's claret, blue and white strip.

Cobblers: Northampton Town (1897). For the city's boot and shoe manufacture.

Cottagers: Fulham (1879). From their home ground, at Craven Cottage.

Dons: Wimbledon (1889). From the district's name, punning on the academic sense.

Filberts: Leicester City (1884). From their home ground, at Filbert Street.

Glaziers: Crystal Palace (1905). From the Crystal Palace, the exhibition building resembling a giant greenhouse, originally in Hyde Park but then moved to Sydenham, where the team's ground was.

GRECIANS

Gulls: Torquay United (1910). From the birds at this seaside town. *See also* Seagulls *below*.

Gunners: Arsenal (1886). For the club's original location near Woolwich Arsenal.

Hammers: West Ham United (1895). From the district name, punning on the punishing instrument.

Hatters: Luton Town (1885). From the town's fame as a centre of straw-hat manufacture.

Hornets: Watford (1891). From the club's yellow and black strip.

Imps: Lincoln City (1883). From the 'Lincoln Imp', a famous carving high up in Lincoln Cathedral.

Iron: Scunthorpe United (1899). From the ironstone beds that brought the town industrial fame.

Ironsides: Middlesbrough (1876). From the heavy industries formerly based in the area.

Latics: (1) Oldham Athletic (1895); (2) Wigan Athletic (1932). A corruption of the second word of the club name. *See also* Addicks *above*.

Magpies: (1) Newcastle United (1881); (2) Notts County (1862). From the black and white strip of each.

Mariners: Grimsby Town (1878). From the town's once famous fishing harbour.

Merry Millers: Rotherham United (1884), From the team's home ground, at the Millmoor Ground.

Minstermen: York City (1922). From York Minster, the city's crowning glory.

Owls: Sheffield Wednesday (1867). The club's ground is located in a district divided into the localities of Hillsborough and Owlerton. The latter gave the punning nickname. *See also* HILLSBOROUGH DISASTER.

Pilgrims: Plymouth Argyle (1886). From the 'Pilgrim Fathers' who set sail for America from Plymouth in 1620.

Pirates: Bristol Rovers (1883). From the club's 'roving' style without a home base, and for Bristol's fame as a port from which pirates set sail.

POSH

Potters: Stoke City (1863). From the location of Stoke-on-Trent at the heart of the Potteries.

Quakers: Darlington (1883). From Darlington's former fame as a railway centre, thanks to the financial backing of John B. Pease, one of the town's prominent Quaker residents.

Railwaymen: Crewe Alexandra (1877). From Crewe's once famous railway junction and workshops.

Rams: Derby County (1884). From the mythical Derby Ram, a beast so huge that it covered an acre with every stride, while eagles built their eyries in its horns. The annual Derby Tup plays, with a man dressed as a tup (a castrated ram), are performed in Derbyshire on Boxing Day.

Robins: Bristol City (1894). From the team's red and white strip.

Red Devils: Manchester United (1892). From the club's colours.

Reds: (1) Nottingham Forest (1865); (2) Liverpool (1892). From the clubs' colours.

Rokermen: Sunderland (1879). From the club's former home ground, Roker Park; following the club's move to the STADIUM OF LIGHT in 1997 supporters were asked to choose a new name. They chose the name Black Cats.

Saints: Southampton (1885). From the club's original name, Southampton St Mary's.

Seagulls: Brighton and Hove Albion (1901). From the club's seaside location. *See also* Gulls *above*.

Seasiders: BLACKPOOL (1887).

Sky Blues: Coventry City (1883). From the club's sky-blue strip, itself reflecting 'Coventry blue' as an old name for a type of blue thread made at Coventry.

Spurs: Tottenham Hotspur (1882). From the club name, punning on the device to urge on a horse.

Throstles: West Bromwich Albion (1879). From the thrushes (throstles) that reputedly flocked in the bushes of the area known as the Hawthorns, now the team home ground. *See also* Baggies *above*.

Toffeemen or Toffees: Everton (1878). From the former well known 'Everton toffee' brand name.

Trotters: Bolton Wanderers (1874). From the team's nomadic style before they had a home ground.

Tykes: Barnsley (1887). From the 'Yorkshire tyke', a nickname for a Yorkshireman.

Valiants: Port Vale (1876). From the club name, punningly.

Villans: Aston Villa (1874). From the club name, punningly.

Whites: Leeds United (1919). From the club colours.

Wolves: Wolverhampton Wanderers (1877). From the club name, punning on the voracious animal.

Among the nicknames of Scottish teams, the following require some explanation:

Bully Wee: Clydebank. 'Bully' meaning 'jolly', and 'wee' meaning 'little', the team not being one of the leading clubs.

Gable-endies: Montrose. Many 19th-century houses in the town are built with their gable ends to the street.

Honest Men: Ayr United. In Burns's poem 'Tam o' Shanter', Ayr is celebrated for 'honest men and bonnie lasses'.

Jags: Partick Thistle. Referring to the prickliness of the plant.

Pars: Dunfermline Athletic. Various theories have been put forward: (1) an abbreviation of 'paralytics'; (2) the team was 'on a par' with other clubs once it was promoted to the League; (3) the black-and-white stripes on the players' jerseys resemble the markings on a parr, a young salmon.

Red Lichties: Arbroath. The great rose window in Arbroath Abbey was long a beacon for shipping.

Spiders: Queen's Park. Referring to the black hoops on their white jerseys.

Teddy Bears (or just Bears): Glasgow Rangers. Rhyming slang for 'Gers', the last syllable of Rangers.

Tims: Celtic. Protestant slang for 'Catholic'.

Wasps: Alloa. Referring to the black and yellow stripes on their jerseys.

Outside Britain, colourful nicknames exist for African football teams, many adopted from animals, as the following:

Atlas Lions: Morocco

Bafana Bafana: South Africa ('The Boys'; the women's team is Banyana Banyana, 'The Girls')

Black Panthers: Angola

Black Stars: Ghana

Cranes: Uganda

Crocodiles: Lesotho

Desert Rats: Namibia (*see also* DESERT RATS)

Desert Warriors: Algeria

Eagles: Mali

Elephants: Côte d'Ivoire (former Ivory Coast)

Indomitable Lions: Cameroon

Leopards: Congo Democratic Republic

Lions: Senegal

Lone Star: Liberia (referring to the single white star in the Liberian flag)

Mambas: Mozambique

Mighty Zambia: Zambia

Pharaohs: Egypt

Red Devils: Congo

Scorpions: Gambia

Super Eagles: Nigeria

Warriors: Zimbabwe

Zebras: Botswana

Jamaica's nickname, the Reggae Boys, is said to have been coined by a journalist in 1995 when the team travelled to Africa to play Zambia in a friendly. *See also* BRAZILIAN FOOTBALLERS.

**Football pools.** An organized system of betting on the results of football matches. Participants bet by postal coupon or through a collection agent (or point) on which matches will finish in a score-draw, i.e. a drawn match in which the sides score at least one goal each. The total prize money, or pool, is distributed to those who have a winning entry, the size of the pay-out depending on the number of winners and the amount of money in the pool. Football pools were launched by Littlewoods in 1923, originally in Manchester. The first £100,000 prize was won in 1950 and the first £1 million prize in 1987. The biggest pay-out by the end of the 20th century was £2,924,622 on 19 November 1994 by Littlewoods Pools to a syndicate from Manchester. Such sums have, however, been dwarfed by those winnable in the NATIONAL LOTTERY.

**Foot in both camps.** To have a foot in both camps is to have an interest or stake concurrently in two parties or sides. The expression dates from the 1930s.

**Foot-in-mouth disease.** The perennial bane of making grossly tactless or embarrassing remarks. The expression dates from the 1960s and puns on both foot-and-mouth disease as the contagious disease of livestock and a continual tendency to PUT ONE'S FOOT IN ONE'S MOUTH. A punningly pedantic term for the affliction is 'dontopedology'.

**Foot in the door.** To get a foot in the door is to gain a first introduction to a business or organization. The allusion is to a door-to-door salesman or canvasser, who when the door is opened, or is about to be closed, blocks it ajar with one foot. *See also* TOE IN THE DOOR.

**Footnotes to Plato.** How the English philosopher and mathematician Alfred North Whitehead (1861–1947) characterized the history of Western philosophy:

> The safest general characterization of the European philosophical tradition is that it consists of a series of footnotes to Plato.
>
> *Process and Reality* (1929)

**Footsie.** The acronymized pronunciation of 'FTSE', the abbreviation of the 'Financial Times-Stock Exchange' 100 share index, influenced by 'footsie', the amorous sport of caressing a person's foot with one's own under the table. One can play footsie just as one 'plays' the stock market. The nickname dates from the mid-1980s.

> Storm-hit Footsie finds calmer waters
> *Evening Standard*, headline (19 May 2006)

***Forbidden Planet.*** A SCIENCE FICTION film (1956), adapted by Cyril Hume from a story by Irving Block and Allen Adler, about a space mission that lands on the remote planet Altair-4 to check on the welfare of the scientist Morbius and his daughter, Altaira, only to be terrorized by an invisible monster. The film, which many years later inspired the hit stage musical *Return to the Forbidden Planet*, was based loosely on Shakespeare's *The Tempest*, Morbius equating with Prospero, Altaira with Miranda, Robby the Robot with Ariel, and the monster with Caliban.

**Forces' Sweetheart.** The nickname of the popular singer Vera Lynn (originally Vera Margaret Welch) (b.1917), who became a household name in the Second World War with her radio show *Sincerely Yours* (1941–7) and who went to Burma in 1944 to entertain the British troops. She is specially associated with sentimentally patriotic songs such as 'The WHITE CLIFFS OF DOVER' (1941) and ''WE'LL MEET AGAIN'' (1939). She was made a Dame of the British Empire in 1975.

**For crying out loud!** An exclamation of frustration or anger, arising in the early 20th century as a US euphemism for 'For Christ's sake!'

**Ford Anglia.** A modest car manufactured in Britain between 1940 and 1967. In the Harry POTTER books and films there is a light blue Ford Anglia 105E, registration number 7990 TD. It can fly. In October 2005 the car used in the films disappeared from the South West Film Studios in St Agnes. Police said it could not have been driven away, as it did not have an engine. (It reappeared in Falmouth, Cornwall, in May 2006, still engineless.)

**Ford Capri.** *See* FORD CORTINA.

**Ford Cortina.** A family saloon car manufactured in Britain between 1962 and 1982. It was named after the fashionable

Italian ski resort, and was the car of choice of the ancestor of MONDEO MAN before being replaced by the Sierra and then by the Mondeo itself. On Ian Dury's first album, *New Boots and Panties!* (1977), Billericay Dickie boasts of his affairs:

'ad a love-affair with Nina
In the back of my Cortina,
A seasoned-up hyena
Could not've been more obscener.

The Cortina's more glamorous contemporary, the coupé Ford Capri (named after the Italian island where the Emperor Tiberius toyed with his catamites), was nicknamed the 'Cortina in drag'.

**Ford Mondeo.** *See* MONDEO MAN.

**Ford Prefect.** A model of saloon car manufactured in Britain from 1938 to 1961. It was replaced by the FORD CORTINA. A character from outer space in Douglas Adams's HITCH-HIKER'S GUIDE TO THE GALAXY adopts the name 'Ford Prefect' for his visit to earth, his inadequate research having led him to believe that the name would be inconspicuous, cars being (so he understood) the dominant life form on the planet.

**Forever Amber.** A bestselling novel (1944) by Kathleen Winsor. The beautiful but promiscuous heroine of the book is Amber St Clair, who has various adventures among the royalty and aristocracy of Restoration England. Her name created a certain vogue for the female first name Amber. In the film version (1947) the title role was taken by Linda Darnell.

> The novel was not called *Forever Amber* when first offered to us. … One of the publicity staff was discussing the manuscript one day. She said, in effect, 'I get a little tired of Amber – it's forever Amber, forever Amber, forever Amber … ' 'Wait a minute,' one of her listeners exclaimed, 'we've been wanting a title. You've given it to us – *Forever Amber*.'
> HAROLD S. LATHAM: *My Life in Publishing*, II (1965)

**Forget it!** An exclamation dating from the 1960s to imply dismissal of an idea or proposal, or to waive an apology or expression of gratitude, or to imply that the previous speaker did not understand the gist of the conversation.

**Forgotten Army.** A name for the British Army in Burma after the fall of Rangoon in 1942, the evacuation west, and subsequent cutting by the Japanese of the supply link from India to Nationalist China. The words are said to derive from Lord Louis Mountbatten's encouragement to his troops when he took over as Supreme Allied Commander Southeast Asia in late 1943:

> Right, now I understand people think you're the Forgotten Army on the Forgotten Front. I've come here to tell you you're quite wrong. You're not the Forgotten Army on the Forgotten Front. No, make no mistake about it. Nobody's ever *heard* of you.
> LORD LOUIS MOUNTBATTEN: quoted in Richard Hough *Mountbatten: Hero of Our Time* (1980)

*See also* D-DAY DODGERS.

**Forgotten Man, The.** A phrase derived from W.G. Summer (1840–1910), a US sociologist, to describe the decent, hard-working, ordinary citizen. It was later popularized by F.D. Roosevelt (*see* FDR) in 1932 during the presidential election campaign, although he actually used the expression before his nomination. He advocated a NEW DEAL and appealed to the 'forgotten man at the bottom of the economic pyramid'.

**Former Naval Person.** A code name used by Winston Churchill to refer to himself in his secret communications with the US president Franklin Roosevelt (FDR) prior to America's entry into the Second World War. Churchill had been First Lord of the Admiralty (1911–15, 1939–40).

**Form follows function.** The slogan of modernism in architecture, coined by the US architect Louis Sullivan (1856–1924) – builder of the first skyscrapers – in *The Tall Office Building Artistically Considered* (1896). *See also* MACHINE FOR LIVING IN.

**Formula One.** Until 1906 international motor racing was open to all kinds of automobile. When it became clear that driving ability could not be fairly tested in cars of different types, races were organized for cars with similar specifications. Types of vehicles were grouped into various formulas, each defined by the characteristics of a car's performance. Formula One eventually applied to cars weighing not less than 505kg, with a maximum width of 200cm, a four-stroke engine with a maximum 12 cylinders, an engine capacity of 3500cc and no turbocharger.

**For Pete's sake!** A mild exclamation of annoyance, exasperation or the like, dating from the 1920s. It may be a euphemistic form of 'For pity's sake!'

**Forrest Gump.** A film (1994) directed by Robert Zemeckis and adapted by Eric Roth from a novel of the same title by Winston Groom about an intellectually challenged Southerner who, largely by accident, witnesses many of the great events of his time and comes face to face with many of the great figures of postwar US history. Played by Tom Hanks, Forrest Gump became a symbol of well-meaning American conservatism whose good nature won the plaudits of leading Republican politicians. However, the film was described by one exasperated critic as 'a well-meaning celebration of stupidity'.

**Fort Apache.** A nickname given in the last quarter of the 20th century to the 41st Police Precinct of New York City, an area of the South Bronx notorious for crime and violence. It was inspired by the 1948 John Ford film *Fort Apache*, a stirring tale of the old and violent West.

**Fortnum–Mason line.** A jocular name for the imaginary geographical line that marks off the supposed 'lush' south of England from the 'lean' north and that thus pinpoints the NORTH–SOUTH DIVIDE or separates the south from all parts of the country north of WATFORD. The phrase adopts the name of the prestigious London store Fortnum and Mason as a pun on the Mason–Dixon Line that is the boundary between Maryland and Pennsylvania in the United States.

**FORTRAN.** *See* PROGRAMMING LANGUAGES.

**Fortress Europe.** (German *Festung Europa*.) A Nazi propaganda image of a heavily fortified mainland Europe, impregnable to attack, especially by the United States and Britain. The propaganda image was not entirely without foundation. The Allied campaign up through Italy had to overcome a succession of heavily fortified positions, such as the GUSTAV LINE and the GOTHIC LINE. Any Allied invasion of northwest Europe had to face the so-called ATLANTIC WALL along the French and Belgian coasts, although German newsreel footage leaked to Allied countries via neutrals carefully exaggerated the strength of the coastal defences. Finally, there were the WEST WALL and SIEGFRIED LINE along Germany's western frontier. Before the D-DAY landings, Nazi radio propagandist AXIS SALLY (US citizen Mildred Gillars) broadcast to Allied troops, warning them of the dire consequences of trying to invade Fortress Europe. (It was this broadcast that led to Gillars serving 12 years for treason.) As it turned out, the German defences in Normandy were much less strong than in the Pas de Calais, where the invasion had been expected.

**Fortune 500.** A list of the 500 largest US industrial corporations, published annually in *Fortune* magazine. From 1970 there has also been a Fortune 1000, including the next 500 largest.

**45-minute warning.** *See* SEPTEMBER DOSSIER.

**Forty Martyrs.** The short name of the Forty Martyrs of England and Wales, a group of representative English and Welsh Roman Catholics who were martyred between 1535 and 1679. They were canonized by Pope Paul VI on 25 October 1970 after being selected from 200 already beatified by earlier popes. They include 13 seminary priests, 10 Jesuits, three Benedictine monks, three Carthusian, one Brigettine, two Franciscans and one Austin Friar. The remaining seven, four men and three women, were lay folk. *See also* BLACK MARTYRS.

**42nd Street.** A street in Manhattan running east from the Hudson through a notorious RED-LIGHT DISTRICT near TIMES SQUARE. Its name is sometimes used for similar districts elsewhere. It is also the title of a film musical (1933) with a score by Harry Warren (1893–1981) about life backstage at a Broadway theatre (a stage version appeared in 1980). 42nd Street is the street in Broadway where the biggest theatres are situated.

**42.** *See* LIFE, THE UNIVERSE AND EVERYTHING.

***For Whom the Bell Tolls.*** A novel (1940) by Ernest Hemingway (1899–1961). It was written out of his experiences as a war correspondent in 1937 during the civil war in Spain. He was in the company of the book's dedicatee, his mistress Martha Gellhorn (1908–98), who during the conflict also acted as a war correspondent (they married in 1940). The mainspring of the plot is the blowing up of a bridge, symbolizing also the futility of the politicization of a country. A stolid film version (1943), directed by Sam Wood, starred Gary Cooper and Ingrid Bergman in key roles. The title is a quotation from John Donne:

> Any man's death diminishes me, because I am involved in Mankind; And therefore never send to know for whom the bell tolls; it tolls for thee.
>
> *Devotions upon Emergent Occasions*, Meditation No. 17 (1624)

**For your tomorrow we gave our today.** A phrase used in many REMEMBRANCE DAY commemorations around Britain. The line is found on the memorial at Kohima, India, to those who lost their lives in the Burma campaigns of the Second World War (Kohima, on the Burmese border, was successfully defended by a small garrison against an entire Japanese division in 1944):

> When you go home, tell them of us and say,
> 'For your tomorrow we gave our today.'

The line has its origins in John Maxwell Edmonds's *Inscriptions Suggested for War Memorials* (1919):

> When you go home, tell them of us and say,
> 'For your tomorrows these gave their today.'

*See also* THEY SHALL GROW NOT OLD.

**Fosbury flop.** In athletics a style of high jump in which the jumper clears the bar headfirst and backwards. It is named for its deviser and perfecter, the US athlete Dick Fosbury (b.1947), who won a gold medal at the 1968 Mexico Olympics using this technique.

**Foucault's Pendulum.** The second novel (1989; in Italian as *Il Pendolo di Foucault*, 1988) by Umberto Eco (b.1932), which he wrote 'because one novel could have been an accident'. Experimental in form, it features computer science and Rosicrucianism. The pendulum devised by Léon Foucault (1819–68) to demonstrate the rotation of the earth is the motif with which the novel opens: 'The sphere, hanging from a long wire set into the ceiling of the choir, swayed back and forth with isochronal majesty.'

**Foul-mouthed Joe.** A nickname of US Republican politician Joseph ('Joe') Gurney Cannon (1836–1926). As speaker of the House of Representatives (1903–11) he controlled Congress in a highly partisan manner with his profane and lashing tongue. Despite his tyrannical methods, he was personally liked by many, earning the fonder nickname Uncle Joe.

**Fountain.** The inspirational title given by the DADAISM artist Marcel Duchamp (1887–1968) to one of his 'ready-mades': a urinal rotated 90 degrees (1917). It was signed 'R. Mutt', the name of a firm of sanitary engineers. As a member of the jury of the first New York *Salon des Indépendants*, Duchamp submitted this work to his fellow jurors for consideration. Predictably enough they rejected it with indignation, and Duchamp resigned. Its shock value wore off in time, however, and at a Dada exhibition in the 1950s it hung over the main entrance, filled with geraniums. In 2004, in a survey of artists, curators, critics and dealers, *Fountain* was voted the most influential work of art of the 20th century.

**4×4.** Shorthand for 'four by four', as a colloquialism for a four-wheel drive vehicle, i.e. one that provides power directly from all four wheels, as distinct from the usual two front wheels or, less commonly, the rear two. Such vehicles were originally designed for driving over rugged terrain or OFF-ROADING generally but by the 1990s became the almost exclusive preserve of middle-class mothers in suburban residential areas, who used them for transporting their children to school and elsewhere and who came to look on them as a social accessory or STATUS SYMBOL. *See also* CHELSEA TRACTOR; SPORT-UTILITY VEHICLE.

**Four-colour problem.** A problem first posed in the early 1850s but not solved until 1976. The puzzle was to find the minimum number of colours required to colour a map in such a way that no two adjacent regions were of the same colour. Three colours are not enough, as can be seen in a map of four regions with each region contacting three others. It had been proved mathematically that five colours would serve, and in practice no map had ever been found in which four colours would not do.

The problem was solved by a group of mathematicians at the University of Illinois by creating a catalogue of 'unavoidable' configurations that must be present in any graph, however large it is. They then showed how each of these configurations could be reduced to a smaller one in such a way that if the smaller one could be coloured with four colours, so could the original catalogue configuration. Thus if a map existed that could not be coloured with four colours, they could use their catalogue to find a smaller map that could not be so coloured, then a smaller one still, and so on. Such a reduction process would lead to a map with only three or four regions, which supposedly could not be coloured with four colours. This absurd result, deriving from the hypothesis that a map coloured with more than four colours might exist, led to the conclusion that no such map exists. All maps can thus in fact be coloured with four colours.

**Four Feathers, The.** A novel (1902) by A.E.W. Mason (1865–1948). The four white feathers, symbols of cowardice, are given to Harry Feversham by three fellow officers and by his fiancée, when, fearful that he cannot measure up to his father's standards of bravery, he resigns his commission after his regiment is ordered to Egypt on active service. Harry follows after the regiment and in disguise performs two acts of incredible heroism, as a result of which the feathers are taken back, and he gets his girl after all. The story has been filmed several times, notably in 1939 under the direction of Zoltan Korda. This was remade in 1956 as *Storm over the Nile*, while an effective television version (1977) starred Beau Bridges, Robert Powell, Simon Ward, Richard Johnson and Jane Seymour.

**4.50 from Paddington.** A detective novel (1957; in the United States as *What Mrs McGillicuddy Saw*, 1957; as *Murder She Said*, 1961) by Agatha Christie (1890–1976), featuring her spinster sleuth Jane MARPLE. From the 4.50 train from London's Paddington Station, Elspeth sees a man strangling a woman in a compartment in another train that is running alongside hers. Then the other train draws away. A disappointing film version, *Murder She Said* (1961), directed by George Pollock, was not even saved by a gallantly British Margaret Rutherford as Miss Marple.

**Four Freedoms.** The formulation of worldwide social and political objectives enunciated by Franklin D. Roosevelt (FDR) in a message delivered to the US Congress on 6 January 1941. The president stated the freedoms to be the freedom of speech and expression, the freedom of every person to worship God in his own way, the freedom from want, and the freedom from fear.

**4-H Club.** One of a number of US clubs for young people aged 10 to 21 who pursue programmes of 'learning by doing' in farming, rearing livestock and the like. Their emblem is the four-leaf clover with the letter H on each leaf, and the designation itself derives from the vow:

> I pledge my head to clearer thinking, my heart to greater loyalty, my hands to larger service, and my health to better living, for my club, my community and my country.

The clubs originated among rural youth in the early 20th century and are sponsored by the Department of Agriculture.

**Four Horsemen of the Apocalypse.** The nickname given to four American football players from the University of Notre Dame who made a big impact in the 1920s. The name was coined by the sports journalist Grantland Rice (1880–1954) in a report in the *New York Tribune* (19 October 1924) of a match between Notre Dame and the US Military Academy at Westpoint:

> Outlined against a blue-grey October sky, the Four Horsemen rode again. In dramatic lore they were known as Famine, Pestilence, Destruction and Death. These are only aliases. Their real names are Stuhldreher, Miller, Crowley and Layden. They formed the crest of the South Bend cyclone before which another fighting Army football team was swept over the precipice.

The original Four Horsemen of the Apocalypse were the four agents of destruction described in Revelation 6, two being agents of war and two of famine and pestilence. The first appeared on a white horse, the second on a red horse, the third on a black horse and the fourth on a pale horse.

**Four legs good, two legs bad.** *See* ANIMAL FARM.

**Four-letter man.** A superannuated euphemism for an obnoxious man, best summed up by the FOUR-LETTER WORD 'shit'.

**Four-letter word.** Any of various short English words relating to sex or excrement. The two words commonly regarded as the grossest are those that came to be widely known in the 1990s as the F-WORD and, perhaps uniquely offensive today, the 'C-word' (cunt). The otherwise liberally minded *Oxford English Dictionary* did not even admit these two to its pages until it issued the first volume of its Supplement (A–G) in 1972. Although such words are still not used in polite society, they have gained an increasing degree of acceptance in the media and in literature. However, many newspapers still resort to dashes or asterisks when printing them, and their occurrence in literature, even of the 'serious' type, still offends many. *The F-Word*, edited by Jesse Sheidlower, was published in 1995 as a study of the history and usage of this particular expletive from the 15th

century to the present day, and in 1999 Channel 4 screened *A Brief History of the F-Word*, a 60-minute documentary on the subject.

Four-letter words are sometimes referred to as 'Anglo-Saxon words', although some are not of Old English origin. 'Crap', for example, comes from Medieval Latin *crappa*, 'chaff', and 'piss' from Old French *pisser*. The term itself is also sometimes punningly applied to everyday words with four letters. Henry Livings's play *Eh?* (1965) was turned into a film under the title *Work is a Four-Letter Word* (1968), while Nicholas Monsarrat's two-volume autobiography was presented to the public as *Life is a Four-Letter Word* (1966, 1970). *See also* FOUR-LETTER MAN; F-WORD; SHIT.

> Good authors too
> Who once used better words
> Now only use four-letter words.
> COLE PORTER: 'Anything Goes' (song) (1934)

**Four-minute men.** The name given in the United States during the First World War to the members of a volunteer organization some 75,000 strong who, in 1917–18, set out to promote the sale of Liberty Loan Bonds and stir up support for the war in Europe. They gave talks of four minutes' duration to church congregations, cinema audiences, lodges and the like.

**Four-minute mile.** The running of a mile in 4 minutes was for many years the eagerly sought goal of professional athletes. The rigorous training and timed pacing of P.J. Nurmi (*see* FLYING FINN) achieved a time of 4 minutes 10.4 seconds in 1924, but Roger Bannister (b.1929) was the first man to achieve the ambition in 1954, when he breached the barrier at Oxford with a time of 3 minutes 59.4 seconds. In 1979 Sebastian Coe set a new world record of 3 minutes 49 seconds, only to be beaten almost immediately by Steve Ovett, who reduced this time by one-fifth of a second. The time has subsequently been gradually eroded. Coe beat his own record in 1981 with a running of 3 minutes 47.33 seconds. In July 1999 the Moroccan athlete Hicham El Guerrouj notched up a new world record with a mile in 3 minutes 43.13 seconds. The current (December 2005) women's record holder for the mile is Svetlana Masterkova of Russia, with a time of 4 minutes 12.56 seconds.

***4' 33".*** A controversial and certainly unusual work by the US composer John Cage (1912–92), scored for any instrument or any combination of instruments. The piece consists of 4 minutes and 33 seconds of silence. It was first performed in 1952. Ten years later Cage went one better with *0' 00"*, designed 'to be performed in any way to anyone'. In his book entitled *Silence* (1961), Cage observed:

nothing is accomplished by writing a piece of music
nothing is accomplished by hearing a piece of music
nothing is accomplished by playing a piece of music

**Four Musketeers, The.** The flamboyant French tennis players Jean Borotra (1898–1994), Jacques 'Toto' Brugnon (1895–1978), Henri Cochet (1901–87) and René Lacoste (1904–96) were thus known. They won the Davis Cup for France in six successive years (1927–32). *See also* BOUNDING BASQUE.

**404.** A slang term for someone who is clueless. It derives from the World Wide Web error message '404 not found', meaning that the requested web page could not be located.

**Fourpenny dark.** A colloquial Australian term for cheap red wine. It dates from the mid-1950s.

**Fourpenny one.** A blow; a hit; a 'clip round the ear'. The term may have its origin in rhyming slang, 'fourpenny bit' giving 'hit', although no coin of this value was current in the 1930s, when the expression is first recorded.

***Four Saints in Three Acts.*** The teasingly misleading title of an opera by Virgil Thomson (1896–1989) to a libretto by Gertrude Stein (1874–1946). The opera, which is set in Spain, actually has four acts, and more than four saints (among whom are St Theresa and St Ignatius). Its first performance in 1934 was given by an all-black cast dressed in Cellophane.

**Fourteen Points.** The 14 conditions laid down by President Woodrow Wilson as those on which the Allies were prepared to make peace with Germany on the conclusion of the First World War. He outlined them in a speech to Congress on 8 January 1918, and they were eventually accepted as the basis for the peace. They were: (1) the renunciation of secret diplomacy; (2) freedom of navigation of the high seas; (3) freedom of trade; (4) the reduction of arms; (5) a settlement accommodating the peoples of the colonies as well as the colonialist powers; (6) respect for Russia's right of self-determination; (7) the restoration of Belgium; (8) German withdrawal from France and a settlement of the Alsace-Lorraine dispute; (9) a readjustment of the frontiers of Italy along ethnic lines; (10) the prospect of autonomy for the peoples of Austria-Hungary; (11) the restoration of Romania, Serbia and Montenegro, including free access to the sea for Serbia and international guarantees for the Balkan states; (12) the prospect of autonomy for the non-Turkish peoples of the Ottoman Empire and the unrestricted opening of the Straits, but at the same time sovereignty for the Turks in their own areas; (13) independence for Poland with access to the sea; and (14) 'a general association of nations' to guarantee every state's integrity.

The French prime minister Georges Clemenceau commented on Wilson's Fourteen Points: 'The good Lord only has ten.' *See also* LEAGUE OF NATIONS; OPEN DIPLOMACY.

**Fourth dimension.** As a mathematical concept, a hypothetical dimension, whose relation to the recognized three of length, breadth and thickness is analogous to their relation with each other. Albert Einstein in 1921 introduced time as the fourth dimension in his theory of relativity. The expression is also occasionally used to describe something beyond the limits of normal experience.

**Fourth leader.** The fourth leading article in *The Times* from 1922 to 1966, usually light or humorous in nature. The role has subsequently been irregularly filled by the third leader.

**Fourth man.** *See* BURGESS AND MACLEAN.

**Fourth Republic.** The French Republic established in 1946 to replace the provisional governments that followed the collapse of the VICHY regime after D-DAY. It gave way to the Fifth Republic in 1958.

**Fourth World.** A name for those countries and communities of the THIRD WORLD that are regarded as the poorest and most underdeveloped. The tag was coined in 1974 by Robert McNamara (b.1916), US president of the World Bank from 1968 to 1981.

***Four Weddings and a Funeral.*** An astonishingly successful British comedy film (1994), written by Richard Curtis and directed by Mike Newell, about a reserved young Englishman's abiding love for an American called Carrie, which survives the four weddings and a funeral of the title before its consummation. Hugh Grant played the young Englishman in what would become his trademark 'charmingly diffident' manner. The film begins, famously, with the repetition by Grant of the F-WORD, and it includes a moving reading of W.H. Auden's 'Funeral Blues' (1936), which briefly took a collection of the poet's verse into the bestseller lists, just as the film of The ENGLISH PATIENT engendered a short-lived interest in Herodotus.

**Fowler.** The short name of *A Dictionary of Modern English Usage*, by H.W. Fowler (1858–1933), first published in 1926 and soon established as a 'bible' for settling matters of dispute in the use of English. Fowler first made his name in 1906 with *The King's English*, a book about good and bad English written together with his brother, F.G. Fowler. A second edition of the *Dictionary*, revised by Sir Ernest Gowers, appeared in 1965, and a more radical revision, edited by R.W. Burchfield, was issued in 1996 under the title *The New Fowler's Modern English Usage*. Fowler's name often occurs in the phrase 'according to Fowler'.

The original Fowler was a well-balanced blend of fogeyish pedantry, sound advice and good-natured humour, and the distinctive style was evident from the headings of some of the general articles, which included 'Battered ornaments', 'Facetious formations', 'Novelty-hunting', 'Pairs & snares', 'Pride of knowledge', 'Sturdy indefensibles', 'Unequal yokefellows' and 'Worn-out humour'. The following is the opening sentence of the general article headed 'Hackneyed phrases':

> When *Punch* set down a heading that might be, & very likely has been, the title of a whole book, 'Advice to those about to marry', & boiled down the whole contents into a single word, & that a surprise, the thinker of the happy thought deserved congratulations for a week; he hardly deserved immortality, but he has – anonymously, indeed – got it; a large percentage of the great British people cannot think of the dissuasive 'don't' without remembering, &, alas! reminding others, of him.

**Fox, The.** The nickname, sometimes self-applied, of various 20th-century criminals, among them the US child murderer Edward Hickman (1907–28), the British murderer, rapist and robber Arthur Hutchinson (b.1941) and the British rapist and burglar Malcolm Fairley (b.1952). The fox is a prime symbol of cunning and trickery. *See also* DESERT FOX; HOLY FOX.

**Foxhole.** A small slit trench or pit for one or more men.

**Foxtrot.** A short, quick walking pace, as of a fox. A foxtrot is also a ballroom dance originating in America, popular from the 1920s until the 1950s.

**Foxy.** As well as meaning 'crafty', as a fox is traditionally said to be, the word has also been used from the early 20th century to mean 'sexually attractive'.

> W/f [white female] … 21 years old and foxy, would like to hear from a gorgeous man with a terrific body.
> *Easyriders* (February 1983)

Jimi Hendrix had a 1967 song entitled 'Foxy Lady'.

**Foyle's.** A name synonymous with bookshops. The store of W. & G. Foyle Ltd in Charing Cross Road, London, arose from the textbook-selling business set up by the brothers William and Gilbert Foyle in 1903. Their initial stock was second-hand, but they added new books in 1912. In 1930 William's daughter, Christina Foyle (1911–99), inaugurated monthly literary luncheons, held at the Grosvenor Hotel, to enable the reading public to meet distinguished writers and artists. She held the reins as managing director until her death, running the business traditionally and ignoring advances in retailing such as credit cards, labour unions,

electronic tills, and computerized billing even into the 1990s, after which the store's trading practices were overhauled. William Foyle died in 1963, Gilbert in 1971.

**F Plan Diet.** The proprietary name of a type of high-fibre diet devised by Audrey Eyton in the early 1980s. F stands for 'fibre', meaning food material such as bran and cellulose that is not broken down by the process of digestion, otherwise what was formerly known as 'roughage'.

**Fraffly.** According to the writer Alistair Morrison, the brand of English spoken in London's West End, humorous examples of which are provided in *Fraffly Well Spoken* (1968) and *Fraffly Suite* (1969), under the supposed authorship of a Professor Afferbeck Lauder. Both volumes present comic dialogues in which upper-class English speech is spelled out phonetically to demonstrate its drawling absurdities. Thus 'York air scissors good as mine' translates as 'Your guess is as good as mine', 'Egg-wetter gree' as 'I quite agree', and 'Rilleh quettex trod nerreh!' as 'Really quite extraordinary!' *See also* STRINE.

**Fragging.** The act of killing one's superior officer, as practised not infrequently by drafted GIs during the VIETNAM War. The favoured means of dispatch was a fragmentation grenade – hence the term. Being intentional, it is thus the opposite of FRIENDLY FIRE.

**Franglais.** (blend of French *français*, 'French', and *anglais*, 'English'). A fusion of French and English, either in the form of French speech that makes excessive use of English expressions, or as pidgin French spoken by an English person, as sometimes rather unsubtly guyed by humorists. The term itself was proposed in 1949 by Maurice Rat in an article reproduced in René Étiemble's seminal study of the subject, *Parlez-vous franglais?* (1964). Similar blends are denoted by names such as Japlish (Japanese + English), Spanglish (Spanish + English) and the like. *See also* HINGLISH.

**Frank, Anne.** A German Jewish girl (1929–45) who kept a lively and moving diary when in hiding from the Nazis with her family in Holland and who perished in the Bergen-BELSEN concentration camp. The only surviving member of her family was her father. Her diary was first published in abridged form in 1947 (in English in 1952). Many of the original entries relating to her repressed sexual feelings were issued separately in 1989 and a full 'definitive' edition appeared in 1997.

> I see the world gradually being turned into a wilderness, I hear the ever approaching thunder, which will destroy us too, I can feel the sufferings of millions and yet, if I look up

into the heavens, I think that it will all come right, that this cruelty too will end, and that peace and tranquillity will return again.

ANNE FRANK: *The Diary of a Young Girl*, from entry for 15 July 1944 (1952)

**Frasier.** The central character of the highly popular US SITCOM named after him, first screened in 1994. He is the psychiatrist Dr Frasier Crane, played by Kelsey Grammer, and appearing earlier in the equally enjoyable comedy *Cheers* (1982–93). He now returns home to Seattle to start a new life following his divorce from his wife Lilith, originally played by Bebe Neuwirth, and embarks on a career as a radio phone-in psychiatrist. A key motif is the volatile relationship between Frasier and his brother Niles, a fellow psychiatrist, played by David Hyde Pierce, and between the two rather precious opera-loving brothers and their down-to-earth ex-cop father Martin, played by John Mahoney. *Frasier* was the first television series to win five consecutive EMMY awards for 'Outstanding Series'.

**Freak out.** To react in a wild and irrational way, as under the influence of drugs or when mentally unbalanced. The expression dates, unsurprisingly, from the SWINGING SIXTIES.

**Freddie Mac.** A US nickname for the Federal Home Loan Mortgage Corporation. *See also* FANNIE MAE; GINNIE MAE.

**Freddie Star Ate My Hamster.** A headline in *The Sun*, 13 March 1986, which has since come to epitomize British tabloid journalism: trivial, and untrue. As far as is known, the 'madcap' comedian Freddie Starr (b.1944) has no particular penchant for snacking on rodents.

**Fred Karno's Army.** A humorous nickname applied to the new British Army raised during the First World War, in allusion to Fred Karno, the popular comedian and producer of stage burlesques, whose real name was Frederick John Westcott (1866–1941). Fred Karno's company was a household name at the time through its high-spirited and eccentric performances. The well-known army chorus, sung to the tune of 'The Church's One Foundation', runs:

We are Fred Karno's army,
Fred Karno's infantry;
We cannot fight, we cannot shoot,
So what damn good are we?
But when we get to Berlin
The Kaiser he will say
Hoch, hoch, mein Gott
Vot a bloody fine lot,
Fred Karno's infantry.

There are variants, of course, and in the Second World War 'Old Hitler' was substituted for 'The Kaiser'. The name is also applied derisively to other nondescript bodies. Karno himself adopted his stage name when he and two gymnast colleagues filled in at a music-hall for an act called 'The Three Carnos'. His agent, Richard Warner, suggested they change the 'C' to a more distinctive 'K'.

**Free and easy.** Casual and carefree. The expression has an implication of moral laxity.

'It's just that I don't believe in this – whatever you call it – this free-and-easy way of going on. It –'
'Anticipation of marriage is probably how they put it in your – in the advice columns.'

KINGSLEY AMIS: *Take a Girl Like You*, ch. 4 (1960)

**Free association.** In psychology a method of investigating a person's unconscious by eliciting spontaneous associations with ideas or words proposed by the examiner. The word 'chair' might thus prompt a response 'table' in one subject, 'high' in another and 'electric' in a third. The second and third of these would alert the examiner more than the first.

**Freebie.** A colloquialism for something provided free, especially as a bonus, 'perk' or inducement. The increasing prevalence of freebies by way of corporate hospitality in the business world has met with some criticism. *See also* FRINGE BENEFITS.

The freebie-culture of certain professions – journalism, showbiz, PR – causes people to start believing, against all reason, that they shouldn't have to pay full price for *anything*.

*The Times* (24 October 1994)

**Freedom fries.** The name suggested in the United States by Republican Representative Bob Ney in March 2003 to replace the term 'French fries' (what the British call chips) in the cafeterias and restaurants of Congress. The move was in angry response to France's opposition to the US plan to invade Iraq, and the term had first been used by a restaurant in North Carolina. French toast was also to be renamed, as 'freedom toast'. Two years later, in June 2005, Representative Ney called for US troops to be pulled out of Iraq.

Freedom Fries??? OK, I have a question – is the War on Terrorism over? Because I sure as hell want to know that ALL THE TERRORISTS IN THE WORLD HAVE BEEN CAPTURED before legislators actually take the time to rename their GODDAMN CAFETERIA FOOD!

DAVID REES: *Get Your War On* (cartoon strip) (2003)

*See also* SURRENDER-MONKEY.

**Freedom of Information Act.** *See* CHARTER 88.

**Freedom's just another word for nothin' left to lose.** Wise and oft-repeated words from the 1969 song 'Me and Bobby McGee' by the US Country and Western singer and actor Kris Kristofferson (b.1936). The words continue:

> Nothin' ain't worth nothin', but it's free.

**Freedom Tower.** The planned replacement for the twin towers of the WORLD TRADE CENTER, New York City, destroyed in the terrorist attack of 9/11. The design, by Daniel Libeskind, consists of a group of angular towers, the highest, a needle-like structure, reaching 541 m (a symbolic 1776 feet, in homage to the date of America's Declaration of Independence). It won a competition held by developer Larry Silverstein, leaseholder of the site, and the Port Authority of New York and New Jersey, which owns the land. Libeskind left the project after Silverstein brought in another architect, David Childs. Controversy continued in May 2005 when billionaire property tycoon Donald Trump said the design 'looks like a junkyard' and continued: 'It is the worst pile of crap architecture I've ever seen in my life.'

**Free fall.** A downward movement due solely to gravity, as of a parachutist before the parachute opens. The term is used for any state of falling rapidly, as of a 'dive' of share prices on the stock market.

*Free Fall* is also the title of a novel (1959) by William Golding (1911–93). The artist Sammy Mountjoy, 'violently searching and self-condemned', looks back on his life, contemplating how he has chosen freedom and fallen from grace, a 'free fall' from the mount of joy that his name implies.

**Free French.** *See* FFL; FIGHTING FRENCH.

**Free running.** *See* PARKOUR.

**Free-Staters.** The Irish supporters of the Anglo-Irish treaty signed on 6 December 1921, which set up the Irish Free State in the southern 26 counties of Ireland as a dominion within the British Commonwealth. The treaty continued to demand an oath of allegiance to the British crown, and left Northern Ireland (six of the nine counties of Ulster) as an integral part of the United Kingdom. The Free-Staters were led by Michael Collins (the BIG FELLA), and opposed by Republicans led by Éamon de Valera (DEV or the Long Fellow), who refused to accept any outcome other than complete independence for the entire island of Ireland. This led to a bloody civil war in which Collins was assassinated (*see* BÉAL NA MBLÁTH). The civil war ended in 1923, and in 1937 a new constitution renamed the country EIRE. In 1949 the Republic of Ireland was established, and it withdrew from the Commonwealth. *See also* FIANNA FÁIL; FINE GAEL.

**Free, white and 21.** A descriptive term, now dated and regarded as racist, for a young white person who has reached their majority and who is thus a free agent. The phrase originally applied to both sexes but subsequently became specifically associated with a young American woman.

> We're all of us free, white, twenty-one, and hairy-chested, and we know how to be kind to a pretty girl.
>
> JOHN BUCHAN: *The Courts of the Morning*, Pt II, ch. 14 (1929)

**Free world.** A nickname for themselves given collectively by non-communist countries during the COLD WAR.

**Freikorps.** (German, 'free corps'.) Any of a number of far-right German paramilitary groups that first emerged in December 1918, just after Germany's defeat in the First World War. The Freikorps were made up of ex-soldiers and unemployed youths, and their numbers grew through 1919. They were used unofficially by the WEIMAR REPUBLIC government to assist in the suppression of left-wing revolts but developed a taste for looting and vandalism. When the government resolved to disband the Freikorps brigades, one brigade marched on Berlin (13 March 1920) and set up a government under the right-wing Prussian politician Wolfgang Kapp (1858–1922), the so-called Kapp Putsch (*Putsch* being the German word for a sudden and violent seizure of power). However, Kapp's government fell within days in the face of a general strike by Berlin workers. Kapp himself fled to Sweden, but then returned to Germany and died awaiting trial. Many Freikorps personnel subsequently joined the NAZI Party, and one Freikorps commander, Ernst Röhm, became head of the BROWNSHIRTS.

**Frelimo.** An acronym for *Frente de Libertação de Moçambique* (Portuguese, 'Mozambique Liberation Front'), the armed political group led by Samora Machel (1933–86) that fought for independence from Portugal from 1963. With independence achieved in 1975, Frelimo set up a one-party socialist state, and from 1977 fought a civil war against the South African-backed Renamo. Renamo is an acronym for *Resistência Nacional Moçambicana* (Portuguese, 'Mozambican National Resistance'). Renamo is also referred to as the MNR. Multi-party democracy was introduced in 1990, and a peace treaty between the warring factions was signed in 1992.

***French and Saunders.*** A television comedy series featuring and written by Dawn French (b.1957) and Jennifer Saunders (b.1958), first screened in 1987. The programmes mix satire and slapstick from a female perspective and essentially bridge the gap between ALTERNATIVE and mainstream comedy. As with many memorable comic couples, much of the humour derives from the contrast between the two and their adopted personalities, French being short, dark, plump and frivolous while Saunders is tall, fair, slim and serious. The two originally created and honed their double act on stage. Saunders went on to create the highly successful ABSOLUTELY FABULOUS.

**French Connection, The.** A film (1971) adapted by Ernest Tidyman from a book of the same title by Robin Moore about a detective's efforts to combat the illegal drug trade in New York. Starring Gene Hackman as Detective 'Popeye' Doyle and Roy Scheider as his partner, both characters were based on actual drug-squad officers. The film contains one of the most memorable chase scenes ever filmed. The title refers to the link between drug dealers in Marseilles and New York that the two detectives uncover, the word 'connection' being doubly significant in that it is also slang for a drug dealer or pusher.

**French cricket.** A simplified form of cricket without stumps in which the 'bowler' gets the 'batsman' out if the ball hits the latter's legs. The name, first mentioned in the early 20th century, is a slighting allusion to the French, who supposedly cannot understand the rules of cricket.

**French flu.** A passion for all things French. The phrase was invented by Arthur Koestler (1905–83).

> The managerial class on Parnassus ... have lately been affected by a new outbreak of that recurrent epidemic, the French 'Flu.
>
> ARTHUR KOESTLER: *The Yogi and the Commissar* (1945)

**French kiss.** A kiss with one's tongue in the other's mouth, as said to be favoured by the French.

**French knickers.** A type of loose-fitting, wide-legged women's knickers that are usually trimmed with lace and generally made of silk or satin. The style is supposedly typically French.

**French Lieutenant's Woman, The.** A novel (1969) by John Fowles (1926–2005), in which a deliberate blend of styles supports an exploration into the historical and subconscious worlds. It opens in Lyme Regis in the 1860s, at a spot overlooked by the 18th-century house in which Fowles lived from 1965. Several alternative endings are suggested. The 'woman' is Sarah Woodruff, believed to have been deserted by a French lieutenant. She is unsuccessfully pursued by Charles Smithson, at the cost of his own engagement. A rather unsatisfactory film version (1981) was directed by Karel Reisz from a screenplay by Harold Pinter.

**French Resistance.** *See* MAQUIS.

**French tickler.** A type of condom with ribbed protrusions. The term evolved in the 1960s from the earlier 'French letter' as a colloquial term for a condom. This, and expressions such as FRENCH KISS and FRENCH KNICKERS, preserve the traditional British notion, not entirely groundless, that the French attach a particular importance to the sensual aspects of sexual pleasure, just as they do to those of food and drink.

**Freudian slip.** An unintentional mistake that appears to reveal a subconscious intention. It takes its name from the Austrian neurologist and psychotherapist Sigmund Freud (1856–1939), famous for his interest in the sexual subconscious. This last gave the term a popular or facetious usage for a slip of the tongue that reveals thoughts of a sexual nature. The term dates from the 1950s.

**Frick and Frack.** In colloquial African-American English, a humorous term for an inseparable pair of individuals or items. It is often used specifically to refer to the testicles. It comes ultimately from the name of a Swiss comedy skating team of the 1920s and 1930s, who performed in the US and Europe. They were famous for a routine in which they put the heels of their skates together, bent their knees and skated in large circles with their bodies leaning outwards.

**Friday Club.** An information association of progressive artists founded in 1905 by the painter and designer Vanessa Bell, its members initially meeting on Fridays at her home, 46 Gordon Square, London. For some years there was a strong BLOOMSBURY GROUP presence and exhibitions were held down to 1922.

**Friedmanism.** An economic doctrine named after the US economist Milton Friedman (b.1912), who won the 1976 Nobel Prize for economics. Friedman opposed KEYNESIANISM and instead emphasized the importance of the free market and control of the money supply. His theories, also known as monetarism, strongly influenced the Conservative government of Margaret Thatcher. *See also* IRON LADY; MAD MONK; NO SUCH THING AS A FREE LUNCH.

**Friendly fire.** A military euphemism for fire coming from one's own side, especially when it results in accidental injury or death among one's own forces. The phrase was current in the VIETNAM War (1964–75) but came into prominence during the First GULF WAR of 1991, when many fatal casualties among Allied troops were attributed to it. 'Friendly bombing' is also found as a variant. *See also* BLUE ON BLUE; FRAGGING.

**Friendly neighbourhood ... .** A jocular formula used to preface, often ironically, a reference to a particular person, establishment, etc., especially one engaged in a particular line of business. Inspired by 'Your friendly neighborhood grocer', a US advertising slogan-turned-cliché of the 1950s, it enjoyed a vogue in the late 1960s and early 1970s, and has stuck around ever since.

> Miklós Sándorfia, friendly neighbourhood pursuivant, interested in period heraldry and tournaments, heraldic display, consulting, SCA heraldic practice and tradition.
>
> http://andrew.draskoy.net (27 July 1998)

**Friendly persuasion.** Gentle coercing; gradual inducement. The phrase became popular from the Western film of 1956 so titled, itself based on Jessamyn West's novel *The Friendly Persuasion* (1945). The sense there is quite different, however, since the book is a series of sketches of the life of a Quaker family during the American Civil War, with 'friendly' punning on the official name of the Quakers as the Society of Friends and 'persuasion' relating to religious beliefs.

**Friend of Dorothy.** A euphemism for a male homosexual. The allusion is to Dorothy Gale, the young heroine of L. Frank Baum's children's novel *The* WIZARD OF OZ (1900), who in the film version of 1939 was played by Judy Garland (1922–69), an actress who subsequently gained cult status in the gay community. The variant 'Dorothy's friend' is also current. *See also* STONEWALL.

**Friends.** A popular US television SITCOM first shown in the United States in 1994. It depicts a sextet of good-looking TWENTY-SOMETHING New Yorkers, three men and three women, and the action takes place mainly in a local coffee bar called Central Perk and the two adjoining apartments above it, occupied by some of the group. The last of 236 episodes was broadcast in 2004, although the ten series are endlessly repeated.

**Friends of the Earth.** An environmental pressure group, originating in the United States and existing in Britain since 1970. It first became publicly prominent in a campaign of 1971, in which thousands of disposable bottles were dumped on the doorstep of the soft drinks manufacturers Schweppes. By the mid-1990s it had branches in more than 30 countries. Protests and propaganda are furthered by public meetings, demonstrations and so on. Members are actively against all forms of pollution, developments that ruin the countryside and the destruction of wildlife. *See also* GREENPEACE.

**Friends thought I was mad.** A journalistic cliché dating from the first half of the 20th century and used when describing some apparently foolhardy venture, such as moving from a spacious and well-appointed town house to the sparse amenities of an isolated country cottage. The pronoun is obviously variable.

> Friends thought they were mad. Family shook their heads as they surveyed the mildew-spotted wall, peeling plaster, rusty radiators, and the gull droppings on the parquet floor.
>
> *Daily Mail* (28 May 1994)

**Frighten the horses.** To alarm people, usually invoked in the negative. The words are attributed to Mrs Patrick Campbell (1865–1940) in Daphne Fielding's *The Duchess of Jermyn Street*, Chapter 2 (1964): 'It doesn't matter what you do in the bedroom as long as you don't do it in the street and frighten the horses.'

> What is equally certain is that Labour's strategy of doing nothing which could 'frighten the horses' will mean their tactics pin-point the 'soft' voters.
>
> BILL BUSH: in *The BBC News General Election Guide* (1997)

**Fringe, The.** The secondary festival held on the periphery ('fringe') of the annual Edinburgh Festival. It was first held in 1947 when eight companies presented plays in venues which they hired themselves. The enterprise has remained faithful to the original open policy and there is no censoring of performers. The result is originality of the highest order on the one hand and time-wasting trivia on the other. At the 2005 Fringe 1800 shows were presented, at 250 different venues. *See also* BEYOND THE FRINGE; HAPPENING.

**Fringe benefits.** Concessions and benefits given to employees; 'perks' that go with a job or appointment such as free fuel, use of a car, pensions, insurances, medical benefits and so forth. *See also* FREEBIE.

**Fringe party.** A British political or quasi-political party with a small or ephemeral membership, as distinct from the Conservative Party, LABOUR PARTY or Liberal Democrats. Many such parties emerge only at the time of a general election and are of narrow, local or frivolous appeal, with policies that may be specific or deliberately nebulous. As such, they add a note of eccentricity to an otherwise serious and even portentous event. One of the best-known fringe parties is the MONSTER RAVING LOONY PARTY, its name aptly echoing its affinity with the LUNATIC FRINGE.

In the British General Election of 2005 the following were among the many fringe parties that fielded one or more candidates:

Baths Party

Bean Party

Blair Must Go Party

Bridge Party

Church of the Militant Elvis Party

Civilization Party

Death, Dungeons and Taxes Party

Get Britain Back

Good Party

Honesty Party

Imperial Party

Iraq War, Not In My Name

Max Power Party

Motorcycle News Party

Northern Progress for You

Personality & Rational Thinking? Yes! Party

Protest Vote Party

Removal of Tetra Masts in Cornwall

St Albans Party

Silent Majority Party

S-O-S Votes Against Overdevelopment of Northampton

Telepathic Partnership

Their Party

Tigers Eye the Party for Kids

UK Pensioners Party

Wessex Regionalist

Xtraordinary Peoples Party

Your Party

**Fringe theatre.** A form of British theatre corresponding to the American off-off-Broadway (*see* OFF-BROADWAY), i.e. devoted to productions that because of their political content or experimental nature are usually staged in non-theatrical buildings such as converted warehouses or factories, or even rooms in pubs. Their audiences have mostly been young and anti-ESTABLISHMENT. The term itself probably derives from the Edinburgh FRINGE.

**Frisbee.** The concave disc designed for skimming through the air evolved in 1957 from the pie tins used similarly that themselves came from the Frisbie bakery in Bridgeport, Connecticut. Frisbees were commercially produced by Wham-O Manufacturing, makers of the HULA HOOP, and they now serve as a fitness fetish in Ultimate Frisbee, a seven-a-side team game invented by students at a New Jersey high school in the late 1960s. The game has been billed as a cross between football, basketball and hockey, and its name implies that it is 'the ultimate sports experience'. The governing body is the World Flying Disc Federation, and a key rule is that a player must not hold the Frisbee for more than 10 seconds before passing it to another member of the side. *See also* BIG FRISBEE.

**Fritz.** A nickname for a German, from the pet form of the common German forename Friedrich (Frederick). It was widely used by British forces in the First World War but in the Second World War was largely replaced by JERRY. Walter Mondale (b.1928), whose middle name is Frederick, was known as Fritz when US vice-president (1977–81) in allusion to his Germanic ancestry. *See also* 'NORWEGIAN WOOD (THIS BIRD HAS FLOWN)'.

**Fritz the Cat.** A character created by the US cartoonist Robert Crumb (b.1943). The anthropomorphic hero, who possesses the morals of a tomcat, appeared in a number of underground comics in the 1960s, and in 1972 starred in a feature-length animated film of the same name, the first such film ever to receive the British film censors' X-rating. A sequel, *The Nine Lives of Fritz the Cat* (1974), found less favour with critics and audiences.

Fritz the Cat is also the nickname of the Austrian skier Fritz Strobl, the 2002 Olympic downhill champion.

**Frodo.** A HOBBIT in J.R.R. Tolkien's *The* LORD OF THE RINGS (1954–5), who goes on a quest to destroy a ring that can make the wearer all-powerful, lest it fall into the hands of an evil lord. 'Frodo Lives' was a HIPPIE slogan of the 1960s.

**Frog in one's throat.** A temporary hoarseness or phlegm in the throat. The allusion may be to the 'croaking' of the voice, although frog is also an old term for various diseases of the mouth or throat. The expression dates from the early 20th century.

**Frog march.** A method of carrying an obstreperous prisoner face downwards by his four limbs, like a frog. The term is now more generally used, however, for a way of making a person walk somewhere by pinning his arms behind him and hustling him forwards.

**From can to can't.** A phrase denoting a long day, used by workers on the prison farms of the American Deep South, who were obliged to work from dawn to dusk, from 'can see' to 'can't see'.

**From go to whoa.** In colloquial Australian and New Zealand English, from start to finish. The expression is first recorded in 1971.

> Each book can be read as a story in itself but … is much more satisfying if you are following the family and their friends from go to whoa.
>
> www.pukeariki.com (2003)

**From hell.** A tag applied to a person or group of people regarded as unusually bad or dangerous, as 'the au pair from hell' or 'the neighbours from hell'. A television exposé of consultants and GPs who continued practising although struck off the register was entitled *Doctors from Hell* (1999). The phrase may also be used to describe a normally mundane event that turns out disastrously, such as a dinner party, interview, holiday, etc.

> She also found herself sharing with three flatmates from hell: three lads, who were pleasant individually, but they never washed up.
>
> *The Times* (26 August 1999)

**From Here to Eternity.** The first novel (1951) by James Jones (1921–77). He was serving in the US infantry in Hawaii when the Japanese bombed PEARL HARBOR in 1941. Twice promoted and twice reduced to private, he fought at Guadalcanal and was wounded in the head by a mortar fragment. The novel, which won a National Book Award, draws on his own experiences in Hawaii and caused a sensation for its exposé of army brutality and its outspokenness about sex and military mores. The film (1952) was a slick, 'cleaned-up' version directed by Fred Zinnemann. The title comes from the poem 'The Gentlemen-Rankers' (1889), about oppressed junior ranks, by Rudyard Kipling:

> Gentlemen-rankers out on the spree,
> Damned from here to Eternity,
> God ha' mercy on such as we.

**From Russia with Love.** The second film (1963) in the long-running series of movies about British secret agent James BOND derived from the spy novels of Ian Fleming (1908–64). Starring Sean Connery as Bond and Robert Shaw as Red Grant, one of the best of all Bond villains, its title was inspired by a standard formula on British holiday postcards.

**From soda to hock.** From beginning to end. The phrase dates from the turn of the 20th century and derives from the game of faro, in which 'soda' is the exposed top card at the beginning of a deal and 'hock' the last card remaining in the box after all the others have been dealt.

**From the get-go.** From the beginning. A phrase of African American origin dating from the 1960s, with 'get-go' a shortened form of 'get going'.

> Let's get one thing straight from the get-go: anyone after a good narrative thriller would be better off reading a book.
>
> *heat* (16 December 1999–5 January 2000)

**From the House of the Dead.** (Czech, *Z Mrtvého Domu.*) A surprisingly up-lifting opera by Leoš Janáček (1854–1928), which has a text by the composer based on Fyodor Dostoyevsky's prison reminiscences, *Memoirs from the House of the Dead* (1862). The 'House of the Dead' in question is a Siberian prison camp. Nothing much happens, although the

Dostoyevsky figure (called Alexander Goryanchikov in the opera) arrives at the beginning and departs at the end. At the head of the score Janáček wrote: 'In every human being there is a divine spark.' He left the work unfinished at the time of his death; it was completed by Břetislav Bakala and O. Zitek and first performed in 1930.

**Front-end loading.** In financial jargon the repayments of a loan arranged in such a way that service charges relating to the whole period of the loan are recovered in the early payments and so form a large proportion of such payments by the investor. The term dates from the 1960s. In literal terms a front-end loader is a machine with a bucket or scoop on an articulated arm at the front for digging and loading earth.

**Front up.** In colloquial Australian and New Zealand English, to put in an appearance, to turn up. The expression dates from the 1960s, and probably evolved from an earlier Australian (originally services') sense of 'front (up)', 'to appear before a court or other disciplinary authority', which itself was a specialized application of 'front', 'to confront'.

> **800 front up for 3.00am Little Flower Mass**
>
> 800 people were present at 3.00am yesterday morning to greet the arrival of the relics of St Therese of Lisieux in Australia.
>
> www.cathtelecom. com (1 February 2002)

**Fruit boots.** In US slang, a jocular term for footwear of a type stereotypically associated with the more flamboyant sort of gay man (a 'fruit' is a male homosexual) – for example, white tennis shoes, or Italian-style shoes with pointed toes.

**Fruit-loop.** In US slang, a crazy, eccentric or stupid person. First recorded in 1984, it was inspired by 'Fruit Loops', the brand name of a type of US breakfast cereal, with a nod to 'loopy' in the sense 'mad'.

**Fruit machine.** A coin-operated gaming machine or ONE-ARMED BANDIT that spins symbols of fruit on a dial. If when the spin stops all the symbols are identical, such as three pears, the player usually wins. The use of fruit as a reward or prize is in a tradition dating from classical times, and fruit has an equally venerable association with the classical cornucopia as a symbol of plenty.

**Fruit salad.** A sardonic term for an ostentatiously abundant display of medal ribbons on a military uniform. The usage arose in services' slang during the Second World War. In the late 1960s it was joined by a new, drug-users' meaning: a random combination of any pills or capsules of drugs available, including psychotropic and medicinal, on which to get intoxicated.

**FUBAR.** A US services' slang acronym based on 'fucked up beyond all recognition', denoting a complete COCK-UP. First recorded in 1944, it recalls and was probably inspired by the more widely known military acronym SNAFU. In later use it was reapplied by US college students to someone completely drunk or under the influence of drugs.

**Fuck you up, your mum and dad, They.** *See* THEY FUCK YOU UP, YOUR MUM AND DAD.

**Fuddy-duddy.** An irredeemably old-fashioned person; an inveterate old fogey. The expression dates from the turn of the 20th century and is probably of dialect origin.

> RIBA, the fuddy-duddy architects' body, has recruited Naomi Campbell's friend to introduce razzle-dazzle into an otherwise dry event.
> *The Times* (19 July 1999)

**Fudge and mudge.** To gloss over differences or blur distinctions; to prevaricate. The phrase is first recorded in a speech made by the politician David Owen at the 1980 LABOUR PARTY conference. 'Mudge' is simply a rhyming jingle on 'fudge'.

> We are fed up with fudging and mudging, with mush and slush. We need courage, conviction, and hard work.
> *The Guardian* (3 October 1980)

**Fudge factor.** A factor speculatively included in a calculation to compensate for the lack of accurate information.

> The market soon recognized the fudge factor – half a point tacked on for the drought effect – and settled back into more familiar expectations on growth.
> *Financial Times* (22 February 1989)

**Führer.** (German, 'leader'.) The title assumed by Adolf Hitler (1889–1945) when he acceded to supreme power in Germany on the death of Hindenburg in 1934. *See also* CAUDILLO; DUCE; EIN VOLK, EIN REICH, EIN FÜHRER.

**Fulbright scholar.** A student receiving an educational grant under an international exchange scholarship programme conceived by US Senator William Fulbright (1905–95) of Arkansas and implemented by the Fulbright Act of 1946, which authorized funds from the sale of surplus war materials overseas to be used for the purpose. Candidates for a Fulbright grant must be under 35 years old, have a Bachelor of Arts degree or equivalent, be proficient in the language of the country in which they plan to study and be generally competent scholastically. Most exchanges to date have been made by university or college students, but teachers and researchers have also qualified.

> A picture of that year's intake
> Of Fulbright Scholars. Just arriving –

> Or arrived. Or some of them.
> Were you among them?
> TED HUGHES: *Birthday Letters*, 'Fulbright Scholars' (1998)

**Full Fathom Five.** The wild action painting by Jackson Pollock (1912–56) dates from 1947. Most of Pollock's subsequent works had numerical titles such as *Number One*, *Number Thirty Two*, or, marginally more original, *Black and White Number Five*. However, this one is a quotation from *The Tempest* (I.ii):

> Full fathom five thy father lies;
> Of his bones are coral made;
> Those are pearls that were his eyes …

These are the words that Ariel sings to Ferdinand, who believes his father has drowned in the storm. While he was still in his teens, Pollock had lost his own father. As he himself said, 'Every good painter paints what he is.'

**Full frontal.** A painting or photograph of a nude person with genitals exposed to full view or an actual person standing thus.

**Full Metal Jacket.** A film (1987) about the training of a squad of US Marines and their subsequent experiences in VIETNAM. It was based on the novel *The Short Timers* by Gustav Hasford and was filmed by Stanley Kubrick entirely in the UK (a gasworks in the East End doubling up for Vietnam, complete with imported palm trees). The title is explained by Anthony Frewin, assistant to Stanley Kubrick from 1965 to 1999, in an e-mail to the present editors:

> What it actually refers to is the casing of a bullet. Lead bullets upon impact flatten like a pancake and have only minimal penetration. Whereas a bullet with a full metal jacket (usually copper) retains its shape and will go right through you and, probably, the person standing behind you too.

The reality of the film was heightened by the presence of R. Lee Ermey as Gunnery Sergeant Hartman. Ermey was a former army drill instructor who was hired initially just to advise but who persuaded Kubrick into letting him play the part himself.

**Full monty.** Everything; the lot; 'the works'. Said of anything done to the utmost or fullest degree. The origin of the expression is uncertain. It may derive from 'the full amount' or the Spanish card game monte (literally 'mountain', i.e. heap of cards), or allude to a full three-piece suit from the men's outfitters Montague Burton. One explanation traces the term to Field Marshal Bernard Montgomery, nicknamed MONTY (1887–1976), said to have begun every day with a full English breakfast when campaigning in the North African desert in the Second World War. Yet another derives it from the city of Montevideo, Uruguay, on the grounds that fleece-packers shipping sheepskins from there graded them as 'full Monte'. In the absence of any early evidence (it is not recorded before 1986) the source is unlikely to be definitively identified, although its frequent use in the context of clothing suggests that 'Montague' Burton may be the most plausible candidate.

The British phrase became familiar generally in the English-speaking world from its use as the title of a successful comedy film (1997) about a group of unemployed British factory workers who raise money by staging a strip act at a local club.

**Full quid, The.** In Australian and New Zealand slang, someone described as 'not quite the full quid' is not in full possession of his or her faculties (a 'quid' is a pound, but in this case there are less than 20 shillings). The expression, which dates from the 1930s, is of a piece with other characterizations of eccentricity or madness as the lack of a full (mental) complement, such as 'not all there' and the multiple variations on the 'X short of a Y' formula (*see* TWO SANDWICHES SHORT OF A PICNIC).

**Full stop.** And that's that; there is no more to be said. A tag placed at the end of a sentence to indicate that further elaboration on a topic is unnecessary. The implication is that a final full stop has been written. 'Period' is used similarly in American English. *See also* END OF STORY.

> Jeff Clark … said: 'Road signs are put up by the relevant divisions. … Any other signs are illegal and have to be removed. We do not put advertising up, full stop.'
> *The Citizen* (4 January 2000)

**Fu Manchu.** The Chinese master villain who is head of the dreaded 'Si-Fan' secret society. He was the creation of Sax Rohmer (real name Arthur Sarsfield Ward) in a series of stories that ran in the *Story-Teller Magazine* from 1912. These were soon collected to form bestselling novels such as *The Mystery of Dr Fu Manchu* (1913). Fu operates internationally, his ultimate aim apparently being to gain mastery of the world, but his evil plans are constantly foiled by the doughty Englishman Dennis Nayland Smith. Fu Manchu's adventures were later transferred to the screen, and he became established as the 'YELLOW PERIL incarnate', a familiar racial stereotype.

**Fun and games.** Enjoyable goings-on. The phrase dates from the early 20th century, often applying to sexual play.

**Fun City.** A nickname, sometimes ironic, of any place of potential or actual pleasure. It came to be associated with New York during the term of office of John V. Lindsay as mayor (1966–73), and was coined in January 1966 by Dick Schaap, a columnist for the New York *Herald Tribune*.

**Fundamentalism.** In Christianity, the maintenance of traditional Protestant Christian beliefs based on a literal acceptance of the Scriptures as fundamentals. Fundamentalism as a religious movement arose in the United States about 1919 among various denominations. What was new was not so much its ideas and attitudes, but its widespread extent and the zeal of its supporters. It opposed all theories of evolution and anthropology, holding that God transcends all laws of nature and that He manifests Himself by exceptional and extraordinary activities, belief in the literal meaning of the Scriptures being an essential tenet. In 1925, John T. Scopes (*see* MONKEY TRIAL), a science teacher of Rhea High School, Dayton, Tennessee, was convicted of violating the state laws by teaching evolution, an incident arousing interest and controversy far beyond the religious circles of the United States. The leading anti-evolutionist of the period was William Jennings Bryan (1860–1925), the lawyer and populist politician. *See also* INTELLIGENT DESIGN.

The term 'Islamic fundamentalism', dating from the 1950s, designates a strict adherence to certain tenets of Koranic teaching, such as was practised by the AYATOLLAHS in Iran in the 1980s, and, in an even more extreme form, by the TALIBAN in Afghanistan in the late 1990s.

**Fungus the Bogeyman.** The lovably loathsome hero of Raymond Briggs's illustrated book for children so titled (1977). Fungus and his family live underground in a dank and noxious world where all things dry and clean are outlawed. The book is full of (literal) dirty jokes and puns that have given it a certain additional appeal to adults.

**Funny bone.** A pun on the word *humerus*, the Latin name for the arm bone. It is the inner condyle or knob at the end of the bone where the ulnar nerve is close to the surface of the skin at the elbow. A knock on this part is naturally painful and produces a tingling sensation.

**Funny-face.** A term of endearment. It is first recorded as, and was very likely inspired by, the title of a 1927 Broadway musical by George and Ira Gershwin (this reappeared in a 1957 film version, starring Fred Astaire and Audrey Hepburn, which bore little resemblance to the original beyond the name *Funny Face*).

**Funny farm.** A colloquial or facetious term for a psychiatric hospital. The expression is said to refer to Friern Hospital, the former mental hospital at Friern Barnet, North London, which had a working farm. Noël Coward has a song 'All the Fun of the Farm' in his musical play *Cavalcade* (1931).

**Funny Girl.** A film musical (1968) based on the stage musical of the same title (1964) by Jule Styne, Bob Merrill and Isobel Lennart about the life of vaudeville star Fanny Brice (1891–1951), who was at one time the wife of the gangster Nicky Arnstein. Brice was played on both stage and in the film and in the sequel, *Funny Lady* (1975), by Barbra Streisand, with whom the title became almost synonymous.

**Funny money.** Counterfeit or worthless money, especially when associated with crime or dubious practices. The term dates from the 1940s. 'Funny' here does not mean amusing but relates to 'funny business' as a term for deceitful or underhand practices. In the money-mad 1980s, the term came to connote money in such ludicrously large amounts that it ceased to have any meaning to the ordinary person.

> It's the Lloyd's Building, and it rises like an exhalation from a City of funny money where … yobs who say 'Yah' transmit notional fortunes round the globe.
> *The Observer* (23 April 1989)

**Funny old game.** Football. A journalistic cliché that sometimes omits the 'old'. It is frequently used by footballers themselves. *See also* BEAUTIFUL GAME.

> Funny old game football, as Greavsie [footballer Jimmy Greaves] might have said … even when it's TV's fantasy kind.
> *Today* (30 August 1994)

**Funny old world.** Said of anything strange or unexpected. The phrase was adopted from the quip spoken by W.C. Fields in the film *You're Telling Me* (1934): 'It's a funny old world – a man's lucky if he gets out of it alive.' Margaret Thatcher also memorably commented: 'It's a funny old world' on being persuaded to withdraw from the contest for leadership of the Conservative Party in 1990.

**Funny-peculiar or funny-ha-ha?** A question put to someone who uses the word 'funny' without making it clear which of the two senses is meant.

> *Chris*: That's funny.
> *Button*: What do you mean, funny? Funny-peculiar, or funny ha-ha?
> IAN HAY: *Housemaster*, III (1936)

**Funny Thing Happened on the Way to the Forum, A.** A film musical (1966) based on a stage show of the same title (1962), with music by Stephen Sondheim and book by Burt Shevelove and Larry Gelbart, about a Roman slave's farcical attempts to gain his freedom. Starring Zero Mostel, Phil Silvers and Buster Keaton, the film was, like the stage show, derived ultimately from the comic writings of Plautus.

**Fun run.** A long run undertaken by a large number of people for pleasure and exercise, and especially a sponsored run, as a marathon to raise money for charity. The term and the activity itself originated in the United States in the mid-1970s.

**Furby.** A furry toy animal with a microchip implant that enables it to make sounds (including those of bodily functions) and respond to and imitate external stimuli. Furbies were the invention of the American Dave Hampton and were the Christmas present craze of 1998.

**Fur coat and no knickers.** In a woman described as being 'all fur coat and no knickers', external respectability is viewed as concealing an underlying lubricity. More generally, it can mean that a certain pretentious and showy exterior belies a lack of substance, a flimsiness, a tawdriness. *See also* ALL MOUTH AND TROUSERS.

> Edinburgh was a schizophrenic city, the place of Jekyll & Hyde sure enough … of fur coats and no knickers (as they said in the west).
> IAN RANKIN: *Knots & Crosses* (1987)

**Furry Boots City.** A nickname bestowed on Aberdeen, Scotland, by the *Glasgow Herald* diarist Tom Shields during the 1980s, owing to the propensity of the inhabitants to find out all about you without giving anything away about themselves; thus they would begin a conversation by asking, in the local accent, 'Fur aboots are ye from?' (i.e. 'Whereabouts do you come from?').

**Fusion food.** A late 20th-century term for restaurant menus, usually at the higher end of the gastronomic scale, that deliberately merge elements from regionally different culinary traditions (e.g. Italian and Southeast Asian) on the same plate. The ethnic mix of cosmopolitan cities such as New York, San Francisco and London has encouraged the trend. 'Fusion' has been used to apply to certain mixing of musical styles too (especially jazz–rock fusion).

**Future, Captain.** *See* CAPTAIN FUTURE.

**Future shock.** A state of distress or disorientation resulting from rapid social or technological change. The expression is first defined by Alvin Toffler in *Horizon* (1965) as 'the dizzying disorientation brought on by the premature arrival of the future'. In 1970 Toffler published a bestselling book entitled *Future Shock*, in which he coined the phrase 'information overload', a state of affairs in which an individual or organization has so much information that decisions or coherent overviews are impossible. *See also* CULTURE SHOCK.

**Futurism.** An art movement that originated at Turin in 1909 under the influence of Filippo Tommaso Marinetti

(1876–1944). Its adherents sought to introduce into paintings a 'poetry of motion' whereby, for example, the painted gesture should become actually 'a dynamic condition'. The Futurists tried to indicate not only the state of mind of the painter but also that of the figures in the picture. It was another movement to shake off the influence of the past. Original members apart from Marinetti included Umberto Boccioni (1882–1916), Carlo Carrà (1881–1966), Luigi Russolo (1885–1947) and Gino Severini (1883–1966), and they first exhibited in 1912 at the Galérie Bernheim-Jeune in Paris. 'Futuristic' is often used as a general term for any 'modern' art, even when not strictly Futurist. *See also* CUBISM; DADAISM; FAUVISM; ORPHISM; RURALISM; SURREALISM; SYNCHROMISM; TACHISM; VORTICISM.

**Fuzz, The.** The police. The colloquialism is of US origin and dates from the 1920s. The source may lie in 'fuss', as a reference to an over-particular person.

**F-word.** A term usually used euphemistically to denote the taboo slang word 'fuck', but adopted by UK Europhobes and Eurosceptics (*see* EUROPHILE) to denote 'federalism', i.e. political union, in the context of the European Union. Supporters of federalism are dubbed Federasts (playing on 'pederast'). *See also* FOUR-LETTER WORD; *The* NAKED AND THE DEAD.

**Fylingdales.** The moorland site near the coast in North Yorkshire of a US early-warning station, built in 1963. It was notable for its radar installations shaped like giant golf balls, designed to give early warning of a nuclear attack. So striking in appearance were these structures that it was suggested in some quarters that they be made listed buildings. However, the golf balls have now been replaced by solid-state phased-array radar (SSPAR) in the form of a three-sided truncated pyramid *c*.36m (120 ft) high.

# G

**Gaia hypothesis.** The theory that the earth is not a collection of independent mechanisms but a single living organism in which everything interacts to regulate the survival and stability of the whole. The hypothesis was put forward in 1969 by the British scientist James Lovelock and at the suggestion of the novelist William Golding was named after Gaia, Greek goddess of the earth, whose name is sometimes used of the earth itself, especially when viewed holistically and reverentially. Adherents of the principle are known as Gaians. Some scientists object to the religious overtones of the theory, but it has gained acceptance among many conservationists. As a girl's name Gaia became fashionable for its environmental connotations from the 1990s and was given among others to the daughter (b.1999) of the OSCAR-winning actress Emma Thompson.

> Gaia is a tough bitch. People think the earth is going to die and they have to save it, that's ridiculous … There's no doubt that Gaia can compensate for our output of green-house gases, but the environment that's left will not be happy for any people.
>
> LYNN MARGULIS: in *New York Times Biographical Service* (January 1996)

**Galah session.** In Australia, a period of time set aside on an outback radio network, particularly that operated by the Flying Doctor service, for people to engage in private conversations, swap gossip, etc. (rather than make emergency calls). The term was inspired by the 'galah', more formally *Cacatua roseicapilla*, a rose-breasted grey-backed Australian cockatoo which is constantly chattering (the word 'galah' itself is of Aboriginal origin). Latterly it has been used more broadly for any gossip session.

**Gallipoli.** A disastrous campaign of the First World War. The plan was for the British fleet to bombard its way through the heavily defended Dardanelles, a narrow strait between Europe and Asiatic Turkey, while an Allied army captured the Gallipoli peninsula, on the European side. Neither happened owing to miscalculation and incompetence. The fleet withdrew after three battleships were sunk in an undetected minefield, and the troop landings on 25 April 1915 were gallant but ineffectual. The Allies withdrew in January 1916 with the loss of more than 200,000 men.

A film of the same name, directed by Peter Weir and starring Mel Gibson, was released in 1981. Despite some inaccuracies, it depicts in moving fashion the courage in the face of death of members of the Australian Tenth Light Horse Regiment. *See also* ANZAC.

**Gallivespians.** A race of diminutive human-like people in Philip Pullman's trilogy HIS DARK MATERIALS. Their stature, along with their resourcefulness and combativeness (they are armed with poisonous spines), makes them excellent spies. They ride on dragonflies.

**Galloping Gourmet.** A semi-facetious nickname for Graham Kerr (b.1934), the popular British-born cookery expert, whose television programmes were made in Canada but were shown in many countries in the late 1960s and early 1970s. He earned the name from his alacrity in the kitchen and his nimbleness in the preparation of dishes.

**'Galloping Major, The'.** A song (1906) by G.H. Bastow, which was popular well into the second half of the 20th century. It was also the title of a 1951 British film comedy film about a racehorse syndicate, and more memorably a nickname for the Hungarian footballer Ferenc Puskás (b.1927), who at one time held the rank of major in the Hungarian army. He was a free-scoring forward, and played a prominent part in the 6–3 Hungarian victory over England at Wembley in 1952 that shook English football to its foundations. The nickname was later applied to Major Ronald Ferguson (1931–2003), the polo-playing father of the Duchess of York (*see* FERGIE). He gave the title *The Galloping Major* to his memoirs, published in 1994.

**Gallup Poll.** The best known of the public opinion surveys, instituted by Dr George H. Gallup (1901–84) of the American Institute of Public Opinion in 1935. Trained interviewers interrogate a small but carefully selected cross-section of the population. For the British general election of 1945, out of 25 million voters, 1809 were interviewed, but the Gallup Poll forecast was within 1 per cent. The forecast was, however, wrong for the US presidential election of 1948. A Labour victory was correctly forecast for the British general elections of 1964 and 1966. It is held that such polls in themselves influence the result. Straw polls and market research surveys were the forerunners of the Gallup Poll. Most electoral polls in Britain are now conducted by MORI (Market and Opinion Research Institute), a joint Anglo-American organization, founded in 1969. *See also* MASS-OBSERVATION.

**Game Boy.** The proprietary name of a hand-held, battery-operated device for playing computer games. It has a small screen, direction and function buttons, and a slot where various game cartridges, such as that for POKÉMON, can be inserted. It was launched on the market in the late 1980s by the Japanese firm Nintendo as a portable version of its popular video game. Its name indicates its function and its usual owner and operator, while also suggesting its small size. See also PLAYSTATION; SEGA.

**Game on!** All necessary preliminaries have been completed, and the action can begin. The expression originated in the game of darts, and began to spread into the general language when it was televised in the 1970s and 80s.

**Game over.** The situation is hopeless. A phrase of US origin probably deriving from the announcement at the end of a computer game.

**Game plan.** A strategy worked out in advance, especially in sport, politics or business. The original sense specifically related to a plan of fixed 'plays' pre-arranged by the coach and the team for winning a game of American football. The term was taken up in Britain in the 1980s when this sport became more familiar from television.

**Game show.** The popular genre of television programme, in which members of the public compete to win prizes, has its origin in US radio shows of the 1930s. American television then adopted the game show in the 1950s, using large cash rewards for correct answers. An indication of the quantum increase was the escalation of one radio programme's highest prize, the SIXTY-FOUR DOLLAR QUESTION, to a sixty-four thousand dollar question on television. The television game show in Britain was launched in the 1960s with series

such as *The* GOLDEN SHOT, *The* GENERATION GAME, *Sale of the Century* (1972–83), *Celebrity Squares* (1975–9) and the more complex *3–2–1* (1978–87). A new plateau of prize money was achieved by WHO WANTS TO BE A MILLIONAIRE?, but contestants on the BBC's less well endowed *The* WEAKEST LINK have to be in it for the glory rather than the cash.

The following transcript of an extract from an early episode of *3–2–1*, compered by the comedian Ted Rogers, offers a taste of the general level of erudition on display in such programmes:

> *Ted Rogers*: 'This is a composer, German by birth, English by
>       adoption, best known for an oratorio published in 1741.'
>       Short pause. 'It was called … Messiah.' Longer pause.
>       'You're bound to know … his handle.'
> Both teams press buzzers.
> *Ted*: 'Who is it?'
> *Female contestant* (shutting eyes): 'Oh God, I used to have it
>       at school … Handel's Water Music.'
> *Ted*: 'So who's the composer?'
> *Female contestant*: 'Chopin.'
> Uproar from audience.
> *Ted* (turning to other team): 'So I can offer it to you.'
> *Male contestant*: 'Beethoven?'
>       MARCUS BERKMANN: *Brain Men* (1999)

**Gamesmanship.** A term popularized by Stephen Potter, whose book *The Theory and Practice of Gamesmanship* (1947) defines the meaning in its subtitle: 'The Art of Winning Games without actually Cheating.'

**Gandalf.** In J.R.R. Tolkien's novels *The* HOBBIT (1937) and *The* LORD OF THE RINGS (1954–5), the tall, good magician who helps Bilbo BAGGINS and FRODO on their quests. In the late 1960s he became something of a cult figure, and a British underground magazine, *Gandalf's Garden*, was named after him.

**G and T.** Gin and tonic, a drink mostly favoured by the better off or those priding themselves on their discernment. *See also* GIN AND IT; GIN AND JAG.

**Gang of Four.** The leaders of a Chinese radical group who unsuccessfully attempted to seize control after the death of Mao Zedong in 1976. The gang, who were imprisoned in 1981, consisted of Jiang Qing (Mao's widow and third wife), Zhang Chungqiao, Wang Hongwen and Yao Wenyuan.

In Britain the name was given to the four MPs who left the Labour Party in 1981 to form the Social Democratic Party (SDP), namely Roy Jenkins (party leader until 1983), David Owen, Shirley Williams and Bill Rodgers.

**Gang show.** A variety show formerly performed annually by

BOY SCOUTS and GIRL GUIDES. The first Boy Scout Gang Show was held in 1932 as the brainchild of the theatrical actor and producer Ralph Reader (1903–82). The last such show ran for a fortnight and closed in October 1974, when Reader retired. He then revealed that that he had worked for British Intelligence in the Second World War and had used Gang Shows as a cover to recruit former Scouts to track down enemy agents. Local gang shows have since been staged intermittently in support of charitable causes.

**Gangsta rap.** A type of RAP MUSIC that evolved in south central Los Angeles in the 1990s. 'Gangsta' is an African American slang word, first appearing in the 1980s, denoting a rebellious individual who refuses to accept the authority of the (white) establishment. The 'gangsta' lifestyle embraces sex, violence, drugs and money. The deliberate misspelling of 'gangsta' ('gangster' in Standard English) reflects the anti-establishment pose. *See also* BLING; HIP-HOP.

**Gang up.** To form a closely knit group, usually in a spirit of antagonism.

**Gannex.** The trademark name of a make of raincoat much favoured by Labour politician Harold Wilson (1916–95), prime minister (1964–70, 1974–6). The maker of Gannex, Joseph Kagan (1915–95), became Lord Kagan in Wilson's controversial 1976 resignation honours list (the LAVENDER LIST) and was subsequently given a prison sentence for evading excise duties.

**Gap year.** A year between secondary and further or higher education, when some school-leavers go out 'into the world' to travel or to find work before resuming their studies. Those who travel often go hitch-hiking or backpacking abroad, especially to exotic or even dangerous places. By the late 1990s some travellers had become something of an unattractive phenomenon, cocooning themselves in a bubble of self-centred hedonism and spurning a genuine voyage of discovery for more ersatz attractions.

Another recent development has been for people to take a gap year after university.

**Garage.** A term applied to various types of modern electronic dance music. The term goes back to the late 1970s and derives from the Paradise Garage nightclub in New York City.

**Garden city.** The garden city movement in England was the inspiration of Sir Ebenezer Howard (1850–1928), who coined a name for his vision in *Tomorrow: A Peaceful Path to Real Reform* (1898), later republished as *Garden Cities of Tomorrow* (1902). His aim was to combine the best aspects of town and country in an environment appropriate for all

members of society, and in practical terms planned a scheme whereby six 'satellite' cities would encircle a central metropolis, each having its own allotments, hospitals and leisure areas. His ambition resulted in the formation of the Garden City Association in 1899 and to the laying out of Letchworth on a green-field site in Hertfordshire in 1903. The new city prospered and others followed, among them Hampstead Garden Suburb in 1907 and Welwyn Garden City in 1919. *See also* NEW TOWN.

**Gardening.** A term used in British espionage for the carrying out of an activity that will force the enemy to send a message in cipher or code, thus giving cryptographers a crib to help their work. A typical ruse in the Second World War was to lay ('plant') mines in an area that the Germans thought they had cleared. When the Germans discovered a new mine, they would report it and deploy minesweepers until the signal 'route cleared' was transmitted. Interception of this single message was enough for cryptographers to isolate the text and discover the daily change in the cipher.

**Gardening leave.** A euphemism for suspension from work on full pay, as if to enable an employee to stay at home and garden. Such suspension is typically made to prevent the employee from seeking work with another employer before the end of their contractual notice period.

**Garden of Remembrance.** A garden commemorating the dead of either or both world wars, typically found in a town that lost many local people thus. Sometimes a whole road or avenue may be so dedicated, and Folkestone, Kent, has a Road of Remembrance planted with rosemary ('That's for remembrance', *Hamlet*, IV.v).

> Across the Garden of Remembrance? No,
> That would be blasphemy and bring bad luck.
>
> JOHN BETJEMAN: *A Few Late Chrysanthemums*, 'Original Sin on the Sussex Coast' (1954)

**Garden suburb.** *See* GARDEN CITY.

**Garfield.** The fat and lazy ginger cartoon cat created by the US illustrator Jim Davis first appeared in a comic strip in 1978 and proved one of the most popular of all cartoon characters over the following decade. Davis gave the cat his grandfather's middle name.

**Garlic Wall.** The satirical name applied by Gibraltarians to the Spanish barrier, which closed the frontier to La Linea in 1969 as a consequence of Spain's claim to the Rock. Spain reopened the frontier in 1985.

**Garnett, Alf.** The working-class Londoner played by Warren Mitchell in the television series *Till Death Us Do Part*

(1964–74). He is an archetypal royalist and racist, and his forthright pronouncements had the unusual effect of simultaneously endearing him to the viewing public, who secretly agreed with some of his views, yet alienating him from them because of his bigoted attitude and his bad language. His appearance in a sequel, *In Sickness and in Health* (1985–6), seemed much less shocking. His US equivalent was Archie BUNKER in *All in the Family* (1971–8), a television series based on *Till Death Us Do Part*.

**Garp.** The mother-fixated hero of John Irving's bestselling novel *The* WORLD ACCORDING TO GARP (1978). He is the offspring of Jenny Fields, a New England heiress, and a brain-damaged airman who can only shout the meaningless exclamation 'Garp!' His initials are T.S., standing for Technical Sergeant. Garp grows up to become the author of a novel called *The World According to Bensenhaver*, while his mother becomes a charismatic feminist leader. Both mother and son are assassinated.

**Garryowen.** In rugby football a very high kick that keeps the ball in the air long enough for the kicker and other members of his team to run up and take it where it falls among the opposition. It is also known as an 'up and under', for obvious reasons, and takes its name from the Irish rugby club in Limerick where it was first deployed. Garryowen is also the name of a 'mangy mongrel' in James Joyce's ULYSSES (1922). The name itself puns on Owen Garry, a legendary 3rd-century king of Leinster.

**Gas guzzler.** A nickname for a large car with a high fuel consumption, especially a US one, which 'guzzles the gasoline'. Cynics claimed that the Second GULF WAR was fought to make the world safe for the gas guzzler.

**Gastarbeiter.** (German, 'guest worker'.) A person who has temporary permission to work in another country, otherwise an immigrant worker. The term arose from those encouraged into West Germany after the Second World War, many of them Turks and Yugoslavians, to assist in its postwar economic revival.

**Gate.** As -*gate*, this is the second element of a noun denoting a scandal associated with the person, animal or place named in the first element. The analogy is with WATERGATE. Irangate was thus a scandal of 1986 following the revelation that members of the Reagan administration had sanctioned arms sales to Iran in exchange for the release of hostages in Lebanon, the proceeds being used to give arms to the CONTRAS in Nicaragua, while Lawsongate was a British scandal of 1988 caused by allegations that the Chancellor of the Exchequer, Nigel Lawson, had deliberately deceived the public about the economy. The format was still in active use in the early 21st century. *See also* CAMILLAGATE; PLAMEGATE; SQUIDGYGATE.

**Gatsby, Jay.** The central character of F. Scott Fitzgerald's classic novel *The* GREAT GATSBY (1925), a wealthy but mysterious man who gives lavish parties but whom nobody really knows. He epitomizes the type of man who has little or no self-esteem and who relies on wealth to enhance his social status.

***Gaudy Night.*** A detective novel (1935) by Dorothy Sayers (1893–1957). The gaudy is an Oxford college reunion for former undergraduates, and the title plays on the following lines from Shakespeare's *Antony and Cleopatra* (III.xi):

> Let's have one other gaudy night: call to me
> All my sad captains; fill our bowls once more;
> Let's mock the midnight bell.

In Sayers's novel, Harriet Vane returns to her college for the occasion and finds herself in a maelstrom of obscene graffiti and poison pen letters. She asks Lord Peter WIMSEY for help. He manages not only to identify the perpetrator but also to overcome Harriet's feminist objections to marriage.

**Gaullist.** A supporter of the French politician Charles de Gaulle (1890–1970) or, more specifically, of any of the various right-wing political parties claiming to represent his political philosophy after his death. Present-day Gaullists follow the RPR or *Rassemblement pour la République* (French, 'Rally for the Republic'), which came into being in 1976.

**Gay.** (Old French *gai*.) Light-hearted; merry; brightly coloured.

> Belinda smiled and all the world was gay.
> ALEXANDER POPE: *The Rape of the Lock*, ii (1714)

French *gai* became associated with effeminate roles in French burlesque theatre, and the English theatre similarly began to apply the word 'gay' to saucy or 'promiscuous' characters. By the 19th century it had taken on specific connotations of prostitution, and it may well be that male prostitutes and their male clients were the vector for the present-day sense 'homosexual' (the earliest reliable printed record of which is from 1933). It underwent an equally violent semantic wrench in the early 21st century, when kids' slang commandeered it (with conscious paradox) for anything 'lame' or 'rubbish'.

**Gay plague.** A (usually homophobic) US nickname for AIDS dating from the early 1980s. When the disease was first identified it seemed to be spreading rapidly and uncontrollably in the United States exclusively among GAY men.

**Gay, proud and angry.** The slogan of the Gay Liberation Front in the early 1970s. It derived from 'Say it loud, we're gay and we're proud', itself based on James Brown's song title from 1968, 'Say It Loud, "I'm Black and I'm Proud"'.

**Gaza Strip.** The strip of territory in Palestine that includes the city of Gaza was administered by Egypt from 1949 until 1967, when it was occupied by Israel (*see* SIX-DAY WAR). It became a self-governing enclave under the PLO–Israel accord of 1994 and elected its own legislative council in 1996. Israeli settlements in the area were abandoned in 2005 on the orders of the Israeli government. *See also* WEST BANK.

**Gazelle Boy.** In 1961 Jean-Claude Armen, travelling by camel through the Spanish Sahara in west Africa, was told by nomad tribesmen of the whereabouts of a young boy living with a herd of gazelles. In due time he sighted the boy and eventually attracted him to close quarters by playing a Berber flute. The boy fed on the same plants as the animals, sometimes eating worms and lizards. On a subsequent expedition in 1963, this time in a Jeep, the speed of the boy when galloping with the herd was established at 50kph (over 30mph).

**Gazumping.** A colloquial term from the early 1970s relating to the property market. It denotes the dubious practice of raising the selling price of a house after agreement has been reached with an intending purchaser. After agreeing a price with the vendor, the purchaser finds that he is gazumped because the vendor has accepted a higher offer from another buyer before contracts have been signed and exchanged. The origin of the word is uncertain. It may derive from a Yiddish verb meaning 'to swindle'. GAZUNDERING is a later variant.

**Gazundering.** Essentially the converse of GAZUMPING, as the practice of lowering the selling price of a house shortly before the exchange of contracts and threatening to withdraw from the sale if the new offer is not accepted. The term dates from the 1980s and substitutes 'under' for the '-ump' of 'gazump', interpreted humorously as 'up'.

**Gazza.** The popular nickname of the English footballer Paul Gascoigne (b.1967), who played for his local team, Newcastle United, before being transferred for £2 million to Tottenham Hotspur in 1988. He gained fame in the semi-final of the 1990 World Cup in Italy, when the referee showed him a YELLOW CARD after a foul against Berthold of West Germany. It was his second card of the tournament and would have prevented his playing in the final if England had won this match. In front of the millions watching on television, Gascoigne wept. The event was a milestone in the maverick player's career and endeared him to many. *See also* G8.

**GCHQ.** The Government Communications Headquarters at Cheltenham, and the centre of Britain's global intelligence-gathering network. After the Second World War it established a partnership with the US National Security Agency and in the 1990s had some 10,000 employees. In 1982 a linguist at GCHQ, Geoffrey Prime, was convicted of handing the secrets of US spy satellites to the USSR and two years later the organization was again in the news when the Conservative government announced that workers there could no longer belong to a trade union. A compensation of £1000 was offered instead to each employee, and within a month 9 out of 10 employees had accepted. A small minority, however, refused to give up membership. Their case was rejected by the European Court of Human Rights in 1987 but the rights of all GCHQ employees to have union representation were restored by the Labour government in 1997. *See also* ROOM 40.

**Gear.** Clothing, equipment and the like, as, for example, sports gear. The word also applies to the combination of toothed wheels and levers, which connect a motor with its work. 'High gear' is the arrangement whereby the driving part moves slowly in relation to the driven part, while 'low gear' is when the driving part moves relatively more quickly than the driven. Colloquially, 'gear' signifies illegal drugs.

**Geddit?** Do you get it? A journalistic device to draw the reader's attention to a pun or joke that might otherwise be missed, or to a particularly 'corny' or unoriginal one.

> Her [Kathy Lette's] paperback titles … have all the subtlety of tabloid bad-pun headlines: Foetal Attraction, Altar Ego. 'Geddit? Geddit?' you can hear her screaming.
> *Sunday Times* (6 June 1999)

**Geek.** A knowledgeable and obsessive enthusiast, or more generally a NERD. The US word originally meant a simpleton or dupe and arose as a variant of 'geck', an English dialect term for a fool. The late 20th-century application is typically to technology.

**Geiger counter.** The German nuclear physicist Hans Geiger (1882–1945) produced the first primitive version of his famous radiation detector in 1908 while working with Ernest Rutherford at Manchester University. His invention was subsequently improved through collaboration with his colleague Walther Müller, and the device is still sometimes known by both men's names.

**G8.** A name for the eight leading industrialized nations: Canada, France, Germany, Italy, Japan, Russia, the United Kingdom and the United States. The full title is Group of Eight. Until Russia joined in 1998 the group was known as the Group of Seven (*see* G7), a label still current for the original seven as a financial entity. Meetings of the group are often attended by anti-globalization protests. *See also* BAND AID.

'G8' was also the new name adopted in October 2004 by former soccer star Paul Gascoigne (a.k.a. GAZZA, b.1967), to mark a break with his troubled past (alcohol abuse, domestic violence, and so on). The new name has nothing to do with the Group of Eight (*see above*), the body representing the world's leading industrial nations, but rather embodies the initial of his surname and the number on the back of his old strip. 'G8 is right for us now,' Gascoigne was reported as saying. 'It sounds a bit like great, or it does with my Geordie accent.'

*See also* ARTIST FORMERLY KNOWN AS PRINCE.

**Gemini.** The name of a series of US spacecraft launched into orbit around the earth between 1964 and 1967, so called from its two-man crew (Latin *gemini*, 'twins'). The programme was chiefly designed to test the ability of astronauts to manoeuvre their spacecraft by manual control and to develop techniques for docking with a target vehicle. Such procedures were vital to the success of the ensuing APOLLO programme.

**Gender bender.** A colloquial term for a person who dresses and behaves in a manner characteristic of the opposite sex, or more generally for an androgyne. The term evolved in the early 1980s in the context of an androgynous fashion among NEW ROMANTIC pop singers such as Boy George.

**Gender gap.** The difference in attitudes or viewpoints that can exist between men and women, especially in the political field.

**Gene pool.** Literally, the stock ('pool') of different genes in an interbreeding population. More generally the term is used for the total of all people in a group or of a kind, especially one of highly rated individuals of varied origin.

> Some of modelling's biggest names have learned the hard way that a beautiful face and big name aren't a passport to Oscar glory … 'Julia Roberts is pretty enough to satisfy most audiences. Hollywood's gene pool just isn't clamouring for a transfusion from the catwalks.'
>
> *heat* (17–23 February 2000)

**General, The.** The English footballer and manager Sir Alf Ramsey (1920–99), under whom England won the World Cup in 1966. Cool, taciturn and somewhat superior in manner, and often criticized for a lack of tactical imagination, Ramsey's achievement earned him a knighthood and the enduring gratitude of a hitherto sceptical nation.

**General Belgrano.** An old Argentinian cruiser named after Manuel Belgrano (1770–1820), a military leader in the Argentinian war of independence against the Spanish. The ship had previously belonged to the US navy, under the name USS *Phoenix*, and had survived the Japanese attack on PEARL HARBOR. But on 2 May 1982 it was sunk with the loss of 362 lives by a British submarine, HMS *Conqueror*, in what turned out to be the most controversial incident in the FALKLANDS WAR. Margaret Thatcher (*see* IRON LADY) and her ministers told the Commons that it had been on course for the Falklands at the time, but it turned out that it had been steaming in the opposite direction for some eight hours. The Labour MP Tam Dalyell (b.1932) campaigned to expose the truth, believing the sinking was a deliberate attempt to scupper the peace plan proposed by Peru; like many, he believed that Thatcher was determined to fight a war to restore her electoral fortunes (*see* FALKLANDS FACTOR). Dalyell's case was strengthened in 1984 when a senior civil servant, Clive Ponting, passed documents to his member of parliament suggesting there had indeed been a cover-up. Ponting was charged under the Official Secrets Act, but in March 1985 was acquitted by the jury against the direction of the judge, establishing the principle that the interests of the state are not necessarily identical with the interests of the government.

**General Strike.** Britain's first and only nationwide strike was called by the Trades Union Congress at midnight on 3 May 1926 in support of the miners' union, which was resisting the mine-owners' demands for longer hours and lower wages (*see* NOT A PENNY OFF THE PAY, NOT A SECOND OFF THE DAY). Stanley Baldwin's Conservative government used troops, volunteers and special constables to maintain food supplies and basic services, and it held a monopoly on the media, including BBC Radio and a specially produced newspaper, *The British Gazette*, edited by Winston Churchill. The TUC ended the strike after nine days, leaving the miners, who felt betrayed by them, unsuccessfully continuing the strike until 12 November. The Trades Disputes Act of 1927 made general strikes illegal.

**General Synod.** The governing body of the Church of England, established in 1969 to achieve a more effective system of control, to give a greater role to the laity, and to avoid the delays caused by the previous diarchy of the Convocations and Church Assembly. Members of its three houses, bishops, clergy and laity, meet twice a year to discuss doctrine and worship. It also has a pastoral role and speaks for the Church on political, social and moral issues. In 1995 a synod committee urged the abandonment of the phrase 'in sin'. Members voted to 'take note' of the request but emphasized the Christian ideal of marriage.

**Generation Game, The.** A popular GAME SHOW screened from 1971 to 1981 and hosted first by a cheery Bruce Forsyth, then by a CAMP Larry Grayson. Two pairs of contestants, related to each other and of different generations, performed 'arts and crafts' feats such as throwing pots and icing cakes after watching an expert. Predictably this rapidly degenerated into farce. The winning couple were then placed beside a 'conveyor belt' and challenged to memorize the GOODIES that passed before them. The items recalled could be taken home as prizes. The show was relaunched in 1990 and was hosted again by Bruce Forsyth and from 1995 to 2002 by the comedian Jim Davidson.

**Generation gap.** The years that separate an older generation from a younger, especially as discernible in a difference of outlook, values and attitudes. In some instances the disparity can lead to a lack of understanding or empathy between the two.

**Generation X.** The generation born after that of the baby boomers (*see* BABY BOOM), i.e. in the 1960s and 1970s, distinguished by their disaffection and general lack of direction. The name comes from a sociological survey of 1964 by Charles Hamblett and Jane Deverson, whose front cover blurb ran: 'What's behind the rebellious anger of Britain's untamed youth? Here – in their own words – is how they really feel about Drugs, Drink, God, Sex, Class, Colour and Kicks.' The theme was continued in a book by the Canadian writer Douglas Coupland, *Generation X: Tales for an Accelerated Culture* (1991), in which he coined the term MCJOB to describe 'low-pay, low-prestige, low-benefit, no-future jobs in the service industry'.

> They are Generation X – resigned to insecure working and wanting a flexible lifestyle, which they see as incompatible with homebuying.
> *The Observer* (10 May 1998)

The formula was later satirically amended to 'Generation XL', alluding to the late 20th-century boom in overweight children and young adults ('XL' in clothing-size nomenclature being 'extra large').

The term Generation Y has subsequently been adopted to refer to the generation born in the last two decades of the 20th century, and following them are so-called 'Millennials'.

**Genetically modified.** Of foodstuffs, containing or consisting of genetically altered plant or animal material. The stocking of supermarket shelves with genetically modified (GM) food products in the late 1990s caused widespread concern among consumer organizations and consumers themselves, since the latter had been largely kept uninformed about the ethical and health implications of such products. Moreover, many foods made with GM organisms were initially not even labelled as such. Members of environmental groups such as FRIENDS OF THE EARTH and GREENPEACE protested by destroying fields where GM crops were being experimentally grown, and the public became increasingly confused and concerned about the issue, despite certain reassurances from politicians and food manufacturers.

**Genetic fingerprinting.** The pattern of DNA unique to each person that can be analyzed in a sample of blood, saliva or tissue, and that is used as a means of identification as conventional fingerprints are.

**Genevieve.** A good-natured film (1953) written by William Rose and directed by Henry Cornelius about two rival couples who enter their classic cars in the annual BRIGHTON RUN rally. Genevieve was the name of the car (a 1904 Darracq) owned by Alan and Wendy McKim (played by John Gregson and Dinah Sheridan). Their rivals, Ambrose Claverhouse and Rosalind Peters, were played by Kenneth More and Kay Kendall.

**Genocide.** A word invented by the US jurist Raphael Lemkin, and used in the drafting of the official indictment of NAZI war criminals in 1945. It is a combination of Greek *genos*, 'race', and Latin *caedere*, 'to kill'. It is defined as acts intended to destroy, in whole or in part, national, ethnic, racial or religious groups, and in 1948 was declared by the General Assembly of the UNITED NATIONS to be a crime in international law. *See also* HOLOCAUST.

**Gentle giant.** A nickname for a tall and strong but kindly person that is first recorded in the 19th century but that came into its own in the 20th. A policeman killed by an IRA bomb outside Harrods store in London in 1983 was so dubbed by the media, and the name has been accorded to various sportsmen, among them the footballer John Charles (1931–2004), centre-half for Leeds United, who helped Wales to the World Cup finals, the US track and field champion James R. Mason (b.1945) and the world heavyweight champion Larry Holmes (b.1950). In the film *The Gentle Giant* (1967) a small boy in Florida befriends a bear that later saves the life of the boy's hitherto disapproving father. The alliteration of the phrase makes it memorable and thus apt for advertising purposes, as in the following jingle promoting Pickfords Removals in the 1930s:

A note from you, a call from us,
The date is fixed, with no worry or fuss,
A Pickfords van, a gentle giant,
The work is done – a satisfied client.

**Gentleman friend.** A genteelly euphemistic and now passé term for a woman's regular male companion.

*Margy*: I'm sick of this town and everything that goes with it. Damn him.
*Gregg*: Oh, the gentleman friend, eh?
*Margy*: Gentleman, hell. You're the first one to ever call him that.
MAE WEST: *Sex* (1926)

**Gentleman's agreement.** An arrangement or understanding that is based on trust or honour rather than a legal obligation. The *Oxford English Dictionary* dates the earliest occurrence of the term as 1929 and claims that it is of US origin.

**Gentlemen Prefer Blondes.** A novel (1925) by Anita Loos (1888–1981), subtitled 'The Diary of a Professional Lady'. Breathless, ungrammatical entries record the heroine's picaresque search for a broader mind, a living and, she hopes, a rich husband. It is said that some of its popularity was due to the fact that young women took it seriously as a how-to-get-rich handbook. The success of the musical comedy (1949) based on the novel made both the title and its best-known number, 'Diamonds are a Girl's Best Friend', into popular catchphrases. The updated film (1953), directed by Howard Hawks, starred Jane Russell and Marilyn MONROE. In 1974 Carol Channing, who had starred as Lorelei LEE when the musical first opened, appeared in a revival of the show entitled *Lorelei*, advertised under the slogan 'Gentlemen Still Prefer Blondes'.

**Gentrification.** The process by which a working-class or decayed urban area, especially in the inner city, is made middle-class. The term has been ascribed to the Marxist urban geographer Ruth Glass, who used it in an article of 1964, but it did not become generally familiar until the early 1970s, when the professional middle classes began to buy homes in traditional working-class city areas. Their aim was to restore and renovate the properties to suit their tastes, and this in turn led to a change in character of the area as a whole, so that shops went upmarket and pubs and cafés became bistros or wine bars.

**Geoff Who?** A nickname of the Labour politician Geoff Hoon (b.1953), who, as secretary of state for defence from 1999 failed to attract much notice until the run-up to the Iraq War in 2003. Subsequently, because of perceived mistakes and errors of judgement, he became known as Hoon the Goon or Buff-Hoon. After the 2005 general election Hoon was demoted to the suitably anonymous post of Leader of the House until being reshuffled out of the cabinet as minister for Europe in May 2006. (To rub it in, he was still allowed to attend cabinet meetings but not allowed to vote on any decisions.)

**Geography.** One of many euphemisms for the lavatory. One may have to explore a building in order to find it. A considerate hostess in a private house would thus tell guests: 'Let me show you the geography.' The now obsolescent (though not obsolete) expression dates from the 1920s.

**Geometry of Fear.** A term coined by the art critic Herbert Read to describe the angst-ridden look of the work of a group of eight British sculptors who exhibited together at the 1952 Venice Biennale. They were Robert Adams (1917–84), Kenneth Armitage (1916–2002), Reg Butler (1913–81), Lynn Chadwick (1914–2003), Geoffrey Clarke (b.1924), Bernard Meadows (1915–2005), Eduardo Paolozzi (1924–2005) and William Turnbull (b.1922). Many of them were influenced by the 'Existentialist' sculptures of Giacometti and Richier, which seemed to encapsulate the anguish and bewilderment of the postwar generation.

**George Cross** and **George Medal.** The George Cross is second only to the Victoria Cross. It consists of a plain silver cross with a medallion showing St George and the Dragon in the centre. The words 'For Gallantry' appear round the medallion, and in the angle of each limb of the cross is the royal cipher. It hangs from a dark blue ribbon. The George Cross was instituted by George VI in 1940 for acts of conspicuous heroism, primarily by civilians. It is awarded to service personnel only for acts of heroism not covered by existing military honours. There have been over 150 recipients, including two collective awards: the island of Malta (*see* GEORGE CROSS ISLAND), and the ROYAL ULSTER CONSTABULARY, which controversially received the medal in 2000.

The George Medal (red ribbon with five narrow blue stripes) is awarded for similar but somewhat less outstanding acts of bravery.

*See also* CARVE HER NAME WITH PRIDE.

**George Cross Island.** Malta is so called from the award of the GEORGE CROSS to the island by George VI in April 1942 in recognition of the steadfastness and fortitude of its people while under siege in the Second World War. It had suffered constant aerial attacks from Italian and German bombers. The George Cross is shown on Malta's flag.

**George Medal.** *See* GEORGE CROSS.

**Georgia Mafia.** A disparaging label applied to the group of advisers that Democratic President Jimmy Carter (b.1924) assembled around him when he went to the White House in 1977. Most of the group had worked with him while he was governor of Georgia (1970–4), and their inexperience in national politics led to considerable problems.

**Georgian Poetry.** This was originally the title of a series of five poetry anthologies published between 1912 and 1922 and named after George V, whose reign began in 1910. The term has since been applied more generally to rural and stylistically conventional verse of the kind the original books mostly contained. Major poets so categorized include W.H. Davies, Walter de la Mare, John Masefield, Ralph Hodgson, Edward Thomas, James Stephens, Andrew Young, Siegfried Sassoon, Rupert Brooke, Wilfred Owen, Robert Graves, Edmund Blunden and D.H. Lawrence. While many of these poets produced works of great merit, much verse of the genre was characterized by pedestrian rhythms, rural sentimentality and imaginative banality, so that 'Georgian' has gained something of a pejorative sense in the modern critical armoury. *See also* WAR POETS.

**Georgia Peach.** A nickname for the outstanding US baseball player Ty Cobb (1886–1961), who was born in Georgia. He played for the Detroit Tigers and the Philadelphia Athletes. The name alludes to his popularity and is said to have been coined by a Detroit sportswriter.

**German racket, A.** The description of the European Union by the Conservative secretary of trade and industry Nicholas Ridley (1929–93), in an interview published in *The Spectator*, 14 July 1990.

> This is all a German racket designed to take over the whole of Europe. It has to be thwarted. This rushed take-over by the Germans on the worst possible basis, with the French behaving like poodles to the Germans, is absolutely intolerable.

Ridley, who had thought his remarks were off the record, was obliged to resign.

**Geronimo!** This cry of exultation, first used by US paratroops in the Second World War, is the name of the Apache Indian chief Geronimo (1829–1900), who warred against the Mexicans when they killed his mother, wife and three children. His Indian name was Goyahkla, 'One Who Yawns'.

**Gerson diet.** A vegetarian diet of fresh fruit and raw food, used successfully in the 1920s by the German physician Max Gerson (1881–1959) to treat patients with chronic conditions such as tuberculosis, arthritis and vascular disease, and later also cancer. It is based on the diet of apes and was first applied by Gerson to himself to cure the severe migraine from which he suffered in his youth.

**Gert and Daisy.** The pair of Cockney gossips were created as a comic duo for BBC Radio in the 1930s by the sisters Elsie (*c.*1895–1990) and Doris (*c.*1904–78) Waters. They became national institutions in the Second World War to the extent that Lord HAW-HAW, in a broadcast from Germany, declared: 'the good folk of Grimsby should not expect Gert and Daisy to protect them from attacks by the Luftwaffe.'

**Gertcha!** GET AWAY WITH YOU! This colloquial form of the phrase, dating from the 1930s, was adopted from a popular song by the Cockney trio Chas and Dave for a television commercial for Courage Best Bitter in the early 1980s. The scene was set in an East End pub, and the drinkers shouted the word out during breaks in the music.

**Gestalt therapy.** A psychotherapeutic approach developed *c.*1950 in New York by Fritz Perls (1893–1970) and his wife Laura. It focuses on insights into so-called gestalts in patients and their relations to the world, and frequently uses role-playing in order to help resolve past conflicts.

The German word *Gestalt* literally means the way a thing has been *gestellt*, i.e. 'placed', and in English use the term was adopted by psychologists to mean an organized whole whose attributes are not deducible from analysis of the parts in isolation.

**Gestapo.** A name shortened from German *Geheime Staatspolizei*, 'secret state police', which acquired sinister fame in NAZI Germany after 1933. It was formed by Hermann Goering (1893–1946) and later controlled by Heinrich Himmler (1900–45), and it was responsible for terrorizing both the Germans and the peoples of occupied territories. It was declared a criminal organization by the Nuremberg Tribunal in 1946.

**Get a guernsey.** In colloquial Australian English, to gain selection for a team or, more broadly, to win approval or approbation. A guernsey in Australia is a football jersey, especially one of the sleeveless sort worn by Australian Rules footballers. The term originally denoted a thick knitted jumper of a type developed on the Channel Island of Guernsey, traditionally worn by sailors.

**Get a handle on.** *See* HAVE A HANDLE ON.

**Get a life!** An adjurement to someone to start living a more purposeful existence, the implication being that their present life is empty or boring or work-obsessed. *See also* GET REAL!

**Get away with you!** You can't be serious! You're having me on! Don't make me laugh! *See also* GERTCHA!

**Get a wiggle on.** To get a move on; to hurry up; to 'look lively'. An expression of US military origin dating from the turn of the 20th century.

**Get cracking.** To get started; to begin work speedily and efficiently. The phrase dates from the 1930s and alludes to cracking one's whip when mustering cattle or geeing-up a team of horses.

**Get in on the act.** To involve oneself in an enterprise or activity, especially one that promises kudos or reward.

**Get it on.** To have sex (together), especially for the first time or after a long period of time. An expression of US origin dating from the 1960s. *See also* HAVE IT OFF WITH SOMEONE.

> Whoo-ooh I'm askin' you, baby
> To get it on with me.
> MARVIN GAYE: 'Let's Get It On' (1973)

> He's a slob. She's dead. Can Mark Ruffalo and Reese Witherspoon still get it on?
> *The Guardian* (30 December 2005)

**Get knotted!** Go away! An expression of contemptuous rejection, perhaps alluding to a sexual liaison.

**Get lost!** Go away! Clear out! A term dating from the 1940s.

> Rover says that all their press demonstrators are booked out until February. And no more reservations are being taken. Roughly translated, this means, 'Get lost, sunshine'.
> *Sunday Times* (5 December 1999)

**Get nowhere fast.** To make no headway after making every effort to do so. The phrase dates from the 1950s.

**Get off** or **out at Gateshead.** To practice coitus interruptus (as a form of birth control). The basis of the euphemistic metaphor is leaving a train just before it arrives at a terminus (Gateshead is the station immediately before Newcastle upon Tyne), and the leading roles have been played by several other penultimate locations in both Britain and Australia, including Clapham Junction (the last major station before London Victoria and London Waterloo), Edge Hill (before Liverpool Lime Street), Haymarket (before Edinburgh Waverley, 'coming' from Glasgow), Paisley (before Glasgow on the West Coast line) and Redfern (before the Sydney terminus). It is first recorded in the 1970s, but may well have been in use long before then.

**Get off one's bike.** In Australian and New Zealand slang, to lose one's temper. The expression dates from the 1930s.

**Get off the ground.** To make a successful start. The allusion is to the take-off of an aircraft or the launch of a spacecraft. The expression dates from the 1960s.

**Get one's act together.** To organize or reorganize one's life or business. The phrase implies an under-rehearsed or poorly performed part in a play that has been worked on until right. The expression dates from the 1960s and originated in African American slang.

**Get one's arse into gear.** To stop being indecisive or lazy and start putting some effort or commitment into what one is doing; to start doing something useful and positive; to bestir oneself. The slang usage dates from the 1950s. In New Zealand English it is euphemistically abbreviated to 'get one's a into g'.

**Get one's cookies off.** *See* GET ONE'S ROCKS OFF.

**Get** or **have (all) one's ducks in row.** To put or have all one's affairs in order, prepared and ready to go. The expression, which seems to have originated in the US in the 1930s, may allude to a mother duck lining her ducklings up in an orderly queue.

**Get one's feet under the table.** To become established in a job. The image is of sitting down to work at a desk and settling oneself there.

> This is the time of the year when foreign diplomats new to London are getting their feet under the table.
> *The Times* (9 October 1999)

**Get one's finger out.** *See* PULL ONE'S FINGER OUT.

**Get one's hands dirty.** To do manual or menial work, especially when normally one is, or regards oneself to be, above such basic labour.

**Get one's head down.** To sleep; to concentrate on the task in hand. In the former case one lays one's head on the pillow; in the latter one lowers one's head over one's task.

**Get one's head round something.** To puzzle it out; to make sense of it. The expression is usually found in the negative.

**Get one's jollies.** To have fun; to get a thrill. 'Jollies' is probably a shortening of 'jollifications'.

**Get one's kit off.** To remove one's clothes, especially as part of a stage or film performance or as an artistic model. The expression dates from the 1970s and partly suggests a sports player's undressing at the end of a game in order to wash or shower and then re-dress in ordinary clothes. Compare the word 'strip' in its dual sense of 'act of undressing' and 'sports player's identifying outfit'.

**Get one's knickers in a twist.** To become unduly concerned or excited about a matter, especially when frustrated. The allusion is to a woman who misaligns the named garment when hastily dressing (or re-dressing). The expression dates from the 1960s.

**Get one's leg over.** To achieve sexual intercourse. The allusion is to the position adopted. The expression dates from the 1970s, although 'to lift one's leg over' in the sense of to seduce is found in the 18th century.

**Get one's rocks off.** To experience an orgasm, 'rocks' here being the testicles, as a pun on medieval 'stones' in this sense. The vulgar expression, which originated in US slang, has gained a wider and more generally acceptable meaning 'to enjoy oneself', 'to obtain satisfaction'. Both senses date from the 1940s. Alternative formulations include 'get one's nuts off' and the euphemistic 'get one's cookies off'. The ROLLING STONES had a song 'Rocks Off'.

**Get** or **sink one's teeth into something.** To become fully engaged or engrossed in it. The analogy is with an animal biting deeply and vigorously into food. The expression dates from the early years of the 20th century.

**Get on your bike.** An exhortation thought to sum up the Thatcherite 1980s, in which self-help was regarded as the highest virtue. The phrase derives from a speech given by Norman (now Lord) Tebbit (the CHINGFORD SKINHEAD) to the Conservative Party Conference on 15 October 1981.

> I grew up in the Thirties with our unemployed father. He did not riot, he got on his bike and looked for work.

Since Mrs Thatcher had led her party to electoral victory in 1979, British manufacturing industry had gone into an apparently terminal decline, unemployment had risen to 3 million, and there had been riots in several of Britain's inner cities.

**Get out more.** To gain greater experience of life and people; to emerge from one's cocooned existence and see the REAL WORLD. The expression is mainly used of a naive or narrow-minded person, or someone so involved in their own interests that they miss the wider picture of things.

> She [television cook Delia Smith] offers up a veritable paean of praise and love to the cauliflower, the dismembering of whose florets is declared to be 'fun'. She should really get out more.
>
> *The Times* (7 February 2000)

**Get out of Dodge.** In US slang, to leave with all speed. The expression, which is typically elaborated to 'get the hell (*or* fuck) out of Dodge', alludes to Dodge City, Kansas, scene of innumerable Wild West stories and films in which the baddies are compelled to make a rapid exit from town by the forces of law and order.

**Get out of someone's face.** To stop pestering them. The expression dates from the 1960s and as may be expected is mostly found in the imperative. *See also* IN YOUR FACE.

> 'People would ask me, "Is your name Mena [Suvari] because you're mean?" What should I say? "Yeah, I'm a bitch. Now get out of my face!"'
>
> *heat* (16 December 1999–5 January 2000)

**Get out of third gear.** To get going properly; to move towards one's peak. The third gear is the one the driver of a motor vehicle engages for manoeuvring before changing up to top gear.

**Get real!** Be realistic! An admonition of US campus origin current from the 1970s. *See also* GET A LIFE!

**Get someone's goat.** To irritate them. A somewhat fanciful story explains the phrase as an allusion to the goat that was traditionally stabled with a racehorse as its 'comforter'. To nobble the horse the trick was to creep into its stable the night before a big race and steal the goat. It would then be restless all night and off form the following day. But one can irritate a person by constantly butting in, and this may be a more likely reference. The expression is first recorded (in the US) in 1908.

**Get the message.** To understand; to take a hint. A phrase dating from the 1950s and originating in jazz jargon.

**Get the show on the road.** To get going; to get started. The expression is of US origin and refers to the times at the turn of the century when companies presenting plays, vaude-villes, circuses and the like toured all over the country.

**Get under someone's neck.** In colloquial Australian English, to get the better of someone, to gain an advantage over them. The metaphor, first recorded in 1953, probably comes from horse racing.

**Get up someone's nose.** To irritate or annoy them. The allusion is to a bad smell, which offends the nostrils. The expression dates from the 1950s.

**Get weaving.** To begin an action; to GET CRACKING. The expression dates from the Second World War and derives from RAF slang. An aircraft was said to 'weave' when flying a devious course, especially to avoid or escape danger.

**GHB.** *See* DATE RAPE.

**Gherkin, The.** The popular nickname given to a glass-clad tower office block shaped like a portly bullet, erected in St Mary Axe in the City of London in 2002–3 to the design of Norman Foster on a site previously occupied by the Baltic Exchange. It was the first building in the Square Mile to break the 600ft (200m) barrier since Tower 42 (the NatWest Tower) in 1979. Its official name is the 30 St Mary Axe Tower, but it is more generally known as the Swiss Re Tower (after the Swiss Reinsurance Company, which commissioned it). Its nickname is a tribute to the extent to which Londoners took its revolutionary appearance to their hearts (fortunately the tower does not curl to one side like a real gherkin).

**Ghetto-blaster.** A large portable radio, especially one used to play loud pop music. The term dates from the early 1980s and alludes to the prevalence of such radios in under-privileged African American precincts, or 'ghettos', of US cities.

**Ghost in the machine.** The mind ('ghost') as distinct from the body ('machine'). The expression was coined by the philosopher Gilbert Ryle in *The Concept of Mind* (1949). The phrase is sometimes used in a derogatory sense by critics of the dualism exemplified by Descartes' distinction between the material body and the immaterial soul.

**Ghost town.** A town that once prospered but that is now in decay with few inhabitants.

**Ghost train.** A train seen running at a time when none is scheduled, especially silently or after dark. Arnold Ridley's comedy thriller *The Ghost Train* (1925) was one of the most successful ever written, and formed the basis of many films, the best being *Oh Mr Porter* (1937). At a fun fair a ghost train is a miniature train that takes riders on a round trip of ghoulish sights, sounds and special effects. In railway jargon a ghost train is a night-running de-icing train on electric railways equipped with conductor rails.

**Ghost turd.** A US term for a ball of dust and fluff, as found in an undusted area of the home; a DUST BUNNY. It dates from at least the mid-1960s.

**Ghost writer.** An anonymous author who writes speeches, articles or books, and especially autobiographies, for which another, better known person gets the credit. The term dates from the 1920s.

**Ghote, Inspector.** The Indian police detective created by H.R.F. Keating for his novel *The Perfect Murder* (1964). He lives and works in Bombay and is amiable and unassuming, but he always cracks his cases. Of his subsequent involvements *Inspector Ghote Trusts the Heart* (1972) is reckoned to be one of the best.

**GI.** During the Second World War US enlisted men called themselves GIs, from an abbreviation of Government (or General) Issue. After becoming accustomed to GI shirts, GI blankets and other army issues, the soldiers began to apply the term to themselves.

**Giant rat of Sumatra.** An enigmatic beast known only through a single reference to it by the great fictional detective Sherlock Holmes, who had dealings with it at some point in his career. It is mentioned (in passing, and with deliberate flesh-creeping intent) in 'The Adventure of the Sussex Vampire' (1924), in connection with the *Matilda Briggs*, 'a ship which is associated with the giant rat of Sumatra, a story for which the world is not yet prepared'. We hear no more of the rodent, so its precise nature and history are left to our imagination in perpetuity. The Firesign Theatre, a US comedy troupe, entitled their 1974 album of pun-filled post-psychedelic pastiche *The Tale of the Giant Rat of Sumatra*.

**GI bride.** A woman who married a US serviceman (GI) after meeting him when he was stationed in England (or some other country) in the Second World War. An estimated 75,000 women became GI brides, and a third of all births in the war were illegitimate.

**Gibson Girl.** A representation of female beauty characteristic of its era depicted by Charles Dana Gibson (1867–1944) in several series of black-and-white drawings dating from 1886 and continuing well into the 20th century. His picture books with drawings of the modern and staunchly US girl enjoyed an enormous vogue. One of the best known was *The Education of Mr Pip* (1899), chronicling the adventures in high society of the wealthy and amiable Mr Pip, his socially ambitious wife and his Gibson Girl daughter, and *A Widow and Her Friends* (1901), following the emergence from mourning of a beautiful young widow and the antics of her six suitors. The Gibson Girl was portrayed in various poses and occupations, her individuality accentuated by the sweeping skirts and large hats of the period. She was based on his wife Irene (née Langhorne), one of whose sisters was Nancy, Viscountess Astor (1879–1964).

**Gibson guitar.** The US guitarist Les Paul (b.1915) took his new solid-bodied electric guitar to the famous Gibson company in 1947. Nicknamed 'the log', it was an adaptation of Adolph Rickenbacker's version of 1931, known as 'the frying pan'. The Gibson was the required instrument for rock 'n' roll guitarists from the late 1960s.

**Gideons.** The organization of Christian business and professional men, familiar to the traveller and tourist from the Bibles they place in hotel rooms, was founded in Janesville, Wisconsin, in 1899. It began placing Bibles in 1908, and during the Second World War supplied the US armed forces with service Testaments. The work of the Gideons is supported by voluntary donations, and their emblem is a two-handled pitcher and torch, in memory of the biblical Gideon's victory over the Midianites (Judges 7:15–23).

**Gidget.** The nickname of Francine Lawrence, a sporty teenage 'California girl' who is the main character in several novels by Frederick Kohner, beginning with *Gidget* (1957). She appeared in a series of films based on the books from 1959, played in turn by Sandra Dee, Deborah Walley and Cindy Carol. In US slang, a gidget is a lithe, pert young woman.

**GIFT.** The semi-punning acronym of *gamete intra-fallopian transfer*, as a technique developed in the 1980s for facilitating human conception. The procedure involves transferring sperm and ova directly into the Fallopian tubes of the mother-to-be.

**Giggle water.** A humorous term for alcoholic drink. It tends to be applied particularly to champagne, well known for its quick-acting hilarity-producing effect. Alternative formulations are 'giggle juice' and 'giggle soup', and in the same vein marijuana has been nicknamed 'giggle weed'.

**Gigi.** The pet name of Gilberte, the young Parisian girl who is the heroine of Colette's novel titled after her (1944), in which she is trained by her aunt to become a courtesan. The story inspired a film of 1948, in which Gigi is played by Danièle Delorme, and a successful screen musical by Frederick Loewe and Alan Jay Lerner (1958), with Leslie Caron in the lead role. The later film has the popular numbers 'Thank heaven for little girls' and 'I remember it well'.

**Gig-line.** In US army slang, a straight vertical line formed by the buttons on one's shirt or jacket, one's belt-buckle and the flies of one's trousers, de rigueur when on parade. Any deviations from the straight may be punished by 'gigging' (putting the offender on a charge).

**GIGO.** In computer jargon, the acronym, pronounced to rhyme with 'my go', of 'garbage in, garbage out'. The sense is that faulty input will always result in faulty output.

**GI Jane.** During the Second World War and afterwards, a female member of the US army. The name was modelled on GI JOE.

**GI Joe.** A Second World War nickname for a US infantryman. It was the name of the soldier in Lieutenant Dave Breger's comic strip for *Yank*, the US Army magazine, and first appeared in the issue of 17 June 1942 (although the term itself is first recorded in another US military publication, *Our Army*, 1935). *See also* ACTION MAN.

**Gilded cage.** A luxurious but restrictive environment. The expression dates from the turn of the 20th century. It was popularized and possibly introduced to the language by Arthur J. Lamb and Harry von Tilzer's song 'A Bird in a Gilded Cage' (1899) about a young girl who marries for wealth instead of love and pays for the luxury with a life of regret.

**Giles.** The pen-name of the cartoonist Carl Ronald Giles (1916–95), whose work appeared regularly in the *Daily Express* and *Sunday Express* from 1943 until his death. His wartime cartoons, often featuring Hitler and Mussolini, were crowded with detail and incident, but he is most closely associated with the large and chaotic 'Giles Family', dominated by Grandma, a squat figure with a bespectacled, pugnacious face only partly visible between her black coat and hat.

**Gill Sans.** This elegant sans serif typeface was created in 1928 for the Monotype Company (later Monotype Corporation) by the sculptor Eric Gill (1882–1940). It was commissioned by the company's consultant, Stanley Morison, as was Gill's subsequent typeface, Perpetua, created in 1930. Both are classics of 20th-century typography. Morison himself designed the typeface now known as Times New Roman for *The Times*, where it first appeared on 3 October 1932.

**Gimmick.** The first use of this word in US slang in the 1920s was to describe some device by which a conjurer or fairground showman worked his trick. In later usage it applied to some distinctive quirk or trick associated with a film or radio star, then to any device. The origin of the word is uncertain. It may be an alteration of 'gimcrack' or even a form of 'magic'.

**Gin and it.** Gin and Italian (bitter-sweet) vermouth, in the middle years of the 20th century a drink mostly favoured by the aspiring or actual upper-middle classes. Slightly higher in the social scale was a gin and French (dry) vermouth. *See also* G AND T.

**Gin and Jag.** Gin and a Jaguar car, two of the desireable perquisites of the upper-middle class and an encapsulation of their lifestyle. The 'gin' is likely to be G AND T or GIN AND IT. The jingle dates from the 1960s.

> The 'gin and Jag' brigade has mobilized against Alan Shearer … After snobbish mutterings in the clubhouse, he has been stuck on a waiting list stretching well into the next millennium.
>
> *The Times* (14 June 1999)

**Ginger Man, The.** The first novel (1955; 1963 unexpurgated) by J.P. Donleavy (b.1926). Sebastian Dangerfield, both a redhead and a man of action ('ginger'), rollicks and frolics drunkenly through Dublin and its society. The play (1959), adapted by the author, was withdrawn from the Dublin stage because of clerical opposition.

**Ginnie Mae.** A US nickname for the Government National Mortgage Association, based on the earlier FANNIE MAE. *See also* FREDDIE MAC.

**Gioconda smile.** An enigmatic smile, as that of the *Mona Lisa*. Leonardo da Vinci's famous painting (1503–6), also known as *La Gioconda* or *La Joconde*, is a portrait of the wife of Francesco del Giocondo. The expression was popularized or even coined by Aldous Huxley, who has a short story, 'The Gioconda Smile', in *Mortal Coils* (1922).

**Gipper.** A regular nickname for Ronald Reagan (1911–2004), film actor and 40th president of the United States (1981–9). The reference is to the part of George Gipp that he played in the film *Knute Rockne – All American* (1940). Gipp himself (1895–1920) had been an American football star coached by Knute Rockne when at Notre Dame University, Indiana. Following Gipp's early death from a mysterious illness, a press story circulated that on his deathbed he had urged his team to 'win one for the Gipper', a phrase that subsequently became legendary. It was famously repeated by Ronald Reagan in the film and subsequently exploited by him at political rallies. *See also* DUTCH; GREAT COMMUNICATOR.

**Gippy tummy.** *See* MONTEZUMA'S REVENGE.

**Gipsy Moth IV.** The 16.75-m (55-foot) yacht in which Francis (subsequently Sir Francis) Chichester (1901–72) made the first solo sailing voyage around the world, making only one stop. The voyage, in 1966–7, took a total of 226 actual sailing days. The gipsy moth (*Lymantria dispar*) is a species of European moth, which also gave its name to a biplane, popular as a trainer. It was in such a plane that Chichester had made a solo flight from Britain to Australia in 1929. In 1960 Chichester won the first transatlantic solo yacht race in *Gypsy Moth III*.

**Girl Friday.** A dated term for a female 'clerk of all work' or personal assistant. The term is a 1950s adman's alteration of Man Friday, as the name of the young savage found on a Friday by the hero of Daniel Defoe's *Robinson Crusoe* (1719) and kept as his servant and companion on the desert island. The name is appropriate for someone whose working week ends (and weekend begins) on this day. The term was popularized by the film *His Girl Friday* (1940) starring Cary Grant and Rosalind Russell, but fell from favour in the 1980s as being sexist.

Person Friday required for this busy Interior Design and Architectural Practice.

*The Times* (advertisement) (26 October 1994)

**Girl Guides.** The female counterpart to the BOY SCOUTS, organized in 1910 by Lord Baden-Powell (1857–1941) and his sister Agnes (1858–1945). Their training and organization is much the same as the Scouts and is based on similar promises and laws. The three sections of the movement, since 2002 called Girlguiding UK rather than Girl Guides, were originally BROWNIES, Guides and Rangers, but the names and groupings have now been modified to: Rainbow Guides (aged 5–7), Brownie Guides (7 and over), Guides (10–14), and a Senior Section that provides a wide range of opportunities for yourng people aged 14–26.

In the United States they are called Girl Scouts (formed 1912), with names and age groups: Daisies (5–6), Brownies (6–8), Juniors (8–11), and Girl Scouts (11–17).

**Girl meets boy.** The paradigm of a conventional love match, fictional or in fact.

**Girl next door.** A young woman, especially one known from childhood, regarded as a pleasant and decent but in the main conventional marriage partner.

**Girl of the Golden West, The.** A play (1905) by David Belasco. It formed the basis of Puccini's opera *La Fanciulla del West*, which was first performed in New York in 1910 with a libretto by Carlo Zangarini and Guelfo Civinini. The story is set in California in 1850 at the time of the first big gold rush. Minnie, keeper of the Polka Saloon and a friend of the gold miners, falls in love with the stranger Dick Johnson, who turns out to be the wanted bandit Ramírez. When Dick is wounded by the guns of a posse she hides him in her cabin, but the sheriff, Jack Rance, discovers him there. Minnie and Rance agree to a game of poker to decide Johnson's fate, and she wins by cheating. Rance leaves, but Johnson is captured by the miners and is about to be hanged. Minnie begs them to spare the man she loves and they release him. Minnie and Dick ride off into the sunset. The Italian opera title lacks the 'Golden' glow of Belasco's English original.

**Girl power.** The social and economic power of young women as individuals in their own right, rather than as sexual stereotypes. The feministic stance of the 1990s was based on the need for young women to make their voices heard and was expanded and expounded in such books as Patty Ellis's *Girl Power: Making Choices and Speaking Out* (1994) and Hillary Carlip's *Girl Power: Young Women Speak Out* (1995), the latter a variety of viewpoints by 'cowgals, lesbians, teen mothers, sorority sisters and girls in gangs'. The 'official book' of the SPICE GIRLS was entitled *Girl Power!* (1997), and the phrase became associated with the group, whose lyrics purported to extol its virtues. At the decidedly harder end of the 'girl power' (or 'grrl power') spectrum were the RIOT GRRLS.

> Girl Power! Girls can do whatever they like, and it's all Girl Power! And as Girl Power is feminism with added fun and hair-mascara, so women dressed as teenagers are feminist statements on sexuality.
> CAITLIN MORAN: in *The Times* (3 August 1999)

**Girls in pearls.** A colloquial term for a 'society portrait' of a fashionably dressed young woman, such as that appearing weekly in *Country Life*.

**Girl's Own Paper, The.** A magazine for girls first published in 1880, a year after *The* BOY'S OWN PAPER. Like its companion publication, it featured material in keeping with contemporary ideas about the correct upbringing of juveniles: features on women's fashions, articles on homemaking skills, such as sewing and cooking, and accounts of 'suitable' female role-models such as Queen Victoria and Florence Nightingale. It ceased publication in 1965.

**Giro.** The word has come to have two main applications, one formal, the other informal. Formally, it is the name of the Girobank, a clearing bank set up as part of the Post Office in 1968. It operates like any other bank, but uses post offices as its outlets. Informally, as an abbreviation for girocheque, it is the name of the social security payment sent by post to those entitled, who then cash the cheque at a post office – hence the title of James Kelman's 1983 collection of stories about working-class life in Glasgow, *Not, Not While the Giro*. The word ultimately goes back to Italian *giro*, 'circulation'.

> 'That my lager?' he inquired, feeling mean even as he uttered the question. 'Yeah, d'you mind?' said Raymond. 'I'll replace it when I get me next giro.'
> DAVID LODGE: *Nice Work*, Pt III, ch. 2 (1988)

**Gitmo.** *See* CAMP X-RAY.

**Give-'em-hell Harry.** A nickname given to the forthright Democratic politician Harry S. Truman (1884–1972), president of the United States (1945–53). In the 1948 presidential election campaign his supporters shouted 'Give 'em hell, Harry'. Truman responded: 'I never give 'em hell; I just tell 'em the truth and they think it's hell.' During his presidency he earned the nickname High-Tax Harry from his opponents (*compare* FDR's nickname of Franklin Deficit Roosevelt). An earlier nickname had been Haberdasher Harry; after the First World War Truman had opened a haberdashery store in Kansas City, which failed after

two years. He was also known as the Man from Missouri (as indeed he was). The 'S' in his name does not stand for anything (as with the 'H' in General H. Norman Schwarzkopf, STORMIN' NORMAN). *See also* NMI.

**Give it up.** An exhortation to give someone, especially a performer, a large and enthusiastic round of applause (as in 'Let's give it up for Will Young'). The expression dates from around 1990.

**Give me strength!** A 'prayer' uttered on hearing some stupid statement. The invocation is for the strength to restrain oneself. The phrase dates from the 1920s.

**Give one's left nut.** In US slang, to 'give everything' (literally, one's left testicle); in other words, to want something very much (as in 'I'd give my left nut to be able to change places with you'). The expression dates from around 1950.

**'Give Peace a Chance'.** The title of a song (1969) by John Lennon (1940–80), recorded under the name of The Plastic Ono Band, during Lennon and Yoko Ono's 1969 'Bed-In', when the couple stayed in bed in the Queen Elizabeth Hotel, Montreal, for a week to promote world peace. Among those present during the recording were such giants of the counter-culture as Timothy Leary (*see* TURN ON, TUNE IN, DROP OUT) and Allen Ginsberg (*see* HOWL). The song was released as a single and reached number 2 in the UK charts. The phrase 'Give peace a chance' has since frequently been used as an anti-war slogan. *See also* MAKE LOVE, NOT WAR.

> Ev'rybody's talking about
> John and Yoko, Timmy Leary, Rosemary,
> Tommy Smothers, Bobby Dylan,
> Tommy Cooper,
> Derek Taylor, Norman Mailer,
> Alan Ginsberg, Hare Krishna,
> Hare Hare Krishna.
> *All we are saying is give peace a chance.*
> *All we are saying is give peace a chance.*

**Give someone a bell** or **a buzz.** To telephone or call them.

**Give** or **slap someone five.** To slap someone's upraised (and sometimes also downturned) palm or palms as a form of greeting or as a signal of often mutual congratulation for a notable feat. The expression originated in the late 1950s, apparently referring to a waist-level palm-slapping ritual among African Americans; its modern application stems from US basketball usage in the 1970s (*see also* HIGH FIVE). 'Five' stands for the five fingers ('ten' is occasionally substituted when both hands are referred to).

**Give someone grey hairs.** To cause them worry or trouble; to annoy or pester them persistently. The expression is logically best applied to a young person whose hair has not yet naturally begun to turn grey.

**Give someone heaps.** In Australian slang, to SOCK IT TO SOMEONE, to stuff them. The expression is first recorded in 1978.

> He [Mark Latham, then leader of the Australian Labor Party] does not need to respond to every bizarre request from the self-important pundits of the media, but at the very least he should avoid being compared unfavourably with the ultra-cosseted Howard, as is starting to happen. It's time to get out there and give them heaps.
>
> www.echonews.com (8 July 2004)

**Give someone something on a plate.** *See* HAND SOMEONE SOMETHING ON A PLATE.

**Give someone the finger.** To make a gesture of contempt. In the United States, and now also in Britain, the gesture is an upward jerk of the middle finger. More commonly in Britain it is a V-SIGN.

**Give someone the large.** To give them their freedom. The expression can equally be applied to animals or to anything living, such as flowers or plants.

> I did a little audition at home planting some clematis, giving it the large, you know, and got the job.
>
> *heat* (6–12 January 2000)

**Give us the tools and we will finish the job.** Winston Churchill's plea to the Americans, before they had entered the Second World War, made in a radio broadcast on 9 February 1941:

> Here is the answer which I will give to President Roosevelt … We shall not fail or falter; we shall not weaken or tire. Neither the sudden shock of battle nor the long-drawn trials of vigilance and exertion will wear us down. Give us the tools and we will finish the job.

Roosevelt was to oblige Britain and the allies with the LEND-LEASE scheme.

**Glad bag.** A US euphemism for a body bag, in which the body of a dead serviceman or woman is returned home from a foreign theatre of war. First recorded in 1983, it is a blackly humorous redeployment of the trade name of a make of plastic sandwich bag.

**Glad eye.** An amorous glance; a look of sexual interest. The phrase dates from the early 20th century and has been humorously associated with the first name Gladys and *vice versa*.

**Glad rags.** One's best clothes, and specifically formal dress. The expression is of US origin.

**Glagolitic Mass.** A setting of the Ordinary of the Mass for solo voices, chorus, organ and orchestra by Leoš Janáček (1854–1928). The title of a piece is a misnomer: the composer thought 'Glagolitic' referred to the Old Slavonic language of the 9th century, the time of St Methodius and St Cyril, but the term only refers to the Old Slavonic alphabet, supposedly invented by St Cyril. Of the work, which was first performed in 1927, Janáček wrote: 'I wanted to portray the faith in the certainty of the nation, not on a religious basis but on a basis of moral strength which takes God for witness.'

**Glamour boy.** A nickname for a Royal Air Force pilot in the Second World War. The RAF had a glamorous image, not only for their exploits but for their appearance. *See also* BRYLCREEM BOYS; the FEW.

**Glamour puss.** A glamorous person, usually female but also sometimes male. The expression dates from the 1950s.

**Glam rock.** A style of rock music of the early 1970s, characterized by the wearing of extravagantly coloured clothes and make-up by the male performers. The aim was perhaps to make a statement about decadence, or simply to draw attention away from the unoriginality of the words and music. 'Glam' is 'glamorous'. *See also* ZIGGY STARDUST.

**Glasnost.** (Russian, 'openness'). The practice of more open consultative government and wider dissemination of information in the former Soviet Union was initiated from 1985 by Mikhail Gorbachev (*see* GORBY). The policy had been only partially implemented by the time of the country's collapse as a communist state in 1991. *See also* PERESTROIKA.

**Glass ceiling.** An invisible barrier on the career ladder that some employees, in particular women and members of minority groups, find they can see through but which they cannot surmount.

**Glasshouse.** Army slang for a military prison. It was originally applied to the prison at North Camp, Aldershot, which had a glass roof.

**Glass menagerie.** A diverse but also meretricious or insubstantial display of people or things. The allusion is to the title of Tennessee Williams's play *The Glass Menagerie* (1944), in which a collection of small glass animals owned by the daughter of the central character, Tom Wingfield, symbolizes the Wingfields themselves as the 'little people', whose poor world is falling apart.

**Glastonbury Festival.** The short name of the Glastonbury Festival of Contemporary Performing Arts, better known as an annual rock festival, held at the end of June on Worthy Farm in the village of Pilton near the ancient Somerset town of Glastonbury, itself a centre of pagan and Christian legend and a magnet for droves of NEW AGE adherents. The festival was the enterprise of a local farmer, Michael Eavis, who in September 1970 leased out his land for a combination of pop festival, country fair and harvest festival. The event has evolved from a fairly primitive affair with rudimentary facilities and an attendance of only 2000 to a highly organized occasion, complete with roads laid specially for the three days, cash points, retail outlets, proper restaurants and flush lavatories for the convenience of the thousands of music fans and performers.

**Glastonbury Romance, A.** A novel (1933) by John Cowper Powys (1872–1963), set in the Somerset town of Glastonbury. To illustrate his central theme of self-fulfilment, Powys draws on the local legend that Joseph of Arimathea came to convert the British, choosing Glastonbury as his base and placing the Holy Grail, the cup used by Christ at the Last Supper, beneath a spring on a hill by the town. The attitude to a symbolic grail of each of the main characters is examined. A climax of the narrative is a pageant depicting details from Arthurian legend and the story of the Crucifixion. *See also* GLASTONBURY FESTIVAL.

**Gleam in one's eye.** *See* TWINKLE IN ONE'S EYE.

**Gleneagles Agreement.** An agreement made at the luxurious Gleneagles Hotel in Perthshire in 1977 between the Commonwealth heads of government to end all official sporting links with South Africa as a protest against the country's APARTHEID regime.

**Glengarry Glen Ross.** A play (1984) by David Mamet (b.1947), who also wrote the screenplay for the film version (1992), directed by James Foley. It is about the pressures sales staff at a real estate office find themselves under when they learn that the two least successful among them will be sacked. Glengarry Glen Ross refers to the useless areas of land that the staff compete to sell.

> Put that coffee down. Coffee's for closers only.
> DAVID MAMET: *Glengarry Glen Ross*

**Glitterati.** A name for fashionable people, especially those conspicuously involved in show business or some other glamorous activity. The term arose in the 1950s as a blend of 'glitter' and 'literati', the latter being a 17th-century word for literate or well-educated people, as the plural of Latin *literatus*, literally 'acquainted with letters'.

**Glitter Gulch.** A nickname for the downtown casino area of Las Vegas, Nevada, around Fremont Street. First recorded in 1953, it was inspired by the lurid neon signs and other sparkling gewgaws of the original Vegas entertainment area, before the Strip developed.

**Glittering Prizes, The.** A six-part TV series and novel (1976) by Frederic Raphael (b.1931) that follows the progress of a group of clever and often self-satisfied Cambridge arts graduates through the 1950s and 1960s to 1972. Cambridge is itself described as the 'CITY OF PERSPIRING DREAMS' – in contrast to the traditional description of Oxford as a place of 'dreaming spires'. The title comes from the address that F.E. Smith (Lord Birkenhead), the Conservative politician and witty lawyer, gave on 7 November 1923 in his capacity as rector of Glasgow University:

> The world continues to offer glittering prizes to those who have stout hearts and sharp swords.

**Globaloney.** *See* BALONEY.

**Global village.** The world regarded as a unified community linked by telecommunications. The implication of the term, originally coined by Marshall McLuhan, is that the mass media reduces national distinctions and creates an element of economic and social interdependence, as in a small village, where everything is accessible to everyone.

> The new electronic interdependence recreates the world in the image of a global village.
> MARSHALL MCLUHAN: *The Gutenberg Galaxy* (1962)

*See also* MCLUHANISM.

**Global warming.** The gradual increase in the overall temperature of the earth's atmosphere due to the GREENHOUSE EFFECT. The two terms are sometimes confused in the public mind.

**Global War on Terror.** *See* WAR ON TERROR.

**Gloom and doom.** *See* DOOM AND GLOOM.

**Gloomy Dean.** The nickname of W.R. Inge (1860–1954), dean of St Paul's Cathedral, London, from 1911 to 1934. The sobriquet sprang from his resistance to current trends and his forcefully expressed doubts regarding political and social reforms that most saw as beneficial.

**Gloriana.** A controversial opera by Benjamin Britten (1913–76) with a libretto by William Plomer. It was commissioned by Covent Garden to celebrate the coronation of Elizabeth II and was first performed in the queen's presence in 1953. It was criticized at the time both for its music and for its depiction of its subject. Gloriana was the name that Edmund Spenser (*c*.1552–99) gave to Queen Elizabeth I in *The Faerie Queene*, and Britten's opera concerns the relationship between Elizabeth I and the Earl of Essex.

**Glorioso mutilado, El.** (Spanish, 'the glorious mutilated one'.) The nickname given by his followers to the extreme right-wing Spanish soldier José Millan Astráy y Terreros (1879–1954), a profoundly sinister, death-obsessed hench-man of General Franco and creator of the Spanish Foreign Legion. The brutal methods of the latter under Astray's leadership contributed much to Franco's victory in the Spanish Civil War. He owed his name to the fact that he was maimed by a number of old war wounds, having but one arm, one eye, a shattered jaw and mutilated fingers on his remaining hand. *See also* CAUDILLO.

**Glory hole.** In gay slang, a hole cut in the side wall of a public-lavatory cubicle, through which a man may push his penis so that another (anonymous) man on the other side of the partition can fellate him. The usage, first recorded in the late 1940s, is a reapplication of a term that had been put to many other more or less scabrous uses in the past, including 'storage place for random unwanted items', 'Salvation Army meeting place' and 'vagina'.

**Gloves are off.** A journalistic cliché to describe a worsening dispute. The metaphor is from boxing, in which removal of the gloves signifies a more serious bare-knuckle fight.

> If Murdoch can offer big bucks and get them, then so can we. The gloves are off now.
>
> *The Guardian* (29 April 1995)

**Glutton for punishment.** A person who welcomes hard or unpleasant tasks. The phrase is often used humorously for a repeated imposition that one is obliged to undergo, such as a training routine or a regular round of domestic chores. The expression dates from the 1970s as an altered form of the earlier 'glutton for work'.

**Glyndebourne.** The country estate, near Lewes in Sussex, where John Christie (1882–1962) opened the Glyndebourne Festival Theatre in 1934 for operatic and musical perfor-mances, which became an annual summer event. A new and larger auditorium opened in 1994, but seats are still in short supply, and this, together with a suspicion that many of the black-tie audience are more interested in their alfresco interval supper in the grounds than in the music, has not helped to dispel the elitist image of opera in Britain. Nor has the helipad. For those who prefer their Puccini without a picnic, Glyndebourne Touring Opera presents productions in theatres around the country in the winter season.

**G-men.** Government men or agents of the FBI. The term originally applied to the agents of the Department of Justice's Bureau of Investigation under J. Edgar Hoover and continued after the establishment of the FBI in 1935.

**Gnomes of Zurich.** An uncomplimentary name given to those financiers of Zurich controlling international monetary funds. The phrase became popular after its use in 1964 by George Brown, then Labour Minister of Economic Affairs, at the time of a sterling crisis. The expression had been used before this, however, by Harold Wilson, when in a speech in the House of Commons on 12 November 1956 he had referred to 'all the little gnomes in Zurich and other finance centres'.

> What most infuriated George Brown, and Labour MPs such as John Mendelson and Ian Mikardo … was that the men they disparaged as the 'gnomes of Zürich' were really giants.
>
> T.R. FEHRENBACH: *The Gnomes of Zürich* (1966)

**Go a bundle on.** To be very keen on. The original sense was to bet a large sum of money (a 'bundle' or 'packet') on a horse. The expression is of US origin and dates from the 1930s.

**Go ape.** To go crazy; to lose one's self-control; to display strong emotion or reaction. The allusion is to the frenzied and panic-stricken behaviour of monkeys and apes when captured and caged, typically involving screaming and defecation.

**Goat-fuck.** Originally, in US slang, a situation of complete disorganization and chaos; a cock-up. The expression reached a rather wider audience towards the end of the 20th century when it began to be applied to the disorderly and somewhat aggressive scrum of press photographers and television camera crews, some of them mounted on step ladders, that assembles round a cornered celebrity or other newsworthy person.

> 'I've never seen anything so amazing', said a young woman, who watched the crowd of TV cameras move in a scrum (the technical term is … 'goatfuck') as Ricco … crossed Pearl Street.
>
> www.marash.tv (31 May 2005)

**Go ballistic.** To fly into a rage. The image is of the launch of a ballistic missile. The expression is of US origin and dates from the 1980s. A stronger variant is 'go nuclear'. *See also* GO APE; GO INTO ORBIT.

**Gobbledygook.** A word invented in the early 1940s by the Texan lawyer Maury Maverick, chairman of the US Smaller War Plants Corporation and a descendant of the cattle-owner Samuel A. Maverick, eponym of the *maverick*, to describe the convoluted, pretentious and often meaningless language of bureaucracy.

> People ask me where I got gobbledygook. I do not know. It must have come in a vision. Perhaps I was thinking of the old bearded turkey gobbler back in Texas, who was always

gobbledy-gobbling and strutting with ludicrous pomposity. At the end of this gobble there was a sort of gook.

*New York Times* (21 May 1944)

Whether deliberately or not, Maverick's account fails to mention the earlier US euphemism 'gobble the goo', meaning to perform fellatio or cunnilingus, which can scarcely fail to have played at least a subconscious part in the genesis of 'gobbledygook'.

**Go belly up.** To go bankrupt. The allusion is to the posture of a dead fish in the water. The expression dates from the 1920s.

**Go-Between, The.** A novel (1953) by L. P. Hartley (1895–1972). The go-between is a boy holidaying at the stately home in Norfolk of his schoolfriend. He agrees to take messages between his friend's elder sister and the local farmer with whom she is in love. The main themes are the destruction of a child's innocence in an adult world and the dangers of sexual relationships between classes in the context of 1900. The film version (1970), an almost palpable re-creation of the EDWARDIAN ERA in the mould of a MERCHANT IVORY FILM, with haunting music by Michel Legrand, was directed by Joseph Losey from a script by Harold Pinter.

The past is a foreign country: they do things differently there.

*The Go-Between*, prologue

This line provided a title, *Another Country*, for the 1984 film starring Rupert Everett and Colin Firth and based on the Julian Mitchell play about an upper-class homosexual defector to the Soviet Union, whose motives are traced to his experiences at public school. *See also* CAMBRIDGE SPY RING.

**Gobsmacked.** Astounded; speechless with amazement. The allusion may be to a slap on the face, or to the involuntary act of clapping a hand over one's mouth ('gob') when taken aback. The term originated in North of England dialect speech but entered general usage only in the 1980s.

I remain, as [former governor of Hong Kong] Chris Patten once famously put it, 'gobsmacked' by the Earl of Snowdon's decision to accept a nomination for a life peerage.

ANTHONY HOWARD: in *The Times* (10 November 1999)

**Go commando.** To go about fully clothed externally, but with no underpants. The subtext may be that 'real' men need no such effete garments.

**Godfather, The.** A film (1972) adapted from a novel (1969) by Mario Puzo (1902–99) about an Italian Mafia family in New York. Directed by Francis Ford Coppola and starring Marlon

Brando as the head (or 'Godfather') of the powerful Corleone clan, it inspired two equally acclaimed sequels and firmly established the use of 'the Godfather' to describe any person at the head of an organization, particularly one suspected of employing dubious, underhand or plain illegal methods.

In business circles a takeover bid for a company that is so generous no one can afford to turn it down is commonly referred to as a 'godfather offer', with reference to the tradition of Mafia gangsters making 'an offer you can't refuse'.

The football manager Don Revie (1928–89) was called 'the Godfather' because of his so-called autocratic style of management. The allusion is to the Mafia boss played by Marlon Brando in the 1972 film. Revie made Leeds United into one of the best club sides in Europe in the early 1970s but was subsequently less successful as manager of the English national side.

**Go directly to jail. Do not pass Go. Do not collect £200.** The instructions on one of the 'Community Chest' cards in MONOPOLY. The injunction is often quoted humorously.

**Go down a storm.** To be enthusiastically received by an audience, who react to one's speech or performance with a storm of applause.

[Chancellor Gordon] Brown's speech went down a storm … In a barnstorming performance, Brown set out the future direction of the Government.

*The Times* (29 September 1999)

The phrase 'to go down a bomb' (from the early 1960s) means the same, and thus has the opposite sense of the US phrase 'to bomb'. It was reported that US teenagers of 1964 were perplexed to hear that the super-successful BEATLES were about to launch themselves on the United States having gone down a bomb in their native land.

**Go down like a lead balloon.** To be poorly received, as of a speech, proposal or the like. A balloon normally goes up, but weighted with lead will do the reverse. The expression is of US origin and dates from the 1950s.

I do not know [who] … came up with this crazy scheme but it would have been catastrophic politics – going down like a lead airship with the vast majority of the electorate if ever implemented.

*The Times* (25 November 1999)

**God particle, The.** The nickname given to the Higg's boson, a hypothetical elementary particle first posited by the British physicist Peter Higgs (b.1929), who had his 'big idea' while walking in the Cairngorm Mountains one weekend in

1964. If it exists, it plays a key role in defining the nature of the universe, as it explains why matter has mass. Hence its nickname. Physicists regard the search for an experimental proof of the particle's existence as something of a holy grail.

**'God Save the Queen'.** A scabrously anarchic song by the short-lived PUNK rock group The Sex Pistols, which was released in 1977, the year of the Silver Jubilee of the accession to the throne of Queen Elizabeth II. The song's provocative title (the name of the national anthem of the UK) and lyrics (at one point the UK is described as a 'fascist regime') led to its being banned by the BBC on grounds of taste, and a number of high-street shops refused to stock it. The sleeve of the single featured a photograph of the queen defaced with the name of the group and the song's title. *See also* ROCK GROUP NAMES.

**God's Eye.** A small cross made of twigs, branches and the like around which coloured yarn or threads is wound in geometric patterns. The artefact is popular in Mexico and the southwestern United States as a decoration or a symbol of good luck. The name translates Mexican Spanish *ojo de dios*, 'eye of a god', and the symbol is so called because it originally represented the eye of a deity among certain Native American peoples.

**God's gift.** A person regarded as a 'godsend', especially a man irresistible to women. The term is often used ironically, as (of an idiosyncratic teacher): 'He thinks he's God's gift to education.' The phrase is sometimes expanded to 'God's own gift'.

> Jessica Hatfield thought she was 'God's gift' to advertising when she dreamt up a scheme to link point-of-sale promotional material across supermarkets in Britain.
> *Sunday Times* (7 November 1999)

**God slot.** A period in a broadcasting schedule regularly reserved for a religious programme, such as BBC radio's daily *Morning Service* or BBC television's *Songs of Praise* each Sunday evening.

**God squad.** A nickname for an evangelical Christian group, especially one proselytizing among college students.

**God's rottweiler.** An epithet applied to the Bavarian cardinal Joseph Ratzinger (b.1927), who became Pope Benedict XVI on 19 April 2005. He acquired the nickname as Pope John Paul II's 'Enforcer' (as he was also called) of Catholic orthodoxy, when he was head of the Congregation for the Doctrine of the Faith (1981–2005); he was thus associated with the more conservative-minded wing of the Roman Catholic Church. On the announcement of his papal election, journalists toyed with other sobriquets, such as the

'Panzer Cardinal' in reference to his brief, involuntary stint in the German Army at the end of the Second World War, and 'Paparatzi' (which appeared in the *Sun* newspaper).

**Godzilla.** A fearsome dinosaur of the cinema that is awakened from its primordial slumbers by H-bomb tests and proceeds to menace Tokyo. It first appeared in the film that bears its name, in the original Japanese *Gojira* (1955). The name itself is a blend of Japanese *kujira*, 'whale', the nickname of a film production company employee at the time, and 'gorilla'. The monster reappeared in a number of sequels, some even more ridiculous than the original, including *King Kong vs. Godzilla* (1962), *Godzilla vs. the Thing* (1964) and *Destroy All Monsters* (1964). An all-new, all-American re-creation was *Godzilla* (1998).

When the 140-million-year-old fossil of an extinct 4-m (13-ft) crocodile, *Dakosaurus andiniensis*, was discovered in Patagonia in 2005, it was nicknamed Godzilla. The ancient reptile had 10-cm (4-in) serrated teeth, and probably fed on plesiosaurs and ichthyosaurs.

**Go for broke.** To risk everything in a venture; to commit oneself unreservedly. The reference is to gambling, when one stakes all. The expression is of US origin and dates from the 1960s.

**Go for it.** To set about a task or accept a challenge whole-heartedly. First recorded in the 1970s, the expression is often used as an exclamation of encouragement to someone weighing up the risks of proceeding further.

> We can look forward to the best and brightest of our society's talented youth choosing careers in chemistry, an essential step to ensuring that chemistry lives up to its potential of improving the quality of life for people everywhere on Earth. That's a tall order, but this is National Chemistry Week. Go for it!
> *Chemistry and Engineering News* (21 October 2002)

**Go for the big spit.** In Australian slang, to vomit. Beer-drinking and its after-effects having been a key feature of 20th-century macho male Aussie culture, this is one of a range of colourful antipodean metaphors for vomiting (*see also* CHUNDER; TECHNICOLOR YAWN). It dates from the 1950s, but was popularized in the 1960s by Barry Humphies's frequently crapulous Barry MCKENZIE.

**Go for the burn.** To push one's body to the extreme when undergoing physical training or 'working out'. Although recommended by such manuals as *Jane Fonda's Workout Book* (1981), the practice is not automatically applicable to all and is positively ill-advised in some cases.

**Go for the doctor.** In colloquial Australian English, to make an all-out effort, to go for broke. The expression, which is first recorded in 1949, is based on the notion of sending for a doctor in a medical emergency.

**Go for the jugular.** To be aggressive when making an attack. The allusion is to the jugular vein in the neck, which carries blood from the head and face. A predator such as a wolf will literally go for the jugular when seizing the throat of a larger animal with the aim of killing it.

**Go-go dancer.** A scantily dressed female dancer who performs energetic and often erotic dances in a nightclub or the like. The term is based on a reduplication of 'go' influenced by French *à gogo*, 'aplenty', 'galore'.

> The fourth floor resembled a hi-tech Bangkok jazz bar, with conveyor belts of Thai nibbles whirring past the stockinged go-go dancers who were gyrating to booming r'n'b.
>
> *heat* (17–23 February 2000)

**Go great guns.** To go well; to perform vigorously. The expression dates from the early 20th century and apparently originated in horse racing, 'great gun' already existing as a term for an eminent or 'go-ahead' person, a BIG SHOT.

**Going on.** Getting on for; nearly. Said of ages, as: 'He must be going on 60.' The phrase, earlier 'going on for', is often used to compare a person's actual age with an apparent one, especially when a young person displays an ability or maturity ahead of their years.

> 'The guy [golfer Sergio García] is hugely talented. I cannot think of any weaknesses in his game. He is 19 going on 30.'
>
> *The Times* (16 August 1999)

**Go into a flat spin** or **tailspin.** To become agitated; to panic; to lose control. A flat spin is one in which an aircraft descends in tight circles while remaining almost horizontal. In a tailspin the aircraft falls nose first, its tail describing a spiral. Both expressions date from the early years of the 20th century.

**Go into orbit.** To lose one's temper. The expression dates from the 1960s and the start of space exploration proper. *See also* GO BALLISTIC; IN ORBIT.

**Golan Heights.** (Arabic *Al Jawlān*, Hebrew *Ha-Golan*.) A strategically important range of hills in southern Syria. From here the Syrian army was able to shell settlements in northern Israel, making it an important objective for the Israelis in the SIX-DAY WAR (1967). They succeeded in capturing most of the Golan Heights, and Israeli settlements were established there. Israel's annexation of the area in 1981 was not recognized internationally, and the status of the Golan Heights has since proved a stumbling block to peace negotiations between Israel and Syria.

**Gold Beach.** The Allied code name for the stretch of beach on the Normandy coast running west from JUNO BEACH at La Rivière to Arromanches. On D-DAY it was where the British XXX Corps came ashore.

**Gold-digger.** A young woman who courts or marries an older man for his money.

**Gold disc.** A record, usually of popular music, that has sold a specified high number of copies. In Britain the term applies to an album that has sold 100,000 copies or a single that has sold 400,000. In the United States the honour is awarded to either an album or a single that has sold 500,000 copies.

**Golden arches.** The logo of MCDONALD'S, the fast-food chain, representing an 'M'. In some branches, the golden arches rise sculpturally above the building.

***Golden Arrow.*** A famous Pullman train service from London to Paris, with a ferry crossing from Dover to Calais. On the French side of the English Channel the train had the equivalent name, *Flèche d'Or*. A train had been leaving Victoria Station at 11 a.m. daily for many years on this route before the name was adopted in 1929. The service was withdrawn in 1972. The name itself comes from folklore, in which the Golden Arrow was the one sought by a pair of lovers in the land of their dreams. The legend is alluded to in the title and story of Mary Webb's early novel *The Golden Arrow* (1916). The name was apt for a train that took passengers to Paris, the 'City of Lovers'. *See also* TITLED TRAINS.

**Goldenballs.** A *Private Eye* nickname for Sir James Goldsmith (1933–97), who filed numerous libel suits against the magazine (*see also* REFERENDUM PARTY). The name itself is an old abusive appellation, recorded in the Domesday Book (1086) as *gildyn ballokes*. In the modern adoption it was naturally suggested by the surname. Victoria Beckham used it, presumably affectionately, for her husband, the footballer David (b.1975), and once she revealed it in 2001 it was widely trumpeted in the British press.

**Golden Bear.** An annual award for the best feature film made by the Berlin Film Festival since 1956, when it went to Gene Kelly's *Invitation to the Dance* (1956). According to legend, Berlin takes its name from the medieval margrave Albert the Bear (Old High German *bero*, modern German *Bär*), and a black bear appears on the city arms. Hence the name of the award.

**Golden boy** or **girl.** A popular or successful person, especially in sport or business. In the former, it is usually implicitly connected with one who wins gold medals, especially when handsome or attractive. Thus the good-looking US boxer Oscar De La Hoya was dubbed the 'Golden Boy of Boxing' after winning the gold medal in the 1992 Olympics. In Clifford Odets's play *Golden Boy* (1937) the hero, a violinist, is also a successful boxer. *The Golden Girls* (1985–92) was an US television SITCOM featuring three middle-aged women and one clearly older. The title was deliberate, as one can still be a 'golden girl' when no longer really young in years. *See also* GOLDEN OLDIE.

> [Michelle] Smith, the golden girl of Ireland, the swimmer who improved … enough to win three gold medals at the last Olympic Games, has paid the inevitable price.
>
> *The Times* (9 June 1999)

**Golden Cockerel Press.** A publishing business founded in 1920 by Harold Taylor (d.1924) to produce works of a high typographic quality. Its first book was A.E. Coppard's collection of short stories, *Adam and Eve and Pinch Me* (1921), and its most famous work was *The Four Gospels* (1931), with wood engravings by Eric Gill, a magnificent quarto volume bound in white pigskin. The much later Golden Cockerel Press, founded in 1980, is quite distinct, as a distributor of titles for the US firm of Associated University Presses. The golden cockerel symbolizes a new dawn or sunrise.

**Golden Delicious.** The greenish-yellow (rather than obviously golden) apple of this name should not be confused with the 'Delicious'. The Golden Delicious is a US apple that appeared as a chance seedling on the West Virginia farm of A.H. Mullins, in 1890. It is now the most widely grown variety in many countries. The 'Delicious', a red apple, began as a chance seedling on the farm of Jesse Hiatt of Peru, Iowa, in 1872. He marketed it as 'Hiatt's Hawkeye', but a fruit-growing company, Stark Brothers, bought Hiatt out and renamed the variety 'Delicious'. It has been the leading US apple since the 1940s and is now widely grown elsewhere. The similarity between the names arose because the same nursery firm bought the rights to both varieties.

**Goldeneye.** A James BOND film (1995), with Pierce Brosnan as the suave secret agent, who goes to Russia to foil the fiendish plots of a criminal mastermind. In temper with the changing times, M is played by Judi Dench (just as, in the 1990s, MI5 was headed by a woman, Stella Rimington). Unlike earlier Bond films, it was not based on any of the Bond novels by Ian Fleming (1908–64), but adapted from a story by Michael France. Goldeneye was the name of Fleming's house in Jamaica, which he had named after one of his Second World War operations, when he worked as a senior officer in naval intelligence.

Originally, goldeneye is a handsome species of duck (*Bucephala clangula*) with striking black and white plumage.

**Golden farewell.** *See* GOLDEN GOODBYE.

**Golden Gate Bridge.** Until the completion of the Verrazano-Narrows Bridge in New York in 1964, the Golden Gate Bridge, completed in 1937 across the Golden Gate, California, was the longest suspension bridge in the world. Its construction involved many difficulties, including frequent storms and fogs, but it remains an inspiring sight in its magnificent setting.

**Golden girl.** *See* GOLDEN BOY.

**Golden Globe.** An annual film award made since 1944 by the Hollywood Foreign Press Association, an organization of journalists and photographers founded in 1943 to cover HOLLYWOOD film and television for foreign publications. It first went to Henry King's *The Song of Bernadette* (1943).

**Golden Gloves.** The amateur boxing competition of this name was initiated by Arch Ward, sports editor of the *Chicago Tribune*, and first sponsored by that paper in 1926. Annual tournaments between Chicago and New York were held from 1927, the New York organizer being Paul Gallico of the *New York Daily News*. The idea was subsequently taken up by other cities. Many Golden Gloves champions went on to become professional world champions, among them Joe Louis (1914–81), Sugar Ray Robinson (1920–89), Floyd Patterson (1935–2006) and Sugar Ray Leonard (b.1956). Cassius Clay, later Muhammad Ali (b.1942), won six Golden Gloves titles, the first at the age of 14.

**Golden goal.** In football, the first goal scored in extra time following a draw. This wins the game under a 'sudden death' system, as distinct from a penalty shoot-out. The modification to the rules was introduced in the first half of the 1990s and has now been extended to hockey. The German striker Oliver Bierhoff was the first player to score a golden goal in the final of a major international tournament in the 94th minute of the 1996 European Championship final against the Czech Republic at Wembley.

**Golden goodbye** or **farewell.** A compensation payment similar to a GOLDEN HANDSHAKE made to a company executive on transferring to non-executive status or to any employee leaving employment under certain conditions. *See also* GOLDEN HELLO.

**Golden handcuffs.** Payments to an employee that are deliberately deferred over a number of years in an attempt to make them stay with a particular company. *See also* GOLDEN HANDSHAKE.

**Golden handshake.** A phrase that is applied to the often considerable terminal payments made to individuals, especially business executives, whose services are prematurely dispensed with. It was coined by Frederick Ellis (d.1979), City Editor of the *Daily Express*. *See also* GOLDEN GOODBYE.

> The average 'golden handshake' to departing directors has risen for the first time since 1994, from £328,000 for the year to October 1997 to £463,000 over the past 12 months.
> *The Times* (2 October 1998)

**Golden hello.** A special payment made by a company or other body to a sought-after recruit when they sign a contract of employment. *See also* GOLDEN GOODBYE; GOLDEN HANDSHAKE.

**Golden hour.** In medical jargon the hour following a person's serious head injury, as in boxing, during which prompt treatment may limit brain damage or prevent death.

**Golden Lion.** An annual award made since 1980 by the Venice Film Festival for the best feature film. The first award went jointly to John Cassavetes' *Gloria* (1980) and Louis Malle's *Atlantic City* (1980). The award's full title is the Golden Lion of St Mark, after the winged lion that appears on the coat of arms of the city, whose patron is St Mark.

**Golden Mile.** The popular name for a promenade or street for strolling in some cities, especially one with places of evening entertainment such as cinemas, theatres, pubs and clubs. One of the most familiar is the seafront promenade at BLACKPOOL, and in particular the section between the Tower and the South Pier. Another Golden Mile is in Belfast, leading down from the Opera House on Great Victoria Street to Queen's University, the Botanic Gardens and the Ulster Museum. The area buzzes with activity most evenings, especially in term time, and its attractions include the Crown Liquor Saloon, a famous Victorian gin palace. 'Golden' refers both to the glamour and glitter of such streets and to the amount of money that changes hands.

**Golden Notebook, The.** A novel (1962) by Doris Lessing (b.1919). The work is experimental in form and ambitious in scope. The writer Anna Wulf keeps four notebooks – coloured black, red, yellow and blue – in which she records different aspects of her experience: her time in Africa during the Second World War, her membership of the Communist Party of Great Britain, a fictionalized version of her love life, and an introspective record of her psychoanalysis. Eventually Anna manages to free herself from this fragmentation and to unite her experiences in a golden notebook. The novel was important in the revival of the women's movement in the 1960s.

> There's only one real sin, and that is to persuade oneself that the second-best is anything but the second-best.
> *The Golden Notebook*

**Golden oldie.** Something that is an old favourite, such as a nostalgic song or piece of music. Also a person who is no longer young but still successful in a particular field.

**Golden Palm.** (French *Palme d'or*.) An annual award for the best film of the year made at the Cannes Film festival since 1955, when the winner was Delbert Mann's *Marty* (1955).

**Golden parachute.** A clause in a senior executive's contract that grants special benefits if he or she loses their post as the result of a takeover. There is a pun on 'bale out' and 'bail out' here. *See also* GOLDEN GOODBYE; GOLDEN HANDSHAKE.

**Golden Raspberry.** One of a number of semi-serious annual awards made for the worst film, actor or actress of the year or some similar category as a counter to the OSCAR awards. Colloquially known as the 'Razzies', they were instituted by John Wilson in 1980. The awards in 2004 included, for worst actress, Halle Berry in *Catwoman* (which also won the 'worst film' Razzie) and, for worst actor, George W. Bush in *Fahrenheit 9/11. See also* BLOW A RASPBERRY.

**Golden Ring of Russia.** (Russian *Zolotoye kol'tso Rossii*.) A famous tourist route northeast of Moscow. It was laid out in the 1970s and takes a looping clock-wise course through the medieval cities of Sergiyev Posad (formerly Zagorsk), Pereslavl-Zalessky, Rostov, Yaroslavl, Kostroma, Suzdal and Vladimir. The name reflects the unique historical and architectural interest of the towns and also mirrors the dazzling golden cupolas of the many churches and monasteries seen along the route.

**Golden rivet.** In US slang, a mythical object with which the legs of newcomers to the navy or merchant marine are pulled. A greenhorn sailor may be asked to go below to find or polish the golden rivet. It turns out to be either non-existent or a euphemism for the penis, in which case the result of the quest may be sexual assault.

**Golden share.** A share in a company that controls at least 51 per cent of the voting rights. Such shares are usually those held by the government on the occasion of a privatization. The figure of 51 per cent is a token one, indicating just over half of the total. In the closing years of the 20th century the Labour government held a golden share in 10 companies.

**Golden Shot, The.** An early television GAME SHOW screened from 1967 to 1975. Contestants were required to guide a blindfolded cameraman on a 'telebow' and instruct him with commands such as 'left a bit', 'up a bit' to fire at targets in return for prizes. The ultimate prize was won by piercing a thread hung before an apple, whereupon a hoard of coins spilled over the studio floor. The idea was adopted from the German game *Der Goldene Schuss* and the series was hosted for most of its run by an unctuous Bob Monkhouse. 'Golden girl' hostesses also participated (the best known was the mathematically challenged Anne Aston), and the telebowloader, who sprang into action at the words 'Bernie, the bolt', became a minor cult figure (none of the men who did it was actually called Bernie).

**Golden shower.** In the colloquial jargon of sexual variation, urolagnia: being urinated on as an act of sexual gratification. The expression is first recorded in the 1940s.

**Golden Triangle.** An approximately triangular area of Southeast Asia, consisting of parts of Myanmar (Burma), Laos and Thailand, where most of the world's raw opium is grown. The name is also found elsewhere for any geographical area characterized by high productivity or social superiority, such as the industrial area that extends from the Midlands of England to the Gulf of Genoa or the wealthy residential region that centres on Wilmslow in Cheshire.

> Cheshire's so-called Golden Triangle owes its existence not to mindless materialists but to its better weather and the beautiful countryside unblemished by the industrial revolution.
>
> *Sunday Times,* letter to the editor (31 October 1999)

***Goldfinger.*** A thriller (1959) by Ian Fleming (1908–64), featuring his secret service agent James BOND. His adversary has gained the sobriquet Goldfinger, not just because he has a passion for the metal but because he has a habit of painting his girlfriends all over with it. The plot includes a classic golf match – and in fact it was on a golf course that Fleming had met the Hungarian-born modernist architect Ernö Goldfinger (1902–87), from whom he borrowed the name of his villain. A lively film version (1964), directed by Guy Hamilton, had Sean Connery as Bond and Honor Blackman as the sexy Pussy Galore.

**Goldfish bowl.** A place or situation in which one has no privacy and in which one can thus be publicly viewed and watched, like goldfish in a bowl. This sense of the term evolved in the 1930s and originally applied specifically to a police interrogation room, where the prisoner is isolated among his interrogators and where a one-way mirror is also often in operation.

**Goldilocks.** *See* TARZAN.

**Gold Microphone in Waiting.** A mocking nickname given to the BBC broadcaster Richard Dimbleby (1913–65), known for his support of royalty and the ESTABLISHMENT generally, and for his sonorous commentaries on state occasions, such as the coronation of Queen Elizabeth II and the funeral of Sir Winston Churchill. His sons David and Jonathan followed him into broadcasting. The latter is a biographer and friend of the Prince of Wales, and thus may be regarded as having inherited his father's title. *See also* DIMBLEDOM.

**Goldwynisms.** Any of a range of incongruous sayings attributed to the Polish-born US film producer Samuel Goldwyn (1882–1974; original name Samuel Goldfish), who established the HOLLYWOOD studio that later became MGM. Some are undoubtedly apocryphal, and most of the 'genuine' ones were probably dreamed up by his publicity staff, but he no doubt established the pattern. A selection of the more celebrated and surreal ones is given here, quoted in Richard Lederer's *Anguished English* (1989).

Include me out.

A verbal contract isn't worth the paper it's written on.

In two words: im-possible.

Every director bites the hand that lays the golden egg.

Anyone who goes to a psychiatrist should have his head examined.

I had a monumental idea last night but I didn't like it.

We have all passed a lot of water since then.

I'll give you a definite maybe.

We're overpaying him, but he's worth it.

I never liked you, and I always will.

Don't talk to me when I'm interrupting.

I may not always be right, but I'm never wrong.

The scene is dull. Tell him to put more life into his dying.

This book has too much plot and not enough story.

It's more than magnificent – it's mediocre.

A bachelor's life is no life for a single man.

Go see it and see for yourself why you shouldn't see it.

It's spreading like wildflowers!

If I could drop dead right now, I'd be the happiest man alive!

You've got to take the bull by the teeth.

This makes me so sore it gets my dandruff up.

When I want your opinion, I'll give it to you.

Colour television! Bah, I won't believe it until I see it in black and white.

I read part of it all the way through.

William? What kind of a name is that? Every Tom, Dick and Harry is called William.

**Golfball.** A nickname for the type-ball or spherical printing element formerly found in some electric typewriters. It was the invention of IBM, which introduced it in the 'Selectric' model of 1961. The innovation was a technological breakthrough in that the machine itself had no type-bars and no movable carriage. The type-ball bore 88 alphabetic characters, numerals and punctuation symbols and was mounted on a small carrier which ran along a cylindrical metal bar while in use. Because the type-ball moved, not the paper-carrying unit, the need for the familiar carriage was eliminated. The 'Selectric' thus required less space, minimized vibration and abolished altogether the noisy and disruptive carriage return jolt.

**Golightly, Holly.** The fascinating young heroine of Truman Capote's novella BREAKFAST AT TIFFANY'S (1958). She has a calling card which states, 'Miss Holiday Golightly. Travelling', and it turns out that she is a farmer's child bride on the run. Her name marks her role as a carefree roving girl. She was memorably portrayed by Audrey Hepburn in the film version of the book.

**Gollancz.** The British publishing house of this name was founded in 1927 by Victor Gollancz (1893–1967) with the stated aim of steering between 'the Scylla of preciousness and dilettantism and the Charybdis of purely commercialized mass production'. Its initial list consisted of histories, biographies and fiction, and it soon established itself on a sound commercial footing, its editions drawing the eye with their distinctive bright yellow dust jackets. It attracted authors such as Daphne du Maurier, A.J. Cronin, Dorothy Sayers and George ORWELL and began to specialize in socialist and pacifist books, a development that led to the formation of the LEFT BOOK CLUB. From the mid-1940s many of its authors were Americans such as John Updike, Vladimir Nabokov, James Agee and John Cheever, and in the 1960s it became noted for its SCIENCE FICTION titles. By the early 21st century it was part of Orion and solely science fiction in orientation.

**Golliwog.** The black-faced doll with a shock of black hair began life as a character in a children's picture book by Bertha and Florence Upton, *The Adventures of Two Dutch Dolls – and a 'Golliwogg'* (1895), with Florence illustrating the verse text written by her mother, Bertha. The character became immensely popular, and a 'golliwogg' (*sic*) craze soon developed. Debussy even included a 'Golliwog's Cakewalk' in his CHILDREN'S CORNER suite (1905–6). The doll also caught on as a rather incongruous commercial symbol for Robertson's jam. However, 100 years after his creation, the golliwog became a serious victim of POLITICAL CORRECTNESS, and his centenary was only mutely marked, if at all. The origin of the name is uncertain. It may be a blend of 'golly' (what a sight!) and 'polliwog', a US term for a

tadpole. It is perhaps itself the source of the also subsequently outlawed slang word WOG.

**Golliwogg's Cakewalk.** *See* CHILDREN'S CORNER.

**Gollum.** A creature in J.R.R. Tolkien's novels *The* HOBBIT (1937) and *The* LORD OF THE RINGS (1954–5). First encountered by Bilbo BAGGINS under the Misty Mountains, he is so named by Bilbo because of the curious glottal noises he makes in his throat. It is revealed in *The Lord of the Rings* that Gollum was formerly a hobbit-like being, originally named Sméagol, who had fled hearth and home after murdering his friend Déagol to gain possession of what turns out to be the One Ring. Gollum succumbs to the power of the ring (which he refers to as 'the Precious'), losing his original appearance and becoming a repellent, slimy, crawling thing.

**Golly gosh.** A form of overblown juvenile exclamation, combining two mild euphemisms for 'God', often used by adults in a facetious or ironic sense (it became a catchphrase of the bumbling chaplain Mervyn Noote, played by Derek Nimmo in the BBC television sitcom *All Gas and Gaiters*; 1967–71).

> The government's Women's Unit has concluded that they [women] find it difficult to strike a balance between home and work. Well, golly gosh; who would have thought it?
> *Sunday Times* (10 October 1999)

**Gondor.** A kingdom of MIDDLE-EARTH in J.R.R. Tolkien's *The* LORD OF THE RINGS (1954–5). Gondor contains the greatest cities of Middle-Earth and stands in contrast to MORDOR, the Land of Shadow. There are Arthurian echoes in Tolkien's depiction of Gondor as a quasi-medieval realm of chivalrous knights. Its capital, Minas Tirith (the Tower of Guard) was formerly known as Minas Anor (the Tower of the Sun) and was the twin city of Minas Ithil (the Tower of the Moon), later renamed MINAS MORGUL. At the time of the events recounted in *The Lord of the Rings* Gondor has fallen into decline, but its fortunes revive spectacularly with the victory of the army of the West over the forces of SAURON described towards the end of the trilogy.

**Gone a million.** In colloquial Australian English, completely ruined, defeated or finished, beyond all hope. The expression is first recorded in 1913.

> They mumbled something about sub judice and I thought we were gone a million on that question.
> www.notes.nt.gov.au (7 May 1991)

**Gone to the big** or **great ... in the sky.** A light-hearted formula to state that someone has died and 'gone to heaven'. The missing word depends on the person's occupation or interest, thus an actor might go 'to the big theatre in the sky',

a seasoned drinker to 'the big pub in the sky' and a horticulturist to 'the great garden in the sky'.

> To Reid Miles, Barney Bubbles, Neon Park and Mike Doud –
> gone to the great studio in the sky.
>
> STORM THORGERSON and AUBREY POWELL: *100 Best Album*
> *Covers*, Dedication (1999)

**Gone With the Wind.** A highly acclaimed film (1939) based
on a romantic historical novel (1936) of the same title by
Margaret Mitchell (1900–49). The film, which depicts the
experiences of thrice-married Southern belle, Scarlett
O'Hara, during the US Civil War, starred Vivien Leigh as
Scarlett O'Hara and Clark Gable as her lover, Rhett Butler,
and has long been the stuff of Hollywood legend. The title
comes from a line in Ernest Dowson's poem 'Non sum
qualis eram' (1896):

> I have forgot much, Cynara! Gone with the wind,
> Flung roses, roses riotously with the throng,
> Dancing, to put thy pale, lost lilies out of mind.

This was itself based on the refrain in one of Horace's *Odes*
(IV.i), with the lines *Non sum qualis eram bona/Sub regno*
*Cynarae* ('I am not as I was when good Cynara was my
queen'). To Dowson, Cynara represented a 12-year-old
Polish girl, Adelaide Foltinowicz ('Missie'), with whom he
fell in love after seeing her serving in her parents' restaurant
in Sherwood Street, London. While still working on the
novel, Mitchell used the working title 'Pansy', the original
name of her heroine. Other titles she considered included
'Tote the Weary Land', 'Tomorrow Is Another Day' and even
'Ba! Ba! Black Sheep'.

> There was a land of Cavaliers and Cotton Fields called the
> Old South. Here in this patrician world the Age of Chivalry
> took its last bows. Here was the last ever seen of the Knights
> and their Ladies fair, of Master and Slave. Look for it only in
> books, for it is no more than a dream remembered, a
> Civilization gone with the wind.
>
> *Gone with the Wind*, prologue (1939)

**Gonzo journalism.** Journalistic writing of an exaggerated,
subjective and fictionalized style, fashionable in the United
States from the 1970s, and deriving out of the New
Journalism of the likes of Tom Wolfe, for example in *The
Electric Kool-Aid Acid Test* (*see* the MERRY PRANKSTERS). The
word was first used by the US journalist Bill Cardosa in
relation to the writing of Hunter S. Thomson (1939–2005),
and the style is epitomized in Thomson's FEAR AND
LOATHING IN LAS VEGAS. The word perhaps derives from
Italian *gonzo*, 'foolish', or Spanish *ganso*, 'fool', literally
'goose', although among the Boston-Irish a *gonzo* is a man
who is still on his feet after an all-night drinking session.

**Goodbye, Mr Chips.** A novella (1934) by James Hilton
(1900–54) about a gruff master of the old tradition at a minor
English public school, Mr Chipping. His response, on his
deathbed, to hearing a colleague say that it was a pity that he
had had no children, is, 'Yes – umph –I have … Thousands
of 'em … all boys.' Equally celebrated is the parting remark,
after one of Chipping's intimate tea-parties, by a small new
boy, who has only heard him referred to by his nickname:
'Goodbye, Mr Chips.' A classic film version (1939), in
MGM's best sentimentally romantic style and with Robert
Donat as the schoolmaster, was directed by Sam Wood. A
less appealing musical version (1969), with Peter O'Toole
in the title role, was directed by Herbert Ross. *See also*
Mr CHIPS.

**Goodbye to All That.** A volume of memoirs (1929) by the poet
and novelist Robert Graves (1895–1985), recalling his
miserable schooldays, the awfulness of trench warfare and
his unhappy first marriage. The title evokes a world lost
forever (with perhaps a suggestion of 'good riddance').

**Goodbye to Berlin.** A novel (1939) by Christopher Isherwood (1904–86), who as himself is the observer and
narrator: 'I am a camera with its shutter open, quite passive,
recording, not thinking.' The book begins and ends with
extracts from 'A Berlin Diary' respectively for Autumn 1930
and Winter 1932–3, the period that he was teaching English
in Berlin. The four linked sketches in between reflect the
situations of various characters and their reactions to the
brittle political situation. Elements concerning the promiscuous cabaret performer, Sally BOWLES, were made into a
play, *I Am a Camera* by John van Druten (1901–57), from
which were derived a musical, CABARET (1966), and a film of
the same title (1972).

**Good cop, bad cop.** An encapsulation of a method of
interrogation (as allegedly sometimes used by the police) in
which periods of amiable and supportive treatment, putting
the questioned person at his or her ease, are alternated with
periods of tough questioning and other psychological
pressure, potentially or actually accompanied by violent
treatment. The expression is frequently put to wider
metaphorical use.

> The agreement between Iran and the International Atomic
> Energy Agency (IAEA) over the control of the Iranian
> nuclear programme represents a success for tough
> diplomacy in which Europeans and Americans found
> themselves playing a good cop/bad cop routine. The
> Europeans … urged Iran to cooperate and offered
> technology and fuel to allow it to develop nuclear power.
> The Americans threatened Tehran with sanctions.
>
> www.bbc.co.uk/news/ (26 November 2003)

**Good Friday Agreement.** An agreement between the British and Irish governments regarding the future of Northern Ireland, reached on Good Friday, 10 April 1998. At the core of the agreement was the principle of consent that Northern Ireland is part of the United Kingdom and would remain so for as long as the people who live there wish it. Conversely, it was agreed that if the people of Northern Ireland were formally to consent to the establishment of a united Ireland, the government of the day would bring forward proposals to implement this. The agreement thus resulted in a formal resolution of the historic differences between Britain and Ireland, a development in principle welcomed by SINN FÉIN. *See also* DIRECT RULE.

**Good girl, bad boy.** Two converse expressions whose alliterative appeal has contributed to the sexual stereotyping of the children (or animals) in question.

**Good Guides.** An alliterative basis for many titles of informative books and radio programmes, the two words sandwiching the subject in question. First and foremost in the field was *The Good Food Guide* (1951), edited by Raymond Postgate. Others to follow, as listed in *British Books in Print* (1982), have included *Good Beer Guide, Good Birth Guide, Good Boat Guide, Good Caff Guide, Good Camera Guide, Good Camps Guide, Good Con Guide, Good Cook's Guide, Good God Guide, Good Health Guide, Good Hotel Guide, Good Job Guide, Good Life Guide, Good Move Guide, Good Museums Guide, Good Pets Guide, Good Plants Guide* and *Good Toy Guide.* A four-part radio series broadcast in 1988 using words and music to celebrate parliament, the law, the church and royalty was entitled *The Good Establishment Guide.* The format is more subtle than it seems, since 'Good' relates not only to the guide, as being supposedly superior to others on the subject, but to the subject itself, singled out for selective appraisal as the best of its kind.

**Goodies.** A term for any tasty titbits. 'Goody' or 'Goody goody' is still used as a sign of approval and a once popular childish expression of satisfaction was 'Goody goody gum drops'. A goody-goody is a smug or unduly virtuous person, however. In a story or film, the 'Goody' is the hero or heroine, as contrasted with the 'Baddy'. There may well be several 'Goodies' lined up against the 'Baddies'.

*The Goodies* was the collective name adopted by three comics in the BBC television series so titled, running from 1970 to 1982. They were Graeme Garden, Tim Brooke-Taylor and Bill Oddie. 'Goodies' actually represented letters from the beginning, middle and end of their surnames: *G*arden, Br*oo*ke-Taylor and Od*die*.

**Good Life, The.** A BBC television SITCOM running from 1975 to 1978. It depicted a middle-class suburban couple, Tom and Barbara Good, and their efforts to go 'back to the land', growing their own food, keeping animals and making their own tools and equipment. Inevitably, the enterprise creates friction with their next-door neighbours, Jerry and Margo Leadbetter. The series owed much to its topicality, its clever scripts and its first-rate acting and casting, with Richard Briers and Felicity Kendal as the Goods and Paul Eddington and Penelope Keith as the Leadbetters.

**Goodman Memorial Theatre.** The oldest regional theatre in the United States, in Chicago, Illinois. It opened on 22 October 1925, when it was donated to the Arts Institute of Chicago by the parents of the playwright Kenneth S. Goodman (1883–1918), author of *Dust of the Road* (1913) and *The Wonder Hat* (1913), the latter one of eight plays written in collaboration with Ben Hecht. The theatre was meant to combine a school of acting with a resident professional company, but the GREAT DEPRESSION forced the company to disband in the 1930s. In the 1960s the Goodman once again housed a fully professional company and in 1977 was incorporated as the Chicago Theatre Group.

**Good Neighbour Policy.** A popular name for the Latin-American policy of President Franklin D. Roosevelt (*see* FDR). It was suggested by his commitment 'to the policy of the good neighbour', as outlined in his first inaugural address of 4 March 1933, and resulted in a renunciation by the United States of its right to intervene in the internal affairs of Latin American states. The success of the policy was measured by the rapidity with which most Latin-American countries rallied to the Allies in the Second World War.

***Goodness Had Nothing To Do With It.*** The autobiography (1959) of the feisty American actress and writer Mae West. The title comes from a line West spoke in the character of Mandie Triplett in the film *Night After Night* (1932), written by Vincent Laurence but 'with additional dialogue' by West. Another character exclaims on seeing her 'Goodness! What beautiful diamonds!', to which West responds: 'Goodness had nothing to do with it, dearie.'

**Good news and the bad news.** The mixed consequences of an action; an outcome that has both a good and a bad side. The implication is generally that the news is good but that it is tempered by an unexpected disadvantage. The dual consequence is typically implied in the such formulations as: 'Do you want the good news or the bad news?' or 'First the good news'. The verbal contrast dates from the 1970s.

The good news is that British Telecom has just conducted the world's first live GPRS data call, and announced that it will be introducing the service next year. The bad news is that things rarely happen when they're supposed to.

*Sunday Times* (5 December 1999)

**Good News Bible.** A version of the Bible produced by the American Bible Society, designed to be easily understood, including those whose first language is not English. The New Testament was published in 1966 and the complete Bible in 1976. It follows the traditional numbering of chapter and verse. The modernized text was not to everyone's taste and was criticized by some for the quality of its translation.

> The accuracy of the latest and much-heralded translation of Holy Scripture, the Good News Bible, the millionth copy of which has just been presented to the Queen, has been challenged by Dr Eric Kemp, Bishop of Chichester. He says he finds it incredulous [*sic*] that those famous words of St Paul about 'flesh' and 'lower nature' have, in his episcopal view, been altogether mistranslated.
>
> *Manchester Guardian Weekly* (6 February 1977)

**Goodnight children … everywhere.** *See* UNCLE MAC.

**Good ole boy.** A traditional white male of the southern US states. It originated as a term of companionable approval in the southern white community, but latterly has come often to be used with connotations of racist bigotry. More generally, it can refer to any hidebound old traditionalist. 'Ole' is 'old', as GRAND OLE OPRY.

> This is the world of the Good Ole Boy, the country hick from down in the hollow, his innocent, God-fearing eyes scanning the world of corruption laid out before him at every crossroad grocery store, supermarket, and shopping center.
>
> *Harper's* (September 1976)

> There is a huge disparity between those who knew what they were doing in the vineyard and the good old boys with big crops and little understanding. Fortunately the sort of growers we buy from come into the former category.
>
> JASPER MORRIS: in Berry Bros. & Rudd's Grand Burgundy Offer (2005)

**Good on you.** An Australian equivalent of 'good for you', dating from the early 20th century.

**Good Person of Setzuan, The.** A play, originally entitled *Der gute Mensch von Sezuan* and sometimes rendered as *The Good Woman of Setzuan* (1938–41), by the German playwright Bertolt Brecht (1898–1956), first performed in 1943. Three gods travel the globe in search of a good person, and they eventually find Shen Te, a prostitute of Setzuan, who uses the money she wins to set up a cigar factory (which she runs in the guise of a man, employing various underhand means). The idea of three gods descending on a town and

finding it wanting is an ancient literary device, but in Brecht's mind it became linked with a visit he and two friends made to Dresden, where they got a cool welcome. He took his revenge by savaging the city in a poem. *See also* EPIC THEATRE.

**Good question.** One that requires careful consideration before answering. A common evasive response to a question which one cannot answer is: 'That's a good question.'

**Good, the Bad and the Ugly, The.** The last film (1966) in Sergio Leone's 'Man With No Name' trilogy of spaghetti Westerns (*see* A FISTFUL OF DOLLARS). Set during the American Civil War, it stars Clint Eastwood as Joe ('the Good'), Lee Van Cleef as Setenza ('the Bad') and Eli Wallach as Tuco ('the Ugly'), all of whom are after a fortune buried in an unmarked grave. The title has become a common journalistic catchphrase, much played on by headline writers.

**Good Time Charlie.** *See* CHAMPAGNE CHARLIE.

**Goodtime George.** A nickname for George Melly (b.1926), jazz singer, critic, connoisseur of excess and devotee of SURREALISM. The name derives from John Chilton's song 'Goodtime George', a Melly favourite.

**Good-time girl.** A young woman who seeks pleasure and 'plenty of action' to go with it, often at the expense of a more mundane commitment such as working, studying or domestic duties. The term, of US origin and dating from the 1920s, can also euphemistically imply sexual promiscuity.

**Good time was had by all, A.** Everybody enjoyed themselves. A supposed traditional conclusion of a descriptive account of a social event in a parish magazine. The words were adopted as the title of a collection of poems by Stevie Smith published in 1937.

**'Good Vibrations'.** A song by The Beach Boys, one of the classic songs of the 1960s. Written by Brian Wilson (over a period of six months) and released in 1966, it marries the HIPPIE notion of 'vibes' (meaning variously atmosphere, feeling or intuition, as in 'I'm getting bad vibes off her') with the time-honoured pop music theme of boy-meets-girl. Glen Campbell, later famous as a star of country music, who worked as a session guitarist on the single, is reported to have remarked to the Beach Boys' Brian Wilson: 'What were you smokin' when you wrote that?' *See also* ROCK GROUP NAMES.

**Goody bag.** A little bag containing GOODIES or other small presents, given to children to take home after a party or to adults at the end (or start) of a social event, conference, business presentation or the like. In the latter case the bag may be big rather than little, and the presents large rather than small. The aim is to express goodwill or hospitality. The concept is of US origin.

**Goody two-shoes.** A smugly virtuous person. The usage arose, probably in the Unites States in the 1930s, from a misunderstanding of the name of the central character in the nursery tale *The History of Little Goody Two-Shoes* (1765), who owned only one shoe and when given a pair was so pleased that she showed them to everyone, saying: 'Two shoes!' 'Goody' is an archaic title for a married woman, without necessarily any implication of moral virtue.

**Go off the deep end.** To succumb to anger; to vent one's emotions violently. The allusion is to a swimmer diving or jumping in where the water is deepest, not simply paddling in the shallows. The expression dates from the 1920s.

**Google.** A US company formed in 1998 that runs the Google INTERNET search engine, which resulted from a research project in 1996 by two postgraduate students from Stanford University, Larry Page and Sergey Brin. Such is the dominance of Google over other search engines that 'to google' has become a generic verb meaning to search for something on the Internet. The story goes that Page and Brin thought they were naming their company after GOOGOL, the vast number, but got the spelling wrong. In the same vein the company's headquarters is called the Googleplex. *See also* YAHOO!

**Googlewhacking.** A game, popular in the early years of the 21st century, consisting of entering two words into the GOOGLE search engine with the aim of getting just a single 'hit'. Such a hit is known as a 'Googlewhack' (an example is – or rather was – 'musclebound okapi'). As the years go by and Google's database gets larger and larger, the chances of success have diminished. The term is based on 'whack', meaning 'to hit hard', probably under the influence of 'whack off', meaning 'to masturbate'.

**Googly.** A cricketing term dating from the early 20th century for an off-break bowled with an apparent leg-break action. The delivery was invented and developed by the Middlesex bowler B.J.T. Bosanquet (1877–1936) in the late 1890s, and he used it against the Australians in 1903. In Australia it is called a 'BOSIE'. The origin of the term 'googly' is uncertain. New Zealand has often been claimed as its place of birth (Bosanquet toured there as well as Australia in 1903 and took his invention with him) – either exploiting an unspecified Maori dialect term or adapting the existing Australianism 'googler' applied to any high-tossed, looping delivery (which made the batsman 'goggle'). *See also* CHINAMAN; DOOSRA.

**Googol.** This word for the number 1 followed by 100 zeroes ($10^{100}$) is explained in *Mathematics and the Imagination* (1940), by the US mathematician Edward Kasner and his student James Newman, as having been invented by Kasner's nine-year-old nephew, who was asked to think up a name for a very big number. The boy may have subconsciously based the word on the name of the comic strip *Barney Google* (*see* HEEBIE-JEEBIES). The name is not in formal use. The word 'googolplex' was subsequently coined for 1 followed by a googol of zeros. *See also* GOOGLE.

**Goo-goo eyes.** Amorous glances. The expression probably relates to 'goggle' although 'goo-goo' is associated with babies and SWEET NOTHINGS on the lines of COOCHY COOCHY COO. The phrase came into vogue at the turn of the 20th century, and Carl Smith and Fanny Wentworth's *The Goo-Goo Song* (1900) popularized the general idea.

**Gook.** US slang (now regarded as highly offensive) for any East Asian person. It was used extensively by the US military during the VIETNAM War to refer to the Vietnamese (of whatever political persuasion). However, its use among the US military dates back to the 1920s, when it was used to refer to Filipinos, and subsequently was also applied to Japanese and Koreans. A number of not entirely plausible etymologies have been proffered. One relates it to the Filipino word *gugu*, meaning 'spirit'. Another suggestion is that it mimics the sound of an incomprehensible language, just as the ancient Greek *barbaros* ('uncivilized', 'barbarian') mimicked the 'ba-ba' sound attributed to foreign speech.

**Goombah.** In US slang, a close male friend or associate. The term was originally Italian-American, and it was popularized by the US boxer and actor Rocky Graziano on the *Martha Raye Show* on NBC-TV in the mid-1950s. It appears to be an alteration of Italian *compare*, 'godfather', and by the end of the 1960s it was also being used in English for 'godfather' in the sense of a mafia boss.

**Goons, The.** A team of four comics who won a wide following for their absurd sense of humour in the weekly radio series *The Goon Show* (1951–60). The crazy quartet comprised Spike Milligan (1918–2002), Peter Sellers (1925–80), Harry Secombe (1921–2001) and Michael Bentine (1921–96). The name Goon betrayed the wartime influence on Milligan and Secombe, who had first met in the North African desert. It was a word often used by prisoners of war for their German guards, and may have been a blend of 'gorilla' and 'baboon'. Milligan claimed, however, that he took the name from the creature called Alice the Goon in the POPEYE comic strip by the US cartoonist Elzie C. Segar. The former origin may have prompted one of the programme's catchphrases: 'Neddie

Seagoon' (Secombe) would offer a cigarette with the words 'Have a gorilla', to which the reply was, 'No thanks, I only smoke baboons.'

**Go overboard.** To be very enthusiastic; to overreact. The evocation is of a vigour or action so extreme that one throws oneself over the side of a ship. The expression dates from the 1930s.

**Go over the wall.** To escape from prison; to leave a religious order; to defect to another country. In all three instances an actual wall may have to be traversed in order to make one's way out. In *I Leap Over the Wall* (1950) Monica Baldwin, a niece of the prime minister Stanley Baldwin, describes her return to the outside world after having spent 28 years in a monastery. She based the title on the Baldwin family motto, *Per Deum meum transilio murum*, 'By the help of my God I leap over a wall', itself from the biblical words, 'By my God have I leaped over a wall' (2 Samuel 22:30; Psalm 18:29). Miss Baldwin recounts in the book how some 400 years earlier her ancestor, Thomas Baldwin of Diddlesbury, had leapt to freedom from behind the walls of the Tower of London, where his name with an inscription 'July 1585' can still be seen where he carved it on the wall of his cell in the Beauchamp Tower.

**Go pear-shaped.** To go wrong. The phrase became current in the 1980s, but despite persistent reports of earlier use, notably in RAF slang, there have been no confirmed sightings of it before 1983. However, the term 'pear-shaped' does crop up in the 1958 British film *The Captain's Table*, where it is used as a colloquialism for 'unorthodox', and that might well be a precursor of the current usage. The ultimate basis of the metaphor remains unclear, but the underlying idea is probably of deviation from a standard or norm (the shape of a pear could be regarded as a sphere that has been partly deflated or 'gone wrong').

**Go places.** To succeed; to do well. The concept is of gaining seniority by moving to different posts. The phrase is of US origin and dates from the 1920s.

**Go public.** To seek a quotation on the stock market. This specific sense, as applied to a privately owned company, came to give a general meaning to reveal oneself, to come out into the open.

**Gorblimey.** A rakish hat, as supposedly worn by a Cockney or anyone prone to exclaiming 'gorblimey', as a slurring of 'God blind me'. ('Blimey' is a short form of this.) The hat so named evolved in the early years of the 20th century as a type of unconventional military headgear in the form of a floppy field-service cap. Gorblimey trousers were in similar

style, and both terms were directly inspired by a ribald Liverpool folk ditty, 'My Old Man's a Fireman on the Elder-Dempster Line', which had the couplet, 'He wears Gorblimey trousers/An a little gorblimey 'at'. This same song was adapted by Lonnie Donegan for his Number 1 hit, 'My Old Man's a Dustman' (1960), which again popularized the garments.

**Gorby.** The nickname of the Soviet communist politician Mikhail Gorbachev (b.1931), general secretary of the Communist Party (1985–91) and president of the Soviet Union (1989–91). The liberalizing reforms he unveiled under the slogans GLASNOST and PERESTROIKA made him popular in the West, and led to a surge of 'Gorbymania'. The Soviet foreign minister Andrei Gromyko (GRIM GROM) described Gorbachev thus in a speech to the Central Committee of the Party on 11 March 1985:

> Comrades, this man has a nice smile, but he's got iron teeth.

**Gordon, Flash.** *See* FLASH GORDON.

**Gordonstoun.** The Scottish public school near Lossiemouth, renowned for its emphasis on physical self-reliance, was founded in 1934 by the German educationist Kurt Hahn after he was forced to flee from NAZI Germany. His aim was to counteract what he saw as the 'four social declines' of physical fitness, initiative, care and compassion. To combat the problems of puberty, he instigated a rigorous routine of morning runs and cold showers. He later devised the Duke of Edinburgh Award scheme. The school won royal approval, and no fewer than three royal princes, Charles, Andrew and Edward, were educated here, the first of these letting it be known subsequently that his time there had not been a happy one. The school has now toned down its ruggedness and rigidity, but much of Hahn's legacy survives. Gordonstoun became coeducational in 1972.

**Gorgeous George.** Originally, the nickname of the US wrestler George Raymond Wagner (1915–63), who was noted for his flamboyant appearance. It was subsequently sometimes applied to the dashing French boxer Georges Carpentier (1894–1975) and more recently, with a degree of irony, to the dapper Scottish MP George Galloway (b.1954), who represented Labour until he was expelled from the party for supporting Iraq during the Coalition invasion of 2003. He then went on to found the left-wing, anti-war Respect Party, under whose banner he won the seat of Bethnal Green and Bow from Labour in the 2005 general election. In January 2006 he astonished the nation by his decision to enter the BIG BROTHER House for a new series of *Celebrity Big Brother*, in which he successfully impersonated a cat. Prior to this development, one of his former Labour colleagues in his old Glasgow Hillhead constituency observed: 'George could start a riot in an empty house.'

**Gorgeous Gussie.** The nickname of the US tennis star Gussie Moran (b.1923), whose lace-trimmed panties caused a sensation on the courts of Wimbledon in 1949. They were designed for her by the Wimbledon fashion expert Ted Tinling. The name has appropriate overtones of GUSSIED UP.

***Gorky Park.*** A crime novel (1981) by Martin Cruz Smith (b.1942) in which a Soviet policeman sets out to solve the mystery of a murder in Moscow's Gorky Park, named after Maxim Gorky (1868–1936), Russian novelist, dramatist and communist social and political agitator. A film version (1983), directed by Michael Apted and shot in Helsinki, failed to capture the authentic detail of Moscow life in the original.

**Gormenghast.** The sprawling, labyrinthine castle which lies at the heart of a trilogy of fantasy novels by Mervyn Peake (1911–68): *Titus Groan* (1946), *Gormenghast* (1950) and *Titus Alone* (1959). The hereditary seat of the Lords of Groan, its aspect is fearful, and the landscape between Gormenghast Mountains and the castle is bleak and desolate. Its inhabitants (which include the murderous Steerpike, the quirky schoolmaster Dr Prunesquallor, the cadaverous servant Flay, the brutal chef Swelter and Sourdust, the Master of Ritual) are simply part of it and have no idea of the world that exists outside its mummified traditions. Only the young heir, TITUS GROAN, eventually breaks free from its bonds. *See also* FIRST LINES OF NOVELS.

**Gort Na Cloca Mora.** The home of the leprechauns in James Stephens's best-known novel *The Crock of Gold* (1912). It lies on the edge of a wood, where a rough field is scattered with grey rocks. Hence its name, which in Irish means 'Field of the Great Stones'.

**Gory details.** An explicit account of some unpleasant episode, such as a business deal or a divorce. A humorous allusion to the 'bloody' content.

**Gotcha!** Got you! Caught you! A notorious front-page headline in *The Sun* newspaper on 4 May 1982, referring to the sinking of the Argentinian cruiser GENERAL BELGRANO in the FALKLANDS WAR. The word itself, dating from the 1930s, was earlier familiar in the form 'gotcher'.

***Go Tell It on the Mountain.*** The first novel, published in 1953, with autobiographical undertones, by the African American writer, James Baldwin (1924–87), the climax of which is the religious conversion of a 14-year-old Harlem boy. At the centre of the book are the boy's troubled relations with his stepfather, a preacher of the store-front Temple of the Fire Baptized. Aspects of the slave era and of life in a dysfunctional family are recounted in flashbacks. Various biblical passages are reflected in the title, the closest perhaps being the following: 'O Zion, that bringest good tidings, get thee up into the high mountain; … say unto the cities of Judah, Behold your God!' (Isaiah 40:9).

**Goth.** Any young person who dresses up in a post-PUNK style in black, with heavy black make-up, and who affects an interest in death, vampires, Satanism, etc. The style first emerged in the early 1980s.

**Gotha raids.** The air raids on Britain by German Gotha G-IV and G-V bombers in the First World War. The Gothas were twin-engined biplanes, with a pencil-shaped fuselage suspended from the upper wing and 'pusher' engines attached to the rear of the lower wing. They had a three-man crew, a range of 480km (290 miles) and could carry 500kg (1100 lb) of bombs on external racks. They were manufactured by the Gothaer Waggonfabrik and named after the town of Gotha in central Germany. The Gotha raids began on 13 June 1917, taking over from the earlier ZEPPELIN raids. The Gothas caused little damage, but caused a public uproar in Britain. Fighters were withdrawn from the WESTERN FRONT to meet the threat, but in fact it was the number of losses due to accidents and anti-aircraft fire that led the Germans to abandon the raids in May 1918.

During the First World War the British royal family changed their surname from Saxe-Coburg-Gotha to WINDSOR.

**Go the distance.** To carry through an action to completion. The expression originated in boxing, in which a boxer who 'goes the distance' lasts for all the scheduled rounds. In baseball the same phrase means to pitch for the entire length of the game. The distance is thus of time, not space.

**Go the extra mile.** To make a special and often prolonged effort to achieve one's aim, especially on behalf of another. The idea is that one is prepared to do more than just GO THE DISTANCE. The expression dates from the 1950s but has a biblical resonance: 'And whosoever shall compel thee to go a mile, go with him twain' (Matthew 5:41).

> For Bill Hitzig, lifelong friend, who has gone more extra miles for more people than even the poets dreamed possible.
> NORMAN COUSINS: *Human Options*, Dedication (1981)

**Go there.** To mention or discuss a particular topic, especially one likely to prove embarrassing or controversial. The usage, which emerged towards the end of the 20th century in American English, almost always occurs in negative contexts, notably the admonition 'Don't go there!'

I would ascribe Evelyn's cold, detached reaction to Bron's pitiful condition as … an attempt, perhaps, to break away from his upbringing etc., etc. However, I am not a psychoanalyst, so I shan't 'go there' as they say. I leave it instead for others to decide.

ALEXANDER WAUGH: *Fathers and Sons* (2004)

**Go the whole nine yards.** *See* WHOLE NINE YARDS.

**Gothic Line.** (German *Gotisch Linie*.) A heavily fortified defensive line built across Italy by the Germans during the Second World War. The line crossed the Italian peninsula north of Florence, running between La Spezia on the west coast to Pesaro, south of Rimini, on the east coast. The Allied operation to breach the line took place in August–September 1944. The name refers to the ancient Gothic tribes, fearsome warriors who were regarded as the ancestors of modern Germans. *See also* FORTRESS EUROPE; GUSTAV LINE.

**Go through the roof.** To lose one's temper suddenly. *See also* HIT THE CEILING.

**Go-to.** Denoting a person or thing one has recourse to ('goes to') as a first choice among a range of others, especially because of their reliability. The usage emerged in the US in the early 21st century.

The way McGrath tipped the scales at Lord's, he looked destined to be Ricky Ponting's go-to guy this series also.

GIDEON HAIGH: *Ashes 2005* (2005)

**Go to town.** To do something thoroughly or extravagantly; to enjoy oneself greatly. The concept is of a rural resident finding reward and fulfilment in 'the big city'. The expression is of US origin and dates from the 1930s.

**Gotrocks.** A facetious surname applied in US slang to a person of unseemly wealth – as, 'Mr Gotrocks' ('rocks' here being a slang term for 'dollars'). It is first recorded in Thomas Wolfe's *The Web and the Rock* (1938), in which he introduces a 'Mr Maecenas Gotrox'.

**Go troppo.** In Australian slang, to become mentally disturbed or unbalanced. The expression was born out of Second World War service in the tropics, which had a damaging psychological effect on many who were caught up in it.

Hmmm, 3 more weeks of school holidays, must find something to amuse these children before I go totally troppo.

www.essentialbaby.com.au (11 January 2005)

**Gottle o' geer.** A representation of the words 'bottle of beer' said without moving the lips, as a supposed typical utterance of a ventriloquist and so a byword for their art.

**Governator, The.** A nickname that was given to Arnold Schwarzenegger (b.1947) when he became Republican governor of California in 2003. Variations include 'Gubernator' and 'Guvernator'. In his earlier career as a film star (*see* the AUSTRIAN OAK) Schwarzenegger played the title roles in the films *The* TERMINATOR (1984) and *Terminator 2* (1991).

Horrified by the Governator's famous self-reinventions, [Gary] Indiana eviscerates Arnie's ascendancy in what he calls 'a society where fetishised images seem more credible than reality'.

*The Observer* (24 July 2005)

**Government Communications Headquarters.** *See* GCHQ.

**Governor Moonbeam.** A nickname given to Jerry Brown (b.1938), governor of California (1975–83), because of his environmentally aware policies, regarded by some as eccentric. His beliefs had developed into a kind of NEW AGE philosophy (he studied Zen in Japan) by the time he tried for the Democratic presidential nomination in 1992, earning him the new nickname, the SPACE CADET.

**Go West, Young Man.** A film (1937) whose title contains a reference to its star Mae West (1892–1980) while punning on a well-known exhortation to new arrivals in the United States in the mid-19th century, when the western territories of the country were being opened up to settlers. The slogan is usually attributed to the newspaperman Horace Greeley, who ran unsuccessfully for the presidency, but it was, in fact, coined by John Babsone Lane Soule, writing in the Terre Haute (Indiana) *Express* in 1851:

Go west, young man, and grow up with the country.

**Go while the going is good.** To get away while one can; to proceed while conditions are favourable. The US expression appears in many popular novels of the first half of the 20th century and relates to horse racing, which is best held when the 'going' or condition of the ground is good.

**Go with a bang.** To be highly successful; to be a 'hit'. *See also* WITH A BANG.

**Go with a swing.** To be a great success; to be lively and enjoyable. The phrase dates from the 1970s and typically applies to a party or other social function where there is vigorous activity or animated conversation. At its height such a party would be in full swing.

**Go with the flow.** To accept a situation rather than trying to control it. The phrase dates from the 1960s and is a succinct resumé of the teaching of the US psychologist Carl R. Rogers (1902–87) that life involves 'floating with a complex streaming of experience'.

**Graceland.** The mansion and burial site of Elvis Presley

(1935–77), the KING, at Memphis, Tennessee, opened as a shrine to his adoring public in 1982. 'Graceland' is also the title of a song and album by Paul Simon, released in 1986, the inspiration behind the song being an actual trip that Simon made to Graceland with his young son. *See also* ELVIS LIVES; ELVIS THE PELVIS.

**Grace under pressure.** How the US novelist Ernest Hemingway (1899–1961) defined 'guts' (i.e. courage) in an interview with Dorothy Parker, published in *The New Yorker*, 30 November 1929.

**Grade.** This word is commonly used to denote a student's assessment or mark of attainment in schools and colleges, as the seven grades A to G in the GCSE (General Certificate of Secondary Education) examination. From 1994 there has been an additional 'starred' A grade (A*) to cater for the highest attainers.

**Graduate, The.** A film (1967) adapted by Calder Willingham and Buck Henry from the autobiographical novel by Charles Webb about a young man's confusion as he approaches adulthood in suburban southern California. Starring Dustin Hoffman and directed by Mike Nichols, the film's title refers as much to his seduction by an older married woman (played by Anne Bancroft) and his grappling with what he wants from life as it does to the recent completion of his college studies. The soundtrack, by Paul Simon and Art Garfunkel, includes such classic songs as 'Mrs Robinson', 'The Sound of Silence' and 'Scarborough Fair'.

**Graffiti.** (Italian *graffito*, 'scratching'.) A name applied originally to the 'wall scribblings' found at Pompeii and other Italian cities, as the work of schoolboys, idlers and the like, many of them obscene and accompanied by rough drawings. Modern graffiti are found on walls, in public toilets, on posters and in other clearly visible places. They are sometimes crude and erotic, but some are genuinely witty. One seen in Manchester in 1978 read: 'If you hate graffiti, sign a partition.'

Political graffiti were formerly common in the 1930s and so-called graffiti art, also known as 'spraycan art', evolved in the 1980s as a semi-abstract, quasi-pictorial manifestation in the New York subway system. A leading exponent of the technique was Jean-Michel Basquiat (1960–88). His brief but bright career was ended by a drugs overdose. *See also* CHAD; KILROY.

**Grammy.** One of a number of annual awards given by the American National Academy of Recording Arts and Sciences for achievement in the record industry, first made

in 1958 and taking its name from a blend of 'gramophone' and EMMY. It was introduced largely as a publicity stunt. The award itself is in the form of a gold-plated disk.

**Granadaland.** The area around Manchester, where Granada Television is based, typically regarded as brash and affluent. The company takes its name from the Granada chain of cinemas opened in 1930 by Sidney Bernstein (1899–1993), who so called them after a holiday in the Spanish city of Granada, where he had much admired the Alhambra Palace.

In 1987 Bernstein received a silver pomegranate from the governor of the Spanish province of Granada in recognition for his company's achievement in 'putting Granada on the map'. *Granada* is the Spanish for 'pomegranate'.

**Granddaddy of them all.** The first, oldest or greatest example of something, as: 'That old TV set is the granddaddy of them all.' The expression dates from the 1950s.

**Grandmother's steps** or **footsteps.** A children's game in which one player stands with his back to the others who approach him stealthily and try to touch his back without him seeing them move. The player at the front is allowed to turn round often and without warning and anyone he sees moving is sent back to the starting line. The name takes a grandmother as a person supposedly hard of hearing or dimly sighted and so unlikely to be aware of anyone's approach. The game dates from the 1920s. *See also* RED LIGHT.

> We, who remember, look back to the blossoming May-time
> On ghosts of servers and thurifers after Mass,
> The slapping of backs, the flapping of cassocks, the play-time,
> A game of Grandmother's Steps on the vicarage grass.
> JOHN BETJEMAN: *High and Low*, 'Anglo-Catholic Congresses' (1966)

**Grand Ole Opry.** This country music show at Nashville, Tennessee, began weekly radio broadcasts in 1925, playing traditional country or hillbilly music. The show was originally known as the 'WSM Barn Dance', but gained its familiar name, a dialect form of 'Grand Old Opera', in 1926. In 1941 the Opry became a live stage show, and in 1974 moved to the Opryland amusement park and entertainment centre in Nashville.

**Grandpa England.** The name given to George V (reigned 1910–36) by his granddaughter Princess Elizabeth (the present Queen) when a child. He was also known as 'the Sailor King', having served in the Royal Navy until the death in 1892 of his elder brother, Albert Victor, made him heir to the throne.

**Grandparents Day.** MOTHER'S DAY and FATHER'S DAY had been observed for much of the 20th century before National Grandparents Day was inaugurated in the United States in 1978 to complement the family commemoration on the Sunday after Labor Day (first Monday in September).

**Grand slam.** A sports term for a win in each of a group of major championships or matches in a given year, and especially in tennis, golf or rugby union. The tennis grand slam refers to winning the four most prestigious tournaments: the Australian Open, the French Open, the US Open and Wimbledon. The golf grand slam refers to winning all four MAJORS in a single year. The rugby union grand slam refers to winning all the matches in the six nations championship, which is contested by England, Scotland, Wales, Ireland, France and Italy. This 20th-century usage evolved from the specific 19th-century term for the bidding and winning of all 13 tricks in the game of bridge. 'Slam' here is not the same as the word for a loud bang but the name of an old card game.

Grand Slam is also the nickname of the largest conventional bomb ever used in action, 8m (26ft 6in) long and weighing 10,000kg (22,000lb). It was developed in 1945 by Barnes Wallis (*see* DAM BUSTERS), and could penetrate 7m (23ft) of reinforced concrete. Over 40 were dropped on targets in Germany before the end of the Second World War.

***Grange Hill.*** A pioneering children's SOAP OPERA first screened in 1978 and set in the (fictional) London comprehensive school of the title. Plot lines included a teenage boy's HEROIN addiction and a teenage girl's pregnancy, and the regular scenes of hair-pulling and shop-lifting outraged many. The producers countered criticism, however, by claiming that the tales were cautionary ones.

**Granita Meeting, The.** The legendary meeting at the Granita restaurant in Upper Street, Islington, in May 1994, at which Tony Blair and Gordon Brown, following the sudden death of John Smith, reputedly resolved the ticklish question as to which of them should become the leader of the Labour Party. It is said that Brown agreed to support Blair for the leadership, on condition that Blair would stand down after two terms. When Blair announced in October 2004 (while Brown was out of the country) that he would run for a third term as prime minister, Brown was reported as saying, 'There is nothing that you could say to me now that I could ever believe.' Blair has always denied that any deal was brokered, while Brown has to date refused to comment. The choice of the Granita, a fashionable 'Cal-Ital' restaurant redolent of rocket and ciabatta, heralded to many the flavour of Blair's NEW LABOUR, a flavour far removed from the beer and sandwiches of the party's traditional roots in working men's clubs. In 2003 Channel 4 screened a drama about the pact entitled *The Deal*, written by Peter Morgan and directed by Stephen Frears.

> Those suspicious of the recent outbreak of love between Blair and Brown [in the run-up to the 2005 election] may enjoy noting that Granita, the trendy, minimalist restaurant where their original, untrustworthy deal was hatched, is now a Tex-Mex establishment called Desperados.
>
> JACK WINKLER: letter to *The Guardian* (25 April 2005)

**Granny dumping.** The deliberate 'dumping' of an elderly relative, usually female, especially one suffering from fits of confusion or other troubling habits, by taking them to a hospital or care centre and abandoning them there. The practice was first observed in the United States in the early 1990s.

**Granny flat.** A self-contained flat or annexe inside or built on to a house, designed as a modest home for an elderly relative. Such flats became less common in the closing years of the 20th century, the elderly largely living in sheltered housing or similar residential accommodation. The term granny annexe is sometimes contracted as 'grannex'.

**Granny glasses.** Spectacles with small circular lenses, which were in fashion in the 1960s during the heyday of The BEATLES and the FLOWER CHILDREN. Their popularity was largely due to John Lennon, who wore glasses of this type.

**Granny lane.** In CB RADIO slang, the inside or slow lane on a highway.

***Grapes of Wrath, The.*** A novel (1939) by John Steinbeck (1902–68), which won the PULITZER PRIZE for fiction. It charts the vicissitudes of a farming family, which migrates from the dustbowls of Oklahoma in search of a better future in California during the GREAT DEPRESSION. The title comes from 'The Battle Hymn of the Republic' by Julia Ward Howe (1819–1900): 'Mine eyes have seen the glory of the coming of the Lord,/ He is trampling out the vintage where the grapes of wrath are stored' (lines 1–2). A superb film version (1940) was directed by John Ford. *See also* OKIES.

**Grasshopper mind.** One unable to concentrate on any single subject for long. The grasshopper is quick to leap from one resting place to another.

**Grassy knoll.** An area in Dallas that was just ahead of President John F. Kennedy when he was assassinated on 22 November 1963. Those conspiracy theorists who do not accept that Lee Harvey Oswald was a lone gunman interpret various bits of evidence to indicate that the shots that killed

Kennedy came from the grassy knoll and not from Oswald in the Texas School Book Repository, as the official WARREN COMMISSION concluded. *See also* JFK.

The phrase has come to be used figuratively:

Virtually every bar of his [J.S.Bach's] music has become a grassy knoll of hidden meaning and message.

JOHN BUTT: in *The Guardian* (12 December 2005)

**Grateful Dead, The.** *See* AMERICAN BEAUTY; DEADHEADS; KEEP ON TRUCKING; MERRY PRANKSTERS; ROCK GROUP NAMES.

**Grauniad, The.** A mostly affectionate media nickname for *The Guardian* newspaper, dating from the 1970s and originating in *Private Eye*. The name is an anagrammatic travesty of the paper's title and alludes to its legendary misprints. In 1997 *The Guardian* launched an entertaining and instructive 'corrections and clarifications column' to set the record straight in such instances. One such item read: 'The film starring Errol Flynn … was *The Master of Ballantrae*, not *The Mask of Gallantry*' (quoted in *The Times* of 10 December 1999).

**Graveyard shift.** In the Second World War the name given by shift workers in munitions factories and other workplaces to the shift covering the midnight hours. The allusion is perhaps to the watchmen who at one time patrolled the graves of the wealthy in order to deter grave robbers. The second word is variable for any similar night work or schedule.

The so-called 'graveyard' slot for the 11pm *Nightly News* has proved quite lively at times.

*The Times* (23 July 1999)

**Gravity's Rainbow.** A novel (1973) by Thomas Pynchon (b.1937). Set in Europe towards the end of the Second World War and immediately after it, the main plot concerns a US soldier who has erections in places in London that are due to be hit by V–2 missiles, which in turn would become the method of delivering the nuclear armaments that were being developed in the United States at the same time. 'Gravity's Rainbow' refers both to the arc of the missile and to the metaphorical trajectory of civilization as it moves towards its own destruction. The novel shared the National Book Award. It was selected for the PULITZER PRIZE only to be thrown out by the advisory board as 'obscene' and 'unreadable', but won the Howells Medal, which the author refused. *See also* FIRST LINES OF NOVELS.

**Gravy train.** A sinecure; a simple situation or nominal position that will give ready profit. The image is of a train of 'gravy' as a pleasing addition to the 'meat' that is one's daily

sustenance. There is doubtless also an association in sense between a 'gravy boat', so called from its shape, and a 'gravy train', both alluding to forms of transport. The expression dates from the 1920s.

**Gray, Cornelia.** The woman detective who appears in P.D. James's novels *An Unsuitable Job for a Woman* (1972) and *The Skull Beneath the Skin* (1982). She is independent, single-minded and intelligent and, in an appealing way, entirely guileless. In a television version (1985) of the former novel she was played by Pippa Guard, and in a later and better version of 1998 by Helen Baxendale.

**Graziano, Rocky.** The US middleweight boxing champion, born Thomas Rocco Barbella (1919–90), who helped to popularize the nickname 'Rocky' for boxers. He was at his best in the 1940s and 1950s, when his brawling style made him popular with the public. He was a model for the ROCKY films starring Sylvester Stallone. *See also* Rocky MARCIANO.

**Grease.** A film musical (1978) based on a stage show (1972) with music by Jim Jacobs and Warren Casey about a group of lively teenagers during the ROCK 'N' ROLL era of the 1950s. Starring John Travolta and Olivia Newton-John, the film was a massive international success, spawning several major pop hits. The title, referring to the grease most young men put in their hair at that time, was changed to *Glease* when the film was released in Japan, to *Vaselino* when released in Mexico, and to *Brilliantine* when shown in France. A sequel, *Grease 2* (1982), was unmemorable.

**Greasy pole.** A form of outdoor entertainment dating from the 19th century in which two people try to knock each other off a horizontal pole covered with an oily substance that makes it difficult to keep one's feet. The traditional 'weapons' for this purpose are pillows. Figuratively a greasy pole is a difficult 'career ladder' that one has to climb. Here the pole is envisaged as vertical.

**Greasy spoon.** A nickname for a cheap café or restaurant, so called from its unwashed cutlery. The expression is of US origin and dates from the 1920s.

**Great American Novel, The.** A novel (1973) by the US writer Philip Roth (b.1933), which uses the decline of a once-great baseball team as an allegory of contemporary developments in American politics and society. Achieving 'The Great American Novel' has long been the Holy Grail of US writers, and the accolade has been bestowed on works as different as *Moby-Dick* and *The* GREAT GATSBY. The US poet William Carlos Williams (1883–1963) published a collection of essays in 1923 entitled *The Great American Novel*.

**Great American Nude.** The series of paintings and mixed-media works by the US Pop artist Tom Wesselmann

(1931–2004) includes *Great American Nude No. 10* (1961) and *Great American Nude No. 54* (1964). In some of the works the flatly painted nude contrasts with the actual room fittings in the assemblage, such as a radiator, a telephone that rings, a window and curtains. The title is a SWINGING SIXTIES dig at the 'great AMERICAN DREAM' and the 'GREAT AMERICAN NOVEL'.

**Great and the good.** Those who are distinguished and worthy, often applied to those members of the ESTABLISH-MENT who are chosen to sit on royal commissions and other such lofty bodies. The term also occurs as 'the good and the great' and frequently has an ironic implication. Further adjectives may be added.

> The great, the good and the ghastly of the Tory party slid over one another to cast the first stone at [Lord] Archer and his lie.
>
> *Sunday Times* (28 November 1999)

*See also The* BEST AND THE BRIGHTEST.

**'Great Balls of Fire'.** A rock 'n' roll song released in 1958, written by Otis Blackwell and performed with manic energy and intensity by Jerry Lee Lewis (nicknamed the 'back-woods wildman'). The 'balls of fire' in question are the fires of passion, but such was the devilish frenzy of Lewis's way with the song (and the piano) that they came in some people's minds to have an almost satanic implication.

> Man, I got the devil in me.
>
> JERRY LEE LEWIS: after recording 'Great Balls of Fire'

**Great Communicator.** A nickname of Republican politician Ronald Reagan (1911–2004), president of the United States (1981–9). Reagan had been an actor in numerous Hollywood B-movies before entering politics and successfully used his communication skills to present himself as a man of humility, warmth, integrity, homespun wisdom and gentle wit, which won him enormous support for his right-wing policies from the US people, including many former Democrats (*see* REAGAN DEMOCRATS). During his tenure of office wags referred to Washington, D.C., as Hollywood East. Reagan's ability to extricate himself from political scrapes led to another nickname, the Great Rondini, after the escapologist Harry HOUDINI. *See also* DUTCH; EVIL EMPIRE; GIPPER; INCH WAR; MURDER ON THE ORIENT EXPRESS.

**Great Crocodile, The.** The English version of *Groot Krokodil*, the Afrikaans nickname of P.W. Botha (b.1916), prime minister (1978–84) and president (1984–9) of South Africa, and the last defender of APARTHEID. Under his successor, F.W. de Klerk (b.1936), South Africa made the transition to majority rule.

**Great Depression.** The economic slump that began in 1929 in North America, Europe and other industrialized regions of the world. It originated in the United States, where it was triggered by a catastrophic collapse of stock market prices on BLACK THURSDAY, resulting in the insolvency of many banks. As the United States was the major creditor and financier of postwar Europe, whose economies had been weakened by the war itself, its effects were soon felt across the Atlantic. *See also* DUST BOWL; NEW DEAL; OKIES.

**Great Dictator, The.** A film comedy (1940) written by, directed by and starring Charles Chaplin (1889–1977) about a nameless Jewish barber who protests against the persecution of the Jews in the fictional country of Tomania under its dictator Adenoid Hynkel (Chaplin playing both main roles). It was the physical similarity between Chaplin's celebrated tramp, complete with toothbrush moustache, and the German dictator Adolf Hitler that inspired the making of the film, Chaplin's first 'talkie'.

**Great Escape, The.** A film (1963) adapted by James Clavell and W.R. Burnett from a book of the same title by Paul Brickhill about a mass escape of Allied prisoners from a German prisoner of war camp during the Second World War. The plot was based on a real mass break-out staged by Allied prisoners from the POW camp Stalag Luft III in 1942. *See also* ESCAPE FILM.

**Greatest Story Ever Told, The.** A biblical film epic (1965) that attempted to make great cinema of the life of Christ, the 'greatest story' of the title. Starring Max von Sydow as Christ and filmed largely in Utah rather than Palestine, it was generally considered a failure, chiefly because of the distracting appearance of well-known HOLLYWOOD stars in bit parts. One such was John Wayne as a Roman centurion, whose drawling delivery of the line 'Truly, this man was the Son of God' provoked hilarity.

**Greatest week in the history of the world since the creation, The.** President Richard Nixon's (*see* TRICKY DICKY) description of the successful landing of men on the moon in 1969. He made the claim while welcoming the returning *Apollo 11* astronauts on board USS *Hornet* on 24 July. The president's hyperbole did not go unadmonished. The evangelist Billy Graham told him: 'I know exactly how you felt, and I understand exactly what you meant, but, even so, I think you may have been a little excessive.'

**Great Game, The.** The rivalry between the British and Russian empires to establish hegemony in Central Asia – in particular in Afghanistan – through the 19th century and into the early 20th century. From the British point of view, the aim was to protect their possessions in India from Russian expansionism. The Russians called it 'the tournament of shadows', and the struggle for strategic dominance involved espionage, covert operations, diplomacy and exploration. The term is attributed to Arthur Connolly (1807–42), a British intelligence agent who travelled in disguise through Central Asia, and became widely known in Rudyard Kipling's novel KIM:

> When he comes to the Great Game he must go alone – alone, and at peril of his head.
>
> *Kim*, ch. 7 (1901)

*See also* DUNSTERFORCE.

**Great Gatsby, The.** A classic novel (1925) by F. Scott Fitzgerald (1896–1940), set on Long Island, New York. Jay GATSBY, one of the wealthy criminal class, has an affair with Daisy, who is married to Tom, rich, dim and violent. Tom takes as his lover Myrtle Wilson, whose husband works in a garage. Daisy, driving Gatsby's car, accidentally kills Myrtle and does not stop. Tom tells Myrtle's husband that it was Gatsby who was driving. Wilson shoots Gatsby and then turns the gun on himself. There have been two rather unsatisfactory film versions, directed respectively by Elliott Nugent (1949) and Jack Clayton (1974), while a televised version (2000) was a handsomely glossy costume drama that never really came to life. *See also* FIRST LINES OF NOVELS.

**Great Leap Forward.** The attempt by Mao Zedong in 1958–60 to speed up the process of industrialization in China and improve agricultural production. The population was organized into large collectives and labour-intensive methods were introduced. The 'great leap' was more a small hop, however, and progress was slow. The CULTURAL REVOLUTION followed soon after.

**Great Masturbator, The.** The probably self-referential painting by Salvador Dalí (1904–89) was executed in 1929. Dalí was himself a lifelong devotee of onanism, an enthusiasm happily tolerated by his wife Gala. Among the more identifiable features of the painting is the head of an attractive young woman sniffing with apparent pleasure at the scantily covered genitalia of an adolescent boy.

**Great Patriotic War.** (Russian, *Velikaya Otechestvennaya voyna*.) The Soviet name for the Second World War from the point of NAZI Germany's invasion of the Soviet Union on 22 June 1941 (*see* BARBAROSSA). The war ended in 1945 with the USSR in control of Eastern Europe and East Germany. According to the *Great Soviet Encyclopedia* (1971), the Great Patriotic War was the 'just, liberating war of the Soviet people for the freedom and independence of the Socialist

homeland against Fascist Germany and its allies (Italy, Hungary, Romania, Finland, and in 1945, Japan)'. *See also* SOVIET SAYINGS.

**Great Rondini.** *See* GREAT COMMUNICATOR.

**Great Satan.** A term applied to the United States by AYATOLLAH Ruholla Khomeini (1902–89), the spiritual leader of the anti-Western Islamic fundamentalist regime in Iran.

**Great she-elephant.** A description of Margaret Thatcher (the IRON LADY) by the Conservative MP Julian Critchley.

**Great Society.** The vision of the United States presented by President Lyndon Johnson during a speech at the University of Michigan in May 1964: 'We have the opportunity to move not only toward the rich and the powerful society, but upward to the Great Society … The Great Society rests on abundance and liberty for all. It demands an end to poverty and racial injustice.' To this end Johnson pursued a 'war on poverty', introduced sweeping civil-rights reforms and established subsidized health care via the Medicaid and Medicare schemes. Unfortunately his immersion in the VIETNAM War deflected attention from his achievements in social reform. The phrase itself was actually coined by Johnson's speechwriter, Richard N. Goodwin. *See also* LBJ.

**Great Storm.** A media nickname for the ferocious winds that battered the southeast of England on the night of 15–16 October 1987. The onslaught caused considerable destruction, uprooting some 15 million trees and inflicting costly ecological damage. At the Royal Botanic Gardens, Kew, the storm destroyed 500 trees and damaged 1000 others, including some rare specimens. The death toll of 18 was relatively low but insurance losses to property amounted to some £800 million.

> Earlier on today, apparently, a woman rang the BBC and said she heard there was a hurricane on the way. Well, if you're watching, don't worry, there isn't!
>
> MICHAEL FISH: presenting the weather forecast on BBC TV (15 October 1987)

**Great Train Robbery.** The most audacious crime in British history was committed on 8 August 1963 when a gang hijacked a Royal Mail train in Buckinghamshire and escaped with mailbags containing £2.6 million in the form of used banknotes on their way to being destroyed. The robbers stopped the train by turning off a green signal and replacing it with a red signal rigged up with batteries. During the raid itself the train driver, Jack Mills, was clubbed over the head and received injuries from which he never fully recovered. Twelve of the fifteen were caught and convicted but one of the gang, Ronnie Biggs, escaped from prison, picked up his share of the haul and made his way to Brazil, which did not then have an extradition treaty with Britain. He finally returned to the UK in 2001 and resumed his sentence, in Belmarsh prison (several appeals for his release on the grounds of ill health have been turned down). Media accounts of the robbery and its long-running aftermath were inspired by *The Great Train Robbery*, the title of a famous silent US film of 1903.

**Great Wallendas.** A famous family of US tightrope walkers, founded by Karl Wallenda (1905–78) and involving his children, grandchildren, cousins, nephews and nieces. The troupe first gained fame in Europe for their four-man pyramid and high-wire cycling act. They then worked in circuses, where they developed a seven-man pyramid in 1947. From then on, they performed independently, always working without a net. Two members of the troupe were killed in a 1962 performance, another in 1963, and yet another in 1972. Karl himself lost his life in 1978 when a gust of wind blew him off the cable he was walking between two hotel buildings in Puerto Rico.

**Great War.** The common name of the First World War (or World War I) from its outbreak in 1914. It might be thought that the name 'First World War' would not have come into use until the outbreak of the Second World War (also known as World War II), but in fact the English soldier and journalist Charles à Court Repington (1858–1925) had rather prophetically used the name in the title of a book published in 1920: *The First World War 1914–18*. The first use of the name 'World War II' is attributed to *Time* magazine, in September 1939:

> World War II began last week at 5.20 a.m. (Polish time) Friday, September 1, when a German bombing plane dropped a projectile on Puck, fishing village and air base in the armpit of the Hel Peninsula.

At this stage most people were simply talking about 'the war in Europe'. The French call the Second World War *La Seconde Guerre mondiale*, the adjective *second* being used for the second of only two (as distinct from *deuxième*, which implies a higher count).

*See also* GREAT PATRIOTIC WAR.

**Great white hope.** A US expression for a person or thing that is expected to succeed. It dates from the early 20th century and alludes specifically to the African American heavyweight boxing champion Jack Johnson (1878–1946), who seemed invincible. The phrase was thus used for any white hopeful who might defeat him. The term was popularized by the title of Howard Sackler's Pulitzer Prize-winning play *The Great White Hope* (1968), based on Johnson's life, and by a 1970 film version of this.

**Great White Way.** A once popular name for Broadway, New York, especially the part that passes through TIMES SQUARE. The name is associated with the area's multitude of electric advertising signs and brilliant street lighting, but was actually given by journalists in December 1901 following a heavy snowfall, as an adoption of the title of Albert Bigelow Paine's novel *The Great White Way* (1901), a tale of adventure at the South Pole.

**Grebo.** A member of a 1980s urban youth cult in Britain characterized by musical tastes ranging from HEAVY METAL to PUNK ROCK, an aggressive or antisocial manner, and long hair and clothes reminiscent of the earlier 'biker' generation. The term is also used for the cult itself and is probably based on 'greaser', as a scruffily dressed member of a motorcycle gang, with '-bo' as in 'dumbo' or 'jumbo'.

**Grecians.** The nickname of Exeter City football club, founded in 1904. In 1726 a re-enactment of the siege of Troy was held at an Exeter fair, with the attacking Greeks played by the residents of St Sidwells, outside the city walls. A tradition of football matches developed between the city dwellers (Blues) and St Sidwells inhabitants (Greeks, subsequently Grecians). A football ground with a 'Grecian' entrance gate was built off Sidwell Street for the matches and the team playing there, originally St Sidwell's Old Boys, became Exeter City and adopted their long-established nickname. *See also* FOOTBALL CLUB NICKNAMES.

**Grecian 2000.** The proprietary name of a hair colouring lotion that 'restores' dark tones to a male head whose locks have greyed with age. The name is invoked slightingly or mockingly of various celebrities who are deemed to have resorted to the product. The name itself is presumably intended to evoke the dark hair of the ancient Greeks in 2000 BC, perhaps with a hint of 'grease'.

**Greed is good.** The doctrine of the ruthless free-marketeer Gordon Gecko (played by Michael Douglas) in the 1987 film *Wall Street* (screenplay by Stanley Weiser and Oliver Stone).

> Greed – for lack of a better word – is good. Greed is right. Greed works.

The slogan became the watchword of the red-braced, striped-shirt stock market yuppies of the Thatcherite/Reaganite 1980s. The lines had their origin in the commencement address at Berkeley given by the US businessman Ivan F. Boesky on 18 May 1986:

> Greed is all right … Greed is healthy. You can be greedy and still feel good about yourself.

Shortly afterwards, Boesky was convicted of insider dealing.

**Greek Colonels.** The three senior army officers who were placed in key posts under prime minister Konstantinos Kollias in the military government of Greece from 1967 to 1974. They were Lieutenant-General Gregorios Spandidakis, Brigadier Stylianos Patakos and Colonel Georgios Papadopoulos. King Constantine fled to Rome in December 1967, whereupon General Georgios Zoitakis was appointed regent while Papadopoulos and Patakos, relinquishing their military ranks, took over as prime minister and deputy prime minister respectively. In 1972 Papadopoulos replaced Zoitakis as regent and in 1973 became president, the junta decreeing the monarchy to be abolished. A civilian government under Konstantinos Karamanlis resumed office in 1974.

**Green belt.** A stretch of country around a large urban area that has been scheduled for comparative preservation and where building development is restricted. The concept was introduced in the 1930s but was adopted only in the 1950s in response to the pressure to expand towns regarded by many to be large enough already. Green belts have no statutory authority and their demarcation is under constant challenge from the conflicting interests of developers, farmers, conservationists and existing residents. *See also* GREENFIELD SITE.

**Green Berets.** A nickname for British or US commandos.

**Green card.** A green-coloured document issued by various authorities in the 20th century, including: (1) a card filled in by a visitor to the Houses of Parliament, requesting an interview with an MP; (2) an international insurance document for motorists taking their cars abroad, and confirming that the driver holds the necessary insurance cover; (3) a permit issued by the US government enabling a foreign national to live and work permanently in the United States. This last is formally known as an 'alien-registration-receipt card', and provided the title for an off-beat 1990 film comedy.

**Green Cross Code.** A code of road safety for children, first published in 1971 and now included in the HIGHWAY CODE as a guide to crossing the road for all pedestrians. A green traffic light or pedestrian crossing light is associated with safety.

**Greeneland.** A name (punning on 'Greenland') for the imaginative world of the novels of Graham Greene (1904–91). It was coined by the writer Arthur Calder-Marshall (1908–92). A Roman Catholic author, Greene's work is much concerned with themes of spiritual and moral struggle.

**Greenfield site.** A rural or undeveloped site that has potential for the building of private houses or for commercial exploitation. *See also* BROWNFIELD SITE; GREEN BELT.

**Green fingers.** To have green fingers is to be unusually successful in making plants grow. The phrase dates from the 1920s and was popularized by Reginald Arkell's book so titled (1934).

**Green form.** The form on which application is made for legal advice and assistance in England and Wales. It is completed by the client and the solicitor then assesses the client's means by referring to a 'key card'. Those whose income and capital are within certain limits are entitled to free advice on most legal matters. The scheme provides initially for up to three hours' work for matrimonial cases where a petition is drafted, and two hours for other work.

**Green goddesses.** A nickname for the green military fire engines (properly, 'Bedford self-propelled pumps') that were brought in when crews of the regular fire services were out on strike. They were introduced, mainly for civil defence use, in 1955, and decommissioned in 2005. The name has been similarly given to other vehicles, such as the double-decked trams running in Liverpool in the 1930s. In this case the adoption seems to have been suggested by William Archer's popular melodrama *The Green Goddess* (1921), then playing at a theatre in the city. The Green Goddess was also a name for the keep-fit demonstrator Diana Moran, who wore a lurid green body stocking on breakfast television in 1983.

**Greenham Common.** A village near Newbury, West Berkshire, that was the site of a United States cruise missile base and that from 1981 until its closure in 1991 was the focal point of a camp of 'peace women' protesting against nuclear weapons. At the peak of the protest in December 1982 some 30,000 women encircled the perimeter fence. The camp was not disbanded until 1999. The 'green' place-name was coincidentally appropriate for the stance. *See also* CND.

**Greenhouse effect.** Literally, an effect occurring in greenhouses in which radiant heat from the sun passes through the glass and, trapped inside by the glass, warms the contents. The term came to apply to an analogous effect on the earth's atmosphere in which carbon dioxide and other gases in the atmosphere absorb the infrared radiation emitted by the earth's surface through being exposed to solar ultraviolet radiation. As a result, the earth's mean temperature rises. The term is first found in G.T. Trewartha's *Introduction to Weather and Climate* (1937). *See also* GLOBAL WARMING.

**Green light.** Permission to proceed. The image is that of a green traffic light or railway signal, authorizing one to go ahead. The phrase dates from the 1970s.

**Green Line.** A boundary line established in the 1970s in the Lebanese capital, BEIRUT, to separate Christian and Muslim factions in East and West Beirut. It became a dangerous barricade permanently dividing the city, somewhat in the manner of the BERLIN WALL.

**Green Machine, The.** A nickname (first recorded in 1969) for the US Marine Corps or the US Army (the reference is probably to the ubiquitous olive-drab colour of US military life). An alternative designation among the disaffected is 'The Green Motherfucker'.

The term has subsequently been variously reapplied, among others to the South African cricket team (green predominates in their colours) and a range of environmentally friendly vehicles and other devices.

**Greenmail.** The stock market practice of buying enough shares in a company to threaten a takeover, so forcing the company concerned to buy them back at a higher price in order to retain control of the business. The term is a variant of 'blackmail' with 'green' here in the sense of money, as in 'greenback', a US $1 bill, so named from its colour.

**Green man.** A popular name, especially as used to children, for the outline of a human figure on the green light of a PELICAN CROSSING, signifying that it is safe to cross the road. He is not to be confused with LITTLE GREEN MEN.

> 'She was absolutely amazed when we came out of Debenham's and she saw the little green man flashing on the lights at the crossing.'
>
> *The Times* (10 December 1999)

**Greenmantle.** A thriller (1916) by John Buchan (1875–1940), employing some of the same characters as in *The* THIRTY-NINE STEPS, including the protagonist Richard Hannay. The setting is the Middle East, and the theme, the danger of Germany sponsoring a Muslim uprising which would destabilize India, was a real one which Buchan knew from his work in Intelligence and from writing the history of the First World War as it happened. The title is the code name for the seer Zimrud ('Emerald'), after a Turkish miracle play, found on a scrap of paper on the body of a dead British agent. Reading the book cheered up the family of Tsar Nicholas II (1868–1918) of Russia as they awaited their fate in captivity. *See also* MR STANDFAST.

**Green Paper.** In British parliamentary parlance, a command paper containing policy proposals for discussion in the Houses of Parliament. When the proposals have been discussed by all the parties concerned, they are published as a White Paper. This in turn usually leads to the introduction of a Bill and finally to an Act of Parliament. An example is the Green Paper introduced by the Home Secretary after the Southall riots of 1979. This led in 1985 to a White Paper called 'The Review of Public Order', which in turn led to the introduction of the Public Order Bill and Act of 1986.

The Green Paper, so called from the colour of its cover, was introduced by the Department of Economic Affairs in 1967, and was defined by Michael Stewart, Senior Economic Adviser to the Treasury, as 'a statement by the Government not of policy already determined but of propositions put before the whole nation for discussion' (*The Times*, 1 March 1969).

**Green Party.** In Britain a political party founded in 1973 after the publication of *Blueprint for Survival*, a work issued by the editors of the *Ecologist* magazine by way of offering radical solutions to environmental problems. The party was known as the Ecology Party until 1985. Despite the importance it attaches to environmental issues, the party has made only a minimal impact on the political scene. It fielded 183 candidates in the 2005 general election, but failed to win any seats.

**Greenpeace.** A movement originating as an anti-nuclear group in British Columbia, Canada, in 1971, initially to oppose US nuclear tests in Alaska. It now aims to persuade governments to change industrial activities that threaten natural resources and the environment. It supports direct non-violent action and has gained wide attention by its efforts to protect whales, among other environmental campaigns. When acting against French nuclear tests in the South Pacific in 1985, its ship *Rainbow Warrior* was sunk by French secret agents. The origin of the name can be traced to a comment made in 1970 by the Canadian environmentalist Bill Darnell at a meeting of the Don't Make a Wave Committee, the predecessor of Greenpeace:

> Make it a *green* peace.

In *Warriors of the Rainbow* (1979), Robert Hunter explained why the name had been adopted:

> The word Greenpeace had a ring to it – it conjured images of Eden; it said ecology and antiwar in two syllables; it fitted easily into even a one-column headline.

*See also* FRIENDS OF THE EARTH.

**Green pound.** The exchange rate for the pound applied to payments for agricultural produce in the EUROPEAN UNION.

**Green revolution.** A term dating from the 1970s for the introduction of new and more productive agricultural techniques in developing countries. New hybrid wheats were first bred in Mexico in the 1950s and new rice varieties in the Philippines in the 1960s. Such new varieties have since spread to other THIRD WORLD countries and have had considerable success, in some cases more than doubling the yields of traditional varieties. It remains unlikely, however, that the green revolution will ever fulfil its original promise because of lack of capital and expertise, lack of time and the will to act quickly, and lack of cooperation on the part of farmers. The degree of resistance of the new strains to attacks of insects and plant diseases is also uncertain.

**Green Shield Stamps.** A popular brand of British trading stamps in the 1960s. They were given to customers with purchases as an incentive to buy more goods and were redeemable for cash or merchandise. They were introduced in 1957 on the lines of the green stamps issued in the United States by the firm of Sperry and Hutchinson.

**Greenshirt.** A supporter of the Social Credit Movement established in England by Major Douglas in the 1920s, and so named from the green uniform shirt adopted.

**Green shoots.** The version most often quoted (and mocked) of a speech to the Conservative Party Conference, 9 October 1991, by the chancellor of the exchequer, Norman Lamont (b.1942):

> The green shoots of economic spring are appearing once again.

The words came back to haunt him, as Britain obstinately refused to pull itself out of recession for several more years, and many homeowners continued to be burdened with NEGATIVE EQUITY. Lamont continued in office through BLACK WEDNESDAY in 1992, eventually resigning in 1993.

**Green weenie, The.** A US slang expression of Second World War military origin, designating anything bad that happens or may happen to one, especially unjustly or undeservedly. Someone who had been unluckily killed might thus be said to have 'eaten the green weenie'. A 'weenie' is a type of sausage, and one that had gone green might well be considered unpropitious.

**Green wellies.** Green wellington boots, as typically worn by SLOANE RANGERS, or those members of the upper classes who practise the country sports of HUNTING, SHOOTING AND FISHING. The 'green welly brigade' is a term dating from the 1970s for such people in the mass.

**Greenwich Village.** The residential area of lower Manhattan, New York, gained a reputation from the early years of the 20th century for its bohemianism, and became established as a meeting-place of unconventional writers, artists and musicians, especially members of the BEAT GENERATION and of students generally. In more recent times it has lost much of its sense of creative originality, although its alternative lifestyle continues to be represented in that of its gay community. Many New Yorkers now wax lyrical about 'the Village', with its former feel of excitement and vitality.

**Gremlin.** One of a number of imaginary gnomes or goblins humorously blamed by the RAF in the Second World War for everything that went wrong in an aircraft or an operation. The name was probably coined at the end of the First World War or in the 1920s and was apparently in use on RAF stations in India and the Middle East in the 1930s. The name is first traced in print in *The Aeroplane* (10 April 1929). One explanation claims that a gremlin was the goblin that came out of Fremlin's beer bottles (Fremlin being a Kent brewer), although there are numerous other origins, some more plausible than others.

***Gremlins.*** A comedy horror film (1984), directed by Joe Dante, about a small furry creature called the MOGWAI that spawns a race of ferocious monsters called gremlins when accidentally wetted. Chris Columbus, who wrote the screenplay, derived the basic idea for the film from a nightmare in which he dreamed his feet were being nibbled by mice. *See also* GREMLIN.

**Grey area.** Generally, an area or situation where distinctions cannot be clearly made or rules precisely determined. In a more specific sense, a grey area is a region of relatively high unemployment, first so called in Britain in 1966. The official term for such a region is a development area. The description 'grey' may have owed something to maps of Britain showing such areas shaded grey.

**Grey-collar worker.** A mostly US term for a mechanic or maintenance man, who usually wears grey overalls. The expression dates from the 1960s and contrasts with the WHITE-COLLAR WORKER and BLUE-COLLAR WORKER. *See also* PINK-COLLAR WORKER.

> By 1975, only one out three jobs is expected to be in production … Blue-collar, gray-collar, and farm employment combined will just barely exceed the white-collar total.
> *World Year Book* (1968)

**Greyfriars.** The imaginary school that is the setting of the long series of school stories by 'Frank Richards' (Charles Hamilton). Its most colourful pupil is Billy BUNTER, but its shining light is the brave, energetic and resourceful Harry Wharton, whose inner circle of friends consists of Frank Nugent, Bob Cherry, Johnny Bull and the rather more exotic Hurree Jamset Ram Singh, the youthful Nabob of Bhanipur.

> The year is 1910 – or 1940, but it is all the same. You are at Greyfriars, a rosy-cheeked boy of fourteen in posh tailor-made clothes, sitting down to tea in your study on the Remove passage after an exciting game of football which was won by the odd goal in the last half-minute. There is a cosy fire in the study and outside the wind is whistling. The ivy clusters thickly round the old grey stones. The King is on his throne and the pound is worth a pound. … Everything is safe, solid and unquestionable. Everything will be the same for ever and ever. That approximately is the atmosphere.
>
> GEORGE ORWELL: in *Horizon* (1940), quoted in E.S. Turner, *Boys Will Be Boys*, ch. 13 (1948)

**Grey goo.** A term applied by scientists in the late 20th century to the homogeneous substance to which all life on earth could be reduced if consumed by millions of rapidly replicating nanorobots (robots the size of a single molecule).

> Life in the nanofuture will not be all roses, Drexler fears: 'gray goo' weapons might be developed – soups of omnivorous nanorobots that could reduce the biosphere to dust.
>
> *Scientific American* (January 1990)

**Grey market.** In the Second World War a transaction regarded as a lesser breach of the rationing regulations than the black market. In Stock Exchange parlance, a grey market is a market in the shares of a new issue by investors who have applied for the shares but not actually received them.

**Grey Owl.** The pen-name of the Sussex-born Canadian author and conservationist Archibald Stansfeld Belaney (1888–1938), who adopted the name when he became a blood brother of the Ojibwa people in 1920. A former trapper, he later became interested in conservation and, in addition to setting up a beaver sanctuary, wrote a novel for children, *The Adventures of Sajo and Her Beaver People* (1935). A film (2000) about the life of Grey Owl, directed by Richard Attenborough, starred a bizarrely miscast Pierce Brosnan.

**Grey water.** Water that has been used domestically (e.g. for washing) but, rather than being dispatched down the drain, is recycled for other purposes (e.g. watering plants). The term became familiar in the early years of the 21st century, as water shortages in Britain began to encourage a less profligate use of existing resources.

> Sounder practice would be to connect your bowser to your downpipe and collect rainwater, or at least use 'grey water' from Cherie's bath or Tony's washing-up.
>
> *The Guardian* (9 June 2006)

**Gricer.** A nickname for a railway enthusiast, especially one who turns a hobby into an obsession. The origins of the term are obscure, but it apparently emerged in the north of England in the 1940s. A variant of 'grouser' has been suggested by some, as has a pun on 'grouse', since TRAIN-SPOTTING is an activity bearing a supposed resemblance to grouse-shooting. Further speculative etymologies are given in the June 1970 number of *Railway World*.

**GRID.** Gay-related immune deficiency, the original name of AIDS in the early 1980s, before it was realized that the HIV virus takes no notice of its victims' sexual orientation.

**Grime.** A genre of black urban music, which emerged from the East End of London in 2002. It derives from garage and hip-hop, and its best-known exponent is Dizzee Rascal. Other performers include Lady Sovereign and The Streets.

**Grim Grom.** A popular media nickname for the Soviet foreign minister Andrey Gromyko (1909–89), who invariably had a solemn expression. English 'grim' and Gromyko's Ukrainian surname, deriving from *grom*, 'thunder', are linguistically related, so the name is not mere alliteration. *See also* GROMYKO OF THE LABOUR PARTY.

**Grin and bare it.** To brave a social function in a revealing costume. A punning expression based on 'grin and bear it', it is applied mostly to BRIGHT YOUNG THINGS or PARTY GIRLS.

**Grind to a halt** or **come to a grinding halt.** To come laboriously to a standstill. The reference is to the clogging up of a piece of machinery until it can no longer function. In the days of the windmill, when the wind dropped, the grinding action of the millstones on the grain stopped the mill, and it literally ground to a halt.

**Grits and Fritz.** A nickname for the successful Democratic ticket in the 1976 US presidential election, comprising Jimmy Carter (b.1924) and his running-mate Walter Mondale (b.1928). Coming from Georgia, Carter was 'Grits' (a kind of maize porridge popular with Southerners), while in the Senate Mondale was known as FRITZ. *See also* GEORGIA MAFIA; 'NORWEGIAN WOOD (THIS BIRD HAS FLOWN)'.

**Grocer, The.** A *Private Eye* nickname for Sir Edward Heath (1916–2005), Conservative prime minister from 1970 to 1974. There is a twofold allusion. The first is to Heath's role as secretary of state for trade and industry in the 1960s, when he was negotiating British entry into the Common Market and so discussing the prices of eggs, butter, bacon and the like. The second is to his modest social background. The name was enthusiastically seized on by *The Guardian* newspaper.

**Grocer's Daughter.** (French *fille d'épicier*.) A description of

Margaret Thatcher, the IRON LADY, by Valéry Giscard d'Estaing (b.1926) while president of France (1974–81), referring not only to the fact that her father was a grocer in Grantham, Lincolnshire, but also to her petit-bourgeois outlook on the world. It should be noted that she followed Edward Heath, the GROCER, as Conservative leader. Westminster wags observed:

> She was only the Grocer's Daughter, but she showed Sir Geoffrey Howe.

*See also* DEAD SHEEP.

**Grockles.** A term used in Devon for visiting tourists and holidaymakers, especially when from the Midlands or the north of England. The word is said to derive from the clown Grock, implying someone who is a 'little clown'. It apparently arose in 1963 from comments about holiday-makers made at the Globe Inn, Brixham, and was used by Peter Draper in his film *The System* (1964), shot at Brixham, Torquay and other parts of the English Riviera. The film itself centres on the system adopted by seaside layabouts for collecting and sharing female visitors. *See also* EMMETS.

**Gromyko of the Labour Party.** A description of himself by the Labour politician Denis (now Lord) Healey (b.1917). Andrey Gromyko (1909–89) was Soviet foreign minister (1957–85) and president (1985–8). Like Healey, despite his enormous power and influence over several decades, he never obtained the job of party leader. Healey himself was secretary of state for defence (1964–70), chancellor of the exchequer (1974–9) and deputy leader of the Labour Party (1981–3). *See also* DEAD SHEEP; GRIM GROM; LADY WITH THE BLOWLAMP.

**Groot Krokodil.** *See* the GREAT CROCODILE.

**Groovy.** Successful; fashionable, exciting. The allusion is to the accurate reproduction of music by a needle in the groove of a gramophone record. The term originally related to the SWINGING SIXTIES but in the 1980s took on the converse sense of passé, out-of-date, referring to that era.

**Gross out.** To disgust or repel. The expression arose in the 1980s from 'gross' in the US campus sense of 'disgusting'. 'Gross me out!' thus became an exclamation of disgust. A 'gross-out movie' is a genre designed to appeal mainly to adolescents (particularly boys), who are amused by sexual and scatological humour. Examples of the genre include *National Lampoon's Animal House* (1978) and AMERICAN PIE (1999).

**Grouch bag.** A hidden pocket or purse where one can keep one's money safe. The implication is that one grouches

when spending or revealing one's money. The comedian Groucho Marx, born Julius Henry Marx, was perhaps so nicknamed because he carried a bag of this type around with him. *See* MARX BROTHERS.

**Groucho Club.** A London club founded in 1985 for writers, artists, publishers and those working generally in the arts and media. Its name alludes to the celebrated comment by the comedian Groucho Marx (1890–1977) that he would never join any club that would have him as a member. *See also* MARX BROTHERS.

**Ground control.** The personnel and equipment at an airbase or launch site that monitor and control the flight of aircraft or spacecraft.

**Groundhog Day.** A film comedy (1993) adapted by Danny Rubin and Harold Ramis from a story by Rubin about an obnoxious television weather presenter (Bill Murray) who finds himself reliving the same day over and over again until he becomes a better person. In the United States Groundhog Day is Candlemas Day (2 February), the name deriving from the saying that the groundhog first appears from hibernation on that day. If he sees his shadow, he goes back to his burrow for another six weeks, indicating six more weeks of winter weather. The general idea is that a sunny day (when he sees his shadow) means a late spring, whereas a cloudy day (when he does not see it) means an early spring.

**Groundnut scheme.** Figuratively, an expensive failure or ill-considered enterprise. The reference is to a hastily organized and badly planned British government scheme (1947) to clear large areas of hitherto unprofitable land in Africa to grow groundnuts. The venture was abandoned three years later at considerable cost to the taxpayer.

**Ground Zero.** The point either just above or below the explosion of an atomic bomb. Figuratively the term is sometimes used to describe the starting point of an activity. Following the cataclysmic terrorist attacks on the United States of 11 September 2001 (*see* 9/11), however, the name began to be used to designate the site of the ruins of the WORLD TRADE CENTER in Lower Manhattan, New York City. *See also* FREEDOM TOWER.

**Group of Eight.** *See* G8.

**Group of Seven.** *See* G7.

**Group therapy.** A form of psychiatric therapy originally introduced in the United States by Joseph H. Pratt (1872–1942). Instead of meeting the therapist individually, several patients come together in a group to describe and discuss their problems. A therapist usually guides the proceedings and in many cases patients have a problem in common, such as alcoholism or bereavement.

**Grove Family, The.** The first authentic British television SOAP OPERA, screened from 1954 to 1957 and centring on the domestic and social concerns of a lower middle-class family from Hendon. The family, named after the BBC's Lime Grove studios, consisted of Mr and Mrs Grove, librarian daughter Pat, National Serviceman son Jack, younger son Lenny and irascible Gran.

**Grovel, grovel.** A phrase first current in the 1960s to express an apology or a fawning request. (The metaphor was actualized in 1976 when the England cricket captain Tony Grieg literally (and ironically) grovelled on all fours after his team had been convincingly beaten by the West Indies, having incautiously boasted on taking over the captaincy that he intended to 'make them grovel'.)

**Growing experience.** US PSYCHOBABBLE for a salutary factor extracted from a misfortune, 'bad turned to good'. The US show business couple David and Talia Shire were quoted in 1984 as saying of their 'very loving separation': 'We're going to rotate the house and we even rotate the cars. We've been separated for four months and it's a growing experience' (quoted by William Safire in the *New York Times Magazine*, 20 January 1980). The reference is to the lessons that a growing child can learn from his or her mistakes.

**Growing pains.** A figurative expression dating from the early 20th century for the difficulties experienced in the early stages of an enterprise, such as the setting up of a new business. Literal growing pains are the vague aches and pains occurring in the limbs of young children. Their cause is unknown, and they do not seem to be related to the process of growth itself. The term is also used for sexual stirrings in one's teens.

**Gruesome Gerty.** *See* OLD SPARKY.

**Gruesome twosome.** A phrase originating with African Americans in the 1940s to express two people in a relationship, neither of them necessarily gruesome. A FEARSOME FOURSOME is also sometimes similarly heard for a group of four, as in mixed doubles at tennis.

**Grumbling appendix.** One that gives intermittent discomfort without actually flaring into appendicitis. The term dates from the 1930s.

**Grunge.** A style of rock music characterized by a raucous guitar sound and lazy vocal delivery. It emerged in the United States in the early 1990s and was typified by

Nirvana's 1992 hit 'Smells Like Teen Spirit'. The term was subsequently extended to apply to clothing evoking impoverishment, such as ill-fitting jackets, moth-eaten sweaters, ripped jeans or 'clumpy' shoes. The word was originally adjectival, as 'grungy', and seems to have evolved as a blend of 'grubby' and 'dingy' with, at least in Britain, a further touch of 'gunge'.

**Grunt work.** Any dull but necessary work, especially when menial or undemanding. The phrase is associated with 'grunt' as a US slang word for an infantry soldier, perhaps referring to his endless muttering and complaining. There is also perhaps a suggestion of 'groundwork', as preliminary or basic work which can be physically and mentally wearing but which is essential for the building of a firm and durable edifice, whether literal or figurative.

**G7.** A name for the seven leading industrialized nations: Germany, Canada, the United States, France, the United Kingdom, Italy and Japan. Russia joined the group in 1998 to form the Group of Eight (*see* G8) but the finance ministers of the original countries still meet independently to coordinate their economic policy and as such continue to be known as the Group of Seven or G7.

**G-spot.** A sensitive area, literal or figurative, that reacts uncontrollably to excitation or stimulation. The origin is in the Gräfenberg spot, a site in the vagina identified by the German-born American gynaecologist Ernst Gräfenberg (1881–1957) as highly erogenous. The transferred use of the term evolved in the late 1980s.

**Guantánamo Bay.** *See* CAMP X-RAY.

**Guardian Angels.** A citizen vigilante group founded in New York City in 1979. Wearing their maroon berets they ride the subway system in order to deter crime. Chapters have been founded in other cities in the world, but an attempt to establish a chapter in London in 1989 came to nothing.

**Gubernator, The.** *See* the GOVERNATOR.

**Guernica.** Perhaps the most famous painting of the 20th century, the great mural was painted by Pablo Picasso (1881–1973) in 1937 in horrified protest at a notorious atrocity in the Spanish Civil War. On 27 April 1937 bombers of the German Kondor Legion, in support of Franco's nationalists, destroyed the ancient Basque capital of Guernica, causing many civilian casualties. Picasso's stark monochromatic painting has become a symbol of the barbarity of modern warfare. The name of the village itself happens to evoke its subject: Spanish *guerra* and French *guerre* both mean 'war'. There is a (probably apocryphal) story that while Picasso was living in Paris in the Second

World War, a Gestapo officer visited his studio. Looking at the canvas of *Guernica*, the Nazi asked: 'Did you do that?' 'No,' Picasso replied, 'You did.'

**Guerrilla Girls.** A group of women artists founded in New York in 1984 to combat what they saw as sexism and racism in the art world. Members appeared on television, wearing gorilla masks to hide their identity, and distributed leaflets and posters to advertise their cause. One of their posters showed a reclining female nude by Ingres with the woman's head replaced by that of a gorilla and an accompanying text: 'Do women have to be naked to get into the Met. Museum? Less than 5 per cent of the artists in the Modern Art Sections are women, but 85 per cent of the nudes are female.' The group's activities were documented in a book called *Confessions of the Guerrilla Girls (Whoever They Really Are)* (1995).

**Guest beer.** A term dating from the 1970s either for a beer available only temporarily in a pub which is a free house, or in the case of a tied house for a beer offered in addition to those produced by the particular brewers. In the latter case the guest beer is usually an independent REAL ALE.

**Guide dogs.** Dogs were first specially trained to guide the blind in the First World War, when they were schooled to work with blinded German soldiers. Special organizations were later set up to provide such dogs, two of the best known being the SEEING EYE in the United States and, from 1931, the Guide Dogs for the Blind Association in Britain. Several breeds are trained for the work, including labrador crosses such as a labradoodle, a cross between a labrador and a poodle.

**Guildford Four.** On 5 October 1974 two IRA bombs killed five people in two Guildford pubs. A month later two were killed in an IRA bomb attack on a Woolwich pub. Patrick Armstrong, Gerald Conlon, Paul Hill and Carole Richardson were subsequently arrested, charged with murder in both incidents and sentenced to life imprisonment. Irregularities in police evidence resulted in the release of all four in 1989. *In the Name of the Father*, a 1993 film based on the case, explored movingly the relationship between Gerald Conlon and his sick father, but was described by one critic as 'unashamed Irish myth-making' on account of the inaccuracies of its court-room denouement. *See also* BIRMINGHAM SIX; BRIDGEWATER THREE; WINCHESTER THREE.

**Guinea pig.** A person or thing used as a subject for experiment, as guinea pigs were formerly by vivisectionists. The use of the animal's name in this way dates from the 1920s. In the Second World War the term was specifically applied to

RAF pilots suffering from burns when treated at the Queen Victoria Hospital, East Grinstead, under the pioneering plastic surgeon Sir Archibald McIndoe. A Guinea Pig Club, headed by a Chief Guinea Pig, was subsequently formed to care for their welfare. The 1948 film entitled *The Guinea Pig* stars Richard Attenborough as a working-class boy who wins a scholarship to a public school. It was based on a play by Walter Chetham Strode, and directed by Roy Boulting.

> We're all of us guinea pigs in the laboratory of God. Humanity is just a work in progress.
> TENNESSEE WILLIAMS: *Camino Real*, Block xii (1953)

**Guinness Book of Records.** An annual record of the superlative or 'mostest' in every conceivable field, first published in 1955. The germ of its creation was a shooting party in County Wexford, Ireland, in 1951, during which Sir Hugh Beaver, managing director of the brewery Arthur Guinness & Co. Ltd, was involved in a dispute as to whether the golden plover was Europe's fastest game bird. He realized that the answer was best found among people in pubs, and that a book which provided the answers for similar pub debates would be of benefit to licensees. The future athlete Chris Chataway, then an underbrewer with Guinness, recommended two friends to produce such a book, the twins Norris and Ross McWhirter, whom he had met at athletics events. They were duly commissioned and the first copy of the book was bound on 27 August 1955. It now appears in its own pages as an all-time bestseller. Since 1999 the editions have been retitled *Guinness World Records*.

**Gulag.** The abbreviation of Russian *Glavnoye upravleniye ispravitel'no-trudovykh lagerey*, 'Chief Administration for Corrective Labour Camps'. Such camps were a notorious feature of the Soviet Union from 1930 to 1955 and resulted in the deaths of thousands of prisoners. Their true nature was revealed to the public at large by Alexander Solzhenitsyn's *The* GULAG ARCHIPELAGO (1973).

**Gulag Archipelago, The.** A three-volume history (1974–78; in Russian as *Arkhipelag Gulag*, 1973–76) of the GULAG, the Soviet administrative department responsible for maintaining prisons and forced labour camps, by Alexander Solzhenitsyn. Having been awarded the NOBEL PRIZE for Literature (1970), the author was in 1974 deported after the publication in Paris of the first two volumes and the suicide of his former assistant who, after five days of interrogation by the KGB, had revealed where she had hidden a copy of the complete work.

**Gulf War.** A term now used particularly to denote the conflict in the Persian Gulf region in January and February 1991, when an international coalition of forces assembled in Saudi Arabia to force the withdrawal of Saddam Hussein's Iraqi forces from Kuwait, which they had invaded the previous year. It is often known as the First Gulf War, even though previously the term had been applied to the Iran–Iraq War of 1980–8, which ended inconclusively after considerable hardship and huge losses on both sides. The US-led invasion of Iraq in 2003 is sometimes referred to as the Second Gulf War. *See also* DESERT RATS; DESERT SHIELD; DESERT STORM; GULF WAR SYNDROME.

**Gulf War syndrome.** A name for a disorder of the nervous system alleged to have been contracted by soldiers serving in the First GULF WAR (1991). It was initially questioned whether such a syndrome actually existed, but when physical evidence was produced, a search for a possible physical cause began. Attribution was made either to anti-nerve-gas medication administered to troops before service in the Gulf or to exposure to harmful chemicals during such service.

**Gummidge, Worzel.** The scarecrow who comes to life in the children's books by Barbara Euphan Todd, beginning with the one that bears his name (1936). He normally stands in the Ten-Acre Field at Scatterbrook Farm but in his alter ego becomes involved in a host of comic adventures. He was a popular figure on CHILDREN'S HOUR and in a television series (1978–81) was convincingly played by Jon Pertwee.

The nickname Worzel Gummidge was at one time applied to Michael Foot (b.1913), left-wing leader of the LABOUR PARTY (1980–3), admired for his convictions, oratory, writings and intellect, but not for his powers of leadership (his stewardship saw Labour at its most divided) or for his sartorial elegance. It was the absence of the latter characteristic that led *Private Eye* and others to confer the nickname. In 1982 Foot appeared at the REMEMBRANCE DAY ceremony dressed in what his opponents unkindly described as a donkey jacket, recalling the shock caused almost a century before when QUEER HARDIE turned up to take his seat in the Commons wearing a cloth cap. The US novelist Norman Mailer likened his appearance to that of 'an eccentric professor of ornithology'.

**Gunboat diplomacy.** A foreign policy supported by the use or threat of military force. Gunboats go back to the 18th century, but the phrase dates only from the 1920s and was originally applied in the US press to foreign intervention in China.

**Gun for.** To 'have it in for' someone. The image is of a Western gun-fighter pursuing his prey.

**Gung-ho.** Excessively or unthinkingly eager, especially in the context of patriotism and military aggression. The term dates from the Second World War when it was adopted as a slogan by US Marines as a pidgin English form of Mandarin Chinese *kung, gonghé*, literally 'work together'.

**Guns of Navarone, The.** A thriller (1957) by Alistair Maclean (1922–87). An international team of commandos in the Second World War attempts to destroy a battery of heavy naval guns at the Greek fortress of Navarone, with the Germans on their trail, before an Allied invasion fleet passes within range. An ambitiously heroic film version (1961) was directed by J. Lee-Thompson.

**Guns or butter.** When a nation is at war a choice of priorities has to be made between material comforts and a contribution to the war effort. In NAZI Germany Hermann Goering summarized the situation in a speech at Hamburg in 1936: 'We have no butter … but I ask you – would you rather have butter or guns? … Preparedness makes us powerful. Butter merely makes us fat' (quoted in W. Frischauer, *Goering*, ch. 10, 1951). Joseph Goebbels had earlier made the same specific comparison in a speech in Berlin on 17 January 1936:

> Ohne Butter werden wir fertig, aber nicht, beispielsweise, ohne Kanonen. Wenn wir einmal überfallen werden, dann können wir uns nicht mit Butter, sondern nur mit Kanonen verteidigen. ('We can manage without butter but not, for example, without guns. If we are attacked we cannot defend ourselves with butter, only with guns.')
>
> *Deutsche Allgemeine Zeitung* (18 January 1936)

**Guomindang.** *See* KUOMINTANG.

**Gurrelieder.** An early Wagnerian-style extravaganza by Arnold Schoenberg (1874–1951). It was completed in 1911 and is scored for five solo singers, three male choruses, one mixed chorus, a narrator and a vast orchestra, which includes a set of iron chains. The title means 'Songs of Gurra', and the text is a German translation of poems by the Danish poet J.P. Jacobsen (1847–85). Gurra itself is a 14th-century castle, in which lives the heroine Tove, who is loved by the Danish king, Waldemar IV. In his memoirs *The Tongs and the Bones* (1981) Lord Harewood wrote of the piece: 'A proof if you want it – and I often do – that Schoenberg could, as they used to say about Picasso, draw when he wanted to.'

**Guru.** Properly, a Hindu spiritual teacher, from a Sanskrit word meaning 'grave', 'weighty', but in modern times a general term for any influential teacher, leader or expert.

**Gussied up.** Dressed up in one's best clothes, as for a night out. The origin may lie in Gussie, a pet form of the name Augustus, current in the early 20th century for an effeminate man. Some see a source in 'gusset', as a piece of material sewn into a garment to allow for freedom of movement. *See also* GORGEOUS GUSSIE.

**Gustav Line.** (German *Gustav Linie*.) A heavily fortified defensive line built across Italy by the Germans in the winter of 1943–4. The line stretched across Italy south of Rome and north of Naples, extending from the mouth of the River Garigliano on the west coast to the mouth of the Sangro on the east coast, and included the key position on the hilltop monastery of Monte Cassino, the capture of which cost so many Allied lives in the first half of 1944. *See also* GOTHIC LINE.

**Gut bomb.** In US slang, any item of food calculated to have a temporarily deleterious effect on the eater's wellbeing. The expression, a product of late 1960s college slang, often designates specifically a very greasy hamburger.

**Gut reaction.** An instinctive or emotional reaction, as opposed to a rational or considered one. A 'gut feeling' is similarly instinctive or intuitive. Expressions of this type date from the 1960s.

> [*Yorkshire Evening Post* editor Neil] Hodgkinson also admits to a gut feeling that a tabloid was the right solution for Britain's ninth bestselling evening paper serving a vibrant city.
> *The Times* (17 September 1999)

**Gut rot.** A colloquial term for stomach ache or an upset stomach. It is also sometimes applied to cheap rough alcoholic drink (more standardly known as 'rotgut').

**Gutted.** Bitterly disappointed; devastated. A colloquialism dating from the 1980s that came to be mainly associated with sports players and media celebrities. The sensation is similar to receiving a blow in the guts.

> They all really wanted to see Gizz's band, but due to Break for the Border's policy of only admitting over 21s, they couldn't go. They were gutted, and we were gutted for them.
> *Stamford Herald and Post* (10 June 1999)

**Gutter press.** A derogatory collective name for the popular tabloid newspapers, seen as trawling the gutters for filth. 'Journalists belong in the gutter because that is where the ruling classes throw their guilty secrets' (Gerald Priestland, himself a journalist, speaking on Radio London, 19 May 1988). *See also* YELLOW PRESS.

**Guvernator, The.** *See* the GOVERNATOR.

***Guys and Dolls.*** A musical comedy (1950) with music and lyrics by Frank Loesser (1910–69) and book by Jo Swerling and Abe Burrows about the romance that develops between a Salvation Army worker (representing the 'dolls') and gambler Sky Masterson (representing the 'guys'). Filmed in 1955 with Frank Sinatra, Marlon Brando and Jean Simmons, it was based on stories by Damon Runyon (1884–1946).

**Guzzle guts.** A greedy person. A term used mainly among children and dating from the 1950s, when it arose as a variant of the much older 'greedy guts'.

**Gymslip mum.** A teenage girl who bears a child while still at school. Gymslips or gym tunics were invented in 1893 by a student at Hampstead College of Physical Education and although originally designed specifically for physical activities in a gymnasium rapidly became a standard girls' school uniform. Their use declined in the Second World War although they were still worn in some of the more traditional schools well into the 1950s. The stock phrase preserves the memory of their existence.

> Today, Clare, Chris and Linda open their hearts to *The People* to reveal how they coped from the moment Linda discovered her daughter was about to become a gymslip mum.
> *People* (30 April 1995)

***Gypsy.*** A musical comedy (1959) with a score by Jule Styne (1905–94), lyrics by Stephen Sondheim (b.1930) and book by Arthur Laurents (b.1918), telling the story of a vaudeville entertainer who with the encouragement of her ambitious mother builds a reputation as a striptease artist. The show, which furnished Ethel Merman with one of her best roles as the mother, was based on the career of the real-life striptease dancer Gypsy Rose Lee (1914-70).

# H

**Haberdasher Harry.** *See* GIVE-'EM-HELL HARRY.

**Hacker.** Someone who illicitly breaks into other people's computers, especially those of companies, governments, etc.

**Hackette.** A mostly derogatory media nickname for a female journalist, with the feminine suffix '-ette', as in 'usherette', added to 'hack' as a term for a male journalist who produces dull or unoriginal work, just as a hack is or was an ordinary horse for riding. The word was popularized by its use in *Private Eye*. The gossip columnist Lady Olga Maitland (b.1944) was nicknamed the 'Fragrant Hackette'.

> Perhaps Mr Cameron was misquoted, or plied with drink and led on by a *Sunday Times* hackette.
>> *The Listener* (16 May 1985)

**Hack it.** To be up to a particular job or task; to be able to cope successfully. The expression originated in the United States and is first recorded in 1952.

> A career in journalism – can you hack it? Do you have a passion for writing?
>> www.learndirect-advice.co.uk

**Haddock, Austin.** The name adopted temporarily in 2001 by Austin Mitchell (b.1934), Labour MP for Grimsby, to demonstrate his solidarity with the the many trawlermen in his constituency.

**Haganah.** (Hebrew, 'defence'). A Zionist military organization set up by Jewish settlers in Palestine in 1920 to protect themselves from attacks by Palestinian Arabs. When the British authorities began to take harsh measures to restrict Jewish immigration after the Second World War the Haganah embarked on a sabotage campaign. In 1947, after the United Nations determined on the partition of Palestine, the Haganah became involved in open conflict with the British and with Palestinian Arabs. On the creation of the State of Israel in 1948 the Haganah was turned into the official army. The Israeli armed forces are called Tzva Haganah le-Yisra'el (Hebrew, 'Israel defence forces'). *See also* DEIR YASSIN; IRGUN; STERN GANG.

**Hagrid, Rubeus.** *See* Harry POTTER.

**Haigspeak.** Obfuscatory or convoluted speech, often producing a surreal effect, of the kind supposedly typified by Alexander Haig (b.1924), especially in his dealings with the press when US secretary of state (1981–2). A representative sample: 'The warning message we sent the Russians was a calculated ambiguity that would be clearly understood.' The term also encompasses the conversion of nouns and other word-classes into verbs, a rhetorical tic to which Haig was particularly prone (e.g. 'Let me caveat that').

The nearest equivalent in modern British public life is probably the often tortured grammar and malapropistic vocabulary of the Labour politician John Prescott (b.1938; *see* TWO JAGS), who in a House of Commons statement on 13 December 2005 about a serious fire at a fuel depot in Hemel Hempstead claimed that the smoke plume was made up of 'carbon dioxide, carbon monoxide and hydrocardigans'.

***Hair.*** *See* ROCK OPERA.

**Hairdressers' names.** Many modern hairdressers devise a punning name for their salon that is as artistically apt as the styles they pride themselves on creating. One need only look under 'Hairdressers' in the local YELLOW PAGES to find premises called 'Cut Above', 'Face Value', 'Hair We Go', 'In the Pink' or 'Turning Heads'. The following real examples of American and British salons with names of this type are from Paul Dickson's *What's In a Name?* (1996):

> About Faces, Best Little Hairhouse in Town, Beyond the Fringe, Clip Joint, Curl Up 'n Dye, Do Yer Nut, Hair Apparent, Headmasters, Julius Scissors, Kiss My Act, Lockworks, Loose Ends, Makin' Waves, Mane Attraction, Off the Top, Shear Artistry, Short Cut, Streaks Ahead.

**Hair up** or **in one's ass, A.** In US slang, someone who has a hair (or a wild hair) up their ass is extremely angry, upset or excited. The expression probably dates from around the Second World War period.

**Hairy eyeball, The.** In US slang, a suspicious or malevolent glance, such as might be characterized by a partial lowering of the eyelids. The vivid metaphor dates from the early 1960s.

**Haka.** A Maori ceremonial war dance involving chanting. The ALL BLACKS rugby team dance a version of it before a match as a challenge to the opposing team and first performed it internationally in 1888, when the 'Natives' toured New Zealand, Australia and Britain. The chanted words are: '*Ka mate ka mate, ka ora ka mate ka mate, ka ora tenie tengata, puhuru huru nana e piki mai, whaka whiti te ra hupanei, hupanei, hupanei kaupanei whiti te ra*' ('There is going to be a fight between us. May it mean death to you and life to us. We will fight on, or until our side is vanquished. So long as the daylight lasts. We are here to continue the battle. To be either killed or to be victorious.').

**HAL.** The computer on board the spaceship *Discovery* in Arthur C. Clarke's novel 2001: A SPACE ODYSSEY (1968), based on his early story 'The Sentinel' (1951), and widely popularized by the spectacular film released simultaneously with it. HAL 9000, an artificial intelligence, has been sent with a three-man crew to locate the origin of an alien monolith found on the moon. HAL malfunctions, plans to take over the mission, and murders two of the crew members. The remaining member, David Bowman, dismantles the computer's memory, effectively 'killing' HAL. The scene in which HAL regresses to infancy, singing 'Daisy, Daisy', is curiously moving. HAL's name is an acronym of '*h*euristically programmed *al*gorithmic computer', and the letters themselves are one alphabetical place short of IBM.

**Haldane principle.** The principle that government research agencies should be completely separated from government departments that benefit from their research. The name is that of the geneticist J.B.S. Haldane (1892–1964), chairman of the committee that formulated the principle in 1918.

**Half a Sixpence.** A musical comedy (1963) with music and lyrics by David Heneker (1906–2001) about a poor young man who wins a fortune, loses it and is finally redeemed by his love for his wife. Based on the novel *Kipps* by H.G. Wells, the title refers to the sixpence that the two lovers split in two, each keeping half to remind themselves of the other.

**Halitosis Hall.** A nickname given to the House of Commons in *Private Eye*'s 'Dear Bill' letters, purportedly written by

Denis Thatcher (1915–2003), husband of the IRON LADY, to William (now Lord) Deedes (b.1913), editor of the *Daily Telegraph* (1974–86). The name echoes the titles of various satirical novels by Thomas Love Peacock (1785–1866), such as *Headlong Hall* (1816), *Nightmare Abbey* (1818), *Crotchet Castle* (1831) and *Gryll Grange* (1860).

**Hall of Fame.** A place where famous persons are commemorated by busts or plaques, especially in the United States. Two of the best known are the Hall of Fame for Great Americans in the Bronx, New York City, founded in 1900 and dedicated on 30 May 1901 by Henry M. MacCracken, president of New York University; and the National Baseball Hall of Fame and Museum at Cooperstown, New York, founded in 1936 and dedicated on 12 June 1939, the centenary of the supposed invention of baseball by the US Army officer Abner Doubleday (1819–93).

**Halloween.** A cult horror film (1978), directed by John Carpenter, about a psychopath on the loose in a small Illinois town on Halloween night. It was one of the most commercially successful independent films of all time and generated a number of inferior sequels.

**Hamas.** (Arabic, 'zeal'.) A Palestinian Islamic fundamentalist movement that calls for the creation of a Palestinian state founded on religious principles. It first came to prominence in the GAZA STRIP in the 1980s. An impetus to its campaign came in 1988 when the Palestinian Liberation Organization (PLO) recognized Israel's right to exist. It has consistently opposed the PLO and denied Israel's right to exist. It boycotted the first Palestinian elections in 1996; however, it participated in and won the 2006 elections, and took over the government of the Palestinian Authority, much to the consternation of Israel, the West, and its Palestinian opponents. Its name has also been interpreted as an acronym of *harakat al-Muqawama al-Islamiyya*, 'Islamic Resistance Movement'.

**Hamburger.** This popular US dish of fried minced beef, onion, egg and so forth, made into a flat cake, takes its name from Hamburg in Germany. It appears to have originated in the Baltic region some centuries ago, but it was introduced into the United States in the 19th century by immigrants from the port of Hamburg and subsequently 'naturalized'. The beefburger came to be so called by caterers to avoid confusion by association with ham. There are now various types of burgers with the first part of the name indicating the chief constituent. Examples are cheeseburger, chickenburger, steakburger, vegeburger. *See also* BIG MAC; FAST FOOD; JUNK FOOD; MCDONALD'S.

**Hammer, Mike.** The tough and amoral detective in a series of violent thrillers by Mickey Spillane, beginning with I, THE JURY (1947). He butts and bludgeons his way through the various cases, is brutal towards women, and has a particular antipathy for communists. Film and television versions of some of the stories followed in due course. *See also* KISS ME DEADLY.

**Hammer, The.** A nickname given by the *Scottish Daily Express* to Sir David McNee (b.1925), Commissioner of the Metropolitan Police from 1977 to 1982, for his tough approach to law and order when a senior detective in Glasgow. The name alludes to the historical 'Hammer of the Scots', otherwise Edward I of England (1272–1307). The nickname has subsequently been applied to Dr John Reid (b.1947), former communist and since 1997 a prominent member of Tony Blair's NEW LABOUR cabinet (and promoted to home secretary in May 2006), known for his no-nonsense ways with impertinent interviewers on BBC Radio 4's *Today* programme.

**Hammer and sickle.** The emblem of communism, symbolic of the union of workers in the factory and peasants on the land. In particular it became the symbol of the former USSR, on whose flag it featured. Soviet citizens themselves always referred to the emblem as 'Sickle and Hammer' (*Serp i molot*).

**Hammer Films.** In financial terms one of the most successful companies in the history of the British cinema. It was founded in 1947 by Will Hammer (real name William Hinds) and Sir James Carreras and first won fame in 1956 when it launched a cycle of low-budget HORROR MOVIES that quickly captured wide markets in Britain and the United States. It emphasized blood and gore in vivid colour, and revived such figures from the US cinema as Frankenstein and Dracula. It then expanded into other genres such as SCIENCE FICTION, psychological thrillers and costume dramas. In 1980 it produced an anthology of spine-chilling 'shockers' for television under the title *Hammer House of Horror*. The name is a byword for any 'grim' situation, literal or metaphorical.

**Hammond organ.** The once ubiquitous electric organ of this name was the invention in 1929 of the US mechanical engineer Laurens Hammond (1895–1973), who in the same year set up the Hammond Instrument Co. of Chicago to manufacture it. It was favoured by dance bands since its varying tones could be used to back a small group of players, while it was popularized as a solo instrument by performers such as Ethel Smith in the United States and Harry Farmer in Britain. Several variations on the original model were subsequently produced.

**Hampstead set.** A term originally applied in the 1950s to a group of supporters of Hugh Gaitskell (1906–63), leader of the Labour Party (1955–63). The group, opposed by NYE Bevan and his followers, lived, like Gaitskell, in the wealthy area of Hampstead in North London. The group included Anthony Crosland, Denis Healey (*see* GROMYKO OF THE LABOUR PARTY), Douglas Jay, Roy Jenkins (*see* WOY) and Frank Pakenham (*see* LORD PORN). Subsequently, journalists have used the term more generally and collectively for liberal and/or left-leaning intellectuals living in and around Hampstead, such as the playwright Harold Pinter (b.1930) and the historical biographer Antonia Fraser (b.1932), who have been involved in fashionable causes such as CHARTER 88, and are deemed a subset of the CHATTERING CLASSES.

**Hamptons, The.** The popular name of the eastern end of Long Island, New York City, where the resort villages of Westhampton, Southampton, Bridgehampton, East Hampton and Hampton Bays are located, among others. Nicknamed 'Hollywood East' (*see also* GREAT COMMUNICATOR), the area is a summer retreat for wealthy New Yorkers, including many celebrities, and the leading summer social event is a glittering charity benefit. The August 1999 issue of *The Tatler* somewhat unexpectedly nominated West Wittering, West Sussex, as the English answer to the Hamptons, but 'without its pretentiousness'.

***Hancock's Half-Hour.*** A classic television comedy series screened from 1956 to 1961 and starring the popular actor Tony Hancock (1924–68), famous for his lugubrious buffoonishness. His gradual decline, alcoholism and suicide added, in hindsight, a note of genuine poignancy to his finely judged roles, one of the most memorable being that of a timorous blood donor. Hancock's fictitious address, 23 Railways Cuttings, East Cheam, was equally savoured by his fans.

**Handbag.** To attack. The colloquialism relates specifically to women (who carry a handbag) and became associated in particular with the prime ministerial period of office (1979–90) of Margaret Thatcher (*see* IRON LADY), who was depicted in cartoons as hitting opponents with her omnipresent handbag. This method of assault is not of course new, and in *The* MUPPET SHOW the leading lady, Miss Piggy, although normally composed, was prone to felling with her handbag anyone who offended her.

**Hand in the till.** *See* FINGERS IN THE TILL.

**Hand it to someone.** To recognize their achievement, as: 'I've got to hand it to you, you were easily the best.' The image is of handing the person an award. The phrase is of US origin.

**Handlebar moustache.** A wide, thick moustache with the ends curving slightly upwards. The term dates from the 1930s and probably relates more to the motorcycle than the bicycle.

> Handle-bar moustaches show the extrovert or suggest an inferiority complex.
> GUY EGMONT: *The Art of Egmontese*, ch. 1 (1961)

**Handmaids's Tale, The.** A novel by the Canadian writer Margaret Atwood (b.1939), published in 1985. It describes a future North American dystopia in which women are subjugated by a male-run fundamentalist Christian theocracy. Freedoms have been suspended, martial law has been declared, and dissidents, abortionists and homosexuals are put to death. Women of the under-classes, known as handmaids, are encouraged to breed for the benefit of the state, as the wives of the ruling elite are often infertile. The novel is narrated by the handmaid Offred. A 1990 film version, directed by Volker Schlöndorff, had a screenplay by Harold Pinter and a performance by Natasha Richardson as Offred. *See also* FIRST LINES OF NOVELS.

**Hand of God.** A name for the goal scored in the 51st minute by the Argentine player Diego Maradona in the football World Cup quarter-final against England at Mexico City in 1986. Maradona quite clearly punched the ball into the net ahead of the England goalkeeper Peter Shilton. The infringement enabled Argentina to win 2–1 and Maradona was quoted afterwards as saying that the goal was 'a little bit of Maradona's head (*sic*), a little bit of the hand of God'.

**Hand of history, The.** Something that Prime Minister Tony Blair claimed to feel on his shoulder on 7 April 1998, at the time of the signing of the GOOD FRIDAY AGREEMENT in Northern Ireland, so coining one of the most successful soundbites of a thoroughly soundbitten career:

> A day like today is not a day for soundbites really. We can leave those at home. But I feel the hand of history upon our shoulder in respect to this. I really do.

**Hands Across America.** A human chain of some 6 million people was formed on 25 May 1986 to raise money and awareness in the cause of homelessness. Apart from some unavoidable breaks in desert areas, the hand-to-hand line extended from New York to Long Beach, California.

**Hand** or **give someone something on a plate.** To give it to them with little or no effort on their part. The allusion is to a plate of food served up ready to eat. The phrase dates from the 1920s.

**Hands-on.** A term originating in the late 1960s and at first applied to the direct operation of a computer by using a keyboard, as distinct from a theoretical understanding of the process. The term then extended in meaning to apply to active participation in any area of knowledge, whether actually using the hands or not, especially one traditionally regarded as academic.

> 'Hands-on archaeology' is being offered [to young people] at Bignor Roman Villa and the Fishbourne Roman Palace, both in West Sussex.
> *The Times* (19 July 1999)

**Handy, Para.** *See* PARA HANDY.

**Hanging and flogging brigade.** An uncomplimentary later 20th-century nickname for those in Britain who invoke fondly the days of official corporal and capital punishment as a way of keeping society in order, and who sometimes agitate for their return. The description is applied particularly to a subset of the Conservative Party.

> He was a conspicuously liberal Tory at a time when that phrase did not seem a contradiction in terms, though, even then, his distaste for his party's hanging and flogging brigade … made him distrusted by many Conservatives.
> GEOFFREY WHEATCROFT: *The Guardian*, obituary of the political biographer John Grigg (2 January 2002)

*See also* FLOGGING AND WHIPPING.

**Hang in there.** To stick with it, even when the going is tough. The allusion is probably to the boxing ring, where a boxer getting the worst of it may seek relief by clinging on to his opponent or to the ropes. After such a brief respite he is better able to continue.

> 'No, no,' said Simon. 'I'll hang in there now that I've waited this long.'
> JEFFREY ARCHER: *First among Equals*, ch. 12 (1984)

**Hang it out.** In US slang, to take risks. The expression is a euphemistic curtailment of the earlier synonymous 'hang one's ass out'.

> In combat you got to hang it out if you want to do your job.
> MARK BERENT: *Steel Tiger* (1990)

*See also* LET IT ALL HANG OUT.

**Hang left** or **right.** To make a left or right turn, especially in motoring or skiing. A variant is 'to hang a left' etc. The expression is of US origin and dates from the 1960s.

> 'Hang a right on Santa Monica Freeway, hang a left on Harbour and another right on Sixth Street.' If you hang lefts where you were told to hang rights, the freeway system is unforgiving.
> *Sunday Telegraph* (29 July 1984)

**Hang loose.** To have a relaxed attitude to everything. The expression probably originated in sport, where one often performs better if one is not tense. *See also* HANG TOUGH.

**Hangman, The.** A nickname given to the high-ranking SS officer Reinhard Heydrich (1904–42), also known as the Butcher of Prague. He became Reichsprotektor for Bohemia and Moravia in 1941, and within five weeks he had ordered the execution of some 300 Czechs. He also headed the notorious Wannsee Conference, which determined the so-called FINAL SOLUTION. His assassination in 1942 by Czech resistance fighters led to hundreds of Czechs being executed in retaliation, and the wiping out of the entire village of LIDICE.

**Hang one on.** To 'hang one on someone' is to punch them hard. On the other hand, simply to 'hang one on' is to get extremely drunk. Both expressions originated in US slang.

**Hang** or **hold on to your hat!** Stand by for a surprise! Get ready for a shock! A stock warning of unexpected news dating from the early years of the 20th century and perhaps having its origins in a rollercoaster ride, where one would indeed need to hold on to one's hat, if wearing one.

**Hangover Square.** A thriller (1941) by Patrick Hamilton (1904–62), subtitled 'A Story of Darkest Earl's Court', an area in West London. A schizophrenic haunts the streets and public houses in an almost perpetual hangover, obsessed, in his lost periods, with murdering the woman he loves. The title puns on Hanover Square.

**Hang right.** *See* HANG LEFT.

**Hang someone out** or **up to dry.** To leave someone unprotected to suffer the consequences of their own actions. The image, which originated in the United States in the 1920s, is probably of washing on a line, left to flap at the whim of a breeze.

> A desperate attempt to save Rove's butt and hang Libby out to dry? We'll see.
> www.thecarpetbaggerreport.com (20 October 2005)

> Defence chiefs have admitted for the first time that they failed to look after soldiers at the centre of Iraq abuse allegations. Troops say the army left them hanging 'out to dry' once they had been accused.
> *The Observer* (6 November 2005)

**Hang ten.** In US surfing slang, to ride on a surfboard with all ten toes of both feet hooked over the edge of the board – a mode that ensures maximum speed. If you can manage only one foot, you are 'hanging five'.

**Hang tough.** In US slang, to persist in a course of action, whatever the problems. The expression, which dates from the 1930s, has also come to be used as an encouraging parting shot. *See also* HANG LOOSE.

> PM plans to hang tough on cabinet jobs [headline]. Prime Minister Ariel Sharon told a festive gathering of Likud MKs … last night that he will not back down on his plan to push through three ministerial appointments as a group.
> www.haaretz.com (31 October 2005)

**Hang-up.** An emotional problem or inhibition; a mental block. A phrase dating from the counterculture of the 1960s.

**Hannay, Richard.** *See The* THIRTY-NINE STEPS.

**Hannibal the Cannibal.** The nickname of Dr Hannibal Lecter, a character in a number of novels by Thomas Harris (b.1940), and the films based on them. Lecter, a psychopath of outstanding intelligence and an insatiable hunger for human flesh, makes his first appearance in *Red Dragon* (1981; filmed as *Manhunter* in 1986 and under the original title in 2002). He subsequently features in *The* SILENCE OF THE LAMBS (1989; film 1990), *Hannibal* (1999; film 2001) and *Behind the Mask* (2006; to be filmed as *Young Hannibal*). Lecter has been played by Anthony Hopkins in the 1990, 1999 and 2002 films.

**Hanoi Hilton.** In US military slang during the VIETNAM War, an ironic name given to a North Vietnamese prison camp, or to time spent incarcerated in one (Hanoi was the capital of North Vietnam from 1954 to 1976, and Hilton Hotels are a US-based international chain of luxurious hotels). *See also* BANGKOK HILTON.

**Hanoi Jane.** A hostile nickname given by right-wing US critics to the film star Jane Fonda (b.1937), whose support for radical and left-wing causes included a visit to Hanoi, the capital of communist North Vietnam, at the time of the VIETNAM War. She made a documentary about this visit, *Introduction to the Enemy*, in 1974. The purpose of her trip was to bear witness to US bombing strikes on the dyke system of the Red River delta, which if breached would threaten the lives of some 200,000 people. The bombing of the dykes stopped within a month of her return to the United States. Fonda herself has said of the nickname:

> I hate it. It's become way bigger than me. I'm like this little pawn in this huge myth created by people who need the myth to flog their right-wing world view.
> Quoted in *The Observer* (10 April 2005)

Earlier Fonda had formed the Anti-War Troupe with the Canadian actor Donald Sutherland, which gave performances at army bases despite the Pentagon's attempts to stop them. Her documentary about this tour (1972) was entitled *F.T.A.* (*Free the Army*).

**Happening.** An all-embracing word describing a partly improvised or spontaneous piece of theatrical or pseudo-theatrical performance, especially when involving audience participation. The term arose in the 1950s in the world of US avant-garde art. Happenings became a regular feature of the FRINGE performances at the Edinburgh Festival. One such, organized by the US director Kenneth Dewey, involved the wheeling of a naked model on a trolley across the organ gallery of the McEwan Hall in the midst of the 1963 International Drama Conference. The conference organizer, John Calder, and the model, Anna Kesselaar, were charged with indecency. The event caused a publicity storm but was a landmark of its kind. The concept of the happening was seized on internationally and the term was adopted un-translated, as French *le happening*, German *das Happening*, Italian *il happening*, Russian *kheppening*, Japanese *hapuningu*.

**'Happiness is a Warm Gun'.** A darkly ironic and ambiguous song by The BEATLES, credited to John Lennon and Paul McCartney. It appears on the so-called WHITE ALBUM, released in November 1968. The title originally derives from a slogan used by the US National Rifle Association ('Happiness is a warm gun in your hand'), which greatly shocked Lennon. Given that 'gun' is an established slang term for both the male member and a hypodermic syringe, the song's title (and its lyrics) are clearly open to a variety of interpretations. *See also* HAPPINESS IS A WARM PUPPY.

**Happiness is a warm puppy.** A twee truism made popular by the title of Charles M. Schulz's bestselling book of 1962 centring on his cartoon puppy SNOOPY and itself evolving from a caption to a panel in an earlier strip showing a small child hugging the dog. The phrase spawned a raft of advertising slogans, since 'happiness' is the goal of all manufacturers and service providers. Among them were 'Happiness is egg-shaped' (British eggs), 'Happiness is a quick-starting car' (Esso petrol), 'Happiness is a cigar called Hamlet' (first in 1964), 'Happiness is a warm ear-piece', 'Happiness is being elected captain – and getting a Bulova watch', 'Happiness is a $49 table' (Brancusi furniture), 'Happiness is giving Dad a Terry Shave Coat for Christmas' (Con Sporterry), 'Happiness is the Sands' (a Las Vegas hotel), 'Happiness is a bathroom by Marion Wieder' (a firm of US decorators) and 'Happiness can be the color of her hair' (Miss Clairol). The words equally suggested themselves to motorists as suitable bumper-sticker fodder, as 'Happiness is being single', 'Happiness is seeing Lubbock, Texas, in the rear view mirror' (a line from a COUNTRY AND WESTERN song), 'Happiness is Slough in my rear-view mirror', 'HAPPINESS IS A WARM GUN' (title of a song of 1968 by John Lennon), 'Happiness is Wren-shaped' (i.e. in the mould

of the WRENS rather than the birds) and dozens on the same lines.

> We have lived through the era when happiness was a warm puppy, and the era when happiness was a dry martini, and now we have come to the era when happiness is 'knowing what your uterus looks like'.
> NORA EPHRON: *Crazy Salad*, 'Vaginal Politics' (1975)

**Happy as Alice.** Very happy. A phrase varying the gender of the male HAPPY AS LARRY.

> For two days I panicked. Then they ran another scan and it had gone. I have been as happy as Alice ever since.
> *The Times* (26 May 1999)

**Happy as Larry.** Very happy. An Australian expression. It is suggested that the original Larry may have been Larry Foley (1847–1917), the noted boxer, but the word may actually derive from 'larrikin', an Australian term for an unruly young man.

**Happy birthday!** A greeting to someone on their birthday. The birthday greeting song 'Happy Birthday to You', with the person's name inserted in the third line after 'Dear', was originally a children's song, 'Good Morning to You', written in 1893, with words by the US kindergarten educator Patty Smith Hill (1868–1946) and music by her sister, Mildred J. Hill. The present words by Clayton F. Summy were substituted in 1935.

**Happy bunny.** A synonym of HAPPY CAMPER, and used in the same sort of contexts: someone who is 'not a happy bunny' is far from gruntled.

**Happy camper.** US campus slang of the 1980s for a contented person, the reference being to a holiday camp. The expression is frequently found in the negative for a dissatisfied or unhappy person, 'not a happy camper'. The flippancy of the phrase may hide a heaviness of heart.

**Happy clappy.** A term descriptive of a type of evangelical religious worship, with joyful hymn singing accompanied by rhythmic clapping. The phrase was established by the early 1990s. Those who participate in such services are referred to as happy clappers.

> Holy Trinity, Brompton, one of the largest happy-clappy (and one of the poshest) churches in London.
> *The Independent* (21 July 1992)

The name Happy Clappers was adopted by a British HOUSE music group in the 1990s.

**Happy Days.** A play (1961) by the Irish playwright Samuel Beckett (1906–89) in which the two characters, Winnie and her husband Willie, babble incoherently but evocatively as they are gradually buried up to their necks in sand. The deeper Winnie is buried in the sand, the more ludicrous her chaotic optimism becomes:

> Oh this is a happy day, this will have been another happy day!

**Happy dust.** A term applied to various euphoria-inducing drugs in powdered or crystalline form, especially cocaine, heroin and morphine. It originated in US drug-users' slang and is first recorded in 1914.

**Happy hour.** An hour when a pub or bar sells drinks at reduced prices, the idea being that patrons will consume more than usual and stay on to buy drinks when they revert to full price. The period may well be longer than just a single hour. The phrase originated in the 1950s as a US Navy term for a scheduled time of entertainment and refreshment.

**Happy landings!** A toast when drinking, especially among aircraft pilots.

**Happy slapping.** A form of aggravated bullying in which a child is assaulted by a group of others, who record the attack on a video-phone and send the footage to friends. The practice and its distastefully incongruous name emerged in Britain in 2004.

The practice can go beyond bullying. In December 2005 three youths and a 15-year-old girl were convicted of manslaughter after a happy-slapping attack on the South Bank in London led to the death of their victim, who was unknown to them. They had later watched the attack at home on a mobile phone.

> 'Our school has already banned phones because of happy slapping,' wrote 12-year-old Arthur. 'I got happy-slapped on my way to the bus by two people from my school, one filming it with a camera phone.'
>
> *The Observer* (26 June 2005)

**Happy Valley.** A place where people live or work in peace and contentment. The term can be applied ironically. In the Second World War RAF pilots so named the Ruhr, as a much bombed area. In Hong Kong, on the other hand, Happy Valley is the site of a famous racecourse, its Chinese name being Wong Nei Chong Valley, while in Labrador, Canada, Happy Valley is a residential district established in 1970 for families of a local military base. The name ultimately comes from Dr Johnson's prose romance *Rasselas* (1759), the story of a prince of Abyssinia who, weary of the joys of the 'happy valley' where the inhabitants know only 'the soft vicissitudes of pleasure and repose', travels far and wide in search of true happiness. In the ROARING TWENTIES Happy Valley was the name of a loose gathering of dissolute aristocrats

and playboys in colonial Kenya headed by the handsome philanderer Lord Erroll, otherwise John Carberry, formerly Baron Carbery of Castle Freke, Ireland, whose murder by Sir Jock Delves Broughton in 1941 was a *cause célèbre* of the day, and formed the subject of the 1987 film *White Mischief. Happy Valley* (1939) is also the ironic title of the first novel of the Australian writer Patrick White.

**Happy Warrior.** The nickname of the US Democratic politician Al (Alfred Emmanuel) Smith (1873–1944). When Franklin Roosevelt, FDR, spoke in support of his bid to win the Democratic nomination to run for president in 1924, he described Smith as 'the happy warrior of the political battlefield'. Smith's bid was unsuccessful.

A cartoon-strip biography of Winston Churchill in the EAGLE comic in the 1950s, written by Clifford Makins, was entitled 'The Happy Warrior', and the nickname was also applied to the liberal Democratic US politician Hubert Humphrey (1911–78). Humphrey was Lyndon Johnson's vice-president (1965–9) and ran unsuccessfully for president against Richard Nixon in 1968. When paying tribute to Humphrey in 1980 President Jimmy Carter eulogized him thus: 'The great president who might have been – Hubert Horatio Hornblower!' (inadvertently confusing Humphrey with the fictional naval hero of C.S. Forester's historical novels, set during the Napoleonic Wars). Humphrey himself was prone to gaffes: on hearing of the failed assassination attempt against President Gerald Ford in 1975 he commented: 'There are too many guns in the hands of people who don't know how to use them.' *See also* TRICKY DICKY.

**Hard** or **tough act to follow.** A performance or feat which it is difficult to emulate. The expression arose in the early 20th century from US vaudeville, originally as a description of a particularly good act that would make the one following it seem mediocre by comparison.

> [David] Attenborough, more than anyone else, has ensured that the second century of the broadcasting age has a hard act to follow.
>
> *Sunday Times* (2 January 2000)

***Hard Day's Night, A.*** The title of a BEATLES film, its soundtrack album and a track on it all of which were released in 1964. The film was still without a title when shooting began in March 1964, and 'A Hard Day's Night' is usually credited to The Beatles' drummer Ringo Starr, who apparently used the phrase to describe a particularly tiring day of filming. Other titles that were considered for the film included 'It's A Daft, Daft, Daft, Daft, Daft World', BEATLEMANIA and 'What Little Old Man?', the last being one of the first lines uttered in the film. The song is credited to John Lennon and Paul McCartney. The soundtrack album included the songs 'Can't Buy Me Love', 'Tell Me Why' and 'And I Love Her'.

**Hard hat.** US slang for someone with reactionary or conservative views. The allusion is to construction workers, known from their protective headgear as 'hard hats', who took a conservative stance during the social upheaval of the 1960s.

**'Hard Rain's A-Gonna Fall, A'.** An anti-war song by Bob Dylan, released in 1963 in the aftermath of the Cuban Missile Crisis, at the height of the COLD WAR. The 'hard rain' of the title is nuclear fallout and the lyrics prefigure the concept of NUCLEAR WINTER.

> Oh, where have you been, my blue-eyed son?
> Oh, where have you been, my darling young one?
> I've stumbled on the side of twelve misty mountains,
> I've walked and I've crawled on six crooked highways,
> I've stepped in the middle of seven sad forests,
> I've been out in front of a dozen dead oceans,
> I've been ten thousand miles in the mouth of a graveyard,
> And it's a hard, and it's a hard, it's a hard, and it's a hard,
> And it's a hard rain's a-gonna fall.

**Hard rock.** A type of highly amplified rock music with a heavy beat, popular in the latter half of the 1960s.

**Hardworkingfamilies.** A constituency to which all three political parties constantly appealed during the 2005 general election campaign, presumably on the basis that shiftless youths in hoodies and single mothers on benefit would not bother to turn out anyway. The fact that the phrase 'hardworkingfamilies' had become such a shibboleth reflected the political paradigm shift wrought by Margaret Thatcher (*see* THERE IS NO SUCH THING AS SOCIETY). Variants on hardworking families include ordinaryhardworkingfamilies and hard-working familiesandpensioners. In the United States, President George W. Bush put it this way:

> Families is where our nation finds hope, where wings take dream.

**Hardy perennial.** Horticulturally a herbaceous plant with a perennial rootstock, i.e. one that lasts for several years and that dies back in winter. Metaphorically a hardy perennial is a thing that irrevocably recurs, especially annually.

**Hare Krishna.** A sect devoted to the worship of the Hindu deity Krishna. It arose in the United States in 1966 as the International Society for Krishna Consciousness and claims a lineage of spiritual masters dating back to Caitanya

(1485–1533), whom it regards as an incarnation of Krishna. It has become familiar to the public from the shaven-headed, saffron-robed young people who chant and clash cymbals as they weave their way along the city streets. The chant, known as the Maha ('Great') Mantra, gave the present name, and in full runs: 'Hare Krishna, Hare Krishna, Krishna, Krishna, Hare Hare.' This is repeated, substituting Rama, as the name of the second most popular Hindu deity, for Krishna every second verse. 'Hare' means 'O god'.

**Harlem Globetrotters.** The African American professional basketball team of this name was founded in 1927 by Abe Saperstein, a sports promoter. As players had no home base, they originally began touring the United States in Saperstein's car but later, as their name implies, travelled widely abroad. They are known for their spectacular ball handling and amusing antics, and play against a team called the 'Opposition', largely made up of white players, which never wins. Famous Globetrotters include Marques Haynes (b.1926), 'Meadowlark' Lemon (b.1933), the 'Clown Prince of Basketball', and Wilt 'the Stilt' Chamberlain (1936–99), 2.18m (7ft 2in) tall, regarded by many as the greatest basketball player of all time.

**Harlem Renaissance.** A term applied to a mainly literary artistic movement centred on New York's Harlem district in the 1920s. During this period, writers and artists generated a new aesthetic within African American culture, one that reflected the opportunities and challenges facing a younger generation that was moving away from the rural South to northern urban areas such as Harlem.

The idea of a 'Harlem Renaissance' gained currency following the publication in 1925 of *The New Negro* by Alain Locke (1885–1954). Locke studied at Oxford as the university's first African American Rhodes Scholar (1907–10) and identified in the work of Harlem's artistic community 'a spiritual coming of age'. The Renaissance attracted criticism from conservative African American community leaders and, at least briefly, the interest of white intellectuals. Always primarily concerned with the aesthetics of self-expression, the Renaissance lost momentum during the GREAT DEPRESSION.

**Harlequin romances.** The US equivalent of MILLS & BOON, in the form of cheaply priced romantic novels, first issued for the mass market in 1949. The protagonists were long in the mould 'dominant male, submissive female', but have recently become more of an equal match.

> The traditional Harlequin heroine is young, vulnerable, in a dead-end job; the hero is ten years older, arrogant and moody, as well as being rich and powerful. Sometimes he's

brutal as well, alternating between kissing and hitting. But in the end the heroine learns that he's mocked her because he really loves her.

EMILY TOTH: in Women's Review of Books (February 1983)

**Harley-Davidson.** The famed US motorcycle, first produced in Milwaukee, Wisconsin, in 1903, is named after its designers, William Harley and the brothers Arthur, Walter and William Davidson. The low, loud Harley 'hog' became a lasting symbol of the wide-open US road.

**Harry Lime.** *See* Harry LIME.

**Harry Potter.** *See* Harry POTTER.

**Harry Potty.** A nickname given to Prince Harry by both *The Sun* and *The Mirror* following a contretemps outside a nightclub at 3 o'clock in the morning on 21 October 2004 in which the PLAYBOY PRINCE physically attacked a photographer and had to be restrained by royal protection officers. As an infant Harry was known as 'Ginger Tot'.

**Harry Ramsden's.** A name synonymous with fish and chips, and with the palatial fish and chip restaurant at White Cross, Guiseley, Yorkshire, where in 1928 Harry Ramsden (1886–1963) started his business in a small wooden hut with a loan of £150. In 1931 he opened the plushest 'chippie' yet seen in Britain, and in 1989 the restaurant was the first of its kind to be floated on the stock market. There are now Harry Ramsden branches elsewhere in Britain, although those in motorway service stations are hardly in the opulent style of the Guiseley prototype.

**Harry starkers.** Stark naked. The prefixing of a word by *Harry*, the word itself taking the ending *-ers*, evolved from upper-class forces slang in the Second World War as a British linguistic quirk. Some words attracted the form more than others. Also common was *Harry flakers*, 'flaked out'. In naval usage *Harry flatters* for a calm sea was popular. The style is still sometimes heard.

**Hartley, J.R.** A fictitious elderly man who figured in advertisements for YELLOW PAGES on British television in the 1980s. The part was played by Norman Lumsden. The scenario was that he was the author of an out-of-print book called *Fly Fishing* and was ringing around a succession of second-hand book shops to try to find a copy. Only when he found one did he reveal that he was J.R. Hartley. It caught the public imagination at the time, and many people attempted to obtain the non-existent book. Naturally enough, the hole in the market was plugged when a book entitled *Fly Fishing: Memories of Angling Days*, under Hartley's name but written by Peter Lapsley, was published in 1991.

**Har-Tru.** The US proprietary name of an artificial surface for tennis courts, made of crushed greenstone. The name represents the physical attributes of such courts, 'hard' and 'true', the latter word in the sense 'level'. *See also* ASTROTURF.

**Harvey.** The invisible six-foot rabbit who befriends the drunken Elwood P. Dowd in Mary C. Chase's comedy of this name (1944). In the delightful film (1950), adapted by Chase and Oscar Brodney from Chase's play, Dowd is played by James Stewart. The imaginary rabbit's name has entered US parlance and in the 1980s the military programme to develop a STEALTH bomber was nicknamed 'Project Harvey'.

**Harvey Nicks.** SLOANE RANGER slang for the fashion store Harvey Nichols, famous for its cosmetics department. Its original, and still flagship, shop is in Knightsbridge, London, but in 1996 it opened a branch in Leeds, and it now also has a presence in Birmingham, Edinburgh, Manchester and Riyadh, Saudi Arabia.

**Harvey Smith.** A V-SIGN. At the Hickstead show-jumping finals in August 1971 it was alleged that the horseman Harvey Smith (b.1938), on completing his last, winning round, made the sign at Douglas Bunn, one of the judges. He was threatened with the loss of all prize money, but claimed that he had merely made a V FOR VICTORY sign to mark his triumph. The matter was subsequently dropped but his name became attached to the gesture.

**Harvey Wallbanger.** A cocktail of gin or vodka and orange juice. It emerged in the United States in the late 1960s and has a name that presumably compliments and commemorates its inventor and alludes to its disorientating effect on those who drink it.

**Háry János.** The central character of Zoltán Kodály's opera that bears his name, set to a libretto by Béla Paulini and Zsolt Harsányi, and premièred at Budapest in 1926. It is the composer's best-known opera, mainly for its incidental music rather than its story, and contains long stretches of spoken dialogue. Háry János himself is the great liar of Hungarian folklore, and the plot centres on his love for Napoleon's second wife, Archduchess Maria-Louisa of Austria.

**Hashbury.** A nickname for the district of Haight-Ashbury in San Francisco, celebrated as a centre of the alternative, drug-using HIPPIE culture in the late 1960s. By the 1970s, however, it had declined into a squalid drug-dealers' paradise. 'Hash' is a slang abbreviation of hashish (cannabis resin).

**Hasta la vista.** (Spanish, literally 'until the seeing'.) A Spanish farewell which found its way into English towards the end of the 20th century thanks to the Austrian-born US film star Arnold Schwarzenegger (*see* the AUSTRIAN OAK), who used it ironically, usually after an act of extreme violence, in the movie *The* TERMINATOR 2 (1991). It proliferated in US college slang, along with the variations 'hasta la bye-bye' and the rhyming 'hasta la pasta'.

**Hastings Day.** An eight-day celebration held every October in Hastings, East Sussex, since 1968. The event had its genesis in 1966, the 900th anniversary of the town's foundation. The current festivities include music, sports and flag ceremonies, with all in the town contributing. A recent addition is the revival of a bonfire tradition, and a torchlight procession culminates in a bonfire and fireworks, featuring the 'largest Guy Fawkes in England', on the Saturday nearest 14 October.

**Hatchet job** or **work.** A vicious verbal attack on someone, especially in print. The term frequently applies to a critic's dismissive review of a new book. The person who carries out such an attack is thus a 'hatchet man', in turn so called from a Chinese assassin of old who used a real hatchet.

**Hate mail.** Hostile and sometimes threatening letters sent, usually anonymously, to an individual or group. The subject of the letters is often controversial and the style of writing frequently crudely abusive. The term is first recorded in the 1960s, but the practice dates from considerably earlier. *See also* POISON PEN LETTER.

**Hatterji.** A nickname given to Roy (now Lord) Hattersley (b.1932), who served in the Labour cabinet (1976–9) and was deputy leader of the Labour Party (1983–92), by analogy with the Indian name Chatterji. The nickname derived from the large number of Indians and Pakistanis in his Birmingham Sparkbrook constituency, which he represented from 1964 to 1997. Hattersley was crudely depicted as an Asian in a long-running *Private Eye* cartoon strip. He has also been lampooned for his alleged fondness for good lunches (Tory politician Norman Fowler observed that he was 'the only man to move from the cabinet table to the restaurant table and consider it a promotion'), and for his somewhat salivating manner of speech. Once regarded as being on the right of the Labour Party, since Tony Blair's government came to power in 1997 Hattersley has presented himself as the guardian of the party's socialist conscience. *See also* TUB OF LARD.

**Hattonistas.** The supporters of Derek Hatton (b.1948), the Trotskyite MILITANT TENDENCY deputy leader of Liverpool City Council (1983–6). The term was coined in allusion to the SANDINISTAS, the left-wing guerrilla movement that had seized power in Nicaragua in 1979. The sharp-suited Hatton was expelled from the Labour Party in 1987 along with other members of the Militant Tendency, and subsequently embarked on a career in broadcasting and public relations. *See also* PORTILLISTAS.

**Have a ball.** To have a good time; to enjoy oneself uninhibitedly. The ball here is a dance. The expression is of US origin and dates from the 1940s.

**Have a bash.** To attempt something; to give it a go. A phrase from the 1940s.

**Have a cow.** In US slang, to become extremely or immoderately upset; to 'have a fit' (as in 'If I'm not back by midnight, my mom'll have a cow!'). The expression dates from the mid-1960s, and presumably invokes the eye-watering notion of giving birth to a cow.

**Have a good war.** To achieve satisfaction or success during a war. The expression dates from the 1960s and is mostly ironic, as in the title of the musical *Oh, What A Lovely War!* (1963), a documentary satire about the First World War, set in a holiday camp.

**Have** or **get a handle on.** To possess a means of understanding or controlling a person or thing, as if grasping them. The expression is of US origin and dates from the 1970s.

> It is Cameron Diaz … who has, perhaps, a better handle on him [film director Oliver Stone]. 'He is,' she says, 'a mad genius.'
> *Sunday Times* (31 October 1999)

**Have a lot on one's plate.** To have much to occupy one. The reference is to a large plateful of food that one has to consume. The expression dates from the 1920s.

> Can you tell me how many times in all she has forbidden you the house? – No, sir. Half a dozen times? – It might have been. I cannot say. I have a lot on my plate … Mr. Justice Horridge: A lot on your plate! What do you mean? Elton Pace: A lot of worry, my lord.
> *Daily Express* (4 July 1928)

**Have a nice day.** A stock expression of goodwill to one departing that reached its heyday in the United States in the 1950s and also subsequently crossed the Atlantic to Britain. The phrase is usually a token politeness, since the speaker rarely cares what sort of day the other will have. *See also* ENJOY YOUR MEAL.

**Have** or **get a snout on (someone** or **something).** In Australian and New Zealand slang, to have a great dislike for someone or something, to get annoyed with them, to have a 'down' on them. The expression dates from the early years of the 20th century.

> If someone does steal cattle in Australia, the owners of the beasts and the cowhands will 'get a snout on' or get angry, in simple English.
>
> www.thinglish.com (8 September 2005)

**Have a tiger by the tail.** *See* RIDE A TIGER.

**Have by the short and curlies.** To have at a disadvantage or under one's complete control. The 'short and curlies' are pubic hair.

**Have had one's chips.** To be dead; to be dying; to be out of the running. The metaphor is from gambling. When one no longer has any chips, as counters representing money, one has lost.

***Have I Got News For You.*** A satirical comedy show (sometimes abbreviated to 'HIGNEFY') first screened on BBC2 in 1990, in which the host (originally Angus Deayton) puts questions on the previous week's news to two regular panellists, Ian Hislop and Paul Merton, and to the celebrity guest accompanying each, usually a politician or an entertainer. The programme's popularity lies in the wit of the two regulars and their put-downs of the hapless guests. Deayton was removed from his chair in 2002, following embarrassing revelations about his private life, and since then there has been a succession of 'guest' hosts. *See also* NEWS TO ME.

**Have it away.** *See* HAVE IT OFF.

**Have it made.** To be in an excellent position; to be set up for life. The idea is that all the necessary work or preparation has been done for one and one can now reap the reward. The phrase dates from the 1920s.

**Have it off** or **away.** To have sexual intercourse. The phrase seems to imply a success or 'score', as if one has won a prize. *See also* GET IT ON.

> 'What's his wife like?'
>
> 'She's been having it off with Arthur, on Tuesday and Thursday afternoons, back of the shop.'
>
> FAY WELDON: *The Heart of the Country* (1987)

**Have kittens.** To be extremely nervous or apprehensive. Pregnant cats are sometimes scared into premature kittening.

**Have** or **eat someone for breakfast.** To deal with them or defeat them with consummate ease.

**Have the hots for someone.** To be sexually attracted to them, 'hots' alluding to the physical arousal involved. The expression dates from the 1940s.

**Have the wood on someone.** In Australian and New Zealand slang, to have the advantage over someone. First recorded in the mid-1920s, the expression may have been inspired by the slang verb 'wooden', meaning 'to knock someone down' or 'to stun them', which in turn probably carried the idea of turning someone into an insensible block of wood.

**Have tickets on someone** or **something.** In Australian and New Zealand slang, to have great admiration for someone or something. The expression, which dates from the early 20th century, is usually self-referential: a person who 'has tickets on' him- or herself is conceited.

> Mariah [Carey], you might have noticed, has tickets on herself. She said the lack of sexual partners was not through lack of opportunity. Mariah said: 'If I even look at a man, he immediately thinks: "Oh, she fancies me."'
>
> http://xrrf.blogspot.com (18 January 2005)

**Have what it takes.** To possess the necessary qualities or commodities that enable one to succeed. The implication is that it may have taken a lot. The phrase dates from the 1930s.

**Haw-haw, Lord.** In the Second World War the name given by Jonah Barrington, a journalist with the *Daily Express*, in allusion to his upper-class accent, to the US-born William Joyce (1906–46), who broadcast anti-British propaganda in English from Germany. His broadcasts usually began 'Germany calling! Germany calling!' with 'Germany' pronounced more like 'Jairmany'. Joyce was hanged for treason. *See also* AXIS SALLY; TOKYO ROSE.

**Hawks and doves.** In foreign affairs the hawks are those who favour war and resolute military action, the doves those who support peace or compromise and negotiation. The pairing became particularly associated with the Cuban Missile Crisis of October 1962, a COLD WAR confrontation that brought the United States and the USSR close to war over the presence of Soviet nuclear missiles in Cuba. US 'hawks' favoured an air strike to eliminate the missiles, while the 'doves' opposed such strikes and favoured a naval blockade. The 'doves' won the day and, after an exchange of messages between John F. Kennedy and Nikita Khrushchev, amidst extreme tension on both sides, the Soviet premier eventually backed down. The terms are also used for similar stances generally.

> 'Doves' on the MPC [Monetary Policy Committee] will also draw comfort from yesterday's … survey, which pointed to a moderation of growth in confidence. However, MPC 'hawks', who would like to see higher rates, will point to recent evidence of stronger economic growth.
>
> *The Times* (5 October 1999)

*See also* BRINKMANSHIP; EYEBALL TO EYEBALL; PEACEFUL COEXISTENCE.

**Hay burner.** A facetious and often dismissive US and Australian term for a horse (which 'burns' hay as its fuel). It has also been used to denote someone who smokes marijuana.

**Hay Fever.** A play (1925) by the British playwright Noël Coward (1899–1973) about a family of sharp-tongued eccentrics who make a habit of treating visitors to their home with total indifference to the normal rules of etiquette and hospitality. Coward reportedly based his portrait of the delicious but impossible Bliss family on the actress Laurette Taylor (1884–1946), who treated visitors to her New York home with similar indifference to their wants and needs, instead obliging them to take part in parlour games.

**Hays Code.** The informal name given to the Production Code issued in 1930 by the Motion Picture Producers and Distributors of America, Inc. (later the Motion Picture Association of America), known as the Hays Office after its president (since 1921), Will H. Hays (1879–1954). The Hays Code (actually drawn up by Martin Quigley, a Catholic publisher, and Daniel Lord, a Jesuit) provided strict guidelines to the movie studios regarding the depiction of sexual, social and criminal behaviour. For example, obscenity and complete nudity were forbidden, no criminals were to be shown profiting from their activities, nor adultery shown in an attractive light, while the institution of marriage and the family was to be promoted positively. The US screenwriter Gene Fowler (1890–1960) greeted the establishment of the Hays Office thus:

> Will Hays is my shepherd, I shall not want. He maketh me to lie down in clean postures.

**Hazel.** The rabbit hero of Richard Adams's bestselling children's novel WATERSHIP DOWN (1972), telling how he and his second-sighted brother Fiver lead a small band of rabbits from their doomed warren to go in search of a new home. An animated film of the book was released in 1978, with Hazel voiced by John Hurt.

**H-Block.** *See* the MAZE.

**Head for the hills.** To make for the rolling open countryside, especially to escape the stress of modern life. The expression is in the US pioneering spirit and may be applied figuratively to allude either to a retreat from the rat-race or to a venture into a major new enterprise.

> Then the school tests, the constant assessments, the looming exams, the league tables. … I'd be there on the sidelines as

ambitious and watchful as every other modern parent. Why on earth didn't I ever shout, 'Let's head for the hills'?
> *The Times* (31 August 1999)

**Headhunt.** To identify and approach a person in a senior managerial post and offer them a similar but usually enhanced position with another company. Such individual recruitment is usually carried out by a special agency. The jargon relates to the practice among some peoples of cutting off the heads of slain enemies and keeping them as trophies. The modern metaphorical sense dates from the 1960s.

**Heads will roll.** People will be dismissed. A journalistic catchphrase denoting that senior members of an organization will be obliged to resign because of some form of gross mismanagement or scandal. In other words, they will be 'axed'. The *Daily Herald* of 26 September 1930 quoted Adolf Hitler as saying: 'If our movement is victorious there will be a revolutionary tribunal which will punish the crimes of November 1918. Then decapitated heads will roll in the sand.'

**Health warning.** In the figurative sense a warning that a thing is not what it should be or normally is. The term applies in particular to radio reports made under restrictive conditions. A more literal health warning is the one placed by law on tobacco products and in tobacco advertising.

> The BBC precedes all Mr Simpson's dispatches with a 'health warning' explaining that they are being monitored by the Serbs.
> *The Times* (16 April 1999)

**Hearing dog.** A dog trained to alert a deaf or hard-of-hearing person to a meaningful sound in the home such as a knock at the door, the bleep of a smoke alarm, the crying of a baby or the ringing of an alarm clock. The name and function are based on those of the SEEING EYE dog.

**Heartbeat.** A television drama series first screened in 1992. It is set in the 1960s and opens when a London policeman, PC Nick Rowan, is transferred to the (fictional) Yorkshire village of Aidensfield, where his wife sets up practice as a rural GP. Its nostalgic tone, picturesque settings, upbeat story lines and period pop music brought it high ratings from the first. Its title is a gently subtle pun on a country bobby's beat in the heart of the community, and on the human heart that needs both a doctor's physical care and the loving support of friends and family.

**Heartbeat away from the presidency.** A description of the circumstance of the US vice-president, who, by the US Constitution, succeeds to the presidency on the death of the incumbent and serves for the rest of the term. The phrase has been current since the 1950s, when Richard Nixon was Eisenhower's vice-president. Since that time only one vice-president, Lyndon Johnson (LBJ), has succeeded to the presidency in this fashion. The United States was luckily spared the likes of Spiro Agnew and T. Dan Quayle; indeed, there was an apocryphal story that Quayle was always accompanied by two CIA men with orders to shoot him should anything happen to President Bush.

> The young man [Richard Nixon] who asks you to set him one heart-beat from the presidency of the United States.
>
> ADLAI STEVENSON: speech at Cleveland, Ohio (23 October 1952)

**'Heartbreak Hotel'.** A moody rock 'n' roll song performed by Elvis Presley, written by Tommy Durden and Mae Axton. Released in 1956, it was the first song recorded by Elvis to reach the top of the US charts. The song had its roots in a real-life newspaper report in the *Miami Herald* of a suicide victim who left a note containing the words 'I walk a lonely street'. Fittingly, the hotel of the title is metaphorically located at the end of 'Lonely Street'.

**Heartbreak House.** A play (1919) by George Bernard Shaw (1856–1950) about the disastrous consequences that result from the arrival of the youthful Ellie Dunn in the household of the 88-year-old Captain Shotover. The play, which may be interpreted as an allegory for the state of modern civilization, was inspired in part by the chaotic home life of Hubert Bland (1856–1914), a brush manufacturer and member of the Fabian Society who divided his time between his wife, the writer Edith Nesbit, and his mistress Alice Hoatson, and had several children by both, all three of them living in the same house at one point.

> *Ellie* [musically]: This silly house, this strangely happy house, this agonizing house, this house without foundations.
>
> GEORGE BERNARD SHAW: *Heartbreak House*, III

**Heart is a Lonely Hunter, The.** A novel (1940) by Carson McCullers (1917–67) of the 'Southern grotesque' school. It features a deaf mute to whom the other main characters wrongly attribute the faculty of inner serenity that they lack. The title is from the poem 'The Lonely Hunter' (1896) by Fiona Macleod (pen-name of William Sharp; 1855–1905): 'My heart is a lonely hunter that hunts on a lonely hill.' A rather pale film version (1968) was directed by Robert Ellis Miller.

**'Heart of Darkness'.** A short story, written in 1899 and first published in *Youth: A Narrative, with Two Other Stories* (1902), by Joseph Conrad (1857–1924). It is based on the author's own experience of a voyage up the River Congo in 1890 and is told by Marlow, commander of a French coasting steamer. He finds a corrupt and depraved regime under the control of the monstrous figure of Kurtz, who finally dies on board Marlow's boat. In an epilogue Marlow tells of visiting Kurtz's fiancée and pretending that he died with her name on his lips. The story ends: 'The offing was barred by a black bank of clouds, and the tranquil waterway leading to the uttermost ends of the earth flowed sombre under an overcast sky – seemed to lead into the heart of an immense darkness.' Kurtz's words 'The horror! The horror' (ch. 3) inspired Francis Ford Coppola's controversial film APOCALYPSE NOW (1979) set during the VIETNAM War, which has parallels with Conrad's story. *See also* FIRST LINES OF NOVELS.

**Heart of England.** A touristic name for the West Midlands of England, extending north to Cheshire with its GOLDEN TRIANGLE, west to the Welsh borders, east to Shakespeare Country (*see* COUNTRY) and south to the Cotswolds, the whole presenting an idyllic image of picturesque houses, pubs and churches, despite the presence of industrial Birmingham and Stoke-on-Trent. The implication is that this is the 'essence' of England. Geographically the region lies more or less in the centre of the country and politically it may even be identified with MIDDLE ENGLAND.

**Hearts and flowers.** Mawkish sentimentality. The named objects are traditional symbols of love and affection. The phrase dates from the early 20th century and was popularized by a song of 1891 by Mary C. Brine so titled. *See also* MILLS & BOON.

**Hearts and minds.** Both people's emotions and their rational faculties. The phrase is usually used in the context of attracting the approval of the public, for example for a government policy, and it is particularly prevalent in military usage for gaining the cooperation of a civilian populace in a theatre of conflict and for enabling local intelligence-gathering. It seems to have originated in the Bible:

> And the peace of God, which passeth all understanding, shall keep your hearts and minds through Christ Jesus.
>
> Philippians 4:7

**Heart-to-heart.** An intimate talk. A phrase of US origin dating from the early years of the 20th century. The idea is that each speaks openly, 'from the heart'.

**Heath Robinson.** A term sometimes applied to an absurdly complicated mechanical contraption, especially one performing a basically simple function. The name is that of William Heath Robinson (1872–1944), whose amusing drawings of such absurdities appeared in *Punch* and elsewhere. *See also* Professor BRANESTAWM; RUBE GOLDBERG.

**Heathrow.** London Airport, as it is officially known, takes its popular name from the small settlement that was formerly in that place, west of London, itself so called as it was simply a row of cottages at the western edge of Hounslow Heath. The site was acquired by the Ministry of Civil Aviation in 1946 and in 1955 Queen Elizabeth II opened the Europa Building, the first of the airport's permanent buildings, now Terminal 2. The Oceanic Terminal, now Terminal 3, opened in 1962, and Terminal 1 was formally opened in 1969. Terminal 4 followed in 1986. In 2001, after the longest public inquiry in British history, lasting 46 months, government approval was given for a fifth terminal. The first phase of the project is due for completion in 2008, and the second phase in 2011. *See also* THIEFROW.

**Heave-ho.** Expulsion or dismissal by a person or organization. The phrase is most commonly used of a jilted lover or a sacked employee: 'I was given the old heave-ho.' As 'heave-ho' is associated with pulling, so there is an analogy with pushing: 'I was given the push.' The original 'Heave-ho' was a cry of sailors when hauling on a rope to raise the anchor, pull in sails or the like.

**Heaven's Gate.** A small Californian cult led by Marshall Applewhite. In 1997 the members killed themselves, believing that this was the only way that they could board a UFO taking to them to the Hale-Bopp comet then visible in the sky.

**Heaven's Gate.** The WESTERN film (1980), written and directed by Michael Cimino (b.1940), is set against the 1892 Johnson County wars in Wyoming. Starring Kris Kristofferson, the film cost somewhere between $35 million and $50 million but lost more than any other film ever made. It was slated by critics and public alike, but the doomed extravagance of the project entered movie legend. Within the film Heaven's Gate is the name of a local roller-skating rink popular with settlers in Wyoming in the early 1890s. The phrase 'Heaven's gate' also crops up in the Bible, Shakespeare and William Blake's 'Jerusalem' (1815):

I give you the end of a golden string;
Only wind it into a ball:
It will lead you in at Heaven's gate,
Built in Jerusalem's wall.

*See also* DANCES WITH WOLVES.

**Heavies.** A colloquial term dating from the 1950s for the serious newspapers, which contain weightier or more intellectually demanding material than the others. Such papers, especially the Sunday editions, have now also become physically heavier, with many having several parts or sections and usually including one or more magazines. *See also* TABLOID.

**Heavy hitter.** An important person or celebrity, especially in business, politics or the social world. The metaphor is from baseball and dates from the 1970s.

Most modern actresses are what would have been called starlets in the days of the real Hollywood heavy-hitters.
*Sunday Times* (2 January 2000)

**Heavy metal.** A type of rock music emerging in the early 1970s. It is characterized by its high amplification, its harsh, brutal sound, its repetitive rhythms and its frequent use of violent or fantastic imagery. 'Heavy' may relate to the music's heavy beat and 'metal' either to its metallic sound or to the metal decorations of the leather gear worn by its performers and adherents. The phrase goes back to the 19th century in the sense of large pieces of ordnance (*Heavy Metal* is the title of a 2005 memoir of Captain Jason Conroy, a US tank commander in the Iraq War), but in the musical sense it first appears in the phrase 'heavy metal thunder', from the Steppenwolf song 'Born to Be Wild' (1968). The lyricist, Mars Bonfire (Dennis Edmonton), took the phrase from the SF novel *The Ticket That Exploded* (1962) by William S. Burroughs. In addition to Steppenwolf, other seminal heavy metal bands included Black Sabbath, Iron Maiden and Led Zeppelin, although the last-named eschewed the label. *See also* ROCK GROUP NAMES.

**Heavy water.** Water that has been enriched with deuterium oxide. Deuterium, or 'heavy hydrogen', is an isotope of hydrogen with two neutrons in its nucleus (rather than the one neutron found in common hydrogen). Heavy water is used as a moderator in some nuclear reactions. During the Second World War the Germans, as part of their programme to develop atomic weapons, prepared stocks of heavy water at a plant in Norway. This was destroyed by a British commando raid on 19–20 November 1942. The operation was the subject of the film *The Heroes of Telemark* (1965).

**Heavy weather.** To make heavy weather of something is to do it ineptly or magnify its difficulties, which may hardly exist in the first place. The expression dates from the early 20th century and derives from the nautical sense relating to the hard passage of a ship in a storm or rough seas.

**Hedgers and Ditchers.** The two opposing Conservative groups in the House of Lords that split over the bill that was to become the 1911 Parliament Act, which restricted the Lords' power of veto over bills passed by the Commons. The

Hedgers, also known as the Judas group, were prepared to 'hedge' (hedge their bets or dodge expressing their true feelings) by voting in favour of the bill, by which they hoped to avoid the government's threat to create a large number of new Liberal peers. The Ditchers, also know as the DIEHARDS, claimed that they would die in 'the last ditch' rather than give in. Hedging and ditching are important activities in the countryside, maintaining hedgerows and clearing ditches. In the Commons, meanwhile, the bill's Conservative opponents, whom Lady Violet Bonham Carter later described as behaving 'like mad baboons', were known as Hughligans, after their leader Lord Hugh Cecil.

**Heebie-jeebies.** An US slang term for a state of nervousness or jitters, attributed to the cartoonist Billy DeBeck and first noted in his strip *Barney Google* in the *New York American* on 26 October 1923.

**Heffalump.** A child's (and now also adult's) word for an elephant, popularized if not actually invented by A.A. Milne in his books about WINNIE-THE-POOH. The apt name ('lump') provides a challenge for translators of these stories into other languages. One Russian version has the Heffalump as a *Slonopotam*, blending *slon*, 'elephant', with *gippopotam*, 'hippopotamus'. The word is sometimes applied to a large person or animal in general.

> I could not help feeling more than my usual desperation to lose the extra 15lb that clings to me as tenaciously as a limpet. … I am a Heffalump.
> *The Times* (16 August 1999)

A 'heffalump trap' (based on an incident in *Winnie-the-Pooh* (1926), when Pooh attempts to construct such a device; there is now a 'Heffalump Trap' feature in Ashdown Forest) is a trap for the foolishly unwary, especially one that ensnares its creators as happens to Pooh in *The House at Pooh Corner* (1928).

> The Conservatives are not going to leap into the heffalump-trap in which their opponents … reside.
> *Spectator* (22 August 1958)

The Disney cartoon extravaganza *Pooh's Heffalump Movie* appeared in 2005.

**Heidelberg man.** A type of prehistoric man found near Heidelberg, Germany, in 1907, possibly of the genus *Pithecanthropus*. A single lower jaw was found along with other extinct mammal fossils of the Pleistocene period.

**Heidi headscarf.** A peasant-style red headscarf fashionable in the late 1990s, resembling that worn by the young Swiss orphan Heidi in illustrations for Johanna Spyri's novel that bears her name (1881).

**Heil Hitler.** (German, 'Hail Hitler'.) The familiar salutation to the FÜHRER, often used derisively of one adopting dictatorial methods or attempting dictatorial policies. *See also* HITLERISM; SIEG HEIL.

**Heimlich manoeuvre.** An emergency technique to treat someone who is choking. The rescuer embraces the choking victim from behind, beneath the rib cage, then presses a closed fist under the breastbone with a quick upward thrust. This should dislodge food or any other object from the person's windpipe. There is also a 'Heimlich's sign' to indicate that one is choking, made by grasping one's neck between the thumb and index finger of one hand, a natural reaction for many victims in any case. The name is that of Henry J. Heimlich (b.1920), the US surgeon who devised the procedure.

**Heligan, The Lost Gardens of.** *See* LOST GARDENS OF HELIGAN.

**Hell is other people.** A line, which has since become proverbial, from the play *Huis Clos* (1944; known as *In Camera* in Britain, and *No Exit* in the United States) by the French existentialist philosopher Jean-Paul Sartre (1905–80): '*Vous vous rappelez: le soufre, le bûcher, le gril … Ah! quelle plaisanterie. Pas besoin de gril, l'Enfer, c'est les Autres.*' ('Do you remember, brimstone, the stake, the gridiron? … What a joke! No need of a gridiron, Hell is other people.') The play involves three people shut together in a room for eternity. The French term *huis clos*, like the English 'in camera', is used to describe a trial or judicial hearing from which the public are barred.

It is possible that Sartre's construction may have been influenced by the famous line (recorded in his diary, 28 January 1890) by the French novelist and playwright Jules Renard:

> *Les bourgeois, ce sont les autres.*
> (The bourgeoisie are other people.)

**Hello?** A sarcastic expression deployed by members of the WHATEVER GENERATION to indicate that the speaker's interlocutor is thought of as irremediably stupid. An example of usage might be: 'I'm like Hello? And he's like Wah?'

> I'm like, hello record company, do you NOT want us to listen to the music?
> www.girlcomic.net (2001)

***Hello!*** A weekly colour magazine, founded in 1988, specializing in photographs of celebrities such as POSH AND BECKS, many of whom have been paid handsome sums to graciously invite *Hello!*'s photographers into their elegant homes (*see* MCMANSION). The magazine is bought by ESSEX GIRLS and those of a similar intellectual calibre.

A rival magazine called *OK!* sued *Hello!* in 2003 for publishing unauthorized photographs of the wedding of film stars Michael Douglas and Catherine Zeta-Jones, who had given exclusive rights to *OK!* for £1 million. Douglas and Zeta-Jones also sued *Hello!* A number of lawyers made a large amount of money.

Following the wedding blessing of Prince Charles and Camilla Parker Bowles (*see* ROTTWEILER) at St George's Chapel, Windsor, in April 2005, one newspaper's verdict on the guests was, 'More *Hello!* than *Debrett's*.'

*See also* CELEBRITY CULTURE; HELLO?

**Hello, good evening, and welcome.** David Frost's trademark introduction to BBC TV's *The Frost Programme* (1966–7). The oleaginous greeting was much mocked by impersonators, and featured in sketches on MONTY PYTHON'S FLYING CIRCUS, for example:

> *Compère:* Hello, good evening, and welcome to 'It's A Living'. The rules are very simple: each week we get a large fee; at the end of that week we get another large fee; if there's been no interruption at the end of the year we get a repeat fee which can be added on for tax purposes to the previous year or the following year if there's no new series…

**Hello, sailor!** A camp greeting born of sailors' reputation for homosexuality induced by long spells at sea, but no doubt originally a prostitute's call to a sailor on shore leave. The phrase was made familiar by various radio and television programmes, such as *The Goon Show* (*see* The GOONS) and MONTY PYTHON'S FLYING CIRCUS (1969–74).

**Hell's Angels.** Members of a group of unruly motorcyclists originating in California in the 1950s. They typically wear denim or leather jackets, and their symbol is a death's head. In due course Hell's Angels appeared in Britain and Europe. They are often tattooed, flaunt NAZI symbols and badges and are noted for their lawlessness and initiation rites. Hell's Angels are depicted in the film *The Wild One* (1954), starring Marlon Brando, although they are there called 'Black Rebels'. *See also* MODS AND ROCKERS.

**Hell's bells!** A fairly mild expletive dating from the 1920s, expressing irritation or disappointment. The phrase is sometimes expanded to 'Hell's bells and buckets of blood!' *See also* LIKE THE CLAPPERS.

**Hell's Corner.** The triangle of Kent centring on Dover was so called in the Second World War from being both the recipient of German bombardment from across the English Channel and the scene of much of the fiercest air combat during the BATTLE OF BRITAIN.

**Helpline.** A telephone service that can provide specialized information, advice or assistance. The facility originated in the United States in the 1970s and soon spread to other countries. Although the service can be provided by a commercial company or organization, it is most familiar as that available from a charity or government authority, usually in the form of a name incorporating the nature or scope of the help and with a memorable number. Examples of British helplines at the end of the 20th century were thus DrinkLine, ChildLine, Parentline and Seniorline.

**Help the police with their enquiries.** To be interviewed by the police in connection with a crime. A nice euphemistic turn of phrase dating from the 1950s.

> A 17-year-old girl … was found battered to death … Later, a man was helping police with their enquiries.
> *Sunday Times* (14 October 1973)

**'Helter-Skelter'.** An undistinguished foray into heavy rock by The BEATLES, credited to John Lennon and Paul McCartney. It is one of the tracks on the so-called WHITE ALBUM, released in November 1968. Bizarre to relate, the psychopathic HIPPIE godfather Charles Manson, notorious for the grisly murders of the actress Sharon Tate and four others at the California home of the film director Roman Polanski in August 1969 (*see* MANSON MURDERS), unaware that 'helter-skelter' signifies in British English a type of spiral fairground slide, interpreted the term as having something to do with 'hell' and used it as a codeword for the mayhem he hoped to unleash.

**Henman Hill.** An informal name bestowed by tennis journalists on a grassy bank at the All England Tennis Club at Wimbledon in the late 1990s and early 2000s. It was from there that those (mainly female) fans of Britain's number-one tennis player Tim Henman (b.1974) who found themselves without tickets for the show courts were able to watch the progress of their boyish hero on a large screen. The perennially hopeful Henman, a fine grass-court player but of often limited effectiveness on other surfaces, reached the Wimbledon quarter finals eight times and the semi-finals four times between 1996 and 2006. Henman's fans are said by the press to suffer from 'Henmania'.

**Hen night.** An all-women party for a bride the night before her wedding. *See also* STAG NIGHT.

**Henry the Fourth.** *See* HIV-POSITIVE.

**Here be dragons.** A cliché indicating a hidden risk, from the supposed traditional indication on early maps that a region was unexplored and potentially dangerous.

No doubt there are problems … with new techniques. But if we are denied the benefits of experiment by a culture which pins a 'Here Be Dragons' warning on anything new, we will never know.

*The Times* (28 December 1999)

**Here's looking at you.** A drinking toast. A clichéd variant, 'Here's looking at you, kid', has its origin in words addressed by Humphrey Bogart (as Rick Blaine) to Ingrid Bergman (as Ilse Lund) in the film CASABLANCA (1942).

**Here's mud in your eye.** A jocular drinking toast dating from the First World War and perhaps originating among army officers, with reference to the mud of the trenches.

**Here's one I made earlier.** A catchphrase popularized from the 1960s by the children's television programme BLUE PETER, as the culmination of a set of directions for making a model from everyday household items, such as empty yoghurt pots and coat hangers. It is now associated particularly with cookery programmes, in which, in order to present the result of a lengthy cooking process (and eliminate the risk of disasters), the TV chef must pre-cook a sample of the dish he or she is demonstrating.

**Here today, gone tomorrow.** The words that came to define Conservative politician and businessman (Sir) John Nott (b.1932). They were applied to him by Robin Day, the BBC broadcaster, during a 1982 interview at the Conservative Party Conference in Brighton:

But why should the public, on this issue, as regards the future of the Royal Navy, believe you, a transient, here-today and, if I may say so, gone-tomorrow politician, rather than a senior officer of many years?

The insulted Nott, secretary of state for defence at the time, ripped off his microphone and left the studio. The description stuck, and in 2002 Nott published his autobiography as *Here Today, Gone Tomorrow*, reflecting ruefully that 'the irony is that I shall be remembered only for a media event' (*Daily Telegraph*, 14 March 2002).

**Her Indoors.** A man's wife, especially when regarded as taking charge or 'wearing the trousers'. The expression was popularized by the television series MINDER, in which the leading character, Arthur Daley, regularly refers to his wife (who never appears on screen) by this name. The phrase is sometimes spelt ''Er Indoors' to suggest a Cockney tone. *See also* NICE LITTLE EARNER.

**Heritage.** A vogue word from the 1970s for any feature of historical, cultural or touristic interest regarded as worth protecting and preserving for future generations before it is destroyed or damaged by the present one. A heritage coast is thus a section of officially protected coastline, and a heritage centre is a museum of local cultural 'heritage'. *See also* HERITAGE INDUSTRY; HERITAGE RAILWAYS.

'Heritage' – a word he [Sir Neil Cossons, chairman of English Heritage] dislikes, but for which, like all of us, he cannot think of a good synonym.

*Sunday Times* (5 December 1999)

**Heritage industry.** A term arising in the 1980s for the commercial exploitation of historic buildings or sites, or anything loosely termed HERITAGE. Opinions are divided regarding the activity. On the positive side it may be said that such commercialization preserves and popularizes evidence of the country's history. On the negative side the argument is often made that it cheapens and distorts it, reducing all to the level of a mere tourist attraction. The latter view tends to predominate, and the expression is thus usually understood in a dismissive sense. 'Heritage', according to this view, is not simply that which is inherited but that which additionally can be packaged and marketed. *See also* EXPERIENCE.

**Heritage railways.** Special privately owned railways catering for the tourist and holidaymaker. They mostly run through scenic regions and some are known by nicknames. The Bluebell Line, first so named in *c.*1955 by a journalist, runs between Sheffield Park and Kingscote in Sussex, while the Watercress Line runs between Alton and Alresford in Hampshire, the latter town being noted for its watercress beds. The Tarka Line, though no longer taking passengers, is named after Henry Williamson's *Tarka the Otter* (1927) (*see* TARKA) and runs between Exeter and Barnstaple in Devon, where the novel is set. There are many heritage railways in Wales, mostly narrow gauge, while Kent has the famous Romney, Hythe and Dymchurch 15in-gauge miniature railway. The Snowdon mountain railway, opened in 1896, is Britain's only rack and pinion railway. The majority of such trains are powered by steam or vintage diesel, adding to their nostalgic appeal.

**Herland.** The imaginary country populated solely by women that is the setting of Charlotte Perkins Gilman's feminist utopian novel of the same name, published serially in 1915. Its inhabitants are strong and athletic, while the older women have an ageless quality of power and beauty. All wear their hair short, and their clothes are comfortable and practical, in the form of close-fitting tunics worn over knee-breeches. The culture of Herland revolves around motherhood and the raising of children, and the language is simple and rational.

**Heroin.** An opiate drug used for pain relief in extreme cases, such as those suffering from terminal cancer. It was introduced in the 1890s by the German company Friedrich Bayer as a supposedly less addictive substitute for morphine, of which it is a derivative, and is also known as diamorphine or diacetylmorphine. Heroin is in fact extremely addictive, and gives an extraordinary sense of euphoria, suggesting that its name may derive from Greek *hērōs*, 'hero'. As a so-called RECREATIONAL DRUG it can be 'snorted', injected into veins or smoked. The hazards of heroin abuse are appalling, and involve loss of appetite, convulsions, vomiting, loss of bowel control, sleeplessness, impotence in men, infertility in women and ultimately death. *See also* DRUG NICKNAMES; GOLDEN TRIANGLE; HEROIN CHIC; JUNKIE.

**Heroin chic.** A term evolving in the mid-1990s for the glamorization of the culture and appearance of HEROIN users, characterized in particular by the use of thin, wan models.

> In the press in recent days, we've seen reports that many of our fashion leaders are now admitting – and I honor them for doing this – they're admitting flat out that images projected in fashion photos in the last few years have made heroin addiction seem glamorous and sexy and cool. And as some of those people in those images start to die now, it has become obvious that that is not true. You do not need to glamorize addiction to sell clothes.
>
> PRESIDENT BILL CLINTON: reported remarks (May 1997), in response to the death by overdose of fashion photographer Davide Sorrenti, at the age of 20.

**Herrenvolk.** A German word meaning broadly 'master race'. In NAZI usage it implied the superiority of the German peoples. *See also* UNTERMENSCHEN.

**Hershey bar.** In the United States, a well-known make of chocolate bar, which was available only to the troops in the Second World War. The name is that of Milton S. Hershey (1857–1945), who founded the Hershey Chocolate Corporation in 1903. General Lewis B. Hershey (1893–1977) was Director of the Selective Service System (1941–70), the agency that drafted millions of young US men into the armed forces. In US army slang the term 'Hershey bar' was thus applied to the narrow gold bar worn by troops on the left sleeve to indicate that they had done six months' overseas service.

**Herzog.** A novel (1964) by Saul Bellow (1915–2005), in which Moses Herzog, a Jewish scholar, addresses a voluminous series of letters to the living and the dead, which are never sent. His sufferings reflect the break-up of Bellow's second marriage, to Sondra Tschacbasov, a Catholic convert. *See also* FIRST LINES OF NOVELS.

**He was my North, my South, my East and West.** The opening of W.H. Auden's 'Funeral Blues' (1936), a poem brought to a wider audience by the romantic comedy film FOUR WEDDINGS AND A FUNERAL (1994), in which it is spoken at the funeral of Gareth (Simon Callow) by his lover Matthew (John Hannah).

> He was my North, my South, my East and West,
> My working week and my Sunday rest,
> My noon, my midnight, my talk, my song;
> I thought that love would last for ever: I was wrong.

**He would, wouldn't he?** The response by the courtesan and night-club chanteuse Mandy Rice-Davies (b.1944) when told at the trial of Stephen Ward for pimping that Lord Astor denied any association with her. Ms Rice-Davies was a colleague of Christine Keeler, a central figure in the PROFUMO AFFAIR. Ward, who was found guilty, was generally regarded as the Establishment's scapegoat in the scandal. He committed suicide before sentence could be passed.

**'Hey Jude'.** A song by The BEATLES with weighty orchestral backing, one of their longest (7 minutes and 15 seconds in length). Credited to John Lennon and Paul McCartney (but mostly by McCartney), it was released in Britain in November 1968. The title was originally intended to be 'Hey Jules' (after Lennon's son Julian) but later became 'Hey Jude'.

**Hezza.** A not unaffectionate nickname for the Conservative politician Michael Heseltine (b.1933), more dashingly and originally known as TARZAN. The name is similar to that of GAZZA.

**Hidden agenda.** An ulterior or secret motive for something; an 'agenda' that is deliberately not spelled out. The term originated in the jargon of business management training in the mid-1970s. The agenda of a meeting is normally the official, written statement of issues for discussion.

**Hidden persuaders.** Those involved in the advertising business. The term is from Vance Packard's book *The Hidden Persuaders* (1957), which sets out to demonstrate how advertisers influence and manipulate consumers by means of psychological techniques, many of which take place below the level of human awareness. The appeals that prompt a response are thus largely 'hidden'.

**Hi-de-Hi!** A period-piece television SITCOM running from 1981 to 1988 and centring on the trials and tribulations endured by an entertainment troupe at a typical British holiday camp in the late 1950s. The series was in effect a pastiche of real-life camps such as BUTLIN'S and PONTIN'S with their respective REDCOATS and Bluecoats, as implied by the fictional Maplin's and its Yellowcoats. Much of the humour lay in the relations between the troupe's newly appointed manager, the dreamy academic Jeffrey Fairbrother, played by Simon Cadell, and the individual members of his team. The title represents the campers' rallying call, broadcast over the public address system. The response, at first enthusiastic, soon lapsed into a weary 'Ho-de-Ho.'

**Hide the weenie.** In US slang, to 'hide the weenie', or to 'play hide the weenie', is to have sexual intercourse. A 'weenie' is a type of sausage, and the metaphor has been realized with a number of alternative 'sausage' words, including 'hide the hot dog', 'hide the salami', 'hide the baloney' and, in Australian English, plain 'hide the sausage'.

**Hiding to nothing.** To be on a hiding to nothing is to be unlikely to succeed, or to be unlikely to gain much advantage if one does. The expression dates from the early 20th century and apparently derives from horse racing, in allusion to giving a horse a 'hiding' (whipping) to no avail.

**Hi-fi.** *See* HIGH FIDELITY.

**Highbrow.** In the literal sense, having a lofty brow or forehead, a supposed sign of superior intellectual powers or the possession of esoteric cultural interests. The term is of US origin and dates from the turn of the 20th century. 'Lowbrow', denoting the converse, followed soon after, while 'middlebrow', relating to average or moderate cultural interests, dates from the 1920s.

**Highbury, Battle of.** *See* BATTLE OF HIGHBURY.

**High Fidelity.** The first novel (1995) by Nick Hornby (b.1957). It follows the varied route towards self-discovery of its NEW LAD, THIRTY-SOMETHING narrator, a pop-music obsessive and struggling record shop owner, after he has been discarded (on the first page) by Laura. The title reflects fidelity of musical reproduction as well as faithfulness in relationships. It was the basis of a film (2000), which moved the location from London to Chicago. *See also* FEVER PITCH.

**High fidelity** or **hi-fi.** Sound reproduction on electronic equipment that gives faithful reproduction with a minimum of distortion. High-fidelity sound systems assembled by specialists from individual components were first in use in the 1920s, while complete systems housed in cabinets appeared in the 1950s.

**High five.** A form of greeting or mutual congratulation of US origin in which two people slap each other's raised right hand. 'Five' refers to the five fingers (the metaphor had already been used in GIVE SOMEONE FIVE). The term and practice originated among US basketball players in the late 1970s, although a similar palm-slapping ritual at waist height, first with one hand, then with the other, existed earlier among African Americans.

> 'And what are these girls after, O knowledgeable one?' McDermott asks, bowing slightly as he walks. Van Patten laughs and still in motion they give each other high-five.
> BRET EASTON ELLIS: *American Psycho* (1991)

**High-maintenance.** An adjective used to denote something or someone that takes a lot of looking after. Its present-day high-profile application to an emotionally demanding person was popularized by its use in the film WHEN HARRY MET SALLY (1989).

**High Noon.** A WESTERN film (1952), based on the story 'The Tin Star' by John W. Cunningham. It stars Gary Cooper as a marshal deserted by all his fellow-townsfolk as he awaits the hour (noon) when he will have to fight a returning desperado and his gang. The importance of the hour of noon in the film is underlined by the fact that the film takes place in 'real' time, beginning at 10.40 in the morning and ending at five past midday. Although director Fred Zinnemann denied it, the writer of the screenplay, Carl Foreman, claimed that it was an allegory of the need for individual opposition to the work of the House Un-American Activities Committee (*see also* MCCARTHYISM), which was then busy rooting out suspected communists in HOLLYWOOD (including Foreman himself). The phrase 'high noon' has since been quoted on innumerable occa-sions whenever someone or something faces a moment of crisis.

**High society.** The fashionable sector of the upper classes. *The Philadelphia Story* (1940), one of the America's finest comedy films, was remade as *High Society* (1956), a musical version that fell far short of the wit and glamour of the original.

**High-Tax Harry.** *See* GIVE-'EM-HELL HARRY.

**Highway Code.** A booklet giving guidance and rules on all aspects of road use in Britain, from drivers and passengers to cyclists and pedestrians, although intended primarily for motorists. It was first published in 1931. Knowledge of the *Highway Code* forms an essential part of the driving test.

> If you have to herd animals after dark, wear reflective clothing and ensure that white lights are carried at the front and red lights at the rear of the herd.
> *Highway Code* (Rule 215) (1996)

**Highway of Death.** *See* TURKEY SHOOT.

**High, wide and handsome.** Happy; carefree. The expression is of US origin and became specifically associated with cowboys at a rodeo.

**High Wind in Jamaica, A.** The first novel (1929; in the United States as *The Innocent Voyage*) by Richard Hughes (1900–76) was inspired by a real event in 1822, recounted in a manuscript that was passed on to his mother. Seven amoral children, whose parents think they will be safer in England after a high wind and storm have ravaged their Jamaican home, are unintentionally hijacked by a band of incompetent pirates. The film version (1965) was directed by Alexander Mackendrick.

**High-wire act.** One requiring great skill or judgement, like that demanded of a tightrope walker.

**Hijacker.** A term of US origin now applied to a person who seizes a vehicle in transit to force it to go to a different destination or to commandeer it for another purpose. The name is popularly said to derive from the gunman's command to his victim, 'Stick 'em up high, Jack,' meaning that the arms were to be raised well above the head. *See also* CARJACKING; SKYJACKER.

**Hill, The.** A shorthand used by US politicians to refer to Congress, which is situated on Capitol Hill in Washington, D.C.

**Hillbilly.** A nickname from the turn of the 20th century for an inhabitant of a remote or rural region of the United States and in particular of the Appalachian Mountains of the southeast. The name became attached to a form of COUNTRY MUSIC from that area, in which string bands with banjos and guitars predominate. The basic meaning of the name is a 'Billy' or person who comes from the hills. For *The Beverly Hillbillies, see under* BEVERLY HILLS.

**Hillsborough Declaration.** The joint statement in April 1999 by Tony Blair and Bertie Aherne, the respective British and Irish prime ministers, at Hillsborough Castle near Belfast. It proposed a plan to break the impasse in the Northern Ireland peace process by removing any connotations of surrender in the looked-for DECOMMISSIONING of weapons by the IRA. The latter rejected the plan. The 1985 Anglo-Irish Agreement was signed at Hillsborough, and the mansion was the residence of the governor of Northern Ireland from 1925 to 1973. The village owes its name to Sir Arthur Hill, who built the fort here in 1650. Its Irish name is Cromghlinn, 'winding valley'.

**Hillsborough disaster.** The deaths of 96 football fans on 15 April 1989 at the FA Cup semi-final between Liverpool and Nottingham Forest at Hillsborough in Sheffield were caused when Liverpool supporters rushed onto the already crowded centre section of the west stand. Victims were crushed in the entrance tunnel, on the steps up to the terraces and against the perimeter fence. The tragedy resulted in the removal of fences from all football fields.

**Himbo.** A male BIMBO, whose main asset is good looks rather than intelligence, 'brawn' rather than 'brain'.

**Hindenburg Line.** The German fortified line of defence in northeastern France set up by Field Marshal Paul von Hindenburg (1847–1934) in the First World War. It resisted all Allied attacks in 1917 and was not breached until late 1918. *See also* SIEGFRIED LINE.

**Hinglish.** A blend of Hindi and English spoken in India. It uses English parts of speech for more complicated functions, as in the following: 'Dekho great democratic institutions kaise India main develop ho rahi hain', meaning 'See how the great democratic institutions are developing here in India' (quoted *The New Yorker*, 9 September 1967). The name itself is a blend of 'Hindi' and 'English'. *See also* FRANGLAIS.

**Hip-hop.** A street subculture originating among African American urban teenagers in the late 1970s and involving RAP MUSIC, GRAFFITI art and BREAK-DANCING as well as particular codes of dress and speech. The term combines 'hip' in the sense of fashionable (*see* HIPPIE) and 'hop' in the sense of dance. *See also* GANGSTA RAP.

**Hippie.** The hippie 'movement' emerged in San Francisco during the SUMMER OF LOVE of 1967. The hippies – whose style and values rapidly spread to western Europe – were peaceful anarchists with a care for the environment and a fondness for recreational drugs, rock music, beads, long hair and flowery clothes. Their slogans included FLOWER POWER and MAKE LOVE, NOT WAR. They were the successors to the Beatniks of the BEAT GENERATION, and their immediate precursors were the MERRY PRANKSTERS. A decade later the hippies had become eclipsed by PUNK, but the values of the movement are to some extent maintained by NEW AGE travellers and those involved in the BACK TO THE LAND movement. The word probably comes from 'hip' in the sense of fashionable. For politicized hippies, *see* YIPPIES.

**Hire and fire.** To engage and dismiss employees, especially as a way of indicating one's authority.

**Hired gun.** A person with special knowledge or expertise employed to resolve a complex problem, especially in business. The allusion is to a gunman or HITMAN employed to kill someone, not always a straightforward task. The expression is of US origin and dates from the 1950s.

**Hiroshima.** A Japanese city and military base, the target of the first atomic bomb dropped in warfare (6 August 1945). More than 160,000 people were killed or injured and far more rendered homeless. The flash of the explosion was seen 275km (170 miles) away and a column of black smoke rose over the city to a height of 12,190m (40,000ft). Hiroshima remains a solemn portent of the fate overshadowing mankind in the event of major world conflict. There is now an annual Peace Festival there. *See also* ENOLA GAY.

**Hiroshima mon amour.** The first feature film (1959) by the French New Wave director Alain Resnais, with a screenplay by Marguerite Duras. While a French actress is making a film in HIROSHIMA, she embarks on an affair with a Japanese man. This brings back memories of her wartime affair in occupied France with a German soldier, who is killed. The film was much admired for its formal innovations and for its sensitive explorations of a variety of themes. The title (literally 'Hiroshima my love') is open to a variety of interpretations relating to love and death.

In 2001 Malcolm Pryce published a novel called *Aberystwyth Mon Amour*, about a private eye investigating schoolboy deaths in the Welsh resort.

**His Dark Materials.** A highly praised trilogy of fantasy novels for children by Philip Pullman (b.1946) consisting of *Northern Lights* (1995; US *The Golden Compass*), *The Subtle Knife* (1997) and *The Amber Spyglass* (2000). Set in numerous parallel universes, and drawing on influences as diverse as Milton, Blake and modern particle physics, they centre on the quest of a young girl called Lyra (joined after *Northern Lights* by a boy called Will) as it interweaves with great events that threaten the very future of creation. Assisting or hindering the child heroes as they make their way from universe to universe are a range of natural and supernatural beings, including witches, angels, armoured bears (led by their king, IOREK BYRNISON), the diminutive GALLIVESPIANS and the wheel-propelled MULEFA. The narrative is compelling, but does not obscure more abstract issues that are touched on, such as the origins of consciousness and the nature of free will. The trilogy's title comes from Milton's *Paradise Lost* (1667), of which it is in part a reworking:

Unless the almighty maker them ordain
His dark materials to create more worlds…

*See also* DARK MATTER.

**Hiss affair.** An early episode in the REDS UNDER THE BED

scares in the United States as the COLD WAR got under way. On 3 August 1948 Whittaker Chambers (1901–61), an ex-communist, testified before the House Un-American Activities Committee (HUAC) that Alger Hiss (1904–96), a former employee of the US State Department, had given secret documents to him to pass on to the Soviets in the 1930s. A prominent member of HUAC, Richard Nixon (*see* TRICKY DICKY), used the allegations to smear the State Department, anticipating Senator Joe McCarthy's subsequent allegations of communist infiltration of government (*see* MCCARTHYISM) and vaunting his own red-baiting credentials. Hiss denied the charges and sued Chambers for slander when he repeated them outside the privileged setting of the House. However, Chambers produced documents that he alleged Hiss had supplied to him; Chambers had hidden the documents in a pumpkin on Chambers's Maryland farm. Hiss was indicted on two charges of perjury and, after a first trial in 1949 ended with a hung jury, was retried and sentenced in 1950 to five years in prison. He was released in 1954. In 1992, at Hiss's request, Russian officials went through the Soviet archives and could find no evidence of Hiss's involvement in a spy ring, although experts did not regard this as conclusive.

**His Shadowship.** A nickname given to the US politician and civil-rights activist Reverend Jesse Jackson (b.1941) when in 1990 he became one of the two Washington, D.C., 'shadow senators' (officially 'statehood senators'), posts created by Washington City Council to campaign for statehood for the District of Columbia. It was Jackson's first elective office, as he had failed to win the nomination as Democratic candidate for the presidential election in both 1984 and 1988. His 1984 bid had been damaged by his reference to New York City as 'Hymietown', which was taken as evidence of anti-Semitism.

**Hissy fit.** An outburst of temper, a tantrum. 'Hissy' comes from 'hiss' or possibly 'hysterical'. The term originated in the United States in the 1970s.

Director Ridley Scott needed to give little instruction this week as [Russell] Crowe repeatedly threw a hissy fit over a missed phone call.

www.heraldsun.news.com.au (16 October 2005)

**History, To be.** An originally US expression meaning 'to be no longer relevant or remembered', as may be used of a former romantic partner or a past event or, threateningly, to someone about to be eliminated. A recent notable use of the phrase was England fast bowler Devon Malcolm's remark, on being roughed up by South Africa's pace attack at the Oval in 1994, 'You guys are history!' He went on to back up his words with action by bowling South Africa out with 9 for 57. In the early 21st century initiatives to eliminate THIRD WORLD poverty have been pursued under the motto 'Make Poverty History'.

**History is bunk.** The verdict of the US motorcar manufacturer, Henry Ford (1863–1947); in a 1916 interview with Charles N. Wheeler of the *Chicago Tribune*, he stated, 'History is more or less bunk. It's tradition.' In 1919, when Ford sued the *Tribune* for calling him an 'ignorant idealist' and an 'anarchist', the defending counsel proceeded to demonstrate Ford's ignorance by showing that he could not give the date of the foundation of the United States (he suggested 1812). His 1916 statement to Wheeler was also proffered as evidence, to which Ford retorted, 'I did not say it was bunk. It was bunk to me … but I did not need it very bad.' The *Tribune* lost the case and damages of 6 cents were awarded.

Other things that Ford thought were bunk included exercise – which he presumably regarded as bad for business, although he (allegedly) explained it thus: 'If you are healthy, you don't need it. If you are sick, you shouldn't take it.'

**History Man, The.** A novel (1975) by Malcolm Bradbury (1932–2000) that, like his two earlier books, *Eating People is Wrong* (1959) and *Stepping Westward* (1965), has a university campus setting. He described Howard Kirk, the trendy Marxist lecturer who is its principal character, as a 'sociologist, but also a "history man" because he believes he can act to change history and transform individual lives, challenging humanism as an old philosophy of individualism and innocence'. The novel was brilliantly adapted for television (1981) by Christopher Hampton, with Anthony Sher, sporting a ZAPATA MOUSTACHE, as the sexually adventurous Kirk.

**History of Mr Polly, The.** A comic novel (1910) by H.G. Wells (1866–1946). The book is intended as a reflection on the popular education of the times. Mr Polly goes from dissatisfaction with his shop and his marriage to freedom in an unexpected way, and, finally, through a stroke of good fortune, to contentment. A gentle film version (1948), typically 'English' in style, starred John Mills in the title role and was directed by Anthony Pelissier.

**History of the World in 10½ Chapters, A.** A novel (1989) by Julian Barnes (b.1946) consisting of ten linked pieces and a 'half-chapter' inserted two-thirds of the way through, in which the author expounds his theories on the nature of love. The biblical, historical and imaginative incidents that are chosen to illustrate his thesis have thematic links.

**Hit-and-run.** Descriptive of a road accident in which the driver of a motor vehicle has hit or knocked down a person, then driven on without stopping.

**Hitch-Hiker's Guide to the Galaxy, The.** A cult radio classic by Douglas Adams (1952–2001), broadcast in 1978 and 1979. The story begins with the imminent destruction of the earth to make way for a hyperspace express route and centres on the attempts of the earthling Arthur Dent and his friend FORD PREFECT to escape the apocalypse by hitching a ride on a Vogon spacecraft. Prefect is a researcher on a cosmic reference work called *The Hitchhiker's Guide to the Galaxy*, 'probably the most remarkable book to come out of the great publishing corporations of Ursa Minor'. The programme combined the comic with the surreal and introduced a host of eccentric characters, including the two-headed renegade Zaphod Beeblebrox and the lugubrious android Marvin.

Adams turned the series into two books, *The Hitchhiker's Guide to the Galaxy* (1979) and *The Restaurant at the End of the Universe* (1980), in the latter of which it was famously revealed that the answer to life, the universe and everything is '42', and later followed them up with *Life, the Universe and Everything* (1982), *So Long and Thanks for All the Fish* (1984) and *Mostly Harmless* (1992). The radio series was also adapted for television in 1981, with some success. A film version of the *Guide* appeared in 2005, to modest acclaim.

**Hit for six.** *See* KNOCK FOR SIX.

**Hitler diaries.** *See under* FAKES.

**Hitlerism.** A generic term for the whole doctrine and practice of FASCISM as exemplified by the NAZI regime of Adolf Hitler (1889–1945), who became German Chancellor in 1933 and ruled until his death. His regime was marked by tyranny, aggression and mass persecution of leftists and Jews.

**Hitler moustache.** A narrow moustache in the centre of the upper lip, as regularly worn by Adolf Hitler (*see* HITLERISM).

**Hitler Youth.** The *Hitlerjugend* was initiated by Hitler in 1933 for the education and training of male youth in NAZI principles. By 1935 it included almost 60 per cent of all German boys and in 1936 it was decreed that all young 'Aryan' Germans were expected to join. On reaching his tenth birthday a German boy was registered and investigated for 'racial purity' and, if qualifying, was inducted into the *Deutsches Jungvolk* or German Youth People. At the age of 13 he became eligible for the Hitler Youth, from which he graduated when he was 18. He then progressed to membership of the Nazi Party and served in the state labour service or the armed forces until he was at least 21. The *Bund Deutscher Mädel* or League of German Girls was a parallel organization.

**Hit list.** Originally, a list of people to be assassinated for criminal or political reasons. The term, dating from the 1970s, then passed to a list of people against whom action is to be taken, as typically a dismissal or demotion.

**Hitman.** A hired assassin, especially one engaged by a criminal or political organization. *See also* HIRED GUN.

**Hit Man.** The nickname of the US welterweight, light-middleweight, middleweight and light-heavyweight boxer Thomas Hearns (b.1958), who possessed a devastatingly effective punch.

**Hit on.** In colloquial American English, to make romantic or sexual advances to someone; to try to chat someone up. The expression dates back at least to the mid-1950s, but did not become widespread until the late 1960s.

**Hit parade.** Formerly, a list of the most popular songs, as the forerunner of the TOP 10. The term is US in origin and dates from the 1930s, but was used by the *New Musical Express* to announce Britain's first 'Record Hit Parade' in its issue of 14 November 1952. There were actually 15 records occupying 12 positions in this prototype 'Top Ten', with Al Martino and 'Here in My Heart' at Number 1 and Johnnie Ray with 'Walkin' My Baby Back Home' at Number 12. The chart was extended to a Top 20 in 1954 and to a Top 30 in 1956, the year generally regarded as that of the birth of ROCK 'N' ROLL in Britain. A Top 50 ensued in 1983 and has remained since.

**Hit the ceiling** or **roof.** To lose one's temper. The image is of leaping so high in one's rage that one hits the object named. The expression dates from the early years of the 20th century. *See also* GO THROUGH THE ROOF.

**Hit the deck.** To get out of bed; to throw oneself to the ground.

**Hit the ground running.** To proceed with energy and enthusiasm. The imagery is military, of a person who has jumped from a landing craft or helicopter or even landed by parachute and who instantly springs into action. The expression dates from the 1960s.

**Hit the hay** or **sack.** To go to bed. The image is of a weary wanderer in a hay barn or granary.

**Hit the headlines.** To receive prominent attention in the newspapers or the news media generally. The phrase dates from the 1930s. *See also* MAKE THE FRONT PAGE.

**Hit the jackpot.** To win any great prize or unexpected 'bonanza'. The expression dates from the 1930s and comes from a form of poker in which the pool or pot accumulated until a player could open the bidding with at least a pair of jacks or higher.

**Hit the panic button.** *See* PANIC BUTTON.

**Hit the roof.** *See* HIT THE CEILING.

**Hit the sack.** *See* HIT THE HAY.

**Hit the silk.** *See* TAKE THE SILK.

**Hit the wall.** In marathon running, to reach the point of extreme fatigue at which the body's stores of energy are virtually exhausted. The 'wall' is thus the barrier that one runs into and that must be surmounted if the course is to be completed. The expression dates from the 1970s.

**HIV-positive.** A term used of a person who has had a positive result in a test to determine whether they are infected with the AIDS virus HIV (human immunodeficiency virus). The expression dates from the Aids-anxious 1980s and loosely means simply 'liable to develop Aids' (although more recently drug treatments have been developed that can prevent or delay the onset of full-blown Aids). A rather dark euphemism is 'Henry the Fourth' (from 'H' plus 'IV', the latin numerals for 'four'). *See also* GRID.

**HMS Ulysses.** The first novel (1955) by Alistair Maclean (1922–88) reflects his own experience as a leading torpedo operator in a destroyer on the terrifying convoys of supplies to Murmansk during the Second World War. It is a record of just such a convoy, and of the endurance of the officers and crew of the ship most involved. The screen rights to the novel were sold, but no film has so far resulted.

**HMV.** The music stores so called take their name from the abbreviation of His Master's Voice, registered as an official trademark in 1911 but in use on a record label two years earlier. The name itself is properly the title of a picture of a dog listening to an old-fashioned phonograph, an early type of US wind-up gramophone. The picture was painted in 1898 by the photographer and artist Francis Barraud, and the dog itself, named Nipper, belonged to his brother. In 1899 Barraud visited the Gramophone Company, formed in London in 1897 as an offshoot of the American Berliner Gramophone Company, and left a photograph of his painting. The company bought the picture on condition that Barraud paint out the phonograph and replace it with a gramophone. The picture was duly altered and assigned to the Gramophone Company on 31 January 1900 together with its title, 'His Master's Voice', to be adopted for commercial use in due course.

**Hobbit.** One of an imaginary race of benevolent, half-sized people, the creation of Professor J.R.R. Tolkien. Sturdy and determined, they resemble human beings except in having hairy feet. They feature in two of his works, *The Hobbit* (1937) and *The* LORD OF THE RINGS (1954–5). The name is their own for themselves and according to them means 'hole-dweller'. They are also known as 'halflings'. *See also* Bilbo BAGGINS; FIRST LINES OF NOVELS; FRODO; GOLLUM; the SHIRE.

> In a hole in the ground there lived a hobbit.
>
> J.R.R. TOLKIEN: *The Hobbit* (1937)

The informal designation 'hobbit' has been applied to a presumed early, extremely small hominid, the fossilized remains of which were discovered on the Indonesian island of Flores (whence its official name *Homo floresiensis*) in 2004. It was only about 1m (3ft) tall. It is thought to have evolved from *Homo erectus* and lived as recently as 13,000 years ago. Some authorities, however, insist that it is merely a very tiny, possibly microcephalic example of *Homo sapiens*.

> Following the discovery of the remains of up to seven 1m-high hominids in an Indonesian cave, presumably Snow White is assisting the police with their inquiries.
>
> HARRY WHEELDON: letter to *The Guardian* (29 October 2004)

**Hobble skirt.** A long skirt with a wide band below the knees and above the ankles, in fashion just before the First World War. The style impeded the wearer in walking, much as a horse is hobbled.

**Hobson's Choice.** A play (1916) by the British playwright Harold Brighouse (1882–1958) about a tyrannical shoe-shop owner who is eventually obliged to succumb to the wishes of his equally strong-willed daughter after she takes up with his gormless apprentice, Willie Mossop. The title refers to the proverbial 'Hobson's choice' available to those who have no choice at all. The play was filmed in 1955, with Charles Laughton as the patriarch.

The original Hobson was a Cambridge liveryman, Thomas Hobson (*c*.1544–1631), who always offered his customers the horse nearest the door of the stable, and no other.

**Ho Chi Minh Trail.** A route from North Vietnam through neighbouring Laos and Cambodia used by the communists in the VIETNAM War (1964–75) to supply the VIET CONG guerrillas fighting in South Vietnam. The US attacks on Cambodia (1970) and Laos (1971) were principally aimed at the trail, which had started as a network of jungle paths and had developed into an elaborate and efficient supply system. It was named after the North Vietnamese leader Ho Chi Minh (1890–1969). After the North Vietnamese victory and the unification of Vietnam in 1975 Saigon, the former capital of the South, was merged with neighbouring towns as Ho Chi Minh City.

**Hog heaven.** A situation of blissful but sometimes illusory happiness. The expression, which recalls the simile 'as happy as a pig in shit', is characteristic particularly of the southern and western states of the United States.

> The rules of the [Bohemian] Grove forbid the conduct of business; but it is hog heaven for the professional networker like an ambassador.
>
> CHRISTOPHER MEYER: *DC Confidential* (2005)

**Hogs Norton.** A village in Oxfordshire, now long called Hook Norton, 8km (5 miles) northeast of Chipping Norton. The name owes its more recent fame to Gillie Potter, an English comedian and radio broadcaster, who in the 1930s described in mock erudite fashion a long series of unlikely events taking place in this village.

> The humorous corruption to Hogs Norton, recently employed by Mr Gillie Potter, goes back to at least the 16th century, when the village had become proverbial for rusticity and boorishness … There was evidently a jingle about Hogs Norton, where pigs play on the organ.
>
> MARGARET GELLING: *The Place-Names of Oxfordshire*, ii (1954)

**Hog the limelight.** To keep the focus of attention on oneself. The limelight is the theatrical spotlight, so called because its intense white light was originally produced by directing an oxyhydrogen flame against a block of lime. The hog or pig is a famously gluttonous animal.

**Hogwarts.** The boarding school for wizards and witches in the Harry POTTER novels of J.K. Rowling. It has its own house system (the four houses are Ravenclaw, Hufflepuff, Slytherin and Gryffindor, the last-named being Harry's house); a traditional sport (a fast and violent game known as QUIDDITCH, played in the air by teams mounted on broomsticks); and a curriculum that includes Potions (a nightmare version of chemistry), History of Magic, Charms, Care of Magical Creatures, Divination, Transfiguration, and Defence Against the Dark Arts. For Harry, whose MUGGLE guardians loathe everything to do with wizarding, Hogwarts becomes effectively his home, yet, although the place is protected by powerful charms, it invariably brings him into contact with the dark forces that seek to destroy him.

For most of the first six novels its affable and magisterial headmaster is Albus Dumbledore, whose name combines Latin *albus* and the dialect word *dumbledore* to produce a name meaning either 'white bumblebee' or 'white hedgehog'. Other members of staff include the sinister Professor Snape, the sherry-loving, crystal-ball-gazing Professor Trelawney and the strict yet kindly Professor Minerva McGonagall. Rubeus Hagrid, a half-giant, is the Keeper of Keys and Grounds as well as, in the later novels, teacher of Care of Magical Creatures. The post of teacher of Defence Against the Dark Arts seems to be blighted, its incumbents coming to various unhappy ends. Pupils travelling to the school by train must catch the Hogwarts Express (every boy's dream steam engine) from Platform 9¾ at King's Cross. It passes through a mountainous landscape to reach the school: Hogwarts' surroundings appear to locate it in a place topographically similar, at least, to the Highlands of Scotland.

The 'Potter' films to date have used as locations for the school scenes Alnwick Castle in Northumberland, Glencoe in Scotland, Durham Cathedral and Castle, and the Bodleian Library, Oxford. Hogwarts' local station, Hogsmeade, is played by Goathland station in the North York Moors, although to get to it from King's Cross it appears necessary to use the West Highland Line between Fort William and Mallaig.

**Hog-whimpering.** An expressive phrase of 20th-century US origin denoting an extreme level of drunkenness ('hog-whimpering drunk' is the usual collocation). The image of a pig in alcohol-fuelled distress is a powerfully evocative one.

> To avoid complete, staggering, hog-whimpering inebriation at big tastings I just take tiny sips – and a second if the first seems promising.
>
> SIMON HOGGART: in *The Guardian* (8 December 2001)

**Hokey-cokey.** A light-hearted Cockney dance, popular during the 1940s, with a song and tune of this name to go with it. It is also known as the 'Cokey-Cokey', especially in the version written by Jimmy Kennedy in 1945 and recorded by Billy Cotton and His Band, among others.

> You put your left foot in,
> You put your left foot out,
> In, out, in, out, shake it all about,
> You do the Hokey-cokey
> And you turn around,
> That's what it's all about.

Troubled graffitists have been known to ask:

> What if the Hokey-cokey *is* what it's all about?

**Hokey-pokey.** An early form of cheap ice cream, sold by street vendors until the 1920s with the cry 'Hokey-pokey penny a lump'. The name is probably derived from 'hocus pocus' (there is evidence of 'hokey-pokey' being used to mean 'nonsense' in the 19th century), although it has also been suggested that it came from the Italian *Ecco un poco* ('Here is a little') or *O che poco* ('Oh how little'), Italian street vendors being associated with ice cream.

**Hold on to your hat!** *See* HANG ON TO YOUR HAT!

**Hold someone's hand.** To give them moral support; to comfort them. The expression dates from the 1930s.

**Hold the fort.** To look after something in a person's temporary absence. The phrase became current from the 1930s, but has been traced to an order given by General William T. Sherman in 1864: 'Hold the fort [against the enemy at Allatoona] at all costs, for I am coming.' These words were subsequently familiar as the first line of a popular hymn:

> 'Hold the fort, for I am coming',
> Jesus signals still,
> Wave the answer back to heaven,
> 'By Thy grace we will'.
>
> PHILIP BLISS: *Sacred Songs and Solos sung by Ira D. Sankey*, 'Hold the Fort' (1874)

**Hole in one.** A perfect achievement. The reference is to a stroke in golf in which the ball is driven straight from the tee into the hole with a single stroke.

**Hole in the wall.** A colloquial term for a cash machine in the wall of a bank. The phrase has several prior applications. In the 19th century it was an US term for an illicit liquor store, then more generally came to be used for any small or cramped place, such as a tiny apartment. The Hole in the Wall Gang was a gang of outlaws in the American Wild West, taking its name from the Hole-in-the-Wall Pass in Wyoming. It included among its members at various times Jesse James and Butch Cassidy. As a proper name the Hole in the Wall is now used for several restaurants and pubs (a notable example was the Hole in the Wall restaurant in Bath, which under George Perry-Smith in the 1960s and 70s was one of the outriders of the late 20th-century English gastronomic renaissance). In some of these there may be a reference to a particular spy-hole or similar site, but the name also has overtones of the earliest US sense, agreeably combining a notion of cosiness with one of covert drinking.

**Holiday of a lifetime.** A travel company's lure that in most cases promises more than it actually delivers. 'Win the holiday of a lifetime' is a typical promotional enticement.

**Holier than thou.** Having the appearance of being morally superior. The phrase is first recorded only in the early years of the 20th century but its origin is biblical: 'Stand by thyself, come not near to me; for I am holier than thou' (Isaiah 65:5).

**Holism.** (Greek *holos*, 'whole'.) A term coined by General J.C. Smuts in the 1920s when defining his philosophical belief that the fundamental principle of the cosmos is the creation of self-contained systems or 'wholes'. In current usage holism tends to refer more to an attitude than to a philosophical principle and 'holistic' relates to the consideration of a system in its entirety rather than focusing on individual parts of it. Holism has a recognized application in medicine, the idea being that the doctor considers the whole person, both as a 'whole' of body, mind and spirit, and as a 'whole' within the systems of family, community, culture and environment. To some extent all general practitioners would probably regard themselves as holistic.

**HOLLAND.** *See* LOVERS' ACRONYMS.

**Hollywood.** The internationally famous byname of the US film industry and of the glamorous actors and actresses who are its vital exponents. Geographically it is the suburb of Los Angeles where a number of independent producers set up their studios in 1912 and to the casual visitor it looks far from glamorous. The location's actual name is said to have been given by Horace Wilcox, who laid it out in 1886. *See also* SODOM BY THE SEA; TINSELTOWN.

**Hollywood Bowl.** A huge natural amphitheatre in HOLLYWOOD, noted for its remarkable acoustics. It has seating for 25,000 and was purchased in 1919. Since 1922 it has staged the so-called 'Symphonies Under the Stars' in the form of concerts given over nine weeks every summer by the Los Angeles Philharmonic Orchestra.

**Hollywood 10.** The 10 American screenwriters, film producers and directors who in 1947 refused to tell the Un-American Activities Committee whether or not they were communists. They were Alvah Bessie (1904–85), Herbert Biberman (1900–71), Lester Cole (1905–85), Edward Dmytryk (1908–99), Ring Lardner Jr (b.1915), John Howard Lawson (1894–1977), Albert Maltz (1908–85), Samuel Ornitz (1891–1957), Adrian Scott (1912–73) and Dalton Trumbo (1905–76). All served prison sentences and for several years had difficulty obtaining work in HOLLYWOOD.

**Hollywood East.** *See* GREAT COMMUNICATOR.

**Holmes, Sherlock.** *See The* HOUND OF THE BASKERVILLES.

**Holocaust.** The name given to the murder of some 6 million Jews by Hitler in the Second World War. The terror began within a month of Hitler's becoming German chancellor in January 1933. The Nuremberg Laws of 1935 deprived Jews of German citizenship, and the night of 9–10 November 1938 saw the *Kristallnacht*, a night of violence against Jewish persons and property, so called ironically from the litter of broken glass left in the aftermath (*see also* CHILD OF OUR TIME). Discussion of the *Endlösung* or FINAL SOLUTION was held on 20 January 1942, when it was agreed that the Jews of central and western Europe would be deported to camps in eastern Poland, where they would be exterminated or made

to work as slave labourers until they perished. Gypsies and homosexuals were among the other victims of Nazi genocide.

The word holocaust literally means 'burned whole', from the Greek, and originally applied to a sacrifice wholly consumed by fire. This is the 'burned offering' of the Old Testament, when slaughtered sacrificial animals or birds were burned on the altar, the skin being given to the priest who performed the ritual. The current use of the word was introduced by historians in the 1950s as an equivalent of the Hebrew *Shoah* ('Catastrophe') or *Hurban* ('Destruction'). This particular word was probably suggested by the crematoria in which the bodies of the victims were burned. *See also* AUSCHWITZ; EINSATZGRUPPEN.

**Holy cow!** An exclamation of surprise of US origin, dating from the 1920s. The words presumably pun on the 'sacred cow' of the Hindus while rhyming on 'Wow!' The phrase is a variant of such earlier exclamations as 'Holy mackerel!' or 'Holy smoke!'

**Holy Fox.** A punning nickname given by the Churchill family to Edward Frederick Lindley Wood, 1st earl of Halifax (1881–1959), viceroy of India (1925–31) and Conservative foreign secretary (1938–40). Halifax's father had been a leader of the Anglo-Catholic movement, and Halifax was himself a devout high churchman. While he was viceroy of India his profound religious faith helped him to get on well with the nationalist leader MAHATMA Gandhi. Halifax's reputation was later tarnished when, as foreign secretary, he supported Neville Chamberlain's policy of appeasement, and advocated that Britain should seek to make peace with Germany in 1940. In December of that year he was sent to Washington, D.C., as the British ambassador.

**Holy moley!** An exclamation of surprise used by US teenagers from the late 1950s. It was popularized by its use by the comic-book hero CAPTAIN MARVEL. It appears to be essentially a euphemistic alteration of 'Holy Moses!', but there may also be a reference to 'moly', the name of a magical herb in Greek mythology (Captain Marvel's extraordinary powers are ascribed to mythological sources).

**Homburg.** A soft felt hat popularized by Edward VII (reigned 1901–10). It was originally made at Homburg in Prussia where the king 'took the waters'.

**Home alone.** Said of a child left at home unsupervised while the parents are out or away. The expression was popularized by the US film *Home Alone* (1990), in which a young boy is inadvertently left behind when his parents go on holiday. The phrase can be extended to anyone left after family members have departed, such as EMPTY NESTERS. *See also* LATCHKEY CHILD.

**Home and dry.** Safe and successful, having satisfactorily completed some endeavour. The allusion is to a horse race home, when the winning rider has such a good lead that he can rub down his mount before the rest of the field arrive. The expression dates from the 1930s.

**Homeboy.** A person from one's own home town or region, or a member of one's own peer group. The term is of African American origin and became associated in the 1980s with the HIP-HOP subculture. The female equivalent is a homegirl, although here the word may also apply to a shy or domesticated girl or young woman, one who likes to 'stay home'.

**Home economics.** A school subject usually studied by girls rather than boys and including diet management, budgeting, child care and other aspects of running a home. It was formerly familiar as domestic science.

**Home Guard.** In Britain, the force of volunteers raised early in the Second World War and trained for defence against the threat of invasion. It was originally known as the Local Defence Volunteers, but was renamed the Home Guard at Winston Churchill's suggestion. It soon came to be affectionately known as DAD'S ARMY and at its peak, in about June 1943, consisted of around 2 million men. The Home Guard was officially disbanded in 1957.

**Home, James!** A light-hearted instruction to a driver to set off for home. A fuller version is 'Home, James, and don't spare the horses', the title of a popular song of 1934 by Fred Hillebrand.

**Home page.** In computing, the document on the WORLD WIDE WEB that serves either as a point of introduction to a person or organization or that is a focus of information on a particular topic. It usually contains links to other related documents.

**Home Rule.** The name given by Isaac Butt (1813–79), its first leader, to the movement for securing governmental independence for Ireland under the British crown. The Home Government Association was founded in 1870 (renamed the Home Rule Association in 1873), and after Charles Stewart Parnell (1846–91) became its leader in 1879 its policy of obstruction in parliament became a thorn in the flesh of British governments. A Home Rule Bill was eventually passed in 1914, but its implementation was postponed by the First World War. The EASTER RISING in 1916, the activities of SINN FÉIN and resistance in Ulster led to the establishment of the Irish Free State in 1921, but Northern Ireland continues to be represented in the British

parliament. *See also* CURRAGH MUTINY; DEVOLUTION; DIRECT RULE; FREE-STATERS.

**Home Service.** The main BBC broadcast service from September 1939, when it was formed by a merger of the National Programme and the Regional Programme. On 30 September 1967 it was renamed Radio 4. *See also* LIGHT PROGRAMME; THIRD PROGRAMME.

**Home shopping.** Shopping carried out from home by means of mail order catalogues, satellite television channels, the INTERNET and the like. Although having apparent advantages, the procedure can nevertheless be frustrating and unsatisfactory, as the purchaser cannot see or handle the goods directly and can incur inconvenience and expense when returning unsuitable items.

**Homicide Hank.** The nickname of the US boxer Henry Armstrong (1912–88), who simultaneously held the world featherweight (1937), welterweight (1938) and lightweight (1938) titles.

**Homme moyen sensuel.** (French, 'average sensual man'.) The average man, the man in the street. The expression implies a person with normal appetites and desires, neither an intellectual on the one hand nor an idiot on the other. The expression dates from the early 20th century.

***Honest to God.*** A work of radical theology (1963) by John Robinson (1919–83), Bishop of Woolwich. Robinson had already caused a stir when he appeared for the defence in the LADY CHATTERLEY TRIAL in 1960. His book, which rejected the language and concepts of traditional Christianity as unsuited to the modern scientific, secular world, sparked off the so-called 'Honest to God Debate', which was said to have brought religion out of the churches and on to the high street. *Honest to God* was the bestselling religious work since *The Pilgrim's Progress* and was translated into many languages.

**Honey-do.** A jocular US term, punning on 'honeydew' (which in American English is pronounced identically), for a household chore, especially one allotted to a husband by his wife. First recorded in 1990, it mimics such injunctions as 'Honey, do the dishes!'

**Honeypot.** A nickname for a person or thing regarded as attractive or in some way 'sweet'. This sense does not apply, however, to the 'honeypot' that is a children's term, dating from the 1940s, for a jump into a swimming pool with one's knees drawn up and one's hands clasped round them. The name alludes to the posture, resembling the shape of a honeypot. The term itself apparently comes from a children's game of 19th-century origin:

One of the players, called a honey-pot, sits with his hands locked under his hams, while the 'honey-merchants' lift him by the arm-pits as handles, pretend to carry him to market, and shake him, with the aim of making him let go his hold.

*Oxford English Dictionary* (1933)

**Honey trap.** A scheme to lure a person into a compromising sexual situation in order to blackmail them. The scenario typically involves a seductive woman as the 'honey' and a senior civil servant or intelligence agent as the victim.

**Hong Kong dog.** *See* MONTEZUMA'S REVENGE.

**Honkers.** A nickname for Hong Kong current among British expatriates from the 1920s. The *-ers* is similar to that in HARRY STARKERS and similar concoctions.

**Honky-tonk.** A disreputable nightclub or low roadhouse; a place of cheap entertainment. A honky-tonk piano is one from which the felts of the hammers have been removed, thus making the instrument more percussive and giving its notes a tinny quality. Such pianos are often used for playing ragtime and popular melodies in public houses.

**Hoodie.** A garment for the upper body consisting of a sweatshirt with attached hood. Towards the end of the 20th century it became something of a badge of membership to youths aspiring to black street culture, and in the early 21st century its often threatening aspect (disguising the wearer and suggesting, to the nervously disposed, a propensity for violence) led to its being banned in some schools and public places (e.g. shopping centres).

**Hooked on.** Addicted to. A US expression dating from the 1920s, originally referring to drugs. An addict has been 'caught' and finds it hard to escape.

**Hoon the Goon.** *See* GEOFF WHO?

**Hooray Henry.** A loud and lively but 'wet' upper-class young man, whose bray is better than his brain. A female equivalent is a 'Hooray Henrietta'. The term dates from the 1930s and, rather unexpectedly for a peculiarly British phenomenon, is of US origin. It appears, for example, though in a slightly different form, in Damon Runyon's story 'Tight Shoes' (1936), in which a young man called Calvin Colby is described as 'without doubt strictly a Hoorah Henry'.

**Hooter.** A term for the nose in British slang, but in US slang (in the plural) for the female breasts. The former refers to the sound of a nose being blown or 'trumpeted'. The latter alludes to the supposed resemblance to an old-fashioned car horn with its bulbous end.

**Hoover.** The tradename of a firm of vacuum cleaner makers, which, to the company's displeasure, has come to be used as a noun and a verb relating to vacuum cleaners and

vacuuming in general. The name was patented by the company in 1927, although this cannot legally stop people using it in a generic sense. The name is that of William H. Hoover (1849–1932), a saddler of North Canton, Ohio, who saw the potential of an 'electric suction cleaner' invented in 1907 by Murray Spangler, a department store guard.

**Hoover hog.** A jocular US term during the GREAT DEPRESSION years of the 1930s for a wild rabbit or armadillo, which in country areas were much in demand as meat in those straitened times. On the rationale of the name, *see* HOOVERVILLE.

**Hooverville.** A nickname for a shanty town in the United States built by the unemployed and destitute during the GREAT DEPRESSION of the 1930s during the presidency of Herbert Hoover (1874–1964).

**Hopalong Cassidy.** The black-garbed hero of the Old West was created by the American writer Clarence E. Mulford for his novel named after him (1910). Sequels followed and he then re-emerged on the cinema screen in the 1930s in a series of 60 cheaply made movies, in which he was played by William Boyd. Many Western fans regard his film persona as an improvement on the original.

**Hop in.** To get into a car, especially when being given a lift, as: 'Come on, hop in.'

**Hop it!** Clear off! A phrase dating from the early 20th century.

**Horlicks.** To make a Horlicks of a thing is to make a mess of it. The word uses the proprietary name of the malted milk drink as a pun on 'bollocks', itself a (related) synonym of 'balls'. The use of the name in this sense dates from the 1980s. *See also* NIGHT STARVATION.

They made a Horlicks of the casting: the plain sister was far better-looking than the pretty one.

*Sunday Times* (12 September 1999)

**Hormones.** Internal secretions that stimulate a specific physiological action on reaching a particular part of the body. Their existence was discovered by the British researchers William Bayliss and Ernest Starling in 1902 and they coined the word from Greek *horman*, 'to stir up'. A comment such as 'It's her hormones' to explain a person's mood or uncharacteristic behaviour is taken to refer to their sex hormones. Hormone replacement therapy (HRT) involves the use of oestrogen hormones to alleviate menopausal symptoms such as HOT FLUSHES.

**Hornblower, Horatio.** The naval officer hero of a series of eleven books by C.S. Forester, beginning with *The Happy Return* (1937). The novels chart his career from midshipman to admiral at the time of the Napoleonic Wars, and throughout he is calm, taciturn, intelligent, a first-class seaman and an excellent strategist. He was portrayed by Gregory Peck in a film based on the books, *Captain Horatio Hornblower RN* (1951), by Michael Redgrave in a radio series of the early 1950s and by Ioan Gruffudd in a television series (*Hornblower*) first broadcast in 1998. *See also* HAPPY WARRIOR.

**Horror movie.** A film made to shock or scare its audience by means of a fearful or gruesome subject treated in such a way as to emphasize its unpleasant or macabre aspects. The genre was initiated in the early 20th century by the Germans and was only slowly taken up by HOLLYWOOD. Early classic examples are *The Cabinet of Dr* CALIGARI (1919), *Dracula* (1931) and *The Mummy* (1932), while in more recent times a notorious box-office hit was *The* EXORCIST (1973). After 1950 many of the story lines were influenced by SCIENCE FICTION. *See also* DISASTER MOVIE; HAMMER FILMS; SLASHER MOVIE.

**Horse designed by a committee, A.** The camel, according to Alec Issigonis (1906–88), the British engineer and designer of the Mini. Issigonis was not a team player and the saying is popular among creative types who dislike compromise.

**Horsefeathers.** A US colloquialism for nonsense. The notion of a horse having feathers is ridiculous. Hence *Horse Feathers* (1932), the title of one of the MARX BROTHERS' wildest films.

**Horse-holder.** In US Army slang, a functionary in a subordinate role (such as a senior officer's aide-de-camp), especially a sycophantic one. The image is of a servant who holds on to a horse while his master mounts or dismounts, or is absent. The expression is first recorded in 1982.

**Horse opera.** A WESTERN film or television series, in which horses play a prominent role. The expression dates from the 1920s. *See also* SOAP OPERA.

**Horse's Mouth, The.** The third (1944) in a trilogy of novels by Joyce Cary (1888–1957) about artistic expression, each of which is told from the point of view of a different protagonist. The painter Gulley Jimson, based on an amalgam of William Blake and Stanley Spencer, verges violently between rage and creative expression as he tries to wheedle some of his early canvases out of his one-time mistress, while engaged in illicitly covering walls with ambitious murals. According to Cary, the title refers to the 'voice that commands Gulley to be an artist, and makes him struggle to realize his imagination in spite of all discouragement'. This itself evokes the title of the second novel in the trilogy, *To Be a Pilgrim*, which comes from the famous song in John Bunyan's *The Pilgrim's Progress* (1684): 'There's no

discouragement/Shall make him once relent/His first avow'd intent/To be a pilgrim.' The first novel in the series was *Herself Surprised* (1940). An amusing film version of *The Horse's Mouth* (1958) with a screenplay by Alec Guinness, who also starred as Jimson, and with paintings by John Bratby, was directed by Ronald Neame.

**Horst Wessel Song.** *Die Fahne Hoch* ('Raise the Flag'), the party anthem of the NAZIS. It was written by a student, Horst Wessel (1907–30), killed in the communist quarter of Berlin where he lived as commander of an SA section. The tune was a music-hall song popular at the German Front in 1914.

**Hospice.** A hospice was originally a medieval house of rest and entertainment for pilgrims, travellers and strangers run by a religious order, as those set up by the monks of St Bernard and St Gotthard in the Alps. In its modern sense as a home for the terminally ill the word dates from the late 19th century. The modern hospice movement, however, was founded by Dame Cicely Saunders (1918–2005) in 1967 in response to her concern that many terminally ill people have no choice but to spend their last days in a noisy hospital surrounded by strangers. There are now more than 200 hospices in Britain admitting some 60,000 patients a year, and offering them peace, privacy and care as they approach death. The word is directly related to 'host', 'hostel', 'hospital' and 'hotel'.

**Hospital pass.** In rugby, a pass that arrives at a player when he is in a position that is vulnerable to a heavy tackle, and that therefore risks getting him seriously injured. The term is first recorded in 1981, but probably predates that; it may have originated in New Zealand English.

**Hot button.** A crucial issue, especially one that is highly charged emotionally or politically. The 'button' is the one that must be identified and pressed in each individual if their favourable response is to be obtained, so that they back the contentious cause or give the politician their vote. The image is perhaps that of a PANIC BUTTON rather than a starter button, 'hot' implying urgency. The expression dates from the 1970s. *See also* HOTLINE.

**Hot dog.** A sausage, especially a frankfurter, served in a hot roll split lengthways. The following story is told to account for its origins. A Bavarian sausage seller, Anton Ludwig Feuchtwanger, began selling hot wieners at the World's Columbian Exposition, Chicago, in 1893, giving his customers white gloves to keep them from burning their fingers as they devoured the tasty meat. When the gloves started disappearing as handy souvenirs, Feuchtwanger then substituted elongated bread rolls to hold the frankfurters. The fashion later caught on at baseball stadiums. Circumstantial as the account is, it does not explain where the name 'hot dog' came from. In fact 'dog' had been a facetious US term for a sausage since the mid-19th century (perhaps alluding to the often dubious contents), and the earliest known reference to 'hot dog' for a hot sausage in a bun is from 1895, apparently as a usage among Yale University students. The name was popularized further by the US cartoonist and sportswriter Tad Dorgan (*see* CAT'S PYJAMAS), who included a dachshund inside a frankfurter among his many animal inventions.

**Hotel California.** The title of a song and album by the US West Coast country rock group The Eagles, which was released in 1976. The album's theme is the hedonistic lifestyle of southern California, of which the hotel is a symbol.

**Hotel du Lac.** A novel (1984) by Anita Brookner (b.1928), which won the BOOKER PRIZE for fiction. Brookner began writing fiction in 1981, when she embarked on a range of subtly observed stories of blighted female lives. *Hotel du Lac*, her fourth novel, is set in a fashionable hotel in Switzerland, the place of retreat of a young woman in disgrace with her family for having a mind of her own about marriage.

**Hot flushes.** A sudden sensation of heat in the skin, especially in the face, neck and upper trunk, experienced by many women at the time of the menopause. The cause is decreased oestrogen hormone production by the ovaries. The term dates from the early 20th century. The US equivalent is 'hot flashes'. *See also* HORMONES.

**Hot from** or **off the press.** Just printed. The phrase dates from the turn of the 20th century, a time when hot (i.e. molten) metal was used for printing. Hence 'hot news' as the latest news.

**Hotline.** A special direct telephone line, for use in emergencies. In commercial usage the term is applied to an ordinary line over which a customer can place an order.

**Hot off the press.** *See* HOT FROM THE PRESS.

**Hot on.** Strict on, as in the phrase: 'The boss is very hot on punctuality.'

**Hot pants.** Very brief skin-tight shorts, as worn by young women in the early 1970s as a sort of development of the MINISKIRT, although even more revealing. They were first so called by the US periodical *Women's Wear Daily*. The name evokes the 'hot pants' of a sexually aroused person. The first flush of fashion soon passed but the style is subject

to revival, as at the close of the 1990s, and has been fairly consistently preserved by prostitutes and American CHEERLEADERS.

**Hot potato.** A delicate or tricky situation, which, as the term suggests, has to be handled with great care. The expression dates from the 1950s.

**Hot rod.** An old car stripped and tuned for speed and, by transference, the owner of such a vehicle. The expression dates from the 1940s and has an implied sexual imagery.

**Hot seat.** A difficult or precarious position. The hot seat is also US slang for the electric chair (*see also* HOT SQUAT).

**Hot spot.** A region of potential violence or danger, as a war zone.

**Hotspur.** An adventure paper for boys published by D.C. Thomson from 1933 until the early 1980s. It featured the heroic Wilson, the Wonder Athlete, who is 128 years old but, thanks to his healthy lifestyle and diet of 'gruel, nuts and berries', does not appear even to have reached middle age.

**Hot squat.** In US prison slang, a blackly humorous nickname for the electric chair, or for execution in one. *See also* HOT SEAT.

**Hot stuff.** A thing or person that is outstandingly good or, specifically, sexually exciting.

**Hot ticket.** A person or thing that is very fashionable or in great demand. The US term dates from the 1940s and originally applied to a successful theatre show or performer.

> Proust and Shakespeare are box-office dynamite and Elizabeth Gaskell and Jane Austen are TV hot tickets.
> *The Times* (25 February 2000)

**Hot to trot.** Ready and eager to get started on something; up for something; and in particular, needing no second invitation to sexual activity ('hot' is a well-worn metaphor for sexiness). The expression originated in US English around 1950.

> These guys are hot to trot. They are like little boys in a candy store, and apparently have high libidos.
> *Reality News Online* (10 July 2002)

**Hot-wire.** To start a car or other vehicle by improvising a connection between two electrical wires, bypassing the standard ignition procedure, typically in order to steal the car. The expression originated in US slang of the 1950s. In more recent times it has also been used to denote an illegal connection to the mains electricity supply.

**Houdini, Harry.** The stage name of Ehrich Weiss (1874–1926), the most celebrated illusionist and escapologist to date. Born in Budapest to Jewish parents, who emigrated to New

York, he began his career as a magician in 1890, but world fame began with his appearance in London in 1900. No lock could hold him, not even that of the condemned cell in Washington jail. He escaped from handcuffs, ropes, safes and similar restraints and was nicknamed the 'King of Handcuffs'. In 1907 he introduced an escape in under three minutes from a sealed milk can filled with liquid and in 1912 he got out of a locked, roped packing case submerged in New York Harbour. In 1915 he freed himself from a straitjacket while dangling head first from a skyscraper. He repeated these feats often and the straitjacket escape drew outdoor crowds of up to 100,000. He took his professional name from the French illusionist Jean-Eugène Robert-Houdin (1805–71), with Ehrich anglicized as Harry. He died from a punch to the stomach, delivered before he had tensed his muscles. A biopic, directed by George Marshall and starring Tony Curtis as Houdini, was released in 1953.

**'Hound Dog'.** A song, released in 1953, written by Jerry Leiber and Mike Stoller for the African American lesbian rhythm-and-blues singer Willie Mae 'Big Mama' Thornton (1926–84). The song was later recorded by Elvis Presley, The KING, who turned the sexually ambiguous flavour of Thornton's original performance into a bright and breezy number that became a worldwide hit.

**Hound of the Baskervilles, The.** A novel (1902) by Arthur Conan Doyle (1859–1930), featuring his intellectual detective Sherlock Holmes, Holmes's worthy henchman Dr Watson and mysterious activities around the isolated Devonshire mansion of the Baskerville family, which seem to be connected to the appearances of a fearsome black dog. The stories of Sherlock Holmes were serialized in the *Strand Magazine* from July 1891 until December 1893, when Doyle killed off Holmes and his arch-enemy, Professor Moriarty. Public pressure prevailed, and Holmes was miraculously resurrected in the magazine in October 1903. In the meantime Doyle had written *The Hound of the Baskervilles* as a longer story, serialized from August 1901 to April 1902. There have been several film versions, but the first and arguably best is that of 1939, with Basil Rathbone as Holmes and Nigel Bruce as Watson.

**House.** An electronic development of disco music, first emerging in Chicago in the mid-1980s and characterized by electronic drum machines, synthesized bass lines, sparse vocals and a fast beat. The term is short for Warehouse, the name of the Chicago nightclub where it was first played.

**House church.** A term used either for a group meeting for Christian worship in a private house or for a church within the CHARISMATIC MOVEMENT that is independent of traditional denominations. In the latter case services were originally held in private houses although subsequently many congregations acquired their own buildings.

**House for Mr Biswas, A.** A tragi-comic novel (1961) by the Trinidadian novelist V.S. Naipaul (b.1932). Set in the Indian community of Trinidad, it covers three generations and features the convergent and mixed fortunes of two families. At the centre of the story is Mohan Biswas's obsession with having a house of his own. His difficulties, and the corruption and ingenuous incompetence that he encounters on the way, are presented as symptomatic of the colonial culture in which Naipaul was brought up.

**House husband.** A married man who carries out household duties traditionally undertaken by a housewife, including the care of children. The term originated in the United States in the 1950s, and John Lennon notably became one in New York during the later 1970s as an antidote to his frenetic BEATLE years. *See also* NEW MAN.

**House is Not a Home, A.** The title of the autobiography of Polly Adler (1900–62), one of the most successful madams in 1920s New York. It formed the basis of a docudrama film of the same title made in 1964. A 'house' in this context is, of course, one of ill repute.

**'House of the Rising Sun'.** A traditional folk song arranged by Alan Price, the keyboard player with the Animals, and released by the group in 1964. The 'House of the Rising Sun' is a brothel that has 'been the ruin of many a poor boy'. The song originated in Jacobean England, later crossing the Atlantic to the United States with emigrants to become an Appalachian folk song. A earlier version of 'House of Rising Sun' had been sung on Bob Dylan's first album in 1962. *See also* ROCK GROUP NAMES.

**House will in no circumstances fight for its King and Country, This.** *See* THIS HOUSE WILL IN NO CIRCUMSTANCES FIGHT FOR ITS KING OR COUNTRY.

**Housewives' choice** or **favourite.** A male radio or television personality admired by older women who are largely home- and family-centred. The phrase owes much to the popular radio programme *Housewives' Choice* (1946–67), a record request show aimed at women at home. Recent examples have included the former Labour-politician-turned-talkshow-host-turned-UK-Independence-campaigner-turned-VERITAS-party-leader Robert Kilroy-Silk (*see* ROBERT THE PUCE) and television-gardener-turned-talkshow-host-turned-novelist Alan Titchmarsh.

**Houston, we've had a problem.** The words of the American astronaut James A. Lovell Jnr (b.1928) spoken to ground control on 14 April 1970 from the APOLLO 13 spacecraft heading towards the moon. Lovell's words were notably understated, as there had been a major malfunction, and it took the best part of a week for the crippled craft to make its way back to earth while much of the world held its breath. The story formed the basis of the feature film *Apollo 13* (1995), starring Tom Hanks as Lovell. The line is often quoted in less serious situations, usually in the form 'Houston, we have a problem.'

Numerologists of a paranoid persuasion point out that the *Apollo 13* spacecraft was launched at 13:13 and that the root of the problem – an explosion that damaged an oxygen tank – took place on 13 April.

**Hove into view.** A fairly common journalistic variant of the correctly nautical 'to heave into view', meaning to come into view. 'Hove' is really the past tense or past participle of this verb, which is also subject to other irregularities.

> As the solar surface hoves into view, the daylight quickly resumes.
>
> *The Times* (21 July 1999)
>
> Because he can live by his wit, a more attractive set of options hoved into view for McCoist.
>
> *The Times Magazine* (27 November 1999)

**Hovercraft.** The first air-cushion vehicle so named 'took off' in 1955 as the invention of the engineer Christopher Cockerell (1910–99). It was only a balsa wood model powered by a model-aircraft petrol engine, but it worked, and Cockerell filed his patent the same year. The following year he founded Hovercraft Ltd, using a name that he and his wife devised. The first hovercraft proper successfully crossed the English Channel in 1959 with the inventor on board.

**Howards End.** A novel (1910) by E.M. Forster (1879–1970). Howards End is a country house, based on Forster's early home in Hertfordshire. The question of who will inherit it underlies the basic conflict, which is between culture and commerce. The germ of the idea seems to have occurred to Forster in 1906, as a result of visiting a newly wed couple who lived in rural isolation. The wife was pretty, pleasant, clever and cultured, the husband boorish and philistine. A noted MERCHANT IVORY FILM (1991) was made of the novel.

**How did you feel?** A crass and clichéd question put by a television journalist to a person who has suffered a devastating loss or other personal blow, from the death of a loved one to an unposted winning pools coupon. News editors frequently claim that the question is legitimate and of real interest to the public, although some accept that the response alone should be broadcast. When the civil rights

lawyer Thurgood Marshall (1908–93) retired from the US Supreme Court in 1991 he was asked at a press conference, 'How do you feel?' His reply was, 'With my hands.'

**How do you like them apples?** In US slang, an ironical, rhetorical demand, amounting to 'What do you think about that then, and what are you going to do about it?' The implication is that, whatever one thinks, there is little or nothing one can do.

**How Green Was My Valley.** A novel (1939) by Richard Llewellyn (pen-name of Dafydd Vivian Llewellyn Lloyd; 1906–83). It is a first-person narrative of a Welsh mining community, for whom coal has destroyed the rural environment but brought employment, at a cost. The rhythm and structure of the language correspond to the English spoken in Wales. The film version (1941), an effective TEARJERKER, was directed by John Ford.

**How is it** or **are they hanging?** A jocular hearty male-to-male greeting: the 'it' refers to the penis, the 'they' to the testicles (the traditional answer to the latter is 'One in front, for speed'). The plural form can also be addressed to females, in which case 'they' equals breasts.

**Howl.** A long poem by the BEAT GENERATION writer Allen Ginsberg (1926–97). It has become an icon of beat writing and of the hipper, more dangerous side of the AMERICAN DREAM, attacking as it did the conventional, suburban values of the Eisenhower years. Ginsberg first recited the poem in 1955 at the Six Gallery in San Francisco , while Jack Kerouac chanted 'Go, go, go' from the front row of the audience. Ginsberg was later charged with obscenity, but cleared.

> I saw the best minds of my generation destroyed by madness, starving hysterical naked, dragging themselves through the negro streets at dawn looking for an angry fix, angelheaded hipsters burning for the ancient heavenly connection to the starry dynamo in the machinery of night ...
>
> *Howl* (published 1956), opening lines

**Howler.** A glaring and unintentionally amusing mistake, as typically perpetrated by a school student in written work. The error may simply be the result of sloppy expression, such as the definition of a gynaecologist as 'a specialist in women and other diseases'. But it may equally come from a misuse of words, or by confusion between similar words, such as: 'The whole story was a virago of lies' (for 'farrago'). Translators and interpreters fear howlers like the plague, as do copywriters employed by companies marketing products overseas. One food company promoted its *burrito* (a type of filled tortilla) in Spanish-speaking countries as a *burrada*. This was something of a *faux pas*, because *burrada* is Spanish for 'big mistake'. Even the slip of a single letter can produce a howler, as that of the US motor company that advertised two new models with the words, 'Cars that break tradition, now your bank account' (instead of 'not'). Collections of genuine howlers like these make enjoyable but salutary reading.

**How old is Ann?** Who knows? A US catchphrase current in the early years of the 20th century and deriving from a 'brain-twister' published in the *New York Press* of 16 October 1903: 'Mary is 24 years old. She is twice as old as Ann was when Mary was as old as Ann is now. How old is Ann?' (Answer: Ann is 18.)

**How's your father?** A purely rhetorical question that originated as a humorous catchphrase in the music-halls before the First World War. It later came to be a synonym for 'nonsense' or meaningless ritual, so that the Northern Ireland MP Bernadette Devlin was reported in the *Daily Mail* of 23 April 1969, following her maiden speech, as saying: 'All this stand up, sit down, kneel down and how's-your-father was so funny.' Later still, the phrase acquired a sexual connotation on the lines of hanky-panky, as 'a bit of the old how's-your-father'.

**How to ....** The stock opening words of the title of a book offering practical help or advice. Two famous titles of this type are Dale Carnegie's HOW TO WIN FRIENDS AND INFLUENCE PEOPLE (1936) and Shepherd Mead's *How to Succeed in Business Without Really Trying* (1953), the latter turned into a musical by Frank Loesser in 1961. On the fictional front there is also Erica Jong's novel *How To Save Your Own Life* (1978), a tale of the personal pilgrimage of a pornographic writer. More recently there have been such humorous compilations as *How to Become Ridiculously Well-Read in One Evening* (1985), *How to Become Absurdly Well-Informed about the Famous and Infamous* (1987), *How to Be Tremendously Tuned-in to Opera* (1989) and the like.

**How to Win Friends and Influence People.** The title of a self-help book published in 1936 by Dale Carnegie (1888–1955), a US lecturer and writer who specialized in teaching public speaking. The book, which sought to show how anybody could make a success of their lives, became an immense bestseller, and its title a hardy perennial of catchphrases and clichés. *See also* HOW TO ...

**Hoxne Treasure.** In November 1992 an extensive hoard of Roman coins, jewellery and tableware was dug up in a field at Hoxne near Eye in Suffolk, and was found to include the largest collection of Roman coins yet discovered in Britain,

originally buried in the 5th century. The find was declared a treasure trove in September 1993 and bought by the British Museum in April 1994.

**HP Sauce.** A commercial brand of sauce first made in the 1870s. The initials that form its name are traditionally supposed to stand for 'Houses of Parliament', a picture of which appears on the label. However, the name was adopted by the Midland Vinegar Company, its original manufacturers, from that of another firm's product, 'Garton's H.P. Sauce', and it was thus ready-made, whatever the letters themselves might have actually meant. The name was registered as a trademark in 1912.

**HTML.** Hypertext Mark-up Language, in computing a specification for generating WORLD WIDE WEB pages that enables the viewing software to display text, images and other resources, and to execute links to other such pages. It also allows the user to create and print out documents. *See also* HYPERTEXT.

**http.** *See* HYPERTEXT.

**Hubba hubba.** Among US teenagers, an exclamation of excitement or approval, especially one directed at an attractive passing girl or young man. First recorded in 1941, it seems to have originated as a college cheer at a sports match, but its derivation remains a mystery. One account traces it back to a sergeant on a US Second World War training base who used to shout out 'A hub, a hub, a hub' on the parade ground. One of his cadets reputedly adopted it as a discreet formula for alerting colleagues to passing female pulchritude.

**Huggy bear.** In colloquial American English, a cuddlesome person. First recorded in 1964, the expression was brought to a wider public by the character Huggy Bear (played by Antonio Fargas), who was the two cops' street contact in the US television police drama STARSKY AND HUTCH(1976–81).

**Hughligans.** See HEDGERS AND DITCHERS.

**Hugh the Drover.** An opera by Ralph Vaughan Williams, first performed in 1924 with a libretto by Harold Child. The scene is set in the early 19th century in a small Cotswold town where Hugh the Drover and John the Butcher are rivals for the hand of Mary, the constable's daughter. She loves Hugh, but her father wants her to marry the wealthy John. A boxing match is held by way of a duel. Hugh wins, but is accused by John of being a Napoleonic spy and is placed in the village stocks by Mary's father. He is released by the sergeant, who turns out to be an old friend, and Hugh and Mary leave together. The composer used the work as a vehicle for a variety of English folk songs, some of them set to his own music.

**Hugo award.** One of several awards made annually from 1955 by the World Science Fiction Convention for the best new SCIENCE FICTION novel, short story or the like. The name is that of the American editor and publisher Hugo Gernsback (1884–1967), founder of the first science fiction magazine, *Amazing Stories*, in 1926. The names of winning authors and titles are mainly unfamiliar to those to whom the genre is a closed book.

**Hula hoop.** The large hoop spun round the body by gyrating the hips, whether for pleasure or exercise, became all the rage in 1958. It was the brainchild of the Wham-O Manufacturing company, creator of the FRISBEE, which copied it from a hoop used by Australian children in gym class. The simplicity and cheapness of the hoop assured it instant international fame. The first word alludes to the hula, the Hawaiian women's dance, which involves undulation of the hips.

**Hulot, Monsieur.** The comic hero of films by the French film director and actor Jacques Tati (1908–82). He made his first appearance in *Les Vacances de Monsieur Hulot* (1953), bringing Tati instant fame, and set forth on a second outing in *Mon Oncle* (1958), a film that made his creator rich. M. Hulot reappeared in *Playtime* (1967) and *Traffic* (1971). The gawky, accident-prone character, eagerly apologetic in soft hat and triangular raincoat, with pipe, furled umbrella and striped socks, became one of cinema's most enduring creations. The films have very little dialogue, and depend for their humour largely on subtle visual gags, which often find the hero baffled by modern technology.

**Human shield.** A person or group of people held near a potential target to deter an attack. The term became prominent in the Second GULF WAR when the Iraqi government forcibly deployed Western citizens in military and other installations that were expected to be targets.

**Hump day.** In colloquial US English, the day that is at the centre, literally or metaphorically, of a period or enterprise, after which one is coasting insouciantly 'downhill' towards its conclusion. The expression is often used specifically to refer to Wednesday, as the middle of the working week.

**Hun.** An uncivilized brute, from the barbarian tribe of Huns who invaded the East Roman Empire in the 4th and 5th centuries. In the First World War it became a colloquial name for the Germans. Ironically, it was a speech by Wilhelm II that promoted the latter sense. On 27 July 1900 the German emperor addressed troops at Bremerhaven about to set sail for China. As reported in the English press, the speech contained the following passage:

No quarter will be given, no prisoners will be taken. Let all who fall into your hands be at your mercy. Just as the Huns a thousand years ago, under the leadership of Etzel [Attila], gained a reputation in virtue of which they still live in historical tradition, so may the name of Germany become known in such a manner in China that no Chinaman will ever again even dare to look askance at a German.

*The Times* (30 July 1900)

**Hundertwasser, Fritz.** The eccentric and blatantly self-promoting Austrian artist of this name was born in Vienna in 1928 as Friedrich Stowasser. After studying briefly at the Academy in 1948 he adopted the name Hundertwasser, translating the initial 'Sto-', the Czech word for 'hundred', to German *Hundert*. From about 1969 he signed his work 'Friedensreich Hundertwasser', the extended first name, German for 'kingdom of peace', being his boast that through his painting he would introduce the viewer to a new life of peace and happiness. He often subsequently added 'Regenstag', German for 'rainy day', so that his full name was now Friedensreich Hundertwasser Regenstag. This further expansion symbolized his happy mood on rainy days because colours then have an extra sparkle. Hundertwasser has been an outspoken critic of modern architecture but has made his own contribution in the fantastic, polychromatic Hundertwasser House in Vienna, completed in 1986.

***Hundred and One Dalmatians, The.*** A fantasy (1956) for children by 'Dodie' (Dorothy Gladys) Smith (1896–1990), in which the villainous Cruella DE VIL kidnaps Dalmatian puppies for their fur. The story was made into a popular Disney cartoon film, *One Hundred and One Dalmatians* (1961), and subsequently into a live-action film, *101 Dalmatians* (1996), in which Cruella De Vil was played by Glenn Close. Dalmatians were the author's passion.

**Hundred days.** A term used by supporters of President Franklin Roosevelt to refer to his first three months in office in 1933, during which he pushed through an avalanche of legislation to establish the NEW DEAL. The phrase echoes Napoleon's 'hundred days', between his escape from Elba and his defeat at Waterloo (1815). *See also* FDR; THOUSAND DAYS.

**Hundred Flowers campaign.** A campaign initiated by Mao Zedong in China in 1956 apparently to encourage constructive criticism of government and the Communist Party, following the classical Chinese slogan: 'Let a hundred flowers bloom, and a hundred schools of thought contend.' Mao may have been inspired by the 'thaw' in the Soviet Union that had followed Nikita Khrushchev's denunciation of STALIN in February 1956, and in May of that year told a group of party leaders:

> I hope that everybody will express his opinions openly. It's no crime to talk, and nobody will be punished for it. We must let a hundred flowers bloom and a hundred schools of thought contend, and see which flowers are the best and which school of thought is best expressed, and we shall applaud the best blooms and the best thoughts.

By April 1957, however, intellectuals were voicing such strong criticisms that Mao called off the campaign, replacing it with an 'anti-rightist' campaign against the critics.

**Hungerford Massacre.** The shooting of 28 people, of whom 13 died, by an unbalanced gunman, Michael Ryan. The massacre took place at Hungerford, a small town in Berkshire, on 20 August 1987. Ryan, whose victims included his own mother, ended his killing spree by shooting himself. *See also* DUNBLANE MASSACRE.

**Hunger march.** A march of the unemployed to call attention to their grievances, as that of 1932, the year in which Wal Hannington, the leader of the communist-backed National Union of Unemployed Workers, led a march on London. The biggest of the marches organized by the union was the Jarrow Crusade of 1936, led by the local MP, 'Red Ellen' Wilkinson, when 200 men from the unemployment black-spot of Jarrow on the Tyne marched to London to seek aid for their town. The march received much sympathetic publicity and a petition was presented to parliament, but little practical help was forthcoming.

**Hunt, Laura.** *See* LAURA.

**Hunting, shooting and fishing.** The traditional sporting trinity of the British landed gentry, centring on the capturing, wounding and killing of animals. The phrase is sometimes written 'huntin', shootin' and fishin'' to convey the clipped accent of some of the more venerable practitioners. *See also* GREEN WELLIES.

> Mr [Alan] Clark, a vegetarian, sided with the hunting, shooting and fishing set and declared: 'I could not countenance legislation to block hunting.'
> *The Times* (8 September 1998)

**Hunt the Shunt.** A nickname of the world champion racing driver James Hunt (1947–93), so called early in his career from his propensity to propel his vehicle into the path of others.

**Hurricane Higgins.** *See* SPORTING NICKNAMES.

**Hurricane names.** The modern custom of assigning names to hurricanes originated with the Australian meteorologist Clement Wragge (1852–1922), who gave women's names to tropical storms and men's to non-tropical. The practice was officially adopted by US meteorologists in 1953, when an alphabet of women's names was created for the purpose: Alice, Barbara, Carol, Dolly, Edna, Florence, Gilda, Hazel, Irene, Jill, Katherine, Lucy, Mabel, Norma, Orpha, Patsy, Queen, Rachel, Susie, Tina, Una, Vickie and Wallis. These names were also used in 1954, when the severity of hurricanes Carol, Edna and Hazel prompted some to suggest that men's names would have been more suitable. Women's names remained, however, until the 1970s, when feminist pressure led to the adoption of alternate men's and women's names in 1977.

**Hurry Upkins.** A nickname given in Britain to the US special envoy to Britain Harry Hopkins (1890–1946) before America's entry into the Second World War. The name referred to both Hopkins's whistle-stop visits to London and the British desire that the United States 'hurry up' and enter the war. Hopkins had been a NEW DEAL administrator, and throughout the Second World War was FDR's closest personal adviser, heading the LEND-LEASE programme from 1941.

**Hurtin' for certain.** In African-American English, in serious trouble or distress. The expression dates from the 1950s, and has subsequently also come to mean 'extremely ugly'.

> 'We're hurtin' for certain,' Mary Groen said. 'We need 6,000 applications for enumerators. We only have 3,200.'
> www.enquirer.com (17 March 2000)

**Hush-hush.** A term that came into use in the First World War to describe very secret operations, designs, or inventions, from the exclamation 'hush' demanding silence.

**Hush money.** Money given as a bribe for silence or hushing a matter up.

**Hush puppy.** An American aliment of deep-fried corn meal batter, often served with fried fish in the Southern states. Pieces thrown to hungry barking dogs with the injunction 'Hush, Puppy!' were said to effect an instant silence. 'Hush Puppies' became familiar in the 1960s as the trade name of a type of soft shoe. The allusion is to shoes that comfort 'barking dogs', slang for tired or sore feet.

**Hustle.** A dance devised by African American youths in East Harlem in the early 1970s. It had a lively and strenuous style in which the male span his partner and tossed her in the air. Its steps were akin to those of the foxtrot. It was brought before the public at large by the hit instrumental song 'The Hustle' released in 1975 by Van McCoy and The Soul City Symphony.

**Hustler.** The title of a popular US porn magazine founded by Larry Flynt in the early 1970s. The magazine pushed the boundaries of what was acceptable: its second issue published photographs of Jacqueline Onassis (JACKIE O) sunbathing naked on a Greek beach, after which sales soared. Flynt was soon surrounded by a rising and hostile tide of puritanism from the US religious right, and was sued by the Reverend Jerry Falwell over a *Hustler* satire on the TV evangelist's first sexual experience. The case went all the way to the Supreme Court, which upheld Flynt's right to free speech. Flynt's career was the subject of the 1996 film *The People vs. Larry Flynt*.

In US slang 'hustler' has several meanings, but 'successful womanizer' is presumably what Flynt had in mind (following the model of PLAYBOY, but with appropriately raunchier overtones). Other meanings include: (1) a prostitute of either sex (as in Andy Warhol's 1965 film *My Hustler*); (2) a person who pursues life and business aggressively and successfully; (3) a gambler or pool player or similar who makes a living beating less talented players (as in the 1961 Paul Newman film, *The Hustler*).

**Hutber's Law.** Improvement means deterioration, a cynical construct proposed by Patrick Hutber (1928–80), originator of the 'Questor' column in the *Daily Telegraph* and City Editor of the *Sunday Telegraph* from 1966 to 1979.

> Ask [British Telecom] for the telephone number of someone who has moved house and you will be told that it is not listed ... 'It takes at least three weeks to get on to the computer'. With computers, Hutber's law doubles in force.
> *Daily Telegraph* (2 May 1992)

**Hype.** Extravagant publicity; exaggerated promotion, especially in flowery, convoluted or even ungrammatical language. The word, perhaps a shortening of 'hyperbole', is of US origin and initially meant a swindle. It began to gain its present sense in the 1920s. The following, quoted in *The Times* of 24 January 2000, is a sample, as part of a press release by the firm Procter & Gamble promoting its new site on the INTERNET.

> This site is a great opportunity for P&G to further increase the relevance of our brands to the teenage audience. The internet gives us a unique platform to leverage the scale of our portfolio to better meet the needs of specific target groups.

**Hypertext.** A term coined in 1974 by the American computer expert Theodor Nelson to describe electronic texts with embedded links to other texts. It now denotes a software system that allows cross-referencing between such texts and associated graphic material. It is the 'h' of 'http' (hypertext transfer protocol), providing file access on the WORLD WIDE WEB, and of HTML.

**Hyphenate.** A person who combines two or more roles, so called because these are often joined with a hyphen, as 'writer-director'.

> [Dominic] Anciano and [Ray] Burdis ... are the ultimate multi-hyphenates: they are writer-producer-directors who also act in their work.
> *The Times* (25 September 1999)

Similarly, a hyphenated American is one who can trace their ancestry to another part of the world, such as an African-American or Irish-American. Not all Americans have approved:

> There is no room in this country for hyphenated Americanism ... The one absolutely certain way of bringing this nation to ruin ... would be to permit it to become a tangle of squabbling nationalities.
> THEODORE ROOSEVELT: speech in New York (12 October 1915)

# I

*I Am a Camera. See* GOODBYE TO BERLIN.

**I am become death, the destroyer of worlds.** The line from the Bhagavadgita, the ancient Hindu poem (2nd century BC–2nd century AD), that occurred to Robert J. Oppenheimer (1904–67), the leading scientist on the MANHATTAN PROJECT, as he watched the first atomic test explosion in the New Mexico desert, 16 July 1945. Two years later Oppenheimer told an audience at the Massachusetts Institute of Technology:

> The physicists have known sin; and this is a knowledge that they cannot lose.

Oppenheimer opposed the development of the hydrogen bomb, and was named as a security risk by Senator Joe McCarthy (*see* MCCARTHYISM). As a result, in 1954 he was dismissed from his post as chairman of the advisory committee of the Atomic Energy Commission. *See also* ENOLA GAY; HIROSHIMA.

*I Am Curious – Yellow.* A film (1967) by the Swedish novelist and director Vilgot Sjöman (b.1924), who had already made a number of films exploring taboos such as incest (*My Sister, My Love*, 1966) and bestiality (*491*, 1964). The curiosity of the title is evinced by the protagonist, a drama student (Lena Nyman) who plays the role of a sociologist. While questioning her fellow Swedes about their attitudes to a range of political and social issues, she also indulges in some frankly depicted sexual experimentation. There are also appearances by, among others, Olaf Palme, Yevgeni Yevtushenko and Martin Luther King. The film was seized by US Customs, but its clearance by the courts opened the way for more explicit sex in US cinema. There is a companion piece entitled *I Am Curious – Blue* (1968), using footage not employed in the Yellow edition. The colours referred to are those of the Swedish flag: a yellow cross on a blue background.

**'I am the Walrus'.** A bizarre, anarchically anti-establishment song by The BEATLES, credited to John Lennon and Paul McCartney (though mostly by Lennon) and released in Britain in November 1967. The song and its title reflect Lennon's love of schoolboy nonsense lyrics (witness 'yellow matter custard dripping from a dead dog's eye'), but also includes grotesque and scurrilous invective targeted against conventional institutions and morality. Edgar Allan Poe (1809–49), the enigmatic US poet, short-story writer, part-time alcoholic and hero of the 1960s counter-culture, is 'kicked' at one point in the song's lyrics. The song featured in the film of MAGICAL MYSTERY TOUR.

**'(I Can't Get No) Satisfaction'.** A blues-influenced anti-establishment song by The ROLLING STONES, released in 1965. The satisfaction that eludes the singer is both sexual and existential, the lyrics railing against society in general, the claims of advertising ('some man comes on and tells me how white my shirts could be / but he can't be a man 'cos he doesn't smoke the same cigarettes as me') and problems with girls ('I can't get no girl reaction'). Its message of adolescent protest captured the mood of the 1960s in a similar manner to The Who's 'MY GENERATION' . The phrase 'trying to make some girl' was bleeped when the group made an appearance on the *Ed Sullivan Show* in the United States.

**ICBM.** The abbreviation for *i*ntercontinental *b*allistic *m*issile. Nuclear-armed ICBMs threatening Armageddon have hung over the world like the sword of Damocles since the 1950s, although with the ending of the COLD WAR the threat has, in the eyes of many, receded. With ranges up to 12,000km (8000 miles) or more, they were designed to hit targets in the Soviet Union if launched from the United States and vice versa. They can also be launched from submarines, although in such cases they are usually referred to as SLBMs (*s*ubmarine-*l*aunched *b*allistic *m*issiles). *See also* ABM; MAD; POLARIS; SALT; STAR WARS; TRIDENT.

**Ice beer.** A type of strong lager. 'Ice' refers to the brewing process, in which the beer is cooled to sub-zero temperatures so that ice crystals form. These are then filtered out. Breweries claim that the process produces a smoother taste as well a higher alcoholic content. Beer of this type was introduced in the early 1990s as a marketing gimmick.

**Iceberg, The.** A nickname of the US film star Grace Kelly (1929–82), famed for her performances in such films as *High Noon* (1952), *Rear Window* (1954) and *High Society* (1956). She abandoned her screen career to marry Prince Rainier III of Monaco in 1956. The name derives from her blond hair and cool demeanour. The director Alfred Hitchcock, who directed her in three films, spoke of her 'sexual elegance'. She died following a driving accident.

**Ice Cold in Alex.** A classic adventure film (1958) set in North Africa in 1942, during the Second World War. The commander of an ambulance (John Mills) tries to get his passengers across the desert and back to safety in Alexandria (Alex), where they are promised ice-cold beers on arrival. The promise is duly kept. The beer in question was Carlsberg lager and the drinking scene later featured in a Carlsberg advertising campaign.

**Ice cream pants.** A US term of the early 20th century for white flannel trousers, especially when worn with a blue blazer as a 'uniform' for a young man going out on a date.

**Ice maiden** or **queen.** A 'cold' and apparently emotionless woman. The expressions became current from the 1950s but evoke folkloric figures such as the Russian 'Snow Maiden' (Snegurochka). *The Ice Maiden* (1927), a ballet choreographed by Fydor Lopokov and based on Grieg's *Peer Gynt* suite, tells the story of the Ice Maiden, who disguises herself as a beautiful girl to attract young men and bring them death.

> *Second Voice*: Sinbad Sailors watches her [Gossamer Beynon] go by, demure and proud and schoolmarm in her crisp flower dress and sun-defying hat, … the butcher's unmelting icemaiden daughter veiled for ever from the hungry hug of his eyes.
> DYLAN THOMAS: *Under Milk Wood* (1954)

**Iceman Cometh, The.** A play (1946) by the US playwright Eugene O'Neill (1888–1953) in which a disparate group of characters gather in Harry Hole's saloon to lament the death of their collective illusions. The play was inspired by the down-at-heel characters O'Neill encountered in the bars of Lower Manhattan during his own early years of disillusion and depression. The mysterious 'iceman' of the title (the man bringing ice to the saloon) is referred to several times in the script and comes to represent death. The choice of the word 'cometh' suggests biblical overtones, and Hickey the cheery salesman is commonly interpreted as a Christ figure.

**Ice queen.** *See* ICE MAIDEN.

**Ich bin ein Berliner.** *See* BERLINER.

**Icing on the cake.** An attractive but inessential addition to something already good. A US equivalent is 'frosting on the cake'. The expression dates from the 1960s.

***I, Claudius.*** A historical novel (1934) by Robert Graves (1895–1985) about the emperor Claudius (10 BC–AD 54), who in AD 41 succeeded his nephew Caligula in unlikely fashion as ruler of the Roman Empire. It begins: 'I, Tiberius Claudius Drusus Nero Germanicus This-that-and-the-other (for I shall not trouble you yet with all my titles) … .' *Claudius the God and His Wife Messalina* (1934) is a sequel. Their timely appearance in 1976 as a television drama series, directed by Herbert Wise and written by Jack Pulman, saved the author from financial embarrassment. The stammering but wily Claudius was memorably played by Derek Jacobi.

**Icon.** Apart from its original use to denote a painting of a holy figure, by the early 1990s 'icon' had acquired two new meanings: first, and generally, as a word for a famous person regarded as a cult figure (as if worshipped, like the holy icon); second, and specifically, as a term for a small symbolic figure on a computer screen that represents a particular facility and that can be activated to provide it. By the end of the 1990s the word in the former sense had itself become an 'icon'.

**I couldn't care less.** I am quite indifferent. The cliché may in fact mean the opposite, since the speaker has reacted with some passion to a situation. The expression dates from the 1940s. A US variant of the 1960s was 'I could care less', perhaps influenced by 'I should care'.

> Never say 'I couldn't care less'. It's rude, common, and usually untrue.
> GUY EGMONT: *The Art of Egmontese*, ch. 6 (1961)

**I couldn't possibly comment.** *See* YOU MIGHT VERY WELL THINK THAT. I COULDN'T POSSIBLY COMMENT.

**I counted them all out and I counted them all back.** The words used by Brian Hanrahan (b.1949) in a BBC television broadcast from the Falkland Islands during the FALKLANDS WAR, referring to the British Harrier jets that had taken part in a raid on Port Stanley, 1 May 1982. Hanrahan prefaced the phrase with an explanation that he was subject to military censorship: 'I'm not allowed to say how many planes joined the raid, but …' The phrase has often since been parodied or used in less serious contexts.

**ICT.** *See* IT.

**Ideal Home Exhibition.** An annual exhibition of the latest home comforts at Earl's Court, London. The popular show, famous for its spectacular displays, including a full-size house of the future, evolved from the exhibition first held in 1908 by the *Daily Mail* as an advertising gimmick.

**Identikit.** A method of identifying criminals from composite photographs based on an assemblage of individual features selected by witnesses from a wide variety of drawings. The method was developed by Hugh C. McDonald and first used in Los Angeles in 1959.

**Identity cards.** While identity cards (or 'ID cards', as they are more familiarly known) have long been a regular fact of life in many countries, they were first issued in Britain only in the early days of the Second World War. They were abolished in 1952, but in the latter part of the 20th century British governments developed an itch to reintroduce them. Taking the need for protection against terrorism as its cue, the Labour government introduced its Identity Cards Bill in 2005 amid much parliamentary and media opposition but apparent public support or apathy. Potential provisions include the encoding of biometric data on a SMART CARD (for which the owner will be required to pay) and the setting up of a National Identity Register.

**Identity theft.** An expanding sector of the criminal industry in the early 21st century. Identity theft involves any form of fraud that cheats the victim by acquiring details of their bank account, credit cards, online passwords or other personal details, whether by PHISHING or by obtaining transaction receipts.

**Idiot savant.** (French, 'knowledgeable idiot'.) A psychological term current in English from the 1920s for a person with a mental disability who nevertheless displays a remarkable talent in some respect, typically memorizing or rapid calculation. The expression has also gained a more general sense to apply to an otherwise unworldly person who displays natural wisdom and insight.

**Idiot Son, The.** The name given to President George W. Bush (DUBYA) by Iraqi propagandists in Saddam Hussein's government prior to the Second GULF WAR. Bush's father, George Bush Snr, was US president during the First Gulf War between Iraq and a US-led international coalition.

**Idiot zone.** An Americanism for a time or place devoid of worthwhile activity; a 'silly season'.

Summer is more traditionally the 'idiot zone' in American cinemas when all the big popcorn movies clog up thousands of air-conditioned theatres.
*heat* (14–20 October 1999)

**Idlewild.** The former popular name of the New York International Airport, situated at Idlewild on the northeast shore of Jamaica Bay, Long Island. In 1963 it was renamed the John F. Kennedy International Airport, popularly referred to as JFK.

**I don't believe it!** How could it have happened? An exclamation of disbelief that such a situation could have arisen (and been caused by my or someone else's action). It became famous as the catchphrase (with the stress firmly on the '-lieve') of the irascible pensioner Victor Meldrew in the BBC television sitcom ONE FOOT IN THE GRAVE.

**'I Don't Like Mondays'.** A song by the Irish PUNK ROCK group the Boomtown Rats, released in 1979. The title of the song derives from the explanation given by the US schoolgirl Brenda Spencer for her shooting dead several of her classmates on 29 January 1979. When asked why she had carried out the shootings she replied: 'I don't like Mondays.' A Number 1 hit in Britain, the song unsurprisingly fared less well in the United States, where many radio stations chose not to play the single on grounds of taste. *See also* ROCK GROUP NAMES.

**I don't think so.** Certainly not. A catchphrase current since the early 1990s to denote that in the speaker's view the statement just made, the question just asked or the situation described is patently untrue. In spoken form the phrase is usually stressed on the 'I'.

I am sure she [Jade Jagger] is as sweet as she is pretty, but a role model for grown-up women? I don't think so.
*Sunday Times* (9 January 2000)

**IDS.** The conveniently shortened name by which the British politician Iain Duncan Smith (*see* the QUIET MAN) chose to be known after his brief elevation to the leadership of the Conservative Party (2001–3). It was modelled on such US presidential initialisms as FDR and JFK.

**'If'.** 'If —', the title of a famous moralistic poem by Rudyard Kipling, originally appeared in *Rewards and Fairies* (1910). It enumerates 12 conditions, the successful fulfilment of which will bring the doer 'the Earth and everything that's in it, / And – which is more – you'll be a Man, my son!' The poem gave the ironic title of the highly praised film *If* ….

As someone pointed out recently, if you can keep your head when all about you are losing theirs, it's just possible you haven't grasped the situation.
JEAN KERR: *Please Don't Eat the Daisies* (1957)

**If ….** The film (1968), written by David Sherwin and John Howlett, is an allegory about the violent rebellion of pupils at an English public school against the authority of their masters. Directed by Lindsay Anderson and starring Malcolm McDowell, the script was originally titled *The Crusaders* but acquired its final title in ironic reference to Rudyard Kipling's celebrated poem 'If —' (*see* 'IF'). *If …* is also the name of a satirical cartoon strip by the illustrator Steve Bell, which first appeared in the *Guardian* newspaper in 1981.

**If it ain't broke, don't fix it.** A modern proverb, possibly first coined by the US government official Bert Lance (b.1931) and quoted in *Nation's Business*, May 1977. It has also been attributed to Henry Ford. In the 1991 animated Disney film, *Beauty and the Beast*, the character Cogsworth conducts a tour of the castle:

> This is yet another example of the late neo-classical baroque period and, as I always say, if it's not baroque, don't fix it.

**If it isn't hurting, it isn't working.** The policy towards controlling inflation enunciated by the Conservative politician John Major (b.1943) while chancellor of the exchequer. At a speech in Northampton on 27 October 1989, Major said: 'If the policy isn't hurting, it isn't working.' The Conservative Party picked this up as the basis for a slogan in 1996: 'Yes it hurt, yes it worked.' The following year they were slung out of office. *See also* NO PAIN, NO GAIN.

**If it looks like a duck, walks like a duck and quacks like a duck, then it just may be a duck.** A test devised by the US labour leader Walter Reuther (1907–70) in the McCarthy era (*see* MCCARTHYISM) as to whether someone was a communist. The expression has become proverbial. The British comic writer Douglas Adams (1952–2001) offered this variant:

> If it looks like a duck, and quacks like a duck, we have at least to consider the possibility that we have a small aquatic bird of the family Anatidae on our hands.

Sceptics have pointed out that the subject of the inquiry could, in fact, be just a decoy.

**I forgot to duck.** The explanation given to his wife by the boxer Jack Dempsey (1895–1983) as to why he lost the World Heavyweight title on 23 September 1923.

President Ronald Reagan, whose conversation and speeches were larded with second-hand lines (largely from the movies), used the same phrase to his wife Nancy after being shot by John Hinkley in a failed assassination attempt on 30 March 1981.

**If voting changed anything, they'd abolish it.** A common graffito in the 1970s, which became the title of a 1987 book by the Labour politician Ken Livingstone (RED KEN).

**If you ask me.** If you want to know my opinion (whether you actually ask for it or not).

**If you can't beat them, join them.** The pragmatist's credo: fall in with the prevailing state of affairs if it is clear that nothing can be done to change it. The modern proverb is first recorded in 1955.

**If you can't stand the heat, get out of the kitchen.** Advice to those contemplating the ascent of any GREASY POLE planted in shark-infested waters. The saying is often attributed to US President Harry S. Truman (1884–1972), although Truman credited the saying to one of his generals, Harry Vaughan (1893–1981).

**Ig Nobel prizes.** Annual science awards founded in 1991 by Marc Abrahams, editor of *The Annals of Improbable Research*, and presented (by actual NOBEL PRIZE winners) each year to the scientists who have undertaken the most (apparently) useless but nevertheless fascinating research projects – those that 'first make people laugh, and then make them think'. Winners over the years have included Vice-President J. Danforth Quayle (Education prize, 1991), 'for demonstrating, better than anyone else, the need for science education'; Edward Teller, the father of the hydrogen bomb and champion of STAR WARS (Peace, 1991), 'for his lifelong efforts to change the meaning of peace as we know it'; a team from the Shiseido Research Centre, Yokohama (Medicine, 1992), 'for their conclusion that people who think they have foot odour do, and those who don't, don't'; T. Yagyu and an international team (Biology, 1997), 'for measuring people's brainwave patterns while they chewed different flavours of gum'; Dr Mara Sidoli of Washington, D.C. (Literature, 1998), 'for her illuminating report, "Farting as a Defence Against Unspeakable Dread"' (published in *Journal of Analytical Psychology*, vol. 41, no. 2, 1996, pp. 165–78); and, more recently, Victor Benno Meyer-Rochow of the International University Bremen, Germany, and Jozsef Gal of Lorand Eotvos University, Hungary (*Fluid Dynamics*, 2005), for their paper 'Pressures Produced When Penguins Poo: Calculations on Avian Defecation'. Every March, to coincide with National Science Week in Britain, the British Association for the Advancement of Science and *The Guardian* sponsor an 'Ig Nobel Tour of the UK'; there is also an Ig-Nobel Tour in Australia every August.

**I have a dream.** The refrain of the most famous speech given by Martin Luther King (1929–68), addressing a civil rights march in Washington, D.C., on 28 August 1963.

I have a dream that one day this nation will rise up and live out the true meaning of its creed: 'We hold these truths to be self-evident, that all men are created equal.'

I have a dream that one day on the red hills of Georgia, the sons of former slaves and the sons of former slave owners will be able to sit down together at the table of brotherhood. I have a dream that one day even the state of Mississippi, a state sweltering with the heat of injustice, sweltering with the heat of oppression, will be transformed into an oasis of freedom and justice.

I have a dream that my four little children will one day live in a nation where they will not be judged by the color of their skin but by the content of their character.

I have a *dream* today!

**Ike.** The nickname of Dwight D. Eisenhower (1890–1972), US general and 34th president of the United States (1953–61). The name, originally a school tag based on Eisenhower's surname, was in regular use throughout his military career and formed the basis of his winning slogan, 'I like Ike', first appearing on buttons as early as 1947. It seemed irrelevant that 'ike' was 19th-century US slang for an ignorant rustic, or that 'Ikey' is a derogatory name for a Jew. *See also* MONTY.

**IKEA.** The brand of self-assembly furniture, giving a semblance of stability and style at a reasonable cost, was first produced in 1947 by the Swedish manufacturer Ingvar Kamprad. The name is a blend of his initials and those of the farm where he was born, Elmtaryd, and his village, Agunnaryd. The acronym is interpreted by cynical Germans as *Idioten kaufen eben alles*, 'Some fools will buy anything.'

Thousands throng to IKEA stores at weekends, and the 2005 opening of a new outlet at Edmonton, North London, resulted in the emergency services being called to help those crushed in the crowds. The company maintains low prices through emphasizing self-service (customers must load products on to trolleys, as in a supermarket) and through minimal concessions to regional cultures: labels remain in Swedish wherever the goods are sold.

**I kid you not.** I am perfectly serious. The jocular expression, of US origin and current from the 1950s, has been attributed to the entertainer and talk show host Jack Paar (b.1918).

> David Boreanaz and (I kid you not) Charisma Carpenter head the good-looking young cast.
> *The Times* (7 January 2000)

**I Know Where I'm Going.** A film (1945) co-written and directed by Michael Powell (1905–90) and Emeric Pressburger (1902–88) about a headstrong young woman's plan to marry her wealthy elderly employer. The scheme is thrown awry when she falls for a young naval officer while on her way to be married in the Hebrides. Starring Wendy Hiller and Roger Livesey, it took its title from an Irish song that Powell's wife sang to him as they travelled on a London bus to Piccadilly Circus:

> I know where I'm going
> And I know who goes with me
> I know whom I love
> But the dear Lord (or Devil) knows whom I'll marry.

On Powell's instructions, music from the film was played at his funeral.

**I Know Why the Caged Bird Sings.** A volume of memoirs (1970) by the African-American writer, singer and actress Maya Angelou (b.1928). Angelou borrowed her title from a line in the poem 'Sympathy' by the US poet Paul Lawrence Dunbar (1872–1906).

> We think caged birds sing, when indeed they cry.
> JOHN WEBSTER: *The White Devil* (1612), V.iv

**Il Cavaliere.** *See* Il CAVALIERE.

**Illegitimate child of Karl Marx and Catherine the Great, the.** The description of Soviet communism by the Labour statesman Clement Attlee (1883–1967) in a speech at Aarhus University, 11 April 1956.

**Illegitimi non carborundum.** A facetious cod-Latin translation of DON'T LET THE BASTARDS GRIND YOU DOWN (despite appearances, 'carborundum' is not a Latin word at all; it is the name of a type of abrasive substance made from silicon carbide, coined in English and registered as a trademark in 1892). It seems to have emerged around the time of the Second World War – according to some reports, among members of British Army intelligence.

**I'll make him an offer he can't refuse.** A line spoken by Don Corleone in Mario Puzo's classic Mafia novel, *The Godfather* (1969). In the film version (1972), in which Marlon Brando plays Don Corleone, the line is slightly altered: 'I'm gonna make him an offer he can't refuse.' The phrase has become proverbial.

**Illywhacker.** An Australian slang word of 1940s provenance for a confidence trickster, especially one who follows fairs around the country. *Illywhacker* (1985) by the Australian novelist Peter Carey (b.1943), is the epic fictional autobiography of a 109-year-old boaster, aviator and conman.

**I'm a Celebrity, Get Me Out of Here!** *See* REALITY TV.

**Imagism.** A school of poetry founded by Ezra Pound (1885–1972), derived from the ideas of the philosopher T.E. Hulme (1883–1917). The imagist poets were in revolt against excessive romanticism and proclaimed that poetry should use the language of common speech, create new rhythms, be uninhibited in choice of subject and present a precise image. Imagism was a key influence on MODERNISM in English-language verse.

***I'm All Right Jack.*** A film (1959) adapted by John Boulting and Frank Harvey from Alan Hackney's novel *Private Life* about the comical clashes between a communist trade unionist and factory management during a strike. Starring Peter Sellers as the shop steward in question and Ian Carmichael as a management representative caught in the middle of the dispute, the film was retitled in reference to the traditional English saying 'I'm all right, Jack' (the expurgated version of 'Fuck you, Jack, I'm all right'), denoting the selfishness of a man who does not care what happens to those around him as long as his own interests have been taken care of. A nautical equivalent of the phrase is: 'Pull up the ladder, Jack, I'm inboard.'

***I Married a … / I Was a …*** Both of these title formulas have proved popular for films, echoing sensational headlines in the tabloid press. Examples of 'I Was a …' include:

*I Was a Spy* (1933)

*I Was an Adventuress* (1940)

*I Was a Prisoner on Devil's Island* (1941)

*I Was a Male War Bride* (1949)

*I Was a Communist for the FBI* (1951)

*I Was an American Spy* (1951)

*I Was a Teenage Frankenstein* (1957)

*I Was a Teenage Werewolf* (1957)

*I Was Monty's Double* (1958)

Examples of 'I Married a …' include:

*I Married a Nazi* (1940)

*I Married an Angel* (1942)

*I Married a Witch* (1942)

*I Married a Communist* (1949)

*I Married a Woman* (1956)

*I Married a Monster from Outer Space* (1958)

*I Married a Dead Man* (1983)

**IMAX.** A proprietary name for a technique of cinematography developed in Canada which produces an image approximately ten times larger than that from standard 35mm film. The name is a blend of 'image' and 'maximum', and the system was first introduced in 1970. To watch a film made by this method, viewers sit on a series of elevated rows angled 30 to 45 degrees in such a way that they feel fully involved in the picture, which is on a screen ten times the normal size

and up to eight storeys high. The British Film Institute's IMAX cinema at Waterloo, London, has Britain's largest screen.

**I may be some time.** The last recorded words of the English explorer Captain Lawrence Edward Oates (1880–1912), spoken just before he walked to his death on the Antarctic expedition of Captain Robert Falcon Scott on 16 March 1912. Oates, who had decided that his illness was slowing down his companions, walked calmly out into a blizzard with the remark 'I am just going outside, and I may be some time.' The words were recorded by Scott and appeared in his journals, published as *Scott's Last Expedition* in 1913. Oates's statement, interpreted by succeeding generations as the essense of stiff-upper-lipped British courage, has since become widely disseminated as a catchphrase used when someone absents themselves from a gathering for any reason. *See also* SOUTH POLE.

**I'm backing Britain.** The slogan of a national campaign to buy British goods and increase productivity, launched in 1968 by the prime minister, Harold Wilson. As it happened, with the pound having just been devalued, buying imported goods had suddenly become much less attractive. The spirit of the campaign was picked up by a group of women secretaries at a factory in Surbiton, Surrey, who volunteered to work an extra 30 minutes per day without pay (to the horror of the trade unions). The slogan itself was emblazoned over a union jack, and printed on badges and T-shirts. The campaign rather flagged when it came to light that a batch of 'I'm backing Britain' T-shirts had, in fact, been manufactured in Portugal. *See also* 'BACK IN THE USSR'.

**IMF.** The abbreviation for the International Monetary Fund, a specialized agency of the United Nations set up at the BRETTON WOODS Conference in 1944. The purpose of the IMF is to promote trade expansion, the stabilization of currencies and international monetary cooperation. Along with its sister organization, the WORLD BANK, it has been criticized for promoting policies unfavourable towards the environment and the THIRD WORLD, and for undermining national sovereignty by dictating economic policies to governments as a condition for making loans.

**I'm just going out.** *See* I MAY BE SOME TIME.

**Imperial Conference.** The name given to the conferences held in London between the prime ministers of the various dominions of the British Empire between 1907 and 1946. These conferences had their origin in the first Colonial Conference, which met in 1887 on the occasion of Queen Victoria's Jubilee. Since 1948 the Commonwealth Prime Ministers' Conference has replaced the Imperial Conference.

**Imperial presidency.** A term for the office of the president of the United States viewed as exceeding in power and authority the executive role provided by the Constitution. The term derives from the book *The Imperial Presidency* (1973) by the American historian Arthur M. Schlesinger Jr.

> One area in which the imperial presidency is as regal as ever is the matter of international airline routes: by law the President can bestow on any airline of his choice the right to fly between any American city and any foreign one and he need not bother to state a reason.
>
> *Time* (16 January 1978)

**Impulse buyer.** A person who buys something on a whim or the spur of the moment, especially when doing so without consideration of cost, quality or usefulness. Many supermarkets place confectionery and other attractive or useful items at the entrance to a checkout in the hope of tempting such shoppers to make a purchase.

> A new range of McVitie and Price cake packages … will be on display in supermarkets this week, designed to attract the 'impulse' buyer.
>
> *The Times* (11 March 1970)

**I'm Sorry, I Haven't a Clue.** *See* MORNINGTON CRESCENT; NOT HAVE A CLUE.

**I'm Sorry, I'll Read That Again.** A chaotically cheerful and crudely comic radio programme broadcast from 1964 to 1973, its title based on the stock apology of a stumbling or stuttering newsreader. Billed as 'a radio custard pie', it was full of groan-inducing puns and mildly smutty sketches and helped to launch the careers of many of its participants, including John Cleese of FAWLTY TOWERS and the three comedians who later cast themselves as the GOODIES.

**In a bad way.** Suffering; in difficulties. There is no contrary 'in a good way'.

**Inch war.** Dieting; the 'fight against flab', when the struggle is to lose inches round the waistline. The term can also apply to any gradual campaign. The *Evening Standard* of 8 June 1994 had a sub-heading 'Battle of the inch war' that referred to a plan by airlines to provide more passenger accommodation by dropping first-class seating.

**In Cold Blood.** Subtitled 'A True Account of a Multiple Murder and Its Consequences', this book (1966) by the US author Truman Capote (1924–84) has been described both as 'a non-fiction novel' and as 'creative reporting'. Capote worked from 1959 to 1965 on his investigation into the motiveless murder of a Kansas family and accompanied the two perpetrators on their way to the gallows several years after they had been convicted. An action carried out 'in cold blood' is performed in a cool and calculated manner, not in the heat of passion. A complex and brutal film version (1967), directed by Richard Brooks, was remade as a television mini-series (1990) directed by Jonathan Kaplan and starring Anthony Edwards and Eric Roberts. Truman Capote's investigation is retold in the film *Capote* (2005), with Philip Seymour Hoffman playing the part of Capote, for which he won an OSCAR for Best Actor in 2006.

**Incredible Hulk, The.** The huge green humanoid into which the humble scientist Dr David Bruce Banner metamorphoses whenever he is possessed by anger. The creature was the brainchild of the US writer Stan Lee and first featured in Marvel Comics in 1962. It (he) later appeared in a television version screened from 1978 to 1982, with Lou Ferrigno in the role of the man-beast, and in 2003 the Hulk was played by Eric Bana in a big-budget film version.

**Incredible Sulk, The.** A nickname given to a number of people, playing on the name of the US cartoon character, the INCREDIBLE HULK. Holders of the title have included Edward Heath (*see* the GROCER), who, after he lost the leadership of the Conservative Party in 1975, until his death in 2005, carried out a bilious campaign against his successor, Margaret Thatcher (*see* GROCER'S DAUGHTER). Another notable holder of the title is Gordon Brown (*see* IRON CHANCELLOR; MISERY FROM THE MANSE), who has long been thought of as coveting the premiership and whose body language in the presence of the incumbent, Tony Blair, is thought to betray his true feelings. In the area of sport, the epithet has been applied to people such as the tennis player John McEnroe (*see* SUPERBRAT) and the French footballers Thierry Henry and Nicolas Anelka.

**In deep kimchi.** In US military slang, in serious trouble. The expression, a humorous bowdlerization of 'in deep shit', was born during the Korean War (*kimchi* is a Korean delicacy consisting of pickled cabbage).

**Indie.** An abbreviation of 'independent' used for a pop group or record label that does not belong to a major record company and whose music in many cases is intentionally unpolished. Indie rock is strictly speaking rock music released on such labels, but the term has come to apply more generally to guitar bands that descended from the PUNK groups of the 1970s and, by extension, to the youth subculture coalescing around such bands from the late 1980s.

'Indie' is also the nickname of *The Independent*, a top-end-of-the-market British daily newspaper launched in 1986 (the Sunday version is known as the 'Sindie').

**Industrial action.** A strike or stoppage. The expression seems curiously contradictory, since what is involved is a ceasing of work, otherwise inaction. On 14 May 1980 the Trades Union Congress even called a 'Day of Action' for such a tactic. But those resorting to the strategy see it as a positive move rather than a negative stance. The term itself dates from the 1970s, a decade in which strikes loomed large in Britain.

**Industrial-strength.** Of the most powerful, formidable or serious grade or type (as in 'an industrial-grade crisis'). The usage was inspired in the United States in the late 1960s by a television advertising campaign for 'Janitor In A Drum' (a trademark of Texize Chemicals, Inc.) as 'the industrial-strength floor cleaner' – the implication being of greater power than is usually available for domestic use.

**Indy 500.** The popular name of the Indianapolis 500 motor race, held annually with the exception of war years from 1911 at the Indianapolis Motor Speedway, near Indianapolis, Indiana. It was originally held on Memorial Day, 30 May, but later took place on the preceding Saturday or Sunday. It is 805km (500 miles) in length, which means that drivers of the 33 participating cars need to circuit the near-oblong 4km (2½ mile) track 200 times, starting three abreast from the initial line-up. The Indy 500 draws more spectators than any other US sporting event, and an attendance of 300,000 is not unusual.

**Inextinguishable, The.** The title of the symphony No. 4 (1916) by the Danish composer Carl Nielsen (1865–1931). During the course of the piece a side-drum attempts to drown out the rest of the orchestra, but does not in the end succeed.

> Music is life, and, like it, inextinguishable.
> CARL NIELSEN: motto of his symphony No. 4

**Inferiority complex.** A psychiatric term for a complex resulting from a sense of inferiority dating from childhood. Attempts to compensate for the sense of worthlessness may take an aggressive or violent form, or manifest themselves in an overzealous involvement in activities. The term dates from the 1920s, when it was coined by the Austrian psychoanalyst Alfred Adler (1870–1937):

> Individual psychology holds that the most important key to the understanding of both personal and mass problems is the so-called sense of inferiority, or inferiority complex, and its consequences.
> Quoted in the *New York Times* (20 September 1925)

**Information overload.** *See* FUTURE SHOCK.

**In good nick.** In good condition. A phrase of dialect origin, with 'nick' here the same word as that for a notch or cut, and as in other phrases, as 'in the nick of time'. The converse, 'in bad nick', is not often encountered.

> He looked the woman up and down. She was a little older, perhaps in her forties, but still in good nick, he noticed.
> DERMOT BOLGER (ed.): *Finbar's Hotel*, 'No Pets Please' (1997)

**Inhaling or not inhaling.** Bill Clinton, when admitting that he had experimented with marijuana in his youth, confessed in March 1992 that:

> When I was in England, I experimented with marijuana a time or two, and I didn't like it. I didn't inhale and never tried it again.

Later that year he was duly elected president of the United States. The phrase was much taken up and adapted by satirists, while in 2004 Mark Latham, leader of the Australian Labor Party, admitted he *had* inhaled.

**In-joke.** A joke shared exclusively by a small group of people. 'In' here originally had rather the sense of 'fashionable' than simply meaning 'within the group'. The expression dates from the mid-1960s.

**Inkatha.** The Zulu political organization of this name was originally founded in 1928, but was revived by Chief Buthelezi in 1973. It claims an aim of racial equality and universal franchise in South Africa, but has been subject to clashes both with the rival African National Congress (ANC) and among factions within the party itself. Its name is a Zulu word for a crown of woven grass, a tribal emblem representing the force that unites the Zulu nation.

**Inklings.** A group of Oxford friends, centring on the literary scholar and critic C.S. Lewis (1898–1963), who met from the 1930s to the 1960s to talk and to read their compositions aloud to one another. Other members were the philologist and writer J.R.R. Tolkien (1892–1973), the poet and theological writer Charles Williams (1886–1945), the medieval literary scholar Nevill Coghill (1899–1980) and the academic H.V.D. Dyson (1896–1975). Many of their meetings were held at The Eagle and Child pub in St Giles. The group name puns rather obviously on 'ink'. Humphrey Carpenter's *The Inklings* (1977) is a study of the circle.

**In like Flynn.** Most decidedly or rapidly 'in'. Originally a US usage, first recorded in 1945, it often refers specifically to a speedy and successful sexual conquest. It is traditionally associated with the actor Errol Flynn (1909–59), who was renowned for his sexual prowess, and is said to have been coined following his acquittal in February 1943 of the charge of statutory rape of a teenage girl. However, examples of what seem like precursors of the phrase (e.g. 'you're Flynn, meaning you're in') have been found from before 1943, and it may be that the Errol Flynn attribution only got tacked on to it later. An alternative candidate for the original Flynn is Edward J. Flynn, known as 'Boss' Flynn, who was a campaign manager for the Democratic Party during Franklin D. Roosevelt's presidency.

**'In My Life'.** A reflective and affectionate song by The BEATLES, credited to John Lennon and Paul McCartney and released in Britain in December 1965 on the album RUBBER SOUL. The 'Life' in question is John Lennon's, the roots of the song lying in a previously attempted lyric in which Lennon proposed to describe the sights and sounds he saw during the course of a bus journey from his home into Liverpool city centre. 'In My Life' represents a leaner and less ambitious version of this original idea. A curious feature of the song is the appearance halfway through it of a witty piece of baroque pastiche played on the electric piano by George Martin, The Beatles' producer (*see* FIFTH BEATLE).

**Inner cabinet.** A name dating from the turn of the 20th century for a decision-making group of ministers within the regular cabinet, or for a similar group within another body, such as a council.

**Inner city.** A central or innermost area of a city regarded as having social problems such as inadequate housing and high levels of crime and unemployment. The term is of US origin and dates from the 1960s. In Britain, as well as being locations of poverty, some inner cities in the 1980s experienced violence and rioting, exacerbated by racial tensions, as in Brixton in London, Toxteth in Liverpool, Handsworth in Birmingham and the St Paul's district of Bristol.

Responses by governments to deal with the problem have included the establishment in 1981 of so-called 'enterprise zones', designed to encourage new commercial and industrial enterprises, and the setting up in 1993 of an Urban Regeneration Agency with the aim of reclaiming derelict land in decayed inner cities.

**Inner space.** A term introduced in the late 1950s for the part of the human mind that is not normally accessible to consciousness. Attempts have been made to explore this region, since ancient times through meditation and in the psychedelic 1960s and 1970s through drugs, but results have remained unsatisfactory or at best inconclusive. The term itself was probably prompted by the then current interest in the exploration of outer space.

**Innit.** A representation of a casual British pronunciation of 'isn't it', usually as a tag question (as in 'Cold, innit?'). The

form dates from the 1950s, though the pronunciation it represents is no doubt of far greater antiquity. Grammatically it emulated its full form in referring back specifically to the subject of the preceding sentence (as in 'That's nice, isn't it?'), but in the latter part of the 20th century, in the street slang of London, it broadened out into an all-purpose tag, rather like French *n'est-ce pas?* (as in 'I've got a lot of work on, innit?').

**Innocent bystander.** A bystander who is not responsible for or directly involved in an event or incident yet suffers as a result of it. An innocent victim is similar. The terms evolved in the 1950s.

**In no uncertain terms.** Very clearly; emphatically. A meiotic turn of phrase that seems to have become popular only from the 1950s.

> When I asked her to calm down, she informed me, in no uncertain terms, of my place in the scheme of things.
> *Today* (15 February 1995)

**In office but not in power.** A comment made by the former Conservative chancellor of the exchequer, Norman Lamont (b.1942), in his 1993 resignation speech about his erstwhile boss, prime minister John Major. He was referring to the widespread dissidence thought to exist within both the parliamentary party and the cabinet. Conservative leader Michael Howard used the same phrase about Tony Blair in November 2005, following the second resignation of David Blunkett (*see* BIG BLUNKETT) from the cabinet.

**Inoperative statement.** A euphemism for a lie, coined by the White House press spokesman Ron Ziegler (b.1939) at the time of the Watergate scandal.

> This is the operative statement. The others are inoperative.
> Press conference (17 April 1973)

**In orbit.** In a state of great excitement; exhilarated; 'high'. The phrase dates from the 1960s and ultimately alludes to the launch of the first Soviet SPUTNIK in 1957. See also GO INTO ORBIT.

> I have recently found the man of my dreams … I'm in orbit and feel as if all my Christmases have come at once.
> TARA PALMER-TOMKINSON: in *Sunday Times* (8 August 1999)

**In Place of Strife.** A government White Paper on trade-union reform, issued on 17 January 1969. The title was suggested by the journalist Ted Castle (1907–79) to his wife Barbara Castle (1910–2002), who was at the time secretary of state for employment in Harold Wilson's Labour government. The proposals were withdrawn in the face of fierce opposition from the unions and senior cabinet figures such as Jim Callaghan.

**Inside every fat man there's a thin one trying to get out.**

A phrase probably originating with George Orwell:

> I'm fat, but I'm thin inside. Has it ever struck you that there's a thin man inside every fat man, just as they say there's a statue inside every block of stone?
>
> *Coming up for Air* (1939)

The saying influenced later writers:

> Imprisoned in every fat man a thin one is wildly signalling to be let out.
>
> CYRIL CONNOLLY: *The Unquiet Grave* (1944)

> Outside every fat man there was an even fatter man trying to close in.
>
> KINGSLEY AMIS: *One Fat Englishman* (1963)

The American jazz pianist Oscar Levant (1906–72) admitted in *Memoirs of an Amnesiac* (1965):

> Underneath this flabby exterior is an enormous lack of character

while the English journalist Katherine Whitehorn (b.1928) held that:

> Outside every thin girl there is a fat man trying to get in.

**Inside job.** A crime committed by someone familiar with the layout and routine of the place where it happens. *See also* OUTSIDE JOB.

**Insider dealing.** A Stock Exchange term for the buying or selling of shares when in possession of 'inside' information that will affect the price. The practice was made illegal by the Company Securities (Insider Dealing) Act of 1985 and the first person to be prosecuted under it, in 1987, was Geoffrey Collier, joint manager of Morgan Grenfell Securities, who was fined £25,000.

**Inside the tent pissing out.** *See* BIG TENT.

**In space no one can hear you scream.** *See* ALIEN.

**Inspector Appleby.** *See* Inspector APPLEBY.

**Inspector Calls, An.** A play (1946) by J.B. Priestley (1894–1984) in which a complacent Yorkshire industrialist and his family are quizzed about their individual involvement in the suicide of a poor young woman. The inspector of the title is merciless in his exposure of each person's guilt, but towards the end of the play his own identity comes into question as it is revealed that he is not an official inspector at all. A film version (1954), in which the inspector was played by Alastair Sim, was directed by Guy Hamilton. In 1993 an inventive, dreamlike production of the play, staged by Stephen Daldry for the National Theatre, reinvigorated Priestley's drama for late 20th-century audiences and won awards internationally.

**Inspector Clouseau.** *See* Inspector CLOUSEAU.

**Inspector Gadget.** A nickname for a mechanical expert or 'techno-whiz'. The name is that of an American animated cartoon character of the late 1980s who is the first 'gadgetized' and bionic inspector to work for INTERPOL.

> Peter Snow, in charge of maps and gadgets for the BBC, was hero of the hour … To call him Inspector Gadget would be making light of his talent. He is Deputy Assistant Commissioner Gadget.
>
> *Sunday Times* (2 January 2000)

**Inspector Ghote.** *See* Inspector GHOTE.

**Inspector Morse.** An elegantly filmed television crime series, screened from 1987, centring on the investigations of Chief Inspector Morse of Thames Valley Police, a complex character originally created in novels by Colin Dexter (b.1930). Accompanied by his Geordie sidekick, Sergeant Lewis (played by Kevin Whately), the curmudgeonly, pedantic, crossword-solving, REAL ALE-drinking, music-loving Morse (played by John Thaw) pursues plots that bridge the gap between a regular WHODUNIT and a sophisticated allegory. One episode, 'Promised Land', was not only a murder mystery but also a parody on Mozart's opera *The Magic Flute*. The series was filmed in and around Oxford, which added to the nostalgic feel and cerebral charm of the whole. In the 1997 story 'Death is Now My Neighbour' Morse's Christian name was finally revealed to be Endeavour. In the last story, 'The Remorseful Day', broadcast on 15 November 2000, he dies, as did John Thaw (of cancer) in 2002. In 2006 a pilot drama, *Lewis*, followed the return of the now-promoted Inspector Lewis to Oxford following several years working abroad. Now a grieving widower, and with his children flown from the nest, his solitariness and personal demons partially evoked the character of his mentor.

**Inspector Rebus.** *See* Inspector REBUS.

**Instant messaging.** On the INTERNET, a system of 'dialogue' by which two or more computer users can have a 'conversation' in real time by typing their words, which are instantly relayed to their interlocutors' screens, often in the environment of a CHAT ROOM.

**Intelligence quotient** or **IQ.** The ratio, expressed as a percentage, of a person's mental age to his or her actual age, the former being the level of test performance that is median for that age tested by the Binet type scale or some similar system. Thus if a ten-year-old has a mental age of nine years, the IQ is ninety. 100 indicates average intelligence. The term was introduced by the German educationist Wilhelm Stern as *Intelligenz-Quotient* in 1912 and popularized by Cyril Burt (1883–1971), Lewis M. Terman (1877–1956) and others.

**Intelligent design.** The theory, proposed by a small minority of scientists (mostly Christians and mostly in the United States), that the complexity of life, the universe and everything requires the existence of an intelligent, supernatural designer, and cannot be explained by orthodox scientific ideas such as Darwin's theory of natural selection. The vast majority of scientists reject intelligent design as no more than 'creationism in a cheap tuxedo' (a phrase coined by Leonard Krishtalka, director of the Natural History Museum, University of Kansas), in other words as religious belief rather than science. (Creationism is the belief that the earth and life were formed exactly as described in the Bible.) The National Academy of Sciences in the United States has stated that intelligent design 'and other claims of supernatural intervention in the origin of life' are not science because they cannot be tested, and because they do not generate predictions. In 2005 President George W. Bush (DUBYA) was reported as saying that schools should teach both natural selection and intelligent design. Those of a satirical bent have claimed that the president is himself a living proof of the fallacy of the latter theory. *See also* FLAT EARTH SOCIETY.

**InterCity train.** A brand name introduced by British Railways in the mid-1950s for what was formerly known as an express train. The word 'intercity' meaning 'linking cities' was not new, nor was its application to the BR trains original, as the North British Railway was running 'intercity expresses' between Edinburgh and Aberdeen as early as 1906.

**International Brigades.** The units of foreigners who volunteered to fight on the Republican side in the Spanish Civil War (1936–9). Most of the volunteers, who came from around 50 countries, were communists, and the International Brigades were organized by the COMINTERN, the Soviet-led Communist (or Third) International. In all, some 37,000 men and women volunteered, and each of the seven brigades was organized into battalions according to nationality: for example, many Americans were in the Abraham Lincoln Battalion and there was also a John Brown Battery, named after two heroes of the antislavery movement in the United States. The International Brigades were withdrawn in 1938 as the USSR slimmed down its support for the Republic. Not all anti-fascist foreign volunteers joined the International Brigades: George ORWELL, for example, joined the militia of the Marxist but anti-Stalinist POUM (Partido Obrero de Unificación Marxista) in 1936,

and ended up fighting the Soviet-controlled communists who set out to destroy the POUM and other ideological opponents within the Republican camp.

**International Monetary Fund.** *See* IMF.

**International Standard Book Number.** *See* ISBN.

**International Women's Day.** The day so named was proclaimed in 1910 at the Second International Socialist Women's Conference in Copenhagen on the suggestion of the German socialist (later communist) leader Clara Zetkin (1857–1933). It was first observed the following year by comrades in Germany, Austria-Hungary, Switzerland and Denmark and subsequently other countries. At first the date varied but from 1914 it settled as 8 March. It was fully celebrated in the Soviet Union, where the Presidium of the Supreme Soviet, in a decree of 8 May (VE DAY) 1965, declared it a public holiday 'in honour of the outstanding services of Soviet women in the building of communism and the defence of the Motherland during the GREAT PATRIOTIC WAR, and of their heroism and selflessness at the front and in the rear, and also to mark the great contribution of women to the cementing of friendship between nations and the struggle for peace'. Satellite states took a similar line, but the demise of communism in eastern Europe in the early 1990s allowed the day to be taken up more openly in the United States and elsewhere.

**Internet.** The international system of computer networks, often just termed 'the Net', that enable academic, business, government and home computers to communicate with each other via cables or wireless means. It had its origins in the COLD WAR, when in 1969 the US Defense Department built an experimental computer network designed to withstand a nuclear attack. The expansion of this network eventually came to provide E-MAIL, as well as information in the form of HYPERTEXT on the WORLD WIDE WEB, and other IT services. So thoroughgoing is its impact on the modern world that few areas of life remain unaffected, from shopping to learning to dating. In the early 21st century, in tandem with the IPOD and similar devices, the burgeoning downloading of music began to threaten even the relatively recent technology of the compact disc (CD).

In the 1990s concern was expressed regarding the ease with which users, especially children, gained access (sometimes unwittingly) to pornography on the Net, either through websites devoted to the subject or via a CHAT ROOM ostensibly treating an innocent topic but in fact having a sexual basis; nowadays 'parental controls' software is available as a censor. Internet 'grooming' of children by adults intent on sexual exploitation has featured in some high-profile criminal cases that have had tragic consequences. The Internet also provides support to other forms of criminal and terrorist activity, but as internet service providers (ISPs) point out, the Internet is the electronic equivalent of a postal service, and they claim it is not possible (or, according to some, desirable) to attempt to impose controls. As with many transforming technologies, the Net's uses and abuses go hand in hand.

> Previously the domain of techie anoraks and boffins in lab coats, the Internet is now part of everyday life.
>
> *The Times* (25 September 1999)

**Interpol.** The short name of the International Criminal Police Organization, set up in Vienna in 1923 to facilitate the cooperation of the police forces of different countries in the international fight against crime. In 1938 NAZI Germany seized Austria and Interpol with it, and took all its records to Berlin. It was reorganized immediately after the Second World War and is now based in Paris.

**In the bag.** Settled; made certain. The allusion is to game that has been shot and placed in the game bag. The expression is of US origin and dates from the 1920s.

**In the club.** Pregnant. The expression is short for 'in the pudding club', the 'pudding' being the foetus in the womb. *See also* BUN IN THE OVEN; UP THE DUFF.

**In the doghouse.** In trouble or disgrace, as a dog is confined to its kennel after misbehaving. The phrase is traditionally applied to an errant husband. In J.M. Barrie's PETER PAN (1904) Mr Darling lives in the dog kennel until his children return as a penance for his treatment of NANA. The term dates from the 1930s.

**In the frame.** Eligible. The allusion is either to the racetrack, where the names of the winning horses are displayed in a frame, or to snooker, where the balls ready for play are positioned in a frame. The phrase is often expanded as 'names in the frame' to refer to particular eligible individuals.

**In the front row.** In the best seats; in the place of privilege. The term applies specifically to the front row at a fashion show. A political equivalent exists in the House of Commons as the front bench, i.e. the foremost seats, occupied by members of the cabinet and shadow cabinet. Either term has potential for figurative use.

> 'You're either in the front row, or you're just at the show.' A friend at *Vogue* said the very same thing to me recently … And make no mistake, the front row it has to be. Fighting it out for a second- or third-row seat is pointless.
>
> *Sunday Times Magazine* (19 September 1999)

**In the Heat of the Night.** A film (1967) adapted by Stirling Silliphant from a novel by John Ball about the conflict that develops between a bigoted Mississippi sheriff (Bill Gillespie) and the African American detective (Virgil Tibbs) with whom he has to collaborate while investigating a racial murder. Directed by Norman Jewison and starring Rod Steiger as Gillespie and Sidney Poitier as Tibbs, the film is set in a sweltering cotton town, hence the title. Such was the political 'heat' involved in racist issues in Mississippi in the 1960s that it was felt necessary to make the film some distance away, in Illinois. The film won OSCARS for best picture and best actor (Steiger).

**In the house.** In rappers' slang, excellent, 'cool' (for an additional authentic touch, spell it 'in da house'). The usage arose in the late 1980s from the earlier sense of being present, and hence aware or 'hip'.

**In the loop.** Belonging to the circle of people who are influential or well informed. To be 'out of the loop' is conversely to be excluded from the circle of those in the know. The expression arose as US political jargon of the 1990s but can apply to a social, business or any other circle.

**In the Night Kitchen.** A picture book (1970) by the US illustrator Maurice Sendak (b.1928). A boy called Michael is mixed into a batter by three identical fat bakers (drawn to resemble the comedian Oliver Hardy) after he falls from his bed into a Night Kitchen. He manages to escape on a flying machine made of dough and returns to his bed. The inspiration for the book's title came from Sendak's childhood memory of a New York bakery that displayed the slogan 'We bake while you sleep!' The book has frequently been banned in the United States, on account of the nakedness of the boy.

**In the pipeline.** Forthcoming; about to happen; in the process of being prepared. The phrase dates from the 1950s and perhaps alludes to oil or gas that is processed and about to be delivered.

**In the right ballpark.** Approximately accurate; within reasonable bounds. A US phrase of the 1960s referring to a baseball stadium. *See also* BALLPARK FIGURE.

**In the sticks.** In a remote rural location; in the 'back of beyond'. 'The sticks' are the world of trees and nature. More specifically, in US theatrical jargon 'the sticks' refers to any town outside the regular touring circuit, far removed from New York. A headline in *Variety* for 17 July 1935 ran: 'Sticks nix hick pix', meaning that rural residents gave the thumbs down to films about farms.

**In this day and age.** Now. A meaningless piece of journalistic padding that apparently dates from the early 20th century and that has the merit of seeming more sonorous and dignified than it actually is. Cecil B. de Mille's film *This Day and Age* (1933) describes how, during an American youth week, boys put a gangster on trial and by his own methods force him to confess to murder. The movie was condemned by some at the time as an incitement to FASCISM.

'We knew drug-dealing was going on … but I thought that, in this day and age, you just had to learn to accept that sort of thing.'

*People* (4 December 1994)

**Intifada.** (Arabic, 'a jumping up'). This term for an Arab uprising or revolt, as a 'jumping up' in reaction to something, became familiar in the West from 1987, when the PLO began its campaign of sustained unrest in the Israeli-occupied WEST BANK and GAZA STRIP. The first Intifada ended with the Oslo Accords and the signing of the Israel–Palestine Declaration in Washington in 1993, which gave the Palestinians a degree of autonomy in the Occupied Territories. A second Intifada started in 2000, following the provocative visit of Ariel Sharon, then leader of the Israeli opposition, to the al-Aqsa mosque on the Temple Mount, Jerusalem, a Muslim holy place.

**Intranet.** A internal communications network belonging to a particular organization, and employing similar technology to that of the INTERNET.

**Invisible Man, (The).** The title of two very different novels. The first is a work of science fiction by H.G. Wells (1866–1946), published in 1897. In this story a scientist finds the secret of invisibility, which lures him into temptation. The first film version (1933), starring Claud Rains, was highly regarded, but its several sequels less so.

Another novel, lacking the 'The', was by the African American writer Ralph Ellison (1914–94). Published in 1952, it won the 1953 National Book Award for fiction. The novel tells the story of a Southern African American who moves to New York, participates in the struggle against white oppression, and ends up ignored and living in a coal hole.

I am an invisible man, I am a man of substance, of flesh and bone, fibre and liquids – and I might even be said to possess a mind. I am invisible, understand, simply because people refuse to see me.

*Invisible Man*, prologue

**In your face.** Bold and aggressive; blatant and provocative. The image is of a thing thrown or thrust directly into a person's face. The phrase originated partly among the African American population in the United States and partly from basketball jargon, in which a defensive player closely marking an attacker is said to be 'in the face of' that player. A spelling reflecting a colloquial pronunciation is 'in yer face'. *See also* GET OUT OF SOMEONE'S FACE.

**Iorek Byrnison.** The king of the armoured bears in Philip Pullman's trilogy HIS DARK MATERIALS. A pitiless warrior and master of metals (attributes symbolically combined in his mighty suit of armour), he is a force for good in the story and a staunch friend of its heroine Lyra.

**Ipcress File, The.** A film (1965) based on a spy thriller (1962) of the same title by the novelist Len Deighton (b.1929) about a reluctant counter-intelligence agent who finds himself caught up in a convoluted spy plot involving the kidnapping of top scientists. Starring Michael Caine as the antihero Harry Palmer (who is not named in the books), the film spawned two sequels, *Funeral in Berlin* (1966) and *Billion Dollar Brain* (1967). The Ipcress File of the title is a mysterious tape simply labelled 'Ipcress' that Palmer turns up during his investigations.

**iPod.** The proprietary name of various types of small, portable music players produced by Apple (*see* APPLE MACINTOSH). Larger versions use a hard disk to store data, while the most compact versions use a rewritable memory chip. Introduced in 2001, the iPod soon became a must-have item for cool youth, thanks to both its classically simple and elegant design and the fact that very large amounts of data can be downloaded onto it, facilitating the personalized portability of vastly more songs and other items than the previous generation of CD-players. The 'i', which may be short for INTERNET, was inherited from previous Apple products (e.g. iBook, iMac), while 'Pod' stands for '*p*ersonal *o*n demand'. *See also* MP3; PODCAST.

**IQ.** *See* INTELLIGENCE QUOTIENT.

**IRA.** The Irish Republican Army, a guerrilla force largely reorganized by Michael Collins (1890–1922; *see* BIG FELLA) from the former Irish Volunteers, which confronted the Royal Irish Constabulary and the BLACK AND TANS from 1919 to 1921. After the Irish Civil War (1922–3) extremists kept it in being as a secret organization and, although it was proscribed in 1936, the IRA continued to make occasional raids into Northern Ireland, in pursuit of its aim of establishing a united Irish republic. After a period of quiescence, violence steadily increased from the mid-1950s. From 1969 to 1994, when it announced a ceasefire, its commission of acts of terrorism in Northern Ireland, mainland Britain and elsewhere made a settlement of Northern Ireland's TROUBLES increasingly difficult. It ended the

ceasefire in 1996, when a bomb in London's DOCKLANDS killed 2 and injured 100, but announced its restoration in 1997.

The GOOD FRIDAY AGREEMENT of 1998 seemed to bring a peace settlement nearer, but the disarmament of the IRA (a process characterized as the 'DECOMMISSIONING' of their weapons) remained a sticking point and the deadlock was not broken by further discussions in the summer of 1999, despite the creation in December that year of Northern Ireland's first devolved government since 1974.The power-sharing assembly was suspended in February 2000 and DIRECT RULE reimposed after the IRA and other paramilitary groups failed to decommission their weapons by a deadline set by the British government. However, the IRA's decision to open their arms dumps to inspection by a team of inter-national observers allowed the assembly to recommence its functions in the early summer of 2000. The assembly was once again suspended in October 2002, this time over allegations of a SINN FÉIN spy ring in STORMONT (Sinn Féin being the IRA's political wing). On 28 July 2005 the IRA formally declared the 'armed struggle' over. Accusations of IRA involvement in general criminality, notably the huge Northern Bank Raid in 2004 (which netted £26.5 million) and the pub murder in 2005 of Robert McCartney by IRA members, have continued to dog the organization.

In the aftermath of the Good Friday Agreement there emerged two dissident Republican groups opposed to the Accord: the 'Real IRA' and the 'Continuity IRA', the former responsible for the Omagh bombing of 1998. The names of both groups reflect their claims to be the true inheritors of Irish Republican tradition. The Real IRA broke away from the Provisional IRA, while the Continuity IRA is associated with Republican Sinn Féin, a faction that broke away from Provisional Sinn Féin in the 1980s. The 'continuity' implied is that of strict Republican orthodoxy in keeping with the aims and methods of the instigators of the 1916 EASTER RISING. See also HILLSBOROUGH DECLARATION; PROVOS; STICKIES.

**Iran-Contra Affair.** A more formal name for Irangate. See GATE.

**Iraqi Freedom.** The US operational code name for its part in the 2003 invasion of Iraq. The UK military operation was code-named Telic and the Australian operation was Falconer. When President George W. Bush (DUBYA) was asked in December 2005 whether he thought the affair had gone as well as originally planned, he replied:

I think we were welcomed, but it was not a peaceful welcome.

See also COALITION OF THE WILLING; ENDURING FREEDOM; WAR ON TERROR.

**Irascibles.** A group of US artists who in 1950 protested against the exhibition policy of the Metropolitan Museum, New York, demanding the setting up of a department to show modern American art. Their number included many leading lights of ABSTRACT EXPRESSIONISM such as de Kooning, Newman, Pollock, Rothko and Still, and a subsequently much reproduced photograph of 15 of the original 18 members appeared in Life magazine on 15 January 1951.

**Irgun.** In full, Irgun Zvai Leumi (Hebrew, 'national military organization'), an underground anti-socialist Zionist military organization established by right-wing Jewish settlers in Palestine in 1931 as a rival organization to the HAGANAH. Its aim was to establish a Jewish state in Palestine, and to this end it carried out acts of terrorism against both Arabs and the British, who were administrators of the League of Nations mandate. Its leader from 1943 to 1948 was Menachem Begin (1913–92) the future prime minister of Israel (1977–83). The Irgun was responsible for the bomb attack on the King David Hotel in Jerusalem in 1946, which resulted in the deaths of 91 military and civilian personnel, including Britons, Arabs and Jews. The following year its commandos killed all 254 inhabitants of an Arab village (see DEIR YASSIN). The Irgun disbanded on the establishment of the State of Israel in 1948, and Begin founded the Herut ('freedom') Party. The STERN GANG was a splinter group of the Irgun.

**Irish** or **Belfast confetti.** Stones, bricks, etc. used as ammunition in a street fight. First recorded in 1913, the expression plays on a stereotypical view of the Irish as drunken brawlers, and as such is now decidedly politically incorrect.

**Irish Free State.** See FREE-STATERS.

**Irish Republican Army.** See IRA.

**Irish R.M., The.** A compendium (1956) of stories by E.O. Somerville (1858–1949) and her cousin Martin Ross (pen name of Violet Martin; 1862–1915), consisting of Some Experiences of an Irish R.M. (1899), Further Experiences of an Irish R.M. (1908) and In Mr Knox's Country (1915). The R.M. (resident magistrate) is Major Sinclair Yeates, appointed to Skebawn, Co. Cork, where he meets robust and ingenious opposition to his application of the law, while occasionally turning the tables on his tormentors.

**I, Robot.** The first volume of short stories (1950) by Isaac Asimov (1920–92), in which he promulgated his three 'laws of robotics', presaging the science of artificial intelligence.

**'Iron Ass' LeMay.** *See* BOMB THEM BACK INTO THE STONE AGE.

**Iron Brew.** A patent carbonated soft drink popular in Scotland and said to have curative properties with regard to a hangover. It originated in the early part of the 20th century under the impetus of the temperance movement, and derived some of its inspiration from the tradition of tonics and health drinks prepared by herbalists. The name is something of a misnomer, since it often contained no iron and was hardly a 'brew' in the traditional manner. A commercial brand, dubbed 'Scotland's other drink' (the prime being Scotch), is now sold under the registered name of Irn Bru. The first word of this represents 'eye-rin' as a local pronunciation of 'iron'.

**Iron Butterfly.** The nickname of the US singer and actress Jeanette MacDonald (1901–65), who teamed up with Nelson Eddy (1901–67) in a string of successful if high-camp screen musicals in the 1930s. The two were referred to as America's Sweethearts, or, less charitably, as the Iron Butterfly and the Singing Capon.

It is also the nickname (alternatively 'Steel Butterfly') of Imelda Marcos (b.1930), wife of President Ferdinand Marcos (1917–89) of the Philippines. As a young woman she had been a singer, and she was notorious for her vanity and greed. She was accused of benefiting from her husband's corrupt rule, for example by accumulating an astonishingly large collection of shoes. When her husband was ousted from power in 1986 she went into exile with him, but she subsequently returned to the Philippines, where she unsuccessfully ran for the presidency in 1992. She was subsequently charged with corruption and extortion, relating to the period of her husband's presidency.

In the 1960s a US rock group took the name Iron Butterfly and the nickname has sometimes also been applied to the straight-laced UK actress and singer Julie Andrews (b.1935). *See also* FILM STAR NICKNAMES.

**Iron Chancellor.** Originally the name given to Prince Otto von Bismarck (1815–98), the creator of the German Empire. A century later, Gordon Brown (b.1951), chancellor of the exchequer in the Labour government since it was elected in 1997, was also so dubbed for his proverbial frugality with the nation's resources. See also INCREDIBLE SULK; MISERY FROM THE MANSE.

**Iron Curtain.** The phrase denoting the barrier of secrecy created by the former USSR and its satellites along the Stettin–Trieste line, the communist countries east of this line having cut themselves off from western Europe after the Second World War. The name was popularized by Winston Churchill in his Fulton Speech (5 March 1946), but it was used previously in Germany by Josef Goebbels in *Das Reich* (25 February 1945) and by Churchill himself in a cable to President Truman (4 June 1945): 'What is to happen about Russia? … An iron curtain is drawn down upon that front.' It has earlier antecedents: Ethel Snowden used it in 1920 with reference to BOLSHEVIK Russia; Lord D'Abernon used it in 1925 with regard to the proposed Locarno Treaties; and in 1914 Elisabeth, queen of the Belgians, spoke of a 'bloody iron curtain' between her and the Germans. The phrase occurs in the Earl of Munster's journal as far back as 1819.

> From Stettin, in the Baltic, to Trieste, in the Adriatic, an iron curtain has descended across the Continent.
> WINSTON CHURCHILL: Fulton Speech (1946)

*See also* BAMBOO CURTAIN.

**Iron Guard.** (Romanian *Garda de fier*.) A Romanian fascist organization that constituted a major social and political force between 1930 and 1941. It evolved from the Legion of the Archangel Michael founded in 1927 by Corneliu Zela Codreanu, was committed to the 'Christian and radical' renovation of Romania, and fed on anti-Semitism and mystical nationalism. Repeated attempts to suppress it were unsuccessful until its final discrediting in 1941.

**Iron Lady.** The name bestowed on Margaret Thatcher (b.1925), when leader of the Conservative opposition in the House of Commons, by the Soviet Defence Ministry newspaper *Red Star* (24 January 1976). After she had warned the Commons of the increasing Russian threat to the West, the *Red Star* accused the 'Iron Lady' of trying to revive the COLD WAR, referring to her 'viciously anti-Soviet speech' and to 'the peace-loving policy of the Soviet Union'. Her speech (made on 19 January) had included the words: 'The Russians are bent on world dominance … the Russians put guns before butter.' Thatcher herself revelled in the label and on 31 January, in the course of a speech in her Finchley constituency, declared:

> Ladies and gentlemen, I stand before you tonight in my green chiffon evening gown, my face softly made up, my fair hair gently waved ... the Iron Lady of the Western World. Me? A Cold War warrior? Well, yes – if that is how they wish to interpret my defence of values, and freedoms fundamental to our way of life.

*See also* ATTILA THE HEN; COLD WAR WARRIOR; GUNS OR BUTTER; LEADERENE; SHE WHO MUST BE OBEYED.

**Iron lung.** An airtight metal cylinder that encloses a person's body and that provides artificial respiration in cases where the patient's respiratory muscles are paralysed, as in poliomyelitis. The artificial respirator, as it is more formally known, was the invention in 1927 of the brothers Cecil and Philip Drinker of Harvard University, Cambridge, Massachusetts.

**Iron Mike.** Originally, in the 1920s, a personification of an automated piloting device used on board ship or in an aircraft. The name was subsequently also used in the United States, from the 1950s, for an automatic baseball pitching machine, but it was introduced to a wider audience when it was adopted as a nickname of the US heavyweight boxer Mike Tyson (b.1966), a brutally powerful puncher and the youngest ever world heavyweight champion, notorious as much for his activities outside the boxing ring, including a prison term for rape, as for his boxing prowess.

**Ironside.** The chief of detectives in the San Francisco police force, with full name Robert Ironside. He was the creation of scriptwriter Collier Young and was played by Raymond Burr in the long-running television series named after him (1967–75). Although confined to a wheelchair, Ironside always gets his man. *See also* Perry MASON.

**ISBN.** The abbreviation of International Standard Book Number, a 10-digit number (from 1 January 2007, a 13-digit number) assigned to every book before publication. The system, necessitated by computerization, was introduced to Britain in 1967 as the SBN and in 1970 became the ISBN. The main part of an ISBN consists of three groups of digits identifying the geographic, language or other area of the work in question together with its publisher, title, edition and volume number. A single 'check digit' in the form of a final figure or letter is then added to this, as for a BARCODE.

**I shall return.** The famous words spoken on 20 March 1942 by the American soldier, General Douglas MacArthur (1880–1964), commander of US forces in the Philippines. He had just arrived in Australia, having escaped from the besieged American redoubt at Corregidor, which fell to the Japanese the following month. On 20 October 1944 MacArthur did return, retaking the islands. *See also* OLD SOLDIERS NEVER DIE.

**Ish kabbible.** An exclamation of indifference, nonchalance or the like, the equivalent of 'I should worry.' It is presumably of Yiddish origin, although the precise sense is obscure. Possibly none was ever intended, although the 'ish' is certainly 'I'. It was apparently introduced, and perhaps even invented, by the American Jewish comedienne Fanny Brice (1891–1951) in the 1930s.

**Ishmaelia.** The fictional African country featuring in Evelyn Waugh's novel *Scoop* (1938). It is a mountainous, isolated land to the south of Sudan, and its capital, a shoddy place, is

Jacksonville. There is another town, Laku, shown prominently on the map, but it cannot be visited as it does not exist. The Ishmaelites are Christians, but polygamy is still practised. The people themselves are fond of oratory in all forms, whether sermons, lectures or even charity appeals. *See also* FIRST LINES OF NOVELS.

**Is it a bird? Is it a plane?** A slogan associated with the punch line 'No, it's Superman!' However, the preamble to the US radio show from the 1940s actually went:

> Faster than a speeding bullet! … Look! Up in the sky! It's a bird! It's a plane! It's Superman!

**Islington Man.** A middle-class socially aware person of left-wing views, regarded as typical of the wealthier sections of the North London borough of Islington. This is a usage that is more jibe than compliment.

> Just as Essex Man … represented the 1980s, Islington Man – more properly Islington Person – may turn out to be the most potent composite of the late 1990s.
> *Independent on Sunday* (17 July 1994)

**ISP.** In computing, the abbreviation of 'internet service provider' as a company that provides, usually for a fee, access to the INTERNET and E-MAIL services. These are often companies that also provide normal telephone services. Connecting to an ISP used to involve telephone wires and cables, but the development of wireless access technology such as BLUETOOTH is making that obsolete.

**Istanbul.** Turkey's former capital officially received its present name in 1930. Until then it was known outside Turkey as Constantinople, after Constantine the Great, who rebuilt ancient Byzantium and made it his capital in AD 330. The European part of Istanbul contains the old city of Stamboul. All three names are in fact identical, although Istanbul and Stamboul have lost the first syllable of Constantine's name.

**Is that a gun in your pocket, or are you just pleased to see me?** A provocative and much quoted line traditionally ascribed to the raunchy American film actress Mae West (1892–1980), although not traced in her *oeuvre*.

**Is the pope a Catholic?** *See* DO BEARS SHIT IN THE WOODS?

**Is your journey really necessary?** An official anti-travel slogan in the Second World War, originally issued in 1939 to dissuade evacuated civil servants from going home for Christmas. The question was put to civilians generally from 1941, when the government decided against the introduction of any positive measure, such as a ban on travel without a permit over more than 80km (50 miles), but instead relied on voluntary compliance. To encourage this it took to making travel uncomfortable by reducing the number of trains.

**IT.** Information technology, the use of computer and telecommunications systems for storing, receiving and distributing information. The rise of the INTERNET and the WORLD WIDE WEB has elaborated the phrase, in the early 21st century, into ICT (information and communications technology), and the subject has became part of the school curriculum.

**It Ain't Half Hot Mum.** A television SITCOM screened in eight series from 1974 to 1981 and depicting the exploits of a Royal Artillery Concert Party based in India in the Second World War. It was written by Jimmy Perry (*see* DAD'S ARMY) and based on his own wartime experiences in India. The focus was the antagonistic relationship between Sergeant-Major Williams, played by Windsor Davies, and his charges, who included the somewhat feminine 'Gloria' Beaumont, played by Melvyn Hayes, the intellectual pianist Graham, played by John Clegg, the diminutive lead singer 'Lofty' Sugden, acted by Don Estelle, and Christopher Mitchell's dense Parkins, whose use of the phrase 'It ain't half hot Mum' in his letters home gave the title of the series. Michael Bates blacked up to play the central character of Rangi Ram, an Indian who lauds everything British – a characterization that to some viewers seemed the embodiment of political incorrectness (*see* POLITICAL CORRECTNESS).

**Italia irredenta.** (Italian, 'unredeemed Italy'.) Those parts of Italy remaining under foreign domination after the war of 1866. The phrase gave the name of the Irredentists, the Italian patriots who sought to deliver Italian lands from foreign rule in the late 19th and early 20th centuries. Many areas at that time were still controlled by Austria. The phrase dates from the early years of the 20th century.

**Italian salute.** In American English, an obscene gesture of derision or contempt, in which one arm is bent and jerked abruptly upwards while the other hand grasps the bicep. It originated in Italy and was imported into the US by immigrants.

**It all depends what you mean by ...** The perennial catchphrase of Professor C.E.M. Joad, panel member on *The* BRAINS TRUST, when answering questions. The phrase is often heard in the mouths of philosophers, lawyers and politicians:

> It all depends on what the meaning of the word 'is' is.
>
> PRESIDENT BILL CLINTON: while giving testimony regarding his relationship with Monica Lewinsky to a grand jury in 1998

**ITALY.** *See* LOVERS' ACRONYMS.

**Itchy feet.** To have or get itchy feet is to be restless and to have a desire to travel.

> When I'm on the road for any length of time, I start to look forward to the odd day in the office. Then, as soon as I've been cooped up for more than two days, I get itchy feet.
>
> *The Times* (14 February 2000)

**Item.** A colloquialism for a couple, who if famous will provide more than one item of gossip for the media. The term dates from the 1980s.

> Natalie [Appleton] was quoted in the *Sun* as saying: 'We want to remain friends but we are no longer an item.'
>
> *heat* (13–19 January 2000)

**'It' Girl.** The American film actress Clara Bow (1905–65), an embodiment of the FLAPPER. She was so promoted following her appearance in the film *It* (1927), based on Elinor Glyn's novel titled by this word, itself already in use as a euphemism for sex appeal. The term has since been applied by the media to other PARTY GIRLS and supposed sex symbols. *See also* OOMPH.

> The tattlers called Tara [Palmer-Tomkinson] an It Girl, meaning a professional partygoer, a member of a privileged, hedonistic sub-cult among Thatcher's children.
>
> *The Times* (17 June 1999)

**It had to happen.** A more or less meaningless journalistic phrase used to introduce a news item or piece of gossip. The implication is that it was an inevitable consequence of something.

**I, the Jury.** A crime novel (1947) by 'Mickey' (Frank Morrison) Spillane (1918–2006), in which he introduced his hardboiled detective Mike HAMMER. At the denouement Hammer addresses the murderess, unmasked and also naked: 'I'm the jury, now, and the judge, and I have a promise to keep. Beautiful as you are, as much as I almost loved you, I sentence you to death.' There were two tough film versions, directed respectively by Harry Essex (1953) and Richard T. Heffron (1982), the latter more in line with the tone of the original.

**-itis.** A suffix of Greek origin properly used to form the name of an inflammatory disease, the first part of the word naming the organ affected. Thus hepatitis is inflammation of the liver, arthritis of the joints and appendicitis of the appendix. In the 20th century the suffix came to be appended to any word or phrase regarded as causing a figurative 'disease', so that politicians are periodically prone to 'electionitis' and schoolchildren become feverish with 'end-of-term-itis'.

When in 1997 Mr Ashdown attacked Labour's spending plans, Peter Mandelson savaged him for 'oppositionitis' and he shut up.

*The Times* (22 September 1999)

**It is not.** A phrase common in an idiosyncratic linguistic inversion popular in the 1990s, the preceding word usually being a noun or adjective and the whole designed for emphasis, often by way of a comparison. Thus a run-down resort might be described as 'Tuscany it is not' or a poor landscape painter derided as 'Constable he is not'. The verb is invariably some form of 'to be', and when a contrast is involved an affirmative statement may precede the negative. The contraction 'isn't' may be used.

A virgin home buyer I may be. Stupid I am not.

*The Times* (14 August 1999)

**It'll Be Alright On The Night.** A popular long-running television series consisting of a series of amusing or embarrassing 'out-takes' from the cutting room floor, first shown in 1977 and always good-humouredly presented by Denis Norden. The title is an old theatrical catchphrase, as an optimistic reassurance that however dire the dress rehearsal all will go well when it comes to the first performance. The populist spelling of 'Alright' has concerned some pedants.

**ITMA.** (Initials of *It's That Man Again.*) This highly popular radio comedy series did much to brighten the dreariness of the BLACKOUT years in Britain during the Second World War. It was devised and maintained by the comedian Tommy Handley (1896–1949), the scripts being written by Ted Kavanagh, and ran from 1939 until Handley's death. Among the characters were the char MRS MOPP, Funf the spy, Claude and Cecil the polite handymen, Ali Oop the saucy SEASIDE POSTCARDS seller, the bibulous Colonel Chinstrap, Signor Soso the funny foreigner, and the lugubrious laundress Mona Lott. Each character had a memorable catchphrase. Mrs Mopp's was 'Can I do yer now, sir?', Colonel Chinstrap's was 'I don't mind if I do', Mona Lott's was 'It's being so cheerful as keeps me going', Funf's was 'Ziss iss Funf speakink.' Mrs Mopp's farewell was 'Ta-ta for now', abbreviated as 'TTFN'. 'That man' was Handley. Kavanagh took the full title from a *Daily Express* headline of 2 May 1939 referring to Hitler.

It is sometimes forgotten that the full title of the opening broadcast, It's That Man Again, was merely the use of a catchphrase already established. Hitler might not yet, on July 12, 1939, have made one territorial grab too many. But he had long exceeded what even the patient British thought was any reasonable speech ration.

*The Times* (18 September 1958)

**It's a Knockout.** A series of televised open-air comic team games screened from 1966 to 1982 and set in towns competing for the right to represent Britain in the European finals of *Jeux sans frontières*. The title puns on the two senses of 'knockout', as a sporting elimination on the one hand and a 'hit' on the other. The programme's most notorious manifestation was the one-off *It's a Royal Knockout* of 1987, organized by Prince Edward, in which he and other royal personages participated to general derision. The series was revived in 1999 in a pale imitation of the original.

**It's a Wonderful Life.** A film (1946) based on the story 'The Greatest Gift' by Philip Van Doren Stern, about a suicide who is dissuaded from killing himself by an angel who shows him what the world would have been like without him. Directed by Frank Capra and starring James Stewart, it was hailed as one of the most life-affirming movies ever made. Philip Van Doren Stern's original story was penned to send to his friends as a Christmas card.

**It's life, Jim, but not as we know it.** The oracular pronouncement of Dr SPOCK, addressed to Captain James T. Kirk, on encountering an alien life-form in the long-running space saga STAR TREK. It was uttered in the first television series and established itself as his catchphrase. It appeared in *Star Trek: the Motion Picture* (1979) as 'It's life, Captain, but not life as we know it.' It has become a template for referring to anything that presents itself in an unfamiliar guise:

It was journalism, Jim, but not as I knew it.

ANDREW MARR: *My Trade* (2004)

**It's not over until the fat lady sings.** *See* the OPERA ISN'T OVER UNTIL THE FAT LADY SINGS.

**It's the economy, stupid.** A slogan devised by James Carville, Democratic campaign manager in 1992, during the lead-up to the presidential election in which Carville's boss, Bill Clinton, was victorious. Carville was referring to the recession that the United States had entered under President Bush, and emphasizing that this was the issue above all others that voters would respond to. The slogan has been frequently invoked by political commentators ever since, for example in relation to the stability and success of the British economy under Gordon Brown, chancellor of the exchequer since 1997.

**It takes two to tango.** Both parties in a situation are equally responsible for it. The reference may be to anything from a simple agreement to an act of adulterous sexual intercourse. The tango is usually regarded as a sexually charged dance, perhaps partly from the suggestion of 'tangle'. The phrase became popular from the 1950s.

There are lots of things you can do alone!

But, it takes two to tango.

AL HOFFMAN and DICK MANNING: 'Takes Two to Tango' (song) (1952)

**IVF.** *See* TEST-TUBE BABY.

**Ivory tower.** To live in an ivory tower is to live in seclusion, divorced from everyday life, and wilfully or unwittingly excluding the harsh realities of the outside world. The phrase is first recorded in English in 1911 as a translation of French *tour d'ivoire*, a term used by the critic and poet Charles Sainte-Beuve to refer to his fellow poet Alfred de Vigny. The English phrase was then used by Henry James for the title of his novel *The Ivory Tower* (1916), and was popularized by the writings of Hart Crane, Ezra Pound, H.G. Wells, Aldous Huxley and others.

Et Vigny plus secret,

Comme en sa tour d'ivoire, avant midi rentrait.

(And Vigny more discreet,

As if in his ivory tower, retired before noon.)

CHARLES SAINTE-BEUVE: *Les Pensées d'août, à M. Villemain* (1837)

**Ivy League.** The eight US universities that have a similar academic and social reputation to Oxford and Cambridge in England. They are all in the northeastern states and are, with year of foundation: Harvard (1636), Yale (1701), Pennsylvania (1740), Princeton (1746), Columbia (1754), Brown (1764), Dartmouth (1769) and Cornell (1853). The Ivy League is also the name of the athletic conference for intercollegiate (American) football and other sports to which they belong. Various explanations have been offered to account for the name, such as a derivation in the Roman numeral IV for an early sports league formed by four of them, but it seems likely that the allusion is simply to the ivy-clad walls that the buildings of some of them have or had. The term is first recorded in the 1930s. *See also* SEVEN SISTERS.

The fates which govern [football] play among the ivy colleges and academic boiler-factories alike seem to be going around the circuit.

*New York Herald Tribune* (16 October 1933)

**I want to be alone.** A phrase forever associated with the Swedish film actress Greta Garbo (1905–90), who on the whole managed to keep her private life private. The phrase was already associated with Garbo by the time she spoke it in the film *Grand Hotel* (1932), although there appears to be no evidence that she had actually said it in this form before. In an interview in *Life* magazine (24 January 1955), Garbo clarified the matter:

I only said, 'I want to be *let* alone.'

**IWW.** *See* WOBBLIES.

**Izvestia.** (Russian, 'news'). The official newspaper of the government of the former Soviet Union, founded in 1917 as the organ of the revolution. In 1991, when the Soviet Union collapsed, *Izvestia* became an independent newspaper. *See also* PRAVDA.

# J

**Jackal, The.** A journalistic name for the Venezuelan-born assassin Illich Ramirez Sanchez (b.1949), who himself used the *nom de guerre* Carlos. He has worked with various terrorist gangs in different countries. In the 1970s he was involved in various acts of international terrorism in the cause of Palestinian liberation, including the 1972 massacre at Tel Aviv airport and the 1975 kidnapping of oil ministers at the OPEC meeting in Vienna. In 1997 he was sentenced to life imprisonment by a French court for the murder of two policemen in Paris in 1975. The nickname is drawn from Frederick Forsyth's thriller *The* DAY OF THE JACKAL (1971), whose central character is a professional assassin hired to kill President de Gaulle. A forgettable remake of the 1973 film appeared in 1997, entitled *The Jackal*.

**Jackanory.** A long-running series of stories for young children read on television from 1965 by various famous actors and actresses. The title represents modern rhyming slang for 'story'.

**Jackie O.** A nickname of Jacqueline Bouvier Kennedy Onassis (1929–94), the glamorous widow of President John F. Kennedy. She married Greek shipping magnate Aristotle Onassis (1906–75) in 1968, he having cast off his long-term mistress, opera diva Maria Callas. *See also* CAMELOT; JACK THE LAD; JACK THE ZIPPER; JFK; THEATRE OF CRUELTY.

**Jacko.** The nickname of the US pop singer and songwriter Michael Jackson (b.1958). His often eccentric behaviour, and persistent speculation aroused by the curious change in the colour and shape of his face, led to the nickname being extended by the press to WACKO JACKO.

'Jacko' was also the nickname of the British golfer Tony Jacklin (b.1944).

**Jack the Lad.** A self-assured and carefree young man, especially when bold and brash. The nickname is said to have been that of the thief Jack Sheppard (1702–24), the subject of numerous ballads and popular plays. He was imprisoned four times and on each occasion effected a spectacular escape, even when manacled to the floor of his cell in solitary confinement. After his fifth arrest he was hanged, reputedly before a gathering of some 200,000 people. The popular hornpipe in Sir Henry Wood's *Fantasia on British Sea Songs* (1905), which is traditionally performed at the LAST NIGHT OF THE PROMS, is known as *Jack's the Lad*, but here Jack is a 'tar'.

**Jack the Zipper.** A posthumous nickname given to President John ('Jack') Fitzgerald Kennedy (1917–63) after it emerged that during his period of office (1961–3), despite being married to a beautiful wife (the future JACKIE O), he had frequent sexual liaisons in the White House with a succession of young women visitors, including, it has been rumoured, Marilyn MONROE. The name puns on the nickname of the unidentified Victorian serial killer Jack the Ripper, who murdered and mutilated at least seven women prostitutes in the East End of London in 1888. *See also* ACTION PAINTING; JFK.

**Jacuzzi.** The 'whirlpool' bath takes its name from its Italian-born American inventor, Candido Jacuzzi (1903–86), who devised it in 1949 for his seven-year-old son, a victim of rheumatoid arthritis. He subsequently patented his invention and began to market the finished product in the early 1950s as a hydromassage unit for bathtubs of conventional size. The whirlpool pump system that evolved was subsequently incorporated into specially large baths, known as 'hot tubs'.

**Jaffa cake.** A small sponge cake coated in chocolate and with a jelly-type filling made from Jaffa oranges. Jaffa (Haifa), on the Mediterranean coast of Israel, is the biblical Joppa.

**Jai alai.** A game like pelota played with a hard ball and a basket-like racket strapped to the arm. It is of Basque origin, in which language its name means 'jolly feast', and it was introduced to the United States at the World's Fair in St Louis in 1904. The name is pronounced 'high-a-lie'.

**Jailbait.** A boy or girl below the AGE OF CONSENT, sexual intercourse with whom would constitute statutory rape and in most cases result in the jailing of the perpetrator.

**Jailhouse Rock.** The title of a rock 'n' roll film and its title song, sung by Elvis Presley, the KING, and released in 1957. The song was written by Jerry Leiber (b.1933) and Mike Stoller (b.1933). The possibly homosexual implication of the words appears to have been lost on Elvis himself.

**Jalopy.** A dilapidated old car. The word is US in origin and dates from the 1920s. Its derivation is unknown, but it could be partly imitative of the car's unsteady progress while also suggesting a blend of 'jolt' and 'lollop'.

> We got a ride from a couple of young fellows – wranglers, teenagers, country boys in a put-together jalopy.
>
> JACK KEROUAC: *On the Road*, Pt I, ch. 3 (1957)

**Jamaica Inn.** A hotel in the middle of Bodmin Moor, near the Cornish village of Bolventor. In earlier centuries it was a coaching inn, and its romantically isolated position inspired the novelist Daphne du Maurier (1907–89) to make it the focus of her historical romance *Jamaica Inn* (1936). In the story the inn is the centre of the activities of a gang of smugglers, while divided loyalties inform the romantic aspects of the plot. A stilted film version (1939), starring Charles Laughton and Maureen O'Hara, was directed by Alfred Hitchcock.

**Jam and Jerusalem.** A traditional epithet of the Women's Institute. The movement originated in Canada in 1897 and was introduced to Britain in 1915 by a Canadian, Mrs Alfred Watt (1868–1948), who founded a branch in Anglesey. The aim of the first WI members was to help the war effort, and an early lecture was on jam-making. A competition was held in the 1920s to find a theme song. No decision was made, but Hubert Parry's *Jerusalem* (1916), a setting of William Blake's poem, was sung at the 1924 annual WI meeting and has been associated with the movement ever since. WI stalls selling homemade jam are still a feature at weekly markets.

**Jamdung.** A Jamaican nickname for the island of Jamaica, punning on a local pronunciation of 'jam down' and alluding to the oppression of ordinary Jamaicans by their political masters.

**Jammy dodger.** A type of small cake with a jam filling. 'Dodger' was originally a US term for a hard-baked corn-cake, but in the early 20th century it came to apply to other kinds of bread and cake. The origin is probably in a dialect word 'dodge' meaning 'piece', 'lump'.

**Jane.** A strip cartoon heroine popular in the Second World War. She was created by the artist Norman Pett in 1932 for a strip in the *Daily Mirror*. She began as a reasonably recognizable BRIGHT YOUNG THING, but in the war years she progressed to more exotic roles, in many of which she managed to lose most of her clothes. The newspaper strip ran until 1959, but she was revived in 1982 for a semi-animated television series in which she was played by Glynis Barber. The comic strip was also the inspiration for the 1988 film *Jane and the Lost City*.

**Janet and John.** The stereotypical two children of a middle-class British family. They take their names from the *Janet and John* graded readers for small children first published in 1949 and described at the time by their publishers as 'true to the best in the life of modern children'. The series was adopted in British primary schools as late as the 1970s before it fell out of use. In 2001 an updated series was republished.

**Jankers.** A military nickname for a punishment. The term dates from the First World War but is of uncertain origin. A possible source is 'jangle', referring to the locking of a prisoner in a cell.

**Janus word.** A word that has two opposite meanings, such as 'cleave' (both 'stick' and 'split') and CHUFFED. The allusion is to Janus, the Roman god of doorways and gates, who is represented with two faces, one looking forwards, the other back.

**JAP.** *See* JEWISH PRINCESS.

**Japanimation.** *See* ANIME.

**Jarhead.** American military slang for a US Marine. It originated in the Second World War and is said to refer to the Marines' blue dress uniform with its high collar, said to resemble a Mason jar, the type of glass jar with a metal screwcap used for bottling fruit, developed by John Landis Mason in 1858. The term jarhead is also taken to refer to the severely cropped hairstyle favoured by the Marines. Anthony Swofford gave the title *Jarhead* to his 2003 memoir of serving with the Marines in the First GULF WAR (1991). This became the basis of a film (2005) with the same title, directed by Sam Mendes.

Earlier than the Second World War, the word 'jughead' was applied by the US Marines to any member of the US Army. This usage is first recorded in 1933, and may derive from the mule mascot of the US Army football team. The slang 'jughead' for a mule or horse with an oversized head goes back to the late 19th century, such a head being thought to reflect the animal's stubborn and unintelligent nature.

**Jarrow Crusade.** *See* HUNGER MARCH.

**Java.** The proprietary name of a computer programming language used to create networking applications, especially interactive elements within WORLD WIDE WEB pages. The name alludes to Java coffee, a favourite drink of many US computer programmers, and was chosen to suggest the richness and strength of the language.

**Javal, Camille.** A name stated by many reference works to be the original name of the French film actress Brigitte Bardot (b.1934). The misinformation is given in such otherwise reputable authorities as David Thomson's *A Biographical Dictionary of Film* (1994) and *The Penguin Biographical Dictionary of Women* (1998) and even appeared in earlier editions of Leslie Halliwell's famous *Halliwell's Who's Who in the Movies* (1999). In reality the name is that of the character Bardot played in *Le Mépris* (1963), a film based on Alberto Moravia's novel *Il Disprezzo* (1954), but cinema historians seized on it and chose to promote it as her 'real' name. The facts of the matter are given in Jeffrey Robinson's *Bardot: An Intimate Portrait* (1994).

**Jaw-dropping.** Amazing. A person struck with amazement or other strong emotion may well drop their jaw and gape open-mouthed. An extreme reaction of this kind is sometimes expressed in a kind of cartoon imagery by saying that 'their jaw hit the ground'.

**Jaw-jaw.** To talk; to discuss; to negotiate. The slang term comes from a speech made by British prime minister Harold Macmillan (SUPERMAC) at Canberra, Australia, on 30 January 1958: 'Jaw-jaw is better than war-war.' Macmillan was echoing Winston Churchill, who had uttered the phrase 'To jaw-jaw is always better than to war-war' at the White House on 26 June 1954. The slang term 'jaw' on its own (meaning much the same thing) dates from the mid-18th century.

**Jaws.** A film (1975) based on a novel of the same title by Peter Benchley (the grandson of the humorist Robert Benchley) about a man-eating great white shark that terrorizes a small seaside resort on the western seaboard of the United States. The title of Benchley's book was a last-minute inspiration that neither author nor publisher was immediately very happy with. Previous suggestions had included *Great White*, *The Shark*, *Leviathan Rising*, *The Jaws of Death*, *A Silence in the Water* and the rather less seriously intended *What's That Noshin' on My Laig?* Superfluous film sequels were *Jaws 2* (1978), *Jaws 3-D* (1983) and *Jaws: The Revenge* (1987).

Just when you thought it was safe to go back in the water.
Publicity slogan for the sequels to *Jaws*

**Jaws of Life.** An US proprietary name for a hydraulic device shaped like a pair of scissors in which the jaws are used to prise apart the wreckage of crashed vehicles to rescue people trapped inside. The name is probably based on KISS OF LIFE. The device dates from the 1970s.

**Jaywalker.** A person who crosses or walks in a street thoughtlessly, regardless of passing traffic. The word alludes both to the bird, which hops in an erratic fashion, and to the jay that is a foolish person. The term is of US origin and dates from the early 20th century. A periodic series of half-hour television documentaries on social and religious matters presented by Susan Jay in the 1970s was inevitably titled *Jaywalking* in the punning manner beloved of television producers.

**Jazz.** A type of dance music originating in the folk music of the African Americans of the cotton fields. It first developed in New Orleans and reached Chicago by 1914 where it gained its name. It is characterized by syncopation and the noisy use of percussion instruments, together with the trombone, trumpet and saxophone. Its impact grew steadily and it has had many notable exponents. The name has been somewhat loosely appropriated by popular dance orchestras playing their own conception of the jazz idiom.

The origins of the word 'jazz' (first recorded in 1913) continue to remain mysterious. It emerged from African-American English, apparently originally in the sense 'copulation', so determined but ultimately unconvincing attempts have been made to find a source in a West African language. The underlying scenario of the word crossing the Atlantic in the slave ships first appeared in a 1917 article in the New York *Sun*, but it seems to have been purely the invention of a press agent.

*See also* ALL THAT JAZZ; BLUES; BOOGIE-WOOGIE; JAZZ AGE; SWING.

**Jazz Age.** The era, especially in the United States, between the end of the First World War in 1918 and the WALL STREET CRASH in 1929 that marked the onset of the GREAT DEPRESSION. The term, popularized by F. Scott Fitzgerald (1896–1940) in the title of a short-story collection, *Tales of the Jazz Age* (1922), reflected the growing popularity of JAZZ in the 1920s. The period was one of relative prosperity and, for the middle-class young at least, liberation from earlier social and sexual mores, for this was the era of the emancipated young woman, the FLAPPER. *See also* ROARING TWENTIES.

**Jedi, The.** A fictional ancient knighthood that figures in the STAR WARS films. The name is based on that of Jed or Jeddak, the lords of Barsoom in Edgar Rice Burroughs' *A Princess of Mars* (1912).

**Jeep.** The registered name of an all-purpose car suited to rugged terrain first developed by the United States during the Second World War and known as GP, i.e. General Purpose, the US Army designation for this type of car. The name probably derives from this, although it was influenced by 'Eugene the Jeep', a versatile cartoon character that had a cry of 'Jeep'. It was introduced in the comic strip 'Thimble Theater' (the forerunner of POPEYE) by the cartoonist Elzie C. Segar in 1936 and used briefly for the name of a commercial vehicle the following year. According to another account, the name came from the exclamation, 'Jeepers creepers!', made by Major General George Lynch, US Army chief of infantry, when he first rode in a prototype of the vehicle at Fort Myer, Virginia, in 1939, and accordingly adopted then by the vehicle's designer, Charles H. Payne. The experimental models were also called Beeps, Peeps and Blitz Buggies, but the name Jeep arrived to stay in 1941. Jeep is now the marque of a range of SPORT-UTILITY VEHICLES and is sometimes applied generically to such vehicles.

**Jeeves.** Bertie WOOSTER's dignified and loyal butler in the books by P.G. Wodehouse. He is as intelligent as his master is vacuous, and as soberly resourceful as he is cheerfully inept. Wodehouse took his name from a Warwickshire county cricketer, Percy Jeeves (1888–1916), killed in the First World War. The name is generally applied to any loyal manservant or faithful personal attendant. Jeeves has appeared in a number of films and television series, the latter including *The World of Wooster* (1965–8), in which he was played by the urbane Dennis Price, and *Jeeves and Wooster* (1990–3), in which Jeeves was portrayed by Stephen Fry and Bertie Wooster by Hugh Laurie.

**Jeffrey Bernard is Unwell.** A play (1991) by Keith Waterhouse (b.1929) in which an alcoholic journalist recalls his past career in Fleet Street. Jeffrey Bernard (1932–97) was a real Fleet Street journalist famed for his ill-health as much as for the dissolute ways that so grievously affected his health. The title refers to the announcement that regularly appeared in the place of his *Spectator* column when he was 'indisposed'.

**'Je ne regrette rien'.** (French, 'I regret nothing'). The refrain of the song '*Non, je ne regrette rien*', written in 1960 by Michel Vaucaire and sung by Edith Giovanna Gassion (1915–63), whose tiny stature suggested the stage name Piaf, the Parisian slang for 'sparrow'. The song is similar in sentiment to 'MY WAY', and is almost as popular with drunken old has-beens in karaoke bars.

**Jennifer's Ear.** *See* WAR OF MARGARET'S SHOULDER.

**Jennings.** The spirited schoolboy hero of a long series of books by Anthony Buckeridge (1912–2004), starting with *Jennings Goes to School* (1950). He attends Linbury Court preparatory school, where he gets into a number of comic scrapes, and his best friend is Darbishire, a staid, bespectacled foil to his unruly persona. His full name is John Christopher Timothy Jennings, and he first appeared in the radio play *Jennings Learns the Ropes*, broadcast on 16 October 1948 in CHILDREN'S HOUR. The books containing his adventures and antics have been translated into a number of languages, and in French he is known as Bennett, in German as Fredy and in Norwegian as Stompa.

**Jerry.** Since the First World War a nickname for a German or Germans collectively. Also an old colloquialism for a chamber pot, said by some to allude to the shape of an upturned German helmet, although the word may actually be a shortening of 'jeroboam'. *See also* FRITZ.

**Jerrycan.** A 4½-gallon- (20.5-litre) petrol or water container, which would stand rough handling and stack easily, developed by the Germans for the AFRIKA KORPS in the Second World War. It was borrowed by the British in Libya and became the standard unit of fuel replenishment throughout the Allied armies. The name is an allusion to its origin.

**Jersey, Beast of.** *See* BEAST OF JERSEY.

**Jersey Lily.** The nickname of the British actress and famous beauty Lillie Langtry (1853–1929), who was born as Emilie Charlotte le Breton on the island of Jersey in the Channel Islands. Her nickname comes from the title of a portrait of her by John Everett Millais (1829–96), in which she is holding a Jersey lily. In 1874 she married Edward Langtry, and two years after his death in 1897 she married Hugo de Bathe, who became a baronet in 1907, making her Lady de Bathe. There was a sensation in 1881 when she made her stage debut – she was the first society lady to embark on a stage career. Among her admirers was the Prince of Wales, the future Edward VII.

**Jerusalem Bible.** A modern Roman Catholic translation of the Bible, published in 1966 as the English version of the French *La Bible de Jérusalem*, so called as the work of the faculty of the *École Biblique* in Jerusalem, a Dominican biblical and archaeological graduate school founded in 1890. The *New Jerusalem Bible*, based on the revised French edition of 1973, appeared in 1985, with some books extensively retranslated to give a more readable style.

**Jesus, more popular than.** *See* MORE POPULAR THAN JESUS.

**Jesus boots, shoes** or **slippers.** Simple sandals, of the kind that Jesus is popularly portrayed as wearing. The terms are of US origin and date from the 1940s.

> He [rock singer Mick Hucknall] wears Jesus sandals, incontinence trousers and a scruffy white shirt. Oddly, he doesn't look like a vagrant.
>
> *heat* (7–13 October 1999)

***Jesus Christ Superstar.*** *See* ROCK OPERA.

**Jesus freak.** A fervent Christian evangelist, especially one adopting a lifestyle similar to that of a HIPPIE. The term originated in the United States and dates from the 1970s.

> On leaving … she [Victoria Adams, of the SPICE GIRLS] was accosted by a proud Jesus Freak in the car park, telling her that she needed God in her life.
>
> *heat* (20–26 January 2000)

**Jesus movement** or **revolution.** A Protestant fundamentalist (*see* FUNDAMENTALISM) movement in the United States in the 1960s. It consisted mainly of young people who spread the Christian message independently of any established churches or organizations and had a peculiarly US flavour. *See also* CHILDREN OF GOD.

**Jesus nut.** A jocular term among helicopter pilots, engineers, etc. for the large retaining nut that fastens a helicopter's rotor-blade assembly to its mast. Without it the aircraft would be in serious trouble.

**Jesus shoes** or **slippers.** *See* JESUS BOOTS.

**Jesus wept!** A general and blasphemous oath, current from the 1920s (the eminently respectable BBC commentator Richard Dimbleby shocked the nation in the early 1960s by using it on the air, unaware that his microphone was live). The words are those of the shortest verse in the Bible (John 11:35) in a passage describing the raising of Lazarus.

**'Je t'aime … moi non plus'.** A notorious pop song written in 1967 by the dissolute, chain-smoking French singer Serge Gainsbourg (1928–91). The song was originally written as a duet for Gainsbourg and Brigitte Bardot, but the latter's husband refused to allow its release because of the sounds of sexual groaning it contained. Gainsbourg then re-recorded the song with his girlfriend Jane Birkin. The resulting record, with background noises of orgasm, was banned by the BBC and condemned by the Vatican. The song's French title means 'I love you … nor do I.'

**Jet lag.** The lassitude and sense of temporal disorientation experienced after a long flight across different time zones.

The sufferer's BIOLOGICAL CLOCK does not adjust to the new time for some days but lags behind it. The phenomenon arose with the development of long-distance flights by passenger jet in the 1960s. Opinions vary regarding the best remedy for the disturbance.

**Jet set.** Wealthy and fashionable people who travel widely for business or pleasure, typically by jet. The expression dates from the 1950s and generally superseded the earlier 'smart set'.

***Jeux sans frontières.*** *See* IT'S A KNOCKOUT.

**Jew canoe.** A decidedly non-politically correct US slang term, dating from the early 1970s, for a large luxurious car, especially a Cadillac, as supposedly driven by rich Jews. Alternative formulations are 'Jew buggy' and 'Jewish submarine'. In the 1980s the term crossed the Atlantic to be applied to Jaguar cars.

***Jewel in the Crown, The.*** The first (1966) in the Raj Quartet of novels by Paul Scott (1920–78), set in the five years leading up to the independence of India in 1947. 'The Jewel in Her Crown' is a painting of Queen Victoria with some of her Indian subjects, owned by the elderly mission schools' supervisor in Mayapore, who commits suicide after her house is ransacked by a mob. Events in Mayapore are a microcosm of what will happen nationally during the next few years. The remaining three novels are *The Day of the Scorpion* (1968), *The Towers of Silence* (1971) and *A Division of Spoils* (1975). A stunningly scenic televised version (1985), with star performances by Peggy Ashcroft, Susan Wooldridge, Art Malik, Tim Piggott-Smith, Geraldine James, Charles Dance and Rachel Kempson, rightly won an International EMMY for 'Best Drama'. *See also* FIRST LINES OF NOVELS.

**Jewish Alps, The.** A jocular US nickname for the Catskill Mountain resort area, in southeastern New York State, which is patronized by Jewish New Yorkers. The name has also been applied to Washington Heights, New York City, the home of many successful Jews.

**Jewish penicillin.** A humorous name for chicken soup, which by reputation is regarded by Jews, and especially Jewish mothers, as a sovereign remedy for all ailments.

**Jewish piano.** An offensively humorous term, dating from the 1930s, for a cash register. It plays on the stereotype of the Jew as an accumulator of money.

**Jewish princess.** A primarily US nickname dating from the 1970s for a rich or spoiled girl or woman in a Jewish family. An alternative form of the nickname is 'JAP', standing for 'Jewish American princess'.

To add the necessary dramatic tension, he's lower class and a bit of a slob while she's rich and Jewish-princess chic.

*Maclean's* (16 March 1981)

**Jew Süss.** The English title of *Jud Süss*, a historical novel (1925) by Lion Feuchtwanger (1884–1958). Feuchtwanger was a German novelist and playwright, born of a Jewish family, known for his historical romances. He went into exile in France in 1933 and in 1940, after spending some time in a concentration camp, he escaped to the United States. Set in 18th-century Württemberg, *Jud Süss* tells the story of Josef Süss Oppenheimer, a Jew who rises to a position of power to help his people but is destroyed by his enemies. In the process he finds he is a Gentile, and the novel points up the meaninglessness of racial distinctions. The book was made into a play and a British film (1934). It became notorious when the Nazi propaganda minister, Josef Goebbels, revised the script for an anti-Semitic film version (1940) directed by Veit Harlan. In this version, 'to serve the politics of the state', the Jew is depicted as entirely evil, ravishing Aryan girls.

**JFK.** The commonest nickname of John Fitzgerald Kennedy (1917–63), Democratic president of the United States from 1961 until his assassination on 22 November 1963. The use of the initials was modelled on FDR, the nickname of President Franklin Delano Roosevelt. The style was also taken up by Kennedy's successor, LBJ. JFK has also become the popular name for the John F. Kennedy International Airport, New York City's main airport (formerly known as IDLEWILD). *JFK* is also the title of a much-excoriated film (1991) based on the book *On the Trail of the Assassins* by New Orleans district attorney Jim Garrison. The film is based on Garrison's interpretation of the events surrounding Kennedy's assassination, which rejects the findings of the WARREN COMMISSION. It was directed by Oliver Stone and starred Kevin Costner as Garrison. *See also* GRASSY KNOLL; JACKIE O; JACK THE ZIPPER; KENNEDY CURSE.

**Jigger.** *See* SHOT GLASS.

**Jiggle show.** A dismissive US colloquial term for a television show that relies for its appeal mainly on nubile young women in revealing clothing. The archetype is generally considered to be *Charlie's Angels* (1977–82). It was probably inspired by the frequent absence of bras, although 'jiggle' also has a long history as a euphemism for 'to have sexual intercourse'.

**Jihad.** *See* MUJAHEDIN.

**Jim Crow.** A name coined by Winston Churchill in 1940 for a roof-top spotter of enemy aircraft, punning on 'crow' as thieves' slang for a person who keeps watch while another steals and 'crow's nest' for a lookout's platform at a ship's masthead, but ultimately deriving from Jim Crow as a former nickname for an African American. Jim Crow was also a shorthand for the systematized discrimination against the African American population in the southern US states from the 1870s.

**Jim'll fix it.** The catchphrase of a BBC children's television series of the same title, screened from 1975 to 1978, in which the disc jockey Jimmy Savile arranged for the pipe dreams of his young viewers to be realized.

**Jimmy.** A name used by the Scots increasingly commonly from the 1980s as an address to a stranger, to some extent replacing the time-honoured 'Jock'.

**Jitterbug.** Originally a SWING enthusiast in the late 1930s, with the name probably coming from Cab Calloway's song 'Jitter Bug' (1934), in which a 'jitter bug' was a person who drank regularly and so 'has the jitters ev'ry morning'. The name passed to a person who danced the jitterbug, a fast, twirling, whirling US dance to a JAZZ accompaniment, popular in the 1940s. Hence also more generally, a nervous person, one who 'has the jitters'.

**Jive.** A type of fast, lively JAZZ, or the jerky dancing to it, popular in the 1920s and revived, to ROCK 'N' ROLL, in the 1940s and 1950s. Hand jive, with synchronized movement of the hands and forearms, was a British development, as seen, for example, in the popular television series *Rock Follies* (1976–7). Jive talk is the specialized vocabulary of its adepts.

**Jix.** The nickname of Sir William Joynson-Hicks, 1st Viscount Brentford (1865–1932), noted puritan and tactless speaker. He was home secretary (1924–9) and was prominent in defeating the adoption of the Revised Prayer Book of 1928. A short-lived term for a type of two-seater taxicab licensed in 1926 during his secretaryship was 'Jixie'.

> We mean to tread the Primrose Path,
> In spite of Mr Joynson-Hicks.
> We're People of the Aftermath
> We're girls of 1926.
>
> JACQUES REVAL: *The Woman of 1926*, 'Mother's Advice on Father's Fears' (1926)

**Job satisfaction.** The factor in one's work that brings fulfilment to one's hopes and desires.

**Jobseeker.** A euphemism for an unemployed person, whether actively seeking a job or not.

When we began calling the unemployed 'jobseekers', it was clear we were forgetting the English tradition of saying what you mean.

JOHN MORTIMER: in *Sunday Times* (10 May 1998)

**Jobs for the boys.** A form of favouritism giving jobs and appointments to friends and acquaintances or through the OLD BOY NETWORK, regardless of their qualifications or ability and not by fair and open competition.

**Jobsworth.** A minor official or underling who insists on the letter of the law being applied in all cases, however un-reasonable or unsympathetic this may seem. He dare not deviate or accommodate, because 'It's more than my job's worth.'

**Jockey for position.** To manoeuvre or manipulate for one's own benefit. The reference is to a horse race, in which a jockey will aim to manoeuvre his horse into a better position for winning. The figurative sense of the phrase dates from the 1950s.

**Joe Bloggs.** A nickname for an average man, frequently used as a random name in examples of form-filling and the like. Despite its somewhat disparaging overtones, the name was seized on by an immigrant Manchester businessman, Shami Ahmed, to found the highly successful Joe Bloggs Clothing Company in 1985.

**Joe Blow.** An US equivalent of JOE BLOGGS, perhaps so called because originally an 'oompah man' or supporting player in a wind band.

**Joe Public.** A member of the general public, and specifically a member of an audience. Performers will usually be keen to see what 'Joe Public' thinks of their act.

**Joe Six-pack.** An US nickname for an ordinary beer-drinking man, so called from the popularity of SIX-PACKS of beer among working males.

To bring all these new people into its ranks, however, the G.O.P. [Grand Old Party, i.e. Republican Party] is going to have to modify its country club image: Joe Sixpack does not belong to a country club.

*Time* (21 July 1980)

**Joe Soap.** A foolish or gullible person, who is easily swayed by smooth talk or 'soft soap'.

**Joe Who?** A nickname of the Canadian politician Joe (Charles Joseph) Clark (b.1939), who became leader of the Progressive Conservatives in 1976 and in June 1979 became Canada's youngest-ever prime minister. His minority government lasted only until March 1980, however. Clark, regarded as well meaning but ineffective, continued as party leader until 1983.

**Jogger's nipple.** Soreness of the nipple caused by the rubbing of clothing against it while jogging or running a long distance. It can affect men as well as women and can be prevented by applying petroleum jelly to the nipple before setting out. The term dates from the 1970s, when jogging itself was already becoming established as a popular sport in its own right.

**John Birch Society.** A reactionary US organization founded in 1958 to combat communism. It was named after John Birch (1918–45), a Baptist missionary and US intelligence officer killed by Chinese communists and regarded by the Society as the 'first casualty' of the COLD WAR.

**John Macnab.** A novel (1925) by John Buchan (1875–1940), inspired by the exploits of Captain James Brander Dunbar in 1897, when he caught a salmon or killed a stag on three separate Scottish estates without being apprehended. Three bored, respectable, middle-aged men concoct a bet on similar lines, with the twist that each landowner is to be warned of what is to happen in a note signed 'John Macnab'. The story was updated in Andrew Greig's novel *The Return of John Macnab* (1996).

**Johnny Foreigner.** A not unfriendly nickname for someone from another country, even if speaking the same language, as an American from the point of view of a Briton, or vice versa.

**Johnny no-stars.** An inept or foolish person. The allusion, from the late 20th century, is to the system of skill ratings used in MCDONALD'S fast-food outlets, where many young-sters take temporary MCJOBS. An employee who has failed to garner even one star is clearly a lost cause.

**John o'London's Weekly.** A magazine of literary articles and book reviews founded in 1919. It was aimed at a popular readership who normally steered clear of the weightier literary press and took its title from the pen-name of its editor, Wilfred Whitten (d.1942). It ceased publication in 1936.

**Johnson, Pussyfoot.** William E. Johnson (1862–1945), a temperance advocate, gained his nickname from his 'cat-like' policies in pursuing law breakers in gambling saloons and elsewhere in Indian territory when serving as Chief Special Officer of the US Indian Service (1908–11). After this he devoted his energies to the cause of PROHIBITION and gave many lectures on temperance.

**Joined at the hip.** Inseparable. Said of two intimate friends or close colleagues who see eye-to-eye on everything. The allusion is to conjoined (or 'Siamese') twins, who are typically joined at the waist.

**Joined-up writing.** Literacy; coherent written expression. The phrase alludes to a child's early efforts to write, when letters at first formed separately in a word progress to the cursive stage. The expression has variants in other fields.

> There will be an excellent opportunity in the House of Commons … for some joined-up thinking to be translated into legislation.
>
> *The Times*, letter to the editor (16 April 1999)

**Join up the dots.** To complete the picture; to fill in the details; to recall in entirety. The allusion is to the child's (or adult's) diversion of drawing a line through a succession of numbered dots that form an outline picture on completion.

**Jokari.** The proprietary name of a type of bat and ball game in which the ball is attached to the bat with a long length of rubber cord. The name dates from the 1940s and presumably derives from Italian *giocare*, 'to play', or its source, Latin *jocari*, 'to jest'.

**Joker, The.** *See* BATMAN.

**Jolly d.** Jolly decent (of you). A middle-class slang term of the mid-20th century. 'Oh, jolly d!' was a catchphrase popularized by Maurice Denham as Dudley Davenport in the radio comedy series MUCH-BINDING-IN-THE-MARSH.

**Jolly Green Giant.** A nickname (often shortened to 'Jolly Green' or simply 'Jolly') in the American military for any of a range of large, standardly green-painted transport or air-rescue helicopters (e.g. the CH-47 Chinook). Dating from the Vietnam War period, it was inspired by the jovial outsized character who was the trademark of Green Giant Foods, Inc. (producers most notably of canned sweetcorn and other vegetables) and who featured in many animated television advertisements in the 1960s.

**Jolly hockeysticks.** Said of a woman who is (often) public-school educated, and who is brightly enthusiastic and optimistic in her approach to the world, and 'sporty' in her interests and code of moral decency and fair play. The catchphrase 'Jolly hockey sticks!', epitomizing such a person, was first heard in the late 1940s in the radio comedy series *Educating Archie*, in which it was uttered by Monica, Archie's schoolgirl friend. *See also* DIMSIE.

> The painstakingly put-together facsimile of project leader Heather's diary, allowing you to trace her descent from early jolly hockeysticks-style excitement to later demented hysteria.
>
> *heat* (18–24 November 1999)

**Jolly Jack.** An ironic nickname for the Yorkshire writer and actor J.B. Priestley (1894–1984), who was notoriously grumpy.

**Joltin' Joe.** The nickname of the legendary baseball player Joe Dimaggio (1914–99), whose feats with the New York Yankees made him the hero of a generation. His fame is reflected in references to him in contexts as diverse as Hemingway's *The Old Man and the Sea* (1952) and the Simon and Garfunkel lyric 'Mrs Robinson' for the soundtrack of the film *The* GRADUATE (1968). Dimaggio was also known as 'The Yankee Clipper'. His younger brother Dom Dimaggio (b.1917), a successful player with the Boston Red Sox, was known as the 'Little Professor'.

> What's that you say, Mrs Robinson?
> Joltin' Joe has left and gone away.
>
> SIMON and GARFUNKEL: 'Mrs Robinson' (song) (1968)

**Jonah word.** A colloquial term for a word that a chronic stutterer finds difficult to utter in ordinary conversation. The allusion is to the biblical Jonah, who brought bad luck (and who was thus thrown overboard to be swallowed by a whale). A notorious Jonah word is 'mother', whose initial 'm' can be a fearsome obstacle since it involves sealed lips that must be opened.

**Jones, Bridget.** The independent, unattached woman in her 30s who recounts the ups and (mostly) downs of her life in the humorous fictional *Bridget Jones's Diary* by Helen Fielding, in which she counts her calories, cigarettes, glasses of Chardonnay, weight and other obsessions. The diary first appeared as a column in *The Independent* in 1995, and was transformed into a book in 1996. Bridget is shallow and neurotic, but also endearingly amusing in her manic enthusiasms and petulant disappointments. Her name became a synonym for any real female relationship-obsessed THIRTY-SOMETHING of this type. A sequel, *Bridget Jones: The Edge of Reason* (1999), was a further affectionate portrayal of the original comic creation. A successful film version (2001), directed by Sharon Maguire, starred Renée Zellweger as Bridget. A film of the sequel followed in 2004, again starring Renée Zellweger.

**Jonestown.** The site in northwestern Guyana of the mass suicide/murder on 18 November 1978 of 913 members of the People's Temple cult led by Jim Jones (1931–78). Jones set up his cult in northern California in the 1960s, but, after allegations that he was appropriating the income of his members, he and his followers left the United States to set up a commune at Jonestown in 1977. After further allegations of appropriation of funds and tyrannical behaviour on the part of Jones, US Representative Leo Ryan arrived in Guyana, accompanied by journalists and relatives of cult members, to carry out an investigation. Four days later, as they were about to leave Jonestown, cult members attacked the visiting group, killing five of them, including Ryan. The others managed to escape. Jones then ordered his members to drink a punch laced with cyanide, which most of them, including 276 children, duly did. Jones himself was found dead, having been shot in the head.

**Journey's End.** A play (1929) by R.C. Sherriff (1896–1975) depicting the horror of trench warfare during the First World War. The central character, Captain Stanhope, is on the verge of mental collapse after three years at the front, while 18-year-old 2nd Lieutenant Raleigh actually reaches 'journey's end' at the end of the play when he is mortally wounded. The play drew on Sherriff's own experiences as a captain in the trenches, although he wrote the piece only in order to raise money for his rowing club. He planned originally to call the play *Suspense*, changed his mind when he admitted that it did not have any, then considered *Waiting* before settling on the final title after coming across the following line in a book he was reading: 'It was late in the evening when we came at last to our Journey's End.'

**Journey to the End of the Night.** (French title: *Voyage au bout de la nuit.*) The first novel (1932) by the French writer Louis Ferdinand Céline (1894–1961). The central character, Ferdinand, wanders aimlessly and despairingly through the First World War and afterwards. The work was praised by some for its innovatory style, and excoriated by others for its savage pessimism and coarse language. Céline went on to become even more misanthropic, anti-French and anti-Semitic, and was suspected, though later exonerated, of collaboration with the Nazis in the Second World War.

**Joy.** The first word of various book titles alluding to a specific that presumably gave the writer pleasure and that he or she wishes to share with readers. The vogue was apparently launched with *The Joy of Cooking* (1931) by the US cookery expert Irma S. Rombauer. Forty years on Alex Comfort rejuvenated the formula with *The Joy of Sex* (1972), following it with a companion volume, *More Joy of Sex* (1974), and at the age of 70 finally updating it as *The New Joy of Sex* (1991). Titles listed in *British Books in Print* (1982) include *Joy of a Home Fruit Garden, Joy of Beauty, Joy of Building, Joy of Flying, Joy of Hand-Weaving,* Leonard Bernstein's *Joy of Music* and Margaret Allan's *Joy of Slimming*. In 1984 Nigel Rees published the ironically titled *Joy of Clichés* and soon after came Fritz Spiegl's *The Joy of Words* (1986). A book that is a joy to write is not necessarily, however, a joy to read.

**Joyriding.** Driving and riding in a car for pleasure, especially a stolen one. Joyriding gained notoriety in the early 1990s when teenage African Americans in Newark, New Jersey, took to racing and crashing model sports cars taken from

the white suburbs. It soon became a popular pastime of errant youth in Britain too. A later development was CARJACKING.

**Joystick.** The control column of an aircraft, which is linked to the elevators and ailerons. It is so nicknamed from the great pleasure and 'kicks' it gives to the pilot who operates it. The term was later extended to the control lever used to play computer games.

> Lewis sat on the pilot's right, trying to make sense of all the dials and gauges.
>
> 'And this one?' he ventured. 'Joystick, I suppose?'
>
> The plane was a trainer and had dual controls. Alex corrected him: 'We call it the control column nowadays. One for me and one for you if I faint.'
>
> BRUCE CHATWIN: *On the Black Hill*, ch. 48 (1982)

**Judge a book by its cover.** To assess the nature of a person or thing by outward appearances alone. The expression often appears in the proverbial form: 'You can't judge a book by its cover.' Most publishers are aware that potential readers often do illogically judge a book in this way.

**Judges' Rules.** Rules that concern the questioning of suspects by the police and the taking of statements. They were first formulated in 1912, revised in 1918 and reformulated in 1964. They were superseded by provisions of the Police and Criminal Evidence Act of 1984, Part V, and the Secretary of State's Code of Practice.

**Jud Süss.** *See* JEW SÜSS.

**Juggernaut.** A word for a large lorry, especially one that travels throughout Europe. Such lorries or HGVs (heavy goods vehicles) have become increasingly common in Britain with the expansion of the EUROPEAN UNION, and 'juggernaut' for this reason has become a dirty word with environmentalists. The word itself has become popularly associated with -naut in its application to long-distance voyagers such as the Argonauts or an ASTRONAUT, while jugger- is in some cases misapprehended as a form of 'judder'. The name derives from that of a Hindu god, whose name is an alteration of Hindi *Jagannath*, from Sanskrit *Jagannā tha*, 'lord of the world'. The name is a title of Vishnu, chief of the Hindu gods. Juggernaut is also sometimes used to denote a regime or institution beneath which people are ruthlessly crushed.

**Jughead.** *See* JARHEAD.

**Juke box.** A kind of large automatic record player, usually in a public place such as a public house or bar, in which coins are inserted and buttons pressed to select the relevant tunes. 'Juke' was an African American slang term of the 1930s, denoting an establishment offering food, drink, music, dancing and perhaps baser pleasures as well. It ultimately derives from the word *juke* or *joog* in the Gullah language of West Africa, meaning 'disorderly', 'wicked'.

**Juliet Bravo.** A television crime drama series screened from 1980 to 1985 with a central character in the policewoman Jean Darblay who, although a victim of sexism from her male colleagues at the (fictional) Hartley station in Lancashire, manages to solve a number of realistic cases. The title represents the letters JB as her police call sign. *See also* ROGER.

**July Bomb Plot.** The attempted assassination of Adolf Hitler on 20 July 1944 by senior German officers. The conspirators, alarmed at the deteriorating military situation, sought to take power in Germany and seek favourable peace terms with the Allies. The plot, which was first hatched towards the end of 1943 and code-named *Walküre* ('Valkyrie'), is also referred to as the Stauffenberg Plot or the Rastenburg Assassination Plot. The conspirators included General Ludwig Beck (formerly chief of the general staff), Colonel Claus Philipp Schenk (usually referred to by his title, Graf von Stauffenberg) and Field Marshal Erwin Rommel (*see* DESERT FOX). Rommel, however, had been seriously ounded three days before and was unable to take a direct part. It was Stauffenberg who prepared and carried out the plan, depositing a briefcase containing a bomb in a conference room at Hitler's 'Wolf's Lair' headquarters at Rastenburg in East Prussia. An aide moved the briefcase away from where Hitler sat, however, so that when it went off Hitler received only minor injuries, although four other people in the room died. Meanwhile Stauffenberg had flown to Berlin to meet the other conspirators. However, they were betrayed by one of their number, General Friedrich Fromm, and over the next few months some 200 plotters (including Fromm) were arrested, tortured and executed in a variety of gruesome ways. Beck and Rommel were forced to commit suicide. Apparently Hitler watched films of some of the executions.

**Jumbo jet.** Although now applied generally to any large airliner, the nickname was originally bestowed on the Boeing 747, developed in the 1960s and making its maiden flight on 9 February 1969. The early version accommodated 350–490 passengers, but later types could take up to 650 people. Jumbo was the name of an elephant at the London Zoo from 1865 to 1882.

**Jumpers.** A play (1972) by Tom Stoppard (b.1937) in which a professor of ethics struggles to cope with a variety of misfortunes, from the body of a dead politician to the death of his pet hare. The jumpers of the title are the gymnasts of the play's opening scene, who are subsequently revealed to be professional philosophers, leaping under the direction of the distinguished Sir Archibald Jumper.

**'Jumpin' Jack Flash'.** A song by The ROLLING STONES, released in 1968 and credited to Mick Jagger and Keith Richards. The name Jumpin' Jack Flash evinces a number of verbal influences, from JACK THE LAD (a roguish and adventurous youth), to jumping jack (a type of firework). It also reflects the almost demonic energy of Mick Jagger as a vocalist. The song dates from the same period as 'SYMPATHY FOR THE DEVIL', and its lyrics have much of the latter's darkly aggressive nature:

> I was raised by a toothless, bearded hag
> I was schooled with a strap right across my back
> But it's all right now, in fact it's a gas
> But it's all right, I'm Jumpin' Jack Flash
> It's a gas, gas, gas.

A comedy film of the same title was released in 1986, starring Whoopi Goldberg. 'Jack Flash' is also an Australian slang term for the drug hashish.

**Jump in the lake!** Go away! GET LOST! The expression dates from the early 20th century and is frequently preceded by 'Go'. A person who jumps in a lake will disappear from sight.

**Jump into bed with someone.** To have sexual intercourse readily with them.

**Jump jet.** A nickname for a VTOL (vertical take-off and landing) aircraft, and specifically for the Harrier fighter that in 1969 became the first fixed-wing VTOL type in service with the RAF. The latter's own sobriquet for it was the 'Leaping Heap'.

**Jump jockey.** Racing parlance for a jockey in a steeplechase. The term dates from the 1970s.

**Jump leads.** A pair of cables fitted with crocodile clips that are used to start a motor vehicle when the battery is flat by connecting the battery to another battery.

**Jump start.** A method of starting a car when the engine cannot be started by the ignition in the normal way. The car is pushed along or allowed to freewheel downhill and the gears are suddenly engaged. The term is also used for a similar start using JUMP LEADS.

**Jumpsuit.** A one-piece garment of trousers and a sleeved top, worn as a fashion garment or as protective clothing or uniform. The name was originally given to the garment worn by American parachutists in the Second World War. Hence 'jump'.

**Jump the gun.** To act prematurely. The allusion is to a false start in a race, when a runner sets off before the starting pistol has been fired. The phrase dates from the 1930s.

**Jump through hoops.** To go through an elaborate procedure in order to achieve an objective; to go to great lengths to please someone. The allusion is to circus animals trained to jump through hoops. The expression dates from the early 20th century.

**Jump up and down.** To bring oneself into notice by one's movements or actions; to be busy or physically active.

**June War.** *See* SIX-DAY WAR.

**Jungle.** *See* DRUM'N' BASS.

**Jungle Book, The.** The Disney cartoon (1967), based on Rudyard Kipling's *The Jungle Book* (1894), was the last animated film to be personally supervised by Walt Disney. The similarities between the movie and Kipling's book are few, but the film brought Kipling's books and characters of Mowgli, Shere Khan (the tiger), Bagheera (the panther), Kaa (the snake) and Baloo (the bear) to a wider audience. The film is particularly admired for its songs in a traditional jazz idiom, mainly by Richard M. and Robert B. Sherman, including 'Bare Necessities', 'I wanna be like you' and 'King of the Swingers'.

**Jungle gym.** A type of climbing frame for young children, originating in the United States in the 1920s. It was originally a proprietary name and in turn gave the name of the comic strip character Jungle Jim, created by Alex Raymond in the 1930s.

**Jungle juice.** Strong, rough alcoholic drink. The term arose among the armed forces in the Second World War to apply to various homemade alcoholic drinks, but originally to a kind made of jungle-grown fruits and plants.

**Jungle music.** A style of dance music popular in Britain from the early 1990s, also known simply as 'jungle'. It incorporates elements of RAGGA, HIP-HOP and hard core, and mainly consists of very fast electronic drum tracks and slower synthesized bass lines. It is presumably named from its drumming and chanting, sounds associated with the jungle, although there could also be a more subtle reference to the CONCRETE JUNGLE.

**Junk bond.** A high-yielding, high-risk security, typically issued to raise capital speedily in order to finance a takeover. Such bonds first emerged on Wall Street in the 1970s and were so called because of doubts whether the issuing company would be able to pay the promised interest. If it could not, the bonds would be worthless, or 'junk'. The US financier Michael Milken (b.1947) was known as the 'junk bond king' from his ability to raise millions in minutes by selling junk bonds that came with his personal commendation and interest rates that older hands would have considered usurious. All ended in tears when he filed for bankruptcy in 1990.

**Junket Jack.** The nickname of the Labour politician Jack Cunningham (b.1939), a member of Tony Blair's New Labour cabinet from 1997 to 1999, first as agriculture minister and then as 'cabinet enforcer'. The nickname was awarded by the tabloid press on account of his apparent enthusiasm for foreign trips.

**Junk food.** Food of low nutritional value, such as potato crisps, sugar-coated cereals and the like, or as typically sold by FAST FOOD outlets such as McDONALD'S. Other popular junk food items include chips, pizza, popcorn, doughnuts, ice cream, hot dogs, burgers (e.g. BIG MACS), fried chicken (e.g. KFC) and all kinds of confectionery. Junk food, including a bewildering variety of sweet fizzy drinks, is usually irresistible to children, who are thus the consumers mainly targeted by the manufacturers. By the early 21st century considerable concern was being expressed that the popularity of junk food was leading to an epidemic of childhood obesity in the West, especially in the United States. *See also* E-NUMBERS.

**Junkie.** An impressionistic novel (1953) by William Lee (pen-name of William Burroughs; 1914–97). Subtitled 'Confessions of an Unrepented Drug Addict', it reflects the progress of his own addiction to HEROIN ('junk') from 1944. He was finally cured of the habit in London in 1957. *See also* BEAT GENERATION.

**Junk in the** or **one's trunk.** Excessively large buttocks; an expression of African American origin that came on the scene in the early to mid-1990s ('trunk' in this context is what British-speakers would refer to as the 'boot' of a car).

> I like a little junk in my trunk. So today I read an article in the *New York Times* about the recent rise of mannequins who have a little bootay [i.e. bottom].
> www.skinnykat.com (17 November 2004)

**Junk mail.** Unsolicited or unwanted material, typically attempting to sell a product or service, that is sent by post. *See also* SPAM.

**Junkyard dog.** In US political slang of the 1980s, a politician who is adept at or zealous in investigating corruption. It was inspired by the expression 'meaner [i.e. more aggressive] than a junkyard dog'.

**Juno.** A Canadian award presented annually for outstanding achievements in music, on the lines of the US GRAMMY. The name is derived from that of the broadcaster Pierre Juneau (b.1922) and has no connection with the code name of the beach in Normandy on which Canadian forces landed in Operation OVERLORD (*see* JUNO BEACH).

**Juno and the Paycock.** A play (1924) by the Irish playwright Sean O'Casey (1880–1964), first performed at the ABBEY THEATRE, Dublin. It concerns the fate of a Dublin family, the Boyles, during the Irish Civil War (1922–3). 'Juno' is Juno Boyle, the long-suffering but resilient wife of the workshy 'Captain' Boyle, who spends his time 'strutting about the town like a paycock' (peacock).

**Juno Beach.** The Allied code name for the stretch of beach on the Normandy coast between GOLD BEACH to the west and SWORD BEACH to the east. On D-DAY Juno Beach was where the 3rd Canadian Division and the 2nd Canadian Armoured Brigade came ashore. In Roman mythology Juno was the wife of Jupiter, ruler of the gods.

**Jurassic Park.** A film (1993) directed by Steven Spielberg, based on a novel by Michael Crichton about the chaos that overtakes an ambitious island THEME PARK in which the main attractions are dinosaurs from the Jurassic era (208–146 million years ago) recreated by scientists using the DNA (*see* DOUBLE HELIX) of dinosaur blood supposedly found in the guts of mosquitoes fossilized in amber. The novel idea that a Jurassic Park could be created in real life provoked much discussion among audiences at the time of the film's release, although the suggestion was panned by scientists. There have been two film sequels, *The Lost World: Jurassic Park* (1997) and *Jurassic Park III* (2001), neither approaching the quality of the original. A third sequel is due for release in 2006.

**Jury is out.** A decision has yet to be made; the general opinion of the public is unknown. The implication is that the subject is controversial. A fuller form of the phrase is 'The jury is still out.' The reference is to a jury debating their verdict before returning to the courtroom.

> Six months after the official launch of the individual savings account (Isa), the jury is still out.
>
> *The Times* (2 October 1999)

**Just deserts.** Deserved reward; 'comeuppance'. A quasi-biblical phrase that caught on as a 20th-century cliché.

> The father thumps the yob, pulls out his warrant card to reveal he's a policeman, and arrests him. Just deserts for the yob and cheers for the PC?
>
> ANDREW NEIL: in *Daily Mail* (9 March 1995)

**Just So Stories.** Animal fables for children (1902) by Rudyard Kipling (1865–1936). These amusing beast myths explain, for instance, how the leopard got his spots, the camel his hump, and the rhinoceros his folded skin and bad temper. They are accompanied by uplifting verses:

> The Camel's hump is an ugly lump
> Which well you may see at the Zoo;
> But uglier yet is the hump we get
> From having too little to do.

The 'Best Beloved' to whom each story is addressed was Kipling's eldest child Josephine, to whom he read the stories aloud. She died in 1899 at the age of six. *See also* JUNGLE BOOK.

**Just What Is It that Makes Today's Homes So Different, So Appealing?** The satirical and influential collage by Richard Hamilton (b.1922) was a pioneering work of British POP ART. Dating from 1956, the picture includes photographs of a muscleman, a woman with impossible breasts, a tape recorder and other consumer durables, various brand labels and so on. The title is in the style of an article heading from a home-interiors magazine. *See also* $HE.

**Just what the doctor ordered.** Just right; exactly what is needed, like the precise prescription made by a doctor for a specific treatment or cure. The catchphrase dates from the early 20th century. *See also* YOU'RE THE DOCTOR.

**Just when you thought it was safe to go back in the water.** *See* JAWS.

**Just William.** *See* WILLIAM.

**Jutland.** The Battle of Jutland was one of the major naval events of the First World War. It took place on 31 May 1916 when the British Grand Fleet under Admiral Jellicoe engaged the German High Seas Fleet in the North Sea west of Jutland. The outcome was a tactical victory for the Germans but a strategic victory for the British, and the German fleet never again sought a full-scale engagement with the British.

# K

**Kabbalah.** (Hebrew *qabbālāh*, 'tradition'.) A Jewish mystical system of theology and metaphysics, dating from the 11th and 12th centuries, but with much older antecedents in the teachings of, among others, the neo-Platonists and neo-Pythagoreans. Its aim is to relate the finite and the infinite, which was brought about by emanations from the Absolute Being. A modern organization called the Kabbalah Centre, partly based on the traditional Kabbalah, and mixed with various Jewish rites and NEW AGE beliefs, was founded in Los Angeles in 1984 by Rabbi Philip Berg as a partly commercial enterprise. It has attracted a number of celebrity adherents, many of them not Jewish, including Madonna, Elizabeth Taylor, Winona Ryder, Mick Jagger, and David and Victoria Beckham. Sectaries can be identified by the red strings round their wrists.

**Kafkaesque.** An adjective used to describe a work of litera-ture, drama or film, or a real situation, in which an innocent individual is at the mercy of anonymous, bizarre and frightening forces, usually in the form of a malevolent or indifferent state bureaucracy. The word derives from Franz Kafka (1883–1924), who grew up in Prague, but wrote in German, and whose posthumously published novels and stories embody such situations. In *The* TRIAL (1925), for example, Joseph K. is arrested and brought before a court, but the charges against him are never stated. He is driven to find out what he is supposed to have done wrong and to seek acquittal, but is taken to the edge of the city and killed 'like a dog'. Kafka himself is supposed to have said: 'In the fight between you and the world, back the world.' *See also* FIRST LINES OF NOVELS.

**Kai Lung.** The Chinese sage and tale-teller who is the central character of an entertaining series of short stories by Ernest Bramah (real name Ernest Bramah Smith). They abound in mock-Chinese aphorisms of the kind popularized by Charlie CHAN and are collected in five volumes: *The Wallet of Kai Lung* (1900), *Kai Lung's Golden Hours* (1922), *Kai Lung Unrolls His Mat* (1928), *The Moon of Much Gladness* (1932) and *Kai Lung Beneath the Mulberry Tree* (1940).

**Kaiser, The.** The nickname accorded to Franz Beckenbauer (b.1945), a gifted football player for Bayern Munich and West Germany in the 1960s and 1970s. The German word *Kaiser* ('emperor') is, like the Russian 'tsar', derived from the Latin word *Caesar*. The nickname reflects Beckenbauer's imperious skills as a player and the respect in which he is held.

**Kaiser Bill.** A British nickname for Wilhelm II (1859–1941), king of Prussia, German emperor (*Kaiser*) (1888–1918) and nephew of Queen Victoria. Like many German military figures and their conservative supporters he believed that a short victorious European war would solve Germany's problems. As the First World War dragged on, however, he was sidelined by the right-wing military-industrial complex and the virtual dictatorship of Generals Hindenburg and Ludendorff that controlled Germany from 1916. He abdicated and went into exile in the Netherlands on the defeat of Germany in November 1918. *See also* HUN; LAUGHING MURDERER OF VERDUN.

**Kalashnikov.** The popular name for the AK-47, a Soviet make of assault rifle designed by Mikhail Timofeyevich Kalash-nikov (b.1919), who ended up as a major-general in the Red Army. AK stands for *Avtomat Kalashnikova* ('automatic Kalashnikov'), and 47 for 1947, the year in which the weapon was adopted by Soviet forces. It went on to be manufactured in many communist countries and was the standard infantry weapon in communist armies for some four decades. It has also been widely used by nationalist, guerrilla and terrorist groups, including the IRA, and features on the flag of Mozambique.

**Kamerad.** (German, 'comrade'.) A word used by the

Germans in the First World War as an appeal for mercy. For a while it was taken up in English to mean 'I surrender'.

> 'Kamerad, Bull! I'll come in,' said Loftie. Vaughan's hands had gone up first.
>
> RUDYARD KIPLING: *Limits and Renewals* (1930)

**Kamikaze.** A Japanese word meaning 'divine wind', referring to the providential typhoon that on a night in August 1281 baulked a Mongol invasion. In the Second World War it was applied to the 'suicide' aircraft attacks organized under Vice-Admiral Onishi in the Philippines between October 1944 and January 1945. Some 5000 young pilots gave their lives when their bomb-loaded fighters crashed into their targets.

**Kampuchea.** The official name of Cambodia for international purposes between 1976 and 1989. 'Kampuchea' is a more precise transliteration of the traditional Khmer name of the country, of which 'Cambodia' (and the French *Cambodge*) are Westernized alterations. The name 'Democratic Kampuchea' was given to the country by the KHMER ROUGE, who had taken power the previous year. After the Vietnamese invaded the country in 1978 and set up a puppet regime the country was renamed the 'People's Republic of Kampuchea'. When the Vietnamese withdrew in 1989 the official name was changed again to 'State of Cambodia' (Khmer *Roat Kampuchea*).

***Kandy-Kolored Tangerine Flake Streamline Baby, The.*** The dazzling debut (1965) by the US journalist Tom Wolfe (b.1931). The book is a collection of essays in which the author introduced the United States to the1960s – to the TWIST, The BEATLES, Bouffant Hairdos, Kar Kustomizers and much more. The provocative title caught the zeitgeist by combining the hip and cool with crass commercialism.

**Kanga.** A media nickname for Lady Tryon (1948–97), at one time an 'adviser' to Prince Charles, so called from her Australian background and bouncy personality. The name may have been coined by the prince himself.

**Kangaroo.** In British parliamentary procedure, the process by which the Speaker, on the report stage of a bill, selects the amendments to be debated, rather than having all the amendments discussed. The procedure was first used on the discussion of the Financial Bill of 1909. It is so named because the debate leaps from clause to clause. The word is also applied when the chairperson of a parliamentary committee selects some amendments for discussion but not others.

**Kangaroo court.** A term applied to an irregular court or tribunal that is conducted in disregard of proper legal procedure, as, for example, a mock court held among prisoners in a jail. 'To kangaroo' means to convict a person on false evidence. The term, which probably arose from some resemblance of the 'jumps' of the kangaroo to the progress of 'justice' in such courts, was common in the United States during the 19th century. It obtained wide currency in Britain in 1966 when it was applied to the irregular punitive measures taken by certain trade unions against their members who were regarded as strikebreakers.

**Kangaroo ticket.** In US political slang, a pair of candidates for office (e.g. president and vice-president) in which the minor partner (the running mate) has more popular appeal than the major one. First recorded in 1971, the expression is said to go back to the 1930s. It may be based on the notion that the kangaroo's hind limbs are far more formidable than its fore limbs.

**Kangaroo Valley.** A nickname given in the 1960s to the Earl's Court area of West London, the allusion being to the large number of temporary or permanent Australian immigrants living there.

**Kangol.** The proprietary name of a range of headwear, safety harnesses and seat belts traces its origins back to the Polish-born British beret manufacturer Jacques Spreiregen and his nephew, Jo Meisner, who in 1937 set up a factory at Cleator, near Whitehaven, Cumbria, to make berets for schoolwear, GIRL GUIDES uniforms and fashion wear. They devised the name from the three original raw materials used for the headgear, sil*k*, *ang*ora and woo*l*, and after the Second World War extended the range to military berets and subsequently to related fabric-based items. In the 1980s the brand suddenly became cool. It was sported by the rap star LL Cool J, and rap fans in their thousands followed the trend. The now familiar kangaroo logo was introduced in 1984, making a virtue of the fact that in the United States most customers asked for a 'kangaroo' rather than a 'Kangol'.

**Kansas Coolidge** or **Kansas Sunflower.** A nickname of the US politician Alf (Alfred Mossman) Landon (1887–1987), governor of Kansas (1933–7). As the Republican candidate in the 1936 presidential election he was annihilated by Franklin D. Roosevelt, winning only eight votes in the electoral college. One of the Democrats' slogans in the election was 'Sunflowers wilt in November.' The charismatically challenged Calvin Coolidge, SILENT CAL, had been Republican president of the United States (1923–9).

**Kapp Putsch.** *See* FREIKORPS.

**Karaoke.** A popular feature of British pubs and clubs from the early 1980s, in the form of a pre-recorded track of popular music without the vocal part, enabling a person to sing along with it and, as desired, record the resulting performance on tape or video. The system derives from Japan (the word means literally 'empty orchestra' – Japanese *oke* is a much eroded form of English 'orchestra') and caught on among business people in that country visiting bars and clubs on their way home from work. Karaoke machines can now be bought for family entertainment in the home. An elaboration of the idea is the television WANNABE show POP IDOL.

> The idea of the karaoke bar is very simple. You get roaring drunk, chat up the bar girls and sing maudlin popular songs, dreadfully out of tune.
>
> *Daily Telegraph* (19 May 1989)

*See also* 'MY WAY'.

**Karloff, Doris.** A rather unkind nickname bestowed on the British Conservative politician Anne Widdecombe (b.1947), shadow home secretary (1997–2001). The name puns on the name of Boris Karloff (1887–1969), star of HORROR MOVIES in the 1930s and 1940s, and reflects both the supposed frumpiness and fierceness of her appearance ('Doris' is generally regarded as an old-fashioned and faintly comic name) and her forthright and uncompromising manner. She achieved particular notoriety as a junior Home Office minister (1995–7) in John Major's government, when she ordered that a woman prisoner be shackled while giving birth. *See also* SOMETHING OF THE NIGHT. In later years she has attempted to embrace a mellower image.

**Katanga.** A mineral-rich Congolese province whose secession from the newly independent Congo in 1960 precipitated the so-called Congo Crisis (1960–5). Katanga was reintegrated into the Congo, with the assistance of UNITED NATIONS forces, in 1962, but bloody chaos still reigned elsewhere. Central authority was finally imposed in 1965 by the iron fist of Colonel Mobutu, who was to rule the Congo (as Zaire) in an increasingly corrupt manner until 1997.

**Kat stitch.** A stitch in lace-making that forms a star-shaped ground net. The name dates from the early 20th century, but the reference is historically much earlier. 'Kat' is Catherine of Aragon (1485–1536), the first wife of Henry VIII, who is said to have invented the stitch.

**Katyn Massacre.** On 12 April 1943 German radio announced that the bodies of 4143 Polish officers had been found in eight communal graves in the Katyn Forest near Smolensk in western Russia. The Soviet authorities long maintained that the Germans had killed the Poles during Operation BARBAROSSA and only in 1989 began to admit that the murders had, in fact, been carried out in the spring of 1940 by the NKVD (*see* KGB). The reason for the pogrom is still not clear. Some claim it was ordered by STALIN simply through his hatred of Poles. Others hold that the NKVD was evacuating prison camps to make way for deportees from the Baltic States. The massacre left a deep scar on Polish–Soviet relations during the remainder of the Second World War and afterwards.

**Katyusha.** *See* STALIN ORGAN.

**KBO.** A humorously euphemistic abbreviation of 'keep buggering on', an injunction to persist in spite of all obstacles. It was reputedly, and fittingly, a favourite of Winston Churchill.

**Keedoozle.** *See* PIGGLY WIGGLY.

**Keep ahead of the game.** *See* AHEAD OF THE GAME.

**Keep Britain tidy.** This simple anti-litter slogan was first promoted in 1952 through the Central Office of Information by means of a sticker produced for the Ministry of Housing and Local Government. Litter louts have largely ignored the plea, despite the plentiful provision of litter bins.

***Keeping Up Appearances.*** A television SITCOM first broadcast on BBC1 in 1990 and centring on the outrageously snobbish Hyacinth Bucket (pronounced 'bouquet'), played by Patricia Routledge, and her hen-pecked husband Richard, played by Clive Swift. Much of the programme's mostly rather unsubtle humour lay in Hyacinth's barnstorming efforts to order the lives of others.

**Keep one's chin up.** To remain cheerful in difficult circumstances. To raise one's chin is to tilt the head back in an attitude of bravery or defiance. The expression dates from the 1930s and is often found in the simple exhortation 'Chin up!'

**Keep one's eye on the ball.** To remain alert and attentive. In most sports it is important to follow the path of the ball to plan or make one's next move.

**Keep one's fingers crossed.** To hope for success. The expression dates from the 1920s, but the ultimate allusion is to making the sign of the cross in order to banish evil and invite good. Many people actually cross their index finger and forefinger when saying 'Keep your fingers crossed', meaning 'Wish me luck', and children cross their fingers in some games to mean they are 'safe'.

**Keep one's head down.** To remain inconspicuous in difficult times; to concentrate on one's work.

**Keep on trucking.** Keep going; don't give up. A general term of encouragement, originally US, from 'to truck' in the sense 'to move', 'to travel'. This meaning of 'truck' may go back to the 1930s Depression-era United States, when hoboes would ride the railroads by clinging onto the 'trucking' equipment between the wheels of the rolling stock. It may be from this that the African American dance known as 'The Truck' or 'Trucking', which burst out of Harlem in 1934, took its name. The slogan 'Keep on truckin" was popularized in the 1960s by the US satirical cartoonist Robert Crumb (b.1943), who in his drawings associated it with a *very* laid-back mode of walking.

> Truckin', got my chips cashed in,
> Keep truckin', like the doo-dah man,
> Together, more or less in line,
> Just keep truckin' on.
>
> ROBERT HUNTER: lyrics of 'Truckin", on The Grateful Dead's album AMERICAN BEAUTY (1970)

**Keep the Aspidistra Flying.** A novel by George ORWELL (1903–50), published in 1936. It tells the story of an assistant in a bookshop who has literary ambitions and a contempt for bourgeois materialism. In the end, however, he ends up being obliged to marry the girl he loves and accepting the comforts of middle-class life. *See also* ASPIDISTRA.

**Keep up with the Joneses.** To endeavour to maintain one's social level; to keep up appearances with one's neighbours. The phrase was invented by the cartoonist Arthur R. Momand ('Pop') for a comic-strip series ('Keeping up with the Joneses – by Pop'), which began in the New York *Globe* on 1 April 1913 and ran for 28 years. He based it on his own experiences as a newly married young artist living in an affluent New York suburb on a limited salary.

**Keepy-uppy.** An informal game of skill involving keeping a football in the air without the use of the hands (i.e. by kicking it, heading it, chesting it, etc.). The term, first recorded in 1983, evolved from the synonymous *keepy-up*, which dates from the 1950s.

**Keg party.** In Australian English, a party in which the liquid refreshment is sourced mainly from a barrel of beer, which has been bought with contributions from the partygoers. The term is first recorded in 1950.

**Keith.** A nickname given to Prince Philip (*see* PHIL THE GREEK) by *Private Eye* (*compare* BRENDA).

**Keller plan** or **course.** An American method of college instruction in which the subject matter of a course is divided into study units that students are allowed to master at their own pace. The name is that of the US psychologist Fred S. Keller, who proposed the plan in 1968.

**Kelly, Ned.** The hero of Australian folklore became a favourite subject of the great Australian painter Sidney Nolan (1917–92). Kelly (1855–80) was a notorious bushranger, who wore homemade armour for his armed escapades. He was hanged after being captured following a shoot-out in 1880. Nolan started his series of paintings of Kelly in 1946. In most of these paintings Kelly is part of what Nolan described as 'the great purity and implacability' of the Australian landscape. Kelly has been the subject of a number of films, including *The Story of the Kelly Gang* (1906), the first ever feature-length film, and *Ned Kelly* (1970), directed by Tony Richardson and with Mick Jagger playing the outlaw. Peter Carey's novel *True History of the Kelly Gang* won the 2001 Booker Prize.

**Kelvinside.** A well-off residential area of west Glasgow that has given its name to the affected and over-refined form of Scottish English spoken by its genteel, middle-class inhabitants. A characteristic is the pronunciation of 'a' as 'e' in such words as 'fancy' ('fency') and 'actually' ('ectually'); hence 'sex' are what you put potatoes in. The area takes its name from the River Kelvin. *See also* MORNINGSIDE.

**Kemo Sabe.** A phrase supposedly meaning 'faithful friend' by which the LONE RANGER was addressed by his Native American companion Tonto. Although presented as being from a genuine NATIVE AMERICAN language, it was the creation of the Lone Ranger's inventor, George W. Trendle.

**Kennedy curse.** The US Kennedy dynasty, whose brightest star was President John F. Kennedy, suffered an extraordinary series of tragedies during the 20th century. The dynasty began with Joseph Patrick Kennedy (1888–1969) and Rose Elizabeth Fitzgerald (1890–1995), who had nine children. In 1944 their son Joseph Kennedy Jr was killed in an air crash while flying a secret wartime mission. In 1948 Joseph's sister, Kathleen Agnes Kennedy, was killed in a plane crash in France. In 1963 Patrick Bouvier Kennedy, son of John and Jacqueline Kennedy, died days after his premature birth. On 22 November 1963 President John Fitzgerald Kennedy (1917–63) was assassinated in Dallas. On 6 June 1968 his brother, Robert Francis Kennedy (1925–68), was assassinated in Los Angeles. In 1969 Senator Edward M. Kennedy was involved in a car accident on the island of CHAPPAQUIDDICK, killing his passenger. In 1973 his son, Edward Kennedy Jr, had his right leg amputated in a successful attempt to halt the spread of cancer. In 1984 one of Robert's 11 children, David Kennedy, died of a HEROIN overdose. In 1997 Robert's son Michael was killed while playing ski football in Colorado. In 1999 President John F. Kennedy's only son, John F. Kennedy Jr (1960–99), died in an air crash off the Massachusetts coast. His wife, Carolyn Bessette Kennedy, and her sister, Lauren Bessette, perished with him. It was Edward M. Kennedy who first voiced the suspicion that the Kennedys seemed to be living in the shadow of a curse. *See also* JFK.

**Kenwood.** The well-known make of electric food mixer takes its name from Kenneth Wood (1916–97), who launched its prototype in 1948, basing it on existing models. His most popular model, the Kenwood Chef, made him a millionaire at the age of 42, although a misguided foray into refrigerators in the early 1960s was the cause of a notable financial setback. His company was taken over by Thorn Electrical Industries in 1968.

**Kerb-crawling.** The action of driving slowly close to the kerb in order to pick up a prostitute or indeed any woman on the pavement or by the roadside. The term dates from the early 1970s in this sense, although it existed earlier in spoken slang and police jargon as an expression for walking along the pavement for this same purpose.

**Kermit.** The garrulous, green-garbed puppet frog was the mainstay of the Muppets, created by Jim Henson. He first appeared on US television in 1957, but did not become generally familiar until 1969, when he featured in the children's educational programme *Sesame Street*. This in turn led to *The* MUPPET SHOW, running from 1976 to 1981, in which Kermit pranced and parleyed with his equally esoteric friends, among them Miss Piggy and Fozzie Bear. His name is not uncommon as a first name in the United States and is familiar as that of the businessman and explorer Kermit Roosevelt (1889–1943), the son of Theodore Roosevelt, the 26th president.

**Kerr's Cur.** A description of Australian Liberal politician Malcolm Fraser (b.1930) by Gough Whitlam (b.1916). The occasion was on 11 November 1975 when the governor general of Australia, Sir John Kerr (1914–91), dismissed Whitlam and his Labor administration and appointed Fraser as caretaker prime minister. As leader of the opposition Fraser had blocked Whitlam's money bills and the crisis came when Whitlam refused to call a general election. Fraser won the election that followed Whitlam's dismissal and remained in office until 1983.

**Kes.** *See* KESTREL FOR A KNAVE.

**Kestrel for a Knave, A.** A novel (1968) by Barry Hines (b.1939). The only consolation for a boy from a council estate in northeast England, whose family background and environment are responsible for the trouble into which he gets, is the kestrel that he caught and has raised. The film

version (1969), one of the key British films of the period, was directed by Ken Loach with the title *Kes*, which was subsequently used for new editions of the book. The original title is a quotation from *The Boke of St Albans* (1486):

> An Eagle for an Emperor, a Gyrfalcon for a King, a Peregrine for a Prince, a Saker for a Knight, a Merlin for a Lady, a Goshawk for a Yeoman, a Sparrowhawk for a Priest, a Musket for a Holy water Clerk, a Kestrel for a Knave.

**Kevin.** A name applied from the 1990s to any grumpy, graceless, grunting, spotty, smelly and thoroughly hormonal adolescent boy. The prototypical Kevin was a character created by the British comedian Harry Enfield in his television series *Harry Enfield and Chums* (from 1994). Kevin is at permanent loggerheads with his parents ('I hate you, I wish I'd never been born'), and his only friend is a Kevin-clone called Perry (played by Kathy Burke).

**Kewpie doll.** The US celluloid doll, designed by Joseph Kallus and made by George Borgfeldt, evolved from Rose O'Neill's drawings of chubby, top-knotted cherubs, first appearing in the *Ladies' Home Journal* (1909). By 1913 the dolls had become a commercial phenomenon, decorating soaps, fabrics and stationery. The name comes from 'Cupid', with perhaps a dash of 'cute'. The dolls' latter-day descendants were the TELETUBBIES.

**Keyhole Kate.** The nosy schoolgirl whose insatiable curiosity leads to a host of comic disasters in the DANDY comic, in which she appeared from 1937 to 1955. She was the creation of the artist Allan Morley. In 1965 she was revived by other hands for the new paper *Sparky*.

**Keyhole surgery.** The colloquial term for a surgical technique that involves operations being performed with minimal external incision through a small opening (the 'keyhole') and monitored via fibre optics on a screen. The formal term for the technique is 'minimally invasive surgery'. The procedure was introduced in the late 1980s.

**Keynesianism.** The economic doctrine named after the British economist John Maynard Keynes (1883–1946). Broadly, Keynesian theories argue that high unemployment can be avoided by government intervention in the free-market economy, for example by manipulating demand through the use of fiscal and monetary policies. Keynesianism dominated the economic policies of many Western governments in the decades after the Second World War, but was later challenged by FRIEDMANISM.

**Keystone Kops.** A troupe of slapstick film comedians led by Ford Sterling, and including Charlie Chaplin (1889–1977), Fatty Arbuckle (1887–1933) and Chester Conklin

(1888–1971), who, from 1912 to 1920, under the inspiration of Mack Sennett (1880–1960), made a number of action-packed comedies at the Keystone Studios, HOLLYWOOD, complete with crazy chases and trick effects. The 35 Keystone films starring Charlie Chaplin are particularly significant, especially *Tilly's Punctured Romance* (1914), regarded as the first feature-length comedy. Sennett's Bathing Beauties were added in 1915 to complement the Kops and introduce a note of glamour.

**KFC.** The registered abbreviation of Kentucky Fried Chicken, a style of batter-dipped chicken sold by the company of this name. It was founded by 'Colonel Sanders', otherwise Harland D. Sanders (1890–1980), a US farmer's son from Indiana whose catering career began in 1930 when he opened Sanders' Café behind a petrol station at North Corbin, Kentucky, and who five years later was awarded his honorary colonel's title from the governor of Kentucky. The company expanded into a worldwide FAST FOOD chain.

**KGB.** The secret police of the USSR, the initials standing for *Komitet gosudarstvennoy bezopasnosti* (Committee of State Security). Russia's original secret police was set up in 1917 as the Cheka, *Chrezvychaynaya komissiya* (Extraordinary Commission i.e. to combat counter-revolution). In 1922 this became the GPU, *Gosudarstvennoe politicheskoe upravlenie* (State Political Directorate), and the following year Ogpu, adding *Obyedinynnoye* (United) to the previous title. In 1934 it was renamed the NKVD, *Narodnyy komissariat vnutrennykh del* (People's Commissariat for Internal Affairs). In 1946 this was superseded by the MGB, *Ministerstvo gosudarstvennoy bezopasnosti* (Ministry of State Security), which in 1953 was renamed the MVD, *Ministerstvo vnutrennykh del* (Ministry of Internal Affairs). The KGB was formed in 1954 but ceased to exist in 1991 on the demise of the Soviet Union (except in Belarus, where its name was retained). It was succeeded by the FSK, *Federal'naya sluzhba kontrrazvedki* (Federal Counter-Intelligence Service). In 1995 this was renamed the FSB, *Federal'naya sluzhba bezopasnosti* (Federal Security Service).

**Khaki Cup Final.** A nickname for the 1915 FA Cup Final at Old Trafford, which Sheffield United won 3–1 against Chelsea. The name alludes to the large number of servicemen in the crowd, a year after the outbreak of the First World War. On presenting the trophy Lord Derby said that it was 'now the duty of everyone to join with each other and play a sterner game for England'.

**Khaki Election.** The name given to the general election of 1900 (28 September to 24 October) by which the Conservatives sought to profit from the recent military victories in the Second BOER WAR (1899–1902), when khaki was first generally familiar as the colour of active service uniforms. It was promoted by Joseph Chamberlain (1836–1914) and the Conservatives won, although their gain in seats was slight.

**Khaki fever.** The supposedly uncontrollable erotic yearnings unleashed among young women during the First World War by the presence in British society of so many attractive men in uniform. The syndrome persists, and in eastern and southern Africa the term refers to the attraction experienced by certain female tourists for their safari guides.

**Khmer Rouge.** A communist movement in Cambodia, initially backed by North VIETNAM. It opposed the Cambodian government in the 1960s and waged civil war from 1970 to 1975, when it gained total power. For the next four years it exercised a regime of terror under Pol Pot (1926–98), resulting in the deaths of at least 2 million. It was overthrown by the Vietnamese in 1979 and became a guerrilla movement until 1991, when it declared itself 'reformed'. Since then it has maintained its guerrilla activities from bases in Thailand. The Khmer are the indigenous people of Cambodia. These particular ones were *rouge* (French, 'red') because of the party's espousal of communism. Cambodia was a French protectorate until 1955. *See also* KAMPUCHEA; KILLING FIELD.

**Kibbutz.** (Modern Hebrew *qibbūṣ*, 'gathering'.) A Jewish communal settlement in Israel organized on socialist lines by which land and property are shared. Work and meals are arranged collectively. Adults have private quarters but children are housed together. Kibbutzim were originally agricultural only, but various factories and industries later developed. The first kibbutz was set up in the Jordan Valley in 1909 by Jewish immigrants from Europe. They played a considerable part in the creation and defence of the State of Israel, but by the 21st century the collectivist ideology of the movement had been somewhat diluted.

**Kickapoo juice.** In US slang, strong alcoholic drink, especially as brewed at home or in prison. The expression was coined in 1941 by the American cartoonist Al Capp in his strip *L'il Abner*. It comes ultimately from the Kickapoo tribe, an Algonquian Indian nation of the US Midwest, but Capp would have come across the word in the names of various patent medicines around the turn of the 20th century (e.g. 'Kickapoo Indian Worm Killer'). The ingredients of the drink, according to the comic strip, included 'a barr'l o' kerosene, two dozen chicken haids, a bucket o' somethin' sloppy we swiped off a passin' truck, a motorman's glove, three pairs o' old socks, a dash o' axlegrease, turpentine', so no doubt the notion of 'kick' contributed to the name as well.

**Kick ass.** To act roughly or aggressively; to be impressive or assertive. The expression is of US origin and evolved in the 1980s from the earlier literal sense of beating or defeating someone by booting their backside. The hawks in the US government and military became notorious for encapsulating their enthusiasm for the First GULF WAR in the rallying cry 'We've got to go in there and kick ass!'

**Kickback.** An American slang term dating from the 1950s, denoting a bribe or other illicit payment. An earlier sense was of a negative reaction, or repercussion.

**Kick in.** To begin to start working or take effect. The 'kick' was originally the sharp stimulus afforded by a drug. To kick in with a payment, on the other hand, is to make a contribution. The distinction in sense is usually clear from the context.

**Kick someone when they are down.** To cause further misfortune to someone who is already in an unfortunate or disadvantageous situation. The image is of a person knocked down in a fight who is then kicked by the victor.

**Kick something into touch.** To remove it from the centre of attention; to 'sideline' it. The metaphor dates from the 1980s and is from football. If a ball is kicked over the touchline (at the side of the field) it goes out of play. 'To kick something into the long grass' is similar in sense and origin.

**Kick the tin.** In Australian slang, to make a contribution of money to some particular cause or for a particular purpose (e.g. buying a round of drinks). The reference is to a tin container into which people put money for charity or as a kitty.

> The bottom line remains a concern, with local business yet to really kick the tin for the region's only national professional sports team.
> www.smh.com.au (15 October 2005)

**Kick up one's heels.** An expression that together with variants such as 'to turn up one's heels' or 'to turn up one's toes' originally meant to die. In the 20th century a virtually converse sense emerged of to enjoy oneself, to 'have a fling'. The later imagery is of a horse freed from its harness or of an exuberant dancer.

**Kid brother** or **sister.** One's younger brother or sister. A 20th-century Americanism.

**Kiddie-fiddler.** A late 20th-century colloquialization of 'child-molester', no doubt called into being by the paedophilia panics of the 1990s. The positive of its euphemizing force evidently outweighed the negative of its trivializing tendency, for it has remained in use in the 21st century and has even gained some wider currency as a generalized playground insult.

> All of you who thought books were just room insulation and a hobby for weird kiddie-fiddlers and smelly rural wrinklies – look again! This Dickens fella, he's the man!
> A.A. GILL: *Sunday Times* (30 October 2005)

**Kiddy porn.** Pornographic representations or descriptions of children; child pornography. The term is first recorded in 1979, and was in increasing demand in succeeding decades as the INTERNET became a high-profile conduit for such material.

**Kids and cars.** A stock succinctness to describe a council housing estate, where children are everywhere and where cars and vehicles of various kinds are parked on most grass verges.

**Kid sister.** *See* KID BROTHER.

**Kids' stuff.** Anything very simple, such as something a child could handle. The expression dates from the 1920s.

**Kiki of Montparnasse.** The most famous artists' model of the 20th century was born in 1901 as Marie Prin, a French farmer's daughter who settled in Paris at the end of the First World War. Her original intention was to find work in a shoe factory, but she was discovered by the painter Moïse Kisling and began a career posing for him and other artists. The most notable of these was Man Ray (1890–1977), with whom she lived for six years, and he immortalized her in a photograph entitled *Le Violon d'Ingres* (1924) in which he painted a violin's two *f*-holes on her naked back. The title was a pun on the French phrase VIOLON D'INGRES. From 1926 Kiki exhibited her own paintings and made a name for herself as a nightclub singer. She latterly lost her looks and died in drunken poverty in 1953. The name Montparnasse, that of the famous artists' quarter of Paris, remains as a reminder of her youthful fame and beauty.

**Kildare, Dr.** The young doctor originally created by the US pulp-magazine writer Max Brand (real name Frederick Schiller Faust) for a series of stories with titles such as *The Secret of Dr Kildare* or *Calling Dr Kildare*, from which MGM produced seven films (1938–41). Dr James Kildare works at Blair General Hospital under the supervision of the tetchy Dr Gillespie, who is confined to a wheelchair. A popular television series bearing his name followed (1961–6) with Richard Chamberlain as Kildare and Raymond Massey as his boss.

**Killer fact.** A fact that, when revealed, definitively clinches a matter that has been in dispute. The usage is first recorded in 1994.

Tony Blair today reveals a dossier to justify war on Iraq – but there is not one 'killer fact' proving Saddam Hussein is an immediate threat.

www.mirror.co.uk (24 September 2002)

**Killer instinct.** A ruthless determination to succeed or win. The phrase dates from the 1920s, and was in particular applied by the press to the US world heavyweight champion Jack Dempsey (1895–1983). The allusion is to a predatory animal that lives by killing.

**Killer submarine.** A small submarine designed for searching out and sinking enemy submarines. The analogy is with a predatory animal, such as a shark or a killer whale, which hunts down and kills its prey.

**Killing field.** A place of mass slaughter. The term was originally applied to Cambodia under the KHMER ROUGE regime in the mid-1970s, when thousands of so-called 'bourgeois elements' were deported from the cities to the countryside and executed in what became known as the 'killing fields'. The phrase passed generally into the language following the film on this grim subject, *The* KILLING FIELDS (1984). The term later came to apply to any large-scale killing, whether in the countryside or not.

**Killing Fields, The.** A film (1984) based on the real-life relationship between US journalist Sidney Schanberg and his Cambodian translator Dith Pran following the US withdrawal from Phnom Penh in 1975. The plot recounts Schanberg's attempts to locate Pran after the latter is seized for 're-education' by the KHMER ROUGE. The 'killing fields' of the title were the paddy fields around Phnom Penh in which the Khmer Rouge executed their opponents. The part of Dith Pran was played by Haing S. Ngor, a doctor who had himself fled from the Khmer Rouge. In reality Dith Pran saw the killing fields himself for the first time only when he visited them as mayor of his home town, long after the Khmer Rouge had been thrown out. *See also* KILLING FIELD.

**Kilroy.** During the Second World War the phrase 'Kilroy was here' was found written up wherever the US troops (particularly Air Transport Command) had been. Its origin is a matter of conjecture. One suggestion is that a certain shipyard inspector at Quincy, Massachusetts, chalked up the words on material he had inspected. Pictorially Kilroy was a wide-eyed, bald-headed face peering over a fence, something like Mr CHAD. The outrageousness of the GRAFFITI was not so much what it said but its ubiquity, as Kilroy's presence was marked in such sacred sites as the torch of the Statue of Liberty in New York Harbour and the walls of the Arc de Triomphe in Paris.

**Kim.** The orphan boy, Kimball O'Hara, who is the hero of the novel by Rudyard Kipling that bears his name (1901), regarded by many as the writer's finest. He passes as a native Indian boy nicknamed 'Little Friend of All the World', takes up with a wise old Tibetan lama, and eventually becomes a secret agent on behalf of the British government. The British spy Kim Philby (*see* CAMBRIDGE SPY RING) was nicknamed after him, his original forenames being Harold Adrian Russell.

**Kim's game.** A memory-testing game introduced to BOY SCOUTS by their founder, Robert Baden-Powell, as a development of the 'Jewel Game' described in Rudyard Kipling's KIM, chapter 9 (1901). As explained in *Scouting for Boys* (1908), it consists in placing a number of small articles on a tray, covering them up, then uncovering them for one minute, at the end of which they are covered again. Whoever recalls the greatest number of articles wins the game. The principle lies behind more recent games and contests, such as the prize-winning procedure in *The* GENERATION GAME on television.

**Kinder, Kirche, Küche.** (German, 'children, church, kitchen'.) A traditional slogan, dating from the early years of the 20th century, regarding the place of women in Germany. The phrase was adopted by the NAZIS, who emphasized the role of women as home-makers and breeders of little Aryans. From 1933 German women were actively discouraged from going to university or taking employment, and during the Second World War women were not mobilized on anything like the same scale as they were in Britain or the Soviet Union, an ideological reservation that certainly put constraints on industrial output.

**Kindertotenlieder.** A moving cycle of five songs with orchestral accompaniment, composed in 1901–4 by Gustav Mahler (1860–1911) with words by Friedrich Rückert. The title means 'songs on the death of children'. The work was sadly prophetic, for in 1907 Mahler's adored eldest daughter died at the age of four, one of a number of tragedies to beset his family.

**Kind Hearts and Coronets.** A celebrated British film comedy (1949), loosely based by Robert Hamer and John Dighton on the turn-of-the-century novel *Israel Rank* by Roy Horniman, about a lowly relation of the aristocratic D'Ascoyne family who murders his way to the dukedom he believes is rightfully his. Starring Dennis Price as Louis Mazzini, the amoral murderer, and Alec Guinness as eight of his blueblooded victims, the film owes its title to a poem by Tennyson:

Trust me, Clara Vere de Vere,

From yon blue heavens above us bent

The grand old gardener and his wife

Smile at the claims of long descent.

Howe'er it be, it seems to me,

'Tis only noble to be good.

Kind hearts are more than coronets,

And simple faith than Norman blood.

'Lady Clara Vere de Vere' (1842)

**Kindness of strangers, The.** *See* Blanche DUBOIS.

**King, The.** The nickname of Elvis Presley (1935–77), regarded by many people as the first and greatest rock 'n' roll star. It is also the nickname of the Welsh rugby union international Barry John (b.1945), a fly-half of regal skill. *See also* KING KENNY.

**King and Country, for.** *See* THIS HOUSE WILL IN NO CIRCUMSTANCES FIGHT FOR ITS KING OR COUNTRY.

***King and I, The.*** A musical play (1951) with a score by Richard Rodgers (1902–79) and book by Oscar Hammerstein II (1895–1960) about the experiences of an English governess who is engaged to care for the children of the King of Siam. Filmed with Yul Brynner and Deborah Kerr in 1956, the play was based on the biographical book *Anna and the King of Siam* by Margaret Landon, in which she related the experiences of Anna Leonowens as governess to the king of Siam's 67 children. The story was filmed for the first time in 1946, with the same title as Landon's book. It was the actress Gertrude Lawrence, who played Anna in the first stage production, who first suggested that the book would make a good musical. Among the memorable numbers are 'Hello, Young Lovers' and 'Shall We Dance?'

**King Arthur.** A hostile nickname given to Arthur Scargill (b.1938), militant president of the National Union of Mineworkers from 1981. Margaret Thatcher described the miners as 'the ENEMY WITHIN' during their bitter and protracted 1984–5 strike, which ended in the closure of most of Britain's pits. *See also* PLUTONIUM BLONDE.

**King David Hotel.** *See* IRGUN.

**Kingfish.** A nickname of populist and charismatic US politician Huey Long (1893–1935). He was governor of Louisiana from 1928 and a US senator from 1931, and became virtual dictator of the state. The nickname was drawn from the popular radio show AMOS 'N' ANDY. Long himself is quoted (in Arthur M. Schlesinger Jnr, *The Politics of Upheaval*, 1960) as saying:

I looked around at the little fishes present and said, 'I'm the Kingfish.'

Long was also known as the Prince of Piffle. He proposed to run against Franklin D. Roosevelt in the 1936 presidential election on the 'Share Our Wealth' platform, an alternative to Roosevelt's NEW DEAL. One of his own slogans was 'Every man a king, but no man wears a crown.' He was so confident of victory that he published a book entitled *My First Days in the White House* (1935). However, Long was assassinated by a New Orleans doctor, Carl Austin Weiss, on 10 September 1935. His life was fictionalized by Robert Penn Warren (1905–89) in his PULITZER PRIZE-winning novel, *All the King's Men* (1946), which was adapted as a stage play and as an Oscar-winning film (1949) in which the Long character was named Willie Stark.

**King Kenny.** The nickname of the Scottish footballer and football club manager Kenny Dalglish (b.1951). His successes as a player and as a manager are probably without parallel in British football. Quite apart from winning 102 caps for Scotland and a Scottish league and cup double with Glasgow Celtic, during his time at Liverpool as a player (from 1977) and a manager (from 1985), Liverpool won the league championship nine times, the European Cup four times, the League Cup four times and the FA Cup twice. Small wonder that a Liverpool supporter's banner in the 1970s was seen to carry the punning message 'Kenny's from heaven.'

**King Kong.** The giant ape who is the fearsome yet curiously touching star of the HORROR MOVIE (1933) that bears his name – both parts of which suggest that he is a king (Danish *Kong*). He is discovered on a Pacific island and brought to the United States as a circus attraction. He breaks loose there, runs riot in New York and climbs the Empire State Building. He is finally gunned down by fighter planes, but not before he has gently carried a young woman (played by Fay Wray, one of the WAMPAS BABY STARS) in his hairy hand to the top of the skyscraper. 'It was Beauty killed the Beast', observes one of the characters, in the closing line of the film. The story was written by Merian Cooper and Edgar Wallace. Jessica Lange played Wray's part in the 1976 remake (in which Kong climbs the TWIN TOWERS), and in the 2005 version, directed by Peter Jackson and much invigorated by computer-generated imagery, it was taken by Naomi Watts.

**Kingledon.** A name for the Wimbledon tennis courts coined in 1972 by the *Daily Mirror* as a tribute to the US player Billie Jean King (b.1943) when she won the women's singles title there for the fourth time.

**King of Calypso.** A nickname for the US singer Harry Belafonte (b.1927). A calypso is a type of West Indian ballad, often satirical. As a child Belafonte spent five years in

Jamaica, and subsequently had a great popular success with calypsos, such as 'Banana Boat Song' ('Day-O, day-O, daylight come an' I wanna go home').

**King of Chavs.** A sobriquet awarded to the youthful English footballer Wayne Rooney (b.1985), regarded by the snobbish as the epitome of the CHAV, and by cultural commentators as a key figure in contemporary CELEBRITY CULTURE. Appropriately enough, his girlfriend Colleen McLoughlin, famed for her need of RETAIL THERAPY, is dubbed the 'Queen of Chavs'. Rooney has played for Everton, Manchester United and England with considerable success, but he has let himself down by unfortunate tantrums on (and sometimes off) the pitch. In March 2005 the president of the National Union of Teachers said that footballers such as Rooney provided a 'bad example' for children, after Rooney was shown on camera during a match against Arsenal swearing at the referee. Like many high-earning footballers, he lives in a McMANSION in Cheshire.

> Rooney has a mission to support the indigent sex workers of his native Liverpool, where a CCTV camera recorded his charitable efforts outside a brothel. 'I'll shag you for £50,' he shouted. Not all the prospective recipients of his bounty are as grateful as they might be. Curvy brunette Gina McCarrick told the *Sunday Mirror* that young Rooney has a face 'like a smacked arse'. Inexplicably, Rooney was voted most fanciable footballer in a survey of women fans carried out by research agency TNS Sport.
>
> HERMIONE EYRE and WILLIAM DONALDSON: *The Dictionary of National Celebrity* (2005)

In another survey from 2005, this time conducted among the under-10s, Rooney came second only to God in the 'most famous person' category. In the 2006 World Cup, he was sent off for treading on an opponent's testicles.

**King of Fop.** The press's sobriquet for Michael Jackson (*see* WACKO JACKO), the *soi-disant* 'King of Pop', on the occasion of his trial for child molestation in 2005. The surgically adjusted Jackson appeared in a succession of dandyish outfits, involving frock coats, armbands, multicoloured waistcoats, medallions, in a style that the journalist Dan Glaister dubbed the 'Peter-Pan-meets-bell-hop look' (*The Guardian*, 19 March 2005). Jackson was acquitted of all the charges.

**King of Hollywood.** A title awarded in the 1930s to the US film star Clark Gable (1901–60), whose most famous role was as Rhett Butler in GONE WITH THE WIND (1939). It was the columnist Ed Sullivan who polled his readers as to who was the 'King of Hollywood', and Gable won by an enormous margin. However, Gable did not have an auspicious start:

after a screen test in the 1920s the MGM producer Irving Thalberg had exclaimed, 'It's awful – take it away!', and Howard Hughes, Darryl F. Zanuck and Jack L. Warner had all been put off by the famous Gable ears.

**King of Pop.** *See* KING OF FOP.

**King of Rock 'n' Roll.** *See* the KING.

**King of Spain.** *See* WHEELIE BIN.

**King of Spin.** *See* BUSH'S POODLE.

**King of Swing.** A nickname of Benny Goodman (1909–86), the US clarinettist and band leader, who made his name playing swing, a style of jazz popular in the 1930s and 1940s.

**King Rat.** The name given to an individual rat of unusually impressive size and aggression. Hence *King Rat*, the title of a novel (1962) by James Clavell, the eponymous rat being a pragmatic US corporal imprisoned by the Japanese in Singapore's notorious Changi Jail during the Second World War. The novel provided the basis for a film (1965).

'King Rat' was also the nickname of the Ulster Protestant paramilitary leader Billy Wright (1960–97), who became the leader of his own breakaway group named the Loyalist Volunteer Force. He was implicated in the deaths of a number of Catholics and was shot dead by three INLA prisoners in the Maze. *See also* MAD DOG.

> Great King Rat died today
> Born on the twenty first of May
> Died of syphilis forty four on his birthday
> Every second word he swore
> Yes he was the son of a whore
> Always wanted by the law.
>
> FREDDIE MERCURY: 'Great King Rat'

The term 'king rat' also refers to a bizarre phenomenon in which a number of rats become mutually entangled by their tails, their struggles only serving to tighten the knots. There is a description of such a tangle in E. Annie Proulx's novel *Accordion Crimes* (1996).

**King-sized.** Extra large. The term arose in the 1940s to refer to extra-long cigarettes but subsequently came to apply to anything specially grand, as a very big bed or a huge hamburger. The idea is that the size is fit for a king. A queen-sized bed is similar, but slightly less large.

> She found herself pondering the word king-sized. What did it mean, really? A king could be any size, when it came down to it. Richard III, for example, was almost a midget, whereas Henry VIII was six foot tall and could have worn his stomach as a kilt.
>
> DERMOT BOLGER (ed.): *Finbar's Hotel*, 'The Test' (1997)

***King Solomon's Ring.*** A popular book (1949) on animal behaviour by the pioneering Austrian ethologist Konrad Lorenz (1903–89). In it he describes many of his discoveries and experiments, including that involving the imprinting of ducklings and goslings: it was Lorenz who found that at a certain stage after hatching the young birds adopt the nearest living creature as their mother and follow it around as long as it makes the appropriate quacks. Thus Lorenz himself became 'mother' to many. The original Solomon's ring enabled the ancient king of Israel (10th century BC) to understand and converse with the animal world. In addition, it helped him to overcome all opponents and to transpose himself to the celestial spheres, where he learned the secrets of the universe. The ring also sealed up the refractory jinn in jars and cast them into the Red Sea.

***Kingston bypass.*** One of Britain's earliest urban bypasses, south of Kingston-upon-Thames, and now part of the A3. Planning of the bypass began in the 1920s, and the name came to encapsulate the mixed pleasures and frustrations of motoring in and around London.

> Give me the Kingston By-Pass
> And a thoroughly 'posh' machine
> Like a Healey three-litre
> All complete with heater
> Or a shiny grey Chevrolet Limousine.
>
> NOËL COWARD: *The Globe Revue*, 'Give Me the Kingston By-Pass' (1952)

***King Street.*** A name for the executive committee of the Communist Party of Great Britain, from its former location in the London street of this name leading to the present Covent Garden Market.

***Kinnockio.*** A hostile nickname given to Neil Kinnock (b.1942), leader of the Labour Party (1983–92) and subsequently a European Union commissioner. The nickname was modelled on Pinocchio, the childlike puppet hero of a children's story by the Italian writer C. Collodi (pseudonym of Carlo Lorenzini; 1826–90). Pinocchio, whose nose grows whenever he tells a lie, was also the subject of a 1940 Walt Disney cartoon film. Kinnock is also known as the WELSH WINDBAG and after he was elevated to the peerage in 2005 became known as Lord Kinnockio of Windbag.

***Kinsey Report.*** When the US zoologist Dr Alfred C. Kinsey (1894–1956) found himself short of answers to his students' questions about human sexual behaviour he set out to compile the sexual life history of the human species. The result in 1948, after ten years of research and thousands of interviews, was his landmark study *Sexual Behaviour in the Human Male*, otherwise the Kinsey Report. What shocked its readers was not so much the varieties of sexual experience it detailed as the explicit nature of the research. A second volume on female sexuality followed in 1953. Kinsey was known to colleagues as 'Prok' (*Professor Kinsey*) and to the press as 'Dr Sex'. The 2004 biopic *Kinsey* starred Liam Neeson as the doctor.

***Kippers.*** An acronym to denote the increasing numbers of TWENTY-SOMETHINGS who still live with their parents, saddled as they are with student debt and the difficulty of placing a foot on the bottom rung of the housing ladder. The acronym stands for '*k*ids *i*n *p*arents' *p*ockets *e*roding *r*etirement *s*avings'. A survey by the Prudential insurance company in 2005 found that there were some 6.8 million Kippers in Britain.

***Kipper tie.*** A very wide and brightly coloured tie popular in the 1960s, so named punningly because it was promoted by the London menswear designer Michael Fish.

***Kir.*** A drink made from dry white wine and crème de cassis, named after and perhaps even devised by Canon Félix Kir (1876–1968), the resistance hero and mayor of Dijon during the Second World War. It was first sampled in Britain in the mid-1960s. A 'kir royale' is made with sparkling wine.

***Kirlian photography.*** A technique said to record directly on photographic film the field radiation of electricity emitted by an object to which an electric charge has been applied. It was developed in the 1930s by the Russian technicians Semyon D. and Valentina K. Kirlian and continues to attract both claims and counterclaims regarding its efficacy, especially as a tool in psychotherapy.

***Kirov Ballet.*** The best-known name of a Russian ballet company that developed from the Bolshoi Theatre of St Petersburg, which housed the city's opera and ballet company from 1783 to 1860, and the Maryinsky Theatre, which opened in 1860. After the October Revolution of 1917 it became the State Academic Theatre for Opera and Ballet, and in 1935 it was renamed, in honour of the Russian revolutionary Sergei Kirov (1886–1934), head of the Leningrad Communist Party, assassinated the previous year. It retained the name until the demise of the Soviet Union in 1991, since it was the one by which it won international renown, but it has since been renamed the Maryinsky Ballet. Its reputation suffered in the 1960s when its repertory became sterile, resulting in the mass defection to the West of some of its top dancers, including the finest, Rudolf Nureyev (1938–93).

***Kismet.*** A musical play (1953) based on a play (1911) by Edward Knoblock about a poet turned beggar who has a series of adventures reminiscent of *The Arabian Nights*. The music of Alexander Borodin was arranged by Robert Wright and George Forrest, and the show's most popular numbers include 'Baubles, Bangles and Beads', 'Stranger in Paradise' and 'This is My Beloved'. The title came from the Turkish *kismet* ('portion' or 'lot') and is now commonly understood to mean 'fate'.

**Kiss.** An acronym standing for 'keep it simple, stupid'. The maxim is of US origin, and is said to have been much used by the scientists and technicians on the APOLLO space programme of the 1960s, though it may well be earlier than that. A modern Occam's razor, it warns those foolish enough to think that complexity is clever that the best results can usually be achieved by reducing things to their essentials. It is often invoked in such fields as engineering and software development. The formula of direct address to an uncomprehending person was successfully repeated in the slogan IT'S THE ECONOMY, STUPID.

**Kiss and make up.** To become reconciled. The image is of two children resuming a friendship after a quarrel or fight, or two lovers resuming their attachment after a tiff. The expression emerged in the 1940s as an alternative to the much older and still current 'to kiss and be friends'.

**Kiss goodbye to something.** To accept its loss or non-realization, as: 'When the children went down with flu we had to kiss goodbye to our holiday.' The expression dates from the early years of the 20th century and relates to a genuine kiss on parting. The ironic touch was probably intensified by the First World War, in which a farewell kiss may well have been a final one.

> Wretched Derby can surely kiss the play-offs good-bye after being outgunned by Burnley, going down 3–1.
>
> *People* (16 April 1995)

**Kissing garden.** A garden designed for private use by its owner's family and friends. It typically consists of a small enclosed paved area with seats and potted plants or shrubs arranged semi-formally around a rectangular pond, and takes its name from the title of Charlotte Bingham's romantic novel *The Kissing Garden* (1999), set in the English countryside in the years following the First World War. The sentimental analogy is an old one. *See also* HEARTS AND FLOWERS.

**Kiss Kiss Bang Bang.** A phrase used to denote the sexy super-spy genre in both fiction and film, and sometimes more broadly to sum up the very essence of the movies. The phrase appears to have originated in 1962, when an Italian journalist dubbed James BOND Mr Kiss Kiss Bang Bang.

However, Ian Fleming himself, in a letter to Raymond Chandler (*c*.1955), described his books as 'straight pillow fantasies of the bang-bang, kiss-kiss variety'. The US film critic Pauline Kael published a book on the movies in 1968 with the title *Kiss Kiss Bang Bang*, and explained it thus:

> The words 'Kiss Kiss Bang Bang', which I saw on an Italian movie poster, are perhaps the briefest statement imaginable of the basic appeal of the movies. This appeal is what attracts us and ultimately what makes us despair when we begin to understand how seldom movies are more than this.

The original title credit music to the Bond film *Thunderball* (1965) was a song entitled 'Mr Kiss Kiss Bang Bang', written by John Barry and Leslie Bricusse, and sung by Shirley Bassey, but, as this did not have the film's title in it, it was used elsewhere in the film instead, and replaced at the beginning by a song called 'Thunderball', written by John Barry and Don Black, and sung by Tom Jones – who reputedly fainted in the recording studio while singing the final long high note.

The title *Kiss Kiss Bang Bang* has also been used for at least three films: (1) a 1966 Italian production, directed by Duccio Tessari, about a former spy who is spared from death if he can steal a secret formula; (2) a 2000 US production, written and directed by Ray Brady, about a science-fiction writer whose obsession with the girl next door turns to madness; and (3) a 2005 US production written and directed by Shane Black about a New York crook who is cast to play the part of a private detective in a film and ends up becoming involved in a murder mystery.

***Kiss Me Deadly.*** A crime novel (1953) by 'Mickey' (Frank Morrison) Spillane (1918–2006). Detective Mike HAMMER, having destroyed a crime syndicate and killed its boss, finds himself up against a blonde armed with a gun and wearing just a robe after her bath. She says, 'You're going to die now … but first you can do it. Deadly … deadly … kiss me.' Instead Hammer ignites her with his cigarette lighter. An exuberant film version (1955), with brutal close-ups and unusual camera angles, was directed by Robert Aldrich with Ralph Meeker as Hammer.

***Kiss Me Kate.*** A musical comedy (1948) with a score by Cole Porter (1892–1964), loosely based on William Shakespeare's *The Taming of the Shrew*. The show interweaves elements of the original play with the backstage goings-on of a company supposedly rehearsing it. The title was based on a line in Shakespeare's play:

> *Katharina*: Husband, let's follow, to see the end of this ado.
> *Petruchio*: First kiss me, Kate, and we will.
> *Katharina*: What! in the midst of the street?
>
> WILLIAM SHAKESPEARE: *The Taming of the Shrew*, V i.

**Kiss-me-quick.** A type of small hat sold at the seaside and perhaps even bearing the words of the invitation or some similar device. In the 19th century the name was in use for a small bonnet worn on the back of the head. The implication is that the hat leaves the face open for the desired action, unlike more ornate or veiled articles of millinery.

**Kiss my arse** or **ass.** A crude challenge or rejection, inviting a person to perform the stated obsequious and degrading act. *See also* Pogues *under* ROCK GROUP NAMES.

**Kiss of death.** Anything certain to cause the end of an enterprise, as: 'The new regulation was the kiss of death for our farming experiment.' The phrase dates from the 1940s. The original 'kiss of death' must have been that given treacherously by Judas to Jesus (Matthew 26:49), but the phrase in this form is attributed to the American Democratic politician Al Smith (1873–1944), referring in a 1926 speech to the support given to a political opponent by the newspapers of William Randolph Hearst. There is also a tradition in the Mafia that when one is kissed by the boss one is being sentenced to death. *Kiss of Death* is the title of a 1947 US crime melodrama, remade with the same title in 1995.

**Kiss of life.** A name originally used in the 1960s for mouth-to-mouth resuscitation. Sleeping Beauty was awakened from her deathlike sleep by the Prince's kiss. The expression is also used metaphorically for anything that revives or reinvigorates. *See also* KISS OF DEATH.

**Kiss of peace.** A mutual greeting between members of the congregation in the Eucharist. It is not an actual kiss but a shaking of hands, usually accompanied by words such as 'Peace be with you'. It is a revival of a custom in the primitive church and is not welcomed by some of the faithful, who claim that it is artificial and disrupts the progression of the service.

***Kiss of the Spider Woman.*** A film (1985) based on a novel *El beso de la mujer araña* (1976) by the Argentinian writer Manuel Puig. It is about the unlikely friendship that develops between a gay man and a political prisoner when they are thrown into the same cell in a South American prison. The title refers to a B-MOVIE about 'Spider Woman' that the two discuss between sessions of torture at the hands of their captors.

**Kissogram.** A greetings service for a party or celebration, in which a person, typically a provocatively dressed young woman, is hired to come and kiss the celebrator. The word is a blend of 'kiss' and 'telegram'. *See also* STRIPPERGRAM.

**Kitchener's Army.** The mass volunteer army recruited in Britain by Field Marshal Earl Kitchener (1850–1916) in the First World War. The recruits were also referred to as the New Army or New Armies. Kitchener, who had become a British national hero after his campaigns in the Sudan and the Boer War, was appointed war minister on the outbreak of the First World War. Between 1914 and the introduction of conscription in January 1916 some 2.6 million men had volunteered. Kitchener's enormously successful campaign was aided by the famous poster with his uniformed and moustachioed portrait pointing towards the viewer, accompanied by the slogan 'Your King and Country Need You' (devised by Eric Field of the Caxton Advertising Agency a month before the outbreak of war). However, this success created problems in training and equipping so many men, and in filling the gaps in the labour force that they left behind. Kitchener himself died when the cruiser *Hampshire*, on which he was sailing on a diplomatic mission to Russia, struck a mine off the Orkneys. *See also* OLD CONTEMPTIBLES.

**Kitchen sink drama.** A type of drama popular in the 1950s, in which the plot centres on the more sordid aspects of working-class or lower-middle-class domestic life, much of which is spent at the kitchen sink. Examples of the genre include John Osborne's LOOK BACK IN ANGER (1956), set in a cluttered bedsitter, Shelagh Delaney's *A* TASTE OF HONEY (1958), set in a cheerless flat in Salford, and Arnold Wesker's *The Kitchen* (1959), set in the chaotic kitchen of a busy restaurant. *See also* ANGRY YOUNG MAN; KITCHEN SINK SCHOOL.

**Kitchen Sink School.** A group of artists active in the 1950s who specialized in drab working-class subjects, especially interiors and still-lifes of domestic clutter. The main artists covered by the term were John Bratby (1928–92), Derrick Greaves (b.1927), Edward Middleditch (1923–87) and Jack Smith (b.1928). The name was coined by the critic David Sylvester in the December 1954 number of *Encounter*. *See also* KITCHEN SINK DRAMA.

**Kitemark.** The label on a manufactured product that says it meets with the approval of the British Standards Institution. It consists of a kite-shaped monogram of the letters BSI, the Institution's initials. The BSI was founded in 1901 and the Kitemark was already in use in 1903 on tram rails.

**Kitsch.** A term first recorded in English in the 1920s for any art, object or design that is considered to be lacking in taste because of its garishness or sentimentality but that, because of these attributes, may well have gained a value in its own right. The word is German for 'vulgar trash', and derives from *verkitschen*, 'to cheapen', 'to sentimentalize'. It was originally applied to sentimental German novels and novelettes but was then extended to cover other forms of expression.

**Kitten heel.** A type of low heel on a woman's shoe, or a shoe with such a heel. The heel is so called because it supposedly suggests that its wearer is a SEX KITTEN. Such heels were in fashion in the early 1960s and again in the 1990s.

**Kitty Hawk.** A town in North Carolina, situated on a sandy stretch of Atlantic coast. It was just south of the town, in the Kill Devil Hills, on 17 December 1903 that Orville (1871–1948) and Wilbur Wright (1867–1912) made the first sustained, manned, powered and controllable flight in a heavier-than-air aircraft. Their aeroplane was named *The Flyer*. The name Kitty Hawk, which has become almost synonymous with that first flight, probably derives from the Algonkian name Chickahauk, the meaning of which is unknown.

**Kiwanis.** An organization founded in Detroit in 1915 aiming to improve business ethics and provide leadership for raising the level of business and professional ideals. There are many Kiwanis clubs in the United States and Canada, and also several in Britain. The name is said to come from a Native American language and to mean 'to make oneself known'.

**Kiwi.** A native of New Zealand, especially a soldier or member of a sports team, from the indigenous Maori name of the flightless bird that is the country's symbol or mascot.

**KKK.** *See* KU KLUX KLAN.

**Kleenex.** The trade name of a type of soft paper tissue, used for paper handkerchiefs. Kleenex (originally known as Celluwipes) were the world's first paper handkerchiefs (1924), and were manufactured by Kimberly-Clark in the United States. The task of selling the concept to the public was entrusted to the advertising guru Albert Lasker (1880–1952), who, with his 1921 Kotex campaign, had already introduced the world at large to the sanitary towel.

**Kludge.** A term coined around 1962 by the US writer J.W. Granholm for what he described as 'an ill-assorted collection of poorly matching parts, forming a distressing whole'. It contains an ironic reference to German *klug*, 'clever'. At first it was applied to improvised and unreliable computer set-ups, but it soon broadened out to cover anything thrown together more by luck than judgement and with little style or sophistication.

**Kneecapping.** A form of punishment used by paramilitary groups in Northern Ireland, especially the IRA. Used against informers, defectors or minor criminals, kneecapping involves shooting or drilling through the victim's kneecaps, so crippling them. Such punishments continued even after the 1997 cease-fire. In Italy kneecappings were carried out by left-wing terror groups in the 1970s against businessmen and judges, along with kidnappings and shootings. *See also* PADRE PIO.

**Knee-jerk reaction.** An automatic and unthinking response. The allusion is to the test of the nervous system known as the knee-jerk reflex. A tap with a rubber hammer just below the kneecap stretches a tendon of one of the thigh muscles, causing it to contract and jerk the lower leg up.

> Divorce specialist Vanessa Lloyd Platt advises: 'Many people see a solicitor before they're psychologically ready to deal with it [divorce] – it's a knee-jerk reaction.'
> *Independent on Sunday* (3 October 1999)

**Kneesies.** Amorous play with the knees, usually covertly under the table. *See also* FOOTSIE.

**Knee-slapper.** An uproarious joke of the kind that makes the listener slap their knee with delight. The US expression dates from the 1960s.

**Knees-up.** A boisterous and energetic dance, in which the dancers raise alternate knees. Hence any lively party or celebration. The dance gets its name from 'Knees up, Mother Brown!', the song to which it is traditionally performed. Both date back to at least 1918, and the dance was widely performed in squares, streets and pubs on Armistice Night (11 November) that year, but the first published version of the song seems to be as below. It was widely popularized by the Cockney duo GERT AND DAISY.

> Ooh! Knees up Mother Brown!
> Well! Knees up Mother Brown!
> … knees up, knees up!
> Don't get the breeze up
> Knees up Mother Brown.
> HARRIS WESTON, BERT LEE and IRVING TAYLOR: 'Knees up, Mother Brown!' (1938)

**Knickerbocker Glory.** A dessert consisting of ice cream served with fruit, cream and other ingredients in a tall glass. It is uncertain what relationship it has, if any, with knickerbockers. The name first became familiar in the 1930s.

> 'Have a *parfait* … They do a very good Maiden's Dream. Not to speak of Alpine Glow. Or the Knickerbocker Glory.'
> GRAHAME GREENE: *Gun for Sale*, ch. 1 (1936)

**Knievel, Evel.** The adopted name of the US motorcycle stunt performer Robert C. Knievel (b.1938). He began to perform stunts as a teenager and after a succession of varied jobs, from hockey player to safecracker, formed Evel Knievel's

Motorcyle Devils in 1965. He soon gained fame for his spectacular and dangerous performances, one of which resulted in spinal injuries when in May 1975 his car failed to clear 13 buses. His son, Robbie Knievel, followed him in his hazardous career.

**Knight in shining armour.** An idealized chivalrous man who comes to the aid of a DAMSEL IN DISTRESS. The image of a dashing knight in glittering armour on a white charger is an old one, but the expression dates only from the 1960s. *See also* WHITE KNIGHT.

**Knight of the shire.** A Conservative MP for a country consistency who has been knighted for political services. The designation derives from the term for a gentleman representing a shire or county in parliament in medieval times, originally one of two of the rank of knight.

**Knightsbridge.** The nickname given by British forces to a crossroads in the desert south of Tobruk, during the North African campaign in the Second World War. There were fierce tank battles here in May–June 1942 prior to the German advance to El ALAMEIN. The name comes from an affluent area of London that includes the department store Harrods.

**Knock back.** To drink or eat, especially quickly and/or in large quantities. The expression can be traced back to the 1910s, but does not seem to have become widespread until the 1950s. It often connotes the rapid draining of a glass of alcoholic drink.

> I knocked back the last of my brandy and went out.
>
> JOHN WYNDHAM: *Day of the Triffids* (1951)

In British slang, 'knock back' can also have financial implications: if a purchase 'knocked you back' £50, it cost you that much.

**Knock boots.** In US college slang from the mid-1980s, to have sexual intercourse.

**Knocked the bastard off.** *See* WELL, WE KNOCKED THE BASTARD OFF.

**Knock** or **hit for six.** To demolish utterly an argument or to defeat completely an opponent, figuratively or literally. In cricket the ball is 'knocked for six' when the batsman, by hitting it full pitch over the boundary of the field, scores six runs, so 'punishing' the bowler. The expression dates from the early 20th century: a hit over the boundary scored only four runs until 1910, when six runs were allotted to such a stroke. In the quotation below, the expression is applied punningly to England's 6–0 football win over Luxembourg in 1999.

> A hat-trick for [England's captain Alan] Shearer, as England knock Luxembourg for six.
>
> *BBC1 Television News*, headline (4 September 1999)

**Knock, knock!** An invitation to respond to a riddle punning on a personal name. An old example is: 'Knock, knock!' 'Who's there?' 'Roland.' 'Roland who?' 'Roland mow the lawn.' More sophisticated examples may be allusive: 'Knock, knock!' 'Who's there?' 'Sam and Janet.' 'Sam and Janet who?' 'Sam and Janet evening.' A restriction to personal names is not essential: 'Knock, knock!' 'Who's there?' 'A little old lady.' 'A little old lady who?' 'I didn't know you could yodel.'

**Knock-on effect.** A secondary or indirect effect; a consequence of an earlier action. The image is of a 'pile-up', in which one vehicle runs into another, which in turn strikes a third.

**Knock someone's block off.** To hit them hard on the head. The expression is mostly used in general threats that are not implemented, as: 'If he does that again I'll knock his block off.'

**Knock** or **blow someone's socks off.** To impress them. The image is of a stunning or explosive effect that causes the socks to fly from the feet.

**Knole sofa** or **settee.** A type of sofa designed in the style of an early 17th-century model, with adjustable sides that can be lowered to make it into a 'day bed'. It was first fashionable in the 1940s and takes its name from the prototype at Knole House, Kent.

**Knot Garden, The.** A semi-mystical opera by Michael Tippett (1905–98) with a libretto by the composer. It was first performed in 1974. The symbolic knot garden of the title is a revolving stage device in which the various characters work out their relationships. The characters include a benevolent analyst, Mangus (a variant of 'magus'?), who sets up an elaborate charade based on Shakespeare's *The Tempest* to help the others to work through their problems.

**Know all the answers.** To be knowledgeable or expert on something. The expression dates from the 1930s and is often sarcastically used of a 'know-all': 'You know all the answers, don't you?'

**Knowledge, The.** The test that drivers of London BLACK CABS must pass to show that they know the name and location of every street and the shortest or quickest route to it. Drivers have typically prepared for the test by riding a moped around the streets while memorizing routes from a plan clipped to the handlebars. This particular method formed the subject of Jack Rosenthal's enjoyable television play *The Knowledge* (1979), with Nigel Hawthorne as the sadistic examiner.

**Known unknowns.** *See* UNKNOWN UNKNOWNS.

**Know one's onions.** To be knowledgeable in a particular field. The expression dates from the 1920s and is sometimes said to refer to the lexicographer C.T. Onions (1873–1965), co-editor of the *Oxford English Dictionary* and author of books on English. This seems unlikely, however, because its earliest record is in US usage. Also unlikely is a proposed source in rhyming slang, with 'onions' short for 'onion rings', meaning 'things'. It may be simply a whimsical variant on 'to know one's stuff', perhaps with an implied pun on 'stuffing', of which (sage and) onions were by the 1920s a stock ingredient.

**Know the score.** To understand the situation; to appreciate what is happening. The expression dates from the 1930s and alludes to someone who keeps up with the score in a particular sport.

**Know what I mean, Harry?** A possibly apocryphal remark by the British boxer Frank Bruno (b.1961) to the BBC TV sports commentator Harry Carpenter. The catchphrase became forever after associated with Bruno.

**Knuckle-duster.** A loop of heavy metal, gripped in the hand and fitting over the knuckles, used as an offensive weapon. Its origin goes back to the days of Roman pugilism.

**Knuckle sandwich.** A punch in the mouth.

**Kojak.** The tough New York policeman played by Telly Savalas in the popular television series that bore his name (1973–8). He was the creation of the writer Abby Mann, and his 'trademarks' were his bald head, his habit of sucking lollipops and his catchphrase, 'Who loves ya, baby?' In a new series, first aired in 2005, the part of Kojak was played by the African American actor Ving Rhames.

**Kon-Tiki expedition.** The unique voyage made in 1947 by the Norwegian Thor Heyerdahl (1914–2002) with five companions, who sailed a balsa raft from Callao in Peru to Tuamotu Island in the South Pacific. Their object was to support the theory that the Polynesian race reached the Pacific islands in this fashion and were descendants of the Incas of Peru. Their raft was called *Kon-Tiki* after the Inca sun-god.

> The original name of the sun-god Virakocha, which seems to have been more used in Peru in old times, was Kon-Tiki or Illa-Tiki, which means Sun-Tiki or Illa-Tiki. Kon-Tiki was a high priest and sun-king of the Incas' legendary 'white men'

who had left the enormous ruins on the shores of Lake Titicaca.
> THOR HEYERDAHL: *The Kon-Tiki Expedition* (1950)

**Kop, The.** The former terrace at the south end of the Anfield stadium, the home ground of Liverpool football club, was opened on 1 September 1906 and within weeks was dubbed the Spion Kop, or simply the Kop, after the BOER WAR battle of 24 January 1900 at Spion Kop ('Lookout Hill') that arose from repeated British attempts to relieve the siege of Ladysmith. The battle resulted in some 250 British casualties, including many Merseysiders. The Kop was roofed in 1928 and became the largest covered terrace in Britain, with room for 28,000 people. It was demolished following the club's final home match of the 1993–4 season on 30 April 1994 against Norwich City and a concert on 1 May featuring Merseybeat bands of the 1960s, such as Gerry and the Pacemakers and The Searchers. It was replaced by a new stand seating 12,000 and housing a club shop and a branch of McDONALD'S, the first at a sports stadium in Britain. The initiator of the original nickname is said to have been Ernest Edwards, sports editor of the *Liverpool Daily Post*. The name was also in use elsewhere, as at Arsenal's Plumstead ground and Birmingham's Tilton Road. Bradford City's Valley Parade ground had a 'Nunn's Kop', named after one of the club's founders.

**Korean War.** A conflict between North and South Korea. In 1950 the communist North, supported by the USSR, invaded the South, but a counterattack by mainly US forces sent by the UNITED NATIONS Security Council pushed the communists back over the 38th parallel of latitude (the original dividing line between the two Koreas, established in 1945), and pressed as far north as North Korea's border with China. Chinese intervention on the North Korean side then drove the UN forces as far south as the South Korean capital, Seoul, in early 1951. After two more years of fighting, an armistice was signed in 1953, restoring the territorial status quo. The threats to bomb China uttered by General Douglas MacArthur, commander of the UN forces, seemed to some to be likely to start a THIRD WORLD WAR and led to his sacking by President Harry S. Truman. *See also* COLD WAR.

**Korfball.** (Dutch *korfbal*, literally 'basket ball'). A combination of NETBALL and basketball invented in 1901 by an Amsterdam schoolmaster, Nico Broekhuysen, and soon after adopted in Britain and elsewhere. It is played out of doors by two teams of six, usually women against men, and goals are scored by throwing the ball into an open-ended basket at the top of a goalpost. Action consists almost entirely in passing the ball from hand to hand; kicking or punching the ball, or running with it, are illegal. Correct play is courteous and considerate, and the fact that the game was devised for both sexes has caused it to be both gentlemanly and even at times ladylike.

**Kraken Wakes, The.** A SCIENCE FICTION novel (1953) by John Wyndham (pen-name of John Wyndham Parkes Lucas Beynon Harris; 1903–69). As a result of a global disaster interstellar invaders settle on the seabed and flood Britain. The title was inspired by Tennyson's poem 'The Kraken' (1830):

> Below the thunders of the upper deep;
> Far, far beneath in the abysmal sea,
> His ancient, dreamless, uninvaded sleep
> The Kraken sleepeth.

**Krankies, The.** A Scottish comic double act consisting of the husband-and-wife team Ian and Janette Tough, the latter in the role of 'wee Jimmy', a naughty schoolboy. The pair were established as regulars on the children's television programme CRACKERJACK and then had their own television show in *The Krankies Klub* (1982–4). Their humour consists largely of juvenile 'anti-authoritarian' routines with raucously delivered quips and the inevitable slapstick.

**Krapp's Last Tape.** A short play (1958), though by no means one of his shortest, by the Irish writer Samuel Beckett (1906–89). The scatologically named Krapp listens obsessively to monologues recorded by his younger self – who seems a stranger and a fool to the pessimistic old man. At one point he eats a banana. The play was written for the Irish actor Patrick Magee. Krapp's later incarnations have included Max Wall, Albert Finney and more recently John Hurt.

> Perhaps my best years are gone … but I wouldn't want them back.
>
> *Krapp's Last Tape*

**K ration.** An emergency food ration consisting of a single prepared meal, supplied to US soldiers in combat in the Second World War. It was named after the American physiologist who instigated it, Ancel B. Keys (1904–2004).

**Kray twins.** The murderers Ronnie (1933–95) and Reggie (1933–2000) Kray were born in the East End of London, where they ran a criminal Mafia-style operation in the 1960s. Their 'firm' collected protection money, organized illegal gambling and drinking clubs, and participated in gang warfare. The dominant twin was Ronnie, who modelled himself on Chicago gangsters. In the late 1960s he entered The Blind Beggar, a pub on Mile End Road, and shot dead

George Cornell, a member of a rival gang, while Reggie lured another, Jack 'The Hat' McVitie, to a flat and stabbed him to death. The twins were tried at the Old Bailey in 1969 and given prison sentences of not less than 30 years. A campaign to free them failed, and Ronnie died in prison. In 1999 a further campaign to free Reggie was mounted on the grounds that he had now served the full prison term. Both received FULL MONTY East End funerals. A memorable biopic, *The Krays*, appeared in 1990, directed by Peter Medak and starring Gary and Martin Kemp as the brothers.

**Krazy Kat.** The comic-strip alley cat so known was invented by the cartoonist George Herriman in 1910, and his adventures with his friend Ignatz Mouse were syndicated in US newspapers until the artist's death in 1944. The mad moggy has also led a long life in animated films.

**Kremlin.** The walled palace complex of the tsars of Russia in Moscow, mostly dating from the 15th to the 18th centuries. The Kremlin subsequently became the centre of government of the Soviet Union and since 1991 of the Russian Federation. 'The Kremlin' thus became synonymous with the Soviet government, and Western analysts of Soviet affairs became known as Kremlinologists or Kremlin-watchers.

**Kriegspiel.** (German, 'war play'.) A word adopted in English for a game introduced in the British Army after the Franco-Prussian War of 1870. It arose in Switzerland earlier in the 19th century and was played by moving blocks representing parts of armies, guns and the like about on maps. As such it provided useful strategical and tactical training for military students. In *c*.1900 the word was applied by H.M. Temple to a form of chess in which two players at separate boards play without seeing each other or even being told each other's moves. They may, however, put a restricted number of questions to an umpire, who sits at a third board. This variant on the traditional form of the game is, however, hardly a 'war game'.

**Kristallnacht.** *See* HOLOCAUST.

**Kronstadt Mutiny.** A revolt in 1921 by the Soviet garrison of the naval base at Kronstadt in northwest Russia. Kronstadt is situated on Kotlin Island in the Gulf of Finland. The mutineers demanded greater democratic freedom, a free market for peasants to sell their produce and an end to the requisitioning of grain. Although the mutiny was put down, this and other disturbances encouraged LENIN to change direction and adopt the NEW ECONOMIC POLICY.

**Krueger, Freddy.** *See* ELM STREET.

**Krypton Factor, The.** A popular television programme in the form of a combined quiz and physical endurance test, screened from 1976 to 1995. Competitors were tested for brawn on a military assault course and for brain in a series of IQ, observational and general knowledge questions. The prize was a trophy. The title had nothing to do with the gas so called but was taken from the name of the home planet of the comic-book hero SUPERMAN.

**Kryptonite.** *See* SUPERMAN.

**Ku Klux Klan.** A secret US society of white supremacists, noted for acts of violence against Jews and African Americans. It is often referred to as the KKK or the Klan. The name possibly derives from the Greek *kuklos* ('circle') with *Klan* ('clan') spelt thus for the sake of orthographic alliteration, although another theory is that the name echoes the sound of a rifle bolt being drawn back ready for firing. The Klan was originally formed in Tennessee in 1866 to resist the introduction of civil rights for African Americans in the South in the wake of the American Civil War. A combination of anti-Klan federal legislation and the fact that it had managed to achieve most of its objectives led to its virtual disappearance by the late 1870s. However, the Klan was revived in 1915 by Colonel William J. Simmons (1880–1945), and added anti-socialism, anti-Semitism, anti-Catholicism and general xenophobia to its portfolio of hatreds. It received a further boost from the white backlash against the civil rights movement and federal civil rights legislation introduced in the 1950s and 1960s, but it has subsequently declined and fragmented. Some members are thought to be associated with neo-NAZI groups. When in action, Klan members light fiery crosses and dress up in long white robes and long pointed caps that also cover their faces. The top Klansman is traditionally known as the grand wizard, and other officers in the hierarchy go by such titles as grand dragon, grand titan and grand cyclops. *See also The* BIRTH OF A NATION.

**Kulaks.** Those wealthier peasant farmers in Russia who owned their own land and were important figures in the social structure of village life. The word *kulak* derives from the Russian for 'fist' and means 'a tight-fisted person'. After the Bolshevik Revolution of 1917 the kulaks' position was eroded, but the introduction of the NEW ECONOMIC POLICY in 1921 favoured them. They opposed the drive to collectivize agriculture from 1929, and as a result were 'liquidated' as a class on STALIN's orders (the process was called 'dekulakization'). By 1934 most kulaks had been arrested, exiled to remote parts of the Soviet Union or executed, and their property taken over by the state.

**Kultur.** (German, 'culture'.) A word taken up in English in a derogatory sense for the German view of civilization in the First and Second World Wars, the latter necessarily from a darker NAZI angle. It involved notions of racial and cultural superiority, militarism and imperialism, and became popularly associated with the remark attributed to Hermann Goering: 'Whenever I heard the word culture, I reach for my pistol.' The words correctly belong to the dramatist Hanns Johst: *Wenn ich Kultur höre entsichere ich meine Browning* ('When I hear the word "culture" I release the safety-catch of my Browning') (*Schlageter*, 1933).

**Kumbayah.** The title and key word of a Gullah spiritual, originating some time in the 1920s or even earlier and first published in the 1930s. It was then rediscovered in Angola, where it may have been taken by missionaries, and was revived in the folk-singing boom of the 1950s and 1960s, being recorded by the likes of Joan Baez and Peter, Paul and Mary. It also became popular with Girl Guides singing round the camp fire. The word itself is Creole for 'come by here'. It ends every line of the song, one version of which runs as follows:

Someone's crying, Lord, kumbayah,
Someone's singing, Lord, kumbayah,
Someone's praying, Lord, kumbayah,
Sinners need you, Lord, kumbayah,
Someone's sleeping, Lord, kumbayah,
Come by here, my Lord, kumbayah.

**Kuomintang.** (Chinese, 'National People's Party'.) A Chinese political party formed by Sun Yat-sen (1867–1925) in 1912, which, after his death, passed to the control of General Chiang Kai-shek (1887–1975). From 1927 to 1949 the Kuomintang was in power in China when it was driven out by the Communist Party under Mao Zedong (1893–1976). The Nationalists still maintain themselves in Taiwan (formerly Formosa). *See also* CASH-MY-CHEQUE, GENERAL; GENERAL BELGRANO.

**Kwok's disease.** *See* CHINESE RESTAURANT SYNDROME.

**Kyoto Protocol.** An international agreement (in full, the Kyoto Protocol to the United Nations Framework Convention on Climate Change) committing its signatories to reducing emissions of carbon dioxide and other greenhouse gases (*see* GREENHOUSE EFFECT). It was concluded in Kyoto, Japan, in 1997 and came into force in 2005. It has not been ratified by the United States, however, which effectively precludes any chance of its success.

# L

**Labanotation.** A system of recording human movement, invented by the Hungarian dance theorist Rudolf Laban (1879–1958) and first published in1928. The basic symbol is the rectangle, which is modified in shape to show direction of movement, in length to show duration of movement, and in shade to show level. It is written on a vertical, three-line stave, with the centre line representing the division of the body into left and right and the two columns used as symbols to indicate means of support and left and right leg gestures. Additional columns of symbols show positions for the body, arms, hands and head. Thestave is read from top to bottom and written from the performer's point of view. The most frequent application of Labanotation is for recording dance choreographies.

**Labour Party.** One of the major political parties of Britain, established with the aim of promoting socialism. It has been so called since 1906 but was originally formed as the Labour Representation Committee in 1900 from such elements as the Independent Labour Party, the trade unions, and the Fabian Society. The first Labour government was that of Ramsay MacDonald in 1924; the second lasted from 1929 to 1931, when the party split over the cuts in unemployment benefit. It was not returned to power again until 1945 and was replaced by the Conservatives in 1951. It was again in office from 1964 to 1970, 1974 to 1979, and from 1997 having, as NEW LABOUR, been reborn in the image of its leader, Tony Blair (*see* BLAIRISM; BLATCHERISM; BUSH'S POODLE), ridding itself of its commitment to state socialism (*see* CLAUSE FOUR) and generally making itself more appealing to that part of the electorate that had previously voted for the Conservative Party (*see* MONDEO MAN; WORCESTER WOMAN).

**Ladette.** The female equivalent of the NEW LAD of the late 1990s, as an embodiment of the type of up-front feminism displayed by RIOT GRRLS. The term became particularly attached to the television presenter Zoë Ball (b.1970).

'I [television presenter Denise Van Outen (b.1974)] don't drink pints and I'm not a ladette. People say I'm a ladette just because I'm an outspoken girl. But I don't down pints and go to pubs and snooker halls.'

> *The Times Magazine* (11 September 1999)

**Ladies who lunch.** A term for the wealthy set of dowagers, countesses, heiresses and Trophy wives (*see* TROPHY WIFE) who inhabit Manhattan's fashionable Upper East Side, one of whose staple pleasures is to meet up for lunch and gossip at expensive restaurants. The term is also used for such women generally, and less critically for those who raise money for charity by organizing lunches.

> A toast to that invincible bunch
> The dinosaurs surviving the crunch
> Let's hear it for the ladies who lunch.
>
> STEPHEN SONDHEIM: *Company*, 'The Ladies who Lunch' (song) (1970)

**Lady and the Tramp.** A 1955 animated feature film from Walt Disney, concerning the relationship of Lady, a snooty spaniel, and Tramp, a scruffy mongrel. The title refers to Lorenz Hart's 1937 song 'The Lady is a Tramp' from *Babe in Arms*:

> Doesn't like crap games with barons or earls,
> Won't go to Harlem in ermine and pearls,
> Won't dish the dirt with the rest of the girls,
> That's why the lady is a tramp.

**Lady Bird.** A name given to Claudia Johnson (b.1912), wife of President Lyndon Johnson, by her childhood nurse. The name stuck, and when she married Johnson both had the initials LBJ. The 1965 Highway Beautification Act restricting billboard advertising was prompted by her, and became known as the Lady Bird Act. She also pioneered the planting of native wild flowers along the highways of her native Texas. The name Lady Bird does not have the connotations that it would have in Britain, as in North America a ladybird is called a 'ladybug'.

**Ladybird Books.** A series of small-format illustrated children's books. The first book, *Bunnikin's Picnic Party*, was published in 1940 and over the years the Ladybird series expanded to embrace a wide range of subject matter, including fairly tales, history and natural history books. Price was always important and for 29 years the books remained at half a crown (12½p).

The Key Words Reading Scheme – started in 1962 and still in print – features the lives of two JANET AND JOHN-like, middle-class children, Peter and Jane, and has sold over 100 million copies round the world.

**Lady Blamey.** In Australian English of the mid-20th century, a crude drinking vessel consisting of the lower half of a beer bottle, its edge rounded off with sandpaper. It took its name from the redoubtable wife of the soldier Sir Henry Blamey (1884–1951), who was well known for her welfare work among the troops. She taught them how to make such a glass by tying kerosene-soaked string around a bottle, setting light to it and plunging the bottle into cold water, where-upon it would break cleanly in two.

**Ladyboy.** A euphemism for a young male transvestite, especially an oriental one.

Once inside, there were gyrating Thai ladyboys.
*heat* (17–23 February 2000)

**Lady Chatterley's Lover.** A novel (1960; privately printed 1928) by D.H. Lawrence (1885–1930). Written in Italy after Lawrence had been diagnosed as having terminal cancer, it is an intense study of human relationships and sexuality. Lady Chatterley's husband, after they have had only one month together, is wounded in the First World War and paralyzed from the waist down. After one unsatisfactory affair with an outsider, she responds to the advances of Mellors, the gamekeeper, who has an intriguing back-ground. There is much steamy sex, but a moral ending. On 2 November 1960, after a six-day trial, a jury of nine men and three women found PENGUIN BOOKS not guilty of publishing 'an obscene article' (*see* LADY CHATTERLEY TRIAL). *See also* FIRST LINES OF NOVELS.

**Lady Chatterley trial.** The trial in 1960 of PENGUIN BOOKS on a charge of obscenity for publishing LADY CHATTERLEY'S LOVER, written by D.H. Lawrence in 1928. The book, which contains detailed descriptions of sex acts and makes liberal use of FOUR-LETTER WORDS, had been published privately in 1928. In 1960 Penguin deliberately published the book in an uncut version to test the English law of obscenity, and called

a number of distinguished expert witnesses, including Richard Hoggart, to testify on its behalf as to the literary merits of the work. The defence team, Gerald Gardiner, Jeremy Hutchinson and Edward du Cann, might have believed that the case was lost on the first day when Mervyn Griffith-Jones, counsel for the prosecution, uttered the words, much derided since: 'Is it a book that you would have lying around in your own house? Is it a book that you would even wish your wife or your servants to read?'

The jury found that the work was neither obscene nor corrupting. A similar verdict had been returned by a US court the previous year. Penguin went on to sell more than 3.5 million copies, and the verdict opened the way to a much greater freedom in the treatment of sex in literature. *See also* Lady CHATTERLEY.

> Sexual intercourse began
> In nineteen sixty-three
> (Which was rather late for me) –
> Between the end of the Chatterley ban
> And the Beatles' first LP.
> PHILIP LARKIN: 'Annus Mirabilis' (1974)

**Lady Di.** A popular name for Diana, Princess of Wales, who before her marriage to Prince Charles in 1981 was Lady Diana Spencer. *See also* DISCO DI; PEOPLE'S PRINCESS; PRINCESS OF HEARTS; QUEEN OF HEARTS.

**Lady Forkbender.** A nickname given by *Private Eye* to Marcia Falkender, née Williams (b.1932), who was Harold Wilson's private and political secretary from 1956 to 1983. She became Baroness Falkender in 1974, and was said to have influenced Wilson's notorious 1976 resignation honours list, nicknamed the LAVENDER LIST because it was typed on Lady Falkender's lavender-coloured note paper. The nickname, which first appeared in 'Mrs Wilson's Diary' in *Private Eye* in 1975, was presumably inspired by the widespread publicity given to the supposedly magical ability of Israeli showman Uri Geller to bend forks and spoons by gently manipulating them. *See also* GANNEX.

**Ladykillers, The.** A sublime and enduring Ealing Comedy (1955) (*see* EALING COMEDIES) about a criminal gang, which hides up after a big robbery in the quiet house of a little old lady, pretending for her benefit to be amateur classical musicians. The irony in the title lies in the fact that none of the criminals (Alec Guinness, Peter Sellers, Cecil Parker, Herbert Lom and Danny Green) turns out to be prepared to murder the old lady (Katie Johnson) after she discovers what they have really been up to, and they are instead obliged to kill each other. A pale and superfluous remake appeared in 2004.

**Lady Macbeth of the Mtsensk District.** A formerly controversial opera by Dmitri Shostakovich (1906–75), with a libretto by the composer and A. Preys, after an 1865 story by Nikolai Leskov (1831–95) about a woman who, somewhat in the manner of the wife of Shakespeare's Macbeth, lives and dies by violence. It was first performed in 1934 and proved popular until the Soviet authorities started to show their disapproval of MODERNISM in 1936. In that year *Pravda* sinisterly commented: 'It is a leftist bedlam instead of human music. The inspiring quality of good music is sacrificed in favour of petty-bourgeois clowning. This game may end badly.' The work was not revived in the Soviet Union until 1963, when it was staged under the title *Katerina Izmailova*. It was, however, performed in the United States in 1935. One American critic described the music as 'pornophony'.

**Lady Muck.** A nickname for a pompous or self-opinionated woman. *See also* LORD MUCK.

**Lady of the night.** A euphemism for a prostitute.

**Lady's Not For Burning, The.** A historical play (1948) by Christopher Fry (1907–2005) about a beautiful alchemist who finds herself accused of witchcraft and is threatened with death by burning. The play is perhaps now best remembered for having furnished Margaret Thatcher, then prime minister, with her most famous quote (*see* LADY'S NOT FOR TURNING).

**Lady's not for turning.** A declaration by Margaret Thatcher, the IRON LADY, to the 1980 Conservative Party Conference, asserting her determination not to perform a U-turn in her economic policies, which were inflicting so much discomfort. The phrase, coined by speechwriter Sir Ronald Millar, plays on the title of a poetic drama, The LADY'S NOT FOR BURNING (1948), by Christopher Fry. It is said that Mrs Thatcher was unaware of its source. *See also* TINA.

> To those waiting with bated breath for that favourite media catchphrase, the U-turn, I have only one thing to say. You turn if you want to. The lady is not for turning.

**Lady Vanishes, The.** A film thriller (1938) adapted by Sidney Gilliat from a novel *The Wheel Spins* by Ethel Lina White about the mystery surrounding the apparent disappearance of an elderly lady on board a trans-European train. Directed by Alfred Hitchcock, the film concentrates on the efforts of the hero and heroine to unravel the truth behind the woman's disappearance. The title of the film refers to a traditional magician's trick in which a woman is apparently made to disappear before the audience's very eyes. Anthony Page directed a dire remake (1979).

**Lady with the Blowlamp.** A description of Margaret Thatcher, the IRON LADY, by Denis Healey, the GROMYKO OF THE LABOUR PARTY, giving a sinister twist to the by-name of Florence Nightingale (1820–1910), 'the Lady with the Lamp', who nursed wounded British soldiers during the Crimean War (1853–6). The ever-imaginative Healey also called Thatcher Miss Floggie, Rhoda the Rhino, La Pasionara of Middle-Class Privilege (*see* THEY SHALL NOT PASS), and a Pétain in petticoats (*see* PÉTAINISTS).

**Laff.** A source or occasion of amusement. The word is a jocular or journalistic respelling of 'laugh', as in 'a bit of a laff', and pronounced to rhyme with 'caff' rather than 'calf'. Another re-spelling of the same word, but with a pronunciation closer to the norm, is 'larf', as in the title of Len Deighton's novel about three confidence tricksters, *Only When I Larf* (1968).

**Lager lout.** A term in use from the late 1980s and applied to a young hooligan who creates disturbances, damages property and the like after drinking too much lager or beer. The phrase may owe something to the earlier 'litter lout'. *See also* ESSEX MAN.

**Lagerphone.** A wryly humorous Australian term (first recorded in 1956) for a rude 'musical instrument' made by nailing beer-bottle tops to a stick. It is played by banging one end on the floor, or alternatively with an improvised 'bow'. It can also be called a 'jingling johnnie'.

**Laid-back.** Relaxed; unconcerned; peacefully passive. The expression arose in the SWINGING SIXTIES and came to be particularly associated with HIPPIES.

**Laika.** The first living creature to go into orbit (although various animals had earlier made sub-orbital flights). Laika ('Barker') was a mongrel bitch, who had been found wandering the streets of Moscow. In 3 November 1957 she was fired into space by the Soviets on board SPUTNIK 2. At the time, the Soviet authorities said that Laika died peacefully while orbiting the earth a week after launch. However, in 2002 it was revealed that she died of overheating, as a result of stress, a few hours into her flight. *Sputnik 2* continued to orbit the earth until 4 April 1958, when it burnt up on re-entry. The American press dubbed Laika 'Muttnik'. *See also* ABLE AND BAKER.

**Lake Wobegon.** An imaginary small town in Minnesota that first appeared in *Lake Wobegon Days* (1985), a bestselling collection of gently humorous but acutely observed short stories about the lives of the town's inhabitants by Garrison Keillor (b.1942). His later *Wobegon Boy* (1997) tells the story of John Tollefson, an unmarried man in his forties, first encountered in *Lake Wobegon Days*, who leaves his family behind in Minnesota for a job as a public radio station manager in upstate New York. A radio broadcaster also famed for his public readings of his fictional works, Keillor has hosted the hugely popular nationally syndicated radio show *A Prairie Home Companion* since 1974.

**La-La land.** A nickname for Los Angeles (known as L.A.) or HOLLYWOOD, evoking the alleged eccentricities of the people who live and work there. The name puns on 'la-la-land' as a term for a person's fantasy world or dreamworld, especially one brought on by drink or drugs.

**Lambada.** A fast erotic dance of Brazilian origin which couples perform with their stomachs touching. It was a logical development of DIRTY DANCING in the late 1980s and takes its name from the Brazilian Portuguese word meaning 'beating', 'lashing'.

**Lambeth Walk.** A thoroughfare in Lambeth leading from Black Prince Road to the Lambeth Road. It gave its name to the popular Cockney dance featured by Lupino Lane (from 1937) in the musical show *Me and My Gal* at the Victoria Palace. The dance has couples strutting forward, arms linked, then strutting back and jerking their thumbs in the air to the exclamation 'Oi!' Many council housing estates now have a Lambeth Walk as a memento.

> Any time you're Lambeth way,
> Any evening, any day,
> You'll find us all
> Doin' the Lambeth walk.
>
> DOUGLAS FURBER and ARTHUR ROSE: 'Doin' the Lambeth Walk' (1937)

**Lambretta.** A type of motor scooter made by the Italian firm Innocenti from 1947 to 1972 (and then sold to the Indian government), which, along with the VESPA, became the standard transport of Britain's Mods. The name 'Lambretta' derives from the Lambrate district of Milan, where the scooter was manufactured. *See also* MODS AND ROCKERS.

**Lame duck.** Any weak or ineffectual person, institution, etc. unable to keep up with its peers. In business, it is applied specifically to a large and prestigious company that cannot meet foreign competition without government support. Edward Heath's Conservative government elected in 1970 famously declared that it would not support any more lame ducks. However, it did, bailing out firms such as Rolls Royce and Upper Clyde Shipbuilders. In the United States the phrase 'lame duck' refers to a president who has been defeated in the November presidential election but is still in office – albeit effectively powerless – until the following January. It is also more broadly applied to any politician who is considered to be IN OFFICE BUT NOT IN POWER. The phrase originated in the mid-18th century, when it was applied to a stockjobber or dealer who would not, or could not, pay his losses, so that he had to 'waddle out the alley like a lame duck'.

**Lamington.** A confection more familiar in Australia and New Zealand than elsewhere in the English-speaking world, in the form of a small cake covered with chocolate icing and rolled in coconut. Its name, first recorded in the early 20th century, is believed to come from Lord Lamington, governor of Queensland from 1896 to 1901, or else from his wife, in whose kitchen it may have been created. Fund-raising Lamington drives still thrive in Australia and testify to the popularity of the cake.

**Lamps are going out all over Europe, The.** The mordantly elegiac phrase with which the British foreign secretary, Edward Grey (Lord Grey of Fallodon; 1862–1933), greeted the imminent prospect of war in 1914. He continued: 'We shall not see them lit again in our lifetime.' His tone was very much at odds with that of the general populace, who were wildly enthused on the outbreak of war. Grey's words have an echo of those of an earlier statesman, Pitt the Younger, who, after Napoleon's victory at Austerlitz in 1805, referring to a map of Europe, said: 'Roll up that map; it will not be wanted these ten years.' In his memoirs, *Twenty-five Years* (1925), Grey recalled:

> A friend came to see me on one of the evenings of the last week – he thinks it was on Monday August 3. We were standing at a window of my room in the Foreign Office. It was getting dusk, and the lamps were being lit in the space below on which we were looking. My friend recalls that I remarked on this with the words, 'The lamps are going out all over Europe; we shall not see them lit again in our lifetime.'

**Lanark.** The first novel (1981) by Alasdair Gray (b.1934) was begun when he was 18 years old. It is subtitled 'A Life in Four Books', Book Three preceding the Prologue and Book One. Set in the disintegrating city of Unthank, which represents Glasgow, it interweaves both fantastically and naturalistically episodes from the lives of Duncan Thaw and of Lanark, Thaw's alter ego, the early experiences of both of whom echo those of Gray himself.

**Lance the boil.** To make a bold stroke with the aim of solving a problem or ending an undesirable situation such as an occurrence of corruption. The allusion is to the cutting open of a boil to release the purulent matter inside.

**Land camera.** The proprietary name of a camera that can

produce a near instant picture. It takes its name from the US scientist Edwin H. Land (1909–91), the inventor in 1936 of Polaroid, as a material which in the form of thin sheets produces a high degree of plane polarization in light passing through it. The camera evolved as the result of a holiday trip in 1943 to New Mexico, when Land's three-year-old daughter asked why she could not immediately see a photograph he had taken of her. The first public demonstration of a sepia-and-white Polaroid camera was in 1947. Black-and-white cameras followed in 1950 and a popular low-price colour camera, the Swinger, was launched in 1965.

**Land girls.** Young women recruited for agricultural work during the two world wars. The first land girls were the members of the Women's Land Army, first established in 1917. In June 1939 the organization was re-formed, and more than 10,000 young women volunteered to do what had previously been regarded as exclusively male jobs. Their duties included driving tractors, milking cows, planting, harvesting, cleaning pigsties and cowsheds and reclaiming land. It was not unusual to work a 14-hour day. At the end of the war they were demobbed on a 'first-come-first-leave' basis. They were obliged to return their uniforms but were allowed to keep their shoes and greatcoat so long as they dyed the latter from brown to navy blue. Each woman was allocated six clothing coupons, enough to buy a hat, a tie and some knickers. The WLA was disbanded in 1951. The sexual freedom supposedly enjoyed by the young women during the Second World War was reflected in the gibing slogan 'Backs to the land, girls.' A sentimental film *The Land Girls*, based on a novel (1995) of the same name by Angela Huth, was released in 1998.

**Land of a thousand contrasts.** A travel agent's overblown lure to attract the potential tourist to a foreign country, especially one regarded as 'exotic'. An advertisement in Austin Reed's spring and summer catalogue for 1995 described Morocco as 'this beautiful land of a thousand contrasts'. More factually, Finland is sometimes promoted as the 'land of a thousand lakes'.

**'Land of Hope and Glory'.** Great Britain was so portrayed in the heyday of imperialism in Sir Edward Elgar's famous melody with words by A.C. Benson. It was sung by Dame Clara Butt in 1902 and widely used at EMPIRE DAY celebrations and other occasions. It is now a traditional item at the LAST NIGHT OF THE PROMS. The tune was taken from Elgar's POMP AND CIRCUMSTANCE march, No. 1 (1901). The words were originally written to be sung as the finale to Elgar's *Coronation Ode* of 1902.

Land of Hope and Glory, Mother of the Free,
How shall we extol thee who are born of thee?
Wider still and wider shall thy bounds be set;
God who made thee mighty, make thee mightier yet.

**Land of the Long White Cloud.** A nickname for New Zealand, as a translation of the country's Maori name, Aotearoa, from *ao*, 'cloud', *tea*, 'white', and *roa*, 'long'. The native name itself now has a certain official status, appearing in the New Zealand passport and on some postage stamps. The reference is to the cloud that hangs over many of the mountains of North Island. The country's highest peak, Mount Cook, has the Maori name of Aorangi, 'cloud piercer'.

**Landslide Lyndon.** *See* LBJ.

**Lane, Lois.** *See* SUPERMAN.

**La Niña.** The weather system that is the counterpart of EL NIÑO. Whereas El Niño is characterized by unusually warm ocean temperatures in the Equatorial Pacific, La Niña causes cold temperatures. Its name, Spanish for 'the little girl', indicates its contradistinction from El Niño, 'the little boy'. There is some confusion about the nomenclature, especially as La Niña is also known as El Viejo, 'the old one', the contrast in this case being between an old man (who is cold) and a young boy (who is warm).

**Lap dancer.** A woman who performs an erotic dance or striptease close to, or actually sitting on, the lap of a paying customer in a club or bar. The dance itself is of US origin. *See also* POLE DANCING.

**Lap of honour.** A celebratory circuit of a racetrack or sports field by a winner or winning team to receive applause. The expression and practice date from the 1950s and originated among cyclists.

**Lara Croft.** *See* Lara CROFT.

**'Lark Ascending, The'.** A popular and lyrical 'romance' for violin and orchestra by Ralph Vaughan Williams (1872–1958), composed in 1914 and revised in 1920. It was inspired by a poem of the same name by George Meredith (1828–1909).

**Larkin family.** Pop and Ma Larkin are a happy-go-lucky farming couple who appear in a series of comically rustic novels by H.E. Bates, beginning with *The* DARLING BUDS OF MAY (1958). They live on a ramshackle farm deep in the Kent countryside and have a brood of six children with horticultural sounding names such as Zinnia, Petunia and Primrose. Surprisingly, the stories were not brought to the television screen until 1991, when they appeared to popular acclaim under the title of the first novel, with David Jason playing Pop Larkin, Pam Ferris as Ma and Catherine Zeta-Jones as their eldest daughter, Mariette. They are not to be confused with the Larkins, the family that featured in the eponymous ITV sitcom (1958–64), with Peggy Mount as Ada Larkins and David Kossoff as Alf Larkins.

**Larks and owls.** Someone who works best early in the day is frequently known as a 'lark' or 'morning person', while one who does not begin functioning fully until the afternoon or early evening is an 'owl' or 'evening person'. Psychologists claim that there is a real difference between the two types, but medical evidence is largely lacking for the supposed distinction. *See also* DAY PERSON.

**Larry Parnes's Stable of Stars.** Larry Parnes (1930–89), regarded by many as the pre-eminent manager and impresario of British ROCK 'N' ROLL, was responsible for promoting and in many cases rechristening a string of pop and rock successes, beginning with Tommy Steele (b.1936), whose real name was Thomas Hicks. Steele devised his own stage name, but among those renamed by Parnes were Marty Wilde (b.1936), born Reginald Smith, Billy Fury (1941–83), born Ronald Wycherley, Johnny Gentle (b.1941), formerly John Askew, Dickie Pride (*c.*1940–*c.*1970), earlier Richard Knellar, Vince Eager (b.*c.*1940), originally Roy Taylor, and Georgie Fame (b.1943), born Clive Powell. The Cockney guitarist Joe Brown (b.1941), however, refused to become Almer Twitch. Parnes's business approach and financial acuity earned him his own nickname of 'Parnes, Shillings and Pence'. His supremacy as kingmaker was ended by The BEATLES, whose potential he had seriously underestimated some time before.

**Larry the Lamb.** The wooden toy lamb that first appeared in 1925 in a series of story books for young children by S.G. Hulme Beaman. From 1929, together with his friends, Dennis the Dachshund and Ernest the Policeman, Larry appeared regularly on BBC Radio's CHILDREN'S HOUR, his voice bleatingly rendered by 'Uncle Mac' (Derek McCulloch). *See also* TOYTOWN.

**Lascaux caves.** On a day in September 1940 four French schoolboys were hunting rabbits near the village of Montignac in the Dordogne when their dog disappeared down a hole. Climbing down to retrieve him, they found themselves in a grotto filled with delicate paintings of animals. An examination by archaeologists revealed a magnificently decorated main cavern, dubbed *la grande salle des taureaux* (Great Hall of Bulls), connected by passageways to side galleries. They dated the paintings to about 18,000 BC and declared the cave one of the richest treasure troves of Palaeolithic art ever discovered. The find rapidly became a tourist attraction, but by 1963 the colours were fading and fungus beginning to spot the frescoes, necessitating its closure to the public. A replica cave has since been built nearby for tourists to visit.

**Laser.** The device generating an intense beam of light of a very pure single colour was first constructed in the United States in 1960 by Theodore H. Maiman, using a rod of ruby. The name is an acronym of 'light amplification by stimulated emission of radiation'. A forerunner, operating on the same basic principle, was the maser, the first letter standing for 'microwave'. The application of lasers is wide, and ranges from supermarket BARCODE scanners to CD and DVD players. They are also used in surgery, fibre optics, laser printers and weapons guidance systems.

**Lassa fever.** This acute and often fatal viral disease, occurring chiefly in West Africa, takes its name from the village of Lassa, near Mubi in northeast Nigeria, where it was first reported in 1969. It is usually acquired from infected rats.

**Lasseter's Lost Reef.** In 1929 the Australian writer and explorer Lewis Hubert 'Harold Bell' Lasseter (1880–1931) claimed that in about 1911 he had discovered 'a vast gold-bearing reef in Central Australia'. The government of the day were not interested in his story, but when he repeated it in 1930 he interested one John Bailey, of the Australian Workers' Union, and a small expeditionary party, led by Fred Blakeley and guided by Lasseter, set off to find it. In September 1930 the expedition abandoned the search but Lasseter went on alone, only to meet his death in the Petermann Ranges in the centre of the continent. The key to one of Australia's greatest enigmas continued to be sought, and versions of Lasseter's story were retold in such popular books as Ion Idriess's *Lasseter's Last Ride* (1931) and Fred Blakeley's *Dream Millions* (1972). The true facts about Lasseter and his reef seem to have been finally settled by the research of Gerald Walsh for the *Australian Dictionary of Biography* (1983) but the mystery of the reef has never been solved.

**Lassie.** One of the most popular dogs in the cinema. The first film starring her (played by a male dog called Pal) was in 1943, and was itself based on Eric Knight's children's novel *Lassie Come Home* (1940). Lassie is an intelligent collie who is sold by her owners in Yorkshire when they cannot afford to keep her, much to the distress of their young son. She promptly runs away from her new home in Scotland until, after travelling hundreds of miles, she 'comes home', and is reunited with the family she loves. In the *Lassie* TV series

(1954–74), the stories were transferred to the United States, and the heroine was usually played by male dogs. There have been several other Lassie TV series and films. A remake of the original film, repatriated to Britain, was released in 2006. *See also* RIN TIN TIN.

**Last chance saloon.** A legendary bar where one has a last chance to drink before meeting one's fate. Many US casinos bear the name, such as the one in Deadwood, South Dakota, the town that gave the name of the dime novel hero 'Deadwood Dick'. In the famous Western DESTRY RIDES AGAIN (1939) Marlene Dietrich stands on a bar in the Last Chance Saloon to sing 'See What the Boys in the Back Room Will Have' (*see* BACKROOM BOYS). The phrase now alludes to any final opportunity or seemingly irrevocable annihilation.

> This is … a critical week for the Conservatives. It is almost closing time in their last chance saloon.
>
> *The Times* (2 October 1999)

**Last Exit to Brooklyn.** A bleak novel (1964) by Hubert Selby Jr (1928–2004). The British publisher was found guilty of issuing an obscene publication in 1967, but a successful appeal against the judgement, led by John Mortimer QC, was made the following year. The book consists of a series of loosely connected episodes, evoking the harshness of life in the criminal and sexual underworld of the district of Brooklyn in New York city. There are some moments of tenderness among descriptions of violence and hetero-sexual and homosexual sex. The title is a road sign on the motorway giving drivers a final chance to turn off for Brooklyn. An equally gloomy film version (1989) was directed by Uli Edel.

**Last hurrah.** The final act in a politician's career or, more generally, any final performance or flourish. The phrase comes from the title of Edwin O'Connor's bestselling novel of 1956 about the political boss of an eastern city in the United States. It was filmed in 1958.

**Last in, first out.** A method of accounting in which all goods of the same kind are valued at the price paid for those most recently acquired. In business the phrase can also apply to a redundancy scheme whereby those who have most recently joined as employees are the first to leave, the theory being that their youth or inexperience makes them more readily 'expendable'.

**Last Night of the Proms.** The final evening of the annual Promenade Concerts at the Royal Albert Hall, London, in September, popularly regarded as the apotheosis of the series. The audience is mainly made up of young promenaders who enthusiastically join in the traditional choruses of 'LAND OF HOPE AND GLORY' and 'Rule, Britannia' while waving Union Jacks, bursting balloons, throwing streamers, and displaying other signs of patriotic fervour and good humour. The FIRST NIGHT OF THE PROMS may also be something of an occasion, if only as a prelude to this rousing finale.

**Last of the Red-Hot Mamas.** The nickname of the big-voiced, big-bodied Russian-born US vaudeville singer Sophie Tucker (1884–1966), after the title of one of the songs she recorded, the lyrics written in 1928 by Jack Yellen (1892–1991). Tucker traded on her physical appearance, singing songs such as 'I Don't Want to Be Thin' and 'Nobody Loves a Fat Girl, But Oh How a Fat Girl Can Love'.

> The week before sailing for London [in 1930] I played the Palace in New York again. I was billed as 'SOPHIE TUCKER, THE LAST OF THE RED-HOT MAMAS!' This was the first time I carried this billing, which was to become so closely associated with me that it has persisted through all the years since that season when I introduced Jack Yellen's song hit, 'I'm the Last of the Red-hot Mamas'.
>
> SOPHIE TUCKER: *Some of These Days: An Autobiography*, ch. 13 (1948)

**Last of the Summer Wine.** The longest running SITCOM on British television, first screened in 1973 and still running, after over 200 episodes, a third of a century later. It is set in the Yorkshire Pennines and centres on three old school friends who, now elderly and unemployed, set about enjoying a second childhood in a series of mischievous escapades. The original trio consisted of the pompous Cyril Blamire, played by Michael Bates, the unobtrusive and wary Norman Clegg, played by Peter Sallis, and the small and fearless Compo, played by Bill Owen, who usually came down to earth with a bump or ended up to his neck in water (Clegg remains, but the other two's places are now taken by Herbert 'Truly' Truelove (Frank Thornton) and Compo's 'son', Tom, played by Bill Owen's actual son Tom). A fourth character is the daunting, wrinkled-stocking housewife NORA Batty, played by Kathy Staff. The title is almost too lyrical for its purpose. The writer Roy Clarke dreamt it up 'to suit the age group and location', and was surprised the BBC did not change it. He may have been influenced by the 1969 song 'If I Thought You'd Ever Change Your Mind' by John Cameron (sung by Kathe Green), in which the offer is made to 'feed you winter fruits and summer wine'; and by the title of Mary Renault's novel set in ancient Crete, *The Last of the Wine* (1956).

**Last taboo.** A subject or condition regarded as so sordid, shameful or otherwise offensive that it is still not openly discussed or written about. The term is traditionally applied to drug abuse, although it may also be used of a deviant sexual practice such as incest, bestiality or paedophilia.

**Last Tango in Paris.** A film (1972) co-written and directed by Italian director Bernardo Bertolucci (b.1940) about the sexual relationship that develops between Paul, a recently widowed American (played by Marlon Brando), and Jeanne, a young French woman (played by Maria Schneider), who is engaged to a NOUVELLE VAGUE film-maker, after they meet while flat-hunting in Paris. The affair ends with Paul's suicide. The title of the film, evoking the potent sexuality of the tango, underlines the passion of the couple's affair. The appearance of a pat of butter as an aid to sodomy was for many their abiding memory of a film described in *Halliwell's Film Guide* as a 'pretentious sex melodrama mainly notable for being banned'.

**Last Year at Marienbad.** A film (1961) written by Alain Robbe-Grillet (b.1922) and directed by Alain Resnais (b.1922) in which a man apparently tries to persuade a woman that they know each other and may have had an affair. The truth of their relationship is left obscure: the suggestion is that they met 'last year in Marienbad' and planned to run away together. One critic described the film as 'elaborate, ponderous and meaningless'. *See also* NOUVELLE VAGUE.

**Latchkey child.** A child left at home without adult super-vision for some of the day. The term dates from the 1960s and originated in the United States in the 1940s with reference to children who let themselves into their home after school because the parents were still out at work. The US source explains the use of 'latchkey' instead of the more usual British front door key. *See also* HOME ALONE.

**Lateral thinking.** The solving of problems by an indirect or creative approach, typically by viewing the problem in a new light or approaching it from a different angle. The term was coined by Professor Edward de Bono in his account of the method, *The Use of Lateral Thinking* (1967). His term for the conventional, direct method of reasoning was 'vertical thinking'.

**Lateran Treaty.** A treaty concluded between the Holy See and the kingdom of Italy on 11 February 1929, settling the 'Roman Question', which had resulted from the fall of the city of Rome as the last territory of the Papal States. The Holy See was financially compensated for the loss of property, the Vatican City State was established as a political entity independent of Italy, and a concordat was agreed upon that guaranteed and regulated the role of the Roman Catholic

Church in the life of Italy, making it the official religion of the country. The concordat was renegotiated and formally ratified on 3 June 1985. Catholic instruction is no longer mandatory in state schools, and the clergy are no longer paid salaries by the state.

**Laugh all the way to the bank.** To be so fortunate or wealthy that one can afford to ignore criticism. The image is of someone happily hastening to deposit a large sum of money in the bank. The US pianist and entertainer Liberace (1919–87) joked in the 1950s that bad reviews made him 'cry all the way to the bank'.

**Laughing, To be.** To be in a fortunate or successful position, especially by comparison with others. A typical use of the expression might be, 'Once I get that contract I'll be laughing'. No actual laughter is normally involved although a smile of satisfaction may be evidenced. The phrase dates from the 1930s.

**Laughing boy.** An ironic term of reference or address for someone of a morose disposition or gloomy countenance. First recorded in 1940, it may have been inspired by the song 'A Laughing Boy But Yesterday' from the Gilbert and Sullivan operetta *The Yeomen of the Guard* (1888).

**Laughing Murderer of Verdun.** A nickname given to Crown Prince Wilhelm of Germany (1882–1951), who held various commands on the WESTERN FRONT throughout the First World War, and was associated with the most militaristic sectors of German society. The nickname was earned from his command of the hugely costly German offensive at VERDUN from February 1916. British troops also referred to him as LITTLE WILLIE, in contrast to his father, Kaiser Wilhelm II, KAISER BILL, whom he joined in exile after the armistice in 1918.

**Laugh like a drain.** To laugh heartily; to chuckle inordinately. The sound of a guffaw can suggest that of water gurgling down a drain.

**Laughter lines.** A name dating from the 1930s for the small lines or wrinkles at the corners of the eyes that are supposed to have been produced by years of intermittent laughter. An older and less flattering term for the feature, going back to the time of Chaucer, is crow's feet.

**Laura.** The eponymous heroine (Laura Hunt) of the Otto Preminger film *Laura* (1944), a murder mystery based on a novel (1943) of the same name by Vera Caspary and featuring Clifton Webb as the fastidious and acerbic man-about-town and society columnist Waldo Lydecker. It was a forerunner of the notable Hollywood FILM NOIRS of the later 1940s. (Laura (played by Gene Tierney) turns out not to have been murdered. The policeman assigned to investigate her supposed death falls in love with her.)

**Laura Norder.** *See* Laura NORDER.

**Lavender and old lace.** Old-fashioned gentility. The phrase comes from the title of a novel by Myrtle Reed published in 1902. A dramatized version by Rose Warner appeared in 1938. This was given a new twist as a black comedy by Joseph Kesselring under the title ARSENIC AND OLD LACE (1941), and an enjoyable film version was screened in 1942.

**Lavender Hill Mob, The.** A sparkling Ealing comedy (*see* EALING COMEDIES) (1951), written by T.E.B. Clarke and directed by Charles Crichton, about a mild-mannered civil servant who decides to use his inside knowledge of bullion transport to steal a million pounds' worth of gold and then spirit it out of the country after melting it down into miniature Eiffel Towers. The ludicrous notion that such a retiring, dull individual could pull off this breathtaking crime is underlined by the film's title, which cheekily conveys the unlikelihood of hardened criminals hailing from such a respectable part of London as Lavender Hill (a southwestern inner suburb, in Battersea). The film stars Alec Guinness as the criminal mastermind, and Stanley Holloway as his right-hand man.

**Lavender List.** The dissolution honours awarded by Harold Wilson (1916–95) after his resignation as Labour prime minister in 1976. The name is said to stem from the fact that the list was written on lavender-coloured paper by Marcia Williams (later Lady Falkender; b.1932), Wilson's private and political secretary, with only a few corrections added by Wilson himself. The implication was thus that the choice had been hers. The journalist John Junor remarked of Wilson's resignation, and the list:

> Such a graceful exit. And then he had to go and do this on the doorstep.

*See also* LADY FORKBENDER.

**Laverstock Panda.** Many of the figures cut out of the chalk hillside in central and southern England are ancient. The white horses of Wiltshire, however, were joined by a newcomer to the county in the early hours of Sunday 26 January 1970 when a group of students from the University College of North Wales, Bangor, delineated the figure of a panda in a hillside to the left of the A30 road to Exeter, 1.6km (1 mile) north of Salisbury, just before the turn to Laverstock. The operation was executed by removing the topsoil and filling the resultant shallow excavation with chalk dug from nearby pits. When discovered, it was at first supposed that the cutting celebrated the meeting of the two pandas Chi-

and An-An in the London Zoo. In fact it was a rag week stunt, the panda being Bangor's rag symbol, while the particular location was chosen because one of the instigators lived nearby and knew the site would be suitable. Today the Laverstock Panda is overgrown and no longer visible except for the face.

**Law of Martinis.** A rule of thumb among scuba divers, based on the fact that the deeper one goes beneath the surface of the water, the greater the sense of euphoria, similar to drunkenness. In roughly equivalent terms, a descent of one atmosphere (a unit of pressure equal to mean atmospheric pressure at sea level), reached at approximately 10m (33ft), has an effect similar to that of imbibing a single Martini cocktail. Two atmospheres thus equals two Martinis and so on. The deeper one goes, however, the greater the danger of vertigo (through disorientation) and 'the bends', which in some cases can lead to death, as can an equivalent excessive intake of Martinis.

**Law of the jungle.** Ruthless competition, especially when motivated by self-interest. The phrase became current from the 1920s and derives from Rudyard Kipling's *The* JUNGLE BOOK (1894):

> The Law of the Jungle, which never orders anything without a reason, forbids every beast to eat Man except when he is killing to show his children how to kill.
>
> 'Mowgli's Brothers'

**Lawrence of Arabia.** The name by which the British soldier, archaeologist, Arabist, classical scholar and writer T(homas) E(dward) Lawrence (1888–1935) is popularly known. During the First World War Lawrence went to Arabia (October 1916) to assess the chances of success of the revolt of the Arabs against their Turkish Ottoman rulers. Judging the outcome to be promising, he became a key military commander in the revolt and conducted an innovative and successful guerrilla campaign against the Turks. His success in commanding the respect of the Arabs was partially due to a deliberate cultivation of his own image as a legendary hero. The Arabs themselves had their own name for their extraordinary leader, calling him 'El Aurens' and coming to treat him very much as one of their own. After the war Lawrence found his celebrity back home difficult to deal with, and public fascination was increased by the obvious psychological complexity of his character (he claimed to have been homosexually raped by his Turkish captors in the Syrian town of Deraa in 1916). He was also disillusioned by the failure of the Western powers to grant Arab independence. In 1922, to escape the limelight, he enlisted in the RAF as Aircraftsman Ross (having assumed the name John Hume Ross), but he was found out by journalists and had to leave shortly afterwards. He then enlisted in the Royal Tank Corps as Private T.E. Shaw (borrowing the surname from his friend George Bernard Shaw) but was later transferred back to the RAF. He recounted his wartime adventures in *The Seven Pillars of Wisdom* (1926), which served to increase his mythic status. Within three months of retiring from the RAF in 1935 he was killed while riding his motorcycle BOANERGES.

A play by Terence Rattigan (1911–77) entitled *Ross* (1960) deals with Lawrence's life. The epic historical film *Lawrence of Arabia* (1962), adapted by Robert Bolt (1924–95) from Lawrence's *The Seven Pillars of Wisdom* (1926), follows Lawrence's maverick career as a commander of the Arab revolt. Directed by David Lean and starring Peter O'Toole as Lawrence, the film would probably not have met with its subject's approval had he been still alive as he developed a pathological dislike of the fame his exploits brought him.

**Laxton's Superb.** This popular variety of late-ripening eating apple takes its name from Messrs Laxton of Bedford, sons of the horticulturist William Laxton (1830–90), who introduced it in 1921. The brothers produced thousands of cross-bred apples, other well-known varieties including 'Laxton's Pearmain', 'Laxton's Fortune' and 'Laxton's Exquisite'.

**Lay an egg.** To fail absolutely, especially in a variety performance. The implication is presumably that one has laid a bad egg. The origin is not likely to be in the 'duck's egg' or zero score in cricket, as sometimes explained.

**Layer cut.** A style first in fashion in the 1960s in which the hair is cut in overlapping layers.

**Layered look.** A fashion in clothes since the 1970s in which garments of various types and lengths are worn on top of one another. The term 'layering' to describe this mode of dressing was coined in 1950 by the US fashion designer Bonnie Cashin.

**Lay it on the line.** To speak frankly and directly. The image is of setting one's words on a line, where all can see their true value, as when placing a bet. The expression dates from the 1940s.

**'Layla'.** An anguished love song by Derek and The Dominos (the guitarist Eric Clapton accompanied by an ad hoc group of instrumentalists), released in 1972 and featuring one of the best-known guitar 'riffs' in pop music. The title comes from a story by the 12th-century Persian poet Nizami, entitled *The Story of Layla and Majnun*, concerning an ill-starred love affair. It reflects Clapton's feelings for Patti

Harrison, the wife of his friend, the Beatle George Harrison. Clapton eventually married Patti Harrison, but the couple divorced in 1988, although not before Clapton had written another decidedly uxorious love song for her, entitled 'Wonderful Tonight'.

**Lazy daisy stitch.** An embroidery stitch used in making flower patterns, and consisting of a long chain stitch. It first caught on in the 1920s.

**Lazy dog.** In US military jargon a fragmentation bomb that detonates in mid-air and scatters steel pellets over a wide target area.

**Lazy eight.** An aerobatic manoeuvre in which the aircraft executes an S-shaped path which, when viewed laterally, resembles a figure 8 lying on its side.

**Lazy eye.** An ambiguous term dating from the 1930s for an eye that has poor vision and so is little used, with the result that its sight deteriorates even further. It is most commonly the unused eye in a squint.

**Lazy susan.** A type of revolving stand or tray on a table for holding condiments and the like. The device is of US origin and dates from the early 20th century. Susan is taken as a typical maidservant's name.

**LBJ.** A nickname of Lyndon Baines Johnson (1908–73), Democratic president of the United States (1963–9). The use of initials as a nickname was by then well established by Democratic presidents (*see* JFK; FDR). One of Johnson's slogans during the 1964 presidential election was 'All the way with LBJ'. Subsequently, demonstrators opposed to his pursuance of the VIETNAM War chanted: 'Hey, hey, LBJ, / How many kids did you kill today?' Johnson's earlier nickname was Landslide Lyndon, earned after his narrow win in the US Senate election of 1948. *See also* LADY BIRD.

**L-committee.** A short form of legislative committee, as a committee formed annually from members of the British cabinet to decide which legislation should be introduced in the following session (beginning in November). The workings and composition of this committee are secret, but it is known that it includes the leaders of both Houses and the Government whips of both Houses.

**Leaderene.** A media nickname for Margaret Thatcher both as leader of the opposition and as prime minister (1979–90). The term is a jocular (or ironic) feminine form of 'leader', perhaps partly based on French *speakerine*, a female radio or television announcer. It has also been suggested that the nickname refers to the Gadarene swine, into whom Christ cast the devils possessing a 'man with an unclean spirit'

(Mark 5). The swine subsequently 'ran violently down a steep place into the sea … and were choked in the sea'. The word can also be applied to any female leader. *See also* ATTILA THE HEN; IRON LADY.

**Lead in one's pencil.** Male sexual vigour. To put lead in someone's pencil is thus to boost or bolster them. A pencil is useless without lead. The resemblance of 'pencil' to 'penis' is etymologically justified, since the words are related, both ultimately deriving from Latin *penis*, 'tail'.

**Lead someone up the aisle.** To marry them. The bride in fact goes up the nave of a church, not one of the aisles which run parallel to it. The use of the word in this sense perhaps springs from an association with 'alley'.

**Lead with one's chin.** To act incautiously. The reference is to a boxer who leaves his chin unprotected, thus rendering him dangerously vulnerable. The expression dates from the 1940s.

**Leaf-peeping.** The pastime of touring to see the colours of the trees change in autumn, a popular activity in New England. Those who travel for this pleasant purpose are known as leaf-peepers.

**League of Nations.** A league, having at one time about 60 member nations with headquarters at Geneva, with the essential aim of preventing war as well as promoting other forms of international cooperation. It was formed on 10 January 1920 as a consequence of the TREATY OF VERSAILLES but was weakened from the outset by the refusal of the United States to participate (although President Woodrow Wilson of the United States had played a major part in its foundation) and the exclusion of Russia. Its achievements were considerable in many fields, but it failed in its primary purpose. It last met on 18 April 1946, being replaced by the UNITED NATIONS Organization, which had been established on 24 October 1945. *See also* MANDATE.

**Lean and mean.** An adjective, of US origin, that encapsulates late 20th-century admiration for spare, focussed aggression. It appears to have started life in the US Marine Corps, and spread from there to general use. It is often used in a commercial context, to praise a company that is run economically (with perhaps a subtext of the ruthless culling of excess employees) and behaves robustly.

**Lean over backwards.** *See* BEND OVER BACKWARDS.

**Learjet.** The small passenger jet aircraft, popular among the rich and famous, takes its name from its designer, the US electrical engineer William Lear (1902–78), the first of the fleet being launched from his base at Wichita, Kansas, in 1962. It has since come to be regarded as one of the most glamorous aircraft, its name entering the language as a symbol of affluence and power.

**Learner's dictionary.** A monolingual dictionary for foreign learners of a language. A pioneer in the field was A.S. Hornby's *A Learner's Dictionary of Current English* (1948), followed by the same author's *Advanced Learner's Dictionary of Current English* (1963).

**Learning curve.** The rate of a person's progress in learning a new skill. The literal reference is to a curve on a graph indicating an animal's or human's rate of learning, as of a rat in a maze or an unskilled worker in a new job. The term dates from the 1920s and arose as psychological jargon.

**Lease-Lend.** *See* LEND-LEASE.

**Leave it out!** Stop it! Cut it out! A request dating from the 1960s directed at someone who talks nonsense or behaves undesirably.

**Lebensraum.** (German, 'living space'.) A term used in NAZI ideology for vast areas of eastern Europe, particularly the 'breadbasket' of the Ukraine, earmarked for German settlement. This 'living space' would allow the German population to expand and dominate the world. This use of the term originated in Adolf Hitler's MEIN KAMPF, and the area targeted was considered suitable by Hitler as its Slavic inhabitants were deemed UNTERMENSCHEN (sub-humans), ruled by BOLSHEVIKS, themselves the puppets of a world Jewish conspiracy. The achievement of *Lebensraum* lay behind German military and foreign policy through the 1930s, and the invasions of Poland (1939) and the Soviet Union (1941). The origin of the term *Lebensraum*, is however, rather different. It was the German geographer and ethnologist Friedrich Ratzel (1844–1904) who first developed the concept, which he used as a way of relating groups of humans to the geographical location where they develop; his essay *Lebensraum* (1901) is regarded as a seminal work in geopolitics. The Nazi idea was based on the reinterpretation of Ratzel's concept by the Swedish political scientist Rudolf Kjellén (1864–1922), whose *The State as a Life Form* (1916) was influential in Germany.

**Leboyer birth.** A manner of childbirth involving as little pain and disturbance to the baby as possible. Forceps are not used, a quiet, softly lit room is provided for the delivery, and the infant is placed in a warm bath upon birth. The technique was recommended by the French obstetrician Frédérick Leboyer (b.1918) in his book *Birth Without Violence* (1975).

**Lecter, Hannibal.** *See* HANNIBAL THE CANNIBAL.

**Lee, Lorelei.** An archetypal GOLD-DIGGER of the FLAPPER era in Anita Loos's comic novels GENTLEMEN PREFER BLONDES (1925) and *But Gentlemen Marry Brunettes* (1928). The first of these became a stage play (1925), a silent film (1928), a stage musical (1949) and a musical movie (1953), in the last of which Marilyn MONROE starred as Lorelei. A high spot was her rendering of the song 'Diamonds Are a Girl's Best Friend'.

**Lee, Terry.** The young blond hero of the popular US comic strip *Terry and the Pirates*, created in 1934 by Milton Caniff. Terry goes treasure-hunting in China and falls foul of a band of pirates led by the infamous DRAGON LADY. His chief ally is the manly, pipe-smoking Pat Ryan, while another friend is the brassy blonde known as Burma. Connoisseurs of comic strips rate *Terry and the Pirates*, which ran until 1973, as one of the finest ever.

**Left Book Club.** A publishing venture launched in 1936 by Victor GOLLANCZ in association with John Strachey and Harold Laski. It was modelled on commercial book club lines and aimed to counter the rise of FASCISM and Nazism by providing politically educative left-wing literature. Early titles included André Malraux's *Days of Contempt* (1936), Stephen Spender's *Forward from Liberalism* (1937) and J.B.S. Haldane's *A.R.P.* (1938). By 1939 it had over 56,000 subscribers and more than a thousand 'left discussion groups' in Britain, with major rallies held at the Albert Hall. The outbreak of the Second World War that year initiated a sharp decline in membership and it closed in 1948 with the publication of G.D.H. Cole's *The Meaning of Marxism*. Few of the orange cloth-bound books have survived, with the exception of George ORWELL's *The* ROAD TO WIGAN PIER (1937), a title about which, ironically, Gollancz had profound misgivings.

**Left-field.** Unorthodox; experimental; out of the ordinary. A US jazz jargon term picked up by British journalists and musicians in the 1970s. It derives from the phrase 'out of left field', relating to baseball, in which the left field is the area to the batter's left, beyond third base, which rarely sees any action and from which the ball rarely arrives.

**Left-footer.** A nickname for a Roman Catholic, current from the 1930s. The allusion seems to be to an Irish turf-cutter who uses a special left-footed spade, many Irish being Catholics. *See also* TAIG.

**Legal eagle.** A keen and astute lawyer. The phrase dates from the 1940s.

**Legend in one's lifetime.** A person so famous that they are the subject of popular repeated stories in their lifetime. The expression derives from Lytton Strachey's *Eminent Victorians* (1918), in which he applied it to Florence Nightingale (1820–1910): 'She was a legend in her lifetime, and she knew it.' Veteran journalists of a certain type are sometimes punningly known as 'a legend in their lunchtime' (the phrase was allegedly applied originally by Christopher Wordsworth in the 1970s to Clifford Makins (1924–90), one time editor of the EAGLE and sports editor of the *Observer*, who liked a liquid lunch). *See also* EMINENT VICTORIAN.

> Leading libel lawyer Peter Carter-Ruck once said of him [Lord Goodman]: 'He became a legend in his lifetime.'
> *Sunday Express* (14 May 1995)

**Legionnaires' disease.** A form of pneumonia that was first identified in 1976 as being caused by a previously unknown bacillus, *Legionella pneumophila*, which thrives in contaminated air-conditioning units. The name comes from a convention held that year at a Philadelphia hotel by members of the American Legion, an organization of retired US servicemen. A total of 192 Legionnaires contracted the disease, 29 of them fatally.

**Lego.** The construction toy consisting of interlocking plastic building blocks arose from a business set up in 1932 at Billund, Denmark, by Ole Kirk Christiansen, a master carpenter and joiner, who originally made and sold stepladders, ironing boards and wooden toys. In 1934 he named the latter Lego, from Danish *leg godt*, 'play well', a name that it was later realized was also Latin for 'I study'. The business introduced plastic toys in 1947, and began to perfect what were at first known as 'Automatic Binding Bricks'. The firm's products grew in variety and in 1958 the coupling system for the blocks was patented. In 1960 the company opened Legoland, an entire village made of Lego at Billund. It remained the sole Lego Mecca until 1996 when a second Legoland opened at Windsor, close to London. A third was added in 1999 at Carlsbad, California, and a fourth in 2002 near Günzburg in Germany. The company's products now range from Disney characters to working models of all kinds. Various ingenious Lego fans have created some spectacular constructions. Henry Lim, for example, has built a full-size playable harpsichord, using an estimated 100,000 pieces, and in which only the strings are not made of Lego.

**Legs.** If a product or idea is said to have legs it is successful and popular, enjoying a long run. The expression typically applies to television programmes or books and particularly to films that are 'good box office'.

**Leg show.** A now dated term first current at the turn of the

20th century for a theatrical production in which dancing girls displayed their legs.

**Leg warmers.** A pair of tubular knitted garments designed to cover the leg from ankle to knee or thigh. They are typically worn by dancers during rehearsal but in the 1970s also became generally fashionable.

**Le Mans.** A town in northwest France famous for its motor-racing circuit, on which an annual 24-hour endurance race, *les Vingt-Quatre Heures du Mans*, has from 1923 been the high spot.

**LeMay, 'Bombs Away'.** *See* BOMB THEM BACK INTO THE STONE AGE.

**Lemmy Caution.** *See* Lemmy CAUTION.

**Lemon, Answer's a.** *See* ANSWER'S A LEMON.

**Lender of last resort.** In the world of finance an institution that will lend to a borrower when no one else will. More generally a lender of last resort is a central bank that will lend to other banks when they run low on funds because of heavy withdrawals.

**Lend-Lease** or **Lease-Lend.** Reciprocal agreements made by the United States with Britain and the Allied nations in the Second World War to foster the pooling of resources. The policy began with the destroyers sent to Britain in return for naval and air bases in parts of the British Commonwealth and was formalized by the Lend-Lease Act of March 1941. When Lend-Lease ended in 1945 the United States had received somewhat less than one-sixth, in monetary terms, of what they had expended in aid to their allies, over 60 per cent of which went to the British Commonwealth.

**Lenin.** The assumed name of Vladimir Ilyich Ulyanov (1870–1924), founder of the Soviet Union and propagator of its guiding doctrine of Marxism-Leninism. The origin of his pseudonym remains uncertain. It is popularly said to derive from the Siberian River Lena, but although he had been exiled to Siberia, it was not to this river. He first used the name in 1901.

**Leningrad.** The name given in 1924 on the death of LENIN to Petrograd which, until 1914, was known as St Petersburg, the former capital of Tsarist Russia founded by Peter the Great in 1703. In 1991 it reverted to its original name of St Petersburg. The siege of Leningrad in the Second World War (August 1941–January 1944) caused more than one million deaths from cold and famine. It was the inspiration for Shostakovich's symphony No. 7 (the LENINGRAD SYMPHONY). The Nazis were determined to obliterate Shostakovich's native city, as noted in a directive from General Walter

Warlimont: 'The Führer has decided to raze the city of St Petersburg from the face of the earth. After the defeat of Soviet Russia there will be not the slightest reason for the future existence of this large city.'

***Leningrad Symphony.*** The title given to Shostakovich's symphony No. 7, which the composer wrote in 1941–2, during the German siege of Leningrad (St Petersburg), which began in August 1941. As well as working on his symphony, Shostakovich joined the Leningrad fire brigade. At first the authorities requested that he leave the city, along with the rest of Leningrad's cultural elite, but Shostakovich refused until 29 September, when he was ordered to go. He left on 1 October, taking his unfinished score with him. Through that winter hundreds of thousands died in the besieged city, as Shostakovich worked to complete his symphony. The first performance took place on 5 March 1942 in Kuibyshev, but the first performance in Leningrad itself had to wait until 9 August 1942, when the starving remnants of the Leningrad Radio Orchestra, joined by Red Army musicians, gave a broadcast concert. Along the front line around the city, speakers were mounted to direct the defiant music towards the enemy positions.

> To the historic confrontation now taking place between reason and obscurantism, culture and barbarity, light and darkness. I dedicate my Seventh Symphony to our struggle against fascism, to our coming victory and to my native city of Leningrad.
>
> DMITRI SHOSTAKOVICH: dedication of the *Leningrad Symphony* (1942)

**Leninspart, Ken.** *See* RED KEN.

***Leopard, The.*** A novel (1960; in Italian as *Il Gattopardo*, 1958) by Giuseppe di Lampedusa (1896–1957), Duke of Palma and Prince of Lampedusa. It is set in Sicily, to which in May 1860 Giuseppe Garibaldi (1807–82) sailed with 1000 volunteers to win the island from the Bourbons. The narrative describes the reactions to historical events of Fabrizio, Prince of Salina, and the Salina family between 1860 and 1910. The leopard is the family motif, which appears as the centrepiece of a vaulted ceiling in the family convent and, at the book's end, 'in red thread' on the border of a towel. The author died of cancer a week after the manuscript had been rejected by the house of Mondadori. He left instructions that his family should pursue publication. It appeared under the imprint of Feltrinelli, to become the highest selling and most widely translated 20th-century Italian novel.

**Leotard.** The close-fitting garment so called, worn by acrobats and dancers, takes its name from the French trapeze artist Jules Léotard (1839–70), who wore something similar.

The costume is first recorded in the United States in the 1920s, its design presumably based on the particular original. It subsequently became a fashion garment.

**Less is more.** Restraint or moderation is more effective than overemphasis or exaggeration. The aphorism was a favourite of the German-born US modernist architect Ludwig Mies van der Rohe (1886–1969), but the words come from Browning.

> Yet do much less, so much less, Someone says,
> (I know his name, no matter) – so much less!
> Well, less is more, Lucrezia: I am judged.
>
> ROBERT BROWNING: *Andrea del Sarto* (1855)

According to the American architect Robert Venturi (b.1925), one of the seminal figures of the postmodernist movement, 'Less is a bore' (*Complexity and Contradiction in Architecture*, 1966). Venturi was criticizing architectural modernism for its lack of irony and complexity.

**Let George do it.** Let someone else do the work or take the responsibility. The expression is of US origin and dates from the turn of the 20th century. The source of the phrase is uncertain but it is possibly a learned adoption of the French *Laissez faire à Georges* in the same sense, where the reference is to Cardinal Georges d'Amboise (1460–1510), a church and government official under Louis XII responsible for major tax and judicial reforms. It was the English phrase that gave 'George' as the colloquial term for an automatic pilot in an aircraft.

**Let it all hang out.** To do just what one wants; to be quite uninhibited. The allusion is probably to a naked or 'unbuttoned' person. The expression gained popularity in the counterculture of the 1960s and originated with African Americans.

> It's a fellow with hair curling over his neck shrieking: 'Uptight–outasight! What you gonna doo–boogaloo! Let it all hang out!'
>
> RICHARD GILBERT: in *Anatomy of Pop* (1970)

**Let It Be.** The thirteenth and last album by The BEATLES, released in Britain in May 1970. It included the tracks 'Across the Universe', 'Let It Be', MAGGIE MAE, 'The Long and Winding Road' and 'Get Back', the last having been the original title of a project that was cancelled in favour of *Let It Be*. The Beatles' final album has a markedly spiritual and reflective flavour, exemplified by the overtly religious stamp of its title song. A film of the same title was released in the same month as the album. The similarity of its title to that of The Rolling Stones' song and album LET IT BLEED (released the previous year) appears to be coincidental.

**Let it Bleed.** A song and album by The ROLLING STONES, released in 1969. The album includes such tracks as 'Gimme Shelter', 'Let It Bleed', 'Midnight Rambler', 'Monkey Man' and 'You Can't Always Get What You Want'. The cover featured a garishly decorated cake, baked by DELIA Smith, then a little-known freelance home economist. *See also* LET IT BE.

**Let's be having you.** A stock order to respond by a sergeant to his men or a police officer to a suspect or criminal. A street outside the police station at Sheffield Airport is called 'Letsby Avenue', the outcome of a prank perpetrated on the Ordnance Survey by an anonymous policeman. *See also* DELIA.

**Let's face it.** Let's face the facts. The hackneyed phrase does not normally imply any challenge.

**Letter from America.** The longest running radio programme in the world, in the form of a weekly talk on a US topic given for 58 years by the British-born broadcaster Alistair Cooke (1908–2004), who took US citizenship in 1941. The first talk was broadcast in 1946 in what was originally commissioned as a series of 13. Ill health finally forced Cooke to retire from the programme on 2 March, 2004, and he died on 30 March. In 2005 the BBC announced a revamped *Letter from America*, with the journalist Sir Harold Evans (b.1928) as the correspondent.

**Level playing field.** An area of activity that offers no advantage to any particular side. In real terms, a field that is not level may serve to favour a home team, who will be familiar with it. The metaphorical use of the expression is chiefly found in the worlds of business and politics.

**Levittown.** The name applied to a type of pioneering postwar suburban housing tract in the United States constructed by the building firm William Levitt and Sons. The first Levittown was built in Hempstead, New York, between 1947 and 1951. It eventually provided more than 17,000 private homes. Although the houses were extremely basic, the privacy they offered was greatly valued, and the company subsequently built a second Levittown on the outskirts of Philadelphia and a third in southern New Jersey. The name came to be applied to similar housing developments all over the United States, and not just those built by Levitt and Sons.

**Lewinsky, Monica.** *See* MONICA.

**Ley lines.** Imaginary mystic lines running across Britain, said to connect places of power such as churches and different types of ANCIENT MONUMENTS and so to form 'power grids'. Stonehenge is one of several monuments said to lie at the intersection of at least two ley lines. The idea of such lines was introduced to the public by Alfred Watkins in his *Early British Trackways* (1922). His original theory 'that mounds, moats, beacons and mark stones fall into straight lines throughout Britain' was firmly rejected by archaeologists and historians but in more recent times has generated a lively NEW AGE cult. The longest ley line is the St Michael Line, extending from Cornwall to East Anglia, and running past many churches dedicated to St Michael, including St Michael's Mount itself and those at Brentor in Devon, Trull, Othery and Stoke St Michael in Somerset, Clifton Hampden in Oxfordshire and Hopton in Suffolk. 'Ley' is a variant of 'lea', meaning 'field', 'meadow'.

**LG.** A nickname for David Lloyd George, the WELSH WIZARD.

**LHOOQ.** The letters inscribed beneath a reproduction of the *Mona Lisa*, on whose upper lip a moustache has been drawn, on the front cover of a 1920 Dada manifesto by Marcel Duchamp (1887–1968) and Francis Picabia (1879–1953). If the letters are read in French, they sound like *elle a chaud au cul*, which means 'she's got a hot arse'.

**Lib Dems.** A short name, favoured by the news media, for the LIBERAL DEMOCRATS.

**Liberal Democrats.** Britain's third main political party, after the LABOUR PARTY and the Conservatives. It was formed from the old Liberal Party in May 1988 as a merger between that party and the Social Democrats and was at first known as the Liberal and Social Democrats. In 1989 the cumbersome title was shortened to the Liberal Democrats or, colloquially, the Lib Dems. Its first leader (to 1999) was Paddy Ashdown (b.1941); he was succeeded by Charles Kennedy (b.1959), followed by Sir Menzies Campbell (b.1941) (also known as MING Campbell, MING THE MERCILESS and Old Father Time) in 2006. In the political spectrum it is mainly left of centre, and it came to support several of the measures introduced by NEW LABOUR under Tony Blair.

> By-elections are what the Lib-Dems are good at.
> *Sunday Express* (27 February 2000)

**Liberation Day.** The annual holiday (9 May) in the Channel Islands to mark the liberation of the islands in 1945 from the Second World War German occupation. The Channel Islands were the only part of the British Isles to be conquered by the NAZIS, being occupied unopposed following the fall of France in 1940. The German garrison surrendered as part of the overall surrender of German forces at the end of the European war (*see* VE DAY).

**Liberation theology.** The theory originating among Roman Catholic theologians in South America that liberation from social, political, and economic oppression is a vital constituent of the Christian message. The term translates Spanish *teología de la liberación*, coined by the Peruvian Gustavo Guttierez in 1968 and used for the title of his book published in 1971. 'Liberation' expresses a dislike of 'development', meaning an imposed solution to South America's problems, determined by the industrialized nations and involving little initiative on the part of the people.

**Liberty bodice.** A type of sleeveless vest formerly worn by young children. The name was a commercial one given to suggest a greater freedom of movement than that provided by the conventional bodice. It was first manufactured in the early 20th century by the firm of R. & W.H. Symington, of Market Harborough, Leicestershire, but ceased to be produced in the 1960s.

**Liberty Bonds.** Between 24 April 1917 and 2 March 1919 the US government authorized five issues of gold bonds in aid of the war effort. The sales of these Liberty Bonds, as they were known, peaked in 1918, their appeal enhanced by endorsements from such HOLLYWOOD stars as Charlie Chaplin, Mary Pickford and Douglas Fairbanks. A patriotic poster for the 3rd Liberty Loan bore the words: 'Remember the Flag of Liberty! Support It! Buy U.S. Government Bonds.'

**Lib-Lab Pact.** The agreement in 1977–8 between the Liberals led by David Steel (the BOY DAVID) and the Labour government of James Callaghan (SUNNY JIM). The government, to shore up its slim majority, agreed to follow moderate policies and to consult the Liberals on important issues in return for their support. The Liberals ended the pact in the autumn of 1978, and in March 1979 the government lost a vote of no confidence and was obliged to call a general election.

**Librium.** The proprietary name of a white crystalline compound used as a tranquillizer. Together with VALIUM it was a prime resort of the stressed and superanxious in the 1960s and the 1970s; it is still prescribed but the effects of dependency are better understood. The name may derive from Latin *libra*, 'balance'.

**Licence to print money.** A description of any highly profitable enterprise, especially one requiring little effort. The expression was famously used by the Canadian-born newspaper tycoon Roy Thomson (1894–1976) in relation to commercial television in Britain. He had just (August 1957) founded Scottish Television (STV), and, according to Russell Braddon's biography of Thomson (1965), he made the remark to a neighbour in Edinburgh.

**Lidice.** This village of about 450 inhabitants near Prague was 'liquidated' by the Germans on 10 June 1942 as part of a massive reprisal for the assassination by Czech underground fighters of Reinhard Heydrich (1904–42), deputy leader of the SS. The 172 men were shot and the women were transported to the Ravensbrück concentration camp. The 90 children, after being screened and found to be 'racially pure', were dispersed throughout Germany to be renamed and brought up as Germans. When the massacre and deportation were complete, the SS burned the village, dynamited anything that was left standing and levelled the rubble. In 1947 a new village site was designated nearby, while a museum, with a monument and rose garden, marks the original site. *See also* the HANGMAN; ORADOUR-SUR-GLANE.

**Lie back and think of England.** To submit to unavoidable sexual intercourse. The phrase seems to blend two different expressions: 'to close one's eyes and think of England' and 'to lie back and enjoy it'. The former is usually attributed to Alice, Lady Hillingdon's *Journal* of 1912: 'I am happy now that Charles calls on my bedchamber less frequently than of old. As it is, I now endure but two calls a week and when I hear his steps outside my door I lie down on my bed, close my eyes, open my legs and think of England.' Alice, Lady Hillingdon (1857–1940) married the 2nd Baron Hillingdon in 1886, but the whereabouts or even existence of her *Journal* is unknown. The latter expression is of more uncertain origin. In his novel *The* JEWEL IN THE CROWN (1966), Paul Scott refers to it as 'that old, disreputable saying', but quite how ancient it is remains a mystery.

**Lie detector.** An informal name for the polygraph, a US invention that records the physiological changes of a person under questioning. It is based on the assumption that a human being cannot tell a lie without changes in breathing, blood pressure, pulse rate and palm perspiration, and the knowledge that these can be recorded. The rare instances when individuals have succeeded in duping a lie detector point to the fact that automatic physiological responses can with practice be brought under conscious control. US courts have consistently ruled against lie detector evidence. In the intelligence community, however, security officials have just as consistently upheld its use.

**Lie down in a darkened room.** Metaphorically to recover one's composure or regain one's sanity. The described action is often recommended to someone expressing an eccentric notion.

> In response to the hon. Gentleman, I ask him to go away, lie down in a dark room, keep taking the tablets and think

carefully about whether the Liberal Democrats have an opinion one way or the other on the merits of any of the proposals that I have just announced
> Conservative home secretary KENNETH CLARKE: replying to Liberal Democrat Robert Maclennan during a Commons debate on criminal justice (13 May 1993)

**Lied von der Erde, Das.** The posthumously performed 'song-symphony' by Gustav Mahler (1860–1911), composed in 1908 and featuring German translations of six Chinese poems from the 8th century. The title means 'Song of the Earth', and the final song is entitled 'Der Abschied', the farewell. Although Mahler called the work a symphony he did not give it a number as it would have been his ninth, and he was superstitiously aware that Beethoven, Schubert and other composers had died after completing their ninth symphonies. Nevertheless, he appears to have overcome his anxieties, and went on to write a ninth and parts of a tenth symphony; the latter lay uncompleted at his death. In his memory, Bruno Walter gave the first performance of *Das Lied von der Erde* in 1911.

**Lie follows.** *See* CANNOT COME. LIE FOLLOWS.

**Life after death.** This phrase typically found in the form of a question, 'Is there life after death?', has become a catchphrase in the 20th century. As such it was memorably caricatured in an episode of the television comedy MONTY PYTHON'S FLYING CIRCUS on 21 December 1972: 'Tonight on "Is There" we examine the question, "Is there life after death?" And here to discuss it are three dead people.' Film titles such as *Is There Sex After Death?* (1971) and *Is There Sex After Marriage?* (1973) vary the formula, while a graffito seen in Ballymurphy, Ireland, in the early 1970s was recorded as, 'Is there life *before* death?' Seamus Heaney quotes this in his poem 'Whatever You Say You Say Nothing' in *North* (1975).

> Is there life after redundancy?
> *Sunday Times Magazine*, headline (14 October 1984)

**Life and Death of Colonel Blimp, The.** A film (1943) written and directed by Michael Powell (1905–90) and Emeric Pressburger (1902–88) about the life of a British colonel from his early army days in the Boer War through to 1943 and the Second World War. Starring Roger Livesey as Colonel Blimp, the film was controversial in sending up the pomposity of a certain type of elderly senior officer and consequently incurred the wrath of Prime Minister Winston Churchill, who feared it would damage wartime morale: he had its exportation banned and only relented two years later, by which time the film had enjoyed huge success with British audiences. The 'Colonel Blimp' character was not original to the film but was derived from the cartoons of David Low in the *London Evening Standard*. *See also* BLIMP.

**Life and Loves of a She-Devil, The.** A blackly comic novel (1983) by Fay Weldon (b.1931), in which the macabre and ugly Ruth Patchett takes her revenge on bestselling author Mary Fisher, who she feels has stolen her husband, Bobbo. In the triumphant televised version (1986), directed by Philip Saville, Julie T. Wallace played Ruth in a physically and emotionally memorable performance.

**Life and Times of Michael K.** A novel (1983) by J.M. Coetzee (b.1940), which won the BOOKER PRIZE for fiction. A political fable, it concerns Michael's journey with his mother to the farm of her birth. When she dies on the way, he carries on, tries to live in isolation, but is overtaken by a civil war, captured and imprisoned as a guerrilla. The name of the central character echoes that of Josef K., the protagonist of Franz Kafka's *The* TRIAL BY TELEVISION (1925).

**Life begins at 40.** A view held generally by optimists and an increasing number of realists, whereas pessimists are inclined to opine that at this age one is OVER THE HILL. The words come from the book *Life Begins at Forty* (1932) by the US writer Walter B. Pitkin.

**Life of Riley.** The good life; a comfortable existence. Riley or Reilly, a common Irish surname, is said to be a character in a 19th-century song. Two possible candidates are Pat Rooney's 'Are You the O'Reilly?', originally 'Is That Mr Reilly?' (1883), and Charles B. Lawlor's 'The Best Man in the House' (1898). The first certain use of the name is in Harry Pease's 'My Name is Kelly' (1919), which has two lines as follows:

Faith and my name is Kelly, Michael Kelly,
But I'm living the life of Reilly just the same.

**Life sentence.** A sentence of imprisonment for life, awarded in Britain as the mandatory sentence for murder and the maximum penalty for a number of serious offences such as robbery, rape, arson and manslaughter. Since 1997 courts in England and Wales have been required to impose life sentences also on those convicted for a second time on a serious violent or sexual offence. Unless 'life means life', people serving life sentences are normally detained for at least 20 years. They are then released but remain on licence for the rest of their lives and are subject to recall if their behaviour suggests that they could again be a danger to the public.

**Life's rich pageant.** A phrase much favoured by the Dr Panglosses and JOLLY HOCKEYSTICKS of this world when faced with any sort of unpleasantness. 'Life's rich tapestry' is an alternative version.

What, knocked a tooth out? Never mind, dear, laugh it off, laugh it off; it's all part of life's rich pageant.
    ARTHUR MARSHALL: monologue *The Games Mistress* (1937)

**Life, the Universe and Everything.** That which some people forever seek the meaning of. The phrase famously occurs in *The* HITCH-HIKER'S GUIDE TO THE GALAXY:

'O Deep Thought Computer,' he said, 'the task we have designed for you to perform is this. We want you to tell us ...' he paused, ' ... the Answer!'

'The Answer?' said Deep Thought. 'The Answer to what?'
'Life!' urged Fook.
'The Universe!' said Lunkwill. 'Everything!' they said in chorus.

It turns out that the answer is, in fact, 42.

**Light at the end of the tunnel.** A long-awaited indication that a period of hardship or lengthy endeavour is nearing an end. The allusion is to the distant light at the exit of a railway tunnel, which is all that is seen while the train travels in darkness. The expression apparently dates no earlier than the 1920s and is chiefly used by politicians or journalists with reference to a slight upturn in an economic or other situation. It is on record as having been resorted to by Stanley Baldwin in 1929 and by Neville Chamberlain in 1937 and is said to have been exploited by Winston Churchill in 1941. At some point in the 1960s a jocular variant emerged: 'If we see the light at the end of the tunnel, it's the light of the oncoming train.' This is quoted by Robert Lowell in his poem 'Since 1939' (1977) and was repeated as 'Rowe's Rule' by Paul Dickson in an article in the *Washingtonian* of November 1978: 'The odds are five to six that the light at the end of the tunnel is the headlight of an oncoming train.' *See also* GREEN SHOOTS.

**Light of one's life.** A dearly loved person. The expression has now mostly superseded, at first ironically or semi-seriously, the much older 'light of one's eye'.

Lolita, light of my life, fire of my loins.
    VLADIMIR NABOKOV: *Lolita*, Pt I, ch. 1 (1955)

**Light Programme.** The BBC Radio service inaugurated in 1945 as the peacetime successor to the Forces Programme. It continued the same mixture of broad comedy and light music that had made it so popular in the Second World War and the essential ingredients were maintained when it changed its name to Radio 2 on 30 September 1967. *See also* HOME SERVICE; THIRD PROGRAMME.

**Lights are on but there's no one at home.** A sardonic comment on someone who shows little or no sign of a developed intellect or who is suffering from dementia. It dates from the 1970s.

**Lightyear, Buzz.** One of the heroes of the computer-animated films *Toy Story* (1995) and *Toy Story 2* (2000). He is a toy action figure of an astronaut, and suffers from hubris of a forgivable sort. His first name echoes that of Buzz Aldrin (b.1930), the second man on the moon, and his surname is a unit of length used in astronomy, being the distance that light travels in a year at a speed of 300,000 km (186,000 miles) per second.

Buzz Lightyear's slogan is 'To Infinity and Beyond'. This had previously been the title of a book (1987) by Eli Maor, subtitled 'A Cultural History of the Infinite'. Maor explains in his preface:

> I took the title *To Infinity and Beyond*, from a telescope manual that listed among the many virtues of the instrument the following: 'The range of focus of your telescope is from fifteen feet to infinity and beyond.'

**Like a bag of spanners.** In British slang, extremely ugly. The metaphor is usually applied to a person's face.

> Paul sets out on his quest to leave singledom behind... Including: The date with the psycho weirdo nutter. The date who didn't turn up. The world's shortest date. And the date with a face like a bag of spanners.
> www.guardianbookshop.co.uk (2005)

**Like a bat out of hell.** Very fast. The expression is said to have originated among US fighter pilots in the First World War. An alternative image is of bats fleeing the glare of the fires of hell. The expression dates from the 1920s.

**Like a bomb.** Very successfully. The phrase is often used ironically.

**Like a fish needs a bicycle.** Not in the least; the exact opposite. A fish does not need a bicycle. The colourful simile derives from the comment attributed in *c.*1970 to the US feminist Gloria Steinem (b.1934) that 'a woman without a man is like a fish without a bicycle'.

**Like a rat up a drainpipe.** With unseemly alacrity. The phrase originated in Australia in the 1940s, and is often used with a sexual connotation.

**Like a stunned mullet.** With a dazed, vacant or uncomprehending expression, (as if) stupefied. The phrase originated in colloquial Australian English, and is first recorded in 1953.

> He looks at me with that stunned mullet look only highly experienced cameramen can make when one of life's great dramas is about to unleash and you realize that something important is not there.
> www.tvcameramen.com (September 2001)

**Like gangbusters.** With great and successful force or vigour. The US expression, which usually occurs in such phrases as 'go like gangbusters' and 'come on like gangbusters', was inspired by the gunshots, police sirens and other ear-assaulting sound effects that were broadcast at the start of each episode of *Gangbusters*, a US radio series that ran from 1936 to 1957.

**Like, hello?** *See* HELLO?

**Likely lad.** An able or smart youth. 'Likely' in this sense goes back to the 15th century but the particular alliterative combination dates from the 20th century as a friendly north of England phrase for a young man of promise or enterprise. It was popularized by the title of the television SITCOM *The Likely Lads* (1965–9) about the friendship between two working-class young men in northeast England, Terry Collier, played by James Bolam, and Bob Ferris, played by Rodney Bewes. A sequel was *Whatever Happened to the Likely Lads* (1973–4).

**Like nobody's business.** To an extraordinary extent; like mad, as: 'She was pedalling along like nobody's business.' An unusual phrase dating from the 1930s.

**Like the clappers.** Very fast; very hard. The phrase dates from the 1940s and is a shortening of 'like the clappers of hell', meaning those of HELL'S BELLS!

**Li'l Abner.** The handsome HILLBILLY created by the US newspaper cartoonist Al Capp in 1934. He comes from the dead-end town of Dogpatch and has a DUMB BLONDE girlfriend, Daisy Mae. His adventures have been represented in both stage and screen versions. *See also* SADIE HAWKINS DAY.

**'Lili Marlene'.** A German song of the Second World War. It was based on a poem written in 1917 by a German soldier, Hans Leip (1894–1983), and was composed by Norbert Schultze in 1938. The German singer Lale Andersen initially made it known in 1939. It became increasingly popular, especially with the AFRIKA KORPS, and the recorded version was played nightly by Radio Belgrade from the late summer of 1941 virtually until the end of hostilities in 1945. Other German stations relayed it, and it was picked up and adopted by the 8TH ARMY, the English version of the lyric being by Tommy Connor (who deleted an implication in the original that Lili Marlene was a prostitute). There were French, Italian and other renderings of what became the classic song of the war, and it was one of the theme songs of its namesake, the German-born actress Marlene Dietrich. A recording of the song by Ann Shelton in 1944 sold a million copies. Leip subsequently said he had based Lili Marlene on two girls, Lili and Marlene, whom he had known in Berlin when on leave.

> Bei der Kaserne
>
> Vor dem grossen Tor,
>
> Stand eine Lanterne
>
> Und steht sie noch davor …
>
> Mit dir, Lili Marlene,
>
> Mit dir, Lili Marlen'.
>
> (Underneath the lantern
>
> By the barrack gate,
>
> Darling, I remember
>
> The way you used to wait …
>
> My Lili of the lamplight,
>
> My own Lili Marlene.)

**Limbo dancing.** A dance of West Indian origin popular from the 1950s in which the dancer bends backwards to pass under a horizontal bar, which is progressively lowered until it is barely off the ground. The word derives from 'limber' in the sense lithe, supple.

**Lime, Harry.** The intriguing villain who runs a drugs racket in postwar Vienna in the film The THIRD MAN (1949), scripted by Graham Greene (1904–91). He was played by Orson Welles (1915–85), and although he does not appear until halfway through the film, all Welles's obituary notices mentioned his memorable portrayal of the role. The radio series The Lives of Harry Lime (from 1951) also starred Orson Welles, but in the television series The Third Man (1959–65) the part was played by Michael Rennie. An authentic Harry Lime is depicted in David Thomson's book Suspects (1985), in which he is shown as a South London WIDE BOY who makes a killing from a crooked salvage business during the BLITZ before going to Vienna to meet a literally dirty end in the city's sewers.

**Limousine liberal.** A US term for a wealthy person who professes sympathy for the deprived. The term's conflicting image of a person who drives an expensive car while pitying the poor is intended to imply the hypocrisy of the stance. The British equivalent is a CHAMPAGNE SOCIALIST.

**Limp-wristed.** Effeminate; affected; CAMP. The phrase dates from the 1950s and refers to the supposedly typical gestures or poses of male homosexuals.

**Lindbergh, Charles Augustus.** The US aviator (1902–74), nicknamed 'The Lone Eagle', who was the first to make a solo nonstop flight across the Atlantic (New York to Paris), in his monoplane SPIRIT OF ST LOUIS. The flight, on 20–21 May 1927, took 33½ hours, made Lindbergh into an instant hero and earned him his nickname. The waist-length aviation jacket he wore inspired a fashion, and the so-called Lindbergh jacket was popular in the 1930s. In 1932 Lindbergh's two-year-old son was kidnapped and murdered, and the Lindbergh baby case became one of the most notorious of the decade. In 1936 Bruno Richard Hauptmann was executed for the murder. Lindbergh's speeches in favour of US isolationism in 1940–1 led to criticism from President Franklin D. Roosevelt, and Lindbergh resigned his commission in the Air Corps Reserve in April 1941. However, once the United States entered the war, Lindbergh was active in the Allied cause. See also LINDY HOP.

**Lindy hop.** The frenzied dance of this name originated in the Savoy Ballroom, Harlem, New York, in the late 1920s and was inspired by Charles LINDBERGH's pioneering solo transatlantic flight of 1927, reported in the news headline 'Lindy hops the Atlantic'. The dance re-enacted the flight, with the couple standing face to face and the man tossing the woman in a whirl of solo turns and supported leaps. After a 'landing', she was ready for the next 'flight'. According to legend, the dance began with a group of men and women leaping and yelling, 'Look, I'm flying like Lindy!'

**Lindy's.** A restaurant opened by Leo Lindemann on Broadway, New York, in 1921 and frequented by many celebrities from the world of sport and entertainment. Lindemann opened a second Lindy's on Broadway in 1930 and both restaurants became known for their sandwiches, sturgeon, herring and cheesecake. As 'Mindy's' they were immortalized in the short stories of Damon Runyon. The original restaurant closed in 1949 and the second in 1957.

**Linear B.** The bald academic designation of a form of Bronze Age writing discovered on clay tablets in Crete and deciphered as an early form of Greek (now known as Mycenaean Greek) by Michael Ventris (in collaboration with the Cambridge philologist John Chadwick) in 1952. It proved to be a syllabic script composed of linear signs dating from c.1400 to c.1200 BC (the late Minoan period) and is believed by some scholars to have developed from the earlier, undeciphered Linear A. Ventris died in a car accident in 1956 at the age of 34.

**Line dancing.** A dance craze of the 1990s similar to COUNTRY AND WESTERN dancing. Dancers line up without partners and follow a fixed pattern of steps to music. The sight of the dancers kicking and turning in unison is almost as satisfying to the viewer as the actions themselves are to the dancers.

**Link trainer.** A flight simulator, as a device enabling pilots to learn and practise flying techniques while still on the ground. It was the invention in 1929 of the US pilot Edward A. Link (1904–81). Hence the name, which also happens to suggest a link between ground and air.

**Lion of Judah.** The title of Hailie Selassie (1892–1975), emperor of Ethiopia from 1930 until his overthrow in 1974. Before becoming emperor he was known as Ras (Prince) Tafari Makonnen, the origin of the name of the RASTAFARIANS cult, which worships him as the Messiah.

**Lions Clubs.** Civilian service clubs that comprise the International Association of Lions Clubs, founded in Dallas, Texas, in 1917 to foster a spirit of 'generous consideration' among the peoples of the world and to promote good government, good citizenship and active interest in social and moral welfare. Lions Clubs activities include general community welfare projects, aid to the blind and support of the UNITED NATIONS. There are now Lions Clubs in over 150 countries and the headquarters of the association is in Oakbrook, Illinois.

**Lions led by donkeys.** A metaphor traditionally associated with British soldiers in the First World War, with reference to their complaints about their generals. Alan Clark in *The Donkeys* (1961) attributes the saying to Max Hoffman (1869–1927), but the phrase was already known by the 1870s.

**Lion, the Witch and the Wardrobe, The.** A fantasy (1950) for children by C.S. Lewis (1898–1963), the first to be published of seven books about the mythical land of NARNIA. The lion, known as ASLAN, is a Christ-like figure. The witch has held Narnia in thrall for a hundred years. The wardrobe is the means through which four children enter Narnia. The series upholds Lewis's dictum that 'a book which is enjoyed only by children is a bad children's book'. A faithful televised version was made in 1963, to be followed by a less satisfactory re-creation, full of technical wizardry, in the series *Chronicles of Narnia* (1988–90), and a visually striking feature film, *The Chronicles of Narnia: The Lion, the Witch and the Wardrobe* (2005), directed by Andrew Adamson and replete with computer-generated imagery. *See also* FIRST LINES OF NOVELS.

**Liquid lunch.** A midday meal in which the consumption of alcoholic liquor is greater than that of solid food.

**Lisbon Lions.** The nickname given to the Glasgow Celtic football team who on 25 May 1967 defeated Inter Milan 2-1 in Lisbon to become the first British club to win the European Cup.

**LISP.** *See* PROGRAMMING LANGUAGES.

**Listed building.** *See* ANCIENT MONUMENT.

**Listen with Mother.** A popular radio programme for very young children, broadcast from 1950 to 1982. It consisted of 15 minutes of stories, songs and nursery rhymes and the opening words were always the same: 'Are you sitting comfortably? Then I'll begin.' *See also* WATCH WITH MOTHER.

**Lite.** A respelling of 'light', especially with reference to a low-calorie light beer. The first such beer, Miller Lite, was marketed in the United States in 1975.

**Litmus test.** Figuratively, a decisively indicative test. This sense of the phrase dates from the 1950s and derives from the physical litmus test, in which a piece of blue litmus paper turns red under acid conditions and back to blue again under alkaline ones.

**Little Black Banda.** A highly offensive nickname bestowed on Dr Hastings Kamuzu Banda (1905–97), the autocratic leader of Malawi from 1963 to 1994. The nickname, based on the now-frowned-upon children's story LITTLE BLACK SAMBO, was coined by David Frost on THAT WAS THE WEEK THAT WAS.

**Little black book.** A notebook in which men supposedly keep a list of potential dates.

**Little black dress.** A woman's short or medium-length black dress, deemed to be suitable for almost any social engagement. It was created in the 1920s by the French dress designer Coco Chanel (1883–1971) who made it out of jersey wool, then an unfashionable material associated with maids' uniforms, and adorned it with lavish costume jewellery. Amy Holman Edelman's book *The Little Black Dress* (1998) is a study of the style.

**Little Black Sambo.** The now controversial tale of a small African American boy, written and illustrated by Helen Bannerman (1862–1946) and first published in 1899 by the publishers Grant Richards of London. Little Black Sambo encounters a group of menacing tigers in the jungle, but bribes them by offering them his clothes, shoes and umbrella. The tigers argue among themselves for possession of the objects and, racing round a tree, are turned into a pool of melted butter, which is later used by Sambo's mother to cook delicious pancakes. In the 1970s *Little Black Sambo* was criticized for its apparent racism in Britain by, among others, Teachers against Racism and in the United States by the National Association for the Advancement of Colored People. It nevertheless continued to sell in significant numbers. The book popularized the use of the word 'Sambo', which had been used as a term for a black person as early as the 18th century, but the term, like the book, has long ceased to be acceptable.

**Little Book of ..., The.** A title formula popularized in the later 1990s by Paul Wilson's *The Little Book of Calm* (1996), a pocket-sized guide to dealing with life's upsetting moments. It offers advice such as: 'Write down your worry', 'Breathe deeply', 'Avoid tense people' and 'Massage your forehead'. Other NEW-AGE titles along these lines include *A Little Book of Eternal Wisdom*.

In 1998 Rohan Candappa published *The Little Book of Stress*, with the slogan 'Calm is for wimps. Get real. Get stressed.' It offers such advice as:

Really tense up all your muscles
Try to stay this way all day.
If this proves impossible, you have yet
again failed at a really simple task.

Other little books along these lines include *The Little Book of Bollocks* and *The Little Book of Farting*.

**Little Boy.** *See* ENOLA GAY.

**Little boys' room.** A coy euphemism for a men's lavatory, dating from the 1930s.

**Little Britain.** A British comedy programme, written and performed by Matt Lucas and David Walliams, that first appeared on BBC Radio in 2001 and was transferred to television in 2003. It consisted of a series of brief unconnected sketches featuring a cast of regularly recurring characters, such as Daffyd Thomas ('The Only Gay in the Village'), the quintessential chavette Vicky Pollard (*see* CHAV) and the extravagantly bedecked transvestites Emily and Florence ('We are ladies'). The programme was a considerable popular hit, and many of the characters' catchphrases (notably Vicky's quickfire 'Yeah, but no, but yeah, but no, but...') achieved instant recogizability.

**Little Caesar.** A gangster film (1930) based on the novel (1929) by W.R. Burnett about the career and ultimate demise of the ambitious mobster Rico Bandello (played by Edward G. Robinson). It was the first 'talkie' gangster film. Rico's vicious and unrepentant campaign to establish himself as a latterday Caesar in the underworld caused considerable controversy at the time of the film's release, not least because of the clear parallels that could be made with the career of the real-life gangster Al CAPONE.

Mother of God, is this the end of Rico?

EDWARD G. ROBINSON: as Rico Bandello (his last words)

**Little Entente.** The name given to the political alliance formed between Czechoslovakia, Yugoslavia and Romania (1920–2). It was originally designed to prevent the restoration of Habsburg power but became broader in scope. It was brought to an end by the destruction of Czechoslovakia after the MUNICH Agreement (1938).

**Little Foxes, The.** A play (1939) by the US playwright Lillian Hellman (1907–84) about the machinations of the ambitious Regina Hubbard, who is prepared to sacrifice all those around her in the pursuit of material gain. The biblical title comes from the Song of Solomon 2:15: 'Take us the foxes, the little foxes, that spoil the vines; for our vines have tender grapes.'

**'Little Gidding'.** The last part of *Four Quartets* (1942), a poetical work by the Anglo-American poet T.S. Eliot (1888–1965) exploring the theme of 'time past and time present'. Following 'Burnt Norton', 'East Coker' and 'The Dry Salvages', 'Little Gidding' took as its subject the religious community established at Little Gidding in 1625 by Nicholas Ferrar (1592–1637) and finally broken up by the Puritans in 1646. Little Gidding is a hamlet in Cambridgeshire, a few miles northwest of Huntingdon.

You are here to kneel
Where prayer has been valid.

T.S. ELIOT: 'Little Gidding'

**Little girls' room.** A coy euphemism for a women's lavatory, dating from the 1940s and based on the LITTLE BOYS' ROOM that is its male counterpart.

**Little green men.** Imaginary people of peculiar appearance, supposedly landed from outer space. The description (first recorded in 1961) derives from cartoons of such creatures emerging from FLYING SAUCERS. *See also* ALIENS; SETI.

**Little Grey Men, The.** A Carnegie Medal-winning fantasy novel (1942) by B.B. It is the tale of three Warwickshire gnomes named Sneezewort, Baldermoney and Dodder who search for a missing brother.

**Little Grey Rabbit.** The name of the main character in a series of more than 30 illustrated books for young children by Alison Uttley (1884–1976), which began with *The Squirrel, the Hare and the Little Grey Rabbit* (1929), illustrated by Margaret Tempest. The last book in the series was *Hare and the Rainbow* (1975). The Little Grey Rabbit works tirelessly for the lazy Hare and Squirrel, who remain unappreciative of her efforts.

**Little House in the Big Woods.** The first (1932) of eight autobiographical studies by the US writer Laura Ingalls Wilder (1867–1957) of her pioneering family. Told in the third person, the sequence covers her life from the age of four to her marriage at 18, as the family moves westward from Wisconsin, through Minnesota to South Dakota. The best-known title in the series is *Little House on the Prairie* (1935), which was also the title of the popular television series (1974–82) based on Wilder's books.

**Little local difficulty.** A euphemism for a major problem. The expression was popularized by Harold Macmillan's statement at London Airport on 7 January 1958. The prime minister was about to leave for a Commonwealth tour following the resignation of the chancellor of the exchequer, among others.

> I thought the best thing to do was to settle up these little local difficulties and then turn to the wider vision of the Commonwealth.
>
> HAROLD MACMILLAN: quoted in *The Times* (8 January 1958)

**Little man.** An insignificant man. The expression is also used of a local handyman who operates on a small scale.

**Little Mary.** A former euphemism for the stomach, from the play of that name by J.M. Barrie (1903).

> And what is the subject of the piece? Who is Little Mary? It is nobody; it is simply a nursery name that the child-doctor invents as a kind of polite equivalent to what children ordinarily allude to as their 'tum-tum'.
>
> *Punch* (14 October 1903)

**Little Mo.** The US tennis star Maureen Connolly (1934–69) was so dubbed by the media, 'Mo' being a pet form of her first name and 'Little' alluding to her small size and slight figure. The name also punned on 'Big Mo', the US battleship *Missouri*, flagship of the US Pacific Fleet in the Second World War and scene of the Japanese surrender in 1945, four years before 'Little Mo' became the youngest female to win the National Junior Championships. She went on to win nine 'grand slam' titles between 1951 and 1954, when injury ended her meteoric career.

**Little old ladies in tennis shoes.** A nickname for conservative Republican women voters in US elections, said to be typified by an elderly resident in the western states who does not care about her appearance and who 'votes for values'. Their support did much to boost the position of the conservative Republican Senator Barry Goldwater in the late 1950s and 1960s. *See also* BLUE RINSE BRIGADE.

> 'Burt Reynolds has done more for little old ladies in tennis shoes than anyone else in the history of the world,' said Dinah Shore at the annual Friars Club roast, where Reynolds was the guest of honor.
>
> *Newsweek* (1 June 1981)

**Little Orphan Annie.** The archetypal US waif in Harold Gray's comic strip in the *New York Daily News* from 1924. She is adopted by a billionaire businessman, Daddy Warbucks, and has many adventures during his regular absences from home. Her name if not her persona appears to have been adopted from a poem of 1885 by James W. Riley entitled

'Little Orphant Annie'. She has subsequently appeared in films and on the radio and she was the subject of Charles Strouse's musical *Annie* (1977), itself filmed in 1982 with Aileen Quinn in the name part.

**Little Red Book.** The popular name of *Quotations from Chairman Mao*, Lin Biao's simplified and dogmatized version of the thoughts of Mao Zedong, a vade mecum of the RED GUARD during the CULTURAL REVOLUTION. One 'thought' included in Section 2 but originally written in 1927 was: 'A revolution is not a dinner party.' The name simply described the work's physical form. Some 800 million copies of the booklet were said to have been sold or distributed from 1966 to 1971, when possession became virtually mandatory. A European equivalent but with an educational agenda was the Danish *Den lille røde bog for skoleelever* by Søren Hansen and Jesper Jensen, published in 1969 and appearing in English translation in 1971 as *The Little Red Schoolbook*. It gave frank advice to schoolchildren on sex and drugs as well as routine matters such as lessons and homework and was condemned as obscene or at best subversive in its day.

***Little Red Engine, The.*** A series of picture books, recounting the adventures of an anthropomorphized railway engine, by the British writer Diana Ross (1910–2000), of which the first to be published was *The Little Red Engine Gets a Name* (1942).

**Little Ships, The.** The fleet of fishing boats, barges, yachts, pleasure cruisers and other small craft that in May–June 1940 set off from England across the Channel to help evacuate the British Expeditionary Force from the beaches of DUNKIRK, where their shallow draughts enabled them to come close to the shore.

> This little steamer, like all her brave and battered sisters, is immortal. She'll go sailing proudly down the years in the epic of Dunkirk. And our great-grandchildren, when they learn how we began this war by snatching glory out of defeat, and then swept on to victory, may also learn how the little holiday steamers made an excursion to hell and came back glorious.
>
> J.B. PRIESTLEY: radio broadcast, 5 June 1940

> The little ships, the unforgotten Homeric catalogue of *Mary Jane* and *Peggy IV*, of *Folkestone Belle*, *Boy Billy* and *Ethel Maud*, of *Lady Haig* and *Skylark* ... the little ships of England brought the Army home.
>
> PHILIP GUEDALLA: *Mr Churchill* (1941)

It is a myth that most of the boats were sailed across by their owners. Apart from a few vessels, most of the crews comprised naval officers, ratings and experienced volunteers.

**Little Shop of Horrors.** A very funny cult HORROR MOVIE (1960) directed by Roger Corman (b.1926) about a carnivorous talking plant that quickly outgrows the flower shop of its dimwitted owner and becomes a voracious man-eating monster. Corman's film was dreamed up and filmed in just two days and three nights after he was offered the chance to make a low-budget movie on the street set used for another film in the two days remaining before it was due to be torn down. The film includes one of Jack Nicholson's earliest performances, as a masochistic dental patient. The success of Corman's original inspired a stage musical with the same title in the 1980s and an inferior film remake in 1986, in which the fully grown plant was over 3.5m (12ft) tall and required almost 20km (12 miles) of cable.

**Little Venice.** A small area of West London centring on the western end of the Regent's Canal. Its leafy limpid charm makes it a haven in this somewhat unprepossessing part of London. Its tone has been moderately artistic and bohemian (musicians and painters such as Lennox Berkeley, Lucien Freud and Feliks Topolsky made it their home, and Lady Diana Cooper was also a resident). Its name was coined apparently in the period between the two world wars, although in the 19th century both Lord Byron and Robert Browning had noted a resemblance to the canal-dominated townscape of Venice.

**Little Willie.** A nickname of Crown Prince Wilhelm of Germany and Prussia (1882–1951), also known as the LAUGHING MURDERER OF VERDUN. It was later applied disparagingly to various people and by army personnel to a range of weapons. In the 1990s it was used tongue-in-cheek by Baroness Thatcher to refer to John Major's successor as Conservative leader, William Hague (*see* MEKON). Before all this, in 1905 Donald McGill had produced one of his 'naughty' seaside postcards, showing a fat man looking down in vain over his paunch to try to see a little boy at his feet. The caption reads:

Can't see my little Willy.

**Live Aid.** *See* BAND AID.

**Live 8.** *See* BAND AID.

**Live high on the hog.** To have a luxurious lifestyle. An expression of US origin alluding to the best part of a pig to provide a cut of rich and succulent pork.

**Live in each other's pockets.** To live in close dependence on someone or be closely involved with them. The expression dates from the 1950s.

**Liver bird.** A nickname for a young woman from Liverpool, especially when working-class or lower-middle-class. The name puns on 'Liver', rhyming with 'fiver', the fanciful bird appearing in Liverpool's coat of arms (and on the twin towers of the Royal Liver Exchange Building), and 'bird' as a colloquialism for a young woman. The term was popularized by Carla Lane's television SITCOM *The Liver Birds* (1969–78) about the exploits of two young female friends in Liverpool, Sandra Hutchinson, played by Nerys Hughes, and Beryl Hennessey, played by Polly James.

**Liverpool Poets.** A group of Liverpool writers prominent in the 1960s whose poetry was in the same self-ironizing spirit as the lyrics of The BEATLES and like them intended for public performance, often with a musical accompaniment. They were also known as the Merseyside Poets. Core exponents were Brian Patten (b.1946), Roger McGough (b.1937) and Adrian Henri (1932–2000). *See also* MERSEY.

**Living National Treasure.** *See* NATIONAL TREASURE.

**Living Theatre.** A US avant-garde theatre company founded in 1947 by Judith Malina and her husband Julian Beck. Its original commitment was to poetic drama and modernist plays that had little chance of commercial success, such as T.S. Eliot's *Sweeney Agonistes* (1932), but it later progressed to subversive social politics and to the promotion of street performances as a way of dissociating itself from the traditional elitism of the conventional theatre. It subsequently modified its political extremism and effectively ceased to exist when Beck left the company in the mid-1980s.

**Living Treasures, Australian.** *See* NATIONAL TREASURE.

**Living will.** A document drawn up by a person giving instructions that they are not to be kept alive by artificial means in the event of becoming severely disabled or terminally ill. The concept is of a will that defines acceptable living conditions. The idea was originally mooted in the United States in the 1960s, and the first living will was drawn up by a Chicago lawyer in 1969. Such wills were regarded as legally binding in most US States by 1990, but have yet to be tested in British courts. Their use has, however, been endorsed by the British Medical Association. *See also* EXIT.

**Lizard of Oz.** A nickname given by the *Sun* newspaper to the Australian Labour politician Paul Keating (b.1944), prime minister from 1991 to 1996. The name is a play on the children's story *The* WIZARD OF OZ (1900) by L. Frank Baum, the basis of the perennially popular 1939 film. Keating had incurred the tabloid's wrath through his forthright anti-British republicanism. He particularly incensed royalists when he touched the Queen's arm during a visit to Australia. *See also* CULTURAL CRINGE.

I'm a bastard. But I'm a bastard who gets the mail through.

PAUL KEATING: remark to a colleague, quoted in the *Sunday Telegraph* (20 November 1994)

**Llareggub.** The little town by the sea that is the fictional setting for Dylan Thomas's 'play for voices', UNDER MILK WOOD (1954). The original title of the work was *Llareggub (A Piece for Radio Perhaps)*, but the spelling of the town's palingrammatic name was altered after the author's death to the more delicate Llaregyb. The play was written in Thomas's home town of Laugharne, and its own name may have been the initial inspiration for the literary invention. Both places, real and fictional, are harbour towns at the mouth of a river on the Welsh coast.

**Lloyd George knew my father.** The first line of a two-line comic song, sung to the tune of 'Onward, Christian Soldiers' and sometimes attributed to Tommy Rhys Roberts (1910–75). The words may refer to the Liberal prime minister's fondness for womanizing, and to the euphemism 'How's your father' for sexual intercourse.

Lloyd George knew my father,
My father knew Lloyd George.

**Loaded question.** One charged with an underlying meaning or hidden implication, as: 'When did you stop beating your wife?' The expression dates from the 1940s.

**Loadsamoney.** A character created by the British comedian Harry Enfield, first appearing on Channel 4's *Saturday Live* in 1986–7. Loadsamoney was an obnoxious skilled or semi-skilled working-class type in his 20s, an archetypal ESSEX MAN, who had done well under THATCHERISM and liked nothing better than to rub his wad in one's face. The catch-phrase 'Loadsamoney!' was seized on by journalists and taken up by the Labour leader Neil Kinnock, who in May 1988 accused Margaret Thatcher's Conservative administration of fostering an uncaring 'loadsamoney mentality'.

**Lobby.** The most general meaning of 'lobby' is an entrance hall, but in politics it has come to have a number of related meanings. In the Houses of Parliament and various other legislatures, the 'division lobbies' are corridors on either side of the two chambers, through which members pass to record their votes. Backbenchers who always vote unthinkingly for their own party are collectively known as 'lobby fodder' (on the model of 'cannon fodder', infantry who are sacrificed in an attack). At Westminster, the lobby is an informal group of journalists ('lobby correspondents') who are given briefings by politicians on a non-attributable basis (on 'lobby terms'); the name derives from the Members' Lobby at the entrance to the Commons chamber, where only MPs, officers of the House and lobby correspondents are allowed. More generally, a lobby can be a hall in a legislative building where the public can meet politicians, hence the verb 'to lobby', meaning to try to influence legislators over a particular policy; those who do this professionally are known as 'lobbyists'.

**Local Defence Volunteers.** *See* HOME GUARD.

**Local talent.** The attractive women in a region. The colloquialism dates from the Second World War.

**Local yokel.** A local resident, especially in a rural locality. The potentially belittling term dates from the 1950s. *See also* VILLAGE IDIOT.

**Loch Ness Monster.** On 22 July 1933 a grey monster some 1.8m (6ft) long was spotted crossing a road near Loch Ness, Scotland, and subsequent 'sightings' reported a strange object some distance out in the water. Descriptions of it varied, so that two years later its length was said to be nearer 6m (20ft) and its appearance a cross between a seal and a plesiosaur, with a snake-like head at the end of a long neck and two flippers near the middle of its body. From then on it became a continual object of media attention. Investigations showed no substantial evidence of the existence of the supposed monster but more recent observations have increased the belief in the presence of 'Nessie', and in 1987 a sonar scan of the loch revealed a moving object some 181kg (400lb) in weight which scientists could not identify. The ornithologist Sir Peter Scott dubbed the creature *Nessiteras rhombopteryx*, after its appearance on a photograph taken by some Americans. The name was taken to mean 'Ness monster with the diamond-shaped fin', but crossword fans soon pointed out that it was in fact an anagram of 'monster hoax by Sir Peter S'.

**Lockerbie air disaster.** On 21 December 1988 a Boeing 727 aircraft, PanAm flight PA 103, en route from London to New York, was blown up by a terrorist bomb as it passed over Lockerbie, southwest Scotland, killing all 259 passengers on board and 11 on the ground. Two Libyan suspects were named in 1991 and brought to Europe in 1999 for trial by a Scottish court at Camp Zeist in the Netherlands in 2000. One of them was found guilty and sentenced to life in a Scottish prison.

**Logic bomb.** A set of instructions secretly incorporated into a computer program so that when a particular set of conditions occurs the instructions will cause the system to break down. The term evolved in the 1980s in connection with the type of computer sabotage that was then becoming prevalent. Some logic bombs were inserted by disgruntled employees, who were well away by the time the fault was triggered off. Others were planted in an attempt to blackmail or to suppress evidence of fraud. The expression itself is based on 'time bomb', with 'logic' the technical term for the principles that underlie the arrangements of elements in a computer system.

**Log in** or **on.** To go through the appropriate procedures to start using a computer system. The operation in particular often involves establishing one's identity, via a username and password. The converse, on completion of a session, is 'to log off' or 'to log out'. *See also* CLOCK IN.

**Loiner.** A colloquial name for a resident or native of the city of Leeds. The word dates from the 1950s and is of uncertain origin, although the Venerable Bede recorded the placename as *Loidis* in the 8th century.

**Loins of Longleat.** A lubriciously punning nickname for the Marquess of Bath (b.1932), from his residence, famous for its SAFARI PARK of lions, and his many WIFELETS.

**Lolita.** The 12-year-old NYMPHET who is the beloved of Humbert Humbert in Vladimir Nabokov's brilliant but controversial novel that bears her name, a name subsequently used for any underage sexpot. Her full name is Dolores Haze. The book was filmed by Stanley Kubrick (1962) and Adrian Lyne (1997) but neither picture did proper justice to the original, partly because the actresses in the name part, respectively Sue Lyon and Dominique Swain, were necessarily some years older than the prototype.

> She was Lo, plain Lo, in the morning … She was Lola in slacks. She was Dolly at school. She was Dolores on the dotted line. But in my arms she was always Lolita.
>
> VLADIMIR NABOKOV: *Lolita*, Pt I, ch. 1 (1955)

*See also* FIRST LINES OF NOVELS.

**Lollipop lady** or **man.** A friendly name for a school crossing patrol, so called from the pole with a red warning disc on top to halt the traffic, suggesting the lollipop confection of youthful delight. The term dates from the 1960s.

**Lollywood.** *See* BOLLYWOOD.

**London Bridge.** The present bridge of three spans over the Thames was built in 1967–72 and replaced the earlier five-arched one, completed in 1831. This was dismantled and in 1968 sold for $1.8 million to the McCulloch Oil Corporation of the United States, who re-erected it to span an inlet on the Colorado at Lake Havasu City, Arizona. It was long rumoured that the Americans thought they were buying Tower Bridge, a canard hotly denied by the company chairman, George McCulloch. The first London Bridge was

probably made of wood and built during the Roman occupation.

**London calling.** *See* THIS IS LONDON CALLING.

**London Eye.** *See* MILLENNIUM.

**London Group.** A society of artists founded in 1913 by an amalgamation of the CAMDEN TOWN GROUP with various small groups and individuals. The first president was Harold Gilman (1876–1919) and apart from other former Camden Town Group artists there were those who would subsequently be associated with VORTICISM, including David Bomberg (1890–1957), Sir Jacob Epstein (1880–1959), C.R.W. Nevinson (1889–1946) and Edward Wadsworth (1889–1949). The group's aim was to break away from academic tradition and to draw inspiration from French Post-impressionism.

**Londonistan.** A nickname given to London from the end of the 20th century by foreign intelligence agencies, who see it as a refuge for Islamist radicals plotting terrorist activities around the world. Those using the nickname believe that Britain has been too tolerant in providing asylum to such people. The city has also been dubbed Beirut-on-Thames. The name came to prominence in the British Press following the London bombings of July 2005 (*see* 7/7).

***London's Burning.*** A SOAP OPERA about the firefighters of Blue Watch B25, Blackwall, London, first screened in 1988. It has its origin in a one-off television play of the same name by Jack Rosenthal (1931–2004), broadcast in 1986. The series dwelt as much on the fighters' heroics in the many spectacular conflagrations as on their domestic problems. The title comes from the old round about the Great Fire of London (1666): 'London's burning,/Look yonder,/Fire, fire,/And we have no water'.

**Lone Eagle.** *See* Charles LINDBERGH.

***Loneliness of the Long-Distance Runner, The.*** A novella (1959) by Alan Sillitoe (b.1928), published as the title piece of his first collection of stories. The long-distance runner is the protagonist and narrator, a lad in BORSTAL because of a 'bakery job', carrying on a running battle of wits with the governor, who sees him purely as a means to win the inter-institution cross-country race. Smith, as he is called, enters the sports ground for the final lap far ahead of his nearest rival, and then runs on the spot until he is overtaken. A compelling film version (1962) was directed by Tony Richardson and starred Tom Courtenay and Michael Redgrave.

**Lonely Planet.** The guidebooks of this name had their

genesis in the early 1970s, when Tony Wheeler and his wife Maureen travelled as backpackers from London across Europe, the Middle East and Asia to Australia. They were soon being asked for advice from other would-be travellers, so sat down at their kitchen table in Sydney, Australia, to write an account of their trip, publishing it in 1973 as a guide to backpacking on the cheap. By the beginning of the 21st century more than 400 Lonely Planet travel books had won repute for their well-researched, up-to-date information and were regarded as indispensable *vade mecums* by many independent travellers. *See also* ROUGH GUIDES.

The name arose by way of a mistake. Wheeler had liked a line in Joe Cocker's song 'Space Captain', 'Once while travelling across the sky this lovely planet caught my eye', but had misheard 'lovely' as 'lonely'.

**Lone Piners.** The group of teenagers who feature in many of the children's adventure novels by the British writer Malcolm Saville (1902–82), the first being *Mystery at Witchend* (1943). The name reflects the wild settings, including rural Shropshire and the English Lake District, of many of Saville's novels.

**Lone Ranger, The.** The masked adventurer of the American West, whose 'real' name was John Reid. He was the creation of George W. Trendle and Fran Striker for a US radio series that began in 1933. The Lone Ranger is an ex-Texas Ranger, who has become an enforcer of law. He is honest, upright and well-spoken, and he shoots only to wound, using special silver bullets. He has an Indian friend, Tonto, who addresses him as 'KEMO SABE', and a horse, Silver, whom he urges off with a cry of 'Hi-ho, Silver, awaaaaay!' The Lone Ranger was also a nickname of the Democratic US senator Wayne Morse (1900–74), because he so often voted on the minority side. *See also* SLOANE RANGER.

**Lone wolf.** A person who prefers to do without the company or assistance of others. Wolves usually live in packs but some species tend to hunt alone. The term is of US origin and at the turn of the 20th century originally applied to a criminal operating alone. In the novels by Louis Joseph Vance, The Lone Wolf is a gentleman thief. His real name is Michael Lanyard, and he first appears in *The Lone Wolf* (1914). Several films followed, in which he was played by various actors including Francis Lederer, Warren William, Gerald Mohr and Ron Randell.

**Long and the Short and the Tall, The.** A film melodrama (1960) set in Malaya during the Second World War, with a screenplay by Wolf Mankowitz after a play by Willis Hall. The title comes from the 1940 song 'Bless 'Em All' by Jimmy Hughes and Frank Lake:

You'll get no promotion this side of the ocean,
So cheer up, my lads, Bless 'em all!
Bless 'em all! Bless 'em all!
The long and the short and the tall.

**Long con.** A complex confidence trick that involves extensive pre-planning. The term originated in US underworld slang of the 1930s. *See also* SHORT CON.

**Long Dark Tea-Time of the Soul, The.** A humorous fantasy novel (1988) by Douglas Adams (1952–2001), begetter of *The* HITCH-HIKER'S GUIDE TO THE GALAXY, in which 'holistic' private eye Dirk Gently attempts to solve the mysteries of the universe. An explosion at Heathrow Airport, London, is designated an Act of God – but, wonders, Dirk,

What God would be hanging around Terminal Two of Heathrow Airport trying to catch the 15.37 to Oslo?

The title is an understated English swipe at the phrase 'the dark night of the soul', originally the title of a poem (Spanish *Noche oscura del alma*) by St John of the Cross (1542–91), and it was subsequently associated with the experiences of other mystics. *The Oxford Dictionary of Quotations* (1999 edition) suggests that the phrase was actually introduced by David Lewis, the translator of St John of the Cross's *Complete Works* (1864).

**Long Day's Journey into Night.** A PULITZER-PRIZE-winning play (1956) by the US playwright Eugene O'Neill (1888–1953) depicting the four self-destructive members of the Tyrone family, who variously seek salvation in drugs and drink. The partly autobiographical work was written by O'Neill in the early 1940s but not produced until after his death. Its title reflects the time sequence within the play, which begins at 8.30 in the morning and ends around midnight on the same hot August day in 1912.

A play of old sorrow, written in tears and blood.
EUGENE O'NEILL: description of *Long Day's Journey into Night*

**Longest Day, The.** A film (1962) based on the novel of the same title by Cornelius Ryan about the Allied invasion of occupied France during the Second World War. The day in question is D-DAY, 6 June 1944, when a huge Allied force landed on the beaches of Normandy and began the liberation of Europe. In an effort to ensure authenticity filming only took place when weather conditions matched those that prevailed during the actual invasion. *See also* OVERLORD.

**Longest suicide note in history, The.** The description by Labour MP Gerald Kaufman (b.1930) of Labour's 1983 election manifesto *New Hope for Britain*, which, with Michael Foot as party leader, was one of the more Left-leaning manifestos in the history of the party, and included a commitment to UNILATERAL NUCLEAR DISARMAMENT. Margaret Thatcher's Conservative Party, flush with victory in the Falklands, swept back to power.

**Long Fellow.** *See* DEV.

***Long Good Friday, The.*** A highly regarded film (1980), written by Barrie Keeffe, about a London gangster boss who embarks on a mission to find out who is murdering his henchmen. Starring Bob Hoskins as crime boss Harold and Helen Mirren as his wife, Victoria, the film follows what happens in the course of a Good Friday in the early 1980s after Harold is given just 24 hours by his Mafia contacts to solve the mystery or risk a major deal with them falling through.

**Long hot summer.** A period of civil unrest, as that in the summer of 1967 in the United States, when riots erupted among underprivileged blacks in several cities. In June of that year Martin Luther King warned:

> Everyone is worrying about the long hot summer with its threat of riots. We had a long cold winter when little was done about the conditions that create riots.

*The Long Hot Summer* was the title of a film of 1958 based on William Faulkner's story *The Hamlet* (1928), in which one of the chapters is headed 'The Long Summer'. The expression later evolved to denote any difficult period or enterprise, especially if it actually takes place in summer. *See also* SUMMER OF LOVE.

> It looks as if it will be a long hot summer for the dons of Christ's College, Cambridge, who are once again faced with the tricky business of electing a Master.
> LADY OLGA MAITLAND: in *Sunday Express* (11 July 1982)

**Long johns.** A US colloquialism of Second World War vintage for long woollen underpants. Half a century later *The Long Johns* was the title of a series of satirical sketches by John Bird and John Fortune in the form of face-to-face television interviews. The two took it in turn to be interviewer and interviewee, the former putting a number of forthright questions on a topical business or political issue, the latter, usually called George Parr, either evading the answer or responding shamelessly in a way that revealed startling hypocrisy, greed or inefficiency. The sketches first appeared in the 1990s in the satirical shows of the impressionist Rory Bremner on the BBC, later on Channel 4.

**Long March, The.** The journey of about 9650km (6000 miles) made in 1934–5 by about 100,000 Chinese communists when they were forced out of their base at Kiangsi in southeastern China. They made their way to Shensi in northwestern China, with only some 8000 surviving the ordeal.

**Longstocking, Pippi.** The gawky, red-headed, athletic young girl who first appeared in the Swedish children's novel by Astrid Lindgren that bears her name (1945). (In the original she is known as Pippi Langstrump.) Pippi is an orphan who believes that her father is a South Sea cannibal king. She is so strong that she can lift policemen and horses, is very untidy and, as her name suggests, wears mismatched stockings. In a word, she is the ideal children's fantasy figure, entirely free of adult constraints or restraints and with superhuman strength. A number of sequels followed, as did four Swedish films (1969–71), in which she is played by Inger Nilsson. One of these was dubbed in English as *Pippi in the South Seas* (1974) but is so poorly made and badly dubbed that it is virtually unwatchable.

**Long time no see.** A mock traditional greeting to a person one has not seen for a long time. It is a form of pidgin English based on Chinese Neville17 *haŏ jiŭ méi jiàn. See also* NO CAN DO.

> Phil, faced by Janet – Claire's friend – trembles:
> 'Hi, Jan, long time no see!'
> VIKRAM SETH: *The Golden Gate*, 4.9 (1986)

***Long Walk to Freedom.*** The autobiography (1994) of Nelson Mandela (b.1918), the first black president of South Africa, who, under the apartheid regime, had been jailed for three decades, largely on Robben Island. The title is said to have been inspired by the words in 'From Lucknow to Tripuri', an essay (1939) by Jawaharlal Nehru, who was to become the first prime minister of independent India:

> There is no easy walk-over to freedom anywhere, and many of us will have to pass through the valley of the shadow again and again before we reach the mountain-tops of our desire.

**Lonrho.** A multinational company run for many years by Tiny Rowland (born Roland Fuhrhop; 1917–98). The name of the company derives from the London and Rhodesian Mining and Land Company, with which Rowland merged his own business interests in 1961, becoming co-chief executive and managing director of the firm. In 1973 a corruption scandal involving Lonrho attracted the observation from the Conservative prime minister, Edward Heath, that this was the UNACCEPTABLE FACE OF CAPITALISM. From 1981 to 1993 Rowland owned *The Observer* Sunday newspaper and was criticized for attempting to influence editorial policy to protect his business interests in Africa. He also became involved in a vitriolic feud with the Al Fayed brothers, his successful rivals in a bid to buy Harrods. He ceased being managing director of Lonrho in 1994, following a long-running row within the company.

**Loo.** This common euphemism for a lavatory or toilet dates from the 1940s but is of much disputed origin. One theory is that the word puns on *Waterloo* as the trade name of a make of iron water cistern in the early years of the 20th century. Professor A.S.C. Ross appears to favour this origin in his examination of possible sources in *Blackwood's Magazine* for October 1974. Other proposals, which should almost all be taken with a grain of salt, include the following:

1. From French *lieu*, 'place', as in the now dated euphemism, *lieux d'aisances*, 'places of ease'. Among the least unlikely derivations.

2. From French *l'eau*, 'water'

3. From *gardyloo*, from French *gardez l'eau*, 'beware of the water', a cry in old Edinburgh when emptying the contents of a chamber pot from a high window into the street below. A much touted source, but chronologically untenable.

4. From *bordalou*, a type of 18th-century portable commode carried by ladies in their muff when travelling, supposedly from the name of Louis Bourdaloue (1632–1704), a fashionable but prolix Jesuit preacher

5. From the name of Lady Louise Hamilton, said to have been fixed to a lavatory door in Dublin in 1870

6. From *louvre*, referring to the slatted doors of some lavatories

7. From *leeward*, as the side of a boat (downwind) from which one would logically urinate

8. From an abbreviated form of the word 'lavatory' itself

Yet one more ingenious explanation is offered by Peter Lyon, writer of a letter to William and Mary Morris, authors of the *Morris Dictionary of Word and Phrase Origins* (1977), and reproduced in their second edition (1988):

> When I was in England researching a biography of Eisenhower, I spent a day with Brigadier Sir James Gault, who had been Eisenhower's British aide during the war. When I mentioned that I had researched *loo* in the British Museum and found your theories and a couple of others, Lady Gault said they were all wrong. She explained that after the first Great War, when the Bright Young People began to cross the Channel again to France, they naturally stopped at French hotels. The French numbered the rooms from 1, say, to 12 on the first floor, picking up with 13 through 25 on the second, then on to 26 through 40 on the third. On each floor would be one room marked 00, which, of course, was the bathroom. Now, said Lady Gault, the British visitors simply prefaced that 00 with the appropriate French *l*, and so fetched up with *l'00* or *loo*. That certainly is a more elegant explanation.

**Lookalike.** A person who looks like another, especially when the other is a celebrity. A surprising number of people aspire to be convincing impersonators of the famous and may be seen in pubs and clubs and on stage and television as the alter ego of their idol. Some manage a convincing evocation in more than just appearance. In 1979 Susan Scott Lookalikes was set up to exploit the commercial potential of the concept, engaging Jeanette Charles to impersonate Queen Elizabeth, Vicki Scott to incarnate Marilyn Monroe and Kenny Whymark to pose as Humphrey Bogart. Other agencies followed and celebrity lookalikes were soon a standard feature at corporate functions, their fee being a mere tithe of that demanded by their eponym for a personal appearance.

**Look away now.** A light-hearted request for someone to avert their eyes, from the catchphrase used by television sports reporters – in full, 'Look away now if you don't want to know the score' – when about to show the result of a match yet to be broadcast, so as not to spoil the anticipation of intending viewers.

***Look Back In Anger.*** A play (1956) by John Osborne (1929–94) about a young man's dissatisfaction with his marriage, his life and the world in general, in particular the hidebound conventions of the older generation. Jimmy Porter, the play's protagonist, represented the restless, frustrated youth of the immediate postwar generation, and the controversial play helped to establish Osborne as the archetypal ANGRY YOUNG MAN. The title of the play resurfaced in 1996 in 'Don't Look Back in Anger', a hit song by the British rock band Oasis.

> I doubt if I could love anyone who did not wish to see *Look Back in Anger*. It is the best play of its decade.
> KENNETH TYNAN: review of the premiere at the Royal Court (1957)

**Lookie-lou.** In US slang, a nosy or inquisitive person, especially a peeping Tom. The expression seems to have originated in California in the late 1970s as an exasperated name for someone who views houses for sale with no intention of buying.

**Look like death warmed up.** FEEL LIKE DEATH WARMED UP.

**Look over someone's shoulder.** To be uninterested in them or in what they are saying or doing; to have one's mind on something else. The image is of a bored lover in an embrace.

> Supermodels refused to sleep with him. Even the bog-standard girl about town looked over his shoulder at parties.
> *The Times* (4 February 2000)

**Look who's talking!** You're a fine one to say that! A phrase implying that the original speaker is in no position to judge the other. The expression became current in the 1940s.

**Looney Tunes.** The title under which WARNER BROTHERS released their many cartoon shorts from the 1930s, featuring such characters as BUGS BUNNY, Daffy Duck, Porky the Pig and Tweetie Pie.

> We are especially not going to tolerate these attacks from outlaw states run by the strangest collection of misfits, Looney Tunes, and squalid criminals since the advent of the Third Reich.
>
> RONALD REAGAN: speech following the hijack of a US plane (8 July 1985)

**Loon pants.** Close-fitting flared trousers, popular in the 1970s. The name derives either from the slang verb 'to loon', to fool around, to act irresponsibly, itself perhaps from 'loony', or from 'pantaloon'.

**Loony Benn.** *See* BERTIE WOOSTER OF MARXISM; LOONY LEFT.

**Loony Left.** A term coined by the popular press in the late 1970s to describe the more hard-line activists of the LABOUR PARTY, whether MPs or trade union activists. Notable among them were Tony Benn (b.1925), Ken Livingstone (b.1945) and Bernie Grant (1944–2000). Their influence had largely evaporated by the general election of 1992. 'Loony' is 'lunatic'. *See also* RED KEN.

**Loop the loop.** The air pilot's term for the manoeuvre that consists of describing a perpendicular circle in the air. At the top of the circle, or loop, the pilot is upside down. The term is from a kind of switchback once popular at fairs in which a moving car or bicycle performed a similar revolution on a perpendicularly circular track.

**Loose cannon.** An unpredictable or uncontrolled person who may unintentionally cause damage. The phrase dates only from the 1970s but alludes to an unsecured cannon on a warship, which is liable to career unpredictably across the deck with the rolling or pitching of the ship. The expression is of US origin and is frequently applied to military personnel. It was used of General Alexander Haig (*see* HAIGSPEAK) in the Reagan administration and of Colonel Oliver North (b.1943), implicated in the Irangate scandal (*see* GATE), under the same administration.

**Loose lips sink ships.** A US government security slogan in the Second World War. *See also* BE LIKE DAD, KEEP MUM.

**Lord Emsworth.** *See* Lord EMSWORTH.

**Lord Haw-Haw.** *See* lords HAW-HAW and EMSWORTH.

**Lord Jim.** A novel (1900) by Joseph Conrad (1857–1924). Jim (we never know his second name) is a young ship's officer who leaps overboard in a crisis to save himself. In order to expiate his guilt, he wanders from place to place in the East, finally settling in a remote part of Malaya, where his integrity earns him the respect he has craved. A visitor asks:

> 'What's his name? Jim! Jim! That's not enough for a man's name.'
> 'They call him,' said Cornelius, scornfully, 'Tuan Jim here. As you may say Lord Jim.'

A worthy film version (1964) of the novel was directed by Richard Brooks.

**Lord love a duck!** Good Lord! A mild expression of surprise dating from the early years of the 20th century. The words are an elaboration of 'Lord lumme' ('Lord love me').

**Lord Love-a-Duck of Limehouse.** The title that Clement Attlee (1883–1967), Labour prime minister (1945–51), said he would take should he ever be elevated to the peerage. LORD LOVE A DUCK! is a Cockney expression of disbelief, and Limehouse is an area in the Cockney East End of London. When Attlee resigned as LABOUR PARTY leader in 1955 he actually became 1st Earl Attlee of Walthamstow, Viscount Prestwood.

**Lord Lucan.** *See* Lord LUCAN.

**Lord Muck.** A pompous or self-opinionated man. He assumes the air of a lord but is 'as common as muck'. The expression, first recorded in Australia in 1901, is a variant of the earlier 'Lord High Muck-a-Muck', where the name probably represents Chinook *hiyu muckamuck*, 'plenty of food'. *See also* LADY MUCK.

**Lord of the Flies.** A novel (1954) by William Golding (1911–93), illustrating how internal and external pressures can cause a society to disintegrate, exemplified in this case by a group of schoolboys marooned on an island. The title represents one interpretation of the Hebrew term for Beelzebub, who appears in 2 Kings 1:2 as Baal-zebub, a Caananite god whose shrine is at Ekron, and in the New Testament as 'prince of the devils' (Matthew 12:24). In the story itself, the name 'Lord of the Flies' is applied to the fly-infested pig's head that the boys impale on a stick. A rather crude film version (1963) was directed by Peter Brook, and a US remake (1990) was little better. *See also* FIRST LINES OF NOVELS.

**Lord of the Rings, The.** The title of J.R.R. Tolkien's sequel (1954–5) to *The* HOBBIT (1937). A trilogy, it comprises *The Fellowship of the Ring*, *The Two Towers* and *The Return of the King*. It is also the title of SAURON the Great, the ruler of MORDOR, whose power depends on the possession of certain rings, especially the One Ring, the Ruling Ring, the Master Ring, which he lost many years ago and which he now seeks to regain to give him strength to cover the land in a second darkness. This ring eventually comes into the hands of the hobbit Bilbo BAGGINS, who passes it on to FRODO Baggins, his adopted heir. If Sauron recovers it, the Hobbits will be doomed, and the only way to destroy the ring is to find the Cracks of Doom and cast it into the volcano Orodruin, the 'Fire-mountain'. The saga essentially concerns Frodo's struggles, trials and adventures to achieve this. A film trilogy of Tolkien's epic, directed by Peter Jackson, was released in 2001, 2002 and 2003, and went on to win a record number of 17 OSCARS. *See also* FIRST LINES OF NOVELS; GONDOR; MINAS MORGUL; MORDOR; the SHIRE.

**Lord Peter Wimsey.** *See* Lord Peter WIMSEY.

**Lord Porn.** A media nickname for Frank Pakenham, 7th Earl of Longford (1905–2001). The name derived from his campaigns against pornography and other aspects of the PERMISSIVE SOCIETY, which took him on a 'fact-finding' mission to investigate the sex industry in Scandinavia, accompanied by a mob of gleeful journalists.

**Lord's Resistance Army.** A millenarian armed group, led by the mystic psychopath Joseph Kony, which has been in rebellion against the Ugandan government since 1987. The LRA is notorious for its brutality, its massacres and mutilations, and its abduction of thousands of children to fight as soldiers or work as sex slaves. Its victims are mainly among the Acholi people of northern Uganda.

**Lord's Taverners.** An association of cricket-lovers founded in 1950 by Martin Boddey. It stages matches and other events to raise funds for charity. There is a large 'stage-and-screen' element in its membership and its patron is the Duke of Edinburgh. Its name commemorates the Tavern at Lord's cricket ground in London, a hostelry to the right of the pavilion which was demolished in the early 1960s (the Tavern Stand now occupies its site).

**Lord Suit.** *Private Eye*'s nickname for the successful business-man David Ivor Young (b.1932), one of the MEN IN SUITS, on whom Margaret Thatcher bestowed the title Lord Young of Graffham in 1984 in order to bring him into her government. He was initially minister without portfolio (1984–5) and subsequently served as secretary of state for employment (1985–7), and then for trade and industry (1987–9). He was deputy chairman of the Conservative Party (1989–90) before returning to the private sector.

**Lorelei Lee.** *See* Lorelei LEE.

**Lose it.** To lose one's temper or self-control momentarily, 'it' being either of these. The expression dates from the 1970s. *See also* LOSE ONE'S COOL.

Dale told police there had been ill feeling between the two girls dating from this year's Mid Lent Fair. 'She said the girl was laughing at her and she just lost it,' Mr Grys said.
*Stamford Mercury* (28 May 1999)

**Lose one's cherry.** To lose one's virginity. The image is of ripeness rather than any physical resemblance. The expression dates from the 1930s. To take (or pop) someone's cherry is thus the converse. The metaphor has led some modern academics to reach a purely sexual construal for J.E. Millais' well-known painting *Cherry Ripe* (1879), a portrait of a small girl seated next to a bunch of cherries, not merely on the basis of the title but also from certain supposedly sexually significant details in the picture itself (Pamela Tamarkin Reis and Laurel Bailey in *Victorian Studies*, vol. 24 no. 2, Winter 1991). More directly, however, the title could simply derive from Robert Herrick's poem *Cherry-Ripe* (1648), beginning 'Cherry-ripe, ripe, ripe, I cry', itself the call of a street vendor. The visual imagery is, even so, familiar enough to many and has been drawn upon in modern times by cartoonists, advertisers and others to impart a salacious gloss to their work.

**Lose one's cool.** To lose one's temper or self-control. 'Cool' here means 'composure', 'poise', and originated as a term used in the 1960s among US street gangs for a temporary armistice between rival gangs, who were thus for a time no longer heated. *See also* COOL IT; LOSE IT.

**Lose one's gills.** To mature; to gain experience and wisdom as one grows older. The analogy is with a tadpole, which loses its gills soon after hatching as it grows into a frog.

**Lose one's marbles.** To become mentally unhinged. The origin of the phrase is uncertain. One suggestion is that it derives from a story about a boy whose marbles were carried off by a monkey. An unlikely derivation is in rhyming slang, as if 'marbles and conkers', two popular children's games, represented BONKERS. The expression dates from the 1920s.

**Lose one's rag.** To lose one's temper. The allusion is to the 'red rag' or tongue, which is unbridled when one is in a rage.

**Lose the plot.** To lose one's way in a situation; to miss the meaning. The expression dates from the 1980s and may allude to a film director who, after an auspicious debut, lost his sense of direction.

As the elite of America gorge on an unprecedented run of spectacular stock market flotations, one question begs to be asked. Have Wall Street bankers lost the plot?
*The Times* (20 December 1999)

**Loss leader.** A term of US origin dating from the 1920s for an article offered for sale below normal price, usually in department stores and supermarkets, with the aim of attracting customers, who will then be drawn to make other purchases at unreduced prices. The theory is that the losses incurred will be more than made up by the greater number of sales at normal prices.

**Lost Gardens of Heligan.** In early 1990 a group of entrepreneurs looking for land near St Austell, Cornwall, to start a rare breeds farm stumbled across the remains of an extensive area of gardens and woodland, neglected for half a century. The gardens, occupying some 63ha (157 acres), were created by the Tremayne family over the years from 1780 to 1914, but the death of many estate workers in the First World War brought ruin, and new tenants after the war could not afford to maintain the grounds. Painstaking restoration and reconstruction began following the discovery, and in 1992 the gardens were open in all their re-created glory to the public.

**Lost Generation, The.** A name sometimes applied to the young men, especially of the cultivated upper and middle classes, who lost their lives in the First World War. According to James R. Mellow's *Charmed Circle* (1974) the phrase originated with Gertrude Stein (1874–1946), who on one occasion in the south of France heard a French garage owner address his incompetent mechanics as *une génération perdue*. She herself applied the term to the disillusioned US writers, such as F. Scott Fitzgerald, Ezra Pound and Ernest Hemingway, who went to live in Paris in the 1920s, and Hemingway himself used the words 'You are all a lost generation' to preface *The Sun Also Rises* (1924).

**Lost in the shuffle.** Overlooked or missed in the mêlée or multitude. The reference is to a card missed in a shuffle of the pack. The expression is of US origin and dates from the 1930s.

**Lost weekend.** A weekend spent in dissolute living or drunkenness. The expression was popularized by Charles Jackson's bestselling novel *The Lost Weekend* (1944), which was adapted into film by director Billy Wilder and Charles Brackett in 1945. The tale concerns a struggling writer who surrenders to alcoholism one weekend after he falls victim to writer's block. Starring Ray Milland, the film caused a considerable stir: representatives of the liquor industry offered $5 million for the negative, so that it could be destroyed, fearing the effect it would have upon sales of alcohol, and members of the temperance movement also tried to have the film banned, suspecting that it might actually encourage people to drink.

*Lost World, The.* An adventure novel (1912) by Sir Arthur Conan Doyle (1859–1930), in which the irascible and bearded Professor Challenger, accompanied by the explorer Lord John Roxton and the young newspaper reporter Edward Malone, goes in search of the 'Lost World' where he believes dinosaurs and ape-men still survive. The 'Lost World' is an imaginary volcanic plateau north of the Amazon in Brazil, but it is based on the real cliff-girt plateaux, such as Mount Roraima, that stud the rainforests on the Venezuela–Brazil–Guyana border. In the novel the remote plateau has been given the name MAPLE WHITE LAND, after its discoverer, an artist and poet from Detroit, Michigan.

The first, silent, film version (1925) deployed special effects that were remarkable for their time; the 1960 remake was derisory. The second of the JURASSIC PARK films, on a similar theme, was also entitled *The Lost World* (1997).

**LOTS.** The acronym of 'Left On The Shelf', the name (alluding to the expression 'on the shelf', meaning 'put to one side, out of action') of a campaign group formed by Tottenham Hotspur football club supporters in 1988 to prevent the club from replacing the middle terrace area of the East Stand, known as 'The Shelf', at their home ground, White Hart Lane, with seating and executive boxes. The campaign delayed the work and meant that Tottenham were unable to play their opening fixture of the 1988–9 season against Coventry City. As a result they had two points deducted, although this penalty was later commuted to a £15,000 fine. LOTS and the club eventually reached a compromise, albeit a short-lived one, whereby some of the area would be retained for standing spectators. In 1994 the area was finally converted to seating.

**Lotto.** *See* NATIONAL LOTTERY.

**Lotus position.** A sitting position with the legs folded and intertwined and the hands resting on the knees, an important part of the Hindu yoga tradition. The expression, first recorded in 1962, translates Sanskrit *padmasana*, from *padma*, 'lotus', and *asana*, 'posture'. The allusion is to the lotus leaf, which rests on water without becoming wet, so giving an impression of detachment.

**Lounge lizard.** A popular phrase in the 1920s to describe a young man, a gigolo, who spends his time dancing and waiting upon rich women, typically in the lounge of a grand hotel. A lizard is colourful, reptilian, and 'suns' itself as if lazily lounging. The term has been attributed by some to the US cartoonist Tad Dorgan (*see* CAT'S PYJAMAS).

**Lovat green.** A muted green colour found mainly in tweed

and woollen garments. The name is that of the hamlet of Lovat on the River Beauly west of Inverness, Scotland, where the cloth was made at the turn of the 20th century.

**♥** . Pictorial shorthand for 'love' in such slogans as 'I♥ DOGS', using the playing-card 'heart' symbol. It was originally popularized as 'I♥ New York', a slogan promoted in 1977 by the New York State Department of Commerce.

> 'I ♥ winos', 'I ♥ L.A.'
> Or 'Have you hugged your whale today?'
> VIKRAM SETH: *The Golden Gate*, 2.12 (1986)

**Love-bombing.** A style of recruitment practised by some religious cults, notably in the United States. Potential members are saturated with expressions of love, care and beguiling idealism. The term expresses the intensive CHARM OFFENSIVE used to bring about a capitulation. The strategy is also known as FLIRTY FISHING.

**Love for** or **of Three Oranges, The.** The comic opera by Sergei Prokofiev (1891–1953) with a text by the composer was based on a 1761 comedy by Carlo Gozzi (1720–1806). The oranges of the title are taken into the desert by a prince; each contains a princess, two of whom die of thirst, but the third survives and is united with the prince. The work was first performed in 1921.

**Love handles.** Bunches of excess fat at the waist, which one's lover can grasp. The term dates from the 1970s. *See also* SADDLEBAGS.

> Eating chocolate, so far from melting away the pounds, will give you unattractive love handles.
> *New Statesman* (10 May 1999)

**Love–hate relationship.** A relationship characterized by ambivalent feelings of love and hate by one or both of two people. It frequently exists within families and between romantic partners. The term originated as psychoanalysts' jargon in the 1920s. The two words form one of the commonest pairs of antonyms. Certain macho males have 'LOVE' tattooed on the knuckles of one hand and 'HATE' on the other, the idea presumably being that one can stroke with the one and strike with the other. The concept itself is an ancient one, as expressed in the 1st century BC by Catullus: *Odi et amo* ('I hate and I love') (*Carmina* No. 85). *See also* MAN YOU LOVE TO HATE.

> My relationship with him [the writer's father] is complicated. It's love-hate – but with far more emphasis on the love. We've had flaming rows, but always make it up with tears and hugs.
> *Sunday Times Magazine* (19 September 1999)

**Love in a Cold Climate.** A light novel (1949) by Nancy Mitford (1904–1973), whose narrative takes place at about the same time as that of her first novel, *The Pursuit of Love* (1945), and which concerns some of the same characters. The environment is that of the eccentric, impoverished, aristocratic society in which she was brought up. The novel was originally to have been called 'Diversion'. The final title recalls the remark made by the poet Robert Southey (1774–1843) in a letter to his brother about Mary Wollstonecraft's letters from Sweden and Norway: 'She has made me in love with a cold climate, and frost and snow, with a northern moonlight' (28 April 1797).

**Love is a Many-Splendored Thing.** A film (1955) based on a novel (1952) by Han Suyin depicting the doomed relationship between a US journalist (played in the film by William Holden) and a Eurasian doctor (Jennifer Jones). Han Suyin disliked the film, as did most of the critics, which is remembered mainly for the OSCAR-winning theme song. The title came originally from a poem by Francis Thompson:

> The angels keep their ancient places;
> Turn but a stone and start a wing!
> 'Tis ye, 'tis your estrangèd faces,
> That miss the many-splendoured thing.
> FRANCIS THOMPSON: 'The Kingdom of God' (1913)

**Lovejoy.** An antiques dealer who doubles as an amateur detective in the comic mystery novels by Jonathan Gash (real name John Grant). He narrates his own adventures but does not reveal his first name. Titles in the series include *The Judas Pair* (1977), *Gold from Gemini* (1978), *The Grail Tree* (1979), *Spend Game* (1980), *The Vatican Rip* (1981), *Firefly Gadroon* (1982), *The Sleepers of Erin* (1983), *The Gondola Scam* (1984) and *The Tartan Ringers* (1986). A somewhat sanitized version of the raunchy original stories was screened as a television series from 1986 to 1994, with Ian McShane in the name part.

**Lovely jubbly!** Good! Excellent! From the 1990s a general term of approval, popularized by the character 'Del Boy' in the television sitcom ONLY FOOLS AND HORSES, and subsequently given an extended life by Jamie Oliver, the NAKED CHEF. The phrase is more narrowly used as a slang term for money or wealth, and has its roots in an advertizing slogan of the 1950s for an orange drink called 'Jubbly' (presumably a blend of 'juice' and 'bubbly'). The second word is not thus simply a meaningless rhyme on the first.

**'Lovely Rita'.** A jolly song that appears on The BEATLES album SERGEANT PEPPER'S LONELY HEARTS CLUB BAND, credited to John Lennon and Paul McCartney. The Rita (METER MAID) of the title is based on a real-life encounter McCartney had with a traffic warden called Meta Davis in St John's Wood, London.

**Love means never having to say you're sorry.** A line from LOVE STORY (1970). The construction 'Love means …' has, like a virus, found a continuing life in many mutations, frequently found on the sort of sentimental, flower-strewn posters put up on their bedroom walls by adolescent girls of all ages.

**Love of Three Oranges.** *See The* LOVE FOR THREE ORANGES.

**Love on the Dole.** The first novel (1933) by Walter Greenwood (1903–74), set in the industrial town of Salford, where he was brought up. For one man, an apprenticeship leads only to the dole queue and a life of poverty when his girlfriend becomes pregnant. For another, marriage is on the cards when he is made redundant, and he dies after being beaten up while participating in a mass protest. His fiancée, who has to support an out-of-work brother and father, chooses to be the mistress of a local businessman rather than plumb the depths of poverty. A depressing film version (1941) was directed by John Baxter.

**Love rat.** A condemnatory nickname for a man who abandons his wife or girlfriend for another.

> The handsome captain of the England rugby team [Will Carling] went from being a likeable lad to a loathsome 'love rat' for walking out on his girlfriend Ali Cockayne and their 21-month-old baby Henry.
> *Sunday Times* (26 September 1999)

**Lover boy.** A lover; an attractive man or boy; a woman-chaser. The phrase is frequently used as a term of address to one who is this last.

**Lovers' acronyms.** Love letters between couples or spouses have long carried coded messages of passion, in particular when the man is away from home on military service. The following are some of the more modern examples, mostly based on names of countries:

BOLTOP: Better on lips than on paper (of a kiss)

BURMA: Be undressed ready, my angel

EGYPT: Eager to grab your pretty tits

HOLLAND: Hope our love lasts and never dies

ITALY: I trust and love you

MALAYA: My anxious lips await your arrival

NORWICH: (K)nickers off ready when I come home

POLAND: Please open lovingly and never destroy

*See also* SWALK.

**'Love Song of J. Alfred Prufrock, The'.** A poem by the Anglo-American poet T.S. Eliot (1888–1965), first published in the United States in 1915 in the magazine *Poetry* and in

Britain in 1917 in the collection *Prufrock and Other Observations*. It depicts the doubts and sexual inhibitions of a shy Bostonian by the name of J. Alfred Prufrock. Eliot took the name of his celebrated central character from that of a St Louis furniture company.

> I grow old ... I grow old ...
> I shall wear the bottoms of my trousers rolled ...
> I have heard the mermaids singing, each to each.
> I do not think that they will sing to me.
> T.S. ELIOT: 'The Love Song of J. Alfred Prufrock'

**Love Story.** A tear-jerking film (1970) based on the novel of the same title by Erich Segal about the romance that blossoms between a young man and woman but that ends prematurely with her death. Starring Ryan O'Neal as Oliver and Ali MacGraw as Jenny, the film was publicized as the ultimate 'weepie', and stories were told of boxes of tissues being sold in cinema foyers for the use of distraught audiences. A sequel, *Oliver's Story* (1979), failed to excite much interest. *See also* LOVE MEANS NEVER HAVING TO SAY YOU'RE SORRY; TEARJERKER.

> Love means never having to say you're sorry.
> ERICH SEGAL: *Love Story* (Oliver speaking)

**Love that dares not speak its name, The.** Homosexual love. The expression originated in the poem 'Two Loves' (1896) by Lord Alfred Douglas, intimate of Oscar Wilde: 'I am the Love that dare (*sic*) not speak its name.' The phrase was later adopted to apply to any 'secret' love or loyalty.

**Love Thy Neighbour.** A television SITCOM screened from 1972 to 1976 and centring on the relationships that develop between Eddie Booth, a jingoistic, beer-swilling socialist, played by Jack Smethurst, and his wife Joan, played by Kate Williams, and their newly arrived next-door neighbours, the West Indian couple Bill and Barbie Reynolds, played by Rudolph Walker and Nina Baden-Semper. The script's blatantly racist content, although intended comically, would never have been tolerated in the climate of POLITICAL CORRECTNESS that prevailed a decade later, despite the title's biblical adjuration (Mark 12:31).

**Love you!** A more or less meaningless 'sign-off' on parting or at the end of a telephone conversation.

**Lower 48, The.** A name for the 48 states of the continental United States excluding Alaska, so called as all lying south of or below the latter.

> People arrive steadily. And people go. They go from Anchorage and Fairbanks [in Alaska] ... Some, of course, are interested only in a year or two's work, then to return with saved high wages to the Lower Forty-eight.
> *The New Yorker* (20 June 1977)

**Lowest form of animal life.** Literally the simplest form of biological life, generally taken to be protozoa. In the 20th century the phrase came to apply figuratively to any despised person or group of people, 'the lowest of the low'. In the film *Mutiny on the Bounty* (1935) a midshipman is described as the 'lowest form of animal life in the navy'.

**LSD.** Lysergic acid diethylamide, a powerful hallucinogenic drug, colloquially known as acid. It was formulated in 1943 by the Swiss biochemist Albert Hoffman, who notoriously experienced its disorientating effect when riding his bicycle through the streets of Basel (Basle). During the Cold War, the American military and the CIA experimented with it (sometimes on uninformed subjects) to see whether it would be an aid in interrogation. It wasn't. By the later 1960s LSD had become the favoured PSYCHEDELIC drug among the young (*see* 'LUCY IN THE SKY WITH DIAMONDS'; MERRY PRANKSTERS; TURN ON, TUNE IN, DROP OUT).

> LSD? Nothing much happened, but I did get the distinct impression that some birds were trying to communicate with me.
>
> W.H. AUDEN: on his experiment with the drug, quoted in George Plimpton (ed.), *The Writer's Chapbook* (1989)

**L7.** SQUARE. If the thumb and forefinger of the left hand form a letter L and the thumb and forefinger of the right hand form a figure 7, the two joined together will form a square. The expression arose as African American or teenage US slang in the 1950s. A RIOT GRRLS rock band of this name was formed in Los Angeles in 1985.

**Lubbock's Law.** In literature the principle that the point of view of a novel's heroine must be such that a female reader can readily identify with it. The concept was formulated by the critic and biographer Percy Lubbock (1879–1965), author of *The Craft of Fiction* (1921). The narratives of most MILLS & BOON novels obey Lubbock's Law at a popular level.

**Lubyanka.** The building off Dzerzhinsky Square, Moscow, that was the headquarters of the KGB and other Russian-Soviet state security organs. It also served as a prison and execution centre. Before the 1917 Revolution the building housed two insurance companies, 'Anchor' and 'Russia'. After 1917 these were taken over by the Soviet insurance company *Gosstrakh*, short for *gosudarstvennoye strakhovaniye*, 'state insurance'. In Russian the second half of the acronym, *strakh*, happens to mean 'terror', and with typical wry humour Soviet citizens would pun, 'It used to be *Gosstrakh* but now it's *Gosuzhas*', i.e. 'It used to be state terror but now it's state horror.'

The art deco offices of the *Daily Express* in Fleet Street, all chrome and black glass, were known with grim facetious-ness as the 'Black Lubyanka' while the newspaper was in residence there (at the start of the 21st century they were occupied by Goldman Sachs).

**Lucan, Lord.** Richard John Bingham, 7th Earl of Lucan (b.1934), nicknamed 'Lucky' for his success at the gaming table. He allegedly murdered the family nanny, Sandra Rivett, following an attack on his estranged wife in 1974. He then disappeared, and was long sought without success. In 1999 his family was granted probate by the High Court and he was officially declared dead in a document stating: 'Be it known that the Right Honourable Richard John Bingham, Seventh Earl of Lucan, of 72a Elizabeth Street, London SW1, died on or since the 8th day of November 1974.'

**Luck of the draw.** The outcome of chance rather than of design. The allusion is to the random drawing of a playing card. The expression dates from the 1950s.

**Luck out.** An American expression with two diametrically opposed meanings. The original one, dating from the 1940s, seems counter-intuitive to British-speakers: 'to succeed by good fortune alone'. 'Out' usually has negative connotations in British English, and the later sense 'to be unlucky' (first recorded in 1957) is more in tune with this.

**Lucky Country.** A nickname for Australia, originating from the title of *The Lucky Country* (1964) by Donald Horne (1921–2005), a critique of contemporary Australian society and a considered definition of the 'Australian dream'. The name was originally intended ironically, and Horne saw Australia as 'a lucky country run mainly by second-rate people who share its luck'. More recently, though, people have tended to take the phrase at face value.

*Lucky Jim.* The first novel (1954) by Kingsley Amis (1922–95), recording the tribulations of Jim Dixon, a lecturer in history at a recently established provincial university. 'Lucky' is in turn a justifiable and an ironic description of his fortunes. Although it was not the first of the wave of novels that gave their authors the sobriquet ANGRY YOUNG MAN, it was the one that did most to suggest the existence of such a movement. The title comes from an American song by Frederick Bowen and Charles Horwitz, which tells how a man waited for his childhood friend to die so that he could marry the girl they both wanted. Unhappily married, however, he wishes he were also dead: 'Oh, lucky Jim, how I envy him.'

A film version (1957) was directed by John Boulting, with Ian Carmichael in the title role. *See also* FIRST LINES OF NOVELS.

**'Lucy in the Sky with Diamonds'.** A dreamily PSYCHEDELIC

song that appears on The BEATLES album SERGEANT PEPPER'S LONELY HEARTS CLUB BAND and is credited to John Lennon and Paul McCartney (though mostly by Lennon). The title comes from a drawing by Lennon's four-year-old son Julian. Despite the patently psychedelic nature of the lyric and its musical ambience, and the coincidence of the song's initials with those of the hallucinogenic drug LSD, it seems that no allusion to LSD was intended by The Beatles. This notwithstanding, the song was banned by the BBC for the alleged reference. The song also reflects Lennon's obsession with the hallucinatory world of Lewis Carroll in *Through the Looking-Glass* (1872), the latter being a favourite text of the counterculture of the 1960s.

**Lucy Stoner.** A woman who declines to adopt her husband's surname when she marries. The exemplar for this action was the US feminist Lucy Stone (1818–93), who continued to use her own name on marrying Henry Blackwell in 1855. In 1879, when women in Massachusetts were allowed to vote in school district elections, Lucy Stone registered in her own name, but the Board of Registrars removed her name from the voting list. The Lucy Stone League was subsequently founded by Ruth Hale, who similarly refused to change her name after marrying Heywood Broun in 1917. The term Lucy Stoner appears in some pre-1960 American dictionaries.

**Luftwaffe.** (German, 'air weapon'.) The German Air Force, first officially mentioned in a proclamation by Goering in May 1935, although it had in fact existed since 1933. It was configured primarily to fly in support of ground forces, and its Ju–87 STUKA dive-bomber was its principal ground-attack aircraft in the Spanish Civil War (1936–9) and the opening years of the Second World War. The postwar Luftwaffe was formed in 1956. *See also* BATTLE OF BRITAIN.

**LUG.** In US college slang of the 1990s, a female student who is not necessarily a lesbian, but who experiments with feminism and lesbian politics and culture. The abbreviation is short for 'lesbian until graduation'.

**Luke Skywalker.** *See* STAR WARS.

**Lulu.** The central character in a duet of plays, *The Earth Spirit*, originally *Erdgeist* (1895), and *Pandora's Box*, originally *Die Büchse der Pandora* (1903), by the German playwright Frank Wedekind (1864–1918). The plays are about the sexual career of Lulu, a dancer, and although her uninhibited enjoyment of sex is essentially innocent, her character has gone down as a symbol of feminine guile and eroticism, whose licentiousness proves fatal to the men who fall for her. At the close of the second play she is reduced to working as a prostitute in London and meets her end at the hands of

Jack the Ripper. The character was suggested to Wedekind by the women he met while he was working on a ballet for the Folies Bergère in Paris around the turn of the century. Her name was probably intended to recall that of the biblical Lilith, Adam's rebellious first wife.

The opera, also named *Lulu*, by Alban Berg (1885–1935) was based on Wedekind's two plays, and it was first performed in Zurich in 1937 in the original two-act form in which the composer had left it at the time of his death. The missing third act was supplied by the Viennese composer Friedrich Cerha (b.1926), and the full work finally emerged in Paris in 1979 under the baton of the French composer and conductor Pierre Boulez.

Lulu is also the stage name of the diminutive but feisty Scottish pop singer Marie McDonald McLaughlin Lawrie (b.1948), and who first came to national attention at the age of 15 with her single 'Shout!'. Her stage name was presumably chosen to alliterate with her first backing band, The Luvvers, rather than as an allusion to Wedekind's tragic *femme fatale*. Lulu's solo career continued successfully into the 21st century.

**Lumpectomy.** A surgical operation to remove a tumour ('lump') from the breast, typically when cancer is present but has not yet spread. The procedure, employed since the early 1970s, is obviously an improvement on the traditional mastectomy, which entails the amputation of the entire breast. The term is an ugly combination of English 'lump' and classical Greek '-ectomy', from the root word meaning 'excision' (literally 'cutting out'). Most medical terms with this element have a Greek specific, as 'mastectomy' itself (Greek *mastos*, 'breast'). Although *phuma* exists as Greek for 'tumour', presumably the English word was preferred as less intimidating.

**Lumps or bumps.** A medical euphemism for growths or swellings on or in the human body. 'Lumps and bumps' is also a colloquialism for a woman's breasts and the natural curves of the female figure, especially when regarded as disproportionate.

> It's for the rest of the gender, those of us who are an average size 14–16 and have lumps and bumps that can be disguised only with the help of clever clothing.
> *Sunday Times* (7 November 1999)

**Luna Park.** An amusement centre opened on Coney Island, New York, in 1903. It presented a world of fantasy in which, as the name implies, the moon played a key role. In 1904 a highly popular show 'Trip to the Moon' opened, in which visitors in a darkened theatre watched passengers embarking on an imaginary trip through outer space. The park burned down in 1944 but meanwhile the name had been adopted for amusement centres elsewhere, such as a fun parlour that opened in Sydney, Australia, in 1935, and that in its day was regarded as a classic example of fairground art.

**Lunar landscape.** An alliterative cliché for any bleak or barren-looking region, the imagery being that of the moon during its close-up photographic observation in the 1960s.

**Lunatic fringe.** The small section of the community who follow and originate extremist ideas and whose behaviour is sometimes eccentric by conventional standards but whose influence on the majority is mostly minimal. The expression is attributed to President Theodore Roosevelt, who in a letter of 1913 to Henry Cabot Lodge commenting on the defeat of the Bull Moose Party, a faction of the Republican Party, in the previous year's election, wrote: 'There is apt to be a lunatic fringe among the votaries of any forward movement.' *See also* LOONY LEFT; MONSTER RAVING LOONY PARTY.

**Lunatics have taken over the asylum, The.** A line used by the American film producer Richard Rowland (1881–1947) to refer to the formation in 1919 of United Artists by the actors Charlie Chaplin, Mary Pickford and Douglas Fairbanks, and the director D.W. Griffith, with the aim of producing and distributing their own films. The phrase has since been used in many other contexts. For example, in 1933 David Lloyd George declared: 'The world is becoming like a lunatic asylum run by lunatics.' More recently, in 2003, the Conservative leader Iain Duncan Smith (*see* IDS), in relation to the Labour government's policy towards asylum-seekers, told parliament:

> On Sunday the Home Office announced its new policy … on Monday that was reversed. On Tuesday ministers blamed officials. It seems another week when the lunatics took over the asylum policy of this government.

**Lunatic soup.** Cheap, low-quality alcoholic drink. The slang term, which originated in Australia in the 1930s, is often applied specifically to cheap red wine, and also to methylated spirits as drunk by alcoholics.

**Lunchbox.** A mildly amusing term for the male genitals, especially when prominently outlined beneath tight trousers or shorts. The word is an elaboration of 'box' as a term for a light shield to protect a sports player's genitals and was applied by *The Sun* in various headlines of the mid-1990s to the athlete Linford Christie (b.1960). The alliteration with his first name afforded an added attraction.

> He pranced around the stage with co-host Jenna Elfman but, unlike Elfman, who had a modest and tiny skirt-effect

covering her, David [Hyde Pierce] bravely exposed his lunchbox area.
> *heat* (23–29 September 1999)

**Lupin, Arsène.** The gentleman thief turned gentleman detective in the stories and novels of Maurice Leblanc, beginning with *Arsène Lupin, gentleman cambrioleur* (1908). He is a French blend of E.W. Hornung's Raffles and Arthur Conan Doyle's Sherlock Holmes and the latter actually appears in some of the stories under the name 'Herlock Sholmès'. Many of the books have been translated into English and there have been movie versions of Lupin's exploits, beginning with five German films of 1910–11. A French television series duly followed in the 1970s.

*Lusitania.* The Cunard liner made its last voyage on 1 May 1915, carrying 1959 passengers from Liverpool to New York, its regular run since 1907. Approaching the Irish coast the vessel was struck by two German torpedoes and sank in 18 minutes with the tragic loss of 1198 lives. Both the *Lusitania* and the TITANIC became unforgettable 20th-century symbols of maritime disaster.

**Luther, Lex.** *See* SUPERMAN.

**Luv.** A colloquial written form of 'love' adopted from the 1950s to indicate casual or local speech ('There you are, luv') or to sign off a private note or letter ('Luv, Nick'). *See also* LUVVY.

**Luvvy.** A humorous or with some speakers even derogatory term for an actor or actress, as a form of the affectionate vocative 'lovey'. The word first began to appear in print in the early 1990s. It encapsulates the supposed demonstrativeness or flamboyance of theatre folk and the frequent terms of endearment used by and between them. The film director Richard Attenborough (Lord Attenborough; b.1923) is sometimes cited as a prime example of the type, with his regular recourse to 'darling' as a stock form of address to males and females alike.

*Luxe, calme et volupté.* The hedonistic painting of nude bathers on a beach by Henri Matisse (1869–1954). It was painted with a free pointillist technique in St Tropez in 1904–5. The title comes from the refrain of the poem *L'Invitation au voyage* by Charles Baudelaire (1821–67): *Là, tout n'est qu'ordre et beauté, / Luxe, calme et volupté* ('There, all is simply order and beauty, / Luxury, calm and delight'). The painting was bought in 1905 by the painter Paul Signac (1863–1935), one of the originators of the pointillist technique. Another painter, Raoul Dufy (1877–1953), wrote in 1925: 'On looking at that picture I grasped all the new reasons for painting; the realism of the impressionists lost its charm for me as I contemplated the miracle of the imagination introduced into draughtsmanship and colour.' Matisse returned to the theme in 1907–8. *Le Luxe* is still quite painterly, but *Le Luxe II* is characterized by flat planes of colour and hard outlines.

**Lycra.** This lightweight stretchy polyurethane fibre or fabric, patented in the US by E.I. du Pont de Nemours and Co. in 1958, was originally used for underwear and swimming costumes but later gave rise to the body-hugging designs of the sportswear worn in the fitness fetish of the 1980s. The name seems to suggest a partial anagram of 'acrylic'.

**Lyin' and testifyin'.** Misleading talk; persuasive badinage. The expression originated in the 1990s in African American street talk and was included in so-called EBONICS. 'Lyin'' is positive, not negative, and denotes skilful story-telling.

**Lyme disease.** A form of arthritis caused by bacteria that are transmitted by deer ticks. It takes its name from Lyme, Connecticut, where an outbreak occurred in 1975.

**Lymeswold.** A British make of blue creamy cheese, on sale for 10 years from 1982. Its name, suggesting 'slime' and 'mould', may have contributed to its uncertain reception, although it was apparently intended to evoke 'limes' and 'wold', as words of rural imagery. It may have been suggested by Wymeswold, a village near Loughborough in Leicestershire, a county noted for its cheese. It was actually produced at Aston in Cheshire, similarly famed.

**Lysenkoism.** *See* MICHURINISM.

# M

**M.** The designation of James BOND's boss at the fictional 'British Secret Service' in the books and films. Ian Fleming based his fictional M on a real character, the right-wing MI5 officer Maxwell Knight (1900–68), who had joined the British Fascisti in 1924. In his role at MI5 he recruited many agents from far-right organizations such as the British Union of Fascists, who were then infiltrated into left-wing organizations. One of Knight's agents was William Joyce (Lord HAW-HAW) – and another was Fleming himself. In 1940 Knight helped to crack a pro-Nazi cell.

In the more recent Bond films M has been played by Dame Judi Dench (MI5 itself had its first female director general in the form of Dame Stella Rimington, from 1992 to 1996).

**M.** A classic film (1931) by Fritz Lang, his first exercise using sound. A child murderer (played by Peter Lorre) is terrorizing Berlin, driving the citizenry to hysteria. The police are getting nowhere, so the underworld decides to take on the job of catching the killer. He is eventually identified because a witness has managed to put on his back the mark 'M' (for *Mörder*, 'murderer'). In 1951 Joseph Losey directed a remake, transferring the story to Los Angeles.

**Maastricht Treaty.** The agreement reached between the heads of government of the (then) 12 members of the European Community (*see* EUROPEAN UNION) at Maastricht in the Netherlands in 1991. It was designed to prepare the way for economic, monetary and political union within the EC, and contained a protocol regarding social and employment policy in member states. Ratification of the treaty was hampered by various factors, one being Britain's reluctance to accept certain directives set out in the SOCIAL CHAPTER. The treaty was regarded by some as a threat to national sovereignty. It was eventually ratified in 1993.

**McCarthyism.** Political witch-hunting, such as the hounding of communist suspects to secure their removal from office and public affairs. The name is that of US Republican Senator Joseph McCarthy (1908–57), who declared in the early 1950s, at the height of the COLD WAR, that there existed an orchestrated communist campaign to infiltrate the US government at all levels and embarked on a campaign to root out 'un-American' activity in all walks of life. *See also The* CRUCIBLE; HISS AFFAIR.

> McCarthyism is Americanism with its sleeves rolled.
> JOSEPH MCCARTHY: speech in Wisconsin (1952)

**McDonald's.** The chain of FAST FOOD outlets grew from a germ planted in April 1955 when Ray A. Kroc (1902–84), a former jazz pianist, opened a franchise in the Chicago suburb of Des Plaines. He joined Richard and Maurice McDonald to set up assembly-line production of HAMBURGERS, French fries and milk shakes, and in 1961 bought out the brothers, by which time his business had grown to a chain of over 200 branches. The company's trademark letter M and golden arches are now a worldwide symbol of American consumerism, and as the COLD WAR was ending McDonald's opened its first branch in Moscow. The early 21st century saw glimmers of a slowdown in what had seemed the inexorable advance of the brand: in the UK the company announced that 25 branches were closing and over 70 were being relocated. Responding to slowing sales, McDonald's bought 33 per cent of the Prêt à Manger chain of sandwich shops to 'diversify'. *See also* BIG MAC; GOLDEN ARCHES; JUNK FOOD; MAC OUT; MCJOB; MCMANSION.

**Macfarlane.** A type of overcoat incorporating a shoulder cape and with slits at the waist to allow access to pockets in clothing worn beneath. The name is presumably that of its original Scottish designer or manufacturer. The word is first recorded in English in 1920, but is found in French much earlier, in an issue of *Le Monde illustré* for 1859.

**McGee, Fibber.** The compulsive liar who lives with his wife

Molly at 79 Wistful Vista somewhere in the United States in the radio comedy series *Fibber McGee and Molly* (1935–7) and the television series of the same title (1959–60), starring Bob Sweeney and Cathy Lewis. The characters also appeared in various films, among them *Look Who's Laughing* (1941) and *Here We Go Again* (1942), in which they were played by Bob and Marian Jordan. Every time Fibber opened his built-in wardrobe its contents debouched in deafening disarray. To say 'It's like Fibber McGee's closet in here' is to comment on a state of spectacular untidiness.

**McGuffin.** A name devised by the film director Alfred Hitchcock (1899–1980) for an object or event, of little interest in itself, such as secret plans or stolen papers, that serves to trigger the action. The term was later extended to a similar device in fiction. The origin of the name is uncertain, but it purportedly comes from a Scotsman who appeared in a story about two men in a train. On the other hand 'guff', as a word for anything trivial or worthless, may lie at the root.

**Machine for living in, A.** The definition of a house by the French architect Le Corbusier (1887–1965), summing up the functional, no-frills approach of international modernism.

> *Une maison est une machine-à-habiter.*
> LE CORBUSIER: *Vers une architecture* (1923)

Le Corbusier may have been influenced by Tolstoy's line in *War and Peace* (1868–9), translated by A. and L. Maude: 'Our body is a machine for living.' Le Corbusier himself did not like the word 'function' (*see* FORM FOLLOWS FUNCTION):

> This frightful word was born under other skies than those I have loved – those where the sun reigns supreme.

**Machismo.** (Spanish *macho*, 'male'.) A usage of American origin denoting assertive masculinity that emphasizes such features as bravery, virility and the domination of the opposite sex.

**Mach number.** An expression of the ratio of flight speed to the speed of sound, devised by the Austrian physicist and psychologist Ernst Mach (1838–1916). An aircraft that is flying at Mach 2 is travelling at twice the speed of sound.

**Macintosh.** *See* APPLE MACINTOSH.

**McJob.** A low-paid or menial job with few prospects and little job satisfaction. The expression, combining the name of MCDONALD'S with 'job', was coined by Douglas Coupland in his book GENERATION X (1991) and alludes both to the type of job available in the named fast-food chain and to the JUNK FOOD it sells.

**McKenzie, Barry.** A fictitious sex-hungry, frequently drunken OCKER created by the Australian humorist and actor Barry Humphries (b.1934). He first appeared in a cartoon strip (drawn by Nicholas Garland) in the magazine *Private Eye* in the late 1960s, and was later immortalized on celluloid (played by Barry Crocker) in *The Adventures of Barry McKenzie* (1972) and *Barry McKenzie Holds His Own* (1974). Lantern-jawed and wearing the traditional cork-hung Aussie hat, and with bodily effluvia figuring largely in his life, he contributed several colourful expressions in this area to Australian English (many of them invented by Humphries, who played McKenzie's aunt, Edna EVERAGE, in the films) (*see* GO FOR THE BIG SPIT; SIPHON THE PYTHON; STRAIN THE POTATOES; TECHNICOLOR YAWN).

**McKenzie friend.** A person who attends a court of law to help a party to a case by making notes, quietly giving advice and the like. The name is that of the litigants in the case of McKenzie v. McKenzie (1970), in which the Court of Appeal ruled that such a helper had a right to attend a trial to assist a person who did not wish to use the services of a lawyer.

**McLuhanism.** The ideas of the influential Canadian media and communications theorist Marshall McLuhan (1911–80). In books such as *The Gutenberg Galaxy* (1962) he predicted the death of the book as the world became a GLOBAL VILLAGE linked by instant electronic media such as TV and computers. He also held that these new media would dominate and shape the content that they carried, summed up in his aphorism 'The MEDIUM IS THE MESSAGE.'

**McMansion.** A pejorative name given to any large modern house that is at once lavish and tasteless, and thus imaginatively cheap while being ostentatiously expensive. Favoured 'styles' include mock-Georgian and fake-hacienda. McMansions are much favoured by high-earning (or overpaid) football players (*see also* KING OF CHAVS; ROASTING). The name is modelled on that of MCDONALD'S, the fast-food chain. *See also* CELEBRITY CULTURE; MCJOB.

**Mac out.** To overeat. American teenage slang of the 1980s, implying that one has over-indulged in BIG MACs and other forms of fast food at MCDONALD'S.

**Mac the Knife.** A nickname of Harold Macmillan (1894–1986), prime minister from 1957 to 1963, following his sacking in 1962 of seven cabinet ministers, including the chancellor of the exchequer, in the NIGHT OF THE LONG KNIVES. Mack the Knife is a character in Kurt Weill and Bertolt Brecht's *The* THREEPENNY OPERA (1928), and its jazzy song so titled was familiar at the time from Bobby Darin's Number 1 hit recording of it in 1959. *See also* SUPERMAC; WIND OF CHANGE.

**MAD.** The appropriate acronym for 'mutually assured destruction', the doctrine that ensured the deterrent effect of nuclear weapons throughout much of the COLD WAR. If one side were to launch a nuclear attack, it could be confident that it would be wiped out in retaliation. See also ABM; BALANCE OF TERROR; ICBM; STAR WARS.

**Madam Cyn.** The self-styled nickname of Cynthia Payne (b.1933), a London brothel-keeper who was revealed in the 1970s as selling £25 luncheon vouchers to her clients by way of an entitlement to food, drink, a STRIPTEASE and a spell upstairs with a girl of their choice. In 1987 she was cleared by an Old Bailey jury of technically running a brothel in the so-called 'sex on the stairs' case. Julie Walters played her in the biopic *Personal Services* (1986) as did Emily Lloyd in a more fictionalized prequel, *Wish You Were Here* (1987).

> Welcome to my house of Cyn
>
> www.cynthia-payne.co.uk, homepage (2006)

**Madame Butterfly.** The central character of Giacomo Puccini's opera *Madama Butterfly*, first performed at La Scala, Milan, in 1903, with a libretto by Giuseppe Giacosa and Luigi Illica based on David Belasco's play *Madame Butterfly* (1900), in turn taken from John Luther Long's short story so titled (1898), itself inspired by an actual event. The scene is set in Nagasaki in the early 20th century. The young and pretty geisha Cio-Cio-San (Madame Butterfly) marries Lieutenant Pinkerton of the US Navy, an arrangement that he treats lightly despite the warnings of the US consul, Sharpless. Deserted by her husband soon after the wedding, Butterfly awaits his return. She now has a son, 'Trouble'. She remains insistent that Pinkerton will return, so Sharpless hesitates to read her a letter from her husband saying that he now has an American wife. She refuses to listen when he does read it and undertakes an all-night vigil with her loyal servant Suzuki. The next day, when Pinkerton returns with his new wife, Kate, Butterfly is obliged to face reality. Giving her young child a US flag to play with, she commits hara-kiri.

**Madame X.** The title of at least seven multi-handkerchief US TEARJERKERS, based on *La Femme X* (1908), a play by the French dramatist Alexandre Bisson (1848–1912). It tells the story of a woman who after a scandal is forced by her jealous husband to leave her young son with him while she disappears from society. Her life thereafter goes downhill until she finds herself being defended on a murder charge by the son she was forced to abandon all those years before. The title role has been played by Sarah Bernhardt (in the original stage production), Ruth Chatterton (1929), Gladys George (1937) and Lana Turner (1966), among others.

**Mad cow disease.** The colloquial name of bovine spongiform encephalopathy (BSE), a disease of cattle that affects the central nervous system, causing staggering and usually resulting in death. It is believed to be caused by prions (protein particles) and to be related to Creutzfeldt-Jakob disease (CJD), a fatal degenerative disease affecting nerve cells in the human brain. Both BSE and CJD became major concerns in Britian in the 1990s, and many countries banned British beef imports for years afterwards.

When its profile was at its height, the name served as a model for other, more facetious designations (e.g. 'mad chicken disease').

> For years, the English were lulled into thinking the only Mad Cow threatening them was Margaret Thatcher when it seems their entire land was full of them.
>
> WILL DURST: on www.alternet.org, 26 April 2000

**Maddermarket Theatre.** An unusual theatre in Norwich, built in 1921 as a replica of an Elizabethan playhouse. Its amateur company puts on a new production every month for just nine performances and the actors are always anonymous. It takes its name from the former medieval market there, itself so called from the locally growing madder, a plant whose root yields a red dye or pigment.

**Mad Dog.** The nickname of the Ulster Protestant paramilitary leader Johnny Adair (b.1964), leader of the Belfast Company of the Ulster Freedom Fighters, which is affiliated to the Ulster Defence Association. Associated with a number of atrocities against Catholic civilians, he was released from prison following the GOOD FRIDAY AGREEMENT, but became involved in violent internecine strife within the UDA, was rearrested and later was forced to move to England. *See also* KING RAT.

**Madeleine.** A small cockle-shaped sponge cake, possibly named after the 19th-century French pastry cook Madeleine Paulmier. The madeleine is the most iconic food item in modern literature, playing a key role in Proust's novel sequence REMEMBRANCE OF THINGS PAST:

> And suddenly the memory revealed itself. The taste was that of the little piece of madeleine which on Sunday mornings at Combray … my aunt Léonie used to give me, dipping it first in her own cup of tea or tisane.
>
> MARCEL PROUST: *Swann's Way* (1913)

The madeleine thus provides the novelist with a way into the world of his past. Since then this modest cake (not to be confused with the jam- and desiccated-coconut-coated British madeleine) has frequently been invoked in discussions of the power of taste and smell to bring back lost memories.

**'Mademoiselle from Armenteers'.** In the First World War Armentières in northern France was held by the British until the great German spring offensive of 1918. The popular army song 'Mademoiselle from Armenteers' originated *c.*1915 as a modification of the much earlier song 'The Landlady's Little Daughter', otherwise known as 'Three Prussian Officers Crossed the Rhine', with words by Ludwig Uhland set to a traditional air. It readily lent itself to improvisation, especially of a scurrilous nature. One version ran:

> O Madam, have you any good wine?
> Parlez-vous;
> O Madam, have you any good wine?
> Parlez-vous.
> O Madam, have you any good wine?
> Fit for a soldier of the line?
> Hinky-dinky, parlez-vous.

**Madge.** A deflationary nickname for the glamorous American pop singer Madonna (b.1959 as Madonna Louise Veronica Ciccone). Madonna is rated by some critics more as a fashion innovator and post-feminist icon than as a musician, although her songs, according to one commentator, are 'enjoyed by eight-year-olds at jelly and ice-cream discos' (Eyre, H., and Donaldson, W., *The Dictionary of National Celebrity*, 2005). In regard to her non-musical achievements, mention must be made of *Sex*, her photographic oeuvre of 1993. In this she is to be seen in a number of challenging situations, such as clambering over a wall having forgotten to put her knickers on. *See also* DESPERATELY SEEKING SUSAN; KABBALAH.

'Madge' is also the name of the long-suffering companion and foil of Dame Edna EVERAGE, the very drabness of her name and appearance contrasting with the outré personality and dress of the international superstar. This Madge is often seen knitting, on the sidelines, while Edna holds court.

**Madison Avenue.** A street in New York that was formerly the centre of the US advertising and public relations business. The name is still used allusively in this connection and first came into use in this sense in 1944 when an article on the contribution of advertising to the war effort appeared in the *New Republic* magazine by a writer signing himself 'Madison Avenue'.

**Mad Max.** The violent hero, played by Mel Gibson, of the futuristic Australian film *Mad Max* (1979) and its sequels, *Mad Max 2* (1981) and *Mad Max beyond Thunderdome* (1985), depicting violently anarchic combat between motorcycle gangs and the police. The character's name has in some cases come to be applied to people and objects, such as vehicles or clothing, similar to those in the films.

**Mad money.** In the 1920s, money kept by a woman for use in an emergency, in particular when abandoned far from home by a boyfriend. 'Mad' denotes more the anger of the man than that of the woman. The phrase was subsequently adopted to mean money set aside for some frivolous or self-indulgent purpose. Here 'mad' indicates the crazy spending. Both uses of this American phrase are now dated but not quite obsolete.

**Mad Monk.** A nickname of the Conservative politician Sir Keith Joseph (1918–94), regarded by many as the *éminence grise* behind Thatcherite (*see* THATCHERISM) ideology. The name, first applied to RASPUTIN, was awarded to Joseph because of his generally crazed look, his inability to communicate effectively with the public and the purity (or extremity) of his free-market beliefs (*see also* FRIEDMANISM).

**Mad Mullah.** A nickname given to Mohammed bin Abdullah, a mullah who caused great problems for the British in Somaliland at various times between 1899 and 1920. He claimed to be the Mahdi and made extensive raids on tribes friendly to the British. The dervish power was not finally broken until 1920 when the Mad Mullah escaped to Ethiopia, where he died in 1921.

***Madness of George III, The.*** A play (1991) by Alan Bennett (b.1934), depicting the political and personal turmoil arising from one of King George III's periodic bouts of insanity (believed by modern doctors to have been caused by porphyria). The play was subsequently filmed as *The Madness of King George*. An apocryphal anecdote ascribes the alteration of the title to the concerns of the film's US backers who feared that US audiences would assume that the film was the third in a series of 'George' movies.

**Madonna.** *See* MADGE.

**Mae West.** The name given by RAF personnel early in the Second World War to the inflatable life jacket worn when there was danger of being forced into the sea. The allusion was to the full figure of the American film actress of this name (1892–1980), who apparently approved the adoption.

> I've been in *Who's Who*, and I know what's what, but it'll be the first time I ever made the dictionary.
>
> MAE WEST: letter to the RAF of the early 1940s, quoted in Fergus Cashin, *Mae West*, ch. 9 (1981)

**Mafeking Night.** 18 May 1900, when news reached London that Mafeking in South Africa, now Mafikeng, had been relieved by British forces after a seven-month siege by the

Boers during the South African War (Second BOER WAR). The resultant jubilation led to the coining of the word 'maffick', meaning 'to indulge in extravagant demonstrations of exultation on occasions of national rejoicing' (*Oxford English Dictionary*). The usage was chiefly confined to journalism and was almost extinct by the end of the First World War.

**Maggie.** One of the more affectionate nicknames given to Margaret Thatcher, the IRON LADY, by her supporters. It was also taken up by her opponents, and many anti-Thatcher demonstrations rang to the cry of 'Maggie, Maggie, Maggie – Out, out, out!'

**Maggie Mae.** A version of a traditional sailors' song about a Liverpool prostitute that appeared on The BEATLES album LET IT BE, released in Britain in May 1970. The Beatles' version is credited as 'trad. arr. John Lennon, Paul McCartney, George Harrison and Richard Starkey' (Ringo Starr). She also features in Rod Stewart's 1971 hit 'Maggie'. The original Maggie Mae operated in the notorious Lime Street area in the 1890s.

**Magical Mystery Tour.** A television film, EP ('extended play') recording based on it, and title song by The BEATLES, credited to John Lennon and Paul McCartney and released in the UK in December 1967. The concept was based on the idea of a PSYCHEDELIC roadshow in a brightly coloured coach. The film and EP notably contain the song 'I AM THE WALRUS'.

The title derives from the 'mystery tour', in which tourists board a coach without knowing what their route or destination is going to be. Such mystery tours have been run since the 1920s.

**Magic bullet.** A medicine or other remedy with highly specific properties that can serve as a simple cure for a particular disease. The fact that in some cases one particular drug does knock out a disease, as penicillin can syphilis, has lent disproportionate support to the theory that a similar remedy can be found for any disease, whether treated by conventional or ALTERNATIVE medicine. As a result many sufferers either look to the doctor for a single prescribed 'quick fix' that will clear up their condition or attribute undue efficacy to a supposed 'tried and trusted' home remedy, as adherents of herbal medicine, for example, may do with evening primrose oil.

**Magic Circle.** The British society of magicians was founded in 1905 with the famous David Devant (real name David Wighton; 1868–1941) and Nevil Maskelyne (1839–1917) as its earliest presidents. Its journal, *The Magic Circular*, was started the following year. The society's headquarters are in Stephenson Way off North Gower Street, London, where there are libraries, a small theatre and a museum of historic conjuring apparatus. The highest distinction is to be a member of the Inner Magic Circle. The motto of the Circle is *Indocilis privata loqui*, 'Not apt to disclose secrets', and its symbol is the circular sign of the zodiac, which appears on the floor of the club room. The name ultimately puns on the magic circle invented by Benjamin Franklin in 1749 as an arrangement of numbers in radially divided concentric circles with arithmetical properties similar to those of a magic square.

In politics the 'magic circle' is a term for the inner group of Conservative politicians viewed as choosing the party leader in the days before this was an electoral matter. The name was coined by Iain Macleod in a critical article in the *Spectator* of 17 January 1964 on the 'emergence' of Alec Douglas-Home (*see* BAILIE VASS) in succession to Harold Macmillan in 1963.

**Magic Mountain, The.** A novel (1927; in German as *Der Zauberberg*, 1924) by Thomas Mann (1875–1955). The densely symbolic story of the young Hans Castorp's search for self-knowledge while undergoing treatment for tuberculosis in a sanatorium in the Swiss Alps is ultimately a study of the uneasy situation in Europe before the outbreak of the First World War. The theme is the application of art and philosophy (the mountain) to the crisis of contemporary existence below. *See also* FIRST LINES OF NOVELS.

**Magic realism.** A style of fiction writing in which the realistic and everyday are blended with the unexpected or inexplicable. The term was adopted in this sense in the 1970s by a number of young British writers, such as Emma Tennant (b.1937), Angela Carter (1940–92) and Salman Rushdie (b.1947). Rushdie's MIDNIGHT'S CHILDREN (1981) and *Shame* (1983) are regarded as typical of the genre.

The exact origin of the term is uncertain, but it may have lain in the question posed by the Cuban novelist Alejo Carpentier: 'What is the story of Latin America if it is not a chronicle of the marvellous in the real?' It was first employed as a literary definition by the US critic Alastair Reid with reference to the large body of fantastic fiction produced in South American countries after the Second World War. Gabriel García Márquez' novel *Cien años de soledad* (1967; *see* FIRST LINES OF NOVELS), familiar in Gregory Rabassa's translation from the Spanish as *One Hundred Years of Solitude* (1970), is generally regarded as the paradigm.

**Magic Roundabout, The.** A popular children's television puppet series that became cult viewing for many adults. It was written by Eric Thompson (1929–82), who based it on a French programme, *Le Manège enchanté* (1963), by Serge Danot. It ran from 1965 to 1977, and its characters included Dougal the dog, BRIAN the snail, Ermintrude the cow, Dylan the rabbit, Zebedee the spring-man and Florence, a little girl. A computer-animated feature film of the same title (2005) revived the characters for a new generation.

On the A4259 the English town of Swindon boasts a pentagonal roundabout dubbed, in homage to the puppet show, the 'Magic Roundabout'. It inspired a song, 'English Roundabout', by the Swindon pop group XTC.

**Magic sponge.** A footballer's term for the wet sponge traditionally wielded by the trainer when administering first aid to an injured player. It has now been outlawed following concern regarding the risk of blood-borne infections, and has been mostly replaced by ice packs, 'deep-heat' treatment and muscle sprays.

**Maginot Line.** A zone of fortifications built along the eastern frontier of France between 1929 and 1934 and named after André Maginot (1877–1932), minister of war, who sponsored its construction. The line, essentially to cover the returned territories of Alsace-Lorraine, extended from the Swiss border to that with Belgium and lulled the French into a belief that they were secure from any German threat of invasion. In the event, Hitler's troops entered France through Belgium in 1940. *See also* SIEGFRIED LINE.

**Magnificent Seven, The.** A WESTERN (1960) that was inspired by Akira Kurosawa's film *The Seven Samurai* (1954) and its theme of a small band of rough-hewn heroes defending a village against hordes of blood-thirsty bandits. The success with which director John Sturges transposed the story to the Wild West inspired numerous imitations, not least four lesser sequels featuring survivors of the original seven. The title itself has since been aped not only by subsequent movies (*The Seven Deadly Magnificent Sins*, starring Spike Milligan and others, or *The Magnificent Two*, starring Eric Morecambe and Ernie Wise, for instance) but in many other spheres of human activity, including international espionage (the 'Magnificent Five' were, to the Soviets, the notorious British spies involved in the BURGESS AND MACLEAN spy scandal that erupted in the early 1960s).

**Magoo, Mr.** The incompetent, myopic cartoon character was the creation of animators John Hubley and Robert Cannon. He first appeared in the late 1940s and 'played' various famous fictional characters, such as Dr Jekyll and Long John Silver, in a television series of the 1960s. His lugubrious voice was provided by Jim Backus.

**Mahagonny.** An imaginary city of material pleasure, with a capitalist morality, which features in the savagely satirical opera *The Rise and Fall of the City of Mahagonny (Aufstieg und Fall der Stadt Mahagonny)* by Kurt Weill (1900–50), with a libretto by Bertolt Brecht (1898–1956). The opera was first produced in 1930, following an earlier, simpler version of 1927.

**Mahatma.** (Sanksrit, 'great soul'). The title bestowed by his followers on the Indian nationalist leader Mohandas Karamchand Gandhi (1869–1948), owing to his great spirituality and emphasis on non-violence. A hagiographic film version of the life of Gandhi, directed by Richard Attenborough and starring Ben Kingsley as Gandhi, was released in 1982. *See also* NON-VIOLENCE.

**Mah-jongg.** A Chinese game played with 'tiles' like dominoes, made of ivory and bamboo, with usually four players. The tiles, 136 or 144 in all, are made up of numbered bamboo, circle and character suits, honours (red, green and white dragons), winds (north, east, south and west) and, additionally, numbered flowers and seasons.

The game itself is probably of 19th-century origin but was brought from Shanghai to the United States after the First World War by a US missionary, Joseph P. Babcock, under the tradename Mah-jongg, which he coined. It is Chinese dialect for 'sparrows', referring to the 'bird of a hundred intelligences' that appears on one of the tiles. At the peak of the fad, in 1923, some 10 million US women were meeting regularly for mah-jongg parties as an escape from housework.

**Maiden's prayer, Answer to a.** *See* ANSWER TO A MAIDEN'S PRAYER.

**Maigret, Inspector.** The pipe-smoking police detective who features in a long series of novels and stories by the Belgian writer Georges Simenon, who conceived him in 1929. His full name is Jules Maigret, and he solves mysteries by analyzing character rather than by examining physical clues. He first appeared in *Pietr le Letton* ('Peter the Latvian') (1930). The first Maigret titles to be published in Britain were *Introducing Inspector Maigret* (1933), *Inspector Maigret Investigates* (1933) and *The Triumph of Inspector Maigret* (1934). Each book contained two short novels, a scheme that continued until the 1950s, when the stories began to appear singly. Maigret was portrayed on film by Jean Gabin (1904–76), but many British television viewers remember him best as played by Rupert Davies between 1960 and 1963 or Michael Gambon between 1992 and 1993.

**Main squeeze.** A US colloquialism for a boyfriend or girlfriend, the allusion being to a tight hug or embrace, representing a close or intimate relationship. The term dates from the 1970s.

**Main Street.** The principal thoroughfare in many of the smaller towns and cities of the United States. Sinclair Lewis's novel of this name (1920) epitomized the social and cultural life of these towns, and the term came to denote the mediocrity, parochialism and materialism of small-town existence.

**Mainwaring, Captain.** *See* DAD'S ARMY.

**Major Barbara.** A play (1905) by the Irish playwright George Bernard Shaw (1856–1950) about a Salvation Army officer who debates the role that capitalism plays in supporting charity. Major Barbara is Barbara Undershaft, the daughter of an arms manufacturer who struggles with the idea that her charitable efforts are underwritten by the capitalism her father represents.

> *Bill Walker*: Wot prawce selvytion nah?
>
> GEORGE BERNARD SHAW: *Major Barbara*, II

**Majors, The.** Golfing jargon for the four most important tournaments: the Open, played annually in Britain since 1860, the US Open, first held in 1895, the US PGA (Professional Golfers' Association), dating from 1916, and the US Masters, first played in 1934. *See also* GRAND SLAM.

**Make all the right noises.** To talk in generally positive terms but without any real indication of action. The expression, which sometimes omits 'all', dates from the 1950s.

**Make a meal of something.** To treat it with greater attention to detail than is necessary. A retort to an elaborate description of some exploit might thus be: 'There's no need to make a meal of it.'

**Make an issue of something.** To turn it into a subject of contention; to make a fuss about it. The expression dates from the 1920s.

**Make a pass at someone.** To make an amorous advance to them. The expression dates from the 1920s.

> Men seldom make passes
> At girls who wear glasses.
>
> DOROTHY PARKER: 'News Item' (1937)

**Make a pig of oneself.** To overeat; to be extremely greedy. The pig has long symbolized gluttony, more for its manner of eating than for the amount it consumes. The phrase is of US origin and dates from the 1940s. *See also* PIG OUT.

**Make a statement.** To deliberately indicate one's attitude or point of view by one's actions.

> If the Tories had been making a statement, in the modish

phrase, it was a curious one. Having gone down to another disastrous defeat under an old-fashioned, balding, right-wing leader, they had now chosen a man who was more old-fashioned, even balder, and still further to the right.
>
> GEOFFREY WHEATCROFT: *The Strange Death of Tory England* (2005)

**Make babies.** To engage in sexual intercourse. A coy euphemism dating from the 1960s.

**Make do and mend.** An exhortation to thrift that has become proverbial, but which originated as an official slogan in the Second World War, when clothing and textiles were severely rationed. The Board of Trade issued a pamphlet called *Make Do and Mend*, which contained advice on how to patch, unpick and knit again. Among the sartorial achievements of the era were 'scanties', baggy women's underpants made from old flour bags.

**Make him an offer he can't refuse.** *See* I'LL MAKE HIM AN OFFER HE CAN'T REFUSE.

**Make it snappy!** Hurry up! Get on with it! A US phrase dating from the 1920s.

**Make it up as one goes along.** To improvise or 'ham'; to present information in an idiosyncratic or informal manner. The phrase need not imply that one is fabricating the facts.

**Make like a tree and leave.** To leave; to depart. The punning phrase is of US origin and has a number of equivalents, such as 'to make like a drum and beat it', 'to make like a banana and split'. These all date from the 1950s.

**Make love, not war.** The rallying cry of late 1960s and early 1970s hippiedom, encapsulating FLOWER POWER's attachment to 'peace and love' and its adherents' opposition to nuclear weapons and the VIETNAM War. The slogan is first recorded in 1969. *See also* 'GIVE PEACE A CHANCE'.

> I want you to make love, not war
> I know you've heard it before
>
> JOHN LENNON: 'Mind Games' (song) (1973)

**Make music together.** To engage in sexual intercourse. The adjective 'beautiful' is sometimes added. The expression implies a sweet harmony.

**Make my day.** Do what you threaten to do so that I have the satisfaction of doing what I have to do. The catchphrase is of US origin and is particularly associated with a scene in the film *Sudden Impact* (1983) in which Clint Eastwood, as the tough San Francisco police detective Harry Callahan, known as DIRTY HARRY, points his gun at a criminal and says: 'Go ahead, make my day.' If the criminal proceeds with the crime, Callahan will have the justification he wants for shooting him. More straightforwardly, to say of a person or thing that they 'made my day' is to say that they made it a success. Even here, however, the usage may be ironic. A variation on the familiar notice 'Beware of the dog' is a picture of a guard dog with the words: 'Break in. Make my day.'

**Make nice.** To behave pleasantly, agreeably or considerately. The expression, often addressed as an admonition to someone who is doing precisely the opposite, is an American one and may have originated as an imitation of Jewish American/Yiddish usage. It is first recorded in 1957.

**Make out with someone.** To engage in sexual activity with them.

**Makeover TV.** A subgenre of REALITY TV in which members of the public have some aspect of their lives transformed by 'experts' from its former banal or unsatisfactory state into something wondrously fashionable, desirable, sexy, empowering, etc. The first makeover targets were dowdy houses, on which television producers delighted to unleash teams of professional interior decorators. Much of the entertainment value of such programmes lay in seeing whether the householder was entranced or appalled by the result. A pioneer show in the US was *This Old House* (1979). That was followed by, among others, *Trading Spaces, Extreme Makeover: Home Edition, Guess Who's Coming to Decorate* and, in the UK, *Homefront* and *Changing Rooms*. Other aspects of people's lives to have been subjected to the televised transformative treatment include personal appearance or apparel (*What Not to Wear, How Do I Look?, Queer Eye for the Straight Guy, Fashion Police*), gardens (*Ground Force*), cars (*Pimp My Ride*) and marital arrangements (*Trading Spouses*). Many of the experts have achieved cult status (e.g. the fashion martinets Trinny Woodall and Susannah Constantine, of *What Not to Wear*, and the interior designer Laurence Llewelyn Bowen). *See also* NIP AND TUCK.

**Make the cut.** To do well; to come up to standard. The expression dates from the 1990s and was adopted from golfing jargon, in which the sense is to equal or better a required score, thus avoiding elimination from the last two rounds of a four-round tournament.

> This … Modern Library decided that *The Charterhouse of Parma* no longer made the cut, and deleted the novel from its list of the world's great literature in reprint.
> *Times Literary Supplement* (22 October 1999)

**Make the front page.** To be important enough to appear on a newspaper's front page. *See also* HIT THE HEADLINES.

**Make the grade.** To rise to the occasion; to reach the required

standard or level; to overcome obstacles. The allusion is to climbing a hill or gradient. The expression is of US origin and dates from the early 20th century.

**Make waves.** To cause trouble by 'rocking the boat' (*see* ROCK THE BOAT). A phrase of US origin that became current in the 1970s.

**Make with.** To proceed to use or supply, as: 'Come on, make with the drinks.' The phrase is an adoption of Yiddish *machen mit*, 'to brandish something'.

**Making the trains run on time.** What the admirers of the Fascist dictator Benito Mussolini (1883–1945) said he had achieved in Italy, a proverbially unpunctual land.

> The first benefit of Benito Mussolini's direction in Italy begins to be felt when one crosses the Italian frontier and hears '*Il treno arriva all'orario* [The train is arriving on time].'
> INFANTA EULALIA OF SPAIN: *Courts and Countries after the War* (1925)

**Malarkey.** This US term for meaningless talk or nonsense is first recorded in the 1920s in J.P. McEvoy's novel *Hollywood Girl*: 'It's a wonder you notice me, I told him. There's a lot of malarky (*sic*), says he' (ch. 7). The origin of the word is uncertain, but Irish *mullachán*, 'large-headed person', hence 'fathead', 'idiot', has been suggested.

**MALAYA.** *See* LOVERS' ACRONYMS.

**Malcolm X.** The name adopted by the African American activist Malcolm Little (1925–65), who in 1952 joined the NATION OF ISLAM, while in prison for burglary, and disowned his original surname as a 'slave name'. Malcolm X rejected the civil rights movement's aim of integration, which he described as cultural suicide, and was suspicious of the cult of personality that he saw growing up around the movement's leader, Martin Luther King (1929–68). He also rejected the movement's emphasis on non-violence, asserting the right of African Americans to defend themselves. However, he broke with the Nation of Islam in the winter of 1963–4 and set up the Organization of Afro-American Unity. He also converted to orthodox Islam, took the name Malik El-Shabazz and initiated a dialogue with Martin Luther King with the aim of creating a broader front in the struggle for equality between the races. On 21 February 1965 he was assassinated at a rally in New York by Nation of Islam loyalists. A film starring Denzel Washington as Malcolm X and directed by Spike Lee was released in 1992.

**Male chauvinist pig.** A man who believes in and actively proclaims the supposed superiority of men over women. The phrase, frequently abbreviated to 'MCP', arose in the US women's liberation movement of the 1970s.

'Pig' has long been established as a derogatory term for a male member of some unpopular group and the police were already known as 'pigs' in the early 19th century. In addition feminists regard such a man as not 'kosher'.

**Male menopause.** A stage in a middle-aged man's life supposedly corresponding to the menopause of a woman. It is generally accompanied by, or even caused by, a loss of potency and typically manifests itself in a crisis of confidence and identity, and occasionally in the purchase of a sports car. The term dates from the late 1940s but is not in strict medical use.

**Malice Aforethought.** A crime novel (1931) by Francis Iles (pen-name of Anthony Berkeley Cox; 1893–1971). It is a forerunner of the psychological murder story. The murderer is named on the first page and the suspense derives from following his thoughts before, during and after the crime and from his ultimate fate. 'Malice aforethought' is criminal law jargon for the determination to perform an unlawful act.

**Mall rat.** A young person who hangs around apparently aimlessly in a shopping centre, giving the impression of being up to no good. The expression originated in the United States, home of the shopping mall, in the early 1980s.

**Maltese Falcon, The.** A thriller (1930) by Dashiell Hammett (1894–1961), an early example of the 'hard-boiled' genre of US detective novels. A complex story of deception and self-deception, it features the PRIVATE EYE Sam Spade. The Maltese falcon is, or purports to be, an ancient artefact in the form of a jewel-encrusted falcon, emanating from Malta. The film of 1941, directed by John Huston as a remake of the 1931 version, was a triumph in every respect. It was Huston's first film as director, and it starred Humphrey Bogart as Sam Spade, Sydney Greenstreet as the politely villainous Gutman and Peter Lorre as his henchman Joel Cairo. A 1936 film version of the story was entitled *Satan Met a Lady*.

**Mama of dada, The.** The US critic Clifton Fadiman's somewhat inaccurate, but nevertheless satisfying, description of the US modernist writer Gertrude Stein (1874–1946), who, though resident in Paris, was not particularly associated with DADAISM. Fadiman coined the phrase in *Party of One* (1955).

**Mambo.** A Latin American dance (and musical form) similar in rhythm to the rumba. It emerged in North America in the 1940s and became a craze of the 1950s, its appeal enhanced by such popular songs as 'Mambo Italiano' and 'Papa Loves Mambo'. A spin-off was the CHA-CHA. Like all such dances

both have enjoyed periods of revival. 'Mambo' itself is a word of Yoruba origin meaning literally 'to talk'.

**Mamelles de Tirésias, Les.** A surrealistic *opéra burlesque* by Francis Poulenc (1899–1963) with texts by the modernist poet Guillaume Apollinaire (1880–1918). It was first performed in 1947. The title means 'the breasts of Tiresias'. The story tells of a couple who each change their sex, the woman getting rid of her breasts while her husband gives birth to 40,000 children. In Greek mythology Tiresias was a Theban man who spent seven years of his life as a woman. Zeus and Hera consulted him to resolve the argument as to whether men or women get more pleasure out of sex. Tiresias declared in favour of women and was struck blind by Hera. Tiresias became a seer and informed Oedipus of his true parentage. Tiresias also makes an appearance in Part 3 of T.S. Eliot's *The* WASTE LAND (1926):

> I Tiresias, though blind, throbbing between two lives,
> Old man with wrinkled female breasts, can see …

**Management buyout.** The purchase of a company by its own managers, usually with financial assistance from a bank or other institution and almost always when the company concerned is experiencing financial difficulties. The term is of US origin and dates from the late 1970s.

**Man and Superman.** A play (1903) by the Irish playwright George Bernard Shaw (1856–1950) in which the author discusses the notion of the Nietzschean SUPERMAN, a superior race who represent the future of mankind. The superman of the title is John Tanner, an intelligent but haughty man who resists, but finally succumbs to, the primacy of women (in Shavian terms, the victory of instinct over intellect).

**Manassa Mauler, The.** The nickname of the US heavyweight boxer Jack Dempsey (1895–1983), who was born in Manassa, Colorado. He was world champion from 1919 to 1926.

**Manchester School.** A collective name for the playwrights who wrote for Annie Horniman's company at the Gaiety Theatre, Manchester, between 1907 and 1921. Chief among them were Stanley Houghton (1881–1913), author of *Hindle Wakes* (1912), and Harold Brighouse (1882–1958), writer of the acclaimed comedy HOBSON'S CHOICE (1916).

A later Manchester School was the group of avant-garde composers who studied at the Royal Manchester College of Music in the 1950s. The leading figures were Harrison Birtwistle, Peter Maxwell Davies, Alexander Goehr and John Ogden.

The original Manchester School was a group of political economists in the earlier 19th century, including John Bright and Richard Cobden, who campaigned for the repeal of the Corn Laws.

**Manchukuo.** A state set up in Manchuria in 1932 by the Japanese, who seized the territory from China in 1931–2 following the MUKDEN INCIDENT. Henry Pu-Yi (1906–67), who had been deposed as the last emperor of China in 1912 while still a child, was made the puppet ruler. A LEAGUE OF NATIONS Commission condemned the Japanese occupation, leading to Japan's withdrawal from the League in 1933. Manchukuo ceased to exist after the Japanese surrender in 1945, and the area came once again under Chinese rule.

**Manchurian candidate.** A term for a person who has been brainwashed by some organization or foreign power and programmed to carry out its orders automatically. The allusion is to Richard Condon's novel *The Manchurian Candidate* (1959) and the memorable film based on it (1962), telling the story of a KOREAN WAR 'hero' (played in the film by Laurence Harvey) who returns as a brainwashed zombie triggered to kill a liberal politician, his 'control' being his ambitious mother. A 2004 remake starred Denzel Washington.

**Mandate.** The authority conferred on certain nations by the LEAGUE OF NATIONS after the First World War to administer the former German colonies and Ottoman Turkish dependencies outside Europe. By the Treaty of Sèvres (August 1920) France received 'Greater Syria' (modern Syria and Lebanon) while Britain gained Palestine, Transjordan (now Jordan) and Iraq. Other mandated territories included German East Africa (to Britain), Togo and Cameroon (partitioned between Britain and France), Southwest Africa (to South Africa), German New Guinea and the Bismarck Islands (to Australia), German Samoa (to New Zealand), the Mariana, Caroline and Marshall Islands (to Japan), and Nauru (to Britain).

**Mandy.** A nickname of Peter Mandelson (b.1953), widely regarded as the *éminence grise* and presentational enforcer of Tony Blair's Labour government, whose election he did much to ensure in 1997. The nickname Mandy (usually a girl's name) alludes to Mandelson's homosexuality, which was revealed to the world at large by a former Tory MP, Matthew Parris, himself gay, during the course of a TV discussion. Subsequently the BBC decreed that no mention of Mandelson's sexuality should be made on its programmes. He is also known as Mandy Pandy, in ironic *hommage* to ANDY PANDY. Other nicknames include the Sultan of Spin (a play on 'SULTANS OF SWING') and PRINCE OF DARKNESS, both on account of his mastery of the 'dark arts' of spin (*see* SPIN DOCTOR). Among Mandelson's government responsibilities

was the completion of the MILLENNIUM DOME in Greenwich, earning him the title of Dome Secretary. Mandelson resigned as secretary of state for trade and industry in 1998 following revelations that he had obtained a loan to purchase a house from fellow minister Geoffrey Robinson, into whose business affairs his department was carrying out an investigation. In 1999 he was back in government as secretary of state for Northern Ireland, but in 2001 he was forced to resign yet again, following allegations of improper interference in the application for a British passport of the Indian billionaire Srichand Hinduja. In 2004 he was appointed as the EU Commissioner for Trade.

**Maneater.** A sexually predatory woman. The analogy is with a man-eating tiger.

***Man For All Seasons, A.*** A play (1960), later a film (1967), by Robert Bolt (1924–95) about the Tudor statesman Sir Thomas More and his opposition to Henry VIII's divorce from Catherine of Aragon. The title was derived by Bolt from a description of More by his contemporary Robert Whittington (*c.*1480–*c.*1530), who wrote:

> More is a man of angel's wit and singular learning; I know not his fellow. For where is the man of that gentleness, lowliness and affability? And as time requireth, a man of marvellous mirth and pastimes; and sometimes of as sad a gravity: as who say: a man for all seasons.
>
> *Vulgaria* (1521)

Whittington in turn borrowed the tag from Erasmus, a friend of More's, who had described More in his preface to *In Praise of Folly* (1509) with the words *omnium horarum hominem* ('a man of all hours'). The construction caught on after the success of Bolt's play and film, and many leading personalities of the day have since been eulogized as 'men (or women) for all seasons'.

**Man from Missouri.** *See* GIVE-'EM-HELL HARRY.

**Man from the ministry.** A tag dating from the 1960s for a government official or bureaucrat, especially of the officious kind. The phrase was adopted from the title of a radio SITCOM, *The Men from the Ministry* (1962–77), about two timorous and incompetent civil servants, played by Richard Murdoch and Deryck Guyler, forever trying to placate their irritable boss, Sir Gregory.

***Man from U.N.C.L.E., The.*** A long-running US TV series (1964–8), conceived of as a spoof of the James Bond films (*see* James BOND), and similarly filled with glamour and hi-tech gadgetry. As if to anticipate DÉTENTE, the American Napoleon Solo (the eponymous 'Man' of the title, played by Robert Vaughn) works with the Russian Illya Kuryakin

(David McCallum). Both are agents of U.N.C.L.E., which stands for 'United Network Command for Law Enforcement', an organization whose job it is to take on the enemies of peace. Chief among these is the sinister T.H.R.U.S.H., an acronym whose true meaning is never revealed, although it is clearly an irritant of some kind. The series had a considerable fan-base among the sub- and proto-teens, blond mop-head David McCallum in particular being the object of girlish adulation akin to that bestowed on The BEATLES.

**Manga.** A Japanese genre of comic book, usually with a SCIENCE FICTION or fantasy theme, and often containing violent or sexually explicit material. Typical titles (in translation) are *Battle Angel Alita*, *Oh My Goddess!* and *You're Under Arrest!* The word literally means 'indiscriminate picture'. *See also* ANIME.

**Manhattan.** A cocktail made from whisky and vermouth, with a dash of Angostura bitters and Curaçao or Maraschino. It is named from Manhattan Island, New York.

**Manhattan Project.** The US government research project of 1942 to 1945 that produced the first atomic bomb, so named because it was undertaken by the Manhattan District of the US Army Corps of Engineers. It was headed by Brigadier General Leslie R. Groves. 'Manhattan Project' subsequently became the code name for similar research work right across the country. The first atomic bomb was exploded at 5.30 a.m. on 16 July 1945 at a site on the Alamogordo air base south of Albuquerque, New Mexico. *See also* ENOLA GAY; HIROSHIMA; I AM BECOME DEATH, THE DESTROYER OF WORLDS.

**Man in black.** A nickname for a football referee, who generally wears black to be distinguished from the shirts of the two teams. Where a team's strip is itself black he will naturally wear a different colour. Referees originally wore a jacket top and PLUS FOURS, but this was replaced by a blazer and shorts, then by a tunic top, which ultimately evolved into the all-black outfit of today.

'The Man in Black' was also the sobriquet of the deep-voiced English actor Valentine Dyall (1908–85), who made something of a speciality of flesh-creeping roles. It came from the persona created for him for the BBC radio series *Appointment with Fear*, first broadcast in 1943, in which he narrated a range of chilling stories. Another performer known as 'The Man in Black' was the American country-music singer Johnny Cash (1932–2003), who was known for his deep voice, dark clothes and brooding manner. *See also* MEN IN BLACK.

**Man in white.** In Australian English, a colloquial term for a (white-clad) referee or umpire in an Australian Rules football match. It is first recorded in 1968.

**Man mountain.** A fat man, who seems mountainous by comparison with most other men.

**Mannerheim Line.** *See* WINTER WAR.

**Manny.** A nickname of Emanuel Shinwell (1884–1986), the astonishingly long-lived and sharp-tongued Labour politician. He started his political career as a militant agitator (in 1919 he was jailed for five months for incitement to riot during a dockers' strike) and ended it as Baron Shinwell of Easington in the House of Lords, where from 1982 he sat with the independents in protest against 'left-wing militancy' in the Labour Party. *See also* CLYDESIDERS.

**Man of the match.** The player adjudged to have played the best in a particular game.

**Man of the moment.** A person who is currently popular or in the news. The phrase is sometimes misused to mean a person who acts spontaneously (on the spur of the moment) or instantly (in the same moment that the need for action is apparent.) The first word may vary according to gender.

> 'Someone told me two seasons ago that I was the girl of the moment,' she [model Gisele Bundchen] says, 'and now I still am.'
>
> *The Times* (2 October 1999)

**Man o' War.** The most famous thoroughbred racehorse in the United States and the greatest horse of the first half of the 20th century was foaled in 1917. In a brief career of only two seasons (1919–20), the chestnut colt, nicknamed 'Big Red', won 20 out of 21 races. His sole loss was to Upset on 13 August 1919 at Saratoga, New York, and occurred only because he was facing the wrong way when the race started. He was retired to stud in 1930 and died in 1947.

**Manson murders.** A series of gruesome murders in California in 1969 that saw the HIPPIE dream turn to nightmare. The murders were perpetrated by a mini-cult called 'The Family', led by Charles Manson (b.1934), an unbalanced ex-convict who encouraged his followers into sexual excess and experimentation with LSD. Their first victims were Leno LaBianca, the millionaire owner of a supermarket chain, and his wife. They then raided the mansion of the film director Roman Polanski in BEVERLY HILLS and in a frenzied attack killed five people, including Polanski's wife, the actress Sharon Tate, who was eight months pregnant. During their subsequent trial the four accused members of the Family claimed that they had been inspired by listening to

The BEATLES song 'HELTER-SKELTER'. Also during the trial President Nixon (*see* TRICKY DICKY) attracted criticism for apparently breaking *sub judice* rules by declaring Manson's guilt prior to the verdict, which turned out to be 'guilty' anyway. The defendants ended up serving indefinite sentences. *See also* ALTAMONT.

**Man the lifeboats.** To prepare to extricate oneself from a difficult situation.

**Man Upstairs.** A euphemism or nickname for God, dating from the 1960s. Its level of mild humour is similar to that of 'the big round shiny thing in the sky' for the sun and similar conceits.

**Man Who Came to Dinner, The.** A film comedy (1941) adapted by Julius and Philip Epstein from a successful stage play by George S. Kaufman (1889–1961) and Moss Hart (1904–61) about an opinionated radio host, called Sheridan Whiteside, who is obliged by injury to outstay his welcome at the home of a suburban family. The original 'man who came to dinner' was the real-life US theatre critic Alexander Woollcott (1887–1943), who was renowned for his eccentric, domineering character. Far from being offended by his portrayal, Woollcott enjoyed the notoriety (he had long pleaded with Hart to be preserved for posterity in one of his plays) and ultimately played the part of Whiteside himself when the play went on tour.

> I'm perfect for the part. I'm the only man you know who can strut sitting down.
>
> ALEXANDER WOOLLCOTT: lobbying Hart for the role of Sheridan Whiteside

**Man Who Mistook His Wife for a Hat, The.** A collection of case studies (1985) by Oliver Sacks (b.1933), a clinical neurologist. The title piece concerns a musician suffering from visual agnosia:

> He reached out his hand, and took hold of his wife's head, tried to lift it off, to put it on. He had apparently mistaken his wife for a hat! His wife looked as if she was used to such things.

**Man Who Never Was, The.** A film (1955) based on the true Second World War story of one of the many disinformation efforts hatched by the Allies prior to D-DAY. The aim was to mislead the Germans into thinking that the 'Second Front' would be opened somewhere other than Normandy. To this end British naval intelligence persuade a grieving father to part with the body of his son, who has died of pneumonia. They give the body the identity of a senior naval officer and jettison it into the sea with false documents off neutral Portugal, where they know the currents will wash it ashore,

and where they are confident that German spies will manage to see the documents. The plan works more or less perfectly, although in a fictional twist at the end a German spy in London almost finds out the truth.

> But I hae dream'd a dreary dream,
> Beyond the Isle of Skye;
> I saw a dead man win a fight,
> And I think that man was I.
>
> ANONYMOUS: 'The Battle of Otterbourne'. These words from the old ballad are spoken at the beginning and end of the film.

**Man Who Was Thursday, The.** A novel (1908), subtitled 'A Nightmare', by G.K. Chesterton (1874–1936). The book, much like Conrad's *The* SECRET AGENT, is much concerned with anarchists, although the tone is lighter. Gabriel Syme is a detective posing as an anarchist poet in order to infiltrate the underground movement of real anarchists. He succeeds in penetrating a shady secret organization, whose various high office holders are known by days of the week; he himself is elected as Thursday. As the plot deepens, events become increasingly bizarre and dreamlike.

**Man Who Would Be King, The.** A film (1975) adapted by its director John Huston and Gladys Hill from a short story by Rudyard Kipling (1865–1936) about two British adventurers who set themselves up as rulers of a remote region of Afghanistan. A pet project of John Huston (he first planned the film in the 1940s, with Clark Gable and Humphrey Bogart in mind), it was eventually filmed with Sean Connery and Michael Caine in the lead roles. The film had to be shot on location in Morocco rather than Afghanistan because of violent unrest in the area.

**Man with No Name.** The mysterious avenger of the American West played by Clint Eastwood in a series of SPAGHETTI WESTERNS, beginning with *A* FISTFUL OF DOLLARS (1964) and continuing with *For a Few Dollars More* (1965) and *The Good, the Bad and the Ugly* (1966). He wears a poncho, smokes a cheroot and says very little. Eastwood played essentially the same character in *Hang 'Em High* (1968) and *High Plains Drifter* (1973). The credits of *A Fistful of Dollars* reveal that the drifter's name is Joe.

**Man with the Golden Arm, The.** A novel (1949) by Nelson Algren (born Nelson Algren Abraham; 1909–81), set in the Polish slums of Chicago. Francis Majcinek (known as Frankie Machine), a dealer in a gambling den, is said to have a 'golden arm', so sure is his handling of playing cards, his cue when playing pool, dice and drumsticks. He is unable, however, to break out of his social environment, and this and his heroin addiction lead to his suicide. A rather muddled film version (1956) was directed by Otto Preminger, with Frank Sinatra in the title role.

**Man you love to hate.** A nickname for any villainous or unpleasant type whom one nevertheless finds attractive or alluring, as in a LOVE-HATE RELATIONSHIP. The description was specifically associated with the Austrian-born US actor Erich von Stroheim (1885–1957) following his appearance in the First World War propaganda film *The Heart of Humanity* (1918), in which he not only attempts to rape the leading lady but casually tosses a baby out of a window.

**Mao suit.** A suit of the type worn by China's communist leader Mao Zedong (1893–1976). He usually appeared in a cotton suit of loose trousers and a straight jacket with a close-fitting, upright collar, a style indistinguishable from the clothing commonly worn in China at the time (1949–76). Mao's name was given to the so-called mandarin collar style taken up in Paris in 1967 and in later years applied to other items, including the distinctive peaked cap. *See also* NEHRU JACKET.

> Out, apparently, are Mao caps, Guevara beards, Maharishi gowns and Zapata moustaches.
>
> *Punch* (24 July 1968)

**Maple White Land.** A fictional volcanic plateau north of the Amazon in Brazil. It is the subject of Arthur Conan Doyle's novel *The* LOST WORLD (1912), as which it is also commonly known, and it is named after its discoverer, an artist and poet from Detroit, Michigan. It was first explored by Professor CHALLENGER, who gave his name to Fort Challenger, now ruined.

**Mapp and Lucia.** The comic novel (1935) by E.F. Benson (1867–1940) in which the scheming Elizabeth Mapp, who first appeared in *Miss Mapp* (1922), and the formidable Emmeline Lucas (Lucia), of *Queen Lucia* (1920) and sequels, come together in Mapp's home town of Tilling. Mapp's home is modelled on Benson's house, previously owned by the novelist Henry James (1843–1916), and Tilling on the town of Rye, Sussex, where the house is. A television series (1985–6) based on the stories had Prunella Scales as the dowdy Mapp and Geraldine McEwan as Lucia.

**Maquis.** The name by which the French Resistance in the Second World War came to be known. *Maquis* is the thick, impenetrable shrubby vegetation found in southern France which formed useful cover for resistance fighters. After the fall of France in 1940 resistance was at first haphazard, but gradually it became more organized, partially through the efforts of the British SOE. The French Resistance became involved in helping Allied airmen to escape, in sheltering Jews and in carrying out acts of sabotage.

Three distinct resistance groups emerged. The supporters of General de Gaulle, who had formed a government-in-exile in London, formed L'Armée Secrète (the Secret Army). The French communists formed the National Liberation Front, whose military wing was called the Francs-Tireurs et Partisans Français (*francs-tireurs* had been the name given to civilian snipers who had resisted the German invasions of 1870 and 1914). A third group, the Organisation de Résistance de l'Armée (ORA, Army Resistance Organization), rallied round General Henri Giraud, who became the leader of the Free French (FFL) in North Africa in 1942, and who was favoured by the United States and Britain over de Gaulle, who was regarded as 'difficult'. The three groups formed the Conseil National de la Résistance (National Council of the Resistance) and declared de Gaulle to be their overall leader in 1943. Early in 1944, with the prospect of an Allied invasion, the groups merged their military resources into the FFI (French Forces of the Interior), which played an important role in disrupting German communications before and during the Normandy landings. The symbol of the French Resistance was the Cross of Lorraine, the two-barred cross that was the emblem of Joan of Arc. Such crosses mark memorials to the Resistance all over France. Winston Churchill, who had a difficult relationship with de Gaulle, is said to have quipped: 'The Cross of Lorraine is the heaviest cross I have had to bear.' He later denied having said it, but said he wished he had.

**Maradona of the Carpathians.** The Romanian footballer Gheorghe Hagi (b.1965), a talented midfield player of the 1980s and 1990s and a hero in both his country and Turkey. The flawed but brilliant Argentinian Diego Maradona (b.1960) was probably the best player of the 1980s (*see* HAND OF GOD), while the Carpathians are a Central European mountain system that form a semicircle through Slovakia, Poland, Ukraine, Moldova and Romania.

**Marchioness disaster.** A fatal accident on the River Thames in London on 20 August 1989 involving a pleasure boat, the *Marchioness*. On the night in question the boat had been hired for a birthday party by a young City businessman. In the early hours of the morning a Thames dredger, the *Bowbelle*, collided with the *Marchioness*, which rapidly sank, resulting in the deaths of 51 people.

**March on Rome.** The means by which Mussolini (the DUCE) came to power in Italy. With many in Italy disappointed by the country's meagre gains in the First World War and with the middle classes fearful of a communist revolution, Mussolini's fascists received increasing support. In the summer of 1922 a general strike was threatened, and

Mussolini declared that either the government should stop it or the fascists would. On 24 October 1922, with the country on the verge of civil war, Mussolini ordered his BLACKSHIRTS to take control of various key localities throughout Italy and to converge on the capital. On 28 October the government declared Rome to be under siege, but King Victor Emmanuel III refused to sign the order that would have obliged the army to resist the fascists. The king's motives have been the subject of debate and controversy, but on 29 October he invited Mussolini to form a cabinet. Mussolini arrived in Rome from Milan the following day. Although the March on Rome was subsequently portrayed by the fascists as a seizure of power by force, the transition of power was entirely within the constitution, and it was not until 1925 that Mussolini suspended democratic rights and began to establish a dictatorship.

**Marciano, Rocky.** The US heavyweight boxer, born Rocco Francis Marchegiano (1923–69), helped to popularize ROCKY as a nickname for boxers. Marciano served in Britain in the Second World War, and it was during this period that he took up boxing. When he retired from the ring in 1956 he was undefeated and had 49 victories out of 49 bouts to his name, including 43 knockouts. He died in an aircrash. *See also* BROCKTON BOMBER; Rocky GRAZIANO.

**Marconi scandal.** A scandal involving the Liberal politician David Lloyd George that broke in 1913 and almost ended the WELSH WIZARD's career. In April 1912 Lloyd George, then chancellor of the exchequer, together with the attorney general Rufus Isaacs, had purchased shares in the US Marconi company at a price below that available to the public. The deal was made via Isaacs's brother, who was managing director of the company. The British Marconi company, closely connected with the US company, had just received the go-ahead from the British government for the construction of a relay of radio stations throughout the British Empire, and its share price leapt upwards. The affair came before a Commons select committee. Lloyd George and Isaacs denied speculating in 'the Marconi company', which technically referred to the British company, and were cleared of charges of corruption by the Liberal-dominated committee. The prime minister, H.H. Asquith, refused to accept Lloyd George's proffered resignation. *See also* OLD SQUIFFY.

**Mardi Gra.** The code name of Edgar Pearce, a 61-year-old former advertising employee, who for five years from 1994 waged a campaign across London and the Home Counties in an attempt to extort millions of pounds from Barclays Bank and Sainsbury's supermarkets. He planted some 36 explosive devices, injuring six, and took his name because he began his campaign on a Tuesday, alluding to the French *Mardi Gras* or Shrove Tuesday festival. He omitted the final 's' so that the police would recognize the bombs as his work. He was finally arrested in April 1999 moments after withdrawing £700 in cash from a bank machine in southwest London. In some respects he was a paler version of the American UNABOMBER.

**Margaret's Shoulder.** *See* WAR OF MARGARET'S SHOULDER.

**Marianne.** The female figure who symbolizes the French republic. She first appeared in 1792 during the French Revolution, the name then being that of a secret republican society formed to overturn the Second Empire (1852–70). The name was at first derisory but soon lost its pejorative sense. The lightly clothed figure wears a Phrygian cap, a symbol of liberty at the time of the Revolution, and appears on French coins and stamps. Her bust similarly has a place in every French town hall. The models for the figure were at first anonymous, but in 1969 the authorities decided that Marianne would henceforth be based on the film star Brigitte Bardot (b.1934). Her successor in this role in 1984 was another actress, Catherine Deneuve (b.1943), and she has been followed by, among others, the actress Isabelle Adjani, the singer Mireille Mathieu, the model Laetitia Casta and the chat-show hostess Evelyne Thomas. Marianne's transatlantic counterpart exists in the figure of the Statue of Liberty at the entrance to New York Harbour, dedicated in 1886. It was the work of the French sculptor Frédéric-Auguste Bartholdi, and commemorates the friendship of the peoples of the United States and France.

The reason for the choice of this particular name is uncertain. It may have been intended to honour the Spanish Jesuit historian Juan de Mariana (1532–1624), a campaigner for the assassination of tyrant monarchs. Other sources claim it to be a mystical representation of the French words *République démocratique et sociale*. From a religious viewpoint the name can be seen as a twofold tribute to the Virgin Mary and her mother, St Anne.

**Marie Celeste.** To say that a place is 'like the *Marie Celeste*' is to say that it gives the appearance of having been suddenly and inexplicably deserted. The expression dates from the 1930s and refers to the US cargo ship, properly named *Mary Celeste*, that in December 1872 was found mysteriously abandoned with sails set in the North Atlantic.

**Marketese.** The abbreviated names of fruit, flowers and vegetables, used not only on the price labels of market stalls and in the shops of fruiterers, florists, greengrocers, etc, but also on domestic shopping lists. Examples are 'strawbs' for strawberries, 'toms' for tomatoes, 'pots' for potatoes and 'mums' or 'xanths' for chrysanthemums. This last is a linguistic curiosity, since although 'xanth' represents an abbreviated pronunciation, based on the second syllable, the full name means 'golden flower', from the Greek, yet Greek *xanthos* means 'yellow', which is equally appropriate.

**Mark of Zorro, The.** A film (1940) based on 'The Curse of Capistrano' by Johnston McCulley about a masked swordsman who rights wrongs and combats evil in 19th-century Los Angeles. Starring Tyrone Power as ZORRO, this was just one of several cinematic treatments of the same story, others starring the likes of Douglas Fairbanks, Yakima Canutt, Frank Langella, George Hamilton and, in 1998, Antonio Banderas. The 'mark of Zorro' is the slashed Z he habitually slices into his victims.

**Mark 1 eyeball.** The unaided human eye as a means of visual perception (as opposed to a radar screen, telescope, etc.). The expression seems to have originated during the Korean War and taps into the convention of designating the original model of a particular weapon, military vehicle, etc. as 'Mark 1'.

**Marks and Sparks.** A colloquial jingling name for the Marks & Spencer clothes and food stores, current from about the 1940s.

> In their Marks and Sparks' woollies and living in what looks like a remarkably nice housing estate, Topsy and Tim clearly stand in for classless society.
>
> *Sunday Times* (5 April 1964)

**Mark someone's card.** To provide them with information; to tip them off; to put them right. The expression dates from the 1960s and derives from horse racing, in which the 'card' is the programme of events that the punter or tipster will annotate ('mark') to indicate possible winners.

> After *The Mail on Sunday* article [favouring support for an alleged murderer] I orchestrated local coverage and spoke to columnists on national papers. I call it marking people's cards.
>
> MAX CLIFFORD: in *The Times* (17 September 1999)

**Marlboro country.** In colloquial American English, remote, wild country, far from the city. The expression was suggested by the landscapes (redolent of a macho Old West) featured in advertisements for Marlboro cigarettes (the cigarettes in turn got their name from Great Marlborough Street in the West End of London, where their manufacturer had its original headquarters).

**Marlowe, Philip.** The Californian PRIVATE EYE in the stories and novels of Raymond Chandler. He is probably the most famous of all fictional private eyes, an oddly noble figure who moves incorruptibly through the 'mean streets' of the United State's West Coast underworld. He first appears in *The* BIG SLEEP (1939), and continues in FAREWELL, MY LOVELY, (1940), *The High Window* (1942), *The Lady in the Lake* (1943), *The Little Sister* (1949), *The Long Goodbye* (1953) and *Playback* (1959). He has been played by various actors in different films, ranging from Dick Powell in *Murder My Sweet* (1944) to Robert Mitchum in *The Big Sleep* (1977), and in 1984 Powers Boothe portrayed him in the British television series *Marlowe – Private Eye.*

**Marmalize.** To thrash or crush; to defeat decisively. The slang word, first recorded in the 1960s, may be a blend of 'marmalade' and 'pulverize', and although there is no English verb 'to marmalade' the sense of crushing is clear, as in the pseudo-English words of the Wedgwood Teapot to the Chinese Cup in Colette's French libretto for Ravel's opera *L'Enfant et les Sortilèges* (1925): 'I boxe you, I marm'lad' you.' French *marmelade* does not in fact mean marmalade but a mixture of fruits cooked in sugar. The image is even so equally valid.

**Marmite.** The proprietary name for a tangy yeast spread, usually eaten on bread or toast. It is made from brewers' yeast and was first produced in 1902 in the brewery town of Burton-upon-Trent, Staffordshire. Its name is represented pictorially on its label, as the French word for a cooking pot. *See also* VEGEMITE.

**Marple, Miss.** The elderly spinster detective, full name Jane Marple, who is the heroine of a number of crime novels by Agatha Christie (1890–1976), beginning with *Murder at the Vicarage* (1930), in which she is 74 years old. She bases her methods on the belief that 'human nature is much the same everywhere' and regards her village, St Mary Mead, as a microcosm of the world. She has been played by various well-known actresses in film and television versions of the stories, including Margaret Rutherford in the former medium and Joan Hickson and Geraldine McEwan in the latter. *See also* 4.50 FROM PADDINGTON.

**Mars Bar.** The chocolate bar ultimately takes its name from the company set up in 1911 by the US candy maker Frank C. Mars. Its predecessors were the Mar-O-Bar, launched by Mars in 1922 but only tepidly received by the public, and the much more successful Milky Way, first on the market in 1924. Frank's son Forrest Mars (1904–99) was a partner in the business, but in 1932 the two fell out and Forrest, armed with the foreign rights to the Milky Way, moved to Europe, at first working for Nestlé in Switzerland. He then moved to England, where he started his own confectionery business in Slough and, in 1933, launched his father's product as the Mars Bar. Towards the end of the 20th century the semi-mythical deep-fried Mars Bar (coated, like fried fish, in batter and, aficionados insist, fried in beef fat) achieved a cult-like status as representative of the depraved diet of the Scots.

**Marshall Plan.** The popular name for the European Recovery Programme sponsored by US Secretary of State George C. Marshall (1880–1959), to bring economic aid to stricken Europe after the Second World War. It was inaugurated in June 1947. Most states, apart from the Soviet Union and its satellites, participated. Britain ceased to receive Marshall Aid in 1950. The name has subsequently been applied allusively to any scheme in which countries group together to aid a stricken state. *See also* LEND-LEASE.

> The idea of a new Marshall Plan as part of the peace deal with Serbia [after its confrontation with ethnic Albanians in Kosovo in 1999] is music to the ear of Balkan countries.
>
> *The World Today* (July 1999)

**Marteau sans maître, Le.** The musical gauntlet thrown down by the one-time *enfant terrible* of the musical avant-garde, Pierre Boulez (b.1925). The work was first performed in 1955 and established Boulez's reputation as a fiercely cerebral modernist. The title means 'the hammer without a master'. Scored for contralto and instruments, Boulez's piece is a setting of René Char's surrealist poems of the same title (1934). One critic described the work as 'Webern sounding like Debussy'.

**Martha Stewart syndrome.** A wry name for a housewife's state of awareness that her household falls short of the standard exemplified by the US millionaire homemaker Martha Stewart (b.1941). The latter's very name suggests her perfection in this respect, Martha being the eager and attentive biblical hostess who was 'cumbered about with much serving' (Luke 10:38) and Stewart meaning 'steward'.

> I still have a month to worry about Christmas decorations, but Olive's festive display has brought on an attack of Martha Stewart syndrome.
>
> *The Times* (26 November 1999)

Stewart's reputation was tarnished (although not, apparently, among her most diehard fans) when in 2004 she was jailed for five months for lying to an investigation into suspect share dealings.

**Martial arts.** The ancient Japanese sports of judo and ju-jitsu as forms of unarmed combat have been familiar in the West since the 19th century. More recently other martial arts have been added to the Western armoury, and include the following:

*aikido* (Japanese, 'way of adapting the spirit'): uses locks, holds and throws

*hapkido* (Korean, 'art of coordinated power'): uses locks, throws and high kicks

*karate* (Japanese, 'empty hand'): uses hands and feet to deliver and block blows

*kendo* (Japanese, 'way of the sword'): a form of fencing with two-handed bamboo swords

*kung fu* (Chinese, 'master of merit'): similar to *karate*

*ninjutsu* (Japanese, 'art of stealth'): a method of espionage using stealth and camouflage

*qigong* (Chinese, 'energy exercise'): *see* FALUN GONG

*tae kwon do* (Korean, 'art of hand and foot fighting'): similar to *karate*

*t'ai chi ch'uan* (Chinese, 'great ultimate boxing'): uses very slow controlled movements

**Martian poetry.** A term introduced by the poet James Fenton (b.1949) for a mode of writing that uses strikingly original metaphors and similes produced by transposing visual information. The style sprang from the publication in 1979 of Craig Raine's poem 'A Martian sends a Postcard Home', its title serving as key example of the idiom and giving the name of the genre itself. The matching of an image and its origin can involve the reader in a task as complex as the solving of a crossword puzzle, as in the following from this same poem:

> In homes, a haunted apparatus sleeps,
> that snores when you pick it up.
> If the ghost cries, they carry it
> to their lips and soothe it to sleep
> with sounds. And yet, they wake it up
> deliberately, but tickling it with a finger.

**Martini shot.** In film production, a nickname for the last shot of the day, after which one goes home and has a Martini. *See also* ABBY SINGER SHOT.

**Marvel.** An adventure paper for boys published from 1893 until 1922. It included the adventures of the fictional detective Sexton BLAKE'S 7. It is not to be confused with Marvel Comics, the US publishers of SPIDERMAN, The INCREDIBLE HULK, CAPTAIN AMERICA, etc., which was founded in 1939.

**Marvel, Captain.** *See* CAPTAIN MARVEL.

**Marx Brothers.** The four brothers who formed one of the finest comic teams in the history of the cinema: Leonard Marx, known as Chico (1886–1961), Adolph Marx, otherwise Harpo (1888–1964), Julius Marx, familiar as Groucho

(1890–1977), and Herbert Marx, otherwise Zeppo (1901–79), who left the act in due course. A fifth brother, Milton Marx, known as Gummo (1897–1977), left the team early. Their names mostly grew out of their characters: Chico was always chasing the 'chicks', Harpo played the harp, Groucho had a GROUCH BAG, Zeppo was born about the time the first ZEPPELIN was built and Gummo had holes in his shoes so wore gum shoes over them. The least madcap and most human of the four was Groucho, memorable for his wisecracks. Their first film was *The Cocoanuts* (1929); their best perhaps *A* NIGHT AT THE OPERA (1935). *See also* ANIMAL CRACKERS; DUCK SOUP; HORSEFEATHERS; *A* NIGHT IN CASABLANCA.

**Mary Poppins.** *See* Mary POPPINS.

**MASH.** A US acronym for a mobile army surgical hospital, the word gruesomely evoking some of the casualties treated. The term became familiar to the British from the television comedy series *M\*A\*S\*H* (1973–84) centring on events in such a hospital. It was essentially a dark, anti-war satire developed from Robert Altman's award-winning film of the same name (1970) about the weary surgeons and staff of the 4077th mobile hospital during the Korean War. This was itself based on a book by Richard Hooker, who disowned the televised version because of its liberalism.

**Mason, Perry.** The investigating lawyer in a series of 89 crime novels by Erle Stanley Gardner, starting with *The Case of the Velvet Claws* (1933). Much of the action takes place in the courtroom, and Mason is assisted in his work by his legman Paul Drake and secretary Della Street. A Perry Mason series was broadcast on US radio from 1943 to 1955 and he successfully transferred to television, where from 1957 to 1966 (1961 to 1967 in Britain) he was played by the Canadian actor Raymond Burr, who later portrayed IRONSIDE.

**Masquerade.** A bestselling children's picture book (1979) by the British illustrator Kit Williams (b.1946). *Masquerade* is a treasure-hunt, the pictures in the book being clues to the discovery of a golden hare made and actually buried by the author himself. The mystery was solved (by an unnamed reader) and the hare dug up in 1982.

**Massage parlour.** Strictly, commercial premises providing massage. Since many such establishments also offered various types of sexual services, the term was tacitly understood from the first as a euphemism for a brothel. The name dates from the early years of the 20th century.

**Mass hysteria.** In July 1982 at an annual jazz festival at Hollinwell, Nottinghamshire, there was a sudden unexplained outbreak of nausea, vomiting, stomach pains,

burning eyes and a metallic taste in the mouth among children. Food poisoning was ruled out as there had been no communal meal. Crop-spraying was considered as a cause, but there had been none. The only explanation was mass hysteria, a manifestation of psychologically produced symptoms that passes from person to person. It usually occurs in large groups of young women in an emotionally charged atmosphere, and in this case arose in a parade of young females marching and blowing musical instruments with a risk of hyperventilation. Some 500 people were treated either at the site or in hospital and several victims were still unconscious two hours after the onset of the attack.

**Massive.** Black teenage slang dating from the 1980s for a group of people who share social interests such as music. The word is usually prefixed by a name that geographically identifies the group or by that of the cult object, such as a dance or pop group. *See also* ALI G.

> What will the Steps massive think in the playground?
>
> *heat* (16 December 1999–5 January 2000)

**Mass-Observation.** A British tradename for a system of obtaining information as to popular opinion, similar to the GALLUP POLL. It grew out of a voluntary organization started by Tom Harrison, Charles Madge and Humphry Jennings in 1937 and continued into the 1950s. The enterprise was revived in 1981 under the auspices of the University of Sussex.

**Master, The.** A sobriquet applied to a number of men regarded as magisterially pre-eminent in their field, notably the English dramatist, actor and singer Noël Coward (1899–1973), the US film director D.W. Griffith (1875–1948), the English writer Somerset Maugham (1874–1965) and the English batsman Jack Hobbs (1882–1963):

> The Master: records prove the title good:
> Yet figures fail you, for they cannot say
> How many men whose names you never knew
> Are proud to tell their sons they saw you play.
>
> JOHN ARLOTT: 'To John Berry Hobbs on his Seventieth Birthday' (16 December 1952)

More sinisterly, the renegade, evil-doing Time Lord opposed to fellow Time Lord DOCTOR WHO was also called 'the Master'.

**Master and Margarita, The.** (Russian title: *Master i Margarita*.) A novel by Mikhail Bulgakov (1891–1940), combining dark humour, satire, fantasy and philosophy. It was completed in 1938, but not published in Russia until 1966–7 (in serial form); the English edition was published in

1967. In the 1930s the Devil visits Moscow, and, with the aid of a naked girl and a gun-toting, cigar-smoking man-sized cat, spreads chaos and mayhem, showing up the moral inadequacies of Soviet society. Standing apart from all this is the Master, a novelist of great integrity, and his beloved, Margarita. He is writing a book about the appearance of Jesus before Pontius Pilate in Jerusalem, long sections of which are included by Bulgakov. The book is prefaced by a quotation from Goethe's *Faust*. A TV mini-series based on the book had Russian viewers gripped in 2005–6. It was regarded as the most faithful of various film and TV adaptations over the years.

**Master bedroom.** An estate agent's name for the main bedroom in a house, usually containing a double bed. The implication is that the master of the house sleeps here with his mistress. The term dates from the 1920s.

**Master blaster.** A term with a multiplicity of disparate applications: in the US Army, it denotes the recipient of a Master Parachutist Badge; for drug users it means a large quantity of freebase cocaine; and cricket-followers are familiar with it as a nickname of the Somerset and West Indies batsman Sir Vivian Richards (b.1952), noted for the savage power of his hitting.

***Mastermind.*** A BBC television quiz for individual contestants who sit on a spotlit black chair and answer two rounds of questions, the first on a specialized subject of their own choice, the second on general knowledge. It ran initially from 1972 to 1997 and always had the same question-master, Icelandic-born Magnus Magnusson (b.1929). His routine formula when caught in mid-question by the timeout buzzer, 'I've started, so I'll finish', became a familiar catchphrase. The programme was revived in 2003 with the journalist John Humphrys (b.1943) asking the questions. Since contestants are required to regurgitate facts and figures rather than respond with original reasoning, it has been suggested that a more appropriate title might be *Master Memory*.

**Master of the universe.** In late 20th-century US business jargon, a pre-eminently successful person, a high achiever. The usage was coined by Tom Wolfe in his novel *Bonfire of the Vanities* (1987). He got the idea for it from Masters of the Universe, the trade name of a series of US superhero dolls.

**Mata Hari.** The assumed name of the Dutch dancer and courtesan Margaretha Gertruida MacLeod, née Zelle (1876–1917), from a Malay expression for the sun, meaning 'eye of the day'. She was shot by the French on charges of spying for the Germans in the First World War, although precise details of her espionage activities remain rather obscure. Her own story was that she had agreed to act as a French spy in occupied Belgium without telling the French intelligence authorities of her agreement with the Germans. Her physical allure and glamorous role meant that her stage name was afterwards used for any seductive female spy. She first danced in Paris in 1905, billed as the 'Hindu dancer', in the library of the Musée Guimet, a repository of Asiatic art refitted as an Indian temple for the occasion. Parisians later recalled that they had never seen anything like it.

**Matchstick men.** Simple human figures drawn with short, thin, straight lines, like matchsticks. Such figures are associated with the works of the painter L.S. Lowry (1887–1976), to whom the pop duo Brian and Michael dedicated their Number 1 hit 'Matchstalk Men (*sic*) and Matchstalk Cats and Dogs' (1978).

**Matinée idol.** A handsome actor of the type supposed to be attractive to women attending a matinée performance. The term dates from the turn of the 20th century, and soon became associated with the cinema as well as the stage. It can also be used, usually ironically, of any theatrically handsome man.

**Matryoshka.** *See* RUSSIAN DOLL.

**Matthew effect.** A term introduced in 1968 by the US sociologist Robert K. Merton for the tendency whereby more is given to those who already have, and in particular whereby established individuals and institutions receive continued or even excessive recognition to the detriment of their less well-established counterparts. The allusion is to the words in St Matthew's Gospel: 'Unto every one that hath shall be given, and he shall have abundance; but from him that hath not shall be taken away even that which he hath' (25:29).

**Mau Mau.** This African secret society, originating among the Kikuyu, came to the fore in the 1950s when it used violence and terror in the cause of expelling European settlers and ending British rule in Kenya. In 1952 Jomo Kenyatta (*c*.1891–1978), Kenya's future president, was sentenced to life imprisonment for leading the Mau Mau and by 1957 the movement had been crushed by the British. Kenyatta was released in 1961 and Kenya gained independence two years later. The origin of the name is uncertain.

**Mauve Decade.** A now little heard or used nickname for the 1890s, deriving from Thomas Beer's 1926 book of the same title, in which he views it as a peaceful and prosperous but decadent decade. Mauve, like purple, suggests idle self-indulgence. *See also* NAUGHTY NINETIES.

**Max Factor.** The cosmetics of this name owe their origin to the Polish-born entrepreneur Max Faktor (*c.*1872–1938), who after four years in the Russian army opened a small shop in Ryazan, near Moscow, making and selling his own creams, fragrances and wigs. In 1904 he and his family emigrated to New York, where he adjusted his name to Factor and opened a barber's shop. In 1909 he founded Max Factor and Company, producing his own line of theatre make-up products, and his cosmetics empire grew from there, much of its wealth coming from his work for HOLLYWOOD.

**Maximum John.** A nickname for the US federal judge John J. Sirica (1904–92), famous from his participation in the WATERGATE prosecutions of the 1970s. The allusion was to his reputation for awarding the stiffest penalties.

**'Maxwell's Silver Hammer'.** A blackly comic BEATLES song about a homicidal maniac, credited to John Lennon and Paul McCartney (but mostly by McCartney) and appearing on the album ABBEY ROAD, released in September 1969. The song includes a reference to 'pataphysical science', the latter being a 'science of imaginary solutions' devised by the French writer Alfred Jarry (1873–1907), author of the grotesque avant-garde drama *Ubu Roi* (1896).

**Maze, The.** A former prison in County Armagh, near Lisburn. It was originally an RAF base called Long Kesh, a name still used by Republicans (often abbreviated to the Kesh). During the TROUBLES it was turned into a prison camp, following the introduction on 9 August 1971 of internment without trial in Northern Ireland, and many suspected of political violence were held in NISSEN HUTS here, 'behind the wire'.

> Armoured cars and tanks and guns
> Came to take away our sons
> But every man will stand behind
> The men behind the wire.
>
> PADDY MCGUIGAN: chorus from the song 'The Men Behind the Wire'

The huts were subsequently replaced by new accommodation, the famous H-blocks (named from their H-shaped layout), surrounded by zones known as 'inertias' and 'steriles'.

Although internment without trial was abandoned, the Maze still held paramilitary prisoners (of both persuasions) who maintained that their actions had been politically motivated. In the late 1970s Republican inmates, demanding they be recognized as political prisoners, began a BLANKET PROTEST, in which they refused to wear prison uniform and would wear only blankets.

> So I'll wear no convict's uniform
> Nor meekly serve my time
> That Britain might brand Ireland's fight
> Eight hundred years of crime.
>
> ANON.: chorus from 'The H-Block Song'

Some prisoners went on to mount a DIRTY PROTEST, smearing their cell walls with excrement. In 1981 a number of Republican prisoners embarked on a hunger strike: Bobby Sands (who during his protest was elected as an MP) was the first of ten to die. Although the British government refused to grant political status to the prisoners, the hunger strikes led to a surge in support in the Nationalist community for the IRA and its political wing, Sinn Féin. In 1983 the Maze witnessed the biggest breakout in UK prison history, when 38 IRA inmates hijacked a lorry and smashed their way out; only 19 were recaptured. Subsequently conditions were relaxed and prisoners were housed according to their paramilitary affiliation, different groups controlling different H-Blocks.

After the GOOD FRIDAY AGREEMENT of 1998 those paramilitary prisoners whose groups had agreed to a ceasefire were gradually released and the Maze was closed down in 2000. In 2003 it was proposed to turn the site into a sports stadium, although there has been controversy about this and other proposals, such as that the site be made into a museum of the Troubles. Meanwhile, nature is gradually taking the place back.

**MBE.** *See* MEMBER OF THE ORDER OF THE BRITISH EMPIRE.

**Mean machine.** A sports team of high ability. The term, sometimes extended to 'lean, mean machine', is of US origin and arose in the 1970s. In the mid-1980s it was specifically applied to the Australian men's 4 × 100m freestyle relay swimming team. It is also used of a fast or stylish car. 'Mean' here has its African American sense of attractive or fashionable.

**Means test.** The principle of supplying evidence of need before qualifying for relief from public funds, i.e. a test of one's means. Such a test was introduced by the first of the NATIONAL GOVERNMENTS in 1931 when a person's unemployment benefit was exhausted, and the resulting inquisition was much resented by those concerned. It took note of any earnings by members of the household and all monetary assets, and penalized the provident. The regulations governing public assistance were modified after the Second World War.

**Mean Streets.** A film (1973) written and directed by Martin

Scorsese (b.1942) about the violence of New York's criminal underworld. Starring Robert De Niro and Harvey Keitel, it took its title from a much-quoted line in 'The Simple Art of Murder' (1944) by the US crime thriller writer Raymond Chandler (1888–1959):

> Down these mean streets a man must go who is not himself mean; who is neither tarnished nor afraid.

**Meat and potatoes.** The ordinary but fundamental part or parts of something; the essential ingredients, as: 'These two clauses are the meat and potatoes of the contract.' Meat and potatoes have long been the basic ingredients of a cooked meal, and 'meat' has long been synonymous for the essence or chief part of something.

> Their detractors refer to them as a meat and potatoes band – in other words, doggedly ordinary.
>
> *heat* (18–24 November 1999)

**Mebyon Kernow.** (Cornish, 'Sons of Cornwall'.) A society of Cornish nationalists, established in 1951. Their flag is the emblem of St Piran: a white cross, which symbolizes tin, on a black field, which represents the ground rock from which it is extracted.

**Meccano.** The familiar construction set evolved from a toy kit of perforated metal strips devised by Frank Hornby (1863–1936) for his children at the turn of the 20th century. After failing to interest manufacturers, Hornby set up his own business together with a partner, D.H. Elliott, who provided financial support. The earliest kits were sold under the name of Mechanics Made Easy, but by 1907 the name Meccano had been registered and the business grew rapidly at its Liverpool base. Despite legal wrangles over patents, particularly in the United States, Meccano soon outstripped all competitors to become widely acknowledged as 'The World's Most Famous Toy'. Hornby introduced the clockwork trains named after him in 1920. These were known as gauge '0', but later the smaller gauge '00', or Hornby Dublo, was the one that took the fancy of most fanatics. *See also* DINKY TOYS.

**Med, The.** A nickname for the Mediterranean, dating from the Second World War.

**Medallion man.** A man, or type of man, who wears a neck chain and a large gold medallion, often with his shirt opened by several buttons to reveal this display on an extravagantly hirsute chest. The exhibition is or was intended to signify style, wealth and of course virility. The phenomenon was a macho manifestation of the 1970s and mercifully began to fade from the late 1980s.

> While it is easy to mock him [popular singer Tom Jones] as a

Medallion Man ... his longevity has now brought him 'elder statesman' status.

> *heat* (23–29 September 1999)

**Medical abbreviations.** Doctors in their surgeries and surgeons in their hospitals have evolved a host of abbreviations and acronyms for use in the world of medicine. The following examples typify some of the laconicism and wry humour of the profession. *See also* TIB AND FIB; TLC.

BIBA: brought in by ambulance

BID: brought in dead

DNA: did not attend

DOA: dead on arrival

FLK: funny-looking kid

FOOH: fell on outstretched hand

GOMER: get out of my emergency room

HBD: has been drinking

HPC: history of presenting complaint

I-PSS: international prostate symptoms score (for measuring ease of urination)

LOLNAD: little old lady with no actual disease

NFN: normal for Norwich (a supposedly typical provincial city), or normal for Norfolk (supposedly a county with a lower-than-average IQ, due to inbreeding)

NLM: nice-looking mother (used by paediatricians)

OAP: over-anxious parent

OD'd: took an overdose of a drug (and died)

O-sign: the rounded open mouth of a dead person (pictorial); (*see also* Q-sign *below*)

PAFO: pissed and fell over

PP: plumbum pendulans (sham Latin for 'swinging the lead')

PVN: patient very nervous

Q-sign: the rounded open mouth of a dead person with the tongue lolling out (pictorial)

RICE: rest, ice, compression, elevation (treatment for soft tissue injury, typically in sport)

SIG: stroppy ignorant git

T&E: TIRED AND EMOTIONAL

TEETH: tried everything else, try homeopathy

TUBE: totally unnecessary breast examination (*see also* BOOB TUBE)

UQ: useless quack

**'Medium is the Message, The'.** The playfully paradoxical title of the first chapter of *Understanding Media* (1964) by the Canadian philosopher of communications Marshall

McLuhan (1911–80). His point appears to be that the form of the electronic media (television, computers, etc.) plays a key role in shaping our thought, in that a 'message' is 'the change of scale or pace or pattern' that new technology 'introduces into human affairs'.

**Medjugorje.** On 24 June 1981 four teenage girls and two boys in this Croatian village claimed to have seen a vision of the Virgin Mary. Various apparitions have been reported since then, although the local bishop, Pavao Zanic, dismissed them as a case of 'collective hallucination' and accused the Franciscans of exploiting the situation for self-interest. Medjugorje soon became a popular place of pilgrimage, and in 1986 Pope John Paul II approved travel there for prayer, fasting and conversion.

**Meeja.** A humorous respelling of 'media', meant to represent a colloquial pronunciation of the word, which arose in the 1980s as a term for the print and electronic media seen as a social group.

**Meeter and greeter.** A person employed to greet and deal with customers or clients, as at the entrance to a club or store. A commissionaire at the entrance to a hotel or theatre performs a somewhat similar function but more formally. The term dates from the 1980s.

**Meeting of minds.** An agreement or understanding; a 'seeing eye to eye'. The expression has been current from at least the 1960s.

**Meet one's maker.** To die. One's maker is God. The expression, which dates from the 1930s, is also used frivolously of the destruction of something, as: 'It's time this old toaster met its maker.'

**Megan's Law.** A US law requiring that communities should be notified if a convicted sex offender becomes resident locally. It takes its name from Megan Kanka, a seven-year-old girl raped and murdered in New Jersey in 1994 by a convicted paedophile who had moved into the street where she lived. The principle was subsequently taken up in Britain, where it is more usually known as 'community notification'. The murder in Sussex in 2000 of the eight-year-old Sarah Payne by the paedophile Roy Whiting led to calls for a so-called 'Sarah's Law' in Britain, encompassing many of the same provisions as 'Megan's Law' and also providing for indefinite life sentences for paedophile murderers.

**Me generation.** The young generation of the 1980s and its concomitant creed of THATCHERISM, widely perceived as a period of selfishness and materialistic greed. The expression arose as a broadening of the 'me decade' identified by the US writer Tom Wolfe in the 1970s as an age of narcissism among the young, manifested in a cult of therapy, health clubs and the like, and an almost pathological obsession with self-improvement.

> We are now in the Me Decade – seeing the upward roll of … the third great religious wave in American history … and this one has the mightiest, holiest roll of all, the beat that goes … Me … Me … Me … Me.
>
> TOM WOLFE: *Mauve Gloves and Madmen*, 'The Me Decade and the Third Great Awakening' (1976)

**Meibion Glyndŵr.** (Welsh, 'sons of Glyndŵr'.) A clandestine Welsh nationalist organization, opposed to the loss of Welsh language and culture, that claimed responsibility for waging a campaign of arson against holiday homes owned by English people in Welsh-speaking districts of north and west Wales from 1979 to the mid-1990s. The name of the group refers to the Welsh prince Owain Glendŵr (or, anglicized, Owen Glendower) who in the early 15th century led a nationwide Welsh revolt against the English rule of Henry IV. *See also* MUDIAD AMDDIFFYN CYMRU.

**Mein Kampf.** (German, 'My Struggle'.) The title adopted by Adolf Hitler (1889–1945) for the book embodying his political and racial theories and misreadings of history, which in due course became the NAZI 'bible'. The first part was written when he was in prison after the abortive BEER HALL PUTSCH of 1923. It was published in two parts (1925 and 1927). *See also* HITLERISM.

> *Der breite Masse eines Volkes … fällt einer grossen Lüge leichter zum Opfer als einer kleinen.*
> (The broad mass of a nation … will more easily fall victim to a big lie than to a small one.)
> ADOLF HITLER: *Mein Kampf*, Pt 1, ch. 10 (1925)

After World War II and Hitler's suicide, copyright was declared to rest with the state of Bavaria, and this power has been used to ensure that the book remains officially unpublished and untranslated. There are a few exceptions, for example an English translation that occurred as a result of a pre-war publishing deal and, perhaps surprisingly, a postwar Hebrew edition authorized to enable Jewish historical analysis of the whole NAZI trauma.

**Mekon.** The deadly foe of DAN DARE in the comic strip by Frank Hampson in the EAGLE. The Mekon is a 'Treen' from the planet Venus. He is green-skinned and slitty-eyed, with a small body and a huge head, and generally resembles, perhaps intentionally, a monstrous human foetus. In the late 1970s the Conservative politician Angus Maude (1912–93) was dubbed 'The Mekon' by his junior parliamentary colleagues, from a supposed physical similarity to the creature. Two decades later the nickname was applied to

William Hague (LITTLE WILLIE), leader of the Conservative Party from 1997 to 2001.

**Melancholy.** An atmospheric early 'metaphysical' painting by Giorgio de Chirico (1888–1978). The picture, painted in 1912, features an almost empty classical townscape, in which the lengthened shadows emphasize the perspective. Two silhouetted figures lurk in the background, while in the foreground square is a statue of a reclining Roman lady, leaning her head on her hand.

Both the title and the composition suggest a number of cultural references. The posture of the statue recalls that of the figure in Albrecht Dürer's famous engraving *Melancholia* (1514), while Giorgio Vasari in his *Lives of the Painters* (1568 edition) seems to have voiced a common belief when he claimed that any painter who pays excessive attention to perspective 'becomes solitary, eccentric, melancholy and poor'.

**Meldrew, Victor.** *See* ONE FOOT IN THE GRAVE.

**Melissa virus.** A computer virus, in full W97M/Melissa.A, which caused chaos in a number of company E-MAIL systems in 1999. The name 'Melissa' is said to have been taken by its creator, 30-year-old hacker David L. Smith, from that of a topless dancer in Florida. *See also* WORM.

**Mellow yellow.** In the HIPPIE years of the 1960s and 1970s, dried banana peel, which, according to contemporary rumour, could have a hallucinogenic effect when smoked. The term was introduced by the Scottish singer Donovan, who in 1966 had a hit song of that name.

> They call it mellow yellow,
> Quite rightly.

It is not clear where he got it from, but he may have been aware of the previously existing African American slang term 'mellow yellow', referring to an attractive mixed-race woman. It was subsequently also applied in South Africa to a type of yellow-painted armoured truck used to keep order in the black townships during the apartheid era.

**Melvin.** A forename that for some reason has gained 'nerdish' overtones. Hence its adoption in the 1950s for a studious or stupid person and in the 1980s for a state in which someone's clothing rides up high between their buttocks. It is assumed that anyone called Melvin would be so unaware that he would be happy with this arrangement. 'To give someone a melvin' is thus to tug a person's underwear up suddenly with the aim of jerking them off the ground. The prank originated on US campuses. *See also* NERD.

**Member of the Order of the British Empire.** The lowest of the five classes of the ORDER OF THE BRITISH EMPIRE and similarly awarded for service in a wide range of fields. The BEATLES were invested with the MBE on 26 October 1965, but on 26 November 1969 John Lennon notoriously returned his award to the Queen with the following note:

> Your Majesty, I am returning this in protest against Britain's involvement in the Nigeria-Biafra thing, against our support of America in Vietnam, and against *Cold Turkey* slipping down the charts. With love. John Lennon of Bag.

**Men Are from Mars, Women Are from Venus.** A bestselling self-help book (1992) by the US family therapist Dr John Gray (b.1951) on improving relationships, based on the premise that difficulties arise when men, forgetting they come from a different planet, expect women to think, communicate and react as they do, and vice versa. Dr Gray also has his own website (marsvenus.com), which covers such topics as 'How to Cure the Resentment Flu' and seeks to deal with complaints such as 'My husband invalidates me'.

**Men Behaving Badly.** A television SITCOM written by Simon Nye. It was first shown in 1991 and conceived as a slap in the face to POLITICAL CORRECTNESS in general and to the cult of the NEW MAN in particular, and thus as an encomium to the NEW LAD in all his bawdy glory. The story centres on the antics of Gary Strang, played by Martin Clunes, and Dermot, played by Harry Enfield (later Tony, played by Neil Morrissey), who share a chaotic London flat. They swig beer, talk out their fantasies and try to avoid work by opening another tin or heading off to their private room for the pleasures of *Playboy*. Two 'girls', Deborah, played by Leslie Ash, and Dorothy, played by Caroline Quentin, are embroiled in the goings-on. The episode screened as a 'Christmas special' in 1998 drew criticism for its explicit sexual content.

**Men in Black.** Black-suited, highly secretive government agents in dark glasses whose job it supposedly is to prevent the American public learning the truth about UFOs. The existence of the 'Men in Black' (MIBs for short, also known as 'Men in Grey') has long been asserted by US conspiracy theorists, convinced that their government has for decades covered up numerous sightings of flying saucers, alien abductions and so on. Anyone experiencing one of these varieties of CLOSE ENCOUNTER is likely to be paid a visit by gentlemen in dark suits, who sinisterly arrive in their big black cars and as sinisterly depart. The existence of the 'Men in Black' was given additional credence as far as the more gullible were concerned by their appearance in the long-running, hokum-ridden television series *The* X-FILES. The whole notion is sent up in the hit comedy film *Men in*

*Black* (1997) starring Tommy Lee Jones and Will Smith, whose job it is not only to conceal from the public the presence on earth of a host of ALIENS of all shapes and sizes, from every corner of the cosmos, but also to keep the more mischievous elements among the extraterrestrials in order. The theme song, sung by Will Smith, reached Number 1 in the UK. A sequel, *Men in Black II* (a.k.a. *M.II.B.*), came out in 2002.

> Protecting the Earth form the Scum of the Universe.
>
> Slogan for *Men in Black*

*See also* MAN IN BLACK.

**Menin Gate.** A massive arched war memorial built in 1927 near the Belgian town of Ypres (WIPERS, Flemish *Ieper*), site of three great battles (1914, 1915 and 1917) in the First World War. The third battle of Ypres is also called PASSCHENDAELE. The memorial is covered with the names of 55,000 British soldiers whose bodies were never found and is surrounded by the graves of those who were identified. Running eastwards from Ypres to the town of Menin (Flemish *Menen*) is the Menin Road, scene of some of the heaviest fighting involving British forces on the WESTERN FRONT. To the British it became a symbol of national sacrifice. Its stark, shattered landscape was the subject of a number of paintings by the official war artist Paul Nash (1889–1946), such as *The Menin Road* (1918), now in the Imperial War Museum in London. *See also* THIEPVAL MEMORIAL.

**Men in suits.** High-ranking executives in a business or organization, especially when influential in some way. The term, describing their efficient, conformist dress, is sometimes contracted to 'the suits' or expanded to include 'grey' as the typical 'faceless' colour of a business suit. In South Africa 'men in grey suits' is a propitiatory euphemism for great white sharks (another euphemism is 'tax collectors'). *See also* LORD SUIT.

**Men in white coats.** Psychiatrists or psychiatric workers, who are traditionally regarded as wearing such coats. The phrase is usually found in a light-hearted statement about a person's mental state.

> People who claim that the Earth is flat can expect men in white coats to come and take them away.
>
> *The Times* (1 December 1999)

**Mensa.** The society of this name was founded in Oxford in 1946 by Roland Berrill, a barrister, and Dr Lance Ware, a scientist and lawyer, with the aim of providing a social organization for the mentally gifted. Accordingly membership is restricted to those with an IQ equal to the top 2 per cent of the population. The name seeks to play down any implied elitism by representing the Latin word for 'table', the allusion being to a round table at which all have equal status. The founders may further have meant Latin *mens*, 'mind', to be apprehended as a secondary sense. The society grew rapidly from the 1960s in the United States and in the early 21st century had about 100,000 members worldwide (over 25,000 in the UK).

**Mensheviks.** A Russian word for a minority party (Russian *men'she*, 'less'). The name was applied to the moderate Russian social democrats who opposed the BOLSHEVIKS in the Russian Revolution of 1917.

**Merchant Ivory film.** A so called 'heritage film' that is typically a rich visual dramatization of an Edwardian novel but that replaces its original irony with a lovingly nostalgic re-creation of the past. The name combines those of the Indian producer Ismail Merchant (1936–2005) and the US director James Ivory (b.1928), who became Indian on marriage to the novelist and screenwriter Ruth Prawer Jhabvala (b.1927). The first Merchant Ivory film was *Shakespeare Wallah* (1965). Adaptations of novels include Henry James's *The Bostonians* (1984), E.M. Forster's *A* ROOM WITH A VIEW (1986) and HOWARDS END (1991), and Kazuo Ishiguro's *The Remains of the Day* (1993). *See also* EDWARDIAN ERA.

**Merchants of death.** A phrase often applied by their critics to arms dealers, tobacco companies, etc. It was originally coined in 1934 as the title of a book by H.C. Englebrecht and F.C. Hanighen about arms manufacturers who profited from war. In 2005 Lord Tebbit (*see* CHINGFORD SKINHEAD) warned the (generally Tory-voting) readers of the *Mail on Sunday* against selecting Ken Clarke (*see* BIG BEAST; PIE, PINT AND PANATELLA MAN) as the next leader of the Conservative Party:

> He will be smeared up hill and down dale as a merchant of death because of his long-standing connections with the tobacco industry. And he is just too lazy.

**Merkin.** An archaic term for a female pubic-hair wig which began an unexpected new double career in the 1990s. Exploiting the notion of a wig concealing the truth, it was applied to a man who poses as the husband or lover of a lesbian who wishes to hide her real sexual preference. Exploiting no more than an accidental phonetic resemblance, in the United States it came to be used as a punning replacement for 'American', referring especially to the American English language or to an American person (particularly President George W. Bush, with whom the pronunciation has latterly become associated).

With Rove gone, Bush will likely not be left to deal with the 'Merkin' public without some other mouthpiece in tow.

www.watchblog.com (11 October 2005)

**Mermaid Theatre.** The theatre at Puddle Dock by the Thames developed from that created in 1951 by Sir Bernard Miles and his wife in the garden of their house in St John's Wood. They named it after the historic Mermaid Tavern, famous for its literary connections.

**Merry Pranksters, The.** A group of BEAT GENERATION proto-hippies who gathered around the writer Ken Kesey (*see* ONE FLEW OVER THE CUCKOO'S NEST) and in 1964 set off on the first-ever psychedelic bus on a long journey across the United States, ending up at WOODSTOCK in 1969. On the way they turned many on to marijuana and LSD, inviting the uninitiated to take the 'acid test', to the music of The Grateful Dead (*see* DEADHEADS). Parts of the journey were chronicled by the US journalist Tom Wolfe in his book *The Electric Kool-Aid Acid Test* (1968).

**Merry widow.** An amorous or designing widow. The phrase comes from the English title of Franz Lehár's operetta *Die Lustige Witwe* (1905), in which the widow is Hanna Glawari.

**Mers-el-Kébir.** A former French naval base on the Mediterranean coast of Algeria, near Oran. It was here that much of the French fleet concentrated after the fall of France in June 1940. The British, fearing that the fleet would fall into German hands, sent a powerful naval force to demand that the French fleet surrender or scuttle itself, otherwise the Royal Navy would attack. On 3 July, after hours of unsuccessful negotiations, the British opened fire, sinking one battleship and seriously damaging two others, with the loss of 1147 French sailors. Three days later British aircraft from the *Ark Royal* finished off one of the damaged battleships and strafed the survivors, killing a further 150 men. The controversial engagement seriously damaged Anglo-French relations.

**Mersey.** A river synonymous with Liverpool, and giving its name not only in 1974 to the new county of Merseyside but some ten years earlier to the Mersey beat and the Mersey sound, the English type of rhythm 'n' blues music associated with The BEATLES, and with such groups as Gerry and the Pacemakers (*see* 'FERRY ACROSS THE MERSEY'), The Searchers, and The Swinging Blue Jeans. The river name itself derives from Old English words for 'boundary river'. The Mersey formed the boundary between the counties of Cheshire and Lancashire, and before that between the Anglo-Saxon kingdoms of Mercia and Northumbria. This long historic link was broken overnight when the new county was created. It has in its turn now been deconstructed into five 'unitary authorities' as administrative divisions of local government.

**Merseyside Poets.** *See* LIVERPOOL POETS.

**Merz.** A generic term (tantamount to 'trash') applied by the German Dadaist poet and artist Kurt Schwitters (1887–1948) to his elaborate constructions of bits and pieces he picked up from dustbins and gutters. 'I am a painter and I nail my pictures together', said Schwitters. The term forms part of the title of many of Schwitters' works, for example, *Merzbild Einunddreissig* (1920; 'Merz Picture 31').

**Mess of plottage.** A theatre critic's punning term for a play with a poorly constructed plot. The phrase dates from the 1940s and alludes to the 'mess of pottage' as the price for which the biblical Esau sold his birthright to his brother Jacob (Genesis 25:29–34).

**Metamorphosen.** The mournful and dense piece of music by Richard Strauss (1864–1949) is scored for 23 solo strings. The work was composed in 1945 and first performed in 1946. The title is German for 'metamorphoses', and the piece is inscribed 'In Memoriam'. Strauss's activities during the NAZI era were the subject of controversy: his opera *Friedenstag* (1938) was enjoyed by Hitler and he stayed in Germany throughout the Second World War. On the other hand, Strauss was supportive of his Jewish librettist Stefan Zweig. Many saw *Metamorphosen* as a lament for Hitler (it was even banned in the Netherlands after the war), but most have seen it more sympathetically and accurately as a threnody for the destruction of German culture.

**Meter maid.** A nickname of US origin for a female traffic warden, originating in the 1950s.

> When I caught a glimpse of Rita,
> Filling in a ticket in her little white book.
> In a cap she looked much older,
> And the bag across her shoulder
> Made her look a little like a milit'ry man.
> Lovely Rita, Meter Maid.
>
> JOHN LENNON and PAUL McCARTNEY :'Lovely Rita' (1967)

*See also* 'LOVELY RITA'.

**Method acting.** A technique of acting in which the actor aims to lose himself in the part he is playing and identify completely with the character being played. It is based on the system evolved by Konstantin Stanislavsky, propounded in his *An Actor Prepares* (1926), and first became prominent in the United States in the 1930s. The technique was fostered by such institutions as the Actors' Studio, New

York, especially by Elia Kazan (b.1909) and Lee Strasberg (1901–81), and it became particularly associated with the actors Marlon Brando (b.1924) and Dustin Hoffman (b.1937).

**Metroland.** An early 20th-century term for the region around a metropolis. As a proper name, Metroland is the region northwest of London served by the Metropolitan Railway, lovingly evoked in John Betjeman's poem 'The Metropolitan Railway' (1954) and further explored in his television programme *Metro-land* (1973). The name was adopted by the railway in 1915 as a term for the districts through which it ran, and *Metro-Land* was the title of its guidebook, issued annually from that year to 1932, the last full year of its existence as an independent company. Lady Metroland, née Margot Beste-Chetwynde, is the wife of Lord Metroland, né Sir Humphrey Maltravers, Minister of Transportation, in Evelyn Waugh's DECLINE AND FALL (1928), while in his first novel, *Metroland* (1980), Julian Barnes drew on memories of his suburban childhood.

> Metro-Land is a country with elastic borders which every visitor can draw for himself, as Stevenson drew his map of Treasure Island.
>
> *Metro-Land* (1932)

**Metrosexual.** A heterosexual man whose care for his appearance, dress, etc. is likened to that of a gay man. The term appears to have been coined around 1994 by the journalist and author Mark Simpson.

> The metrosexual – by which I mean narcissistic, sensitive, modern man – is anything but dead. Barring a nuclear winter or a strike by personal fitness trainers, the process of metrosexualisation, which has been under way since the 1980s and which introduced us to the male striptease in advertising (all those Levi's ads) and men's magazines (*GQ, Arena, FHM*), is going to continue. The global economy depends on it.
>
> MARK SIMPSON: *The Times* (31 August 2005)

A more recent synonym (first recorded in 2002) is 'gay-adjacent'.

In *The Future of Men* (2005), one of the co-authors, trend-spotter Marian Salzman, declared, however, that the metrosexual – typified by the likes of Jude Law, Orlando Bloom and David Beckham (*see* POSH AND BECKS) – was giving way to the 'übersexual' ('super-sexual'):

> Übersexuals are confident, masculine and stylish, and committed to uncompromising quality in all areas of life.

According to Salzman, while the metrosexual grooms his hair, the übersexual grooms his mind. Examples of the latter

apparently include Bono, George Clooney, Pierce Brosnan and Bill Clinton (SLICK WILLIE). Not all women bemoan the supposed passing of the metrosexual – as Jenice Armstrong commented in the *Philadelphia Daily News*:

> What woman wants to compete with a man for mirror time?

Those, meanwhile, who resolutely adhere to the traditional model of masculinity have been termed 'retro-sexuals'.

**Metro-Tory.** A term explained by Simon Hoggart in *The Guardian*, 9 October 2004, reporting from that year's Conservative Party Conference, where the expression was apparently in vogue:

> It means all those, hip, happening young Tories who see themselves as the party's future. They often live in Notting Hill (as always, the Conservatives tend to latch on to something just after it's stopped being fashionable), they eat in good restaurants, dress in designer clothes, would never go hunting (does Armani make hunting pink? I think not) but regard it as a useful symbol of liberty and freedom. They look down on older Tories with amused contempt. No wonder those who still wear tweed jackets, Viyella shirts and 'frocks', as opposed to dresses, can't stand them in return.

It was the Metro-Tories – also known as the NOTTING HILL SET, and later as the CAMEROONIANS – who helped to ensure that the young David Cameron (*see* BOY DAVID) took over the party leadership in December 2005.

**Mexican overdrive.** Coasting or freewheeling a motor vehicle downhill to save petrol. An US expression of the 1960s. Mexicans have a generally negative or risible image in the United States. Hence other phrases with the word, such as a 'Mexican breakfast', as a cigarette and a glass of water, or 'Mexican rig', as anything poorly constructed.

**Mexican wave.** A stunt periodically indulged in by spectators at sporting events such as the Olympic Games or a football match. Successive sections of the crowd stand up with their arms raised then sit down with them lowered, causing a rising and falling 'wave' effect. The procedure was repeatedly carried out at the World Cup football competition at Mexico City in 1986, from which the name is derived, but was practised before this by fans of American football. *See also* WALLY.

**MGM.** Metro-Goldwyn-Mayer, the legendary HOLLYWOOD film studio, was founded in 1924 when the struggling companies started by Samuel Goldwyn (1882–1974) and Louis B. Mayer (1885–1957) merged with the theatre chain owned by Marcus Loew (1870–1927), owner also of Metro

Pictures. The new studio promptly released one of the most important films in the history of cinematic realism, Erich von Stroheim's *Greed* (1925), a drama of human degradation. Now a brand, rather than an independent company, MGM was acquired by a consortium led by Sony in 2005. Leo the lion, the studio's trademark, still growls before the opening credits to an MGM film.

**Michelin guide.** The series of guidebooks was launched in 1900 as the French *Guide Michelin*, the first systematic survey of European restaurants. It was published by the Michelin Tyre Company, founded in 1888 by the brothers André (1853–1931) and Édouard (1858–1940) Michelin. There are now editions covering 20 European countries and in 2005 a Michelin guide to New York City was launched. The guides grade restaurants with one, two or three stars, the last being widely regarded as the ultimate accolade of gastronomic excellence (in 2006 there were 59 three-star restaurants, including 26 in France and 3 in the UK – of which two, the Waterside Inn and the Fat Duck, are in the Berkshire village of Bray).

**Michelin man.** A nickname for an obese person, from the rotund figure made of motor tyres so named as an advertising 'mascot' for the Michelin Tyre Company. *See also* MICHELIN GUIDE.

**Michurinism.** A genetic theory, named after the Soviet horticulturist I.V. Michurin (1855–1935), repudiating the laws of Mendel and essentially claiming that acquired characteristics can be inherited. It is alternatively called Lysenkoism, after T.D. Lysenko (1898–1976), the Soviet agriculturist, whose pamphlet *Heredity and its Variability* attempted to discredit orthodox genetics. Its revolutionary character was due more to Marxist wishful thinking than to scientific proof and the acceptability of such teaching to the Soviet government. Lysenkoism replaced orthodox genetics in the USSR in 1948 but after 1952 lost ground. Lysenko was dismissed from his key position in 1965.

**Mickey Finn.** A surreptitiously doctored or drugged drink, used to render someone insensible. The name dates from the 1920s and according to one theory is that of a notorious Chicago saloon-keeper active at the turn of the 20th century.

**Mickey Mouse.** One of the best-known cartoon characters of all time. He is the hero of Walt Disney films and first appeared in the short silent movie *Plane Crazy* (1928), followed soon after the same year by a sound cartoon, *Steamboat Willie*. His main friends are Minnie Mouse and the clumsy dog Pluto. They were joined in the 1930s by another

dog, Goofy, and by Mickey's closest rival in popularity, DONALD DUCK. He is represented 'live' by a costumed human at DISNEYLAND and elsewhere, and has a whole host of toys, games and artefacts bearing his cheery image around the world, including in France where he is known as *Michel Souris*, Germany where he is *Mickey-Maus*, Italy where he is *Topolino* and Japan where he is *Miki Mausu*. The term 'Mickey Mouse' is also used for anything of inferior quality, such as a 'Mickey Mouse radio' or a 'Mickey Mouse business agreement'.

> Fancy being remembered around the world for the invention of a mouse!
> WALT DISNEY: (almost) last words, 1966

When King George V was asked what film he would like to see, he apparently replied:

> Anything except that damn Mouse.

**Mick the Miller.** One of the most successful of all racing greyhounds. He was bred by a parish priest in Ireland and won 15 out of 20 races before going to England in 1929, where he became the first dog to win the Greyhound Derby twice, in 1929 and 1930. In this same golden two-year period he also won 46 of his 61 races in Britain, 19 of them consecutively. His fame resulted in his appearance as the star in the film of his life, *Wild Boy* (1935), and when he died in 1939 his body was embalmed and sent for display to the Natural History Museum in London.

**Microsoft.** *See* COMMERCIAL INVENTIONS; PLAYSTATION.

**Middle-age spread.** A name dating from the 1930s for the paunchiness that can appear in a middle-aged person, especially one leading a sedentary lifestyle. Since the interpretation of 'middle-aged' is variable (*see* CHAMBERSISMS) and 'spread' hardly specific, the term is really a euphemism designed to hide the reality of an undesirable development.

**Middle America.** The central and western states of the United States, which are generally regarded as typifying the 'model' US citizen, with his conservative political views and unadventurous way of life. *See also* FLYOVER ZONE; MIDDLE BRITAIN; MIDDLE ENGLAND.

> Laid out like a sheet of rolled steel on the Great Miami River, a major industrial center plopped down on the placid, undulating farmland of southwestern Ohio, Dayton is about as Middle America as you can get.
> *The Atlantic* (September 1971)

**Middle Britain.** A more broadly representative equivalent of MIDDLE ENGLAND.

> 'Middle Britain' is easy to make fun of, but it constitutes most of the nation, does most of the work, pays most of the

taxes, and mans the organizations … which knit the country together.

*The Times* (21 September 1999)

**Middle-Earth.** The fantasy world that is the setting of J.R.R. Tolkien's trilogy *The* LORD OF THE RINGS (1954–5). It is menaced by SAURON the Great and in the canon the name is said to translate *Endorë* or *Ennor*, meaning 'Mortal Lands'. Middle Earth is also an old Anglo-Saxon name for the world, regarded as situated midway between heaven and hell. The name is a corruption of Old English *middangeard*, from words related to modern 'mid' and 'yard', and as such is directly related to the Midgard of Scandinavian mythology. *See also* GONDOR; HOBBIT; MORDOR; the SHIRE.

**Middle East.** A geographical name dating from the turn of the 20th century for an area approximating to southwestern Asia and northern Africa, extending from the Mediterranean to Pakistan and including the Arabian peninsula. A designation was necessary for this region owing to its increasing importance as a source of oil for Western countries. It is the 'Middle' East because it was originally regarded as lying between the Near East, at a time when that designation applied to the Balkan states of southeastern Europe, and the Far East, or the countries of eastern Asia such as China and Japan. Confusingly, the Middle East and Near East are now synonymous.

> Geographical names are rarely open to dispute at law, though I once waited all day in Court on the chance of being called to make a discouraging statement on the names Near, Middle, and Far East.
>
> M. AUROUSSEAU: *The Rendering of Geographical Names*, ch. 6 (1957)

**Middle eight.** A short section, typically of eight bars, in the middle of a conventionally structured popular song. As such, it is generally of a different character from the rest of the song. The term dates from the 1960s.

**Middle England.** The middle classes in England outside London, regarded as representing a conservative political viewpoint. They are said to be self-reliant in their outlook, hold national values higher than international, dislike change and aspire to self-improvement. It was arguably Middle England that brought NEW LABOUR into power in the 1997 general election. The concept is thus not a geographical one, despite the analogy with MIDDLE AMERICA. *See also* HEART OF ENGLAND; MIDDLE BRITAIN; MONDEO MAN; WORCESTER WOMAN.

> While Middle England is in vogue with politicians, research suggests that the traditional values it is seen as espousing may be under threat.
>
> *Sunday Times* (4 October 1998)

**Middle name.** A personal name following the first name and preceding the surname, as typically found for Americans, where it is often represented by an initial. The middle name of Dwight D. Eisenhower (1890–1956) was thus David. *See also* NMI.

The expression is also used to denote a person's most characteristic quality, as: 'Caution is my middle name.' The quality or attribute may actually serve as a sobriquet in the manner of a middle name, as typically with gangsters. George 'Machine Gun' Kelly (1895–1954) is an example.

**Middle of nowhere.** A remote and isolated place. The expression dates from the early 20th century.

**Middle of the road.** Moderate; not extreme; especially in political views.

> We know what happens to people who stay in the middle of the road. They get run down.
>
> ANEURIN BEVAN: quoted in *The Observer* (6 December 1953)

The phrase also denotes pop and rock music that is neither too anodyne nor too demanding. In this respect the name of the early-1970s UK pop group Middle of the Road is a misnomer, its greatest hit being the saccharine 'Chirpy Chirpy Cheep Cheep' (*see* BUBBLEGUM MUSIC).

**Middlesex Twins.** The nickname of the Middlesex and England batsmen Denis Compton (*see* BRYLCREEM BOY) and Bill Edrich (W.J. Edrich; 1916–86), who enjoyed record-breaking success in the 1947 English season, both men scoring over 3000 runs and often batting together. They gave every sign of enjoying life to the full.

**Midinettes.** Young French female shop assistants, especially in the Paris fashion or millinery business, are so known, from their thronging of the parks and cafés at midday. The word is a blend of *midi*, 'midday' and *dînette*, 'snack'.

> The midinettes are working girls who appear (for their lunch hour) at noon. The place to see them in crowds is in the Jardin de la Trinité, about half-past twelve.
>
> E.I. ROBSON: *A Guide to French Fêtes*, ch. 4 (1930)

**Midlife crisis.** An emotional rather than a physical crisis that can occur in one's late 40s or early 50s, especially among men. Its cause is the realization that life may be passing one by. The psychologist who coined the term in 1965, Elliott Jaques, referred to the typical age of crisis as 35, but this biblical mean hardly matches the popular conception of 'midlife'.

**Midnight, Captain.** *See* CAPTAIN MIDNIGHT.

**Midnight Express.** A film (1978) adapted by Oliver Stone from a book by Billy Hayes and William Hoffer based on

Hayes's experiences in a Turkish prison after he was found guilty of smuggling hashish out of the country. Directed by Alan Parker and starring Brad Davis as Billy Hayes, the film owed its title to prison slang, 'taking the midnight express' meaning simply 'to escape'.

**Midnight feast.** A secret snack eaten late at night by children, usually neither at midnight nor in the ritualized manner of a feast. It was a frequent feature in school stories of the 1930s and later, when it was typically held in a dormitory after lights-out. The thrill was the risk run as much as the unusual hour and the concealed comestibles. It is now often held openly in a child's home when a friend comes to stay, as in a SLEEPOVER.

**Midnight's Children.** A novel (1981) by Salman Rushdie (b.1947; *see* NAUGHTY BUT NICE), which won the BOOKER PRIZE for fiction. The midnight is 15 August 1947, when India became independent. The children are the 581 born at that midnight. The narrator, who is one of them, is, like Rushdie himself, on the borderline between cultures. The book, which has been read as history and as fantasy, encompasses the post-independence of the nation. *See also* FIRST LINES OF NOVELS; MAGIC REALISM.

**Midsummer Marriage, The.** A mystical 'quest' opera by Michael Tippett (1905–98) with a libretto by the composer. The work, which was first performed in 1955, is consciously modelled on Mozart's *The Magic Flute*. The parts of Tamino and Pamina are taken by Mark and Jennifer, who quarrel on their wedding day and are obliged to undergo a series of trials, after which they are reunited. This also has echoes of the lovers' tiffs, transmutations and reconciliations in Shakespeare's *A Midsummer Night's Dream*. Another couple in Tippett's opera, Jack and Bella, take the parts of Mozart's Papageno and Papagena.

**Midwich Cuckoos, The.** A SCIENCE FICTION novel (1957) by John Wyndham (pen-name of John Wyndham Parkes Lucas Beynon Harris; 1903–69). All the women in the English village of Midwich are impregnated at the same time by an astral force, resulting in the births of a breed of children with frightening powers. They are 'cuckoos' in the sense that they are alien, like the chicks that hatch from eggs laid by cuckoos in the nests of other birds. A memorable film version appeared as *Village of the Damned* (1960). A remake (1995) was entirely forgettable.

**MI5.** The British intelligence service responsible for counter-espionage and other internal threats such as terrorism. It was first organized by Captain Vernon Kell (1873–1942) when, in 1909, the Admiralty established the Secret Service Bureau to counter the threat posed by the expanding German fleet. Kell became responsible for counter-espionage within the British Isles, and in 1915 his service was incorporated in the Directorate of Military Intelligence as MI5. The number originally indicated Europe as its area of operations, as distinct from MI1, MI2, MI3 and MI4, which covered the other continents. MI5 played a major role in both world wars and in countering the subsequent communist threat. *See also* MI6.

**MiG.** A type of Russian fighter aircraft first familiar in the Second World War. It takes its name from its designers, Artyom Mikoyan (M) and Mikhail Gurevich (G), with *i* the Russian for 'and'. The wartime MiGs were all propeller-driven, but the MiG–9 of 1946 was a jet. The MiG–15, which first flew in 1947, was the Soviet Union's standard jet fighter of the early Cold War period. Appropriately for a fast plane, Russian *mig* means 'instant', 'moment', while *migom* means 'in a flash'.

**Mighty Wurlitzer.** The majestic electric theatre organ takes its name from its manufacturers, the Rudolf Wurlitzer Company of Cincinnati, Ohio. Rudolf Wurlitzer (1831–1924), a German instrument-maker, went to the United States in 1853 and founded the company that bears his name in 1890. In 1910 it acquired the Hope-Jones Organ Company of Elmira, New York, and moved its operations to North Tonawanda, New York. It was there where the organ originally known as the 'Unit Orchestra' and now familiar as the 'Mighty Wurlitzer' was developed to become, in the 1920s and 1930s, almost as great an attraction in a cinema auditorium as the film on the screen.

**Miguelito.** *See* PORTILLISTAS.

**Mikrokosmos.** A challengingly modernist collection of 153 piano pieces by Béla Bartók (1881–1945), intended as an instructional course in piano technique. The pieces were written between 1926 and 1939. The title is German for 'microcosm', a concept reflected in the titles of some of the pieces, such as 'From the Diary of a Fly'.

**Mildenhall treasure.** In 1944 a hoard of Roman silver tableware was discovered in a field near the remains of a 4th-century Roman building northwest of Mildenhall, Suffolk. It included a great dish showing Bacchus and Hercules, and was presumably buried for safety by the building's occupants during the troubled days of the Anglo-Saxon invasions. It is now in the British Museum.

**Mile a minute.** Very fast or rapidly, as: 'He talks a mile a minute.' The expression dates from the 1950s when British Railways took to advertising trips at this speed, although trains had been travelling at 60mph (97kph) long before this.

The 'mile-a-minute weed' or 'mile-a-minute vine' (*Polygonum perfoliatum*) is a rapidly growing Asian plant with sharp spines and bright blue fruit that has invaded large areas of the eastern United States.

**Mile-high club.** A notional 'club' evolving in the 1970s of those who have coupled sexually while in an aeroplane. The first recorded incident of this type is said to have taken place in 1916, when Lawrence Sperry, an aircraft designer flying a biplane over New York, lost control and crashed, although he and his lover lived to tell the tale. A more recent equivalent is the 'mile-deep club', whose members have followed their example while travelling through the CHANNEL TUNNEL.

**Miles away.** Lost in thought; inattentive. The expression dates from the 1940s and is typically used of a person whose thoughts wander while waiting or with others: 'Sorry, I was miles away.'

**Militant Tendency.** This left-wing grouping, Trotskyite in its policies but aiming to work within the LABOUR PARTY, was formed in the early 1960s as the Revolutionary Socialist League but came to be known by the shorter name, based on that of its newspaper, *Militant*. Considerable damage was done to the image of the Labour Party when evidence emerged in 1980 that Militant had worked to gain control of Labour constituency and regional organizations, as well as trade union branches and trade councils. It was subsequently judged by Labour to be a distinct party, making its adherents ineligible for Labour Party membership. Neil Kinnock, on becoming Labour leader in 1983, undertook the task of rooting out Militant, beginning with the expulsion of five leading members. The peak of Militant's power was its control of Liverpool City Council in the 1980s, with Derek Hatton as deputy council leader. He was expelled from Labour in 1986. *See also* HATTONISTAS; TROT.

**Military-industrial complex.** The mutually beneficial association between the defence establishment and manufacturing industry, especially in the United States. Even President Dwight E. Eisenhower was suspicious of its influence, and in his farewell address to the American people on 17 January 1961, as he left office, he warned:

> [The] conjunction of an immense military establishment and large arms industry is new in the American experience … In the councils of government we must guard against the acquisition of unwarranted influence, whether sought or unsought, by the military-industrial complex. The potential for the disastrous rise of misplaced power exists and will persist.

The idea wasn't entirely original to Eisenhower, as the political scientist Malcolm Moos had a hand in drafting this part of the speech. As Eisenhower's predecessor, Harry S. Truman, observed: 'I'm not sure he understood what he was saying.' Under Eisenhower's successors, John F. Kennedy and Lyndon B. Johnson, the United States committed more and more troops and materiel to the Vietnam War, seemingly fulfilling Eisenhower's (or Moos's) prophecy. *See also* BIGGER BANG FOR YOUR BUCK; WHAT'S GOOD FOR GENERAL MOTORS IS GOOD FOR THE COUNTRY.

**Milk Race.** The popular name of the Tour of Britain, the country's leading long-distance cycle race, so called because originally sponsored by the Milk Marketing Board in 1958. It had actually been launched seven years earlier, on the basis of the TOUR DE FRANCE, with sponsorship from the *Daily Express*. It takes place over 12 days with distances that have varied from 1475km (922 miles) to 2424km (1515 miles). As in its French equivalent, the yellow jersey is awarded to the daily race leader. The red jersey is the 'King of the Mountain' trophy, awarded to the rider who makes the fastest ascent of the hill peaks.

**Milk round.** An expression dating from the 1970s for the annual tour of universities and college made by recruiting staff from large companies. A milk round is normally the milkman's daily delivery of milk, but here the idea is presumably to 'milk' the best talent from the universities or to find the 'cream' of business potential.

**Milk run.** An RAF expression of the Second World War for any sortie flown regularly day after day, or a sortie against an easy target on which inexperienced pilots could be used with impunity. It was as safe and simple as a milkman's early morning round.

**Milk Snatcher.** A nickname given to Margaret Thatcher, the IRON LADY, while she was secretary of state for education and science (1970–4) in Edward Heath's government (*see* GROCER'S DAUGHTER). In this capacity she ended the provision of free milk to schoolchildren, hence the playground rhyme, 'Thatcher, Thatcher, / Milk Snatcher.' *See also* ATTILA THE HEN.

**Millbank Tendency.** A contemptuous nickname coined by adherents of 'Old Labour' for the NEW LABOUR apparatchiks whose tentacles spread over the Labour party from their former headquarters in Millbank Tower. It was based on MILITANT TENDENCY, the name of the Trotskyite group that infiltrated the party in the 1980s. *See also* TRANSPORT HOUSE.

**Millennium.** The arrival of the year 2000 (strictly speaking a bimillennium) fired the imagination of many countries, and special ceremonies were devised to mark the event. In Britain the focus was on the Millennium Experience exhibition by the Thames in London, where the two talking points were the MILLENNIUM DOME and, at the western end of the SOUTH BANK, a huge Millennium Wheel officially called the London Eye. Many events for the millennium weekend itself were held throughout the country, millennial postage stamps were issued, and special grants were made to a whole host of organizations and enterprises. *See also* MILLENNIUM BUG.

**Millennium Bridge.** A name bestowed in honour of the Millennium on three English bridges intended to be opened in the year 2000.

In London it denotes a footbridge over the River Thames, linking Blackfriars with Southwark. Built to the design of Norman Foster, the bridge was opened by Queen Elizabeth II on 10 June 2000, but had to be closed almost immediately when it was discovered that large numbers of people walking across it made it sway alarmingly. After the necessary adjustments had been made it was reopened in 2002. The northern approach to the bridge opens up a new vista of St Paul's Cathedral, and a 180° turn offers an imposing view of Tate Modern (formerly Bankside Power Station).

On Tyneside the Millennium Bridge links Newcastle and Gateshead. It is a tilting span bridge (the world's first), which pivots to allow ships to pass. It is for cyclists and pedestrians only. Its outline is somewhat eye-shaped – whence its local nickname, 'the Blinking Eye'.

The Millennium Bridge in York opened tardily in 2001. It is a foot and cycle bridge over the River Ouse, and its design is described as 'offset suspension'.

**Millennium bug.** The name given to the nightmare that threatened the correct operation of computer systems in the first second after midnight on 31 December 1999, the opening moment of the year 2000 and of the new MILLENNIUM. The problem arose because most computers manufactured before 1993 used only two digits instead of four to represent the year portion of the date. The danger was thus that as the new era dawned, the untreated computer chips would register the year as 1900, not 2000. In consequence the closing years of the 20th century witnessed a sort of MASS HYSTERIA, with companies racing against the clock to debug their 'non-compliant' systems in order to avert widespread chaos. The measures were either successful or unnecessary in the first place, there was little or no disruption to business or inconvenience to the public.

**Millennium Dome.** The showpiece and centrepiece of the

Millennium Experience exhibition in London marking the new MILLENNIUM. It was erected on a tract of previously derelict land on the Greenwich peninsula as the largest structure of its kind ever built and was divided into 14 exhibition zones, each sponsored by a well-known company: Body, Faith, Home Planet, Journey, Talk, Learning, Living Island, Mind, Money, Work, Play, Rest, Self Portrait and Shared Ground. The Dome was opened by Queen Elizabeth II on 31 December 1999. It initially disappointed many visitors, who endured long waits to see poorly explained or even malfunctioning exhibits. It closed on 1 January 2001, having made a heavy financial loss and proved something of an embarrassment to the Conservatives and the New Labour government, who had both supported it. It was widely perceived as a white elephant. In 2003 permission was granted to turn it into a 20,000-seater arena, projected to open in 2007 (it is planned to hold the gymnastic events and the basketball finals there in the 2012 Olympic Games). In 2005 the telecommunications company $O_2$ assumed sponsorship of it and it was officially renamed 'The $O_2$'.

For the so-called Dome Secretary, *see* MANDY.

**Millennium Island.** On 11 August 1997 the Republic of Kiribati, in the southwest Pacific, declared the International Date Line to pass east of Caroline Island, instead of west, at the same time renaming it 'Millennium Island' so that it would be the first place in the world to see in the MILLENNIUM. The uninhabited island gained brief fame in consequence and featured on television around the world.

**Millennium Wheel.** *See* MILLENNIUM.

**Million Man March.** A march on Washington, D.C., on 16 October 1995 by a large number of African American men, organized by the NATION OF ISLAM. The aim was to encourage black participation in elections and in civil society generally, particularly in the voluntary sector and in community action. Various aspects of the march were controversial: the actual numbers taking part; the participation of the Nation of Islam leader Louis Farrakhan, who has been accused of anti-Semitism; the religious flavour of the event; and the absence of black women. However, following the march, there was a sharp increase in voter registration by African American men.

**Mills, Bertram.** *See* BERTRAM MILLS.

**Mills & Boon.** The byname for accessible, affordable romantic fiction had its origin in the publishing partnership in 1908 of Gerald Mills (1877–1928) and Charles Boon (1877–1943). They began with editions of standard popular authors such as P.G. Wodehouse, Jack London and Hugh Walpole. Later, during the depressed 1930s, when more people took to reading as a form of escapism, they decided that the genre to cultivate was romantic fiction. Their combined name is now generic for a GIRL MEETS BOY love story or even a real-life 'love match'. All Mills & Boons are written to a formula, described in a manual for the authors called *Behind the Hearts and Flowers*. See also HARLEQUIN ROMANCES; LUBBOCK'S LAW.

**Mills bomb.** A type of hand grenade used by the British Army for several decades. It was designed in 1915 by William Mills (1856–1932) and entered service in the First World War as Grenade No. 5. Later models (designated Grenade No. 23 and No. 36) could be fired from a rifle. It continued in use until the 1960s. Mills bombs were also popularly referred to as 'pineapples', from their shape.

**Milly-Molly-Mandy.** A character created by the British writer and artist Joyce Lankester Brisley (1896–1978). Milly-Molly-Mandy, a little girl who lives in a cottage with her parents, grandparents, aunt and uncle, first appeared in *Milly-Molly-Mandy Stories* (1928) and many other titles followed.

**Milner's Kindergarten.** A nickname given to a group of young men associated with Sir Alfred Milner (Viscount Milner from 1902) in the period after the BOER WARS. Milner (1854–1925) was the aggressively imperialist British high commissioner in South Africa (1897–1905), who had done much to precipitate the war. His 'Kindergarten', which included the future novelist John Buchan, was involved with him in the task of postwar reconstruction, employing policies aimed at encouraging British immigration and creating a British majority in South Africa. The group went on to become ardent advocates of the British imperial idea.

**Minas Morgul.** A sinister fortress-city in J.R.R. Tolkien's epic *The* LORD OF THE RINGS (1954–5), situated on the borders of MORDOR. Formerly known as Minas Ithil (the Tower of the Moon), it was renamed Minas Morgul (the Tower of Sorcery) after its capture by SAURON, the Dark Lord. *See also* GONDOR.

**Mind-boggling.** Overwhelming; startling. The literal sense of the term, which dates from the 1960s, is 'causing the mind to boggle', i.e. to be alarmed or scared, from a word related to 'bogey'. The catchphrase 'The mind boggles' is used to describe a reaction to anything unusual or unlikely.

> Barry Cryer singing in a West End musical? The mind boggles.
>
> *The Times* (10 September 1999)

**Minder.** An ITV comedy-drama series of 1979–94 about a well-meaning bodyguard or 'minder', Terry McCann, played by Dennis Waterman (later replaced by Gary Webster as Terry's cousin), and his boss, a shady second-hand car dealer, Arthur Daley, played by George Cole. The series began as a thriller but low ratings and critical disfavour caused a reduction in its violence and an increase in its humour, to the benefit of all concerned. Daley popularized the catchphrases HER INDOORS, NICE LITTLE EARNER and the WORLD IS YOUR LOBSTER.

**Mind game.** An act of psychological manipulation calculated to confuse or deceive someone. The term originated in the United States in the early 1970s; it is first recorded (in the plural) as the title of a 1973 song and album by John Lennon.

> Mind games force drivers to slow down ... Now local authorities are to be allowed to use more subtle and psychological tricks to get motorists to take their foot off the accelerator.
>
> *The Observer* (6 November 2005)

**Ming.** A nickname of Australian politician Sir Robert Menzies (1894–1978), Liberal prime minister of Australia (1939–41, 1949–66), the Scottish pronunciation of the name 'Menzies' being 'Mingis'. The evil Emperor Ming was a character in the US space opera FLASH GORDON. Menzies's long tenure of office became known as the Ming dynasty (the original Ming dynasty ruled China from 1368 to 1644). The leader of the UK LIBERAL DEMOCRATS since 2006, Sir Menzies Campbell (b.1941), is also known informally as Ming (and less kindly as MING THE MERCILESS).

**Ming the Merciless.** The name bestowed by the press on Sir Menzies (pronounced 'Mingis') Campbell (b.1941), deputy leader of the Liberal Democrats, in regard to his role in the toppling of his leader, Charles Kennedy (CHAMPAGNE CHARLIE), in January 2006, following the latter's admission of a drink problem. Campbell was elected leader of the party in March 2006. The original Ming the Merciless was the despotic ruler of the Planet Mongo, and the arch-enemy of the strip-cartoon hero FLASH GORDON.

**Mini.** The popular British car was an instant success when launched by the British Motor Corporation in 1959. It cost just under £500, achieved maximum room for its small size by placing its engine sideways under the bonnet, and owed its good road-holding property to its front-wheel drive and independent suspension. It was originally marketed under the Morris and Austin labels, the former marked by straight lines on its radiator grille, the latter by wavy. A speedier version, designed by John Cooper, was available from 1961 as the Mini-Cooper. Forty years on the Mini was still regarded with nostalgic affection and was still seen on the road. In 2000 a new, wholly redesigned Mini was launched by its new owners, BMW.

**Miniature for Sport.** A nickname given to the diminutive Conservative politician Colin (now Lord) Moynihan (b.1955) when he became minister for sport in 1987.

**Minimalism.** A trend in abstract art, and especially sculpture, of the 1960s, involving an emphasis on simple geometric shapes, the use of primary colours and a minimum of meaning, emotion or illusion. In the next decade mini-malism emerged as an avant-garde movement in music, where it is characterized by the repetition of very short phrases that gradually change, producing a hypnotic effect. Leading minimalist sculptors include Carl Andre (b.1935), Donald Judd (1928–94) and Tony Smith (1912–80), while Philip Glass (b.1937), Steve Reich (b.1936) and Terry Riley (b.1935) may be named as major minimalist com-posers. All six are American.

The term is also applied to modernist architecture and design that adheres to the principle of LESS IS MORE.

**Mini-Me.** In the spy-spoof Austin Powers films of Mike Myers, a diminutive character (played by Verne Troyer) who is a one-eighth-sized clone of Dr Evil. He first appeared in *Austin Powers: The Spy Who Shagged Me* (1999). The term 'mini-me' is actually first recorded in 1996, denoting any small-scale version of someone, but it was the Powers films that popularized it. It is now particularly used, especially in American English, for anyone who apes or is viewed as an inferior substitute for another, and also, more benevolently, for a person's child.

> Beware of Fidel's Mini-Me [headline]. Venezuelans have a chance to head off Cuban style repression in today's recall election.
> www.opinionjournal.com (15 August 2004)

**Miniskirt.** The skirt with the daringly high hemline, at its peak reaching heights of up to 9in (23cm) above the knee, was created in 1965 by the Parisian couturier André Courrèges, popularized by British designers such as Mary Quant, and publicized by the model Jean Shrimpton, the SHRIMP. Moral watchdogs condemned the rising hem, which often revealed more than a flash of thigh, as a sign of falling standards, but many young women, and some older ones, saw it as the epitome of the new freedoms, particularly since the advent of the PILL. The maxiskirt, reaching to the ankles, soon followed as if in reaction, and the midiskirt, reaching to midcalf, evolved soon after to balance the two extremes.

**Minister of Fun.** A nickname given to the Conservative politician David Mellor (b.1949) when appointed in 1992 as the first secretary of state for the national heritage, whose portfolio included sport and the arts. It was then revealed that Mellor, an avid football fan, had had an affair with a young actress and had allegedly made love to her wearing a Chelsea strip. Just as Mellor seemed to be riding this scandal, it emerged that he had accepted a holiday from the daughter of a senior figure in the PLO, and he was obliged to resign. Earlier in his career, while a junior Foreign Office minister, he had publicly criticized what he said was Israeli brutality in dealing with the Palestinian INTIFADA. Mellor lost his seat in the 1997 general election, and later described himself as a 'broadcaster and international business adviser'. *See also* MINISTRY OF … .

**Ministry of ….** A nickname for an organization or authority of some kind, its nature indicated by the appropriate word or phrase, such as the Ministry of Silly Walks in the comedy series MONTY PYTHON'S FLYING CIRCUS or the Ministry of Sound nightclub in Southeast London. The formula is based on political titles such as the Ministry of Transport or Ministry of Agriculture. The usage is facetious or decorative rather than satirical.

> The Ministry of Silly Names has been at it again. Corus, the moniker for merged British Steel and Koninklijke Hoo-govens, is not the worst of its ilk. But like most of these rebranding exercises Corus brings the usual, inexplicable, neo-classical pretensions.
> *The Times* (1 October 1999)

**Minor public school.** A somewhat demeaning term dating from the 1930s for an English public school that is not one of the ancient foundations, such as Eton, Harrow, Rugby or Winchester.

**Mint condition.** Perfect condition; new or good as new. The expression derives from philately, in which a stamp in mint condition is one 'retaining all the freshness and perfection with which it was endowed at the time it left the manufacturers' (B.W.H. Poole and Willard O. Wylie, *The Standard Philatelic Dictionary*, 1922). Philatelists in turn adopted the term from numismatists. The phrase was subsequently taken up by used-car salesmen and second-hand dealers, not always with the greatest degree of veracity.

**Mir.** (Russian, 'peace', 'world'.) The core module of the Soviet space station so named was launched on 19 February 1986 and was first occupied a month later by the cosmonauts Leonid Kizim and Vladimir Solovyev, who spent 53 days adjusting equipment and bringing the complex into working order. In March 1987 the module Kvant

('Quantum') 1 was added for work in astrophysics, and Kvant 2 and 3 followed in February and March 1990 respectively. *Mir* was designed to last five years, but it survived until 1999 when it was abandoned after more than 77,000 orbits and 1600 breakdowns, marking the end of a heroic episode in Russian space exploration.

**Miracle in the Gorbals.** A ballet by Arthur Bliss (1891–1975) with choreography by Robert Helpmann (1909–86). The work was first performed in 1944. The Gorbals is an area of Glasgow, to the south of the River Clyde, and was then a notoriously rough slum district, hence the expression a 'Gorbals kiss' for a head butt.

**Miracle Mile.** A nickname applied by the developer A.W. Ross in the 1930s to a stretch of Wilshire Boulevard, Los Angeles, extending about 1.5km (1 mile) from La Brea Avenue to Fairfax Avenue. The aim was to promote the Boulevard's commercial potential.

**Miracle on 34th Street.** A film (1947) adapted by George Seaton from a story by Valentine Davies about the extraordinary events that follow after a kindly old man calling himself 'Kris Kringle' (a play on CHRIST KINGLE) is recruited as Macy's Santa Claus during New York's Christmas rush. The 'miracle' that takes place in the film is the influence this latter-day Santa Claus (played by Edmund Gwenn) has in reminding busy shoppers of the true meaning of Christmas. There was an unnecessary remake in 1994.

**Miramax.** A film company based in New York that has done much to raise the profile of American independent cinema. It was founded in 1979 by brothers Bob and Harvey Weinstein, the name combining the first names of their parents, Miriam and Max. It started off by distributing and marketing a number of critically acclaimed films, among them *The Thin Blue Line* (1988), SEX, LIES, AND VIDEOTAPE (1989), *My Left Foot* (1989), *Reservoir Dogs* (1991) and *The Piano* (1993). In 1989 it began to make its own films, such as the SLASHER MOVIE *Scream* (1996), *The* ENGLISH PATIENT (1996), *Good Will Hunting* (1997), *Sliding Doors* (1998), *Shakespeare in Love* (1999), *Cold Mountain* (2003) and *The Aviator* (2004). The company was bought by Walt Disney in 1993, but the Weinsteins continued to run it until 2005. There was some controversy in 2004 when Disney refused to allow Miramax to distribute Michael Moore's polemical documentary *Fahrenheit 9/11* (*see* FAHRENHEIT 451).

**Miranda Rights.** In US law the rights of an arrested person to have access to legal counsel and to remain silent under questioning. The rights resulted from the four cases of 1966

known collectively as Miranda v. State of Arizona. Ernesto Miranda, a 23-year-old dropout arrested for rape and kidnap, had signed a written confession without being aware of his rights and had not been informed of them by the arresting officers. The US Supreme Court thus ruled that the explicit statement of the rights must become a required part of the arrest procedure.

> You have a right to remain silent, the Constitution requires that I so inform you of this right and you need not talk to me if you do not wish to do so. You do not have to answer any of my questions.
>
> *Miranda Rights* (Clause 1) (1966)

**Misérables, Les.** A musical tragedy (1980) with a score by Claude-Michel Schönberg (b.1944), lyrics by Herbert Kretzmer and libretto by Alain Boublil about the life of Jean Valjean, a former prisoner who rises to become the leader of a revolutionary movement in France. The show was based on Victor Hugo's novel of the same name (1862), the title referring to the oppressed people whom Valjean represents. The show became familiarly known as *Les Miz* as it established itself as one of the West End's longest running entertainments (another nickname, facetiously translating the French and recalling the lugubrious family in the 1950s BBC radio comedy series *Take It From Here*, was *The Glums*).

**Misery from the Manse, The.** A nickname given to Gordon Brown (b.1951), chancellor of the exchequer in Britain's New Labour government since 1997. Brown's father was a minister of the Church of Scotland, making Brown Jnr a 'son of the manse' (manse being the Scottish equivalent of a vicarage or rectory); Brown is not known for his light touch in public, but rather as chancellor gives an impression of dour prudence. *See also* IRON CHANCELLOR; INCREDIBLE SULK.

**Misery Line.** A former nickname for the railway line from Fenchurch Street, London, to Southend, given by commuters for its crowded, dirty and frequently late trains. The Northern Line of the London Underground is still referred to as the Misery Line, as, despite new rolling stock, the line is notorious for delays.

**Misfits, The.** A film (1961) based on a screenplay by US playwright Arthur Miller (1915–2005) about a small group of lonely souls whose lives become intertwined through their mutual sympathy. Starring Clark Gable and Montgomery Clift as drifting rodeo riders and Marilyn MONROE as a recently divorced former stripper, the film entered movie legend if only on the strength of the fact that all three stars died not long after. The title, which clearly reflects upon the main characters, also refers to the 'misfit' horses Gable is often hired to round up, 'misfits' being wild mustangs considered too small to be used for rodeo or ranch work and suitable only as an ingredient in dog food.

**MI6.** The British secret service responsible for overseas activities, especiall espionage and intelligence gathering. It is also known as the Secret Intelligence Service (SIS). In its modern form it dates from 1909 when Captain Mansfield Cumming (1859–1923) was put in charge of overseas intelligence operations. *See also* 'C'; FIFTH MAN; MI5.

**Misper.** Police slang for a missing person. The term was publicized in 1994 following the horrific discovery of the bodies of several young women in Gloucester, killed and buried over a number of years. Concern was expressed that many of the victims had become 'mispers' without their disappearance being registered by family or friends. The word has become familiar by its frequent use in the television drama series *The* BILL and was even the title of a 1997 opera.

**Miss America.** The first beauty pageant of this name was held in Atlantic City, New Jersey, in 1921, mainly as a publicity stunt to extend the tourist season beyond Labor Day (the first Monday in September). There were only eight contestants, representing towns rather than states, and in 1928 the annual event was discontinued, only to be revived in 1935. In 1954 the pageant was first televised, and since then it has known both fame and shame. In 1984 Vanessa Williams, the first African American Miss America, was deprived of her crown when explicit photographs of her appeared in *Penthouse* magazine. *See also* MISS WORLD.

**Miss a trick.** To fail to see an opportunity; to be unaware of a potential advantage. The expression is mostly found in the negative, as: 'He never misses a trick.' The allusion is to a card game such as whist or bridge, in which a trick is a group of cards played in a given round and either won ('taken') or lost ('missed'). The phrase dates from the 1920s.

**Miss Frigidaire.** A media nickname for the US tennis champion Chris Evert (b.1954), given on account of her cool and unsmiling style. The derivation is in the refrigerator so named, itself suggesting 'frigid air'. Hillary Clinton (b.1947), New York senator and wife of former US President Bill Clinton, was dubbed 'Sister Frigidaire' by the media for her cold exterior. *See also* ICE MAIDEN.

**Missionary position.** The usual position for sexual intercourse, in which the woman lies underneath the man. Early missionaries are said to have recommended this position as the 'proper' one to Polynesian people, to whom the practice was unknown. The term dates from the 1960s.

**Mission creep.** A gradual deviation from the original strategic or political aim of an enterprise (originally of a military campaign). The implication of the phrase is that the departure from the plan is deleterious, and may lead to an unwanted long-term commitment. It is first recorded (in American English) in 1991.

> Nothing in the [Congress] resolution allows the United States to use force to protect one militia (be it pro-Karzai or not) from another militia. This appears to be unconstitutional mission creep.
> www.thenation.com (20 February 2002)

**Mission impossible.** Any impossible or seemingly impossible task. The catchphrase was popularized by the title of a US television spy thriller broadcast from 1966 to 1972 (in Britain from 1967 to 1974). Each week's instalment opened with the following words spoken on a tape recorder that self-destructed five seconds later: 'Your mission, Jim, should you decide to accept it … .' Jim was Jim Phelps, played by Peter Graves, head of the elite espionage agency Impossible Missions Force (IMF). A feature film version, *Mission: Impossible*, appeared in 1996, followed by sequels (2 and 3) in 2000 and 2006.

> She said there was no fish on the menu. So Brogan took out a fiver and discreetly approached the porter who said he would look into it. Mission Impossible.
> DERMOT BOLGER (ed.): *Finbar's Hotel*, 'No Pets Please' (1997)

**Mission statement.** A formal summary of the policy and objectives of a business firm, government organization or the like. The expression is of US origin and was first taken up in Britain in the early 1990s. 'Mission' here carries deliberate associations of vocation or even a religious calling, as well as simply denoting an intention. Some mission statements are brief and pithy, while others are rambling and repetitive, such as the following, that of the Football League:

> The role of the Football League is to provide a nationwide membership organization and structure for professional football through which the Football League can facilitate financial success, stability and development of professional football clubs, administer and regulate the professional game and promote the values and contribution of the professional game to our national life.

Towards the end of the 20th century the practice grew of increasing the supposed pithiness of such statements by dispensing with a main verb, leaving only what has been described as a 'disembodied present participle':

> The Metropolitan Police: Working together for a safer London.

**Miss Marple.** *See* Miss MARPLE.

**Miss Smilla's Feeling for Snow.** A novel (1993; in the United States as *Smilla's Sense of Snow*; in Danish as *Frøken Smillas Fornemmelse for Sne*, 1992) by Peter Høeg (b.1957). Part mystery story on land and part adventure thriller at sea, it is told in the first person by a personable Inuit academic whose special study is snow. A film version was released in 1997.

**Miss Thing.** A colloquial term of address to a gay man. Originating in the United States in the 1960s, it is used mainly within the homosexual community, either neutrally or affectionately, or occasionally censoriously, to put down arrogance or uppitiness.

**Miss World.** The annual beauty contest was inaugurated by Eric Morley in 1951 as a British equivalent of the American Miss Universe. It was regularly televised until 1988, when mounting feminist protests resulted in its transfer from Britain to Asia and Latin America. It reverted to London in 1999. A Mr World competition was introduced in 1996. *See also* MISS AMERICA.

**Mister ..., Miss ..., Mrs ...** *See* entries alphabetized by letter under 'Mr', 'Miss', 'Mrs'; *see also* MS.

**Mitty, Walter.** *See* WALTER MITTY.

**Mix and match.** A term for the selection and combination of any different but complementary items, such as clothing or pieces of equipment. A social gathering of supposedly compatible individuals may also be so described.

> At an experimental mix 'n' match do the other day, an Old Etonian friend of mine, when asked where the loos were, replied: 'They don't have any loos here. Only toilets.'
>
> *Sunday Times* (13 June 1999)

**Miz Lillian.** The nickname of the much-respected Lillian Carter (1898–1983), wife of a Georgia peanut warehouser and mother of Jimmy Carter, Democratic president of the United States (1977–81). Her other son, Billy Carter, was a hard-drinking Southern redneck and on-going embarrassment for his brother.

**Miznerisms.** The US dramatist Wilson Mizner (1876–1933) is best remembered for his philosophical maxims, many of which are included in Alva Johnston's *The Legendary Mizners* (1953). The following three are probably the best known: 'Be nice to people on your way up because you'll meet 'em on your way down', 'Treat a whore like a lady and a lady like a whore', and 'If you steal from one author, it's plagiarism; if you steal from many, it's research.'

**Moaning Minnie.** A First World War term for a medium German trench-mortar. The first word alludes to the rising shriek when it was fired; the second was based on the German word for 'mortar', *Minenwerfer* (literally 'mine thrower'). The name was also given in the Second World War to the air-raid warning siren, from its repetitive wail, and it is colloquially applied to any constant moaner or habitual 'whinger' or complainer. The latter became particularly associated with Margaret Thatcher (b.1923), who during her prime ministership was wont to refer to complainers, especially those of a liberal or 'wet' (*see* WETS) cast, as 'Moaning Minnies'.

**Mob, The.** A nickname for the US Mafia, dating from the 1920s.

**Mobile phone.** A type of telephone with access to a cellular radio system, enabling it to be used over a wide area without being physically connected to a network. In the United States and Canada it is more commonly known as a cellphone. A 'cell' is a particular local area covered by a short-range transmitter: calls are automatically switched from one transmitter to the next as the caller enters an adjoining cell. In 1990 only a handful of people owned a mobile phone in Britain, but 16 years later three out of four Britons own one, as do nine out of ten young people. In Germany a mobile phine is a *handy*.

**Mockney.** An affected imitation of Cockney speech or vocabulary, or a person who adopts such speech, often with the aim of winning STREET CRED. The name is a felicitous blend of 'mock' and 'Cockney'.

> Recent television interviews with Princes William and Harry showed that the ... blunt, casual, glottal-stopping strains of 'Mockney' are endemic, even at Highgrove.
>
> www.telegraph.co.uk. (8 October 2005)

**Mock-up.** A phrase originating in the Second World War for a trial model or full-size working model. In the US Air Force a panel mounted with models of aircraft parts and used for instructional purposes was so called.

**Modelizer.** A term of the late 1990s for a man who dates models or SUPERMODELS. It is based on 'womanizer' and arose in New York City bars frequented by models, such as Lot 61 and the Bowery, but caught on more widely when the television series SEX AND THE CITY (1998), starring Sarah Jessica Parker, devoted an entire episode to men who compete to date models. Modelizers are equally active in Britain, especially in clubs such as ANNABEL'S and TRAMP. The phenomenon saw the supermodel shifting her emphasis from the furtherance of her career to the desirable social cachet of public recognition in the company of a rich but relatively unknown 'nice young man'.

**Modern classic.** A modern literary work that is seen or promoted as one that will be come to be regarded as of high or lasting quality. The phrase was popularized by PENGUIN BOOKS' Modern Classics of the 1960s, which complement the Penguin Classics of the 1940s. *See also* FIRST LINES OF NOVELS.

**Modernism.** An umbrella term for the various movements in the arts developing in the 20th century that were characterized by a rejection of traditional subjects, attitudes and techniques. In literature it is associated with the STREAM OF CONSCIOUSNESS style, in music with SERIALISM and in the visual arts with the various movements of non-representational or abstract art (*see* CUBISM; DADAISM; FUTURISM). *See also* POSTMODERNISM.

The term also denotes a movement in the Roman Catholic Church that sought to interpret the ancient teachings of the church with due regard to the current teachings of science, modern philosophy and history. It arose in the late 19th century and was formally condemned by Pope Pius X in 1907 in the encyclical *Pascendi*, which stigmatized it as the 'synthesis of all heresies'.

**Modesty Blaise.** *See* Modesty BLAISE.

**Mods and rockers.** The mods (from 'modern') developed as a teenage cult in London in the early 1960s, initially putting their emphasis on fastidiousness and extravagance in dress and fashion. The rise of CARNABY STREET as their dress centre was a consequence. Mainly devoid of social conscience, they had some association with homosexuality and drugs, and their mode of life reflected what many saw as the less desirable results of the AFFLUENT SOCIETY. With the rise of the rival gangs of leather-jacketed rockers (from ROCK 'N' ROLL), akin to the TEDDY BOYS of the 1950s and modelling themselves on the American HELL'S ANGELS, trouble began. Bank holiday clashes between mods and rockers, who arrived in their hordes on scooters and motorcycles, made some seaside resorts, notably Brighton, hazardous places.

**Mogadon Man.** A nickname for the politician Sir Geoffrey Howe, later Baron Howe of Aberavon (b.1926), chancellor of the exchequer (1979–83) and foreign secretary (1983–9), from his measured manner and somnolent appearance. Mogadon is the name of a proprietary soporific, and Anthony Howard, in *The Independent*, 29 July 1989, credited Harold Macmillan as the originator of the phrase. The Labour politician Denis Healey, when criticized by Howe, said it was 'like being savaged by a DEAD SHEEP' (House of Commons, 14 June 1978). Howe held his cabinet posts under Margaret Thatcher, the IRON LADY, with whom he

eventually fell out over Europe. His resignation speech in 1990 criticizing her leadership style led to her downfall.

**Mogwai.** (Cantonese, 'demon', 'monster'.) Any of a race of small furry creatures that appeared in the films *Gremlins* (1984) (written by Chris Columbus) and *Gremlins 2: The New Batch* (1990). If exposed to daylight or water or allowed to eat after midnight they spawn a numerous and distinctly less pleasant brood of malevolent scaly GREMLINS.

**Mohican.** A style of haircut current from the early 1980s in which the head is shaved except for a brush-like strip of hair over the top of the head to the back of the neck. It derives its name from its supposed resemblance to that worn by the Mohican Indians.

**Mole, Adrian.** The intellectually ambitious schoolboy in Sue Townsend's humorous novel *The Secret Diary of Adrian Mole Aged 13¾* (1982) and its sequels *The Growing Pains of Adrian Mole* (1984), *True Confessions of Adrian Albert Mole* (1989), *Adrian Mole from Minor to Major* (1991), *Adrian Mole: The Wilderness Years* (1993), *Adrian Mole: The Cappuccino Years* (1999) and *Adrian Mole and the Weapons of Mass Destruction* (2004; *see also* WEAPONS OF MASS DESTRUCTION). In the first of these he is faced with a precarious family life and beset by various emotional problems and fantasies, the latter mainly involving the beautiful Pandora Braithwaite (who by the late 1990s has become a member of the NEW LABOUR government).

**Molesworth, Nigel.** The inky schoolboy who is 'the curse of St Custard's'. He was the creation of the writer Geoffrey Willans and the artist Ronald Searle, and his adventures and misadventures are recounted in *Down with Skool!* (1953), *How To Be Topp* (1954) and other books. One of his distinctive attributes is his quirky, quasi-phonetic spelling in phrases such as 'as any fule kno'.

> Still xmas is a good time with all those presents and good food and i hope it will never die out or at any rate not until i am grown up and hav to pay for it all.
> *How To Be Topp*, ch. 11

**Molotov.** The alias (meaning 'hammer') of the Soviet statesman Vyacheslav Mikhailovich Skryabin (1890–1986), commissar (later minister) for foreign affairs (1939–49). In the Second World War the name became associated with the MOLOTOV BREADBASKET and MOLOTOV COCKTAIL.

**Molotov breadbasket.** A canister of incendiary bombs which, on being launched from a plane, opened and showered the bombs over a wide area. It took its name from V.M. MOLOTOV.

**Molotov cocktail.** A homemade anti-tank bomb, invented and first used by the Finns against the Soviets in 1940 during the WINTER WAR and developed in Britain as one of the weapons of the HOME GUARD. It consisted of a bottle filled with inflammable and glutinous liquid, with a slow match protruding from the top. When thrown at a tank, the bottle burst, then the liquid ignited and spread over the plating of the tank. It was named after the Soviet foreign minister, V.M. MOLOTOV.

**Moment of truth.** The time when a person is put to the test or a decision must be made. The expression translates Spanish *el momento de la verdad*, which refers to the time of the final sword-thrust in a bullfight. The English equivalent is first found in Ernest Hemingway's *Death in the Afternoon* (1932) with reference to the literal meaning:

> The whole end of the bullfight was the final sword thrust, the actual encounter between the man and the animal, what the Spanish call the moment of truth.
>
> ch. 7

**Monday Club.** A club of right-wing Conservatives founded in 1961, so named because they originally met regularly for lunch on a Monday. They chose this day to mourn BLACK MONDAY, the day of Harold Macmillan's WIND OF CHANGE speech, which to them was anathema. They are regarded, or regard themselves, as the proper guardians of true Conservatism.

**Monday morning blues** or **feeling.** Disinclination to start work after the weekend. The perception that one feels unhappier on Mondays than on other days of the week is a myth. It is simply that the day follows directly after the weekend, when one is usually more cheerful and relaxed. *See also* 'I DON'T LIKE MONDAYS'.

**Monday morning quarterback.** A person who criticizes with the benefit of hindsight. The term derives from American football and originated in the 1930s when the game as a SPECTATOR SPORT was mostly watched at weekends. Office discussions of the past weekend's game would take place on Mondays and be dominated by various 'experts' who would revise the quarterback's instructions to his team in such a way as to optimize the results.

**Mondegreen.** A phantom word or phrase that arises from a mishearing or misinterpretation of what was actually said (or sung: the term is often used in the context of the lyrics of a song). The word was introduced in the early 1950s by Sylvia Wright, and is itself an example of the phenomenon it names. Wright describes how on hearing the ballad 'The Bonny Earl of Murray', she misanalysed 'laid him on the green' as 'Lady Mondegreen':

> When I was a child, my mother used to read aloud to me from Percy's *Reliques*, and one of my favourite poems began, as I remember: Ye Highlands and ye Lowlands, Oh, where hae ye been? They hae slain the Earl Amurray, And Lady Mondegreen.
>
> *Harper's Magazine* (November 1954)

**Mondeo Man.** A British sociological and psephological type, named after the Ford Mondeo car (often a company vehicle) favoured by suburban, middle-aged middle-managers, typically with 2.4 young children and a modest detached house in an executive estate. Prior to 1997 they would have voted Tory, but in that year Tony Blair, seeing a 30-something man polishing his Mondeo, decided he was the kind of MIDDLE ENGLAND 'bloke' NEW LABOUR needed to win over. *See also* FORD CORTINA.

**Mondo.** (Italian, 'world'.) A word used as an intensive when coupled with another word, the latter given the Italian-style ending *-o*. Examples are 'mondo weirdo' for something very unusual, 'mondo cheapo' for something impressively cheap. The linguistic quirk arose among US students in the 1960s and specifically derives from the title of the Italian documentary film *Mondo Cane* (1961), literally 'Dog's World', depicting eccentric human behaviour.

**Money shot.** That part of a film, television programme, etc. for the sake of which people are prepared to watch (and hence pay for) the entire thing. The term originally referred to the most taboo-breaking sequence in a pornographic film (typically a man's ejaculation – a female orgasm being somewhat less verifiable).

**Money talks.** A proverb that only found its current form in the 20th century, although the sentiment is much older. For example, in Henry Fielding's *The Miser* (1733) there is: 'Money will say more in one moment than the most eloquent lover can in years.' Earlier than this is the Italian proverb 'The tongue hath no force when gold speaketh.'

> Money doesn't talk, it swears.
>
> BOB DYLAN: 'It's Alright, Ma (I'm Only Bleeding)' (1965)

**Monica.** A female first name tarnished in the latter half of the 20th century from its association with prostitutes and illicit sexual relationships, as notably by Monica Coghlan, a prostitute with whom the Conservative politician Jeffrey Archer was alleged to have been involved in 1986, and by Monica Lewinsky, an American White House employee with whom President Clinton was similarly associated in 1998. The sleazy overtones were increased by the media's regular use of the name in connection with such contexts. *See also* ORAL OFFICE.

**Monkey see, monkey do.** A comment to or about a person who is imitating another's action or whose action might itself be imitated. It is mostly used as a criticism or admonition and arose in the United States in the 1920s, probably from a children's game.

**Monkey shines.** In colloquial American English, mischievous pranks. 'Shines' comes from an earlier use of 'shine', meaning 'brilliant display'.

**Monkey suit.** A uniform or formal suit; a man's evening dress. The allusion is probably to performing monkeys that were dressed or rigged out in such suits.

**Monkey Trial.** The highly publicized trial from 10 to 21 June 1925 of John T. Scopes, a high-school teacher in Dayton, Tennessee, charged with violating state law by teaching the theory of evolution. The nickname alludes to the Darwinians' belief that human beings are related to monkeys. Scopes was convicted and fined $100, but was subsequently acquitted on the technicality that the fine was excessive.

**Monocled Mutineer, The.** The nickname of Private Percy Toplis (c.1897–1920), who deserted from the British Army in 1917 and was alleged to have come out of hiding to join the mutiny at the training camp at Étaples, France, that year. He is said to have passed as an officer wearing a monocle. After the First World War he was pursued by the police for the shooting of two police officers and a taxi driver in Andover, Hampshire, and was shot dead in the Lake District. Despite his long criminal record, he was glorified in a 1986 television drama entitled *The Monocled Mutineer*, in which he was dashingly portrayed by Paul McGann. The play drew official condemnation for its suggestion that British soldiers had been executed for desertion, although this is known to have been the case.

**Monopoly.** The well-known board game, based on the acquisition of real estate, was patented in 1933 as the brainchild of Charles B. Darrow, a US heating equipment engineer from Germantown, Pennsylvania. Its origins, however, date back to the late 19th century, when property games began to become popular, and it in fact bears a close similarity to 'The Landlord's Game', invented by Elizabeth Magie in 1904. Magie had developed her game as a piece of anti-capitalistic propaganda, with the aim of showing how unscrupulous landlords could charge exorbitant rents. It is thus somewhat ironic that Monopoly evolved to become one of the great symbols of capitalism. It sells in over 20 languages around the world and the properties on the board are named after the streets of a city in the appropriate

country. This is usually the capital, so that the British version has London streets, the French those of Paris and so on. The American game has streets in Atlantic City, New Jersey, as there was where the Darrows spent their holidays.

**Monroe, Marilyn.** The US actress who became a symbol of HOLLYWOOD's ruthless exploitation of beauty and youth, born Norma Jean Mortensen in Los Angeles in 1926. She had a disturbed childhood spent for the most part in foster homes as the result of the mental illness suffered by her mother. She was married for the first time at 16, to James Dougherty, partly to prevent her return to an orphanage. They were divorced four years later and that same year, 1946, she had her first screen test, adopting the name Marilyn Monroe. It has been suggested that she became a prostitute to support herself. After several small film parts she starred as a sexy DUMB BLONDE in *How to Marry a Millionaire* and GENTLEMEN PREFER BLONDES (both 1953). Wanting more serious roles, she studied at Lee Strasberg's Actors' Studio, and appeared to critical acclaim in *Bus Stop* (1956) and *The* MISFITS (1961). The latter was her last film, written for her by the playwright Arthur Miller, whom she had married in 1956. She had a close relationship with John F. Kennedy and Robert F. Kennedy (*see* JACK THE ZIPPER; KENNEDY CURSE), and famously sang 'Happy Birthday, Mr President'. She was divorced from Miller in 1961 and the following year died of an overdose of sleeping pills. *See also* CANDLE IN THE WIND; SOME LIKE IT HOT.

> Marilyn Monroe was a legend. In her own lifetime she created a myth of what a poor girl from a deprived background could attain. For the entire world she became a symbol of the eternal feminine.
>
> LEE STRASBERG (at Monroe's funeral): quoted in Ephraim Katz, *The Macmillan International Film Encyclopedia* (1994)

**Monroe effect.** A term for any sudden gust of wind or draught that lifts women's skirts. It derives from the famous publicity photograph of the actress Marilyn MONROE (1926–62) from the film *The* SEVEN-YEAR ITCH (1955), in which she is shown standing on a subway (underground railway) grating just as a train passes underneath, blowing her skirt high in the air.

**Mons, Angels of.** *See* ANGELS OF MONS.

**Monsieur Hulot.** *See* Monsieur HULOT.

**Monsieur Non.** The nickname given to the Conservative politician David Davis (b.1948) when he was Minister for Europe in John Major's government. The name alludes to his Eurosceptical intransigence. In 2005 he ran unsuccessfully for the Tory Party leadership.

**Monster Raving Loony Party.** The best-known British FRINGE PARTY was the brain child of David 'Screaming Lord' Sutch (1940–99), a former pop musician and eccentric stage artist who on a whim in 1963, when the PROFUMO AFFAIR caused a by-election in Stratford-upon-Avon, decided to enter the political fray and set himself up as the National Teenage Party candidate. The one-man band was the germ of the Official Monster Raving Loony Party, Sutch himself being by implication the 'raving loony'. The party regularly met the challenge of subsequent elections, and its absurd policies injected a note of welcome zaniness and levity into the traditionally po-faced proceedings. They included the abolition of all work before lunchtime, the decimalization of time, with 100 minutes to the hour, 10 hours to the day, and 10 days to the week, and the turning upside down of Battersea Power Station to make a snooker table. At first, inevitably, Sutch polled minimal votes, but in the 1990s he did rather better, reaching a peak of 1114 at Rotherham in 1994. Beset by personal problems that few knew about, Sutch took his own life at the age of 58, but his loyal supporters elected a new leader, Alan 'Howling Laud' Hope (assisted, until his death in 2002, by his cat, Cat Mandu, allegedly the real winner of the leadership ballot.

**Monstrous carbuncle.** A phrase famously used by Prince Charles of the proposed ultramodern design by Ahrends, Burton and Koralek for an extension to the National Gallery in London:

> A monstrous carbuncle on the face of a much-loved and elegant friend.
>
> Speech to the Royal Institute of British Architects, 30 May 1984

The design was subsequently scrapped in favour of something more classical by Robert Venturi, and the extension, opened in 1991, is now called the Sainsbury Wing. As in so many other cases, Charles was not being original, but rather borrowing a phrase from his then step-mother-in-law:

> Alas, for our towns and cities. Monstrous carbuncles of concrete have erupted in gentle Georgian Squares.
>
> RAINE, COUNTESS SPENCER: *The Spencers on Spas* (1983)

**Monte Cassino.** *See* GUSTAV LINE.

**Montessori method.** A system of training and educating young children evolved by the Italian educationist Dr Maria Montessori (1870–1952). Based on 'free discipline', and the use of specially devised 'educational apparatus' and 'didactic material', it has exercised considerable influence on work with young children. In 1907 Dr Montessori opened the first *Casa dei Bambini* (Children's House), a school for young children from the San Lorenzo slum district of Rome, and in 1909 she set forth her theories in *Il metodo della pedagogica scientifica* (1909), a work appearing in English translation as *The Montessori Method* (1912).

**Montezuma's revenge.** One of several colourful euphemisms for diarrhoea suffered by visitors to Mexico or abroad in general, in allusion to the Aztec emperor's supposed reprisal after his defeat. Others of similar local reference are Aztec two-step, Cairo crud, Delhi belly, gippy (i.e. Egyptian) tummy, Hong Kong dog and Rangoon runs.

**Montoneros.** A left-wing urban guerrilla group active in Argentina in the 1970s. The group was founded by Juan Perón (1895–1974), populist president of Argentina, before his overthrow and exile in 1955. In 1970 the Montoneros set about eliminating the moderate Perónista union leadership. When Perón returned to power as president in 1973 he condemned the Montoneros, who embarked on a wider campaign of political violence. Under the right-wing military junta that overthrew Perón in 1976 the Montoneros became a target of the 'Dirty War' and many joined the DISAPPEARED. In South American Spanish *montonero* is a generic term for a guerrilla fighter.

**Mont Sainte-Victoire.** The small rocky mountain in Provence became the favourite subject of the painter Paul Cézanne (1839–1906). He started painting it in the 1880s and his last version was completed in 1902. In this late period, the fruits of which were to influence the course of art in the 20th century, Cézanne described how: 'The landscape becomes human, becomes a thinking, living being within me. I become one with my picture ... We merge in an iridescent chaos.' However, he was not always so effusive: on being asked what he was going to paint for his next submission to the Salon he replied, 'A pot of shit.'

**Monty.** The affectionate nickname of the British public's favourite Second World War commander, Field Marshal Bernard Law Montgomery (1887–1976), who was created 1st Viscount Montgomery of Alamein in 1946. He first came to prominence as commander of the 8th Army at the third Battle of ALAMEIN (23 October– 4 November 1942), Britain's first significant victory of the war. After the successful conclusion of the North African campaign, Montgomery went on to serve (somewhat irritably) under General Eisenhower in Operation OVERLORD and the subsequent campaign in northwest Europe. Although Montgomery's relations with other senior commanders (including Eisenhower) were poor, his attention to the morale of his men made him popular with the troops. He is also known for the respect he showed to his enemies: in the caravan that served as his HQ in the Western Desert he placed on the wall a portrait of the German commander of the AFRIKA KORPS, Erwin Rommel. *See also* DESERT FOX; FULL MONTY; IKE.

**Monty Python's Flying Circus.** A cult BBC television comedy series screened in three series between 1969 and 1974. Each programme consisted of a succession of finely honed sketches with situations and settings of an imaginative or often surreal nature, yet involving characters whose odd credibility made them memorable. By their subtle juxtaposition of real and unreal, lifelike and dreamlike, the programmes stood the traditional tenets of television comedy on their head, and soon won a wide following. The title was suggestive rather than significant (alternatives originally under consideration were 'Gwen Dibley's Flying Circus' and 'Owl-Stretching Time'). The series spawned a number of catchphrases, the most familiar being the link line: AND NOW FOR SOMETHING COMPLETELY DIFFERENT. *See also* BLEEDIN' OBVIOUS; BRIAN; FLYING CIRCUS; NUDGE, NUDGE, WINK, WINK; SPAM.

The Python team moved on to the cinema with *Monty Python and the Holy Grail* (1975), *Monty Python's Life of Brian* (1979) (a controversially anarchic take on the life of Christ) and *Monty Python's The Meaning of Life* (1983).

**Moog synthesizer.** The synthesizer, as an electronic musical instrument so called because it originally 'synthesized' or combined different items of equipment, was at first a large and cumbersome device based on valve technology. In 1966 two US engineers, Robert Moog (1934–2005) and Donald Buchla, formed separate companies to manufacture a more compact instrument, and the former gave his name to the model that prevailed.

**Moominland.** A region on the coast of the Gulf of Finland that is the fictional setting of the Moomintroll books by the Finnish writer Tove Jansson (1914–2001), beginning with *The Moomins and the Great Flood* (1945). To the north lies Daddy Jones's Kingdom, while to the south is Moominpapa's Island. The Moomins or Moomintrolls themselves are small, white, hibernating animals with large snouts, short tails and smooth, hairless skin. However, they walk on their hind legs and speak human languages.

**Moonball.** In tennis, a shot that sends the ball in a high, gently looping arc. The cumulative effect of such shots on the receiver is frustrating, and they are generally viewed with disapproval if the perpetrator is not a beginner. The term dates from the mid-1970s.

**Moonies.** A religious sect, properly called the Unification Church, founded by Sun Myung Moon (b.1920) in South Korea in 1954. It spread to the United States in the 1960s and subsequently to Britain, Australia and elsewhere. Moon claims that he is the Second Messiah and that his devotees will save mankind from Satan. Funds built up by his followers by selling artificial flowers and other items were used by Moon to create a large property and business organization in the United States where he has lived since 1973. Tax avoidance led to his prosecution and imprisonment (1984–5). In 1995 he conducted a wedding service in South Korea in which he simultaneously married 35,000 couples present in the stadium before him and another 325,000 couples linked in by satellite. The Rev. Moon has been banned from entering the United Kingdom since 1995, on the grounds that his presence would not be 'conducive to the public good'.

**Mooning.** The displaying of one's bare buttocks as a taunt or insult or simply to amuse. The practice seems to have originated among US women students in the mid-1950s as some sort of sexual statement, although it would be ingenuous to adduce an allusion to the moon and its traditional femininity. When done by men the act is typically associated with football teams travelling on coaches. The word refers to the round shape and pale hue of the exposed anatomy.

**Moonlight and roses.** A situation or atmosphere characterized by sentimentality or romance. The phrase comes from the title of a 1925 song by Neil Moret and Ben Black.

**Moonlighter.** A person who takes up a second job, especially one undeclared for tax purposes and notionally carried on in the evening or at night by moonlight. This usage of the word dates from the 1950s and derives from an original 19th-century sense for a thief who operates at night.

**Moon of Gomrath, The.** A fantasy (1963) for children by Alan Garner (b.1934), the sequel to *The* WEIRDSTONE OF BRISINGAMEN. The bracelet containing the weirdstone is again the pivot of a plot with Arthurian undertones. The children unwittingly release the forces of the Old Magic by lighting a fire on a hill while they wait for the moon to rise on the eve of Gomrath.

**Moonraker.** The name by which Detective Inspector George Smith (1906–70), a noted spycatcher, was regularly known inside Scotland Yard. *The Times* obituary of him states that 'none of his senior contemporaries … is able to remember how he got the name' (27 October 1970), although the answer is straightforward. Smith lived at Edington, Wiltshire, and native or long-established residents of that county are called 'Moonrakers' with reference to a legend telling how local yokels, when raking a pond to retrieve kegs of smuggled brandy, pretended to be raking for the moon when surprised by excisemen.

**Moon's a Balloon, The.** The actor David Niven's first volume of memoirs (1972). It takes its title from e.e. cummings's poem '& N &' (1925):

> who knows if the moon's
> a balloon, coming out of a keen city
> in the sky – filled with pretty people?

**Moors Murders.** A particularly horrifying series of crimes between 1963 and 1965 in which Ian Brady (b.1938) and his mistress Myra Hindley (1942–2002) collaborated on five child murders. The children, among them 12-year-old John Kilbride and ten-year-old Lesley Ann Downey, were raped and tortured, in some cases being tape-recorded and photographed in their final moments, and then buried on Saddleworth Moor near Oldham, northeast of Manchester. Brady and Hindley were convicted of the crimes, and sentenced to life imprisonment, in 1966. Campaigners for the release of Hindley on compassionate grounds consistently had their case repudiated.

**Mopp, Mrs.** *See* MRS MOPP.

**Moral high ground.** A position of advantage or superiority in a moral debate or issue. The phrase 'high ground' was first used figuratively in this sense, but the fuller form dates from the 1980s. The literal 'high ground' was originally elevated terrain in a military campaign that afforded an important strategic advantage to those who occupied it.

> This Government chooses its moral high ground with curious selectivity.
> *The Times*, letter to the editor (18 August 1999)

**Moral Majority.** In the United States an association of fundamentalist Christians (*see* FUNDAMENTALISM) founded in 1979 in Lynchburg, Virginia, by the Baptist minister Jerry Falwell with the aim of promoting 'traditional values' and reversing what he saw as the godless advance of liberal political and social attitudes.

> The Moral Majority, an organization that once struck fear into the hearts of liberals and inspired bumper stickers like 'The Moral Majority is Neither', has been laid to rest. It came in like a lion in March 1979 and went out like a lamb. Jerry Falwell, who proclaimed its creation, announced its demise in Las Vegas, Nevada, a city that shows off many sins he tried to fight. The Moral Majority never lived up to its supporters' highest expectations or its detractors' worst fears.
> *International Herald Tribune* (15 June 1989)

**Moral Rearmament.** A movement, known as MRA, which was founded in 1938 by the US evangelist Frank Buchman (1878–1961). Its purpose was to counter the materialism of present-day society by persuading people to live according to the highest standards of morality and love, to obey God, and to unite in a worldwide association according to these principles.

**Mordor.** The mountain-ringed land of darkness in J.R.R. Tolkien's *The* LORD OF THE RINGS (1954–5), ruled over by SAURON, the Dark Lord, and contrasting with the realm of GONDOR to the west. Mordor is a barren land with the volcano Orodruin (Mount Doom) at its centre. The casting of the One Ring into the volcano, which successfully concludes the quest of FRODO the ring-bearer, causes Orodruin to erupt, laying Mordor to waste. *See also* MINAS MORGUL.

**More bang for your bucks.** *See* BIGGER BANG FOR YOUR BUCK, A.

**Morecambe and Wise Show, The.** A series of memorable television comedy shows broadcast first by ITV from 1961 to 1968, then by the BBC from 1968 to 1977, and finally again by ITV from 1978 to 1983. Its core was the longstanding double act perfected by Eric Morecambe (real name Eric Bartholomew; 1926–85) and Ernie Wise (real name Ernest Wiseman; 1925–99), Morecambe assuming the role of a droll, pipe-smoking sceptic and Wise that of his pompous foil. The humour lay in the wit of their lines and the insouciance of their delivery, as well as in the classic contrast between the tall, imposing Morecambe and the shorter, unassuming Wise. The close rapport between the two in their respective personae made every sketch and stand-up routine a delight.

**More dash than cash.** A catchphrase of the fashion world popularized by *Vogue* in the 1950s. It refers to clothes that are stylish but cheap and was subsequently taken up by the media generally.

> The march of Waterstone's bookshops through the 1980s high streets owed more to dash than cash.
> *The Observer* (4 September 1994)

**More popular than Jesus.** What John Lennon (1940–80) claimed The BEATLES were, in an interview published in the *Evening Standard*, 4 March 1966:

> We're more popular than Jesus now; I don't know which will go first – rock 'n' roll or Christianity.

Not to be outdone in the stakes of vainglory, Noel Gallagher (b.1967) of Oasis told the *New Musical Express* (12 July 1997):

> I would hope we mean more to people than putting money in a church basket and saying ten Hail Marys on a Sunday. Has God played Knebworth yet?

The following month, Mel C. (Sporty Spice, a.k.a. Melanie Chisholm; b.1974) of The Spice Girls, with a hutzpah that owed more to girl power than knowledge of comparative religion, was quoted as telling a reporter:

> If Oasis are bigger than God, what does that make us? Bigger than Buddha?

**More Pricks than Kicks.** A collection of short stories (1934), the first prose work by Samuel Beckett (1906–89). They all concern a student called Belacqua Shuah, whose first name is that of a Florentine musical instrument maker and friend of the Italian poet and philosopher Dante Alighieri (1265–1321), who used him in his *Divina Commedia* as a symbol of indolence. The title reflects the answer given by Jesus to Paul: 'I am Jesus whom thou persecutest: it is hard for thee to kick against the pricks' (Acts 9:5). *See also* FIRST LINES OF NOVELS.

**More will mean worse.** A typically morose comment from the novelist Kingsley Amis (1922–95), first enunciated in July 1960 in the CIA-sponsored magazine *Encounter* and subsequently taken up by those of a *Spectator*-ish, dystopian disposition:

> The delusion that there are thousands of young people about who are capable of benefiting from university training, but have somehow failed to find their way there, is … a necessary component of the expansionist case … More will mean worse.

**Morning-after pill.** A contraceptive PILL that is effective if taken within 72 hours after intercourse (assumed to have taken place at night) but preferably much sooner to ensure its effectiveness.

> The morning after pill is an increasingly popular form of contraception despite unpleasant side-effects and concern that it encourages unprotected sex.
>
> *Daily Mail* (27 February 1999)

**Morning breath.** A euphemism for bad breath experienced and probably sensed by others 'the morning after the night before', i.e. typically after drinking and smoking the previous evening.

**Morningside.** A prosperous residential area of south Edinburgh that has given its name to the widely mocked upper-middle-class Scottish accent supposedly spoken by its inhabitants. A characteristic is the pronunciation of 'a' as 'e' in such words as 'back' ('beck') and 'marry' ('merry'), much as in KELVINSIDE, its Glasgow equivalent. The name is also used generally in allusion to the strait-laced, conservative attitudes traditionally attributed to the upper middle class in Edinburgh. Both accent and attitude are nicely

reflected in Muriel Spark's novel *The* PRIME OF MISS JEAN BRODIE (1961), about a schoolmistress who tries to mould her select group of girls, the 'Brodie set', into proper young ladies. The televised version of the novel (1978) conveyed the speech and style much more effectively than the film version (1969). The name of the area itself dates no earlier than the 17th century and appears to mean what it says, 'morning side'.

**Mornington Crescent.** An improvised parlour game played by panel members on the BBC radio programme *I'm Sorry, I Haven't a Clue* (1972– ). The ostensible 'aim' of the game is to move from station to station around the London Underground system according to a set of obscure and indeterminate rules and conventions (about which the players argue and upon which they learnedly digress), and to be the first to get to Mornington Crescent Station (a task even more surreally difficult from 1992 to 1998, when it was closed).

The name is that of a residential street in London (NW1), to the east of Regent's Park. It was built in 1821. In the 19th century it was known as a favourite residence of artists and writers.

> I acted so tragic the house rose like magic,
> The audience yelled 'You're sublime!'
> They made me a present of Mornington Crescent,
> They threw it a brick at a time.
>
> W.F. HARGREAVES: 'The Night I Appeared as Macbeth' (1922)

**Moron.** Now a colloquial word for a stupid person, 'moron' was originally a specific medical term for an adult with a mental age of about 8 to 12. It was proposed in 1910 by the US psychologist Henry H. Goddard (1866–1957) and was formally adopted by the American Association for the Study of the Feeble-Minded in May that year. The word itself is the neuter form of Greek *moros*, 'foolish'.

**Morrison shelter.** Whereas the Second World War ANDERSON SHELTER was erected outdoors and was more or less permanent, the Morrison shelter was a transportable indoor refuge against bombs and falling masonry. It was made of steel and table-shaped, so that it could actually be used as a table when people were not sheltering under it. It took its name from Herbert Morrison (1888–1965), home secretary during the war.

**Morse, Inspector.** *See* INSPECTOR MORSE.

**Moscow Theatre Siege.** In October 2002 a group of Chechen fighters (including several women) took control of a theatre in Moscow during a performance, taking more than 700 hostages. They demanded the withdrawal of Russian troops from Chechnya, a predominantly Muslim part of the

Russian Federation, where a bloody war of independence had started in the early 1990s. On the third day, Russian special forces used a secret gas to render those inside the theatre unconscious. All the hostage-takers were killed, but 130 hostages also died from the effect of the gas. *See also* BESLAN MASSACRE.

**Moses basket.** A portable cot for young babies in the form of a basket with handles. The name alludes to the 'ark of bulrushes' in which the baby Moses was left by the Nile (Exodus 2:3).

**Moshing.** A type of frenzied dancing that involves jumping up and down and colliding deliberately with other dancers. At rock concerts a special moshpit by the stage may be available for this mostly male indulgence. Dancers may pack together to support a person 'surfing' overhead on raised arms; diving off a platform or stage onto the crowd is another variant. The dance form appeared in the early 1980s at PUNK ROCK concerts but later spread to the HEAVY METAL scene. The word perhaps evolved from 'mash' or 'mush' with a further suggestion of 'mass'.

**Mosleyites.** The supporters of Sir Oswald Mosley (1896–1980), who founded (1932) and led the British Union of Fascists (BUF). His followers, also known as BLACKSHIRTS, numbered some 20,000 and became involved in violent demonstrations, often directed at Jews. Among Mosley's supporters was the newspaper proprietor Viscount Rothermere. The BUF was banned in 1940 and Mosley was interned from 1940 to 1943. In 1948 Mosley became the leader of the Union Movement, the successor of the BUF.

**Mosquito Coast.** A novel (1981) by the US-born Paul Theroux (b.1941) in which a mentally unbalanced inventor abandons civilization in protest against modern culture and takes his family to Honduras, which has a coastal region called Mosquitia. Habitually leaving chaos behind him, he travels inland in an attempt to find an environment untouched by humans, where he can work unhampered by outside influences. Bungling to the last, he meets his death, and the family struggle back to civilization. A visually striking film version (1986), starring Harrison Ford and Helen Mirren, was directed by Peter Weir.

**Mosquito State.** A nickname for the US state of New Jersey, apparently alluding to an abundance of the troublesome insects. The name dates from the 1920s and is distinctly less flattering than its improbable official nickname, the Garden State.

**Mossad.** The principal secret intelligence service of Israel, established in 1951, three years after the creation of the

Jewish state itself. The name is Hebrew for 'institute', as the first word of the organization's full name *Mosad 'Elyon le-Modi'in u-Bitahon* (Supreme Institute for Intelligence and Security). The name was earlier in use for an underground organization formed in 1938 for the purpose of bringing Jews from Europe to Palestine. Here the full name was *Mosad le-'Aliyah Bet* (Institute for the Second Immigration).

**Motel.** The roadside hotel for motorists, its name an obvious blend of 'motor' and 'hotel', originated with the 'Mo-tel Inn', San Luis Obispo, California, which opened in 1925. Initially a motel was simply an administration building with a small group of cottages or chalets, each with its garage. Later it became a more regular hotel with ample parking space, so that a modern hotel, which usually also caters for motorists, is a 'motel' in all but name. A development of the 1950s was the 'botel' or 'boatel', a waterside hotel with facilities for mooring boats.

> To any other type of tourist accommodation I soon grew to prefer the Functional Motel – clean, neat, safe nooks, ideal places for sleep, argument, reconciliation, insatiable illicit love.
> VLADIMIR NABOKOV: *Lolita*, Pt II, ch. 1 (1955)

**Mother.** An affectionate if somewhat fearful nickname given to Margaret Thatcher, the IRON LADY, by her loyalists, who referred to those Conservatives who engineered her downfall in 1990 as 'matricides'.

**Mother Courage and her Children.** A play (1961) by the German playwright Bertolt Brecht (1898–1956), in German as *Mutter Courage und ihre Kinder* (1941), first staged in Zurich. It is about an indomitable woman who fights to protect her family at the time of the Thirty Years War (1618–48). Mother Courage is the nickname of a canteen-woman called Anna Fierling. Her courage avails her little, however, as she declines to become politically involved in the events that threaten her family and is thus doomed to lose them all. Brecht based his play loosely on *Trutz Simplex* (1670), by the German author Hans Jacob Christoffel von Grimmelshausen (c.1622–76), who had served in the Thirty Years War before writing of the sufferings of German peasants and townsfolk during that conflict. *See also* EPIC THEATRE.

**Mother of ....** The biggest of; the most extreme example of. The expression originated during the Second GULF WAR as a translation of the Iraqi dictator Saddam Hussein's phrase *umm al-ma'arik*, 'mother of battles', made in a speech in the Iraqi capital city of Baghdad on 6 January 1991 in which he declared that Iraq had no intention of relinquishing Kuwait and was prepared for a major conflict.

(Arabic *umm*, 'mother (of)', is a figurative term for 'the best', 'the biggest', as if meaning one that had engendered all others.) The phrase was popularly rendered by the media as 'mother of all battles' and came to apply to other examples of extremes, for example, Dr Ian Paisley, leader of the Democratic Unionist Party in Northern Ireland, described the 1998 GOOD FRIDAY AGREEMENT as 'the mother of all treachery'.

**Mothers and fathers.** A young children's game in which the roles of mothers and fathers are acted out, not perhaps without some unconscious or subconscious sexual role-playing.

**Mother's Day.** The modern and secular equivalent of Mothering Sunday. The campaign for such a day was led in the United States by Anna May Jarvis (1864–1948), a Philadelphia suffragist and temperance worker, who was troubled by the fact that she had neglected her mother in her youth. Its origin is dated to 1908, when she observed the anniversary of her mother's death (9 May 1906) at the Andrews Methodist Church in Grafton, West Virginia. In 1914 the second Sunday in May was officially designated Mother's Day by President Woodrow Wilson. *See also* FATHER'S DAY.

**Mother's ruin.** Gin. The nickname dates from the 1930s.

**Mother Teresa.** An Albanian Roman Catholic missionary (1910–97; real name Agnes Gonxha Bojaxhiu) who became an Indian citizen in 1948 and founded the Order of Missionaries of Charity to help the destitute and dying. Her work in Calcutta and elsewhere became famous around the world, and by the time of her death she was a widely revered figure. She was awarded the Nobel peace prize in 1979 and beatified in 2003.

**Motormouth.** A mostly derogatory colloquialism originating in African American slang of the 1960s for anyone who talks rapidly and incessantly. A running motor cannot turn itself off.

> She [television director Janet Street-Porter] cultivated the image of a Cockney motormouth to provide a burst of colour at the monochrome BBC.
> *The Times* (1 July 1999)

**Motorway madness.** Irresponsible or reckless driving on a motorway, especially in bad weather. The expression dates from the 1960s, when motorways first experienced behaviour of this kind.

**Motown.** A shortening of 'Motor Town' as a nickname for Detroit, Michigan, a city that thanks to the enterprise of Henry Ford became the 'automobile capital of the world'.

Detroit has a high African American population. Hence TAMLA MOTOWN as the name of the first African-American-owned record company in the United States.

**Moulton bicycle.** An unusual type of 'foldaway' bicycle invented in the 1960s by the engineer Alex Moulton (b.1920), who had earlier designed the suspension for the MINI. The bicycles were portable, easy to store and, thanks to the innovative rubber suspension on both front and back wheels, easy to handle and comfortable to ride. A popular model was the 'Stowaway' of 1965.

**Mountain bike.** A sturdy type of bicycle with broad, deep-treaded tyres, small wheels, straight handlebars and multiple gears. It was developed in California by Charlie Kelly and Gary Fisher during the 1970s for use on rough cross-country or mountain tracks. In various parts of the world there are specially constructed downhill mountain-bike tracks, which involve all kinds of obstacles, jumps, etc. Mountain biking is now a competitive sport. 'Hybrid' bikes have since been developed, which combine elements of the mountain bike (many gears, wider treads) with more traditional features for everyday town and country riding, for those who have ambitions neither to enter the Tour de France nor to scale mountain tracks.

***Mourning Becomes Electra.*** A play (1931) by Eugene O'Neill (1888–1953) consisting of a trilogy of dramas set in New England during the US Civil War. The central character, Lavinia, wears mourning black in the first two dramas, then in the third appears in bright colours until her lover Peter shoots himself and she dons black once again. Deliberately evoking links with the ancient Greek legend of Agamemnon's daughter Electra, whose life is similarly beset with tragedy and death, the title did not initially find favour with O'Neill's publishers, Harper & Brothers, who complained that it was 'meaningless', failing to understand that here O'Neill used the word 'becomes' in its rather old-fashioned sense of 'flatters'.

**Mouse potato.** A person who spends an inordinate amount of time at a computer (using its mouse). The term arose in the mid-1990s as a pun on the earlier COUCH POTATO.

**Mousetrap.** Ordinary cheese, such as is used to bait a mousetrap. The term dates from the 1940s, when more refined varieties of cheese were in short supply. Cheddar cheese is sometimes dismissed as 'mousetrap'.

***Mousetrap, The.*** A murder mystery by Agatha Christie that holds the record for the world's longest-running play. It opened in London on 25 November 1952 at the Ambassador's Theatre and in 1974 moved next door to St Martin's. The Royal Gala evening of its 50th anniversary, in

2002, was the 20,807th performance. The audience, typically composed of tourists, is asked not to reveal the identity of the murderer, but a few have unsportingly divulged the secret. The title comes from the 'play within a play' in *Hamlet*.

> *King*: What do you call the play?
>
> *Hamlet*: The Mouse-trap. Marry, how? Tropically. This play is the image of a murder done in Vienna.
>
> WILLIAM SHAKESPEARE: *Hamlet*, III, ii (1601)

**Mouth-breather.** A derisive colloquialism applied to people of low intelligence. Breathing through the mouth rather than the unaided nose is supposedly a sign of impaired mental development.

**Movers and shakers.** Powerful people who initiate events and influence people. The phrase in this sense dates from the early 1970s, yet derives from the poem 'Music and Moonlight' (1874) by the minor English poet Arthur O'Shaughnessy (1844–81), where it specifically refers to poets. The adoption of the words a whole century later is curious. The rather fine lines are as follows:

> We are the music-makers
> And we are the dreamers of dreams,
> Wandering by lone sea-breakers,
> And sitting by desolate streams;
> World-losers and world-forsakers,
> On whom the pale moon gleams:
> Yet we are the movers and shakers
> Of the world forever, it seems.

The poem was set to music by Edward Elgar as *The Music Makers* (1912).

**Move the goalposts.** To alter the basis of a procedure, especially in order to accommodate unfavourable developments. The idea is of a fixed aim or goal whose agreed parameters are changed after action has begun. The more vivid image is of a football goal whose posts have been shifted nearer each other, so narrowing the goal mouth to the disadvantage of the opposing side.

**Moving Church.** In 1951 Major the Rev. Vivian Symonds was appointed to the living of St Mark's, BIGGIN HILL, the church then being a 50-year-old iron building that had never been consecrated. In order to rebuild it he obtained permission to use material from a war-damaged church, All Saints, Peckham, 27km (17 miles) away. Standing on a lorry facing the latter, he is said to have commanded in a loud voice, 'In the name of Jesus Christ be thou removed to Biggin Hill.' Working with volunteer labour, but often quite alone, he rebuilt St Mark's, the 'Moving Church', over a period of three years.

**MP3.** In full, the unprepossessing 'MPEG-1 Audio Layer 3', a European-devised format for digitally capturing and compressing sound, hence the ubiquity of small portable MP3 players whose mostly younger owners can save large amounts of music, via a computer, and listen to it on earpieces or speakers. The Fraunhofer Society, a German research organization, is credited with making the technology public in the mid-1990s. 'MP3 player' has come to define, generically, the varieties of digital audio player (DAPs) on the market, in the way that in Britain 'Hoover' defines vacuum cleaner. *See also* IPOD.

**MRA.** *See* MORAL REARMAMENT.

***Mr and Mrs Clark and Percy.*** One of the best-known post-Pop, 'cool', naturalistic portraits by David Hockney (b.1937), painted in 1970–1. It is one of a series of double portraits of Hockney's friends and features the British fashion designer Ossie Clark (1942–96) and his (then) wife, the fabric designer Celia Birtwell, together with Percy, the cat. Hockney painted the work from photographs and drawings, and simplified the interior of the Clarks' sitting room in Bayswater. Of the positions of the sitters Hockney has commented: 'It's odd that Ossie is sitting down; it should really be the lady who's sitting down, but Celia's standing up. That alone causes a slight disturbance, because you know it should be reversed.' Hockney made the portrait as a wedding present, but the marriage ended in 1974. Clark was murdered by his Italian lover, Diego Cogolato.

***Mr Bean.*** The first of a series of television comedies starring Rowan Atkinson (b.1955) in the name part and running from 1990 to 1996. Mr Bean is essentially a NERD in a sports jacket with leather elbow patches and owns a small temperamental car. His involvement with the highs and lows of life either ends in chaos or progresses to a point of acute embarrassment. Each of the episodes is virtually dialogue-free and thus reminiscent of the comedy classics of the silent cinema. Atkinson wanted the character to be named after a vegetable. 'Mr Cauliflower' and 'Mr Cabbage' were considered, but 'Mr Bean' eventually won the day. The final episode, *Goodnight Mr Bean*, was shown in 1995, whereupon Mr Bean moved to the big screen as the hero of *Bean – The Ultimate Disaster Movie* (1997), a worldwide box-office hit.

***Mr Big.*** The head of an organization of criminals; any important person.

> It is less obvious that Tom Parker Bowles or the now former England rugby captain Lawrence Dallaglio ... are quite the Mr Bigs of the drug world that would justify such sophisticated forms of entrapment.
>
> *The Times* (28 May 1999)

Mr Big (but always known as 'Big', actual name: John) is also the character in SEX AND THE CITY who finally wins the heart of Carrie Bradshaw, played by Sarah Jessica Parker, at the end of the last series. He is a sizeable individual, at least heightwise.

**Mr Blobby.** A grotesque, egg-shaped figure in the form of a pink plastic dummy with leering lips, lascivious lashes and yellow spots, introduced by the BBC in 1992 as a source of amusement in the knock-about television comedy series NOEL'S HOUSE PARTY (1991), compèred by Noel Edmonds. The figure was operated by a human inside the costume and went on to record a hit pop song, with lines, 'Blobby, oh Mr Blobby,/ You're the guy who put the 'do' in 'do or die'./ Blobby, oh Mr Blobby,/Your deeds are guaranteed to stupefy', lyrics so inane that Radio 1 refused to broadcast them. The figure must even so have touched something of a chord in the critical media, since he was the subject of an open letter by John Lyttle in *The Independent*, an article by Bryan Appleyard in the *Mail on Sunday*'s 'Day and Night' section and a piece by Cosmo Landesman in the *Sunday Times*. In theological student circles the nickname 'Mr Blobby' has also been applied, purely from a supposed facial resemblance, to George Carey (b.1935), Archbishop of Canterbury from 1991 to 2002.

> What *is* it about the English? What *is* Mr Blobby – just a gormless colossus or something of far grander import? I don't know. As someone said on the wireless just the other day, 'It's just far too big to get your intellectual hands around.'
>
> Q (February 1994)

**Mr Chad.** *See* CHAD.

**Mr Chips.** *Se*e Mr CHIPS; GOODBYE, MR CHIPS.

**Mr Clean.** An honourable or incorruptible politician, with a clean reputation. The name has specifically been applied to John Lindsay, mayor of New York from 1965 to 1973, and the US attorney general Elliot Richardson, who resigned in 1973 rather than agree to the restrictions then being imposed by President Nixon on investigations into the WATERGATE affair. The term dates from the early 1970s and derives from the brand name of a US cleanser.

**Mr Five Per Cent.** A name applied shortly before the First World War to the Turkish-born oil millionaire and philanthropist Calouste Gulbenkian (1869–1955) when his share of the Turkish Petroleum Company was reduced from 40 per cent to 5 per cent following an Anglo-German agreement. He claimed, however, it was better to have a small slice of a big cake than a big slice of a small cake.

**Mr Fixit.** Literally a person who fixes things by repairing them, otherwise a handyman, but metaphorically a TROUBLESHOOTER or someone who arranges deals by underhand methods. The term is of US origin and dates from the 1960s. *See also* BOB THE BUILDER; JIM'LL FIX IT.

**Mr Kiss Kiss Bang Bang.** *See* KISS KISS BANG BANG.

**Mr Nice Guy.** An amiable and pleasant person. The nickname is often found in a negative context, especially when a 'nice' person becomes 'nasty'. Hence the catchphrase, sometimes bearing an ironic implication, 'no more Mr Nice Guy', applied in 1972 by his aides to Senator Edmund S. Muskie as challenger for the presidency and more recently the title of Howard Jacobson's novel *No More Mister Nice Guy* (1998).

***Mr Norris Changes Trains.*** A novel (1935; in the United States as *The Last of Mr Norris*) by Christopher Isherwood (1904–86), reflecting the uneasy political situation in the early 1930s in Germany, where Isherwood taught English in Berlin from 1930 to 1933. The observer and narrator William Bradshaw (who is Isherwood himself, under his second and third names) meets Arthur Norris, a suspicious character, on a train, and through him is involved in sinister activities.

**Mr Perfecto.** A nickname for a handsome film star, popular singer or the like, especially when of the 'Latin lover' type. *Perfecto* is Spanish for 'perfect'.

**Mr Plastic Fantastic.** The nickname of Walter Cavanagh (b.1943) of Santa Clara, California, owner of the world's biggest collection of valid credit cards. His total in 2005 was recorded at 1497. *See also* PLASTIC.

**Mr Rising Price.** *See* DESICCATED CALCULATING MACHINE.

***Mrs Dale's Diary.*** A radio SOAP OPERA broadcast from 1948 to 1969 depicting the placid, middle-class life of Mary Dale and her husband Jim, a doctor, in the fictional South London suburb of Parkwood Hill. The title was changed to *The Dales* in 1962 when the family moved to the expanding new town of Exton somewhere in the Home Counties. Despite the blandness of the action and paleness of the characters, the programme was generally regarded with affection and attracted many regular listeners.

***Mrs Dalloway.*** A novel (1925) by Virginia Woolf (1882–1941), with which she introduced the STREAM OF CONSCIOUSNESS technique into her *oeuvre*. The action takes place on a single day, on which Clarissa Dalloway, the fashionable wife of a member of parliament, is due to hold a party. A sub-plot tells of the shell-shocked Septimus Smith, who at the end of the day commits suicide. A gripping film version (1997) was directed by Marleen Gorris, with Vanessa Redgrave in the title role.

**Mrs Miniver.** A film (1942) that aimed to celebrate the patient heroism of British women during the Second World War. Mrs Miniver, played by Greer Garson, was the archetypal middle-class English gentlewoman, who presided over the home front while her husband (Walter Pidgeon) went off to help to rescue the British army at DUNKIRK. Briefly fêted as a fitting tribute to England's wartime resilience, the film's HOLLYWOOD origins hit a false note with postwar audiences and a sequel, *The Miniver Story* (1950), in which Mrs Miniver fought terminal cancer, failed to win approval. Mrs Miniver herself was originally conceived by the writer Joyce Anstruther, who (using the pen-name Jan Struther) published what purported to be Mrs Miniver's diary recollections of the war years as *Mrs Miniver*. Winston Churchill claimed that the film did more to win the war than the efforts of six divisions.

**Mrs Mopp.** A cleaning lady or 'daily'. The name dates from the 1940s and was adopted from that of a character in the radio comedy show ITMA.

**Mr Standfast.** A thriller (1919) by John Buchan (1875–1940), the third in which Richard Hannay appears. German spies are still the problem, and the action ranges from London to Skye, Switzerland to the South Tyrol, and a French château to the battlefields of the First World War. One of the novel's themes is the significance of fortitude, loyalty and moral strength, represented in *The Pilgrim's Progress* (1678) by John Bunyan (1628–88) by Mr Standfast, and in *Mr Standfast* by Peter Pienaar who is reading Bunyan's book, references to which recur throughout the novel. *See also* GREENMANTLE; *The* THIRTY-NINE STEPS.

**'Mr Tambourine Man'.** An infectiously good-humoured, folksy song with a catchy chorus by Bob Dylan, released in 1965 on the album *Bringing It All Back Home*. Mr Tambourine Man is a kind of HIPPIE minstrel, and the song's lyrics accordingly contain much hallucinatory imagery ('Take me on a trip upon your magic swirling ship' ) and intriguing wordplay. The song became a hit for the Byrds (*see* ROCK GROUP NAMES), who recorded a shortened version of the song and released an album of the same name.

> Hey! Mr Tambourine Man, play a song for me,
> I'm not sleepy and there is no place I'm going to.
> Hey! Mr Tambourine Man, play a song for me,
> In the jingle jangle morning
> I'll come followin' you.

**Mr Teasie Weasie.** The byname of the hairdresser Raymond (1911–92), whose original name was Raymond Pierre Carlo Bessone. He earned his sobriquet as a result of his appearances on the television programme *Quite Contrary* (1953), in which he would demonstrate his art by holding up a lock of hair and saying: 'A teasie-weasie here and a teasie-weasie there'. He later commented: 'Teasie Weasie may be a rotten name, but the man behind it is not what he is purported to be' (*Daily Telegraph*, obituary, 2 April 1992).

**Ms.** An abbreviation, pronounced 'Miz', of either Mrs or Miss, designed to avoid distinguishing between married and unmarried women. The title first arose in the United States in the 1950s. The feminist magazine *Ms.*, founded by Gloria Steinem 'for the liberated female human being', first appeared in January 1972.

> As an old-fashioned man, the President [Richard Nixon] prefers the old conventions, such as addressing a woman as 'Miss' or 'Mrs' rather than the new, liberated, statusless 'Ms' – not pronounced 'Muss' or 'Mess' as certain fastidious male chauvinists have suggested. No, for reasons that elude me, 'Ms' is pronounced 'Miz'.
> *New York Post* (3 January 1972)

> If *Miss* means respectably unmarried, and *Mrs* respectably married, then *Ms* means nudge, nudge, wink, wink.
> ANGELA CARTER: 'The Language of Sisterhood', in Christopher Ricks (ed.), *The State of the Language* (1982)

**MTV.** Music Television, the first 24-hour music channel, introduced in 1981 by the Warner Amex Satellite Entertainment Company, at the time the largest cable entertainment programmers in the United States. It proved hugely popular, tripling its subscribership in just over a year, but was initially criticized for its neglect of African American performers and the sexist nature of its videos, in which male artists were usually surrounded by scantily clad females. It was MTV that launched the careers of such superstars as Madonna (*see* MADGE) and Michael Jackson (*see* WACKO JACKO), and the channel was parodied by some who had achieved their success the more traditional way:

> Now look at them yo-yo's that's the way you do it
> You play the guitar on the MTV
> That ain't workin' that's the way you do it
> Money for nothin' and your chicks for free
> DIRE STRAITS: 'Money for Nothing', from the album *Brothers in Arms* (1985)

By 2000 original shows had become a major part of MTV's programming. *The Osbournes*, based on the 'everyday' life of rock star Ozzy Osbourne, his wife Sharon, and two of their children, Jack and Kelly, and launched in 2002, proved one of its greatest successes.

**Much-Binding-in-the-Marsh.** A radio comedy series that ran from 1947 to 1953. It was written by and starred Kenneth Horne (1907–69) and Richard Murdoch (1907–90), who had met in the Air Ministry during the Second World War, and was supposedly set in an RAF station doubling as a country club. Each programme ended with the whole cast singing a humorous ditty about the location that gave the title, a mock rural place-name that itself puns on 'binding' in the sense of complaining, an activity associated with service life on a remote RAF base.

**Muck and magic.** A derisory nickname in the 1990s for organic farming, especially among practitioners of scientifically based farming, with its use of industrial feedstuffs and antibiotics. Public support for the organic lobby was boosted at this time following several incidents of MAD COW DISEASE and media reports of contaminated beef imports.

**Muck in.** To share tasks or accommodation without expecting any privileges; to DO ONE'S BIT. The expression dates from the First World War and originally applied specifically to sharing one's army rations with a comrade in arms. Hence 'mucker' as a slang term for a friend or companion.

**Muckraking.** In 1903 *McClure's* magazine in the United States began to publish a series of articles that exposed corruption and greed in business and politics, pricking the consciences of their middle-class readers in the process. President Theodore Roosevelt dubbed them 'muckrakers' after the man with the muckrake in John Bunyan's *The Pilgrim's Progress* (1684), who pursues worldly gain at the expense of celestial rewards by raking filth from the ground and not looking up to see the celestial crown he was being offered for the muckrake he was using. The articles in *McClure's* planted the seeds of modern investigative journalism.

**Mudiad Amddiffyn Cymru.** (Welsh, 'Movement for the Defence of Wales'.) A Welsh nationalist group responsible for explosions in various parts of Wales in the late 1960s, mainly as a protest against the investiture of the Prince of Wales in 1969. Buildings damaged included the Temple of Peace in Cathays Park, Cardiff. *See also* ABERGELE MARTYRS; MEIBION GLYND?R.

**Muesli belt.** A general nickname for a middle-class district where people are or were likely to eat muesli and other health foods. (More specifically, the North London suburb of Muswell Hill has been nicknamed 'Muesli Hill' by some.)

The term arose in the late 1970s. Children who are thought to be undernourished as a result of the health food diet imposed on them by their well-meaning parents are sometimes said to suffer from 'muesli-belt malnutrition'. The debilitation is probably caused not so much by the diet itself but by the fact that the food takes longer to chew, so that the children do not eat enough.

**Muggle.** In the Harry POTTER novels of J.K. Rowling, an ordinary human being, with no magic powers.

**Mug's game.** An activity in which it is unwise to engage oneself as it is likely to be unsuccessful or dangerous. The term dates from the early years of the 20th century, with 'mug' in its already existing sense of a foolish person.

> *Nicobar*: I am going out of politics. Politics is a mug's game.
> GEORGE BERNARD SHAW: *The Apple Cart*, II (1929)

**Mugshot.** A photograph of a person's face ('mug'), especially for official purposes.

**Mujahedin.** A plural form of Arabic *mujahid*, a person who fights a *jihad*, a holy Muslim war against unbelievers. The name first became familiar in the West as that of the Islamic guerrillas fighting the Marxist government of Afghanistan following the Soviet invasion in 1979. They were eventually victorious in 1992. The name is also used by other groups of militant Muslim fighters.

**Mukden Incident.** An incident in Manchuria in 1931, engineered by right-wing Japanese officers as an excuse for the Japanese occupation of the region, which they renamed MANCHUKUO. Since the end of the Russo-Japanese War in 1905 the Japanese had exercised certain rights in Manchuria, including the right to station troops there to protect the South Manchurian Railway. When an explosion occurred on the railway near the city of Mukden (now called Shenyang) on 18 September 1931 the Japanese military in Manchuria blamed the Chinese army, and, without reference to the civilian government in Japan, occupied Mukden and then the rest of Manchuria. The Tokyo government fell and its successor retrospectively authorized the military's actions.

**Mulberry.** In the Second World War this was the code name given to the prefabricated ports towed across to the Normandy coast to make possible the supply of the Allied armies in France in 1944 consequent upon the D-DAY landings. Submersible sections of concrete formed a breakwater and quay alongside which the transports were unloaded. The name was chosen at the time because it was the next in rotation on the British Admiralty's list of names available for warships. Two such Mulberries were set up, but the one serving the US beaches was wrecked by a storm (19 June). That serving the British beaches was kept in service until Antwerp was available.

**Mulefa.** In Philip Pullman's trilogy HIS DARK MATERIALS, graceful quadrupeds in another universe, whose bodies are based on a diamond-shaped framework rather than a backbone and which have spoken language, augmented by a sign language in which their trunks (in the elephantine sense) play a major role. Their means of locomotion is a pair of massive wheel-shaped seedpods attached to their front and rear legs.

**Mulligan.** An extra stroke in golf awarded after a poor shot and not counted on the score card. The name dates from the 1940s and according to one account derives from a bottle called a 'Mulligan' kept on the bar in American family-type saloons. It contained a concoction of pepper seeds and water that could be added to 'spice up' one's beer, the effect being a shock to the system similar to the humiliating blow of being granted an extra shot at one's ball.

**Mummerset.** A mock West Country accent as adopted by actors or by speakers in real life. The essence is to burr the letter 'r' ('barrrn'), sound 'f' as 'v' and 's' as 'z' ('varm', 'Zummerzet') and pronounce 'i' in 'bite' or 'y' in 'my' as 'oi' ('Oi be boidin' moi toim'). Liberties are also taken with verbs and pronouns ('Er be allus after we'). The word itself blends 'mumble' and 'Somerset'. *See also* OO-AR!

**Mummy's boy.** A young male who is excessively influenced by or attached to his mother. The phrase is a variant on the earlier 'mother's boy' in this sense.

> I was very family oriented and my family were there all the time, they probably thought, 'He's a mummy's boy, daddy's boy – we won't offer it [marijuana] to him.'
>
> *heat* (9–15 December 1999)

**Munchausen's syndrome.** A type of mental disorder in which a person repeatedly feigns illness so as to obtain hospital treatment. It was first recognized in the 1950s among people who had travelled a good deal, like Baron Münchhausen (in full, Karl Friedrich Hieronymus, Freiherr von Münchhausen (1720–97)), the hero of a book of fantastic travellers' tales written in 1785 by Baron Raspe. The condition known as 'Munchausen's syndrome by proxy', in which another person is harmed by the sufferer, has been controversially diagnosed in cases where someone, typically a woman, has killed or otherwise harmed a child.

**Munchies, The.** A craving for food, often sweet or in an otherwise unlikely combination of flavours, that can be an after-effect of smoking hashish or marijuana. First recorded in the United States in the late 1950s, the usage is probably a development of an earlier sense 'snacks'.

**Munchkin.** An US colloquialism for a young child, from the Munchkins, the race of small childlike creatures who help Dorothy in her quest for the city of OZ in L. Frank Baum's children's fantasy *The* WIZARD OF OZ (1900). Public awareness of these grew as a result of the 1939 film of the book, in which the Munchkins are played by midgets. In 1999 pop singer Britney Spears was described as a '17-year-old munchkin turned Madonna-lookalike' (*heat*, 18–24 November).

**Munich.** A common shorthand for the Munich Agreement, signed in 30 September 1938 on behalf of Germany, Britain and France by Hitler, Neville Chamberlain and Édouard Daladier. The Italians were also present at the conference. The agreement, which has come to be seen as the low point of Britain and France's APPEASEMENT of Nazi Germany, ceded to Germany the right to the Czechoslovak territory of the SUDETENLAND, which contained a large German-speaking population. Chamberlain returned to Britain claiming that he had achieved PEACE IN OUR TIME, while Winston Churchill commented: 'We have sustained a defeat without a war.' The following year the Nazis occupied the rest of Czechoslovakia. Since then the phrase 'another Munich' has been used for any potentially disastrous, humiliating or dishonourable act of appeasement or surrender.

**Munich air crash.** *See* BUSBY'S BABES.

**Munich Putsch.** *See* BEER HALL PUTSCH.

**Munro.** A Scottish mountain over 914m (3000ft) in height. The name is that of Hugh T. Munro (1856–1919), who published a list of them in the *Scottish Mountaineering Club Journal* for 1891. The list is revised now and again, in the light of new survey information; it now includes 284 such peaks, eight of them over 1220m (4000ft) and the highest of all Ben Nevis (1343m/4406ft). A climber who attempts to ascend all 284 is known disparagingly among hillwalkers and mountaineers as a 'Munro-bagger', a term implying an emphasis purely on the height of the hill rather than on the activity itself. There are also Corbetts, between 762 and 914m (2500–3000ft), listed by J.R. Corbett, and Grahams, between 610m (2000ft) and 762 m (2500 ft), listed by Fiona Graham. Donalds, named after Percy Donald, are those mountains in Scotland south of the Highland Line over 610m (2000ft).

**Muppet Show, The.** A television comedy series screened

from 1976 to 1981 and featuring puppets of all shapes and sizes. They were the creation of the US puppeteer Jim Henson (1936–90) and originally appeared on the US children's programme *Sesame Street*, first screened in 1969. They were then adapted in Britain to adult entertainment. Each show was ostensibly put on by the puppets in a theatre, the compere being KERMIT, a garrulous green-garbed frog. Other characters were the cosy Fozzie Bear and the impossibly vain Miss Piggy. A human was usually introduced as a victim of their pranks. The name 'Muppet' seems to be a blend of 'marionette' and 'puppet', although Henson himself said that it was 'simply a word that sounded good to him' (*Time*, 25 December 1978).

**Murder, Inc.** A name given by President Ronald Reagan to Iran under the AYATOLLAHS, referring to that state's involvement in anti-US terrorism. Like so much of the GREAT COMMUNICATOR's phraseology, the term derives from the movies: *Murder, Incorporated* was a 1960 Hollywood film about 1930s gangsters. *See also* IRAN-CONTRA AFFAIR.

***Murder on the Orient Express.*** A detective novel (originally as *Murder on the Calais Coach*, 1934) by Agatha Christie (1890–1976), involving her retired Belgian policeman Hercule POIROT, who first appears in *The Mysterious Affair at Styles* (1920). The original Orient Express ran from Paris via Vienna to Istanbul and other Balkan cities between 1883 and 1961. A film version (1974) directed by Sidney Lumet was disappointing, despite the cast, which included Albert Finney (as Poirot), Ingrid Bergman, Lauren Bacall, Sean Connery and Vanessa Redgrave.

**Murphy bed.** The type of folding bed so known from the 1920s takes its name from the US manufacturer William L. Murphy (1876–1959), its original designer. In its earliest form the bed folded or swung into a cupboard when not needed and was thus mainly found in small apartments, where space was at a premium.

**Murphy's law.** 'If anything can go wrong, it will.' If a slice of bread and jam is dropped on the floor, it is bound to land jam side down. The expression is said to derive from a remark made in 1949 by Captain E. Murphy of the Wright Field Aircraft Laboratory. More likely, it is simply a use of the common Irish surname, in allusion to the alleged illogicality of the Irish. *See also* SOD'S LAW.

**Muscle car.** A high-powered car, especially one with a souped-up engine. The term, which originated in the US in the 1960s, tends to connote ridicule rather than admiration.

**Museumland.** A nickname for South Kensington, London, and in particular for the area south of the Royal Albert Hall where the Victoria and Albert Museum, the Science Museum and the Natural History Museum are located.

**Museum piece.** An old-fashioned or decrepit person or thing. The term passed early in the 20th century from a genuine description of an item of value or rarity to this pejorative sense.

**Mushroom cloud.** The standard description of the shape of the cloud formed after an atomic or thermonuclear detonation. The phrase became a metonym for global nuclear apocalypse in the angst-ridden years of the Cold War. It derives from the account of the first atomic test in New Mexico on 16 July 1945 by the US journalist William L. Laurence (1888–1977), published in the *New York Times*, 26 September 1945:

> At first it was a giant column that soon took the shape of a supramundane mushroom.

**Music to one's ears.** Something that is very pleasant to hear, typically good news.

***Music While You Work.*** A BBC radio programme first broadcast in 1940. It consisted of a medley of popular tunes, played by a different band each day, and was introduced in the dark days at the beginning of the Second World War to keep factory workers contented and therefore productive. It continued in the happier years of peacetime until 1967.

> Though 'Music while you work' is now our wont,
> It's not so nice as 'Music while you don't'.
> JOHN BETJEMAN: *A Few Late Chrysanthemums*, 'The Dear Old Village' (1958)

**Musso's Lake.** A Second World War nickname for the Mediterranean, 'Musso' being the Italian dictator Benito Mussolini (1883–1945), who entered the war on Germany's side in 1940. His attempt to chase the British out of the Mediterranean that year proved fruitless.

**Mutt and Jeff.** A nickname for a stupid pair of men, especially one tall and one short. The names are those of two such characters in US comic strips drawn by Bud Fisher from 1907 and soon after appearing in short cartoon films. Mutt was tall and lanky; Jeff was short and bald. 'Mutt and Jeff' went on to achieve rhyming-slang status, meaning 'deaf'.

**Muzak.** The proprietary name of a system of recorded light background music played through speakers in public places such as supermarkets, restaurants, factories and the like. It is objected to by some, but providers of the service claim it relaxes people and so encourages the customer to buy more, the diner to order more and the worker to produce more. The name, based on 'music', was registered as a trademark by Rediffusion Ltd in 1938.

> We shall have muzak wherever we go.
> *The Listener* (16 June 1965)

**Mwah.** A representation dating from the mid-1990s of the sound made by someone giving an air kiss, i.e. a social kiss made without lip contact but often with cheek contact, typically once on each cheek. The utterance is most common among media people and luvvies (*see* LUVVY). When first encountered in print it was mistaken by some as a respelling of French *moi*, as in 'Pretentious, *moi*?'

> Not all the post is depressing. I've also been sent the [television gardener] Charlie Dimmock calendar, personally signed to me by her. Thank you, mwah, mwah. What a way to see in the new century.
> *Sunday Times* (19 September 1999)

**My Fair Lady.** A film musical (1964) based on a stage musical by Alan Lerner (1918–86) and Frederick Loewe (1901–88) depicting the transformation of roughly spoken cockney FLOWER GIRL Eliza DOOLITTLE into a well-groomed society lady through the efforts of the arrogant linguist Professor Henry Higgins. Starring Audrey Hepburn and Rex Harrison, the film was derived ultimately from the play PYGMALION (1913) by George Bernard Shaw (1856–1950). Shaw had reservations about the film and the musical was given a different title partly to differentiate it from the original play. The new title was extracted from a traditional rhyme:

> London Bridge is falling down, falling down, falling down,
> London Bridge is falling down, my fair lady.
> 'London Bridge is falling down'

**My Family and Other Animals.** An autobiographical study (1956) by the zoologist Gerald Durrell (1925–95) of the unorthodox household in Corfu in the 1930s, of which his brother Lawrence Durrell (1912–90), the poet and novelist, was also a member.

**My feet are killing me.** My shoes are uncomfortably tight. A complaint mostly voiced by women, for whom fashion frequently takes precedence over fit in matters of footwear.

**My foot!** I don't believe it! You can't be serious! The phrase dates from the 1920s, as does its variant, 'My left foot!' *My Left Foot* (1954) was the title of the autobiography of the Irish writer Christy Brown (1932–81), a cerebral palsy victim who was able to write only by using his left foot to operate a specially adapted typewriter. This provided the basis of a

1989 film of the same name, in which Daniel Day-Lewis won an Oscar for his portrayal of Brown.

**'My Generation'.** A frenziedly anti-establishment song by The Who, released in 1965 and described by its writer Pete Townshend as 'anti-middle age, anti-boss class, and anti-young marrieds'. Its title comes from a line in a Bob Dylan song, 'Talkin' New York, Talkin' 'bout my genera-tion'. A sort of PUNK anthem *avant la lettre*, the song includes the nihilistic wish 'Hope I die before I get old' and the near-expletive of the line 'why don't you all f-fade away'.

> People try to put us d-down (Talkin' 'bout my generation)
> Just because we get around (Talkin' 'bout my generation)
> Things they do look awful c-c-cold (Talkin' 'bout my generation)
> I hope I die before I get old (Talkin' 'bout my generation)

**My Lai Massacre.** A more than shameful incident during the VIETNAM War (1964–75), when on 16 March 1968 US troops killed 109 civilians in My Lai, a small village in South Vietnam. An investigation into the atrocity in 1969 produced enough evidence to charge 30 soldiers with war crimes, but the only one to be convicted was Lieutenant William Calley, the unintelligent and inexperienced platoon commander. He was sentenced to life imprisonment but was released after only three years, thanks to the intervention of President Nixon.

**My Little Pony.** A range of brightly coloured toy ponies with manes and tails that little girls can brush; the equine equivalent of a BARBIE DOLL. The range was launched in 1983, and has spawned a number of animated TV programmes. Hence 'My Little Tony', as George W. Bush (DUBYA) is said to call Tony Blair (according to the comedy show *Bremner, Bird and Fortune*, Channel 4 TV, 27 March 2005). *See also* BUSH'S POODLE.

**My Little Tony.** *See* BUSH'S POODLE; MY LITTLE PONY.

**Myra Breckenridge.** *See* Myra BRECKENRIDGE.

**Mystic Marquess.** A nickname of Spencer Compton, 7th Marquess of Northampton (b.1946), given for his interest in spiritualism. Said to be Britain's wealthiest Buddhist, he married his fifth wife in 1990, and is currently Pro Grand Master of the United Grand Lodge of England (the main governing body of the Freemasons).

**'My Way'.** The title of a song by the Canadian singer and songwriter Paul Anka (b.1941), who wrote the lyrics in 1968 to the tune of a French song '*Comme d'habitude*' ('as usual') by Claude François and Jacques Revaux, and released it in 1969 on his album entitled *My Way*. The song was most famously associated with Frank Sinatra (OL' BLUE EYES), but has been recorded by a huge number of other artists – perhaps most surprisingly by Sid Vicious of The Sex Pistols, whose punk version (1978) was later used to accompany the closing credits of the dark Mafia movie *Goodfellas* (1990), perhaps in ironic homage to Sinatra's alleged Mafia links. 'My Way' is often to be heard in KARAOKE bars, being particularly popular with those who believe that by belting it out they somehow justify whatever mess they've made of their lives.

And now the end is near
And so I face the final curtain,
My friend, I'll say it clear,
I'll state my case of which I'm certain.
I've lived a life that's full,
I've travelled each and every highway
And more, much more than this,
I did it my way.

*See also* 'JE NE REGRETTE RIEN'; SINATRA DOCTRINE.

# N

**NAAFI.** The popular acronym for the Navy, Army, and Air Force Institutes, set up in 1921 to provide canteens for servicemen and later developing to run shops and recreational facilities for service personnel wherever they are posted.

> The NAAFI is a sort of caafi
> Where soldiers are rude
> About the food.
> *The Spectator* (23 January 1959)

**Nab.** A nickname for Conservative backbencher Sir Gerald Nabarro (1913–73), best remembered for his handlebar moustache and his Rolls Royce, registration number NAB 1. Nabarro in fact owned not just NAB 1 but the series NAB 1 to NAB 8, and also NAB 10, NAB 99 and NAB 555. *See also* CHERISHED NUMBER.

**Nabob of Sob, The.** A sobriquet of the 1950s American crooner Johnnie Ray (1927–90), who was able to produce actual tears during his performances. His other nicknames included the Cry Guy, the Prince of Wails and Mr Emotion. The name 'Nabob of Sob' has also been applied to Morrissey (b.1959), the miserablist lead singer of the 1980s Mancunian band The Smiths.

**Nadsat.** The jargon spoken by 15-year-old Alex and his teenage friends in Anthony Burgess's black comedy *A* CLOCKWORK ORANGE (1962). The words are based on Russian, as is *nadsat* itself, representing the equivalent of '-teen', and some of them have entered youth slang generally. Examples are *droog*, 'friend', *horrowshow*, 'good', and *gloopy*, 'stupid'. Burgess often adds the English equivalent in the narrative, but even where he does not the sense is usually perceptible. *See also* COPYCAT KILLING.

> Then we slooshied the sirens and knew the millicents were coming with pooshkas pushing out of the police-auto-windows at the ready. That little weepy devotchka had told them, no doubt.
> *A Clockwork Orange*, ch. 2

**Naff.** Lacking taste or style. The slang word surfaced in the 1950s but its origin remains uncertain. It is not likely to derive from NAAFI, as sometimes suggested, and may be a euphemistic formation. It appears not to be related to 'naff off' meaning 'go away', which is probably based on the 'F-word' (*see* FOUR-LETTER WORD). In 1982 Princess Anne famously lost her temper with pestering PAPARAZZI and told them to 'naff off'.

> Davina McCall … gets away with presenting programmes that are the naffest of the naff.
> *heat* (6–12 January 2000)

**Naked and the Dead, The.** The first novel (1948) by Norman Mailer (b.1923). Mailer enlisted in the US Army in the Second World War with the idea of writing 'a short novel about a long patrol'. *The Naked and the Dead* is a long novel about a long patrol during the US assault on the Philippines, whose 14 members represent a microcosm of American society. The term 'naked' in the title is referred to in the text: 'A shell sighed overhead, and unconsciously [Sergeant] Martinez drew back against a gunhousing. He felt naked.' The title phrase also recalls a phrase in the Apostle's Creed:

> He ascended into heaven, And sitteth on the right hand of God the Father Almighty; From thence he shall come to judge the quick and the dead.
> The Book of Common Prayer (in this context, 'the quick' means 'the living')

A further possible influence on the title is the 1921 novel by F. Scott Fitzgerald, *The Beautiful and Damned*. The borrowing would be ironic, given that Fitzgerald's novel portrays a world in which the ultimate aim is 'the final polish of the shoe, the ultimate dab of the clothes brush, and a sort of intellectual There!' – whereas Mailer's gritty novel strips men down to their basic selves, facing them with their own weaknesses and with the reality of death. Mailer's publishers put some restraint on his grittiness, however, obliging him to replace the F-WORD with the euphemistic but unambiguous 'fug' – supposedly leading Tallulah Bankhead, on being introduced to Mailer, to say: 'So you're the young man who can't spell *fuck*.' In the film version (1958), directed by Raoul Walsh, not even 'fug' was heard. *See also* FIRST LINES OF NOVELS.

**Naked ape.** A human being. The term was introduced by the ethnologist Desmond Morris (b.1928):

> There are one hundred and ninety-three living species of monkeys and apes. One hundred and ninety-two of them are covered with hair. The exception is a naked ape self-named *Homo sapiens*.
>
> DESMOND MORRIS: *The Naked Ape*, Introduction (1967)

**Naked as nature intended.** Nude; unclothed. The phrase was popularized as the title of a British nudist film of 1961, originally to have been entitled *Cornish Holiday*. The equation of nakedness with naturalness is an old one, and Rudyard Kipling has a passage in *Stalky & Co.* (1899) in which he describes a group of schoolboys 'stripping as they ran, till, when they touched the sands, they were naked as God had made them, and as happy as He intended them to be'.

> He [Prince Charles] must have felt like he was caught in one of those terrible nightmares – you know, the ones where you find yourself in the High Street as naked as unforgiving Mother Nature intended.
>
> *Daily Mirror* (8 September 1994)

**Naked Chef, The.** A BBC television series featuring Jamie Oliver (b.1975), an amiable young chef from Essex. It was first broadcast in 1998, since when he has presented a number of other cookery series. The title refers not to Oliver's state of dress, but to the simplicity of his recipes. His campaigning 2005 series, *Jamie's School Dinners*, resulted in the government giving a commitment to provide more nutritious lunches for schoolchildren (*see* TURKEY TWIZZLER). Oliver is noted for his MOCKNEY banter, involving expressions such as 'pukka' and 'LOVELY JUBBLY!', laced (as is fashionable for the 21st-century celebrity chef) with a good dash of FOUR-LETTER WORDS in moments of stress.

**Naked into the conference chamber.** A phrase coined by Aneurin Bevan (1897–1960) in a speech to the Labour Party Conference in Brighton on 3 October 1957, opposing a resolution that the party adopt a policy of UNILATERAL NUCLEAR DISARMAMENT.

> If you carry the resolution you will send Britain's foreign secretary naked into the conference chamber.

Bevan's point was that unilateralism would result in a loss of allies, hence the predicted nakedness.

**Naked Lunch, The.** A surreal novel (1959, Paris; US title *Naked Lunch*, 1962) by William Burroughs (1914–97), which was the last book to be censored by local authorities in the United States. It was created by a form of linguistic collage from thousands of pages of notes that Burroughs made while addicted to HEROIN. The Nobel prize-winning author Samuel Beckett (1906–89) commented on the technique: 'That's not writing, it's plumbing.' The title was suggested to Burroughs by the BEAT GENERATION author Jack Kerouac (1922–69), who helped with the manuscript, and implies, according to Burroughs, 'that frozen moment when everyone sees what is on the end of every fork'. David Cronenberg's film of the same title (1991) explored the creation of the novel through the hallucinatory experiences of a writer. *See also* FIRST LINES OF NOVELS.

**Naked Rambler, The.** The sobriquet applied by the press to Stephen (or Steve) Gough, who, beginning in 2004, attempted to walk from Land's End to John o' Groats wearing nothing but his boots (and occasionally a hat). He was arrested on numerous occasions. He eventually reached his goal in February 2006, accompanied by his equally naked girlfriend.

**Nam** or **'Nam.** The regular short name for VIETNAM as used by US armed forces during the Vietnam War (1964–75).

**Name and shame.** To make a public disclosure of a person's or group of people's perceived or actual wrongdoing. The phrase arose in the United States in the climate of moral reformativism of the early 1990s.

> A dentist became the first health professional to be 'named and shamed' by the Health Service Ombudsman for bad treatment of a patient yesterday.
>
> *The Times* (25 November 1999)

**Name of the game.** What matters most; the way things are supposed to be. The phrase became current from the 1960s and is of US origin, perhaps arising from sports journalism. It was popularized by an American television melodrama, *Fame is the Name of the Game* (1966), and by a series of films following from this, *The Name of the Game* (1968–70). In the UK, 'Life', according to the trenchantly philosophical theme song of The GENERATION GAME, 'is the name of the game.' 'The Name of the Game', by the Scandinavian pop group Abba, was a catchy chart-topping number of the late 1970s. Lovers of apt personal names like to play 'the game of the name', finding doctors called C. Fitt and dentists named I. Pulham.

> Anything that interrupts the vital flow of e-mails is fuddy-duddy. Instant communication is the name of the game.
>
> *Sunday Times* (26 December 1999)

**Name of the Rose, The.** A historical novel (1983; in Italian as *Il nome della rosa*, 1980) by Umberto Eco (b.1932), Professor of Semiotics at the University of Bologna. It is a metaphysical quest for truth and meaning in the form of a whodunnit set in a medieval Benedictine monastery in a mountain castle, in which a learned English Franciscan, William of Baskerville, seeks the serial murderer of several monks. According to Eco, the cryptic Latin hexameter with which the book closes, '*Stat rosa pristina nomine, nomina nuda tenemus*' (from *De contemptu mundi*, a 12th-century satirical poem by Bernard of Cluny), implies that 'departed things leave (only, or at least) pure names behind them'. The title 'came to me virtually by chance, and I liked it because the rose is a symbolic figure so rich in meanings that now it hardly has any meaning left. ... A title must muddle the reader's ideas, not regiment them.'

A curiously muted film version (1986) was directed by Jean-Jacques Annaud, with Sean Connery in the role of Baskerville, and Christian Slater in the role of Adso of Melk, the tale's youthful narrator.

**Nana.** In the story of PETER PAN the gentle and faithful old dog who always looks after the children of the Darling family. (Hence her name, as 'nana' is a children's word for 'nurse'.) When Mr Darling plays a trick on Nana by giving her unpleasant medicine, which he himself has promised to drink, the family does not appreciate his humour. This puts him out of temper, and Nana is chained up in the yard before he goes out for the evening. As a consequence Peter Pan effects an entry into the children's bedroom. *See also* IN THE DOGHOUSE.

**Nancy boy.** A derogatory nickname for an effeminate man or male homosexual, dating from the early 20th century and evolving from the earlier 'Miss Nancy'. It is also common as 'nancy', which in turn is shortened to 'nance'.

**Nanking, Rape of.** *See* RAPE OF NANKING.

**Nanny Jowell.** A nickname of the Labour politician Tessa Jowell (1947), who became secretary of state for culture, media and sport in 2001. The political commentator Matthew Norman has explained that the nickname is:

> ... born of her penchant for trying to mould our behaviour, albeit more with a spoonful of sugar than with the firm hand so mythically popular with members on the Tory benches opposite.

*See also* NANNY STATE.

**Nanny state.** A nickname for the government and government institutions, seen as authoritarian and paternalistic, and as imposing on people what is good for them, for 'nanny

knows best'. The term is particularly invoked in relation to legislation concerning social and cultural matters. It is first recorded in a *Spectator* article of 1965 by the Conservative politician Iain Macleod (writing under the pseudonym 'Quoodle'), at a time when Labour was in power. But the term is politically transferable, and for many the 'nanny' herself was epitomized by Margaret Thatcher (*see* IRON LADY) who, when prime minister (1979–90), despite her free-market individualistic principles, oversaw a concentration of power in central government and maintained a firmly authoritarian attitude towards many social issues.

> This new victory for the Nanny State represents the wrong approach. It is certainly the duty of ministers to make sure that there is a full knowledge of risks thought to be involved in heavy cigarette smoking – and this duty was discharged by Conservative ministers of health and education. If this is done, the decision to smoke or not is for the individual, and it should be left to him.
>
> IAIN MACLEOD: in *The Spectator*, 12 February 1965

> The nanny state has found its way into the mother of parliaments. Pint drinkers in the bars of the House of Commons now find a stark message staring at them from the bottom of the glass – 'Don't drink and drive.'
>
> *Sunday Times* (20 February 2000)

**Nansen passport.** An identification document issued after the First World War to a stateless person ineligible for a formal passport. It took its name from the Norwegian diplomat and explorer Fridtjof Nansen (1861–1930), who was responsible for the issue of these papers.

**Napalm.** The highly inflammable sticky jelly of this name, used in incendiary bombs and flame-throwers and consisting of petrol thickened with special soaps, takes its name from a combination of *na*phthenic acid and *palm*itic acid. It is so called because the aluminium salts of these acids are used in the manufacture of the chemical that thickens petroleum. It was invented in 1942 and first gained notoriety in 1966 when 20 US soldiers died in South VIETNAM as a result of one of their own aircraft bombarding them with napalm. One of the most haunting images of the Vietnam War is a widely reproduced photograph of 1972 showing children fleeing from their burning homes, one girl with her clothes burned off her back, after an American napalm attack. The attack was targeted at a VIET CONG village, but instead it devastated the 'friendly' South Vietnamese village of Trang Bang. Napalm was also used with extremely destructive effect by Iraq in the Iran–Iraq War of 1980–8.

**Napoo.** Soldier slang of the First World War for something that is of no use or does not exist. It represents the French phrase *il n'y en a plus* ('there is no more of it'). It occurs in a popular song in which the returning British soldier bids a fond farewell to his French mam'zelle:

> Good-bye-ee! good-bye-ee!
> Wipe the tear, baby dear, from your eye-ee.
> Tho' it's hard to part, I know,
> I'll be tickled to death to go.
> Don't cry-ee! – don't sigh-ee! –
> There's a silver lining in the sky-ee! –
> Bonsoir, old thing! cheerio! chin-chin!
> Nahpoo! Toodle-oo! Good-bye-ee!
>
> ROBERT P. WESTON and BERT LEE: 'Good-Bye-Ee' (1917)

*See also* FIRST WORLD WAR SLANG.

**Nappy brain.** A colloquial term for the fuzzy memory and loss of concentration said to be characteristic of pregnant women and new mothers. It is sometimes attributed to the mother's besottedness with her unborn or newborn child. Some recent neurological research denies its existence, suggesting that mothers' instincts and abilities either remain intact or even become sharper, at least with regard to the necessary skills for bringing up a child. In today's world of equal opportunities, however, men also become eligible for the condition, whether it is real or imagined.

> NAPPY BRAIN – No-sleep Kennedy loses plot big time
> *Daily Star* (15 April 2005), on the then Liberal Democrat
> leader Charles Kennedy (a new father) during the 2005
> general election

**Nappy Valley.** A facetious designation in New Zealand for a dormitory suburb, full of families with young babies. It was modelled on HAPPY VALLEY, with perhaps a nod also towards the Napa Valley in California. In the UK the name is applied to Crouch End in North London.

**Narnia.** The fictional land in which are set the seven children's books by C.S. Lewis, beginning with *The* LION, THE WITCH AND THE WARDROBE (1950). It is visited only by select children, and peopled by talking beasts, giants, witches and other characters of myth and legend. To the north lie Ettinsmoor and the Wild Lands of the North; to the south, Archenland and Calormen. It seems that Lewis chose the name simply because he liked the sound, although as a classicist he may well have come across the various Roman places so called, the best known of which is the Umbrian hill town of Narnia (now Narni in Italy), formerly Nequinum. *See also* ASLAN.

**Narziss und Goldmund.** A novel (1930; translated from German as *Death and the Lover*, 1932, and as *Narcissus and Goldmund*, 1968) by Hermann Hesse (1877–1962). It is a medieval allegory of an artist and an intellectual on their way to self-discovery.

**Nasa.** The National Aeronautics and Space Administration, an independent American government agency founded in 1958 to research and develop vehicles and activities for the exploration of space. It was created largely in response to the Soviet launch of the first SPUTNIK in 1957 and accepted President John F. Kennedy's challenge to put a man on the moon by the end of the 1960s. It designed the APOLLO programme to that end, and achieved its aim when the US astronaut Neil Armstrong became the first man on the moon in 1969.

**Nasty bit** or **piece of work.** An unpleasant person. The expression dates from the 1920s.

**Nasty Party, The.** A nickname for the Conservative Party. At the Party Conference in October 2002, the party's first woman chairman, Theresa May (b.1956), addressed delegates thus:

> Let's not kid ourselves. There's a way to go before we can
> return to government. There's a lot we need to do in this
> party of ours. Our base is too narrow and so, occasionally,
> are our sympathies. You know what some people call us: the
> nasty party.

May went on castigate unnamed colleagues for 'trying to make political capital out of demonizing minorities'. The former party chairman Norman Tebbit (the CHINGFORD SKINHEAD; *see also* SEMI-HOUSETRAINED POLECAT) commented that when the party was truly 'nasty' it used to win elections. May ceased to be chairman the following year, but at the end of 2005 the election of David Cameron to lead the party signalled an effort to kick the 'nasty' label in favour of greater cuddliness.

**National Forest.** A planned forest of some 520 sq. km (200 square miles) in central England, covering parts of Staffordshire, Derbyshire and Leicestershire, on the site of old coal tips and other damaged land. Planting got underway in the 1990s, and tree cover had increased from 6 per cent of the area in 1991 to 16 per cent in 2005.

**National Front.** An extremist organization formed in 1967 from various small right-wing groups. It came to prominence in the 1970s in the wake of concern about the increasing number of immigrants to Britain, a fear fanned by Enoch Powell and other Conservative politicians. It had strong support in various parts of London, the Midlands and some northern cities. This support declined after 1977, however, and in the 1979 general election the National Front received only 1.3 per cent of the vote. In 1982 its chairman,

John Tyndall, left to form the British National Party (BNP), which has since supplanted the National Front on the extreme right-wing edge of British politics. In local council elections in 2006 the BNP won a sizeable number of seats in East London, a source of concern to all the mainstream political parties.

**National governments.** As a result of financial crises and the collapse of the Labour government in 1931 a COALITION GOVERNMENT was formed under J. Ramsay MacDonald (1931–5), the first of a series of governments called 'National' that held office in succession until 1940, under MacDonald, then Stanley Baldwin (1935–7) and lastly Neville Chamberlain (1937–40). Those Liberal and Labour MPs who supported these governments called themselves National Liberal candidates and National Labour candidates. The administrations became increasingly Conservative in character.

**National Lottery.** The biggest lottery in the UK, now called Lotto, established by the government in 1993 and administered by CAMELOT. The weekly draws are shown live on BBC Television every Saturday night. Of every £1 spent by the punters, 28p goes to good causes, with the remainder being split between the prize fund, the organizers and ticket sellers, and the government. The chances of winning the jackpot are 1 in 13,983,816.

> The Lottery, with its weekly pay-out of enormous prizes, was the one public event to which the proles paid serious attention … It was their delight, their folly, their anodyne, their intellectual stimulant.
>
> GEORGE ORWELL: *Nineteen Eighty-Four* (1949)

**National Service.** Until the First World War Britain relied on volunteer forces to fight its wars. The carnage on the WESTERN FRONT caused a severe shortage of fighting men, however, and in February 1916 the government introduced conscription for men aged between 18 and 40 (later the upper limit was raised to 50 and married men were included as well as single men). Compulsory military service ended in 1918, but as war again threatened in 1939 it was reintroduced under the National Service Act for men aged between 18 and 41 (later 51). From 1942 unmarried women were also made available for service. The call-up continued after the Second World War until 1960 for men of 18, who served a period of 18 to 24 months' service. *See also* KITCHENER'S ARMY.

**National treasure.** A nickname for any widely respected or admired celebrity, such as an actor, writer or sportsman or woman, especially one who is 'getting on'. In Japan there is an official status of 'Living National Treasure', applied to a number of distinguished traditional craftsman, such as potters and woodblock printers. The list of 'Australian Living Treasures' (first published in 1997 by the National Trust of Australia) is somewhat broader in scope, and includes such names as the actors Russell Crowe, Judy Davis and Nicole Kidman, the Nobel laureate for physics Peter Docherty, the feminist Germaine Greer, the entertainers Rolf Harris and Barry Humphries, the tennis players Evonne Goolagong, John Newcombe, Ken Rosewall and Rod Laver, the art critic Robert Hughes, the writers Thomas Keneally and Colleen McCullough, the golfer Greg Norman, the singer Joan Sutherland, the cricketer Steve Waugh, plus a number of Australian Aboriginal leaders and former prime ministers.

**National Trust.** The short name of the National Trust for Places of Historic Interest or Natural Beauty, the foremost conservation body for England, Wales and Northern Ireland (Scotland has the National Trust for Scotland, founded in 1931). It began as a private venture, founded by the housing reform pioneer Octavia Hill and others in 1895. Its first two properties came through the gift of a small scenic coastal area in North Wales and the purchase for £10 of a 14th-century timber-framed clergy house in Alfriston, East Sussex. Open spaces and small houses remained the key interest until the 1930s, when it became evident that the country's stately homes must have priority. The first to be given was Blickling Hall in Norfolk, together with its contents, gardens and estate. By the close of the 20th century the Trust had come to own some 300 houses open to the public, as well as complete villages, such as Lacock, Wiltshire, given in 1944 by Matilda Talbot (a descendant of the photographic pioneer William Fox Talbot), and extensive areas of countryside.

***National Velvet.*** A novel (1935) by Enid Bagnold (1889–1981). Velvet, a butcher's daughter, wins a piebald horse in a raffle. Disguised as a boy, she rides it in the Grand National, Britain's premier steeplechase, and is first past the winning post, but is disqualified for dismounting before the weighing-in. A popular film version (1945), directed by Clarence Brown, starred the 14-year-old Elizabeth Taylor.

**Nation of Islam.** An African American nationalist religion, also known as Black Muslims, which evolved in the United States in the 20th century. The movement proper was founded by Wallace Fard, who established a temple in Detroit in 1931. The chief developer of the movement, however, was Elijah Muhammad (1897–1975), who founded a second temple in Chicago. The movement urges blacks to drop the 'slave religion' of Christianity and return to their native Islamic faith. The current leader is Louis Farrakhan (b.1933), a controversial figure who has been accused of anti-Semitism and who has been denied permission to enter the UK by the Home Office. *See also* FIVE PERCENTERS; MALCOLM X; MILLION MAN MARCH.

**Nation shall speak peace unto nation.** The motto of the BBC, suggested by Dr Montague Rendall, one of the first five governors, when the original company was incorporated in 1927. It is based on a phrase in a biblical verse: 'They shall beat their swords into ploughshares, and their spears into pruning hooks: nation shall not lift up sword against nation, neither shall they learn war any more' (Isaiah 2:4). There is something similar in Micah 4:3: 'Nation shall not lift up a sword against nation.'

**Native American.** A term for the indigenous peoples of the United States, favoured by many from the early 1970s for the formerly familiar Red Indians, whose skin is not uniformly copper-coloured and who are not Indians, although dubbed as such following Christopher Columbus's mistaken assumption that he had reached the East Indies. An intermediate variant, 'American Indian' or 'Amerindian', was also at one time a preferred designation, though these still have some currency in Central and South America. In Canada the equivalent term is 'First Nations', which usually excludes both the Inuit (formerly Eskimos) and the (originally mixed-race) Métis people. *See also* AFRICAN AMERICAN.

**Nato.** The North Atlantic Treaty Organization, set up in 1950 at the time of the COLD WAR for the defence of Europe and the North Atlantic against the perceived threat of Soviet aggression. Its founding members were the signatories of the North Atlantic Treaty of 1949: Britain, Canada, the United States, France (which became semi-detached from 1959, causing the headquarters to be moved from Paris to Brussels, before returning to the fold in the mid-1990s), Belgium, the Netherlands, Luxembourg, Norway, Denmark, Iceland, Italy and Portugal. Greece and Turkey joined Nato in 1952, West Germany in 1955 (unified Germany in 1990), and Spain in 1982. In response the Soviet Union and its allies signed the WARSAW PACT. The number of Nato members grew to 19 in 1999 with the accession of the Czech Republic, Hungary and Poland, and to 26 in 2004, when Bulgaria, Estonia, Latvia, Lithuania, Romania, Slovakia and Slovenia all joined.

**Nattering nabobs of negativism, The.** A phrase coined by Republican Vice President Spiro T. Agnew in a speech in San Diego, 11 September 1970:

In the United States today, we have more than our share of the nattering nabobs of negativism.

Agnew himself was obliged to resign on 10 October 1973 to avoid prosecution for corruption. *See also* CHATTERING CLASSES.

**Natural Law Party.** A body of TRANSCENDENTAL MEDITATION practitioners who came into the public eye in Britain in 1992 when they contested every seat in the general election and lost every one. They have their base at Mentmore Towers, Buckinghamshire, where they practise yogic flying, and their avowed aim is 'for everyone to enjoy Heaven on Earth through the implementation of Maharishi's Master Plan to Create Heaven on Earth'.

**Naturism.** Nudism, as practised for health, quasi-mystical or hedonistic reasons in holiday camps or other centres, typically by the seaside. The term dates from the 1930s, and implies both a 'state of nature' and an identity of the unclothed human body with the unadorned world of nature. The word is felt to have a respectability clearly not present in 'nudism', a word itself dating from the previous decade, and in 1961 members of the British Sun Bathing Association voted to substitute 'naturism' for 'nudism' in their official literature. *See also* NAKED AS NATURE INTENDED.

**Naughty bits.** A jocular euphemism for the male or female genitals or female breasts, popularized and possibly even coined by the creators of MONTY PYTHON'S FLYING CIRCUS. *See also* WOBBLY BITS.

**Naughty but nice.** Disobedient or forbidden (which is bad) but delectable (which is good). The phrase was the title of an American film of 1939, but was later familiar as an advertising slogan for various tasty products, such as cream cakes in the late 1970s (the novelist Salman Rushdie once claimed to have coined the phrase at this time as a slogan to promote fresh cream in cakes for the National Dairy Council). The ultimate source is undoubtedly the fuller phrase 'It's naughty but it's nice', found as the title of a song of 1873 by Arthur Lloyd. The words are sexually suggestive.

**Naughty Nineties.** The 1890s, when the puritanical Victorian code of behaviour and conduct gave way in certain wealthy and fashionable circles to growing laxity in sexual morals, a cult of hedonism, and a more light-hearted approach to life generally. The expression is first recorded only in the 1920s. A nickname for the 1990s has yet to be established. *See also* MAUVE DECADE; the NOUGHTIES.

***Nausea.*** (French title: *La Nausée*; alternative English title: *The Diary of Antoine Roquentin*.) A novel (1938; English translation 1949) by the French existential philosopher Jean-

Paul Sartre (1905–80). Roquentin, the protagonist, experiences nausea when he realizes that there is no reason for the existence of people or things:

> Things are entirely what they appear to be and *behind them …* there is nothing.

However, in the end he realizes that the very purposelessness of existence makes him absolutely free.

**Nautilus, USS.** A US submarine, the world's first nuclear-powered vessel (launched in 1954), which in 1958 sailed across the Arctic Ocean, under the polar ice cap and directly beneath the North Pole. *Nautilus* had also been the name of one of the first-ever submersible craft, designed by the American Robert Fulton in 1800. It is also the name of Captain Nemo's submarine in Jules Verne's *Twenty Thousand Leagues under the Sea* (1870). The name derives from the nautilus, a kind of marine mollusc related to squids and cuttlefish; this in turn owes its etymology to the Greek *nautilos*, 'sailor', from *naus*, 'ship'.

**Navel-gazing.** Complacent self-absorption; concentration on a single issue at the expense of a wider view. The allusion is to mystic religions such as Buddhism, in which the navel is venerated as the source of birth and being. To contemplate one's own navel, in the sense of spending time complacently considering one's own interests, is a similar concept. Such figurative expressions date from the turn of the 20th century.

**Nazi.** A shortened form for a member of the National-sozialistische Deutsche Arbeiterpartei or NSDAP (National Socialist German Workers' Party), founded in 1919 and led by Adolf Hitler from 1921 to 1945. The term is now used colloquially and derogatorily to describe any person of extreme right-wing views. *See also* MEIN KAMPF; NIGHT OF THE LONG KNIVES; SA; SS.

**Near miss.** A narrowly avoided mishap; an attempt that almost succeeds. The expression is first recorded in the Second World War with reference to a bomb exploding in the water near enough to a ship to cause damage but not to sink it. It could have been a hit, but was fortunately a miss, and 'a miss is a good as a mile'. The phrase was probably based on the earlier 'near thing'.

**Neasden.** A district of the North London borough of Brent that in the mid-20th century came to be regarded as a typical London suburb, faceless and formless. It was satirically pictured as such by *Private Eye*, no doubt partly on account of its name, which, though actually meaning 'nose-shaped hill', suggests 'Nilsdon' or in US terms 'Nowheresville'.

**Neddy.** The popular name for the National Economic Development Council set up by the British government in 1962 and functioning until 1992. The numerous economic development committees for particular industries that appeared were called 'Little Neddies'.

**Needle park.** A small open space in a city frequented by drug users, who gather there to inject heroin. The term was originally applied, in the early 1960s, to the traffic roundabout at Broadway and 71st Street, New York City, and was brought to wider notice by James Mills's book *The Panic in Needle Park* (1966).

**Needless Markup.** A jocular nickname, first recorded in the mid-1990s, for the US department store Neiman-Marcus, reflecting many customers' views of its prices. Its reputation was no doubt not helped by an URBAN LEGEND, widely dispersed in the United States, that the store once charged a customer $250 for a $2.50 cookie recipe.

**Need no introduction.** To be known to all concerned. The expression is popular among those who introduce a speaker to a meeting, although some negate its import by following it with a potted biography of the individual in question.

**Need something like a hole in the head.** Not to need it at all. The expression dates from the 1940s and renders the Yiddish phrase *ich darf es vi a loch in kop*, 'I need it like a hole in the head'.

**Neets.** An acronymic social category in the 15-to-24-year-old age group, in full 'not in education, employment or training'. In 2005 it was estimated that there were over 1 million Neets in Britain. *See also* TWENTY-SOMETHING.

**Negative equity.** A situation in which a homeowner is burdened with a mortgage greater than the market value of the house. This was a common situation in the UK recession of the early 1990s, following the house-price boom of the later 1980s. *See also* GREEN SHOOTS.

**Nehru jacket.** A type of lapel-less jacket that button down the front, popular in the 1960s. It was based on that worn by Jawaharlal Nehru (1889–1964), the first prime minister of independent India, and was promoted in modified form by the French couturier Pierre Cardin. *See also* MAO SUIT.

**Neighbourhood Watch.** A scheme to dissuade suburban criminals from their nefarious deeds. As a result of increasing crime, especially burglary, residents in particular areas began organizing Neighbourhood Watch groups from the early 1980s with police cooperation. Stickers in their windows alert passers-by that a Watch scheme is in operation, the theory being that they provide a disincentive to thieves. Suspicious activities and circumstances are reported to the police, and some worthwhile effect on burglary has often resulted. The idea was copied from similar schemes in the United States.

**Neocon.** A colloquial abbreviation (first recorded in 1979) of 'neoconservative', a member of a group of mostly US Republican politicians, POLICY WONKS and academics who have reacted against the socially progressive and leftish values that came to dominate public discourse in the United States in the 1960s and 1970s, as well as the foreign-policy realpolitik of Republican luminaries such as Henry Kissinger, who advocated the backing of distasteful regimes in order to maintain balances of power. The 'neo' prefix reflects the fact that many neocons were originally liberals, Democrats or even socialists, a lineage apparent in their strong desire to change the world. Neocons are known for their unilateralist and interventionist stance on foreign affairs, in which they advocate the expansion of freedom and democracy in the Third World, sometimes backed by military force (as in Iraq in 2003). The German-born US political scientist Leo Strauss (1898–1973) is often regarded as the 'father' or 'godfather' of neoconservatism, with his assertion that the relativism inherent in liberalism is essentially nihilistic, and this he blamed for what he perceived as the aimlessness of modern US society.

The administration of President George W. Bush is particularly associated with neoconservative values in foreign policy, unlike the presidency of his father. Prominent neocons include Vice-President Dick Cheney, Secretary of Defense Donald Rumsfeld, and his former deputy, Paul Wolfowitz, once described as 'the neocon's neocon' (in 2005 he became president of the World Bank).

> Although it was normal at first to distinguish the neo-conservatives from the traditional conservatives, whose power-base is rural and whose ideal is of a moral majority, the two currents of US conservatism have increasingly flowed together, and are now almost indistinguishable.
>
> ROGER SCRUTON: *A Dictionary of Political Thought* (2nd edn, 1996)

*See also* CHICKENHAWKS.

**NEP.** *See* NEW ECONOMIC POLICY.

**Nerd.** This term for a studious but tedious person dates from the 1950s but only fully came into its own in the 1980s, when a T-shirt reading 'I'm a Nerd, and I'm Proud' was popular. A typical nerd wears a white shirt, baggy trousers and black-rimmed glasses, and carries a pack of pens in his shirt pocket. The term itself apparently derives from Californian surfers' jargon. *See also* ANORAK; BOGAN; GEEK; MELVIN; NIGEL.

> And the jock shall dwell with the nerd and the cheerleader lie down with the wimp and there will be peace upon the campus.
>
> *The Observer* (29 May 1988)

**Nervous Nelly.** A nickname for a foolish or timid person. It was originally used of Frank B. Kellogg (1856–1937), the US secretary of state from 1925 to 1929. He was so dubbed by isolationists when he negotiated the Kellogg–Briand Pact (1928) to outlaw war.

> He called her 'flibbertigibbet' and 'nervous Nellie', according to the not-always-accurate *National Enquirer*.
>
> *heat* (13–19 January 2000)

**Nervous wreck.** A person suffering from stress or emotional exhaustion. The phrase dates from the early 20th century with 'nervous' qualifying 'wreck' in the sense of a physically or mentally broken person.

**Nesbitt, Rab C.** The string-vested Scottish philosopher of this name, created by Ian Pattison, was wonderfully embodied by the actor Gregor Fisher, who first assumed his persona in the television sketch series *Naked Video* (1986–91). He burgeoned to his full foul-mouthed, beer-boozing self in the series that bore his name, first screened in 1990, where he appears with his wife, Mary, his teenage sons, Gash and Burney, his devious drinking pal, Jamesie, and the latter's baby-craving wife, Ella. Beneath his crude exterior Rab is patently a vulnerable individual and at the very least a loveable rogue. He soon endeared himself to viewers, even if many of them could make little of his slang-ridden speech and his almost impenetrable musings, delivered in a strong Glasgow accent.

**Netball.** The sport of this name originated at a physical training college for girls in Hampstead, where in 1895 a visiting American introduced a version of basketball that the girls played with wastepaper baskets at each end of the hall. The rules were at first imprecise, but were codified in 1901. Netball's association with girls' schools stems entirely from this particular place of origin. In modern times the game has become familiar to Londoners and visitors to London from the lunchtime games played by office staff in Lincoln's Inn Fields. *See also* KORFBALL.

**Net Book Agreement.** The agreement set up in Britain in 1900 between booksellers and publishers, by which, with a few exceptions, the former undertook not to sell books at less than the price marked on the cover. The agreement effectively collapsed in 1995 when three major publishers, HarperCollins, Random Century and PENGUIN BOOKS, withdrew their support. Since then, while the so-called 'deep discounting' of some bestsellers and selected other titles by bookshops and, increasingly, supermarkets has altered the expectations of book buyers, the vast majority of books in bookshops remain at their cover prices. However, the emergence of Amazon and similar INTERNET booksellers, which discount across a wide range of titles, has mounted a challenge to all physical bookshops.

**Net-head.** A nickname for an enthusiastic or compulsive user of the computer INTERNET. The term originated in the early 1990s as US jargon. *See also* NETIQUETTE.

**Nether regions.** A genteel euphemism for the genital and excretory area, adopted from an earlier term for the underworld or hell. *See also* DOWN THERE.

**Netiquette.** A punning semi-serious coinage of the 1990s for the largely unwritten rules of behaviour on the INTERNET, especially with regard to using E-MAIL and CHAT ROOMS. The coinage has developed into an established term. *See also* FLAMING.

**Neue Sachlichkeit.** (German, 'New Objectivity'.) A movement in German art in the 1920s and 1930s that reflected the resignation and cynicism of the postwar period. It had no unified style or group affiliation, but its main trend involved the use of meticulous detail and violent satire to portray the face of evil. Its leading exponents were Otto Dix (1891–1969) and George Grosz (1893–1959). The name of the movement, which dissipated in the 1930s with the rise of the NAZIS, was coined in 1923 by Gustav Hartlaub, director of the Kunsthalle, Mannheim, and was used by him as the title of an exhibition he staged there in 1925.

**Never a dull moment.** A phrase used positively to indicate the constant variety of a full life but also negatively or ironically in allusion to something difficult or dangerous. The expression apparently arose in the Royal Navy in the 1930s and from there spread to civilian use.

**Never Give a Sucker an Even Break.** A film comedy (1941) written by and starring the US comedian W.C. Fields (1879–1946). Its absurd plot, which begins with Fields falling out of an aeroplane in pursuit of his bottle of whisky, was allegedly jotted down by Fields ON THE BACK OF AN ENVELOPE and sold to Universal Studios for $25,000. Released in the UK under the less memorable title *What a Man!*, the film is now known chiefly for its title, which has long been quoted as a quintessentially Fieldsian piece of advice. Fields himself suggested shortening it to *Fields: Sucker*, thinking the longer version might be a trifle unwieldy.

**Never had it so good.** A phrase popularized in Britain by its use by Harold Macmillan, Conservative prime minister (1957–63), in a speech at Bedford (20 July 1957):

> Let's be frank about it. Most of our people have never had it so good. Go around the country, go to the industrial towns, go to the farms, and you'll see a state of prosperity such as we have never had in my lifetime – nor indeed ever in the history of this country. What is beginning to worry some of us is 'Is it too good to be true?'

It was not original, though. It appears to have been coined by the American labour leader George Meany (1894–1980) and was used as a Democratic Party slogan in the 1952 US presidential election.

**Neverland.** *See* NEVER NEVER LAND.

**Never Mind the Bollocks, Here's the Sex Pistols.** The title of a famous/infamous PUNK album by The Sex Pistols released in 1977, including the songs 'Anarchy in the UK', 'GOD SAVE THE QUEEN', 'Pretty Vacant' and 'Holidays in the Sun'. An apocryphal story tells that Malcolm McLaren, the manager of the Sex Pistols, was in a pub with the guitarist Steve Jones and was anxious because Virgin, the company to which they had just signed, was demanding a title for the album and they didn't have one. Jones commented: 'Never mind all that bollocks', and thus a title was found. Jamie Reid, who designed the album's cover, gives a different account, claiming that he and Jones were discussing possible titles with John Varnom of Virgin, one possibility being 'God Save the Sex Pistols', when Jones, unimpressed, said 'Never mind the bollocks.' *See also* ROCK GROUP NAMES.

**Never Mind the Quality, Feel the Width.** A television SITCOM broadcast from 1967 to 1971, centring on the unlikely business partnership formed in the East End of London between Patrick Kelly, an Irish Catholic trousermaker, played by Joe Lynch (initially by Frank Finlay), and Emmanuel Cohen, a Jewish jacketmaker, played by John Bluthal. The humour largely devolves on the inability of each to understand the other's religious beliefs, patriotic loyalties or philosophy of life. Yet, although they are apparently incompatible, the two need each other to succeed in their enterprise, just as a jacket needs trousers. The title is said to have derived from a phrase that one of the scriptwriters, Vince Powell, had heard an Irish tailor use, but it may have been a deliberate inversion of a cloth trade saying: 'Never mind the width, feel the quality.'

**Never-never.** To get or buy something on the never-never is to obtain it on hire purchase, a system of deferred payment.

**Never Never Land.** The land (originally 'the Never Land') where the Lost Boys and Red Indians live, and where Pirates sail up the lake, in J.M. Barrie's PETER PAN (1904). *Neverland* is the title of a 2004 film about J.M. Barrie and the real-life Lost Boys, starring Johnny Depp. The phrase 'Never Never Land' was also applied to the whole of the Australian outback, but since the publication of Jeannie Gunn's *We of the Never-Never* (1908), an affectionate portrait of life in the back of beyond at the turn of the 20th century, it has been restricted to northwest Queensland and the Northern Territory.

Michael Jackson (*see* WACKO JACKO), the Peter Pan of pop, calls his Californian ranch Neverland.

**Never Say Never Again.** A film (1983) starring Sean Connery as secret agent James BOND, based on the spy novels of Ian Fleming (1908–64). The title was an in-joke between the movie producers and Connery himself, who had sworn that his appearance in the earlier Bond movie, DIAMONDS ARE FOREVER (1971), would be his last.

**New ..., The.** The fashionable alternative to the stated thing at any given time. The expression first found popularity among fashion writers, enthusiastically identifying 'the new black' (as in 'Orange is the new black'). A particular (now clichéd) collocation is 'the NEW ROCK 'N' ROLL', applied to every transient fad deemed to be COOL.

**New Age.** A world view of the late 1980s centring on ALTERNATIVE medicine, astrology, spiritualism, animism and the like. Two notable phenomena of the period were New Age music, a type of gentle melodic music combining elements of jazz, folk and classical music, played largely on electronic instruments, and New Age travellers, groups of latter-day HIPPIES who lead a nomadic existence, travelling the country with their children and animals in ancient vehicles to set up camp at such spiritually significant sites as Stonehenge or Glastonbury (*see* GLASTONBURY FESTIVAL). The name itself evokes the AGE OF AQUARIUS.

**New black, The.** *See* NEW ROCK 'N' ROLL.

**New Boots and Panties!!** A characterful pop album by Ian Dury (1942–2000) and The Blockheads, released in 1977. The album contains a series of witty musical portraits of characters such as 'Plaistow Patricia', 'Billericay Dickie' and 'Clevor Trever', the last two being a pair of Essex men (*see* ESSEX MAN) *avant la lettre*. Blending music-hall vulgarity with elements of PUNK, the songs owe much of their impact to Dury's playfully sinister cockney voice and his imaginatively crude lyrics. 'Plaistow Patricia' is a seedy East End drug-addict, killing herself through a life of excess; 'Billericay Dickie' tells the sordid tale of the

conquests of an Essex WIDE BOY; while 'Clevor Trever' (the misspellings are intentional), represents the sorry attempts at self-expression of the hopelessly inarticulate Trevor of the title.

> Had a love-affair with Nina in the back of my Cortina,
> A seasoned-up hyena could not have been more obscener.
> IAN DURY: 'Billericay Dickie' (1977)

**New Criticism.** A school of literary critical theory that emerged after the First World War. It insisted on the intrinsic value of a work of art and concentrated attention on the individual work as an independent unit of meaning, apart from the circumstances of its writing or its author's biography. The technique employed in the approach, involving a close, analytical reading of the text, is the subject of I.A. Richards' *The Principles of Literary Criticism* (1924) and William Empson's *Seven Types of Ambiguity* (1930). The movement did not have a name, however, until it was further treated in John Crowe Ransom's *The New Criticism* (1941).

**New Deal.** The name given to US President Franklin D. Roosevelt's (*see* FDR) policy of economic reconstruction to tackle the effects of the GREAT DEPRESSION, announced in his first presidential campaign (1932): 'I pledge you, I pledge myself, to a new deal for the American people.' A relief and recovery programme known as the 'First New Deal' was inaugurated in March 1933, and a 'Second New Deal', which was concerned with social reform, in January 1935. The 'Third New Deal' of 1938 sought to preserve gains made by its predecessors. In Britain in the late 1990s NEW LABOUR introduced a number of 'New Deals' as special initiatives intended to improve the country's social, economic and educational status.

**New Economic Policy.** A policy introduced in the Soviet Union by LENIN in 1921, to replace the 'war communism' that had been official policy since the 1917 OCTOBER REVOLUTION. The NEP was introduced in the wake of economic difficulties and disturbances such as the KRONSTADT MUTINY. It allowed a degree of private enterprise and internal trade, and established state banks. It was replaced under STALIN in 1929 by the first of the FIVE-YEAR PLANs. *See also* KULAKS.

**New Europe.** *See* OLD EUROPE.

**New Frontier.** The phrase coined by John F. Kennedy (1917–63) to encapsulate the spirit of what he intended to do as president of the United States. He used it in Los Angeles in his speech accepting the Democratic Party nomination, on 15 July 1960:

We stand today on the edge of a new frontier – the frontier of the 1960s – a frontier of unknown opportunities and perils – a frontier of unfulfilled hopes and threats.

The reference was to the 'frontier spirit' of the 19th-century American pioneers, and Kennedy deliberately contrasted his ambitions with what many regarded as the complacency of the Eisenhower years (what the American poet Robert Lowell called 'the tranquillized Fifties'). In particular, Kennedy set the country the challenge of sending a man to the moon. The escalation of the war in VIETNAM was to be another symptom of the restlessness of the era. *See also* GREAT AND THE GOOD.

**New jack.** In rappers' slang, a young newcomer or novice, a NEW KID ON THE BLOCK, as yet inexperienced in the ways of the streets. Hence, 'new-jack swing', a style of rhythm and blues influenced by rap music. In US drugs slang, the term also refers to a mixture of heroin and morphine.

**New kids on the block.** Newcomers to a particular place or activity, especially those who have yet to prove themselves. The American phrase was popularized by New Kids on the Block, a pop group of five New England teenagers who enjoyed a brilliant but brief career in the first half of the 1990s. 'Block' here is an urban area centring on a block of buildings.

**New Labour.** The LABOUR PARTY as restyled under Tony Blair, who became its leader in 1994. While paying lip service to the party's traditional socialist values (characterized as 'Old Labour'), it stressed the importance of the individual in society and indicated its receptiveness to new ideals and aspirations and its willingness to modernize. Its acceptance of many aspects of market-based economics overturned the Old Labour policy of nationalization. *See also* BLAIRISM; BLATCHERISM; CLAUSE FOUR; COOL BRITANNIA; EDUCATION, EDUCATION, EDUCATION; MANDY; SPIN DOCTOR.

Everybody should have a taste of the good life. A decade ago it was the Tories; now it is New Labour.
*Sunday Times* (10 October 1999)

**New lad.** A young man who embraces sexist attitudes and who pointedly eschews POLITICAL CORRECTNESS and the apparent effeteness of the NEW MAN. The concept of the new lad evolved in the early 1990s and later came to be associated with young rock bands and BRITPOP. The use of 'lad' evokes such phrases as 'a bit of a lad' and 'one of the lads'. *See also* LADETTE.

**New Look.** The name given to the long-skirted women's dress of 1947 that was launched as the DIOR LOOK. The style was reminiscent of the EDWARDIAN ERA and was shortlived.

The phrase is also used generally for a redesigned periodical or restructured radio or television programme. An annual 'makeover' of this kind usually takes place in the autumn.

Next week, your *New Statesman* will have a new look. Alongside a brighter, easier-to-read design, we shall bring you an extended arts, culture and books section.
*New Statesman* (11 September 1998)

**New man.** In late-20th-century terms, a man who actively expresses his latent caring nature by helping with domestic work and young children in the home. *See also* HOUSE HUSBAND; NEW LAD; METROSEXUAL; NEW WOMAN.

Laddish [television chef] Jamie Oliver may be, but he's New Man enough to offer to cook for his sister's hen night and offer his utterly cool Central London apartment for the occasion.
*The Times* (21 April 1999)

**New morality.** A popular term of the 1960s, implying that the hitherto publicly accepted canons of morality were no longer relevant to contemporary society, owing to the rapid spread of social and technical change, the advent of the PILL, and more 'enlightened' attitudes generally. Such thinking was, it was argued, induced by the growth of the AFFLUENT SOCIETY, the diminishing of individual responsibility occasioned by the WELFARE STATE, the declining influence of Christian standards and 'middle-class morality', and the championship of hedonism and self-indulgence by certain writers and theorists. *See also* NEW WOMAN.

**New Order.** *See* NEW WORLD ORDER.

**New rock 'n' roll.** Something new, highly fashionable and, potentially, profitable. The term draws on the impact made by ROCK 'N' ROLL in the 1950s, when the new style of music was seen as the quintessence of all that was modish and exciting. In the 1990s, as the BABY BOOM generation hit middle age, both gardening and cookery became 'the new rock 'n' roll'. More generally, 'X is the new Y' has become a dreary journalistic cliché. *See also* the NEW ....

**New Romantic.** A follower of a style of popular music and fashion in vogue in the early 1980s, post-PUNK ROCK, in which both men and women wore make-up (often black) and dressed in flamboyant clothes (lacy cuffs and frilly shirts on men, playing on the cod-Romantic theme). Androgyny was a key feature, and groups such as Culture Club, Duran Duran, New Order (*see* NEW WORLD ORDER) and Soft Cell were typical of the genre, while Boy George (b.1961) was one of its more outré exponents. The lifestyle, with the usual crop of CRASH AND BURN casualties, faded out of fashion by the end of the decade, but the music saw a revived popularity in the early 21st century.

**News of the Screws.** A frivolous nickname for the *News of the World*, a Sunday newspaper specializing in sensational stories of sexual shenanigans.

**Newsom Report.** The report *Half Our Future* (1963) by Sir John Newsom (1910–71) considered the education of 13- to 16-year-olds of average and less than average ability attending full-time courses at school or in further education establishments. It recommended a raising of the school age to 16 for all pupils entering secondary schools from 1965 and certain other measures, ranging from the replacement of slum secondary schools by new schools to positive guidance on sexual behaviour. The report was compassionate and practical and the policies it advocated were taken up again in the PLOWDEN REPORT, when Newsom served as chairman.

**Newspeak.** A language in which words change their meaning to accord with the official views of the state. The word was coined by George ORWELL in his novel *Nineteen Eighty-Four* (*see* 1984). An example of Newspeak is 'War is peace. Freedom is slavery. Ignorance is strength.'

> Don't you see that the whole aim of Newspeak is to narrow the range of thought? In the end we shall make thought-crime literally impossible, because there will be no words in which to express it.
> Pt 1, ch. 5

*See also* DOUBLETHINK.

**New Statesman, The.** A moderate left-wing weekly magazine founded in 1913 by the social reformers and Fabian Society founders Sidney (1859–1947) and Beatrice Webb (1858–1943).

A television SITCOM of the same title, screened on ITV from 1987 to 1992, centred on the blatant machinations and depravities of the newly elected Conservative MP Alan B'Stard, played by Rik Mayall. Despite the outrageous travesty of political life, the series nevertheless reflected some truths of 1980s Britain. The story owed much of its success to Mayall's full engagement with his obnoxious persona, allowing his character's latent boyish charm to shine through the sleaze.

**News to me.** Something I was not aware of. The expression dates from the beginning of the 20th century, typically in the phrase 'That's news to me.' One may similarly apprise a person of a fact by saying 'I have news for you', especially when one believes they are misinformed or mistaken. *See also* HAVE I GOT NEWS FOR YOU.

**New town.** A town established as a new settlement with the aim of relocating populations away from large cities. The first new towns in Britain were inspired by the GARDEN CITY concept formulated at the end of the 19th century. They were proposed in the New Towns Act of 1946, and 12 were designated in England and Wales over the next four years, with a further two in Scotland. Each had its own development corporation financed by the government. Further new towns were set up in the 1960s. Many new towns are based on existing towns or villages. The general tally is:

ENGLAND: Basildon, Bracknell, Central Lancashire, Crawley, Harlow, Hatfield, Hemel Hempstead, Stevenage, Welwyn Garden City, Newton Aycliffe, Corby, Milton Keynes, Northampton, Peterborough, Peterlee, Redditch, Runcorn, Skelmersdale, Telford, Warrington, Washington

WALES: Cwmbran, Newtown

SCOTLAND: Cumbernauld, East Kilbride, Glenrothes, Irvine, Livingston

Northern Ireland had a separate New Towns scheme (Antrim and Ballymena, Craigavon, Derry/Londonderry). New Towns have, technically, ceased to exist, the responsibilities of their development corporations passing to local authorities and other bodies in 1992–6.

**New wave.** A type of rock music in vogue in the late 1970s. It derived from PUNK ROCK but was generally more melodious in sound and less aggressive in performance. 'New Wave' is also used as the English equivalent of NOUVELLE VAGUE.

**New woman.** A type of 'liberated', independently minded and self-motivated woman who emerged in the late 19th century as a successor to the feminist crusaders of the 1860s. Her successors in the 20th century include the 'career girl' or 'career woman' of the 1950s and, in the backlash against the open promiscuity and AIDS scares of the 1980s, the NEW MORALITY 'virgin' or sexual abstainer of the 1990s. The term has largely been a creation of the media. *See also* NEW MAN.

**New World Order.** A state of affairs held by some commentators to have arrived with the ending of the COLD WAR and the collapse of the Soviet Union in 1991. In this New World Order there was only one superpower, the United States, which would act as 'the world's policeman'. The apparent unity of so many countries in following the US lead in condemning Iraq's invasion of Kuwait in 1990, and in the First GULF WAR (1991), seemed to confirm this view. In a much- discussed book, the US academic Francis Fukuyama proclaimed *The* END OF HISTORY (1992) and the final victory of Western-style capitalism and liberal democracy.

Subsequent events have cast a shadow over this triumph-alism and the United States has been criticized for acting as 'the world's policeman' only where US interests are affected. The term has unfortunate echoes of Hitler's plans for a 'New Order' in Europe, and the 'New Order in East Asia' declared by the Japanese government in 1938.

In 1940 H.G. Wells published a book with the title *The New World Order*. New Order was also the name of a British band founded in 1980 as a successor to Joy Division, after the suicide of lead singer Ian Curtis.

**New Year's resolution.** A decision made on New Year's Eve to abandon a bad habit or adopt a good one in the New Year. A survey in 1997 showed that two people out of three make such resolutions, but most soon break them. The most popular resolutions are to give up smoking and to diet.

***New Yorker, The.*** An influential weekly American magazine launched in February 1925 by Harold Ross (who edited it until his death, in 1951) and Jane Grant with funds from the family that owned the Fleischmann Yeast Company. It was aimed at an urbane and literate readership, and became famous for certain regular features, such as its 'Profiles' or biographical sketches of prominent living men and women, its short stories, and its generally liberal-leaning political coverage. Cartoons and comic drawings in the magazine have also had a widespread influence on artists and editors elsewhere. It underwent significant changes in style and editorial practice in the late 1980s and early 1990s, parti-cularly under the somewhat controversial and 'glitzy' editorship (1992–8) of Englishwoman Tina Brown, but on the whole it retained its high-profile image and the loyalty of its longstanding readers (as well as some lovable editorial quirks, such as the use of a diaresis to aid pronunciation in double-vowelled words such as 'reënact' or 'coöperate'). In 2004 *The New Yorker* hit the headlines when Seymour Hersh (*see also* MY LAI MASSACRE) revealed in its pages the recent US abuse of Iraqi prisoners at Abu Ghraib prison, west of Baghdad. The magazine's editor since 1998 is David Remnick, only the fifth in its history.

**Nice guys finish last.** A phrase that originated in 1946, in a remark by the US baseball coach Leo Durocher (1906–91), and recorded thus by journalists present:

All nice guys. They'll finish last. Nice guys. Finish last.

The phrase has since been adapted into a rule of sexual etiquette.

**Nice little earner.** Money earned easily or effortlessly, possibly but not necessarily illicitly. The colloquialism was popularized by the main character, Arthur Daley, in the television series MINDER. *See also* HER INDOORS.

**Nice Nellyism.** Excessive prudishness. A US expression emerging in the 1930s and based on 'nice Nelly' as a conventional nickname for an ultra-respectable woman.

**Nice one.** A general term of approval, popularized in the 1970s by 'Nice one, Cyril', originally used in a television commercial of 1972 for Wonderloaf bread, and subsequently taken up by football fans in a chant dedicated to the Tottenham Hotspur player Cyril Knowles. The Spurs team went on to record, under the name Cockerel Chorus, a song based on the phrase:

Nice one, Cyril.
Nice one, son!
Nice one, Cyril.
Let's have another one.
SPIRO and CLARKE: 'Nice One, Cyril' (1973)

**Nice work if you can get it.** An envious reaction to what is seen as someone's more favourable situation, especially one easily obtained. The words quote the title of a song by Ira Gershwin:

Holding hands at midnight
'Neath a starry sky,
Nice work if you can get it,
And you can get it if you try.
IRA GERSHWIN: *Damsel in Distress*, 'Nice Work If You Can Get It' (1937)

The expression gave David Lodge the title of his campus novel *Nice Work* (1988), about an affair between a university English lecturer and a factory manager.

**Niche marketing.** The selling of a product or service in a profitable corner of a commercial market. The con-cept evolved from the 1960s, and the art of identifying and exploiting this type of market became known as nichemanship.

**Nickelodeon.** The first cinema theatre called a 'Nickelodeon' (i.e. 'Nickel Odeon', because the admission price was only five cents), was that opened by John P. Harris and Harry Davis at McKeesport, near Pittsburgh, Pennsylvania, in 1905. The picture shown was *The Great Train Robbery*. It was the first real motion-picture theatre and thousands more nickelodeons soon sprang up throughout the United States. Hence, a cheap entertainment, and also its application to a JUKE BOX.

Put another nickel in,
In the nickelodeon,
All I want is loving you
And music, music, music.
STEPHEN WEISS and BERNIE BAUM: 'Music, Music, Music' (1950)

**Nicknames.** *See* DRUG NICKNAMES; FILM STAR NICKNAMES; SPORTING NICKNAMES.

**Nicorette.** A proprietary name familiar from the 1980s for a type of nicotine-flavoured chewing-gum used to reduce dependency on tobacco. The name is apparently a blend of 'nicotine' and 'cigarette', thus seemingly delivering the very objects of desire that the taker seeks to abandon.

**Nigel.** A male forename that for some reason gained a pejorative patina in the 1960s. It came to be regarded as typical of the British upper-middle-class or upper-class male, and was seen as epitomizing young men who drive sports cars and wear flat caps and tweed jackets. It has since acquired NERD overtones.

> I am proud of never quite managing to live up to the awfulness of being Nigel. I think that was one of the reasons I wrote my first situation comedy under a false name.
>
> NIGEL WILLIAMS: in *Sunday Times* (7 November 1999)

**Nigel Molesworth.** *See* Nigel MOLESWORTH.

**Night at the Opera, A.** A film comedy (1935) written by George S. Kaufman and Morrie Ryskind and starring the MARX BROTHERS. As the title suggests, the film has an operatic setting and culminates in the hilarious sabotaging of a performance of Verdi's opera *Il Trovatore*. The title enjoyed a new lease of life in the 1970s as the title of a bestselling album released by the British rock group Queen.

**Nighthawks.** A painting (1942) by the US artist Edward Hopper (1882–1967), showing people at an all-night coffee stand. A nighthawk is the same as a 'night owl', i.e. someone who likes to stay up all night. A nighthawk – also called a mosquito hawk or bulbat – is also any of a group of American nightjars.

*Nighthawks* has also been used as the title of two films, one (1978) about the night-time cruising of a gay British schoolteacher, and the other (1981) about American policemen pursuing a terrorist.

**Night in Casablanca, A.** A film comedy (1946) featuring the MARX BROTHERS. Starring Groucho Marx as the manager of a hotel in Casablanca much frequented by spies, it clearly owed a great deal to the Bogart classic CASABLANCA. Warner Brothers, which had released *Casablanca*, threatened to sue over the use of the word 'Casablanca' in the title, only for Groucho to retort that if they did then he would sue them in return over their use of the word 'Brothers'.

**Night Mail.** A landmark British documentary film (1936), directed by John Grierson of the GPO Film Unit. The film follows the journey of the mail train from London to Glasgow, with specially commissioned music by Benjamin Britten and verse by W.H. Auden:

> This is the Night Mail crossing the Border,
> Bringing the cheque and the postal order,
> Letters for the rich, letters for the poor,
> The shop at the corner, the girl next door.

***Nightmare on Elm Street.*** *See* ELM STREET.

**Night of the Barricades.** The name given to the night of 10 May 1968, when students of the Sorbonne in Paris, locked out of their campus, fought the tear gas of the riot police with barricades, bricks, paving stones and MOLOTOV COCKTAILS. The unrest was the climax of a nationwide movement of protest against the authoritarianism of the GAULLIST regime. The name recalls earlier occasions of Parisian unrest, notably the three-day 'war of the barricades' during the Revolution of July 1830.

**Night of the Long Knives.** A descriptive phrase applied to the night of 30 June 1934, when Hitler, assisted by Himmler's SS, secured the murder of the leaders of the SA. The shootings (mainly at Munich and Berlin) actually began on the Friday night of the 29th and continued through the Sunday. The estimates of those killed vary between 60 and 400; Ernst Röhm and Kurt von Schleicher were among them. Hitler had decided to rely on the *Reichswehr* (the army) rather than risk dependence on the SA. Himmler presented the assassins with 'daggers of honour' inscribed with his name. On 13 July Hitler addressed the Reichstag:

> It was no secret that this time the revolution would have to be bloody … When we spoke of it, we called it 'The Night of the Long Knives [*Die Nacht der langen Messer*]'.

In British politics the term is used of 13 July 1962, when Harold Macmillan sacked a third of his cabinet following a disastrous by-election (*see also* MAC THE KNIFE). It was this event that prompted Liberal MP Jeremy Thorpe's verdict (echoing St John 15:13):

> Greater love hath no man than this, that he lay down his friends for his life.

When on 14 August 1981 Margaret Thatcher dismissed some WETS from her own cabinet, some commentators referred to the cull as 'the night of the long hatpin'. Macmillan's cull was in turn evoked by journalists to describe Tony Blair's May 2006 cabinet reshuffle (*see* BLAIR DITCH PROJECT). The term has its antecedents. George Borrow, referring to a treacherous murder of South British chieftains by Hengist in 472, wrote:

> This infernal carnage the Welsh have appropriately denominated the treachery of the long knives. It will be as

well to observe that the Saxons derived their name from the saxes, or long knives, which they wore at their sides, and at the use of which they were terribly proficient.

*Wild Wales*, ch lii (1862)

**Night starvation.** A phrase created and promoted in the early 1930s by the manufacturers of HORLICKS malted milk powder drink, the theory being that a cup of their product just before bedtime would maintain blood and sugar levels throughout the night and so give restful sleep. A healthy person does not, of course, normally starve or go hungry in the night, although the suggestion of abstinence from food is present in the word 'breakfast', meaning the meal with which one breaks one's fast. Horlicks itself takes its name from William A. Horlick (1846–1936), a saddler's son from Gloucestershire who emigrated to the United States in 1869 and together with his brother James, a chemist, began to manufacture baby food in Chicago in 1873.

**Night to Remember, A.** A DISASTER MOVIE (1958) adapted by Eric Ambler from a book by Walter Lord about the sinking of the TITANIC on the night of 14 April 1912. The *Titanic* had by then already sunk once, in a film simply entitled *Titanic* in 1953, and went down once more, under the same title, in 1997, with Leonardo DiCaprio and Kate Winslet on board. In 1980 Lew Grade attempted to reverse the process in his film *Raise the Titanic*, the financial cost of which prompted Grade himself to observe that it would have been cheaper to have lowered the Atlantic.

**Nightwatchman.** In cricket a term (first recorded in 1948) for an inferior batsman sent in to bat when a wicket falls just before the end of the day. The aim is to avoid the dismissal of a better batsman, who thus remains 'protected' for the following day's play, just as a nightwatchman guards a building overnight.

**Nike.** A make of training shoes, first on sale in 1972 and soon becoming a fashionable item of footwear, even among non-sporting fans. The name is that of the goddess of victory in Greek mythology, who on vases of the classical period is depicted striding, running or flying. The name is pronounced to rhyme with 'spiky', not 'spike'.

**Nikkei index.** The figure indicating the price of shares on the Tokyo Stock Exchange. The name is an abbreviation of Japanese *Nihon Keizai Shimbun*, 'Japanese Economic Newspaper', which has calculated the index since 1974. An earlier index was calculated by the Tokyo Stock Exchange itself.

**Nimby.** An acronym of 'not in my back yard', expressing the stance adopted by someone who objects to a development

perceived as undesirable or hazardous in their own neighbourhood, while not raising the same objection about a similar development elsewhere. The expression often relates to environmental issues, such as the proposed location of a nuclear waste disposal site or the construction of a new bypass. The term dates from the 1980s and the use of 'yard' betrays its US origin. A Briton would be more likely to say 'not in my back garden'.

**9½ Weeks.** A film (1986) in which Mickey Rourke and Kim Bassinger spend the specified period having a steamy affair. The film stirred some at the time, but left others dozing.

> One great hole on the screen for two hours.
> *Variety* magazine, 1986

**9/11.** The predominant shorthand way of referring to SEPTEMBER 11 2001, the day on which AL-QAIDA launched airborne attacks on the United States. The usage had no difficulty in establishing itself in British English, despite its being configured in the US way, with the month preceding the day. On that day hijacked passenger aircraft were deliberately flown into the TWIN TOWERS of the WORLD TRADE CENTER and into the PENTAGON. More than 80 people were killed in the latter assault, 2749 in the former. A fourth plane was destined for the White House, but the hijackers were overpowered by its passengers, and it crashed prematurely. The images of the two planes hitting the Twin Towers and their subsequent collapse were seen live on television by an audience of millions, and seared themselves into the world's memory. In retaliation the United States launched its WAR ON TERROR, striking at Afghanistan, toppling the TALIBAN regime and destroying Al-Qaida bases there, and searching unsuccessfully for its leading figure, Osama BIN LADEN (b.1957).

British newspapers re-used the formula to refer to the tube and bus suicide-bomb attacks on London on 7 July 2005 as 7/7.

> His [David Davis's] speech, which starts off with the 7/7 bombings, moves on to the need to chuck out Labour's human rights legislation.
> *The Observer* (9 October 2005)

**999.** In Britain and Ireland the telephone number for summoning the emergency services (police, ambulance or fire brigade). It was introduced in London in July 1937. The number is popularly said to have been chosen because on the old dial telephones the finger-hole for the number 9 was easy to find in the dark or in smoke. The real reason was more practical. The number 0 was already in use to call the operator free of charge from public call boxes, and it was relatively simple to modify the mechanism so as to extend coin-free dialling to 9, the dial number next to it. Today the standard EU emergency number, 112, can also be used. In North America the emergency number is 911.

**Nine Tailors, The.** A detective novel (1934) by Dorothy Sayers (1893–1957). The Nine Tailors, perhaps standing for 'nine tellers', is a peal performed on the eight bells of the church of Fenchurch St Paul, where Lord Peter WIMSEY is stranded and where he investigates two deaths.

**1984.** A year of the 20th century long regarded as apocalyptic and entered as such in the *Oxford English Dictionary*. It derives from the title of George ORWELL's novel *Nineteen Eighty-Four* (1949), a prophecy of the totalitarian future of mankind, portraying a society in which government propaganda and terrorism destroy the human awareness of reality. It is generally thought that Orwell named the novel by reversing the last two figures of the year in which it was written, 1948, but an article by Sally Coniam in the *Times Literary Supplement* of 31 December 1999 proposed another theory. In 1934 Orwell's first wife, Eileen O'Shaughnessy, published a poem, 'End of the Century 1984', in *The Chronicle*, the school magazine of Sunderland Church High School, where she had been a pupil in the 1920s. The poem was written to mark the school's 50th anniversary, looking back then forward to the future and to the school's centenary in 1984. It seems likely that Orwell could have adopted the year accordingly, although for him it was a random date. Support for this theory lies in the poem's mention of 'telesalesmanship' and 'Telepathic Station 9', terms strangely modern for their time, which seem to prefigure Orwell's own NEWSPEAK, 'teleprogrammes' and 'telescreen'. *See also* BIG BROTHER; DOUBLETHINK; FIRST LINES OF NOVELS.

**19th hole.** The bar in the club house of a golf club, to which players resort after playing the 18 holes of the course. There is an implied pun on 'sink', since after sinking a putt one sinks a drink.

**1922 Committee.** A term for the entire body of backbenchers in the Conservative Party. It takes its name from a meeting of Conservative MPs in the Carlton Club in October 1922, when those present voted against Austen Chamberlain's policy of remaining in Lloyd George's COALITION GOVERN-MENT, even though the meeting was chaired by Chamberlain himself. The decision caused his downfall as party leader and the sudden taste of power suggested the need for a body through which backbenchers might exert influence. The executive of the Committee now meets weekly when the Commons is sitting, and the chairman has direct access to the Conservative Party leader.

**Nine-to-five job.** A standard working day of eight hours, from 9 a.m. to 5 p.m., with one hour off for lunch.

> Working nine to five
> What a way to make a living
> Barely getting by
> It's all taking and no giving
>> DOLLY PARTON: 'Nine to Five' (theme song to the film of the same title) (1980)

With the relaxation of labour laws, and more of an open-all-hours culture, the nine-to-five job has begun to be something of a rarity.

> We now work longer hours than any other country in Europe – weekends, evenings and nights. 24-hour Britain has arrived.
>> www.bbc.co.uk/news/, 'Bye Bye Nine to Five' (24 March 2006)

**99.** An ice cream with a chocolate flake in it. The '99' was originally so called because the flake it carried was 99mm long. Such flakes were specially made for the ice cream trade and were sturdier than the traditional crumbly flake chocolate.

**97-pound weakling.** A physically or morally puny person. The term comes from one of the many striking pronouncements made by the US bodybuilder Charles Atlas, real name Angelo Siciliano (1893–1972), who boasted, 'I was once a 97-pound weakling'. The stated weight equals 7st 13lb, and the phrase is sometimes adjusted to '98-pound weakling' to make 8st exactly.

**92 Club.** A loose association of football fans who have visited every one of the 92 Premier League and Football League grounds in Britain. It was formed in 1978.

**Nintendo.** *See* GAME BOY.

**Nip and tuck.** A 19th-century phrase of US origin meaning neck and neck, as in a close-run race, that was adopted in the 20th century for a cosmetic surgical operation to reduce an area of sagging skin. The latter sense is perhaps closer than the former to the source of the expression, which is probably in a process of sewing or tailoring.

*Nip/Tuck* is the title of a US televison drama series about a pair of plastic surgeons in Miami, first broadcast in 2003. Cosmetic surgery has also featured in an increasing number of MAKEOVER TV series.

> Hardly a night passes without some programme or other featuring ordinary folk having bits nipped, tucked, pinched, stretched or sliced out of their bodies in glorious colour.
>> BRENDA POWER: *Sunday Times*, 'Why not a nip and tuck for Mullingar heifers?' (6 February 2005)

**Nippies.** Waitresses in teashops run by J. Lyons & Co. Ltd of London, so known from the 1920s to the 1950s from their nimbleness and adroitness as they sped from table to table. The name was registered by Lyons in 1924.

**Nisei.** (Japanese, 'second generation'.) An American whose parents were immigrants from Japan. Many were interned during the Second World War, following Japan's attack on PEARL HARBOR. A famous example was TOKYO ROSE.

**Nissen hut.** A type of semi-cylindrical, corrugated-iron hut, named after its inventor, Colonel Peter N. Nissen (1831–1930). *See also* QUONSET HUT.

**Nitty-gritty.** The realities or practical details of a situation; 'brass tacks'. The origin of the phrase is uncertain, although nits are tiny and grit is composed of minute particles. It is first recorded in 1956, which makes it highly unlikely that it has (as has sometimes been claimed) any connection with the slave trade.

**Nixon in China.** A 'post-minimalist' (*see* MINIMALISM) political opera by John Adams (b.1947), first performed in 1987. The opera concerns the visit that US President Richard Nixon (*see* TRICKY DICKY) made to China in 1972 as part of his strategy of DÉTENTE, which led to the establishment of diplomatic relations between the United States and the People's Republic. One critic has commented of the opera that it 'proved to some listeners that there is more to minimalism than at first meets the ears'.

**NKVD.** *See* KGB.

**NMFP.** In the language of early 21st-century solipsism, 'not my fucking problem'. If treated as an acronym it can be vocalized as 'nomfup'. *See also* RTFM.

**NMI.** An American abbreviation for 'no middle initial', thus breaking the norm, since most Americans have three names, the middle one often simply appearing as an initial, as Franklin D. Roosevelt, John F. Kennedy. Some Americans choose to be known by first and last name alone, however, in the British tradition. Very rarely an American's middle name is IO (initial only). This was famously the case with President Harry S. Truman (1884-1972), where the letter alone was a compromise designed to appease his maternal grandfather, Solomon Young, and his paternal grandfather, Anderson Shippe Truman. 'Although it could be said to stand for nothing, Truman customarily placed a period after it, thus tacitly recognizing it as the dual-purpose abbreviation his parents had intended' (*American National Biography*, 1999).

**Nobel prize.** One of six international prizes awarded annually for outstanding work in physics, chemistry, physiology or medicine, literature, economics and the promotion of peace. They were endowed by Alfred Nobel (1833–96), the Swedish inventor of dynamite, and were first awarded in 1901. Public interest centres mostly on the winners of the literature and peace prizes. The former have included Eugene O'Neill (1936), T.S. Eliot (1948), Sir Winston Churchill (1953), Ernest Hemingway (1954), Samuel Beckett (1969), Alexander Solzhenitsyn (1970), Seamus Heaney (1995) and Harold Pinter (2005). It was declined by Boris Pasternak in 1958.

The peace prize has been awarded to Albert Schweitzer (1952), Martin Luther King Jr (1964), Mother Teresa of Calcutta (1979), the Dalai Lama (1989) and Mikhail Gorbachev (1990), among others, and to the International Red Cross Committee three times (1917, 1944, 1963), but in some years it has not been awarded at all. A developing tradition has been to award the peace prize jointly to former antagonists who seem to have overcome their antipathies, as with Nelson Mandela and F.W. De Klerk (1993), Yasser Arafat, Shimon Peres and Yitzhak Rabin (1994), and John Hume and David Trimble (1998).

*See also* IG NOBEL PRIZES.

**No big deal.** Nothing much; not worth bothering about. A phrase originating in US teenage slang of the 1960s. *See also* BIG DEAL!

**No-brainer.** Something so simple or straightforward that little or no intelligence is required to cope with it or understand it – for example, an easy question or decision, or something obvious. The expression originated in the United States in the early 1970s.

> 'It confirms what we've long suspected,' said a (male) writer in the *Sun*. 'The male of the species is cleverer than the female. It's a no-brainer.'
> *The Observer* (6 November 2005)

**No can do.** I am unable to do that. A pidgin-English-style phrase of US origin and mostly with apologetic overtones. It became familiar as the title of a popular song by Charles Tobias and Nat Simon, first performed in 1945. *See also* LONG TIME NO SEE.

**No comment.** A statement of refusal to comment on a situation, especially in response to questions from a reporter or interviewer. The phrase dates from the 1950s.

**Nodding donkey.** A type of pump for pumping oil from land-based oil-wells, as typically in the United States. The shape and up-and-down motion of the pump gave its colloquial name.

**Noddy.** The wooden figure of a small boy whose head nods when he speaks, the creation of Enid Blyton (1897–1968). He lives in Toyland, drives a bright red motor car, and has friends who include BIG EARS, a bearded gnome, and PC PLOD. Noddy first appeared in *Little Noddy Goes to Toyland* (1949). He and his friends have subsequently been criticized by teachers, librarians and others as infantile stereotypes, and the stories in which they appear as undesirable and patronizing (some of their more sensational elements, such as Noddy regularly sharing a bed with Big Ears, have been suppressed). They remain popular with their young readers, however. Animated television series in 1998 and 2001 brought Noddy to a new audience.

In the jargon of television journalism, 'noddy' is a term for the recording of footage of an interviewer (showing him or her, as it might be, nodding sagely) that can later be inserted into an interview recorded separately. Such brief clips are known as 'noddy shots'.

> In these programmes, the reporters' pieces-to-camera, and the basic art of fitting together words and pictures, with cutaways, 'noddies' and the rest of the bag of tricks, were first tried out.
>
> ANDREW MARR: *My Trade* (2004)

**Noddy bike.** In the days before the PANDA CAR a lightweight motorcycle used by police officers on patrol duty. The name has nothing to do with the puppet NODDY but came about because an officer riding such a bike could not safely salute but had to nod his head instead.

**No dice.** Nothing doing; out of the question. An expression of US origin dating from the 1930s and presumably referring to the refusal of a gambling-house proprietor to allow a player to start or continue playing.

**Nod the nut.** In Australian slang, to plead guilty in court (the 'nut' is the head, nodding in acknowledgement of wrongdoing). The expression is first recorded in 1950. *See also* PUT ONE'S HAND UP.

**Noel's House Party.** A live television show hosted by a constantly genial Noel Edmonds and first screened in 1991. It was set in a mock manor house in the (obviously fictional) village of Crinkley Bottom and subjected its guests, both famous and unknown, to a variety of pranks and performances for the delectation of the delirious audience. A regular feature was a tank that poured a torrent of gaudy 'gunge' over guests. A later addition was a pink plastic dummy with yellow spots called MR BLOBBY.

**No-fly zone.** An area over which military aircraft are forbidden to fly, mainly during and even for some time after an armed conflict. The United States and Britain maintained no-fly zones in Iraq for some years after the First GULF WAR.

**No-go area.** An area that is dangerous or impossible to enter, or to which entry is restricted or forbidden. The term came to the fore in the early 1970s to apply to parts of Northern Ireland that were dominated by the IRA. *See also* BANDIT COUNTRY; BOGSIDE.

**NoHo.** A nickname given to a neighbourhood in Lower Manhattan, New York, so called as it is 'north of Houston Street'. The name puns on SOHO. The area became fashionable in the 1970s after artists such as Robert Rauschenberg and Frank Stella moved into converted loft buildings here.

In London, 'Noho' is estate-agentese for the FITZROVIA area.

**No holds barred.** With all restrictions relaxed; anything goes. The US expression is first recorded in the 1940s and derives from wrestling terminology.

**No-Mates.** A pitying or mocking nickname (first recorded in 1993) applied to someone who seems friendless or a loner. Typically it is prefixed by an arbitrary (usually male) forename (e.g. 'Billy No-Mates', 'Norman No-Mates').

> Alone in the library like a real Norman No-Mates.
>
> *The Scotsman* (13 October 1995)

**Nomenklatura.** A Russian term (from the Latin *nomenclatura*, 'summoning of names') applied in the former Soviet Union and its satellites in the eastern bloc to those who played key roles in the state and Communist Party machines. The term became synonymous with the privileged ruling class. The term was also used for the system, controlled by Communist Party committees, by which people were appointed to such key roles. It is sometimes used colloquially to refer to any ruling elite, of whatever political persuasion. *See also* GREAT AND THE GOOD.

**No more Mr Nice Guy.** *See* MR NICE GUY.

**No names, no pack drill.** The identity in question will not be revealed. The allusion is to military punishment. Offenders may be sent on a forced march in full kit, but if the drill sergeant does not have the names of the miscreants, he is unable to impose this ordeal on them.

**None But the Lonely Heart.** A film (1944) adapted by US playwright Clifford Odets from a novel of the same title by the Welsh writer Richard Llewellyn (1906–83). It tells the story of a shiftless young cockney who drifts into a life of crime. Starring Cary Grant and Ethel Barrymore, it took its title from a song of 1869 written by Tchaikovsky, which was itself based on 'Mignon's Song' in the novel *Wilhelm Meisters*

*Lehrjahre* (1795–6) by Goethe. In Tchaikovsky's song the relevant lyric is usually translated as:

> None but the weary heart can understand how I have suffered and how I am tormented.

**Nonesuch Press.** A distinctive and distinguished private press founded in 1923 by Francis Meynell (1891–1975) with the aim of demonstrating that machine-produced books could be as good as those hitherto hand-produced by private presses and yet be sold for a fraction of the price. It relied on the best commercially available type and issued both limited and 'unlimited' editions. Its first production, John Donne's *Love Poems*, issued on 3 May 1923, appeared in an edition of 1250 copies. One of its most popular productions was *The Week-End Book* (1924), an anthology edited by Meynell and his wife Vera, and it went on to produce works by writers such as Wycherley, Rochester, Otway, Vanbrugh, Farquhar and Dryden as well as illustrated books. It later became an imprint of Reinhardt Books Ltd, a firm acquired by Max Reinhardt in 1947.

**Non-event.** A disappointing or insignificant occurrence or occasion, especially one that was expected to be important or original. The expression dates from the early 1960s.

**No-no.** A thing that is NOT ON or impossible, as: 'Mowing the lawn was a no-no after the night's rain.' The expression dates from the 1940s.

> A big no-no is liquid eyeliner. 'Avoid it at all costs, one drop of rain will send it running down your face,' cautions the make-up artist Adam De Cruz.
>
> *The Times* (23 August 1999)

**No! No! No!** The constructive contribution made to the European debate by Margaret Thatcher (the IRON LADY) in a speech in the House of Commons, 30 October 1990. In particular she was expressing her opposition to a single European currency and greater powers being taken on by the European Commission in Brussels. The resignation of the deputy prime minister Geoffrey Howe (*see* DEAD SHEEP) two weeks later was prompted by her style of leadership, and in particular the difficulties her belligerent anti-Europeanism had given him in his earlier role of foreign secretary (1983–9):

> It is rather like sending your opening batsmen to the crease only for them to find the moment that the first balls are bowled that their bats have been broken before the game by the team captain.
>
> GEOFFREY HOWE: resignation speech to the House of Commons, 13 November 1990

Thatcher's fall from office followed soon afterwards.

**Non-violence.** A philosophy of political action that rejects the use of armed struggle. It is also known as 'passive resistance', and may involve such tactics as civil disobedience, sit-ins, marches and other forms of peaceful demonstration. An early theoretician of non-violence was the American writer Henry David Thoreau, who in his essay 'Civil Disobedience' (1849) argued that to cooperate with the government, for example by paying taxes, was to condone its actions. Thoreau was incensed with the US government over its war with Mexico, its treatment of Native Americans and its toleration of slavery. It was MAHATMA Gandhi who organized the first great campaign of non-violence, in his long struggle to achieve independence for India. His policy of *satyagraha* (non-cooperation) began in 1919 and independence was eventually achieved in 1947. The civil rights movement in America in the 1950s and 1960s, led by Martin Luther King, also pursued a policy of non-violence, but by the later 1960s groups such as the BLACK PANTHERS were arming themselves. In South Africa the policy of non-violence adopted by the ANC (a body founded by Gandhi among others) in its struggle against APARTHEID was abandoned following the SHARPEVILLE MASSACRE of 1960.

> Non-violence is the first article of my faith. It is also the last article of my creed.
>
> MAHATMA GANDHI: speech at Shahi Bag (18 March 1922)
>
> In my humble opinion, non-cooperation with evil is as much a duty as is cooperation with good.
>
> MAHATMA GANDHI: speech in Ahmadabad (23 March 1922)

***No Orchids for Miss Blandish.*** A salacious novel (1939) by James Hadley Chase in which Barbara Blandish, a millionaire's daughter, is kidnapped, tortured and raped by the villainous Slim Grissom. 'Chase' was in fact an Englishman, named René Raymond, who attempted to write in the American vernacular. The story subsequently spawned stage and screen versions of dubious merit.

> Miss Blandish belongs forever in the Forties schoolboys' prurient pantheon as part of the unholy trinity completed by Fanny Hill and Lady Chatterley: to be joined shortly after the war by Amber St Clair. Their names were enough to raise a laugh in any desperate music-hall comedian's act.
>
> PHILIP FRENCH: in the *New Statesman* (5 November 1971)

**No pain, no gain.** A motto of bodybuilders, perhaps deriving from Adlai Stevenson's slogan 'There are no gains without pain', first voiced when accepting the Democratic nomination for the US presidency in 1952. The words can apply to any situation to indicate that no progress is possible without effort.

**No problem.** It's all right; that is easily done. A catchphrase of the latter half of the 20th century, often used as a stock response to 'Thank you'. There is usually no question of a problem existing in the first place. *See also* NO SWEAT.

**No purchase necessary.** A phrase familiar in the text of promotional competitions. It indicates that the promotion is not legally a competition since it is not based on skill and does not require, for example, the writing of a slogan. The wording arose in order to avoid falling foul of the Lotteries and Amusement Act 1976, which prohibits games of chance. Potential entrants are thus offered a way of participating without purchasing. The usual method is to enter the draw by sending one's name and address on a plain piece of paper or by writing in to request a person in a handling house to open an actual product to see if the required symbol or notice is inside. Such promotions are successful because most people cannot be bothered with such a rigmarole but instead buy the product to discover instantly if they have won.

**No questions asked.** I suspect that what you are doing may be illegal but I shall say nothing since I am interested myself. A phrase that might apply to certain street traders, for example.

**Nora.** A female forename that, in the 1990s, came to evoke a dull or unattractive woman. The sense may have specifically evolved from Nora Batty, the untidy housewife in the popular television SITCOM *The* LAST OF THE SUMMER WINE.

**Noraid.** The informal name of the Irish *Northern Aid* Committee, an American organization founded in 1969 whose principal objective was to raise funds for the Republican cause in Northern Ireland, and in particular the IRA.

**Norder, Laura.** A jocular personification of 'law and order', the shibboleth of the *Daily Mail*-reading classes and of all those whose solution to society's ills is to round up all the thieves, muggers, druggies and other malcontents, then 'bang 'em up and throw away the key'. Ms Norder possibly first appeared in graffiti in the early 1970s. Laura Norder is also the name adopted by the British anarcho-punk artist Laura Oldfield-Ford. *See also* HARDWORKINGFAMILIES; SHORT SHARP SHOCK; TOUGH ON CRIME AND TOUGH ON THE CAUSES OF CRIME.

**Normal for Norfolk.** A non-politically-correct doctors' categorization of patients whose behaviour or intelligence level are accounted for by the sort of backwardness stereotypically attributed to country areas like Norfolk. Usually euphemistically disguised as 'NFN'. *See also* MEDICAL ABBREVIATIONS.

**Norman.** A male forename that is supposedly characteristic of a dull and typically bourgeois or even petit bourgeois person. An evocation of 'normal' is strong, and 'Norman Normal' is a nickname dating from the 1960s for a notably conventional or conformist person. Bucking the trend are the outsized personalities of Norman Tebbit, the CHINGFORD SKINHEAD, and STORMIN' NORMAN Schwarzkopf.

***North by Northwest.*** A classic film thriller (1959), directed by Alfred Hitchcock and written by Ernest Lehman, about an advertising executive who becomes confused with another man and consequently finds himself pursued across the United States by people trying to kill him. Starring Cary Grant as the businessman driven to the point of madness by his experiences, the film derived its title from Shakespeare's *Hamlet*, specifically the passage in which the 'gloomy prince' denies the fact that he is actually mad:

> I am but mad north-northwest; when the wind is southerly I know a hawk from a handsaw.
> II.ii

**North of Watford.** *See* WATFORD.

**North Pole.** The pole was first reached on 6 April 1909 by the US explorer Robert Edwin Peary (1856–1920). In May 1933 it was claimed by the Soviets and four years later they established a polar station there under Professor Otto Schmidt. *See also* SOUTH POLE.

**North–South divide.** The division of England into regions north or south of a line running approximately between the Severn and the Wash. A severe economic recession with consequent depression of house prices above the line in the 1980s, especially in the Northeast, made the residents of that region the effective poor relations of those below it, where the recession was less marked and where property prices were booming. In the early 1990s much of the distinction between North and South dissolved, but later in the decade the former differences re-emerged, with a reduction in industrial output in the North and a growing economy in London and the Southeast. Galloping house prices in the 21st century, although a country-wide phenomenon, were much more intense further south, and in that sense the divide has sharpened considerably.

> The North–South divide is so stubborn a pattern in the British economy that it seems to have become a geographical feature snaking across the Midlands ... with boom to the south and bust to the north.
> *Independent on Sunday* (10 October 1999)

A social and political distinction between the 'hard' North and 'soft' South has long been popularly implicit, and Elizabeth Gaskell drew on the concept for her novel

*North and South* (1854), contrasting the 'satanic mills' of Manchester with the easy country life of Hampshire. The notion of such a divide can be taken back to Roman times, when the construction of Hadrian's Wall in the 2nd century AD separated colonized and settled Britannia from the wilder provinces north of the border. The same duality was later present in the Scandinavian Danelaw, of northern and eastern England, and the settled Saxon kingdoms of Mercia and Wessex in the West and South. *See also* FORTNUM–MASON LINE.

**Norway spruce.** A long-coned European spruce widely grown for timber and pulp and often used in Britain as a Christmas tree. A giant specimen is donated every year by Norway to London as a mark of the country's appreciation for the role Britain played in defeating the NAZIS in the Second World War. The tree is erected in Trafalgar Square in December and the annual ceremony in which the Norwegian ambassador turns on the lights is one of the most popular in the Christmas calendar. Norway donates another giant tree to Edinburgh, which stands upon the Mound.

**'Norwegian Wood (This Bird has Flown)'.** A folk-influenced song by The BEATLES, credited to John Lennon and Paul McCartney and released in Britain in December 1965. It appears on RUBBER SOUL. 'Norwegian Wood' concerns an affair that John Lennon was conducting with a female journalist and features the first use of a sitar in a pop single. The true meaning of the song's title (and its lyrics) is nonetheless obscure and may simply reflect the contemporary predilection for teasingly elusive lyrics *à la* Bob Dylan. The subtitle was originally intended to be the song's actual title.

Norwegian Wood was also a nickname given to the US Democratic politician Walter Mondale (b.1928) on account of his expressionless delivery and Scandinavian origins. Mondale was vice-president (1977–81) under Jimmy Carter (*see* GRITS AND FRITZ) and was trounced in the 1980 presidential election by the GREAT COMMUNICATOR, Ronald Reagan.

**NORWICH.** *See* LOVERS' ACRONYMS.

**Nose candy.** A narcotic drug, such as cocaine or heroin, in crystalline form, suitable for taking by inhalation. The slang term dates from the 1920s, but is still at the beginning of the 21st century. It is of US origin. *See also* EYE CANDY.

**Nosey Parker.** A prying person. The name is popularly said to allude to Matthew Parker, Archbishop of Canterbury (1504–75), who was noted for the detailed articles of inquiry concerning ecclesiastical affairs generally and the conduct of the clergy that he issued for the visitations of his province and diocese. However, the term is first recorded only in the early 20th century, so such a reference seems unlikely. According to one account, it was the nickname given to a man who spied on courting couples in Hyde Park, London. An alteration of 'nose-poker' is a possibility.

**No skin off one's nose.** Said of something that has no adverse effect on oneself. The allusion may be to a fight, in which one has scratched one's adversary while remaining unscathed oneself. The expression dates from the 1920s.

**Nostalgia isn't what it used to be.** Graffito dating from the 1960s/1970s. It was used by the French actress Simone Signoret (1921–85) as the title of her memoirs: *La Nostalgie n'est plus qu'elle était* (1976; *Nostalgia Isn't What It Used to Be*, 1978).

**No strings attached.** Said of an offer that carries no special conditions or restrictions. The reference is to a puppet that is free to move of its own volition when not manipulated by strings.

> 'We're entering a float for the Carnival. Needs someone to be in charge – what's wrong with you?'
> 'No, thank you,' said Natalie.
> 'No strings attached,' he pleaded.
> FAY WELDON: *The Heart of the Country* (1987)

**Nostromo.** A novel by Joseph Conrad (1857–1924), published in 1904. The story is set in an imaginary and unstable South American republic called Costaguana. (*Costa* is Spanish for 'coast'; *guano* is the excrement of seabirds, harvested off the cost of Chile and used as a fertilizer; in South American Spanish it is also a slang word for money.) Costaguano's wealth depends on its silver, which ends up corrupting even the best of men – notably Nostromo himself, an Italian sailor who is now *capatez de cargadores* (head of the dockers). *Nostromo* is the Italian word for 'boatswain', from *nostro uomo*, 'our man'.

**No such animal.** 'There ain't no such animal' is often said to mean that something does not exist. The catchphrase originated as the caption of a cartoon in *Life* magazine of 7 November 1907 showing a farmer at the circus looking at a dromedary.

**No such thing as a free lunch.** To say that there's no such thing as a free lunch is to repeat the popular truism that one cannot get something for nothing. A lunch involves preparation and expense, otherwise time and money. The words were particularly associated with the US economist Milton Friedman (b.1912; *see* FRIEDMANISM), but have been recorded since 1938.

'Oh, "tanstaafl". Means "There ain't no such thing as a free lunch". And isn't,' I added, pointing to a FREE LUNCH sign across room, 'or these drinks would cost half as much. Was reminding her that anything free costs twice as much in the long run or turns out worthless.'

ROBERT A. HEINLEIN: *The Moon is a Harsh Mistress*, ch. 11 (1966)

**No such thing as society.** *See* THERE IS NO SUCH THING AS SOCIETY.

**No Surrender!** The slogan of the Protestant Unionists of Ulster, often to be heard on the lips of the likes of Dr Ian Paisley, leader of the Democratic Unionist Party. The slogan originates in the siege of Derry in 1689, when the Protestant defenders shouted it at the besieging Jacobites.

**No sweat.** No trouble; no bother; NO PROBLEM. A phrase from the 1950s. The implication is that there is no need to make an effort that would produce perspiration.

**Not!** A word added at the end of a statement to negate it, the statement itself often being ironic. An example might be: 'He's one of the smartest people I know – not!' The usage was originally American, but it has since spread to English-speaking teenagers elsewhere. It appears to have stemmed from VALSPEAK, but was popularized by the American film *Wayne's World* (1992) about a chaotic cable TV show devised by two girl-mad, rock-crazed teenagers.

**Not a happy bunny.** Displeased, especially as a reaction to a piece of news or a situation. The description is often applied by one person to another euphemistically, as:

Diogenes of Sinope – perhaps the wisest and most authentic human being in recorded history – was not a happy bunny.

SWAMI VRKHA BABA: review of *Happiness: A Physician/Biologist Looks at Life* by Joseph N. Abraham, posted on www.beyond-thepale.co.uk (May 2005)

**Not a hope in hell.** No chance whatsoever. A phrase from the early years of the 20th century. The implication is that one is so deeply damned that one has no chance for heavenly salvation.

**Not a penny off the pay, not a second off the day.** The slogan of the striking miners in 1926, first uttered by A.J. Cook (1885–1931), secretary of the Miners' Federation of Great Britain, in a speech at York on 3 April. The miners' action – which briefly escalated into the GENERAL STRIKE – was provoked by the imposition by the employers of wage cuts in return for longer hours.

**Not a pretty sight.** Unpleasant to look at. The ironic phrase, current from the 1980s, was at first used to describe the body of a person who had met a sudden death. It was later applied to any particularly unprepossessing person.

**No-Tell Motel.** A colloquial US rhyming term for a cheap motel of the sort traditionally selected for illicit or clandestine sexual liaisons. It dates from the mid-1970s.

**Not give a monkey's.** To be completely indifferent or unconcerned; to NOT GIVE A STUFF. The missing word is the 'F-word' (*see* FOUR-LETTER WORD) or alternatively 'toss'. The expression dates from the 1960s.

**Not give a stuff.** To be completely indifferent or unconcerned; to NOT GIVE A MONKEY'S. 'Stuff' is a euphemism for the 'F-word' (*see* FOUR-LETTER WORD). The expression dates from the 1970s.

**Not give someone the time of day.** To have no time for them; to refuse even to exchange civilities with them. The expression emerged in the 1950s, although in its now rare positive form to give someone the time of day dates from the time of Shakespeare. The modern negative phrase is typically found in a statement such as 'I wouldn't give him the time of day.'

**Not have a clue.** To have absolutely no idea. The expression dates from the 1920s. *I'm Sorry I Haven't a Clue* is the title of a long-running comedy programme on BBC Radio 4 presented by the veteran jazz musician Humphrey Lyttleton. The programme, first broadcast in 1972, is described as 'the antidote to panel games', and the regular 'contestants' have included Barry Cryer, Tim Brooke-Taylor, Graeme Garden and the late Willie Rushton.

**Nothing to write home about.** Unremarkable or insignificant, despite reports or rumours to the contrary, as: 'The hotel was nothing to write home about.' The expression arose at the start of the 20th century and probably originated among troops stationed overseas.

**Not just a pretty face.** Intelligent as well as attractive. The expression, which dates from the 1950s, is often used humorously by someone who has achieved something praiseworthy: 'I'm not just a pretty face, you know!'

**Not know one's arse from one's elbow.** To be ignorant or stupid; to be quite incompetent. The two parts of the anatomy are unmistakably distinctive, but the comparison seems random.

**Not know shit from Shinola.** To be ignorant or innocent. The expression dates from the early 20th century, with Shinola (based on 'shine') the proprietary name of a US brand of boot polish. Similar is 'neither shit nor Shinola', with the sense 'neither one thing nor the other'.

**Not know what has hit one.** To be taken entirely unawares by an event; to be dealt an unexpected blow or awarded an unexpected benefit.

**Not me guv.** It's nothing to do with me. A representation of a response from an employee when charged with avoiding responsibility for a duty or the like, 'guv' (for 'governor') being a working man's supposedly stock form of address to a superior.

**Not much chop.** Not very satisfactory; not up to much. The phrase dates from the start of the 20th century, with 'chop' here in the sense 'seal', 'stamp'. The word is of Hindi origin and subsequently passed to China, whence it came into Australian and New Zealand usage.

**Not my cup of tea.** Not to my taste; of no interest to me. This negative phrase evolved in the 1930s from the positive '(just) my cup of tea', referring to a person or thing that is right or suitable.

**Not on.** Socially or otherwise unacceptable; impossible. The allusion is perhaps to a military operation that was first 'on' then cancelled because of unforeseen circumstances.

**Not one's day.** A day when one has a succession of misfortunes. The possessive is obviously variable, as 'not my day', 'not your day', etc. The expression dates from the 1920s.

***Not Only … But Also ….*** A revue-style television comedy series screened from 1965 to 1966 and 1970 to 1973. Its absurdist skits won it instant cult status, and its regular high spot was a routine in which Peter Cook and Dudley Moore (*see* BEYOND THE FRINGE) as 'Pete and Dud', a pair of cloth-capped proletarian philosophers, discussed the vanity of the world in a sequence of nicely inconsequential musings. 'Pete and Dud' also spawned the characters of 'Derek and Clive', two ageing perverts whose lavatorial exploits are recorded in three obscenity-laden albums, *Derek And Clive (Live)* (1976), *Derek and Clive Come Again* (1977) and *Derek and Clive ad Nauseam* (1978), the first of which included the 'tracks' 'In The Lav' and 'Winkie Wanky Woo'.

**Not on your nelly.** Certainly not. A variant of 'not on your life'. The phrase gained popularity in the 1940s as a shortening of 'not on your Nelly Duff', a name used as rhyming slang for 'puff', i.e. breath of life.

**Not Pygmalion likely!** A somewhat dated euphemism for 'not bloody likely!' In Shaw's play PYGMALION (1913) the Cockney flower girl Eliza Doolittle simultaneously shocked and delighted the audiences of her day by uttering the then taboo emphatic negative.

> Freddy [*opening the door for her*]: Are you walking across the Park, Miss Doolittle? If so –
>
> Liza: Walk! Not bloody likely. [*Sensation*]. I am going in a taxi. [*She goes out*].
>
> GEORGE BERNARD SHAW: *Pygmalion*, III (1913)

**No Trousers Charlie.** *See* BIG EARS.

***Not So Much a Programme More a Way of Life.*** A television comedy programme of the mid-1960s that packed the same satirical punch as its predecessor, THAT WAS THE WEEK THAT WAS. Its most contentious sketch, featuring John Bird as President Jomo Kenyatta of Kenya, drew an official complaint from that country's High Commission.

***Not the Nine O'Clock News.*** A topically satirical television sketch series running from 1979 to 1982 and scheduled on BBC2 at the same time as the *Nine O'Clock News* on BBC1. The series launched the careers of the comedians Rowan Atkinson (*see* MR BEAN), Mel Smith, Chris Langham (later replaced by Griff Rhys Jones) and Pamela Stephenson. Jones and Smith went on to collaborate in the BBC sketch series *Alas Smith and Jones* (1982–7), while Stephenson married comedian Billy Connolly, the BIG YIN, gained a doctorate in clinical psychology and began a counselling practice; she also wrote a bestselling biography of Connolly.

**Not the only pebble on the beach.** Not unique or irreplaceable. The expression originally referred to an eligible young man or woman and became popular at the start of the 20th century following its occurrence in Harry Braisted's song 'You're Not the Only Pebble on the Beach' (1896):

> If you want to win her hand,
> Let the maiden understand
> That she's not the only pebble on the beach!

***Notting Hill.*** A film (1999) written by Richard Curtis about a celebrated US film actress who falls for a humble British bookshop manager while on a visit to London. Starring Julia Roberts and Hugh Grant as the hesitant lovers, the pair first meet in Grant's bookshop in Notting Hill, the area where Curtis lives and where most of the action takes place (with the consequence that the district eagerly looked forward to a flood of tourists inspecting the locations used in the film). The sunny conceit, that despite numerous problems a transatlantic relationship could blossom between a global celebrity and a nonentity, had wide appeal.

**Notting Hillbillies.** A jocular name for residents of Notting Hill, London. The expression dates back to the end of the 20th century when the already bohemian status of the area was altered by the influx of a trendy, creative crowd.

> Sienna Miller … her style is Notting Hillbilly mixed with a little Los Angeles boho.
>
> www.telegraph.co.uk (30 December 2003)

**Notting Hill Carnival.** Europe's largest street festival, held annually in the district of Notting Hill, northwest central London, on the last (bank holiday) weekend of August as a celebration of the West Indian way of life. It had its origins in a street party held in 1964 for the children of Trinidadian immigrants who had settled in the area. Two years later the party evolved into a regular event, with steel bands providing the music, and food and drink donated by local traders. In due course the colour and extravagance of costumes, volume and variety of music, and originality and ingenuity of the floats rivalled the panache of New Orleans or Rio de Janeiro and a huge amount of trade was generated. The carnival was dogged by violence and disorder for many years, notably in 1976, when black youths clashed with police, but since the 1990s it has been mostly peaceful.

**Notting Hill set.** A description in the summer of 2004 by the Conservative MP Derek Conway of certain younger members of the parliamentary party (the *Guardian* news- paper called them 'a coterie of young turks surrounding [the Tory Party leader] Michael Howard'), whom he accused of mounting a whispering campaign against older Tory MPs and specifically of suggesting that the latter were prevent- ing younger Tories from standing for parliament:

> This is what we call the Notting Hill Tory set. They sit around in these curious little bistros in parts of London, drink themselves silly and wish they were doing what the rest of us are getting on with. They'll just have to be a little more patient.
>
> DEREK CONWAY: MP for Old Bexley and Sidcup (July 2004)

Over the following year the Notting Hill set evolved into the so-called CAMEROONIANS, who successfully secured the party leadership for David Cameron (*see* BOY DAVID). *See also* METRO-TORY.

**Not to worry.** Don't worry. The implication is that the diffi- culty can be easily resolved. A phrase dating from the 1950s.

**Not want to know.** To be uninterested; to prefer not to be told. The phrase frequently applies in a situation where one person does not wish to hear what another says or does, either because it is irrelevant and irksome, or because it is illegal and 'ignorance is bliss'.

> Don't bother telling your boss that you have got in early all week and that your prediction about the Boots share price was right. He won't want to know.
>
> *The Times* (4 October 1999)

**Not waving but drowning.** A phrase describing a situation in which a gesture may be misinterpreted. It derives from a poem of this name by Stevie (Florence Margaret) Smith (1901–71), written in 1953 when its author was suffering from clinical depression. Much of Smith's verse was

characterized by an eccentric directness. In a poll conducted in 1995 'Not Waving But Drowning' emerged as Britain's fourth favourite poem:

> Nobody heard him, the dead man,
> But still he lay moaning:
> he was much further out than you thought
> And not waving but drowning.

*See also* NOVEL ON YELLOW PAPER.

**Not with a bang but a whimper.** The conclusion of T.S. Eliot's poem 'The Hollow Men' (1925):

> This is the way the world ends
> This is the way the world ends
> This is the way the world ends
> Not with a bang but a whimper.

The phrase has been much borrowed by those – especially journalists – in need of an image of bathos.

**Noughties, The.** A nickname for the first decade of the 21st century, from 2000 to 2009, so called from the prominent noughts (zeros) in the dates. The suggestion of 'naughties' may have promoted the (limited) popularity of the name. *See also* NAUGHTY NINETIES.

> If the 90s will be remembered as the decade when everyone stopped worrying about nuclear war and began to care about the environment, the 'noughties' are the decade that will see people going into space for recreation.
>
> *heat* (6–12 January 2000)

**Nouveau roman.** (French, 'new novel'.) An alternative term for the French ANTI-NOVEL, adopted in Britain in the 1960s.

**Nouvelle cuisine.** (French, 'new cookery'.) A style of French cooking that was developed by French chefs in the 1970s. It involves the use of fresh and healthy ingredients, light sauces, quick cooking to retain the colour and texture of the ingredients, and artistic presentation. This last feature was initially a cause of some derision, since it apparently involved the arrangement of minute portions of brightly coloured items on the plate for purposes of admiration rather than actual consumption. The style was subsequently modified, with the preparation of more sustaining portions and the reintroduction of some traditional elements of French cooking.

**Nouvelle vague.** (French, 'new wave'.) A movement in French cinema beginning in the late 1950s that sought innovation in subject matter and technique as a reaction to the moribund French film industry. Exponents included the former film critics François Truffaut (1932–84), Claude Chabrol (b.1930), Jean-Luc Godard (b.1930), Éric Rohmer (b.1920) and Alain Resnais (b.1922). The first film of the type is generally reckoned to be Chabrol's *Le beau Serge* (1958), although the true rise of the movement was marked by Truffaut's *Les quatre cents coups* (1959), an unsentimental autobiographical portrait of an alienated youth, Resnais's *Hiroshima mon amour* (1959), centring on a love affair between a Japanese man and a Frenchwoman ravaged by memories of the Second World War, and Godard's *À Bout de souffle* (1959), known in English as BREATHLESS, paying homage to the American gangster film. *See also* LAST YEAR AT MARIENBAD.

**Novel on Yellow Paper.** A novel (1936) by Stevie (Florence Margaret) Smith (1902–71). After trying to get some of her poems published and being advised instead to 'go away and write a novel', Smith did just that, typing it in the firm's time (she worked for a publisher) on the firm's 'very yellow' carbon-copy paper. The book itself is an autobiographical exercise in the free association of ideas and experience. *See also* NOT WAVING BUT DROWNING.

**No way.** It is impossible or NOT ON. There is no way in which it can be done or I will not do it. The expression became current in the late 1960s. An extended form is 'in no way, shape or form' and a stock rhyming variant is 'No way, José'.

> No panto for me this New Year, thank God. I do it every year, but this year, I just thought, no way.
>
> *The Times* (20 November 1999)

**'Nowhere Man'.** An introspective and mildly nihilistic song by The BEATLES, credited to John Lennon and Paul McCartney (but mainly by Lennon) and released in Britain in December 1965. It appears on RUBBER SOUL. The title and lyrics ('He's a real nowhere man, sitting in his nowhere land, making all his nowhere plans for nobody') reflect John Lennon's sense of aimlessness and inadequacy during a time of personal difficulty.

**No-win situation.** One in which one loses whatever one does. The phrase dates from the 1960s and perhaps originally had a military relevance. *See also* YOU CAN'T WIN; WIN-WIN SITUATION.

**Now, Voyager.** A film (1942) based on a novel (1941) of the same title by Olive Higgins Prouty about a repressed New England spinster who finds love with a married man while on a recuperative cruise. Prouty derived her title from the poetry collection *Leaves of Grass* (1855) by the US poet Walt Whitman:

> Now voyager, sail thou forth to seek and find.

**Nuclear-free zone.** A term that became current as the Cold War warmed up again in the 1980s and the United States

began to deploy cruise missiles in Europe. In a number of places left-wing local councils erected signs on their boundaries declaring the borough to be a nuclear-free zone. Elsewhere, the whole of New Zealand declared itself a nuclear-free zone (*see* ANZUS PACT).

The phrase led to many jocular derivatives, such as describing Geoffrey Howe (*see* DEAD SHEEP) as being 'a charisma-free zone'.

**Nuclear winter.** A term describing the conjectured period of extreme cold and environmental devastation that would follow a nuclear war, caused by the blocking out of the sun's rays by smoke and dust particles in the upper atmosphere. It was coined by the scientist Richard Turco in December 1983 and was popularized by the science writer Carl Sagan in an article in the *Washington Post*.

**Nude Descending a Staircase, No. 2.** The remarkably kinetic painting (1912) by the Dadaist (*see* DADAISM) Marcel Duchamp (1887–1968) has become as much an icon of early MODERNISM as Picasso's *Les* DEMOISELLES D'AVIGNON. In a Cubist (*see* CUBISM) style, the picture evokes a sense of motion by repeating fragments of the same figure down a diagonal. Duchamp himself later remarked: 'When the vision of the *Nude* flashed upon me, I knew that it would break for ever the enslaving chains of Naturalism.' The poet X.J. Kennedy wrote of the painting:

> One-woman waterfall, she wears
> Her slow descent like a long cape
> And pausing, on the final stair
> Collects her motions into shape.

**Nudge, nudge, wink, wink.** A phrase expressive of heavy-handed sexual innuendo, often quoted with ironic reference to its source, a 1969 sketch in the BBC television comedy show MONTY PYTHON'S FLYING CIRCUS in which Eric Idle obscurely but salaciously quizzes a bemused Terry Jones about his wife's sexual habits. In full the phrase is 'Nudge, nudge, wink, wink, know what I mean, say no more.'

**Number cruncher.** A nickname for any powerful computer that can handle large numerical calculations, especially when the machine itself is large or operates ponderously. The term dates from the 1970s and has since come to apply to a human calculator or manipulator of such numbers, sometimes in a derogatory way (e.g. 'a mere number-cruncher') to imply someone who can quantify without having any insight into the meaning or value of what is being calculated.

**Nuremberg Laws.** The infamous NAZI laws promulgated in

September 1935. Jews, and all those of Jewish extraction, were deprived of all rights of German citizenship, and regulations were made against those of partial Jewish ancestry. Marriage between Jew and 'German' was forbidden. Nuremberg (Nürnberg) was the centre of the annual Nazi Party rallies.

**Nuremberg Rally.** The name of any of the massive NAZI rallies held in 1923, 1927, 1929 and from 1933 to 1938 in Nuremberg (Nürnberg), mainly as propaganda events, carefully staged to reinforce party enthusiasm and to showcase the might of Nazism to Germany and the world. The first major rally was that of 1929, which included most of the overblown ingredients that featured in future rallies, such as blaring brass-band music, goose-step marches, human swastika formations, torchlight processions, bonfires and dazzling fireworks displays. Hitler and other Nazi leaders delivered ranting orations, and buildings were festooned with giant flags and Nazi insignia. The events of the 1934 rally were captured in Leni Riefenstahl's classic film *Triumph of the Will* (1936; *Triumph des Willens*), its opening sequence showing the FÜHRER descending by plane from the skies. A planned 'peace' rally for 1939 was cancelled because of preparations for war with Poland. The Germans themselves knew the rallies as the *Nürnberger Parteitage*, 'Nuremberg Party Days'. *See also* CATHEDRAL OF LIGHT.

**Nuremberg Trials.** The trial of 22 NAZI leaders conducted by an international military tribunal at Nuremberg (Nürnberg) after the Second World War (November 1945 to October 1946). Three were acquitted; Goering, Ribbentrop and ten others were condemned to death; three, including Rudolf Hess, were sentenced to life imprisonment; and four, including Speer, were sentenced to terms ranging from 10 to 20 years. Goering avoided retribution by committing suicide. The trials created the concept of 'war crimes' and established precedents for judicial proceedings under international law against former figures of a regime, as seen more recently in the cases of Slobodan Milosevic (the BUTCHER OF THE BALKANS) and others at the International Criminal Tribunal for the Former Yugoslavia in The Hague, and a similar International Criminal Tribunal for Rwanda, trying the perpetrators of the 1994 genocide in that country. *See also* SPANDAU.

**Nutmeg.** In football a ball played between an opponent's legs. The term is sometimes shortened to 'nuts' or 'megs' but ultimately derives from 'nutmegs' as a former slang word for the testicles. The mascot of the 1999 Women's World Cup football tournament in the United States was a figure of a fox named Nutmeg.

**Nutopia.** The fictional country that is the setting of ex-BEATLE John Lennon's album *Mind Games* (1973). It has no land, no boundaries and no passports but only people. It also has no laws other than cosmic laws. Its international anthem is *Bring on the Lucie*. Further information can be obtained from the Nutopian Embassy, 1 White Street, New York, New York 10013, USA.

**Nuts!** An expression of defiance or contempt; a statement of refusal or negation. A story of the Second World War tells how General Anthony C. McAuliffe, acting commander of the US 101st Airborne Division at Bastogne in the Ardennes at the time of the BATTLE OF THE BULGE (December 1944), when surrounded by enemy forces, was informed by the Germans that they would accept a surrender. His terse response to this proposal was 'Nuts!', a message that the Germans initially interpreted to mean 'crazy'. Agence France Presse later reported the incident, translating the General's retort more expansively but not altogether accurately as *Vous n'êtes que de vieilles noix* ('You're just old fogeys'). A British officer in the same situation might well have said 'Balls!', the actual sense of McAuliffe's retort.

**Nuts and bolts.** The essentials of a situation. Nuts screwed onto bolts can serve to hold a basic structure together. The expression dates from the 1960s.

**Nuts and sluts.** Eccentric men and promiscuous women, regarded as typically making up the most provocative type of guests or audience in a television talk show.

> Poor Vanessa Feltz was crucified for having spoof guests on her nuts 'n' sluts show. But what did it matter? They were seen, they performed, they were as real as anything else in the 1990s.
>
> *Sunday Times* (26 December 1999)

**Nutty as a fruitcake.** Completely crazy; quite mad. A fruitcake normally contains nuts as well as fruit. 'Nutty' meaning 'insane' dates from the early 19th century, but the elaborated expression from the 1930s.

**Nye.** The nickname of the left-wing Labour politician and noted orator Aneurin Bevan (1897–1960), who resigned from Clement Attlee's postwar government over prescription charges in 1951, having established free medical care in the form of the National Health Service three years earlier. *See also* DESICCATED CALCULATING MACHINE.

**Nylon.** The synthetic polymer, originally known as superpolymer 66, was first produced by the Du Pont Company in the United States in the 1930s. Nylon stockings were displayed in 1939 at the New York World's Fair and the San

Francisco Golden Gate International Exposition and were in instant demand, even though 'nylons' cost twice as much as silk stockings. Their great attraction was that they were shrinkproof, mothproof and resistant to mildew, whereas silk stockings were subject to all three hazards. When nylon was taken up in the Second World War for the manufacture of parachutes, nylon stockings could be had only on the black market. The word itself is popularly said to derive from the initials of New York, but it was actually patterned on 'cotton' and 'rayon'.

**Nymphet.** A sexually attractive young girl. Although already existing as a word for a young or small (classical) nymph, the term was first used in the current sense by Vladimir Nabokov in his novel LOLITA (1955). A spelling 'nymphette' is sometimes found, as if to emphasize the bearer's diminutiveness or femininity.

# O

**OAO.** An abbreviation of 'one and only', signifying in US college slang one's sweetheart or girlfriend (steady girlfriend, that is, as opposed to any incidental, temporary ones). It is first recorded in 1928.

**OAS.** An abbreviation for l'Organisation de l'Armée Secrète (French, 'the secret army organization'), a right-wing organization of French settlers in colonial Algeria opposed to Algerian independence. It was formed in 1961 and led by General Raoul Salan (1899–1984). He and other high-ranking French officers who had assisted President de Gaulle's return to power in 1958 now felt betrayed by de Gaulle's apparent willingness to consider Algerian independence. They staged an attempted coup in Algiers in 1961 and then mounted a terrorist campaign in both Algeria and France, including a number of attempts on de Gaulle's life. However, with Algerian independence granted in 1962 and Salan's imprisonment in the same year (he was released in 1968), the OAS campaign fizzled out.

OAS is also an abbreviation for the Organization of American States, an international body of countries in North, Central and South America, and the Caribbean, founded in 1948 to foster cooperation in the social, economic and security fields.

**OBE.** *See* ORDER OF THE BRITISH EMPIRE.

**Obi-Wan Kenobi.** The wise JEDI knight who advises Luke Skywalker in the STAR WARS films. The role was played, most lucratively, by Sir Alec Guinness, and later, in the three 'prequel' films, by Ewan McGregor.

The first part of his name comes from Japanese *obi* 'sash', and the following element may have been suggested by the Japanese honorific suffix *san*.

**Objective correlative.** A somewhat obfuscatory term introduced by T.S. Eliot in a famous essay on *Hamlet* to denote the literary and artistic technique of representing a particular emotion by means of symbols, which then indicate the emotion and become associated with it.

> The only way of expressing emotion in the form of art is by finding an 'objective correlative'; in other words, a set of objects, a situation, a chain of events which shall be the formula of that *particular* emotion; such that when the external facts, which must terminate in sensory experience, are given, the emotion is immediately evoked.
> T.S. ELIOT: in *Atheneum* (26 September 1919)

**Obolensky's try.** The classic try scored for England by Prince Alexander Obolensky (1916–40) in a rugby international against New Zealand in 1936.

**Ocker.** A boorish or aggressive Australian, an Antipodean version of the UGLY AMERICAN. The term dates from the early 1970s and derives from an alteration of 'Oscar' used for a character devised and played by Ron Frazer in an Australian television series, *The Mavis Bramston Show* (1965–8). *See also* Barry MCKENZIE.

**O'clock.** Apart from its regular use for naming an hour, this term has been employed in military parlance since the start of the 20th century to denote a bearing corresponding to the position of the hands on a clockface, from the standpoint of a person facing twelve o'clock. Thus three o'clock is due east and nine o'clock due west. The usage is most familiar in naming a target to be fired at, so that a shot ending up below the bull will be at six o'clock and one to its right at three o'clock. In the Second World War the term became more widely familiar from the radio communications of fighter pilots, with 'six o'clock' indicating a location under the speaker, so that 'bandits at six o'clock' meant 'enemy aircraft below me'. In more prosaic forms of travel, the metaphor is sometimes invoked to describe exits off roundabouts for drivers. *See also* TEN TO TWO.

**October Revolution.** In Russian history, the BOLSHEVIK

revolution of October 1917 (November in the Western calendar), which led to the overthrow of Kerensky and the MENSHEVIKS and the triumph of LENIN. *See also* ALL POWER TO THE SOVIETS!

**Octobrists.** A 'constitutionalist' centre party in Russia supported by the landlords and wealthy mercantile interests, prominent in the duma between 1907 and 1914, after the Tsar's liberal manifesto published in October 1905.

**Octopush.** A game resembling underwater hockey, first played in the early 1970s. The name combines 'octopus' and 'push' and the game itself consists in propelling a lead puck, or 'squid', along the bottom of a swimming pool and trying to push it into the opposing goal, or 'gulley'.

**'Octopus's Garden'.** A song by The BEATLES credited to Richard Starkey (Ringo Starr) and appearing on the album ABBEY ROAD, released in September 1969. Starkey's inspiration for the song came from a holiday he spent in Sardinia during which he learned that octopuses roam the seabed, picking up stones and shiny objects with which they build gardens. Like the earlier 'YELLOW SUBMARINE', the song includes various underwater sound effects created in the recording studio.

**Odds and sods.** Miscellaneous people or things; odds and ends. The expression originated as services slang in the 1930s.

**Odeon.** The British cinemas so called arose in the 1930s as a chain owned by the film distributor Oscar Deutsch (1893–1941), who named them partly after the odeon or odeum of ancient Greece and Rome, a building used for musical performances, and partly after his own initials. The first cinema to bear the name opened in Perry Barr, Birmingham, in 1930. *See also* ROXY.

**Oder–Neisse Line.** The frontier between Poland and East Germany (initially the Soviet zone of occupation of Germany) established at the Potsdam Conference of the victorious Allies in 1945, after the end of the Second World War in Europe. The frontier, which now forms the border between unified Germany and Poland, follows the course of the River Oder south to its junction with the River Neisse, which it then follows to the Czech border. As the new border awarded substantial areas of what had been Germany to Poland, West Germany did not recognize it until 1970. The change of policy was part of the OSTPOLITIK pursued by Chancellor Willy Brandt.

**Odessa.** An acronym for Organisation der Ehemaligen SS-Angehörigen (German, 'organization of former SS members'), sometimes rendered as ODESSA, the best known of a number of secret organizations that sought to smuggle Nazis out of Germany to safety after the Second World War. It was founded in 1947, and among those it helped to escape was Adolf Eichmann (*see* BANALITY OF EVIL). Favoured destinations were Franco's Spain, Arab countries in the Middle East, and South American countries such as Argentina and Paraguay. Odessa, which inspired Frederick Forsyth's 1972 thriller *The Odessa File*, was wound up in 1952 and replaced by the Kameradenwerke ('comrade workshop'). *See also* SS.

**Odessa Steps.** One of the most famous sequences in the history of cinema, from the silent classic *The* BATTLESHIP POTEMKIN (1925), directed by Sergei Eisenstein (1898–1948). The film is a partly fictionalized account of the mutiny of the Russian Black Sea fleet at the Crimean port of Odessa during the failed 1905 Revolution. In the sequence, which features much cross-cutting, innocent civilians are slaughtered by Tsarist forces. A particularly celebrated image is that of a baby in a pram, bouncing unattended down the steps.

The sequence has been celebrated and parodied through visual references in later films. The gangster movie *The* UNTOUCHABLES (1987), featuring a shoot-out on a station staircase, is an example of the former, while the police send-up *Naked Gun*, directed by David Zucker (1988), exemplifies the comic treatment.

**Oedipus complex.** The psychoanalytical term introduced by Sigmund Freud for the sexual desire (usually unrecognized by himself) of a son for his mother and conversely an equally unrecognized jealous hatred of his father. The situation may lead to repression, feelings of guilt and an inability to form normal emotional or sexual relationships. The allusion is to Oedipus in Greek tragedy, who unknowingly killed his father, King Laius, and married his mother, Jocasta. *See also* ELECTRA COMPLEX.

**Of-.** *See* OFSTED.

**Off-Broadway.** In the US theatre, a term relating to productions that are in generally smaller venues (and thus cheaper) than mainstream Broadway shows. The term also used to denote experimental, low-budget or not commercially viable productions, but the late-20th-century development of the tripartite theatre hierarchy, now also including 'off-off-Broadway', has largely devolved those attributes to this latter category. Off-off-Broadway shows are often staged in small halls, cafés, churches and the like.

> For proof that the theme of sexual diversion can be honestly and yet dramatically treated, one has to go, not to off-Broadway but to what is called off-off-Broadway. Actually the distinction between the two is quite real.
> *Manchester Guardian Weekly* (17 October 1968)

'Off Broadway' inspired London's 'Off West End', so that London theatre is now classified by such magazines as *Time Out* into three categories too. *See also* the FRINGE.

**Office, The.** A BBC television SITCOM portraying in quasi-documentary FLY ON THE WALL style the office lives of the employees of Wernham Hogg, a Slough stationery-supply firm. It was written by Ricky Gervais and Stephen Merchant. The former played the part of David Brent, the regional manager whose excruciatingly self-centred tactlessness and boorishness propelled the action of this acclaimed comedy of embarrassment. It was broadcast in two series in 2001 and 2002, with a Christmas special at the end of 2003. It was also a hit in the United States, inspiring a customized US version.

**Office party.** A party for members of the staff of an office or the employees of a company, especially one held just before Christmas. The office party became an established feature from the 1950s and soon came to be regarded as an occasion when the usual hierarchy of authority was set aside and traditional social constraints were abandoned. The norm instead became an overindulgence in alcohol, a careless indiscretion of speech and an eager exploitation of amorous opportunities.

> An office party is not, as is sometimes supposed, the Managing Director's chance to kiss the tea-girl. It is the tea-girl's chance to kiss the Managing Director.
> KATHARINE WHITEHORN: *Roundabout*, 'The Office Party' (1962)

**Officers' groundsheets.** A nickname give to members of the ATS, the Auxiliary Territorial Service, the women's branch of the Army during the Second World War. The women of the ATS had a reputation for easy virtue (by the standards of the day), though the other women's forces also suffered slurs: the slogan of the LAND GIRLS was said to be 'Backs to the land', and there was also the adapted proverb, 'Up with the lark, to bed with a Wren.' Princess Elizabeth (now Queen Elizabeth II) served with the ATS during the war.

**Official Secrets Act.** The legislation that controls access to confidential information important for national security in Britain originated as the Official Secrets Act of 1911. There have been several amended versions since. Apart from its general prohibition on spying, the essence of the Act is contained in Section 2, which makes it a criminal offence for government employees to divulge certain categories of information. It was under this Act that the civil service 'moles' Sarah Tisdall and Clive Ponting were charged in 1983. Tisdall, working in the Foreign Office, was jailed for six months for passing secret papers to *The Guardian* relating to the arrival in Britain of cruise missiles. Ponting, employed by the Ministry of Defence, leaked documents about the sinking of the GENERAL BELGRANO in the FALKLANDS WAR. He was eventually acquitted. Twenty years later Katharine Gun, an employee at GCHQ, Britain's secret communications centre, was charged under the Act after she leaked a request by the US government that the UK secret services bug foreign diplomats at the UN in an effort to obtain their support for the war in Iraq. The apparently watertight case against Gun was dropped in February 2004, following the demand by her counsel that the court be shown the attorney general's advice to the government regarding the legality of the war.

> The concept of the 'official secret' is the particular invention of bureaucracy.
> MAX WEBER: 'Politik als Beruf' (1919)

**Off message.** Departing from the official party line. The term is chiefly used of politicians who stray in this way, and who are thus more newsworthy than those who remain 'ON MESSAGE'. The 'message' is the party line itself. *See also* GET THE MESSAGE.

**Off-roading.** The sport of driving or racing a vehicle over rough terrain or along unmade roads, i.e. off the main road. An off-roader is a vehicle, usually having a four-wheel drive, used in such a pursuit. The sport originated in the United States in the late 1960s but has existed in Britain as an organized activity since the late 1970s. The use of off-road vehicles for non-off-road purposes (*see* CHELSEA TRACTOR) has become an increasingly controversial activity in the 21st century. *See also* 4×4.

**Offshore.** In finance, an account, such as a building society savings account, based abroad, where tax arrangements are more advantageous than in one's own country. In Britain 'offshore' in this sense applies to the Channel Islands and the Isle of Man, as well as further afield.

**Off the cuff.** Without previous preparation. The phrase, of US origin and dating from the 1930s, refers to the (largely mythical) habit of some after-dinner speakers of making jottings on their stiff shirt cuffs as ideas occur to them during the meal.

**Off the hook.** When a telephone is off the hook the receiver is not on the rest and no incoming calls can be received. This expedient is commonly resorted to by those who do not wish to be disturbed or to hear from a particular caller, although these days it is equally possible to switch off the ringer. There is now no actual hook as such, but in the early days of telephony, when it was not in use, the receiver hung from a hook next to the mouthpiece.

**Off the record.** Unofficially; confidentially. A term originating in the United States in the 1930s and taken up by spokesmen for public bodies when giving the media information that is either not for publication or not to be attributed (generally a convention that journalists respect in order to gain the information in the first place). The phrase may have a legal origin and refer to evidence that the judge has ordered to be struck off the court record as irrelevant or improper and thus to be ignored by the jury.

**Off the top of one's head.** Spontaneously; impromptu. An American phrase dating from the 1930s. Anything said or done spontaneously will not have been considered inside one's head but allowed to emerge uncontrolled.

**Off the wall.** Unorthodox; bizarre. The allusion may be to the unpredictable angle of return of a ball rebounding from a wall, as in baseball or squash. The phrase dates from the 1950s.

***Of Human Bondage.*** A semi-autobiographical novel (1915) by W. Somerset Maugham (1874–1965). The action is held together by the character of Philip Carey, who has a club foot. His is a largely tragic, isolated life, with two disastrous affairs, one without feeling and the other without sex, until Philip, with the encouragement of a friend, takes up his medical studies again, marries his friend's daughter and becomes a country general practitioner. The title is that of one of the five parts of *Ethics* by the Dutch philosopher and theologian Benedict de Spinoza (1632–77), issued posthumously by his friends in 1677 in an anonymous volume.

***Of Mice and Men.*** A novella (1937) by John Steinbeck (1902–68). It centres on two casual labourers, Lennie, a simple, sentimental giant who loves small animals but does not know his own strength, and his friend George. In a tragic ending, George's efforts are not enough to keep Lennie out of the trouble that he has unwittingly brought upon himself. The title is from 'To a Mouse' (1786) by Robert Burns (1759–96):

> The best laid schemes o' mice an' men
> Gang aft a-gley,
> An' lea'e us nought but grief an' pain,
> For promis'd joy.

A persuasive film version (1939) was directed by Lewis Milestone. *See also* FIRST LINES OF NOVELS.

**Ofsted.** The *Of*fice for *St*andards in *Ed*ucation, a government body set up in 1992 to monitor standards in schools by means of regular inspections. It answers directly to the secretary of state for education. The name aligns with those of similar bodies emerging in Britain from the 1980s, including Offer (the Office of Electricity Regulation), Ofgas (the Office of Gas Supply), Ofrail (the Office of the Railway Regulator), Oftel (the Office of Telecommunications, since 2003 part of Ofcom, the Office of Communications), and Ofwat (the Office of Water Services). The fact that the last five abbreviations sound as if they contain 'off', and thus suggest negation or disruption, does not seem to have occurred to their creators.

> Perhaps the best idea would be to privatise the Church of England, to get in a regulator – OfGod or something like that – and a few consultants, and then start marketing the Lord who is suitable to the 21st century.
> Labour MP TONY BANKS: speaking in parliament on reversing the decline in church attendance (December 1995)

**Ogopogo.** A water monster supposedly inhabiting Okanagan Lake, British Columbia, Canada. The name is said to come from a music-hall song of the 1920s sung by Davy Burnaby (1881–1949), with lines as follows, quoted in Peter Costello, *In Search of Lake Monsters*, chapter 10 (1974): *See also* LOCH NESS MONSTER.

> His mother was an earwig,
> His father was a whale.
> A little bit of head,
> And hardly any tail,
> And Ogopogo was his name.

**Ogpu.** *See under* KGB.

***Oh, Calcutta!*** A stage revue (1969) devised by the British theatre critic Kenneth Tynan (1927–80), which caused a considerable furore for its sexual explicitness. It came about just as theatre censorship had ended in Britain. The title was suggested to Tynan by his wife, Kathleen Tynan, who was writing an article about a painting of a nude by the French surrealist Clovis Trouille entitled *Oh! Calcutta! Calcutta!* (1946). Unbeknown to the Tynans at the time, the French title was a pun on *oh, quel cul t'as* (meaning 'oh, what a lovely arse you've got').

**Oh-so.** An intensive phrase prefixed to an adjective or adverb, the 'oh' representing a hesitation while searching for an appropriate word or else simply an expression of emotion before the 'so'. Thus the statement 'he is oh-so-ordinary' would have originated as 'he is, oh, so ordinary!' The phrase is recorded from the 1920s.

> Julian Sands … saunters in for his fitting and is incredibly laid back and oh-so-ca-su-al compared to my oh-so-strung-up state.
> RICHARD E. GRANT: *With Nails* (1996)

**Oh, What a Lovely War!** A musical (1963) created by Joan Littlewood's Theatre Workshop at the Theatre Royal, Stratford East, London, as a satirical commentary on the huge losses suffered in the First World War. The show featured lampoons of popular songs of the day, as sung by soldiers in the trenches.

> Oh, oh, oh, it's a lovely war,
> Who wouldn't be a soldier, eh?
> Oh, it's a shame to take the pay;
> As soon as reveille is gone,
> We feel just as heavy as lead,
> But we never get up till the sergeant
> Brings our breakfast up to bed …
> 'Oh, What a Lovely War!' (the title song)

**Okely-dokely.** A variation on 'okey-dokey' (itself an expanded form of 'OK') popularized in the United States from around 1990 by the character Ned Flanders in the television cartoon series *The Simpsons* (see Bart SIMPSON).

**Okies.** A derogatory term for American migrant workers, and especially those from Oklahoma who were forced off their farms in the 1930s during the GREAT DEPRESSION and who sought a new life in a hostile California. They are the subject of John Steinbeck's novel *The* GRAPES OF WRATH (1939) and of John Ford's powerful film based on it (1940). Ford said that the subject of the book reminded him of the famine years of his ancestral Ireland. *See also* DUST BOWL.

**Oklahoma!** A musical (1943) by Richard Rodgers (1902–79) and Oscar Hammerstein (1895–1960) set among the cowboys and farmers of the American West. Based on Lynn Rigg's play *Green Grow the Lilacs* (1931), it was originally to be titled *Oklahoma and Away We Go!* It was of *Oklahoma!* that one dismissive critic commented of its prospects: 'No legs, no jokes, no chance.' It became a classic of the genre.

**Okun's Law.** A law devised in 1962 by the US economist Arthur M. Okun (1928–80). It states that as the gross national product of a country declines because of recession, debt or inefficiency, there is a proportional rise in unemployment, statistically calculable according to specific indices.

**Olbers' Paradox.** The paradox propounded by the German astronomer Heinrich Olbers (1758–1840) that if stars were distributed evenly in sufficient numbers throughout an infinite static universe, the sky ought to be as bright at night as in the daytime, since, although the apparent brightness of a star decreases with distance, the actual number of stars increases in the same proportion. The anomaly is first recorded under this name in the 1950s. The paradox can be resolved by identifying its incorrect assumptions, the chief of which is that, as shown by the BIG BANG theory, the universe is not infinite.

**Ol' Blue Eyes.** A publicity-oriented nickname for the popular US singer Frank Sinatra (1915–98), a teenage idol in his twenties. He announced his retirement in 1971 but two years later returned with the slogan, 'Ol' Blue Eyes is back', adopted as the title of a television special. Posthumously, he (or rather giant projected images of him in performance) has starred in the 2006 tribute musical *Sinatra* at the London Palladium, accompanied by (living) orchestra, backing singers and dancers.

**Old bag.** A term dating from the 1940s for an elderly and unattractive or slovenly woman or for a 'lady of easy virtue'.

> Ah reckon you must have fired that old bag you had in the kitchen and got yourself a hundred per cent American cook.
> PAUL GALLICO: *Mrs Harris Goes to New York*, ch. 16 (1960)

**Old bean.** A familiar form of address to a man, dating from the First World War. *See also* OLD FRUIT.

**Old Bill.** A nickname for the police force, or a member of it. *See also* BETTER 'OLE.

**Old boy network.** To arrange something on the old boy network is to fix it through a social contact (properly someone from one's old school) instead of through the usual channels. The expression dates from the late 1950s, although the system obviously goes further back than that. *See also* OLD SCHOOL TIE.

**Old codger.** An old or eccentric person who is, even so, regarded with affection and even respected for his worldly wisdom. From 1936 to 1990 the *Daily Mirror* ran a 'Live Letters' column in which a couple of supposed 'Old Codgers' answered readers' questions on a variety of subjects in an entertaining and anecdotal way. 'Codger' is perhaps a variant of 'cadger'.

> This sprightly old codger [Prince Philip] has one major regret: that the Queen has never named him 'Prince Consort'.
> COMPTON MILLER: *Who's REALLY! Who* (1997)

**Old Contemptibles.** Members of the British Expeditionary Force of 160,000 men that left Britain in 1914 to join the French and Belgians against Germany. The soldiers are said to have given themselves this name from an army order (almost certainly apocryphal) issued by the German Kaiser (*see* KAISER BILL) at Aix on 19 August and published in an annexe to BEF Routine Orders of 24 September 1914:

> It is my royal and imperial command that you exterminate the treacherous English, and walk over General French's contemptible little army.

He may have actually called the BEF 'a contemptibly little army', which is not nearly so disparaging.

The surviving veterans held their last parade at the garrison church of All Saints, Aldershot, on Sunday, 4 August 1974 in the presence of Elizabeth II, who took tea with them before their final dispersal.

**Old Dun Cow.** A derisive nickname given by the troops to the steamer *River Clyde* beached at GALLIPOLI in 1915 during the First World War. It was probably a reference to the song of this name, popularized by Harry Champion, that contains the words, 'The Old Dun Cow she's done for now', the Old Dun Cow in question being a public house that had run dry.

**Old Europe.** US Defense Secretary Donald Rumsfeld's description of those European countries, particularly France and Germany, opposed to the invasion of Iraq by US and British forces in 2003. 'Old Europe' implies a contrast with 'New Europe', i.e. those former eastern-bloc countries such as Poland, plus countries such as Italy and Spain with right-wing governments, that supported the invasion. The idea of a perfidious 'Old Europe' may derive from the 'strong traditional distrust of old-world politics and a habit of isolation from old-world entanglements' that H.G. Wells detected in the United States in his *Short History of the World* (1922); the phrase itself is found in Hegel's description of the United States:

> It is a land of desire for all those who are weary of the historical arsenal of old Europe.
>
> G.F.W. HEGEL: *Lectures on the Philosophy of World History: Introduction* (1830), trans. H.B. Nisbet, 1975

**Olde worlde.** Old-fashioned in style; quaintly attractive. A pseudo-archaic phrase that is supposedly suggestive of 'the good old days'. It dates from the 1920s and is typically applied to a tea shop. *See also* OLD-TIME DANCE.

> Dymchurch is full of olde-worlde seaside charm – lovely.
>
> *Sunday Times* (26 December 1999)

**Old Firm, The.** The collective name for Glasgow's two top football teams, Celtic and Rangers. Thus an 'Old Firm game' is a Glasgow derby. The term originated in the early 20th century, and suggested the dominance the two clubs had (and continue to have) over Scottish football, and the financial success that this dominance brought.

**Old fogy.** An old-fashioned person; a 'stick in the mud'. *See also* YOUNG FOGY.

**Old fruit.** A familiar form of address to a man, dating from the 1920s. It is now as dated or mannered as OLD BEAN.

**Old grey whistle test.** A phrase that was adopted for the title of a weekly television pop music programme broadcast from 1971 to 1983 on BBC2 as a 'serious' partner to *Top of the Pops* on BBC1. The gravitas of the former programme was evidenced in the style of the laid-back MC 'Whispering' Bob Harris as opposed to the pumped-up disc jockeys who mostly compered the latter. The phrase derives from New York's 'Tin Pan Alley', where popular music was at one time published. Songwriters used to play their compositions to the 'old greys', the elderly doorkeepers and other employees in the publishing houses. If the 'old greys' were still whistling the tunes after a week or so, they were likely to be worth publishing.

**Old Groaner.** A nickname of the popular US singer Bing Crosby (1904–77), a pioneer of CROONING.

***Old Man and the Sea, The.*** A novella (1952) by Ernest Hemingway (1899–1961), which won the PULITZER PRIZE for fiction and was instrumental in Hemingway being awarded the NOBEL PRIZE for Literature in 1954. It tells of an elderly fisherman who, after 84 days going out in his skiff without a catch, and 44 without his boy assistant, who has abandoned him, hooks an enormous marlin. The battle with the fish and the struggle to get it back to land in the face of the predations of sharks, have been interpreted as an allegory of the contribution of courage and endurance to survival in the natural world. A rather disappointing film version (1958), starring Spencer Tracy, was directed by John Sturges.

**Old Man River.** A nickname for the Mississippi, originating in the song of this name by Oscar Hammerstein II for the musical *Showboat* (1927) and subsequently popularized by Paul Robeson. The name is not inappropriate, for the river's Native American name means 'great water', similarly suggesting seniority and implying veneration. The title could apply equally or even more aptly to other major rivers. The name of Ireland's longest river, the Shannon, is thus related to Irish *sean*, 'old', and probably refers to the ancient water god, or 'old man', who was at one time believed to inhabit it.

> Ol' man river, dat ol' man river,
> He must know sumpin', but don't say nothin',
> He jus' keeps rollin',
> He jus' keeps rollin' along.
>
> OSCAR HAMMERSTEIN II: 'Ol' Man River' (song)

Anticipating the age of POLITICAL CORRECTNESS, in 1957 Stan Freberg and Daws Butler produced a satirically 'polite' version of the song, which began:

> Elderly man river, that elderly man river,
> He must know something, but he doesn't say anything.

**Old Mother Riley.** The garrulous old washerwoman was the creation and persona of the music-hall comedian Arthur Lucan (born Arthur Towle; 1887–1954), whose Irish wife, Kitty McShane (1897–1964), stood in as her daughter. Her heyday was the 1930s, when she appeared on the stage of the London Palladium. She then transferred to the cinema and a number of radio series.

**Old school tie.** Literally, a distinguishing neck-tie worn by the former pupils of a particular school. Such ties being essentially associated with the public schools and the older grammar schools led to 'old school tie' being given a pejorative use as a symbol of class distinction, e.g. 'the old school tie brigade', meaning the members of a privileged class. The phrase is first recorded in Rudyard Kipling's *Limits and Renewals* (1932) but would have already then been current. A suggestion of 'tie' in the sense 'bond', 'association' is also perhaps present. *See also* OLD BOY NETWORK.

> If you are entitled to wear what is generically known as an Old School Tie, whether it represents your public school, university, regiment, golf club, rowing club, or any other sporting or social associations, wear it sparingly.
>
> GUY EGMONT: *The Art of Egmontese*, ch. 1 (1961)

**Old Smoky.** A grimly humorous nickname for the electric chair (*see* OLD SPARKY), from the effects caused when operated.

**Old soldiers never die.** A modern proverb that may originate in the First World War and certainly formed the title of a song copyrighted in 1920 by the British songwriter J. Foley:

> Old soldiers never die,
> They simply fade away.

The song was a parody of the hymn 'Kind Words Can Never Die'. In 1951 General Douglas MacArthur was relieved of his command in the Korean War for insubordination, but President Truman was obliged to allow MacArthur, on his return, to address Congress (19 April). MacArthur, as ever, played to the gallery:

> I still remember the refrain of one of the most popular barrack ballads of that day, which proclaimed, most proudly, that old soldiers never die. They just fade away. And like the old soldier of that ballad, I now close my military career and just fade away – an old soldier who tried to do his duty as God gave him the light to see that duty. Goodbye.

*See also* I SHALL RETURN.

**Old Spanish custom.** A longstanding but unauthorized practice. The phrase dates from at least the 1930s and in the

1980s came to describe the irregular behaviour of newspaper production workers, especially with regard to cheating over pay packets. The reason for the particular national attribution is uncertain, although the Spanish have come to be associated with casual working practices and what might be called the '*mañana* syndrome'. 'Spanish practices' is a variant of the term.

**Old Sparky.** A nickname for the electric chair, long the executioner's tool of choice in the United States – it was first used in 1890. It is also known as the Florida Flambée, that state being notably partial to capital punishment. The electric chair sometimes leads to an unintended conflagration (it turned out that in Florida the prison staff were not dampening the electrode attached to the head sufficiently, so that the victim's brains caught fire). Alternative nicknames include Sizzling Sally, Gruesome Gerty and Old Smoky. These days death by lethal injection is more fashionable in the United States, although a few states hang on to the old ways.

**Old Squiffy.** A nickname given to H.H. Asquith (1852–1928), British Liberal prime minister (1908–16), by Lord Alfred Douglas on account of Asquith's tippling skills, 'squiffy' being an informal term for 'drunk'. However, the Conservative politician Andrew Bonar Law (1858–1923), who helped to engineer the downfall of Asquith's wartime coalition, observed that 'Asquith, when drunk, could make a better speech than any of us sober.' *See also* OLD WAIT AND SEE; SQUIFFITES.

**Old sweat.** An experienced soldier of long service, or even any old soldier. The expression dates from the First World War.

**Old thing.** A formerly familiar mode of address between friends. Preceded by a descriptive, as 'funny old thing', 'poor old thing', it is still current. In Britain the phrase has become especially associated with the fruity-voiced cricket commentator Henry Blofeld, an Old Etonian, who uses it (generally in the form 'my dear old thing') to address his fellow-commentators on BBC Radio's *Test Match Special*. *See also* NAPOO.

**Old Timber.** A punning nickname of the English conductor Sir Henry Wood (1869–1944), who founded the London Promenade Concerts ('the Proms') in 1895 and continued to conduct them until his death. He was knighted in 1911.

**Old-time dance.** A formal or formation dance of the kind danced in the 19th century or the early years of the 20th. To indicate its nostalgic nature the term is sometimes spelled 'olde-tyme dance'.

**Old Vic.** The London theatre opened in 1818 as the Royal Coburg Theatre, taking its name from its chief patrons, Prince Leopold of Saxe-Coburg (1790–1865), the future King Leopold I of Belgium and uncle of Queen Victoria, and his wife Princess Charlotte (d.1817). In 1833 it was renamed the Royal Victoria Theatre in honour of 14-year-old Princess Victoria, later Queen Victoria. It was soon popularly known as the 'Vic', but by the start of the 20th century this name had been expanded to 'Old Vic', partly in reference to Victoria's age and reign (she died aged 81 after 64 years on the throne, longer than any other British monarch), but mainly as a token of affection. The name later became effectively official and in 1970 the 'Young Vic' was founded nearby as a counterpart to provide good theatre for young people at cheap prices.

**Old Wait and See.** Another nickname for the Liberal prime minister H.H. Asquith (*see* OLD SQUIFFY), from his frequent use of the response 'Wait and see' in parliament, notably at the time of the Lords' rejection of the 1909 PEOPLE'S BUDGET, when questioned as to whether he was going to pack the Upper House with new Liberal peers. Later, when his opponents became critical of his perceived lack of decisive action in the conduct of the First World War, the nickname came to haunt him. Matches that failed to produce a flame were known as 'Asquiths' or 'Wait and sees'.

**Olympic Games.** The modern games, a revival of the ancient Greek festival held every four years at Olympia, were organized in 1896 as international sporting contests. The first Summer Olympics were held at Athens, and subsequently at Paris (1900), St Louis (1904), London (1908), Stockholm (1912), Antwerp (1920), Paris (1924), Amsterdam (1928), Los Angeles (1932), Berlin (1936), London (1948), Helsinki (1952), Melbourne (1956), Rome (1960), Tokyo (1964), Mexico City (1968), Munich (1972), Montreal (1976), Moscow (1980), Los Angeles (1984), Seoul (1988), Barcelona (1992), Atlanta (1996), Sydney (2000), Athens (2004) and Beijing (2008). The 2012 Games were awarded to London, the announcement (6 July 2005) enthusing many in that city the day before terrorists bombed it (*see* 7/7).

The Winter Olympic Games were inaugurated in 1924 at Chamonix, France, with subsequent sites at St Moritz (1928), Lake Placid (1932), Garmisch-Partenkirchen (1936), St Moritz (1948), Oslo (1952), Cortina d'Ampezzo (1956), Squaw Valley (1960), Innsbruck (1964), Grenoble (1968), Sapporo (1972), Innsbruck (1976), Lake Placid (1980), Sarajevo (1984), Calgary (1988), Albertville (1992), Lillehammer (1994), Nagano (1998), Salt Lake City (2002) and Turin (2006). The 2010 Winter Games have been awarded to Vancouver.

**Omaha Beach.** The Allied code name for the stretch of beach on the Normandy coast between the Vire River and Port-en-Bressin, where the US 5th Corps landed on D-DAY. The beach became known as 'Bloody Omaha' for the stiff German opposition there. The Allied army also landed on four other Normandy beaches, code-named UTAH BEACH, GOLD BEACH, JUNO BEACH and SWORD BEACH. Steven Spielberg's film *Saving Private Ryan* (1998) sought to convey the full horror of the Omaha landing in its opening scenes.

**Ombudsman.** (Swedish, 'legal representative'.) In Scandinavian countries, an official appointed by the legislature whose duty it is to protect the rights of the citizen against infringement by the government. Sweden has had one since 1809, Denmark since 1955, and Norway since 1962. New Zealand was the first Commonwealth country to appoint such a commissioner (1962) and Britain appointed a Parliamentary Commissioner for Administration in 1967, commonly known as the 'Ombudsman'. Local Commissioners, or local government ombudsmen, were later appointed to investigate complaints from the public against local authorities, and independent ombudsmen schemes were similarly set up for banks, building societies, insurance companies, financial institutions and independent financial advisers.

In Britain, since the 1980s, regulatory bodies have sprouted up charged with supervising education and the privatized ultities, and with protecting the consumers thereof: *see* OFSTED; QUANGO.

**OMOV.** An acronym, rhyming with 'home of', of 'one member, one vote', as a principle of democratic election within an organization. It was achieved in the LABOUR PARTY in 1993, so ending the block vote of the trade unions, and was first used in 1994 for the election of Tony Blair as leader. The term ultimately derives from 'one man, one vote' as a principle of universal suffrage dating from the mid-19th century.

**On a collision course.** Adopting an approach or following a line that is bound to lead to conflict with another person or group of people. The expression dates from the Second World War and originally applied literally to two ships on converging courses. The figurative sense became current from the 1960s.

> The great powers are now headed on a collision course over Berlin.
>
> *New Statesman* (21 July 1961)

**On a roll.** Experiencing luck; enjoying success; doing well. The American expression originates from gambling (specifically crapshooting), and dates from the 1970s. The roll is that of the dice, which keep falling favourably.

**On a wing and a prayer.** With only a small hope or chance of success. The phrase comes from a Second World War song based on the words that the pilot of a damaged aircraft radioed to ground control as he prepared to come in to land:

> Tho' there's one motor gone, we can still carry on
> Comin' in on a wing and a pray'r.
>
> HAROLD ADAMSON: 'Comin' in on a Wing and a Pray'r' (1943)

**Once and Future King, The.** A tetralogy (1958) by T.H. White (1906–64), consisting of revised versions of *The Sword in the Stone* (1938), *The Witch in the Wood* (1939), and *The Ill-Made Knight* (1940) with *The Candle in the Wind* (1958) added. It is a reworking of the Arthurian legend, beginning with Arthur's childhood, and offering with wit and pathos a parable for modern times and a commentary on the *Morte D'Arthur* of Thomas Malory (*c.*1410–71), which has the following passage: 'And many men say that there is written on his tomb this verse: *Hic iacet Arthurus, rex quondam, rexque futurus*' ('Here lies Arthur, once a king and a future king') (Bk 21, ch. 7). *The Sword in the Stone* was turned into an unsubtle cartoon film (1963), which was directed by Wolfgang Reitherman.

**Ondes Martenot.** (French, 'Martenot waves'.) This unusual electronic instrument, originally known as *ondes musicales*, 'musical waves', was developed by the French musician Maurice Martenot (1898–1980) and first demonstrated by him at the Paris Opéra on 20 April 1928. It somewhat resembles a spinet, with a keyboard of five octaves, but can produce only one note at a time. It is operated by a wire across the keyboard, which the player manipulates to produce the desired pitch. The signal is then amplified through a loudspeaker. Tone colour and timbre are obtained by pressing a button and volume is controlled by a key. The instrument may be heard in Olivier Messiaen's TURANGALÎLA SYMPHONY (1949) and Arthur Honegger's dramatic oratorio *Jeanne d'Arc au bûcher* (1935).

**One-armed bandit.** A FRUIT MACHINE operated by the insertion of coins and the pulling of an arm or lever and so called because it 'robs' one of change. It has now mostly been superseded by electronic machines.

**One damned thing after another.** What life is, according to the US writer Elbert Hubbard (1859–1915), writing in the December 1909 issue of *Philistine*. The sentiment has since been shared by many others.

**One Day in the Life of Ivan Denisovich.** A novella (1963; in Russian as *Odin den' Ivana Denisovicha*, 1962) by Alexander Solzhenitsyn (b.1918), first published outside the USSR. Life in one of STALIN's labour camps is seen through the eyes of an inmate. The author was himself in such a camp from 1950 to 1953. A film version (1971) directed by Caspar Wrede was a fairly faithful adaptation of the original, with all its harrowing detail.

**Onedin Line, The.** A BBC television drama of the sea, running from 1971 to 1980. The story concerned the ruses devised by James Onedin, a 19th-century ship's master, to own a fleet of sailing vessels. The combination of salt-sprayed action, romantic intrigue and costume drama made the series required regular Sunday evening viewing.

**One Flew Over the Cuckoo's Nest.** A novel (1962) by Ken Kesey (b.1935). The narrator is the Chief, whose father was the last chief of his tribe. He is a patient in a mental hospital (the 'cuckoo's nest'), in which authority is represented by 'Big Nurse'. The admission of McMurphy from prison precipitates a struggle between 'good' (the patients) and 'evil' (Big Nurse), with the 'liberation' of the patients from institutional restrictions as the stake. The film version (1975), directed by Milos Forman and starring Jack Nicholson, was amusing and horrifying in equal parts, but had an unexpected commercial success. The title comes from the nursery rhyme:

> One flew east, one flew west,
> One flew over the cuckoo's nest.

**One Foot in the Grave.** A BBC television SITCOM running from 1990 to 2000. The story centres on the cantankerous Scotsman Victor Meldrew, forced into early retirement and trying to adjust to his final years of leisure with his wife Margaret. His well-meaning attempts to take on odd jobs, help with good causes and generally offer help to others invariably end in disaster or at best misunderstanding and confusion. Embroiled in the muddles of his own making, Meldrew's already simmering temper usually becomes explosive. In the final episode he is killed by a hit-and-run driver. The series elevated the comic bit-part actor Richard Wilson, as Meldrew, to star status almost overnight. Subsequently, calling someone a 'Victor Meldrew' implies that he is a grumpy old man. *See also* I DON'T BELIEVE IT!

An attempt was made at a US version (1996–2000), starring Bill Cosby and entitled *Cosby*, but (in typical Meldrew style) it managed to shoot itself in the foot. Assuming that American audiences would be too upset by the original's lack of cheerful payoff and Meldrew's thorough-going misanthropy, it softened the character's edges, made the storylines more heartwarming, traded on its star's name – and eventually disappeared, unmourned.

**One for the book.** Anything noteworthy or remarkable. The expression, of US origin and dating from the early

20th century, originally referred to record books kept for sports.

**One for the road.** A final drink before departure to fortify one for the journey ahead. The expression (and the practice) fell victim to the increasing enforcement of DRINK-DRIVING legislation from the 1980s. A similar enticement exists in the phrase 'Afore ye go', found (as a registered trademark) on bottles of Bell's whisky, and from the equally Scottish *doch an doris* (from the Gaelic for 'a drink at the door').

**One Hundred Years of Solitude.** *See* FIRST LINES OF NOVELS; MAGIC REALISM.

**One is not born a woman, one becomes one.** An epigram from Simone de Beauvoir's *The Second Sex* (1949), the book that trumpeted the arrival of the second wave of feminism, which followed the winning of the vote for women. The phrase reflects de Beauvoir's existentialist position.

**One-liner.** A short joke or witty remark. The term is of US origin and dates from the start of the 20th century.

> [President] Reagan's substitute for strong emotions seems to be humor, both memorized and spontaneous. He is a walking repertory theater of show-biz anecdotes, one-liners, elaborate routines.
> *Time* (20 October 1980)

**One-man band.** Properly, a street entertainer who plays several instruments at the same time. Metaphorically a one-man band is a person who runs a business alone. The phrase dates from the 1920s and was made familiar by the title of Ted Weems's bestselling record hit 'The One-Man Band' (1931).

**One Million Years B.C.** A film (1939) depicting the lives of a band of cave-dwellers in prehistoric times. Based on an earlier silent movie called *Man's Genesis*, directed by D.W. Griffith in 1912, and also known by the alternative titles *The Cave Dwellers*, *Cave Man* and *Man and His Mate*, this version of human existence in prehistoric times diverges wildly from scientific fact, with men pitting themselves against dinosaurs that were extinct millions of years before. This did not prevent a remake of the film, complete with dinosaurs, appearing in 1966, starring Raquel Welch (in a fur bikini) and John Richardson in the roles originally taken by Carole Landis and Victor Mature. 'This is the way it was!' shrieked the posters. It wasn't.

**One-night stand.** A single performance by a touring theatrical company or the like at a town that will probably provide an audience for only one night. Also, a sexual liaison lasting only one night. The latter sense evolved from the former in the 1930s.

**One-off.** An unusual or unique person, especially positively so. The expression dates from the 1930s and originally applied to a single manufactured object of some kind, often produced as a sample or specimen.

> [Conservative MP Alan] Clark was a one-off. In a political party where 'sound' is the strongest expression of approval … Clark was his own man, and very unsound indeed.
> *The Times*: obituary of Alan Clark (8 September 1999)

**One of Our Aircraft is Missing.** A film (1941) co-written and directed by Michael Powell (1905–90) and Emeric Pressburger (1902–88) about the crew of a Wellington bomber during the Second World War who are shot down but make their way back to England with the help of the Dutch underground. The title was inspired by a stock formula of wartime broadcasts about recent raids on enemy territory. The original title was *One of Our Aircraft Failed to Return*. In 1975 Walt Disney released a comedy adventure entitled *One of Our Dinosaurs is Missing*, apparently under the influence of the Powell/Pressburger film.

**One of the boys.** One who mixes well socially; an equal member of a team or group. The phrase dates from the start of the 20th century and is frequently applied to a 'woman in a man's world'.

**One picture is worth a thousand words.** This supposed traditional maxim was the creation of Fred R. Barnard of the American magazine *Printer's Ink*. He first published it in the issue for 8 December 1921 but with 'look', not 'picture'. He changed the phrase to its present form for the edition of 10 March 1927, calling it 'a Chinese proverb, so that people would take it seriously'. The story behind the familiar saying is given in Burton Stevenson's *The Home Book of Proverbs, Maxims, and Familiar Phrases* (1948).

> If a picture paints a thousand words,
> then why can't I paint you?
> The words will never show
> the you I've come to know.
> DAVID GATES: 'If' (song) (1971)

**One small step …** The first words spoken by a man on the moon, uttered as Neil Armstrong (b.1930) stepped off the lunar module *Eagle* onto the moon's surface:

> That's one small step for [a] man, one giant leap for mankind.

Unfortunately, radio interference lost the indefinite article.

If the *Apollo 11* mission had ended in tragedy and the astronauts had been stranded on the moon, President Nixon, like any politician worth his salt, had a contingency plan. He would have broadcast the following words, scripted by William Safire, to the nation:

Fate has ordained that the men who went to the moon to explore in peace will stay on the moon to rest in peace. These brave men, Neil Armstrong and Buzz Aldrin, know that there is no hope for their recovery. But they also know that there is hope for mankind in their sacrifice … For every human being who looks up at the moon in the nights to come will know that there is some corner of another world that is forever mankind.

> Quoted in Lee Clarke, *Worst Cases: Terror and Catastrophe in the Popular Imagination* (2005)

*See also The* EAGLE HAS LANDED.

**One-stop shop.** A shop providing a wide range of goods, so that a customer can make various purchases in a single visit. Such shops arose in the United States in the 1930s and are now found in British suburban streets and as village stores. The phrase has now moved beyond retail, so that other phnenomena that seem to offer a comprehensive service may be termed thus.

**One that got away.** The prize that one only just missed and that was better than all the others. The metaphor is from fishing mythology, according to which it is always the biggest fish that just manages to elude capture: 'You should have seen the one that got away!'

**One-track mind.** A mind with one dominant preoccupation (usually, in modern usage, sex), which constantly reverts to the one subject, as a single-track railway allows traffic in only one direction at a time. The expression is first recorded in D.H. Lawrence's LADY CHATTERLEY'S LOVER (1928) but must date from before this.

> That's the only way to solve the industrial problem: train the people to be able to live and live in handsomeness, without needing to spend. But you can't do it. They're all one-track minds nowadays.
>
> D.H. LAWRENCE: *Lady Chatterley's Lover*, ch. 19 (1928)

**One-upmanship.** The art or knack of being 'one up', or gaining an advantage over other people. The term was popularized by Stephen Potter in his book of this title (1952). *See also* GAMESMANSHIP.

**On Hearing the First Cuckoo in Spring.** The orchestral piece by Frederick Delius (1862–1934) is not as English as one might think, in that it makes use of a Norwegian folk song that had previously been drawn on by Edvard Grieg (1843–1907) in his *Nineteen Norwegian Folk Tunes*. The work was first performed in 1913, and the cuckoo itself is played by the clarinet.

**Only Fools and Horses.** A long-running BBC television

SITCOM, written by John Sullivan, who also sang the theme tune. It was screened from 1981 to 1991, with several Christmas specials thereafter. It centres on the comic adventures of WHEELER-DEALER Derek ('Del Boy') Trotter and his put-upon younger brother Rodney, played by David Jason and Nicholas Lyndhurst respectively, as they eke out a living in the streets of London. The title derives from the Cockney saying 'Only fools and horses work.' The series is memorable for its colourful writing, and the dialogues of the two are peppered with slang words such as 'dipstick' and 'plonker' for an idiot and LOVELY JUBBLY! as a term of approval. *See also* RELIANT ROBIN.

**Only game in town, The.** The sole option, especially an unsatisfactory one that one must accept for lack of any alternative. The expression, first recorded in 1942, originated in American English.

> 'If you want to attach your network to the Internet, but you don't like the Network Solutions Inc.'s (NSI) policies, for whatever reason, you quickly learn that NSI is the only game in town,' said Catherine Simmons-Gill at a Congressional hearing in 1996.
>
> *Computer Law Review & Technology Journal* (VIII) (2004)

**Only joking.** I didn't mean it. A phrase said after one has cracked a joke or made a (supposedly) witty remark which might be taken seriously by some.

> One of the band went into an Irish pub and was called a 'faggot' and I swear I saw someone knitting at the front of our gig. Only joking!
>
> BOY GEORGE: in *Sunday Express* (27 February 2000)

**Only thing we have to fear is fear itself, The.** A line, subsequently proverbial, from the 1933 inaugural address of President Franklin D. Roosevelt (1882–1945). The NEW DEAL that FDR introduced did much to alleviate the suffering of the American people during the Depression.

**On message.** What politicians are encouraged to be by their press officers (*see* SPIN DOCTOR), i.e. they are to present a united front on all areas of policy, and push forward the same agenda; in other words, the opposite of OFF MESSAGE. The phrase has become widespread since the election of the NEW LABOUR government in 1997. It was said that Alastair Campbell, Director of Communications and Strategy at No. 10 Downing Street (the prime minister's office) from 1997 to 2003, would use pagers, text messages and abrasive phone calls to keep potentially errant ministers in line.

No government in history has been as obsessed with public

relations as this one … Speaking for myself, if there is a message I want to be off it.

JEREMY PAXMAN: quoted in the *Daily Telegraph* (3 July 1998), after Alastair Campbell had criticized the style of interviewing on various BBC news and current affairs programmes

*See also* SING FROM THE SAME HYMN SHEET.

**On one's own time and own dime.** Entirely at one's own expense. The American expression is often shortened to 'on one's own dime'. 'Dime', properly a 10-cent coin, here simply means 'money'.

'I live in Los Angeles, and Kimberly [Peirce] was conducting interviews in New York,' she [actress Hilary Swank] says. 'I got over there on my own dime, put myself up and read for her.'
*Sunday Times* (27 February 2000)

**On one's tod.** On one's own. The origin of the expression, which dates from the 1930s, is in rhyming slang, with 'own' from the name of the US jockey Tod Sloan (1874–1933), who came to England in 1897 and was the leading winner of 1900. He was as much noted for his gambling and social climbing as his innovative racing style and success on the course itself.

**On one's toes.** Alert; ready for any eventuality. The image is of a runner set to race or of a dancer poised to perform. The expression was popularized by the Rodgers and Hart musical *On Your Toes* (1936).

In modern Cockney slang, to 'have it on one's toes' is to run away, especially from the danger of imminent arrest. The expression dates from the 1950s.

**On someone's ginger.** In Australian slang, hotly pursuing someone, 'on someone's tail'. 'Ginger' is short for 'ginger ale', Australian rhyming slang for 'tail'.

**On the back burner.** Having low priority; available in reserve. The allusion is to the back burners (hotplates, rings) of a stove, which cook more slowly than the front ones. The phrase dates from the 1960s.

**On the back of.** Resulting from; following as a consequence. An expression often associated with the business world.

Share prices rallied in London on the back of the overnight rebound on Wall Street. But it was a half-hearted affair, lacking conviction.
*The Times* (3 September 1998)

**On the back of an envelope.** The traditional location for an initial calculation or sketch that may well evolve into a major feat or invention.

The chairman asked Major Bill Tillman, the notorious lightweight explorer and mountaineer, if he would like to say a few words. 'Yes,' said Bill, 'in my experience, any worthwhile expedition can be organized on the back of an envelope.'
*The Times* (10 June 1999)

**On the ball.** Alert; well informed. The expression is American in origin and dates from the early 20th century. The reference is to baseball, in which to put something on the ball is to pitch with extra speed or a special spin in order to strike out more batters.

**On the bugle.** *See* ON THE NOSE.

**On the buroo.** Receiving unemployment benefit. A Scottish phrase dating from the 1930s, in which 'buroo' is a pronunciation of 'bureau', meaning the Labour Bureau or social security office.

**On the button.** Exactly right; precisely correct. The expression derives from boxing slang, in which the 'button' is the chin, the part of the body a boxer aims to punch to score a knockout blow.

**On the case.** Actively looking into or dealing with a matter. If someone complains that someone else is always 'on their case', they mean that that person is always harrassing or criticizing them.

**On the club.** Off work sick, especially when receiving sickness benefit. If the illness is morning sickness, the person concerned will also be IN THE CLUB.

**On the coat.** In Australian slang, in the condition of being ostracized or sent to Coventry. The expression, first recorded in 1940, is applied particularly by strikers to blacklegs, and may come from the former practice, in the Australian docks, of grasping a strike-breaker by the right lapel to indicate his ostracized status to fellow workers.

**On the dot.** Precisely on time. The reference is to the minute hand of the clock being exactly over the dot marking the hour (or one of the five-minute intervals) on the dial of an analogue clock or watch.

**On the job.** Actively at work; engaged in sexual intercourse.

**On the lam.** On the run from prison; in flight from the police. The phrase originated as American underworld slang in the 1920s. 'Lam' is probably from the more familiar verb meaning 'to beat'. There may thus be a pun on 'beat it'.

**On the money.** Completely accurate(ly) or precise(ly). The expression originated (perhaps with reference to an accurate shot that wins first prize) in 1940s America.

Computer forecast models ... have been consistently right on the money for this slow-moving storm.

*Richmond* (Virginia) *Times-Dispatch* (23 December 1994)

**On the nose.** In Australian and New Zealand slang, having a bad smell, and hence by extension morally dubious or criminal. 'Bugle' being an Australian slang synonym for 'nose', 'on the bugle' has the same meaning. Both expressions probably date from the 1930s.

**On the pull.** Seeking a sexual liaison. The 'pull' is the endeavour to attract or draw to oneself. The expression dates from the 1960s.

**On the Q.T.** Secretly; unofficially. 'Q.T.' stands for 'quiet'.

**On the receiving end.** Bearing the brunt; 'taking the rap'. The allusion is to being the recipient of a blow or punishment, by implication unjustly so. The expression dates from the 1930s.

**On the Road.** A novel (1957) by Jack Kerouac (1922–69), based on several wild trips across the United States with Neal Cassady (1926–68). In it Kerouac uses the term BEAT GENERATION 'to describe guys who run around the country in cars looking for odd jobs, girlfriends, and kicks'. The book became the prose manifesto of the culture it evokes, although Truman Capote dismissed it with the remark:

That's not writing, that's typing.

*See also* FIRST LINES OF NOVELS; ROAD MOVIE.

**On the same wavelength.** In complete agreement; in full rapport. The expression alludes to radio waves carrying a broadcast.

**On the wagon.** Voluntarily abstaining from alcohol. Such a person is 'on the water wagon' as distinct from the wine bottle.

**On the Waterfront.** A COLUMBIA PICTURES film (1954) with a screenplay by Budd Schulberg from his own novel, which was based on a series of articles by Malcolm Johnson about corruption in New York's docklands (hence the title). Starring Marlon Brando, Rod Steiger and Lee J. Cobb, the film depicts Brando's character, Terry, a former boxer, as a stool pigeon who nonetheless achieves heroic status in the struggle against the waterfront mafiosi. Many critics interpreted this approach as a defence on behalf of Schulberg and the director, Elia Kazan, who had both controversially testified before the McCarthyite (*see* MCCARTHYISM) House Un-American Activities Committee and had thus caused problems for left-wing colleagues in the film business.

See! You don't understand! I could've been a contender. I could've had class and been somebody.

Terry, in *On the Waterfront*

**On top of the world.** Happy and elated. The allusion is to a peak of happiness or success. The expression dates from the 1920s.

**On your bike!** Go away! Clear off! The phrase dates from the 1960s, but later gained the implication that one should go and look for work. This sense was popularized in a speech at the Conservative Party Conference in 1981 by Norman Tebbit, then Employment Secretary, when he said that his father had not rioted in the 1930s, when unemployed, but had instead 'got on his bike and looked for work'. *See also* CHINGFORD SKINHEAD; SEMI-HOUSETRAINED POLECAT.

The gut instinct of this Government is no different from the last. It yearns to support the cause of the motorist, the shopping mall, the rural housing estate, the enterprise ideology of 'on your bike'.

*The Times* (22 September 1999)

**Oo-ar!** A representation of a stock MUMMERSET equivalent of 'oh yes!'.

**Oo-er!** An exclamation of surprise or alarm, representing an 'ooh' of surprise followed by an 'er' of hesitation.

'Oo-er!' cried Jenny. 'We aren't going to sleep in the dark?'

COMPTON MACKENZIE: *Carnival*, ch. 9 (1912)

Followed by 'Missus', it is a rather heavy-handed signal of a double entendre, associated particularly with the confiding stand-up comedy style of Frankie Howerd.

At a lunch last week he [David Cameron] first spilt food down his tie before a waitress plunged his cafetiere so vigorously – ooh er, missus – that she splashed coffee all over his white shirt.

*Sunday Times* (9 October 2005)

Front zip difficult to get right with a woman's lumpy bits, so a rear entry would be better (oo-er missus, brace yerself love, this might smart a bit).

www.yorkshire-divers.co.uk

**Ooh-la-la** or **oh-la-la.** A phrase intended to evoke a French-style 'naughtiness'. It dates from the 1940s and represents French *ô là! là!*, literally 'Oh there, there!'

**Ooh, you are awful.** *See The* DICK EMERY SHOW.

**Oomph.** Sex appeal; attractiveness; energy or 'go'. The word is imitative of something that has 'punch'. The US film star Ann Sheridan (1915–67) was promoted by WARNER BROTHERS as the 'Oomph Girl' for her sex appeal, just as Clara Bow before her was the 'IT' GIRL.

**Oor Wullie.** 'Our Willie', the shock-headed little boy whose strip-cartoon adventures appear in the Scottish *Sunday Post*. He wears dungarees and sits on an upturned bucket and his speech is scripted in broad Scots dialect. He was the creation in 1936 of Dudley D. Watkins and has become part of Scotland's popular mythology.

**Op art.** A form of abstract art that evolved in the 1960s. It gives an illusion of movement by the precise use of pattern and colour, or by creating conflicting patterns that emerge and overlap. The name, while patterned on POP ART, is intended as an abbreviation of 'optical art' and was first used in print in the US magazine *Time* in October 1964. The term was popularized by the exhibition 'The Responsive Eye', held in 1965 at the Museum of Modern Art, New York, as the first international exhibition with a predominance of Op art paintings. Leading exponents are Victor Vasarely (1908–97) and Bridget Riley (b.1931). Op art became something of a fad in the world of fashion and in 1965 Riley unsuccessfully tried to sue an American clothing company that had used one of her paintings as a fabric design.

**Op-Ed.** The abbreviation of 'opposite editorial', as an American term for a page in a newspaper opposite the editorial page and devoted to personal comment, feature articles and the like. It was the creation of the US newspaper editor Herbert B. Swope, who introduced it to the *New York World* soon after becoming that paper's executive editor in 1920.

**Open All Hours.** A BBC television SITCOM running from 1976 to 1985 and starring Ronnie Barker (1929–2005) as the stuttering, miserly, lustful shopkeeper Arkwright. The humour was as much physical as verbal, and Barker was supported by strongly drawn contrasting characters, the chief being Arkwright's dreamy nephew, Granville, played by David Jason (*see* ONLY FOOLS AND HORSES).

**Open diplomacy.** The opposite of secret diplomacy, as defined in the first of US President Woodrow Wilson's FOURTEEN POINTS, 'open covenants of peace openly arrived at, after which there shall be no private international understandings of any kind'. It is perhaps significant that the TREATY OF VERSAILLES was an 'open treaty' negotiated in secret.

**Open Skies Treaty.** The treaty signed in March 1992 between the United States, Russia, Britain and France and a number of former republics of the USSR. It sanctioned each country's right to fly reconnaissance aircraft over the territory of the others in order to photograph military installations. Former WARSAW PACT members later joined the accord, and by 1996 42 nations had signed.

**Open slather.** In Australian slang, a situation in which there are no restrictions or limits to what one may do; a free-for-all. The expression is first recorded in 1919, and 'slather' comes from a dialect verb, once current in British and American English, meaning 'to squander'.

**Open University.** A distance-learning institution founded in 1969 to provide adult education up to degree level, using correspondence courses, radio and TV programmes, and residential summer schools. The Open University came into being under the Labour administration of Harold Wilson, who dubbed it 'The University of the Air'. The first courses commenced in 1971. The development of the INTERNET and the WORLD WIDE WEB has interested many of the more traditional universities in the concept of distance learning or E-LEARNING, often aimed at those older than school-leavers.

**Opera isn't over until the fat lady sings, The.** A phrase, often used in sporting contexts, to mean that the eventual outcome won't be known until the end of the contest. It is also a warning against jumping to conclusions. The reference is to the final aria in an opera, often delivered by a well-upholstered diva (in particular, it is said to refer to Brünnhilde's 'Fire Song' at the end of Wagner's very long *Die Walküre*). It has been attributed to the American baseball player Yogi Berra, but what he is reported to have said in 1973 is 'It's not over till it's over.' The phrase certainly came to wide prominence in 1978 when the San Antonio sports commentator Dan Cook used it (*Washington Post*, 3 June): 'The opera ain't over 'til the fat lady sings.' However, the phrase 'Church ain't out till the fat lady sings' is said to have been current in the American South for several decades before this.

**Operation ...** For military operations, *see under* the second part of the name, for example, BARBAROSSA; DESERT STORM; ENDURING FREEDOM; IRAQI FREEDOM; OVERLORD. *See also* SECOND WORLD WAR OPERATIONAL CODE NAMES.

**OPP.** In rappers' slang, another person's steady sexual partner. The abbreviation (the subtext of which is 'no trespassing') stands for 'other people's property' or, in the unexpurgated version, 'other people's pussy *or* penis'. It was popularized, or perhaps even originated, by the US rap group Naughty by Nature in 1991.

**Opportunity Knocks.** A long-running television talent show screened by ITV from 1956 to 1978, when it was hosted by a genial Hughie Greene, and by the BBC from 1987 to 1990, when the host was Bob Monkhouse. A popular feature of the first series was Greene's 'clapometer', which registered the volume of applause from the audience. The show launched

the careers of many celebrities, among them the comedians Freddie Starr and Little and Large and the singers Mary Hopkin and Bonnie Langford. 'Opportunity knocks' itself is a catchphrase of US origin dating from the 1940s. It was earlier common in the fuller form 'Opportunity knocks but once.'

**Opposite number.** A person's equivalent in an organization or system, their 'number' being the same in the hierarchy. The expression dates from the early 20th century and later gave 'oppo' as a colloquialism for a best friend or 'mate'.

**Opus Dei.** (Latin, 'God's work'.) An international Roman Catholic organization of lay people and priests founded in Spain in 1928 by Monsignor Josemaría Escrivá de Balaguer (1902–75) with the aim of spreading Christian principles. The activity of the organization is shaped by Escrivá's work *The Way* (1935), a series of 999 spiritual maxims. Opus Dei members have at times been controversial in the Catholic Church, among other things for their advocacy of the mortification of the flesh (*see* CILICE). The organization is unfavourably portrayed in Dan Brown's bestselling novel *The* DA VINCI CODE (2003). Escrivá himself was canonized by Pope John Paul II in 2002.

**Oradour-sur-Glane.** A village in south-central France, northwest of Limoges, destroyed by the Germans on 10 June 1944, exactly two years after a similar fate had befallen the Czechoslovakian village of LIDICE. All 652 inhabitants were routed from their homes and into the village square. The men were then herded into barns, and the women and children into the church. German troops barred the doors and set fire to the whole village. The death toll was 642, with 10 somehow managing to survive the fire and feign death until the ss had departed. After the war the gutted church and its cemetery were left as a memorial and a new village was built nearby.

**Oral Office.** The OVAL OFFICE in the White House, as renamed by wags in the wake of the MONICA Lewinsky affair. The quip was suggested by the acts of fellatio performed on President Clinton by the love-struck intern. *See also* COMEBACK KID; SLICK WILLIE.

**Orange Revolution.** *See* REVOLUTION NAMES.

***Oranges Are Not the Only Fruit.*** A semi-autobiographical first novel (1985) by Jeanette Winterson (b.1959) about the childhood and growing up of a fictional Jeanette against the background of the religious fanaticism of her Pentecostal mother. The oranges of the title represent her mother's attitude to life, in which 'everything in the natural world was a symbol of the Great Struggle between good and evil'.

The crunch comes when Jeanette abandons the forces of good, which she was destined to promote as a missionary, in favour of those of evil, having been discovered *in flagrante delicto* in bed with another girl. In a memorable televised version (1990), adapted by Winterson from her own novel, the central character, Jess, was played as a teenager by Charlotte Coleman.

**Orcs.** The name used to refer to goblins in J.R.R. Tolkien's epic *The* LORD OF THE RINGS (1954–5), in which they are employed as soldiers by SAURON. They are first encountered as 'goblins' beneath the Misty Mountains by Bilbo BAGGINS in *The* HOBBIT (1937), but in Tolkien's later works they are referred to as Orcs. Brutal, dirty and grotesquely ugly, with long arms, bow legs and long fangs, the Orcs present a stark contrast to the home-loving and gentle hobbits.

**Order of Lenin.** The highest award in the former Soviet Union, named after V.I. LENIN, the leader of the 1917 OCTOBER REVOLUTION. It was established in 1930 and awarded to individuals or institutions that had made outstanding contributions to science and technology, medicine, the arts or economics, or to the service of the state. It was also awarded to foreigners for the promotion of good relations with the USSR. Notable recipients included Yuri Gagarin, the first man in space (*see* VOSTOK), and Marshal Zhukhov, the victorious RED ARMY commander in the Second World War.

**Order of Merit.** An order for distinguished achievement in all callings founded by Edward VII in 1902, with two classes, civil and military. It is limited to 24 men and women and confers no precedence. The badge is a red and blue cross with a blue medallion in the centre surrounded by a laurel wreath, and it bears the words 'For Merit'. The ribbon is blue and crimson. Crossed swords are added to the badge for military members. *See also* COMPANION OF HONOUR.

**Order of the boot.** A rejection or dismissal. 'I was given the order of the boot' could thus mean that I was rejected by a lover or sacked from a job. To reject or dismiss someone is to boot them out. The phrase puns on genuine orders of honour, such as Order of the Bath, Order of the Garter.

**Order of the British Empire.** The Order of the British Empire was instituted by George V on 4 June 1917, in the darkest days of the First World War, as a way of rewarding British and Allied subjects who had rendered conspicuous service at home, in India, and in the Dominions and Colonies other than that rendered by the Navy or Army. It was divided into civil and military divisions in 1918 and was subsequently used to reward service in every field. For the first time it enabled a large number of women to be admitted to honours, but in some years was so generously granted that to remain undecorated seemed almost a greater distinction. There are also those who feel that the name is increasingly anachronistic, the British Empire having effectively ceased to exist in the aftermath of the Second World War, when the process of decolonization began. In 2003 the black British poet Benjamin Zephaniah publicly announced that he had rejected an offer of an OBE, saying that the name of the honour 'reminds me of how my foremothers were raped and my forefathers brutalized'. The cynical claim that the letters OBE stand for 'other buggers' efforts'. *See also* MEMBER OF THE ORDER OF THE BRITISH EMPIRE.

**Order of the Frozen Flesh.** The nickname given by embittered German soldiers to the German winter-campaign medal in Russia, 1941–2.

**Oreo.** An AFRICAN AMERICAN despised by other African Americans for seeking to integrate with whites. The nickname comes from the commercially marketed Oreo biscuit, which consists of two chocolate wafers containing a white sugar cream filling. An 'Oreo' is thus 'brown outside but white inside' (Alan Dundes, *Mother Wit from the Laughing Barrel*, 1973).

**Organization man.** A species of employee, a sort of corporate equivalent of the political APPARATCHIK. The term was coined by the US writer William H. Whyte in his book *The Organization Man* (1956):

> This book is about the organization man … I can think of no other way to describe the people I am talking about. They are not the workers, nor are they the white-collar people in the usual, clerk sense of the word. These people only work for the Organization. The ones I am talking about *belong* to it as well.

*Orlando.* A novel (1928), subtitled 'A Biography', by Virginia Woolf (1882–1941). It is a literary fantasy whose central character 'was a man till the age of thirty; when he became a woman and has remained so ever since'. The book is dedicated to Vita Sackville-West (1892–1962), who has been identified as the original of Orlando. A visually striking film version (1992) was directed by Sally Potter.

**Orphism.** A movement in painting started by Robert Delaunay (1885–1941) as a development from CUBISM and characterized by patches and swirls of intense and contrasting colours. The name, given by the poet Guillaume Apollinaire in 1912, alludes to the poetry of the mythological Greek poet Orpheus. Artists associated with the movement apart from Delaunay include Marcel Duchamp (1887–1968),

František Kupka (1871–1957), Fernand Léger (1881–1955) and Francis Picabia (1879–1953). *See also* CUBISM; DADAISM; FAUVISM; FUTURISM; RURALISM; SURREALISM; SYNCHROMISM; VORTICISM.

**Orpington man.** A term that enjoyed a currency in the 1960s following the victory of the Liberal candidate in the Orpington by-election of 1962. Orpington, in Kent, is an outer London suburb, and 'Orpington man' was the typical home-county commuter who abandoned the habits of a lifetime to vote Liberal rather than Conservative. *See also* ESSEX MAN; ISLINGTON MAN; SELSDON MAN; WORCESTER WOMAN.

**Or three.** A semi-humorous substitution for 'or two', in such contexts as 'a glass or two', to denote an even greater quantity.

> Whenever football is discussed in pubs or clubs over a beer or three, the question is nearly always raised as to how the standard of football has improved (or otherwise) over the years.
>
> PETER OSGOOD: foreword to Micheal Heatley and Ian Welch, *History of Football* (1997)

**Orwell, George.** The pen-name adopted by Eric Arthur Blair (1903–50), Old Etonian and socialist, author of The ROAD TO WIGAN PIER (1937), ANIMAL FARM (1945) and *Nineteen Eighty-Four* (1949) (*see* 1984), among other works. His derived his pen-name from St George, patron saint of England, and the River Orwell in Suffolk, on whose banks he had once lived. *See also* BIG BROTHER; DOUBLETHINK; DOWN AND OUT IN PARIS AND LONDON; FIRST LINES OF NOVELS; NEWSPEAK.

**Oscar.** A gold-plated figurine awarded annually by the American Academy of Motion Picture Arts and Sciences for the best film acting, writing, production and so on of the year. There are two claims for the origin of this name. One is that in 1931 the future executive secretary of the Academy, Mrs Margaret Herrick, joined as librarian and, on seeing the then nameless gold statue for the first time, exclaimed: 'It reminds me of my Uncle Oscar.' The other is that it derives indirectly from Oscar Wilde (1854–1900). When on a lecture tour of the United States he was asked if he had won the Newdigate Prize for Poetry, and he replied: 'Yes, but while many people have won the Newdigate, it is seldom that the Newdigate gets an Oscar.' When Helen Hayes was presented with the award, her husband Charles MacArthur, a noted wit and playwright, said: 'Ah, I see you've got an Oscar,' and the name stuck.

There is a story about the Academy-Award-winning German actor Emil Jannings, who, after a bried career in Hollywood, returned to Germany. As the Nazi regime collapsed in 1945 Jannings approached suspicious US soldiers holding the statuette above his head and shouting, 'Don't shoot! I have Oscar!'

*See also* BAFTA AWARD; EMMY.

**Oscar and Lucinda.** A period novel (1988), with elements of MAGIC REALISM, by Peter Carey (b.1943), which won the BOOKER PRIZE for fiction. Oscar sees in gambling a way of providing the essentials of education and family background, having rejected those provided by his father, a figure based on the father in FATHER AND SON (1907) by Edmund Gosse (1849–1928). Oscar's compulsion is shared by Lucinda, whose ambition is to run a successful glassworks in Sydney. The result is a mad wager to transport a glass church into the Australian bush, which ends in violence. A film version (1997), directed by Gillian Armstrong, did not quite capture the spirit of the original. *See also* FIRST LINES OF NOVELS.

**Ossi.** A nickname in Germany for a citizen of the former German Democratic Republic, as an abbreviation of *Ostdeutsch*, 'East German'. East and West Germany were unified in 1990.

**Ostpolitik.** (German, 'east politics'.) The foreign policy of DÉTENTE among Western countries in the 1960s with regard to the former Soviet Union and communist bloc. It was implemented by Willy Brandt, socialist chancellor of West Germany, in 1970, when his government signed a 'renunciation of force' treaty with the USSR. *See also* ODER–NEISSE LINE.

**Other Club.** A dining club founded in 1911 by Sir Winston Churchill and F.E. Smith (Lord Birkenhead) and said to be so called because they were not wanted at an existing fraternity known as The Club. It still meets at the Savoy, and membership is not confined to Tories or politicians.

**Other guy, The.** One's opponent or rival. The expression belittles him by not naming him and by trivializing his status as simply 'guy'.

> Autobiography offers the chance to draw across the past a warm duvet, or knee the other guy in the stomach.
> *The Times* (12 October 1999)

**Other Place, The.** A studio theatre in Stratford-upon-Avon, opened in 1974 and owned by the Royal Shakespeare Company. It showcases modern and experimental works, as well as revivals of rarely performed plays, and has a name based on that of its forerunner, The Place, a small London theatre where the RSC staged plays for three seasons from 1971 to 1973.

**OTT.** *See* OVER THE TOP.

**Our Gang.** A group of American child film actors first appearing in the 1920s in short slapstick comedies produced by Hal Roach. Their personnel changed over the years but the originals included 'Fat' Joe Cobb, Jackie Condon, Mickey Daniels, Mary Kornman and Ernie 'Sunshine Sammy' Morrison. In the 1930s the gang was led by Spanky McFarland. Production continued until 1944, after which many of the shorts appeared on television and were released on video, with the gang renamed in the latter medium as The Little Rascals.

**Our Gracie.** An affectionate nickname for the popular singer Gracie Fields (1898–1979; *see also* ASPIDISTRA). 'Our' is a typical north of England possessive for a family member, as 'Our Jack', and it came to be applied to various personalities, especially in show business or sport, or as a bantering term in the media. Others are 'Our Marie' for the music-hall entertainer Marie Lloyd (1870–1922), 'Our 'Enery' as a nickname for the boxer Henry Cooper (b.1934), and 'Our Shirl' as a *Private Eye* name for the Labour (now Liberal Democrat) politician Shirley Williams (b.1930).

**Our Island Story.** An enormously popular children's history book (1905), subtitled 'A Child's History of England', by H(enrietta) E(lizabeth) Marshall, who retold stories from English history (including some, such as that of King Arthur, that properly belong in the domain of legend) to two Australian children. The title reflects without embarrassment the untroubled Anglocentric mindset of the period, for the book deals almost exclusively with tales from English history.

> Not once or twice in our rough island-story,
> The path of duty was the way to glory.
> ALFRED, LORD TENNYSON: *Ode on the Death of the Duke of Wellington* (1852)

A hundred years on, the book was republished in 2005 by Civitas, to popular acclaim and a generally positive response from newspaper reviewers, some of them reliving their childhoods.

**Our Lady of the Flowers.** A novel (1943) by Jean Genet (1910–86), written with a pencil on brown paper while the author was in prison for theft. It portrays the underworld of Montmartre, inhabited by 'the girl-queens and boy-queens, the aunties, fags and nellies', among them 'Our Lady of the Flowers'. The 'dark and lovely flowers' are murders and treasons and executions that Genet hears about in his prison cell, from scraps of newspaper or prisoners' gossip; there is presumably an allusion to Baudelaire's *Fleurs du mal*

('Flowers of Evil'). 'Our Lady of the Flowers' is a creature called Divine, 'Lady of High Pansiness', 'Divine the Gaytime Girl', who 'died holy and murdered – by consumption' – and who was once a village youngster named Louis Culafroy.

**Our Val.** *See* PRINCESS PUSHY.

**Outing.** In its modern sense, the word denotes the act of making it publicly known that a particular well-known person is homosexual, i.e. when they have not themselves chosen to 'come out'. The verb for this action is thus 'to out'. There was a small spate of political outings in the late 1990s, many of them inspired by the militant British organization OutRage!, founded by the gay-rights activist Peter Tatchell and others in 1990.

> Chris Smith, Labour's national heritage spokesman, who is homosexual, said: 'I don't believe that outing is either just or sensible. More is gained by gay people coming out voluntarily.'
>
> *Sunday Times* (4 December 1994)

*See also* COME OUT OF THE CLOSET.

**Out like a light.** Instantly asleep or unconscious, as if a light had been extinguished or turned off. Switching off the bedside light is usually the last conscious act of the day before falling asleep. The metaphor dates from the 1930s.

**Out of Africa.** An autobiographical memoir (1937) by Karen Blixen (1885–1962), who also wrote novels in her native language, Danish, as Isak Dinesen. Rejected by a cousin with whom she had fallen in love, in 1914 she married instead his twin brother, Baron Bror Blixen-Finecke. They settled on a farm near Nairobi in Kenya, but after a year she returned to Denmark for treatment for syphilis, which she had contracted from him. They were divorced in 1921. *Out of Africa* is the story of her struggle to keep the farm going and of her love for Denys Finch-Hatton, a safari conductor, who died when his plane crashed in 1931, just after she had been forced to sell up. She subsequently left Africa for good. The title is based on a line from Pliny's *Historia Naturalis* (1st century AD): *Semper aliquid novi Africam adferre* ('Africa always brings [us] something new'), often quoted as *Ex Africa semper aliquid novi* ('Always something new out of Africa'). Blixen's own Afrikaans title for her book was *Den afrikanske farm* ('The African Farm').

A critically acclaimed film version (1985), starring Meryl Streep as Blixen and Robert Redford as Finch-Hatton, was directed by Sydney Pollack.

**Out of here.** Since the 1970s expressions such as 'I'm out of here!' (or more informally, 'outta here') have been used to signal the intention of making an (often hasty) departure.

> If he keeps the faster bowlers on, the umpires will say 'Listen, Inzi, if you do that, we're out of here!'
>
> JONATHAN AGNEW: *Test Match Special* (BBC Radio 4)
> (15 November 2005)

**Out of one's skull.** Extremely bored; intoxicated by drink or drugs; crazy. The expression dates from the 1960s.

> Since my teens I have wondered why people use alcohol or drugs to get out of their skulls. ... For the trip of a lifetime, get 'right' outside your skull. ... The best-known OOBE [out-of-body experience] is the near-death experience.
>
> URI GELLER: in *The Times* (6 October 1999)

**Out of one's tiny mind.** Mentally unbalanced; completely crazy. The phrase evolved in the 1960s as an elaboration of 'out of one's mind'. The implication is that one's mind was inadequate or deficient to begin with.

**Out of order.** Apart from its everyday senses of not working or not according to the rules this phrase has a colloquial meaning 'unacceptable', 'in bad taste'. The new sense evolved in the 1980s.

> 'I think you're well out of order,' he said. Apparently he had been waiting for seven years to see Grace [Jones] again, and was peeved about the extra four hours standing around.
>
> *The Independent* (30 March 1990)

**Out of the bag.** In colloquial Australian English, something that is 'out of the bag' is unexpected or startling.

**Out of the box.** In 21st-century management-speak, to 'think out of the box' is to think originally or creatively, unfettered by conventional assumptions or models. *See also* BLUE-SKY THINKING; PUSH THE ENVELOPE.

> The NBC Entertainment Idea Box is a website we developed in an effort to give you a platform to express your out-of-the-box ideas and creativity.
>
> www.defamer.com (3 October 2005)

A rather earlier application of 'out of the box', in colloquial Australian English, was to something exceptionally good. First recorded in the 1920s, it may have been inspired by the American usage in which someone or something smart is said to have 'come out of a bandbox'.

**Out of this world.** Fantastic; amazing; wonderful. The implication is of something too good for this world. The phrase dates from the 1920s.

**Out on one's ear.** Ejected unceremoniously; summarily dismissed. The image is of being thrown out head first. The expression dates from the 1920s.

**Outside job.** A crime committed by someone not associated with the place where it occurred. The opposite, which is generally more effective, is an INSIDE JOB.

**Outsider.** A person who is not a member of a particular circle or group, or one who is not considered a socially desirable companion; also a horse or person not thought to be in the running. The usage comes from coaching days when the humbler passengers travelled outside (other than on the box next to the coachman). In more recent times the word has been specifically applied to a person who in some way is alienated from society, and *The Outsider* in this sense is the title of a novel (1953) by the African American writer Richard Wright, of a study (1956) by Colin Wilson of the alienation of a man of genius, and as the English rendering (1946) of the title of Albert Camus' novel *L'Étranger* (1942), about a rebel or misfit who is out of tune with the times.

**Out to lunch.** Crazy; eccentric; absent-minded. The implication is that one is temporarily 'out of one's mind' in the same way that a person who is out to lunch is temporarily absent from work. The phrase arose as US campus slang in the 1950s.

**Oval Office.** The official office of the president of the United States, in the White House, so named for its shape. It was added to the West Wing of the building in 1909, during the presidency of Theodore Roosevelt, and is the place where key meetings are held, interviews are granted and important policy decisions are made. *See also* ORAL OFFICE.

> With the convention still in progress, an aide to the President's media man, Gerald Rafshoon, plastered a hotel-room wall with ideas for negative T.V. spots – 'Empty Oval Office', 'Places He Would Attack' and 'He Is Not Active, He Means It'.
>
> *Newsweek* (25 August 1980)

**Ovaltine.** The food drink so named was launched by Dr George Wander in Bern, Switzerland, in the 19th century and was originally called 'Ovomaltine', alluding to two of its main ingredients, eggs (Latin *ovum*, 'egg') and malt. The name was then shortened as now and was registered in Britain in 1906. The drink itself became the archetypal soothing nightcap and its popularity was enhanced by *The Ovaltineys*, a children's radio show sponsored by the manufacturers and first broadcast on RADIO LUXEMBOURG in 1935. It was complemented by a club, the League of Ovaltineys, which had its own secret codes and Seven Rules. By 1939 some 5 million children had joined and Ovaltiney comics were included free with *Chuckler* and *Dazzler*. Today, Ovaltine tends to be more associated with the elderly (*see* POLITICS OF OVALTINE AND BRANDY).

> He gives his Ovaltine a stir
> And nibbles at a 'petit beurre'.
> JOHN BETJEMAN: *Mount Zion*, 'The Wykehamist' (1932)

**Over a barrel.** In a helpless position; at someone's mercy. The allusion is said to be to the practice of draping over a barrel someone who has been rescued from the water when close to drowning, so encouraging the ejection of water from the lungs. A more likely reference may be to a form of punishment in which the victim is bent over a barrel and beaten. The expression is of US origin and dates from the 1930s.

**Over easy.** Of a fried egg, turned over carefully without breaking the yolk, as distinct from 'sunny side up', with the yolk left uppermost. An Americanism. *See also* DINERESE.

**Overlord.** The code name given to the Allied operation for the invasion of German-occupied Normandy, which began on D-DAY 1944. It was so named as it was regarded as the overriding operation of the day. *See also* SECOND WORLD WAR OPERATIONAL CODE NAMES.

**Over my dead body.** Not if I can help it. The implication is that you cannot do what you propose as long as I am alive to prevent it.

**Overpaid, overfed, oversexed and over here.** A humorous description of US troops in Britain in the Second World War. The words are attributed to the comedian Tommy Trinder (1909–89) but are probably not original. The phrase lends itself to variants applicable to other American visitors to the UK.

> The San Francisco Ballet: overdue, overtalented and over here.
> *Sunday Times* (31 October 1999)

**Over the fence.** In general colloquial English, someone who has escaped from prison or a prison-camp is said to have gone 'over the fence'. In Australian slang, the phrase has a more abstractly metaphorical use (first recorded in 1918): 'beyond the bounds of acceptable behaviour'.

> Some publications which unduly emphasize sex were 'entirely over the fence', the Chief Secretary, Mr C.A. Kelly, said yesterday.
> *Sydney Morning Herald* (18 September 1964)

**Over the hill.** Escaped from custody; middle-aged. In the former sense the escapee has vanished over the hill. In the latter the person has passed life's high point and is beginning to go downhill. *See also* LIFE BEGINS AT 40.

**Over the moon.** Very happy. An expression that came to be a standard expression of delight and satisfaction among sports players after a win or a promotion. It comes from the phrase 'to jump over the moon', in turn from the familiar nursery rhyme about the cow that jumped over the moon, dating from at least the 18th century. *See also* SICK AS A PARROT.

> A hospital spokeswoman yesterday said Martin was in a 'stable but serious condition'. Mrs Hunisett said: 'I am over the moon. I never thought I would see my son alive again.'
> *The Independent* (21 June 1995)

**Over the top.** Excessive; gross. The expression is often shortened to OTT. The allusion is probably to troops going 'over the top' of the trenches in the First World War. *OTT* was the title of an 'adult' version of TISWAS, shown on ITV in 1982 and comprising comic sketches. The show was created by Chris Tarrant.

**OVRA.** The acronym for Opera di vigilanza e repressione antifascista (Italian, 'organization of vigilance and repression of antifascism'). OVRA was the secret police of Fascist Italy, set up in 1927 and modelled on Lenin's Cheka (*see* KGB) in the USSR, which had shown how effective state terror could be in suppressing dissent.

**Owl Service, The.** A fantasy (1967) for young adults by Alan Garner (b.1934), in which dialogue predominates. The moving force behind this story of passions and possession, with a violent climax, is a tale from the medieval Welsh storehouse of folklore, *The Mabinogion*. It is reflected in modern times by a set of dinner plates bearing a floral pattern that resembles the form of owls.

**Own goal.** An act that unintentionally harms one's own interests or puts one at a disadvantage. The term is from football, in which a goal scored when a player inadvertently strikes or deflects the ball into his own team's goal is awarded to the other side. In practice own goals are attributed only if a genuine error has been made and not, for instance, if a player merely makes contact with a shot towards the goal. A diverting collection of blunders, gaffes and 'goofs' of the metaphorical type of own goal is to be found in Graham Jones' *Own Goals* (1985).

**Oxfam.** The Oxford Committee for Famine Relief was founded in Oxford in 1942 to raise funds for the feeding of hungry children in Greece. After the Second World War it concentrated on providing aid to refugees, but in the 1960s it broadened its scope to help to improve agriculture and food production in THIRD WORLD countries. More generally it provides emergency aid for areas stricken by natural disasters such as droughts, floods and earthquakes.

**Oxford accent.** A term in use from the early 20th century to denote a supposedly educated English accent, although the phrase has long also implied the affected tones of Oxford undergraduates. The accent now regarded as that of standard southern English is usually known as Received Pronunciation.

**Oxford bags.** Wide baggy trousers, as typically worn by Oxford undergraduates in the years between the two world wars.

**Oxford comma.** A comma before the 'and' in a listing, as 'bread, butter, cakes, and jam', so called in the house style of Oxford University Press. It is also the standard North American style. It is uncommon among the British, who would normally write 'bread, butter, cakes and jam' unless any ambiguity would result from excluding a comma.

**Oxford English.** English spoken with an OXFORD ACCENT.

**Oxford Group.** The name until about 1938 of the MORAL REARMAMENT movement, so called because it was first popularized in Oxford in the 1920s.

**Oxfordianism.** The literary conceit that the works of William Shakespeare were in fact written by Edward de Vere, 17th Earl of Oxford (1550–1604). The theory was propounded in 1920 by J. Thomas Looney, a schoolmaster, on the basis of four main tenets: (1) that the few facts known about Shakespeare's life give little indication of poetic or literary activity (despite the fact that to Ben Jonson he was the 'Sweet Swan of Avon'); (2) that the many details of Oxford's life show him to have been a poet, a playwright and a patron of writers and actors; (3) that the works themselves are full of references to exclusively aristocratic pastimes and sports, with 36 of the 37 plays set in courtly or wealthy society; (4) that the noble sentiments expressed in the works could only have proceeded from a nobleman's heart. The popularity of Oxfordianism lay in its romantic and nostalgic appeal to a war-disoriented generation who longed for a return to the class-based hedonism of the EDWARDIAN ERA.

**Oxford marmalade.** A type of dark, thick-cut marmalade originally made in the 1870s at 84 High Street, Oxford. The name, registered as a trademark in 1908 and 1931 by the manufacturers, Frank Cooper, is redolent of the archetypal genteel English breakfast.

**Oxygen of publicity, the.** What Margaret Thatcher (the IRON LADY) intended to starve the IRA of:

> We must try to find ways to starve the terrorist and the hijacker of the oxygen of publicity on which they depend.
> Speech to the American Bar Association in London (15 July 1985)

To this end, in 1988 Thatcher's home secretary, Douglas Hurd, introduced a ban on the broadcast media transmitting the actual voices of members of the IRA's political wing, Sinn Féin. The result was that when film of the Sinn Féin leader Gerry Adams, for example, was broadcast, his words were spoken by an actor on voice-over. The ban was lifted in 1994.

**Oz.** (1) A colloquialism for Australia, as a phonetic rendering of 'Aus', an abbreviation frequently used for that country. *See also* LIZARD OF OZ; STRINE.

(2) The name of the magical country inhabited by *The* WIZARD OF OZ, with the Emerald City as its capital and the seat of its ruler, Princess Ozma. The Land of Oz is surrounded by four small countries: MUNCHKIN Country, Winkie Country, Quadling Country and Gillikin Country. These in turn are flanked by four deserts: Shifting Sands, the Great Sandy Waste, the Deadly Desert and the Impassable Desert. To the north lies the Kingdom of Ix, to the northeast Merryland, to the southwest the Land of the Mangaboos, and to the northwest Nomeland. These last two are underground.

(3) *Oz* was also the title of a HIPPIE-style 'underground' magazine of the late 1960s, so named as it was founded by an Australian, Richard Neville. It gained notoriety through a court case in 1971, when it was charged with 'conspiracy to corrupt the morals of liege subjects of Her Majesty the Queen by raising in their minds inordinate and lustful desires'. The offending issue had not, in fact, been edited by Neville and his two co-editors but by schoolchildren, and this so-called 'schoolkids' issue' caused particular offence by dealing with the sex life of RUPERT BEAR. The editors were convicted and given prison sentences, but these were quashed on appeal. *See also* RUMPOLE OF THE BAILEY.

**Ozone Man.** A nickname given during the 1992 presidential election by sitting president and Republican presidential candidate George Bush to Al Gore (b.1948), the Democratic vice-presidential candidate, on account of the latter's airing of environmental concerns. Gore and his presidential running mate Bill Clinton, the COMEBACK KID, went on to win the election.

# P

**Pacific Rim.** A name for the nations of Asia that border on the Pacific Ocean, including the island nations actually located in the ocean and, in the fullest sense of the term, the shorelines of Central and South America. The name dates from the 1960s, when the nations in question began to form an increasingly important and interconnected economic region.

**Pacific 231.** The 'symphonic movement' by Arthur Honegger (1892–1955) evokes the 'visual impression and physical enjoyment' produced by a steam locomotive (*Pacific 231* being the name of a US engine). The piece dates from 1923. Honegger seems to have felt a particular affinity with locomotives. In his book *I am a Composer* (1951) he wrote:

> I am like a steam engine: I need to be stoked up, it takes me a long time to get ready for genuine work.

**Package deal.** A settlement including a number of conditions that must be accepted in its entirety by the parties concerned. The allusion is to a parcel or package containing in one wrapping a number of different items. Similarly, a package tour or holiday includes provision for meals, entertainment, gratuities, lodging and the like for a single payment. These and similar terms date from the 1950s and are of US origin.

**Pack a punch.** To deliver a skilful or forceful blow; to have a powerful effect. The expression is of US origin and dates from the 1920s.

**Packet of Woodbines.** The nickname given to the Russian cruiser *Askold* from its five long thin funnels, Woodbine cigarettes being thin and sold in packets of five. The ship was taken from the BOLSHEVIKS after the OCTOBER REVOLUTION of 1917 and used by the Royal Navy against the revolutionaries in the White Sea. *See also* WOODBINE WILLIE.

**Pack it in.** To stop doing something. The expression, dating from the 1920s, is usually heard as a command, as: 'Stop that! Pack it in, will you?' The notion is of 'putting away' one's action.

**Pack up your troubles in your old kit-bag.** The opening line of one of the most memorable choruses of the First World War. It was written by George Asaf, whose real name was George Powell, and composed by his brother, Felix Powell, in 1915. Ironically, Felix committed suicide in 1942, despairing at the world's apparent commitment to fight a war to end all wars.

> Pack up your troubles in your old kit-bag,
> And smile, smile, smile.
> While you've a lucifer to light your fag,
> Smile, boys, that's the style.
> What's the use of worrying?
> It never was worth while,
> So, pack up your troubles in your old kit-bag,
> And smile, smile, smile.

**Pac-Man.** A video game popular in the early 1980s, in which Pac-Man is a voracious 'munching menace', devouring enemies who attack him. He was based on a Japanese folk hero and his name apparently relates to the way he 'packed away' his opponents. In US business parlance a 'Pac-Man defence' is a tactic in which a company threatened by a hostile takeover bid launches its own takeover bid for the company that threatens it. The allusion is obvious if one is familiar with the game.

**Pact of Steel.** *See* AXIS.

**Paddington Bear.** The small, ursine hero of numerous children's books by Michael Bond (b.1926). He wears a sou'wester, wellington boots and a duffle coat and is so called because he was found by the Brown family at Paddington Station, London, with a label saying 'Please look after this bear'. He first appeared in *A Bear Called Paddington* (1958). The name is apt for an animal that 'pads'. In 1999 the original story was published in a Latin version by Michael Needham under the title *Ursus Nomine Paddington*, following the example of Dr Alexander Lennard's more ambitious rendering of the first WINNIE-THE-POOH book as *Winnie Ille Pu* (1961).

**Paddy Clarke Ha Ha Ha.** A novel (1993) by Roddy Doyle (b.1958), which won the BOOKER PRIZE for fiction. It records the day-to-day life in a Dublin suburb of a ten-year-old boy, with his reactions to the break-up of his parents' marriage, reflected in the chant of boys at his school:

Paddy Clarke
Has no da.
Ha ha ha!

**Paddy Pantsdown.** A nickname given in 1992 by a *Sun* headline writer to Paddy Ashdown (b.1941), leader of the Liberal Democrats (1988–99), after Ashdown revealed a long-dead affair with a former secretary. The revelation resulted in a significant boost in the Liberal Democrats' poll rating.

**Padre Pio.** The nickname given to a style of punishment inflicted by the IRA in Northern Ireland in the 2000s, involving the victim being shot through the hands. Padre Pio was an Italian priest who carried signs of the stigmata from 1918 until shortly before his death in 1968. *See also* KNEECAPPING.

**Pageboy.** A woman's hairstyle consisting of a shoulder-length bob curling slightly under at the ends and with a fringe at the front. The style was adopted from historical depictions of court pages.

**Page Three girl.** A euphemistic term for a nude female model, so called from the daily photo of a topless young woman that first appeared on page 3 of *The Sun* newspaper on 17 November 1970. The feature was so popular that other tabloids copied it. The publishers of *The Sun* have now registered the term as a trademark.

**Page-turner.** A gripping novel such as a thriller that encourages the reader to turn its pages. The expression dates from the 1970s.

**Pain in the neck.** A difficult or annoying person. The expression, dating from the 1930s, is probably a euphemism for 'pain in the arse' (or 'ass'). Anyone or anything annoying or tiresome can similarly be called simply 'a pain', and the word is typically applied to an unwelcome task or bore, as: 'It's a pain having to wash the floor each time'.

**Paintball.** A war game of US origin that first became popular in the 1980s. Participants use weapons that fire capsules of brightly coloured paint which burst on impact, and a player marked in this way is immediately eliminated from the game.

The game has become particularly associated with the team-building exercises beloved of contemporary management theorists, in which corporate executives spend time together outside the workplace engaged in outdoor activities intended to foster cooperation and a sense of collective identity.

**Paint oneself into a corner.** To end up in a situation from which it is difficult to escape or in which one has little room to manoeuvre. If one paints a floor to finish in a corner, one will find it hard to extricate oneself.

Why are we still dropping bombs on power stations and bridges? As punishment for the atrocities or because Nato has painted itself into a corner from which it can only bomb?
*The Observer* (30 May 1999)

**Paint the Forth Bridge.** To carry out an apparently endless task that has to be started again as soon as it is finished. The reference is to the railway bridge over the Firth of Forth in southeast Scotland, built in 1890 and legendary for its continuous painting process, each session of which traditionally takes four years to complete. The introduction of a new type of paint in the early 21st century means that a new coat is only required every ten years, so rendering the saying obsolescent.

**Paisleyites.** Supporters of the Rev. Ian Paisley (b.1926), Northern Ireland Free Presbyterian minister and Unionist politician, since 1970 MP for North Antrim and co-founder in 1971 of the Democratic Unionist Party as a hardline rival to the ULSTER UNIONIST PARTY, which it replaced as the dominant Unionist party in Northern Ireland in 2003. He has long been a vociferous and outspoken defender of the Protestant Unionist position in Northern Ireland and his party has taken a more intransigent stance than the Ulster Unionists on sectarian issues and on relationships with the Republic of Ireland. Paisley's dire warnings of the supposedly imminent betrayal of Ulster's Protestants (by perfidious British politicians and Unionists of lesser mettle than he) are expressed in language of a distinctly biblical hue and have been a constant factor in Northern Irish politics since the start of the TROUBLES. He was particularly hostile to the Anglo-Irish Agreement of 1985 and the GOOD FRIDAY AGREEMENT of 1998. In Northern Ireland he is sometimes known as the 'Big Man', for his considerable physical presence and stentorian voice. He is also nicknamed PAPA

DOC, in reference to the former dictator of Haiti, François Duvalier (1907–71). Paisley's politician son, Ian Paisley Jnr, is known as Baby Doc, the nickname of Duvalier's son and successor, Jean-Claude (b.1951).

**Pakistan.** The name of this state formed in 1947 was coined in 1933 by a Cambridge Muslim student, Chaudhari Rahmat Ali, to represent the units that should be included when the time came: P for Punjab, A for the Afghan border states, K for Kashmir, S for Sind and 'stan' for Baluchistan. At the same time the name can be understood to mean 'land of the pure', from Iranian or Afghani *pāk*, 'pure', and Old Persian *stān*, 'land' (as in Afghanistan itself).

**Pak pai.** A term for a car illegally used as a taxi in Hong Kong. The words are Chinese for 'white licence', referring to the white registration plates bearing black numerals, like those on private cars. The nickname was taken up in English from the 1970s.

**Palais glide.** A type of ballroom dance that came into being in the 1930s. It was not exactly a dance in the accepted sense but something like the gallop popular at hunt balls. It was usually performed to the foxtrot. 'Palais' is short for French *palais de danse*, a grand-sounding designation adopted in English for any type of dance hall, however unpalatial.

**Pale Fire.** A novel (1962) by Vladimir Nabokov (1899–1977) in the form of a 999-line poem ('Pale Fire'), purporting to be by a recently murdered academic, John Shade, with foreword, notes, commentary and index by an exiled European who was his neighbour. The title of both the novel and the poem comes from Shakespeare's *Timon of Athens*:

> The moon's an arrant thief,
> And her pale fire she snatches from the sun.
> IV.iii

**Palestine Liberation Organization.** *See* PLO.

**Palm Court.** From the early years of the 20th century many fashionable hotels had a courtyard or tea room decorated with potted palms, where a string ensemble played to provide light background music for guests. Such players gave the name to the various palm court orchestras that evolved, one of them broadcasting regularly even in the years after the Second World War.

**Palmer, Laura.** *See* TWIN PEAKS.

**Palookaville.** An imaginary town or community of idiots or incompetents. The name arose in the 1990s from US slang 'palooka' as a term for a stupid person, or more precisely a slow and stupid boxer. It was itself coined in the 1920s by Jack Conway of *Variety* magazine, and popularized by Ham

Fisher's comic strip 'Joe Palooka', launched on 19 April 1930, and brought before a wider audience in the 1934 film *Palooka*. In the film *Joe Palooka, Champ* (1946), a boxing promoter grooms a young dope for the ring.

> So what happens? He gets the title shot outdoors in the ball park – and whadda I get? A one-way ticket to Palookaville.
> BUDD SCHULBERG: screenplay for *On the Waterfront* (1954)

The 1995 film *Palookaville* is a comedy drama about three incompetent small-time New Jersey crooks.

**Panda car.** A small police patrol car. Such cars, generally blue or black in colour, originally bore a broad white stripe, evoking the markings of the giant panda. The name dates from the 1960s and may have been suggested by the former panda pedestrian crossing, which was marked with black and white chevrons. The term, often shortened to 'panda', is now rarely used.

> It was felt that panda drivers should be warned that the vehicles were not meant to be pursuit cars.
> *Daily Telegraph* (19 May 1971)

**Panic attack.** A sudden spell of acute anxiety. The laconic phrase belies the unpleasantness of the experience and its real physical symptoms, which can include sweating, a feeling of choking, a pounding heart, and a terror of losing control or even one's reason. The cause of such attacks is unknown but they may be associated with particular phobias.

**Panic button.** A button to be pressed in the event of an emergency, as in an office or bank, a hospital ward or a private home, usually by means of a telephone-linked emergency response service. Figuratively to push, press or hit the panic button is to call for or take emergency action, often over-hastily and even unnecessarily. *See also* HOT BUTTON.

> It may all look uncomfortably like a rerun of Wall Street in the Thirties, but don't hit the panic button yet.
> *The Times* (27 September 1999)

**Panic stations.** A state of alarm or emergency. The colloquialism dates from the 1960s and puns on ACTION STATIONS.

> While getting our makeup done and costumes donned, we hear that the Art Department has been fired and it's PANIC STATIONS.
> RICHARD E. GRANT: *With Nails* (1996)

**Panorama.** The flagship current affairs programme of BBC Television, first screened in 1957 and presenting each week a documentary on a matter of topical concern. Its edition of

10 May 1982 notoriously presented opposing views on the FALKLANDS WAR from both Labour and Conservative politicians. *See also* DIMBLEDOM.

**Pansy.** A derogatory nickname for a male homosexual or effeminate man, dating from the 1920s. An association with the flower is uncertain, and it is possible that the word is a variant of the earlier 'nancy' (from the girl's name) in the same sense. *See also* NANCY BOY.

**Panzer divisions.** This term entered the English language in the Second World War as a part-translation of German *Panzerdivisionen*, referring in particular to Rommel's tanks and armoured troop-carriers in the North African desert. The first three panzer divisions were created in October 1935, and by the outbreak of the war in 1939 there were six. In the campaign against France there were ten panzer divisions incorporating all the German tanks in that campaign, 2474 out of the 3400 tanks that Germany possessed. Soon after, in 1941, 17 panzer divisions, grouped in four panzer armies, spearheaded the German invasion of the Soviet Union (*see* BARBAROSSA). 'Panzer' came to be regarded as a name of some kind to English speakers, perhaps meaning 'panther', but it is simply the German word for 'armour', deriving from Latin *pantex*, 'paunch', and in turn related to English 'paunch' itself.

**Papa Doc.** The nickname given to François Duvalier (1907–71), the brutal dictator of Haiti from 1957 until his death. He was succeeded by his son Jean-Claude Duvalier (b.1951), known as Baby Doc, who was overthrown in 1986. *See also* PAISLEYITES.

**Papa Dop.** A nickname, by analogy with the brutal Haitian dictator PAPA DOC, given to Georgios Papadopoulos (1919–96), leader of the GREEK COLONELS who seized power in 1967.

**Paparazzi.** The Italian term for press photographers who pester celebrities is not related to any form of the word 'paper'. The word, in the singular *paparazzo*, comes from the name of such a photographer in Federico Fellini's famous film *La Dolce Vita* (1960), a cynical evocation of modern Roman high life. It was supplied by Fellini's scenarist, Ennio Flaiano, who himself took the 'prestigious' name, as he called it, from *Sulle rive dello Ionio* (1957), Margherita Guidacci's translation of George Gissing's travel narrative *By the Ionian Sea* (1901). In this, Gissing devotes two paragraphs to the worthy proprietor of the Albergo Centrale, Catanzaro, where he spent a few days in 1897. He noted that the owner, Coriolano Paparazzo, had put up a notice on the door of each room expressing his regret that some of his clients chose to dine in other establishments.

**'Paperback Writer'.** A humorous song about ambition by The BEATLES, credited to John Lennon and Paul McCartney and released in Britain in June 1966. The 'paperback writer' of the title is a naively aspiring writer who wishes to tempt a publisher into accepting his novel ('Dear sir or madam, will you read my book/ It took me years to write, will you take a look?'). The allusion in the fourth line of the lyric ('It's based on a novel by a man named Lear') is to the nonsense writer Edward Lear (1812–88).

**Paper Moon.** A film (1973) directed by Peter Bogdanovich and starring Ryan and Tatum O'Neal as a clergyman and orphan who travel the Mid-West in the 1930s, perpetrating a series of con tricks. Tatum O'Neal won an Oscar for best supporting actress. The film was based on the novel *Addie Pray* (1971) by Joe David Brown, and its title was inspired by the 1933 song 'It's Only a Paper Moon' by Yip Harburg and Billy Rose:

> Say, it's only a paper moon,
> Sailing over a cardboard sea.

**Paper over the cracks.** To resort to a temporary expedient; to create a mere semblance of order or arrangement. The shorter form 'to paper over' subsequently evolved in the sense of disguising problems rather than solving them. The original expression translated a phrase by the German Chancellor, Otto von Bismarck, in a letter of 14 August 1865 at a time when he was attempting to unite Germany under Prussian leadership shortly before the Convention of Gastein, which provided for Schleswig to be administered by Prussia and Holstein by Austria: *Wir arbeiten eifrig an Erhaltung des Friedens und Verklebung der Risse im Bau* ('We are working keenly for the preservation of peace and the papering over of the cracks in the building').

**Paper tiger.** A person or thing that seems strong, forceful or powerful, but that is, in fact, feeble or ineffective; a balloon when pricked. The expression arose from a Chinese saying applied by Chairman Mao in the 1940s to the United States (in the original, *zhǐ lǎohǔ*).

> The atom bomb is a paper tiger which the United States reactionaries use to scare people. It looks terrible, but in fact it isn't ... All reactionaries are paper tigers.
>
> MAO ZEDONG: interview (1946) in *Selected Works*, IV (1961)

**Pap test.** A diagnostic test made on a cervical smear to detect cancer of the cervix or womb. The procedure was set out by the Greek-born US anatomist and oncologist George N. Papanicolaou (1883–1962) in a book written jointly with

Herbert F. Traut, *The Diagnosis of Uterine Cancer by the Vaginal Smear* (1943). The test has resulted in a marked decrease in the death rate from the disease.

**Parade's End.** A tetralogy of novels (1924–8) by Ford Madox Ford (1873–1939), comprising *Some Do Not* (1924), *No More Parades* (1925), *A Man Could Stand Up* (1926) and *The Last Post* (1928), telling the story of an English gentleman before, during and after the First World War. In 1950 they were published together in one volume as *Parade's End*, the title referring to the disillusion and social changes brought about by the war.

**Paradise.** An evocative word increasingly associated in the 20th century with an exotic foreign holiday, as 'A stunning island paradise' (Bermuda Tourism advertisement in *The Times*, 25 September 1999). The religious overtone of the word is significant, and is found equally in the converse, a ruined holiday that is 'hell'. In his novel *Paradise News* (1991), set in Hawaii, David Lodge describes an anthropologist who is carrying out research for an academic study of the tourist industry. The thesis of his book is that 'tourism is the new world religion'. Sightseeing is a substitute religious ritual, souvenirs are relics and guidebooks are devotional aids. The holiday itself is thus both pilgrimage and paradise, with the beach holiday resort a place where the subject 'strives to get back to a state of nature, or prelapsarian innocence', otherwise the Garden of Eden. The simile is extended in the ultimate origin of the word in Persian *pairidaeza*, 'enclosed park', 'pleasure ground', a description equally appropriate for a 20th-century THEME PARK.

**Para Handy.** This modern Scottish folk hero, skipper of the 'puffer' or small cargo boat *The Vital Spark,* with real name Peter McFarlane, first appeared in the *Glasgow Evening News* on 16 January 1905 as the creation of the writer Neil Munro. He eventually progressed to a weekly column in which his anecdotal tales of seafaring life were a regular delight to his readers. Munro considered him lightweight fare compared to his main literary contributions, however, and when his columns were published in book form masked his identity as 'Hugh Foulis'. Para Handy's gentle drollery was seen as suitable fare for television and he duly made an appearance in that medium in 1959, with *Para Handy – Master Mariner* set in the very locations that Munro had used in his original stories and shot on a 'puffer' of a similar vintage to the one described. The hero was played by Duncan Macrae in this first series, and subsequently by Roddy McMillan in *The Vital Spark* (1965–74) and Gregor Fisher in *The Tales of Para Handy* (1994–5).

**Paralympics.** An international athletic competition for disabled athletes, modelled on the OLYMPIC GAMES. The name is short for Paraplegic Olympics, and the contest evolved from that originally held for paraplegic athletes at Stoke Mandeville hospital, Buckinghamshire, in the early 1950s. The element 'para-' in the name could also be appropriately interpreted as 'beside', referring to a person or thing distinct from, but analogous to, what is named. Thus the Paralympics are analogous to the Olympics in the same way that paramedics are analogous to qualified doctors. The latter, however, should not be confused with the paramedics who are parachuted in to give emergency aid. *See also* PARAMILITARY.

**Paramilitary.** A term in use from the 1970s to refer to an armed force that has a military structure but not a professional personnel and that in many cases operates outside the law. The word has become generally familiar as a result of the TROUBLES in Northern Ireland, and the IRA together with various armed Protestant groups may be properly described as paramilitary. *See also* ULSTER VOLUNTEER FORCE.

**Pardon me for breathing!** An ironic exclamation countering some minor or annoying criticism. The phrase dates from the 1940s.

**Pardon my French.** Excuse my swearing or FOUR-LETTER WORDS. Real French is unlikely to be involved. The French are unfairly associated with anything 'naughty' in the British mind. *Pardon My French!* (1998) is the title of a pocket French slang dictionary published by Harrap.

> 'If you really want to get married and have children and cook, well, you better get a move on, little sister … You should shit or get off the pot, pardon my French.'
> 'Beautiful French,' said Suzanne. 'Is that some Berlitz thing I'm not aware of?'
> CARRIE FISHER: *Postcards from the Edge* (1987)

**Parent Trap, The.** A film (1961) based on the novel *Das Doppelte Lottchen* by Erich Kästner (better known as the author of EMIL AND THE DETECTIVES (1928)) about identical twins who plot to reunite their divorced parents. Starring Hayley Mills in the dual starring role, the film was unnecessarily remade in 1998 with Lindsay Lohan as the twins.

**Par for the course.** As expected or predicted, given the circumstances, as: 'He's half an hour late but that's par for the course, knowing him.' The phrase dates from the 1940s and alludes to a golf player's expected score for a particular course.

Some midnight assignations, a bit of bonking and a good deal of philosophizing are obviously par for the course.

*Venue* (26 April 1985)

**Parfumée, La.** (French, 'the perfumed one'.) A nickname of Edith Cresson (b.1934), unpopular Socialist prime minister of France (1991–2). She subsequently became a European Union commissioner, and allegations of corruption against her and other commissioners led to the resignation of the entire commission in 1999.

**Parkinson's Law.** As satirically promulgated by C. Northcote Parkinson (1909–93) in his book with this title (1958), the proposition states that 'work expands so as to fill the time available for its completion'. The 'law' is mainly directed at public administration, but it is also aimed at inefficient business administration.

As Parkinson's Law observes, work expands to fill the time available for doing it. With twice as much time at its disposal, Congress created twice as much work, which meant twice as much governing.

*New York Times Magazine* (9 July 1978)

**Parkour.** A form of EXTREME SPORT that involves making one's way through an urban environment above ground level, by jumping off buildings, over walls, etc. It was developed in the suburbs of Paris by David Belle around 1990. The name is short for *parcours du combatant*, denoting the type of assault course used by the French military. In English it is sometimes alternatively known as 'free running' or 'obstacle-coursing'. Those who take part are called *traceurs* or, in English, 'free-runners'. They value the 'buzz' produced by fluid, uninhibited movement rather than the achievement of record times or numbers of jumps.

**Parkway.** As part of a railway station name, such as Didcot Parkway, this word denotes a mainline station with a large car park. The station itself is close to the named town or city, which is either within easy driving distance or easily reached by bus or taxi. It may also serve an important catchment area of some kind. The term was coined by British Railways and first applied to Bristol Parkway in 1972.

**Part of the furniture.** As familiar as a piece of furniture that one takes for granted in one's home. The expression dates from the early years of the 20th century.

Consider Yourself at home,
Consider Yourself one of the family …
Consider Yourself well in:
Consider Yourself part of the furniture.

LIONEL BART: *Oliver!*, 'Consider Yourself' (song) (1960)

**Partridge, Alan.** A comic character created by the Scottish satirist Armando Iannucci (b.1964) and played by the actor Steve Coogan (b.1965). Partridge is a rather sad and ultimately vacuous radio and TV presenter of a certain age, who attempts to ingratiate himself with those he regards as worth sucking up to, while behaving disgracefully to those who he thinks are not. Partridge has appeared in a number of spoof radio and TV programmes, such as *Knowing Me, Knowing You* (1992), a chat show with fictional guests, and *The Day Today* (1994), on which Partridge was the sports correspondent. By the time of the mock documentary, *I'm Alan Partridge* (1997), Partridge's career had gone seriously downhill, and he was struggling to keep his job on Radio Norwich, while still succeeding in giving offence.

**Party animal.** A regular partygoer; a frequenter of the social scene.

**Party girl.** A young woman who regularly attends parties, especially as a celebrity or star who is already a frequenter of the social scene and in the public eye. The expression dates from the early 1930s, the age of the BRIGHT YOUNG THINGS.

Serious party girls such as Elizabeth Hurley, Donatella Versace and Victoria Beckham can still be spotted nipping out in nothing but small scraps of very expensive cloth.

*Sunday Times* (2 January 2000)

**Party pooper.** A person whose behaviour or attitude spoils other people's enjoyment; a 'wet blanket'. An antidote to a party pooper might be a PARTY POPPER.

**Party popper.** An amusing device which throws forth a paper streamer with a strident wail, used at parties as a diversion and as a corrective to a PARTY POOPER.

**Party's over, The.** The good times have come to an end. The phrase was popularized by the 1956 song of the same title by Betty Comden and Adolph Green with the line: 'The party's over, it's time to call it a day.' The words were famously repeated by the Labour Environment Secretary Anthony Crosland when cutting back central government's support for housing rates in the 1970s.

**PASCAL.** *See* PROGRAMMING LANGUAGES.

**Pas devant les enfants.** (French, 'not in front of the children'.) A phrase used with reference to a remark or action that is regarded as inappropriate for children (or other present company) to hear. The warning is expressed in French so as not to be understood by the person(s) in question. It is often shortened to *pas devant*. In former days the vernacular 'Not in front of the servants' served a similar function.

**Pasionaria, La.** *See* THEY SHALL NOT PASS.

**Passage to India, A.** A novel (1924) by E.M. Forster (1879–1970) whose three parts represent respectively the Muslim, Western and Hindu approaches to truth, rationality and spirituality. Forster visited India in 1912–13, when he saw the Barabar Hills, which became in his novel the Marabar Caves, where the fateful encounter takes place that is at the heart of the book. He returned to India for six months in 1921, to act as secretary to the Maharaja of Dewas, after which he went back to writing the novel, which he had begun in 1913. The title comes from the poem of the same name by Walt Whitman (1819–92), of whom Forster wrote that there was 'no-one who can so suddenly ravish us into communion with all humanity or with death' (*Two Cheers for Democracy*). An intelligent film version (1984) of the novel was directed by David Lean. *See also* Dr AZIZ; FIRST LINES OF NOVELS.

**Passchendaele.** A village in western Belgium whose name became synonymous with the appalling loss of life inflicted by the First World War. From July to November 1917 British, Canadian and Australian troops fought an unsuccessful offensive battle, also known as the Third Battle of Ypres, resulting in more than 350,000 casualties. Much of the fighting took place in appalling weather conditions, and the battle achieved only minimal territorial gains. The poignancy of the name is increased by its coincidental evocation of 'passion'. *See also* WESTERN FRONT; WIPERS.

**Passive resistance.** *See* NON-VIOLENCE.

**Passive smoking.** The involuntary inhalation by non-smokers of smoke from the cigarettes, cigars and pipes that others are smoking. Passive smoking has been shown to increase the risk of lung cancer and those in the vicinity of smokers can at the least also suffer considerable immediate discomfort in the form of coughing, wheezing and watering eyes. The term dates from the 1970s.

**Pass Laws.** A notorious and much-resented aspect of APARTHEID-era South Africa. The laws, introduced in 1948, strengthened existing regulations by imposing stringent restrictions on the movements of non-white people and demanded that non-whites in 'white' areas had to carry an appropriate 'pass' authorizing them to be there. It was a demonstration against the Pass Laws that resulted in the SHARPEVILLE MASSACRE in 1960. The Pass Laws were among the institutions of apartheid that began to be dismantled in the later 1980s.

**Passport to Pimlico.** A delightful film comedy (1948) about a district of London that declares itself to be an independent state after the discovery of an ancient charter identifying the area as part of Burgundy. Starring Stanley Holloway and Margaret Rutherford among the citizens of the breakaway republic, it was the first of the EALING COMEDIES, and its title is still commonly quoted whenever a British village, town or city threatens to exert political independence in some form or other.

**Past is another country, The.** *See The* GO-BETWEEN.

**Past one's sell-by date.** *See* SELL-BY DATE.

**Pastry, Mr.** The much loved alter ego of the comedian Richard Hearne (1908–79), as a bumbling, accident-prone old man forever involved in slapstick and physical comedy in a host of films and television sketches. His name, based on a character Hearne had played in *Big Boy* (1945), a stage comedy by Fred Emney, was reflected in his appearance, with his GRANNY GLASSES, white moustache and flour-sprinkled hair.

**Pataphysics.** *See* 'MAXWELL'S SILVER HAMMER'.

**Pathé.** The name of a popular cinema newsreel, founded in France in 1909 as *Pathé Gazette* by Charles Pathé (1863–1957). Pathé newsreels were introduced in the United States in 1910, and in Britain in 1911, and continued until 1956.

**Pathological liar.** An inveterate or habitual one. The implication is that such a person lies as the result of a mental abnormality. The term dates from the 1940s.

**Patience and Fortitude.** The names of the two marble lions lying before the New York Public Library at Fifth Avenue and 42nd Street. They were so named by the mayor of New York, Fiorello La Guardia, who always ended his Sunday radio broadcasts in the 1940s with the exhortation, 'Patience and fortitude'. They were originally named Leo Astor and Leo Lenox, after the Astor and Lenox libraries on which the new library was based. They had also been known as Lord Lenox and Lady Astor, or Leo and Leonora, despite the fact that they are obviously males, as indicated by their manes. They were set on their pedestals a few days before the building was dedicated by President Taft on 25 May 1911 but were disliked by the public who called them 'absurd' or 'squash-faced'. They have since become a popular landmark, especially at Christmas, when each sports a big red bow. Their presence also enables library users to joke punningly about 'reading between the lions'.

**Patrial.** This rare 17th-century word, from Latin *patria*, 'fatherland', was reintroduced by the Immigration Bill of 1971 to refer to a person who has the right to live in Britain through the British birth of a parent or grandparent. The term became a subject of controversy, as it was seen as a thin disguise for 'white person'. It is now chiefly used in the context of immigration control.

**Patriot Act.** The common name for a piece of US federal legislation introduced in October 2001, in the wake of the events of 9/11. Its formal name is the 'Uniting and Strengthening America by Providing Appropriate Tools Required to Intercept and Obstruct Terrorism Act of 2001', and it is seen by its supporters as a key element in the WAR ON TERROR. The Patriot Act was passed by Congress with virtually no dissent. Among other things the act gave the federal government the power to search people's homes without notifying them, and to examine their medical, business and even library-borrowing records. Some regarded the act as an assault on civil liberties. For example, the comedian Robin Williams told the people of Iraq, attempting to agree on a new constitution: 'Here, take our Constitution. We're not using it anyway.'

**Patriotism is not enough.** A statement by the British nurse, Edith Cavell (1865–1915), on the eve of her execution in Belgium by a German firing squad for helping Allied soldiers to escape:

> Standing, as I do, in view of God and eternity, I realize that patriotism is not enough. I must have no hatred or bitterness towards anyone.

The words are inscribed on her monument at the junction of Charing Cross Road and St Martin's Lane, near the north-east side of Trafalgar Square, London.

**Patron saints for the modern era.** There have been patron saints for particular groups of people, things or occupations for centuries, such as St Dunstan for the blind, St Nicholas for children, St Andrew for fishermen or St Valentine for lovers. The categories listed below all arose or became established in the 20th century and duly acquired their individual patron saints. The list is necessarily only a selection of the many that exist and not all are official.

Advertisers and advertising: St Bernardino of Siena (1380–1444), named patron saint by Pope Pius XII in 1956 because of the powers of his sermons, which he enlivened with anecdotes and mimicry

Aircraft pilots and crews: the Virgin Mary, depictions of whose Assumption (celebrated 15 August) often show her ascending through the clouds. Declared a patron by France in 1952

Astronauts: St Joseph of Cupertino (1602–63) is popularly so named, from his ability to levitate

Blood banks: St Januarius (3rd century), for the miraculous liquefaction of his blood, first reported in 1389; his relics were translated to Naples in the 5th century

BOY SCOUTS or SCOUTS: St George, patron saint of England, where the movement was founded

Cavers: St Benedict of Nursia (6th century), declared patron of Italian cavers by Pope Pius XII in 1954 for the three days the saint spent in an inaccessible cave

Ecologists and ecology: St Francis of Assisi (1181–1226), so named by Pope John Paul II in 1979

Flight attendants: St Bona of Pisa (1156–1207), so named by Pope John XXIII in 1962 for her pilgrimages to Jerusalem, Santiago de Compostela and Rome

Motorists: St Frances of Rome (1384–1440), who was named the patron saint of Roman motorists by Pope Pius XI (reigned 1922–39) from her continuous vision of her guardian angel, which enabled her to see at night; the decree was confirmed in 1951

Motorways: St John the Baptist, who proclaimed, 'Make straight the way of the Lord' (John 1:23); the patronage has so far been only provisionally proposed

Petrol-station attendants: St Eligius (7th century), earlier the patron of blacksmiths and farriers

Telecommunications: St Gabriel the Archangel, so named by Pope Benedict XV in 1921; 'archangel' literally means 'chief messenger'

Television writers: St Clare of Assisi (1193–1253), so named by Pope Pius XII in 1958 from the vision that she had of a matins service, complete with singers and organ, which she was too ill to attend; SOAP OPERA fans often claim their addiction stems from watching television while off work sick

YUPPIES: St Bathild (7th century), an Anglo-Saxon saint who is portrayed as ascending a ladder; the patronage has been provisionally proposed for those who are 'upwardly mobile'

**Patter of tiny feet.** A sentimental or ironic poeticism for the forthcoming birth of a child. An earlier form was 'the patter of little feet', made popular by Longfellow:

> I hear in the chamber above me
> The patter of little feet,
> The sound of a door that is opened,
> And voices soft and sweet.
> H.W. LONGFELLOW: *Birds of Passage*, 'The Children's Hour' (1860)

**Patterson, Sir Les.** An Australian 'attaché for cultural affairs' created by the comedian Barry Humphries (b.1934), the begetter of Dame Edna EVERAGE. He is a literally filthy figure of fun, forever swilling alcohol and spilling food down his front, and appeared regularly on television in the 1970s and 1980s. He has supposedly written a book, *The Traveller's Tool* (1985), and has released an LP of songs, *Twelve Inches of Sir Les* (1985).

**Paul Jones.** A dance popular in Britain in the 1920s, in which the ladies formed an outward-facing circle moving in the opposite direction to the men, who faced inwards. The couples facing each other when the music stopped became partners for the next part of the dance, this pattern being repeated several times. It was earlier one of the 'sets' in US barn-dancing, and is said to be named after John Paul Jones (1747–92), a Scottish-born naval officer noted for his victories for the Americans during the War of Independence (1775–83).

***Pavane pour une infante défunte.*** (French, 'Pavan for a Dead Infanta'.) A solo piano composition (1899; later in an orchestrated version) by Maurice Ravel (1875–1937), the name of which recalls the Spanish court custom of performing solemn dances at periods of royal mourning. Its pronunciation, with three different French nasal vowels, often presents an insurmountable stumbling block to English-speaking radio announcers.

The *infanta* is an eldest daughter of a ruling monarch of Spain who is not the heir to the throne. A pavan or pavin is a stately dance of the 16th and 17th centuries. The origin of the name is uncertain. One theory has it originating in Spain and so called because in it the dancers stalk like peacocks (Latin *pavones*). Another traces its derivation to the Italian town of *Padova* (Padua). The pavan was especially popular with English composers of the late 16th and early 17th centuries, and in the compositions of Byrd, Bull, Gibbons, Dowland and others was generally followed by a faster dance, the galliard.

**Pavlova.** A dessert consisting of a meringue base or shell filled with whipped cream and fruit. It was created as a compliment to the Russian ballerina Anna Pavlova (*see The* DYING SWAN) during her visit to Australia and New Zealand in 1926. It is uncertain which of the two countries has the true right to the honour. Australians claim that the dessert was invented in 1935 by Herbert Sachse, an Australian chef, and named by Harry Nairn of the Esplanade Hotel, Perth. The built-up sides of the pavlova are said to suggest the shape of a tutu. New Zealanders, however, claim that the name was being used as early as 1927, a date supported by the *Oxford English Dictionary*, but this use apparently relates to a different dessert.

**Pavlovian response.** Ivan Petrovich Pavlov (1849–1936) pioneered the study of the conditioned reflex in animals. In his classic experiment, he first rang a bell when feeding a hungry dog, then trained the dog to salivate on hearing the bell even when there was no sight of food. A Pavlovian response is now generally regarded as any automatic or 'knee-jerk' reaction.

The report does not hesitate to name names, a procedure that will inevitably touch off a Pavlovian response from Leftist circles to deride it as a 'Reds under the Beds' scare.
*Daily Telegraph* (8 February 1974)

**Pax Americana.** (Latin, 'American peace'.) A term based on *Pax Britannica*, denoting the peace formerly imposed by Britain in her colonial empire. The latter phrase is in turn modelled on the Latin *Pax Romana*, the peace existing between the different parts of the Roman Empire. The phrase *Pax Americana* came into vogue from the 1960s, a time when the United States was increasingly taking over Britain's former role.

Never in the history of the world had any single nation dominated the international system as fully as the United States did for almost a quarter of a century after the Second World War. But the logic of Pax Americana led to the war in Vietnam, and the American people have learned their lesson.
*Newsweek* (28 November 1983)

**Paxo.** The nickname of the political interviewer, Jeremy Paxman (b.1950), the 'attack dog' of BBC2's *Newsnight* programme. Paxman famously asked Michael Howard (SOMETHING OF THE NIGHT), when the latter was home secretary, the same question 15 times, as he felt, quite rightly, that it had not been satisfactorily answered. Paxman is said to say to himself while interviewing politicians, 'Why is this lying bastard lying to me?'

**Payola.** A bribe given to gain a special favour, such as a payment made to a disc jockey to 'plug' certain records or tapes, or to promote a particular commercial product. The word arose in the 1930s as a blend of 'pay' and either 'Pianola' or 'Victrola', the latter being an American make of gramophone.

**PC 49.** A rather dated nickname for a policeman, especially a 'bobby on the beat'. It derives from the central character of a radio series of over 100 adventures broadcast from 1947 to 1953, in which the improbably upper-class constable so numbered was actually named Archibald Berkeley-Willoughby. 'P.C. 49' was earlier the title of a popular song of 1913 by William Hargreaves, author of 'Burlington Bertie from Bow'. *See* BURLINGTON BERTIE.

**PC Plod.** A nickname for a policeman, from Mr Plod in Enid Blyton's NODDY books for children (who was modelled on the village policeman in Studland, Dorset, in the mid-20th century). The name is also shortened to simply 'plod', the ultimate reference being to the policeman's measured walk along his beat.

**PDA.** *See* BLACKBERRY; PSION.

**Peace Corps.** The US government agency of volunteers so named was set up in 1961 by President John F. Kennedy to assist other countries in their development efforts by providing skilled workers in a wide range of fields. Once abroad, the volunteer is expected to remain as a good neighbour in the host country for at least two years, speaking its language and living on a level comparable to that of his or her counterparts in the United States. The initial intake of 900 volunteers served in 16 countries, but the latter number was nearer 90 by the 1990s.

**Peaceful coexistence.** A phrase applied by historians to the new COLD WAR dispensation following the 1962 Cuban Missile Crisis (*see* HAWKS AND DOVES), after which there was a lessening of superpower tension, marked, for example, by the signing of the 1963 Nuclear Test-Ban Treaty. Although the phrase had earlier been used in other contexts, in this particular sense it was first employed by the US Democratic politician J. William Fulbright (1905–95), who in a speech to the Senate on 27 March 1964 spoke of:

> A policy that can be accurately, though perhaps not prudently, defined as one of 'peaceful coexistence'.

*See also* DÉTENTE.

**Peacehaven.** This tranquilly named East Sussex town, a near neighbour of Newhaven, is a relatively recent creation. It arose in the First World War as a PLOTLANDS development, as happened elsewhere along the south coast, and was originally called New Anzac-on-Sea, a name resulting from a competition: '£2,600 in prizes for a Name of a New South Coast Resort' (*The Times*, 10 January 1916). The name was intended as a tribute to the ANZAC troops who were stationed locally. In 1917, however, the original planner of the plotland, Charles Neville, announced a new name, Peacehaven, both denoting a 'haven of peace' and expressing the common desire for peace to end the war. The name also matched that of nearby Newhaven.

**Peace in our time.** The form (influenced by the versicle in Morning Prayer: 'Give peace in our time, O Lord') in which the naive phrase used by Prime Minister Neville Chamberlain (1869–1940) on his return from the Munich Conference with Adolf Hitler on 30 September 1938 is now familiar. What he actually said, in a speech from 10 Downing Street (and alluding to Disraeli's phrase 'peace with honour' on his return from the Congress of Berlin in 1878), was:

> This is the second time in our history that there has come back from Germany to Downing Street peace with honour. I believe it is peace for our time.

**Peaceniks.** A derisive term applied by the American right to those who opposed US policy and campaigned for peace during the COLD WAR. The coinage is on the model of BEATNIK, with the '-nik' suffix suggesting a Russian connection (as in SPUTNIK, for example). Those peaceniks who opposed US involvement in the VIETNAM War were sometimes disparagingly referred to as Vietniks. *See also* BETTER RED THAN DEAD; REFUSENIK.

**Peace Pledge Union.** A body pledged to renounce war, organized by Canon Dick Sheppard of St Martin-in-the-Fields in 1936.

**Peace sign.** *See* V FOR VICTORY.

**Peaches and cream complexion.** A fair complexion with delicately white skin and pink cheeks. The phrase also implies a sweetness and 'lusciousness', as of the dessert itself.

**Peak District.** Britain's first national park, over half of which lies in northern Derbyshire. It opened in 1951 and is a highly popular tourist area, with the gritstone-edged moors of the so-called 'Dark Peak' and limestone dales of the 'White Peak'.

**Pearl Harbor.** The US naval base at this harbour on Oahu Island, Hawaii, was the object of a surprise air attack by the Japanese on 7 December 1941. Much of the US Pacific Fleet was damaged or destroyed, including the USS *Arizona*, which sank with the loss of more than 1100 men. Overall casualties totalled more than 3400, with over 2300 killed. The action brought the United States into the Second World War on the Allied side. The film *Pearl Harbor* (2001), a three-way (and three-hour) love story set against events leading up to 7 December, starred Ben Affleck, Josh Hartnett and Kate Beckinsale. *See also* DAY OF INFAMY; TORA! TORA! TORA!

> I fear we have only awakened a sleeping giant, and his reaction will be terrible.
> ADMIRAL YAMAMOTO: remark after the attack on Pearl Harbor, which he himself, as commander-in-chief of the combined fleet, had devised, despite his opposition to Japan entering the Second World War

**Pearly king.** The so called pearly kings and queens, princes and princesses of the London boroughs are named from their glittering attire studded with innumerable pearl buttons. There has been a pearly king of London since the FESTIVAL OF BRITAIN. They were originally elected by the street traders of London to safeguard their rights from interlopers and bullies, but they now devote their efforts to collecting and working for charities. Their tradition is said to have stemmed from an incident in the 1880s when a boat spilled its cargo of Japanese pearl buttons after foundering in the Thames. Henry Croft, a local roadsweeper, decorated his suit, hat and stick with his share of the salvage, thus becoming the first 'pearly king'. On his death in 1930 some 400 'pearlies' followed his coffin to St Pancras cemetery.

**Pecking order.** A term translating German *Hackliste*, literally 'peck list', applied in the 1920s by animal psychologists to a pattern of behaviour originally observed in hens whereby those of high rank within the group are able to attack (peck) those of lower rank without provoking an attack in return. The phenomenon was later recognized in other groups of social animals. In the 1950s the term was adopted to apply to any form of human hierarchy based on rank or status. The concept is sometimes popularly misunderstood to refer to pecking at food, as if those at the top were able to pick the choicest morsels while the underlings had to wait their turn and take what was left.

**Pedal-pushers.** Women's cropped tight trousers or jeans similar to CAPRI PANTS, so called as suitable for wear when riding a bicycle.

**Peekaboo.** Apart from the hiding game played with young children the word in the 1940s came to apply to a woman's hairstyle in which the hair, worn long, is allowed to fall over one eye. The style was popularized by the US film star Veronica Lake (1919–73), who first wore it during the Busby Berkeley film *Forty Little Mothers* (1940). Its introduction created a national fashion trend and established her as Hollywood's newest sex symbol.

**Peel, Emma.** The neat and nimble black-dressed heroine of the television series *The* AVENGERS (1961–8) who is the assistant of the secret agent John Steed. She was played by Diana Rigg. Her name is meant to suggest 'M appeal', i.e. 'man appeal', in which role she undoubtedly succeeded.

**Peel me a grape.** The archetypal request of the pampered decadent, perhaps deriving from Mae West's line in her film *I'm No Angel* (1933):

> Beulah, peel me a grape.

**Pelican crossing.** A type of road crossing that can be controlled by pedestrians. Hence its name, from '*pe*destrian *li*ght *con*trolled crossing', with the acronym assimilated to 'pelican'. *See also* GREEN MAN; PUFFIN CROSSING; ZEBRA CROSSING.

> It is safer to cross at subways, footbridges, islands, Zebra, Pelican and Puffin crossings, traffic lights or where there is a police officer, school crossing patrol or traffic warden.
>
> *The Highway Code*, The Green Cross Code, 7a (1996)

**Pelmanism.** A system of mind and memory training. It takes its name from Christopher Louis Pelman, who in 1899 founded the Pelman Institute for the Scientific Development of Mind, Memory and Personality in London. Owing to its extensive advertising, the verb 'to pelmanize', meaning to obtain good results by training the memory, was coined. It also gave its name to a card game, popular with children, which largely depends on mental concentration and memory.

The game is also known as 'Pairs' or 'Concentration' and is played as follows. The cards are shuffled and placed face down on a table or the floor, preferably at random rather than in rows. The first player turns over any two cards. If they make a pair, as two 7s, the player wins them. The same player then turns up another two cards, and continues until the cards are different. Having thus given the other players time to see which cards have been turned face-up, the player then turns the two odd cards face down again, in exactly the same position as they were in before. The next player to the left then has a turn. The player who has the most pairs when all the cards have been picked up wins the game.

**Pelvis, The.** *See* ELVIS THE PELVIS.

**PEN Club.** The international organization of writers takes its apt acronymic name from the poets, playwrights, editors, essayists and novelists who form its members. It was founded in London in 1921 by Mrs C.A. Dawson Scott, and its first president was the novelist John Galsworthy. It has since grown to include writers worldwide, and now has 130 centres in 91 countries. The club promotes international intellectual exchanges among writers and is particularly active in defending and supporting writers who are being harassed, persecuted or oppressed by their government.

**Penfriend** or **pen pal.** The notion of a friend with whom one keeps in touch by correspondence evolved in the 1930s. Many such correspondents never meet, although cases are known of happy marriages resulting from a sharing of news and views in this manner. 'Penfriend' is the commoner term in England, and 'pen pal' in the United Statess.

**Penguin, The.** *See* BATMAN.

**Penguin Books.** The paperbacks so called take their name from the publishing firm founded in 1935 by Allen Lane, the name itself being one suggested by his secretary, Joan Coles. According to Sir Allen, the logo appealed because it 'had an air of dignified flippancy and was easy to draw in black and white'. Earlier considered names were 'Dolphin' and 'Porpoise', but another publisher, FABER AND FABER, already owned the latter. Among the first ten Penguins to be published, priced at sixpence each, were Ernest Hemingway's *A Farewell to Arms*, Dorothy L. Sayers' *The Unpleasantness at the Bellona Club*, André Maurois's *Ariel* and Eric Linklater's *Poet's Pub*. In 1960 Penguin was prosecuted for publishing an uncut version of D.H. Lawrence's sexually explicit LADY CHATTERLEY'S LOVER, but after intense publicity won a historic victory against censorship. The novel sold two million copies in six weeks, overtaking Penguin's previous bestseller, E.V. Rieu's translation of Homer's *Odyssey* (1946), the first of the 'Penguin Classics'. *See also* MODERN CLASSIC; PEVSNER GUIDES.

**Penguin suit.** A man's evening dress, so nicknamed from its black and white colours and because it makes the wearer look stiff and formal, like a strutting penguin.

**Penicillin.** One of the first and still one of the most widely used antibiotic drugs, derived from the *Penicillium* mould in 1928 by Sir Alexander Fleming, who had observed that colonies of the pus-producing bacterium *Staphylococcus aureus* failed to grow in those areas of a culture that had been accidentally contaminated by the green mould *Penicillium notatum*. He isolated the mould, grew it in a fluid medium, and found it capable of producing a substance that killed many of the common bacteria that infect humans. The mould derives its name from Latin *penicillum*, 'paintbrush', since the penicillium cells resemble small brushes.

**Pennies and pence.** Whereas 'p' is now the standard abbreviation for 'pence' in stating amounts under £1, such as 10p, 25p, 80p and so on, before decimalization in 1971 the written abbreviation was 'd', for Latin *denarius*, 'penny', and the spoken word 'pence'. The latter invariably formed a single word with the amount, so that one had twopence (pronounced 'tuppence' and written thus colloquially), threepence (similarly 'thruppence'), fourpence, fivepence, sixpence and so on up to elevenpence. The same held for adjectival twopenny ('tuppenny'), threepenny ('thruppenny'), fourpenny, etc. Although now historical in their literal sense, these words survive in phrases such as 'twopenny-halfpenny' for anything worthless, 'fourpenny one' for a blow, 'right as ninepence' meaning in perfect condition etc. In the 21st century the original 'penny' and its conventional plural 'pennies' have almost been forgotten, and when a unitary amount or single coin has to be referred to it is usually as 'one pence'. *See also* TURN ON A SIXPENCE or A DIME; TWOPENNY TUBE.

> I've got sixpence, jolly, jolly sixpence,
> I've got sixpence to last me all my life:
> I've got twopence to spend, and twopence to lend,
> And twopence to send home to my wife.
>
> DESMOND COX: 'I've Got Sixpence' (song) (1941)

**Pennies from heaven.** Unexpected financial benefits; a windfall. The expression seems to have originated from the song of this title popularized by Bing Crosby, who first sang it in the film of the same name (1936).

> Every time it rains, it rains
> Pennies from heaven.
> Don't you know each cloud contains
> Pennies from heaven?
>
> JOHNNY BURKE: 'Pennies from Heaven' (1936)

*Pennies from Heaven* was also the title of a critically lauded television drama (1978) by Dennis Potter. It starred Bob Hoskins and featured a number of popular songs of the 1920s and 1930s.

**Penny dropped, The.** It became clear. The phrase indicating a person's final realization of something alludes to the old penny-in-a-slot machine, as on the door of a public lavatory. The expression dates from the 1940s. *See also* SPEND A PENNY.

**'Penny Lane'.** A song of charm, vigour and no little musical sophistication by The BEATLES, credited to John Lennon and Paul McCartney and released in February 1967. Inspired by The Beatles' Liverpool childhood and incorporating motifs as diverse as a fireman's handbell and a reference to the second *Brandenburg Concerto* by J.S. Bach, 'Penny Lane' evokes a kaleidoscope of images of the city, from the banker 'waiting for a trim' in a barber's shop to the rhapsodic celebration of its 'blue suburban skies'. The reference to 'fish and finger pie' at one point in the song is a smuttily nostalgic allusion to adolescent sexual experimentation. Penny Lane is both a Liverpool street name and an area of the city. *See also* 'STRAWBERRY FIELDS FOREVER'.

**Pen pal.** *See* PENFRIEND.

**Pentagon.** A vast five-sided building erected in Washington, D.C., in 1943 to house government officials. It now houses the US Department of Defense, and Pentagon is a synonym for the official American line in military matters. Part of the Pentagon was destroyed and more than 80 people killed in the terrorist assault of 11 September 2001, when a hijacked airliner was flown into the building. *See also* 9/11; PUZZLE PALACE; WORLD TRADE CENTER.

**Pentagon Papers.** Official documents detailing a history of the US role in Indochina from the Second World War until 1968. They were commissioned in 1967 by Robert S. McNamara, the US Secretary of Defense, and were leaked to the press by Daniel Ellsberg, a government official, in 1971. They revealed, among other things, that the Harry S. Truman administration had given military aid to France in its colonial war against the Viet Minh, thus directly involving the United States in VIETNAM. The *New York Times* began publishing the papers on 13 June 1971 and they were subsequently commercially issued in book form in four volumes. Their release stirred controversy not only throughout the United States but also internationally.

**People carrier** or **mover.** A form of transport for several people. The two terms are sometimes used indifferently but are not properly synonymous. A people carrier is a vehicle with (usually) three rows of seats, affording greater accommodation than the average car, while a people mover is an automated transport system, such as a moving pavement or driverless car. Both types of transport came to the fore in the 1990s and, confusingly, are each also known as a multipurpose vehicle.

> So that's it. High summer is over, the last caravans and people-carriers have crawled back up the dual carriageway for the new term.
> *The Times* (31 August 1999)

**People person.** A person who interacts well with others and enjoys doing so. The expression is intended to have a positive application both socially and in business circles, but can easily come across as shallow PSYCHOBABBLE (tellingly guyed in the person of Tom, Reginald PERRIN's ineffectual and unworldly son-in-law in the television sitcom *The Fall and Rise of Reginald Perrin*, who was constantly claiming to be a 'people person').

> Friendly & informal yet highly professional Nanny agency based in South Kensington require a dynamic and organized 'people person' to run own department in a busy and often hectic office.
> *The Times* (advertisement) (16 September 1999)

**People power.** Political or other pressure exerted by ordinary people, as distinct from politicians and other influential individuals. The term arose in the mid-1970s and originally applied to physical effort exercised by people rather than machines. The present sense dates from the early 1980s.

**People's Budget.** The radical budget brought before parliament in 1909 by David Lloyd George (*see* WELSH WIZARD), chancellor of the exchequer in Asquith's Liberal government. To fund social reform measures, such as the proposed old-age pensions, and also to raise money for more battleships to challenge the German naval expansion programme (*see* DREADNOUGHT), Lloyd George proposed taxes on land sales and land values, higher death duties and a supertax on higher incomes. All this was anathema to the Conservative landed interests which dominated the House of Lords, which refused to pass the budget, so breaking with constitutional convention. Asquith retaliated by

introducing the Parliament Act (1911), which put severe restrictions on the powers of the Lords. The Lords agreed to pass the act only when Asquith threatened to swamp the Lords with new Liberal peers. *See also* DIEHARDS; HEDGERS AND DITCHERS; OLD SQUIFFY.

**People's Homewrecker, The.** *See* the ROTTWEILER.

**People's Princess.** A media nickname for Diana, Princess of Wales (1961–97), noted for her charity work and her special interest in children and the sick, in particular AIDS victims. The term was popularized by the New Labour prime minister Tony Blair, giving his first (no doubt scripted, and certainly well acted) response on 31 August 1997 to Diana's death in a car crash in Paris:

> People everywhere, not just here in Britain, kept faith with Princess Diana. They liked her, they loved her, they regarded her as one of the people. She was the People's Princess, and that is how she will stay, how she will remain in our hearts and in our memories for ever.

**People's Republic.** A title assumed by various socialist or communist states from the late 1940s. The most familiar example is the People's Republic of China, formed in 1949, when Hungary also adopted the title. Despite the decline of communism from the late 1980s, People's Republic remained a designation at the dawn of the 21st century, sometimes together with a political 'Socialist' or a tautological 'Democratic', for Bangladesh, China, North Korea and Laos.

**Peoria.** *See* PLAY IN PEORIA.

**PEP.** The Personal Equity Plan was introduced in Britain in 1987 as a type of investment scheme that allowed relatively small investors to own shares in British companies free from income tax and capital gains tax. The PEP had its enthusiasts, but was replaced in 1999 by the less enterprising ISA (Individual Savings Account). *See also* TESSA.

**Pepsi-Cola.** The familiar cola drink was the invention of a North Carolina pharmacist, Caleb D. Bradham, who named it in 1898 and who incorporated the Pepsi-Cola Company in 1902. He based the name on that of COCA-COLA, with 'Pepsi-' implying that his concoction could relieve dyspepsia. The real founder of modern Pepsi-Cola, however, was Charles G. Guth, who established a new company under the same name in 1931, got a chemist to formulate a better drink, and set up bottling operations. His 12-ounce bottle of Pepsi-Cola, costing 5 cents, realized spectacular sales.

**Pep talk.** An inspirational address aimed at boosting morale. The phrase dates from the 1920s and is based on the 20th-century word 'pep' meaning 'energy', as a shortened form of 'pepper'.

**Per ardua ad astra.** (Latin, 'through difficulties to the stars'.) The motto of the Royal Air Force. The phrase, originally the motto of the Mulvany family, was adopted as the motto of the RAF (then the Royal Flying Corps) in 1914. The headquarters of the former Air Ministry (now part of the Ministry of Defence) was set up at Adastral House, London, in 1955.

**Percy.** Like CUTHBERT, a nickname in the First World War for a CONSCIENTIOUS OBJECTOR. The name was apparently chosen for its suggestion of effeteness, perhaps from some sort of folk memory of the noble north of England Percy family, many of whom fell in battle or were executed. *See also* FIRST WORLD WAR SLANG.

**Perestroika.** (Russian, 'restructuring'.) The policy of restructuring or reforming the economic and political system of the former Soviet Union was first proposed by Leonid Brezhnev in 1979 and actively promoted by Mikhail Gorbachev. The original concept was of increased automation and labour efficiency but the term subsequently came to denote a greater awareness of economic markets and the phasing out of central planning. *See also* GLASNOST; GORBY.

> The idea of *perestroika* ... combines continuity and innovation, the historical experience of bolshevism and the contemporaneity of socialism.
> MIKHAIL GORBACHEV: speech, 2 November 1987 (the 70th anniversary of the October Revolution)

**Performance art.** An art form combining elements of theatre and music with the visual arts. It dates from the late 1960s and has involved a wide range of expression, from self-inflicted discomfort and humiliation to surreal whimsicality. An example of the latter was staged in 1975 when the three-man Ddart Performance Group walked around East Anglia in a 240km (150 mile) circle with a pole attached to their heads. The style has also been linked to rock music, a field in which Laurie Anderson (b.1947) is the most noted exponent. Other artists in this variable arena are Joseph Beuys (1921–86), Gilbert and George (b.1943 and 1942) and Bruce Nauman (b.1941).

**Perm.** A shortening of permanent wave, as a method of setting the hair in waves or curls and then treating it with chemicals so that the style lasts for several months, although hardly 'permanently'. The procedure was introduced in 1906 and initially took between 8 and 12 hours.

**Permissive society.** A term widely used in Britain from the 1960s (the first recorded use dates from 1960) to denote the increasingly tolerant and liberal attitudes in society that tend to blur the distinctions between right and wrong.

Gambling clubs, strip clubs, the legalizing of homosexual practices between 'consenting adults', the liberalization of the divorce laws, the abolition of theatre censorship and the growing use of 'bad language' and obscenities in publications, in the theatre and on television, were typical manifestations. *See also* NEW MORALITY; SWINGING SIXTIES.

> The permissive society has been allowed to become a dirty phrase. A better phrase is the civilized society.
> ROY JENKINS: speech in Abingdon (19 July 1969). As home secretary, Jenkins had been responsible for the reforms of the laws on censorship, divorce and homosexuality.

**Perpetua.** *See* GILL SANS.

**Perrin, Reginald.** The frustrated businessman who attempts to remake his life by faking suicide and starting afresh in the comic novels by David Nobbs, beginning with *The Death of Reginald Perrin* (1975). He made a memorable translation to television in the talented hands of Leonard Rossiter in *The Fall and Rise of Reginald Perrin* (1976–9), a SITCOM unusually cerebral for its time.

**Perry Mason.** *See* Perry MASON.

**Pershing missile.** A type of US intermediate-range ballistic missile (IRBM), first developed in the 1960s. Pershing II missiles were controversially deployed in western Europe in 1984, during a particularly chilly period of the COLD WAR, to face the Soviet equivalent, the SS-20. The Pershing II had a range of 1760km (1100 miles) and could carry a 15-kiloton warhead. They were withdrawn following the INF (intermediate nuclear forces) treaty of December 1987. The Pershing missile, like the US Pershing heavy tank of the Second World War, was named after General John J. Pershing (1860–1948), commander of the American Expeditionary Force in Europe in the First World War, who in 1919 became the United States's first General of the Armies (*see also* BLACK JACK).

***Persistence of Memory, The.*** The famous 'soft watches' painting by Salvador Dalí (1904–89) was executed in 1931. As Dalí helpfully explained in *Conquest of the Irrational* (1969): 'The famous soft watches are nothing else than the tender, extravagant, solitary, paranoic-critical camembert of time and space.'

**Pester power.** A nickname for the persistent pressure that children put on parents or other adults to buy them an object of desire seen in a shop, television commercial or elsewhere. The mania is particularly rife at Christmas, when commercial HYPE is at its height.

**Pétainists.** The supporters of Marshal Pétain, head of the VICHY regime in France (1940–44), which collaborated with the Nazis after the fall of France. Philippe Pétain (1856–1951) had been a French hero in the First World War, leading the defence of VERDUN. Having become a military figurehead of enormous prestige, he was summoned to join the French cabinet as the German armies poured through Belgium in 1940. When France fell in June 1940, Pétain persuaded his colleagues to reject the proffered military union with Britain and to seek an armistice with the Germans. The prime minister, Paul Reynaud, resigned, and Pétain took his place, agreeing to the German terms at COMPIÈGNE on 22 June. Pétain attempted a reactionary National Revolution to establish a quasi-fascist state, with the slogan 'work, family and fatherland' replacing the French Republican 'liberty, equality, fraternity'. Pétain attempted to maintain a semblance of independence and rejected calls for France to join Germany in its war against Britain. However, he found his position steadily eroded by more ardent collaborationists and by the Germans, who eventually arrested him in August 1944. He returned to France in 1945 and was sentenced to death, although General de Gaulle commuted the sentence to life imprisonment.

**Peter and the Wolf.** The charming musical tale for children by Sergei Prokofiev (1891–1953) was first performed in 1936. The narration is interspersed with orchestral interludes, in which each character is portrayed by a different solo instrument, the duck by the oboe, for example, making the piece a perennially popular way of teaching the sounds of different orchestral instruments. Needless to say, the boy Peter triumphs over the fierce wolf, which is taken to a zoo.

**Peter Grimes.** The moody and gloomy opera by Benjamin Britten (1913–76) with a libretto by Montagu Slater was first performed in London in 1945 and was Britten's first major success. The story is based on one of the dark verse tales from *The Borough* (1810) by George Crabbe (1754–1832), set in his native Aldeburgh, Suffolk, which was also to become Britten's home. Grimes is a fisherman and a loner. Suspected by the townspeople of murdering a boy, he escapes to sea in fog and sinks his boat.

**Peter Pan.** The little boy who never grew up, the central character of J.M. Barrie's famous play of this name (1904). The story begins when Peter enters the nursery window of the house of the Darling family to recover his shadow. He flies back to NEVER NEVER LAND accompanied by the Darling children, to rejoin the Lost Boys. Eventually all are captured by the pirates, except Peter, who secures their release and the defeat of the pirates. The children, by now homesick, fly back to the nursery with their new friends, but Peter refuses to stay as he does not wish to grow up. In their

absence Mr Darling lives in the dog kennel as penance for having taken NANA away, thus making possible the children's disappearance in the first place.

The name of Barrie's hero resulted from the combination of those of the Greek god Pan and of Peter Llewelyn Davies, one of the five young sons of Barrie's friends Arthur and Sylvia Llewelyn Davies (who became Mr and Mrs Darling in the play). Barrie explained to the boys that he made Peter Pan 'by rubbing the five of you violently together, as savages with two sticks produce a flame', but it was Peter Llewelyn Davies who came to be most closely associated with the character. He was named Peter after the title character in his grandfather George Du Maurier's novel *Peter Ibbetson* (1891). The five brothers generally met unhappy fates: one (George) died fighting in the First World War; another (Michael) drowned while at Oxford; and Peter himself (by then a publisher) committed suicide in 1960 by throwing himself under a train in the London Underground. Sir George Frampton's statue of Peter Pan in Kensington Gardens was not, incidentally, modelled on Peter Llewelyn Davies, but on his brother, Michael. The name of WENDY, the little girl who befriended Peter, was invented by Barrie and soon caught on as a new girl's name.

In 1929 Barrie donated the lucrative royalty rights to the play to the Great Ormond Street Hospital for Sick Children. *See also* FIRST LINES OF NOVELS; IN THE DOGHOUSE; WENDY HOUSE.

> To die will be an awfully big adventure.
>
> J.M. BARRIE: *Peter Pan*, III

**Peter Pan collar.** A flat collar with rounded points, as traditionally worn by PETER PAN in the play that bears his name and in illustrations to the book based on it. The style was popularized in the 1930s by the child film star Shirley Temple (b.1928), whose dresses had collars of this type.

**Peter Principle.** The theory, usually taken not too seriously, that all members of a hierarchy rise to their own levels of incompetence. It is named after the Canadian-born American educationist Dr Laurence J. Peter (1919–90), who, with Raymond Hull, first propounded it in *The Peter Principle* (1969).

**Peter Rabbit.** The most familiar of the animal characters created by Beatrix Potter (1866–1943) for her nursery tales. He is small and harmless, and first appears in *The* TALE OF PETER RABBIT (1901).

**Petit Prince, Le.** An allegorical story for children (1943; in English as *The Little Prince*, 1944) by Antoine de Saint-Exupéry (1900–44), in which he explores his personal philosophical convictions about values. A film version

(1974), directed by Stanley Donen, turned the charming original into an arch musical. *See also* WIND, SAND AND STARS.

**Petrified Forest, The.** A play (1935) by the US playwright Robert Sherwood (1896–1955) about a group of gangsters who hide up in a rundown desert roadhouse. Filmed in 1936 with Leslie Howard, Bette Davis and Humphrey Bogart, the play owed its title to a roadmap, which Sherwood found in the otherwise bare office that he occupied while writing the text. It was while looking at the map that Sherwood decided to set his story in the Arizona desert, and when one of the characters subsequently referred to his destination up the road, the author automatically checked the map to see where it led in reality: it led straight to a place identified as the Petrified Forest.

**Petrolhead.** A person with an excessive or obsessional interest in cars and driving. The standard model is male and ageingly laddish (think Jeremy Clarkson), but the term can also encompass BOY RACERS. It originated in Australia around 1980, but quickly spread to other varieties of English.

**Petrushka.** The ballet of this name, with an innovative Modernist (*see* MODERNISM) score by Igor Stravinsky (1882–1971) and choreography by Michel Fokine (1880–1942), was first performed by Diaghilev's BALLETS RUSSES in 1911 in Paris. The ballet tells of the fate of Petrushka, a puppet who comes to life. Stravinksy's music makes much use of the chord of C against F sharp, which has become known as 'the Petrushka chord'.

**Petting zoo.** A US term dating from the 1970s for a zoo where children are allowed to handle and feed the animals.

**Pevsner guides.** The magisterial series *The Buildings of England*, published by PENGUIN BOOKS, was inaugurated in 1951. Its author was Nikolaus Pevsner (1902–83), a German-born art historian who fled to Britain when the NAZIS came to power in 1933. The series of 46 volumes, of which 32 were written single-handedly by Pevsner, ran until 1974 and covered a wide range of buildings of architectural interest throughout England, with at least one volume to a county. Later authors have revised Pevsner's text, adding newer buildings, but respecting the personally authoritative, and often censorious, tone of the originals.

**Phalange.** *See* FALANGE.

**Phantom goal.** In football a goal awarded although not actually scored. In a Division One match against Ipswich Town on 26 September 1970 Alan Hudson of Chelsea was awarded such a goal although the ball in fact hit the metal stanchion outside the net and bounced back into play. The referee, Roy Capey, awarded a goal rather than a goal kick to Ipswich in the belief that the ball had struck the stanchion inside the goal. Although BBC television cameras showed that it was not a goal, the Football League ruled that a replay could not be ordered, as Ipswich demanded, because the laws of football state categorically that the referee's decision is final.

Perhaps the most hotly debated of all goals, with the possible exception of the HAND OF GOD, was the second goal of Geoff Hurst's hat-trick for England against West Germany in the 1966 World Cup final. Hurst's shot hit the underside of the bar and dropped straight down. After consultation with a Russian linesman, the referee allowed the goal, giving England a 3–2 lead. Renewed study of archive films in 2006 led experts to conclude that the ball had not in fact crossed the line. *See also* THEY THINK IT'S ALL OVER.

**Phantom Major.** The nickname of Major (later Colonel) James Stirling (1915–90), who founded the Special Air Service (SAS) in 1941 to conduct sabotage missions behind enemy lines during the North Africa campaign in the Second World War. The nickname was given to Stirling by the German AFRIKA KORPS, who were amazed by the ability of his force to appear out of the desert and disappear again. In 1943 Stirling was captured in Tunisia, escaped four times and was finally imprisoned in COLDITZ. He was knighted in 1990.

**Phantom of the Opera, The.** A novel by Gaston Leroux (1911). The real name of the eponymous phantom is Erik, and he is a man with a hideous skull-like face who lives in seclusion beneath a Paris opera house. He falls in love with a singer, masking his deformity and committing a number of murders to achieve his desire, but in the end fails to get the girl. The unusual story was made into a film of 1925 with Lon Chaney, 'the man of a thousand faces', in the name part, and following further cinematic versions was given a new lease of life in Andrew Lloyd Webber's identically titled hit musical (1986), still running in London and New York in 2006, when it became the longest-running musical on Broadway ever.

**Phantom pregnancy.** An uncommon psychological disorder, also known as false pregnancy and medically as pseudocyesis, in which there are all the usual physical signs of pregnancy without any foetus being present. Many women experiencing the condition are childless or approaching the menopause, and an intense desire to have children is a concomitant. Treatment usually consists of counselling or psychotherapy.

**Philadelphia Story, The.** A film (1940) based on a play by

Philip Barry (1896–1949) about a spoiled Philadelphia heiress, Tracy Lord, who begins to have doubts about her forthcoming marriage to a dull company executive in the face of the taunts of her ex-husband and the growing interest of a magazine reporter, Mike Conner. Starring Katharine Hepburn (in a role specially written for her) alongside Cary Grant and James Stewart, the film was remade as the musical *High Society* (1956), with Bing Crosby, Frank Sinatra and Grace Kelly.

**Philosophy in the Boudoir.** The disturbing painting by the Belgian surrealist René Magritte (1898–1967) was executed in 1947. The picture features a nightdress with breasts and a pair of high-heeled shoes with human toes. The title presumably refers to the notorious *La Philosophie dans le boudoir* (1793) by the Marquis de Sade.

**Phil the Greek.** A nickname for Prince Philip, Duke of Edinburgh (b.1921), consort to Queen Elizabeth II. Philip's father was Prince Andrew of Greece and Philip was born in Corfu, although he is actually of Germanic stock (he changed his surname to Mountbatten from Schleswig-Holstein-Sonderburg-Glücksburg on his marriage). *See also* KEITH.

**Phishing.** A form of electronic scam, by which fraudsters attempt, often by E-MAIL, to acquire details of the victim's bank account, credit cards, passwords, etc., often by offering some sort of a 'bait'. A common ploy, particularly popular with Nigerian fraudsters, is to offer the victim a large fee for allowing their UK bank account to be used to deposit some enormous sum of (imaginary) money on a temporary basis. If the victim 'bites', and provides their bank details, they will quickly find that their account has been emptied. Phishing is one form of IDENTITY THEFT, and the term was coined in the mid-1990s by computer hackers on the model of phone PHREAKING, and with a reference to FISHING EXPEDITIONS.

**Phone a friend.** *See* WHO WANTS TO BE A MILLIONAIRE?

**Phoney.** Fraudulent, bogus or insincere. The word is a US colloquialism and slang term that became anglicized about 1920. It is said to derive from 'fawney', an obsolete underworld cant word meaning the imitation gold ring used by confidence tricksters, itself from Irish *fáinne*, 'ring'.

**Phoney Quid.** An ingenious nickname for Admiral of the Fleet Sir Dudley Pound (1877–1943), First Sea Lord in the Second World War. 'Quid' is a general naval nickname for anyone called Pound, while 'Phoney' derives from the admiral's first name, which is popularly shortened as 'Dud'.

**Phoney Tony.** *See* BUSH'S POODLE.

**Phoney War.** The name given by US journalists to the period between Britain and France's declaration of war on Germany in September 1939 and the Nazi invasions of Denmark, Norway, the Low Countries and then France in April–May 1940. The period was marked by a virtual absence of fighting on what was to become the Western Front. The Germans called this period the *Sitzkrieg*, 'sitting war', while the French name was *la drôle de guerre*, 'the joke or strange war'. Neville Chamberlain, the British prime minister, referred to the period as a 'Twilight War'. The Phoney War ended with German BLITZKRIEG attacks on western Europe.

**Photo opportunity.** A staged opportunity for the press to take photographs of famous people. The expression originated in the United States as media jargon in the 1970s but did not became generally familiar until the 1980s, when it was used of newsworthy pictures of President Reagan and Mrs Thatcher by public relations advisers who realized the advantages of giving press photographers what they wanted instead of simply leaving matters to chance. A negative aspect of the photo opportunity is its trivialization of politics by treating it almost as an offshoot of show business.

**Phreaking.** The manipulation by hackers of the telephone system to enable them to make free calls. The practice – and the word, combining 'phone' and 'freak' – emerged in the United States in the 1950s.

**Phwoar!** An exclamation dating from the 1980s, found mostly in the media, to express male sexual desire. The suggestion is of a blend of 'phew!' and 'wow!' There are variant spellings. *See also* WOLF WHISTLE.

**Physical Impossibility of Death in the Mind of Someone Living, The.** The notorious shark in formaldehyde by Damien Hirst (b.1965) dates from 1991. Hirst said of the work: 'I wanted the real thing, I wanted people to think "that could … eat me".' The same could not be said of *Away From the Flock*, Hirst's 1994 sheep in formaldehyde. When exhibited at the Serpentine Gallery in London, someone poured ink into the sheep's tank; Hirst was not unduly upset.

**Piano Man, The.** The name given by the media to the mysterious young man found by the police in April 2005 wandering around Sheerness in Kent in a soaking wet suit. The man, who refused to talk, was taken to a mental health unit, where, still refusing to speak, he drew a picture of a grand piano. Presented with a piano, he then proceeded to play a range of music, from Tchaikovsky to The Beatles, non-stop for four hours. Over the months that followed there was intense speculation as to the man's identity, and a number of people from various parts of Europe claimed they knew who he was (one Danish woman claimed he was her Algerian husband). In August the health authorities in England said the man was no longer in their care, following 'a marked improvement in his condition'. The man turned out to be a Bavarian called Andreas Grassl.

**Pick-and-mix** or **pick'n'mix.** Assembled or collected by choosing different items from an overall variety. The term can apply to a method of selecting confectionery or other goods from a store's display to a blending of elements in an undertaking such as the compilation of an educational course or the drafting of a political programme.

**Pick up the tab.** To pay the bill; to meet the cost. 'Tab' is perhaps a shortening of 'tabulation'. The phrase is of US origin and dates from the 1950s.

**Pick your own.** A marketing arrangement whereby customers purchase fruit or vegetables by picking or digging them at the site where they are commercially grown. The system is ingenious, since the customer exercises quality control and therefore cannot subsequently complain. The term is often abbreviated to PYO.

**Picture window.** A large window consisting of a single pane of glass, through which the view appears like a picture in a frame. The term is of US origin and dates from the 1930s.

> If you have a large picture window, we suggest sill-length casement drawn curtains.
> *American Home* (20 November 1938)

**Piece of cake.** Something easy, or easily obtained. The allusion is to the ease with which a slice of cake is taken and eaten. The RAF appropriated the expression in the Second World War, and a cartoon at the time of the Berlin airlift in 1948 depicted a pilot saying, 'Piece of Gatow, old boy'. (Gatow was a strategic Berlin airfield used for this operation.) A less polite alternative formulation is 'piece of piss'.

**Piece of the action.** Involvement in a profitable activity, or one that promises to be so. The expression is associated with the criminal or gambling world and dates from the 1950s.

**Pie-eater.** In Australian slang, a term of abuse for an inconsequential or contemptible person. Meat pies are a stereotypical staple of the Australian diet (*see* AS AUSTRALIAN AS A MEAT PIE), and a perception of their lowly status vis-à-vis more sophisticated European cuisine (*see* CULTURAL CRINGE) may have contributed to the usage. The

main underlying idea, though, is probably a reprehensible self-indulgence.

The Australian cricketer Rodney Marsh (b.1947) may have been inspired by the same stereotype when he dismissed English bowlers as mere 'pie-throwers' (although a clown throwing a custard pie may also have been in his mind). The term caught on as a way of insulting a bowler.

> The spinners were not that great – Dharmasena, to be honest, is a pie thrower, and Chandana bowls rubbish quite often.
> www.forum.cricketweb.net (12 June 2004)

In the UK the term 'pie-eater' is applied to an inhabitant of the Lancashire town of Wigan, not because Wigan is famed for its pies (although it is), but because during the Miners' Strike of 1926 (*see* NOT A PENNY OFF THE PAY, NOT A SECOND OFF THE DAY) the Wigan miners returned to work before their comrades elsewhere in the country, and were thus said to have 'eaten humble pie'.

**Pie in the sky.** A 'reward in heaven' (Matthew 5:12), here taken to mean the good time or good things promised that will never come. The term comes from a rallying song of the WOBBLIES attributed to their martyred organizer, Joe Hill (*c.*1872–1915).

> You will eat, bye and bye,
> In the glorious land above the sky;
> Work and pray, live on hay,
> You'll get pie in the sky when you die.
> JOE HILL: *Songs of the Workers*, 'The Preacher and the Slave' (1911)

**Pie, pint and panatella man.** A description by Simon Hoggart in *The Guardian*, 18 July 2001, of the Conservative politician Kenneth Clarke (b.1940). Describing the elimination of Michael Portillo (*see* PORTILLISTAS) from the Conservative leadership contest by the casting of votes for Clarke, he commented: 'Portillo has been destroyed by the pie, pint and panatella man.' The ample-girthed Clarke is often caricatured as a lover of beer and cigars. He failed to win the party leadership again in 2005. *See also* BIG BEAST; MERCHANTS OF DEATH.

***Pierrot Lunaire.*** A landmark Modernist (*see* MODERNISM) musical 'melodrama' by Arnold Schoenberg (1874–1951). It was written in 1912 for solo female voice and a small instrumental group. The title means 'Moonstruck Pierrot', and the work consists of settings of 21 poems by Albert Giraud, translated into German by Otto Erich Hartleben. The vocal part features *Sprechgesang*, a technique between singing and speaking. In a letter in 1931 Schoenberg wrote: '*Pierrot Lunaire* is not to be sung! Song melodies must be balanced and shaped in quite a different way from spoken melodies.'

**Piggly Wiggly.** The proprietary name of a chain of US self-service stores founded in Memphis, Tennessee, in 1916 by Clarence Saunders (1881–1953) and a forerunner of the modern supermarket. When asked by a business associate why he had chosen the name, Saunders replied, 'So people would ask me what you just did' (*The New Yorker*, 6 June 1959). He later devised the Keedoozle, from 'key does all', a type of automated grocery store in which the customer selected merchandise by placing a 'key' into a slot beside the desired item and pushing a button. This perforated a tape inside the key. On completing the trip, the customer handed the tape to a clerk who ran it through a machine that added up the bill. This in turn was thus an early equivalent of the modern EFTPOS and 'card swipe'.

**Piggy bank.** A child's money box, especially one in the shape of a pig. In a transferred sense 'piggy bank' is used for one's savings, as: 'I'll have to draw on my piggy bank.'

**Pig Island.** A nickname for New Zealand dating from the early 20th century. The reference is to the pigs introduced by Captain Cook when he surveyed the islands in 1769. They later went wild.

**Pig out.** To overeat; to MAKE A PIG OF ONESELF. An expression evolving in the 1970s.

> Popcorn, ice-cream, chocolate and cappuccino or Coke to drink. If you're going to sit on the sofa and pig out, do it properly!
> *The Times* (25 September 1999)

**Pig's bladder on a stick.** A description of the right-wing Tory MP Terry Dicks (b.1937) by the Labour MP Tony Banks (1943–2006), who was infuriated by Dicks's opposition to state funding of the arts. Dicks lost his seat in the 1997 election.

> When he leaves the chamber he probably goes to vandalize a few paintings somewhere. He is to the arts what Vlad the Impaler was to origami … He is undoubtedly living proof that a pig's bladder on a stick can be elected as a Member of Parliament.

**Pig's ear** or **breakfast.** A mess; an inept handling. 'You've made a right pig's ear of that' means you have made a complete muddle of it or have indeed failed to do it at all. It is possible 'ear' may be a euphemistic form of 'arse'. The phrases date from the 1930s. *See also* DOG'S DINNER.

**Pigs might fly.** The concept of pigs flying as an unlikely occurrence dates from the 16th century but in the 19th century settled to proverbial form as 'Pigs may fly, but they are very unlikely birds'. The current shorter and modified form of this is a 20th-century creation.

**Pilates.** A system of gentle exercises performed lying down that stretches and lengthens the muscles, making the body long, lean, supple and strong. It came into vogue on both sides of the Atlantic in the 1990s and was invented in the 1920s by Joseph Pilates (1880–1967), a German entrepreneur who studied different exercise routines to strengthen his body after a sickly childhood. The name is pronounced 'Pi-lah-teez'.

**Pile it high, sell it cheap.** The byword of Sir John ('Jack') Cohen (1898–1979), founder of the Tesco supermarket chain in 1931. The '-co' of the store name derives from his surname, while the 'Tes-' represents the initials of T.E. Stockwell, of Messrs Torring & Stockwell, his original tea suppliers.

**Pilgrim Trust.** The US philanthropist Edward S. Harkness (1874–1940) set up the $10-million trust of this name in 1930. It was inspired by his interest in Britain and the British and supports such projects as the preservation of historic sites and training for the unemployed.

**Pill, The.** Since the introduction of the oral contraceptive in the early 1960s, its impact has caused it to be known as *the* pill, to the exclusion of all others, for whatever ailment or condition. *See also* MORNING-AFTER PILL.

**Pillbox.** A name given to the small concrete outposts erected in Britain at the start of the Second World War in case of a German invasion. It is estimated that about 28,000 were built, some of which still survive.

**Pillbox hat.** A woman's hat something like the cylindrical box formerly used for medicinal pills. It first came into fashion in the 1930s but was given social cachet when worn by Jackie Kennedy (*see* JACKIE O) at the presidential inauguration of John F. Kennedy in 1961. She was wearing it again when sitting next to her husband in the open-top car in which he was assassinated in Dallas in 1963.

**Pilote de Guerre.** *See* WIND, SAND AND STARS.

**Piltdown man.** *See under* FAKES.

***Pincher Martin.*** A philosophical novel (1956) by William Golding (1911–93), set on a rock in the Atlantic. Realistic flashbacks are combined with the surrealistic efforts of Martin's dead persona to survive; a 'pincher' in this context can be read as an identity-preserver. In the British armed forces and elsewhere, 'Pincher' has been a nickname for anyone surnamed Martin since the mid-19th century, when Admiral Sir William F. Martin was notorious for 'pinching' (arresting) sailors even for trivial offences. In the United States Golding's novel was published as *The Two Deaths of*

*Christopher Martin*. It is possible that his choice of title was influenced by that of *Pincher Martin, O.D.* (1915), an early volume of stories and sketches of life in the Royal Navy by the naval officer and writer 'Taffrail' (Captain Henry Taprell Dorling) (1883–1968). Golding himself served in the Royal Navy in the Second World War.

**Pinch oneself.** If you say you 'have to pinch yourself', you are incredulous, you are unable to appreciate the reality of a situation. The image is of someone pinching their own body to be reassured that they actually exist.

**Pindown.** A practice in some children's homes in the 1980s, whereby 'difficult' children were kept in solitary confinement, often dressed in just their night-clothes or underwear. The reference was supposedly not to physically 'pinning down' the children but to pinning down the problem they caused by means of so-called 'behaviour modification therapy'. The treatment as used in Staffordshire was halted by High Court order in 1989 and came to light in a report published in 1991, achieving instant notoriety.

**Pineapple.** *See* MILLS BOMB.

**Pinewood Studios.** The film studios near Iver, Buckinghamshire, date from 1934 when Charles Boot, a wealthy local builder, bought Heatherden Hall and named what he hoped would become the most advanced film studio in the world after the tall pines in the grounds. The name also compliments (and complements) that of HOLLYWOOD, which Boot saw his enterprise as rivalling. He formed a partnership with J. Arthur Rank and the studios went on to achieve several blockbuster successes, among them *The Red Shoes* and *Oliver Twist*, both made in 1948. US production companies were attracted to Pinewood from the 1960s and the CARRY ON FILMS and James BOND films were made there, as were television series such as MINDER. In 2001 Pinewood bought up and joined forces with Shepperton film studios.

**Ping-pong.** The game of table tennis took its popular name at the turn of the 20th century, 'ping' representing the sound made when the bat strikes the ball and 'pong' the sound when the ball hits the table. According to the *Daily Chronicle* of 2 May 1901 the inventor of Ping-Pong was one James Gibb, a former Cambridge athlete. The game was originally sold under various names, such as 'Gossima', 'Whiff Whaff' and 'Flim Flam', and like these 'Ping Pong' was a proprietary name, registered in Britain in 1900 and in the United States in 1901. The US rights to the name were sold to Parker Brothers of Salem, Massachusetts, soon after and it is still a trademark there.

'Ping-pong diplomacy' is a former term for the establishment of trade and other relations between the United States and China, begun when a US table tennis team went to China in 1971. *See also* AERIAL PINGPONG.

**Pink.** A colour associated with homosexuals from the time of the Second World War, when NAZI concentration camp prisoners identified as such were obliged to wear a pink triangle. The colour is readily accepted by the gay community, and *The Pink Paper* is a weekly national newspaper for lesbians and gay men founded in 1987. The adoption of this particular colour probably comes from its traditional feminine associations, as distinct from 'masculine' blue. *See also* PINKO; PINK POUND.

**Pink-collar worker.** A US term for a working woman, especially one in a job where women predominate, such as teaching, clerical and retail sales. The expression dates from the 1970s and arose by contrast with the WHITE-COLLAR WORKER, BLUE-COLLAR WORKER and GREY-COLLAR WORKER.

**Pink elephants.** The hallucinatory creatures supposedly seen by those in the throes of delirium tremens. 'Pink spiders' are an earlier variant manifestation. The phrase dates from the 1930s.

**Pinko.** A socialist sympathizer, tending to the red of communism but holding moderate or liberal views that merit a paler tone than the full-blown colour. The colloquialism dates from the 1930s.

> Down here in the West Country they wouldn't understand why … No one but puffy pale pinkos in sight down here, and racism's rampant.
>
> FAY WELDON: *The Heart of the Country* (1987)

**Pink Panther, The.** A film comedy (1963) starring Peter Sellers as the incompetent Inspector CLOUSEAU, a French policeman on the trail of a notorious diamond thief (played by David Niven). The 'Pink Panther' of the title is, in fact, the name of the famous diamond that Niven's character plots to steal, although audiences quickly came to identify the name instead with the pink-hued cartoon panther which appeared in the animated title credits and which quickly became a hugely successful film and television character in his own right. No mention was made of the 'Pink Panther' diamond in the various sequels that followed in the *Pink Panther* series, although most included the words 'Pink Panther' in their titles.

**Pink pound.** A term arising in the 1990s for the combined purchasing power of homosexuals considered as a consumer group. *See* PINK.

The pink pound has never been more fiercely chased. The

spending power and brand loyalty of gay consumers are not to be ignored lightly.

*Independent on Sunday* (6 February 1994)

**Pink slip.** In the United States a notice of dismissal, printed on pink paper. Hence a term for the dismissal itself. In some US states a pink slip is also a learner's permit for driving a car.

**Pin one's ears back.** To listen attentively. The expression dates from the 1940s and in its imperative form is often heard in the light-hearted form 'Pin back your lugholes'. This became a catchphrase of the comic broadcaster Cyril Fletcher (1913–2005) who used it to preface one of his humorous poems or 'Odd Odes'.

**Pin-up.** In the Second World War servicemen used to pin up in their quarters pictures of film stars and actresses (often scantily clad) or their own particular girlfriends. These were called 'pin-up girls'. The most popular pin-up picture among US forces was a photograph of the actress Betty Grable (1916–73) turning towards the camera with a smile and a wink in high heels and a white swimsuit, a pose that earned her $300,000 in one year. The term 'pin-up girl' itself first appeared in the armed forces newspaper *Yank* on 30 April 1943 and was reinforced by the film *Pin-Up Girl* (1944), in which Grable was the central character. The art form was subsequently taken up in such specialized publications as PLAYBOY and the PIRELLI CALENDAR. *See also* PAGE THREE GIRL.

**Pinyin.** A system for transliterating Chinese into Roman characters, introduced in China in 1958 as a teaching aid but not utilized to communicate with foreigners until 1979. Until then, the most widespread romanized system had been the Wade-Giles system, devised by Sir Thomas Wade (1818–95) and modified by Herbert Giles (1845–1935). In the Pinyin system the name of Chairman Mao Tse-tung is rendered Mao Zedong, and that of Premier Chou En-lai as Zhou Enlai. The system is most readily observed in Chinese place-names, so that Canton become Guangzhou, Nanking is Nanjing, Peking is Beijing and Tientsin is Tianjin. The term is Chinese for 'transcription', literally 'spell-sound'.

**Piña colada.** (Spanish, 'strained pineapple'.) A type of long drink popular in the latter half of the 1970s and made with pineapple juice, rum and coconut. Its name is as exotic as its content.

**Pip emma.** Signalese for p.m. (post meridiem) in the First World War. The equivalent for a.m. was ack emma. Emma was replaced by Monkey in 1921. *See also* ACK-ACK; ROGER.

**Pippi Longstocking.** *See* Pippi LONGSTOCKING.

**Pip-pip.** Dated slang for 'goodbye', representing a toot on a motor horn from a departing guest.

**Pips.** The term for the time signal on BBC Radio, consisting of five short pips and one longer one on the hour, the exact hour beginning at the start of the latter. The pips were first broadcast at 9.30 p.m. on 5 February 1924 and until 1990 were officially known as the Greenwich Time Signal. Originally each pip was 0.10 seconds long: the last one was lengthened to 0.5 seconds in 1971. The BBC owns the pips themselves, while the Royal Observatory owns the spaces between them.

**Pipsqueak.** A nickname for an insignificant person, especially when small or young (or both). The term dates from the early 20th century and each half of the word represents its respective sound.

**Pip, Squeak and Wilfrid.** A term for any group of three things or people, such as the three First World War medals 1914–15 Star, War Medal and VICTORY MEDAL. The names are those of three animal characters, a dog, a penguin and a baby rabbit, in a *Daily Mirror* children's comic strip that ran from 1919 to 1953. Wilfrid, the baby, could only say 'Gug' and 'Nunc' (for 'Uncle') and a fan club was formed with members known as 'Gugnuncs'. *See also* PIPSQUEAK; SQUEEZE SOMEONE UNTIL THE PIPS SQUEAK.

**Pirate radio.** A term for the radio stations that in the 1960s began broadcasting without official authorization from offshore sites. Many such stations were located on ships or boats anchored in international waters in the North Sea, an area chosen because the low-lying coast of eastern England offered no hindrance to radio signals. They broadcast pop music, eagerly lapped up by a young audience who were not yet catered for by the BBC. They attracted rewarding advertising until this development was banned by Harold Wilson's Labour government under the Marine Etc Broadcasting (Offences) Act 1967, whereupon many of the ships gave up. The most famous and persistent of these pioneers was RADIO CAROLINE. Pirate radio stations later surfaced on the mainland, such as those run by reggae enthusiasts from council tower blocks in the mid-1980s, but again the government moved in and ordered all pirates to close in 1988. Most obeyed, but a third generation of pirates emerged in the 1990s, transmitting HOUSE and other types of music.

**Pirelli calendar.** A famous annual PIN-UP calendar published by the tyre manufacturers Pirelli from 1964. The original intention was to enhance the mostly sleazy photographs found on greasy garage walls to a proper art form. Professional photographers were employed for the purpose and were so successful that the calendars became better known than the firm itself. Only a limited number were issued to favoured clients each year and as a result became collectors' items.

**Piss and vinegar.** In US slang, someone described as being 'full of piss and vinegar' is full of energy or vigour, especially of an aggressive sort. The phrase dates from the 1920s.

**Piss artist.** Originally, in the 1940s, a regular drunkard, but subsequently used mainly as a term for someone the speaker has profound contempt for.

**Pissholes in the snow.** Someone whose eyes are likened to 'two pissholes in the snow' is in a bad way, quite possibly as a result of excessive alcohol intake. Their eyes are dark-ringed, hollow and bloodshot. The vivid metaphor dates from the 1960s.

**Pissing contest.** A term of US origin for any form of rivalry in which the participants are keener to assert their individual superiority than to achieve the best overall result. The image is of small boys seeing who can 'do it' farthest or highest.

**Piss in someone's pocket.** To ingratiate oneself with someone, to curry favour with them. A slang expression that originated in Australia in the 1940s.

**Piss in** or **into the wind.** To waste one's time in futile effort (much as King Canute tried to defy nature by turning back the waves). The expression dates from the 1960s.

**Piss money against** or **up the wall.** To spend one's money wastefully or with no good result. The original target of the expression was expenditure on alcohol, but it is now used more generally.

**Piss off.** Intransitively, to make a rapid departure. Transitively, something that pisses you off makes you really annoyed. Both slang usages date from at least the 1930s.

**Piss oneself.** To laugh uproariously. A reference to the releasing effect of uncontrollable laughter on the bladder.

**Piss poor.** Extremely poor. Originally, in the 1920s, the slang expression referred literally to lack of funds, but subsequently it has more commonly been used metaphorically to denote abysmally low quality.

**Pistol Pete.** Originally, in US slang, a nickname given to a zealous and effective male lover. It was inherited by the US tennis player Pete Sampras (b.1971), but more as a tribute to the power and accuracy of his serve than to his amatory expertise.

**Pit lizard.** An American colloquialism for a female fan or follower of racing drivers. The term dates from the 1970s and arose on an analogy with the LOUNGE LIZARD, the pit here being the area beside a racetrack where cars are serviced and fuelled and where the drivers are thus obliged to stop and can be fleetingly admired.

> 'Pit lizards', camp followers, or dedicated racing fans, whatever you choose to call them, they are part of the scene and their presence is pleasing to racing men.
> *Atlantic* (June 1973)

**Pits, The.** Anyone or anything that is the worst of its kind or absolutely unbearable. The Americanism was brought before a wide British public by the tennis player John McEnroe (b.1959) in 1981, the year in which he first won the Wimbledon men's singles title, when he characterized a Wimbledon umpire as 'the pits of the world'. The allusion is to something hellish or 'dark and deep' rather than to the armpits, as sometimes explained. *See also* BRAT PACK.

**Pittura colta.** (Italian, 'cultured painting'.) A movement in Italian painting dating from the 1980s, in which artists imitate certain stylistic features of the Old Masters in an ironic manner regarded as characteristic of POSTMODERNISM. A leading exponent is Carlo Maria Mariani (b.1931), while others associated with the genre are Alberto Abate (b.1946), Bruno d'Arcevia (b.1946), Antonella Cappuccio (b.1946) and Vittio Scialoja (b.1942), all of whom paint mythological or pseudo-mythological subjects in a gaudy reworking of the historical conventions. The name of the movement was coined by the Italian critic Italo Mussa for the title of his book *La Pittura colta* (1983).

**Pixilation.** A film-making technique whereby the movements of real people are filmed in such a way that they appear to move like animated characters. The method involves taking the shots one frame at a time with the person moving slightly between each shot. Special effects such as flying can be achieved in this way, and pixilation was used to good effect in *The Secret Adventures of Tom Thumb* (1993), a film that combined animated and human figures. The term itself derives from 'pixilated' in the sense 'crazy', 'confused'.

**Plaid Cymru.** (Welsh, 'Party of Wales'.) The Welsh nationalist party, set up in 1925 by six men in Pwllheli with the object of achieving self-government for Wales. Support grew from the 1960s and the party gained three seats in the House of Commons in 1974, two in 1979 and 1983, three in 1987, four in 1992, 1997 and 2001, but only three in 2005. Plaid Cymru reaped the first fruits of its objectives when a National Assembly for Wales was set up in 1999 following a referendum on DEVOLUTION. *See also* SNP.

**Plamegate.** The scandal surrounding the illegal outing by the US administration of Valerie Plame (b.1963) as a covert CIA agent. The name is modelled on WATERGATE. Plame is the wife of Joseph Wilson, a former US ambassador who in 2003 was critical of the reliability of the intelligence used by the Bush administration to justify its war on Iraq. The administration subsequently leaked the information about Wilson's wife to the press. In 2005, Lewis 'Scooter' Libby, chief of staff to vice-president Dick Cheney, was indicted by a grand jury on charges that he lied to investigators looking into the leak. Investigations are continuing into the role played by other members of the administration.

**Plan B.** An alternative strategy; another option. The expression derives from military jargon. 'Plan A' is usually implicit as the prime intention or scheme, although not always designated as such, even when there is a declared 'Plan B'.

> As the Hour of the Abyss approaches, Tony Blair claims that there is no Plan B for Ulster. As far as he is concerned, it is Plan A or Armageddon.
>
> *The Times* (30 June 1999)

Plan B is also the brand name of a popular US morning-after pill.

**Planets, The.** A much-played orchestral suite by Gustav Holst (1874–1934). The seven movements are: 'Mars, the Bringer of War', 'Venus, the Bringer of Peace', 'Mercury, the Winged Messenger', 'Jupiter, the Bringer of Jollity', 'Saturn, the Bringer of Old Age', 'Uranus, the Magician' and 'Neptune, the Mystic' (which also features a wordless female chorus). Astronomers will note the unastronomical order of the first three and the absence of the earth, PLUTO and SEDNA, of which the last two were unknown at the time of composition (the non-appearance of Pluto was rectified by the composer Colin Matthews, who wrote a new final movement for the piece, 'Pluto – The Renewer', first performed in 2000). The work had its first full public performance in 1920. The theme from 'Jupiter' provided the music for the hymn 'I vow to thee, my country'.

**Planet X.** Originally the provisional name for an as yet undiscovered planet predicted in 1902 by the US astronomer Percival Lowell (1855–1916). He began searching for it in 1905 but it was not discovered until 1930, some years after his death, when it was named PLUTO. In 1972 the name was revived for a supposed tenth planet in the solar system, the 'X' standing for both 'ten' and 'unknown'. Recent candidates have included Quaoar (2002), named after the creation deity of the Native American Tongva people; SEDNA (2004); and 2003UB[313], a large planetlike object discovered in 2003 and made public in 2005. None proved eligible in the 2006 Astronomical Union's (IAU) redefinition of 'planet'.

**Planned obsolescence.** The policy of deliberately giving manufactured goods a short usage life by introducing changes in design, ceasing to supply spare parts, using materials of poor quality or the like, so encouraging consumers to purchase a replacement. The practice dates from at least the early 1960s. The term 'built-in obsolescence' is also sometimes used.

> Our whole economy is based on planned obsolescence.
>
> BROOKS STEVENS: quoted in Vance Packard, *The Waste Makers* (1960)

**Plastic.** A colloquialism for a payment made by plastic card, as distinct from cash, cheque or credit. By the end of the 20th century the proliferation of various types of plastic card such as credit card, bank card, debit card, charge card, store card and the like made it relatively easy for the routine shopper to say 'I prefer to pay with plastic'. *See also* FLEXIBLE FRIEND.

**Plastic bag moment.** A whimsical term for the moment when one suddenly glimpses a touch of beauty in a normally utilitarian object. The reference is to an empty plastic bag such as a dustbin liner lying in the street that suddenly fills and floats up in a gust of wind. The concept may seem pretentious but the experience is not unusual and other examples readily suggest themselves.

**Plasticine.** Commercial production of this modelling material was begun in 1900 by William Harbutt (1844–1921), an art teacher, in an old flour mill at Bathampton, near Bath. Its name indicates its nature as a plastic substitute for modelling clay, intended for creative educational and recreational purposes. At first it was available only in grey, but a three-colour pack of red, blue and yellow Plasticine called 'The Complete Modeller' soon followed.

**Plate glass universities.** The universities of East Anglia, Essex, Kent, Lancaster, Sussex, Warwick and York, built in the 1960s with plate-glass windows, in marked contrast to the earlier REDBRICK universities.

> The collective academic phenomenon now known as the Plateglass universities coincides with a break in the great graduate bull market of the 1950s and 1960s.
>
> *Manchester Guardian Weekly* (22 May 1971)

**Platform shoes.** Shoes with thick raised soles, notably in vogue in the 1970s (although such trends had appeared previously) and favoured by both sexes. The 1970s were the forerunner of the 'clumpy' shoes popular among young women in the 1990s. Entertainers such as Elton John (*see* *under* PSEUDONYMS) took the platform shoe to ludicrous and dangerous heights.

**Platinum blonde.** A woman with silvery-blonde hair. The vogue for hair of this colour was at its height in the 1930s and the English actress Binnie Barnes appeared as a platinum blonde in Noël Coward's musical *Cavalcade* (1931) although her natural hair colour was auburn. The epithet was primarily associated, however, with the US film actress Jean Harlow (1911–37), who was so dubbed by Columbia Pictures for a film originally to have been called *Gallagher* but retitled in her image as *Platinum Blonde* (1931). The result was a craze of 'peroxide blondes' among the public in general that was also taken up by such actresses as Joan Crawford (1908–73) and Alice Faye (1912–98). *See also* PLUTONIUM BLONDE.

**Play ball.** To cooperate; to respect the requirements of another. The phrase implies a mutual understanding: 'You play ball with me and I'll play ball with you.'

**Playboy.** A monthly magazine famous for its 'girly' pictures. It was launched by the US publisher Hugh Hefner (b.1926) in December 1953, the first issue depicting Marilyn MONROE posing nude. The combination of high-quality photographs of nude or semi-nude models, practical advice on sexual problems, men's talk and articles of high literary standard soon made Hefner a millionaire and the magazine itself a conspicuous success. The *Playboy* empire subsequently extended into real estate, clubs with BUNNY GIRL hostesses, and sundry related products. The magazine did much to pioneer the CENTREFOLD, calling its subject 'Playmate of the Month'.

**Playboy of the Western World, The.** A play by the Irish playwright J.M. Synge (1871–1909), which provoked demonstrations when it was first staged at the ABBEY THEATRE, Dublin, in January 1907. It is about the disruption that follows when a feckless young man, Christy Mahon, arrives in a country pub in Mayo in the west of Ireland boasting that he is on the run after killing his own father. Although it is subsequently learned that he has done no such thing, he retains the spurious glamour he has acquired in the eyes of Pegeen Mike, the daughter of the landlord, and after he is driven out of the village she laments:

> Oh, my grief, I've lost him surely. I've lost the only Playboy of the Western World.

**Playboy Prince, The.** A nickname applied both to Edward VIII when Prince of Wales, and to the present Prince Harry (*see* HARRY POTTY), on account of their respective lifestyles.

**Play catch-up.** To attempt to catch up (usually metaphorically), having fallen behind others or suffered a setback. The expression originated in American English in the 1940s.

> Is Windows now playing catchup to Linux?
> www.itworld.com (22 November 2000)

**Playgroup.** A group of pre-school children or RISING FIVES, organized to provide basic care and an opportunity to socialize before compulsory schooling begins. Playgroups are run mainly by volunteers and usually operate in rented accommodation such as the local town hall. The movement grew in the 1960s out of the acute shortage of nursery school places.

**Play hardball.** To be ruthless in the pursuit of one's goal, especially in politics. The allusion is to baseball, alternatively called hardball to be distinguished from softball, a variant form of the game. The US phrase dates from the 1960s.

**Play hard to get.** To appear aloof and dispassionate in order to make oneself more attractive or desirable. The expression, traditionally but by no means exclusively used of women, dates from the 1920s. The conceit is: 'The harder the chase, the greater the catch.'

**Play in Peoria.** To be acceptable to the average consumer. The expression originated in the 1930s among touring theatre companies keen to ensure that their productions would find favour in MIDDLE AMERICA, represented by the town of Peoria, Illinois. 'It'll play in Peoria' subsequently became a catchphrase of the Nixon administration (1969–74).

**Play It Again Sam.** A film comedy (1972), based on a stage play (1969), written by and starring US comedian Woody Allen (b.1935). Allen plays a film critic who receives advice about his love life from the ghost of Humphrey Bogart, complete with trench coat. The title comes from a line in the classic Bogart movie CASABLANCA (1942), although it does not appear exactly in that form in the original film. The closest anyone gets to it is: 'Play it, Sam. Play "As Time Goes By",' as directed to the pianist Sam, played by Dooley Wilson. The song, dating from 1931, was nearly left out of the film at the request of its composer, Max Steiner, who begged Warner Brothers to drop it, fearing it would not work. The lyricist was Herman Hupfeld.

> You must remember this, a kiss is just a kiss,
> A sigh is just a sigh;
> The fundamental things apply,
> As time goes by.

**Play one's cards close to one's chest.** To be secretive or cautious about one's intentions. The metaphor derives from card-playing, in which a player may hold his cards close to his chest so that others cannot see his hand. The phrase dates from the 1950s.

**Play one's cards right.** To make the best use of one's assets or knowledge. The metaphor is obviously from card games. An earlier form of the expression was 'to play one's cards well'.

**PlayStation.** A brand of home video gaming technology involving a console, which swept the world from its launch by SONY in 1994, and for which thousands of software options on CD and DVD were subsequently developed. Its success, and the degree to which the (mostly young) 'PlayStation generation' become absorbed into its games, was blamed in some quarters for the decline in family life, dinnertime conversation, etc., in the manner that once television programmes used to be pilloried.

> Mr Dyke said he was keen to fire the popular imagination and bring learning to all rather than just an intellectual and cultural elite and said he wanted to 'rise to the challenge of the Playstation generation'.
>
> www.bbc.co.uk/news/, 'Blunkett welcomes Dyke's education commitment' (19 November 1999)

Eager to get a slice of the lucrative action, Microsoft came up with its own version, the Xbox, in 2001.
*See also* GAME BOY; SEGA.

**Play the field.** To indulge in a number of sexual relationships without committing oneself to any single one of them. The expression dates from the 1930s and takes its image from horse racing, where it means to bet on all the horses with the exception of the favourite.

**Plc.** The abbreviation of 'public limited company', replacing 'Ltd' ('Limited') as the official designation of a British limited-liability company under the terms of the 1980 Companies Act. All British companies are registered with the Registrar of Companies and most corporate businesses are 'limited liability' companies, meaning that their liability is restricted to contributing an amount related to their shareholding. Companies may be public or private. Before a company becomes a plc it must be limited by shares and have a share capital, state in its memorandum of association that it is to be a plc, meet specified minimum capital requirements, and add 'plc' to its name. All other British companies are private companies which are generally prohibited from offering their shares to the public. *See also* BRITAIN PLC.

**Please, Sir!** One of the top television SITCOMS of its day (1968–71), centring on the experiences of a newly qualified

teacher at a tough south London secondary modern school. His lofty idealism is predictably blunted, not least by the ineducable Class 5C, whose form teacher he is. The hapless hero, Bernard Hedges, nicknamed 'Privet' by his pupils, was played by John Alderton.

**Pleidiol wyf I'm gwlad.** (Welsh, 'loyal am I to my country'.) These words from the Welsh national anthem *Hen Wlad Fy Nhadau* ('Land of my Fathers') have appeared on the milled edge of the Welsh one-pound coin since 1985. 'Land of my Fathers' was written by Evan James, a weaver from Mid Glamorgan, in 1856, and the song was adopted as the Welsh national anthem in the late 19th century.

**Plinge, Walter.** A fictitious name used on English playbills for an actor who is 'doubling' or playing two parts. There are two stories to account for the name. The first derives it from the landlord of a public house near the stage door of the Lyceum Theatre, London, in c.1900. The second takes it from a phrase 'Mr Plinge is waiting', used by an actor for a supposedly convivial acquaintance who has invited him out for a drink. The first to use the name on a playbill may have been the actor and producer Oscar Asche (1871–1936), who took over the management of His Majesty's Theatre in 1907. The American equivalent of Walter Plinge is George Spelvin, a name first found in New York in 1886 in the cast list of Charles A. Gardiner's *Karl the Peddler*.

**PLO.** The Palestine Liberation Organization, formed in 1964 from AL FATAH to unite various Palestinian Arab groups and ultimately bring about an independent state of Palestine. Yasser Arafat (1929–2004) became its leader in 1969. In the early 1970s it made its base in Lebanon but when PLO forces were expelled from that country in 1982 it set up its headquarters in Tunisia. Frustration at Israel's continued occupation of its claimed territory led to the start of the INTIFADA in 1987 but since then it has recognized Israel's rights to exist in secure borders. Israel, for its part, has in turn recognized the PLO as the legitimate representative of the Palestinian people. An accord with Israel in 1994 enabled the GAZA STRIP to become self-governing and a similar agreement in 1995 gained autonomy for the WEST BANK. Arafat was succeeded as chairman by Abu Mazen (Mahmoud Abbas; b.1935). In 2005, Israel pulled out of the Gaza Strip, passing it over to Palestinian control. Israeli settlers were forced to move out. Some Israeli settlements in the West Bank were also evacuated. *See also* BEIRUT.

**Plonk.** A term of Australian origin for any cheap or unsophisticated wine, especially red. Despite this, the derivation of the word is probably from French *vin blanc*, 'white wine'. In Australian English it also denotes cheap red wine fortified by methylated spirit.

**Plotlands.** A name given in the 1920s to the settlements that sprang up along the south and southeast coasts of England after the First World War. Houses in such places were at first little more than shacks or shanties, in some cases built out of old buses or railway carriages or based on deserted army camps, while the plots of land themselves could be obtained at little cost or even free if occupied by squatters. Despite the initial primitive conditions, as well as tussles with the local authorities, the settlers themselves were delighted with their enterprise, which offered them fresh air, a sea view, tranquillity and a sense of freedom. They were criticized in many quarters for their desecration of the countryside, much as the NEW AGE travellers have been in more recent times. But while some of the settlements have remained rudimentary, others, such as PEACEHAVEN, have grown into respectable, thriving townships.

**Plough and the Stars, The.** A play (1926) by the Irish playwright Sean O'Casey (1880–1964), first produced at the ABBEY THEATRE, Dublin, when its depiction of the sufferings of Dublin slum-dwellers during the EASTER RISING of 1916 caused a riot. The title refers to the designs on the flag of the Irish Citizen Army, the working-class organization behind the Rising, but was also intended by the author to suggest the contrast between the real and the ideal in life.

**Ploughman's lunch.** A meal of bread and cheese, typically served with pickle and salad and consumed in or outside a pub as a bar snack. The name arose as a marketing ploy of the English Country Cheese Council in the early 1960s. The lauded film *The Ploughman's Lunch* (1983) tells of the deepening cynicism experienced by members of the media as a result of the FALKLANDS WAR.

**Plowden Report.** The report *Children and the Primary Schools* (1967) by Lady Bridget Plowden (1907–2000) marked a watershed in the development of English primary education. It considered such education in all its aspects, including the transition to secondary schools, and recommended that schools, local education authorities and the Department of Education should encourage parents to become more actively involved in their children's education and that increased resources be made available for nursery education and 'educational priority areas', or areas starved of new investment. Child-centred approaches should be taken to their logical limits and the teaching-learning process should be completely individualized. *See also* NEWSOM REPORT.

**Plum.** An inevitable nickname for a person whose first name is Pelham, as the cricketer Pelham Francis Warner (1873–

1963) or the novelist P.G. (Pelham Grenville) Wodehouse (1881–1975), creator of JEEVES and Bertie WOOSTER.

**Plunging neckline.** A very deep-cut neckline on a woman's garment, so called as it 'dives' into the cleavage. The term is first recorded in the 1940s but the style itself dates from much earlier, and the craze for plunging necklines in 1910 caused concern that the female population could be decimated as a result of pneumonia.

**Plus fours.** Loose knickerbockers overlapping the knee and thereby giving added freedom for active outdoor sports. They were particularly popular with golfers in the 1920s. The name derives from the four extra inches (about 10cm) of cloth required below the knee in tailoring. Plus twos also exist as a shorter variant, and are favoured by some current golfers. *See also* MAN IN BLACK.

**PLUTO.** Pipe Line Under the Ocean, a project essential to the Normandy invasion in the Second World War. In its original version pipelines from out at sea ran to the beachheads, so enabling ships to deliver fuel without docking. Later undersea pipelines were laid to carry petrol the full distance from Dungeness to Boulogne and from the Isle of Wight to Cherbourg. The acronym has an appropriate reference to Pluto, the Greek god of the underworld, whose name means 'wealth'. *See also* D-DAY; OVERLORD.

**Pluto.** A dwarf planet in the solar system, discovered only in 1930 by the US astronomer Clyde W. Tombaugh during a systematic search for a planet beyond Neptune, itself discovered in 1846. Tombaugh recognized the new planet in a series of photographs he had taken at the Lowell Observatory at Flagstaff, Arizona. Continuing the tradition of naming planets after Roman gods, Vesto M. Slipher, the director of the observatory, chose the name Pluto, god of the regions of darkness. The name also embodies the initials of Tombaugh's fellow astronomer, Percival Lowell, who had long sought his PLANET X, and Pluto's planetary symbol is a superimposed 'P' and 'L'.

After its discovery, Pluto was classified as the ninth full planet (and the furthest from the sun), but at the beginning of the 21st century its status was seriously reviewed. After much wrangling in scientific circles, Pluto was demoted to a dwarf planet in August 2006.

Gustav Holst's popular orchestral suite *The Planets* (1920) was composed before the discovery of Pluto, and naturally contains no portrayal of it (*see under* PLANETS). The gap was filled by the composer Colin Matthews, who wrote a new final movement for the piece, 'Pluto – The Renewer', first performed in 2000.

**Plutonium Blonde.** A nickname given to Margaret Thatcher (the IRON LADY) by Arthur Scargill (KING ARTHUR), the left-wing leader of the bitter 1984–5 miners' strike. Thatcher successfully crushed the strike, and subsequently closed down most of Britain's pits. The nickname, a play on PLATINUM BLONDE, refers both to Thatcher's liking for nuclear energy in preference to coal and to her partiality for nuclear weapons.

**Podcast.** A digital audio or video file that can be downloaded onto a computer or a digital music player such as an IPOD (or MP3 player) – whence the term. The most popular 'podcasts' are of talk-based radio programmes, but they are now working their way into many spheres of activity, such as E-LEARNING. The term was supposedly coined in 2004 by the writer Ben Hammersly.

**Poet's day.** The weary worker's acronymic name for Friday: 'Push off early, tomorrow's Saturday.'

**Po-faced.** Solemn and humourless; serious where one might have expected a show of amusement. The term probably derives from 'poker-faced', referring to the expressionless face of a poker player, but with a suggestion of 'po', a chamber pot.

**Pogo stick.** A toy for jumping about on, consisting of a long, spring-loaded pole with a handle at the top and a rest at the bottom for the feet. The name may be a blend of 'pole' and 'go'. The device itself is first recorded in 1919.

**Point Counter Point.** A satirical novel (1928) by Aldous Huxley (1894–1963), often epigrammatic in style and cynical in tone, portraying 'modern' London life in the 1920s. It is also a roman à clef, featuring a large number of mostly unsympathetic characters drawn from the British upper classes and intelligentsia: there are thinly disguised portraits of, among others, D.H. and Frieda Lawrence, Augustus John, Sir Oswald Mosley, John Middleton Murry, Katherine Mansfield and Huxley himself. The title's reference to musical counterpoint (in which two or more melodic lines occur simultaneously, complementing one another) is reflected in some of the structural features of the novel, for example, the relationships between and among the various couples, and the fact that the novel planned by the Huxley character, Philip Quarles, parallels the real life going on around him; indeed, the overall structure of the book is said to be based on J.S. Bach's Suite No. 2 in B minor.

**Point of no return.** The point in an aircraft's flight at which it has not enough fuel to return to its point of departure and must continue. Hence the figurative application of the expression to a point or situation from which there is no going back. The phrase originated among pilots in the Second World War.

**Points.** A term from the Second World War relating to the system of rationing food, clothing and other commodities. Apart from direct rationing of meat, bacon, sugar, fats and tea, miscellaneous groceries were given 'points' values and each ration-book holder was given a certain number of points to spend in an allotted period. Hence 'it's on points' was a common reference to many commodities.

**Point someone in the direction of something.** To show them where it is. An expression apparently arising as a facetious military or civil service circumlocution.

**Points system.** A system used by a local authority for granting a council house to a tenant. Points are awarded according to the person's status, depending on such factors as length of residence in the area, number of children in the family and so on.

**Pointy head.** A nickname for an intellectual, on an analogy with an EGGHEAD. The term 'pointy-headed' is said to have been coined in 1968 by the anti-integrationist US politician George C. Wallace (1919–98), following his first term of four as governor of Alabama.

**Poirot, Hercule.** The small and unassuming Belgian detective, with his waxed moustache and comically fastidious manner, was the creation of Agatha Christie (1890–1976) and appeared in her first detective novel, *The Mysterious Affair at Styles* (1920). He went on to play a key role in some 40 further novels, including the famous MURDER ON THE ORIENT EXPRESS (1934). He has since appeared in the cinema and on television in a number of popular adaptations of the stories, being played by such disparate actors as Austin Trevor, Albert Finney, Peter Ustinov, Ian Holm and David Suchet. *See also* DEATH ON THE NILE.

> 'This affair must all be unravelled from within.' He tapped his forehead. 'These little grey cells. It is "up to them" – as you say over here.'
>
> AGATHA CHRISTIE: *The Mysterious Affair at Styles*, ch. 10 (1920)

**Poison pen letter.** An anonymous letter that is abusive, libellous or malicious. The suggestion is that the pen to write the letter has been dipped in poisonous ink, and will wound or kill the recipient in the manner of a poison-tipped arrow. The expression dates from the early 20th century. *See also* HATE MAIL.

**Poison pill.** A pill containing a fast-acting poison such as cyanide, a traditional resort by captives in some countries as a means of suicide when defeat in combat is inevitable. In financial jargon a poison pill is a ploy used by a company to deter a bidder when faced with an unwelcome takeover bid. The term is said to have been first used in the latter sense by a US lawyer in 1982.

**Pokémon.** These toy monsters so named (Pokémon functions as both singular and plural) were launched worldwide by the Japanese in 1999 as the annual children's Christmas fetish. The object is to collect every one of nearly 400 named models to become 'Pokémon Master'. Pokémon is also a multimedia toy and exists as a card game (collecting and swapping soon became a craze), a television series, and a video game. In this last, played on a GAME BOY or the equivalent, the player takes the role of Ash, a Pokémon trainer. With the aid of Pikachu, a helpful Pokémon, Ash moves around Pokémon Island fighting other Pokémon, disabling them with his trusty ball so that they lose their energy. When a Pokémon is captured, its powers can be used to fight other Pokémon, although some Pokémon turn into others when captured. The name itself, pronounced 'po-kay-moan', is pidgin Japanese, derived from '*Pocket Mon*ster'.

**POLAND.** *See* LOVERS' ACRONYMS.

**Polaris.** A type of US nuclear-armed SLBM (submarine-launched ballistic missile) with a range of 4800km (3000 miles) that entered service with the US Navy in 1960. By the 1962 Nassau Agreement the United States agreed to supply Britain with the missiles. (This led President de Gaulle of France to veto Britain's application to join the COMMON MARKET in 1963, on the grounds that the UK was not sufficiently oriented towards Europe.) In the United States Polaris was replaced by Poseidon missiles in 1969, which in turn were replaced by TRIDENT missiles in the 1980s. In the UK Polaris was replaced by Trident in the 1990s. Polaris is the astronomers' name for the North or Pole Star.

**Polaroid.** *See* LAND CAMERA.

**Poldark.** *See* ROSS POLDARK.

**Polecat, semi-housetrained.** *See* SEMI-HOUSETRAINED POLECAT.

**Pole dancing.** A form of dancing, often erotic and involving striptease, in which mostly young women (though sometimes older women, and sometimes men) perform gymnastic routines up, down and around a vertical pole. Pole dancing is performed in such venues as nightclubs and strip joints, although the World Pole Sport Federation has attempted to desexualize the activity by putting on competitions involving fully clothed participants. In 2005 the RAF, as part of its retraining programme for former

service personnel, gave Senior Aircraftwoman Stephanie Hulme a grant to go on a pole-dancing course. *See also* LAP DANCER.

**Pole position.** In motor racing the starting position in the front row and on the inside of the first bend, usually regarded as the best and most advantageous. The reference is to the pole as the term for the inside fence on a racecourse and also the starting position closest to it. A horse was said to 'have the pole' if the jockey had drawn this position. Hence 'to be in pole position', meaning to have the advantage generally.

> Ipswich relinquished their hold on the pole position to champions Liverpool.
> *News of the World* (17 April 1977)

**Poles apart.** In complete opposition; having nothing in common. The poles here are the earth's geographical extremities, the North and South poles. The expression dates from the early 20th century.

**Policy wonk.** Someone who takes an excessive interest in the minor details of political policy. The expression dates from the 1980s, using 'wonk' as an existing derogatory term for a studious person or NERD.

**Polish Corridor.** The territory returned to Poland by the TREATY OF VERSAILLES (1919) to give the re-formed country access to the Baltic Sea west of Danzig (Gdansk). It had been Polish territory for most of the 10th–18th centuries, before its annexation by Prussia. It followed roughly the line of the River Vistula. The Corridor, with its high preponderance of German-speakers, cut off East Prussia from the rest of Germany and proved to be a bone of contention from the outset, and one exploited by NAZI warmongers.

**Polish the apple.** To curry favour; to seek to flatter. The allusion is to the bright and shiny apple that a schoolchild traditionally gives a teacher in the hope of winning approval.

**Politburo.** Formerly, the chief policy-making body of the Communist Party in the USSR, set up by LENIN in 1917 to direct the revolution. It examined matters before they were submitted to the government and consisted of five members. It was superseded by the PRESIDIUM of the Central Committee of the Communist Party in 1952. The word is a typical Soviet abbreviation, here for *Politicheskoye byuro*, 'political bureau'.

**Political correctness.** A philosophy of the 1990s, of US origin, that promoted the avoidance of expressions or actions that could be understood to denigrate groups or minorities traditionally regarded as disadvantaged in some way, as by race, gender, class, disability, religious or political leanings, or sexual orientation. Propagandists of this new morality recommended particular expressions that can and should be substituted for the traditional ones, such as 'the common citizen' for 'the common man' and 'childcare worker' for 'nursemaid'.

Dictionaries of such terms have been published, such as Henry Beard and Christopher Cerf's *The Official Politically Correct Dictionary and Handbook* (1992). Such revisionism extended even to the rewriting of established religious texts, such as the Bible, one version of which, published in 1994, not only avoided most 'gender-specific' words but substituted 'God's mighty hand' for 'God's right hand' for fear of offending the left-handed.

According to Nigel Rees's *The Politically Correct Phrasebook* (1993), the following '-isms' are politically *in*correct:

ableism: discrimination in favour of able-bodied people

ageism: discrimination on grounds of age, especially against the middle-aged and elderly

alphabetism: discrimination according to the alphabetical position of a person's surname

animalism: discrimination against animals on the grounds that they are inferior to humans

classism: discrimination on grounds of social status

disableism: discrimination against the disabled

diseaseism: discrimination against the sick

fattism: discrimination against fat or overweight people

hairism: discrimination on the grounds of hair colour or length

handism: discrimination against the left-handed

heightism: discrimination against tall women or short men

heterosexism: discrimination against homosexuals

lookism: discrimination on the grounds of (supposed) unpleasant looks

racism: discrimination on grounds of race

sexism: discrimination against a person's sex (usually male against female)

sightism: discrimination against the blind

sizeism: discrimination on the grounds of size, i.e. weight and/or height

smellism: discrimination on the grounds of body odour

smokeism: discrimination against smokers (by non-smokers)

uglyism: discrimination on the grounds of (supposed) unfavourable appearance

weightism: discrimination on the grounds of (excessive) weight

**Political power grows out of the barrel of a gun.** A slogan coined by the Chinese communist leader Mao Zedong in a

speech given on 6 November 1938. It was taken up by many New Left revolutionaries in the 1960s.

**Politics of Ovaltine and brandy, The.** A phrase coined by Andrew Marr, chief political editor of the BBC from 2000 to 2005, on 10 March 2005 to refer to an attempt to push legislation through the House of Lords after many of their lordships have retired for the night. On this particular occasion the legislation was the government's controversial Terrorism Bill, which allows for house arrest of suspects without charge or trial. However, the gerontocrats managed to stay awake long enough to throw out the bill. *See also* OVALTINE.

**Pollyanna.** The cheerfully optimistic young heroine of the novel named after her (1913) by Eleanor H. Porter (1868–1920). Her full name is Pollyanna Whittier, and she is known as the 'glad girl' for her determination to remain cheerful whatever happens. She is orphaned at the age of 11, and sent to live with a grim spinster aunt, but melts the hearts of everyone she meets, however sour and dour. Her name has entered the language to describe anyone who is unduly optimistic or who is able to remain happy through self-delusion.

> I feel like an embarrassingly unfashionable Pollyanna when I admit that our family grinned our way through Central London and then had a wholly wonderful time.
>
> LIBBY PURVES: in *The Times* (4 January 2000)

**Polytechnics.** The former institutions of higher education originated from the Polytechnic Institution founded in London in 1838 for the exhibition of objects connected with the industrial arts, the name itself deriving from the Greek for 'many arts'. In 1989 the British 'polys' gained autonomy from local education authorities and in 1992 were able to call themselves universities. This led to a number of name changes, especially where there was an existing university, as at Birmingham, Leicester, Liverpool, Nottingham, Oxford and Sheffield. Some of the new names are noted below, the earlier name given in brackets.

De Montfort University (Leicester Polytechnic)

Liverpool John Moores University (Liverpool Polytechnic)

Nottingham Trent University (Nottingham Polytechnic)

Oxford Brookes University (Oxford Polytechnic)

Sheffield Hallam University (Sheffield Polytechnic)

Thames Valley University (Polytechnic of West London)

University of Central England in Birmingham (Birmingham Polytechnic)

University of Glamorgan (Polytechnic of Wales)

University of Greenwich (Thames Polytechnic)

University of Hertfordshire (Hatfield Polytechnic)

University of Northumbria at Newcastle (Newcastle Polytechnic)

University of Plymouth (Polytechnic South West, earlier Plymouth Polytechnic)

University of the West of England, Bristol (Bristol Polytechnic)

University of Westminster (Polytechnic of Central London)

**Pommy** or **Pommie.** An Australian and New Zealand term for an Englishman, used both affectionately and disparagingly. The name is of uncertain origin. Evidence suggests that it arose as a blend of 'pomegranate' and 'immigrant', the former word referring to the ruddy complexions of the English. Other notably less convincing explanations are that it was formed from the initials POME, 'prisoner of Mother England', or POM, 'prisoner of Millbank', alluding to the transportation of English convicts to Australia (Millbank was a penitentiary in London through which such convicts were processed), or that it came from 'pom-me-soul', a dig at the "Pon my soul' that was presumably constantly on the lips of English toffs in 19th-century Australia. Expansions of the name are 'Pommy Bastard' and 'Whingeing Pom', the latter with reference to the supposed British national pastime of 'grousing'. The name first gained currency in the First World War.

**Pomp and Circumstance.** The collective title given by Edward Elgar (1857–1934) to five marches for orchestra, first performed separately between 1901 and 1930. The title comes from Shakespeare's *Othello* III.iii:

> Farewell the neighing steed and the shrill trump,
> The spirit-stirring drum, the ear-piercing fife,
> The royal banner, and all quality,
> Pride, pomp, and circumstance of glorious war!

With slight alterations, the trio section of the first march became the finale of Elgar's *Coronation Ode* (1902), with words by A.C. Benson beginning 'LAND OF HOPE AND GLORY'. This was later published as a separate song under that title. The song is traditionally performed with audience participation at the LAST NIGHT OF THE PROMS and has also become associated with right-wing English nationalism.

**Pontin's.** The main rival to BUTLIN'S in the holiday camp business takes its name from its founder, Fred Pontin, who opened his first centre in 1946 on a former army training site at Brean Sands near Weston-super-Mare, Somerset. The staff are known as Bluecoats, as distinct from the Butlin's REDCOATS.

**Pont Street Dutch.** A term coined by the cartoonist and architectural writer Osbert Lancaster (1908–86) for a 19th-century architectural style typified by the large gabled redbrick mansions that line Pont Street and nearby streets in Knightsbridge, London.

**Pony car.** An American term dating from the 1970s for a medium-sized car. The name originally applied specifically to certain small and sporty cars that were modelled on the Ford Mustang, the latter word of which suggested 'pony'.

**Ponzi scheme.** A type of investment fraud in which initial investors are paid off with funds taken from subsequent investors attracted by the prospect of sizeable profits. The term arose in the 1970s and takes its name from the US swindler Charles Ponzi, who devised such a scheme in 1919 and within six months had defrauded investors of more than $10 million.

**Poo.** Children's slang for excrement, dating from the 1950s and deriving from the involuntary exclamation on reacting to an unpleasant smell. From the 1980s 'poo' was also US student slang for champagne. Here the origin is in a shortening of 'shampoo', as an extension of 'sham', itself a 19th-century abbreviation of the name.

> Yes, I admit it, me, the ultimate party girl, was never a big fan of 'poo'. Indeed, in my experience, it always gave me the most frightful headache.
>
> TARA PALMER-TOMKINSON: in *Sunday Times* (2 January 2000)

**Poodle-faker.** A term current at the turn of the 20th century for a man who cultivates female society, especially for purposes of personal advancement. The image is of one who poses like a poodle, a fashionable pet. The expression originated as army slang.

**Poohsticks.** A game originating from A.A. Milne's stories about WINNIE-THE-POOH. Players simultaneously drop sticks into the upstream side of a bridge over a stream or river. The winner is the player whose stick emerges first on the downstream side. Pooh originally played the game alone with two fir cones, one large and one small, but later switched to sticks because they were easier to mark. The sport has gained something of a cult status, especially among college students, and 'virtual' Poohsticks can be played on the INTERNET.

**Poontang.** Sexual activity, or a woman or women regarded solely in terms of this. The Americanism dates from the 1920s and is a corruption of French *putain*, 'prostitute'. The French word itself is ultimately related to English 'putrid'.

**Pooper scooper.** An implement for clearing up dog excrement, as a 'scoop' for its 'poop'. The expression is of US origin and dates from the 1970s.

**Poor but honest.** Penniless but principled; modest but moral. The words are familiar from the song 'She Was Poor

But She Was Honest' popular among troops in the First World War. Its provenance and date are uncertain and its verses variable, but one version of the chorus is given below. The phrase itself is found much earlier, and in Shakespeare's *All's Well That Ends Well* (1602) Helena says, 'My friends were poor, but honest; so's my love' (I, iii).

> It's the same the whole world over,
> It's the poor wot gets the blame,
> It's the rich wot gets the pleasure,
> Ain't it all a bloomin' shame?

**Poor little rich girl.** A wealthy young woman whose fortune brings her no contentment. The phrase was famously applied by the press to the heiress Barbara Hutton (1912–79), whose life was a series of misfortunes after she inherited $50 million at the age of 21. It was already familiar, however, as the title of a film of 1917 starring Mary Pickford, and later brought before the public again by a film of 1936, starring Shirley Temple. Noël Coward also popularized the term:

> Poor little rich girl,
> You're a bewitched girl,
> Better beware!
> Laughing at danger,
> Virtue a stranger,
> Better take care!
>
> NOËL COWARD: *On With the Dance*, 'Poor Little Rich Girl' (1925)

**Pootie-Poot.** US President George W. Bush's affectionate nickname for his 'soul mate', Vladimir Putin (b.1952), president of the Russian Federation since 1999.

**Pop art.** A movement in painting and sculpture which began independently in Britain and the United States in the 1950s. It was largely a reaction against the self-centred seriousness of 'high art' and the remoteness of abstract art. The images were gaudy and vulgar, owing much to contemporary advertising and commercial packaging. 'Pop' refers as much to an explosiveness as to 'popular', and the first recorded use of the word in art is in a collage by Eduardo Paolozzi (1924–2005) entitled *I Was a Rich Man's Plaything* (1947) which shows a gun firing 'POP!' at the sexy plaything in question. Other leading exponents are Peter Blake (b.1932), David Hockney (b.1937), Richard Hamilton (b.1922), Jasper Johns (b.1930), Robert Rauschenberg (b.1925), Roy Lichtenstein (1923–97) and Andy Warhol (1928–87). *See also* OP ART.

**Popcorn movie.** An undemanding film watched purely for amusement or diversion by a popcorn-eating audience, this confection being as transitorily satisfying or nutritious as the entertainment itself. The attribute can be attached to other media areas, such as 'popcorn television', 'popcorn press' or 'popcorn music'. The word itself has appropriate overtones of 'pop' or 'popular'.

> Summer is more traditionally the 'idiot zone' in American cinemas when all the big popcorn movies clog up thousands of air-conditioned theatres.
>
> *heat* (14–20 October 1999)

**Popemobile.** The special vehicle used by the pope on official visits. The word is modelled on the 'Batmobile', BATMAN's vehicle of choice, a sleek, black, rocket-powered monster. The first Popemobile was a white Toyota off-roader (*see* OFF-ROADING), introduced by Pope Paul VI in 1976. Pope John Paul II acquired a customized Mercedes 500 in 1997, and in 1999 used an open-top Cadillac DeVille while visiting St Louis in the United States, which had escalator-type steps at the back, an elevated platform to raise the pontiff while waving to the crowds, and a revolving white leather papal throne. Later the same year the increasingly frail John Paul added a 'Pope-Kart' in the form of an adapted golf buggy to his range of Popemobiles for use both inside and outside the Vatican. When John Paul II was succeeded in 2005 by Benedict XVI (GOD'S ROTTWEILER), it was suggested that he would be using his own fleet of papal Fiats.

**Popeye.** The muscle-bound sailor man came into the cartoon world in 1919 when the American comic strip artist Elzie C. Segar created him for his classic *Thimble Theatre* strip. He was at first known as Ham Gravy, but was renamed with his familiar sobriquet in 1929. He gains his muscular might from the can of spinach that he carries with him. His girlfriend is the stick-like Olive Oyl. Popeye's first appearance in a film was in the Betty BOOP cartoon, *Popeye the Sailor* (1933). He has a unique, strangulated delivery, with catch lines such as 'Blow me down' or 'I eats my spinach', and his jaws are constantly clamped jauntily on his pipe, even when eating or speaking.

**Pop group names.** *See* ROCK GROUP NAMES.

**Pop Idol.** A British television show – a cross between REALITY TV, a talent contest, and an extended KARAOKE session – to find the best new singer, in which contestants performed the songs of various musical stars in the manner of those stars. Devised by Simon Fuller, manager of the SPICE GIRLS, it ran for only two years (2002 and 2003) in Britain, but became possibly Britain's most lucrative cultural export with spin-off shows in about 30 countries. In 2006 *American Idol* viewers cast nearly 64 million votes in the final, more than the 62 million votes received by President Bush in the 2004 election.

**Popmobility.** One of many keep-fit fads of the late 20th

century, in this case fashionable in the late 1970s and consisting of the performance of movements to pop music.

**Pop one's clogs.** To die. The incongruous euphemism is particularly favoured in the media and is typically used in light-hearted fashion by television presenters and disc jockeys. The image seems to be that of 'popping' (pawning) a person's clogs after their death. The expression itself is first recorded in the 1970s but probably dates from some time before this.

**Popos.** An acronym used by officials in the UK to denote 'prolific and persistent offenders'. In 2005 Stephen Shaw, the prisons and probation ombudsman, requested, via the columns of *Prison Service News*, that the word no longer be used, as in Turkish it can be interpreted as meaning 'babies' bottoms'.

**Poppins, Mary.** The children's nanny who possesses magical powers in the stories by P.L. Travers (1899–1996), beginning with the one named after her (1934). She can not only slide *up* the banisters but walk into a picture, understand what dogs are saying and travel round the world in seconds. She was played by Julie Andrews in the film of 1964, also named after her. *See also* SUPERCALIFRAGILISTICEXPIALIDOCIOUS.

**Poppy Day.** After the First World War the Allies adopted the poppy as a symbol of sacrifice, both from its blood red colour and from its prominence on the fields of Flanders where many soldiers lost their lives. Poppy Day for this reason became a popular name for REMEMBRANCE DAY, when artificial poppies are worn. *See also* ARMISTICE DAY; BRITISH LEGION.

**Popski's Private Army.** A British raiding and reconnaissance force of about 120 men formed in October 1942 under Lieutenant Colonel Vladimir Peniakoff (1897–1951), who had previously worked with the Libyan Arab Force. He was familiarly known as 'Popski', and his men wore the initials PPA on their shoulders. He was born in Belgium of Russian parents, educated at Cambridge and resident in Egypt from 1924. Popski and a small element of his force, together with the Long Range Desert Group, reconnoitred the route by which Montgomery conducted his surprise attack around the Mareth Line, and subsequently operated in Italy and Austria.

**Popsocks.** Women's short stockings reaching up to the knee, fashionable in the 1990s and popularized by the actress Alicia Silverstone, who wore them in the film *Clueless* (1995). They are usually worn under trousers and are so called as they are easy to pop on and off, unlike full-length stockings.

**Popular Front.** A political alliance of left-wing parties (communists, socialists, liberals, radicals and so on) against reactionary government, especially dictatorship. The idea of an anti-Fascist Popular Front was proposed by the Communist International in 1935 (*see* COMINTERN). Such a government was set up in Spain in 1936, but the Civil War (1936–9) soon followed. The French Popular Front government, set up by Léon Blum in 1936, ended in 1938.

**Porgy and Bess.** The pioneering work by George Gershwin (1898–1937) was the first opera written for an all-African American cast. The libretto was by Du Bose Heyward and Ira Gershwin, and the numbers include the immortal 'Summertime'. The disabled Porgy competes with Crown for the favours of Bess, who, however, goes off to New York with Sportin' Life. Porgy kills Crown and pursues Bess. The work was first performed in 1935, and in 1955 it became the first US opera to be staged at La Scala, Milan. It has also been staged in Russia in 1955 and at Glyndebourne, Sussex, in 1988. It was filmed in 1959. Gershwin's will requires that all stage performances be given with an all-African American cast.

**Porkies.** Lies, as rhyming slang from 'pork pies'. The London working-class expression suddenly became popular from the 1970s, when policemen in television programmes always seemed to be questioning suspects with lines such as, 'You wouldn't be telling me porkies, would you, son?'

> It's a pity, really, Lord Archer didn't go into show-business. He would have made a good luvvie and no one would have minded that he tells porkies.
>
> *The Times* (4 December 1999)

**Porridge.** A colloquial term for imprisonment, punning on earlier 'stir' as a slang word of Romany origin for prison while also referring to a supposedly typical prison break-fast. The expression, dating from the 1940s, was brought before a wider public as the title of a television SITCOM series of 1973–7 starring Ronnie Barker as the wily old London lag Norman Stanley Fletcher.

**Portage scheme.** A scheme designed to help children of pre-school age with learning or developmental difficulties. It involves parents and teachers working together to support the child in the home and takes its name from Portage, Wisconsin, where it originally evolved in 1978.

**Porter, Jimmy.** The voluble and vituperative university-educated anti-hero of John Osborne's groundbreaking play LOOK BACK IN ANGER (1956), who rails against his parents, his wife, his world. He and his creator were both described as ANGRY YOUNG MEN, thus lending the name to the dis-affected of the era.

**Porterhouse Blue.** A satirical novel (1974) by Tom Sharpe (b.1928), set in the imaginary Cambridge college of Porterhouse, based (if only in name) on Peterhouse. The main plot concerns the political infighting between rival factions of academics over proposed changes to the running of the college, culminating in a furore over the succession to the position of head of the college. The irascible college porter, Skullion, stops at nothing to preserve tradition but is dismissed after 45 years' loyal service. Another strand of the plot charts the grotesque sexual efforts of Zipser, a frustrated postgraduate, which culminate in his seduction by his bedder and their subsequent incineration in an explosion caused by gas-filled condoms becoming stuck in a college chimney. The novel generally is a satire on Oxbridge rituals, with its paraphernalia of dons, porters, bedders (gyps), high-table dining and the like. A 'Porterhouse blue' is a cerebral stroke, such as is suffered by one of the principal characters at a critical moment, leading to a bizarre denouement. A television version (1987) by Malcolm Bradbury featured David Jason, who played Skullion to the hilt. *See also* BLOT ON THE LANDSCAPE.

**Portillistas.** A nickname given to supporters of the Conservative politician Michael Portillo (b.1953), modelled on Spanish terms such as Peronistas, supporters of Juan Perón, populist president of Argentina (1946–55, 1973–4), and SANDINISTAS, the left-wing guerrillas who took power in Nicaragua in 1979. Portillo's father was Spanish and fought on the Republican side in the Spanish Civil War. In contrast, Portillo (apparently known as Miguelito to his more intimate friends) is on the right of his party and was regarded as a dangerous threat to the leadership of John Major, in whose cabinet he served from 1992 until he lost his Enfield and Southgate seat in the 1997 general election. Portillo has subsequently attempted to present a more caring image and has admitted to homosexual experiences while a student at Cambridge. He returned to parliament in November 1999, winning the seat of Kensington and Chelsea in a by-election, and became shadow chancellor in 2000. When William Hague (*see* LITTLE WILLIE) resigned following the Conservatives' defeat in the 2001 general election, Portillo was expected to succeed him as party leader. He was eliminated, however, at an early stage of the leadership contest, dismaying the Portillistas and leaving the Tories with what Jonathon Freedland in *The Guardian* described as 'a duel between the lean captain and the Midlands butterball' or, in plainer English, a choice in the final round of voting between the ramrod-straight Eurosceptic former army officer Iain Duncan Smith (*see the* QUIET MAN) and the rotund veteran Europhile and

Nottingham MP Kenneth Clarke (*see* PIE, PINT AND PANATELLA MAN). To the bafflement of many, Duncan Smith emerged the victor. Portillo subsequently left politics, not contesting his Kensington and Chelsea seat in the 2005 general election and seeking a new career in the media (in which he had previously dabbled). *See also* HATTONISTAS.

> At one point Portillo was polishing his jackboots and planning the next advance. And the next thing is he shows up as a TV presenter. It is rather like Pol Pot presenting the Teletubbies.
>
> TONY BANKS: speech at a Tribune rally, 1997

**Portmeirion.** This remarkable Italianate village near Porthmadog in northwest Wales, described variously as 'the last nobleman's folly', 'a Welsh Xanadu' and 'a home for fallen buildings', was the creation in the 1920s of the inspired Welsh architect Clough Williams-Ellis (1883–1978), a campaigner against the ever-encroaching spoliation of the natural landscape. He purchased the old mansion of Aber Ia here, added Castell Deudraeth and its grounds to the property, then began the transformation of the site into something on the lines of Portofino in northwest Italy. The locality is one of the showplaces of North Wales and its eccentricity made it an ideal setting for the cult television spy series *The Prisoner* (1967–8). The name of the village partly reflects that of Portofino itself, as well as of nearby Porthmadog, but also geographically identifies it as a port in the former county of Merioneth, Welsh *Meirionnydd*, now an administrative district in the county of Gwynedd.

**Portnoy's Complaint.** A novel (1969) by Philip Roth (b.1935). It is prefaced with a spoof definition of Portnoy's Complaint: 'A disorder in which strongly felt ethical and altruistic impulses are perpetually warring with extreme sexual longings, often of a perverse nature.' The main thrust of Alexander Portnoy's argument, outlined as a confession to his psychiatrist, concerns the repressive attitude of his mother, with whom he carried on into manhood a war of attrition (his main 'complaint'). His condition manifested itself in his compulsive masturbation as a boy (another 'complaint') and his subsequent obsession with having sex with Gentile women. With this novel, Roth claims that he finally managed to absorb his 'ideas about sex, guilt, childhood, about Jewish men and their Gentile women' into 'an overall fictional strategy'. A lacklustre and ill-judged film version (1972), starring Richard Benjamin, was directed by Ernest Lehman.

**Porton Down.** The site on Salisbury Plain of the Ministry of Defence's Chemical and Biological Defence Establishment, which was set up in 1916 to develop and manufacture chemical weapons (including poison gas) for use by the British Army in the First World War. Porton Down is now part of the MOD's Defence Evaluation and Research Agency.

**Portrait of the Artist as a Young Man, A.** An auto-biographical novel (1916) by James Joyce (1882–1941), extracted from a long work called *Stephen Hero*, a fragment of which was published in 1944. Stephen Dedalus, the protagonist, is not Joyce, but his consciousness is the means through which the author filters the relationship between imagination and reality. The five chapters cover events from infancy to 1902, when Joyce made his first visit to Paris. The beginning is in the third person in what corresponds to the language of childhood. The narrative ends with diary entries of the artist, whose soul has been 'born' through experience. The title suggested that of Dylan Thomas's *A Portrait of the Artist as a Young Dog* (1940), a collection of autobiographical short stories. *See also* FIRST LINES OF NOVELS; ULYSSES.

**Posh.** This colloquial word meaning stylish or elegant is first recorded in *Punch* of 25 September 1918: 'Oh, yes, Mater, we had a posh time of it down there.' It is popularly said to be an acronym of 'port out, starboard home', referring to cabins on the north-facing, cooler side of ships on voyages between England and India, but this origin lacks substantiation. The source in an identical but now obsolete word for a dandy is a more plausible possibility and a contraction of 'polished' has also been proposed. The word is sometimes humorously pronounced to rhyme with 'gauche'.

Posh is also the nickname of Peterborough United football club, founded in 1934 from the remnants of Peterborough & Fletton United. There are various accounts purportedly explaining the name. The most widely accepted claims that supporters referred to the team as looking 'posh' when they kicked off in the Southern League against Gainsborough on 1 September 1934 wearing a new strip. According to another account, in 1921 the manager of Fletton United said that he wanted 'posh players for a posh new team' and the name stuck when Peterborough & Fletton United was established in 1923. But on its formal founding in 1934 Peterborough United gained professional status and 'posh' may thus actually derive from 'profes-sional'. In 2003 the club was presumptuously challenged by the singer 'Posh Spice' (Victoria Beckham) over its legal right to register the name as a trademark (*see also* POSH AND BECKS; SPICE GIRLS).

**Posh and Becks.** The nickname for Victoria Beckham, née Adams ('Posh Spice' of the former SPICE GIRLS pop group)

and her husband, footballer David Beckham, captain of the England team from 2000 to 2006. They were married on 4 July 1999. With their obsession with fashion and love of BLING they are regarded as Britain's premier celebrity couple. Posh has brought out Becks's more feminine side (an innovation in the world of football), and the latter has been seen in a sarong and a variety of different hairstyles, including one involving an ALICE BAND. Their three children all have names suited to the sons of celebrities: Brooklyn, Romeo and Cruz. *See also* BECKINGHAM PALACE.

> I haven't read a book in my life. I haven't got enough time. I prefer to listen to music, although I do love fashion magazines.
> VICTORIA BECKHAM: interview with *Chic* magazine, August 2005. Her autobiography, *Learning to Fly*, was published in 2001

**Posh totty.** Upper- and upper-middle-class young women (or sometimes men) as objects of (lower- and lower-middle-class) male (or female) fantasy and desire. 'Totty' as a British colloquialism (derived from 'tot' meaning 'young child') for a sexually desirable young woman dates from the late 19th century, but it was not until the 1980s that it embarked on a new career as a collective noun (gradually taking over much of the territory previously occupied by 'crumpet').

> He [Gary Lineker] saved the best bit until last, when he handed back [after interviewing Zara Phillips, Princess Anne's daughter] to [Sue] Barker with the soon-to-be-legendary link line: 'And now for some more posh totty – Sue!'
> www.theroyalforum.com (14 December 2005)

**Position paper.** A written statement of views, attitudes or intentions. The US term originated in the 1960s and has its chief application in business and politics.

**Positive thinking.** The expedient of concentrating one's mind on the good and positive aspects of a matter in order to eliminate destructive attitudes and emotions. The expression comes from the title of Norman Vincent Peale's book *The Power of Positive Thinking* (1952).

**Posslq.** An acronym, pronounced 'possle-kew', of 'person of the opposite sex sharing living quarters', as a euphemism for one half of an unmarried couple living together. The term was coined in 1979 by the US Census Bureau and despite its artificiality gained currency for a time.

**Possum.** The proprietary name of an electronic device that enables a disabled person to telephone or operate a keyboard. It was introduced in the early 1960s and was officially known as a patient-operated selector mechanism, the initial letters of which, POSM, were reinterpreted as Latin *possum*, 'I am able'.

**Possum-eater.** An Australian slang term applied to both a country bumpkin and a stingy person. It is first recorded in 1942.

**Postal.** In US slang, to 'go postal' is to fly into a violent rage. The usage arose out of news stories in the 1990s of deranged US postal workers who shot people and then committed suicide.

**Postcode.** The British postal addressing system, consisting of a combination of letters and numbers, dates back to the division of London into postal districts in the mid-19th century. These were denoted by letters representing compass points, as N for Northern, E for Eastern, and WC for West Central. Numerical suffixes were then added as a labour-saving device in the First World War to denote sub-districts, so that the Eastern District became E1, Bethnal Green Sub-District became E2 and Bow became E3. This system prevailed until after the Second World War, when a more sophisticated method was needed. Experiments based on Norwich from 1959 led to the decision to use an alpha-numeric postcode. Despite considerable publicity, however, mail senders in the areas concerned proved reluctant to adopt the device. A revised system was accordingly introduced in Croydon in 1966 and proved more successful, so that by 1974 the whole of the UK had been allocated post-codes and Norwich had been recoded.

The postcode itself is now divided into two halves, the first being the inward code and the second the outward. In the postcode AL6 9QA, used for a small group of houses in New Place, Welwyn, Hertfordshire, AL indicates the postal area (St Albans), 6 indicates the postcode district within that area, 9 is the postcode sector within the district, and QA is the postman's 'walk'. *See also* ZIP CODE.

**Postcode lottery.** A situation in which supposedly uniform national treatment in fact varies from area to area. The term is most widely used with reference to the National Health Service, to characterize variations in patient care, drug provision, etc. in different health authorities.

A leading health charity has welcomed a study of stroke care by the Royal College of Physicians – but says a 'postcode lottery' still exists in Northern Ireland. The NI Chest, Heart and Stroke Association points to the fact that everyone treated for stroke in the Erne Hospital in Enniskillen can expect to be admitted to a specialist stroke unit, while the figure is zero in the Causeway Trust area because no such unit exists.

www.nichsa.com (14 March 2004)

**Postillion Struck by Lightning, A.** The title of the first volume of memoirs (1977) by the actor Dirk Bogarde (1921–99). Bogarde explains the title as coming from an old foreign-language phrase book encountered during a childhood holiday, in which he found the useful expression, 'The postillion has been struck by lightning.' (A postillion is a person whose job it is to ride one of the horses drawing a coach.)

**Post-It Notes.** The handy adhesive notes of this name were the invention in 1975 of the US chemical engineer Art Fry, an employee of the company 3M. Annoyed by the fact that the scrap of paper he used to mark his hymn book kept falling out, he saw a solution in a bookmark with a light adhesive that would stay in place but that could be easily removed and reapplied. His 'Press and Peel Pads', as they were originally called, did not immediately catch on because people did not know what to do with them, but with the backing of his employers, who gave away sheets of the notes with instructions how to use them, his innovation was at last successfully launched in 1979.

**Postman Always Rings Twice, The.** A film thriller (1946) based on the book (1934) by James M. Cain (1892–1977) about the liaison between a hobo and a bored waitress, which culminates in the murder of the latter's husband. Also made into a play and an opera, the film version starred Lana Turner and John Garfield. It was remade in 1981, with a screenplay by David Mamet and starring Jessica Lange and Jack Nicholson. Cain offered two explanations for the title of this, his first novel. The first was that while he was writing the book the postman always rang his doorbell twice if he was bringing bills, but only once if he had personal mail. The second was that the postman would ring the bell twice if he was delivering one of Cain's manuscripts after it had been rejected by a publisher: this happened so often that when the postman finally rang just once, to signify that the work had been accepted, the author gratefully altered the title to celebrate the fact.

**Postman Pat.** The eponymous hero of a BBC animated series for very young children. The programme was devised by John Cunliffe, directed by Ivor Wood and first broadcast in 1981. Postman Pat and his black-and-white cat Jess, together with a cast of characters including Mrs Goggins the postmistress, Granny Dryden and the Rev. Timms, live blameless and generally untroubled lives in the valley of Greendale, inspired by Longsleddale in the Lake Disctrict. Further series were made in the 1990s and 2000s.

**Postmodernism.** A style and concept in the arts, architecture, literature and criticism of the late 20th century, representing a departure from MODERNISM and having at its root a general distrust of grand theories and ideologies as well as suspicion of anything smacking of 'art'. The style is best seen in architecture, and one famous example is the Lloyd's Building in London, designed by Richard Rogers. Another is the AT&T skyscraper in New York, completed in 1984. Whereas the predominant style of modern architecture was formerly geometrical, functional and unornamented, postmodernist architecture borrows from many styles, especially the Classical, with playful, colourful and even intentionally vulgar use of decoration. In literature, postmodernism is characterized by self-consciousness, irony, game-playing and reference to other texts.

**Post-traumatic stress disorder.** A psychological disorder suffered by a person who has experienced a traumatic event such as a major disaster. The term was invented by US psychologists dealing with casualties of the VIETNAM War in the early 1970s. Disturbance of sleep and a constant vivid recall of the experience are typical symptoms, resulting in a dulled response to others and the outside world generally. The term is ponderous but more precise than the equivalent 'shell shock' of the First World War.

**Potatohead.** One of many terms for an idiot, in this case one whose head is as 'thick' as a potato.

**Potato Jones.** Captain D.J. Jones, who died in 1962 aged 92. In 1937, with his steamer *Marie Llewellyn* loaded with potatoes, he tried to run General Franco's blockade off Spain, but was prevented by a British warship. Two other blockade-running captains were called 'Ham-and-Egg' Jones and 'Corncob' Jones.

**Potato Pete.** A human figure in the form of a potato publicized in posters by the Ministry of Food in the Second World War with the aim of encouraging people to make the most of available vegetables. He had a fellow in Doctor Carrot. The London department store John Lewis held a 'Potato Christmas Fair' sponsored by Potato Pete in their bombed-out premises in Oxford Street. Children received hot baked potatoes as they pledged, 'I promise as my Christmas gift to the sailors who have to bring us our bread that I will do all I can to eat home-grown potatoes instead.'

**Pot Noodles.** A proprietary name for a fast-food dish consisting of a plastic tub of flavoured noodles, which can be prepared for eating by adding hot water. The product dates from the late 1980s and was regarded as a step up from the existing ubiquitous but barely nutritious JUNK FOOD.

**Potter, Harry.** A boy-wizard whose adventures are chronicled in a massively commercially successful sequence of children's novels by J.K. Rowling (b.1965). The first novel in the series, *Harry Potter and the Philosopher's Stone* (1997), describes the orphaned Harry's rescue from the everyday world of boorish 'Muggles' (ordinary human beings) by Rubeus Hagrid, Keeper of Keys and Grounds at HOGWARTS School of Witchcraft and Wizardry, and his subsequent experiences during his first year at the magical boarding-school. *Harry Potter and the Chamber of Secrets* (1998) and *Harry Potter and the Prisoner of Azkaban* (1999; *see also* AZKABAN) describe, respectively, Harry's second and third years at Hogwarts. They were followed by *Harry Potter and the Goblet of Fire* (2000), *Harry Potter and the Order of the Phoenix* (2003) and *Harry Potter and the Half-Blood Prince* (2005). One final volume is planned in the sequence, bringing Harry up to the age of 17 (the last chapter of the last book is said to have already been written, and locked away in a bank vault). The strictly coordinated release of a new Harry Potter title has become a uniquely newsworthy publishing event, with potential buyers camping outside bookstores overnight to be among the first to lay their hands on the young wizard's latest adventure.

The novels combine elements of the school story, the adventure story and the fantasy novel, and their imaginative richness and playful humour attracted an adulatory readership, both child and adult, from the outset. Hogwarts is both a fully realized imaginary world and a humorous reflection of the 'real', non-magical, world. The stories' strange blend of slapstick and menace is evident in many of the characters' names. Thus, Cornelius Fudge is 'Minister of Magic'; Draco Malfoy, Harry's rival in Slytherin house, hints at Transylvanian malevolence and bad faith; while Voldemort, sinister 'fallen' alumnus of Hogwarts and mortal enemy of Harry Potter, translates from the French as 'flight of death' or 'theft of death'.

A much-anticipated film version of *Harry Potter and the Philosopher's Stone* (in the US *Harry Potter and the Sorcerer's Stone*), directed by Christopher Columbus and starring Daniel Radcliffe as Harry, opened in the UK in 2001, and was strikingly faithful to the original book. This was followed by film versions of *Harry Potter and the Chamber of Secrets* (2002), *Harry Potter and the Prisoner of Azkaban* (2004) and *Harry Potter and the Goblet of Fire* (2005).

*See also* DEATH EATER; FIRST LINES OF NOVELS; FORD ANGLIA; HARRY POTTY; QUIDDITCH.

**POTUS.** An acronymic designation of the 'President of the United States'. It is most closely associated with Franklin D. Roosevelt (*see* FDR), but it has continued in use since his time.

The USA's greatest-never chief … the heroic, dynamic, enlightened yet intriguingly vulnerable POTUS, Josiah

'Jed' Bartlet (1999–2006) [in the US television drama *The West Wing*].

*The Observer* (29 January 2006)

**Poujadistes.** The supporters, chiefly shopkeepers and peasants, of Pierre Poujade (1920–2003), a French bookseller who in the 1950s led a right-wing populist movement that campaigned against high taxes. He founded the Union de Défense des Commerçants et des Artisans (Union for the Defence of Traders and Artisans), and in the 1956 elections Poujadistes won 52 of the 595 seats in the National Assembly. In the 1958 elections, however, Poujadistes won no seats, and Poujadisme was a spent force.

**Pound in your pocket, The.** Following the financial crisis of 1967 and the devaluation of the pound, on 19 November Prime Minister Harold Wilson sought to reassure the nation in a television broadcast:

From now the pound abroad is worth 14 per cent or so less in terms of other currencies. It does not mean, of course, that the pound here in Britain, in your pocket or purse or in your bank, has been devalued.

The speech was the subject of much mockery by those who viewed devaluation as a national disgrace, and Jim Callaghan was obliged to swop his post as chancellor of the exchequer with the home secretary Roy Jenkins.

**Pound the pavement.** To walk the streets in search of work. An expression of US origin dating from the 1950s.

**Pour on the coal.** To speed up. The phrase is of US origin and alludes to the coal-burning fireboxes of railway engines. The application of the phrase can be figurative as well as literal.

**Poverty trap.** A situation arising when a person's increase in income is offset by a resultant loss in state benefits, so that they are no better off.

**Powder one's nose.** To go to the lavatory, one of many euphemistic phrases for the action, here (usually) applicable to a woman, who might well literally powder her nose among other cosmetic adjustments while in the place in question. The expression, dating from the 1920s, is now rather old-fashioned but 'powder room' is still sometimes found as a term for a women's lavatory.

**Powellism.** The political and economic policies advocated by the controversial Conservative politician Enoch Powell (1912–98), especially that of restricting or terminating the immigration of people into Britain. In 1968 Powell lost his Conservative shadow cabinet post as a result of his infamous 'Rivers of Blood' speech (*see* RIVER TIBER FOAMING WITH MUCH BLOOD), in which he argued that Britain was

building 'its own funeral pyre' by allowing such people to claim British citizenship through their Commonwealth status.

**Power dressing.** A style of dressing for work and business in such a way that an impression of efficiency and self-assurance is conveyed. The term is applied more to women than to men, and can further the intention of breaking through the GLASS CEILING. *See also* POWER SUIT.

Power dressing is definitely out, open shirts and chinos in. This has filtered through to many organisations where Friday is now casual day.

*Sunday Express* (27 February 2000)

**Power grows out of the barrel of a gun.** *See* POLITICAL POWER GROWS OUT OF THE BARREL OF A GUN.

**Power is the great aphrodisiac.** A truth long held to be self-evident, but first articulated in this form in 1971 by the US politician and diplomat Henry Kissinger (b.1923), President Nixon's national security adviser and then secretary of state. His one-time companion, Barbara Howar, commented: 'Henry's idea of sex is to slow down to 30 miles an hour when he drops you off at the door.'

**Power lunch.** A working lunch at which top-level business or political discussions are held. The devoting of one's meal or leisure hours to business came to be regarded by many Americans in the 1980s as a symbol of commercial or political success. A 'power nap', as a brief daytime sleep in the working day, bestows a similar status, and the high-flying lifestyle also involves POWER DRESSING.

**Power Ranger.** The proprietary name of a plastic toy figure resembling a character from the US children's television series *Mighty Morphin Power Rangers* (1993–6), about five teenagers able to 'morph' (transmute) into kung-fu super-heroes to do battle with evil ALIENS.

**Power-sharing.** A key term in the political lexicon of Northern Ireland's TROUBLES, denoting the sharing of power between the province's Unionist and Nationalist communities and referring specifically to attempts to create a devolved government for Northern Ireland in the early 1970s. The SUNNINGDALE AGREEMENT of December 1973 included provisions for a power-sharing executive, and the Northern Ireland Executive Council, a coalition of Protestants and Catholics including representatives from all Northern Ireland's political parties and led by the Ulster Unionist leader Brian Faulkner, took office in 1974. However, it was rejected soon afterwards by the ULSTER UNIONIST PARTY and was eventually brought down six months later after a strike by the Protestant Ulster Workers' Council (organized with the connivance of hardline PAISLEYITES and Loyalist Paramilitaries (*see* PARAMILITARY)) had paralysed Northern Ireland. DIRECT RULE from Westminster was then reimposed.

**Power suit.** A woman's tailored business suit, conventionally with shoulder pads and a knee-length skirt, the former intended to give the outfit a more masculine outline. Such suits were in favour in the 1980s and early 1990s and were an essential part of the fashion for POWER DRESSING.

**Power to the people.** The slogan of the BLACK PANTHERS from 1969, subsequently adopted by other groups. It echoes the call of the Petrograd workers in the months before the Russian Revolution, 'All power to the Soviets!' In 1971 John Lennon attempted to portray himself as a working-class hero by singing 'Power to the People (Right On!)'.

**Power without responsibility.** A phrase used by Rudyard Kipling (1865–1936) in relation to press barons, especially Lord Beaverbrook, proprietor of the *Daily Express*:

> Power without responsibility: the prerogative of the harlot throughout the ages.

The phrase was used by the Conservative leader Stanley Baldwin (1867–1947) in a speech on 18 March 1931, and played upon by Tom Stoppard (b.1937) in his novel *Lord Malquist and Mr Moon* (1966):

> The House of Lords, an illusion to which I have never been able to subscribe – responsibility without power, the prerogative of the eunuch throughout the ages.

**Prague Spring.** The brief period of liberalizing and democratizing reform in Czechoslovakia in 1968 after Alexander Dubček (1921–92) became first secretary of the Communist Party (January 1968). The reforms were dismantled following the invasion of Soviet-led WARSAW PACT forces on the night of 20–21 August 1968. Prague was the capital of Czechoslovakia (and is now the capital of the Czech Republic), while 'spring' suggests an ending of COLD WAR oppression and echoes the short-lived liberalizing 'thaw' in the USSR under Nikita Khrushchev in the late 1950s.

**Praise the Lord and pass the ammunition.** A phrase from the Second World War, said to have been used by a US naval chaplain during the Japanese attack on PEARL HARBOR, although the actual identity of the chaplain has since been in dispute. One candidate is Lieutenant Howell M. Forgy; another is Captain William H. Maguire. It was made the subject of a popular song by Frank Loesser in 1942. It is said to date from the American Civil War (1861–5).

**Prang.** RAF slang in the Second World War meaning to bomb a target with evident success, to shoot down another or to crash one's own aircraft, and generally to collide with, or bump into, any vehicle. Hence, also, 'wizard prang', for an accurate hit or other successful strike. According to Eric Partridge in *A Dictionary of RAF Slang* (1945), the word may be a blend of 'paste' and 'bang', but it is more likely to be simply imitative.

***Pravda.*** A play (1985) by the British playwrights Howard Brenton (b.1942) and David Hare (b.1947) depicting the unprincipled behaviour of Lambert Leroux, a South African newspaper magnate, after he buys up two daily British newspapers. The play profited from the parallels that could be drawn with the media empires of Robert Maxwell and Rupert Murdoch, and it offered a bleak picture of how the truth can be manipulated by egocentric press barons. The title *Pravda* is an ironic reference to the Russian newspaper of the same name (meaning 'truth' in Russian), in which the propagandist influence over what was printed during the Soviet era was obvious even to the casual reader.

**Prawn night.** A traditional Australian social occasion at which the male members of a club, often accompanied by females not their wives, get together to consume prawns and beer and be regaled by such entertainments as strippers and off-colour comedians. The expression is first recorded in 1976.

***Precious Bane.*** A rural novel (1924) by Mary Webb (1881–1927), featuring a heroine, Prudence Sarn, who is disfigured by a hare-lip, as was the author herself. The plot abounds with romance and melodrama. The title, from John Milton's *Paradise Lost* (1667), has a rustic ring:

> Let none admire
> That riches grow in hell; that soil may best
> Deserve the precious bane.
> Bk I

The book received posthumous publicity when the then prime minister, Stanley Baldwin, praised it at a Royal Literary Society dinner in 1928. Stella Gibbons wrote a parody of it, COLD COMFORT FARM.

**Prefect, Ford.** *See* FORD PREFECT.

***Premonition of Civil War.*** One of the more repellent paintings of Salvador Dalí (1904–89), this bears the alternative title *Soft Construction with Boiled Beans*. It was painted in 1936, the year that the Spanish Civil War broke out. The composition largely consists of two humanoid constructions made of various limbs and other body parts. The lower figure is fiercely squeezing the breast of the grimacing upper figure, while various pieces of soft offal lie around, along with the eponymous beans. Dalí's support for Franco in the Civil War led to his expulsion from the Surrealist (*see* SURREALISM) movement in 1938. As Herbert Read commented 30 years later: '[His] theatricality ... is now at the service of those reactionary forces in Spain whose triumph had been the greatest affront to humanism which, in spite of all its extravagance, had been the consistent concern of the surrealist movement.'

**Preppy.** Stylish in dress or appearance, like the aspirational students at a US prep school, the equivalent of a British public school. The vogue reached its height in the early 1980s, its connotations promoted by Lisa Birnbach's *The Preppy Handbook* (1981). *See also* SLOANE RANGER.

> He is variously described as 'Ivy League' or 'preppy' and he is instantly recognized by his blue button-down Oxford cloth shirt, navy blazer, club tie and penny loafers. He might be viewed as an American Hooray Henry, except that he is quietly-spoken, excessively polite and never throws muffins.
> *The Independent* (12 March 1988)

**Presidium.** In the former USSR the Presidium of the Supreme Soviet was a body elected by the Supreme Soviet to fulfil the role of constitutional head of the state. Its chairman was its representative in ceremonial affairs and it issued ordinances when the Supreme Soviet was not in session. Apart from its chairman, it consisted of 15 deputies (one for each of the republics), a secretary and 20 members. The term itself was adopted from Latin *praesidium*, 'garrison'. *See also* POLITBURO.

**Press the flesh.** To shake hands, especially formally or repeatedly.

> Donald Trump, a self-confessed 'germ freak' who once wrote of his loathing for handshakes, will have to press a lot of flesh in the coming months.
> *The Times* (21 October 1999)

**Press the panic button.** *See* PANIC BUTTON.

**Prestel.** The proprietary name of a computerized visual information system introduced in the late 1970s as a form of teletext. It was pioneered by BT (British Telecommunications) and enabled data selected from one or more databases to appear on a television screen by dialling the appropriate telephone number. The word presumably combined 'press', or perhaps 'presto', with 'telephone' or 'television'.

**Pretty as a picture.** Very pretty. A pretty person or thing will often be depicted with an idealized prettiness in a painting. The expression is American and dates from the turn of the 20th century.

**Pretty please.** An intensified form of 'please', implying a request made deliberately decorously or even decoratively, as if 'gift-wrapped'. The somewhat cloying phrase dates from the 1950s.

**Prezza.** *See* TWO JAGS.

**Price is right, The.** The price is reasonable; whatever is being sold is good value. The phrase was the title of a popular television GAME SHOW screened from 1984 to 1988, in which members of the public had to guess the retail price of various consumer goods. Whoever came closest to the correct amount won the object in question.

**Primal scene.** A term for the first time that a young child is emotionally aware of his or her parents having sexual intercourse. The expression originated with Sigmund Freud and became familiar in English from James Strachey's translation of Freud's work (1925).

**Primal scream therapy.** A type of psychotherapy in which patients, often in groups, are encouraged to scream and behave violently to relive birth and the sufferings of infancy and to express aggressive emotions about their parents. The treatment was developed by the US psychologist Arthur Janov and named by him in his book *The Primal Scream* (1970). John Lennon and Yoko Ono were among the more well-known experimenters with it.

**Primary Colors.** An anonymously published novel (1996), about a Southern governor running for US president; the subtitle is 'A Novel of Politics'. The fact that the governor was a philanderer and his wife fiercely ambitious left readers in no doubt that the book was based on Bill Clinton's first presidential campaign, in 1992. Publication of this *roman à clef* caused much speculation among the American chattering classes as to the identity of the author. It was Donald W. Foster, professor of English at Vassar College, who first came up with the correct answer, as the result of computer-aided textual-comparison techniques. He pointed the finger at Joe Klein, a veteran New York journalist, who at first angrily denied authorship, but some months later admitted to the truth.

The 'primary' in the title refers to a US preliminary election in which voters in a state select which candidate of their party they would like to run for president; while in painting, 'primary colours' are the three pigments, red, yellow and blue, from which all other pigments may be mixed. The novel was turned into a film (1998) starring John Travolta and Emma Thompson.

**Prime Minister of Mirth.** The billboard byname of the music-hall entertainer George Robey (originally George Edward

Wade) (1869–1954), given when he was well established in his career. The analogy is perhaps not so much with a political prime minister as with a person supremely skilled in ministering (i.e. providing) laughter.

> He was billed later on as 'The Prime Minister of Mirth', but prime ministers are the dominant figures of democracies, ruling by persuasion. Robey could more accurately have been called the dictator of laughter, so firmly did he grip and subdue his audiences.
>
> IVOR BROWN: in *Twentieth-Century Dictionary of National Biography*, vol. 6 (1951–60)

**Prime of Miss Jean Brodie, The.** A novel (1961) by Muriel Spark (1918–2006), set, and reflecting her upbringing, in Edinburgh. It recounts the influence on five impressionable schoolgirls of Jean Brodie, their stylish teacher in the junior department of the Marcia Blane School during the 1930s. There have been both film (1969, starring Maggie Smith) and television versions. *See also* MORNINGSIDE.

> 'Next year,' she said, 'you will have the specialists to teach you history and mathematics and languages, a teacher for this and a teacher for that, a period of forty-five minutes for this and another for that. But in this your last year with me you will receive the fruits of my prime. They will remain with you all your days.'
>
> ch. 1

**Prime Suspect.** A gripping television thriller series by Lynda La Plante first screened in 1991. The plot focused on the sexism that cramped the career of the ambitious CID officer DCI Jane Tennison in her pursuit of high-profile crimes, among them a serial prostitute murderer and a case of paedophilia. The series owed much of its success to the genius of Helen Mirren as Tennison.

**Prime time.** The time of day when a radio or television audience is expected to be at its greatest. For television this is usually mid-evening. The concept is American in origin and dates from the 1960s.

**Primordial soup.** A scientific name dating from the 1950s for the solution rich in organic compounds which is thought to have formerly made up the oceans or lakes of the earth and to have been the environment in which cellular life originated.

> We can't say why the elements in the primordial soup knitted themselves into DNA any more than the ancient Egyptians could say where the Sun went at night.
>
> *The Times* (24 December 1999)

**Prince of Darkness.** A nickname for any dubious or 'shady' character, especially if dark haired or swarthy. The source is

ultimately biblical, with a reference to Satan: 'For we wrestle … against principalities, against powers, against the rulers of the darkness of this world' (Ephesians 6:21). The precise phrase occurs in Shakespeare: 'The black prince, sir; *alias*, the prince of darkness; *alias*, the devil' (*All's Well That Ends Well*, IV.v, 1601). In modern times it has been applied, among others, to Douglas Haig (1861–1928), commander-in-chief of British forces in France in the First World War, for his strategy that led to the loss of so many men's lives (the slaughter on the SOMME led to his being dubbed 'the Butcher'); to Richard N. Perle (b.1941) assistant secretary of defense from 1981 to 1987 in the Reagan administration, for his hostility to the Soviet Union; and, a shade more lightly, to the New Labour politician Peter Mandelson (*see* MANDY), on account of his mastery of the 'dark arts' of spin (*see* SPIN DOCTOR):

> Peter Mandelson's a sweet guy, you know. But I eat lots of garlic and I sleep with garlic flowers round my neck. So I'm safe … for the moment.
>
> TONY BANKS: quoted in *The Guardian* (May 1998)

More trivially, the name has also been used of the US television chat-show host Johnny Carson (1925–2005), simply because his programme went out at night. *See also* SOMETHING OF THE NIGHT.

**Prince of Wails.** *See* NABOB OF SOB.

**Princess Consort.** The title that Camilla, Duchess of Cornwall (née Parker Bowles; *see* the ROTTWEILER) will carry when her husband, Prince Charles, becomes king. The FIRM apparently thought that the public, still soft on the late Princess Diana (*see* PEOPLE'S PRINCESS; PRINCESS OF HEARTS), would not stomach her becoming Queen Camilla, so came up with this innovative title.

> But the agonizing that will have taken place to produce the spanking new title of Princess Consort! How perfect it is for the British royal family, which loves ritual and ceremony that seem ancient, but in reality are as newly minted as last week's copy of *Hello!* magazine.
>
> SIMON HOGGART: in *The Guardian* (12 February 2005)

Several commentators remarked that the title reminded them of one of British Leyland's less charismatic cars of the 1970s. This is in keeping with Camilla's lapses of dress sense: when she visited Washington with her husband in 2005, the *New York Post* called her a 'dumpy frump fashion disaster'.

**Princess Diana.** *See* DISCO DI; PEOPLE'S PRINCESS; PRINCESS OF HEARTS.

**Princess of Hearts.** A title claimed by Princess Diana (the PEOPLE'S PRINCESS) in her PANORAMA interview on BBC TV in 1995, following her separation from the Prince of Wales, but prior to their divorce. Asked whether she thought she'd ever be queen, she replied:

> I'd like to be a queen of people's hearts, in people's hearts, but I don't see myself being queen of this country. I don't think many people will want me to be queen. Actually, when I say many people I mean the establishment that I married into, because they have decided that I'm a non-starter.

**Princess Pushy.** A nickname of Princess Michael of Kent, née Baroness Marie-Christine von Reibnitz (b.1945), the daughter of an Austrian father with connections to the Nazi Party and the wife of Prince Michael of Kent, the Queen's first cousin. It is said that it is the other members of the royal family who find Princess Michael 'pushy', and in some quarters she has a reputation for 'demanding behaviour and an unduly privileged lifestyle'. Tall and blond, she is also apparently referred to by the Queen as 'Our Val', with reference to the Valkyries, warrior-maidens of Germanic myth. Princess Michael has denied allegations that she made regrettable comments about a group of African American diners in a restaurant in New York in 2004. In 2005 she told the German newspaper *Welt am Sonntag* that she felt sorry for Prince Harry (*see* HARRY POTTY) when he was criticized for wearing Nazi uniform to a fancy-dress party. She continued:

> The English take the breeding of their horses and dogs more seriously than they do their children. God forbid that the wrong drop of blood should get into their Labrador, but their children marry however they wish. Perhaps arranged marriages were not the worst option.

**Princess Sourpuss.** A former nickname of Princess Anne, the Princess Royal, on account of her somewhat grumpy demeanour. However, she is now one of the more popular royals.

**Princeton Plan.** In the United States a plan to give college students a recess, usually of two weeks, in an election year in order to enable them to work for the election candidate of their choice. It was first implemented in the early 1970s at Princeton University, New Jersey. This same university had pioneered another Princeton Plan in the 1960s, as a scheme to achieve racial balance in public schools by pairing a school of mainly white students with one of black students, so that all students in certain grades attended the same school.

**Prisoner, The.** A cult British television fantasy series of the late 1960s starring Patrick McGoohan as a former secret agent imprisoned in a bizarre village. All inmates have numbers rather than names, and all apart from McGoohan (Number 6) seem docilely content with their lot. The head of the village is the mysterious and unseen Number 1 (who in a surreal twist in the final episode turns out to be identical with McGoohan's character), and escape is prevented by a guard in the shape of a large bouncing white balloon. The symbolic or allegorical significance (or lack of it) of various elements in the programme aroused considerable controversy at the time, and it has continued to excite speculation ever since. The village used for filming was PORTMEIRION in North Wales, created as an Italian fantasy by Sir Clough Williams-Ellis.

**Prisoner of conscience.** A person imprisoned or detained because of their political or religious beliefs, where these run counter to the official line of the state in which they live. The term was made familiar following its adoption by AMNESTY INTERNATIONAL in the early 1960s.

**Private eye.** A private detective. 'Eye' as a term for a detective dates from the 19th century, and an all-seeing eye was adopted as the badge of Pinkerton's National Detective Agency, founded in 1855. The British satirical magazine *Private Eye*, founded in 1961, gave the phrase further familiarity.

**Private Lives.** A play (1930) by the British playwright Noël Coward (1899–1973) about two divorcés, Elyot and Amanda, who find themselves staying in the same hotel on their honeymoons following their marriages to new partners. The film version (1931), which was somewhat lifeless, starred Robert Montgomery and Norma Shearer. The title occurs early in the first act when Amanda reflects upon the nature of normality:

> I think very few people are completely normal really, deep down in their private lives. It all depends upon a combination of circumstances. If all the various cosmic thingummys fuse at the same moment, and the right spark is struck, there's no telling what one mightn't do.

**Prix Goncourt.** The most prestigious French literary prize, awarded by the *Académie des Goncourt*, founded in 1902 under the will of the novelist Edmond de Goncourt (1822–96). The annual prize, first awarded in 1903, is given to what is judged to be the best imaginative prose work of the year, a verdict not always justified by posterity but nevertheless usually generating good sales. Winners have included Marcel Proust, *À l'ombre des jeunes filles en fleurs* (1919), André Malraux, *La Condition humaine* (1933), Marguerite Duras, *L'Amant* (1984) and Pascale Roze, *Le Chasseur Zéro* (1996). The award was declined by Julien Gracq for *Le Rivage des Syrtes* (1951) and by Vintila Horia for *Dieu est né en exil* (1960).

**Proactive.** 'Making things happen.' This BUZZWORD of the 1990s, typically in a management or business context, originated in the 1930s as the converse of 'reactive', as applied to someone who, instead of reacting to a situation, anticipates it (Greek *pro*, 'before') and takes action to create or control it.

**Product placement.** A practice whereby firms use films or television programmes to promote their products or services, either visually or by inclusion in the dialogue. The ploy arose in the 1980s, an early classic example being the promotion of Reese's Pieces in *E.T.* (1982), resulting in a tripling of sales for these sweets, produced by the makers of the HERSHEY BAR. (Universal Studios had originally suggested to the makers of the MARS BAR that a trail of their M&M chocolate buttons lead the alien out of the brush, but the company had turned down the proposal.) Later 'plugs' were for the US 'Taco Bell' restaurant chain in *Demolition Man* (1993) and 'Red Stripe' beer in *The Firm* (1993). The US television series SEX AND THE CITY (1998–2004) was particularly notorious for blatant product placement, while in his novel *American Psycho* (1991) Bret Easton Ellis takes the idea to satirical excess, the eponymous yuppie narrator endlessly listing luxury brand after luxury brand:

> Courtney opens the door and she's wearing a Krizia cream silk blouse and Krizia rust tweed skirt and silk-satin d'Orsay pumps from Manolo Blahnik.

An interesting new development occurred during the British general election campaign of 2005, when, in a party political broadcast (27 April) by the Labour Party directed at mothers of HARDWORKINGFAMILIES, a container of Utterly Butterly was clearly to be seen, with no attempt made to conceal the label.

New technology, from videorecorders to view-on-demand, have undermined the traditional dependence by television advertisers on commercial breaks in programmes: viewers simply bypass them with their ZAPPERS. Thus, under pressure from broadcasters and advertisers alike, in December 2005 the European Union began relaxing the ban on product placement for European channels. *See also* SOAP OPERA.

**Professional foul.** In football a deliberate foul committed, usually as a last resort, to prevent an opponent from scoring. The euphemism was greeted with widespread derision when it first became public in the 1970s. The term can also be applied to a similar tactic in business or politics. Tom Stoppard's television play *Professional Foul* (1977) tells what happens when an academic attending a conference in Prague is asked by a former student to smuggle a manuscript out to the free world. The metaphor of the play, as well as its title, came specifically from the football international that was being played in the city.

**Professor Challenger.** *See* Professor CHALLENGER.

**Profumo Affair.** Perhaps the most extensive political scandal in Britain in the postwar years takes its name from the Conservative politician John Profumo (1915–2006), secretary of state for war under Harold Macmillan (*see* MAC THE KNIFE). Rumours began circulating that he was consorting with a young model and showgirl, Christine Keeler (b.1942), mistress of the Soviet assistant naval attaché, Yevgeny Ivanov (1926–94). In March 1963 Profumo assured the House of Commons that there was no truth in the allegation, but three months later he confessed that he had lied and resigned his seat. The doubts cast upon the efficiency of the security service almost resulted in the downfall of the government. However, in July 1963 Macmillan commented:

> I was determined that no British government should be brought down by the action of two tarts.
>
>> Quoted in Anthony Sampson, *Macmillan* (1967). The other 'tart' was Keeler's colleague, Mandy Rice-Davies (*see* HE WOULD, WOULDN'T HE?).

Profumo retired from public life, and became a voluntary worker at Toynbee Hall, a social-outreach centre in London's East End. *See also* MONSTER RAVING LOONY PARTY.

**Programming languages.** Even the non-computerate will be familiar with many of the names of languages used for writing computer programs. FORTRAN was the first, invented in 1956. It appears below together with a selection of more recent names, most of them acronyms.

Ada: from Ada Augusta King, Countess of Lovelace (1815–52), daughter of the poet Lord Byron, who became assistant to the machine computing pioneer Charles Babbage (1791–1871) and worked with him on his early mechanical model

ALGOL: acronym of *algo*rithmic *l*anguage or *alg*ebraic *o*riented *l*anguage

BASIC: acronym of *b*eginners' *a*ll-purpose *s*ymbolic *i*nstruction *c*ode, punning on 'basic'

C: developed from *B*, short for *BCPL*, abbreviation of *b*asic *c*omputer *p*rogramming *l*anguage

COBOL: acronym of *co*mmon *b*usiness-*o*riented *l*anguage

FORTRAN: acronym of *for*mula *tran*slation

LISP: acronym of *lis*t *p*rocessing

PASCAL: acronym of French *p*rogramme *a*ppliqué à la *s*élection et la *c*ompilation *a*utomatique de la *l*ittérature ('program for the selection and automatic compilation of literature'), but also from the name of the French mathematician and physicist Blaise Pascal (1623–62)

PL/1: abbreviation of *program language* 1

PROLOG: acronym of *programming in logic*, punning on 'prologue'

**Prog rock.** 'Progressive' rock, a style of rock music that developed in the earlier 1970s, characterized by the CONCEPT ALBUM, extensive use of electronic effects and (in the opinion of its critics) a goodly dollop of HIPPIE-ish drug-inspired pretentiousness. Prog rock bands included Emerson, Lake and Palmer, Genesis, King Crimson and Pink Floyd. When PUNK ROCK arrived in the mid-1970s, Prog rock suddenly seemed very middle-aged.

**Prohibition.** The prevention by law of the manufacture and sale of alcohol in the United States from 1919 to 1933. The legislation ultimately arose out of the intense religious revivalism of the 1820s and 1830s but was more immediately aimed at improving efficiency in the workplace and reducing the level of corruption in saloons. Prohibition brought the bootlegger into being as a new kind of criminal, epitomized by the career of the notorious Al CAPONE.

> This is the time to acquire your Wines and Liquors. Prices are advancing daily and will continue to advance whether Prohibition becomes effective July 1, 1919, or January 20, 1920.
>
> *New York Times* (advertisement) (4 May 1919)

**Project, The.** Tony Blair's term for the transformation of the LABOUR PARTY into the Middle-England-friendly NEW LABOUR, for example by revising CLAUSE FOUR and accommodating himself to the Thatcherite paradigm shift that occurred in UK politics in the 1980s (*see* BLATCHERISM). *The Project* was the title of a 2002 BBC TV drama about the young activists who helped to engineer New Labour's election victory in 1997.

**PROLOG.** *See* PROGRAMMING LANGUAGES.

**Prom queen.** The most outstanding girl or young woman at a prom, a dance held by a high school class at the end of the academic year in American schools. Stephen King's first novel *Carrie* (1974) concerns a gawky 16-year-old girl who is elected prom queen as a malicious prank but who uses her supernatural powers to exact her revenge on her tormentors.

**Propeller-head.** A person with an obsessive interest in computers or technology. The reference is to a BEANIE hat with a propeller on top, as popularized by SCIENCE FICTION enthusiasts and as actually worn by some children. The propeller suggests that the wearer has some sort of cerebral 'lift-off' or specialized technical knowledge. The usage dates from the early 1980s.

**Property-owning democracy.** A democratic society characterized by private home ownership. The phrase is often associated with Sir Anthony Eden, Conservative prime minister in the mid-1950s, and it became a mantra of the Thatcher administration of the 1980s, but in fact it is first recorded in 1923. This coincided with a marked rise in owner-occupation in the first 20 years of the 20th century. In 1900 over 90 per cent of the British population lived in rented or tied accommodation, but new housing developments such as those that followed in the wake of the Metropolitan Railway in northwest London encouraged people to buy their own homes.

**Prop up the bar.** To drink alone at the bar of a public house. 'Prop' refers to the bar as supporting the drinker, rather than the drinker the bar.

**Protestant work ethic.** An interpretative concept derived from Max Weber's work, *The Protestant Ethic and the Spirit of Capitalism* (1904–5), in which Weber pointed out that the most successful German capitalists had been Protestants. He ascribed their worldly success to the psychological anxiety of Calvin's dogma of predestination, by which only God knows who is destined for salvation. Looking for some sign of divine favour, the anxious businessman would see the accumulation of capital (and the puritanical avoidance of blowing it on fripperies) as an indication that he might not, after all, be damned.

**Protocols of the Elders of Zion.** *See under* FAKES.

**Provos.** A nickname for members of the Provisional IRA, a faction favouring terrorist action that broke away from the 'Official' IRA in 1969. The name was probably patterned on *provo*, from French *provocateur*, as a term for a member of a group of young Dutch activists in the 1960s. The name 'Provisional IRA' derives from the Dublin EASTER RISING of 1916, when Irish Republicans rose against the British and proclaimed a 'provisional government'. For Irish Republicans, therefore, the name created a link between the present-day IRA and their 'heroes' of 1916. The Provisionals are also referred to as Provies (this has a slightly softer nuance than Provos) or occasionally as 'pinheads'. *See also* STICKIES.

**Prozac.** A trade name for fluoxetine, a drug used to treat depression by inhibiting the uptake of serotonin in the brain. It first went on the market in 1987 and rapidly became the 'wonder drug' of the decade. Its proponents believe that its ability to enhance confidence, self-image and energy levels outweigh its known side-effects, which include nausea, diarrhoea and sexual dysfunction.

**Prufrock, J. Alfred.** *See* 'LOVE SONG OF J. ALFRED PRUFROCK'.

**Psammead, The.** The sand fairy created by E. Nesbit for her children's books *Five Children and It* (1902) – 'It' being the fairy – *The Phoenix and the Carpet* (1904) and *The Story of the Amulet* (1906). The Psammead is an unattractive creature, with a fat furry body, bat-like ears and eyes on stalks. It is also bad-tempered, but it can at least grant wishes. In the former book, this creates chaos, while in the latter the Psammead's powers permit the children to travel back in time to ancient Egypt and Babylon. The Psammead's name comes from Greek *psammos*, 'sand'.

**Pseud.** A pretentious person or poseur. The term, an abbreviation of 'pseudo', became a BUZZWORD in the 1960s, partly because of its use by the magazine *Private Eye*, whose long-running column *Pseud's Corner* reprints instances of pretentiousness. This latter phrase is also used as a general label for anything regarded as absurdly exaggerated or overwrought.

> Occasionally out of nowhere comes a band bursting at the seams with great songs. A band that prompts the average critic to make a determined bid for a place in Pseud's Corner.
> *The Times* (16 October 1999)

**Pseudonyms.** The 20th and 21st centuries can with some justification be called the Age of the Pseudonym, especially in the worlds of popular fiction, the cinema, the theatre and pop music. The crime novelist John Creasey (1908–73) generously exemplifies the phenomenon, with two dozen pen-names for different novels and genres: Gordon Ashe, Margaret Cooke, M.E. Cooke, Norman Deane, Elise Fecamps, Robert Caine Frazer, Patrick Gill, Michael Halliday, Charles Hogarth, Brian Hope, Colin Hughes, Kyle Hunt, Abel Mann, Peter Manton, J.J. Marric, James Marsden, Richard Martin, Rodney Mattheson, Antony Morton, Ken Ranger, William K. Reilly, Tex Riley, Henry St John and Jeremy York. Pseudonyms can be counted in thousands but the following is a selection of over 100 of the most familiar of the period, together with their (usually less well known) originals. *See also* LARRY PARNES'S STABLE OF STARS.

Woody Allen, US actor (b.1935): Allan Stewart Konigsberg

Julie Andrews, English actress (b.1935): Julia Elizabeth Wells

Fred Astaire, US dancer and actor (1899–1987): Frederick Austerlitz

Charles Atlas, US bodybuilder (1893–1972): Angelo Siciliano

Lauren Bacall, US actress (b.1924): Betty Joan Perske

Anne Bancroft, US actress (1931–2005): Anna Maria Luisa Italiano

Jack Benny, US comedian (1894–1974): Benjamin Kubelsky

Cilla Black, English television presenter (b.1943): Priscilla Maria Veronica White

Dirk Bogarde, English actor and writer (1921–99): Derek Gentron Gaspart Ulric van den Bogaerde

Mark Bolan, English pop musician (1947–77): Mark Feld

Bourvil, French comic actor (1917–70): André Raimbourg

David Bowie, English rock musician (b.1947): David Robert Hayward-Jones

Boy George, English pop singer (b.1961): George Alan O'Dowd

Bricktop, US cabaret singer (1894–1984): Ada Beatrice Queen Victoria Louise Virginia Smith

Elkie Brooks, English popular singer (b.1946): Elaine Bookbinder

Anthony Burgess, English novelist (1917–93): John Burgess Wilson

Richard Burton, Welsh actor (1925–84): Richard Walter Jenkins

Red Buttons, US comic actor (1918–2006): Aaron Schwatt

Marti Caine, English singer and entertainer (1945–95): Lynda Denise Ives, née Crapper

Michael Caine, English actor (b.1933): Maurice Joseph Micklewhite

Cantinflas, Mexican clown, bullfighter, comic actor (1911–93): Mario Moreno Reyes

Truman Capote, US writer (1924–84): Truman Streckfus Persons

Diahann Carroll, US singer and actress (b.1935): Carol Diann Johnson

Jasper Carrott, English comedian (b.1945): Robert Davies

Christopher Caudwell, English writer (1907–37): Christopher St John Sprigg

Blaise Cendrars, French writer (1887–1961): Frédéric Louis Sauser

Cyd Charisse, US actress (b.1921): Tula Ellice Finklea

Chubby Checker, US pop musician (b.1941): Ernest Evans

Judy Chicago, US artist (b.1939): Judy Cohen

Upton Close, US journalist and writer (1894–1960): Josef Washington Hall

Nat 'King' Cole, US jazz musician (1919–65): Nathaniel Adams Coles

Colette, French writer (1873–1954): Sidonie Gabrielle

Robbie Coltrane, Scottish television actor (b.1950): Anthony Robert McMillan

Russ Conway, English popular pianist (1927–2000): Trevor Herbert Stanford

Alice Cooper, US rock singer (b.1945): Vincent Damon Furnier

Elvis Costello, English rock singer (b.1954): Declan MacManus

Joan Crawford, US actress (1904–77): Lucille Fay Le Sueur

Tony Curtis, US actor (b.1925): Bernard Schwartz

Clemence Dane, English writer (1888–1965): Winifred Ashton

Skeeter Davis, US country singer (b.1931): Mary Frances Penick

Doris Day, US actress and singer (b.1924): Doris von Kappelhoff

Chris De Burgh, Irish-born popular singer (b.1948): Christopher John Davidson

Bo Diddley, US jazz musician (b.1928): Otha Ellas Bates, later McDaniel

Marlene Dietrich, German-born US actress (1901–92): Maria Magdalene Dietrich von Losch

Diana Dors, English actress (1931–84): Diana Mary Fluck

Fifi D'Orsay, Canadian-born US actress (1904–83): Angelina Yvonne Cecil Lussier D'Sablon

Kirk Douglas, US actor (b.1916): originally Issur Danielovitch, then Isidore Demsky

O. Douglas, Scottish writer (1875–1940): Anna Buchan

Fabia Drake, English actress (1904–90): Ethel McGlinchy

Bob Dylan, US rock musician (b.1941): Robert Allen Zimmerman

Adam Faith, English pop singer and actor (1940–2003): Terence Nelhams

Georgie Fame, English pop singer (b.1943): Clive Powell

M.J. Farrell, Irish writer (1904–96): Mary ('Molly') Nesta Keane, née Skrine

Fernandel, French comic actor (1903–71): Fernand-Joseph-Désiré Contandin

Stepin Fetchit, US actor (1902–85): Lincoln Theodore Monroe Andrew Perry

Gracie Fields, English popular singer (1898–1979): Grace Stansfield (*see also* OUR GRACIE)

W.C. Fields, US comic actor (1879–1946): William Claude Dukinfield

Margot Fonteyn, English ballerina (1919–91): Margaret Hookham

Nicci French, English 'writer': British husband-and-wife crime writers *Nicci* Gerrard (b.1958) and Sean *French* (b.1959)

Greta Garbo, Swedish-born US actress (1905–90): Greta Lovisa Gustafsson

Cary Grant, English actor (1904–86): Alexander Archibald Leach

David Hamilton, English radio and television compère (b.1939): David Pilditch

Jean Harlow, US actress (1911–37): Harlean Carpentier

James Herriot, English writer (1916–95): James Alfred Wight

Jack Higgins, English writer (b.1929): Henry Patterson

William Holden, US actor (1918–81): William Beedle

Billie Holiday, US jazz singer (1915–59): Eleanora Gough McKay, née Fagan

Buddy Holly, US rock musician (1936–59): Charles Hardin Holley (*see also* AMERICAN PIE)

Rock Hudson, US actor (1925–85): Roy Harold Fitzgerald, originally Roy Scherer

Engelbert Humperdinck, English pop singer (b.1936): Arnold George Dorsey

Elton John, English pop musician (b.1947): Reginald Kenneth Dwight

Tom Jones, Welsh popular singer (b.1940): Thomas Jones Woodward

Boris Karloff, English actor (1887–1969): William Henry Pratt

Penelope Keith, English actress (b.1940): Penelope Timson, née Hatfield

Alexander Korda, Hungarian-born film producer (1893–1956): Sándor László Kellner

Veronica Lake, US actress (1919–73): Constance Frances Marie Ockleman

Dorothy Lamour, US actress (1914–96): Dorothy Mary Leta Lambour, earlier Slaton

Lupino Lane, English comic actor (1892–1959): Henry Lane George Lupino

Mario Lanza, Italian-born US opera singer (1921–59): Alfredo Cocozza

John Le Carré, English writer (b.1931): David John Moore Cornwell

Vanessa Lee, English actress and singer (1920–92): Winifred Ruby Moule

Sophia Loren, Italian actress (b.1934): Sofia Scicolone

Lulu, Scottish popular singer, television presenter (b.1948): Marie McDonald McLaughlin Lawrie

Vera Lynn, English popular singer (b.1917): Vera Margaret Welch

Hugh MacDiarmid, Scottish poet (1892–1978): Christopher Murray Grieve

Madonna: US pop singer (b.1958): Mary Louise Ciccione

Marilyn MONROE, US actress (1926–62): Norma Jeane Dougherty, née Mortensen, later Baker

Ivor Novello, Welsh actor and playwright (1893–1951): David Ivor Davies

Maureen O'Hara, Irish-born US actress (b.1920): Maureen FitzSimons

Patti Page, US pop singer (b.1927): Clara Ann Fowler

Nicola Pagett, English actress (b.1945): Nicola Mary Scott

Jean Plaidy *and* Victoria Holt, English novelist (1906–93): Eleanor Alice Hibbert, née Burford

Ted Ray, English comedian (1905–77): Charles Olden

Miss Read, English writer (b.1913): Dora Jessie Saint, née Shafe

Mary Renault, British writer (1905–83): Eileen Mary Challans

Frank Richards, English writer (1875–1961): Charles Hamilton (*see also* Billy BUNTER)

Roy Rogers, US actor (1912–98): Leonard Franklin Slye

Sax Rohmer, English writer (1886–1959): Arthur Sarsfield Ward

Omar Sharif, Egyptian actor (b.1932): Michael Shalhoub

Ringo Starr, English drummer (b.1940): Richard Starkey

Alvin Stardust, English rock singer (b.1942): Bernard William Jewry

Sting, English rock singer (b.1951): Gordon Matthew Sumner

Sophie Tucker, US actress (1884–1966): Sophia Abuza, originally Kalish

Arthur M. Winfield, US writer (1863–1930): Edward L. Stratemeyer

John Wyndham, English writer (1903–69): John Wyndham Parkes Lucas Beynon Harris

Ximenes, English crossword compiler (1902–71): Derrick Somerset Macnutt

*See also* Theda BARA; Camille JAVAL; LENIN; George ORWELL; SAKI; STALIN.

**Psion.** The proprietary name of an early make of palmtop computer. The company that made it was set up in 1980 by David Potter, originally a designer of computer games, and it folded in 2001. The acronymic name represents 'Potter Scientific Instruments', with the final '-on' allegedly originating in Potter's last word in an argument about what the company should be called: 'It's Potter Scientific Instruments or nothing'. 'Psion' itself happens also to be a scientific term for a psi particle.

Psions were amongst the first PDAs (*personal digital assistants*), of which the portable E-MAIL devices such as the BLACKBERRY are a development.

**Psmith.** The eccentric young snob created by P.G. Wodehouse for a series of stories, and first appearing in a boys' paper, the *Captain*, in 1908. His full name is Rupert (or Ronald) Eustace Smith, and the initial P is an affectation, as is the monocle he sports. Although educated at Eton, he claims to be a socialist and calls everyone 'Comrade'. He is the leading character in three novels, *Psmith in the City* (1910), *Psmith Journalist* (1910) and *Leave it to Psmith* (1923), in the last of which he visits Blandings Castle and makes the acquaintance of Lord EMSWORTH. Wodehouse based Psmith on Rupert D'Oyly Carte (1876–1948), son of Richard D'Oyly Carte, the impresario and producer of Gilbert and Sullivan operas.

**Psychedelic.** The term relating to hallucinogenic drugs such as LSD was on the lips of many in the 1960s but was coined in 1956 in a letter to Aldous Huxley by Humphry Osmond, a British research scientist, then living in Canada. It represents Greek *psukhé*, 'mind', and *dēlos*, 'clear', since he regarded such drugs as 'enriching the mind and enlarging the vision'. Purists argued that 'psychodelic' would have been a better formation. The BEATLES album SERGEANT PEPPER'S LONELY HEARTS CLUB BAND (1967) was described at the time as 'psychedelic' music but the word came to be mostly used as a general term for anything perceived as remotely avant-garde.

**Psycho.** A suspenseful film (1960) adapted by Joseph Stefano from a novel by Robert Bloch about the deranged Norman BATES, a psychopath (hence the title) who murders visitors to the Bates Motel that he runs. Arguably the most famous of all Alfred Hitchcock's thrillers, it is best remembered for the much-imitated scene in which Janet Leigh is knifed to death in a shower. It spawned two lesser sequels, both starring Anthony Perkins, who played Norman in Hitchcock's original, and a particularly egregious remake, which followed the original script almost exactly, appeared in 1998, directed by Gus Van Sant.

> Don't give away the ending – it's the only one we have!
> Alfred Hitchcock

**Psychobabble.** A derogatory term for the jargon of popular psychology, especially as used by lay people with regard to their own personality or relationships. The word dates from the 1970s and was popularized by the title of R.D. Rosen's book *Psychobabble: Fast Talk and Quick Cure in the Era of Feeling* (1977).

> 'Borderline personality disorder', a term of American psychobabble that embraces a multitude of miseries.
> *Sunday Times* (19 September 1999)

**Psych oneself up.** To gird up one's mental loins for an important or challenging enterprise. The phrase originated in the United States in the 1960s in the context of self-expression or GROUP THERAPY.

**Psych someone out.** To intimidate them by outmanoeuvring them. The implication is that one is using psychology to seek out one's opponent's weak points.

**Pub bore.** A solitary drinker in a pub who importunes others with lengthy reminiscences or other tedious monologues. He has come for the company, but usually succeeds in alienating it. The type has long provided good material for comedians and has been portrayed in various shows and programmes, such as television's *The* FAST SHOW, in which he is played by Paul Whitehouse.

**Pub crawl.** To go on a pub crawl is to partake in a drinking session in which one progresses, after suitable refreshment, from one public house to another, the number of such visited obviously depending on the length of stay at each and the capacity of the 'crawler' to stay the course.

**Pub grub.** Commercial jargon for meals served in a pub. For many years the British public house was simply a dedicated beer bar and 'boozer', but by the end of the 1970s had become a place of civilized refreshment. The use of 'grub' rather than 'food' is an earnest of a friendly welcome.

**Public enemy number one.** The designation by which the US bank robber and murderer John Dillinger (1903–34) came to be known. It was officially applied to him in 1933 by the US attorney general, Homer Cummings. Once coined it was used subsequently for a wide range of people badly wanted by the police (notably the African American activist Angela Davis (b.1944), so named by the FBI for her championship of black prisoners and in particular for her association with the revolutionary George Jackson, one of the so-called Soledad (Prison) Brothers), and it became almost a generic term for a notorious criminal at large. The basic formula also permits variations:

> I think you're a bit hard on Bruce Mitchell, and in case you don't know, in the Transvaal he's public heart-throb number one.
>
> Unnamed South African woman: in 1939, quoted in
> D. Rayvern Allen, *Jim: The Life of E.W. Swanton* (2004)

**Pub quiz.** This peculiarly British and predominantly male pastime has become an essential weekly ritual in many pubs. It evolved in the 1980s with the introduction of the board game TRIVIAL PURSUIT and quiz machines in pubs, the quiz itself having its roots in US GAME SHOWS. Typical pub quiz questions are: 'What colour is the flight recorder in aeroplanes?' or 'Which way did Dickens always face when writing?' (The respective answers are 'Orange' and 'North'.) The real point of such quizzes is for participants to show how intelligent they are, although it is normally a limited sort of intelligence that is expected, as these examples illustrate.

**Puckoon.** A comic novella (1963) by Spike Milligan (1918–2002). 'Several and a half metric miles North East of Sligo, split by a cascading stream, her body on earth, her feet in water, dwells the microcephalic community of Puckoon.'

**Pudding bowl** or **basin.** A term used for a hairstyle in which the hair is cut, or looks as if it has been cut, by inverting a pudding bowl on the person's head and trimming off the hair that protrudes underneath. The style is popularly or pictorially associated with holy or saintly individuals.

**Puffin crossing.** A pedestrian crossing with traffic lights that revert to showing green only when infrared detectors and mats on the crossing detect that no pedestrians are present. The name derives from 'pedestrian user-friendly intelligent', assimilated to 'puffin' in the manner of the earlier PELICAN CROSSING.

**Pugwash.** An international organization of scientists, academics and other prominent figures who work for the avoidance of armed conflict, and for nuclear disarmament. It was founded in 1957 in Pugwash, a town in Nova Scotia, by the physicist Joseph Rotblat (1908–2005) and the philosopher Bertrand Russell (1872–1970). Rotblat and Pugwash were jointly awarded the 1995 Nobel Peace Prize.

**Pugwash, Captain.** *See* CAPTAIN PUGWASH.

**Puleeze.** Don't give me that! A sarcastic two-syllable distortion of 'please' (with numerous spelling variations, including 'per-leeze', 'pur-leeze' and 'puh-leeze') indicative of pained incredulity.

> Alix embarrassed? Vulnerable? Oh, puleeeze, Mr Connery, do *not* be so patronizing!
>
> *The Times Magazine* (20 November 1999)

> A young, cloistered, prematurely wealthy white male – and he thought he knew the street? *Purlease*.
>
> GIDEON HAIGH: *Ashes 2005* (2005)

**Pulitzer prizes.** Prizes for literary work, journalism, drama and music, which are awarded annually from funds left for the purpose by the Hungarian-born US newspaper magnate Joseph Pulitzer (1847–1911). The prizes are administered by the trustees of Columbia University and were first awarded in 1917.

**Pull a fast one.** To obtain an advantage by trickery or deception. The phrase is generally said to have its origin in cricket matches of the 1930s, when the English captain, Douglas Jardine, instructed his fast bowlers, Larwood and Voce, to abandon gentlemanly deliveries and bowl fast and short at the batsman's body. Such BODYLINE BOWLING produced the desired results, and the intimidated batsmen were speedily dismissed. The expression is recorded in US texts of the 1920s, however, and may in fact allude to a fast shuffle of the cards in gambling.

**Pull a swiftie.** The Australian equivalent of PULL A FAST ONE. It dates from the 1940s.

**Pull** or **get** or **take one's finger out.** To stop being lazy or procrastinating and start to apply oneself energetically to what one ought to be doing. The expression (which is first recorded in 1941, in Australian English) presumably relies on the image of someone vacantly scratching their anus as the epitome of idleness. The underlying notion was enough to cause some tremors of shock when Prince Philip used the phrase publicly in the early 1960s (see the quote below), but it has since become reasonably respectable. It is sometimes facetiously formalized to 'remove *or* extricate the digit', or even 'dedigitate', and in New Zealand slang it has been reduced to the much terser 'pull finger'.

> Just at the moment we are suffering a national defeat comparable to any lost military campaign and, what is more, it is self-inflicted ... I think it is time we pulled our finger out.
>
> PRINCE PHILIP: speech to businessmen (17 October 1961)

**Pull one's punches.** To restrain oneself. A phrase of the 1930s that originated in the boxing ring. When a boxer 'pulls his punches' he pulls back during a punch just before the full force of the blow is felt, so landing a lighter blow than usual on his opponent. The usage is mainly negative, as: 'He didn't pull his punches when it came to saying what he thought.'

**Pull rank.** To use one's senior status within a hierarchy to unfair advantage. The expression is of US military origin and dates from the 1920s.

> No one at *The Spectator* pulls rank at work.
>
> *The Times* (4 February 2000)

**Pull the plug.** To terminate; to cancel. The image is now usually of an electric plug being pulled from its socket but the reference is in fact to an early type of lavatory flush which involved the pulling out of a plug to empty the pan into the soil pipe. 'To pull the plug' is also to commit suicide, as if disconnecting oneself from a life-support machine.

> Earlier this year Mirror Group pulled the plug on its accident-prone plan to relaunch *The Sporting Life* as a daily sports newspaper.
>
> *The Times* (13 August 1999)

**Pull the rug from under someone.** To withdraw abruptly one's support for them. The image is similar to the childish trick of pulling away a person's chair as they are about to sit down on it. The expression dates from the 1940s.

**Pulp Fiction.** A violent but entertaining film thriller (1994) written and directed by Quentin Tarantino (b.1963) in which four tales about the underworld are cleverly interwoven in circular fashion. The title deliberately evokes the kind of trashy, violent crime fiction published in PULP MAGAZINES.

**Pulp magazines.** A genre of popular US magazines at their height in the 1920s and 1930s. They contained sensationalist crime writing, often highly erotic in nature, and helped create the character of the laconic 'tough guy'. The most influential of the kind was *Black Mask*, founded in 1930 and publishing Raymond Chandler's first short story, 'Blackmailers Don't Shoot' (1933). Others were *Popular Detective* and *Dime Detective Magazine*. The magazines were so called as they were originally printed on rough paper made of cheap wood pulp.

**Pump iron.** To exercise with weights in fitness training or for purposes of body-building. 'Pump' refers to the up-and-down movements of the exerciser's arms, and 'iron' to the weights. The term is of US origin and dates from the early 1970s.

**Punch-drunk.** Stupefied, like a boxer who has sustained brain damage from repeated blows to the head and who thus resembles a drunkard. The expression dates from the early years of the 20th century and is usually applied literally to any state of physical confusion or disorientation.

**Punk.** An old word for a harlot, a worthless person or thing. From the mid-1970s it came to be applied to certain young people who reacted against the HIPPIE ethos by adopting an aggressive mien (involving much swearing and spitting), producing raucous PUNK ROCK and wearing shabby, torn clothes (sometimes held together with safety pins and/or incorporating black bin liners) and short, spiky hairstyles (especially the mohican). *See also* GOTH; HELL'S ANGELS; MODS AND ROCKERS; RIOT GRRLS; SKINHEADS.

**Punk rock.** A form of rock music of a raw and (to some ears) cacophonous nature, as typified by British bands such as the Sex Pistols. Punk burst on the music scene in the mid-1970s, in reaction to the sometimes overblown and pretentious PROG ROCK that had preceded it. Some punk lyrics were politically engaged, others nihilistic. Although punk was succeeded by the end of the decade by a rather more melodious 'post-punk' idiom, notably NEW WAVE, its influence persists. *See also* 'CALIFORNIA ÜBER ALLES'; NEVER MIND THE BOLLOCKS, HERE'S THE SEX PISTOLS; ROCK GROUP NAMES.

> You just pick a chord, go twang, and you've got music.
>
> SID VICIOUS: quoted in J. Green, *The Book of Rock Quotes* (1982)

***Puppetry of the Penis.*** A cabaret show conceived by Simon Morley and David Friend, and first performed by them in Australia in 1998. The two men, who claim the show is a revival of 'the ancient art of genital origami', manipulate their penises, scrotums and testicles into a variety of objects, such as a hamburger, a windsurfer and a mollusc. The official publicity describes the show as 'an over 18 non-sexual show'. *See also* the VAGINA MONOLOGUES.

**Puppy fat.** Chubbiness in a young child, which usually disappears at adolescence. The phrase dates from the 1930s and can also be used generally of any young person's plumpness. Nutritionists claim that the amount of puppy fat on an 11-year-old gives the best indication of the size of subsequent MIDDLE-AGE SPREAD.

**Purple Heart.** The original US military decoration of this name was instituted by George Washington in 1782 and awarded for bravery in action. It was simply a purple heart-shaped piece of cloth edged with silver braid and sewn onto the coat. Records show that only three men received it during the War of American Independence (1775–83), after which it was forgotten about for some 150 years. It was revived on 22 February 1932, the bicentenary of Washington's birth, this time as a medal in the form of a purple heart-shaped badge with bronze edges and a relief bust of Washington in military uniform. The reverse side has the inscription 'For Military Merit' and the recipient's name. Purple hearts was also a 1960s slang term for amphetamines.

**Purple prose.** Over-elaborate prose. The term is based on 'purple patch' or 'purple passage' for an excessively ornate passage in a literary composition. This in turn derives from Horace's reference to *purpureus pannus*, 'purple patch', in his *Ars Poetica* (1st century BC), as the purple piece of cloth which is an irrelevant insertion of a grandiloquent passage into a work.

**Pusher.** A supplier of illicit drugs. The expression, dating from the 1930s, takes 'push' as a verb meaning 'to promote', 'to attempt to sell'. The term is only rarely used by pushers or dealers themselves.

**Push one's luck.** To act rashly on the assumption that one will continue to be successful; to seek to gain greater favour than one has already been granted. The expression is frequently found in a negative warning: 'Don't push your luck.'

**Push paper about.** To engage in paperwork; to do petty office jobs.

**Push someone around.** To treat them roughly or inconsiderately; to browbeat or dominate them. The expression dates from the 1920s.

**Push the boat out.** To be lavish in one's spending, especially when entertaining other people. The reference is to a shore party setting off to the mother ship, an operation in which one member of the group is usually soaked while freeing the boat from the beach. The expression dates from the 1930s.

**Push the envelope.** To go beyond normal limits; to pioneer. The phrase comes from aviation, in which an 'envelope' is the known limit of an aircraft's range and powers, so called from their appearance on a graph. 'Pushing' such an envelope could thus mean flying fast enough to break the sound barrier.

> The start of a second [television] series for Alexander and Ben, who are staying faithful to the sketch-show format while pushing the envelope in an appealing manner.
> *The Times* (7 August 1999)

**Push the panic button.** *See* PANIC BUTTON.

**Push tin.** To work as an air traffic controller, the 'tin' being the aircraft. The US colloquialism was popularized by the film *Pushing Tin* (1999), about the stresses and strains in the professional and private life of an operator at New York's Terminal Radar Approach Control.

**Push up the daisies.** To be dead and buried. The idea is that the dead body fertilizes the soil, so stimulating the growth of the daisies in the churchyard. The expression is first recorded in a poem by Wilfred Owen written in the First World War. Keats had earlier written of 'daisies growing over me' in a letter of 1821, the year of his death.

**Put a sock in it.** To be quiet; to shut up. The mouth can be gagged with a sock. The expression dates from the First World War.

**Put down roots.** To settle in a locality; to make a place one's home. The expression dates from the 1920s and likens human settlement to the rooting of a plant.

**Put lead in one's pencil.** *See* LEAD IN ONE'S PENCIL.

**Put oneself about.** To be socially active or, depending on context, sexually promiscuous. The expression dates from the 1970s.

**Put one's foot down.** Apart from the established sense to adopt a firm position a more recent meaning of the phrase is to speed up a motor vehicle by pressing on the accelerator. *See also* STEP ON IT.

> I put my foot down and the Zephyr gathered speed up the slope.
> JOHN BRAINE: *Life at the Top*, ch. 2 (1962)

**Put one's foot in one's mouth.** To make a verbal gaffe; to say something that embarrasses oneself as much as the hearer. The expression is an elaboration of the older 'to put one's foot in it'. *See also* FOOT-IN-MOUTH DISEASE.

**Put one's hands together.** To applaud; to clap. A stock phrase with a master of ceremonies, as: 'I now ask you to put your hands together for [the person announced].'

**Put one's hand** or **hands up.** To confess. An underworld expression originating in the 1950s from the classroom, as a child's response to a question such as 'Who knows?' or 'Whose is this?' *See also* NOD THE NUT.

**Put** or **raise one's head above the parapet.** To speak out and make one's views heard, especially with regard to a controversial issue about which one might otherwise have stayed silent. The image is of raising one's head above the protective wall of a trench, so exposing oneself to possible enemy fire.

> Any woman who puts her head above the parapet in public life still tends to find that she attracts a degree of hatred, suspicion and antagonism that would be thought remarkable for a man.
>
> AMANDA CRAIG: in *Sunday Times* (26 December 1999)

**Put one's money where one's mouth is.** To support one's statements or opinions with suitable action. The expression relates to gambling in the general context of 'deeds, not words'.

**Putsch.** *See* BEER HALL PUTSCH; FREIKORPS.

**Put someone down.** To belittle them by criticizing or deriding them before others. Hence 'put-down' as a term for such criticism or derision.

**Put someone in the picture.** To inform them what is happening; to include them as an active participant in an undertaking. The idea is that one can add a person to the existing scenario. The expression dates from the turn of the 20th century.

**Put someone off their stroke.** To disconcert them; to disrupt the pattern of their work. The expression dates from the early 20th century and alludes to a player's stroke in a game of golf.

**Put someone through the wringer.** To pressurize them; to subject them to severe interrogation. The wringer here is the old-fashioned mangle used to wring water from rinsed clothes after washing. The expression dates from the 1940s.

**Put something on hold.** To postpone or defer it. The term dates from the 1960s and alludes to the period in which one waits for a connection during a telephone call.

**Put the arm on.** To attempt to force someone to do something, especially to hand over money. The reference is to an attack from the rear by a robber who hooks his arm around his victim's throat. The expression dates from the 1930s.

**Put the boot in.** Literally, to kick hard and brutally. Metaphorically, to treat someone harshly, especially when they are vulnerable. The phrase dates from the First World War but was taken up by SKINHEADs in the 1960s.

**Put** or **set the cat among the pigeons.** To say or do something that causes trouble or alarm. The allusion is obvious.

**Put the finger on.** To betray; to inform; to identify a target or possible victim. The image is of pointing one's finger at the person concerned. The phrase originated in US underworld slang and dates from the 1920s.

**Put the frighteners on.** To intimidate; to menace. An underworld expression of the 1960s. The frighteners are any threatening things or people that will scare a person into complying.

> A key-jangling oaf in tanned acrylic and a brown peak cap might put the frighteners on the bumbling British shoplifter but in Rio de Janeiro … protecting your property requires a little more attention to detail.
>
> *Maxim* (April 2000)

**Put the hard word on.** In Australian slang, to make importunate requests of someone; to PUT THE SCREWS ON someone. The expression is first recorded in 1923.

> ASIC puts the hard word on licence applicants [headline]. The Australian Securities and Investments Commission last week sent out a confidential 'hurry up' message to corporate and compliance chiefs.
>
> www.theage.com.au (27 January 2004)

**Put the mockers on.** To put a stop to; to put a jinx on. The expression was in Australian use in the early years of the 20th century but may have originally come from the language of English market traders and be based on Yiddish *makkes*, ultimately from Hebrew *makot*, 'plagues', 'visitations'. It is hard to see 'the mockers' as 'the people who mock' for no such regular class exists.

**Put the mouth on.** To appear to bring bad luck on someone by saying something positive about them. For example, a cricket commentator praising the play of a batsman who then is immediately dismissed might be said to have 'put the mouth on' him. The expression is of Australian origin.

**Put the moz on.** The Australian version of PUT THE MOCKERS ON. It dates from the 1920s. 'Moz' is short for 'mozzle', meaning 'luck', which in turn came from Hebrew *mazzāl*, 'luck'.

**Put the screws on.** To pressure. The screws are the thumbscrews, formerly used in tortures to extract information.

**Put the squeeze on.** To put the pressure on; to coerce. The phrase dates from the 1940s.

**Putty in someone's hands.** Easily swayed or manipulated by them. An expression dating from the 1920s that transfers the malleable quality of putty to human behaviour.

**Put up or shut up.** A pugilistic twist on the injunction to 'put your money where your mouth is', i.e. 'put up your fists for a fight, or stop arguing with me'. (In the United States, the phrase is taken to mean, 'put up your wager'.) On 22 June 1995 John Major, suffering from hostility and dissidence within both the parliamentary party and the cabinet, resigned as Tory leader in order to stand for re-election. In his statement he declared:

> The Conservative Party must make its choice. Every leader is leader only with the support of his party. That is true of me as well. That is why I am no longer prepared to tolerate the present situation. In short, it is time to put up or shut up.

**Puzzle Palace.** A US nickname dating from the 1950s for any place of decision-making and in particular the White House and the PENTAGON. The term was used for the title of James Bamford's book *The Puzzle Palace* (1982), a definitive and revealing account of the work of the National Security Agency, the principal US signals intelligence organization.

***Pygmalion.*** A play (1913) by George Bernard Shaw (1856–1950) about a phonetician's campaign to transform a roughly spoken cockney FLOWER GIRL into a sophisticated society lady. The play was the basis of the popular musical MY FAIR LADY (1956; film 1964). The title refers to Ovid's story of Pygmalion, the sculptor whose statue of a beautiful woman comes to life so that he can marry her. The inclusion of the word 'bloody' in the script, the first time it had been heard on the English stage, caused a sensation and for some years later the title of the play itself entered use as a euphemism for 'bloody' (*see* NOT PYGMALION LIKELY!).

**Pyjama cricket.** A derisive term for professional one-day limited-overs cricket, in which since around 1980 the players have worn coloured clothing rather than the traditional whites.

**Pyjama party.** A party at which the guests wear pyjamas, as if prepared for the nocturnal fun to come. The expression and activity date from the early years of the 20th century.

**Pylon school.** A name applied to various poets of the 1930s whose writing contained imagery reflecting the impact of industry and technology on Britain's countryside and culture. Pylons themselves feature in several works of the period, with Stephen Spender's 'The Pylons' (1933) being typical of the genre and providing its name:

> Now over these small hills, they have built the concrete
> That trails black wire;
> Pylons, those pillars
> Bare like nude, giant girls that have no secret.

**PYO.** *See* PICK YOUR OWN.

**Pyramid selling.** A system of selling goods whereby distributors recruit other distributors and sell them the goods at a profit. The second batch of distributors does the same, and the process proceeds similarly, as if down the side of a pyramid. The inevitable consequence is that the final distributors, at the lowest level, are likely to find themselves with stock that is too expensive to sell. In a particularly egregious recent instance, two-thirds of the Albanian population invested in pyramid schemes in 1996–7, and when they collapsed the already parlous national economy went into a downward spiral. The system is illegal in Britain. The term itself dates from the mid-1970s.

**Pyrex.** The heat-resistant glass ovenware of this name was first manufactured in 1915 by the Corning Glass Works, established in Corning, New York, in 1868. The name itself is popularly explained as blending Greek *pur*, 'fire', with Latin *rex*, 'king', but the company has a different explanation:

> The assistant secretary of the [Corning Glass] company wrote me as follows: The word *pyrex* is a purely arbitrary word which was devised in 1915 as a trademark for products manufactured and sold by Corning Glass Works … We had a number of prior trademarks ending in the letters *ex*. One of the first commercial products to be sold under the new mark was a pie plate and in the interests of euphonism the letter *r* was inserted between *pie* and *ex* and the whole thing condensed to *pyrex*.
>
> *American Speech*, XXXII (1957)

# Q

**Q.** The master of gadgetry in the James BOND films, who provides Bond with a range of devices, from an exploding pen to an Aston Martin equipped with an ejector seat. Q stands for 'Quartermaster', and the character's name is actually Major Boothroyd. Q has been played in the films mostly by Desmond Llewelyn and then more recently by John Cleese. He is often heard to say, 'Oh do grow up, 007.'

**QALY.** The acronym of *quality-adjusted life year*, a term invented by economists at the Centre for Health Economics at the University of York as a way of assigning a numerical value to the quality of extra years of life that a particular person's medical treatment will yield if successful. The procedure enables administrators to decide who to treat by dividing the expected cost of the treatment by the number of QALYs. Although not yet used as an official yardstick by the NHS, it was taken seriously enough to be the subject of a BMA seminar in 1986.

**QE2.** The short name of the *Queen Elizabeth 2*, the passenger liner launched in 1967 that made its maiden voyage in 1969. The ship was launched by Queen Elizabeth II but is not named after her. Its name commemorates its predecessor, the *Queen Elizabeth*, launched in 1938 and named after the wife of George VI, i.e. the future Queen Elizabeth the Queen Mother. While being built the *QE2* was actually known as the 'Q3', as the third of the 'Queens', the first being the QUEEN MARY.

**Q fever.** An infectious disease caused by rickettsiae and transmitted to humans from cattle, sheep and goats by unpasteurized milk. It was first recorded in 1935 in Queensland, Australia, among slaughtermen, cattle ranchers and dairy farmers, when its causative organism was unknown. Hence the name, with Q standing for 'query'.

**Q ships.** In the First World War the name given to warships camouflaged as tramp steamers. These 'mystery ships' were used to lure U-BOATs to their destruction. 'Q' represents 'query'.

**Quality circle.** A group of employers who meet to discuss ways of improving production, resolving problems and so on, within their organization, especially in factories. The concept evolved in Japan and was adopted in Britain from the early 1980s, partly as a result of Japanese ownership of some businesses and the consequent introduction of certain Japanese management techniques.

**Quality of life.** The degree of satisfaction or contentment afforded to an individual by their everyday existence and circumstances. The term dates back to the 1940s (it is first recorded in the context of speculation as to how people would live their lives after the Second World War). There is often some expressed or implied contrast in its use – for example, with the length or continuation of existence (e.g. in discussions over the desirability of prolonging the life of a terminally ill person) or with sheer material prosperity.

> He [David Cameron] has spoken about 'quality of life' being more important to people than 'quantity of money'. That's a promising theme, but not perhaps the speech to make the morning after attending the Beckhams' £500,000 party.
> *The Observer* (11 June 2006)

**Quality Street.** The confectionery assortment of this name was introduced in 1936 by John Mackintosh & Sons Ltd (*see* ROWNTREE MACKINTOSH). The name was adopted from the title of J.M. Barrie's play *Quality Street* (1902), set in *c*.1805, and the product's identity was based on the play's main characters, a soldier and his young lady. Early advertisements depicted the couple, renamed 'Miss Sweetly' and 'Major Quality', dressed in period costume, with Miss Sweetly opening a tin of the assortment to show to the Major and with dialogue beginning as follows:

> *Major Quality*: Sweets to the Sweet, Miss Sweetly.

*Miss Sweetly*: Spare my blushes, Major Quality. Feast your eyes rather on this sumptuous array of Toffees and Chocolates.

*Major Q.*: A feast, indeed. What is this wonderful confection?

*Miss S.*: 'Tis the most momentous thing that has yet happened in the world of sweetness. It is a box of Mackintosh's 'Quality Street' Assortment.

*Major Q.*: The fame of Mackintosh for Quality I know well.

*Miss S.*: And that, dear Major, is just why they have called this, their very latest and greatest achievement – 'Quality Street' – for Quality is its keynote through and through.

> *Daily Mail*, advertisement (2 May 1936)

**Quality time.** An American phrase and concept of the 1970s, meaning time spent productively or profitably, either with a partner or especially by parents with their children. The expression subsequently gained a euphemistic veneer for the limited time available for this. Many working parents are too tired at the end of the day to spend much time, 'quality' or otherwise, with their children.

**Quango.** An acronym for quasi (or quasi-autonomous) non-governmental organization, as a cumbersome term for a type of semi-administrative body that is outside the civil service but that is financially supported by the government, which also appoints its members. Quangos originated in the United States in 1967 and first emerged in Britain in 1973. They multiplied rapidly, so that by the end of the 1970s they numbered over 3000. Despite government promises to review the proliferation, there were still more than 2000 quangos in the mid-1990s. The name gained a derogatory taint, and in the 21st century 'quango' was (officially) replaced by 'NDPB' (Non-Departmental Public Body). In 2005 there were 861 NDPBs, such as the Architects Registration Board and the Dairy Produce Quota Tribunal.

**Quantum leap.** A sudden large advance; a spectacular leap forward. The term evolved in the 1970s as a variant of the older 'quantum jump', which properly and originally described the abrupt transition of an electron, atom or molecule from one energy state to another. Such a 'leap' is not of course large in the traditional sense, however spectacular it may have seemed to physicists. The present sense may have come about through a wrong association of 'quantum' with 'quantity'.

> The imperial Presidency did not begin with Richard Nixon although under him abuses of the offices took a quantum leap.
>
> *The New Yorker* (13 June 1977)

**Quare Fellow, The.** A play (1954) by the Irish playwright Brendan Behan (1923–64) about events in a Dublin prison on the eve of an execution. The 'quare fellow' (in Irish English, a 'queer' or eccentric man) of the title is the man due to be hanged, a pork butcher who butchered his own brother with a meat cleaver.

**Quark.** A term in physics for any of a group of subatomic particles, originally three in number, believed to be among the fundamental constituents of matter. Quarks have not been directly observed but theoretical predictions based on their existence have been confirmed experimentally. There are six types or 'flavours': up, down, top, bottom, strange and charm, each of which has three varieties or 'colours': red, yellow and blue. To each quark there is an antiparticle, called an antiquark. The name of the particle was coined in 1964 by the US physicist Murray Gell-Mann and based on the line 'Three quarks for Muster Mark' in James Joyce's novel FINNEGANS WAKE (1939), words that are said to be a whimsical perversion of 'Three quarts for Mr Mark'.

Quark Xpress is a leading software package in use in the publishing and printing industries for graphic design and for laying out pages of books.

**Quarry Men.** The SKIFFLE group founded by John Lennon that was eventually to metamorphose into The BEATLES.

**Quartet for the End of Time.** A presumably eschatological chamber work for violin, clarinet, cello and piano by Olivier Messiaen (1908–92). The work was written in 1941 while Messiaen was a prisoner of war of the Germans in Silesia, which explains the unusual combination of instruments and perhaps also the title.

**Quatermass.** A pioneering BBC television series of SCIENCE FICTION dramas, written by Nigel Kneale and featuring a scientist called Professor Bernard Quatermass. The first, *The Quatermass Experiment* (1953), concerned an experimental spacecraft, which returned to earth with its sole occupant contaminated by an alien virus that subsequently transmuted him into a vast vegetable. Later in the series came *Quatermass II* (1955) and *Quatermass and the Pit* (1958–9). The dramas owed their considerable impact both to their unsettling scripts and to Rudolph Cartier's inspired production and direction. All three were subsequently filmed for the cinema. An additional series, called simply *Quatermass*, followed in 1979 on ITV.

**Queen Elizabeth.** *See* QE2.

**Queen Mary.** A former nickname for a long, low-loading road trailer, comparing it to the huge passenger liner of this name, launched in 1938 but in 1967 turned into a floating hotel.

**Queen Mary hat.** A type of toque popularized by Queen

Mary (1867–1953), wife of George V, and favoured by her because it enabled the public to have a clear view of her face.

**Queen of Crime.** A promotional nickname given to the crime novelist Agatha Christie (1891–1976), and subsequently to her successors in this role, P.D. James (b.1920) and Ruth Rendell (b.1930).

**Queen of Hearts.** A sentimental sobriquet applied by the British media to Diana, Princess of Wales (1961–97) for her charity work and concern for the victims of misfortune.

> The BBC last night defended its decision to cut footage of the Princess Royal reacting angrily to a comparison with the late Diana, Princess of Wales. The film apparently showed the Princess's clear resentment of her former sister-in-law's popular image as a 'Queen of Hearts'.
> *The Times* (3 October 1998)

*See also* PRINCESS OF HEARTS.

**Queen of the Air.** A nickname given by journalists to the pioneer British aviator Amy Johnson (1903–41). She came into the public eye in 1930 when she flew solo from Britain to Darwin in Australia, although she failed to beat the record by three days. Her flights to Tokyo (1931) and to Cape Town (1932) did break records, however. In the Second World War she served with the Air Transport Auxiliary and disappeared while on a mission somewhere over the Thames estuary.

**Queen of the Halls.** A nickname of the music-hall singer and comedienne Marie Lloyd (originally Matilda Alice Victoria Wood; 1870–1922). She made her debut in 1885 and collapsed on stage in 1922, dying a few days later. Her brand of risqué Cockney comedy was highly popular, and her songs included 'Oh, Mr Porter', 'I'm One of the Ruins that Cromwell Knocked About a Bit' and 'A Little of What You Fancy Does You Good'.

**Queenybopper.** A nickname given in his teenage years to Prince Edward (b.1964; now the Earl of Wessex). The name puns on 'teenybopper'.

**Queer.** The sense 'homosexual' for this word emerged only in the 1920s, its origin perhaps not so much in the established English sense of 'strange', 'unusual', but closer to the possible source in German *quer*, 'oblique', 'perverse'. Homosexuals long found the word offensive, but later came to adopt it as an alternative for GAY, and it was readily promoted in the 1990s by the homosexual liberation movement Queer Nation, their motto being: 'We're here, we're queer. Get used to it.'

The term has now gone mainstream. In 1999, the Russell T. Davies-authored (*see also* DOCTOR WHO) drama series *Queer as Folk*, about gay men's lives on the Manchester scene, premiered on Channel 4, and the following year a US version (set in Pittsburgh) was broadcast. In the MAKEOVER TV-obsessed 21st century, *A Queer Eye for the Straight Guy* is a lighhearted television series in which five gay men reform many aspects of a heterosexual man's life, from his wardrobe to his conversation.

**Queer Hardie.** A nickname of Keir Hardie (1856–1915), the former coalminer who in 1892 became the first socialist member of parliament, founding the Independent Labour Party the following year. He lost his seat in 1895 but was re-elected in 1900, holding his seat until his death. The nickname refers to his quirks of manner and dress, such as attending parliament in a cloth cap rather than the conventional top hat and dress coat. *See also* Worzel GUMMIDGE.

**Question mark.** To say that a question mark hangs or is over something is to express doubt or uncertainty about it. The cliché dates from the 1920s.

**Quick and dirty.** Makeshift; done or produced hastily. The term arose in the 1960s as an American colloquialism for a cheap café, where food preparation was perfunctory and hygiene deficient.

**Quick buck.** *See* FAST BUCK.

**Quick fix.** A quick but probably none too permanent or satisfactory solution to a problem. The expression dates from the 1960s.

**Quick on the draw.** Quick to act or react. The allusion is to the gunslinger of the American West who was adept at drawing his gun instantly from its holster when necessary. An earlier variant was 'quick on the trigger'.

**Quidditch.** In the Harry POTTER novels of J.K. Rowling, the wizarding team sport that is also the school sport of HOGWARTS. It is a fast and violent aerial game, played by two teams of seven players mounted on broomsticks. There are four balls, one of which, the Quaffle, must be put through a hoop to score a goal. In *Harry Potter and the Goblet of Fire* wizards and witches from around the world descend on England variously to take part in or watch the finals of the Quidditch World Cup: Irish and Bulgarian wizards seem to be particularly good at it. *See also* SNITCH.

**Quids in.** In luck or money; in profit; up on a deal. The phrase dates from the First World War.

**Quiet American.** A nickname for a person suspected of being an undercover agent or spy. The name comes from the title of Graham Greene's novel *The Quiet American* (1955), in which Alden Pyle, an idealistic graduate who becomes involved in US-sponsored political terrorism during the Indochinese War of the early 1950s, is the 'quiet American'. The book is prophetic of the future US involvement in VIETNAM.

**Quiet Man, The.** A sobriquet applied to himself by Iain Duncan Smith (b.1954), the here-today-and-gone-tomorrow leader of the Conservative Party (2001–3), also known as IDS. The name referred to his quiet voice: he was often troubled with a sore throat while debating in parliament. At the 2002 Conservative Party Conference he told delegates:

> Don't underestimate the determination of the quiet man.

At the 2003 Conservative Party Conference he decided it was NO MORE MR NICE GUY and told delegates: 'The Quiet Man is going to turn up the volume.' He resigned shortly afterwards.

*The Quiet Man* was a 1952 John Ford film starring John Wayne.

**Quiller Memorandum, The.** A mystery thriller (1964) by Adam Hall (pen-name of Elleston Trevor; 1920–95). It is the first in a series of 19 books, told in the first person, about Quiller, a peripatetic executive for an ultra-secret international agency in London.

**Quisling.** A traitor or fifth columnist, from Vidkun Quisling (1887–1945), the Norwegian admirer of Mussolini and Hitler, who acted as advance agent for the German invasion of Norway in 1940. He duly became puppet minister-president. He surrendered (9 May 1945) after the German defeat and was tried and shot (24 October).

**Quonset hut.** The US equivalent of a NISSEN HUT as a type of military shelter. It takes its name from Quonset Point, Rhode Island, where such huts were first erected at a US Air Force base in the Second World War.

**Quorn.** A type of textured vegetable protein made from an edible fungus and used as a meat substitute. It was launched on the market in Britain in 1984 and takes its name from its original manufacturers, Quorn Specialities Ltd, located in the Leicestershire village of Quorn or Quorndon, best known as the home of a famous hunt. The provenance of a meatless product from a place associated precisely with the pursuit of live flesh has a somewhat unpalatable irony.

**Quote, unquote.** A parenthetical expression said before a word or phrase to indicate that if written the latter would be in quotation marks, as: 'I gave him a little quote, unquote talking-to.' A variant is to say 'quote' before and 'unquote' after. An alternative is to mime quotation marks by twitching one's raised forefingers as one says the word or phrase. The expression dates from the 1930s and has its origin in the oral formula for quotation marks in a dictation.

*Quote … Unquote* is a panel-game, based on quotations, which has been broadcast on BBC Radio 4 since 1976. The show is devised and hosted by Nigel Rees.

**Quo Vadis?** A biblical film epic (1951) based on the book (1896) of the same title by Henryk Sienkiewicz about the martyrdom of St Peter during the reign of the Emperor Nero. Starring Robert Taylor, Deborah Kerr and Peter Ustinov, the film followed two earlier versions (1912 and 1924). The title was derived from the word *Domine, quo vadis?* ('Master, whither goest thou?') reputedly uttered by St Peter when he encountered Christ on the Appian Way during his flight from Nero's Rome. Christ replied that he was on his way to Rome 'to be crucified again', on which the shamefaced Peter turned around and went back to Rome to meet his death. According to tradition he asked to be crucified head downwards and related his meeting with Christ as he was nailed to the cross.

The 'Quo Vadis' Italian restaurant was founded in London's Soho in 1926 by Peppino Leoni, in premises in Dean Street formerly occupied by Karl Marx. Over the decades it became a notable fixture in the Soho scene. At the end of the 20th century it became part of the Marco Pierre White empire.

**QWERTY.** The standard layout on English-language typewriter keyboards, representing the first six letters from the left on the top row. The layout, still found even on modern computer keyboards, was originally designed to slow down typing and so prevent jamming of the keys on the early manual machines. This was effected by having the typebars come up from opposite directions and so not clashing together. It so happens that all the letters needed to type the word 'typewriter' are in the top line of the layout (QWERTYUIOP), but the theory that this was intended to help non-skilled sales staff demonstrate the machine is an old secretaries' tale. The French equivalent is AZERTY. In 1986 Anthony Burgess published a collection of his reviews under the title *Homage to QWERTYUIOP*. *See also* DSK.

# R

**Rab.** The popular initialism of R.A. Butler (1902–82), Conservative minister of education (1941–5) in the Second World War, when he introduced the radical Education Act of 1944. His political career then progressed to chancellor of the exchequer (1951) and Lord Privy Seal (1955). He was widely expected to succeed Anthony Eden as prime minister in 1957 after the SUEZ CRISIS, but Harold Macmillan was chosen and Butler instead became home secretary. He again narrowly lost the premiership to Alec Douglas-Home in 1963 and was appointed foreign secretary. Butler was epitomized in political circles as 'both irreproachable and unapproachable'. *See also* ART OF THE POSSIBLE; BEST PRIME MINISTER WE NEVER HAD.

**Rabbit.** The nickname of Harry Angstrom, the hero of a series of four novels by John Updike: *Rabbit, Run* (1960), *Rabbit, Redux* (1971), *Rabbit Is Rich* (1981) and *Rabbit at Rest* (1990). His byname comes from his former glory days as a high school basketball champion. He subsequently becomes the owner of a car sales agency, but is generally limited and complacent in his attitudes, as a sort of latter-day BABBITT. (The resemblance between the names is presumably coincidental.) He finally dies of a heart attack during a playground game of basketball.

**Rabbit on.** To talk at length; to chatter away. 'Rabbit' here represents rhyming slang for 'rabbit and pork', i.e. 'talk', although happening to suggest similar words relating to talking such as 'babble', 'gabble', 'ramble' and the like. The expression dates from the Second World War.

**Rabbit punch.** A sharp chop with the edge of the hand to the back of the neck, like that traditionally given by a gamekeeper to put a rabbit out of its misery. The term dates from the early 20th century.

**Rabbits.** A charm-word traditionally said by children on the first day of the month. An alternative is or was 'white rabbits', and the ritual is sometimes extended by saying 'hares' on the last day of the month. No response to the utterance is now normally expected, although it apparently once was, when first recorded in the early 20th century.

> On the first day of the month you have to say 'Rabbits'. If you say it to me first, I have to give you a present, and if I say it to you first, you have to give me a present.
>
> DORNFORD YATES: *The Courts of Idleness*, Pt 2, ch. 2 (1920)

**Race to the sea, The.** The rapid development of trenches in the First World War. Following the First Battle of the Aisne (13–28 September 1914), both the French and German sides realized that they lacked the manpower for frontal assaults and that the only alternative was for each side to try and overlap and envelop the flank of the other, in this case the one on the side pointing towards the North Sea and the English Channel. The trench networks of both sides were thus extended in a northwesterly direction in a 'race to the sea' until they reached the coast at a point just inside Belgium, west of Ostend, creating the WESTERN FRONT.

**Rachmanism.** The exploitation and intimidation of tenants by unscrupulous landlords. The name comes from that of Peter Rachman (1919–62), a Polish immigrant whose undesirable activities of this kind in the Paddington area of London were brought to light in the early 1960s. His name was brought to public attention from a former connection with the women in the PROFUMO AFFAIR.

**Rack off.** In Australian slang, to go away; clear out; fuck off. Its usual mode is the imperative. First recorded in 1975, its basis may be 'rack' as a term for a horse's ungainly gait in which both feet on one side are lifted at the same time.

> Rack off Hoges [i.e. Paul Hogan, archetypal Aussie], we just don't like the way you speak.
>
> headline, quoted on www.smh.com.au (25 January 2005)

**Rack something up.** To achieve it, typically as a score or amount. The expression probably alludes to the accumulation of points in pool-playing. At the beginning of the game the balls are placed in a triangular wooden frame called a rack. When the frame is removed, the balls themselves are also known as the rack. Players are then in a position to start playing and so accumulate points. The phrase dates from the 1950s and is distinct from the more recent 'to ratchet up', meaning to make something rise in a step that is part of an irreversible progress.

**RADA.** The Royal Academy of Dramatic Art, Britain's leading drama school. It was founded in 1904 by the actor Sir Herbert Beerbohm Tree in the dome of His Majesty's Theatre in the Haymarket, London, but later that year was transferred to the Georgian house in Gower Street that it has occupied ever since. It was granted a royal charter by George V in 1920 and for many years was run by Sir Kenneth Barnes (1878–1957), under whom its theatre, the Vanburgh, named after his sisters, the actresses Irene (1872–1949) and Violet (1867–1942) Vanburgh, was built to replace an earlier one, destroyed in the BLITZ of 1941.

**Radar.** A term formed from *r*adio *d*etection *a*nd *r*anging, a means of detecting the direction and range of aircraft, ships and the like by the reflection of radio waves. It is particularly valuable at night or in fog when the eye is of no avail. It was first developed effectively for the purposes by Sir Robert Watson-Watt in 1934–5 (and independently in the United States, France and Germany) and was of great importance during the Second World War, especially during the BATTLE OF BRITAIN.

**Radical chic.** The fashionable affectation of radical left-wing views. The expression was coined by the American writer Tom Wolfe in 1970 to denote high society's adoption of radicals and radical issues as fashion accessories. The term subsequently came to apply to anything left-wing that seemed to be embraced on the grounds of being modish rather than through personal conviction. *See also* SHABBY CHIC.

> Radical Chic … is only radical in Style; in its heart it is part of Society and its tradition – Politics, like Rock, Pop, and Camp, has its uses.
>
> TOM WOLFE: in *New York* (8 June 1970)

**Radiocarbon dating.** A scientific method of estimating the age of organic materials. Carbon dioxide from the atmosphere, which contains the radioactive isotope carbon 14, is taken up by all living matter. After the animal or plant from which the material comes has died, the amount of carbon 14 diminishes at a known rate, thus permitting the age of the material to be dated approximately. The method was devised in 1946 by the American chemist Willard F. Libby (1908–80).

**Radio Caroline.** The first and most famous of Britain's North Sea PIRATE RADIO stations went on the air on Easter Day, 29 March 1964, with the following welcome from its disc jockey, Simon Dee: 'Good morning, ladies and gentlemen. This is Radio Caroline broadcasting on 199, your all-day music station.' Its initiator was a young Irishman, Ronan O'Rahilly, who claimed that he named the station after Caroline Kennedy, daughter of President John F. Kennedy, assassinated the previous October. Cynics, however, suggested he hoped to curry favour with the then chancellor of the exchequer, Reginald Maudling, who also had a daughter named Caroline. The station soon attracted millions of fans, who saw it as a symbol of freedom and rebellion, and although it later ran into troubled waters, sometimes literally so, it survived several setbacks until it finally fell silent in 1990.

**Radio City Music Hall.** The largest and most prestigious theatre in the United States, at Rockefeller Center, New York, was conceived by Samuel Rothafel (*see* ROXY) as a palatial entertainment centre affordable to the general public and opened on 27 December 1932 with a gala performance by Martha Graham, Ray Bolger and Gertrude Niesen. The ceiling of the auditorium gives the impression of a giant sunset, and the opulence of the foyer stunned theatregoers during the GREAT DEPRESSION, with its ceiling 18m (60ft) high, ornate mirrors and slender chandeliers. Soon after its opening the theatre presented programmes combining feature films with stage shows, a format that remained popular for almost 50 years. It subsequently became a principal venue for live spectacles and television events, and the GRAMMY awards were staged there from the 1980s. The theatre's best-known institution is the precision dance troupe The ROCKETTES.

**Radio Doctor.** The by-name of Dr Charles Hill (1904–89), who was the BBC's 'Radio Doctor' from 1942 to 1950. He went on to became a Conservative health minister in the 1950s, then chairman of the Independent Television Authority and finally chairman of the BBC.

**Radio Luxembourg.** A famous commercial radio station that helped to train some later well-known disc jockeys in British broadcasting in the 1950s to 1980s, among them David Jacobs, Pete Murray, Jimmy Savile, Jimmy Young, Noel Edmonds, Mike Read and Peter Powell. It began its nightly English-language service in 1933, when its first DJ was Stephen Williams. The station took the lead in developing sponsored programmes with shows such as *The Ovaltineys* (*see* OVALTINE) and its entertainers and singers included such famous names as George Formby and Gracie Fields (*see* OUR GRACIE). During the Second World War the NAZIs used Radio Luxembourg as a propaganda outlet, employing such stooges as Lord HAW-HAW, but after the war it entered its golden age, delighting pop music fans who were not catered for by the BBC until the advent of Radio 1 in 1967. Its audience shrank when PIRATE RADIO lured listeners away from its wavelength of 208 metres on medium wave, and its last English-language broadcast went out in 1992.

**Radio Priest.** The by-name of the US priest Father Charles Edward Coughlin (1891–1979), whose regular radio show in the 1930s became notorious for its increasingly extreme denunciations of Franklin D. Roosevelt (FDR) and the NEW DEAL as a conspiracy of communists and Jewish bankers. He was disowned by Catholic leaders in 1937 and in 1942 his broadcasts were suppressed for opposing the entry of the United States into the Second World War.

**Raft of the Medusa, The.** A controversial oratorio by Hans Werner Henze (b.1926). Its title in German is *Das Floss der Medusa*, and it was described by the composer as an *oratorio volgare e militare*. It was commissioned by Hamburg Radio, and its first performance in 1968 was disrupted by demonstrators and police intervention. The work certainly had a radical agenda: it was dedicated to Che Guevara and commemorated a shocking episode in French naval history, when in 1816 the officers of the wrecked *Medusa* abandoned their men to float on a raft, leading to the deaths of 139 of the 154 originally set adrift. The story is also the subject of a famous painting (1818–19) by Théodore Géricault.

**Ragga.** A style of music similar to dance hall in which a DJ improvises lyrics over an electronic backing track. It arose in the 1990s as a fusion of REGGAE and urban HIP-HOP and takes its name from 'ragamuffin', alluding to the casual dress of its followers.

**Ragged-Trousered Philanthropists, The.** A fable (1914, in full 1955) by Robert Tressell (pen-name of Robert Noonan; 1870–1911). Subtitled 'Being the story of twelve months in Hell, told by one of the damned, and written down by Robert Tressell', it was written between 1907 and 1910 to give his only daughter some financial security. It takes the form of an account of the lives of a band of men who work for an unscrupulous decorating firm, and it reflects the attitudes of the philanthropists (the working class) towards their capitalist exploiters.

**Raging Bull.** A film (1980) based on the autobiography of US middleweight boxer Jake LaMotta. Directed by Martin Scorsese and starring Robert De Niro as LaMotta, the film's title indicates its theme of uncompromisingly violent masculinity and male values. De Niro reputedly put on more than 20kg (50lb) in weight in order to play the older, bloated LaMotta.

**Rags to riches.** From poverty to wealth; from nonentity to fame. The phrase, often found as an adjectival phrase, became current in the Second World War. The allusion is to the heroine of a fairy tale who makes such a transition, such as Cinderella, who met and married Prince Charming.

**Rah-rah skirt.** *See* RA-RA SKIRT.

**Raiders of the Lost Ark.** A film (1981) adapted by Lawrence Kasdan from a story by George Lucas and Philip Kaufman about the adventures of an archaeologist, Indiana Jones, as he struggles in 1936 to locate the biblical Ark of the Covenant, allegedly still containing the Ten Commandments, before the Nazis do. The film was inspired by the cliffhanger adventure series shown in cinemas in the 1930s and starred Harrison Ford as 'Indy' (although Tom Selleck was director Steven Spielberg's first choice). Its success led to two sequels, *Indiana Jones and the Temple of Doom* (1984) and *Indiana Jones and the Last Crusade* (1989).

**Railway Children, The.** A much-loved children's novel (1906) by E. Nesbit (1858–1924). It tells of three siblings who move to a country cottage with their mother after their father is mysteriously taken away. Their adventures centre on the railway line that runs close to their new home. It emerges that their father has been wrongly imprisoned for passing secrets to the enemy, but he is released when the true culprit is identified. The novel's enduring popularity is reflected in a number of film and television versions. A nostalgically textured film version (1970), directed by Lionel Jeffries, has many memorable moments, not least that of 17-year-old Jenny Agutter whipping off her petticoat to avert tragedy on the railway line. A remake (2000), directed by Charles Elton, is a more measured version of the original, with 18-year-old Jemima Rooper in Agutter's role as Roberta and Agutter herself as the mother of the three children. *See also* FIRST LINES OF NOVELS.

**Rainbow coalition.** A term arising in the United States for a political grouping of minority peoples and other disadvantaged elements, especially in order to elect a candidate. The allusion is both to the diversity of political shades, 'all the colours of the rainbow', and to the connotations of hope associated with a rainbow ('where the rainbow ends', 'somewhere over the rainbow'). The concept was embraced by the politician Jesse Jackson (*see* HIS SHADOWSHIP) when running for the 1984 Democratic presidential nomination, the first African American to mount a serious campaign for this office.

> When I look out at this convention, I see the face of America, red, yellow, brown, black and white. We are all precious in God's sight – the real rainbow coalition.
>
> JESSE JACKSON: speech at Democratic National Convention, Atlanta (19 July 1988)

**Rainbow Corner.** In the Second World War Messrs Lyons' Corner House in Shaftesbury Avenue, London, was taken over and turned into a large café and lounge for American servicemen under this name, and it became a general meeting place for Americans in London. The name was in reference to the 42nd Infantry Division of the US Army, nicknamed the Rainbow, and the rainbow in the insignia of SHAEF (Supreme Headquarters Allied Expeditionary Forces). The division itself was so called because it was composed of military groups from the District of Columbia and 25 US states, representing several sections, nationalities, religions and viewpoints. They blended themselves into a single harmonious unit and a First World War major, noting its various origins, said: 'This division will stretch over the land like a rainbow.'

**Rainbow Nation.** A nickname for South Africa, alluding to its multiracial population. The term was coined by Nelson Mandela, South African president (1994–99), following the end of APARTHEID in 1991. *See also* RAINBOW COALITION.

**Rainbow Warrior.** *See* GREENPEACE.

**Rain on someone's parade.** To prevent them from enjoying an occasion; to spoil their plans. The expression is of US origin and dates from the beginning of the 20th century.

**Rain or shine.** No matter what happens. A figurative use, dating from the beginning of the 20th century, of the much older phrase meaning 'whatever the weather'.

**Raise one's eyebrows.** To show surprise, disbelief or mild disapproval by the described movement of the features. 'Raised eyebrows' are thus a general expression of this kind. The phrase dates from the early years of the 20th century.

**Raise one's head above the parapet.** *See* PUT ONE'S HEAD ABOVE THE PARAPET.

**Raise one's sights.** To become more ambitious; to increase one's expectations. The sights are those on a gun through which one takes aim after raising the gun to one's shoulder. The converse, literally and figuratively, is 'to lower one's sights'.

**Rake's Progress, The.** The 'neoclassical' opera by Igor Stravinsky (1882–1971) has a libretto by W.H. Auden and Chester Kallmann, loosely based on the 'moral narrative' of William Hogarth (1697–1764), painted in 1733–5 and subsequently made into popular engravings. The story concerns the decline and fall of one Tom Rakewell, who deserts Anne Trulove for the delights of London in the company of Nick Shadow, who turns out to be the Devil. Tom ends up in Bedlam, and the moral of the tale is: 'For idle hearts and hands and minds the Devil finds a work to do.' The opera was first performed in 1951. For the 1975 Glyndebourne revival, striking sets and costumes were designed by David Hockney (b.1937).

**Rambert Dance Company.** The oldest existing British ballet company arose from the dance studio opened in London in 1920 by Marie Rambert (1888–1982), a Polish-born dancer whose original name was Cyvia Rambam. By 1931 regular Saturday matinée performances were being given under the name of the Ballet Club, and in 1934 this became the Ballet Rambert. Its base was the minute Mercury Theatre in Notting Hill, a former Victorian school building, and this remained its home until the 1960s. Early choreographers were Frederick Ashton (1904–88) and Antony Tudor (1908–87). Rambert herself remained director until 1966. The company adopted its present name in 1987, after Richard Alston became director. Of all the established London dance companies the Rambert has consistently enjoyed a progressive and young-minded public.

**Ramblers.** The word is generally used for anyone who enjoys walking for pleasure in the countryside or even through city streets. More specifically it is associated with the Ramblers' Association, a pressure group formed in 1935 with the twin aims of encouraging people to enjoy the countryside, as they had always done, and ensuring that there is public access to it, as there has not always been (*see* RIGHT TO ROAM). It has thus campaigned to prevent the closure of footpaths and rights of way, in some cases trespassing on private land in order to do so, and so in 2000 it welcomed the RIGHT TO ROAM legislation. Many landowners and farmers are ambivalent about the Association: it shares their rural interests but seeks to deprive them of their traditional proprietorial rights, or what they hold to be such.

**Rambo.** The tough VIETNAM War veteran first appeared in David Morrell's violent thriller, *First Blood* (1971), in which he runs into trouble with a local sheriff, takes to the hills and finally massacres an entire unit of the National Guard single-handed. He was brought before a wide public by the film of the same title (1982), in which he is played by Sylvester Stallone, and by its unashamedly melodramatic sequels, *Rambo First Blood Part II* (1985) and *Rambo III* (1988). His name became a household word when President Reagan praised the second film in one of his speeches, as a result of which 'Rambo' became a nickname for Reagan himself, especially with regard to his policy of foreign military intervention. The nickname is also applied to others adopting an aggressive, gun-toting militaristic stance.

> Given the bomb-'em-kill-'em suggestions pulsing from the typewriters of 100 literate Rambos, a boycott of the airport was the most reasonable act suggested.
> *Washington Post* (6 July 1985)

**Ram raid.** A robbery carried out by ramming a vehicle into the wall or window of the building to be robbed, typically commercial premises.

**Ramsay Mac.** A nickname of (James) Ramsay MacDonald (1866–1937), Britain's first Labour prime minister (1924). He became prime minister of a second Labour government in 1929, then in 1931 broadened it into a National Government coalition, which was increasingly dominated by Conservatives, and which resulted in his condemnation as a traitor by most socialists. *See also* BONELESS WONDER; COALITION GOVERNMENT.

**R & B.** Rhythm and blues. Originally, R & B was the raw, blues- and jazz-influenced seminal rock music played by African American bands from the late 1940s. The term was coined by Jerry Wexler of *Billboard* magazine, and applied to such performers as Muddy Waters, Fats Domino and Jerry Lee Lewis. ROCK 'N' ROLL is often regarded as a sanitized version of R & B played by white kids, although white bands such as The Rolling Stones brought genuine R & B to a wider audience. Since the 1980s the term R & B has been applied to a more anodyne style of (generally) black pop music deriving from soul and disco.

**Random Harvest.** A film (1942) based on a novel (1941) by the British writer James Hilton (1900–54) about a First World War veteran who has lost his memory in battle but later regains it after being hit by a car, only to find that he has forgotten all that happened in the intervening period. The title was derived from wartime German propaganda claims that German planes had successfully dropped bombs on the English town of Random (a claim based on misinterpretation of a British communiqué that German bombs had been 'dropped at random').

**Random House.** This noted US publishing firm was founded in New York in 1927 by Bennett Cerf (1898–1971) and Donald S. Klopfer (1902–86), owners of the Modern Library, to publish their own luxury editions 'at random'. It soon developed into a trade publisher and gained a reputation for its substantial and highly profitable children's department and for its commitment to publishing dramatic works. Its authors have included such disparate writers as William Faulkner, Robert Penn Warren, Eugene O'Neill, Lillian Hellman and Gertrude Stein.

**R and R.** Rest and recreation, an abbreviation of US military origin dating from the 1990s. The reference is to off-duty time as a positive and integral ingredient of regular military routine.

**Randy Andy.** A nickname given to Prince Andrew prior to his marriage to Sarah Ferguson (*see* FERGIE), on account of his dalliances with such models/actresses as Vicky Hodge and Koo Stark.

**Rangoon runs.** *See* MONTEZUMA'S REVENGE.

**Ranji.** The Indian-born Sussex and England batsman His Highness the Maharajah Jam Sahib of Nawanagar (Kumar Shri Ranjitsinhji; 1872–1933). The Ranji Trophy competition in India is named after him. Ranjitsinhji's is one of a number of cricketers' names that appear in punning versions in the cricket-loving James Joyce's esoteric novel FINNEGANS WAKE:

> At half-past quick in the morning. And her lamp was all askew and trumbly-wick-in-her, ringeysingey.

**Rape of Nanking.** The name commonly given to the massacres, rapes, arson and looting carried out in the Chinese city of Nanking (Nanjing in the modern pinyin transliteration) by Japanese troops after they took the city on 13 December 1937. Estimates of the numbers of dead vary: Chinese sources give a civilian death toll as high as 300,000 (including tens of thousands of women and girls who were raped before they were killed), while some rightwing Japanese politicians have denied that Japanese forces were responsible for any wartime atrocities at all. There was an international outcry when in 1982 the Japanese Ministry of Education removed all mention of the Nanking massacres from a school textbook. Such attitudes have led to a re-emergence of anti-Japanese feeling in China.

**Rapists, All men are.** *See* ALL MEN ARE RAPISTS.

**Rap music.** A style of music, originally dating from the 1970s when it was established by African American musicians in New York, in which the often improvised lyrics are sung or chanted against a heavy bass line (the latter being often created by a drum machine or synthesizer). The use of the word 'rap' in this context is probably a 1960s usage meaning to indulge in repartee or street talk. *See also* GANGSTA RAP; HIP-HOP.

**Ra-ra** or **rah-rah skirt.** A short skirt with multiple layered flounces, of the kind worn by American CHEERLEADERS, who are colloquially known as 'ra-ra girls', from their cries of 'ra-ra' (from 'hurrah'). The heyday of the ra-ra as a fashion fetish was the early 1980s, when it was popularized by such all-girl pop groups as The Belle Stars and Bananarama. One reason for its early demise was its impracticality.

**Rarin' to go.** Keen to get started. The verb is an American dialect form of 'rearing', alluding to a horse that rears up when anxious to be off. The expression dates from the early 20th century.

**Rasputin.** Grigoriy Yefimovich Novykh (*c*.1871–1916), the Siberian 'holy man' notorious for his baneful influence over the Russian monarchy in its last years, was apparently so called by his fellow villagers. *Rasputin* means 'dissolute' and he lived up to his nickname until the end. His easy conquests of women were helped by his assertion that physical contact with him was itself a purification. His gross indecencies and disgusting coarseness did not prevent his excessive familiarity with the Empress Alexandra and Tsar Nicholas II, which arose from his undoubted success in healing and sustaining the Tsarevich Alexis, a victim of haemophilia. Rasputin was first called to the palace in 1905, and his power increased steadily until his murder by Prince Felix Yusupov and his associates.

The method of dispatch was a sorry saga. On the night of 29 December 1916 Rasputin was invited to Yusupov's home in St Petersburg and there given poisoned wine and tea cakes. When he did not die, the desperate Yusupov shot him. Rasputin collapsed but managed to run into the courtyard, allegedly shouting 'Felix, Felix, I'll tell the Tsarina!' There he was shot again by Vladimir Purishkevich, a member of the Duma. The conspirators then bound Rasputin and bundled him through a hole in the ice into the River Neva, where he at last drowned.

Although Rasputin was in fact a *starets*, an unordained religious man, not a monk, the nickname 'the MAD MONK' has attached itself firmly to him.

> Ra-ra Rasputin
> Russia's greatest love machine
> FRANK FARIAN, FRED JAY and GEORGE REYAM: 'Rasputin' (from
> The Boney M album *Nighflight to Venus*) (1978)

*See also* YORKSHIRE RASPUTIN.

**Rastafarians.** Members of the Ras Tafari, a black political and religious group originating in the 1920s in Jamaica, recognizing Haile Selassie (1892–1975), emperor of Ethiopia, as a god. They consider that blacks are superior to whites, that Ethiopia is heaven and that Haile Selassie would arrange

that all of African origin will find a homeland in Ethiopia. *Ras* means 'duke' and *Tafari* was a family name of Haile Selassie ('Might of the Trinity'). There are now Rastafarians in the West Indies, the United States, Canada and Europe, conspicuous by their DREADLOCKS. *See also* LION OF JUDAH.

**Rat fink.** An unpleasant person, especially one suspected of being an informer ('rat'). 'Fink' probably derives from the identical German word meaning 'finch', in the sense of someone who 'sings' or informs. The term dates from the 1960s.

**Rationing.** *See* POINTS.

**Ratner, doing a.** *See* DOING A RATNER.

**Rat pack.** A juvenile gang. The earliest such group, although not of juveniles, was the Holmby Hills Rat Pack of HOLLY-WOOD, consisting of Humphrey Bogart and his drinking friends. Its successor (from the mid-1950s to the mid-1960s) was the Rat Pack, a name given by *Time* magazine to the showbiz entourage of Frank Sinatra, OL' BLUE EYES. Its other main members, besides Sinatra, were the singer Dean Martin, the entertainer Sammy Davis Jr, the actor Peter Lawford, and the actor and comedian Joey Bishop. They usually referred to themselves as 'The Clan'. A later development was the BRAT PACK.

**Rat race.** The relentless struggle to get ahead of one's rivals, particularly in professional and commercial occupations.

> Even if you win the rat race, you're still a rat.
> REV. WILLIAM SLOANE COFFIN (b.1924): comment
> (*c*.1950s–1960s)

**Rat run.** A residential street used by drivers as a short cut or to avoid a congested main road, especially during the rush hour. A rat run is a maze of small passages used by rats when running about their territory. The term was also applied (with particular stress on the supposed pusillanimousness and sneakiness of the rat) to the various routes, especially to South America, used by leading Nazis escaping from Europe at the end of the Second World War.

**Rats with good PR.** A disparaging term for grey squirrels. The North American species (*Sciurus carolinensis*) was introduced into the UK at the start of the 20th century, since when it has successfully taken over much of the territory of the native and less aggressive red squirrel (*Sciurus vulgaris*), which is now confined to small pockets, such as the Lake District and the Highlands of Scotland.

**Rattle one's dags.** In Australian and New Zealand slang, to hurry up; to get a move on; to 'look lively'. 'Dags' are lumps of dried excrement around a sheep's anus, so the underlying image is of the animal bestirring itself sufficiently to agitate these. The expression is first recorded in 1968.

**Rattle someone's cage.** To irritate or annoy them. The image is of a caged bird or animal being provoked in this manner. The expression dates from the 1970s and is mostly found in the form of a rhetorical question, as: 'Who rattled his cage?'

**Rave.** The word passed from its use to mean an enthusiastic recommendation for someone or something (a 'rave review') before gaining the more specific sense of a party attended by large numbers of young people, typically one with energetic dancing fuelled by drugs such as ECSTASY.

**Rave from the grave.** *See* BLAST FROM THE PAST.

**Raw deal.** A transaction that is harsh or unfair to a person, perhaps from the idea that it leaves them feeling 'raw' or hurt. The expression is American in origin.

***Reader's Digest.*** A US-based monthly magazine with one of the largest circulations of any periodical in the world. It was first published in February 1922 as a digest of condensed articles of topical interest and entertainment value taken from other periodicals. The founders, working on a low budget, were DeWitt Wallace (1889–1981) and his wife, Lila Acheson, who had at first failed to interest publishers in their plan. The pocket format appealed to many, however, and sales gradually rose. The magazine began publishing condensed versions of current books in 1934. It then took to commissioning articles that it would offer to other publications only to reprint them in due course, offering the other magazine a fee for reprint rights. It has been criticized by some for its unadventurous content and conservative point of view, but its circulation has rarely faltered.

**Read my lips.** An exhortation to pay close attention, as if the speaker is talking to a deaf person. The phrase was popularized by the US Republican statesman George Bush Snr (b.1924) on 19 August 1988 during the presidential election campaign:

Read my lips: no new taxes.

He won his election and subsequently introduced new taxes. Since then the phrase has often been invoked in an ironic sense ('I say I'm not going to do it, but both you and I know that I will').

**Ready, steady, go!** A formula for starting a race, especially among children. At the word 'ready' the runners prepare themselves, at 'steady' they brace themselves, at 'go!' they start to run. In professional athletics, when contestants are UNDER STARTER'S ORDERS, the formula is usually 'On your marks, get set, go!', or simply 'Marks, set', with 'go!' replaced by the firing of the starter's pistol. The *Oxford English Dictionary* records the former phrase no earlier than the 1960s and the latter first in the 1930s. An earlier equivalent, still in use, was simply 'One, two, three, go!'

In the SWINGING SIXTIES *Ready, Steady, Go!* (commonly shortened to *RSG!*) became well known as the name of a pioneering pop-music programme first broadcast on ITV in 1963. It went out on Friday evenings, and its slogan was 'The Weekend Starts Here'.

**Reaganauts.** The nickname of a clique of right-wing ideologues who strongly influenced the policies in office of President Ronald Reagan, the GREAT COMMUNICATOR. The name comes by analogy with 'astronaut', with a suggestion both of bold, pioneering spirit and of being not of this world.

**Reagan Democrats.** A name given to those former Democratic voters in the United States, mostly white, male, blue-collar workers, who voted for the Republican presidential candidate Ronald Reagan in 1980 and 1984.

**Reagan Doctrine.** A COLD WAR policy espoused by Ronald Reagan during his presidency of the United States (1981–9). It held that what was seen as Soviet influence and/or aggression around the world should be countered at every instance, and it involved the supply of military aid to various anti-communist insurgent groups in the Third World, such as the CONTRAS in Nicaragua, Unita in Angola and the Mujahadeen in Soviet-occupied Afghanistan.

**Reaganomics.** The economic policies of Ronald Reagan, the GREAT COMMUNICATOR, during his presidency (1981–9). Cuts in taxes and social-services budgets were their centrepiece, along with increased military expenditure, and they led to a record rise in the national budget deficit. The name, originally intended derisively, was a variation on 'Reaganism', coined during an earlier phase of the president's career to denote his politics in general. *See also* VOODOO ECONOMICS.

**Real ale.** Cask-conditioned beer that is served traditionally, not from metal kegs under gas pressure. The term implies that beer produced by mass-production methods is not 'real', whereas 'ale' has agreeable historical or 'heritage' associations. The Campaign for Real Ale (CAMRA), founded in 1972, has done a great deal to preserve and promote the original kind of beer, to the extent that many pubs have come to advertise it as a lure to potential customers. *See also* GUEST BEER.

**Real deal, The.** The 'genuine article'; the truth. The expression originated in African-American English in the early 1970s.

Yes, we're the real deal, with lawyers, accountants, bankers, a board, the whole enchilada.

www.blahblahblog.newzguy.com (1 October 2005)

**Reality TV.** A 21st-century television genre that first emerged in Europe before quickly spreading to the United States and becoming a popular global phenomenon. Although the term can cover a wide variety of programmes, at the core of most of them are 'real' people (i.e. not actors or television professionals) who are tracked by camera and microphone as they engage in whatever quotidian activity is involved, whether it be renovating a house, driving a police car, enduring cosmetic surgery, swapping marital partners, or living in a hothouse atmosphere with a group of perfect strangers (i.e. BIG BROTHER). The appeal to television companies is an obvious one: reality is much cheaper to produce than drama. The appeal to the participants is sometimes material gain or simply just the 15 minutes of fame (*see* FAMOUS FOR 15 MINUTES), important if one is a WANNABE.

The genre's detractors deplore its reliance on voyeurism and the tendency of some of its output to exploit humiliation and embarrassing exposure. However, reality TV has offered an opportunity for a number of half-remembered television faces to put themselves in the public eye again via the show *I'm a Celebrity, Get Me Out of Here!* (2002– ), a kind of jungle-based *Big Brother*, where the challenge is to survive boredom, a host of creepy-crawlies and (perhaps worse than either of these) one's fellow semi-celebrities.

The main elements of reality TV were presciently adumbrated in Nigel Kneale's 1968 BBC television play *The Year of the Sex Olympics*, in which a television producer has the brainwave of putting a man, woman and child alone on an island, televising their doings 24 hours a day and, when the audience's interest begins to flag, adding a murderer to the mix. A later satirical fictional treatment of the genre is Peter Weir's film *The Truman Show* (1998), in which a man living apparently in zombie-like happiness in an island community suddenly discovers that in fact he is the star of a 24-hour television soap opera. *See also* CELEBRITY CULTURE; VOYEURVISION; ZOO TV.

**Real Madrid.** The leading Spanish football club was founded by students in 1902 as the Madrid Club de Fútbol. In 1920 it was given its royal (Spanish *real*) blessing by King Alfonso XIII and it turned professional in 1929 when the Spanish national league began. Real's rise to prominence began in earnest after the Spanish Civil War (1936–9) and in the late 1950s it achieved European dominance, winning five European Cups between 1956 and 1960. The ultimate accolade came when General Franco (*see* CAUDILLO) let it be known that Real Madrid was his favourite team.

***Real Thing, The.*** A play (1982) by Tom Stoppard (b.1937) in which a married playwright debates whether his love for an actress (also married) is the 'real thing' or not. The phrase has been used with relation to 'genuine' love as distinct from mere infatuation or sexual desire for many years, with records of its appearance going back as far as 1857. Since 1942, however, it has also become well known as an advertising slogan for COCA-COLA, an association that Stoppard almost certainly had in mind when he was selecting the title for his play.

**Real world, The.** The reality of everyday life and routine, as distinct from the world of one's imagination, innocence or ignorance. *See also* GET OUT MORE.

At the end of a working day I [novelist Rose Tremain] do 45 minutes of yoga. Then I switch off and return to the real world. I go to the kitchen, pour myself a drink and cook.

*The Times* (11 September 1999)

**Rearrange someone's face.** To hit or punch it so that its features are unrecognizable.

***Rear Window.*** A claustrophobic suspense film (1954) directed by Alfred Hitchcock and starring James Stewart and Grace Kelly. The rear window is a window through which a photographer, recuperating after breaking his leg, sees a murder committed. The film is based on a short story by Cornell Woolrich entitled 'It Had to be Murder' (1942).

***Rebecca.*** A novel (1938) by Daphne du Maurier (1907–89). Although the unnamed Mrs de Winter is at the centre of this study of psychological jealousy, it is Rebecca, her husband's first and dead wife, who dominates the action. The book grew out of the author's jealousy of an ex-fiancée of her husband, Lieutenant-General Frederick Browning (1896–1965), whom she married in 1932. It has been adapted for screen, stage and television, but the classic version remains the 1940 film, directed by Alfred Hitchcock, in which key roles were played by Laurence Olivier, Joan Fontaine, George Sanders, Judith Anderson, Nigel Bruce and Gladys Cooper. *See also* FIRST LINES OF NOVELS.

***Rebel Without a Cause.*** A film (1955) adapted by Stewart Stern and Irving Shulman from the story 'Blind Run' by Robert M. Lindner about a rebellious teenager whose unruly behaviour culminates in a death-defying challenge in which he and a rival drive their cars full speed towards the edge of a cliff. Starring James Dean, Natalie Wood and Sal Mineo, the film acquired iconic status among the restless young of the 1950s, Dean in particular often being referred to as the 'rebel without a cause'. The tragedy of the characters in the film was reflected in the premature deaths of all three stars: Dean died in a car crash eerily reminiscent of the climax of the film in 1955, Mineo was murdered in West Hollywood in 1976, and Wood drowned in obscure circumstances in 1981.

**Rebirthing.** A form of ALTERNATIVE therapy using yogic breathing techniques to release the trauma that, according to specialists, can manifest itself as physical pain or negative behaviour. It was developed in San Francisco in the 1970s and involves talking to a therapist about the circumstances of one's birth, as far as one can recall them, then lying in a darkened room and breathing in a particular way, inhaling and exhaling through the mouth. Tingling in areas where trauma is stored should then be felt. The technique has gained some credence in scientific circles.

**Rebus, Inspector.** The hard-drinking, somewhat dour yet ultimately sympathetic Edinburgh policeman (first name John) who is the central figure in a series of popular detective novels by Ian Rankin (b.1960), beginning with *Knots and Crosses* (1987). A number of the Rebus novels have been dramatized for television, with John Hannah in the star role, although in a new series, broadcast in 2006, the part was taken by Ken Stott. Regarding the Inspector's name, a rebus is a kind of puzzle in which pictures represent syllables or whole words. For example, H with a picture of a painting on an easel ('art') would give 'heart'. Prior to this, a rebus was an armorial device in heraldry that provided a pun on its bearer's name.

**Received Pronunciation.** *See* OXFORD ACCENT.

**Recharge one's batteries.** To regain one's strength and energy by resting and relaxing for a time. The fairly obvious allusion is to the restoring of an electrical charge to a battery. The expression dates from the 1920s.

**Recipe for disaster.** A plan or course of action that could lead to injury or collapse.

> 'I'm not happy about the incorporation of three regulation fences including an open ditch,' said Nicholson. 'I think they should stick to cross-country fences, otherwise it could be a recipe for disaster.'
> *The Guardian* (24 November 1994)

**Reclaim the night.** The slogan of an annual march by women first made on 23 November 1977 in Leeds, Manchester, Newcastle and other English cities to protest against men's control of the streets at night. Similar marches were held in the United States under the slogan TAKE BACK THE NIGHT and the organized protests developed in some cases into political campaigns such as 'Women against Violence against Women'.

**Recreational drug.** A drug taken for pleasure rather than for medical reasons. The implication is that drug use (or abuse) is optional, and not the consequence of addiction. The expression became current from the early 1970s. *See also* ECSTASY; HEROIN; LSD.

**Rector of Stiffkey.** The Reverend Harold Francis Davidson (1875–1937), who achieved a certain notoriety as rector of Stiffkey, Norfolk, in the early 20th century. He considered the most important part of his religious vocation to be saving the souls of fallen women, to which he devoted most of his energies. His neglected parishioners viewed his activities askance, particularly after, in the early 1930s, stories about him began to appear in the tabloid press and crowds of sightseers turned up in charabancs to hear him preach. He was unfrocked in 1932 and decided to become a music-hall entertainer. This turned out not to be a good career move, as in 1937 he was mauled by the partner in his act, a lion called Freddy, and died of his injuries.

**Red alert.** A warning of danger; an instruction to be prepared for an emergency. The term dates from the 1950s and chiefly finds application in military establishments and hospitals. In the latter it is an instruction that emergency cases only are to be admitted. *See also* DEFCON.

**Red Army.** The combined Soviet army and air force were officially so named from 1918 to 1946, when the forces were renamed the Soviet Army. The original name was long preferred by the Western media, however. *See also* WHITE ARMY.

**Red Army Faction.** *See* BAADER-MEINHOF GANG.

**Red Arrows.** The aerobatic display team of the RAF, formed in 1965. They are familiar from the nine red aircraft with which they perform complex coordinated manoeuvres at high speed and from the trails of coloured vapour that they release to add to the already breathtaking spectacle.

**Red Badge of Courage, The.** The novel (1895) by Stephen Crane (1871–1900), about the experiences of a naive young recruit in the Union forces during the American Civil War, was adapted as a film (1951) by director John Huston and Albert Band. Although Crane had no personal experience of war, the star of the film, Audie Murphy, was the most decorated US soldier of the Second World War. The making of the film, which was cut to ribbons by studio executives after Huston abandoned it to start work on *The African Queen*, has long been the subject of legend, as related in Lillian Ross's book *Picture*. The 'red badge' of the title refers to the bloody wounds of soldiers hurt in battle.

**Red Baron.** The First World War German fighter pilot Manfred Freiherr von Richthofen (1892–1918) was so known from his red Fokker aircraft. He led what became known as Richthofen's Circus, creating havoc and destroying some 80 planes. When eventually shot down over Allied lines he was given a military funeral, with a firing party provided by the Australian Flying Corps. Germans know him as *der rote Kampfflieger*, 'the red fighter pilot', rather than the Red Baron.

**Redbrick.** A term that came to be loosely applied to all English universities of a late 19th- or early 20th-century foundation. The name was introduced by 'Bruce Truscot' (Professor E. Allison Peers) in his book *Redbrick University* (1943). He was primarily dealing with the universities of Birmingham, Bristol, Leeds, Liverpool, Manchester, Reading and Sheffield, and expressly excluded London. In his Introduction he says: 'Though red brick, rather than dingy stone, has been chosen as the symbol of the new foundations, it must be categorically stated that no one university alone has been in the author's mind.'

> I don't think one 'comes down' from Jimmy's university. According to him, it's not even red brick, but white tile.
>
> JOHN OSBORNE: *Look Back in Anger* (1956)

*See also* PLATE GLASS UNIVERSITIES.

**Red Brigades.** (Italian *Brigate rosse*.) The group of URBAN GUERRILLAS who in 1978 kidnapped and murdered the former Italian prime minister Aldo Moro. Their reputed founder was Renato Curcio (b.1945), who set up a left-wing group at the University of Trento in 1967, married a fellow radical, Margherita Cagol, in 1969, and moved with her to Milan. They proclaimed the existence of the Red Brigades in 1970, fire-bombing factories and warehouses, then began kidnappings in 1971 and murders in 1974. By the late 1980s they had ceased to be a major force.

**Redcap.** A name for a member of the British military police, who wear such a cap as part of their uniform. An ITV drama series (1964–66) based on the military police and starring John Thaw was called *Redcap*. The BBC ploughed the same furrow in 2002 with a drama series starring Tamzin Outhwaite, and titled with even less originality *Red Cap*.

> So we sang the Stein Song stumbling along the blacked-out streets until a couple of red caps suddenly flashed a torch on Brooke and asked to see his pay book.
>
> JULIAN MACLAREN-ROSS: *Memoirs of the Forties* (1965)

**Red card.** In football, a card shown by the referee to a player who is to be sent off the field for a repeated or serious infringement. Red cards were introduced to English football on 2 October 1976. That same day the first red cards in the English league were shown to David Wagstaffe of Blackburn Rovers, in their match against Leyton Orient, and also to George Best, for foul and abusive language when playing for Fulham in their game at Southampton. *See also* YELLOW CARD.

**Red carpet.** A ceremonial carpet unrolled for the arrival or departure of an important visitor. In British tradition red is used to signify importance and dignity. Hence its use for so called 'red books' such as court guides, peerage lists, official regulations and the like, or for a government minister's 'red box' in which official papers are held. To roll out the red carpet for someone is thus to lavish hospitality on them, to give them a 'right royal welcome'.

**Red Clydeside.** *See* CLYDESIDERS.

**Redcoats.** The entertainers and organizers at BUTLIN'S holiday camps, so named from their red jackets. Redcoats were also British soldiers of the 16th century and later, similarly so dubbed from their uniform.

> Her beach house at Middleton-on-Sea was ridiculed as 'Bognor', where she was supposedly woken by Butlin's redcoats shouting wakey-wakey every morning.
>
> *Sunday Times Magazine* (29 August 1999)

**Red Dean.** Dr Hewlett Johnson (1874–1966), Dean of Canterbury from 1931 to 1963. The name alludes to his left-wing views and his genuine belief that the communist ideal was compatible with Christian ethics. He visited Russia in 1938 and launched his public lauding of Sovietism in *The Socialist Sixth of the World* (1939). In 1951 he was awarded the Stalin Peace Prize. His sobriquet was a self-bestowed title when, during the Spanish Civil War, he said: 'I saw red – you can call me red.'

**Red Devils.** The freefall display team of the Parachute Regiment, formed in 1963. Dressed in red jumpsuits and trailing plumes of coloured smoke, they 'swim' into a succession of formations as they fall, passing through hoops that they hold for one another and landing on or near a narrowly defined target area in front of the public.

**Red Duster.** A nickname for the Red Ensign, the flag flown by British merchant ships.

**Red Dwarf.** A long-running SCIENCE FICTION space SITCOM, first screened in 1988 and soon developing a keen international cult following. The premise is that the crew of a 21st-century spaceship, the *Red Dwarf*, have all, with one exception, been wiped out following a radiation leak. The sole survivor is David Lister, who after remaining in suspended animation for 3 million years is joined by a motley assortment of characters, including 'Ace', a hologram of Arnold Rimmer, his former shift leader; Holly, the now senile shipboard computer; and 'Cat', a strange humanoid creature. The story devolves on their adventures as they roam the universe.

**Red-eye.** A colloquialism dating from the 1960s for a plane flight that deprives passengers of proper sleep as a result of take-off or arrival times or because of differences in time zones.

**Red flag.** A sign generally used to indicate danger or as a stop signal. It is also the symbol of international socialism and *The Red Flag* is a socialist anthem still used, somewhat incongruously, by the British LABOUR PARTY. It is not the same as the *Internationale* (French *chanson internationale*, 'international song'), the official international socialist anthem, and the Soviet national anthem until 1944, whose words were written in 1871 by Eugène Pottier, a Parisian transport worker, and set to music by Pierre Degeyter, a woodworker of Lille (1848–1932).

> Then raise the scarlet standard high!
> Within its shade we'll live or die.
> Tho' cowards flinch and traitors sneer,
> We'll keep the red flag flying here.
> JAMES CONNELL: 'The Red Flag' (1889)

**Red Friday.** Friday, 31 July 1925, when a stoppage in the coal industry, planned to meet the threat of wage cuts, was averted by promise of government subsidies to support wages. It was so called by the Labour press to distinguish it from BLACK FRIDAY of 1921.

**Red gold.** Payment made by the KGB in the former Soviet Union to Western spies and informants.

> In his resignation letter … [he] admitted taking 'red gold' in the form of expenses for foreign trips paid for by the KGB, but not cash for information.
> *Sunday Times* (11 December 1994)

**Red Guard.** A movement of armed workers in Russia prior to the October Revolution of 1917. A militant youth movement of the name also existed in China from 1966 to 1976 (*see* CULTURAL REVOLUTION). Its members wore red armbands and carried copies of Chairman Mao's LITTLE RED BOOK. Their name was probably a conscious copying of the Russian original (*Krasnaya gvardiya*).

**Red-hot momma** or **mama.** A name for an 'earthy' female jazz singer, especially given to African American singers. The vaudeville singer Sophie Tucker (1884–1966) was known as 'The LAST OF THE RED-HOT MAMAS', and in her latter years billed herself as such.

**Red Ken.** A fairly obvious media nickname for Ken Livingstone (b.1945), Labour leader of the Greater London Council (GLC) from 1981 to its dissolution in 1986. He transformed the GLC from a mainly administrative body into an instrument of left-wing policies and a key tool in Labour's consistent criticism of the Conservative national programme. The right-wing press, in conjunction with Margaret Thatcher's government, launched a concerted campaign against him, portraying him and his policies as the epitome of the LOONY LEFT. At this time *Private Eye* dubbed him 'Ken Leninspart'.However, Thatcher's decision to abolish the GLC in 1983 (implemented in 1986), together with Livingstone's self-deprecatory wit and GLC policies such as cutting fares on London Transport, made him popular with Londoners, even with Tory voters. In 1987 Livingstone became Labour MP for Brent. In 2000 he stood in Labour's contest to select its candidate for mayor of London but narrowly lost to Frank Dobson, then secretary of state for health. He then stood as an independent, easily defeating his (official) Labour, Conservative and Liberal Democrat rivals to become London's first elected mayor.

In January 2004 Livingstone was readmitted to the party and stood as the official Labour Party candidate for mayor in the June 2004 elections, which he won. While his policies as mayor have relatively little in common with those of the Red Ken of GLC days, his verbal forthrightness still ensures regular headlines.

> It would actually be quite nice if the American ambassador in Britain could pay the [traffic congestion] charge that everybody else is paying and not actually try and skive out of it like some chiselling little crook.
> KEN LIVINGSTONE: in interview on the *London Today* programme (28 March 2006)

**Red Kennedy.** *See* CHAMPAGNE CHARLIE.

**Red light.** A children's game of US origin in which one player turns his back on the others and counts rapidly to ten. While he is doing so the others try to sneak up to him without being seen moving. When he reaches ten he calls out 'red light!', whereupon each advancer must stop in his tracks and hold the position in which he was caught. The allusion is to the red light that halts a railway train. *See also* GRANDMOTHER'S STEPS.

**Red-light district.** The district of a town or city where prostitution or other commercialized sexual activities are concentrated. The allusion is to a red light as a sign of a brothel.

**Red mafia.** A name current in the 1990s for the organized criminal gangs of Russia and eastern Europe, who after siphoning millions of dollars from the former Soviet bloc through fraud, extortion and smuggling invested heavily in London stocks and shares. The gangs were linked to the murder in 1999 of the billionaire banker Edmond Safra, one of the world's richest men.

**Red menace.** A term arising in the 1920s for the political or military threat apprehended as emanating from the Soviet Union. An alternative was 'red peril', based on the earlier YELLOW PERIL.

**Redneck foreplay.** A US slang expression, dating from the 1960s, denoting a complete absence of preliminaries before sexual congress. (In the United States, 'redneck' is a disparaging term for one of the 'uneducated' masses, or for a racist Southerner who supports segregation.) *See also* WHAM, BAM, THANK YOU MA'AM.

**Red Ned.** In Australian and New Zealand slang, cheap and fairly unpalatable red wine. The expression dates from the 1940s.

**Red Nose Day.** A day once a year when people wear a small red nose or sport a large one on the front of their car. A red nose is a badge of the clown, and in this instance it is a symbol of the charitable enterprise COMIC RELIEF that the nose-buyers have supported.

**Red Robbo.** A nickname given by the right-wing tabloid press to Derek Robinson (b.1937), hard-left union convenor at British Leyland's Longbridge plant in Birmingham. Robinson was sacked in 1976 following a succession of unofficial strikes.

**Red Rum.** The bay gelding that won the Grand National an unprecedented three times, in 1973, 1974 and 1977, was foaled in 1965 and bought in 1972 when crippled with a form of equine arthritis, a condition eased by being trotted in the sea along Southport beach. He was to have been entered for the 1978 National but was withdrawn because of injury less than 24 hours before the start. He was retired from racing that year but continued to earn money until 1994, when he retired altogether from public life. He died the following year.

**Reds under the bed.** Undisclosed communist sympathizers. The phrase was current in the COLD WAR with mocking reference to those obsessed with hunting down real or supposed communists (*see* MCCARTHYISM). A person hiding under a bed may overhear the most intimate or closely guarded secrets.

**Red-tops.** Media jargon for the TABLOID press, referring to the red-coloured mastheads of newspapers such as the *Daily*

*Mirror* and *The Sun*. The term became current in the late 1990s.

> A tabloid paper had a story about his private life. 'I can't talk about it,' said the 50-year-old Labour peer … But the redtops could – and did.
>
> *Sunday Times* (24 October 1999)

**Reeperbahn.** 'Ropewalk', a street in Hamburg's RED-LIGHT DISTRICT. The name is sometimes used of similar districts elsewhere.

> The Reeperbahn or 42nd Street of Sydney is King's Cross.
>
> JAN MORRIS: *Journeys* (1985)

**Reese's Pieces.** *See* PRODUCT PLACEMENT.

**Referendum Party.** A single-issue party founded in 1994 by the billionaire Anglo-French financier Sir James Goldsmith (1933–97; *see also* GOLDENBALLS). His aim was to force the government to hold a plebiscite on the issue of whether Britain should be part of a federal Europe or a bloc of independent trading nations. The party attracted several high-profile defectors from the right wing of the Conservative Party, such as Alan Walters (b.1926), a former economics adviser to Margaret Thatcher, and for a brief spell the MP Sir George Gardiner (b.1935). Despite extensive media advertising, however, funded by Goldsmith with £20 million from his personal fortune, the party's support in national opinion polls failed to rise above 1 per cent. After the 1997 general election, in which it failed to win a single seat, it suffered a humiliating demise. Goldsmith himself stood in the Putney consituency in London, helping to topple the sitting MP David Mellor (*see* MINISTER OF FUN), who responded with a vituperative speech against the Referendum Party. See also GOLDENBALLS; UKIP.

**Reflexology.** A technique for relief of tension by massaging the feet, popular as an ALTERNATIVE therapy from the 1980s. The premise is that pressure points on the feet are linked to various parts of the body, so that action on a pressure point has a reflex ('reflected') action on some other organs.

**Refusenik.** A term in the 1970s for a Jew in the Soviet Union who was refused permission to emigrate to Israel, the *-nik* being as in BEATNIK. The word is now used more generally for anyone who refuses to obey orders, especially as a protest.

**Reggae.** A style of popular music with a strongly accented subsidiary beat, originating in Jamaica. It evolved in the late 1960s from ska music and other local variations on the calypso and rhythm and blues, and was widely popularized in the 1970s by Bob Marley and the Wailers. The word itself perhaps derives from Jamaican English *rege-rege*, meaning 'row', 'quarrel', literally 'ragged clothes', from the casual dress of its performers. *See also* RAGGA.

**Regime change.** A term for the overthrow (not necessarily violent) of a government that is in some way disapproved of by the state or states involved in its overthrow. Those that bring about the overthrow then help to install a government more to their liking. Regime change does not appear to be legitimate under international law, infringing as it arguably does another nation's sovereignty. Regime change *vis à vis* Saddam Hussein's rule in Iraq became US policy under the Iraq Liberation Act of 1998, and the phrase itself became increasingly current in the early years of the presidency of George W. Bush (*see* DUBYA), under whom it became an overriding foreign-policy objective, culminating in the invasion of Iraq in 2003. Prior to the Iraq War, Bush's ally, British prime minister Tony Blair (*see* BUSH'S POODLE), insisted that his principal war aim in Iraq was the removal of WEAPONS OF MASS DESTRUCTION (WMDs), which he claimed presented a threat to British security, not regime change. However, with the failure to find any WMDs, Blair has confirmed that regime change was, in his view, sufficient justification.

**Reinvent oneself.** To take on a new or radically different character or guise, often as a result of altered circumstances. In the case of a public figure, the move may be made in order to refresh and refurbish one's public image. The term dates from the late 1980s.

> As Archibald Delaney, the son of a Sussex doctor who reinvented himself in the Thirties as a campaigning American Indian, [Pierce] Brosnan's prospects weren't aided by his pony-tail.
>
> *Sunday Express* (27 February 2000)

**Reinvent the wheel.** To waste time or effort in creating something that already exists. The wheel is one of mankind's earliest and most radical inventions, dating from at least 3500 BC.

> 'It used to be you almost had to reinvent the wheel to get funding,' said Daniel Cobb, dean of the faculty at the small liberal arts college in West Virginia.
>
> *Washington Post* (16 July 1984)

**Reith Lectures.** An annual series of radio lectures broadcast by the BBC and named after its first director general, John Reith (1889–1971), a Scottish Presbyterian minister's son famous for his championing of the moral and intellectual role of broadcasting. The series was inaugurated in 1948, when the philosopher Bertrand Russell spoke on 'Authority and the Individual'. Each series consists of six lectures, the speakers until recently being mostly white English male

academics. In 2006 the Reith Lecturer was the pianist and conductor Daniel Barenboim, and his 'lectures' were conversational and unscripted, causing a stir among traditionalists.

**Rejoice! Rejoice!** The phrase usually attributed to Margaret Thatcher (the IRON LADY) when she told the press on 25 April 1982 of the recapture of South Georgia, the first success of the Falklands War. Her actual words were:

> Just rejoice at that news and congratulate our armed forces and the Marines. Rejoice!

**Relais routier.** (French, 'transport café'.) The roadside restaurants so known in France were originally designed for lorry drivers, like the old British 'pull-ups', but since the 1960s they have been sought out by tourists and travellers for their high-class food at reasonable prices (attributes often alien to British transport cafés).

**Reliant Robin.** A well-known make of three-wheeled car, regarded with amused disdain by many 'real' car drivers but with loyalty and affection by their owners. The Reliant Motor Company had its beginnings in the workshop set up in 1935 by T.L. Williams in his garden at Tamworth, Staffordshire, to make three-wheeled delivery vehicles. The first passenger tricar was the Regal, launched in 1953. The Robin superseded it in 1972 and soon found favour for its low road tax and the fact that it could be driven on a motorcycle licence. The use of a yellow Reliant Robin (carrying the legend 'New York – Paris – Peckham') by Del Boy in the television comedy ONLY FOOLS AND HORSES enhanced rather than diminished its cult status; a Corgi diecast model followed in the wake of the show's success. A new model was introduced in 1989, with a fibreglass body (it was nicknamed 'the plastic pig'). The Robin finally ceased production in 2002.

**Remembrance Day.** After the First World War ARMISTICE DAY, or Remembrance Day, commemorating the fallen, was observed on 11 November. From 1945 to 1956 it was observed on the first or second Sunday of November, now commemorating the fallen of both world wars. In 1956 Remembrance Day was fixed on the second Sunday of November. *See also* FOR YOUR TOMORROW WE GAVE OUR TODAY; POPPY DAY; THEY SHALL GROW NOT OLD; TWO-MINUTE SILENCE; VETERANS DAY.

**Remembrance of Things Past.** The title of a sequence of seven novels (1922–31; in French as *À la recherche du temps perdu*, 1913–27) by Marcel Proust (1871–1922). Together, they constitute a deeply significant, quasi-autobiographical study of people and the society in which they move, in the course of which the protagonist, Marcel, assumes a variety of roles before ultimately regaining his lost vocation as a writer. When G.K. Scott-Moncrieff started publishing the first famous English translation of the work in 1922, the year of Proust's death, he gave it an evocative but not entirely accurate title taken from Shakespeare: 'when to the sessions of sweet silent thought / I summon up remembrance of things past' (Sonnet 30). The title was well in keeping with the florid tone of his translation, and its poetic resonance doubtless helped to sell his work. Proust, however, was not writing about idle remembrance but about arduous research (*recherche*), as he himself exemplified in the 12 years of illness and solitude that he spent writing the sequence. When, therefore, a freshly revised translation of the work was published in 1992, it was given a title much closer to the intention of the original: *In Search of Lost Time*.

In the face of such a dauntingly long work of literature, MONTY PYTHON'S FLYING CIRCUS memorably created the All-England Summarize Proust Competition, in which, for example, a male voice choir never quite got past a beautifully rendered 'Proust wrote about ...' before running out of time.

*See also* FIRST LINES OF NOVELS.

**Renaissance man.** A man with many talents and interests, especially in the humanities. The expression goes back to the 1940s, and makes an explicit contrast with the narrow specialism often considered typical of the modern age. The underlying model may be Leonardo da Vinci (1452–1519), man of genius in many areas of the arts and sciences and outstanding figure of the Italian Renaissance.

**Renamo.** *See* FRELIMO.

**Rendition.** *See* EXTRAORDINARY RENDITION.

**Rent-a-crowd** or **mob.** A crowd of demonstrators. The implication is that they have been paid to demonstrate and that they will happily do so for or against any cause, simply for the financial reward. The term derives from the American car hire company Rentacar, established in 1921.

> The day that rent-a-mob came to the City of London did have its comical side. The thuggish anarchists and Trotskyists who were intent on causing violent confrontation with the police were accompanied by such unlikely groups as the Association of Autonomous Astronauts and the Biotic Baking Brigade.
>
> *Sunday Times* (20 June 1999)

**Rentaquote.** A term applied by the press to those backbench MPs who always seem to be willing to sound off to journalists on any subject that is required, particularly on days when there is little 'real' news.

**Rent boy.** A young male prostitute, a 'boy' available for 'rent'. The term, but not the phenomenon, dates from the 1960s.

**Repetitive strain injury.** A rather grand term (commonly abbreviated to 'RSI') for a medical condition in which injury to muscles or tendons is caused by the repeated use of particular muscles, as when operating a keyboard. Many employers are now aware of it as an occupational health hazard.

**Repo man.** A repossession man, employed by finance companies to repossess goods whose buyer has defaulted on payments. In US parlance a repo man is usually associated with cars. The term dates from the 1960s. Alex Cox's comic FILM NOIR, *Repo Man*, was made in 1984.

**Representative on Earth.** The usual mouthpiece of the particular powerful personage named. The usage has an ancient religious lineage: in the Roman Catholic Church the pope is commonly identified as 'God's representative on Earth'. In the latter part of the 20th century, however, it began to be applied sarcastically to the somewhat menial spokesperson for any extremely powerful and influential figure who did not to enter the public arena in person.

> Irwin Stelzer, Rupert Murdoch's representative on Earth, recently commended Mr Cameron to readers of *The Weekly Standard*, the house journal of the right wing of the American Republican party.
>
> *The Observer* (23 October 2005)

**Resistible Rise of Arturo Ui, The.** A play, originally entitled *Der aufhaltsame Aufstieg des Arturo Ui* (1958), by the German playwright Bertolt Brecht (1898–1956) about the career of a small-time Chicago gangster as he seeks to establish a stranglehold over the city's cauliflower business. Arturo Ui himself is a thinly disguised portrait of the NAZI dictator Adolf Hitler, although the character was first suggested to Brecht when he read newspaper reports in New York about the killing of a real-life gangster called Dutch Schulz. These he combined with details culled from his reading of a biography of Al CAPONE and his viewing of numerous American gangster movies. The role made the name of Ekkehard Schall (1930–2005), one of Brecht's leading performers, and in the English-speaking theatre Leonard Rossiter (*see* RISING DAMP), Christopher Plummer and (in 2002) Al Pacino have been among those to take the part.

**Rest is history, The.** You know what happened later. A stock formula for breaking off a biographical anecdote, either because the outcome is generally familiar or because the speaker cannot be bothered to repeat it. When describing his transition from Oxford history don to Broadway revue artist the writer Alan Bennett, speaking at a seminar at Nuffield College, Oxford, in 1986, said: 'The rest, one might say pompously, is history. Except that in my case the opposite was true. What it had been was history. What it was to be was not history at all.'

> There across all the papers was the photograph of me presenting the Queen Mother with her chart, under the caption 'Astrologer Royal'. Well, the rest, as they say, is history.
>
> RUSSELL GRANT: in *TV Times* (15 October 1983)

**Retail therapy.** Shopping as a method of alleviating anxiety, stress or ennui. An ironic term, first recorded in 1986, it satirizes the shallowness of modern consumer society, but perhaps there are few who, if pressed, would not admit to having occasionally been psychologically lifted by a particular purchase. *See also* SHOPPING AND FUCKING.

> Stop for a reviving cafe au lait or a glass of wine ... at Place de General de Gaulle, before setting out for more retail therapy.
>
> *Cosmopolitan* (August 1998)

**Retro.** A vogue word of the 1980s and 1990s, indicating little more than a nostalgic harking back to the past, a sentimental retrospection. The term particularly caught on in the worlds of popular music and fashion, and was prefixed to other words to form impressive-looking compounds such as 'retro-chic' or 'retro-culture'.

> Black patent Grace Kelly handbags, long black gloves and high-heeled slingbacks are retro accessories to the elegant look.
>
> *The Times* (1 July 1986)

**Reuben sandwich.** A type of sandwich popular in the United States in the 1960s, containing a combination of corned beef, Swiss cheese and sauerkraut served hot. It is said to take its name from Arnold Reuben (1883–1970), a restaurant owner.

**Rev. A.R.P. Blair MA (Oxon), The.** *See* BUSH'S POODLE.

**Rev. Dubya Bush of the Church of Latter Day Morons, The.** *See* DUBYA.

**Revised Standard Version.** A modern translation of the Bible produced in the United States and published between 1946 and 1957. It was in the tradition of the Authorized (King James) Version of 1611, but aimed to eliminate excessively archaic language. It became the standard text in many churches and communities, and remained in widespread use until 1990, when a further revision, the New Revised Standard Version, was published, with the text presented in a more contemporary idiom. An anglicized edition was published in 1995.

**Revolution names.** Various REGIME CHANGES in recent decades have been achieved peaceably and have acquired appropriately peaceful names:

**Carnation Revolution.** The overthrow of the quasi-fascist regime in Portugal by the armed forces in 1974. The people – the vast majority of whom supported the change – presented the soldiers with carnations. The broadcast of Portugal's entry in the Eurovision Song Contest that year was the signal to the armed forces for the revolution to begin.

**Velvet Revolution.** The peaceful demise of the communist regime in Czechoslovakia in 1989, followed by a smooth transition to democracy. The term Velvet Revolution is a translation of the Czech *sametová revoluce*, the former word being related to English 'samite'. The peaceful secession was signalled when vast crowds gathered in Wenceslas Square in Prague, and rattled their keys.

**Rose Revolution.** The peaceful overthrow of President Schevardnadze of Georgia in November 2003. The opposition marched on parliament carrying roses as a symbol of non-violence. Schevardnadze, a former key Soviet figure, was offered asylum in Germany.

**Orange Revolution.** The change of leadership in Ukraine in November 2004. Following a notably corrupt presidential election, followers of the unfairly defeated pro-Western candidate Viktor Yushchenko took to the streets of Kiev to demonstrate, wearing orange scarves, hats, etc. The government fell and Yushchenko took over the presidency.

**Tulip Revolution.** The largely peaceful overthrow of the pro-Russian regime of President Askar Akayev in Kyrgyzstan in spring 2005 – the time when tulips are in bloom. It was also known as the Silk Revolution, as protestors wore pink and yellow silk scarves, although this term is also applied to the upheaval in 1990 when the then pro-democracy Akayev came to power.

**Revolver.** A critically acclaimed album by The BEATLES, released in the UK in August 1966 and favoured by some over its better-known successor SERGEANT PEPPER'S LONELY HEARTS CLUB BAND. The title of the album refers to the revolutions of an LP on a record turntable, rather than to a gun, and was chosen over such earlier candidate names as 'Freewheelin' Beatles', 'Bubble and Squeak' and 'Four Sides to the Circle'. *Revolver* includes the tracks 'ELEANOR RIGBY', some specifically drug-evoking songs ('Dr Robert', 'Got to Get You into My Life' and 'Tomorrow Never Knows'), the satirical 'Taxman', the languid 'I'm Only Sleeping', and the beautiful 'Here, There and Everywhere'. It confirmed the creative progress of The Beatles, which had begun with RUBBER SOUL, from pop group to PSYCHEDELIC rock band.

Post-psychedelia, *Revolver* was to prove influential for new generations of bands, such as The Jam, Blur and Oasis.

In 1976 George Harrison revisted the mechanics of LP turntables by entitling an album *33 & ⅓* (plus it was his age at the time).

**Rexists.** A group of Belgian fascists who collaborated with the NAZIS during the German occupation in the Second World War. The Rexist Movement was founded in 1930 by Léon Degrelle (1906–94) as a branch of the Catholic Party, with the aim of purging politics from the Catholic Church. The name derives from *Christus Rex* (Latin, 'Christ the King'), the slogan of the Catholic Young People's Action Society, which had been established in 1925. The Rexists went on to establish their own political party, which, subsidized by Mussolini, became a fascist organization. During the German occupation Rexists took control of local government and the press, and also organized Belgian units to fight for the Germans on the Eastern Front. After the liberation Degrelle fled to Franco's Spain, where he remained for the rest of his life.

***Rhapsody in Blue.*** A work for piano and orchestra by George Gershwin (1898–1937), orchestrated by Ferde Grofé (1892–1972) and first performed in New York in 1924 by Paul Whiteman's jazz orchestra, with Gershwin on piano. As the title suggests, the work successfully fuses jazz and classical music – the first concert work to do so. The title plays with the convention of naming a classical composition 'sonata in F', 'symphony in G minor', and so on. The opening sequence of Gershwin's *Rhapsody*, beginning with a wailing call on the clarinet, accompanies the start of the film *Manhattan* (1979), written and directed by and starring Woody Allen, himself a jazz clarinettist.

> The *Rhapsody* is not a composition at all. It's a string of separate paragraphs stuck together – with a thin paste of flour and water … I don't think there's been such an inspired melodist since Tchaikovsky … but if you want to speak of a *composer*, that's another matter.
> LEONARD BERNSTEIN: in *Atlantic Monthly* (1955)

***Rhinoceros.*** A play (1959), characteristic of the THEATRE OF THE ABSURD, by the Romanian-born French playwright Eugène Ionesco (1912–94) depicting how an ordinary man in a small French town discovers that everyone he knows is gradually turning into a rhinoceros. In Ionesco's hands the disease 'rhinoceritis' became an allegory for the spread of FASCISM through the populations of Europe in the years before the Second World War.

**Rhubarb.** A word conventionally repeated by actors to represent the murmur of conversation in a crowd scene. The

practice, dating from the 1930s, is not unknown in Shakespeare productions, especially at an amateur level. Other languages have similar dodges: Russian actors repeat *govoryu, ne govoryu*, 'I speak, I don't speak'.

> And in the next-door room is heard the tramp
> And 'rhubarb, rhubarb' as the crowd rehearse
> A one-act play in verse.
> JOHN BETJEMAN: *Summoned by Bells*, ch. 9 (1960)

**Rhythm and blues.** *See* R & B.

**Rich bitch.** A derogatory nickname of US origin for a wealthy woman, especially one who dresses or deports herself ostentatiously.

**Richter scale.** The numerical scale for expressing the magnitude of an earthquake on the basis of seismograph oscillations takes its name from the US geologist Charles F. Richter (1900–85). The scale is logarithmic, and the numerical value assigned to an earthquake measures its overall size, not its intensity at a given point. Richter's own name for his invention, created in 1927 and perfected in 1935, was 'the magnitude scale', and he regretted that the new name did not reflect the contribution to his work made by his fellow seismologist Beno Gutenberg (1889–1960). Earthquakes had previously been measured in subjective terms, by recording the damage sustained by structures of different types. The scale itself begins at 1, detected only by seismographs, and has no theoretical upper limit, although the largest earthquakes have not exceeded a scale value of 9. The term has also enjoyed some metaphorical use, for any notional scale of rising and potentially explosive seriousness:

> In an arm of government as seismologically sensitive as the Foreign Service, the news was a shock on the level of six or seven on the diplomatic Richter scale.
> HARRIS GREENE: *FSO-1* (1977)

***Riddle of the Sands, The.*** A thriller (1903) by Erskine Childers (1870–1922), set against the background of the Anglo-German Great Naval Race of the early 20th century. The 'sands' are the sandbanks of the Friesian Islands, and the 'riddle' is to resolve the mystery that lies there. Ultimately two Englishmen thwart the traitorous aim of a former British naval officer who is preparing for a German invasion of Britain. An ardent Irish nationalist, Childers became a minister in the self-constituted Irish parliament (DÁIL Éireann) in 1921. During the Irish Civil War he was captured, court-martialled and shot on the orders of the Irish Free State government for the illegal possession of a revolver. This, his only novel, is memorable as much for its descriptive passages about sailing as for its gripping story line. A rather tame film version (1978) was directed by Tony Maylam. *See also* FIRST LINES OF NOVELS.

**Ride a tiger.** To embark on a course of action that turns out to be unexpectedly difficult but cannot be safely abandoned. The expression comes from the modern proverb: 'He who rides a tiger is afraid to dismount,' itself apparently of Chinese origin. A tiger is a dangerous beast. One may ride it in an attempt to capture it, but it may turn on one at any moment and one cannot readily dismount.

**Ride off into the sunset.** To conclude an episode or experience with a happy resolution. The reference is to the classic final scene of certain Western films of the 1930s in which the cowboy hero, having vanquished the 'baddies', literally rides off into the sunset.

***Riders to the Sea.*** A play (1904) by the Irish playwright J.M. Synge (1871–1909) about the grieving of an old peasant woman, Maurya, for her husband and five of her six sons, lost at sea. It is realized that the last son has been claimed by the sea when the old woman reports having seen his image riding a grey horse by the sea, the grey horse recalling the 'pale horse' of the Apocalypse: 'his name that sat on him was Death'. The play was turned into an opera (1932) of the same name by Ralph Vaughan Williams.

**Ride shotgun.** To guard a person or thing in transit. The US expression alludes to the armed assistant on a stagecoach who sat beside the coachman to protect him from marauding Indians, bandits and the like. The term was later used of any person riding in the front passenger seat of a motor vehicle.

**Ride the clutch.** In driving a motor vehicle to keep one's foot too long on the clutch pedal, depressing it slightly. If persisted in the tactic will soon wear out the friction lining.

**Ride the cushions.** To travel luxuriously by public transport, as by train with a first-class ticket. It is a US expression dating from the early 20th century. *See also* RIDE THE RAILS.

**Ride the lightning.** To be executed in OLD SPARKY. It is a vivid American metaphor dating from the 1940s.

**Ride the rails.** To travel by train, especially on a freight train without paying. A mostly Canadian expression dating from the 1940s. *See also* RIDE THE CUSHIONS.

**Right on.** Modern; fashionable; politically sound; ideologically correct. The expression dates from the 1950s and originated from an African American shortening of 'right on time'. The transference of sense was thus from temporality to topicality.

**Right stuff, The.** Shorthand for the manly virtues of stiff-upper-lip and spunk. Ian Hay published a novel called *The Right Stuff* in 1908, subtitled 'Some episodes in the career of a North Briton'. The phrase was revived by the American writer Tom Wolfe as the title of a book (1979), referring to the qualities required by US test pilots and the first US astronauts (turned into a film in 1983).

**Right to roam.** Although there has long been no automatic right of public access to open country in England and Wales, the Countryside and Rights of Way Act 2000 gave walkers in England and Wales a new right to explore the countryside. This 'right to roam' for the purpose of recreation applies to scheduled areas of mountain, moor, heath, down and registered common land and can be extended to other types of open country such as some woodland. At the same time walkers have a clear responsibility to respect the rights of landowners and managers. The Land Reform Act (Scotland) 2003 provides less restricted rights in Scotland. *See also* RAMBLERS.

**Rillington Place.** A former cul-de-sac in Notting Hill, West London, where No. 10, a shabby terraced house, was the location of the murders of at least eight women over the period 1943–53. John Christie had moved into the ground-floor flat with his wife in 1938 and ten years later Timothy Evans moved into the second-floor flat with his pregnant wife. In 1949 Evans, who was mentally retarded, confessed to the murder of his wife and baby girl, and was hanged. In 1953 the mouldering bodies of three young women were found in Christie's kitchen cupboard. His wife's body was then discovered under the kitchen floorboards and the skeletons of two women buried some ten years earlier in the garden. Christie, a necrophiliac, confessed to these murders and to that of Mrs Evans, and was also hanged. Evans was granted a posthumous pardon in 1966. The house has now been demolished and the street renamed. The film *Ten Rillington Place* (1971), based on a book by Ludovic Kennedy, offered a realistically sordid reconstruction of the *cause célèbre* with Richard Attenborough in the role of the murderer and John Hurt as Evans.

**Ring a bell.** To jog one's memory; to sound familiar, as: 'That name rings a bell.' The expression dates from the 1930s and may have derived from the fairground 'try-your-strength' machine, in which a bell on top of a tall column could be struck by hammering a pivot at the base and sending a projectile upwards. Alternatively the reference may be to a summoning of the memory in the same way that a ring at the door or the ring of a telephone summons one to answer. *See also* CLOSE, BUT NO CIGAR.

**Ring of Bright Water.** A moving account (1960) by the naturalist Gavin Maxwell of his life with two otters on the west coast of Scotland. The book became the basis of the 1969 film of the same name. The title is from Kathleen Raine's 1952 poem 'The Marriage of Psyche':

> He has married me with a ring, a ring of bright water
> Whose ripples spread from the heart of the sea,
> He has married me with a ring of light, the glitter
> Broadcast on the swift river.

**Ring of steel.** A surrounding armed defence, especially one preventing escape. In a speech on the Italian armistice in 1943 Adolf Hitler said, 'Tactical necessity may compel us … to give up something on some front in this gigantic fateful struggle, but it will never break the ring of steel that protects the Reich' (translated from Gordon W. Prange, ed., *Hitler's Words*, 1944). In the early 1990s the term became associated particularly with the stringent security measures put in place to protect the City of London against IRA attack, including police checkpoints on all major routes into the City.

**Rinky-dink.** Cheap and shoddy; outdated and unfashionable. The American term dates from the early years of the 20th century but is of uncertain origin. It perhaps represents the repetitive percussive sounds of an uninspired musical group.

> The range of discontinued old rockets with chipped paint, spare parts from Skylab and rusting moon-buggies brought one (American) phrase to mind: rinky dink.
>
> *The Times Magazine* (5 June 1999)

**Rin Tin Tin.** The talented German shepherd (Alsatian) dog that became a star of HOLLYWOOD movies in the 1920s. The original dog that bore the name was real, not fictional, and was one of a litter that US airmen rescued from an abandoned German dugout in France in September 1918. Corporal Lee Duncan named the pup after a tiny doll that the French soldiers carried for luck, and took him home to California. At first trained for dog shows, 'Rinty' was so successful in his first film, *Where the North Begins* (1923), that over the next nine years he made more than 40 movies, earned over £1 million and kept WARNER BROTHERS solvent. After he died in 1932 his son, Rin Tin Tin Jr, starred in Westerns until 1938, and another descendant appeared in *The Return of Rin Tin Tin* (1947). *See also* LASSIE.

**Riot grrls.** A loose-knit grouping of feminist PUNKS formed in Washington, D.C., in the early 1990s. Their rallying cry was 'Revolution Girl Style Now!' and a chief aim was to combat the male dominance of the punk scene. Their overall platform was that of GIRL POWER. The term subsequently became attached to any aggressive or overtly sexual female rock group.

**Ripley.** The anti-hero of a series of five thrillers (collectively known by fans as *The Ripliad*) by Patricia Highsmith (1921–95). Tom Ripley is a plausible young man with a pathological criminal mind who is not averse to murder in order to maintain a comfortable existence in his château near Fontainebleau. He makes his first appearance in *The Talented Mr Ripley* (1956), which was the basis of the 1959 film *Plein Soleil* (*Purple Noon*), directed by René Clément and starring Alain Delon as Ripley. The story was remade in 1999 under its original title by director Anthony Minghella, with Matt Damon in the title role. The third novel in the series, *Ripley's Game* (1974), was the basis of Wim Wenders' film *Der amerikanische Freund* (*The American Friend*; 1977); a more recent film version under the original title (2002) starred John Malkovich as Ripley.

**Rip-off.** A fraud or swindle in which something is stolen from or 'ripped off' the victim.

**Ripping Yarns.** A series of television comedies broadcast in 1977 and 1979 as a spoof of the type of stirring adventure stories found in boys' publications such as *The BOY'S OWN PAPER*. The nine episodes were created by Michael Palin and Terry Jones of MONTY PYTHON'S FLYING CIRCUS and their surreal humour is evident throughout. Two of the episodes, *The Testing of Eric Olthwaite* and *Golden Gordon*, are almost without peer in the realm of British comedy half-hours. *Across the Andes by Frog* was perhaps the most memorably titled episode.

**Rise and Fall of the City of Mahagonny.** A ferocious political satire of an opera, *Aufstieg und Fall der Stadt Mahagonny*, by Kurt Weill (1900–50), with a libretto by Bertolt Brecht (1898–1956). It was first produced in 1930, following an earlier, simpler version of 1927. Mahagonny is an imaginary city of material pleasure, with a capitalist morality: when the hero, Jimmy Mahoney, is arrested and brought to trial, he is sentenced to two days' imprisonment for indirect murder and four years for seduction by means of money, and is condemned to die for failing to pay his whisky bill.

**Rise and shine.** To get smartly out of bed. The phrase (commonly preceded by 'Wakey, wakey!') was originally a military command at the start of the 20th century. The rather obvious analogy is with the sun.

> I was due to go on picquet outside at four in the morning, and the sergeant banged on the door then and said, Wakey, wakey, rise and shine.
>
> JULIAN MACLAREN-ROSS: 'Gas', from *The Stuff to Give the Troops* (1944)

**Rising Damp.** The ITV SITCOM of this name, screened from 1974 to 1978, owed its success to the performance of Leonard Rossiter (1926–84) in the role of its central character, Rupert Rigsby, the landlord of a run-down boarding-house in a northern university town. Rigsby is reactionary, racist, lecherous, interfering and generally obnoxious, but in Rossiter's talented hands he is almost lovable. His tenants include the lovelorn spinster Ruth Jones, played by Frances de la Tour, and two young men who often perplex or goad him: the carefree medical student Alan Moore, played by Richard Beckinsale, and the wise black student Philip Smith, played by Don Warrington.

**Rising fives.** Educational jargon for young children just below the compulsory school age of five. At the close of the 20th century many such children were attending nursery schools and classes or reception classes in primary schools, or else received pre-school education at private day nurseries and pre-school PLAYGROUPS, largely organized by parents. From 1998 the government provided free nursery education in England and Wales for all four-year-olds whose parents wanted it.

**Rite of passage.** A ceremony or event marking an important stage in someone's life, such as birth, initiation, marriage or death. The term translates French *rite de passage*, coined by the French ethnographer Arnold van Gennep in his major work *Les Rites de passage* (1909), in which he considered such ceremonies. The title of William Golding's prize-winning novel *Rites of Passage* (1980), the first of a trilogy, puns on 'passage' in the sense of sea journey, and all three books are set in the 18th century on a ship travelling to Australia.

**Rite of Spring, The.** The throbbingly rhythmic ballet with music by Igor Stravinsky (1882–1971) and choreography by Vaslav Nijinsky (1890–1950) was first performed by Diaghilev's BALLETS RUSSES in 1913 at the Théâtre des Champs-Elysées, Paris. It is often referred to by its French title, *Le Sacre du printemps*. The subtitle of the work is 'Pictures from Pagan Russia', and its two parts are titled 'The Adoration of the Earth' and 'The Sacrifice'. The unprecedented ferocity of the music's grinding discords and rhythms caused a riot at the first performance. One contemporary critic commented that it was 'rather a *Massacre du printemps*'; Diaghilev himself called it 'the 20th-century's Ninth Symphony'.

**Ritzy.** In colloquial usage, fashionable and luxurious; ostentatiously smart. The allusion is to one or other of the Ritz-Carlton Hotel, New York, the Ritz Hotel, Paris, or the Ritz Hotel, London, which all became identified with wealth. The last of these was established in 1906 by the Swiss hotelier César Ritz (1850–1918). Hence 'to put on the Ritz', meaning to make a display of riches or luxury. The phrase was popularized by Irving Berlin's song 'Puttin' on the Ritz' (1929):

> If you're blue and you don't know what to do
> Why don't you go where Harlem sits
> Puttin' on the Ritz.

**River Tiber foaming with much blood, The.** The notorious warning of future racial violence in the UK by the Conservative politician Enoch Powell (1912–98), at a Conservative Party meeting in Birmingham, 21 April 1968:

> As I look ahead, I am filled with foreboding. Like the Roman, I seem to see 'the River Tiber foaming with much blood'.

He was promptly sacked from the shadow cabinet, and later joined the Ulster Unionist Party. Powell, a classical scholar, was referring to a passage in Virgil's *Aeneid* (book 6):

> *Bella, horrida bella,*
> *Et Thybrim multo spumantem sanguine cerno.*
> (I see wars, horrible wars,
> and the Tiber foaming with much blood.)

*See also* POWELLISM.

**RNVR.** *See* WAVY NAVY.

**Road kill.** An animal that has been run over and killed by a road vehicle. Such items, when not unrecognizably flattened, have been known to make a useful dietary supplement in rural areas. The usage emerged in North America in the late 1970s, and has come to enjoy a wider metaphorical role, denoting something irretrievably ruined or hopeless:

> We all know any number of men who can cook a virtuoso dish or two, but outside of this they are strictly roadkills in the kitchen.
> *Esquire* (December 1993)

*See also* SMART CAR.

**Road map.** Metaphorically, an outline of a course of action to be pursued. The expression came into its own in the early years of the 21st century when it began to be applied to a plan (hovering somewhere between outline and detailed) for the resolution of the long-running conflict between Israel and the Palestinians.

> A performance-based roadmap to a permanent two-state solution to the Israeli-Palestinian conflict.
> www.state. gov (US Department of State) (30 April 2003)

**Road movie.** A type of film in which the main character takes to the road or travels, usually in a car, either as an escape from something or in a search for something, typically in a journey of self-discovery. The form was best defined in print in Jack Kerouac's novel ON THE ROAD (1957), in which the characters seek fulfilment as they travel. Road movies such as *Easy Rider* (1969) had an instant appeal to American youth, and to some extent replaced the Western as entertainment. Male bonding was an integral feature until the 1990s, when feminism found its voice in *Thelma and Louise* (1991) and later films.

**Road numbers.** The roads in England are numbered by the Department of Transport according to a system, introduced in 1919, which divides the country into sectors. The six major routes leaving London are numbered A1 to A6 and the same number, 1 to 6, is given to the sector of country adjacent to each route, going clockwise. The A1 thus runs north to Berwick-upon-Tweed, the A2 southeast to Dover, the A3 southwest to Portsmouth, the A4 west to Bristol, and to the northwest the A5 to Holyhead and the A6 to Carlisle (which now starts in Luton). All main roads in sector 1 have 1 as the first digit of their number, with A or B as a prefix depending on their greater or lesser importance. Thus in sector 1 the A12 runs northeast to Great Yarmouth and in sector 4 the A40 runs northwest to Cheltenham and Wales. The subsequent digits are random, a new road being given the next unallocated number in its own sector. A road originating in one sector but passing through others keeps its original number for its entire length. The same system applies in Scotland, where the sectors are defined by the routes A7 to A9 radiating from Edinburgh. Motorway numbers are organized similarly, with the prefix M.

**Road rage.** A driver's uncontrolled aggressive behaviour towards other road users. It is supposedly caused by the stress of modern driving, and can range from the brandishing of a fist or the mouthing of a curse to a full-scale beating-up or even, in a few cases, to an actual killing. The term has been evoked by some drivers in mitigation of their behaviour, as if a medical condition. See also WHITE VAN MAN.

**Road to Wigan Pier, The.** A sociological investigation (1937) by George ORWELL into the conditions of the unemployed in the towns of Wigan, Sheffield and Barnsley in the north of England. In the second half of the book he took a revolutionary stance that opposed Stalinism, embarrassing members of the LEFT BOOK CLUB, of which it was a choice. The title is ironic, as Wigan is more than 30km (20 miles) from the sea. *See also* WIGAN PIER.

**Roaring twenties, The.** The 1920s, a time of liberation and buoyancy after the First World War. The decade was characterized in the United States by the BRIGHT YOUNG THINGS and their flamboyant fashions, by PROHIBITION,

with its speakeasies (*see* SPEAKEASY) and gangsters, and by its financial boom that continued until the GREAT DEPRESSION.

**Roasting.** A slang phrase for several men having sex with one woman, an increasingly popular post-match activity among footballers in the early 21st century.0

> Top young footballers driven by lust regularly lure young girls for group sex – and they call their sick post match sex games 'roasting' … 'It's not unusual for a girl to s**g all of us,' said Meikle, who explained that the game gets it name from roasting a chicken. 'It gets stuffed.'
> *Daily Star* (5 October 2003)

*See also* DOGGING.

**Robert the Puce.** A nickname given to the politician Robert Kilroy-Silk, the permanently tanned leader of VERITAS, with a play on the 14th-century Scottish king, Robert the Bruce.

**Robot.** (Czech *robota*, 'forced labour'). An automaton with semi-human powers and intelligence. From this the term is often extended to mean a person who works automatically without employing initiative. The name comes from the mechanical creatures in Karel Čapek's play R.U.R (*Rossum's Universal Robots*), which was successfully produced in London in 1923.

> The three fundamental Rules of Robotics … One, a robot may not injure a human being, or, through inaction, allow a human being to come to harm … Two … a robot must obey the orders given it by human beings except where such orders would conflict with the First Law … Three, a robot must protect its own existence as long as such protection does not conflict with the First or Second Laws.
> ISAAC ASIMOV: 'Runaround' in *I, Robot* (1950),

**Rob the coach.** In Australian slang, 'Who's robbing this coach?' is an affronted inquiry as to who is in charge, implying that the person addressed has been getting above him- or herself. First recorded in 1945, the expression may hark back to the old bushranging days, when coach-robbing was a common occupation.

**'Rock Around the Clock'.** The song usually (though not necessarily correctly) identified as the first ROCK 'N' ROLL record, first released in 1954 by Bill Haley and his Comets. The song's title derived from an earlier song written by Bill Haley's manager Jimmy Myers entitled 'Dance Around the Clock', the title of which was changed for the new song to the happily rhyming 'Rock Around the Clock'. The song first appeared as the B-side of a song called 'Thirteen Women'. It later appeared in the teenage rebellion film *The* BLACKBOARD JUNGLE and when reissued reached the top of the charts in both the United States and Britain. 'Rock Around the Clock' was associated by the conservative-minded with what they saw as a rising tide of juvenile delinquency. *The Blackboard Jungle* provoked the following reaction from the Scottish Conversative politician Robert (nowLord) Boothby:

> What worries me is that a fourth-rate film with fifth-rate music can pierce the shell of a civilization. The sooner this ridiculous film is banned the better.

**Rock Drill, The.** An aggressively mechanistic sculpture of a robot-like figure by Jacob Epstein (1880–1959). It is one of the most famous works of early British MODERNISM (sculpted in 1913–14). The figure has certain drill-like qualities and was originally displayed on a real drill. Epstein himself commented: 'Here is the armed, sinister figure of today and tomorrow. No humanity, only the terrible Frankenstein's monster we have made ourselves into.'

**Rocket science** or **rocket scientist.** Terms generally used in negative constructions expressing the extreme simplicity of a task, such as 'It's hardly rocket science' or 'You don't have to be a rocket scientist to understand how the internal combustion engine works.' The implication is that, in contrast with the intellectually unchallenging nature of the matter alluded to, understanding the workings of rockets demands a great deal of specialist knowledge and mental prowess.

**Rockettes, The.** A team of 36 high-kicking, bejewelled dancers who first appeared at the RADIO CITY MUSIC HALL in 1933, and soon became icons of New York and 'showbiz' generally. They originated as a 16-member troupe from St Louis called the Missouri Rockets. They then became the Rockets and, when appearing at the ROXY Theatre, New York, the Roxyettes. This name was modified as now in 1934, since when a highlight has been the dancers' performance of their 'Parade of the Wooden Soldiers' routine at the annual Christmas show.

**Rock group names.** No one growing up since the 1950s can have failed to be struck by the many distinctive names of pop and rock groups, ranging from the apparently meaningless to the seemingly surreal. Like the covers of their albums and CDs, they have become almost an art form in themselves, although with an appeal that is verbal rather than visual. The following are the origins of the names of some of the most familiar groups, mostly based on information in Mark Beech's *The A–Z of Names in Rock* (1998). Each group name is followed by the dates of its existence (still ongoing in many cases, if only notionally so), many drawn from the *Guinness Rockopedia* (1998).

Abba (1972–83): a palindromic acronym of the names of its four Swedish members: *A*gnetha Fältskog, *B*jörn Ulvaeus, *B*enny Andersson, *A*nni-Frid Lyngstad.

AC/DC (from 1973): from the standard abbreviation meaning 'alternating current/direct current', referring to a musical instrument that can be switched to either in any country.

Aerosmith (from 1970): a blend of 'aerospace' and 'songsmith'.

a-ha (from 1982): an exclamation of satisfaction.

Animals, The (1962–83): from 'Animal' Hogg, the nickname of a friend of the lead singer Eric Burden. The name was appropriate for the group's wild stage act.

Anthrax (from 1981): a word adopted by the heavy metal group for its unpleasant associations.

Arctic Monkeys (from 2003): in the words of guitarist Alex Turner, 'We've made up so many stories about how and why we chose the name that I can't even remember the truth'. (www.toronto.now.com, 10–16 November 2005)

Aztec Camera (from 1980): a combination of 'Aztec', adopted simply for its surreal sound and appearance, and 'Camera', a song by The Teardrop Explodes (*see below*).

Bananarama (from 1981): a blend of 'banana', a fruit with sexual associations, and the Roxy Music single 'Pyjamarama'.

Bay City Rollers (from 1967): from *Bay City*, Oregon, Texas (or Rochester, Michigan), and 'roller', for its association with surf and ROCK 'N' ROLL.

Beach Boys (from 1961): for the California group's surfing associations.

BEATLES, THE.

Bee Gees (from 1955): from the initials of the *B*rothers *G*ibb, its three members, or of its lead singer, *B*arry *G*ibb, or of the group's promoter, *B*ill *G*ates.

B-52s, The (from 1976): for the beehive hairstyle of two of its members, Kate Pierson and Cindy Wilson, the style in turn being named after the US Air Force's B-52 bomber.

Black Sabbath (from 1969): from one of the group's own songs, based on bass player Terry 'Geezer' Butler's interest in black magic.

BLONDIE.

Blue Öyster Cult (from 1969): for bluepoint oysters (from Blue Point, Long Island, New York), the subject of a song by the group's manager Sandy Pearlman, with an umlaut added to enhance the name's mystery.

Blur (from 1988): a name chose for its suggestion of the effect of alcohol, drugs or simply the passage of time, as well as vagueness of vision or memory.

Bonzo Dog (Doo Dah) Band, The (1965–71): *see* BONZO.

Boomtown Rats, The (1975–86): from the name of a gang in Woody Guthrie's autobiographical novel *Bound for Glory* (1943), read by the group's lead singer, Bob Geldof.

Boo Radleys, The (from 1988): from the town idiot, Boo Radley, in Harper Lee's novel *To Kill a Mockingbird* (1960).

Boyzone (from 1993): from the boys' magazine *The* BOY'S OWN PAPER with a presumed pun on 'boy zone'.

Bread (from 1968): for the money ('bread') that the group hoped to make.

Byrds, The (1964–73): for the group's 'lofty' ambition, coupled with the interest in aeronautics of its founder, Roger McGuinn.

Canned Heat (from 1966): for Tommy Johnson's song 'Canned Heat Blues', itself punning on canned' in the sense 'drunk'.

Chemical Brothers, The (from 1989): said to allude to the 'chemical bond' of the group's music, although its two members are not brothers.

Chicago (from 1966): for the group's city of origin.

Clannad (from 1970): from Irish *clan na Dobhair*, 'family of Dore', referring to Gweedore, Co. Donegal, the Irish group's place of origin.

Clash, The (1976–86): a general word to evoke the PUNK group's music and its members' aggressive view of life.

Cranberries, The (from 1990): from 'cranberry sauce' via the puerile pun 'the cranberry saw us'.

Cream (1966–8): for the group's exalted view of themselves as an elite band.

Creedence Clearwater Revival (1967–72): from a mutual friend, Creedence Nuball, coupled with 'Clearwater' in an advertisement about the use of pure drinking water in a brand of beer, and a 'revival' of the group's original musical direction.

Cult, The (1982–95): originally the Southern Death Cult, from the title of an anthropological study of Native Americans from Mississippi.

Culture Club (1981–6): for the group's love of night-clubbing and its mixed background or 'culture'.

Cure, The (from 1976): a shortening of Easy Cure, from a song by the group's original drummer Laurence Tolhurst, who (like others before him) thought love a cure for all ills.

Deep Purple (from 1968): a 'colour' name on the lines of Black Sabbath and Pink Floyd; possibly an unconscious echo of the lyric 'Deep Purple' (1939) by Mitchell Parish, added to a 1934 melody by Peter de Rose:

> When the deep purple falls over sleepy garden walls,
> And the stars begin to flicker in the sky,
> Thru' the mist of a memory you wander back to me,
> Breathing my name with a sigh.

Def Leppard (from 1977): an allusion to deafness as an occupational hazard of heavy metal fans combined with 'leopard' as a fashionable animal name, both words being phonetically respelled.

Depeche Mode (from 1980): apparently an adoption of *Dépêche Mode*, 'Dispatch Mode', the title of a French trade and general interest fashion magazine.

Dire Straits (from 1977): an allusion to the group's initial impecunious status.

Doors, The (1965–73): ultimately from William Blake's *The Marriage of Heaven and Hell* (1790): 'If the doors of perception were cleansed everything would appear to man as it is, infinite.' Aldous Huxley borrowed the words for the title of *The Doors of Perception* (1954), an essay on experiments with mescaline and LSD, and this was a more immediate source for the group name.

Duran Duran (from 1978): from the mad scientist Durand Durand played by Milo O'Shea in the cult film BARBARELLA (1967).

East 17 (from 1990): from the postal district, E17, of the group's London homes.

Echobelly (from 1993): according to the band's lead singer, Sonya Aurora Madan, a name was chosen that was 'quite female and organic and voluptuous', and suggested a hunger for something.

Electric Light Orchestra, The (from 1971): a reference to the group's electric instruments playing light music in combination with the stringed instruments normally associated with a classical orchestra.

Everything But the Girl (from 1984): said to derive from a notice in a second-hand furniture shop in Hull reading: 'For your bedroom needs we sell everything but the girl.'

Fairport Convention (from 1966): from a house named Fairport in Muswell Hill, North London, where the group originally rehearsed as a 'convention' of musicians.

Fine Young Cannibals, The (1985–92): from the title of the film *All the Fine Young Cannibals* (1960).

Fleetwood Mac (from 1967): from the names of two of the group's members, drummer Mick Fleetwood and bass player John McVie.

Foo Fighters, The (from 1994): an early term for UFOs, used by Allied pilots in the Second World War, and possibly deriving from the catchphrase of Smokey Stover, a 1930s comic-strip fireman: 'Where's there's foo there's fire.'

Frankie Goes to Hollywood (1982–7): from a *New Yorker* headline about Frank Sinatra's move from Las Vegas to Los Angeles: 'Frankie Goes to Hollywood'.

Fugee, The (from 1987): an abbreviation of 'refugees'.

Genesis (from 1967): an allusion to the first book of the Bible, to denote the group's debut.

Grateful Dead, The (1965–95): said by some to have been picked at random from a dictionary, and by others to derive from the old legend telling of those who return from the dead to help those still living who had helped them while they were alive.

Hawkwind (from 1969): not a mystic or esoteric reference but simply a nickname given singer Nik Turner for his aquiline features and troublesome flatulence.

Heaven 17 (1980): from a fictional pop group in Anthony Burgess's novel *A* CLOCKWORK ORANGE (1962): 'The Heaven Seventeen? Luke Sterne? Goggly Gogol?' (Pt 1, ch. 4).

Hootie and the Blowfish (from 1986): the nicknames of two of the band's friends, Ervin 'Hootie' Harris and Donald 'Blowfish' Feaster.

Hot Chocolate (1969–87): for the group's 'hot' music and its Jamaican-born lead singer, Errol Brown.

Human League (from 1977): the name of one of two rival empires in a SCIENCE FICTION computer game.

Hüsker Dü (1979–88): the name of a Swedish children's board game meaning 'Do you remember?'

INXS (1977–97): a representation of 'in excess'.

Iron Butterfly (from 1967): based on the name of the Aztec god Izpapaloti, literally 'stone butterfly'.

Iron Maiden (from 1976): from the instrument of torture, a coffin-shaped box lined with iron spikes.

Jam, The (1976–82): from the 'jam sessions' that the band's members held when at school.

Japan (1974–83): a name chosen simply for its orientally exotic associations.

Jefferson Airplane (from 1965): from the Jefferson Airplane Company. From 1970 to 1989 the group was known as Jefferson Starship, the latter word a reference to the SCIENCE FICTION cult of the day.

Jethro Tull (from 1967): from the English farmer Jethro Tull (1674–1741), inventor of the seed drill.

Kaiser Chiefs, The (from 2003): According to the band, from the South African football team Kaizer Chiefs, from which Lucas Radebe transferred to become captain of Leeds United, the band's home-town team.

Kinks, The (from 1963): said to allude to the 'kinky boots' worn by Honor Blackman in the television series *The* AVENGERS.

Kiss (from 1972): a basic amatory or sexual reference.

Kraftwerk (from 1970): the German band produced music that reflected their industrial environment. Hence the name, meaning 'power plant'.

Kula Shaker (from 1995): from a Krishna mystic named Kula Sekhara.

Led Zeppelin (1968–80): said to derive from a prediction by Keith Moon, drummer of the *Who*, that the group would GO DOWN LIKE A LEAD BALLOON; *see also* ZEPPELIN.

Level 42 (1980–94): from '42', the answer to the question 'What is the meaning of life, the universe and everything' posed in Douglas Adams's novel *The* HITCH-HIKER'S GUIDE TO THE GALAXY (1979).

Lindisfarne (from 1969): the group was founded in Newcastle and took its name from the island off the coast to the north, also known as Holy Island.

Lovin' Spoonful (1965–8): from the words 'I love my baby by the lovin' spoonful' in Mississippi John Hurt's song 'Coffee Blues'.

Lynyrd Skynyrd (from 1965): a corruption of Leonard Skinner, the name of the unpopular gym coach at the high school in Jacksonville, Florida, that most of the group's members originally attended.

Madness (from 1979): from Prince Buster's song of the same name (1964).

Mamas and the Papas, The (1965–8): a San Francisco colloquialism for men and women, with specific reference to the band's two couples.

Manic Street Preachers, The (from 1988): allegedly a term for a fanatical evangelist, a 'manic street preacher', perhaps with reference to the band's enthusiastic guitarist, James Dean Bradfield.

Marillion (from 1979): from the title of J.R.R.Tolkien's posthumous cult novel *The* SILMARILLION (1977).

Monkees, The (from 1966): a respelling of 'Monkeys', with particular allusion to the group's drummer Mickey Dolenz, who had earlier 'monkeyed about' in roles as a juvenile film actor.

Mötley Crüe (from 1981): a respelling of 'motley crew' as an allusion to the HEAVY METAL band's mixed background and musical style.

Motörhead (from 1975): from the US slang term for an amphetamine user or 'speed freak'.

Mott the Hoople (1969–76): from the title of an obscure novel by Willard Manus.

Nazareth (from 1968): from the song 'The Weight' by The Band, about the trials and tribulations of Joseph and Mary, whose home town according to the biblical account was Nazareth.

Nirvana (1987–94): from the transcendent state of being that is the final goal of Buddhism, with an implication of the word's literal meaning of 'extinction' as a form of total self-absorption.

Oasis (from 1991): allegedly from a club named the Swindon Oasis where the group's lead guitarist, Noel Gallagher, once performed.

Orchestral Manoeuvres in the Dark (from 1978): from an early act in which a tape recorder played sound effects in the form of tank noises and battlefield explosions.

Pearl Jam (from 1990): apparently from Pearl, the Native American great-grandmother of the lead singer, Eddie Vedder, and the supposedly hallucinogenic jam that she made.

Pet Shop Boys (from 1981): said to derive from a suggestion by the group's lead singer, Neil Tennant, that three young men working in an Ealing pet shop should start their own band.

Pink Floyd (from 1964): usually said to compliment two of the group's musical heroes, Pink Anderson (1900–74) and Floyd Council (1911–76), but perhaps in fact from two cats, Pink and Floyd.

Pogues, The (1982–96): originally Pogue Mahone, representing Irish *póg mo thón*, 'kiss my arse', an intentionally irreverent name chosen by the group's Irish lead singer, Shane MacGowan.

Police, The (1977–86): a reference to the fact that the group's American drummer, Stewart Copeland, was the son of a former senior CIA officer.

Prefab Sprout (from 1982): from a mishearing by the group's lead singer, Paddy MacAloon, of the words 'pepper sprout' in Nancy Sinatra and Lee Hazlewood's song 'Jackson', in which the two sing that their love for each other is stronger than the plant in question.

Pretenders, The (from 1978): from The Platters' hit song 'The Great Pretender' (1956), admired by the group's lead singer, Chrissie Hynde.

Pretty Things, The (from 1962): from Bo Diddley's hit 'Pretty Thing' (1963). The name was intended as an ironic reference to the group's unprepossessing appearance, with long, unkempt hair.

Procol Harum (from 1967): said to derive from the name of a friend's cat, although classicists posit an (ungrammatical) origin in a Latin phrase supposedly meaning 'far from these things'.

Psychedelic Furs, The (1977–92): from The Velvet Underground's song 'Venus in Furs', itself the English title of the pornographic novel *Venus im Pelz* (1870) by the Austrian writer Leopold von Sacher-Masoch (who gave his name to masochism).

Queen (from 1970): a name chosen by the group's flamboyant gay lead singer, Freddie Mercury, for its evocation of royal grandeur and as a tongue-in-cheek allusion to his own sexuality.

R.E.M. (from 1980): an allegedly random name but popularly interpreted as the standard abbreviation for 'rapid eye movement', a term for the movement of a person's eyes when asleep and dreaming.

REO Speedwagon (from 1968): from a make of American truck manufactured in the 1920s by Ransom E. Olds, father of the Oldsmobile, the letters being his initials.

ROLLING STONES, THE.

Rose Royce (from 1976): from ROLLS-ROYCE, with the name appropriately given by the group's MOTOWN producer, Norman Whitfield.

Roxy Music (1970–82): given by the group's lead singer, Bryan Ferry, as a blend of the ROXY cinema name and 'rock music'.

Run D.M.C. (from 1982): from the nicknames of two of the group's singers, 'Run' being Joseph Simmons and 'DMC' Darryl McDaniels.

Runrig (from 1973): a Scots dialect word for the Scottish band's name, 'runrig' being (historically) a ridge ('rig') of land running among others held by joint tenure but now a ridge between furrows.

Santana (from 1966): the name of the group's Mexican-born lead singer, Carlos Santana.

Scritti Politti (from 1977): from Italian *scritti politichi*, 'political writing', a phrase used in a work by the Italian communist and political theorist Antonio Gramsci (1891–1937).

Searchers, The (from 1963): from the title of the John Wayne Western *The Searchers* (1956).

Sex Pistols, The (1975–8): from Sex, the Chelsea clothes store run by the group's manager, Malcolm McLaren, and a perversion of 'pistil', the term for a flower's female reproductive organs.

Shakespear's Sister (from 1989): from The Smiths' song 'Shakespeare's Sister' (1985), itself named after Virginia Woolf's fictional character Judith Shakespeare in her feminist essay so titled (1929), in which she ponders the possible consequences of Shakespeare being a woman.

Shalamar (from 1978): from a travel brochure describing the Shalamar garden in Lahore, India.

Shangri-Las, The (1963–9): from the SHANGRI LA of James Hilton's novel *Lost Horizon* (1933).

Simple Minds (from 1978): a jocularly self-deprecatory name for the group, taken from David Bowie's song 'The Jean Genie' about an astronaut 'so simple-minded' that he cannot operate his module.

Simply Red (from 1984): for the band's red-haired lead singer, Mick Hucknall, and a pun on 'simply read'.

Skunk Anansie (from 1994): from the skunk and spider characters in Jamaican folk tales.

Slade (from 1966): originally Ambrose Slade, the latter word deriving from Slade Heath, north of Wolverhampton, West Midlands, the group's town of origin.

Smiths, The (1982–7): a name chosen for its commonness to counter the pretentious portentousness of names such as Orchestral Manoeuvres in the Dark. There were no actual Smiths in the group.

Soft Cell (1979–84): a blend of 'soft sell' and 'padded cell'.

Soft Machine (1966–76): from the title of William Burroughs's novel (1961), a sequel to *The* NAKED LUNCH (1959).

Spandau Ballet (from 1979): from a graffito seen on a wall in Berlin, the location of SPANDAU prison, the place of confinement of the Nazi leader Rudolf Hess until his death in 1987. SPICE GIRLS.

Status Quo (from 1962): from the standard Latin phrase meaning 'the existing state of affairs'.

Stone Roses, The (1984–96): from the Jam song 'English Rose' (1978) and The ROLLING STONES.

Suede (from 1990): a 'fabric' name in the mould of The Chiffons, Felt, etc., with perhaps a punning reference to the slightly 'swayed' appearance of the group's lead singer, Brett Anderson.

Supertramp (from 1969): ostensibly from the title of W.H. Davies's *The Autobiography of a Super-Tramp* (1910) but more directly a reference to the group's initial 'super-scruffy' appearance.

Sweet (1968–81): for the group's aim to attract young fans through its BUBBLEGUM MUSIC.

Take That (1991–6): a phrase implying a sexual invitation to the group's young female fans.

Talking Heads (1975–91): from the term for people conversing on television; *see* TALKING HEAD.

Tangerine Dream (from 1967): a surreal creation suggested by the titles of paintings by Salvador Dalí, one of the more extravagant being *Dream Caused by the Flight of a Bee around a Pomegranate One Second before Waking Up* (1944).

Teardrop Explodes, The (1978–83): from the caption to a cartoon in a D.C. Marvel comic: 'Filling the wintered glades of Central Park with an unearthly whine … painting the leaf-bare branches with golden fire … THE TEARDROP EXPLODES!! … for echoing seconds the sky is filled with silver webs of lightning – and, with the glow's fading, a new menace is revealed!' (*Prince Namor*, No 77, June 1971). The PSYCHEDELIC name was chosen by the group's lead singer, Julian Cope.

Tears for Fears (from 1981): a term from the jargon of PRIMAL SCREAM THERAPY for a method of releasing emotion ('tears') to relieve depression ('fears').

10cc (1972): a random name, as if 'ten cubic centimetres', given the group by Jonathan King, the entrepreneur who signed the group up.

The The (from 1979): a name chosen purely for its memorability, but also serving as an ironic allusion to the trend for names beginning with a definite article as if to imply uniqueness.

Thin Lizzy (1969–83): *see* TIN LIZZIE.

Thompson Twins, The (from 1977): from the detective twins, Thompson and Thomson, in Hergé's comic strips about the adventures of the cub reporter TINTIN (from 1930). No members of the group had the name.

TLC (from 1991): partly from the familiar abbreviation (*see* TLC) but more specifically from the initials of the nicknames of the group's three female members, Tionne 'T-Boz' Watkins, Lisa 'Left-Eye' Lopes and Rozonda 'Chilli' Thomas.

T Rex (1969–77): a shortening of the group's original name, Tyrannosaurus Rex, from the scientific name of the species of dinosaur.

Troggs, The (from 1964): from 'trog', a nickname for a contemptible person, as an abbreviation of 'troglodyte', properly a primitive cave-dweller.

UB40 (from 1978): from the designation of the former British *u*nemployment *b*enefit form, before it was replaced by the euphemised 'jobseeker's allowance'.

Ultravox (from 1976): from Latin *ultra*, 'beyond', and *vox*, 'voice', the intended meaning being 'the ultimate voice' or more precisely 'the voice from beyond'.

U2 (from 1978): allegedly a pun on 'you too' or 'you two', implying that all fans could share the Irish band's music, whether individually or as couples.

Velvet Underground, The (1965–73): from Michael Leigh's book about sadomasochism so titled. The name was chosen because it seemed to imply an involvement with the underground film scene.

Wet Wet Wet (from 1982): from the words 'his face is wet, wet with tears' in the *Scritti Politti* song 'Gettin', Havin' and Holdin'' (1982).

Wham! (1981–6): from the line WHAM, BAM, THANK YOU MA'AM in a song by the group's lead singer, George Michael.

Who, The (from 1964): a name chosen for its potential to bemuse and amuse, especially in a verbal exchange such as: 'Have you heard The Who?' 'The who?' 'The Who.'

XTC (from 1975): a representation of 'ecstasy', meaning happiness rather than the drug ECSTASY.

Yardbirds, The (from 1963): a tribute to the American saxophonist Charlie 'Bird' Parker (1920–55), himself so nicknamed for his fondness for chicken (a 'yardbird').

Yes (from 1968): a word chosen for its positive quality and its brevity on posters.

**Rockhampton Rocket.** The nickname of the great Australian tennis player Rod Laver (b.1938), who was born in

Rockhampton, Queensland. The nickname reflects his speed around the tennis court. Laver won the GRAND SLAM of tennis tournaments twice in his career, in 1962 and 1969.

**Rocking-horse manure.** In colloquial Australian English, something so scarce as to be virtually unobtainable. First recorded in 1944, the phrase is usually found in the simile 'as rare as rocking-horse manure'.

**Rock 'n' roll.** Rock and roll, or just rock, was *the* pop music of the latter half of the 1950s, characterized by its swing or rhythm and the style of dancing that went with it. Its fans were called rockers and they belonged to the days of the TEDDY BOYS, before the advent of the mods (*see* MODS AND ROCKERS). Famous practitioners included Elvis Presley (1935–77) and Bill Haley (1925–81) and the Comets, and the latter's hit 'ROCK AROUND THE CLOCK' (1954) was the first to popularize the style. The term itself probably alludes to the vigorous movements of the dancers, swaying the body backwards and forwards ('rocking') and from side to side ('rolling'). The music itself derives from African American R & B. *See also* HIT PARADE; ROCK GROUP NAMES.

**Rock opera.** A somewhat pretentious term for a drama set to rock music. The first successful examples of the genre were *Hair* (1969) and *Jesus Christ Superstar* (1970). Later compositions have mostly been simply known as musicals rather than 'operas'.

**Rock the boat.** To disturb a stable situation, especially when it is potentially to one's advantage. A small craft such as a canoe can be capsized by moving carelessly about. The phrase is commonly found in the negative advice, 'Don't rock the boat.' The song 'Sit Down, You're Rocking the Boat' sung by Stubby Kaye in Frank Loesser's musical *Guys and Dolls* (1950) further popularized the phrase, which dates from the early years of the 20th century. *See also* MAKE WAVES.

**Rocky.** The professional boxer created by Sylvester Stallone as the hero of the film named for him (1976) and of its three sequels: *Rocky II* (1976), *Rocky III* (1982) and *Rocky IV* (1985). His full name is Rocky Balboa, and although he is not very intelligent his physical prowess and grim determination to win brought him many fans. The first of the series was directed by John G. Avildsen and the remainder by Stallone himself, who also played him. *See also* Rocky GRAZIANO.

Rocky was also a nickname of the moderate Republican politician Nelson Rockefeller (1908–79), governor of New York (1959–73) and vice-president of the United States under Gerald Ford (1974–7). He unsuccessfully sought his party's nomination as presidential candidate in 1960, 1964 and 1968.

**Rocky Graziano.** *See* Rocky GRAZIANO; ROCKY.

**Rocky Horror Picture Show, The.** A film (1975) based on the successful stage rock musical *The Rocky Horror Show* (1973), written by Richard O'Brien. The title reflects the show's anarchic mixture of ROCK 'N' ROLL music and horror film clichés, all delivered in a high CAMP style. The show quickly attracted a cult following and both live performances and showings of the film (often at midnight) were commonly attended by audiences wearing the outlandish costumes of such favourite characters as Dr Frank N. Furter and Riff Raff the hunchbacked butler.

**Rocky Marciano.** *See* Rocky MARCIANO.

**Rodney.** A foolish or stupid person. The male first name was adopted to mean this by schoolchildren in the 1980s from the character Rodney Trotter, played by Nicholas Lyndhurst, in the television comedy ONLY FOOLS AND HORSES.

***Roes among the Lilies.*** A novella (1935) by the US writer Braun D. Heffer (1884–1939), a passionate and doomed love story in which, during a sticky *fin-de-siècle* summer in Mississippi, Arabella Wickwire, the descendant of an antebellum plantation owner, has a brief but steamy fling with Mencken Plutarch, a handsome and well-read octoroon, in the wrecked garden of her family's plundered mansion.

> Thy two breasts are like two young roes that are twins, which feed among lilies.
>
> Song of Solomon 4:5

**Rogallo.** A mainly American alternative term for a hang-glider, a type of one-man aircraft that evolved from the kite-like device used to slow down the re-entry of a space probe, the invention in *c.*1962 of Francis M. Rogallo, an engineer working for NASA.

**Roger.** In radio communications, a term meaning 'message received and understood'. It represents a former telephonic name for the letter R, the initial of 'received'. The signalling alphabet current in the period 1921–41, based on that used in the First World War, was:

A = Ack, B = Beer, C = Charlie, D = Don, E = Edward, F = Freddie, G = George, H = Harry, I = Ink, J = Johnnie, K = King, L = London, M = Monkey, N = Nuts, O = Orange, P = Pip, Q = Queen, R = Roger, S = Sugar, T = Toc, U = Uncle, V = Vic, W = William, X = X-ray, Y = Yellow, Z = Zebra

In 1942 the following was introduced:

A = Able, B = Baker, C = Charlie, D = Dog, E = Easy, F = Fox, G = George, H = How, I = Item, J = Jig, K = King, L = Love, M = Mike, N = Nan, O = Oboe, P = Peter, Q = Queen, R = Roger, S = Sugar, T = Tare, U = Uncle, V = Victor, W = William, X = X-ray, Y = Yoke, Z = Zebra

In 1956 the NATO alphabet was generally adopted (although Roger was kept for 'received'):

A = Alpha, B = Bravo, C = Charlie, D = Delta, E = Echo, F = Foxtrot, G = Golf, H = Hotel, I = India, J = Juliet, K = Kilo, L = Lima, M = Mike, N = November, O = Oscar, P = Papa, Q = Quebec, R = Romeo, S = Sierra, T = Tango, U = Uniform, V = Victor, W = Whiskey, X = X-ray, Y = Yankee, Z = Zulu

**Rogers, Buck.** *See* BUCK ROGERS.

**Rogue Male.** A thriller (1939) by Geoffrey Household (1900–88). Published in the very month in which the Second World War was declared, this topical story begins with an unsuccessful attempt by the narrator to assassinate an unnamed dictator, who has affinities with Adolf Hitler. The rest of the story concerns his attempts to avoid being killed by a secret agent of the dictator or being arrested by the British police after he has had to kill an accomplice of the agent at Aldwych Underground station in London. The title is a reference to beasts who, through pain or having lost their mate, isolate themselves from their fellows and act with increased cunning and ferocity, as is the case with the narrator.

**Rogue state.** A term used after the end of the COLD WAR to denote a state that does not play by the normal 'rules' of international conduct, e.g. by ignoring UN Security Council resolutions, disregarding international agreements, invading other countries, acquiring WEAPONS OF MASS DESTRUCTION or supporting terrorism abroad. The application of the term is obviously subjective: the US government has used the term in relation to such countries as Iran, North Korea and Iraq (*see* AXIS OF EVIL), while critics of US foreign policy, such as Noam Chomsky (*Rogues States: The Rule of Force in World Affairs*, 2000), have turned the phrase on the United States itself. *See also* WAR ON TERROR.

**Roland Rat.** A rodent puppet 'superstar' on British breakfast television in the 1980s. He was credited with saving the commercial breakfast television company TV-am by boosting its falling ratings and was promoted in this role by Greg Dyke, subsequently director general (2000–4) of the BBC.

**Role model.** A person regarded by others as an example to be followed, as a teacher by a pupil or an officer by his subordinates. The term emerged from sociological jargon in the 1950s.

**Role-playing game.** A form of game in which players act out the part of imaginary characters in an imaginary setting. The exercise as a technique in psychiatry dates back to the 1940s, but in its modern form it evolved in the 1970s when a number of new games, notably 'Dungeons and Dragons', were devised to involve the participants as characters in a particular setting. Computer games in similar style came on the market in the 1980s and are also known as role-playing games.

**Rolfing.** A massage technique aimed at the vertical realignment of the body and deep enough to release muscular tension at skeletal level. It was developed by the Swiss-born US biochemist Dr Ida Rolf (1896–1979) and adopted from the 1950s. A typical Rolfer devotes ten one-hour sessions to a client to achieve this alignment, and various emotional and psychological insights may be achieved during the course. The release of emotional pain may also be involved.

**Rollerblading.** A roller-skating fad of the late 1980s and early 1990s in which the old 'quad' wheel design was replaced by 'in-line' wheels to give the acceleration and manoeuvrability of ice skates. In-line skates first appeared on the highways of the United States in 1980.

**Roller coaster.** The THEME PARK attraction originated in the late 19th century but reached its apogee in the late 20th, with at least a dozen of the devices vying to provide the greatest thrills. The most intense experience in Britain is by general agreement offered by Nemesis at Alton Towers, while its neighbour there, Oblivion, is notorious for its awesome drop. In BLACKPOOL the Pepsi Max Big One is one of the highest, while the Grand National is an exhilarating wooden racing coaster built in 1935. The Traumatizer at Southport and the Millennium Roller Coaster near Skegness also pull the public, but the wooden Megafobia at Narberth, Pembrokeshire, has been generally judged to give the best 'shake, rattle and roll' ride in the country.

'Rollercoaster ride' became a fashionable cliché of the late 20th and early 21st centuries, referring to sudden violent and often repeated changes of circumstance. A frequent variant is 'emotional rollercoaster'.

> I would love to think that England can ... be up in the series at the end of this next Test, in which case we can all prepare for a real roller coaster ride at the Oval.
>
> DAVID GOWER: in *Sunday Times* (21 August 2005)

**Rolling Stones, The.** The rock group so named was formed in 1962 with Mick Jagger (b.1943) as lead singer and Keith Richards (b.1943) as guitarist. The other original members were Brian Jones (guitarist, 1942–69), Charlie Watts drummer, b.1941) and Bill Wyman (bassist, b.1941). Their R & B music was derivative but distinctive, and their raunchy style won them many fans. In the 1960s they vied with The BEATLES for pre-eminence in the rock music aristocracy, until the latter disbanded leaving them free to claim the crown. Jones, who famously drowned in his swimming pool, was replaced by Mick Taylor (from 1969 to 1974) and then by Ron Wood. In 2006 the 60-somethings were still touring.

The group (abbreviated often to simply 'The Stones') took their name from Muddy Waters's song 'Rollin' Stone' (1950), and their format was initially influenced by the American blues musician's electrically amplified band. *See also* ALTAMONT; BROWN SUGAR; 'JUMPIN' JACK FLASH'; LET IT BLEED; '(I CAN'T GET NO) SATISFACTION'; STICKY FINGERS; 'SYMPATHY FOR THE DEVIL'.

**Roll one's own.** To make one's own cigarettes (by rolling loose tobacco in cigarette papers). Hence the subsequent figurative sense, 'to do something without assistance'.

**Roll something out.** In the language of politicians, to present the first stage of a plan or policy, the rest of which is to be introduced subsequently, often at some unspecified date, hence a 'rollout'. The reference is to the first public showing of the prototype of a new aircraft, which is rolled out of its hangar but has yet to fly or even make its first test flight. The phrase was current in the late 1990s.

**Rolls-Royce.** The automobile name first came before the public in 1906 when the motoring and aviation pioneer Charles S. Rolls (1877–1910) and the electrical engineer Henry Royce (1863–1933) formed a company to produce a high-quality car. Models such as the Silver Ghost and Silver Shadow became equal names of excellence, and the car's bonnet figure, Charles Sykes's 'Spirit of Ecstasy', was part of the prestigious image. Rolls, the first Englishman to fly across the Channel, lost his life in an air crash and when Royce died in 1933 the colour of the monogram RR on the car's bonnet was changed from red to black. The name came to be used allusively to describe a person or thing that is the best of its kind.

> It [*Animal Fair*] is the Rolls-Royce of dog magazines which will focus on the pashmina-wrapped lifestyles of celebrities and their beloved pets.
> *The Times* (9 October 1999)

**Roll up one's sleeves.** To get down to work; to tackle the matter in hand. One rolls up one's sleeves both to free one's hands and arms for action and to keep the sleeves themselves clean.

> You'll see me on TV, getting on and off planes, meeting Presidents and Prime Ministers, Kings and Queens. It's all part of the job. But the part that matters most to me is getting my sleeves rolled up and pushing through the changes to our country that will give to others, by right, what I achieved by good fortune.
> TONY BLAIR: speech at Labour Party conference (28 September 1999)

**Roll with the punches.** To adapt to adversity; to deal with events and problems as they come. The image is from boxing, in which a contestant will bend (roll) his body to one side when deflecting the full force of his opponent's blow. The expression dates from the 1950s.

**Rom-com.** 'Romantic comedy', the specifically cinematic genre thereof. Usually, as in traditional theatrical comedies of love, boy meets girl, difficulties ensue and are resolved, and troth is plighted, as in the recent successful British rom-coms *Four Weddings and a Funeral* (1994) and *Notting Hill* (1999). There are occasional exceptions to the standard plot, with characters ultimately finding themselves or friendship rather than the love they thought they had wanted, as in the case of the Julia Roberts vehicle *My Best Friend's Wedding* (1997) and the romantic musical chairs of another British film, *This Year's Love* (1999). *See also* CHICK FLICK.

> The fringe (his), the sweet smile (hers), the laughter (ours), the tears (everybody's): it's all here in the rom-com that outgrossed *Four Weddings And a Funeral*.
> heat: review of *Notting Hill* (3–9 February 2000)

**Romper room.** A place for lively meetings or gatherings. The term arose as US campus slang in the 1980s, the allusion being to young children in rompers playing and brawling.

> Dress is polos, chinos and loafers, and office colours are bright and stimulating. There's a romper room for meetings and break-out space for chats.
> *The Times* (27 September 1999)

**Ronde, La.** A wry comedy (1903) by the Austrian playwright Arthur Schnitzler (1862–1931) in which the action traces a series of ten sexual liaisons, each containing a character from the previous encounter. It begins with a prostitute having sex with a soldier and ends with a count picking up the same prostitute, thus traversing the social scale and creating the circle reflected in the title. The play has been filmed twice, once in 1950 and once, with a screenplay by Jean Anouilh, in 1964. David Hare's play *The Blue Room* (1998) is an updated version. Its production in London's West End starred Nicole Kidman, whose performance was described as 'theatrical VIAGRA'.

**R 101.** The world's biggest airship was commissioned by the British government in 1924 and made its maiden flight in 1929, taking off from Cardington, Bedfordshire, with 52 people on board, and circling over London and the Southeast of England. On 1 October 1930, following a successful maiden transatlantic flight earlier that year, it set off for India, the official party now including Lord Thomson, secretary of state for air. At 2 a.m. the following morning it touched the ground on its approach to Beauvais, France, caught fire and exploded. A total of 44 people died, including the minister. The cause of the tragedy was heavy rain, which forced the dirigible to lose height. The disaster put an end to the use of airships in Britain.

**Ronnie Scott's.** London's best-known jazz venue. Club Eleven, the first club set up in 1958 by the saxophonist Ronnie Scott (original name Ronald Schatt; 1927–97), closed after a few months following a drugs raid. In 1959 Scott opened a second club in Gerrard Street, Soho, where he and his fellow jazz musicians could play. It attracted major figures from the world of jazz, and its heyday was in the latter half of the 1960s, following its move to larger premises in Frith Street. It remains a centre of British jazz today.

**Room 40.** A euphemistic nickname for the code-breaking work undertaken by the Royal Navy in the First World War, originating as the number of the room in the Old Admiralty Building, Whitehall, that was assigned to cryptanalysts for the purpose. After the war Room 40 evolved into the Government Code and Cypher School (GC&CS), which was itself the forerunner of GCHQ.

**Room 101.** In George Orwell's *Nineteen Eighty-Four* (1949), the room in which people are tortured by being confronted with their ultimate terror (for the hero, Winston Smith, it was rats). More lightheartedly, the term has been used as the title of a series (originally on BBC Radio 5 and later, from 1994, on BBC 2) in which celebrity guests discuss their pet hates and make a case for having them consigned to destruction in 'Room 101'. The original Room 101 was supposedly a conference room in Broadcasting House in which Orwell had to sit through many boring meetings when he was employed by the BBC during the Second World War.

**Room at the Top.** The first novel (1957) by John Braine (1922–86) is an iconoclastic story of an opportunist, amoral, working-class young man, Joe Lampton, who achieves social acceptance and material prosperity. Braine returned to this formula and to his original characters in *Life at the Top* (1962). The words 'There is always room at the top' are attributed to the US politician Daniel Webster (1782–1852), said when he was advised against joining the overcrowded legal profession. Simone Signoret won an Oscar for her part in the film (1958), when she played the married woman with whom Lampton has a brief affair. *See also* FIRST LINES OF NOVELS.

**'Room of One's Own, A'.** A long essay by Virginia Woolf (1882–1941), published in 1929. The essay grew out of two lectures that Woolf had delivered to female students at Newnham College, Cambridge, the previous year, in which she addressed the difficulties that women writers would continue to face until they had the freedom and security of 'a room of one's own' and 'five hundred a year'. For Woolf herself the 'room of one's own' was the attic room of J.M. Keynes's house at 46 Gordon Square in London.

> A room of one's own can be a womb, but it can also be an ivory tower, a prison and a grave. Its dangers and promise are inherent in all Virginia Woolf's work.
> STEPHEN COOTE: *The Penguin Short History of English Literature* (1993)

**Room with a View, A.** A novel (1908) by E.M. Forster (1879–1970). It is a domestic comedy, set in Florence and England, and explores the differences between Italian and English temperaments. It opens with a contretemps in a *pension* largely occupied by English visitors to Italy about the rooms with a view that had been promised, instead of which they have 'north rooms, looking into a courtyard, and a long way apart'. The model for Mrs Honeychurch, the mother of Lucy, who is the book's female protagonist, was Forster's maternal grandmother, Louisa Whichelo, who died in 1912. The novel was the subject of a MERCHANT IVORY FILM in 1985.

**Roosevelt Corollary.** *See* SPEAK SOFTLY AND CARRY A BIG STICK.

**Roots.** A sociological study (1976), with fictional interpolations, by US author Alex Haley (1921–92). It purports to be a chronicle of his family through seven generations, beginning with the African, Kunte Kinte, who was brought as a slave from Gambia to Annapolis in 1767. The bestseller won a PULITZER PRIZES and had an even greater impact when it was made into a gripping television mini-series (1977).

**Rope-a-dope.** In boxing the tactic of feigning to be trapped against the ropes, so goading an opponent (the 'dope') into throwing tiring, ineffectual punches. The phrase was coined in the 1970s by the US heavyweight Muhammad Ali with reference to his use of the dodge in a match with his great rival, George Foreman. *See also* FLOAT LIKE A BUTTERFLY, STING LIKE A BEE.

**Roping and doping.** Taking drugs, 'rope' being a slang term for marijuana, from the use of hemp in rope-making, and also a word for a vein, so called from its appearance when 'shooting up'.

**Rorschach test.** A type of psychological personality test in which the subject looks at a series of ink-blots and describes what they suggest or resemble. The test was devised by the Swiss psychologist Hermann Rorschach, who introduced it in 1921. The ink-blots in the test are usually symmetrical, which to some extent restricts the degree of subjectivity of their interpretation.

**Roseanne.** The central character of the top-rank US television SITCOM running from 1988 (in Britain from 1989) to 1997. Roseanne Conner is the smart, wisecracking and overweight wife of the equally well-rounded Dan, her high-school sweetheart, and mother of David Jacob ('DJ'), Darlene and Becky. The family's involvements and relationships were remarkable for their social realism, with Roseanne played by the talented stand-up comic Roseanne Barr as a variation of a character she developed for the stage.

**Rose Bowl.** The annual American college football contest, held on New Year's Day in Pasadena, California. The contest and the name derive from the Battle of the Flowers, first held on New Year's Day in 1890, in which local residents decorated their buggies and carriages with flowers and drove round a planned route. The parade was followed by amateur athletic events. In 1902 the first Tournament of Roses American football game was held and in 1922 a stadium was opened for this annual contest. The morning parade still takes place with many decorated floats. *See also* SUPER BOWL.

The Rose Bowl is also the name of the stadium in Southampton that is the headquarters of Hampshire County Cricket Club. Opened in 2001, it has been used for one-day internationals.

**Rosemary's Baby.** A horror film (1968) based on a novel by Ira Levin about a young New York couple whose happiness about the forthcoming birth of their first child is undermined by the wife's growing conviction that she is carrying the Devil's child. Directed by Roman Polanski and starring Mia Farrow as the expectant mother, the movie did much to revitalize the HORROR MOVIE genre in the modern cinema.

**Rosenberg case.** The case of Julius (1918–53) and Ethel (1915–53) Rosenberg, the first US civilians to be executed for espionage. Julius Rosenberg, originally named Greenglass, became an engineer with the US Army Signal Corps in 1940 and from this point of vantage he, together with his wife, aimed to turn over to the Soviet Union military secrets that came into their possession. Ethel's brother, assigned to the atomic bomb project at Los Alamos, New Mexico, gave the couple data on nuclear weapons. This information was passed on to Harry Gold, a courier for the US espionage ring, and by him to the Soviet vice-consul in New York. The Rosenbergs were brought to trial in New York on 6 March 1951, found guilty under the Espionage Act of 1917 and, despite several appeals and a worldwide campaign for mercy, executed at Sing Sing on 19 June. The case fuelled McCarthyite (*see* MCCARTHYISM) paranoia in the United States during a tense period of the COLD WAR. It formed the subject-matter of a novel by E.L. Doctorow, *The Book of Daniel* (1971), in which the Rosenbergs' story is told by their fictional son.

**Rosencrantz and Guildenstern are Dead.** A play (1966) by Tom Stoppard (b.1937) focusing on the fate of two minor characters from William Shakespeare's *Hamlet* (1601). Rosencrantz and Guildenstern are the two 'attendant lords' who accompany Hamlet to England, while secretly carrying letters asking the English king to execute their master, but they end up being executed themselves after Hamlet inserts their names in the fatal document. The names Rosencrantz and Guildenstern were fairly common in Denmark in Shakespeare's time, and the full title is a straight quotation from the last scene of the original play, in which news of their demise is perfunctorily reported by the First Ambassador in the aftermath of Hamlet's own death and that of the king, Claudius:

> The sight is dismal;
> And our affairs from England come too late:
> The ears are senseless that should give us hearing,
> To tell him his commandment is fulfill'd,
> That Rosencrantz and Guildenstern are dead.

**Rosenkavalier, Der.** The lushly romantic and highly popular opera by Richard Strauss (1864–1949), which has a libretto by Hugo von Hofmannsthal. It was first performed in 1911. The title is German for 'the knight of the rose'. Old Baron Ochs, looking for a messenger to take a silver rose as a betrothal token to the young Sophie, visits his cousin the Marschallin. The Marschallin's husband is away and she is entertaining her young lover, Oktavian. Aware that she is growing too old for him, the Marschallin gives Oktavian the rose to take to the young Sophie. The two fall in love and, following various complications, the Marshallin persuades Sophie's father to bless the pair.

**Rose Revolution, The.** *See* REVOLUTION NAMES.

**Rose Tattoo, The.** A play (1951) by Tennessee Williams (1911–83) about a Sicilian widow's quest for love. The title of the play refers to the rose tattoo that is described as adorning the chest of the widow's dead husband, but it also relates to the name of the widow, Serafina Delle Rose, and that of her spouse, Rosario. The prevalence of rose imagery in the play reflected the author's preoccupation with his sister Rose, who was troubled by mental illness throughout her life. Other 'rose' titles that he considered included *Novena to a Rose, A Candle to a Rose, A Rose for Our Lady, A Rose from the Hand of Our Lady* and *Perpetual Novena to a Rose*. However, the play began its life under the alternative titles *The Eclipse of May 29, 1919* and *Stornella*.

**Rosie the Riveter.** While GI JOE was on the battlefront in the Second World War his other half was busy on the home front in the weapons industry. The American women engaged in such work were embodied by the fictional Rosie the Riveter, a young woman wearing slacks and armed with a rivet gun. She was commemorated in song and depicted by Norman Rockwell on the cover of the *Saturday Evening Post*, where she rolled up her sleeves beneath the words 'We Can Do It!' (which would have pleased BOB THE BUILDER).

***Ross Poldark.*** A novel (1945; US title as *The Renegade*, 1951) by Winston Graham (b.1912). Subtitled 'A Novel of Cornwall 1783–1787', it is the first of a sequence of ten historical adventure novels featuring members of the Poldark family, of which the last is *The Loving Cup*, subtitled 'A Novel of Cornwall 1813–1815' (1984). A television series, *Poldark* (1976–7), was based on the novels as a popular Sunday evening BODICE-RIPPER, with Robin Ellis as Ross Poldark and Angharad Rees as the urchin servant girl, Demelza, for whom he has a passion.

**Rotary Club.** A movement among businessmen, which takes for its motto 'Service above Self'. The idea originated with Paul Harris, a Chicago lawyer, in 1905. In 1911 it took root in Britain and there are now clubs in most towns, membership being limited to one member each of any trade, calling or profession. Lectures are delivered at weekly meetings by guest speakers and the clubs engage in charity fundraising. The name derives from the early practice of holding meetings in rotation at the business premises of its members. The Rotary Clubs are now members of one association called Rotary International. *See also* SOROPTIMISTS.

**Rottweiler, The.** Princess Diana's name for Camilla Parker Bowles (1947), née Shand, now Mountbatten-Windsor, long the mistress and since 2005 the wife of Prince Charles. She first introduced herself to Charles at a polo match in 1970, allegedly with the words 'My great-grandmother was the mistress of your great-grandfather. How about it?' (The references were to Alice Keppel and Edward VII.) The prince was apparently game, but unfortunately his great-uncle, Lord Mountbatten, insisted that 'bedded can't be wedded' was a constitutional principle, and the course of true love was further thwarted when she married Andrew Parker Bowles in 1973. Nevertheless, the relationship continued even after Charles himself married, Princess Diana wistfully telling an interviewer and the nation after her divorce: 'There were three of us in the marriage – it was rather crowded.' (Camilla also had greater academic success than Diana, managing to pass one O-level.) With Diana divorced, and dead, Charles felt able to wed his sweetheart

at last, and when the marriage was announced in February 2005 the *Daily Star* echoed the sentiments of many with the headline 'Boring Old Gits to Wed'. Less charitably, one US television network styled Camilla 'The People's Home-wrecker' (referring to Diana being dubbed 'The PEOPLE'S PRINCESS'). It was announced that the Prince of Wales's wife would not be known as the Princess of Wales, for fear of upsetting the millions of devotees of the previous bearer of the name. Instead she is known as the Duchess of Cornwall (or, if in Scotland, the Duchess of Rothesay). When Charles becomes king, she is to be PRINCESS CONSORT. To her husband, she is 'Gladys', while to her he is 'Fred'. *See also* CAMILLAGATE; GOD'S ROTTWEILER.

**Rough** or **wrong end of the pineapple, The.** In Australian slang, unfair treatment; a raw deal; the 'rough end of the stick'. The expression dates from the 1960s.

**Rough Guides.** A series of unglossy but text-heavy travel guides to all parts of the world. The first guide was published in 1982, when Mark Ellingham, a graduate just out of university, was travelling in Greece. Although he had brought with him many of the popular guides of the day, he found that they were all deficient in some way. Their priority was the visitor's standard Mecca of ruins and museums, and they said little about the country's contemporary world, its politics, culture and people. He therefore set about writing his own book, aiming to give the sort of practical information that the traveller really wanted. By the end of the 1990s there were 100 such titles, aimed mainly at the more youthful end of the travelling spectrum. In 2002 the company was acquired by PENGUIN BOOKS, which had already been distributing the titles. *See also* LONELY PLANET.

**Rough trade.** Male homosexuality or prostitution, especially when involving brutality or sadism. The expression dates from the 1930s. Hence the related expression 'a bit of rough', originally applied to a female sexual partner but subsequently to a male whose attraction lies in his lack of sophistication.

**Roundhouse, The.** The London theatre so named evolved from Arnold Wesker's CENTRE 42, set up in 1961. The building was originally a 'roundhouse', a locomotive shed with tracks radiating from a central turntable, which for a hundred years had languished as a warehouse. Hence the name, which was further appropriate for the THEATRE-IN-THE-ROUND productions subsequently staged here, such as Peter Brook's experimental version of Shakespeare's *The Tempest* in 1968. The building subsequently sank again into desuetude, but at the beginning of the 21st century it was back in business, playing host to, for example, the Royal Shakespeare Company.

**Round the bend** or **twist.** Crazy; eccentric. The implication is that one is not 'straight'.

**Route One.** In football a long pass upfield as an attacking tactic, usually by way of exploiting the heading skills of tall attackers. The name comes from a television football quiz show of the 1960s, *Quiz Ball*, in which questions, graded in difficulty, led to scoring a goal, Route One being the direct path.

**Route 66.** The major highway that runs for some 3540km (2200 miles) across America from Chicago to Los Angeles, an important westward migration route during the Depression, but also a symbol of romance and adventure. It is celebrated in Bobby Troup's song '(Get Your Kicks On) Route 66' (1946), performed by, among others, Nat King Cole, The Rolling Stones and Van Morrison. The name 'Route 66' has become metaphorical for any road with similar associations.

> Winding through a grim, polluted landscape of new wrecks, new graffiti, new drug dealers and new prostitutes, Europastrasse-55 is the Route 66 of the lands that communism betrayed.
>
> *Independent on Sunday* (21 June 1992)

**Rowan and Martin's Laugh-In.** A US television comedy series running from 1968 to 1973 (1971 in the UK) and hosted by the gifted comedians Dan Rowan and Dick Martin. It launched the careers of Hollywood actress Goldie Hawn and English-born comedienne Judy Carne (b.1939). The programme presented a kaleidoscope of sketches and skits, with many recurring characters, and popularized a number of catchphrases, such as SOCK IT TO SOMEONE (Carne's catchphrase), 'You bet your bippy' and 'Look that up in your Funk and Wagnalls'. The second of these is a euphemistic form of 'You bet your ass', the final word of which was 'bipped' or 'bleeped' on television. Funk and Wagnalls, despite their suggestive name, are the publishers of *A New Standard Dictionary of the English Language*, sales of which are said to have soared as a result of this unusual PRODUCT PLACEMENT.

**Rowntree Mackintosh.** The confectionery company of this name was formed in 1969 following a merger of Rowntree & Co. Ltd, founded in 1869 by Henry Isaac Rowntree, a York tea dealer and chocolate manufacturer, and John Mackintosh & Sons Ltd, founded in 1890 by John Mackintosh, a Halifax confectioner. Rowntree introduced a number of popular brands of confectionery to the public, all of them still selling today. The following is a list of the best known, with year of introduction (*see also* QUALITY STREET):

Rowntree's Fruit Gums (1893)

Black Magic (1933)

Kit Kat (originally Chocolate Crisp) (1935)

Aero (1935)

Dairy Box (1936)

Smarties (1937)

Polo (1948)

After Eight (1962)

The company was acquired by Nestlé in 1988.

**Roxy.** A chain of cinemas. They were so called because they took their name from the US radio host and movie theatre impresario Samuel L. Rothafel (1881–1936), known as 'Roxy'. (His original surname was Rothapfel, but the family dropped the 'p' at the end of the First World War when Germanic names were in disfavour.) The name was originally that of the sumptuous Roxy Theater, New York, constructed by Rothafel in 1927 as a 'cathedral of the motion picture'. *See also* ODEON; The ROCKETTES.

**Roy.** In Australia, the archetype of a chic, sophisticated, 'trendy' man. The term (from the male forename, which was evidently 'smart' in Australia when it was first thus used, around 1960) is not complimentary. *See also* ALF.

**Royal Borough.** A name sometimes applied to the London borough of Kensington and Chelsea. Royal status was granted to Kensington in 1901 by Edward VII in honour of Queen Victoria, who died that year and who had been born at Kensington Palace, and when the boroughs of Kensington and Chelsea merged in 1965 the honorific title passed to them jointly. Other English boroughs currently so designated, but of much more ancient pedigree, are Kingston upon Thames and Windsor (since 1974, Windsor and Maidenhead).

**Royal Hunt of the Sun, The.** A play (1964) by Peter Shaffer (b.1926) about the conquest of the Inca nation by the Spanish conquistadors. The Spaniards, led by Pizarro, come on a hunt for gold, but during the course of the play it becomes clear that Pizarro is obsessed by the hunt for a god-figure, as personified by the sun-god Ahahuallpa (hence the title of the play).

> *Pizarro*: I've gone god-hunting and caught one.
>
> PETER SHAFFER: *The Royal Hunt of the Sun*

**Royal Mile.** A name for the road in Edinburgh that runs from Edinburgh Castle down to the royal palace of Holyrood House. It is first recorded in W.M. Gilbert's *Edinburgh in the Nineteenth Century* (1901), in which it appears in inverted commas, and it was further popularized as the title of a 1920 guidebook by Robert T. Skinner. The name is not only historically meaningless but also falsely implies that the road was created as a royal route between the castle and the palace. It is in fact a modern translation of medieval Latin *via regia*, 'king's street', a term for any public highway and in this case for the Canongate and the High Street that now form part of the route.

**Royal Ulster Constabulary.** The former name for the police force of Northern Ireland, created in 1922 and patterned on the former Royal Irish Constabulary. The initial establishment was 3000 men. Although it was intended that one third of the total be allocated to Roman Catholics, the quota was never filled. The RUC lost just under 200 men and over 100 reserves killed during the TROUBLES, and circumstances brought radical changes to its structure, one consequence being an increase in members to almost 8500 by 1991. In 2001, following the GOOD FRIDAY AGREEMENT, it was replaced by the Police Service of Northern Ireland, with the intention that the new force be half Catholic and half Protestant. *See also* BATTLE OF THE BOGSIDE; B SPECIALS.

**Royle Family, The.** An acclaimed BBC television SITCOM first screened in 1998, and intended as a subtle parody on the British royal family, as the punningly ironic title indicates. There is little in the way of action and the story concentrates on the gentle chattering and bickering between members of a working-class Manchester family as they sit slumped in their living room idly watching television. The programme is remarkable for its observational detail and for the naturalistic performances of the cast, headed by Ricky Tomlinson as the jaded, beer-bellied paterfamilias and Caroline Aherne as his starry-eyed, bride-to-be daughter.

**Roy of the Rovers.** Roy Race, fictitious blond-haired footballer extraordinaire for Melchester Rovers and star of the cartoon strip 'Roy of the Rovers', which first appeared in the *Tiger* comic in 1954 and continued there until 1983. From 1976 to 1993 he had his own *Roy of the Rovers Comic*.

**Rozelle rule.** In American football, the provision in a contract between a free agent and a professional team that requires the team to give the free agent's former team either a negotiated compensation or a compensation set by the commissioner of the National Football League. The name is that of Alvin Ray ('Pete') Rozelle (1926–96), league commissioner from 1960, who established the rule in 1974.

**RTFM.** In computer parlance, the irritated retort of an IT sophisticate when faced with a question that has an obvious answer. It stands for 'read the fucking manual'.

RTFM – Straight Talk for Developers – No Bull
homepage of www.readthefuckingmanual.co.uk

*See also* NMFP.

**Rubber cheque.** A cheque drawn on an account without the funds to pay it, and so one that 'bounces'. The punning expression dates from the 1920s. Various persons, including the record-breaking runner Emile Zatopek (1922–2000) and the crooked businessman Robert Maxwell, have been dubbed 'the BOUNCING CZECH'.

**Rubber chicken circuit.** The circuit followed by professional speakers. The US expression dates from the 1950s and alludes to the supposedly customary dish of tough chicken in the meal that precedes the speech.

***Rubber Soul.*** An album by The BEATLES released in December 1965, hailed at the time as their most substantial collection of songs to date. The title, invented by Paul McCartney, is a humorous allusion to white musicians who attempt to perform in a soul idiom and also puns on 'rubber sole' in the sense of the underside of a shoe. The album includes the tracks 'NORWEGIAN WOOD (THIS BIRD HAS FLOWN)', 'NOWHERE MAN', 'Michelle', 'Girl' and 'IN MY LIFE'. *See also* REVOLVER.

**Rube Goldberg.** An American name used from the early 20th century for any complicated machine or arrangement, especially one devised for the accomplishing of a simple task. It is that of the cartoonist Rube Goldberg (1883–1970), whose drawings and characters were soon familiar to many. His absurdly complicated devices, however, were designed not only to amuse but also to satirize the American mania for gadgets. A typical device was a 'simple' alarm clock, operated as follows: a bird on a bedroom windowsill catches a worm, a string attached to the worm pulls the trigger of a pistol, the pistol fires a bullet that bursts a balloon, the balloon drops a brick on an atomizer, the atomizer squirts liquid onto a sponge, the weighted sponge pulls a string, the string tilts a board, and a cannon ball rolls off the board to fall on the chest of a sleeper and by an attached string pull the cork off a vacuum flask filled with iced water, which falls on the sleeper's face to aid the wake-up blow delivered by the cannon ball. The whole is in the style of the British HEATH ROBINSON.

**Rubik's Cube.** A teasing puzzle invented by the Hungarian Ernö Rubik (b.1944) in 1974. A cube, apparently composed of 27 cubelets, initially has each of its six faces made up of nine cubelets of the same colour. An interior system of pivots allows any layer of nine cubelets to be rotated with respect to the rest, so that repeated rotations cause the cubelet faces to become scrambled. The challenge is to restore a scrambled cube to its initial configuration. With millions of combinations, there is only one possible way of achieving the desired solution. There was a brief but intense craze for the puzzle in the early 1980s.

**Rub salt into someone's wounds.** To make a painful experience even more painful. Salt will sting an open wound, although it may also help to heal it. The expression dates from the 1940s.

**Rub someone's nose in it.** To draw their attention to an embarrassing or painful fact by constantly or repeatedly drawing attention to it. The allusion is to the practice of rubbing a puppy's or kitten's nose in its misplaced excreta ('it') in an attempt to house-train it. The expression dates from the 1960s and variants are frequently found.

**Rude boy.** Originally, in Jamaica in the 1960s, a snappily dressed ska fan (*rude* being Jamaican slang for 'cool, hip', while *rudeness* was a synonym for sexual intercourse; ska was a musical style out of which REGGAE evolved). The term (sometimes reduced to plain 'rude') came to be applied to any 'young, Black Jamaican male who is an aggressive social dropout' (J. Green, *The Cassell Dictionary of Slang*, 1998). In early 21st-century British slang, 'rudes', 'rude boys' or 'rude girls' are terms sometimes applied to young Afro-Caribbeans with a penchant for BLING and music genres such as GANGSTA RAP, DRUM'N' BASS, HIP-HOP or GARAGE.

**Rudolph the Red-Nosed Reindeer.** The most famous of the reindeer that haul Santa Claus's sleigh at Christmas. He is chosen by Santa because his red nose, though laughed at by the other reindeer, lights up the foggy night like a light bulb. The words of the song were written by Robert May, an American advertising executive, to be given away to children by the Father Christmases in department stores. In 1949 the American composer Johnny Marks (1909–85) set the words to music, and the song was recorded by Gene Autry. The 1964 animated television film of the story, directed by Kizo Nagashima, is broadcast on US network television every Christmas.

> Rudoph the Red-Nosed Reindeer
> Had a very shiny nose,
> And if you ever saw it,
> You would even say it glows.

**RU 18.** A mock car number plate displayed in some pubs as a reminder that alcoholic drinks cannot be served to minors. Before the age of majority was lowered to 18 in 1970 the sign was RU 21.

**Rufty-tufty.** A person involved in any basic fieldwork or groundwork, especially when it is both physically and mentally demanding. The phrase, unrecorded in many dictionaries, combines 'rough' with 'tough'.

> The pool boys are known among the rest of the hacks as 'the rufty tufties' because they are supposed to travel with their army units and have, therefore, to resort to sleeping in odd places on occasions, including out in the open.
> *The Times* (18 June 1999)

**Rugged individualism.** A phrase famously used by US Republican politician Herbert Hoover (1874–1964) in a speech in New York city on 22 October 1928 during the run-up to the presidential election (which he won):

> We are challenged with a peacetime choice between the American system of rugged individualism and a European philosophy of diametrically opposed doctrines – doctrines of paternalism and state socialism.

Hoover himself disclaimed credit for the coinage; in 1934 he commented: 'It has been used by American leaders for over half a century in eulogy of those God-fearing men and women of honesty whose stamina and character and fearless assertion of rights led them to make their own way in life.' 'Rugged individualism' continues to be a leitmotif in the American way of life; those of a more collectivist persuasion have interpreted the cult of 'rugged indivi-dualism' as an assertion of ruthless economic self-interest of the I'M ALL RIGHT JACK variety.

**Rug rat.** A small child, especially one who cannot walk yet but crawls on the carpet. The nickname dates from the 1970s. The children's television cartoon series *Rugrats*, first screened in 1996, depicts life and adults as seen through the eyes of a gang of children and animals.

**Rule 43.** A prison regulation whereby prisoners, especially sex offenders, can be isolated for their own protection.

**Rules** or **rule, OK?** A stock formula in graffiti slogans from the 1970s, preceded by whoever or whatever the writer wishes to promote, as: 'Big Mal rules, OK?', 'Three-wheelers rule, OK?' As with much graffiti, the wording is subject to punning variation and corruption, as 'Queen Elizabeth rules UK', 'Rodgers and Hammerstein rule OK, lahoma' and 'Dyslexia rules, KO?' In 1981 Virginian rubbed tobacco was advertised with the slogan 'Virginian Rolls OK' and a well-known brand of French cigarette with *Gauloises à rouler, OK*.

> Gold rules OK?
> *The Observer*, headline (13 November 1983)

**Rumble in the Jungle.** A near-rhyming nickname given to the epic heavyweight boxing bout fought on 30 October 1974 in Kinshasa, Zaïre (now Democratic Republic of the

Congo) between George Foreman and Muhammad Ali (*see* FLOAT LIKE A BUTTERFLY, STING LIKE A BEE) and won by the latter. The rhymed pairing caught on as a formula for naming supposedly stupendous head-to-head contests – for example, the verbal showdown between George Galloway (*see* GORGEOUS GEORGE) and his opponent, the polemical journalist Christopher Hitchens, in New York on 14 September 2005 was billed as 'the Grapple in the Apple' (*see* BIG APPLE). *See also* THRILLER IN MANILA.

**Rumpole of the Bailey.** A television drama series running from 1975 to 1992 and centring on defence lawyer Horace Rumpole and the cases in which he is involved. The series owed its success in equal measure to the bibulously Dickensian performance of Leo McKern as Rumpole, henpecked by Hilda, 'SHE WHO MUST BE OBEYED', and to John Mortimer's richly ironic script. (Mortimer himself was a barrister, and worked for the defence in the OZ trial.)

Rumpole also appeared in short-story form, and in *Rumpole and the Penge Bungalow Murders* (2004), the first full-length Rumpole novel, Mortimer told in 50-year flashback the story of how his involvement in the case of a young man accused of killing his father and his father's friend made his name. The affair was frequently referred to in the Rumpole stories over the years, as a sort of in-joke for aficionados, but the details (as with Sherlock Holmes's GIANT RAT OF SUMATRA) never emerged. All was now revealed.

**Rumpy-pumpy.** Surreptitious sexual intercourse. The semi-humorous euphemism is an elaboration of 'rump', alluding to the male backside, and 'pump', alluding to the action.

**Rum, sodomy and the lash.** Winston Churchill's characterization of the Royal Navy, in response to an argumentative naval officer: 'Don't talk to me about naval tradition. It's nothing but rum, sodomy and the lash.' The remark has been reported as dating from 1911 and from the Second World War. The version quoted above comes from Peter Gretton, *Former Naval Person* (1968), while Harold Nicolson in his diary entry for 17 August 1950 has: 'Naval tradition? Monstrous! Nothing but rum, sodomy, prayers and the lash.' The version 'rum, buggery and the lash' may predate Churchill altogether.

In 1884 the US politician Samuel Dickinson Burchard (1812–91) had said in a speech: 'We are Republicans and don't propose to leave our party and identify ourselves with the party whose antecedents are rum, Romanism and rebellion.' *Rum, Sodomy and the Lash* was the title of an album by the punk-folk band The Pogues in the 1980s. The jazz musician and writer George Melly used *Rum, Bum, and Concertina* as the title of one volume of his autobiography (1977).

**Run around in circles.** To be fussily busy with little result. The 20th-century phrase is of US origin.

**Runaway success.** A journalistic and promotional cliché for anything selling well, or showing promise of doing so. The phrase is typically applied to a novel that is a 'runaway bestseller'. The term dates from the 1950s and was adopted to apply to anything regarded as giving good results, as: 'His plan was a runaway success.'

**Running on empty.** At the end of one's resources. The reference is to a car that is about to run out of petrol. The phrase was popularized by Jackson Browne's award-winning 'road' album *Running on Empty* (1978).

**Running start.** An initial advantage. The allusion is to an athletic event such as the long jump, in which the person runs up to the point of take-off, so having an advantage over anyone who attempts the jump from a standing position. The expression dates from the 1920s.

**Run of the mill.** Ordinary or undistinguished. The allusion is to materials or fabrics as they emerge from the production process in a mill and before they have been sorted or inspected for quality. The expression dates from the beginning of the 20th century.

**Run out of road.** Of a motor vehicle, to fail to negotiate a bend and to skid off the road. The expression dates from the 1960s and gave a figurative sense along the lines of 'to go off the rails'.

**Run out of steam.** To lose energy; to tire. Although steam engines were an 18th-century invention, the phrase dates from the 1960s.

**Run someone ragged.** To exhaust them or wear them out. The image is of working so hard that one is reduced to rags. The expression is American in origin and dates from the 1920s.

**Run something past someone.** To present it to them for their opinion or reaction, as: 'I'd like to run these figures past you.'

**Run something up the flagpole and see if anyone salutes.** To float an idea to see what kind of a response it gets. The phrase, originally 'Let's run it up the flagpole and see if anyone salutes it', comes from Reginald Rose's TV courtroom drama *Twelve Angry Men* (1955), later turned into the classic 1957 film starring Henry Fonda. It subsequently became popular among advertising types.

**Rupert Bear.** The distinctive strip cartoon bear, with his check trousers, red jersey and scarf, was the creation of the illustrator Mary Tourtel, who introduced him in the pages of the *Daily Express* in 1920. The picture books with his adventures in rhyme began to appear in the mid-1920s, and the famous Rupert Annuals in 1936, the latter illustrated by Alfred Bestall. Rupert's world centres on his village of Nutwood, but he travels far and wide and has companions in the form of Bill Badger, Algy Pug, Edward Trunk, Bingo the Brainy Pup and others. *See also* OZ.

**R.U.R.** A play (1920) by the Czech playwright Karel Čapek (1890–1938) about a rebellion by robots against their human masters. Standing for 'Rossum's Universal Robots', *R.U.R.* inaugurated a new genre in SCIENCE FICTION and incidentally introduced a new word to the English language: ROBOT (derived by Karel's brother Josef from the Czech *robota*, meaning 'drudgery' or 'forced labour').

**Ruralism.** The Brotherhood of Ruralists arose in 1975 as a group of seven British painters then living in the rural West of England: Ann and Graham Arnold (b.1936 and 1932), Peter Blake (b.1931; *see also* 'SERGEANT PEPPER'S LONELY HEARTS CLUB BAND') and his former American-born wife Jann Haworth (b.1942), David Inshaw (b.1943), and Annie and Graham Ovenden (b.1945 and 1943). They held that the country offered a potent source of inspiration and imagery that artists should not ignore, and sought to bring to it their experience and subjective perception of poetry, literature, music, history and myth. Their name (a coinage of the writer Laurie Lee) and to some extent their concepts echo those of the Pre-Raphaelite Brotherhood, founded in 1848. *See also* CUBISM; DADAISM; FAUVISM; FUTURISM; ORPHISM; SURREALISM; SYNCHROMISM; TACHISM; VORTICISM.

**Rushed off one's feet.** Extremely busy. The expression dates from the 1930s and derives from the slightly earlier phrase 'to rush someone off their feet', meaning to hurry or pressure them.

> Dear Dorothy, I give you back your word. I have been prepared for this. It has all been a mistake. It was my fault for having rushed you off your feet.
>
> ARNOLD VILLIERS: *Everybody's Letter Writer*, 'Love Letters' (*c.*1930)

**Russell Flint.** The name of the artist Sir William Russell Flint (1880–1969), a byword in his own lifetime for his mildly erotic nudes and Spanish gypsy scenes, painted in a distinctive but rather garish style. John Betjeman's poem 'A Russell Flint' in *High and Low* (1966) is an evocation of a beautiful woman with grey-green eyes whom he had met at the Garrick Club in London.

**Russian doll.** A type of wooden doll, known in Russia from *c.*1890 but actually copied from Japan. It is a nest of hollow dolls, each doll containing a smaller one inside it. 'Like a Russian doll' is thus often used as a simile for a complex, many-layered situation, in which the answer to one question just leads to another question. It may have been this image that inspired Winston Churchill's famous words in a radio broadcast on 1 October 1939:

> I cannot forecast to you the action of Russia. It is a riddle wrapped in a mystery inside an enigma.

In Russian, the doll is called *Matryoshka*, one of the many diminutives of the Russian woman's name Matrona, itself directly related to English 'matron'.

**Russian roulette.** A potentially fatal game of chance in which a 'player' loads a bullet into one chamber of a revolver, spins the cylinder, puts the gun to his head and pulls the trigger. The practice was popularized by Russian officers at the Tsar's court in the months before and during the 1917 Revolution, when the term is first recorded. It subsequently gained a figurative sense to apply to any potentially dangerous activity.

A notable fictional game of Russian roulette is played in the film *The Deer Hunter* (1978), in which three American POWs are forced by their Vietnamese captors to take it in turns with the revolver.

**Rust Belt.** A nickname in the 1980s for the declining industrial areas of the American Midwest and northeastern states. The cause of the decline was recession on the one hand and foreign competition on the other. The name, patterned on SUN BELT, alludes to the decaying steel industry.

**Rust bucket.** A jocular term for a rusty old car, but earlier for a dilapidated ship or aeroplane. The original sense dates from the 1940s.

**Ruth, 'Babe'.** *See* The BABE.

**Rutland.** England's smallest county, which, although still a historic entity, was removed from the political map when it was absorbed by Leicestershire in the local government county boundary changes of 1974, much to the annoyance of the local people. The name itself means 'Rōta's land', referring to an Anglo-Saxon landowner, and the county motto is *Multum in parvo*, 'Much in little'. The county was reinstated as a unitary authority in 1997.

*Rutland Weekend Television*, a television comedy show (1974–5), was a spoof of a low-budget independent channel (the name being based on the real London Weekend Television). It was the brainchild of Eric Idle, formerly of MONTY PYTHON'S FLYING CIRCUS, with songs provided by

Neil Innes, formerly of The Bonzo Dog (Doo Dah) Band (*see* BONZO), and it spawned a parody of The BEATLES named The Rutles.

**Rutland Panther.** A mysterious large animal with black fur and a long tail glimpsed on several occasions in different parts of RUTLAND from 1994. It is probably a big cat released into the wild either because it grew too large to be kept as a pet or as a consequence of the Dangerous Animals Act 1976, which ruled that animals such as lynxes, panthers and pumas must not be kept as pets. *See also* BEAST OF BODMIN MOOR.

**Ryder Cup.** The golfing trophy so named was presented by the English seed merchant Samuel Ryder (1856–1936), and was first competed for by British and US teams in 1927. The contest is held every two years and until 1979 was dominated by the Americans. The opposing team then became Europe, whereupon the balance began to be redressed. *See also* SOLHEIM CUP.

# S

**SA.** (German *Sturmabteilung*, 'assault division'.) Hitler's NAZI paramilitary organization, founded in 1921 and drawing its early members chiefly from the FREIKORPS ('Free Corps'), armed freebooter groups consisting mainly of former soldiers. It was kitted out in brown uniforms after the fashion of Mussolini's BLACKSHIRTS and accordingly became known as the Brownshirts. It was notorious for its methods of violent intimidation, both before and after its reorganization in 1925. Its leadership was purged in the NIGHT OF THE LONG KNIVES. *See also* SS.

**Sabotage.** Wilful and malicious destruction of machinery or plant by strikers, rebels, fifth columnists and the like. The term came into use after the great French railway strike in 1912. The word is traditionally said to have referred to the action of the strikers, who threw *sabots* (a type of wooden shoe or clog) into the machinery to damage it. This explanation cannot be sustained, however, and the allusion is probably to the noise made by the wooden shoes in walking, evoking a clumsy or bungling action.

**Sabra and Chatila.** *See* BEIRUT.

**Sabre-rattling.** A display or threat of military force, alluding to the sabres brandished by the Hungarian cavalry in the 18th century before an armed conflict. The term was much in evidence in the COLD WAR and in one form or another entered the languages of the countries concerned, as French *bruits de sabre*, German *Säbelrasseln* and Russian *bryatsanie oruzhiem*.

**Sabrina neckline.** A neckline with ties at the shoulders, as that of the dress worn by Audrey Hepburn (1929–93) in the role of Sabrina Fairchild in the film *Sabrina* (1954; in the UK titled *Sabrina Fair*).

**Sacco–Vanzetti case.** A highly controversial US legal case that culminated in the execution of two Italian-born anarchists, Nicola Sacco and Bartolomeo Vanzetti, for the murder during an armed robbery of two employees of the firm of Slater & Morrill in Braintree, Massachusetts, on 15 April 1920. Controversy arose from the fact that the evidence on which the two men were condemned was largely circumstantial and from the patent intolerance of the men's radical politics displayed by the legal system. The trial judge, Webster Thayer, apparently referred to the men as 'dagos' and 'anarchist bastards'. The men remained on death row for six years and, despite pleas for clemency from Albert Einstein, George Bernard Shaw and others, were executed by electric chair on 23 August 1927. In 1977 the state of Massachusetts declared that the two men had been improperly tried.

**Sack dress.** A woman's short, loose, unwaisted dress, somewhat resembling a sack, fashionable in the 1950s.

**Sacred cow.** A term dating from the early years of the 20th century for a person or thing held to be above criticism. The cow is venerated by the Hindus from its association with certain deities, and verses of the Rig Veda refer to the animal as Devi (goddess).

**Sacred mushroom.** A name given to various hallucinogenic mushrooms, especially species of *Psilocybe* and *Amanita*, which have been ritually eaten in different parts of the world. John Allegro, author of books on the DEAD SEA SCROLLS, aimed to prove in *The Sacred Mushroom and the Cross* (1970) that an intrinsic interrelationship exists between the mushroom, as cause and catalyst of heightened spiritual awareness, and the essentially mystic mainspring of Christianity.

**SAD.** An appropriate acronym for the depressive state known officially as seasonal affective disorder. It is associated with the autumn and winter seasons and is believed to be caused by a lack of light. The condition was first identified in the 1980s.

**Saddlebags.** A euphemism dating from the 1960s for folds of excess flesh round the stomach. *See also* LOVE HANDLES.

> I do a 10-minute workout with a Cindy Crawford video every other day and am pleased with the results. Which video would have exercises to get rid of saddlebags?
>
> *Sunday Times* (3 October 1999)

**Sadie Hawkins Day.** 9 November, in the United States a day corresponding to the English Leap Day (29 February) on which, according to a 'tradition' begun by the cartoon series LI'L ABNER in 1938, women can propose marriage to men. In modern times the custom usually centres on a college dance, with the girls issuing invitations to the boys. Sadie Hawkins herself is a character in the cartoon, in which on the day named after her the unmarried women of Dogpatch chase the unmarried men across the countryside like hounds after a hare, marrying those whom they catch.

**Sad sack.** A colloquialism for an incompetent person who is well-intentioned but cannot help making mistakes. The name was originally that of a US cartoon character, a lugubrious little GI, created by the artist George Baker in the Second World War for the US Army magazine *Yank*. The implied full expression is 'sad sack of shit', a demeaning description of a human being as simply a container of excrement.

**Safari park.** As an imitation of an African game park, where lions and other large wild animals are kept in open spaces for public viewing, the safari park in Britain was the brainchild of the circus owner Jimmy Chipperfield (1912–90). The first such park opened at Longleat in 1966 and was soon copied elsewhere. Safari itself is a Swahili word deriving from Arabic *safara*, 'to travel'.

**Safari suit.** A lightweight suit, typically with short sleeves and four pleated pockets in the jacket, as originally worn by quasi-colonials or military men on safari. The safari jacket was particularly associated with the writer Ernest Hemingway (1899–1961) and he is depicted wearing one in many of his photographs. In the 1970s Roger Moore, in his role as James BOND, sported the garment.

**Safe haven.** A place of refuge or security, especially for members of a religious or ethnic minority. The apparently tautological term gained prominence in the aftermath of the First GULF WAR when protected zones were set up in northern Iraq for the Kurds, many of whom had fled to Turkey and Iran after coming under attack by Saddam Hussein's troops. Similar zones were later set up by the United Nations in the former Yugoslavia following the implementation of ETHNIC CLEANSING. The expression is not limited to this specific sense, however.

**Saga.** A UK-based company that specializes in providing holidays and other services (such as insurance) for those over 50. The company was founded in the early 1950s by Sidney de Haan and it initially offered off-peak trips to Folkestone.

**Sailor King, The.** *See* GRANDPA ENGLAND.

**Sailor Who Fell from Grace with the Sea, The.** A novel (1965; in Japanese as *Gogo no eiko*, 1963) by Mishima Yukio (1925–70) in which a group of boys rejects the adult world. When the mother of one of them begins an affair with a naval officer, at first the boy reacts with hero-worship. Subsequently, after spying on them in bed, he turns vindictive and castrates his former hero. Mishima, having mounted an unsuccessful coup in favour of the Emperor against the prevailing administration, disembowelled himself with his sword. A film version (1976) of the novel, directed by Lewis John Carlino, was set in Dartmouth and described by the critic Benny Green in *Punch* as an 'everyday tale of torture, scopophilia, copulation, masturbation, dismemberment and antique dealing'.

**Saint, The.** The 'Robin Hood of modern crime' created by the Anglo-Chinese thriller writer Leslie Charteris. 'The Saint' is his crime name, his real name being Simon Templar. His symbol is a haloed stick-figure. He lives beyond the law, but he is otherwise a perfect English gentleman, a rescuer of damsels in distress and a jolly joker. He first appeared in the novel *Meet the Tiger* (1928), and went on to star in a long series of stories and books, as well as in film and television versions, the best known of the latter running from 1963 to 1968 and starring Roger Moore in the title role.

**St Clair, Amber.** *See* FOREVER AMBER.

**St Ives School.** A loose group of artists associated with the Cornish fishing port of St Ives. The town had long been popular with artists, as had the fishing village of Newlyn near Penzance, but St Ives remained only of local artistic importance until the sculptor Barbara Hepworth (1903–75) and the painter Ben Nicholson (1894–1982) moved there in 1939, just before the Second World War. Hepworth lived in St Ives for the rest of her life and Nicholson stayed there until 1958. The two formed a nucleus of avant-garde artists who made St Ives an internationally recognized centre of abstract art. The heyday of the St Ives School was in the 1950s and 1960s. In 1993 the Tate Gallery opened a branch museum there housing displays of 20th-century artists associated with the town.

**St Mugg.** A nickname of the writer and broadcaster Malcolm Muggeridge (1903–90), who became a fervent Roman Catholic in 1982.

**St Trinian's.** An outrageous girls' school, the exact converse of a genteel and well-ordered 'seminary for young ladies', in the cartoons by Ronald Searle (b.1920), first collected in *Hurrah for St Trinian's* (1948). The riotous scenarios were subsequently transferred to the screen in a series of films, the first and best of which is *The Belles of St Trinian's* (1954), with Alastair Sim in the role of the headmistress. Searle's own daughters attended St Trinnean's School, Edinburgh, and this probably inspired the name of the fictional establishment, which subsequently became a byword for any lawless behaviour on the part of uniformed schoolgirls, real or imaginary.

> Nina, Beth and Lou are three latter-day belles of St Trinians. Bosom chums at a girls' boarding school in the late Eighties, they flout the rules, smoking, ... bamboozling off-licences into selling them bottles of cider and licking Hula Hoops off their fingers in the dormitory.
>
> *Sunday Times:* review of Kate Bingham, *Slipstream*
> (15 January 2000)

**St Valentine's Day Massacre.** The murder of a group of bootlegging gangsters in Chicago on 14 February 1929. Disguising themselves as policemen, members of the Al CAPONE gang entered a garage on North Street run by members of the George 'Bugs' Moran gang, lined their opponents up against the wall and gunned the seven men down. Moran himself was not there, and neither was Capone, who had gone to Florida. The bloody incident dramatized the intense rivalry for control of the illegal liquor traffic during the PROHIBITION era in the United States. The massacre features in a number of movies and is the starting point for the classic cross-dressing comedy SOME LIKE IT HOT (1959).

**Saki.** The pseudonym of Hector Hugh Munro (1870–1916), the author of many short stories, such as the collections *Reginald* (1904), *The Chronicles of Clovis* (1911), *Beasts and Super-Beasts* (1914) and *The Toys of Peace* (1919), and three novels, of which the best is *The* UNBEARABLE BASSINGTON (1912). He took his pen-name either from a line in Edward FitzGerald's *The Rubáiyát of Omar Khayyám* (1859) ('And when like her, O Saki, you shall pass') or as a contraction of Sakya Muni, one of the names of the Buddha. He was killed in the First World War in France, shot in the head while resting in a crater. His style is often wickedly but wittily satirical. His stories frequently involve animals that take their revenge on humans and children who display their superiority of spirit over feckless adults. Much of the enjoyment comes from the names of his characters, as in story titles such as 'The Jesting Arlington Stringham', 'Filboid Studge, the Story of a Mouse That Helped', 'The

Secret Sin of Septimus Brope' and 'The Remoulding of Groby Lington'.

**Salami technique.** A method of carrying out a plan by means of a series of small or imperceptible steps, and specifically a type of computer fraud in which small amounts of money are transferred from several accounts into an account under a false name. The term dates from the 1970s and refers to the gradual steps of the operation, like successive thin slices of salami.

**Salop.** An abbreviated name of the county of Shropshire, representing a contraction of *Salopescira*, a Norman form of the original Old English name, recorded in the Domesday Book as *Sciropescire*. The name was officially adopted for the county in 1974 but was disliked by many local people and was particularly unpopular with the Euro-MP for Salop and Staffordshire, who discovered when attending conferences in continental Europe that *Salop* is uncomfortably close to French *salope*, meaning 'slut'. The original name was thus readopted in 1980. Despite these objections, the adjective 'Salopian' continues in use to describe the county's inhabitants and remains the name for past and present members of Shrewsbury School. It was Shrewsbury, the county town, that gave the name of the county in the first place, so that it is effectively 'Shrewsburyshire'.

**SALT.** The Strategic Arms Limitation Talks, organized from 1968 as a series of negotiations between the United States and the Soviet Union with the aim of reducing, or at any rate limiting, nuclear armaments. They resulted in two treaties, signed respectively in 1972 and 1979, although the second was never ratified by the US Senate. They were superseded by START.

**Saltash luck.** An unwelcome task that involves getting soaked through. The phrase dates from the early years of the 20th century and supposedly alludes to the poor catches of the fishermen of Saltash in Cornwall, a port that is now essentially a suburb of Plymouth. It has been used especially in the Royal Navy and Merchant Navy, where it is more succinctly summed up as 'a wet arse and no fish'.

**Samaritans.** An organization founded in 1953 by the Rev. Chad Varah (b.1911) of St Stephen Walbrook, London, to help the despairing and suicidal. By the early 1990s there were more than 180 centres in the British Isles as well as some overseas. Trained volunteers give their help at any hour to those who make their needs known, mostly by telephone. The name alludes to the New Testament parable of the Good Samaritan, who tended the victim of a robbery (in modern terms, a mugging) where others 'passed by on the other side' (Luke 10:30–37).

**Same difference.** Essentially the same; not different despite appearances. The expression dates from the 1940s.

**Same old story.** The latest bad situation is monotonously familiar. The expression was popularized in the Second World War by its occurrence in Herman Hupfeld's song 'As Time Goes By' (1931), performed by Dooley Wilson in the film CASABLANCA (1942):

> It's still the same old story,
> A fight for love and glory,
> A case of do or die!
> The world will always welcome lovers,
> As time goes by.

An extra note of bored fatalism is added by the modern variant 'Same old same old'.

**Samizdat.** Banned dissident literature in the former Soviet bloc, or the system by which it was printed and distributed. Printing was often in the form of photocopying. The term is Russian, and literally means 'self-publishing house'.

**Samson and Delilah.** A biblical film epic (1949) depicting the doomed liaison between Samson, who was famed for his great strength, and the beautiful but treacherous Delilah. Starring Victor Mature and Hedy Lamarr, it was the impressive expanse of Mature's chest that prompted one of Groucho Marx's most famous observations:

> You can't expect the public to get excited about a film where the leading man's bust is bigger than the leading lady's.

**Sandbagger.** A term of US origin dating from the 1960s for a person who deliberately under-performs in a sport in order to gain an unfair handicap or other advantage.

**Sandinistas.** Members of a left-wing Nicaraguan political organization, the Sandinista National Liberation Front (Spanish *Frente Sandinista de Liberación Nacional*), commonly known as FSLN, which came to power in 1979 after overthrowing the dictator Anastasio Somoza (1925–80). They were opposed during much of their rule by the US-backed CONTRAS and were voted out of office in 1990. They took their name from Augusto César Sandino (1893–1934), the nationalist leader of a similar earlier organization. *See also* PORTILLISTAS.

**Sanpaku.** The name for a condition of the eye in which the white is visible below the iris as well as on both sides. It is said to result from a failure to follow a macrobiotic diet, with its organically grown sugar, fruit and vegetables, in favour of a traditional diet of meat, eggs and the like. The term derives from Japanese *san*, 'three', and *haku*, 'white', and was adopted in English in the 1960s.

The publicist introduces a girl of about twenty who is very sanpaku – in fact, an inordinate amount of veinless white shows beneath the lampblack pupils – and almost intimidatingly beautiful.

> *Esquire* (January 1972)

**Sarajevo.** The capital of Bosnia-Herzegovina twice gained particular notoriety during the course of the 20th century.

(1) On 28 June 1914 the Archduke Franz Ferdinand, heir of the Austro-Hungarian Empire, and his wife were assassinated in Sarajevo by Gavrilo Princip, a Bosnian Serb student and member of the secret Serbian nationalist organization, the BLACK HAND. The shooting lit the 'powder-keg' of a system of national alliances that had developed during the last decades of the 19th century and has thus been described as 'the shot heard round the world'. Austria-Hungary, which had long perceived Serbia to be a sponsor of nationalist unrest in its Balkan provinces, used the assassination as a pretext to make unreasonable demands on Serbia. When Serbia, acting on the advice of its Slav ally, Russia, refused to comply with these demands, the Austrian army was mobilized and the Serbian capital city, Belgrade, bombarded. When Russia mobilized in response, Germany, fearing the disintegration of its Austro-Hungarian ally, demanded that Russian mobilization cease and asked France, Russia's ally, to guarantee that it would remain neutral in the event of a Russo-German war. The stage was now set for the outbreak of a coalition war. Germany put into action the SCHLIEFFEN PLAN and declared war on Russia and France. When the German army crossed into neutral Belgium as a preliminary to its attack on France, Britain, guarantor of Belgian neutrality since 1831, declared war on Germany and the WAR TO END WAR was under way. *See also* CENTRAL POWERS; ENTENTE CORDIALE; SCRAP OF PAPER; SHOT HEARD AROUND THE WORLD; TRIPLE ENTENTE.

> We come to Sarajevo, Herr Burgomeister, and have a bomb thrown at us.
>
> ARCHDUKE FRANZ FERDINAND: last words before he was assassinated (28 June 1914)

(2) From 1992 to 1994 Sarajevo was subjected to a hellish siege during the Bosnian war that followed the break-up of the former Yugoslavia. Sarajevo was besieged and bombarded from high points overlooking the city by the Bosnian Serb army (with the effective backing of the Serbian army), as part of its efforts to carve up in its favour the newly independent, multi-ethnic republic of Bosnia-Herzegovina. However, a United Nations ultimatum, allied to a threat of bombing by NATO, led to a ceasefire in February 1994, and the Bosnian Serb artillery withdrew.

**Sardines.** A party game dating from the 1920s and played mainly by children. One person hides somewhere in the house and is looked for by everyone else. When someone finds the hider they join him, so that ultimately all except the final searcher are packed tight, like sardines, in a single hiding place. The last finder then becomes the next seeker. The game is also played by adults, since it provides a legitimate excuse for close physical contact. The US version is generally known more fully as 'sardines-in-the-box' or alternatively as 'hide-and-go-seek'.

**SAS.** The British Special Air Service traces its origins to the Second World War, when it was formed to operate behind enemy lines, conducting raids, sabotaging aircraft and disrupting communications and lines of supply. It was disbanded in 1945 but reborn four years later as the Malayan Scouts. In 1951 it officially became 22 Special Air Service. It was in action in Malaya, Oman, Borneo and Aden in the 1950s and 1960s, and was first sent to Northern Ireland in 1969. In 1980 the normally clandestine force was on public view when television cameras filmed an SAS team storming the besieged Iranian Embassy. Five of the six terrorists were killed. *See also* WHO DARES WINS.

**Satanic Verses, The.** A novel (1988) by Salman Rushdie (b.1947). Questions of faith and doubt underlie this panoramic vision of Britain during the Thatcherite era, India, and the mystical landscape in which the Prophet Mahound does battle, through which Rushdie explores the clash of cultures between East and West. The satanic verses are whispered by Shaitan in the ear of Mahound, who then repudiates them: 'The Devil came to him in the guise of the archangel, so that the verses he memorized ... were not the real thing but its diabolical opposite, not godly, but satanic.' The novel caused offence to many Muslims for certain remarks put into the mouths of its characters. As a result, a Muslim FATWA (legal ruling) was issued by Iran's AYATOLLAH Khomeini, declaring Rushdie an apostate who should be killed for insulting the Prophet Muhammad. On 24 September 1998, after Rushdie had spent the intervening time in hiding, the government of the Islamic Republic of Iran announced that it had no intention, nor would it take any action, to threaten Rushdie's life or that of anybody associated with his work, or encourage or assist anybody to do so. *See also* FIRST LINES OF NOVELS.

**'Satisfaction'.** *See* ('I Can't Get No) Satisfaction'.

**Saturday girl.** A girl or young woman who helps out in a shop or store on Saturdays, one of the busiest shopping days of the week (though, in the 21st century, hotly followed by Sunday after relaxation of the trading laws).

**Saturday Night and Sunday Morning.** The first novel (1958) by Alan Sillitoe (b.1928), a gritty story of working-class Nottingham, based on his own background. Arthur (DON'T LET THE BASTARDS GRIND YOU DOWN) Seaton makes the most of what life has to offer, including the wives of his workmates, though ultimately he settles for marriage. The title refers to the period spent with a married woman while her husband is away. The award-winning film version (1960), starring Albert Finney and Rachel Roberts, was imaginatively directed by Karel Reisz.

**Saturday Night Fever.** The title of a film and its soundtrack album, both released in 1978, and featuring music by The Bee Gees, The Tavares and Kool and The Gang. The album and its songs, including 'Stayin' Alive', 'How Deep is Your Love', 'Jive Talkin'' and 'Night Fever', are seen as the essence of the sound of 1970s disco music. The film starred John Travolta, whose dance routine was much imitated.

**Saturday night special.** A cheap pistol or revolver, as used by petty criminals in the United States. The allusion is to the use of the weapon in barroom and street fights at the weekend.

**Saudi Arabia.** The kingdom in southwestern Asia was founded in 1932 by the Muslim leader Ibn Saud (1880–1953), and named after him. His name derives from an Arabic word meaning 'good fortune', 'happiness', but it is purely a coincidence that the main part of the Arabian peninsula was known to the Romans as Arabia Felix, 'Arabia the fortunate'.

**Sauron.** The Lord of Darkness in J.R.R. Tolkien's *The* LORD OF THE RINGS (1954–5). Sauron is ruler of the land of MORDOR and dwells at Barad-dûr, the Dark Tower. The deep sense of evil and menace with which Tolkien invests him is heightened by his never actually appearing in physical form in the novel. Sauron's efforts to regain the One Ring from FRODO, the ring-bearer, are the motor of the plot, and the Ring's destruction leads to the shattering of his power. The name Sauron, coincidentally or otherwise, is reminiscent of the Greek word *sauros* ('lizard').

**Sausage sizzle.** In New Zealand, an outdoor social event marked by the cooking of sausages, typically on a barbecue or campfire. The term dates from the early 1970s.

**Saved by the bell.** Extricated from an unpleasant or undesirable situation by the intervention of someone or something. The reference is to the sounding of a bell at the end of a round in a boxing match, rescuing the loser from further punishment. Schoolchildren are sometimes similarly saved from answering an awkward question in class by the sounding of the bell at the end of a lesson.

**Save the Children Fund.** A charity founded in Britain in 1919 by a Shropshire woman, Eglantyne Jebb (1875–1928), in response to the famine among children in Europe caused by the First World War. It now operates to improve the lives of children in 70 countries.

**Save the town it became necessary to destroy it, To.** The words reportedly used by an unnamed US Army major in relation to the town of Ben Tre during the 1968 Tet Offensive in the VIETNAM War. The Associated Press reported the words in the form: 'It became necessary to destroy the town to save it' (*New York Times*, 8 February 1968). Variations on the theme have been sounded by others over the years. In 2005 Karen Hughes, public-relations adviser to President George W. Bush, told her audience on a trip to Turkey:

> To preserve the peace, sometimes my country believes war is necessary.
>
> Quoted in *The Observer* (2 October 2005)

**Save the whale.** An environmental slogan of the early 1980s alerting the public to the rapid decline of the whale population. It was instrumental in bringing about the moratorium on commercial whaling introduced in 1985.

**Savoy Hill.** The site of the first studios of the British Broadcasting Company (1922) and until 1932 the headquarters of the British Broadcasting Corporation, the original BBC call sign being 2LO (i.e. No. 2, London).

**Say cheese!** A traditional injunction from a photographer to a group of people about to be photographed, in order to make them smile (by saying the word 'cheese').

**Say it ain't so, Joe.** The attributed words of a young fan to the US baseball star 'Shoeless Joe' Jackson of the Chicago White Sox as he emerged from a grand jury session at the time of the BLACK SOX SCANDAL of 1919. Jackson always maintained his innocence, but he and seven others were barred from baseball for life.

**Scamperdale.** A type of Pelham bit for horses, having a combined snaffle and bit but angled back to prevent chafing. It was invented in the 1930s and takes its name from Lord Scamperdale in R.S. Surtees's *Mr Sponge's Sporting Tour* (1853).

**Scanties.** *See* MAKE DO AND MEND.

**Scapa Flow.** This sea basin in the Orkneys was the main base of the British fleet in the First World War. The surrendered German fleet scuttled itself here in 1919, but most of the ships were salvaged over the following 20 years. It was again a fleet base in the Second World War. On 14 October 1939 a U-BOAT penetrated the anchorage and sank the battleship *Royal Oak* with the loss of 810 lives.

**Scare the living daylights out of someone.** *See* BEAT THE LIVING DAYLIGHTS OUT OF SOMEONE.

**Scarface.** A nickname of the gangster Al CAPONE (1899–1947), from the scar on his left cheek, caused by a razor slash sustained in a Brooklyn gang fight in his younger days. *Scarface* is also the title of a 1932 film directed by Howard Hawks and written by Ben Hecht, in which the Capone character is called Tony Camonte. In Brian de Palma's 1983 version, the character is renamed Tony Montana, and is played by Al Pacino.

**Scarlet Pimpernel.** The fictional spy hero created by Baroness Orczy for her bestselling novel *The Scarlet Pimpernel* (1905). His real name is Sir Percy Blakeney and he is the head of the League of the Scarlet Pimpernel, a band of young Englishmen pledged to rescue the aristocratic victims of the Reign of Terror that followed the French Revolution. He outwits his French opponents through his courage and ingenious disguises, identifying himself in his secret rescue missions by a signet ring with the image of a scarlet pimpernel flower. The verse with which Blakeney mocks his chief enemy, Citizen Chauvelin, one of Robespierre's most cunning agents, is well known:

> We seek him here, we seek him there,
> Those Frenchies seek him everywhere.
> Is he in heaven? – Is he in hell?
> That demmed, elusive Pimpernel?
>
> ch. 12

A first-class period film version (1934), starring Leslie Howard, Merle Oberon and Raymond Massey, was directed by Harold Young.

**Scaryana.** The nickname of Ariana, the Afghanistan airline, with the reputation of being the worst in the world. Its safety record has led to Ariana flights being banned from most US and European airports, and UN officials and the diplomats of most countries are forbidden to fly Ariana. Dr Muhammad Atash, who became the airline's new boss in 2005, has said that Ariana faces a number of difficulties:

> Embezzlement. Nepotism. Red tape. Lack of qualified staff. And a general attitude not to work. ... [But] I believe we are starting to make progress.
>
> Quoted in *The Guardian* (7 November 2005)

**Scat singing.** In JAZZ a form of singing without words, using the voice as a musical instrument. It is said to have been started by Louis Armstrong in the 1920s when he forgot the words or accidentally dropped the paper on which they were written while singing a number. Jelly Roll Morton, on the other hand, claimed to have sung scat as early as 1906. The word itself is presumably imitative.

**Schicklgruber, Herr.** A contemptuous nickname that was applied occasionally by Winston Churchill to Adolf Hitler (1889–1945), the Nazi FÜHRER. Hitler's father, Alois Schicklgruber (1837–1903), used his mother's surname until the later 1870s, when he started to use the surname Hitler, based on a local priest's mistranscription of his father's name, Johann Georg Heidler, who had fathered him five years before marrying his mother. The Schicklgruber connection was discovered by Hitler's opponents in Germany and Austria in the 1930s. *See also* AUSTRIAN CORPORAL.

**Schindler's Ark.** A novel with historical interpolations (1982; in the United States as *Schindler's List*) by the Australian novelist Thomas Keneally (b.1935), which won the BOOKER PRIZE for fiction. It describes the life and times of Oskar Schindler (1908–74), an ethnic German born into a Catholic family living in Moravia (incorporated in the new republic of Czechoslovakia in 1918 and now part of the Czech Republic). During the Second World War Schindler, playboy industrialist and 'discoverer of unprocurables', saved some 1100 Polish Jews by the device of setting up at his own expense a personal 'labour camp' within the forced labour camp of Plaszów, near Cracow, and passing the men and women off as 'skilled workers'. The film version (1993), entitled *Schindler's List* and directed by Steven Spielberg, was acclaimed by Terrence Rafferty of *The New Yorker* as the finest film ever made about the HOLOCAUST.

**Schindler's List.** *See* SCHINDLER'S ARK.

**Schlieffen Plan.** The German military's strategic plan for achieving victory in a war against France and Russia, developed between 1899 and 1905 by Count Alfred von Schlieffen (1833–1913), chief of the general staff (1891–1905). The plan was devised in response to the 1892 alliance between France and Russia, and it was based on the premise that Russia would be much slower to mobilize than either France or Germany. Germany would make its main attack on France through neutral Belgium, while smaller German forces withdrew along France's eastern frontier, drawing after them the bulk of the French army, which would then be attacked in the rear by the main German force. Having surrounded and destroyed the French army, German forces would be transferred to the east, to defeat Russia. The whole plan was to follow a detailed timetable, but when it came to it a number of unpredicted events, such as determined Belgian resistance, a quick British intervention and a rapid Russian offensive, served to thwart the outcome. The successful German offensive on the Low Countries and France in 1940 followed a variant of the Schlieffen Plan. *See also* SARAJEVO.

**Schlock.** Cheap or inferior; trashy. The term is one of several words of Yiddish origin that came to denote a shoddy or defective object or a stupid or boorish person. Examples of the latter include 'schlemiel', 'schlep', 'shlub', 'schlump', 'schmo', 'schmuck' and 'schnook'. *See also* SCHM-.

**Schm-.** This initial element of various words of Yiddish origin, such as 'schmaltz', 'schmooz' and 'schmuck', can be prefixed to any word to express one's disparagement, dismissal or derision of the word in question, which is quoted before it, as in the old joke about the psychiatrist and the fond Jewish mother: 'I have to tell you, madam, that your son is suffering from an Oedipus complex.' 'Oedipus, Schmoedipus! What does it matter so long as he loves his mother?'

> To consider in what particulars they [prime ministers] were wise or unwise … is so much trickier than to chin-wag about 'honour' and 'personal integrity'. Honour, schmhonour; integrity be damned.
>
> *The Times* (4 September 1999)

**Schneider Trophy.** An international trophy for aviation, presented in 1913 by Jacques Schneider, a French patron of aviation. It was open to seaplanes of all nations and was won outright by Britain in 1931, when contests ceased.

**Schoolgirl complexion.** Beautiful skin and colouring, without any wrinkles, lines or signs of ageing. The expression derives from a US advertising slogan for Palmolive soap from 1917, more fully: 'Keep that schoolgirl complexion.' The slogan was coined by Charles S. Pearce, a Palmolive executive. The healthy image of a young person's clear skin and radiant features has long been traditional, as for example in Shakespeare's 'schoolboy, with … shining morning face' (*As You Like It*, II, vii). *See also* PEACHES AND CREAM COMPLEXION.

**School of hard knocks.** The painful or difficult experiences that are regarded as providing a salutary lesson on the realities of life. The US expression dates from the early 20th century.

**Schweppes.** The manufacturers of the mineral waters and soft drinks of this name used its sibilance to create a number of amusing neologisms in the 20th century, such as 'Schweppervescence', introduced in 1946. The company produced its own newspaper, the *Schweppshire Post*, published in 'Cirenschwepster' and costing 'Schweppence', to report such incidents as 'Councillor collides with cow' (in 'Schwepton Mallet') or 'Streetcar kidnapped in Hove, Pa.', and to print its own weather forecast, promising a 'Schweppitome of dullness' in the Midlands. The name itself, for all its onomatopoeic evocation, derives from the German entrepreneur Jacob Schweppe (1740–1821), who moved to Britain in 1792.

**Science fiction.** A fiction based on imagined future developments in science, especially with regard to space or time travel, life on other planets, visits to earth from ALIENS and the like. Much science fiction is sophisticated and fires the imagination, but the worst types of the genre are mostly risible and fit only for crude comic strips or picture stories. The term first gained general currency in the 1920s.

**Scientology.** A religious system, in full the Church of Scientology, based on the seeking of self-knowledge and spiritual fulfilment by means of special courses and training. It was founded in 1955 by the US SCIENCE FICTION writer L. Ron Hubbard, developer of DIANETICS. It has been the subject of considerable criticism, to which it has responded with vigorous lawsuits.

**Scofflaw.** An US term for a person who flouts ('scoffs at') the law, especially one who fails to comply with a law that is difficult to enforce. The word dates from 1923, when many law-enforcement officers were concerned at the increasing disrespect shown for the newly enacted Eighteenth Amendment, the PROHIBITION law, on the grounds that an attitude of defiance to one federal law could lead to gradual loss of respect for the whole body of laws. They therefore sought a word to describe people who derided the National Prohibition Act. A Massachusetts millionaire, Delcevare King, announced a prize contest for the most appropriate word. The prize was a mere $200 but it attracted 25,000 entries. In January 1924 King announced that the winning entry, 'scofflaw', had been submitted independently by Henry Irving Shaw and Kate Butler, both residents of Massachusetts. The neologism was soon entered in the dictionaries.

**Scooby-Doo.** The cowardly Great Dane created in 1969 by Hanna-Barbera Productions for television cartoons. He helps four teenage detectives tour the country in their 'Mystery Machine' mobile van in search of the supernatural and gained his name from the meaningless phrase 'scooby-dooby-doo' in Bert Kaempfert's song 'Strangers in the Night' (1966), made into a hit by Frank Sinatra. A live-action feature film entitled *Scooby-Doo* was released in 2002, and a sequel in 2004.

Among the divers of the Royal Navy, a 'scooby-doo' is a 'civilian sport scuba diver'. A 'scooby' is also rhyming slang for both 'clue' and 'Subaru' (a marque of car). In the United States, a 'scooby-doo' can be either a cannabis cigarette or a person who eats voraciously without gaining weight.

**Scoop.** A novel by Evelyn Waugh (1903–66), published in 1938. The novel draws on Waugh's own experiences as a war correspondent for the *Daily Mail* during the Italian campaign in Abyssinia (Ethiopia) in 1936. In the novel, the *Daily Beast* intends to send out the novelist John Boot as its man-in-the-thick-of-it in the war-torn African state of Ishmaelia. In error, the job goes to the *Beast*'s retiring writer of nature notes, William Boot. This Boot is more accustomed to penning lines such as:

> Feather-footed through the plashy fen passes the questing vole …

Waugh based some aspects of William Boot on W.F. (Bill) Deedes, then reporting for the *Morning Post*. Deedes, like Boot, arrived in Abyssinia with an extraordinary quantity of luggage (his paper didn't expect him to return, or at least not for a long time), causing Waugh much mirth. Deedes himself, in a BBC Radio interview in 2001, said that he indeed shared Boot's naivety (and his volume of luggage), but that he was much less 'shambolic'. Deedes went on to become one of Britain's most distinguished journalists and was for many years editor of the *Daily Telegraph* (*see also* HALITOSIS HALL)

William Boot lives on in another guise – as the pseudonymous author of 'Unauthorised Returns', a humorous column in *The Bookseller* magazine.

*See also* UP TO A POINT, LORD COPPER.

**Scorched earth policy.** A policy of burning and destroying crops and anything that may be of use to an invading force. The term arose in the late 1930s and apparently translates Chinese *shāotǔ zhèngcè*, from *shāo*, 'to burn', *tǔ*, 'earth' and *zhèngcè*, 'policy'.

**Score.** A verb that has acquired various colloquial meanings in the 20th century, among them to commit a crime, to steal, to obtain an illegal drug and, usually of a man, to find a sexual partner.

**Scorpion kick.** A style of kick in football pioneered by the Colombian goalkeeper René Higuita (b.1966). His technique has been to wait for a high, goal-bound ball then dive forward and kick the ball away with his heels, in the process adopting a scorpion shape. He used the trick effectively at Wembley in Colombia's 0–0 draw with England on 6 September 1995.

**Scotch tape.** In 1930 the Minnesota Mining and Manufacturing Company of St Paul, Missouri, now known as 3M, introduced a specialized new product in the form of a transparent, adhesive cellulose tape. As 'a little went a long way' when it came to sealing packages, they gave it a name that complimented the reputed thriftiness of the Scots. By 1935, when a dispenser was added, the tape was already an institution and its name is as familiar as that of its British rival, SELLOTAPE.

**'Scotland the Brave'.** A traditional tune to which new words were written in the 1950s by a Scottish journalist, Cliff Hanley. For several years it was the unofficial Scottish national anthem, sung by sports spectators, but was subsequently replaced in popularity by 'FLOWER OF SCOTLAND'.

**Scottish Colourists.** A term used for four Scottish painters who in the years before the First World War each spent some time in France, where they were influenced by the rich colours and bold handling of recent French painting, especially FAUVISM. They were F.C.B. Cadell (1883–1937), J.D. Fergusson (1874–1961), Leslie Hunter (1877–1931) and S.J. Peploe (1871–1935). The name was popularized by T.J. Honeyman's book *Three Scottish Colourists* (1950), dealing with Cadell, Hunter and Peploe. The four did not form a group but knew one another individually.

**Scottish National Party.** *See* SNP.

**Scottish Renaissance.** A term coined in 1924 by the French literary critic Denis Saurat to describe the interwar revival of consciousness and culture in Scotland. The name became loosely associated with such writers as Hugh MacDiarmid (1892–1978), Lewis Grassic Gibbon (1901–35), Edwin Muir (1887–1959) and Neil M. Gunn (1891–1973). The resurgence itself was prompted partly by the growth of national awareness in Scotland after the First World War, partly as a reaction against the sentimental trend in 19th-century Scottish writing. The first major work of the genre was MacDiarmid's long semi-STREAM OF CONSCIOUSNESS poem *A Drunk Man Looks at the Thistle* (1926).

**Scott of the Antarctic.** *See* SOUTH POLE.

**Scouse** or **Scouser.** A nickname for an inhabitant of Liverpool, so called from the lobscouse, or sailor's meat stew, formerly popular as a local dish. The name also serves for the form of English spoken in Liverpool. Characteristics of this are the pronunciation of words such as 'fair' and 'spare' as 'fur' and 'spur', the separate sounding of the 'g' in 'long' (as normally in 'longer'), and the sounding of 't' as 'r' in words such as 'matter', giving 'marrer'. In a publicity drive for the Liverpool clean streets campaign, litter was described as 'norra lorra fun'. The voice quality of the Scouse speaker is markedly adenoidal, a feature that has puzzled phoneticians.

***Scouting for Boys.*** A book, published in fortnightly parts in 1908, by Robert Baden-Powell (1857–1941), the founder of the Scout Movement. It includes advice on healthy living (particularly camping in the wild), and a number of 'camp fire yarns'. Its reissue in 2004 proved a surprising success (perhaps partly to be accounted for by the title's whiff of innuendo, which modern nostrils picked up). *See also* BOY SCOUTS.

**Scouts.** *See* BOY SCOUTS.

**Scout's honour.** I am telling the truth; trust me. The allusion is to the honour on which BOY SCOUTSor SCOUTS promise to obey the Scout Law, as originally defined by Robert Baden-Powell in SCOUTING FOR BOYS (1908): 'A Scout's Honour is to be trusted.' The phrase is now used as an asseveration that what one says is true, as: 'I won't tell anyone, scout's honour.'

**Scrabble.** The well-known game, in which players compete in forming words with lettered tiles on a board of 225 squares, was invented in 1931 by a New York architect, Alfred M. Butts (1900–93), who called it 'Criss Cross' with reference to the way the words interlock on the board, as in a crossword puzzle. It was redesigned and renamed Scrabble by Jim Brunot, a social worker, in 1948, and he and his wife began to manufacture sets by hand the following year. They failed to make a profit, however, and it was only when Jack Strauss, chairman of Macy's, the New York department store, became interested in 1952 that the Brunots finally achieved a breakthrough. Each lettered tile is worth a given number of points, the commonest letters having the lowest value and the rarest the highest. Words are scored by adding up the values of their letters, multiplied by any of the 'premium' squares that may be covered, such as double letter, triple letter, double word or triple word. The player who scores the most points is the winner. The game has gained a serious enough status to be played in official tournaments.

**Scrambled egg.** Services slang dating from the Second World War for the gold braid on an officer's cap, hence for an officer himself.

**Scrape the barrel** or **the bottom of the barrel.** To be reduced to using the most mediocre things or people simply because there is none other available. The expression dates, significantly, from the Second World War.

**Scrap of paper.** A treaty or pledge that one does not intend to honour. The phrase is said to have been used by the German Chancellor, Theobald von Bethmann Hollweg, in connection with the German violation of Belgian neutrality in August 1914 (*see* SARAJEVO).

The Chancellor said that … just for a word – 'neutrality', –

just for a scrap of paper Great Britain was going to make war on a kindred nation.

EDWARD GOSCHEN: letter of 8 August 1914 in *Collected Diplomatic Documents relating to the Outbreak of the European War* (1915)

**Scratch card.** A card with a section (or sections) covered in a waxy coating that can be scratched off, usually with a coin, to reveal a possible winning symbol. Scratch cards were introduced in the United States in the 1980s and the flutterer's delight (or downfall) soon spread to Britain, where they could either be bought or were given free as a consumer incentive. Some of the most popular purchasable cards are those linked to the NATIONAL LOTTERY.

**Scratch one's head.** To think hard in order to find a solution; to express puzzlement. The gesture is traditionally regarded as accompanying these mental processes, presumably as it symbolizes a 'stirring of the brain'.

**Scratch the surface.** To deal with or investigate only superficially. The implication is that one must dig deeper to resolve the matter properly or fully.

**Screaming habdabs** or **abdabs.** A fit of great anxiety; the 'heebie-jeebies'. The origin of the latter word is uncertain – it may represent a stuttering or gulping – but the phrase dates from the 1940s.

**Screaming Lord Sutch.** *See* MONSTER RAVING LOONY PARTY.

**Screaming Popes, The.** A series of paintings executed between 1949 and the mid-1950s by Francis Bacon (1909–92). They were inspired by the portrait of Pope Innocent X by Velázquez (1599–1660), a painting described by Sir Joshua Reynolds in the 18th century as 'the most beautiful picture in Rome'. Sir Joshua would not have appreciated Bacon's reworkings, which are nightmarish depictions of hysterical terror, sometimes accompanied by hunks of meat. As one critic put it: 'The major influence on Bacon has been his own surname.'

**Scream queen.** A term for an actress who plays a part in a HORROR MOVIE, in which she will be invariably required to scream. The colloquialism became particularly attached to Jamie Lee Curtis (b.1958), who appeared in such films as *Prom Night, Terror Train* and *The Fog* (all 1980). Another candidate for the title is Barbara Shelley (b.1933), who shrieked her way through many British horror films of the 1960s.

**Screw around.** To be sexually promiscuous; to fool about or behave aimlessly. The former usage dates from the 1930s, the latter from the 1950s.

**Screw up.** To mess up; to ruin; to blunder, as: 'I really screwed up that time' or, transitively, 'I really screwed things up'. The phrase is of US origin and dates from the 1920s.

**Scrumpy.** Rough cider made from 'scrumps', withered or stunted apples, and a drink particularly associated with the West Country. The word itself is of dialect origin and first recorded in the early 20th century.

**Scrunchy.** A circular band of fabric-covered elastic used for holding a bunch of hair, especially a pony tail, and so called from its crumpled ('scrunched') appearance. 'Scrunchies' is also sometimes used for 'crunches', gymnastic exercises used to strengthen the abdominal muscles by means of 'sit-ups'.

He did go to the same gym as Mel [C of the SPICE GIRLS], he was on the exercise bike while she did scrunchies.

*heat* (23–29 September 1999)

**Scud.** The NATO code name for a type of long-range surface-to-surface guided missile developed in the Soviet Union. They came into the news in 1991 during the First GULF WAR when they were launched against Allied forces in SAUDI ARABIA. The name is not an acronym but a conventional word beginning with S used for a type of Soviet surface-to-surface missile. Other types were Savage, Scapegoat and Scrooge. Names beginning with G were chosen for surface-to-air missiles (SAMs), with K for air-to-surface missiles and with A for air-to-air missiles.

**Scud stud.** A sobriquet originally bestowed on the handsome NBC television reporter Arthur Kent (b.1953), who while covering the 1991 GULF WAR was present during an Iraqi SCUD missile attack on Dhahran, Saudi Arabia. It was subsequently also applied to the BBC's Rageh Omaar (b.1967), who in 2003 was constantly to be seen on British television screens reporting from the roof of a Baghdad hotel while the explosions prefacing the US-led invasion burst all around him. He acquired a large clutch of admirers.

**SCUM.** The Society for Cutting Up Men, a hypothetical organization originating in the *SCUM Manifesto*, published in 1968 by the US feminist Valerie Solanas (1936–88). That same year Solanas shot the pop artist Andy Warhol (who had refused to produce her play *Up Your Ass*) and the art critic Mario Amaya, and was jailed for attempted murder. In the *SCUM Manifesto* Solanas argues for a communistic society inhabited solely by women:

Life in this society being, at best, an utter bore and no aspect of society being at all relevant to women, there remains to civic-minded, responsible, thrill-seeking females only to overthrow the government, eliminate the money system, institute complete automation and destroy the male sex.

It is now technically feasible to reproduce without the aid of males (or, for that matter, females) and to produce only females. We must begin immediately to do so …

**Sea and sangria.** An encapsulation of the pleasures of a holiday in Spain for the British tourist. The latter word, the name of a drink of red wine mixed with lemonade and fruit, became familiar in English only in the 1960s. A similar earlier drink was known as 'sangaree', and the origin of both is apparently in Spanish *sangría*, 'bleeding'. *See also* SUN BELT; SUN, SEA AND SAND.

**Seagull.** The nickname of the Moroccan footballer Abdeslam Ouaddou (b.1978) while at Fulham FC, from the punning line 'Ouaddou like to be beside the seaside.'

**Sealed Knot.** An organization founded in 1971 to re-enact battles of the English Civil War between Charles I and his parliamentary opponents (1642–9). The enterprise is enacted both for pleasure and for charitable purposes, and the name derives from a Royalist secret society active during the Protectorate (1654–9) and dedicated to the restoration of the Stuart line. Its modern namesake cuts more of a dash than the original.

**Sea Lion.** On 2 August 1940 Hermann Goering, head of the German LUFTWAFFE, issued a directive laying down a plan of attack in which a few massive blows from the air would destroy British air power and so open the way for an amphibious invasion, termed Operation Sea Lion (German, *Seelöwe*). Victory by RAF Fighter Command in the BATTLE OF BRITAIN blocked this possibility, however, and essentially created the conditions for Britain's survival, for the extension of the Second World War and for the eventual defeat of NAZI Germany.

**Seals.** The elite special-operations force of the US Navy. The name stands for 'Sea, Air And Land (forces)'. Such a unit was brought into being in the Second World War, but it was not called the 'Seals' until 1962. Its exploits during the VIETNAM War established its reputation for unconventional warfare.

**Sean Connery is James Bond.** A promotional device identifying an actor with his screen role, in this case for the James BOND film YOU ONLY LIVE TWICE (1967). The somewhat misleading formula was repeated with 'Paul Hogan *is* Crocodile Dundee' (1987), and is not restricted to actors. 'The Sunday Times *is* the Sunday papers' was carried regularly by the newspaper in question.

**Searchlight tattoo.** A military entertainment, carried out at night in the open air with illuminations, military exercises

and martial music. The best known is that at Edinburgh Castle, staged during the Edinburgh Festival on the Castle Esplanade, with the floodlit castle as a dramatic backdrop.

**Search me!** I've no idea! Don't ask me! The expression dates from the early years of the 20th century and is of US origin. The suggestion is that one may search the speaker for the answer but it will not be found there.

**Seaside postcards.** The collecting of picture postcards while on holiday by the sea has been a British hobby since the EDWARDIAN ERA. A particular development has been the gaudily coloured comic postcard with a caption involving a mildly ribald *double entendre*. Such cards owe much to the talents of Donald McGill, an English artist whose original name was Fraser Gould (1875–1962). Outsized women in bathing costumes paddling alongside weedy husbands are typical of his subjects, while salacious girls and cheeky children also feature. An example of the music-hall humour is a scenario in which a big-bosomed customer buying a brassiere is asked by the assistant 'What bust, Madam?' only to receive the rejoinder 'Ee luv, nothing bust, it just wore out.'

**Sea, the Sea, The.** A visionary novel (1978) by Iris Murdoch (1919–99), which won the BOOKER PRIZE for fiction. It is set in and around an isolated house by the sea to which a theatrical director, Charles Arrowby, retires in order to write his autobiography. He is beset by welcome and unwelcome people from his past. There are parallels with Shakespeare's play *The Tempest*, and always the influence of the sea and its changing moods. The title comes from the *Anabasis* of the Greek historian Xenophon (*c*.430–*c*.355 BC), recounting his epic march to bring the defeated army of Greek mercenaries from Babylon to the sea in 401 BC. It is their cry as they reach their objective. *See also* FIRST LINES OF NOVELS.

**Secondary picketing.** Picketing by strikers of the premises of a firm that trades with their employer but that is not otherwise involved in the dispute in question.

**Second banana.** A supporting comedian, the leading performer being a TOP BANANA.

**Second front.** In the Second World War, a front in NAZI-occupied Europe additional to the Russian sector of fighting, and as such a reality much desired by the Soviet Union, to disburden it of what it saw as its unfair share of the land war against Germany. Despite various schemes proposed by Winston Churchill and others, it did not begin to achieve realization until D-DAY.

**Second honeymoon.** A holiday, something like a honeymoon, that a couple take after they have been married for some years. The aim, if possible, is to 'recapture that first fine careless rapture' (Robert Browning).

**Second World War.** For the origins of this name, *see* GREAT WAR.

**Second World War operational code names.** The following is a list of the military code names of some of the most significant military operations of the Second World War.

A: the Japanese counter-offensive in June 1944 following the US capture of the Marshall Islands. The plan ended disastrously for the Japanese in the Battle of the Philippine Sea, 'the Great Marianas Turkey Shoot'.

Adlerangriff ('eagle attack'): the German air offensive against RAF bases in Britain during August–September 1940. The air battles that followed became known as the BATTLE OF BRITAIN.

Anvil: the planning stage of Operation Dragoon (*see below*).

Archery: the British commando raid on the Lofoten and other Norwegian islands in December 1941–January 1942 (*see also* Claymore *below*).

Avalanche: the first Allied landings in mainland Italy, near Salerno, on 9 September 1943.

Bagration: the major and successful Soviet offensive in June–August 1944 through Belarus and into Poland.

BARBAROSSA: the German invasion of the Soviet Union, launched on 22 June 1941.

Battleaxe: the unsuccessful British offensive in the Western Desert in June 1941.

Big Scheme: the Polish resistance plan for a rising in the summer of 1944 that resulted in Operation Burza (*see below*).

Blau I–III ('blue'): the German offensive in the Soviet Union in the summer of 1942.

Burza: the ill-fated WARSAW RISINGS of the Polish resistance in August–October 1944.

Catapult: the controversial British naval attack on the French fleet at MERS-EL-KÉBIR in Algeria on 3 July 1940, to prevent the fleet falling into German hands.

Catchpole: the US capture of Eniwetok Atoll in the Marshall Islands during February 1944.

Chariot: the 'St Nazaire raid' of 28 March 1942 by British commandos and naval forces, which succeeded in destroying a strategic dry dock.

Claymore: the successful British commando attack on the Norwegian Lofoten Islands in March 1941, the first major commando operation of the war.

Cobra: the Allied break-out from the hedgerows of Normandy in July 1944, following the D-DAY landings.

Compass: the successful British and Commonwealth offensive in December 1940–February 1941 against the Italians in Egypt and Libya, which prompted the arrival of German forces in North Africa.

Coronet: the planned follow-up to Operation Olympic (*see below*), aimed at ending all Japanese resistance in the home islands.

Crusader: the British and Commonwealth offensive in the Western Desert in November 1941–January 1942. It achieved limited success.

Demon: the British withdrawal from Greece in April 1941.

Dragoon: the Allied invasion of southern France in August 1944. Planning for the operation was under the code name Anvil.

Dynamo: the British withdrawal from DUNKIRK and the adjacent coast in May–June 1940.

Eiche ('oak'): the daring raid by German commandos in September 1943 to rescue Mussolini (*see* DUCE) from imprisonment on the Gran Sasso in the high Apennines.

Elkton: the overall code name for Allied operations in the southwest Pacific in 1943–4, involving offensives in the Bismarck Archipelago, the Solomon Islands and New Guinea.

Extended Capital: the major and successful British offensive in central Burma in November 1944–March 1945.

Fischreiher ('heron'): the strategically disastrous German offensive to capture STALINGRAD, launched in July 1942.

Flintlock: the US capture of the southern Marshall Islands in January–February 1944.

Forager: the US capture of the Marianas Islands in June–August 1944, bringing the Japanese home islands within range of Allied bombers.

Freshman: the British commando raid in November 1942 that succeeded in destroying a crucial German HEAVY WATER plant in Norway.

Frühlingserwachen ('spring awakening'): the optimistically chosen code name for the last German offensive on the Eastern Front in March 1945. It failed to stem the Soviet advance.

Frühlingswind ('spring breeze'): the German offensive in North Africa in February 1943. Although temporarily successful, in the end it failed to prevent AXIS forces from being trapped between Allied armies advancing from both east and west.

Georg: the German siege of Leningrad (St Petersburg), which began in September 1941 and was not ended until January 1944.

Granite: the US Admiral Chester Nimitz's 1944 strategic plan for defeating Japan by cutting its empire in two. It was abandoned in favour of General Douglas MacArthur's plan for a direct offensive towards the Japanese home islands.

Grapefruit: the final, successful Allied offensive in northern Italy in April–May 1945.

Herbstnebel ('autumn mist'): the German offensive in the Ardennes in December 1944–February 1945, resulting in the BATTLE OF THE BULGE.

Himmler: the German operation involving the staging of a hoaxed Polish raid against a German radio station, providing the immediate pretext for the German invasion of Poland on 31 August 1939.

Husky: the Allied invasion of Sicily on 9 July 1943.

Iceberg: the US invasion of Okinawa, launched on 1 April 1945. However, it was not until 21 June that organized resistance ended.

Impact: the British and Commonwealth offensive across Lake Comacchio in northern Italy in April 1945.

Ironclad: the British capture of the port of Diego Suarez in the VICHY-held island of Madagascar in May 1942 to prevent the port from falling into Japanese hands. The whole island was under Allied control by November.

Jubilee: the controversial Canadian and British raid on Dieppe in August 1942, carried out as an experiment in landing techniques. The raid resulted in two-thirds of the attackers being killed, wounded or taken prisoner.

Judgement: the attack by 21 Fleet Air Arm Fairey Swordfish on the Italian naval base at Taranto on 11 November 1940. It was the world's first carrier-based air attack and resulted in three Italian battleships being disabled.

Ketsu ('excellence'): the Japanese plan for defending the home islands from the expected US assault.

Kikushi ('floating chrysanthemum'): the Japanese kamikaze campaign against US naval forces off Okinawa in April–May 1945.

King II: the US invasion of Leyte Island in October–December 1944, the first step in the reconquest of the Philippines.

Koltso ('ring'): the successful Soviet operation to wipe out the encircled German army in STALINGRAD in January–February 1943.

Kugelblitz ('ball lightning'): the temporarily successful German campaign against the Yugoslav partisans in December 1943–February 1944.

Lightfoot and Supercharge: the two phases of the British and Commonwealth offensive during the Second Battle of El ALAMEIN in October–November 1942.

Loincloth: the first CHINDITS expedition behind Japanese lines in Burma, February–April 1943.

Love III: the US recapture of Mindanao in the Philippines, December 1944–January 1945.

Lumberjack: the Allied offensive towards the Rhine in March 1945, which resulted in the establishment of a bridgehead on the far side at Remagen.

Madison: the Allied offensive in eastern France in November–December 1944, which took US forces to the SIEGFRIED LINE.

Margarethe I: the German occupation of Hungary on 9 March 1944.

Margarethe II: the planned German occupation of Romania should it go over to the Allied side. When it did, in August 1944, it was too late, as Soviet forces were sweeping through the country.

Marita: the German conquest of Yugoslavia and Greece in April 1941.

Market Garden: the unsuccessful Allied campaign at Arnhem in September 1944, aimed at securing a bridgehead over the lower Rhine. The airborne component was Operation Market, while the advance by ground forces to relieve the airborne forces was called Operation Garden. It was a BRIDGE TOO FAR.

Menace: the unsuccessful attempt by the British and Free French to capture the VICHY-held naval base at Dakar in French West Africa, August–September 1940.

Merkur ('Mercury'): the German conquest of Crete in May 1941, including a notable early use of airborne troops, perhaps the reason the operation was named after the winged messenger of the gods.

MI: the Japanese naval offensive against the US base at Midway Island that led to the Battle of Midway (May–June 1942), the turning point in the war in the Pacific.

Micki Maus ('Mickey Mouse'): the German abduction of the regent of Hungary, Admiral Horthy, on 15 October 1944, after he went over to the Allies.

Mike I–VII: the US recapture of Luzon in the Philippines, January–April 1945.

Millennium: the first RAF THOUSAND-BOMBER RAIDS, against Cologne, on 30 May 1942.

Mincemeat: the Allied plan to deceive the Germans that the invasion of southern Europe would take place in Sardinia and Greece, rather than in Sicily (Operation Husky; *see above*). The plan, carried out in May 1943, involved planting phoney secret documents on the body of a drowned man, and was the subject of the classic film *The Man Who Never Was* (1955).

MO: the Japanese plan to capture Tulagi in the Solomon Islands, Port Moresby in New Guinea and the Louisiade Islands. The operation was thwarted at the Battle of the Coral Sea in May 1942.

Montclair: the operation in which US forces retook Mindanao and the Visayas (Panay, Cebu, Negros and Bohol) in the Philippines and Australian forces retook Borneo, in April–July 1945.

Morgenluft ('morning air'): the German operation in Tunisia in February 1943, to complement Operation Frühlingswind (*see above*).

Morgenrote ('dawn'): the German counter-offensive against the Allied landings at Anzio in February 1944.

Neptune: the code name for all the naval operations within Operation OVERLORD, the Allied invasion of Normandy in June 1944.

Noball: the Allied air operations against V-1 launching sites in northwest Europe in 1944.

Nordwind ('north wind'): the fruitless German counter-offensive in Alsace in December 1944–January 1945.

Oboe I–III: the three phases of the Australian recapture of Borneo (part of Operation Montclair; *see above*) in May–July 1945. (*see* HIROSHIMA).

Ochsenkopf ('ox head'): the ineffective German offensive in North Africa in February–March 1943.

Olive: successful Allied assault in August–September 1944 on the GOTHIC LINE, the line of German defences stretching across Italy north of Florence.

Olympic: the plan for the Allied invasion of the Japanese home islands, due to start on 1 November 1945 but abandoned following the dropping of the atomic bombs in August 1945 (*see* HIROSHIMA).

Orkan: the successful German operation to take the Crimea in May–July 1942.

OVERLORD: the Allied invasion of northwest Europe via the Normandy beaches in June 1944.

Pedestal: perhaps the best known of several heroic convoys to Malta. Pedestal took place in August 1942 and brought the first significant supplies to get through that year. Perhaps its most important delivery was the 10,000 tonnes of oil on board the tanker *Ohio*. *See also* GEORGE CROSS ISLAND.

Persecution: the US landings in northern New Guinea in April 1944, which, in combination with the Australian advance up the coast, succeeded in encircling the Japanese forces on the island.

Plans X, Y and Z: the Allied plans for the recapture of three main sectors of Burma, hatched in 1943 but not carried out until 1944–5.

Plunder: the massive British offensive across the Rhine north of the Ruhr in March 1945 (*see also* Varsity *below*).

Pointblank: the overall code name for the strategy of bombing German military, economic, industrial and civilian targets after January 1943.

Postern: the US-Australian attack on the Huon peninsula of New Guinea in September 1943–April 1944.

Princeton: the overall US strategic plan for the recapture of parts of the Philippines, Borneo and Indonesia in 1943–4.

Providence: the operation in which the Allies recaptured part of the northern coast of Papua in November 1942–January 1944.

Pugilist-Gallop: the British advance that broke through the German Mareth Line in Tunisia in March 1943.

Queen: the Allied offensive from eastern Belgium towards the Rhine across the plain of the River Ruhr. Launched in November 1944, the advance ground to a standstill in December.

Quick Anger: the Canadian offensive through the Netherlands and into Germany in April 1945.

R: the capture by the Japanese of the strategically important Australian base at Rabaul in New Britain, along with Kavieng in New Ireland, in January 1942.

Rainbow: the Chinese offensive through southern China into Burma in May–August 1944.

Raincoat: the only partially successful Allied offensive towards the GUSTAV LINE and the Anzio beach-head in southern Italy in December 1943.

Raubtier ('beast of prey'): the successful German counter-offensive between Novgorod and Leningrad (St Petersburg) in March 1942.

Regenbogen ('rainbow'): the German naval operation against Arctic convoys heading for the Soviet Union, in which the battle cruiser *Scharnhorst* was sunk by the Royal Navy on 31 December 1943.

Reno: the strategic plan for US forces in the Pacific in 1942–4, involving advances through the Bismarck Archipelago, New Guinea and eastern Indonesia, culminating in the invasion of the Philippines.

Rheinübung ('Rhine exercise'): the commerce-raiding sortie into the Atlantic by the German battleship BISMARCK and the heavy cruiser *Prinz Eugen* in May 1941, during which the *Bismarck* was sunk by the Royal Navy.

RI: the Japanese landings in Papua in July 1942 before the offensive against Port Moresby.

Rösselsprung ('knight's move'): the German attack by air and sea in July 1942 on the Arctic convoy PQ17, resulting in only 13 of the 34 Allied ships reaching northern Russia.

Rot ('red'): the second part of the German conquest of France in June 1940 (part one being entitled Tiger; *see below*).

Rupert: the seizure by British and French forces of the strategic port of Narvik in northern Norway in May 1940. However, the crisis in France led to the Allied withdrawal in June.

Saturn: the major Soviet offensive in southern Russia, including the STALINGRAD front, in December 1942.

Schwarz ('black'): the German plan for the military take-over of Italy in the event of Italian capitulation. It was duly put into effect, with some modification, in 1943.

Scipio: the successful British and Commonwealth offensive in southern Tunisia in April 1943. The name was particularly appropriate, as it was in Tunisia that the Roman general Scipio Africanus won his decisive victory over the Carthaginians, at Zama in 202 BC.

SEA LION (German 'Seelöwe'): the German plan for the invasion of Britain in 1940.

Setting Sun: the US bombing campaign against Japan in 1944. The name played on Japan as 'the land of the rising sun', as depicted on its wartime flag.

Shingle: the Allied landings at Anzio in central Italy in January 1944, which failed in their strategic objective.

Sho: the Japanese defensive strategy from mid-1944, including Sho-1 for the Philippines, Sho-2 for Taiwan and the Ryukyu Islands, Sho-3 for Kyushu and Honshu and Sho-4 for the Kurile Islands and Hokkaido.

Sonnenblume ('sunflower'): the commitment of German troops to North Africa in January–February 1941 following the failures of the Italians in the Western Desert.

Source: the attack by British midget submarines on the *Tirpitz* in northern Norway on 22 September 1943, which succeeded in seriously damaging the German battleship.

Star: the major Soviet offensive in February–March 1943 that succeeded in taking Kharkov only to lose it again to the Germans.

Steinbock ('ibex'): the German bombing campaign in January–May 1944 against London and various British ports, also known as the 'baby BLITZ'.

Strike: the final Allied offensive against AXIS forces in Tunisia in May 1943, ending the campaign in North Africa.

Sunrise: the secret negotiations between the Allies and the SS commander in Italy leading to the surrender of German forces there on 2 May 1945.

Supercharge: *see* Lightfoot *above*.

Taifun ('typhoon'): the German offensive against Moscow, which began on 2 November 1941 and was abandoned on 5 December.

Talon: the British and Indian offensive in central Burma in early 1945.

Thunderclap: the Allied strategic plan to bring about a German surrender by the all-out bombing of Berlin, Chemnitz, Leipzig, Dresden and other German cities in 1945. Only DRESDEN had been completely destroyed by the time of the German surrender.

Thursday: the second CHINDITS expedition behind Japanese lines in Burma, March–August 1944.

Tidal Wave: the costly and ineffective attack on the Ploeşti oilfields in Romania by US bombers on 1 August 1943.

Tiger: the first part of the German conquest of France in June 1940. It struck through the MAGINOT LINE from the north and was complemented by Operation Bär ('Bear') through Alsace further south to make a pincer movement. It was followed by Operation Rot (*see above*).

Toenails: the US invasion of the central Solomon Islands in June–October 1943.

Torch: the Allied landings in French North Africa on 8 November 1942.

U: the attempted Japanese invasion of India via Imphal and Kohima in Assam in March–June 1944.

Undertone: the US offensive south of the Mosel as part of the drive to the Rhine in March 1945.

Uranus: the Soviet offensive that trapped the German 6th Army in STALINGRAD in November 1942.

Varsity: the airborne operation to cross the Rhine on 24 March 1945, in conjuction with the ground-based Operation Plunder (*see above*).

Veritable: the British and Canadian offensive between the Maas and the Rhine in February 1945.

Vert ('green'): the disruption of rail traffic by French railway workers at the time of the D-DAY landings.

Vesuvius: the recapture of Corsica by Free French forces in September–October 1943.

Victor I–V: the US recapture of the southern and central Philippines in February–July 1945.

Violet: the disruption of communications by French telephone workers at the time of the D-DAY landings.

Watchtower: the US operation to recapture the southeastern Solomon Islands, including Guadalcanal, in August 1942. The battle for Guadalcanal did not end till February 1943.

Weiss ('white'): the German invasion and conquest of Poland in September–October 1939.

Weserübung ('Weser exercise'): the German invasion and conquest of Denmark and Norway in April–June 1940.

Wintergewitter ('winter storm'): the failed German attempt to relieve STALINGRAD in December 1942.

Z: the Japanese attack on PEARL HARBOR on 7 December 1941.

Zitadelle ('citadel'): the German offensive in the Soviet Union that ended in devastating defeat at the Battle of Kursk in July 1943.

**Secret Agent, The.** A novel by Joseph Conrad (1857–1924), published in 1907. The setting is London, and the 'secret agent' is Verloc, an *agent provocateur* for a foreign power anxious to discredit anarchist groups, and also an informer for the Home Office. Stevie, the younger brother of Verloc's wife, ends up being blown up while carrying a bomb. This part of the plot was based on an incident that took place on 18 February 1894, when Marcel Boudin, an anarchist, blew himself up in error near Greenwich Observatory.

**Secret Garden, The.** A much-loved children's novel (1911) by Frances Hodgson Burnett (1849–1924). It charts the gradual transformation of the character of Mary Lennox, the daughter of a British civil servant in India, who is sent to Misselthwaite Manor, the Yorkshire home of her reclusive uncle. Mary discovers a secret garden, neglected for ten years, and starts gardening there. She also effects a miraculous cure of Colin, her uncle's invalid-hypochondriac son, and their friendship blossoms as the garden itself starts to bloom. The fictional garden is based on the Rose Garden at Maytham Hall in Kent, where Burnett spent the years 1898–1907. Film versions of the story appeared in 1949 and (starring Maggie Smith) in 1993.

**Secret Seven, The.** The central characters in 15 novels by Enid Blyton (1897–1968), beginning with *The Secret Seven* (1949). The novels recount the adventures of seven children and their dog, Scamper, and are aimed at a younger age group than the books about the FAMOUS FIVE.

**Secret weapon.** A weapon officially classified as secret, especially one with the power to end a conflict by a decisive strike. The term emerged in the 1930s during the build-up to the Second World War, during which Winston Churchill described the magnetic mine as Germany's 'secret weapon'. Figuratively the term can allude to any person or thing potentially available to achieve a result.

Women are the secret weapon for [political] recovery.
*Independent on Sunday*, headline (28 November 1999)

**Section 28.** A law (known before its official enactment as 'Clause 28') banning the 'promotion' of homosexuality by British local authorities, and hence in British schools, libraries, etc. It was introduced by the Conservative government in 1988 as an amendment to its Local Government Bill following a sexual error committed by a Tory backbencher and was passed in the midst of a political storm surrounding a book, *Jenny Lives with Eric and Martin*, that the then Inner London Education Authority had decided to put into a reference library for teachers. Section 28 provoked considerable controversy, not only because it implicitly attacked gay rights but also because it threatened the sponsorship of a number of cultural activities that could be said to have some kind of homosexual content or association. In 2000 the newly devolved Scottish parliament voted to abolish it, and in 2003 it was repealed in England and Wales.

**Securicor.** The ubiquitous security services company began its career in 1935 as a small private guard business called Night Watch Services. Contracts were at first hard to come by, and at the outbreak of the Second World War it had just 12 patrol guards. After the war its luck changed following a move into industrial security and the return into the jobs market of hundreds of soldiers. It changed its name to Securicor, a contraction of Security Corps, in the early 1950s, by which time it employed nearly 200 guards. It subsequently entered the 'cash-in-transit' business, as well as parcels delivery and detective work. In 2004 Securicor merged with Group 4, another security firm.

**Securitate.** The secret police of communist Romania. The Securitate became the main support of the tyrannical rule of Nicolae Ceauşescu (1918–89), who by the 1980s had turned Romania into a police state. The downfall of Ceauşescu within a week in December 1989 resulted from a combination of popular unrest and a conspiracy by dissident party members and Securitate and army personnel. Even after Ceauşescu's execution on 25 December, however, loyalist Securitate forces continued to mount a short-lived but violent resistance, leading to many civilian and military deaths.

**Security blanket.** Something that dispels anxiety, such as an appointment diary carried on the person. The expression evolved in the 1960s from the blanket or piece of cloth held by a young child to reduce anxiety. An entirely different security blanket is an official sanction imposed on information to maintain secrecy on a particular matter.

**Securocrat.** Originally a South African term, used to denote a military or police officer with excessive and covert influence on government. Hence securocracy. The term (a conflation of 'security' and 'bureaucrat') has been taken up by Republicans in Northern Ireland to denote those members of the security establishment (the RUC and its replacement, the Police Service of Northern Ireland, together with Special Branch, MI5 and the Army) whom they see as having a vested interest in putting a brake on the peace process.

**Sedna.** When the discovery of a new planet in the Solar System was announced on 15 March 2004, precedent was modified by naming it after not a Roman deity but after a sea goddess mistakenly claimed to be Inuit. It is the most distant object in the Solar System, three times further from the Sun than PLUTO. Its planetary status is not universally accepted by astronomers. *See also* PLANET X.

**See a man about a dog.** To excuse oneself abruptly from a meeting, party or the like in order to visit the lavatory. The fiction is that one is going to place a bet on a dog in a race. The expression dates from the 1930s.

**Seeing Eye.** A US organization that provides GUIDE DOGS, corresponding to the Guide Dogs for the Blind Association in Britain. It was founded in January 1929 by Mrs Dorothy Harrison Eustis, a dog breeder. The first Seeing Eye dog was a German shepherd (Alsatian) bitch named Buddy, assigned to guide Morris Frank, a young blind man in Tennessee. *See also* HEARING DOG.

> The hearing ear, and the seeing eye, the Lord hath made even both of them.
>
> Proverbs 20:12

**See red.** To suddenly become angry. The phrase is popularly said to allude to a bull's angry reaction to a red cape waved by a matador. A more likely association is with the reddened face and heated blood of anger, as one similarly speaks of a fiery temper.

**See stars.** To see what seem to be flashes or darts of light as a result of a blow on the head.

**See things.** To experience hallucinations. The phrase is usually found in participial form, as: 'I thought I was seeing things.'

**See where someone is coming from.** To understand or appreciate their meaning or motives. The expression originated in African American slang in the 1960s.

> Clearly, as with all relationships, areas open themselves up for abuse – but I suddenly see where [actress] Patsy Kensit is coming from. And it doesn't seem quite as deep a pit as it once did.
>
> *Ms London* (27 September 1999)

**See you later, alligator.** A stock pleasantry current from the 1950s when taking one's leave. The one left conventionally replied: 'In a while, crocodile'. The popularity of the expression stemmed from a hit song performed by Bill Haley and the Comets, but 'alligator' was already a term in the 1930s for a jazz or swing fan, as someone who 'swallowed up' everything on offer.

> See you later, alligator,
> After 'while, crocodile, –
> Can't you see you're in my way, now,
> Don't you know you cramp my style?
>
> R.C. GUIDRY: 'See You Later, Alligator' (song) (1957)

**Sega.** The coin-operated computer games so named are made by the company Service Games founded around 1940 with the aim of producing and managing amusement arcade machines. The name was shortened to Sega in 1965. Business long brought in steady revenue and the company expanded into home video gaming, but it began to be adversely affected in the 1990s by competition from consoles such as PLAYSTATION. In the 21st century it moved to concentrate on software. *See also* GAME BOY.

**Seinfeld.** The US television SITCOM of this name, which ran from 1989 to 1998 (and was first shown in the UK from 1993), was based on the stage act of the stand-up comic Jerry Seinfeld (b.1955). It is essentially a series of episodes about the minutiae of daily living, as experienced by four single New Yorkers who are obsessed about such minor matters as queuing for the theatre, getting caught in traffic jams, meeting friends and the like. The quartet are Seinfeld as himself, Julia Louis-Dreyfus as the feisty Elaine Benes, Jason Alexander as the intense, nervy George Costanza and Michael Richards as the eternally optimistic Cosmo Kramer. The series came to be billed as 'the show about nothing', and its unique observational style soon won it a cult following on both sides of the Atlantic.

**Selfish gene.** In genetics, a gene that exploits the organism in which it occurs as a vehicle for its own self-perpetuation. A gene of this type was posited by the evolutionary biologist William Hamilton (1936–2000) and given its memorable name by Richard Dawkins in his book *The Selfish Gene* (1976). The theory overturned the traditional concept of the gene as a vehicle of inheritance for the organism and did much to popularize the study of sociobiology.

**Selfridges.** The London store of this name was opened on 15 March 1909 as the creation of the US entrepreneur Harry Gordon Selfridge (1858–1947), the son of the owner of a dry-goods business. The grandiose emporium on the north side of Oxford Street originally had 130 departments and a wide range of facilities for its customers, including its own library, a post office, rooms for foreign visitors, an American soda room, a department for the clergy and a 'silence room' with a notice reading 'Ladies Will Refrain From Conversation'. Miss Selfridge, providing for teenage fashions, opened as a spin-off in 1966.

**Self-starter.** Originally a term for the electric motor that started the engine of a motor vehicle, a self-starter in business jargon was later a term for a well-motivated person capable of exercising initiative. The latter sense arose in the 1960s in the vocabulary of job advertisements.

**Sellafield.** A nuclear power plant and reprocessing centre on the coast of Cumbria. It was known as Windscale until 1971, when management of the site was transferred from the UK Atomic Energy Authority to British Nuclear Fuels Ltd. Calder Hall, the world's first industrial-scale nuclear power station, was opened here in 1956. Britain's worst nuclear accident took place at Sellafield in 1957, when a fire destroyed the core of a reactor and released large amounts of radioactive iodine into the atmosphere. The activities at Sellafield continue to be controversial, provoking criticism from anti-nuclear campaigners, and from the Irish and Norwegian governments. However, the operation here is a major source of local employment.

**Sell-by date.** The date by which a perishable item, such as a food product, must be sold if it is to be consumed in a fresh or fit state. It is not the same as a use-by or best-before date, which is usually a day or two later. The expression has gained a facetious figurative sense to refer to a person who is 'getting on', so that if one is 'past one's sell-by date' one is past one's prime. *See also* BEST-BEFORE DATE.

> Once described by an over-enthusiastic newspaper as 'one of London's most eligible bachelors', Stacpoole is now grey, portly and, at 55, looking rather past his sell-by date.
> *Today* (1 September 1994)

**Sell off the family silver.** To dispose of valuable assets that, once gone, cannot be retrieved. The phrase is said to have been popularized by Sir Harold Macmillan's speech of 8 November 1985 to the Tory Reform Group attacking the Thatcher government's programme of privatization of nationalized industries, although his actual words were: 'First of all the Georgian silver goes, and then all that nice furniture that used to be in the saloon. Then the Canalettos go.'

**Sellotape.** A name sometimes used for any 'sticky tape' but one that properly belongs to the British company that first marketed it in 1937. The name is based on Cellophane, but with the initial C changed to S for purposes of trademark registration. A famous US rival is SCOTCH TAPE.

**Sell someone short.** To fail to recognize or state their true value. To sell oneself short is thus to underrate oneself, to be silent or unduly modest about one's achievements or abilities.

**Selsdon man.** A nickname given to a supposed supporter of the proto-Thatcherite (*see* THATCHERISM) policies outlined at a conference of Conservative Party leaders at the Selsdon Park Hotel near Croydon in 1970. They included support for a market economy as opposed to state intervention, rejection of compulsory wage control and a refusal to rescue industrial 'lame ducks'. The coinage is based on PILTDOWN MAN (*see under* FAKES).

**Semi-housetrained polecat.** A description of Norman Tebbit, the Conservative politician also known as the CHINGFORD SKINHEAD, by Labour politician Michael Foot in the House of Commons, 2 March 1978:

> It is not necessary that every time he rises he should give his famous imitation of a semi-housetrained polecat.

**Seminal work.** A written work that may or may not be original but that strongly influences later developments. The use of the adjective in this sense dates from the 1960s and it can equally apply to anything similarly influential, such as an article, a piece of research or even a person, as a 'seminal pianist'. The literal sense is 'sowing seed', from Latin *semen*, 'seed'.

> Though this dish has a long history in Burgundy, it was not really introduced to Britain until 1960, by Elizabeth David in her seminal work, *French Provincial Cooking*.
> *Independent on Sunday Magazine* (14 May 1995)

**Semtex.** A type of plastic explosive originally manufactured near the village of Semtín in the Czech Republic and familiar from its use by terrorists in the mid-1980s, in some cases in letter bombs. In 1991 Czechoslovakia announced that Semtex was no longer being made, but it was estimated that worldwide stocks could last for several decades.

**Senderista.** *See* SHINING PATH.

**Send her** or **it down, Hughie!** In colloquial Australian English, an appeal to the gods for rain, deployed when drought strikes in the outback or, conceivably, when rain might save Australia from defeat by England at cricket. Hughie has been Australia's mythical rain deity since at least the beginning of the 20th century, but his antecedents are mysterious (an early claim that he was an amateur meteorologist called Mr Huie is unsubstantiated). Surfers have also adopted him as a tutelary deity, and 'Send 'em up, Hughie!' is an appeal for surfable waves.

**Send someone up the wall.** *See* DRIVE SOMEONE UP THE WALL.

**Senior citizen.** A somewhat patronizing euphemism for a retired person or pensioner. The term arose in the United States in the 1930s but did not reach Britain until the 1960s. It is now commonly found in notices relating to admission charges, concessionary rates and the like. The use of 'citizen' betrays the US origin, as a word found only in formal British English.

**Senior moment.** An incident (e.g. forgetting why one has come into a particular room) humorously attributed to the effects of advancing age.

**Sensory deprivation.** A process developed by Dr John Lilly in the 1950s by which a person floats in a special isolation tank, naked, enclosed and completely cut off from all external stimuli. Without stimulation the brain eventually begins to hallucinate. Initially Lilly used the method to investigate altered states of consciousness but a later purpose was to reduce stress and tension through relaxation. Meditation can achieve the same end by mental control rather than mechanical means.

**Sensurround.** The tradename of a system of special effects which are used to enhance the physical impact of a DISASTER MOVIE or similar 'action' film. It was developed by the Universal film company in 1974 to magnify the tremor scenes in *Earthquake* (1974) by adding air vibrations to the sound track during the dubbing process. The vibrations then 'blast' the body and ears of members of the audience to create the illusion of participation in the scene on the screen. Subsequent episodes using Sensurround (a combination of 'sense' and 'surround') include a battle scene in *Midway* (1976) and a roller coaster ride in *Rollercoaster* (1977).

**Separate** or **sort out the men from the boys.** To distinguish those who are brave, mature, professional, etc., from those who are weak, immature, amateur, etc. The expression dates from the 1930s and is always used figuratively.

**Separate Tables.** A pair of plays (1954) by Terence Rattigan (1911–77) about the hidden lives of a variety of guests in a Bournemouth hotel. The plays are separately entitled *Table by the Window* and *Table Number 7*, after the tables in the dining room where the characters concerned sit. A film version (1958) starred Burt Lancaster and David Niven, who won an OSCAR for his portrayal of the ersatz hero Major Pollack. An unnecessary remake (1983) starred Alan Bates and Julie Christie.

**September Dossier, The.** An informal name for the paper entitled *Iraq's Weapons of Mass Destruction: The Assessment of the British Government*, published on 24 September 2002, some six months before US, British and other forces invaded Iraq. The prime minister Tony Blair (*see* BUSH'S POODLE) had been assuring the country for some time that his government had evidence that the Iraqi dictator Saddam Hussein presented a threat to the security of the UK via his accumulation of WEAPONS OF MASS DESTRUCTION. When the September Dossier was published critics commented that it contained little new information. Exceptions included the claim that Iraq was attempting to obtain uranium for nuclear weapons from Africa (a claim still disputed), and that, in Blair's words, Saddam Hussein's 'military planning allows for some of the WMD to be ready within 45 minutes'.

This latter claim led *The Sun* to scream 'Brits 45 Mins from Doom'. Subsequent to the war no weapons of mass destruction have been found in Iraq, let alone those capable of being launched within 45 minutes. Critics subsequently claimed that the dossier had been 'sexed-up' (dubiously made more 'sexy', i.e. persuasive, powerful). *See also* DODGY DOSSIER.

**September 11.** A somewhat fuller, though now less widely used, way of referring to the events of 9/11.

**Septic tank.** Rhyming slang (often abbreviated to simply 'septic' or, in Australia, 'seppo') for 'Yank' (i.e. an American). The usage originated in Australia in the 1960s, but soon spread to other varieties of English.

**Sequel numbers in film titles.** The practice of titling a film sequel with the name of the original followed by a number appears to have originated with *Quatermass II* (1957), a simplified version of the television series QUATERMASS. It did not become fashionable until the 1970s, however, which saw, among others, *French Connection II* (1975) following *The* FRENCH CONNECTION (1971) and *Jaws 2* (1978) following JAWS (1975), in turn followed by *Jaws 3-D* (1983). Some spawnings are prolific, as with ROCKY (1976), which produced *Rocky II* (1979), *Rocky III* (1982), *Rocky IV* (1985) and *Rocky V* (1990), although none of these was up to the standard of the original. A more recent example has been the *Scream* series (*see* SLASHER MOVIE). The procedure was nicely guyed by *Naked Gun 2½: The Smell of Fear* (1991) and *Naked Gun 33⅓: The Final Insult* (1994) in the wake of *The Naked Gun: From the Files of Police Squad* (1988). *See also The* MADNESS OF GEORGE III; SLASHER MOVIE.

**Sergeant Pepper's Lonely Hearts Club Band.** The title (and title track) of a celebrated BEATLES album, one of the most fêted in the history of popular music, which was released in June 1967. The name 'Sergeant Pepper's Lonely Hearts Club Band' (a mythical band that forms a kind of alter ego for The Beatles), was influenced by the often vaudeville-tinged names of contemporary US West Coast groups. The album's 13 tracks include 'LUCY IN THE SKY WITH DIAMONDS', 'WITH A LITTLE HELP FROM MY FRIENDS', 'When I'm Sixty-Four', 'LOVELY RITA' and 'DAY IN THE LIFE'. The title song, credited to John Lennon and Paul McCartney, combines a 'big band' sound with thunderous electric guitar textures that were to be an influence on the development of HEAVY METAL music.

The album is a milestone in the history of 20th-century popular music and a seminal popular cultural document of the SWINGING SIXTIES. It was the first album to have a gatefold sleeve and to offer a set of printed lyrics, and it is also sometimes described as the first CONCEPT ALBUM.

The much-imitated cover of the album was designed by the pop artist Peter Blake (*see* RURALISM). It focuses on period fashion, and features an array of celebrities past and present (not all of them recognizable) including Mae West, W.C. Fields, Edgar Allan Poe (*see also* 'I AM THE WALRUS'), Sir Robert Peel, Stuart Sutcliffe (the original FIFTH BEATLE), Marilyn MONROE, Dr David Livingstone, LAWRENCE OF ARABIA and Diana Dors. The cover includes a number of waxworks lent by Madame Tussaud's museum in London. *See also* SUMMER OF LOVE.

> A decisive moment in the history of Western Civilization.
> KENNETH TYNAN: quoted in Howard Elson, *McCartney* (1986)

**Serialism.** A technique of musical MODERNISM, in which the traditional rules of melody, harmony and rhythm are replaced by a structural 'series' of notes that dictate the development of a piece. The series or 'tone row' consists of the 12 notes of the chromatic scale arranged in a fixed order and used by the composer to generate melodies and harmonies. The first fully realized works of serialism were composed by Arnold Schoenberg (1874–1951) in 1923. The technique is also known as the 12-tone or 12-note system. The melodic strangeness of music composed in this vein can make for uncomfortable listening, but serialism nonetheless influenced most 20th-century composers.

**Serial killer.** A term arising in the 1970s for what until then had been known as a mass murderer (or multiple murderer). It implies that the murderer used a similar weapon or method for killing each of his individual victims, and was prompted by crimes of this type in the 1960s and early 1970s. The term itself is said to have been coined at the FBI's behavioural unit at Quantico, Virginia. *See also* DR DEATH.

**Serious.** Meaningful or important; not trivial or ephemeral. A BUZZWORD of the 1990s to denote someone or something that runs counter to the hedonistic superficiality and self-centredness of the decade, and which is precisely what it claims to be, such as a 'serious' boyfriend or a 'serious' hobby.

**Serjeant Musgrave's Dance.** A play (1959) by John Arden (b.1930) about a group of soldiers who arrive in a mining town in northern England apparently on a recruiting drive, but who are subsequently revealed to be deserters traumatized by their involvement in an atrocity while on service overseas. Serjeant Musgrave, the leader of the soldiers, dances a wild dance in front of the skeleton of a former comrade before threatening to kill 25 people of the town when they fail to rally to his cause. Following Musgrave's arrest, the miners join in their own celebratory dance. The play shows the influence of the EPIC THEATRE of Bertolt Brecht.

**Servant problem.** A fly in the golden ointment of the EDWARDIAN ERA, caused by the increasing number of people unwilling to enter domestic service. The problem was subsequently exacerbated by the First World War, after which those who had been in service, or who at one time might have entered it, saw the alternatives available and sought employment elsewhere.

**Set alarm bells ringing.** To alert to a problem or danger. The bells in question are presumably those set off by a fire or a break-in.

> The decision early this summer to cut the price from £1.5m to £750,000, however, sent [*sic*] alarm bells ringing through the business. Is English wine facing a crisis?
> *Independent on Sunday* (14 August 1994)

**SETI.** An acronym for Search for Extraterrestrial Intelligence, a project that began in 1960 with Project Ozma, in which a giant radio telescope at Green Bank, West Virginia, was directed at two nearby stars, Epsilon Eridani and Tau Ceti. No meaningful signals were detected. In 1967 the astronomers Jocelyn Bell and Antony Hewish of Cambridge University were astonished when their instruments picked up extremely regular pulses of radio waves. They initially thought that these could be signals from an alien civilization, and they dubbed the source LGM-1 (for LITTLE GREEN MEN). However, it was soon realized that these pulses came from rotating neutron stars, known as pulsars. The search for extraterrestrial intelligence has continued, and the vast quantity of signals received by radio telescopes is broken up and distributed to thousands of volunteers round the world, who use spare computing capacity to analyse the data. So far, nothing more than bursts of radiation from distant stars and the background echo of the Big Bang have been detected. *See also* ALIENS.

**Set one's sights on something.** To aim at achieving it. The sights are those of a gun or rifle through which one looks when aiming.

**Set one's watch by someone.** To note their unfailing punctuality. The expression may be approbatory, in admiration of such correctness and orderliness, or derisory, in contempt of such calculated and possibly unfeeling lack of flexibility.

> 'Where's Daddy?' Ben asked, at seven o'clock. 'He said he'd be back at six-thirty. He's always punctual. I set my watch by him.' He didn't, of course, but he liked the ring of the phrase.
> FAY WELDON: *The Heart of the Country* (1987)

**Set someone up.** To lead them on in order to cheat or incriminate them; to frame them. Hence a set-up as a scheme or trick to incriminate or deceive someone.

**Seuss, Dr.** The pseudonym of the US writer and illustrator Theodor Seuss Geisel (1904–91), a prolific and successful author of children's picture books, such as *The Cat in the Hat* (1947), aimed at the early reading market. Geisel invented the doctorate for himself but his alma mater, Dartmouth College, conferred an authentic doctorate on him in 1955.

**Seven Dwarfs.** The dwarfs who try to protect Snow White in the Walt Disney film *Snow White and the Seven Dwarfs* (1937). They whistle while they work, and individually they are Happy, Sleepy, Doc, Bashful, Sneezy, Grumpy and Dopey.

**7:84.** A radical touring theatre company founded in 1971 by the left-wing British playwright John McGrath (1935–2002). The name reflects the statistic published in *The Economist* in 1966, that 7 per cent of the population of the UK owned 84 per cent of the wealth. In 1973 it split into Scottish and English companies.

**Seven Samurai, The.** *See The* MAGNIFICENT SEVEN.

**Seven-session slide.** A stock market tongue-twisting term for a fall in the value of leading company shares on seven consecutive trading days, regarded as a possible portent of further collapse.

**7/7.** The designation given by the press to the London bombings of 7 July 2005, on the model of 9/11. During the morning rush hour, four young British-born Islamist suicide bombers detonated their explosives on three London Underground trains and a bus, killing 52 people (plus the perpetrators) and injuring 700. The bombings, in which AL-QAIDA claimed to have had a hand, came the day after the announcement that London was to host the 2012 Olympics. Two weeks later, on 21 July, four more Islamist terrorists attempted a repeat attack on London's transport system (three Underground trains and a bus), but, although the detonators went off, the main devices failed to explode. The perpetrators fled, but were later arrested. The following day armed police followed a suspected suicide bomber into Stockwell Underground station and shot him dead; it later transpired that the victim was an entirely innocent Brazilian electrician, Jean Charles de Menezes.

**Seven Sisters.** The alliterative term has long been used for a grouping of seven things or people. In the 20th century it was notably applied to the seven international oil companies (Exxon, Mobil, Gulf, Standard Oil of California, Texaco, British Petroleum and Royal Dutch Shell) that had a dominant influence on the production and marketing of petroleum in the 1960s, and to the long-established group of women's colleges (Barnard, Bryn Mawr, Mount Holyoke, Radcliffe, Smith, Vassar and Wellesley) regarded as being the most prestigious in the United States. *See also* IVY LEAGUE.

**Seventh art.** The art of the cinema. The phrase was coined in 1916 by the Italian poet and film critic Ricciotto Canudo (1879–1923).

**Seventh Seal, The.** A highly regarded film (1957) directed by the Swedish director Ingmar Bergman (b.1918). A vision of a medieval land ravaged by the Black Death, the film impressed and mystified audiences around the world. The title refers to a verse that appears in the Bible:

> And when he had opened the seventh seal, there was silence in heaven about the space of half an hour
>
> Revelation 8:1

**Seven-year itch.** A tendency towards infidelity, said to set in after about seven years of marriage. The expression was popularized by George Axelrod's comedy of this name (1952), made into a film (1955), in which a married man has a fling with the girl upstairs.

**Severed Head, A.** A novel (1961) by Iris Murdoch (1919–99). In spite of its macabre title and solemn themes, which include adultery, incest, castration, violence and suicide, this is also a comedy about valuing relationships. The narrator is told by Honor Klein, with whom he is in love: 'I am a severed head such as primitive tribes and old alchemists used to use, anointing it with oil and putting a morsel of gold upon its tongue to make it utter prophecies.' A stage version of the novel by J.B. Priestley, written in collaboration with Murdoch, was produced in 1963, and an unduly boisterous film version, written by Frederic Raphael and directed by Dick Clement, followed in 1970.

**Sew something up.** To bring it to a satisfactory conclusion; to gain exclusive control over it. In both cases the image is of completing a garment or other item of needlework or embroidery.

**'Sex and Drugs and Rock and Roll'.** An encapsulation of the late SWINGING SIXTIES and early 1970s in a song title of 1977 by the British rock musician Ian Dury (1942–2000).

**Sex and shopping.** A type of popular fiction in which the characters enjoy the pleasure of fashionable consumer goods and frequent explicit sexual encounters. A more forthright synonym is SHOPPING AND FUCKING. *See also* BONKBUSTER.

This trivial sex-and-shopping confection flaunts superior pretensions on every page. The sex, of which there is a lot, comes gift-wrapped in cultural allusions ... But more often it is a matter of brandnames.

*Sunday Times*: review of Jonathan Keates, *Smile Please* (20 February 2000)

*See also* PRODUCT PLACEMENT.

**Sex and the City.** A US television comedy (1998–2004), based on the book of the same name by Candace Bushnell, which in turn was based on her column in the *New York Observer*. The show concentrated on the volatile love lives of four best friends – the show's narrator Carrie Bradshaw (a journalist), the sexually flamboyant female rake Samantha Jones, the domestically aspirant and relatively shy Charlotte York, and the spiky, semi-rebellious Miranda Hobbes. They were played respectively by Sarah Jessica Parker, Kim Cattrall, Kristin Davis and Cynthia Nixon. Set firmly at the affluently modish end of New York City's social scale, the stylish show fed, and was fed by, a myriad of trends (where to eat, what to drink, what to wear) – figuring largely as PRODUCT PLACEMENT – and became cult viewing for TWENTY-SOMETHING and THIRTY-SOMETHING girls who saw that the single life (so long as there was enough money) could be fun. Disarmingly frank for US television, the show broke boundaries, and its success lay in the fact that so many women watching could relate to at least one of the characters – and even think it was all right to spend all their salary on a pair of shoes. *See also* DESPERATE HOUSEWIVES; MODELIZER; MR BIG.

**Sex and the Single Girl.** A feminist study (1962) by Helen Gurley Brown (b.1922). She was brought up to believe that: 'I would have to make do on whatever brains I had, because I was told I would never be pretty enough to get a rich husband and succeed that way.' The book was written after her marriage to a film producer when she was 36: 'I knew I wanted to write a book about sex being okay for single women.' In 1965 she was appointed editor-in-chief of *Cosmopolitan*, a popular magazine appealing to career women and those looking for personal emancipation. She held the post until 1996, when she retired, at the age of 73. On the eve of her 78th birthday she was photographed lying on a sofa with a cushion embroidered with the legend: 'Good girls go to heaven, bad girls go everywhere.'

**Sex bomb.** An 'explosively' attractive person (usually a woman). The expression dates from the 1960s. At the turn of the 21st century the singer Tom Jones (since 2006 Sir Tom) had a hit with a song called 'Sex Bomb', accompanied by his trademark thrusting and gyrating stage movements:

Sex bomb, sex bomb, you're a sex bomb,
You can give it to me when I need to come along.

*See also* BIKINI; BLONDE BOMBSHELL.

**Sexed-up.** *See* SEPTEMBER DOSSIER.

**Sex kitten.** A young woman who asserts her sex appeal. The appellation came to be particularly associated with the film actress Brigitte Bardot (b.1934), who established her reputation as an international sex symbol by posing and pouting in sun-tanned nudity in *Et Dieu créa la femme* (*And God Created Woman*) (1956). *See also* Camille JAVAL.

**Sex, Lies, and Videotape.** A film (1989) written and directed by Steven Soderbergh about an impotent film-maker who becomes emotionally involved in the marital discord that has developed between an old college friend and his wife. The catalyst for trouble is his collection of videotapes he has made of his interviews with women about their sex lives. Critical acclaim at the Cannes film festival was matched by commercial success, which was much promoted by the prurient interest evoked by its title (although relatively little sex is actually portrayed on screen). The film starred James Spader and Andie MacDowell.

**Sex object.** A person considered solely in terms of their sexual attractiveness, with any other personal attributes ignored. The expression originated in the terminology of psychology in the early years of the 20th century (it is first recorded in 1911), but it entered the public domain in the 1960s as feminists sought to draw attention to the objectification and depersonalization of women in imagery (for example, in advertising) that concentrates on their physical attractions.

It's a sex object if you're pretty
and no love
or love and no sex if you're fat.

NIKKI GIOVANNI: 'Woman Poem' (1970)

**Sex on legs.** A colloquialism for a sexually attractive person, the latter part of the phrase denoting that they are 'walking sex', i.e. personify it wherever they go, just as a 'walking dictionary' is a person with an impressive store of words or a 'walking encyclopaedia' is one with a mine of facts. There is probably also an implicit allusion to the location of the sex organs themselves. The term is more often used by women of men than the converse.

The concert was out of this world. I come every time he [popular singer Barry Manilow] comes here. He is brilliant. I am a devoted fan ... He is sex on legs.

*heat* (20–26 January 2000)

I even like watching toddler telly, especially *Come Outside* with the gorgeous Auntie Mabel, and *Step Inside* with sex-on-legs Mr Mopple/Chris from Cbeebies.

JO BRAND: in *Radio Times* (3 September 2005)

*See also* ART ON LEGS.

**Sex something up.** To make something more sexy or, metaphorically, more exciting, interesting or trendy. The latter usage came into prominence in the early 21st century with allegations that official reports on Iraq's military capability were manipulated to make them more sensational (*see also* DODGY DOSSIER).

Bush denies sexing up Iraq brief.

www.theaustralian.news.au (12 November 2005)

Sexing up Canadian ethnic identity. Seven Canadian authors and poets will take Taipei by storm next week ... They'll be 'projecting Canadian excellence, values, and a Canada that is "intellectually sexy".'

www.taipeitimes.com (11 November 2005)

**Sex-starved boa constrictor.** A description of Margaret Thatcher (the IRON LADY) by the Labour politician Tony Banks (1943–2006):

She behaves with all the sensitivity of a sex-starved boa constrictor.

Quoted in *The Independent* (October 1997)

**Sexton Blake.** *See* Sexton BLAKE.

**Sexual politics.** The principles determining the relationship of the sexes and the role of gender in society, especially with regard to feminism, gay rights, sexual discrimination and the like. The term originated as the title of a classic study (1970) by the US feminist Kate Millett.

**Sez you.** That's what you say (but I don't believe it or think much of it). The phrase and spelling are of US origin.

**Shabby chic.** A type of stylishness derived through being old and worn. The term alludes chiefly to dress but can also apply to anything untidy or neglected or to an object such as a dilapidated building or run-down residential area. The style came into vogue in the late 20th century, partly in reaction to the smart and 'trendy' fashions of earlier years. *See also* HEROIN CHIC; RADICAL CHIC.

**Shack up with someone.** To make one's home or cohabit with them, as if sharing a shack.

**Shadow cabinet.** A group of members of an opposition party nominated as counterparts of the governing cabinet. The expression dates from the beginning of the 20th century but was not widely in use until after the Second World War, by which time 'shadow' had also come to apply to an individual counterpart, as the 'shadow chancellor' or 'shadow transport minister'.

**Shagger Norris.** A nickname of the Conservative politician Steven Norris (b.1945), secretary of state for transport in John Major's government, after it was revealed that he maintained several mistresses as well as a wife. This was at the time of Major's ill-fated BACK TO BASICS campaign. Norris was subsequently defeated by Ken Livingstone (RED KEN) twice (2000 and 2004) in his attempt to become mayor of London.

**Shaggy dog story.** A supposedly funny story told laboriously and at great length with an unexpected twist at the end. It is usually more amusing to the teller than the hearer and is so called from the shaggy dog that featured in many stories of this genre in the 1940s. The following classic shaggy dog story is recounted by Eric Partridge:

Travelling by train to London from one of its outer dormitories, a businessman got into a compartment and was amazed to see a middle-aged passenger playing chess with a handsome Newfoundland. The players moved the pieces swiftly and surely. Just before the train pulled in at the London terminus, the game ended, with the dog victorious. 'That's an extraordinary dog, beating you like that – and obviously you're pretty good yourself.' – 'Oh, I don't think he's so hot; I beat him in the two games before that.'

ERIC PARTRIDGE: *A Charm of Words*, 'The Shaggy Dog' (1960)

**Shaken not stirred.** How James BOND likes his vodka martinis; he himself is rarely shaken, and only stirred by the likes of Pussy Galore. The phrase first appears in the following passage:

The waiter brought the Martinis, shaken and not stirred, as Bond had stipulated.

IAN FLEMING: *Diamonds are Forever* (1956)

**Shanghai grip.** A sexual technique, allegedly mastered by the American divorcée Wallis Simpson, that 'makes a matchstick feel like a cigar'. It is said that this is what endeared her to the poorly endowed Edward VIII, a state of affairs that culminated in the ABDICATION CRISIS.

**Shangri La.** A fictional Buddhist lama paradise hidden somewhere in the Himalaya Mountains, described in James Hilton's novel *Lost Horizon* (1933). In 1942 the name was adopted as a code name for the US aircraft carrier *Hornet*, from which the great air raid on Tokyo was launched on 18 April. In 1945 it was further applied by President Franklin D. Roosevelt to CAMP DAVID in order to avoid identifying its location. The name is now used similarly for any imagined earthly 'paradise' or utopia.

*Shangri* is an invented name, but *la* is the Tibetan word for a mountain pass. In real geographical terms the Indian state of Sikkim, between Nepal, Tibet and Bhutan, has been so dubbed and when in 1963, before its annexation by India, Palden Thondup Namgyal, the crown prince, announced his marriage to Hope Cooke, a 23-year-old American debutante, the match was described in the foreign press as 'The Fairy-Tale Wedding in Shangri-La'.

**Shankill Butchers.** The grimly appropriate name given to a Loyalist gang responsible for a series of grisly sectarian murders of Catholics in the SHANKILL ROAD area of West Belfast at the height of the TROUBLES in the mid-1970s. In 1979 11 members of the gang were given life sentences for the murders by a Belfast court. The gang was led by 'Lenny' Murphy, a renegade member of the ULSTER VOLUNTEER FORCE. He was shot dead outside his home in 1983, probably by the Provisional IRA. The gang's activities were meticulously chronicled by Martin Dillon in his book *The Shankill Butchers* (1990). *Resurrection Man* (1995), a novel by Eoin McNamee, was based on Murphy's murderous exploits, and a film version of the novel, directed by Marc Evans and starring Stuart Townsend, was released in 1998.

**Shankill Road.** An exclusively Protestant working-class street of industrial West Belfast, Northern Ireland. During the TROUBLES 'the Shankill', the road and its adjacent streets, became synonymous with hard-line Loyalism. In the same way 'the Falls' around the nearby Catholic FALLS ROAD became synonymous with hard-line nationalism.

**Shape of things to come.** The way the future is likely to develop. The phrase derives from the title of a novel of 1933 by H.G. Wells chillingly predicting war in 1939 followed by plague, rebellion, a new glass-based society, the first rocketship to the moon and the establishment of a world government in 2059. The work formed the basis of Alexander Korda's acclaimed film *Things to Come* (1935), with a memorable musical score by Arthur Bliss.

**Shape up.** To improve; to reform; to develop satisfactorily. The sense is of gaining a full satisfactory shape. The expression dates from the 1930s.

**Shape up or ship out.** To do properly what one is supposed to do or, if one cannot manage this, stop doing it altogether. The expression originated in the US armed forces in the Second World War, when any soldier, sailor or marine judged to be unworthy of the name was liable to be sent overseas to a combat zone.

**Shapwick Hoard.** The largest hoard of early Roman coins ever discovered in Britain came to light in a field at Shapwick, Somerset, in 1999 when Kevin Elliott, a dairy farmer's son, tried out a metal detector lent him by his cousin, Martin Elliott, a self-employed welder. The 9000 or so silver *denarii* date from between the time of Mark Antony (31 BC) and the emperor Severus Maximus (AD 222–235), and are calculated to have been buried in about AD 230 and to be the equivalent of ten years' pay for a legionary soldier in the Roman army. The find is now in the British Museum.

**Sharon.** A female forename of biblical origin: 'I am the rose of Sharon, and the lily of the valley' (Song of Solomon 2:1). The name was adopted by the attraction of the rose that here accompanies it, although Sharon itself is not a person but a plain in the north of Palestine. The forename had became very popular by the 1970s but subsequently came to gain a pejorative patina, especially when coupled with the name TRACY. To say, for example, that a club was full of Sharons and Tracys is to say that it was full of ESSEX GIRL types. In the 1990s television comedy series BIRDS OF A FEATHER the two main characters, Sharon and Tracey, are sisters of this kind.

> There was a forest of spindly tables carrying drinks, populated by Sharon and Tracy.
> *Financial Times* (4–5 December 1999)

'Sharon fruit' is the name given to a variety of persimmon developed in the Sharon area of Israel.

**Sharpeville Massacre.** The shooting of unarmed civilian demonstrators by South African police on 21 March 1960, resulting in the deaths of 67 blacks and the wounding of a further 186, including women and children. The demonstration, organized by the Pan-African Congress (PAC, a splinter and rival of the ANC), was held in the Transvaal township of Sharpeville, and was to protest against the hated PASS LAWS. Following the incident both the ANC and the PAC were banned; the ANC went underground and turned to armed struggle. The incident drew international attention to the iniquities of APARTHEID and provoked worldwide condemnation of the South African government.

**She.** The picture of a toaster and a fridge with a woman styled to match by Richard Hamilton (b.1922) was executed in 1958–61, and the work had a major influence on POP ART in Britain. Presumably the punning title refers to the commodification of human beings in the consumer society. *See also* JUST WHAT IS IT THAT MAKES TODAY'S HOMES SO DIFFERENT, SO APPEALING?.

**Sheena.** Essentially the female counterpart of TARZAN, the jungle girl of US comic books has the real name Janet Ames. She is a white foundling raised by an African tribe who teach her MARTIAL ARTS and shamanistic skills. She was the creation of Will Eisner and S.M. Iger for *Jumbo Comics*, and made her debut in 1938. She subsequently appeared in a television series and in a film of 1984, named after her, in which she was played by Tanya Roberts.

**Sheep in sheep's clothing, A.** Supposedly Winston Churchill's description of Clement Attlee, leader of the Labour Party and deputy prime minister during the Second World War. Attlee belied this description when he defeated Churchill in the 1945 election and went on to lead one of the most energetic British governments ever, which founded the National Health Service, nationalized swathes of industry and laid the foundations of the modern welfare state. Churchill himself denied that he ever called Attlee a 'sheep in sheep's clothing', a phrase that had in 1936 been applied to Ramsay MacDonald, an earlier leader of the Labour Party, by BEACHCOMBER.

The phrase plays, of course, on 'a wolf in sheep's clothing', which made its debut in the fables of Aesop. *See also* DEAD SHEEP.

**Shell suit.** A casual and typically garish outfit consisting of a loose jacket and trousers with an elasticated waist, or else cut all in one. It was a fashion garment of the late 1980s and early 1990s at a time when sportswear was popular as general leisurewear and was so called from its shiny polyester outer shell. It was worn mainly but not exclusively by males of the ESSEX MAN type.

**Shergar.** The three-year-old bay colt, by Val de Loir out of Sharmeen, that won the Derby by a record ten lengths in 1981, ridden by Walter Swinburn. After winning several other races, he retired to stud in Co. Kildare, Ireland, but was abducted there in February 1983 by armed and masked men, never to be seen again. The melancholy conclusion was that he had been taken by members of the IRA and probably killed soon afterwards.

**She's apples.** In colloquial Australian English, everything is all right or perfect. The usage dates from the early 1940s. 'Apples' is short for 'apples and spice', rhyming slang for 'nice'.

**She who must be obeyed.** A description of Margaret Thatcher, the IRON LADY, by Julian Critchley (1930–2000), a Conservative backbench MP from 1970 to 1997. The name derives from the heroine of the novel *She* (1887) by Sir Henry Rider Haggard (1856–1925), the long-lived white queen Ayesha (properly 'She Who Must Be Obeyed'). It was also half-jokingly applied to his formidable wife Hilda by Horace Rumpole (*see* RUMPOLE OF THE BAILEY).

**Shiatsu.** A form of ALTERNATIVE therapy of Japanese origin in vogue from the 1960s and based on the same principles as acupuncture but without the use of needles. The word is Japanese for 'finger pressure'. Central to the technique is *chi*, meaning literally 'air', 'breath', representing the circulating life force that each person possesses and which, according to oriental medicine, can be lightly replenished or heavily taxed. Shiatsu practitioners thus begin a subject's first session by assessing the two most extreme meridians in their body in terms of *chi*.

'Shiatsu' is not to be confused with 'shitzu', the name (in Chinese literally 'lion son') of a small breed of dog of oriental origin.

**Shin Bet.** The principal security service of Israel, which was established on 30 June 1948, only six weeks after Israeli independence. Its successes, unlike those of MOSSAD, have rarely been publicized. It is so called from the Hebrew letters that begin the first two words of its full name, *Sherut Bittahon Kelali*, General Security Service.

**Shining city on a hill, A.** A favourite image of Ronald Reagan, the GREAT COMMUNICATOR, to evoke all that he thought best about the United States. He seems to have used it as early as 1969 and frequently deployed it through his tenure as president in the 1980s. At the Democratic Convention in 1984 Mario Cuomo, governor of New York, criticized the blinkered nature of Reagan's vision:

> There is despair, Mr President, in the faces that you don't see, in the places that you don't visit in your shining city ... This nation is more a tale of two cities than it is just a shining city on a hill.

Reagan borrowed the image from John Winthrop, governor of the Massachusetts Bay Colony, who in 1630 told the settlers:

> We shall be as a city upon a hill, the eyes of all people are upon us.

Winthrop in turn was inspired by Matthew 5:14:

> A city that is set on a hill cannot be hid ... Let your light so shine before men that they may see your good works.

**Shining Path.** A translation of Spanish *Sendero Luminoso*, the name of a neo-Maoist Peruvian revolutionary movement. It was founded in 1970 following a split in the Communist Party of Peru and subsequently became a secret guerrilla organization involved in widepread terrorist activities, including brutal attacks on ordinary civilians. Its name refers to the maxim of José Carlos Mariátegui, founder of Peru's original Communist Party in 1928: *El Marxismo-Leninismo abrirá el sendero luminoso hacia la revolución*, 'Marxism-Leninism will open the shining path to revolution.' Members are known as Senderistas. Since its leader Abimael Guzmán was imprisoned in 1992 it has been largely dormant, apart from the activities of a small group of hardliners.

**Shipping forecast.** A regular feature of BBC Radio, information provided four times a day by the Meteorological Office on wind conditions and visibility at sea, given individually for each of the 31 forecasting areas around the British Isles. The mesmeric names of the latter are mostly based on geographical features, such as rivers (Tyne, Humber), bays (Biscay, German Bight), islands (Hebrides, Rockall) or underwater sandbanks (Dogger, Forties). Since it was first broadcast in something approximating its current format on 1 January 1924 the litany has grown from 13 names to 31, the latest additions (1984) being North and South Utsire, off the southwestern coast of Norway. German Bight was renamed from Heligoland in 1956 and in 2002 the name Finisterre, which was, confusingly, used by the Spanish for a completely different area, was changed to FitzRoy.

> This nightly recitation of troublesome wind in Dogger and Fisher has all the calming qualities of a repeated mantra or, for traditionalists, a favourite part of the Book of Common Prayer.
>
> KEN BRUCE: in Paul Donovan, *The Radio Companion* (1991)
>
> Darkness outside. Inside, the radio's prayer –
> Rockall. Malin. Dogger. Finisterre.
>
> CAROL ANNE DUFFY: 'Prayer', from *Mean Time* (1993)

**Shipping News, The.** A tragi-comic novel (1993) by the US writer E. Annie Proulx (b.1935), which won the PULITZER PRIZE for fiction. Quoyle, a newspaper reporter in Mockingbird, New York, takes refuge in Newfoundland with his aunt and his two small delinquent daughters after his wife is killed in a car crash while absconding with her lover. The aunt opens a shop and Quoyle gets a job on the local paper. 'I want you to cover local car wrecks … We run a front-page photo of a car-wreck every week, whether we have a wreck or not … And the shipping news.' A film version was released in 2002.

**Shire, The.** A region of MIDDLE-EARTH in J.R.R Tolkien's *The* HOBBIT (1937) and *The* LORD OF THE RINGS (1954–5). The Shire is the home of the hobbits. Bilbo BAGGINS and later his nephew FRODO live at Bag End in the village of Hobbiton. As is implied by its name, the Shire bears many of the characteristics of a long-gone rural England, its gentle landscapes and rustic homeliness contrasting with the epic landscapes found elsewhere in Middle Earth. Many place-names in the Shire, coincidentally or otherwise, seem to echo English village-names. Buckland, the home of the

Brandybuck family of hobbits, is actually the name of a village in western Oxfordshire.

**Shit.** This FOUR-LETTER WORD in its basic sense of 'to void excrement' goes back to medieval times. Its figurative applications mostly date from the 20th century, however, and include 'in the shit' (in trouble), 'up shit creek' (in difficulties) and 'shit-scared' (very frightened). As an exclamation, 'shit' can express anything from a keen annoyance to a mild deprecation. In this role it has a mainly Irish variant form, 'shite', a stylized American representation, 'she-ite', and a euphemistic equivalent, 'sugar'. In slang usage (from the 1940s), 'shit' denotes both drugs in general and HEROIN and cannabis in particular.

**Shit happens.** A fatalistic formula for times when things go wrong: 'Bad things happen; what can you do about it?' It dates from the 1980s. The euphemistic version is STUFF HAPPENS.

**Shit hits the fan, The.** When the shit hits the fan, the difficulties really begin in earnest, especially as repercussions of an earlier action. Various substitutes for 'shit' are on record, both synonymous ('doo-doo') and more vaguely euphemistic ('stuff'), and the mock-pompous 'the excrement *or* solids hit(s) the air conditioning' has a down-toning effect. Indeed, there is some evidence to suggest that the original object hitting the fan (probably some time in the 1930s, in the United States) may have been an egg. The outcome of the encounter, however, remains the same: a sudden catastrophic dispersal that affects everyone.

An interesting reversal occurs as 'when the fan hits the shit', i.e. when a disgruntled supporter punches a former object of admiration.

**Shit or get off the pot.** To take a decisive and committed step or remove oneself from the scene of the action. The pungent injunction against prevarication probably originated in North American forces slang of the Second World War period.

> You better tell some of those limousine liberals back in Langley Virginia it's time for them to shit or get off the pot.
>
> JOHN LE CARRÉ: *The Honourable Schoolboy* (1977)

**Shock and awe.** A US military strategy, an update of BLITZKRIEG, aimed at the rapid physical and psychological destruction of the enemy's will to resist by using overwhelming force and technological superiority, for example by deploying SMART BOMBS and cruise missiles. COLLATERAL DAMAGE (a euphemism for civilian casualties) cannot be ruled out, but is not intended. The strategy was first enunciated at the National Defense University in 1996 and employed in Iraq in 2003. *See also* DECAPITATION STRATEGY.

**Shock, horror** or **Shock! Horror!** An ironic exclamation made in response to something that supposedly shocks. 'Shock-horror' headlines are sensationalistic banner headlines, as typically found in the press. The expression dates from the 1970s.

> Recently there has been a lot of fuss about ten-year-old girls wearing make-up and even having – shock, horror – facials.
> *The Times* (14 August 1999)

**Shocking pink.** A vibrant shade of pink, introduced by the Italian-born French fashion designer Elsa Schiaparelli (1890–1973) in February 1937. 'Shocking' here means little more than 'vivid', but the word derives its impact from its use to describe a colour normally regarded as soft and gentle.

**Shock jock.** A radio disc-jockey who is intentionally offensive or provocative. The phenomenon arose in the United States in the latter half of the 1980s, but was less well tolerated when it crossed to Britain in the 1990s.

**Shock of the new, The.** A phrase first applied to modernism in art in the title of a 1972 book by Ian Dunlop (b.1925): *The Shock of the New: Seven Historic Exhibitions of Modern Art*. The title was subsequently borrowed for a 1980 BBC2 television series on modern art, written and presented by Robert Hughes (b.1938), which was in turn made into a book (1981) with the same title.

***Shogun.*** A historical novel (1975) by James Clavell (1924–94). There is a clash of cultures in early modern Japan when a shipwrecked Englishman is compelled, in return for his survival, to serve as secretary to a war lord (*shogun*) and has to reconsider his personal principles. A mini-series, starring Richard Chamberlain, was shown on BBC1 in 1982.

**Shoo-fly pie.** A rich tart of treacle baked in a pastry case with a crumble topping, so called because of the (real or imagined) need to shoo flies away from the sweet treacle. American 'pie' here equates to British 'tart', and the confection as a whole is thus a modern equivalent of the much older British treacle tart. The name dates from the 1930s.

**Shoo-in.** A person or thing that is sure to succeed, especially to win a contest. The expression dates from the 1930s and originally referred to a horse in a rigged horse race that one metaphorically merely needed to 'shoo in' to win. The term is often misspelled 'shoe-in' by writers unaware of the origin, presumably from an image of being kicked in, like a successful shot at goal: 'Muhammad Ali … who was a shoe-in for sportsman of the last millennium' (*The Times*,

1 January 2000); 'With these names, I'd have thought lottery cash was a shoe-in' (*Sunday Times*, 9 January 2000).

> Politics directly intervened in literature with the appointment of [Ted] Hughes's successor as poet laureate … Once [Seamus] Heaney had declared himself Irish … Andrew Motion was a shoo-in.
> *Independent on Sunday* (28 November 1999)

**Shoot a beaver.** 'Beaver' being a colloquial euphemism for the female pubic hair, and by extension for the female external genitalia, there is more to 'shooting a beaver' than pulling a trigger. In US college slang of the 1960s, it denoted taking a sly look up a woman's skirt in hopes of erotic revelation, but by the 1970s its focus had been switched round so that it could also refer to a woman deliberately exposing her genitals to view, and hence more generally to sitting with the legs provocatively apart.

**Shoot from the hip.** To react hastily or inconsiderately; to respond aggressively. The imagery derives from Western films, in which a rider faced with a challenge would respond with a shot from a gun drawn quickly from the holster on his hip.

**Shoot oneself in the foot.** To harm one's own cause inadvertently; to damage one's chances. The allusion is to an accidental shooting of this type as distinct from the deliberate shooting of oneself in the foot in order to avoid military service, a ruse entered in various army records.

**Shoot someone** or **something down.** To crush a person or reject their opinions by means of forceful criticism or argument. The metaphor derives from aerial combat in the First World War. An emphatic form is 'to shoot down in flames', as: 'I was shot down in flames for my trouble.'

**Shoot someone's fox.** To take the wind out of someone's sails by stymieing a particular course of action, typically by taking that action oneself before they can. The metaphor comes from the hunting field, where shooting a fox (a heinous crime among the pink-coated fraternity) ruins everyone's sport (including no doubt the fox's). It enjoyed some popularity among politicians in the early 21st century.

> His [Sir Menzies Campbell's] typed notes … included a 'reserve' set of questions on the cost of the Government's identity cards scheme for use in case David Cameron, who is called first, shot his fox.
> *The Times* (18 January 2006)

**Shoot the breeze** or **the bull.** To chat idly; to gossip. A 'breeze' is a rumour, which is wafted from one person to another, as when one 'gets wind of' something. 'Bull' is short for 'bullshit'. The phrases are of US origin and date from the early 20th century.

**Shoot the Pianist.** (French title: *Tirez sur le pianiste.*) A film (1960) by François Truffaut, intended as an *homage* to the US B-feature *film noir*. The story, based on a novel by David Goodis, follows the adventures of a café pianist (played by Charles Aznavour) who becomes involved with a bunch of criminals. The title recalls the notice seen by Oscar Wilde in a dancing saloon in the United States:

> Please do not shoot the pianist. He is doing his best.
> Quoted in Oscar Wilde, *Impressions of America* (c.1882–3), 'Leadville'

**Shoot through like a Bondi tram.** In Australian slang, to make an extremely rapid exit. The characteristic Australian use of 'shoot through' to denote a departure or disappearance dates from the 1940s, and this embellishment, citing a well-known Sydney suburb, is roughly contemporary.

**Shop around.** Literally, to go from shop to shop searching out where prices are lowest or the best bargains are to be had. More generally, to shop around is to compare any products or services with such an aim. A slang sense of the phrase, which dates from the 1920s, is to engage in a number of sexual relationships before selecting the one that will serve for a longer term or even marriage.

**Shopping and fucking.** A derisive term (often abbreviated to 'S&F') from the last decade of the 20th century for a lifestyle dominated by acquisitiveness and sensuality, and also for a literary genre featuring lives in which shopping and sexual intercourse loom large. The use of the phrase by Mark Ravenhill as the title of a play (1996), about five misfits in an uncertain drug society, caused much consternation to its publicists, and in many places it appeared as *Shopping and ****ing*. A less abrasive synonym is SEX AND SHOPPING. *See also* BONKBUSTER.

**Shopping days to Christmas.** Preceded by a figure, such as 50, the phrase is an irritating reminder of the decreasing opportunities to buy Christmas presents. The commercial countdown was first promoted by SELFRIDGES department store in London, and its US founder, Gordon Selfridge (1856–1947; *see also* CUSTOMER IS ALWAYS RIGHT), when still in his native Chicago, is said to have sent out an instruction to Marshall Field's heads of departments and assistants reading: 'The Christmas season has begun and twenty-three more shopping days remain in which to make our holiday sales record.' As virtually every day of the week is now a shopping day, the figure is essentially the number of days to 25 December. The countdown usually begins in earnest from October, and there are 85 shopping days from the 1st of that month.

**Shop till one drops.** To indulge in a shopping spree, especially after coming into money. A phrase that epitomized the hedonistic commercialism of the 1980s and 1990s.

**Short con.** A confidence trick that can be performed spontaneously and on the spot, without any elaborate preparation. The term originated in US underworld slang of the 1930s. *See also* LONG CON.

**Short sharp shock.** A phrase associated with the punishment of young criminals. The phrase gained popular currency from the 1950s, but in fact has a Gilbertian genesis:

> Awaiting the sensation of a short, sharp shock,
> From a cheap and chippy chopper on a big black block.
> W.S. GILBERT: *The Mikado*, I (1885)

The phrase was used by Margaret Thatcher in parliament in 1961 when giving evidence to a standing committee in support of the restoration of corporal punishment of young offenders:

> If, instead of giving him [an offender] a short, sharp lesson, we encourage in him a feeling of self-justification, we may completely blot out all feeling of guilt or shame ... The method of a short, sharp shock ... no longer seems to be the aim of detention centres.

The phrase acquired a more enduring life when in a speech to the Tory Party Conference in October 1979 the home secretary, William Whitelaw, proposed a new punitive, military-style regime for young offenders, which he described as a 'short, sharp shock'. The idea was that the severity of the treatment would deter youths from repeat offences. Doubts were subsequently raised regarding the efficacy of this approach.

**Shot glass.** A small glass for serving spirits, traditionally one containing a 'shot' of 1½ US fluid oz (44.5ml). Such a glass is also known as a 'jigger', probably so called because it goes up and down ('jigs') between the bottle and the customer's glass.

> Proof of a successful party, empty glasses, beer bottles and shot glasses littered every available space.
> *heat* (17–23 February 2000)

**Shotgun wedding.** One forced upon the couple, usually by the bride's parents, when the bride is pregnant. The image is of the bride's father threatening the groom with a shotgun, itself perhaps serving as a symbol of the act that caused her condition. The expression dates from the 1920s.

**Shot heard round the world, The.** A phrase applied to the assassination in SARAJEVO of Archduke Franz Ferdinand, heir apparent to the Austro-Hungarian Empire, by the Serb nationalist Gavrilo Princip on 28 June 1914. The assassination precipitated a succession of events culminating in the outbreak of the First World War. The phrase originally referred to the outbreak of the American War of Independence at Concord, Massachusetts, in 1775, and was coined by Ralph Waldo Emerson in a commemorative poem, 'Concord Hymn', written for the opening of a memorial on the site in 1837:

> By the rude bridge that arched the flood,
> Their flag to April's breeze unfurled,
> Here once the embattled farmers stood,
> And fired the shot heard round the world.

**Shot in the arm.** An encouraging stimulus. The allusion is to the injection of a stimulant. The expression dates from the 1920s.

> 'Hopefully it will bring Ilfracombe out of the Sixties. It needs a shot in the arm, something to bring it into the real world,' said restaurateur John Clemence.
> *Evening Standard* (27 September 1999)

**Shoulder surfing.** The practice of hovering surreptitiously behind someone's back as they use an ATM or similar device in order to observe their PIN number. The expression dates from the 1990s.

**Shoulder to cry on.** A person who listens sympathetically to one's problems. The phrase evokes both the resting of a weeping person's head on the shoulder of another, and also the shoulder itself as a traditional source of strength and support. Hence the pleasant dedication of Claire Rayner's novel *Long Acre* (1978): 'For Joan Chapman, with gratitude for her ever-patient rusty shoulder'.

**Showa.** The auspicious name or reign title given to the period of rule (1926–89) of the Japanese Emperor Hirohito (1901–89). It means 'Enlightened Peace' and became the emperor's name after his death. He was succeeded by his son, Akihito (b.1933), whose reign is designated Heisei, meaning 'Achieving Peace'.

**Show and tell.** An elaborate public presentation or display, as of a couple's photographs of their round-the-world cruise. The expression arose in the 1940s from the US teaching method for young children, in which each child brings some object to class to show and describe to the others.

**Show must go on, The.** The activity in progress must continue; we must keep going. The expression appears to have originally applied to a circus, which, despite difficulties such as sick animals or absent performers, must continue to hold its performances in order not to disappoint the public. A film of 1937, *The Show Goes On*, tells how a mill-girl becomes a star singer with the help of a dying composer, and 'The Show Must Go On' is a song by Ira Gershwin in Jerome Kern's musical *Cover Girl* (1944).

> Why must the show go on?
> Why not announce the closing night of it?
> The public seem to hate the sight of it.
> NOËL COWARD: 'Why Must the Show Go On?' (1950s)

**Show, carry, fly** or **wave the flag.** To demonstrate support for one's country or organization, especially when abroad. A ship of the Royal Navy literally 'flies the flag' of the White Ensign when in a foreign port. A reluctant but dutiful attender of a social function may also be said to 'show the flag'.

**Show trial.** A judicial trial attended by great publicity. The term usually relates to the prejudged trial of political dissidents by a totalitarian government. The Stalinist show trials in the Soviet Union in the 1930s, with the sinister Andrei Vyshinsky (1883–1954) as prosecutor (1936–8), are a well-known example. The expression itself dates from the 1930s. *See also* U–2.

**Shrek.** An ugly smelly green ogre with a heart of gold, the eponymous hero of a gently satiric fairy tale (1990) written by William Steig (1907–2003). When his swamp is invaded by refugeed fairy-tale characters he agrees to rescue a princess in return for being left alone and falls in love with her. He was brought to wider fame by the Walt Disney computer-animated films *Shrek* (2001) and *Shrek 2* (2004), which took elements of the original stories and intermingled them with contemporary humour, parody and satire.

**Shrimp, The.** A media nickname for the model Jean Shrimpton (b.1943), who introduced the MINISKIRT to a delighted or dismayed public. She was one of the first SUPERMODELS and at the centre of the London scene that shook the world in the SWINGING SIXTIES. Her boyfriends included the photographer David Bailey, the man who made her, and the actor Terence Stamp. She retired from modelling at the age of 28 and became a virtual recluse, telling one interviewer, 'The trouble is I really hate clothes.'

**Shrink.** A psychiatrist. The word is a shortening of 'head-shrinker' in the same sense, adopting the term used historically for a headhunter who preserved and shrank the heads of his dead enemies. The term sheds interesting light on the extent to which people may feel diminished as individuals by the process of psychoanalysis and psychotherapy.

> I wonder if my shrink (sorry, psychiatrist) was a woman not a man I'd be in a better or worse state, after three months in this place?
> FAY WELDON: *The Heart of the Country* (1987)

**Shrinking violet.** A unduly shy or modest person. The violet, although nobly coloured and sweetly scented, grows in secluded spots, as if anxious to hide these two attributes. The expression, dating from the early years of the 20th century, is often found in the negative, as: 'She's no shrinking violet.' In a positive sense it can imply a reluctance to face one's responsibilities.

> In his 24 years in the post [of Master of the Queen's Music, Malcolm] Williamson has not overtaxed his talents. But surely this shrinking violet should now be prodded into collaborating with our new Poet Laureate, Andrew Motion.
>
> *The Times* (31 August 1999)

**Shuttle diplomacy.** Diplomatic negotiations conducted by a mediator who travels between two or more parties that are themselves reluctant to meet for direct discussions. Henry Kissinger, US secretary of state in the 1970s, was a master of the method. *See also* FLYING PEACEMAKER.

**Sick as a parrot.** Very disappointed or glum; terminally dejected. The expression came to prominence in the 1970s and came to be regarded as the stock response of a footballer or team manager after losing a match. However, its origins may be much older:

> Jacinta: Lord, Madam, you are melancholy as a sick Parrot.
> Julia: And can you blame me, Jacinta? Have I not many
> Reasons to be sad?
>
> APHRA BEHN: *The False Count* (1682).

*See also* OVER THE MOON.

**Sick building syndrome.** A condition affecting office workers, typically manifesting itself in headaches and respiratory problems. Its cause is attributed to unhealthy or stressful factors in the working environment, such as poor ventilation, air conditioning, absence of natural light and a frustration at being unable to control the ambient physical conditions. A 'sick' building is one that is not functioning properly. The expression dates from the 1980s.

**Sick joke.** An insensitive, morbid or sadistic joke, not amusing in the normal way but the product of warped wit. An example is the following:

> What's a thousand metres long and eats vegetables? A Moscow meat queue.
>
> 'NORMA P. LAMONT': *The Official Ministry of Fun Joke Book* (1992)

**Sid.** A name selected for the average small investor when encouraged to take part in the share issue of British Gas on its privatization in 1986. The full form of the lure then posted everywhere was: 'If you see Sid, tell him.' The name was taken up in the media for any typical small-scale share-buyer or shareholder and was itself presumably chosen for its 'plebeian' associations.

House of Fraser stores groups will be embarking on a 'Sid-style' marketing campaign to woo private investors and shoppers.

> *Sunday Telegraph* (30 January 1994)

**Sidney Street Siege.** An incident on 3 January 1911 when police and soldiers, on the orders of the home secretary Winston Churchill, who personally (and somewhat ostentatiously) attended the siege, surrounded 100 Sidney Street in London's East End. Inside the house were three Latvian anarchists who had killed three policemen during a raid on a jeweller a few weeks earlier. Two of the gang were killed in the siege, but the leader, 'Peter the Painter' (a sign painter by trade), escaped.

**Siegfried Line.** The defences built by the Germans on their western frontier before and after 1939 as a reply to France's MAGINOT LINE. The British song, popular in 1939, 'We're Gonna Hang Out the Washing on the Siegfried Line' was somewhat premature. When Canadian troops penetrated the Line in 1945 they hung up a number of sheets with a large notice on which was written 'The Washing'. The name is that of the hero of Wagner's *Ring* cycle and of the medieval epic on which that work is based, the *Nibelungenlied*, and many Germans will have been aware of its literal significance, from *Sieg*, 'victory', and *Fried*, 'peace'. The Germans had already used the name in the First World War for what other countries knew as the HINDENBURG LINE.

**Sieg Heil.** A German phrase with the literal meaning 'hail victory', from the German *Sieg* ('victory') and *Heil* ('hail'), used as a victory salute at NAZI political rallies. The phrase became familiar from films about the Second World War. *See also* HEIL HITLER.

**Signature tune.** A musical theme played regularly as a means of identification to introduce a particular artist or regularly broadcast programme. One of the best-known signature tunes in the days of STEAM RADIO was 'Here's To the Next Time', played in the 1930s at the close of every broadcast by Henry Hall and the BBC Dance Orchestra. *See also* THEME MUSIC.

> If one wished to be facetious, one could say that the *leitmotive* of characters in Wagner's *Ring* are their 'signature-tunes'.
>
> MICHAEL KENNEDY: *The Oxford Dictionary of Music* (1994)

**Significant other.** A person with whom one has a romantic or sexual relationship; a boyfriend or girlfriend. The expression is of US origin, dating from the 1970s, and was adopted from the jargon of sociology as a term for a person who directly influences an individual's self-evaluation and behaviour, as a parent does a child or an employer an employee. *See also* ROLE MODEL.

**Significant Others.** A volume (1988) in a series of novels by the US writer Armistead Maupin (b.1944), chronicling, through a wide range of characters and rapid changes of plot, life in San Francisco in the 1980s. *Significant Others* introduces three new characters to Maupin's regular cast of characters, known to television audiences through the serialization of his *Tales of the City* (1978): Wren Douglas, 'the world's most beautiful fat woman', Polly Berendt, a lesbian, and Thack Sweeney, a restorer of old houses. *See also* SIGNIFICANT OTHER.

**Sign one's own death warrant.** To bring about one's own downfall; to do oneself irreparable harm. In 1921 the Irish nationalist leader Michael Collins, after signing the treaty establishing the Irish Free State, wrote in a letter: 'I tell you – early this morning I signed my death warrant.' The following year he was ambushed and assassinated by anti-treaty Republicans. *See also* BÉAL NA MBLÁTH; BIG FELLA; FREE-STATERS.

**Sign on the dotted line.** To indicate one's acceptance of the terms agreed, literally by writing one's signature on the line allotted for it in a contract. The term dates from the early 20th century.

**Silence of the Lambs, The.** A horror novel (1989) by Thomas Harris (b.1940) about a homicidal genius and cannibal, Hannibal Lecter (*see* HANNIBAL THE CANNIBAL). The title refers to a childhood experience of his potential victim, a female trainee investigator, who recalls the lambs on the farm where she was brought up being rounded up and taken away for slaughter. At the book's enigmatic ending, 'she sleeps deeply, sweetly in the silence of the lambs'. A tense and sometimes gruesome film version (1990) was directed by Jonathan Demme.

> *Hannibal*: A census taker once tried to test me. I ate his liver with some fava beans and a nice chianti.

**Silent Cal.** A nickname of Republican politician Calvin Coolidge (1872–1933), president of the United States (1923–9). Noted for his taciturnity, Coolidge was allegedly once approached by a guest at the White House who informed him that she had just made a bet that she could elicit more than three words from the great conversationalist. Coolidge replied: 'You lose.' Dorothy Parker famously responded to the news that the former president was dead with the words: 'How could they tell?' Coolidge himself admitted, 'I always figured the American public wanted a solemn ass for President, so I went along with them.'

**Silent majority.** The majority of people, who hold moderate opinions but rarely express them. President Richard Nixon gave the expression a political emphasis when using it in speeches of 1969–70 appealing for support from MIDDLE AMERICA. The implication was that such people did not bother to make their opinions known but should do so.

**Silent Spring.** A book (1962) by the US zoologist Rachel Carson (1907–64), one of the first to alert the world to the dangers to the natural environment of excessive use of pesticides in agriculture, especially the insecticide DDT, which accumulated in birds and mammals higher up the food chain with disastrous effects.

> Over increasingly large areas of the United States, spring now comes unheralded by the return of the birds, and the early mornings are strangely silent where once they were filled with the beauty of bird song.

**Silicon Fen.** England's answer to America's SILICON VALLEY, meaning the Fenland city of Cambridge with its many electronics companies. The name puns on that of SILICON GLEN.

> For more than a decade, the Cambridge phenomenon has been illuminating Silicon Fen by spawning a legion of biotechnology and electronics groups originating in the university's laboratories and lecture theatres.
>
> *Sunday Times* (6 June 1999)

**Silicon Glen.** Scotland's answer to America's SILICON VALLEY. Silicon Glen broadly coincides with that section of the Central Belt between Glasgow and Edinburgh, including such towns as Stirling, Linlithgow, Livingston and East Kilbride, but also extending northeast to Glenrothes and Dundee.

**Silicon Prairie.** A nickname for a region near Dallas, Texas, that is the site of many high-technology and computer companies. *See also* SILICON FEN; SILICON GLEN; SILICON VALLEY.

**Silicon Valley.** A name given to the Santa Clara Valley, south of San Francisco, California, where a number of electronics and computing industries are located. The name, alluding to the use of silicon in the manufacture of microchips, was subsequently extended to similar sites elsewhere, both in the United States and in other countries. *See also* SILICON FEN; SILICON GLEN; SILICON PRAIRIE.

**Silly ass.** A stupid person. The ass or donkey is traditionally regarded as a stupid animal. The expression is first recorded only at the turn of the 20th century, in G.B. Shaw's *Captain Brassbound's Conversion* (1899). A 'silly ass' was later established as the stereotype of the effete, upper-class, braying Englishman, nicely described by George Orwell as 'the silly-ass Englishman with his spats and monocle' ('In Defence of P.G. Wodehouse', in *Windmill*, July 1946).

**Silly me.** A facetiously ironic or gently self-deprecating rebuke following a slip or error, as: 'Silly old me, I thought today was Tuesday.'

**Silly Putty.** A US plaything first marketed in 1949 as a form of 'putty' that could be stretched, shattered and bounced if appropriately manipulated. A later British equivalent was Potty Putty.

**Silly Symphonies.** A series of animated character cartoons produced by Walt Disney from 1928, their aim being to evoke settings, seasons and events in the style of Aesop's *Fables*. Animals thus regularly featured (though not MICKEY MOUSE or DONALD DUCK), as in *Birds of a Feather* (1931), *Three Little Pigs* (1933), *The Tortoise and the Hare* (1935) and *The Country Cousin* (1936). The overall title refers to the humorously appropriate musical accompaniment.

**Silmarillion, The.** A posthumously published collection (1977), edited by his son, of imaginative tales by J.R.R. Tolkien (1892–1973). They constitute the storehouse of materials from which he developed his children's novel, *The* HOBBIT (1937), and the saga *The* LORD OF THE RINGS (1954–5). The Silmarils are 'the three jewels made by Fëanor before the destruction of the Two Trees of Valinor, and filled with their light'.

**Silver Bodgie.** A nickname of Australian politician Bob (Robert) Hawke (b.1929), Labour prime minister (1983–91). A 'bodgie' is Australian slang for a TEDDY BOY, and Hawke earned the name from his mane of silver hair, which the novelist Patrick White described as 'his cockatoo hairdo'.

**Silver screen.** An early hyperbolic metaphor for the cinema, from the days when cinema screens were covered with metallic paint to produce a highly reflective silver-coloured surface (in publicists' puffs, movie stars would be 'stars of the silver screen'). Screens are now usually made of white opaque plastic, although glass-beaded screens and platinum screens are used for special daylight presentations.

**Silver surfer.** An older user of the INTERNET and the WORLD WIDE WEB, 'silver' because of the greying hair those of advancing years are prone to sport. Generally more sedentary than younger generations (and therefore more likely to turn to online shopping, for example), silver surfers are now being seen as potentially rich pickings by Internet advertisers and marketeers.

**Silver Sword, The.** A novel (1956) by Ian Serraillier (1912–94) relating the efforts of three Polish refugee children to reunite themselves with their parents after their family is broken up by the NAZI invasion of Poland. The sword of the title refers to a sword-shaped silver penknife, which was given by the children's father to another child, named Jan, and which he knows will be recognized by his own children.

**Silver Tassie, The.** A play (1928) by the Irish playwright Sean O'Casey (1880–1964) in which the author laments the loss of life in the First World War. The 'silver tassie' of the title is a silver cup brought home in victory by Dublin footballer Harry Hegan in the first act.

**Simpson, Bart.** The brash, spiky-haired, school-hating 'bad boy' hero of the television cartoon series *The Simpsons*, created in 1987 by the US cartoonist Matt Groening. Each episode opens with ten-year-old Bart (an anagram of 'brat') at a school blackboard writing as punishment such lines as 'I will not drive the principal's car' or 'I did not see Elvis.' The show's humour is primarily aimed at adults, but Bart himself has a direct appeal for younger viewers, who delight in his catchphrases such as 'Aye, caramba' and 'EAT MY SHORTS!' Other members of the Simpson family are Homer, the thick-headed, beer-swilling father (whose frequent exclamation of frustration and despair, 'Doh!', is now recorded in the *OED*), Marge, his sensible, down-to-earth wife, Lisa, their young hyper-intelligent daughter, and Maggie, their perpetually dummy-sucking infant.

**Sinatra doctrine.** A phrase coined on 25 October 1989 by the Soviet foreign ministry spokesman, Gennadi Gerasimov, to describe the policy of the reforming Soviet leader Mikhail Gorbachev (*see* GORBY) towards the USSR's allies in Eastern Europe. These countries would now be free to pursue their own destinies, 'to do it their way', after the song 'MY WAY' popularized by the US singer Frank Sinatra (1915–98). The Sinatra doctrine was in contrast to the earlier BREZHNEV DOCTRINE. According to early-1970s graffitists, Sinatra was also responsible for a significant contribution to philosophy.

> 'To do is to be – Rousseau. To be is to do – Sartre.
> Doobedoobedoobedoo – Sinatra.'
>> Quoted by Ronald Fletcher in BBC Radio programme
>> *Quote … Unquote* (5 April 1978)

*See also* OL' BLUE EYES.

**Sin bin.** In ice hockey and some other sports such as rugby, an enclosure where offending players have to sit out for a stated time. Hence a term for a centre where offenders are sent for detention or rehabilitation.

**Since when?** Since when has that been so? A phrase casting doubt on the veracity of a statement.

> *Broadbent* [*very solemnly*]: No: I am a teetotaller.
> *Aunt Judy* [*incredulously*]: Arra since when?
> *Broadbent*: Since this morning, Miss Doyle.
>> G.B. SHAW: *John Bull's Other Island*, (1904)

**Since you ask.** A phrase preceding an answer to a spoken or unspoken question, in the latter case often to pre-empt an actual inquiry. The question itself usually seeks clarification regarding a possibly dubious or devious aspect of the matter, and the implication is that if the question had not been put or presumed, the information would not have been given.

> Did we hear rumours, before his appointment, that the outcome had been decided in advance of the interviews? Yes, since you're asking, but it can only have been a coincidence.
>
> *Times Literary Supplement* (30 July 1999)

**Sinfonia Antartica.** The atmospheric seventh symphony of Ralph Vaughan Williams (1872–1958). The title is Italian for 'Antarctic Symphony'. The piece was adapted from Vaughan Williams's music for the film *Scott of the Antarctic* (1948; *see* SOUTH POLE), starring John Mills, James Robertson Justice and Kenneth More. The symphony, which was first performed in Manchester in 1953, includes parts for wind machine, vibraphone, wordless soprano solo and women's chorus. At a rehearsal of the piece the conductor Sir John Barbirolli instructed the chorus: 'I want you to sound like twenty-two women having babies *without* chloroform.'

**Sing from the same hymn sheet.** To present a united front in public by not disagreeing with one another. The image is of people of different religious groups or even faiths joined in worship. The phrase has become widespread in political circles since the election of NEW LABOUR to power in 1997, since when the government has often been criticized for prioritizing presentation over policy. A recent variant is to be 'on the same page'. See also BIG TENT; ON MESSAGE.

**Singing Butler, The.** An enormously popular work by the Scottish painter Jack Vettriano (originally Jack Hoggan, b.1951), depicting a young couple in 1930s evening dress dancing on a beach while a butler holds an umbrella above them. Like all Vettriano's work *The Singing Butler* is dismissed as kitsch by most critics and in 1992 was rejected by the Royal Academy's annual summer exhibition. However, in 2004 it sold at auction for nearly £750,000 and as a print it is the bestselling reproduction of a painting in the UK. Neither Vettriano nor his fans were troubled when in 2005 it was alleged that he had copied the figures out of an old book, *The Illustrator's Figure Reference Manual.*

**Singing Detective, The.** A controversial BBC television drama series (1986) written by Dennis Potter. Its central character, an author of pulp fiction (played by Michael Gambon), is confined to hospital with a debilitating skin disease (not unlike the one Potter himself suffered from). As he lies in bed, scenes from his life are played out in flashback. The programme's obscurity of narrative and imagery annoyed many; its ground-breaking portrayal of a naked male bottom in enthusiastic coital rise and fall scandalized more. An underwhelming US film version appeared in 2003.

**Singing Nun, The.** The English stage-name of the Belgian nun Jeanne Deckers (Sister Luc-Gabrielle; 1933–85), who in 1964 had a surprise UK chart hit with 'Dominique', which she sang to her own guitar accompaniment. She gave up the veil not long afterwards, but never repeated her initial success. Her French stage-name was 'Soeur Sourire' (Sister Smile).

**Singing Postman, The.** The stage-name of the Norfolk postman Allan Smethurst (1927–2000), who in 1966 had a surprise UK chart hit with 'Hev Yew Gotta Loight, Bor?', sung in his local dialect. He was never able to repeat the successful formula and eventually died an alcoholic in a hostel.

**Singin' in the Rain.** A film musical (1952) written by Adolph Green and Betty Comden about the struggles of a top Hollywood production team to adapt from silent movies to talkies in the late 1920s. It starred Gene Kelly, Donald O'Connor, Debbie Reynolds and Jean Hagen. The idea for the film grew out of the song 'Singin' in the Rain', which remains the highlight of the movie, with Kelly dancing with joy in the puddles (despite the fact that he made much of the movie while suffering from a heavy cold).

**Single currency.** A unified currency proposed for all member states of the EUROPEAN UNION, the currency itself being the EURO. More generally the term symbolizes the relationship between national sovereignty and economic and monetary union. *See also* WAIT AND SEE.

**Sinister Street.** A novel (1913–14) by Compton Mackenzie (born Edward Montague Compton; 1883–1972), originally published in two volumes. It is divided into four books: 'The Prison House' (Michael's childhood), 'Classical Education' (school), 'Dreaming Spires' (Oxford) and 'Romantic Education'. The last book largely concerns Michael's ultimately fruitless efforts to find and redeem a former girl-friend who has become a prostitute, in the course of which he takes lodgings in London and traverses streets that are the haunts of the city's lowest life. In a dedication, the author states: '*Sinister Street* is a symbolic title which bears no reference to an heraldic euphemism.'

**Sink one's teeth into something.** *See* GET ONE'S TEETH INTO SOMETHING.

**Sink without trace.** To disappear and not be seen or heard of again. The expression dates from the 1920s and translates German *spurlos versenkt*, 'sunk without trace'. This phrase became widely known during the First World War following the publication in September 1917 of a secret telegram sent to Berlin in May that year by Count Luxburg, the German minister in Buenos Aires, advising that Argentine shipping should be either turned back or sunk without trace.

**Sinn Féin.** (Irish, 'ourselves alone'.) A political party formed in 1905 with the aim of establishing a united Irish republic. After winning a majority of Irish seats in the 1918 British general election, it set up a secessionist Irish Republic (1919) under Éamon de Valera (*see* DEV). It carried on guerrilla warfare (*see* BLACK AND TANS) against British forces until the Anglo-Irish Treaty of 1921, which created the Irish Free State and partitioned Ireland. Led by de Valera, a section of Sinn Féin refused to accept the treaty, triggering armed conflict between anti-treaty Republicans and FREE-STATERS. De Valera's resignation of the presidency of Sinn Féin in 1926 and his creation of a new party, FIANNA FÁIL, began a period of marginalization for the party, but it returned to prominence with the outbreak of Northern Ireland's TROUBLES. Sinn Féin's links with the IRA prompted the British government in 1988 to ban the broadcasting of speeches by its members, including its leader, Gerry Adams. In return for a ceasefire in 1997, however, it was allowed to take part in talks on the future of Northern Ireland and in 1999 became part of the province's first devolved government since 1974. The devolved government has been suspended since 2002. *See also* ARMALITE; DIRECT RULE; GOOD FRIDAY AGREEMENT.

**Siphon the python.** Originally in Australian slang, of a man, to urinate; one of the many colourful images introduced to the English language (in the mid-1960s) by Barry Humphries's creation Barry MCKENZIE. *See also* TECHNI-COLOR YAWN.

**Siren suit.** A one-piece lined and warm garment on the lines of a boiler suit, sometimes worn in London in air-raid shelters during the bombing raids of the Second World War. It was famously worn by Winston Churchill, who referred to his blue siren suit as his 'rompers', and was so named from its being slipped on over nightclothes at the first wail of the air-raid siren.

**Sister Frigidaire.** *See* MISS FRIGIDAIRE.

**Sitcom.** A situation comedy in the form of a radio or television series in which the same characters are involved in various amusing situations. Classic British examples of the latter are PORRIDGE and *The* GOOD LIFE. The first television sitcom is generally held to be CBS's *The Goldbergs*, first shown in 1949.

**Sit next to Nellie.** To learn an occupation by watching an experienced worker.

**Sit on one's hands.** To withhold one's approval; to take no action. The expression arose in the 1920s and originally applied to members of an audience who withheld their applause.

**Sitting duck.** An easy target. A duck that is sitting is much easier to hit than one in flight. The phrase dates from the 1940s.

**Sitting pretty.** Doing very nicely; enjoying the material comforts of life. The image is of being handsomely placed. The phrase dates from the 1920s and was popularized as the title of two musicals, one of 1924 with lyrics by Jerome Kern, the other of 1933.

**Sit-up-and-beg bike.** An old-fashioned bicycle on which the rider sits upright, like a dog begging.

**Sitzkrieg.** (pseudo-German.) The 'sitting war', the descriptive term applied (in contrast to BLITZKRIEG) to the period of comparative quiet and seeming military inactivity at the outset of the Second World War (September 1939 to April 1940), the period also known as the PHONEY WAR.

**Six, Les.** A group of French composers formed in Paris in 1918 under the aegis of Jean Cocteau and Erik Satie to further their innovative ideas and those of modern music generally. Its members were Arthur Honegger (1892–1955), Darius Milhaud (1892–1974), Francis Poulenc (1899–1963), Louis Durey (1888–1979), Georges Auric (1899–1983) and Germaine Tailleferre (1892–1983). The name was given in 1920 by the French music critic Henri Collet, but the group lost cohesion soon after.

**Six, The.** The six countries Belgium, France, Germany, Italy, the Netherlands and Luxembourg, the original participants in three international organizations: the European Coal and Steel Community (ECSC; 1952), the European Economic Community (EEC; 1957), and the European Atomic Energy Community or Euratom (1957). In 1967 these combined to form the European Communities (EC), but until 1987 the grouping was commonly known as the EEC. *See also* EUROPEAN UNION.

***Six Characters in Search of an Author.*** A play, originally titled *Sei personaggi in cerca d'autore*, by the Italian playwright Luigi Pirandello (1867–1936), first performed in 1921, in which the actors in a theatre act out the destiny of a family of six strangers who have interrupted their rehearsal.

When they first appear the family believe they are merely characters in a play and are in search of the author to find out what is to become of them. After the actors show them their fate they are appalled, despite the actors' insistence that their fate is not real.

**Six Counties.** A term mainly used by Republicans for Northern Ireland, which consists of six of the nine counties of the ancient province and kingdom of Ulster. The remaining three counties are part of the Republic of Ireland, often referred to by Republicans as the Twenty-six Counties. The use of these terms reflects the commitment of Irish Republicans to a 32-county Irish Republic and their reluctance to accept the legitimacy of any state structures that fall short of their ideal. *See also* FREE-STATERS; SINN FÉIN.

**Six-Day War.** The war of 5–10 June 1967 in which Israel occupied the Sinai peninsula, Old Jerusalem, the WEST BANK and the GOLAN HEIGHTS, and defeated the alliance formed between Egypt, Lebanon, Jordan, Syria and Iraq. The conflict is also known as the June War.

**Six feet under.** Dead and buried. A phrase of US origin dating from the 1930s. *Six Feet Under* is the title of a US television drama series (2001–5) about a family of undertakers. *See also* DEEP SIX.

**Six Million Dollar Man, The.** *See* Steve AUSTIN.

**Six o'clock swill.** A somewhat contemptuous term applied to the frenzied consumption of alcohol that in former times preceded the set pub closing time of 6 pm in New South Wales and parts of New Zealand (the law was changed in Australia in 1955 and in New Zealand in 1967). Allowing a smidgin more drinking-up time, it was also termed in New Zealand the 'five-to-six rush' or 'five-to-six swill'.

**Six of the best.** Six strokes of the cane, a once regular ration of corporal punishment in schools. They are 'the best' since they are or were of the best quality.

> 'You'll get six of the very best, over the back of a chair,' said one.
> 'They'll draw a chalk line across you, of course, you know,' said another.
> 'A chalk line?'
> 'Rather. So that every cut can be aimed exactly at the same spot. It hurts much more that way.'
> 'SAKI' (H.H. MUNRO): *The Unbearable Bassington*, ch .2 (1912)

**Six-pack.** A colloquial term for pack of six cans of beer. Hence also, from their resemblance to such cans, a set of well-developed abdominal muscles ('abs').

**Sixty-four** or **sixty-four thousand dollar question.** The last and most difficult question; the crux of the problem. The allusion is to a prize awarded in a US GAME SHOW for answering the final question, the stake having doubled seven times. The expression dates from the 1950s.

> Did that mean the whole area had extractable tin underneath it? 'That's the 64,000 dollar question.'
> *Sunday Telegraph* (5 August 1979)

**Sizzling Sally.** *See* OLD SPARKY.

**Skateboarding.** A sport in which a person 'skates' along pavements or other asphalt surfaces on a narrow wheeled board, propulsion being effected by occasionally pushing one foot against the ground, as in riding a scooter. It has been a popular teenage activity from the 1970s, and initially fell foul of the law and the public for the accidents it caused and the damage it did to walls, benches and passers-by. However, since then it has been embraced as a socially acceptable leisure activity and many parks now provide specially constructed skateboarding areas.

**Skegness is so bracing.** The wording on a famous railway poster first issued by the Great Northern Railway in 1908. It depicts a jolly, pipe-smoking fisherman bounding along the beach at Skegness, the Lincolnshire resort that later became the home of the first BUTLIN'S holiday camp.

**Skid row.** A US expression applied to a district abounding in vicious characters and down-and-outs. In the lumber industry, a skid row was a skidway or grass track down which felled timber was hauled to the river that would carry it down to the sawmill. Early on, Tacoma, near Seattle, flourished on its lumber production, and in due course liquor (in taverns) and women (in brothels) became available for loggers descending the skid row. In time the part of a town where loggers lived or spent their free time came to be known generally as Skid Road. In the mid-20th century this name reverted to 'skid row' and was applied to any area of cheap bar-rooms and seedy hotels frequented by vagrants and alcoholics.

**Skiffle.** A name given to a style of JAZZ of the 1920s, and subsequently to a type of jazz folk music current in Britain in the late 1950s played by a skiffle group, consisting of guitar, drums, kazoo, washboard and other improvised instruments. The word is perhaps of imitative origin. *See also* QUARRY MEN.

**Skin flick.** A pornographic film, featuring (usually female) nudity ('skin'). 'Flick' derives from the FLICKS as an old term for the cinema. The phrase is played with in *Kinflicks*, the title of a 1975 novel by the US writer Lisa Alther.

**Skinhead.** A young person with closely cropped or shaved head, typically the member of an aggressive or racist gang and originally prevalent in the latter half of the 1960s. The term was originally applied in the United States to an army recruit with an extreme CREW CUT. *See also* BOVVER BOY; MODS AND ROCKERS; PUNK.

> It is at these shows that Rosko the brash, shrieking voice, becomes flesh and blood to his different fans – reggae-loving skin-heads, draped and winkle-pickered rockers, tumescent girls.
> RICHARD GILBERT: in *Anatomy of Pop* (1970)

**Skin is cracking.** In colloquial Australian English, when someone's skin is said to be cracking they are dying for a drink, preferably alcoholic. The expression dates from the 1950s.

**Skinny-dipping.** Swimming in the nude, when all one has on is one's skin.

**Skin of Our Teeth, The.** A play (1942) by the US playwright Thornton Wilder (1897–1975) in which the characters jump about almost at whim through the whole range of human history. The title appears in the text when one of the characters describes how they came through the Napoleonic Wars 'by the skin of our teeth' (in other words, very narrowly indeed), but it also expresses the aggressive stance the author was taking in the play against the conventional middle-class drawing-room drama that he himself had already rejected. The saying is an old one, appearing in Job 19:20: 'My bone cleaveth to my skin and to my flesh, and I am escaped with the skin of my teeth.'

**Skirt-chaser.** A man who compulsively pursues women; a dedicated ladies' man. The term dates from the 1940s.

**Sky art.** A term coined in 1969 by the German artist Otto Piene (b.1928) to describe works of art that are viewed in or from the sky. The tag has been used to embrace kite-flying and fireworks displays as well as works using advanced technology. Two noted examples are Piene's own *Olympic Rainbow* (1972), consisting of five helium-filled polythene tubes each 600m long, produced for the Munich Olympic Games, and Charlotte Moorman's *Sky Kiss* (1981–6), in which the artist played her cello while suspended from helium-filled tubes. A high-technology work is Tom Van Sant's *Desert Sun* (1986), in which a series of mirrors reflected sunlight to the sensors of a satellite orbiting the earth.

**Skyhook.** An imaginary device by which something could be suspended in the air. In mountaineering, a skyhook is a small metal device that can be hooked over a tiny flake of rock, enabling upward progress to be made on an otherwise holdless wall.

**Skyjacker.** A criminal who secures passage on an airliner with the intent to terrorize the crew into flying him to a particular destination. Skyjackers are often terrorists but robbers and deranged individuals are also among them. *See also* CARJACKING; HIJACKER.

**Skylab.** The first US space station, launched into orbit round the earth on 14 May 1973. Three successive teams of astronauts conducted experiments on board in the period to February 1974. Its orbit was then adjusted to an altitude which was judged to be sufficient to keep it in space until 1983. It wandered from its orbit in 1978, however, and on 11 July 1979 it burned up and disintegrated as it plunged back into the earth's atmosphere.

**Skylon.** A futuristic sculpture consisting of a large stream-lined spindle-shaped object pointed at each end, somewhat reminiscent of a space projectile, held upright in the air by wires. It was made for the South Bank exhibition as part of the 1951 FESTIVAL OF BRITAIN.

**Skytrain.** The name of a service of cheap-rate 'no-frills' transatlantic flights with unreserved single-class seating operated in the 1970s by Laker Airways Ltd, the enterprise of Freddie Laker (1922–2006). His career suffered following the failure of the project in 1982, but in 1995 he founded Laker Airways, Inc. and started a service of daily trans-atlantic flights from Gatwick to Miami.

**Slag someone off.** To criticize them abusively. The sense is that one is calling them a slag, a term for a contemptible person dating from the 18th century and ultimately deriving from 'slag' in its common sense of refuse or waste material. The current sense dates from the 1970s.

> The following day, Johnny's back on the phone, checking he hadn't got carried away and slagged anybody off.
> *heat* (6–12 January 2000)

**Slam dancing.** A type of dancing to rock music in vogue in the 1980s in which participants deliberately collide with ('slam into') one another. The violent variant arose at PUNK ROCK concerts. *See also* MOSHING.

**Slam dunk.** Something reliable or certain; a foregone con-clusion. The imagery is from baseball, in which a slam dunk is a forceful shot ('dunk') in which the player thrusts ('slams') the ball down through the basket with both hands from above the rim.

**Slap and tickle.** Amorous play or sexual foreplay. The expression dates from the 1920s.

**Slap** or **smack on the wrist.** A reprimand, as administered to a naughty child. An adult who has made some slip may make the gesture to their own wrist by way of self-rebuke. The expression dates from the early 20th century.

**Slapsie Maxie.** The nickname of Maxie Rosenbloom (1904–76), the US boxer and actor in boxing and gangster films. The name was given him by the New York journalist and sportswriter Damon Runyon for his unorthodox style, which consisted in slapping his opponents with open gloves rather than punching them. The use of such blows was subsequently banned by New York's State Athletic Commission.

**Slap someone five.** *See* GIVE SOMEONE FIVE.

**Slash.** A slang word of opposite meanings: on the one hand an alcoholic drink; on the other an act of urination. The former is more common in American than in British usage. Both date from the 1930s.

**Slasher movie.** A sadistic genre of HORROR MOVIE in which victims, typically women or teenage girls, are slashed with knives or razors. A famous example is MIRAMAX's *Scream* (1996), about a psychopathic killer who targets high school students, which was followed by two sequels, *Scream 2* (1997) and *Scream 3* (2000). *See also* ELM STREET; SPLATTER MOVIE.

**Slaughterhouse-Five.** A novel (1969) by the US writer Kurt Vonnegut Jr (b.1922), drawing on his experience of witnessing, as a prisoner of war, the Allied destruction of DRESDEN by fire bombs during the Second World War. The framework of the book concerns Billy Pilgrim, who is transported by ALIENS through a TIME WARP, enabling him to witness events in the past of which he has foreknowledge. So it is that, with other US prisoners, he finds himself shut up in a slaughterhouse (Slaughterhouse-Five) in Dresden when the city is bombed. A film version (1972) was directed by George Roy Hill.

**Sleaze factor.** The sleazy or sordid aspect of a situation, especially in politics. The term originated in the United States, and in Britain it became associated with various scandals and alleged malpractices in the 1980s and 1990s, one of which was the CASH FOR QUESTIONS affair. 'Sleaze' as an alternative form of 'sleaziness' is a relatively recent linguistic development, first recorded in the 1960s.

> Fairly or not … this was the [Conservative] parliament which added the word 'sleaze' to the lexicon of political scribes, and the 'sleaze factor' to the textbooks of political pundits.
> JOHN PIENAAR: in *The BBC News General Election Guide* (1997)

**Sleep around.** To have a number of casual sexual partners. The expression is American in origin and dates from the 1920s. 'To sleep' implying to engage in sexual intercourse dates from Anglo-Saxon times, and it occurs thus in Chaucer and Shakespeare.

> People in London are far more concerned with safe sex; if you sleep around you get a reputation for being a slut.
> *Sunday Times Magazine* (2 January 2000)

**Sleeping policeman.** A slight bump built across a road in order to slow the speed of traffic. The image is of a recumbent but law-enforcing police officer and for this reason other names are now mostly used, such as (unofficially) speed bump or (officially) TRAFFIC CALMING measure. The device was introduced in the 1970s and the name is said to derive from Caribbean English.

**Sleeping with an elephant.** The simile deployed by the Canadian prime minister Pierre Trudeau (b.1919) to describe Canada's relationship with the United States:

> Living with you is in some ways like sleeping with an elephant. No matter how friendly and even-tempered the beast, one is affected by every twitch and grunt.
> Speech to the National Press Club, Washington, D.C.
> (25 March 1969)

The image has been borrowed by others. For example, Ludovic Kennedy gave the title *In Bed with an Elephant* to his 1995 book about Scotland's past and present, the pachyderm in this instance being England.

**Sleepover.** A night spent away from home, especially by a child or young person at a friend's house. The practice took a commercial turn when in the late 1990s the Science Museum, London, organized a 'Science Sleepover' for groups of young visitors, who after attending a series of workshops and lectures were allowed to sleep in the museum following a picnic feast.

**Slick Willie.** A nickname given to Bill Clinton, also known as the COMEBACK KID, by George H.W. Bush (b.1924), his unsuccessful Republican rival in the 1992 US presidential election. Since then Clinton has proved himself as slick as TEFLON. Other hostile nicknames include DOLLAR BILL, the Bill We'll Be Paying for Years, Willy the Weasel and Big Dog (this last suggesting a slobbering, woman-chasing hound dog).

**Slingback.** A type of woman's shoe fashionable from the 1940s, so called because it is held in place by a strap ('sling') around the ankle above the heel.

> [Actress Jennifer] Aniston swept the glam stakes in a multipetticoated, black satin dress, black-and-white pointed sling-backs and an over-the-arm granny bag.
> *heat* (20–26 January 2000)

**Slipped disc.** An anatomical misnomer dating from the 1950s for a disorder of the spine properly known as disc prolapse, in which an intervertebral disc ruptures and part of its pulpy core protrudes, causing pressure on a nerve and pain in the back. The condition, most frequently experienced in the lumbar region, became almost fashionable for a time.

**Slippery slope.** A risky course of action. The image is of traversing a slithery hillside, where one is in danger of losing one's footing and sliding to the bottom. The expression dates from the 1950s. The two words are often associated in sense but quite unrelated in origin.

**Slip, slap, slop.** The slogan used in Australia from 1981 to encourage people to protect themselves from the sun, in the light of the high incidence of skin cancer in the country. The idea was to 'slip' on a T-shirt, 'slap' on a hat, 'slop on some sun cream'. The slogan was originally used in Queensland in the form 'Slip Slop Shove', but was refined into its present form by an advertising copywriter, Philip Adams. Sung on television by Sid the Seagull, it was an instant hit with both children and adults.

**Sloane Ranger.** An expression from the 1980s and early 1990s, describing a young upper class or upper-middle class person who is conservative, well-mannered and educated at boarding school. Part of the GREEN WELLY brigade, those in London live around Sloane Square, Holland Park and Kensington – with the more impoverished living in Fulham or SWONE-ONE. The term was coined in October 1975 by Martina Margetts, a sub-editor on *Harpers and Queen*, and was taken up by the magazine's style editor Peter York (real name Peter Wallis). The name puns on the LONE RANGER. The *Official Sloane Ranger Handbook* (1982) by Ann Barr and Peter York elaborated the theme.See also HOORAY HENRY; PREPPY.

**Sloppy Joe.** A US colloquialism dating from the 1940s for three different objects: (1) a long, loose sweater or pull-over worn by women; (2) a dish made from minced meat cooked in a barbecue sauce and spread on an open bun; (3) a multi-layered sandwich filled with meats, cheeses and mayonnaise. The two lavish comestibles are difficult to eat without getting the fingers and face messy, so they essentially justify their name.

**Slow burn.** An US term dating from the 1930s for gradually increasing anger, as distinct from a sudden outburst of rage. It was associated with the comedian Edgar Kennedy (1890–1948), 'Master of the Slow Burn' and one of the original KEYSTONE KOPS who predated the arrival of Charlie Chaplin.

**Slow learner.** One of a number of euphemisms for a school

pupil of below-average intelligence. This one dates from the 1930s.

**Smack on the wrist.** *See* SLAP ON THE WRIST.

**Small Back Room, The.** A suspense novel (1943) by Nigel Balchin (1908–70) about a disabled bomb-disposal expert in the Second World War whose efficiency and nerve are eroded by drink, emotional problems and bureaucracy. It draws on Balchin's experience as a psychologist in the War Office and as deputy scientific adviser to the Army Council, with the rank of brigadier. The title echoes Lord Beaverbrook's famous speech about BACKROOM BOYS. A film version (1949) was directed by Michael Powell and Emeric Pressburger.

**Small but perfectly formed.** Said of someone or something noticeably small but compensating for this by a perfection of quality. The phrase occurs in a letter written in October 1914 by the Conservative MP and diplomat Duff Cooper to Lady Diana Manners, later his wife, and quoted in Artemis Cooper's *Durable Fire* (1983): 'Your two stout lovers frowning at one another across the hearth rug, while your small, but perfectly formed one kept the party in a roar.' The expression was probably not original to Cooper but drawn from the fashionable talk of the period. The usage is often tongue-in-cheek or journalistically formulaic for anything small.

**Small is beautiful.** A phrase popularized by the German-born British economist E.F. Schumacher in the title of his book subtitled 'A Study of Economics as if People Mattered' (1973). The concept is of opposition to large-scale institutions, bureaucratic centralization, expansionist businesses and all that is blind to the human scale. Schumacher was originally going to call his book *The Homecomers*; it was his publisher Desmond Briggs who came up with the catchy final phrase. *See also* BLACK IS BEAUTIFUL; SMALL BUT PERFECTLY FORMED.

**Small print.** *See* FINE PRINT.

**Smart bomb.** A type of radio- or laser-guided bomb that can accurately home on a target. It is 'smart' because it is seemingly intelligent. The general public awareness of such weapons arose from media descriptions of their deployment in the First GULF WAR (1991), although they date from the 1970s. Bombs that do not possess such sophisticated guidance systems, such as the DAISY-CUTTER, are sometimes referred to as 'dumb bombs'. *See also* BRILLIANT PEBBLES; SMART CARD.

**Smart Car.** A brand of diminutive two-seater car with a very short body length, shorter than a MINI and scarcely longer than the car's width. It was launched by Daimler-Chrysler in Europe in 1998 and is intended for urban use and for parking in spaces impossible for other cars. Its introduction into the United States looked a challenging prospect:

> Anything that size in this country is basically SUV road kill.
>
> MICHELLE BARAN, a New York resident: quoted in 'Can the Smart Car Move America?', BBC News World Edition website (27 April 2004)

A longer-bodied sports model has already appeared in Europe.

**Smart card.** A plastic card (*see* PLASTIC) with a built-in microprocessor, holding personal data or financial information and thus able to serve as an IDENTITY CARD. It dates from the 1980s.

**Smarts.** Intelligence; know-how; nous; 'brains'. A US colloquialism, often used in conjunction with a defining term (e.g. 'street smarts', the quality of being streetwise, 'book smarts', a modern equivalent of 'book learning', 'money smarts', 'web smarts').

> *Car Smarts: An Easy-to-Use Guide to Understanding Your Car and Communicating With Your Mechanic*
>
> MARY JACKSON: title (1998)

**Smash-and-grab raid.** A directly descriptive phrase of the 1920s for a robbery in which the thief smashes a shop window and grabs some of the objects on display. A later development, evolving partly as a result of the deterrent presented by toughened glass, is the RAM RAID.

**Smear campaign.** An attempt to ruin a person's reputation by slander or vilification. The expression dates from the 1930s, with 'smear' in the sense of an unpleasant mark that 'sticks'.

**Smersh.** Acronym for Smert Shpionam (Russian, 'death to spies'), originally created as the Special Department of the NKVD (*see* KGB) by Lavrenty Beria in 1941. Its job was to deal with 'traitors, cowards and deserters' in the Red Army and the intelligence services. From 1943 to 1946 it functioned as a separate agency directly under STALIN.

In the James BOND novels, SMERSH is a Soviet organization dedicated to subverting the West and assassinating its agents (especially Bond). In the first Bond novel, *Casino Royale* (1953), a Soviet agent carves an initial representing SMERSH on the back of Bond's hand, and references to the resulting scar appear in subsequent novels. In many of the Bond films SMERSH becomes the less politically loaded S.P.E.C.T.R.E.

**Smiley, George.** The British intelligence chief who features in various novels by John Le Carré, beginning with *Call for the Dead* (1961) and *A Murder of Quality* (1962). He plays a relatively small part in Le Carré's early spy stories, *The Spy Who Came in From the Cold* (1963) and *The Looking Glass War* (1965) but comes to the fore in TINKER, TAILOR, SOLDIER, SPY (1974) and its immediate sequels, *The Honourable Schoolboy* (1977) and *Smiley's People* (1980), in the last of which his deadly enemy is a Russian master-spy known as Karla. The novels raised Smiley to a cult figure appropriate to the age of the CAMBRIDGE SPY RING. In the television version of *Tinker, Tailor, Soldier, Spy* (1979) Smiley was played with great subtlety by Alec Guinness, who again took the role in *Smiley's People* (1982).

> Smiley is his [Le Carré's] best known and best loved character because he is a still point in the turn-around world, a figure of stability amid so much that is confused and provisional.
>
> BLAKE MORRISON: in *Times Literary Supplement* (11 April 1986)

**Smiley face.** A circular smiling yellow face (also known simply as 'smiley'), with a curve for the smile and two dots for the eyes, and originating in the youth culture of the 1970s as an international symbol of hope, peace or solidarity. The face can also be created on a computer keyboard using punctuation marks and is used in this form in E-MAIL, when it appears sideways. Its basic form is :–), denoting that the writer is pleased or joking. There are many variants, such as ;–) to denote lasciviousness and 0:–) for innocence. The symbol is also known as an emoticon (from 'emotion' and 'icon').

**Smith Square.** A Westminster square that long had contrasting political associations, and at one time held the headquarters of the Conservative, Labour and Liberal Parties. Until 1980 the LABOUR PARTY was at Transport House, the former headquarters of the Transport and General Workers' Union, and between 1958 and 2004 the Conservative Party was at No. 32. *See also* TRANSPORT HOUSE.

**Smog.** A linguistic and literal blend of 'smoke' and 'fog', as an insidious form of polluted air. The word appears to have been first used in 1905 by H.A. des Voeux of the Coal Smoke Abatement Society to describe atmospheric conditions over British towns. It was popularized by his report to the Manchester conference of the Society in 1911 on the many deaths caused by the pall that paralyzed Glasgow and Edinburgh during the autumn of 1909. The dense smoke-laden fogs that afflicted London and other major cities in the 1950s and 1960s are now a thing of the past, but they have been succeeded by the so-called 'summertime smogs' and 'wintertime smogs' periodically produced by emissions from the growing number of motor vehicles. Measures to control pollution of this type as well as that resulting from industrial processes have had some success, but the nuisance has still not been reduced to acceptable levels, let alone abolished.

**Smoke and mirrors.** An explanation or evincement that is essentially misleading. The allusion is to the smoke and mirrors used by conjurors in order to create an illusion.

> When confronted with the sort of fiscal numbers that [Chancellor of the Exchequer] Gordon Brown laid out last week, professional cynics are bound to search high and low for the catch. Has it been done with smoke and mirrors?
>
> *The Times* (15 November 1999)

**Smoke-filled room.** A room filled with tobacco smoke from which political leaders emerge with a decision after long hours of discussion or bargaining. The original smoke-filled room was a suite in the Blackstone Hotel, Chicago, in which Warren Harding was selected as the Republican presidential candidate in June 1920. The phrase itself appears to have come from a comment by Harding's chief supporter, Harry Daugherty, that the meeting would not be able to decide between the two obvious candidates and that a group of bleary-eyed senators would 'sit down about two o'clock in the morning around a table in a smoke-filled room in some hotel and decide the nomination'. That was what actually happened and Warren Harding was duly selected. The smoke in this instance was probably emitted by cigars. *See also* BEER AND SANDWICHES.

**Smokestack industries.** A US term dating from the 1970s for the heavy manufacturing industries, especially when coal-powered and associated with high levels of pollution and old-fashioned technology.

**Smokey Bear.** An American nickname for a policeman, especially a state highway patrol officer. The allusion is to the broad-brimmed ranger's hat worn by such officers, resembling that worn by Smokey Bear, an animal character used in US fire-prevention campaigns. The familiar poster figure, with ranger hat, blue jeans and shovel, was created in 1944 by the US Forest Service. There was also a real bear of this name, found in 1950 as a badly burned cub in the Lincoln National Forest, New Mexico, after a five-day fire. He was nursed back to health, adopted by the Forest Service, and taken to Washington, D.C., where he became one of the most popular inhabitants of the National Zoo. He died in 1976 and was buried in the Smokey Bear National Park at Capitan, New Mexico, near the site where he had been originally found.

**Smoking can seriously damage your health.** A government health warning printed on cigarette packets and tobacco advertisements in the UK since 1971 (the word 'seriously' was added in 1977). A variety of other slogans are now also used and the size of the warning in relation to the size of the packet has increased dramatically. Journalists and politicians endlessly play on the phrase, usually in the form of 'X can seriously damage your wealth'.

**Smoking gun.** A piece of incontrovertible incriminating evidence. The allusion is to a gun that has obviously only just been fired after being used to commit a crime. The expression is particularly applied to the incriminating tape of 23 June 1973 in the WATERGATE affair, on which President Nixon can be heard approving a plan to direct the CIA to request that the FBI halt its investigation into the source of the cash possessed by the Watergate burglars and into the 'silence' money promised them by the administration. Nixon would almost certainly not have been threatened with impeachment if the tape had remained undiscovered.

The phrase acquired a particularly apt association with the widely diverging views, before, during and after the invasion of Iraq in 2003, about whether Saddam Hussein still possessed WEAPONS OF MASS DESTRUCTION. Their discovery would have been hailed by the finders as a 'smoking gun'.

**Smokin' Joe.** A nickname for the heavyweight boxer Joe Frazier (b.1944), winner of the 'fight of the century' against Muhammad Ali in 1971 (when he became the first boxer to defeat Ali in a professional fight) and possessor of a ferociously powerful punch. The name has sometimes been applied to the great West Indian batsman Sir Viv Richards (Isaac Vivian Alexander Richards; b.1952), because of his brooding demeanour and powerful batting style. *See also* THRILLER IN MANILA.

**Smorgasbord.** (Swedish, 'bread and butter table'.) A Swedish-style range of open sandwiches and delicacies served as hors d'oeuvres or a buffet. The term dates from the 1920s and gained a figurative sense for any wide range or variety, whether of things or people.

> But what really stands out are the women, a smorgasbord of international female talent.
>
> *heat* (23–29 September 1999)

**Smurfs.** These blue pixies with white stocking caps were created by the Belgian illustrator Pierre 'Peyo' Culliford and first appeared in the comic *Le Journal de Spirou* in 1958. They came before a wider public in the late 1970s, when they featured in a series of promotions by British Petroleum, and the peak of their popularity was in 1982. Their name varied in different countries. To the French they were *Les Schtroumpfs*, to the Germans *Die Schlümpfe*, to the Dutch *De smurfen*, to the Spanish *Los Pitufos*, to the Italians *I Puffi*, to the Czechs *Šmoulové* and to the Finns *Smurffit*.

**SNAFU.** A US services slang acronym denoting a complete COCK-UP. First recorded in 1942, it is based on 'situation normal: all fucked up' (often tidied up for family audiences as 'all fouled up'). *See also* FUBAR.

**Snail mail.** A jocular term for conventional mail, which is by its very nature slower than E-MAIL.

**Snake.** A former nickname for the European Monetary System (EMS), inaugurated in 1979, under which the exchange rates of the currencies of member states fluctuate within certain limits. The name derived from the earlier 'snake in the tunnel', or narrow fluctuation in rates of exchange agreed by the SIX and countries awaiting membership of the COMMON MARKET, so called by contrast with the wider range of fluctuation in the foreign exchange markets.

**Snake eyes.** A throw of two at dice, regarded as unlucky. The two white dots suggest the eyes of a snake about to strike.

**Snakes and ladders.** A favourite board game among children, evolving at the beginning of the 20th century from an Indian game called *moksha patamu* ('heaven and hell', literally 'salvation by flight'), used as a means of religious instruction. The board is divided into 100 numbered squares and decorated with snakes and ladders running respectively from a higher number to a lower and vice versa. A counter landing at the foot of a ladder thus takes the player nearer to the finish, while one landing on the head of snake is a setback or reversal. The symbolism is vaguely biblical, the ladder going up to heaven and the snake representing a 'fall'.

**Snap out of it!** Pull yourself together! Cheer up! An exhortation to a person to quit their mood of depression or despair and revert to normal. The expression dates from the 1920s.

**Snatch squad.** A group of personnel trained to operate as a unit in riot control by identifying ringleaders and arresting ('snatching') them. The technique was first used by the army in Northern Ireland in the early 1970s (*see* TROUBLES) and was later adopted by the police generally.

**Sneak preview.** The screening of a film in advance of its general release to test audience reaction. More generally a sneak preview is an advance sighting of any forthcoming work or event, as the viewing of a new car model before it is officially revealed.

**Snettisham Treasure.** A ploughman working near this Norfolk village in 1948 turned up a metal object that his foreman pronounced to be a bit of brass bedstead. It turned out to be a gold torque and the beginning of the discovery of the richest Iron Age hoard in Britain. Further finds were made over the years, that in 1991 yielding a treasure trove of 1st-century BC Celtic coins. The location of the hoard is a mystery, as there is no sign of any contemporary settlement.

**Snitch.** In the Harry POTTER novels of J.K. Rowling, a small, winged golden ball (in full, the 'Golden Snitch') that features in the game of QUIDDITCH. It flies at great speed, and a member of each team (called the 'Seeker'; Potter is one) is assigned to catch it. Its capture earns an extra 150 points and brings the game to an end.

**Snoopy.** The day-dreaming beagle first appeared in Charles M. Schulz's comic strip *Peanuts* in 1950. He is Charlie Brown's dog and, although he never speaks, he makes up for it by his endless dreams of glory, enacting in his imagination roles that will make him world famous. *See also* HAPPINESS IS A WARM PUPPY.

**Snowball's chance in hell.** No chance at all. The phrase is usually found in the negative, as: 'He doesn't have a snowball's chance in hell of passing.' The expression dates from the 1950s. *See also* TILL HELL FREEZES OVER.

**Snow bunny.** Skiers' slang for an inexperienced female skier or alternatively for an attractive young woman who frequents ski slopes.

***Snow Goose, The.*** A novella (1941) by the US writer Paul Gallico (1897–1976). It is a love story, in which a goose flies over the rescue craft at the evacuation of the Allied troops from DUNKIRK in 1940.

**Snow job.** A deception or concealment of one's real motive in an attempt to flatter or persuade. The image is of an object concealed under innocent-looking snow. The expression arose among American GIs in the Second World War, when it was typically applied to an elaborate fiction presented to a superior officer with the aim of excusing some misdemeanour.

**SNP.** The Scottish National Party, which evolved from the National Party of Scotland formed in 1928 by Hugh MacDiarmid and others. The name was changed in 1934 when it merged with the Scottish Party, a rival nationalist party founded two years earlier. It has had mixed fortunes in elections and made several policy shifts, but it has consistently campaigned for the establishment of an independent Scottish parliament, a goal finally achieved in 1999. *See also* PLAID CYMRU; TARTAN TORIES.

**Snuff movie.** A pornographic film supposedly recording the actual death of one of the participants. The genuineness of such films remains in doubt. 'To snuff it' is a 19th-century colloquialism meaning 'to die', in allusion to the sudden extinction of life, like a snuffed candle.

**Soap opera.** A term for a sentimental type of play, usually in serial form, originally used by commercial radio and television in advertising soap and other commodities. Such programmes were sponsored by soap manufacturers as an early form of PRODUCT PLACEMENT, perhaps because they were obviously 'clean'. Radio producers then nicknamed the plays 'soaps'. When they were taken up by television 'opera' was added as a humorous allusion to their increasingly 'heavy' content.

Noted British soap operas at the beginning of the 21st century, apart from CORONATION STREET and EASTENDERS, have been *Brookside* (1982–2003), set on a private housing estate in Liverpool, and *Emmerdale* (from 1972), centring on a Yorkshire Dales farm. Australian soaps include *Home and Away* (1988), set in a fictional seaside town, and *Neighbours* (1985), located in Ramsay Street in the fictional Melbourne suburb of Erinsborough, the latter's name being a near anagram of the title.

**Sob sister.** A now dated nickname for a female journalist who writes the answers to readers' personal problems, so called because of the tear-provoking sentimentality involved. The expression dates from the early years of the 20th century.

**Sob story.** An explanation, especially an excuse, that plays on the emotions. The phrase dates from the early 20th century and presumably represents a reaction to Victorian sentimentality.

**Sob stuff.** A phrase describing newspaper, film or other stories of a highly sentimental kind, otherwise cheap or tear-jerking pathos.

**Socceroos.** The nickname of the Australian international soccer team, as a blend of 'soccer' and 'roo', the colloquial abbreviation of 'kangaroo'.

**Social chapter.** The part of the MAASTRICHT TREATY that dealt with social policy, and in particular workers' rights and welfare, and that among other points recommended a minimum wage. Its basis was the so-called social charter, signed in December 1989 by 11 EUROPEAN UNION member states.

**Social Contract.** A concept in political philosophy that goes back to Hobbes, Locke and Rousseau, denoting the agreement between a people and their rulers, and

establishing the principle that the latter rule through the consent of the former. The phrase was revived in a more limited sense in the 1970s to describe a compact agreed in 1973 between the Labour Party and the trade unions, by which, in return for wage restraint, the next Labour government would introduce legislation favourable to the unions. Jim Callaghan used the phrase in 1972, when he referred to the document entitled *Labour's Programme*:

> We say that what Britain needs is a new Social Contract. That is what this document is all about.

When Labour came to power in 1974 it proceeded to repeal anti-union legislation and introduced such measures as the Health and Safety at Work Act 1974, and the Employment Protection Acts 1975 and 1978. The Social Contract came apart in 1978 when a wave of public-sector strikes ushered in the WINTER OF DISCONTENT.

**Social Credit.** An economic theory introduced by the Scottish engineer Clifford Douglas (1879–1952), according to which consumer spending power should be increased either by subsiding producers so that they can lower prices or by distributing the profits of industry to consumers. Most economists doubted the efficacy of such a system. Social Credit parties in Alberta and British Columbia, Canada, won provincial elections between the 1930s and the 1980s.

**Socialism with a human face.** What the liberal, reforming communist government of Alexander Dubček attempted to introduce to Czechoslovakia during the PRAGUE SPRING of 1968:

> In the service of the people we followed such a policy that socialism would not lose its human face.
>
> ALEXANDER DUBČEK: in *Rudé Právo*, 19 July 1968.

The WARSAW PACT tanks rolled in the following month.

**Socialist realism.** A term used to describe the official artistic doctrine adopted by the Congress of Soviet Writers in 1924 and approved by STALIN, Gorky, Bukharin and Zhdanov. It required the creative artist to 'serve the Revolution' by presenting images of socialist possibility and enterprise, and condemned the bourgeois artist, together with all forms of experimentalism and formalism, as degenerate and pessimistic. The works of James Joyce (*see* ULYSSES) were singled out for particular denigration.

**Socionyms.** Such may be called the acronyms, mainly of US origin, devised by marketing men from the 1980s to designate particular social groups, especially from the point of view of age, income, marital status and professional placing. The designations were originally those of aspirational young people, the so-called YUPPIES, climbing the ladder of fame and fortune, but the emphasis then shifted to the older groups, which are the fastest-growing and potentially most profitable categories in Britain. The acronyms themselves are often evocative, and range from the factual to the facetious, the latter punningly devised for the purpose. A selection of some of the better-known is given below.

DING: double income, no girlfriend (typically a professional sportsman with a regular job)

DINK: double income, no kids

DINKY: double income, no kids – yet

DUMP: downwardly mobile urban middle-class professional

GLAM: grey, leisured, affluent middle class

KIPPERS

NEETS

PIPPY: person inheriting parents' property

SINBAD: single income, no boyfriend and desperate

SITCOM: single income, two children, oppressive mortgage

TRIFFID: three recent infants, falling further into debt

WOOP: well-off older person

YUMP: young upwardly mobile manual person

*See also* TWENTY-SOMETHING; WRINKLY; YUCKIES.

**Sock it to someone.** To deal with someone vigorously; hence, to amaze them. To 'sock' (not related to the garment) is to hit forcefully. The catchphrase 'Sock it to me!', meaning 'Amaze me!', 'Surprise me!', 'Let's hear it!' was popularized by the US television comedy series ROWAN AND MARTIN'S LAUGH-IN.

**Sodom by the Sea.** A nickname given to HOLLYWOOD by those who regard it as a den of sexual depravity. The allusion is to Sodom and Gomorrah, the 'cities of the plain' destroyed by God with fire and brimstone 'because their sin is very grievous' (Genesis 18–19).

**Sod's law.** Essentially the same as MURPHY'S LAW but dating later, from the 1970s. 'Sod' here is simply a name for an awkward or frustrating situation that provokes one to think or say 'Sod it!' Some linguistic legalists discern a fine distinction between the two laws. If a piece of bread lands buttered side down when dropped, they say, that is Sod's law. Murphy's law, on the other hand, dictates that as a piece of bread can land this way, sooner or later it will. Viewed thus, Sod's law can be seen as a corollary of Murphy's law.

**Sod this for a game of soldiers.** An expression of irritation or exasperation at a situation, especially one that seems pointless or a waste of time. One common variant is: 'Blow this for a lark.'

**SOE.** The Special Operations Executive, a branch of the British intelligence services in the Second World War that specialized in sending agents to foster and support resistance movements in occupied Europe. SOE was set up in July 1940 and disbanded in 1946. One of its major successes was in helping Tito's communist partisans in Yugoslavia, but its most important theatre was France, where SOE agents worked with the MAQUIS. One of the many SOE agents who died in France was Violette Szabo, whose story is the subject of the 1958 film CARVE HER NAME WITH PRIDE.

**Sofa sitcom.** A disparaging term for a mild, middle-class, domestic television SITCOM in which the characters mostly exchange banter and humour while sitting around on sofas. Such sitcoms were particularly common from the late 1960s, and included *Father Dear Father* (1968–1973) and *Terry and June* (1979–87), but the term was turned on its head overnight with the screening in the late 1990s of *The* ROYLE FAMILY, in which the sofas essentially epitomize the characters seated on them.

**Soft art.** A term for sculpture that uses non-rigid materials, such as rope, cloth, leather, paper or canvas. Such works were in vogue in the 1960s and 1970s, and an early and influential exponent was the Swedish-born American sculptor Claes Oldenburg (b.1929), famous for giant replicas of foodstuffs such as hamburgers made from stuffed vinyl and canvas.

**Soft focus.** A slight and deliberate blurring of the focus in a photograph, often used for advertising effect or to tone down an otherwise pornographic image. In a film it may be used to photograph a person who may not stand up to sharper definition, or to enhance an exotic shot in a musical number. In F.W. Murnau's silent film *Sunrise* (1927) soft focus is used to create a romantic mood, while it evokes nostalgia and idealism in the picnic scene in Arthur Penn's BONNIE AND CLYDE (1967).

**Softly-softly.** Said of any action that is cautious and patient. The term comes from the quasi-proverb, 'Softly, softly, catchee monkey', recorded in the early years of the 20th century. The present phrase was popularized by the television series *Softly, Softly* (1966–76), about the work of a fictional Midlands crime squad. 'Softly, Softly' is the motto of the Lancashire police. *See also* Z-CARS.

**Soft-shoe dance.** A form of tap dance performed in soft-soled shoes instead of shoes with metal taps. It first became popular in the United States in the 1920s, and one of its most watchable practitioners was the American actor and dancer Ray Bolger (1904–87).

**Soft touch.** A person who is easily imposed upon, especially to give or lend money. The expression is of US origin and gained currency in the GREAT DEPRESSION.

**Soft underbelly.** The most weakly defended part of something, where it is most vulnerable to attack. The metaphor was born of Winston Churchill's obsession with an attack on Nazi Europe via its southern coast, which he thought would have a greater chance of quick success than an invasion of northern France, and hence shorten the war. In the House of Commons he announced:

> We make this wide encircling movement in the Mediterranean ... having for its object the exposure of the underbelly of the Axis, especially Italy, to heavy attack.
>
> *Hansard* (11 November 1942)

In the event the underbelly proved harder than expected and the invasion became seriously bogged down, but by the end of the 1940s the expression 'soft underbelly' had established a wider metaphorical application.

> I gave him [John Betjeman] a lift back to Radnor Walk and as we bowled along Royal Avenue I called it 'the soft underbelly of Chelsea', which made him laugh a lot.
>
> NED SHERRIN (referring to the 1970s): quoted in Bevis Hillier, *Betjeman: The Bonus of Laughter* (2004)
>
> Batteries, the soft underbelly of pervasive computing.
>
> *IFTF's Future Now* (21 July 2005)

**SoHo.** An American acronym of the 1990s for 'small office, home office', meaning the small-business sector of the economy, especially the part of it that is home-based. The spelling with capital 'S' and 'H' derives from SoHo, the nickname of an area in Manhattan, New York City, itself an abbreviation of 'south of Houston Street' and in turn evoking London's Soho. *See also* NOHO.

**So last century.** A dismissive term for anything regarded as old hat, deployed by would-be trend-setters as soon as the new millennium dawned (and building on the existing expression 'so last year'). A quick trawl of the Internet will find that among the things deemed 'so last century' are socks (as Christmas gifts for men), coffins (why not have one's ashes fired into space?) and certainty (this is apparently the era of the disorderly system).

**Soldiers.** Strips of bread or toast dipped into a soft-boiled egg, so called as the yolk gives them a yellow 'coat' or uniform. The colloquial term, popular with children, like the breakfast *bonne bouche* itself, dates from the 1960s.

> What better ... than a glorious boiled egg with soldier dipped in yolk, which if started from boiling water will take only four minutes to prepare (toast included).
>
> *The Times*, letter to the editor (28 December 1999)

**Solheim Cup.** The women's golfing trophy corresponding to the RYDER CUP, awarded to the winners of a biennial match between European professionals and those of the United States. It takes its name from the Norwegian-born American inventor of the Ping putter, Karsten Solheim (1911–2000), who together with his wife Louise first presented it in 1990.

**Solidarity.** An independent trade union in Poland, which evolved into a mass movement for political change and which lit the touchpaper for sweeping opposition to communist regimes right across central and eastern Europe. It was formed in 1980 under Lech Wałesa (b.1943), banned in 1981, following the imposition of martial law, and legalized again in 1989, when it won a majority in elections. Its name translates the Polish original (*Solidarność*).

**Somebody up there loves me.** I am having a good run of luck at the moment. 'Somebody' is God; 'up there' is heaven. The expression is of US origin and dates from the 1960s. *Somebody Up There Likes Me* (1956), starring Paul Newman and Pier Angeli, is a sentimental film based on the life of the boxer Rocky GRAZIANO.

**Some chicken! Some neck!** The conclusion of a defiant speech made by Winston Churchill to the Canadian parliament, 30 December 1941:

> When I warned them [the French government] that Britain would fight on alone whatever they did, their generals told their prime minister and his divided cabinet: 'In three weeks England will have her neck wrung like a chicken.' Some chicken! Some neck!

***Some Like It Hot.*** A sparkling film comedy (1959), written by Billy Wilder (1906–2002) and I.A.L. Diamond (1920–88). Jack Lemmon and Tony Curtis star as two jazz musicians who disguise themselves as women and join an all-girl band en route to Miami in order to escape the murderous attentions of some gangsters after they accidentally witness the ST VALENTINE'S DAY MASSACRE. The title of the film relates as much to the heat of the situation in which the two heroes find themselves as to the 'hot' jazz they like to play. In retrospect, it also came to symbolize aspects of the film that caused it to receive a heated reception in conservative quarters, especially the sensual performance of Marilyn MONROE and the dubious relationship that develops between the disguised Lemmon and a besotted millionaire, played by Joe E. Brown. Brown's character delivers the film's celebrated closing line, 'Nobody's perfect', on discovering that his fiancée is in fact a man.

There may be a link between the film's title and the 18th-century nursery rhyme 'Pease porridge hot':

> Some like it hot

Some like it cold
Some like it in the pot
Nine days old.

**Some Mothers Do 'Ave 'Em.** A television SITCOM broadcast from 1973 to 1978 and starring Michael Crawford as the well-meaning but disastrously accident-prone wimp Frank Spencer, typically wearing mac and beret. His long-suffering, sympathetic wife, Betty, was played by Michelle Dotrice. Crawford's interpretation of his role as Spencer imbued him with a nature that was as childlike as it was comical, earning him an affectionate place in the public psyche. The title adopted a 1920s catchphrase implying that some mothers seem to have a simpleton for a son.

**Some Tame Gazelle.** The first novel (1950) by Barbara Pym (1913–80). It is a *roman à clef* in that Harriet and Belinda, two spinster sisters, are based on Pym's sister and herself, and other characters on people she knew as an undergraduate at Oxford, represented now in middle age. Both sisters turn down offers of marriage, preferring their known routine to the uncertainties of the married state: 'Some tame gazelle or some gentle dove or even a poodle dog – something to love, that was the point.' The title and the reference are from a song by Thomas Haynes Bayly (1797–1839):

Some tame gazelle, or some gentle dove:
Something to love, oh, something to love!

They also recall the parody by Charles Dickens of lines of Thomas Moore (1779–1852), put into the mouth of Dick Swiveller: 'I never loved a tree or flower, but 'twas the first to fade away; I never nursed a dear Gazelle, to glad me with its soft black eye, but when it came to know me well, and love me, it was sure to marry a market-gardener' (*The Old Curiosity Shop*, ch. 56).

**Something else.** An exceptional person or thing. It is a slang usage, which can be traced back to early 20th-century America.

As a group they are something else, but off-stage they're pretty untogether, and they need someone like me to get them to the top.
JENNY FABIAN and JOHNNY BYRNE: *Groupie* (1969)

'Something else again', on the other hand, is used when a comparison, typically disadvantageous, is made with what is already noteworthy.

Getting out of a car is always an ordeal for women in the public eye. When you're heavily pregnant it's something else again.
*Sunday Times* (6 June 1999)

**Something for the weekend.** 'Something for the weekend,

Sir?' was a supposedly stock question put to a male customer by a barber after a haircut, the 'something' implicitly being a packet of condoms. The euphemistic catchphrase still exists in various contexts and was the title of a spectacularly NAFF television series of 1999, in which members of the public were interviewed about their sex lives and participated in a range of suggestive games and stunts.

The days when a Friday night visit to the barber's shop ended with the whispered enquiry: 'Anything for the weekend, Sir?' are long past.
*The Times* (11 August 1999)

**Something in the water.** 'It must be something in the water' is a humorous way of accounting for the unusual fecundity of a place's population or for any eccentric human or animal behaviour.

Teachers at High Crags Nursery, West Yorkshire, have to deal daily with five sets of twins in the same class … Joanne Light, a nursery nurse, said: 'There must be something in the water round here.'
*The Times* (29 November 1999)

**Something nasty in the woodshed.** Something shocking or distasteful in a person's past that has been kept secret. The phrase comes from Stella Gibbons's novel COLD COMFORT FARM (1932), in which Aunt Ada Doom's repeated assertion that she has seen 'something nasty in the woodshed' ensures that her family continually attend her. There is a curious echo of the 19th-century 'nigger in the woodpile', although the sense there is of a hidden snag or drawback.

**Something of the night.** A description of Conservative politician Michael Howard (b.1941) by Anne Widdecombe (*see* Doris KARLOFF), who had served under him when he was home secretary (1993–7) in John Major's government. The actual phrase she used, quoted in the *Sunday Times* of 11 May 1997 after the Tory defeat in the 1997 general election, was: 'He has something of the night in him.' It hinted at darkly sinister personal qualities (reflected for some in his somewhat saturnine demeanour), and dogged him for some years afterwards.

In many cartoons, especially during his time as party leader (2003–5), Howard was depicted as Count Dracula, and he played up to this image one Christmas by sending his friends copies of Bram Stoker's novel *Dracula* with his own picture on the cover. The journalist and broadcaster Anne Robinson, a family friend, says that Howard gives a passable impression of someone who would 'like to kick your cat or put your baby in prison if it cried'.

**Something Wicked This Way Comes.** A SCIENCE FICTION

fantasy (1962) by Ray Bradbury (b.1920). When a circus comes to town, two boys watch an old woman becoming young again and a man's severed leg being put back. The transformations are a deep mystery to them. The title quotes the words of the Second Witch about Macbeth in Shakespeare's *Macbeth*:

> By the pricking of my thumbs
> Something wicked this way comes.
> IV.i

A film version (1983) directed by Jack Clayton presented the original as a grim fairy tale.

**Somewhere in X.** In the First World War, a reference to a locality in the theatre of war that could not be named directly for security reasons. It was thus said to be 'somewhere in' a larger region, such as 'somewhere in Flanders', 'somewhere in France'. In the Second World War 'somewhere in England' was similarly current, and the expression is still in use for any undivulged location.

**'Somewhere Over the Rainbow'.** A song by Yip Harburg (1898–1981), with music by Harold Arlen, for the 1939 film of *The* WIZARD OF OZ, sung by Dorothy (Judy Garland). It has come to epitomize longing for a never-never land.

> Somewhere over the rainbow
> Way up high,
> There's a land that I heard of
> Once in a lullaby.

**Somewhere to the right of Genghis Khan.** Said of right-wing views of the most extreme kind. Genghis Khan (1162–1227), the founder of the Mongol Empire, is generally regarded as the archetype of a repressive and tyrannical ruler.

> Of course, in those days, the union leaders were well to the right of Genghis Khan.
> ARTHUR SCARGILL: quoted by John Mortimer in *Sunday Times* (10 January 1982)

**Somme.** The name of a river and *département* in northern France, notorious in British folk memory as the location of an extended and costly Allied offensive on the WESTERN FRONT in the First World War. Launched on 1 July 1916, the battle dragged on until 18 November. Initially the plan called for the involvement of large numbers of French troops, but with the French army being 'bled white' at VERDUN the burden fell largely on their British allies, commanded by Sir Douglas Haig (1861–1928). By the time it was launched the operation had become a large-scale diversion, intended not only to gain territory but to drain German manpower.

The offensive took place along a 30-km (18-mile) front running more or less northwards from the River Somme between Amiens and Péronne. Despite a massive preliminary bombardment lasting eight days, the deeply entrenched German defences were left largely intact, as was the barbed wire. On the first day of the attack the British lost 58,000 casualties, a third of them killed, making this the worst day in the history of the British Army. By the end of the day nearly all the attackers had been forced back to their own trenches. However, the Allies continued to attack throughout the summer and autumn, and by the time operations were suspended, owing to the winter weather, they had gained a maximum of 12km (7 miles).

Total British casualties were 420,000, while the French total was nearly 200,000. The Germans suffered an estimated 500,000, and never really recovered from the loss of junior officers and NCOs, in some ways justifying Haig's unimaginative war of attrition. However, the Somme has subsequently become synonymous with senseless slaughter.

*See also* THIEPVAL MEMORIAL; ULSTER VOLUNTEER FORCE.

**Son et lumière.** (French, 'sound and light'.) Pageantry and dramatic spectacles presented after dark in an appropriate natural or historic setting, particularly in vogue in Britain during the 1960s, and adopted from enactments of this type at French châteaux such as Chambord (where *son et lumière* originated in the early 1950s). They are accompanied by, and dependent on, lighting effects, suitable music and narrative.

**Song in one's heart, A.** A feeling of joy or pleasure. The phrase comes from a song by Lorenz Hart in the musical *Spring is Here* (1929), which became familiar to British radio listeners after the Second World War as the signature tune of the long-running BBC record-request programme *Family Favourites*.

> With a song in my heart, –
> I behold your adorable face.
> LORENZ HART: 'With a Song in My Heart' (song)

**Sonny Jim.** *See* SUNNY JIM.

**Sony.** The consumer electronics and entertainment company of this name was founded in Tokyo in 1946 by Ibuka Masaru, whose Japan Precision Instruments Company had supplied electronic devices in the Second World War, and Akio Morita, an applied sciences instructor. Their company was called the Tokyo Tsushin Kogyo Kabushiki Kaisha, or Tokyo Telecommunications Engineering Corporation, and clearly a shorter name was desirable. They thought of Latin *sonus*, 'sound', and at first considered adapting this as 'Sony' or 'Sonny Boy', for homeliness. But 'Sonny' in Japanese would suggest *son-ni*, 'at a loss', so they instead adjusted the spelling to 'Sony', rhyming with 'bony' rather than 'bunny'. *See also* BETAMAX; PLAYSTATION; WALKMAN.

**Sooner State.** A nickname for Oklahoma, which became the 46th US state in 1907. 'Sooners' was already a name for those who endeavoured to get into government territory in the West before (sooner than) the time appointed for the settlement. This was particularly common in the area now known as Oklahoma before its official opening to settlers on 22 April 1889.

**Sooty.** A TEDDY BEAR with black ears, manipulated as a glove puppet on children's television by his creator in the 1950s, Harry Corbett, and inherited by the inventor's son, Matthew. Sooty's sidekick was Sweep, a grey spaniel, and the two took a succession of roles in a range of adult locations such as hospitals, law courts, workshops and gymnasiums. Corbett helped them resolve their problems in these grown-up situations. The mute Sooty whispered 'confidentially' in his ear, while Sweep 'spoke' in staccato yelps. Corbett's endless patience was rewarded by being pelted with various messy missiles and his invariable 'Bye-bye, everybody' was delivered with mournful resignation.

**Sophie's Choice.** A novel (1979) by the US novelist William Styron (b.1925), a dark story of love and loss. Sophie's choice is not so much between the two men in her life, with one of whom she chooses to commit suicide, but the agonizing experience of having been forced, by a Nazi officer in AUSCHWITZ, to select which of her two children will be taken from her. An honourable film version (1982) was directed by Alan J. Pakula.

**Sophie's World.** A novel (1995; in Norwegian as *Sofies verden*, 1991), subtitled 'A Novel about the History of Philosophy', by Jostein Gaarder (b.1952). A philosopher guides 14-year-old Sophie Amundsen through a tour of Western philosophy after leaving two questions in her letterbox: 'Who are you?' and 'Where does the world come from?'

**Soroptimists.** Members of an international service club for professional and business women, founded in California in 1921 on lines similar to those of the ROTARY CLUB. The name comes from Latin *soror*, 'sister', and the earlier Optimist Club, founded in Buffalo, New York, in 1911.

**Sort out the men from the boys.** *See* SEPARATE THE MEN FROM THE BOYS.

**SOS.** The Morse code signal (three dots, three dashes, three dots, $\cdots--\cdots$) used by shipping and the like in distress to summon immediate aid, hence any urgent appeal for help. The signal was recommended at the Radio Telegraph Conference in 1906 and officially adopted two years later. It replaced the call 'CQD', standing for 'call to quarters' or 'come quickly', or representing 'seek you' and the initial of 'distress'. The letters are simply a convenient and readily recognizable combination, and are not an abbreviation, although they have been held to stand for 'save our souls' or 'save our ship'.

**'Sosban Fach'.** (Welsh, 'Little Saucepan'.) The Welsh rugby song of this name is usually associated with the town of Llanelli, whose civic emblem is a saucepan. The first verse was written in 1873 by Richard Davies (1833–77), known by the bardic name of Mynyddog ('Man of the Mountain'), as part of a poem. It was later altered by Talog Williams, an accountant from Dowlais, who added four verses and the chorus, the whole forming a sort of parody of a nursery rhyme or even a nonsense song. Characters mentioned include Meri Ann, Dafydd the servant, Joni Bach and Dai Bach the soldier, although it is not clear what relevance they have, if any, to the story, which involves a boiling saucepan and a crying baby. The tune to which the song is sung, reminiscent of a Welsh hymn, is one of those most frequently heard at rugby matches.

**Sot-Weed Factor, The.** A novel (1960; revised edition 1967) by John Barth (b.1930). The starting point is Ebenezer Cook's *The Sot-Weed Factor: or, A Voyage to Maryland* (1708), a satirical poem purporting to describe the exploits of an Englishman who comes to North America to work as an agent (or factor) for a dealer in sot-weed (tobacco). The novel, which is written in an 18th-century style, reconstructs the activities of the factor and comments on aspects of the poem, with historical and critical digressions.

**Soul food.** A term dating from the 1960s for food that is traditionally associated with African Americans who live in the southern states. Typical examples of soul food are hominy, corn breads, black-eyed peas and chitterlings.

**Sound and the Fury, The.** A novel (1929) by William Faulkner (1897–1962). A tragic family situation, stemming originally from a brother's obsession with his sister, is told from four different points of view, employing STREAM OF CONSCIOUSNESS techniques. The brother's own account suggests:

> a tale
> Told by an idiot, full of sound and fury,
> Signifying nothing.
>     SHAKESPEARE: *Macbeth* (V.v)

An unimaginative film version (1959) was directed by Martin Ritt.

**Sound bite.** A short, succinct extract (sometimes rendered as 'soundbite') from an interview or speech, used to summarize a stance or policy as part of a news or party political broadcast. Politicians and others now make frequent use of the device to capture the attention of a public either too inattentive to respond to anything longer or too nimble with their television remote controls. The expression itself dates from the 1980s. *See also* SPIN.

**Sound of Music, The.** A musical (1959), with a score by Richard Rodgers (1902–79) and Oscar Hammerstein II (1895–1960) and book by Howard Lindsay (1889–1968) and Russel Crouse (1893–1966), about a postulant nun who becomes governess to the aristocratic Von Trapp family in Austria at the time of the NAZI takeover. Filmed in 1965 with Julie Andrews as Maria, the show was based on *The Trapp Family Singers*, the memoirs of the real Maria Von Trapp, who left Austria in similar circumstances. The title refers not only to Maria's love of music but to the fame of the Trapp family singing troupe she organized with her youthful charges. Such was the success of the show, both on stage and in the cinema, that it acquired cult status, and since the 1990s 'singalong' presentations of the film, with the audience dressing up as members of the cast, have proved highly popular. The film opens with the title song:

> The hills are alive with the sound of music,
> With songs they have sung for a thousand years.
> The hills fill my heart with the sound of music,
> My heart wants to sing ev'ry song it hears.

The discordant version performed by the Bonzo Dog (Doo Dah) Band on their *Gorilla* album (1967) provides an antidote for those for whom this adulation is all too much.

**Sound of silence.** A pseudo-poetic term for the stillness and peace found in an isolated or sheltered place, increasingly sought after in the frenetic bustle and stress of contemporary life. The phrase comes from Paul Simon's song 'Sound of Silence' (1964).

**Souped-up.** Of a car, modified by its owner to produce a higher power or acceleration than it had when it left the manufacturer. The phrase probably derives from 'supercharged', perhaps reinforced by 'soup' as colloquialism for fuel for a powerful motor or for a substance injected into a horse to change its speed or temperament. The expression dates from the 1930s.

**Soup run.** A periodical delivery of soup or other sustenance to homeless 'street people', undertaken by a members of a charitable organization.

**South Bank.** A stretch of the Thames in London across the river from the Victoria Embankment, from Westminster Bridge to London Bridge. It was the site of the FESTIVAL OF BRITAIN, held on derelict land here in 1951, and now extends eastwards from the South Bank Centre, a composite of venues devoted to the arts, including the Royal Festival Hall, Queen Elizabeth Hall, Purcell Room, Hayward Gallery, National Theatre and National Film Theatre. More recent buildings are the Tate Modern gallery in the disused Bankside power station, the new Globe Theatre and, at the western end, the giant wheel of the LONDON EYE. In the 1980s the South Bank gained notoriety for the 'home for the homeless' in CARDBOARD CITY. *See also* BRUTALISM.

**South Bank religion.** A journalistic label for religious activities in the diocese of Southwark in London, south of the Thames. It was associated with Mervyn Stockwood, Bishop of Southwark (1959–80), John Robinson, Suffragan Bishop of Woolwich (1959–69) and author of HONEST TO GOD (1963), and some of their diocesan clergy. Characterized by outspokenness on moral and political issues, often from a socialist angle, and energetic attempts to bring the Church into closer relation with contemporary society and its problems, South Bank religion was not without its critics and the label was often applied disparagingly by opponents. *See also* SOUTH BANK.

> That is rather the new idea inside the Church. I should definitely say you were a South Banker.
> AUBERON WAUGH: *Consider the Lilies*, ch. 9 (1968)

**South Ken.** A familiar name of South Kensington, London, famous on the one hand as MUSEUMLAND and on the other for its opulent shops and residences.

**South Pacific.** A musical (1949), with a score by Richard Rodgers (1902–79) and Oscar Hammerstein II (1895–1960) and book by Hammerstein and Joshua Logan (1908–88), about a US Navy nurse who falls in love with a French planter while stationed on a South Pacific island. The plot was based on 'Fo' Dolla', a story from James A. Michener's *Tales of the South Pacific* (1947), combined with 'Our Heroine', another story from the same collection, about a US lieutenant's love for a Polynesian girl.

**South Park.** A scatological and surreal US television cartoon series first screened in 1998 and featuring four anything-but-cute kids from South Park, Colorado: Waspy Stan, the permanently hooded and regularly killed Kenny, the fiendish fat boy Eric Cartman and the mixed-up Jew Kyle. The vivid language ensured a late-night scheduling on most networks, but did not prevent the series from becoming a predictable playground hit.

**South Pole.** The South Pole was first reached by a Norwegian expedition under Roald Amundsen (1872–1928) on 14 December 1911. A party led by Captain Robert Falcon Scott ('Scott of the Antarctic'; 1868–1912) reached the Pole on 17 January 1912, only to discover that Amundsen had beaten them to it. All members of Scott's party perished in appalling weather conditions on the return journey to their ship, the *Terra Nova*. The deaths of Scott and his companions were quickly mythologized as the epitome of selfless heroism, and extracts from Scott's journals (published in 1913) were cited as matchless statements of British pluck in adversity: 'Had we lived, I should have a tale to tell of the hardihood, endurance and courage of my companions which would have stirred the hearts of every Englishman. These rough notes and our dead bodies must tell the tale.' Scott is now generally seen as having made errors of planning that made the demise of his expedition inevitable, notably his reliance on horses rather than teams of dogs.

A 1948 film, *Scott of the Antarctic* (starring John Mills as Captain Scott), in what was clearly a piece of propagandist fable-making tailored to the austerity of postwar Britain, reinvents the expedition as a moving tale of the integration of different social classes. A television adaptation of Roland Huntsford's *Scott and Amundsen* (1979) depicted Scott as an Edwardian amateur and representative of a class-ridden British 'Establishment', defeated in the race for the South Pole by a group of efficient, 'classless' Norwegians.

*See also* I MAY BE SOME TIME.

**South Riding.** A regional novel (1936) by Winifred Holtby (1898–1935), finished a month before its author's death from kidney cancer, which had been diagnosed in 1932. The complexities and conflicts of local government are explored, and the characters of those involved in the decision-making revealed. South Riding is a fictional creation, but has affinities with the East Riding of Yorkshire, where Holtby was born and brought up. A satisfying film version (1937) was directed by Victor Saville.

**Soviet calendar.** Somewhat on the lines of the French Republican calendar of 1793–1806, a rationalized, secular calendar was introduced in the Soviet Union on 1 October 1929. Each month was allocated 30 days, with five extra days as national holidays: LENIN Day following 30 January, two Workers' First of May days after 30 April and two Industry Days after 7 November (the day of the 1917 revolution in the New Style calendar). In a leap year 30 February was to be followed by Leap Day. The seven-day week was replaced by a five-day cycle from Monday to Friday, and each day was a rest day for one-fifth of the population, symbolized by a slip in one of five colours, yellow, pink, red, purple and green,

given to each citizen. The national holidays remained outside the cycle. The aim was not only to combine personal leisure with continuous industrial production, but also to disrupt religious observance. The Western months were restored from 1 December 1931 but with a six-day week of five working days followed by a rest day on the 6th, 12th, 18th, 24th and (except in February) 30th of the month. The 31st was outside the cycle. This system was in turn abandoned on 26 June 1940, supposedly to increase production but in fact because the peasantry had sabotaged the new system by taking Sundays off as well as the new free days. The old weekdays had meanwhile never really been forgotten, even in official documents.

**Soviet sayings.** As one of the world's major geographical and political systems to rise, flourish and fall within the historical parameters of the 20th century (1918–91), the Soviet Union saw the creation of a number of catchphrases, slogans, Leninisms and propagandistic precepts that became familiar to most Russians. They are less familiar in the West, however, and by way of preserving their memory, but not necessarily endorsing their message, a selection is offered below.

'Attacking class': a metaphor for the ideal revolutionary class in its spearhead role in bourgeois society, from Vladimir Mayakovsky's poem *Vladimir Ilyich Lenin* (1924).

'At the top of one's voice': a phrase to emphasize the force, rightness or frankness of a saying or action, from the title of a poem of 1930 by Vladimir Mayakovsky.

'Broad is my native land': the first line of the chorus of the 'Song of the Motherland' from the film *The Circus* (1936), alluding to the vastness of the Soviet Union. The musical notes accompanying the words were used by Radio Moscow as a call sign for its foreign broadcasts.

'Communism is Soviet power plus the electrification of the whole country': LENIN's famous practical definition of communism, from his report to the 8th party congress of 1920.

'Dr Ouch-It-Hurts': a children's nickname for a doctor, from Korney Chukovsky's children's verses of 1929, in the original Russian *Aybolit*, from *ay*, 'ouch!', and *bolit*, 'it hurts'.

'Dress rehearsal for the October Revolution': LENIN's term in his *'Left Wing' Communism: An Infantile Disorder* (1920) for the first Russian revolution (1905–6), which opened with BLOODY SUNDAY.

'Great initiative': a name for the enterprise of the communist *subbotniki* (*see* Red Saturday *below*), from the title of a tract by Lenin published in 1919.

'How the steel was tempered': a metaphor for the moulding of the ideal Soviet citizen, from the title of Nikolay Ostrovsky's novel of 1932–4, telling how the young worker Pavel Korchagin fights for his country in the Civil War and becomes a Komsomol (Communist Youth League) leader.

'In the name of man, for the good of man': a phrase encapsulating communist aims for Soviet society. A phrase from the Communist Party Programme of 1961.

*My Universities*: the title of Maxim Gorky's autobiographical novel of 1923, telling of the SCHOOL OF HARD KNOCKS that in his youth shaped him as an adult.

'Nobody is forgotten and nothing is forgotten': a tribute to the fallen of the Second World War, or in Soviet terms, the GREAT PATRIOTIC WAR (1941–5). The words, by Olga Berggoltz, are engraved on the main memorial at the Piskarev Cemetery, St Petersburg, the burial place of Leningraders who lost their lives in the blockade of 1941–3 and of troops killed on the Leningrad front during the war, some 470,000 in all.

*Path to life, A*: the title of Nikolay Ekk's highly praised film of 1931 about the communal re-education of homeless orphans left after the OCTOBER REVOLUTION and the Civil War (1917–21). The term was adopted for any 'gateway' to a person's career or future generally.

'Red Saturday': A specified Saturday when young workers known as *subbotniki* (from *subbota*, 'Saturday') undertook voluntary unpaid work as part of the Great Initiative (*see above*).

'Road through purgatory': a metaphor for the difficulties of life, sometimes used jocularly for difficulties that are really negligible. The words form the title of Aleksey Tolstoy's trilogy of 1920–42, a study of Russian intellectuals converting to the BOLSHEVIK cause in the Civil War. The title itself derives from the old religious story of the Virgin Mary's visit to hell.

'Scarlet sails': an expression of the romantic and ambitious dreams of youth, from the title of a novel of 1923 by Alexander Grin.

'State is us, The': a term from LENIN's report of the Communist Party Congress of 1922, as a reminder that ultimately the effectiveness and authority of the state depend on each of its individual members. The statement paraphrases Louis XIV's famous *L'état, c'est moi* (1651).

*Story of a real man, The*: the title of a novel of 1946 by Boris Polevoy about the exploits of a Soviet airforce pilot in the Second World War. The words came to be used for any story of heroic deeds.

'Study, study and study': *see* EDUCATION, EDUCATION, EDUCATION.

*Tempest-born, The*: the title of a novel of 1934–6 by Nikolay Ostrovsky about young revolutionaries battling to establish Soviet rule in the Ukraine in the 1920s. The phrase was used for members of the Komsomol (Communist Youth League) born then and for the YOUNG GUARD subsequently.

'What is good and what is bad': the title of a poem of 1925 for children by Vladimir Mayakovsky, as applied to a situation where the positive must be distinguished from the negative. The words were often applied humorously or trivially, since their source in a children's poem was well known.

'Your mother country calls you!': a patriotic slogan on a poster of 1941, at the start of the GREAT PATRIOTIC WAR, calling Soviet citizens to fight for their homeland against the enemy.

**SP.** In racing terminology, starting price, meaning the final odds at the start of a horse race. Hence from the 1950s the more general sense 'information', 'facts'.

> 'So I'm showin' this Pakistani all the catalogues and givin' him the full SP and he's noddin' away at me.'
> DERMOT BOLGER: (ed.): *Finbar's Hotel*, 'The Test' (1997)

**Space age.** The age of space exploration, generally regarded as beginning on 4 October 1957 with the launch of SPUTNIK 1, the world's first artificial satellite, but foreseen by scientists and visualized by fantasists long before this.

**Space cadet.** An eccentric person, especially one who seems permanently 'high' on drugs. The phrase dates from the 1970s and may have its origin in the 1950s US television programme *Tom Corbett, Space Cadet*, which showed the adventures of a group of teenage cadets at a futuristic space academy, regarded as being 'far out'. The term is also used for a real drug addict. *See also* GOVERNOR MOONBEAM.

**Spaced out.** 'High' on drugs. The imagery is of one 'flying' in space, or perhaps of a person whose regular chain of existence has been broken by blanks and 'spaces'. The expression arose in the HIPPIE counterculture of the SWINGING SIXTIES. *See also* SPACE CADET.

**Space Invaders.** An animated computer game of the late 1970s, in which players attempt to defend themselves against a fleet of enemy spaceships. No pun appears to be intended on the expression 'to invade someone's space', meaning to encroach on their personal way of life.

*Space Oddity.* The title of an album and song by David Bowie first released in 1969. The song concerns an astronaut who is so disillusioned by what he sees on earth that he decides to stay in space. The title puns on Stanley Kubrick's film 2001: A SPACE ODYSSEY, which also concerns an astronaut lost in space. The song was re-released in 1975, when it reached Number 1 in the charts in Britain.

**Space opera.** A genre of unsophisticated science-fiction adventure stories, films and TV series involving spacemen, rockets and LITTLE GREEN MEN. FLASH GORDON is a classic of the genre. The term is modelled on SOAP OPERA and HORSE OPERA.

**Spaceship Earth.** A name for the planet earth and its inhabitants regarded as a spacecraft and its passengers, who depend on its resources to survive. The concept dates from the 1960s, at a time when the first photographs of the earth from space were being taken by astronauts. In 1965 Adlai Stevenson told a UNESCO meeting:

> We travel together, passengers on a little space ship, dependent on its vulnerable reserves of air and soil.

The term was popularized by the US inventor and environmentalist R. Buckminster Fuller (1895–1983) in his book *Operating Manual for Spaceship Earth* (1969), in which he stated: 'I am a passenger on the spaceship, Earth.' Marshall McLuhan commented, 'There are no passengers on Spaceship Earth. Only crew.'

> We also demonstrate our respect for 'spaceship earth', the concept of accepting that there are limitations on the world's resources and that their use is a matter of common international concern. The more enlightened oil exporters, by the way, endorse 'spaceship earth' themselves.
>
> *Guardian Weekly* (8 May 1977)

**SPAD.** Signal (or signals) passed at danger. An acronym, current in the railway industry since at least the late 1980s, denoting an incident in which a driver has crossed a red signal. It first impinged largely on the public consciousness following the Ladbroke Grove (Paddington) rail crash of 5 October 1999, which was caused by such an incident.

**Spaghetti Junction.** The nickname of the Gravelly Hill Interchange, the junction between the M1 and M6 motorways near Birmingham, where the many winding and intersecting roads, underpasses and overpasses bear a fanciful resemblance to spaghetti. It was opened in 1971.

**Spaghetti western.** A dismissive name for the Italian imitations of American WESTERN films that became popular in the 1960s, using such actors as Lee Van Cleef and Clint Eastwood. They gained an international repute and in the process made Eastwood a star through the work of Sergio Leone, beginning with his *A* FISTFUL OF DOLLARS (1964), in which the actor plays an avenging stranger who cleans up a Mexican border town. The genre had lost much of its impact by the early 1970s. The name alludes to the Italian fondness for spaghetti. *See also* MAN WITH NO NAME.

**Spam.** The tradename of a tinned meat product, first marketed in the United States by George A. Hormel & Co. in 1937. A competition was held for a neat name for the new product and the $100 prize was won by the entry 'Spam', standing for 'spiced ham'. However, years later its low culinary status made it a byword for cheap convenience food, and the product motivated a sketch in the BBC Television comedy series MONTY PYTHON'S FLYING CIRCUS in which every item on the menu in a desultory café includes Spam. (In 2005 a stage musical based on the film *Monty Python and the Holy Grail* opened on Broadway: it was entitled *Spamalot*, punning on 'Camelot'.)

More recently spam has become computer jargon for inappropriate or unwanted messages sent by E-MAIL on the INTERNET, the equivalent of 'junk mail' in standard postal terms. The term apparently derives from the Monty Python sketch. The nuisance grew steadily in the 1990s, to such an extent that various forms of software have been developed to defeat it. Anti-spam laws have been introduced in a number of countries.

**Spandau.** A prison in the Spandau district of Berlin that after 1946 was used to incarcerate Nazi war criminals. Among the prisoners was Albert Speer (1905–81), Hitler's architect (*see* CATHEDRAL OF LIGHT), who was released in 1966. After 1966 the sole inmate was Rudolf Hess (1894–1987), Hitler's deputy, who died in the prison, according to some in suspicious circumstances. Spandau Ballet was the name of a 1980s pop group. *See under* ROCK GROUP NAMES.

**Spanglish.** *See* FRANGLAIS.

**Spanish flu.** A misnomer for the influenza pandemic of 1918, the worst in history, in which some 21 million people died. The outbreak did not begin in Spain but received its name simply because a news agency in Madrid issued the first uncensored wartime report of its existence. The epicentre was in fact probably southern China, as it was for the Asian flu epidemic of 1957, the Hong Kong influenza epidemic of 1968 and the recent outbreak of avian flu (*see* BIRD FLU).

**Spanish Lady, The.** Another name for SPANISH FLU, and also the title of an opera by Edward Elgar (1857–1934), unfinished at the time of his death. The libretto by Barry Jackson was based on Ben Jonson's play *The Devil is an Ass* (1616).

**Spanish practices.** *See* OLD SPANISH CUSTOM.

**Spanner in the works.** Something that prevents the successful implementation of a task; a 'spoke in one's wheel'. The suggestion is of a person who deliberately throws a spanner into smooth-running machinery in order to stall it. John Lennon's *A Spaniard in the Works* (1965) was a bestselling collection of stories and drawings.

**Spare someone's blushes.** To avoid embarrassing them by praise.

**Spare tyre.** A roll of fat round the midriff, especially as a consequence of MIDDLE-AGE SPREAD. It is 'spare' because it is additional to the body, like the extra tyre carried around by a car in case of a puncture.

**Sparrow units** or **squads.** Small guerrilla squads in the Philippines. They arose in the 1980s as militant communist activists, conducting attacks on policemen, government ministers and other persons in authority. Their name alludes to their rapid 'in-and-out' tactics.

**Spartacists.** An extreme socialist group in Germany that flourished between 1916 and 1919. It was founded by Karl Liebknecht (1871–1919) who, with Rosa Luxemburg (1871–1919), led an attempted revolution in January 1919 when they were both killed. The movement was finally crushed by Friedrich Ebert's government in April. It took its name from the Thracian gladiator Spartacus, who in 73 BC led a slave rebellion against Rome, which was not suppressed until 71 BC. During the uprising he defeated five Roman armies and devastated whole tracts of Italy. *See also* WEIMAR REPUBLIC.

**Speakeasy.** A place where alcoholic liquors are sold illegally. A US term widely current in the years of PROHIBITION. 'Easy' here means 'softly', and the name refers either to the fact that such places were spoken about quietly or that people spoke quietly in them, to avoid attracting the attention of police or neighbours. *See also* Al CAPONE.

**Speakers' Corner.** A small area near Marble Arch in the northeast corner of Hyde Park, London, where a motley band of speakers holds forth every Sunday. The name is relatively recent but the practice dates from 1855, when a large crowd gathered here to protest against Lord Robert Grosvenor's Sunday Trading Bill. There was no right of assembly then, but it was granted in 1872 and anyone may now indulge in soapbox oratory on any subject they choose, so long as it is not obscene or blasphemous, or does not constitute an incitement to a breach of the peace. By the beginning of the 21st century most of the speakers were religious extremists. *See also* BUGHOUSE SQUARE.

> Speakers' Corner is a mixed grill of apostles and propa-
> gators, of oddities and crudities, of fanatics and eccentrics.
>
> J.C. GOODWIN: *One of the Crowd*, ch. 19 (1936)

**Speak for England.** An exhortation in the House of Commons by the Conservative MP Leo Amery (1873–1955) to Arthur Greenwood, leader of the Labour Party, on 2 September 1939, as he rose to speak in the debate that followed the German invasion of Poland. The Prime Minister, Neville Chamberlain, was criticized for prevarication, but the next morning his government declared war.

**Speak softly and carry a big stick.** America's foreign policy under President Theodore Roosevelt (1858–1919), who used the expression in a speech in Chicago on 3 April 1903:

> There is a homely old adage which runs: 'Speak softly and
> carry a big stick; you will go far.' If the American nation will
> speak softly, and yet build and keep at a pitch of the highest
> training a thoroughly efficient navy, the Monroe Doctrine
> will go far.

The Monroe Doctrine (enunciated by President James Monroe in 1823) warned the European powers that the United States would resist any new colonial adventures in the Western Hemisphere. By the so-called Roosevelt Corollary of 1904 Roosevelt virtually declared US hegemony in the region, and this was used to justify a number of military interventions by Roosevelt and his successors.

**Spear-carrier.** An actor with a walk-on part. Hence any minor participant in a group effort.

**Spear tackle.** In rugby, an illegal tackle in which a player lifts an opponent off his feet and then throws him to the ground head first. The term and the practice were brought forcefully to public attention in June 2005 when the British and Irish Lions captain Brian O'Driscoll was the victim of such a tackle by the New Zealanders Tana Umaga and Keven Mealamu at an international match in Christchurch, and suffered a dislocated shoulder.

> Briefly, the crowd got excited after a dreadful spear tackle on
> Gordon D'Arcy.
>
> *Sunday Times* (13 November 2005)

**Special needs.** A euphemistic formulation for referring to those who are markedly below the average level of competence in a particular aspect of life (what would formerly have been termed 'handicapped'). It was initially used by educationalists for children who have particular requirements at school because they are physically disabled, emotionally disturbed or have 'learning difficulties' (the phrase can also be taken as implying that such children are 'special'). Its increasing use in other fields, however (e.g. 'special-needs transport' for the physically disabled), has meant that 'special educational needs' (often abbreviated to SEN) is now standardly specified. *See also* STATEMENTED.

> I realized she'd picked up on the phrase 'special needs' and
> she liked that. So, we've gone from the word 'mongol' to
> 'mentally handicapped' to 'special' – and I think that's about
> right.
>
> *Sunday Times Magazine* (30 May 1999)

**Special Operations Executive.** *See* SOE.

**Special relationship.** The relationship between Britain and the United States, regarded as particularly close because of common origins and language. The term is associated with Winston Churchill, who in the House of Commons on 7 November 1945 declared that 'we should not abandon our special relationship with the United States and Canada'. In a speech at Fulton, Missouri, on 5 March 1946, Churchill declared:

> Neither the sure prevention of war, nor the continuous rise of world organization will be gained without what I have called the fraternal association of the English-speaking peoples. This means a special relationship between the British Commonwealth and Empire and the United States.

The special relationship has at times come under strain, for example at the time of the SUEZ CRISIS and the 1983 US invasion of Grenada. Things have been cosier in recent years, however. In his 2005 memoir *DC Confidential* the former British Ambassador in Washington, Sir Christopher Meyer, claims to have been instructed by Jonathan Powell, Tony Blair's foreign affairs adviser, in 1997:

> We want you to get up the arse of the White House and stay there.

*See also* BUSH'S POODLE; FIFTY-FIRST STATE.

**Spectator sport.** A sport such as football that provides as much entertainment and excitement for the spectators as it does for the players. The phrase is of US origin and dates from the 1940s.

> The reduction of politics to a spectator sport … has been one of the more malign accomplishments of television.
> J.K. GALBRAITH: *A Life in Our Times* (1981)

**S.P.E.C.T.R.E.** A fictional criminal/terrorist organization combated by James BOND. It first appears in Ian Fleming's novel *Thunderball* (1961), and in the Bond films it replaces SMERSH. It is led by Ernst Stavro Blofeld, and it is an acronym for *S*pecial *E*xecutive for *C*ounterintelligence, *T*errorism, *R*evenge and *E*xtortion.

**Speed merchant.** Anyone who moves fast, as a driver, runner, bowler, pitcher, swimmer or the like.

**Speedy Gonzalez.** A Mexican mouse character who featured in a series of Warner Bros animated cartoons. He was created in the early 1950s by Friz Freleng. Subsequently his name came to be used, often as a form of address, for someone who moves or works very fast (or, ironically, very slowly).

**Spelvin, George.** *See* Walter PLINGE.

**Spencer, Frank.** *See* SOME MOTHERS DO 'AVE 'EM.

**Spend a penny.** To urinate. The allusion is to the door lock on a cubicle in a public lavatory, which in the pre-decimal era was opened by inserting a penny (1d). *See also* the PENNY DROPPED.

**Spend more time with one's family.** The frequent reason offered by politicians, chief executives, etc., as to why they have resigned. The formula became popular following Norman Fowler's letter of resignation to Margaret Thatcher, 3 January 1990:

> I have a young family and for the next few years I should like to devote more time to them while they are so young.

Although in Fowler's case the reason appears to have been genuine, it is often used as cover for a forced resignation or sacking. When the Blairite health secretary Alan Milburn gave the standard reason when he resigned from the cabinet in June 2003 some commentators were puzzled, as he was regarded as one of Tony's golden boys and no dark secret was suspected. Normality was restored when Milburn decided he wanted to spend more time with his prime minister and returned to the cabinet in September 2004. After Greg Dyke was forced to resign as director general of the BBC in 2004 after the Hutton Report, he later recalled:

> I announced that I wanted to spend more time with my family. I soon discovered, however, that my family did not want to spend more time with me.
> Quoted in *The Observer* (6 March 2005)

**Spice Girls, The.** A phenomenally popular British pop group of the late 1990s. Taking their name from an early song 'Sugar and Spice', the five young women released their first single in 1996 and were instantly nicknamed. Emma Bunton was 'Baby Spice' for her innocent air and youth, Victoria Adams was 'Posh Spice' for her aloof demeanour and designer clothes, Melanie Brown ('Mel B') was 'Scary Spice' for her spiky hair and BODY PIERCING, Melanie Chisholm ('Mel C') was 'Sporty Spice' for her keep-fit interests and sports gear, and Geraldine Halliwell ('Geri') was 'Ginger Spice' for her hair colour. The lives and loves of the women were long a titillating topic of interest to the media, and Adams's marriage to the glamorous footballer David Beckham in 1999 was a gaudy social event. *See also* POP IDOL; POSH AND BECKS.

**Spiderman.** A comic strip hero of the 1960s, the creation of writer Stan Lee and artist Steve Ditko. His real name is Peter Parker, who as a youth had been bitten by a mutant spider and acquired its characteristics. He has great strength, can climb almost anything, especially New York skyscrapers, and pursues villains with a 'webshooter'. His costume, which extends to a face mask, is a red and blue uniform decorated with black webbing. A film version, *Spider-Man*, directed by Sam Raimi, appeared in 2002, with Toby Maguire as the arachnidiform hero. *Spider-Man 2* followed in 2004.

Spiderman is not to be confused with Spider Woman, a female arch-criminal who kills her victims with spiders and who first appeared, pitted against the forensic skills of Sherlock Holmes, in a 1944 film of the same name.

**Spill the beans.** To divulge information, especially under pressure or unintentionally. The allusion is to vomiting, as when one is urged to 'cough it up' or 'spit it out'. The expression is of US origin and dates from the early 20th century.

**Spin.** To give a news story a particular slant, in the manner of a SPIN DOCTOR. The past tense of this verb is normally 'spun' but the archaic form 'span' is frequently found in the media.

> They span she was exhausted, they span she'd no eye for detail … She span back.
>
> *The Times* (28 July 1999)

**Spin doctor.** An expression originating in the United States in the mid-1980s to refer to a politician or public relations expert employed to give a favourable interpretation of events to the media. Its origin is in baseball, from the spin put on the ball by a pitcher to make it go in the desired direction. The idiom later passed into British usage.

> The spin doctors, the PR [public relations] generals, argued after the Reykjavik talks that Reagan still stands by Star Wars and within reach. The White House's primary target was opinion-makers in Washington and New York, but a special spin patrol will descend on 15 other cities this week.
>
> *Newsweek* (27 October 1986)

> We should put the spin-doctors in spin clinics, where they can meet other spin patients and be treated by spin consultants. The rest of us can get on with the proper democratic process.
>
> TONY BENN: quoted in *The Independent* (25 October 1997)

*See also* ON MESSAGE; SING FROM THE SAME HYMN SHEET.

**Spion Kop.** *See* KOP.

**Spirit of St Louis.** The aeroplane in which Charles A. LINDBERGH made the first nonstop solo flight from New York to Paris on 20–21 May 1927, taking 33 hours 33 minutes. The plane was a single-engine high-wing monoplane, adapted by Lindbergh so that the space normally used for four passengers was occupied by fuel tanks, and was named in tribute to the St Louis businessmen who had financed its construction. The plane is now in the Smithsonian Institution in Washington, D.C.

**Spit-and-sawdust.** Said of a run-down or dirty pub or bar. The allusion is to the sawdust formerly strewn on the floor of the general bar of a public house and to the spitting of drinkers onto it.

**Spitting Image.** A satirical television series screened from 1984 to 1996 in which famous people in British and international life were re-created in the form of latex puppets that, in the manner of political cartoons, exaggerated the particular person's most obvious physical features or personality characteristics. Each programme consisted of a series of topical sketches, the voices of the unseen actors often providing uncannily convincing versions of those portrayed. The series specifically lampooned politicians, foreign heads of state and media personalities, and even the British royal family were not spared. The creators of the puppets were the model-makers Peter Fluck and Roger Law, whose effigies of politicians had earlier appeared in the press.

The title puns on 'spitting image' as a term for an exact likeness (as if one person is 'spit' by another), the 'spitting' being the satire and the 'image' the programme itself.

**Spiv.** A man, typically flashily dressed, who makes his living by disreputable dealings. The slang term came to the fore in the Second World War with reference to black market negotiations, but it undoubtedly dates from much earlier. Its origin is problematic, but it may be related in some way to 'spiffing'. Popular theories derive it from a reversal of 'VIPs' (very important persons) or from a police abbreviation for 'suspected person and itinerant vagrant'. *See also* WIDE BOY.

**Splash out.** To spend money extravagantly or ostentatiously. The image is of emptying a bucket of water in a single throw. The expression dates from the 1930s.

**Splatter movie.** A genre of film in which characters die in a violent or gruesome manner. The allusion is to the physical disintegration of bodies, which appear to be splattered across the screen. The first film to earn the title was *The* TEXAS CHAINSAW MASSACRE (1974). Aspects of the genre were parodied in Quentin Tarantino's highly lauded PULP FICTION (1994). *See also* SLASHER MOVIE.

**Splendor in the Grass.** A film (1961) directed by Elia Kazan with Natalie Wood and Warren Beatty as sexually frustrated high-school kids in 1920s Kansas. The title comes from Wordsworth:

> Though nothing can bring back the hour
> Of splendour in the grass, of glory in the flower;
> We will grieve not, rather find
> Strength in what remains behind …
>
> WILLIAM WORDSWORTH: 'Ode. Intimations of Immortality' (1807)

**Spock, Dr.** The popular name of the US paediatrician Benjamin Spock (1903–98), author of the influential bestseller *The Common Sense Book of Baby and Child Care* (1946), which challenged traditional methods of child-rearing by telling parents to follow their instincts instead of imposing set routines and rigorous discipline. His name became a literal household word in the art of parenting. *See also* SPOCK-MARKED.

> A single woman, even if she is a file clerk, moves in the world of men … Her world is a far more colorful world than the one of P.T.A., Dr Spock and the jammed clothes dryer.
> HELEN GURLEY BROWN: *Sex and the Single Girl* (1962)

**Spock, Mr.** The impassive, pointy-eared member of the Starship *Enterprise* played by Leonard Nimoy in the cult US television series STAR TREK. Being from the planet Vulcan (though with a human mother), he is almost entirely logical and emotionless – hence the nickname of the Conservative politician John Redwood (*see* VULCAN). Mr Spock became the most famous character of the series and featured prominently in the books that were based on it.

**Spock-marked.** A punning colloquialism, based on 'pock-marked', for a baby felt to be hampered rather than helped by an upbringing based on the recommendations of Dr SPOCK.

**Spoiler.** In journalism, a news story or other newspaper item published to spoil the impact of a related item published in another paper. The usual way of doing this is to present it 'bigger and better', and if possible sooner, with a more detailed text coverage and a greater number of photos.

**Spoonerism.** A form of metathesis that consists of transposing the initial sounds of words so as to form some ludicrous combination, often the accidental result of mental tiredness or absentmindedness. It is so called from the Rev. W.A. Spooner (1844–1930), Warden of New College, Oxford. Some of the best (but possibly apocryphal) attributed to him are: 'We all know what it is to have a half-warmed fish within us' (for 'half-formed wish'). 'Yes, indeed; the Lord is a shoving leopard', and 'Kinkering Kongs their titles take.' Sometimes the term is applied to the accidental transposition of whole words, as when a teashop waitress was asked for 'a glass bun and a bath of milk'. This sort of spoonerism can lend itself to deliberate word play, as when Oscar Wilde said: 'Work is the curse of the drinking classes' (quoted in Hesketh Pearson, *Life of Oscar Wilde*, ch. 12; 1946). The word itself is first recorded in 1900 but was colloquially current at Oxford for some years before this.

**Sporting nicknames.** Many sportsmen and women have acquired nicknames, some more flattering than others. A selection is included here.

Air Jordan: the basketball player Michael Jordan (b.1963), reflecting his legendary jumping ability

AMBLING ALP

Anfield Iron: the footballer Tommy Smith (b.1945), a 'hard man' in the Liverpool sides of the 1960s and 1970s

BABE, The

Baby-faced Assassin: the Norwegian and Manchester United footballer Ole Gunnar Soljskaer (b.1973), in recognition of his youthful appearance and goal-scoring ability

BANDITO

BARNACLE BAILEY

BEEFY

Big Bill: the tall and imposing US tennis player Bill Tilden (1893–1953), a leading player of the 1920s; *see also* Little Bill *below*.

Big Bird: the Barbados, West Indies and Somerset cricketer Joel Garner (b.1952), a towering fast bowler who stood 2m (6ft 9in) tall

BIG MAN

BIG O

BIG TRAIN

Bites Yer Legs: the Leeds United and England footballer Norman Hunter (b.1943), so called for his fearsome tackling

BLACK BRADMAN

Black Diamond: the Brazilian footballer Leonidas (Leonidas da Silva; 1913–2004); *see also* BRAZILIAN FOOTBALLERS

Black Octopus or Black Spider: the footballer Lev Yashin (1929–90), a mobile-limbed goalkeeper for Moscow Dynamo and the Soviet Union in the 1950s and 1960s

Black Panther: *see* EUROPEAN PELÉ

BLACK PEARL

Blockbuster: *see* BROCKTON BOMBER

Bobby-dazzler: the Yorkshire and England fast bowler Darren Gough (b.1970). Usually shortened to simply 'the Dazzler'.

Boil: *see* BARNACLE BAILEY

Both: *see* BEEFY

BOUNDING BASQUE

BROCKTON BOMBER

BROWN BOMBER

BRYLCREEM BOY

CANNIBAL

Cannonball Kid: the US tennis player Roscoe Tanner (b.1951), famous for his fast serves

CAPTAIN MARVEL

CAT, The

CHARIOTS OFFIAH

Chin: the English footballer, club manager and commentator Jimmy Hill (b.1928), so called for his very prominent lower jaw

Chopper: the hard-tackling Chelsea footballer Ron Harris (b.1944), a much-feared member of the successful Chelsea sides of the 1960s and 1970s

Clones Cyclone: the fast-punching Irish boxer Barry McGuigan (b.1961), born in Clones, Co. Monaghan, in the Republic of Ireland

Crafty Cockney: Eric Bristow (b.1957), a London-born darts player who was the most skilful and successful exponent of the sport during its high noon of popularity in the 1980s

CROUCHER, The

DEADLY DEREK

DIVINO

DR J

DON, The

Durable Dane: the Copenhagen-born US lightweight boxer Oscar Nelson (born Oscar Nielsen; 1882–1954), famed for his ability to take punches

Electric Eel or Electric Heel: the Blackpool, Hull City, Southampton and England footballer Stan Mortensen (1922–91), a forward of slippery skill

ERIC THE EEL

EUROPEAN PELÉ

FEARSOME FOURSOME

FIERY FRED

Flo-Jo: the flamboyant US sprinter Florence Griffith Joyner (née Delorez Florence Griffith; 1959–98), winner of the 100m and 200m at the 1988 Olympics, and famous for her colourful attire and long, painted fingernails

FLYING FINN

FRITZ THE CAT

FOUR MUSKETEERS, The

Freddie Flintoff: the Lancashire and England all-rounder Andrew Flintoff (b.1977). The allusion is to Fred Flintstone (*see The* FLINTSTONES).

GALLOPING MAJOR

GAZZA

GENERAL, The

GENTLE GIANT

GODFATHER, The

GORGEOUS GUSSIE

Governor General: the cricketer Charles Macartney (1886–1958), an authoritative strokemaking batsman for New South Wales and Australia

Great One: the Canadian ice hockey player Wayne Gretzky (b.1961), Canada's greatest ever goal scorer

Great White Shark: the Australian golfer Greg Norman (b.1955), one of the best players of the 1980s and 1990s, so named for his striking blond hair

Guy the Gorilla: *see* BEEFY

Herminator: the Austrian skier Hermann Maier (b.1972) (*see* TERMINATOR)

HIT MAN

Hollywood: the Australian leg-spinner Shane Warne (b.1969), for his film-star-like high media profile

HOMICIDE HANK

HUNT THE SHUNT

Hurricane: the Northern Irish snooker player Alex Higgins (b.1949), so called because of the phenomenal speed of his potting

Iron Gloves: an unflattering nickname applied to the record-breaking Australian wicketkeeper Rodney Marsh (b.1947) during the early part of his career, when catches often seemed to bounce straight out of his gloves

IRON MIKE

JOLTIN' JOE

J.P.R.: the Welsh rugby union fullback J.P.R. Williams (John Peter Rhys Williams; b.1949)

KAISER

KING, The

KING KENNY

King of East Anglia: the football club manager Bobby Robson (b.1933), so called for his successful period as manager of Ipswich during which the team won the FA Cup (1978) and the UEFA Cup (1981)

King of Spain: *see* WHEELIE BIN

Kipper: the Kent and England batsman Colin Cowdrey (1932–2000), from his habit of taking a nap in the dressing room

Little Bill: the US tennis player William Johnson (1894–1946), who lost six times to Big Bill (*see above*) Tilden in US championship finals

Little Miss Poker Face: the US tennis player Helen Wills Moody (1905–98), so called for her lack of any display of emotion on court

LITTLE MO

Livermore Larruper: the US heavyweight boxer Max Bauer (1909–59), who was known as much for his fast-paced lifestyle as for his powerful punching. 'Larrup' is a slang term meaning to beat or thrash.

Lloyd George of Welsh Football: *see* WELSH WIZARD

Lord Ted: the Sussex and England cricketer Ted Dexter (b.1935), a powerful stroke-making batsman of aristocratic bearing at the wicket

Magic Johnson: the US basketball player born Earvin Johnson (b.1959), one of the greatest all-round players in history

Manster: the US football player Randy White (b.1953), a strong defensive tackler. The name is a portmanteau word combining 'man' and 'monster'.

MARADONA OF THE CARPATHIANS

Marvelous Marvin: the US middleweight boxer Marvin Hagler (b.1952), who was so enamoured of this nickname that he had his name legally changed to 'Marvelous Marvin Hagler'

MASTER, The

MASTER BLASTER

Michigan Assassin: the US middleweight boxer Stanley Ketchel (born Stanislaus Kiecal; 1886–1910), who was born in Grand Rapids, Michigan

MIDDLESEX TWINS

Mighty Mouse: the English footballer Kevin Keegan (b.1951), the leading forward of his generation, so called for the power and energy of his game, which belied his relatively small size

Multiple Mac: the US field athlete Mac Wilkins (b.1950), who threw the discus, javelin and hammer, as well as throwing the shot

Nugget: the Australian cricketer Keith Miller (1919–2004), a dynamic all-rounder who formed a fearsome new-ball partnership with Ray Lindwall (1921–96)

Orchid Man: the French light-heavyweight boxer Georges Carpentier (1894–1975), so called because of his debonair appearance

Pistol Pete: (1) the US basketball player Pete Maravich (1947–88); (2) the US tennis player Pete Sampras (b.1971)

Preston Plumber: the footballer Tom Finney (b.1922), a fleet-footed winger for Preston North End and England, who ran a plumbing business both during and after his career as a professional footballer

Psycho: the footballer Stuart Pearce (b.1962), a 'hard man' in defence for Nottingham Forest and England

RANJI

ROCKHAMPTON ROCKET

ROCKY

Rumble of Thunder: the Italian footballer Luigi Riva (b.1944), a prolific goalscorer with Legnano, Cagliari and Italy

SEAGULL

Shoeless Joe: the US baseball star Joe Jackson (1887–1951); *see also* BLACK SOX SCANDAL; SAY IT AIN'T SO, JOE

Sicknote: the Tottenham Hotspur and England footballer Darren Anderton (b.1972), who has the reputation of missing games through injury

SMOKIN' JOE

SUGAR RAY ROBINSON

SUPERBRAT

TARMAC

THOMMO

THREE WS

Tich Freeman: the Kent and England leg-spinner Alfred Freeman (1888–1965), who stood just 1.57m (5ft 2in) tall

Tiger O'Reilly: the Australian cricketer Bill O'Reilly (1905–92), an aggressive bowler of leg-breaks and googlies in the 1930s and 1940s

Tiger Pataudi: the Nawab of Pataudi (b.1941), captain of India in the 1960s and 1970s, who was known for his predatory fielding

Toey Tayfield: the South African cricketer Hugh Tayfield (1929–94), an off-spin bowler who earned his nickname from his habit of grinding his toe into the ground before each ball he bowled

Tugga Waugh: the Australian cricketer Steve Waugh (b.1965), punning on 'tug of war', with reference to his gritty pugnacity

Turbanator: the Indian spin bowler Harbhajan Singh (b.1980), who, in compliance with the demands of his Sikh religion, always wears a patka (a simple turban) on the field of play (*see* TERMINATOR)

Tylerstown Terror: the Welsh flyweight boxer Jimmy Wilde (1892–1969), who was born in Tylerstown, Wales, and the power of whose punching belied his diminutive size

Typhoon Tyson: the Northamptonshire and England cricketer Frank Tyson (b.1930), a fast bowler of lightning pace

Vaulting Vicar: the US pole vaulter Bob Richards (b.1926), who was ordained as a minister in 1948

WELSH WIZARD

W.G

WHEELIE BIN

WHISPERING DEATH

WHITE PELÉ

Wor Jackie: the footballer Jackie Milburn (1924–88), a star with Newcastle United and England in the 1940s and 1950s. Wor Jackie is a Geordie rendition of 'Our Jackie'.

Yifter the Shifter: the Ethiopian middle-distance runner Miruts Yifter (b.1944), winner of the 5000m and 10,000m at the 1980 Olympic Games

*See also* BEAUTIFUL GAME.

**Sport-utility vehicle.** A four-wheel-drive vehicle designed and marketed for urban use but with features (e.g. robust construction and high traction capability) that make it more suitable for rough terrain. The term (often abbreviated to SUV) originated in the United States. *See also* CHELSEA TRACTOR; 4×4; SMART CAR.

**Spot the ball.** A type of weekly competition run by some newspapers and FOOTBALL POOLS companies. For a small fee, the competitor is given a photograph of a football game from which the ball has been erased and places a cross where he judges or guesses its original position to have been. The winner is the entrant who places the cross closest to the centre of the ball. In 1975 a levy was placed on spot-the-ball competitions operated by pools companies in order to finance the Football Grounds Improvement Trust and later the Football Trust.

**Spotting.** A technique among ballet dancers to prevent giddiness while turning. It consists in fixing one's eyes on a spot in the auditorium or the wings for as long as possible to ensure one's sense of orientation. Hence the frequent frozen look on the face of a twirling dancer.

**Spratt, Sir Lancelot.** The senior surgeon at St Swithin's general hospital in the series of humorous novels by Richard Gordon, beginning with *Doctor in the House* (1952). He is a 'surgeon of the grand old school' referred to behind his back as 'that bloody old butcher'. He is said to have earned his knighthood by performing 'a small but essential operation on a cabinet minister that allowed him to take his seat in the House with greater ease'. He does not feature in the second novel of the series, *Doctor at Sea* (1953), but reappears in the later volumes. He was played with extravert panache by the red-bearded actor James Robertson Justice in the films based on the books, starting with *Doctor in the House* (1954).

**Spread betting.** A form of betting popular in the 1990s in which the amount of money won or lost depends on the degree to which a score or result in a sporting contest exceeds or falls short of a level decided by the gambler. Such betting is particularly suited to football. If the bookmakers thus offer the time of Manchester United scoring their first goal against Sheffield Wednesday as between 14 minutes and 20 minutes, and the gambler thinks they will score before 14 minutes, he will 'buy' the spread. If he puts £10 on this, and the first goal is in fact scored in the ninth minute, he will win £50. But if he 'sells' the spread, betting that the goal will be later, he will lose £50.

**Spreadsheet.** In computer jargon, a program used chiefly for accounting, in which figures arranged in the rows and columns of a grid can be manipulated and used in calculations. The term dates from the early 1980s.

**Spring chicken.** A young person. The phrase is usually found in the negative, as: 'She's no spring chicken.' The implication is that she has reached an age when she is no longer a chick. A spring chicken is a young fowl ready for eating, which was originally in the spring. The expression is of US origin and dates from the early years of the 20th century.

**Spruce Goose.** The nickname given to the giant eight-engined Hughes H-4 Hercules, the world's biggest flying boat, with the largest wingspan of any aeroplane ever built (97.54 m / 319 ft 11 in). It was commissioned in 1942 by the US Department of War, which required an aircraft to carry troops and materiel across the Atlantic and Pacific Oceans in large quantities, safe from submarine attack. The plane, designed and built by the US tycoon Howard Hughes, was largely built of birchwood (not spruce) owing to a wartime shortage of metals. It was intended that it should carry 750 men or two tanks. As the project dragged on until after the end of the war, in 1947 Hughes was called before Congress to explain himself. During a break in the hearings Hughes piloted the plane on its first and only flight, in which the mammoth 'Flying Lumberyard' (as its critics called it) managed to cover only 1.5 km (1 mile), at a height of 20 m (65 ft). Shortly afterwards Congress ended funding for the project, and the plane was put into mothballs.

**Spud-bashing.** Potato-peeling, especially when done in a lengthy session. The term dates from the Second World War, and is associated with army routine and JANKERS. *See also* SQUARE-BASHING.

**Sputnik.** (Russian, 'fellow traveller'.) The Soviet artificial satellite, Sputnik 1, was launched on 4 October 1957 as the first of its kind to be projected successfully into orbit around the earth. Achieving an apogee of 942km (548 miles) and a perigee of 230km (143 miles), it circled the earth every 96 minutes and remained in orbit until early 1958. Sputnik 2, launched on 3 November 1957, carried the dog LAIKA, the first living creature to be shot into space and orbit the earth. *See also* FELLOW TRAVELLER; SPACE AGE.

**Spycatcher trial.** A legal case of 1986 in which the British government sought to suppress publication of the book *Spycatcher*, an account by Peter Wright (1916–95), then living in Australia, of his experiences as a senior MI5 officer. The course of justice hardly ran smoothly. The cabinet secretary, Sir Robert Armstrong, was obliged to apologize to the Australian court for unintentionally giving misleading evidence (*see* ECONOMICAL WITH THE TRUTH), while in 1987 contempt proceedings were brought against the *Sunday Times* for publishing extracts from the book. The bid to ban Wright's memoirs ended ignominiously in 1988.

**Spy in the cab.** A term for a tachograph, as an instrument that makes a record of engine speed over a period in a commercial road vehicle. The device has been resented by many lorry drivers, even though in recording their driving hours it is designed to enhance their productivity and efficiency.

**Spy in the sky.** A nickname dating from the COLD WAR for a satellite or aircraft used to gather military intelligence.

**Spy Who Came in from the Cold, The.** A COLD WAR thriller (1963) by John Le Carré (b.1931), inspired by the recent building of the Berlin Wall, and concerned with the story of a British agent who apparently defects to East Germany. The title refers to an agent returning from active service to a desk job, or a rogue spy returning to his original loyalties. Graham Greene said that it was the best spy novel he had read. It was turned into a film in 1965, starring Richard Burton. The formula 'the X who came in from the cold' has since become popular with headline writers: for example, an article in *The Guardian* in 2004 about the fifth generation of the Vauxhall Astra was headed 'The Car that Came in from the Cold'. *See also* CHECKPOINT CHARLIE.

**Squander bug.** A symbol of reckless extravagance and waste, familiar in Britain in the Second World War from a series of publicity campaigns promoted by the National Savings Committee to encourage economy. It was graphically portrayed as an evil-looking insect.

**Square.** A slang term for a person who is not in with current trends or fashions and is hence old-fashioned. There are several suggestions for the origin of the term, none of which is particularly convincing. One explanation derives the word from a JAZZ musician's and standard conductor's hand gesture that beats out a regular rhythm, the hand describing a square figure in the air. The term originated in African American slang and has been current from the 1940s. *See also* L7.

> [Actor] Joseph Fiennes was voted Britain's most stylish man. He laughs when I bring this up. 'Actually, I'm a bit of a square,' he says. This is not false modesty. He *is* a bit of a square. The look he's wearing today … is more 80s than new millennium man.
>
> *heat* (20–26 January 2000)

**Square-bashing.** Army drill on a parade ground, when one bashes the ground with one's boots. The term dates from the Second World War.

**Square Deal.** Theodore Roosevelt succeeded to the US presidency in 1901 and the following year used this term for his personal approach to current social problems and the individual. At its core was the ideal of peaceful coexistence between big business and labour unions. The concept was subsequently incorporated into the platform of the short-lived Progressive Party when Roosevelt was its presidential candidate in 1912.

**Square-eyed.** Affected by or given to watching too much television, as if to make one's eyes the same shape as the screen. A light-hearted phrase dating from the 1960s.

**Squarial.** A square dish aerial for receiving satellite television broadcasts. It enjoyed a brief moment of fame at the end of the 1980s, but production ceased in 1990 when the company that manufactured it, British Satellite Broadcasting, merged with Sky Television.

**Squeaky clean.** Above criticism; beyond reproach. The suggestion is of the squeaking of one's shoes when walking over a newly washed floor or of one's finger when rubbed over a clean glass. Army sergeant majors sometimes demand that boots be highly polished so that they squeak when worn.

**Squeegee merchant.** A person with a squeegee (a rubber-edged blade on a handle) who willy-nilly cleans the windscreen of a car stopped in traffic and demands payment from the driver. The ploy arose in American downtown streets in the 1980s. The second word can vary and the importuners are often simply referred to as 'squeegees'.

> This one-time left-wing student radical [Jack Straw] was now calling for the streets to be reclaimed from aggressive 'winos, addicts, and squeegee merchants' (September 1995).
>
> JANE PEEL: in *The BBC News General Election Guide* (1997)

**Squeeze play.** A US term dating from the early 20th century for a situation in which one must apply force or pressure to get what one wants. The allusion is to a baseball tactic in which the runner on third base breaks for home plate (dashes to the base by the batter) while the batter himself bunts (helps him by tapping the ball gently so that it does not roll beyond the infield).

**Squeeze someone until the pips squeak.** To exact the maximum payment from them. The expression originated in a speech on 10 December 1918 at the Beaconsfield Club, Cambridge, by Sir Eric Geddes, First Lord of the Admiralty and Unionist MP for Cambridge, with reference to Germany's indemnity after the First World War.

> Sir Eric said: The Germans, if this Government is returned, are going to pay every penny; they are going to be squeezed

as a lemon is squeezed – until the pips squeak. My only doubt is not whether we can squeeze hard enough, but whether there is enough juice.

*Cambridge Daily News* (11 December 1918)

Denis Healey, Labour chancellor of the exchequer, is famously supposed to have used the phrase in the 1970s, saying he would 'squeeze the rich until the pips squeak'. However, Healey denies ever having used the phrase. But in a speech to the Labour Party Conference on 1 October 1973, Healey, then shadow chancellor, *did* say:

I warn you there are going to be howls of anguish from the 80,000 people who are rich enough to pay over 75 per cent [tax] on the last slice of their income.

**Squidgygate.** The name given by the *Sun* newspaper to the leaking in 1992 of taped telephone conversations between Diana, Princess of Wales, and her lover, James Gilbey, who addressed her as 'Squidgy'. The tapes are thought to have been made in 1989 by elements in the intelligence services and leaked to the press by someone in the Prince of Wales's circle, as the royal marriage spiralled towards divorce. Howevever, public sympathy for Diana appeared to increase as a result, and the Princess of Wales's Royal Regiment unofficially began to refer to itself as 'Squidgy's Own'. The name Squidgygate itself is modelled on WATER-GATE, the seminal scandal involving taped conversations. *See also* CAMILLAGATE.

**Squiffites.** The supporters of the Liberal politician H.H. Asquith, OLD SQUIFFY, after he had been ousted from the premiership by fellow Liberal David Lloyd George, the WELSH WIZARD, in December 1916. The Squiffites were at odds with the rest of the Liberal Party until Asquith resigned as party leader in 1926. The split marked the terminal decline of the Liberal Party's fortunes.

**Squillions.** A very large number. The word emerged in the 1940s as a fanciful form of 'millions', 'billions', 'trillions' and the like, perhaps with the idea of one of these 'squared'. *See also* ZILLIONS.

Squillions of steaming wet people squeeze into a space the size of my kitchen.

*Evening Standard* (27 September 1999)

**SS.** (German *Schutzstaffel*, 'protection squad'.) An armed force that originated as part of Hitler's bodyguard in 1925, two years after the formation of the SA, to which it was initially subordinate. In 1929 Heinrich Himmler took on the SS and, defining its duties as 'to find out, to fight and to destroy all open and secret enemies of the FÜHRER, the National Socialist Movement, and our racial resurrection', raised it to

a position of power and great numerical strength. During the Second World War, SS divisions fought with fanatical zeal. The sleek black uniforms of the SS men earned them the name BLACKSHIRTS and made them feel superior to the Brownshirts (*see* SA). *See also* ABWEHR; NIGHT OF THE LONG KNIVES; WAFFEN SS.

**Stab in the back.** A treacherous act. The expression dates only from the early years of the 20th century, but the image is ancient and popularly applies to the conspiratorial assassination of Julius Caesar on 15 March (the Ides of March) 44 BC.

The phrase came to prominence in the wake of the First World War. In Germany the so-called *Dolchstosslegende* ('stab-in-the-back myth') was propagated by the Nazis and other right-wing nationalists, who asserted that Germany had not been defeated militarily, but that the army had been betrayed by Jews and socialists in the government. General Erich Ludendorff, one of Germany's military leaders during the war, stated in February 1919:

The political leadership disarmed the unconquered army and delivered over Germany to the destructive will of the enemy.

**Stack on a turn.** In colloquial Australian English, to make a fuss or a scene. 'Stack on' in this context means 'to make or produce'. The usage dates from the 1940s.

**Stack up.** To measure up; to compare; to make sense. The allusion is to piling up one's chips in a game of poker.

**Stadium of Light.** The impressive home ground of Sunderland Football Club, built in 1997 on the site of the former Wearmouth Colliery, which closed in 1993, as the largest all-seater stadium in Britain since the Second World War. Its name was not adopted from Benfica's ESTÁDIO DA LUZ but reflects both the Davy lamps worn by the miners of old and the desire of the club to be in the limelight and to serve as a beacon in the world of football. The ground is also close to the National Glass Centre, suggesting a further association with light. There is also a practical realization, for the whole stadium was illuminated from twilight to midnight as a symbol of the regeneration of Sunderland itself. The name remained a secret until it was unveiled by the club's directors at a midnight news conference on 29 July 1997. The new stadium has provided STATE-OF-THE-ART pre-match entertainment for its spectators, and before the home side's Division One match against Portsmouth on 21 March 1998 the Northern Symphony Orchestra played music from Prokofiev's ballet *Romeo and Juliet* complete with a troupe of dancers. In 2003 the stadium hosted its first competitive football international, between England and Turkey.

**Stagecoach.** A WESTERN film (1939) directed by John Ford and starring John Wayne, set in a stagecoach making its way through hostile American Indian territory. The film rises above the conventional western thanks to the excellence of the characterization of the seven individuals brought together in the stagecoach. The scenery of Arizona's Monument Valley adds much to the visual excitement of the film, which is based on a short story, 'Stage to Lordsburg', by Ernest Haycox.

> The basic western, a template for everything that followed.
> JOHN BAXTER (1968): quoted in *Halliwell's Film & Video Guide* (1999)

**Stage-door Johnny.** A man who hangs around stage doors to waylay actresses as they leave.

**Stagflation.** An economic term coined by the Conservative politician Iain Macleod (1913–70) in a speech to the House of Commons on 17 November 1965, while in opposition to Harold Wilson's Labour government:

> We now have the worst of both worlds – not just inflation on the one side or stagnation on the other side, but both of them together. We have a sort of 'stagflation' situation.

**Stag night.** A festive, usually alcohol-fuelled, gathering of men only, especially on the eve of a wedding (or the weekend before), the guest of honour then being the groom. *See also* HEN NIGHT.

**'Stairway to Heaven'.** An eight-minute acoustic-meets-HEAVY METAL anthem by the rock group Led Zeppelin. It appeared on the album *Led Zeppelin IV*, released in 1971. The song's obscurely Tolkienesque and metaphor-laden lyrics are, according to one's viewpoint, insufferably pretentious or excitingly and allusively ambiguous ('Sometimes words have two meanings', sings Robert Plant). *See also* ROCK GROUP NAMES.

Bizarrely, the song was a top ten single for the Australian entertainer Rolf Harris in the 1990s. Harris had responded to an invitation to singers from the Australian alternative comedy show *The Money or the Gun* to perform the song in any way they wanted.

**Stakeholder.** A word that became fashionable among politicians in the last decade of the 20th century, to denote any individual or organization with an interest in some project or institution. The concept of 'stakeholder capitalism' was discussed by Will Hutton in *The State We're In* (1995), a book that was briefly influential among NEW LABOUR policy-makers. The following year Tony Blair gave a speech in Derby entitled 'The Stakeholder Economy'. In 2001 the Labour government introduced what it called

'stakeholder pension schemes', essentially private pension schemes that met certain standards. In the 'stakeholder society' everyone is to be given opportunities, but must also take responsibilities.

> The stakeholders in a corporation are the individuals and constituencies that contribute, either voluntarily or involuntarily, to its wealth-creating capacity and activities, and that are therefore its potential beneficiaries and/or risk bearers.
> JAMES E. POST, LEE E. PRESTON and SYBILLE SACHS: *Redefining the Corporation: Stakeholder Management and Organizational Wealth* (2002)

**Stake-out.** A period of police surveillance over a defined area, as if one marked out with stakes.

**Stakhanovite.** In the former USSR a worker whose productivity exceeds the norm and who thus earns special privileges and rewards. The name is that of Aleksei Grigoryevich Stakhanov (1906–77), a Donbass coalminer who substantially increased his daily output by rationalization. His record output was 102 tons of coal in a 5¾-hour night shift on 30 August 1935, 14 times the norm. That same year STALIN held a conference of Stakhanovites in which he extolled the working man.

**Stalin.** The Soviet leader, who succeeded LENIN as head of the Communist Party, was born Iosif Vissarionovich Dzhugashvili (1879–1953), his surname being Georgian in origin. He adopted his well-known party name in 1913, from Russian *stal'*, 'steel', perhaps originally to indicate his unbroken spirit after repeated arrest, banishment and imprisonment. He had various other pen-names, including Soso, Koba (a short form of Yakoba, the name of a Georgian fictional patriotic hero), David, Nizheradze, Chizhikov and Ivanovich. *See also* UNCLE JOE.

**Stalingrad.** Formerly Tsaritsyn, on the Volga, renamed in 1925 to commemorate its defence by Stalin, in 1917, against the WHITE RUSSIANS. Stalin died in 1953 and in 1961 the name was changed to Volgograd. In 1943 it was the scene of the decisive defeat of the German 6th Army, a turning point of the Second World War. The ferocious battle for Stalingrad had begun in August 1942, with the Germans in the ascendant. In November, however, the Soviets launched 'Operation Uranus', encircling and trapping the German 6th Army, which finally surrendered on 31 January 1943. The horrors of the battle were graphically recreated in Antony Beevor's bestselling book *Stalingrad* (1997).

**Stalin organ.** The nickname given by German soldiers in the Second World War to the Soviet Katyusha multiple rocket launcher, usually mounted on the back of a lorry. Katyusha ('little Katya') itself was the name given by Red Army soldiers to the device after the crescendo in the popular wartime Russian song entitled 'Katyusha', in which the eponymous young woman promises to her lover at the front that she'll keep her love for him alive in her heart.

**Stalin's Granny.** The nickname of the formidable Labour politician Helen Liddell (b.1950), who at the age of 26 became secretary general of the Scottish Labour Party. She was secretary of state for Scotland from 2001 to 2003.

**Stalking.** The following or pestering of a person, especially a celebrity, with whom the follower has become obsessed. The obsession may climax in violence to the victim. Although stalking has been recognized as an unpleasant fact of famous lives, most cases involve ordinary people who have fallen out with a partner, colleague or friend. The phenomenon came to prominence in the 1990s.

**Stalking horse.** Originally in the 16th century a screen made in the shape of a horse behind which a hunter took concealment when stalking prey, the term later came to apply to any false pretext that concealed a person's true intention and specifically from the late 1980s to a candidate in an election for the leadership of a political party who stands simply in order to provoke the election and so allow a stronger candidate to come forward. Thus in 1999 Calum Miller was put forward as a 'stalking horse' to test the strength of the opposition in an election to replace Alex Salmond as leader of the SNP. In 1989 the media described Sir Anthony Meyer as the 'stalking donkey' in the first Conservative leadership challenge against Margaret Thatcher.

**Stamping ground.** A place where one regularly spends time; a favourite haunt; one's home territory or area of operation. The phrase originally referred to a location frequented by animals.

**Stand-off.** An uneasy deadlock or impasse, when each of two sides 'stands off' the other.

> Trouble erupted across Northern Ireland last night after security forces blocked the biggest Drumcree parade in its 191-year history and hundreds of Orangemen embarked on a stand-off that could last weeks.
>
> *The Times* (6 July 1998)

**Stand on someone's shoulders.** To base one's beliefs or principles on those of a predecessor. The image is of a person raised to greater heights by standing on the shoulders of another.

**Stand up and be counted.** To make one's presence known and one's views felt, often at some risk to oneself. The image is of rising to one's feet at a meeting when a count of supporters for a controversial motion is taken. The phrase is of US origin and dates from the early years of the 20th century.

**Stand-up comedy.** Comedy in the form of jokes told by a comedian standing on stage before an audience. The term dates from the 1960s, when comedians of this type first became familiar on television, although they were long familiar before this in the music hall. Examples of British stand-up comedians are Max Miller, Max Bygraves, Frankie Howerd, Ken Dodd, Billy Connolly and Eddie Izzard, each of whom found early on the knack of holding his audience in the hollow of his hand with his particular brand of humour. Although the genre went out of fashion in favour of the sketch-based comedy of university wits such as the members of MONTY PYTHON'S FLYING CIRCUS, the advent of a new generation of often political comedians from the 1980s, such as Ben Elton, brought about a resurgence, aided by a proliferation of comedy venues around the UK, and 'standup' flourished once more.

**Starlight Express, The.** A play by Violet Pearn, with incidental music (including wind machine and cowbells) by Edward Elgar, first produced in 1915. The play was based on the mystery tale *A Prisoner in Fairyland* by Algernon Blackwood (1869–1951), and Elgar's music quotes from his own *Wand of Youth* suites for orchestra, which are themselves based on music Elgar wrote at the age of 12 for a family play. Andrew Lloyd Webber recycled Pearn's title for his roller-skating spectacle *Starlight Express* (1984).

**Starsky and Hutch.** A pair of US plain-clothes policemen, with the full names Dave Starsky and Ken Hutchinson, played by dark-haired Paul Michael Glaser and blond David Soul in the successful and popular television series named after them (1976–81). They spend much of the time jumping in and out of fast cars with squealing tyres in an unidentified US city that is presumed to be Los Angeles, on a mission to put ne'er-do-wells behind bars.

**START.** The Strategic Arms Reduction Talks that evolved from SALT. The first negotiations between the United States and the Soviet Union were in 1982. The Intermediate Nuclear Forces (INF) treaty was signed as a result in 1987 and the Strategic Arms Reduction Treaty in 1991. The talks continued after the disintegration of the Soviet Union in the latter year.

**Starter home.** A house or flat designed to suit a young couple or family buying their first home. The implication is that it is a start, and that they will move on to something bigger and better a few years later. There may also be a secondary allusion to their wish to start a family.

**Star Trek.** The cult US space fiction television series, first screened in 1966 and set in the future, tells how the crew of the Starship *Enterprise* reconnoitre the universe, finding monsters and mysteries at every turn. The best-known crew member is Mr SPOCK, the Starship's first officer, and others include Captain Kirk (played by William Shatner) and Captain Picard (Patrick Stewart). The creator of the whole series was Gene Roddenberry (1921–91). Its many fans, or 'Trekkers' (earlier 'Trekkies'), express their rapturous devotion in conventions in both North America and Britain, and eagerly await the latest *Star Trek* book, film or DVD. In 1995 Paramount Pictures chose a fourth *Star Trek* series, *Voyager*, as the flagship programme of its new network, UPN, and in 2002 the tenth *Star Trek* movie, *Nemesis*, was released. *See also* BEAM ME UP, SCOTTY!; BOLDLY GO WHERE NO MAN HAS GONE BEFORE; IT'S LIFE, JIM, BUT NOT AS WE KNOW IT.

**Start-rite.** The children's shoes so named evolved in 1921 as a patent design of the firm of Henry Quant & Son of Bury St Edmunds. The patent was later sold to James Smith of Norwich. The well-known advertisement depicting the Start-rite twins walking hand in hand down a long, tree-lined road dates from 1947 and was suggested by Rudyard Kipling's own illustration for his story 'The Cat that Walked by Himself' in the JUST SO STORIES (1902).

**Star Wars.** A blockbuster SCIENCE FICTION movie (1977), conceived, written and directed by George Lucas, was the first part of a trilogy, sequels being *The Empire Strikes Back* (1980) and *Return of the Jedi* (1983). It tells how a rebel princess in a distant galaxy escapes and with the help of her robots and a young farmer overcomes the threatening forces of evil. The strange names of the characters are more meaningful than they seem. That of the villainous DARTH VADER may suggest 'Death Invader', but was intended to mean 'Dark Father'. The first name of the youthful hero LUKE SKYWALKER evokes Greek *leukos*, 'light', appropriately for a boy who discovers the power of 'the Force' that can activate light sabres. The surname of the heroine, Princess Leia Organa, reflects the conflict of nature and technology seen in the forest-dwelling heroes ranged against 'the Empire'. The roughneck space pilot Han Solo has a name suggesting 'John' and 'solo', implying a 'loner' in an older world. The robot R2-D2 took his name from a sound editor's shorthand for 'Reel Two, Dialogue Two'. The hairy Wookie, Chewbacca, has a name inspired by Lucas's malamute dog

Indiana (which also gave the hero's name in his Indiana Jones films). The name of the ancient knighthood of the Jedi is based on that of Jed or Jeddak, the lords of Barsoom in Edgar Rice Burroughs' *A Princess of Mars* (1912). The Jedi knight OBI-WAN KENOBI takes the first part of his name from *obi*, a Japanese sash, and perhaps *san*, the Japanese honorary suffix. *Star Wars* was re-released using digital technology in 1997. 'Prequels', *The Phantom Menace*, *Attack of the Clones* and *Revenge of the Sith*, followed in 1999, 2002 and 2005.

The Strategic Defense Initiative (SDI) of the United States, first adumbrated by President Reagan in 1983 as a means of defending the United States against attack from Soviet intercontinental ballistic missiles (ICBMs), was also dubbed 'Star Wars', in allusion to the film series, because parts of the system proposed would be based in space. The US government spent $30 million on the project before finally abandoning it in 1993, two years after the demise of the Soviet Union.

**Stasi.** An abbreviation of German *Staatssicherheitsdienst*, 'State Security Service', as the name of the East German secret police. It was formed in 1950 and disbanded in 1990 following the reunification of Germany. At its peak it employed some 85,000 full-time officers and kept files on 5 million East German citizens, roughly one in three of the population. It maintained close ties with the KGB in Moscow and had links with various terrorist organizations.

**Statemented.** Of a school pupil, having SPECIAL NEEDS. The statement is the legally binding assessment made by a local education authority (LEA) defining the child's requirements. The process for statementing is fairly straightforward. The child is first referred to an educational psychologist for an assessment. After initial testing other experts such as occupational therapists or social workers may be called in. The LEA then responds by issuing the statement detailing the extra help it intends to provide. The procedure was introduced by the Education Act of 1981.

**State-of-the-art.** Sophisticated and up to date. The phrase emerged in the 1970s as a general adoption of the narrower 1950s sense, as applied to the current conditions of practical or technological knowledge in a given field. 'Art' here is thus used in its broadest implication, relating to any creative or imaginative process.

> Aside from the luxury trimmings, the liner will also boast a state-of-the-art security system including trained guards and a heliport with a hi-tech cover hood.
>
> *heat* (18–24 November 1999)

**Stateside.** In (or towards) the United States, a term of US origin dating from the 1940s.

**Status symbol.** A term of US origin dating from the 1950s for a possession or asset that supposedly enhances a person's social prestige. Status symbols are most readily found in the world of business or fashion. Typical examples are a grossly outsized office desk, a designer label, or an ostentatiously displayed item of electronic equipment (such as the most up-to-date MOBILE PHONE) or jewellery (a diamond-encrusted watch often suffices). Their owners would naturally claim that these were essential accoutrements.

> It is a status symbol to have a bookmaker, even if you always ask him for Tote odds.
>
> GUY EGMONT: *The Art of Egmontese*, ch. 1 (1961)

*See also* TROPHY WIFE.

**Stauffenberg Plot.** *See* JULY BOMB PLOT.

**Stay tuned.** Watch or listen for further developments. The phrase originated as a formula spoken before a radio commercial. A printed equivalent is WATCH THIS SPACE!

**Steady state theory.** A theory explaining the origin of the universe, and contrasting with the more popular BIG BANG theory. It claims that the universe exists in time in a 'steady state', i.e. in such a way that the average density of matter does not vary with distance or time. Matter is thus continually being created in the space left by the receding stars and galaxies of the expanding universe. The theory was propounded in 1948 as the 'perfect cosmological principle' by three British scientists: Fred Hoyle, Hermann Bondi and Thomas Gold.

**Stealth.** A term applied to military vehicles and devices designed specifically to evade radar detection at normal combat ranges. The first operational example was the Lockheed F-117 Nighthawk, a ground-attack aircraft of flying-wing design, which entered service with the US Air Force in 1982, although so secret was it that its existence was denied until 1988. The F-117 was followed by the so-called 'Stealth bomber', the Northrop Grumman B2 Spirit strategic bomber (which, at $2.2 billion each, is the most expensive plane ever). Also of flying wing design, the B2 made its first flight in 1989 and saw action in the 1999 Kosovo conflict, in operations in Afghanistan in 2001–2 and in the 2003 invasion of Iraq, flying non-stop from bases in the United States. Stealth technology has also been applied to naval design. Stealth warships have plain slablike sides and an outline simplified drastically from the traditional forest of turrets, funnels, aerials, etc. The equivalent French term is *furtif*.

**Steal the show.** To be the centre of attraction. The expression dates from the 1930s and originated in theatre talk. The idea is that the person 'stole' the limelight from the rest of the cast.

**Stealth tax.** A tax introduced or levied in such a way that those subject to it (supposedly) do not realize they are paying it. The term itself (in active use from around the start of the 21st century, and inspired no doubt by the notion of STEALTH weaponry) is largely an insult hurled at governments by their critics, but the idea of raising revenue in a less obvious and therefore perhaps less painful way is one that has increasingly appealed to vote-hungry politicians since electorates began to revolt against tax-and-spend governments in the latter part of the 20th century.

> A succession of 'stealth taxes', which actually saw most individuals' tax burden increase over the course of the past parliament …
>
> *Country* (May–June 2002)

**Steam radio.** Sound broadcasting, as the original basic medium, by contrast with the later and more sophisticated television. The expression evokes the steam age of rail travel, which preceded that of the diesel and electric train. The phrase was attributed by Asa Briggs, in volume 3 (1970) of *A History of Broadcasting in the United Kingdom*, to the novelist and BBC executive Norman Collins (1907–82).

**Steel Magnolia.** A nickname given to Rosalynn Carter, wife of Jimmy Carter (b.1924), Democratic president of the United States (1977–81), on account of her 'steely' temperament and southern origins (magnolia being associated with the South). *Steel Magnolias* is also the title of a popular play by US writer Robert Harling. Set in a southern beauty salon, it was first performed in 1987 and turned into a film in 1989. The Steel Magnolias are also a rock group (with a name of the IRON BUTTERFLY type).

**Sten gun.** The lightweight sub-machine gun takes its name from the initials of its designers, R.V. Shepherd and H.J. Turpin, with the *-en* from the name of the BREN GUN. It was first in use in the Second World War.

**Stepford wives.** Uncannily perfect women, like those in Ira Levin's novel *The Stepford Wives* (1952), about the wives in Stepford, a commuter village outside New York, who to a newcomer seem all too good to be true. They are in fact computerized models, substituted by their husbands for the human originals. A film version appeared in 1974 and a less-admired remake in 2005. In 1998 the Labour MP Brian Sedgemore notoriously compared many of NEW LABOUR's women MPs to Stepford wives, suggesting that they had microprocessors implanted in their brains to keep them ON MESSAGE.

> 'Then there's the Stepford Wives,' veteran Left-winger Brian Sedgemore said in an outburst that earned him a rebuke from the party leadership. 'That's those female New Labour

MPs who've had the chip inserted into their brains to keep them on-message.'

*Sunday Express* (27 February 2000)

*See also* BLAIR BABES.

**Step forward.** Let me introduce … . Here now is … . Journalistic jargon for a person or organization forming the next or even the main topic of one's piece. The image is of inviting a person to step out of a group in order to be identified and introduced to the present company.

There is always some corner of our operatic field that is forever esoteric. Step forward, the reformed Royal Opera House.

*The Times* (2 November 1999)

**Stepinfetchit.** A US name, now a discredited stereotype, dating from the 1960s for a supposedly typical shuffling, fawning, eye-rolling black servant or more generally for any servile African American. The term comes from Stepin Fetchit, the stage name of the African American actor Lincoln Perry (1902–85), who before he became a film actor danced in a vaudeville as half of a team called 'Step 'n' Fetchit, the Two Dancing Fools from Dixie', taking the name of a horse that Perry had bet on and won. After the act split up, Perry kept the name for his solo act. The name itself spells out as 'step and fetch it', i.e. 'go and get it'.

The driver, from a small town outside Houston, though white, seemed to have taken a course at the Stepin Fetchit school of etiquette. No matter what I said, or asked, his answer was the same: 'Yassuh.'

*Maclean's* (March 1974)

**Stepney wheel.** A former type of spare wheel for a motor vehicle, in the form of an already inflated tyre on a spokeless metal rim, which could be temporarily clamped over a punctured wheel. The devices existed in the early years of the 20th century and took their name from Stepney Street, Llanelli, where they were first made. The name persists in the Indian subcontinent for any kind of spare wheel.

**Step on it** or **on the gas.** To speed up, as in a motor vehicle by putting one's foot on the accelerator. *See also* PUT ONE'S FOOT DOWN.

**Step out of the shadows.** To enter the public gaze from a position of obscurity or reticence; to speak out and clarify one's position.

**Steptoe and Son.** A classic television SITCOM running from 1964 to 1973 and centring on the relationship between a father and son in the rag-and-bone trade. The wilful, manipulative and eccentric old father, Albert Steptoe, played by Wilfrid Brambell (1912–85), and the perpetually exasperated son, Harold, struggling for independence, played by Harry H. Corbett (1925–82), invariably end up by thwarting each other's dearest aspirations. The genius of the series lay in its finely balanced blend of humour and pathos.

**Stern Gang.** A right-wing Zionist terrorist group founded in Palestine in 1940 by Abraham Stern (1907–42). Stern objected to the decision by the IRGUN to stop attacking the British in Palestine for the duration of the Second World War. One of the Stern Gang's most notorious acts was the assassination in 1948 of the United Nations mediator Count Folke Bernadotte (1895–1948), the nephew of King Gustaf VI of Sweden. The gang disbanded later in the same year. *See also* DEIR YASSIN.

**Stick 'em up!** Hands up! An armed robber's command that dates from the 1930s but is now rarely heard in real life.

**Stickies.** A nickname for the 'Official' IRA, a faction that came into being as a result of a split in the ranks of the Irish Republican Army, mirrored by a similar split in the ranks of SINN FÉIN, in 1969. The Stickies were so named for their habit of affixing their Easter lilies (worn by Irish Republicans in memory of the 1916 EASTER RISING) to their lapels with gum, unlike supporters of the Provisional IRA who used pins for the purpose (hence 'pinheads', a derisive nickname for the Provisionals). *See also* PROVOS.

**Stick one's bib in.** In colloquial Australian English, to interfere; to 'stick one's oar in'. To do the opposite – minding one's own business – is to 'keep one's bib out'. A 'bib' in this context is the upper part of a garment. The usages date from the 1940s.

**Stick one's neck out.** To take a rash risk; to ask for trouble. The expression is of US origin and dates from the early years of the 20th century, the reference probably being to a chicken that extends its neck in preparation for slaughter by decapitation.

**Stick out like a sore thumb.** To be very conspicuous. A sore thumb will be held out to avoid contact with the fingers, making it and its owner conspicuous. The simile dates from the 1930s.

**Sticks Nix Hick Pix.** The classically euphonic headline in *Variety*, the US movie magazine, on 17 July 1935, referring to the lack of popularity of rural dramas among backwoods audiences.

**Sticky Fingers.** An album released by The ROLLING STONES in 1971. The key to its salacious title lies in the audacious cover, designed by the Pop artist Andy Warhol (1928–87) and featuring a pair of jeans with a real zip. The album includes the songs 'BROWN SUGAR', 'Wild Horses' and 'You Gotta Move'.

**Sticky wicket.** A tricky or awkward situation. The reference is to a cricket pitch that is drying after rain and is difficult for the batsman (in cricketing parlance also known as a 'sticky dog'). The expression dates from the Second World War. An amusing misexplanation of the term is unintentionally offered by William and Mary Morris in their *Morris Dictionary of Words and Phrases* (1988). Having read somewhere that the allusion is to a soft pitch, they write: 'In cricket – so we are told – a soft pitch can cause the batsman more trouble than one smartly delivered.' The error results from an understanding of 'pitch' as it is used in baseball, meaning a delivery of the ball by the pitcher, corresponding to the bowl of a bowler.

**Stig of the Dump.** The name of a Stone Age man who is found living in a rubbish dump by a boy in a highly successful novel (1963) of the same name by Clive King (b.1924).

**Stijl, De.** (Dutch, 'The Style'.) The name of an organization of mainly Dutch artists founded in 1917 by Theo van Doesburg (1883–1931) and Piet Mondrian (1872–1944), as well as of the journal they published to announce their ideas. They hardly had any cohesive force and did not exhibit together, but the particular 'style' they promoted was one of austere abstract clarity.

**Sting, The.** A film (1973) written by David S. Ward about an elaborate 'numbers racket' set up by two conmen to cheat a gangster out of a fortune. Starring Paul Newman and Robert Redford as the conmen and featuring the ragtime music of Scott Joplin, the film was a huge success and revived the word 'sting' (in disuse since the 1930s) as slang for a con trick or robbery. *See also* BUDDY MOVIE.

**Stir-crazy.** Mentally disturbed, especially as a result of being imprisoned. The expression is of US origin, although 'stir' is British 19th-century jargon for a prison, perhaps from Romany *sturbin*. *Stir Crazy* is the title of a US film of 1980 about two New Yorkers who plan their escape from prison when wrongly convicted of a bank robbery.

**Stitch someone up.** To betray a person by fabricating evidence against them; to manipulate a situation to one's own advantage. The idea is of completing a garment by sewing it up.

> Openshaw, 41, allegedly said on his arrest: 'I'm being stitched up.' The trial goes on.
> *Daily Mirror* (14 July 1989)

The noun derived from the verb is 'stitch-up'.

**Stockbroker belt.** A term for the area outside a city, and especially London, as the stereotypical abode of stockbrokers and other wealthy people.

> Henk Huffener's house, off the Guildford–Dorking road, is not merely in the Surrey stockbroker belt – it is at its very buckle.
> *The Times* (1 March 1999)

**Stockbrokers' Tudor.** A facetious term coined in the 1930s by the writer and cartoonist Osbert Lancaster for a style of mock-Tudor architecture supposedly favoured by stockbrokers. *See also* TUDORBETHAN.

**Stock car.** A car that has been specially strengthened and modified for a form of racing in which the cars deliberately collide. Such cars have a standard or stock chassis, hence the name.

**Stockholm syndrome.** A term dating from the 1970s for the observed tendency of hostages to try to cooperate with their captors. The phenomenon takes its name from a robbery of the Sveriges Kreditbank in Stockholm in 1973, remarkable for the bonds formed between hostages and captors. The story of a woman suffering from Stockholm syndrome is the subject of the film *Blue Velvet* (1986), directed by David Lynch and starring Isabella Rossellini. The kidnapping of the heiress Patti Hearst by the SYMBIONESE LIBERATION ARMY in 1974 led to what may be described as an extreme example of the syndrome.

**Stocking filler** or **stuffer.** A small gift suitable for putting in a Christmas stocking.

**Stoker Jim.** *See* SUNNY JIM.

**Stone the crows!** An exclamation of surprise, dismay, disgust or the like. It originated in Australian English around the time of the First World War. Alliterative alternatives (e.g. 'starve', 'stiffen') have taken the place of 'stone' and other animals (rats, lizards and 'bardies', the latter being edible grubs) have substituted for crows, but it is 'stone the crows' that made the transition to British English.

**Stonewall.** On the night of 27 June 1969, the day of Judy Garland's funeral, police from the Public Morals Section of the New York City Police raided the Stonewall Inn, a gay bar on Christopher Street, Greenwich Village. The operation was supposedly routine, since the bar had no liquor licence. Instead of passively accepting the situation, however, the patrons reacted angrily, taunting the police and sparking off a confrontation that lasted several days. The outcome was the birth of the gay liberation movement, and the name Stonewall was adopted worldwide by organizations campaigning for lesbian and gay rights. *See also* FRIEND OF DOROTHY.

**Stop and search.** The British police are empowered to stop and search people and vehicles if they have reasonable grounds for suspecting that they may find stolen goods, offensive weapons or implements that could be used for burglary. Senior police officers can further authorize stop and search operations in specified localities if they believe that serious incidents of violence may take place, or in order to prevent acts of terrorism. The practice is based on the 'stop and frisk' procedure carried out in the United States in the 1960s.

**Stormin' Norman.** A nickname of General H. Norman Schwarzkopf (b.1934), US commander-in-chief of Allied forces during the 1991 GULF WAR. Also known as the Bear, the temperamentally unpredictable Schwarzkopf became a national hero after the war, was awarded an honorary knighthood by the Queen and retired from the US Army later in 1991. As with the S in Harry S. Truman (*see* GIVE-'EM-HELL HARRY) the H in his name does not stand for anything. *See also* DESERT STORM; NMI.

**Stormont.** The eastern suburb of Belfast that is the location of Parliament House, built in 1928–32 in a Greek classical style and the seat of the Northern Ireland parliament until the introduction of DIRECT RULE in 1972, and of Stormont Castle, the former official residence of the Northern Ireland prime minister, built in 1858 from the original house erected *c*.1830 by the Rev. John Cleland. In 1998, following the GOOD FRIDAY AGREEMENT, Parliament House became the seat of the Northern Ireland Assembly (when not in suspension; *see* DIRECT RULE) and Stormont House the office of the Northern Ireland first minister.

**Story of my life.** Said ruefully of a recurring misfortune, as: 'Stood up again – that's the story of my life.' *The Story of My Life* is a standard title for an autobiography.

**Strafe.** This expressive verb, meaning to attack repeatedly with bombs or machine-gun fire from low-flying aircraft, is not English in origin but was derisively adopted from the German First World War catchphrase, *Gott strafe England*, 'May God punish England'. The source of this execration is uncertain, but it is in Alfred Funke's book *Schwert und Myrte* ('Sword and Myrtle') (1914).

**Straight from the horse's mouth.** Directly from the source; entirely reliable. The phrase applies to news, information and the like and comes from racing jargon. A racing tip that comes straight from the horse's own mouth must be dependable.

**Straight man.** The half of a comedy duo whose lines and actions are designed to give his partner most of the laughs. Examples are Bud Abbot for Lou Costello or Dean Martin for Jerry Lewis in the cinema, or Ernie Wise for Eric Morecambe on television.

**Straight up.** Truthfully; honestly. A phrase emphasizing that a statement is honest and genuine, since it is 'straight' or direct, not 'angled' or devious.

**Strain the potatoes** or **spuds** or **taters.** In Australian euphemistic slang, of a male, to urinate. The usage is one of a number of colourful expressions introduced into the language in the 1960s by Barry Humphries's Barry MCKENZIE.

**'Strange Fruit'.** A song (1939) performed by Billie Holiday (1915–59), about lynchings in the southern United States:

> Southern trees bear strange fruit,
> Blood on the leaves and blood at the root,
> Black bodies swinging in the Southern breeze,
> Strange fruit hanging from the poplar trees.

**Strangers and Brothers.** A novel (1940) by C.P. Snow, later Lord Snow (1905–80). It was reissued (1973) as *George Passant*, to allow the original title to encompass a sequence of 11 novels, reflecting the author's professional experiences over the years as scientist, academic and civil servant, and narrated by a kind of alter ego, the lawyer Lewis Eliot. The title indicates the divided world that Eliot enters: he and his brothers and two friends who have an almost fraternal relationship with him are the 'brothers', while other people are the 'strangers'.

**Strangers on a train.** A stock metaphor for a relationship that is doomed to end as suddenly as it began. Two strangers seated next to or opposite one another on a train may strike up a conversation and achieve a degree of intimacy, but the association will end when the train reaches its destination or when one of the two leaves the train before the other. The phrase itself was popularized by the title of Patricia Highsmith's first novel, a psychological thriller, *Strangers on a Train* (1950), the story of two men who 'swap' murders, made into a classic film the following year by Alfred Hitchcock from a screenplay by Raymond Chandler. The image here is hardly romantic, but the phrase is now usually thought of in such terms. The situation itself has formed the basis for various literary works and has a pre-echo in David Lean's equally memorable film BRIEF ENCOUNTER (1945), set on a railway station.

**Strawberry box.** In colloquial New Zealand English, a small receptacle given to boat passengers to vomit into in case of sea sickness. The term is first recorded in 1936, and reflects a resemblance to the punnets in which strawberries and other soft fruits are sold.

**'Strawberry Fields Forever'.** An innovatively recorded PSYCHEDELIC song by The BEATLES, credited to John Lennon and Paul McCartney and released in February 1967 as the B-side of 'PENNY LANE'. The lyrics evoke a lost world of childhood in a quasi-pastoral manner that was to become popular with a number of English pop groups of the late 1960s. Strawberry Fields is the name of an actual girls' reform school in Woolton, Liverpool. There is a Strawberry Fields memorial garden to John Lennon in New York's Central Park, near the spot where Lennon was fatally shot on 8 December 1980.

**Streaking.** The act of running naked in a public place by way of a stunt, sometimes under the influence of a stimulant other than a bet or the buzz of bravado. The feat is usually staged out of doors, typically at a sporting venue, but may also be enacted in a public building such as a restaurant. The practice first emerged on US college campuses in the early 1970s, and male streakers at first outnumbered female. In Britain the activity caught the attention of the public in 1974, when the Australian Michael O'Brien was escorted off the pitch at Twickenham during an England vs France rugby match, a policeman using his helmet to restore the culprit's modesty. The following year, during the Ashes series, Michael Angelow jumped over the stumps at Lord's cricket ground, wearing only his plimsolls. According to John Ballard and Paul Suff's *Dictionary of Football* (1999) the first female streaker at a major football match was Variana Scotney, who ran on to the pitch at Highbury when Arsenal were playing Tottenham Hotspur in 1981. More memorably, in 1982 Erica Row ran topless across the pitch at Twickenham during a match between England and Australia. The enthusiasm for streaking at great sporting events (including the Derby, the Open and Wimbledon) had not diminished by the early 21st century, although the police continue to take an unamused view. *See also* FAMOUS FOR 15 MINUTES; NAKED RAMBLER.

**Stream of consciousness.** A Modernist (*see* MODERNISM) technique of novel-writing, first deliberately employed by Dorothy Richardson (1873–1957) in *Pointed Roofs* (1915), and developed by James Joyce (1882–1941) and Virginia Woolf (1882–1941). By this technique the writer presents life as seen through a flow of thoughts and impressions in the mind of a single character. The term itself was coined by William James in *Principles of Psychology* (1890). *See also* MRS DALLOWAY; ULYSSES.

**Streetcar Named Desire, A.** A play (1947) by Tennessee Williams (1911–83) that was subsequently turned into a successful film, directed by Elia Kazan, starring Marlon Brando and Vivien Leigh. An intense drama about the relationship between faded Southern belle Blanche DUBOIS and her brother-in-law Stanley Kowalski, the play had several titles before the final one, including *The Moth*, *Blanche's Chair in the Moon* and *The Poker Night*. The eventual title was inspired by a streetcar called 'Desire' (now preserved) that, together with another called 'Cemeteries', plied the main street in the district of New Orleans where Williams lived. The play is a leitmotif in Pedro Almodóvar's film *Todo sobre mi madre* (*All about My Mother*) (1999). *See also* DESIRE STREET.

> They told me to take a streetcar named Desire, then transfer to one called Cemeteries.
>
> TENNESSEE WILLIAMS: *A Streetcar Named Desire* (Blanche's first line)

**Street cred.** In full, street credibility, or a *persona grata* status among one's young urban peers. The expression arose in the popular music industry in the 1970s and embodies the tenet that the 'artist' must relate genuinely to the 'people', meaning the working-class youth of the streets and housing estates. Many police officers aim to gain 'street cred' for the greater efficiency of their duties.

> Crime writers and television producers have never doubted the value of the ageing detective with a well-worn patina of street cred.
>
> *The Times* (12 July 1999)

**Street film.** A type of silent film made in Germany during the 1920s. It laid emphasis on the depressing and dehumanizing aspects of urban life for the lower middle class and usually featured a sensitive individual seeking to rise above the limitations of his environment. The first such film was Carl Grune's *Die Strasse* ('The Street') (1923) and the best-known is probably G.W. Pabst's *Die freudlose Gasse* ('Joyless Street') (1925).

**Strength through Joy.** (German *Kraft durch Freude*.) The name of the Nazi leisure organization, a subsidiary of the German Labour Front. It was founded in 1934, and the name was coined by Robert Ley (1890–1945), leader of the German Labour Front. The organization mainly concerned itself with organizing holidays for the working class. Ley committed suicide at the end of the war.

**Stressed out.** Colloquially, exhausted or debilitated as a result of stress. The term emerged in the 1980s, an era when stress received recognition as a hazard of the pressures of modern life.

**Stretch limo.** A limousine that has been 'stretched' by the incorporation of an extended seating area. Such cars originated in the United States and became associated with pop stars and other celebrities from the 1980s, but in the 21st century they are regularly hired by the wider population for celebrations such as HEN NIGHTS.

**Strictly for the birds.** Unimportant; worthless. A phrase of US origin that became current in the 1950s. The reference is to horse manure, which is good only for picking over by birds.

*Strife.* A play (1909) by John Galsworthy (1867–1933) about the conflict between management and labour in the course of an industrial strike. A production of the play at the National Theatre on the SOUTH BANK in 1978 was especially poignant as the theatre was involved in a bitter dispute with its stage staff at the time.

**Strikes again.** Said tongue-in-cheek of someone or something repeating a characteristic action. The expression probably arose from a SCIENCE FICTION story involving an evil power. One of the six sequels to the comedy film *The* PINK PANTHER (1963), starring Peter Sellers as the incompetent Inspector CLOUSEAU, was *The Pink Panther Strikes Again* (1976).

> Harold Pinter Strikes Again [headline] ... Ailing British playwright Harold Pinter used his Nobel prize lecture ... to deliver a fierce attack on US foreign policy.
>
> michellemalkin.com (7 December 2005)

**Strine.** According to the writer Alistair Morrison, the brand of English spoken by Australians, a humorous survey of which is provided in *Let's Talk Strine* (1965), subtitled 'a lexicon of modern Strine usage'. The clipped tones of Australian speech are spelled out phonetically, with amusing and linguistically playful results. Thus 'Fried eye car nelpew' translates as 'I'm afraid I can't help you'; 'Hacker chufa get?' as 'How could you forget?'; and 'Nwotsa taller bat?' as 'What's it all about?'. 'Strine', of course, means 'Australian', and the baffling name of the book's supposed author, Professor Afferbeck Lauder (described as 'Professor of Strine Studies, University of Sinny; Fellow of the Yarnurdov Foundation') on closer examination turns out to be an Australian rendering of 'alphabetical order'. A later volume of Strine, *Nose Turn Unturned*, followed in 1966. *See also* FRAFFLY.

**String along with someone.** To accompany them generally or casually. The allusion is to a train of pack-mules, each 'strung' to the one in front. The expression dates from the 1920s.

> You may not be an angel
> 'Cause angels are so few,
> But until the day that one comes along
> I'll string along with you.
>
> AL DUBIN: 'You'll Never Be an Angel' (song) (1934)

**Stringfellows.** A famous London nightclub opened in 1980 by the self-proclaimed 'world's greatest disco owner' Peter Stringfellow (b.1940). It is brash and garish by comparison with ANNABEL'S or TRAMP, but it has several celebrities among its mostly middle-aged businessmen members.

> ... the dominating image is of a pot-bellied unashamed voluptuary in a powder-blue *cache-sexe* posing on a beach in the Caribbean with a woman forty years his junior. Is it a Port Said pimp? An Italian pandar? No. It is Peter Stringfellow, strip-show entrepreneur and enemy of *le vie en gris*. But here is a conundrum. Is he at one and the same time the furtive Anglo-Saxon voyeur and the tit-squeezing Gallic-style sexual extrovert? Achilles and the Hare in but a single form? A Zeno's Paradox *pour nos jours*?
>
> HERMIONE EYRE and WILLIAM DONALDSON: *The Dictionary of National Celebrity* (2005)

*See also* BRIEF HISTORY OF TIME.

**String quartets.** Many Western countries saw the creation of new string quartets in the 20th century, either to promote and popularize modern music or to concentrate on a particular period of music or even a particular composer. The following is a selection of some of the better-known British quartets, with the date of their formation (and demise) and the origin of their name.

Aeolian Quartet (1944–82) (originally Stratton Quartet, from its leader, George Stratton): for Aeolus, Greek god of the winds, also the Aeolian harp, a stringed instrument named after him

Alban Berg Quartet (from 1971): after the Austrian composer Alban Berg (1885–1935)

Allegri Quartet (from 1953): after the Italian composer Gregorio Allegri (1582–1652)

AMADEUS QUARTET

Arditti Quartet (from 1974): from one of its original four members, Irvine Arditti

Belcea Quartet (from 1994): from its first violinist, Corina Belcea

Blech Quartet (1934–50): from its leader, Harry Blech (1910–99)

Brodsky Quartet (from 1973): in honour of the Russian violinst Adolph Brodsky (1851–1929)

Brosa Quartet (1924–38): from its leader, Spanish-born Antonio Brosa (1894–1979)

Chilingirian Quartet (from 1971): founded by the Cypriot violinist Levon Chilingirian (b.1948)

Endellion Quartet (from 1979): after the Cornish village of St Endellion

Fitzwilliam Quartet (from 1975): after the 17th-century Fitzwilliam Virginal Book

Gabrieli Quartet (from 1966): after the Italian composer Giovanni Gabrieli (c.1554–1612)

Griller Quartet (1928–61): founded by Sidney Griller (1911–93)

Lindsay Quartet (1967–2005; latterly known as The Lindsays): in honour of Alexander Dunlop Lindsay, 1st Baron Lindsay of Birker (1879–1952), first Principal of the University College of North Staffordshire, later Keele University, where it was quartet in residence 1967–72

London String Quartet (1908–35): London-based, and originally the New String Quartet

London String Quartet (1958–61): London-based, and originally the New London Quartet

Maggini Quartet (from 1988): after the 16th-century Brescian violin-maker Giovanni Paulo Maggini

Medici Quartet (from 1974): after the noted 17th-century Italian art patrons

Quartetto Italiano ('Italian Quartet') (1945–80): from the nationality of its members

Smetana Quartet (1945–89): after the Czech composer Bedřich Smetana (1824–84)

Takács Quartet (from 1975): after the Hungarian violinist Gabor Takács-Nagy, one of its founder-members

**Strip, The.** The main street or central area of a US city, and especially Las Vegas, where the name is applied to the street where most of the gambling casinos are found.

> Not many performers can survive Las Vegas … It got to Frank Sinatra; his years on the Strip gave him disastrous delusions of grandeur.
>
> *heat* (23–29 September 1999)

**Strip city.** A US term dating from the 1950s for a long, narrow stretch of urban development between two or more relatively distant cities.

> By 1980 or so, 80 per cent of us will live in cities, and the strip city – Boston to Washington, Los Angeles to San Diego, and Milwaukee to Cleveland – will have made its appearance.
>
> *Saturday Review* (13 January 1968)

**Strippergram.** A form of 'greetings telegram' delivered by a messenger who performs a STRIPTEASE for the benefit of the recipient, sometimes attired (to begin with) in the uniform of a traffic warden or policeman (-woman) or some other kind of authority figure. Now just called 'a stripper', the show is popular at both STAG NIGHTS and HEN NIGHTS,

often to the embarrassment of the person getting married. *See also* KISSOGRAM.

**Strip poker.** A game of poker in which a player with a losing hand removes an item of clothing as a penalty or forfeit.

**Strip search.** A search of a person involving the removal of all their clothes. The aim is to find drugs or the like concealed in body cavities.

**Striptease.** A club or cabaret performance in which a woman or (less often) a man slowly and provocatively undresses, i.e. teases by stripping. Striptease is said to have originated at the *Bal des Quat'z Arts* held at midnight on 9 February 1893 at the Moulin Rouge in Paris, when a group of students rented the music hall for their celebrated Four Arts Ball. The event was notorious for its debauchery and drunkenness, and on this occasion the personal attractions of two girls were debated by their admirers. The young women then stood on tables for their ankles to be judged. Competition extended to their legs, thighs, hips, buttocks, breasts and shoulders, until one of the two ended up completely naked. News of the performance reached directors of other music halls and on 13 March 1894 a short sketch entitled *Le Coucher d'Yvette* ('Yvette Goes to Bed') was staged at Le Divan Fayouau on the Rue des Martyrs. The act relied on the spectator's lubricious imagination being one jump ahead of actuality, so that when the actress reached the final stage of her gradual disrobing the audience would already see her as naked, although she had not yet removed her last drapes. The vogue caught on like wildfire, and soon every variety house in Paris had its own version of *Le Coucher d'Yvette* with titles such as *Le Bain de la Maid* ('The Maid Takes a Bath'), *Suzanne et la Grande Chaleur* ('Suzanne in a Heatwave') and *Liane chez le Médecin* ('Liane at the Doctor's'). *See also* LAP DANCING; POLE DANCING.

**Stroke City.** A Northern Ireland nickname for the city of Derry/Londonderry, alluding to the stroke ('/') that separates the alternative names. The basic and historic name is Derry, from Irish *doire*, 'oak grove', but in 1609 James I granted a charter authorizing a plantation by merchants from London on the site of the city following its burning by the English. Hence the addition of the English name. Today, 'Derry' is preferred by Catholics and 'Londonderry' by many Protestants. Official authorities, such as the Post Office, are generally non-committal when it comes to advising which of the two is 'correct', and entrance routes to the city have road signs showing both names. 'Stroke City' may be a partial pun on 'Stoke City' as the name of a football club. *See also* BOGSIDE.

**Stroll on!** Get away with you! You must be joking! An expression of astonishment or incredulity dating from the 1950s.

**Strong silent type.** A man of few words but effective action. The expression, now often used ironically, dates from the early 20th century when it was taken up by various women novelists to describe a romantic male character of some kind.

**Stroppy.** Bad-tempered and argumentative. The word dates from the 1950s and may derive from 'obstreperous', although there is perhaps also a suggestion of Greek *strophē*, 'a turning', 'a twisting'. (An older equivalent is 'wayward', which originally meant 'turned away'.) Hence 'strop' as a slang term for a bad mood or temper.

**Strut one's stuff.** To display one's ability; to show what one has to offer. The expression dates from the 1920s and has its origin in African American slang for flaunting one's sexual attraction. Some birds literally 'strut their stuff' in their courting rituals.

> Groups simply register with the Shakespeare Centre, strut their stuff during April, then send a record of the event.
> *The Times* (28 December 1999)

**Stuart Little.** An anthropomorphized mouse, the eponymous hero of a classic children's novel (1945) by E.B. White. He is supposedly the second son of Mr and Mrs Frederick C. Little, with a perfectly normal-sized human-looking older brother, but his diminutiveness and rodent qualities are never got to the bottom of. The film (1999) of the same name, obviously impatient with such genetic mysteries, had Stuart instead adopted by a New York couple called Little who had promised their young son a brother. In both the original film and the sequel *Stuart Little 2* (2002), which mixed real actors with animation, the voice of the mouse was provided by Michael J. Fox.

**Stuckism.** The name adopted in 1999 by a group of British figurative painters who decry the dominance of conceptual artists such as Tracey Emin (*see* EVERYONE I'VE EVER SLEPT WITH 1963–95) and Damien Hurst (*see* PHYSICAL IMPOSSIBILITY OF DEATH IN THE MIND OF SOMEONE LIVING) in contemporary British art fashion (*see* BRIT ART), as patronized by such figures as the collector Charles Saatchi or Sir Nicholas Serota, director of the Tate Gallery. The phrase was coined by the painter Charles Thomson, recording what Emin had said to the painter Billy Childish, her then boyfriend: 'Your paintings are stuck. You are stuck. Stuck! Stuck! Stuck!' In their first manifesto, abominating the tricksiness and sensationalism of the YBAs ('Young

British Artists', as exponents of Brit Art are known), the Stuckists declared:

> Artists who don't paint aren't artists.

Among the exhibitions and events held by the Stuckists are those entitled *The Resignation of Sir Nicholas Serota* and *The Real Turner Prize*, the latter held in 2000 at the time of the TURNER PRIZE. Billy Childish has since distanced himself from the movement, whose fame has spread far and wide: in Colombia, for example, they are known as Los Stuckistas.

**Stud muffin.** A very sexually attractive male. This addition to the armoury of equal-opportunity sexual stereotyping came into vogue in 2005.

> Andie Harper, BBC Radio Cambridgeshire Drivetime presenter and token 'stud muffin', admits he's a bit hopeless when it comes to wooing the women.
> www.bbc.co.uk/cambridgeshire (22 October 2005)

**Studs Lonigan.** A trilogy (1935) by the US novelist James T. Farrell (1904–79), consisting of *Young Lonigan: A Boyhood on the Chicago Streets* (1932), *The Young Manhood of Studs Lonigan* (1934) and *Judgment Day* (1935). The starting point was the story 'Studs' in *This Quarter* in 1930. William (Studs) Lonigan is the son of a lower-middle-class Irish Catholic family in Chicago. The trilogy, written in a naturalistic style, follows Lonigan from the age of 15 to his 30s, when pneumonia cuts short a life tainted by ill-fortune, dissipation and joblessness. An unpolished film version (1960) was directed by Irving Lerner.

**Stuffed owl.** An expression applied to poetry that treats trivial or inconsequential subjects in a grandiose manner. It comes from *The Stuffed Owl*, 'an anthology of bad verse' published by Percy Wyndham Lewis in 1930 and taking its title from a line by Wordsworth:

> The presence even of a stuffed Owl for her
> Can cheat the time; sending her out
> To ivied castles and to moonlight skies,
> Though he can neither stir a plume, nor shout;
> Nor veil, with restless film, his staring eyes.
> *Miscellaneous Sonnets*, III, xiii (1827)

**Stuffed shirt.** A pompous but vacuous person. The allusion is to a dummy displaying a dress shirt in a menswear store. The figure is pompous-looking but in fact hollow.

**Stuffed their mouths with gold.** What the Labour politician Aneurin Bevan (1897–1960) claimed to have done to the hospital consultants who had previously opposed his introduction of the National Health Service in 1948.

**Stuff happens.** A euphemistic alternative to SHIT HAPPENS, as deployed, for example, by US secretary of defense Donald Rumsfeld at a press conference (11 April 2003) in response to the looting of Baghdad following the Anglo-American capture of the Iraqi capital:

> Stuff happens ... and it's untidy, and freedom's untidy, and free people are free to make mistakes and commit crimes and do bad things.

Subsequently, David Hare gave the title *Stuff Happens* to his 2004 play about the lead-up to the Iraq War.

> Stuff was happening during Duncan Smith's brief reign as Tory leader. War drums rolled, diplomatic manoeuvres continued at the United Nations, and Blair claimed still more absurdly that he was doing everything he possibly could to work for peace.
>
> GEOFFREY WHEATCROFT: *The Strange Death of Tory England* (2005)

**Stuff to give the troops.** Just what is needed; exactly what should be given. Often occurring in the stock sentence 'That's the stuff to give the troops', the expression probably arose in the First World War but is first recorded only in the 1920s. 'Stuff' does not necessarily mean food.

**Stuka.** The popular name (derived from the generic German term for a dive bomber, *Sturzkampfflugzeug*) of the Junkers Ju-87, which first entered service with the German LUFTWAFFE in 1937. It was tested successfully during the Spanish Civil War and became a key component of the BLITZKRIEG tactics that brought about rapid German victory in Poland in 1939 and western Europe in 1940. The terror of its steep dive towards its targets was enhanced by the attachment of screaming sirens (*Jericho-Trompeten*, 'trumpets of Jericho'). The Stuka proved no match for British fighters such as the Spitfire and Hurricane, however, and was soon rendered obsolete. Nevertheless, it continued in service in some theatres, and production did not end until 1944.

**Stunt girl.** A US term for a woman reporter in the early years of the 20th century who went to great lengths, often in disguise, to get a story. The prime example was Winifred S. Black (1863–1936), who wrote under the pen-name 'Annie Laurie', from the popular song of this name. Her first major story was in 1890, when she faked an accident in order to be admitted to the San Francisco Receiving Hospital and so report on the rough treatment given to women vagrants there. In 1892 she secured an exclusive interview with President Benjamin Harrison by sneaking aboard his private train and hiding under a table. Her greatest story was in 1900, when she disguised herself as a boy to mingle among soldiers and write about a flood in Galveston, Texas.

**Stupenda, La.** (Italian, 'the stupendous one'.) The sobriquet of the Australian operatic soprano Dame Joan Sutherland (b.1926), who thrilled audiences with her spectacular coloratura. It was originally awarded to her by the Italian press after her performance in Donizetti's *Lucia di Lammermoor* at La Scala, Milan, in 1961.

**Subbuteo.** This popular game of table football dates from 1947 as the creation of Peter Adolph, who originally wanted to call it 'Hobby'. This name was not acceptable for registration purposes, however, so instead he took the Latin name of the hobby hawk, *Falco subbuteo*, adopting the second word of this by default. The suggestion of 'boot' in the name is thus fortuitous but apt.

**Subsidiarity.** A term used in politics for the principle that a central authority should have a subsidiary function and perform only those tasks that cannot be performed at a more local level. The word was first made familiar to the general public in 1990 as the result of controversy about the speed of progress towards European union, but it is found in the specialized vocabulary of Eurocrats before this date and ultimately arose in the 1930s as a translation of German *Subsidiarität*, used in a paraphrase of Pope Pius XI's encyclical *Quadragesimo Anno* (1931). This articulated the modern Catholic social teaching that the best institutions for responding to a particular social task are those that are most proximate to it.

**Subtext.** The meanings or ideas that underlie the surface text of a literary work, drama or film. The term originated in the 1950s as theatrical jargon for the unspoken in a play, and especially what was implied by a pause or by silence. In the cinema the subtext is often suggested by the juxtaposition of scenes or by background sound or music. The text of Ingmar Bergman's *The Virgin Spring* (1959), for instance, deals with the rape of a young girl and the revenge of her father, while the subtext elicits the viewer's awareness of the struggle of Christianity to overcome paganism and of the need for faith. The subtext of a work is always implicit, not explicit.

**Subtopia.** A word coined (from 'suburb' and 'Utopia') by the architectural journalist Ian Nairn to denote the sprawling suburban housing estates built to satisfy the urban workers' yearning for country surroundings while clinging to the amenities of the town. The term includes all the paraphernalia of concrete posts, lamp standards, chain link fencing and other uglinesses associated with a disfigured landscape.

> There will be no real distinction between town and country. Both will consist of a limbo of shacks, bogus rusticities, wire

and aerodromes, set in some fir-poled fields … Upon this new Britain the *Review* bestows a name in the hope that it will stick – *Subtopia*.

IAN NAIRN: *Architectural Review*, cxvii (1955)

**Such Sweet Thunder.** The title of the Shakespearian suite by Duke Ellington (1899–1974), dating from 1957, comes from *A Midsummer Night's Dream* (IV.i):

I was with Hercules and Cadmus once,
When in a wood of Crete they bay'd the bear
With hounds of Sparta: never did I hear
Such gallant chiding; for, besides the groves,
The skies, the fountains, every region near
Seem'd all one mutual cry. I never heard
So musical a discord, such sweet thunder.

In the series of vignettes Ellington matches Shakespearian characters to the individual style of his soloists: for example, Johnny Hodges on saxophone is a fervent Cleopatra and Jimmy Hamilton on clarinet a haughty Caesar, while Cat Anderson on trumpet reaches wildly high notes as Hamlet in 'Madness in Great Ones'. It was said that only a dog could hear his highest notes.

**Sudetenland.** An area, also called the Sudeten, in the north of what is now the Czech Republic. Formerly part of the Austro-Hungarian Empire, it became part of the new state of Czechoslovakia following the Treaty of St Germain (1919). There were some 3.25 million German-speakers in the Sudetenland, and in the 1930s Hitler exploited the grievances of these people, sponsoring the formation of a quasi-NAZI Sudeten Party that agitated against the Czechoslovak government. The escalating violence led to the MUNICH Agreement, by which Britain and France allowed Hitler to annex the Sudetenland (September 1938). The following year the Nazis occupied the whole of Czechoslovakia. At the end of the Second World War Czechoslovakia took back the Sudetenland and expelled the German-speaking population. *See also* PEACE IN OUR TIME; SUDETEN SCOTS.

**Sudeten Scots.** A nickname for expatriate Scots in England who opposed DEVOLUTION, alluding to the German presence in Czech SUDETENLAND. The phrase, which happens to suggest 'southern Scots', was coined by William Ross, later Lord Ross of Marnock (1911–88), secretary of state for Scotland (1964–70 and 1974–6).

**Sudoku.** A puzzle that involves filling in a 9×9 matrix with numbers. Every digit from 1 to 9 must be inserted once into each of nine vertical columns and nine horizontal rows, and into each of nine 3×3 boxes (known as 'regions'). The game

was invented in the United States in 1979 by Howard Garns and was published in *Dell Magazine* under the name 'number place puzzle' (which it still often goes by in the United States). It first appeared in Japan in 1984 under the slogan *Suuji wa dokushin ni kagiru*, meaning 'The numbers must be single'. The rather unwieldy appellation was subsequently shortened to *sudoku*. The puzzle arrived in Britain in November 2004, when *The Times* published one under the name Sudoku. Other newspapers followed suit early in 2005 and a craze got under way, earning Sudoku the honorary title of the RUBIK'S CUBE of the 21st century.

**Suedehead.** A young person similar to a SKINHEAD but with slightly longer hair and smarter clothes.

**Suez Crisis.** A brief conflict that erupted in 1956 following the nationalization of the Suez Canal by President Nasser of Egypt in retaliation for the withdrawal of financial support from the United States and Britain for the building of the Aswan High Dam. Israel attacked Egypt on 29 October 1956, and the following day Britain and France (who had secretly been in negotiation with Israel) demanded that both sides withdraw from the canal. When Egypt refused, the British and French launched air attacks and landed troops. The action was strongly condemned by the United Nations and the United States, the latter putting pressure on Britain and France to withdraw. The conflict is often referred to as simply 'Suez'.

Suez – a smash and grab raid that was all smash and no grab.
SIR HAROLD NICOLSON: in conversation with Antony Jay (November 1956).

**Suffer the little children.** A media catchphrase frequently adopted to head a report of child ABUSE, a charity appeal or some similar item involving the suffering of children. The words are biblical, but with 'suffer', properly meaning 'allow', 'let', misapplied in its modern sense of 'experience pain': 'Jesus said, suffer little children, and forbid them not, to come to me' (Matthew 19:14).

**Suffragette.** The suffragette movement in Britain dates from the early 20th century, when women organized a campaign of demonstrations and militant action in their bid for the right to vote. The campaign was prompted by the repeated defeat of women's suffrage bills in parliament in the 19th century, and was led by Mrs Emmeline Pankhurst (1858–1928) and her daughters Christabel (1880–1958) and Sylvia (1882–1960), who in 1903 founded the Women's Social and Political Union, with its motto 'Votes for Women'. Women over the age of 30 won the vote in 1918, and in 1929 the franchise was extended to all women of majority age, then 21. The word itself, first recorded in 1906, was the first in

English to use the French feminine suffix -*ette*, and it spawned later terms such as usherette and drum majorette, where it is added to the masculine original. *See also* CAT AND MOUSE ACT.

> 'Very well ... Suffragettes if you like. To get an abuse listened to is the first thing; to get it understood is the next. Rather than not have our cause stand out clear and unmistakable before a preoccupied, careless world, we accept the clumsy label; we wear it proudly. And it won't be the first time in history that a name given in derision has become a badge of honour!'
>
> ELIZABETH ROBINS: *The Convert* (1907)

**Sugar Bowl.** The post-season American collegiate football game that has been played every New Year's Day at New Orleans, Louisiana, since 1935. It was originally played at the stadium of Tulane University but in 1976 moved to the Louisiana Superdome. The name alludes to 'Sugar State' as the nickname of Louisiana, so called from its many sugar plantations and sugar refineries. *See also* SUPER BOWL.

**Sugar daddy.** A rich, middle-aged or elderly man who lavishes expensive gifts on a much younger woman, usually in the hope of sexual favours. The expression is of US origin and arose in the 1920s. A derivation in rhyming slang, 'sugar and honey' meaning 'money', has been proposed, but 'sugar' has long been a word associated with affection and luxury. *See also* TOY BOY.

> The morning papers had come aboard, reassuring citizens ... that sugar daddies were still being surprised in love-nests.
>
> P.G. WODEHOUSE: *The Luck of the Bodkins*, ch. 21 (1935)

**Sugar Ray Robinson.** The US middleweight boxer (1921–89) was born Walker Smith. He became 'Ray Robinson' when he substituted for another boxer of that name, the word 'Sugar' being added later when his trainer was told that his boxer was 'sweet as sugar'. The US welterweight and middleweight boxer Ray Leonard (b.1956) took the name 'Sugar Ray' Leonard.

**Suicide blonde.** A woman with dyed blonde hair or peroxide blonde hair. The allusion may be to its 'killing' effect on men. *See also* PLATINUM BLONDE.

**Suitable Boy, A.** A novel (1993) by Vikram Seth (b.1952). The action begins in India in 1950, just after independence, and chiefly involves the members of four families. The central plot concerns the efforts of Mrs Mehta to find an appropriate husband ('a suitable boy') for her younger daughter, Lata. Lata finally makes her own choice from three men: a fellow student who is a Muslim, a factory manager and a poet, each of whom has good qualities. Subplots illustrate the general political situation at the time.

**Suitable Case for Treatment, A.** A television play (1962) by David Mercer (1928–80), turned into a film in 1966 (directed by Karel Reisz) with the title *Morgan – A Suitable Case for Treatment*. Morgan (played by David Warner in the film) is an angry young man living in a fantasy world, a working-class artist married to an upper-class woman (played by Vanessa Redgrave). When she divorces him, he embarks on an increasingly crazy campaign to win her back.

**Suited and booted.** Originally, and literally, fully supplied with all the necessary clothing and footwear, and hence ready to face the world. The implication is often that a person who usually dresses casually has put on more formal wear. Latterly the expression has also come to mean more generally 'fully equipped and ready to go'.

> A suited and booted [poker] player tends to have, at the very least, a decent grasp of maths and a fairly analytical brain. More so than the guy in the Hawaiian shirt, anyway.
>
> VICTORIA COREN: www.paradisepoker.com (5 November 2005)

**Sultan of Spin.** *See* MANDY.

**Sultans of Bling.** A nickname given to Tony and Cherie Blair by the Italian press following revelations in 2005 that they had accepted presents of jewellery and expensive watches from the Italian prime minister, Silvio Berlusconi. The reference is to the song 'SULTANS OF SWING' and to the slang word BLING.

> The Italian newspaper *Corriere della Sera* recently shed another little shaft of light onto our prime minister's personality – and that of his wife. Cherie Blair is now under attack for the size of her fee for a charity tour of Australia in comparison with the funds actually raised for the children's cancer charity. *Corriere*'s story concerned the steady flow of jewellery and gifts from premier Silvio Berlusconi to Tony and Cherie Blair since they were famously feted at his Sardinian villa and treated to a fireworks display reading 'Viva Tony'.
>
> Gifts between government leaders are as old as history. Berlusconi's, however, are apparently aimed to satisfy some insatiable lust for the trappings of wealth: watches, earrings, a necklace, ring and bracelet. *Corriere* duly dubbed the Blairs 'The Sultans of Bling'. Under protocol, Berlusconi's gifts can be worn, but remain the property of Downing Street – apart from two watches, which caught the Blairs' fancy so much that they invoked Whitehall procedure to purchase them for £350 each.
>
> ED VULLIAMY: in *The Guardian* (26 October 2005)

In the same year articles in a number of US and UK newspapers about an exhibition of Ottoman treasures were headlined 'Sultans of Bling'.

**'Sultans of Swing'.** A song written by Mark Knopfler and released by Dire Straits in 1979. It tells of the pleasures of being a part-time musician 'living it up for Friday night'. The wit of its lyrics and the sinuous elegance of its music (particularly the accomplished guitar-playing of Mark Knopfler) contrasted with the contemporary fashion for the angry voice of PUNK.

**Summerhill.** A coeducational 'progressive' school set up near Leiston, Suffolk, in 1927 by A.S. Neill (1883–1973), a radical Scottish educationalist. The basic tenet is that children need attend lessons only if they feel like it and that they themselves should formulate their rules of conduct. The scheme was seen as anarchic and degenerate by many, and the school has been criticized for its rudimentary facilities and poor academic standards. It was subsequently taken over by the founder's daughter, Zoë Neill Redhead.

**Summer of love.** The summer of 1967, which saw the birth of the HIPPIE movement. Peace, love and flowers in the hair were particularly on display in San Francisco, although the phenomenon was apparent in other Western countries. As it was the height of the VIETNAM War, the slogan of the summer was 'Make love not war', while the theme album was The Beatles' SERGEANT PEPPER'S LONELY HEARTS CLUB BAND. *See also* 'ALL YOU NEED IS LOVE'; HASHBURY; LONG HOT SUMMER.

**Summer pudding.** The dessert so known, made of soft summer fruits such as redcurrants and raspberries with bread, has had this name only since the early 20th century. It was earlier known as 'hydropathic pudding', as it was served at health resorts where pastry was forbidden.

**Summer's Lease.** A novel (1988), part social comedy, part mystery story, by John Mortimer (b.1923). The plot centres on the villa in Tuscany on temporary lease for the summer holidays to an accident-prone, articulate family. The title is from Shakespeare:

> Shall I compare thee to a summer's day?
> Thou art more lovely and more temperate:
> Rough winds do shake the darling buds of May,
> And summer's lease hath all too short a date.
> Sonnet 18

**Summer Time.** The idea of making fuller use of the hours of daylight by advancing the clock originated with Benjamin Franklin (1706–90), but its introduction was due to its advocacy from 1907 by William Willett (1856–1915), a Chelsea builder. It was adopted in 1916 in Germany, then in Britain as a wartime measure, when clocks were advanced one hour. In Britain it became permanent by an Act of 1925. Summer Time, as it was called, began on the day following the third Saturday in April, unless that was Easter Day, in which case it was the day following the second Saturday in April. It ended on the day following the first Saturday in October. During the Second World War it ran from 25 February to 31 December in 1940 and from 1 January in the four years from 1941. In 1945 it ended in October. Double Summer Time (i.e. two hours in advance of GMT instead of one) was in force from 1941 to 1945 and in 1947 to save fuel. After the war Summer Time was in force in the years from 1948 to 1952 and from 1961 to 1964. In 1961 Summer Time was extended by six weeks, beginning in March and ending in October, and similar extensions were made in 1962 and subsequent years. From 27 October 1969 until 31 October 1971, clocks were kept one hour ahead of GMT continuously in what was known as British Standard Time (BST). The end of Summer Time on the last Sunday in October has been marked since 1972 at Merton College, Oxford, with a backward procession round Fellows' Quad between 2 a.m. BST, as the moment when GMT is restored, and 2 a.m. GMT itself.

In the United States Summer Time (March to October) was in force in 1917 and 1918, and again from 1942 to 1945 (all the year round and known as War Time). The Uniform Time Act of 1967 reintroduced Summer Time from the last Sunday in April until the last Sunday in October, while allowing individual states the right of option. The oil crisis of 1973 caused Congress to legislate for continuous Daylight Saving Time from 6 January 1974 to 26 October 1975. The Act was not renewed, but in 1986 the start of Daylight Saving Time was moved to the first Sunday in April with effect from 5 April 1987.

**'Summertime Blues'.** A pop anthem by Eddie Cochran, released in 1958, concerning a teenager experiencing problems with his girfriend, his boss and his parents ('There ain't no cure for the Summertime blues'). At one point in the song, a congressman responds to the tortured teenager 'I'd like to help you, son, but you're too young to vote.' 'Summertime Blues' is one of the first in a line of pop-music expressions of teenage angst that would later include The Who's 'MY GENERATION' and '(I CAN'T GET NO) SATIS-FACTION' by The Rolling Stones. The Who in fact later sang a version of 'Summertime Blues' on their album *Live At Leeds*.

**Summit meeting.** A summit meeting or summit conference is where the leaders of two or more countries come together to discuss some issue of mutual concern. There were a number of important summits of Allied leaders during the

Second World War (for example, the YALTA CONFERENCE), but the actual term in its modern sense seems to have been coined by Winston Churchill a few years after the war, as quoted in *The Times* (15 February 1950):

> It is not easy to see how things could be worsened by a parley at the summit, if such a thing were possible.

It is possible that Churchill was recalling a passage in Walter Bagehot's *The English Constitution* (1867): 'Nations touch at their summits.'

**Sun Belt.** The southern states of the United States, which are generally sunnier and drier than the northern. The name implies not merely a favourable climate, but a high standard of living, a high population density and generally conservative attitudes. The term was coined in 1969 by the US writer Kevin P. Phillips, who based it on 'corn belt' or BIBLE BELT. *See also* RUST BELT.

> That growth of small towns is distributed from region to region but national in scope: it is highest in the Sun Belt states of the West and South, lowest in the Middle West, but steady and substantial even in the Northeast, where the big cities are losing population.
>
> *Newsweek* (6 July 1981)

**Sun City.** The name of two very different communities, one for the elderly, the other for the young. Sun City, Arizona, was founded in 1960 as a residential suburb of Phoenix for retired people. By 1990 its population had grown to almost 40,000. Sun City in what is now North-West Province, South Africa, was built in the early 1980s as a gambling, entertainment and sporting area in what was then the Bophuthatswana homeland, the aim being to attract tourists from the Rand area. The concept of a wealthy white man's playground in a predominantly impoverished black country is still grotesque. *See also* BANTUSTAN.

**Sundae.** The dish of ice cream with added ingredients first became popular at the beginning of the 20th century. Its name remains of uncertain origin, although it appears to be associated with 'Sunday'. According to Harva Hachten, in *The Flavor of Wisconsin* (1981), it was the creation in 1881 of Ed Berners, owner of an ice cream parlour in Two Rivers, Michigan, and a customer called George Hallauer. Initially it had no distinctive name but was simply a 'chocolate-topped ice cream'. Another ice cream parlour then opened up in nearby Manitowoc, and its owner, George Giffy, began serving similarly embellished ice creams on Sundays. One weekday a little girl came in and ordered a dish of ice cream 'with stuff on it'. When told it was only served on Sundays, the young customer is reported to have said, 'Why, then, this must be Sunday, for it's the kind of ice cream

I want.' Giffy gave it to her, and henceforth called the dish a 'Sunday'. This does not explain the present spelling, however, which may have been made out of respect for Sunday churchgoers.

In 1973 the State Historical Society of Wisconsin erected a marker at Two Rivers in recognition of its status as the birthplace of the confection, which is now traditionally served in a tall glass.

**Sunday artist.** An amateur artist, thought of as painting only on Sundays as a hobby.

**Sunday driver.** A person regarded as driving a car erratically or amateurishly, like one who drives only on Sundays for a 'spin', frequently slowing to see or point out the view.

**Sunday lunch.** The specially large and lengthy midday meal served on Sundays. The British Sunday lunch has a traditional main dish of roast beef, Yorkshire pudding, roast potatoes, a green (and perhaps another colour) vegetable and gravy, all cooked by a devoted wife, and is followed by a period of protracted inertia. Nowadays a Sunday roast is probably more often chicken, but may be lamb, pork or even game, and a household's menfolk may involve themselves in the preparation or even handle it exclusively. However, with Sunday increasingly resembling Saturday (shopping, eating out, etc.) the whole Sunday lunch tradition has taken a battering in the early 21st century.

**Sunday punch.** A powerful or destructive blow. It is one's 'best', like a Sunday suit.

**Sunlit uplands.** A phrase much used in his wartime speeches by Winston Churchill, and by others since, to denote a happy, peaceful and prosperous future. A variant is 'sunny uplands'. A famous Churchillian usage was in his FINEST HOUR speech (18 June 1940):

> Hitler knows that he will have to break us in this island or lose the war. If we can stand up to him, all Europe may be free and the life of the world may move forward into broad, sunlit uplands. But if we fail, the whole world, including the United States, including all that we have known and cared for, will sink into the abyss of a new Dark Age …

**Sunningdale Agreement.** An agreement in 1973 that resulted in the short-lived POWER-SHARING experiment in Northern Ireland, ended by a Protestant general strike in 1974. The agreement resulted from talks between the Irish and British premiers, Liam Cosgrave and Edward Heath, together with representatives from the Northern Ireland political parties. The talks were held at Sunningdale in Berkshire. *See also* DIRECT RULE.

**Sunny** or **Sonny Jim.** A form of address to a man or boy, especially patronizingly or humorously. The name is obviously influenced by 'son' but specifically derives from Sunny Jim, a sprightly character adopted as a mascot by the manufacturers of Force breakfast cereal at the start of the 20th century. It is believed that he arose as the winning entry of a competition run by the Force Food Company to find a character to promote their cereal, and it is known that his creator was a US schoolgirl named Ficken. The jingles that accompanied his antics were written by Minnie Hanff. The best known, as it appeared on a poster of 1903, is:

> High o'er the fence leaps Sunny Jim,
> 'Force' is the food that raises him.

Sunny Jim was also a media nickname for the Labour politician James (later Lord) Callaghan (1912–2005), chancellor of the exchequer (1964–7), home secretary (1967–70), foreign secretary (1974–6) and prime minister (1976–9). Callaghan was defeated in the 1979 general election after the far-from-sunny WINTER OF DISCONTENT. The nickname was awarded because of his continuing smile in the face of adversity (although he was often tetchy and prey to melancholia in private). Another nickname for Callaghan was 'Stoker Jim', Callaghan having served in the Royal Navy during the Second World War, not as a stoker, but as a sub-lieutenant. Callaghan's successor as leader of the Labour Party, Michael Foot, called him 'PC Callaghan' because of his work on behalf of the Police Federation, while the Beatle John Lennon called him 'Mr Caravans'. *See also* Worsel GUMMIDGE.

**Sunrise industry.** A new and growing industry, typically in electronics or telecommunications. The term dates from the early 1980s. The converse, 'sunset industry', is less commonly found to denote traditional heavy industry. 'Sunrise' implies the dawn of a new era.

**Sun, sea and sand.** A travel agent's alliterative lure to the holidaymaker. Many southern European destinations can offer the required ingredients in abundance, notably Spain. The order of the second two nouns may be reversed in the phrase, and 'sex' is often implied as a further bait. *See also* SEA AND SANGRIA.

> Sun, sand and sea are no longer enough for the Yuppie generation of fun-seekers.
> *The Observer* (26 June 1988)

**Sunset Boulevard.** A broad and handsome street in downtown Los Angeles, so called as it runs from the city centre westward to the Pacific. The section of the street to the west of HOLLYWOOD is known as the Sunset Strip and is the centre of the city's night life. *Sunset Boulevard* is also the name of a successful Hollywood melodrama of 1950, featuring Gloria Swanson as a faded star of the silent era, and of Andrew Lloyd Webber's musical of 1993 based on it.

**Sunshine.** A colloquial form of address to an unknown person, perhaps as an embellishment of 'son'.

**Sunshine State.** A nickname for New Mexico, which became the 47th state of the United States in 1912. The allusion is obvious. The name also applies to other states, such as California and South Dakota.

**Super Bowl.** In American football, the championship game of the National Football League, played by the winners of the league's American Football Conference and National Football Conference every January. The game resulted from the merger in 1966 of the American Football League (AFL) and the older National Football League (NFL), and was originally called the AFL-NFL World Championship Game. The first game was played on 15 January 1967 in the Los Angeles Coliseum, with a win for the NFL's Green Bay Packers over the AFL's Kansas City Chiefs by 35–10. The present name, suggested by Lamar Hunt, owner of the Kansas City Chiefs, was based on that of the ROSE BOWL. *See also* SUGAR BOWL.

**Superbrat.** An opprobrious nickname applied, mainly by the press, to the US tennis player John McEnroe (b.1959), who was notorious for his tantrums on court when he felt that he had suffered injustice at the hands of the umpire, a linesman, his opponent or the world in general (he was disqualified from the 1990 Australian Open for verbal abuse of officials). Among his other nicknames are 'Mac the Mouth', 'King Sneer' (after Shakespeare's *King Lear*), 'The Merchant of Menace' (his *Merchant of Venice*), 'The Prince of Petulance', 'The Rude Dude' and 'The INCREDIBLE SULK'. *See also* YOU CANNOT BE SERIOUS.

**Supercalifragilisticexpialidocious.** Amazing; wonderful. A fantastic invention popularized by the Walt Disney film *Mary Poppins* (1964) but apparently originating, although with different spelling, in an unpublished song title of 1949. Life Music Co. and the two writers of the song, named Parker and Young, brought a copyright-infringement suit in 1965 against the Disney organization, but in view of earlier oral uses of the word sworn to in affidavits and dissimilarity between the songs the judge ruled against the plaintiffs. If meaningful, the elements of the name may perhaps be taken as *supercali* ('boiling hot') *fragilistic* ('inclined to fragility') *expialidocious* ('inclined to explode'), in other words very volatile. The word was still in use at the beginning of the 21st century. *See also* Mary POPPINS.

In 2000 the *Sun* newspaper met a longstanding challenge among sub-editors to come up with a headline playing on the word when it reported on Celtic's defeat by Caledonian Thistle in the Scottish Cup:

Super Cally Go Ballistic, Celtic Are Atrocious

**Supergirl.** *See* SUPERMAN.

**Superhooligans.** A term for certain groups of football supporters with a reputation for violence towards fans from other clubs. They differ from ordinary fans because they typically sport no club colours, travel to matches by regular transport rather than 'football specials' and not infrequently leave 'calling cards' on their victims. Noted gangs of the 1980s were the 'Baby Squad', supporting Leicester City, the 'Bushwhackers' for Millwall, the 'Gooners' for Arsenal, the 'Headhunters' for Chelsea, the 'Inter City Firm' for West Ham United and the 'Service Crew' for Leeds United.

**Supermac.** A nickname of the Conservative statesman Harold Macmillan, 1st Earl of Stockton (1894–1986), prime minister from 1957 to 1963. The name was the creation of the political cartoonist VICKY, who in a drawing for the *Evening Standard* of 6 November 1958 showed Macmillan dressed as SUPERMAN. The sobriquet was originally intended ironically, but as Macmillan's premiership evolved it came to apply more realistically to his particular style of relaxed showmanship. In the 1990s the *Guardian* cartoonist Steve Bell, in a back-handed homage to Vicky, depicted the Conservative prime minister John Major wearing his Y-FRONTS over his trousers as a weedy would-be Superman. *See also* MAC THE KNIFE.

**Superman.** A hypothetical superior human being of high intellectual and moral attainment, fancied as evolved from the normally existing type. The term (*Übermensch*) was invented by the German philosopher Friedrich Nietzsche (1844–1900), and was popularized in English by George Bernard Shaw's play MAN AND SUPERMAN (1903). *See also* UNTERMENSCHEN.

In the world of US comics, Superman is one of the most popular heroes. He can fly, has X-ray vision, can move mountains single-handed and is invulnerable – apart from a proneness to the negative effects of kryptonite, a mineral from his home planet Krypton, from which he is a refugee. By day he is the mild-mannered human newspaper reporter Clark Kent. When the occasion requires, however, he changes from his sober suit and spectacles into his blue tights and red cape and is 'up, up and away', soaring into the sky, often to do battle with his arch-enemy, Lex Luthor. His tragedy is that his attractive journalist colleague Lois Lane never realizes that Clark Kent, whom she does not fancy but

who is available, is the very same person as Superman, whom she does but who isn't.

Superman was the creation of two SCIENCE FICTION fans, Jerry Siegel and Joe Schuster, who introduced him in *Action Comics* in 1938. He has appeared in several films and a radio and television series, and there has even been a musical, *It's a Bird, It's a Plane, It's Superman* (a catchphrase from the radio series), turned into a television movie (1975).

The wide popularity of the term has given rise to many compounds, such as 'superwoman', 'superstar', 'SUPER-MODEL' and the like, while Superman's cousin, Supergirl, has her own adventures, first appearing in *Action Comics* in 1959. Her real name is Kara, alias Linda Lee Danvers. *See also* BATMAN; IS IT A BIRD? IS IT A PLANE?

**Supermodel.** A fashion model who has gained the status of a celebrity. In the 1990s many such models were seen as successors to the traditional film and pop stars, their glamour on a par with that of the silent movie stars of the 1920s. The genesis of the supermodel is usually dated to January 1990, when Peter Lindbergh's photograph of five models, Cindy Crawford, Linda Evangelista, Tatjana Patitz, Christy Turlington and Naomi Campbell, appeared on the cover of that month's British *Vogue* magazine. Since then stars such as Claudia Schiffer and Kate Moss have been added to the galaxy. *See also* MODELIZER.

**Supply siders.** A US term for those economists, particularly prominent since the 1980s, who believe in limiting the money supply as a way of controlling inflation and regulating a country's economy. *See also* FRIEDMANISM.

***Suppose They Gave a War and Nobody Came?*** A would-be satirical US film (1969) starring Tony Curtis and Ernest Borgnine. The title refers to a phrase common at the time of the anti-Vietnam War demonstrations, and which was the title of an article by Charlotte Keyes in *McCall's* magazine (October 1966). The origin of the saying is in Carl Sandburg's epic poem *The People, Yes* (1936):

Little girl … Sometime they'll give a war and nobody will come.

After the film Alan Ginsberg worked the question into his poem 'Graffiti' (1972):

What if someone gave a war & Nobody came?
Life would ring the bells of Ecstasy and Forever be Itself again.

**Supreme sacrifice.** To make the supreme sacrifice is to die for one's country in battle. The expression dates from the First World War and is first recorded in W.M. Clow's *The Evangel of the Strait Gate* (1916): 'These young men … have gone down not only to the horror of the battlefield but to the gates of death as they made the supreme sacrifice.' The phrasing may seem pompous now but was entirely appropriate for the spirit of its time.

**Surf and turf.** A combination of seafood and steak in the same course or on the same plate. The concept originated in the United States in the 1960s and soon spread around the Pacific Rim to Australia. More conservative European diners have yet to take it to their hearts (what wine to choose with it?).

**Surf the Net.** To move from site to site on the INTERNET, especially in order to explore its diversities or sample its wares. The image is of riding on a surfboard. An alternate term for this computer activity is 'browsing', because one has to use the software of a 'browser', such as Microsoft's Internet Explorer. *See also* SILVER SURFER.

**Surprise, surprise!** A phrase said either when giving someone a surprise or, ironically, when something happens that was entirely predictable. The expression dates from the 1960s.

> 'You again!' he said. 'Surprise, surprise!' He'd been up and down the road four times, waiting for her.
>
> FAY WELDON: *The Heart of the Country* (1987)

**Surrealism.** A movement in art, literature and film that began in the mid-1920s, emerging out of DADAISM, and which flourished in the interwar years under the leadership of the poet André Breton (1896–1966). In painting it falls into two groups: hand-painted dream scenes, as exemplified by Giorgio de Chirico (1888–1978), Salvador Dalí (1904–89) and René Magritte (1898–1967); and the creation of abstract forms by the practice of complete spontaneity of technique as well as subject matter by the use of contrast, as with Jean Arp (1888–1966), Man Ray (1890–1976), Joan Miró (1893–1983) and Dalí. Prime examples of surrealist films are Man Ray's *L'Étoile de mer* (1928) and Luis Buñuel and Dalí's *Un Chien andalou* (1928). The latter includes shots of dead donkeys on pianos and opens shockingly with the slicing of a young woman's eyeball by a razor. *See also* CUBISM; FAUVISM; FUTURISM; ORPHISM; RURALISM; SYNCHROMISM; TACHISM; VORTICISM.

**Surrender-monkey.** A US term of withering contempt for a French person, prompted by French opposition to the US-led invasion of Iraq in 2003 but harking back to the French capitulation to Germany in 1940. The full insult used at the later date was usually 'cheese-eating surrender-monkey'. The expression was widely taken in Britain to be a reference to France's rich cheese heritage – General de Gaulle once famously asked how it was possible to govern a country that produced 246 different types of cheese – but in fact 'cheese-eating' is an allusion to rats and dates back in US slang to at least the 1880s. *See also* FREEDOM FRIES.

**Surrogate mother.** A woman who bears a child on behalf of another woman, either from her own egg fertilized by the other woman's partner, or from the implantation in her womb of a fertilized egg from the other woman. The ethics of surrogacy were a key factor in the BABY M case.

**Surtitles.** Captions projected onto a screen or otherwise displayed above the stage during the performance of an opera, either to translate the libretto or simply to enable the audience to follow the words being sung. The device, its name based on 'subtitles', was invented in 1983 by John Leberg as part of a move to popularize opera generally.

**Survivalism.** In its specialized sense, the practising of outdoor survival skills as a sport or hobby. By the late 1980s the term had become associated with the carrying of weaponry and, in the United States, with participation in paramilitary activity. The death by shooting of 16 people in Hungerford, Berkshire, in 1987 at the hands of a self-styled survivalist, Michael Ryan, brought the term before a wide public and associated it with deranged behaviour and an obsession with militaria. *See also* HUNGERFORD MASSACRE.

**Susie-Q.** *See* SUZI-Q.

**Sutch, Screaming Lord.** *See* MONSTER RAVING LOONY PARTY.

**Sutton Hoo Treasure.** An Anglo-Saxon ship burial of the early 7th century, discovered at Sutton Hoo near Woodbridge, Suffolk, in 1939. It is one of the richest ever found and the treasure, consisting of a sword and sheath, helmet, bowls and other objects in precious metals, is now in the British Museum. Further excavations were carried out on the site in the 1980s, and by 1992 six more mounds had come to light.

**SUV.** *See* SPORT-UTILITY VEHICLE.

**'Suzanne'.** A lugubrious song by the Canadian poet, novelist and singer Leonard Cohen, released in 1968. First recorded by Judy Collins, the song appeared on Leonard Cohen's debut album *Songs of Leonard Cohen*. The Suzanne of the title, and Cohen's muse on this occasion, was a dancer whom Cohen once visited in her loft near the St Lawrence River in Montreal. The song's deeply personal lyrics include the line 'I touched her perfect body with my mind', and its baffling second verse has Jesus Christ walking on the waters of Montreal Harbour.

**Suzi-Q** or **Susie-Q.** A dance of African American origin popular in the 1930s, in which the dancer interlaced fingers of both hands at chest height, then with elbows akimbo made a sawing motion across the body while performing cross-over footwork. The origin of the name is uncertain.

**Suzuki method.** A method of teaching the violin to very young children, typically in large groups. It was developed by the Japanese music teacher Suzuki Shin'ichi (1898–1998) and is based on his belief that any child can attain a high standard of ability as a violinist by adapting to external stimuli.

**Svengali.** A person who exercises a controlling or mesmeric influence on another. The name is that of the musician in George du Maurier's novel *Trilby* (1894) who trains Trilby's voice and controls her stage singing by his sinister hypnotic powers.

> It's a mistake to write off [modern art patron Charles] Saatchi, or to view him as a Svengali figure, conjuring artists and movements out of the air.
> *Sunday Times* (22 August 1999)

**SWALK.** An acronym of 'sealed with a loving kiss', traditionally placed on the back of envelopes, where the physical act of licking the flap approximates to the kissing of the loved addressee. The full phrase dates back to at least the 17th century. *See also* LOVERS' ACRONYMS.

**Swallowers and stuffers.** Customs officers' jargon for those who smuggle drugs into a country either by swallowing them sealed in a bag, which is subsequently excreted, or by concealing them in a body orifice such as the rectum or vagina. The terms date from the 1980s.

**Swallows and Amazons.** The first of a series of 12 children's novels by Arthur Ransome (1884–1967), writer, journalist and, briefly, husband of Evgenia Shelepin, Leon Trotsky's secretary. *Swallows and Amazons* (1930) is set in the English Lake District and, like the novels that followed it, deals with the adventures of children on holiday, reflecting its author's love of sailing and other outdoor pursuits. The Swallows are the four children of the Walker family, John, Susan, Titty and Roger, and they are named after their boat, *Swallow*; the Amazons are Nancy and Peggy Blackett, who are named after their boat, *Amazon*. The eleven novels that followed were, in order of publication: *Swallowdale* (1931), *Peter Duck* (1932), *Winter Holiday* (1933), *Coot Club* (1934), *Pigeon Post* (1936), *We Didn't Mean to Go to Sea* (1937), *Secret Water* (1939), *The Big Six* (1940), *Missee Lee* (1941), *The Picts and the Martyrs* (1943) and *Great Northern?* (1947). These later novels introduce new characters and settings as diverse as the Norfolk Broads, the North Sea, the South China Sea and the

Outer Hebrides. A rather tame film version (1974) of the first novel was directed by Claude Whatham.

> I have never read the Arthur Ransome classic but, if it is as dull as the film, I doubt I ever will … Everyone is frightfully prissy and well behaved.
> KEN RUSSELL: *Fire over England* (1994)

*See also* FIRST LINES OF NOVELS.

**Swallow the dictionary.** To say that someone has swallowed the dictionary is to accuse them of using long and recondite words. The expression is first recorded in the 1930s.

**Swampy.** The *nom de guerre* of the dreadlocked environmental protester Daniel Hooper, who briefly came to fame in 1996 for his attempts to frustrate an extension to the A30 road just outside Exeter. His excavation and occupation of a system of tunnels captured the public imagination, and the name subsequently achieved a certain generic status.

> They have underestimated the potential of an environmental campaign. My neighbouring Conservative MP, John Randall, has threatened to lie down in front of the bulldozers. We're getting Tory Swampys ... on this.
> JOHN MCDONNELL: quoted in *The Observer* (1 January 2006)

**Swan about** or **around.** To move around aimlessly. The phrase is first recorded among troops in the Second World War to describe a tank moving apparently aimlessly across the battlefield, like a swan swimming idly about the waters or meandering with others in an aimless convoy. The tank's long gun barrel additionally evoked the bird's long neck. The expression caught on and is now variably directed, so that one can 'swan in', or enter in an ostentatiously relaxed way, and even 'swan out', or exit similarly.

> I play Kate. I'm a cocaine dealer and I swan in and seduce the hostess's husband and then tease him about it.
> *The Times* (12 January 2000)

**Swastika.** The fylfot, an elaborate cross-shaped design used as a charm to ward off evil and bring good luck. It was adopted by Hitler as the NAZI emblem about 1920, probably from the German Baltic Corps, who wore it on their helmets after service in Finland, where it was used as a distinguishing mark on Finnish aeroplanes. The word is from Sanskrit *svasti*, 'well-being'.

> The swastika was used in such a way that it represented something more than itself: a relic of an Aryan culture, peculiarly German and Indian and possessing special and exclusive virtues.
> PETER CALVOCORESSI: in *Times Literary Supplement* (review of Malcolm Quinn, *The Swastika*) (16 December 1994)

**SWAT.** An acronymic designation applied to a paramilitary police unit that is deployed on dangerous operations. It originally stood for 'special weapons attack team', but is now generally interpreted as 'special weapons and tactics'. The concept appears to have originated in the city of Delano, California, in 1960, and was quickly followed up and developed in Los Angeles.

**Swatch.** Nothing to do with a sample of fabric but a term for a disposable Swiss watch. The timepiece was developed in 1983 by the Swiss watchmakers Ernst Thonke, Jacques Müller and Elmer Mock and was the first integrated watch, in which the action is not a separate component from the case. The original model was the 'Delirium', and both it and later models have gained cult status, in some cases even becoming collectors' items.

**Sweat bullets.** To suffer mental anguish; to work extremely hard. The allusion is to drops of perspiration the size of bullets. The Americanism dates from the 1950s.

**Sweater girl.** A dated term for a young woman with a generous bust, which is made apparent by the wearing of a tight sweater. The 'Sweater Girl' was the US film actress Lana Turner (1920–95), and her promotion by this name at the beginning of her career in the late 1930s popularized the expression.

**Swedish massage.** A particularly vigorous form of massage involving *effleurage* (stroking), friction and rubbing, *petrissage* (kneading and squeezing) and *tapotement* (slapping and pounding), all of which stimulate blood circulation through the soft tissues of the body. The term dates only from the 20th century but probably derives from the tradition established by the Swedish fencing master and pioneer of massaging techniques Peter Henrik Ling (1776–1839).

**Sweeney.** A shortening of 'Sweeney Todd', rhyming slang for FLYING SQUAD. The name is that of a fictitious barber who murders his customers in George Dibdin's play *A String of Pearls, or the Fiend of Fleet Street* (1847), later known as *Sweeney Todd, the Demon Barber of Fleet Street*. The character's grim persona and grisly deeds presumably appealed to the cockney coiners of the term, which dates from the 1930s. It was brought before a wide public by the television crime drama series *The Sweeney* (1975–82), centring on Detective Inspector Jack Regan, played by John Thaw, and his sidekick George Carter, played by Dennis Waterman. Both characters regularly ignored the rule book, associated with villains, swore and drank to excess and generally presented an unflattering portrait of their templates in their pursuit of various villains and 'bad boys'.

**Sweep something under the carpet.** To conceal something embarrassing or unpleasant in the hope that it will be overlooked. One may hide household dust by sweeping it under the carpet, but one will not have removed it. The figurative expression dates from the 1960s.

**Sweet Fanny Adams.** The phrase, meaning 'nothing at all', dates from the early 20th century. On 21 August 1867 eight-year-old Fanny Adams was raped and hacked to death in a hop garden at Alton, Hampshire. A 21-year-old solicitor's clerk, Frederick Baker, was tried soon after and hanged on Christmas Eve at Winchester. The Royal Navy, with grim humour, adopted her name as a synonym for tinned mutton, first issued at this time, with reference to its negligible nutritious value. Sweet Fanny Adams became, as a consequence, a phrase for anything worthless, and then for 'nothing at all'. The phrase is often abbreviated as 'Sweet FA' or simply 'SFA', the 'F' often being taken as the 'F-word'. *See* FOUR-LETTER WORD.

**Sweetheart arrangement.** A secret business arrangement for mutual advantage, especially between employers and trade-union leaders, and on terms that are beneficial to both these sides but not to the employees. The use of 'sweetheart' in this sense arose in the United States in the 1950s.

**Sweetie-pie.** A term of endearment that is first recorded in the 1920s but was still in regular use at the end of the 20th century. The allusion is to a tasty dish such as an apple pie. A person to whom one is attracted is similarly 'toothsome'. The phrase was punningly adopted for the name of the canary Tweety Pie pursued by the 'puddy tat' Sylvester in the long series of Warner Brothers cartoons made between 1947 and 1964.

**Sweet nothings.** Sentimental trivia; formulaic phrases of amorous import. The expression dates from the start of the 20th century. *See also* COOCHY COOCHY COO; GOO-GOO EYES.

**Sweet Smell of Success.** A much-admired film melodrama (1957) set in the world of New York journalism, written by Clifford Odets and Ernest Lehman, directed by Alexander Mackendrick, and starring Burt Lancaster and Tony Curtis. Lancaster played J.J. Hunsacker, who, in search of a light, memorably says: 'Match me, Sidney.' The *Oxford Dictionary of Quotations* (1999 edition) appears to suggest the film's title as the origin of the well-known phrase. Pauline Kael described the film as 'A sweet smell of perversity, a study of dollar and power worship'.

**Sweet spot.** The point on a tennis racket believed by players to deliver the maximum power to the ball. In 1997 a physicist in Australia claimed to have disproved its existence. The term was originally used with reference to a golf club. In a broader sense the sweet spot is used of an especially fortunate or beneficial circumstance or factor. The term is first recorded in the 1970s.

**Swing.** With reference to JAZZ, swing is solo or ensemble playing over a regular pulse beat in such a way as to give the impression of a 'swinging' (forward-moving) rhythmic momentum. 'To swing' is to play jazz music in this particular way and the term, although not new, gained a wide currency in the early 1930s from a popular number beginning: 'It don't mean a thing if it ain't got that swing.' The bandleader Glen Miller (1904–44) is often known as 'The King of Swing'. *See also* BOOGIE-WOOGIE.

**Swing both ways.** To be bisexual. The expression dates from the 1970s.

**Swinging London.** A nickname for London in the SWINGING SIXTIES, when it was regarded as the fashion and music capital of the world, with CARNABY STREET as its focus.

**Swinging sixties.** The 1960s, regarded as a period when all was lively, fashionable and exciting. The phrase reflects not only the general sense of freedom following the constraints and hardships of the postwar period but also the mood of rebellion among the young, who rose against the ESTABLISHMENT to demand peace and a 'brave new world'. *See also* SUMMER OF LOVE.

**Swingometer.** A device used to demonstrate the effect of a political swing at the time of an election. The best known was that first used in the mid-1960s by the BBC broadcaster Robert McKenzie. It was shaped like a large inverted metronome and pushed to left or right, marking the percentage swing in votes to one side or the other. Its function was soon taken over by computer graphics, but its sophisticated successors in later general elections, demonstrated by the broadcaster Peter Snow, were still known by the name.

> Once again the BBC's swingometer will be our earliest guide to the likely outcome. From the moment the first seat is declared, its pendulum will instantly and automatically swing to the party that has gained the advantage over the other since the last election.
>
> PETER SNOW: in *The BBC News General Election Guide* (1997)

**Swings and roundabouts.** A situation in which a gain in one direction is balanced by a loss in the other. The allusion is to the fairground owner's mixed fortunes on the two attractions. The expression 'to gain on the swings and lose on the roundabouts' dates from the early 20th century.

> For 'up an' down an' round', said 'e, goes all appointed things,
> An' losses on the roundabouts means profits on the swings!
> PATRICK CHALMERS: *Green Days and Blue Days* (1912)

**Swing the lead.** To malinger. A leadsman on a ship required skill rather than strength when taking soundings, so was taunted for not pulling his weight with the rest of the crew. The expression dates from the early 20th century.

**Swiss army knife.** A form of penknife incorporating various gadgets and so noteworthy for its versatility. The term may be used figuratively for a 'Jack-of-all-trades' or other handy person.

**Swiss itch.** A technique of drinking tequila that involves licking a pinch of salt from the back of one's hand, knocking back the tequila and immediately biting into a slice of lime.

**Switched on.** Well informed on contemporary fashionable and popular cults; thoroughly up to date and responsive to current trends and tendencies. The expression dates from the 1960s and in 21st-century usage often refers more generally to someone who is bright or intelligent. *See also* TURN SOMEONE ON.

**Swone-one.** Society slang (pronounced 'swun-wun') in the 1970s and 1980s for Battersea in South London, an area to which SLOANE RANGERS and the like who could not afford Belgravia had recourse. A verbalization of SW11, the locality's postal district, it made it sound a little like SW1 (Belgravia's district). Battersea has also been referred to as South Chelsea, a nod to the diaspora from the more chic address.

**Swoose.** A cross between a swan and a goose. The hybrid name dates from the 1920s. Animal names of this kind have an ancient pedigree that includes the *camelopard* or giraffe, believed at one time to be a cross between a camel and leopard, and the *leopard* itself, thought to be half lion, half pard (male panther). The 20th century has seen the *tigon* as the offspring of a male tiger and a lioness, a *liger*, conversely, as that of a male lion and a tigress, a *shoat* as the fruit of a sheep and a goat, and its own opposite number, a *geep*. In livestock breeding there is the *beefalo*, a beast that is three-eighths bison and five-eighths domestic cow, and the much older *catalo*, as a cross between a cow ('cattle') and a buffalo.

In man-made flight, the *Swoose* was the B-17 FLYING FORTRESS flown by Colonel Frank Kurtz, the most decorated US pilot of the Second World War, and he preserved the name in that of his actress daughter, Swoosie Kurtz (b.1943). The plane now resides at the National Air and Space Museum in Washington, D.C.

**Sword Beach.** The Allied code name for the stretch of beach on the Normandy coast running from the River Orne in the east to JUNO BEACH in the west. It was the easternmost of the Normandy landing beaches, and on D-DAY it was where the British 3rd Division came ashore. By the end of the day the British held a stretch of beach 6.5km (4 miles) wide and had penetrated the same distance inland.

**Sword opera.** A term of the 1990s for a television drama series set in ancient times, with much swordplay and other stylized action of a more or less violent nature. An example is *Xena: Warrior Princess*, first shown on satellite television in 1996, in which the title character campaigns against wicked warlords, man-eating centaurs and the like. The term itself is based on SOAP OPERA. *See also* XENA.

**Sydney or the bush.** All or nothing. An Australian phrase dating from the 1920s. Sydney, as Australia's largest city and chief port, is 'all', while the bush, as uncultivated or unsettled land, is 'nothing'. The bush for Australians is country as opposed to town, rural life as opposed to urban.

**Sykes.** A much-loved television SITCOM screened from 1960 to 1965 and 1971 to 1979, featuring the self-improving Sykes, played by Eric Sykes, and his twin sister Hattie, played by Hattie Jacques (in real life the wife of John le Mesurier of DAD'S ARMY fame), the two sharing a house at 24 Sebastopol Terrace, Suburbia. Early episodes opened with the arrival of some new gadget or new goods, but later plots centred on a series of domestic crises. Deryck Guyler played Corky, a pompous police constable, to add to the gentle humour.

**Symbionese Liberation Army.** A corps of US revolutionaries who first surfaced in 1973, when they killed a school official with cyanide-tipped bullets. The following year they gained worldwide notoriety following their kidnapping of the 19-year-old newspaper heiress Patricia Hearst, demanding that her parents distribute free food to the Californian poor. When they complied Hearst joined her captors, took the name Tania and participated in a bank robbery. She eventually married her SLA bodyguard. The name derives from the Greek for 'living together'. *See also* STOCKHOLM SYNDROME.

**'Sympathy for the Devil'.** A controversial song by The ROLLING STONES, credited to Mick Jagger and Keith Richards, and released in 1968. Mick Jagger sings in the persona of a knowing and sinisterly sophisticated Satan ('Pleased to meet you, hope you guess my name / But what's puzzling you is the nature of my game'), chronicling his impact on the history of the human race to the demonic rhythms of electric guitar, bongo drums and maracas. The song appears on the album *Beggar's Banquet*. *See also* ALTAMONT.

> Please allow me to introduce myself
> I'm a man of wealth and taste
> I've been around for a long, long year
> Stole many a man's soul and faith.

**Synchromism.** (Greek *sun*, 'with', and *khrōma*, 'colour'.) A form of abstract art resembling ORPHISM begun in 1912 by two young US artists living in Paris, Morgan Russell (1886–1953) and Stanton Macdonald-Wright (1890–1973). It was characterized by movements of pure colour evolving by gradations or rhythms from the primaries to the intermediary colours. Russell's *Synchromy in Green* (1913) was the first painting to bear the name. *See also* CUBISM; DADAISM; FAUVISM; FUTURISM; RURALISM; SURREALISM; VORTICISM.

# T

**Tabloid.** A nickname dating from the early 20th century for a newspaper having pages half the size of the average broadsheet. It is usually popular in style and dominated by huge headlines, a plethora of photographs and a slew of sensational stories. The name was originally a proprietary term, registered on 14 March 1884 by Messrs Burroughs, Wellcome & Co., for a medicine sold in the form of a tablet. The term then came to denote any medicinal tablet and finally the newspaper as described, which presents news in a reduced format and a 'concentrated', easily assimilable form. The name was first applied in this new sense to the *Daily Mail*, founded in 1896, referring not to its format (it was originally a broadsheet) but to its brief and pithy paragraphs, which it promoted as 'all the news in the smallest space'. The latest newspapers in the UK to change to a tabloid format (but preferring to call it 'compact') are *The Independent*, *The Times* and *The Scotsman*. *See also* BERLINER HEAVIES; RED-TOPS.

**Tachism.** (French *tache*, 'spot', 'splotch'.) A style of abstract painting popular in the late 1940s and 1950s, characterized by the use of irregular dabs or splotches of colour. The term was first used in this sense in *c.*1951 by the French art critics Charles Estienne and Pierre Guéguen and it was given wider currency by Michel Tapié in his book *Un art autre* (1952). The genre has affinities with ABSTRACT EXPRESSIONISM and leading exponents include Jean Fautrier (1898–1964), Georges Mathieu (b.1921) and Pierre Soulages (b.1919). *See also* CUBISM; DADAISM; FAUVISM; FUTURISM; RURALISM; SURREALISM; VORTICISM.

**Tactical voting.** The practice of transferring one's normal political allegiance to another party when voting at an election, the aim being to deny victory to a third party. The tactic was first widely in evidence during the general election of February 1974, when many people who would have voted Labour if there had been a full number of parties in their constituency, voted Liberal where the Labour candidate had little or no chance of winning, thus hoping to deny a win to the Conservatives.

**Ta-da!** Take a look at this! Presenting …! A phrase imitating a fanfare, drawing attention to a person or thing, as: 'Ta-da! How do you like my hairstyle?' The word dates from the 1970s.

**Taffia.** A network of influential Welsh people, especially those of marked nationalistic stance. The term is or was intended humorously as a blend of Taffy (a Welshman) and Mafia.

**Taff Vale judgement.** The verdict in a civil suit brought by the Taff Vale Railway Company in 1901 against the Amalgamated Society of Railway Workers. The judge granted the company £23,000 damages against the union as compensation for losses incurred by the company during a strike. The precedent established by the judgement potentially threatened the ability of unions to carry out industrial action, and resentment over this was a factor in the formation of the Labour Party in 1906. In the same year the Trades Dispute Act granted trade unions immunity from such actions.

**Taft-Hartley Act.** A controversial Act of Congress of 1947, limiting the power of trade unions in the United States. Sponsored by Senator Robert A. Taft of Ohio and Representative Fred A. Hartley Jr of New Jersey, it outlawed closed shops, proscribed the political use of union funds and allowed the government to bring injunctions against strikes that endangered national health or safety. The legislation was prompted by various factors, among them a fear of communist infiltration of the unions, the rapid growth in power and membership of the unions themselves, and a series of large-scale strikes, together leading to an anti-union climate in the United States after the Second World War.

**Taggart.** A television crime drama series first screened in 1983 and centring on the cases investigated by the Glasgow DCI Jim Taggart, played by Mark McManus. Following McManus's premature death in 1994, the series continued with Taggart's sidekick, DI Jardine, played by James McPherson, and WDC Jackie Reid, played by Blythe Duff, leading the investigations. McManus's dour anti-hero image left a lasting impression on the screen and the episodes without him were to a large extent imbued with his unseen presence.

**Taig.** A derogatory Protestant nickname for a Roman Catholic in Northern Ireland. It is an anglicized spelling of the Irish name *Tadhg* (English Teague), itself a nickname for an Irish person.

**Tail-end Charlie.** An RAF phrase in the Second World War for the rear gunner in the tail of an aircraft; also for the aircraft at the rear of a group, or the last ship in a flotilla.

**Tail wags the dog, The.** The less important or subsidiary factor dominates the situation, and the normal roles are thus reversed. The expression dates from the 1930s. In the satirical film *Wag the Dog* (1997), a US president diverts public attention away from the sex scandal in which he is involved by manufacturing a war with Albania. Thus 'wag the dog syndrome' came to apply to any scenario in which the US president uses foreign military adventurism as a smokescreen to divert attention from personal embarrassments: in recent times both presidents Clinton and Bush (the younger) have been accused of indulging in this.

**Take a bath.** To suffer loss, especially in business, sport or gambling, The allusion is to being 'cleaned out'. The expression dates from the 1930s. *See also* TAKE SOMEONE TO THE CLEANERS.

> *Scream* distributor Miramax took a bath on *The Faculty* when it was released in December '98, so might be running scared this time.
> *heat* (7–13 October 1999)

**Take a dim view of.** To regard with disapproval. The expression dates from the 1930s and is of military origin.

**Take a gander.** To take a look. The reference is to the bird's long neck.

**Take a leak.** To urinate, of a male. The expression dates from the early 20th century, although 'leak' in this sense goes back to at least the time of Shakespeare: 'Why, they will allow us ne'er a jordan, and then we leak in the chimney' (*Henry IV, Part I*, IV, i; 1598).

**Take a page out of someone's book.** To imitate them; to follow their example.

**Take a powder.** To leave quickly, especially in order to avoid a difficult situation. The US expression dates from the 1930s and is a shortening of 'to take a run-out powder', meaning to escape, with 'powder' probably alluding to the dust that one raises as one leaves.

**Take a raincheck.** To politely decline an offer while implying that one may take it up later. The phrase is of US origin, a raincheck being a voucher entitling one to see another baseball game if the original for which a ticket was purchased is rained off. The noun alone may be used figuratively for a courteous or diplomatic refusal of the type described.

**Take a running jump at yourself!** An expression of contempt, dislike or indifference. The phrase may have a veiled sexual import, as 'jump' is an old word for sexual intercourse.

**Take back the night.** A slogan first used in the United States in the 1970s as a theme for a women's protest march at night through San Francisco's red-light district. It was made in the cause of halting the tide of violence against women and of promoting their demand that the perpetrators of such violence should be held responsible for their actions. *See also* RECLAIM THE NIGHT.

> We have to take back the night every night, or the night will never be ours. And once we have conquered the dark, we have to reach for the light, to take the day and make it ours.
> ANDREA DWORKIN: *Take Back the Night* (1978)

**Take care.** Look after yourself. A general expression of goodwill on parting, signing off a letter, ending a telephone call or the like. There is normally no suggestion that the person needs to be particularly careful. The catchphrase became current in the late 1960s or early 1970s.

**Take five.** To take a short break, notionally one of five minutes. The expression arose in the Second World War.

**Take gas.** Originally, in US 1950s slang, to be subjected to verbal abuse, taunting or scolding (the lineage is 'gas' in the sense 'inconsequential or tiresome talk'). In the 1960s the expression branched out to signify, in US campus slang, 'to do badly or fail, especially in an exam' and, among surfers, 'to lose control of one's board and fall off'.

**Take it.** To suffer mental or physical hardship without complaint. The expression is often found in the negative, as: 'I just can't take it any more.' The phrase dates from the 1930s.

**Take It from Here.** A radio comedy series that ran from 1948 to 1959, created by Frank Muir and Denis Norden. It blended skits, sketches and songs and its most popular item was 'The Glums', a comic SOAP OPERA about the everlasting engagement between the absurdly gormless Ron and the eternally optimistic Eth. The title of the series is a common phrase used in rehearsing a script.

**Take it on the chin.** To endure hardship and adversity without complaint. A metaphor from boxing dating from the 1920s.

**Take some** or **a bit of doing.** To require special effort or planning. The phrase dates from the 1930s.

**Take someone for a ride.** To trick or deceive them, especially for financial gain. The expression derives from US underworld slang of the 1920s, in which it was a euphemism for 'to kill'. Assassins would take their victim out in a car, kill them at some stage, then dump the body.

**Take someone to the cleaners.** To deprive them of their money or possessions, especially fraudulently. One 'cleans them out'. A later meaning of the phrase is to defeat or to criticize, as: 'The Dutch team were taken to the cleaners', 'She really took him to the cleaners over the loan.'

**Take something in one's stride.** To deal with something unpleasant or difficult as if it were part of one's normal routine. The figurative expression evolved at the turn of the 20th century from the literal, as applied to a horse that cleared an obstacle (jumped a fence) without checking its gallop.

**Take the fifth.** In American usage to refuse to testify to a US legislative committee under the protection of the Fifth Amendment to the US Constitution (1789), which states, in part, that: 'No person … shall be compelled in any criminal case to be a witness against himself … without due process of law.'

**Take the heat off someone.** To relieve the pressure on them. A phrase dating from the 1960s.

**Take the mickey out of someone.** To tease them. 'Mickey' probably represents 'Mickey Bliss', rhyming slang for 'piss', so that the expression is a euphemism for 'to take the piss'. This in turn alludes to the deflating of a person, as a bladder deflates when emptying.

**Take** or **hit the silk.** To bale out of an aircraft by parachute. The expression dates from the 1930s and although of US origin perhaps partly puns on the legal phrase 'to take silk', said of a barrister who becomes a Queen's (or King's) Counsel.

**Take the weight off one's feet.** To sit down; to relax. An expression dating from the 1930s.

**Take to the hills.** To run off; to disappear. The expression dates from the 1930s and derives from Western or adventure films. *See also* HEAD FOR THE HILLS.

**Taleban.** *See* TALIBAN.

***Talented Mr Ripley, The.*** *See* RIPLEY.

**Talent scout** or **spotter.** A person who searches out individuals who seem to have potential in a field such as entertainment, sport, modelling, or the like. In the world of espionage a talent spotter is a person who alerts an intelligence officer to someone who is a potential agent. The officer will then gather background information on the proposed agent and if appropriate make an approach.

***Tale of Peter Rabbit, The.*** A story for young children (1900) written and illustrated by Beatrix Potter (1866–1943), first published privately. It became the forerunner of many similar books, whose success is due not just to her story-telling ability and command of language, but also to her shrewd characterization and ecological accuracy. She was a noted botanical artist and a mycologist whose work was in 1897 wrongly dismissed by the Linnaean Society as nonsense, causing her to abandon any further attempt to publicize the findings of her scientific research. She wrote in her secret diary: 'It is odious to a shy person to be snubbed as conceited, especially when the shy person happens to be right.'

**Taliban.** (Persian, 'students'.) A fundamentalist Muslim militia formed in Afghanistan in 1994 as a force of youthful fighters from religious schools in Pakistan. The Taliban (or Taleban) pledged to replace with Islamic law the factionalism that had marked Afghan political life since the demise of the communist regime in 1992. Boosted by popular support and military success, they captured the capital, Kabul, within two years and by 1997 had come to control two thirds of Afghanistan. They interpret Islamic law in the strictest terms, calling for public floggings and stoning to enforce social restrictions, banning music, television and even kite-flying, and prohibiting many activities by women, who could not attend school, work or appear in public unless accompanied by a male relative. Following the attacks on the WORLD TRADE CENTER and the PENTAGON on 11 September 2001, the US government identified Osama BIN LADEN – whom the Taliban had sheltered since 1996 – as the culprit, and launched Operation ENDURING FREEDOM against the Taliban and AL-QAIDA training camps in Afghanistan. The Taliban were overthrown and the training camps destroyed, but bin Laden was not found. Taliban fighters continue to wage guerrilla war in parts of the country.

**Talking head.** A television presenter or speaker, who appears only in head-and-shoulders close-up, without any distracting background. The expression dates from the 1960s and has a derogatory tone, implying passivity rather than activity. By contrast *Talking Heads* (1988) was a series of six moving monologues for television by Alan Bennett. *See also* ROCK GROUP NAMES.

**Talks about talks.** Preliminary discussions held before entering into formal negotiations. The expression dates from the 1970s and typically relates to political debates or labour disputes.

**Talk the talk and walk the walk.** To perform in practice what one has claimed to be able to perform verbally. The usage generally takes such interrogative forms as 'He talks the talk, but can he walk the walk?' *See also* WALK THE TALK.

**Tall Blacks.** A nickname, punning on ALL BLACKS, given in the 1990s to the New Zealand national basketball team.

**Tall, dark and handsome.** Winningly good-looking. A stock phrase current from the 1930s and typically applied to an admired or romantically viewed film actor such as Cary Grant (1904–86).

> After sending the pop world into a dizzy fit last year with an excess of latinate wiggling, Ricky Martin looks to have turned his back on the whole Tall, Dark And Handsome act by bleaching his hair.
>
> *heat* (13–19 January 2000)

**Tall poppy.** In Australian English, someone who has achieved public eminence. The expression 'tall poppy syndrome' denotes the supposed Australian tendency to denigrate or 'cut down to size' prominent or famous people – diagnosed by some as a symptom of an ingrained national fear and suspicion of success.

**Tall Ships race.** An international sailing race held in the summer every two years over different courses, such as Plymouth to Tenerife or Falmouth to Copenhagen. The ships may be square-riggers (with sails set at right angles) or fore-and-afters (with sails set lengthwise) and half the crew must be trainees in order to prevent domination by the professionals. Most of the crews are young – at least two have been all-female – and entrants include navies, governments, cadet training establishments and the like. The first such race was held in 1956. The term 'tall ship' for a high-masted ship dates from at least the 16th century, long pre-dating the opening lines of John Masefield's poem 'Sea Fever':

> I must go down to the sea again, to the lonely sea and the sky,

> And all I ask is a tall ship and a star to steer her by.
>
> JOHN MASEFIELD: 'Sea Fever' (1902)

**Tamagotchi.** An electronic toy that was all the rage in Britain for a year or two after 1997. It displayed a digital image of a creature that had to be looked after and responded to by its owner as if it were a pet. The original Tamagotchi was ovoid. Hence its name, based on Japanese *tamago*, 'egg'. The Japanese manufacturer released a new version in 2004.

**Tamil Tigers.** The short name of the Liberation Tigers of Tamil Eelam (LTTE), a Sri Lankan guerrilla organization formed in 1972 with the aim of establishing an independent state in the northeast of the country, where there is a Tamil majority. Its members display a tiger-like ferocity and strength in their determination, and a brutal civil war has continued for decades on the island. Eelam is the name of the desired Tamil homeland.

**Tamla Motown.** The first African-American-owned record company in the United States, set up by Berry Gordy in Detroit (MOTOWN) in 1959. It was originally two separate companies, Tamla and Motown, the former taking its name from the song 'Tammy' sung by Ray Evans in the film *Tammy and the Bachelor* (1957), in which Tammy is a tomboy played by Debbie Reynolds.

**Tamworth Two.** Two pig siblings of the Tamworth breed whose escape from a Malmesbury abattoir in January 1998 excited considerable media interest in a slow news week. The pair, christened 'Butch' and 'Sundance' by the *Daily Mail*, swam the Wiltshire Avon and hid out on a wooded hillside. Butch was swiftly recaptured, but Sundance managed to keep the media circus going until the end of the week. The Two were understandably not returned to the abattoir, and were settled comfortably in a rare-breeds centre in Kent.

**Tánaiste.** *See* TAOISEACH.

**Tank.** The heavy armoured combat vehicle running on caterpillar tracks was first introduced on the battlefield by the British in the Battle of the SOMME (1916), although the first effective use of tanks was at the Battle of Cambrai the following year. The vehicle was called by the code name 'tank' in order not to arouse enemy suspicions. The term came about partly because the vehicle resembled a water tank, partly because it was supposedly designed for use in desert warfare. British tanks are usually given names beginning with C. Examples are the Churchill, Cromwell and Comet during the Second World War and the Centurion, Chieftain and Challenger after it.

'Tanks' is what these new machines are generally called, and the name has the evident official advantage of being quite undescriptive.

*The Times* (18 September 1916)

**Tankies.** A derogatory nickname of the 1980s for members of the British Communist Party who supported hardline Soviet policies, and specifically that of military intervention using tanks, as in Afghanistan.

**Tank top.** The close-fitting sleeveless top, typically made of wool and worn over a shirt or blouse, came into fashion in the late 1960s. It was named after the tank suits of the 1950s, as one-piece bathing costumes worn in a tank (swimming pool), and is often known simply as a tank. *See also* BIKINI.

**Tank up.** To fill a vehicle's petrol tank; to drink copiously. The latter sense is typically found in the passive, as: 'By now he was really tanked up.' The expressions date from the 1930s.

**Tante Yvonne.** (French, 'Aunt Yvonne'.) A nickname of Yvonne de Gaulle, née Vendroux (1900–79), wife of Charles de Gaulle (1890–1970), president of France (1958–69). She was so named for her homeliness.

**Taoiseach.** The prime minister of the Republic of Ireland, from an Irish word meaning 'chief', 'leader'. In the 1937 Constitution of Ireland (mainly the work of Éamon de Valera; *see* DEV) the *taoiseach* replaced the president of the executive council (the name given to the prime minister of the Irish Free State from 1922). *Tánaiste*, the name given to the deputy prime minister under the 1937 constitution, was in Gaelic Ireland a king or chief's designated successor. *See also* EIRE.

**Tapiola.** The terse and monothematic tone poem by Jean Sibelius (1865–1957) was composed in 1925. It was his last great orchestral work, as he gave up composition for the last thirty years of his life. Tapio was a god of the forests in Finnish mythology, and the following sunny lines are written at the head of the score:

Wide-spread they stand, the Northland's dusky forests
Ancient, mysterious, brooding savage dreams;
Within them dwells the Forest's mighty God,
And wood sprites in the gloom weave magic secrets.

**Tapping up.** In sport, especially football, the practice of approaching a professional player without the permission of the club he is contracted to with a view to enticing him to join another club, which is against the rules of the sport.

The fines will be a deterrent to blatant illegal meetings but they won't stop tapping up, because it's so widespread and undetectable if you're subtle.

TONY CASCARINO: www.timesonline.co.uk (3 June 2005)

**Taras Bulba.** A stirring rhapsody for orchestra by Leoš Janáček (1854–1928). Taras Bulba was a 15th-century Ukrainian Cossack leader who fought the Poles. Janáček was inspired by an 1835 story about him by Nikolai Gogol (1809–52).

**Tardis.** The vehicle in which DOCTOR WHO wends his way through the universe and across time. The word is an acronym for '*t*ime *a*nd *r*elative *d*imension *i*n *s*pace'. The Tardis is bigger on the inside than out, and is 'disguised' on the outside to resemble a London police telephone box. In theory it should metamorphose into a different exterior shape to fit in with the varied environments in which it lands, but that particular facility went on the blink eons ago.

**Targa roof.** A type of roof hood on a sports car. The forward, rigid section can be detached, when it leaves a soft, convertible rear section and a central transverse roll-bar for structural support. The name comes from a model of Porsche car with this feature, introduced in 1965, and taking its own name from Italian *targa*, 'plate', 'shield', probably with reference to the *Targa Florio*, 'Florio Shield', a motor time-trial held annually in Sicily.

**Tarka.** The otter that is the subject of Henry Williamson's moving novel *Tarka the Otter* (1927), set in north Devon, telling the story of his life and concluding with his hunt to the death. A HERITAGE RAILWAYS line in his home country has been named after him.

**Tarmac.** An ingenious nickname given to the Jamaican-born footballer John Barnes (b.1963) during his period at Liverpool Football Club in the late 1980s and early 1990s. 'Tarmac' is an extension of the nickname the 'Black Heighway', conferred on Barnes by Liverpool in recognition of his supposed similarity to Steve Heighway, a Liverpool star of the 1970s.

**Tartan Army.** Scottish football supporters, famed for following their team's fortunes wherever they play and for visibly and audibly advertising their national allegiance. A typical contingent will wear tartan costumes or bonnets, sport ginger wigs, paint blue St Andrew's saltires on their faces, and fearlessly flaunt the Scottish flag in the territory of the enemy. *See also* BARMY ARMY.

**Tartan Tories.** A dismissive former nickname for the Scottish National Party, the SNP, originating with Willie Ross (later Lord Ross of Marnock; 1911–88), secretary of state for Scotland (1964–70, 1974–6) at a time when the SNP was achieving significant electoral successes. Ross himself lost office over his opposition to DEVOLUTION. Since then the SNP has moved to the left.

**Tart with a heart.** A prostitute with a generous nature. The full form of the phrase is 'tart with a heart of gold'.

> Salma Hayek plays a stripper who just happens to be an angel – an unfamiliar twist on the old tart with a heart cliché – in director Kevin Smith's new film *Dogma*.
>
> *heat* (7–13 October 1999)

**Tarzan.** The famous foundling reared by apes in the African jungle was created in 1912 by Edgar Rice Burroughs (1875–1950). He has countless adventures in novels and films, in which he communes with animals, rescues damsels in distress and discovers lost civilizations. The first novel of 24 in which he appears is *Tarzan of the Apes* (1914). In the 'monkey language' that Burroughs invented for him, his name means 'white skin', from *tar*, 'white', and *zan*, 'skin'. He is given this name by his foster-mother, Kala the ape. The name came to be adopted for any apparent 'he-man' and was bestowed by the media on the Conservative politician Michael Heseltine (b.1933), not only for his height and blond hair but also with reference to an incident of 1976 when he brandished the House of Commons mace to protect it. Heseltine apparently relished the nickname, entitling his autobiography *My Life in the Jungle*. Tarzana, now a suburban residential section of Los Angeles, was named in honour of Tarzan. *See also* HEZZA; SHEENA.

> The power that makes us respond to the wanderings of Odysseus is also at work in Burroughs' Tarzan, and the two great popular heroes speak openly to our most cherished fantasies.
>
> ERLING B. HOLTSMARK: *Tarzan and Tradition: Classical Myth in Popular Literature* (1981)

**Task force.** An armed force set up for a special operation, the latter being the 'task'. The term, of US origin and dating from the Second World War, was generally brought before the public in 1982 at the time of the FALKLANDS WAR, when the British government sent a naval task force to liberate the islands from the Argentinians.

**TASS.** The official news agency of the former Soviet Union, founded in 1925. The initials stand for *Telegrafnoe agentstvo Sovetskogo Soyuza* (Russian, 'Telegraphic Agency of the Soviet Union'). It had bureaux in many foreign countries (some used as covers for KGB activities), and Western analysts regarded its pronouncements as following the official Soviet line. In January 1992, shortly after the collapse of the Soviet Union, TASS became an independent commercial news agency, renaming itself ITAR (Information Telegraph Agency of Russia), although the name TASS was preserved for the domestic wire service. In Britain TASS was an acronym for the former Technical and Supervisory

Staff union, now part of the MSF (Manufacturing, Scientific and Finance union).

**Taste of Honey, A.** A play (1958) by Shelagh Delaney (b.1939) about the experiences of a young working-class girl, Jo, who finds herself pregnant after a brief affair with a black naval rating. The film (1961), directed by Tony Richardson and starring Rita Tushingham as Jo, was admired as a fine example of KITCHEN SINK DRAMA. The title echoes a line in 1 Samuel 14:43: 'I did but taste a little honey with the end of the rod that was in mine hand, and, lo, I must die.'

**Tate bricks.** The name by which the installation entitled *Equivalent VIII*, by the US sculptor and poet Carl Andre (b.1935), has become popularly known. The installation, consisting of 120 firebricks arranged in a rectangle two bricks deep, was first created in 1966 and purchased by the Tate Gallery, London, in 1972. The work was vandalized in 1976 when a visitor threw dye over it in protest at what he considered to be a waste of public money.

**Tautonym.** (Greek *tauto*, 'same'.) In biological nomenclature this term indicates a taxonomic name in which the generic repeats the specific, as *Martes martes*, the pine marten. It could equally be applied, however, to the growing rank of designations, mainly in the business world, in which the generic word repeats a word that has become absorbed in an abbreviation whose original meaning is forgotten. A familiar example is 'PIN number', where 'number' repeats the word in 'personal identification number', the origin of the abbreviated 'PIN'. Other examples are 'ATM machine' (from 'automated teller machine'), 'APR rate' ('annual percentage rate'), 'TSB bank' ('Trustee Savings Bank') and, as its own official name, 'HSBC Bank' ('Hongkong and Shanghai Banking Corporation'). Also not uncommon in the media are 'AGM meeting' ('annual general meeting') and 'HIV virus' ('human immunodeficiency virus') (*see* HIV-POSITIVE).

**Tawny Owl.** *See* BROWN OWL.

**Taxi Driver.** A bleakly realistic film (1976), directed by Martin Scorsese, about an inarticulate VIETNAM veteran, Travis Bickle, who becomes a taxi driver and who is dehumanized by the urban landscape of violent crime and brutality around him. The film starred Robert DeNiro as Bickle and, controversially, 12-year-old Jodie Foster as the drug-addicted teenage whore, Iris, whom he determines to save.

**Taxi Kennedy.** *See* CHAMPAGNE CHARLIE.

**Taxi squad.** In American football a group of players who are not listed on a club's roster but who take part in practices and who are available as reserves for the team. The term owes its origin to Arthur McBride, founder of the Cleveland Browns football team, who also ran a taxi company, and who would give such players jobs with his business to support them and keep them available.

**Tea and Sympathy.** A play (1953) by the US writer Robert Anderson about the problems faced by a sensitive teenage boy at an elite New England boarding school who is accused of homosexuality. The 'tea and sympathy' in question is provided by the housemaster's wife. A bowdlerized film version followed in 1956.

> All you're supposed to do is every once in a while give the boys a little tea and sympathy.
>
> ROBERT ANDERSON: *Tea and Sympathy* (1953), Act I

The phrase 'tea and sympathy' has come into more general usage to denote caring and hospitable behaviour towards a troubled person.

**Tea boy.** The boy whose job it is to make the tea. The designation is a paradigm for the lowliest employee in an organization, especially in the context of its chain of authority.

**Teacher's pet.** A person regarded with (undue) favour. The original sense, as applied to a teacher's favourite pupil, dates from the 1920s.

**Teach-in.** A US term for a series of lectures and discussions on a particular theme led by experts. The expression became current in England in the 1960s.

**Teamster.** A US term for a lorry driver, and specifically one who belongs to the Teamsters Union, the largest labour union in the United States. It was founded in 1903 as the International Brotherhood of Teamsters, Chauffeurs, Stablemen and Helpers of America but in 1940 'Stablemen' became 'Warehousemen'. It has had a chequered career, and between 1957 and 1988 three of its presidents were convicted of various criminal charges and sentenced to prison terms. Among their number was Jimmy Hoffa (1913–c.1975), leader of the Teamsters from 1957, who was imprisoned in 1967 for the attempted bribery of a federal court judge after he was charged with corruption. Released by President Nixon in 1971, Hoffa disappeared in 1975 and is generally believed to have been murdered. His controversial career was the subject of a lengthy and tedious biopic, *Hoffa* (1992), starring Jack Nicholson.

**Teapot Dome scandal.** A corruption scandal that affected US President Warren Harding's administration in the 1920s. For strategic reasons the government had acquired a number of US oil fields, and from 1921 the administration of these assets came under Albert B. Fall (1861–1944), secretary of the interior. Fall, in return for more than $300,000 (and a herd of cattle), secretly allowed the Mammoth Oil Company to drill on one of the government's oil fields, at Teapot Dome in Wyoming in 1922. He also did similar illegal deals with the Pan American Petroleum Company for the Elk Hills and Buena Vista Hills fields in California (the scandal is also called the Elk Hills scandal). Fall was eventually convicted and imprisoned.

**Teapot Toulouse.** The nickname given to the artist Henri Toulouse-Lautrec (1864–1901) by the Paris whores, on account of his squat stature and impressive endowment.

**Tear into someone.** To attack or scold them; to attack them physically.

**Tearjerker.** A sentimental or romantic film evoking sadness, sympathy, yearning or the like. The term, of US origin and dating from the 1920s, can also apply to a novel, play, story, song or even person or event, such as a farewell occasion. Whatever it is, it can bring tears to the eyes. *See also* LOVE STORY.

**Teasmade.** The automatic tea-making machine of this name was invented by one Brenner Thornton in 1936 and the following year bought by the firm of Goblin, who made vacuum cleaners. The name is a neat pun on 'tea's maid' and 'tea's made', both indicating a personal service. Goblin's original model was rather more lavish than in later years, incorporating not only a clock and a bedside light but including two earthenware cups and saucers, a cream jug and a sugar basin.

**Technicolor.** Since the inception of the cinema filmmakers had sought to create a colour film. Early attempts were crude and unsatisfactory until 1922, when HOLLYWOOD produced its first Technicolor feature, a version of *Madama Butterfly* entitled *Toll of the Sea*. The process involved a camera containing two strips of film, one for red, the other for green, and a prism to split the incoming light into the primary colours. When the film was developed the two strips were combined, producing pleasing, natural results. The technique was further improved subsequently.

**Technicolor yawn.** An act of vomiting. A piece of Australian slang of the early 1960s, expressive of a multicoloured effluvium, which like several others of the same general sort (*see also* GO FOR THE BIG SPIT) was made familiar to British speakers via the character Barry MCKENZIE. An alternative formulation is 'technicolor spit'.

**Techno.** A type of popular music with a dance beat first appearing in the late 1980s, so called from its heavy use of technology in the form of synthesized sounds and electronic effects. TRANCE was a development.

**Technobabble.** Pretentious scientific or pseudo-scientific jargon, especially in the world of computers. The word is based on the earlier PSYCHOBABBLE, as the jargon of popular psychology.

**Teddy bear.** A child's toy bear, named after US President Theodore (Teddy) Roosevelt (1858–1919), who was fond of bear-hunting. Roosevelt was shown sparing the life of a bear-cub in a cartoon drawn by C.K. Berryman in 1902 as a spoof on the president's role as an ardent conservationist. In 1906 the *New York Times* published a humorous poem about the adventures of two bears named Teddy B and Teddy G in his honour. These names were then given to two bears newly presented to the Bronx Zoo and manufacturers seized on the event to put toy bears called teddy bears on the market. *See also* BRIDESHEAD REVISITED; TEDDY BEARS' PICNIC; WINNIE-THE-POOH.

**Teddy bears' picnic.** An occasion of innocent merriment. The phrase comes from the popular song of this name, which originated as a piece composed by John W. Bratton in 1907 as a tribute to President Theodore Roosevelt (*see* TEDDY BEAR). Words by Jimmy Kennedy were added in 1930 at the request of the publisher, B. Feldman and Co., for use in a Manchester pantomime. Val Rosing's famous recording with Henry Hall's Orchestra, made in 1932, was nominated by the 1933 International Radio Convention as ideal for testing broadcasting equipment.

> If you go down in the woods today
> You're sure of a big surprise
> If you go down in the woods today
> You'd better go in disguise.
> For every Bear that ever there was
> Will gather there for certain because,
> Today's the day the Teddy Bears have their Picnic.
>
> JIMMY KENNEDY: 'The Teddy Bears' Picnic' (1930)

**Teddy Boys.** A name arising in the 1950s for working-class youths who affected a style of dress and appearance supposedly reminiscent of the EDWARDIAN ERA, 'Teddy' being a pet form of the name Edward. Their costume typically consisted of a brightly coloured and velvet trimmed frock coat, an ornamental waistcoat, DRAINPIPES, and a narrow tie. Footwear could vary but often took the form of shiny lace-ups, BROTHEL CREEPERS or WINKLE-PICKERS. Hair styles were important, and were mostly based on a variant of the quiff. Two favourites were the DUCK'S ARSE and the so called 'elephant trunk', the latter being a large and long quiff swept forward over the face. Teds were often regarded as trouble-

makers, and the media carried stories of gang violence and antisocial behaviour. The flamboyance of dress and demeanour, however, to some extent compensated for the associated aggravation and aggressiveness, while it was the advent of the new pop music that took the teen cult into the mainstream. *See also* ROCK 'N' ROLL.

**Teds.** A colloquial name for TEDDY BOYS, dating almost from the first.

**Teenage Mutant Ninja Turtles.** A popular children's television cartoon series screened from 1988 to 1995. The characters were four turtles named Michelangelo, Raphael, Leonardo and Donatello, who with the aid of a ninja mask, as worn by Japanese ninjutsu, became swift martial arts experts. They were 'mutant' because when accidentally dropped down the New York sewer system they grew to human size and gained the power of speech. They were conceived in 1983 by Kevin Eastman and Peter Laird as a parody of the Japanese samurai-style heroes then prominent in comic strips. When they were launched in Britain 'ninja' was altered to 'hero', because it was feared British children would be baffled by the word 'ninja'.

**Teenybopper.** An American colloquialism applied from the 1960s and 1970s to girls in their early teens who adopted current fashions in dress and were devotees of pop music and the latest crazes generally. Although deriving from 'teen' the term has been influenced by 'teeny' (in the sense of small).

**Tee-shirt.** *See* T-SHIRT.

**Teething troubles.** Short-term problems that occur in the early stages of an enterprise. The expression dates from the 1930s and rather obviously alludes to the difficulty or discomfort sometimes experienced by young children when cutting or growing their teeth.

**Teflon.** A patent non-stick coating for cooking vessels marketed from the mid-1950s. The word combines letters from the substance's scientific name, poly*tetra*fluoroethylene, with '-on' as in nylon or rayon.

The name Teflon has been taken up by the media to apply to anyone, but especially a politician, who is 'non-stick' in terms of blame, criticism, scandal and the like. In 1983 'Teflon-coated' was memorably applied by the Democratic Congresswoman Patricia Schroeder to President Reagan:

> Ronald Reagan … is attempting a great breakthrough in political technology – he has been perfecting the Teflon-coated presidency. He sees to it that nothing sticks to him.
>
> Speech in the House of Representatives (2 August 1983)

The US Mafia boss, John Gotti, became known as the Teflon Don, as the authorities could not make any charges stick – until in 1992 he was jailed for life for racketeering and five counts of murder.

In Ireland, Bertie Aherne, *taoiseach* (prime minister) since 1997, is known as the Teflon Taoiseach, having managed to remain relatively untarnished by the various scandals that rocked his Fianna Fáil Party in the 1990s.

Tony Blair no longer commands. Teflon Tony is dead.

PETER RIDDELL: www.timesonline.co.uk (10 November 2005)

**Telecom Valley.** A nickname for the Côte d'Azur in southeast France, as the location of several French and foreign telecommunications companies. The name is patterned on America's SILICON VALLEY.

**Telecottage.** Not usually a cottage in the normal sense but a room or building in a rural area containing computer equipment for the use of local people. The concept is of Swedish origin and the word translates Swedish *telestuga*. The first telecottage in Britain was opened in 1989 at a school in Warslow, Staffordshire.

**Telethon.** A mammoth television programme, or 'television marathon', especially one designed to raise money for charity. Telethons have been broadcast on BBC Television since 1980 with viewers making donations by telephoned pledges. 'Children in Need', dating back to a five-minute radio appeal on Christmas Day in 1927, was the first charity that raised money in this way. COMIC RELIEF, which raises money through RED NOSE DAY, held its first telethon in 1988.

**Teletourism.** The last quarter of the 20th century saw the start of the growth of television tourism, as the visiting of places where popular television programmes were filmed, especially SOAP OPERAS and dramatizations of novels. The places are invariably renamed in their televisual reincarnation, and this is part of the attraction for the fans, who as in the story itself are happy to blur the distinction between real and fictional. Even when the fictional place is unnamed, the location of filming still draws the crowds, as did Holmfirth, Kirklees, the setting of *The* LAST OF THE SUMMER WINE (since 1973). The following are some of the better known, fictional name first. *See also* COUNTRY.

Aidensfield (HEARTBEAT, from 1990): Goathland, North Yorkshire

Arnscote (*By the Sword Divided*, 1983, 1985): Rockingham Castle, Leicestershire

Beckindale (*Emmerdale*, from 1989): Esholt, Bradford

Balamory (*Balamory*, from 2003): Tobermory, Isle of Mull

Ballykissangel (*Ballykissangel*, 1996–2001): Avoca, County Wicklow

Brideshead (BRIDESHEAD REVISITED, 1981): Castle Howard, North Yorkshire

Cardale (*Peak Practice*, 1993–2002): Crich, Derbyshire

Darrowby (*All Creatures Great and Small*, 1978–90): Askrigg, North Yorkshire

Dibley (*The Vicar of Dibley*, 1994–2006): Turville, Buckinghamshire

Emmerdale (*Emmerdale Farm*, 1972–89): Arncliffe, North Yorkshire (*see also* Beckindale)

Fawlty Towers (FAWLTY TOWERS, 1975–9): Wooburn Grange, Bourne End, Buckinghamshire

Grantleigh Manor (*To the Manor Born*, 1979–81): Cricket House, Cricket St Thomas, Somerset

Home Farm (*The* DARLING BUDS OF MAY, 1991–3): Bliss Farm, Pluckley, Kent

Loch Dubh (*Hamish Macbeth*, 1995–7): Plockton, Highland

Middlemarch (*Middlemarch*, 1994): Stamford, Lincolnshire

Millstone Manor (*Grace and Favour*, 1992): Chavenage House, Tetbury, Gloucestershire

Royston Vasey (*The League of Gentlemen*, 1999–2002; Royston Vasey is the real name of the comedian Roy 'Chubby' Brown): Hadfield, Derbyshire

Skelthwaite (*Where the Heart Is*, from 1997): Slaithwaite, West Yorkshire

Strathbogle House (*Monarch of the Glen*, 2000–5): Ardverikie House, Ardverikie, Highland

Sun Hill (*The* BILL, from 1984): Blackwall, London

Tannochbrae (1) (*Doctor Finlay's Casebook*, 1962–71): Callander, Scotland

Tannochbrae (2) (*Doctor Finlay*, 1993–6): Auchtermuchty, Scotland

Tarrant (*Howards' Way*, 1985–90 ): Bursledon, Hampshire

The Village (*The* PRISONER, 1967–8): Portmeirion, Gwynedd

Walmington-on-Sea (DAD'S ARMY, 1968–77): Thetford, Norfolk

**Teletubbies.** The four 'techno-babies', Tinky Winky, Dipsy, La La and Po, who first appeared on BBC children's television in 1997 as the creation of the children's television producer Anne Wood. They are distinctively coloured and resemble miniature spacemen, with aerials on their heads and televisions in their stomachs. They live in a magical land and have a friend in the Noo Noo, a vacuum cleaner character, who cleans up after them. They speak baby language and mostly run about, play, dance and eat custard and toast.

Their fans came to include both young viewers and students, the latter awarding them cult status, but many parents regarded them with disfavour because of their apparently deleterious effect on the speech-learning processes of their offspring. Similar charges had been levelled by a previous generation of parents in regard to the FLOWERPOT MEN.

**Tell it like it is.** To give the facts realistically or honestly. The expression originated from black English in the 1960s.

**Tell me another!** You can't expect me to believe that! The implication is that the speaker is telling a lie or a joke rather than relating a fact.

**Tell someone what to do with something.** To reject something vehemently. 'What they can do with it' is stick it up their backside.

**Tell someone where to get off** or **where to go.** To scold them for interfering; to tell them off. 'Where they get off' or 'where they go' is hell.

> Someone suggested he [BBC chief political correspondent John Sergeant] present the late Sunday night God slot *Everyman*. Sergeant … told his BBC bosses where to go.
> *The Times* (21 January 2000)

**Telstar.** The name given to the satellite launched by the United States in 1962 for relaying transatlantic telephone messages and television pictures. It was something of a pioneer of its time and that same year was even the subject of a popular musical hit by the British group The Tornados.

**Temple, Paul.** The English detective-novelist created by Francis Durbridge for the radio serial *Send for Paul Temple* (1938) and its many sequels broadcast over the next 30 years. He soon appeared in novels, the first of which appeared in the same year as the radio serial under the same title. Temple was the leading fictional detective on BBC Radio in the Second World War, and he then graduated to films such as *Calling Paul Temple* (1948) and *Paul Temple Returns* (1952), all starring John Bentley.

**Temporary gentleman.** A condescending nickname in the First World War for an officer commissioned only for the duration of the war. The allusion is to the hallowed phrase 'an officer and a gentleman'.

**10.** A comedy film (1979) starring Dudley Moore as a sexually obsessed middle-aged composer who marks his girls 1 to 10 depending on their performance. His co-star, Bo Derek, scores 11, provoking Moore into embarrassing pursuit.

**Ten Days That Shook the World.** The title of a book (1919) by the US journalist John Reed (1887–1920), an eyewitness account of the BOLSHEVIK Revolution in Russia in November 1917. Reed, who came from a wealthy background, was one of the leading radical figures in the United States, became a friend of LENIN and helped to found the US Communist Party. Accused of treason in the United States, he fled to Soviet Russia, where he died of typhus. After his death the US Communist Party established many 'John Reed' clubs for writers and artists in US cities. His life is the subject of the film *Reds* (1981), directed by and starring Warren Beatty.

**Tender is the Night.** A novel (1934) by F. Scott Fitzgerald (1896–1940). Written and rewritten under various titles several times, it in some respects complements the autobiographical novel, *Save Me the Waltz* (1932), by Fitzgerald's wife, Zelda (Sayre) (1900–48), whom he married in 1920 and who was from 1937 almost permanently in a home for the mentally ill. The novel charts the deterioration of a psychiatrist, Dick Diver, who marries one of his patients, a schizophrenic. The title comes from 'Ode to a Nightingale' by John Keats (1795–1821): 'Already with thee! Tender is the night, / And haply the Queen-Moon is on her throne.' A patchy film version (1961) was directed by Henry King.

**Ten for 66 and All That.** The title of the autobiography of the Australian leg-spin bowler Arthur Mailey (1886–1967) punning on the title of Sellar and Yeatman's celebrated 1066 AND ALL THAT and celebrating his feat of taking 10 wickets for 66 runs for the Australians against Gloucestershire in 1921.

**Tenko.** A grimly realistic television drama by Lavinia Warner running from 1981 to 1984 and telling of the trials and tribulations of a disparate group of British and Dutch women in a Japanese prison camp after the fall of Singapore in 1942. The title is the Japanese for 'rollcall'.

**Ten Little Niggers.** A detective novel (1939; as *And Then There Were None*, 1940; also published as *Ten Little Indians* and *The Nursery Rhyme Murders*) by Agatha Christie (1890–1976). The changes of title were largely due to POLITICAL CORRECTNESS. The references are to the familiar nursery rhyme, written as a song by Frank Green in 1868 or 1869: 'Ten little nigger boys went out to dine; / One choked his little self, and then there were nine [etc.] … One little nigger boy living all alone; / He got married, and then there were none.' It was undoubtedly inspired by Septimus Winner's 'Ten Little Injuns', published in England a short while earlier, and still remembered in American nurseries. A classic film version (1945), with some splendid acting cameos, was meticulously directed by René Clair as an enjoyable black comedy.

**10 out of 10.** Complete success. A term of admiration or approval for something perfectly done. The allusion is to 10 out of 10 marks in a piece of schoolwork, 'full marks'. Hence '10' as a colloquialism for the ideal man or woman, reinforced by the film 10. Assessing a possible romantic or sexual partner on such a scale is a common practice among young people and is found in socializing settings such as clubs, pubs, television dating shows and the like.

> One of my favourite things there is that the girls would always go '6, 7', something like that. The guys would always add on halves. They'd be like '8, 8 and a half'. And I'd go, 'What's the half for?' What's that about?
>
> *heat* (16 December 1999–5 January 2000)

**1066 and all that.** Britain's past history, popularly viewed as explaining the nation's heterogeneous heritage. The phrase is the title of W.C. Sellar and R.J. Yeatman's humorous survey of British history, published in 1930 as 'a subtle mixture of schoolboy howlers, witty distortions and artful puns'. The book was designed to satirize the smugness of the English and the teaching of history by rote, but ironically itself became a historical icon. A typical definition is 'The Cavaliers (Wrong but Wromantic) and the Roundheads (Right but Repulsive)'. 1066, as the date of the Norman Conquest, probably still remains the best-known date in British history, 'all that' being the blur of dates and events that occurred before and after it.

> The earl's own name undermined the solidity of his Anglo-Saxon lineage. Charles Francis Topham de Vere Beauclerk is an elision of British and French, a reminder of 1066 and all that.
>
> *The Times* (28 October 1999)

**Ten to two.** With one's hands on the steering wheel of a car in the position of the hands of a clock showing ten minutes to two. The phrase is equally used of a person's feet so placed. The stated time is also that at which clocks and watches are set when offered for sale, the position of the hands supposedly representing a smile in order to encourage a purchase.

**Tequila sunrise.** A cocktail of tequila and grenadine, popular in the 1970s. Its name alluded to its lurid hue, which placed it in the lower range of the social scale.

**Terminate with extreme prejudice.** A secret-service euphemism, originating in the CIA, for the assassination of an individual. First recorded in 1972, various other circumlocutions (e.g. 'dismiss', 'eliminate') can take the place of 'terminate'.

> [Senator Howard Metzenbaum] was a critic of the 'rogue elephant' that the CIA became during the years of targeting a Lamumba or a Castro for 'elimination with extreme prejudice'.
>
> *Washington Post* (12 January 1986)

**Terminator, The.** A film thriller (1984) about a lethal cyborg robot that is sent back in time to the present day in order to kill the mother of a future leader of mankind in the battle against machines that seek to take over the planet. Starring Arnold Schwarzenegger as the 'Terminator', the film was followed by the equally successful sequel *Terminator 2: Judgment Day* (1991), which at $100 million was then the most expensive film ever made. The films established 'terminator' as a stock phrase for any person hired to kill or otherwise reduce the opposition, from assassins and mercenaries to officials and industrial managers ordered to make cuts in staffing levels. Austrian-born Schwarzenegger became so closely associated with the name 'Terminator' that when he was elected governor of California in 2003, he was dubbed 'the GOVERNATOR'.

Adapting the original, the all-conquering Austrian skier Hermann Maier (b.1972) has been nicknamed 'the Herminator', and the Indian Sikh spin bowler Harbhajan Singh (b.1980) has been called 'the Turbanator'.

**Terminological inexactitude.** A mock-pompous euphemism for a downright lie, sometimes resorted to in parliament for this purpose. It was first so used in a speech about labour contracts by Winston Churchill:

> It cannot in the opinion of His Majesty's Government be classified as slavery in the extreme acceptance of the word without some risk of terminological inexactitude.
>
> *Hansard* (22 February 1906)

**Terran.** A SCIENCE FICTION name for an inhabitant of the planet earth, from Latin *terra*, 'earth'. The term dates from the 1950s, with the spelling and capital differentiating the word from the much earlier 'terrene', as applied to the dry land or to the world in the sense 'secular'.

**Terrence Higgins Trust.** Britain's leading AIDS charity, founded in 1982 in memory of one of the first British gay men to die of the disease. Terrence Higgins had joined the navy as an 18-year-old but sought release on discovering his sexuality. Denied this legitimate loophole, he painted hammer and sickle symbols all over the ship on which he was serving and was finally asked to leave. In the late 1960s he made his way to SWINGING LONDON and spent much of his time partying. Things began to go wrong in the early 1980s, when he started to lose weight, and a collapse on the dance floor resulted in his admission to hospital. He discharged himself but was soon readmitted. Doctors diagnosed a parasitic pneumonia but were at a loss to identify its cause. Friends were expecting Higgins to make a full recovery but on 4 July 1982 death supervened.

**Terrible beauty.** *See* EASTER RISING.

**Terrible twos.** The age of two, recognized by generations of harrassed and haggard parents as the time when infant behaviour is at its most antisocial.

**Terriers.** The Territorial Army was established in 1908 as part of the military reforms of Lord Haldane, then secretary of state for war, and within months had been semi-officially dubbed with the apt nickname. 'Terrors' and 'Torrals' were also considered but wisely rejected. The TA is now part of the wider Reserve Forces but has retained its identity and its sobriquet.

**Terry and the Pirates.** *See* Terry LEE.

**Tesco.** *See* PILE IT HIGH, SELL IT CHEAP.

**TESSA.** The popular, friendly sounding Tax-Exempt Special Savings Account, introduced in 1991, allowed savers to invest a stated amount in a bank or building society and pay no tax on the interest, so long as the capital remained in the account for five years. Together with the PEP, it yielded to the blander ISA (Individual Savings Account) in 1999.

**Test-tube baby.** A baby conceived by *in vitro* fertilization. The world's first child to be born in this way was Louise Brown, delivered by Caesarian operation at Oldham District Hospital, Greater Manchester, on 26 July 1978. The embryo had been implanted in Mrs Brown's womb the previous November, after one of her eggs was fertilized in a test-tube by her husband's sperm. The procedure was the subject of considerable criticism at the time, both within the scientific establishment and from groups opposed on religious and ethical grounds.

**Tet offensive.** An attack carried out by North Vietnamese forces and VIET CONG in early 1968, during the VIETNAM War (1964–75). The offensive was aimed at major towns and cities throughout South Vietnam and was launched on 31 January, the Vietnamese Tet (new year) holiday, when many South Vietnamese troops were on leave. The communists managed to seize a number of symbolic targets in the South Vietnamese capital, Saigon, including the US embassy itself. Although through February US and South Vietnamese forces took a terrible toll of the Viet Cong, the determined and coordinated nature of the attack shocked many Americans, who viewed the fighting nightly on their television sets. The negative reaction of the US public persuaded President Johnson (*see* LBJ) to try to find a way out of the war.

**Tetra Pak.** The ubiquitous plastic-coated paper-board cartons for milk and other liquids were the invention in 1951 of the Swiss entrepreneur Dr Ruben Rausing, who chose the original tetrahedon shape that gave the name because it used a small amount of material to enclose a large volume. It was awkward to handle, however, and was superseded by several other configurations, including the 'Tetra Brik'. These were developed by the inventor's son, Gad Rausing, who bought the rights to the product in 1965 and together with his brother, Hans, built up the new business into the world's largest food packaging group.

**Texas.** The name of the US state came to be used in various belittling culinary senses in the 20th century. Thus Texas butter is gravy made with flour and water in dripping, Texas strawberries are red beans and Texas toast is a thick slice of bread warmed (but not toasted) and spread with butter. Texas tea, however, is a nickname for marijuana, easily available in the state.

**Texas Chainsaw Massacre, The.** A notorious HORROR MOVIE (1974) written by Kim Henkel and Tobe Hooper in which a family of chainsaw-wielding unemployed slaughterhouse workers terrorize a Texas community, desecrating the local cemetery and decorating their house with human and animal remains. The title proclaimed the film's horror credentials, although it contains few scenes with much gore. It was loosely based upon the atrocities committed in real life by deranged Wisconsin farmer Ed Gein, whose bloodthirsty activities also influenced Alfred Hitchcock's PSYCHO. *See also* SPLATTER MOVIE.

**TGIF.** 'Thank God it's Friday', an utterance of relief from the world-weary worker. 'TGI Friday's' is the name of a chain of casual-dining restaurants, the first of which opened in New York City in 1965. *See also* POET'S DAY.

A youth-TV show presented by Chris Evans on Channel 4 on Friday evenings between 1996 and 2000 was titled *TFI Friday*, standing (officially) for 'Thank Four It's Friday'.

**TGV train.** The first *train à grande vitesse* or French high-speed electric train ran from Paris to Lyon in 1981. Its cruising speed is about 300kph (185mph).

**Thalidomide.** A sedative and anti-sickness drug that was prescribed in West Germany and the UK between 1959 and 1962. However, it was found that if taken by pregnant women it badly affected the development of the foetus, leading to children being born with 'seal limbs' and other deformities. More than 2000 such children were born in West Germany, and around 500 in the UK, until the drug was withdrawn.

**Thames and Hudson.** A still-independent publishing house famous for its art books. It was founded in 1949 with offices in London and New York, hoping to attract an English-speaking readership on both sides of the Atlantic. Hence its name, from the rivers Thames and Hudson, on which London and New York respectively stand. The origin is also pictorially represented in its colophon of two dolphins, the upper one facing left or west, the lower right or east.

**Thankful villages.** Those villages in England where all the men who went off to fight in the First World War came back safely (or at least alive). Arthur Mee, in his book *The Enchanted Land* (1936), lists 23 such villages, but more have since come to light.

**Thanks a million.** Thank you very much. The usage is mostly ironic: 'Thanks a million, talking to you has made me late for work.' The same goes for variants such as 'Thanks a bunch'.

**Thanks, but no thanks.** I appreciate your offer but do not wish to accept it. A catchphrase from the 1970s. The implication is often that the offer is unacceptable rather than unwanted.

**Thanks for nothing.** An ironic response to an act of meanness or selfishness.

> Hey, world: Thanks for nothing. Do you know what the definition of ungrateful is? It is being clearly spelled out for us in the world's response – or rather, its lack of response – to the carnage wrought by Hurricane Katrina earlier this week.
>
> JON DOUGHERTY: *WorldNetDaily* (2 September 2005)

**Thatcherism.** A term for the policies and style of government of Margaret Thatcher (*see* IRON LADY) as Conservative prime minister (1979–90). It denoted an emphasis on monetarism as a means of controlling the economy, the privatization of nationalized industries and anti-union legislation. In a broader sense Thatcherism connoted a stress on individual responsibility and enterprise. The Conservative MP Julian Critchley had this to say about Thatcher and Thatcherism:

> Like Marxism, Thatcherism is, in fact, riddled with contradictions. Mrs Thatcher, on the other hand, is free of doubt; she is the label on the can of worms.

*See also* BLATCHERISM.

**Thatcher's Britain.** A mainly derogative media nickname for Britain under the premiership of Margaret Thatcher (*see* THATCHERISM), especially as a society moulded or affected by the policies of her successive governments. The term was current for the whole of the 1980s.

**Thatcher's children.** The rising generation of the 21st century, especially the young Britons born in 1982, in the early days of THATCHERISM, and coming of age in the hallmark year 2000. Media pundits inevitably gave confused and conflicting interpretations of their attitudes and aspirations.

They are confident, consumerist, content. But do Thatcher's children – proud of their country but unwilling to vote – have some nasty surprises in store?

*Sunday Times Magazine* (2 January 2000)

**That'll be the day.** That will be worth waiting for. The usage is mainly ironic, implying that the day will never come. The phrase is of New Zealand origin and dates from the 1930s. 'That'll Be The Day' was the title of a song by Buddy Holly and The Crickets (1957), and was also the title of a film (1975), starring David Essex, about a fairground worker's ascent to pop stardom.

**That'll do nicely, sir.** An advertising slogan used by American Express for its credit card in the 1970s and 1980s, suggesting global and much-welcomed acceptance. It was later adopted in other contexts, sometimes parodically.

> *Customer (offering card)*: American Express?
> *Sales assistant*: That'll do nicely, sir – and would you like to rub my tits?
> *Not the Nine O'Clock News* (BBC Television, 1979–82)

**That makes two of us.** I quite agree; I know all about that. A catchphrase dating from the 1950s and typically said by someone who has experienced the same misfortune or unpleasantness as another.

***That Obscure Object of Desire.*** A film, originally entitled *Cet obscur objet du désir* (1977), written and directed by the Spanish film director Luis Buñuel (1900–83), about a French businessman's obsessive love for a beautiful young Spanish woman called Conchita, the object of his desire. The obscurity of Conchita's character and her feelings for her admirer were cleverly emphasized by Buñuel's trick of casting two actresses, Carole Bouquet and Angela Molina, in the same role.

**That's about the size of it.** That's the way it looks. The phrase implies both an agreement and an assessment of a situation that is probably bad rather than good.

**That's all I need.** That is the last straw, on top of what I have already endured. The ironic phrase dates from the 1950s.

***That's Life!*** A television programme broadcast by the BBC from 1973 to 1994. Presented by Esther Rantzen, it was a popular blend of consumer complaints, staged stunts, *double-entendres* and crudely comic street interviews.

**That's the way the cookie crumbles.** That's how things turn out. When you break or bite a cookie (biscuit) it may crumble anywhere. The US expression dates from the 1950s.

***That Was the Week That Was.*** British television's first satirical show, screened by the BBC from 1962 to 1963. *TW3*, as it came to be known, was produced late on Saturday nights by Ned Sherrin and was characterized by a tone of irreverent informality. Features included revue sketches and songs, impromptu cartoons, and provocative monologues delivered from a high stool by Bernard Levin, who on one occasion was assaulted by an irate member of the audience. The presenter was David (now Sir David) Frost.

**Theatre-in-the-round.** A form of play presentation in which the audience is seated all round the acting area. It is one of the oldest forms of theatre but was revived in the 20th century as a conscious art form by those rebelling against the 'tyranny' of the proscenium arch, which can form a barrier between actors and audience. It was pioneered in the Soviet Union but then taken up elsewhere, some theatres being specifically designed for the purpose. *See also* the ROUND-HOUSE.

**Theatreland.** A term for the district of a city where its theatres are concentrated, applied in Britain particularly to a segment of the West End of London fanning eastwards from Shaftesbury Avenue across Leicester Square to Charing Cross Road and St Martin's Lane. This is where since the mid- to late 19th century the majority of the capital's commercial theatres have been concentrated. Local road signs now carry the sub-identification 'Theatreland'. In this sense the name was introduced by the *Daily Chronicle* in its issue of 28 December 1905.

**Theatre of Cruelty.** A term for plays in which the dramatist seeks to communicate a sense of pain, suffering and evil through the portrayal of extreme violence. The expression translates French *théâtre de la cruauté*, coined by the French poet, actor and director Antonin Artaud in his *Manifeste du théâtre de la cruauté* (1932). Artaud's theory was that theatre should not be simply entertainment but genuine action with real effects on the real world, a typical scenario being a police raid on a RED-LIGHT DISTRICT, with prostitutes being rounded up on the streets and flushed out of brothels. All the ingredients of the genre are here, including not just violence but sexuality, social taboos and the eruption of dramatic action outside the safe confines of the stage.

**Theatre of the Absurd.** A term for a type of mainly French theatre portraying the futility and anguish of an individual's struggle in a meaningless and inexplicable world. '*L'absurde*' arose as Albert Camus's designation for the situation of modern humanity, a stranger in an inhuman universe. Samuel Beckett's play WAITING FOR GODOT (1955) typifies the genre and introduced the term to the public at large. It was seized on by journalists, who unfortunately confused it with the everyday sense of the word as applied

to something outrageously comic. Other leading French absurdist dramatists are Arthur Adamov (1908–70), Eugène Ionesco (1912–94) and Jean Genet (1910–86), while the US theatre has Edward Albee (b.1928) and the British stage Harold Pinter (b.1930). A key study of the subject was Martin Esslin's *Theatre of the Absurd* (1961). *See also The* BALD PRIMA DONNA; RHINOCEROS.

**Thé dansant.** (French, 'tea dancing'.) An afternoon tea party with dancing. Such genteel entertainments were popular in the 1920s and 1930s.

> How restful to putt, when the strains of a band
> Announced a *thé dansant* was on at the Grand.
> JOHN BETJEMAN: *New Bats in Old Belfries*, 'Margate, 1940' (1945)

***Thelma and Louise.*** *See* ROAD MOVIE.

**Them and us.** *See* 'THEY'.

**Theme music.** A recurrent musical melody in a film, play or musical, often heard at the beginning of the work as a foretaste and serving as a final reprise at the end. It may relate to a specific character or place, as 'Tara's Theme' in Victor Fleming's film GONE WITH THE WIND (1939), 'The Harry Lime Theme' in Carol Reed's film *The* THIRD MAN (1949) and 'Lara's Theme' in David Lean's film DOCTOR ZHIVAGO (1965). *See also* SIGNATURE TUNE.

**Theme park.** An amusement park organized around a unifying idea ('theme') or group of ideas. The concept is American in origin and dates from the 1960s, taking its cue from DISNEYLAND. The realization first became popular in Europe in the 1980s. Most theme parks have a ROLLER COASTER as a leading attraction. The film JURASSIC PARK (1993) tells of the ordeal of a group of visitors in a theme park where the main attractions are genetically engineered dinosaurs.

**There is no such thing as society.** An infamous statement by Margaret Thatcher (the IRON LADY), in *Women's Own* (31 October 1987). She continued:

> There are individual men and women, and there are families. And no government can do anything except through people, and people must look to themselves first. It's our duty to look after ourselves and then to look after our neighbour.

In an attempt to bury THATCHERISM, David Cameron (*see* BOY DAVID), after his election to the Conservative Party leadership in December 2005, declared:

> There is such a thing as society. It's just not the same thing as the state.
> Quoted in *The Observer* (11 December 2005)

**There you go.** Here you are. A phrase used when giving a person something, as change from a purchase. The suggestion is that you take it and go off with it. The expression is also used, as if with a sigh of resignation, to signify fatalistic regret over something that has gone wrong. In the form 'There you go again' it can imply exasperation with one's interlocutor. In this sense it was a key weapon in the debating armoury of Ronald Reagan (the GREAT COMMUNI-CATOR), who in a televised debate with Jimmy Carter in the 1980 presidential election countered Carter's masterly deployment of facts and figures with a repeated 'There you go again.' It was the same story in the 1984 election, this time confronted with Walter Mondale's criticism of Reagan's VOODOO ECONOMICS:

> You know, I wasn't going to say this at all, but I can't help it
> – There you go again.

**Thermolactyl.** *See* DAMART.

**These islands.** A purposely vague term that came into use towards the end of the 20th century to refer to the archipelago consisting of Britain, Ireland and their associated islands and islets. Its traditional designation, 'the British Isles', has proved increasingly irksome to the Irish (who have sometimes suggested 'the Hibernian Archipelago' instead). Alternatives widely favoured in academic circles, 'the Atlantic Isles' or 'the North Atlantic Archipelago', have made little headway in general usage.

**'They'.** Those in authority, especially when seen as faceless and oppressive. The quotation marks emphasize their remoteness and express the speaker's implied criticism or resentment.

> This time 'they' may have gone too far. 'They' are putting the price of petrol up to £3.35 a gallon.
>
> FAY WELDON: in *Sunday Times* (22 August 1999)

The contrast with those over whom 'they' have authority is encapsulated in the phrase 'them and us', first recorded in 1948.

**They fuck you up, your mum and dad.** The opening line of a rather late (1974) but not untypically misanthropic poem, 'This Be the Verse', by Philip Larkin, which, largely because of its demotic opening, was to become one of his most famous.

> They fuck you up, your mum and dad.
> They may not mean to, but they do.
> They fill you with the faults they had
> And add some extra, just for you.

**They shall grow not old.** The opening of the poem 'For the Fallen' (1914) by Laurence Binyon (1869–1943), spoken at many annual REMEMBRANCE DAY services around Britain.

> They shall grow not old, as we that are left grow old.
> Age shall not weary them, nor the years condemn.
> At the going down of the sun and in the morning
> We will remember them.

It is frequently misquoted as 'They shall not grow old'. *See also* FOR YOUR TOMORROW WE GAVE OUR TODAY.

**They shall not pass.** The English version of French *Ils ne passeront pas*, a slogan of the French army at the defence of VERDUN in 1916. The words are variously attributed to Marshal Pétain and General Robert Nivelle and are first recorded in slightly different form in the latter's Order of the Day (23 June 1916) to his troops at the height of battle: *Vous ne les laisserez pas passer!* ('You will not let them pass!'). The actual inscription on the Verdun medal is *On ne passe pas* ('No one passes'). The words were adopted in the Spanish form *No pasarán* as a Republican watchword in the Spanish Civil War (1936–9) and ended a radio speech of 19 July 1936 by Dolores Ibarruri (La Pasionaria) calling on the women of Spain to help defend the Republic.

**They Shoot Horses, Don't They?** A film (1969) adapted by James Poe and Robert E. Thompson from a novel of the same title (1935) by Horace McCoy that depicts the hardships suffered during the era of the GREAT DEPRESSION. The action revolves around a Chicago dance marathon where the prize is three meals a day and $1500 in cash. The title turns up in the script as the reply given when the drifter Robert, one of the dancers, is asked why he has murdered an opponent. It encapsulates the prevailing belief that when times are so hard there is little room for losers, who like horses with broken legs should be put out of their misery.

**They think it's all over.** Words spoken by the BBC television commentator Kenneth Wolstenholme in the closing seconds of the 1966 Wembley World Cup final, when England were leading West Germany by three goals to two. Wolstenholme's comment was prompted by the appearance on the pitch of England fans, who believed the match to be over. As he was speaking, the England forward Geoff Hurst scored a fourth goal for England, and Wolstenholme finished his sentence with the words 'it is now!' *They Think It's All Over* is also the title of an irreverent BBC Television sports quiz show, first screened in the 1990s (prior to which it was on the radio). *See also* PHANTOM GOAL.

**Thiefrow.** A nickname for London's HEATHROW Airport, from its reputation for lax security and lost or purloined luggage.

**Thiepval memorial.** The Memorial to the Missing of the

Battle of the SOMME, designed by Sir Edwin Lutyens (1869–1944) and constructed at Thiepval, northern France, in 1928–30. The battle of Thiepval Ridge, fought in September 1916, was one of the actions during the Somme offensive.

**THIGMOO.** A nickname for the British trade-union movement, being an acronym for 'this great movement of ours', a phrase used in many a speech.

**Things ain't what they used to be.** A phrase, now proverbial, that was originally the title of a 1941 song by Ted Persons. The phrase has also provided the title of songs and/or albums by jazzmen Duke Ellington, Johnny Hodges and McCoy Tyner, of a number of rap songs (e.g. by Mo B. Dick and Master P.), of a volume of musical memoirs (1987) by Al Young, and (Cockneyfied as *Fings Ain't What They Used T'Be*) of a musical (1959) by Lionel Bart.

**Things that go bump in the night.** Supernatural manifestations as a source of night-time terror. The phrase is part of the anonymous 'Cornish or West Country Litany' recorded in Francis T. Nettleinghame's *Polperro Proverbs and Others* (1926): 'From ghoulies and ghosties and long-leggety beasties / And things that go bump in the night, / Good Lord, deliver us!' The verse itself is obviously older than this but its precise date of origin remains uncertain.

**Thingy.** A shortening of 'thingummy' in vogue from the 1930s used to refer to a person or thing whose name one has forgotten, does not know, or prefers not to mention for some reason.

> Mick Jagger, Liz Hurley, Camilla Parker-Bowles and Tamara Thingy [Beckwith] were among the guests, which gives you some idea about the tone.
> *The Times* (27 November 1999)

**Think globally, act locally.** The slogan of FRIENDS OF THE EARTH, adopted *c*.1985.

**Thinking man's crumpet.** A nickname for the television presenter Joan Bakewell (b.1933), so ungallantly dubbed in the 1960s by the writer and broadcaster Frank Muir, implying an appeal both intellectual and sexual. The formula caught on, so that the film actor Peter Coyote (b.1942) was referred to in *The Observer* (13 September 1987) as 'the thinking woman's West Coast crumpet', while the same newspaper, in its issue of 29 January 1998, described the youthful-looking television presenter Nick Ross (b.1947) as 'the thinking woman's newspaper boy'.

**Think on one's feet.** To react to a situation quickly and effectively, without prior planning. Much thinking is done in a leisurely way while seated, but here one thinks while

working or walking. The expression dates from the 1930s and is often found in the world of business and commerce.

**Think-tank.** A popular term for a group of people with specialized knowledge and ability, set up to carry out research into particular problems (usually social, political and technological) and to provide ideas and possible solutions. The expression is of US origin and arose in the mid-20th century, although 50 years earlier it was already current to mean a brain. Many think-tanks have a political purpose. UK examples include the Adam Smith Institute (right of centre) and the Fabian Society (left of centre). Think-tanks are thus often the breeding ground of POLICY WONKS.

> We propose things which people regard as on the edge of lunacy. The next thing you know, they're on the edge of policy.
> MADSEN PIRIE (president of the Adam Smith Institute): quoted in *The Guardian* (10 May 2005)

**Think the unthinkable.** To give serious consideration to possibilities, courses of action, etc. that hitherto had appeared too fanciful, idealistic, difficult, distressing, etc. to be worthy of it. In 1997, Tony Blair famously appointed Frank Field to a ministerial post to 'think the unthinkable' about welfare reform (i.e. to come up with completely new and possibly uncomfortable solutions to the politically sensitive problem of updating Britain's social-security system); his thoughts proved too unthinkable, and he left his post in 1998.

> What does a president do if he believes a war is just and necessary, but the people come to believe it is the wrong war, in the wrong place, at the wrong time, with the wrong enemy? We are not at that point yet, but we are getting there. And President Bush had best begin to think the unthinkable.
> PAT BUCHANAN: on www.antiwar.com (19 April 2004)

***Thin Man, The.*** A comedy mystery film (1934), starring William Powell and Myrna Loy as the ever-bantering and happily tippling husband-and-wife sleuth team Nick and Nora Charles, who, with the aid of their wire-haired terrier Asta, investigate the disappearance of the tall, eccentric inventor Clyde Wynant (Edward Ellis), who is the 'Thin Man' of the title. The screenwriters Albert Hackett and Frances Goodrich based their sparkling script on the novel *The Thin Man* (1932) by Dashiell Hammet (1894–1961), who is said to have based the wisecracking and mutual teasing of Nick and Nora on his own relationship with the playwright Lillian Hellman (1905–84). There were several more *Thin Man* films, generally less successful than the first.

**Third age.** Old age, regarded positively as an opportunity for travel, further education and the like. The expression translates French *troisième âge*, and was first current in Britain after 1983, when the University of the Third Age (U3A), founded in France 10 years earlier, was established to provide learning opportunities for retired people.

> 'Third Agers' will soon be so large a proportion of the population that they will exert huge influence on everything from politics to TV schedules.
>
> *The Times* (23 July 1999)

**Third Man, The.** A thriller (1950) by Graham Greene (1904–91) from his own script for the stylish film (1949), directed by Carol Reed. Set in postwar Vienna, it concerns a US writer who arrives to stay with his friend, Harry LIME, only to discover that Lime has apparently been murdered. His chauffeur was driving the car that ran him down, and his doctor was on the scene. According to a witness, however, a third man was there when the body was moved. There are plots and a romantic sub-plot. The book has a happy outcome, and the film's ending is both poignant and scenic. In the film Lime was played by Orson Welles, who also contributed some of the dialogue. The film was influenced by the FILM NOIR, and one of its many memorable features was its atmospheric musical score performed on the zither by the Viennese composer/performer Anton Karas, which became know as 'The Harry Lime Theme'. The title 'the third man' was aped by the press in the early 1960s during the BURGESS AND MACLEAN spy scandal, in the course of which Kim Philby was thus identified.

**Third Programme.** The uncompromisingly highbrow service of broadcast speech and music introduced by the BBC in September 1946 and so named as the third station after the HOME SERVICE and LIGHT PROGRAMME. It initially went out in the evenings only but in 1953 began broadcasting at 3 p.m. on Sundays. Other services such as Network Three and the Music Programme were subsequently added to the frequency, diminishing its impact, and in 1967 they all combined under the umbrella title of Radio 3. The Third Programme kept a separate editorial team until 1970, however, when it was absorbed into its new Radio 3 parent, the less esoteric parts of its speech output going to Radio 4. Whatever its designation it has always had a very tiny audience, some 2 per cent of the total, although Radio 3 controllers have latterly striven to make the service more 'listener-friendly'.

**Third Reich.** The German state under the rule of Hitler and the NAZI Party (1933–45). The term was adopted from the title of Arthur Moeller van den Bruck's cultural study of Germany, *Das Dritte Reich* ('The Third Empire') (1923). In

terms of German history the 'First Reich' was the Holy Roman Empire and the 'Second Reich' that under the Hohenzollern emperors (1871–1918). *See also* THOUSAND-YEAR REICH.

**Third wave.** A term coined in the early 1980s by the US futurist Alvin Toffler (b.1928) to denote the age of information technology, as a development of the agrarian first wave and the industrial second wave.

**Third way.** A 'middle way' between the political left and right, especially as evolving through the moral, social or economic failure of either of these. The expression came to be particularly associated with the NEW LABOUR policies of Tony Blair after the 1997 general election. However, there were many 'third ways' long before this. Examples may be found in the FASCISM of the 1920s, in Harold Macmillan's 'capitalism with a human face' in the 1930s, in the path between capitalism and communism sought by the Socialist International in the 1950s, in the German GREEN PARTY in the 1970s, and in the Swedish Social Democrats in the 1980s. Tony Blair's 'third way' followed two decades of THATCHERISM on the one hand and the collapse of communism on the other. *See also* BLATCHERISM.

**Third wheel.** An unwanted or superfluous person, often on the principle that 'two's company, three's a crowd'. Such a person is as desirable as a third wheel on a bicycle.

**Third World.** (French *tiers monde*.) An expression coined in 1952 by the French demographer Alfred Sauvy (1898–1990), when he compared the developing countries of Asia, Africa and Latin America to the pre-Revolutionary Third Estate (the bourgeoisie and working class) in France. The term was subsequently applied to these same countries regarded as distinct from the capitalist ('first') world and communist ('second') world. Sauvy's thesis was that 'the third world is nothing, but wants to be something'.

**Third World War.** The war that it was feared would break out between the United States and its NATO allies and the USSR and its WARSAW PACT allies as a result of the tensions of the COLD WAR. The term, first used in the late 1940s, is still used to refer to any hypothetical future global conflict, and is also used figuratively to describe a scene of extreme violence or mayhem.

**38th parallel.** *See* KOREAN WAR.

**Thirty-Nine Steps, The.** A thriller (1915) by John Buchan (1875–1940), later, as Lord Tweedsmuir, governor general of Canada (1935–40). Defined by Buchan himself as a 'shocker' and written while its author recovered from illness, it was originally to have been called 'The Black Stone'. It is a picaresque story of a chase and marks the introduction of the character Richard Hannay, who reappears in other novels by Buchan. Against a background of German spy scares, Hannay has to prove his innocence when charged with murder as he is pursued by both the police and foreign spies the length and breadth of Britain. The resolution of the plot turns on Hannay's recognizing that a cryptic message about 'the thirty-nine steps' must refer to a set of steps down to the sea at a coastal town. Richard Hannay has been played by three different actors in film versions of the novel: Robert Donat in 1935, Kenneth More in 1959 and Robert Powell in 1978. The 1935 version was directed by Alfred Hitchcock, and the 1978 version was the first to be set in the correct EDWARDIAN ERA of Buchan's novel, and has a memorable scene in which Hannay clings to the clock hands of Big Ben in order to stop the detonation of a bomb. The site of the 'thirty-nine steps' themselves is a genuine one in Kent, on the low cliffs not far from Broadstairs (whose own name means 'broad steps'). *See also* FIRST LINES OF NOVELS; GREENMANTLE; MR STANDFAST.

**Thirty-something.** In one's 30s, an age when aims and ambitions crystallize and relationships 'make or break'. The expression was popularized by a US television series so titled, which from 1989 to 1992 recounted the stories of the family lives of a group of baby boomers (*see* BABY BOOM). The second part of the term is freely attached to any age decade:

> I have tea with some women from Shrewsbury, one in her eighties … 'He's just got it, Cameron, hasn't he?' the eighty-something tells me. 'Davis reminds me of an oily used-car salesman.'
>
> *The Observer* (9 October 2005)

*See also* TWENTY-SOMETHING.

**30-year rule.** The rule in Britain that public records may be open to public inspection after a lapse of 30 years. The rule, introduced by the Public Records Act 1967, allowed a fresh batch of material to become available at the Public Record Office (PRO, now subsumed into the National Archives at Kew) on the first working day in each January. Some papers are regarded as too sensitive even for this delay and are subject to a longer restriction. A similar 50-year rule was earlier in force for much of the 20th century.

The Freedom of Information Act 2000 replaced many of the provisions of the 30-year rule, with some exemptions (e.g. for the intelligence services).

**This House will in no circumstances fight for its King or Country.** A motion debated at the Oxford Union on 9 February 1933, and carried by 275 votes to 153. The motion was drafted by D.M. Graham, librarian of the Union at the

time, and it reflected the wave of pacifist sentiment that swept the country following the slaughter of the First World War. Opinions are divided as to whether the carrying of the motion encouraged Hitler (who had just come to power) in his territorial ambitions, but it seems unlikely that it played a significant role.

**This is London calling.** The call sign of BBC Radio from the 1920s, and through the Second World War, when the US journalist Ed Murrow began his famous radio reports for CBS with the line 'This … is … London', including his trademark pauses. *London Calling* was the name of a 1979 album by the British PUNK band The Clash.

**This is Not a Pipe.** *See* CECI N'EST PAS UNE PIPE.

**This is Spinal Tap.** A spoof documentary (1984) written by Christopher Guest, Michael McKean, Harry Shearer and Rob Reiner about an ageing British HEAVY METAL band on a disastrous tour of the United States. The accuracy of this satire about the rock business fooled many into thinking that Spinal Tap was a real rock group. The wheel turned full circle when the band actually conducted a US tour with their second album *Break Like the Wind* in the early 1990s.

**This is the end.** The opening line of the doom-laden 1967 song 'The End' by the US rock group The Doors, and sung by Jim Morrison (1943–71):

> This is the end
> Beautiful friend
> This is the end
> My only friend, the end.

While most bands were celebrating the SUMMER OF LOVE, The Doors were exploring the dark flip side of the AMERICAN DREAM. In the lyrics of 'The End' (described by one critic as 'an 11-minute Oedipal drama') a father is killed and a mother 'fucked'.

The song was used to great effect on the soundtrack of another Oedipal masterpiece, APOCALYPSE NOW.

**This is where we came in.** We have come full circle; we are back where we started. The expression dates from the 1940s and refers to the former type of continuous cinema performance where one could enter at any point in the film and stay until the same point was reached in the next showing.

**This is Your Life.** A long-running series of television programmes first broadcast in 1951 in each of which an unsuspecting victim, often but not exclusively a celebrity, is ambushed by the presenter in disguise and presented with a big red book encapsulating their life. They are then taken back to the studio to be faced with an unexpected succession of people from their often distant past. The programmes, combining sentiment and embarrassment in equal measure, were presented engagingly by Eamonn Andrews until his death in 1987, when Michael Aspel assumed his mantle.

**'This Ole House'.** A jaunty, country-influenced song released in 1954, written by Stuart Hamblen and performed by Rosemary Clooney (the aunt of former ER-turned-Hollywood-heartthrob George Clooney). The poignant inspiration for the song came from Hamblen's discovery, in the backwoods of rural Texas, of a deserted hut containing, along with heaps of broken furniture, the dead body of an old man. The song describes how the house might have been during the last stages of the old man's life. A version of the song was released, successfully, by Shakin' Stevens in Britain in 1981.

***This Sporting Life.*** The first novel (1960) by David Storey (b.1933). Rugby league football, which Storey played as a professional for Leeds, is the background of a story in which the conflict is between working-class origins and modern aspirations. That the title is intended ironically is revealed at the end of the book, when Arthur Machin, who has seen the game as a means to attain social position, realizes that it is only one facet of life. A moving film version (1963) was directed by Lindsay Anderson, with Richard Harris and Rachel Roberts in leading roles.

***Thomas the Tank Engine.*** One of the 26 highly popular picture books in the 'Railway Series' for children by the Rev. W. Awdry (1911–97), begun in the 1940s and continued by Awdry's son Christopher from the 1980s. The stories are set on the imaginary British island of Sodor. Other titles in the series included *The Three Railway Engines* (1945), *James, the Red Engine* (1947) and *Tank Engine Thomas Again* (1948). Thomas, a shunting engine, is bossed about by the FAT CONTROLLER and attracts the disdain of other larger locomotives such as Gordon, the Big Engine, but eventually acquires his own branch line. He is, after all, 'a Really Useful Engine'. The series spawned a mass of franchised merchandise, a feature film and a TV series narrated by the ex-Beatle Ringo Starr.

**Thommo.** The Australian cricketer Jeff Thomson (b.1950) who, with fellow fast bowler Dennis Lillee (b.1949), formed one of the most feared fast-bowling attacks in test cricket history. Their contribution to Australia's defeat of England in the 1974–5 Ashes series in Australia gave birth to the rhyme:

> Ashes to ashes, dust to dust –
> If Lillee don't get ya, Thommo must.
> *Sydney Telegraph* (1975)

**Thoughtcrime.** *See* NEWSPEAK.

**Thought for the Day.** A brief daily religious programme on BBC Radio 4 first broadcast in 1970, in which the speaker has three minutes to 'reflect on the events of the day from a perspective of faith'. Most of the regular speakers have been Christian, but Jewish speakers have also been heard (notably Rabbi Lionel Blue, a frequent contributor) and less often those of other faiths. Prince Charles used the programme in 1995 to reflect on the 50th anniversary of VE DAY, and again on 1 January 2000 to consider the new MILLENNIUM.

**Thousand-bomber raids.** A name for the massive night-time bombing raids carried out by the RAF against German cities in the Second World War. The first such raid, Operation Millennium, took place on 30 May 1942, and the target was Cologne.

**Thousand days.** A term used by former members of his administration to refer to the period that President Kennedy held office (20 January 1961–22 November 1963). The phrase echoed President Roosevelt's HUNDRED DAYS and also suggested the tragic brevity and lost promise of the CAMELOT era. The phrase occurs in the title of Arthur Schlesinger's Pulitzer-winning inside account of the administration, *A Thousand Days: John F. Kennedy in the White House* (1965). *See also* JFK.

**Thousand island dressing.** A pink mayonnaise-based salad dressing flavoured with tomatoes, chilli, green peppers and the like. The name alludes to the multitude of ingredients and dates from the early 20th century, apparently being adopted from the Thousand Islands, a group of almost 2000 small islands in the St Lawrence River between the United States and Canada.

**Thousand-yard stare.** A syndrome suffered by shell-shocked soldiers returning from the First World War, who were unable to focus on their immediate surroundings. It has since been applied to soldiers in other wars. The war artist Tom Lea, working for *Life* magazine in the Pacific during the Second World War, painted a portrait of a US Marine entitled *The Two Thousand Yard Stare*. On 15 May 1967 photojournalist Frank Johnston found himself under heavy enemy fire in Nha Tho An Hoa, Vietnam:

> I looked up and saw a Marine with what they call the thousand-yard stare, and I lifted my Leica and snapped his picture. The soldier's gaze never left my lens.

The next day the resulting photograph was splashed across the front pages of papers across the United States.

**Thousand-Year Reich.** Hitler's somewhat inaccurate description of his THIRD REICH, which, as it turned out, only managed to last a dozen years (1933–45).

**Three-Cornered Hat, The.** The popular ballet by Manuel de Falla (1876–1946) was based on a short novel, *El sombrero de tres picos* (1874), by Pedro de Alarcón. Alarcón's story satirizes the *corregidores*, the Spanish government officials or magistrates, often regarded as overbearing and prone to intrigue. Falla's first version of the music was in the form of a pantomime entitled *El corregidor y la molinera* ('The Magistrate and the Miller's Wife'), which was first performed in 1917. The ballet version with the present title was first staged by Diaghilev's BALLETS RUSSES in 1919, with choreography by Leonide Massine and costume designs by Pablo Picasso. Alarcón's story also forms the basis of the 1895 opera *Der Corregidor* by Hugo Wolf (1860–1903).

**Three-day event.** A horse-riding contest held over three days, originating in 1949 at Badminton House, the seat of the Duke of Beaufort in Gloucestershire. The first day is devoted to dressage, the second to cross-country riding and the third to show-jumping. The major annual contests in the UK are the Burghley Horse Trials, near Stamford, Lincolnshire, the Badminton Horse Trials in Gloucestershire, and the British Open Horse Trials at Gatcombe Park, near Stroud, Gloucestershire.

**Three-day week.** The economic crisis of 1973 in Britain caused by labour disputes. It involved the coal mines, railways and power stations, and industry and commerce were restricted to three days' electricity consumption a week, obliging all television services to close at 10.30 p.m. The energy minister Patrick Jenkin famously advised the public that they could clean their teeth in the dark. The three-day week resulted in two general elections in 1974, both won by Labour with a narrow majority.

**Three Graces, The.** *See* TITANIC.

**Three Graces of Liverpool, The.** The three fine Edwardian buildings on the Pier Head at Liverpool: the Port of Liverpool Building (1907), the Royal Liver Exchange Building (1911) and the Cunard Building (1916). It was planned to add a fourth Grace, a futuristic building called The Cloud, a 10-storey irregular globe designed by Will Alsop, which was to function as an exhibition space and conference centre. The project was scrapped in July 2004.

**3HO.** A form of Sikhism practised mainly in North America. It was founded in 1969 by the Indian Sikh Yogi Bhajan and sometimes incorporates elements of yoga and vegetarianism. Full-time members of the group, who are almost always young Westerners, and often former HIPPIES, are readily distinguished by their traditional Sikh dress. The basic ideals of Sikhism are followed, so that only natural, pure foods are eaten, drugs and alcohol are banned, and males do not cut their hair. The name itself is an abbreviation of 'Happy, Healthy and Holy Organization'.

**Three-Martini lunch.** A term suggestive of the alcohol-fuelled US business lunches of the 1950s and 1960s, in the days before health-conscious executives learned to love water. The Martini in question was of course the cocktail of that name, an apparently simple marriage of gin and dry vermouth (aficionados who agonize over precise proportions, the validity of an olive, to stir or to shake, etc., would of course argue about 'simple'). The higher the gin-ratio, the more it is entitled to be called a 'dry martini'. It appears originally (in the early 1880s) to have been called a 'Martinez cocktail', after the town of that name in California, but this soon changed to 'Martini', presumably under the influence of the brand of Italian vermouth produced by the firm of Martini and Rossi (their name was registered as a trademark in the United States in 1882).

**Three Mile Island.** An island in the Susquehanna River near Harrisburg, Pennsylvania, that was the scene of the most serious accident in the history of the US nuclear power industry. At 4 a.m. on 28 March 1979 a valve in the nuclear reactor of the power station closed in error, blocking the water supply to the main feedwater system and causing the reactor core to shut down. This was an automatic procedure that itself caused no hazard, but a series of equipment and instrument malfunctions, combined with human errors and mistaken decisions, led to a serious loss of water coolant from the reactor core. As a result the core was partially exposed and a quantity of hydrogen gas escaped into the reactor building. Though having negligible health consequences, the incident had profound effects on the US nuclear power industry, resulting in the closure of seven similar reactors and increased public fears about the safety of nuclear reactors in general. Coincidentally, 1979 also witnessed the release of *The* CHINA SYNDROME, a film in which an operational flaw in a nuclear power station is covered up by the authorities.

**Threepenny Opera, The.** The best known of the collaborations of the playwright Bertolt Brecht (1898–1956) and the composer Kurt Weill (1900–50). It was first performed in 1928. *Der Dreigroschenoper* (to give its German title) is a modern version of John Gay's *The Beggar's Opera* (1728), the biggest musical hit of 18th-century London, and is set in the criminal underworld of Soho at the beginning of the 20th century. The German text of *The Threepenny Opera* is based on a translation of Gay by Gerhart Hauptmann, and some of the lyrics are drawn from Rudyard Kipling and from François Villon (the 15th-century criminal-poet). One of the best-known songs is 'Mack the Knife', the name given by Brecht to Gay's original character, Macheath. *See also* MAC THE KNIFE.

**Three Stooges.** Three US knockabout comedians who appeared in hundreds of short films from the 1930s. They were Larry Fine (1911–75), Moe Howard (1895–1975) and Moe's brother Jerry (Curly) Howard (1906–52). In 1947 Curly was replaced by another brother, Shemp Howard (Samuel Howard; 1891–1955). The form of slapstick they indulged in was peculiarly violent.

**Three strikes and you're out.** A popular term for a law in the United States whereby a person convicted of three serious felonies is subject to mandatory life imprisonment. The phrase, often shortened to 'three strikes', is from baseball, in which a batter who has had three strikes, or three successive opportunities of hitting a fairly pitched ball without doing so, is out.

**Three Studies at the Base of a Crucifixion.** The unsettling painting (1944) with which Francis Bacon (1909–92) first came to prominence. The canvas displays disturbingly contorted grey figures against a harsh orange background. 'I deform and dislocate people into appearance; or hope to … I don't think of it as horror. I think of it as life,' said Bacon.

**Three Tenors, The.** A collective label for Luciano Pavarotti, José Carreras and Placido Domingo, who first performed together under this banner at a charity gala in Rome in 1990, on the eve of the World Cup final. They have subsequently performed during other World Cup finals (Los Angeles 1994, Paris 1998, Yokohama 2002), and at various other venues. A recording of the Three Tenors became the best-selling classical album of all time. Their repertoire includes 'lollipops' from Puccini, Verdi and Donizetti, numbers from Broadway musicals, and various pop songs.

A British singing ensemble has followed the pattern in calling itself Four Poofs and a Piano.

**Three Ws.** The collective nickname given to the Barbados and West Indies cricketers Sir Frank Worrell (1924–67), Sir Everton Weekes (b.1925) and Sir Clyde Walcott (b.1926), all of whom were successful batsmen in the West Indies sides of the 1950s.

**Thriller in Manila.** A rhyming nickname given to the epic heavyweight boxing bout fought on 1 October 1975 in Manila, capital of the Philippines, between Joe Frazier and Muhammad Ali and won by the latter. *See also* RUMBLE IN THE JUNGLE.

**Thrills and spills.** The excitement of a dangerous sport or entertainment, especially as experienced by spectators. The 'spills' are the mishaps and accidents and possibly even deaths. (The original meaning of 'to spill' was in fact 'to kill', from Old English *spillan*.)

**Throw a curve.** To surprise or outwit someone; to act unexpectedly. An Americanism from baseball, in which a pitcher tries to fool the batter by means of a curve ball, i.e. one delivered with sufficient spin to make it deviate from its expected path.

**Throw a wobbly.** To display a fit of temper; to panic. The latter word relates to the person's uncontrolled deviation from the norm. The expression dates from the 1960s.

**Throw one's toys out of the pram.** In colloquial British English, to lose one's temper spectacularly; to have a tantrum (as a baby in a pram might).

> So you're saying I can't have an opinion? If I said the same to you, you'd cry blue murder and throw your toys out of the pram.
> www.dvdtimes.co.uk (8 August 2005)

**Throw one's weight about.** To act arrogantly or aggressively, as if adding physical weight to any authority one has. The expression dates from the early 20th century.

**Throw someone in at the deep end.** To plunge them straight into a task or undertaking without any previous experience of it. The analogy is with a novice swimmer thrown in at the deep end of a swimming pool on a 'sink or swim' basis. The expression dates from the 1970s.

**Throw someone to the wolves.** To sacrifice a subordinate, friend or colleague in order to avert danger or difficulties for oneself. The allusion is probably to stories of wolves in a pack pursuing travellers in a horse-drawn sleigh, one of whom to check the horde pushes a fellow-passenger off the vehicle. The expression dates from the 1920s.

**Throw the baby out with the bathwater.** To discard or reject what is essential or valuable along with the inessential or useless. The vivid expression dates from the turn of the 20th century and has its equivalent in German *das Kind mit dem Bade ausschütten*.

**Throw the book at someone.** To charge them with a particular offence; to inflict a severe punishment on them. The 'book' is an imaginary book of rules or of offences and their prescribed penalties. The expression dates from the 1930s and is of US origin.

**Thumb a lift.** To ask for or 'scrounge' a ride from a passing vehicle by holding out the hand with the thumb pointing in the direction of intended travel. The phrase and the practice are of US origin and date from the 1930s.

**Thumb index.** A series of rounded notches or indentations cut in the pages of a book showing initial letters or other particulars to enable the reader to find a reference easily. The device dates from the turn of the 20th century and in its issue for July 1903 *The Periodical* described the newly published *Oxford Thumb-Index Bible* as 'the latest novelty'.

**Thumper.** A nickname of the Labour politician John Prescott (b.1938), deputy prime minister from 1997. The allusion is not so much to his heavy figure and forceful manner but more subtly to Thumper, the rabbit in Walt Disney's cartoon film *Bambi* (1928), as a close colleague of Tony Blair, known as BAMBI. The nickname acquired an unexpected relevance during the general election campaign of 2001, when Prescott – infuriated at being struck by an egg thrown at point-blank range by a protester – landed a well-aimed punch on his assailant, with whom he then become entangled in an unseemly brawl. *See also* TWO JAGS.

**Thunderbirds.** A series of puppet films televised from 1965 to 1966 and depicting the explosive missions of the family-based members of International Rescue. The main characters are Jeff Tracey and his five sons, Scott (pilot of Thunderbird 1), Virgil (Thunderbird 2), Alan (Thunderbird 3), Gordon (co-pilot of Thunderbird 2, pilot of Thunderbird 4 for underwater work), and John (Thunderbird 5 space satellite), together with the blonde London agent Lady Penelope and her chauffeur Parker (catchphrase: 'yes m'lady'). The series, intended for children but annexed as cult adult viewing, was created by Gerry and Sylvia Anderson using their 'supermarionation' technique.

**Thunder-thighs.** A nickname for an overweight person, who has heavy thighs. The suggestion is that they cause the person's steps to crash like thunder, or more vividly that their ponderous rubbing together when walking resembles the collision of clouds, as the popular cause of thunder. The name was at one time applied, before she slimmed, to Christina Onassis (1951–88), daughter of the Greek millionaire ship-owner Aristotle Onassis (1906–75).

**Tiananmen Square.** One of the largest squares in the world, situated in the centre of Beijing and famous as the site of pro-democracy demonstrations in May– June 1989, which were brutally suppressed by the Chinese authorities. The square takes its name from the Tiananmen ('Gate of Heavenly Peace') at the northern end of the square, which was once the entrance to the Imperial Palace. The pro-democracy movement had first come to the fore in April at the funeral of Hu Yaobang, who in 1987 had been forced to resign as secretary general of the Chinese Communist Party following student demonstrations demanding reform. At one point in May 1989 there were over a million demonstrators in Tiananmen Square, and many students established themselves there permanently. However, on 3–4 June tanks and troops entered the square, killing hundreds of demonstrators, and a period of harsh repression followed throughout China. The massacre and subsequent events were condemned by the international community.

**Tib and fib.** Medical jargon for a compound fracture of the tibia and fibula, or for a person who has suffered this. *See also* MEDICAL ABBREVIATIONS.

**Tibbs, Virgil.** *See* IN THE HEAT OF THE NIGHT.

**Tiber foaming with much blood.** *See* RIVER TIBER FOAMING WITH MUCH BLOOD.

**Tickety-boo.** In good order; all right. The phrase, now somewhat dated, goes back to at least the 1930s and may be an elaboration of 'that's the ticket'. A putative source in Hindi *thik hai babu*, 'It's all right, sir', seems rather contrived.

**Tickled pink.** Highly amused. A tickled person goes red in the face. The phrase dates from the 1920s.

**Tickle the dragon's tail.** To undertake something dangerous or hazardous.

**Tickle the ivories.** To play the piano, especially idly or lightly. The allusion is to the ivory keys. The phrase dates from the 1940s.

**Tie-in.** A book, film or other product produced to take commercial advantage of a related work in another medium. A common example is the 'book of the film' as an antithesis to the established 'film of the book'. Some cult films or film series, such as STAR WARS and STAR TREK, generate a plethora of books, games, toys, models and artefacts of all kinds. *See also* AS SEEN ON TV.

**Tiger, The.** A nickname of Georges Clemenceau (1841–1929), radical prime minister of France (1906–9, 1917–20). Prior to his return to the premiership he was a strident critic of successive French governments over their conduct of the First World War. He came to power in November 1917 at a time when France was polarized in its attitudes to the war in the wake of the disastrous 1917 spring offensive (*see* CHEMIN DES DAMES) and the subsequent mutinies in the French army. Clemenceau advocated 'war to the end', suppressed dissent and pacifist literature, and put several leading politicians on trial for treason. He insisted that the French army pursue a strategy of attack, and at the Paris Peace Conference was fierce in his demands of the defeated Germany, although the resulting TREATY OF VERSAILLES was not fierce enough for many in France. *See also* SPORTING NICKNAMES.

**Tiger in one's tank.** Energy; vitality; 'go'. The phrase comes from an advertising slogan of 1965 by the Esso Petroleum Co.: 'Put a tiger in your tank.' The words were made more memorable by the accompanying drawing of a pouncing tiger.

**Tiger Tim.** The mild little cartoon tiger, leader of the Bruin Boys, first appeared in the *Daily Mirror* in 1904 as the creation of the artist Julius Stafford Baker. For many years he and his chums appeared in the children's weekly comic *Rainbow* and subsequently in *Jack and Jill*, as well as various annuals. The name has also been used, not without a certain irony, as a nickname of the British tennis player Tim Henman (b.1974).

**Tigger.** The toy tiger that, with WINNIE-THE-POOH, is one of the animal friends of CHRISTOPHER ROBIN in the children's stories by A.A. Milne. He makes his first appearance in *The House at Pooh Corner* (1928), in which three of the ten stories concern him. He suddenly shows up in the forest as 'a Very Bouncy Animal, with a way of saying How-do-you-do, which always left your ears full of sand'.

**Tight ship.** Literally a ship in which ropes, rigging and so on are tied and taut and ready for use, hence a strictly run ship. The expression is mostly used figuratively, as: 'He runs a tight ship.'

**Tiki bar.** A bar on a beach in the style of such a bar on one of the tropical islands of the South Pacific. The term comes from the Californian tourist industry. A tiki is an image of a human figure in the form of a small greenstone ornament. The word is of Maori origin.

**Till Death Us Do Part.** *See* Alf GARNETT.

**Till hell freezes over.** Forever; endlessly. Hell will never freeze over. The expression dates from the early 20th century.

**Tim.** A Scottish Protestant nickname for a Roman Catholic, especially one who supports Glasgow Celtic football club. The name is simply the pet form of Timothy. *See also* TAIG.

**Time and Tide.** An influential British news magazine founded by Lady Rhonnda in 1920. It continued to publish until 1979. The title came from the old proverb (traced back to the 14th century), 'Time and tide wait for no man.' *Time and Tide* is also a novel (1992) by Edna O'Brien.

**Time for a Little Something.** A phrase used by WINNIE-THE-POOH when his craving for honey gets the better of him. The words are often heard on the lips of those who need a literary justification for their next visit to the biscuit tin.

**Time of the month.** A common euphemism for a period of menstruation, a word itself implying 'month', from Latin *mensis*.

> Then, surprising herself as much as him, she drew back and away.
> 'I can't', she said.
> 'Time of the month?' he asked. 'I don't mind.' He didn't either, unlike Harry, whom menstruation made nervous.
> FAY WELDON: *The Heart of the Country* (1987)

**Time's arrow.** The notion of time travelling from past to future as if in a physical dimension. The expression was coined by the astronomer Arthur Eddington. Martin Amis's novel *Time's Arrow* (1991) ingeniously plays with the concept.

> Let us draw an arrow arbitrarily. If as we follow the arrow we find more and more of the random element in the world, then the arrow is pointing towards the future; if the random element decreases the arrow points towards the past … I shall use the phrase 'time's arrow' to express this one-way property of time which has no analogue in space.
> ARTHUR EDDINGTON: *The Nature of the Physical World* (1928)

**Time-share.** A property used as a holiday home for a fixed limited time each year. The term was adopted in the 1970s from computer jargon, in which 'time sharing' denoted simultaneous access to a central processor by more than one user.

**Times New Roman.** *See* GILL SANS.

**Times Square.** A New York City square famous as one of the world's major entertainment centres. It is located in midtown Manhattan at the intersection of 7th Avenue, 42ND STREET and Broadway (*see* GREAT WHITE WAY) and was originally known as Longacre Square, but was renamed in 1903 when the *New York Times* set up its offices nearby. When the site of the original offices of the London *Times* at Printing House Square, Blackfriars, was redeveloped in the 1990s the location was renamed Times Square, partly to commemorate the newspaper but partly also to attract US corporate clients. *See also The* CRICKET IN TIMES SQUARE.

**Times They Are a Changin', The.** A song and album by Bob Dylan, released in 1964. Its title refers both to the political change desired by 1960s radicals and also, possibly, to imminent changes in the direction of Dylan's music (the album is generally considered Dylan's last release as a purely folk artist). The song 'Only a Pawn in Their Game' makes reference to the assassination of the civil rights leader Medgar Evers (1925–63).

**Time warp.** An imaginary distortion of space in relation to time whereby people or objects of one period can be moved to another. The concept arose in the 1950s and originally applied to SCIENCE FICTION. The notion was later extended to anything 'out of time', especially a realistic 're-creation' or re-enactment of the past or the pristine preservation of a particular location.

> Duxford … has been preserved in a time warp. Douglas Bader served here and the old RAF station is still alive with the ghosts of pilots pitching up at the beautiful original brick and sash-window guard house in their wire-wheeled MGs.
> *The Times* (25 September 1999)

The 'Time Warp' was a dance in *The* ROCKY HORROR PICTURE SHOW.

**Tina.** A nickname for Margaret Thatcher (b.1925), Conservative prime minister from 1979 to 1990, as an acronym of 'There *is* *n*o *a*lternative'. The words became a popular encapsulation of her response when government cuts in public spending were opposed. Her actual words were:

> We have to get our production and our earnings in balance. There's no easy popularity in what we are proposing, but it is fundamentally sound. Yet I believe people accept there is no real alternative.
> MARGARET THATCHER: speech at Conservative Women's Conference (21 May 1980)

*See also* ATTILA THE HEN; LADY'S NOT FOR TURNING.

**Tin Drum, The.** The first novel (1962; in German as *Die Blechtrommel*, 1959) by Günter Grass (b.1927). It is the first of a picaresque trilogy, which begins in his native city of Langfuhr (Danzig) three years before he was born and reflects the growth of Nazism. The tin drum of the title is the metaphorical means whereby the dwarf Oskar Matzerath, from a mental hospital bed, 'drums up' experiences in his life. A film version (1979) was directed by Volker Schlöndorff. *See also* FIRST LINES OF NOVELS.

**Tin ear.** One who is tone deaf or unable to perceive subtleties in speech. Tin is a metal incapable of sensation. The phrase dates from the 1930s. *See also* CLOTH EARS.

**Tin fish.** Naval slang for a torpedo (which itself took its name from the fish known as the torpedo ray or electric ray).

**Tin hat.** A soldier's name for his protective metal helmet, dating from the turn of the 20th century. To 'put the tin hat' on something is to bring it to an abrupt and conclusive end.

**Tinker, Tailor, Soldier, Spy.** A spy thriller (1974) by John Le Carré (pen-name of David Cornwell; b.1931). It is the first of a trilogy in which the enigmatic spy-master George SMILEY closes in on his adversary, the Russian Karla. The title reflects the children's fortune-telling rhyme when counting cherry stones or other small objects: 'Tinker, Tailor, Soldier, Sailor, Rich man, Poor man, Beggarman, Thief.'

**Tin Lizzie.** An old car; a jalopy or 'banger'. The name was originally a US nickname for the highly popular Model T Ford, launched in 1908. It was so called as it was sturdy, dependable and black, like the traditional Southern servant, called Elizabeth. Many people believed the car was made of tin, hence the descriptive, although its body was in fact of heavier-gauge sheet metal. The Irish pop group Thin Lizzy, formed in 1969, took its name from a robot cartoon character called Tin Lizzie in the comic BEANO. The band respelled both words, pointing out that many Irish do not pronounce the 'h' in *th*.

**Tinny.** An Australian slang word for a can of beer, dating from the 1970s.

**Tin Pan Alley.** The district of New York, originally in the area of Broadway and 14th Street, where popular music is published. In London, Denmark Street, off Charing Cross Road, was so called as the centre of the popular music industry. The name probably derives from the 19th-century musicians' nickname 'tin pan' for an old tinny piano. The 'Alley' is now largely deserted by song writers and music publishers who have moved to bigger premises.

**Tinseltown.** HOLLYWOOD, so dubbed for its superficial glamour and meretricious allure. The nickname first became popular in the 1970s and is said to have originated in a derisive remark made by the actor and composer Oscar Levant in the 1940s.

> British talent takes Tinseltown by storm.
> *Daily Telegraph*, headline (23 March 1999)

**Tintin.** A cub reporter who is the main character of the comic strip stories by the Belgian artist Hergé (Georges Rémi; 1907–83). He has a constantly worried expression beneath his quiff of red hair, and is accompanied by his faithful dog, Milou (Snowy, in the English versions). He first appeared in 1929. His name relates to French slang *tintin*, 'nothing at all'. *See also* 'Thompson Twins' *under* ROCK GROUP NAMES.

**Tip and run raid.** A phrase used in the Second World War to denote a hurried and often indiscriminate air raid when the enemy sped homeward after jettisoning their bombs. Its origin is in the light-hearted form of cricket in which the batsman is forced to run every time he hits ('tips') the ball.

**Tip of the** or **an iceberg.** The small perceptible part of a much larger situation or problem that remains hidden. Six-sevenths of an iceberg remain unseen below the surface. The expression dates from the 1960s.

**Tip one's hand.** To reveal one's intentions inadvertently. The expression is of US origin and alludes to a hand of cards held in such a way that others can see them.

**Tipperary.** The perennially popular song 'It's a Long Way to Tipperary' is inseparably associated with the First World War. The music is credited to Jack Judge, of Oldbury, Birmingham, and the words to Harry Williams of Temple Balsall, Solihull. Judge subsequently claimed that he wrote both words and music, the credit to Williams being made in repayment for a loan. The song was actually composed one day early in 1912 at the New Market Inn in Stalybridge, Manchester, and sung by Judge at the Grand Theatre that evening. It was popularized in the music hall by Florrie Forde in a pantomime of 1914 and tells of an Irishman on a visit to London who longs to return to his homeland and his girl despite the lure of the legendary streets paved with gold.

> It's a long way to Tipperary,
> It's a long way to go;
> It's a long way to Tipperary,
> To the sweetest girl I know!
> Goodbye, Piccadilly,
> Farewell, Leicester Square;
> It's a long, long way to Tipperary,
> But my heart's right there!

**Tipton Three.** A name bestowed by the media on Asif Iqbal, Ruhal Ahmed and Shafiq Rasul, three British Muslims from Tipton in the West Midlands who were held in the US prison camp at Guantánamo Bay in Cuba, having been captured in Afghanistan in November 2001. They were returned to Britain in March 2004. *See also* CAMP X-RAY.

**Tiramisu.** An Italian dessert of layers of sponge cake soaked in coffee and brandy or liqueur and filled with mascarpone cheese. The word represents Italian *tira mi sù*, literally 'pick me up', and gained its first foothold in English in the 1980s.

**Tired and emotional.** A euphemism for 'drunk', said to have originated with a BBC press officer when describing the behaviour of George Brown, then deputy leader of the Labour Party, on the night of President Kennedy's assassination in 1963. The phrase was a useful way of avoiding a libel case, and was soon picked up gleefully by *Private Eye*, which did much to popularize the expression. An inebriated person easily falls asleep and readily becomes maudlin or 'weepy'.

**Tiswas.** A state of confusion of flustered excitement. To be 'all of a tiswas' is thus to be 'in a real state'. The word may be an elaboration of 'tizzy' or possibly a shortening of 'it is, it was', alluding to something that is no sooner present than it is gone. As the title of an anarchic Saturday morning television programme for young children, originally shown by ATV in the Birmingham area, *Tiswas* (1974–82) was proclaimed to mean 'This is Saturday Wear a Smile.'

**Titanic.** The British luxury passenger liner, the largest ship in the world when built, set sail from Southampton on 10 April 1912 on its maiden voyage to New York. In the early hours of 15 April it struck an iceberg off Newfoundland and sank with the loss of 1515 lives, including those of the captain and the ship's designer. Its 16 watertight compartments had been intended to make it unsinkable. In 1985 the wreck was located and explored by an unmanned submersible under the direction of American and French scientists. The tragedy and its aftermath inspired several re-creations, including the films A NIGHT TO REMEMBER (1958), the award-winning *Titanic* (1997) and *Raise the Titanic!* (1980), which cost $40 million to make and prompted its producer Lew Grade to observe that it would have been cheaper to lower the Atlantic.

Titanic was one of three huge Olympic-class passenger liners built for the White Star Line early in the 20th century, the others being the RMS *Olympic* and RMS *Britannic*. Together they were known as the 'Three Graces'. *Britannic* was sunk, probably by a mine, while serving as a hospital ship in the Mediterranean in 1916. *See also* LUSITANIA.

**Titled trains.** Many long-distance trains in Britain have gained names relating to their destinations or routes, or to the (royal) occasion of their first journey. Some Scotland-bound trains have names alluding to the novelist Sir Walter Scott. A few have historical titles. The following were still running at the beginning of the 21st century:

*Armada*: Leeds–Plymouth

*Atlantic Coast Express*: London–Newquay

*Bristolian*: London–Bristol

*Broadsman*: London–Norwich

*Caledonian*: London–Glasgow

*Cathedrals Express*: London–Oxford–Hereford–Worcester

*Cornishman*: Edinburgh–Penzance

CORNISH RIVIERA

*Devonian*: Newcastle–Paignton

*Devon Scot*: Aberdeen–Plymouth

*Dorset Scot*: Edinburgh–Bournemouth

*East Anglian*: London–Norwich

FLYING SCOTSMAN

*Golden Hind*: London–Plymouth

*Highland Chieftain*: London–Inverness

*Irish Mail*: London–Holyhead

*Master Cutler*: Leeds–Sheffield

*Mayflower*: London–Plymouth

*Midland Scot*: Edinburgh–Birmingham

*Norfolkman*: London–Norwich

*Northern Lights*: London–Aberdeen

*Pines Express*: Manchester–Poole

*Red Dragon*: London–Swansea

*Regatta Express*: London–Henley-on-Thames

*Robin Hood*: London–Nottingham

*Royal Duchy*: London–Penzance

*Royal Scot*: London–Glasgow

*St David*: London–Swansea

*Sussex Scot*: Edinburgh–Brighton

*Thames-Avon Express*: London–Stratford-upon-Avon

*Torbay Express*: London–Torquay

*Wessex Scot*: Edinburgh–Bournemouth

*Y Ddraig Gymreig/The Welsh Dragon*: London–Holyhead

The following trains formerly ran under the names given below:

*Aberdonian*: London–Aberdeen

*Bournemouth Belle*: London–Bournemouth

*Brighton Belle*: London–Brighton

*Cambrian Coast Express*: London–Aberystwyth

*Cheltenham Flyer*: London–Cheltenham

*Clansman*: London–Perth

*Coronation*: London–Edinburgh

*Coronation Scot*: London–Glasgow

*Devon Belle*: London–Plymouth/Ilfracombe

*Elizabethan*: London–Edinburgh

*Emerald Isle Express*: London–Holyhead

*Fenman*: London–King's Lynn

GOLDEN ARROW

*Heart of Midlothian*: London–Edinburgh

*Irishman*: Glasgow–Stranraer

*Lakes Express*: London–Maryport

*Lancastrian*: London–Manchester

*Mancunian*: Manchester–London

*North Briton*: Leeds–Edinburgh

*Palatine*: Manchester–Derby–London

*Peak Express*: London–Derby–Manchester

*Ports-to-Ports Express*: Newcastle–Barry

*Queen of Scots*: London–Glasgow

*Royal Highlander*: London–Aberdeen

*Royal Wessex*: London–Bournemouth

*Silver Jubilee*: London–Newcastle

*Sunny South Express*: Manchester–Hastings

*Talisman*: London–Edinburgh

*Tynesider*: London–Newcastle

*Waverley*: London–Edinburgh

*White Rose*: London–Leeds

*Yorkshireman*: London–Bradford

**Titus Groan.** The young protagonist of the GORMENGHAST novels of Mervyn Peake. Still a baby at the end of the first book, he inherits the title of 77th Earl of Groan, but he can never be reconciled with the stifling ritual of Gormenghast Castle, and eventually he leaves and ventures out into the wide world.

**TLC.** Tender loving care, as shown to a sick person being nursed back to health on the one hand or to a pampered pot plant on the other. The use of the abbreviation is now mostly facetious or ironic, but the phrase itself has a vaguely biblical ring: 'Remember, O Lord, thy tender mercies and thy loving kindnesses' (Psalm 25:6). The phrase is more precisely to be found in Shakespeare, *Henry VI, Part II*, III. ii:

> *Commons (Within)*: An answer from the King, or we will all break in!
> *King*: Go, Salisbury, and tell them all from me,
> I thank them for their tender loving care.

*See also* MEDICAL ABBREVIATIONS; 'TLC' *under* ROCK GROUP NAMES.

**TM.** *See* TRANSCENDENTAL MEDITATION.

**Toad Hall.** The ancestral home of Mr Toad in Kenneth Grahame's children's novel The WIND IN THE WILLOWS (1908). It stands by the river that flows past River Bank, has every modern convenience and is an exceedingly comfortable gentleman's residence. Mr Toad himself, although basically kind-hearted, can seem conceited and boastful. He is given to short-lived enthusiasms for expensive or dangerous hobbies, the most recent of which is a passion for motorcars. Imprisoned for stealing a car, he contrives to escape and returns to Toad Hall only to find it occupied by a group of weasels, toads and ferrets from the Wild Wood.

**Tobacco baron.** A prisoner who controls the supply of cigarettes to other prisoners and so dominates them. The term is more commonly used by the media than by inmates themselves.

**Tobacco Road.** A novel (1932) by the US writer Erskine Caldwell (1903–87) about a dysfunctional family who live in extreme poverty on Tobacco Road in rural Georgia. This slice of low life and earthy sex became a bestseller after its acquittal in a New York court of obscenity and the success of the dramatization (1934), which almost closed after a fortnight and then ran for over six years. An excellent but bowdlerized film version (1941) was directed by John Ford.

**To Birmingham by way of Beachy Head.** Metaphorically, a roundabout approach. It is a quotation from G.K. Chesterton's poem 'The Rolling English Road' (1914):

A merry road, a mazy road, and such as we did tread
The night we went to Birmingham by way of Beachy Head.

**To bits.** Very much, as: 'I was thrilled to bits', 'she loves him to bits'. The suggestion is of an action so intense that it 'shatters' the one involved.

The man [rock musician Ian Dury] is sheer pounding, good-willed energy. *New Boots and Panties!!* was the best album of the late Seventies/early Eighties. We love him to bits.
*Evening Standard*, letter to the editor (27 September 1999)

**Toblerone.** The chocolate bars of this name were the creation in 1899 of the Swiss manufacturer Johann Tobler (1830–1905). This explains the main part of the name but not its modification, which is based on Italian *torrone*, a kind of nougat. The name was devised in 1908 by the firm's production manager, Emil Baumann, and was patented the following year. The triangular shape of the bar, with its practical serrations, is intended to suggest the peaks of Swiss mountains.

**Toc H.** The old telegraphy code for the letter T (*see* ROGER) and H, as the initials of Talbot House. The term was used in the First World War, when the first Talbot House was founded in December 1915 at Poperinghe, Belgium, in memory of Gilbert Talbot, third son of Edward Stuart Talbot (1844–1934), bishop of Winchester, who had been killed at Hooge earlier that year. The Rev. P.T.B. 'Tubby' Clayton made it a rest and recreation centre. In 1920 he founded a similar centre in London, also known as Toc H, which developed into an interdenominational association for Christian social service.

**Toddlers' truce.** In British television in the early 1950s, a break in transmission between 6 and 7 pm, avowedly to enable parents to get their children off to bed without either party being exposed to the temptations of televiewing.

**To die for.** Said of something extremely good or desirable, as if worth dying for. The phrase was already current at the turn of the 20th century but suddenly came into vogue in the

1990s, when it was popularized by its punning use as the title of two films: the first British and released in 1994, about the ghost of a gay man's lover who had died of AIDS, the second American and first screened in 1996, about a small-town television weathergirl who murders her husband.

A few years ago there was a kind of fashion explosion in Antwerp and Belgium suddenly started producing to-die-for, avant-garde clothing.
*Sunday Times* (24 October 1999)

**Toe-cover.** An inexpensive and useless present. The term is the creation of the US writer Betty MacDonald in her book *The Plague and I* (1948) in which she describes it as a 'family word' and gives as an example of such a present a crocheted napkin ring.

**Toe in the door.** To have a toe in the door is to be in a position from which progress can be made. The expression dates from the 1970s. *See also* FOOT IN THE DOOR.

**Toff, The.** The suave but roguish hero of more than 50 crime novels by John Creasey, beginning with *Introducing the Toff* (1938). His real name is the Honourable Richard Rollison, and he is a young man 'down from Cambridge with half a million and a hatred of dullness'. He first appeared in *The Thriller* magazine in 1933, standing in for the SAINT.

**To infinity and beyond.** *See* Buzz LIGHTYEAR.

**Tokenism.** The practice or policy of making merely a token effort or granting only minimal concessions, especially to minority or suppressed groups. The term is of US origin and dates from the 1960s.

**To Kill a Mocking-Bird.** A novel (1960) by the US writer Harper Lee (b.1926), which won the PULITZER PRIZE for fiction. The trial of a black man accused of raping a white woman, and the events that follow the trial, are seen through the eyes of Scout, the six-year-old daughter of the white defence lawyer, Atticus Finch. Although clearly innocent, the man is found guilty and is subsequently shot seventeen times by prison guards while, it is claimed, he was trying to escape. The editor of the local paper writes a courageous leader comparing the death to 'the senseless slaughter of songbirds by hunters and children'. A film version (1962) was directed by Robert Mulligan, with an OSCAR-winning performance by Gregory Peck as Finch.

**Tokoism.** The doctrine propounded by the Angolan missionary Simao Toko (1918–84). Raised in Luanda, and later a teacher in Baptist schools in Kibokolo and Bembo, Toko went in 1943 to the Belgian Congo (now Congo) to help bring aid to the Congolese. In 1949 he declared himself to be

a prophet and began to preach his promise that Africans would throw off the status of slave and assume that of master. His words won many adherents, who formed groups of peaceful resistance to the Portuguese powers. In 1955 Toko was outlawed to the post of lighthouse keeper near Porto Alexandre (now Tombua) and in 1963 banished to the Azores. He died in his native Luanda.

**Tokyo Rose.** The name given by US servicemen to a woman broadcaster of propaganda from Japan during the Second World War. Several American-born Japanese women were suspected of taking part in these broadcasts but only one, Iva Ikuko Toguri d'Aquino (b.1916) was found guilty and in 1949 charged on eight counts of treason in San Francisco. She served six years in prison, but in 1977 was granted a pardon by President Gerald Ford. In the 1940s and 1950s Tokyo Rose was also rhyming slang for 'nose'. *See also* AXIS SALLY; Lord HAW-HAW.

**Tom and Jerry.** The well-known cat and mouse cartoon characters first appeared in an animated cartoon called *Puss Gets the Boot* (1940), as the creations of the veteran animators, William Hanna and Joseph Barbera. Their names were chosen from hundreds of suggestions submitted by studio employees in a contest held at MGM, the film company that launched them. The names were not original, however, and existed earlier for the pair of roystering young men about town in Pierce Egan's *Life in London; or, The Day and Night Scenes of Jerry Hawthorn, Esq, and His Elegant Friend Corinthian Tom* (1821).

**Tombeau de Couperin, Le.** A piano suite by Maurice Ravel (1875–1937), written in 1917, and in which each of the six movements is dedicated to a friend killed in the First World War. The title means 'the tomb (or tombstone) of Couperin', referring to the great French composer and harpsichordist François Couperin (1668–1733). A number of 17th-century French composers used *tombeau* in the titles of works lamenting the death of some notable person; for example, Denis Gaultier's *Tombeau* for lute in memory of the lutenist de Lenclos. Ravel later orchestrated four of the six movements, which have provided music for two ballets.

**Tom Keating's pictures.** *See under* FAKES.

**Tommy.** *See* Tommy ATKINS.

**Tommy gun.** A Thompson short-barrelled sub-machine-gun, so named after its co-inventor (with John N. Blish), US General John T. Thompson (1860–1940), who patented it in 1920.

**Tomorrow is another day.** A phrase of tautological vacuity which nevertheless has taken on board a great emotional

freight (as far as the susceptible are concerned) since its use as the last line of GONE WITH THE WIND, in which Scarlet O'Hara brings down the curtain by declaiming:

After all, tomorrow is another day.

Apparently Margaret Mitchell at one point considered calling her blockbuster *Tomorrow is Another Day*.

**Tomorrow is the first day of the rest of your life.** A thought-provoking truism dating from the late 1960s and said to have been coined by Charles Dederich, US founder of the Synanon drug and alcohol addiction centres. 'Today' sometimes replaces 'Tomorrow'. The sentiment is similar to the less personally oriented TOMORROW IS ANOTHER DAY.

**Tom's Midnight Garden.** A much-admired novel (1958) for children by the British writer Philippa Pearce (b.1920). Tom is sent away to stay with his aunt and uncle in a country house when his brother falls ill with measles. The 'Midnight garden' is a secret garden that appears only after the grandfather clock in the house has struck the 13th hour, and in it Tom makes the acquaintance of a Victorian family who formerly occupied the house.

**Tom Swifties.** A mildly amusing linguistic trick, in which an adverb relates both properly and punningly to a sentence of reported speech. An example is: '"What can I get you?" asked the waitress fetchingly.' The quip takes its name from Tom Swift, a boy's adventure hero created by the prolific US writer Edward L. Stratemeyer in the early 20th century. Tom Swift rarely passed a remark without a qualifying adverb, as 'Tom added eagerly' or 'Tom smiled ruefully', and the wordplay arose as a pastiche of this.

**Tono-Bungay.** A novel (1909) by H.G. Wells (1866–1946), in which ideas about society are blended with scientific projections of the future. Wells himself described it as a 'social panorama in the vein of Balzac'. Tono-Bungay is a patent medicine, by means of which George Ponderevo's uncle Edward, having lost everything on the stock exchange, builds up a business empire, before going bankrupt again and being charged with forgery. In the meantime George has been designing aeroplanes and airships, in one of which he takes Edward to France to escape justice.

**Tonton.** A nickname of the French Socialist politician François Mitterrand (1916–96) when he was president of France (1981–95). 'Tonton' is a French child's word for 'uncle'.

**Tonton Macoutes.** Members of a notoriously brutal militia formed by President François PAPA DOC Duvalier of Haiti (1907–71) as a private force to terrorize and liquidate alleged enemies of his regime. They were officially known as

National Security Volunteers and were active from 1961 to 1986. The Haitian French name approximates to 'bogeymen'.

**Ton-up.** A speed of 100mph, especially on a motorcycle. A 'ton-up boy' is a rider who achieves this, or more generally a member of a motorcycle gang. The term dates from the 1950s.

> The BBC broadcast of 'Morning Service' from Keele University, Staffs, yesterday was interrupted when a record about 'ton-up' boys was heard above the hymn singing. A loudspeaker was found hidden behind a stage in the chapel.
> *Daily Telegraph* (25 January 1965)

**Tony.** The name of a number of awards made annually from 1947 in the American theatre in various categories. The name is that of the US actress and manager Antoinette ('Tony') Perry (1888–1946). The word fortuitously echoes 'tony' in the colloquial sense of chic or sophisticated, literally having 'tone'.

**Tony Curtis.** A male hairstyle popular in the 1950s in which the hair at the sides of the head is combed back and that on the forehead combed forwards. The style takes its name from the US film actor Tony Curtis (b.1925), whose real name is Bernard Schwartz.

**Tony's cronies.** A derisive nickname for the INNER CABINET of Tony Blair, Labour prime minister from 1997, some of whom were supposedly appointed as personal friends rather than as skilful politicians. In 1998 the opposition leader, William Hague, accused NEW LABOUR of CRONYISM, his criticism centring on revelations about the supposedly corrupt activities of influential 'insiders'. Blair's cabinets have included such unelected figures as Derry Irvine, Blair's head of chambers when he was a barrister, whom Blair appointed as his first lord chancellor; and Charlie Falconer, one of Blair's old schoolfriends, who succeeded Irving as lord chancellor. Both were created peers to enable them to sit in parliament. *See also* BLAIR BABES.

The term is also applied to various prominent businessmen courted by Tony Blair. Some of these have become donors to Labour Party funds, and some have been awarded peerages (for example, Paul Drayson and Kumar Battacharyya). The fact that wealthy individuals had made undeclared 'loans' to political parties, and that some of them had subsequently gained peerages, became a political hot potato in 2006.

> The growing power exercised by 'Tony's cronies' is threatening parliamentary democracy and undermining the Civil Service by handing government over to an unaccountable new elite.
> *The Times* (25 February 2000)

**Toodle-oo.** Goodbye. The word is more likely to represent a parting toot on a motor horn than to be a corruption of French *à tout à l'heure*, 'see you soon', as sometimes explained. 'Toodle-pip' is a variant, and 'tooraloo' (of Australian origin) another.

**Too many chiefs, not enough Indians.** A characterization of a situation in which there is an unwieldy number of people notionally in charge, probably getting in each other's way, and too few people available to carry out the actual work that needs to be done – resulting in confusion and failure.

**Too much geography.** What Canada has, according to the Canadian Liberal statesman William Lyon Mackenzie King (1874–1950). He made the point in a speech to the Canadian House of Commons on 18 June 1936, during his third premiership:

> If some countries have too much history, we have too much geography.

**Toon, The.** A nickname for Newcastle upon Tyne, especially as the home of the celebrated football club Newcastle United, whose supporters, in their replica black-and-white team shirts, are known as the 'Toon Army' (*see also* TARTAN ARMY). 'Toon' is a northern dialect form of 'town'.

**Too posh to push.** An encapsulation of the attitude of an affluent and 'sophisticated' mother-to-be (*see* YUMMY MUMMY) who would rather have a Caesarian section than give birth in the ordinary effortful and painful way.

In recent years there has been a big increase in women undergoing elective Caesarians, and some 10,000 are now carried out in the UK annually. Among celebrities who have opted for the operation are Victoria Beckham (*see* POSH AND BECKS) and Liz Hurley.

**Tooth fairy.** A desired or imaginary source of riches, as: 'Let's hope a tooth fairy can help with the funding.' The allusion is to the fairy said to take children's milk teeth after they have fallen out and to leave a coin under their pillow as payment.

> 'No doubt Solomon and David Morgan will continue to trap victims' … concluded MacIntyre. 'But perhaps after tonight they might find it a little more difficult.' If MacIntyre truly believes this, he probably believes in the tooth fairy, too.
> *The Times* (1 December 1999)

**Too True to Be Good.** A play (1932) by the Irish playwright George Bernard Shaw (1856–1950) in which a Burglar teams up with a Nurse in an attempt to steal an invalid's necklace but then befriends the intended victim to the extent that all three share the proceeds of the necklace's sale and set up home together on a tropical beach. The title results from a mangling of the proverbial 'too good to be true'.

**Top banana.** The leading comic in a performance; a chief or boss generally. The expression apparently derives from a skit involving the sharing of a banana. *See also* SECOND BANANA.

**Top Cat.** *See* ALLEY CAT.

**Top dog.** A person who by skill, personality or violence obtains the mastery. The analogy is with a dog who is on top of another in a fight. The expression dates from the turn of the 20th century.

**Top drawer.** To be out of the top drawer is to have a high social status or be specially proficient. The allusion is to the uppermost drawer of a bureau or dresser, where jewellery and other valuables are kept.

**Top End.** A laconic nickname for the northern part of Northern Territory, Australia, dating from the 1930s. The southern part of the state is sometimes known as 'the Centre', with Alice Springs as its 'capital', just as Darwin, the capital of the state as a whole, is specifically associated with the 'Top End'.

**Top-of-the-range.** The best there is of its kind. The term is typically applied to a manufactured article that is superior to all others of its type and that is frequently promoted as such.

**Top shelf.** The top shelf in a newsagent's shop, where pornographic magazines are placed to keep them out of view of the general public and out of reach of children. The phrase formerly denoted high quality or excellence, in the manner of 'top hole'.

**Topsy and Tim.** The names of two children used to represent gender stereotypes or the attitudes of a typical middle-class British family. The names are those of the small girl and boy who feature in a series of picture books for young children by Jean and Gareth Adamson, first published in 1959.

**Top 10.** The 10 bestselling recordings of pop or rock music in the weekly charts. Attention usually focuses on the Number 1 spot. *See also* HIT PARADE.

**Tora! Tora! Tora!** A film about the Japanese attack on PEARL HARBOR, made in 1970 by a joint US-Japanese production team. Reconstructing events on both the American and Japanese sides, the film concentrates on the attack itself and the reasons why it was not prevented by the US military, rather than looking at the wider political context of the events of 7 December 1941. 'Tora, Tora, Tora' was the code name used by the Japanese to indicate the success of their mission. *Tora* is Japanese for 'tiger'.

**Torch Song Trilogy.** A trio of plays (1981) by the US playwright Harvey Fierstein (b.1954) in which the common link is a professional drag queen called Arnold. The title refers to the 'torch song' genre of intense love songs commonly delivered by singers in the bars and clubs that Arnold and his friends frequent. The genre in turn owes its name to the expression to CARRY A TORCH FOR SOMEONE.

**Torrey Canyon.** An oil tanker that on 18 March 1967 struck a reef between the Scilly Isles and Cornwall, resulting in one of Britain's worst environmental disasters, with some 130 km (80 miles) of Cornish coast being polluted by crude oil. The ship took its name from the Torrey Canyon Oil Company, one of three 'wildcatter' companies that in 1890 formed the Union Oil Company of California (now the Unocal Corporation). *See also* EXXON VALDEZ.

> This is the greatest ever peacetime threat to Britain.
> HAROLD WILSON: commenting on the *Torrey Canyon* disaster (30 March 1967)

**Torschlusspanik.** A German word, dating from the mid-20th century, designating a sense of alarm or anxiety at the passing of life's opportunities. The literal meaning of the word is 'door-closing panic', from the German words *Tor*, 'door', 'gate', *Schluss* 'closure', and *Panik* 'panic'.

**Tortoise Recalling the Drone of the Holy Numbers ..., The.** In full, *The Tortoise Recalling the Drone of the Holy Numbers as They Were Revealed in the Dreams of the Whirlwind and the Obsidian Gong, Illuminated by the Sawmill, the Green Sawtooth Ocelot, and the High-tension Line Stepdown Transformer*. It is an avant-garde musical work (1964) by the US composer LaMonte Young (b.1935), a pupil of Stockhausen. The piece, which is governed by the principles of indeterminacy, is part of the ongoing performance for voices and electronic devices entitled *The Tortoise, His Dreams and Journeys*. Another piece from the main work is entitled *The Tortoise Droning Selected Pitches from the Holy Numbers for the Two Black Tigers, the Green Tiger and the Hermit* (1964).

**Torvill and Dean.** Jayne Torvill (b.1957) and Christopher Dean (b.1958) entranced the British public in the 1980s as a romantically dashing and talented pair of ice-skaters. They formed their partnership in 1975 and were soon setting new standards in the sport. They were six times British champions and won the grand slam of World, Olympic and European ice-dance titles in 1984, receiving a total of 136 perfect 'sixes', the highest award a judge can give. The high spot of their act was a haunting interpretation of Ravel's BOLÉRO. They later performed together in their own ice shows, and made a brief comeback to the sport at the 1994 Winter Olympics, in which they won bronze medals. In 2006 they acted as coaches in ITV's *Dancing on Ice* (*see* CELEBRITY CULTURE).

**Torygraph, The.** A media nickname for the *Daily Telegraph*, alluding to its more or less consistent support for the Conservative Party.

**Tosca.** The heroine of Puccini's opera that bears her name, premièred at Rome in 1900. The libretto, by Giuseppe Giacosa and Luigi Illica, is based on Victorien Sardou's drama *La Tosca* (1887). The story is set in Rome in June 1800. Baron Scarpia, chief of police, lusts after Floria Tosca, the self-centred actress lover of the artist and republican loyalist, Mario Cavaradossi, who has aided the escape of Cesare Angelotti, former consul of the Roman Republic. He has Cavaradossi arrested and tortured until Tosca reveals Angelotti's hiding-place. Scarpia agrees to release Cavaradossi and provide both him and Tosca with a safe conduct after Cavaradossi has been subjected to a mock execution. Scarpia's price is Tosca herself. She agrees, but stabs him with a knife snatched from his desk when he begins to embrace her. Scarpia's so-called 'mock' execution squad turns out to have live bullets, and Cavaradossi is killed. By this time Scarpia's murder has been discovered, and in grief Tosca flings herself from the battlements. The US musicologist and critic Joseph Kernan (b.1924) memorably described the opera as a 'shabby little shocker'.

**Totes Meer.** This is one of several paintings by Paul Nash (1889–1946) depicting the air war in the Second World War, during which he was an official war artist, as he had been in the First World War. The title is German for 'dead sea', and the picture shows a sea of shot-down German aeroplanes in which the wings become waves. Painted in 1940–1, the work was reproduced on a Royal Mail stamp in 1965 to commemorate the BATTLE OF BRITAIN (1940). The poet Anna Adams wrote of the painting: 'This clear eye records the waste, does not insist on pain.' *See also* WE ARE MAKING A NEW WORLD.

**To the Lighthouse.** A novel (1927) by Virginia Woolf (1882–1941). The novel explores, via stream-of-consciousness narration, the ambiguities of time and the contrast between the sexes, as embodied in Mrs and Mr Ramsay – said to be based on Woolf's mother and her father, Sir Leslie Stephen. Although the book is set on the west coast of Scotland, the lighthouse in question is modelled on the lighthouse on a little rocky island off Godrevy Point, across the bay from St Ives, Cornwall, where Woolf had spent childhood holidays. In the first part of the book the Ramsays' youngest son, James, is eager to visit the lighthouse, but this is not achieved until years later, by which time his brother and mother are dead.

**Tottenham Three.** The collective name given to Winston Silcott, Engin Raghip and Mark Braithwaite, who were sentenced to life imprisonment in 1987 for 'having common cause' with the mob who murdered PC Keith Blakelock during the October 1985 Broadwater Farm riots in Tottenham, North London. Their convictions were quashed in 1991 after tests revealed that Silcott's confession had been tampered with. Braithwaite and Raghip were released, though Silcott remained in jail until 2003 as he was serving a sentence for another murder as well.

**Totting up.** A system introduced in 1988 by which penalty points for driving offences accumulate until they lead to disqualification. Originally three endorsements on a driver's licence led to this, but it is now the consequence if twelve points are incurred within three years. The number of points awarded for an offence is at the discretion of the court. For careless driving the figure may range from three to nine, while for speeding it is from three to six.

**Touchy-feely.** Expressing one's emotions openly and through physical contact. The phrase implies both senses of 'touch' (make physical contact, affect emotionally) and of 'feel' (perceive by touch, be emotionally affected). The term arose in the 1970s from the encounter groups of the 1960s, whose members sought physical benefit by close mutual contact.

**Tough act to follow.** *See* HARD ACT TO FOLLOW.

**Tough cookie.** A tough person; a survivor. 'Cookie' here simply means 'person'. The phrase is of US origin and dates from the 1930s. The variant 'one tough cookie' is also found.

> Lisa Anderson is one tough cookie. You can hear it in her plummy, confident voice. You can see it in the set of her mouth. If you want to know something, she will tell you straight.
>
> *Sunday Express* (27 February 2000)

**Tough love.** A method of promoting the welfare of a person such as an addict or criminal by enforcing certain constraints on them or requiring them to take responsibility for themselves, stressing the importance of self-help rather than the indulgence of others. The US concept dates from the 1980s and was readily embraced by politicians seeking to restrict state benefits.

**Tough on crime and tough on the causes of crime.** A slogan enunciated by Tony Blair (b.1953) as shadow home secretary in a speech to the Labour Party Conference, 30 September 1993. He prefaced the soundbite with the claim: 'Labour is the party of law and order in Britain today.' The slogan was much parodied; for example, the following year Blair's colleague, Chris Smith MP, talked about the Labour

Party's policy regarding the cleaning of old buildings: 'Tough on grime and tough on the causes of grime.' *See also* Laura NORDER.

**Tough shit** or **titty.** So what; too bad. The crude American responses to express a lack of sympathy date from the 1950s, the mammary variant perhaps based on an African American folk saying: 'It's tough titty, but the milk is good.'

> 'Even if you get away with it, you'll never be able to come home.'

> 'Well, so, tough titty.'

> TRUMAN CAPOTE: *Breakfast at Tiffany's* (1958)

**Tour de France.** The world's first and best-known cycle race was established in 1903 by the French cyclist and journalist Henri Desgrange (1865–1940) as a six-stage race of 2410km (1497 miles). This distance was later extended so that it is now about 4000km (2500 miles). The route now runs mainly through France and Belgium with occasional brief visits to Italy, Spain, Germany and Switzerland. In 1994 part of the race took place in England to mark the opening of the CHANNEL TUNNEL. From 1971 the race was restricted to 20 shorter stages. The winner of each stage is awarded the *maillot jaune* (yellow jersey) and the riders are accompanied by a vast fleet of official, press and support vehicles. The race has been won five times by Jacques Anquetil (France), Eddy Merckx (Belgium), Bernard Hinault (France) and Miguel Induráin (Spain). *See also* MILK RACE.

**Towers of Trebizond, The.** The last novel (1956) by Rose Macaulay (1881–1958), a witty account of a party of eccentric Anglo-Catholics attempting to spread the Christian faith in Turkey. The disused Byzantine churches of the ancient city of Trebizond (Trabzon) that they visit symbolize the nostalgia for the Christian faith in which the narrator indulges, having forfeited it by reason of her adulterous affair. The situation also reflects Macaulay's private grief. Her own 25-year affair with the Irish novelist Gerald O'Donovan (1871–1942) prevented her from practising her strict Anglo-Catholicism. *See also* FIRST LINES OF NOVELS.

**Townie.** A disparaging term applied by some country people in the UK to city-dwellers or ex-city-dwellers, thought of as indifferent to the traditions and troubles of rural-dwellers (such as fox-hunting and depressed agricultural prices); furthermore, townies are thought of as treating the countryside as no more than a pretty playground. The term is also applied by the students of some universities to the non-academic population of the town in which the university is situated (the 'town vs gown' conflict in Oxford goes back to the Middle Ages). Finally, the term is used in some parts of the UK as a synonym for CHAV.

**Town Like Alice, A.** A novel (1949) by Nevil Shute (1899–1960). A young Englishwoman, who has, with her group, suffered incredible privations in Malaya during the Second World War at the hands of the Japanese, uses an inheritance to transform Willstown, a depressed settlement in the Australian Gulf of Carpentaria country, into 'a town like Alice [Springs]'. A film version (1956), directed by Jack Lee and starring Peter Finch and Virginia McKenna, was freely adapted from the first part of the novel, and was followed by a popular television mini-series (1981) starring Helen Morse and Bryan Brown.

**Toy boy.** A young man who is 'kept' as a lover by an older woman. The term has also been used of gay relationships. A sort of converse is the 'boy toy', a young woman regarded as sexually attractive to young men. The rock star Madonna (b.1958) was so described in 1989. *See also* SUGAR BOWL.

**Toytown.** A name used figuratively of a thing that apparently or actually lacks real value or substance. The word originated in the 19th century in the literal sense of a model town for a child to play with. It subsequently became familiar as a proper name in a series of children's stories by the toymaker and illustrator S.G. Hulme Beaman (1886–1932), first in books, beginning with *The Road to Toytown* (1925), then from 1929 as radio plays on CHILDREN'S HOUR.

**Tracey.** *See* TRACY .

**Trachtenberg system.** A system of speedy mathematical calculations based upon simple counting according to prescribed keys or formulae, which need to be memorized. There is no division or multiplication as such, and complicated calculations can be more easily and rapidly handled than by normal processes. The system was devised by Jakow Trachtenberg (1888–*c*.1960) during his seven long years in a NAZI concentration camp. He was born at Odessa and trained as an engineer and became a refugee in Germany after the Russian Revolution. The method still had its adherents at the turn of the 21st century.

**Track record.** Literally and originally, the record of an athlete or horse on a particular running track. This sense dates from the 1950s. The term was then adopted to denote the past record of a person or business, especially as a guide to likely future performance.

**Tracy** or **Tracey.** A female forename highly popular in the 1960s and 1970s. It was at one time a male forename, as were the surnames of other English noble families such as Clifford, Dudley and Stanley. As a female name it later took on overtones of a BIMBO or AIRHEAD, and when coupled with SHARON served subsequently to personify an ESSEX GIRL type. *See also* BIRDS OF A FEATHER.

**Tracy, Dick.** The newspaper comic-strip detective created by Chester Gould from 1931, and in his day one of the best-known 'dicks' in the United States. He was played by Ralph Byrd in four film serials and later by Morgan Conway in two feature films before moving to television and to a stage musical in 1970. Of all the films in which he has appeared the most memorable was the lavishly produced *Dick Tracy* (1990), in which he was played by Warren Beatty. *See also* DICKLESS TRACY.

**Trade plates.** Temporary number plates used by car dealers or manufacturers on unlicensed cars, and usually recognizable by their *ad hoc* fixing and red and white colours. Such cars are delivered for the motor trade by 'trade platers', who are generally paid the return train fare but who mostly find it advantageous to hitch-hike back.

**Traduttori traditori.** An early 20th-century Italian phrase, the literal meaning of which is 'translators (are) traitors', indicating that is impossible to translate without misrepresenting the original. The phrase is also found in the singular: *traduttore traditore*, (a) translator (is a) traitor.

**Traffic calming.** The deliberate slowing of traffic in a residential area by means of SLEEPING POLICEMEN and other measures. The technique was introduced to Britain in the late 1980s and the expression is a literal translation of German *Verkehrsberuhigung*.

**Trahison des clercs.** (French, 'treason of the clerks'.) The betrayal of standards by intellectuals influenced by politics. An early 20th-century French phrase, it originated in *La Trahison des Clercs* ('The Treachery of the Intellectuals'), a work (1927) by Julien Benda, in which he denounces as moral traitors those who betray truth and justice for racial and political considerations.

**Trailer trash.** A US term current from the 1990s for poor whites who live in large stationary caravans ('trailers') and who are regarded as being unsociable, uncouth and unsightly. An older expression is 'white trash', although the latter do not necessarily live in trailers. The expression 'trailer trash' came to be used generally as a term of scornful or semi-serious abuse.

> Eminem, aka Marshall Mathers, is white trailer trash, America's worst nightmare after black ghetto trash.
> *The Times* (31 December 1999)

**Trainspotting.** In the narrow sense, the collecting of railway locomotive numbers, a pursuit regarded by the uninvolved or uncomprehending as fit only for ANORAKS. The term subsequently broadened to apply to any obsessive occupation, especially one regarded as trivial or at best of minority interest. This second sense was popularized by the title of Irvine Welsh's cult novel of 1993, filmed to much acclaim in 1996. ('Trainspotting' refers to the veins ('tracks') into which addicts inject heroin.) Written largely in a phonetic Scottish patois, Welsh's book consists of a series of loosely connected episodes illustrative of the lives of Edinburgh junkies, wideboys and psychopaths. On Leith Central Station 'an auld drunkard ... lurched up tae us, wine boatil in his hand ... "What yis up tae, lads? Trainspottin, eh?" he sais, laughing uncontrollably at his ain fucking wit.' *See also* FIRST LINES OF NOVELS.

**Trains run on time, making the.** *See* MAKING THE TRAINS RUN ON TIME.

**Tramp.** A famous London nightclub opened in 1969 by Johnny Gold, who took its name from a television documentary describing Charlie Chaplin as 'the greatest tramp of them all'. Its 6000 members include many celebrities, some of whom still pay its original £10.50 entry fee. It has a rule 'no tramps without birds', meaning that male members must be accompanied by females, and despite some colourful incidents has always stayed away from controversy or scandal.

**Trance.** A type of electronic dance music evolving in the 1990s from TECHNO, so named from its hypnotic 'tribal' rhythms and sounds. The music was also seen as possessing a spiritual dimension.

**Transcendental Meditation.** A movement based on special techniques of meditation. TM, as it is usually known, was introduced to the West in the 1960s by the Maharishi Mahesh Yogi (b.c.1911) in his book *The Science of Being and Art of Loving*. It uses one of a number of Sanskrit mantras, each being a short word or phrase that is repeated in the mind to help the user quiet the activity of thought and so attain a deeper level of consciousness. This process, it is claimed, gives the practitioner deep relaxation, leading to inner joy, vitality and creativity. TM became particularly popular when The BEATLES embraced it in 1967.

**Transit van.** This general-purpose vehicle, despite its seemingly generic name, was launched by Ford in 1965 and was originally to have been called the 'V-series'. At the last minute, however, Sir William Batty, then chairman of Ford of Britain, decided that the name Transit would make the van more marketable. It was an immediate success, with a 'chunky' and businesslike look that its predecessor, the Thames, had lacked. Transits were soon being adapted for a wide range of tasks and the roomy and reliable vehicle was readily adopted for a host of transportation purposes. *See also* WHITE VAN MAN.

**Transport House.** A former name for the leadership of the LABOUR PARTY, from its headquarters in SMITH SQUARE, London. The building was also the head office of the Transport and General Workers' Union. Hence its name. The Labour Party moved from Smith Square to Walworth Road in 1980 and subsequently to Old Queen Street – and is now in Victoria Street – while the TGWU (also known as T & G) is now based in a new Transport House in Theobalds Road. *See also* MILLBANK TENDENCY.

**Travelogue.** A film or illustrated lecture about travel. The word suggests a blend of 'travel' and 'monologue'. Travelogues were a staple of early silent cinema before the advent of the feature film and later became popular short films accompanying the main film. Their purpose was essentially to increase tourism, and many presented a glamorized and often vulgarized view of life in the country or region depicted.

**Treasure of the Sierra Madre, The.** A novel (1935; in German as *Der Schatz der Sierra Madre*, 1927) by the Polish-born German (or possibly Austrian) novelist B. Traven. Traven was the pen-name of Berick Traven Torsvan (*c.*1890–1969), whose name was originally Albert Otto Max Feige and who was also known as Ret Marut. Traven was an actor and anarchist, who settled in Mexico, where he was a union activist, eventually being listed as an enemy of the state. His best-known book is an analysis of greed as three Americans search for a lost gold mine in the mountains of central Mexico. An unforgettable film version (1948) was directed by John Huston and starred Humphrey Bogart, Walter Huston and Tim Holt.

**Treat someone** or **something with ignore.** In Australian English, to disregard someone or something; to treat them with disdain. Finding a nominalization of the verb 'ignore' has long been problematical in English: 'ignorance' means something else; 'ignoral' has been tried but failed to convince; Australians plumped for a straight category shift (known technically as a 'conversion') in the 1930s, and the usage has survived.

**Treaty of Versailles.** A treaty between Germany and the Allies that brought a formal end to the First World War. It was signed in the Palace of Mirrors in the Palace of Versailles on 28 June 1919 by Lloyd George of Britain, Georges Clemenceau of France, Woodrow Wilson of the United States and Vittorio Orlando of Italy and took force on 10 January 1920. By the terms of the treaty, Germany suffered considerable territorial losses, had the size of its armed forces restricted, and was obliged to pay massive reparations. The treaty also established the LEAGUE OF NATIONS. It

was bitterly criticized by the Germans, who complained that it had been 'dictated' to them, that it violated the spirit of the FOURTEEN POINTS and that it demanded intolerable sacrifices that would wreck their economy. It was subsequently revised and altered, mostly in Germany's favour. Nevertheless, Germany's resentment at the treaty, and its desire to regain its lost territories, were major reasons behind the outbreak of the Second World War. At the signing of the treaty, Marshal Foch, the Allied commander in chief, percipiently remarked:

> This is not a peace treaty, it is an armistice for twenty years.

The Treaty of Versailles was just one of several treaties signed at the Paris Peace Conference by the Allies and the defeated CENTRAL POWERS, among whom Austria and Turkey in particular also lost significant amounts of territory.

*See also* PEACE IN OUR TIME; POLISH CORRIDOR; STAB IN THE BACK.

**Tree hugger.** A contemptuous term for an environmental campaigner, typically regarded as hugging trees in order to love them and protect them.

**Trekkie** or **Trekker.** A fan of the cult US SCIENCE FICTION television programme STAR TREK.

**Trench coat.** A long, loose-belted, double-breasted raincoat in a military style, so called as originally worn by British army officers in the trenches during the First World War. It soon became fashionable among men and later also among women, and has more than once been revived in the latter style.

**Trench fever.** A remittent or relapsing fever affecting men living in trenches, dugouts and the like, and transmitted by the excrement of lice. It first appeared in the First World War, in the static warfare on the WESTERN FRONT.

**Trent's Last Case.** A novel (1913) by E.C. Bentley (1875–1956), regarded as the prototype of the realistic detective story. Philip Trent, an artistic and literary figure with a gift for solving crimes, works on the mystery of the murder of an American millionaire. When the truth is finally revealed, he decides it is time to withdraw from being an amateur detective. Bentley was also the inventor of the CLERIHEW. A film version (1952) was directed by Herbert Wilcox.

**Trial, The.** A fragmentary novel (1937; in German as *Der Prozess*, 1925) by Franz Kafka (1883–1924). It concerns the tribulations of Josef K., arrested and imprisoned by an unnamed bureaucracy, and accused of a crime which is never specified. K's attempts to discover the reasons for his arrest come to nothing, and he is eventually led away by two men in black and executed by knifing. The novel has generally been interpreted as an allegory of existential guilt, and its depiction of a shadowy and menacing bureaucracy as an eerie premonition of the methods of 20th-century totalitarianism. Orson Welles directed a film version of the novel (1963). *See also* KAFKAESQUE.

**Trial by television.** The questioning of someone on a controversial matter in a television interview, especially when the questions are felt to be over-severe or unfair. The expression evokes 'trial by fire' and the experience involves a similar 'grilling'.

**Triangle Shirtwaist fire.** The most serious factory fire in the history of New York. It occurred on 25 March 1911 in the Asch building at the corner of Washington Street and Greene Street, where the Triangle Shirtwaist Company occupied the top three floors of 10. Some 500 young Jewish women and girls were employed there at the time and were unable to escape when fire broke out in the cutting room on the eighth floor. A total of 146 women died in less than 15 minutes, some as a result of jumping from open windows. The owners of the company, who had resisted government safety regulations, were charged with manslaughter but later acquitted.

**Tribeca.** A name adopted by property developers in the 1970s for an area of land in the West Side of New York City, as an acronym of '*tri*angle *be*low *Ca*nal Street'. Dilapidated factories and warehouses have been converted to residential lofts, many of them inhabited by artists, and Tribeca is now a fashionable neighbourhood with a generally affluent population.

**Tribute group** or **band.** A group of amateur pop musicians who imitate a (usually well-known) band that has officially dissolved, partly to pay tribute to its former popularity, partly to please its nostalgic fans.

**Trick cyclist.** A punning jocularism for a psychiatrist, who may indeed cultivate a delicate balancing act similar to that of the bicycling expert.

**Trick or treat.** A Halloween custom of US origin, in which children in fancy dress call at houses and threaten to play a prank ('trick') if they are not given sweets or a small gift ('treat'). In most cases the latter is usually proffered and the former rarely realized. A good example of the practice can be seen in the musical film *Meet Me in St Louis* (1944).

**Tricks of the trade.** The ingenious devices or 'dodges' known only to the members of a craft or profession. There is no necessary implication of trickery.

**Tricky Dicky.** The nickname of Richard M. Nixon (1913–94), Republican vice-president (1953–61) and 37th president of the United States, so called from his combined political adroitness and evasiveness. The nickname was awarded to him long before his final disgrace and resignation over WATERGATE. It first appeared in 1950, when he was so dubbed by Helen Gahagan Douglas in the Californian *Independent Review* after Nixon, during his bid to become a senator, had inaccurately smeared his opponent as a communist fellow traveller. Various incidents in his subsequent career meant that the nickname stuck.

Once in the Senate, Nixon helped Joseph McCarthy's anti-communist witch-hunt (*see* MCCARTHYISM). Allegations that he was secretly funded by Californian businessmen almost scuppered Nixon's successful bid to become Eisenhower's running-mate in the 1952 presidential election. He got out of this scrape by making a tear-jerking television speech in which he admitted accepting, as a gift for his children, a dog named Checkers. Nixon stood for the presidency against J.F. Kennedy (JFK) in 1960, and, perhaps boosted by his success with the Checkers speech, agreed to a televised debate with his opponent. However, Nixon refused to wear make-up, and his FIVE O'CLOCK SHADOW made him look shifty and shady. His next bid for the presidency, in 1968, was successful, and during his first term he moved towards ending US involvement in the VIETNAM War and pursued a policy of DÉTENTE with China and the Soviet Union. However, as the Watergate scandal broke in his second term, he fully lived up to his nickname, desperately trying to cover up his involvement in illegal activities.

*See also* WOULD YOU BUY A USED CAR FROM THIS MAN?

**Trident.** A type of US nuclear-armed SLBM (submarine-launched ballistic missile). The first version of Trident, which entered US service in the early 1980s, was based on its predecessor, the Poseidon 3, with the addition of a third-stage rocket motor. The name alludes to the trident wielded by Poseidon, the Greek god of the sea. The UK government's original decision to go ahead with Trident, at enormous cost, was the subject of considerable controversy in Britain, particularly as the COLD WAR was by then over.

Trident 2, the version adopted by Britain in the 1990s to replace its aged POLARIS missiles, has a range of 12,000km (7400 miles). It will become obsolete around 2020 and it is uncertain whether it will be replaced.

**Trigger-happy.** Ready or over-ready to shoot at anything at sight on the slightest provocation. The expression dates from the Second World War. The comedy series *Trigger Happy TV*, featuring Dom Joly and broadcast on Channel 4

2000–2, is a surreal version of CANDID CAMERA. A US version was broadcast in 2003. *See also* BOMB-HAPPY.

**Triple Alliance.** *See* TRIPLE ENTENTE.

**Triple Crown.** An award or honour for winning a group of three events in various sports. In Britain the Triple Crown in rugby union denotes a victory in the Five Nations Championship (renamed the Six Nations Championship in 2000 when Italy joined the competition) by one of the four home countries (known as the Home Nations) over all the other three in the same season, as happened in 2006, when Ireland won their matches against England, Wales and Scotland. In the United States the Triple Crown means a win in the Kentucky Derby, the Preakness and the Belmont Stakes, as famously occurred in 1919 when the chestnut colt Sir Barton swept the board, a feat that would not be repeated until 1930.

**Triple Entente.** A military alliance (1914–17) between Britain, France and Russia in the First World War. It was based on three earlier agreements: the Franco-Russian Alliance (1894), the ENTENTE CORDIALE between Britain and France (1904) and the Anglo-Russian Entente (1907). These agreements were drawn up in response to the Triple Alliance of Germany, Austria-Hungary and Italy formed in 1882, and the effect was to divide Europe into two armed camps. Romania allied itself with the Triple Alliance in 1883, and Italy withdrew in 1914 (*see* CENTRAL POWERS). Russia withdrew from the Triple Entente after the OCTOBER REVOLUTION in 1917. *See also* SARAJEVO.

**Triple threat.** An Americanism for a person adept in three skills or abilities. The expression comes from American football, in which a triple threat (to the opposition) is a player who is good at running, passing and kicking.

**Triple-witching hour.** In financial jargon the time when stock options, stock index futures and options on such futures all mature at once. Triple-witching hours occur quarterly and are usually accompanied by highly volatile trading. The allusion is to 'witching hour' as a term for midnight, the time when witches are active and magic takes place. The phrase derives from Shakespeare: ''Tis now the very witching time of night, / When churchyards yawn and hell itself breathes out / Contagion to this world' (*Hamlet*, III. ii). The term originated with reference to a one-day fall in share prices on Wall Street in September 1986, a year before BLACK MONDAY.

**Triumph of the embalmer's art, The.** Gore Vidal's description of Ronald Reagan, the GREAT COMMUNICATOR, quoted in *The Observer*, 26 April 1981. Being a former Hollywood actor, the aged Reagan was not unfamiliar with pancake and rouge.

**Trivial Pursuit.** The commercially packaged quiz game of this name was born in 1979 when two Canadians, photo editor Chris Haney and sportswriter Scott Abbott, bought their eighth game of SCRABBLE, having worked through seven previous sets, and began to wonder how many other people had bought multiple copies of the game. The realization of a potential market led them to devise their own game, and as their job was reporting news it was natural for them to be interested in current affairs, and to present this from the time-honoured angles of 'who, what, when, where and why'. They originally planned to call the game 'Trivia Pursuit' but Haney's wife jokingly called it 'Trivial Pursuit', and this was the name adopted. Sales were initially discouraging, but a breakthrough came when the game was taken up by the American company Selchow and Righter, who gave it a major promotion at the 1983 New York Toy Fair. It is played with dice and question cards, the questions themselves falling into six colour categories: in the standard 'genus' edition blue is for geography, pink for entertainment, yellow for history, brown for art and literature, green for science and nature, and orange for sport and leisure. *See also* PUB QUIZ.

**Trolley dash.** A consumer-oriented prize awarded by some competition organizers, commercial companies and the like. It consists in racing frenziedly around the aisles of a supermarket with a trolley and filling it with as many products as possible in a given time. The stunt usually attracts a cheering crowd of shoppers and brings welcome publicity to the sponsors right in the marketplace.

**Trophy art.** Works of art looted in time of war. The term particularly applies to art looted by the RED ARMY from NAZI Germany at the end of the Second World War and, conversely, to Russian art looted by the Germans. Russia's biggest loss of this type is generally considered to be the lavish Amber Room in the Yekaterinsky (Catherine's) Palace, Tsarskoye Selo (formerly Pushkin), destroyed by the Germans during the Nazi siege of LENINGRAD (now St Petersburg) (1941–4), during which many amber panels were looted. Much art of this type has still not been returned to its country of origin, and the Pushkin Museum, Moscow, continues to display a collection of Germany's Trojan gold, brought to the Soviet Union at the end of the war.

**Trophy wife.** A derogatory term for a person's wife regarded as a status symbol for her husband. She is typically seen as a BIMBO, perhaps an example of ARM CANDY, who has married an older man, often as his second wife. The arrangement is not without its rewards for the wife, who gains access to her husband's wealth. *See also* LADIES WHO LUNCH.

**Tropic of Cancer.** A semi-autobiographical novel (1934) in experimental form by Henry Miller (1891–1980). Unashamedly exhibitionistic, it covers his activities and other forms of low life in Paris during the 1930s. *Tropic of Capricorn* (1939) is a companion volume, reflecting his childhood and earlier life in the United States. Both books were banned in the United States until the 1960s. Of *Tropic of Cancer*, the poet and critic Ezra Pound (1885–1972) commented: 'At last an unprintable book which is readable.' The tropics of Cancer and Capricorn are two parallel lines of latitude between which the sun can be vertical over the earth's surface. Miller commented that 'Cancer is separated from Capricorn only by an imaginary line … You live like a rock in the midst of the ocean; you are fixed while everything about you is in turbulent motion.' An unsatisfactory film version (1970) was directed by Joseph Strick.

**Trot.** A term of abuse in the 1960s for anyone vaguely left-wing and so politically suspect. The word is an abbreviation of 'Trotskyite' as a nickname for a radical socialist, especially one inspired by the political and economic principles of the Russian revolutionary Leon Trotsky (1879–1940), who advocated the establishment of world socialism by means of continuing revolution. *See also* HATTONISTAS; MILITANT TENDENCY.

**Troubles.** A term used for various periods of unrest in Irish history. In the 20th century the name became particularly associated with the Anglo-Irish War (War of Independence) of 1919–21 and the period of terrorism in Northern Ireland which began in the late 1960s. A novel entitled *Troubles* (1970), by J.G. Farrell (1935–79), uses the symbol of a rundown hotel (the ironically named 'Majestic'), to paint a vivid and tragicomic picture of events in southern Ireland in the stormy year of 1919, as British rule in southern Ireland began its final collapse. *The Troubles* (1996) was the title of an account of events in Northern Ireland since 1969 by Tim Pat Coogan. *See also* BIG FELLA; BOGSIDE; DIRECT RULE; FREESTATERS; IRA; POWER-SHARING; ULSTER VOLUNTEER FORCE.

**Troubleshooter.** An American coinage for someone expert in locating and mending 'trouble', mechanical or otherwise. The original application at the turn of the 20th century was specifically to an engineer who traced and corrected faults on a telegraph or telephone line. The term was later adopted for a person brought into an industry to mend relations between employer and employee.

**Trout Fishing in America.** An experimental novel (1967) by Richard Brautigan (1935–84). It represents a quest for an alternative lifestyle, free from the constraints of modern living, in the form of a search for the perfect trout stream.

**Trout pout.** The characteristic appearance of lips that have been 'enhanced' (perhaps inexpertly) by the introduction of tissue implants, especially collagen. Numerous celebrities have undergone the treatment, including Elizabeth Hurley and Kylie Minogue, but it was apparently the actress Leslie Ash who originally inspired the phrase: people are said to have shouted it at her in the street after the surgery resulted in a mouth unfortunately like an inflatable rubber ring.

> Mockingly termed the 'trout pout', a collagen lip injection is one of the most common treatments, which costs as little as £300.
> www.timesonline.co.uk (29 January 2005)

**True Grit.** A film WESTERN (1969) based on a novel (1968) of the same title by Charles Portis. The film starred John Wayne as an indomitable one-eyed marshal, 'Rooster' Cogburn, who is eventually persuaded to help a determined teenage girl avenge herself upon her father's murderers. According to Portis, he picked up the phrase while researching memoirs about the old West, in which all manner of heroes were praised for their 'grit' (meaning their determination or courage): 'I had never seen it in such profusion as in these books. There was grit, plain grit, plain old grit, clear grit, pure grit, pure dee grit (a euphemism for damned) and true grit. Thus the hard little word was in my head when I began the story.' He jotted the phrase down on the title page of his script for use within the text when it became appropriate, and then realized it would make a good title itself. Portis was not, as he admitted himself, the first writer to make use of the phrase, and as early as 1897 Bram Stoker quoted it in his novel *Dracula*.

**Truman Doctrine.** The pronouncement by US President Harry S. Truman on 12 March 1947 in which he declared immediate economic and military aid to the governments of Greece, threatened by communist insurrection, and Turkey, under pressure from Soviet expansion in the Mediterranean. Congress responded by promptly appropriating $400 million for this purpose. The move led to the establishment of the first US military bases abroad. *See also* EISENHOWER DOCTRINE.

**Trustafarian.** A vogue word of the 1990s for a young person from a wealthy background who affects the lifestyle and attitudes of the inner-city ghetto. The term combines 'trust fund', as a frequent means of support for such people, and RASTAFARIANS.

> A posh accent could be classed as a handicap in the employment market … Hence the Trustafarian's attempt to adopt Estuary English: 'Seriously cool, yah?'
> *Independent on Sunday* (28 November 1999)

**Trust-busting.** In 1902, as part of his SQUARE DEAL, President Theodore Roosevelt was determined to restrict the excessive power wielded by certain monopolies. Congress was reluctant to grant the necessary regulatory authority, but he circumvented the opposition by reviving the almost forgotten Sherman Anti-Trust Act (1890) and bringing successful suit against the Northern Securities Company. He pursued his policy of 'trust-busting' by bringing suit against 43 other corporations over the next seven years.

**Truth drug.** A drug claimed to make a person tell the truth under questioning. A US doctor, R.E. House (1875–1930), used alkaloid scopolamine to induce a state of lethargic intoxication in which the patient lost many of his defences and spoke the truth concerning matters about which he would normally have lied or prevaricated. The value of this and other drugs in penology has by no means been established.

**Truth or Consequences.** The small American town and health resort of this name in New Mexico was originally called Hot Springs for its warm mineral waters. In 1950 the city council collaborated with the radio and television personality Ralph Edwards, host of the GAME SHOW *Truth or Consequences*, in a promotion effort to hold a yearly programme and fiesta there. Residents approved the new name, but it remains controversial and many still prefer Hot Springs.

**Truth 24 times a second.** The French film director Jean-Luc Godard's definition of cinema in *Le Petit Soldat* (1960):

> Photography is truth. The cinema is truth 24 times per second.

**Tsar.** *See* DRUG CZAR.

**T-shirt** or **tee-shirt.** The familiar short-sleeved top, usually made of cotton, is so named as it has the shape of the letter T when spread out flat. The shirt is of US origin and first came into vogue in the 1940s when the US Navy introduced a knitted cotton undershirt of this style. It was initially worn by soldiers and marines but later evolved as a general garment, especially after being popularized by the film actor James Dean, who wore one in REBEL WITHOUT A CAUSE (1955).

**Tsukahara.** In gymnastics a style of vaulting consisting of a quarter or half turn onto the horse followed by one and a half back somersaults. It was introduced in international competition in 1970 by the Japanese gymnast Mitsuo Tsukahara (b.1947) and was a speciality of the teenage Romanian gymnast Nadia Comaneci in the late 1970s.

**TTFN.** *See* ITMA.

**Tube Alloys.** The Second World War code name for a section of the Department of Scientific and Industrial Research formed in 1940 to examine methods of producing an atomic bomb. The section was placed under the charge of William Akers, a director of ICI.

**Tub of lard.** An uncomplimentary nickname for a plump person. When the Labour politician Roy Hattersley failed to turn up to take part in the satirical television quiz HAVE I GOT NEWS FOR YOU an actual carton of lard was placed on the desk before his empty chair. *See also* HATTERJI.

**Tudorbethan.** An architectural style imitative of Tudor and Elizabethan. It was characteristic of the 1930s, when a rash of half-timbered suburban villas broke out in Britain. A similar term and style was Jacobethan, blending Jacobean and Elizabethan. *See also* STOCKBROKERS' TUDOR.

> The style in which Gothic predominates may be called, inaccurately enough, Elizabethan, and the style in which the classical predominates over the Gothic, equally inaccurately, may be called Jacobean. To save the time of those who do not wish to distinguish between these periods of architectural uncertainty, I will henceforward use the term 'Jacobethan'.
>
> JOHN BETJEMAN: *Ghastly Good Taste*, ch. 4 (1933)

**Tug of love.** A dispute over the custody of a child, who is thus torn between his or her parents, or between each of the adults who claims custody. This sense arose in the 1970s as a sort of punning converse of 'tug of war' although the expression is found earlier as the title of one of Israel Zangwill's *Ghetto Comedies* (1907).

**Tulip revolution.** *See* REVOLUTION NAMES.

**Tum-Tum.** *See* EDWARD THE CARESSER.

**Tunnel of love.** A fairground attraction of US origin designed for couples and consisting of a boat or train ride through a darkened tunnel. The concept has a certain sexual symbolism.

**Tupamaros.** A left-wing URBAN GUERRILLA group in Uruguay, founded as the Movimiento de Liberación Nacional (Spanish, 'National Liberation Movement') in around 1963 by Raúl Sendic (*c*.1925–89). Their terrorist activities escalated from around 1968, but they were ruthlessly crushed by the military regime that came to power in 1973. Following the restoration of democracy in 1985 thousands of imprisoned Tupamaros were released, including Sendic, who reorganized the Tupamaros as a legal political party. The name Tupamaro was derived from the native Peruvian Tupac Amaru II (originally José Gabriel Condorcanqui; *c*.1740–81), a descendant of Tupac Amaru, the last Inca ruler, who was executed by the Spanish in 1571. In 1780–81 Tupac Amaru II led an unsuccessful revolt against Spanish rule that spread from Peru to Bolivia and Argentina. Tupac Amaru II was captured, and forced to watch his wife and sons being killed before he himself was brutally put to death.

**Tupperware.** The plastic food containers take their name from Earl S. Tupper (1907–83), an American farmer's son from New Hampshire, who formed the Tupper Plastics Company in 1938. He developed methods to refine and purify polyethylene slag, until then regarded as a waste product, into a usable product that he called 'Poly-T'. He opened his first manufacturing plant in Farnumsville, Massachusetts, in 1942 and produced a range of dishes, bowls and cups to sell to hardware stores. The first sealed food storage containers followed in 1947, their waterproof and airtight lids based on an inverted paint tin lid. When sales slumped, Tupper took to selling his wares in people's homes. Tupperware 'parties' soon became staples of American life and a firmly established feature of suburban culture, opening economic as well as social doors for women. The brand received an unexpected boost in Britain in 2004 when it was revealed that the Queen uses Tupperware containers for her breakfast cereals.

**Turandot.** The opera by Giacomo Puccini of this name (1926) has a story that can be traced back to a tale given by Antoine Galland as part of his translation of *The Arabian Nights* (1704–8), but Puccini's libretto (written by Giuseppe Adami and Renato Simoni) was based on the play (1762) by the Italian dramatist Carlo Gozzi. The central character of the title is a Chinese princess who vows vengeance on all men for some past grievance but offers to marry any nobleman who can solve three riddles. If he cannot, she will kill him. A prince does solve them, but she refuses to marry him after all. A final change of heart, however, is also a change of mind. The opera is unpopular with many, who point to the torture and death of the loyal slave-girl Liu, the only genuinely good character. The princess's name is of Persian origin and means 'daughter of the Turanians', i.e. of the northern people (to the Arabians) who inhabit ancient Turkestan. The final '-dot' is related to English 'daughter'. Ferruccio Busoni also wrote an opera (1917) with this title, which was similarly based on Gozzi's play.

**Turangalîla Symphony.** The massive and mystical symphony by Olivier Messiaen (1908–92) was composed between 1946 and 1948 and first performed in 1949. *Turangalîla* is Sanskrit, the composer translating it as 'a love song, a hymn to joy, time, movement, rhythm, life and

death'. Apparently the word should be pronounced with a heavy emphasis on the last two syllables. The music includes Indian influences and features parts for piano and ONDES MARTENOT, an early form of electronic keyboard.

**Turf war.** A dispute over territory between rival groups. The allusion is to the territory or 'patch' controlled by a street gang or criminal.

> The debate over mortgages has degenerated into a bitter turf war between the Treasury … and the Department of Trade and Industry.
> *The Times* (6 January 2000)

**Turing machine.** A hypothetical computing machine for performing simple reading, writing and shifting operations in accordance with a prescribed set of rules. It is invoked in theories of computability and automata and takes its name from the British mathematician Alan Turing (1912–54), who described such a machine in 1936. During the Second World War Turing was one of the team that cracked the German ENIGMA code.

**Turin Shroud.** *See under* FAKES.

**Turkeys don't vote for Christmas.** A modern proverb encapsulating the notion that people are highly unlikely to endorse any course of action that will be seriously detrimental to their interests.

> He [Tony Benn] predicted the Parliamentary Labour Party would never vote 'to destroy 50 of its own members … turkeys do not vote for Christmas'.
> www.bbc.co.uk/news/ (5 November 1998)

As that quotation suggests, it began as and continues mainly to be a politicians' joke, and it seems first to have come on the public stage in a House of Commons speech by James Callaghan on 28 March 1979, in the no-confidence debate that prefaced the fall of his government, in which he derided the Liberal and Scottish Nationalist parties for supporting the motion:

> The minority parties have walked into a trap … It is the first time in recorded history that turkeys have been known to vote for an early Christmas.
> Quoted in NIGEL REES: *Cassell Companion to Quotations* (1997)

**Turkey shoot.** Anything very easy, and specifically a military situation where the attacker has an overwhelming advantage. The term is of US origin and alludes to former marksmanship contests in which a live turkey was tied behind a log with just its head showing as the target. It became familiar to British speakers when it was much used to characterize the Coalition attacks on the retreating Iraqi forces as they moved north out of Kuwait on the so-called

'Highway of Death', on the way back to Baghdad, at the end of the 1991 GULF WAR.

**Turkey trot.** A type of ballroom dance to ragtime music originating in the United States and popular in the early 20th century. The steps of the dancers suggest the stiff but rapid gait of a trotting turkey.

**Turkey Twizzler.** A much-derided brand of cheap processed 'cutlet'. It shot to notoriety as the epitome of poor-quality school catering identified by chef Jamie Oliver, when he undertook to transform an education authority's school meals service in the television series *Jamie's School Dinners* (2005). The then education secretary Charles Clarke was forced to eat one on camera, before diplomatically pronouncing it 'fine'. Subsequently, 'turkey twizzler' spread to become a metaphor for the lowest quality-level of a product or activity, as in 'the turkey twizzler of tourism'.

> British audiences are forever being served up the cinematic equivalent of the Turkey Twizzler, and film-makers everywhere must ask themselves: 'Before I make it, would I buy it?'
>
> *The Guardian*, 'The Turkey Twizzler Film' (13 August 2005)

**Turner Prize.** A prize established in 1984 by the Patrons of New Art to encourage the collection of contemporary British art. Since 1991 it has been restricted to artists aged under 50. In 1993 it was controversially awarded to Rachel Whiteread (b.1963) for her work *Untitled (House)*, a concrete cast of the interior of a house in London's East End. Later awards attracted similar debate, such as that of 1998, won by Chris Ofili (b.1968) for his work *The Adoration of Captain Shit and the Legend of the Black Star Part Two*, incorporating his 'trademark' elephant dung. The prize is named after the English painter J.M.W. Turner (1775–1851).

**Turn of the century.** The beginning or end of a particular century. The turn of the 20th century is thus the period about the year 1900, when the 19th century turned into the 20th. The expression is first recorded in 1926.

**Turn of the Screw, The.** A ghostly psychological opera by Benjamin Britten (1913–76) with a libretto by Myfanwy Piper, based on the short story (1898) by Henry James (1843–1916). It was first performed in Venice in 1954. James's story, which concerns a governess who becomes convinced that her young charges are possessed, also inspired a film, *The Innocents* (1961), directed by Jack Clayton and with a screenplay by William Archibald and Truman Capote.

**Turn on a sixpence** or **a dime.** To turn a vehicle round in a tightly restricted area, represented by the US dime and the former English sixpence, both very small coins. The term is also figuratively applied to a business that can be similarly 'turned round' or reoriented at short notice.

**Turn on, tune in, drop out.** The epigrammatic title of a lecture given in June 1966 by the US drug-culture GURU and advocate of LSD Timothy Leary (1920–96). The sense is: 'Heighten your awareness through drugs (*see* TURN SOMEONE ON), set yourself on my (or the universe's) wavelength, and reject conventional society' (*see* DROPOUT). Leary explored the theme further in his book *The Politics of Ecstasy* (1968), in which the lecture was published.

> If you take the game of life seriously, if you take your nervous system seriously, if you take your sense organs seriously, if you take the energy process seriously, you must turn on, tune in and drop out.

**Turn someone on.** To excite them; to stimulate their interest, especially sexually. 'Whatever turns you on' is a stock response to a person's description of some unusual experience or plan, however mild. *See also* SWITCHED ON.

**Turn the knife.** *See* TWIST THE KNIFE.

**Turn-up for the book.** A completely unexpected result or occurrence, especially a welcome one. 'Turn-up' alludes to the turning up of a particular card in a game, while the 'book' is the one kept by a bookmaker on a racecourse. The expression dates from the 1940s.

**Tutankhamun's curse.** A legend arising from the death of the 5th Earl of Carnarvon (1866–1923) following his sponsorship of the archaeologist Howard Carter and his assistance during the latter's excavations of the tomb of the pharaoh Tutankhamun (d.c.1352 BC). He died after an infection from a mosquito bite, but the writer Sir Arthur Conan Doyle, by then a convinced spiritualist, suggested that the death might be attributed to elementals created by the priests of Tutankhamun.

Coincidentally there was a power failure at Cairo when Carnarvon died, and his dog in England expired at the same time. Carter survived until 1939.

**Tweenies.** Children of primary school age, who are between toddlerhood and teenhood. A tweeny was originally a colloquialism for a between-maid, i.e. a maid between a cook and a housemaid.

> Let's start with the 'tweenie' market, the hugely successful … enclave for six to 11-year-old girls and boys.
>
> *The Times* (17 December 1999)

There is also a highly popular television show for three-to-five-year-old children, called *The Tweenies*, first screened in 1999. The characters are four brightly coloured rag doll 'children', Bella, Milo, Fizz and Jake, played by actors in costume. Bella and Fizz are two females who love ballet and dressing up, while Milo and Jake, the two males, enjoy dismantling toys. They were the creation of Iain Lauchlan, a former pantomime dame, and their audience were preschoolers who had outgrown TELETUBBIES.

**Twelve-tone system.** *See* SERIALISM.

**Twentieth-century blues.** A feeling of despair or world weariness with regard to the 20th century, which opened with the golden glow of the EDWARDIAN ERA but went on to witness two world wars and, between them, the GREAT DEPRESSION. The *mal du siècle* was at its height in the latter period, and the phrase itself comes from a song in Noël Coward's musical play *Cavalcade*.

> Twentieth Century Blues
> Are getting me down.
> Who's
> Escaped those weary
> Twentieth Century Blues.
>
> NOËL COWARD: *Cavalcade*, 'Twentieth Century Blues' (1931)

**24 carat.** Entirely trustworthy; the finest. The purity of gold is measured in carats, 24 being the purest. The figurative use of the term dates from the 1930s. 'Twenty-two carat' is sometimes used similarly.

**24/7.** Every day; all the time. The reference is to something that occurs or is available 24 hours a day, seven days a week, i.e. round the clock. The expression dates from the 1980s and sometimes appears as 24/7/365.

> This is the city that never sleeps. New York is a veritable 24/7 souk.
>
> *The Times* (24 January 2000)

**Twenty-six Counties.** *See* SIX COUNTIES.

**Twenty-something.** A modern term for a person aged, technically, between 20 and 29. As with THIRTY-SOMETHING, the term has a particularly urban aspect and is part of the currency of advertising and marketing, in that it is viewed as a target market: post-school, post-university, pre-marriage and pre-offspring young people, beginning their careers but with, as yet, little fixed in their lives. A reasonably high disposable income – money that is much sought after by providers of entertainment, alcohol, sport, clothes and cars – self-doubt and an instability in personal relationships are seen to characterize this life phase. It is not necessarily a happy time:

> Born in the 1970s? Then you earn more than the children of the 60s, but you are also more miserable … It's a surprise you can find time to gloat over your wage slip, what with your

increased propensity for headaches, fatigue, indigestion, violent rages and other worries.

> RYAN DILLEY: 'Behind the Twenty-something Malaise', www.bbc.co.uk/news/ (27 November 2002)

I suspect a generation gap has opened up between twentysomethings and the middle-aged baby-boomers who thought *they* had created the sexual revolution.

> *The Times* (19 September 1998)

**Twenty-three skiddoo.** Go away; clear off. 'Skidoo' means 'skedaddle', but the reason for the particular number is uncertain. According to one theory, the reference is to air currents that would blow up women's skirts on the corner of Broadway and 23rd Street, New York. Police would shoo away gleeful male spectators with a shout of 'skiddoo!' Another source attributes the number to railway jargon, in which 23 denoted a message of urgency.

**Twenty-twenty vision.** Perfect vision. The term alludes to the Snellen chart used when measuring visual acuity. The patient reads rows of letters printed in successively decreasing sizes. Twenty-twenty (20/20) vision means that a row of letters near the bottom of the chart can be read at a distance of 20 feet. Measurements are now metric, so that the chart is placed 6 metres from the patient and normal vision is expressed as 6/6. If the patient can read only the letters twice as large as those on the 6/6 line (which a normal eye could read at 12 metres) the acuity is said to be 6/12. The technical term gave 'twenty-twenty hindsight' to mean perfect understanding or appreciation of what has been seen. Hindsight, with its certain knowledge, is always superior to foresight.

**Twiggy.** The nickname that became the professional name of the 1960s model Lesley Hornby (b.1946). It referred to her stick-thin body, which at school had similarly caused her to be dubbed Sticks. She later took up a career as a singer and dancer. In 1988 she married Leigh Lawson and has since performed as Lesley Lawson.

> Twiggy is a stupid name for a woman in her 40s, but it would be hard to drop. At least a full name makes me sound like a person, instead of a strange animal.
>
> LESLEY LAWSON: interviewed in *Telegraph Magazine* (6 July 1991)

**Twiglet.** The nickname of Stephen Twigg (b.1966), the New Labour MP who famously defeated Michael Portillo in the previously safe Conservative seat of Enfield and Southgate in 1997, and subsequently shot up the greasy pole and into government, until he lost his seat in the 2005 general election. The name (that of a brand of twig-shaped savoury snack) refers to Twigg's youth and stature.

**Twilight sleep.** A state of semi-consciousness produced by injection of scopolamine and morphia in which a woman can undergo childbirth with comparatively little pain. *See also* TRUTH DRUG.

**Twilight zone.** The run-down area that sometimes develops around the central business district of a city. The expression took on a more general sense to mean any ambiguous or unsettled state between two opposing states and was popularized by the cult US SCIENCE FICTION television series *The Twilight Zone* (1959–63), created and often narrated by Rod Serling. Favourite themes in the 151 stories were TIME WARPS, Faustian pacts, doppelgängers and machines with minds of their own.

> There is a fifth dimension beyond that which is known to men. It is a dimension as vast as space and as timeless as infinity. It is the middle ground between light and shadow, between science and superstition, and it lies between the pit of man's fears and the summit of his knowledge. This is the dimension of imagination. It is an area we call The Twilight Zone.
>
> ROD SERLING: *The Twilight Zone*, Introduction (1959)

**Twinkie.** An American nickname for a male homosexual or effeminate man, also a young and sexually attractive person, a 'tempting teenager'. The allusion is apparently to the Twinkie, a type of cupcake with a soft centre, popular among young people.

**Twinkie defence.** An American colloquialism for an unlikely excuse, and originally for a legal defence of diminished responsibility in which the defendant's criminal behaviour is attributed to the effects of an unbalanced diet of convenience food, a typical example of which is the TWINKIE cupcake. The defence so known was first employed in 1979 in a San Francisco Supreme Court murder trial, the grounds being that the defendant's compulsive diet of candy bars, cupcakes and Cokes had built up an excessive sugar level which had aggravated a chemical imbalance in his brain. The defence was subsequently disallowed by the US Congress in 1981.

**Twinkle** or **gleam in one's eye.** A barely formed idea, and specifically that of a child that has not yet even been conceived. The expression dates from the 1960s.

**Twin Peaks.** A somewhat surreal television drama series, set in the lumber town of the title in the American Pacific Northwest, which was broadcast to an intrigued audience from 1990 to 1991. The story centred on the question, 'Who killed Laura Palmer?', Laura being a beautiful high-school student. The main investigator was the FBI agent Dale Cooper, whose methods of detection included Tibetan mysticism, dreams and ESP. As the series progressed, viewers learned that Palmer was not the innocent she seemed and that Twin Peaks was a murky pool of drugs, adultery, pornography and satanism. Most of the town's inhabitants were cast as potential suspects before it was finally revealed that the culprit was Palmer's own father, possessed by the demonic 'Killer Bob'. Directed by David Lynch, *Twin Peaks* rapidly acquired cult status.

**Twinset and pearls.** Apparel taken as symbolic of middle- to upper-middle-class female respectability in the middle years of the 20th century (a twinset was a matching cardigan and jumper).

**Twin Towers, The.** A journalistic name given after their destruction on 9/11 to the two tower blocks of the World Trade Center in Lower Manhattan, New York City. They were 381m (1250ft) high. The name was also given to the iconically distinctive pair of towers that adorned Wembley Stadium in northwest London, before it was demolished to make way for a new stadium at the beginning of the 21st century. *See also* FREEDOM TOWER.

**Twin town.** A town in an overseas country that has established an official link with a town or community in one's own country. Many European towns set up such links after the Second World War as an earnest of the postwar mood of international amity and cooperation. Representatives of each place in the relevant country frequently make an annual visit to their opposite number in order to maintain the tie. Some twinnings are multiple, so that by 1991 the London borough of Lambeth was twinned with Vincennes, France (1954), Moskvoretsky, USSR (1962), Bluefields, Nicaragua (1984), Kenema, Sierra Leone (1989), and Shinjuku, Japan (1989). Coventry twinned with Volgograd, USSR, in 1944, actually during the war.

**Twist, The.** A dance popular in the 1960s, so called from the contortions performed. 'The Twist', a rhythm-and-blues number by Hank Ballard and The Midnighters, released in 1959 as the B-side of 'Teardrops on Your Letter', soon afterwards became a major international hit for Chubby Checker.

**Twist in the wind.** To suffer protracted humiliation, regret or the like. The phrase presents the gruesome image of a hanging body in the open air. A variant includes 'slowly' after 'twist'.

**Twist someone's arm.** To compel them to do something against their will. The expression, which dates from the 1950s, is often used jocularly, as: 'Another drink?' 'You can twist my arm.'

**Twist** or **turn the knife.** To intensify a person's suffering deliberately. The image is of stabbing someone, then twisting the knife in the wound.

**Twitcher.** A colloquialism for a birdwatcher (called a birder in the United States), presumably so called from becoming 'twitchy' or nervously excited at the prospect of another sighting. There is also a suggestion of 'twitter' or 'tweeter', for the chirp that can equally indicate a bird's presence. The term dates from the 1970s.

**Twitch the net curtains.** To express puritanical disapproval. The allusion is to the genteel or prudish inhabitants of a respectable residential district who supposedly tweak aside the curtains preserving their privacy to peep at some scandalous scene, which then forms a topic of outraged gossip. The reaction is traditionally regarded as typical of MIDDLE ENGLAND.

**Two Brains.** The nickname of the supposedly brilliant Conservative politician and ideologue David Willetts (b.1956), who worked as an adviser to Nigel Lawson and Margaret Thatcher and at the Thatcherite Centre for Policy Studies, before entering parliament in 1992. He was known as 'the court philosopher' of John Major's government, and became paymaster general in 1996, although he had to resign the same year after it emerged that he had earlier attempted to influence the outcome of a Commons inquiry into the Neil Hamilton affair (*see* CASH FOR QUESTIONS). He played an important role in the Tory election campaign of 1997 and after the landslide Labour victory sat on the Opposition front bench under William Hague – and subsequently under Iain Duncan Smith, Michael Howard and David Cameron. *See also* TWO JAGS.

**Twocking.** The act of stealing a car, from the police acronym TWOCK, 'taking without owner's consent'. Those who commit such an offence, often disaffected teenagers, are thus twockers. The term dates from the early 1990s.

**Two cultures.** The existence in England, and to a great extent in western Europe, of two separate cultures with few points of contact between them, one based on the arts and the other on the sciences. The phrase gained immediate popularity after C.P. Snow's Rede Lecture, subsequently published as *The Two Cultures and the Scientific Revolution* (1959).

> I believe the intellectual life of the whole of western society is increasingly being split into two polar groups … Literary intellectuals at one pole – at the other scientists, and as the most representative, the physical scientists. Between the two a gulf of mutual incomprehension.
>
> C.P. SNOW: *The Two Cultures and the Scientific Revolution* (1959)

**Two fingers.** A V-SIGN. To put two fingers up at (or to) a person or thing, or show two fingers to them, is thus to make this obscene gesture of scorn or defiance, literally or figuratively.

> He [Donald Sinden] is meant to be the play's 'giver of life', a genial Falstaff energetically showing two fingers to senility and death.
>
> *The Times* (10 September 1999)

**Two Jags.** A nickname, one of several, applied to the Labour politician John Prescott (b.1938), deputy prime minister and (until May 2006; *see* BLAIR DITCH PROJECT) secretary of state for transport and the regions in Tony Blair's government since 1997. The likeable but at times verbally challenged minister has struggled to bring forth transport policies that reduce the role of private cars. The barbed nickname derives from the fact that he has two official Jaguar cars at his disposal, one of which he used to carry himself and his wife a few hundred metres from his hotel to the conference centre during the 1999 Labour Party Conference (in order, according to him, to protect her hair-do against the high winds of Bournemouth). After his pugilistic contretemps with an elector during the 2001 general election (*see* THUMPER), the nickname was modified by *The Sun* to Two Jabs Prescott.

When in April 2006 Prescott admitted to having had an affair with one of his secretaries, Tracey Temple, it was inevitable that the press would metamorphose his nickname once more, this time to 'Two Shags' Prescott. Much criticized in 2006 for retaining his salary and perks despite being relieved of his department, the deputy prime minister gave up his official residence at Dorneywood after photographs of him enjoying a game of croquet presented a somewhat over-relaxed image of the public servant.

Prescott is also known as Prezza, on the model of HEZZA and GAZZA.

*See also* ADMIRALTY ARCH.

**Two left feet.** To have two left feet is to be clumsy. Most people are right-footed in matters of stepping and kicking, so to have not just one left foot but (supposedly) two is to be anything but adroit. The expression dates from the early 20th century.

**Two-minute silence.** The cessation of traffic and all other activities for two minutes at 11 a.m. on 11 November to commemorate those who died in the First World War. First observed in 1919, it remained a central feature of REMEMBRANCE DAY. A special nationwide two-minute silence began at 8.38 p.m. (sunset) on 8 May 1995 to mark the 50th anniversary of VE DAY. Two-minute silences have also been held in Britain to remember the victims of 9/11 and 7/7. *See also* ARMISTICE DAY.

At the going down of the sun and in the morning
We will remember them.

LAURENCE BINYON: 'For the Fallen' (1914)

**Twopenny Tube.** A nickname for the Central London Railway, opened as part of the Underground network in 1900. The fare was originally 2d but the name lingered on for several years after it was raised to 3d in 1907.

*2 Point 4 Children.* A television SITCOM shown from 1991 to 1998 and centring on the life of the Porter family of East Chiswick. The series differed from the norm in that the main character was not the husband, Ben, played by Gary Olsen, but his wife, Bill, played by Belinda Lang, depicted not as a traditional wife and mother but as a person in her own right, unconfined by her family. The title refers to the supposed size of the average British family.

*Two Ronnies, The.* A television comedy series screened from 1971 to 1986, featuring the large and laid-back Ronnie Barker (1919–2005) and the small and vivacious Ronnie Corbett (b.1930). The humour derived as much from the contrast between the two as from their mildly 'naughty' scripts. Each programme included a song by a female singer, a humorous monologue by the diminutive Corbett in a large armchair, and an episode of a spoof serial. Barker's tag-out line, 'It's goodnight from me, and it's goodnight from him', became something of a catchphrase.

**Two sandwiches short of a picnic.** Stupid; crazy; 'not all there'. The phrase dates from the 1980s. Similar expressions of identical meaning include the following:

Three bricks shy of a load.
Several currants short of a bun.
A few trolleys short of a supermarket.
A slice short of a full loaf.
A nosebag short of a sack of oats.
A few pence short of a first-class stamp.
A few cans short of a six-pack.
A sheaf short of a stook.
Three diamond clusters short of a tiara.
One player short of a cricket team.

*2001: A Space Odyssey.* A SCIENCE FICTION novel (1968, from his own screenplay) by Arthur C. Clarke (b.1917). While the novel demonstrates Clarke's ability to extrapolate from known data, it also represents a philosophical quest for the meaning of life and an investigation into the evolutionary process. The film version (1968), directed by Stanley Kubrick, was a masterly blend of technical wizardry and obscure symbolism, criticized by some for its tedium but praised by others for its moments of striking imagery. The

music was by various composers but most memorable of all was the 'Sunrise' opening of Richard Strauss's *Also sprach Zarathustra* (1895). The film acquired cult status as a vision of the technological future, even if space exploration had not advanced nearly as far in reality by 2001. The film inspired a sequel (1984) directed by Peter Hyams under the title *2010*, but fans of the original movie were not impressed and gave it the alternative title *Ten Past Eight*. *See also* HAL.

**Two-time.** To deceive or betray, especially one's spouse or lover by consorting with someone else. The reference may be to having two lovers at a time or to 'making time' (sexually succeeding) with two at once. The term, of US origin, dates from the 1920s.

**Two-Ton Tessie.** The nickname of Tessie O'Shea (1914–95), an amply proportioned British music-hall singer, noted for her jollity and general 'full-of-fun' style. The name is sometimes applied to any plump or overweight person. Another such was 'Two-Ton Tony', otherwise Tony Galento (1910–79), a US heavyweight boxer noted for his adiposity.

If you're worried about clogging your arteries or turning into a two-ton Tessie, have a wodge of heavenly butter on your toast only once in a while.

*Sunday Times* (30 May 1999)

**Two-up, two-down.** A house with two reception rooms downstairs and two bedrooms upstairs. The term is first recorded in the 1950s but houses of this type date from at least the 19th century.

**Two-way mirror.** A somewhat misleading name for a pane of glass which serves as a mirror one side but which can be seen through the other like a window. A person looking through from the second side can thus see or 'spy' without being seen.

**Type A and Type B.** The two types into which psychologists divide the personality. 'Type A' is characterized by ambition, impatience and competitiveness, but is susceptible to stress and heart disease; 'Type B' is easy-going and believed to have low susceptibility to stress. The two types thus posit specific links between a person's mental make-up and their physical condition.

**Typhoid Mary.** The nickname of Mary Mallon (1869–1938), an Irish-born carrier of typhoid fever in the New York area. Her case first arose in 1904, when an epidemic of typhoid spread over Oyster Bay and nearby towns on Long Island. The sources were traced to households where Mary had been a cook. She was apprehended, but escaped.

She was eventually committed to an isolation centre and released only in 1910 on condition that she never worked with food again. But she resumed her occupation, and in 1914 a further epidemic broke out at Newfoundland, New Jersey, and at a Manhattan maternity hospital, both places where Mary had worked. Altogether 51 cases of typhoid, including three deaths, were directly attributed to her, although she herself was immune to the typhoid bacillus. The nickname became a metaphor for pollution and for the evil a single person can inflict on society.

**Typhoo.** The proprietary brand of tea was first produced by John Sumner in Birmingham in 1903 as 'Typhoo Tipps', the first word being a meaningless oriental-style creation, perhaps suggested by 'typhoon', the latter being a printer's misprint for 'tips', meaning the top leaves and buds of the tea plant that make the drink.

# U

**U and Non-U.** A former semi-humorous mark of distinction between social classes in England based on the usage of certain words. 'U' is Upper Class and 'Non-U' is non-Upper Class. It is 'U' to say 'luncheon' for what 'Non-U' folk call 'lunch', 'U' to say 'napkin' instead of 'serviette', and 'U' to prefer 'cycle' to 'bike'. The terms owe their popularity to Nancy Mitford (1904–73), who quoted them in an article in the magazine *Encounter* in September 1955, but they were invented by Professor Alan Ross in 1954 and appeared in his article 'Linguistic class-indicators in present-day English' in the Finnish philological journal *Neuphilologische Mitteilungen*. A simplified and condensed version of this, entitled 'U and Non-U: An Essay in Sociological Linguistics', was later included in *Noblesse Oblige* (1956), edited by Nancy Mitford.

> No wonder show-jumping had recently attracted so many enthusiasts: it is the gypsy life of modern times, nomadic, transitory and glamorous, in which the gentry can take part as legitimately as the professional, where it is just as 'U' to sleep on straw in a horse-box as it is in the smartest hotel.
>
> MOYRA WILLIAMS: *Adventures Unbridled*, ch. 11 (1960)

**U-bend.** A section of piping or tubing in the form of a letter U, and particularly that of a waste pipe or toilet bowl outlet. The term has a figurative use for anything sinister, suspect or 'dirty'.

**Übermenschen.** *See* UNTERMENSCHEN.

**Übersexual.** *See* METROSEXUAL.

**UB 40.** The designation of the card that was issued by the government to a person registered as unemployed, the initials standing for 'unemployment benefit'. UB 40 is also the name of a white-and-black reggae group formed in 1979. The name originally denoted the workless status of its members but they later promoted it positively as a political stance, and in 1980 their album cover for *Signing Off* was a UB 40 card stamped in red with the titular words. Their

record 'One in Ten' (1981) was barbed comment on the level of British unemployment at the time.

**U-boat.** A German submarine. The term is adapted from German *Unterseeboot*, 'underwater vessel'. *See also* E-BOAT.

**UDA.** *See* ULSTER DEFENCE ASSOCIATION.

**UDI.** The unilateral declaration of independence by the Rhodesian government of Ian Smith (b.1919), made on 11 November 1965. The declaration was made in the face of the demand of Britain, the colonial power, that independence was conditional on black majority rule. White minority rule continued illegally in Rhodesia, however, until the escalation of guerrilla activity forced the Smith government into talks in 1979, which resulted in the establishment of black majority rule and the independence of the country as Zimbabwe in 1980.

**UFO.** Unidentified flying object, the name given to objects claimed to have been sighted in the sky such as FLYING SAUCERS, or picked up on radar screens, the exact nature of which is uncertain. Study and observation of UFOs is termed ufology by enthusiasts. The peak of interest in such phenomena was in the 1950s and 1960s. By the close of the 20th century astronomers were generally agreed that there was no evidence for the visitation of earth by ALIENS and that obsession with UFOs had actually delayed legitimate research into the possibility of intelligent life elsewhere. *See also* CLOSE ENCOUNTER; FOO FIGHTER; LITTLE GREEN MEN.

**Ugandan affairs** or **practices.** A euphemism for sexual intercourse popularized by *Private Eye* in the 1970s. The term 'talking about Uganda' first appeared in a gossip item in the magazine's issue of 9 March 1973, describing a fashionable party held by Neal and Corinne Ascherson at which a former cabinet colleague of President Obote of Uganda had a 'meaningful confrontation' with the former

# 787

features editor, Mary Kenny. In a letter to *The Times* of 13 September 1983 Corinne Ascherson, now Adam, identified the coiner of the phrase as the poet and critic James Fenton.

**Ugli.** The proprietary name of a hybrid citrus fruit, first produced in Jamaica by crossing a Seville orange, a grapefruit and a tangerine. The name was registered in 1938 and reflects the resulting fruit's unprepossessing appearance.

**Ugly American.** An American who behaves objectionably abroad. The expression derives from the title of William J. Lederer and Eugene Burdick's bestselling novel *The Ugly American* (1958), telling of tragic American misadventures in Southeast Asia during the COLD WAR. The parallel 'ugly Australian' was coined in the 1970s (*see also* OCKER).

**Ugly Rumours.** The rock band in which Tony Blair (*see* BUSH'S POODLE) performed while an undergraduate at Oxford in the 1970s. Subsequently, he has rarely passed up an opportunity to be photographed with his guitar.

**Uhu.** The adhesive so named was first formulated in 1932 by Hugo and August Fischer in Bühl, southwest Germany. Their chemical company already produced goods with brand names based on birds, such as *Pelikan* and *Schwan*, and for this new product they selected *Uhu*, 'eagle-owl', a bird found in the nearby Black Forest, its own name based on its cry.

**UKIP.** The United Kingdom Independence Party, a right-wing political party formed in 1993. It campaigns on a platform of 'Five Freedoms': 'freedom from the European Union, freedom from crime, freedom from overcrowding [i.e. freedom from 'mass immigration'], freedom from bureaucratic politicians, freedom from political correctness'. It is seen by some of its opponents as a middle-class, *Daily Mail* version of the British National Party (*see* NATIONAL FRONT). *See also* REFERENDUM PARTY; VERITAS.

**UK plc.** A jargonistic synonym for BRITAIN PLC.

**Ukridge.** An idle opportunist (in full, Stanley Featherstonehaugh Ukridge), who is one of the less appealing characters created by the comic writer P.G. Wodehouse. Constantly coming up with get-rich-quick schemes that never succeed and usually leave others in the lurch, he appears in several novels and short stories, including *Ukridge* (1924). In a BBC television version of his misadventures (1968), he was played by Anton Rogers.

**Ulster Defence Association.** The largest Loyalist/Protestant paramilitary group in Northern Ireland, formed in 1971, and banned in 1993. Under its alternative name, the Ulster Freedom Fighters, it engaged in violence against Catholics and the IRA, and the organization frequently fomented civil disruption during the TROUBLES. The UDA/UFF called ceasefires in the mid–late 1990s, and later paralleled such IRA moves, but it opposed the GOOD FRIDAY AGREEMENT and then became embroiled in internecine conflict with the ULSTER VOLUNTEER FORCE.

**Ulster Defence Regiment.** The reserve force of soldiers, many of them part-time, that was established in 1970 in response to the upsurge of terrorism in Northern Ireland. Its predominantly Protestant membership made it controversial in any crisis caused by sectarian rivalry. In 1992 the UDR was merged with the two battalions of the Royal Irish Rangers to form a new Royal Irish Regiment, and for the first time it became a part of the regular British Army.

**Ulster Freedom Fighters.** *See* ULSTER DEFENCE ASSOCIATION.

**Ulster Unionist Party.** A political party in Northern Ireland, founded in 1905 to resist the threat of all-Ireland HOME RULE. It is right-of-centre in orientation and advocates equality for Northern Ireland within the United Kingdom and so opposes union with the Republic of Ireland. For long it had the broadest support of any party in the province, reflecting the majority Protestant 'British' population of Northern Ireland, and for many years it consistently won a large proportion of parliamentary and local seats. The UUP opposed the Anglo-Irish Agreement of 1985 but cautiously welcomed the DOWNING STREET DECLARATION of 1993. Under David Trimble (its leader 1995–2005), it supported the GOOD FRIDAY AGREEMENT of 1998.

The party is sometimes known as the Official Unionist Party to distinguish it from the more hard-line Democratic Unionist Party (DUP), which, in the 2003 election for the Legislative Assembly, gained more seats than the Ulster Unionist Party. In the UK general election of 2005 the UUP was trounced by the DUP, retaining just one seat at Westminster; Trimble lost his seat and resigned, entering the House of Lords in 2006. *See also* NOBEL PRIZE; PAISLEYITES.

**Ulster Volunteer Force.** The UVF was formed in 1913 by Sir Edward Carson, an ultra-Unionist Dublin barrister, with the military assistance of senior officers in the British Army, its aim being to provide military support for the resistance of Ulster's (Protestant) Loyalists to the third (Irish) HOME RULE Bill. During the First World War members of the UVF fought with the 36th (Ulster) Division on the battlefields of the SOMME, gaining a reputation for bravery that still resonates in the folk memory of Northern Ireland's Protestants. The UVF was active in sectarian warfare in Belfast during the early 1920s, but by the Second World War had virtually ceased to exist. Its veterans, however, formed the basis of the notorious B SPECIALS.

The name was subsequently revived in the 1960s for a clandestine Protestant paramilitary force that was responsible for sectarian assassinations preceding the TROUBLES. The UVF was outlawed in the 1970s, when it remained less popular and active than the ULSTER DEFENCE ASSOCIATION (UDA), with which it frequently clashed. Its public image was boosted by the prominence of its long-imprisoned leader, Gusty Spence, in the announcement of the UVF ceasefire that followed the IRA ceasefire of 1994.

**Ultra.** *See* ENIGMA.

**Ulysses.** James Joyce's Modernist (*see* MODERNISM) novel of 1922, regarded by many as the 20th century's most important work of fiction in the English language. The book was published by a small press in Paris in 1922, after three US judges had banned further publication of chapters in the United States. The narrative centres on a single day, 16 June 1904, the day on which Joyce had his first formal date with Nora Barnacle (1884–1951), a barmaid with whom in October that year he went to Zurich and then lived in Pola and Trieste. They married in 1931, after they had had a son in 1905 and a daughter in 1907. The book tells of a day in the life of its Jewish-Irish hero, Leopold Bloom, his wife, Molly, and Stephen Dedalus, the protagonist of the author's *A PORTRAIT OF THE ARTIST AS A YOUNG MAN* (1916). The structure of the book is intended to parallel that of Homer's *Odyssey*, with Odysseus's 19 years of wandering compared to Bloom's single day of roaming in Dublin. Bloom thus represents Odysseus (Ulysses), Molly answers approximately to Penelope and Dedalus corresponds to Telemachus. The work is famous for its STREAM OF CONSCIOUSNESS style and for Molly's lengthy, unpunctuated monologue that concludes it. T.S. Eliot commented: 'James Joyce has no style but is the vacuum into which all styles rush.' The variety of styles and of narrative and typographical techniques in *Ulysses* express the different ways in which different people perceive. It was eventually cleared for publication in the United States, the judge concluding: 'whilst in many places the effect of *Ulysses* on the reader undoubtedly is somewhat emetic, nowhere does it tend to be an aphrodisiac.' *Ulysses* was published in the United States in 1934, and in Britain in 1936. *See also* BLOOMSDAY; FINNEGANS WAKE; FIRST LINES OF NOVELS.

**Umpteen.** Many; countless. The word is a blend of *umpty*, military slang for a dash in reading the Morse code, and *-teen* in the numbers 13 to 19. It dates from the First World War period.

**Unabomber.** The byname of Theodore Kaczynski, a US professor at the University of California at Berkeley, who in 1998 was given three life sentences for his 17-year reign of terror in the United States. He killed three people and injured 28 in a series of bomb attacks, although the reasons for these remained unclear. The main motivation seems to have been a conservation issue. The *una-* of the name refers to the *u*niversities and *a*irlines where his bombs first exploded.

**Unacceptable face of capitalism.** A phrase used by the Conservative prime minister, Edward Heath, in a parliamentary answer on 15 May 1973 alluding to the so-called 'LONRHO affair'. This concerned a large payment made to the former Tory cabinet minister, Duncan Sandys, as compensation for leaving his consultancy post with the Lonrho Company, and in turn paid by him into an account in the Cayman Islands in order to avoid British tax. Heath's actual words (apparently drafted by Douglas Hurd) were:

> It is the unpleasant and unacceptable face of capitalism, but one should not suggest that the whole of British industry consists of practices of this kind.

The expression subsequently came to apply to the 'unacceptable face' of almost anything. *See also* ACCEPTABLE FACE.

**Unanswered Question, The.** A short 'philosophical' orchestral work by Charles Ives (1874–1954). It was composed in 1906. The subtitle of the work is 'A Contemplation of a Serious Matter', and in it the two instrumental groups represent the Real and the Transcendental, and are obliged to deploy an element of improvisation. As Ives observed elsewhere: 'Beauty in music is too often confused with something that lets the ears lie back in an easy chair.'

**Unbearable Bassington, The.** A satirical novella (1912) by SAKI (H.H. Munro). The title of the book refers to Comus Bassington, who flouts his mother's attempts to marry him off in order to maintain her materialistic existence in the self-serving society of the EDWARDIAN ERA. Its bleak ending symbolizes the doomed generation who were shortly to lose their lives in the First World War, as Saki himself did.

**Unbearable Lightness of Being, The.** A novel (1984; in Czech as *Nesnesitelná lehkost bytí*, 1984) of the MAGIC REALISM school, by Milan Kundera (b.1929), in which the fates of two couples are played out against a background of communist rule in Czechoslovakia. In such circumstances, there is an unbearable foreboding even when the 'sweet lightness of being' rises 'out of the depths of the future'. An unsatisfying film version (1987), starring Daniel Day-Lewis and Juliette Binoche, was directed by Philip Kaufman.

**Uncertainty principle.** A principle in quantum mechanics

enunciated in 1927 by the German physicist Werner Heisenberg (1901–76). The principle, also known as Heisenberg's uncertainty principle or the indeterminacy principle, states that it is not possible to measure accurately the position and momentum of a particle at any one time, as the very act of observing alters the outcome. Although the principle is significant only at the level of subatomic particles, it serves to undermine Newton's mechanistic account of the universe. It has important philosophical implications, not least because it casts doubt on the concept of causation. As a graffito seen in London in the 1970s has it, 'Heisenberg probably rules OK.'

**Uncle Joe.** A nickname for Joseph STALIN (1879–1953), supreme leader of the Soviet Union from 1929 until his death. The nickname was awarded to Stalin by his British allies during the Second World War, but his avuncular appearance belied the true nature of the tyrant responsible for the deaths of millions of his own people. More appropriate was his adopted name (he was born Iosif Vissarionovich Dzhugashvili): Stalin means 'man of steel'. *See also* FOUL-MOUTHED JOE.

**Uncle Mac.** The name adopted by Derek McCulloch (1892–1978), presenter of children's programmes on BBC Radio from the 1930s, first on CHILDREN'S HOUR and then on the Saturday morning *Children's Favourites* (which died with the Light Programme in 1967). On *Children's Hour* during the Second World War Uncle Mac would end the programme – which went out to an audience around the world – with the words 'Goodnight, children … everywhere.' This would be followed by the chimes of Big Ben and the V-for-victory theme. *Goodnight Children Everywhere* became the title of a play (1997) by Richard Nelson, about a boy evacuated to Canada who returns to Britain, an orphan, in 1945.

**Uncle of Europe, The.** *See* EDWARD THE CARESSER.

**Uncle Sam.** A personification of the United States. It originated in the neighbourhood of Troy, New York, in about 1812, partly from the frequent appearance of the initials US on government supplies to the army and others, but its prevalence derives from the 20th century. (The other contributory factor to the derivation is puzzling, but some have maintained that there was a local resident who had a connection with army supplies and who was actually known as Uncle Sam.)

Uncle Sam is typically depicted as a rather disreputable-looking travelling showman, in stripy trousers and a top hat with stars in the band. In recruiting posters in both world wars, he points fiercely at the viewer, with the slogan 'I want *you*'. In antiwar posters from the Vietnam era, the face of Uncle Sam becomes a skull.

**Underclass.** In the jargon of sociology a term for the lowest social stratum of society, mainly consisting of the poor, the uneducated and the unemployed, the latter in many cases being unemployable. The term dates from the 1960s as a translation of Swedish *underklass*.

**Underground mutton.** A jocular Australian term (first recorded in 1946) for rabbit meat. Rabbits are (excessively) plentiful in the outback, and are a useful resource when times are hard.

**Under Milk Wood.** A radio play by Dylan Thomas (1914–53), first broadcast on BBC Radio on 25 January 1954. The original title of the first part was LLAREGGUB ('bugger all' spelt backwards), the name of the Welsh seaside town in which the author introduces such characters as Myfanwy Price the dressmaker, her lover Mog Edwards the draper, the Rev. Eli Jenkins and Captain Cat. Friends persuaded the poet to opt for *Under Milk Wood* as the title, having convinced him that US readers would not understand his joke. Milk Wood is the wood above the town where Polly Garter has illicit meetings with the 'gandering hubbies' of other women. Laugharne, the Carmarthenshire town where Thomas is buried, is often identified as the model for his Llareggub.

> To begin at the beginning:
> It is spring, moonless night in the small town, starless and bible-black …
> DYLAN THOMAS: *Under Milk Wood* (opening lines)

*See also* BOYO.

**Under one's own steam.** Alone and unaided. The expression dates from the 1940s and alludes to the power provided by a steam engine.

**Under starter's orders.** Of racehorses or other runners, awaiting the starter's signal to depart. The expression dates from the 1960s. *See also* READY, STEADY, GO!

**Under the counter.** A phrase first current in the Second World War in connection with an illegal practice in some shops. Articles in short supply were kept out of sight, under the counter, for sale to favoured customers, often at inflated prices.

> Chief goods to 'go under the counter' are fully fashioned silk stockings, watches and silk handkerchiefs.
> *Evening Standard* (20 December 1945)

**Under the Volcano.** A novel (1947) by Malcolm Lowry (1909–57), intended to be one part of a Dante-esque novel sequence to be called 'The Voyage that Never Ends'. The first draft was written in Mexico in sight of the volcano Popocatepetl, after a spell in hospital in the United States, which failed to cure Lowry's alcoholism. The presence of the volcano looms over the account of a disillusioned British consul, destroyed by drink and drugs, during the Mexican Day of the Dead. A film version (1984), starring Albert Finney and directed by John Huston, sacrificed the subtlety of the original in favour of a seemingly endless drunken monologue.

**Underwhelmed.** Unimpressed; disappointed. This facetious counterpart to 'overwhelmed' began to emerge in English from the 1950s.

**Under wraps.** Concealed; hidden away. The term, which dates from the 1930s, is typically used of a new project, such as an innovative design or a new car model, which is kept secret until completion.

**Uni.** Student slang for a university, especially when of the REDBRICK variety.

**Unilateral declaration of independence.** *See* UDI.

**Unilateral nuclear disarmament.** The aim of CND and other anti-nuclear organizations, which believe that the world will be freed from the threat of a nuclear holocaust only if nuclear disarmament is started by one country; others will then follow. Unilateral nuclear disarmament or unilateralism was for long a topic of fierce debate within the British LABOUR PARTY (*see also* NAKED INTO THE CONFERENCE CHAMBER): it was briefly the policy of the Labour Party in 1960, and again in the 1980s (*see* LONGEST SUICIDE NOTE IN HISTORY) until abandoned by the then party leader Neil Kinnock in 1987. Despite the impassioned commitment of its supporters, unilateral nuclear disarmament never became a majority view among the wider public, and so it proved to be a vote-loser.

The ending of the COLD WAR to some extent made the issue recede; but in the 21st century the rising concern about ROGUE STATES with WEAPONS OF MASS DESTRUCTION revivified concerns.

**Unilever.** The name of the manufacturers and sellers of a wide range of soaps and foods was created on 1 January 1930 as a result of a merger between the Dutch company Margarine Union and the British firm of Lever Brothers Ltd. The latter took its name from William Hesketh Lever (1851–1921), later Lord Leverhulme, a retail grocer's son born in Bolton, Lancashire, and his brother, James D'Arcy Lever, who set up Lever Brothers in 1885 to make and sell Sunlight Soap and, from 1894, Lifebuoy Carbolic Soap.

**Unisex.** Designed to be suitable for both sexes. The term arose in the late 1960s and particularly applied to dress, hairstyles and the like. Unisex clothing was pioneered by the French fashion designer André Courrèges (b.1923). By the end of the century unisex hairdressers were universal, although similar provision did not always extend to all areas of equal personal requirements.

> Wendy Shillam, an architect with a reputation for speaking her mind on 'feminist' issues, initially laughed when I raised the topic … Her own preferred solution would be unisex loos.
>
> *The Times* (6 September 1999)

**UNITA.** An acronym for the *União Nacional para a Independência Total de Angola* (Portuguese, 'National Union for the Total Independence of Angola'), a political and guerrilla group in Angola founded in 1966 by Jonas Savimbi (1934–2002). UNITA played an important part in the struggle for independence against the colonial power, Portugal, along with two other liberation groups: the *Movimento Popular de Libertação de Angola* (MPLA; 'Popular Movement for the Liberation of Angola') and the *Frente Nacional de Libertação de Angola* (FNLA; 'National Front for the Liberation of Angola'). When Portugal suddenly withdrew from the country in November 1975 it left the capital, Luanda, in the hands of the Soviet-backed MPLA, while UNITA and the FNLA set up a rival government in Huambo. Civil war followed, with the MPLA being supported by a large Cuban force, while UNITA was helped by South African raids, and, from 1985, US military aid. Angola had become a pawn in the COLD WAR. By this time the FNLA had ceased to be a player. Eventually a ceasefire was agreed in 1991, and multiparty elections were held the following year. The MPLA beat UNITA in the elections, but Savimbi refused to accept the results, and civil war broke out again. Another peace agreement came in 1994, but Savimbi subsequently rejected the offer of the vice-presidency in a coalition government. In 1998 UNITA, which had supposedly been demilitarized, was expelled from the government for failing to hand over its weapons, and fighting broke out once more. Savimbi was killed in action in 2002, and shortly after his death a ceasefire was declared.

**United Nations.** The successor to the LEAGUE OF NATIONS as a world organization primarily concerned with the maintenance of peace but with numerous other functions, funds and agencies. They include UNHCR (UN High Commission for Refugees), the confusingly similar UNHCHR (UN High Commission on Human Rights), UNICEF (formerly UN Children's International Emergency Fund, now just UN Children's Fund), the WFP (World Food Programme), and UNESCO (UN Educational, Scientific and Cultural Organization).

The United Nations sprang from the DUMBARTON OAKS

talks (1944) between the United States, Britain and the Soviet Union and was formally inaugurated in 1945. Its headquarters are in New York City, though there are other principal UN offices in Geneva, Vienna and Nairobi. The term 'United Nations' was originally used earlier in the Second World War as a name for the Allied nations, in particular the United States, the Soviet Union and members of the British Commonwealth, which united against the AXIS powers. Its most powerful body is the Security Council, whose five permanent members reflect the outcome of the Second World War: China, France, Russia (previously the Soviet Union), the UK and the United States.

In the *Supplement* (1945) to the massive fourth edition of his book *The American Language* (1936), the US linguistic historian H.L. Mencken recounts the origin of the name as follows:

> *United Nations* was coined by President Franklin Roosevelt. This was during Winston Churchill's visit to Washington at the end of December, 1941. He was a guest at the White House, and he and Churchill discussed the choice of a name for the new alliance. One morning, lying in bed, Roosevelt thought of *United Nations*, and at once sought Churchill, who was in his bath. 'How about *United Nations*?' he called through the door. 'That', replied Churchill, 'should do it'. And so it was.

**United Reformed Church.** The church formed in 1972 from the union of a large majority of the Congregational Church of England and Wales with the Presbyterian Church of England. It was joined in 1981 by the majority of the Disciples of Christ, a religious body set up among Scottish Presbyterians in the United States in the 19th century, and as some of these congregations were in Scotland took the name United Reformed Church in the United Kingdom.

**Unit One.** The name of a group of 11 avant-garde British artists formed in 1933, its creation being announced by Paul Nash (1889–1946) in a letter to *The Times* of 12 June that year. The name was intended to denote that while each artist was an individual unit, their common interests were one. The group consisted of seven painters: John Armstrong (1893–1973), John Bigge (1892–1973), Edward Burra (1905–76), Tristram Hillier (1905–83), Nash himself, Ben Nicholson (1894–1982) and Edward Wadsworth (1889–1949); two sculptors: Barbara Hepworth (1903–75) and Henry Moore (1898–1986); and two architects: Colin Lucas (1906–84) and Wells Coates (1895–1958). Hillier replaced Frances Hodgkins (1869–1947), who had been originally named in Nash's letter. Although Unit One was short lived, it had considerable impact in its promotion of abstract art and SURREALISM.

**Universal Declaration of Human Rights.** A document adopted by the General Assembly of the UNITED NATIONS in 1948 setting forth basic rights and fundamental freedoms to which all are entitled. They include the right to life, liberty, freedom from servitude and torture, fair trial, marriage, ownership of property, freedom of thought and conscience, freedom of expression and the rights to vote, work and to be educated.

**University Challenge.** A television student challenge quiz programme running from 1962 to 1987 on ITV and again from 1994 on BBC2. The questions are largely but not entirely academic in nature and the answers sometimes embarrassingly naive. The quizmaster for the first series was the amiable Bamber Gascoigne, while the second series was presented somewhat more acerbically by Jeremy Paxman (*see* PAXO).

The introduction of a greater number of popular-culture questions into the second series, on topics such as pop hits and REALITY TV, prompted some to wonder if dumbing down (*see* DUMB DOWN) was taking place. Defenders, however, could point to the continued preponderance of baffling mathematical and chemical formulae in the overall mix. A recent summer innovation has been a separate battle of competing professionals, representing their particular fields: winners have included teams from the Inland Revenue (2003), the British Library (2004), the Privy Council Office (2005) and the Bodleian Library (2006).

**University of Life.** That institution to which those without a degree claim to owe their success.

> What poor education I have received has been gained in the University of Life.
> HORATIO BOTTOMLEY: speech at the Oxford Union (2 December 1920). Bottomley, a politician and rich businessman, was subsequently jailed for fraud.

The Russian writer Maxim Gorky entitled the third volume of his autobiography *My Universities* (1923), referring to his education in the university of life, his ambition to study for a degree having been thwarted.

In the 1970s, when sweatshirts with the name of one's university were popular among the heartier sort of student, both in the UK and America, a clever entrepreneur came up with a line of sweatshirts emblazoned with:

> Idontgoto
> University

**University of the Air.** *See* OPEN UNIVERSITY.

**Unknown Political Prisoner, The.** A sculpture (1951–2) by Reg Butler (1913–81), which in 1953 won an international competition for a piece with such a title, against competition from established figures like Alexander Calder, Naum Gabo and Barbara Hepworth. Actually, the piece only exists as a maquette in the Tate; it proved impractical to build the full-sized version, which would have been gigantic, so what we are left with is more properly entitled *Project for Monument to the Unknown Political Prisoner*. Butler, whose name the piece made, described it as 'an iron cage, a transmuted gallows or guillotine on an outcrop of rock'.

**Unknown Prime Minister.** A sobriquet of Andrew Bonar Law (1858–1923), Conservative politician and prime minister for 209 days in 1922–3 in succession to Lloyd George. His premiership was cut short by ill health: he resigned in May 1923 and died six months later. His funeral service was held in Westminster Abbey.

> It is fitting that we should have buried the Unknown Prime Minister by the side of the Unknown Soldier.
>
> HERBERT ASQUITH: quoted in Robert Blake, *The Unknown Prime Minister* (1955)

**Unknown unknowns.** The stuff of nightmares for Donald Rumsfeld, US secretary of defense from 2001, who in a news conference on 12 February 2002 discussed the threats posed to the United States:

> As we know, there are known knowns. There are things we know we know. We also know there are known unknowns. That is to say we know there are some things we do not know. But there are also unknown unknowns, the ones we don't know we don't know.

*See also* WAR ON TERROR.

**Unknown Warrior.** The body of an unknown British soldier of the First World War brought home from one of the battlefields of the WESTERN FRONT and 'buried among the kings' in Westminster Abbey (11 November 1920). The inscription, in capital letters, begins: 'Beneath this stone rests the body of a British warrior unknown by name or rank brought from France to lie among the most illustrious of the land and buried here on Armistice Day.' Similar tombs were set up in the Arlington National Cemetery, Virginia, beneath the Arc de Triomphe in Paris, in the Unter den Linden in Berlin, and by the walls of the Kremlin in Moscow. In 1958 the bodies of two more unknown US servicemen were placed in the Tomb of the Unknown Soldier at Arlington, one who died in the Second World War and one who died in the KOREAN WAR (1950–3). Casualties of later conflicts have also been housed there. DNA testing has since confirmed that the VIETNAM 'Unknown' is US Air Force Lieutenant Michael J. Blassie, who was killed in action in 1972.

***Unofficial Rose, An.*** A novel by Irish Murdoch (1919–99), published in 1962. Randall, a rose grower (like the author), leaves his wife for a young woman with whom he is smitten. The title comes from:

> Unkempt about those hedges blows
> An English unofficial rose;
> And there the unregulated sun
> Slopes down to rest when day is done …
>
> RUPERT BROOKE: *The Old Vicarage, Grantchester* (1912)

**Untermenschen.** (German, 'subhumans'.) A term applied by NAZI racial theorists to Jews, Slavs, gypsies and other groups regarded as inferior. The term thus served to help justify the appalling treatment inflicted on these peoples. The idea was in contrast to *Übermenschen* (German, 'supermen'), the Nazi ideal of powerful, physically perfect Nordic 'Aryans', who had the right to dominate and exploit lesser humans. The *Übermensch* was first conceived by the German philosopher Friedrich Nietzsche (1844–1900) as an elitist rather than racist idea: the superman is one of those rare humans who are capable of rising above the 'herd' to achieve the 'enhancement of life'. The 'will to power' Nietzsche talked about in relation to the *Übermensch* seems to have involved self-affirmation rather than the oppression of others. It seems that it was Nietzsche's sister who reinterpreted the philosopher's thinking in line with Nazi ideology. *See also* FINAL SOLUTION; HOLOCAUST; SUPERMAN.

***Untouchables, The.*** A 1959 television drama about the struggle between the gangster Al CAPONE and Eliot Ness of the Bureau of Prohibition in Chicago. It was based on Ness's own book of that name (1947), the 'untouchables' being Ness's incorruptible agents. The drama was followed by two series and a 1987 feature film, starring Kevin Costner as Ness and Robert de Niro as Capone, and directed by Brian De Palma (*see also* ODESSA STEPS).

**Up and running.** Operating; functioning. The phrase is particularly associated with computers that have been 'booted up' and that are running normally, but it has been extended to other activities requiring an initial opening or starting procedure.

**Up a storm.** In colloquial American English, 'with great vehemence, enthusiasm or energy'. It is probably most commonly encountered in the expression 'to cook up a storm':

> Right now she's cooking up a storm in preparation for the rash of friends who will be stopping by on their way to Expo.
>
> *Boston Sunday Herald Magazine* (30 April 1967)

But it also occurs in a range of other contexts:

Bryn Terfel ... sings up a storm as Wotan, ruler of the gods.
*Radio Times* (26 March 2005)

**Up for grabs.** Easily obtainable; ready to be taken. The image is of something being tossed in the air for anyone to grasp or catch. The expression dates from the 1920s.

**Up for it.** Ready for any activity, especially when dangerous or exciting.

If you thought Ibiza was simply a place where battalions of up-for-it clubbers go every summer to get out of it, think again.
*heat* (6–12 January 2000)

**Upside.** The positive or advantageous aspect of something, as opposed to the 'downside', the negative or disadvantageous aspect. The term evolved in the 1960s and originally applied to the upward movement of share prices.

**Upside-down cake.** A sponge cake that is turned out after baking so that the base becomes the top, displaying a decorative pattern composed of fruit. The name implies that the cake is the wrong side up, which of course is not the case. A number of culinary dishes involve an inversion from a mould or the like, such as a blancmange, and are 'right side up' when they emerge.

***Upstairs, Downstairs.*** A highly regarded television series of period drama screened on ITV from 1971 to 1975. It was based on the sharp social divisions that existed in the EDWARDIAN ERA between a well-to-do household and its domestic staff, the respective 'upstairs' and 'downstairs' of the title. The 'downstairs' characters were much more roundly developed than the 'upstairs' Bellamy family, and included Hudson the butler, played by Gordon Jackson, Mrs Bridges the housekeeper, played by Angela Baddeley, and one of the housemaids, Rose, played by Jean Marsh, who together with Eileen Atkins devised the series as a whole.

**Up the creek.** In trouble; facing problems; pregnant. A fuller form is 'up the creek without a paddle'. One is thus in a difficult situation without the means of extricating oneself from it. *See also* SHIT.

**Up the duff.** Pregnant. 'Duff' has the sense of 'pudding'. The expression dates from the 1940s. *See also* BUN IN THE OVEN; IN THE CLUB.

At 19, he was married ('only because she was up the duff' he explains gallantly).
*Daily Telegraph* (26 September 1994)

**Up there.** On a level with others in high esteem. The phrase dates from the 1970s and is often expanded to 'up there with the best of them'. The image is almost of a 'board of honour' or a displayed notice of awards.

Ten inches of pink plastic perfection with a wardrobe to die for, Barbie is up there with Coca-Cola and McDonald's as one of the icons of the last century.
*heat* (6–12 January 2000)

**Uptight.** Nervous, tense; angry, irritated; straitlaced, conventional. All senses date from the 1960s and have the general idea of being 'wound up' and the converse of relaxed.

What this ability to ridicule ourselves tells us about our national [British] character is reassuring. Certainly, it goes directly against the common view ... that we are 'uptight'.
*Sunday Express* (27 February 2000)

**Up to a point, Lord Copper.** An expression of polite or deferential disagreement. It derives from Evelyn Waugh's novel *Scoop* (1938), in which Lord Copper is a newspaper proprietor: 'Mr Salter's side of the conversation was limited to expressions of assent. When Lord Copper was right he said, "Definitely, Lord Copper"; when he was wrong, "Up to a point".' *See also* FIRST LINES OF NOVELS.

'Pardoe's of Netherton, Theakston's of Masham, Adnam's of Southwold, Young's of Wandsworth ... These are the great chateaux of British beer.' Well, up to a point, Lord Copper.
*Sunday Times* (26 September 1999)

**Up to here.** As much as one can stand. The phrase dates from the 1940s and is usually found in a statement such as: 'I've had it up to here.' A gesture of the back of the hand to the chin, indicating that one is 'fed up' to that point, frequently accompanies the comment.

**Up to putty.** In Australian slang, below the required standard; useless. The expression dates from the First World War period, and may well have been coined in deliberate contrast with 'up to snuff', a phrase of 19th-century origin meaning 'of an adequate standard' (snuff is a powder, and in the past 'putty' often denoted a powder from which the now familiar putty paste is made).

I had a beaut result with a lady who couldn't read her kitchen scales so her cooking was 'up to putty'.
www.aris.com.au (9 November 1999)

**Up yours.** A crude exclamation of contemptuous rejection, in spoken form often accompanied by a V-SIGN. The implied full phrase is 'Up your arse'. In November 1990 *The Sun* famously flaunted a front-page heading 'UP YOURS DELORS' for the benefit of Jacques Delors, president of the European Commission.

**Urban guerrilla.** A guerrilla operating in towns or cities and involved in kidnapping, bombing or the like. The term dates from the 1960s, 'urban' indicating the particular area of operations, as distinct from the more usual rural terrain. *See* *also* ASYMMETRIC WARFARE; BAADER-MEINHOF GANG; RED BRIGADES; TUPAMAROS.

**Urban myth** or **legend.** A term current from the 1980s to describe a piece of modern folkore in the form of a widely known story, often macabre in nature. Such stories are called urban because they relate to modern urban society. They are largely apocryphal, but may contain elements of reality or plausibility, and usually take the form of an anecdote, told as if actually experienced by someone known to the teller or at any rate to 'a friend of a friend'. One of the best known is 'The Stolen Corpse', told in many variants but essentially involving a family holidaying in Spain who find one morning that their grandmother has died. Concerned about the formalities, they place the body in a hamper on the roof of the car and set off to find the British consul. On the way they stop for a snack, but on returning to the car find that it has been stolen, complete with the grandmother. Further examples are related in Roy Palmer's *Britain's Living Folklore* (1991) and in *The Vanishing Hitchhiker* (1988) by Jan Harold Brunvand.

**Urinals, Artistic.** *See* FOUNTAIN.

**URL.** In computing the abbreviation of 'universal resource locator', an address that gives each page on the WORLD WIDE WEB a unique location.

**_U.S.A._** A trilogy of novels (1930–6) by the US writer John Dos Passos (1896–1970), presenting from a left-wing perspective a sprawling and somewhat embittered panorama of the United States in the first three decades of the 20th century. As a background to the fictional stories of a wide range of characters there is a documentary assemblage of biographies of real people, such as Henry Ford, Woodrow Wilson, Eugene Debs, J.P. Morgan and Joe Hill, plus the 'newsreel' – news clippings, popular songs, advertisements and headlines. A third form of narrative, the 'camera eye', presents the author's own stream-of-consciousness impressions of his subject. The trilogy comprises: *The 42nd Parallel* (1930), covering the period up to the First World War; *1919* (1932), covering the war and the Paris Peace Conference; and *The Big Money* (1936), covering the 1920s JAZZ AGE boom and the GREAT DEPRESSION of the 1930s.

**User-friendly.** Easy to use or operate. The expression arose in the 1970s, originally with reference to computers, but its range of applications soon broadened, the second part of the term going on to give new formations such as 'environment-friendly', meaning not harmful to the environment.

**Usual suspects, The.** A term (usually now humorously applied) for the sort of people one would expect to be involved in the affair in question. The phrase originates from a line in the film CASABLANCA. When Major Strasser, a German, is shot, the local Vichy police chief, Louis Renault (who is by this stage clearly sympathetic to the Allied cause, and who has seen who killed Strasser) issues the famous order:

> Round up the usual suspects!
>
> JULIUS and PHILIP EPSTEIN: screenplay for *Casablanca* (1942)

The phrase received a boost when *The Usual Suspects* became the title of a crime-thriller feature film (1995) starring Gabriel Byrne and Kevin Spacey, with a clever and complex Oscar-winning screenplay by Christopher McQuarrie.

**Utah Beach.** The Allied code name for a stretch of beach on the east side of the Cotentin peninsula on the Normandy coast. On D-DAY the US 4th Infantry Division landed here. Utah is a state in the Rocky Mountains in the western United States.

**Utility.** The official term given during and after the Second World War to clothing, furniture and the like made according to government specification and sold at controlled prices. The name was a sign of the austerity of the times, practical qualities being more important than ornamentation. The goods bore a symbol consisting of two circles with a wedge removed from each, representing a reduction, and the figure 41, representing the year 1941, that of the scheme's introduction.

**U-turn.** A reversal of policy; a volte face, especially by a leading politician or even head of state. The expression dates from the 1950s and derives from the literal U-turn made by the driver of a motor vehicle when changing direction. A noted political U-turn was made by Edward Heath, Conservative prime minister from 1970 to 1974, when a growing economic crisis obliged him to abandon free-market reforms in favour of a more interventionist approach in 1971. Margaret Thatcher, prime minister from 1979 to 1990, famously invoked the term in order to deny it: *see* the LADY'S NOT FOR TURNING.

> Yesterday the Tories undertook a breathtaking U-turn. John Redwood paraded in Parliament as a defender of the countryside.
>
> *The Times* (3 November 1999)

In 2003 Tony Blair implicitly referred to U-turns when he told the Labour Party Conference: 'I can only go one way, I've not got a reverse gear.'

**U-2.** On 5 May 1960 President Khrushchev of the USSR told the Supreme Soviet that a US high-altitude Lockheed U-2 aircraft had been shot down over Soviet territory on 1 May and its pilot captured. On 7 May the US government admitted it had been carrying out a spying mission. The incident was used by Khrushchev to humiliate the US president, Dwight D. Eisenhower, and to break up the summit conference in Paris on 17 May. The pilot, Gary Powers (1929–77), was convicted at a SHOW TRIAL in Moscow but in 1962 was released in exchange for Rudolf Abel, a Russian spy held by the United States. Powers published his view of the incident in *Operation Overflight* (1970). *See also* ROCK GROUP NAMES.

**UVF.** *See* ULSTER VOLUNTEER FORCE.

# V

**V.** The first novel (1963) by Thomas Pynchon (b.1937), an author of such reclusive habits that the only known photograph of him was taken in 1955. The title initial is the name under which a mysterious woman manifests herself at key moments of disaster that have contributed to the formation of modern Europe and America. V appears in various guises, including Victoria Wren, Vera Meroving, Venus, Virgin and Void. (The shape of the letter V may also symbolize the collision course of two otherwise unrelated chains of events.) The two protagonists, among 200 named characters, are Herbert Stencil, obsessed with finding V, which he never does, and Benny Profane, an accident-prone realist. As Stencil's father notes in his journal: 'There is more behind and inside V than any of us had suspected. Not who, but what: what is she.'

*V* is also the title of a long poem by Tony Harrison (b.1937) written during the Miners' Strike in 1985, and broadcast on television in 1987.

***Vagina Monologues, The.*** A stage show (1998) by the US feminist Eve Ensler, based on a large number of interviews she conducted in various parts of the world with women, asking them about their relationships with their vaginas. Topics covered include smell, pubic hair, sex, masturbation, orgasms, rape, mutilation, secretions, periods, birth, the names given to vaginas, what vaginas might wear if they dressed up, what they might say, and so on.

Celebrities have queued up to speak the monologues on stage, memorably on 'V-day' (St Valentine's Day) 2001, before 18,000 people in Madison Square Garden, New York, when the many speakers included the likes of Glenn Close, Brooke Shields, Isabella Rossellini, Gloria Steinem, Calista Flockhart, Oprah Winfrey, Phoebe Snow and Jane Fonda. Other women criticized the show for equating sex with violence rather than pleasure, while Camille Paglia lambasted the 'psychological poison of Ensler's

archaic creed of victimization'. *See also* PUPPETRY OF THE PENIS.

**Valentine State.** A nickname of Arizona, so called with reference to the date of its entry into the Union, 14 February 1912, Valentine's Day.

**Valium.** A proprietary name for diazepam, an anti-anxiety drug, hypnotic and muscle relaxant. Together with LIBRIUM it was the notorious dependency sedative of the 1960s and the 1970s. The name may derive from Latin *valere*, 'to be strong'.

**Valley Girl.** Originally, in the early 1980s, a fashionable and affluent teenage girl from the San Fernando Valley, near Los Angeles, California, where VALSPEAK was spoken. Over the ensuing decades in US slang the term broke its original geographical connections and came to denote any fairly airheaded affluent young woman whose main concerns were shopping, personal appearance and popularity in her peer group.

**Valley of Ten Thousand Smokes.** A volcanic valley in the region of Mount Katmai, Alaska. Shortly before Mount Katmai erupted on 6 June 1912 there were many bursts of molten matter in the valley, and these fissures have since discharged hot gases. It has been a National Monument since 1918.

***Valley of the Dolls.*** A film (1967), based on a book of the same title (1966) by Jacqueline Susann (*c*.1918–74), about drug-taking among aspiring Hollywood film stars. The 'dolls' of the title are the pills on which the three main characters, all struggling actresses, are dependent. The expression 'valley of the dolls', a mainly US term for drug dependence, comes from the title of the book. The similarly titled film *Beyond the Valley of the Dolls* (1970) had little in common with the first film other than a theme of drug and alcohol addiction in show business.

**Valspeak.** Valspeak or Valleyspeak arose in the early 1980s as the jargon adopted by well-to-do teenagers in the San Fernando Valley near Los Angeles. It was specifically popularized by the rock musician Frank Zappa and his daughter, Moon Unit, in the novelty song 'Valley Girl' (1982), and its words and turns of phrase were characterized by sarcasm and exaggeration, as well as by an underlying ironic tone in expressions such as 'for sure' and 'as if'. Much of its content consisted of 'filler' words such as 'like' and 'totally', and it employed set phrases such as 'grody to the max' (grotty in the extreme). It was typically heard in the speech of the VALLEY GIRL, with her disenchanted view of the world, and has been preserved in the dialogue of several novels and films. A good example of the latter is *Clueless* (1995), a clever re-working of Jane Austen's novel of manners *Emma* (1816), in which a BEVERLY HILLS teenager worries about losing her status as the most popular girl in the school and about winning the boy of her dreams. *See also* NOT!

**Vamp.** A shortening of vampire, as a word for a woman who uses her sexual wiles to attract men. The term arose in the early 20th century and became particularly identified with the US film actress Theda BARA, who first cast her sensual spell in the silent film *A Fool There Was* (1915), based on Kipling's poem 'The Vampire' (1897).

> A fool there was and he made his prayer
> (Even as you and I!)
> To a rag and a bone and a hank of hair
> (We called her the woman who did not care)
> But the fool he called her his lady fair –
> (Even as you and I!)
> RUDYARD KIPLING: 'The Vampire' (1897)

**Vanilla.** Plain and basic, without BELLS AND WHISTLES. The reference is to a plain vanilla ice cream, the most common kind. The metaphor was born, apparently among the US gay community in the early 1970s, in the context of sexual activity, connoting the eschewal of anything more adventurous than basic intercourse, and 'vanilla sex' remains its commonest manifestation, but it has spread to other areas (e.g. computers).

**Vanishing cream.** A cosmetic cream that is readily absorbed by the skin, i.e. it 'vanishes' into it. The name dates from the early 20th century.

**Vanity plate.** A personalized number plate on a private motor vehicle, as the US equivalent of a British CHERISHED NUMBER. The scope is greater, however, since any combination of letters or numbers can be used, provided it does not exceed six characters. This means that whole words can appear without any numbers at all. Thus Paul Rawden, of New Haven, Vermont, acquired a vanity plate reading simply 'PAULR'. Each plate also bears the name of the issuing state.

**Vanity publishing.** The publishing of a book in return for a fee from the author, resorted to by one desperate to see their name in print at any price. The cost is usually exorbitant, the quality of the finished product frequently inferior, and the writer often disappointed and disillusioned. The practice is generally discouraged by professional bodies and literary editors.

> Authors considering vanity publishing should exercise caution.
> *Writers' and Artists' Yearbook 1999*

With the advent of the Internet BLOG, however, one no longer needs to get into print at all to disseminate one's observations, experiences and prejudices.

**VAT.** Value added tax, as essentially a sales tax on various goods and services. In practice it means that a tax is levied on a product each time it changes hands on its route to the point of sale. It was introduced in 1973, and in the mid-2000s there were two rates – 5% and (more commonly) 17½ per cent. The lower rate applies to domestic fuel, house renovations, children's car seats, condoms and other contraceptives, and tampons. There are inconsistencies. Newspapers and books are not subject to VAT, although the processes involved in their production are. Food and drink are generally not subject to VAT, but again there are anomalies. For example, a pie sold cold is not subject to VAT, but the same pie, heated by the vendor and sold as 'takeaway' food, is subject to the tax. Ice creams, chocolates, sweets, potato crisps and alcoholic drinks are also taxable. Further, while public transport in general is not subject to VAT, public transport designed to carry fewer than 12 people is. This means that standard bus and train journeys are zero-rated for VAT, but public minibus trips are not.

**Vatican II.** The short name of Vatican Council II, as the 21st general or ecumenical council of the Roman Catholic Church, held from 11 October 1962 to 8 December 1965. It is regarded by many as the most significant religious event since the Reformation of the 16th century and certainly since Vatican Council I of 1869–70. The proposal to hold the council was apparently entirely due to Pope John XXIII, who attributed the idea of convening such an assembly to a sudden inspiration of the Holy Spirit. He defined its immediate task as the renewal of the life of the Church and of bringing up to date its teaching, discipline and organization, with the unity of all Christians as the ultimate goal. The consequences of the Council have been far-reaching, one being the almost complete replacement of Latin by the vernacular in the liturgy. Communion in both kinds was also extended to the laity, and the relationship with other Churches became warm rather than frigid as hitherto.

**Vatican roulette.** A nickname for the rhythm or calendar method of birth control, in which sexual intercourse is restricted to the times of the woman's menstrual cycle, when ovulation is least likely to occur. It is so called because it is permitted by the Roman Catholic Church and because, like Russian roulette, its efficacy is unpredictable.

**Va-va boom or** or **va-va voom.** A representation of a revving engine and rapid take-off, adopted in the 1960s to suggest sexual allure or 'go' generally. ('Va-va voom' was adopted by the French car manufacturer Renault for its advertising in the late 1990s, to suggest the zippiness and chicness of its cars.) 'Vroom', or a variant of it, is also so used, while *Va Va Voom* is the title of a 'girlie' magazine published by Hugh Hefner, founder of PLAYBOY.

**V-bomber.** One of the three types of long-range jet bomber forming Britain's main nuclear weapons delivery system in the 1950s. The 'V' represents their respective names, as the Avro Vulcan, Handley Page Victor and Vickers Valiant. They were gradually superseded from the 1960s by submarine-based missiles, although some elderly Vulcans took part in the FALKLANDS WAR.

**VC.** *See* VICTOR CHARLIE.

**V-chip.** A device of the 1990s by which a television set can be programmed to block or encrypt a programme containing an unacceptable level of violence, sex or offensive language, usually with children in mind. The 'V' stands for 'viewer' but is popularly thought to represent 'violence'.

**VE Day.** 'Victory in Europe' Day. The end of hostilities in Europe after the Second World War, 8 May 1945. France has an annual public holiday on this day called *Fête de la Liberté et de la Paix* (Freedom and Peace Day). *See also* ARMISTICE DAY; LIBERATION DAY; TWO-MINUTE SILENCE; VJ DAY.

**Veganism.** The adherence to a plant-based diet, avoiding all foods derived from animals, including meat, fish, poultry, eggs, milk and honey. In this strict regime vegans differ from vegetarians, some of whom eat dairy products. Veganism is often adopted in response to the exploitation of animals, although others become vegans for health, ecological or spiritual reasons.

**Vegemite.** A proprietary name for a type of spread made from a concentrated yeast extract. It is regarded as a typical or even prototypical Australian foodstuff, on which all AUSSIES are weaned and reared. The name was coined from a blend of 'vegetable' and MARMITE.

**Veggieburger.** A flat savoury cake (sometimes 'vegeburger') similar to a hamburger, but containing vegetables instead of meat. In 2003 German animal rights activists offered childcare groups in the city of Hamburg 10,000 euros worth of vegetarian burgers if the city changed its name to Veggieburg.

**Velcro.** A proprietary name, registered in Britain in 1960, for a fabric made in narrow strips for use as a fastener. One strip has tiny loops and the other hooks so that they can be fastened by simply being pressed together and unfastened by being pulled apart. The fabric is particularly useful as a quick-release closure for outerwear and footwear such as waterproof jackets and children's shoes. Velcro was invented in 1957 by a Swiss engineer, Georges de Mestral (1902–90), who was inspired by the way burrs stuck to his dog's coat. The name is a shortening of French *velours croché*, 'hooked velvet'.

**Velvet Fog.** A nickname for the popular US singer Mel Tormé (1925–99), alluding to his soft and slightly husky voice and smooth CROONING style.

**Velvet Revolution.** *See* REVOLUTION NAMES.

**Velvet Underground.** *See under* ROCK GROUP NAMES.

**Venture capitalist.** A person engaged in investment, finance or business that is based on so called 'venture capital', now more usually known as risk capital, meaning capital invested in a highly speculative enterprise. The encouragement of small businesses in the 1980s produced a demand for high-risk investment in new ideas and entrepreneurs, with the result that venture capitalism became a regular feature in the world of finance rather than an occasional aspect of traditional financial trading. The downside of the process, for new companies, is that venture capitalists may wish to make their money back (perhaps by selling off the company) rather quicker than traditional, longer-term investors.

**Verbal diarrhoea.** Excessive talk; meaningless monologizing. The phrase arose in the 1940s but 'diarrhoea' as a term for a prolix flow of words was current as early as the 17th century. 'Logorrhoea', based on it and having the same sense, dates from the early 20th century.

> He opens his mouth and lets this noise come out. It's not so much verbal diarrhoea as verbal incontinence.
>
> DERMOT BOLGER (ed.): *Finbar's Hotel*, 'The Test' (1997)

**Verdun.** A French garrison town some 200km (120 miles) east of Paris. During the First World War Verdun came to have an awful significance, as the town and its ring of fortresses (which had remained a French salient since 1914) became the site of the longest and bloodiest battle of the war, lasting from 21 February to 18 December 1916. The stated intention of the Germans in attacking Verdun was to 'bleed the French army white', knowing that the French would defend Verdun at all costs. In command of the German forces was Crown Prince Wilhelm, the LAUGHING MURDERER OF VERDUN, while the French were commanded by General (later Marshal) Philippe Pétain (*see* PÉTAINISTS).

The defence of Verdun became a national crusade in France of almost religious intensity, and both the government and the army high command forbade French withdrawal, despite two recommendations to do so from Pétain. In public Pétain famously promised *'Ils ne passeront pas'* ('THEY SHALL NOT PASS'), and built up a major supply operation along the only road that remained open to Verdun. This small road, under constant German artillery bombardment, carried 90,000 French soldiers to the battle every week. Its popular name in France, *la Voie sacrée*, 'the sacred way', evoked the terrible sacrifices made by French soldiers, and entered French national mythology. Probably more than a quarter of a million Frenchmen died at Verdun, and the same number were wounded. The Germans suffered some 434,000 casualties, half of them killed. In the autumn the French retook the forts they had lost, and in all the Germans had only advanced a few kilometres. The main result of the battle was the terrible and irreplaceable toll of manpower on both sides. *See also* SOMME.

**Verfremdungseffekt.** *See* EPIC THEATRE.

**Veritas.** The name of Robert Kilroy-Silk's political party, which he launched in early 2005 after flouncing out of the United Kingdom Independence Party (UKIP). Kilroy-Silk (b.1942) made little impact as a Labour MP from 1974 to 1986, but after he left parliament (claiming victimization by MILITANT TENDENCY) came to prominence as a host of a BBC daytime TV show, modestly known as *Kilroy*. The BBC sacked him after he penned an article published in the *Sunday Express* in 2004 entitled 'We owe Arabs nothing'. After his departure a UKIP member commented that the famously vain Kilroy-Silk's new party should be called not Veritas ('truth') but Vanitas ('vanity'). Kilroy-Silk banned the wearing of cravats in his new party. Regarding his perma-tan, wags commented, 'The future's bright, the future's orange' (playing on the slogan of the mobile phone company Orange). He was also dubbed ROBERT THE PUCE.

I think it's called Veritas – or at least some kind of arse.
    ALAN COREN: on BBC Radio 4's *The News Quiz* (21 January 2005)

**Verlan.** A French form of back slang which became, in the late 20th century, a popular type of talk among young people. It is formed by inverting the syllables or letters of a word and incorporating any spelling changes to facilitate pronunciation. Thus *pourri*, 'rotten', becomes *ripou*, *femme*, 'woman', is *meuf* and *chaud*, 'hot', is *auch*. The name itself is an inversion of *l'envers*, 'the other way round'.

**Vermeer forgeries.** *See under* FAKES.

**Veronica.** In bullfighting, a movement in which the matador swings the cape in a slow circle round himself to encourage the charging bull to follow the cape rather than attack his person. The ploy is so called since the pose of the matador holding the cape out in his two hands resembles that in paintings of St Veronica holding out a towel to Christ for him to wipe his face as he proceeds on the road to Calvary.

**Versailles, Treaty of.** *See* TREATY OF VERSAILLES.

**Vertigo.** A suspense film (1958) directed by Alfred Hitchcock and starring James Stewart and Kim Novak, based on a novel *D'entre les morts* by Pierre Boileau and Thomas Narcejac (the book was written specifically for Hitchcock to adapt). It concerns a detective with a fear of heights, who falls in love with a woman who falls to her death. The detective is then startled to see what is apparently her double.

**Very gallant gentleman, A.** The description of Captain Oates, one of Scott's companions on his fatal expedition to the South Pole (*see* I MAY BE SOME TIME), in his epitaph, composed by E.L. Atkinson (1882–1929) and Apsley Cherry-Garrard (1882–1959), and placed on a cairn in Antarctica:

> Hereabouts died a very gallant gentleman, Captain L.E.G. Oates of the Inniskilling Dragoons. In March 1912, returning from the Pole, he walked willingly to his death in a blizzard to try and save his comrades, beset by hardships.

**Vespa.** An Italian make of motor scooter popular among the young and (reasonably) affluent from the 1950s and early 1960s. The splutter of a Vespa's engine occasionally shatters the peace of siesta time in the quieter towns of Italy. The name is Italian for 'wasp'.

**Veteran car.** *See* VINTAGE CAR.

**Veterans Day.** An annual holiday in the United States honouring veterans (ex-servicemen) of the armed forces and all men and women killed in the country's wars. It originated as ARMISTICE DAY, commemorating the end of the First

World War on 11 November 1918. In 1954, after the KOREAN WAR, this date was officially designated Veterans Day. The day itself is usually observed with parades, speeches and the placing of floral tributes on servicemen's graves or at memorials. Special services are also held at Arlington National Cemetery, Virginia.

> They have this day, Veterans' Day, that all the jerks that graduated from Pency around 1776 come back and walk all over the place, with their wives and children and everybody.
>
> J.D. SALINGER: *The Catcher in the Rye* (1951)

**V for Victory.** On 14 January 1941 Victor de Lavaleye, a member of the exiled Belgian government in London, proposed in a broadcast to Belgium that the letter V, standing for 'Victory' in many European languages, be substituted for the letters RAF, which were being chalked up on walls and other places in Belgium. The plan was immediately adopted, and the Morse code V (· · · –) was featured in every BBC broadcast to Europe, followed by the opening bar of Beethoven's fifth symphony, which has the same rhythm. 'Colonel Britton'(D.E. Ritchie), director of the BBC European news service, was responsible for the diffusion of the V-sign propaganda, which gave hope to those under the NAZI yoke. Winston Churchill greatly popularized the sign of two upraised fingers in the form of a V, the palm facing outwards. This is now usually known as the peace sign. *See also* V-SIGN.

**Viagra.** A 'wonder drug' claimed to cure male impotence. It was launched by Pfizer in the United States in 1998 and almost immediately became the world's fastest selling prescription drug, although not all doctors favoured its use. The name appears to have been an arbitrary coinage. The first syllable may have been suggested by Latin *vir* 'man' or its English descendants 'virile' or 'virility', but any resemblance to 'Niagara' (a popular destination for American honeymooners), which has often been noted, is according to the manufacturers entirely coincidental. Viagra is also known, jocularly, as the 'Pfizer riser'.

Several older celebrities and public figures have taken part in advertisement campaigns for Viagra, a lack of potency in their public profiles presumably being seen as helpful (Bob Dole, failed Republican candidate for the US presidency, was one such). Its popularity has spread beyond the technically impotent, and is favoured by such professionals as male escorts who wish to ensure a satisfactory outcome to an evening's business. *See also La* RONDE.

**Vice anglais, le.** (French, 'the English vice'.) Flagellation or corporal punishment, regarded with some justification by the French as a typically English interest, especially of the upper classes. The phrase dates only from the 1940s, but the practice is much older and in English terms is particularly associated with Victorian times and the poems of Algernon Swinburne (1837–1909).

**Vichy.** A spa town in central France, on the River Allier, known for its bottled mineral water. It became notorious, however, as the seat of the French collaborationist government during the Second World War, popularly referred to as 'the Vichy government', or just 'Vichy'. Marshal Philippe Pétain, the last premier of the Third Republic, had agreed the German armistice terms at COMPIÈGNE (22 June 1940) after the fall of France and became head of state of the Vichy regime, formally known as *l'État français* ('French State'). While German forces occupied northern France, Vichy was left to administer the unoccupied south. Vichy regimes also held power in most of France's overseas colonies. The government was made up of a mixture of Catholic conservatives and far-right extremists and was authoritarian and quasi-fascist in character. As well as attempting to suppress resistance movements, the Vichy regime was involved in the deportation of French Jews to the Nazi death camps. Pétain's position was gradually eroded, and Pierre Laval (1883–1945), who had been dismissed as Pétain's deputy in December 1940, was installed as head of government on German orders in April 1942. Vichy ceased to have any effective power in southern France in November 1942 when the Germans occupied the zone, following the Allied landings in northwest Africa. The Vichy regime finally dissolved when the Allies landed in Normandy in June 1944. *See also* FIGHTING FRENCH; MAQUIS; PÉTAINISTS; VERDUN.

**Vichyssoise.** The chilled potato and leek cream soup of this name was the creation in the early 20th century of the French chef Louis Diat in New York. He came from the Bourbonnais region of France, not far from Vichy, and the soup was based on a similar dish served by his mother, but hot. In the Second World War some French chefs in New York attempted to change the name to *Crème gauloise*, from their aversion to the VICHY government, but the original name was the one that prevailed.

**Vick.** The decongestant ointment of this name was the invention of a US pharmacist, Lunsford Richardson, born in 1854 in North Carolina. It began as one of his home remedies, the name coming partly from an advertisement for Vicks Seeds that he had seen in a magazine, partly from Vick, the name of his brother-in-law. The product is now marketed under the name 'Vicks VapoRub'. Its homely reputation and reassuring olfactory reminders of childhood were dealt something of a blow when (in the form of the VapoRub and inhaler) it became popular as a stimulatory enhancement of the effects of the drug ECSTASY at parties in the late 1980s and 1990s.

**Vicky.** The pen name of the political cartoonist Victor Weisz (1913–66). A German Jew of Hungarian extraction, he fled the Nazis in the 1930s and came to England. He was best known for his work in the *Evening Standard* newspaper, and in particular for his portrayal of Harold Macmillan as SUPERMAC.

**Victor Charlie.** US military slang for the VIET CONG, 'Victor' being the standard code word for 'V', and 'Charlie' for 'C'. The Viet Cong were also often referred to simply as the VC or Charlie (sometimes spelt Charley).

**Victorian values.** What Margaret Thatcher (the IRON LADY) said she was trying to restore in Britain. She confirmed this in an interview with Brian Walden on 17 January 1983:

> Victorian values … those were the values when our country became great, not only internationally but at home.

It was assumed that what she meant by Victorian values were things such as individual self-reliance and self-improvement, a reversal of liberal and progressive reforms in the social sphere in favour of a paternalistic authoritarianism, a distinction between the 'deserving' and the 'undeserving' poor, and a rolling-back of the state in areas such as welfare and economic intervention. Her critics believed that she intended to dismantle the entire structure of the welfare state, and to remove most of the rights that the trade union movement had gained over the previous century. *See also* BACK TO BASICS.

**Victory Medal.** A bronze medal with a winged figure of Victory on the obverse, awarded in 1919 to all Allied service personnel who had served in a theatre of war in the First World War, also to certain women's formations.

**Victory roll.** A rotational manoeuvre about a longitudinal axis performed by an aircraft as a sign of triumph. The term dates from the Second World War.

**Video nasty.** A video horror film or one depicting violence, sadism, killing or the like. The term became current from the early 1980s at a time when videos themselves, as a major new commercial activity, were beginning to incorporate dubious material that evaded normal censorship procedures. Films issued in home formats, more usually now DVD rather than video, are now classified in Britain by the British Board of Film Classification (BBFC) under a system similar to that for films shown in cinemas. *See also* SNUFF MOVIE.

**Viet Cong.** The communist guerrilla force active in the VIETNAM War (1964–75) against the South Vietnamese government and US forces with the support of the North Vietnamese army. The name means 'Vietnamese communist'. *See also* HO CHI MINH TRAIL; TET OFFENSIVE; VIET MINH.

**Viet Minh.** The communist-dominated nationalist movement that led the struggle for Vietnamese independence from French rule. It was founded in China in 1941 by Ho Chi Minh (1890–1969), and many of its members supported the VIET CONG during the Vietnam War (1964–75). It takes its name from the first and last elements of *Viet-Nam Dôc-Lâp Dông-Minh*, 'Vietnamese Independence League'. *See also* DIEN BIEN PHU; HO CHI MINH TRAIL.

**Vietnam.** This southeast Asian country was the scene of almost continual conflict from 1945 to 1975. The wars in Vietnam constituted perhaps the 'hottest' manifestation of the COLD WAR, and witnessed the humiliation first of France and then of the United States. Indeed, the US failure in Vietnam was to leave a scar on the collective American consciousness and foreign policy for the remainder of the century.

Vietnam had been colonized by the French in the later 19th century. Nationalist resistance began in the 1930s, led by the communist Ho Chi Minh (1892–1969). During the Second World War it came under VICHY French rule, and then under Japanese occupation. The nationalists organized themselves as the VIET MINH, and when the Japanese surrendered in 1945 Ho Chi Minh declared the independence of Vietnam. However, French military forces returned to restore colonial rule, and the Viet Minh withdrew from the cities. All-out conflict began in 1950, and ended in May 1954 with the humiliating French defeat at DIEN BIEN PHU.

At the subsequent Geneva Accords in July 1954, Vietnam was divided into two independent countries, with Ho Chi Minh leading communist North Vietnam, while a Western-aligned government was established in South Vietnam. Shortly afterwards, US President Eisenhower (*see* IKE), fearing the extension of communist power in the region, sent military advisers to South Vietnam, and supported the South's refusal to participate in a referendum on reunification. The North, intent on reunification, supported communist guerrillas in the South (*see* VIET CONG), supplying them via the HO CHI MINH TRAIL. President Kennedy (*see* JFK) stepped up US military aid, but by 1963 much of the South was under Viet Cong control.

In 1964 President Johnson (*see* LBJ) used the North's attack on US warships in the Gulf of Tonkin as the pretext for the escalation of US military involvement. Subsequently some 2 million US troops saw service in Vietnam, and US bombers launched massive raids on the North. However, US forces proved incapable of defeating the guerrilla tactics of the

Viet Cong, or of winning over the 'hearts and minds' of the South Vietnamese peasants who gave them support. Large numbers of US troops were conscripted unwillingly through the 'draft' and this, combined with atrocities against civilians (*see* MY LAI MASSACRE) and the military stalemate, led to the formation of a large antiwar movement in the United States. The nightly showing of uncensored newsreel footage of the war on US television also played its part. In the wake of the 1968 TET OFFENSIVE Johnson initiated peace talks.

Johnson's successor, Richard Nixon (*see* TRICKY DICKY), began US troop withdrawals, and at the same time authorized covert bombing raids and ground incursions into Cambodia (1970) and Laos (1971), aimed at the Ho Chi Minh Trail. Such actions strengthened US antiwar sentiment. A cease-fire was agreed in 1973, and the United States completed its withdrawal. North Vietnamese forces renewed their offensive in 1975, and following the communist victory the two Vietnams were reunited. In all, 47,000 US servicemen died in the conflict, compared to 450,000 South Vietnamese civilians, and nearly one million Viet Cong and North Vietnamese troops.

*See also* AIKEN'S SOLUTION; NAM.

**View from the Bridge, A.** A play (1955) by the US playwright Arthur Miller (1915–2005) about a Brooklyn longshoreman, Eddie Carbone, who takes two illegal immigrants into his home but subsequently informs the authorities of their presence after one of them falls in love with his wife's niece, for whom he has a liking himself. The title reflects both the immediate environment of the play (the Brooklyn waterfront) and the detached observation of events as delivered by the local lawyer, Alfieri, who narrates the story. In the UK, Michael Gambon's portrayal of Carbone for a production directed by Alan Ayckbourn at the National Theatre (1987) was widely considered a *tour de force*.

**View to a Kill, A.** An unexciting film (1985) in the long-running series of James BOND secret agent movies based on the novels of Ian Fleming (1906–64). Roger Moore played Bond. Fleming's original story was published in 1960 with the rather more meaningful title 'From a View to a Kill', which may have been suggested by Anthony Powell's novel *From a View to a Death* (1933), which in turn took the idea from the traditional foxhunting ballad 'D'ye ken John Peel', written in 1832 by John Woodcock Graves:

> Yes, I ken John Peel, and Ruby too,
> Ranter and Ringwood, Bellman and True,
> From a find to a check, from a check to a view,
> From a view to a death in the morning.

A 'check' in foxhunting language signifies a loss of scent, while a 'view' is the cry that signals the actual sighting of a fox.

**Viking.** The names of two unmanned US spacecraft launched respectively on 29 August and 9 September 1975. Ten months later they entered orbits round Mars and released landers to relay measurements of properties of the atmosphere and soil of the planet and colour photographs of its rocky surface. Experiments designed to detect evidence of life on Mars were inconclusive.

**Vile Bodies.** A novel (1930) by Evelyn Waugh (1903–66), satirizing the manners of the BRIGHT YOUNG THINGS in a recognizable but fantasized political and social setting. The 'vile bodies' are those of the characters who spend their time going from party to party, to the fury and puzzlement of their elders. The words have a biblical echo: 'Who shall change our vile body, that it may be fashioned like unto his glorious body' (Philippians 3:21).

**Village England.** Rural England, with its close-knit village communities that in the face of urban growth have retained their age-old associations of pubs, church bells and cricket matches. Many new estates at the close of the 20th century were being planned on the lines of such communities, one high-profile example being the MILLENNIUM Village at Greenwich in southeast London. There is a 'Gazetteer of Village England' listing various fictional locations in the novels and stories of P.G. Wodehouse in Geoffrey Jaggard's *Wooster's World* (1967).

> We are the Village Green Preservation Society
> God save Donald Duck, vaudeville and variety
> RAY DAVIES: 'Village Green Preservation Society', from the
> album of the same name by The Kinks (1968)

**Village idiot.** A comparatively modern term for what was long seen as a regular feature of country life, in the form of a feeble-minded middle-aged or elderly man who supposedly resided in every village. He was traditionally thought of as sitting on a bench outside the village inn, where he readily regaled strangers with lurid local tales in return for a steady supply of ale. There may have been a germ of truth in this imagery, but the precise picture has now faded, leaving the term to persist as simply a light-hearted phrase for a slow or dim-witted person.

> Somewhere in Texas, a village is missing its idiot.
> Bumper sticker during the 2004 US presidential election

*See also* DUBYA; IDIOT SON.

**Vinegar Joe.** A nickname of the acerbic US general Joseph Stilwell (1883–1946), as famous for his tongue-lashing as for his Second World War exploits in China, Burma, India and on the Japanese island of Okinawa. He earned the sobriquet when he was head of the Infantry School at Fort Benning, Georgia, between 1929 and 1933.

**Vinland Map.** *See under* FAKES.

**Vintage car.** An early style or model of motor car, specifically one made between 1917 and 1930. A veteran car is older and to a connoisseur is one made before 1916 or, in some logbooks, 1905. *See also* BRIGHTON RUN; GENEVIEVE.

**Violon d'Ingres.** (French, 'Ingres' violin'.) An activity or pastime for which a person is not primarily known. The French painter Ingres (1780–1867) was said to have been more proud of his violin-playing than of the paintings by which he made his name.

**VIP.** Very Important Person. This well-established abbreviation was popularized by a station commander of Transport Command in 1944 who was responsible for the movement of a plane-load of important individuals, including Lord Mountbatten, to the Middle East. He so described them in his movement orders to avoid disclosing their identity.

The 1963 film *The VIPs*, scripted by Terence Rattigan, centred on a group of notables stranded by fog at London Airport. The main stars, Elizabeth Taylor and Richard Burton, lent a suitably VIPish touch to the proceedings.

**Virgin Soldiers, The.** A novel (1966) by Leslie Thomas (b.1931). Set in Malaysia during the years 1948–52, it reflects the experiences of British soldiers garrisoned there to combat the threat of communist guerrillas: 'Some of this army were good soldiers; others were not.' A significant strand of the story concerns the sexual initiation of a 19-year-old private by a Chinese prostitute, with whom he falls in love. A film version (1969) was directed by John Dexter.

**Virtual reality.** A computer-generated simulation of a three-dimensional image or environment that can be interacted with in a seemingly real way by someone wearing a head-mounted display screen and special gloves. The term was originally used by computer programmers in the 1980s to describe any interactive technology but took on its present sense in 1989, when a US musician, Jaron Lanier, designed the equipment that allows users to participate in the simulation. *See also* CYBERSEX.

**Vision thing, the.** Idealism as opposed to pragmatism. The term usually relates to politicians who see themselves as managers rather than ideologists. It derives from the first President Bush's response 'Oh, the vision thing' (reported in *Time* magazine on 26 January 1987) to the suggestion that he turn his attention from short-term campaign objectives and look to the longer term.

**Visit, The.** A play (1956) by the Swiss dramatist Friedrich Dürrenmatt (1921–90), in German *Der Besuch der alten Dame* ('The Old Lady's Visit'), about public self-delusion and human willingness to submerge moral conscience in favour of material advantage. The old lady of the title, once poor but now a millionairess, returns to her home town Güllen (Swiss German, 'liquid manure') to offer its citizens vast sums as long as her former lover is punished for abandoning her in her youth. This they do, the lover is publicly strangled, and the old lady leaves to resounding cheers. A classic of German-language theatre, the play is a grimly comic parable about both the willing embrace of NAZI ideology in Germany and the contradictions in Swiss attempts to remain aloof from Europe's cataclysms in the 20th century.

**Visiting fireman.** A US term current from the 1920s for a visitor who receives a cordial welcome. The concept is of one set of firemen visiting another fire station and receiving such a welcome.

**Vital statistics.** Properly, population statistics concerned with births, marriages, deaths, divorces and the like (Latin *vita*, 'life'). From the 1950s the term has been applied semi-seriously to a woman's bust, waist and hip measurements, usually given in inches.

**Vitamin.** The word as proposed in 1912 by the US biochemist Casimir Funk was originally 'vitamine', from Latin *vita*, 'life', and English 'amine', the latter referring to the amino acid that the substance was believed to contain. When it was found that this was not the case, the term was modified to its present spelling in 1920.

Vitamins are generally classified as water-soluble (B and C) or fat-soluble (A, D, E and K), and each of the letter-names has its chemical equivalent. Thus vitamin A is another name for retinol, vitamin $B_1$ is thiamine, vitamin $B_2$ is riboflavin, vitamin C is ascorbic acid, vitamin $D_3$ is cholecalciferol and so on.

**Vive la différence.** (French, 'Long live the difference'.) Hurray for the difference between the sexes. A humorous approval of diversity adopted by English from French in the 1960s.

**Vive le Québec. Vive le Québec libre.** (French, 'Long live Quebec. Long live Free Quebec'). The culmination of a speech by Charles de Gaulle, the president of France, made in Montreal on 24 July 1967, at a time when Quebec separatists were agitating (sometimes violently) for independence from Anglophone Canada. The speech caused something of a rumpus, and de Gaulle was obliged to curtail his visit.

**Viz.** A coarsely humorous and rudely satirical comic aimed mainly at young and uninhibited readers. The first issue, published in November 1979, was launched in the bedroom of its founder, Chris Brown, for distribution around the pubs of his native Newcastle upon Tyne. By 1983 local sales had reached 3000 and steadily grew to reach a national peak of over a million in 1990. Its larger-than-life characters include the Fat Slags, two gross women; Johnny Fartpants, a crude juvenile; Billy the Fish, a libidinous OWN GOAL scorer; Roger Mellie, a foul-mouthed television anchorman; Biffa Bacon, a belligerent Geordie; Sid the Sexist, a happily chauvinist Geordie; BUSTER Gonad, with his unfeasibly large testicles; and Finbarr Saunders, a purveyor of double entendres of the most sexually suggestive nature. The name comes from slang 'viz' meaning 'face' (visage).

**VJ Day.** 'Victory in Japan' Day. The end of hostilities in the Far East, 15 August 1945, and thus the end of the Second World War. *See also* VE DAY.

**V-mail.** A system of mail transmission in the United States during the Second World War. To conserve shipping space, a letter written on a letter sheet was reproduced in photographic microfilm and forwarded in this form to be enlarged on photographic paper for delivery. A 'V-letter' was a letter sent by this method. The 'V' is for 'Victory'.

> The same source made it evident that she received V-letters by the bale. They were always torn into strips like bookmarks.
>
> TRUMAN CAPOTE: *Breakfast at Tiffany's* (1958)

**Vodafone.** A manipulated contraction of 'voice data phone'. One of Britain's largest international companies, and one of the biggest mobile phone operators in the world, Vodaphone's recent experience in the treacherous world of hi-tech industries has witnessed spectacular acquisitions of foreign rivals followed by, in 2006, the biggest loss in British corporate history (almost £15 billion).

**Vo-do-deo-do.** A meaningless refrain appearing in popular jazz songs of the 1920s and 1930s and used subsequently to denote a style of singing or song characterized by speed, energy and an insistent rhythm. It is first recorded in Jack Yellen's song 'Crazy Words, Crazy Tune' (1927):

> Sings the same words to ev'ry song.
> Vo-do-de-o. Vo-do-do-de-o-do.

**Voicemail.** A system of US origin dating from the 1980s for electronically storing, processing and reproducing verbal messages left through the conventional telephone network.

**Voie sacrée, La.** *See* VERDUN.

**Voldemort, Lord.** *See* Harry POTTER.

**Volkswagen.** *See* BEETLE.

**Volvo.** The first Swedish car of this name made its test run from Stockholm to Göteborg in 1926 and was produced by a company set up by two engineers, Assar Gabrielsson and Gustaf Larson. The name is Latin for 'I roll', although this did not originally apply to the car but to a subsidiary of the firm where the two men worked, SKF (Svenska Kullager-fabriken), a ball-bearing concern. The name is, however, equally applicable for a vehicle that 'rolls' or runs on wheels along the road.

**V-1.** A type of flying bomb sent against Britain by the Germans, June to August 1944, and subsequently against Antwerp. The droning sound of its flight intimidated its target populations, though British defensive tactics eventually downed a good proportion of V–1s. The V stood for *Vergeltungswaffe* ('reprisal weapon'). *See also* DOODLEBUG; V–2.

**Voodoo economics.** A disparaging term for a macro-economic approach that emphasizes the importance of tax cuts and incentives for businesses in encouraging economic growth. In 1980, when George Bush Snr was vying with Ronald Reagan for the Republican nomination in that year's US general election, Bush derided Reagan's belief that tax cuts would actually lead to increased tax revenues as 'voodoo economics'. The term has been used since to mock any wishful thinking in the economic sphere – for example, the proposal in 2003 by the administration of President George W. Bush to abolish tax on shareholder dividends, which they claimed would benefit working people. Two years earlier, on 4 October 2001, shortly after 9/11, Bush explained his position on tax cuts as a weapon in the WAR ON TERROR:

> We need to counter the shockwave of the evildoer by having individual rate cuts and by thinking about tax rebates.

*See also* REAGANOMICS; SUPPLY SIDERS.

**Vorsprung durch Technik.** A phrase (German, literally 'progress by means of technology') that since 1971 has been the chief advertising slogan of the German motor-manufacturer AUDI. It made a considerable impact on British audiences, and came to be widely used, in appropriate circumstances, well beyond its original application.

**Vorticism.** An avant-garde art movement launched in Britain in 1914. It was related to CUBISM and FUTURISM and was mainly concerned with the visual arts but also embraced literature. Its designs were in straight lines and angular patterns, while machine-like forms were a frequent feature. Among its representatives, Wyndham Lewis (1882–1957) and Edward Wadsworth (1889–1949) were the most notable. The name was bestowed by the US poet Ezra Pound (1885–1972), for whom the vortex represented 'the point of maximum energy', an expression of the dynamism of modern life. *See also* DADAISM; FAUVISM; ORPHISM; RURALISM; SURREALISM; SYNCHROMISM; TACHISM.

**Voss.** A novel (1957) by the Australian writer Patrick White (1912–90). Johann Ulrich Voss, a German explorer who has affinities with Ludwig Leichhardt (1813–*c*.1848), sets out from Sydney to explore the Australian interior, having established an intense intellectual bond with Laura Trevelyan, the niece of one of his patrons. The disasters and sufferings that befall the party, and differing conceptions of Voss's contribution to history, have their counterparts in the experiences of Laura.

**Vostok.** (Russian, 'east'.) The first type of Soviet manned space rocket. On 12 April 1961 *Vostok 1* took Yuri Gagarin (1934–68) into space, where, in a 90-minute flight, he made a single orbit of the earth, the first ever manned space flight. Over the next two years there were a further five Vostok flights. The last, on 16 June 1963, carried Valentina Tereshkova (b.1937), the first woman in space.

**Votes for Women.** The slogan of the SUFFRAGETTE movement, adopted on 13 October 1905 when it was realized that the previous effort, 'Will the Liberal Party Give Votes for Women?', was a bit longwinded for a banner.

**Vote with one's feet.** To indicate one's approval or disapproval of a thing by associating oneself with it (walking in) or dissociating oneself from it (walking out). The latter is the more usual interpretation. The expression dates from the 1960s.

> Britain's consumers are voting with their feet against high prices. Cheap has become chic.
>
> *Sunday Times* (20 June 1999)

**Vox pop.** A term for interviews with members of the public conducted by radio or television reporters. The expression is a shortening of Latin *vox populi*, 'voice of the people'.

> A few days ago, a BBC camera crew went round Washington collecting vox pops – close-ups of men in the street saying pithily what they think of things.
>
> *The Listener* (8 February 1968)

**Voyager.** The name of two US unmanned space probes, which have sent back large amounts of new information about the outer planets, and discovered many new moons and planetary rings. Both were launched in 1977. *Voyager 1*

passed Jupiter in March 1979 and Saturn in November 1980. *Voyager 2* passed Jupiter in July 1979, Saturn in August 1981, Uranus in January 1986 and Neptune in August 1989. Both probes are now heading beyond the Solar System, carrying information about their home planet.

**Voyeurvision.** A prurient form of television in which the private lives of young women are filmed continuously for entertainment. The genre arose in the United States in the 1990s and evolved from *Sliver* (1993), a video-surveillance film starring Sharon Stone. It subsequently became big business on the INTERNET, with such sites as *The Dolls' House* (1998), filming three North London flat-sharers around the clock, and the more explicit American *Voyeur-Dorm* (1997), in which 48 cameras capture the uncensored daily and nightly activities of seven girls. *See also* BIG BROTHER; REALITY TV.

**VPL.** An abbreviation of the 1980s phrase 'visible pantie line', indicating that the line of a person's underwear is perceptible through a tight skirt, dress or pair of trousers. In the early 21st century there has been a fashion among Western teenagers and TWENTY-SOMETHINGS for deliberately visible underwear popping above trousers and skirts, preferably to reveal a designer label (Calvin Klein briefs being popular among men) or (for women) an artfully positioned thong – thus reversing the rationale for the latter garment, which once used to be a way of avoiding VPL.

**V-sign.** A sign of the letter V made with the first two fingers pointing up and the back of the hand facing outwards. It is a crude gesture of abuse or contempt, and is not to be confused with the peace sign, which is made with the palm of the hand facing outwards (*see* V FOR VICTORY). The sign is sometimes said on somewhat dubious evidence to have originated in medieval battles between the English and the French, when English archers captured by the French would have their second and third fingers removed to ensure they would not draw the bow again. In defiance, the English soldiers stuck up their fingers at the French. *See also* GIVE SOMEONE THE FINGER; HARVEY SMITH; TWO FINGERS; UP YOURS.

**V-2.** A long-range rocket with an explosive warhead, which was projected against Britain and other countries by the Germans in the autumn of 1944. V had the same origin as for the V-1. The V-2's flight was inaudible to those on the ground, so its fall to earth was sudden and without warning. There was no effective anti-aircraft defence against it, so the fear factor among British civilians was high. Eventually the German lines were pushed back so far as to make Britain out of range. The V-2's designer, Wernher von Braun (1912–77), and his team would become integral to the US space programme in the postwar years.

**Vulcan.** A member of a fictional race of highly intelligent, coldly unemotional and pointy-eared humanoid beings to which Mr SPOCK (who, technically, is half human via his mother) belongs in the television and cinema series STAR TREK. In the mid-1990s the nickname 'The Vulcan' began to be used for the Conservative politician John Redwood (b.1951), former secretary of state for Wales and member of William Hague's and Michael Howard's shadow cabinets, on account of his fixed stare and somewhat sinisterly otherworldly air.

> In the end, even Vulcans die. John Redwood yesterday left the bridge of the Tory starship for perhaps the last time when William Hague beamed him off the Shadow Cabinet.
>
> *The Times* (2 February 2000)

# W

**WAAC.** The familiar name of a member of the Women's Army Auxiliary Corps, a body of women raised for non-combatant army service in the First World War. In the Second World War they were termed the ATS. This became the Women's Royal Army Corps (WRAC) in 1949. The WRAC was disbanded in 1992, when women wishing to enlist began joining the regular army.

**WAAF.** The familiar name of a member of the Women's Auxiliary Air Force, or the force itself, which was originally set up in 1918 as the Women's Royal Air Force (WRAF). It was disbanded in 1920, but re-formed in 1939 as the WAAF. It once again became the WRAF in 1949 and was finally disbanded in 1994. Women are now able to enlist in the regular RAF.

**WAC.** In the Second World War, the Women's Army Corps, the US equivalent of the British ATS. *See also* WAVES.

**Wacko Jacko.** A nickname for the pop singer Michael Jackson (b.1958). He started his career at the age of 11 with his brothers as one of the Jackson Five, a MOTOWN group, and subsequently became an immensely successful solo artist with albums such as *Thriller* (1982; the bestselling album ever). The richer and more famous he became, the more eccentricities he developed, such as changing colour from black to white (though he blames this on a skin disorder), undergoing cosmetic plastic surgery to reduce the size of his nose, and indulging a penchant for sleepovers with pre-pubescent boys at his Neverland ranch in California (*see* NEVER NEVER LAND). In 2005 he was acquitted of charges of child sexual abuse. He is also known as the King of Pop (or, because of his dress sense, the KING OF FOP).

**Waco.** A town in Texas that in 1993 was the scene of an FBI siege of a compound containing armed and unarmed members of an extreme religious group, the Branch Davidian cult, led by David Koresh, who believed himself to be 'the Lamb of God'. The siege began on 18 February and ended on 19 April with the mass suicide of the 80 cult members still in the compound. The dead included Koresh himself and more than 17 children.

**Waffen SS.** (German, 'Armed SS'.) The combat units of the SS in NAZI Germany during the Second World War. They attempted to recruit British prisoners into an anti-Soviet unit known originally as the Legion of St George and later as the *Britische Freikorps* (British Free Corps). Few enlisted, and it was formed largely from Oswald Mosley's BLACKSHIRTS and British ex-servicemen with divided loyalties resulting from German parentage (*see also* MOSLEYITES).

**Wags.** An acronym based on 'wives and girlfriends', which came to prominence in the summer of 2006, when the consorts of the England World Cup football team were frequently featured in the tabloid press undergoing bouts of serious retail therapy in German.

> Throwing caution and dry-cleaning bills to the wind the WAGS held a wild day out ....
>
> www.thesun.co.uk (30 June 2006)

**Wag the Dog syndrome.** *See* TAIL WAGS THE DOG

**Wait and see.** A phrase at one time humorously used with reference to the Liberal politician H.H. Asquith, 1st Earl of Oxford and Asquith (1852–1928). Thus, 'What did Asquith say?' was formerly another way of saying 'Wait and see', and Asquith himself became known as OLD WAIT AND SEE. The phrase 'Wait and see' was also associated with the stalling policy of John Major when prime minister (1990–7) with regard to Britain's joining the SINGLE CURRENCY.

**Waitangi Day.** Since 1960, 6 February has been celebrated as New Zealand's national day. It is a public holiday and commemorates the day on which the Treaty of Waitangi was made in 1840 by the British governor, William Hobson, with the Maori chiefs. They recognized British sovereignty in return for the tribes being guaranteed possession of their lands. In postcolonial times the treaty (and thus the holiday) has become somewhat controversial among Maori and there have been moves to rename the day 'New Zealand Day' to blur its relationship to the treaty.

**Wait for it!** A parenthetical warning that what follows is a surprise or, ironically, is exactly what one was expecting. The allusion is to the drill sergeant's command on the parade ground to anyone showing signs of making the required move prematurely. The phrase dates from the 1930s.

> Lucy Gannon's new drama serial stars Kevin Whately as an overworked GP whose wife … embarks on an affair with (wait for it) the window-cleaner.
>
> *The Times* (11 September 1999)

**Waiting for Godot.** A play, originally *En attendant Godot*, by Samuel Beckett (1906–89). Perhaps the best-known example of the THEATRE OF THE ABSURD, it was first performed in Paris in 1953 and opened to acclaim in Britain, in a translation from the French by the author, at the Arts Theatre, London, in August 1955. The performance was directed by Peter Hall. The play is ostensibly about a pair of tramps, Estragon and Vladimir, who wait interminably for the arrival of the mysterious Godot. The only other characters are Lucky, Pozzo and a Boy. Beckett dismissed suggestions that Godot was in fact God ('If Godot were God, I would have called him that'), and there has been much debate over Godot's identity and significance. Because the play was written originally in French, other theories have suggested a link with the French *godillot* or *godasse* (slang words for 'boot'), as boots are discussed in the text, and with a tale that the author once came across a crowd watching the Tour de France cycle race and, on asking what they were doing, was informed: 'We are waiting for Godot' (that being the name of the slowest rider in the field). Alternatively, it was claimed, Beckett was once accosted by a prostitute while loitering in the Rue Godot de Mauroy in Paris and, on declining her advances, was asked impatiently what he was hanging about there for; was he perhaps 'waiting for Godot?' (as in the name of the street).

> Beckett's *Waiting for Godot* … arrived in London ten years ago like a sword burying itself in an over-upholstered sofa.
>
> PENELOPE GILLIATT: review

**Waiting for Lefty.** A play (1935) by the US playwright Clifford Odets (1906–63) about the events that led up to a trade union vote to strike in the 1930s. The Lefty of the title is the leader of the union, whose arrival is impatiently expected. News eventually comes of Lefty's murder and the decision to strike follows. Odets deliberately chose the name in order to try to break down traditional hostility towards the political left. It was published in Britain in 1937 by the LEFT BOOK CLUB.

> We're stormbirds of the working class. Workers of the world. … And when we die they'll know what we did to make a new world.
>
> CLIFFORD ODETS: *Waiting for Lefty*

**Wake up and smell the coffee.** To come to a proper and realistic appreciation of the true state of affairs, having previously been ignorant, negligent or self-deceiving. To 'get real'. An expression of US origin, first recorded in 1955. It was popularized and may have been originated by the syndicated advice columnist Ann Landers (1918–2002; real name Esther Pauline Friedman).

**Wake-up call.** In the figurative sense a person or thing that arouses people's awareness of an unsatisfactory situation and that prompts them to do something about it.

**Waldorf salad.** A salad made from apples, walnuts, lettuce and (or) celery and dressed with mayonnaise. It takes its name from the former Waldorf-Astoria Hotel on Fifth Avenue, New York, where it was first served in the early 20th century. The hotel was originally two separate hotels built by two feuding cousins: the Waldorf, built in 1893 by the US-born British financier William Waldorf Astor (1848–1919) on the site of his father's mansion, and the Astoria, erected in 1897 by John Jacob Astor IV (1864–1912) on the site of his mother's mansion to the north. The combined hotel was demolished in 1929 to make way for the Empire State Building. The present hotel of the same name on Park Avenue opened in 1931.

**Walkabout.** An informal stroll among a crowd by an important visitor. The word first gained public attention in this sense in March 1970 when Queen Elizabeth and the Duke of Edinburgh left their car when touring Wellington, New Zealand, and walked along the street to talk to local people. The event was immediately dubbed a royal 'walkabout' by Vincent Mulchrone of the *Daily Mail*. He in fact misused the term, which is Australian English in origin, meaning a periodic journey into the bush by an Aborigine in order to live in the traditional manner for a while and to make a temporary withdrawal from white society. This original sense was popularized by the highly rated Australian film *Walkabout* (1970), directed by Nicholas Roeg, telling how two white children trek among the Aborigines to safety after their father kills himself in the desert.

**Walk and chew gum.** Tasks that the stupid, proverbially

speaking, are incapable of doing simultaneously. For example, in the House of Commons in 1994 the Labour MP Tony Banks (1943–2006) said of the fragrant Tory MP Lady Olga Maitland that she was 'scarcely capable of walking and chewing gum at the same time'. The original version of the phrase has been traced to the earthy President Lyndon B. Johnson (1908–73), who made the following comment regarding the future president, Gerald Ford:

> So dumb he can't fart and chew gum at the same time.
>
> Quoted in Richard Reeves, *A Ford, Not a Lincoln* (1975)

**Walk away from.** To escape with one's life, as when literally walking away from a road accident (*see* WALKING WOUNDED). Also, to withdraw from a situation with which one is (or should be) involved.

**Walk free.** To be released from custody, e.g. after being acquitted of a criminal charge. The implication of the cliché (originally American and first recorded in 1925) is that the person referred to ought, in the speaker's opinion, to still be confined.

> A virtually impromptu rally ... was prompted by judges' decisions to let the rapists walk free.
>
> *Sunday Herald Sun* (Melbourne) (5 December 2004)

**Walkies!** A command to a dog (and sometimes a human) to get ready for a walk. The word became enduringly and endearingly associated with the animal trainer Barbara Woodhouse (1910–88) following her popular television series of 1980 on the training of dogs. Similar commands such as 'Sit!' and 'Wait!' were not far behind.

**Walkie-talkie.** A small radio transmitter and receiver that can be carried on the person to enable one to talk as one walks. The term arose from West Indian speech in the 1930s as US Army slang and passed into other languages, the French preferred form being *talkie-walkie*, pronounced 'tokiwoki'. A walkie-talkie is also a type of doll that can walk and talk. *See also* WALKMAN.

**Walking on two legs.** In modern China, the use of small-scale, local methods in production and education, as distinct from large-scale or capital-intensive ones. The term translates the Chinese original and first became current in English in the 1960s.

**Walking wounded.** A term originating in the First World War for casualties able to make their own way on foot to the treatment stations, not needing to be carried there on a stretcher.

**Walk in the park.** Something very easy to accomplish or cope with; a 'breeze'.

> If I say anything ... this trouble's gonna look like a walk in the park, believe me.
>
> *The Bill* (18 August 2005)

**Walkman.** The SONY brand of personal stereo popular from the 1980s, so called because it could be played while walking (or cycling) along the street or riding in public transport, supposedly without disturbing others. The name became a generic shorthand for the type. The first Walkman was on sale in the West in 1979. Originally they played cassettes, then were developed for CDs, and the latest models double as MP3 players.

***Walk on the Wild Side.*** A novel (1956) by Nelson Algren (1909–81), which is set in New Orleans during the GREAT DEPRESSION. It reflects the author's preoccupation with the criminal underworld and poverty-stricken vagrants, whose experiences he investigated and shared as a journalist. There is an emphasis on alternative sexual lifestyles. A dreary film version was directed by Edward Dmytryk in 1962, the most memorable part of the movie being the opening credits. Lou Reed's hit song 'Walk on the Wild Side' (1972) is an ode to the denizens of Andy Warhol's entourage, of which he was one (with The VELVET UNDERGROUND) in the 1960s.

**Walk the talk.** To suit one's actions to one's words. It is an Americanism dating from the 1980s.

> It's essential that those in authority walk the talk or they risk being pilloried by an increasingly incredulous public.
>
> *Sunday Times* (2 January 2000)

*See also* TALK THE TALK AND WALK THE WALK.

**Wallace and Gromit.** These two puppet characters, an inventor (and cheese fanatic) and his clever dog, were developed by Nick Park and Aardman Animations, and appeared from 1990 onwards as the stars of a number of animated films made by the Claymation process, in which moulded clay models are filmed in a 'stop-action' technique, with minute movements given to the models in between each shot. The films *The Wrong Trousers* and *A Close Shave* both won OSCARS, and in January 2006 *The Curse of the Were-Rabbit* received an Oscar nomination.

**Wall of death.** A fairground or amusement park sideshow in which a motorcyclist uses gravitational force to ride around the inside walls of a vertical cylinder. The act is often performed blindfold. *See also* WHEEL OF DEATH

**Wallpaper.** In a figurative sense, anything that provides a bland or undemanding background to an activity, such as MUSIC WHILE YOU WORK. In computer jargon, wallpaper is an optional background pattern or picture on the screen.

**Wall Street Crash.** The collapse of prices on the New York Stock Exchange on BLACK THURSDAY, leading to the GREAT DEPRESSION.

**Wall-to-wall.** When it arose in the 1950s this expression originally applied to fitted carpets that covered a whole floor from one wall to another. From the 1960s the term gained a figurative sense to describe anything extensive or even excessive, whether numerically countable or not, such as 'wall-to-wall piped music' or 'wall-to-wall customers'.

> After eight years spent in retirement in Gascony, I am delighted to have exchanged wall-to-wall sunshine for this country [Britain] where liberty, common courtesies and healthcare are free.
>
> *The Times*, letter to the editor (25 October 1999)

**Wally.** A term for a stupid or inept person, first current in the 1960s. There are various stories accounting for the name. One tells of a person who lost his dog named Wally at a GLASTONBURY FESTIVAL. The owner walked around calling 'Wally!' and his cry was taken up by the crowd. Over the next few years the habit of calling 'Wally!' became established at rock concerts during a lull in the proceedings, in the manner of a MEXICAN WAVE at a sports event.

Starting in 1987, the British illustrator Martin Handford created a series of children's picture books called *Where's Wally?*, in which, on each double-page spread, children had to find the tiny figure of Wally, a bespectacled young man in a stripy jumper and bobble hat, lurking somewhere in a very crowded and detailed picture.

**Walrus moustache.** A large moustache overhanging the lips and so resembling the drooping whiskers of a walrus. Such moustaches, now considered old-fashioned, were fairly common in the late 19th and early 20th centuries. An example appears in Bruce Bairnsfather's drawing of Old Bill (*see* BETTER 'OLE).

**Walter Mitty.** A fantasist who daydreams of achievements that he can never realize in ordinary life and who in some cases may try to gain them by illicit means. The model was the creation of the US writer James Thurber and appears in his short story 'The Secret Life of Walter Mitty' (1939). The comedy film of the same title (1947), starring Danny Kaye, has only a loose connection with the book.

**Walter Plinge.** *See* PLINGE, WALTER.

**WAMPAS baby stars.** The 13 young US film actresses who were selected annually from 1922 to 1934 by the Western Association of Motion Picture Advertisers (WAMPAS) for showing signs of promise. Among those who fulfilled such promise were Clara Bow, selected in 1924, Mary Astor, Joan

Crawford, Janet Gaynor and Fay Wray (1926), Jean Arthur and Loretta Young (1929), Joan Blondell (1931) and Ginger Rogers (1932). 'Baby' is simply an affectionate if somewhat belittling descriptive, since many of the women were at least 20 when chosen and already established in their careers. The enterprise received much publicity and aroused considerable attention among film fans.

**Wannabe.** A fan of a celebrity who aims to emulate their idol, or more generally anyone who seeks fame. The word represents '(I) want to be' and originated in the United States in the 1980s among white youths who dressed and behaved like members of black gangs. The term subsequently became specifically associated with the rock star Madonna, who early in her career had many emulators and LOOKA-LIKES.

'Wannabe' was the title of a 1996 hit song by The Spice Girls (with a little help from Matthew Rowbottom and Richard Stannard):

> Yo I'll tell you what I want, what I really really want
> So tell me what you want, what you really really want.

*See also* A-LIST; CELEBRITY CULTURE; REALITY TV.

**Want to make something of it?** Do you want to fight over it? A ritual challenge of US origin that arose in the 1930s. It is less menacing than it seems since it gives the other the chance to back down. A folksy variant is: 'Wanna make sumpin' of it?'

**War and peace pudding.** An austerity substitute for Christmas pudding promoted in Canada in the First World War and by the Ministry of Food in Britain in the Second World War. It was made by mixing flour, breadcrumbs, suet, dried fruit, grated raw carrot and bicarbonate of soda, turning all into a well-greased pudding bowl, and boiling or steaming the result for at least two hours. The meaning of the name is obvious, with a pun also implied on 'pease pudding'.

**War baby.** A baby born in wartime, especially the illegitimate offspring of a serviceman.

**War bride.** A soldier's foreign bride, met as a result of wartime postings or operations.

**War chest.** Originally and literally a chest or strong-box containing funds with which to fight a war, but from the later 20th century the term denotes funds set aside by a political party or company for a campaign of some kind. The term is of US origin.

> The news that the Prime Minister is insisting he keeps the 'lid' on a supposed £10 million 'war chest' has enraged those

who dreamed that the money might be spent on schools, roads, hospitals and all the other things which … we supposed it to be in the 'gift' of the politicians.

*Evening Standard* (27 September 1999)

**Wardour Street.** A street in central London that was formerly famous for its antique dealers, but which from the 1930s has contained the offices of several film companies. The name is thus sometimes used allusively for the British film industry. Because some of the antique dealers specialized in imitation antiques, the term 'Wardour-Street English' came into vogue at the turn of the 20th century for pseudo-archaic English, as typically found in historical romances. The nuclear destruction of the street was playfully considered by The Jam in their 1978 song '"A" Bomb in Wardour Street'.

**Warm-up man.** A man who 'warms up' an audience before a show or programme, especially one that is to be televised or recorded for television, by amusing them or entertaining them so that they are 'thawed' and more receptive to the material to come. The term dates from the 1960s.

**Warner Brothers.** The famous US film production company takes its name from the brothers Harry (1881–1958), Jack (1892–1978), Sam (1887–1927) and Albert (1884–1967) Warner. They were of Polish origin and were the sons of Benjamin, of unknown surname, and Pearl Eichelbaum, who emigrated to the United States in the 1880s and changed the family name to Warner in 1907. Harry was the leading light, beginning his career by opening a NICKELO-DEON, the first of a chain, in New Castle, Pennsylvania, in 1905. He abandoned film distribution for production in 1912, and his first film of note was *My Four Years in Germany* (1917). He set up studios in HOLLYWOOD in 1918 and with the cooperation of his brothers and himself as president incorporated the business as Warner Brothers Pictures in 1923. He was president until 1956, when Jack took over, until 1966. The firm produced the first *Don Juan* film with a synchronized musical score (1926), the first 'talkie', *The Jazz Singer* (1927), the first full-length all-talking picture, *Lights of New York* (1928), and the first all-talking colour movie, *On With the Show* (1929). In the 1930s it established a reputation for melodramas and gangster movies, and in the 21st century, as part of the Time-Warner conglomerate, the company enjoyed its meal ticket with the cinematic rights to the Harry POTTER books.

**War of attrition.** A war in which each side seeks to wear the other out by unremitting harassment. The expression dates from the First World War.

**War of Margaret's Shoulder.** A storm in a teacup in February 2005, in the run-up to that year's British general election. The Conservative leader, Michael Howard, pulled out of his hat, as a critique of the New Labour government's management of the NHS, one Margaret Dixon, a 69-year-old pensioner from Warrington, who had had a shoulder operation postponed seven times in a period of several months. Tetchiness between Howard, Tony Blair and health secretary John Reid followed. (Ms Dixon had the operation on 17 March 2005.) The press coined the phrase 'the War of Margaret's Shoulder' on the model of the War of Jenkins's Ear (1739–42), launched against Spain on the pretext that the dastardly Dons had some years earlier (in 1731) seized Captain Jenkins's ship and cut off his ear. On the same model, Louis de Bernières called one of his early, pre-Captain Corelli, novels *The War of Don Emmanuel's Nether Parts* (1991).

The War of Margaret's Shoulder was effectively a re-run of the War of Jennifer's Ear, which erupted in the 1992 general election after the Labour Party anonymously featured the five-year-old Jennifer Bennett in an election broadcast, stating that she had waited 11 months for an operation to treat glue ear. Considerable unpleasantness ensued.

**War of nerves.** A conflict that employs psychological techniques rather than physical violence. Typical ingredients of a war of nerves are propaganda, threats, false rumours and SABOTAGE, all calculated to demoralize the enemy. The expression dates from the early part of the Second World War, although it is also now used in stressful but non-combat situations (such as the workplace).

**War on Terror.** The ongoing campaign against international terrorism, particularly that which threatens the United States and the West, announced by US President George W. Bush following the 9/11 attacks on New York and Washington in 2001. On 20 September 2001 the president inaugurated the doctrine before Congress:

Americans should not expect one battle, but a lengthy campaign, unlike any other we have ever seen. It may include dramatic strikes, visible on TV, and covert operations, secret even in success. We will starve terrorists of funding, turn them one against another, drive them from place to place, until there is no refuge or no rest. And we will pursue nations that provide aid or safe haven to terrorism.

Its full name is the 'Global War on Terror', abbreviated in political and military circles to 'GWOT', and its principal overt manifestations have been the war in Afghanistan (2001), to topple the TALIBAN regime and destroy AL-QAIDA bases, and the invasion of Iraq in 2003 (despite no known links with al-Qaida). Both the term and its practical consequences have been much debated. It has been argued that one cannot make war on an abstract concept, and therefore that the term 'hijacks' military language as a way of justifying controversial policies. Defenders of the doctrine and its implementation argue that international terrorism presents a diffuse and dangerous enemy, in some ways more threatening than the nation states and power-blocs of old, and that existing vocabulary and thinking must be brought up to date.

Critics have also claimed that the very phrase instils fear, so that the citizen will gladly surrender traditional liberties to the state (as in the PATRIOT ACT in the United States, the establishment of CAMP X-RAY, the use of EXTRAORDINARY RENDITION and the attempt by the British government to introduce detention without trial). Others have criticized the whole strategy and tactics of the United States and its allies, suggesting that Western attacks on Muslim nations not only fail to target the loose global networks of terror groups, but also fail to address the causes of terrorism at the same time as alienating large swathes of the Muslim population around the world.
*See also* BUSH DOCTRINE; UNKNOWN UNKNOWNS.

**War poets, The.** A term for those poets who served in the armed forces in the First World War and who wrote about their experiences, often in realistic and harrowing terms. The greatest of their number were Wilfred Owen (1893–1918), Siegfried Sassoon (1886–1967), Robert Graves (1895–1985), Isaac Rosenberg (1890–1918) and Edmund Blunden (1896–1974). Their condemnation of the war, with its whole-sale carnage and final futility, was coupled with a desire to disabuse the public of the aura of glamour that surrounded war as a cause to be fought and won for the honour of one's country and oneself, if need be as an 'ultimate sacrifice'. Many of the war poets had also been Georgian poets (*see* GEORGIAN POETRY), and at first there was no incompatibility between the celebration of the English countryside and the patriotic sentiment of the early years of the war. When the latter gave way to grim realism, however, the two schools became sharply distinguished. The poems of Rupert Brooke (1887–1915), although often about war, were in contrast largely devoted to the theme of idealistic self-sacrifice and thus do not place him among the war poets as generally understood. *See also* 'DULCE ET DECORUM EST'.

**Warren Commission.** The official commission of inquiry into the assassination of President John F. Kennedy (JFK), who was shot in Dallas, Texas, on 22 November 1963. The seven-man commission was headed by Earl Warren (1891–1974), chief justice of the Supreme Court. The inquiry's report was published on 27 September 1964 and concluded that Lee Harvey Oswald (1939–63) had been a lone assassin. Oswald was not available for comment, as he had been shot dead a few days after the assassination by night-club owner Jack Ruby (1911–67) while in police custody. Critics have pointed to a number of pieces of evidence that appear to cast doubt on the Commission's conclusion (*see* GRASSY KNOLL), and conspiracy theorists have come up with a range of culprits, the favourites being the CIA and the COSA NOSTRA. *See also* KENNEDY CURSE.

**War Requiem.** A sombre, anti-war choral work by Benjamin Britten (1913–76), which combines nine poems by the WAR POET Wilfred Owen (1893–1918) with the words of the Latin requiem mass. The work was first performed in 1962 in the new COVENTRY Cathedral, which replaced the medieval cathedral destroyed in a German bombing raid in 1940. Britten, a lifelong pacifist, saw it as a work of recon-ciliation. At that first performance the soloists were Galina Vishnevskaya (a Russian), Dietrich Fischer-Dieskau (a German) and Peter Pears (a Briton). Stravinsky described the requiem as 'Kleenex music'.

**Warrington Bomb.** An IRA action on 20 March 1993 in which two bombs hidden in litter bins in a busy shopping centre in Warrington, near Manchester, exploded, killing a three-year-old boy and injuring more than 50 people; a 12-year-old boy died of his injuries five days later. The bad publicity accruing from the incident was arguably one of a number of factors that led to the first IRA ceasefire of 1994.

**Warsaw Concerto.** The stirring musical score written by Richard Addinsell (1904–77) for the film *Dangerous Moonlight* (1941). The film centres on a Polish pianist who escapes from the NAZIS, flies with the Polish Air Force in the BATTLE OF BRITAIN and loses his memory. This romantic melodrama was a huge hit with wartime audiences.

**Warsaw Pact.** The informal name for the treaty signed in Warsaw in 1955 between the Soviet Union and the eastern bloc countries of Albania (which formally left in 1968), Bulgaria, Czechoslovakia, Hungary, East Germany (membership ceased on German reunification), Poland and Romania as the Soviet response to NATO. Popularly perceived in the West as a contrivance of international cooperation masking a Soviet dominance of servile eastern Europe, its actual internal relations were occasionally pricklier than that image might suggest. Albania was disenchanted in the early 1960s and left in 1968. Romania grew increasingly rebellious, and attempted to impede the Pact's putting down of the PRAGUE SPRING the same year. The Treaty of Friendship, Cooperation and Mutual Assistance (to use its formal name) was annulled in 1991 following the dissolution of eastern-bloc communism.

**Warsaw risings.** Two uprisings against the NAZIS in Warsaw, the Polish capital, during the Second World War. The first uprising, in April–May 1943, was by the Jews who had been confined in a sealed ghetto since 1940. Perhaps 100,000 Jews had died from starvation and disease, and hundreds of thousands had been deported to extermination camps. On 19 April a large SS force set about clearing the ghetto to make the city 'Jew-free' by the next day, the FÜHRER's birthday. However, it met with unexpectedly strong resistance. Two Jewish underground military organizations were in operation in the ghetto: the Farband (Jewish Military Union) and the communist ZOB (Jewish Fighting Organization). After the first day's fighting the Germans were forced to retreat, but over the next 20 days they gradually fought their way across the ghetto, until all but 100 or so of the 60,000 Jews in the ghetto were dead.

The second Warsaw rising, code-named Operation Burza (Polish, 'storm') and initiated by the Home Army (the Polish resistance), broke out on 1 August 1944. With the Red Army having reached the far bank of the River Vistula, the Polish commander, General Tadeusz Bór-Komorowski, assumed he would receive Soviet support once the uprising got under way. However, after the long summer offensive STALIN ordered his forces to recuperate. It is almost certain that he also saw a political advantage in allowing the Home Army to be destroyed, as this would eliminate any possibility of Polish resistance to future Soviet occupation. The Poles were initially successful and had taken most of Warsaw by 4 August. However, the German counterattack began on 10 August. Two months of bitter fighting followed, in which between 150,000 and 180,000 Poles died, before Bór-Komorowski surrendered on 5 October. When the Red Army did eventually enter Warsaw they found it virtually razed to the ground.

**War to end war.** A naively optimistic term applied to the First World War. The phrase may have been suggested by H.G. Wells's *The War That Will End War* (1914), as a prelude to the 'World State' that he envisaged.

> I hope we may say that thus, this fateful morning, came to an end all wars.
>
> DAVID LLOYD GEORGE: announcing the terms of the Armistice to parliament, on the afternoon of 11 November 1918

**Wash and brush-up.** In the literal sense, dating from the start of the 20th century, a quick wash and tidying of one's hair. The phrase later gained a metaphorical sense for any figurative cleaning or cleansing, as of the removal of offensive passages from a literary work.

**Wash one's hands.** One of many euphemisms for visiting the lavatory, in this case dating from the 1930s. The expression does at least preserve the etymological origin of 'lavatory', in Latin *lavare*, 'to wash', and such a visit often concludes with the washing of one's hands in any case.

**Wasp.** A middle- or upper-class American white Protestant, regarded as highly influential in society. The word is an acronym of *w*hite *A*nglo-*S*axon *P*rotestant, originally used in statistical and sociological studies of US ethnic groups in the 1960s, and a term that was popularized by the Philadelphia historian and sociologist E. Digby Baltzell (1915–96). The suggestion of the name of the stinging insect is in all likelihood not coincidental, since such people are reputed to use their social superiority as a 'weapon'.

> Brooks Brothers is the natural habitat of the W.A.S.P. The image of the store is synonymous with the white, Anglo-Saxon Protestant male – a virile but wholesome species flourishing in middle America.
>
> *The Independent* (12 March 1988)

In the demographic trends of the US melting pot in the early 21st century the Wasp is a dwindling species.

**Wasp Factory, The.** The first novel (1984) by Iain Banks (b.1954), a study of insanity, which veers between psychological acuity and grotesque fantasy. The central character, 16-year-old Frank, has already been responsible for three violent murders. He lives with his father on a remote Scottish island, where he constructs a 'wasp factory' out of an old clock face to which he has added various tunnels and compartments, each with a special significance. From time to time he introduces a live wasp into this, using the route it takes and the fate it suffers as a prediction of the future. If it enters the fire compartments, for example, this means there will be a fire; if it enters the water compartments, there will be a drowning. The whole device is, up to a point, symbolic of Frank's true identity, which is eventually revealed.

**Wassup?** *See* WHAT'S HAPPENING?

**Waste Land, The.** A densely allusive poem (1922) by T.S. Eliot (1888–1965) that is now recognized as one of the landmarks of literary MODERNISM. The title, like the poem itself, expresses the sense of futility and disillusion that followed in the wake of the First World War. More specifically, it refers to an incident in the second book of Malory's *Le Morte d'Arthur*, in which the knight Balyn deals King Pellam the 'Dolorous Stroke' that causes the 'Waste Land', a disaster that devastates three kingdoms and whose effects can only be alleviated by the quest for the Holy Grail. Many lines from the poem have become familiar as quotations (and misquotations), including its opening words, 'April is the cruellest month' (*see* CRUELLEST MONTH), and

> When lovely woman stoops to folly and
> Paces about her room again, alone,
> She smoothes her hair with automatic hand,
> And puts a record on the gramophone.

It has also furnished titles for several subsequent literary works, including Evelyn Waugh's novel *A Handful of Dust* (1934) and Iain M. Banks's novel *Consider Phlebas* (1987). In the years following its publication, the poem attracted numerous admirers, including university undergraduates, who allegedly chanted it from college windows as an act of artistic rebellion:

> After luncheon he stood on the balcony with a megaphone which had appeared surprisingly among the bric-a-brac of Sebastian's room, and in languishing tones recited passages from The Waste Land to the sweatered and muffled throng that was on its way to the river.
>
> EVELYN WAUGH: *Brideshead Revisited* (1945)

**Watchful waiting.** The phrase used by President Woodrow Wilson in 1913 to describe his policy of non-recognition of the Mexican government of General Huerta. It did not last long, since US forces occupied Vera Cruz in 1914. The words were earlier used by President Andrew Jackson, in 1836.

**Watch it!** Be careful! A warning to watch one's words or actions before going too far. The phrase dates from the early 20th century.

**Watch someone's back.** To look after or protect them. A phrase dating from the 1950s.

> Robert Downey Jr recruits inmates to watch his back while he does time in America's deadliest jail.
>
> *heat* (23–29 September 1999)

**Watch someone's smoke.** To observe their activity; to see where they are going or what they are up to. The allusion is to a railway engine, whose passage in the days of steam could be followed by its smoke. The phrase usually occurs in the form 'Watch my smoke!' The expression is of US origin and dates from the beginning of the 20th century.

**Watch this space!** Be alert for more news on this topic. The reference is properly to the section of a newspaper page that is reserved for a particular purpose, and especially for an advertisement, although the phrase is also used as a hint that more on a topic may follow in a later edition.

> It remains to be seen whether [Courtney] Love will shave her head. Watch this space.
>
> *The Times* (1 January 2000)

*See also* STAY TUNED.

**Watch with Mother.** A highly regarded television series for pre-school children, running from 1950 to 1980, i.e. the era before the likes of the TELETUBBIES and the TWEENIES. It soon settled into a regular routine of stories and puppets for each day of the week, with *Picture Book* on Monday, ANDY PANDY on Tuesday, *The* FLOWERPOT MEN on Wednesday, *Rag, Tag and Bobtail* on Thursday and *The Woodentops* on Friday. Later contents were rather more varied. *See also* LISTEN WITH MOTHER; WOODENTOP.

**Water cooler.** An iced-water dispenser, as found in offices and other public places. People tend to stop for a conversation when they meet by it, and the late 20th century saw this role lexicalized in such expressions as 'water-cooler moment' (meaning a striking passage in the previous evening's television which people would discuss round the water cooler).

**Watergate.** In the United States, an area of flats and offices beside the River Potomac, Washington, D.C., which gave its name to a major political scandal. An illegal bugging attempt was made by Republicans at the Watergate headquarters of the Democratic Party during the 1972 elections, and this was followed by attempts to cover up the affair. The subsequent resignation and prosecution of senior White House officials, and further evidence of corruption, eventually led to the resignation of the Republican President Richard Nixon (1913–94, President 1968–74) when threatened with impeachment. *See also* ALL THE PRESIDENT'S MEN; DEEP THROAT; GATE; MAXIMUM JOHN; SMOKING GUN; TRICKY DICKY.

> Once the toothpaste is out of the tube, it is awfully difficult to get it back in.
>
> H.R. HALDEMAN: presidential assistant to Richard Nixon, referring to the Watergate affair in a conversation with White House counsel John Dean (8 April 1973)

**Watering hole.** A pool where animals drink, or, in human terms, a favourite pub or bar. The latter sense dates from the 1970s.

**Waterland.** A regional novel (1983) by Graham Swift (b.1949), distinguished by its remarkably atmospheric evocation of the East Anglian Fens (Waterland) and for a technically intricate but skilfully handled plot involving incest, abortion and murder. Its central character, a history teacher, sets aside the syllabus and embarks on a historical and social survey of the Fens. Into this he weaves the dark details of his own family history and of himself and his wife. A glumly melodramatic film version (1992), starring Jeremy Irons, was directed by Stephen Gyllenhaal.

**'Waterloo'.** The irresistibly effervescent song, written by Benny Andersson, Stig Anderson and Björn Ulvaeus, with which the Swedish pop group Abba, clad in garb that hinted more than a little at the style of GLAM ROCK, won the EUROVISION SONG CONTEST in 1974. The song, which dramatically equates the lovelorn subordination of a besotted lover with the final defeat of Napoleon Bonaparte at the Battle of Waterloo in 1815, is memorable for its thunderous piano chords, catchy melody, abysmal rhymes ('the history book on the shelf, is always repeating itself') and the group's audibly Scandinavian pronunciation of the song's English lyrics. It launched a career that would confer cult and gay-icon status on the Swedish foursome. *See also* ROCK GROUP NAMES.

**'Waterloo Sunset'.** A song by The Kinks about loneliness, isolation and the consolations of the London scenes invoked by its lyrics. It was released in 1967 and written by Ray Davies, observing the world from his window. The song was originally intended to be titled 'Liverpool Sunset', but 'Waterloo Sunset' was chosen because the native North Londoner Davies had walked over Waterloo Bridge in London several times a week on his way to art school. It appeared on the album *Something Else*.

**Watershed.** A media term for the time, usually understood as 9 p.m., after which television programmes regarded as unsuitable for children are broadcast. Complaints are sometimes made about unsuitable material transmitted 'before the watershed'. *See also* FAMILY HOUR.

**Watership Down.** An immensely popular animal novel (1972) by Richard Adams (b.1920). It concerns a community of rabbits that sets out in search of a new home on the downs when their Berkshire warren is destroyed by construction workers, and can also be read as a political or environmental allegory. Adams created a complete world and convincing speech for his animal characters, particularly memorable among which are HAZEL, Fiver and Bigwig. The title is the name of a part of the downs near Whitchurch, Hampshire, where Adams lives. A two-dimensional (in every sense) cartoon film version (1978) was directed by Tony Guy. *See also* FIRST LINES OF NOVELS.

**Watford.** This Hertfordshire town, 26km (16 miles) northwest of London, is popularly reckoned to mark the outer limit of urban-based civilization, so that everything and everybody 'north of Watford' are in a supposed cultural wilderness. Watford was itself presumably chosen for this key role as it lies on the M1, the main thoroughfare to London. This Watford is sometimes confused, especially by non-motorists, with the Watford Gap, which is a service station,

also on the M1, but north of Daventry in Northamptonshire. It lies in a broad valley at the northern end of the Cotswolds at the point where road, rail and canal routes run in parallel through the hills. It also has a 'border' role, and is sometimes regarded as the southern boundary of the Midlands.

**Wave of the future.** The inevitable future fashion or trend; the coming thing. The expression was popularized by the title of Anne Morrow Lindbergh's book *The Wave of the Future: A Confession of Faith* (1940), advocating that the advance of fascism should not be resisted.

**WAVES.** Until 1942 the women's section of the US Naval Reserve or, since 1948, of the US Navy. The name is formed by the initial letters of Women Accepted for Volunteer Emergency Service.

**Waves, The.** A novel by Virginia Woolf (1882–1941), published in 1931. The novel is highly experimental, dissolving the world into the streams of consciousness of six characters, followed from childhood to old age. Nothing is fixed, all is flux, like the waves of the recurring seascapes that give some shape to the novel. Waves can also be seen as a figure for the human experience, an analogy of consciousness moving through time and space.

**Wave the flag.** *See* SHOW THE FLAG.

**Wavy Navy.** The popular name for the former Royal Naval Volunteer Reserve (RNVR), whose officers wore gold distinction lace made in wavy lines instead of straight, as worn on the sleeves of regular officers belonging to the 'Straight Navy'. The RNVR lost its separate existence, after a fine wartime record, in 1957, when it was combined with the Royal Naval Reserve (RNR). *See also* WAVES; WRENS.

**Wayne's World.** *See* NOT!

**Way off beam.** Wholly incorrect; altogether on the wrong track. The phrase originated in the US Air Force in the Second World War, the allusion being to radio beams that guide aircraft.

**Way-out.** Unusual; eccentric; avant-garde. A term that gained popularity in the SWINGING SIXTIES. 'Way-in' soon followed to mean 'conventional' or 'sophisticated'.

**Way to go!** Well done! A US exclamation of approval and encouragement, originally to athletes. It is short for 'That's the right way to go' and was first current in the 1940s, when it is said to have been coined for the film *Knute Rockne* (1940; *see* GIPPER).

**Wazzup?** *See* WHAT'S HAPPENING?

**Weakest Link, The.** The title of a BBC television quiz show, first broadcast in 2000, in which one contestant is eliminated (by the votes of the others) in each round. The curt words of dismissal pronounced by the stony-faced presenter Anne Robinson, 'You are the weakest link. Goodbye!', became a popular catchphrase.

**Weapons of mass destruction.** A collective term (often abbreviated to 'WMD') used in military and political jargon to denote weapons (particularly nuclear, chemical and biological weapons) capable of causing massive damage and loss of life. The term enjoyed a high profile in the 1990s and early 2000s, when the question of whether Saddam Hussein's Iraq possessed such weapons was a hotly contested issue. The US-led invasion of Iraq in 2003 was largely justified by the assumption (later shown to be in error) that it did possess them.

Sue Townsend satirized the affair in *Adrain Mole and the Weapons of Mass Destruction* (2004; *see* Adrian MOLE), while those opposed to the war, and suspicious of the motives for the invasion, talked of 'weapons of mass distraction'. Greg Dyke, after losing his job as director general of the BBC over a BBC journalist's allegations that reports of Saddam Hussein's WMD had been exaggerated, acquired a silver Lexus car with the registration plate M16 WMD.

> The world's biggest weapon of mass destruction is the cigarette.
>
> FRANK DOBSON (former Labour health secretary): on the *Today* programme, BBC Radio 4 (16 November 2004)

*See also* DODGY DOSSIER; REGIME CHANGE; SEPTEMBER DOSSIER; SMOKING GUN.

**Wear another hat.** To function in a different role or position. The allusion is to headgear worn for different occupations. The form of the phrase is variable, so that one can 'wear a different hat', 'wear two hats' and so on. The concept dates from the 1960s and arose as civil service jargon.

> Wearing his new 'economic overlord' hat the Prime Minister [Harold Wilson] summoned three key figures to Downing Street today.
>
> *Evening Standard* (29 August 1967)

**We Are Making a New World.** The stark painting by Paul Nash (1889–1946) has become as iconic of the wastefulness of war as the poems of Wilfred Owen or Siegfried Sassoon. After being injured in the First World War, Nash became an official war artist (a role he took on again in the Second World War). The title of this painting is heavily ironic: a low pale sun radiates tenuous beams of light over a shattered landscape of craters and splintered trees. The work, which dates from 1918, hangs in the Imperial War Museum, London. *See also* TOTES MEER.

**We are not alone ... .** *See* CLOSE ENCOUNTER.

**We are the masters now.** The version usually quoted of Labour politician Hartley Shawcross's assertion in the House of Commons on 24 April 1946, following Labour's landslide victory in the July 1945 general election:

> We are the masters at the moment, and not only at the moment, but for a very long time to come.

Shawcross may have been echoing the speech of the Whig MP Edmund Burke in the House of Commons (11 February 1780) in which he declared:

> The people are the masters.

On 7 May 1997, the first day of the new parliament after New Labour's election victory, Tony Blair, quoting the founder of modern conservatism, told the House of Commons:

> We are not the masters. The people are the masters. We are the servants of the people ... What the electorate gives, the electorate takes away.

**We Are The People Our Parents Warned Us About.** A book (1968) about the hippie phenomenon by Nicholas Von Hoffman. The title is based on the remark that the bohemian painter Augustus John made to his fellow bohemian painter Nina Hamnett: 'We have become, Nina, the sort of people our parents warned us about.'

**Wearside Jack.** A media nickname given to the hoaxer who pretended to be the YORKSHIRE RIPPER. His campaign of deception began in 1978 with taunting letters to the police signed 'Jack the Ripper', and in 1979 he sent a message on tape (phoneticians localized the accent to the Castletown area of Sunderland – whence 'Wearside'). The police believed him, and their search for a killer from the Northeast is thought to have significantly delayed the capture of the real 'Ripper'. A new DNA-based inquiry in 2005 revealed 'Wearside Jack' to have been John Humble (b. 1956), an unemployed alcoholic. In 2006 he was convicted of perverting the course of justice and imprisoned for eight years.

**Wear the trousers.** To dominate. Said of a woman, and especially a wife, who assumes a domineering household role that was formerly believed to belong to the husband (who normally wears trousers). The expression dates from the 1930s. *See also* HER INDOORS.

**Weary Willie and Tired Tim.** A phrase still sometimes used for a pair of loafers or idlers. The names are those of two comical tramps, one fat, one thin, created by the cartoonist Tom Browne in 1896 for the weekly *Illustrated Chips*. Their adventures continued on the front page of this paper until it ceased publication in 1953.

**Weasel under the cocktail cabinet, The.** What Harold Pinter once said his plays were about, as recorded by J. Russell Taylor in *Anger and After* (1962).

**Weasel words.** Words of convenient ambiguity, or a statement from which the original meaning has been sucked or retracted. Theodore Roosevelt popularized the term by using it in a speech in 1916 when criticizing President Woodrow Wilson. A quotation from the speech provides a good example: 'You can have universal training, or you can have voluntary training, but when you use the word *voluntary* to qualify the word *universal*, you are using a weasel word; it has sucked all the meaning out of *universal*. The two words flatly contradict one another.'

Roosevelt was indebted to a story by Stewart Chaplin, 'Stained-glass Political Platform', which appeared in the *Century Magazine* in June 1900 and in which occurs the sentence: 'Why, weasel words are words that suck the life out of the words next to them, just as a weasel sucks the egg and leaves the shell.'

**Weathermen.** A terrorist group that evolved in 1969 from the US student organization Students for a Democratic Society, best known for its activity against the VIETNAM War. The Weathermen were the most radical of the factions, vowing to 'lead white kids into armed revolution'. They took their name from a line in Bob Dylan's song 'Subterranean Homesick Blues' (1965): 'You don't need a weatherman to know which way the wind blows.'

**Wedgie.** *See* BERTIE WOOSTER OF MARXISM.

**Wee Frees.** A disparaging nickname for the minority of the Free Church of Scotland that in 1900 refused to unite with the United Presbyterian Church to form the United Free Church, which itself reunited with the Church of Scotland in 1929. The vestigial Free Church of Scotland, which is sternly Sabbatarian, remains strong in some parts of the Highlands and Islands.

**Weekend warrior.** A term for a person who engages in a part-time activity, whether literally at the weekend or not. The use of 'warrior' implies that the activity may be fairly strenuous.

> Don't be a 'weekend warrior'. If your job is sedentary, you must exercise a little in the week as well as at the weekend or the shock to your body could lead to strains and injuries.
> *The Times* (3 January 2000)

**Week is a long time in politics, A.** An epigram attributed to the Labour prime minister Harold Wilson (1916–95) and said to have been uttered by him on more than one occasion in the 1960s, the first time to lobby correspondents just after the 1964 general election. It has been taken to imply that politicians' policies and principles change with circumstances, and/or that unpopular actions are rapidly forgotten by the electorate. Wilson himself claimed later that he meant that politicians and the public should take a longer-term view than they normally do.

**Wehrmacht.** (German, 'Defensive Force'.) The German armed forces, and especially the army, from 1921 to the end of the Second World War.

**Weight Watchers.** An organization, in full Weight Watchers International Inc., founded in the United States in 1961 to promote dieting and exercise as a means of slimming, and serving a similar purpose for compulsive eaters to that provided by ALCOHOLICS ANONYMOUS for compulsive drinkers.

**Weimar Republic.** The German federal republic established under the constitution of 1919, which lasted until it was overthrown by Hitler in 1933. It was so called from the Thuringian town, particularly associated with Goethe, where the constitution was adopted by the National Assembly. *See also* SPARTACISTS.

**Weird and wacky.** Unusual; eccentric; WAY-OUT. An epithet for any unconventional person or 'free spirit'. The phrase is of US origin, and it is a variant on the older 'weird and wonderful'.

**Weirdstone of Brisingamen, The.** This fantasy for children (1960; US title *The Weirdstone*) was the first novel by Alan Garner (b.1934). It is subtitled 'A Tale of Alderley', meaning Alderley Edge, the Cheshire village where Garner was born and from where the tradition behind the story emanates. The story concerns the lost weirdstone, a piece of crystal shaped like a raindrop, which resurfaces in a bracelet, and involves two children with the Wizard of Alderley and his struggle against the forces of evil. A sequel, *The* MOON OF GOMRATH, was published in 1963.

**Welcome mat.** To put down the welcome mat for someone is to make them feel wanted or at home, especially after a period of absence or a time when they have been out of favour. The reference is to the doormat at the entrance to a house, which may actually have the word 'Welcome' on it.

> Hague puts down welcome mat for Ken [Clarke].
> *Sunday Express*, headline (27 February 2000)

**Welfare state.** A term applied to Britain after the implementation of the BEVERIDGE REPORT, providing for social security services for sickness, unemployment, retirement and the like, and essentially based on the National Insurance Act of

1946. The system depends on compulsory contributions and taxation, and was built upon the less sweeping Liberal legislation of 1908–14. Many features were 'reformed' from 1979 under successive Conservative and New Labour governments.

**'Well all right! Well ALL RIGHT!'** Labour leader Neil Kinnock's jubilant, air-punching message to Labour's US-style rally at Sheffield on the eve of the 1992 general election. The triumphalism of the occasion is thought by some to have robbed Labour of the victory they were so sure would be theirs.

**Well-endowed.** Having noticeably large genitals (of a man) or breasts (of a woman). The telling euphemism dates from the 1940s.

**'We'll Meet Again'.** A song written in 1943 by Ross Parker and Hughie Charles, and made famous as sung by Vera Lynn, the FORCES' SWEETHEART, as a bitter-sweet evocation of wartime separation. She first sang it in the musical film of the same title.

> We'll meet again,
> Don't know where,
> Don't know when,
> But I know we'll meet again some sunny day.

The song was used to blackly ironic effect in the film DR STRANGELOVE, in which it is sung while the world is destroyed in a nuclear holocaust.

**Well of Loneliness, The.** A novel (1928) by Radclyffe Hall (pseudonym of Marguerite Radclyffe-Hall; 1880–1943). This study of lesbian love, written by a lesbian partly to demonstrate the isolation of those of similar sexuality, was banned in Britain for many years and finally published in a small, high-priced edition in a plain cover. Its heroine is the 'invert', Stephen Gordon, who is obliged to release her lovers to a conventional world while she herself remains trapped inside a 'well of loneliness'.

**Well, we knocked the bastard off.** The phrase used by the New Zealand mountaineer Edmund Hillary (b.1919) to announce that he and Tenzing Norgay had made the first successful ascent of Mount Everest, on 29 May 1953. He made the remark to a fellow member of the expedition, George Lowe, on descending to their high camp. Hillary recalled in his memoirs, *Nothing Venture, Nothing Win* (1975):

> My comment was not specially prepared for public consumption but for George ... He nodded with pleasure ... 'Thought you must have.'

*See also* BECAUSE IT'S THERE.

**Welsh Windbag.** A media nickname for the Welsh politician Neil Kinnock (b.1942), LABOUR PARTY leader from 1983 to 1992, alluding to his perceived verbosity and garrulousness. *See also* KINNOCKIO.

**Welsh Wizard.** A nickname of the Liberal politician David Lloyd George (1863–1945). As chancellor of the exchequer (1908–15) he laid the foundations of the WELFARE STATE and produced the PEOPLE'S BUDGET of 1909, and as prime minister (1916–22) he led Britain to a hard-won and costly victory in the First World War. The nickname referred to his powers as an orator and his inventive mind, while his enemies identified in him the supposedly pagan and magical qualities of cunning, deviousness and a lack of principles. Margot Asquith (1864–1945) observed, 'He couldn't see a belt without hitting below it,' and John Maynard Keynes (1883–1946) somewhat mysteriously stated, 'When he's alone in a room, there's nobody there.' *See also* LG.

The nickname 'Welsh Wizard' was also applied to the Welsh footballer Billy Meredith (1875–1958), likening his mercurial gifts to those of his famous countryman. The analogy was stated even more explicitly in one of Meredith's other nicknames, the Lloyd George of Welsh Football. He was also known as the Prince of Wingers.

**We must love one another or die.** The conclusion of W.H. Auden's poem 'September 1, 1939' (1940), the title of which refers to the date on which Nazi Germany invaded Poland, so precipitating the Second World War.

> There is no such thing as the State
> And no one exists alone;
> Hunger allows no choice
> To the citizen or the police;
> We must love one another or die.

**Wendy.** This girl's name was the invention of J.M. Barrie for his play PETER PAN. The poet and playwright W.E. Henley (1849–1903) was a friend of Barrie and used to address him as 'Friend'. Henley's young daughter, Margaret, copied this but pronounced the word 'Fwend' and duplicated it childishly as 'Fwendy-Wendy'. The latter half of this gave the name of Wendy Darling in the play. It soon caught on generally, as for the actresses Wendy Barrie (1912–78), Wendy Hiller (1912–2003) and Wendy Toye (b.1917). Wendy Barrie, born Marguerite Wendy Jenkins, was Barrie's goddaughter and was named by him. She later took his surname as her stage name.

**Wendy house.** A toy house large enough for children to play in. It takes its name from the house built around the little girl WENDY Darling in J.M. Barrie's play PETER PAN. In prison slang 'wendy house' is the period of the day and the place in which prisoners are allowed to socialize.

**We never closed.** The boast of Vivian van Damm (c.1889–1960), manager of the WINDMILL THEATRE, London, during the Second World War. Even when a bomb landed next door, killing an electrician and injuring one of the performers, the show went ahead. Among the theatre's morale-boosting specialities were groups of unclothed women arranged in 'artistic' tableaux, with strict instructions not to move as much as an eyelid. When the doors opened for each performance there was a stampede of men to the front six rows, where the seats had constantly to be repaired. The theatre's motto was said to have been interpreted by one showgirl with a lisp as 'We never clothe.'

**We're here because we're here because we're here because we're here.** Words sung to the tune of 'Auld Lang Syne' by British soldiers during the First World War, embodying their fatalistic acceptance of a world gone mad.

**We shall never surrender.** The conclusion of Winston Churchill's speech to the House of Commons, 4 June 1940 – the day that the last British troops were withdrawn from DUNKIRK:

> We shall not flag or fail. We shall fight in France, we shall fight on the seas and oceans, we shall fight with growing confidence and growing strength in the air, we shall defend our island, whatever the cost may be, we shall fight on the beaches, we shall fight on the landing grounds, we shall fight in the fields and in the streets, we shall fight in the hills; we shall never surrender.

**'We Shall Not Be Moved'.** The title of a labour and civil rights hymn of 1931, adapted from an earlier anonymous gospel hymn or spiritual. The words evoke a biblical verse: 'God is in the midst of her; she shall not be moved: God shall help her, and that right early' (Psalm 46:5).

**'We Shall Overcome'.** The title of a song originating from before the American Civil War (1861–5) and adopted for a hymn of 1901 by the Methodist minister C. Albert Tindley entitled 'I'll Overcome Some Day'. It was revived in 1946 as a protest song by black tobacco workers on picket lines in Charleston, South Carolina, and again during the black civil rights campaign of 1963.

**West Bank.** A region on the west bank of the River Jordan, populated by Arabs and a base of Palestinian resistance since its capture by the Israelis in 1967. It was granted to the Arabs at the time of the partition of Palestine in 1948 and became part of Jordan. In 1988 Jordan gave up all claims, ceding the territory to the PLO. Negotiations for the withdrawal of Israeli troops from Arab areas of the West Bank were settled by an agreement between Israel and the PLO in 1995, although its implementation to the satisfaction of both sides continued to be a sticking point. The presence of large numbers of Israeli settlers in the area has provoked considerable resentment among the Palestinians, as has the building by the Israelis of a high wall close to the border with Israel, which has caused much disruption to many Palestinians. *See also* GAZA STRIP.

**Western.** A distinct genre of film or novel in which life in the American West of the latter half of the 19th century is portrayed. The situations are usually formulaic and the characters are often stereotyped, with gun fights and cowboys predominant, but the genre nevertheless came to embody elements of cultural history and helped to shape the nation's image of itself. It is the western of the cinema rather than the novel that has become the more familiar, and its world has been additionally popularized through the medium of COUNTRY MUSIC. *See also The* MAGNIFICENT SEVEN; STAGECOACH; *The* WILD BUNCH.

**Western Approaches.** A mainly maritime name for the area of sea immediately to the west of the British Isles, and in particular for the western end of the English Channel. Admiral Sir Reginald Tupper was appointed Commander-in-Chief, Western Approaches, Queenstown, in 1919, and the name became familiar to many in the Second World War from the speeches of Winston Churchill and from radio news bulletins and newspaper reports. The film *Western Approaches* (1944), played to great documentary effect by men of the Allied navies, was a fictional story, telling how torpedoed merchantmen in the Atlantic were used by a U-BOAT as a decoy. Sir Fitzroy Maclean gave the title *Eastern Approaches* to a 1949 memoir dealing with his pre-war diplomatic life in the USSR and his mission to Partisan leader Tito in Yugoslavia during the Second World War.

**Western Front.** The general term for the front in Belgium and northern France in both world wars. Erich Maria Remarque's anti-war novel *Im Westen nichts Neues* (1929), literally 'Nothing new in the west', became familiar in English translation as ALL QUIET ON THE WESTERN FRONT. The title was an ironic reproduction of a phrase repeatedly used in official communiqués relating to operations in France and Flanders.

**Westland affair.** A major political row during the Conservative administration of Margaret Thatcher, centring on the Westland helicopter company at Yeovil in Somerset. Michael Heseltine, then defence minister, favoured a rescue bid by a European consortium, but was opposed by Leon

Brittan, trade and industry secretary, who sided with the Westland directors in preferring a deal with the US firm of Sikorski. In January 1986 Heseltine caused a sensation by resigning in the middle of a cabinet meeting when Mrs Thatcher insisted that ministerial statements on the affair should be approved by the Cabinet Office. A letter critical of Heseltine was subsequently leaked from the solicitor general. By the end of the month Brittan had also resigned, admitting that he had approved the leak. The opposition claimed that the leak must have been ordered at a higher level, by the prime minister herself, but she stated that she had not been informed of the matter.

The deal with Sikorski went through, and some years later Heseltine mounted a challenge for the Conservative leadership, starting a chain of events that brought Mrs Thatcher's premiership to an end in November 1990.

**West Lothian question.** A nice constitutional point raised in discussion of the proposed DEVOLUTION of Scotland and Wales from the late 1970s onwards by Tam Dalyell, MP for West Lothian in Central Scotland. It highlights an apparent anomaly of representation in the Westminster parliament vis-à-vis the devolved parliaments and assemblies: Westminster MPs for Scottish and Welsh constituencies can vote on matters that concern only England, but MPs for English constituencies no longer have the opportunity to vote on Scottish or Welsh matters.

**West Side Story.** The much performed musical by Leonard Bernstein (1918–90) has lyrics by Stephen Sondheim (b.1930). It was first staged in 1957. The story is an updated version of *Romeo and Juliet* set in New York's West Side dockland area, with the Montagues and the Capulets replaced by rival teenage gangs, the Sharks and the Jets. The rivalry erupts into violence as a result of the love between Tony, one of the Jets, and Maria, the sister of the leader of the Sharks.

The 1961 film version won an OSCAR for best picture.

**West Wall.** (German *Westwall*.) The extension of the SIEGFRIED LINE defences on Germany's western frontier, constructed following an order by Hitler in August 1944, as a belated part of his FORTRESS EUROPE. The West Wall incorporated parts of the MAGINOT LINE and was also built along the German North Sea coast between Denmark and the Netherlands.

**West Wing, The.** The title of an EMMY-winning US television drama series broadcast from 1999 to 2006. Devised by Aaron Sorkin, it chronicles the fortunes of a fictional president, Josiah Bartlet, and members of his White House staff. Bartlet, a liberal New Hampshire Democrat of charm,

humour and intelligence, was played by Martin Sheen. Some commentators have claimed that the series portrayed the kind of Democratic US presidency that many US liberals wished had been provided by Bill Clinton (*see* SLICK WILLIE).

**Wet behind the ears.** Inexperienced; naive; as innocent as a newborn child. When young animals are born the last place to become dry after birth is the small depression behind each ear. The figurative expression dates from the 1920s.

**Wets.** This 19th-century term for a weak or spineless person, familiar to some from the talk of middle-class prep schoolboys, took on a new edge in the summer of 1979 when it came to be applied to members of Margaret Thatcher's Conservative cabinet and party who were opposed to the hard-line monetarist policies then being espoused. Many of those so dubbed actively embraced the name. Those who deviated less sharply from the line were known as Dries. *See also* MOANING MINNIE; NIGHT OF THE LONG KNIVES.

**We Two Boys Together Clinging.** This early painting by David Hockney (b.1937) dates from 1961. The homoerotic subject is executed in Hockney's distinctive early Pop art style. Hockney himself has written about the painting in *David Hockney by David Hockney* (1976):

> *We Two Boys Together Clinging* is from Walt Whitman:
> We two boys together clinging,
> One the other never leaving …
> Arm'd and fearless, eating, drinking, sleeping, loving.
> The emphasis of the painting is on 'clinging'; not only are the arms clinging but small tentacles help keep the bodies close together as well. At the time of the painting I had a newspaper clipping on the wall with the headline 'TWO BOYS CLING TO CLIFF ALL NIGHT'. There were also a few pictures of Cliff Richard pinned up nearby, although the headline was actually referring to a Bank Holiday mountaineering accident.

**We wuz robbed!** We've been cheated! The saying is attributed to the US boxing manager Joe Jacobs following Jack Sharkey's win on points over the German world heavyweight champion Max Schmeling, of whom Jacobs was manager, in the heavyweight title fight of 21 June 1932.

**Wexford, Chief Inspector.** The rural police inspector (full name Reginald Wexford) who appears in a series of detective novels by Ruth Rendell, starting with *From Doon with Death* (1965), in which he investigates gruesome murders in the sleepy country town of Kingsmarkham. He was memorably portrayed by George Baker in a television series based on the stories with the overall title *The Ruth Rendell Mysteries* (1987–92).

**W.G.** The nickname of the prodigiously bearded Gloucestershire and England cricketer Dr William Gilbert Grace (1848–1915), also known as the Doctor and the Champion, who single-handedly invented modern batsmanship.

***Whaam!*** One of several paintings of jet fighters in action executed in enlarged comic-book style by Roy Lichtenstein (1923–97), the Peter Pan of POP ART. *Whaam!*, which dates from 1963, includes the words 'I pressed the fire control … and ahead of me rockets blazed through the sky … '. This results in the 'Whaam!' of the title as the enemy fighter explodes in flames. Similar works by Lichtenstein include *Blam* (1962). He also had a gentler side, and in such works as *Good Morning, Darling* (1964) drew on teenage romances for his inspiration. Hans Richter, the old Dadaist, recalled a conversation with Lichtenstein:

> His little son's schoolfellows asked him what his father was. An artist? What kind of artist? An abstract expressionist! Oh, said the children, somebody who paints abstracts because he's no good at drawing. Lichtenstein Junior came home crying and told his father he couldn't draw. Lichtenstein Senior assured him that this wasn't true and drew him a great big Mickey Mouse, just like in the comic strips. This didn't satisfy him: his father had to prove that he could draw people too. So Papa L. drew him a big George Washington in comic-strip style. That satisfied him! But the strange thing was that not only L. Junior, but L. Senior too, liked it.

**Whacko the diddle oh!** A somewhat eccentric Australian exclamation of enthusiastic approval (especially at the sight of an attractive female). 'Whacko' on its own, first recorded in 1937, has spread to other varieties of English, but the embellishment 'the diddle oh' remains peculiarly Australian. The expression has also been used as an adjective, meaning 'splendid, first-rate', in which role it has been joined latterly by the equally bizarre 'whacko-the-chook' (to an Australian, a chicken is a 'chook') and 'whacko-the-goose'.

> Ample Petrolillium, the all-Aussie you-beaut whacko-the-goose petrol pedlar, tonight admitted it encouraged drunken driving.
> *Kings Cross Whisper* (Sydney) (1970)

**Whale in the bay.** In Australian slang, a person who has money to spend and with luck may put some of it your way. The scenario is of a wealthy (and, one hopes, generous) person who has just arrived in town and, like a whale that has just swum into your local bay, offers the prospect of rich pickings. The expression goes back to the 1930s, and more recently it has also come to be used with connotations of underhanded behind-the-scenes goings-on.

**Wham, bam, thank you ma'am.** An encapsulation of an act of sexual intercourse performed perfunctorily and without emotion. The expression arose among US servicemen in the Second World War and may have been originally adopted from cowboy parlance.

> I can't just fuck. I can't wham bam get rid of my dirty water man. I have to be in love.
> Roger, a convicted killer in Kingston prison, quoted in *The Guardian* (4 January 2006)

*See also* REDNECK FOREPLAY.

**What do you know?** A US expression of surprise dating from the early years of the 20th century, as: 'Hey, what do you know? Steve's gotten himself a new car!'

**Whatever Generation, The.** A term that emerged in the 2000s for the current generation of young people, regarded by their less tolerant elders as insolent, ignorant and uncaring, the type who spit out their chewing gum anywhere without blinking an eye. Those who utter the I-don't-give-a-damn 'Whatever' (pronounced 'wo'evuh') sometimes accompany this with a gesture, holding three fingers upright (to form a W), followed by holding the three horizontally (to form an E). Alternative expressions of bored alienation are 'Am I bothered?', 'Do I look bothered?' and the like, which in 2004 became popular catchphrases thanks to their constant use by Lauren, the teenager with an attitude problem in *The Catherine Tate Show*, a BBC television comedy programme. By those who cannot summon up the energy for an entire phrase, these expressions are often curtailed to simply 'Bothered!' (pronounced 'bovvered').

**What gives?** What's the news? What's happening? An expression of US origin dating from the 1940s. Hence 'What gives with … ?' naming a person or thing, as: 'What gives with the bike?', i.e. 'How is the bike going?' The phrase probably derives from Yiddish *vi geht's?* 'how goes it?' (German *wie geht's?*) *See also* WHAT'S WITH?

**What goes around, comes around.** A fatalistic 20th-century encapsulation of the principles of fortune's wheel: there is nothing entirely new under the sun and, if you are patient, opportunities will re-present themselves. It originated in the United States in the 1960s.

> What goes around, comes around. Everything old is new again. In the world of fashion, most 'new' looks have been around before.
> www.factmonster.com (2005)

***What is to Be Done?*** The title of a 1902 pamphlet, subtitled 'Burning Questions of Our Movement', by the Russian revolutionary leader V.I. Lenin (1870–1924). The phrase was originally the title of an 1863 novel by N.G. Chernyshevsky. In the pamphlet Lenin recounts the various periods in the history of Russian Social Democracy. He concludes (ultimately somewhat bathetically):

> When the third period will come to an end and the fourth (now heralded by many portents) will begin we do not know. We are passing from the sphere of history to the sphere of the present and, partly, of the future. But we firmly believe that the fourth period will lead to the consolidation of militant Marxism, that Russian Social-Democracy will emerge from the crisis in the full flower of manhood, that the opportunist rearguard will be 'replaced' by the genuine vanguard of the most revolutionary class.
>
> In the sense of calling for such a 'replacement' and by way of summing up what has been expounded above, we may meet the question, What is to be done? with the brief reply:
>
> Put an End to the Third Period.

The pamphlet played a part in the split between the BOLSHEVIKS and the MENSHEVIKS in the Russian Social Democrats.

**What Not to Wear.** *See* MAKEOVER TV.

**What planet are you on?** Didn't you know that? Do you really think that? A question put to someone apparently out of touch with reality, as if inhabiting a different planet from earth. The concept can be variously expressed.

> 'The upper-class people are the multimillionaire people who … are such a strata [*sic*] above what I have experienced in life as to be on a different planet.'
>
> ERIC JACOBS and ROBERT WORCESTER: *We British*, ch. 13 (1990)

**What's good for General Motors is good for the country.** A dictum summing up the close relationship that often exists in the United States between government and big business, especially under Republican administrations. The phrase is actually a misquotation from Charles E. Wilson (1890–1961), formerly President of General Motors, whom President Eisenhower had nominated as his secretary of defense. Questioned upon his suitability for the post by the Senate Armed Services Committee on 15 January 1953, Wilson was asked whether he would be able to resolve any conflict of interest between his new job and his continuing investment in General Motors. He replied:

> Yes, sir, I could. I cannot conceive of one because for years I thought what was good for our country was good for General Motors, and vice versa. The difference did not exist.

The sentiment was not new: in 1925 President Calvin Coolidge had declared in a speech that 'The business of America is business', and in the film *Stagecoach* (1939) one of the characters declares, 'What's good for the banks is good for the country.'

*See also* BIGGER BANG FOR YOUR BUCK; MILITARY-INDUSTRIAL COMPLEX.

**What's happening?** A friendly greeting, originally (in the 1950s) among American jazz musicians but subsequently widespread in African-American slang and its imitators. Semantically it mirrors the greeting 'What's up?', which dates back to the 19th century and in the late 20th century metamorphosed into the cooler 'Wassup?' or 'Wazzup?'

**What's My Line?** One of the first British television panel games, originally screened from 1951 to 1963 and featuring some of Britain's earliest television personalities as its regular panellists: Lady Isobel Barnett (1918–81), David Nixon (1919–78), Gilbert Harding (1907–60) and Barbara Kelly (b.1924). The panel, chaired by Eamonn Andrews (1922–87), posed oblique questions to establish the occupation of each guest contestant. The programme was revived in 1973–4 and 1984–90.

**What's not to like?** A rhetorical question, suggesting to a doubter that something or someone is eminently likeable. The construction came into American English from Yiddish, and in the latter part of the 20th century showed some signs of spreading to other varieties of English. The verb can be replaced by near synonyms ('love', 'fall for', etc.), antonyms ('hate') or verbs in altogether different semantic ballparks (e.g. 'understand').

> Reese Witherspoon and Mark Ruffalo in a high-concept romcom about falling for a ghost – what's not to love about that?
>
> *The Guardian* (30 December 2005)

**What's that in aid of?** What is the point of that? What is that all about? A stock query dating from the 1930s. The phrase 'in aid of', meaning 'in support of', is much older.

**What's the haps?** A variation on WHAT'S HAPPENING?.

**What's with?** What's the matter with? What's the reason for? A US phrase enquiring about something, as: 'What's with the hurry?' ('Why the hurry?') or 'What's with that guy?' ('What's wrong with that person?'). The phrase is also expanded to 'What is it with?' *See also* WHAT GIVES?

> What is it with the super-rich? They rarely look as if life is worth living.
>
> *The Times*, letter to the editor (24 June 1999)

**What's your poison?** What would you like to drink? Alcohol actually is a poison, so the expression is not quite the euphemism it appears to be.

**What the Butler Saw.** A farcical comedy (1969) by the British playwright Joe Orton (1933–67) in which life in an asylum run by psychiatrist Dr Prentice is greatly disrupted by the errors and confusions arising from a range of sexual improprieties involving Prentice, his wife and sundry other characters. The title refers to the naughty seaside 'peep-show' machines, which often bore the legend 'What the Butler Saw'.

**Wheeler-dealer.** A person who 'wheels and deals'. 'Wheel' has its sense in the US expression BIG WHEEL. Hence one of great influence in a particular field (usually business or politics), a shrewd and influential operator and manipulator.

**Wheelie.** A stunt whereby the front wheel of a bicycle or motorcycle is lifted off the ground while being ridden.

**Wheelie bin.** A large refuse bin on wheels. Both the term and the object are of Australian origin, and the bins were first in use in Britain in the 1980s.

The cricket writer and broadcaster Henry Blofeld (b.1939) applied the nickname 'The Wheelie Bin' to the Warwickshire and England spin bowler Ashley Giles (b.1973), apparently with reference to his somewhat cumbersome progress in the field. (Giles's other nickname, 'The King of Spain', arose from a typographical error on a large batch of mugs, produced in 2004 in aid of Giles's benefit and intended to be printed with the legend 'The King of Spin'.)

**Wheel of death.** A hazardous circus act in which a performer spins in and on a large 'hamster wheel' as it is gradually lowered to the ground from a 15m (50ft) high wire. *See also* WALL OF DEATH.

**Wheel someone in** or **on.** To introduce a person to a meeting, debate or broadcast programme simply to provide impersonal backing or to support an uncontroversial argument. The image is of wheeling in a dummy figure that can be manipulated accordingly.

**Whelk stall.** To say that someone could not even run a whelk stall is to indicate their complete organizational incompetence. The reason for the choice of this particular trade is uncertain, but as whelk stalls are normally found at seaside resorts the implication may be that little effort or expertise is required to make ready money from happy holidaymakers.

**Wheneye.** A slang term for a self-centred person who is forever reminiscing or recounting tales or experiences of past times, frequently with the opening words 'When I ...'. The implication is usually that the speaker can outdo the (unwilling) listener.

**When Harry Met Sally.** A film comedy (1989), written by Nora Ephron, about a man and a woman (played by Billy Crystal and Meg Ryan) whose relationship changes over a number of years from antipathy to friendship and finally love. Remembered primarily for the much-imitated but never equalled restaurant scene in which Meg Ryan noisily demonstrates her skill at faking an orgasm, the film was originally to have been titled *It Had To Be You*, but this was dropped when it was discovered that another movie was being made with that title. Another suggestion was *Boy Meets Girl*.

> I'll have what she's having.
> ESTELLE REINER: in her role as a diner at the restaurant

*See also* HIGH-MAINTENANCE.

**When push comes to shove.** When it comes down to it; when matters become critical. If a simple push does not produce results, one must resort to a more forceful shove. The expression is of US origin and dates from the 1950s.

> The suspicion that [composer Percy] Grainger is, when push comes to shove, not really that important, still lingers.
> *Times Literary Supplement* (6 August 1999)

**When the balloon goes up.** When the action starts; when the trouble begins. The expression dates from the First World War, when the artillery sent up a balloon as a signal for gunners to open fire, using this visual method as one more reliable than a courier or the field telephone.

**When the fat lady sings.** An abbreviated version of the OPERA ISN'T OVER UNTIL THE FAT LADY SINGS.

**When the going gets tough, the tough gets going.** A proverbial declaration of macho bravura, favoured by those who are testosterone-rich and caution-poor. The phrase has been attributed both to the ruthless financier and diplomat Joseph P. Kennedy (1888–1969), father of President J.F. Kennedy, and to Knute Rockne (1888–1931), the American football coach.

**Where Angels Fear to Tread.** A novel (1905) by E.M. Forster (1879–1970), the inspiration for which was a piece of gossip, overheard while he was in Italy, about an English tourist who formed a *mésalliance* with an Italian. The plot centres on the efforts of the members of an English family to 'rescue', from his Italian father, the baby whose mother, related to them by a former marriage, has died in childhood. The title is from Alexander Pope (1688–1744): 'For Fools rush in where Angels fear to tread' (*An Essay on Criticism*, 1711). A disappointing film version (1991) was directed by Charles Sturridge.

**Where Eagles Dare.** A thriller (1967) by Alistair Maclean (1922–87). Seven men and a young woman are parachuted onto the side of a mountain in Germany in the Second World War. Their mission is to infiltrate themselves into an apparently inaccessible and impregnable castle on the heights, in which a US general in being held for questioning after an air crash. A predictable film version (1969) of the 'schoolboy adventure' type was directed by Brian G. Hutton.

**'Where Have All the Flowers Gone?'** The title of a 1961 anti-war song by the American folk musician Pete Seeger (b.1919):

> Where have all the flowers gone?
> Long time passing
> Where have all the flowers gone?
> Long time ago
> Where have all the flowers gone?
> Girls have picked them every one
> When will they ever learn?
> When will they ever learn?

The girls pick the flowers for their young men, who go off to become soldiers. The soldiers have 'gone to graveyards', and, to the question 'Where have all the graveyards gone?' the singer replies 'Covered with flowers every one.'

**Where it's at.** The real thing; the true state of affairs. The phrase is typically applied to a centre of fashionable activity, where it is desirable to be seen.

> Sydney is where it's at, the place to see if you are a sightseer, and the place to write about if you are a writer.
> *Sunday Times* (8 August 1999)

**Where someone is coming from.** What motivates someone's words or actions. The phrase, which usually occurs in such contexts as 'know or understand where someone is coming from', emerged in the United States in the late 1960s, and has for many people achieved the high irritation factor of a cliché.

**Where's the beef?** Where is the substance in what you say? The phrase has its origin in a television commercial first screened in the United States on 9 January 1984 by the Wendy International hamburger chain: an outraged old lady, patronizing a non-Wendy establishment that serves buns with salad and little else, demands of the manager: 'Where's the beef?' The words were subsequently taken up by Walter Mondale in a televised debate with Gary Hart from Atlanta on 11 March that year: 'When I hear your new ideas I'm reminded of that ad, "Where's the beef?"'

**Where's the fire?** What's the hurry? Why are you going so fast? The phrase dates from the 1920s.

> 'Where's the fire, dear boy?' he drawled. 'Do we really have to run for it?'
> J.F. STRAKER: *Final Witness*, ch. 16 (1963)

**Where the action is.** In the centre of some important or fashionable activity; WHERE IT'S AT.

**Where the bodies are buried.** The long-hidden and probably discreditable secrets of an organization or group. Someone who 'knows where the bodies are buried' is in a position to reveal such secrets and cause much consternation.

**Whiffenpoofs.** This was the name of a famous band of 'gentlemen songsters' at Yale University early in the 20th century, made up of the best singers in the senior class. Their key piece was 'The Whiffenpoof Song', with words by two Yalemen, Meade Minnigerode and Guy S. Pomeroy, that were a part-parody of Rudyard Kipling's poem 'Gentlemen-Rankers' from his *Barrack Room Ballads* (1892). The music was by Guy H. Scull of Harvard in an adaptation by Tod B. Galloway of Amherst. The song itself was composed in 1909 and took its name from the Whiffenpoof, an imaginary fish in Victor Herbert's operetta *Little Nemo* (1908). The Whiffenpoofs still exist, although now their number is limited to 14 seniors.

**Whilst.** A British English alternative form of 'while', dating from medieval times and found in Shakespeare but in modern usage favoured in official documents, letters to the press and the like as bearing a greater degree of perceived dignity or authority than its everyday equivalent. It mostly occurs in the sense 'although' or 'whereas' rather than 'during the time that', and the following opening sentences of letters to the *The Times* (11 August 1999) are typical of the usage: 'Whilst I hold no brief for new Labour …', 'Whilst I agree that "The Church is people, not old stones" …'. Predictably enough, the result is usually an impression of straining after an unattainable gravitas.

**Whirlybird.** A US nickname for a helicopter, dating from the 1950s. The colloquialism linguistically mirrors the standard word, which translates literally from the Greek as 'spiral wing'.

**Whisky Galore.** A novel (1947) by Compton Mackenzie (born Edward Montague Compton; 1883–1972). Said by him to be based loosely on the wreck of the SS *Cabinet Minister* off Eriskay with a cargo of whisky, it is a satire on Scottish life, manners, religion and superstitions, whose starting point is a wreck in similar circumstances during a grave shortage in the Second World War of *uisge beatha* (water of life). A wonderful film version (1948), fast paced and excellently acted, was directed by Alexander Mackendrick.

**Whispering campaign.** A deliberate dissemination of derogatory rumours about someone, specifically a candidate for election. The expression is of US origin and dates from the 1920s.

**Whispering Death.** A nickname for the Jamaica, West Indies, Lancashire and Derbyshire cricketer Michael Holding (b.1954). A fast bowler, his smooth and silent run-up produced deliveries of terrifying velocity. He is particularly remembered for an over bowled in 1981 to the England opening batsman Geoffrey Boycott (a master of defensive play), in which he defeated Boycott with a succession of unplayable balls before clean-bowling him.

**Whispering Giant.** A nickname given to the Bristol Britannia airliner, which entered commercial service in the late 1950s. The reference was to its innovative turboprop engines, which made much less noise than the traditional piston engines of the day.

**Whistle-blower.** A person who informs on someone who is engaged in an illicit activity. *See also* BLOW THE WHISTLE ON; OFFICIAL SECRETS ACT.

> Some of Britain's biggest train companies are refusing to back plans for a national 'whistle-blower' scheme allowing staff to report safety defects confidentially.
> *The Times* (22 October 1999)

**Whistle Down the Wind.** A film (1961) adapted by Keith Waterhouse and Willis Hall from a novel of the same title by Mary Hayley Bell about three motherless children in rural Lancashire who find a fugitive criminal in their barn and become convinced that he is Jesus Christ. The film starred Hayley Mills (the author's daughter), Bernard Lee and Alan Bates, who played the fugitive. The title (generally interpreted as to talk or argue purposelessly) comes from a proverbial saying connected with falconry, referring to the releasing of a hawk down wind. In the 1990s the story was adapted to make a musical by Andrew Lloyd Webber and Jim Steinman.

**Whistle in the dark.** To hazard a guess; to speculate wildly; to appear more confident than one really is. The expression dates from the 1930s.

**Whistle-stop tour.** A fast tour with only brief pauses on the way. A whistle-stop is a US term for a minor station that trains approach with a whistle signal, not stopping unless a flag or lamp is displayed. In political parlance, a whistle-stop tour became the term for a full-scale tour of the United States by a presidential candidate, during which stops were made at communities with a whistle-stop. The train had private cars and the candidate addressed the assembled crowd from the platform of the rear car. Harry S. Truman was the last presidential candidate to undertake a full whistle-stop tour, in 1948. Later candidates have undertaken abbreviated tours, such as that made by Jimmy Carter in 1976. Britain's equivalent is a campaign by BATTLEBUS.

**Whitbread Awards.** A set of literary prizes founded in 1971 and named after their sponsor, Whitbread plc (previously brewers and distillers). Awards are made in two stages. First, nominations are selected in the five categories of novel, first novel, biography, poetry and children's. One of these is then voted by the panel of judges as Whitbread Book of the Year. In 2006 Costa Coffee took over the sponsorship of the award, changing the name to the Costa Book Awards.

***White Album.*** The name generally used to describe a double album by The BEATLES, officially entitled *The Beatles* and released in November 1968. It acquired the name the White Album because of the stark simplicity of its plain white cover. The album's 30 tracks include 'BACK IN THE USSR', the civil-rights influenced 'Blackbird', the satirical 'Piggies', the children's song 'The Continuing Story of Bungalow Bill', 'HAPPINESS IS A WARM GUN', 'Rocky Racoon', 'Sexy Sadie' and 'HELTER-SKELTER'. The extraordinary eight-minute track 'Revolution 9' represents The Beatles at their most avant-garde. Unwittingly some of the songs, bizarrely interpreted, inspired the MANSON MURDERS.

**White Army.** A name for the counter-revolutionary or anti-BOLSHEVIK forces that opposed the RED ARMY in the Russian Civil War of 1918–20. The main groups were the army commanded on the southern front by General Anton I. Denikin, the forces of Admiral Alexander V. Kolchak in Siberia and the troops of General Pyotr N. Wrangel in the Crimea. The Red Army were the eventual victors.

**White Australia policy.** A policy that had its roots in the 19th-century Australian gold rushes, which attracted numerous Chinese workers. The presence of these immigrants led to resentment among white Australians, who feared competition and a lowering in their standard of living. Other resented immigrants included Japanese, Pacific islanders and East Indians. The desire for uniform immigration laws to exclude Asian immigrants was one of the factors that brought the colonies together into the Commonwealth of Australia in 1901. Federal laws soon followed to implement the White Australia policy. For decades immigration was almost entirely from the British Isles, although after the Second World War large numbers of non-English-speaking Europeans were welcomed. Immigration restrictions against non-Europeans began to be relaxed from 1966, and the White Australia policy was formally abandoned in 1973.

**White City.** A famous stadium in Shepherd's Bush, northwest London, completed in 1908 as part of a complex for the Franco-British Exhibition. That same summer it staged the fourth Olympic Games, and it was here that the modern length of the marathon was fixed at 26 miles 385 yards (42.195km). The length was originally planned at 26 miles (41.84km), but the extra yards were added to bring the finishing line before the royal box. Greyhound racing began at White City in 1927, and until its demolition in the 1980s it was the site of the Greyhound Derby. The name alludes to its white-stuccoed buildings and continues in use for the surrounding area, which at the beginning of the 21st century is being developed as a vast new shopping centre.

**White Cliffs of Dover.** The chalk cliffs near Dover, Kent, serving as a patriotic or nostalgic landmark for those returning home from abroad. They were popularized from a morale-boosting song sung by the FORCES' SWEETHEART, Vera Lynn, in the Second World War:

> There'll be bluebirds over
> The white cliffs of Dover,
> Tomorrow, just you wait and see.
> NAT BURTON: 'The White Cliffs of Dover' (1941)

*See also* AUSTERITY.

**White-collar worker.** A professional or clerical worker, whose calling demands or at one time demanded a certain nicety of attire, typified by the wearing of a white collar. The term dates from the 1920s. *See also* BLUE-COLLAR WORKER; GREY-COLLAR WORKER; PINK-COLLAR WORKER.

**White goods.** Originally a term for household linens, such as sheets and towels, which are, of course, not necessarily white. The term later came to apply to electrical goods that are conventionally white, such as washing machines and refrigerators.

**Whitehall Warrior.** A nickname for an officer in the armed forces employed as a civil servant, typically on retirement, rather than on active service. His 'battle' is thus with administrative matters rather than military. Whitehall in London is the location of several government offices.

**White hat.** A US colloquialism for a good man or hero, dating from the 1970s. The reference is to the white hats worn by the 'goodies' in early western films, as distinct from the black ones worn by the 'baddies'. *See also* GOODIES.

**White heat of technology.** A version of a phrase in the Labour leader Harold Wilson's speech to the Party Conference, 1 October 1963. What he actually said was:

> The Britain that is going to be forged in the white heat of this

revolution will be no place for restrictive practices or for outdated methods on either side of industry.

The widespread misquotation encapsulated the image of the Labour Party in the early 1960s as youthful and progressive, in comparison to the fuddyduddiness of the Tories. The following year Wilson became prime minister.

**White hope.** A person expected to bring success to a team or organization. The term dates from the early years of the 20th century and originally applied to a white boxer who might have been able to beat Jack Johnson (1878–1946), the first black boxer to be world heavyweight champion (1908–15).

**White Horse Final.** In footballing history, a nickname for the Cup Final of 1923 between Bolton Wanderers and West Ham United at Wembley. Thousands of fans spilled on to the pitch before the start of the game, and it required mounted police, and in particular Constable George Scorey on his 13-year-old white horse, Billy, to clear it before the match could begin. Although Scorey was only one of several mounted policemen on duty that day, his conspicuous white horse gave the name by which the final has always been referred to since.

**White knight.** A champion or rescuer, especially one who comes to the aid of a company in financial difficulties. The expression dates from the 1980s and appears to derive not from the enthusiastic but ineffectual White Knight in Lewis Carroll's *Through the Looking-Glass* (1871) but from the KNIGHT IN SHINING ARMOUR on a white charger who rescues a DAMSEL IN DISTRESS. *See also* BLACK KNIGHT.

**White-knuckle ride.** A fairground or amusement park ride aiming to give a 'thrill of a lifetime' to its intrepid travellers, who grasp the rail before them so tightly that their knuckles turn white. The expression can be figuratively used of any similar stressful experience.

> Bluewater … is a shoppers' theme park in which the only white-knuckle ride you will experience will take place four weeks later when you open your credit card bills.
> *The Times* (15 September 1999)

**White label.** A musical recording for which the fully printed commercial label is not yet available. It has thus been supplied with a plain white label before any general release of the recording, either for promotional purposes or as a limited-edition pressing to test the market. The term dates from the 1920s.

> Ibiza is … a musical melting pot which attracts producers from all over Europe, who turn up with white labels of their latest tune and distribute them to DJs in the island's innumerable bars and clubs.
> *heat* (6–12 January 2000)

**White list.** The opposite of a black list, as a list of people or products viewed with approval. The term dates from the beginning of the 20th century.

**White man's burden.** In the days of imperialism, the duty supposed to be imposed upon the white races, especially the British, to govern and to educate the more 'backward' coloured peoples. The expression was the creation of Kipling, the original reference being specifically to the role of the United States in the Philippines.

> Take up the White Man's burden –
> Send forth the best ye breed –
> Go bind your sons to exile
> To serve your captives' need.
>
> RUDYARD KIPLING: 'The White Man's Burden' (1899)

**White Mischief.** *See* HAPPY VALLEY.

**White Noise.** In physics, a sound or electronic signal that has equal intensity at a wide range of frequencies. Some such signals occur in the atmosphere. The American writer Don DeLillo (b.1936) adopted the title *White Noise* for a novel (1985) centring on an 'airborne toxic event' and the manufacture of an experimental drug to cure the fear of death.

**White Pelé.** A nickname applied to two Brazilian footballers: Tostão (Eduardo Gonçalves de Andrade; b.1947), a member of his country's World Cup-winning team in 1970; and Zico (Artur Antunes Coimbra; b.1953), a formidable successor to Pelé in the Brazilian national sides of the 1970s and 80s. *See also* BLACK PEARL; BRAZILIAN FOOTBALLERS; EUROPEAN PELÉ.

**White Rose, The.** (German *Die weisse Rose*.) A Christian anti-Nazi group at Munich University during the Second World War. From June 1942 the students issued a number of leaflets critical of the regime, and by February 1943 they were calling for active resistance. On 22 February 1943 three members of the group, Sophie Schöll and her brother Hans, together with Christoph Probst, all young students, were sentenced to death. They were guillotined that same day. Other members of the group were executed later in the year.

**Whiter shade of pale, A.** Paler in complexion than usual. The phrase was popularized by the song of this name performed by the pop group Procol Harum in the late 1960s, with lyrics by Keith Reid and music by Gary Brooker. Its title comes from a phrase used by the song's producer Guy Stevens while talking to his exhausted wife. The song, a worldwide hit, was released in 1967 during the SUMMER OF LOVE. Its melody evokes that of J.S Bach's so-called *Air on a G String* (from his Orchestral Suite No. 3 in D Major), an impression increased by the prominent use of an organ. The lyrics, including references to '16 vestal virgins' and Chaucer's *Miller's Tale*, represent the pop lyric of the 1960s at its most obscurely allusive and, some might say, pretentious.

> And it was later, as the Miller told his tale,
> That her face, at first just ghostly,
> Turned a whiter shade of pale.
>
> KEITH REID: 'A Whiter Shade of Pale' (1967)

**Whiter than white.** Free from taint; beyond reproach; absolutely pure and innocent. The phrase dates from the 1920s and was popularized as a slogan for Persil soap powder.

**White Russian.** An inhabitant of White Russia or Belorussia (now Belarus; Russian *bely*, 'white'), a former republic of the USSR. 'White Russian' is also a term for a counter-revolutionary or *émigré* at the time of the BOLSHEVIK revolution, and their army was known as the WHITE ARMY, in direct contrast to the communist RED ARMY.

For tipplers, a White Russian is a cocktail containing vodka, Kahlua and cream; its cousin, the Black Russian, lacks the cream.

**White settlers.** A term applied by some Scots to English people living in Scotland. The term is also used elsewhere of incomers. The implication is that such people take advantage of their wealth to buy up the best property and have no concern for the local people. The term, which came into popular use in the 1990s, contains within it an echo of the resentment of European settlers that was felt by their subjects in the colonial era.

**White-suit candidate.** A term applied to an independent candidate standing for a particular constituency in a UK election with the aim of ousting the incumbent, often over a particular issue. The term derives from the white suits favoured by the former BBC war correspondent Martin Bell, who in 1997 stood against the sitting MP for Tatton, the former Conservative minister Neil Hamilton, who had been involved in a CASH FOR QUESTIONS scandal. On this basis Bell campaigned on an anti-sleaze platform (*see* SLEAZE FACTOR) and was duly elected.

Among the white-suit candidates at the 2005 election was Reg Keys of Military Families against the War, whose son, a military policeman, had been killed in 2003 while serving in Iraq. Keys, with the support of Bell, unsuccessfully stood against prime minister Tony Blair in his Sedgefield constituency – an example of a failed DECAPITATION STRATEGY.

**White trash.** *See* TRAILER TRASH.

**White van man.** A man with an anonymous white van (including, among others, the TRANSIT VAN) who undertakes various errands and is generally regarded, mostly quite without justification, as a 'shady character' and as a notoriously bad driver given to ROAD RAGE. The term was popularized in the 1990s by the BBC Radio 2 presenter Sarah Kennedy and for a while the *Sun* newspaper ran a 'White Van Man of the Week' column. In due course the expression came to be applied indiscriminately to repair men and delivery men in general, as well as to plumbers and decorators, whether qualified and competent or simply bungling COWBOYS. The individual described is also known as a 'man with a white van' or simply a 'man with a van', its colour being implicit.

**Whitewall.** A style of haircut in which the sides of the head are shaved and the top and back left longer. The appearance is that of a whitewall tyre, which has a white stripe round the outside.

**Whitewater Affair.** A US government scandal based on the alleged dealings of President Clinton and his wife Hillary before Clinton became president in 1993. The action began in 1978 when the Clintons and their partners, James McDougal and his wife Susan, bought a plot of land north of Little Rock, Arkansas, and set up the Whitewater Development Corporation to build holiday homes. The enterprise failed when McDougal went bankrupt and was charged with bank fraud, although he was subsequently acquitted. There was no evidence that the Clintons were aware of any wrongdoing, but critics made much of Clinton's association with McDougal at a time when the future president was state attorney-general in Arkansas. The scandal surfaced when Clinton became president, and it resulted in the resignations of some of his aides.

**White wedding.** A traditional wedding at which the bride wears a long white dress. The term dates only from the 1940s, although white, as a symbol of purity, has been the customary colour for the bridal gown since the 18th century. In the 21st century the purity tends to be notional.

**White Wednesday.** *See* BLACK WEDNESDAY.

**Whizz** or **whiz kid.** A highly intelligent young person, one who achieves rapid success, the onomatopoeic word 'whizz' being the sound of something moving through the air with great rapidity. The term has probably also been influenced by 'wizard'.

**Who ate all the pies?** A taunting question directed at a fat person, typically by a barracking crowd at a sports match. It is said that the original target was the English footballer

William Henry ('Fatty') Foulke (1874–1916), who was noted for his unappeasable appetite.

**Who dares wins.** The motto of the SAS from 1942, adopted from that of Brigadier Robert Yerburgh, Lord Alvingham (1889–1955). *Who Dares Wins* was also the title of a derided action thriller (1982), cashing in on SAS's success in the 1980 Iranian embassy siege, and of a more satirical Channel 4 TV comedy sketch show broadcast between 1983 and 1988, featuring, among others, Rory McGrath and Tony Robinson. In the Australian television game show entitled *Who Dares Wins* (broadcast from 1996) contestants have to perform various difficult and adventurous tasks.

In 1995 the Conservative defence secretary Michael Portillo (*see* PORTILLISTAS) embarrassed himself at the Party Conference by hijacking the SAS motto for crowd-pleasing political purposes: 'Who dares? We dare. We will win.'

**Whodunit.** A colloquialism originating in the United States for a detective story. The word is said to have been coined by Donald Gordon in the American *News of Books* of 10 July 1930, in which he described Milward Kennedy's novel *Half-Mast Murder* as 'a satisfactory *whodunit*'. *See also* WHYDUNIT.

> The detective story is easily identifiable, because despite the ingenuity of writers who prevent the reader from guessing 'Whodunit', it has only one plot, basically: the solution of a mystery, usually murder.
>
> JERRY PALMER: in H.R.F. Keating (ed.), *Whodunit?: A Guide to Crime, Suspense & Spy Fiction* (1982)

**Who Framed Roger Rabbit?** A film (1988) in which animation and live action were cleverly combined to tell the story of a private detective (played by Bob Hoskins) who is hired to investigate the private life of Roger Rabbit's sexy wife Jessica (both cartoon characters). Hence the widely repeated alternative title 'Who Rogered Jessica Rabbit?' When the film was shown in Golders Green, the heart of London's Jewish community, a storm allegedly damaged the title on display at the local cinema so that it read 'Who Framed Roger Rabbi?'

**Who he?** An editorial query written besides the name of a supposedly little-known person. The expression is particularly associated with Harold Ross, founding editor (1925–51) of *The* NEW YORKER. It was subsequently popularized by its use in the satirical magazine *Private Eye*, while Jonathan Goodman's *Who He?* (1984) is an entertaining 'Dictionary of the Unknown Famous'.

**Whole ball of wax.** Absolutely everything; 'the works'. The US expression dates from the 1950s but is of uncertain origin. According to one theory, the reference may be to a former method of distributing the land of an estate to heirs, in which the amount of each portion was concealed in a ball of wax. This was then drawn out of a hat in a sort of lottery. *See also* WHOLE ENCHILADA; WHOLE NINE YARDS.

**Whole enchilada.** The whole thing; everything. The expression originated in US slang in the 1950s, probably as a fanciful variant of earlier synonymous phrases such as 'the whole bag of tricks', 'the whole shooting match' and 'the WHOLE BALL OF WAX'. An enchilada is a Mexican dish.

> Yes, we're the real deal, with lawyers, accountants, bankers, a board, the whole enchilada.
>
> www.blahblahblog.newzguy.com (1 October 2005)

*See also* WHOLE NINE YARDS.

**Whole megillah.** A long or tedious story; a 'rigmarole'. The Megillah, from the Hebrew for 'scroll', is any of the five Hebrew scriptures (The Song of Solomon, Ruth, Lamentations, Ecclesiastes and Esther) appointed to be read on certain Jewish feast-days. The phrase, dating from the 1950s, alludes to the length of the books and translates Yiddish *a gantse Megillah*.

**Whole new ball game.** A totally new or revised situation. The term comes from baseball, in which it is used to mean a sharp turn of events, as when the team that was ahead falls behind. The expression dates from the 1960s.

> This makes molecular anthropology 'a whole new ball game', says Zegura.
>
> *New Scientist* (11 July 1998)

**Whole nine yards.** The complete package, everything; to 'go the whole nine yards' is to attempt or do everything. The phrase, which emerged in the United States in the 1960s, has been explained with reference to all manner of bizarre measurements and quantities, from the length of a hangman's noose and the capacity (in cubic yards) of a ready-mixed cement truck to the dimensions of a nun's habit and the length of a Spitfire's ammunition belt, none of which stands up to close examination. A plausible derivation remains tantalizingly out of reach. The expression was popularized by the title of the comedy film *The Whole Nine Yards* (1999), starring Bruce Willis as a hitman in suburbia.

> I went to the City and Islington sixth-form college after that. … I was there to retake my GCSEs but I left after five months. Stupid. I wanted to go the whole nine yards, be a total graduate.
>
> *Sunday Times Magazine* (2 January 2000)

**Whoop-de-do.** A motorcycling term for a very bumpy road, inspired by the exclamation of the rider.

**Whoopee cushion.** A joke cushion that makes a sound like the breaking of wind when someone sits on it. The allusion is to 'making whoopee' as a synonym for boisterous merry-making. The device was first put to use in the 1960s.

> George was a great one for whoopee cushions when he was a drinking man and a cutup, but I'd be surprised if he was into that sort of thing any more.
>
> JONATHAN S. BUSH (cousin of President George W. Bush): quoted in *The Observer* (2004)

**Who's Afraid of Virginia Woolf?** A play (1962) by US playwright Edward Albee (b.1928) depicting the tense relationship between a sharp-tongued East Coast college professor and his embittered wife, as it is played out in front of two bewildered dinner guests at their home. Filmed in 1966 with Richard Burton and Elizabeth Taylor in the two main roles (their own volatile marriages filled the gossip columns for many years), the play owed its memorable title to a line of graffiti scribbled in soap on a mirror in a bar in New York's Greenwich Village that the author happened to visit in the 1950s. The quip, evidently derived from the song title 'Who's Afraid of the Big Bad Wolf' from the Disney cartoon *The Three Little Pigs* (1933), was later redefined by Albee as meaning 'Who's afraid of living without false illusions?'

**Who's he when he's at home?** A semi-humorous enquiry about a person's identity, especially when that person has no claim to fame or one feels that they are presuming a fame they have not earned. The pronoun is obviously variable.

**Who Wants to be a Millionaire?** A British television quiz show, hosted by Chris Tarrant and broadcast since 1998. Contestants double their prize money with each question correctly answered, but can lose their gains if they get an answer wrong. If they are troubled by a particular question, they have various options, including asking the audience or phoning a nominated friend for help – hence 'Phone a friend', which has become something of a catchphrase. The format has been exported to many other countries. The title comes from the Cole Porter song 'Who Wants to be a Millionaire?', in the film *High Society* (1956), where it is sung by Frank Sinatra and Celeste Holm.

**Why?** A single written query often accompanying a floral tribute at the scene of a fatal accident. The cliché presumably seeks to interrogate the Almighty as to his reasons for allowing the death.

> The congregation … filed slowly … across the road to look at the … floral tributes. … Many bore cards asking simply: 'Why?'
>
> *The Times* (11 October 1999)

On a less metaphysical level, the equally clichéd 'Why, oh why?' has become the stock in trade of writers of letters of ostensibly mystified complaint. It is first recorded in 1865, but not until the second half of the 20th century did it begin to pepper newspaper correspondence columns and, latterly, weblogs.

> Why, oh why does Rolls-Royce ... name its latest product after an area of French marsh-land?
>
> *The Times* (8 March 1975)
>
> Why oh why, of all people, does Lindsay Lohan have to star in Gossip Girl?
>
> *Teen Vogue Forums* (21 September 2005)

**Why don't you come up and see me sometime.** *See* COME UP AND SEE ME SOMETIME.

**Whydunit.** A mystery novel, play or film that deals primarily with the motivation for the crime, as distinct from the WHODUNIT, which concentrates on establishing the identity of the perpetrator.

> [Sean] Connery takes over the interrogation and in the process beats the man to death. This much we know almost from the beginning, so the film [*The Offence*] is less of a whodunit than a whydunit.
>
> *Time* (4 June 1973)

**Why, oh why?** *See* WHY?

**Wicca.** The religious cult of modern witchcraft. It was founded in Britain in the mid-20th century and claims to originate from pre-Christian pagan religions. The word is Old English for 'witch', meaning originally a man (not a woman) who practises witchcraft.

**Wicked Witch of the West Wing.** A hostile nickname for Hilary Rodham Clinton, wife of President SLICK WILLIE Clinton, when she was First Lady (1993–2001). The West Wing is the part of the White House where the president lives and works, and the Wicked Witch of the West is a character in *The* WIZARD OF OZ. Other hostile nicknames include Hilla the Hun and Robbery Hillham.

**Wide boy.** A man who lives by his wits, usually dishonestly; a SPIV or petty criminal. 'Wide' here has its former slang sense of 'sharp', meaning wide awake and alert. The phrase gained popular currency in the Second World War.

**Wide Sargasso Sea.** A novel (1966) by Jean Rhys (pseudonym of Ella Gwendoline Rees Williams; 1890–1979). Set in Dominica, where Rhys was born and lived until she was 16 years old, Jamaica and (in the last of the three parts) England, it is the story of the mad wife of Mr Rochester in *Jane Eyre* by Charlotte Brontë, from her childhood in Jamaica to the moment of truth of the conflagration at Thornfield Hall. The Sargasso Sea is a part of the Atlantic full of seaweed to the north of the West Indies. A lush Australian film version (1992), directed by John Duigan, recast the subtle original as a saga of sex and revenge.

**Widgie.** In Australia in the 1950s, the female equivalent of the BODGIE (Australia's answer to the TEDDY BOY). The origin of the term remains a mystery, although it may be related to Australian English 'ridgie-didgie', meaning 'genuine' or 'honest'.

**Wifelet.** A girlfriend, regarded as fulfilling the role of a wife without having the actual status of one. The word is particularly associated with the partners of Alexander Thynn, the idiosyncratic 7th Marquess of Bath (b.1932), whose residence at Longleat, Wiltshire, is adorned with his own portraits of around 70 such women. Thynn apparently invented the term, its *-let* suffix doubtless intended to denote affection but equally capable of being understood as diminishing or dismissive. *See also* LOINS OF LONGLEAT.

> 'The wifelet is a flexible definition. If somebody is a girlfriend but hasn't been sexually active for some years, I still count them in.'
>
> ALEXANDER THYNN: interviewed in *Sunday Times Magazine* (29 August 1999)

**Wigan Pier.** There are fine piers in several British seaside resorts, notably Eastbourne, Brighton, Blackpool, Weston-super-Mare and Southend. Wigan, however, is an inland town and does not have a pier. What passes for a pier is the remains of a gantry, now little more than a few iron girders, protruding from a wall by the Liverpool–Leeds Canal. As such, it is a curiosity and a tourist attraction in its own right. The story goes that the name arose when a trainload of miners was delayed in Wigan next to a coal-wagon gantry. The area was flooded at the time, and when a miner asked a local where they were, the facetious reply came: 'Wigan Pier.' The tale spread and was soon picked up by music-hall performers who used it to mock the middle classes and their holidays at resorts that had proper piers. George ORWELL's *The* ROAD TO WIGAN PIER (1937) is an account of industrial poverty in Wigan, Sheffield and Barnsley.

**Wightman Cup.** The trophy awarded to the winner of tennis matches held annually between teams of women from Britain and the United States. It was donated in 1923 by the US tennis champion Hazel Hotchkiss Wightman (1886–1974), and the first contest was held at Forest Hills, New York, on 11 and 13 August 1923 with a win for the Americans. Latterly the United States won with embarrassing regularity and after 1989 the unequal contest was abandoned.

**Wiki.** A collaborative website that allows its content to be created or edited by many hands over the INTERNET. The first such is credited to an American programmer, Ward Cunningham (b.1949), in 1995. The name 'wiki' alludes both to a Hawaiian word for 'quick' and, acronymically, to the phrase 'what I know is'. Its best-known realization is *Wikipedia*, a free online encyclopedia to which anyone can contribute. A debate continues about its integrity, critics saying that its absence of editorial vetting or peer review means that it cannot be trusted, while supporters point to favourable comparisons, in some studies, with established online encyclopedias such as *Britannica*.

**Wilco.** Military jargon for '(I) will comply', denoting acceptance of a message received by radio or telephone. The phrase became familiar from its use by the RAF in the Second World War.

**Wild blue yonder.** The far distance; a remote place. The metaphor is aeronautical and derives from Robert Crawford's song 'The Army Air Corps' in Moss Hart's musical *Winged Victory* (1943), the official show of the US Air Force.

> Off we go into the wild blue yonder,
> Climbing high into the sun.

**Wild Bunch, The.** An elegiac, blood-soaked WESTERN (1969) directed by Sam Peckinpah, and starring William Holden, Warren Oates, Ernest Borgnine and Robert Ryan. Set in the twilight years of the Wild West and on the eve of the Mexican Revolution, the film was considered exceptionally violent at the time of its release. The 'Wild Bunch' are a group of ageing outlaws who move into a southern Texan town to carry out a robbery, but are set up and ambushed by bounty hunters (among whose number is a former member of the bunch, forced to pursue his former accomplices or face a life behind bars). Pursued by the bounty hunters, the bunch flee to Mexico, where they become involved with a corrupt and vicious Mexican general who enlists their help in stealing a consignment of US Army weapons. When the youngest member of the bunch is captured and tortured for stealing weapons to supply revolutionaries in his home village, the bunch decide to do battle with the Mexicans to rescue their stricken friend. The words of the bunch's leader, 'I wouldn't have it any other way,' precipitate a final shootout of quite extraordinary ferocity.

**Wild card.** An unpredictable person or thing. More specifically, in computing a wild card is a symbol (often an asterisk) that will match any of a number of characters, of use in searching for, and within, files. The term comes from card games, especially poker, where it refers to a card that can have any value, suit or colour chosen by the player that holds it.

**Wild child.** An unconventional or 'rebellious' young person. The expression is typically associated with the FLOWER CHILDREN of the SWINGING SIXTIES, although the type at its most positive and beguiling is rather more than this. A fine literary example is Hazel Woodus in Mary Webb's *Gone to Earth* (1917), a gypsy's daughter who 'stands for un-adulterated nature in all its bounty and beauty' (Patricia Craig in *Times Literary Supplement*, 24 December 1999).

**Wilderness of mirrors.** A phrase descriptive of the confusing world of espionage. It is said to have been first used in this sense by James J. Angleton (1917–87), the leading counter-intelligence specialist of the CIA, who described it as the 'myriad of stratagems, deceptions, artifices and all the other devices of disinformation which the Soviet bloc and its coordinated intelligence services use to confuse and split the West'. The term originally comes from T.S. Eliot's poem 'Gerontion' (1920). It was also used by David C. Martin as the title of his book about Angleton, *Wilderness of Mirrors* (1980).

**Wild One, The.** A film (1953) adapted by John Paxton from a story, 'The Cyclists' Raid', by Frank Rooney about the chaos that ensues after a gang of motorbike riders, led in the film by Marlon Brando (the 'wild one' of the title), descends on a small country town. The plot was based on an actual incident that took place during the Fourth of July weekend of 1947, when 4000 bikers occupied the small town of Hollister, California, and destroyed it.

> *Murphy*: What are you rebelling against?
> *Brando*: What have you got?

**William.** The grubby-kneed, 11-year-old schoolboy William Brown is the hero of an engaging series of 38 books by Richmal Crompton (1890–1969). He and his pals 'the Outlaws', Ginger, Henry and Douglas, bring a note of welcome anarchy into the select middle-class setting in which they live. Together with William's dog, Jumble, they are involved in a variety of escapades in which they frequently fall foul of adult authority. William also has an ongoing love-hate relationship with Violet Elizabeth Bott, a precious, lisping six-year-old who is forever threatening to 'thcream an' thcream an' thcream till I'm thick'. The first story of his exploits was 'Rice-Mould', which was published in *Home Magazine* in February 1919. The series of novels opened with *Just William* (1922) and closed posthumously with *William the Lawless* (1970). Illustrations by Thomas Henry did much to enhance the lively text.

**Willie.** An affectionate nickname for William Whitelaw (1918–99), the Tory grandee who served as deputy prime minister (1979–88) to Margaret Thatcher, the IRON LADY. When he was elevated to the House of Lords as Viscount Whitelaw in 1983 Thatcher memorably observed that 'every prime minister should have a Willie', apparently in reference to his ability to spot and avoid political BANANA SKINS. *See also* LITTLE WILLIE; WOBBLING WILLIE.

**Willy the Weasel.** *See* SLICK WILLIE.

**Willy-waving.** An instance of competitive aggression or macho showing-off over something essentially trivial, held to be analogous to a male displaying his genitalia in order to gain attention.

> We are genuinely interested in asking the kinds of questions that our viewers want answered and try not to indulge in what is known in the business as 'willy waving' – showing off.
> RICHARD MADELEY: *Richard and Judy's Webchat* (12 July 2004)

**Wilshire Boulevard.** A broad street that passes through the centre of Los Angeles and leads to the Pacific coast in the region of Santa Monica. It is famous for its Miracle Mile, close to HOLLYWOOD, a glamorously glittering stretch of stores, boutiques, hotels, restaurants and nightclubs, and takes its name from a local developer, H.G. Wilshire (1861–1927).

**Wimmin.** A respelling of 'women', adopted by some feminists from the late 1970s as a means of avoiding the undesirable '-men'. The term became particularly associated with the 'peace women' at GREENHAM COMMON.

> We have spelt it this way because we are not w*omen* neither are we f*emale* … You may find it trivial – it's just another part of the deep, very deep rooted sexist attitudes.
> *This Magazine is For, About, and By Young Wimmin* (August 1979)

**Wimp.** A weak or ineffectual person, especially a male. The word may have originated in an Oxford University slang term for a female student and derive from a blend of 'woman' and 'whimperer'. In computer jargon a WIMP, suggesting this word, is an acronym of *w*indows, *i*cons, *m*ice and *p*ull-down menus, devices designed to help the novice or the faint-hearted.

**Wimpy.** A proprietary name for a hamburger, as served in a Wimpy restaurant. The name comes from that of J. Wellington Wimpy, a character who is always portrayed eating a hamburger in Elzie C. Segar's POPEYE comic strip. The name was patented in the United States in 1935.

**Wimsey, Lord Peter.** The aristocratic private detective is the central character of the crime novels of Dorothy L. Sayers (1893–1957). He first appears in *Whose Body?* (1923). In many of his manners he is similar to Bertie WOOSTER: he has a manservant, Mervyn Bunter, a private income and a number of acquaintances among the idle rich. Film versions of Wimsey followed, and he was played on television by Ian Carmichael in *Lord Peter Wimsey* (1972–9) and by Edward Petherbridge in *A Dorothy L. Sayers Mystery* (1987). He is said to be based on the travel writer Eric Whelpton (1894–1981). *See also* GAUDY NIGHT; *The* NINE TAILORS.

**Winchester Three.** In 1988 three young Irish people, Martina Shanahan, Finbar Cullen and John McCann, were sentenced at Winchester Crown Court to 25 years' imprisonment on charges of conspiracy to murder Tom King, then secretary of state for Northern Ireland. They were freed on appeal in 1990. *See also* BIRMINGHAM SIX; BRIDGEWATER THREE; GUILDFORD FOUR.

***Wind in the Willows, The.*** An animal fantasy (1908) by Kenneth Grahame (1859–1932). The book was developed from stories told by Grahame to his son Alastair, born in 1900, and inspired by the river and wood at Cookham Dean, Berkshire, where Grahame was brought up by his grandmother. Opinion is divided as to whether the character of Toad, 'the motor-car snatcher, the prison-breaker, the Toad who always escapes', was created as a means of deflating his rather bumptious son or served as an imaginative extension of the outwardly quiet, respectable Bank of England executive that Grahame was. On its publication the anonymous reviewer in *The Times Literary Supplement* reported: 'As a contribution to natural history the work is negligible.' The story was originally called *The Mole and the Water-Rat* in the author's first draft. It was then retitled *The Wind in the Willows*, itself the original title of the chapter called 'The Piper at the Gates of Dawn', in which Mole and Rat have a vision of Pan. Grahame finally decided in favour of the alliterative title, itself evocative of his earlier lyrical essays on the English countryside. A disappointing film version (1996), directed by Terry Jones, turned the original into little more than a pantomime. *See also* TOAD HALL.

**Windmill Theatre.** A theatre in Soho that was famous in the 1930s and during the Second World War for its shows with nude women, who were allowed to appear so long as they remained still. The logic behind this was that movement would have given them a sexual import, whereas if they posed stationary they were regarded as artistic displays.

The Windmill remained open right through the war, leading it to boast the proud slogan, 'WE NEVER CLOSED'. It closed in 1964, becoming a cinema and casino, and although re-opening for a time in the 1980s for 'nude entertainment' it was taken over for television productions in 1990.

> Windmill: always nude but never rude
>
> *Daily Telegraph*, headline (24 November 2005)

In 2005 the film *Mrs Henderson Presents* offered a version of the history of the shows' beginnings, concentrating on Laura Henderson (played by Judi Dench), who first organized the performances in 1932.

**Wind of change.** A new current of opinion; a reformist trend. The phrase was popularized by Harold Macmillan (1894–1986; *see* MAC THE KNIFE; SUPERMAC) in his speech to the South African parliament (3 February 1960), with reference to the social and political ferment in the African continent. *Winds of Change* was also the title of the first book (1966) of his seven volumes of memoirs, completed in 1975.

> The wind of change is blowing through this continent, and, whether we like it or not, this growth of [African] national consciousness is a political fact.

It is not clear whether the inspiration for the phrase was Macmillan's own or that of David Hunt, the diplomat who wrote his speech, but either way it was a variation on a theme that had been played many times before; in 1934, for example, Stanley Baldwin (1867–1947) had said: 'There is a wind of nationalism and freedom blowing around the world.' *See also* AT THE END OF THE DAY.

**Window of opportunity.** A favourable opportunity for doing something that must be acted on instantly if it is not to be missed. The image is of seeing an opportunity through an open window and seizing it before it shuts. The expression dates from the 1970s. 'Window' alone was in earlier use in the 1960s for an interval in which atmospheric and astronomical circumstances were favourable for the launch of a spacecraft. Earlier still, in the Second World War, the word 'Window' was a code name for 'chaff', strips of metal foil that were released from aircraft to obstruct radar detection.

**Window shopping.** The pastime of looking at goods displayed in shop windows without actually buying any of them. The phrase is of US origin and dates from the 1920s.

**Wind, Sand and Stars.** An autobiographical volume (1939; French title *Terre des hommes*) by the pioneer French aviator Antoine de Saint-Exupéry (1900–44), recounting his flights in the 1920s and 1930s across the Sahara and over the Andes in the course of establishing new airmail routes. The writing is remarkable for its heroically romantic intensity, a flavour Saint-Exupéry also brought to a later volume, *Flight to Arras* (1942; French title *Pilote de guerre*), about the role of the pilot in the Second World War. He also wrote a couple of novels, notably *Night Flight* (1932; *Vol de Nuit*, 1931) and a classic children's book, *Le PETIT PRINCE*. In 1944 he disappeared without trace while making a reconnaissance flight from Sardinia.

**Wind someone up.** To tease or irritate them. The image is of winding up a spring mechanism to increase the tension. An act of teasing in this way is thus a 'wind-up'.

**Windsor.** The name of the British royal family dates from 17 July 1917 when, in a wartime climate of revulsion against all things German, George V (1865–1936) changed his German name, Saxe-Coburg-Gotha, inherited from his grandfather, Prince Albert (1819–61), consort of Queen Victoria, to the more British-sounding Windsor. He adopted this name partly because Edward III (1312–77) had used it, but chiefly as a symbolic reflection of the importance of Windsor Castle, a royal residence since William the Conqueror chose the site for a fortress after his conquest of England in 1066. In 1960 Queen Elizabeth II declared that those of her descendants not entitled to the style of Royal Highness or of Prince or Princess would in future use the surname Mountbatten-Windsor, so linking the surname of her husband (before their marriage the Duke of Edinburgh was known as Lieutenant Philip Mountbatten) with their descendants without changing the name of the house established by her grandfather. The first use of the new name on an official document was at the marriage of Princess Anne to Captain Mark Phillips on 14 November 1973. *See also* GOTHA RAIDS.

**Windsor knot.** A large loose knot in a tie, as sported in the 1950s by the Duke of Windsor, formerly Edward VIII (1894–1972). The half-Windsor is a less extravagant, and now more common, version.

**Winkle one's way.** To worm one's way; to insinuate oneself.

**Winkle-pickers.** Shoes with very elongated and pointed toes, affected by TEDDY BOYS in the 1950s. The allusion is to the use of a pin for picking winkles out of their shells.

**Winnie.** A fond if slightly patronizing nickname given to Winston Churchill (1874–1965) during his last period as prime minister (1951–5), when his powers were visibly failing. His attempts to revive the 'special relationship' with the United States led to a cartoon in which President Eisenhower (*see* IKE) was portrayed as Hiawatha and Churchill as 'Winniehaha' (playing on Minnehaha).

**Winnie-the-Pooh.** The 'Bear of Very Little Brain' who appears in the nursery verses and children's stories by A.A. Milne (1882–1956). He made his bow in 1924 and has gained near cult status since. He had his genesis in a TEDDY BEAR named Winnie belonging to Milne's young son, CHRISTOPHER ROBIN, who also appears in the narratives. 'Pooh' was a nickname for a swan that the little boy fed every morning. The original Winnie was a North American black bear, the mascot of a Canadian regiment. When the regiment was sent to France in 1914 Winnie was left in the care of the Royal Zoological Society and lived in London Zoo until her death in 1934. The popular Russian versions of the stories have Winnie-the-Pooh as *Vinni-Pukh* and by a linguistic quirk *pukh* happens to mean 'swansdown'. *Winnie-the-Pooh* (1926) was translated into Latin by Alexander Lenard as *Winnie Ille Pu* (1960).

The rights to Winnie-the-Pooh were sold in 1961 to the Walt Disney Organization, to the consternation of many of his fans. Disney produced a number of short Pooh cartoon films, beginning with *Winnie-the-Pooh and the Honey-Tree* (1966). Its first feature-length cartoon was *The Many Adventures of Winnie-the-Pooh* (1977). In 2005 it announced, to the dismay of Pooh traditionalists, that in future the bear would have a young girl rather than Christopher Robin as his companion. *See also* HEFFALUMP; PADDINGTON BEAR; POOHSTICKS; TIGGER.

> Pooh woke up suddenly with a sinking feeling. He had had that sinking feeling before, and he knew what it was. *He was hungry.*
>
> A.A. MILNE: *Winnie-the-Pooh*, ch. 5 (1926)

**Win on points.** To succeed, but only just. The term comes from boxing, in which one of the contestants wins by scoring more points than his opponent rather than winning by a knockout.

**Winslow Boy, The.** A play (1946) by the British playwright Terence Rattigan (1911–77) about the trial of a young naval cadet who has been accused of stealing a postal order and whose father is determined to clear his name at any cost. The play was based on a real case, that of George Archer-Shee, a cadet who was expelled from Osborne Naval College in 1908 on charges of petty theft. He was found not guilty of the charges, thanks largely to the brilliant defence of Sir Edward Carson, and received £7000 compensation from the Admiralty. He died at Ypres during the First World War.

**Winter of discontent.** The winter of 1978–9, marked in Britain by serious strikes. The phrase is from Shakespeare's *Richard III* (1592) and was originally applied in this sense in January 1979 by the political journalist Peter Jenkins. It was then taken up a month later in a television interview by the Labour prime minister, James Callaghan (*see* SUNNY JIM). The strikes are generally believed to have been a determining factor in the fall of the Labour government and the election of Margaret Thatcher's first Conservative administration in May 1979.

**Winter War.** The war between Finland and the USSR (30 November 1939 to 12 March 1940), fought in the appalling conditions of the Arctic winter, for which the Finns were much better equipped than the Soviets. The war is also called the Russo–Finnish War or the Soviet–Finnish War. Despite the Nazi–Soviet Non-Aggression Pact of August 1939, Stalin was still fearful of a German attack. To protect the Baltic approaches to the USSR, and to Leningrad (St Petersburg) in particular, the Soviets drew up demands for certain Finnish territories, including part of the Karelian isthmus and a naval base at Hangö, in exchange for a large area of Soviet territory. Negotiations broke down and the Red Army attacked. However, the Finnish forces under Marshal Mannerheim (1867–1951) put up a stiff resistance that cost the Soviets dearly and it was not until March 1940 that the Red Army broke through the so-called Mannerheim Line across the Karelian isthmus. The mooted expeditionary force from Britain and France never materialized, and the Finns were obliged to agree to the Soviet peace terms, ceding western Karelia and giving the USSR a 30-year lease on the Hangö peninsula. Soviet casualties in the conflict were 200,000, while the Finns lost 25,000 men.

**Win ugly.** To succeed through thoroughness, application and hard work rather than with flamboyance and effortlessness. The expression was popularized by the title of the book *Winning Ugly: Mental Warfare in Tennis* (1993) by the Australian tennis player and coach Brad Gilbert (b.1961) and Steve Jamison, and it was not long before it began to seep out into non-sporting contexts.

> Far from losing heart, Americans should accommodate themselves to winning ugly again. Yes, it is at times heartbreaking but it could be worse, we could be losing beautifully.
>
> JUDITH A. KLINGHOFFER: History News Network (10 May 2004)

**Win-win situation.** A situation in which each party benefits in some way from an outcome. The phrase arose as business jargon in the 1990s, presumably as an adaptation of NO-WIN SITUATION.

**Wipers.** A nickname for the town of Ypres in Belgium, from the pronunciation of its name by British servicemen in the First World War. The town was the site of three significant battles involving great loss of life, and the name may have become subconsciously associated with 'wipe (out)'. Some of the men may also have been familiar with the old town fort known as the Ypres Tower at Rye, Sussex. This was originally the Badding Tower but was later renamed when it was sold to a John de Ypres. It now houses a museum as part of Rye Castle. *See also* FIRST WORLD WAR SLANG; MENIN GATE; PASSCHENDAELE.

**Wipe the smile off someone's face.** To make them stop smiling; to 'sober' them by means of a serious remark or action. The expression dates from the beginning of the 20th century.

**Wirewalkers.** Not funambulists, but boys employed by the Post Office during the BLITZ to walk around the City of London as roving post offices. They could take telegrams ('wires'), charge customers and give change, and to announce their services they wore signs saying 'Telegrams Accepted'. The general aim was to maintain a semblance of normality with BUSINESS AS USUAL.

**Wise man.** A colloquial term for a special adviser or expert, especially one consulted or brought in by a government department or a business.

> Scotland Yard is planning to appoint a team of 'wise men' to look for fresh leads in the hunt for [television presenter] Jill Dando's killer.
> *The Times* (10 May 1999)

**Wish book.** A US term for a mail order catalogue.

**Wishful thinking.** A desire or hope for something impractical or unfeasible. The term arose from Freudian psychology in the 1920s and translates German *Wunschdenken*.

**Wish list.** A mental or written list of objects of desire, especially as planned and in many cases realized by the well-off. The term and concept date from the 1970s.

**Wish me luck.** Said when one is about to embark on a risky or difficult enterprise. The expression was popularized by Gracie Fields' song (written by Phil Park and Harry Parr Davies) 'Wish Me Luck as You Wave Me Goodbye', which she first sang in the film *Shipyard Sally* (1939) and which went well into the years of the Second World War.

**Wish you were here.** A phrase dating from the EDWARDIAN ERA, when it was conventionally written on a SEASIDE POSTCARDS and sent to one's family or friends at home. The words have had various applications since then, and *Wish You Were Here* was the title of a film (1987) about the GROWING PAINS of a teenage girl in a seaside town in the 1950s: *see* MADAME CYN.

**With a bang.** Abruptly or spectacularly, as if accompanied by

an explosion, as: 'His words brought me down to earth with a bang', 'The holiday began with a bang.' *See also* GO WITH A BANG.

> This is the way the world ends
> Not with a bang but a whimper.
> T.S. ELIOT: *Poems 1909–1925*, 'The Hollow Men' (1925)

**With a capital ....** A speaker or writer may emphasize a word by referring to it as if spelt 'with a capital', as: 'She is musical with a capital M', 'He's a failure with a capital F.' *See also* CONSERVATIVE WITH A SMALL 'C'.

> He is not a personality with a capital P, not flamboyant, not it seems an angry man.
> NESTA WYN ELLIS: *John Major*, ch. 3 (1991)

**'With a Little Help from My Friends'.** A song by The BEATLES, credited to John Lennon and Paul McCartney, sung by Ringo Starr, and released on the album SERGEANT PEPPER'S LONELY HEARTS CLUB BAND in June 1967. Its mildly narcotic sentimentality epitomizes the communal spirit of the SUMMER OF LOVE, of which it became a favourite anthem, and the title entered common parlance.

> Oh I get by with a little help from my friends,
> Mm, I get high with a little help from my friends.

The song was memorably performed by Joe Cocker at WOODSTOCK in 1969, and it went on to receive around 100 further cover versions by performers as diverse as Count Basie and Ike and Tina Turner.

**Withdrawal symptoms.** A term dating from the 1920s for the unpleasant physiological reactions resulting from the process of ceasing to take an addictive drug. *See also* COLD TURKEY.

**With it.** Fashionable; up to date; trendy; *au fait*. The phrase dates from the 1930s and came into its own in the SWINGING SIXTIES. It is now itself less 'with it' than it was.

**With knobs on.** The same to you and more so. A schoolboy retort dating from the 1920s. A fuller version is: 'The same to you with brass knobs on.' The reference is to an embellishment and perhaps specifically to the brass knobs at the head and foot of an old-fashioned iron bedstead.

**Without batting an eyelid.** Showing no concern or emotion; remarking nothing abnormal. 'Batting' is 'blinking'. The expression dates from the beginning of the 20th century.

**Wizard of Dribble.** A nickname of Sir Stanley Matthews (1915–2000), the renowned English footballer, whose paramount gift on the field lay in dribbling. His almost magical skill carried him clean past the best defenders in over a quarter of a century of world football.

**Wizard of Earthsea, A.** The first (1968) in a trilogy of fantasies for young adults by Ursula Le Guin (b.1929), set in an invented world called EARTHSEA, which consists of a vast and elaborate group of islands. Magic abounds, but, though the perils may be fantastical, the adventures and predicaments are realistic. Further volumes have been added to the trilogy since 1990.

**Wizard of Ooze.** A nickname for Senator Everett M. Dirksen (1896–1969) of Illinois, famous for his flamboyant oratory and colourful phrases. He once upbraided a colleague with the words 'that idea has as much effect as a snowflake on the bosom of the Potomac', and in a floor debate, when an opponent started to filibuster, he said that he would 'invoke upon him every condign imprecation'. His motto was: 'The oilcan is mightier than the sword.'

**Wizard of Oz, The.** The central figure in the popular children's book *The Wonderful Wizard of Oz* (1900), by L. Frank Baum, a US journalist. The musical comedy of the same name (1901) was a great success, which was repeated in the film of 1939, which starred Judy Garland as Dorothy. *See also* FIRST LINES OF NOVELS; OZ; 'SOMEWHERE OVER THE RAINBOW'; YELLOW BRICK ROAD; LIZARD OF OZ.

> We're off to see the Wizard,
> The wonderful Wizard of Oz.
> We hear he is a whiz of a wiz
> If ever a wiz there was.
>
> YIP HARBURG: 'Yellow Brick Road', sung in the film by Dorothy, the Cowardly Lion, the Scarecrow and the Tin Man

**WMD.** *See* WEAPONS OF MASS DESTRUCTION.

**Wobblies.** A nickname for the Industrial Workers of the World (IWW). This US revolutionary labour organization was formed in 1905 at a meeting of labour activists in Chicago and reached its peak before the First World War but largely petered out after it. They aimed to gather the country's poorest and most exploited workers into 'one big union' that would ultimately challenge capitalism itself, and they drew their main support from migratory farmers, textile workers and dockers. Their songs include 'The Preacher and the Slave' (*see* PIE IN THE SKY) and Harry McClintock's 'Hallelujah, I'm a Bum'. They were also known as the Bummery. 'Wobbly' may be from a Chinese-American pronunciation of IWW as 'I wobbly wobbly'.

**Wobbling Willie.** A media nickname for the Conservative politician William Whitelaw (1918–99), current in 1983 when he was made a viscount and had to fend off embarrassing questions from the LABOUR PARTY. *See also* WILLIE.

**Wobbly bits.** A colloquialism or euphemism for the male genitalia or female breasts. The phrase also describes excess areas of unmuscular flesh that possess a momentum of their own. *See also* NAUGHTY BITS.

> Once upon a time actresses used to show off their wobbly bits to attract the attention of the press.
>
> *The Times* (15 September 1999)

**Wog.** A derogatory colloquial name applied to blacks, Arabs, and other non-whites. It is possibly a contraction of 'golliwog', but in popular naval parlance it is held to stand for 'wily Oriental gentleman'. Another assertion is that it was formerly applied by the British Army to its Egyptian labourers and is an abbreviation of 'workers on government service'. The chauvinistic catchphrase 'Wogs begin at Calais' first made itself evident after the Second World War.

**Wolf Cub.** The long-established and original name for a member of the junior branch of the BOY SCOUTS or SCOUTS Movement, now called Cub Scouts (age range 8–10½ years). The conception owes much to Rudyard Kipling's *Jungle Books* (1894, 1895). *See also* AKELA.

**Wolf pack.** A term applied in the Second World War to German submarines in a group.

**Wolf whistle.** A whistle made by a male at the sight of a female, expressing sexual admiration. It usually consists of two notes, one rising, the other descending. The name implies that the male is 'hungry', like a wolf. The expression dates from the 1950s. *See also* PHWOAR!

> Local builders wolf-whistled as [actress] Catherine Zeta Jones took to the Old Course in St Andrews with golf-loving Michael Douglas.
>
> *heat* (14–20 October 1999)

**Woman, not born a.** *See* ONE IS NOT BORN A WOMAN, ONE BECOMES ONE.

**Woman in Black, The.** A ghost story (1983) by Susan Hill (b.1942), in a timeless, period setting. A ghost takes revenge for the death of her child by taking the lives of other children. The title recalls that of the Victorian mystery story *The Woman in White* (1860) by Wilkie Collins.

**Womanist.** A black feminist. The word was originally in use in the 17th century as a term for a womanizer. This meaning then became obsolete, and the term was adopted in its modern sense in the 1970s by the African American novelist Alice Walker (b.1944) as being more relevant to black people than 'feminist' and also for its suggestion of 'womanish'.

**Woman's Hour.** A weekday BBC radio programme for women, first broadcast in 1946. It has gradually but radically changed its content over the years, keeping pace with the equally radical changes in women's lives. It has openly explored formerly taboo subjects on radio, typically sexual matters, but has never quite shaken off its middle-class Home Counties tone. A serialized book has always been a popular feature. The programme long went out at 2 p.m, an hour when women were presumed to be at home and have some time to themselves. In 1990 the schedulers of Radio 4 ruffled the feathers of more than a few when it was moved to 10.30 a.m. and subsequently 10.00 a.m. Jenni Murray has presented it since 1987.

**Woman without a man is like a fish without a bicycle, A.** A slogan from the 1970s, variously attributed to the American feminist Gloria Steinem (b.1934) and to a piece of anonymous German graffiti: *'Eine Frau ohne Mann ist wie ein Fisch ohne Velo!'* It may be predated by a less well-remembered saying, 'A man without God is like a fish without a bicycle.'

**Wombles.** Small, hairy, bear-like creatures that live underground, originally beneath Wimbledon Common in London. Individually they are Great Uncle Bulgaria, Orinoco, Wellington, Bungo, Tomsk, Madame Cholet, Miss Adelaide and the eccentric inventor Tobermory. They were the creation of Elisabeth Beresford, and after taking their bow in the children's book *The Wombles* (1968) they went on to be popular in animated form on television. They are dedicated conservationists and make ingenious use of the litter left by humans. The cult of the cuddly creatures was raised to greater heights by a pop group of the same name who dressed the part and took the charts by storm in 1974 with hits such as 'The Wombling Song' and 'Remember You're a Womble'.

> Underground, overground, wombling free,
> The Wombles of Wimbledon Common are we.
> Making good use of the things that we find,
> Things that the everyday folks leave behind.
> MIKE BATT: 'The Wombling Song' (1974)

**Women's lib.** A trivializing abbreviation of 'women's liberation', a feminist movement arising in the 1960s to campaign for the liberation of women from subservient social status and all forms of sexism. The term was gradually abandoned from the 1970s to be replaced by 'feminism'. Women themselves generally prefer 'women's movement'.

**Wonderbra.** The proprietary name of a type of lacy low-cut brassiere introduced by the US company Gossard in 1968, replacing the earlier cumbersome 'bra-slip'. It was an instant bestseller and remained an object of desire for many young women for the next 20 years. The name may have been intended as a pun on German *wunderbar*, 'wonderful'.

Increasingly politically unsound, because frowned on by some feminists, the brand re-embraced its sexy image wholeheartedly in 1994 through posters in which a bra-clad beauty tempted admirers with the words 'Hello boys'.

**Wonder State.** The official nickname of the state of Arkansas, introduced in 1923 to mask its prevalent chronic unemployment and economic backwardness. The recent rapid growth of private enterprise has to some extent justified the earlier optimistic description.

**Woodbine Willie.** The Rev. G.A. Studdert Kennedy (1883–1929) was so called from the popular brand of small cigarettes named Woodbines, which he gave to the men in the trenches in the First World War when serving as chaplain to the forces (1916–19). *See also* PACKET OF WOODBINES.

**Wooden cross.** A wooden cross on the grave of a serviceman killed in action. Hence an ironic term for death in action, regarded as an 'award of merit'. The phrase arose in the First World War.

**Woodentop.** A nickname for a policeman or a slow-witted person, the former being disparagingly regarded as the latter by comparison with sharp-witted detectives. Both terms date from the 1980s and may have been suggested by the children's television puppet programme *The Woodentops* (1955–8).

**Woods are full, The.** A 20th-century Americanism denoting an abundance, as: 'The woods are full of computer magazines these days.' The imagery is from hunting.

**Woodstock.** A small town near Albany in the state of New York, which gave its name to a huge rock festival held nearby in the summer of 1969. In 1994 a 25th anniversary restaging of the original event, commercially sponsored, attracted some 350,000 young (and not so young) people. *See also* ALTAMONT; AMERICAN PIE.

**Woolton pie.** A vegetable dish of carrots, parsnips, turnips and potatoes, covered with white sauce and pastry, named after Frederick James Marquis, 1st Earl Woolton (1883–1964), minister of food during the Second World War. Woolton encouraged British housewives to make use of whatever foodstuffs were available, but his pie mostly failed to excite the already jaded domestic appetite.

> The London crowd shuffled past, surfeited with tea and Woolton pies.
> EVELYN WAUGH: *Officers and Gentlemen*, Pt II, ch. 6 (1955)

**Woolworth Building.** A 60-storey neo-Gothic office building on Broadway in New York City, erected in 1911 by the chain-store magnate F.W. Woolworth (1852–1919), effectively as a monument to himself. It was the tallest building in the world until it was surpassed by the Chrysler Building in 1926. It is popularly known as the Cathedral of Commerce, a term used of it at the time of its dedication.

**Woomera.** The name of the rocket testing range in South Australia, appropriately an Aborigine word for a spear-throwing stick.

**Woop Woop.** In Australian usage, a humorous name for a remote outback town or district. It probably imitates a typical Aboriginal place-name with its characteristic duplication, such as Wagga Wagga, although according to one theory it derives from the 'geelorious town o' Whoop-Up' in E.L. Wheeler's *Deadwood Dick on Deck* (1878), in which 'Whoop-Up' is the name of a back-country US mining town. The term itself is first recorded only in the 1920s, however.

**Wooster, Bertie.** The amiable young man-about-town who, with his manservant JEEVES, has various comic and amorous adventures in the stories and novels by P.G. Wodehouse, of which he is the narrator. He is as vacuous as Jeeves is clever, and his speech is a goldmine of fashionable pre-1914 slang. His indolent existence is marred chiefly by his fearsome aunts. He made his literary début in the short story 'The Artistic Career of Corky' (1916) and is said to be based on John Wodehouse Kimberley, the 3rd Earl of Kimberley (1883–1941), Wodehouse's cousin.

> It is no use telling me that there are bad aunts and good aunts. At the core they are all alike. Sooner or later, out pops the cloven hoof.
>
> P.G. WODEHOUSE: *The Code of the Woosters*, ch. 2 (1938).

*See also* BERTIE WOOSTER OF MARXISM.

**Wop.** In the original US slang usage this meant an uncouth or aggressive person. The term was later used as a derogatory name for Italians and those of similar complexion. It is probably derived from southern Italian dialect *guappo*, 'braggart', 'dandy', itself from Spanish *guapo*.

**Worcester woman.** A hypothetical psephological woman, identified in the run-up to the 2001 British general election as a THIRTY-SOMETHING school-run mother from a reason-ably well-off part of southern England, married to a plumber or an electrician and likely to buy the children computer games for Christmas. She had voted Labour (perhaps for the first time) in 1997, but was now having second thoughts, so the two main political parties courted her assiduously. Worcester was a Labour seat vulnerable to such vacillations – hence the name (the city had reverted to

Conservative control in the local-government elections of May 2000, but in the 2001 and 2005 general elections it remained in Labour hands).*See also* ESSEX MAN; ISLINGTON MAN; MONDEO MAN; ORPINGTON MAN; SELSDON MAN.

**Words of one syllable.** To speak to someone in words of one syllable is to say what one means plainly and directly, even bluntly. Most so-called FOUR-LETTER WORDS are mono-syllabic. The expression dates from the 1920s.

**Workaholic.** A compulsive worker, who is addicted to work as an alcoholic is to drink. The term, first recorded in 1968, is the earliest of the '-aholics' and was coined by Wayne Oates, an American pastoral counsellor, who popularized it in his *Confessions of a Workaholic* (1971). It was followed in due course by the 'chocaholic', 'shopaholic' and similar obsessives.

**Working girl.** A young woman who goes out to work rather than remaining at home. The term can have disparaging overtones and is also one of many euphemisms for a prostitute. The latter is the sense in the film *Working Girls* (1986), about a prostitute in a New York brothel, but not in *Working Girl* (1988), about a secretary who outsmarts her female boss in business and in love.

> Never having enjoyed the company of Sophie Rhys-Jones [Countess of Wessex], as this working girl no longer wishes to be known, I cannot gainsay those who testify to her gamesome charm.
>
> *The Times* (21 September 1999)

***World According to Garp, The.*** A novel (1978), in experi-mental narrative form, by the US novelist John Irving (b.1942). It follows the unorthodox life of T.S. GARP. A somewhat uneasy film version (1981), directed by George Roy Hill, failed to convey the drama of the original. *See also* FIRST LINES OF NOVELS.

**World Bank.** The informal name for the International Bank for Reconstruction and Development, a specialized agency of the United Nations that was set up in 1945. Its purpose is to use capital investment to aid development, especially in poorer countries, but it has been criticized in a similar way to its sister organization, the IMF.

**World first.** An occurrence that has never taken place anywhere in the world before.

> 'We're performing a 30-minute version of every Shakespeare play and we've got more than 1,000 children involved,' he explains. 'We think it's a world first.'
>
> *The Times* (28 December 1999)

***World is Not Enough, The.*** *See* James BOND.

**World is your lobster, The.** A humorous malapropism of the latter part of the 20th century, based on 'the world is your oyster'. It is particularly associated with the character Arthur Daley in the television series MINDER.

**World music.** The traditional music of Africa, Latin America and Asia. It emerged as a distinct genre at the first annual World of Music, Arts and Dance Festival (WOMAD), held at Pilton near Shepton Mallet, Somerset, in the summer of 1982, and came to embrace everything from field recordings of isolated peoples to new urban styles, traditional revivals to NEW AGE explorations.

> 'World Music' – What Is It? The dawning of a new musical 'global village' or an unfocused, unsuccessful marketing ploy? The realization of time-honoured cultural traditions or cynical pop exploitation and New Age natterings? Old field recordings or brave new electronic blends? It may, in fact, be all those things, none of them, and perhaps something more.
>
> CHRIS HEIM: in *Britannica Book of the Year* (1998)

**World's policeman.** *See* NEW WORLD ORDER.

**World Trade Center.** A building complex in Lower Manhattan, New York City, whose 381m (1250ft) 'twin towers' – until then the tallest buildings in the city – were destroyed on the morning of 11 September 2001 (9/11) when two hijacked passenger airliners were deliberately flown, one after the other, into each of the towers (*see also* PENTAGON). The impact of the second plane with the south tower and the ensuing collapse of both towers were watched live on television by a worldwide audience of millions. Over 3000 people were killed. Horrified New Yorkers likened the scenes they had witnessed to a DISASTER MOVIE, while others, stunned by the scale and unexpectedness of the assault on US home territory, compared it with the events of 7 December 1941 (*see* PEARL HARBOR).

Responsibility for the attacks was swiftly laid at the door of the AL-QAIDA organization of Osama BIN LADEN, whose operatives had launched an earlier attack on the World Trade Center in 1993. After a hiatus of four weeks – during which attention was focused on the heroic efforts of New York's firemen to clear the débris at GROUND ZERO, and on President George W. Bush's attempts to build an international coalition against terrorism – in early October the United States launched a military campaign against Afghanistan, whose ruling TALIBAN regime had harboured Bin Laden since 1996. *See* WAR ON TERROR.
*See also* FREEDOM TOWER.

**World War I and II.** For the origins of these labels, *see* GREAT WAR.

**World Wide Web.** The information system on the INTERNET emerged in 1994 as the world's largest example of HYPERTEXT. The Web, familiar as the 'www' of Internet addresses such as the BBC's www.bbc.co.uk, consists of many thousands of pages of information or 'websites'. Users can move from page to page in search of information by using a 'browser', a program providing a window on a computer screen on which the pages are displayed. In general, the more specialized the website, the longer its address. One for R.D. Blackmore's novel *Lorna Doone* (1869), for example, is http://src.doc.ic.ac.uk/media/literary/ collection/ project-utenberg/gutenberg/etext97/lorna10.txt. The World Wide Web itself, with its cumbersome name, was the invention in 1990 of the British computer scientist (Sir) Tim Berners-Lee (b.1955), who also devised the URL and wrote the two protocols 'http' and 'html' (*see* HYPERTEXT). *See also* DUB DUB DUB.

**Worm.** In computer jargon, a self-replicating virus program able to worm its way across a network. Notable worms have included Explore, Netsky, Bagle, Sasser and MyDoom. The term was introduced in this sense in *The Shockwave Rider*, a novel by the US SCIENCE FICTION writer John Brunner.

> I'm just assuming that you have the biggest-ever worm loose in the net, and that it automatically sabotages any attempt to monitor a call to the ten nines.
>
> JOHN BRUNNER: *The Shockwave Rider*, II (1975)

**Worry beads.** A string of beads that one can manipulate as a means of occupying one's hands and calming one's nerves. They date from the 1960s and originated among the Greeks.

> 'Pardon?' said the foreigner … and the man replied, 'Ah, and there was me thinking you were Greek. It was the way you were using the worry beads. Between the middle fingers, just like a Greek, but I suppose that you are French.'
>
> LOUIS DE BERNIÈRES: 'Greek Legends', in *Times Magazine* (8 January 2000)

**Worse for wear.** In its literal sense, dating from the 18th century, the expression means showing signs of damage or deterioration by being worn. It is now commonly used as a euphemism for 'drunk' or 'suffering from a hangover'.

**Worst-case scenario.** A possibility characterized by circumstances of the worst foreseeable type. The expression was popularized by military bureaucrats during the COLD WAR.

**Worzel Gummidge.** *See* Worzel GUMMIDGE.

**Wot, no …?** *See* CHAD.

**Wouldn't it?** In colloquial Australian and New Zealand

English, an all-purpose exclamation of exasperation, frustration, disgust, etc. It is a shortened and perhaps euphemized version of a range of colourful synonyms that all probably originated during or just before the Second World War, including 'wouldn't it rip you?' and 'wouldn't it root you?' ('root' = 'fuck').

**Would you buy a used car from this man?** A US Democratic Party slogan aimed at the Republican presidential candidate, Richard Nixon, in 1968. The slogan built on the image of Nixon as untrustworthy that had emerged from his televised debate with John F. Kennedy during the 1960 presidential election campaign, when he had come over as shifty, unshaven and sweaty. In 1960 the American voters did not buy. In 1968 they did. *See also* TRICKY DICKY.

**Wow factor.** An attribute of something that catches the admiring attention of anyone who sees it. The term is used particularly in the marketing industry, where the 'wow factor' is the holy grail of publicists seeking to make their product stand out from the crowd.

**Woy.** A *Private Eye* nickname for Roy Jenkins (later Lord Jenkins of Hillhead; 1920–2003) on account of his inability to pronounce the letter 'r'. Jenkins, known for his fondness for claret and Europe, served in Labour governments as chancellor of the exchequer (1967–70) and home secretary (1974–6) before becoming president of the European Commission (1977–81), where he was punningly known as Le Roi Jean Quinze. On returning to Britain he co-founded, and was the first leader of, the Social Democratic Party.

**WRAC.** *See* WAAC.

**WRAF.** *See* WAAF.

**Wrap one's car round something.** To crash it. The image is of a wrecked car encircling a tree or pole, although the phrase is used for even a minor collision or 'encounter'. The expression is American in origin and dates from the 1950s.

> I crash on a weekly basis. Even if I really concentrate, I manage to wrap the car around something – a pillar, a traffic cone, even a cat once.
>
> *Sunday Times* (26 September 1999)

**Wrap up.** To be quiet; to shut up. The image is of parcelling up one's words. The phrase dates from the 1940s.

**Wrens.** Acronymically, members of the Women's Royal Naval Service, formed in 1917. It was temporarily disbanded between the wars, then finally disbanded in 1993 when women were able to enlist in the regular Royal Navy. Wrens were long restricted to shore duties and first went to sea only in 1990, when 16 joined the crew of HMS *Brilliant* for

five weeks' operational training. The Wrens' quarters were often jocularly known as 'The Wrennery' and their barracks at Devonport, in the manner of the Royal Navy, was given the ship's name HMS *Impregnable*, punning somewhat salaciously on the contrary senses of the word. See *also* WAAC; WAAF.

**Wright brothers.** *See* KITTY HAWK.

**Wrinkly.** A casually dismissive or patronizing term for an old person. First recorded in 1972, it superficially resembles many of the SOCIONYMS of the late 20th century (e.g. 'yuppie' or 'dinky'), but it fact it was simply based on 'wrinkle'.

**Write one's own ticket.** To stipulate one's own conditions; to dictate one's own terms. 'Ticket' here has its basic sense of a document that gives its holder a particular right, such as admission to a show or authority to travel. The originally US expression dates from the 1920s.

**Writer's block.** A periodic lack of inspiration that can descend on the most experienced of writers and that results in an almost pathological inability to put pen to paper.

**Write the book on something.** To be an expert on it, as: 'Does he know anything about microlights?' 'He wrote the book on microlights.' The phrase is American in origin.

***WR – Mysteries of the Organism.*** A film (1971) by the Yugoslav writer and director Dusan Makavajev (b.1932). 'WR' is Wilhelm Reich (1897–1957), the Austrian psycho-analyst who, in *The Function of Orgasm* (1927), argued that frequent orgasms are necessary for the avoidance of neurosis. He advocated both sexual and political liberation, left Germany in 1933 and settled in the United States in 1939, where his ideas became increasingly unusual. He built (and rented out) special 'orgone' boxes to concentrate 'orgones', units of cosmic energy he believed were necessary for health. This led to his prosecution by the US Food and Drugs Administration, and he died in prison. Sympathizers believed that the prosecution was politically motivated.

Makavajev's film intersperses an account of Reich's career with a satirical look at contemporary politics, sexual and otherwise, in both the Eastern and Western blocs. It was the first film featuring an erect penis to be passed by the British Board of Film Censors, although when the film was shown later on television the penis (which is being wrapped in plaster of paris to make a mould for a sculpture) was heavily pixillated.

**Wrong side of the tracks.** To be on the wrong side of the tracks is to be socially inferior. The expression is of US origin, dating from the 1930s, and alludes to the fact that poor and industrial areas in many towns were at one time located to one side of the main railway line, partly because the prevailing wind would carry smoke into them, away from the better-off neighbourhoods. The poorer districts of British cities are similarly often found east of the centre, since the prevailing wind is usually west or southwest. A familiar example is London's East End.

> I thought at first that she was from the wrong side of the railroad tracks, but she seems to have settled down to being a nice little lady and a good war worker.
>
> SINCLAIR LEWIS: *Cass Timberlane*, ch. 34 (1945)

**Wrong sort of snow.** The notorious excuse offered by British Rail's director of operations in February 1991 after heavy snowfalls had caused widespread delays and cancellations on the railway system. It was not actually as lame as it sounded (the Norwegian snow-clearing equipment acquired by BR did not cope well with dry powdery snow), but the phrase struck such a chord that it became embedded in the national psyche and was later often adapted, with mordant wit (and with 'kind' or 'type' frequently substituting for 'sort'), to other circumstances:

> Train passengers were left sweltering in hot carriages when the air conditioning stopped working – because of the wrong kind of sunshine.
>
> www.manchesteronline.co.uk (16 July 2003)

> The wrong sort of government.
>
> *The Economist*, headline referring to the governance of California (29 April 2004)

> Wembley was delayed by the use of 'wrong concrete'.
>
> *The Guardian*, headline (13 January 2003)

**WRVS.** The Women's Voluntary Service (WVS) was set up in 1938, primarily to help with air raid precautions. It became the Women's Royal Voluntary Service (WRVS) in 1949. It continues to do valuable social and welfare work with the aged and infirm, and it gives help in emergencies. It is particularly noted for its 'meals on wheels' service.

**www.** *See* WORLD WIDE WEB.

**Wysiwyg.** Computer slang for 'What you see is what you get', i.e. what you see on the screen is exactly what will appear on the print-out. The word, pronounced 'wiziwig', is also used for a person or thing taken 'warts and all'. In 1992 it was adopted as the title of a children's SCIENCE FICTION television comedy series, in which it is the name of a reporter from outer space.

> Look at Ken Clarke. He is a classic 'wysiwyg' politician …
> Click on Ken Clarke, and you get exactly what you see.
>
> *The Times* (29 October 1999)

# X

**X.** At one time a classification for 'adult' films, meaning in the main those of a specifically sexual or violent nature. The designation was replaced in Britain in 1983 by '18', the legal age of majority, and in the United States in 1990 by 'NC-17', i.e. 'no children under 17'. *See also* X-RATED.

**X, Malcolm.** *See* MALCOLM X.

**Xbox.** *See* PLAYSTATION.

**X-craft.** A code name for the Royal Navy's midget submarines that were in action against the German battleship *Tirpitz* in 1943. Each submarine was designated 'X' followed by a distinguishing number.

> Of the six attacking craft X9 was lost on passage and X8 … had to be scuttled. X10 found that *Scharnhorst* had left the fiord and X5 was sunk by gunfire, leaving X6 … and X7 to make their way up Altenfiord.
>
> *The Times*: obituary of Rear-Admiral Godfrey Place
> (30 December 1994)

**Xena.** The feisty fighter who sets forth in quest of wicked warlords, man-eating centaurs and the like in the television series *Xena: Warrior Princess*, screened on satellite television from 1995 to 2001. She is played by the New Zealand actress Lucy Lawless and has a sidekick in the sharp-tongued runaway Gabrielle, played by Renee O'Connor. *See also* SWORD OPERA.

**Xerox.** A proprietary name, registered in 1952, for a make of photocopiers. The name itself is based on a respelling of Greek *xeros*, 'dry', in allusion to xerography, the dry copying process that such copiers employ. From the 1960s the name became virtually generic to mean both 'a photocopy' and 'to photocopy', a development that the manufacturing company rigorously resisted but was powerless to prevent.

**X Factor, The.** A British pop music talent show, first broadcast on ITV in 2004. *See also* CELEBRITY CULTURE.

**X-Files, The.** A television series in which a pair of fictional FBI agents, Fox Mulder and Dana Scully, played respectively by David Duchovny and Gillian Anderson, investigate the paranormal. It was screened from 1993 to 2002 and, along with a film adaptation (1998), retains a cult following. *See also* MEN IN BLACK.

**X marks the spot.** This is the place; this is the exact location. The reference is to the marking of a location on a map or the scene of a crime in a plan or photograph with a cross or 'X'. The catchphrase dates from the 1920s.

**X-rated.** Indecent; pornographic, as 'X-rated humour'. The allusion is to the former X film classification.

**XXXX.** The tradename of a brand of Australian lager, produced by the Brisbane brewers Castlemaine Perkins. It is pronounced 'four-x'. It was later taken up as a humorous euphemism for a FOUR-LETTER WORD (typically as in 'I don't give a XXXX').

**XYZ.** 'Examine your zip', an initialism serving as a caution to a man before he steps forth.

# Y

**Yabba-dabba-doo!** *See The* FLINTSTONES.

**Yackety-yack.** A phrase imitative of incessant chatter dating from the 1950s.

**Yah boo!** An exclamation of derision or scorn, originating from children's slang in the 1920s. 'Yah boo sucks!' is a later expansion. The phrase has gained some currency to express an attitude of mocking superiority.

> In the late 20th century … a distinct yah-boo-sucks attitude has developed on the part of celebrity tyrants towards the politicians who seek to court them.
>
> *The Times* (6 November 1999)

**Yahoo!** This search engine for the INTERNET was set up in 1994 by two American electrical engineering graduate students at Stanford University, David Filo and Jerry Yang, initially to track their favourite sites on the burgeoning WORLD WIDE WEB. The name is supposed to be an acronym for 'Yet Another Hierarchical Officious Oracle', but Filo and Wang claimed that they regarded themselves as yahoos (rude, noisy or violent people). More appropriately, the word is an exclamation of joy or excitement, as on making a happy discovery or thinking a happy thought.

> We started off with a few extra-size beers … I let out a yahoo. The night was on.
>
> JACK KEROUAC: *On the Road*, Pt I, ch. 9 (1957)

*See also* GOOGLE.

**Yalta Conference.** A meeting between Winston Churchill of Britain, Franklin D. Roosevelt of the United States and Joseph Stalin of the Soviet Union from 4 to 11 February 1945 at Livadiya, a Black Sea resort 3km (2 miles) from Yalta in the Crimea. The BIG THREE heads of government planned the final stages of the Second World War and agreed the subsequent division of the defeated countries of eastern Europe. It had already been decided that Germany would be divided into occupied zones administered by British, French, US and Soviet forces.

**Yardie.** A member of a Jamaican or West Indian gang that is engaged in worldwide organized crime, especially in illegal drug-trafficking. The name comes from the Jamaican use of 'yard' to mean a house or home: 'yard' was adopted by Jamaicans in England and elsewhere as a term for their home country.

**Yarg.** The name of a full-cream cow's milk cheese first produced in 1983 in Cornwall by a couple named Gray. Hence its name, as a reversal of theirs. Names formed in this particular way usually indicate an inferior version of the original, as 'Klim', a type of powdered milk available in the Second World War, or even 'yob', as a 'backward' boy, but this does not apparently apply with Yarg.

**YBAs.** Young British Artists; *see* BRIT ART.

**Years young.** A coy substitution for 'years old' in stating the age of older people, designed to emphasize their youthfulness of spirit if not of body. A television documentary on centenarians in Britain was predictably titled *100 Years Young* (1999). The term dates from the beginning of the 20th century.

> To the lovely women, sixty years young, whose noble womanhood wins beauty from the passing years, this book is inscribed in loving esteem and admiration.
>
> ELLA ADELIA FLETCHER: *The Woman Beautiful*, Dedication (1900)

**Year Zero.** What 1975 became to the KHMER ROUGE, which in that year came to power in Cambodia, unleashing a campaign of terror and genocide against everyone associated with the previous regime, and indeed anyone who might have an independent thought. *See The* KILLING FIELDS.

**Yellow brick road.** A metaphorical road to happiness. The allusion is to the Yellow Brick Road along which Dorothy and her friends go on their way to see the WIZARD OF OZ. The pop singer Elton John released a highly successful song and album entitled 'Goodbye Yellow Brick Road' in 1973.

> The road to the City of Emeralds is paved with yellow brick.
>
> L. FRANK BAUM: *The Wonderful Wizard of Oz* (1900)

**Yellow card.** In football a card shown by the referee as a caution to a player who has committed an offence. A repetition of the offence, or a more serious infringement, is likely to result in a RED CARD. The system, based on the amber and red traffic-light signals, was introduced on 2 October 1976. The yellow card was withdrawn by the Football Association in January 1981 but reinstated in 1987.

**Yellow dog contract.** A US term dating from the early 20th century for an employee's work contract (now illegal) that forbids membership of a trade union. 'Yellow dog' was formerly a term for a contemptible person or thing, ultimately referring to a mongrel with a dingy tawny coat.

**Yellow Pages.** The registered tradename of a classified telephone directory. It originated in the United States in the early 20th century as the name of an index printed on yellow paper, as at the back of a mail order catalogue. The name's application to the telephone directory dates from the 1950s. Subscribers are listed alphabetically by their product, occupation or service – e.g. (under B) Baby goods, Background music, Bags, Bailiffs, Bait merchants, Ballet shoes. *See also* J.R. HARTLEY.

**Yellow peril.** A scare, originally raised in Germany in the late 1890s, that the 'yellow' races of China and Japan would rapidly increase in population and overrun the territories occupied by the white races, with fearful consequences. *See also* HUN.

> But Japan was Asia, part of the Yellow Peril, poised like a descending pendulum above Australia's rich, empty, underpopulated pit.
>
> COLLEEN MCCULLOUGH: *The Thorn Birds*, ch. 15 (1977)

**Yellow press.** The sensationalist newspapers. The term derives from an issue of Joseph Pulitzer's *New York World* in 1895 containing a comic strip by Richard Outcault whose central figure was a child in a yellow dress, 'The Yellow Kid'. This experiment in colour printing was Pulitzer's shot in the circulation war against William Randolph Hearst's recently launched *New York Journal*. The rivalry, dubbed 'yellow journalism', came to be characterized by scare headlines, sensational articles, lavish illustrations, comic features, Sunday supplements and the like.

**Yellow ribbon.** A tradition has evolved in the United States of using yellow ribbons to decorate the home or home town of a person or group of people returning from danger. The custom was publicized by the media in 1981 following the safe return of 52 US Embassy hostages from Iran. The observance goes back to the days when a yellow ribbon, a decoration on US cavalrymen's tunics, was given to a sweetheart as a favour.

**'Yellow Submarine'.** A comic song by The BEATLES, credited to John Lennon and Paul McCartney, and released in August 1966. Originally written as a children's song, it involves an array of amusing nautical effects, including bubbles and rattling chains. An animated film called *Yellow Submarine* was released in July 1968, and a soundtrack album with songs by The Beatles and an instrumental score by George Martin (the band's producer) appeared in 1969.

> In the town where I was born
> Lived a man who sailed to sea
> And he told us of his life
> In the land of submarines.

**Yerma.** A play (1934) by the Spanish playwright Federico García Lorca (1898–1935) about a woman trapped in a loveless marriage. Yerma, which means 'barren' in Spanish, is the name of the wife whose husband Juan has no interest in having children, ignoring the fact that she longs to be a mother:

> A woman who doesn't bear children is as useless as a bunch of thistles – something fit for God's rubbish heap.

**Yes, Minister.** A witty BBC TV SITCOM, written by Anthony Jay and Jonathan Lynn, that combines farce with satire. First broadcast from 1980 to 1982, it follows the respective struggles to gain and retain power of an unscrupulous senior civil servant, Sir Humphrey Appleby, played by Nigel Hawthorne, and his ineffectual but occasionally wily minister, the Rt Hon. James Hacker, MP, played by Paul Eddington. The plot lines are suitably convoluted and the dialogue is acutely credible for its ESTABLISHMENT setting. Hacker eventually becomes prime minister, as depicted in a subsequent series, *Yes, Prime Minister* (1986–8). The title may have been inspired by this entry (for 22 October 1964) from the Labour politician Richard Crossman's diary:

> The Civil Service is profoundly deferential – 'Yes, Minister! No, Minister! If you wish it, Minister!'
>
> *Diaries of a Cabinet Minister*, vol. 1 (1975)

**'Yesterday'.** A song by The BEATLES in which the singer (Paul McCartney) reflects on a lost love. Credited to John Lennon and Paul McCartney (though written by the latter), it was released in the UK in August 1965. McCartney's voice is accompanied on the song by a guitar and a string quartet.

The song had the very unromantic working title of 'Scrambled Eggs'. John Lennon makes a bitter reference to the song in a track on his 1971 album *Imagine*, where the lyrics of 'How Do You Sleep' include the line 'The only thing you done was Yesterday', a decidedly unjust allusion to the supposed paucity of McCartney's creative input into The Beatles' songs. For good measure, Lennon's cheeky song continues 'And since you've gone you're just another day', a belittling of a post-Beatles solo record by McCartney entitled 'Another Day'.

**Yesterday's men.** Men, especially politicians, whose career is over or past its peak. The expression was popularized (but not invented) by a LABOUR PARTY slogan of 1970, 'Yesterday's men (they failed before!)', referring to the Conservatives. It was later turned against them by the television programme *Yesterday's Men* (1971), a sardonic documentary on Labour cabinet ministers who had lost office in the 1970 election. The style and content of the programme, written and presented by David Dimbleby, led to the threat of lawsuits, a major political row and the setting up of the Broadcasting Complaints Commission (which became the Broadcasting Standards Commission, but when it ceased to exist at the end of 2003 its duties were assumed by Ofcom, the Office of Communications).

**Yes, Virginia.** A cliché sometimes prefixed to a reply to a naïve or childish question, as: 'Yes, Virginia, tea does contain caffeine, just as coffee does.' It originated in the United States in December 1897, when Francis P. Church, an editor on the New York *Sun*, received a letter from eight-year-old Virginia O'Hanlon asking about Santa Claus, who many of her friends had said did not exist. Church's reply contained the words, 'Yes, Virginia, there *is* a Santa Claus.' The line became a favourite with readers and was reprinted annually by the *Sun* until the paper went out of business in 1949. Virginia O'Hanlon went on to become a headteacher and throughout her life received a steady stream of correspondence about her Santa Claus letter. She died on 13 May 1971, aged 81.

**'Yes, We Have No Bananas'.** The memorable title of a song of 1923 by Frank Silver and Irving Cohen, the latter of whom apparently heard the remark from the lips of a Greek fruit seller. *Punch*, in its issue of 1 August 1923, described the title as 'the latest catchword', and the banana importers Elders & Fyffes distributed 10,000 hands of bananas to music sellers with the slogan, 'Yes! We have no bananas! On sale here.' The words work well in other languages to the notes of Cohen's tune, as French *Si, on n'a pas d' bananes*, German *Ja, wir hab'n kein' Bananen* and Russian *Da, u nas nyet bananov*.

**Y-fronts.** The proprietary name, registered in 1953, of a make of boys' or men's underpants in the form of close-fitting briefs with a front opening within an inverted Y-shape. The first trial Y-fronts were produced in 1934 by Coopers Inc. of Kenosha, USA, under the name 'Brief Style 1001', and the style itself was suggested by a pair of swimming trunks worn by a bather on the French Riviera that one of the firm's senior vice-presidents had seen in a magazine photograph.

**Yippies.** Members of the Youth International Party, an anarcho-absurdist organization that in 1968 together with Students for a Democratic Society (*see* WEATHERMEN) led a demonstration in Chicago against the VIETNAM War, racism and other blights of a blinkered US government. The name alludes to HIPPIE, although the Yippies were highly politicized.

**Yogi Bear.** The cartoon bear who starred in the US animated television series named after him. It was first screened from 1958 to 1963 and produced by the Hanna–Barbera team. He lives in Jellystone Park and has a little friend in Boo-Boo. There have been Yogi Bear comics, and a feature-length cartoon film, *Hey There! It's Yogi Bear!*, was released in 1964.

**Yom Kippur War.** The Israeli and common Western name for the 1973 Arab–Israeli War. The name is not accepted in much of the Arab world, as Yom Kippur is a Jewish religious holiday, the Day of Atonement. In 1973 Yom Kippur fell on 6 October, and it was on this day that Egypt and Syria launched a surprise attack on Sinai and the GOLAN HEIGHTS, territories that had been seized by Israel during the 1967 SIX-DAY WAR. Fierce fighting continued for two weeks, during which the Israelis established a bridgehead on the west bank of the Suez Canal, while the Egyptians crossed in the opposite direction to take part of Sinai. On 22 October a ceasefire was arranged through the mediation of the United Nations, the United States and the Soviet Union.

**Yonks.** The slang word meaning 'a long time', especially in the phrase 'for yonks', first emerged in general use in the 1960s. Its origin is uncertain, although it may relate to 'donkey's years'.

**Yoof culture.** The cultural scene of young people in the raw mass, especially as experienced in the field of broadcasting. The use of 'yoof' for 'youth', originally reflecting a non-standard pronunciation, soon gained a veneer of disparagement. It was particularly associated with the MOCK-NEY speech of the television producer and presenter Janet Street-Porter (b.1946), who was appointed the BBC's commissioning editor for youth television in 1988.

As long ago as 1987 Channel 4 had a 'desert island' strand in its groundbreaking 'yoof' TV show *Network 7*.

*heat* (13–19 January 2000)

**Yorkshire Rasputin.** A nickname given by the press corps to Bernard Ingham (b.1932), former journalist and Labour candidate, who was press secretary to the IRON LADY, Margaret Thatcher, throughout her premiership (1979–90). His nickname derives from the Mad Monk, RASPUTIN, who had a powerful and supposedly sinister influence over the last tsar of Russia, Nicholas II, and his wife. The nickname referred to Ingham's mastery of the 'black arts' of spin doctoring (*see* SPIN DOCTOR), which he combined with a rebarbative, no-nonsense Yorkshire style that kept both press and government ministers in order.

**Yorkshire Ripper.** A media nickname for Peter Sutcliffe (b.1946), murderer of 13 women over a five-year period from 1975. The name was based on that of Jack the Ripper, the unknown murderer of several prostitutes in the East End of London in the late 1880s, the term relating to the gross mutilation of the bodies. *See also* WEARSIDE JACK.

**Yosser.** A nickname for a MOONLIGHTER, from Yosser Hughes, one of the main characters in Alan Bleasdale's television black comedy *The Boys from the Black Stuff* (1982), about a gang of unemployed tarmac-layers in wasteland Liverpool. Hughes drives himself into a psychotic state as he begs for work, and his often-repeated pleas 'Gissa job' and 'I could do that' became national catchphrases, not least because of the political situation of the time.

**You ain't seen nothing yet.** A US catchphrase dating from the 1920s. In its variant form, 'You ain't heard nothing yet', it was spoken by Al Jolson in the first full-length talkie *The Jazz Singer* (1927), in which he was actually promoting the title of one of his songs, recorded in 1919. Ronald Reagan used the 'seen' version during his successful presidential campaign of 1984.

**You are what you eat.** A saying, current in this form from the mid-20th century, that can be traced to Anthelme Brillat-Savarin's *Physiologie du goût* (1825):

Tell me what you eat and I will tell you what you are.

Later in the 19th century the German philosopher Ludwig Feuerbach refined the proposition thus:

*Der Mensch ist, was er isst.*

(Man is what he eats.)

Quoted in Jacob Moleschott, *Lehre der Nahrungsmittel* (1850)

In the early 21st century the proverb was hijacked by Dr Gillian McKeith, who received her doctorate from the American Holistic College of Nutrition, a non-accredited

establishment in Alabama. In 2004 McKeith published a bestselling diet book called *You Are What You Eat* and presented a Channel 4 TV series with the same title. She received *The Guardian*'s Bad Science Award in 2004.

**You cannot be serious.** One of the most celebrated and imitated outbreaks of petulance of the tennis player and SUPERBRAT John McEnroe (b.1959). This one occurred at Wimbledon in June 1981, and was addressed to the umpire – although linesmen were just as likely to feel the stamp of his metaphorical foot. Despite his frequent tantrums McEnroe, one of the most naturally gifted players ever, went on to win three Wimbledon singles titles. These days McEnroe is an amiable and highly entertaining commentator for the BBC at Wimbledon fortnight.

**You can run, but you can't hide.** A semi-jocular way of threatening someone, possibly originating in the words of the US heavyweight boxer Joe Louis (1914–81), spoken on 19 June 1946:

He can run. But he can't hide.

Louis was referring to Billy Conn, whom he was about to face in a title fight. More recently, the following advice has been offered to those parents who have just had their first child:

You can play peek-a-boo, but you can't hide.

**You can say that again.** You are stating the obvious. The expression is often used ironically to refer to an unintentional understatement. The phrase dates from the 1930s.

**You can't get there from here.** The problem is too hard to solve. The phrase can have a literal sense, meaning that the place you want to go to is hard or impossible to get to from here.

**You can't win.** A stock expression said, usually in exasperation, when one realizes or feels that, whatever one does, one will not succeed or manage to please a particular person or group of people. The phrase dates from the 1920s and is the title of Jack Black's novel *You Can't Win* (1926).

An electric wheelchair would really help, but my local authority won't pay for one because I'm not disabled enough. You can't win.

*Sunday Times Magazine* (2 January 2000)

**You can't win 'em all.** You cannot succeed every time. The phrase is a standard expression of comfort to someone who has lost or been unsuccessful, especially after a promising beginning.

**You could have fooled me.** You can't expect me to believe that. A comment expressing scepticism or mild contradiction, dating from the 1970s.

**You dirty rat.** The phrase used by all who seek to impersonate the US film actor James Cagney (1899–1986), star of many gangster movies. However, the phrase does not occur in any of his films.

**You don't know the half of it.** There's more to it than that. The expression dates from the 1930s and implies that the speaker knows everything about a situation, whereas the other does not.

**You guessed it.** There is no need for me to tell you. A journalistic tag preceding a piece of information or an outcome that the reader is likely to expect or deduce.

> Many people are throwing their resources into another scheme that upsets the townies: to turn the old cattle market into – you've guessed it – a multiplex.
> *The Times* (4 August 1999)

**You heard!** Don't pretend you didn't hear what I said! The phrase, dating from the 1950s, is typically addressed to someone who pretends not to have heard a particular statement or question.

**'You'll Never Walk Alone'.** A song by Oscar Hammerstein II in the musical *Carousel* (1945), later taken up by fans of Liverpool Football Club and adopted as its anthem. The song became a Number 1 hit for the SCOUSE group Gerry and the Pacemakers in 1963. The words of the title appear on the gates of the club's home ground at Anfield.

**You might very well think that. I couldn't possibly comment.** The frequent response to journalists and others of the Machiavellian Francis Urquhart, Tory chief whip and would-be prime minister in Michael Dobbs's novel *House of Cards*, turned into a highly regarded television series in 1990, in which Urquhart is played by Ian Richardson. The phrase 'I couldn't possibly comment' has since become a popular catchphrase.

**You must be joking.** You can't expect me to believe that. The expression dates from the 1960s and exists in variants such as 'You've got to be joking' or simply 'You're joking.'

**You name it.** Whatever you can think of. A formula dating from the 1960s to express the extent or variety of something, in a typical fuller form: 'You name it, we've got it.'

> Brooms, sink plungers, dustbins, newspapers, matchboxes – you name it and they'll knock, rip or scrape some sort of rhythmic sense out of the thing.
> *heat* (18–24 November 1999)

**Young British Artists.** *See* BRIT ART.

**Young fogy.** A young or youngish person who has the outlook and mannerisms of an OLD FOGY. The stance was adopted by some in the 1980s as a 'throwback' to the 1950s generation. The novelist and biographer A.N. Wilson (b.1950) was generally regarded as an archetypal young fogy, before he became a middle-aged one.

**'Young, Gifted and Black'.** The title of a song (1969) by the American songwriter Weldon J. Irvine (1942–2002) and sung by Nina Simone. The song became an anthem of those involved in boosting black pride. It was written for *To Be Young, Gifted and Black: Lorraine Hansberry in Her Own Words* (1969), a play about the life of the American dramatist Lorraine Hansberry (1930–65) by her husband Robert Nemiroff. The play includes the following quotation from Hansberry, author of *A Raisin in the Sun* (1959):

> Though it be a thrilling and marvellous thing to be merely young and gifted in such times, it is doubly so, doubly dynamic – to be young, gifted and *black*.

Irvine went on to write a successful musical, *Young, Gifted and Broke*, which ran at the Billie Holiday Theatre, Brooklyn, for eight months.

**Young Guard.** A group of young Russian guerrilla fighters based in Krasnodon in German-occupied Ukraine in the Second World War. They were 91 in number, including factory workers, students and government employees, and had four radio receivers, an underground printing press, weapons and explosives at their disposal. They distributed hundreds of anti-NAZI leaflets and on the eve of the 25th anniversary of the October Revolution set up eight Soviet flags in the city. Other operations included the blowing up of German troop-carrying vehicles and the burning down of the Nazi labour exchange with its lists of local people earmarked for transportation to Germany. On 15 November 1942 they freed 70 Soviet prisoners of war from a concentration camp and evacuated a further 20 from hospital. They were planning to blow up the German garrison when their activities were revealed by one of their company, as a result of which they were captured and tortured, and 71 of their number were thrown, alive or dead, down a 53m (174ft) mineshaft. Five of the original ringleaders were shot in a nearby forest on 9 February 1943, and only 11 escaped.

Their dramatic story was retold by Alexander Fadeyev in his novel *Molodaya gvardiya*, 'The Young Guard' (1946), and the new town of Molodogvardeysk, founded in 1954, was named in their honour.

**Young gun.** An assertive and aggressively self-confident young man, as if making his way in life by shooting with a gun. 'Young Guns (Go For It)' was a hit for the pop group Wham! in late 1982.

Wrinklies like the [Rolling] Stones and Elton [John] lead the rich list but young guns are gaining.

*heat* (13–19 January 2000)

**Young hopeful.** A young or youngish person who is deemed likely to succeed.

**Young Ones, The.** The first real showing of undiluted ALTERNATIVE comedy on television, featuring the chaotic antics of a group of four students sharing a squat in a rambling house. There is no story line to speak of, simply a series of grotesque situations, some verging on the offensive. The four consist of the loud-mouthed Cliff Richard fan Rick, played by Rik Mayall, the dim-witted HIPPIE Neil, nicely evoked by Nigel Planer, the stud-headed, spiky-haired PUNK Vivien, played by Adrian Edmondson, and the rather remote Mike, personified by Christopher Ryan. There were two series, the first in 1982, the second in 1984.

*The Young Ones* (1961) was originally the title of a film starring Cliff (now Sir Cliff) Richard, featuring a song of the same name.

**Young thing.** A young person, especially one seen to possess any or all of the desirable characteristics of youth, as verve, style, good looks, physical prowess and the like. The expression is typically used of the socially advantaged, and the BRIGHT YOUNG THINGS and FLAPPERS of the 1920s and 1930s were prominent on the social scene for their exuberance and often outrageous behaviour.

**Young Turks.** A Turkish reforming party seeking to transform the decadent Ottoman Empire into a modern European state and to give it a parliamentary constitution. It had its origins in a committee formed at Geneva in 1891, and the party, considerably supported by students, raised the standard of revolt at Salonika in 1908, deposed Sultan Abdul Hamid and replaced him by his brother, as Mohammed V (1909). Their 'liberalism' was not dominant, but they remained the major force in Turkish politics until the end of the First World War, when the party was dissolved. Turkey was proclaimed a republic in 1923.

'Young Turks' is also used generally for young people eager for radical change to the established order.

**You Only Live Twice.** The fifth film (1967) in the long-running series of James BOND films based on the secret agent novels of Ian Fleming (1906–64). Scripted by Roald Dahl and starring Sean Connery as Bond, the film derived its title from the proverbial tag 'you only live once', as used in a Fritz Lang crime thriller as early as 1937. It is justified within the script by Bond faking his own death and then reappearing to thwart the plans of arch-villain Blofeld, played in this instance by Donald Pleasence.

**Your actual ….** The real or genuine thing specified, as: 'This is your actual vintage Rolls Royce.' The turn of phrase became popular following its use in the dialogue of two gay characters, Julian and Sandy, in the radio comedy *Round the Horne* (1965–9). Typically, they would introduce some French phrase into their lines and then say: 'That's your actual French, you know.' *See also* YOUR AVERAGE.

**Your average.** The average or typical thing specified, 'your' implying that the reader or listener will be familiar with it. The expression may equally be used of people. *See also* YOUR ACTUAL.

Black on White is not your usual concert, nor is it your average piece of performance art.

*The Times* (5 July 1999)

**Your Country Needs You.** *See* KITCHENER'S ARMY.

**You're a poet and you don't know it.** A catchphrase said, with appropriate variation of pronoun, when someone makes an unwitting rhyme, as: 'If it comes on to rain, we can go on the train.'

**You're telling me.** There is no need to tell me that, I am aware of it already. The phrase expressing agreement dates from the 1930s and may owe something to a 1932 song of the same title by Gus Kahn.

**You're the doctor.** You know best; whatever you say. A catchphrase dating from the early 20th century. *See also* JUST WHAT THE DOCTOR ORDERED.

**Your guess is as good as mine.** I don't know either. A phrase dating from the 1930s.

**Your King and Country Need You.** *See* KITCHENER'S ARMY.

**Your place or mine?** A stock phrase evolving among young people in the 1970s as the key question after a period of time engaged in 'chat'. The implication is of a more intimate engagement.

**You've lost me.** I don't follow what you're saying. The idea is that your reasoning or narrative is so tortuous that I have lost the thread. The phrase dates from the 1960s.

**You win.** Said when conceding agreement to another's demand or choice, usually after a discussion or even argument, as: 'All right, you win, we'll go there later.' *See also* YOU CAN'T WIN.

**You wouldn't read about it.** An expression of pained incredulity, originating in Australian English in the 1940s, and expressing the philosophy that nature is infinitely more various and bizarre than mere art.

They are now ... out of stock again!!!! They (again) have no

ETA for the next shipment of XDA2s ... You wouldn't read about it! At least they said they would credit my OPTUS account $50 for my troubles. And they said they were sorry.
www.mtekk.com.au (19 May 2004)

**Yowie.** A monster resembling an ape, sightings of which were reported in eastern Australia in the last quarter of the 20th century. The word itself means 'dream spirit' in the Yuwaalaraay language of New South Wales.

**Yo-yo.** The familiar toy that falls and rises on an adroitly manipulated string is first recorded in 1915 as a Filipino device of this type. The word was registered as a tradename in Canada in 1932, and it was then that a sudden craze for the toy spread through the Western world. Subsequent vogues followed in the 1950s and the late 1990s. The origin of the name is uncertain, although a meaning 'come-come' is adduced in some dictionaries.

**Ypres.** *See* MENIN GATE; WIPERS.

**Yuck** or **yuk.** A word expressive of disgust or distaste, as an imitative variant of 'ugh'. Hence 'yucky' to denote anything unpleasant or cloyingly sentimental. *See also* YUCKIES.

**Yuckies.** A term for a couple in an embarrassingly close or 'clonish' relationship, of the kind that makes one say YUCK, especially when each was formerly idolized as a media or sports figure. The expression, based on YUPPIES, dates from the late 1990s, and has been applied to, among others, POSH AND BECKS.

It's a rare thing even to see them apart ... Hip as they may try to be, Posh and Becks are sadly what's known as Yuckies.
*Sunday Times* (29 August 1999)

**Yuk.** *See* YUCK.

**Yummy mummy.** A young middle-class mother who is chic, elegant, well-groomed, sexually attractive, etc., in defiance of the stereotypical TWENTY- or THIRTY-SOMETHING ground

down by the cares of motherhood. The term dates from the early years of the 21st century.

It beggars belief that Gordon [Brown] has so misjudged the yummy mummies he's attempting to target [by increasing the road tax on four-wheel drive vehicles] ... women who live by one rule: if it makes my life easier, I'll pay, and bugger the consequences.
*Sunday Times* (2 April 2006)

*See also* CHELSEA TRACTOR; TOO POSH TO PUSH.

**Yuppie flu.** A slighting nickname for the malady known more formally as chronic fatigue syndrome and medically as myalgic encephalomyelitis (ME). The condition, once thought of as typical among YUPPIES, usually occurs after a viral infection, and involves fever, aching and tiredness and depression. The diagnosis became more frequent in the late 1980s as a result of media publicity.

**Yuppies.** Young urban (or upwardly mobile) professional people. A popular acronym from the 1980s, partly of US origin. *See also* SOCIONYMS.

'The Yuppie Handbook' [1984] defined the yuppie as a fast-track baby-boomer between 25 and 46 residing in or near a major city and living on aspirations of glory and power or 'anyone who brunches on the weekend or works out after work'.
*International Herald Tribune* (March 1986)

**Yvette.** Canadian slang for an old-fashioned French Canadian woman or girl, as the name of a character in a Quebec school primer. Its use in this sense was popularized by Lise Payette, a Parti Québecois provincial cabinet minister, during the campaign leading up to the referendum of 1980 on independence for Quebec.

**Yvonne.** A nickname given to Princess Margaret (1930–2002) by *Private Eye* (*compare* BRENDA). *See also* TANTE YVONNE.

# Z

**Zambuck** or **Zambuk.** In colloquial Australian English, a member of the St John Ambulance Brigade, especially one attending a sports match as a first-aid worker. The term, which is first recorded in 1941, is an adaptation of the tradename of a make of antiseptic ointment, originally manufactured in New Zealand.

**Zapata moustache.** A thick moustache that curves down around the edges of the mouth, like that worn by the Mexican revolutionary Emiliano Zapata (1879–1919).

**Zaphod Beeblebrox.** The two-headed renegade in Douglas Adams's *The* HITCH-HIKER'S GUIDE TO THE GALAXY.

**Zapper.** A colloquial term for a remote-control unit for a television or other home enterntainment device.

**Zazie dans le Métro.** A novel (1959; in English as *Zazie in the Metro*, 1960) by Raymond Queneau (1903–76). The mind of the philosopher-poet is behind the clowning in this ostensibly light novel, in which a provincial girl's ambition to travel on the Paris Métro is thwarted by a typical French one-day strike. A film version (1960), directed by Louis Malle, is full of comic action, with a zestful young Catherine Demongeot in the title role.

**Z-Cars.** A seminal television drama series screened from 1962 to 1978. It was set in the docklands of Liverpool and depicted in gritty detail the professional lives of a squad of PANDA CAR drivers, some of whom, controversially for the day, were depicted as fallible human beings. Thus the first episode showed one policeman beating his wife and another asking for the result of a horse race. Many of the actors, such as Colin Welland, Brian Blessed and Leonard Rossiter, became household names, and a spin-off was the police drama *Softly, Softly* (*see* SOFTLY-SOFTLY). The cars used were Ford Zephyrs. Hence the 'Z'.

**Zebra crossing.** A type of road crossing marked by broad black and white stripes on the road, accompanied by BELISHA BEACON at the side of the road. The term dates from the early 1950s. *See also* PELICAN CROSSING.

**Zen and the Art of Motorcycle Maintenance.** A bestselling philosophical tract (1974), subtitled 'An Inquiry into Values', by the US writer Robert M. Pirsig (b.1928). In it Pirsig proposes that to live a full and integrated life we should be able to change the oil and the sparkplugs on our 1000 cc Kawasakis, before roaring off across the United States at an unseemly speed. George Steiner compared the book to *Moby Dick*, but it has not outlived its own time in the way that Melville's masterpiece has. However, Persig's title has been extensively filched, and the shelves of the world's bookstores now groan under volumes with titles such as *Zen and the Art of Archery, Zen and the Art of Making a Living, Zen and the Art of Stand-Up Comedy, Zen and the Art of Writing, Zen and the Art of Knitting, Zen and the Art of Postmodern Philosophy, Zen and the Art of Public School Teaching, Zen and the Art of Pottery*, etc., etc.

**Zeppelin.** The imposing German airship used during the First World War for reconnaissance and bombing and after the war for passenger transport. It took its name from its constructor, Count Ferdinand von Zeppelin (1838–1917). The *Graf Zeppelin* was completed in 1928 and was in commercial passenger service for ten years, making 590 flights before being decommissioned in 1937. In the latter year the *Hindenburg*, the largest Zeppelin ever built, suddenly exploded while landing at Lakehurst, New Jersey, at the end of a transatlantic crossing, killing 36 of its 97 passengers. The disaster was attributed by some to anti-NAZI saboteurs. A second *Graf Zeppelin* was completed in 1938 and was the most advanced commercial airship ever built. It was used by the Germans for surveillance in the months before the Second World War but was grounded after the outbreak of war. Both of the *Graf Zeppelin* airships were broken up in 1940 when Goering, head of the LUFTWAFFE, wanted their aluminium for combat aircraft.

**Zero hour.** A military term, first used in the First World War, for the exact time at which an attack or operation is to be begun. From this are timed the subsequent operations, e.g. 'zero + 3' means three minutes after zero hour. The term was succeeded in the Second World War by 'H-hour'.

**Zero option.** A disarmament proposal by one side to reduce the number of nuclear missiles, or not to deploy them, if the other will do the same. The expression originated in the early 1980s with specific reference to the US proposal that, if the Soviet Union would withdraw its medium-range SS-20 missiles from Europe, the United States would abandon its plan to deploy Pershing and cruise missiles there. The expression itself evolved from the *Null-lösung*, 'zero solution', put forward in 1981 by the German Chancellor Helmut Schmidt. 'Zero' implies reduction to nothing.

**Zero-sum game.** A game in which the sum of the winnings of all the players is always zero and hence any situation in which an advantage to one participant necessarily leads to a disadvantage to one or more of the others. The expression was introduced by the US economists John von Neumann and Oscar Morgenstern in their influential study *Theory of Games and Economic Behavior* (1944).

**Zero tolerance.** The total non-acceptance of antisocial behaviour, with laws or penalties applied rigorously to even minor infringements. The policy was introduced in the United States in the early 1980s to cover a crackdown on even the mildest forms of street crime, such as graffiti, vandalism, obstruction, aggressive begging or spitting. The concept crossed to Britain in the 1990s.

**Ziegfeld Follies.** The American theatrical producer Florenz Ziegfeld (1867–1932) first mounted his *Follies* revue in 1907 at the New York Theatre Roof, his name becoming a permanent part of the title in 1911. The show was loosely based on the Parisian *Folies Bergère*, but, knowing that he could not display the dancing nudes of his French counterpart, Ziegfeld posed the near naked 'girls' in what he called 'living tableaux', or motionless poses. He thus adroitly blurred the distinction between art on the one hand and soft pornography on the other. The extravagantly staged shows ran continuously up to Ziegfeld's death and then periodically thereafter until 1957.

**Zigger-zagger.** The onomatopoeic nickname of the large rattle that football fans formerly brandished at matches. As it was swung round a handle it made a loud rasping or clacking sound. Peter Terson's play *Zigger Zagger*

(1967) is about a football fan named Zigger and a football crowd.

**Ziggy Stardust.** An alien hermaphrodite with blood-red hair, an alter ego of the rock singer David Bowie. Ziggy Stardust appears on the CONCEPT ALBUM *The Rise and Fall of Ziggy Stardust and the Spiders from Mars*, released in 1972, at the height of Bowie's GLAM ROCK phase. The basis of the album resided in the idea of a supergroup (the Spiders) with a five-year lifespan. The concept, with its undertones of SCIENCE FICTION and androgyny, was a feeble one, but many of the songs on the album, such as 'Moonage Daydream', 'Starman', 'Rock and Roll Suicide' and 'Suffragette City', were critically acclaimed. The Spiders from Mars also appeared on the album *Aladdin Sane* (1973).

**Zillions.** A very large number. The word emerged in the 1940s as a fanciful alteration of 'millions', 'billions' and the like, with 'z' perhaps representing the sound of 'x' (as in 'xylophone') in its mathematical role as an unknown number, or even as itself in this role. *See also* SQUILLIONS.

**Zimmer frame.** The make of walking frame for elderly or disabled people takes its proprietary name from its manufacturing company, Zimmer Orthopaedic Ltd. The company's own name comes from Mongolian *zhima*, a sledge drawn by a *zho*, a hybrid of a yak and a cow, which is guided by a man walking at the rear holding an upright frame.

**Zimmermann Telegram.** On 16 January 1917 Arthur Zimmermann (1864–1940), German foreign secretary, sent a telegram to the German minister in Mexico with the terms of an alliance between Mexico and Germany by which Mexico was to attack the United States with German and Japanese assistance in return for the US states of New Mexico, Texas and Arizona. The telegram, originally sent in code, was decoded by British Admiralty intelligence and made available to President Woodrow Wilson, who published it on 1 March 1917. In convincing Americans of German hostility towards the United States, the telegram became one of the principal factors leading to the US declaration of war against Germany five weeks later.

**Zinoviev Letter.** *See under* FAKES.

**Zionism.** The Jewish movement for the establishment of the 'national home' in Palestine. The Zionist movement was founded in 1895 by the Austrian Theodor Herzl (1860–1904), and the BALFOUR DECLARATION of 1917 recognized Zionist aspirations. From 1920 to 1948 Palestine was a British MANDATE, administered under great difficulties arising from the friction between Jews and Arabs. The independent State of Israel was established in 1948. The Palestine

Liberation Organization (PLO), founded in 1964, first fought, often at a high cost, then later negotiated to gain Palestinian statehood in what it regards as Israeli-occupied territory. *See also* HAGANNAH; IRGUN.

**Zip code.** In the United States, the system introduced in 1963 to facilitate the sorting and delivery of mail, based on five-digit (or, since the late 1970s, nine-digit) numbers. The first three of the five digits identified the section of the country to which the item was destined, and the last two the specific post office or zone of the addressee. 'Zip', while suggesting speed, is an acronym of Zone Improvement Plan, the formal name of the system. The British POSTCODE is similar.

**Zoo daddy.** An American colloquialism dating from the 1970s for a divorced or separated father who rarely sees his children. On occasions, when he does see them, he frequently seeks to hold their interest and affection for the brief time available by taking them to the zoo or some other place of public entertainment. Hence 'Disneyland daddy' as an alternative term for the situation.

**Zoo Story, The.** A one-act play (1959) by the US playwright Edward Albee (b.1928) about a chance meeting between two men on a public bench that culminates in one of them being knifed to death after they clash over possession of the bench. The title refers to the visit one of the men has just made to a zoo, although it is the 'human zoo' that is really under discussion:

> You have everything in the world you want; you've told me about your home, and your family, and your own little zoo. You have everything, and now you want this bench. Are these the things men fight for?

**Zoot suit.** An exaggerated style of clothing adopted in the late 1930s by followers of fashionable SWING music. It usually consisted of baggy trousers caught in at the bottom, a long coat resembling a frock coat, a broad-brimmed hat and a flowing tie, all in vivid colours. An essential adjunct was a long watch chain looping across the trousers. The outfit made a comeback in the 1990s and was complemented by a feminine version. 'Zoot' is simply a rhyming jingle on 'suit'.

**Zoot suit riot.** A race riot in Los Angeles in June 1943, in which there was fighting between white servicemen and zoot-suited Mexican American youths.

**Zoo TV.** A type of television programme that encourages emotional and often uncontrolled reactions from the participants, as a debate before a live audience or a scene involving personal disclosures. A typical example is *The Jerry Springer Show*, an American talk show first screened in 1991 that evolved to include outrageous topics and physical fisticuffs among the guests. The analogy is with the untrammelled behaviour of zoo animals, especially monkeys, before the gaze of visitors. *See also* REALITY TV.

> A gaggle of teenagers whooping and hollering in full 'zoo' TV mode.
> *heat* (20–26 January 2000)

**Zorba the Greek.** A novel (1952; in Greek as *Vios kai Politeia tou Alexi Zormpa*, 'The Life and Times of Alexis Zorbas', 1946) of the MAGIC REALISM school by the Greek writer Nikos Kazantzakis (1883–1957). The character of the passive, contemplative narrator contrasts with that of the larger-than-life Greek of the old tradition, whose actions are unpremeditated and often irrational.

> 'I went off all of a sudden, got hold of the boss, who had come that day to inspect the place, and just beat him up.'
> 'But what had he done to you?'
> 'Nothing at all …'
> 'Well?'
> '… It just came over me. You know the tale of the miller's wife? Well, you don't expect to learn spelling from her backside, do you? The backside of the miller's wife, that's human reason.'

An enjoyable film version (1964), with memorable music by Mikis Theodorakis, was directed by Michael Cacoyannis.

**Zorbing.** An EXTREME SPORT that emerged in New Zealand in the mid-1990s, which consists in hurling oneself down hills or fast-flowing streams in a 'zorb', a large perspex ball.

**Zorro.** The black-masked, black-caped master swordsman and avenger of old California was the creation of Johnston McCulley (1883–1958). He first appeared in 1919 in the magazine story 'The Curse of Capistrano'. His 'trademark' is the letter Z, which he slashes on the clothes or skin of his enemies. He soon transferred to the cinema screen, where he was played by such actors as Douglas Fairbanks in *The* MARK OF ZORRO (1920) and Tyrone Power in the 1940 version . His name is the Spanish for 'fox', from a word that originally meant 'cunning'.

**Zuleika Dobson.** The only novel (1911) by Max Beerbohm (1872–1956), essayist, critic, parodist, and caricaturist. Subtitled 'An Oxford Love Story', it describes delicately and wittily the passionate and ultimately apocalyptic response of the undergraduate population to Zuleika DOBSON, the beautiful and predatory niece of the head of one of the colleges.

**Zuppa inglese.** (Italian, 'English soup'.) Not a soup, but a rich Italian dessert resembling trifle. The dish first became familiar to the English themselves in the 1970s.

**Zut alors!** An expression of surprise, annoyance, impatience etc, supposedly typical of the French. It represents *zut*, an imitative word approximating to English 'tut' or 'tch', and *alors*, 'then'.

> Zut alors! You British can have your secrets back.
> *Sunday Times*, headline (12 December 1999)

**Zyklon-B.** A tradename for hydrogen cyanide, the quick-acting, lethal gas used by the NAZIS to kill millions of Jews and other 'UNTERMENSCHEN' during the Second World War. The effectiveness of Zyklon-B in achieving the FINAL SOLUTION was first demonstrated at the Belżec extermination camp in Poland in August 1942 and subsequently employed on an industrial scale at AUSCHWITZ and elsewhere. *See also* HOLOCAUST.

**Zzz.** A representation of the sound of a person sleeping or snoring, typically found in cartoons and comics. The choice of the last letter of the alphabet for this is apt in both sound and sense, since sleeping implies a 'closing down' of activity. *See also* BAG SOME ZS.